Bill James Presents

THE GREAT AMERICAN BASEBALL STAT BOOK

Bill James Presents

THE GREAT AMERICAN BASEBALL STAT BOOK

by
**Bill James,
Don Zminda, Executive Editor,
Gary Gillette, Associate Editor**

Editors

Geoff Beckman	Fred Percival
Mike Duca	Gary Skoog
Bill James	Craig Wright

Mike O'Donnell

Computer Programmers

David Nichols	Tom Tippett

Luke Kraemer, Data Editor

Villard Books • New York

Table of Contents

Acknowledgments

A book like this is an enormous undertaking, involving the efforts of literally hundreds of people. The structure of Project Scoresheet begins, at the grass roots level, with those dedicated volunteers who score our games. We have so many scorers—which is not to say we have enough scorers—that it is impossible to list all of them. However, all of the following people scored a significant amount of games for the Project. Without them there wouldn't be a Project Scoresheet, much less this book.

1987 Scorers

Mitchell Abidor
Paul Adomites
Sunil Agarwal
David Annis
Peter Barnett
Catherine Below
Tom Benner
Ron Blake
Don Bowman
Marc Bowman
David Bradley
Arnie Braunstein
Dennis Bretz
David Broughton
Paul Brown
Ken Burbick
J. Randolph Burnham
Mark Capaldi
Jack Carlson
Michael Cassin
Michael Cervantes
Clem Comly
Allen Copenheaver
Carmen Corica
Tony Darkin
Liane P. Davis
Walter De Soi
Paul Debbas
Pete DeCoursey
Dan Dothat

David Driscoll
Jessie Drucker
Steve Elsberry
Larry Epke
Bernie Esser
Frank Fincken Jr.
Gord Fitzgerald
Michael Fitzgerald
Ray Flemming
Alan Foonberg
Tony Formo
Michael Fraser
Gregory Funk
Greg Gajus
Mike Galbreath
Jim Gartung
Agnes Geraghty
Stan Gilchrist
Gary Gillette
Robin Gipson
Dave Gordon
Jay Gregory
Rick Guzman
Stu Hall
Scott Hanson
Don Hartack
Jim Haug
Victor Hestor
Brigg Hewitt
Kevin Hoare

Joe Holt
Keung Hui
Dic Humphrey
Bill James
Bill Jensen
Bob Jones
Stacy Kaneshiro
Ernie Karm
Bernard Kesten
Jack Kettles
Arthur Kimes
Keith Knopf
Steve Kolk
Mike Kopf
Luke Kraemer
Larry Kreger
Theo Lambos
Thomas P. Lash
Bob Leeper
Rollie Loewen
Ed Loss Jr.
Andre Lower
Steve Lysogorski
Brent MacInnes
Gary Magee
Frank Markotich
Mike Marrero
Steven Marsh
Steve Mattan
John Matthew IV
Welford McCaffrey
Pat McCormick
Jim McDonald
Don McKennan
Sherri Menees Nichols
Andrew Menown
Michael Millet
Clint Mueller
Al Nakamura
Christine Nelson
Susan Nelson
Jim Netter
John Nielsen
Joe Nunziata III
Dennis Orr

Bruce Osterweil
Robert Ostrove
Mike O'Donnell
Peter Palmieri
Rodney Paul
Fred Percival
Tom Peters
Chris Pohl
Claude Racine
Ann Reimer
Fred Reisser
John Rickert
Marc Rivlin
David H. Robinson
Ira Saltz
Paul Schwarzenbar
Phil Scott
Skip Seeger
Scott Segrin
Jeff Sewall
Paul Seybold
Jim Shaarda
Scott Sharp
Stuart Shea
Sanford Sklansky
Chris Smith
James A. Smith, Jr.
Mike Sopp
Ginny Soybel
Steve Stern
Thomas Stillman
Steve Taylor
John Tedford
Wes Teno
John Terrell
Al Them
Bill Thomas
Pam Tomczak
Chris Towne
Wayne Townsend
Mark S. Unger
Vince Vrotny
Dan Walsh
Kevin Warren
Chuck Waselski

Katherine Wayne
Mike Webb
Roger Weber
Bob Wertzberger
Bob Whitemore
Hank Widmer

Wendy Wilson
Barry Wolven
Chuck Wood
Don Yeager
Don Zminda

1987 Team Captains

The scorers need to be organized so we can insure that each game is covered. For that reason we have a captain for each major league team. These are the people who make the scoring assignments and insure that the flow of data keeps running. They are truly the lifeblood of the Project.

Geoff Beckman
Russell Bell
Tom Benner
Ron Blake
Dennis Bretz
Craig Christmann
Clem Comly
Joe Cook
Gord Fitzgerald
Gary Gillette
Dave Gordon
Dic Humphrey
Mike Kopf
Luke Kraemer
Rollie Loewen

Brent MacInnes
Mike Marrero
Clint Mueller
Susan Nelson
Chris Pohl
Greg Pryor
Jim Rogde
Steve Russell
Scott Segrin
Gary Skoog
John Ungashick
Chuck Waseleski
Bob Whitmore
Don Zminda

1987 Division Captains

The division captains choose the team captains, help them and the inputters with their problems, and try their best to answer any and all questions about the workings of the Project.

Gary Gillete
Dennis Bretz

Don Zminda
Gary Skoog

1987 League Coordinators

The league coordinators receive the scoresheets our members send them, try to track down any missing games, then pass the scoresheets on to our inputters for processing. Like the division and team captains, they work closely with the scorers and inputters and answer a ton of mail.

Bud Podrazik

Sue Dewan

Proofers

At the end of the season we are buried under a mound of scoresheets and floppy disks. The inputted games are processed to produce box scores, which are then compared with newspaper box scores for accuracy. Our sharp-eyed (and by the time their job is done, red-eyed) proofers check line by line, twice, to insure that our data is accurate. Under the heroic leadership of Luke Kraemer, this group worked through the holidays to finish a massive job.

Paul Adler
Andrew Berman
Jack Carlson
Carmen Corica
Dan Dobbins
Russ Eagle
Steve Elsberry
Bernie Esser
Stan Gilchrist
Don Gunning
Luke Kraemer

Patricia Morgan
Susan Nelson
Michael O'Donnell
Bruce Osterweil
Bud Podrazik
Gary Renaud
Stuart Shea
Tom Tippett
Chris and Valerie Towne
& the guys from Pursue the Pennant

Data Editors

Once the data has been proofed there comes the job affectionately known as "data clean up." The data editors, again led by Luke Kraemer, go through the disk files and correct the errors caught by our proofers. It's a dirty job, says Luke, but someone has to do it.

Pete Barnett
Luke Kraemer
Ira Saltz

Tom Tippett
Wayne Townsend

Computer Programmers

The games have been scored, the scoresheets inputted, the disk files checked and edited. But we're still not done; we need programs to turn the data files into the statistics we use in this book. It's a long and exacting task, one which we required the efforts of two very talented people. During those last hectic days before the publisher's Absolute and Final Deadline, these fellows put everything aside to see that work was done . . . and done right.

David Nichols

Tom Tippett

Writers

I trust that the most pleasant task involved in putting together this book fell to our writers. Over a hundred people submitted essays to our editorial board, and almost all the submissions were excellent. You'll see the fine work of these people bylined throughout the book.

Manuscript Preparation

The final task in putting together this book involved gathering up all the manuscripts, proofing and re-typing them when necessary, and making one last check to be sure we hadn't confused Billy Bean with Billy Beane. These fellows spent many a late night checking and rechecking the work.

Paul Adler   Scott Hanson
Andrew Berman   Rollie Loewen
Mark Bowman   Jim Morrow
Don Gunning

Typesetting

Special thanks go to the professionals at ComCom in Allentown, Pennsylvania, who typeset the huge manuscript for this book. In particular, Pete Koval and Bill Millberger, both avid baseball fans, were of great help to us in making layout, format, and typesetting decisions. The fact that the hundreds of essays and hundreds of thousands of statistics in this book are well laid out and readable is largely to their credit. The text was set in 10/11 Times Roman and all the stats were set in 7/7 Helvetica Bold.

Career Data

The career data which appears in our book was provided by Pete Palmer; we'd like to express our appreciation to Pete for supplying it. Pete is not only a friend to the Project; he is a friend to anyone who knows and loves baseball statistics. Thanks, Pete.

Project Scoresheet Board of Directors

Coordinating the entire work of Project Scoresheet—not only producing this book, but all our other efforts to provide information to the baseball fans of America—is the job of our Board of Directors. The Board meets at least twice a year in person, and numerous other times by conference call, working to achieve the goals of the Project and the needs of its members. John Dewan served as executive director until the end of the 1987 season, at which time Gary Gillette succeeded him. The following people served on the Project's Board during 1987.

Dennis Bretz   Bill James
John Dewan   Pete Palmer
Sue Dewan   Gary Skoog
Michael Duca   Craig Wright
Gary Gillette   Don Zminda

And Others . . .

For several years the heart and soul of Project Scoresheet were John and Sue Dewan. Under their dedicated leadership the Project grew by leaps and bounds; it was largely through their efforts that this book became a reality. Everyone in the Project owes them a deep debt of gratitude; we can never repay them for all they have done, but we can offer our heartfelt thanks.

Before I finish, I'd like to offer a few final acknowledgments of my own. To Bill James, thanks for sparking my interest in sabermetrics and for supporting my work. To John and Sue, thanks for giving me the opportunity to express myself in print. To Craig Wright, thanks for being a friend from way back. To Luke Kraemer, thanks for hanging in there during a crazy period. To Rollie Loewen and Don Gunning and John Benson, thanks for never saying no when I needed a hand. To Paul Adler, thanks for being the best assistant an editor could have. To Gary Gillette, thanks for your friendship and for your total dedication to this task. To my wife Sharon, thanks for just being there.

And to the scorers, team captains, inputters and other workers of Project Scoresheet, thanks for making all of this possible.

My apologies to anyone I have inadvertently omitted from the above lists.

Don Zminda

A Note from the Editor

This is the second edition of *The Great American Baseball Stat Book* . . . hopefully the second of many. A good number of you bought the inaugural edition last year, and from the comments we've received, most of you seemed to like it. Some of you were thoughtful enough to send suggestions on how to change or improve the book. We appreciate the feedback and, since we like to think of *GABSB* as a fans' book, we've adopted many of those suggestions for this edition.

From your comments we quickly deduced that the most popular part of the book last year was the player essay section. So we've expanded it from 260 players to 338, or thirteen per team. This year we have essays for the eight regulars on each team, the four top pitchers, and one wildcard player. There was one exception to this rule—we felt that none of the Pirate shortstops put in enough playing time to justify an essay, so we substituted one on outfielder R. J. Reynolds. In cases where significant players were traded during the season, we used our own judgment as to which team he made his most important contribution. Thus we included Bill Buckner with the Red Sox and Johnny Ray and Rick Reuschel with the Pirates in counting the thirteen per team. This may cause a bit of grumbling on the part of fans of certain teams, but, believe me, we weren't trying to slight anyone . . . least of all the up-and-coming Pirates.

In response to another of your requests, we're increasing the total number of players for which we offer stats by over 100, to 780. The 442 players who don't receive player essays will have their own section with left/right and home/road breakdowns, both for 1987 and for the 1984-87 period. That should help you make your own personal player evaluations.

Many of you wrote and complained that there were no team essays last year. We agreed, and this year you'll find a section with essays and statistics for each team—one on hitting, one on pitching; there are also stats and commentary for the league hitting and pitching totals. Others wanted some commentary on the managers, so we've got a managers' section this year, one that's bound to stir up a little controversy.

For those of you who feel we neglected the defensive aspect of the game, there's a section compiled by Gary Gillette and Dave Nichols with some new data that should help pinpoint who the best fielders at each position are. Gary and Dave also supplied us with some baserunning figures that should help unlock some of the mysteries of the game.

Of course, including all this new material meant that something had to give; otherwise our book would have been the length of the Manhattan phone directory. We decided, with some regret, to eliminate the player register and its year-by-year breakdowns; most of the material from that section is available from other sources, though not in as much detail as ours. You may miss that section, and rest assured that we do too. We are including complete statistical lines with 1987 and lifetime totals for each of our 750 players; that should at least partially make up for the loss of that section. We're considering running the player register every few years from now on, or maybe even making it into a separate book of its own.

In case you're wondering, we haven't started pulling our punches yet, either. Last year's book was the only major baseball annual to compare Bill Buckner's hitting talent with that of Brooke Shields; this year we compare Donnie Hill with Donny Osmond. And if you're under the impression that the addition of Alfredo Griffin is going to guarantee the Dodgers a pennant, just read what we have to say about him.

We like to think there's a little something for everyone here. The general essay section includes a piece by Brock Hanke which asserts that if Whitey Herzog had come up through today's Cardinal farm system, he would have become an All-Star centerfielder. (Marv Albert's piece asserting that Whitey would have become president of Yale was rejected by our editors.) In another essay Bill Jensen attempts to unlock the mystery of how the Twins won the world championship; among the experts he quotes are Tony Kubek, Billy Martin and Herman Melville. In one of two essays on pitching, Dave Gordon argues, with impressive evidence, that the quality start (or "Johnson Game," as Dave calls it) is a valid measure of pitching excellence; in the other, Merrianna McCully counters with massive evidence of her own indicating that today's starting pitching is just plain lousy. For those of you who stayed awake during math class, there are technical essays by Matt Lieff and Mark Pankin—gee, I always thought "Markov Chains" were what Joaquin Andujar wore around his neck.

And Art Margulis and Robert Merrilees explain how computers in the dugout will soon be enriching Don Zimmer's life.

This is, as I stated before, a fan's book. It's written by fans *for* fans, and though it includes a wealth of statistical evidence, it's also meant to be fun. We hope you'll enjoy it.

Don Zminda

KEY TO ABBREVIATIONS

STATISTICS

PITCHING AND BATTING: G—Games, H—Hits, R—Runs, HR—Home Runs, TBB or BB—Total Bases on Balls, IBB—Intentional Bases on Balls, SO—Strikeouts.

BATTING ONLY: AB—At-Bats, 2B—Doubles, 3B—Triples, TB—Total Bases, RBI—Runs Batted In, HBP—Hit by Pitch, SH—Sacrifice Hits, SF—Sacrifice Flies, SB—Stolen Bases, CS—Caught Stealing, SB%—Stolen Base Percentage [SB/(SB+CS)], GDP or GIDP—Grounded into Double Play, AVE or AVG or BA—Batting Average [H/AB], OBP or OBA—On Base Percentage or On-Base Average [(H+TBB+HBP)/(AB+TBB+HBP+SF)], SLG or SA—Slugging Percentage or Slugging Average (TB/AB).

PITCHING ONLY: GS—Games Started, CG—Complete Games, GF—Games Finished in Relief, IP—Innings Pitched, BFP—Batters Facing Pitcher, ER—Earned Runs, HB—Hit Batsmen, WP—Wild Pitches, Bk—Balks, W—Wins, L—Losses, Pct—Winning Percentage [W/(W+L)], ShO—Shutouts, Sv—Saves, ERA—Earned Run Average [(ER/IP)×9].

FIELDING ONLY: G—Games at Position, PO—Put Outs, A—Assists, E—Errors, TC—Total Chances (PO+A+E), DP—Double Plays, TP—Triple Plays, PCT or FA—Fielding Average [(PO+A)/(TC)], PB—Passed Balls.

TEAMS

ATL—Atlanta
BAL—Baltimore
BOS—Boston
CAL—California
CHA—Chicago (American League)
CHN—Chicago (National League)
CIN—Cincinnati
CLE—Cleveland
DET—Detroit
HOU—Houston
KC—Kansas City
LA—Los Angeles
MIL—Milwaukee
MIN—Minnesota
MON—Montreal
NYA—New York (American League)
NYN—New York (National League)
OAK—Oakland
PHI—Philadelphia
PIT—Pittsburgh
SEA—Seattle
SD—San Diego
SF—San Francisco
SL or STL—St. Louis
TEX—Texas
TOR—Toronto

I

THE PLAYERS

INTRODUCTION

This section contains statistics for 780 players who appeared in the major leagues in 1987. Every batter who played in 15 or more games or who had 40 or more plate appearances in 1987 is included in this section; every pitcher who appeared in 15 or more games or who had 40 or more innings pitched is also included. For 338 of these players, 13 per team (generally the regulars at each position and the most important pitchers), you will find a full page devoted to their exploits, organized as follows:

—A 400–500 word essay, usually about that player
—The player's full name, how he bats and throws, and his date of birth
—The player's 1987 official statistics
—The player's major league career totals
—For pitchers only, their Power/Finesse and Groundball/Flyball classifications for the past four years
—The player's situational statistics for 1987, broken down into various categories (in the left-hand column)
—The player's situational statistical totals for the past four years, 1984–1987 (in the right-hand column)

Following these 338 players comes data for another 442 players. For these 442, the following information is provided:

—The player's full name, how he bats and throws, and his date of birth
—The player's 1987 official statistics
—For pitchers only, their Power or Finesse and Groundball or Flyball classifications for the past four years
—The player's major league career totals
—The player's situational statistics for 1987 for Left/Right breakdowns and Home/Road breakdowns (in the left-hand column)
—The player's situational statistical totals for the past

four years, 1984–1987, for the Left/Right and Home/Road categories (in the right-hand column)

Note that for a small percentage of the 780 players, only two year totals (1986–87) are provided.

Explanations of the categories used for the situational statistics for batters are listed below. A key of abbreviations for statistics used throughout the book can be found on page xiii.

"Vs. Left" and "vs. Right" break the player's statistics down into how he batted against left-handed pitchers and how he batted against right-handed pitchers.

"At Home" and "On Road" break the player's statistics into how he batted in games at his home ballpark and how he batted in games at other team's ballparks.

"Vs. Groundball" and "vs. Flyball" break the player's statistics down into how he batted against pitchers classified as "Groundball" pitchers and how he batted against pitchers classified as "Flyball" pitchers. In order to be classified "Groundball," a pitcher had to have his ratio of ground outs to fly outs be greater than the league ground out/fly out ratio for that season. "Flyball" pitchers are those pitchers whose ground out/fly out ratio is at or below the league average.

"Vs. Finesse" and "vs. Power" break the player's statistics down into how he batted against pitchers classified as "Finesse" pitchers and how he batted against pitchers classified as "Power" pitchers. In order to be classified "Finesse," a pitcher had to be at or below the league average for that season in his total of Walks and Strikeouts per Inning Pitched. "Power" pitchers are those pitchers above the league average in total Walks and Strikeouts per Inning Pitched.

"On Grass" and "On Artificial Turf" break the player's statistics into how he batted in games at ballparks with turf cows can eat and how he batted in games at ballparks with artificial turf that cows can't eat. (Thanks to Dick Allen for this distinction.)

"Day Games" and "Night Games" break down the player's statistics into how he batted in—what else?—games that were played in daylight and games that were played in the dark under artificial light.

The categories labeled with the names of the months break down a player's statistics by the calendar, with all September and October regular-season games being included in the "September-October" line.

The "Bases Empty" line and the two lines under it break down the player's statistics into how he batted when there was no runner on base, further broken down by when he was the first batter in an inning ("Leadoff") and when he was not the first batter in an inning ("Not Leadoff").

The "Runners On Base" line and the two lines under it break down the player's statistics into how he batted when there was a runner or runners on the bases, further broken down by when there was a runner on "First Base Only" and when there was a runner or runners in "Scoring Position" (i.e., on second base and/or third base).

The "Late Innings, Close" line sums up a player's statistics for those instances when he batted in the 7th inning or later with his team ahead by only one run, with the score tied, or with his team behind with the tying run at-bat, on-base or on-deck. This means that the game is always "Close" if his team is behind by only one run, and that the game can never be close if his team is behind by more than five runs. While the definition of a "Close" situation does not change, "Close" situations can change from one at-bat to the next as the score and the number of runners on base change. Essentially, the game is considered "Close" for an at-bat if

it is currently tied, if there is only a one-run difference in the score, or if the team that is currently behind would take the lead, tie the game, or come within one run of tying the game if the batter hit a home run and all runners on base scored.

The "RBI/RBI Opportunities" section at the bottom of the page gives the numbers and percentages of a batter's RBIs in various situations along with the numbers of opportunities he had to drive in runners. First, it breaks down his RBIs into those that drove runners in from second or third base ("Scoring Positon"), then from second or third base with two outs when he batted ("Scoring Position, 2 Out"), then by runners on third base only when he batted with 0 or 1 Out ("On Third, Less than 2 Out"), then by his RBIs in situations which meet the definition of "Close" above, but is not limited to late innings, compared to his total RBIs in all situations ("RBIs in Close Situations/RBI Total"). For example, a single at-bat with the bases loaded and one out would produce the following "RBI Opportunities" by category: two RBI opportunities with runners in scoring position (one for the runner on second base and one for the runner on third base) and one RBI Opportunity for the runner on third base with less than 2 out.

Explanations of the categories used for the situational statistics for pitchers are directly analogous to those for batters. However, a pitcher's statistics section is divided into two parts. The first part shows the traditional pitching statistics for the Home/Road, Grass/Artificial Turf, Day/Night, and Monthly breakdowns. The second part shows how the "Opposing Batters" hit against that pitcher in the various situational categories. Here "vs. Left" shows how left-handed batters hit against that pitcher, and "vs. Right" shows how right-handed batters hit against that pitcher. The "RBI / RBI Opportunities" section is computed for those batters facing that pitcher in the appropriate situation.

Gary Gillette

Mike Aldrete
San Francisco Giants

Sandlot ball in Mike Aldrete's neighborhood must have been exciting, as Mike and Pete Incaviglia grew up on the same block. Not much of a pitchers' league. Aldrete's matinee idol looks and pleasant demeanor belie a very bright Stanford graduate (BA in Communications, Class of '83). In his junior and senior years at Stanford, Mike led the Cardinal to NCAA College World Series berths, driving in 126 runs in 124 games. In the Pioneer League in '83, he hit .417.

In 1984, in the Class A California League, he led the league in total bases (225), slugging (.492), and OBA (.464), was second in hitting (.339), hits (155) and walks (109), was named to *Baseball America*'s Class A All-Star team, and finished with a .994 fielding average at first.

In 1985 he moved up to the AA Texas League, where he finished second in hitting (.333), first in OBA (.447), third in walks (94), fourth in slugging (.512) and fifth in doubles (32). He fielded .992 at first, and committed only 2 errors in 42 games in the outfield. He hit .426 for the month of May.

In 1986, he had 2 stints with the big club. In his second trip up, on July 31, he hit .294, including .354 in 19 games during August, when Danny Gladden was injured, and committed just 1 error.

In 1987, he was the designated "Candy Maldonado." Starting the year as a sub, he filled in magnificently for Maldonado and Leonard. In 29 outfield starts during Candy's DL visit, he hit .330 with 16 RBIs. He hit .348 in his last

36 games, and led the Giants with a .325 average, but was 97 plate appearances short of qualifying. Never, even for a single at-bat, did his average drop below .301. His longest "slump" of the season was an 0-for-8. As a starter, he hit .335, and led the club with a .412 average with men in scoring position.

Make no mistake about it, folks. This man can hit. What probably amazed Giants fans most last year was his ball-hawking defense. He committed only 2 outfield errors and only 1 error at first base. All NL outfielders combined had a Range Factor of 1.90; Aldrete, playing the wings, had a Range Factor of 1.84 on a ball club that was heavily weighted to ground ball pitchers. In addition, he threw out two baserunners in the same inning at New York on May 16. And, of course, his tremendous catch in game 4 of the LCS stole the series momentum for the Giants.

The one rap against Mike thus far is that he hasn't hit many home runs. In the Giant lineup, he hasn't been called on for power, but, rather, for OBA. On August 14, the last day the Giants spent out of first place, Mike had his first 2-homer day. He stroked 9 for the Giants last year, and hit 7 of them to the opposite field, with more at home than on the road. Left field at Candlestick is not home run heaven, so it appears that Mike is learning to drive outside pitches with authority. At age 27, he could be a most valuable member of the Giants for years to come.

Michael Duca

Aldrete, Michael Peter "Mike"   **Bats: Left**   **Throws: Left**   **Born 01/29/61**

1987 SEASON AND MAJOR-LEAGUE CAREER BATTING TOTALS

	G	AB	H	2B	3B	HR	TB	R	RBI	TBB	IBB	SO	HP	SH	SF	SB	CS	SB%	GDP	AVG	OBP	SLG
87 SF	126	357	116	18	2	9	165	50	51	43	5	50	0	4	2	6	0	1.00	6	.325	.396	.462
2 YEARS	210	573	170	36	5	11	249	77	76	76	9	84	2	8	3	7	3	.70	9	.297	.379	.435

	1987 SEASON											FOUR YEAR TOTALS (1984 – 1987)										
	Ave.	OBP	SLG	AB	H	2B	3B	HR	RBI	BB	SO	Ave.	OBP	SLG	AB	H	2B	3B	HR	RBI	BB	SO
Totals	.325	.396	.462	357	116	18	2	9	51	43	50	.297	.379	.435	573	170	36	5	11	76	76	84
vs. Left	.314	.342	.443	70	22	5	2	0	6	3	7	.281	.310	.385	96	27	6	2	0	7	4	13
vs. Right	.328	.407	.467	287	94	13	0	9	45	40	43	.300	.392	.444	477	143	30	3	11	69	72	71
at Home	.335	.421	.506	176	59	7	1	7	25	26	24	.321	.413	.478	293	94	16	3	8	40	46	40
on Road	.315	.370	.420	181	57	11	1	2	26	17	26	.271	.343	.389	280	76	20	2	3	36	30	44
vs. Groundball	.306	.373	.367	147	45	7	1	0	16	17	20	.266	.342	.361	252	67	14	2	2	25	29	38
vs. Flyball	.338	.411	.529	210	71	11	1	9	35	26	30	.321	.408	.492	321	103	22	3	9	51	47	46
vs. Finesse	.333	.397	.422	192	64	9	1	2	23	21	28	.292	.365	.403	318	93	19	2	4	37	35	43
vs. Power	.315	.394	.509	165	52	9	1	7	28	22	22	.302	.396	.475	255	77	17	3	7	39	41	41
on Grass	.306	.390	.442	242	74	10	1	7	33	34	41	.290	.382	.430	407	118	22	4	9	53	60	65
on Artificial Turf	.365	.408	.504	115	42	8	1	2	18	9	9	.313	.373	.446	166	52	14	1	2	23	16	19
Day Games	.294	.370	.441	143	42	9	0	4	19	18	27	.272	.378	.420	243	66	19	1	5	32	41	47
Night Games	.346	.412	.477	214	74	9	2	5	32	25	23	.315	.380	.445	330	104	17	4	6	44	35	37
April	.375	.407	.417	24	9	1	0	0	2	2	5	.375	.407	.417	24	9	1	0	0	2	2	5
May	.333	.393	.392	51	17	3	0	0	6	5	8	.295	.358	.344	61	18	3	0	0	6	6	9
June	.269	.321	.385	26	7	0	0	1	3	2	4	.230	.325	.350	100	23	6	0	2	11	14	16
July	.311	.357	.489	90	28	5	1	3	13	7	12	.286	.356	.457	105	30	7	1	3	13	12	17
August	.352	.416	.527	91	32	5	1	3	14	10	7	.353	.408	.547	139	49	9	3	4	23	13	15
Sept/Oct	.307	.435	.440	75	23	4	0	2	13	17	14	.285	.405	.410	144	41	10	1	2	21	29	22
Bases Empty	.271	.353	.407	214	58	12	1	5	5	27	27	.267	.345	.407	329	88	21	2	7	7	39	44
Leadoff	.259	.315	.388	85	22	5	0	2	2	7	9	.256	.316	.392	125	32	8	0	3	3	11	15
Not Leadoff	.279	.376	.419	129	36	7	1	3	3	20	18	.275	.362	.417	204	56	13	2	4	4	28	29
Runners On	.406	.460	.545	143	58	6	1	4	46	16	23	.336	.420	.471	244	82	15	3	4	69	37	40
First Base Only	.386	.407	.509	57	22	2	1	1	4	2	10	.330	.365	.440	91	30	5	1	1	6	5	16
Scoring Position	.419	.490	.570	86	36	4	0	3	42	14	13	.340	.449	.490	153	52	10	2	3	63	32	24
Late Innings, Close	.293	.349	.448	58	17	3	0	2	9	5	8	.307	.386	.485	101	31	7	1	3	17	13	12

RBI/Opportunities

Scoring Position	38 / 117 (32%)	58 / 229 (25%)
Scoring Position, 2 Out	16 / 53 (30%)	25 / 116 (22%)
On Third, Less than 2 Out	10 / 15 (67%)	17 / 27 (63%)
RBI in close games / RBI Total	32 / 51 (63%)	54 / 76 (71%)

Doyle Alexander
Atlanta Braves/Detroit Tigers

Instead of flying from Atlanta to Detroit after the late season Braves-Tigers trade, Doyle Alexander must have ridden from Georgia to Michigan on a horse named Bucephalus. In the friendly confines of old Tiger Stadium, not-so-friendly Doyle, apparently confusing himself with the legendary Alexander the Great who pitched in the old (Middle) Eastern League, led the team to the divisional title in a torrid race with the frozen blue birds from the Great White North. For a while, in fact, Doyle was clearly the ace of the Tigers' staff, temporarily replacing hard-luck Jack Morris. It's been a long time since any starter in Detroit has been better than Morris.

When the trade was announced to the press, the Detroit brain trust kept talking about how Alexander was a proven winner, a veteran who had an excellent September-October record in the last three years (11–4, 133 IP, 133 H, 37 BB, 2.42 ERA), a guy who had pitched on several championship clubs and in post-season play—blah, blah, blah. *No one could have predicted what Alex would do*, and to his great credit, he candidly admitted as much.

When Alexander was asked in September why he was pitching so awesomely in Detroit, he shrugged and said that he was still the same pitcher, he just had a lot better offensive support, a better defense behind him, and a lot of luck. Unfortunately for those who believe in character, guts, heroic performances and the power of the will, Doyle was right. His performance in Atlanta in 1987 was quite typical of his career:

	G	GS	CG	IP	R	ER	H	HR	TBB	SO	W	L	S	ERA
ATL	16	16	3	117.2	57	54	115	21	27	64	5	10	0	4.13
DET	11	11	3	88.1	16	15	63	3	26	44	11	0	0	1.53

One other key factor, which Doyle mentioned indirectly, is this: Doyle went from one of the best hitter's parks in the majors in Atlanta to one of the better pitcher's parks in the AL in Detroit. Since most everyone still believes that Tiger Stadium is a good hitter's park, it is easy to understand why this would be overlooked. Alexander's indirect reference to the difference in ballparks came in this way: He stated that he was consciously trying to get the hitters to hit straight up the middle in Detroit, because that was the biggest part of the park. What he *didn't* say was that Tiger Stadium's center field is the deepest in the majors (at 440 feet to dead center), and the infield grass in Detroit is high enough to lose Freddie Patek in, and the Tigers' best fielders are located at second, short and center. Pretty smart, huh? Nevertheless, this doesn't make Alexander a better or different pitcher, it just makes him look dramatically better because the circumstances favored him so much.

If there ever was a better example of how circumstances, especially ballparks, mold individual players' performances and statistics in major league baseball, I'd sure as hell like to see it.

Gary Gillette

Alexander, Doyle Lafayette   Bats: Right   Throws: Right   Born 09/04/50

1987 SEASON AND MAJOR-LEAGUE CAREER PITCHING TOTALS

	G	GS	CG	GF	IP	BFP	H	R	ER	HR	SH	SF	HB	TBB	IBB	SO	WP	Bk	W	L	Pct	ShO	Sv	ERA
87 ATL-DET	27	27	6	0	206	821	178	73	69	24	2	3	2	53	5	108	3	0	14	10	.583	3	0	3.01
17 YEARS	494	397	88	56	2915	12200	2871	1301	1186	266	103	78	43	856	50	1307	68	8	174	145	.545	16	3	3.66

1987: Finesse, Flyball   1986: Finesse, Flyball   1985: Finesse, Flyball   1984: Finesse, Flyball

1987 SEASON

	G	IP	H	BB	SO	SB	CS	W	L	S	ERA
Totals	27	206.0	178	53	108	15	8	14	10	0	3.01
at Home	14	108.1	103	33	60	6	5	8	5	0	3.16
on Road	13	97.2	75	20	48	9	3	6	5	0	2.86
on Grass	8	67.0	52	19	31	4	1	4	2	0	2.55
on Artificial Turf	19	139.0	127	34	77	11	7	10	8	0	3.24
Day Games	21	162.0	137	42	84	9	6	12	8	0	2.67
Night Games	6	44.0	41	11	24	6	2	2	2	0	4.30
April	0	0.0	0	0	0	0	0	0	0	0	0.00
May	2	15.0	12	2	9	1	1	1	0	0	3.00
June	6	44.2	40	9	27	0	1	3	3	0	3.43
July	6	44.0	48	14	24	6	2	1	5	0	4.91
August	6	44.1	37	8	18	3	2	3	2	0	3.25
Sept/Oct	7	58.0	41	20	30	5	2	6	0	0	1.09

vs. Opponent Batters	Ave.	OBP	SLG	AB	H	2B	3B	HR	RBI	BB	SO
Totals	.234	.284	.368	761	178	26	2	24	67	53	108
vs. Left	.260	.322	.434	362	94	13	1	16	40	33	44
vs. Right	.211	.249	.308	399	84	13	1	8	27	20	64
Bases Empty	.219	.262	.343	508	111	19	1	14	14	28	70
Leadoff	.222	.255	.325	203	45	4	1	5	5	9	26
Not Leadoff	.216	.267	.354	305	66	15	0	9	9	19	44
Runners On Base	.265	.327	.419	253	67	7	1	10	53	25	38
First Base Only	.250	.284	.414	128	32	4	1	5	12	6	14
Scoring Position	.280	.367	.424	125	35	3	0	5	41	19	24
Late Innings, Close	.368	.442	.647	68	25	2	1	5	14	9	6

FOUR YEAR TOTALS (1984 – 1987)

	G	IP	H	BB	SO	SB	CS	W	L	S	ERA
	133	956.2	939	216	528	52	25	59	36	0	3.43
	72	557.2	517	129	325	26	12	37	17	0	3.03
	61	399.0	422	87	203	26	13	22	19	0	3.97
	48	361.2	337	80	192	22	10	21	15	0	3.11
	85	595.0	603	136	336	30	15	38	21	0	3.63
	65	441.0	462	107	244	28	12	26	20	0	3.76
	68	515.2	477	109	284	24	13	33	16	0	3.14
	15	101.2	91	22	63	3	4	7	1	0	2.83
	19	123.1	143	28	63	6	7	7	4	0	4.89
	23	164.2	172	35	93	3	3	8	9	0	3.55
	24	167.0	183	44	99	15	3	8	12	0	4.26
	25	182.1	176	30	96	12	4	12	6	0	3.55
	27	217.2	174	57	114	13	4	17	4	0	2.07

	Ave.	OBP	SLG	AB	H	2B	3B	HR	RBI	BB	SO
	.256	.298	.397	3662	939	174	20	100	346	216	528
	.265	.318	.420	1833	486	94	5	60	180	141	241
	.248	.277	.373	1829	453	80	15	40	166	75	287
	.255	.294	.394	2270	578	106	14	61	61	125	305
	.246	.277	.386	954	235	39	8	26	26	40	121
	.261	.306	.400	1316	343	67	6	35	35	85	184
	.259	.304	.401	1392	361	68	6	39	285	91	223
	.265	.296	.437	679	180	39	3	24	63	30	92
	.254	.311	.366	713	181	29	3	15	222	61	131
	.295	.338	.501	403	119	17	3	20	56	26	43

RBI/Opportunities

Scoring Position	33 / 165 (20%)
Scoring Position, 2 Out	16 / 85 (19%)
On Third, Less than 2 Out	7 / 22 (32%)
RBI in close games / RBI Total	53 / 67 (79%)

	192 / 917 (21%)
	72 / 425 (17%)
	74 / 153 (48%)
	266 / 346 (77%)

Andy Allanson
Cleveland Indians

Andy Allanson is an object lesson to anyone who believes that all players and teams know what they're doing. At best, he's wasted two years of his career; at worst, he won't have a career after 1988. When Andy reached the majors in 1986, he was the subject of a lot of hype. His boosters claimed that he was a great catcher who, though he didn't have much power, led the Eastern (AA) League in hitting in 1985, had good strike zone judgment and ran well for a backstop. They predicted an excellent future for him. Sensible observers did not. Though he seemed to have many strengths, Allanson's limp bat was an overwhelming weakness. In 890 minor league at-bats, he'd hit 29 doubles, one triple and *no homers*. A man with so little sock would have to be a .300 hitter, draw 80+ walks and play Gold Glove defense in order to be useful; since Andy's career bests were .312 with 52 walks, he was clearly a very long shot.

The furor increased when people saw Allanson in person. At 6' 5" and 220 pounds, he's as tall as and five pounds heavier than Mark McGwire. When asked why he'd never homered as a professional, Andy calmly replied that he never tried to hit homers; that he thought (and his coaches agreed) that his speed, defense and average were all he needed to succeed.

They were wrong. When 1986 began, pitchers treated Andy with the respect that any formidable looking rookie gets. When they saw that his swing produced only weak grounders and pop flies, they began to challenge him. He hit .208 after May 1; that, naturally, began to affect his fielding. He was fourth in the AL with 12 passed balls; his 20 errors were the most for any catcher since 1983. When 1986 ended, even Andy's diehard supporters admitted that he had no hope to succeed in the majors unless he increased his power; only a few thought that he could do it. As the Angels learned with Gary Pettis, players usually can't magically develop a skill that they have never had before.

But, when Rick Dempsey was hurt last year, Andy had to return. He fielded well and—amazingly—was sporting a new swing. He hit nothing but line drives in 1987; when, in September, they finally began falling in, Andy looked very impressive. If he keeps it up, he could be quite a player. So my question is this: If September showed what the real Andy Allanson can do—and, since he's a good athlete (11 steals in 13 tries), it may very well be—then what took him so long to start doing it? Was he truly that naive? Anyway, why didn't someone in the Indians' farm system do anything about it? Even if things all work out in the end, someone has a lot to answer for. If they don't, then new GM Hank Peters should take scalps for the egregious waste of a player with such potential.

Geoff Beckman

Allanson, Andrew Neal "Andy"

Bats: Right   Throws: Right   Born 12/22/61

1987 SEASON AND MAJOR-LEAGUE CAREER BATTING TOTALS

	G	AB	H	2B	3B	HR	TB	R	RBI	TBB	IBB	SO	HP	SH	SF	SB	CS	SB%	GDP	AVG	OBP	SLG
87 CLE	50	154	41	6	0	3	56	17	16	9	0	30	0	4	5	1	1	.50	2	.266	.298	.364
2 YEARS	151	447	107	13	3	4	138	47	45	23	0	66	1	15	9	11	2	.85	9	.239	.273	.309

	1987 SEASON											FOUR YEAR TOTALS (1984 – 1987)										
	Ave.	OBP	SLG	AB	H	2B	3B	HR	RBI	BB	SO	Ave.	OBP	SLG	AB	H	2B	3B	HR	RBI	BB	SO
Totals	.266	.298	.364	154	41	6	0	3	16	9	30	.239	.273	.309	447	107	13	3	4	45	23	66
vs. Left	.277	.309	.362	47	13	4	0	0	7	4	9	.275	.308	.344	131	36	7	1	0	14	8	21
vs. Right	.262	.292	.364	107	28	2	0	3	9	5	21	.225	.258	.294	316	71	6	2	4	31	15	45
at Home	.200	.250	.320	75	15	3	0	2	8	6	13	.225	.262	.297	222	50	6	2	2	24	12	26
on Road	.329	.345	.405	79	26	3	0	1	8	3	17	.253	.284	.320	225	57	7	1	2	21	11	40
vs. Groundball	.240	.269	.360	75	18	3	0	2	7	3	16	.240	.269	.318	192	46	4	1	3	20	8	30
vs. Flyball	.291	.322	.367	79	23	3	0	1	9	6	14	.239	.276	.302	255	61	9	2	1	25	15	36
vs. Finesse	.339	.379	.424	59	20	5	0	0	8	5	6	.268	.305	.339	239	64	10	2	1	27	14	23
vs. Power	.221	.245	.326	95	21	1	0	3	8	4	24	.207	.235	.274	208	43	3	1	3	18	9	43
on Grass	.287	.320	.397	136	39	6	0	3	16	9	27	.244	.278	.309	398	97	11	3	3	42	21	58
on Artificial Turf	.111	.111	.111	18	2	0	0	0	0	0	3	.204	.231	.306	49	10	2	0	1	3	2	8
Day Games	.224	.270	.310	58	13	2	0	1	4	4	11	.235	.279	.294	170	40	5	1	1	14	11	23
Night Games	.292	.314	.396	96	28	4	0	2	12	5	19	.242	.269	.318	277	67	8	2	3	31	12	43
April	.000	.000	.000	0	0	0	0	0	0	0	0	.388	.400	.429	49	19	0	1	0	6	1	2
May	.000	.000	.000	0	0	0	0	0	0	0	0	.203	.239	.281	64	13	3	1	0	4	3	7
June	.000	.000	.000	0	0	0	0	0	0	0	0	.208	.250	.340	53	11	2	1	1	9	3	11
July	.100	.130	.150	20	2	1	0	0	3	1	7	.177	.243	.194	62	11	1	0	0	9	6	9
August	.268	.287	.378	82	22	3	0	2	9	3	15	.217	.237	.295	129	28	4	0	2	9	4	25
Sept/Oct	.327	.379	.423	52	17	2	0	1	4	5	8	.278	.320	.344	90	25	3	0	1	8	6	12
Bases Empty	.306	.330	.412	85	26	3	0	2	2	3	15	.231	.271	.282	234	54	6	0	2	2	13	31
Leadoff	.282	.282	.410	39	11	2	0	1	1	0	5	.284	.298	.343	102	29	3	0	1	1	2	8
Not Leadoff	.326	.367	.413	46	15	1	0	1	1	3	10	.189	.252	.235	132	25	3	0	1	1	11	23
Runners On	.217	.262	.304	69	15	3	0	1	14	6	15	.249	.276	.338	213	53	7	3	2	43	10	35
First Base Only	.393	.433	.607	28	11	3	0	1	2	2	5	.314	.344	.430	86	27	7	0	1	3	4	16
Scoring Position	.098	.160	.098	41	4	0	0	0	12	4	10	.205	.232	.276	127	26	0	3	1	40	6	19
Late Innings, Close	.304	.304	.304	23	7	0	0	0	1	0	4	.328	.338	.391	64	21	2	1	0	4	1	9

RBI/Opportunities

Scoring Position	12 / 61 (20%)	37 / 166 (22%)
Scoring Position, 2 Out	2 / 22 (9%)	14 / 77 (18%)
On Third, Less than 2 Out	10 / 15 (67%)	18 / 31 (58%)
RBI in close games / RBI Total	10 / 16 (63%)	19 / 45 (42%)

Dave Anderson
Los Angeles Dodgers

I was an early subscriber to *Baseball America*, back in the days when it was still called the *All American Baseball News*. The paper, in case you're not familiar with it, covers the minor leagues in great, almost reverent, detail. It also evaluates the top prospects in each organization, usually with a good deal of accuracy. If this publication had been around in the fifties, I might not have spent my childhood thinking Sammy Esposito was a hot prospect.

Back in 1982, when I started reading it, the pages of the *All American Baseball News* were filled with raves about the great L.A. Dodger farm system—especially the club's Triple-A farm team at Albuquerque. Managed by Del Crandall, the Dukes were in the process of winning their fifth straight division championship while compiling a gaudy .313 team batting average, and were loaded with exciting prospects like Mike Marshall, Greg Brock, Candy Maldonado, Orel Hershiser and Sid Fernandez. But the most glittering prospect of all, I was sure, was Dave Anderson. Only 22, Anderson had been the Dodgers' number-one draft choice out of Memphis State University a year earlier. After a half season in A ball, he'd been promoted to the Dukes for '82. And he was performing brilliantly, hitting .343 with 100 runs scored. Best of all, he was a shortstop, and reputed to be an excellent fielder. Anderson was the logical successor to Bill Russell, possibly as soon as 1983.

Anderson did make the big club in '83, as Russell's caddie. The Dodgers didn't mind when he batted only .165 in 115 at bats; the club was winning a division title, and the kid needed to get his feet wet. It was in 1984, the Orwellian year, that things began to get a little shaky. The club went 79-83, and none of those hot Albuquerque prospects was hitting .343, or anywhere near it. Brock was already being looked on as a failure, Marshall wasn't living up to his promise, Maldonado was on the bench, and Fernandez was gone to the Mets, for Carlos Diaz and Bob Bailor. Only Hershiser was having a good year. Anderson? He did replace Russell as the regular, and hit .251. Not horrible, but not what we all expected either.

The Dodgers bounced back in '85, making the playoffs again, but without much help from Anderson. A back injury put him on the disabled list twice, and when he played, he hit .199; Mariano Duncan was suddenly the hot young prospect. In '86 he was hurt again, with a broken finger, but it didn't matter; a .245 average with no power convinced the Dodgers once and for all that Dave was a utility man. So in '87 he filled in, getting into 108 games at second, short and third, and no one was surprised when he only hit .234. His role now seems clear—a fill-in with good speed and a decent glove. Hey, just like Sammy Esposito!

Don Zminda

Anderson, David Carter "Dave"   Bats: Right   Throws: Right   Born 08/01/60

1987 SEASON AND MAJOR-LEAGUE CAREER BATTING TOTALS

	G	AB	H	2B	3B	HR	TB	R	RBI	TBB	IBB	SO	HP	SH	SF	SB	CS	SB%	GDP	AVG	OBP	SLG
87 LA	108	265	62	12	3	1	83	32	13	24	1	43	1	6	1	9	5	.64	2	.234	.299	.313
5 YEARS	459	1191	272	47	7	10	363	150	82	138	10	194	4	23	8	40	18	.69	26	.228	.309	.305

	1987 SEASON											FOUR YEAR TOTALS (1984 – 1987)									
	Ave.	OBP	SLG	AB	H	2B	3B	HR	RBI	BB	SO	Ave.	OBP	SLG	AB	H	2B	3B	HR	RBI	BB	SO
Totals	.234	.299	.313	265	62	12	3	1	13	24	43	.235	.315	.309	1076	253	43	5	9	80	126	180
vs. Left	.250	.316	.333	72	18	2	2	0	6	7	8	.251	.348	.341	334	84	12	3	4	31	49	54
vs. Right	.228	.292	.306	193	44	10	1	1	7	17	35	.228	.300	.295	742	169	31	2	5	49	77	126
at Home	.250	.316	.321	140	35	6	2	0	6	14	24	.253	.331	.309	521	132	16	2	3	34	60	84
on Road	.216	.279	.304	125	27	6	1	1	7	10	19	.218	.301	.310	555	121	27	3	6	46	66	96
vs. Groundball	.248	.315	.333	129	32	5	3	0	8	12	15	.247	.326	.324	490	121	16	5	4	44	58	65
vs. Flyball	.221	.284	.294	136	30	7	0	1	5	12	28	.225	.306	.297	586	132	27	0	5	36	68	115
vs. Finesse	.213	.265	.284	155	33	7	2	0	7	11	18	.233	.304	.307	631	147	24	4	5	46	63	88
vs. Power	.264	.344	.355	110	29	5	1	1	6	13	25	.238	.331	.312	445	106	19	1	4	34	63	92
on Grass	.225	.295	.289	187	42	8	2	0	8	18	32	.229	.314	.294	790	181	26	2	7	49	97	126
on Artificial Turf	.256	.310	.372	78	20	4	1	1	5	6	11	.252	.319	.353	286	72	17	3	2	31	29	54
Day Games	.236	.321	.347	72	17	3	1	1	5	9	17	.235	.325	.329	371	87	21	1	4	28	49	65
Night Games	.233	.290	.301	193	45	9	2	0	8	15	26	.235	.311	.299	705	166	22	4	5	52	77	115
April	.167	.211	.167	18	3	0	0	0	1	1	3	.198	.272	.234	167	33	0	0	2	8	17	27
May	.357	.357	.500	14	5	2	0	0	1	0	0	.286	.337	.385	91	26	7	1	0	7	7	9
June	.265	.330	.434	83	22	5	3	1	3	8	10	.260	.338	.353	235	61	10	3	2	12	28	39
July	.222	.276	.244	90	20	2	0	0	6	7	14	.233	.316	.313	227	53	12	0	2	19	28	43
August	.313	.421	.375	32	10	2	0	0	1	5	7	.253	.348	.348	158	40	9	0	2	14	22	25
Sept/Oct	.071	.161	.107	28	2	1	0	0	1	3	9	.202	.288	.253	198	40	5	1	1	20	24	37
Bases Empty	.202	.285	.277	173	35	6	2	1	1	20	26	.230	.321	.311	643	148	27	2	7	7	86	121
Leadoff	.216	.269	.309	97	21	2	2	1	1	7	13	.213	.300	.299	314	67	14	2	3	3	39	65
Not Leadoff	.184	.303	.237	76	14	4	0	0	0	13	13	.246	.340	.322	329	81	13	0	4	4	47	56
Runners On	.293	.327	.380	92	27	6	1	0	12	4	17	.242	.307	.307	433	105	16	3	2	73	40	59
First Base Only	.395	.409	.581	43	17	6	1	0	4	1	7	.279	.323	.383	183	51	11	1	2	12	12	20
Scoring Position	.204	.259	.204	49	10	0	0	0	8	3	10	.216	.296	.252	250	54	5	2	0	61	28	39
Late Innings, Close	.310	.348	.476	42	13	5	1	0	5	3	9	.247	.324	.338	198	49	13	1	1	19	23	30

RBI/Opportunities

	1987		Four Year	
Scoring Position	8 / 68	(12%)	61 / 359	(17%)
Scoring Position, 2 Out	3 / 27	(11%)	19 / 155	(12%)
On Third, Less than 2 Out	4 / 14	(29%)	31 / 77	(40%)
RBI in close games / RBI Total	7 / 13	(54%)	49 / 80	(61%)

Alan Ashby
Houston Astros

You never know what inspires a ballplayer—put down in this book a year ago, Alan Ashby had the best season of his 15-year career in 1987. He played in more games than ever before (125), with his second most at-bats (386), most hits (111), most homers (14), most runs (53) and RBIs (63), tied for most walks (50) and best batting average (.288). He not only established himself as the regular catcher for the Astros, he was also moved up to the number-four position in the batting order against right-handed pitching.

Ashby suffered a finger injury on September 11. He played in only six games with six more at-bats the rest of the season. However, his hitting had taken a dive after it reached its peak of .310 in mid-August. From August 14 to the end of the season Ashby batted .217, drove in 15 runs (in 20 games), and hit 4 home runs.

Ashby played a major role in keeping the Astros in contention with his hitting until he got tired and injured. Defensively, the opposition appeared to be able to run at will on Alan. The other catchers may have held the opposition running game some, but they made more errors in less games than Ashby. Only Afenir (.300 batting average), up from the minors, showed any potential to hit well. The other catchers batted .203 (Bailey), .167 (Ronn Reynolds), and .103 (Wine). Conventional wisdom holds that, if you want your kid to get to the big leagues, teach him the short-stop's position. Well, since Houston signed Ronn Reynolds as a free agent, despite his having a 5-year batting average *below his weight,* it's clear to me that there is a market for anyone who is willing to don the "tools of ignorance." (Is that why Bobby Wine, the old shortstop, taught his Robbie to be a catcher?)

The Astros need a backup catcher for Ashby next year if they hope to be in contention. Marc Sullivan, with a .200 lifetime average, does not look like the answer. Alan will be 37 next year. While he is coming off his best season ever, the Astros should not count on him for next year, though it appears they will be doing just that. Alan is injury-prone, having missed parts of '83, '84, '85 and '87, and he will need frequent rest. Further, it is unlikely that he can duplicate his 1987 season. He hit way above his career averages. Was it a fluke? Houston fans can only hope Alan finds another year like last year as the search continues for another catcher.

Welford McCaffrey

Ashby, Alan Dean — Bats: Both — Throws: Right — Born 07/08/51

1987 SEASON AND MAJOR-LEAGUE CAREER BATTING TOTALS

	G	AB	H	2B	3B	HR	TB	R	RBI	TBB	IBB	SO	HP	SH	SF	SB	CS	SB%	GDP	AVG	OBP	SLG
87 HOU	125	386	111	16	0	14	169	53	63	50	2	52	1	0	4	0	1	.00	14	.288	.367	.438
15 YEARS	1275	3835	946	172	12	83	1391	374	477	425	63	578	10	53	36	7	10	.41	118	.247	.321	.363

	1987 SEASON											FOUR YEAR TOTALS (1984 – 1987)									
	Ave.	OBP	SLG	AB	H	2B	3B	HR	RBI	BB	SO	Ave.	OBP	SLG	AB	H	2B	3B	HR	RBI	BB	SO
Totals	.288	.367	.438	386	111	16	0	14	63	50	52	.273	.350	.407	1081	295	46	0	33	153	133	157
vs. Left	.255	.318	.277	141	36	3	0	0	10	13	12	.256	.315	.337	403	103	15	0	6	42	36	45
vs. Right	.306	.394	.531	245	75	13	0	14	53	37	40	.283	.370	.448	678	192	31	0	27	111	97	112
at Home	.335	.412	.495	200	67	8	0	8	40	26	29	.286	.363	.402	525	150	25	0	12	79	64	76
on Road	.237	.319	.376	186	44	8	0	6	23	24	23	.261	.338	.412	556	145	21	0	21	74	69	81
vs. Groundball	.308	.376	.465	185	57	5	0	8	38	21	22	.258	.331	.373	520	134	15	0	15	70	58	79
vs. Flyball	.269	.359	.413	201	54	11	0	6	25	29	30	.287	.367	.439	561	161	31	0	18	83	75	78
vs. Finesse	.304	.373	.418	194	59	7	0	5	34	22	23	.295	.358	.427	560	165	23	0	17	79	58	81
vs. Power	.271	.362	.458	192	52	9	0	9	29	28	29	.250	.342	.386	521	130	23	0	16	74	75	76
on Grass	.216	.311	.304	102	22	3	0	2	10	15	16	.250	.332	.375	336	84	9	0	11	41	44	58
on Artificial Turf	.313	.388	.486	284	89	13	0	12	53	35	36	.283	.358	.421	745	211	37	0	22	112	89	99
Day Games	.241	.316	.379	87	21	6	0	2	12	10	16	.258	.352	.408	260	67	9	0	10	37	39	43
Night Games	.301	.382	.455	299	90	10	0	12	51	40	36	.278	.350	.407	821	228	37	0	23	116	94	114
April	.268	.328	.357	56	15	2	0	1	7	5	4	.246	.329	.379	195	48	11	0	5	20	24	22
May	.338	.427	.481	77	26	5	0	2	12	12	6	.283	.385	.399	138	39	7	0	3	19	23	18
June	.250	.372	.528	36	9	1	0	3	8	7	9	.274	.364	.415	135	37	4	0	5	19	19	27
July	.313	.414	.494	83	26	6	0	3	14	14	10	.315	.404	.452	197	62	9	0	6	31	29	26
August	.289	.359	.400	90	26	1	0	3	17	11	16	.284	.339	.368	201	57	8	0	3	28	18	36
Sept/Oct	.205	.217	.364	44	9	1	0	2	5	1	7	.242	.305	.428	215	52	7	0	11	36	20	28
Bases Empty	.301	.379	.471	206	62	8	0	9	9	25	27	.282	.353	.437	579	163	21	0	23	23	63	90
Leadoff	.333	.402	.609	87	29	3	0	7	7	10	12	.280	.340	.476	246	69	6	0	14	14	22	39
Not Leadoff	.277	.363	.370	119	33	5	0	2	2	15	15	.282	.363	.408	333	94	15	0	9	9	41	51
Runners On	.272	.354	.400	180	49	8	0	5	54	25	25	.263	.351	.373	502	132	25	0	10	130	70	67
First Base Only	.240	.305	.293	75	18	4	0	0	2	7	11	.240	.309	.317	221	53	11	0	2	9	22	30
Scoring Position	.295	.386	.476	105	31	4	0	5	52	18	14	.281	.381	.416	281	79	14	0	8	121	48	37
Late Innings, Close	.299	.360	.429	77	23	1	0	3	7	8	11	.253	.326	.387	217	55	5	0	8	28	24	35

RBI/Opportunities

Scoring Position	44 / 152 (29%)	107 / 405 (26%)
Scoring Position, 2 Out	15 / 63 (24%)	36 / 182 (20%)
On Third, Less than 2 Out	17 / 34 (50%)	46 / 87 (53%)
RBI in close games / RBI Total	42 / 63 (67%)	105 / 153 (69%)

Wally Backman
New York Mets

As high as Wally Backman was in 1986, he was just as low in 1987. Doing a flip-flop with Tim Teufel, Backman hit less and played less in 1987, while Teufel hit more and played more. A preponderance of opposition left-handed starters and a nagging hamstring pull kept Wally from ever really getting started in 1987. Luckily for the Mets, Teufel's offense emergence balanced the Backman demise, so that the two second basemen, batting 599 times, still scored 98 runs and drove in 84, with 15 homers, 14 stolen bases and 69 walks. It was a good combination, but mostly because of Teufel.

One adjustment that the opposition made on Wally because of his propensity for slapping the ball to left and centerfields, was for everyone except the first baseman and rightfielder to play him as an opposite field hitter; that deprived him of much of his '86 hit territory. Backman hadn't compensated for this by the time the injuries struck, and his final stats for '87 show it; his average tumbled 70 points from his '86 mark of .320, the second biggest decline in the majors next to Tony Pena. Backman's .250 average was the lowest of his career except for 1983, when he batted only 42 times.

Another sore point in Backman's season was his low walk total. He drew only 26 passes in 335 plate appearances; that, combined with his hitting problems, gave him an on base average of only .309, which is unacceptable even for a middle infielder. Unlike most players, Backman's walk frequency was very high in his early years but has declined (with some fluctuations) as he's gotten older. Backman seems to take fewer pitches when he's in a slump, with disastrous results—he walks less and doesn't help his average, either.

Wally's fielding was only slightly affected by his problems with the bat and if he bounces back, all should be OK. He still doesn't have the greatest range but knows the hitters and anticipates well. Of course, Hernandez at first helps immeasurably.

Backman's traditionally good on base percentage, pesky aggressiveness, and team spirit make him an ideal leadoff or number two hitter but he must rediscover his personal success formula and stay healthy. Teufel had an outstanding year in '87, and Tim generally has hit well against righties; the main reason he's been platooned with Backman has been that Wally has hit righthanders even better. Backman's '87 performance brings that into question, and with young Keith Miller ready to battle for a major league job, Wally could well find himself the odd man out.

Jay Gregory and Don Zminda

Backman, Walter Wayne "Wally" — Bats: Both — Throws: Right — Born 09/22/59

1987 SEASON AND MAJOR-LEAGUE CAREER BATTING TOTALS

	G	AB	H	2B	3B	HR	TB	R	RBI	TBB	IBB	SO	HP	SH	SF	SB	CS	SB%	GDP	AVG	OBP	SLG
87 NYN	94	300	75	6	1	1	86	43	23	25	0	43	0	9	1	11	3	.79	5	.250	.307	.287
8 YEARS	666	2075	581	83	14	7	713	315	148	219	6	286	2	51	10	97	41	.70	35	.280	.348	.344

1987 SEASON

	Ave.	OBP	SLG	AB	H	2B	3B	HR	RBI	BB	SO
Totals	.250	.309	.287	300	75	6	1	1	23	26	43
vs. Left	.086	.179	.086	35	3	0	0	0	2	4	5
vs. Right	.272	.326	.313	265	72	6	1	1	21	22	38
at Home	.284	.322	.314	169	48	5	0	0	15	10	15
on Road	.206	.293	.252	131	27	1	1	1	8	16	28
vs. Groundball	.247	.315	.268	97	24	2	0	0	9	10	13
vs. Flyball	.251	.306	.296	203	51	4	1	1	14	16	30
vs. Finesse	.294	.328	.341	170	50	3	1	1	12	9	15
vs. Power	.192	.286	.215	130	25	3	0	0	11	17	28
on Grass	.272	.315	.309	243	66	6	0	1	18	16	32
on Artificial Turf	.158	.284	.193	57	9	0	1	0	5	10	11
Day Games	.270	.318	.300	100	27	3	0	0	6	7	13
Night Games	.240	.305	.280	200	48	3	1	1	17	19	30
April	.224	.296	.265	49	11	2	0	0	5	5	5
May	.266	.275	.291	79	21	2	0	0	3	1	10
June	.261	.346	.261	23	6	0	0	0	0	3	6
July	.250	.317	.286	56	14	0	1	0	7	6	9
August	.191	.286	.250	68	13	1	0	1	5	9	9
Sept/Oct	.400	.444	.440	25	10	1	0	0	3	2	4
Bases Empty	.201	.258	.250	184	37	4	1	1	1	14	28
Leadoff	.235	.328	.294	51	12	3	0	0	0	7	5
Not Leadoff	.188	.229	.233	133	25	1	1	1	1	7	23
Runners On	.328	.388	.345	116	38	2	0	0	22	12	15
First Base Only	.404	.440	.447	47	19	2	0	0	2	3	4
Scoring Position	.275	.354	.275	69	19	0	0	0	20	9	11
Late Innings, Close	.200	.364	.200	35	7	0	0	0	1	9	5

FOUR YEAR TOTALS (1984 – 1987)

	Ave.	OBP	SLG	AB	H	2B	3B	HR	RBI	BB	SO
Totals	.282	.342	.342	1643	463	67	10	4	114	154	210
vs. Left	.141	.238	.176	256	36	7	1	0	18	32	47
vs. Right	.308	.362	.373	1387	427	60	9	4	96	122	163
at Home	.288	.352	.342	803	231	31	5	1	58	81	91
on Road	.276	.333	.342	840	232	36	5	3	56	73	119
vs. Groundball	.275	.341	.334	716	197	29	5	1	52	73	96
vs. Flyball	.287	.343	.348	927	266	38	5	3	62	81	114
vs. Finesse	.276	.325	.341	927	256	36	9	2	50	68	96
vs. Power	.289	.364	.344	716	207	31	1	2	64	86	114
on Grass	.285	.341	.344	1180	336	46	6	4	85	104	145
on Artificial Turf	.274	.344	.337	463	127	21	4	0	29	50	65
Day Games	.280	.331	.339	626	175	29	4	0	40	50	91
Night Games	.283	.348	.344	1017	288	38	6	4	74	104	119
April	.288	.364	.356	191	55	7	3	0	12	23	20
May	.257	.299	.304	253	65	12	0	0	9	15	36
June	.297	.368	.327	266	79	8	0	0	12	30	29
July	.319	.372	.393	313	100	12	4	1	34	27	39
August	.268	.326	.340	347	93	17	1	2	30	30	42
Sept/Oct	.260	.331	.326	273	71	11	2	1	17	29	44
Bases Empty	.272	.329	.340	1035	282	48	8	2	2	88	134
Leadoff	.286	.339	.368	451	129	28	3	1	1	36	60
Not Leadoff	.262	.322	.318	584	153	20	5	1	1	52	74
Runners On	.298	.366	.345	608	181	19	2	2	112	66	76
First Base Only	.322	.374	.371	264	85	8	1	1	9	22	22
Scoring Position	.279	.360	.326	344	96	11	1	1	103	44	54
Late Innings, Close	.290	.370	.337	252	73	7	1	1	21	32	34

RBI/Opportunities

Scoring Position	20 / 94	(21%)
Scoring Position, 2 Out	11 / 39	(28%)
On Third, Less than 2 Out	6 / 14	(43%)
RBI in close games / RBI Total	13 / 23	(57%)

100 / 480	(21%)
45 / 215	(21%)
36 / 77	(47%)
71 / 114	(62%)

Scott Bailes
Cleveland Indians

The secret to breaking into the Cleveland rotation this year was to first fail in the bullpen. Due to that unique application of the Peter Principle, Scott Bailes really had three phases to his 1987. In phase one, he had five starts, pitched 28.2 innings, compiled a 2.82 ERA and left the game with a lead four times. But, thanks to the bullpen, his record was only 1–0; Cleveland lost four of his five games.

For that reason, Indians' manager Pat Corrales decided to move Scott to the bullpen (which had been his home for most of 1986) and insert Steve Carlton into the rotation. The brilliance of this decision may be best illustrated by the following facts:

1. In the previous two years, Carlton had been released by four teams (Philadelphia twice, Chicago and San Francisco), each of whom badly needed starters;

2. Carlton was 2–2, had a 4.91 ERA, had allowed 17 hits in 18.1 innings and boasted a .64–1 K/W ratio (11 walks, 7 whiffs);

3. Scott had the lowest ERA on the team;

4. In 1986, Bailes had as many relief losses as saves. He'd saved only seven games in 23 save opportunities. In the 36 games he entered with either Cleveland ahead or the score tied, he had allowed the tying run to score 15 times;

5. Carlton was 42 while Scott was only 25.

This unique move produced unique results: Corrales simultaneously weakened both the rotation and the bullpen. Carlton went 3–7 with a sparkling 5.46 ERA, allowing 94 hits, 52 walks and 13 homers in 90.2 IP. Bailes, after allowing no earned runs in 12 of his first 13 appearances, began getting hammered; in his last seven outings, he allowed 10 runs and 19 hits in eight innings. His 1987 stats in relief: 22 games, 2–1, six saves, 38 hits in 27 innings, 4.50 ERA.

At that point, Bailes moved back into the rotation, where he made 12 more starts. For the second year in a row, his arm simply couldn't handle the strain of switching gears. In his first six starts, Scott didn't pitch well (41 hits in 37.1 IP, 1–1, 4.58), but that was nothing compared to his final six starts: 41 hits, 12 walks and eight homers allowed in 26.1 innings; a 2–4 record and a 6.84 ERA. As he had done in 1986, Bailes spent the final weeks of the season on the sidelines.

After two years of careful testing, Cleveland has definitively proven that Scott Bailes's arm will fall off if asked to serve both as relief ace and rotation starter in the same year. One hopes that, in 1988, they will avoid repeating the experiment and allow Scott a fair chance to win the 13–17 games that many observers believe that he could win as a starter.

Bill Murphy and Jim Shaarda

Bailes, Scott Alan   Bats: Left   Throws: Left   Born 12/18/61

1987 SEASON AND MAJOR-LEAGUE CAREER PITCHING TOTALS

	G	GS	CG	GF	IP	BFP	H	R	ER	HR	SH	SF	HB	TBB	IBB	SO	WP	Bk	W	L	Pct	ShO	Sv	ERA
87 CLE	39	17	0	15	120	551	145	75	62	21	4	6	4	47	1	65	3	0	7	8	.467	0	6	4.65
2 YEARS	101	27	0	37	233	1051	268	145	124	33	11	10	5	90	6	125	7	2	17	18	.486	0	13	4.79

1987: Finesse, Flyball   1986: Finesse, Groundball

		1987 SEASON											FOUR YEAR TOTALS (1984 – 1987)										
	G	IP	H	BB	SO	SB	CS	W	L	S	ERA		G	IP	H	BB	SO	SB	CS	W	L	S	ERA
Totals	39	120.1	145	47	65	4	4	7	8	6	4.71		101	233.0	268	90	125	11	5	17	18	13	4.83
at Home	18	53.0	72	21	36	1	3	3	5	2	5.43		49	116.0	130	43	63	5	4	8	10	6	4.81
on Road	21	67.1	73	26	29	3	1	4	3	4	4.14		52	117.0	138	47	62	6	1	9	8	7	4.85
on Grass	14	48.1	65	18	37	2	1	3	4	1	4.84		37	91.0	108	34	64	5	1	10	6	4	4.15
on Artificial Turf	25	72.0	80	29	28	2	3	4	4	5	4.63		64	142.0	160	56	61	6	4	7	12	9	5.26
Day Games	32	91.1	115	33	52	4	4	5	7	6	5.03		83	194.2	226	71	103	10	5	15	16	12	4.95
Night Games	7	29.0	30	14	13	0	0	2	1	0	3.72		18	38.1	42	19	22	1	0	2	2	1	4.23
April	5	24.1	21	15	14	1	0	1	0	0	2.22		15	40.1	38	23	28	1	0	4	1	2	3.35
May	10	15.1	14	4	8	2	0	1	0	2	2.35		25	28.2	31	9	15	4	0	3	3	4	3.45
June	9	12.0	21	2	11	0	0	0	1	4	8.25		21	27.2	38	9	19	1	0	2	1	6	6.18
July	7	28.2	35	8	10	1	2	1	3	0	5.97		17	39.2	45	12	15	2	2	2	5	1	4.99
August	6	32.2	42	14	21	0	1	3	3	0	4.41		16	67.0	75	27	36	1	2	4	5	0	4.43
Sept/Oct	2	7.1	12	4	1	0	1	1	1	0	8.59		7	29.2	41	10	12	2	1	2	3	0	7.58

vs. Opponent Batters	Ave.	OBP	SLG	AB	H	2B	3B	HR	RBI	BB	SO		Ave.	OBP	SLG	AB	H	2B	3B	HR	RBI	BB	SO
Totals	.296	.358	.484	490	145	23	3	21	69	47	65		.287	.350	.449	935	268	45	4	33	144	90	125
vs. Left	.276	.324	.398	98	27	0	0	4	18	6	17		.288	.343	.414	215	62	6	0	7	48	17	34
vs. Right	.301	.367	.505	392	118	23	3	17	51	41	48		.286	.352	.460	720	206	39	4	26	96	73	91
Bases Empty	.329	.389	.570	258	85	14	3	14	14	23	30		.308	.367	.493	477	147	23	4	19	19	42	63
Leadoff	.309	.392	.536	110	34	6	2	5	5	15	11		.301	.363	.476	206	62	8	2	8	8	20	25
Not Leadoff	.345	.386	.595	148	51	8	1	9	9	8	19		.314	.369	.506	271	85	15	2	11	11	22	38
Runners On Base	.259	.326	.388	232	60	9	0	7	55	24	35		.264	.333	.404	458	121	22	0	14	125	48	62
First Base Only	.270	.323	.400	115	31	6	0	3	8	9	18		.229	.286	.336	223	51	9	0	5	13	18	34
Scoring Position	.248	.329	.376	117	29	3	0	4	47	15	17		.298	.374	.468	235	70	13	0	9	112	30	28
Late Innings, Close	.286	.311	.378	98	28	3	0	2	16	4	13		.284	.337	.374	243	69	13	0	3	43	20	38

RBI/Opportunities

Scoring Position	39 / 166 (23%)		90 / 344 (26%)
Scoring Position, 2 Out	20 / 83 (24%)		41 / 157 (26%)
On Third, Less than 2 Out	13 / 29 (45%)		32 / 68 (47%)
RBI in close games / RBI Total	45 / 69 (65%)		89 / 144 (62%)

Harold Baines
Chicago White Sox

Harold Baines is famed for never changing his expression, but last year I caught him doing it twice. May 20, against Milwaukee, 8th inning: 2 on, 2 out, and Baines has a chance get the Sox back into the game. Juan Nieves throws three straight breaking pitches in the dirt, and Harold chases all of them. He's in the midst of a bad slump, and after he fans, he winces. Ever so slightly.

The second time comes on July 22, against Baltimore, 3rd inning: Baines rips Mike Boddicker's 2–0 pitch into the center field bullpen. It's his 155th career homer, a new all-time White Sox record. Baines impassively circles the bases, but when he reaches the dugout he smiles. Broadly.

Last year White Sox fans discovered that Harold Baines is human. How much of this came from his knee trouble? Maybe the fans needed to see a little flaw to take him to their hearts as one of their own. Maybe Harold needed to struggle a little more to see why we wince when overmatched in failure and smile in those moments where we triumph.

In September 1986, Baines hurt his knee, requiring arthroscopic surgery during the off-season. In spring training he seemed far from fully recovered, and sure enough, on Opening Day he hurt it again. More surgery followed, and when he came back, he was a different ballplayer. He couldn't play in the field and he couldn't run very well. Still, he adjusted, and had a typical Harold Baines season with a strong finish. We may see more of the same in 1988 as he had to have more off-season arthroscopic work.

Don Zminda

Harold returned to a tough situation after his in-season knee surgery. The White Sox promptly lost seven straight—so much for the return of a star inspiring a team to win. For most of the year Baines ended up being Chicago's designated hitter, which I think confused the rest of the Sox who seemed to think Harold was supposed to do *all* the hitting for the club.

As far as I can tell, Baines spent his time on the disabled list well. Maybe he read Ted William's book on hitting or perhaps he picked up a copy of last year's *GABSB* book and saw the proof that his impatience at the plate was his most significant weakness. Whatever the case, even though he missed 30 games, he drew 44 non-intentional walks. Percentage-wise, it was the best walk average of his career. Not coincidentally, he had the second best on-base average of his career and his third best slugging percentage. If Baines has indeed learned to be more patient at the plate, and if his knee trouble is brought under control, he may well have his best season yet in 1988.

Andrew Berman

Baines, Harold Douglass   Bats: Left   Throws: Left   Born 03/15/59

1987 SEASON AND MAJOR-LEAGUE CAREER BATTING TOTALS

	G	AB	H	2B	3B	HR	TB	R	RBI	TBB	IBB	SO	HP	SH	SF	SB	CS	SB%	GDP	AVG	OBP	SLG
87 CHA	132	505	148	26	4	20	242	59	93	46	2	82	1	0	2	0	0	.00	12	.293	.352	.479
8 YEARS	1124	4259	1225	208	42	160	1997	551	682	309	62	621	8	8	47	29	18	.62	109	.288	.334	.469

	1987 SEASON											FOUR YEAR TOTALS (1984 – 1987)										
	Ave.	OBP	SLG	AB	H	2B	3B	HR	RBI	BB	SO	Ave.	OBP	SLG	AB	H	2B	3B	HR	RBI	BB	SO
Totals	.293	.352	.479	505	148	26	4	20	93	46	82	.301	.350	.488	2284	688	112	19	92	388	179	335
vs. Left	.254	.308	.409	181	46	8	1	6	25	13	45	.286	.324	.436	802	229	30	8	25	107	46	143
vs. Right	.315	.376	.519	324	102	18	3	14	68	33	37	.310	.363	.516	1482	459	82	11	67	281	133	192
at Home	.312	.353	.538	253	79	15	3	12	52	16	37	.313	.357	.515	1104	345	57	10	49	212	82	145
on Road	.274	.351	.421	252	69	11	1	8	41	30	45	.291	.342	.462	1180	343	55	9	43	176	97	190
vs. Groundball	.274	.326	.430	263	72	15	1	8	49	21	45	.307	.352	.484	1069	328	52	7	41	182	77	140
vs. Flyball	.314	.379	.533	242	76	11	3	12	44	25	37	.296	.348	.491	1215	360	60	12	51	206	102	195
vs. Finesse	.317	.353	.544	281	89	19	3	13	55	17	34	.316	.353	.537	1302	411	75	12	63	246	84	151
vs. Power	.263	.350	.397	224	59	7	1	7	38	29	48	.282	.345	.423	982	277	37	7	29	142	95	184
on Grass	.297	.351	.484	438	130	22	3	18	84	37	72	.305	.355	.486	1939	592	97	14	75	334	155	287
on Artificial Turf	.269	.355	.448	67	18	4	1	2	9	9	10	.278	.320	.499	345	96	15	5	17	54	24	48
Day Games	.276	.344	.400	145	40	7	1	3	21	15	28	.294	.347	.460	656	193	33	5	22	105	57	109
Night Games	.300	.355	.511	360	108	19	3	17	72	31	54	.304	.351	.499	1628	495	79	14	70	283	122	226
April	.500	.600	.750	4	2	1	0	0	2	1	0	.253	.303	.418	225	57	7	0	10	36	16	33
May	.298	.366	.440	84	25	3	0	3	17	9	21	.274	.328	.405	380	104	18	1	10	52	31	52
June	.263	.354	.535	99	26	2	2	7	17	13	11	.310	.376	.508	413	128	18	5	18	75	43	56
July	.343	.400	.571	105	36	6	0	6	22	10	16	.324	.381	.522	408	132	26	2	17	74	38	65
August	.196	.255	.299	97	19	5	1	1	15	8	18	.305	.341	.526	430	131	19	8	20	77	24	63
Sept/Oct	.345	.369	.517	116	40	9	1	3	20	5	16	.318	.357	.507	428	136	24	3	17	74	27	66
Bases Empty	.260	.318	.377	289	75	9	2	7	7	25	47	.278	.326	.437	1261	351	56	9	42	42	89	189
Leadoff	.242	.299	.263	99	24	2	0	0	0	8	14	.269	.315	.382	398	107	16	4	7	7	27	54
Not Leadoff	.268	.329	.437	190	51	7	2	7	7	17	33	.283	.331	.462	863	244	40	5	35	35	62	135
Runners On	.338	.396	.616	216	73	17	2	13	86	21	35	.329	.384	.550	1023	337	56	10	50	346	90	146
First Base Only	.321	.360	.631	84	27	8	0	6	17	4	14	.340	.371	.568	435	148	25	4	22	59	20	53
Scoring Position	.348	.417	.606	132	46	9	2	7	69	17	21	.321	.392	.537	588	189	31	6	28	287	70	93
Late Innings, Close	.308	.372	.410	78	24	3	1	1	8	7	14	.297	.370	.497	330	98	16	1	16	53	37	47

RBI/Opportunities

Scoring Position	59 / 171 (35%)	236 / 774 (30%)
Scoring Position, 2 Out	18 / 65 (28%)	79 / 313 (25%)
On Third, Less than 2 Out	26 / 39 (67%)	103 / 177 (58%)
RBI in close games / RBI Total	58 / 93 (62%)	253 / 388 (65%)

Floyd Bannister
Chicago White Sox

Floyd Bannister was a nice surprise in 1987. Best known for his inconsistency, he actually did quite well after his 1986 performance when he had the league's 9th best ERA (3.54). That's Floyd for you—he's not even predictably inconsistent. Does anyone have any real feeling for what he will do in 1988?

It's easy to see where the good seasons come from. Since he first came up in 1977 with the Astros, he had a label of "unlimited potential." A lot of players with that tag never develop into superstars, but usually a fastball in the 90's with good control is enough to send any pitcher over the top. What's so frustrating is that Bannister bounces in and out of that zone all the time. When he first came to the White Sox in 1983, he was 3–9 in the first half and 13–1 in the second half of the season.

For those of us who thought he had put it together, the next two years were a shock. In 1984–85 he was 14–11 and 10–14 with ERA's of 4.83 and 4.87, not exactly superstar material. About the best you could say about him was he went out there every day, even though you never knew what you were going to get. Then he turned in his 3.54 ERA in 1986, and even then he could have done much better if he hadn't fallen apart for a two-month period in the middle of the season (5.66 ERA in June and July).

Almost everybody has a theory as to why he is so inconsistent. There is no doubt he is at his best when his control is sharp (under three walks per 9 innings). In his brilliant finish in 1987, his walk average was just 1.2/9 IP from August on. But why does his command come and go? My pet theory is he simply has imperfect concentration on the mound. Sometimes he focuses too hard and tries to aim the ball, which actually seems to make him wilder. Sometimes he makes a mistake, or somebody behind him makes an error, and he becomes distracted. Then there are days when everything goes perfectly and his opponents are lucky to score a run off of him.

He had a lot of those moments in September when only Doyle Alexander could keep him from Pitcher of the Month honors. I can imagine Kansas City fans celebrating his acquisition. I hope for his sake that he has at long last found his holy grail of consistency, but I, for one, am not sorry to see him leave Chicago. Who knows? In that ball park he might win 20 games; he also might go something like 11–14, with a 4.70 ERA. Yeah, I know he was 4–7 with a 4.58 ERA in the first half versus 12–4, 2.71, in the second half, but I also remember what happened after 1983. I don't want to go through that kind of disappointment again.

Andrew Berman

Bannister, Floyd Franklin

Bats: Left   Throws: Left   Born 06/10/55

1987 SEASON AND MAJOR-LEAGUE CAREER PITCHING TOTALS

	G	GS	CG	GF	IP	BFP	H	R	ER	HR	SH	SF	HB	TBB	IBB	SO	WP	Bk	W	L	Pct	ShO	Sv	ERA
87 CHA	34	34	11	0	229	939	216	100	91	38	9	3	0	49	0	124	5	1	16	11	.593	2	0	3.58
11 YEARS	334	318	60	3	2061	8771	1987	1008	911	253	66	50	31	729	24	1529	73	7	117	128	.478	16	0	3.98

1987: Finesse, Flyball   1986: Finesse, Flyball   1985: Power, Flyball   1984: Power, Flyball

1987 SEASON

	G	IP	H	BB	SO	SB	CS	W	L	S	ERA
Totals	34	228.2	216	49	124	12	4	16	11	0	3.58
at Home	15	91.2	99	27	53	7	3	6	5	0	3.93
on Road	19	137.0	117	22	71	5	1	10	6	0	3.35
on Grass	7	52.1	32	10	38	2	1	4	2	0	2.58
on Artificial Turf	27	176.1	184	39	86	10	3	12	9	0	3.88
Day Games	27	182.0	174	42	98	11	3	13	9	0	3.36
Night Games	7	46.2	42	7	26	1	1	3	2	0	4.44
April	4	24.2	25	5	15	1	1	1	1	0	4.74
May	6	38.0	35	12	19	2	0	2	2	0	2.84
June	5	29.2	35	9	13	2	1	0	4	0	7.89
July	6	41.0	41	10	18	1	0	3	1	0	2.20
August	6	41.2	42	7	14	4	2	4	2	0	4.75
Sept/Oct	7	53.2	38	6	45	2	0	6	1	0	1.34

vs. Opponent Batters	Ave.	OBP	SLG	AB	H	2B	3B	HR	RBI	BB	SO
Totals	.246	.285	.426	878	216	34	5	38	88	49	124
vs. Left	.248	.324	.388	121	30	6	1	3	8	14	18
vs. Right	.246	.278	.432	757	186	28	4	35	80	35	106
Bases Empty	.245	.284	.446	572	140	21	5	28	28	31	80
Leadoff	.225	.274	.360	222	50	6	0	8	8	15	33
Not Leadoff	.257	.290	.500	350	90	15	5	20	20	16	47
Runners On Base	.248	.287	.389	306	76	13	0	10	60	18	44
First Base Only	.280	.303	.447	150	42	7	0	6	15	5	16
Scoring Position	.218	.273	.333	156	34	6	0	4	45	13	28
Late Innings, Close	.236	.276	.431	72	17	3	1	3	4	4	10

FOUR YEAR TOTALS (1984 – 1987)

	G	IP	H	BB	SO	SB	CS	W	L	S	ERA
Totals	130	822.2	800	277	566	51	26	50	50	0	4.22
at Home	59	389.1	353	138	288	27	14	22	21	0	3.72
on Road	71	433.1	447	139	278	24	12	28	29	0	4.67
on Grass	31	192.1	170	73	132	13	7	10	14	0	4.16
on Artificial Turf	99	630.1	630	204	434	38	19	40	36	0	4.25
Day Games	106	678.1	654	233	470	42	23	38	44	0	4.13
Night Games	24	144.1	146	44	96	9	3	12	6	0	4.68
April	17	104.0	109	38	54	2	5	4	8	0	4.76
May	22	133.2	115	58	100	10	3	7	8	0	3.50
June	16	88.2	104	33	63	7	6	4	7	0	6.19
July	24	160.1	149	58	97	12	3	9	8	0	3.76
August	24	158.2	155	42	116	9	5	12	9	0	4.48
Sept/Oct	27	177.1	168	48	136	11	4	14	10	0	3.70

vs. Opponent Batters	Ave.	OBP	SLG	AB	H	2B	3B	HR	RBI	BB	SO
Totals	.254	.314	.424	3145	800	149	20	115	373	277	566
vs. Left	.258	.325	.427	515	133	30	3	17	64	51	88
vs. Right	.254	.312	.424	2630	667	119	17	98	309	226	478
Bases Empty	.251	.304	.420	1939	486	90	14	70	70	149	348
Leadoff	.257	.308	.413	806	207	37	4	27	27	60	141
Not Leadoff	.246	.301	.425	1133	279	53	10	43	43	89	207
Runners On Base	.260	.331	.431	1206	314	59	6	45	303	128	218
First Base Only	.303	.357	.487	542	164	33	2	21	56	46	77
Scoring Position	.226	.310	.386	664	150	26	4	24	247	82	141
Late Innings, Close	.286	.357	.459	220	63	10	2	8	30	24	37

RBI/Opportunities

Scoring Position	37 / 194 (19%)	198 / 893 (22%)
Scoring Position, 2 Out	14 / 98 (14%)	64 / 400 (16%)
On Third, Less than 2 Out	15 / 33 (45%)	86 / 154 (56%)
RBI in close games / RBI Total	64 / 88 (73%)	286 / 373 (77%)

Jesse Barfield
Toronto Blue Jays

Toronto was disappointed by Jesse Barfield's 1987, but only because they expected that he would have an MVP-like season—which he had in 1986 and George Bell had in 1987—this year. It seemed to be a reasonable expectation in spring. 1987 was the first year in his career that Barfield failed to match or top his career high in batting average; he'd set career bests in both on-base and slugging percentages for the last two years.

There are three explanations for Barfield's 1987. First, for the first time since 1982, Barfield's stats against righties did not improve. In fact, his average against northpaws fell 43 points—back to his 1983 level. Also, in the past, Barfield has always had at least one torrid streak, where he hit a dozen homers in ten days and carried the team on his back; that didn't happen this year. Third, he's almost always had his best months in July and August and his worst months in April and September. This year he had a terrific start and trailed off after the break.

Another "disappointing" area for Barfield in 1987 was his defense. Though only one rightfielder (Devon White) had more total chances and only Ruben Sierra had as many assists, Jesse did make some uncharacteristic lapses this season. Nobody begrudged his misplayed single on June 15, which resulted in a 2–1 loss to Detroit (not then at least). But careful observers did notice that it wasn't an isolated mistake. Two errors in back-to-back games in Kansas City in late June helped extend a Toronto losing streak to eight games. Several days before, during a 15–14 loss to New York, Ron Kittle (!) had hit an inside-the-park homer to right field. Jesse appeared to be having trouble seeing the ball; he let a number of extra-base clouts rattle around in the corner.

But whatever was the problem didn't last long. Barfield, who always practices his fielding—he's not one of those men who shags lazy flies and casually lobs the ball in—bore down with a vengeance. The lapses disappeared by the break.

Two minor surprises in Barfield's season were his RBI stats (84 is a bit low for a man with 56 extra-base hits) and walks (down about 10 from 1985 and 1986). Neither should be too surprising. As Jesse's average dropped, he batted lower in the order. With fewer men on base when he batted, he had fewer RBI chances; while he was trying to bring up his average, he became a bit less patient.

Every player is entitled to one off-year; given his past, there's no reason that Barfield can't snap back and go 40, 110, .300 in 1988. But even if he doesn't, 28 homers and 84 RBIs isn't exactly a lousy year. In the 11-year history of the Toronto Blue Jays, a player has hit 25+ homers and had 80+ RBIs only 11 times. Barfield has four of those seasons.

Mike FitzGerald, Tony Formo and John Stryker

Barfield, Jesse Lee　　　　　　Bats: Right　　Throws: Right　　Born 10/29/59

1987 SEASON AND MAJOR-LEAGUE CAREER BATTING TOTALS

	G	AB	H	2B	3B	HR	TB	R	RBI	TBB	IBB	SO	HP	SH	SF	SB	CS	SB%	GDP	AVG	OBP	SLG
87 TOR	159	590	155	25	3	28	270	89	84	58	7	141	3	1	2	3	5	.38	13	.263	.331	.458
7 YEARS	874	2915	789	137	22	156	1438	460	460	296	25	719	25	9	18	48	35	.58	60	.271	.341	.493

	1987 SEASON												FOUR YEAR TOTALS (1984 – 1987)										
	Ave.	OBP	SLG	AB	H	2B	3B	HR	RBI	BB	SO		Ave.	OBP	SLG	AB	H	2B	3B	HR	RBI	BB	SO
Totals	.263	.331	.458	590	155	25	3	28	84	58	141		.281	.356	.509	2038	572	108	15	109	325	228	511
vs. Left	.299	.380	.525	177	53	9	2	9	21	23	43		.302	.384	.513	719	217	43	5	33	106	98	181
vs. Right	.247	.309	.429	413	102	16	1	19	63	35	98		.269	.340	.506	1319	355	65	10	76	219	130	330
at Home	.305	.371	.487	302	92	18	2	11	39	31	59		.290	.366	.526	1014	294	65	9	52	173	120	243
on Road	.219	.288	.427	288	63	7	1	17	45	27	82		.271	.346	.492	1024	278	43	6	57	152	108	268
vs. Groundball	.303	.360	.527	277	84	13	2	15	46	23	56		.301	.373	.522	929	280	48	8	47	155	101	220
vs. Flyball	.227	.306	.396	313	71	12	1	13	38	35	85		.263	.342	.498	1109	292	60	7	62	170	127	291
vs. Finesse	.270	.335	.464	330	89	12	2	16	42	32	60		.273	.344	.502	1142	312	52	10	63	174	118	247
vs. Power	.254	.325	.450	260	66	13	1	12	42	26	81		.290	.372	.518	896	260	56	5	46	151	110	264
on Grass	.230	.302	.482	222	51	5	0	17	42	23	63		.275	.357	.509	763	210	29	4	47	126	92	192
on Artificial Turf	.283	.348	.443	368	104	20	3	11	42	35	78		.284	.355	.509	1275	362	79	11	62	199	136	319
Day Games	.279	.357	.498	215	60	10	2	11	30	26	52		.268	.352	.474	713	191	42	6	31	107	86	179
Night Games	.253	.316	.435	375	95	15	1	17	54	32	89		.288	.358	.528	1325	381	66	9	78	218	142	332
April	.282	.407	.577	71	20	6	0	5	10	14	16		.244	.310	.442	283	69	17	0	13	34	26	76
May	.268	.349	.505	97	26	2	0	7	14	11	23		.295	.371	.563	336	99	16	1	24	61	40	76
June	.304	.328	.536	112	34	3	1	7	25	5	25		.286	.342	.497	350	100	12	4	18	71	31	81
July	.230	.313	.320	100	23	3	0	2	10	11	25		.290	.375	.545	334	97	19	3	20	52	44	82
August	.173	.229	.398	98	17	2	1	6	13	7	31		.292	.373	.512	346	101	24	5	14	55	45	92
Sept/Oct	.313	.369	.438	112	35	9	1	1	12	10	21		.272	.343	.488	389	106	20	2	20	52	42	104
Bases Empty	.267	.321	.495	329	88	13	1	20	20	24	86		.281	.342	.534	1147	322	56	9	72	72	104	294
Leadoff	.261	.286	.478	115	30	5	1	6	6	4	29		.274	.326	.518	452	124	22	2	28	28	35	108
Not Leadoff	.271	.339	.505	214	58	8	0	14	14	20	57		.285	.351	.544	695	198	34	7	44	44	69	186
Runners On	.257	.342	.410	261	67	12	2	8	64	34	55		.281	.368	.477	891	250	52	6	37	253	124	217
First Base Only	.287	.336	.454	108	31	7	1	3	10	7	22		.307	.355	.514	362	111	28	4	13	42	26	87
Scoring Position	.235	.346	.379	153	36	5	1	5	54	27	33		.263	.377	.452	529	139	24	2	24	211	98	130
Late Innings, Close	.267	.333	.376	101	27	5	0	2	16	9	20		.274	.341	.452	354	97	17	2	14	56	35	81

RBI/Opportunities

	1987		FOUR YEAR	
Scoring Position	45 / 206	(22%)	169 / 733	(23%)
Scoring Position, 2 Out	17 / 90	(19%)	63 / 312	(20%)
On Third, Less than 2 Out	16 / 37	(43%)	64 / 152	(42%)
RBI in close games / RBI Total	48 / 84	(57%)	199 / 325	(61%)

Marty Barrett
Boston Red Sox

Q: What do Marty Barrett, Robin Yount, Tommy Herr, Larry Bowa, Buddy Bell, Bucky Dent and Horace Clarke all have in common?

A: Of the 24 infielders (first basemen excluded) who have led their league in both chances per game and fielding percentage in the same season since the Gold Glove awards began in 1957, they are the only ones who did not win the award that year.

That is just one of the many intriguing questions surrounding the hard-headed, soft-handed Boston second baseman, whom many feel deserves Gold Glove consideration. Here is another:

Q: True or false: Over the last four years, Barrett has played nine fewer games than the combined totals of the American League Gold Glove winners in that span. He has made 17 less putouts. He has also made 68 more assists, committed 3 less errors and turned 25 more double plays.

A: True. In that span, Barrett made 2.079 putouts per game; the gold glovers made 2.084. Barrett averaged 3.04 assists per game; the gold glovers averaged 2.88. Barrett turned 107 DPs per 162 games; the gold glovers turned 99. Barrett made 43 errors; the gold glovers made 46.

Despite playing behind a staff that struck out 1034 batters (fifth in the American League), Barrett's 5.53 C/G figure was the best in the majors. He was involved in 28 percent of the outs where the batter put the ball in play against the Red Sox this year. In the last four years, his errors have resulted in only 22 unearned runs.

A wrist injury, which forced Marty to miss virtually all of spring training and forced him to spend time on the disabled list for the first time in his career, hampered his offensive performance for the first several months of the season. But, when healthy, Marty was very offensive indeed. He batted .325 after June 1; only four other players (Tony Gwynn, Alan Trammell, Kevin Seitzer and Robin Yount) collected more hits than he did in that period.

Perhaps it was because Boston didn't face the Orioles until June 8. In 12 games against Baltimore, Marty hit .529, scored 15 runs and drove in 11 of his 43 RBIs. Boston beat Baltimore 12 times in 13 tries; the game that they lost was the one where Marty did not play.

At bat, Barrett did most of his damage against lefties; quite normal for him (.308 lifetime v. lefties; .273 v. normal people). He also moved runners along effectively. He hit .345 with men on (.263 otherwise), led the majors in sacrifice hits for the second straight year and drove in 79 percent (19–24) of the runners on third base with less than two out (best on the team). And he did this despite—not because of—playing in Fenway Park. For the second straight year, Marty hit better on the road.

Chuck Waseleski

Barrett, Martin Glenn "Marty"   Bats: Right   Throws: Right   Born 06/23/58

1987 SEASON AND MAJOR-LEAGUE CAREER BATTING TOTALS

	G	AB	H	2B	3B	HR	TB	R	RBI	TBB	IBB	SO	HP	SH	SF	SB	CS	SB%	GDP	AVG	OBP	SLG
87 BOS	137	559	164	23	0	3	196	72	43	51	0	38	1	22	5	15	2	.88	11	.293	.351	.351
6 YEARS	631	2255	640	112	8	15	813	288	206	217	5	146	5	56	18	42	17	.71	49	.284	.345	.361

	1987 SEASON											FOUR YEAR TOTALS (1984 – 1987)										
	Ave.	OBP	SLG	AB	H	2B	3B	HR	RBI	BB	SO	Ave.	OBP	SLG	AB	H	2B	3B	HR	RBI	BB	SO
Totals	.293	.351	.351	559	164	23	0	3	43	51	39	.287	.349	.364	2193	629	110	7	15	204	214	145
vs. Left	.347	.412	.420	150	52	5	0	2	17	18	5	.316	.384	.410	646	204	36	2	7	72	76	26
vs. Right	.274	.327	.325	409	112	18	0	1	26	33	34	.275	.334	.345	1547	425	74	5	8	132	138	119
at Home	.292	.350	.369	274	80	15	0	2	17	24	19	.288	.354	.379	1066	307	63	2	10	102	110	86
on Road	.295	.351	.333	285	84	8	0	1	26	27	20	.286	.344	.350	1127	322	47	5	5	102	104	59
vs. Groundball	.327	.388	.389	257	84	10	0	2	25	27	15	.285	.349	.355	1050	299	47	3	7	100	106	55
vs. Flyball	.265	.318	.318	302	80	13	0	1	18	24	24	.289	.350	.372	1143	330	63	4	8	104	108	90
vs. Finesse	.339	.382	.405	289	98	13	0	2	21	22	16	.311	.364	.393	1229	382	69	4	8	107	108	64
vs. Power	.244	.318	.293	270	66	10	0	1	22	29	23	.256	.330	.327	964	247	41	3	7	97	106	81
on Grass	.292	.348	.351	487	142	20	0	3	34	42	38	.287	.351	.363	1856	532	91	6	13	170	186	132
on Artificial Turf	.306	.369	.347	72	22	3	0	0	9	9	1	.288	.339	.368	337	97	19	1	2	34	28	13
Day Games	.243	.298	.288	177	43	5	0	1	8	13	13	.274	.334	.339	708	194	30	2	4	56	64	55
Night Games	.317	.374	.380	382	121	18	0	2	35	38	26	.293	.356	.376	1485	435	80	5	11	148	150	90
April	.188	.235	.188	32	6	0	0	0	5	1	3	.272	.353	.355	169	46	6	1	2	19	20	11
May	.196	.282	.250	92	18	2	0	1	6	11	10	.264	.330	.339	348	92	16	2	2	28	34	24
June	.304	.373	.384	112	34	6	0	1	8	13	7	.286	.346	.352	409	117	21	0	2	29	38	25
July	.323	.381	.355	93	30	3	0	0	7	10	6	.305	.376	.366	374	114	14	0	3	36	44	23
August	.274	.336	.321	106	29	5	0	0	7	10	5	.288	.352	.384	437	126	30	0	4	40	43	33
Sept/Oct	.379	.402	.460	124	47	7	0	1	10	6	8	.294	.343	.375	456	134	23	4	2	52	35	29
Bases Empty	.263	.301	.312	353	93	14	0	1	1	19	28	.284	.334	.352	1319	374	63	3	7	7	100	92
Leadoff	.255	.296	.314	102	26	6	0	0	0	6	9	.308	.353	.396	536	165	34	2	3	3	37	31
Not Leadoff	.267	.303	.311	251	67	8	0	1	1	13	19	.267	.322	.322	783	209	29	1	4	4	63	61
Runners On	.345	.426	.417	206	71	9	0	2	42	32	11	.292	.372	.382	874	255	47	4	8	197	114	53
First Base Only	.392	.416	.464	97	38	7	0	0	1	4	2	.288	.352	.354	378	109	19	0	2	8	37	12
Scoring Position	.303	.434	.376	109	33	2	0	2	41	28	9	.294	.387	.403	496	146	28	4	6	189	77	41
Late Innings, Close	.239	.341	.268	71	17	2	0	0	5	11	5	.273	.356	.351	308	84	16	1	2	36	40	24

RBI/Opportunities

Scoring Position	37 / 181 (20%)	169 / 731 (23%)
Scoring Position, 2 Out	11 / 82 (13%)	81 / 347 (23%)
On Third, Less than 2 Out	19 / 24 (79%)	61 / 120 (51%)
RBI in close games / RBI Total	22 / 43 (51%)	105 / 204 (51%)

Kevin Bass
Houston Astros

Kevin Bass is an established star. He has been overlooked and underrated in the past, but the cumulative weight of his consistent performance is becoming undeniable. There may be a few remaining people who are unaware of Kevin Bass, but those who know about him are virtually unanimous in their appreciation of his accomplishments. Bass has a rare combination of speed and power, and plays up to his ability. Over the past three years, only two NL outfielders have more HR and SB than Bass: Eric Davis and Darryl Strawberry (Rotisserie fans take note).

When analyzing players from Houston, it has been fashionable to make apologies for the impacts of the Astrodome, and to translate Houston performances into their theoretical equivalents. Bass may indeed have bigger numbers if he played in some other city, but he needs no excuses or explanation for statistics now on record. From 1985 to 1987, he has averaged .289 with 18 HR, 77 RBI and 21 SB per year. Using the Favorite Toy method to measure established ability, Bass is a .291 hitter from whom we can expect 19 HR, 80 RBI and 21 SB. Note the consistency in these numbers. Kevin is a predictable and reliable performer; that is one of his greatest strengths. Bass turned in a highly consistent performance in 1987. He hit .282 before the All-Star break and .286 after; 9 HR before and 10 HR after; 10 SB before and 11 after.

Comparing 1987 to 1986, some people may have the idea that Bass declined somewhat in '87, but the question is debatable:

	AB	R	H	2B	3B	HR	RBI	BB	SO	SB	CS
'87	592	83	168	31	5	19	85	53	77	21	8
'86	591	83	184	33	5	20	79	38	72	22	13

Kevin had 16 fewer hits in '87, dropping his average from .311 to .284, but he compensated by drawing 15 more walks, for an OBA of .343 compared to .348 the year before. Add to this the consideration that Kevin got 6 more RBI in 1987 and reduced abortive steal attempts by 5, and it becomes arguable that 1987 was actually a better year. I will not bother to make that case. The point is that the above numbers portray two remarkably similar seasons. There can be no doubt that the same player, playing at the same level of his abilities, produced these two lines. Kevin entered the record books this year, becoming (briefly) the only National Leaguer to homer from both sides of the plate in a game more than once in his career, as he did it twice this year. Unfortunately for Kevin, before they got around to printing the record book, Chili Davis duplicated the feat in 1987, tying Bass, Mickey Mantle, and Eddie Murray as the only 4 players to do so twice in a season.

Kevin Bass is in his prime playing age. We can expect several more excellent seasons from this outstanding player and we can expect his reputation to grow each year.

John C. Benson

Bass, Kevin Charles　　　　　Bats: Both　　Throws: Right　　Born 05/12/59

1987 SEASON AND MAJOR-LEAGUE CAREER BATTING TOTALS

	G	AB	H	2B	3B	HR	TB	R	RBI	TBB	IBB	SO	HP	SH	SF	SB	CS	SB%	GDP	AVG	OBP	SLG
87 HOU	157	592	168	31	5	19	266	83	85	53	13	77	4	0	5	21	8	.72	15	.284	.344	.449
6 YEARS	703	2281	630	115	23	59	968	302	280	135	27	305	19	12	12	69	36	.66	45	.276	.320	.424

1987 SEASON

	Ave.	OBP	SLG	AB	H	2B	3B	HR	RBI	BB	SO
Totals	.284	.344	.449	592	168	31	5	19	85	53	77
vs. Left	.282	.315	.507	227	64	13	4	10	37	10	31
vs. Right	.285	.361	.414	365	104	18	1	9	48	43	46
at Home	.285	.348	.454	302	86	17	2	10	52	30	45
on Road	.283	.340	.445	290	82	14	3	9	33	23	32
vs. Groundball	.308	.373	.451	273	84	16	1	7	44	29	34
vs. Flyball	.263	.319	.448	319	84	15	4	12	41	24	43
vs. Finesse	.297	.353	.453	300	89	16	2	9	41	26	30
vs. Power	.271	.334	.445	292	79	15	3	10	44	27	47
on Grass	.291	.342	.458	179	52	10	1	6	24	14	20
on Artificial Turf	.281	.345	.446	413	116	21	4	13	61	39	57
Day Games	.255	.300	.394	188	48	6	1	6	22	13	25
Night Games	.297	.364	.475	404	120	25	4	13	63	40	52
April	.298	.344	.476	84	25	6	0	3	12	5	14
May	.263	.330	.414	99	26	5	2	2	12	9	10
June	.275	.339	.461	102	28	6	2	3	22	11	16
July	.277	.310	.394	94	26	3	1	2	7	4	10
August	.286	.372	.418	98	28	4	0	3	13	13	17
Sept/Oct	.304	.362	.522	115	35	7	0	6	19	11	10
Bases Empty	.285	.339	.438	333	95	18	3	9	9	24	37
Leadoff	.308	.361	.500	146	45	10	0	6	6	11	18
Not Leadoff	.267	.322	.390	187	50	8	3	3	3	13	19
Runners On	.282	.350	.463	259	73	13	2	10	76	29	40
First Base Only	.287	.330	.472	108	31	6	1	4	10	6	20
Scoring Position	.278	.363	.457	151	42	7	1	6	66	23	20
Late Innings, Close	.284	.353	.471	102	29	7	0	4	23	11	15

FOUR YEAR TOTALS (1984 – 1987)

	Ave.	OBP	SLG	AB	H	2B	3B	HR	RBI	BB	SO
Totals	.284	.330	.439	2053	583	108	20	57	261	129	270
vs. Left	.291	.326	.495	852	248	54	9	34	122	35	125
vs. Right	.279	.334	.400	1201	335	54	11	23	139	94	145
at Home	.285	.337	.424	1023	292	49	9	25	133	73	140
on Road	.283	.324	.454	1030	291	59	11	32	128	56	130
vs. Groundball	.271	.319	.396	943	256	48	6	19	118	62	132
vs. Flyball	.295	.340	.477	1110	327	60	14	38	143	67	138
vs. Finesse	.292	.330	.436	1087	317	61	9	26	131	58	117
vs. Power	.275	.331	.443	966	266	47	11	31	130	71	153
on Grass	.285	.319	.467	636	181	41	6	21	82	31	81
on Artificial Turf	.284	.335	.427	1417	402	67	14	36	179	98	189
Day Games	.267	.309	.416	570	152	27	5	16	60	33	80
Night Games	.291	.339	.448	1483	431	81	15	41	201	96	190
April	.283	.328	.439	269	76	12	3	8	31	17	39
May	.249	.285	.371	321	80	14	2	7	35	15	36
June	.285	.331	.461	362	103	22	3	12	49	26	44
July	.283	.318	.411	336	95	13	3	8	36	17	50
August	.271	.324	.426	310	84	13	4	9	43	24	50
Sept/Oct	.319	.360	.501	455	145	34	5	13	67	30	51
Bases Empty	.284	.317	.442	1192	339	60	13	34	34	54	145
Leadoff	.279	.308	.470	502	140	31	7	17	17	20	63
Not Leadoff	.288	.324	.422	690	199	29	6	17	17	34	82
Runners On	.283	.340	.436	861	244	48	7	23	227	75	125
First Base Only	.273	.317	.429	352	96	21	2	10	32	22	46
Scoring Position	.291	.354	.440	509	148	27	5	13	195	53	79
Late Innings, Close	.305	.358	.457	361	110	18	2	11	58	30	54

RBI/Opportunities

	1987	Four Year
Scoring Position	56 / 208 (27%)	173 / 676 (26%)
Scoring Position, 2 Out	23 / 109 (21%)	78 / 336 (23%)
On Third, Less than 2 Out	16 / 30 (53%)	48 / 102 (47%)
RBI in close games / RBI Total	54 / 85 (64%)	157 / 261 (60%)

Don Baylor
Boston Red Sox

One reason that a bad manager is able to stay in the majors is that, all too often, one doesn't notice the effects of his handiwork until it is (a) too late to do anything about it and (b) as a result, impossible to assess the amount of damage that he has done. Don Baylor, for example, has said that Dave Garcia ruined his career; he may well be right.

Baylor's grievance stems from 1977. When Garcia was hired to replace Norm Sherry, one of his first moves was to shift Baylor from right field to DH. At the time, Baylor had played outfield in 541 of his 668 games in the majors. The only year in which he had not played at least 80 percent of his games in the outfield was 1976, when Chuck Tanner (who used Claudell Washington, Bill North and Joe Rudi as his outfield) had played Baylor at first base in 69 games.

Was Baylor a good outfielder? No, but he was an acceptable one. For a big man, Don had excellent speed—he'd stolen 170 bases in 223 tries (76.2 percent) and hit 14 triples at that particular point in his career. His range factors were in the 2.00–2.10 neighborhood—comparable to figures that Darryl Strawberry, Kirk Gibson and Harold Baines have posted in recent years. Using him in the outfield seemed justifiable; since Earl Weaver had done it, it almost certainly was the right decision.

But Garcia decided that 24-year-old Gil Flores (who had a reputation—that his stats do not support—as a defensive whiz) deserved to be in the lineup and moved Baylor to DH to accommodate him. Flores, who had very little power and rarely walked, was out of the majors by 1979; by then, the damage to Baylor's career had been done. Since 1977, he has played in 1532 games; only 281 of them in the outfield.

Is the word "damage" appropriate? I believe so. Players who do not have a chance to use their skills every day tend to lose them. By 1980, Baylor's speed had disappeared; it was no longer possible for him to play the outfield. More importantly, the DH role made heavy offensive demands on a man who, very simply, wasn't that heavy a hitter. Baylor has spent 16 of his 18 years as a regular; he has slugged .440 or better only five times and his OB% has been .340 or better only seven times. Save for his 1979 and his mini-resurgence after joining Billy Martin in 1983, he has not been (compared to his peers) a very effective DH at all. In the outfield, however, his production would have been at least relatively better and, very likely, substantially better.

This, I suppose, is why I rarely savage Baylor's probably undeserved label as a leader. Since, due to his manager, his reputation as a player suffered, it seems only fair that his reputation in other areas should be enhanced.

Geoff Beckman

Baylor, Don Edward Bats: Right Throws: Right Born 06/28/49

1987 SEASON AND MAJOR-LEAGUE CAREER BATTING TOTALS

	G	AB	H	2B	3B	HR	TB	R	RBI	TBB	IBB	SO	HP	SH	SF	SB	CS	SB%	GDP	AVG	OBP	SLG
87 BOS-MIN	128	388	95	9	0	16	152	67	63	45	3	59	28	0	6	5	3	.63	13	.245	.360	.392
18 YEARS	2200	7934	2077	359	28	331	3485	1208	1242	771	89	1025	255	16	11	2 28 5 11	9 .7	1 18		9 .26	2 .34	2 .43

1987 SEASON

	Ave.	OBP	SLG	AB	H	2B	3B	HR	RBI	BB	SO
Totals	.245	.360	.392	388	95	9	0	16	63	45	59
vs. Left	.267	.353	.407	135	36	1	0	6	23	12	15
vs. Right	.233	.363	.383	253	59	8	0	10	40	33	44
at Home	.268	.376	.448	183	49	3	0	10	39	17	31
on Road	.224	.346	.341	205	46	6	0	6	24	28	28
vs. Groundball	.247	.384	.403	186	46	5	0	8	30	27	23
vs. Flyball	.243	.336	.381	202	49	4	0	8	33	18	36
vs. Finesse	.231	.342	.349	195	45	2	0	7	39	19	23
vs. Power	.259	.377	.435	193	50	7	0	9	24	26	36
on Grass	.243	.374	.399	288	70	3	0	14	54	40	41
on Artificial Turf	.250	.312	.370	100	25	6	0	2	9	5	18
Day Games	.284	.380	.447	141	40	5	0	6	30	11	25
Night Games	.223	.349	.360	247	55	4	0	10	33	34	34
April	.247	.376	.455	77	19	4	0	4	13	13	15
May	.200	.327	.389	90	18	2	0	5	12	12	11
June	.300	.407	.478	90	27	1	0	5	17	9	10
July	.152	.222	.239	46	7	1	0	1	6	4	4
August	.278	.409	.361	36	10	0	0	1	9	2	7
Sept/Oct	.286	.397	.306	49	14	1	0	0	6	5	12
Bases Empty	.218	.329	.345	206	45	2	0	8	8	21	28
Leadoff	.231	.340	.473	91	21	1	0	7	7	8	7
Not Leadoff	.209	.321	.243	115	24	1	0	1	1	13	21
Runners On	.275	.392	.445	182	50	7	0	8	55	24	31
First Base Only	.214	.304	.300	70	15	3	0	1	2	7	16
Scoring Position	.313	.439	.536	112	35	4	0	7	53	17	15
Late Innings, Close	.205	.318	.260	73	15	1	0	1	6	10	11

FOUR YEAR TOTALS (1984 – 1987)

	Ave.	OBP	SLG	AB	H	2B	3B	HR	RBI	BB	SO
Totals	.243	.343	.440	1943	473	85	3	97	337	197	328
vs. Left	.259	.365	.446	668	173	30	1	31	116	86	99
vs. Right	.235	.331	.437	1275	300	55	2	66	221	111	229
at Home	.239	.347	.418	916	219	41	0	41	175	97	159
on Road	.247	.339	.460	1027	254	44	3	56	162	100	169
vs. Groundball	.240	.342	.408	941	226	44	0	38	162	92	148
vs. Flyball	.247	.344	.470	1002	247	41	3	59	175	105	180
vs. Finesse	.237	.331	.432	1066	253	43	1	54	191	95	150
vs. Power	.251	.358	.450	877	220	42	2	43	146	102	178
on Grass	.242	.346	.434	1601	387	72	1	78	289	176	265
on Artificial Turf	.251	.328	.468	342	86	13	2	19	48	21	63
Day Games	.239	.331	.424	665	159	26	2	31	117	56	116
Night Games	.246	.349	.448	1278	314	59	1	66	220	141	212
April	.240	.323	.429	287	69	15	0	13	40	32	42
May	.247	.333	.499	361	89	17	1	24	74	42	58
June	.249	.335	.454	350	87	10	1	20	67	38	55
July	.243	.300	.425	301	73	13	0	14	51	25	48
August	.225	.308	.405	316	71	13	1	14	54	32	58
Sept/Oct	.256	.322	.418	328	84	17	0	12	51	28	67
Bases Empty	.234	.307	.423	985	230	31	3	50	50	91	166
Leadoff	.228	.301	.444	439	100	9	1	28	28	39	74
Not Leadoff	.238	.311	.407	546	130	22	2	22	22	52	92
Runners On	.254	.335	.457	958	243	54	0	47	287	106	162
First Base Only	.247	.296	.471	397	98	20	0	23	53	26	73
Scoring Position	.258	.361	.447	561	145	34	0	24	234	80	89
Late Innings, Close	.251	.307	.469	335	84	14	1	19	62	25	51

RBI/Opportunities

Scoring Position	41 / 175 (23%)	195 / 829 (24%)
Scoring Position, 2 Out	17 / 74 (23%)	64 / 374 (17%)
On Third, Less than 2 Out	16 / 33 (48%)	81 / 153 (53%)
RBI in close games / RBI Total	39 / 63 (62%)	216 / 337 (64%)

Steve Bedrosian
Philadelphia Phillies

How strange a season was 1987? We came within an eyelash of having both the MVP and the Cy Young Award winner from the same last-place club. I suspect Steve Bedrosian was as surprised as anyone that he won the Cy Young—but after all, somebody had to. Which is not to say that the numbers racked up by Bedrock were unimpressive. It's just that he seemed to court disaster in every save opportunity. To illustrate, I'll describe one memorable appearance.

As you recall, between May 25 and June 30 Bedrosian appeared in 13 games and earned saves in every one, setting a major league record. On July 2, he took the mound in the eighth holding a 6–4 advantage over the Astros. After a 1–2–3 inning with two strikeouts, Walling singled to open the ninth. Puhl popped out, but Doran dribbled a hit up the middle. A flyball by Bass brought up Glenn Davis with two out and two on. Not one to build the suspense, Davis belted Bedrock's first pitch far over the left field fence, turning his fourteenth straight save into a defeat.

What makes the streak-ending game unusual is that it combined two propensities Bedrosian was generally able to keep separate in 1987—letting men get on base and giving up home runs. Bedrock allowed 10.3 baserunners (hits plus unintentional walks) per nine innings in 1987, a good but not extraordinary number. The five other 40-save seasons I examined produced values ranging from 8.2 (Quiz 1983) to 9.8 (Rags 1986). As it has been throughout his relief ca-

reer, the home run was Steve's special nemesis; he served up 11 in 89 innings, about the same as in 1986 (12 in 90.1). In fact, most of Bedrosian's totals were indistinguishable from 1986. The difference between 29 and 40 saves may result from allowing more solo homers (with two-run leads) in 1987.

Bedrosian is a one-pitch pitcher. Though he is one of the hardest throwers around, his fastball has very little movement. Bedrock definitely needs to come up with another pitch; he should scrap his slider, which he can't control and probably causes his periodic arm problems. Last season he may have tried to introduce the split-finger, which would be a good alternative if he can control it. Perhaps Giles could arrange an off-season seminar with Roger Craig.

Lee Elia tried to minimize the length of Bedrosian's relief stints, which makes sense for two reasons: hitters get less time to catch up with the heater, and Bedrock's arm might not wear out by the end of the season. Even so, he had to sit out for about ten days in August. Bedrosian did come back in September, though, and was fairly effective.

Even without the development of Milt Thompson, giving up Ozzie Virgil for Bedrosian has to be considered a good deal for the Phils. We might even overlook his unabashed support for the Boston Celtics. As long as he can throw that 95 MPH heat, Bedrock will remain an effective bullpen stopper.

Neal Traven

Bedrosian, Stephen Wayne "Steve"

Bats: Right **Throws: Right** **Born 12/06/57**

1987 SEASON AND MAJOR-LEAGUE CAREER PITCHING TOTALS

	G	GS	CG	GF	IP	BFP	H	R	ER	HR	SH	SF	HB	TBB	IBB	SO	WP	Bk	W	L	Pct	ShO	Sv	ERA
87 PHI	65	0	0	56	89	366	79	31	28	11	2	1	1	28	5	74	3	1	5	3	.625	0	40	2.83
7 YEARS	359	46	0	227	752	3176	638	297	269	65	29	19	16	329	41	617	20	3	47	48	.495	0	110	3.22

1987: Power, Flyball   1986: Power, Flyball   1985: Power, Flyball   1984: Power, Flyball

	1987 SEASON												FOUR YEAR TOTALS (1984 – 1987)											
	G	IP	H	BB	SO	SB	CS	W	L	S	ERA		G	IP	H	BB	SO	SB	CS	W	L	S	ERA		
Totals	65	89.0	79	28	74	12	2	5	3	40	2.83		210	469.2	421	206	371	70	18	29	30	80	3.28		
at Home	33	42.2	42	11	39	8	1	2	2	17	3.38		97	224.0	207	74	174	24	11	11	13	35	3.25		
on Road	32	46.1	37	17	35	4	1	3	1	23	2.33		113	245.2	214	132	197	46	7	18	17	45	3.33		
on Grass	21	29.1	29	6	28	6	1	2	1	10	4.60		72	162.0	141	80	137	27	8	12	13	24	3.39		
on Artificial Turf	44	59.2	50	22	46	6	1	3	2	30	1.96		138	307.2	280	126	234	43	10	17	17	56	3.25		
Day Games	15	23.1	20	12	20	1	1	1	0	11	1.54		92	262.0	244	118	201	29	15	14	17	26	3.50		
Night Games	50	65.2	59	16	54	11	1	4	3	29	3.29		118	207.2	177	88	170	41	3	15	13	54	3.03		
April	9	10.1	11	7	7	1	0	2	1	1	7.84		29	57.1	57	28	37	5	2	4	4	7	4.24		
May	12	17.1	9	6	21	2	0	1	0	10	1.04		37	82.1	66	31	76	9	5	6	3	15	1.75		
June	9	13.0	12	5	11	3	0	0	0	9	0.69		41	92.0	83	49	79	22	3	8	8	15	2.84		
July	13	18.1	16	2	10	1	0	0	1	10	1.96		39	83.0	66	37	61	11	2	4	6	16	3.47		
August	10	15.1	18	4	13	2	1	1	0	4	3.52		34	90.0	82	31	67	8	4	4	1	14	2.80		
Sept/Oct	12	14.2	13	4	12	3	1	1	1	6	3.68		30	65.0	67	30	51	15	2	3	8	13	5.54		

vs. Opponent Batters	Ave.	OBP	SLG	AB	H	2B	3B	HR	RBI	BB	SO		Ave.	OBP	SLG	AB	H	2B	3B	HR	RBI	BB	SO
Totals	.237	.297	.362	334	79	5	2	11	35	28	74		.239	.319	.360	1763	421	65	7	45	191	206	371
vs. Left	.249	.315	.394	193	48	4	0	8	24	19	45		.254	.347	.415	933	237	39	3	35	116	134	171
vs. Right	.220	.272	.319	141	31	1	2	3	11	9	29		.222	.285	.299	830	184	26	4	10	75	72	200
Bases Empty	.250	.299	.402	184	46	2	1	8	8	12	42		.238	.308	.368	990	236	39	4	27	27	98	218
Leadoff	.225	.286	.423	71	16	0	1	4	4	6	18		.250	.318	.413	412	103	19	3	14	14	41	89
Not Leadoff	.265	.308	.389	113	30	2	0	4	4	6	24		.230	.300	.336	578	133	20	1	13	13	57	129
Runners On Base	.220	.293	.313	150	33	3	1	3	27	16	32		.239	.332	.351	773	185	26	3	18	164	108	153
First Base Only	.317	.359	.433	60	19	2	1	1	3	4	8		.306	.361	.455	301	92	16	1	9	22	26	44
Scoring Position	.156	.252	.233	90	14	1	0	2	24	12	24		.197	.315	.284	472	93	10	2	9	142	82	109
Late Innings, Close	.251	.304	.352	267	67	2	2	7	30	21	60		.233	.298	.354	678	158	18	2	20	78	63	166

RBI/Opportunities

Scoring Position	20 / 119 (17%)	126 / 703 (18%)
Scoring Position, 2 Out	8 / 61 (13%)	53 / 329 (16%)
On Third, Less than 2 Out	9 / 21 (43%)	45 / 117 (38%)
RBI in close games / RBI Total	30 / 35 (86%)	146 / 191 (76%)

Buddy Bell
Cincinnati Reds

Buddy Bell has really had only one poor season over his 15-year major league career. That came in 1985, which he split between Texas and Cincinnati. Bell's 1987 statistics were nearly identical to 1986, with no significant change in batting average, on-base percentage, or home run or RBI frequency. In 1987 Buddy finished third among Cincinnati regulars, behind Kal Daniels and Eric Davis, in on-base percentage. He finished second to Davis in walks with 71 (with only 39 strikeouts), third in runs scored with 74, fourth in RBIs with 70 and fifth in homers with 17. In fact, at least one influential Cincinnati scribe picked Bell as the team's 1987 MVP, though that pick may say more about the lack of appreciation in Cincinnati for Daniels and Davis than it does about Bell.

So the Reds look set at third base for 1988 with the 36-year-old Bell. Through 1986 Bell had gone onto the Disabled list only twice in his 15-year career. Then, on May 11 of last season, he fell running the bases and strained his left hamstring, and missed 12 days. He aggravated the hamstring on May 29 as he fielded a ground ball. Bell came back to the lineup June 5. The Reds hadn't prepared for Buddy's absence; they played Kurt Stillwell and Dave Concepcion there, both out of position. Evidently the Reds hadn't contemplated Bell's inevitable retirement or decline. His performance didn't warrant concern, but now the Reds may have to get used to giving Buddy a little rest.

Buddy has totalled 2421 hits in his 16 major league years. He did nothing in 1987 to set back his course for the Hall of Fame. As Gary Gillette noted in last year's *Stat Book,* Bell looks like a decent bet for Cooperstown.

Mike Marrero

Those of you who have access to the 1986 *Bill James Baseball Abstract* might want to review the article on page 12, where Bill discusses at great length his point system for predicting who will be enshrined in Cooperstown, and who will buy tickets to get in. Based on Bill's system, Buddy seems to me to be a good bet to finish with about 75 points, which will get him about three quarters of the way to Cooperstown. Depending on where you start from, that's not all bad, but starting from Cincinnati, it puts Buddy right around the New York-Pennsylvania state line. Other players in that vicinity include Winfield and Blyleven, but they both have the advantage of post-season play.

For Buddy to make it in, he will need to play 2500 or more games at third (possible—he needs just under 300 more), and will need to total 3000 hits. Using the Favorite Toy (explained on the last page of that same *Abstract*), Bell's odds of achieving 3000 hits are slightly better than 1 in 3. If he continues to play in the National League and reaches 3000 hits, he will also get his longevity at third. At his recent pace, he'll need about 2100 at bats, which is 4 to 5 more years of full-time work. Buddy is a fine player, and he may well be selected by the Veteran's Committee, but I don't see him being elected by the Baseball Writers at this point, primarily because of his low career HR total (194), lack of post-season play, and failure to dominate even 1 season in several categories.

Michael Duca

Bell, David Gus "Buddy"

Bats: Right   Throws: Right   Born 08/27/51

1987 SEASON AND MAJOR-LEAGUE CAREER BATTING TOTALS

	G	AB	H	2B	3B	HR	TB	R	RBI	TBB	IBB	SO	HP	SH	SF	SB	CS	SB%	GDP	AVG	OBP	SLG
87 CIN	143	522	148	19	2	17	222	74	70	71	3	39	1	1	2	4	1	.80	14	.284	.369	.425
16 YEARS	2276	8590	2421	411	55	194	3524	1120	1063	803	82	734	38	59	77	54	78	.41	241	.282	.343	.410

	1987 SEASON											FOUR YEAR TOTALS (1984 – 1987)										
	Ave.	OBP	SLG	AB	H	2B	3B	HR	RBI	BB	SO	Ave.	OBP	SLG	AB	H	2B	3B	HR	RBI	BB	SO
Totals	.284	.369	.425	522	148	19	2	17	70	71	39	.276	.355	.419	2203	608	112	15	58	296	273	190
vs. Left	.261	.367	.430	142	37	3	0	7	18	24	12	.284	.366	.448	616	175	27	7	20	85	85	45
vs. Right	.292	.370	.424	380	111	16	2	10	52	47	27	.273	.351	.408	1587	433	85	8	38	211	188	145
at Home	.298	.395	.435	262	78	10	1	8	40	41	10	.287	.368	.449	1082	311	53	10	34	169	137	79
on Road	.269	.342	.415	260	70	9	1	9	30	30	29	.265	.343	.391	1121	297	59	5	24	127	136	111
vs. Groundball	.278	.359	.419	248	69	7	2	8	40	31	18	.276	.356	.407	1044	288	49	8	24	140	133	95
vs. Flyball	.288	.378	.431	274	79	12	0	9	30	40	21	.276	.354	.431	1159	320	63	7	34	156	140	95
vs. Finesse	.263	.354	.360	278	73	9	0	6	28	39	12	.269	.338	.406	1223	329	62	9	29	148	130	82
vs. Power	.307	.386	.500	244	75	10	2	11	42	32	27	.285	.375	.437	980	279	50	6	29	148	143	108
on Grass	.266	.344	.420	169	45	6	1	6	22	21	16	.269	.343	.397	1157	311	58	9	24	146	136	115
on Artificial Turf	.292	.381	.428	353	103	13	1	11	48	50	23	.284	.368	.445	1046	297	54	6	34	150	137	75
Day Games	.273	.354	.419	198	54	9	1	6	19	24	20	.261	.335	.396	656	171	33	7	14	70	70	57
Night Games	.290	.378	.429	324	94	10	1	11	51	47	19	.282	.364	.429	1547	437	79	8	44	226	203	133
April	.268	.358	.415	82	22	7	1	1	10	12	7	.258	.328	.368	291	75	20	3	2	29	31	20
May	.333	.379	.463	54	18	1	0	2	8	4	6	.305	.369	.450	302	92	16	2	8	36	31	24
June	.262	.330	.440	84	22	6	0	3	12	9	8	.246	.321	.358	399	98	17	2	8	44	45	34
July	.299	.376	.361	97	29	0	0	2	9	12	3	.277	.362	.392	375	104	18	2	7	42	50	35
August	.260	.388	.350	100	26	3	0	2	12	21	8	.267	.371	.427	405	108	20	0	15	65	67	38
Sept/Oct	.295	.378	.533	105	31	2	1	7	19	13	7	.304	.376	.506	431	131	21	6	18	80	49	39
Bases Empty	.284	.369	.405	306	87	10	0	9	9	41	18	.263	.343	.395	1211	319	53	5	32	32	147	108
Leadoff	.230	.297	.310	126	29	1	0	3	3	12	9	.259	.330	.388	433	112	18	1	12	12	46	44
Not Leadoff	.322	.416	.472	180	58	9	0	6	6	29	9	.266	.350	.398	778	207	35	4	20	20	101	64
Runners On	.282	.369	.454	216	61	9	2	8	61	30	21	.291	.371	.450	992	289	59	10	26	264	126	82
First Base Only	.276	.313	.487	76	21	2	1	4	9	4	5	.308	.351	.458	428	132	24	5	10	33	28	29
Scoring Position	.286	.396	.436	140	40	7	1	4	52	26	16	.278	.385	.443	564	157	35	5	16	231	98	53
Late Innings, Close	.280	.352	.476	82	23	5	1	3	17	9	8	.277	.357	.412	364	101	19	3	8	54	45	45

RBI/Opportunities

Scoring Position	42 / 204 (21%)	191 / 805 (24%)
Scoring Position, 2 Out	23 / 109 (21%)	68 / 377 (18%)
On Third, Less than 2 Out	9 / 24 (38%)	73 / 143 (51%)
RBI in close games / RBI Total	48 / 70 (69%)	211 / 296 (71%)

Eric Bell
Baltimore Orioles

To illustrate the recent decline of Baltimore's once vaunted staff, one need only compare the apprenticeship served by Eric Bell to that of his counterpart of a decade earlier, Scott McGregor. Both are left handed finesse pitchers. Both were drafted at age 18 and reached the majors at age 23. McGregor, however, spent one year in A ball, one in AA and three in AAA developing his skills. When he joined the Orioles in 1977, he was used sparingly (29 appearances, only five starts), while absorbing the lessons taught by Jim Palmer, Rudy May and Mike Flanagan. Not until 1978 did McGregor move into the rotation—and then only as the number four starter.

Bell, by contrast, spent four seasons at the rookie and A levels. He started his fifth professional year in AA, advanced to AAA in mid-season and spent September as a regular starter with the Orioles. In 1987, Baltimore handed him a spot in the rotation. Bell made more starts than any other rookie in baseball (29) this year; he tied Wally Bunker for second place behind Tom Phoebus (33) in the team record book. The results suggest that too much was expected too soon.

A finesse pitcher, who uses an effective changeup and pinpoint control to get hitters out, must have everything working well for him in order to succeed. Bell had trouble with the key parts of his game in 1987. He admitted to having problems keeping his release point consistent and felt that he was overthrowing the ball. As a result, his control was often faulty. Eric issued 4.25 walks per nine innings (unacceptable for even a dominating power pitcher), threw 11 wild pitches (tied for tenth in the AL) and allowed 1.75 homers per nine innings. Unsurprisingly, Bell failed to pitch six innings in 16 starts and did not last four innings in nine others; only four other regular (20+ starts) starters in the league pitched fewer innings per start in 1987. Bell's 5–1 start reflects the offensive support (6.5 runs per start) that he received in that period.

In mid-season, Bell made several adjustments and displayed something of his form; in six starts, he yielded only 34 hits and 10 walks in 43 innings, struck out 31 men and went 3–2 with a 2.72 ERA. But opposing batters readjusted with a vengeance, leaving Bell with a bloated 7.71 ERA in the last two months of 1987. His win on the last day of the 1987 season was his first since July 29.

In September, Oriole executives expressed concern over Bell's "lack of progress"; I suggest that the problem is more their own lack of patience. Like two earlier "disappointments" (Storm Davis and Ken Dixon), Bell did not receive the benefits of a full year's experience in AAA; his 1987 is an effect—not a cause—of the Orioles' mushrooming team ERA.

Tim Mulligan

Bell, Eric Alvin   Bats: Left   Throws: Left   Born 10/27/63

1987 SEASON AND MAJOR-LEAGUE CAREER PITCHING TOTALS

	G	GS	CG	GF	IP	BFP	H	R	ER	HR	SH	SF	HB	TBB	IBB	SO	WP	Bk	W	L	Pct	ShO	Sv	ERA
87 BAL	33	29	2	1	165	729	174	113	100	32	4	2	2	78	0	111	11	1	10	13	.435	0	0	5.45
3 YEARS	41	33	2	4	194	858	201	130	116	37	5	3	2	96	0	133	11	1	11	15	.423	0	0	5.38

1987: Power, Flyball   1986: Finesse, Flyball

1987 SEASON

	G	IP	H	BB	SO	SB	CS	W	L	S	ERA
Totals	33	165.0	174	78	111	12	8	10	13	0	5.45
at Home	12	62.0	70	27	47	3	2	3	6	0	5.95
on Road	21	103.0	104	51	64	9	6	7	7	0	5.16
on Grass	11	56.0	53	35	35	4	4	5	2	0	5.14
on Artificial Turf	22	109.0	121	43	76	8	4	5	11	0	5.61
Day Games	27	135.0	147	68	90	10	8	8	11	0	5.60
Night Games	6	30.0	27	10	21	2	0	2	2	0	4.80
April	4	17.2	19	9	17	1	1	2	1	0	4.58
May	6	33.1	27	19	18	3	1	3	1	0	4.05
June	7	19.1	31	18	10	0	1	1	3	0	9.78
July	5	41.0	34	10	30	3	2	3	2	0	2.85
August	6	36.0	44	14	17	4	2	0	4	0	7.25
Sept/Oct	5	17.2	19	8	19	1	1	1	2	0	6.62

TWO YEAR TOTALS (1986 – 1987)

	G	IP	H	BB	SO	SB	CS	W	L	S	ERA
Totals	37	188.0	197	92	129	14	8	11	15	0	5.41
at Home	14	71.2	82	34	53	4	2	3	7	0	6.15
on Road	23	116.1	115	58	76	10	6	8	8	0	4.95
on Grass	11	56.0	53	35	35	4	4	5	2	0	5.14
on Artificial Turf	26	132.0	144	57	94	10	4	6	13	0	5.52
Day Games	31	158.0	170	82	108	12	8	9	13	0	5.53
Night Games	6	30.0	27	10	21	2	0	2	2	0	4.80
April	4	17.2	19	9	17	1	1	2	1	0	4.58
May	6	33.1	27	19	18	3	1	3	1	0	4.05
June	7	19.1	31	18	10	0	1	1	3	0	9.78
July	5	41.0	34	10	30	3	2	3	2	0	2.85
August	6	36.0	44	14	17	4	2	0	4	0	7.25
Sept/Oct	9	40.2	42	22	37	3	1	2	4	0	5.75

vs. Opponent Batters — 1987 Season

	Ave.	OBP	SLG	AB	H	2B	3B	HR	RBI	BB	SO
Totals	.271	.350	.495	643	174	40	4	32	92	78	111
vs. Left	.326	.389	.523	86	28	5	0	4	14	9	11
vs. Right	.262	.344	.490	557	146	35	4	28	78	69	100
Bases Empty	.250	.319	.475	404	101	27	2	20	20	39	71
Leadoff	.262	.337	.463	160	42	8	0	8	8	17	34
Not Leadoff	.242	.307	.484	244	59	19	2	12	12	22	37
Runners On Base	.305	.400	.527	239	73	13	2	12	72	39	40
First Base Only	.298	.365	.577	104	31	6	1	7	17	11	19
Scoring Position	.311	.424	.489	135	42	7	1	5	55	28	21
Late Innings, Close	.135	.220	.162	37	5	1	0	0	0	4	6

vs. Opponent Batters — Two Year Totals

	Ave.	OBP	SLG	AB	H	2B	3B	HR	RBI	BB	SO
Totals	.269	.351	.489	732	197	45	4	36	106	92	129
vs. Left	.304	.373	.491	112	34	6	0	5	19	13	15
vs. Right	.263	.347	.489	620	163	39	4	31	87	79	114
Bases Empty	.251	.320	.471	459	115	31	2	22	22	45	83
Leadoff	.253	.327	.462	182	46	11	0	9	9	19	38
Not Leadoff	.249	.316	.477	277	69	20	2	13	13	26	45
Runners On Base	.300	.399	.520	273	82	14	2	14	84	47	46
First Base Only	.297	.362	.551	118	35	7	1	7	17	12	20
Scoring Position	.303	.425	.497	155	47	7	1	7	67	35	26
Late Innings, Close	.135	.220	.162	74	10	2	0	0	0	8	12

RBI/Opportunities

	1987		Two Year	
Scoring Position	46 / 196	(23%)	55 / 230	(24%)
Scoring Position, 2 Out	16 / 86	(19%)	32 / 172	(19%)
On Third, Less than 2 Out	17 / 32	(53%)	34 / 64	(53%)
RBI in close games / RBI Total	68 / 92	(74%)	136 / 106	(128%)

George Bell
Toronto Blue Jays

In the winter of 1980, the world champion Philadelphia Phillies had a numbers crunch. They left a 21-year-old Dominican named George Bell off their 40-man roster, hoping that he might be overlooked in the minor league draft. That looks more and more like the worst decision that Philadelphia ever made—and the $25,000 that Toronto spent to obtain him is easily the best bargain they ever made. Bell has hit .291 with 139 homers and 439 RBIs for the Blue Jays since then; after finishing fourth in the MVP voting in 1986, he won the award in 1987.

The impressive thing about Bell are the breadth of his overall offensive skills. He has power—he finished second in the American League in slugging percentage. He hits for average—eleventh in the AL this year. He's an excellent contact hitter; he's missed two 200-hit seasons by a grand total of 14 hits and, of the twenty 30-homer men in the AL last year, only Wally Joyner and Don Mattingly struck out less often. Bell's walk totals aren't very impressive, but they don't need to be—if you can hit .300 and slug .500 every year, 40 walks is all you need to be well above average in every area.

As it has for most of his career, Exhibition Stadium proved to be something of an obstacle for Bell to hurdle last year. Offensively, his home splits are a surprise; he has usually benefited from playing in Toronto in the past.

Defensively, his numbers should surprise no one; as was the case with Andre Dawson, the turf is destroying Bell's knees. Bell's 1.77 range factor was eleventh among regular leftfielders in the AL this year—the third straight year that his figures have dropped. Given his spat with manager Jimy Williams about being the DH, you can't really play George there—but given Willie Upshaw's offensive output, there is no reason not to move Bell to first base. Immediately.

Finally: The award for the most asinine comment of 1987 goes to anyone who thinks that Bell "choked" down the stretch. He did have a bad September, but he had it for two reasons. First, the injuries to Tony Fernandez and Ernie Whitt were a major factor. In 1987, Bell hit .344 and slugged .623 with Whitt batting third. With Fernandez in the 3 spot, Bell hit .337 and slugged .663. With anyone else in front of him, Bell hit .298 and slugged .591.

The other reason is that Bell—consistently—has bad Septembers. Players use their legs to drive the ball; playing on rock-hard turf always erodes Bell's offensive stats late in the year.

As the Alan Trammell comment suggests, there were reasons not to vote for Bell as the MVP. His lack of clutch ability wasn't one of them.

Darren Peterson, Geoff Beckman and Dave Easby

Bell, Jorge (Mathy) "George" Bats: Right   Throws: Right   Born 10/21/59

1987 SEASON AND MAJOR-LEAGUE CAREER BATTING TOTALS

	G	AB	H	2B	3B	HR	TB	R	RBI	TBB	IBB	SO	HP	SH	SF	SB	CS	SB%	GDP	AVG	OBP	SLG
87 TOR	156	610	188	32	4	47	369	111	134	39	9	75	7	0	9	5	1	.83	17	.308	.352	.605
6 YEARS	730	2739	798	144	25	139	1409	408	453	156	22	357	27	0	26	48	20	.71	59	.291	.333	.514

	1987 SEASON											FOUR YEAR TOTALS (1984 – 1987)										
	Ave.	OBP	SLG	AB	H	2B	3B	HR	RBI	BB	SO	Ave.	OBP	SLG	AB	H	2B	3B	HR	RBI	BB	SO
Totals	.308	.352	.605	610	188	32	4	47	134	39	75	.296	.339	.529	2464	730	137	20	132	424	147	313
vs. Left	.343	.385	.686	175	60	8	2	16	46	12	25	.306	.350	.559	778	238	41	6	48	142	51	99
vs. Right	.294	.339	.572	435	128	24	2	31	88	27	50	.292	.334	.515	1686	492	96	14	84	282	96	214
at Home	.291	.346	.543	302	88	13	3	19	56	23	41	.299	.349	.519	1182	353	69	12	56	210	87	150
on Road	.325	.357	.666	308	100	19	1	28	78	16	34	.294	.329	.537	1282	377	68	8	76	214	60	163
vs. Groundball	.343	.382	.636	283	97	19	2	20	64	16	23	.297	.333	.502	1153	342	62	8	53	183	55	138
vs. Flyball	.278	.326	.578	327	91	13	2	27	70	23	52	.296	.344	.552	1311	388	75	12	79	241	92	175
vs. Finesse	.290	.328	.589	338	98	18	4	25	67	17	31	.281	.314	.495	1393	392	75	14	65	199	62	138
vs. Power	.331	.381	.625	272	90	14	0	22	67	22	44	.316	.370	.572	1071	338	62	6	67	225	85	175
on Grass	.311	.351	.639	244	76	14	0	22	62	15	28	.294	.331	.524	995	293	51	3	57	165	50	125
on Artificial Turf	.306	.352	.582	366	112	18	4	25	72	24	47	.297	.345	.532	1469	437	86	17	75	259	97	188
Day Games	.311	.361	.653	196	61	13	3	16	43	13	25	.289	.338	.524	830	240	49	10	42	151	53	114
Night Games	.307	.347	.582	414	127	19	1	31	91	26	50	.300	.339	.531	1634	490	88	10	90	273	94	199
April	.253	.306	.532	79	20	5	1	5	11	4	10	.323	.365	.562	313	101	20	2	17	53	19	45
May	.352	.352	.743	105	37	4	2	11	31	1	14	.299	.332	.531	405	121	21	8	19	75	21	55
June	.273	.322	.600	110	30	3	0	11	27	9	19	.292	.326	.529	448	131	16	3	28	81	23	61
July	.333	.363	.538	93	31	4	0	5	16	5	11	.288	.335	.523	392	113	19	2	23	73	28	51
August	.321	.376	.670	106	34	10	0	9	28	9	8	.321	.366	.597	442	142	35	0	29	85	31	45
Sept/Oct	.308	.379	.530	117	36	6	1	6	21	11	13	.263	.304	.444	464	122	26	5	16	57	25	56
Bases Empty	.313	.349	.645	310	97	19	3	26	26	13	39	.297	.335	.556	1291	383	73	11	80	80	71	183
Leadoff	.341	.386	.695	164	56	13	3	13	13	9	20	.309	.350	.565	582	180	37	5	34	34	33	81
Not Leadoff	.281	.305	.589	146	41	6	0	13	13	4	19	.286	.324	.549	709	203	36	6	46	46	38	102
Runners On	.303	.355	.563	300	91	13	1	21	108	26	36	.296	.338	.499	1173	347	64	9	52	344	76	130
First Base Only	.282	.336	.573	124	35	3	0	11	22	7	18	.294	.322	.481	493	145	24	4	20	56	17	50
Scoring Position	.318	.368	.557	176	56	10	1	10	86	19	18	.297	.349	.512	680	202	40	5	32	288	59	80
Late Innings, Close	.305	.355	.579	95	29	5	0	7	23	7	9	.309	.352	.539	408	126	22	3	22	75	27	46

RBI/Opportunities

Scoring Position	66 / 228 (29%)	228 / 868 (26%)
Scoring Position, 2 Out	24 / 110 (22%)	92 / 409 (22%)
On Third, Less than 2 Out	24 / 42 (57%)	72 / 149 (48%)
RBI in close games / RBI Total	82 / 134 (61%)	280 / 424 (66%)

Tony Bernazard
Cleveland Indians/Oakland A's

Misfortune and Tony Bernazard seem to be joined at the hip. Had just a few things in his career gone differently, Tony might now be renowned as a key man on several fine teams. They haven't, so he now seems fated to end his career with the "loser" tag firmly in place.

Bernazard began his career in Montreal. In 1978, at age 22, he had a AAA season very like a typical Bernazard year. He spent '79 in the minors, got 183 ABs in 1980 and was then traded to Chicago. Since Montreal spent '79–'83 missing the NL East title by inches and their weakness was second base, it's fair to suggest that Tony could have brought Montreal at least one title had he ever gotten an extended chance to play there.

You probably know what comes next. In 1983, after two good years, Tony was traded for Julio Cruz. Chicago improved from 28–32 to 71–31 and won the AL West by 20 games—Cruz got most of the credit.

Now, for the record: Tony was hitting .262, with a .306 OB% and .373 SL% before the trade; Cruz hit .254 with a .311 OB% and .311 SL% after it. Cruz stole 33 bases for his new team; Bernazard stole 21 for his. Cruz's range factor was better (5.26–4.83), but it obviously was not the sole cause of Chicago's 17-game improvement. Chicago simply took out their frustration for a slow start on a convenient target and happened to have it pay off for unrelated reasons—nothing more and nothing less.

Anyway, Tony played well for Seattle, but the M's went from 26–41 to 34–61. After yet another trade and a truly atrocious year in 1984, the book on him was closed. Traded three times, never played for a winner . . . sure he's got good stats, but look at those intangibles.

But Tony is a battler; he kept fighting for respect. He played well in 1985 (naturally Cleveland lost 102 games that year) and great in 1986. Had Cleveland won or had Tony continued to play well, 1987 could have been his breakthrough year.

Of course it wasn't. Cleveland died in the blocks. Tony started slowly, moved to Oakland and the A's (who were 46–41) went 35–40. Tony had an ungodly range factor (4.22; down from 5.43 in 1986), and didn't hit a lick in September; he got the goat horns for Oakland's slide.

Again, for the record: Tony's post-trade stats (.266 BA, .356 OB%, .383 SL%) were the best of the A's second basemen. Other A's (Phillips, Canseco, Nelson, Honeycutt) also had September slumps. Finally, fielders can have slumps too—especially if a team keeps shuffling shortstops. Unless Tony's leg has fallen off, I expect his range to return in 1988.

Given their trades, I think Oakland has a strong chance to win the AL West in 1988. With Tony's luck, they will—but he'll be playing second base for Atlanta on the day the A's clinch.

Geoff Beckman

Bernazard, Antonio (Garcia) "Tony" — Bats: Both Throws: Right Born 08/24/56

1987 SEASON AND MAJOR-LEAGUE CAREER BATTING TOTALS

	G	AB	H	2B	3B	HR	TB	R	RBI	TBB	IBB	SO	HP	SH	SF	SB	CS	SB%	GDP	AVG	OBP	SLG
87 CLE-OAK	140	507	127	26	2	14	199	73	49	55	2	79	1	7	3	11	8	.58	10	.250	.323	.393
9 YEARS	1065	3688	968	177	30	75	1430	523	391	428	22	602	17	63	35	113	55	.67	67	.262	.339	.388

1987 SEASON / FOUR YEAR TOTALS (1984–1987)

	Ave.	OBP	SLG	AB	H	2B	3B	HR	RBI	BB	SO		Ave.	OBP	SLG	AB	H	2B	3B	HR	RBI	BB	SO
Totals	.250	.323	.393	507	127	26	2	14	49	55	79		.264	.336	.390	2008	530	95	13	44	219	220	298
vs. Left	.230	.323	.381	139	32	7	1	4	16	19	22		.268	.358	.391	553	148	31	2	11	61	78	71
vs. Right	.258	.324	.397	368	95	19	1	10	33	36	57		.263	.328	.390	1455	382	64	11	33	158	142	227
at Home	.238	.313	.339	227	54	12	1	3	16	24	31		.283	.355	.407	966	273	49	10	17	105	109	133
on Road	.261	.331	.436	280	73	14	1	11	33	31	48		.247	.319	.374	1042	257	46	3	27	114	111	165
vs. Groundball	.264	.341	.404	280	74	11	2	8	21	32	35		.267	.340	.386	1017	272	39	8	22	114	109	133
vs. Flyball	.233	.302	.379	227	53	15	0	6	28	23	44		.260	.333	.394	991	258	56	5	22	105	111	165
vs. Finesse	.272	.325	.433	268	73	12	2	9	28	21	27		.283	.338	.426	1136	321	56	7	31	136	95	133
vs. Power	.226	.321	.347	239	54	14	0	5	21	34	52		.240	.334	.343	872	209	39	6	13	83	125	165
on Grass	.249	.330	.361	410	102	23	1	7	37	50	66		.267	.343	.390	1676	447	86	11	33	183	195	251
on Artificial Turf	.258	.291	.526	97	25	3	1	7	12	5	13		.250	.303	.389	332	83	9	2	11	36	25	47
Day Games	.232	.307	.343	181	42	11	0	3	20	19	31		.248	.336	.360	652	162	29	4	12	64	87	101
Night Games	.261	.332	.420	326	85	15	2	11	29	36	48		.271	.337	.404	1356	368	66	9	32	155	133	197
April	.219	.240	.370	73	16	5	0	2	8	2	8		.275	.356	.413	247	68	10	3	6	30	31	37
May	.187	.245	.330	91	17	1	0	4	5	6	22		.229	.303	.341	349	80	16	1	7	27	36	65
June	.282	.361	.518	85	24	3	1	5	14	11	15		.281	.343	.415	359	101	14	2	10	48	34	59
July	.341	.402	.462	91	31	8	0	1	6	10	13		.291	.363	.405	375	109	19	0	8	37	43	41
August	.273	.376	.404	99	27	7	0	2	15	17	12		.260	.330	.399	404	105	24	4	8	50	43	56
Sept/Oct	.176	.273	.235	68	12	2	1	0	1	9	9		.245	.326	.365	274	67	12	3	5	27	33	40
Bases Empty	.254	.309	.425	315	80	17	2	11	11	24	45		.261	.326	.407	1185	309	56	9	33	33	113	180
Leadoff	.178	.231	.281	146	26	4	1	3	3	10	27		.239	.303	.380	547	131	26	6	13	13	50	86
Not Leadoff	.320	.375	.550	169	54	13	1	8	8	14	18		.279	.345	.429	638	178	30	3	20	20	63	94
Runners On	.245	.345	.339	192	47	9	0	3	38	31	34		.269	.352	.366	823	221	39	4	11	186	107	118
First Base Only	.279	.347	.349	86	24	3	0	1	4	9	14		.308	.346	.416	344	106	18	2	5	23	20	43
Scoring Position	.217	.344	.330	106	23	6	0	2	34	22	20		.240	.355	.330	479	115	21	2	6	163	87	75
Late Innings, Close	.275	.367	.420	69	19	7	0	1	4	10	13		.241	.332	.350	294	71	23	0	3	24	40	47

RBI/Opportunities

	1987		Four Year	
Scoring Position	30 / 153	(20%)	151 / 696	(22%)
Scoring Position, 2 Out	15 / 81	(19%)	55 / 324	(17%)
On Third, Less than 2 Out	8 / 20	(40%)	54 / 105	(51%)
RBI in close games / RBI Total	24 / 49	(49%)	127 / 219	(58%)

Bert Blyleven
Minnesota Twins

Before I say anything else, let me admit that I thoroughly despise Bert Blyleven. From the minute that he hit Cleveland, he started bitching. The team wasn't any good, he deserved better, he should be traded—Ernie Banks, he wasn't. An example of his class: After his 200th win, he kindly distributed autographed balls to his teammates; it was kind because he wouldn't sign autographs for them otherwise. Bert is perhaps the only topic where my opinion agrees with Calvin Griffith, Brad Corbett, Chuck Tanner, Gabe Paul and Peter Bavasi: a selfish whiner who deserves the nickname "Cryleven."

I should also say that I think less of his record than many people do. Bert's career winning percentage is .539; he's won 60 percent of his decisions only three times. From 1976 (the first year that I have run support data for) through 1986, Blyleven's teams have scored 1327 runs in his 309 starts (4.29 runs per game); he's allowed 860 (3.25 runs per nine innings). A pitcher with those figures should have a .635 winning percentage; Bert's actual figure in that span is .545. When he gets good support and has a strong bullpen behind him, he's three games over .500; when he doesn't, he's two games under it. People give Don Sutton a hard time about not winning games; Bert makes him look like Lefty Grove.

But, to give the devil his due, he's a very durable pitcher. He's been under .500 as often as he has been over .600. He's pitched less than 150 innings once in his 18-year career. His ERA has been under 4.00 in 15 of those years. When he joins a team, you never have to worry about 20 percent of your rotation.

Also, unlike many players who spend their career complaining, Blyleven always takes care of business first. He's been traded twice in mid-season; his stats when he was traded were 13–16, 3.32. In his final years in Texas and Pittsburgh, he was 22–25, with a 3.72 ERA. You won't ever see this guy pulling a Bill Madlock (i.e., going sub-Mendoza with no power or defense while saying that you don't believe that the team can't trade you); I'll give him a gold star for that.

The last three years have shown that Blyleven has lost some hop on his fastball and hard curve. Though he still pitches a ton of innings, allows fewer hits than innings pitched and fans a lot of people, he's slipped from his glory years. His possible refusal to adapt to aging may explain his new career as a tater farmer; 33 percent of the shots that he's surrendered in his career have come since 1985. If Bert plans to get to 300 wins, he'll have to adjust for that in some way. If he does (and he probably will), he has a strong chance to reach his goal; that (gag) will probably (choke) punch his ticket to (urrrpppp) Cooperstown after he retires.

Geoff Beckman

Blyleven, Rik Aalbert "Bert"   Bats: Right   Throws: Right   Born 04/06/51

1987 SEASON AND MAJOR-LEAGUE CAREER PITCHING TOTALS

	G	GS	CG	GF	IP	BFP	H	R	ER	HR	SH	SF	HB	TBB	IBB	SO	WP	Bk	W	L	Pct	ShO	Sv	ERA
87 MIN	37	37	8	0	267	1122	249	132	119	46	4	6	9	101	4	196	13	0	15	12	.556	1	0	4.01
18 YEARS	578	572	224	3	4254	17477	3854	1664	1484	363	158	97	119	1173	66	3286	98	15	244	209	.539	55	0	3.14

1987: Power, Groundball   1986: Finesse, Flyball   1985: Power, Flyball   1984: Power, Flyball

1987 SEASON

	G	IP	H	BB	SO	SB	CS	W	L	S	ERA
Totals	37	267.0	249	101	196	33	10	15	12	0	4.01
at Home	22	164.2	144	66	134	20	3	9	6	0	3.83
on Road	15	102.1	105	35	62	13	7	6	6	0	4.31
on Grass	14	94.2	107	39	78	15	2	5	4	0	4.37
on Artificial Turf	23	172.1	142	62	118	18	8	10	8	0	3.81
Day Games	11	72.2	79	26	42	8	5	4	4	0	5.08
Night Games	26	194.1	170	75	154	25	5	11	8	0	3.61
April	5	34.0	35	10	22	6	1	1	1	0	4.24
May	7	51.2	49	13	36	3	0	3	3	0	5.05
June	6	41.1	36	16	25	5	4	3	2	0	2.83
July	6	46.0	47	22	39	8	3	3	2	0	4.50
August	6	39.1	44	17	30	3	0	3	2	0	5.26
Sept/Oct	7	54.2	38	23	44	8	2	2	2	0	2.47

vs. Opponent Batters	Ave.	OBP	SLG	AB	H	2B	3B	HR	RBI	BB	SO
Totals	.249	.321	.433	1002	249	45	1	46	113	101	196
vs. Left	.234	.313	.447	555	130	22	0	32	70	61	114
vs. Right	.266	.331	.416	447	119	23	1	14	43	40	82
Bases Empty	.250	.320	.463	620	155	28	1	34	34	59	123
Leadoff	.257	.316	.490	253	65	9	1	16	16	20	52
Not Leadoff	.245	.323	.444	367	90	19	0	18	18	39	71
Runners On Base	.246	.323	.385	382	94	17	0	12	79	42	73
First Base Only	.250	.303	.360	172	43	4	0	5	12	10	25
Scoring Position	.243	.337	.405	210	51	13	0	7	67	32	48
Late Innings, Close	.198	.314	.302	86	17	6	0	1	5	15	25

FOUR YEAR TOTALS (1984 – 1987)

	G	IP	H	BB	SO	SB	CS	W	L	S	ERA
Totals	143	1077.1	979	308	787	110	34	68	49	0	3.51
at Home	80	612.1	574	163	479	67	18	42	22	0	3.53
on Road	63	465.0	405	145	308	43	16	26	27	0	3.50
on Grass	49	357.1	348	122	257	37	10	19	16	0	3.75
on Artificial Turf	94	720.0	631	186	530	73	24	49	33	0	3.38
Day Games	75	551.0	494	160	373	51	19	33	28	0	3.56
Night Games	68	526.1	485	148	414	59	15	35	21	0	3.47
April	20	140.2	146	46	97	17	6	6	5	0	4.03
May	23	166.0	170	38	127	19	3	9	10	0	4.61
June	23	158.1	142	50	99	19	8	11	8	0	3.41
July	24	192.0	162	65	141	19	7	12	10	0	3.52
August	25	195.1	162	49	140	10	4	17	5	0	2.76
Sept/Oct	28	225.0	197	60	183	26	6	13	11	0	3.12

vs. Opponent Batters	Ave.	OBP	SLG	AB	H	2B	3B	HR	RBI	BB	SO
Totals	.241	.295	.392	4067	979	153	24	138	420	308	787
vs. Left	.235	.292	.381	2312	543	83	13	76	233	185	457
vs. Right	.248	.299	.407	1755	436	70	11	62	187	123	330
Bases Empty	.240	.291	.394	2517	605	94	16	87	87	173	499
Leadoff	.253	.293	.411	1045	264	37	9	37	37	58	207
Not Leadoff	.232	.289	.382	1472	341	57	7	50	50	115	292
Runners On Base	.241	.303	.388	1550	374	59	8	51	333	135	288
First Base Only	.245	.290	.384	714	175	23	2	24	60	42	101
Scoring Position	.238	.313	.392	836	199	36	6	27	273	93	187
Late Innings, Close	.231	.304	.369	385	89	16	2	11	39	41	85

RBI/Opportunities

	1987			Four Year		
Scoring Position	55 / 276	(20%)		224 / 1123	(20%)	
Scoring Position, 2 Out	22 / 132	(17%)		102 / 529	(19%)	
On Third, Less than 2 Out	20 / 47	(43%)		82 / 197	(42%)	
RBI in close games / RBI Total	76 / 113	(67%)		292 / 420	(70%)	

Mike Boddicker
Baltimore Orioles

In 1985 and 1986, the Orioles were blaming Mike Boddicker for their slide into mediocrity. In 1987, the shoe was on the other foot. Mike had a very solid 1987; his teammates didn't do their jobs.

Mike's 1987 stats don't appear to be much better than 1986; that's due to a statistical illusion. For some reason (see the AL offense comment for one idea), 1987 was a big year for hitters; the totals in every offensive category rose. League averages were way up—so much so that stats that would have been unacceptable in 1986 (*i.e.,* over the league average) were actually better than average in 1987. In order to get a clear picture of how well he pitched, you have to adjust your perspective.

Which is what I did. I computed the AL average for hits, walks, strikeouts, homers and ERA for 1987, figured out how much below the 1987 average Boddicker was and then multiplied that number by the 1986 average. The first line of the chart shows Boddicker's 1987 stats, adjusted to the 1986 league average figures (with unadjusted games, innings, wins and losses added); the second shows what he did in 1986. As you'll see, he was much better this year:

YEAR	G	IP	H	HR	BB	SO	W–L	ERA
1987	33	226.0	208	25	77	148	10–12	3.92
1986	33	218.1	214	30	74	175	14–12	4.70

Mike's poor record is due to his offense and bullpen. Baltimore scored 167 runs in his 33 starts in 1986 (5.06 runs per game); they scored 138 (4.18) in 1987. The bullpen also blew five save chances. If Boddicker had gotten as much help in 1987 as he got in 1986, he'd have gone 16–10.

What happened? In last year's *Stat Book,* Tim Mulligan and I noted that Mike's stats were sliding because he couldn't get hitters to put the ball in play as much as he'd done in his best years—that he was walking and striking out too many men for a finesse pitcher. Maybe that was because he didn't trust his defense in 1986 (rightly so) and was trying to do it all himself. In 1987, with the holes at second and third base filled by good gloves, Mike let his defense get outs instead; he struck out far fewer men and (not surprisingly) had a better year. If he keeps doing that in 1988, he'll pitch well again; if his teammates carry their share of the load, he might even start winning games again.

Geoff Beckman

Boddicker, Michael James "Mike" Bats: Right Throws: Right Born 08/23/57

1987 SEASON AND MAJOR-LEAGUE CAREER PITCHING TOTALS

	G	GS	CG	GF	IP	BFP	H	R	ER	HR	SH	SF	HB	TBB	IBB	SO	WP	Bk	W	L	Pct	ShO	Sv	ERA
87 BAL	33	33	7	0	226	950	212	114	105	29	7	4	7	78	4	152	10	0	10	12	.455	2	0	4.18
8 YEARS	169	159	49	6	1126	4714	1049	523	465	112	26	22	28	393	19	736	35	1	73	61	.545	13	0	3.72

1987: Finesse, Groundball 1986: Power, Groundball 1985: Power, Groundball 1984: Finesse, Groundball

1987 SEASON

	G	IP	H	BB	SO	SB	CS	W	L	S	ERA
Totals	33	225.2	212	78	152	32	3	10	12	0	4.19
at Home	16	116.2	105	33	78	11	1	5	6	0	4.24
on Road	17	109.0	107	45	74	21	2	5	6	0	4.13
on Grass	6	41.0	39	15	26	9	0	1	2	0	3.95
on Artificial Turf	27	184.2	173	63	126	23	3	9	10	0	4.24
Day Games	27	179.2	176	60	127	28	3	7	10	0	4.36
Night Games	6	46.0	36	18	25	4	0	3	2	0	3.52
April	5	36.0	25	9	23	3	1	2	0	0	1.50
May	6	40.0	34	15	28	7	1	2	1	0	3.60
June	6	45.1	40	14	34	5	0	1	3	0	3.38
July	4	26.1	32	9	16	4	0	2	0	0	6.15
August	6	38.1	40	19	26	9	0	2	3	0	6.57
Sept/Oct	6	39.2	41	12	25	4	1	1	5	0	4.54

FOUR YEAR TOTALS (1984 – 1987)

	G	IP	H	BB	SO	SB	CS	W	L	S	ERA
Totals	132	908.2	871	322	590	124	26	56	52	0	3.87
at Home	63	442.2	402	163	290	53	13	25	25	0	3.58
on Road	69	466.0	469	159	300	71	13	31	27	0	4.15
on Grass	36	254.1	235	77	151	33	3	19	12	0	3.26
on Artificial Turf	96	654.1	636	245	439	91	23	37	40	0	4.13
Day Games	111	757.2	737	279	488	106	24	44	46	0	3.96
Night Games	21	151.0	134	43	102	18	2	12	6	0	3.52
April	18	117.0	100	53	85	16	5	7	4	0	2.92
May	22	164.0	138	66	103	19	4	14	5	0	2.91
June	25	174.2	160	61	99	22	3	11	11	0	4.28
July	22	159.0	157	41	104	30	3	10	8	0	4.08
August	23	152.1	151	52	103	24	3	9	10	0	4.67
Sept/Oct	22	141.2	165	49	96	13	8	5	14	0	4.26

vs. Opponent Batters	Ave.	OBP	SLG	AB	H	2B	3B	HR	RBI	BB	SO
Totals	.248	.315	.413	854	212	38	8	29	99	78	152
vs. Left	.239	.303	.416	485	116	20	6	18	61	40	75
vs. Right	.260	.330	.409	369	96	18	2	11	38	38	77
Bases Empty	.250	.311	.421	523	131	22	5	19	19	41	90
Leadoff	.260	.319	.434	219	57	9	1	9	9	17	37
Not Leadoff	.243	.305	.411	304	74	13	4	10	10	24	53
Runners On Base	.245	.321	.402	331	81	16	3	10	80	37	62
First Base Only	.259	.313	.424	139	36	8	0	5	12	11	20
Scoring Position	.234	.326	.385	192	45	8	3	5	68	26	42
Late Innings, Close	.284	.366	.395	81	23	6	0	1	8	11	12

vs. Opponent Batters	Ave.	OBP	SLG	AB	H	2B	3B	HR	RBI	BB	SO
Totals	.253	.318	.387	3444	871	136	20	95	383	322	590
vs. Left	.259	.323	.391	1889	489	82	10	49	207	173	264
vs. Right	.246	.312	.382	1555	382	54	10	46	176	149	326
Bases Empty	.253	.318	.389	2021	511	84	12	56	56	187	324
Leadoff	.285	.341	.435	871	248	44	3	27	27	73	137
Not Leadoff	.229	.300	.355	1150	263	40	9	29	29	114	187
Runners On Base	.253	.318	.383	1423	360	52	8	39	327	135	266
First Base Only	.275	.318	.393	618	170	25	3	14	39	39	101
Scoring Position	.236	.318	.375	805	190	27	5	25	288	96	165
Late Innings, Close	.216	.306	.338	334	72	11	0	10	32	44	53

RBI/Opportunities

Scoring Position	60 / 253 (24%)	246 / 105 (23%)
Scoring Position, 2 Out	28 / 124 (23%)	99 / 482 (21%)
On Third, Less than 2 Out	19 / 40 (48%)	85 / 169 (50%)
RBI in close games / RBI Total	76 / 99 (77%)	284 / 383 (74%)

Wade Boggs
Boston Red Sox

Analyzing Wade Boggs's fielding is a lot like evaluating Kathleen Turner's acting: Given their other talents, the issue really doesn't matter a whole lot, does it?

Well, you saw it here first. The fellow who batted over .300 for five straight years in the minors but allegedly didn't have a position that he could handle has become one of the best defensive third basemen in the game. Let's compare his 1987 stats (games, assists, putouts, errors, double plays, fielding percentage, chances per game, assists per game, double plays per game) to those of two-time Gold Glove winner Gary Gaetti:

	G	A	PO	E	DP	FLD%	CH/G	A/G	DP/G
BOGGS	145	277	111	14	37	.965	2.68	1.91	.26
GAETTI	150	261	134	11	28	.973	2.63	1.74	.19

Wade's 37 DPs weren't simply the best in the majors in 1987—they were the most started by a third baseman since 1983, when Gaetti had 47 and Boggs had 40. Boggs also led the major-league third basemen in DPs in 1984 (30). He has participated at least 30 twin killings in each of the last five years.

Put it another way: Boggs fielded a ground ball with a man on first base and less than two outs 50 times this year. Thirty-one times—62 percent of the time—he turned a double play. And that's regardless of whether the runner was off with the pitch or not.

Boggs also goes back on foul pops as well as any third baseman in the game. In 1987, he hauled in 30 foul flies, even though he played half his games in the restricted foul territory of Fenway Park.

In the last five years, only four third basemen have averaged at least two A/G in a season three or more times. Three of the four—Terry Pendleton, Mike Schmidt and Gaetti—have won Gold Gloves. The fourth—Boggs—has not.

Can Boggs eventually win the award? The man that people said could hit for power if he would only consent to hitting .330 rather than .350 tripled his previous high in homers this year. He raised his slugging percentage over 100 points—and he also raised both his batting average and his on-base percentage in the process. The man can do anything that he puts his mind to.

As for Turner's thespian talents: Who really cares?

Chuck Waseleski

Boggs, Wade Anthony

Bats: Left **Throws: Right** **Born 06/15/58**

1987 SEASON AND MAJOR-LEAGUE CAREER BATTING TOTALS

	G	AB	H	2B	3B	HR	TB	R	RBI	TBB	IBB	SO	HP	SH	SF	SB	CS	SB%	GDP	AVG	OBP	SLG
87 BOS	147	551	200	40	6	24	324	108	89	105	19	48	2	1	8	1	3	.25	13	.363	.461	.588
6 YEARS	872	3329	1178	218	23	56	1610	582	411	522	50	254	7	23	29	10	13	.43	81	.354	.439	.484

1987 SEASON / FOUR YEAR TOTALS (1984 – 1987)

	Ave.	OBP	SLG	AB	H	2B	3B	HR	RBI	BB	SO		Ave.	OBP	SLG	AB	H	2B	3B	HR	RBI	BB	SO
Totals	.363	.461	.588	551	200	40	6	24	89	105	48		.353	.442	.489	2409	850	160	15	46	293	395	197
vs. Left	.331	.403	.544	169	56	11	2	7	36	20	14		.321	.396	.444	730	234	38	5	14	103	90	67
vs. Right	.377	.484	.607	382	144	29	4	17	53	85	34		.367	.461	.509	1679	616	122	10	32	190	305	130
at Home	.411	.500	.638	282	116	28	3	10	50	53	24		.385	.474	.541	1188	457	98	8	24	152	203	108
on Road	.312	.421	.535	269	84	12	3	14	39	52	24		.322	.412	.438	1221	393	62	7	22	141	192	89
vs. Groundball	.375	.476	.588	277	104	20	3	11	41	53	24		.356	.450	.494	1170	417	75	7	24	141	201	88
vs. Flyball	.350	.446	.588	274	96	20	3	13	48	52	24		.349	.435	.484	1239	433	85	8	22	152	194	109
vs. Finesse	.377	.467	.612	273	103	19	3	13	45	46	18		.361	.440	.505	1353	489	89	9	29	158	190	90
vs. Power	.349	.455	.565	278	97	21	3	11	44	59	30		.342	.445	.469	1056	361	71	6	17	135	205	107
on Grass	.369	.471	.577	452	167	33	5	17	70	91	41		.355	.445	.489	2030	721	136	11	38	244	335	172
on Artificial Turf	.333	.412	.636	99	33	7	1	7	19	14	7		.340	.428	.488	379	129	24	4	8	49	60	25
Day Games	.337	.458	.489	184	62	11	1	5	19	42	16		.341	.439	.470	762	260	54	4	12	82	134	53
Night Games	.376	.462	.638	367	138	29	5	19	70	63	32		.358	.444	.498	1647	590	106	11	34	211	261	144
April	.275	.392	.375	80	22	2	0	2	5	16	7		.294	.419	.401	299	88	15	1	5	28	65	30
May	.388	.466	.684	98	38	8	0	7	22	16	14		.372	.466	.525	398	148	24	2	11	63	72	33
June	.485	.581	.762	101	49	8	4	4	19	22	5		.366	.451	.504	399	146	30	5	5	39	61	33
July	.324	.392	.595	111	36	11	2	5	18	12	9		.322	.409	.468	410	132	30	3	8	55	60	37
August	.344	.462	.484	93	32	4	0	3	11	22	8		.356	.435	.498	464	165	29	2	11	56	67	35
Sept/Oct	.338	.460	.574	68	23	7	0	3	14	17	5		.390	.472	.513	439	171	32	2	6	52	70	29
Bases Empty	.366	.446	.587	322	118	26	3	13	13	45	32		.350	.426	.483	1432	501	94	8	27	27	189	119
Leadoff	.369	.457	.615	130	48	8	0	8	8	21	14		.367	.443	.501	641	235	43	2	13	13	88	49
Not Leadoff	.365	.438	.568	192	70	18	3	5	5	24	18		.336	.412	.469	791	266	51	6	14	14	101	70
Runners On	.358	.480	.590	229	82	14	3	11	76	60	16		.357	.466	.497	977	349	66	7	19	266	206	78
First Base Only	.379	.434	.641	103	39	2	2	7	16	10	6		.359	.429	.513	435	156	28	3	11	30	54	33
Scoring Position	.341	.508	.548	126	43	12	1	4	60	50	10		.356	.492	.485	542	193	38	4	8	236	152	45
Late Innings, Close	.272	.388	.383	81	22	4	1	1	9	15	8		.345	.450	.411	333	115	17	1	1	41	63	29

RBI/Opportunities

	1987		Four Year
Scoring Position	51 / 215 (24%)		219 / 844 (26%)
Scoring Position, 2 Out	14 / 88 (16%)		83 / 394 (21%)
On Third, Less than 2 Out	26 / 48 (54%)		83 / 150 (55%)
RBI in close games / RBI Total	62 / 89 (70%)		184 / 293 (63%)

Barry Bonds
Pittsburgh Pirates

In 1987 Barry Bonds made small improvements in almost all of his offensive performance categories, establishing himself as a player to watch over the next few years. Barry raised his batting average and cut his strikeouts, while posting an impressive increase in his slugging average and increasing his home runs per time at bat. This all added up to a season that was, by any measure, more productive than his rookie season. On the down side, Barry accompanied his decline in strikeouts per at bat with an equally impressive decline in walks per at bat, so that his K/W ratio was almost identical in both years, 1.57 strikeouts for every walk in 1986, and 1.63 strikeouts per walk in 1987. This was only a small decline, to be sure, but the drop in walks is something that should be carefully watched. In 138 more at-bats in 1987, Barry walked 11 fewer times, so that despite a 38 point increase in his batting average, his on-base average did not improve, going from .330 in 1986 to .329 in 1987. If Barry had walked with the same frequency in 1987 as he did in 1986, his improvement in batting average would have driven his on-base average to .362, which would have placed him near the top of the league. If Barry can add the frequent walks back into his offensive mix, and continue the

improvement he showed last year, he'll be quite a player in a very short time.

The other decline in Barry's performance from 1986 to 1987 came in the area of base stealing. Barry ran both less frequently and less successfully in 1987. He is still a good percentage base stealer, but it is to be hoped that his decline in this area is only temporary.

These two areas of Barry's performance, his walk frequency and his base stealing, bear directly on the main question concerning Barry in Pittsburgh right now. That is the question of whether he should be leading off for the Pirates, or batting further down in the order. At this time, it seems clear that his on-base average is too low for him to bat leadoff, and if he continues his power development he'll be too powerful a hitter to bat in the leadoff spot, especially for a team with power problems. If Barry's main attributes as a player were the ability to get on base and speed, then his power would add nicely to his run scoring ability. But it is beginning to look like Barry will be a good power hitter who also has speed. To put it another way, if Barry does develop into a great player, he'll be another Darryl Strawberry, not another Rickey Henderson or Tim Raines.

Pete Palmieri

Bonds, Barry Lamar   Bats: Left   Throws: Left   Born 07/24/64

1987 SEASON AND MAJOR-LEAGUE CAREER BATTING TOTALS

	G	AB	H	2B	3B	HR	TB	R	RBI	TBB	IBB	SO	HP	SH	SF	SB	CS	SB%	GDP	AVG	OBP	SLG
87 PIT	150	551	144	34	9	25	271	99	59	54	3	88	3	0	3	32	10	.76	4	.261	.329	.492
2 YEARS	263	964	236	60	12	41	443	171	107	119	5	190	5	2	5	68	17	.80	8	.245	.329	.460

	1987 SEASON											FOUR YEAR TOTALS (1984 – 1987)										
	Ave.	OBP	SLG	AB	H	2B	3B	HR	RBI	BB	SO	Ave.	OBP	SLG	AB	H	2B	3B	HR	RBI	BB	SO
Totals	.261	.329	.492	551	144	34	9	25	59	54	88	.245	.329	.460	964	236	60	12	41	107	119	190
vs. Left	.228	.303	.456	206	47	13	5	8	21	20	42	.224	.323	.420	357	80	23	7	11	35	49	81
vs. Right	.281	.345	.513	345	97	21	4	17	38	34	46	.257	.333	.483	607	156	37	5	30	72	70	109
at Home	.265	.324	.500	268	71	15	6	12	31	22	50	.255	.338	.486	479	122	32	8	21	57	58	106
on Road	.258	.333	.484	283	73	19	3	13	28	32	38	.235	.321	.433	485	114	28	4	20	50	61	84
vs. Groundball	.266	.326	.500	244	65	16	4	11	20	21	39	.250	.320	.446	444	111	27	6	16	46	44	88
vs. Flyball	.257	.331	.485	307	79	18	5	14	39	33	49	.240	.337	.471	520	125	33	6	25	61	75	102
vs. Finesse	.286	.337	.554	287	82	22	5	15	35	21	34	.248	.316	.474	529	131	35	5	25	64	51	84
vs. Power	.235	.321	.424	264	62	12	4	10	24	33	54	.241	.345	.441	435	105	25	7	16	43	68	106
on Grass	.260	.335	.487	154	40	10	2	7	13	17	25	.250	.332	.460	248	62	15	2	11	24	30	54
on Artificial Turf	.262	.326	.494	397	104	24	7	18	46	37	63	.243	.328	.459	716	174	45	10	30	83	89	136
Day Games	.226	.323	.457	164	37	12	4	6	12	24	23	.214	.307	.417	271	58	20	4	9	22	37	52
Night Games	.276	.332	.506	387	107	22	5	19	47	30	65	.257	.338	.476	693	178	40	8	32	85	82	138
April	.231	.338	.431	65	15	3	2	2	8	11	11	.242	.346	.439	66	16	3	2	2	9	11	11
May	.296	.378	.551	98	29	7	3	4	12	12	16	.283	.372	.528	106	30	8	3	4	12	14	19
June	.233	.280	.448	116	27	5	1	6	12	8	16	.238	.320	.476	227	54	14	2	12	26	28	49
July	.272	.337	.489	92	25	6	1	4	7	8	18	.230	.310	.424	165	38	10	2	6	13	18	42
August	.278	.348	.633	79	22	8	1	6	12	8	13	.262	.353	.561	187	49	16	2	12	31	26	33
Sept/Oct	.257	.306	.416	101	26	5	1	3	8	7	14	.230	.302	.352	213	49	9	1	5	16	22	36
Bases Empty	.265	.324	.496	355	94	23	7	15	15	28	48	.239	.321	.460	628	150	40	9	27	27	73	112
Leadoff	.286	.350	.521	213	61	15	4	9	9	18	30	.265	.345	.492	366	97	25	5	16	16	42	65
Not Leadoff	.232	.283	.458	142	33	8	3	6	6	10	18	.202	.287	.416	262	53	15	4	11	11	31	47
Runners On	.255	.338	.485	196	50	11	2	10	44	26	40	.256	.343	.458	336	86	20	3	14	80	46	78
First Base Only	.381	.409	.702	84	32	7	1	6	15	4	14	.375	.416	.680	128	48	13	1	8	21	9	25
Scoring Position	.161	.292	.321	112	18	4	1	4	29	22	26	.183	.302	.322	208	38	7	2	6	59	37	53
Late Innings, Close	.274	.333	.537	95	26	6	2	5	11	9	16	.242	.330	.448	165	40	10	3	6	17	22	39

RBI/Opportunities

Scoring Position	20 / 163 (12%)	47 / 295 (16%)
Scoring Position, 2 Out	10 / 95 (11%)	18 / 160 (11%)
On Third, Less than 2 Out	6 / 23 (26%)	17 / 49 (35%)
RBI in close games / RBI Total	41 / 59 (69%)	70 / 107 (65%)

Bobby Bonilla
Pittsburgh Pirates

Bobby Bonilla opened the season batting and playing right field. Maybe that was the problem.

When the announcers call you "Roberto," as in Clemente, and when the team that drafted you thought they made such a mistake in letting you go that they gave up a (semi-) front line pitcher to get you back, especially when you hadn't gotten out of AA two years before, you might begin to think that they might be expecting just a bit too much from you.

Bonilla didn't give up. When a severe ankle injury nearly ended his career before it began, he didn't give up. When he came off that injury, and was drafted by the White Sox having only minimal time in AA, he didn't give up. When the Pirates traded for him, the world was expected of Bonilla and he didn't give up. When he finished May, 1987, hitting .233 he didn't give up. (Was he stubborn or obstinate?)

Jim Morrison had been playing third base for a year and a half, but he stopped hitting, and began depending on his glove to hold the job. In a matter of weeks the Pirates were casting about for a new third baseman.

Syd Thrift claims he saw Bonilla playing third base "a long time ago"; these statements have to be taken with a grain of salt. But Bonilla had finished 1986 playing third, and he didn't embarrass himself (too much). The Pirates had nothing to lose.

Bonilla had begun to come out of it by then, becoming the first Pirate to hit home runs in the same game from both sides of the plate, and adding 46 points to his average by the end of June.

When you're playing the outfield you've got time to think about everything, including your lousy swing at that curveball last inning. Playing the infield, especially third, no time. Last inning's strikeout could be this inning's error that could cost the team the game.

Bonilla wouldn't have any time to worry about his failures at the plate, and soon he didn't have any to worry about. Bonilla hit .321 after the All-Star break, complete with .385 OBA and 8 home runs.

Defensively he made 10 errors in the second half of the season, roughly on par with some more experienced third basemen (Terry Pendleton made 13; Tim Wallach made 12, and Mike Schmidt made 6 in the same period of time).

Bonilla can't play third base his whole career. His ankle caused him to miss games last year, and the pounding he will take playing on artificial turf almost 3/4th of the year, combined with his size (6' 3", 210 pounds), will cut into his range.

The Pirates tried to get a third baseman as that right-handed power bat, but nothing came of it. Darnell Coles or Jeff King could end up at third, with Bonilla moving to first, but that won't happen for a while yet.

Meanwhile Bonilla will open next year playing third, and probably batting cleanup. Sometimes great expectations do come through.

Mike Sopp

Bonilla, Roberto Martin Antonio "Bobby"

Bats: Both   Throws: Right   Born 02/23/63

1987 SEASON AND MAJOR-LEAGUE CAREER BATTING TOTALS

	G	AB	H	2B	3B	HR	TB	R	RBI	TBB	IBB	SO	HP	SH	SF	SB	CS	SB%	GDP	AVG	OBP	SLG
87 PIT	141	466	140	33	3	15	224	58	77	39	4	64	2	0	8	3	5	.38	8	.300	.351	.481
2 YEARS	279	892	249	49	7	18	366	113	120	101	7	152	4	5	9	11	10	.52	17	.279	.352	.410

	1987 SEASON										FOUR YEAR TOTALS (1984 – 1987)									
	Ave.	OBP	SLG	AB	H	2B	3B	HR	RBI	BB	SO	Ave.	OBP	SLG	AB	H	2B	3B	HR	RBI	BB	SO
Totals	.300	.351	.481	466	140	33	3	15	77	39	64	.279	.352	.410	892	249	49	7	18	120	101	152
vs. Left	.308	.345	.474	234	72	14	2	7	41	14	21	.291	.349	.411	416	121	23	3	7	60	37	46
vs. Right	.293	.357	.487	232	68	19	1	8	36	25	43	.269	.355	.410	476	128	26	4	11	60	64	106
at Home	.265	.327	.430	223	59	14	1	7	33	20	27	.267	.346	.400	423	113	21	4	9	64	49	64
on Road	.333	.374	.527	243	81	19	2	8	44	19	37	.290	.357	.420	469	136	28	3	9	56	52	88
vs. Groundball	.332	.397	.490	208	69	17	2	4	31	24	31	.294	.372	.401	377	111	24	2	4	48	47	58
vs. Flyball	.275	.313	.473	258	71	16	1	11	46	15	33	.268	.337	.417	515	138	25	5	14	72	54	94
vs. Finesse	.320	.363	.478	253	81	15	2	7	43	19	24	.303	.371	.440	498	151	30	4	10	70	54	63
vs. Power	.277	.338	.484	213	59	18	1	8	34	20	40	.249	.327	.373	394	98	19	3	8	50	47	89
on Grass	.336	.405	.504	113	38	11	1	2	15	14	22	.308	.392	.422	351	108	19	3	5	42	49	65
on Artificial Turf	.289	.333	.473	353	102	22	2	13	62	25	42	.261	.325	.403	541	141	30	4	13	78	52	87
Day Games	.321	.360	.481	162	52	12	1	4	21	11	24	.302	.360	.426	298	90	20	1	5	40	27	47
Night Games	.289	.347	.480	304	88	21	2	11	56	28	40	.268	.348	.402	594	159	29	6	13	80	74	105
April	.228	.241	.281	57	13	3	0	0	4	1	6	.260	.306	.327	104	27	5	1	0	8	7	14
May	.261	.370	.457	46	12	0	0	3	8	7	6	.235	.331	.348	132	31	3	0	4	15	18	20
June	.346	.356	.494	81	28	10	1	0	10	2	12	.322	.388	.463	149	48	14	2	1	23	17	31
July	.267	.350	.500	86	23	3	1	5	13	12	8	.275	.349	.435	131	36	4	1	5	15	16	18
August	.333	.355	.539	102	34	9	0	4	22	5	19	.298	.351	.452	188	56	15	1	4	36	17	34
Sept/Oct	.319	.396	.521	94	30	8	1	3	20	12	13	.271	.360	.399	188	51	8	2	4	23	26	35
Bases Empty	.302	.351	.484	225	68	12	1	9	9	16	25	.260	.337	.366	481	125	17	2	10	10	55	81
Leadoff	.274	.330	.411	95	26	4	0	3	3	8	10	.266	.341	.348	184	49	6	0	3	3	21	27
Not Leadoff	.323	.367	.538	130	42	8	1	6	6	8	15	.256	.334	.377	297	76	11	2	7	7	34	54
Runners On	.299	.352	.477	241	72	21	2	6	68	23	39	.302	.367	.462	411	124	32	5	8	110	46	71
First Base Only	.320	.364	.456	103	33	9	1	1	6	7	17	.347	.393	.488	170	59	12	3	2	10	13	27
Scoring Position	.283	.344	.493	138	39	12	1	5	62	16	22	.270	.350	.444	241	65	20	2	6	100	33	44
Late Innings, Close	.321	.391	.506	81	26	10	1	1	14	10	13	.270	.354	.403	159	43	13	1	2	20	21	32

RBI/Opportunities

Scoring Position	50 / 189 (26%)	83 / 331 (25%)
Scoring Position, 2 Out	16 / 80 (20%)	24 / 131 (18%)
On Third, Less than 2 Out	30 / 45 (67%)	43 / 74 (58%)
RBI in close games / RBI Total	49 / 77 (64%)	77 / 120 (64%)

Bob Boone
California Angels

When Bob Boone settled into the catcher's box against Kansas City last September 16, he became the all-time leader in games caught. Game 1919 moved him past Al Lopez, and it looks like game 2,000 will come pretty easily.

Boone caught 127 games in 1987. Only two other AL catchers caught more, Terry Kennedy (142) and Ernie Whitt (132). It was Boone's seventh straight season with over 125 games behind the plate; the 12th time in his 16-year career. Over the past seven years, he's averaged nearly 140 games behind the plate. He now tops the all-time list with 1935 games caught, and he's done it by catching more games past age 35 than any catcher in major league history. Boone turned 40 shortly after the season ended. He can't catch forever,; it just seems like it.

Interestingly, Boone would have reached the top spot a lot earlier except for missing the first 26 games because of his failed free agency bid. (Under the rules, he couldn't be re-signed by the Angels until May 1.) The 1981 strike that stood up for free agency also cost him 60 games.

Boone's free agency actually gave the club a chance to experiment with its catching future. The Angels acquired veteran Butch Wynegar, both to fill in until Boone returned and to ease some of his load afterward. That didn't work. Wynegar caught the team's first 18 games, but injuries effectively sidelined him nearly the rest of the season. Darrel Miller, who is an exceptional athlete, isn't a good catcher, and Boone returned to his normal workhorse role.

Boone's value to the team is his defense and consummate skill in handling pitchers. He's got a good arm and a quick release, and the team teaches its pitchers to keep runners close enough to give the catcher a chance at stealers.

Offensively, Boone is a modest threat. His .242 average in 1987 was actually an improvement over 1986, but his homer and RBI production slipped. Boone is particularly valuable in things that don't show up in a box score. He is an excellent practitioner of manager Gene Mauch's "little ball." The Angels again led the AL in sacrifices with 70, and Boone kicked in 14.

Each year, the Angels say they won't ask Boone to catch as many games as he did the year before. Yet, each year, he is among the leaders in games caught, and 1988 should be no exception. He keeps himself in remarkable shape year-round, and the Angels just don't have anyone better unless Wynegar makes a strong comeback.

Boone has his own special reason for coming back in 1988, and it has nothing to do with going for 2,000 games behind the plate. Boone has 99 career home runs, one more and he and his father Ray become only the second father-son combination to smack 100 homers each in the majors (Gus and Buddy Bell are the others).

Dean Hill

Boone, Robert Raymond "Bob"

Bats: Right   Throws: Right   Born 11/19/47

1987 SEASON AND MAJOR-LEAGUE CAREER BATTING TOTALS

	G	AB	H	2B	3B	HR	TB	R	RBI	TBB	IBB	SO	HP	SH	SF	SB	CS	SB%	GDP	AVG	OBP	SLG
87 CAL	128	389	94	18	0	3	121	42	33	35	0	36	1	14	3	0	2	.00	10	.242	.304	.311
16 YEARS	1971	6371	1595	270	24	99	2210	597	735	568	84	533	16	12	3 7	3 3	2 4	5 .4	2 16	4 .25	0 .31	0 .34

	1987 SEASON											FOUR YEAR TOTALS (1984 – 1987)										
	Ave.	OBP	SLG	AB	H	2B	3B	HR	RBI	BB	SO	Ave.	OBP	SLG	AB	H	2B	3B	HR	RBI	BB	SO
Totals	.239	.301	.306	389	93	17	0	3	33	35	36	.227	.284	.298	1741	396	62	3	18	169	140	145
vs. Left	.284	.333	.321	134	38	5	0	0	13	11	8	.231	.292	.281	580	134	20	0	3	54	52	35
vs. Right	.216	.285	.298	255	55	12	0	3	20	24	28	.226	.279	.306	1161	262	42	3	15	115	88	110
at Home	.242	.316	.296	186	45	7	0	1	14	20	19	.216	.283	.262	839	181	26	2	3	76	79	77
on Road	.236	.288	.315	203	48	10	0	2	19	15	17	.238	.285	.330	902	215	36	1	15	93	61	68
vs. Groundball	.261	.322	.335	188	49	8	0	2	19	18	17	.238	.288	.311	850	202	36	1	8	87	59	70
vs. Flyball	.219	.282	.279	201	44	9	0	1	14	17	19	.218	.280	.285	891	194	26	2	10	82	81	75
vs. Finesse	.245	.299	.303	188	46	8	0	1	18	14	10	.217	.270	.283	985	214	34	2	9	88	70	75
vs. Power	.234	.304	.308	201	47	9	0	2	15	21	26	.241	.301	.316	756	182	28	1	9	81	70	70
on Grass	.246	.307	.310	329	81	15	0	2	27	29	29	.232	.288	.306	1476	343	54	3	16	143	119	124
on Artificial Turf	.200	.269	.283	60	12	2	0	1	6	6	7	.200	.260	.253	265	53	8	0	2	26	21	21
Day Games	.261	.313	.370	119	31	7	0	2	12	9	11	.241	.286	.339	481	116	20	0	9	56	33	43
Night Games	.230	.297	.278	270	62	10	0	1	21	26	25	.222	.283	.282	1260	280	42	3	9	113	107	102
April	.000	.000	.000	0	0	0	0	0	0	0	0	.217	.260	.300	207	45	11	0	2	14	12	17
May	.266	.329	.297	64	17	2	0	0	5	6	6	.244	.315	.263	262	64	3	1	0	26	27	23
June	.250	.348	.325	80	20	3	0	1	7	12	8	.218	.280	.311	312	68	12	1	5	31	27	24
July	.247	.267	.358	81	20	6	0	1	11	3	8	.219	.265	.304	306	67	14	0	4	32	20	23
August	.236	.313	.292	89	21	5	0	0	6	9	8	.226	.296	.304	319	72	10	0	5	33	31	26
Sept/Oct	.200	.247	.253	75	15	1	0	1	4	5	6	.239	.287	.299	335	80	12	1	2	33	23	32
Bases Empty	.226	.300	.288	226	51	5	0	3	3	24	23	.229	.290	.310	961	220	30	3	14	14	82	82
Leadoff	.174	.248	.217	92	16	1	0	1	1	9	9	.223	.285	.320	394	88	11	0	9	9	34	30
Not Leadoff	.261	.336	.336	134	35	4	0	2	2	15	14	.233	.293	.303	567	132	19	3	5	5	48	52
Runners On	.258	.303	.331	163	42	12	0	0	30	11	13	.226	.279	.282	780	176	32	0	4	155	58	63
First Base Only	.242	.265	.288	66	16	3	0	0	0	1	4	.226	.253	.279	301	68	13	0	1	8	10	22
Scoring Position	.268	.327	.361	97	26	9	0	0	30	10	9	.225	.294	.284	479	108	19	0	3	147	48	41
Late Innings, Close	.158	.250	.211	57	9	0	0	1	1	6	8	.219	.283	.305	279	61	6	0	6	29	24	26

RBI/Opportunities

Scoring Position	29 / 132 (22%)	140 / 647 (22%)
Scoring Position, 2 Out	14 / 78 (18%)	56 / 322 (17%)
On Third, Less than 2 Out	10 / 17 (59%)	55 / 105 (52%)
RBI in close games / RBI Total	23 / 33 (70%)	102 / 169 (60%)

Phil Bradley
Seattle Mariners

During the last day of the 1987 winter meetings, a lot of Mariner fans had their "Phil Bradley Crying Towels" out. No, they weren't upset because they were about to lose probably the best pure athlete to wear a Seattle Mariner uniform. They were scared to death that the M's brass was about to blow the deal. Not just the Phillies deal, but any deal involving Bradley. Needless to say, Phil was not too popular in Seattle.

It's hard to fathom any baseball fan that would willingly want to see their team trade away a star with the impressive credentials that Phil Bradley possesses. Hey, this guy was 1.9 hits away from hitting .300 or better for the fourth year in a row! That spans his entire major league career. For crying out loud, nobody does that except Mattingly and Boggs! Bradley hit 38 doubles, 10 triples, 14 homers, walked 84 times, stole 40 bases, drove in 67 runs, and hit .224 with runners in scoring position. Wait a minute . . . hit *what* with runners in scoring position?

After scoring all but just a handful of Mariner games, one becomes well aware of how shallow stats become when scoring opportunities are missed on a consistent basis. However, that was not the crux of the anti-Bradley sentiment. It was his outspoken and blunt disdain toward his club, his teammates, the fans, and the city of Seattle.

As best as I can gather, it all came to light on the last day of the 1986 season, when he publicly blasted his teammates for not playing hard. For talking about fishing, not baseball. For losing the last 9 games of the season. Maybe he was right. In any case, the Mariner brass scampered about all winter trying to find ways to motivate the team, including a positive-thinking seminar.

Keeping in line with the newly founded major league owner austerity program, the M's sent out 1987 contracts reflecting proposed pay cuts to everyone on the team. Bradley was insulted, said so, and took the club to arbitration. Based on his impressive stats, he was granted a $750,000 contract. Was he happy? No. Apparently, the suggested pay cut was the last straw for him. He privately asked for a trade in spring training and made it public later in the year. This time he whined about the team, the fans, and the Kingdome. Some of his teammates responded. So much for positive thinking.

That was the last straw for the fans. The next day, a local radio sports talk show took a poll. The overwhelming results were to ship Phil Bradley elsewhere. Anywhere. And soon. They had put up with his sullen, whimpering attitude long enough. No one can argue his potential or his numbers. If he applies himself, is happy, and is willing to hit in the leadoff position for the Phillies, he will be a great asset to his new team. The big question is . . . will he be happy? In his exit interview with the *Seattle Times* he said, "Happy at last, or at least, happy for a while." So much for positive thinking.

Merrianna McCully

Bradley, Philip Poole "Phil"

Bats: Right   Throws: Right   Born 03/11/59

1987 SEASON AND MAJOR-LEAGUE CAREER BATTING TOTALS

	G	AB	H	2B	3B	HR	TB	R	RBI	TBB	IBB	SO	HP	SH	SF	SB	CS	SB%	GDP	AVG	OBP	SLG
87 SEA	158	603	179	38	10	14	279	101	67	84	2	119	8	1	5	40	10	.80	18	.297	.387	.463
5 YEARS	607	2159	649	112	26	52	969	346	234	258	9	448	31	18	10	107	40	.73	47	.301	.382	.449

	1987 SEASON											FOUR YEAR TOTALS (1984 – 1987)										
	Ave.	OBP	SLG	AB	H	2B	3B	HR	RBI	BB	SO	Ave.	OBP	SLG	AB	H	2B	3B	HR	RBI	BB	SO
Totals	.297	.387	.463	603	179	38	10	14	67	84	119	.302	.383	.454	2092	631	110	26	52	229	250	443
vs. Left	.347	.426	.642	176	61	15	2	11	26	25	30	.292	.370	.478	590	172	30	7	22	67	71	113
vs. Right	.276	.371	.389	427	118	23	8	3	41	59	89	.306	.388	.444	1502	459	80	19	30	162	179	330
at Home	.309	.398	.520	304	94	18	5	12	41	43	64	.315	.398	.492	1075	339	64	15	32	130	134	211
on Road	.284	.376	.405	299	85	20	5	2	26	41	55	.287	.367	.413	1017	292	46	11	20	99	116	232
vs. Groundball	.276	.389	.379	319	88	13	4	4	28	56	54	.290	.377	.439	1027	298	45	12	28	113	131	181
vs. Flyball	.320	.385	.556	284	91	25	6	10	39	28	65	.313	.389	.468	1065	333	65	14	24	116	119	262
vs. Finesse	.281	.359	.461	334	94	23	5	9	32	35	60	.326	.392	.497	1235	403	76	15	35	129	115	195
vs. Power	.316	.420	.465	269	85	15	5	5	35	49	59	.266	.370	.391	857	228	34	11	17	100	135	248
on Grass	.268	.358	.394	231	62	15	4	2	20	30	46	.285	.364	.415	772	220	31	9	17	79	88	182
on Artificial Turf	.315	.405	.505	372	117	23	6	12	47	54	73	.311	.394	.477	1320	411	79	17	35	150	162	261
Day Games	.255	.366	.363	157	40	9	1	2	16	24	43	.294	.386	.407	541	159	33	5	6	48	75	130
Night Games	.312	.395	.498	446	139	29	9	12	51	60	76	.304	.382	.470	1551	472	77	21	46	181	175	313
April	.184	.374	.263	76	14	1	1	1	9	21	18	.250	.349	.378	288	72	13	3	6	32	42	57
May	.252	.322	.456	103	26	8	5	1	10	11	25	.275	.361	.428	313	86	17	8	5	23	43	67
June	.340	.436	.550	100	34	8	2	3	10	16	17	.303	.371	.484	347	105	20	5	11	44	37	70
July	.345	.402	.632	87	30	6	2	5	14	8	14	.333	.398	.466	309	103	11	3	8	34	33	61
August	.319	.391	.496	113	36	8	0	4	11	12	22	.319	.381	.493	404	129	26	4	12	43	39	93
Sept/Oct	.315	.397	.371	124	39	7	0	0	13	16	23	.316	.395	.452	431	136	23	3	10	53	56	95
Bases Empty	.334	.409	.542	356	119	27	7	11	11	40	65	.306	.375	.479	1235	378	64	16	39	39	132	255
Leadoff	.375	.463	.558	104	39	10	3	1	1	17	14	.316	.386	.460	389	123	26	6	6	6	44	76
Not Leadoff	.317	.386	.536	252	80	17	4	10	10	23	51	.301	.371	.487	846	255	38	10	33	33	88	179
Runners On	.243	.358	.348	247	60	11	3	3	56	44	54	.295	.380	.418	857	253	46	10	13	190	118	188
First Base Only	.280	.344	.451	82	23	2	3	2	7	7	10	.332	.393	.460	352	117	19	4	6	22	34	62
Scoring Position	.224	.364	.297	165	37	9	0	1	49	37	44	.269	.372	.388	505	136	27	6	7	168	84	126
Late Innings, Close	.268	.358	.408	71	19	2	1	2	7	9	22	.306	.378	.471	297	91	10	6	9	47	33	71

RBI/Opportunities

Scoring Position	47 / 240 (20%)	150 / 713 (21%)
Scoring Position, 2 Out	14 / 86 (16%)	55 / 278 (20%)
On Third, Less than 2 Out	22 / 43 (51%)	58 / 130 (45%)
RBI in close games / RBI Total	32 / 67 (48%)	140 / 229 (61%)

Glenn Braggs
Milwaukee Brewers

If you aren't a Brewer fan or don't read *Baseball America,* you may not know that Glenn Braggs was supposed to be an All-Star by now, So first let me touch on his past. In Glenn's worst year in the minors, he hit .296, slugged .496 and had a .396 on-base percentage. He's had OB%s over .440 a few times (once over .500) and slugged over .600 twice (.680 once). He's been in the same leagues with Mike Aldrete, Mickey Brantley, Jack Howell, Dave Valle and Devon White. Every one of them save White (who's two months younger) is over a year older. He consistently outhit them all.

Which is why, in mid-season 1987, Brewer fans were wondering what on earth was wrong with the guy. By the All-Star break, Braggs had played 158 major league games in his career, had hit .238, slugged .377 and had 44 walks and 51 RBIs in 469 at-bats. For the year he was batting .240, slugging .402 and had a .333 OBP. His defense was awful (up from godawful in '86). Frankly, he looked like the reincarnation of Mark Brouhard.

Whatever the problems were, extreme pressure wasn't one of them. On the same day that they promoted Glenn in 1986, Milwaukee re-signed Gorman Thomas for his swan song. Nobody noticed Braggs for over a month—until people looked at the stats and said "Hey, this guy hasn't done what they said he was going to." In the spring of '87 he moved to right field (trading places with Rob Deer) in the

hope that the switch to a more familiar position would help his hitting. That improved his defense, but it didn't help one bit at the plate.

If anything, Braggs has gone out of his way to put pressure on himself. He's not a Pete Rose type; the fans don't like his lackadaisical play in the outfield. He never has a lot to say to reporters either—another strike against a player who needs to make good. If he hadn't finished with a flurry (.299 BA, .332 OB%, .458 SL% after the break), you'd really have to wonder how much time he'd have left in Milwaukee.

The things that Braggs has going for him are that he is still fairly young (25 on opening day) and he plays for a good organization. He doesn't have to worry about being benched, sent down to the minors, or getting his butt chewed by the owner every time he goes 0-for-4. Another thing he has going for him is that he is currently one of the three best outfielders on the roster. Until a new prospect arrives, his job is safe.

The key stats for Braggs in 1988 are, to be blunt, everything. He desperately needs to show marked improvement in every aspect of his game. Check his numbers at the end of May. If he's hitting .320 or has a dozen homers, then you'll know that he's a ballplayer after all. If he's done both, then you'll know that *Baseball America* was right; punch his name on the All-Star ballot.

Scott Segrin

Braggs, Glenn Erick

Bats: Right   Throws: Right   Born 10/17/62

1987 SEASON AND MAJOR-LEAGUE CAREER BATTING TOTALS

	G	AB	H	2B	3B	HR	TB	R	RBI	TBB	IBB	SO	HP	SH	SF	SB	CS	SB%	GDP	AVG	OBP	SLG
87 MIL	132	505	136	28	7	13	217	67	77	47	7	96	4	2	7	12	5	.71	20	.269	.332	.430
2 YEARS	190	720	187	36	9	17	292	86	95	58	7	143	5	4	10	13	6	.68	26	.260	.315	.406

	1987 SEASON											FOUR YEAR TOTALS (1984 – 1987)									
	Ave.	OBP	SLG	AB	H	2B	3B	HR	RBI	BB	SO	Ave.	OBP	SLG	AB	H	2B	3B	HR	RBI	BB	SO
Totals	.269	.332	.430	505	136	28	7	13	77	47	96	.260	.315	.406	720	187	36	9	17	95	58	143
vs. Left	.274	.349	.393	168	46	10	2	2	23	18	29	.279	.340	.425	226	63	14	2	5	33	20	42
vs. Right	.267	.324	.448	337	90	18	5	11	54	29	67	.251	.304	.397	494	124	22	7	12	62	38	101
at Home	.261	.323	.383	253	66	11	4	4	42	25	51	.274	.334	.401	339	93	15	5	6	50	32	64
on Road	.278	.342	.476	252	70	17	3	9	35	22	45	.247	.298	.409	381	94	21	4	11	45	26	79
vs. Groundball	.274	.327	.466	277	76	15	4	10	49	20	48	.281	.331	.463	356	100	16	5	13	57	26	64
vs. Flyball	.263	.338	.386	228	60	13	3	3	28	27	48	.239	.300	.349	364	87	20	4	4	38	32	79
vs. Finesse	.266	.301	.434	290	77	12	5	9	46	14	49	.256	.289	.400	403	103	15	5	11	56	18	71
vs. Power	.274	.370	.423	215	59	16	2	4	31	33	47	.265	.346	.413	317	84	21	4	6	39	40	72
on Grass	.278	.341	.442	421	117	25	7	10	68	40	78	.266	.323	.417	605	161	31	9	14	84	51	117
on Artificial Turf	.226	.286	.369	84	19	3	0	3	9	7	18	.226	.270	.348	115	26	5	0	3	11	7	26
Day Games	.280	.322	.429	161	45	8	2	4	22	9	27	.260	.309	.387	204	53	10	2	4	27	14	42
Night Games	.265	.337	.430	344	91	20	5	9	55	38	69	.260	.318	.413	516	134	26	7	13	68	44	101
April	.295	.364	.511	88	26	5	1	4	14	10	18	.295	.364	.511	88	26	5	1	4	14	10	18
May	.200	.310	.347	75	15	3	1	2	8	11	20	.200	.310	.347	75	15	3	1	2	8	11	20
June	.207	.313	.293	58	12	2	0	1	6	7	13	.207	.313	.293	58	12	2	0	1	6	7	13
July	.302	.355	.542	96	29	8	3	3	20	9	13	.295	.338	.489	139	41	12	3	3	24	10	21
August	.256	.296	.367	90	23	5	1	1	13	5	17	.243	.284	.359	181	44	7	1	4	20	10	35
Sept/Oct	.316	.343	.449	98	31	5	1	2	16	5	15	.274	.309	.397	179	49	7	3	3	23	10	36
Bases Empty	.271	.332	.462	273	74	12	5	10	10	24	52	.269	.319	.445	402	108	18	7	13	13	29	80
Leadoff	.278	.363	.478	90	25	4	1	4	4	11	16	.289	.347	.504	135	39	5	3	6	6	11	23
Not Leadoff	.268	.316	.454	183	49	8	4	6	6	13	36	.258	.305	.416	267	69	13	4	7	7	18	57
Runners On	.267	.332	.392	232	62	16	2	3	67	23	44	.248	.311	.355	318	79	18	2	4	82	29	63
First Base Only	.241	.284	.386	83	20	7	1	1	6	3	14	.256	.297	.380	121	31	7	1	2	8	5	23
Scoring Position	.282	.356	.396	149	42	9	1	2	61	20	30	.244	.319	.340	197	48	11	1	2	74	24	40
Late Innings, Close	.256	.327	.395	86	22	5	2	1	10	10	21	.244	.317	.350	123	30	6	2	1	12	14	30

RBI/Opportunities

Scoring Position	57 / 215 (27%)	69 / 283 (24%)
Scoring Position, 2 Out	24 / 111 (22%)	29 / 143 (20%)
On Third, Less than 2 Out	21 / 41 (51%)	26 / 53 (49%)
RBI in close games / RBI Total	43 / 77 (56%)	53 / 95 (56%)

Mickey Brantley
Seattle Mariners

" . . . Leading off the bottom of the first for the Mariners we have Brantley, Bradley and Bradley . . . (pause) . . . This can't be right? Sounds like a law firm to me!"

Listening to visiting announcers call a game against the Mariners was always good for a laugh when Williams penciled in all three of his "B" boys together. The Ranger broadcast crew declared it illegal, said it broke all the standard baseball announcing rules, and the next time they were going to create their own lineup.

Well, the confusion will lessen in 1988 as one of the Bradleys is now better known as "Philly Phil," but there is very little confusion as to who will take over Phil Bradley's number two spot in the batting order. Now I know that the M's have picked up extra outfielders, and the competition at spring training should be intense, but Brantley has a good shot at being their everyday centerfielder. Especially if he can continue the offensive barrage that he displayed in September and October. As you can see by Mick's 1987 totals, his offense is productive, but in his last 106 AB he hit .368 with 7 homers, 1 triple and 9 doubles.

In 252 less at-bats than Phil Bradley, Brantley drove in just 13 fewer runs. If you project that out to 603 AB, we're talking over 90 RBIs. Mick batted .376 with runners in scoring position last year, Phil battled .224. So you can see why the Mariners didn't panic when Bradley, Phil that is, publicly asked for a trade. Mickey is a natural for the number-two spot and the ink hadn't dried on the trade agreement before Dick Williams announced the change in his line-up. Mickey isn't quite as quick on the base paths, but if he gets in a full season, he should have over 30 SB.

Getting in a full season is probably the only problem in this whole scheme. Brantley has been somewhat injury prone and it was nagging injuries that caused his rookie debut to go unheeded.

In the winter of '86, he had to have scar tissue broken loose from a previous shoulder surgery. Other injuries cost him probably 200 AB in 1987. However, he finished up the year looking very strong and I'm sure that the Mariners are hoping that his strength will continue over into the 1988 season.

For those who'll miss the name game, another Mariner trade has created an interesting combo. If Williams were forced into letting his new pitcher Ken Dixon hit, we could have a lineup of Brantley and Bradley and Nixon and Dixon . . . (pause) . . . This can't be right! Sounds like a reindeer team to me!!

Merrianna McCully

Brantley, Michael Charles "Mickey" Bats: Right Throws: Right Born 06/17/61

1987 SEASON AND MAJOR-LEAGUE CAREER BATTING TOTALS

	G	AB	H	2B	3B	HR	TB	R	RBI	TBB	IBB	SO	HP	SH	SF	SB	CS	SB%	GDP	AVG	OBP	SLG
87 SEA	92	351	106	23	2	14	175	52	54	24	0	44	0	0	3	13	4	.76	2	.302	.344	.499
2 YEARS	119	453	126	26	4	17	211	64	61	34	0	65	0	1	3	14	5	.74	5	.278	.327	.466

	1987 SEASON											FOUR YEAR TOTALS (1984 – 1987)										
	Ave.	OBP	SLG	AB	H	2B	3B	HR	RBI	BB	SO	Ave.	OBP	SLG	AB	H	2B	3B	HR	RBI	BB	SO
Totals	.302	.344	.499	351	106	23	2	14	54	24	44	.278	.327	.466	453	126	26	4	17	61	34	65
vs. Left	.283	.324	.528	127	36	8	1	7	26	8	14	.262	.300	.488	160	42	8	2	8	28	9	21
vs. Right	.313	.355	.482	224	70	15	1	7	28	16	30	.287	.341	.454	293	84	18	2	9	33	25	44
at Home	.321	.347	.604	159	51	8	2	11	30	8	17	.290	.326	.555	200	58	10	2	13	36	12	24
on Road	.286	.341	.411	192	55	15	0	3	24	16	27	.269	.327	.395	253	68	16	2	4	25	22	41
vs. Groundball	.291	.355	.478	182	53	12	2	6	27	19	24	.276	.339	.475	221	61	14	3	8	29	22	31
vs. Flyball	.314	.331	.521	169	53	11	0	8	27	5	20	.280	.314	.457	232	65	12	1	9	32	12	34
vs. Finesse	.301	.326	.507	209	63	11	1	10	35	9	24	.290	.319	.502	255	74	13	1	13	39	12	31
vs. Power	.303	.369	.486	142	43	12	1	4	19	15	20	.263	.336	.419	198	52	13	3	4	22	22	34
on Grass	.329	.372	.479	146	48	13	0	3	22	10	19	.303	.355	.453	201	61	14	2	4	23	16	32
on Artificial Turf	.283	.324	.512	205	58	10	2	11	32	14	25	.258	.304	.476	252	65	12	2	13	38	18	33
Day Games	.288	.329	.479	73	21	6	1	2	8	5	7	.253	.314	.432	95	24	6	1	3	9	9	10
Night Games	.306	.348	.504	278	85	17	1	12	46	19	37	.285	.330	.475	358	102	20	3	14	52	25	55
April	.217	.280	.261	23	5	1	0	0	2	2	4	.217	.280	.261	23	5	1	0	0	2	2	4
May	.000	.000	.000	0	0	0	0	0	0	0	0	.000	.000	.000	0	0	0	0	0	0	0	0
June	.267	.293	.453	86	23	5	1	3	16	4	9	.267	.293	.453	86	23	5	1	3	16	4	9
July	.333	.377	.421	57	19	2	0	1	3	4	6	.333	.377	.421	57	19	2	0	1	3	4	6
August	.253	.289	.443	79	20	6	0	3	10	4	11	.222	.277	.389	144	32	7	1	5	16	11	24
Sept/Oct	.368	.419	.670	106	39	9	1	7	23	10	14	.329	.382	.601	143	47	11	2	8	24	13	22
Bases Empty	.290	.335	.457	221	64	12	2	7	7	15	28	.276	.332	.448	286	79	14	4	9	9	24	42
Leadoff	.264	.322	.453	106	28	6	1	4	4	9	9	.261	.327	.472	142	37	6	3	6	6	14	13
Not Leadoff	.313	.347	.461	115	36	6	1	3	3	6	19	.292	.338	.424	144	42	8	1	3	3	10	29
Runners On	.323	.359	.569	130	42	11	0	7	47	9	16	.281	.317	.497	167	47	12	0	8	52	10	23
First Base Only	.222	.300	.489	45	10	3	0	3	6	5	8	.194	.265	.387	62	12	3	0	3	6	6	9
Scoring Position	.376	.391	.612	85	32	8	0	4	41	4	8	.333	.348	.562	105	35	9	0	5	46	4	14
Late Innings, Close	.292	.333	.375	48	14	1	0	1	3	3	6	.254	.309	.381	63	16	2	0	2	4	5	10

RBI/Opportunities

Scoring Position	35 / 104 (34%)		38 / 128 (30%)	
Scoring Position, 2 Out	8 / 36 (22%)		10 / 49 (20%)	
On Third, Less than 2 Out	14 / 24 (58%)		14 / 28 (50%)	
RBI in close games / RBI Total	27 / 54 (50%)		34 / 61 (56%)	

Sid Bream
Pittsburgh Pirates

For Sid Bream, 1987 was a season in which the promise of 1986 did not develop. Sid, who in 1986 was a solid, if unspectacular, hitter and a fine defensive player, declined in almost all offensive categories in 1987, raising his batting average, but lowering both his slugging and on base averages. His defense was good, but given that he plays first base, it seems fair to say that he needs to contribute more with the bat. His production is only marginally above average for the league as a whole, and well below average for a first baseman.

Sid hasn't played many major league games yet, so it is tempting to think about how much he will develop as a hitter. Unfortunately for this line of argument, he will turn 28 this season, and it is questionable how much potential for improvement he really has. At his 1987 level of production, he shouldn't really be able to hold a job. Even his 1986 level of production was impressive primarily as an indicator of what his strengths as a player could be. If Sid had added 3 HR, 12 RBI, 11 walks, and .039 SA points to his 1986 totals, instead of subtracting those amounts from his totals, he would have been a valuable player for the Pirates, and perhaps could have filled a position for several years. As it is now, he is an unproductive player in an important offensive position who is not too many years away from what is likely to be his decline phase.

This season will be a crucial one for Sid. As the Pirates try to consolidate the gains of 1987 and prepare to move into contention, they can ill afford to carry a player who, given the standards of performance for his position, is well below average. By 1989, there is a good chance that Jeff King will be coming out of the minors with very strong credentials. If the Pirates like Bobby Bonilla at third, King would likely push Bream out of a job. If Bonilla's defense doesn't improve, then King (who has played both positions, but who has primarily been a third baseman), may take third, with Bonilla's strong bat moving over to first, and Bream again losing his job. In either case, if he doesn't improve his production, Sid may find himself just filling a space until the Pirates can make the move they will need to make in order to become a championship team.

Peter Palmieri

Bream, Sid

Bats: Left Throws: Left Born 08/03/60

1987 SEASON AND MAJOR-LEAGUE CAREER BATTING TOTALS

	G	AB	H	2B	3B	HR	TB	R	RBI	TBB	IBB	SO	HP	SH	SF	SB	CS	SB%	GDP	AVG	OBP	SLG
87 PIT	149	516	142	25	3	13	212	64	65	49	11	69	0	3	4	9	8	.53	19	.275	.336	.411
5 YEARS	395	1246	327	72	8	35	520	157	171	135	23	177	1	8	15	23	17	.57	39	.262	.331	.417

1987 SEASON / FOUR YEAR TOTALS (1984 – 1987)

	Ave.	OBP	SLG	AB	H	2B	3B	HR	RBI	BB	SO		Ave.	OBP	SLG	AB	H	2B	3B	HR	RBI	BB	SO
Totals	.275	.336	.410	517	142	25	3	13	65	49	69		.263	.332	.419	1236	325	72	8	35	169	133	175
vs. Left	.273	.314	.454	194	53	9	1	8	27	12	29		.242	.287	.388	389	94	20	2	11	53	27	62
vs. Right	.276	.348	.384	323	89	16	2	5	38	37	40		.273	.351	.433	847	231	52	6	24	116	106	113
at Home	.282	.347	.467	259	73	14	2	10	43	27	28		.271	.338	.439	602	163	40	5	17	88	64	74
on Road	.267	.324	.353	258	69	11	1	3	22	22	41		.256	.326	.401	634	162	32	3	18	81	69	101
vs. Groundball	.263	.304	.407	243	64	13	2	6	25	14	26		.269	.325	.417	566	152	37	7	11	66	50	70
vs. Flyball	.285	.362	.412	274	78	12	1	7	40	35	43		.258	.337	.421	670	173	35	1	24	103	83	105
vs. Finesse	.250	.300	.369	260	65	13	0	6	30	19	33		.250	.315	.391	672	168	35	3	18	84	67	83
vs. Power	.300	.370	.451	257	77	12	3	7	35	30	36		.278	.352	.452	564	157	37	5	17	85	66	92
on Grass	.287	.346	.392	143	41	7	1	2	14	13	23		.246	.313	.389	378	93	17	2	11	49	39	63
on Artificial Turf	.270	.332	.417	374	101	18	2	11	51	36	46		.270	.340	.432	858	232	55	6	24	120	94	112
Day Games	.288	.352	.417	163	47	7	1	4	16	16	28		.230	.307	.362	395	91	19	3	9	40	45	72
Night Games	.268	.328	.407	354	95	18	2	9	49	33	41		.278	.343	.446	841	234	53	5	26	129	88	103
April	.317	.406	.600	60	19	3	1	4	7	9	12		.234	.346	.500	158	37	7	1	11	20	27	29
May	.288	.339	.490	104	30	5	2	4	17	8	16		.291	.360	.498	203	59	13	4	7	31	22	26
June	.266	.337	.342	79	21	3	0	1	6	9	8		.254	.335	.385	169	43	8	1	4	19	21	28
July	.259	.315	.353	85	22	5	0	1	11	7	7		.269	.319	.377	175	47	11	1	2	26	13	16
August	.253	.336	.326	95	24	4	0	1	8	12	8		.274	.337	.400	190	52	10	1	4	22	18	19
Sept/Oct	.277	.300	.394	94	26	5	0	2	16	4	18		.255	.317	.384	341	87	23	0	7	51	32	57
Bases Empty	.284	.326	.428	271	77	12	3	7	7	17	37		.254	.306	.417	657	167	35	6	20	20	49	91
Leadoff	.301	.317	.423	123	37	7	1	2	2	3	17		.255	.303	.450	302	77	17	3	12	12	21	34
Not Leadoff	.270	.333	.432	148	40	5	2	5	5	14	20		.254	.308	.389	355	90	18	3	8	8	28	57
Runners On	.264	.345	.390	246	65	13	0	6	58	32	32		.273	.363	.421	579	158	37	2	15	149	84	84
First Base Only	.357	.406	.541	98	35	6	0	4	11	8	12		.309	.354	.494	259	80	18	0	10	28	18	37
Scoring Position	.203	.309	.291	148	30	7	0	2	47	24	20		.244	.370	.363	320	78	19	2	5	121	66	47
Late Innings, Close	.264	.376	.458	72	19	3	1	3	8	13	10		.231	.344	.394	208	48	12	2	6	30	36	37

RBI/Opportunities

Scoring Position	43 / 208 (21%)	108 / 470 (23%)
Scoring Position, 2 Out	21 / 105 (20%)	42 / 213 (20%)
On Third, Less than 2 Out	14 / 37 (38%)	41 / 84 (49%)
RBI in close games / RBI Total	40 / 65 (62%)	112 / 169 (66%)

Bob Brenly
San Francisco Giants

The annual replacement of Bob Brenly from the starting ranks continues in 1988. The roster of hot rookie prospects has included Bob Cummings, Ron Pruitt, Randy Gomez, Jeff Ransom, John Rabb, Phil Ouellette, Matt Nokes and Mackey Sasser. This year's future prospect is Kirt Manwaring. Every year the Giants tout the catcher from their Double A club in Shreveport as just needing some seasoning in Phoenix, their Triple A club. In the meantime they usually pick up a backup catcher who could possibly start if they would just develop. They are usually players who once were prospects, but for some reason never received enough playing time with their former club. These players include Steve Nicosia, Alex Treviño (who became Candy Maldonado, the best investment the Gyros have made in years), Brad Gulden (who has the singular distinction of being the *first* player labeled by Roger Craig as a "Humm-Baby"; he is working in construction in the upper midwest now, but was the cause of one of the more successful marketing campaigns in Bay area history), and Bob Melvin (who almost—almost—became the first catcher in ML history last year to handle 300+ chances with a fielding percentage of 1.000; he handled over 400, and made his only error in August).

The Giants usually find a way to trade their own prospects away. No matter, they have a limitless supply of super catchers in Shreveport. If any of you have a sense of *déjà vu* over this, yes, this is the same franchise that stocked the entire National League with outfielders in the 60's and 70's. There is a major difference, however—Giant catchers, with the exception of Nokes, haven't produced well at any major league stop. Admittedly, Nokes is no defensive whiz, and might never be, but then Detroit (and Philadelphia) fans used to heap abuse on Lance Parrish, too. As for Sasser, he might produce for the Pirates, but not as a backstop.

Bob Brenly has a couple of major distinctions. He committed 4 errors in a single game at third base in September of 1986 against the Braves, 3 in one inning. He also hit 2 HR in that game, including the gamer in the bottom of the ninth. He also broke the career home run record for third basemen at Ohio University. Oh, did I mention it was Mike Schmidt's record he broke?

Bob (known, predictably, as "BB" to his teammates) is a survivor. What he provides for the Giants is leadership on the field and in the clubhouse. Brenly doesn't demonstrate the strength and resolve of a Jeffrey Leonard; he tends to keep the clubhouse loose and even with his quick wit. His ability to laugh at himself and find humor over a six-month season has helped him survive.

Defensively, Brenly has been helped by the pitching staff's emphasis on holding runners close to the bag. In addition, Roger Craig's eerie ability to successfully call pitchouts has dramatically improved Brenly's (and Melvin's) caught stealing ratios against opposition thieves.

Victor Hester

Brenly, Robert Earl "Bob"   Bats: Right   Throws: Right   Born 02/25/54

1987 SEASON AND MAJOR-LEAGUE CAREER BATTING TOTALS

	G	AB	H	2B	3B	HR	TB	R	RBI	TBB	IBB	SO	HP	SH	SF	SB	CS	SB%	GDP	AVG	OBP	SLG
87 SF	123	375	100	19	1	18	175	55	51	47	3	85	3	3	6	10	7	.59	5	.267	.348	.467
7 YEARS	738	2299	589	107	6	85	963	297	302	287	31	374	15	18	21	43	36	.54	44	.256	.340	.419

	1987 SEASON											FOUR YEAR TOTALS (1984 – 1987)									
	Ave.	OBP	SLG	AB	H	2B	3B	HR	RBI	BB	SO	Ave.	OBP	SLG	AB	H	2B	3B	HR	RBI	BB	SO
Totals	.267	.348	.467	375	100	19	1	18	51	47	85	.257	.340	.431	1793	460	89	2	73	249	226	296
vs. Left	.238	.304	.535	101	24	7	1	7	19	11	22	.247	.339	.447	497	123	31	1	22	73	71	71
vs. Right	.277	.364	.442	274	76	12	0	11	32	36	63	.260	.341	.424	1296	337	58	1	51	176	155	225
at Home	.301	.389	.532	173	52	10	0	10	32	25	31	.256	.340	.423	882	226	46	1	33	125	110	134
on Road	.238	.311	.411	202	48	9	1	8	19	22	54	.257	.341	.438	911	234	43	1	40	124	116	162
vs. Groundball	.313	.404	.606	160	50	8	0	13	29	24	32	.285	.380	.488	820	234	52	0	38	117	119	111
vs. Flyball	.233	.305	.363	215	50	11	1	5	22	23	53	.232	.306	.382	973	226	37	2	35	132	107	185
vs. Finesse	.322	.388	.628	183	59	14	0	14	33	18	29	.276	.350	.475	1005	277	57	1	47	138	111	131
vs. Power	.214	.311	.313	192	41	5	1	4	18	29	56	.232	.328	.374	788	183	32	1	26	111	115	165
on Grass	.269	.364	.481	260	70	13	0	14	38	39	50	.260	.348	.441	1314	342	67	1	56	188	174	202
on Artificial Turf	.261	.310	.435	115	30	6	1	4	13	8	35	.246	.321	.403	479	118	22	1	17	61	52	94
Day Games	.281	.359	.497	167	47	9	0	9	27	20	36	.249	.331	.409	831	207	43	0	30	111	100	126
Night Games	.255	.339	.442	208	53	10	1	9	24	27	49	.263	.348	.449	962	253	46	2	43	138	126	170
April	.182	.289	.242	33	6	2	0	0	1	5	11	.222	.339	.343	198	44	7	1	5	13	35	38
May	.310	.442	.452	42	13	3	0	1	10	9	11	.276	.387	.422	232	64	13	0	7	32	41	44
June	.236	.338	.564	55	13	3	0	5	8	9	10	.266	.366	.455	301	80	12	0	15	49	48	41
July	.360	.404	.651	86	31	5	1	6	11	6	16	.284	.335	.508	331	94	24	1	16	50	25	47
August	.247	.320	.424	85	21	3	0	4	13	9	23	.265	.332	.466	358	95	18	0	18	59	36	66
Sept/Oct	.216	.294	.338	74	16	3	0	2	8	9	14	.223	.298	.359	373	83	15	0	12	46	41	60
Bases Empty	.265	.347	.504	230	61	11	1	14	14	27	53	.258	.343	.429	1031	266	49	2	41	41	131	185
Leadoff	.291	.371	.582	79	23	2	0	7	7	10	18	.256	.331	.433	402	103	17	0	18	18	45	64
Not Leadoff	.252	.335	.464	151	38	9	1	7	7	17	35	.259	.350	.426	629	163	32	2	23	23	86	121
Runners On	.269	.349	.407	145	39	8	0	4	37	20	32	.255	.336	.433	762	194	40	0	32	208	95	111
First Base Only	.372	.438	.488	43	16	2	0	1	2	4	9	.276	.319	.418	294	81	15	0	9	26	18	33
Scoring Position	.225	.315	.373	102	23	6	0	3	35	16	23	.241	.345	.442	468	113	25	0	23	182	77	78
Late Innings, Close	.276	.353	.539	76	21	3	1	5	12	8	15	.233	.304	.394	391	91	16	1	15	45	39	65

RBI/Opportunities

Scoring Position	29 / 153 (19%)	142 / 679 (21%)	
Scoring Position, 2 Out	11 / 58 (19%)	52 / 305 (17%)	
On Third, Less than 2 Out	11 / 31 (35%)	50 / 112 (45%)	
RBI in close games / RBI Total	30 / 51 (59%)	158 / 249 (63%)	

George Brett
Kansas City Royals

George had another tough year hitting lefties, and it appears his recent peak as a balanced hitter is past.

	AB	HITS	B.A.	2B/3B/HR	SLUG%	BB	OBA	K
1984-85 VS LHP	328	100	.304	17/ 1/18	.527	35	.372	30
1984-85 VS RHP	599	191	.319	42/ 3/25	.524	106	.421	56
1986-87 VS LHP	297	76	.256	7/ 1/12	.407	31	.326	46
1986-87 VS RHP	571	176	.308	39/ 5/26	.531	121	.429	46

Don't credit this change totally to the aging process. The 1986–87 data is far closer to Brett's career numbers than the 1984–85 numbers. Back when Brett was in his physical prime, ages 27–29, he had a 60-point differential in BA (.297 versus .357) and his homer rate was about 70 percent better versus RHP than LHP.

Despite the common perception of fans and professional baseball men, your .300-hitters and batters who hit line drives to all fields can have huge platoon differences. And a lot of your big-swinging power hitters will surprise you with fairly normal or even small platoon differences. Reggie Jackson is the guy who would get yanked out of the line-up, but the truth is that Reggie has been a more balanced hitter throughout his career than George Brett has, and Dave Kingman was better balanced than both of them. Further, Gorman Thomas had a smaller platoon difference than most switch-hitters.

There has been a lot of focus on 1987 being the first time Brett has had back-to-back full seasons under .300. George himself has been shaken up enough that he is starting a special training regimen to prepare for 1988. Actually it shouldn't have been a surprise at all. Hitters rarely do well in the first season of a major position change. The exceptions are usually when the player is leaving a position which clearly overmatched his skills. That certainly was not the case for Brett who was a good (if not great) defensive third baseman during his career.

Besides switching over to first base, Brett had that spell where he couldn't throw and had to DH several games. The fidgety Brett has never been suited for that role. His previous experience as a DH in this decade was 33 at-bats in which he hit .212. In 1987 he hit .287 in 21 games at DH and .285 in 83 games at first base. In his 11 games at third base he hit .343.

The good news is that things generally pick up in the second year at the new position, especially if the player is enthusiastic about the change. Brett has been suggesting the change, himself, for many years. Even back when he won the Gold Glove at third base, he talked about the day coming soon when the team might be better off moving him to first base. A lot of times this kind of move signals the beginning of the end for a player's career, and George has made some noise from time to time about retiring early. But given his attitude about the shift to first base, I think he's going to break the mold on this one.

Craig R. Wright

Brett, George Howard

Bats: Left   Throws: Right   Born 05/15/53

1987 SEASON AND MAJOR-LEAGUE CAREER BATTING TOTALS

	G	AB	H	2B	3B	HR	TB	R	RBI	TBB	IBB	SO	HP	SH	SF	SB	CS	SB%	GDP	AVG	OBP	SLG
87 KC	115	427	124	18	2	22	212	71	78	72	14	47	1	0	8	6	3	.67	10	.290	.388	.496
15 YEARS	1856	7102	2219	446	114	231	3586	1143	1128	767	161	536	18	25	75	147	77	.66	129	.312	.377	.505

	1987 SEASON											FOUR YEAR TOTALS (1984 – 1987)										
	Ave.	OBP	SLG	AB	H	2B	3B	HR	RBI	BB	SO	Ave.	OBP	SLG	AB	H	2B	3B	HR	RBI	BB	SO
Totals	.290	.388	.496	427	124	18	2	22	77	72	47	.303	.397	.512	1795	543	105	14	81	331	292	178
vs. Left	.268	.317	.430	149	40	3	0	7	25	12	22	.282	.346	.470	625	176	24	2	30	111	66	76
vs. Right	.302	.422	.532	278	84	15	2	15	52	60	25	.314	.423	.534	1170	367	81	12	51	220	226	102
at Home	.268	.364	.494	231	62	6	2	14	47	36	26	.321	.415	.553	893	287	54	12	43	185	152	81
on Road	.316	.415	.500	196	62	12	0	8	30	36	21	.284	.379	.471	902	256	51	2	38	146	140	97
vs. Groundball	.306	.402	.479	219	67	9	1	9	42	36	20	.318	.410	.507	858	273	55	7	31	160	138	80
vs. Flyball	.274	.373	.514	208	57	9	1	13	35	36	27	.288	.386	.517	937	270	50	7	50	171	154	98
vs. Finesse	.289	.375	.474	228	66	10	1	10	35	33	21	.308	.391	.506	1005	310	64	9	39	169	140	86
vs. Power	.291	.402	.523	199	58	8	1	12	42	39	26	.295	.404	.519	790	233	41	5	42	162	152	92
on Grass	.325	.422	.494	160	52	9	0	6	25	29	17	.285	.381	.474	723	206	37	2	32	119	114	81
on Artificial Turf	.270	.367	.498	267	72	9	2	16	52	43	30	.314	.408	.537	1072	337	68	12	49	212	178	97
Day Games	.360	.421	.640	100	36	7	0	7	17	12	8	.304	.388	.517	448	136	32	4	20	79	64	43
Night Games	.269	.378	.453	327	88	11	2	15	60	60	39	.302	.400	.507	1347	407	73	10	61	252	228	135
April	.318	.500	.500	22	7	1	0	1	3	9	2	.270	.447	.500	148	40	9	2	7	22	48	11
May	.385	.467	.462	13	5	1	0	0	2	2	3	.307	.404	.500	264	81	20	2	9	46	43	29
June	.303	.378	.576	66	20	6	0	4	12	7	7	.312	.402	.477	333	104	18	2	11	52	49	25
July	.271	.355	.364	107	29	4	0	2	17	15	12	.314	.403	.492	360	113	21	2	13	63	55	37
August	.309	.418	.609	110	34	1	1	10	23	22	14	.330	.411	.613	382	126	23	5	25	84	54	48
Sept/Oct	.266	.357	.468	109	29	5	1	5	20	17	9	.256	.345	.464	308	79	14	1	16	64	43	28
Bases Empty	.297	.391	.569	195	58	9	1	14	14	29	22	.294	.372	.517	959	282	61	9	45	45	118	89
Leadoff	.275	.333	.638	69	19	1	0	8	8	5	7	.279	.351	.555	344	96	17	3	24	24	37	29
Not Leadoff	.310	.420	.532	126	39	8	1	6	6	24	15	.302	.384	.496	615	186	44	6	21	21	81	60
Runners On	.284	.385	.435	232	66	9	1	8	63	43	25	.312	.427	.506	836	261	44	5	36	286	174	89
First Base Only	.246	.317	.404	114	28	6	0	4	12	12	10	.308	.362	.531	360	111	19	2	19	53	30	27
Scoring Position	.322	.439	.466	118	38	3	1	4	51	31	15	.315	.468	.487	476	150	25	3	17	233	144	62
Late Innings, Close	.328	.432	.525	61	20	3	0	3	12	12	6	.309	.430	.521	259	80	17	1	12	55	56	25

RBI/Opportunities

Scoring Position	46 / 175 (26%)	198 / 729 (27%)
Scoring Position, 2 Out	10 / 71 (14%)	69 / 285 (24%)
On Third, Less than 2 Out	25 / 38 (66%)	83 / 146 (57%)
RBI in close games / RBI Total	52 / 77 (68%)	236 / 331 (71%)

Greg Brock
Milwaukee Brewers

I'm always wary of bestowing the "genius" tag on an executive. Many folks get hype because they either sacrificed a team's future for the present (Dallas Green), got credit for decisions that someone else made (Pat Gillick, not Peter Bavasi, built Toronto) or just ran a team that had a surprising year (John Schuerholz). I like to wait 3–5 years—to see if they can keep winning—before I bow down to them as a temple of wisdom.

Harry Dalton, though, is one of the people that I do respect. He makes a sensible, intelligent move—a deal that helps—every year. He got burned on Dion James this year—but the Greg Brock deal worked out just like a baby's behind.

Brock is another one of those guys who, for various reasons, has never gotten as much respect as he deserves. Most people never bother to look at a player's extra base hits (not just homers) and walk totals; that's where most of Greg's value lies. Lefties give him fits (.180 from '83–'86); he got just enough at-bats against them (311 of 1489 from '83–'86) to drag his average down. Getting injured twice didn't help his development, either.

Then there was the small matter of his team. Playing in LA did three things to his stats. First, it cut into his power (.395 SL% at home; .451 on the road since 1984). Secondly, since L.A., uh, lacked the necessities to see that he wasn't that bad a player (a mistake that they also made with Candy Maldonado and Sid Bream), they kept dumping on him. Last but not least, he was "Steve Garvey's Replacement." It would have taken a Mattingly-type year to get the fans off his neck; since Brock isn't that good, they were crucifying him.

All this may sound like I'm making excuses for Brock—but that's not the point at all. The point is that there were tangible reasons that his output seemed disappointing. That being so, it was logical to assume that eliminating those reasons would improve it. Get him out of the park, keep him away from the tough lefties, give him a fresh start and don't badger him and you might turn a pretty decent player into a really good one. That, basically, is just what Milwaukee did.

The odd thing about Greg's 1987 is that it's almost disappointing. Milwaukee is by no means a good place for power hitters—but compared to LA, it's a paradise. Though Brock hit 20–30 points better than I expected and his walks were up to his normal standards, his power was very low. Brock slugged .438 in 1985 and .422 in 1986; believe it or not, his homer total was the lowest of his career. I don't expect him to be around .300 again (even in the minors he was never a high-average hitter), but I won't be at all surprised if he makes the 25–30 range in circuit clouts in 1988.

Geoff Beckman

Brock, Gregory Allen "Greg"   Bats: Left   Throws: Right   Born 06/14/57

1987 SEASON AND MAJOR-LEAGUE CAREER BATTING TOTALS

	G	AB	H	2B	3B	HR	TB	R	RBI	TBB	IBB	SO	HP	SH	SF	SB	CS	SB%	GDP	AVG	OBP	SLG
87 MIL	141	532	159	29	3	13	233	81	85	57	4	63	6	4	3	5	4	.56	9	.299	.371	.438
6 YEARS	637	2038	510	82	5	84	854	276	304	271	29	318	7	7	16	24	12	.67	42	.250	.338	.419

	1987 SEASON											FOUR YEAR TOTALS (1984 – 1987)									
	Ave.	OBP	SLG	AB	H	2B	3B	HR	RBI	BB	SO	Ave.	OBP	SLG	AB	H	2B	3B	HR	RBI	BB	SO
Totals	.299	.371	.438	532	159	29	3	13	85	57	63	.259	.339	.428	1566	406	67	3	64	237	188	232
vs. Left	.287	.351	.395	157	45	6	1	3	27	14	22	.215	.279	.337	395	85	13	1	11	53	34	78
vs. Right	.304	.380	.456	375	114	23	2	10	58	43	41	.274	.358	.459	1171	321	54	2	53	184	154	154
at Home	.300	.370	.426	270	81	15	2	5	45	26	28	.265	.339	.406	774	205	30	2	25	122	84	107
on Road	.298	.372	.450	262	78	14	1	8	40	31	35	.254	.338	.451	792	201	37	1	39	115	104	125
vs. Groundball	.315	.381	.444	295	93	16	2	6	52	31	28	.281	.358	.445	744	209	34	2	28	130	90	98
vs. Flyball	.278	.359	.430	237	66	13	1	7	33	26	35	.240	.322	.414	822	197	33	1	36	107	98	134
vs. Finesse	.299	.370	.448	281	84	15	3	7	49	30	28	.272	.346	.450	854	232	35	3	37	130	98	96
vs. Power	.299	.372	.426	251	75	14	0	6	36	27	35	.244	.330	.403	712	174	32	0	27	107	90	136
on Grass	.303	.371	.450	456	138	24	2	13	78	45	55	.263	.340	.428	1248	328	49	2	51	201	146	181
on Artificial Turf	.276	.375	.368	76	21	5	1	0	7	12	8	.245	.332	.431	318	78	18	1	13	36	42	51
Day Games	.301	.363	.458	166	50	11	0	5	32	15	21	.280	.348	.481	497	139	22	0	26	93	53	71
Night Games	.298	.375	.429	366	109	18	3	8	53	42	42	.250	.334	.404	1069	267	45	3	38	144	135	161
April	.324	.407	.521	71	23	2	0	4	18	7	9	.236	.322	.410	229	54	4	0	12	34	26	34
May	.203	.250	.380	79	16	5	0	3	12	4	7	.212	.286	.392	222	47	7	0	11	35	22	32
June	.300	.407	.400	50	15	2	0	1	5	9	4	.263	.362	.474	232	61	10	0	13	32	36	33
July	.317	.377	.426	101	32	3	1	2	16	9	14	.312	.371	.462	221	69	7	1	8	46	20	38
August	.318	.370	.455	110	35	7	1	2	16	9	12	.267	.334	.414	345	92	19	1	10	43	35	46
Sept/Oct	.314	.404	.438	121	38	10	1	1	18	19	17	.262	.360	.426	317	83	20	1	10	47	49	49
Bases Empty	.252	.327	.378	270	68	14	1	6	6	27	30	.233	.305	.400	831	194	37	1	33	33	82	115
Leadoff	.243	.313	.360	136	33	5	1	3	3	12	16	.217	.279	.378	360	78	11	1	15	15	29	54
Not Leadoff	.261	.340	.396	134	35	9	0	3	3	15	14	.246	.324	.416	471	116	26	0	18	18	53	61
Runners On	.347	.416	.500	262	91	15	2	7	79	30	33	.288	.379	.461	735	212	30	2	31	204	106	117
First Base Only	.389	.420	.558	95	37	5	1	3	7	5	7	.313	.387	.485	297	93	13	1	12	25	36	45
Scoring Position	.323	.414	.467	167	54	10	1	4	72	25	26	.272	.374	.445	438	119	17	1	19	179	70	72
Late Innings, Close	.284	.366	.358	81	23	6	0	0	8	10	6	.203	.289	.272	261	53	9	0	3	20	31	42

RBI/Opportunities		
Scoring Position	63 / 219 (29%)	144 / 599 (24%)
Scoring Position, 2 Out	30 / 114 (26%)	59 / 305 (19%)
On Third, Less than 2 Out	18 / 32 (56%)	48 / 96 (50%)
RBI in close games / RBI Total	50 / 85 (59%)	141 / 237 (59%)

Tom Brookens
Detroit Tigers

In his 1984 *Abstract,* Bill James noted that managers tend to favor the players who most closely resemble them as players. Of all the Tigers, Tom Brookens—a white, working class, largely untalented gentleman who tries to compensate for his drawbacks by hard work and a respectful attitude—is probably the most similar player to Sparky Anderson. Perhaps this explains why Detroit would give a $350,000 salary and a regular job to a 34-year-old man who was never, is not now and never will be anything but a thoroughly dreadful baseball player.

In 1987, 13 American League players played 81 or more games at third base. Eight men had higher batting averages than Brookens did last year. Ten had better on-base percentages. Twelve had higher slugging percentages. Defensively, Tom was seventh in fielding percentage and tenth in both range factor and double plays per 162 games. The depth of his atrociousness is matched only by the breadth.

1987, moreover, was not a typical season for Brookens. He set career highs in homers and walks; his runs, RBIs and fielding percentage barely missed career bests. Toward the end of 1987, Anderson commented that Brookens was having the best season of his career—horrifying as it sounds, he may very well have been right.

Detroit's passion for Brookens caused them to make several errors in 1987. It prompted them to first give up on Darnell Coles far too early and then make a bad deal for him. It also forced Anderson to make Bill Madlock the right-handed DH, pushing Larry Herndon, a .325 hitter in '87, to the bench. Finally, at season's end, Detroit decided not to offer Madlock a contract, saying that the third base job was taken and that they preferred to use Herndon as right-handed DH in 1988.

The decision to bench Herndon rather than Brookens seemed to be based on the idea that Brookens's glove was so superior to Madlock's that it outstripped the offensive difference between Brookens and Herndon. Based on their career stats, it is grossly untrue. And the idea of releasing a four-time batting champion and future Hall-of-Famer in favor of Brookens, who is approximately the same age, is so absurd it defies explanation. Though Madlock has always been reported to have a bad attitude and no one really knows what goes on behind closed locker room doors, one does wonder if Madlock, like Dick Allen and others before him, would have the same reputation if baseball were dominated by blacks. In any case, it is no excuse for playing Tom Brookens.

In the end I do have one good thing to say about Brookens. In September he hit a home run that won $1200 for my mother in a local contest. She says thanks again, Tom.

Daniel Z. Douthat

Brookens, Thomas Dale "Tom"

Bats: Right   Throws: Right   Born 08/10/53

1987 SEASON AND MAJOR-LEAGUE CAREER BATTING TOTALS

	G	AB	H	2B	3B	HR	TB	R	RBI	TBB	IBB	SO	HP	SH	SF	SB	CS	SB%	GDP	AVG	OBP	SLG
87 DET	143	444	107	15	3	13	167	59	59	33	3	63	2	9	2	7	4	.64	8	.241	.295	.376
9 YEARS	1070	3102	764	139	33	61	1152	383	359	212	8	479	11	49	31	81	53	.60	52	.246	.294	.371

1987 SEASON

	Ave.	OBP	SLG	AB	H	2B	3B	HR	RBI	BB	SO
Totals	.241	.295	.376	444	107	15	3	13	59	33	63
vs. Left	.240	.310	.422	154	37	7	0	7	25	16	24
vs. Right	.241	.287	.352	290	70	8	3	6	34	17	39
at Home	.226	.291	.325	212	48	3	0	6	26	18	32
on Road	.254	.300	.422	232	59	12	3	7	33	15	31
vs. Groundball	.277	.333	.441	220	61	9	3	7	35	18	31
vs. Flyball	.205	.257	.313	224	46	6	0	6	24	15	32
vs. Finesse	.239	.290	.327	226	54	4	2	4	25	15	21
vs. Power	.243	.301	.427	218	53	11	1	9	34	18	42
on Grass	.254	.311	.392	378	96	11	1	13	54	30	55
on Artificial Turf	.167	.203	.288	66	11	4	2	0	5	3	8
Day Games	.234	.289	.371	124	29	4	2	3	14	9	16
Night Games	.244	.298	.378	320	78	11	1	10	45	24	47
April	.259	.317	.448	58	15	4	2	1	9	5	4
May	.266	.347	.422	64	17	1	0	3	9	8	12
June	.225	.281	.404	89	20	5	1	3	13	7	12
July	.230	.261	.276	87	20	1	0	1	7	4	9
August	.224	.291	.286	49	11	0	0	1	7	4	8
Sept/Oct	.247	.291	.412	97	24	4	0	4	14	5	18
Bases Empty	.240	.293	.371	229	55	8	2	6	6	16	25
Leadoff	.231	.307	.308	91	21	2	1	1	1	9	13
Not Leadoff	.246	.283	.413	138	34	6	1	5	5	7	12
Runners On	.242	.298	.381	215	52	7	1	7	53	17	38
First Base Only	.250	.313	.398	88	22	4	0	3	6	7	14
Scoring Position	.236	.288	.370	127	30	3	1	4	47	10	24
Late Innings, Close	.222	.250	.315	54	12	2	0	1	3	2	10

FOUR YEAR TOTALS (1984 – 1987)

	Ave.	OBP	SLG	AB	H	2B	3B	HR	RBI	BB	SO
Totals	.246	.296	.375	1434	353	71	15	28	157	100	216
vs. Left	.274	.329	.432	625	171	35	8	16	70	53	84
vs. Right	.225	.270	.331	809	182	36	7	12	87	47	132
at Home	.238	.293	.365	698	166	32	6	15	74	53	115
on Road	.254	.299	.385	736	187	39	9	13	83	47	101
vs. Groundball	.263	.310	.399	672	177	37	9	12	80	44	97
vs. Flyball	.231	.284	.354	762	176	34	6	16	77	56	119
vs. Finesse	.250	.285	.353	801	200	37	8	10	75	39	85
vs. Power	.242	.309	.403	633	153	34	7	18	82	61	131
on Grass	.248	.301	.379	1213	301	57	9	28	143	90	186
on Artificial Turf	.235	.268	.353	221	52	14	6	0	14	10	30
Day Games	.251	.306	.381	415	104	22	7	6	50	34	54
Night Games	.244	.292	.373	1019	249	49	8	22	107	66	162
April	.271	.320	.429	140	38	9	5	1	23	10	12
May	.247	.308	.344	215	53	8	2	3	19	19	29
June	.266	.325	.443	289	77	21	3	8	42	25	37
July	.200	.252	.275	280	56	11	2	2	15	20	47
August	.250	.295	.373	228	57	8	1	6	28	14	40
Sept/Oct	.255	.288	.404	282	72	14	2	8	30	12	51
Bases Empty	.247	.296	.386	801	198	42	9	17	17	54	113
Leadoff	.235	.295	.340	341	80	13	4	5	5	28	52
Not Leadoff	.257	.296	.420	460	118	29	5	12	12	26	61
Runners On	.245	.296	.362	633	155	29	6	11	140	46	103
First Base Only	.230	.294	.338	269	62	12	1	5	11	23	46
Scoring Position	.255	.298	.379	364	93	17	5	6	129	23	57
Late Innings, Close	.274	.325	.387	186	51	10	1	3	18	14	32

RBI/Opportunities

	1987		Four Year	
Scoring Position	38 / 180	(21%)	113 / 488	(23%)
Scoring Position, 2 Out	22 / 100	(22%)	58 / 249	(23%)
On Third, Less than 2 Out	9 / 28	(32%)	31 / 70	(44%)
RBI in close games / RBI Total	19 / 59	(32%)	65 / 157	(41%)

Hubie Brooks
Montreal Expos

More than three years later, and despite the role Gary Carter played in leading the Mets to the 1986 World Championship, serious Met fans—not the legions who came out of the woodwork in '86—still seem to be nostalgic for Hubie Brooks. As a Met, Hubie didn't show any signs that he was going to become a superstar, but he was a talented, home-grown ballplayer, and the first sign that the franchise was turning around after ten years of indifferent play (and 20 years of bad third basemen). As talented players entered the lineup next to Brooks, the notion grew that maybe good things were finally going to happen. The good things did happen, but without Hubie. Now he's popular in Montreal. Brooks is a good ballplayer, but he isn't Mr. all-around nice guy, or a self promoter like Carter or Reggie. Despite time on the DL the past two years, he comes across as a solid, dependable player who always gives an honest effort, and who keeps his name out of the papers when he's off the field—a rare find these days.

After a terrific start in '86, Brooks missed the second half of the season with torn ligaments in his thumb, and then lasted only three games in '87, before having his wrist broken by a Danny Darwin pitch in Houston. Coming back after missing 44 days, he never got as hot as he had been in '86, and he was bothered by minor hand and foot injuries all year. There were some good times, though. He had two six-RBI games, had a hit during every game of an Expo 8-game winning streak in July (including 3 GWRBIs), and batted .311 with 29 RBIs in September, keeping the team in the pennant race after Tim Wallach cooled off. Still, it had the feel of a wasted year in the prime of a career.

There's no doubt that Hubie can hit. He has a career batting average of .276 and if he stays healthy in the future, it should go up. He was on his way to his first 20 homer season when he was hurt in '86; with the improved visibility in Montreal he should get it this year. He had a 100 RBI season in 1985, a figure he hasn't come close to before or since, but there was no sense of fluke about it—he can and should do it again. That is a lot of should haves and could haves; if '88 isn't a career year we'll have some reevaluating to do.

There has been doubt that Hubie can field. He's improved his game at short over the past year, but now the Expos are talking of moving him to right field. He did play the outfield in the minors, and right seems like a good spot for his arm. If Montreal can find a shortstop it should be a smart move. And a good place for him to have that career year from.

Michael Cassin

Brooks, Hubert "Hubie"

Bats: Right Throws: Right Born 09/24/56

1987 SEASON AND MAJOR-LEAGUE CAREER BATTING TOTALS

	G	AB	H	2B	3B	HR	TB	R	RBI	TBB	IBB	SO	HP	SH	SF	SB	CS	SB%	GDP	AVG	OBP	SLG
87 MON	112	430	113	22	3	14	183	57	72	24	2	72	1	0	4	4	3	.57	7	.263	.301	.426
8 YEARS	899	3384	935	159	26	69	1353	370	449	211	35	536	22	12	33	42	32	.57	90	.276	.320	.400

	1987 SEASON											FOUR YEAR TOTALS (1984 – 1987)									
	Ave.	OBP	SLG	AB	H	2B	3B	HR	RBI	BB	SO	Ave.	OBP	SLG	AB	H	2B	3B	HR	RBI	BB	SO
Totals	.263	.301	.426	430	113	22	3	14	72	24	73	.283	.330	.442	1902	539	97	17	57	303	131	290
vs. Left	.328	.352	.549	122	40	10	1	5	34	5	19	.315	.373	.516	577	182	41	6	21	106	51	78
vs. Right	.237	.281	.377	308	73	12	2	9	38	19	54	.269	.310	.410	1325	357	56	11	36	197	80	212
at Home	.289	.333	.478	228	66	14	1	9	37	16	38	.305	.353	.478	920	281	59	8	28	155	67	143
on Road	.233	.263	.366	202	47	8	2	5	35	8	35	.263	.307	.408	982	258	38	9	29	148	64	147
vs. Groundball	.265	.295	.400	215	57	13	2	4	32	9	32	.312	.359	.476	929	290	60	7	26	167	68	124
vs. Flyball	.260	.306	.451	215	56	9	1	10	40	15	41	.256	.301	.410	973	249	37	10	31	136	63	166
vs. Finesse	.261	.295	.410	261	68	15	0	8	37	12	43	.294	.338	.448	1087	320	60	4	33	175	69	142
vs. Power	.266	.310	.450	169	45	7	3	6	35	12	30	.269	.320	.434	815	219	37	13	24	128	62	148
on Grass	.241	.272	.345	87	21	3	0	2	11	4	12	.296	.343	.463	763	226	33	5	28	105	54	111
on Artificial Turf	.268	.308	.446	343	92	19	3	12	61	20	61	.275	.320	.428	1139	313	64	12	29	198	77	179
Day Games	.219	.252	.286	105	23	4	0	1	10	5	19	.270	.322	.422	663	179	29	9	18	100	51	96
Night Games	.277	.316	.471	325	90	18	3	13	62	19	54	.291	.334	.453	1239	360	68	8	39	203	80	194
April	.091	.167	.091	11	1	0	0	0	0	0	3	.266	.327	.425	233	62	11	1	8	37	20	33
May	.313	.353	.313	16	5	0	0	0	2	1	1	.318	.362	.522	274	87	10	5	12	45	19	45
June	.318	.359	.576	85	27	5	1	5	22	6	19	.318	.371	.509	352	112	22	3	13	59	30	72
July	.277	.315	.465	101	28	8	1	3	11	6	19	.273	.308	.379	388	106	21	1	6	47	20	52
August	.147	.214	.221	95	14	1	0	2	6	8	13	.242	.296	.400	310	75	12	5	9	50	24	36
Sept/Oct	.311	.323	.492	122	38	8	1	4	31	3	18	.281	.315	.432	345	97	21	2	9	65	18	52
Bases Empty	.228	.278	.402	219	50	8	0	10	10	15	42	.276	.314	.453	1027	283	46	8	40	40	58	147
Leadoff	.216	.231	.373	102	22	1	0	5	5	2	15	.294	.321	.453	459	135	24	5	13	13	18	59
Not Leadoff	.239	.315	.427	117	28	7	0	5	5	13	27	.261	.309	.452	568	148	22	3	27	27	40	88
Runners On	.299	.324	.450	211	63	14	3	4	62	9	31	.293	.346	.430	875	256	51	9	17	263	73	143
First Base Only	.296	.324	.451	71	21	5	0	2	6	2	9	.289	.317	.393	336	97	16	2	5	19	13	39
Scoring Position	.300	.325	.450	140	42	9	3	2	56	7	22	.295	.363	.453	539	159	35	7	12	244	60	104
Late Innings, Close	.246	.254	.462	65	16	2	0	4	13	1	11	.291	.334	.458	330	96	13	3	12	57	22	61

RBI/Opportunities

Scoring Position	49 / 173 (28%)	211 / 728 (29%)
Scoring Position, 2 Out	20 / 68 (29%)	85 / 327 (26%)
On Third, Less than 2 Out	15 / 30 (50%)	79 / 147 (54%)
RBI in close games / RBI Total	43 / 72 (60%)	208 / 303 (69%)

Chris Brown
San Diego Padres

Here is a man with a great deal of ability. He has hit for average and with power in the major leagues. He has good speed for a third baseman and is an excellent, at times unbelievable, fielder. At 26 he should have an excellent career ahead of him. However, he often is injured (his nickname among San Francisco writers was "D.L.") and has a reputation for playing only when he's in the mood. When speaking, he sounds like a dedicated player who gives his best at all times. His injuries have been real, with two serious ones in 1987: a left jaw shattered by a Danny Cox fastball, and a broken wrist. However, according to beat writers covering the Giants, Brown sat forlornly in the corner, wrapped in a blanket (in Saint Louis in May) after his beaning—the Giants had just completed a tremendous comeback, sweeping the Cards after being behind 7–0—telling anyone who would listen that they'd "better interview mc now, 'cause I won't be able to talk for six weeks." It seems that Chris felt everyone should be as sad as he.

In last year's *Stat Book,* one writer said that Al Rosen believes "that certain body types, such as Brown's, are so heavily muscled compared to their skeletal size that they are very prone to muscle injuries." Last year's book documented instances of Chris playing while hurt and being injured while hustling. Gary Gillette added evidence that in recent years, most players with "bad attitude" labels are black. These arguments are sound and help to explain (partially) Brown's situation.

So, just what have the Padres got here? A 26-year-old, 6-foot, 185-pound third baseman who has:

1. Played in only 2/3 of his teams' games in three years;
2. A history of injuries that rivals Pete Reiser's;
3. Never exceeded 16 homers or 61 RBI in the majors;
4. Been sent back from AAA to AA for a whole season;
5. A bad reputation;
6. Been selected to an All-Star team;
7. The potential to add 25 HR, 90 RBI, 20 SB and a .300 BA to the anemic Padre offense;
8. Excellent skills at the hot corner;
9. Played on the same amateur team as Darryl Strawberry and Eric Davis.

What should they do with him?

1. Trade him, if a taker can be found?
2. Develop a special fitness program to reduce the chance of injury to his body type?
3. Tell him to shape up or ship out?
4. Bench him and put Randy Ready at third?
5. Tell him that third base is his and go disprove his detractors?

For a young man with such potential, I prefer the latter solution. Many a ballplayer's career has been shattered by a lack of confidence. If Larry Bowa supports Brown as he did Benito Santiago in '87 (and as Frank Lucchesi did Bowa 20 years ago), Chris should become the best third baseman in Padre history (barring injury). If Bowa doesn't, Randy Ready will probably have third to himself.

Bruce Ericson

Brown, John Christopher "Chris"

Bats: Right   Throws: Right   Born 08/15/61

1987 SEASON AND MAJOR-LEAGUE CAREER BATTING TOTALS

	G	AB	H	2B	3B	HR	TB	R	RBI	TBB	IBB	SO	HP	SH	SF	SB	CS	SB%	GDP	AVG	OBP	SLG
87 SF-SD	82	287	68	9	0	12	113	34	40	20	1	46	6	3	1	4	4	.50	14	.237	.299	.394
4 YEARS	352	1219	341	52	6	36	513	147	161	100	9	186	27	4	7	21	17	.55	46	.280	.346	.421

	1987 SEASON											FOUR YEAR TOTALS (1984 – 1987)										
	Ave.	OBP	SLG	AB	H	2B	3B	HR	RBI	BB	SO	Ave.	OBP	SLG	AB	H	2B	3B	HR	RBI	BB	SO
Totals	.237	.299	.394	287	68	9	0	12	40	20	46	.280	.346	.421	1219	341	52	6	36	161	100	186
vs. Left	.265	.339	.449	98	26	3	0	5	14	10	14	.260	.329	.425	358	93	18	1	13	35	31	52
vs. Right	.222	.278	.365	189	42	6	0	7	26	10	32	.288	.353	.419	861	248	34	5	23	126	69	134
at Home	.219	.280	.372	137	30	6	0	5	18	10	20	.280	.348	.403	615	172	31	3	13	85	56	92
on Road	.253	.317	.413	150	38	3	0	7	22	10	26	.280	.343	.439	604	169	21	3	23	76	44	94
vs. Groundball	.178	.256	.331	163	29	4	0	7	21	13	22	.277	.343	.446	574	159	28	3	21	79	46	71
vs. Flyball	.315	.358	.476	124	39	5	0	5	19	7	24	.282	.348	.398	645	182	24	3	15	82	54	115
vs. Finesse	.207	.257	.354	164	34	3	0	7	20	8	19	.290	.347	.449	706	205	35	4	23	91	45	90
vs. Power	.276	.353	.447	123	34	6	0	5	20	12	27	.265	.344	.382	513	136	17	2	13	70	55	96
on Grass	.245	.300	.414	249	61	9	0	11	36	16	39	.287	.352	.422	954	274	43	4	26	132	78	146
on Artificial Turf	.184	.295	.263	38	7	0	0	1	4	4	7	.253	.322	.415	265	67	9	2	10	29	22	40
Day Games	.256	.308	.545	121	31	8	0	9	28	8	21	.285	.356	.430	604	172	30	2	18	88	58	103
Night Games	.223	.293	.283	166	37	1	0	3	12	12	25	.275	.336	.411	615	169	22	4	18	73	42	83
April	.288	.350	.521	73	21	5	0	4	11	5	9	.300	.364	.456	180	54	9	2	5	25	16	22
May	.000	.333	.000	8	0	0	0	0	0	3	2	.255	.313	.382	165	42	5	2	4	19	13	29
June	.125	.125	.125	40	5	0	0	0	1	0	5	.278	.336	.424	205	57	10	1	6	21	18	26
July	.300	.333	.483	60	18	2	0	3	11	3	10	.320	.364	.492	244	78	13	1	9	38	17	35
August	.208	.262	.299	77	16	1	0	2	7	4	11	.263	.303	.343	236	62	4	0	5	24	12	33
Sept/Oct	.276	.400	.621	29	8	1	0	3	10	5	9	.254	.341	.423	189	48	11	0	7	34	24	41
Bases Empty	.219	.271	.323	155	34	1	0	5	5	9	21	.250	.303	.381	704	176	21	4	21	21	52	103
Leadoff	.154	.214	.269	52	8	0	0	2	2	4	8	.221	.279	.385	262	58	7	3	10	10	21	46
Not Leadoff	.252	.300	.350	103	26	1	0	3	3	5	13	.267	.318	.378	442	118	14	1	11	11	31	57
Runners On	.258	.331	.477	132	34	8	0	7	35	11	25	.320	.382	.476	515	165	31	2	15	140	48	83
First Base Only	.260	.288	.520	50	13	4	0	3	7	2	11	.311	.349	.466	219	68	17	1	5	17	13	32
Scoring Position	.256	.354	.451	82	21	4	0	4	28	9	14	.328	.405	.483	296	97	14	1	10	123	35	51
Late Innings, Close	.264	.361	.377	53	14	3	0	1	6	6	5	.318	.396	.442	242	77	9	3	5	31	29	37

RBI/Opportunities

Scoring Position	22 / 113 (19%)	105 / 404 (26%)
Scoring Position, 2 Out	9 / 51 (18%)	46 / 181 (25%)
On Third, Less than 2 Out	7 / 19 (37%)	34 / 75 (45%)
RBI in close games / RBI Total	19 / 40 (48%)	111 / 161 (69%)

Jerry Browne
Texas Rangers

Jerry Browne fits perfectly into the future of the Ranger lineup, a lineup which has lacked a classic leadoff man since Bump Wills was in his prime. You have a 21-year-old switch-hitter ready to play every day; he gets on base (.358 OBA in his rookie year), and he runs well above average despite a sloppy steal success rate (17 caught stealings in 44 attempts).

He looks good defensively, too: a plus arm for the position, good physical range, steady hands, and a decent pivot. I was rather startled by his confidence and range on pop flies into the outfield. Really outstanding.

What intrigued me the most in watching Browne's rookie season was his ability to get the ball call from the umpires. His 61 walks tied for the team lead, and he did it with only 454 at-bats. Okay, he's short (5′ 10″), and being unusually modest and quiet, he isn't the type to inflame the umpires against a rookie, but, hey, what about Oddibe McDowell?

I remember McDowell's rookie year as being full of lousy ball-strike calls, and he was even shorter (5′ 9″) and generally didn't speak unless spoken to. Oddibe continues to get worse calls than Browne even though Little Mac is the three-year veteran and Browne is the rookie. Obviously something else is in operation here.

In this regard Jerry reminds me a bit of Alvin Davis of Seattle, who also impressed me by getting consistent ball calls in his rookie season. How to describe this? They take pitches with a sense of purpose; they project an aura of knowing what they are doing. When they take a strike they do it with a confidence that says, "Yeah, that was a strike, but not what I'm looking for," or "I just wanted to see if he could throw one." And when the pitch is a ball, that same quiet confidence clearly says, "Nah, that's a ball."

I think the umpires eat that up. They say to themselves, "Hey, this guy knows what he's doing. He knows his strike zone, and he ain't going to bitch on a good call. For him a strike's a strike and a ball is a ball."

I also note that both players reinforce their image by rarely starting their swing on a pitch they end up taking. This may be the biggest difference between McDowell and Browne. Oddibe often has a lot of movement when taking a pitch. His weight starts to shift, his hands come down as if starting his swing. The umpire may take such movement as a sign that the batter was unsure whether a close pitch was a strike or not. By contrast, at the same point where McDowell may be stopping a quarter swing, Browne has already relaxed his stance, indicating to the umpire that he thought it was an obvious ball. That may be the difference right there.

Craig R. Wright

Browne, Jerome Austin "Jerry" Bats: Both Throws: Right Born 02/13/66

1987 SEASON AND MAJOR-LEAGUE CAREER BATTING TOTALS

	G	AB	H	2B	3B	HR	TB	R	RBI	TBB	IBB	SO	HP	SH	SF	SB	CS	SB%	GDP	AVG	OBP	SLG
87 TEX	132	454	123	16	6	1	154	63	38	61	0	50	2	7	2	27	17	.61	6	.271	.358	.339
2 YEARS	144	478	133	18	6	1	166	69	41	62	0	54	2	7	2	27	19	.59	6	.278	.362	.347

	1987 SEASON											FOUR YEAR TOTALS (1984 – 1987)										
	Ave.	OBP	SLG	AB	H	2B	3B	HR	RBI	BB	SO	Ave.	OBP	SLG	AB	H	2B	3B	HR	RBI	BB	SO
Totals	.271	.358	.339	454	123	16	6	1	38	61	50	.279	.363	.348	477	133	18	6	1	41	62	54
vs. Left	.311	.403	.420	119	37	4	3	1	16	18	8	.325	.413	.439	123	40	5	3	1	17	18	8
vs. Right	.257	.342	.310	335	86	12	3	0	22	43	42	.263	.345	.316	354	93	13	3	0	24	44	46
at Home	.306	.390	.380	245	75	9	3	1	22	33	29	.315	.393	.390	267	84	11	3	1	24	34	33
on Road	.230	.321	.292	209	48	7	3	0	16	28	21	.233	.324	.295	210	49	7	3	0	17	28	21
vs. Groundball	.303	.402	.362	221	67	8	1	1	20	35	22	.314	.410	.380	229	72	10	1	1	21	36	24
vs. Flyball	.240	.315	.318	233	56	8	5	0	18	26	28	.246	.316	.319	248	61	8	5	0	20	26	30
vs. Finesse	.294	.370	.377	265	78	11	4	1	23	31	17	.299	.371	.381	278	83	12	4	1	25	31	19
vs. Power	.238	.342	.286	189	45	5	2	0	15	30	33	.251	.352	.302	199	50	6	2	0	16	31	35
on Grass	.275	.361	.346	393	108	13	6	1	34	52	41	.282	.364	.354	415	117	15	6	1	36	53	45
on Artificial Turf	.246	.343	.295	61	15	3	0	0	4	9	9	.258	.352	.306	62	16	3	0	0	5	9	9
Day Games	.262	.347	.320	103	27	4	1	0	8	14	10	.262	.347	.320	103	27	4	1	0	8	14	10
Night Games	.274	.362	.345	351	96	12	5	1	30	47	40	.283	.367	.356	374	106	14	5	1	33	48	44
April	.259	.375	.407	54	14	2	3	0	2	10	3	.259	.375	.407	54	14	2	3	0	2	10	3
May	.238	.364	.302	63	15	4	0	0	9	12	5	.238	.364	.302	63	15	4	0	0	9	12	5
June	.238	.322	.287	101	24	1	2	0	8	13	17	.238	.322	.287	101	24	1	2	0	8	13	17
July	.324	.412	.392	74	24	3	1	0	5	11	8	.324	.412	.392	74	24	3	1	0	5	11	8
August	.286	.318	.357	84	24	3	0	1	7	4	7	.286	.318	.357	84	24	3	0	1	7	4	7
Sept/Oct	.282	.378	.321	78	22	3	0	0	7	11	10	.317	.395	.366	101	32	5	0	0	10	12	14
Bases Empty	.278	.356	.342	316	88	11	3	1	1	36	41	.278	.355	.343	327	91	12	3	1	1	37	44
Leadoff	.262	.330	.326	187	49	5	2	1	1	18	29	.258	.327	.325	194	50	6	2	1	1	19	32
Not Leadoff	.302	.392	.364	129	39	6	1	0	0	18	12	.308	.395	.368	133	41	6	1	0	0	18	12
Runners On	.254	.364	.333	138	35	5	3	0	37	25	9	.280	.379	.360	150	42	6	3	0	40	25	10
First Base Only	.191	.309	.255	47	9	1	1	0	1	8	2	.226	.328	.283	53	12	1	1	0	1	8	3
Scoring Position	.286	.391	.374	91	26	4	2	0	36	17	7	.309	.405	.402	97	30	5	2	0	39	17	7
Late Innings, Close	.317	.469	.365	63	20	1	1	0	8	18	4	.317	.469	.365	126	40	2	2	0	16	36	8

RBI/Opportunities

	1987		1984–1987	
Scoring Position	35 / 131	(27%)	38 / 138	(28%)
Scoring Position, 2 Out	15 / 60	(25%)	18 / 63	(29%)
On Third, Less than 2 Out	14 / 24	(58%)	14 / 25	(56%)
RBI in close games / RBI Total	15 / 38	(39%)	30 / 41	(73%)

Tom Browning
Cincinnati Reds

At the start of the '87 season Reds fans were hoping Browning would bounce back from what looked like a poor 1986. Tom had won 20 games in '85, his rookie year, then slumped to a 14–13 record in 1986.

Of course the fact of the matter was that in '86 Browning had posted essentially the same statistics as in '85. In '86 he allowed just about the same number of base runners per inning pitched as in 1985 and his ERA increased from 3.55 only to 3.81. In a sense the sophomore jinx really did victimize Browning because he couldn't muster the same offensive support in '86 as the year before—hence the drop in victories.

Browning got off on the wrong foot in 1987, yielding five earned runs in just three innings on Opening Day. Then, in his next twelve starts through June 8, Browning lasted seven full innings exactly once. Only three of his outings amounted to "quality" starts. At the end of April the Reds' staff had a league leading ERA of 3.19. Browning's was 6.16. He allowed first inning runs in 38 percent of his games before being sent down, and the opposition was on the scoreboard by the third inning 85 percent of the time during that period. Cincinnati demoted Tom and his 7.39 ERA to Nashville in June, where he continued to pitch poorly. Desperate for pitching when Jerry Reuss and Pat Pacillo didn't work out, the Reds recalled him anyway over the Fourth of July weekend.

Pete was very wise to send Browning down to continue starting; he is a finesse and flyball pitcher, not conducive to getting the ground ball or big strikeout to end an inning.

Although few observers noticed it, from July 5 on Browning pitched practically as well as he had in '85 and '86. He posted a 6–7 record with a 3.65 ERA, and 12 quality starts and two complete games in 18 outings. After the call up, his average innings per start increased from 4.8 to 6.4. In fact, he finished with quite a bang, seven quality starts out of eight after August 28, a 5–2 record and an ERA of 1.89. (Browning got hot at the time Ted Power fell apart, interestingly.) His two September losses were killers, though, both at the hands of the Giants as the Reds were excused from the pennant race.

After his return from Nashville Browning let on that his arm had bothered him in April and May, a fact he hadn't disclosed to the Reds until then. If you can write off the first half of Browning's 1987 to his arm miseries and lack of discretion, the rest of his performance last year is consistent with the rest of his career. The Reds supposedly shopped Browning on the Winter Trade market, but he's the one starter on whose performance the Reds can count going into 1988—the true Browning Automatic.

Doug White and Mike Marrero

Browning, Thomas Leo "Tom" Bats: Left   Throws: Left   Born 04/28/60

1987 SEASON AND MAJOR-LEAGUE CAREER PITCHING TOTALS

	G	GS	CG	GF	IP	BFP	H	R	ER	HR	SH	SF	HB	TBB	IBB	SO	WP	Bk	W	L	Pct	ShO	Sv	ERA
87 CIN	32	31	2	1	183	791	201	107	102	27	10	7	5	61	7	117	2	4	10	13	.435	0	0	5.02
4 YEARS	112	111	12	1	710	2985	695	345	312	82	38	26	9	209	21	433	8	4	45	35	.563	6	0	3.95

1987: Finesse, Flyball   1986: Finesse, Flyball   1985: Finesse, Flyball   1984: Finesse, Flyball

1987 SEASON / FOUR YEAR TOTALS (1984 – 1987)

	G	IP	H	BB	SO	SB	CS	W	L	S	ERA	G	IP	H	BB	SO	SB	CS	W	L	S	ERA
Totals	32	182.2	201	61	117	11	9	10	13	0	5.03	112	710.2	695	209	433	46	26	45	35	0	3.95
at Home	18	100.1	99	36	67	9	6	6	6	0	4.93	55	346.1	336	112	199	22	12	23	18	0	4.18
on Road	14	82.1	102	25	50	2	3	4	7	0	5.14	57	364.1	359	97	234	24	14	22	17	0	3.71
on Grass	14	81.2	92	25	56	5	1	4	6	0	5.07	49	301.1	304	87	189	22	7	20	14	0	4.18
on Artificial Turf	18	101.0	109	36	61	6	8	6	7	0	4.99	63	409.1	391	122	244	24	19	25	21	0	3.78
Day Games	9	55.2	63	16	31	1	2	2	4	0	4.04	35	234.2	224	58	145	15	7	12	9	0	3.45
Night Games	23	127.0	138	45	86	10	7	8	9	0	5.46	77	476.0	471	151	288	31	19	33	26	0	4.20
April	6	30.2	36	9	22	0	1	2	3	0	6.16	14	78.1	75	21	47	2	3	4	6	0	4.37
May	5	22.0	36	9	11	3	0	2	3	0	10.23	18	103.2	124	36	60	9	2	6	9	0	5.56
June	3	9.2	12	6	5	4	1	0	0	0	7.45	15	84.1	80	37	54	11	5	6	3	0	4.59
July	5	30.1	39	6	20	0	3	1	2	0	4.75	18	118.0	117	23	72	1	6	7	6	0	3.97
August	6	39.0	33	17	22	3	1	1	3	0	4.38	21	137.2	125	45	76	9	4	8	7	0	3.66
Sept/Oct	7	51.0	45	14	37	1	3	4	2	0	2.29	26	188.2	174	47	124	14	6	14	4	0	2.81

vs. Opponent Batters	Ave.	OBP	SLG	AB	H	2B	3B	HR	RBI	BB	SO	Ave.	OBP	SLG	AB	H	2B	3B	HR	RBI	BB	SO
Totals	.284	.342	.472	708	201	46	3	27	94	61	117	.257	.311	.403	2702	695	135	6	82	301	209	433
vs. Left	.267	.351	.431	116	31	7	0	4	11	15	21	.248	.320	.350	412	102	15	0	9	38	44	78
vs. Right	.287	.340	.480	592	170	39	3	23	83	46	96	.259	.309	.412	2290	593	120	6	73	263	165	355
Bases Empty	.302	.353	.505	410	124	30	1	17	17	31	76	.260	.307	.403	1662	432	74	2	53	53	111	291
Leadoff	.324	.370	.534	176	57	16	0	7	7	12	35	.254	.302	.399	689	175	32	1	22	22	46	126
Not Leadoff	.286	.340	.483	234	67	14	1	10	10	19	41	.264	.310	.405	973	257	42	1	31	31	65	165
Runners On Base	.258	.327	.426	298	77	16	2	10	77	30	41	.253	.318	.403	1040	263	61	4	29	248	98	142
First Base Only	.220	.262	.309	123	27	8	0	1	5	6	14	.233	.271	.349	510	119	30	1	9	31	25	66
Scoring Position	.286	.368	.509	175	50	8	2	9	72	24	27	.272	.359	.455	530	144	31	3	20	217	73	76
Late Innings, Close	.313	.389	.469	32	10	2	0	1	2	4	5	.229	.292	.335	179	41	7	0	4	18	16	28

RBI/Opportunities

Scoring Position	56 / 243	(23%)		177 / 740	(24%)
Scoring Position, 2 Out	20 / 105	(19%)		70 / 344	(20%)
On Third, Less than 2 Out	20 / 40	(50%)		68 / 124	(55%)
RBI in close games / RBI Total	61 / 94	(65%)		211 / 301	(70%)

Tom Brunansky
Minnesota Twins

Baseball America, in their annual review of top prospects in each major league organization, projected Tom Brunansky as the Twins' starting right fielder on opening day 1991. This must come as a shock to many of Brunansky's critics who generally agree that Bruno's fielding is his weakest skill. Last spring, Tom Kelly was facing the prospect of playing Mickey Hatcher in the outfield, and said he would be moving Brunansky to left field because he wanted his best defensive player there. Since right field is generally felt to be the more difficult position of the two, there was some head scratching among Twins fans who probably thought Kelly's tongue had become twisted through lack of exercise.

Now, Kelly was not necessarily wrong if he truly believed in Bruno's defensive prowess. The left field expanse of the dome, where the ball can scoot up the gap in left center or down the third base line into the arc composing the left field corner, puts a premium on speed and defense. Whereas, right field is perfectly suited for an intelligent player with limited range and a strong arm. Bruno has been a fixture in right following his arrival in Minnesota. Any chance of finding out whether Kelly was serious or whether he was just trying to build up Brunansky's confidence ended with the acquisition of Dan Gladden.

Brunansky reminds me of the all-sports athletes you sometimes encounter in high school. He has the height for basketball, the size for football, and the coordination for baseball. Although lacking speed, he tends to be there when you need him with enough skill to complement the team's stars. In the American League you get by with Bruno's deficiencies because there are always more serious problems to address elsewhere.

Brunansky's future, assuming the Twins develop a right fielder with a little more range, will be as a full-time DH. He hits right handed pitching well enough to play every day. He has settled into quiet, consistent production from year to year. He may not travel a consistent route in a specific season, but he usually arrives in the same spot which gets the job done.

Taking a cue from Billy Gardner, Kelly batted Brunansky in the lower part of the order for most of the season. Gardner seemed to tire of trying to recognize Bruno's hot and cold streaks and removed him from the center of the offense. One of the benefits is that pitchers don't like getting past Puckett, Gaetti, and Hrbek only to find another power hitter lurking to clean up any runners left on base.

Before last season, Brunansky was shopped around in an attempt to solve some of the Twins' problems. Instead, the front office was able to obtain Reardon, Gladden, and Berenguer without trading any key players. Both Brunansky and the Twins can say it worked out for the best.

Bill Jensen

Brunansky, Thomas Andrew "Tom"

Bats: Right   Throws: Right   Born 08/20/60

1987 SEASON AND MAJOR-LEAGUE CAREER BATTING TOTALS

	G	AB	H	2B	3B	HR	TB	R	RBI	TBB	IBB	SO	HP	SH	SF	SB	CS	SB%	GDP	AVG	OBP	SLG
87 MIN	155	532	138	22	2	32	260	83	85	74	5	104	4	0	4	11	11	.50	12	.259	.352	.489
7 YEARS	913	3297	825	153	13	165	1499	452	469	395	22	588	17	3	33	36	30	.55	79	.250	.331	.455

	1987 SEASON											FOUR YEAR TOTALS (1984 – 1987)									
	Ave.	OBP	SLG	AB	H	2B	3B	HR	RBI	BB	SO	Ave.	OBP	SLG	AB	H	2B	3B	HR	RBI	BB	SO
Totals	.259	.352	.489	532	138	22	2	32	85	74	104	.253	.326	.454	2259	571	99	7	114	335	255	382
vs. Left	.228	.321	.481	158	36	8	1	10	27	23	20	.248	.329	.493	670	166	33	4	41	111	87	82
vs. Right	.273	.365	.492	374	102	14	1	22	58	51	84	.255	.325	.438	1589	405	66	3	73	224	168	300
at Home	.300	.384	.574	277	83	15	2	19	50	37	57	.264	.336	.479	1133	299	54	5	60	185	129	190
on Road	.216	.318	.396	255	55	7	0	13	35	37	47	.242	.316	.429	1126	272	45	2	54	150	126	192
vs. Groundball	.293	.377	.478	270	79	12	1	12	44	36	39	.264	.343	.469	1102	291	50	4	56	176	137	170
vs. Flyball	.225	.326	.500	262	59	10	1	20	41	38	65	.242	.310	.440	1157	280	49	3	58	159	118	212
vs. Finesse	.264	.341	.500	258	68	11	1	16	43	28	40	.256	.316	.436	1200	307	46	1	56	169	107	168
vs. Power	.255	.361	.478	274	70	11	1	16	42	46	64	.249	.337	.475	1059	264	53	6	58	166	148	214
on Grass	.218	.323	.426	197	43	5	0	12	32	29	38	.227	.309	.421	844	192	32	1	43	110	100	138
on Artificial Turf	.284	.369	.525	335	95	17	2	20	53	45	66	.268	.336	.474	1415	379	67	6	71	225	155	244
Day Games	.231	.342	.417	156	36	5	0	8	19	26	34	.243	.320	.400	668	162	30	0	25	77	79	122
Night Games	.271	.356	.519	376	102	17	2	24	66	48	70	.257	.329	.477	1591	409	69	7	89	258	176	260
April	.239	.320	.328	67	16	0	0	2	7	7	18	.267	.357	.443	307	82	9	0	15	45	42	56
May	.295	.391	.611	95	28	4	1	8	22	14	21	.302	.374	.550	391	118	17	4	24	71	44	65
June	.256	.365	.512	86	22	4	0	6	13	16	15	.241	.327	.472	377	91	18	0	23	59	49	69
July	.256	.356	.477	86	22	4	0	5	12	14	8	.224	.289	.381	370	83	15	2	13	43	34	51
August	.257	.316	.486	105	27	6	0	6	19	9	22	.255	.322	.454	416	106	20	0	21	57	41	64
Sept/Oct	.247	.355	.473	93	23	4	1	5	12	14	20	.229	.309	.420	398	91	20	1	18	60	45	77
Bases Empty	.252	.330	.479	309	78	8	1	20	20	35	65	.256	.325	.477	1219	312	52	5	69	69	124	192
Leadoff	.238	.314	.516	126	30	5	0	10	10	14	22	.250	.309	.454	537	134	19	2	29	29	46	72
Not Leadoff	.262	.341	.454	183	48	3	1	10	10	21	43	.261	.338	.494	682	178	33	3	40	40	78	120
Runners On	.269	.379	.502	223	60	14	1	12	65	39	39	.249	.334	.428	1040	259	47	2	45	266	131	190
First Base Only	.238	.347	.416	101	24	4	1	4	11	17	14	.255	.326	.476	471	120	19	2	27	62	50	75
Scoring Position	.295	.404	.574	122	36	10	0	8	54	22	25	.244	.339	.388	569	139	28	0	18	204	81	115
Late Innings, Close	.282	.371	.449	78	22	4	0	3	8	11	20	.265	.341	.462	344	91	15	1	17	53	40	68

RBI/Opportunities

Scoring Position	43 / 176 (24%)	170 / 784 (22%)
Scoring Position, 2 Out	14 / 84 (17%)	54 / 358 (15%)
On Third, Less than 2 Out	16 / 33 (48%)	68 / 145 (47%)
RBI in close games / RBI Total	44 / 85 (52%)	208 / 335 (62%)

Bill Buckner
Boston Red Sox

If you're a Bill Buckner fan, skip this page; I'm not and I'll only raise your blood pressure. That's right, sports fans—I'm back for another essay on my favorite player. The only problem is that it's no fun now. Last year people were openly claiming that this gentleman bore a vague resemblance to a major leaguer; I thereby enjoyed forcibly disabusing them of that notion. But this year? Even Buckner admitted that he "didn't play very well in 1987"; what can I add to that? Yeah, I could say that his judgement is only slightly less accurate than Robert Bork's self-assessment as a "moderate" . . . but you really have to be a sicko to kick a guy when he's down.

So let's get anecdotal: In June, I ran into a gentleman who had listened to Bill James promoting the *Stat Book* on several Boston-area talk shows. "Gee", he said, "a lot of people wanted to talk about that Buckner piece. Half the callers thought you were right on the money—the rest thought you let him off the hook too easy."

It's a fun story—don't you just love happy endings?—but I think it says a lot more about the callers than it does the piece. I mean, everyone in Beantown thought Billy Buck was the bees' knees in 1986 and slug bait in 1987—when, in fact, there was very little difference at all. When Boston released Buckner in 1987, he'd gotten 287 at-bats, was hitting .273, slugging .322, had a .299 OB% and 42 RBIs. After 297 ABs in 1986, he was hitting .236, slugging .387, his OB% was .278 and had 40 RBIs. Yes, I suppose the '86 Buckner was somewhat better than the '87 version. But be honest—did either one deserve to be playing?

To me, the real difference between the two years is Boston's winning percentage at the time: .469 as opposed to .658. In 1986, while visions of playoff games danced through their heads, nobody wanted to "risk" releasing Buckner—even though Pat Dodson was roaring through AAA pitching at the time. When Buckner got hot in September, all was forgiven (well, at least for a month it was). In 1987, with the word "debacle" appearing rather frequently in discussions of Boston's season, Sam Horn's numbers suddenly began looking very attractive. Buckner got hot in September again, but this time nobody noticed or cared.

You could say—and, hey, I think I will say—that had Roger Clemens and Rich Gedman been promptly signed and Calvin Schiraldi's ERA not become strikingly similar to the Dow Jones Industrial Average, Buckner might still be wearing carmine hosiery. Anyway, I'm not going to apologize to the Boston management for calling them "desperately stupid" last year—even though Horn sure looks like he can outhit Brooke Shields to me.

Geoff Beckman

Buckner, William Joseph "Bill"

Bats: Left   Throws: Left   Born 12/14/49

1987 SEASON AND MAJOR-LEAGUE CAREER BATTING TOTALS

	G	AB	H	2B	3B	HR	TB	R	RBI	TBB	IBB	SO	HP	SH	SF	SB	CS	SB%	GDP	AVG	OBP	SLG
87 BOS-CAL	132	469	134	18	2	5	1/1	39	74	22	2	26	0	1	6	2	3	.40	13	.286	.314	.365
19 YEARS	2308	8893	2598	480	48	169	3681	1047	1146	424	102	421	42	42	90	177	72	.71	234	.292	.324	.414

1987 SEASON

	Ave.	OBP	SLG	AB	H	2B	3B	HR	RBI	BB	SO
Totals	.286	.314	.365	469	134	18	2	5	74	22	26
vs. Left	.261	.272	.286	119	31	1	1	0	16	3	11
vs. Right	.294	.328	.391	350	103	17	1	5	58	19	15
at Home	.303	.333	.378	238	72	8	2	2	42	13	14
on Road	.268	.293	.351	231	62	10	0	3	32	9	12
vs. Groundball	.293	.320	.388	232	68	14	1	2	33	9	11
vs. Flyball	.278	.309	.342	237	66	4	1	3	41	13	15
vs. Finesse	.303	.320	.376	234	71	12	1	1	37	7	13
vs. Power	.268	.308	.353	235	63	6	1	4	37	15	13
on Grass	.275	.303	.349	378	104	12	2	4	61	18	21
on Artificial Turf	.330	.358	.429	91	30	6	0	1	13	4	5
Day Games	.272	.296	.383	162	44	7	1	3	22	6	12
Night Games	.293	.323	.355	307	90	11	1	2	52	16	14
April	.262	.267	.310	84	22	2	1	0	12	1	3
May	.232	.262	.305	95	22	1	0	2	14	5	9
June	.362	.380	.383	47	17	1	0	0	13	2	3
July	.278	.333	.319	72	20	3	0	0	5	6	5
August	.302	.326	.419	86	26	4	0	2	13	3	2
Sept/Oct	.318	.352	.459	85	27	7	1	1	17	5	4
Bases Empty	.262	.289	.319	260	68	9	0	2	2	10	15
Leadoff	.322	.344	.400	90	29	4	0	1	1	3	5
Not Leadoff	.229	.260	.276	170	39	5	0	1	1	7	10
Runners On	.316	.344	.421	209	66	9	2	3	72	12	11
First Base Only	.342	.366	.430	79	27	5	1	0	4	3	2
Scoring Position	.300	.331	.415	130	39	4	1	3	68	9	9
Late Innings, Close	.276	.321	.329	76	21	2	1	0	8	5	6

FOUR YEAR TOTALS (1984 – 1987)

	Ave.	OBP	SLG	AB	H	2B	3B	HR	RBI	BB	SO
Totals	.281	.316	.411	2253	634	124	9	50	355	117	126
vs. Left	.261	.294	.360	700	183	22	4	13	106	29	47
vs. Right	.290	.327	.434	1553	451	102	5	37	249	88	79
at Home	.279	.317	.406	1117	312	60	8	22	179	63	73
on Road	.283	.316	.415	1136	322	64	1	28	176	54	53
vs. Groundball	.298	.332	.423	1102	328	66	3	22	177	57	56
vs. Flyball	.266	.302	.400	1151	306	58	6	28	178	60	70
vs. Finesse	.291	.320	.430	1233	359	73	4	30	201	54	64
vs. Power	.270	.313	.388	1020	275	51	5	20	154	63	62
on Grass	.277	.313	.409	1900	527	107	9	42	301	101	106
on Artificial Turf	.303	.336	.419	353	107	17	0	8	54	16	20
Day Games	.258	.293	.380	753	194	42	4	14	107	39	45
Night Games	.293	.329	.427	1500	440	82	5	36	248	78	81
April	.257	.286	.366	268	69	16	2	3	33	11	12
May	.272	.316	.399	338	92	16	0	9	50	23	18
June	.265	.295	.379	359	95	16	2	7	54	16	23
July	.269	.303	.401	387	104	28	1	7	54	19	26
August	.294	.331	.435	446	131	26	2	11	80	25	18
Sept/Oct	.314	.347	.457	455	143	22	2	13	84	23	29
Bases Empty	.256	.282	.380	1153	295	57	7	24	24	42	62
Leadoff	.257	.288	.386	412	106	19	5	8	8	18	20
Not Leadoff	.255	.278	.377	741	189	38	2	16	16	24	42
Runners On	.308	.351	.444	1100	339	67	2	26	331	75	64
First Base Only	.328	.362	.445	488	160	28	1	9	30	26	26
Scoring Position	.292	.342	.443	612	179	39	1	17	301	49	38
Late Innings, Close	.340	.389	.451	324	110	19	1	5	47	26	18

RBI/Opportunities

Scoring Position	62 / 190 (33%)	262 / 858 (31%)
Scoring Position, 2 Out	18 / 78 (23%)	88 / 352 (25%)
On Third, Less than 2 Out	31 / 44 (70%)	113 / 179 (63%)
RBI in close games / RBI Total	46 / 74 (62%)	225 / 355 (63%)

Steve Buechele
Texas Rangers

At the start of every series in Texas, Eric Nadel of WBAP radio would interview the opposing manager who almost always ended up praising the playing field of Arlington Stadium. Nadel finally had to start asking them *not* to mention the field in their interviews—it was boring their listeners.

It is a great field, and deserves every ounce of respect it gets. It's a little fast on the infield, but it's purposely built that way. What matters is that it's green and true. It wasn't always that way; I used to think Stalin was alive and reenacting his scorched earth policy at the stadium. While fans stuck with artificial fields cried out for grass that was real, Texas fans once thought it would be nice to have grass that was alive.

A few years ago Ranger fans got a terrific surprise when they arrived at the stadium, "Oh look, Honey, they've painted the grass green". Except it wasn't paint; it was Field Superintendent Jim Angela taking over and putting the "park" back in our ballpark.

You want to hear dedication? Early in 1987 Steve Buechele was eaten up by an evil bad hop in a Ranger home game. After the game, Angela got a tape of the play and studied it to find the flaw in his diamond. By game time the next day it was corrected.

A lot of managers will concede that Steve Buechele is the best defensive third baseman in the American League, but they won't give him a Gold Glove vote. That's fine with me. A player's bat *does* have defensive value when it determines the amount of time he can spend in the field. A good fielder who hits well enough to play every day and snares an extra out every 30 innings has more real defensive value than a great fielder who gets an extra out every 25 innings but plays 20 percent less often.

I don't have a lot of hope for Steve ever settling in as a real regular. He doesn't hit for average; he doesn't walk; he doesn't run, and while he has some power, he tends to hit mostly solo homers. So far in his career he has averaged a homer every 22 at-bats with the bases empty; with men on base you get one every 47 at-bats. When all those negatives come together in one player, you often have a worse hitter than appears on the surface. I think Buechele has been skating by on that illusion as is. I expect him to play less in the future, not more.

But he does have real value to a team if placed in the right role. He hits lefties very well (career .279 BA, .467 SLUG%), and he is a good fielder at both third and second. Earl Weaver became a genius appreciating players like that. The trick is to use them where they are an asset rather than a deficit.

Craig R. Wright

Buechele, Steven Bernard "Steve"

Bats: Right Throws: Right Born 09/26/61

1987 SEASON AND MAJOR-LEAGUE CAREER BATTING TOTALS

	G	AB	H	2B	3B	HR	TB	R	RBI	TBB	IBB	SO	HP	SH	SF	SB	CS	SB%	GDP	AVG	OBP	SLG
87 TEX	136	363	86	20	0	13	145	45	50	28	3	66	1	4	4	2	2	.50	7	.237	.290	.399
3 YEARS	358	1043	246	45	5	37	412	121	125	77	6	202	8	13	8	10	12	.45	28	.236	.291	.395

	1987 SEASON											FOUR YEAR TOTALS (1984 – 1987)										
	Ave.	OBP	SLG	AB	H	2B	3B	HR	RBI	BB	SO	Ave.	OBP	SLG	AB	H	2B	3B	HR	RBI	BB	SO
Totals	.237	.290	.399	363	86	20	0	13	50	28	66	.236	.291	.395	1043	246	45	5	37	125	77	202
vs. Left	.288	.333	.497	177	51	13	0	8	28	12	28	.279	.333	.465	391	109	21	2	16	52	32	76
vs. Right	.188	.250	.306	186	35	7	0	5	22	16	38	.210	.266	.353	652	137	24	3	21	73	45	126
at Home	.250	.316	.404	188	47	11	0	6	30	18	32	.238	.294	.383	522	124	23	1	17	62	38	97
on Road	.223	.262	.394	175	39	9	0	7	20	10	34	.234	.289	.407	521	122	22	4	20	63	39	105
vs. Groundball	.220	.271	.382	186	41	9	0	7	17	12	33	.244	.293	.389	496	121	18	3	16	61	32	90
vs. Flyball	.254	.310	.418	177	45	11	0	6	33	16	33	.229	.290	.400	547	125	27	2	21	64	45	112
vs. Finesse	.238	.278	.405	210	50	11	0	8	32	13	32	.229	.285	.379	593	136	28	2	19	76	43	100
vs. Power	.235	.308	.392	153	36	9	0	5	18	15	34	.244	.300	.416	450	110	17	3	18	49	34	102
on Grass	.233	.287	.384	305	71	16	0	10	43	24	56	.234	.291	.383	869	203	32	4	30	107	65	169
on Artificial Turf	.259	.306	.483	58	15	4	0	3	7	4	10	.247	.296	.454	174	43	13	1	7	18	12	33
Day Games	.227	.318	.333	75	17	5	0	1	7	10	14	.220	.278	.345	200	44	10	0	5	18	16	48
Night Games	.240	.283	.417	288	69	15	0	12	43	18	52	.240	.295	.407	843	202	35	5	32	107	61	154
April	.213	.294	.361	61	13	3	0	2	4	6	17	.237	.308	.432	118	28	5	0	6	10	11	27
May	.209	.250	.343	67	14	3	0	2	6	4	14	.222	.261	.389	144	32	6	0	6	15	8	28
June	.213	.247	.440	75	16	8	0	3	12	4	10	.257	.300	.461	167	43	13	0	7	22	11	32
July	.300	.367	.457	70	21	2	0	3	17	8	5	.234	.297	.321	184	43	4	0	4	24	17	29
August	.225	.262	.275	40	9	2	0	0	1	2	9	.234	.303	.354	192	45	8	3	3	21	19	39
Sept/Oct	.260	.315	.480	50	13	2	0	3	10	4	11	.231	.265	.424	238	55	9	2	11	33	11	47
Bases Empty	.246	.300	.446	195	48	9	0	10	10	14	35	.237	.288	.430	616	146	27	4	28	28	43	119
Leadoff	.221	.264	.488	86	19	2	0	7	7	5	17	.253	.285	.487	269	68	10	1	17	17	12	49
Not Leadoff	.266	.328	.413	109	29	7	0	3	3	9	18	.225	.290	.386	347	78	17	3	11	11	31	70
Runners On	.226	.280	.345	168	38	11	0	3	40	14	31	.234	.288	.344	427	100	18	1	9	97	34	83
First Base Only	.205	.241	.349	83	17	6	0	2	6	4	15	.226	.261	.368	190	43	10	1	5	16	9	37
Scoring Position	.247	.313	.341	85	21	5	0	1	34	10	16	.241	.308	.325	237	57	8	0	4	81	25	46
Late Innings, Close	.300	.375	.380	50	15	4	0	0	2	6	10	.281	.325	.418	153	43	9	0	4	13	10	25

RBI/Opportunities

Scoring Position	31 / 120	(26%)	73 / 322	(23%)
Scoring Position, 2 Out	15 / 63	(24%)	30 / 152	(20%)
On Third, Less than 2 Out	13 / 24	(54%)	31 / 55	(56%)
RBI in close games / RBI Total	22 / 50	(44%)	61 / 125	(49%)

DeWayne Buice
California Angels

DeWayne Buice was not your typical rookie pitching sensation. Pre-season favorites tend to be baby-faced phenoms who can really "bring it." The story goes they only need to fine-tune their control, develop another pitch, gain some confidence, and stardom will be assured. Few actually do it.

In this story Buice definitely came from the other side of the tracks. He isn't young; he turned 30 just four months after his major league debut. His heater is lukewarm in the low 80's. He already had superb control with a 2.48 walk average (which is good for any league). He may need another pitch some day, but not until the AL can find names for everything he throws now. His confidence abounds.

Gene Mauch claims Buice can get you 0–2 or 1–2 faster than anyone ever seen. No matter what the count, he throws his diabolic off-speed sinker for strikes. The pitch has been characterized as a curve, a change, a split-finger fastball, and a spitter. Buice calls it a forkball. Almost everybody calls it too high to take and too low to hit.

DeWayne had some trouble making the team, but his 1987 success will keep that from being a problem in 1988. Some highlights: 5th in the AL in saves, more K per IP than Mike Scott or Roger Clemens, and fewer Hits per IP than Reardon, Righetti, or Plesac. His most powerful credential as a stopper was his domination of both righties (.206) and lefties (.219).

A common question about rookies with good stuff but a peculiar motion—Buice winds up with his back to the plate a la Garber or Tiant—is whether they remain effective through the second half of the season. Superficially, there is reason for concern. DeWayne's ERA was 2.81 before the All-Star break, 4.14 after.

In my opinion, however, those numbers are misleading. A theoretical composite batter with 550 AB facing Buice in early '87 would hit .172 with 21 HR and 47 RBI. Based on second half performance, those 550 AB would produce .238 with 8 HR and 63 RBI. It seems the hitters were learning to swing carefully and make contact against his forkball, but with a big loss of power. The bottom line is they remained essentially ineffective. Luck probably created the ERA disparity: unusually low in the first half and unusually high in the second half.

Whatever his personal future, Buice made a significant dent in the traditional form of spring prognostications. We can hope to hear less about kids with major league velocity, and more about mature rookies with excellent control, sharp movement and major league poise. Rookies like DeWayne Buice and Mark Eichhorn should find it easier to get ink in future spring reviews, perhaps something like, "Give this man regular work with a skillful catcher and he could excel."

John C. Benson

Buice, DeWayne Allison "DeWayne"   Bats: Right   Throws: Right   Born 08/20/57

1987 SEASON AND MAJOR-LEAGUE CAREER PITCHING TOTALS

	G	GS	CG	GF	IP	BFP	H	R	ER	HR	SH	SF	HB	TBB	IBB	SO	WP	Bk	W	L	Pct	ShO	Sv	ERA
87 CAL	57	0	0	44	114	457	87	45	43	12	5	2	2	40	3	109	3	0	6	7	.462	0	17	3.39
1 YEAR	57	0	0	44	114	457	87	45	43	12	5	2	2	40	3	109	3	0	6	7	.462	0	17	3.39

1987: Power, Groundball

	1987 SEASON											FOUR YEAR TOTALS (1984 – 1987)										
	G	IP	H	BB	SO	SB	CS	W	L	S	ERA	G	IP	H	BB	SO	SB	CS	W	L	S	ERA
Totals	57	114.1	87	40	109	8	4	6	7	17	3.38	57	114.1	87	40	109	8	4	6	7	17	3.38
at Home	29	58.0	35	17	58	3	3	3	3	8	2.33	29	58.0	35	17	58	3	3	3	3	8	2.33
on Road	28	56.1	52	23	51	5	1	3	4	9	4.47	28	56.1	52	23	51	5	1	3	4	9	4.47
on Grass	16	28.0	16	15	31	2	1	1	2	5	3.54	16	28.0	16	15	31	2	1	1	2	5	3.54
on Artificial Turf	41	86.1	71	25	78	6	3	5	5	12	3.34	41	86.1	71	25	78	6	3	5	5	12	3.34
Day Games	49	100.2	70	31	94	8	4	5	6	16	2.77	49	100.2	70	31	94	8	4	5	6	16	2.77
Night Games	8	13.2	17	9	15	0	0	1	1	1	7.90	8	13.2	17	9	15	0	0	1	1	1	7.90
April	3	8.0	7	4	9	0	0	1	0	0	3.38	3	8.0	7	4	9	0	0	1	0	0	3.38
May	12	22.1	17	7	21	0	0	1	3	2	3.63	12	22.1	17	7	21	0	0	1	3	2	3.63
June	9	20.2	11	5	27	0	2	1	0	4	2.18	9	20.2	11	5	27	0	2	1	0	4	2.18
July	11	24.0	10	6	16	2	1	1	0	5	1.88	11	24.0	10	6	16	2	1	1	0	5	1.88
August	10	21.0	18	9	21	2	1	1	2	3	3.86	10	21.0	18	9	21	2	1	1	2	3	3.86
Sept/Oct	12	18.1	24	9	15	4	0	1	2	3	5.89	12	18.1	24	9	15	4	0	1	2	3	5.89

vs. Opponent Batters	Ave.	OBP	SLG	AB	H	2B	3B	HR	RBI	BB	SO	Ave.	OBP	SLG	AB	H	2B	3B	HR	RBI	BB	SO
Totals	.213	.285	.348	408	87	17	1	12	53	40	109	.213	.285	.348	408	87	17	1	12	53	40	109
vs. Left	.219	.309	.349	192	42	7	0	6	25	25	54	.219	.309	.349	192	42	7	0	6	25	25	54
vs. Right	.208	.264	.347	216	45	10	1	6	28	15	55	.208	.264	.347	216	45	10	1	6	28	15	55
Bases Empty	.185	.261	.309	233	43	6	1	7	7	24	64	.185	.261	.309	233	43	6	1	7	7	24	64
Leadoff	.196	.237	.380	92	18	2	0	5	5	5	20	.196	.237	.380	92	18	2	0	5	5	5	20
Not Leadoff	.177	.275	.262	141	25	4	1	2	2	19	44	.177	.275	.262	141	25	4	1	2	2	19	44
Runners On Base	.251	.318	.400	175	44	11	0	5	46	16	45	.251	.318	.400	175	44	11	0	5	46	16	45
First Base Only	.221	.284	.368	68	15	1	0	3	6	5	22	.221	.284	.368	68	15	1	0	3	6	5	22
Scoring Position	.271	.339	.421	107	29	10	0	2	40	11	23	.271	.339	.421	107	29	10	0	2	40	11	23
Late Innings, Close	.243	.319	.383	235	57	13	1	6	36	26	60	.243	.319	.383	235	57	13	1	6	36	26	60

RBI/Opportunities

Scoring Position	35 / 149 (23%)		35 / 149 (23%)	
Scoring Position, 2 Out	16 / 69 (23%)		16 / 69 (23%)	
On Third, Less than 2 Out	11 / 24 (46%)		11 / 24 (46%)	
RBI in close games / RBI Total	37 / 53 (70%)		37 / 53 (70%)	

Tim Burke
Montreal Expos

When the Montreal Expos traded ace reliever Jeff Reardon to Minnesota, insuring, though no one believed it at the time, that the Twins would be in the World Series, Expos fans couldn't help but to think that management had tossed in the towel on the 1987 season, and was doing so by reducing its inflated payroll wherever it could.

With Andre Dawson on his way to a Most Valuable Player Award in Chicago, and Tim Raines, the .330 hitter that nobody could use, still waiting in the wings while Montreal played financial hardball, the trade of "The Terminator" for a package of nondescript players was certain to assure Montreal of a finish near the bottom of the National League East standings.

Reardon, of course, had been one of the most feared relief pitchers in baseball, compiling 162 saves in a Montreal uniform. He had saved 41 games in 1985, and followed that with 35 in 1986, despite the fact that his ERA that year had jumped ominously to 3.94. Too much warming up in the bullpen, he had said it was.

ERA and suspected arm ailments aside, Reardon had saved 35 games in 1986, and you don't replace that kind of productivity easily. Devoid of his stopper, manager Buck Rodgers went to a bullpen by committee format. Whitey Herzog had made that kind of arrangement work nicely in 1984 when the St. Louis Cardinals lost to Kansas City in seven games at the World Series. It worked for Rodgers, too, and one of the biggest reasons it did was righthander Tim Burke.

Burke was hardly a newcomer to the Montreal pitching staff. He had spent two seasons as Reardon's caddy, posting some impressive numbers along the way, including a league leading 78 appearances in 1985. He put together a combined 18–12 mark with a 2.64 ERA and a dozen saves while playing the set-up man. But with Reardon gone, it was Burke's time to shine.

Early in the 1987 season, Andy McGaffigan had been the primary closer while Burke overcame some injury problems. Healthy, and with McGaffigan slumping, Burke became Rodgers' primary man in the bullpen, and was virtually unhittable.

In 55 games, he went 7–0 with 18 saves and a remarkable earned run average of 1.19. He allowed only 12 earned runs in 91 innings. In fact, in the biggest offensive year that major league baseball has seen in decades, he allowed fewer hits and walks combined than innings pitched.

Overall, the Expos bullpen recorded 50 saves without Reardon, only one fewer than the league-leading Mets bullpen.

Tom Henry

Burke, Timothy Philip "Tim"

Bats: Right   Throws: Right   Born 02/19/59

1987 SEASON AND MAJOR-LEAGUE CAREER PITCHING TOTALS

	G	GS	CG	GF	IP	BFP	H	R	ER	HR	SH	SF	HB	TBB	IBB	SO	WP	Bk	W	L	Pct	ShO	Sv	ERA
87 MON	55	0	0	30	91	354	64	18	12	3	8	2	0	17	6	58	2	0	7	0	1.000	0	18	1.19
3 YEARS	201	2	0	86	312	1288	253	87	77	19	22	7	11	107	33	227	13	0	25	11	.694	0	30	2.22

1987: Finesse, Groundball   1986: Power, Groundball   1985: Power, Groundball

	1987 SEASON										FOUR YEAR TOTALS (1984 – 1987)										
	G	IP	H	BB	SO	SB	CS	W	L	S	ERA	G	IP	H	BB	SO	SB	CS	W	L	S	ERA
Totals	55	91.1	64	17	58	6	4	7	0	18	1.18	201	313.0	252	107	227	37	15	25	11	30	2.21
at Home	30	46.2	32	11	24	1	3	5	0	7	0.96	94	143.1	112	52	102	13	5	13	5	11	1.88
on Road	25	44.2	32	6	34	5	1	2	0	11	1.41	107	169.2	140	55	125	24	10	12	6	19	2.49
on Grass	16	28.2	16	3	24	2	1	0	0	7	0.63	73	126.1	100	47	92	16	6	3	2	13	1.92
on Artificial Turf	39	62.2	48	14	34	4	3	7	0	11	1.44	128	186.2	152	60	135	21	9	22	9	17	2.41
Day Games	13	26.1	16	4	21	3	1	2	0	7	0.34	54	100.0	69	26	75	8	5	8	2	13	1.44
Night Games	42	65.0	48	13	37	3	3	5	0	11	1.52	147	213.0	183	81	152	29	10	17	9	17	2.58
April	4	4.1	5	1	4	0	0	0	0	0	6.23	23	35.0	26	14	32	7	1	1	0	3	2.31
May	10	19.0	11	4	7	0	0	0	0	5	0.00	31	55.1	40	15	30	2	3	2	1	6	1.30
June	11	18.1	15	6	6	1	1	0	0	2	2.95	42	57.0	45	21	37	4	3	6	1	4	2.21
July	9	16.2	12	2	11	1	1	2	0	2	0.54	33	53.0	41	30	32	10	2	5	2	4	2.21
August	11	17.1	12	2	12	0	2	5	0	3	0.52	37	57.1	46	12	47	2	4	9	4	4	1.73
Sept/Oct	10	15.2	9	2	18	4	0	0	0	6	0.57	35	55.1	54	15	49	12	2	2	3	9	3.58

vs. Opponent Batters	Ave.	OBP	SLG	AB	H	2B	3B	HR	RBI	BB	SO	Ave.	OBP	SLG	AB	H	2B	3B	HR	RBI	BB	SO
Totals	.196	.234	.254	327	64	8	1	3	25	17	58	.221	.287	.313	1140	252	44	2	19	108	107	227
vs. Left	.219	.265	.290	169	37	4	1	2	15	11	22	.258	.342	.356	562	145	23	1	10	65	72	89
vs. Right	.171	.200	.215	158	27	4	0	1	10	6	36	.185	.231	.272	578	107	21	1	9	43	35	138
Bases Empty	.207	.236	.277	188	39	5	1	2	2	7	32	.225	.275	.332	626	141	24	2	13	13	43	127
Leadoff	.211	.250	.289	76	16	3	0	1	1	4	7	.264	.324	.402	261	69	13	1	7	7	23	45
Not Leadoff	.205	.226	.268	112	23	2	1	1	1	3	25	.197	.239	.282	365	72	11	1	6	6	20	82
Runners On Base	.180	.232	.223	139	25	3	0	1	23	10	26	.216	.302	.290	514	111	20	0	6	95	64	100
First Base Only	.157	.157	.176	51	8	1	0	0	0	0	11	.274	.300	.360	164	45	8	0	2	9	6	26
Scoring Position	.193	.270	.250	88	17	2	0	1	23	10	15	.189	.302	.257	350	66	12	0	4	86	58	74
Late Innings, Close	.181	.207	.221	199	36	5	0	1	11	7	41	.217	.283	.295	621	135	21	0	9	53	58	125

RBI/Opportunities

Scoring Position	20 / 120 (17%)	75 / 516 (15%)
Scoring Position, 2 Out	7 / 51 (14%)	25 / 226 (11%)
On Third, Less than 2 Out	8 / 22 (36%)	32 / 85 (38%)
RBI in close games / RBI Total	15 / 25 (60%)	71 / 108 (66%)

Ellis Burks
Boston Red Sox

Imagine, if you can, dropping Babe Ruth into the middle of the 1906 White Sox lineup and you have some idea of the impact that Ellis Burks made in Boston in 1987. For the first time in years there was a player in a Boston uniform who could score a run by beating out a bunt for a base hit, stealing second base and scoring on a line single. He took extra bases on opposing outfielders; he drew throws from opposing pitchers whenever he reached first. Beantown got a taste of speed and liked the flavor; Ellis was the biggest New England rookie sensation in this decade even though he didn't start the year on the 24-man roster.

Ellis had to spend a month in AAA, while Dave Henderson proved that he'd sent his Superman costume to the cleaners after the 1986 playoffs and then lost his claim check, but arrived in time to play 133 games, establish himself as The Future and become a media darling. The Red Sox's flagship television station installed a timer on their replay equipment so that everyone could see just how fast this guy got down the line to first base. He had the most stolen bases for a Red Sox rookie since the Age of Steam. Then there was his defense. The sight of a Boston centerfielder racing into the gaps to snag line drives and beating fly balls to the warning track was a sight unseen in Fenway since Fred Lynn went into semi-retirement with the Angels. Ellis also had a passel of assists (15; fifth in the AL) to go along

with those catches. Finally, Burks started to flash some serious power as the summer passed. His 11 homers over the Green Monster in 1987 was second only to Dwight Evans.

Naturally someone this fast had to bat leadoff, and be the rabbit for Marty Barrett to hit and run with. Manager John McNamara dreamed of endless first-and-third situations with Wade Boggs approaching the plate. But this dream rarely materialized in 1987. Though Ellis did some wondrous things in 1987, he also failed to carry out the leadoff man's Prime Directive: Take pitches; get on base. Burks tied Dwight Evans for the team lead in strikeouts despite 50 less plate appearances. His OB% was below the league average; eight other Boston players reached base to start an inning more often. Amazingly, thc Sox led the AL in OB% with a leadoff man whose figure was 28 points below that of the team as a whole. There is no doubt that Boston would have finished higher than fourth in runs scored with someone other than Burks leading off.

The way for Mr. Burks to increase his contribution to the club is simple and obvious: Stop swinging so much! This will hopefully be a case where hitting coach Walt Hriniak can communicate some of his alleged wisdom and really help a young player improve. Watch Ellis' walks total this season—it will be his most important statistic.

Fred Percival

Burks, Ellis Rena

Bats: Right   Throws: Right   Born 09/11/64

1987 SEASON AND MAJOR-LEAGUE CAREER BATTING TOTALS

	G	AB	H	2B	3B	HR	TB	R	RBI	TBB	IBB	SO	HP	SH	SF	SB	CS	SB%	GDP	AVG	OBP	SLG
87 BOS	133	558	152	30	2	20	246	94	59	41	0	98	2	4	1	27	6	.82	1	.272	.324	.441
1 YEAR	133	558	152	30	2	20	246	94	59	41	0	98	2	4	1	27	6	.82	1	.272	.324	.441

	1987 SEASON											FOUR YEAR TOTALS (1984 – 1987)										
	Ave.	OBP	SLG	AB	H	2B	3B	HR	RBI	BB	SO	Ave.	OBP	SLG	AB	H	2B	3B	HR	RBI	BB	SO
Totals	.272	.324	.441	558	152	30	2	20	59	41	97	.272	.324	.441	558	152	30	2	20	59	41	97
vs. Left	.325	.380	.483	151	49	12	0	4	18	14	29	.325	.380	.483	151	49	12	0	4	18	14	29
vs. Right	.253	.303	.425	407	103	18	2	16	41	27	68	.253	.303	.425	407	103	18	2	16	41	27	68
at Home	.289	.365	.480	256	74	14	1	11	30	30	42	.289	.365	.480	256	74	14	1	11	30	30	42
on Road	.258	.287	.407	302	78	16	1	9	29	11	55	.258	.287	.407	302	78	16	1	9	29	11	55
vs. Groundball	.257	.309	.404	265	68	11	2	8	23	18	39	.257	.309	.404	265	68	11	2	8	23	18	39
vs. Flyball	.287	.338	.474	293	84	19	0	12	36	23	58	.287	.338	.474	293	84	19	0	12	36	23	58
vs. Finesse	.286	.314	.481	283	81	14	1	13	32	11	33	.286	.314	.481	283	81	14	1	13	32	11	33
vs. Power	.258	.333	.400	275	71	16	1	7	27	30	64	.258	.333	.400	275	71	16	1	7	27	30	64
on Grass	.279	.335	.448	466	130	24	2	17	55	39	77	.279	.335	.448	466	130	24	2	17	55	39	77
on Artificial Turf	.239	.263	.402	92	22	6	0	3	4	2	20	.239	.263	.402	92	22	6	0	3	4	2	20
Day Games	.249	.312	.405	173	43	6	0	7	14	15	31	.249	.312	.405	173	43	6	0	7	14	15	31
Night Games	.283	.329	.457	385	109	24	2	13	45	26	66	.283	.329	.457	385	109	24	2	13	45	26	66
April	.000	.000	.000	3	0	0	0	0	0	0	1	.000	.000	.000	3	0	0	0	0	0	0	1
May	.239	.277	.442	113	27	8	0	5	13	6	22	.239	.277	.442	113	27	8	0	5	13	6	22
June	.259	.326	.568	81	21	4	0	7	19	8	16	.259	.326	.568	81	21	4	0	7	19	8	16
July	.319	.358	.513	113	36	8	1	4	10	6	22	.319	.358	.513	113	36	8	1	4	10	6	22
August	.270	.359	.405	111	30	4	1	3	12	15	20	.270	.359	.405	111	30	4	1	3	12	15	20
Sept/Oct	.277	.308	.343	137	38	6	0	1	5	6	16	.277	.308	.343	137	38	6	0	1	5	6	16
Bases Empty	.283	.319	.430	381	108	20	0	12	12	20	61	.283	.319	.430	381	108	20	0	12	12	20	61
Leadoff	.316	.350	.456	228	72	11	0	7	7	12	34	.316	.350	.456	228	72	11	0	7	7	12	34
Not Leadoff	.235	.273	.392	153	36	9	0	5	5	8	27	.235	.273	.392	153	36	9	0	5	5	8	27
Runners On	.249	.333	.463	177	44	10	2	8	47	21	36	.249	.333	.463	177	44	10	2	8	47	21	36
First Base Only	.311	.391	.508	61	19	6	0	2	5	7	8	.311	.391	.508	61	19	6	0	2	5	7	8
Scoring Position	.216	.303	.440	116	25	4	2	6	42	14	28	.216	.303	.440	116	25	4	2	6	42	14	28
Late Innings, Close	.184	.262	.263	76	14	1	1	1	9	8	15	.184	.262	.263	76	14	1	1	1	9	8	15

RBI/Opportunities

Scoring Position	33 / 167 (20%)	33 / 167 (20%)
Scoring Position, 2 Out	12 / 82 (15%)	12 / 82 (15%)
On Third, Less than 2 Out	10 / 22 (45%)	10 / 22 (45%)
RBI in close games / RBI Total	34 / 59 (58%)	34 / 59 (58%)

Randy Bush
Minnesota Twins

For several years, former Minnesota Vikings coach Bud Grant kept the steady, if unspectacular, place kicker Fred Cox on his roster while other more gifted players came and went. There were much more pressing problems than becoming engrossed in a weekly debate about field goal kickers; Grant left that to the fans and sportswriters. Randy Bush's career as a major leaguer is a tribute to just such an attitude. As a solution to a small problem, this left-handed hitter, who can pinch hit, play some in the field, and doesn't complain, has posted a longer-than-average career.

Fortunately for Bush, he arrived in Minnesota in 1982. It was a time when the Twins' problems were more obvious than a Billy Gardner lineup card. Bush quickly deposed the incumbent, Randy Johnson, and established himself as the regular left side DH. In '85 and '86, Bush was given the opportunity to prove himself in the outfield as the Twins first tried Mike Stenhouse and then Roy Smalley in Bush's previous position. That pattern continued last season with Randy in the field while Smalley and Gene Larkin frequently shared DH duties.

1987 was a typical Bush year. He hit 11 home runs for the third time in five full seasons (10 and 7 the other two). His 46 RBI fit neatly between a low of 35 and a high of 56. He has reasonable strike zone judgment and his home runs tend to be of the high trajectory "moonshot" variety. With

him, you know what you get, and you get what you pay for.

There is sometimes an assumption that a manager with extensive minor league managing and playing experience will have the ability to develop young players on the major league level. In 1987, Kelly gave little indication of that. He obtained acceptable performances from players like Tom Nieto, Al Newman, Sal Butera, and Randy Bush. Despite limited major league experience, these players have been around and are really not prospects. Of the rookies, only Gene Larkin and Les Straker received considerable playing time.

Incidentally, Tom Kelly managed Bush in 1981 on the Twins' double-A club, Orlando. Both were similar minor league players. Each had some power and neither was hesitant about taking a base on balls. Despite this natural affinity, Kelly will soon reach the decision stage with Bush. Larkin, a good switch hitting first baseman, needs to be taught another position or be used as a full time DH. Bush is an outfielder with limited range; he simply can't be allowed to hold up the development of other players within the organization.

Still, Randy can probably count on another season with the Twins, and there are always other teams. Managers often have a soft spot for reliable solutions to even small problems.

Bill Jensen

Bush, Robert Randall "Randy"   Bats: Left   Throws: Left   Born 10/05/58

1987 SEASON AND MAJOR-LEAGUE CAREER BATTING TOTALS

	G	AB	H	2B	3B	HR	TB	R	RBI	TBB	IBB	SO	HP	SH	SF	SB	CS	SB%	GDP	AVG	OBP	SLG
87 MIN	122	293	74	10	2	11	121	46	46	43	5	49	3	5	5	10	3	.77	6	.253	.349	.413
6 YEARS	641	1687	417	89	17	54	702	224	238	179	22	281	26	6	20	19	9	.68	25	.247	.325	.416

1987 SEASON

	Ave.	OBP	SLG	AB	H	2B	3B	HR	RBI	BB	SO
Totals	.253	.349	.413	293	74	10	2	11	46	43	49
vs. Left	.222	.417	.222	9	2	0	0	0	2	3	2
vs. Right	.254	.346	.419	284	72	10	2	11	44	40	47
at Home	.258	.380	.367	128	33	3	1	3	19	25	21
on Road	.248	.323	.448	165	41	7	1	8	27	18	28
vs. Groundball	.241	.335	.370	162	39	7	1	4	22	22	29
vs. Flyball	.267	.365	.466	131	35	3	1	7	24	21	20
vs. Finesse	.286	.358	.474	133	38	5	1	6	24	15	12
vs. Power	.225	.342	.363	160	36	5	1	5	22	28	37
on Grass	.264	.347	.472	125	33	6	1	6	20	16	20
on Artificial Turf	.244	.350	.369	168	41	4	1	5	26	27	29
Day Games	.225	.337	.287	80	18	5	0	0	8	12	18
Night Games	.263	.353	.460	213	56	5	2	11	38	31	31
April	.222	.306	.407	54	12	2	1	2	6	7	6
May	.211	.375	.263	38	8	2	0	0	5	10	3
June	.324	.359	.595	37	12	1	0	3	8	2	5
July	.182	.229	.303	33	6	1	0	1	5	2	8
August	.258	.343	.371	62	16	1	1	1	4	8	15
Sept/Oct	.290	.411	.493	69	20	2	0	4	18	14	12
Bases Empty	.224	.319	.382	165	37	3	1	7	7	20	32
Leadoff	.266	.347	.453	64	17	1	1	3	3	7	14
Not Leadoff	.198	.302	.337	101	20	2	0	4	4	13	18
Runners On	.289	.385	.453	128	37	7	1	4	39	23	17
First Base Only	.281	.359	.421	57	16	3	1	1	5	7	7
Scoring Position	.296	.402	.479	71	21	4	0	3	34	16	10
Late Innings, Close	.239	.364	.391	46	11	2	1	1	8	9	12

FOUR YEAR TOTALS (1984 – 1987)

	Ave.	OBP	SLG	AB	H	2B	3B	HR	RBI	BB	SO
Totals	.247	.328	.416	1195	295	59	13	39	169	137	202
vs. Left	.139	.279	.194	36	5	2	0	0	3	7	6
vs. Right	.250	.330	.423	1159	290	57	13	39	166	130	196
at Home	.262	.351	.457	599	157	33	9	22	97	75	97
on Road	.232	.304	.374	596	138	26	4	17	72	62	105
vs. Groundball	.236	.308	.395	605	143	34	7	16	80	58	101
vs. Flyball	.258	.348	.437	590	152	25	6	23	89	79	101
vs. Finesse	.263	.329	.454	632	166	41	7	22	101	60	76
vs. Power	.229	.327	.373	563	129	18	6	17	68	77	126
on Grass	.239	.317	.393	461	110	21	4	14	54	54	82
on Artificial Turf	.252	.335	.431	734	185	38	9	25	115	83	120
Day Games	.239	.330	.416	368	88	25	5	10	51	45	67
Night Games	.250	.327	.416	827	207	34	8	29	118	92	135
April	.248	.329	.455	145	36	8	2	6	19	18	21
May	.229	.319	.434	205	47	12	3	8	35	27	28
June	.231	.292	.435	186	43	10	2	8	34	16	28
July	.262	.323	.424	210	55	9	2	7	24	19	40
August	.247	.333	.372	239	59	15	3	3	21	31	49
Sept/Oct	.262	.346	.395	210	55	5	1	7	36	26	36
Bases Empty	.225	.298	.388	662	149	32	5	22	22	66	119
Leadoff	.238	.293	.414	256	61	11	2	10	10	19	42
Not Leadoff	.217	.301	.372	406	88	21	3	12	12	47	77
Runners On	.274	.356	.450	533	146	27	8	17	147	71	83
First Base Only	.315	.373	.483	238	75	12	5	6	22	22	30
Scoring Position	.241	.344	.424	295	71	15	3	11	125	49	53
Late Innings, Close	.255	.345	.403	196	50	10	2	5	28	27	35

RBI/Opportunities

	1987		Four Year	
Scoring Position	29 / 120	(24%)	103 / 434	(24%)
Scoring Position, 2 Out	11 / 55	(20%)	32 / 195	(16%)
On Third, Less than 2 Out	9 / 17	(53%)	43 / 73	(59%)
RBI in close games / RBI Total	28 / 46	(61%)	115 / 169	(68%)

Brett Butler
Cleveland Indians

One of baseball's most cherished clichés is "You win pennants up the middle"; the last line of defense is the centerfielder. The 1987 World Series showcased teams with two fine ones, lending credence to this wisdom. That fact was apparently not lost on San Francisco general manager Al Rosen. In December, seeking a player who could push his club over the top, he used free agency to grab one of the best ones in baseball; after four years, Brett Butler is back in the National League.

Butler has long been recognized by knowledgeable baseball people as one of the top leadoff men in the American League. In 1987, he outdid himself—he set career highs in both on-base percentage (.400) and walks (91). He hit .288 in Cleveland, with 78 walks, 99 runs scored and only 56 strikeouts per year. He led the AL in triples in 1986. In short, he has been the catalyst of the Indian attack during his tenure in Cleveland.

Giants' manager Roger Craig has said that he plans to turn Butler loose on the bases this year; Brett says that he hopes to steal 60 bases in 1988. Butler has the speed to reach that goal, but he'll probably be thrown out 30+ times in the process. Brett stole 33 bases in 49 tries, for an unspectacular 67.3 percent success rate. The problem is his inability to read a pickoff move—most of his outs on the bases are scored "1–3–6." If the extra running is to be of any help, he'll have to correct that flaw. Since Craig has claimed that he can teach runners how to avoid pickoffs, perhaps Butler will improve. But, since the Giants stole bases at a 55 percent rate this year, more likely he won't. Given San Francisco's power, Butler might be better off just staying at first when he reaches base.

Defensively, Butler ranges from good to exceptional. His range factor in Cleveland has never been below 2.79; it was a fine 2.92 in 1987. The one worrying note is his assist figures, which have dropped by half for the last two years. Brett's league-leading 19 in 1985 fell to nine in 1986; it was down to four this year. But, given a new league in which to seek the Gold Glove that he so desperately craves, Butler may make special efforts to bring his fielding numbers up in 1988.

Butler's departure should be no surprise to anyone. He had, over the past two years, repeatedly asked management for the security of a multi- year contract. The Cleveland front office, claiming that it was against club policy, refused to give him one. Butler has gone to arbitration for the last three years—once for a raise and twice to avoid a salary cut. This winter, given a choice between the Giants (who made bold trades in order to secure a division title) and the Indians (who seem incapable of making a commitment to anything), Brett made the obvious choice. While Indians' management fiddled, their ball club burned.

Jim Shaarda

Butler, Brett Morgan Bats: Left Throws: Left Born 06/15/57 Born 06/15/57

1987 SEASON AND MAJOR-LEAGUE CAREER BATTING TOTALS

	G	AB	H	2B	3B	HR	TB	R	RBI	TBB	IBB	SO	HP	SH	SF	SB	CS	SB%	GDP	AVG	OBP	SLG
87 CLE	137	522	154	25	8	9	222	91	41	91	0	55	1	2	2	33	16	.67	3	.295	.399	.425
7 YEARS	889	3217	901	120	61	26	1221	533	239	408	7	332	12	44	21	233	104	.69	31	.280	.361	.380

	1987 SEASON											FOUR YEAR TOTALS (1984 – 1987)									
	Ave.	OBP	SLG	AB	H	2B	3B	HR	RBI	BB	SO	Ave.	OBP	SLG	AB	H	2B	3B	HR	RBI	BB	SO
Totals	.295	.399	.425	522	154	25	8	9	41	91	55	.288	.373	.396	2302	663	95	45	21	191	311	224
vs. Left	.267	.397	.342	146	39	5	0	2	15	32	25	.302	.391	.389	689	208	26	11	4	62	101	93
vs. Right	.306	.400	.457	376	115	20	8	7	26	59	30	.282	.365	.399	1613	455	69	34	17	129	210	131
at Home	.337	.443	.492	246	83	12	7	4	16	47	29	.303	.385	.405	1108	336	39	28	6	75	150	104
on Road	.257	.359	.366	276	71	13	1	5	25	44	26	.274	.361	.387	1194	327	56	17	15	116	161	120
vs. Groundball	.297	.397	.409	269	80	12	6	2	23	45	23	.278	.368	.373	1123	312	39	22	8	93	158	90
vs. Flyball	.292	.401	.443	253	74	13	2	7	18	46	32	.298	.378	.417	1179	351	56	23	13	98	153	134
vs. Finesse	.308	.384	.422	263	81	9	6	3	21	32	21	.306	.369	.420	1278	391	48	28	14	102	127	95
vs. Power	.282	.414	.429	259	73	16	2	6	20	59	34	.266	.377	.365	1024	272	47	17	7	89	184	129
on Grass	.320	.427	.456	425	136	21	8	7	34	80	41	.292	.376	.400	1927	562	78	41	16	159	262	182
on Artificial Turf	.186	.269	.289	97	18	4	0	2	7	11	14	.269	.359	.376	375	101	17	4	5	32	49	42
Day Games	.262	.381	.399	183	48	9	5	2	10	35	20	.264	.357	.373	769	203	27	18	7	59	112	80
Night Games	.313	.410	.440	339	106	16	3	7	31	56	35	.300	.381	.407	1533	460	68	27	14	132	199	144
April	.154	.267	.308	13	2	2	0	0	1	2	1	.262	.357	.364	225	59	12	4	1	14	33	17
May	.301	.424	.427	103	31	6	2	1	9	21	12	.263	.361	.355	414	109	22	5	2	35	62	45
June	.293	.414	.402	92	27	4	3	0	5	19	7	.288	.374	.392	413	119	21	8	2	35	57	33
July	.269	.346	.366	93	25	4	1	1	6	11	6	.281	.352	.362	392	110	12	7	2	25	43	37
August	.321	.406	.438	112	36	4	0	3	9	16	14	.288	.365	.404	413	119	11	8	7	37	50	51
Sept/Oct	.303	.414	.495	109	33	5	2	4	11	22	15	.330	.415	.474	445	147	17	13	7	45	66	41
Bases Empty	.291	.383	.431	357	104	17	6	7	7	53	38	.281	.357	.399	1532	431	67	34	15	15	181	156
Leadoff	.317	.408	.446	202	64	6	4	4	4	31	20	.279	.354	.393	858	239	35	21	7	7	100	90
Not Leadoff	.258	.350	.413	155	40	11	2	3	3	22	18	.285	.362	.407	674	192	32	13	8	8	81	66
Runners On	.303	.432	.412	165	50	8	2	2	34	38	17	.301	.402	.390	770	232	28	11	6	176	130	68
First Base Only	.280	.365	.333	75	21	4	0	0	1	9	8	.277	.356	.333	321	89	7	4	1	8	38	27
Scoring Position	.322	.479	.478	90	29	4	2	2	33	29	9	.318	.433	.430	449	143	21	7	5	168	92	41
Late Innings, Close	.254	.342	.492	63	16	3	0	4	11	9	11	.264	.345	.344	337	89	10	1	5	36	42	36

RBI/Opportunities

Scoring Position	30 / 140 (21%)	155 / 677 (23%)
Scoring Position, 2 Out	8 / 58 (14%)	54 / 277 (19%)
On Third, Less than 2 Out	11 / 26 (42%)	65 / 123 (53%)
RBI in close games / RBI Total	29 / 41 (71%)	124 / 191 (65%)

Ivan Calderon
Chicago White Sox

The general managership of Ken (Hawk) Harrelson was noted primarily for making people laugh, but the Hawk did have a few good moments. If you make enough moves, you're bound to trip over a good player, and in June of 1986 Harrelson made a great one, trading Scott Bradley to Seattle for Ivan Calderon. Not to knock Bradley, a decent player, but Calderon was stunning in his first full season with the White Sox. He led the club in hits (159), doubles (38), home runs (27), runs scored (93), on-base average (.362), and slugging average (.526). While he was at it he tied for the team batting lead with a .293 average and was third in RBIs (83). Calderon's 38 doubles were the third highest in the league and indicative of the aggressive way he played. The sight of Ivan roaring into second, dust and neck chains flying, was one of the happier memories in a dismal White Sox season.

It was an awfully impressive performance, and somewhat unexpected as well, because Calderon came to Chicago with a less-than-sterling reputation. Seattle's Dick Williams has a legendary eye for young talent, but Williams quickly soured on Ivan and heartily endorsed the trade for Bradley. But it wasn't Calderon's talent that Dick gave up on, and he wasn't the only one who doubted Calderon's desire. As recently as last June, this blurb appeared in Moss Klein's *Sporting News* column: "Several front office executives mentioned Chicago's Ivan Calderon as a player making the least of his ability. 'He could be a dominant factor,' said one G.M., 'but he's too laid back, too lazy. He has the potential to be a star, but he'll never make it big.'"

I'm not about to question the judgment of either Williams or the unknown G.M. (reveal yourself, sir, if you have any courage!), but if Ivan has problems, they sure didn't surface last year. On the contrary, to paraphrase Lincoln on General Grant, maybe we should send a case of "Laid Back Lazy" to the other White Sox players. Calderon's Seattle troubles, whatever they were, might be understood if one looked at his background. He was signed out of Puerto Rico at the age of 17, then moved quickly through the Mariner farm system. He hit wherever he played, but towns like Wassau and Chattanooga must have provided some culture shock, and an ill-advised attempt to turn him into a shortstop had to be unsettling.

When he finally arrived in Seattle in '84, toting a .365 Pacific Coast League average, the Mariner outfield was a combination of has-beens (Barry Bonnell, Al Cowens, Gorman Thomas) and faded prospects (Ricky "Hello Mary Lou" Nelson, Al Chambers). Calderon, along with Phil Bradley, was expected to be a savior. One hand injury, one broken wrist and several run-ins with Williams later, he was sent packing. I think he can put away the suitcase now.

Don Zminda

Calderon, Ivan (Perez)   Bats: Right   Throws: Right   Born 03/19/62

1987 SEASON AND MAJOR-LEAGUE CAREER BATTING TOTALS

	G	AB	H	2B	3B	HR	TB	R	RBI	TBB	IBB	SO	HP	SH	SF	SB	CS	SB%	GDP	AVG	OBP	SLG
87 CHA	144	542	159	38	2	28	285	93	83	60	6	109	1	0	4	10	5	.67	13	.293	.362	.526
4 YEARS	272	940	265	62	7	39	458	148	127	90	8	198	4	1	5	18	8	.69	27	.282	.346	.487

1987 SEASON

	Ave.	OBP	SLG	AB	H	2B	3B	HR	RBI	BB	SO
Totals	.293	.362	.526	542	159	38	2	28	84	60	109
vs. Left	.279	.360	.542	190	53	11	0	13	24	24	40
vs. Right	.301	.364	.517	352	106	27	2	15	60	36	69
at Home	.315	.402	.573	260	82	20	1	15	49	39	47
on Road	.273	.324	.482	282	77	18	1	13	35	21	62
vs. Groundball	.341	.423	.594	261	89	20	2	14	41	37	45
vs. Flyball	.249	.303	.463	281	70	18	0	14	43	23	64
vs. Finesse	.327	.382	.612	312	102	27	1	20	53	28	52
vs. Power	.248	.337	.409	230	57	11	1	8	31	32	57
on Grass	.302	.382	.547	450	136	30	1	26	78	59	91
on Artificial Turf	.250	.255	.424	92	23	8	1	2	6	1	18
Day Games	.275	.329	.535	142	39	16	0	7	27	12	31
Night Games	.300	.374	.522	400	120	22	2	21	57	48	78
April	.258	.319	.379	66	17	5	0	1	2	6	10
May	.380	.492	.800	50	19	6	0	5	13	10	11
June	.288	.325	.495	111	32	9	1	4	21	6	23
July	.276	.342	.457	105	29	4	0	5	17	11	22
August	.304	.379	.539	102	31	3	0	7	15	13	24
Sept/Oct	.287	.363	.574	108	31	11	1	6	16	14	19
Bases Empty	.321	.391	.617	287	92	24	2	19	19	32	52
Leadoff	.310	.364	.581	129	40	12	1	7	7	10	25
Not Leadoff	.329	.411	.646	158	52	12	1	12	12	22	27
Runners On	.263	.331	.424	255	67	14	0	9	65	28	57
First Base Only	.250	.308	.433	120	30	7	0	5	12	10	25
Scoring Position	.274	.350	.415	135	37	7	0	4	53	18	32
Late Innings, Close	.342	.426	.506	79	27	7	0	2	12	13	16

FOUR YEAR TOTALS (1984 – 1987)

	Ave.	OBP	SLG	AB	H	2B	3B	HR	RBI	BB	SO
Totals	.282	.346	.487	940	265	62	7	39	128	90	198
vs. Left	.275	.351	.509	324	89	21	2	17	41	37	72
vs. Right	.286	.343	.476	616	176	41	5	22	87	53	126
at Home	.289	.366	.511	446	129	29	2	22	70	54	85
on Road	.275	.326	.466	494	136	33	5	17	58	36	113
vs. Groundball	.308	.379	.512	441	136	31	4	17	58	48	79
vs. Flyball	.259	.316	.465	499	129	31	3	22	70	42	119
vs. Finesse	.305	.358	.529	544	166	42	4	24	76	43	84
vs. Power	.250	.330	.429	396	99	20	3	15	52	47	114
on Grass	.297	.368	.514	617	183	39	4	29	94	71	132
on Artificial Turf	.254	.300	.437	323	82	23	3	10	34	19	66
Day Games	.271	.316	.473	273	74	26	1	9	46	17	59
Night Games	.286	.357	.493	667	191	36	6	30	82	73	139
April	.245	.301	.344	151	37	9	0	2	8	12	31
May	.291	.364	.576	158	46	10	1	11	32	17	33
June	.284	.328	.485	169	48	15	2	5	26	11	33
July	.289	.353	.474	194	56	11	2	7	27	20	44
August	.280	.346	.476	143	40	4	0	8	17	15	34
Sept/Oct	.304	.373	.584	125	38	13	2	6	18	15	23
Bases Empty	.301	.362	.551	515	155	36	6	27	27	48	105
Leadoff	.304	.343	.535	217	66	15	4	9	9	12	39
Not Leadoff	.299	.374	.564	298	89	21	2	18	18	36	66
Runners On	.259	.323	.409	425	110	26	1	12	101	42	93
First Base Only	.247	.298	.397	194	48	12	1	5	15	14	40
Scoring Position	.268	.342	.420	231	62	14	0	7	86	28	53
Late Innings, Close	.309	.382	.477	149	46	10	0	5	18	19	35

RBI/Opportunities

	1987			Four Year		
Scoring Position	44 / 179	(25%)		72 / 306	(24%)	
Scoring Position, 2 Out	13 / 78	(17%)		17 / 120	(14%)	
On Third, Less than 2 Out	15 / 29	(52%)		29 / 56	(52%)	
RBI in close games / RBI Total	48 / 84	(57%)		78 / 128	(61%)	

Casey Candaele
Montreal Expos

Casey Candaele got a lot of attention last year as the Expo supersub, a man capable of playing both the infield and the outfield. He put in a full season of 138 games doing this, but, if you look at his record, it is hard to justify the playing time. He did play a lot of shortstop, but only until Hubie Brooks got off the disabled list. At second the Expos had two other options, and both significantly outplayed Casey. Tom Foley, who like Candaele can also play short-stop, outhit Casey both for average and for power, and is probably a better infielder. Vance Law is not a better defensive player, but was a much better hitter than Candaele. Casey wasn't going to run Tim Raines or Mitch Webster out of an outfield spot and, while Herm Winningham didn't hit any better than Candaele, he played centerfield and stole bases a lot better.

With Brooks injured and Raines fighting his losing free agency battle, Candaele found himself starting at five different positions early in the year—second, short and all three outfield slots. He made the most of the opportunity; through May 28 he was batting .321, and as late as June 11 his average was .304. By then Brooks and Raines were back, and Candaele spent the rest of the season alternating, for the most part, between second base and center field. He also found National League pitching increasingly harder to solve. From June 12 on Casey hit only .244, with a lowly .314 slugging average. Since Candaele didn't draw many walks (38 for the year) and was a very poor base stealer (7 for 17), he obviously was an offensive liability. He did show good bat control, for whatever that's worth, with only 28 strikeouts in 449 at bats.

The Expos are planning on shaking up their lineup for 1988. With Law lost to free agency and Brooks being moved to right field, Candaele could wind up with a lot of playing time in the infield; that's just as well, since his bat doesn't appear strong enough to justify a regular outfield job. How much he plays depends a lot on whether the projected double play combo of Luis Rivera and Johnny Paredes works out. If one or both of the youngsters can't cut it, Candaele may end up seeing nearly as much action as he did in '87. In the meantime he's projected as the supersub, a role in which he has considerable value.

Candaele's play early in '87 suggests that he could still develop as a hitter; it's no small accomplishment to hit over .300, even for a couple of months, while shifting constantly from position to position. He's obviously come a long way in short time; he was signed as an undrafted free agent, and until recently his main claim to fame was that his mom, a former women's league star, was his hitting coach. Mom obviously taught her boy a thing or two about the game. But it won't be any real surprise if Candaele gets half the playing time in '88 that he had in 1987.

Brock J. Hanke and Don Zminda

Candaele, Casey Todd   Bats: Both   Throws: Right   Born 01/12/61

1987 SEASON AND MAJOR-LEAGUE CAREER BATTING TOTALS

	G	AB	H	2B	3B	HR	TB	R	RBI	TBB	IBB	SO	HP	SH	SF	SB	CS	SB%	GDP	AVG	OBP	SLG
87 MON	138	449	122	23	4	1	156	62	23	38	3	28	2	4	2	7	10	.41	5	.272	.330	.347
2 YEARS	168	553	146	27	5	1	186	71	29	43	3	43	2	4	3	10	15	.40	8	.264	.318	.336

	1987 SEASON											FOUR YEAR TOTALS (1984 – 1987)										
	Ave.	OBP	SLG	AB	H	2B	3B	HR	RBI	BB	SO	Ave.	OBP	SLG	AB	H	2B	3B	HR	RBI	BB	SO
Totals	.272	.330	.347	449	122	23	4	1	23	38	28	.264	.318	.336	553	146	27	5	1	29	43	43
vs. Left	.307	.350	.404	114	35	9	1	0	3	8	2	.297	.333	.394	155	46	13	1	0	8	9	9
vs. Right	.260	.323	.328	335	87	14	3	1	20	30	26	.251	.312	.314	398	100	14	4	1	21	34	34
at Home	.270	.321	.344	244	66	9	3	1	12	16	16	.271	.318	.346	306	83	12	4	1	17	19	28
on Road	.273	.341	.351	205	56	14	1	0	11	22	12	.255	.318	.324	247	63	15	1	0	12	24	15
vs. Groundball	.287	.342	.370	181	52	8	2	1	10	14	9	.291	.339	.363	234	68	10	2	1	13	16	14
vs. Flyball	.261	.322	.332	268	70	15	2	0	13	24	19	.245	.303	.317	319	78	17	3	0	16	27	29
vs. Finesse	.269	.322	.343	242	65	13	1	1	12	18	14	.269	.319	.340	312	84	15	2	1	16	22	19
vs. Power	.275	.339	.353	207	57	10	3	0	11	20	14	.257	.317	.332	241	62	12	3	0	13	21	24
on Grass	.286	.331	.378	119	34	9	1	0	8	9	10	.281	.321	.367	128	36	9	1	0	9	9	10
on Artificial Turf	.267	.330	.336	330	88	14	3	1	15	29	18	.259	.317	.327	425	110	18	4	1	20	34	33
Day Games	.262	.327	.376	141	37	11	1	1	9	12	9	.256	.314	.369	176	45	13	2	1	12	14	14
Night Games	.276	.331	.334	308	85	12	3	0	14	26	19	.268	.319	.321	377	101	14	3	0	17	29	29
April	.317	.423	.383	60	19	4	0	0	2	11	1	.317	.423	.383	60	19	4	0	0	2	11	1
May	.318	.356	.409	110	35	6	2	0	5	6	9	.318	.356	.409	110	35	6	2	0	5	6	9
June	.218	.275	.267	101	22	5	0	0	4	8	5	.219	.281	.276	105	23	6	0	0	6	9	7
July	.317	.356	.439	82	26	5	1	1	5	5	6	.317	.356	.439	82	26	5	1	1	5	5	6
August	.193	.288	.228	57	11	0	1	0	3	8	5	.193	.288	.228	57	11	0	1	0	3	8	5
Sept/Oct	.231	.250	.308	39	9	3	0	0	4	0	2	.230	.257	.288	139	32	6	1	0	8	4	15
Bases Empty	.276	.333	.369	312	86	20	3	1	1	26	22	.273	.329	.361	385	105	23	4	1	1	31	33
Leadoff	.251	.311	.314	175	44	7	2	0	0	14	17	.245	.303	.295	220	54	7	2	0	0	17	23
Not Leadoff	.307	.362	.438	137	42	13	1	1	1	12	5	.309	.363	.448	165	51	16	2	1	1	14	10
Runners On	.263	.322	.299	137	36	3	1	0	22	12	6	.244	.295	.280	168	41	4	1	0	28	12	10
First Base Only	.352	.397	.426	54	19	2	1	0	1	3	0	.313	.352	.373	67	21	2	1	0	1	3	3
Scoring Position	.205	.277	.217	83	17	1	0	0	21	9	6	.198	.259	.218	101	20	2	0	0	27	9	7
Late Innings, Close	.296	.338	.423	71	21	4	1	1	3	5	3	.275	.330	.374	91	25	4	1	1	4	8	5

RBI/Opportunities

Scoring Position	21 / 116 (18%)	26 / 141 (18%)
Scoring Position, 2 Out	7 / 58 (12%)	9 / 70 (13%)
On Third, Less than 2 Out	8 / 19 (42%)	11 / 24 (46%)
RBI in close games / RBI Total	12 / 23 (52%)	15 / 29 (52%)

John Candelaria
California Angels/New York Mets

Coming off a strong year in 1986 (10–2, 2.55 ERA), John Candelaria launched his 1987 campaign with every indication that he intended to be one of the dominant lefties in the game today. He quickly established a 3–0 won-lost record with a sparkling 1.33 ERA. Although he did yield some runs in his next couple outings, he reached a standing of 4–0, making him 14–2 in his last 23 games.

When problems came, however, they were serious. Over an eight-week stretch ending June 19, Candelaria gave up 62 hits in 42.7 innings, and posted a horrendous 6.96 ERA, among the worst in any league during that period. June 19 also marks the day on which John was placed on the disabled list for "personal reasons" that obviously were related to his troubled performance.

Candelaria was finally reactivated in early August. He had some modest success including one 8-inning, 6-hit shutout appearance shortly after his return. But he was inconsistent, and it became increasingly obvious that Candy Man was no longer the toast of the town in Anaheim. By mid-September he was gone to the Mets, and his 1987 AL record was history. The second half amounted to a 3–3 record and 4.60 ERA in 47 innings.

Those final weeks in the American League were actually better than the above numbers would indicate. At a troubled time in his career, Candelaria placed a new reliance on his greatest strength, his outstanding control. In the AL after his June 19 trouble, he gave up only 5 walks. That would be just one day's work for some major league pitchers. Candelaria placed himself at the absolute top of the American League in fewest walks per inning after the All-Star Break, ahead of dart-throwers Dale Mohorcic, Dennis Eckersley, Floyd Bannister and Tom Henke. Noted control artists Frank Tanana, Don Sutton, Curt Young, Bret Saberhagen and Jimmy Key were also near the top of the list, but with about double the frequency of walks that Candelaria yielded.

John's brief tour with the Mets wasn't as bad as his ERA (5.84) suggests. It only covered three starts. He was bombed in the first when he may have been pressing too hard to make a good impression. In the remaining two starts he was 2–0 with a 2.45 ERA.

Candy is now 34 years old; it's possible he no longer has what it takes to be a consistent quality starter. However, there is always a great demand for southpaws who can throw the ball over the plate without giving up homers to lefty hitters. I think he would be excellent as a situational pitcher against lefthanders or as a long reliever-spot starter. He should be eminently employable for years to come.

John C. Benson

Candelaria, John Robert "John" Or "Candy"

Bats: Left   Throws: Left   Born 11/06/53

1987 SEASON AND MAJOR-LEAGUE CAREER PITCHING TOTALS

	G	GS	CG	GF	IP	BFP	H	R	ER	HR	SH	SF	HB	TBB	IBB	SO	WP	Bk	W	L	Pct	ShO	Sv	ERA
87 CAL-NYN	23	23	0	0	129	544	144	78	69	18	8	6	1	23	0	84	0	1	10	6	.625	0	0	4.81
13 YEARS	373	323	47	36	2146	8769	2020	853	767	199	92	70	32	500	47	1360	16	12	151	95	.614	11	15	3.22

1987: Finesse, Flyball   1986: Power, Flyball   1985: Power, Flyball   1984: Finesse, Flyball

1987 SEASON

	G	IP	H	BB	SO	SB	CS	W	L	S	ERA
Totals	23	129.0	144	23	84	3	7	10	6	0	4.81
at Home	13	80.1	83	17	54	3	5	7	3	0	4.71
on Road	10	48.2	61	6	30	0	2	3	3	0	4.99
on Grass	5	31.2	27	3	23	1	2	4	1	0	2.27
on Artificial Turf	18	97.1	117	20	61	2	5	6	5	0	5.64
Day Games	16	93.2	100	20	60	3	5	8	4	0	4.90
Night Games	7	35.1	44	3	24	0	2	2	2	0	4.58
April	5	32.1	33	6	21	1	2	3	0	0	2.51
May	4	19.2	26	5	10	1	0	1	2	0	6.86
June	3	17.2	25	4	13	1	2	1	1	0	6.62
July	0	0.0	0	0	0	0	0	0	0	0	0.00
August	6	37.1	31	4	25	0	2	2	2	0	4.10
Sept/Oct	5	22.0	29	4	15	0	1	3	1	0	6.14

vs. Opponent Batters	Ave.	OBP	SLG	AB	H	2B	3B	HR	RBI	BB	SO
Totals	.285	.313	.457	506	144	21	6	18	72	23	84
vs. Left	.324	.363	.446	74	24	3	0	2	5	5	18
vs. Right	.278	.305	.458	432	120	18	6	16	67	18	66
Bases Empty	.257	.289	.395	311	80	13	3	8	8	13	48
Leadoff	.248	.281	.403	129	32	6	1	4	4	6	14
Not Leadoff	.264	.295	.390	182	48	7	2	4	4	7	34
Runners On Base	.328	.351	.554	195	64	8	3	10	64	10	36
First Base Only	.322	.358	.533	90	29	2	1	5	11	5	16
Scoring Position	.333	.345	.571	105	35	6	2	5	53	5	20
Late Innings, Close	.167	.231	.167	24	4	0	0	0	0	2	5

FOUR YEAR TOTALS (1984 – 1987)

	G	IP	H	BB	SO	SB	CS	W	L	S	ERA
	122	531.1	518	121	398	14	20	41	26	11	3.44
	63	284.1	281	69	226	7	12	21	14	7	3.96
	59	247.0	237	52	172	7	8	20	12	4	2.84
	35	142.1	131	31	104	4	8	12	8	4	3.22
	87	389.0	387	90	294	10	12	29	18	7	3.52
	60	297.2	261	77	225	6	10	27	11	4	3.36
	62	233.2	257	44	173	8	10	14	15	7	3.54
	19	78.2	83	14	62	3	3	7	4	4	2.52
	21	67.0	74	20	48	2	4	3	5	3	4.70
	15	44.0	58	9	34	2	2	1	3	0	5.11
	20	91.2	74	20	61	1	2	9	3	2	2.16
	24	140.0	129	36	106	5	5	11	7	0	3.73
	23	110.0	100	22	87	1	4	10	4	2	3.35

	Ave.	OBP	SLG	AB	H	2B	3B	HR	RBI	BB	SO
	.258	.299	.409	2010	518	94	23	55	230	121	398
	.220	.252	.296	314	69	13	1	3	20	14	99
	.265	.308	.430	1696	449	81	22	52	210	107	299
	.251	.292	.391	1221	306	55	15	29	29	70	236
	.253	.292	.396	510	129	23	7	12	12	28	92
	.249	.292	.388	711	177	32	8	17	17	42	144
	.269	.311	.437	789	212	39	8	26	201	51	162
	.274	.315	.433	365	100	17	4	11	32	22	72
	.264	.307	.441	424	112	22	4	15	169	29	90
	.225	.288	.364	258	58	10	4	6	36	23	55

RBI/Opportunities

Scoring Position	43 / 139 (31%)	142 / 553 (26%)
Scoring Position, 2 Out	20 / 61 (33%)	49 / 241 (20%)
On Third, Less than 2 Out	17 / 28 (61%)	61 / 111 (55%)
RBI in close games / RBI Total	43 / 72 (60%)	169 / 230 (73%)

Tom Candiotti
Cleveland Indians

If you didn't live in Cleveland in 1987 (or Texas in '79–'80 or Philly in '82–'83), you may be wondering what happened to Tom Candiotti this year. The answer is simple—Pat Corrales. As he's done so many times before, Son of Torre couldn't resist the urge to fix a non-existent problem; the result was a wasted year for one of the best pitchers in the AL.

The saga began in March, with a vintage Corrales brainstorm. Most knuckleball pitchers grip the ball with the fleshy tips of their fingers—Tom, who'd developed the pitch on his own, gripped it with his fingernails. Since he'd finished tenth in the AL in ERA in 1986 with that grip, you obviously leave the guy alone, right?

Wrong. Corrales reminded everyone that Tom's nails kept cracking in 1986 and that he'd always had to leave games when that happened (the wimp had only finished 17 of his 34 starts). He convinced Tom to adopt the more conventional grip. He even boasted about it, saying that he expected Tom to start pitching like Phil Niekro in 1987.

And, dear lord, he was right. Tom's control of the pitch disappeared, leaving him almost helpless. Now he doesn't have a bad fastball and his curve is pretty good, but they're much more effective as setups for the floater. If Tom can sneak a strike by you with either one, you'll get butterflies in your wheelhouse until he falls behind in the count. But when batters saw that the knuckler wouldn't stay in the strike zone, they quit swinging at it and began crushing his other pitches.

When Tom Brunansky hit a grand salami off Candy's fastball in mid-May, Corrales told Tom to stop throwing anything but knuckleballs in the future. When Tom objected, the excrement hit the cooling device. For once, the meddling was a matter of public record and the pitcher under discussion was clearly a talented one; the resulting uproar didn't get Pat fired, but it sure greased the skids. When new manager Doc Edwards let Tom return to his old grip, the nuclear knuckler returned; when Tom began mixing it in with his other pitches, it was 1986 all over again:

In 1986, Tom had allowed 8.35 hits per nine innings, had a 1.58–1 strikeout to walk ratio and a 3.57 ERA. Under Corrales in 1987, he allowed 9.18 H/9IP, his K/W ratio was .94–1 and his ERA ballooned to 5.57. Under Edwards, Tom's H/9IP fell to 8.08, his K/W ratio rose to 1.53–1 and his ERA was 4.04. Though the Cleveland offense was no help whatsoever (they scored 3.84 runs per start for Tom in 1987), he went 5–9 in the second half. He threw two one-hitters and six complete games in 15 tries after the All-Star game.

There was absolutely nothing wrong with Candy in 1987 other than his manager. Expect him to be the "Comeback Player of the Year" in 1988.

Geoff Beckman and Jim Shaarda

Candiotti, Thomas Caesar "Tom" — Bats: Right   Throws: Right   Born 08/31/57

1987 SEASON AND MAJOR-LEAGUE CAREER PITCHING TOTALS

	G	GS	CG	GF	IP	BFP	H	R	ER	HR	SH	SF	HB	TBB	IBB	SO	WP	Bk	W	L	Pct	ShO	Sv	ERA
87 CLE	32	32	7	0	202	888	193	132	107	28	8	10	4	93	2	111	13	2	7	18	.280	2	0	4.77
4 YEARS	86	80	26	2	542	2346	527	286	246	55	11	21	14	225	2	322	26	6	29	36	.446	6	0	4.08

1987: Finesse, Groundball   1986: Finesse, Groundball

1987 SEASON

	G	IP	H	BB	SO	SB	CS	W	L	S	ERA
Totals	32	201.2	193	93	111	25	5	7	18	0	4.78
at Home	20	135.1	126	47	70	14	5	5	11	0	4.39
on Road	12	66.1	67	46	41	11	0	2	7	0	5.56
on Grass	13	89.2	103	32	47	11	4	2	10	0	5.12
on Artificial Turf	19	112.0	90	61	64	14	1	5	8	0	4.50
Day Games	29	185.1	171	87	101	22	5	7	15	0	4.71
Night Games	3	16.1	22	6	10	3	0	0	3	0	5.51
April	5	25.1	33	11	9	2	1	1	4	0	6.75
May	5	32.0	32	14	23	4	1	0	2	0	4.78
June	5	26.0	22	23	13	4	2	1	3	0	4.85
July	5	35.1	32	15	20	4	0	1	2	0	5.09
August	6	44.0	32	13	17	3	0	4	2	0	2.86
Sept/Oct	6	39.0	42	17	29	8	1	0	5	0	5.31

FOUR YEAR TOTALS (1984 – 1987)

	G	IP	H	BB	SO	SB	CS	W	L	S	ERA
	76	486.1	465	209	301	56	16	25	32	0	4.18
	43	289.0	270	103	178	28	12	17	17	0	3.77
	33	197.1	195	106	123	28	4	8	15	0	4.79
	24	158.0	173	56	90	17	9	5	14	0	4.61
	52	328.1	292	153	211	39	7	20	18	0	3.97
	66	423.1	390	184	253	46	15	24	25	0	3.89
	10	63.0	75	25	48	10	1	1	7	0	6.14
	10	53.0	49	32	33	5	1	2	6	0	4.42
	10	64.2	65	31	47	9	3	2	5	0	4.73
	13	71.0	77	41	52	10	7	4	4	0	4.69
	13	88.1	86	31	47	8	1	6	4	0	4.28
	12	94.0	73	34	38	7	2	7	4	0	3.16
	18	115.1	115	40	84	17	2	4	9	0	4.21

vs. Opponent Batters — 1987

	Ave.	OBP	SLG	AB	H	2B	3B	HR	RBI	BB	SO
Totals	.250	.330	.406	773	193	33	2	28	105	93	111
vs. Left	.237	.319	.366	388	92	10	2	12	48	49	45
vs. Right	.262	.340	.447	385	101	23	0	16	57	44	66
Bases Empty	.256	.317	.433	464	119	22	0	20	20	40	67
Leadoff	.245	.312	.403	196	48	10	0	7	7	18	26
Not Leadoff	.265	.321	.455	268	71	12	0	13	13	22	41
Runners On Base	.239	.347	.366	309	74	11	2	8	85	53	44
First Base Only	.195	.288	.293	123	24	4	1	2	7	14	14
Scoring Position	.269	.381	.414	186	50	7	1	6	78	39	30
Late Innings, Close	.256	.356	.400	90	23	4	0	3	11	13	14

vs. Opponent Batters — Four Year Totals

	Ave.	OBP	SLG	AB	H	2B	3B	HR	RBI	BB	SO
Totals	.250	.325	.383	1862	465	80	8	51	219	209	301
vs. Left	.247	.322	.365	975	241	32	7	23	109	110	133
vs. Right	.253	.329	.404	887	224	48	1	28	110	99	168
Bases Empty	.258	.318	.408	1083	279	51	2	36	36	95	186
Leadoff	.261	.324	.405	467	122	26	1	13	13	42	80
Not Leadoff	.255	.314	.411	616	157	25	1	23	23	53	106
Runners On Base	.239	.334	.349	779	186	29	6	15	183	114	115
First Base Only	.217	.285	.294	337	73	10	2	4	14	30	43
Scoring Position	.256	.369	.391	442	113	19	4	11	169	84	72
Late Innings, Close	.273	.360	.415	176	48	5	1	6	21	23	23

RBI/Opportunities

	1987	Four Year
Scoring Position	64 / 272 (24%)	143 / 635 (23%)
Scoring Position, 2 Out	26 / 130 (20%)	54 / 295 (18%)
On Third, Less than 2 Out	25 / 50 (50%)	59 / 121 (49%)
RBI in close games / RBI Total	85 / 105 (81%)	161 / 219 (74%)

Jose Canseco
Oakland Athletics

The best thing that happened to Jose Canseco in 1987 was Mark McGwire. The former Rookie of the Year came out of spring training with a .375 average, 9 home runs and 25 RBIs, only to fall into the clutches of the "sophomore jinx." In April he managed to bat .284, but had only one homer and just 10 RBIs. He also struck out 27 times with no walks!

But then in May, Mark McGwire went into Detroit and started doing his impersonation of Roy Hobbs. Canseco no longer felt obligated to try and carry the team, and started hitting with a consistency that carried him through the season. He struck out "only" 157 times; and a .257 average with 31 homers and 113 RBIs with the Oakland Coliseum as your home park is nothing to sneeze at, not even in 1987. It's especially satisfying for a player who won't turn 24 till next July. Canseco has been dubbed "the man of a thousand stances" because of his constant experimentation in the batter's box. He abandoned his 1986 wide open stance in the spring, and for the rest of the season used the batter's box as some sort of twister board.

He has all the tools to become a great hitter: quick hands, good bat speed, and destructive arm extension. If he stood in the box the same way every time, he might get a better idea of why he is swinging at pitches over his head one day and swinging a sand wedge the next. If he wasn't playing in the best pitcher's park in the American League, he could probably hit .300 and still keep his power, but he's never gonna get close if he doesn't start making more contact. (He did "hit" .342 when he managed to put the ball in play.) Canseco is surprisingly quick afoot, especially for being 6'3" and 230 pounds, coming up with 15 steals in 18 tries.

His defense is far from polished, even though he showed tremendous improvement from his rookie year where "inept" was a kind description. He tripled his assists from 4 to 12, and his raw range factor ended up among the top five left fielders. Perhaps the leadership and experience of Dave Parker will accelerate his development even more. Overall, Jose Canseco seems like a solid bet to continue to improve. He still has all the skills that tend to turn scouts into Player Development Directors. He is very mild-mannered and seems to get along very well with the rest of the team. Certainly the development of McGwire and the addition of Parker will lessen some of the pressure he felt in his rookie year as the club's main man. I'm looking forward to sitting back for the next decade or so and watching this kid tear the cover off the ball.

Darren E. Peterson

Canseco, Jose (Capas)

Bats: Right   Throws: Right   Born 07/02/64

1987 SEASON AND MAJOR-LEAGUE CAREER BATTING TOTALS

	G	AB	H	2B	3B	HR	TB	R	RBI	TBB	IBB	SO	HP	SH	SF	SB	CS	SB%	GDP	AVG	OBP	SLG
87 OAK	159	630	162	35	3	31	296	81	113	50	2	157	2	0	9	15	3	.83	16	.257	.310	.470
3 YEARS	345	1326	335	67	4	69	617	182	243	119	3	363	10	0	18	31	11	.74	29	.253	.315	.465

	1987 SEASON											FOUR YEAR TOTALS (1984 – 1987)									
	Ave.	OBP	SLG	AB	H	2B	3B	HR	RBI	BB	SO	Ave.	OBP	SLG	AB	H	2B	3B	HR	RBI	BB	SO
Totals	.257	.310	.469	631	162	35	3	31	113	50	157	.252	.315	.465	1327	335	67	4	69	243	119	363
vs. Left	.307	.356	.615	205	63	12	3	15	46	16	46	.292	.336	.536	418	122	24	3	24	85	30	98
vs. Right	.232	.288	.399	426	99	23	0	16	67	34	111	.234	.306	.432	909	213	43	1	45	158	89	265
at Home	.274	.332	.505	299	82	17	2	16	59	28	66	.250	.318	.457	645	161	28	2	34	121	65	164
on Road	.241	.289	.437	332	80	18	1	15	54	22	91	.255	.312	.472	682	174	39	2	35	122	54	199
vs. Groundball	.286	.339	.529	308	88	17	2	18	68	27	57	.268	.336	.492	630	169	30	3	35	122	64	135
vs. Flyball	.229	.281	.412	323	74	18	1	13	45	23	100	.238	.296	.440	697	166	37	1	34	121	55	228
vs. Finesse	.294	.336	.560	323	95	20	0	22	65	22	50	.280	.330	.507	735	206	36	1	43	134	55	146
vs. Power	.218	.282	.373	308	67	15	3	9	48	28	107	.218	.297	.412	592	129	31	3	26	109	64	217
on Grass	.266	.311	.495	531	141	29	3	29	101	38	130	.253	.314	.473	1112	281	51	4	62	208	98	301
on Artificial Turf	.210	.301	.330	100	21	6	0	2	12	12	27	.251	.321	.423	215	54	16	0	7	35	21	62
Day Games	.292	.349	.566	226	66	18	1	14	49	21	46	.247	.324	.475	497	123	27	1	28	99	53	131
Night Games	.237	.287	.415	405	96	17	2	17	64	29	111	.255	.309	.459	830	212	40	3	41	144	66	232
April	.284	.284	.383	81	23	5	0	1	10	0	27	.276	.343	.436	156	43	7	0	6	29	16	53
May	.231	.274	.404	104	24	3	0	5	13	7	22	.254	.315	.502	213	54	8	0	15	40	20	58
June	.286	.361	.571	105	30	4	1	8	23	13	20	.263	.347	.507	213	56	14	1	12	43	28	50
July	.319	.355	.602	113	36	8	0	8	28	6	27	.294	.336	.505	214	63	9	0	12	45	13	57
August	.246	.302	.475	118	29	8	2	5	21	9	29	.210	.256	.425	219	46	14	3	9	37	13	60
Sept/Oct	.182	.273	.355	110	20	7	0	4	18	15	32	.234	.297	.426	312	73	15	0	15	49	29	85
Bases Empty	.247	.295	.479	340	84	20	1	19	19	22	94	.221	.285	.419	723	160	37	2	34	34	63	226
Leadoff	.262	.308	.500	122	32	8	0	7	7	7	27	.241	.301	.435	278	67	15	0	13	13	23	80
Not Leadoff	.239	.288	.468	218	52	12	1	12	12	15	67	.209	.274	.409	445	93	22	2	21	21	40	146
Runners On	.268	.326	.457	291	78	15	2	12	94	28	63	.290	.347	.520	604	175	30	2	35	209	56	137
First Base Only	.284	.336	.490	102	29	9	0	4	15	7	21	.270	.324	.536	248	67	15	0	17	46	15	57
Scoring Position	.259	.321	.439	189	49	6	2	8	79	21	42	.303	.368	.508	356	108	15	2	18	163	41	80
Late Innings, Close	.265	.306	.451	102	27	7	0	4	24	6	26	.283	.333	.495	212	60	15	0	10	55	16	57

RBI/Opportunities

	1987		Four Year	
Scoring Position	64 / 251	(25%)	132 / 477	(28%)
Scoring Position, 2 Out	28 / 112	(25%)	53 / 207	(26%)
On Third, Less than 2 Out	20 / 52	(38%)	43 / 92	(47%)
RBI in close games / RBI Total	81 / 113	(72%)	175 / 243	(72%)

Gary Carter
New York Mets

It's a sign of the times, I guess. Gary Carter has the worst year of his career, causing everyone in New York to all but call for his retirement. And yet he's still one of the best two or three catchers in baseball. Who's better in the National League? Jody Davis? Benito Santiago? Bo Diaz? In the American League? Hell, the American League doesn't have a best catcher.

However, Carter's gradual decline does have even his most loyal supporters wondering. Since 1984 his batting averages have been .294, .280, .255, .235. He went from having at least 100 RBIs in each of the three prior seasons to 83 in 1987. And even Carter's famed reputation in the clutch was dispelled time and time again last year. What Met fan didn't grow weary of Carter coming up in the late innings, with the tying run in scoring position, followed by the familiar sight of him popping up on the infield and slamming his bat down in disgust? In his defense, it should be pointed out that Gary was playing hurt; Joe Nunziata said that Carter used more tape than a bootlegger at a Grateful Dead concert. Carter's tape was on his knees.

But how many other catchers slump to the tune of 20 HRs and 83 RBIs? Despite his and the team's disappointing year, the Mets' need for a new catcher is not as urgent as the fans seem to think. By August, the Metropolitan trade rumors would have had you laughing out loud. For the benefit of those of you not living in the New York area, try Darryl Strawberry for Matt Nokes. I am not kidding. The Mets don't need someone to replace Carter yet. He just needs a few more days off. (He hit over .280 in '87 in games following a day off.) And the way Barry Lyons filled in last year, I don't think the Mets will be hurt any.

Can Carter come back in 1988? To be honest, I don't see him ever hitting .280 again or 30 HR's again. And all the problems with his knees have left him a shadow of his former self defensively. But Carter is a hard worker and his contributions as a leader on and off the field should not be taken lightly. In '88, I think, he may return to the type of player he was in '86 and, if he does that, I doubt anyone will complain.

Jesse Drucker

Carter, Gary Edmund Bats: Right Throws: Right Born 04/08/54

1987 SEASON AND MAJOR-LEAGUE CAREER BATTING TOTALS

	G	AB	H	2B	3B	HR	TB	R	RBI	TBB	IBB	SO	HP	SH	SF	SB	CS	SB%	GDP	AVG	OBP	SLG
87 NYN	139	523	123	18	2	20	205	55	83	42	1	73	1	1	6	0	0	.00	14	.235	.290	.392
14 YEARS	1829	6586	1769	305	28	291	3003	902	1082	722	97	836	50	30	84	36	33	.52	150	.269	.341	.456

	1987 SEASON											FOUR YEAR TOTALS (1984 – 1987)									
	Ave.	OBP	SLG	AB	H	2B	3B	HR	RBI	BB	SO	Ave.	OBP	SLG	AB	H	2B	3B	HR	RBI	BB	SO
Totals	.235	.290	.391	524	123	18	2	20	83	42	73	.267	.341	.453	2165	579	81	6	103	394	237	240
vs. Left	.239	.322	.402	184	44	9	0	7	27	24	15	.296	.390	.501	730	216	37	1	37	128	119	51
vs. Right	.232	.271	.385	340	79	9	2	13	56	18	58	.253	.314	.429	1435	363	44	5	66	266	118	189
at Home	.231	.294	.376	255	59	8	1	9	42	24	39	.267	.351	.447	1032	276	35	3	48	185	132	116
on Road	.238	.286	.405	269	64	10	1	11	41	18	34	.267	.331	.459	1133	303	46	3	55	209	105	124
vs. Groundball	.296	.350	.474	196	58	6	1	9	33	17	24	.289	.363	.449	979	283	28	3	41	168	108	92
vs. Flyball	.198	.254	.341	328	65	12	1	11	50	25	49	.250	.323	.456	1186	296	53	3	62	226	129	148
vs. Finesse	.219	.278	.361	288	63	10	2	9	46	25	26	.258	.321	.450	1217	314	45	6	59	216	109	104
vs. Power	.254	.305	.428	236	60	8	0	11	37	17	47	.280	.366	.457	948	265	36	0	44	178	128	136
on Grass	.243	.305	.388	366	89	12	1	13	56	34	55	.268	.341	.460	1223	328	34	4	64	237	139	155
on Artificial Turf	.215	.254	.399	158	34	6	1	7	27	8	18	.266	.341	.445	942	251	47	2	39	157	98	85
Day Games	.279	.324	.491	165	46	6	1	9	30	11	21	.275	.348	.481	748	206	33	2	39	142	78	85
Night Games	.214	.275	.345	359	77	12	1	11	53	31	52	.263	.337	.438	1417	373	48	4	64	252	159	155
April	.241	.271	.405	79	19	2	1	3	14	4	7	.269	.343	.455	286	77	15	1	12	60	33	31
May	.215	.308	.342	79	17	2	1	2	10	10	14	.233	.325	.414	343	80	15	1	15	60	46	54
June	.267	.333	.442	86	23	3	0	4	13	9	12	.295	.361	.488	373	110	10	1	20	57	39	33
July	.259	.284	.447	85	22	4	0	4	15	3	10	.261	.318	.437	380	99	14	1	17	74	32	35
August	.209	.277	.418	91	19	4	0	5	19	9	13	.258	.338	.441	345	89	13	1	16	66	42	42
Sept/Oct	.221	.270	.308	104	23	3	0	2	12	7	17	.283	.350	.477	438	124	14	1	23	77	45	45
Bases Empty	.229	.284	.382	262	60	8	1	10	10	19	33	.258	.317	.444	1095	283	36	4	53	53	93	117
Leadoff	.195	.235	.363	113	22	4	0	5	5	6	14	.277	.318	.469	524	145	20	0	27	27	32	54
Not Leadoff	.255	.319	.396	149	38	4	1	5	5	13	19	.242	.316	.420	571	138	16	4	26	26	61	63
Runners On	.240	.297	.401	262	63	10	1	10	73	23	40	.277	.361	.463	1070	296	45	2	50	341	144	123
First Base Only	.237	.302	.412	97	23	5	0	4	10	9	13	.248	.301	.460	404	100	20	0	22	51	31	40
Scoring Position	.242	.293	.394	165	40	5	1	6	63	14	27	.294	.394	.464	666	196	25	2	28	290	113	83
Late Innings, Close	.276	.337	.483	87	24	1	1	5	11	7	20	.281	.347	.442	385	108	12	1	16	53	38	60

RBI/Opportunities

	1987	Four Year
Scoring Position	51 / 211 (24%)	236 / 928 (25%)
Scoring Position, 2 Out	23 / 104 (22%)	91 / 452 (20%)
On Third, Less than 2 Out	18 / 42 (43%)	90 / 170 (53%)
RBI in close games / RBI Total	54 / 83 (65%)	262 / 394 (66%)

Joe Carter
Cleveland Indians

Joe Carter is a bit of an enigma. Though he willingly submits to interviews, he hides his feelings behind agreeable smiles and bland platitudes. What he cannot hide is his attitude toward baseball: Carter loves the game more than anything else. The moment that he crosses the white lines, he always gives his team the best he has.

In an era where it seems impossible to avoid hearing overpaid yo-yos complaining about inane things, Carter is a refreshing exception. Last March, for example, Joe went to spring training looking for a $200,000 raise. Since he had led Cleveland to its best record since 1968 by hitting 29 homers, batting .302, stealing 29 bases and leading the AL in RBIs, it seemed a fair request. Cleveland suggested that a $50,000 raise was more than fair. Since Joe was ineligible for arbitration, he did the one thing that he could do—leave camp in disgust. One week later, he returned, saying that it was unfair to jeopardize Cleveland's chances to contend for selfish reasons.

The season proved to be equally frustrating. Carter started well, but with the Indians struggling out of the gate and manager Pat Corrales challenging the offense to carry the team, Joe tried to do the impossible. He went into a horrible slump, which saw his average slide to below .220, and didn't recover until June.

Just as that happened, Carter took yet another blow. In 1986, pitchers allowed him to crowd the plate; this year they began demanding the outside corner. Joe was hit eight times by pitches and had both his nose and his hand broken. Each time, knowing that Cleveland needed him, Joe returned to the lineup as quickly as possible. Though his power was unaffected, the hand injury seemed to affect his swing; some of his drop in average may be due to that.

It may also be due to Carter's liberal strike zone. He drew less than 35 walks for the second straight year. This may be due to the pressure that Joe placed on himself—he said, more than once, that his job was to hit homers, not walk—but, for whatever reasons, it remains a problem. Carter must become more patient if he ever expects to enter the elite ranks of AL hitters.

With Brett Butler gone, Carter inherits the center field job. He has spent most of his time in Cleveland switching between the three outfield spots and first base; though he has adapted well to it, keeping him in one spot would help him to progress defensively. Though Joe sometimes looked lost when he played center in 1987, he has speed, a fine arm and knows what the words "cutoff man" mean. In time, I think he could learn to be as good a player on defense as he already is on offense.

Jim Shaarda

Carter, Joseph "Joe"

Bats: Right **Throws: Right** **Born 03/07/60**

1987 SEASON AND MAJOR-LEAGUE CAREER BATTING TOTALS

	G	AB	H	2B	3B	HR	TB	R	RBI	TBB	IBB	SO	HP	SH	SF	SB	CS	SB%	GDP	AVG	OBP	SLG
87 CLE	149	588	155	27	2	32	282	83	106	27	6	105	9	1	4	31	6	.84	8	.264	.304	.480
5 YEARS	543	2035	559	97	13	89	949	293	328	95	11	343	17	6	17	87	23	.79	28	.275	.310	.466

	1987 SEASON											FOUR YEAR TOTALS (1984 – 1987)									
	Ave.	OBP	SLG	AB	H	2B	3B	HR	RBI	BB	SO	Ave.	OBP	SLG	AB	H	2B	3B	HR	RBI	BB	SO
Totals	.263	.304	.479	589	155	27	2	32	106	27	105	.277	.313	.472	1985	550	96	12	89	327	95	322
vs. Left	.247	.287	.429	154	38	5	1	7	26	7	28	.281	.321	.484	581	163	25	6	27	95	34	111
vs. Right	.269	.310	.497	435	117	22	1	25	80	20	77	.276	.310	.467	1404	387	71	6	62	232	61	211
at Home	.251	.298	.409	279	70	15	1	9	46	17	43	.283	.326	.462	975	276	49	7	37	147	60	158
on Road	.274	.310	.542	310	85	12	1	23	60	10	62	.271	.300	.482	1010	274	47	5	52	180	35	164
vs. Groundball	.235	.274	.418	311	73	16	1	13	55	11	51	.267	.297	.442	955	255	52	2	37	148	35	139
vs. Flyball	.295	.338	.547	278	82	11	1	19	51	16	54	.286	.328	.500	1030	295	44	10	52	179	60	183
vs. Finesse	.273	.319	.457	300	82	10	0	15	53	16	43	.286	.317	.482	1105	316	53	7	50	180	45	133
vs. Power	.253	.289	.502	289	73	17	2	17	53	11	62	.266	.308	.459	880	234	43	5	39	147	50	189
on Grass	.265	.304	.495	509	135	23	2	30	94	24	90	.281	.317	.484	1672	469	81	10	80	280	82	274
on Artificial Turf	.250	.302	.375	80	20	4	0	2	12	3	15	.259	.296	.406	313	81	15	2	9	47	13	48
Day Games	.272	.313	.525	202	55	7	1	14	33	9	34	.286	.323	.507	676	193	31	7	35	117	36	118
Night Games	.258	.300	.455	387	100	20	1	18	73	18	71	.273	.308	.454	1309	357	65	5	54	210	59	204
April	.253	.299	.505	91	23	5	0	6	14	5	19	.235	.282	.432	213	50	9	0	11	32	13	50
May	.236	.274	.464	110	26	3	2	6	18	5	21	.257	.290	.413	288	74	9	3	10	46	13	48
June	.241	.302	.443	79	19	4	0	4	16	2	16	.294	.341	.513	279	82	17	1	14	49	15	41
July	.268	.305	.527	112	30	5	0	8	27	6	15	.266	.296	.419	346	92	15	1	12	50	15	48
August	.275	.302	.418	91	25	1	0	4	11	3	15	.268	.299	.483	377	101	15	3	20	58	16	54
Sept/Oct	.302	.342	.500	106	32	9	0	4	20	6	19	.313	.345	.531	482	151	31	4	22	92	23	81
Bases Empty	.288	.332	.568	285	82	15	1	21	21	14	48	.277	.313	.496	1035	287	47	7	55	55	49	161
Leadoff	.269	.300	.590	134	36	7	0	12	12	4	22	.276	.302	.517	406	112	14	0	28	28	13	64
Not Leadoff	.305	.360	.550	151	46	8	1	9	9	10	26	.278	.320	.482	629	175	33	7	27	27	36	97
Runners On	.240	.278	.395	304	73	12	1	11	85	13	57	.277	.312	.446	950	263	49	5	34	272	46	161
First Base Only	.231	.238	.433	104	24	6	0	5	11	1	18	.293	.308	.510	365	107	22	3	17	47	8	53
Scoring Position	.245	.297	.375	200	49	6	1	6	74	12	39	.267	.314	.407	585	156	27	2	17	225	38	108
Late Innings, Close	.264	.347	.471	87	23	3	0	5	20	8	14	.305	.349	.480	298	91	7	3	13	59	17	51

RBI/Opportunities

Scoring Position	62 / 252 (25%)	192 / 734 (26%)
Scoring Position, 2 Out	23 / 114 (20%)	65 / 307 (21%)
On Third, Less than 2 Out	24 / 50 (48%)	85 / 162 (52%)
RBI in close games / RBI Total	70 / 106 (66%)	215 / 327 (66%)

Rick Cerone

New York Yankees

It's amazing how a few short years can change your perspective. If, in 1980, you had told a typical Yankee fan that Rick Cerone would be New York's starting catcher in 1987, you would have heard sighs of delight. Had you said the same thing to that same fan in 1986, you would have heard moans of despair. Cerone's 1980 stands as an oasis of productivity in a sea of swill; a career year for a man who, quite simply, hasn't had a very good career. To be fair and honest, New York was lucky to have Cerone last year; without him, the catching duties would have fallen to the likes of Joel (no hit) Skinner and Mark (no catch) Salas. As you may already have guessed, New York had a catching problem in 1987.

By Cerone's standards, 1987 was one of his better years. What do you expect if you give 284 at-bats to a man who has batted .238, slugged .338 and had an on-base percentage of .288 during his career? A .243 average with a .334 SL% and .320 OB% sounds about right to me. He was a little bit off in the power department (though it was the fifth-best figure of his 12- year career), but compensated by missing his career high in OB% by a point.

Cerone's stats against lefties may have you wondering why New York didn't platoon him. The reason why they didn't is that his stats against righties—bad as they were—

were the best figures of any Yankee catcher. In 105 ABs, Salas batted .210, slugged .333 and had a .288 OB%. Skinner batted .149 with a .245 SL% and .196 OB% in 33 ABs.

What the Yankees could have done, should have done and didn't do was to keep Rick from playing in Yankee Stadium whenever possible. In his first stretch in New York, his stats showed no clear pattern; this year, for some reason, he played very well in other stadiums. Since Salas outhit Rick in Yankee Stadium (.277 OB%, .321 SL%), New York might as well have let him play there.

One of the two contributions Cerone did make in 1987 was as a case study in the value of a catcher's fielding percentage. Rick's .988 mark led the league, but Yankee pitchers had a 4.42 ERA when he was behind the plate—he was considerably worse than Skinner (3.95) and in tha same class as Salas (4.53) in 1987. Perhaps it was because 51 of the 74 runners (68.9%) who tried to steal on him succeeded. Maybe it was because he committed 13 passed balls (fourth in the AL behind Texas's "Three Amigos"). But, for whatever reasons, he didn't do the job defensively.

His other contribution? Rick allowed no runs and no hits in two innings as an emergency relief pitcher last year; you may already have guessed that the Yankees also had a pitching problem in 1987.

Craig Christmann

Cerone, Richard Aldo "Rick" Bats: Right   Throws: Right   Born 05/19/54

1987 SEASON AND MAJOR-LEAGUE CAREER BATTING TOTALS

	G	AB	H	2B	3B	HR	TB	R	RBI	TBB	IBB	SO	HP	SH	SF	SB	CS	SB%	GDP	AVG	OBP	SLG
87 NYA	113	284	69	12	1	4	95	28	23	30	0	46	4	5	4	0	1	.00	8	.243	.320	.335
13 YEARS	971	3080	734	138	13	47	1039	294	327	228	6	336	17	41	36	4	19	.17	89	.238	.291	.337

	1987 SEASON											FOUR YEAR TOTALS (1984 – 1987)										
	Ave.	OBP	SLG	AB	H	2B	3B	HR	RBI	BB	SO	Ave.	OBP	SLG	AB	H	2B	3B	HR	RBI	BB	SO
Totals	.243	.320	.335	284	69	12	1	4	23	30	46	.234	.300	.322	902	211	38	1	13	79	83	114
vs. Left	.273	.329	.341	132	36	6	0	1	11	10	20	.233	.284	.311	360	84	16	0	4	31	25	42
vs. Right	.217	.313	.329	152	33	6	1	3	12	20	26	.234	.309	.328	542	127	22	1	9	48	58	72
at Home	.189	.282	.250	148	28	4	1	1	12	18	26	.217	.280	.309	470	102	20	1	7	45	42	52
on Road	.301	.362	.426	136	41	8	0	3	11	12	20	.252	.320	.336	432	109	18	0	6	34	41	62
vs. Groundball	.248	.333	.321	137	34	4	0	2	10	17	24	.207	.271	.274	420	87	13	0	5	36	35	61
vs. Flyball	.238	.307	.347	147	35	8	1	2	13	13	22	.257	.325	.363	482	124	25	1	8	43	48	53
vs. Finesse	.215	.305	.299	144	31	7	1	1	9	18	24	.231	.292	.318	528	122	23	1	7	41	47	67
vs. Power	.271	.335	.371	140	38	5	0	3	14	12	22	.238	.310	.326	374	89	15	0	6	38	36	47
on Grass	.231	.304	.326	242	56	9	1	4	23	23	38	.237	.302	.326	739	175	31	1	11	70	68	89
on Artificial Turf	.310	.408	.381	42	13	3	0	0	0	7	8	.221	.287	.301	163	36	7	0	2	9	15	25
Day Games	.226	.298	.301	93	21	2	1	1	5	7	16	.217	.284	.268	272	59	6	1	2	18	22	40
Night Games	.251	.330	.351	191	48	10	0	3	18	23	30	.241	.306	.344	630	152	32	0	11	61	61	74
April	.105	.250	.105	19	2	0	0	0	1	2	3	.200	.264	.274	135	27	1	0	3	13	10	16
May	.289	.341	.368	38	11	3	0	0	2	3	5	.242	.296	.333	132	32	6	0	2	12	10	19
June	.200	.297	.273	55	11	1	0	1	9	8	7	.229	.292	.312	109	25	6	0	1	13	10	13
July	.283	.365	.413	46	13	3	0	1	6	5	7	.230	.287	.311	161	37	10	0	1	12	12	16
August	.254	.292	.343	67	17	3	0	1	2	3	9	.252	.313	.343	210	53	7	0	4	17	18	28
Sept/Oct	.254	.348	.373	59	15	2	1	1	3	9	15	.239	.335	.342	155	37	8	1	2	12	23	22
Bases Empty	.272	.337	.382	173	47	8	1	3	3	16	27	.244	.298	.336	512	125	21	1	8	8	38	68
Leadoff	.324	.403	.456	68	22	3	0	2	2	9	9	.265	.327	.393	196	52	13	0	4	4	18	24
Not Leadoff	.238	.292	.333	105	25	5	1	1	1	7	18	.231	.279	.301	316	73	8	1	4	4	20	44
Runners On	.198	.295	.261	111	22	4	0	1	20	14	19	.221	.303	.303	390	86	17	0	5	71	45	46
First Base Only	.192	.208	.250	52	10	3	0	0	1	0	9	.225	.268	.310	187	42	13	0	1	6	10	22
Scoring Position	.203	.354	.271	59	12	1	0	1	19	14	10	.217	.332	.296	203	44	4	0	4	65	35	24
Late Innings, Close	.206	.341	.235	34	7	1	0	0	2	7	4	.243	.325	.279	140	34	5	0	0	11	17	14

RBI/Opportunities

	1987			Four Year		
Scoring Position	18 / 91	(20%)		58 / 299	(19%)	
Scoring Position, 2 Out	8 / 51	(16%)		23 / 147	(16%)	
On Third, Less than 2 Out	8 / 12	(67%)		26 / 50	(52%)	
RBI in close games / RBI Total	9 / 23	(39%)		45 / 79	(57%)	

56

Jim Clancy
Toronto Blue Jays

Jim Clancy's 1987 was a typical season for him. Once again, he showed the four characteristics that have been the hallmarks of his career: his inconsistency, his durability, his ability to help Toronto win games and his ability to move right to the brink of recognition as one of the best starters in baseball without going over.

In every season, Clancy has a long period when he is as dominant as any pitcher in baseball. Unfortunately, he always couples it with a stretch where he is as dreadful as can be. Between April 28 and May 23, for example, Jim started six games; he went 6–0 with two shutouts and a 1.26 ERA. The flip side came between July 17 and August 20—in eight starts, he went 0–4 with a 5.71 ERA. In 1986, Clancy went 5–0 with a 1.54 ERA in July and 0–7 with a 4.89 ERA in September. There has never been any way of predicting when his streaks will happen—the only pattern so far is that none has ever happened late in the year.

Clancy has spent 11 seasons and 316 games with Toronto since they acquired him in the 1976 expansion draft. That is a much longer stay than any other pitcher in the history of expansion drafts; the runner-up, Al Fitzmorris, lasted only eight years and 243 appearances with the Royals. Clancy has started 314 games and led or tied for the league in games started in 1982 and 1984. In 1987, his 37 starts tied for second—behind only knuckleballer Charlie

Hough—and he was the only pitcher on the Toronto staff to not miss a single start. In 1987, he started six games on short (three days) rest; the results were impressive. Clancy went 3–1 in those games with a 3.96 ERA.

Toronto seems to win consistently when Clancy is on the mound, even when he doesn't get the victory. Jim's 1987 winning percentage was .577; Toronto went .595 in his starts. Over the last four years, his winning percentage is .525; Toronto went .563 in his starts.

Outside of Toronto, Clancy is, thanks to his inconsistency, certainly not a household word. On several occasions, he's looked like he was going to change that; each time, a slump has held him back. In 1986, he was 14–7 in August and seemed to be a good bet to become the first Blue Jay ever to win 20 games; he wound up at 14–14. In 1987, at the All-Star break, he was 10–6 with a 2.92 ERA and had a chance to win 20; he went 5–5 with a 4.38 ERA in his last 17 starts.

Given his tenure in Toronto, it would be only fitting if Clancy were the first Blue Jay ever to win 20—though Jimmy Key is definitely the favorite, don't bet the house against Clancy. In April, 1986, Jim had 88 career wins to Dave Stieb's 95. Clancy became the first Blue Jay to win 100—he made it two months before Stieb did.

Dave Easby

Clancy, James "Jim"
Bats: Right   Throws: Right   Born 12/18/55

1987 SEASON AND MAJOR-LEAGUE CAREER PITCHING TOTALS

	G	GS	CG	GF	IP	BFP	H	R	ER	HR	SH	SF	HB	TBB	IBB	SO	WP	Bk	W	L	Pct	ShO	Sv	ERA
87 TOR	37	37	5	0	241	1008	234	103	95	24	5	4	1	80	5	180	12	1	15	11	.577	1	0	3.55
11 YEARS	316	314	69	0	2010	8570	1978	998	907	193	51	68	19	767	14	1119	75	1	117	127	.480	11	0	4.06

1987: Power, Groundball   1986: Finesse, Flyball   1985: Finesse, Flyball   1984: Power, Flyball

1987 SEASON / FOUR YEAR TOTALS (1984 – 1987)

	G	IP	H	BB	SO	SB	CS	W	L	S	ERA	G	IP	H	BB	SO	SB	CS	W	L	S	ERA
Totals	37	241.1	234	80	180	24	9	15	11	0	3.54	130	809.0	802	268	490	60	23	51	46	0	4.12
at Home	17	120.0	114	35	80	14	4	7	5	0	3.00	55	339.2	347	107	209	31	8	22	21	0	4.24
on Road	20	121.1	120	45	100	10	5	8	6	0	4.08	75	469.1	455	161	281	29	15	29	25	0	4.03
on Grass	12	80.2	71	30	56	9	2	4	5	0	3.01	47	278.0	268	107	148	23	6	16	18	0	3.98
on Artificial Turf	25	160.2	163	50	124	15	7	11	6	0	3.81	83	531.0	534	161	342	37	17	35	28	0	4.19
Day Games	15	89.0	93	38	74	7	5	5	5	0	4.45	58	354.1	358	132	210	22	13	20	22	0	4.27
Night Games	22	152.1	141	42	106	17	4	10	6	0	3.01	72	454.2	444	136	280	38	10	31	24	0	4.00
April	5	28.1	31	15	11	4	0	2	2	0	4.13	15	95.2	93	42	44	11	0	5	5	0	3.20
May	6	47.1	31	8	40	2	1	5	1	0	1.71	23	152.2	153	43	103	8	5	12	7	0	3.95
June	6	43.2	45	17	25	4	3	1	2	0	2.89	24	135.1	152	55	74	7	6	8	10	0	4.92
July	6	37.2	44	8	35	3	3	2	1	0	5.26	22	144.0	122	39	81	11	4	11	4	0	3.69
August	7	42.0	41	17	33	6	1	2	4	0	4.71	20	127.2	126	45	82	11	2	7	8	0	4.16
Sept/Oct	7	42.1	42	15	36	5	1	3	1	0	3.19	26	153.2	156	44	106	12	6	8	12	0	4.51

vs. Opponent Batters	Ave.	OBP	SLG	AB	H	2B	3B	HR	RBI	BB	SO	Ave.	OBP	SLG	AB	H	2B	3B	HR	RBI	BB	SO
Totals	.255	.314	.401	918	234	52	5	24	85	80	180	.259	.317	.402	3102	802	142	20	88	331	268	490
vs. Left	.281	.335	.433	508	143	35	3	12	45	42	98	.270	.333	.400	1632	440	86	11	35	151	156	249
vs. Right	.222	.288	.361	410	91	17	2	12	40	38	82	.246	.300	.405	1470	362	56	9	53	180	112	241
Bases Empty	.266	.325	.418	552	147	27	3	17	17	47	115	.252	.315	.391	1855	468	87	9	51	51	170	316
Leadoff	.296	.347	.496	240	71	11	2	11	11	19	46	.278	.333	.436	801	223	45	3	25	25	65	116
Not Leadoff	.244	.308	.359	312	76	16	1	6	6	28	69	.232	.303	.358	1054	245	42	6	26	26	105	200
Runners On Base	.238	.298	.374	366	87	25	2	7	68	33	65	.268	.320	.419	1247	334	55	11	37	280	98	174
First Base Only	.221	.260	.355	172	38	13	2	2	10	9	28	.269	.314	.402	592	159	24	8	13	39	39	67
Scoring Position	.253	.329	.392	194	49	12	0	5	58	24	37	.267	.326	.434	655	175	31	3	24	241	59	107
Late Innings, Close	.327	.397	.404	52	17	4	0	0	5	6	9	.350	.414	.455	220	77	11	0	4	24	24	28

RBI/Opportunities

Scoring Position	49 / 248 (20%)	199 / 833 (24%)
Scoring Position, 2 Out	17 / 116 (15%)	87 / 396 (22%)
On Third, Less than 2 Out	14 / 42 (33%)	59 / 139 (42%)
RBI in close games / RBI Total	69 / 85 (81%)	254 / 331 (77%)

Jack Clark
St. Louis Cardinals

Jack Clark is one of the most consistent players in the major leagues. Unfortunately, one of his most consistent tendencies is serious injury. Nevertheless, Clark had an impressive season in 1987—one that would have been a career year for many players. He led the NL in slugging (.597), OBA (a remarkable .459) and walks (139); the profile of a power hitter that teams like to pitch around.

And despite his season-ending injury on September 9, Clark was in the NL top ten in HRs (35) and RBI (105) and not too far behind in runs scored (93). Pretty remarkable for a player with 419 at bats! Even more remarkable when you consider that Busch Stadium is one of the toughest HR parks in the country.

Something else remarkable about Clark's offensive stats is related to his 139 strikeouts (one third of his at bats): His walks and strikeouts add up to 50 percent of his plate appearances. That means that when Jack Clark stepped to the plate in 1987 he only put the ball in play 50 percent of the time. Had Clark stayed healthy (the big IF) in '87 there is little doubt he would have posted the numbers that would have ensured him the MVP award (since he played for a contender).

In fact, it can be argued that Clark was denied the MVP because he again demonstrated his one biggest weakness: injury (and not because he didn't have the numbers for the title). Look at it this way: In 1986 the NL MVP went to Mike Schmidt in part because he had a great year and in part because no one on either the Mets or the Astros had MVP-type numbers. Had Strawberry or Carter posted the identical stats that Clark posted in '87, they probably would have been named MVP. And while it's true that Dawson's '87 numbers were a notch above Schmidt's '86 numbers, Wrigley Field had a great deal to do with Dawson's increased power (over the last five years the Cubs and their opponents have hit 40 percent more HRs at Wrigley than away from Wrigley).

Besides, as Branch Rickey told Ralph Kiner when he asked for a raise after leading the league in HRs: "Son, we could have finished last without you." The MVP isn't usually on a non-contender unless the contenders don't have anyone that stands head and shoulders above the rest as a crucial part of the ball club. Yet Jack Clark is generally acknowledged to be the main reason the Cards were in the race last year. It's not that Dawson wasn't deserving; it's just that understanding the criteria for MVP is like trying to nail Jello to the wall.

Andy Finn

Clark, Jack Anthony Bats: Right Throws: Right Born 11/10/55

1987 SEASON AND MAJOR-LEAGUE CAREER BATTING TOTALS

	G	AB	H	2B	3B	HR	TB	R	RBI	TBB	IBB	SO	HP	SH	SF	SB	CS	SB%	GDP	AVG	OBP	SLG
87 STL	131	419	120	23	1	35	250	93	106	136	13	139	0	0	3	1	2	.33	5	.286	.459	.597
13 YEARS	1366	4824	1333	258	36	229	2350	795	811	761	86	844	14	9	61	63	51	.55	117	.276	.372	.487

1987 SEASON / FOUR YEAR TOTALS (1984 – 1987)

	Ave.	OBP	SLG	AB	H	2B	3B	HR	RBI	BB	SO		Ave.	OBP	SLG	AB	H	2B	3B	HR	RBI	BB	SO
Totals	.286	.459	.593	420	120	22	1	35	106	136	138		.281	.417	.523	1297	364	69	7	77	260	307	316
vs. Left	.261	.480	.543	138	36	9	0	10	33	59	45		.294	.463	.570	419	123	25	2	29	88	134	91
vs. Right	.298	.447	.617	282	84	13	1	25	73	77	93		.274	.392	.500	878	241	44	5	48	172	173	225
at Home	.291	.457	.601	203	59	10	1	17	50	63	65		.265	.398	.483	642	170	33	4	33	118	145	155
on Road	.281	.460	.585	217	61	12	0	18	56	73	73		.296	.435	.562	655	194	36	3	44	142	162	161
vs. Groundball	.280	.457	.492	189	53	7	0	11	45	63	61		.286	.424	.481	618	177	32	2	28	116	150	137
vs. Flyball	.290	.461	.675	231	67	15	1	24	61	73	77		.275	.410	.561	679	187	37	5	49	144	157	179
vs. Finesse	.295	.460	.591	220	65	8	0	19	56	68	63		.297	.417	.530	704	209	34	2	42	136	149	128
vs. Power	.275	.457	.595	200	55	14	1	16	50	68	75		.261	.416	.514	593	155	35	5	35	124	158	188
on Grass	.276	.461	.577	123	34	7	0	10	34	43	41		.303	.444	.541	458	139	19	3	28	107	117	95
on Artificial Turf	.290	.458	.599	297	86	15	1	25	72	93	97		.268	.401	.513	839	225	50	4	49	153	190	221
Day Games	.325	.495	.738	160	52	9	0	19	50	54	53		.285	.428	.540	548	156	26	3	36	118	136	129
Night Games	.262	.436	.504	260	68	13	1	16	56	82	85		.278	.408	.510	749	208	43	4	41	142	171	187
April	.309	.420	.662	68	21	4	1	6	13	13	23		.277	.396	.514	282	78	16	3	15	43	56	63
May	.340	.470	.702	94	32	7	0	9	35	23	21		.326	.438	.596	344	112	19	1	24	89	69	65
June	.274	.426	.579	95	26	5	0	8	24	26	30		.258	.386	.498	329	85	18	2	19	63	69	84
July	.264	.531	.556	72	19	3	0	6	19	41	28		.282	.475	.540	163	46	9	0	11	39	60	48
August	.239	.453	.493	67	16	2	0	5	11	27	26		.233	.419	.434	129	30	6	1	6	19	42	41
Sept/Oct	.250	.400	.417	24	6	1	0	1	4	6	10		.260	.393	.400	50	13	1	0	2	7	11	15
Bases Empty	.234	.407	.516	192	45	7	1	15	15	56	73		.274	.402	.517	636	174	30	4	39	39	137	163
Leadoff	.213	.398	.457	94	20	3	1	6	6	29	37		.268	.399	.529	306	82	15	4	19	19	67	80
Not Leadoff	.255	.416	.571	98	25	4	0	9	9	27	36		.279	.405	.506	330	92	15	0	20	20	70	83
Runners On	.329	.500	.658	228	75	15	0	20	91	80	65		.287	.432	.528	661	190	39	3	38	221	170	153
First Base Only	.380	.505	.722	79	30	6	0	7	16	20	18		.294	.388	.544	252	74	12	0	17	38	39	48
Scoring Position	.302	.498	.624	149	45	9	0	13	75	60	47		.284	.456	.518	409	116	27	3	21	183	131	105
Late Innings, Close	.287	.414	.650	80	23	3	1	8	20	18	26		.313	.439	.567	240	75	13	3	14	46	55	63

RBI/Opportunities

Scoring Position	57 / 242 (24%)	148 / 635 (23%)
Scoring Position, 2 Out	20 / 107 (19%)	48 / 281 (17%)
On Third, Less than 2 Out	21 / 53 (40%)	66 / 144 (46%)
RBI in close games / RBI Total	69 / 106 (65%)	161 / 260 (62%)

Will Clark
San Francisco Giants

Will, on his first major league swing, crushed a Nolan Ryan fastball 12 rows deep in the Dome, becoming the third SF Giant to homer in his first AB (who were the other 2?*). No sophomore jinx here, Will led the Giants in hitting (.308, 6th in the league), games (150), hits (163), homers (35) and RBI (91). He tied the franchise record, held by Mays, McCovey and Cepeda, with RBIs in 9 straight games. Clark hit game-winning homers in both ends of a doubleheader sweep over St. Louis in July. He ended 3 games with homers this year. Twice Player of the Week, he became only the seventh player in SF history to exceed 30 homers.

Of all the superlatives I have heard applied to Will Clark, the most interesting came from Stan Musial, who has seen a few thousand ball players in the 50+ years he has been in organized baseball. Last October, Stan simply said "Will Clark reminds me so much of myself I can hardly believe it." High praise indeed from one of the best hitters who ever lived.

Tagged by Bob Brenly with the nickname Will "the Thrill" Clark, Giant announcers have taken to calling him "the Natural." Although Will can look as bad at the plate as anyone (when he guesses wrong on a changeup he looks like a man fencing with a fly rod on the deck of a rowboat in a typhoon), he's got the sweetest pure swing I've ever seen. As GiantsVision announcer Duane Kuiper said "Oh, to be 23, with Will Clark's stats, swing, and future!"

There are many extremely fine players in the game. Most add a brush stroke or two to the picture that is a ball game; some, like Sutton, Brock, and Hernandez, walk up to the canvas and sign their names, frequently in bold, bright strokes. A special few, however, men like Mays, Koufax, and Mattingly, step up to the canvas and rend it asunder, changing forever the essential nature of the art. Some players have a great, but brief, moment in the sun, such as Bucky Dent; others seem to draw the sun out whenever the game is on the line. In 1987, Will Clark was one of those special few. For him, baseball was not a job, not a game—it was theater.

There have only been 9 upper deck home runs at Candlestick. Will Clark hit 3 of them last year. The 1987 season turned on the evening of August 10. The Giants entered the bottom of the ninth trailing 6–5. Joe Morgan, on the telecast, says "How about a bloop and a blast?" Maldonado spoils that scenario with a line drive to left through the wind off a 3–2 fastball, the first non- breaking pitch after 13 off-speed deliveries. Tie game. Clark steps in, takes three breaking balls for a 2–1 count. Windup. Fastball.

It is only a baseball; it is only a swing, but, as the ball soars majestically into the empty upper deck, the crowd swells from 15,000 to 150,000, a moment in time forever fixed, and reluctantly floats home.

Michael Duca
*(Answer—Bobby Bonds and Johnnie LeMaster)

Clark, William Nuschler "Will" | Bats: Left Throws: Left Born 03/17/64

1987 SEASON AND MAJOR-LEAGUE CAREER BATTING TOTALS

	G	AB	H	2B	3B	HR	TB	R	RBI	TBB	IBB	SO	HP	SH	SF	SB	CS	SB%	GDP	AVG	OBP	SLG
87 SF	150	529	163	29	5	35	307	89	91	49	11	98	5	3	2	5	17	.23	2	.308	.371	.580
2 YEARS	261	937	280	56	7	46	488	155	132	83	21	174	8	12	6	9	24	.27	5	.299	.359	.521

	1987 SEASON											FOUR YEAR TOTALS (1984 – 1987)										
	Ave.	OBP	SLG	AB	H	2B	3B	HR	RBI	BB	SO	Ave.	OBP	SLG	AB	H	2B	3B	HR	RBI	BB	SO
Totals	.308	.371	.580	529	163	29	5	35	91	49	98	.299	.359	.521	937	280	56	7	46	132	83	174
vs. Left	.316	.339	.552	174	55	16	2	7	34	5	34	.313	.343	.493	304	95	24	2	9	48	13	61
vs. Right	.304	.386	.594	355	108	13	3	28	57	44	64	.292	.366	.534	633	185	32	5	37	84	70	113
at Home	.339	.393	.657	274	93	17	2	22	54	24	46	.338	.391	.591	494	167	32	3	29	80	43	81
on Road	.275	.347	.498	255	70	12	3	13	37	25	52	.255	.323	.442	443	113	24	4	17	52	40	93
vs. Groundball	.263	.332	.397	232	61	8	1	7	22	22	46	.276	.333	.392	434	120	18	1	10	43	35	81
vs. Flyball	.343	.401	.724	297	102	21	4	28	69	27	52	.318	.381	.632	503	160	38	6	36	89	48	93
vs. Finesse	.337	.399	.682	267	90	14	3	24	53	26	42	.309	.371	.549	472	146	25	5	26	73	45	72
vs. Power	.279	.341	.477	262	73	15	2	11	38	23	56	.288	.346	.492	465	134	31	2	20	59	38	102
on Grass	.311	.373	.588	405	126	22	3	28	70	39	75	.313	.375	.542	716	224	43	5	37	103	70	136
on Artificial Turf	.298	.365	.556	124	37	7	2	7	21	10	23	.253	.305	.452	221	56	13	2	9	29	13	38
Day Games	.339	.415	.679	218	74	11	3	19	48	25	37	.308	.375	.553	412	127	22	5	23	65	41	74
Night Games	.286	.338	.511	311	89	18	2	16	43	24	61	.291	.346	.495	525	153	34	2	23	67	42	100
April	.266	.330	.468	79	21	3	2	3	7	8	17	.292	.354	.484	161	47	9	2	6	14	16	42
May	.343	.378	.700	70	24	3	2	6	13	3	9	.270	.317	.517	174	47	8	4	9	23	11	32
June	.354	.385	.566	99	35	6	0	5	18	4	18	.343	.378	.543	105	36	6	0	5	19	5	18
July	.242	.303	.396	91	22	2	0	4	13	7	15	.260	.324	.427	96	25	4	0	4	13	8	16
August	.286	.366	.653	98	28	7	1	9	19	13	19	.306	.372	.577	196	60	12	1	13	32	21	25
Sept/Oct	.359	.454	.707	92	33	8	0	8	21	14	20	.317	.389	.532	205	65	17	0	9	31	22	41
Bases Empty	.290	.345	.544	331	96	20	2	20	20	26	63	.301	.345	.516	581	175	36	4	27	27	37	107
Leadoff	.277	.336	.533	137	38	9	1	8	8	11	30	.291	.347	.491	220	64	13	2	9	9	18	40
Not Leadoff	.299	.352	.552	194	58	11	1	12	12	15	33	.307	.344	.532	361	111	23	2	18	18	19	67
Runners On	.338	.412	.641	198	67	9	3	15	71	23	35	.295	.378	.528	356	105	20	3	19	105	46	67
First Base Only	.390	.440	.792	77	30	5	1	8	18	5	12	.348	.395	.667	141	49	10	1	11	26	9	24
Scoring Position	.306	.394	.545	121	37	4	2	7	53	18	23	.260	.369	.437	215	56	10	2	8	79	37	43
Late Innings, Close	.292	.370	.490	96	28	8	1	3	11	10	20	.343	.412	.567	178	61	14	1	8	24	19	30

RBI/Opportunities

	1987			FOUR YEAR		
Scoring Position	43 / 164	(26%)		68 / 309	(22%)	
Scoring Position, 2 Out	14 / 81	(17%)		21 / 131	(16%)	
On Third, Less than 2 Out	16 / 31	(52%)		27 / 62	(44%)	
RBI in close games / RBI Total	55 / 91	(60%)		85 / 132	(64%)	

Roger Clemens
Boston Red Sox

Everyone has their little quirks—a prejudice that, even if they know better, they stubbornly cling to. Mine is power pitchers; I hate almost all of them. I dote on things like strategy, matchups, offensive and defensive philosophies; my favorite players are the ones who show you, in a thousand different ways, that they're thinking while they're playing. I'm not one of those whackos who hates anyone with natural talent, but I do like to see more depth to your game than exploitation of purely physical ability. I wouldn't trade Mark Langston for Charlie Leibrandt . . . but I don't enjoy watching Langston pitch at all.

But, since Scott McGregor collapsed, there isn't anyone in the league that I enjoy watching as much as Roger Clemens. The Rocket Man adapts to his opponents as successfully as anyone; his 95-MPH fastball seems to be just another tool in a well-stocked arsenal.

Take, for example, his control. Clemens's K/W ratio is an exceptional 3.08–1; he walked 2.65 men per nine innings pitched and fanned 8.18. Some of that is obviously due to his ability to throw so hard, but a lot of it is not. If Clemens doesn't need to throw strikes to a batter in order to get him out, he won't.

The five teams that walked the least in the AL in 1987 were Chicago, Cleveland, Minnesota, Kansas City and Baltimore. In 106.1 innings against them, Clemens fanned 105 men (8.89 K/9IP) and walked only 25 (2.12 W/9IP), for an astonishing 4.20–1 K/W ratio. As a result, he allowed only 83 hits (7.02 per nine IP; down from 7.92 overall) and went 10–3 with a 2.20 ERA.

Roger "paces himself" very well, too. In 1987, Clemens walked 7.1 percent of the batters he faced and fanned 24.4 percent. Facing the leadoff hitter in an inning, he walked only 6.6 percent and fanned 19.6 percent. As you can see below, he let hitters put the ball in play and didn't worry if it went in the stands. But the minute that a man reached base, he turned into a monster. Of the 100 leadoff hitters who reached base, only 37 scored in 1987.

Maybe the most impressive thing about Clemens is his desire; if he's set his cap for some goal, he's terrifying. Entering October, he was 18–9, with 236 hits, 82 walks, 231 whiffs and a 3.17 ERA in 263.2 IP. He was by no means a lock for the Cy Young Award; I wouldn't have voted for him over Jimmy Key at the time. Clemens got two more starts in 1987; in those games, he threw two shutouts, allowing 12 hits, fanning 25 and walking *one*. You've got to figure that he won the award by doing that.

Which, frankly, is why Roger's comment that he'd like to be the first pitcher ever to win the award three years in a row scares me to death. Even if someone else goes 30–2 with a 1.16 ERA, I expect Clemens to outdo him and win the Cy Young award in 1988.

Geoff Beckman

Clemens, William Roger "Roger" Bats: Right Throws: Right Born 08/04/62

1987 SEASON AND MAJOR-LEAGUE CAREER PITCHING TOTALS

	G	GS	CG	GF	IP	BFP	H	R	ER	HR	SH	SF	HB	TBB	IBB	SO	WP	Bk	W	L	Pct	ShO	Sv	ERA
87 BOS	36	36	18	0	282	1157	248	100	93	19	6	4	9	83	4	256	4	3	20	9	.690	7	0	2.97
4 YEARS	105	104	36	0	767	3136	656	282	263	58	13	15	18	216	7	694	20	9	60	22	.732	10	0	3.09

1987: Power, Flyball   1986: Power, Flyball   1985: Power, Flyball   1984: Power, Groundball

	1987 SEASON											**FOUR YEAR TOTALS (1984 – 1987)**										
	G	IP	H	BB	SO	SB	CS	W	L	S	ERA	G	IP	H	BB	SO	SB	CS	W	L	S	ERA
Totals	36	281.2	247	83	256	26	14	20	9	0	2.97	105	767.1	655	216	694	69	33	60	22	0	3.08
at Home	20	160.1	129	38	135	14	8	11	6	0	2.75	55	408.1	345	96	377	38	19	31	13	0	3.11
on Road	16	121.1	118	45	121	12	6	9	3	0	3.26	50	359.0	310	120	317	31	14	29	9	0	3.06
on Grass	9	69.1	60	25	74	4	5	5	1	0	2.34	32	225.2	183	71	220	18	12	19	5	0	2.71
on Artificial Turf	27	212.1	187	58	182	22	9	15	8	0	3.18	73	541.2	472	145	474	51	21	41	17	0	3.24
Day Games	32	247.1	217	74	227	21	13	17	8	0	3.09	89	649.2	564	181	597	56	30	49	18	0	3.12
Night Games	4	34.1	30	9	29	5	1	3	1	0	2.10	16	117.2	91	35	97	13	3	11	4	0	2.91
April	4	28.1	25	10	28	6	2	1	2	0	2.86	12	90.2	66	31	92	14	6	7	4	0	2.48
May	6	49.2	40	15	40	2	5	3	2	0	2.54	20	153.2	135	46	137	16	8	12	4	0	3.57
June	6	42.1	41	19	38	5	1	2	2	0	5.53	20	138.2	129	36	115	11	3	10	4	0	3.70
July	7	59.2	51	14	38	7	0	5	1	0	2.26	20	140.2	133	33	103	16	4	10	6	0	3.33
August	6	42.0	48	12	42	4	2	3	1	0	4.07	20	143.1	115	47	146	9	6	11	3	0	3.08
Sept/Oct	7	59.2	42	13	70	2	4	6	1	0	1.51	13	100.1	77	23	101	3	6	10	1	0	1.70

vs. Opponent Batters	Ave.	OBP	SLG	AB	H	2B	3B	HR	RBI	BB	SO	Ave.	OBP	SLG	AB	H	2B	3B	HR	RBI	BB	SO
Totals	.234	.295	.347	1054	247	52	5	19	91	83	256	.228	.284	.338	2872	655	119	11	58	249	216	694
vs. Left	.234	.298	.331	602	141	34	3	6	55	50	134	.232	.291	.325	1611	373	81	8	18	136	130	350
vs. Right	.235	.290	.369	452	106	18	2	13	36	33	122	.224	.275	.354	1261	282	38	3	40	113	86	344
Bases Empty	.257	.300	.375	611	157	36	3	10	10	34	143	.231	.278	.341	1751	404	82	6	33	33	111	423
Leadoff	.303	.350	.408	267	81	19	0	3	3	15	57	.252	.297	.360	739	186	32	3	14	14	44	170
Not Leadoff	.221	.262	.349	344	76	17	3	7	7	19	86	.215	.264	.327	1012	218	50	3	19	19	67	253
Runners On Base	.203	.287	.309	443	90	16	2	9	81	49	113	.224	.292	.333	1121	251	37	5	25	216	105	271
First Base Only	.211	.293	.310	171	36	8	0	3	7	18	41	.238	.298	.374	484	115	15	3	15	37	40	111
Scoring Position	.199	.284	.309	272	54	8	2	6	74	31	72	.214	.288	.301	637	136	22	2	10	179	65	160
Late Innings, Close	.241	.305	.380	108	26	1	1	4	12	10	24	.254	.307	.384	279	71	7	1	9	28	21	57

RBI/Opportunities

Scoring Position	63 / 354 (18%)	160 / 823 (19%)
Scoring Position, 2 Out	24 / 157 (15%)	67 / 388 (17%)
On Third, Less than 2 Out	26 / 56 (46%)	60 / 121 (50%)
RBI in close games / RBI Total	62 / 91 (68%)	167 / 249 (67%)

Vince Coleman
St. Louis Cardinals

Vince Coleman burst onto the scene early in the 1985 season and immediately ran his way into the hearts of Cardinal fans. With his 110 stolen bases, in a season in which most people felt they wouldn't contend, Coleman earned a reputation in the media as the man who made the Cardinal offense go. This was cemented in the minds of most when Vince's postseason injury coincided with the disappearance of the Cardinal offense. Through it all, there was little mention of Coleman's .320 on-base percentage, a poor figure for a leadoff hitter. Coleman made a contribution to the Cardinal offense, but not nearly of the magnitude of those made by McGee, Herr, or Clark. His weaknesses were simply overshadowed by the success of the team.

1986 was the other side of the coin. The shortcomings in Coleman's game were magnified not only by the team's offensive collapse but by the fact that he showed no improvement in any of his weak areas. Articles began appearing in various publications questioning Herzog's use of Vince in the leadoff spot. It didn't help that the Mets had a twenty to thirty game lead over St. Louis all season. The man labeled as the main cog in the Cardinal offense in '85 was certainly not lacking for criticism when the '86 campaign ended.

Coleman's reaction to this criticism was admirable. Whereas following the 1985 season he was making remarks about cutting his strikeouts in half and doubling his walks and stealing 200 bases, things that just don't happen between a player's first and second seasons, Vince made no such remarks after the disastrous '86 season. Instead he spent the off-season working on his hitting stroke and patience at the plate. And when the Redbirds were National League Champs in '87, Vince Coleman was one of the team's offensive stars.

He's still no Tim Raines, but Jack Clark's not Babe Ruth either and nobody's complaining. What Coleman did first in 1987 was to quit chasing bad pitches at the plate. This patience enabled him to draw 43 walks in the season's first half. After the pitchers realized that they couldn't get Vince out with bad pitches and began throwing more strikes, be began to hit the ball with more authority than ever before, slugging .375 for the second half of the season and hitting the first three "outside-the-park" home runs of his career. Through it all he kept his average in the .290-.300 range and continued to get on base and score runs.

1988 could again be a key season in Coleman's career. He made remarkable strides in his offensive game last season, but he still had 44 infield hits. If he wants to remain a productive player as his speed starts to diminish in a few years, he still has to continue to improve. Hopefully, this fact will not be overshadowed by the successful '87 season and Coleman will continue to work hard at improving.

Russ Eagle

Coleman, Vincent Maurice "Vince"

Bats: Both   **Throws: Right**   **Born 09/22/61**

1987 SEASON AND MAJOR-LEAGUE CAREER BATTING TOTALS

	G	AB	H	2B	3B	HR	TB	R	RBI	TBB	IBB	SO	HP	SH	SF	SB	CS	SB%	GDP	AVG	OBP	SLG
87 STL	151	623	180	14	10	3	223	121	43	70	0	126	3	5	1	109	22	.83	7	.289	.363	.358
3 YEARS	456	1859	489	47	28	4	604	322	112	180	1	339	5	13	7	326	61	.84	14	.263	.329	.325

	1987 SEASON											FOUR YEAR TOTALS (1984 – 1987)										
	Ave.	OBP	SLG	AB	H	2B	3B	HR	RBI	BB	SO	Ave.	OBP	SLG	AB	H	2B	3B	HR	RBI	BB	SO
Totals	.289	.363	.358	623	180	14	10	3	43	70	126	.263	.329	.325	1859	489	47	28	4	112	180	339
vs. Left	.268	.361	.416	209	56	8	7	3	17	29	46	.247	.325	.343	647	160	23	15	3	41	74	116
vs. Right	.300	.364	.329	414	124	6	3	0	26	41	80	.271	.331	.315	1212	329	24	13	1	71	106	223
at Home	.275	.348	.376	287	79	8	6	3	27	29	59	.283	.350	.359	922	261	24	17	4	62	90	155
on Road	.301	.376	.342	336	101	6	4	0	16	41	67	.243	.308	.291	937	228	23	11	0	50	90	184
vs. Groundball	.316	.373	.385	288	91	11	3	1	24	25	45	.289	.347	.353	890	257	29	11	2	50	77	128
vs. Flyball	.266	.355	.334	335	89	3	7	2	19	45	81	.239	.312	.299	969	232	18	17	2	62	103	211
vs. Finesse	.285	.355	.368	326	93	8	8	1	23	34	47	.268	.326	.333	1028	275	28	18	1	57	87	150
vs. Power	.293	.371	.347	297	87	6	2	2	20	36	79	.258	.332	.315	831	214	19	10	3	55	93	189
on Grass	.335	.413	.341	173	58	1	0	0	10	23	35	.257	.318	.294	486	125	8	5	0	30	45	98
on Artificial Turf	.271	.343	.364	450	122	13	10	3	33	47	91	.265	.332	.336	1373	364	39	23	4	82	135	241
Day Games	.339	.409	.421	221	75	6	3	2	19	25	42	.272	.336	.355	679	185	20	15	2	47	67	124
Night Games	.261	.338	.323	402	105	8	7	1	24	45	84	.258	.324	.308	1180	304	27	13	2	65	113	215
April	.240	.367	.253	75	18	1	0	0	6	14	16	.251	.342	.315	203	51	7	3	0	15	27	36
May	.306	.393	.378	98	30	1	3	0	6	13	22	.294	.367	.372	296	87	6	7	1	21	33	58
June	.316	.370	.376	117	37	1	3	0	10	10	23	.262	.331	.315	324	85	3	7	0	19	33	55
July	.239	.333	.261	92	22	2	0	0	6	12	21	.247	.319	.298	292	72	9	3	0	14	30	56
August	.306	.351	.413	121	37	6	2	1	7	9	19	.281	.321	.350	360	101	12	5	1	18	22	66
Sept/Oct	.300	.364	.408	120	36	3	2	2	8	12	25	.242	.305	.299	384	93	10	3	2	25	35	68
Bases Empty	.273	.359	.342	406	111	8	7	2	2	51	87	.263	.334	.324	1255	330	32	18	3	3	131	241
Leadoff	.297	.390	.373	249	74	6	5	1	1	35	54	.277	.352	.344	790	219	24	13	1	1	88	156
Not Leadoff	.236	.306	.293	157	37	2	2	1	1	16	33	.239	.303	.290	465	111	8	5	2	2	43	85
Runners On	.318	.371	.387	217	69	6	3	1	41	19	39	.263	.318	.326	604	159	15	10	1	109	49	98
First Base Only	.358	.402	.420	81	29	3	1	0	3	6	11	.269	.307	.324	216	58	8	2	0	5	12	27
Scoring Position	.294	.353	.368	136	40	3	2	1	38	13	28	.260	.324	.327	388	101	7	8	1	104	37	71
Late Innings, Close	.368	.417	.406	106	39	4	0	0	12	9	21	.278	.339	.334	302	84	13	2	0	35	28	53

RBI/Opportunities

Scoring Position	35 / 180 (19%)		101 / 515 (20%)
Scoring Position, 2 Out	18 / 94 (19%)		46 / 264 (17%)
On Third, Less than 2 Out	12 / 30 (40%)		36 / 77 (47%)
RBI in close games / RBI Total	28 / 43 (65%)		75 / 112 (67%)

Danny Cox
St. Louis Cardinals

Danny Cox's season in 1987 was a bit of a disappointment for the Cardinals and their fans. Cox had finished among the top eight in the National League in earned run average for the two previous seasons with ERA's of 2.88 and 2.90. In 1987, however, he not only saw his ERA increase by a full run, but his hits allowed per nine innings increased from 7.73 to 10.11 and his walks per nine innings went from 2.45 to 3.21. His home run rate was up slightly also. Thus Cox posted only an 11–9 won-lost record for 1987 despite receiving run support of almost five runs per game.

It's not that Cox wasn't a good pitcher in 1987. But you would have thought he would have had a little more success than he did given his past performance and that he was pitching for a league champion. Actually the Cardinals were 19–12 in Cox's 31 starts, a better percentage than the team's final record. And the run support figure for Cox, 4.87 runs per game, may be slightly misleading. The Cardinals were such an explosive team early in 1987 that they tended to run up the support figures of several pitchers. In 23 of Cox's starts the Redbirds scored three runs or more. Their record in those games was 19–4. However, there were eight games started by Cox in which they scored two runs or less, more such games than for any other pitcher on the staff. St. Louis was 0–8 in these games. So you can see that

for the most part Danny Cox was winning the games he was supposed to win, or at least keeping the team in the game so that they eventually won.

In 1986 Cox began the season on the disabled list and suffered through a subpar first half. He then finished strongly, going 10–6 in the second half with very little offensive support. 1987 was just the opposite. Cox was more effective during the season's first half, and was just hitting his stride in July, posting a 1.20 ERA for the month, when he went down with an injury. His record at the time was 8–3. After returning from the DL in August he struggled, going 3–6 rest of the way. So it remains to be seen what he can accomplish if he can stay healthy for an entire season.

Over 20 percent of Cox's innings last season were pitched against the Cubs, against whom he started six times and posted a 4–2 record and 2.98 ERA. The Reds were the only other team he beat more than once. One of his most remarkable games of the season was a 3–0 win over Atlanta on July 4 in which Cox pitched the first seven innings. Danny didn't have much that day, giving up six hits and seven walks in those seven innings. Graig Nettles batted three times in the first five innings with the bases loaded, and hit the ball hard twice. But the Braves could never get a runner across the plate. They ended up leaving 13 runners on base, just 1 short of the league record for a shutout.

Russ Eagle

Cox, Danny Bradford   Bats: Right   Throws: Right   Born 09/21/59

1987 SEASON AND MAJOR-LEAGUE CAREER PITCHING TOTALS

	G	GS	CG	GF	IP	BFP	H	R	ER	HR	SH	SF	HB	TBB	IBB	SO	WP	Bk	W	L	Pct	ShO	Sv	ERA
87 STL	31	31	2	0	199	864	224	99	86	17	14	4	3	71	6	101	5	1	11	9	.550	0	0	3.89
5 YEARS	139	137	21	0	899	3754	902	394	334	65	50	22	15	272	25	446	15	10	53	48	.525	5	0	3.34

1987: Finesse, Groundball   1986: Finesse, Groundball   1985: Finesse, Groundball   1984: Finesse, Groundball

1987 SEASON											FOUR YEAR TOTALS (1984 – 1987)										
	G	IP	H	BB	SO	SB	CS	W	L	S	ERA	G	IP	H	BB	SO	SB	CS	W	L	S	ERA
Totals	31	199.0	224	71	101	11	8	11	9	0	3.89	127	816.1	810	249	410	47	33	50	42	0	3.35
at Home	17	121.2	136	32	54	6	5	6	3	0	3.40	66	451.2	435	116	211	17	15	27	19	0	3.05
on Road	14	77.1	88	39	47	5	3	5	6	0	4.66	61	364.2	375	133	199	30	18	23	23	0	3.73
on Grass	12	73.1	81	38	43	4	2	8	3	0	3.93	45	276.2	277	108	139	20	12	19	17	0	3.45
on Artificial Turf	19	125.2	143	33	58	7	6	3	6	0	3.87	82	539.2	533	141	271	27	21	31	25	0	3.30
Day Games	8	46.0	48	24	30	3	1	3	3	0	3.91	31	178.0	186	73	95	14	5	10	15	0	4.10
Night Games	23	153.0	176	47	71	8	7	8	6	0	3.88	96	638.1	624	176	315	33	28	40	27	0	3.14
April	5	32.0	31	14	18	2	1	3	0	0	3.38	15	85.0	86	31	40	4	3	6	4	0	3.81
May	6	37.1	51	12	13	2	1	2	2	0	5.06	25	161.0	159	57	75	10	7	7	9	0	3.58
June	6	41.0	42	10	27	3	1	2	1	0	3.51	22	136.2	142	40	78	8	8	8	6	0	3.42
July	2	15.0	16	10	12	0	1	1	0	0	1.20	16	118.2	112	26	62	2	4	9	6	0	2.65
August	5	30.1	36	7	7	2	2	1	1	0	3.56	23	134.1	145	41	61	12	6	7	8	0	3.95
Sept/Oct	7	43.1	48	18	24	2	2	2	5	0	4.78	26	180.2	166	54	94	11	5	13	9	0	2.89

vs. Opponent Batters	Ave.	OBP	SLG	AB	H	2B	3B	HR	RBI	BB	SO	Ave.	OBP	SLG	AB	H	2B	3B	HR	RBI	BB	SO
Totals	.290	.351	.420	773	224	36	7	17	79	71	101	.264	.319	.386	3074	810	154	23	59	293	249	410
vs. Left	.315	.382	.449	381	120	24	3	7	45	42	35	.276	.336	.404	1515	418	80	12	30	148	137	159
vs. Right	.265	.319	.393	392	104	12	4	10	34	29	66	.251	.302	.369	1559	392	74	11	29	145	112	251
Bases Empty	.302	.366	.465	430	130	22	6	12	12	41	51	.264	.322	.396	1809	478	96	14	38	38	153	241
Leadoff	.300	.364	.442	190	57	10	1	5	5	18	23	.283	.338	.425	785	222	44	7	18	18	65	104
Not Leadoff	.304	.367	.483	240	73	12	5	7	7	23	28	.250	.310	.373	1024	256	52	7	20	20	88	137
Runners On Base	.274	.332	.364	343	94	14	1	5	67	30	50	.262	.314	.372	1265	332	58	9	21	255	96	169
First Base Only	.312	.350	.377	154	48	7	0	1	4	9	21	.281	.315	.393	565	159	25	4	10	33	28	66
Scoring Position	.243	.318	.354	189	46	7	1	4	63	21	29	.247	.313	.356	700	173	33	5	11	222	68	103
Late Innings, Close	.288	.347	.439	66	19	2	1	2	7	6	7	.260	.310	.358	285	74	10	3	4	27	21	28

RBI/Opportunities

	1987		Four Year	
Scoring Position	56 / 257	(22%)	201 / 915	(22%)
Scoring Position, 2 Out	25 / 119	(21%)	84 / 424	(20%)
On Third, Less than 2 Out	19 / 47	(40%)	74 / 166	(45%)
RBI in close games / RBI Total	55 / 79	(70%)	232 / 293	(79%)

Kal Daniels
Cincinnati Reds

Kal Daniels, not Eric Davis, is the best hitter on the Cincinnati Reds and one of the best hitters in baseball. Despite losing about six weeks to arthroscopic knee surgery Daniels created 99 runs and 10.5 runs per 27 outs in 1987. Kal had a higher batting average, on base average, and slugging average than Eric but for some reason Daniels is perceived as just another one of the Reds' fine young outfielders. Eric Davis' 1986 season sparked comparisons to Willie Mays; Daniels' 1987 season was superior in every area except runs and stolen bases:

Category	G	ABs	Hits	HR	Runs	RBI	SB	SB%	BA	OBA	SLG
Davis 86	132	415	115	27	97	71	80	.80	.277	.378	.523
Daniels 87	108	368	123	26	73	64	26	.76	.334	.429	.617

The only advantage Eric has over Kal now is speed (in '86 their SB% was the same and Kal had 4 triples in 181 AB). Kal hits for a better average, has more power, strikes out less, and his strike zone judgment is as good.

As the figures show, Daniels is not just another slap singles hitter. Indeed, Daniels slugging average of .617 was the highest in the league among hitters with 10 or more AB, and was virtually identical to Mark McGwire's AL league-leading .618. This has to be one of the quietest .617 slugging averages ever. Only players like Schmidt, Jackson and Brett get to that level, and usually only once in their careers. Kal had 26 HR (2nd to Davis), averaging about one every fourteen at bats. Had he been hitting in the middle of the order, he might well have driven in 100 runs; as it was, he didn't homer with a man on base until August.

The biggest knock on Daniels has been his fielding. With their preferred starting lineup, the Reds' weakest fielder was Daniels. Left field in Riverfront is not an easy place to play. Directly in front of the left fielder's normal position is an area of seams in the turf approximately 3 feet wide and 125 feet long where the football seats are secured. Any time a ground ball is hit to left field, Daniels has to either run over the seams or hope the ball doesn't take a bad bounce.

One of Pete Rose's problems as a manager has been his difficulty in relating to players who are not as outspoken and visible as himself. Rose seems to favor players like Tracy Jones (who would be named Bosworth if he played football) over quiet, even shy players like Eric Davis, Nick Esasky, and Kal Daniels. Just because a player keeps to himself and doesn't run into walls chasing upper deck home runs doesn't mean he isn't hustling or playing up to his ability.

Pete is contemplating moving Kal into the #3 spot in the batting order to begin 1988. Daniels can handle either spot but it may not be a good idea unless the Reds can find another efficient leadoff hitter. Tracy Jones has no strike zone judgement and Barry Larkin is unproven as a hitter. If neither of them works out, the Reds will be better off with Daniels leading off.

Greg Gajus, Sean Lahman, Tom Locker

Daniels, Kalvoski "Kal" Bats: Left Throws: Right Born 08/20/63

1987 SEASON AND MAJOR-LEAGUE CAREER BATTING TOTALS

	G	AB	H	2B	3B	HR	TB	R	RBI	TBB	IBB	SO	HP	SH	SF	SB	CS	SB%	GDP	AVG	OBP	SLG
87 CIN	108	368	123	24	1	26	227	73	64	60	11	62	1	1	0	26	8	.76	6	.334	.429	.617
2 YEARS	182	549	181	34	5	32	321	107	87	82	12	92	3	2	1	41	10	.80	10	.330	.419	.585

	1987 SEASON										FOUR YEAR TOTALS (1984 – 1987)										
	Ave.	OBP	SLG	AB	H	2B	3B	HR	RBI	BB	SO	Ave.	OBP	SLG	AB	H	2B	3B	HR	RBI	BB	SO
Totals	.334	.429	.617	368	123	24	1	26	64	60	62	.330	.419	.585	549	181	34	5	32	87	82	92
vs. Left	.197	.291	.289	76	15	4	0	1	6	9	17	.194	.287	.269	108	21	5	0	1	6	12	24
vs. Right	.370	.464	.702	292	108	20	1	25	58	51	45	.363	.450	.662	441	160	29	5	31	81	70	68
at Home	.309	.398	.600	175	54	12	0	13	29	25	29	.309	.387	.554	285	88	16	3	16	44	35	51
on Road	.358	.456	.632	193	69	12	1	13	35	35	33	.352	.452	.617	264	93	18	2	16	43	47	41
vs. Groundball	.356	.474	.637	160	57	10	1	11	29	36	22	.355	.457	.592	245	87	14	4	12	39	44	40
vs. Flyball	.317	.391	.601	208	66	14	0	15	35	24	40	.309	.387	.579	304	94	20	1	20	48	38	52
vs. Finesse	.369	.443	.690	187	69	12	0	16	35	25	30	.357	.433	.632	269	96	14	3	18	46	35	44
vs. Power	.298	.415	.541	181	54	12	1	10	29	35	32	.304	.406	.539	280	85	20	2	14	41	47	48
on Grass	.324	.429	.581	136	44	6	1	9	25	25	19	.329	.442	.590	173	57	10	1	11	30	34	24
on Artificial Turf	.341	.429	.638	232	79	18	0	17	39	35	43	.330	.407	.582	376	124	24	4	21	57	48	68
Day Games	.338	.429	.689	151	51	11	0	14	30	23	19	.335	.431	.642	212	71	15	1	16	40	35	26
Night Games	.332	.429	.567	217	72	13	1	12	34	37	43	.326	.411	.549	337	110	19	4	16	47	47	66
April	.300	.355	.714	70	21	6	1	7	15	6	14	.317	.372	.692	104	33	8	2	9	20	9	22
May	.358	.463	.522	67	24	2	0	3	9	13	13	.316	.432	.456	79	25	2	0	3	9	16	16
June	.262	.379	.525	80	21	3	0	6	10	15	13	.276	.388	.517	87	24	3	0	6	12	16	16
July	.545	.583	1.182	11	6	4	0	1	3	1	1	.413	.481	.674	46	19	7	1	1	8	6	5
August	.385	.487	.600	65	25	5	0	3	11	13	8	.342	.418	.541	146	50	9	1	6	17	19	18
Sept/Oct	.347	.443	.640	75	26	4	0	6	16	12	13	.345	.452	.667	87	30	5	1	7	21	16	15
Bases Empty	.349	.429	.668	241	84	14	0	21	21	34	41	.343	.419	.626	356	122	22	2	25	25	47	62
Leadoff	.373	.450	.753	150	56	12	0	15	15	21	29	.374	.442	.724	214	80	19	1	18	18	26	42
Not Leadoff	.308	.394	.527	91	28	2	0	6	6	13	12	.296	.387	.479	142	42	3	1	7	7	21	20
Runners On	.307	.429	.520	127	39	10	1	5	43	26	21	.306	.415	.508	193	59	12	3	7	62	35	30
First Base Only	.294	.368	.510	51	15	2	0	3	6	5	6	.317	.371	.561	82	26	3	1	5	12	6	9
Scoring Position	.316	.464	.526	76	24	8	1	2	37	21	15	.297	.443	.468	111	33	9	2	2	50	29	21
Late Innings, Close	.321	.479	.429	56	18	3	0	1	5	16	12	.326	.469	.506	89	29	7	0	3	13	23	17

RBI/Opportunities

Scoring Position	33 / 115 (29%)	46 / 170 (27%)
Scoring Position, 2 Out	5 / 56 (9%)	11 / 81 (14%)
On Third, Less than 2 Out	16 / 23 (70%)	20 / 32 (63%)
RBI in close games / RBI Total	39 / 64 (61%)	55 / 87 (63%)

Ron Darling
New York Mets

Ron Darling had a very up-and-down season in 1987. Early in the year his control was way off from what it was in 1986. There were a number of times when the opposing teams had more runs than hits. Not surprising, but Darling did it enough times for it to be noticeable. Ron even had a 2 and 7 record at one point last season. He came on with a late spurt, however, and finished the season at 12–8. He could have won more games if he had not broken his finger while diving for a bunt on September 11.

Part of Darling's "off-season" could be linked to his sudden appearance on the Hollywood scene. His marriage to model Toni O'Reilly and the birth of his son Tyler Christian were both highly publicized. Darling also was on *Good Morning America* and *Sesame Street,* and seen on the cover of *GQ.* He was also trying to learn the split-fingered fast ball, a pitch that will baffle hitters if thrown properly but baffle the pitcher if not.

Dan Sadowsky

Darling's 1987 is one of the least consistent years I can remember. In '87 Ron was good one month, bad the next. But check out his weekly ERAs from June 17 to August 5, 1987: 6.75, 3.60, 7.50, 1.98, 5.00, 3.00, 4.73. Immediately preceding that period his season ERA was 4.82; his ERA from August 5 until his season ending injury was 3.40. What went on here?

Some would say Darling was injured for much of the year, that he pitched through his troubles. If this is true, then Ron's a lunatic. Just ask Cub fans used to hearing Scott Sanderson telling everyone how good his back feels while being placed on the disabled list. These should be the prime years of Darling's career; if he can get and stay healthy, he might be able to go 15–6 forever.

Well, maybe. Ron's hits and home runs per 9 innings pitched creep up every year, and last year he allowed one home run every 9 innings—a big jump from the .8 of 1986. He completed just 2 of his 32 starts, but that's nothing new for Darling: he's completed just 13 of his 139 career starts, a remarkably low total for a pitcher regarded as a key to his club's staff. He continues to walk people, regressing from his 1986 improvement in this category by over a walk a game.

This last point is an interesting one to examine, because when one looks at Darling's season, one is tempted to say that what hurt him weren't the walks so much as the many more hits he allowed. During the second half his W/9I went down from 4.5 to 3.8 . . . but his H/9I shrunk from 8.8 to 7.0. When Darling pitched his best ball of the year (from August 26 until he busted his thumb), he allowed only 17 hits in 27 innings, fashioning a 2.96 ERA and winning twice. During this period, he allowed 14 walks. For a pitcher as baffling to figure as Ron Darling, that kind of performance seems typical.

Stuart Shea

Darling, Ronald Maurice "Ron"

Bats: Right **Throws: Right** **Born 08/19/60**

1987 SEASON AND MAJOR-LEAGUE CAREER PITCHING TOTALS

	G	GS	CG	GF	IP	BFP	H	R	ER	HR	SH	SF	HB	TBB	IBB	SO	WP	Bk	W	L	Pct	ShO	Sv	ERA
87 NYN	32	32	2	0	208	891	183	111	99	24	5	3	3	96	3	167	6	3	12	8	.600	0	0	4.28
5 YEARS	140	139	13	1	934	3933	810	396	351	83	38	19	17	412	9	677	30	10	56	32	.636	6	0	3.38

1987: Power, Flyball **1986: Power, Flyball** **1985: Power, Flyball** **1984: Power, Flyball**

1987 SEASON											
	G	IP	H	BB	SO	SB	CS	W	L	S	ERA
Totals	32	207.2	183	96	167	33	4	12	8	0	4.29
at Home	13	88.2	79	34	74	11	4	4	6	0	3.86
on Road	19	119.0	104	62	93	22	0	8	2	0	4.61
on Grass	11	72.2	57	37	59	11	4	5	2	0	3.47
on Artificial Turf	21	135.0	126	59	108	22	0	7	6	0	4.73
Day Games	21	137.1	119	62	111	16	4	7	7	0	4.19
Night Games	11	70.1	64	34	56	17	0	5	1	0	4.48
April	5	28.2	39	11	21	4	0	2	1	0	6.28
May	6	37.1	37	19	23	7	2	0	2	0	4.82
June	6	37.2	23	23	39	5	0	0	2	0	3.82
July	6	41.2	42	9	23	7	2	4	2	0	4.10
August	7	48.1	37	28	47	8	0	5	1	0	3.72
Sept/Oct	2	14.0	5	6	14	2	0	1	0	0	2.57

vs. Opponent Batters	Ave.	OBP	SLG	AB	H	2B	3B	HR	RBI	BB	SO
Totals	.233	.318	.380	784	183	31	6	24	98	96	167
vs. Left	.222	.298	.354	446	99	19	5	10	50	48	91
vs. Right	.249	.344	.414	338	84	12	1	14	48	48	76
Bases Empty	.233	.314	.371	455	106	13	4	14	14	52	107
Leadoff	.238	.323	.404	193	46	4	2	8	8	23	45
Not Leadoff	.229	.308	.347	262	60	9	2	6	6	29	62
Runners On Base	.234	.324	.392	329	77	18	2	10	84	44	60
First Base Only	.221	.279	.346	136	30	6	1	3	9	11	31
Scoring Position	.244	.352	.425	193	47	12	1	7	75	33	29
Late Innings, Close	.343	.397	.557	70	24	3	0	4	10	7	13

FOUR YEAR TOTALS (1984 – 1987)											
	G	IP	H	BB	SO	SB	CS	W	L	S	ERA
Totals	135	898.1	779	395	654	93	46	55	29	0	3.41
at Home	65	457.0	395	166	354	38	23	30	15	0	3.01
on Road	70	441.1	384	229	300	55	23	25	14	0	3.79
on Grass	46	294.2	269	141	206	39	13	17	13	0	3.85
on Artificial Turf	89	603.2	510	254	448	54	33	38	16	0	3.19
Day Games	94	628.2	547	266	476	55	29	39	20	0	3.38
Night Games	41	269.2	232	129	178	38	17	16	9	0	3.47
April	18	104.2	111	48	69	13	4	5	3	0	4.99
May	22	150.0	128	60	107	10	6	10	4	0	3.18
June	23	155.2	121	72	125	15	10	9	5	0	2.89
July	25	172.2	153	70	110	13	13	13	5	0	2.97
August	25	168.2	150	88	134	16	8	10	6	0	3.74
Sept/Oct	22	146.2	116	57	109	26	5	8	6	0	3.19

vs. Opponent Batters	Ave.	OBP	SLG	AB	H	2B	3B	HR	RBI	BB	SO
Totals	.235	.316	.363	3321	779	140	18	83	337	395	654
vs. Left	.233	.310	.351	1774	414	82	12	34	168	198	332
vs. Right	.236	.323	.376	1547	365	58	6	49	169	197	322
Bases Empty	.245	.321	.378	1961	480	78	11	54	54	219	392
Leadoff	.251	.321	.383	838	210	28	4	25	25	86	168
Not Leadoff	.240	.321	.375	1123	270	50	7	29	29	133	224
Runners On Base	.220	.309	.340	1360	299	62	7	29	283	176	262
First Base Only	.231	.295	.358	593	137	28	4	13	40	54	110
Scoring Position	.211	.319	.326	767	162	34	3	16	243	122	152
Late Innings, Close	.252	.341	.368	329	83	17	0	7	30	45	50

RBI/Opportunities

Scoring Position	61 / 267 (23%)	213 / 1049 (20%)
Scoring Position, 2 Out	26 / 128 (20%)	81 / 498 (16%)
On Third, Less than 2 Out	21 / 49 (43%)	81 / 172 (47%)
RBI in close games / RBI Total	74 / 98 (76%)	250 / 337 (74%)

Danny Darwin
Houston Astros

Houston sure got a steal when they got Darwin from the Brewers. They wanted another pitcher for the pennant drive in '86, and were able to get Darwin dirt cheap, giving up a couple of mediocre minor leaguers, neither of whom played for Milwaukee last year. Not only did Darwin contribute to Houston's division title in 1986, which would have been enough to justify the trade, he's out to keep producing dividends for the Stro's for some time to come.

Supposedly the Brewers dumped Darwin because he did not fit into their youth movement. Consider that Darwin was only 30 at the time of the trade, and had established himself as a respectable pitcher both as a starter and out of the bullpen, and you realize the trade's purpose was to cut Milwaukee's payroll. The Brewmeisters may have saved themselves a couple of bucks, but now that the youth movement is starting to bloom, it's a shame that they don't have Danny Darwin to lend experience to their rotation.

Darwin is a consistent pitcher, who will get 10 to 15 wins for you, and on the Brewers (in '87 at least), that's good enough to be the number 2 starter. Down in Houston, they have a bit more pitching, but they have to be more than happy with Danny Darwin as their fourth man, and quite possibly still will be long after the Brewers have forgotten Mark Knudson and Don August, but, they were cheap.

It's pretty hard to have too much pitching, and, believe me, the Brewers have never suffered from such a problem; if they keep making deals like the Darwin trade, they never will. The Brewers could have used Darwin in '87, when they struggled to keep their team ERA under 5.00 and were forced to use retreads like Ray Burris, Len Barker, and Paul Mirabella. Yet, in '87, the Brewers managed to win 91 games and finish only 6 games out. Who knows what would have happened if the Brewers would have had Darwin, and his 10 to 15 wins? It ain't nice to second guess, but every year of the next 5 in which the Brewers wind up falling a few well-pitched games short of a flag, we can all wonder what if Harry Dalton wouldn't have been pinching pennies way back in '86. (Even if you disagree with the premise that Harry Dalton was pinching "pennies" when he traded Darwin, it is pretty hard at this point to look very kindly upon this trade. Mark Knudson can not even be labeled a "suspect" any more, and August can only be labeled as a fair prospect.)

Admittedly, Darwin has been helped by the Astrodome, especially considering his tendency to give up the long ball. Darwin's win-loss record could also be knocked, but if you look at the run support he's received, his record is really pretty good, and there is no reason he couldn't win 15+ for a team like the Brewers; that could be the difference between being an exciting young ball club and being an exciting young championship ball club.

Kent Kirchstein

Darwin, Danny Wayne   Bats: Right   Throws: Right   Born 10/25/55

1987 SEASON AND MAJOR-LEAGUE CAREER PITCHING TOTALS

	G	GS	CG	GF	IP	BFP	H	R	ER	HR	SH	SF	HB	TBB	IBB	SO	WP	Bk	W	L	Pct	ShO	Sv	ERA
87 HOU	33	30	3	0	196	833	184	87	78	17	8	3	5	69	12	134	3	1	9	10	.474	1	0	3.58
10 YEARS	328	171	41	98	1437	6058	1359	658	568	122	57	53	34	469	44	923	27	4	81	88	.479	8	17	3.56

1987: Finesse, Flyball   1986: Finesse, Flyball   1985: Finesse, Flyball   1984: Finesse, Flyball

	1987 SEASON											FOUR YEAR TOTALS (1984 – 1987)										
	G	IP	H	BB	SO	SB	CS	W	L	S	ERA	G	IP	H	BB	SO	SB	CS	W	L	S	ERA
Totals	33	195.2	184	69	134	28	7	9	10	0	3.59	146	821.2	815	232	502	83	26	36	50	2	3.65
at Home	16	99.0	92	40	74	18	3	5	4	0	3.09	68	388.2	392	127	247	43	12	13	28	1	3.45
on Road	17	96.2	92	29	60	10	4	4	6	0	4.10	78	433.0	423	105	255	40	14	23	22	1	3.82
on Grass	10	54.1	45	14	39	5	3	2	3	0	3.31	48	233.0	235	68	164	31	9	11	19	1	3.90
on Artificial Turf	23	141.1	139	55	95	23	4	7	7	0	3.69	98	588.2	580	164	338	52	17	25	31	1	3.55
Day Games	9	48.0	38	15	33	5	2	1	1	0	3.38	101	561.2	548	157	335	48	18	22	34	2	3.61
Night Games	24	147.2	146	54	101	23	5	8	9	0	3.66	45	260.0	267	75	167	35	8	14	16	0	3.70
April	4	28.0	27	11	21	1	3	1	1	0	2.89	19	104.0	92	29	57	13	3	6	3	0	2.94
May	6	30.2	37	11	23	4	1	1	3	0	4.99	25	139.0	151	38	74	13	3	6	8	0	4.08
June	7	38.2	29	14	24	7	0	2	0	0	2.33	24	155.2	158	41	97	17	6	7	8	0	3.76
July	7	49.0	38	10	35	3	1	3	3	0	3.49	26	171.1	154	52	103	13	6	6	12	0	3.36
August	6	31.0	42	12	20	5	1	1	2	0	4.65	22	127.0	139	36	88	9	5	4	11	0	4.11
Sept/Oct	3	18.1	11	11	11	8	1	1	1	0	3.44	30	124.2	121	36	83	18	3	7	8	2	3.54

vs. Opponent Batters	Ave.	OBP	SLG	AB	H	2B	3B	HR	RBI	BB	SO	Ave.	OBP	SLG	AB	H	2B	3B	HR	RBI	BB	SO
Totals	.246	.313	.374	748	184	35	5	17	69	69	134	.257	.309	.395	3169	815	140	19	86	358	232	502
vs. Left	.269	.343	.435	372	100	19	5	11	38	41	56	.283	.348	.453	1602	454	89	12	53	201	157	217
vs. Right	.223	.282	.314	376	84	16	0	6	31	28	78	.230	.267	.335	1567	361	51	7	33	157	75	285
Bases Empty	.232	.300	.387	444	103	24	3	13	13	40	80	.241	.290	.386	1894	456	92	9	55	55	127	309
Leadoff	.207	.277	.303	188	39	6	0	4	4	16	32	.238	.285	.380	789	188	37	3	23	23	49	119
Not Leadoff	.250	.317	.449	256	64	18	3	9	9	24	48	.243	.293	.390	1105	268	55	6	32	32	78	190
Runners On Base	.266	.331	.355	304	81	11	2	4	56	29	54	.282	.336	.408	1275	359	48	10	31	303	105	193
First Base Only	.305	.346	.430	128	39	3	2	3	11	7	19	.296	.340	.451	537	159	18	4	19	54	35	73
Scoring Position	.239	.322	.301	176	42	8	0	1	45	22	35	.271	.334	.377	738	200	30	6	12	249	70	120
Late Innings, Close	.317	.377	.492	63	20	6	1	1	7	5	10	.281	.332	.446	395	111	18	4	13	50	29	58

RBI/Opportunities

Scoring Position	43 / 224	(19%)	225 / 948	(24%)
Scoring Position, 2 Out	17 / 119	(14%)	101 / 459	(22%)
On Third, Less than 2 Out	16 / 30	(53%)	76 / 153	(50%)
RBI in close games / RBI Total	54 / 69	(78%)	263 / 358	(73%)

Alvin Davis
Seattle Mariners

After his Rookie of the Year season in 1984, Alvin Davis's production, and especially his defense, dropped off disappointingly the next two seasons. A problem with his eyesight seemed to be the reason, but experiments with both glasses and contact lenses proved to be fruitless. In 1986 Alvin committed fifteen errors, and things had eroded so much for him defensively that he was being erratically platooned at first with Ken Phelps—another lefthander—or being replaced in late inning situations by outfielder John Moses. It was an embarrassing and insulting arrangement for Alvin, and he eventually lost his confidence during this frustrating turn of events.

The Mariners were just as frustrated and there was talk of a trade or of making Davis the permanent DH. Then, just before spring training started in 1987, Alvin was fitted with a special lens for his left eye. According to Davis' optometrist, Dr. Douglas Nikaitani, Alvin has an irregularly shaped cornea. He's not sure why or how, but obviously the problem cropped up after his great '84 season. The special lens has made such an amazing and dramatic improvement in Alvin's sight that he now has 20/15 vision in both eyes.

Because of the lens, Alvin's 1987 season was his best since his big rookie debut, and perhaps even better. He produced more homers, doubles, and hits, and reached his 100th RBI on the last day of the season. He was turning so well on the ball that the old 1984 "Alvin Davis Shift" to the extreme right was reinstated by many teams.

Just as important to Alvin was regaining his starting role as the Mariner first baseman. Alvin, himself, admits that his range at first is not the best; he knows that he can't get to some of the plays that a Mattingly can. However, due to the improved depth perception, he's confident now that he can catch what's in his reach. Before, his perception had gotten so bad that the ball just wasn't where he thought it should be, making him look rather foolish on a consistent basis. The defensive blunders disappeared after the new lens and Alvin is playing a solid first base again.

His only weakness now is being the slowest 28-year-old player in the league. It looks like he'll just have to live with his lack of speed—unless someone, somewhere, comes up with a special pair of shoes.

Merrianna McCully

Davis, Alvin Glenn Bats: Left Throws: Right Born 09/09/60

1987 SEASON AND MAJOR-LEAGUE CAREER BATTING TOTALS

	G	AB	H	2B	3B	HR	TB	R	RBI	TBB	IBB	SO	HP	SH	SF	SB	CS	SB%	GDP	AVG	OBP	SLG
87 SEA	157	580	171	37	2	29	299	86	100	72	6	84	2	0	8	0	0	.00	17	.295	.370	.516
4 YEARS	599	2204	628	122	7	92	1040	310	366	335	39	301	14	2	24	6	9	.40	49	.285	.379	.472

	1987 SEASON											FOUR YEAR TOTALS (1984 – 1987)										
	Ave.	OBP	SLG	AB	H	2B	3B	HR	RBI	BB	SO	Ave.	OBP	SLG	AB	H	2B	3B	HR	RBI	BB	SO
Totals	.294	.370	.514	582	171	37	2	29	100	72	84	.285	.379	.471	2206	628	122	7	92	366	335	301
vs. Left	.240	.301	.380	208	50	14	0	5	26	19	38	.254	.350	.367	712	181	36	1	14	100	104	118
vs. Right	.324	.406	.588	374	121	23	2	24	74	53	46	.299	.393	.521	1494	447	86	6	78	266	231	183
at Home	.306	.402	.568	278	85	17	1	18	55	44	39	.294	.398	.520	1101	324	62	6	58	202	183	134
on Road	.283	.339	.464	304	86	20	1	11	45	28	45	.275	.360	.424	1105	304	60	1	34	164	152	167
vs. Groundball	.297	.368	.510	306	91	19	2	14	49	34	52	.301	.394	.464	1058	318	57	4	36	155	162	147
vs. Flyball	.290	.372	.518	276	80	18	0	15	51	38	32	.270	.365	.478	1148	310	65	3	56	211	173	154
vs. Finesse	.307	.371	.549	319	98	18	1	19	56	33	34	.295	.376	.474	1280	378	65	4	52	205	167	146
vs. Power	.278	.369	.471	263	73	19	1	10	44	39	50	.270	.383	.468	926	250	57	4	40	161	168	155
on Grass	.303	.359	.496	234	71	18	0	9	38	22	31	.274	.355	.435	848	232	47	0	30	130	110	129
on Artificial Turf	.287	.377	.526	348	100	19	2	20	62	50	53	.292	.394	.494	1358	396	75	7	62	236	225	172
Day Games	.267	.320	.447	161	43	12	1	5	30	13	23	.269	.365	.405	553	149	29	2	14	80	84	81
Night Games	.304	.388	.539	421	128	25	1	24	70	59	61	.290	.384	.494	1653	479	93	5	78	286	251	220
April	.250	.337	.382	76	19	7	0	1	9	11	15	.281	.376	.506	263	74	15	1	14	39	41	39
May	.337	.405	.459	98	33	6	0	2	13	12	17	.315	.428	.492	356	112	22	1	13	61	71	57
June	.304	.393	.478	92	28	5	1	3	14	14	12	.260	.356	.411	389	101	18	1	13	68	59	43
July	.337	.394	.673	98	33	7	1	8	18	9	9	.310	.393	.481	345	107	15	1	14	54	47	33
August	.296	.406	.583	108	32	7	0	8	26	20	12	.308	.396	.529	412	127	28	0	21	73	60	54
Sept/Oct	.236	.280	.473	110	26	5	0	7	20	6	19	.243	.330	.426	441	107	24	3	17	71	57	75
Bases Empty	.296	.360	.486	311	92	21	1	12	12	30	48	.285	.366	.461	1190	339	66	3	46	46	152	161
Leadoff	.328	.367	.626	131	43	15	0	8	8	8	17	.300	.362	.496	450	135	33	2	17	17	44	48
Not Leadoff	.272	.355	.383	180	49	6	1	4	4	22	31	.276	.369	.441	740	204	33	1	29	29	108	113
Runners On	.292	.381	.546	271	79	16	1	17	88	42	36	.284	.392	.483	1016	289	56	4	46	320	183	140
First Base Only	.349	.432	.624	109	38	6	0	8	19	16	17	.300	.376	.493	416	125	25	2	17	50	50	57
Scoring Position	.253	.349	.494	162	41	10	1	9	69	26	19	.273	.403	.477	600	164	31	2	29	270	133	83
Late Innings, Close	.274	.386	.507	73	20	5	0	4	11	14	4	.253	.384	.433	312	79	15	1	13	43	67	34

RBI/Opportunities

Scoring Position	53 / 222 (24%)	210 / 884 (24%)
Scoring Position, 2 Out	22 / 107 (21%)	77 / 378 (20%)
On Third, Less than 2 Out	21 / 36 (58%)	87 / 165 (53%)
RBI in close games / RBI Total	60 / 100 (60%)	230 / 366 (63%)

Chili Davis
San Francisco Giants

So, now that we have guaranteed contracts and free agency, the days of the late-season "salary drive" are over, right? Quick, somebody ring Anaheim Stadium and let Chili know.

Chili made an off-the-record remark to a reporter in Philadelphia in 1986, to the effect that he was "going to really put up some numbers in September so I can get out of Candlestick." Well, he sure did. He hit more homers than the previous three months put together, more doubles than the previous two months put together, raised his batting average thirty-eight points above August's, and slugged one hundred and eighty-three points higher than August. Just one catch. The Giants neglected to cooperate during the off-season, so Chili was forced to endure one more miserable season at the 'Stick.

In late '86, Chili blistered San Francisco fans, saying that the team only had "6,000 real fans, with the rest of these (sphincter deleted) just front-running." Well, the 1987 Giants set an all-time franchise attendance record with over 1.9 million, which means that Chili had to endure 1,443,863 of those "other folks" last year. In spite of the "fact" that you "can't put numbers on the board at Candlestick" (*that* must have interested Mays and McCovey), Chili did tie a major league record at the 'Stick, at night on September 15, when he had his second switch-hit homer game of the season. The second blast, hit lefthanded to straightaway center field, nearly dislodged the center field camera from its perch at the base of the scoreboard. Yes, that's right—September—salary drive time. Chili "hit" an abysmal .167 during the Giants pennant push in August; then, as the Giants entered September with a 4+ game lead, and with free agency beckoning, Chili went to work on his market value, hitting nearly 200 points higher than in August.

In his defense, Chili did perform much better on the road—although his batting average was only mildly affected, his HR% was 5.4 on the road, and only 4.0 at home; his RBI/AB swelled from .13 at home to .17 on the road. He hits much better on grass, which should remain constant in Anaheim. Odd trivia: On September 25, as the Giants clinched the division flag against the Padres, both Davis and Leonard hit their 100th career homers. It was Chili's only pinch-hit RBI, and his only pinch-hit extra base hit, in 20 plate appearances. Chili displayed puzzling performance in his non-hitting plate appearances. For the second year in a row, he was in the top 10 in intentional walks, and in the top 15 in total bases on balls; on the other hand, only 3 National League regulars had both a higher strikeout percentage than Chili and hit fewer than 35 homers—Samuel (28 HR, 80 EBH), Parrish (17 HR, 38 EBH), and Andres Galarraga (13 HR, 56 EBH); Chili's numbers: 24 HR, 47 EBH, 21.8% strikeouts. Chili has a lot of talent; we can only hope that he learns a positive attitude in Anaheim.

P.S. Chili had no sac bunts last year—now, that's what I call tailoring your team to your manager's style!

J. Michael Duca

Davis, Charles Theodore "Chili"   Bats: Both   Throws: Right   Born 01/17/60

1987 SEASON AND MAJOR-LEAGUE CAREER BATTING TOTALS

	G	AB	H	2B	3B	HR	TB	R	RBI	TBB	IBB	SO	HP	SH	SF	SB	CS	SB%	GDP	AVG	OBP	SLG
87 SF	149	500	125	22	1	24	221	80	76	72	15	109	2	0	4	16	9	.64	8	.250	.344	.442
7 YEARS	874	3148	840	144	20	101	1327	432	418	361	64	578	6	15	33	95	62	.61	71	.267	.340	.422

	1987 SEASON											FOUR YEAR TOTALS (1984 – 1987)										
	Ave.	OBP	SLG	AB	H	2B	3B	HR	RBI	BB	SO	Ave.	OBP	SLG	AB	H	2B	3B	HR	RBI	BB	SO
Totals	.250	.344	.442	500	125	22	1	24	76	72	109	.278	.359	.444	2006	558	96	12	71	283	260	353
vs. Left	.262	.337	.536	183	48	6	1	14	34	20	48	.248	.302	.408	568	141	21	2	22	78	45	106
vs. Right	.243	.349	.388	317	77	16	0	10	42	52	61	.290	.381	.458	1438	417	75	10	49	205	215	247
at Home	.242	.352	.404	223	54	7	1	9	28	38	50	.276	.358	.426	944	261	43	4	30	127	125	170
on Road	.256	.338	.473	277	71	15	0	15	48	34	59	.280	.360	.460	1062	297	53	8	41	156	135	183
vs. Groundball	.253	.345	.413	225	57	9	0	9	28	31	45	.282	.357	.439	911	257	38	6	31	124	110	131
vs. Flyball	.247	.344	.465	275	68	13	1	15	48	41	64	.275	.361	.448	1095	301	58	6	40	159	150	222
vs. Finesse	.256	.314	.448	250	64	12	0	12	44	21	38	.286	.340	.472	1129	323	52	7	48	174	95	155
vs. Power	.244	.372	.436	250	61	10	1	12	32	51	71	.268	.382	.408	877	235	44	5	23	109	165	198
on Grass	.260	.352	.449	365	95	16	1	17	54	52	81	.280	.362	.436	1480	415	67	7	50	203	195	265
on Artificial Turf	.222	.325	.422	135	30	6	0	7	22	20	28	.272	.352	.466	526	143	29	5	21	80	65	88
Day Games	.254	.357	.459	209	53	11	1	10	25	33	49	.281	.359	.450	937	263	45	6	34	122	121	173
Night Games	.247	.335	.430	291	72	11	0	14	51	39	60	.276	.359	.439	1069	295	51	6	37	161	139	180
April	.302	.365	.453	86	26	4	0	3	14	9	16	.279	.329	.430	298	83	18	0	9	45	23	56
May	.228	.301	.337	101	23	5	0	2	10	11	25	.283	.359	.460	350	99	20	3	12	48	42	53
June	.200	.301	.433	90	18	3	0	6	14	13	20	.256	.334	.437	394	101	16	5	15	58	46	60
July	.276	.360	.563	87	24	5	1	6	19	11	18	.280	.352	.425	339	95	12	2	11	43	37	63
August	.167	.298	.231	78	13	2	0	1	7	14	18	.260	.372	.402	346	90	15	2	10	45	61	69
Sept/Oct	.362	.486	.724	58	21	3	0	6	12	14	12	.323	.427	.527	279	90	15	0	14	44	51	52
Bases Empty	.233	.300	.404	292	68	14	0	12	12	27	64	.265	.328	.423	1171	310	56	6	39	39	110	206
Leadoff	.252	.330	.515	103	26	3	0	8	8	12	17	.269	.332	.445	479	129	21	3	19	19	45	76
Not Leadoff	.222	.283	.344	189	42	11	0	4	4	15	47	.262	.326	.408	692	181	35	3	20	20	65	130
Runners On	.274	.399	.495	208	57	8	1	12	64	45	45	.297	.403	.474	835	248	40	6	32	244	150	147
First Base Only	.284	.337	.420	88	25	3	0	3	8	6	19	.307	.354	.448	348	107	19	2	11	32	24	56
Scoring Position	.267	.436	.550	120	32	5	1	9	56	39	26	.290	.433	.478	487	141	21	4	21	212	126	91
Late Innings, Close	.241	.393	.414	87	21	3	0	4	17	23	18	.247	.374	.429	364	90	15	3	15	61	75	69

RBI/Opportunities

	1987 SEASON	FOUR YEAR TOTALS
Scoring Position	43 / 186 (23%)	174 / 710 (25%)
Scoring Position, 2 Out	15 / 87 (17%)	57 / 319 (18%)
On Third, Less than 2 Out	15 / 33 (45%)	72 / 137 (53%)
RBI in close games / RBI Total	49 / 76 (64%)	218 / 283 (77%)

Eric Davis
Cincinnati Reds

Eric took a lot of heat for not playing much toward the end of the season and maybe it was deserved. There are a couple of things to consider, though. First, he doesn't seem to be a very good September player anyway. The Reds may not have gained much by having him in the lineup.

Davis is a very intense player and this seems to be taking a toll, but when he's in the game, he's in the game! He did something last season which impressed me as much as anything I've seen in baseball. Bottom of the ninth, score tied, 1 out, Giants on first and third, outfield playing shallow. Hard hit ground ball up the middle, Eric fields the ball on the run, but has no play at the plate. He charges the ball, steps on second base for the force, and threw to first. The batter, to his credit, beat the throw by hustling all the way, but it was a helluva smart play.

Plays like that, and the spectacular catches, robbing Jack Clark and others of home runs, are probably the reason he won the Gold Glove. It wasn't just the highlight film plays, though—Eric led all center fielders in Range Factor with 3.04 (Milt Thompson was second at 2.45) and was second in fielding average at .990.

In the 1986 *GABSB*, my colleague Bill Weydig calls Eric's 1984 and 1985 seasons "fairly unsuccessful trials in the majors." Sorry Bill, but I can't see it. In '84 his pace, over an entire season, would have resulted in 100+ runs and RBI, with about 35 HR and Steals. In '85 the pace was 125+ runs, about 90 RBI and SB and close to 40 HR. The BA and OBA weren't as high as you'd like, and he was striking out too much, but Eric was 22 years old in 1984 and playing for a mediocre team. Who would you rather play?

In Davis' case, as often happens with young players, people focused on what he couldn't do—hit for average, make contact, and get on base a lot—and ignored the many pluses—power, speed, a decent arm, more speed.

In *USA Today*'s "Best, worst in the NL, Sept.-Oct.," Davis had the second "worst" batting, even though he scored 10 runs in 43 AB, a rate of .23 runs/at bat, while NL batting champ Tony Gwynn, rated third best, scored 14 in 98 AB, .14 runs/at bat. Since the point of offense is to score runs, who was "worst" here?

Eric is my favorite player, but it's just silly to compare him to Willie Mays. Through age 25 (Eric's age in '87), Willie's career totals are way ahead despite the fact that Mays missed nearly two seasons due to military service. Davis is a fine player and may produce some Mays-like seasons, but his career totals won't be in the same time zone as Willie's.

Tom Locker

Davis, Eric Keith Bats: Right Throws: Right Born 05/29/62

1987 SEASON AND MAJOR-LEAGUE CAREER BATTING TOTALS

	G	AB	H	2B	3B	HR	TB	R	RBI	TBB	IBB	SO	HP	SH	SF	SB	CS	SB%	GDP	AVG	OBP	SLG
87 CIN	129	474	139	23	4	37	281	120	100	84	8	134	1	0	3	50	6	.89	6	.293	.399	.593
4 YEARS	374	1185	323	51	11	82	642	276	219	183	13	321	3	2	7	156	22	.88	14	.273	.369	.542

1987 SEASON

	Ave.	OBP	SLG	AB	H	2B	3B	HR	RBI	BB	SO
Totals	.291	.397	.589	475	138	23	4	37	101	84	134
vs. Left	.331	.434	.730	148	49	8	0	17	39	27	36
vs. Right	.272	.380	.526	327	89	15	4	20	62	57	98
at Home	.279	.394	.558	233	65	10	2	17	43	44	64
on Road	.302	.399	.620	242	73	13	2	20	58	40	70
vs. Groundball	.343	.435	.618	233	80	13	3	15	50	38	53
vs. Flyball	.240	.361	.562	242	58	10	1	22	51	46	81
vs. Finesse	.331	.412	.669	254	84	17	3	21	52	35	70
vs. Power	.244	.380	.498	221	54	6	1	16	49	49	64
on Grass	.299	.419	.571	147	44	8	1	10	28	31	37
on Artificial Turf	.287	.386	.598	328	94	15	3	27	73	53	97
Day Games	.310	.419	.690	142	44	8	2	14	41	28	37
Night Games	.282	.387	.547	333	94	15	2	23	60	56	97
April	.364	.437	.727	77	28	5	1	7	16	10	19
May	.313	.394	.819	83	26	6	0	12	36	11	21
June	.250	.394	.474	76	19	3	1	4	11	18	22
July	.348	.434	.641	92	32	5	2	6	18	14	27
August	.250	.363	.462	104	26	4	0	6	15	19	30
Sept/Oct	.163	.351	.302	43	7	0	0	2	5	12	15
Bases Empty	.295	.386	.579	271	80	9	1	22	22	39	69
Leadoff	.341	.442	.693	88	30	7	0	8	8	16	14
Not Leadoff	.273	.357	.525	183	50	2	1	14	14	23	55
Runners On	.284	.410	.603	204	58	14	3	15	79	45	65
First Base Only	.306	.410	.576	85	26	6	1	5	13	15	23
Scoring Position	.269	.411	.622	119	32	8	2	10	66	30	42
Late Innings, Close	.205	.359	.452	73	15	3	0	5	21	18	24

FOUR YEAR TOTALS (1984 – 1987)

	Ave.	OBP	SLG	AB	H	2B	3B	HR	RBI	BB	SO
Totals	.272	.369	.540	1186	322	51	11	82	220	183	321
vs. Left	.291	.388	.608	426	124	15	3	38	86	69	105
vs. Right	.261	.358	.503	760	198	36	8	44	134	114	216
at Home	.270	.378	.516	556	150	26	6	33	95	96	146
on Road	.273	.360	.562	630	172	25	5	49	125	87	175
vs. Groundball	.308	.396	.556	613	189	32	9	34	105	90	139
vs. Flyball	.232	.339	.524	573	133	19	2	48	115	93	182
vs. Finesse	.299	.372	.608	635	190	36	8	48	114	73	154
vs. Power	.240	.365	.463	551	132	15	3	34	106	110	167
on Grass	.275	.367	.535	385	106	13	3	27	64	56	88
on Artificial Turf	.270	.369	.543	801	216	38	8	55	156	127	233
Day Games	.292	.393	.627	391	114	17	6	34	91	67	99
Night Games	.262	.357	.498	795	208	34	5	48	129	116	222
April	.244	.317	.508	197	48	7	3	13	26	21	54
May	.267	.335	.612	165	44	8	2	15	49	17	46
June	.317	.431	.579	145	46	7	2	9	25	29	36
July	.305	.393	.575	233	71	17	2	14	40	34	67
August	.258	.384	.475	221	57	6	0	14	38	46	57
Sept/Oct	.249	.354	.520	225	56	6	2	17	42	36	61
Bases Empty	.263	.353	.520	688	181	25	7	46	46	95	167
Leadoff	.268	.354	.559	299	80	15	3	22	22	40	57
Not Leadoff	.260	.353	.491	389	101	10	4	24	24	55	110
Runners On	.283	.389	.568	498	141	26	4	36	174	88	154
First Base Only	.289	.367	.547	201	58	14	1	12	28	25	58
Scoring Position	.279	.403	.582	297	83	12	3	24	146	63	96
Late Innings, Close	.248	.363	.475	202	50	4	0	14	53	37	57

RBI/Opportunities

	1987			Four Year		
Scoring Position	45 / 179	(25%)		102 / 439	(23%)	
Scoring Position, 2 Out	15 / 75	(20%)		45 / 199	(23%)	
On Third, Less than 2 Out	14 / 35	(40%)		29 / 84	(35%)	
RBI in close games / RBI Total	72 / 101	(71%)		154 / 220	(70%)	

Glenn Davis
Houston Astros

Is Glenn Davis the second most valuable player in the NL, or is he just an average first baseman? Nothing personal against this fine young player, but I think the latter description is far more accurate. Compare Davis to a composite of all 12 regular NL first sackers in 1987:

	BA	AB	R	H	2B	3B	HR	RBI	BB	SB
Davis	.251	578	70	145	35	2	27	93	47	4
Composite	.280	578	86	162	32	3	25	94	74	11

Davis is slower, gets on base less often, and scores fewer runs than his peers. His power is at least average, but not clearly superior. Glenn's 1987 numbers were down slightly from 1986, but the difference was minor. In '86 he had 2 more extra-base hits, 8 more RBI, and his average was 1.4 percent higher.

It seems reasonable to reopen the question of why Davis finished 2nd in '86 MVP voting. The most obvious factor is that the Astros had a great year. Another obvious element is that Davis was an interesting story for the media. Less obvious is the lack of attention to other Astros who contributed about as much as Davis to the '86 championship. Based on the Project Scoresheet poll (probably a better yardstick than MVP ballots), Houston in '86 had the league's third best first baseman, third best second baseman, fourth best third baseman, fourth best shortstop, third best left fielder, fourth best right fielder, best starting pitcher, and Dave Smith (relief pitchers were not rated, but he must have been in the top three). How did Glenn Davis manage to stand out in this crowd?

My theory is that Glenn's 17 home runs in the Astrodome impressed more people than any other Astro's accomplishment. The "17" was rare, easy to understand and simple to describe: a sort of Ruthian number, from a team with no Ruths. When the 1965 Dodgers won a world championship with pitching, speed and defense, Lou Johnson and Jim Lefebvre led the team with 12 HR each, proving with their tiny stats that power was not a factor. Glenn Davis simply obfuscated a similar situation in 1986. His 31 HR were extraneous and might have been dismissed, if not for the fluke that 17 of them came in a park where such an output was all but unprecedented. In addition, his RBI count of 101 had a nice sound to it. In all probability, however, Davis' difficult childhood situation probably garnered a few votes, and the mere fact that the Astros had finally produced a legitimate power hitter (as everyone had said they needed for 15 years) and nearly went to the World Series was "proof" that the big slugger must have been the "difference."

Glenn Davis is good enough to be a fixture at first base for several years to come, especially if he remains with Houston. He might even improve some. But he is never going to be an MVP, and not likely to come close again.

John C. Benson

Davis, Glenn Earl Bats: Right Throws: Right Born 03/28/61

1987 SEASON AND MAJOR-LEAGUE CAREER BATTING TOTALS

	G	AB	H	2B	3B	HR	TB	R	RBI	TBB	IBB	SO	HP	SH	SF	SB	CS	SB%	GDP	AVG	OBP	SLG
87 HOU	151	578	145	35	2	27	265	70	93	47	10	84	5	0	5	4	1	.80	16	.251	.310	.458
4 YEARS	427	1563	405	83	5	80	738	218	266	142	22	236	21	4	17	7	2	.78	39	.259	.326	.472

	1987 SEASON											FOUR YEAR TOTALS (1984 – 1987)										
	Ave.	OBP	SLG	AB	H	2B	3B	HR	RBI	BB	SO	Ave.	OBP	SLG	AB	H	2B	3B	HR	RBI	BB	SO
Totals	.251	.310	.458	578	145	35	2	27	93	47	84	.259	.326	.472	1563	405	82	5	80	266	142	236
vs. Left	.244	.323	.477	193	47	13	1	10	28	20	30	.262	.340	.504	581	152	35	2	34	106	64	82
vs. Right	.255	.304	.449	385	98	22	1	17	65	27	54	.258	.317	.452	982	253	47	3	46	160	78	154
at Home	.249	.312	.439	285	71	16	1	12	45	24	41	.280	.343	.486	774	217	39	3	38	141	69	112
on Road	.253	.308	.478	293	74	19	1	15	48	23	43	.238	.308	.458	789	188	43	2	42	125	73	124
vs. Groundball	.263	.332	.511	278	73	17	2	16	51	28	40	.262	.332	.493	741	194	33	3	44	120	67	119
vs. Flyball	.240	.289	.410	300	72	18	0	11	42	19	44	.257	.320	.453	822	211	49	2	36	146	75	117
vs. Finesse	.274	.328	.465	299	82	17	2	12	41	24	40	.282	.341	.502	848	239	44	4	45	146	69	103
vs. Power	.226	.291	.452	279	63	18	0	15	52	23	44	.232	.308	.435	715	166	38	1	35	120	73	133
on Grass	.269	.323	.522	182	49	13	0	11	36	14	24	.243	.305	.447	486	118	27	0	24	74	41	70
on Artificial Turf	.242	.304	.429	396	96	22	2	16	57	33	60	.266	.335	.483	1077	287	55	5	56	192	101	166
Day Games	.237	.297	.441	177	42	12	0	8	21	15	25	.246	.314	.438	480	118	27	1	21	67	44	70
Night Games	.257	.316	.466	401	103	23	2	19	72	32	59	.265	.331	.487	1083	287	55	4	59	199	98	166
April	.247	.256	.393	89	22	4	0	3	9	1	13	.238	.265	.427	164	39	8	1	7	23	6	23
May	.292	.375	.583	96	28	7	0	7	20	14	17	.296	.372	.534	189	56	12	0	11	34	24	30
June	.315	.376	.522	92	29	10	0	3	13	8	12	.283	.335	.502	247	70	16	1	12	36	18	30
July	.223	.272	.404	94	21	3	1	4	15	6	12	.254	.311	.496	276	70	11	1	18	60	23	50
August	.182	.226	.374	99	18	7	0	4	14	5	16	.210	.282	.374	286	60	17	0	10	37	28	41
Sept/Oct	.250	.341	.472	108	27	4	1	6	22	13	14	.274	.348	.494	401	110	18	2	22	76	43	62
Bases Empty	.253	.293	.473	300	76	16	1	16	16	15	40	.256	.301	.479	841	215	41	3	47	47	53	125
Leadoff	.266	.291	.545	143	38	7	0	11	11	4	19	.265	.304	.527	393	104	17	1	28	28	21	54
Not Leadoff	.242	.296	.408	157	38	9	1	5	5	11	21	.248	.299	.438	448	111	24	2	19	19	32	71
Runners On	.248	.327	.442	278	69	19	1	11	77	32	44	.263	.344	.463	722	190	41	2	33	219	89	111
First Base Only	.252	.326	.454	119	30	6	0	6	15	11	16	.254	.327	.484	287	73	15	0	17	44	29	38
Scoring Position	.245	.328	.434	159	39	13	1	5	62	21	28	.269	.355	.448	435	117	26	2	16	175	60	73
Late Innings, Close	.192	.286	.356	104	20	8	0	3	17	13	20	.223	.294	.396	265	59	16	0	10	42	26	56

RBI/Opportunities

Scoring Position	50 / 218 (23%)	143 / 604 (24%)
Scoring Position, 2 Out	23 / 106 (22%)	58 / 295 (20%)
On Third, Less than 2 Out	15 / 39 (38%)	50 / 106 (47%)
RBI in close games / RBI Total	67 / 93 (72%)	186 / 266 (70%)

Jody Davis
Chicago Cubs

For four years, from 1983 to 1986, Jody Davis bore the full brunt of Cub catching duties. He averaged 147 games per year during that stretch, and his second-half offensive totals always tailed off after good starts. The obvious conclusion was that Jody was simply wearing down; if the Cubs could find a reliable back-up and cut Jody back to 120 games or so, his valuable offense should be able to sustain itself longer. In 1987 the acquisition of Jim Sundberg allowed the Cubs to do precisely that. Jody played in a mere 124 games. As a result, how was his offense affected?

Cub fans, the Jody Davis of 1983–87 is as good as we are going to get. He turns 32 in 1988, which means that improvement is highly unlikely. In addition, his 1987 season seems to have shot down the "wearing out" theory. To recap: Jody got off to a good start, as usual. At the end of May he was hitting .282 with 10 homers and a .519 slugging percentage. Following a June slump he was down to usual Jody Davis numbers: .247 batting average, .314 on-base percentage and .414 slugging percentage. These compare evenly with his final season numbers, so he doesn't appear to have worn out. However, it is obvious that the extra rest in 1987 didn't result in greater offensive totals.

Jody's 1987 stats were perfectly in line with previous seasons:

	AVG	OBP	SLG
1987	.248	.331	.418
1986	.250	.300	.428
1985	.232	.300	.400
1984	.256	.315	.418
1983	.271	.315	.480

So Jody's numbers are likely to remain about the same no matter how much rest he gets. Days off, however, are still extremely important to the big redhead's career longevity. One hundred and twenty games per year as opposed to 145 will give Jody a few extra years in the majors. If the Cubs keep him this will be of vital importance.

As I write this, Jody Davis' name is prominent in trade rumors. If I ran the Cubs I would be hesitant to trade him. We all know how rare good catchers are in the major leagues; about half of the teams just get by with two-or three-man platoons. Once in a while these combinations provide excellent results, the most notable example being the Whitt/Martinez platoon Toronto had. More often they are barely adequate. If Jody Davis was traded, the Cub catching situation would suffer terribly. His principal back-up, Jim Sundberg, is close to retirement. Sunny hits just well enough to surprise the opposition once in a blue moon, but at least he can still play defense. The chief youngster waiting in the wings, Damon Berryhill, is an apparently good hitter who has yet to demonstrate any sort of defensive prowess. Jody's offense is decent, even given Wrigley Field inflation. His defense is vital. Unless a quality front-line pitcher could be acquired in trade, Jody Davis should remain a Chicago Cub.

Pat McCormick

Davis, Jody Richard Bats: Right Throws: Right Born 11/12/56

1987 SEASON AND MAJOR-LEAGUE CAREER BATTING TOTALS

	G	AB	H	2B	3B	HR	TB	R	RBI	TBB	IBB	SO	HP	SH	SF	SB	CS	SB%	GDP	AVG	OBP	SLG
87 CHN	125	428	106	12	2	19	179	57	51	52	2	91	2	1	2	1	2	.33	14	.248	.331	.418
7 YEARS	902	3069	777	150	11	116	1297	331	434	278	38	596	7	15	35	7	13	.35	90	.253	.313	.423

	1987 SEASON										FOUR YEAR TOTALS (1984 – 1987)									
	Ave.	OBP	SLG	AB	H	2B	3B	HR	RBI	BB	SO	Ave.	OBP	SLG	AB	H	2B	3B	HR	RBI	BB	SO
Totals	.248	.331	.418	428	106	12	2	19	51	52	91	.247	.311	.417	1961	484	94	6	76	277	188	383
vs. Left	.252	.325	.430	107	27	2	1	5	11	11	19	.248	.316	.437	499	124	31	3	19	61	51	73
vs. Right	.246	.332	.414	321	79	10	1	14	40	41	72	.246	.309	.410	1462	360	63	3	57	216	137	310
at Home	.256	.347	.411	207	53	9	1	7	21	28	41	.265	.335	.456	976	259	50	2	44	162	107	183
on Road	.240	.315	.425	221	53	3	1	12	30	24	50	.228	.286	.379	985	225	44	4	32	115	81	200
vs. Groundball	.230	.328	.343	178	41	3	1	5	15	25	32	.260	.329	.419	921	239	49	4	30	143	99	177
vs. Flyball	.260	.332	.472	250	65	9	1	14	36	27	59	.236	.294	.415	1040	245	45	2	46	134	89	206
vs. Finesse	.234	.313	.395	256	60	9	1	10	28	29	49	.246	.303	.405	1119	275	52	3	40	151	98	186
vs. Power	.267	.357	.453	172	46	3	1	9	23	23	42	.248	.321	.433	842	209	42	3	36	126	90	197
on Grass	.257	.345	.444	304	78	10	1	15	37	40	64	.252	.320	.432	1410	356	70	3	59	208	144	274
on Artificial Turf	.226	.295	.355	124	28	2	1	4	14	12	27	.232	.287	.379	551	128	24	3	17	69	44	109
Day Games	.247	.336	.382	259	64	9	1	8	29	34	52	.258	.327	.431	1268	327	64	3	50	198	135	227
Night Games	.249	.323	.473	169	42	3	1	11	22	18	39	.227	.280	.391	693	157	30	3	26	79	53	156
April	.333	.385	.600	60	20	4	0	4	10	5	10	.292	.347	.460	250	73	15	0	9	38	21	48
May	.250	.308	.469	96	24	1	1	6	14	8	14	.252	.317	.477	365	92	15	2	21	61	35	72
June	.181	.274	.217	83	15	3	0	0	3	10	21	.256	.328	.407	332	85	19	2	9	52	35	62
July	.250	.366	.400	60	15	1	1	2	7	11	11	.215	.263	.350	349	75	13	2	10	34	23	61
August	.299	.389	.558	77	23	2	0	6	15	12	21	.221	.294	.401	344	76	17	0	15	49	36	69
Sept/Oct	.173	.271	.250	52	9	1	0	1	2	6	14	.259	.339	.417	321	83	15	0	12	43	38	71
Bases Empty	.282	.362	.508	238	67	7	1	15	15	28	55	.253	.314	.425	1045	264	47	2	43	43	92	223
Leadoff	.274	.371	.476	84	23	5	0	4	4	12	15	.254	.314	.421	413	105	24	0	15	15	35	78
Not Leadoff	.286	.357	.526	154	44	2	1	11	11	16	40	.252	.314	.427	632	159	23	2	28	28	57	145
Runners On	.205	.292	.305	190	39	5	1	4	36	24	36	.240	.312	.408	916	220	47	4	33	234	96	160
First Base Only	.213	.280	.347	75	16	4	0	2	5	7	12	.260	.309	.445	393	102	23	1	16	39	28	62
Scoring Position	.200	.299	.278	115	23	1	1	2	31	17	24	.226	.314	.380	523	118	24	3	17	195	68	98
Late Innings, Close| .359	.406	.625	64	23	2	0	5	11	4	12	.240	.313	.377	329	79	9	0	12	44	34	75

RBI/Opportunities

Scoring Position	28 / 152 (18%)	164 / 723 (23%)
Scoring Position, 2 Out	12 / 72 (17%)	60 / 339 (18%)
On Third, Less than 2 Out	10 / 29 (34%)	63 / 128 (49%)
RBI in close games / RBI Total	31 / 51 (61%)	160 / 277 (58%)

Mike Davis
Oakland Athletics

It is both exhilarating and frustrating to be a fan of Mike Davis. He is a tremendously gifted athlete who has long streaks where he produces superstar numbers. His problem is he has been chronically inconsistent. If anyone ever does a book about streaks, slumps, and great half-seasons, Mike will have his own chapter.

Davis is known for his combination of power and speed. In 1987 only five AL players (Joe Carter, Kirk Gibson, Lloyd Moseby, Alan Trammell, and Devon White) surpassed him in homers and steals. The crazy footnote is that Davis basically accomplished this in just half a season. At the All-Star break no one was ahead of Davis in power-speed numbers, but then he turned in one of the worst extended slumps baseball has ever tolerated.

In the 1st half he hit .292 and actually had a pace to net 40 homers and 106 RBI's. His second half included a .224 average with 2 homers and 19 RBI's. There has been a lot of speculation linking this to injuries, a sore foot from kicking a door, a hand or wrist injury, a knee injury, blah, blah. Hey folks, this is Mike Davis; he doesn't need excuses for a Yin-Yang performance cycle.

Look, he started the season by hitting .229 through May 3, followed by your typical Mike Davis .455 two-week hot streak. His abysmal second half included a dismal .136 period for over a month, but he finished the season with a flash of brilliance as he hit .363 in his final 15 games. If you want to talk cause-and-effect injuries, in the first half he was hospitalized with a concussion and came back with some of his strongest performances of the year. You don't hear anyone suggesting Lasorda bang him over the head with a bat before every game.

It's nice to dream of his playing in 100 percent physical condition or whatever would be necessary to take the extended slumps out of his season. He might hit .300, steal 40 bases, hit 40 homers, and knock in 120 runs. But it ain't going to happen. A warning to Dodger fans: To keep your sanity you have to learn to live with the wild fluctuations in his level of his play. If you do that, you'll eventually appreciate him as a ballplayer who will, by the bottom line, give you a pretty nice season.

John C. Benson

Davis, Michael Dwayne "Mike" Bats: Left Throws: Left Born 06/11/59

1987 SEASON AND MAJOR-LEAGUE CAREER BATTING TOTALS

	G	AB	H	2B	3B	HR	TB	R	RBI	TBB	IBB	SO	HP	SH	SF	SB	CS	SB%	GDP	AVG	OBP	SLG
87 OAK	139	494	131	32	1	22	231	69	72	42	5	94	1	4	6	19	7	.73	13	.265	.320	.468
8 YEARS	788	2545	680	143	13	84	1101	369	335	195	18	450	10	22	25	121	48	.72	47	.267	.319	.433

	1987 SEASON											FOUR YEAR TOTALS (1984 – 1987)										
	Ave.	OBP	SLG	AB	H	2B	3B	HR	RBI	BB	SO	Ave.	OBP	SLG	AB	H	2B	3B	HR	RBI	BB	SO
Totals	.266	.320	.469	493	131	32	1	22	72	42	94	.265	.319	.448	1911	507	112	8	74	255	157	350
vs. Left	.278	.326	.500	126	35	8	1	6	28	10	31	.270	.322	.467	471	127	28	4	19	80	35	115
vs. Right	.262	.319	.458	367	96	24	0	16	44	32	63	.264	.319	.442	1440	380	84	4	55	175	122	235
at Home	.262	.318	.451	233	61	17	0	9	31	21	45	.262	.327	.453	900	236	54	5	36	119	91	158
on Road	.269	.323	.485	260	70	15	1	13	41	21	49	.268	.313	.444	1011	271	58	3	38	136	66	192
vs. Groundball	.275	.331	.467	255	70	19	0	10	39	23	41	.292	.343	.498	955	279	69	4	40	143	76	157
vs. Flyball	.256	.309	.471	238	61	13	1	12	33	19	53	.238	.296	.399	956	228	43	4	34	112	81	193
vs. Finesse	.244	.293	.440	234	57	11	1	11	33	18	38	.256	.305	.425	1057	271	56	4	38	122	75	170
vs. Power	.286	.345	.494	259	74	21	0	11	39	24	56	.276	.336	.478	854	236	56	4	36	133	82	180
on Grass	.276	.334	.473	402	111	26	1	17	55	37	70	.265	.323	.442	1599	424	89	7	60	207	142	286
on Artificial Turf	.220	.258	.451	91	20	6	0	5	17	5	24	.266	.303	.481	312	83	23	1	14	48	15	64
Day Games	.292	.335	.524	185	54	16	0	9	32	13	28	.266	.328	.476	718	191	48	5	31	115	68	125
Night Games	.250	.312	.435	308	77	16	1	13	40	29	66	.265	.314	.432	1193	316	64	3	43	140	89	225
April	.254	.289	.563	71	18	7	0	5	13	4	12	.273	.314	.527	245	67	20	0	14	41	15	38
May	.325	.385	.687	83	27	7	1	7	17	9	11	.268	.342	.510	314	84	22	3	16	46	36	52
June	.296	.378	.480	98	29	3	0	5	16	13	20	.263	.329	.426	380	100	23	0	13	50	37	74
July	.219	.272	.425	73	16	6	0	3	10	6	19	.237	.281	.404	329	78	17	1	12	41	21	54
August	.205	.267	.269	78	16	5	0	0	8	7	14	.262	.325	.424	302	79	17	1	10	35	29	62
Sept/Oct	.278	.301	.389	90	25	4	0	2	8	3	18	.290	.328	.425	341	99	13	3	9	42	19	70
Bases Empty	.262	.311	.479	282	74	19	0	14	14	19	53	.265	.315	.465	1100	291	67	3	49	49	80	192
Leadoff	.308	.339	.567	104	32	9	0	6	6	5	21	.293	.336	.533	430	126	29	1	24	24	28	67
Not Leadoff	.236	.295	.427	178	42	10	0	8	8	14	32	.246	.302	.421	670	165	38	2	25	25	52	125
Runners On	.270	.332	.455	211	57	13	1	8	58	23	41	.266	.327	.427	811	216	45	5	25	206	77	158
First Base Only	.281	.340	.416	89	25	3	0	3	8	8	15	.286	.336	.440	357	102	17	1	12	31	27	63
Scoring Position	.262	.326	.484	122	32	10	1	5	50	15	26	.251	.321	.416	454	114	28	4	13	175	50	95
Late Innings, Close	.329	.422	.618	76	25	7	0	5	16	13	18	.264	.327	.479	311	82	17	1	16	46	30	69

RBI/Opportunities

Scoring Position	42 / 165 (25%)	150 / 626 (24%)
Scoring Position, 2 Out	20 / 72 (28%)	56 / 292 (19%)
On Third, Less than 2 Out	12 / 28 (43%)	52 / 105 (50%)
RBI in close games / RBI Total	42 / 72 (58%)	148 / 255 (58%)

Andre Dawson
Chicago Cubs

An open letter to Andre Dawson:

Congratulations on that MVP award! Just like you said that day, big guy: "I wanted to convince the baseball world that I would indeed perform better under different circumstances—those circumstances being to get away from the Astroturf and onto a natural playing field." You showed 'em, didn't you? But . . .

I saw that determined glare in your eyes every at bat. Oh, I hated to miss your at bats. Such intensity. I was almost struck with fear as I watched every powerful swing. Mike Schmidt would envy the way you beat poor little Wrigley Field into submission. And there was such fire in your eyes after you had gunned down another foolish baserunner with a perfect rifle throw from right field. You were "possessed" in 1987. But . . .

And I was angry at Peter Gammons' *Sports Illustrated* article (Nov. 30) in which he stated, "Dawson wasn't the most valuable player in the National League." I'd seen you perform all year. I knew better. But . . .

So I set out to use sabermetrics to verify your "obvious" MVP credentials. Thorn and Palmer have the Linear Weights formula (combining the average run value of every offensive event and subtracting the average runs lost value of outs). You contributed about 30 runs better than the average player—outstanding indeed. Boswell uses Total Average (total bases on hits, walks, hit by pitches and stolen bases divided by total outs). Your average was about .88, another fine number. Bill James uses Runs Created (essentially multiplying times on base by total bases and dividing by plate appearances). You earned nearly 114 runs, still superb. But . . .

But . . . Here's the rub, Andre. After doing similar calculations for about 25 other NL players who had good offensive seasons, I must agree with Mr. Gammons. Tony Gwynn had 61, 1.12, and 142 (Linear Weights, Total Average, and Runs Created respectively.) Dale Murphy had 60, 1.12, 136.5; Tim Raines had 56, 1.15, 129; Jack Clark had 61, 1.28, 115; Eric Davis had 54, 1.20, 120. And, I could go on. There's Strawberry, Schmidt, Guerrero, Will Clark, and even Howard Johnson or Andy Van Slyke who had as good a season or better with those numbers. Sorry, big guy, you were great, but others were better.

It must have been the "June swoon." From June 8 to July 4, you hit only .267 (24 of 90) with 3 doubles, no homers, only 8 RBIs, and a feeble slugging percentage of .300. If you were to project your stats for the rest of the season through that time, you would gave hit 58 homers, driven in 153 runs, and scored 102 runs. Wow! What happened for those 4 weeks?

If it's any consolation, Mr. Gammons was wrong in preferring Ozzie Smith or Tim Wallach. Their numbers were way below yours. Even Ozzie's unmistakable, but unmeasurable, defensive skills do not put his 1987 season above yours with your own Gold Glove. You just didn't walk enough (32 in 621 at bats).

Well, I gotta run. Please sign for 1988 with the Cubs. No matter the numbers, you were a thrill in '87. That fire in your eyes. Ooooohh . . .

Robert L. Jones

Dawson, Andre Fernando   **Bats: Right**   **Throws: Right**   **Born 07/10/54**

1987 SEASON AND MAJOR-LEAGUE CAREER BATTING TOTALS

	G	AB	H	2B	3B	HR	TB	R	RBI	TBB	IBB	SO	HP	SH	SF	SB	CS	SB%	GDP	AVG	OBP	SLG
87 CHN	153	621	178	24	2	49	353	90	137	32	7	103	7	0	2	11	3	.79	15	.287	.328	.568
12 YEARS	1596	6249	1753	319	69	274	3032	918	975	386	78	999	69	23	73	264	88	.75	112	.281	.326	.485

	1987 SEASON											FOUR YEAR TOTALS (1984 – 1987)									
	Ave.	OBP	SLG	AB	H	2B	3B	HR	RBI	BB	SO	Ave.	OBP	SLG	AB	H	2B	3B	HR	RBI	BB	SO
Totals	.288	.329	.570	621	179	24	2	49	137	32	103	.269	.316	.479	2179	587	106	12	109	392	138	355
vs. Left	.298	.348	.525	141	42	5	0	9	30	10	22	.296	.347	.537	614	182	31	3	37	110	47	90
vs. Right	.285	.323	.583	480	137	19	2	40	107	22	81	.259	.303	.456	1565	405	75	9	72	282	91	265
at Home	.332	.373	.668	292	97	13	2	27	71	16	47	.274	.324	.485	1040	285	40	7	55	183	71	163
on Road	.249	.291	.483	329	82	11	0	22	66	16	56	.265	.308	.474	1139	302	66	5	54	209	67	192
vs. Groundball	.282	.309	.462	273	77	8	1	13	46	10	39	.277	.323	.454	1001	277	44	5	41	161	67	149
vs. Flyball	.293	.345	.655	348	102	16	1	36	91	22	64	.263	.309	.501	1178	310	62	7	68	231	71	206
vs. Finesse	.283	.316	.547	371	105	13	2	27	75	14	46	.266	.309	.470	1288	343	52	8	65	212	75	161
vs. Power	.296	.348	.604	250	74	11	0	22	62	18	57	.274	.326	.492	891	244	54	4	44	180	63	194
on Grass	.307	.345	.622	423	130	15	2	38	100	21	68	.293	.329	.552	875	256	43	5	58	184	45	149
on Artificial Turf	.247	.296	.460	198	49	9	0	11	37	11	35	.254	.307	.430	1304	331	63	7	51	208	93	206
Day Games	.315	.357	.641	390	123	18	2	35	94	22	66	.305	.354	.581	948	289	46	6	68	208	68	153
Night Games	.242	.282	.450	231	56	6	0	14	43	10	37	.242	.286	.400	1231	298	60	6	41	184	70	202
April	.296	.360	.605	81	24	5	1	6	20	7	13	.308	.373	.575	292	90	14	5	18	56	29	39
May	.273	.302	.518	110	30	3	0	8	21	4	18	.242	.291	.411	384	93	21	1	14	57	26	66
June	.295	.304	.500	112	33	3	1	6	23	1	15	.242	.257	.416	269	65	9	1	12	45	5	42
July	.287	.326	.609	87	25	4	0	8	23	4	13	.265	.313	.434	355	94	15	0	15	64	24	60
August	.309	.361	.736	110	34	2	0	15	28	9	16	.286	.322	.539	419	120	21	2	27	83	22	69
Sept/Oct	.273	.328	.479	121	33	7	0	6	22	7	28	.272	.323	.491	460	125	26	3	23	87	32	79
Bases Empty	.267	.317	.543	311	83	6	1	26	26	19	58	.250	.284	.453	1118	280	46	8	55	55	48	188
Leadoff	.272	.299	.621	103	28	3	0	11	11	4	16	.240	.264	.456	421	101	23	1	22	22	14	60
Not Leadoff	.264	.326	.505	208	55	3	1	15	15	15	42	.257	.295	.452	697	179	23	7	33	33	34	128
Runners On	.310	.341	.597	310	96	18	1	23	111	13	45	.289	.346	.506	1061	307	60	4	54	337	90	167
First Base Only	.282	.288	.519	131	37	7	0	8	20	1	20	.272	.297	.468	412	112	20	2	19	49	15	65
Scoring Position	.330	.378	.654	179	59	11	1	15	91	12	25	.300	.374	.530	649	195	40	2	35	288	75	102
Late Innings, Close	.289	.340	.611	90	26	2	0	9	26	7	12	.257	.315	.450	389	100	14	2	19	75	33	71

RBI/Opportunities

	1987 SEASON		FOUR YEAR TOTALS	
Scoring Position	67 / 227	(30%)	233 / 872	(27%)
Scoring Position, 2 Out	25 / 94	(27%)	86 / 333	(26%)
On Third, Less than 2 Out	25 / 41	(61%)	85 / 177	(48%)
RBI in close games / RBI Total	90 / 137	(66%)	284 / 392	(72%)

Doug DeCinces
California Angels

Aside from the obvious requirement that he remain in good condition with skills essentially intact, an aging hitter needs some other factors to keep his job. The declining player hopes: (1) that there is no younger prospect who can play the same position and produce offensively with such visible skill that fans and management feel compelled to see an honest competition, or (2) that the position of first base will be sufficiently unsettled that a popular veteran can be placed there, or (3) if he is lucky enough to be playing in the American League, that he can become his team's DH.

For Doug DeCinces in 1987, all these factors turned out negative. The Angels produced a promising young third baseman in Jack Howell, whose very appearance seemed to insist that he be given a chance to play. Howell had proven himself unable to hit below .350 in minor league competition, and after shuttling to and from left field, he finally landed the job at third. The Angels' first base job became settled for the next twelve years or more, as far as merit is concerned, when Wally Joyner produced a magnificent season, ending all doubt about the significance of his rookie accomplishments. California was likewise unable to offer the DH assignment to DeCinces, because they had a better and more deserving veteran in Brian Downing. Downing responded very well to DH duty in 1987, producing one of his best seasons ever, and he can expect to keep the DH role full time, as long as he wants it.

DeCinces, symptomatic of the Angels collapse from 1986 heights, came unglued as the season unfolded. His first half was not all bad. Before the All-Star break he hit .241 with 11 HR and 42 RBI, a foundation that might have turned into a successful year. But in the second half, Doug was simply inadequate. He hit .222 with 5 HR and 21 RBI for California. He added one more RBI for St. Louis, while preserving his .222 mark.

Doug's troubles actually started earlier than July. In one eight week stretch encompassing most of May and June, he hit .192 and probably sealed his fate by doing so. Taking a chance on a rookie is not such a daring move when the one replaced has become a liability. As a footnote to his 1987 futility, DeCinces had the highest number of strikeouts in any year of his career, without even counting the ones he picked up for the Cardinals.

After such a struggling season, DeCinces found no takers in his quest for another major league job. Ultimately he signed with the Yakult Swallows of Japan's Central League. For DeCinces it will be a whole new challenge: The man who succeeded Brooks Robinson will now be asked to take the place of Bob Horner.

John C. Benson

DeCinces, Douglas Vernon "Doug"

Bats: Right   Throws: Right   Born 08/29/50

1987 SEASON AND MAJOR-LEAGUE CAREER BATTING TOTALS

	G	AB	H	2B	3B	HR	TB	R	RBI	TBB	IBB	SO	HP	SH	SF	SB	CS	SB%	GDP	AVG	OBP	SLG
87 CAL-STL	137	462	108	25	0	16	181	66	64	70	6	89	2	2	3	3	4	.43	10	.234	.335	.392
15 YEARS	1649	5809	1505	312	29	237	2586	778	879	618	57	904	21	22	64	58	48	.55	176	.259	.329	.445

	1987 SEASON											FOUR YEAR TOTALS (1984 – 1987)										
	Ave.	OBP	SLG	AB	H	2B	3B	HR	RBI	BB	SO	Ave.	OBP	SLG	AB	H	2B	3B	HR	RBI	BB	SO
Totals	.234	.335	.392	462	108	25	0	16	64	70	88	.252	.326	.431	1948	490	90	7	82	320	222	313
vs. Left	.282	.410	.460	163	46	8	0	7	26	36	29	.279	.373	.480	638	178	29	3	31	117	100	89
vs. Right	.207	.291	.355	299	62	17	0	9	38	34	59	.238	.302	.408	1310	312	61	4	51	203	122	224
at Home	.272	.380	.451	235	64	12	0	10	34	40	36	.263	.344	.451	968	255	38	3	46	158	121	143
on Road	.194	.287	.330	227	44	13	0	6	30	30	52	.240	.308	.411	980	235	52	4	36	162	101	170
vs. Groundball	.272	.359	.401	217	59	13	0	5	29	29	36	.287	.357	.462	938	269	47	3	37	160	104	138
vs. Flyball	.200	.315	.384	245	49	12	0	11	35	41	52	.219	.298	.403	1010	221	43	4	45	160	118	175
vs. Finesse	.268	.331	.509	228	61	13	0	14	40	22	39	.260	.316	.460	1062	276	48	4	52	187	91	144
vs. Power	.201	.339	.278	234	47	12	0	2	24	48	49	.242	.337	.397	886	214	42	3	30	133	131	169
on Grass	.246	.357	.401	374	92	19	0	13	51	64	66	.257	.335	.440	1614	414	69	7	71	268	195	240
on Artificial Turf	.182	.234	.352	88	16	6	0	3	13	6	22	.228	.282	.389	334	76	21	0	11	52	27	73
Day Games	.229	.345	.364	140	32	7	0	4	12	24	23	.255	.338	.426	552	141	24	2	22	81	70	87
Night Games	.236	.331	.404	322	76	18	0	12	52	46	65	.250	.321	.433	1396	349	66	5	60	239	152	226
April	.293	.440	.466	58	17	4	0	2	12	15	12	.269	.350	.456	316	85	18	1	13	62	39	41
May	.189	.277	.333	90	17	4	0	3	11	11	17	.210	.290	.349	295	62	11	0	10	33	33	45
June	.209	.320	.384	86	18	3	0	4	9	13	19	.243	.330	.411	338	82	16	1	13	46	43	58
July	.282	.400	.400	85	24	4	0	2	12	18	14	.276	.344	.424	337	93	18	1	10	54	36	53
August	.264	.330	.484	91	24	5	0	5	13	9	15	.285	.359	.529	344	98	17	2	21	75	40	51
Sept/Oct	.154	.214	.250	52	8	5	0	0	7	4	11	.220	.289	.406	318	70	10	2	15	50	31	65
Bases Empty	.238	.323	.410	261	62	15	0	10	10	33	42	.250	.324	.434	1002	250	53	3	42	42	110	141
Leadoff	.291	.386	.527	110	32	8	0	6	6	17	20	.272	.345	.467	430	117	22	1	20	20	48	56
Not Leadoff	.199	.275	.325	151	30	7	0	4	4	16	22	.233	.308	.409	572	133	31	2	22	22	62	85
Runners On	.229	.350	.368	201	46	10	0	6	54	37	46	.254	.333	.428	946	240	37	4	40	278	112	172
First Base Only	.254	.351	.284	67	17	2	0	0	1	9	13	.257	.309	.422	377	97	15	1	15	38	27	65
Scoring Position	.216	.349	.410	134	29	8	0	6	53	28	33	.251	.348	.432	569	143	22	3	25	240	85	107
Late Innings, Close	.205	.341	.342	73	15	4	0	2	7	15	16	.258	.331	.402	326	84	12	1	11	48	36	57

RBI/Opportunities

	1987 Season	Four Year Totals
Scoring Position	40 / 188 (21%)	193 / 797 (24%)
Scoring Position, 2 Out	16 / 83 (19%)	67 / 347 (19%)
On Third, Less than 2 Out	15 / 40 (38%)	84 / 165 (51%)
RBI in close games / RBI Total	40 / 64 (63%)	216 / 320 (68%)

Jeff Dedmon
Atlanta Braves

It is difficult to see why Jeff Dedmon doesn't get a chance in Atlanta. His entire career has been spent in the thankless middle relief role, a role that does not particularly suit him. Dedmon throws four different pitches with below-average control and did not perform well in 1987 when called on with men on base. But on a team that allowed a staggering 829 runs, Dedmon was limited to 90.1 innings despite a 3.89 ERA and allowing only 8.19 hits per nine innings (league average 8.95). In the disaster that was the Braves' 1987, one would think that Tanner would give Dedmon an extended opportunity to show what he could do. With his stuff, he is much better suited to be a fifth starter than a long reliever.

Dedmon made 50 relief appearances for Atlanta last season. His longest outing of the year in relief was 3 2/3 innings (3 times). He pitched 3 innings or longer only 4 times. He had 4 saves, and in another 7 games he finished the game but, due to a loss or a blowout, did not qualify for a save. In most of his remaining 39 relief outings, he came in to bail out the starting pitcher only to be lifted for a pinch hitter within 2 innings. He allowed 2 or more earned runs in only 5 outings. Not great, but then again, not too bad, especially on a staff as pitiful as the Braves'. He struggled a little bit with his control (42 BB, 40 Ks), but he gave up slightly fewer hits than innings pitched (82 hits, 90 1/3 IP), so he pitched at least average compared to other long relievers.

So why did he receive only 3 starts for a team struggling to stay out of last place in the NL West? Granted, he was 0–1 with an ERA of 9.00 in the 3 starts, but how many pitchers make the transition from relief to starting smoothly and quickly? What did Tanner have to lose by giving Dedmon a few more starts? Maybe he could have found a starting pitcher for 1988 (thereby doubling the Braves total).

The Braves intend to commit to a young pitching staff in 1988. With the exception of Zane Smith, the entire rotation could consist of pitchers with very limited professional experience. Derek Lilliquist, Chuck Cary, Tom Glavine, Pete Smith, and Kevin Coffman give the Braves plenty of candidates for the staff, but if two of them pan out the Braves will be lucky. Force feeding young pitchers en masse to the majors is bad baseball—just ask a Cubs fan. A hitters' park like Fulton County Stadium is no place for a young pitcher to develop confidence.

As a result of the youth movement, the Braves will probably use Dedmon in middle relief again. Both Dedmon and Charlie Puleo (another decent pitcher not getting a chance from Tanner) could probably be had from the Braves for two broken bats and a pine tar rag to be named later. Both would benefit from a trade. Jeff Dedmon is not a great pitcher, but he could contribute in a different situation.

Greg Gajus, Doug White

Dedmon, Jeffrey Linden "Jeff"　　　　Bats: Left　　Throws: Right　　Born 03/04/60

1987 SEASON AND MAJOR-LEAGUE CAREER PITCHING TOTALS

	G	GS	CG	GF	IP	BFP	H	R	ER	HR	SH	SF	HB	TBB	IBB	SO	WP	Bk	W	L	Pct	ShO	Sv	ERA
87 ATL	53	3	0	14	90	384	82	46	39	8	2	5	1	42	1	40	2	1	3	4	.429	0	4	3.90
5 YEARS	229	3	0	70	361	1562	352	186	151	27	23	10	8	165	29	193	10	4	19	16	.543	0	11	3.76

1987: Finesse, Groundball　　　1986: Finesse, Groundball　　　1985: Power, Groundball　　　1984: Power, Groundball

	1987 SEASON										FOUR YEAR TOTALS (1984 – 1987)									
	G	IP	H	BB	SO	SB	CS	W	L	S	ERA	G	IP	H	BB	SO	SB	CS	W	L	S	ERA
Totals	53	90.1	82	42	40	19	4	3	4	4	3.89	224	357.0	342	165	190	51	11	19	16	11	3.66
at Home	29	45.0	43	20	21	10	2	2	1	3	3.80	121	190.0	192	71	107	24	7	9	6	6	3.41
on Road	24	45.1	39	22	19	9	2	1	3	1	3.97	103	167.0	150	94	83	27	4	10	10	5	3.93
on Grass	24	35.1	43	18	16	7	1	1	1	2	6.11	80	122.1	117	70	59	17	4	8	4	4	4.41
on Artificial Turf	29	55.0	39	24	24	12	3	2	3	2	2.45	144	234.2	225	95	131	34	7	11	12	7	3.26
Day Games	41	69.2	63	32	33	17	4	2	3	3	3.62	177	284.2	268	134	156	43	9	15	12	9	3.41
Night Games	12	20.2	19	10	7	2	0	1	1	1	4.79	47	72.1	74	31	34	8	2	4	4	2	4.60
April	8	10.2	10	4	4	0	1	0	0	0	6.75	23	36.1	34	17	27	7	1	0	1	2	4.21
May	12	20.0	15	6	7	7	0	2	1	2	2.25	41	69.2	66	29	36	13	0	8	1	5	3.62
June	9	19.0	12	7	12	2	1	0	1	2	1.42	37	61.2	43	25	35	6	2	3	3	3	1.75
July	8	13.2	11	9	4	4	1	1	1	0	1.32	42	65.1	68	34	33	12	5	2	5	0	3.17
August	8	18.0	24	12	9	4	0	0	1	0	8.00	37	60.2	67	30	33	6	1	3	4	0	5.04
Sept/Oct	8	9.0	10	4	4	2	1	0	0	0	5.00	44	63.1	64	30	26	7	2	3	2	1	4.41

vs. Opponent Batters	Ave.	OBP	SLG	AB	H	2B	3B	HR	RBI	BB	SO	Ave.	OBP	SLG	AB	H	2B	3B	HR	RBI	BB	SO
Totals	.246	.327	.368	334	82	13	2	8	53	42	40	.257	.338	.360	1333	342	48	6	26	184	165	190
vs. Left	.222	.311	.323	158	35	2	1	4	21	22	14	.250	.350	.360	625	156	17	5	14	83	98	84
vs. Right	.267	.342	.409	176	47	11	1	4	32	20	26	.263	.326	.360	708	186	31	1	12	101	67	106
Bases Empty	.220	.303	.298	168	37	4	0	3	3	19	20	.262	.326	.360	669	175	25	1	13	13	63	98
Leadoff	.271	.386	.343	70	19	2	0	1	1	13	5	.272	.353	.373	287	78	12	1	5	5	36	33
Not Leadoff	.184	.238	.265	98	18	2	0	2	2	6	15	.254	.305	.351	382	97	13	0	8	8	27	65
Runners On Base	.271	.351	.440	166	45	9	2	5	50	23	20	.252	.349	.360	664	167	23	5	13	171	102	92
First Base Only	.313	.343	.531	64	20	3	1	3	8	3	7	.263	.304	.391	243	64	8	1	7	18	14	36
Scoring Position	.245	.354	.382	102	25	6	1	2	42	20	13	.245	.372	.342	421	103	15	4	6	153	88	56
Late Innings, Close	.281	.377	.371	89	25	5	0	1	11	15	10	.266	.358	.352	418	111	18	0	6	45	61	69

RBI/Opportunities

Scoring Position	36 / 148 (24%)	138 / 651 (21%)
Scoring Position, 2 Out	23 / 75 (31%)	62 / 309 (20%)
On Third, Less than 2 Out	11 / 25 (44%)	52 / 115 (45%)
RBI in close games / RBI Total	25 / 53 (47%)	81 / 184 (44%)

Rob Deer
Milwaukee Brewers

What a difference a year makes. In 1986, with Milwaukee floundering, Rob Deer was the toast of Milwaukee. He was "the new Gorman Thomas"—a low-average, high-power hitter who came out of nowhere to establish himself as a fine player. In 1987, with Milwaukee surging, he was a bust— a man who didn't live up to the promise of 1986.

At least in the eyes of the Milwaukee media, he was; if you look at his 1987 stats, it's a lot harder to see the bust. Deer didn't improve his batting average any, but you had to really be an optimist to expect that. True, his slugging percentage was down 38 points—in the year of the homer, no less—but .456 is still comfortably above the productive point. The plus was Deer's improved strike zone judgement; his on-base percentage was .360 in 1987. That was 20 points higher than in 1986 and four points better than Thomas ever did.

Did you snigger at the words "improved strike zone judgement"? If so, then you're not alone. Deer has a real image problem—because he strikes out a lot and doesn't hit for a high average, people often assume that he's a very impatient hitter who does nothing but swing hard.

That apparently includes his manager; Tom Trebelhorn does not seem to be impressed by Deer at all. Toward the end of the season, Deer was benched for 3–5 games on several occasions so that Mike Felder could play. That doesn't make much sense for two reasons. First, Deer is a streak hitter—when you bench him, you reduce the chance that he'll get hot. Second, Felder has all the offensive potential of Rodney Scott.

Are Deer's strikeouts a problem? They're certainly an eyesore, but that's about all. Contrary to popular belief, a strikeout isn't very much worse than any other kind of out. In the 1986 *Baseball Abstract*, Bill James estimated that you lose about one run for every 100 strikeouts. In his career, Deer has struck out 446 times, meaning that he's cost his teams about 4.5 runs by striking out. Since, unlike many power hitters, he doesn't ground into many double plays (eight in 1126 career at-bats) and he runs pretty well (18 steals in 26 tries), you have to wonder if the strikeouts do any damage at all. It would be nice if he could make more contact and bleed out a few cheap hits, but it's not necessary.

Face facts, folks: Rob Deer had a much higher OBP than either Pete Incaviglia or Jose Canseco, a very comparable SLG and is a much better outfielder than either one—if you wouldn't bench those guys, there's no reason to bench Deer. If Trebelhorn just lets Deer play, the results are going to be positive. There are two things that you want a hitter to do— get on base and hit for power—and Deer is very good at both. Now if he could just make contact a bit more often . . .

Kent Kirchstein

Deer, Robert George "Rob" Bats: Right Throws: Right Born 09/29/60

1987 SEASON AND MAJOR-LEAGUE CAREER BATTING TOTALS

	G	AB	H	2B	3B	HR	TB	R	RBI	TBB	IBB	SO	HP	SH	SF	SB	CS	SB%	GDP	AVG	OBP	SLG
87 MIL	134	474	113	15	2	28	216	71	80	86	6	186	5	0	1	12	4	.75	4	.238	.360	.456
4 YEARS	359	1126	255	37	6	72	520	173	189	188	9	446	9	2	6	18	8	.69	8	.226	.340	.462

	1987 SEASON											FOUR YEAR TOTALS (1984 – 1987)									
	Ave.	OBP	SLG	AB	H	2B	3B	HR	RBI	BB	SO	Ave.	OBP	SLG	AB	H	2B	3B	HR	RBI	BB	SO
Totals	.238	.360	.456	474	113	15	2	28	80	86	186	.226	.340	.462	1126	255	37	6	72	189	188	446
vs. Left	.257	.394	.467	152	39	6	1	8	28	35	48	.256	.383	.536	351	90	14	3	26	68	74	113
vs. Right	.230	.344	.450	322	74	9	1	20	52	51	138	.213	.320	.428	775	165	23	3	46	121	114	333
at Home	.228	.332	.409	232	53	7	1	11	34	33	94	.216	.325	.449	566	122	15	3	37	96	89	222
on Road	.248	.386	.500	242	60	8	1	17	46	53	92	.237	.355	.475	560	133	22	3	35	93	99	224
vs. Groundball	.277	.384	.512	242	67	10	1	15	47	38	96	.254	.364	.515	528	134	22	1	38	103	90	210
vs. Flyball	.198	.337	.397	232	46	5	1	13	33	48	90	.202	.319	.415	598	121	15	5	34	86	98	236
vs. Finesse	.223	.340	.409	269	60	6	1	14	39	45	95	.233	.335	.456	662	154	21	2	41	104	98	231
vs. Power	.259	.387	.517	205	53	9	1	14	41	41	91	.218	.347	.470	464	101	16	4	31	85	90	215
on Grass	.236	.356	.429	403	95	11	2	21	63	72	163	.222	.338	.444	955	212	28	5	58	154	162	379
on Artificial Turf	.254	.384	.606	71	18	4	0	7	17	14	23	.251	.352	.561	171	43	9	1	14	35	26	67
Day Games	.232	.331	.465	155	36	4	1	10	23	23	60	.211	.316	.452	383	81	11	3	25	58	58	159
Night Games	.241	.374	.451	319	77	11	1	18	57	63	126	.234	.352	.467	743	174	26	3	47	131	130	287
April	.338	.444	.770	74	25	1	2	9	22	14	25	.288	.388	.672	125	36	2	2	14	32	20	43
May	.290	.397	.484	62	18	6	0	2	5	11	16	.276	.385	.493	152	42	10	1	7	23	27	48
June	.202	.279	.394	94	19	3	0	5	15	10	39	.191	.265	.373	209	40	3	1	11	31	21	87
July	.250	.394	.488	80	20	1	0	6	10	17	32	.244	.371	.500	164	40	6	0	12	28	31	61
August	.173	.350	.333	81	14	1	0	4	14	21	37	.214	.343	.490	192	41	5	0	16	44	37	77
Sept/Oct	.205	.320	.313	83	17	3	0	2	14	13	37	.197	.323	.377	284	56	11	2	12	31	52	130
Bases Empty	.243	.369	.469	239	58	8	2	14	14	45	84	.231	.344	.470	579	134	17	5	37	37	96	213
Leadoff	.246	.357	.525	122	30	5	1	9	9	18	49	.241	.357	.502	261	63	9	1	19	19	44	93
Not Leadoff	.239	.382	.410	117	28	3	1	5	5	27	35	.223	.332	.443	318	71	8	4	18	18	52	120
Runners On	.234	.351	.443	235	55	7	0	14	66	41	102	.221	.335	.453	547	121	20	1	35	152	92	233
First Base Only	.206	.270	.392	102	21	1	0	6	12	7	47	.210	.292	.460	252	53	9	0	18	37	27	115
Scoring Position	.256	.405	.481	133	34	6	0	8	54	34	55	.231	.368	.447	295	68	11	1	17	115	65	118
Late Innings, Close	.269	.417	.448	67	18	3	0	3	10	15	26	.214	.333	.399	173	37	4	2	8	24	29	74

RBI/Opportunities

Scoring Position	39 / 191 (20%)	83 / 420 (20%)
Scoring Position, 2 Out	18 / 88 (20%)	30 / 196 (15%)
On Third, Less than 2 Out	14 / 39 (36%)	35 / 88 (40%)
RBI in close games / RBI Total	49 / 80 (61%)	116 / 189 (61%)

Jose DeLeon
Chicago White Sox

I have a friend who's a big Pittsburgh Pirate fan, and whenever we talked last year, he kidded me about the Jose DeLeon-for-Bobby Bonilla trade. Bonilla was doing well for Pittsburgh, of course, but when I told him the White Sox were happy with DeLeon, he'd break into laughter. "De-Leon's a loser," my friend would say. "You'll see."

Such is the curse of being a ballplayer with enormous talent but less-than-enormous results. And such is the curse of being Latin American in a white, English-speaking world. The name Jose DeLeon usually conjures up the same images we hold of Joaquin Andujar and Juan Berenguer: storming around the mound, shooting out batters after strikeouts, and, ultimately, letting their emotions get the best of them. The fact that DeLeon doesn't fit this stereotype at all— he is remarkably poised and businesslike when pitching—doesn't seem to matter. People marvel at the talent, which in Jose's case is considerable. But then they recall the 2–19 season and the Latin heritage, and, like my friend, they start shaking their heads.

I have to confess that I wasn't around to watch that 2–19 campaign. The Jose DeLeon I've seen is the one who pitched for the White Sox, and, quite frankly, he's pitched very well. Talk about reliable: Last year he made 31 starts, and in all but six of them he hurled at least six innings. Only twice was he knocked out before the fifth inning. We'll try

to convince you in this book that the quality start is a useful statistic; last year Jose had 19 quality starts, the same number as Bret Saberhagen and Teddy Higuera. (Thanks to Merrianna McCully for this information).

The problems Jose had with Chicago were not due to temperament; they were due to an inability to get the ball over the plate. Last year DeLeon got off to a dime-store start (5 and 10), and the headshaking began again. In point of fact, Jose wasn't pitching that badly—his ERA for his first 21 starts was better than average, 4.11—but there was no question he was pitching below his abilities. Walks were the culprit. For those 21 starts Jose was giving up 5.0 walks per nine innings, and no one excels with numbers like that.

But DeLeon is a diligent worker, and eventually the lessons from pitching coach Dick Bosman began to take effect. Over his last ten starts Jose went 6–3 with a 3.31 ERA. What's remarkable was the improvement in control as he averaged only 2.8 walks per nine innings. Perhaps it was just an illusion that will disappear over the winter, like DeLeon from the White Sox. But Whitey Herzog seems to be believe in him, and there aren't many better judges of character. Jose may never be the pitcher people thought he would be, but he sure doesn't look like a loser to me—not in any way.

Don Zminda

DeLeon, Jose (Chestaro) Bats: Right Throws: Right Born 12/20/60

1987 SEASON AND MAJOR-LEAGUE CAREER PITCHING TOTALS

	G	GS	CG	GF	IP	BFP	H	R	ER	HR	SH	SF	HB	TBB	IBB	SO	WP	Bk	W	L	Pct	ShO	Sv	ERA
87 CHA	33	31	2	0	206	889	177	106	92	24	6	6	10	97	4	153	6	1	11	12	.478	0	0	4.02
5 YEARS	131	113	12	10	764	3230	603	367	332	63	29	21	22	384	17	652	31	6	32	55	.368	3	4	3.91

1987: Power, Flyball   1986: Power, Flyball   1985: Power, Flyball   1984: Power, Flyball

1987 SEASON

	G	IP	H	BB	SO	SB	CS	W	L	S	ERA
Totals	33	205.2	177	97	153	31	8	11	12	0	4.03
at Home	16	94.2	87	46	79	13	4	3	7	0	5.13
on Road	17	111.0	90	51	74	18	4	8	5	0	3.08
on Grass	7	41.0	38	23	20	4	0	0	3	0	4.17
on Artificial Turf	26	164.2	139	74	133	27	8	11	9	0	3.99
Day Games	27	159.2	148	79	112	25	6	7	10	0	4.51
Night Games	6	46.0	29	18	41	6	2	4	2	0	2.35
April	4	27.2	13	20	24	3	1	2	2	0	2.60
May	6	37.2	31	19	20	4	0	2	1	0	3.58
June	5	30.1	30	16	17	6	0	1	4	0	5.64
July	5	30.0	27	16	18	7	3	0	2	0	4.20
August	7	35.1	39	12	33	7	3	3	2	0	5.35
Sept/Oct	6	44.2	37	14	41	4	1	3	1	0	3.02

vs. Opponent Batters	Ave.	OBP	SLG	AB	H	2B	3B	HR	RBI	BB	SO
Totals	.230	.322	.370	770	177	28	4	24	88	97	153
vs. Left	.254	.351	.393	397	101	10	3	13	52	59	64
vs. Right	.204	.290	.346	373	76	18	1	11	36	38	89
Bases Empty	.227	.311	.404	458	104	19	1	20	20	48	91
Leadoff	.247	.330	.402	194	48	9	0	7	7	20	34
Not Leadoff	.212	.297	.405	264	56	10	1	13	13	28	57
Runners On Base	.234	.336	.321	312	73	9	3	4	68	49	62
First Base Only	.211	.322	.236	123	26	1	1	0	1	19	29
Scoring Position	.249	.345	.376	189	47	8	2	4	67	30	33
Late Innings, Close	.271	.381	.429	70	19	3	1	2	10	12	10

FOUR YEAR TOTALS (1984 – 1987)

	G	IP	H	BB	SO	SB	CS	W	L	S	ERA
Totals	116	656.0	528	337	534	107	37	25	52	4	4.09
at Home	59	347.1	273	164	313	56	19	13	30	2	4.17
on Road	57	308.2	255	173	221	51	18	12	22	2	3.99
on Grass	35	186.1	161	109	134	34	9	5	12	0	3.96
on Artificial Turf	81	469.2	367	228	400	73	28	20	40	4	4.14
Day Games	52	293.0	251	155	226	42	14	13	20	1	4.33
Night Games	64	363.0	277	182	308	65	23	12	32	3	3.89
April	11	62.1	48	42	65	9	5	3	5	0	4.04
May	25	119.2	95	69	86	21	4	5	9	1	4.21
June	18	114.1	95	56	87	18	4	5	10	0	4.01
July	16	102.1	82	51	80	20	6	2	9	0	4.22
August	22	125.0	107	63	105	20	11	5	12	0	4.61
Sept/Oct	24	132.1	101	56	111	19	7	5	7	3	3.47

vs. Opponent Batters	Ave.	OBP	SLG	AB	H	2B	3B	HR	RBI	BB	SO
Totals	.221	.319	.343	2391	528	84	17	58	267	337	534
vs. Left	.255	.364	.390	1206	308	45	12	31	158	206	191
vs. Right	.186	.271	.295	1185	220	39	5	27	109	131	343
Bases Empty	.215	.316	.336	1389	298	52	6	35	35	198	318
Leadoff	.236	.334	.350	594	140	24	4	12	12	84	125
Not Leadoff	.199	.302	.326	795	158	28	2	23	23	114	193
Runners On Base	.230	.323	.352	1002	230	32	11	23	232	139	216
First Base Only	.215	.288	.295	410	88	6	3	7	19	41	90
Scoring Position	.240	.346	.392	592	142	26	8	16	213	98	126
Late Innings, Close	.253	.353	.428	229	58	6	5	8	34	35	38

RBI/Opportunities

Scoring Position	61 / 269 (23%)	181 / 829 (22%)
Scoring Position, 2 Out	29 / 126 (23%)	73 / 363 (20%)
On Third, Less than 2 Out	19 / 40 (48%)	73 / 153 (48%)
RBI in close games / RBI Total	64 / 88 (73%)	201 / 267 (75%)

Bo Diaz

Cincinnati Reds

At the age of thirty-four, Bo Diaz was the oldest catcher in the National League last year and, for the first half of the season, he was the best. At the All-Star break, Diaz was hitting .292 with 53 RBI. He was also playing his usual solid defense. Fatigue may have caused his production to decline thereafter—Diaz was just six games behind Benito Santiago for the league lead in games caught—but Bo still wound up with 82 RBIs, the most of any major league catcher.

Despite his age, Diaz has played in only 858 big league games in his eleven year career and had never caught more than 65 games in three consecutive years until 1987. Injuries which forced him to miss so many games earlier in his career have saved his knees so that, much like Carlton Fisk, he can still be productive. Fisk's best years came in his middle thirties; maybe Diaz could do the same?

Rose listed Diaz as untouchable on the trade market, citing him as the Reds' best hitter with men on base (high praise, considering the Reds lineup). In his two full years with Cincinnati, he has averaged 13 HR, 69 RBI, and a .271 BA.

Over the past six years, Bo has hit for a higher average with runners on base than with the bases empty. He seems to have a knack for hooking singles down the left field line when the game is close and runners are in scoring position. His hitting abilities may be overlooked because of his contributions as a catcher, but make no mistake: He is an integral part of the Reds' offense.

The last time that the Reds' farm system produced a legitimate major league catcher was 1968 (Bench), but there are three catchers in the Reds farm system who look very promising. Diaz is not simply filling the gap until they are ready. He is still in the prime of his career and one of the top catchers in the game today. The numbers he put up in 1987 were no fluke. Stay tuned.

Sean Lahman

Did Bo have a good year in 1987? He raised his HR from 10 to 15, his doubles from 21 to 28, and his RBI from 56 to 82.

What suffered in 1987 was OBA, which dropped from a mediocre .327 to a pathetic .300, his bases on balls, which plummeted from 40 to 19, and his strikeouts, which climbed from 52 to 73. His runs scored held steady (50 to 49), which means his ratio of runs scored to RBI, at 59.7 percent, was the lowest for a regular in the National League. Interestingly, nearly all the players in the 60 percent range were catchers—Carter, Diaz, Sundberg, and Andre Dawson, who is excused from this discussion because he scored 90 runs anyway, Bo only reaches base 3 of ten trips; to compound matters, he only scores one-third of the times he reaches base! Diaz is perhaps the slowest runner in baseball, and, hitting behind the leadfooted Buddy Bell, he is a threat to set an all-time GIDP rate record.

Roger Weber

Diaz, Baudilio Jose (Seijas) "Bo"

Bats: Right   Throws: Right   Born 03/23/53

1987 SEASON AND MAJOR-LEAGUE CAREER BATTING TOTALS

	G	AB	H	2B	3B	HR	TB	R	RBI	TBB	IBB	SO	HP	SH	SF	SB	CS	SB%	GDP	AVG	OBP	SLG
87 CIN	140	496	134	28	1	15	209	49	82	19	1	73	5	4	6	1	0	1.00	16	.270	.300	.421
11 YEARS	858	2827	738	148	5	76	1124	295	409	185	15	381	12	23	25	9	13	.41	94	.261	.307	.398

1987 SEASON / FOUR YEAR TOTALS (1984 – 1987)

	Ave.	OBP	SLG	AB	H	2B	3B	HR	RBI	BB	SO	Ave.	OBP	SLG	AB	H	2B	3B	HR	RBI	BB	SO
Totals	.270	.300	.421	496	134	28	1	15	82	19	73	.263	.309	.390	1282	337	66	2	31	178	85	163
vs. Left	.355	.383	.529	138	49	12	0	4	24	7	20	.293	.348	.436	351	103	27	1	7	52	31	38
vs. Right	.237	.268	.380	358	85	16	1	11	58	12	53	.251	.293	.373	931	234	39	1	24	126	54	125
at Home	.306	.338	.488	252	77	20	1	8	52	10	34	.290	.334	.463	600	174	39	1	21	103	37	76
on Road	.234	.261	.352	244	57	8	0	7	30	9	39	.239	.286	.326	682	163	27	1	10	75	48	87
vs. Groundball	.271	.288	.422	225	61	11	1	7	48	7	30	.273	.319	.392	609	166	36	2	11	99	45	77
vs. Flyball	.269	.310	.421	271	73	17	0	8	34	12	43	.254	.300	.388	673	171	30	0	20	79	40	86
vs. Finesse	.257	.273	.395	261	67	13	1	7	41	5	32	.267	.303	.392	688	184	31	2	17	96	35	68
vs. Power	.285	.329	.451	235	67	15	0	8	41	14	41	.258	.316	.387	594	153	35	0	14	82	50	95
on Grass	.245	.275	.381	139	34	7	0	4	19	7	20	.276	.317	.377	387	107	18	0	7	47	25	41
on Artificial Turf	.280	.310	.437	357	100	21	1	11	63	12	53	.257	.305	.396	895	230	48	2	24	131	60	122
Day Games	.282	.303	.397	156	44	9	0	3	26	5	23	.282	.329	.404	394	111	22	1	8	57	29	46
Night Games	.265	.299	.432	340	90	19	1	12	56	14	50	.255	.300	.384	888	226	44	1	23	121	56	117
April	.282	.325	.380	71	20	4	0	1	17	4	15	.266	.317	.386	184	49	10	0	4	32	13	26
May	.204	.229	.290	93	19	2	0	2	9	2	13	.226	.289	.321	159	36	6	0	3	16	13	23
June	.352	.404	.549	91	32	12	0	2	13	7	13	.272	.321	.384	224	61	19	0	2	30	15	31
July	.351	.357	.585	94	33	5	1	5	23	0	16	.306	.337	.515	196	60	10	2	9	40	8	27
August	.192	.219	.323	99	19	4	0	3	15	4	8	.223	.273	.325	292	65	12	0	6	32	21	33
Sept/Oct	.229	.255	.375	48	11	1	0	2	5	2	8	.291	.333	.423	227	66	9	0	7	28	15	23
Bases Empty	.254	.283	.351	279	71	12	0	5	5	8	47	.249	.290	.364	740	184	32	1	17	17	40	106
Leadoff	.295	.315	.438	105	31	6	0	3	3	3	13	.254	.280	.389	311	79	12	0	10	10	11	34
Not Leadoff	.230	.264	.299	174	40	6	0	2	2	5	34	.245	.297	.345	429	105	20	1	7	7	29	72
Runners On	.290	.322	.512	217	63	16	1	10	77	11	26	.282	.336	.426	542	153	34	1	14	161	45	57
First Base Only	.255	.286	.457	94	24	7	0	4	12	2	12	.251	.293	.397	219	55	14	0	6	21	11	21
Scoring Position	.317	.348	.553	123	39	9	1	6	65	9	14	.303	.364	.446	323	98	20	1	8	140	34	36
Late Innings, Close	.232	.257	.362	69	16	6	0	1	7	2	17	.267	.306	.415	217	58	12	1	6	26	12	39

RBI/Opportunities

	1987		Four Year	
Scoring Position	55 / 164	(34%)	126 / 439	(29%)
Scoring Position, 2 Out	24 / 78	(31%)	51 / 206	(25%)
On Third, Less than 2 Out	20 / 26	(77%)	49 / 76	(64%)
RBI in close games / RBI Total	39 / 82	(48%)	96 / 178	(54%)

Ken Dixon
Baltimore Orioles

Behavioral experts often note that intelligent men are, because they're bored easily by mundane things, likely to have a short attention span; how else can we explain Albert Einstein's failing grades in basic math in his school days? Maybe Ken Dixon is equally bright; he often pitches like he's either bored, not paying attention or both. The problem is that Dixon hasn't won any prizes for his pitching so far; the way his career is going, he's not likely to do so in the future.

From the beginning, no one has doubted the quality of Ken's stuff: a fastball in the 90's and a sharp curve. When he got off to a fast start in 1985 (8–4, 3.67), his potential seemed limitless. But he faded in 1986; an ugly penchant for giving up dingers emerged. The Orioles shrugged it off as a sophomore slump and figured Dixon prominently in their plans for 1987. All trade offers were spurned; a spot in the rotation was a given.

Ken's start this year was so awful that it was laughable—he was 1–2 in his first four starts with an 8.53 ERA and seven homers allowed in 19 innings. He'd set the side down masterfully in one inning, using the whole of the plate and changing speeds. Then he'd suddenly seem to forget the purpose of the exercise and groove a fastball on an 0–2 count, giving up a tape-measure blast. With increasing frequency, Dixon pitches were being rocketed to the furthest reaches of AL ballparks.

With Don Aase out for the season and the Tom Niedenfuer trade still a month away, the Orioles tried Ken in the bullpen. The new job opportunity seemed to hold his interest for a while; Ken began getting batters out. By June 1, he had two wins, five saves and a semi-respectable 3.66 ERA in 27 innings as a reliever. At that point, however, Dixon appeared to be bored by it all again. By the end of June, having allowed 10 (!!) homers in his last 19+ innings, he wound up pitching in AAA. He returned in July and won four straight as a starter before his mind began wandering again.

Ken's record seems to demonstrate an ability to perform in a new environment and meet new challenges. But, once he shows some modicum of success, he seems unwilling or incapable to expend the necessary energy to continue to excel. Some people might consider this apparent boredom to be a sign of his great intellect. That's possible; it's possible Einstein was also a lousy righthander. Ken Dixon gets paid to succeed as a pitcher, and thus far he hasn't.

Dixon's tools are such that Seattle traded one of their own enigmas, Mike Morgan, for him this winter. I expect Dixon to start strong with Seattle and then fall apart as his concentration wanes—it should be interesting to see how Dick Williams tries to hold his attention.

Greg Pryor

Dixon, Kenneth John "Ken" Bats: Both Throws: Right Born 10/17/60

1987 SEASON AND MAJOR-LEAGUE CAREER PITCHING TOTALS

	G	GS	CG	GF	IP	BFP	H	R	ER	HR	SH	SF	HB	TBB	IBB	SO	WP	Bk	W	L	Pct	ShO	Sv	ERA
87 BAL	34	15	0	13	105	470	128	81	75	31	1	2	1	27	4	91	5	1	7	10	.412	0	5	6.43
4 YEARS	105	68	5	21	482	2083	480	266	250	85	14	10	4	178	17	377	19	6	26	28	.481	1	6	4.67

1987: Power, Flyball   1986: Power, Flyball   1985: Power, Flyball   1984: Finesse, Groundball

	1987 SEASON										1987 SEASON ERA	FOUR YEAR TOTALS (1984 – 1987)										TOTALS ERA
	G	IP	H	BB	SO	SB	CS	W	L	S	ERA	G	IP	H	BB	SO	SB	CS	W	L	S	ERA
Totals	34	105.1	128	27	91	9	2	7	10	5	6.41	105	482.2	480	178	377	45	11	26	28	6	4.64
at Home	16	54.2	72	15	55	5	0	3	6	1	6.59	57	265.0	279	114	206	28	8	12	20	2	5.13
on Road	18	50.2	56	12	36	4	2	4	4	4	6.22	48	217.2	201	64	171	17	3	14	8	4	4.09
on Grass	13	34.0	44	14	27	5	1	1	5	2	7.41	35	133.0	148	57	111	20	3	4	11	3	5.75
on Artificial Turf	21	71.1	84	13	64	4	1	6	5	3	5.93	70	349.2	332	121	266	25	8	22	17	3	4.25
Day Games	28	87.1	107	23	78	8	2	6	7	4	6.29	88	395.1	414	152	313	39	11	19	24	5	4.94
Night Games	6	18.0	21	4	13	1	0	1	3	1	7.00	17	87.1	66	26	64	6	0	7	4	1	3.40
April	5	24.1	30	6	23	4	0	1	2	0	6.66	11	64.0	58	18	56	8	0	4	3	0	3.80
May	14	22.0	19	8	23	2	2	2	1	5	4.50	25	80.2	76	29	68	9	4	8	4	5	5.13
June	6	19.1	32	7	17	1	0	0	4	0	10.24	21	73.2	97	36	55	8	1	1	9	0	7.70
July	2	11.0	18	3	7	1	0	0	1	0	6.55	14	84.2	66	29	65	6	2	4	3	0	2.98
August	5	27.0	22	1	19	1	0	4	0	0	2.67	16	89.0	80	25	65	6	2	6	2	0	3.74
Sept/Oct	2	1.2	7	2	2	0	0	0	2	0	43.20	18	90.2	103	41	68	8	2	3	7	1	4.86

vs. Opponent Batters	Ave.	OBP	SLG	AB	H	2B	3B	HR	RBI	BB	SO	Ave.	OBP	SLG	AB	H	2B	3B	HR	RBI	BB	SO
Totals	.292	.333	.565	439	128	21	3	31	76	27	91	.256	.320	.452	1876	480	81	16	85	248	178	376
vs. Left	.280	.332	.556	214	60	13	2	14	36	17	40	.247	.323	.435	958	237	46	10	38	110	107	167
vs. Right	.302	.333	.573	225	68	8	1	17	40	10	51	.265	.318	.469	918	243	35	6	47	138	71	209
Bases Empty	.283	.317	.574	265	75	16	2	19	19	13	48	.248	.305	.457	1141	283	52	9	56	56	93	212
Leadoff	.356	.387	.792	101	36	8	0	12	12	5	15	.262	.306	.506	470	123	21	2	30	30	30	85
Not Leadoff	.238	.273	.439	164	39	8	2	7	7	8	33	.238	.304	.422	671	160	31	7	26	26	63	127
Runners On Base	.305	.356	.552	174	53	5	1	12	57	14	43	.268	.344	.445	735	197	29	7	29	192	85	164
First Base Only	.333	.387	.649	57	19	1	1	5	12	5	11	.286	.335	.465	297	85	14	3	11	31	22	59
Scoring Position	.291	.341	.504	117	34	4	0	7	45	9	32	.256	.349	.432	438	112	15	4	18	161	63	105
Late Innings, Close	.253	.311	.411	95	24	1	1	4	16	8	26	.257	.325	.407	226	58	7	3	7	29	23	43

RBI/Opportunities

Scoring Position	37 / 146 (25%)	132 / 602 (22%)
Scoring Position, 2 Out	21 / 70 (30%)	59 / 279 (21%)
On Third, Less than 2 Out	9 / 19 (47%)	51 / 108 (47%)
RBI in close games / RBI Total	49 / 76 (64%)	163 / 248 (66%)

Bill Doran

Houston Astros

Bill James once did an interesting study to determine how many players in this century were above average in the nine major offensive categories and also played a key defensive position (catcher, second base, third base, or center field). Surprisingly, he found only two—one of the all-time greats and a guy whose name was totally unfamiliar to most fans—Willie Mays and George Grantham. Grantham was a National League second baseman in the 1920s and 1930s who had a .302 career batting average, but played in the shadow of Rogers Hornsby and Frankie Frisch.

Bill Doran seems destined to be this generation's George Grantham. A fiery competitor, he does everything well offensively and defensively, but is overshadowed by Ryne Sandberg and Juan Samuel, and even by the inconsistent Steve Sax and Tommy Herr in their good years. Doran has never made the All-Star team nor won a Gold Glove, but he did get a smattering of MVP votes in 1986, finishing 11th, when the 'Stros won the division. He had a better year in 1987 but received only one tenth place vote for MVP. He had a sensational year defensively with his tremendous range and spectacular plays. He made only six errors while playing all 162 games and led National league second basemen with a .992 fielding percentage. In spite of all this, Sandberg won the Gold Glove, while Samuel won the Silver Slugger.

Sandberg has an edge in power, but Doran counters with a higher OBA. Sandberg benefits greatly from Wrigley, where his OBA, BA and SLG are all at least 25 percent higher than on the road, while Doran gets half his at-bats in the best pitcher's park on the planet.

While Doran hit well all year, he was especially effective when he moved to the number three slot in the batting order behind Gerald Young and Billy Hatcher. His 79 RBIs far exceeded his previous high of 59. He should do even better in 1988 if he continues to bat in the number three slot, as appears likely. Doran was the most difficult Astro to strike out in 1987 with only 64 in 625 at bats. He led the team in hits and walks and was voted the team's Most Valuable Player for the second time in the last three years. In addition to RBIs he reached career highs in hits, home runs (16), and total bases.

Surprisingly, Doran scored fewer runs in 1987 than he did in any of the three previous years even though he reached base more times. This is explained by the major decline in productivity by Houston's four and five hitters, Glenn Davis and Kevin Bass. It also helps explain why Nolan Ryan had only an 8–16 record, even though he was, by far, the league's most consistent and effective pitcher.

1988 could be the year that Doran gains some recognition. If Young and Hatcher continue to get on base and Davis and Bass return to their 1986 level of productivity, Doran, batting in the middle, could put up some really impressive numbers.

Bill Gilbert and Kent Kirchstein

Doran, William Donald "Bill" Bats: Right Throws: Right Born 05/28/58

1987 SEASON AND MAJOR-LEAGUE CAREER BATTING TOTALS

	G	AB	H	2B	3B	HR	TB	R	RBI	TBB	IBB	SO	HP	SH	SF	SB	CS	SB%	GDP	AVG	OBP	SLG
87 HOU	162	625	177	23	3	16	254	82	79	82	3	64	3	2	7	31	11	.74	11	.283	.365	.406
6 YEARS	782	2933	810	116	30	48	1130	431	261	390	34	337	7	23	22	134	69	.66	43	.276	.360	.385

	1987 SEASON											FOUR YEAR TOTALS (1984 – 1987)										
	Ave.	OBP	SLG	AB	H	2B	3B	HR	RBI	BB	SO	Ave.	OBP	SLG	AB	H	2B	3B	HR	RBI	BB	SO
Totals	.283	.365	.406	625	177	23	3	16	79	82	64	.277	.360	.393	2301	638	101	23	40	216	300	259
vs. Left	.291	.395	.417	223	65	5	1	7	33	39	19	.298	.382	.414	830	247	38	4	17	87	116	82
vs. Right	.279	.348	.400	402	112	18	2	9	46	43	45	.266	.347	.381	1471	391	63	19	23	129	184	177
at Home	.305	.412	.414	292	89	9	1	7	36	55	31	.274	.371	.393	1098	301	52	14	17	103	169	118
on Road	.264	.320	.399	333	88	14	2	9	43	27	33	.280	.349	.393	1203	337	49	9	23	113	131	141
vs. Groundball	.268	.359	.380	295	79	13	1	6	35	41	23	.272	.353	.377	1089	296	46	9	17	105	138	108
vs. Flyball	.297	.372	.430	330	98	10	2	10	44	41	41	.282	.365	.408	1212	342	55	14	23	111	162	151
vs. Finesse	.287	.354	.412	335	96	13	1	9	48	35	27	.276	.348	.398	1249	345	52	11	26	116	136	112
vs. Power	.279	.378	.400	290	81	10	2	7	31	47	37	.279	.373	.388	1052	293	49	12	14	100	164	147
on Grass	.273	.335	.423	194	53	9	1	6	31	18	22	.288	.356	.416	716	206	32	6	16	80	78	90
on Artificial Turf	.288	.378	.399	431	124	14	2	10	48	64	42	.273	.361	.383	1585	432	69	17	24	136	222	169
Day Games	.271	.330	.427	199	54	5	1	8	32	18	17	.272	.352	.396	599	163	21	4	15	66	74	59
Night Games	.289	.381	.397	426	123	18	2	8	47	64	47	.279	.362	.392	1702	475	80	19	25	150	226	200
April	.200	.274	.388	85	17	1	0	5	10	9	12	.226	.313	.328	296	67	13	1	5	18	38	38
May	.273	.350	.318	110	30	5	0	0	12	13	10	.272	.358	.368	345	94	12	3	5	29	46	34
June	.320	.392	.515	103	33	3	1	5	14	14	16	.293	.376	.440	430	126	14	5	13	50	59	46
July	.287	.361	.444	108	31	5	0	4	13	12	11	.290	.357	.396	427	124	24	3	5	36	44	48
August	.360	.431	.474	114	41	5	1	2	20	15	8	.327	.412	.480	394	129	21	6	9	50	57	47
Sept/Oct	.238	.362	.295	105	25	4	1	0	10	19	7	.240	.333	.328	409	98	17	5	3	33	56	46
Bases Empty	.260	.352	.377	369	96	10	3	9	9	52	44	.273	.353	.398	1507	411	67	19	28	28	186	173
Leadoff	.296	.371	.467	135	40	6	1	5	5	16	12	.287	.355	.417	806	231	34	10	17	17	86	82
Not Leadoff	.239	.341	.325	234	56	4	2	4	4	36	32	.257	.350	.377	701	180	33	9	11	11	100	91
Runners On	.316	.385	.449	256	81	13	0	7	70	30	20	.286	.375	.384	794	227	34	4	12	188	114	86
First Base Only	.351	.400	.536	97	34	6	0	4	12	7	3	.324	.376	.449	321	104	19	0	7	22	26	22
Scoring Position	.296	.377	.396	159	47	7	0	3	58	23	17	.260	.374	.340	473	123	15	4	5	166	88	64
Late Innings, Close	.314	.413	.371	105	33	3	0	1	16	19	9	.275	.359	.369	371	102	13	2	6	41	50	45

RBI/Opportunities

Scoring Position	51 / 228 (22%)	153 / 701 (22%)
Scoring Position, 2 Out	12 / 100 (12%)	59 / 364 (16%)
On Third, Less than 2 Out	21 / 39 (54%)	61 / 111 (55%)
RBI in close games / RBI Total	62 / 79 (78%)	154 / 216 (71%)

Richard Dotson
Chicago White Sox

Remember 1983? A great year for the White Sox and a great year for Richard Dotson. The club won 99 games, reaching postseason play for the first time in 24 years. Even when the Sox lost to Baltimore in the playoffs, the future looked rosy. Bill James was saying the team looked like a dynasty, and Dotson, who'd gone 22–7, was a key reason. He was 24 and loaded with talent. As Curt Gowdy once put it, his whole future was ahead of him.

Those were the days, my friend, we thought they'd never end. But they did. No need to dwell on the misfortunes of the White Sox; it was in all the papers. But Dotson's struggles mirrored those of the club. In '84 his record fell to 14–15, even though he continued to pitch well, with a 3.59 ERA and 14 complete games. Then, early in '85, his right shoulder began to ache. The injury was anything but simple; an overdeveloped muscle in Dotson's chest was causing the pain, and a unique form of surgery had to be performed. There were doubts that Dotson could recover, but remarkably, he showed up in the spring of '86, ready to take his regular turn. Throughout that season he never missed a start. The results, however, were not as impressive. He led the club in innings with 197, but Dotson's record was 10–17, and his ERA was a woeful 5.48. To be frank, he was pitching like someone with a sore arm.

Dotson was on the spot in '87, and he came through magnificently. In mid-August he was 10–9, with a 3.84 ERA, but his work was even better than the ERA indicated; the Sox bullpen was letting numerous Dotson runners score. There was no question about his durability, either. For his first 26 starts Dotson averaged 7.3 innings an appearance, a figure topped only by Roger Clemens, Jack Morris, Bret Saberhagen, Mark Langston and Teddy Higuera. (Thanks to Merrianna McCully for this data.)

Then, just when he seemed fully recovered, Dotson's arm began to ache again. The injury wasn't believed serious; after taking off most of September, he came back during the last week of the season and looked sound during one final start. The Yankees, trusting souls that they are, made a deal for Dotson over the winter.

If healthy, Dotson figures to pitch well for New York. The hype of the big city shouldn't bother him. He's a tough competitor, a natural leader (he was the White Sox player representative) and very secure about his own ability. New Yorkers will find that he's fearless about pitching inside, that he fields his position well, is very hard to run on, and that he isn't likely to let a couple of bad outings or a raving owner get under his skin. I fearlessly predict that Dotson will win more games for the Yanks than Britt Burns and Steve Trout combined, a goal he could probably reach in his first start.

Don Zminda

Dotson, Richard Elliott

Bats: Right   Throws: Right   Born 01/10/59

1987 SEASON AND MAJOR-LEAGUE CAREER PITCHING TOTALS

	G	GS	CG	GF	IP	BFP	H	R	ER	HR	SH	SF	HB	TBB	IBB	SO	WP	Bk	W	L	Pct	ShO	Sv	ERA
87 CHA	31	31	7	0	211	900	201	109	98	24	4	3	0	86	2	114	5	0	11	12	.478	2	0	4.18
9 YEARS	237	233	49	4	1506	6455	1482	748	675	148	48	46	35	596	17	818	37	6	94	88	.516	11	0	4.03

1987: Finesse, Flyball   1986: Finesse, Groundball   1985: Power, Groundball   1984: Finesse, Groundball

1987 SEASON

	G	IP	H	BB	SO	SB	CS	W	L	S	ERA
Totals	31	211.1	201	86	114	2	9	11	12	0	4.17
at Home	16	107.2	109	40	58	0	3	6	8	0	4.35
on Road	15	103.2	92	46	56	2	6	5	4	0	3.99
on Grass	8	63.0	51	20	38	0	1	3	4	0	3.71
on Artificial Turf	23	148.1	150	66	76	2	8	8	8	0	4.37
Day Games	26	185.2	174	72	101	0	8	9	11	0	4.07
Night Games	5	25.2	27	14	13	2	1	2	1	0	4.91
April	5	30.2	35	13	21	0	1	1	2	0	4.99
May	5	39.1	27	15	21	0	2	2	2	0	3.43
June	6	41.2	40	13	28	1	3	2	1	0	4.32
July	6	45.1	38	19	21	0	1	3	2	0	4.57
August	6	44.1	48	20	20	0	2	2	4	0	3.45
Sept/Oct	3	10.0	13	6	3	1	0	1	1	0	5.40

vs. Opponent Batters	Ave.	OBP	SLG	AB	H	2B	3B	HR	RBI	BB	SO
Totals	.249	.320	.399	807	201	35	7	24	89	86	114
vs. Left	.251	.326	.419	430	108	23	2	15	52	48	63
vs. Right	.247	.314	.377	377	93	12	5	9	37	38	51
Bases Empty	.230	.307	.378	474	109	19	3	15	15	53	61
Leadoff	.211	.296	.332	199	42	10	1	4	4	24	20
Not Leadoff	.244	.316	.411	275	67	9	2	11	11	29	41
Runners On Base	.276	.339	.429	333	92	16	4	9	74	33	53
First Base Only	.262	.304	.404	183	48	10	2	4	14	11	30
Scoring Position	.293	.377	.460	150	44	6	2	5	60	22	23
Late Innings, Close	.312	.348	.523	109	34	8	0	5	12	6	14

FOUR YEAR TOTALS (1984 – 1987)

	G	IP	H	BB	SO	SB	CS	W	L	S	ERA
Totals	106	706.1	696	275	377	48	26	38	48	0	4.36
at Home	57	386.1	368	148	211	25	14	22	27	0	4.17
on Road	49	320.0	328	127	166	23	12	16	21	0	4.58
on Grass	35	248.2	236	81	135	19	7	15	13	0	3.66
on Artificial Turf	71	457.2	460	194	242	29	19	23	35	0	4.74
Day Games	90	609.0	587	237	329	39	22	33	41	0	4.20
Night Games	16	97.1	109	38	48	9	4	5	7	0	5.27
April	17	113.1	109	51	58	3	6	5	6	0	4.45
May	20	137.2	113	56	83	11	8	9	8	0	3.53
June	20	138.1	133	43	77	11	4	10	6	0	4.23
July	16	93.1	107	38	34	2	2	5	10	0	6.75
August	19	134.1	146	51	67	11	4	6	9	0	3.62
Sept/Oct	14	89.1	88	36	58	10	2	3	9	0	4.33

vs. Opponent Batters	Ave.	OBP	SLG	AB	H	2B	3B	HR	RBI	BB	SO
Totals	.258	.326	.402	2699	696	106	26	77	321	275	377
vs. Left	.254	.329	.412	1420	360	53	11	50	174	160	210
vs. Right	.263	.323	.391	1279	336	53	15	27	147	115	167
Bases Empty	.248	.316	.397	1606	399	57	17	49	49	158	219
Leadoff	.247	.303	.382	689	170	28	7	17	17	56	75
Not Leadoff	.250	.325	.408	917	229	29	10	32	32	102	144
Runners On Base	.272	.341	.410	1093	297	49	9	28	272	117	158
First Base Only	.281	.330	.424	519	146	25	5	13	43	38	71
Scoring Position	.263	.351	.397	574	151	24	4	15	229	79	87
Late Innings, Close	.291	.340	.477	323	94	15	3	13	37	24	33

RBI/Opportunities

Scoring Position	51 / 216 (24%)	198 / 803 (25%)
Scoring Position, 2 Out	16 / 99 (16%)	61 / 350 (17%)
On Third, Less than 2 Out	25 / 48 (52%)	91 / 165 (55%)
RBI in close games / RBI Total	63 / 89 (71%)	239 / 321 (74%)

Brian Downing
California Angels

Brian Downing is a fun player to watch. You can start right off with his unusual batting stance which gives new definition to the phrase "face the pitcher." His attention is focused toward the mound, not toward the plate, and his posture is more like a boxer than a golfer. You have to wonder if this odd, aggressive stance is disconcerting or even intimidating from the viewpoint of the pitcher.

There is something special to the way Downing plays the game. He sprints with visible intensity, whether running the bases or chasing an outfield hit. His throwing expresses a fine sense of urgency and is consistently accurate. And he can pull a ball into the seats, with stunning power.

To compile an outstanding secondary average, a player needs either overwhelming power (like Mike Schmidt, Jack Clark, and Dale Murphy) or a combination of outstanding speed and respectable power (like Eric Davis, Darryl Strawberry, and Rickey Henderson). Brian Downing fits the slugger stereotype, helped immensely by the walks that come from his fine eye and respectful pitchers. His secondary average was among the top ten in the American league in 1986 (.368) and in 1987 he finished just behind Wade Boggs with a .411 mark.

Brian's 1987 performance (at age 36) was arguably his career year. He served notice of his intentions with April numbers that were among the league leaders in almost every category: .352 average, 19 runs, 9 HR, 22 RBI and .761 slugging percentage. By season's end, he had accumulated 110 runs, the highest total of his career and third best in the American League in 1987, just a shade behind Paul Molitor and George Bell.

Downing tied Dwight Evans for most walks with 106, and even ran a strong second to Don Baylor in the hit-by-pitch category. It appears that Downing finds the DH role quite agreeable. If the Angels keep their promise and put Johnny Ray in left field, Brian can be DH full time in 1988. This opportunity to concentrate on offense (and hopefully avoid injury) should augment his offensive stats and also prolong his career, both of which would be good for baseball and nice for the fans. Personally, I will miss this man's unique fielding efforts; he got everything out of what he had.

Brian Downing has been a very good player, sometimes a great one, and he's been the kind of player who sells tickets and inspires optimistic rooting and team loyalty. But he is not quite Hall of Fame material, and he hasn't gotten to play in a heavy media area or on a dominating team, at least not yet. Chances are the only way he will be remembered decades from now is by the memory we personally carry of him.

John C. Benson

Downing, Brian Jay

Bats: Right   **Throws: Right**   **Born 10/09/50**

1987 SEASON AND MAJOR-LEAGUE CAREER BATTING TOTALS

	G	AB	H	2B	3B	HR	TB	R	RBI	TBB	IBB	SO	HP	SH	SF	SB	CS	SB%	GDP	AVG	OBP	SLG
87 CAL	155	567	154	29	3	29	276	110	77	106	6	85	17	2	3	5	5	.50	10	.272	.400	.487
15 YEARS	1741	5768	1536	264	20	195	2425	873	811	890	36	804	87	54	53	45	37	.55	155	.266	.370	.420

1987 SEASON

	Ave.	OBP	SLG	AB	H	2B	3B	HR	RBI	BB	SO
Totals	.272	.400	.487	567	154	29	3	29	77	106	85
vs. Left	.299	.432	.554	177	53	10	1	11	24	41	35
vs. Right	.259	.384	.456	390	101	19	2	18	53	65	50
at Home	.279	.412	.475	280	78	18	2	11	36	56	43
on Road	.265	.388	.498	287	76	11	1	18	41	50	42
vs. Groundball	.314	.450	.553	264	83	12	0	17	41	58	44
vs. Flyball	.234	.353	.429	303	71	17	3	12	36	48	41
vs. Finesse	.288	.401	.558	278	80	14	2	19	43	46	35
vs. Power	.256	.399	.419	289	74	15	1	10	34	60	50
on Grass	.272	.398	.465	482	131	24	3	21	62	85	69
on Artificial Turf	.271	.411	.612	85	23	5	0	8	15	21	16
Day Games	.312	.436	.618	170	53	8	1	14	32	29	21
Night Games	.254	.384	.431	397	101	21	2	15	45	77	64
April	.352	.472	.761	88	31	7	1	9	22	18	12
May	.231	.358	.429	91	21	3	0	5	12	17	14
June	.260	.388	.430	100	26	6	1	3	8	17	15
July	.263	.370	.384	99	26	4	1	2	11	14	13
August	.247	.355	.430	93	23	5	0	4	9	14	18
Sept/Oct	.281	.452	.510	96	27	4	0	6	13	26	13
Bases Empty	.274	.407	.536	351	96	20	3	22	22	69	53
Leadoff	.308	.433	.647	201	62	13	2	17	17	37	28
Not Leadoff	.227	.373	.387	150	34	7	1	5	5	32	25
Runners On	.269	.388	.407	216	58	9	0	7	55	37	32
First Base Only	.345	.418	.575	87	30	5	0	5	13	8	13
Scoring Position	.217	.370	.295	129	28	4	0	2	42	29	19
Late Innings, Close	.255	.357	.378	98	25	3	0	3	15	15	16

FOUR YEAR TOTALS (1984 – 1987)

	Ave.	OBP	SLG	AB	H	2B	3B	HR	RBI	BB	SO
	.269	.380	.458	2139	576	107	10	92	348	343	296
	.273	.389	.487	706	193	46	3	33	117	133	111
	.267	.376	.443	1433	383	61	7	59	231	210	185
	.263	.379	.444	1052	277	49	6	43	167	180	138
	.275	.381	.471	1087	299	58	4	49	181	163	158
	.284	.395	.470	1017	289	42	6	45	174	161	135
	.256	.366	.447	1122	287	65	4	47	174	182	161
	.284	.382	.477	1173	333	65	7	49	173	163	135
	.252	.378	.435	966	243	42	3	43	175	180	161
	.268	.381	.451	1788	480	86	8	75	286	293	245
	.274	.374	.490	351	96	21	2	17	62	50	51
	.275	.381	.488	637	175	35	4	31	116	93	78
	.267	.380	.445	1502	401	72	6	61	232	250	218
	.291	.402	.550	327	95	18	2	21	74	59	47
	.235	.354	.375	341	80	16	1	10	36	62	46
	.250	.355	.398	332	83	19	3	8	45	50	41
	.259	.350	.427	351	91	13	2	14	56	46	54
	.297	.384	.501	387	115	20	1	19	68	53	52
	.279	.395	.486	401	112	21	1	20	69	73	56
	.259	.361	.440	1226	318	62	6	49	49	184	159
	.279	.374	.512	562	157	33	4	30	30	78	68
	.242	.349	.378	664	161	29	2	19	19	106	91
	.283	.392	.482	913	258	45	4	43	299	159	137
	.297	.384	.496	367	109	19	0	18	47	49	54
	.273	.397	.473	546	149	26	4	25	252	110	83
	.275	.380	.453	331	91	16	2	13	60	56	43

RBI/Opportunities

	1987	Four Year
Scoring Position	39 / 196 (20%)	207 / 808 (26%)
Scoring Position, 2 Out	11 / 82 (13%)	77 / 373 (21%)
On Third, Less than 2 Out	17 / 38 (45%)	82 / 154 (53%)
RBI in close games / RBI Total	51 / 77 (66%)	218 / 348 (63%)

Doug Drabek
Pittsburgh Pirates

It was only a couple of seasons ago that the Pittsburgh Pirates were an over-priced, aging collection of malcontents driving the franchise into the abyss of bankruptcy and the cellar of the National League East. Gems like George Hendrick, Sixto Lezcano, Tim Foli, Lee Mazzilli and Steve Kemp—all either well beyond their prime, expensive damaged goods, or both—were leading the free-fall. In 1984, when the Pirates pitching staff led the National League in earned run average, this group still managed to bring home last place.

Fortunately, the old Buc warhorse and general manager, Joe Brown, was brought back to begin a rebuilding process that would start the Pirates on their way back to respectability, a trend that has continued under the tutelage of current GM Syd Thrift and manager Jim Leyland.

There were times in the beginning of the Thrift administration that folks wondered if he would ever make a deal; if he would ever trade away some of the still marketable veteran talent he had on his hands for some younger souls that might be able to instill some sense of hope back into the hearts of the few remaining Pirate fans. Yet, it was with some discomfiture that Buc partisans responded to the trade with the New York Yankees that exchanged pitchers Rick Rhoden, the only remaining solid starter in the rotation, and Pat Clements for pitchers Brian Fisher, little-known Doug Drabek and Logan Easley.

Funny thing happened, though. While Rhoden was turning in another creditable performance with the Yankees, Clements became ineffective. And all three of the pitchers obtained by the Pirates were on the opening day roster, although Easley has since been released. Rhoden continues to get older (don't we all), while Drabek and Fisher are still young by baseball standards and, if they can avoid injuries, should be able to help the Pirates for years. In case you're wondering, the three young Bucs won a total of 23 games for a sub-.500 club, while Rhoden and Clements won 19 for a Yankee team with vastly more offensive firepower.

Drabek was the key to the deal for Pittsburgh. Slowed by arm problems early in the season, he started out with an unimpressive 1–8 mark. But when the Pirates caught fire in the second half of the season, just finishing below the .500 mark, Drabek was one of the main cogs in the machine. After July 9, Drabek went 10–3 with a 3.11 ERA, and closed with an 11–12 record and a 3.88 ERA. Fisher, Drabek and rookie Mike Dunne, obtained in the Tony Pena deal with the Cardinals, finished 1–2–3 in innings pitched for the Pirates. While this rotation won't remind anyone of the Baltimore rotation in the late 1960s and early '70s, there is reason to think that maybe this youngish trio will blend nicely with all of the youngsters who play every day to develop into a formidable force in the National League in the years to come.

Put another way, would you rather manage the potential of this group, or hope for the best with the Cubs' veterans?

Tom Henry

Drabek, Douglas Dean "Doug"　　　　Bats: Right　　Throws: Right　　Born 07/25/62

1987 SEASON AND MAJOR-LEAGUE CAREER PITCHING TOTALS

	G	GS	CG	GF	IP	BFP	H	R	ER	HR	SH	SF	HB	TBB	IBB	SO	WP	Bk	W	L	Pct	ShO	Sv	ERA
87 PIT	29	28	1	0	176	721	165	86	76	22	3	4	0	46	2	120	5	1	11	12	.478	1	0	3.89
2 YEARS	56	49	1	2	308	1282	291	150	136	35	8	6	3	96	3	196	7	1	18	20	.474	1	0	3.97

1987: Finesse, Flyball　　　1986: Finesse, Flyball

1987 SEASON

	G	IP	H	BB	SO	SB	CS	W	L	S	ERA
Totals	29	176.0	165	46	120	13	10	11	12	0	3.89
at Home	13	78.2	78	16	63	2	2	6	5	0	3.66
on Road	16	97.1	87	30	57	11	8	5	7	0	4.07
on Grass	9	58.2	51	15	40	2	3	3	5	0	3.68
on Artificial Turf	20	117.1	114	31	80	11	7	8	7	0	3.99
Day Games	6	38.1	32	11	21	1	3	2	3	0	3.52
Night Games	23	137.2	133	35	99	12	7	9	9	0	3.99
April	4	23.0	21	4	19	1	1	1	2	0	3.91
May	2	10.1	10	7	4	1	1	0	1	0	5.23
June	6	35.0	43	9	24	5	3	0	4	0	5.14
July	5	28.1	23	10	15	0	3	1	3	0	4.13
August	6	42.0	30	9	29	4	1	5	0	0	2.79
Sept/Oct	6	37.1	38	7	29	2	1	4	2	0	3.38

FOUR YEAR TOTALS (1984 – 1987)

	G	IP	H	BB	SO	SB	CS	W	L	S	ERA
Totals	56	307.2	291	96	196	16	14	18	20	0	3.98
at Home	25	141.0	141	34	102	3	4	8	8	0	3.70
on Road	31	166.2	150	62	94	13	10	10	12	0	4.21
on Grass	17	90.0	89	28	58	3	5	3	8	0	4.30
on Artificial Turf	39	217.2	202	68	138	13	9	15	12	0	3.85
Day Games	28	135.1	126	49	78	3	6	6	10	0	4.19
Night Games	28	172.1	165	47	118	13	8	12	10	0	3.81
April	4	23.0	21	4	19	1	1	1	2	0	3.91
May	3	14.2	11	10	8	1	2	0	1	0	4.30
June	13	53.1	61	19	33	5	3	0	5	0	6.07
July	12	62.1	58	20	29	0	3	3	6	0	4.48
August	12	81.1	72	24	59	6	2	6	3	0	3.21
Sept/Oct	12	73.0	68	19	48	3	3	8	3	0	2.84

vs. Opponent Batters	Ave.	OBP	SLG	AB	H	2B	3B	HR	RBI	BB	SO
Totals	.247	.294	.415	668	165	34	6	22	76	46	120
vs. Left	.274	.332	.479	340	93	17	4	15	46	30	53
vs. Right	.220	.254	.348	328	72	17	2	7	30	16	67
Bases Empty	.234	.296	.372	419	98	19	3	11	11	37	73
Leadoff	.282	.341	.453	170	48	9	1	6	6	15	27
Not Leadoff	.201	.266	.317	249	50	10	2	5	5	22	46
Runners On Base	.269	.290	.486	249	67	15	3	11	65	9	47
First Base Only	.267	.273	.466	131	35	9	1	5	17	1	21
Scoring Position	.271	.308	.508	118	32	6	2	6	48	8	26
Late Innings, Close	.481	.500	.630	27	13	1	0	3	3	1	1

	Ave.	OBP	SLG	AB	H	2B	3B	HR	RBI	BB	SO
	.249	.305	.407	1169	291	60	10	35	132	96	196
	.275	.343	.469	599	165	30	7	24	80	62	84
	.221	.264	.342	570	126	30	3	11	52	34	112
	.241	.305	.392	722	174	33	5	22	22	66	123
	.268	.331	.430	298	80	16	1	10	10	28	47
	.222	.286	.366	424	94	17	4	12	12	38	76
	.262	.306	.432	447	117	27	5	13	110	30	73
	.244	.274	.422	225	55	15	2	7	25	9	32
	.279	.336	.441	222	62	12	3	6	85	21	41
	.346	.433	.538	52	18	1	0	3	6	8	4

RBI/Opportunities

Scoring Position	37 / 142 (26%)	73 / 288 (25%)
Scoring Position, 2 Out	13 / 64 (20%)	26 / 127 (20%)
On Third, Less than 2 Out	15 / 26 (58%)	28 / 59 (47%)
RBI in close games / RBI Total	59 / 76 (78%)	89 / 132 (67%)

Dave Dravecky
San Francisco Giants.

You can kind of understand how Dave Dravecky would belong to such a superpatriotic organization as the John Birch Society. July 4 has been an important date throughout his career. His first major league victory was July 4, 1982, against the Giants. His lowest mid-season ERA was July 4, 1985, at 1.99. And, of course, on the Fourth of July, 1987, he was traded to the Giants as part of the "Chicago Seven" deal also involving Craig Lefferts, Chris Brown, Kevin Mitchell, Mark Davis, Keith Comstock and Mark Grant. Dave was 3–7, with a 3.76 ERA in 20 games (10 starts) to that point. With the Giants, Dave pitched brilliantly, posting a 6–2 record with a 2.68 ERA and three shutouts in his first 13 starts. He won four consecutive starts from August 15 to September 5, including a 21.1 inning scoreless streak (the longest by a Giant in 2 years). He was named NL Player of the Week for August 31–September 6 (2–0, 0.63).

It would be difficult to find a better post-season performer than Dravecky. Bob Gibson, in 9 postseason games, all starts, had an opponents' batting average of .185 and an ERA of 1.89. Dravecky, in 7 postseason appearances, 2 starts, has an opponents' batting average of .126, and an ERA of 0.35. Of course, as we all remember, the only postseason run Dave has given up cost the Giants a 1–0 defeat in game 6, and with it, a trip to Minnesota.

Dravecky saved his professional career in 1981 while pitching for Amarillo when he developed an excellent biting slider, shortly after being traded from the Pirates organization to San Diego for outfielder Bobby Mitchell. (Seems the Padres trade anyone named Mitchell . . .) That same slider is also the cause of his tender elbow and persistent doubts about his durability; only once has he turned in 200 innings in a season. However, he has never been on the Disabled List, and his 191.1 innings pitched in 1987 was his second highest total. If the elbow holds out, he could provide 200 innings to the Giants this year. However, the Giants, with the best team ERA in baseball, may have the luxury of only seeking 150–170 quality innings from Dave this year. Dravecky wants the ball, but he seems willing to fill any role that helps him perform for a winning team.

A hallmark of Dave Dravecky's career has been his low ERA. His won-lost record (60–55) belies his career ERA of 3.13. He is now on a team that should score early and often, and could "blossom" into a dominating pitcher for the Giants. Over his career, batters have only a .234 average against him, and his career walks + hits/innings pitched is an excellent 1.21. (For a reference point, Dwight Gooden's career WHIPs equals 1.08). Dravecky is a tough pitcher with runners in scoring position, but perhaps the most enjoyable thing about watching Dave pitch is seeing him shear off several bats each game—he takes great pride in improving the profitability of Hillerich & Bradsby.

Michael Duca, Victor Hester

Dravecky, David Francis "Dave"

Bats: Right   Throws: Left   Born 02/14/56

1987 SEASON AND MAJOR-LEAGUE CAREER PITCHING TOTALS

	G	GS	CG	GF	IP	BFP	H	R	ER	HR	SH	SF	HB	TBB	IBB	SO	WP	Bk	W	L	Pct	ShO	Sv	ERA
87 SD-SF	48	28	5	8	191	801	186	82	73	18	7	6	5	64	7	138	2	1	10	12	.455	3	0	3.44
6 YEARS	217	137	27	37	1013	4167	927	397	352	91	63	22	15	303	26	534	9	8	60	55	.522	9	10	3.13

1987: Power, Groundball   1986: Finesse, Groundball   1985: Finesse, Flyball   1984: Finesse, Flyball

1987 SEASON

	G	IP	H	BB	SO	SB	CS	W	L	S	ERA
Totals	48	191.1	186	64	138	20	11	10	12	0	3.43
at Home	26	101.2	89	29	77	11	7	6	6	0	2.92
on Road	22	89.2	97	35	61	9	4	4	6	0	4.01
on Grass	14	63.1	49	12	43	6	3	6	1	0	1.42
on Artificial Turf	34	128.0	137	52	95	14	8	4	11	0	4.43
Day Games	35	133.2	117	39	97	12	7	8	8	0	2.96
Night Games	13	57.2	69	25	41	8	4	2	4	0	4.53
April	13	15.0	21	6	17	2	2	0	3	0	4.80
May	11	26.2	23	15	16	3	1	1	2	0	4.39
June	6	37.1	27	10	27	4	0	2	2	0	2.89
July	6	38.2	37	16	26	4	3	2	2	0	3.49
August	6	43.1	43	10	29	0	5	3	0	0	2.08
Sept/Oct	6	30.1	35	7	23	7	0	2	3	0	4.45

FOUR YEAR TOTALS (1984 – 1987)

	G	IP	H	BB	SO	SB	CS	W	L	S	ERA
Totals	158	724.0	660	226	401	57	34	41	42	8	3.08
	81	363.1	318	104	223	37	17	20	19	6	3.12
	77	360.2	342	122	178	20	17	21	23	2	3.07
	55	245.1	208	82	133	17	13	18	11	2	2.60
	103	478.2	452	144	268	40	21	23	31	6	3.35
	116	511.1	454	151	283	45	23	27	29	7	2.97
	42	212.2	206	75	118	12	11	14	13	1	3.34
	32	84.2	74	27	49	5	5	3	7	2	2.66
	33	127.0	108	45	72	9	5	9	7	1	3.26
	29	149.0	115	51	88	12	6	10	8	4	2.17
	24	146.0	129	49	80	12	9	6	6	0	2.71
	21	129.2	132	32	68	5	9	8	7	0	3.19
	19	87.2	102	22	44	14	0	5	7	1	5.34

vs. Opponent Batters — 1987

	Ave.	OBP	SLG	AB	H	2B	3B	HR	RBI	BB	SO
Totals	.259	.321	.378	719	186	30	1	18	81	64	138
vs. Left	.142	.222	.245	106	15	2	0	3	11	11	34
vs. Right	.279	.338	.401	613	171	28	1	15	70	53	104
Bases Empty	.253	.313	.378	431	109	19	1	11	11	35	77
Leadoff	.267	.316	.406	180	48	8	1	5	5	12	33
Not Leadoff	.243	.312	.359	251	61	11	0	6	6	23	44
Runners On Base	.267	.332	.378	288	77	11	0	7	70	29	61
First Base Only	.281	.336	.421	121	34	2	0	5	10	9	21
Scoring Position	.257	.330	.347	167	43	9	0	2	60	20	40
Late Innings, Close	.297	.409	.459	37	11	0	0	2	5	7	10

vs. Opponent Batters — Four Year Totals

	Ave.	OBP	SLG	AB	H	2B	3B	HR	RBI	BB	SO
Totals	.245	.305	.363	2689	660	109	6	65	250	226	401
vs. Left	.204	.271	.283	378	77	10	1	6	34	35	90
vs. Right	.252	.310	.376	2311	583	99	5	59	216	191	311
Bases Empty	.251	.306	.367	1647	414	76	2	37	37	127	232
Leadoff	.241	.291	.359	693	167	32	1	16	16	48	93
Not Leadoff	.259	.317	.373	954	247	44	1	21	21	79	139
Runners On Base	.236	.302	.356	1042	246	33	4	28	213	99	169
First Base Only	.247	.290	.384	469	116	14	1	16	38	27	60
Scoring Position	.227	.311	.333	573	130	19	3	12	175	72	109
Late Innings, Close	.269	.338	.451	297	80	12	0	14	38	31	43

RBI/Opportunities

	1987	Four Year
Scoring Position	53 / 223 (24%)	149 / 779 (19%)
Scoring Position, 2 Out	25 / 103 (24%)	74 / 362 (20%)
On Third, Less than 2 Out	14 / 30 (47%)	43 / 121 (36%)
RBI in close games / RBI Total	50 / 81 (62%)	176 / 250 (70%)

83

Mariano Duncan
Los Angeles Dodgers

Big things have been expected from Mariano Duncan by the Dodgers. He was made a major leaguer at the age of 22 and given the starting shortstop job. In three years as the Dodger shortstop Mariano has used his extraordinary speed to rush to a crossroad in his career.

Mariano spent two full and one partial season in the minors before he came up. He showed flashes of brilliance defensively, and had amazing speed. He stole 97 bases in his two full minor league seasons and led his league both times in triples. The man can flat run. Of course, he also hit 6 triples in Florida in 1986 spring training, which, added to his 0 in League games . . . well, you get the idea.

But despite the speed and the Dodgers' expectations, Duncan has been a disappointment. In his best year he only hit .244. His patience at the plate is lower than his batting average, so he doesn't draw enough walks. This seems to be strong support for environment over genetics—Mariano is one of the legions of impatient hitters to make the major leagues from the tiny hamlet of San Pedro de Macorís in the Dominican Republic. His OBA is intolerably low—only 13 position players racked up 50 or more AB and had an OBA lower than his .267—3 rookies, 4 backup catchers, and 4 Dodger teammates among them. Of players with 200 or more AB, only 2 had lower OBA in the entire league. Nev-

ertheless, Lasorda has tried a couple of times in *each* of the last three years to install Duncan in the leadoff slot. Tommy—maybe you should try reading in the off-season instead of watching so much TV.

Mariano was slowed down due to injuries in 1987 and made fewer than 300 plate appearances. Lucky for the Dodger "attack." He hit .219 to go with his .267 OBA—both career "worsts," both continuing steady slides from his none-too-stellar rookie performances. Because of the injuries and the dearth of opportunities, he only stole 11 bases in 12 tries. If he doesn't steal an arm full of bases he is a complete liability to the Dodgers—his 21 errors in 76 games gave him the lowest fielding average of any shortstop who handled 225 chances in the National League.

Nonetheless the Dodgers seem unwilling to give up on Duncan—because he is from San Pedro de Macorís, they seem certain he will be a great one. Well, there has to be an exception to prove every rule. Thank goodness the Dodgers went out and got Alfredo Griffin, who at least clusters his errors together (he made over a quarter of his 24 for Oakland last year in just 2 games). Mariano won't go into spring training with the shortstop job locked up. If he comes out of spring training with any starting job, management should be locked up.

Carmen Corica

Duncan, Mariano (Nalasco)   Bats: Both   Throws: Right   Born 03/13/63

1987 SEASON AND MAJOR-LEAGUE CAREER BATTING TOTALS

	G	AB	H	2B	3B	HR	TB	R	RBI	TBB	IBB	SO	HP	SH	SF	SB	CS	SB%	GDP	AVG	OBP	SLG
87 LA	76	261	56	8	1	6	84	31	18	17	1	62	2	6	1	11	1	.92	4	.215	.267	.322
3 YEARS	327	1230	286	39	7	20	399	152	87	85	6	253	7	24	6	97	22	.82	19	.233	.285	.324

	1987 SEASON											FOUR YEAR TOTALS (1984 – 1987)									
	Ave.	OBP	SLG	AB	H	2B	3B	HR	RBI	BB	SO	Ave.	OBP	SLG	AB	H	2B	3B	HR	RBI	BB	SO
Totals	.215	.267	.322	261	56	8	1	6	18	17	62	.233	.285	.324	1230	286	39	7	20	87	85	253
vs. Left	.275	.305	.451	91	25	4	0	4	9	4	19	.274	.312	.401	446	122	17	2	12	40	24	82
vs. Right	.182	.247	.253	170	31	4	1	2	9	13	43	.209	.269	.281	784	164	22	5	8	47	61	171
at Home	.227	.277	.336	110	25	3	0	3	9	7	27	.231	.280	.298	590	136	18	2	6	33	38	124
on Road	.205	.259	.311	151	31	5	1	3	9	10	35	.234	.289	.348	640	150	21	5	14	54	47	129
vs. Groundball	.192	.257	.272	125	24	2	1	2	6	10	29	.228	.288	.291	549	125	13	5	4	33	43	101
vs. Flyball	.235	.276	.368	136	32	6	0	4	12	7	33	.236	.282	.351	681	161	26	2	16	54	42	152
vs. Finesse	.168	.223	.270	137	23	5	0	3	6	8	26	.222	.272	.307	685	152	21	2	11	45	44	118
vs. Power	.266	.316	.379	124	33	3	1	3	12	9	36	.246	.301	.347	545	134	18	5	9	42	41	135
on Grass	.221	.273	.326	190	42	6	1	4	14	12	44	.230	.281	.316	941	216	29	5	14	66	63	192
on Artificial Turf	.197	.250	.310	71	14	2	0	2	4	5	18	.242	.295	.353	289	70	10	2	6	21	22	61
Day Games	.181	.220	.287	94	17	2	1	2	9	4	21	.251	.294	.343	399	100	14	1	7	25	23	84
Night Games	.234	.293	.341	167	39	6	0	4	9	13	41	.224	.280	.315	831	186	25	6	13	62	62	169
April	.282	.347	.388	85	24	3	0	2	6	7	22	.239	.305	.340	238	57	9	0	5	12	21	46
May	.161	.188	.215	93	15	2	0	1	6	3	23	.202	.254	.263	243	49	6	0	3	14	17	65
June	.250	.294	.313	16	4	1	0	0	0	1	6	.250	.284	.330	188	47	6	0	3	14	9	30
July	.190	.277	.429	42	8	2	1	2	4	5	7	.230	.281	.362	196	45	8	3	4	16	14	38
August	.200	.231	.320	25	5	0	0	1	2	1	4	.276	.302	.389	185	51	5	2	4	12	7	36
Sept/Oct	.000	.000	.000	0	0	0	0	0	0	0	0	.206	.274	.272	180	37	5	2	1	19	17	38
Bases Empty	.218	.283	.339	165	36	5	0	5	5	13	42	.230	.286	.323	792	182	26	3	14	14	60	169
Leadoff	.179	.250	.238	84	15	2	0	1	1	7	25	.198	.261	.250	424	84	8	1	4	4	35	94
Not Leadoff	.259	.318	.444	81	21	3	0	4	4	6	17	.266	.315	.408	368	98	18	2	10	10	25	75
Runners On	.208	.238	.292	96	20	3	1	1	13	4	20	.237	.278	.326	438	104	13	4	6	73	25	84
First Base Only	.256	.256	.326	43	11	3	0	0	1	0	7	.277	.297	.356	177	49	9	1	1	5	5	33
Scoring Position	.170	.224	.264	53	9	0	1	1	12	4	13	.211	.266	.307	261	55	4	3	5	68	20	51
Late Innings, Close	.302	.400	.419	43	13	3	1	0	4	6	11	.265	.328	.381	181	48	5	2	4	17	16	38

RBI/Opportunities

Scoring Position	11 / 71 (15%)	58 / 355 (16%)	
Scoring Position, 2 Out	4 / 36 (11%)	25 / 176 (14%)	
On Third, Less than 2 Out	4 / 11 (36%)	22 / 61 (36%)	
RBI in close games / RBI Total	14 / 18 (78%)	58 / 87 (67%)	

Mike Dunne
Pittsburgh Pirates

On June 5, Mike Dunne went 6 innings, gave up 4 hits, allowed 3 runs, 1 earned, walked 6, and struck out 1. Not bad for a rookie pitcher making his first major league start/appearance in Shea Stadium against the defending world champion Mets in only his third year of professional baseball. This was just the beginning for Dunne in 1987. He rattled off impressive performance after impressive performance on his way to a 13–6 record and an ERA second in the National League only to Nolan Ryan.

Mike Dunne did everything expected out of a quality major league starting pitcher. Three out of every four times Dunne took the mound (17–23) he lasted into the seventh inning and only twice was he removed from a game before completing the fifth inning, totaling an average of 7.1 innings per start. Dunne never lost to a poor team, with his only loss against a sub-.550 team being to Philadelphia (80–82).

Although Dunne only spent two full seasons in the minors, one might have suspected him to do well in the bigs because of his experience on the Olympic team of 1984. Projecting his numbers over a full season (35 starts), and assuming that he gets decisions in 83 percent of his starts, Dunne can be considered to have a legitimate shot to win 20 games in 1988, especially now that Jeff Robinson enters the picture as the Bucs' number one stopper.

On the basis of his second half performance in 1987 (9–2, 2.54 ERA), Dunne is the logical choice to take the mound on April 5, 1988, in an attempt to lead the Pirates back into the upper half of their division, and all the new, young talent acquired through trades and the farm system, could make them the surprise team in the NL East.

Doug White

Dunne is primarily a sinkerball pitcher, much like his former teammate Rick Reuschel. Dunne and Reuschel were so similar that Leyland had to rework his rotation so that they didn't pitch on successive days.

Dunne pitched very well in 1987, but to repeat his success, there's one major thing he has to do: cut down on those walks. He's not a power pitcher and he can't afford to have as many men on base as he did this year. Among ERA leaders in the National League, the only pitcher who came close to giving up as many walks per game as Dunne was Nolan Ryan, but he gave up quite a bit fewer hits per game. Dunne did handle the walks well, but he was also lucky, and that isn't likely to continue. If he can correct the control problems over the off-season, he'll do fine; if not, Mike Dunne is a prime candidate for sophomore jinx.

Sherri M. Nichols

Dunne, Michael Dennis "Mike"

Bats: Right Throws: Right Born 10/27/62

1987 SEASON AND MAJOR-LEAGUE CAREER PITCHING TOTALS

	G	GS	CG	GF	IP	BFP	H	R	ER	HR	SH	SF	HB	TBB	IBB	SO	WP	Bk	W	L	Pct	ShO	Sv	ERA
87 PIT	23	23	5	0	163	680	143	66	55	10	11	4	1	68	8	72	6	4	13	6	.684	1	0	3.04
1 YEAR	23	23	5	0	163	680	143	66	55	10	11	4	1	68	8	72	6	4	13	6	.684	1	0	3.04

1987: Finesse, Groundball

1987 SEASON

	G	IP	H	BB	SO	SB	CS	W	L	S	ERA
Totals	23	163.1	143	68	72	8	7	13	6	0	3.03
at Home	10	70.2	55	25	36	4	5	6	2	0	2.42
on Road	13	92.2	88	43	36	4	2	7	4	0	3.50
on Grass	7	51.0	47	15	19	3	4	6	1	0	2.47
on Artificial Turf	16	112.1	96	53	53	5	3	7	5	0	3.28
Day Games	5	34.1	33	11	16	0	2	3	2	0	2.88
Night Games	18	129.0	110	57	56	8	5	10	4	0	3.07
April	0	0.0	0	0	0	0	0	0	0	0	0.00
May	0	0.0	0	0	0	0	0	0	0	0	0.00
June	6	42.0	39	25	20	1	2	3	3	0	3.86
July	5	35.0	33	8	20	0	2	3	1	0	2.06
August	6	47.2	34	16	17	2	2	3	1	0	2.45
Sept/Oct	6	38.2	37	19	15	5	1	4	1	0	3.72

vs. Opponent Batters	Ave.	OBP	SLG	AB	H	2B	3B	HR	RBI	BB	SO
Totals	.240	.317	.336	596	143	17	5	10	56	68	72
vs. Left	.277	.367	.408	321	89	8	5	8	30	45	23
vs. Right	.196	.256	.251	275	54	9	0	2	26	23	49
Bases Empty	.254	.319	.375	355	90	9	5	8	8	33	44
Leadoff	.255	.304	.376	157	40	5	1	4	4	11	21
Not Leadoff	.253	.330	.374	198	50	4	4	4	4	22	23
Runners On Base	.220	.314	.278	241	53	8	0	2	48	35	28
First Base Only	.238	.298	.324	105	25	3	0	2	4	9	11
Scoring Position	.206	.325	.243	136	28	5	0	0	44	26	17
Late Innings, Close	.254	.293	.380	71	18	1	1	2	6	4	7

FOUR YEAR TOTALS (1984 – 1987)

	G	IP	H	BB	SO	SB	CS	W	L	S	ERA
Totals	23	163.1	143	68	72	8	7	13	6	0	3.03
at Home	10	70.2	55	25	36	4	5	6	2	0	2.42
on Road	13	92.2	88	43	36	4	2	7	4	0	3.50
on Grass	7	51.0	47	15	19	3	4	6	1	0	2.47
on Artificial Turf	16	112.1	96	53	53	5	3	7	5	0	3.28
Day Games	5	34.1	33	11	16	0	2	3	2	0	2.88
Night Games	18	129.0	110	57	56	8	5	10	4	0	3.07
April	0	0.0	0	0	0	0	0	0	0	0	0.00
May	0	0.0	0	0	0	0	0	0	0	0	0.00
June	6	42.0	39	25	20	1	2	3	3	0	3.86
July	5	35.0	33	8	20	0	2	3	1	0	2.06
August	6	47.2	34	16	17	2	2	3	1	0	2.45
Sept/Oct	6	38.2	37	19	15	5	1	4	1	0	3.72

vs. Opponent Batters	Ave.	OBP	SLG	AB	H	2B	3B	HR	RBI	BB	SO
Totals	.240	.317	.336	596	143	17	5	10	56	68	72
vs. Left	.277	.367	.408	321	89	8	5	8	30	45	23
vs. Right	.196	.256	.251	275	54	9	0	2	26	23	49
Bases Empty	.254	.319	.375	355	90	9	5	8	8	33	44
Leadoff	.255	.304	.376	157	40	5	1	4	4	11	21
Not Leadoff	.253	.330	.374	198	50	4	4	4	4	22	23
Runners On Base	.220	.314	.278	241	53	8	0	2	48	35	28
First Base Only	.238	.298	.324	105	25	3	0	2	4	9	11
Scoring Position	.206	.325	.243	136	28	5	0	0	44	26	17
Late Innings, Close	.254	.293	.380	71	18	1	1	2	6	4	7

RBI/Opportunities

Scoring Position	42 / 203	(21%)
Scoring Position, 2 Out	11 / 72	(15%)
On Third, Less than 2 Out	23 / 46	(50%)
RBI in close games / RBI Total	41 / 56	(73%)

	42 / 203	(21%)
	11 / 72	(15%)
	23 / 46	(50%)
	41 / 56	(73%)

Shawon Dunston
Chicago Cubs

Shawon Dunston emerged as one of the top shortstops in the National League in 1986. As a result expectations were high for the youngster in 1987. Despite a horrid start that saw him drive in *no* runs in April, Shawon began to improve. In the last ten days of May he raised his average from .199 to .230. In June Dunston really sizzled; .358, with a .528 slugging percentage. He was still striking out too much and hardly walking at all, but he was on fire. Cub fans looked for a season similar to 1986 for the up-and-coming shortstop.

Expectations came to a crashing halt on June 15. Sliding headfirst into second base on a steal attempt in the ninth inning of a close game, Shawon broke his finger and was sidelined until late August. When he came back he couldn't find himself at the plate. Shawon's post-injury stats were dismal: .198 batting average, .236 on-base percentage and .241 slugging percentage. The most remarkable dropoff was his power; before the injury Dunston's season slugging percentage was .400. Shawon became an offensive black hole in the middle of the general team collapse.

Even without the concurrent loss of Ryne Sandberg, Dunston's injury would have been difficult to overcome; the combination of the two was devastating. None of his replacements played even close to Dunston offensively. By far the best of the three was Paul Noce, who filled in at second until Ryno returned, then took over at short. Noce's season offensive statistics were a .228 average, .261 on-base percentage, and a .350 slugging percentage. Dunston's initial replacement, Mike Brumley, was far worse: .202 AVG, .276 OBP, .288 SLG. Luis Quinones, called up in desperation after Brumley faltered, was about the same: .218 AVG, .288 OBP, .277 SLG. (This didn't stop Cub management from frequently using Quinones as a pinch-hitter. Okay, so he's lefthanded; does that mean anything if he can't hit? In pinch roles, Quinones batted .174, with 4 singles and one RBI in 23 at bats.)

Defensively, Dunston's range declined to 4.83 chances per nine innings, a sharp drop from '86's 5.38. It is tempting to blame the injury, but wrong; Shawon's range was down even before he was hurt. He was more sure-handed, however, improving his fielding average from .961 in '86 to .969. Noce's range stats were actually better than Dunston's, but he obviously can't hit with Shawon.

In one area, Dunston showed great improvement in 1987: base stealing. In 1986 Shawon was 13 of 26 in stolen base attempts, counting 11 caught stealings and 2 pickoffs. In 1987 he was stealing at an .800 success rate, stealing 12 bases and being caught 3 times with no pickoffs. Even so, all but two of his steals came prior to his injury. Hopefully, the 1987 disaster will not have serious adverse effects on Shawon Dunston. Here's hoping for a banner season from the youngster.

Pat McCormick

Dunston, Shawon Donnell — Bats: Right — Throws: Right — Born 03/21/63

1987 SEASON AND MAJOR-LEAGUE CAREER BATTING TOTALS

	G	AB	H	2B	3B	HR	TB	R	RBI	TBB	IBB	SO	HP	SH	SF	SB	CS	SB%	GDP	AVG	OBP	SLG
87 CHN	95	346	85	18	3	5	124	40	22	10	1	68	1	0	2	12	3	.80	6	.246	.267	.358
3 YEARS	319	1177	295	67	10	26	460	146	108	50	9	224	4	5	6	36	17	.68	14	.251	.282	.391

	1987 SEASON											FOUR YEAR TOTALS (1984 – 1987)										
	Ave.	OBP	SLG	AB	H	2B	3B	HR	RBI	BB	SO	Ave.	OBP	SLG	AB	H	2B	3B	HR	RBI	BB	SO
Totals	.246	.267	.358	346	85	18	3	5	22	10	68	.251	.282	.391	1177	295	67	10	26	108	50	224
vs. Left	.231	.237	.321	78	18	2	1	1	3	0	12	.229	.246	.384	279	64	15	2	8	32	6	44
vs. Right	.250	.276	.369	268	67	16	2	4	19	10	56	.257	.293	.393	898	231	52	8	18	76	44	180
at Home	.221	.239	.337	181	40	8	2	3	15	5	32	.259	.292	.414	633	164	38	6	16	61	29	118
on Road	.273	.298	.382	165	45	10	1	2	7	5	36	.241	.271	.364	544	131	29	4	10	47	21	106
vs. Groundball	.289	.320	.444	142	41	9	2	3	12	7	16	.289	.326	.441	526	152	32	6	12	50	28	69
vs. Flyball	.216	.230	.299	204	44	9	1	2	10	3	52	.220	.246	.350	651	143	35	4	14	58	22	155
vs. Finesse	.275	.303	.408	211	58	15	2	3	15	8	31	.275	.307	.417	691	190	44	6	14	56	29	100
vs. Power	.200	.210	.281	135	27	3	1	2	7	2	37	.216	.248	.354	486	105	23	4	12	52	21	124
on Grass	.227	.248	.348	233	53	12	2	4	20	7	43	.253	.284	.405	825	209	49	8	20	81	35	151
on Artificial Turf	.283	.308	.381	113	32	6	1	1	2	3	25	.244	.278	.358	352	86	18	2	6	27	15	73
Day Games	.237	.257	.352	236	56	11	2	4	16	6	43	.254	.288	.404	814	207	47	6	21	80	37	144
Night Games	.264	.289	.373	110	29	7	1	1	6	4	25	.242	.269	.361	363	88	20	4	5	28	13	80
April	.195	.215	.260	77	15	5	0	0	0	2	13	.226	.258	.353	190	43	13	1	3	9	8	26
May	.255	.265	.436	110	28	9	1	3	13	2	29	.269	.299	.442	249	67	18	2	7	26	11	55
June	.358	.382	.528	53	19	1	1	2	4	2	10	.283	.317	.428	159	45	9	1	4	17	8	34
July	.000	.000	.000	0	0	0	0	0	0	0	0	.240	.263	.438	96	23	6	2	3	14	3	19
August	.316	.381	.368	19	6	1	0	0	1	2	4	.210	.224	.309	162	34	5	1	3	16	3	35
Sept/Oct	.195	.220	.241	87	17	2	1	0	4	2	12	.259	.297	.383	321	83	16	3	6	26	17	55
Bases Empty	.255	.284	.370	216	55	10	3	3	3	9	53	.243	.268	.387	720	175	35	9	17	17	25	152
Leadoff	.266	.303	.351	94	25	4	2	0	0	5	20	.258	.284	.398	322	83	16	4	7	7	12	59
Not Leadoff	.246	.270	.385	122	30	6	1	3	3	4	33	.231	.255	.379	398	92	19	5	10	10	13	93
Runners On	.231	.239	.338	130	30	8	0	2	19	1	15	.263	.301	.396	457	120	32	1	9	91	25	72
First Base Only	.227	.239	.303	66	15	5	0	0	0	0	6	.272	.298	.401	217	59	16	0	4	9	7	32
Scoring Position	.234	.239	.375	64	15	3	0	2	19	1	9	.254	.304	.392	240	61	16	1	5	82	18	40
Late Innings, Close	.297	.324	.344	64	19	3	0	0	2	3	16	.228	.254	.335	197	45	7	1	4	15	7	42

RBI/Opportunities

	1987	Four Year
Scoring Position	15 / 79 (19%)	70 / 320 (22%)
Scoring Position, 2 Out	9 / 38 (24%)	26 / 137 (19%)
On Third, Less than 2 Out	5 / 18 (28%)	28 / 62 (45%)
RBI in close games / RBI Total	15 / 22 (68%)	76 / 108 (70%)

Leon Durham
Chicago Cubs

In the first edition of *GABSB*, Mark Podrazik wrote: "The '87 season ought to be a year of reckoning for Leon Durham." Again in 1987 he was platooned at first base for the Cubs. Manny Trillo or Rafael Palmeiro minded the store while the Bull considered his future in Chicago. If Leon should ever demand a trade—and if I were his agent, I'd *never* so advise—he'd better carefully pick his spots or his career is history immediately.

Relatively few ballplayers are perfectly designed to succeed in one ballpark. Sandy Koufax was perfect for Dodger Stadium in the sixties. Jim Rice and Fenway Park fit like a glove. Willie Mays and centerfield at the Polo Grounds. So, back to the present . . . Leon Durham was built for Wrigley Field. His home/road breakdowns for years have been as unbalanced as any in baseball.

Durham's chance to prove himself came at the start of 1987. Appearing in 64 of the Cubs' first 72 games (through June 25), Durham hit .310 with 14 homers. Then came the fall. A second-half slump (only 13 homers and .235 average) resulted in more days on the pines, and Leon played in only 67 of the last 90 Cub games. His strikeout ratio rose from one every 5.8 at bats to one every 4.0 at bats. The Bull was pressing as he grew disillusioned with the platooning arrangement.

From 1984 to 1986, Durham hit 78 points better at Wrigley than on the road (.312 to .234). He hit nearly three times as many homers at the "friendly confines" (47 to 17).

Doubles were higher at home (49 to 31) as were triples (9 to 4). He even struck out much less at home (one every 6.2 at bats to one every 4.6 on the road). If he wants to go elsewhere, he'd better limit his shopping list to parks suited especially for left-handed sluggers. Maybe he'd best just stay put.

There is a mystique about the Bull. I think it's the glasses. Sort of like Kareem Abdul-Jabbar's goggles. Then there's the mustache and goatee. The arm muscles ripple with each swing as he awaits the pitch. He is a caricature of baseball at the plate. And can he ever send a charge into any pitcher's mistake, depositing souvenirs beyond the confines of Wrigley and onto Sheffield Avenue. But last year I could sense no "magic" when Durham came up in a key offensive situation. Sharing Andre's limelight may have diminished his confidence. His face showed the concern when he was used only late in a game, or only as a pinch-hitter, or when he took his position after the last at bat in an 0-for-4 road game.

Maybe Leon needs to play every day somewhere. If Mark Grace develops in 1988 as many predict he will, the Cubs will not need Mr. Durham. It's so painful to watch how lefties tie him up, and to see how poorly he performs away from home, or at night, or even on Astroturf. Anywhere else he goes, one or more of those negative factors in his resume will likely haunt him.

Robert L. Jones

Durham, Leon

Bats: Left   **Throws: Left**   **Born 07/31/57**

1987 SEASON AND MAJOR-LEAGUE CAREER BATTING TOTALS

	G	AB	H	2B	3B	HR	TB	R	RBI	TBB	IBB	SO	HP	SH	SF	SB	CS	SB%	GDP	AVG	OBP	SLG
87 CHN	131	439	120	22	1	27	225	70	63	51	9	92	0	0	2	2	2	.50	6	.273	.348	.513
8 YEARS	993	3445	964	182	39	143	1653	506	521	428	93	643	8	3	23	106	59	.64	49	.280	.359	.480

	1987 SEASON											FOUR YEAR TOTALS (1984 – 1987)										
	Ave.	OBP	SLG	AB	H	2B	3B	HR	RBI	BB	SO	Ave.	OBP	SLG	AB	H	2B	3B	HR	RBI	BB	SO
Totals	.273	.348	.513	439	120	22	1	27	63	51	92	.275	.356	.482	1938	532	102	14	91	299	251	375
vs. Left	.257	.286	.378	74	19	3	0	2	8	3	19	.251	.319	.390	438	110	20	4	11	60	43	112
vs. Right	.277	.359	.540	365	101	19	1	25	55	48	73	.281	.367	.509	1500	422	82	10	80	239	208	263
at Home	.297	.375	.551	236	70	12	0	16	41	30	48	.309	.391	.572	1017	314	61	9	63	195	141	174
on Road	.246	.316	.468	203	50	10	1	11	22	21	44	.237	.317	.383	921	218	41	5	28	104	110	201
vs. Groundball	.241	.321	.445	191	46	6	0	11	26	23	40	.282	.367	.483	882	249	48	6	39	140	119	165
vs. Flyball	.298	.368	.565	248	74	16	1	16	37	28	52	.268	.347	.482	1056	283	54	8	52	159	132	210
vs. Finesse	.320	.387	.608	250	80	16	1	18	41	28	48	.308	.378	.533	1121	345	65	7	58	175	129	183
vs. Power	.212	.296	.386	189	40	6	0	9	22	23	44	.229	.327	.412	817	187	37	7	33	124	122	192
on Grass	.272	.345	.505	327	89	16	0	20	48	37	69	.293	.370	.519	1363	399	74	11	71	230	173	239
on Artificial Turf	.277	.354	.536	112	31	6	1	7	15	14	23	.231	.323	.395	575	133	28	3	20	69	78	136
Day Games	.302	.373	.570	291	88	15	0	21	50	34	57	.293	.375	.538	1319	386	75	12	75	232	180	239
Night Games	.216	.297	.399	148	32	7	1	6	13	17	35	.236	.314	.363	619	146	27	2	16	67	71	136
April	.311	.381	.568	74	23	1	0	6	10	9	9	.270	.348	.460	248	67	6	1	13	31	30	47
May	.298	.371	.543	94	28	5	0	6	10	11	17	.293	.380	.522	362	106	16	2	21	67	51	65
June	.293	.354	.493	75	22	6	0	3	7	7	19	.280	.353	.432	354	99	23	2	9	47	40	77
July	.214	.267	.386	70	15	6	0	2	11	5	15	.257	.341	.431	304	78	19	2	10	43	39	45
August	.246	.342	.508	65	16	2	0	5	12	10	14	.278	.366	.533	306	85	19	4	17	46	43	72
Sept/Oct	.262	.357	.574	61	16	2	1	5	13	9	15	.266	.352	.508	364	97	19	3	21	65	48	69
Bases Empty	.292	.338	.572	257	75	13	1	19	19	18	54	.272	.332	.480	1076	293	61	8	49	49	96	210
Leadoff	.284	.325	.543	116	33	6	0	8	8	7	31	.258	.315	.477	457	118	28	3	22	22	38	96
Not Leadoff	.298	.349	.596	141	42	7	1	11	11	11	23	.283	.344	.483	619	175	33	5	27	27	58	114
Runners On	.247	.359	.429	182	45	9	0	8	44	33	38	.277	.387	.485	862	239	41	6	42	250	155	165
First Base Only	.292	.364	.551	89	26	5	0	6	13	10	16	.293	.344	.515	392	115	16	4	21	53	30	68
Scoring Position	.204	.356	.312	93	19	4	0	2	31	23	22	.264	.417	.460	470	124	25	2	21	197	125	97
Late Innings, Close	.263	.323	.404	57	15	2	0	2	3	5	10	.260	.366	.450	300	78	18	0	13	41	50	62

RBI/Opportunities

Scoring Position	28 / 135 (21%)	161 / 690 (23%)
Scoring Position, 2 Out	9 / 58 (16%)	56 / 306 (18%)
On Third, Less than 2 Out	10 / 25 (40%)	60 / 132 (45%)
RBI in close games / RBI Total	35 / 63 (56%)	206 / 299 (69%)

Lenny Dykstra
New York Mets

Here he is, the symbol of Met arrogance. Twitching, spitting, jutting, and daring the opposition. He is defiance personified. Behind him and Gary Carter rally the arrogance criers, judging the book by the cover. Among the couple of dozen others are shy ones, humble ones, reclusive ones, moody ones, and no ones. Cocky, indeed. But labels, justified or not, seem to be made of two-sided tape.

It is no secret that both Lenny and Mookie Wilson are unhappy about platooning. At this writing, Mookie's head is on the block and he may be gone by now. Either way, look for Lenny to face a challenge for CF annually. The Mets seem to grow fleet center fielders and I am not sure that Met management is convinced that Lenny is their guy for the long range.

Let's look at the stats, remembering that his role is that of fleet leadoff catalyst. He has had two remarkably similar years since his 1985 rookie half season. Both years were spent platooning and his at bats reflect it (431 both years). Dykstra plays in parts of lots of games. He is often inserted late in a double switch to get 1 or 2 at bats and a couple of innings afield and also removed early in a double switch, of-ten after his fourth at bat. Witness the plate appearances per game: 3.33 in 1986, 3.57 in 1987, awfully low for a leadoff hitter. Here's 1986 vs. 1987:

Year	AB	H	2B	3B	HR	R	RBI	SB	BA	SA
86	431	127	27	7	8	77	45	31	295	.445
87	431	123	37	3	10	86	43	27	285	.455

He did, however, draw 18 less walks in 1987—a serious matter for a leadoff man.

The amazing stat is the doubles. In 1987, he had a double every 11.6 at bats, better than anyone in the league except teammate Tim Teufel (29 2B but only 299 at bats, 1 every 10.3 AB). Eleven of Dykstra's two baggers were in a three week period down the stretch (Sept. 11-Oct. 1).

So, do you want this man as your centerfielder for the '90s? Some good early career stats (better than Joe Morgan in his young Houston days), potential for growth, Pete Rose attitude (nickname *Nails*), good speed, good eye, decent power (and growing), and decent arm. I'll take him, even if Met management may not be convinced.

Dave Gordon

Dykstra, Leonard Kyle "Lenny" Bats: Left Throws: Left Born 02/10/63

1987 SEASON AND MAJOR-LEAGUE CAREER BATTING TOTALS

	G	AB	H	2B	3B	HR	TB	R	RBI	TBB	IBB	SO	HP	SH	SF	SB	CS	SB%	GDP	AVG	OBP	SLG
87 NYN	132	431	123	37	3	10	196	86	43	40	3	67	4	4	0	27	7	.79	1	.285	.352	.455
3 YEARS	362	1098	310	73	13	19	466	203	107	128	4	146	5	15	4	73	16	.82	9	.282	.359	.424

	1987 SEASON											FOUR YEAR TOTALS (1984 – 1987)										
	Ave.	OBP	SLG	AB	H	2B	3B	HR	RBI	BB	SO	Ave.	OBP	SLG	AB	H	2B	3B	HR	RBI	BB	SO
Totals	.285	.352	.455	431	123	37	3	10	43	40	67	.282	.359	.424	1098	310	73	13	19	107	128	146
vs. Left	.203	.289	.324	74	15	6	0	1	7	8	13	.232	.325	.309	233	54	15	0	1	21	30	40
vs. Right	.303	.365	.482	357	108	31	3	9	36	32	54	.296	.368	.455	865	256	58	13	18	86	98	106
at Home	.292	.359	.481	212	62	17	1	7	27	19	27	.293	.367	.447	532	156	37	6	11	59	60	64
on Road	.279	.344	.429	219	61	20	2	3	16	21	40	.272	.351	.403	566	154	36	7	8	48	68	82
vs. Groundball	.309	.374	.463	162	50	17	1	2	16	15	21	.273	.352	.389	465	127	32	5	4	42	57	56
vs. Flyball	.271	.338	.450	269	73	20	2	8	27	25	46	.289	.364	.450	633	183	41	8	15	65	71	90
vs. Finesse	.267	.302	.407	243	65	15	2	5	19	11	35	.298	.348	.430	607	181	36	7	10	55	46	73
vs. Power	.309	.409	.516	188	58	22	1	5	24	29	32	.263	.371	.418	491	129	37	6	9	52	82	73
on Grass	.301	.359	.474	306	92	25	2	8	32	24	46	.291	.362	.432	776	226	53	10	12	74	84	101
on Artificial Turf	.248	.333	.408	125	31	12	1	2	11	16	21	.261	.351	.407	322	84	20	3	7	33	44	45
Day Games	.308	.370	.500	172	53	17	2	4	12	16	31	.297	.364	.457	444	132	33	7	8	36	46	57
Night Games	.270	.339	.425	259	70	20	1	6	31	24	36	.272	.355	.402	654	178	40	6	11	71	82	89
April	.250	.333	.446	56	14	3	1	2	5	7	10	.288	.373	.441	111	32	4	2	3	10	15	17
May	.358	.419	.672	67	24	7	1	4	11	6	7	.297	.358	.486	148	44	9	2	5	15	13	14
June	.247	.284	.299	77	19	4	0	0	1	4	17	.296	.352	.428	152	45	11	3	1	13	13	32
July	.294	.351	.441	68	20	4	0	2	9	6	9	.291	.360	.430	258	75	17	2	5	35	28	29
August	.259	.355	.407	81	21	7	1	1	6	9	12	.252	.343	.370	246	62	14	3	3	18	31	32
Sept/Oct	.305	.367	.488	82	25	12	0	1	11	8	12	.284	.379	.426	183	52	18	1	2	16	28	22
Bases Empty	.278	.335	.441	299	83	25	3	6	6	25	51	.283	.356	.423	750	212	53	8	12	12	85	111
Leadoff	.280	.346	.460	189	53	16	3	4	4	18	33	.284	.362	.437	455	129	33	5	9	9	55	70
Not Leadoff	.273	.316	.409	110	30	9	0	2	2	7	18	.281	.348	.400	295	83	20	3	3	3	30	41
Runners On	.303	.387	.485	132	40	12	0	4	37	15	16	.282	.365	.428	348	98	20	5	7	95	43	35
First Base Only	.353	.389	.627	51	18	5	0	3	7	2	3	.279	.345	.450	129	36	6	2	4	11	12	9
Scoring Position	.272	.385	.395	81	22	7	0	1	30	13	13	.283	.377	.416	219	62	14	3	3	84	31	26
Late Innings, Close	.246	.348	.386	57	14	5	0	1	5	9	8	.274	.364	.396	164	45	12	1	2	16	23	23

RBI/Opportunities

Scoring Position	27 / 112 (24%)	77 / 309 (25%)
Scoring Position, 2 Out	11 / 46 (24%)	38 / 155 (25%)
On Third, Less than 2 Out	9 / 15 (60%)	20 / 38 (53%)
RBI in close games / RBI Total	23 / 43 (53%)	61 / 107 (57%)

Dennis Eckersley
Oakland Athletics

Dennis Eckersley is the kind of guy you can't stand when he plays on another team. He's arrogant, abrasive (pointing his forefinger like a gun barrel at opposing batters after a strikeout) and generally gets on everybody's nerves. But when he's on *your* team, he becomes an amusing flake, a good interview, and a fierce competitor.

With Oakland in 1987, he almost single-handedly rescued the A's bullpen from the loss of Jay Howell. In fact, the combined 32 saves between Eckersley and Howell helped the A's lead their division with 40 saves.

Even the normally somnambulistic Coliseum crowd woke up when Eck got up in the bullpen in crucial situations. Dennis was born to pitch in Oakland, as the following numbers for 1987 illustrate:

	G	IP	ER	W	L	SV	HR	ERA
HOME	28	62.0	9	6	3	9	4	1.31
ROAD	26	53.2	30	0	5	8	7	5.03
TOTAL	54	115.2	39	6	8	17	11	3.03

Eckersley did run into some problems with the long ball and blew a couple of games late in the season. However, his HR/IP ratio is generally quite good. He also inherited a total of 51 runners in his 52 relief appearances and only eleven scored; two of them, unearned.

He had some differences with Athletics Manager Tony LaRussa early in the year about his role as a reliever. To his credit, LaRussa resisted Eckersley's demands to be a starter on the logical grounds that he was more successful in relief. And, to his credit, Dennis did a good job of not pouting over his manager's decision, even though he had been used almost exclusively as a starter for the last ten years (only one appearance in relief in 306 games pitched since 1976).

Eckersley showed tremendous flexibility in the way he moved from role to role according to the needs of the team. He was the designated early reliever when Andujar or Haas took themselves out after the first ten pitches; he worked for awhile as the set-up man for Howell; and he then took over as the stopper when Howell could not pitch in the second half of the year. And he did get his chance to fill in twice as a spot-starter.

Eckersley did it all for Oakland last year, and despite being in his mid-thirties, he should continue to be an important part of the staff, particularly with the trade of Jay Howell to the Dodgers.

Susan Nelson

Eckersley, Dennis Lee   Bats: Right   Throws: Right   Born 10/03/54

1987 SEASON AND MAJOR-LEAGUE CAREER PITCHING TOTALS

	G	GS	CG	GF	IP	BFP	H	R	ER	HR	SH	SF	HB	TBB	IBB	SO	WP	Bk	W	L	Pct	ShO	Sv	ERA
87 OAK	54	2	0	33	116	460	99	41	39	11	3	3	3	17	3	113	1	0	6	8	.429	0	16	3.03
13 YEARS	430	361	100	41	2611	10858	2500	1142	1057	279	95	77	59	641	68	1740	25	14	157	136	.536	20	19	3.64

1987: Power, Flyball   1986: Finesse, Flyball   1985: Finesse, Flyball   1984: Finesse, Flyball

1987 SEASON

	G	IP	H	BB	SO	SB	CS	W	L	S	ERA
Totals	54	115.2	99	17	113	9	1	6	8	17	3.03
at Home	28	62.0	33	10	69	4	0	6	3	9	1.31
on Road	26	53.2	66	7	44	5	1	0	5	8	5.03
on Grass	28	63.2	42	10	71	3	0	3	4	10	2.40
on Artificial Turf	26	52.0	57	7	42	6	1	3	4	7	3.81
Day Games	45	96.1	81	14	94	7	1	6	8	13	3.18
Night Games	9	19.1	18	3	19	2	0	0	0	4	2.33
April	7	16.0	11	3	12	2	0	1	1	1	2.81
May	8	27.0	28	4	22	2	0	2	3	0	4.33
June	8	24.1	18	4	22	2	1	2	0	2	1.11
July	10	12.2	10	2	13	1	0	1	1	4	3.55
August	10	21.2	17	2	26	1	0	0	1	5	2.49
Sept/Oct	11	14.0	15	2	18	1	0	0	2	5	4.50

vs. Opponent Batters	Ave.	OBP	SLG	AB	H	2B	3B	HR	RBI	BB	SO
Totals	.228	.260	.362	434	99	23	1	11	45	17	113
vs. Left	.272	.313	.429	184	50	14	0	5	20	11	32
vs. Right	.196	.220	.312	250	49	9	1	6	25	6	81
Bases Empty	.249	.272	.389	257	64	16	1	6	6	6	70
Leadoff	.231	.245	.365	104	24	3	1	3	3	1	28
Not Leadoff	.261	.289	.405	153	40	13	0	3	3	5	42
Runners On Base	.198	.245	.322	177	35	7	0	5	39	11	43
First Base Only	.239	.271	.463	67	16	3	0	4	8	3	15
Scoring Position	.173	.230	.236	110	19	4	0	1	31	8	28
Late Innings, Close	.231	.256	.376	173	40	7	0	6	19	6	46

FOUR YEAR TOTALS (1984 – 1987)

	G	IP	H	BB	SO	SB	CS	W	L	S	ERA
Totals	145	711.0	693	128	481	72	24	37	38	17	3.66
at Home	68	326.1	308	61	259	32	14	24	17	9	3.64
on Road	77	384.2	385	67	222	40	10	13	21	8	3.65
on Grass	81	412.0	376	75	311	37	16	25	18	10	3.43
on Artificial Turf	64	299.0	317	53	170	35	8	12	20	7	3.94
Day Games	105	491.0	483	85	364	44	20	29	27	13	3.76
Night Games	40	220.0	210	43	117	28	4	8	11	4	3.40
April	21	121.1	112	19	85	9	4	6	6	1	3.93
May	25	140.0	153	22	86	14	7	9	9	0	4.69
June	24	121.0	108	27	72	12	2	4	7	2	4.02
July	25	114.0	92	19	88	9	5	8	4	4	2.45
August	22	101.2	108	21	66	12	3	5	4	5	2.74
Sept/Oct	28	113.0	120	20	84	16	3	5	8	5	3.74

vs. Opponent Batters	Ave.	OBP	SLG	AB	H	2B	3B	HR	RBI	BB	SO
Totals	.255	.289	.398	2719	693	154	15	68	292	128	481
vs. Left	.277	.318	.435	1388	384	90	11	36	165	84	163
vs. Right	.232	.258	.358	1331	309	64	4	32	127	44	318
Bases Empty	.263	.288	.400	1683	443	98	8	39	39	56	313
Leadoff	.271	.289	.413	698	189	42	3	17	17	17	114
Not Leadoff	.258	.287	.392	985	254	56	5	22	22	39	199
Runners On Base	.241	.290	.393	1036	250	56	7	29	253	72	168
First Base Only	.254	.282	.437	410	104	21	3	16	38	16	57
Scoring Position	.233	.296	.364	626	146	35	4	13	215	56	111
Late Innings, Close	.231	.262	.378	347	80	17	2	10	38	15	68

RBI/Opportunities

Scoring Position	30 / 144 (21%)	194 / 825 (24%)
Scoring Position, 2 Out	10 / 72 (14%)	69 / 379 (18%)
On Third, Less than 2 Out	13 / 23 (57%)	85 / 151 (56%)
RBI in close games / RBI Total	31 / 45 (69%)	224 / 292 (77%)

Mark Eichhorn
Toronto Blue Jays

The sharp increase in Mark Eichhorn's ERA between 1986 and 1987 should have been expected. It was affected, moreover, both by one bad stretch and by the way that he was used.

In his excellent annual, *Jays Jazz*, David Driscoll listed every relief pitcher who logged an ERA of 2.00 or less as well as how they did in the subsequent season. 39 of the 44 men in the sample had higher ERAs; the average increase was 1.36 runs. Eichhorn's ERA rose from 1.72 to 3.17; his 1.45-run increase closely matched the norm.

A review of Mark's 1987 shows just how misleading a reliever's statistics can be, given the number of innings that they pitch. In over 65 percent of his innings, he allowed no earned runs; in about 90 percent, he allowed one or less. But Mark went through a very rough stretch between June 14 and June 28, which had a substantial impact on his seasonal totals. In eight appearances, covering 9.2 innings, he allowed 13 earned runs. That bad streak brought his ERA for the year up 73 points.

Overwork was very likely a factor in his poor performance during that period; in the eight days before June 14, Eichhorn worked in six games. But it must be difficult to know when he is tired; he is usually more effective when he works often. When Mark worked with no days rest between appearances was 2.58; it was 2.39 with one day between games and 2.31 with two days. Given three days or more—a

rare occurrence—it jumped to 5.50.

Although Eichhorn pitched 29.2 fewer innings than he did in 1986, he made 20 more appearances this year. He was used much more often in short relief; the role did not agree with him. Eichhorn tends to be vulnerable to the softly hit single; that being so, he is far more effective entering games at the beginning of innings than he is during the middle. Mark converted on only four of nine save chances and allowed 33.3 percent (third-lowest on the team) of his inherited runners to score in 1987.

Eichhorn's unconventional delivery, many observers believe, has a psychological impact that fades with repeated exposure—the more often he faces a team, the less effective he will be. Mark's 1987 suggests that this does appear to be true, but only when a team faces him repeatedly in a very short period of time. The first time that Mark faced a particular team, his ERA was 3.40; if he faced them again within a three-week period, his ERA was 4.22. On his third outing within that period, his ERA dropped to 1.88; on his fourth appearance, it was 2.54. The fifth time, it jumped sharply—to 9.82—but Eichhorn rarely faced a team five times in three weeks in 1987.

To conclude, reports of Mark's demise are somewhat premature. If used correctly, he should continue to be effective in 1988.

Dave Easby

Eichhorn, Mark Anthony — Bats: Right   Throws: Right   Born 10/21/60

1987 SEASON AND MAJOR-LEAGUE CAREER PITCHING TOTALS

	G	GS	CG	GF	IP	BFP	H	R	ER	HR	SH	SF	HB	TBB	IBB	SO	WP	Bk	W	L	Pct	ShO	Sv	ERA
87 TOR	89	0	0	27	128	540	110	47	45	14	7	4	6	52	13	96	3	1	10	6	.625	0	4	3.16
3 YEARS	165	7	0	65	323	1323	255	107	98	26	17	8	13	111	28	278	8	2	24	15	.615	0	14	2.73

1987: Power, Groundball   1986: Power, Groundball

1987 SEASON

	G	IP	H	BB	SO	SB	CS	W	L	S	ERA
Totals	89	127.2	110	52	96	32	4	10	6	4	3.17
at Home	44	67.1	54	16	48	17	1	6	1	2	2.27
on Road	45	60.1	56	36	48	15	3	4	5	2	4.18
on Grass	35	54.1	60	19	45	20	2	4	4	2	4.64
on Artificial Turf	54	73.1	50	33	51	12	2	6	2	2	2.09
Day Games	35	43.2	45	24	39	11	2	3	3	1	4.74
Night Games	54	84.0	65	28	57	21	2	7	3	3	2.36
April	12	24.2	18	10	20	3	1	3	1	1	2.19
May	13	21.0	15	12	18	6	1	3	1	1	2.57
June	18	25.0	31	6	21	7	1	2	1	1	5.40
July	13	14.2	13	13	10	7	0	1	2	0	3.07
August	17	24.2	18	6	14	4	1	1	1	1	2.55
Sept/Oct	16	17.2	15	5	13	5	0	0	0	0	3.06

FOUR YEAR TOTALS (1984 – 1987)

	G	IP	H	BB	SO	SB	CS	W	L	S	ERA
Totals	158	284.2	215	97	262	47	9	24	12	14	2.37
at Home	78	146.1	110	39	138	22	3	13	6	6	2.09
on Road	80	138.1	105	58	124	25	6	11	6	8	2.67
on Grass	57	98.2	86	30	95	24	3	6	5	6	3.01
on Artificial Turf	101	186.0	129	67	167	23	6	18	7	8	2.03
Day Games	62	104.0	82	42	94	20	5	10	4	5	2.86
Night Games	96	180.2	133	55	168	27	4	14	8	9	2.09
April	20	43.1	23	13	40	4	1	5	2	1	1.45
May	25	47.1	30	21	44	9	2	5	2	5	1.90
June	22	38.2	38	12	39	7	1	4	2	1	3.96
July	26	46.1	49	22	44	10	1	2	2	1	3.50
August	34	64.1	39	13	50	5	3	6	2	4	1.68
Sept/Oct	31	44.2	36	16	45	12	1	2	2	2	2.22

vs. Opponent Batters — 1987 SEASON

	Ave.	OBP	SLG	AB	H	2B	3B	HR	RBI	BB	SO
Totals	.234	.315	.374	471	110	20	2	14	57	52	96
vs. Left	.257	.350	.410	183	47	8	1	6	26	25	30
vs. Right	.219	.292	.351	288	63	12	1	8	31	27	66
Bases Empty	.228	.282	.360	267	61	10	2	7	7	16	55
Leadoff	.204	.239	.296	108	22	3	2	1	1	5	23
Not Leadoff	.245	.310	.403	159	39	7	0	6	6	11	32
Runners On Base	.240	.354	.392	204	49	10	0	7	50	36	41
First Base Only	.407	.444	.695	59	24	5	0	4	9	4	10
Scoring Position	.172	.322	.269	145	25	5	0	3	41	32	31
Late Innings, Close	.227	.306	.355	141	32	5	2	3	10	16	36

vs. Opponent Batters — FOUR YEAR TOTALS

	Ave.	OBP	SLG	AB	H	2B	3B	HR	RBI	BB	SO
Totals	.211	.282	.328	1019	215	43	5	22	106	97	262
vs. Left	.258	.342	.424	434	112	25	4	13	60	54	84
vs. Right	.176	.236	.256	585	103	18	1	9	46	43	178
Bases Empty	.212	.251	.337	591	125	25	5	13	13	27	154
Leadoff	.209	.239	.308	234	49	8	3	3	3	9	53
Not Leadoff	.213	.259	.356	357	76	17	2	10	10	18	101
Runners On Base	.210	.321	.315	428	90	18	0	9	93	70	108
First Base Only	.273	.326	.438	128	35	6	0	5	11	10	36
Scoring Position	.183	.320	.263	300	55	12	0	4	82	60	72
Late Innings, Close	.204	.279	.282	426	87	14	2	5	31	44	115

RBI/Opportunities

1987 SEASON		FOUR YEAR TOTALS	
Scoring Position	37 / 241 (15%)	76 / 484 (16%)	
Scoring Position, 2 Out	18 / 128 (14%)	31 / 247 (13%)	
On Third, Less than 2 Out	16 / 47 (34%)	33 / 87 (38%)	
RBI in close games / RBI Total	19 / 57 (33%)	51 / 106 (48%)	

Nick Esasky
Cincinnati Reds

Why do strikeouts bother people so much? If you hit a can of corn to the centerfielder or a grounder to short it seems like you did something, whereas a strikeout . . . But really, an out's an out, isn't it? Esasky's strikeouts have blurred people's perception of him.

The lyric "If it weren't for bad luck, I'd have no luck at all" pretty much summed up Nick Esasky's career up to the All-Star break in 1987. Nick started his career in the impossible position of trying to salvage the wreckage of the Johnny Bench 3B experiment. (It's hard to understand why the Reds didn't trade Driessen after '80 and give John first base for as long as he wanted it, letting him drive in 100+ runs a year. Do you realize Bench is younger than Darrell Evans, Jose Cruz, Gene Garber, Bob Boone, and Nolan Ryan? He turned 40 in December).

Esasky was then platooned extensively, a tough situation for the right-handed half of a platoon combination (How consistent can a power hitter be starting two games a week?). Injuries, and competing with his manager for playing time, limited his 1986 season to 102 games.

Nick started 1987 by breaking his wrist in spring training. To add to his problems, Esasky was the subject of trade rumors, benched briefly in favor of Dave Parker, and platooned with the ridiculously bad Terry Francona. Pete Rose finally committed to Esasky as his every day first baseman in July and Nick responded with his best season.

Working closely with coach Billy DeMars, Nick ho-mered every 15.7 at bats, cut his strikeouts from 29 percent to 22 percent, and set career highs in batting average and slugging. His OWL% (.649) was the third highest on the team behind Kal Daniels and Eric Davis. Mad Marge rewarded DeMars for his fine work with the Reds young hitters by firing him.

One has to wonder what took Rose so long to commit to Esasky. 1987 wasn't the first time Nick has put up solid numbers for Pete after being given an every day job. In mid-1985 Rose put Esasky in LF every day even though Nick had never played the outfield. The results (.262 21 HR/66 RBI) were very similar to his successful 1987 season (.272 22 HR/59 RBI).

1988 looks like the year that Nick Esasky is finally in line for a little good luck. For the first time in his career Nick has a secure role on the team. With the trade of Dave Parker and release of Terry Francona, Nick has no one looking over his shoulder if he hits a temporary slump. Nick should get his first chance to produce for a full season and escape that worst of all possible labels, unfulfilled potential.

1987 may turn out to have been a watershed year for Esasky. After watching what Davis, Daniels, Jones, and Larkin did in '86, Nick decided to just do the things he could do, to stop trying to live up to what others hoped or expected him to be. He knew he was as good as the players around him who were playing well, and this enabled him to stop pressing.

Greg Gajus and Tom Locker

Esasky, Nicholas Andrew "Nick"

Bats: Right   **Throws: Right**   **Born 02/24/60**

1987 SEASON AND MAJOR-LEAGUE CAREER BATTING TOTALS

	G	AB	H	2B	3B	HR	TB	R	RBI	TBB	IBB	SO	HP	SH	SF	SB	CS	SB%	GDP	AVG	OBP	SLG
87 CIN	100	346	94	19	2	22	183	48	59	29	3	76	0	2	1	0	0	.00	10	.272	.327	.529
5 YEARS	525	1713	420	77	14	77	756	215	257	196	10	477	8	9	16	10	10	.50	38	.245	.323	.441

	1987 SEASON											FOUR YEAR TOTALS (1984 – 1987)									
	Ave.	OBP	SLG	AB	H	2B	3B	HR	RBI	BB	SO	Ave.	OBP	SLG	AB	H	2B	3B	HR	RBI	BB	SO
Totals	.272	.327	.529	346	94	19	2	22	59	29	76	.241	.322	.439	1411	340	67	9	65	211	169	378
vs. Left	.253	.370	.505	91	23	5	0	6	15	17	22	.254	.353	.479	493	125	27	6	24	67	77	130
vs. Right	.278	.310	.537	255	71	14	2	16	44	12	54	.234	.304	.418	918	215	40	3	41	144	92	248
at Home	.246	.313	.461	191	47	9	1	10	31	19	42	.228	.304	.424	714	163	39	4	31	109	80	191
on Road	.303	.345	.613	155	47	10	1	12	28	10	34	.254	.340	.455	697	177	28	5	34	102	89	187
vs. Groundball	.273	.325	.538	143	39	6	1	10	21	11	35	.253	.336	.433	675	171	30	5	27	84	85	186
vs. Flyball	.271	.329	.522	203	55	13	1	12	38	18	41	.230	.308	.446	736	169	37	4	38	127	84	192
vs. Finesse	.270	.310	.540	174	47	9	1	12	28	10	28	.237	.306	.452	754	179	38	5	38	115	75	170
vs. Power	.273	.344	.517	172	47	10	1	10	31	19	48	.245	.339	.425	657	161	29	4	27	96	94	208
on Grass	.292	.327	.667	96	28	4	1	10	23	5	21	.254	.348	.463	421	107	16	3	22	70	59	116
on Artificial Turf	.264	.327	.476	250	66	15	1	12	36	24	55	.235	.310	.429	990	233	51	6	43	141	110	262
Day Games	.244	.279	.496	123	30	7	0	8	21	6	26	.223	.313	.394	467	104	26	0	18	65	60	137
Night Games	.287	.352	.547	223	64	12	2	14	38	23	50	.250	.326	.462	944	236	41	9	47	146	109	241
April	.000	.000	.000	0	0	0	0	0	0	0	0	.211	.304	.428	180	38	11	2	8	30	24	59
May	.235	.308	.500	34	8	3	0	2	6	4	7	.214	.315	.353	187	40	11	0	5	22	28	43
June	.241	.293	.630	54	13	1	1	6	16	4	14	.249	.350	.503	173	43	9	1	11	35	27	45
July	.267	.321	.533	75	20	5	0	5	18	6	15	.259	.321	.473	220	57	10	2	11	37	20	58
August	.286	.343	.462	91	26	1	0	5	8	8	22	.250	.317	.434	348	87	10	3	16	44	34	89
Sept/Oct	.293	.343	.543	92	27	9	1	4	11	7	18	.248	.327	.446	303	75	16	1	14	43	36	84
Bases Empty	.253	.295	.449	198	50	9	0	10	10	12	42	.234	.308	.398	796	186	35	3	30	30	86	219
Leadoff	.260	.296	.455	77	20	3	0	4	4	4	14	.236	.297	.385	351	83	14	1	12	12	30	87
Not Leadoff	.248	.295	.446	121	30	6	0	6	6	8	28	.231	.317	.409	445	103	21	2	18	18	56	132
Runners On	.297	.367	.635	148	44	10	2	12	49	17	34	.250	.339	.493	615	154	32	6	35	181	83	159
First Base Only	.315	.359	.685	73	23	5	2	6	14	5	13	.248	.302	.489	270	67	8	3	17	38	21	58
Scoring Position	.280	.375	.587	75	21	5	0	6	35	12	21	.252	.365	.496	345	87	24	3	18	143	62	101
Late Innings, Close	.231	.328	.404	52	12	0	0	3	10	8	13	.217	.315	.394	249	54	3	1	13	42	36	75

RBI/Opportunities

Scoring Position	22 / 103 (21%)	109 / 489 (22%)
Scoring Position, 2 Out	11 / 54 (20%)	38 / 231 (16%)
On Third, Less than 2 Out	6 / 15 (40%)	42 / 89 (47%)
RBI in close games / RBI Total	39 / 59 (66%)	132 / 211 (63%)

Darrell Evans
Detroit Tigers

If you look at longevity and performance level, Darrell Evans may be the most unrecognized player of our time. The term "pretty good player"—which is usually the most lavish praise he gets—rings a bit hollow for a man who joined the 2000-hit club and hit 1250 runs batted in right on the nose this year. At his current pace, he'll reach 400 homers in July. Pending expected retirements, he will have played more games than any other active player in 1988. At age 40, he continues to be an offensive force while most of his contemporaries have long since retired.

Evans's surprisingly low profile stems from two things. First, he's managed to spend almost all of his career on non-playoff teams in media backwaters. After his cup of coffee with the 1969 Braves, he spent 14 years as a key part of good but not great teams. When he finally got to play on a championship team—the 1984 Tigers—he had the third-worst season of his career. If Detroit had beaten Minnesota, it would have been the first year that he'd had a good year for an equally good team.

The other reason is that the things that Evans does well are the ones that people ignore. He's a career .251 hitter with little speed (97 career steals) who's never played a key defensive position. He's hit 40 homers only twice and scored or driven in 100 runs only once in his career. So how good, most people say, can he really be?

The answer is "very." Darrell's lifetime on-base percentage is .363. He's led the league in walks twice. He's drawn 100 walks five times, 90–99 three times and 80–89 three times in a 19-year career. He jumped over six Hall of Famers to thirteenth on the all-time walk list in 1987. He needs 80 more to crack the top ten and 145 to get to seventh; expect him to settle in at that spot or higher. And, unlike most modern sluggers, he draws walks without ungodly strikeout totals. Only Pete Rose, among players who began their careers after World War II, has drawn 1300 free passes without fanning more than he walks. Since the public is now beginning to pay more attention to bases on balls, perhaps Darrell will get more recognition in the future.

Another point that people rarely notice was that Evans was the NL's best defensive third baseman in the mid-'70s. He led the NL in total chances five times, and topped the league in double plays twice. Since moving to first base, he's been one of the more agile ones, too.

Evans showed no signs of decline in 1987; if anything, he is playing better now than ever. Since his game is the walk and the home run, one wonders what kind of totals he might have achieved had he not played such a large portion of his career in Candlestick Park. As it is, he could end up with sufficiently good numbers to make Cooperstown a fair possibility.

John Stryker

Evans, Darrell Wayne Bats: Left   Throws: Right   Born 05/26/47

1987 SEASON AND MAJOR-LEAGUE CAREER BATTING TOTALS

	G	AB	H	2B	3B	HR	TB	R	RBI	TBB	IBB	SO	HP	SH	SF	SB	CS	SB%	GDP	AVG	OBP	SLG
87 DET	150	499	128	20	0	34	250	90	99	100	8	84	2	2	6	6	5	.55	2	.257	.379	.501
19 YEARS	2436	8260	2075	314	35	381	3602	1265	1251	1480	131	1275	34	34	84	97	63	.61	118	.251	.364	.436

	1987 SEASON											FOUR YEAR TOTALS (1984 – 1987)										
	Ave.	OBP	SLG	AB	H	2B	3B	HR	RBI	BB	SO	Ave.	OBP	SLG	AB	H	2B	3B	HR	RBI	BB	SO
Totals	.257	.379	.501	499	128	20	0	34	99	100	84	.245	.362	.465	1912	468	63	1	119	341	354	344
vs. Left	.209	.312	.338	148	31	4	0	5	20	22	31	.238	.340	.412	505	120	16	0	24	81	77	115
vs. Right	.276	.406	.570	351	97	16	0	29	79	78	53	.247	.369	.485	1407	348	47	1	95	260	277	229
at Home	.248	.359	.512	246	61	8	0	19	49	45	43	.242	.357	.470	922	223	27	0	61	172	167	169
on Road	.265	.397	.490	253	67	12	0	15	50	55	41	.247	.366	.462	990	245	36	1	58	169	187	175
vs. Groundball	.279	.389	.509	269	75	11	0	17	51	50	46	.241	.351	.446	938	226	34	1	52	149	161	165
vs. Flyball	.230	.367	.491	230	53	9	0	17	48	50	38	.248	.372	.485	974	242	29	0	67	192	193	179
vs. Finesse	.270	.376	.533	259	70	14	0	18	55	46	39	.249	.358	.479	1055	263	36	1	68	186	182	169
vs. Power	.242	.382	.467	240	58	6	0	16	44	54	45	.239	.366	.449	857	205	27	0	51	155	172	175
on Grass	.255	.370	.497	435	111	18	0	29	88	82	72	.242	.356	.456	1622	392	54	0	98	291	294	287
on Artificial Turf	.266	.434	.531	64	17	2	0	5	11	18	12	.262	.390	.517	290	76	9	1	21	50	60	57
Day Games	.265	.368	.606	170	45	7	0	17	36	30	23	.278	.380	.545	611	170	26	1	45	128	106	103
Night Games	.252	.385	.447	329	83	13	0	17	63	70	61	.229	.353	.428	1301	298	37	0	74	213	248	241
April	.239	.366	.403	67	16	5	0	2	7	13	6	.238	.331	.417	235	56	12	0	10	32	32	31
May	.224	.368	.434	76	17	1	0	5	15	18	9	.251	.362	.443	323	81	8	0	18	53	57	43
June	.293	.413	.667	75	22	7	0	7	21	16	14	.264	.407	.497	288	76	16	0	17	61	70	50
July	.263	.356	.553	76	20	1	0	7	14	11	15	.226	.346	.471	327	74	8	0	24	61	60	59
August	.244	.369	.422	90	22	4	0	4	17	19	21	.246	.362	.489	350	86	11	1	24	69	65	80
Sept/Oct	.270	.393	.522	115	31	2	0	9	25	23	19	.244	.360	.465	389	95	8	0	26	65	70	81
Bases Empty	.226	.359	.453	265	60	6	0	18	18	53	43	.226	.330	.446	1076	243	27	0	70	70	165	193
Leadoff	.232	.328	.518	112	26	2	0	10	10	16	19	.229	.323	.470	445	102	5	0	34	34	62	77
Not Leadoff	.222	.380	.405	153	34	4	0	8	8	37	24	.223	.334	.429	631	141	22	0	36	36	103	116
Runners On	.291	.401	.556	234	68	14	0	16	81	47	41	.269	.402	.490	836	225	36	1	49	271	189	151
First Base Only	.296	.382	.556	108	32	4	0	8	17	15	18	.274	.386	.489	350	96	12	0	21	46	64	60
Scoring Position	.286	.415	.556	126	36	10	0	8	64	32	23	.265	.412	.492	486	129	24	1	28	225	125	91
Late Innings, Close	.257	.360	.405	74	19	2	0	3	8	11	9	.259	.364	.486	290	75	9	0	19	53	47	43

RBI/Opportunities

Scoring Position	46 / 187 (25%)	171 / 737 (23%)
Scoring Position, 2 Out	20 / 80 (25%)	72 / 360 (20%)
On Third, Less than 2 Out	17 / 38 (45%)	60 / 136 (44%)
RBI in close games / RBI Total	53 / 99 (54%)	201 / 341 (59%)

Dwight Evans

Boston Red Sox

In 1987—as he has done so many times in the past—Dwight Evans astounded the observers. This 35-year old man (he turned 36 in November) had by far his best season in the majors last year. Evans set career highs in homers, RBIs, batting average, on-base percentage and slugging percentage and tied his career high in doubles. He tied AL MVP George Bell for the lead (with 198) in that seminal analytical stat, Runs Produced; had Boston been a pennant contender, Evans might very well have been the MVP. In fact, a look at the "Age and Performance" article in the 1986 *Baseball Abstract* (pp. 302–28) suggests that Evans had one of the best seasons ever for a man of his age.

Even more remarkably, Dwight's 1987 ended a two-year decline. Though Evans's 1986 figures (.259 BA, .376 OB%, .476 SL%) were excellent ones, they were (save for the SL%) all lower than his 1985 stats. His 1985 stats, in turn, were lower than his 1984 marks.

What happened? Good question. Part of the answer are his platoon stats. Dwight's left/right splits have been published in the *Baseball Abstract* for every season since 1978. 1986 was the only season in that period where Evans didn't perform much better against lefties than he did against righties—his figures against them were the worst of his career, in fact. His return to normal this year explains some of the surge.

Another factor is his performance on the road. From 1983–86, Evans batted .277 at home, .258 in road grass and .248 on turf. This year, he hit .304 at home, .302 on road grass and .313 on carpets.

A third idea—maybe the best one—is the weather. Dewey is a very pronounced hot weather hitter; June, July and August are almost always his best months of his season. 1987 was one of the warmest seasons in recent memory; the mercury went through the roof in May and stayed there until mid-September. Evans's stats followed the same pattern.

The other notable event in Dwight's 1987 was his long-overdue switch to first base. His range factor, which was once consistently 2.10 or better, has been 1.96 or worse for the last five years; his 1987 figure (1.80) was a career low. Evans frankly admitted that he was not accustomed to his new position (oddly, he said that the throws he had to make were the problem); the stats certainly bear this out. Evans tied Joe Carter and Pat Tabler for the league lead in errors (12) and had the worst fielding percentage of any regular first baseman in the AL. But, as he adjusts to his new position, his fielding should only improve.

Since Evans is 36, one would think that he would be likely to decline in 1988 . . . but, given his past, that is certainly not anything that anyone should be ready to bet on.

Michael Webb and Geoff Beckman

Evans, Dwight Michael "Dwight"

Bats: Right **Throws: Right** **Born 11/03/51**

1987 SEASON AND MAJOR-LEAGUE CAREER BATTING TOTALS

	G	AB	H	2B	3B	HR	TB	R	RBI	TBB	IBB	SO	HP	SH	SF	SB	CS	SB%	GDP	AVG	OBP	SLG
87 BOS	154	541	165	37	2	34	308	109	123	106	6	98	3	0	7	4	6	.40	10	.305	.417	.569
16 YEARS	2087	7202	1950	398	59	325	3441	1191	1072	1095	49	1387	43	48	55	65	48	.58	170	.271	.368	.478

	1987 SEASON										FOUR YEAR TOTALS (1984 – 1987)									
	Ave.	OBP	SLG	AB	H	2B	3B	HR	RBI	BB	SO	Ave.	OBP	SLG	AB	H	2B	3B	HR	RBI	BB	SO
Totals	.305	.417	.569	541	165	37	2	34	123	106	98	.281	.390	.507	2317	650	136	13	121	402	413	435
vs. Left	.368	.465	.688	144	53	10	0	12	37	27	17	.299	.427	.547	592	177	30	3	37	110	135	89
vs. Right	.282	.400	.526	397	112	27	2	22	86	79	81	.274	.376	.493	1725	473	106	10	84	292	278	346
at Home	.304	.399	.567	263	80	23	2	14	65	43	44	.293	.395	.522	1111	326	81	10	51	196	189	183
on Road	.306	.433	.572	278	85	14	0	20	58	63	54	.269	.384	.493	1206	324	55	3	70	206	224	252
vs. Groundball	.324	.440	.614	272	88	20	1	19	73	56	31	.288	.400	.491	1123	323	63	6	51	185	206	160
vs. Flyball	.286	.394	.524	269	77	17	1	15	50	50	67	.274	.379	.523	1194	327	73	7	70	217	207	275
vs. Finesse	.328	.414	.622	262	86	14	0	21	63	41	32	.298	.393	.519	1294	385	85	6	63	208	204	199
vs. Power	.283	.420	.520	279	79	23	2	13	60	65	66	.259	.386	.493	1023	265	51	7	58	194	209	236
on Grass	.303	.414	.563	458	139	34	2	27	105	88	80	.281	.391	.506	1943	546	120	13	97	336	349	357
on Artificial Turf	.313	.436	.602	83	26	3	0	7	18	18	18	.278	.384	.513	374	104	16	0	24	66	64	78
Day Games	.297	.415	.610	182	54	11	2	14	43	39	34	.298	.408	.533	756	225	50	4	40	124	141	135
Night Games	.309	.418	.549	359	111	26	0	20	80	67	64	.272	.380	.495	1561	425	86	9	81	278	272	300
April	.296	.444	.592	71	21	7	1	4	16	19	7	.239	.391	.414	297	71	21	2	9	37	74	44
May	.297	.373	.514	74	22	4	0	4	18	9	15	.231	.348	.419	360	83	23	0	15	50	65	77
June	.317	.403	.545	101	32	8	0	5	24	15	23	.312	.412	.533	394	123	19	4	20	78	67	79
July	.347	.451	.621	95	33	5	0	7	20	18	16	.313	.399	.531	403	126	20	1	22	74	58	78
August	.365	.429	.846	104	38	9	1	13	31	11	19	.307	.389	.623	427	131	32	5	31	88	57	76
Sept/Oct	.198	.398	.271	96	19	4	0	1	14	34	18	.266	.392	.484	436	116	21	1	24	75	92	81
Bases Empty	.288	.385	.558	285	82	19	2	18	18	44	53	.271	.376	.502	1244	337	67	11	66	66	209	229
Leadoff	.274	.346	.479	117	32	6	0	6	6	13	22	.266	.348	.484	556	148	34	3	27	27	70	102
Not Leadoff	.298	.410	.613	168	50	13	2	12	12	31	31	.275	.397	.516	688	189	33	8	39	39	139	127
Runners On	.324	.450	.582	256	83	18	0	16	105	62	45	.292	.404	.514	1073	313	69	2	55	336	204	206
First Base Only	.302	.413	.566	106	32	10	0	6	13	19	16	.305	.395	.550	502	153	42	0	27	63	74	89
Scoring Position	.340	.473	.593	150	51	8	0	10	92	43	29	.280	.410	.482	571	160	27	2	28	273	130	117
Late Innings, Close	.264	.381	.460	87	23	5	0	4	16	16	16	.287	.391	.539	356	102	16	1	24	78	61	65

RBI/Opportunities

Scoring Position	70 / 252 (28%)	219 / 887 (25%)
Scoring Position, 2 Out	27 / 112 (24%)	97 / 401 (24%)
On Third, Less than 2 Out	27 / 54 (50%)	82 / 164 (50%)
RBI in close games / RBI Total	72 / 123 (59%)	264 / 402 (66%)

Sid Fernandez

New York Mets

Sid Fernandez, for no readily apparent reason, suddenly loses it. "It" can be any number of requirements for a good pitcher, among them: location, rhythm, control, concentration and eventually his place on the pitching mound as Davey Johnson must remove him. A Fernandez game is like few others until these lapses occur: few hits, many strikeouts, some but not too many walks, a somewhat slow ballgame, and frequently low scoring as he usually keeps the opposition off balance. Then, he loses it. Furthermore, this mystery apparently can only be solved by Sid himself; Mel Stottlemyre and Johnson have used all tried and true physical and psychological ploys to clear his agenda of potential foibles, but to this point the cigar is not lit easily. Indeed, there are games when everything falls nicely into place; and yet his having only 3 complete games in '87, and not many other "quality starts," simply lends credence to his critics' complaint that he cannot perform capably in pressure situations on a regular basis and therefore doesn't help the team in the overall view.

1988 will be a pivotal year for El Sid. Until now he's been a competent and sometimes brilliant lefthander who has in his career been unable to prove his mettle in any prominent way. His lack of aggressiveness on the mound, and his loss of concentration in key spots (for no apparent reason), allow some detractors to complain of Sid's flakiness or at worst his unwillingness to puthimself on the line.

He has the potential for greatness but so far his tendency toward the negative has greatly undermined a maturity he must reach if he is to become a dominant pitcher either with the Mets or indeed in the major leagues.

Jay Gregory

Have you ever watched Fernandez pitch? You should, because he's got one of the most unique motions you'll ever see. Sid bends way over before he releases the ball, and doesn't seem to let it go until his left arm is practically touching the ground. The result is that, to the hitter, the ball seems to be coming right out of his uniform. Sid's pitches must be extremely tough to pick up.

When Fernandez was in the Dodger farm system, he kept racking up incredible strikeout totals—128 in 76 innings at Lethbridge, 137 in 84.2 innings at Vero Beach, 209 in 153 IP at San Antonio. But a lot of L.A. people were convinced he'd never make it because his radar gun readings were only in the high eighties. Certain that Fernandez had only a "minor league fastball," and convinced also that he'd soon eat his way out of baseball, the Dodgers practically gave him away.

Well, the minor league fastball has served Sid pretty well. But it strikes me that such a motion, depending so much on deception, can go out of sync pretty easily. It might be one reason for the up-and-down performances.

Don Zminda

Fernandez, Charles Sidney "Sid"

Bats: Left   **Throws: Left**   **Born 10/12/62**

1987 SEASON AND MAJOR-LEAGUE CAREER PITCHING TOTALS

	G	GS	CG	GF	IP	BFP	H	R	ER	HR	SH	SF	HB	TBB	IBB	SO	WP	Bk	W	L	Pct	ShO	Sv	ERA
87 NYN	28	27	3	0	156	665	130	75	66	16	3	6	8	67	8	134	2	0	12	8	.600	1	0	3.81
5 YEARS	103	100	8	1	626	2609	480	257	238	51	21	21	13	279	15	585	12	6	43	30	.589	2	1	3.42

1987: Power, Flyball   **1986: Power, Flyball**   **1985: Power, Flyball**   **1984: Power, Flyball**

1987 SEASON

	G	IP	H	BB	SO	SB	CS	W	L	S	ERA
Totals	29	156.0	129	67	134	28	6	12	8	0	3.81
at Home	16	93.2	65	39	89	13	6	9	3	0	2.98
on Road	13	62.1	64	28	45	15	0	3	5	0	5.05
on Grass	10	51.0	48	20	35	15	3	3	2	0	4.59
on Artificial Turf	19	105.0	81	47	99	13	3	9	6	0	3.43
Day Games	20	113.2	81	50	103	14	6	10	5	0	3.09
Night Games	9	42.1	48	17	31	14	0	2	3	0	5.74
April	5	33.0	24	15	35	9	1	4	1	0	2.18
May	5	35.0	22	17	36	5	3	2	1	0	2.06
June	5	28.2	29	7	22	5	0	3	2	0	5.65
July	5	29.0	27	14	17	6	1	1	2	0	4.34
August	3	6.0	8	3	4	0	1	0	2	0	9.00
Sept/Oct	6	24.1	19	11	20	3	0	2	0	0	4.44

vs. Opponent Batters	Ave.	OBP	SLG	AB	H	2B	3B	HR	RBI	BB	SO
Totals	.222	.308	.361	582	129	25	4	16	66	67	134
vs. Left	.219	.284	.397	73	16	5	1	2	9	7	15
vs. Right	.222	.312	.356	509	113	20	3	14	57	60	119
Bases Empty	.213	.300	.352	347	74	14	2	10	10	38	80
Leadoff	.214	.292	.414	145	31	3	1	8	8	14	33
Not Leadoff	.213	.306	.307	202	43	11	1	2	2	24	47
Runners On Base	.234	.320	.374	235	55	11	2	6	56	29	54
First Base Only	.250	.302	.454	108	27	6	2	4	14	6	26
Scoring Position	.220	.333	.307	127	28	5	0	2	42	23	28
Late Innings, Close	.167	.255	.190	42	7	1	0	0	1	4	13

FOUR YEAR TOTALS (1984 – 1987)

	G	IP	H	BB	SO	SB	CS	W	L	S	ERA
Totals	102	620.2	472	272	576	97	22	43	29	1	3.38
at Home	50	312.1	208	133	318	48	13	25	13	1	2.71
on Road	52	308.1	264	139	258	49	9	18	16	0	4.09
on Grass	41	234.1	173	123	208	49	12	16	6	1	3.57
on Artificial Turf	61	386.1	299	149	368	48	10	27	23	0	3.28
Day Games	70	430.0	309	194	409	62	18	31	20	1	3.16
Night Games	32	190.2	163	78	167	35	4	12	9	0	3.92
April	8	53.1	30	27	55	12	2	6	1	0	2.36
May	15	100.1	64	51	96	14	4	6	3	0	2.42
June	15	94.0	77	38	85	14	6	8	6	0	4.12
July	20	126.0	107	50	115	25	2	8	6	0	3.21
August	19	109.0	90	41	97	17	4	6	7	0	3.88
Sept/Oct	25	138.0	104	65	128	15	4	9	6	1	3.78

vs. Opponent Batters	Ave.	OBP	SLG	AB	H	2B	3B	HR	RBI	BB	SO
Totals	.210	.297	.335	2251	472	104	12	51	221	272	576
vs. Left	.201	.279	.316	329	66	18	1	6	25	36	103
vs. Right	.211	.300	.338	1922	406	86	11	45	196	236	473
Bases Empty	.207	.290	.338	1373	284	59	8	35	35	155	351
Leadoff	.200	.289	.343	569	114	19	4	18	18	69	157
Not Leadoff	.211	.290	.335	804	170	40	4	17	17	86	194
Runners On Base	.214	.307	.329	878	188	45	4	16	186	117	225
First Base Only	.227	.299	.364	379	86	22	3	8	35	37	89
Scoring Position	.204	.313	.303	499	102	23	1	8	151	80	136
Late Innings, Close	.223	.306	.386	166	37	8	2	5	19	19	36

RBI/Opportunities

Scoring Position	38 / 189 (20%)	132 / 683 (19%)
Scoring Position, 2 Out	17 / 92 (18%)	49 / 321 (15%)
On Third, Less than 2 Out	14 / 29 (48%)	49 / 100 (49%)
RBI in close games / RBI Total	53 / 66 (80%)	185 / 221 (84%)

Tony Fernandez
Toronto Blue Jays

If anything could have epitomized the 1987 season for the Toronto Blue Jays, the slide by Bill Madlock on September 24 that broke Tony Fernandez's elbow would be it. Without their All-Star and Gold Glove shortstop and number three hitter, who was having the best year of his career, the Blue Jays lost the dramatic race to the wire with the Tigers. They went home after the season with a choke collar wrapped around their collective necks by almost every broadcaster and sportswriter in baseball.

It was on a Thursday night in Toronto that this terrible non-accident happened. The Tigers had just opened a crucial four-game set with the Jays. Madlock came into second on a close play and slid (a generous description of a rolling block) away from the bag to catch Fernandez before he could relay the ball to first. Fernandez was up-ended, coming down hard on his elbow on the seam between the dirt sliding pit and the artificial turf, under which is a wooden slat which borders the dirt pit. Tony's season was over quickly and painfully; the rest of the Blue Jays endured a slower, yet probably more painful, end to their season.

Fernandez's replacement, Manny Lee, played well, even getting a dramatic game-winning triple the next night as the hometown nine beat the Tigers. Of course, Manny also let the game-winning hit (another example of the bizarrely generous hometown scoring in Detroit) roll between his legs in the penultimate game of the season the next weekend. Still, the Jays took the Tigers down to the last game of the season while playing without Fernandez and Ernie Whitt; I wonder how the Tigers would have done if they were playing a full-strength Toronto club without Trammell and Heath, or without Whitaker and Nokes. Losing either of these pairs of players would have hurt them about as badly as Toronto was hurting, and you can be sure that the cries of anguish from Tigertown would have been heard far and wide.

Five or ten years from now, though, no one will remember the injuries, but virtually everyone will remember the Blue Jays' historic collapse— how they "choked" when they had it all within their grasp. Ask Boston fans how many people remember that the Red Sox took the Big Red Machine all the way to the Seventh Game of the 1975 World Series without Jim Rice, whose wrist had been broken before the playoffs by an errant pitch from the Tigers' Vern Ruhle. The story of Toronto's losing the divisional race to Detroit is not a story about "character" or the lack of it, nor is it a story about how the Tigers wanted the title more than the Blue Jays. It is a simple story of how one very good team, after losing two key regulars, was not quite as good as another very good, and quite healthy team.

Gary Gillette

Fernandez, Octavio Antonio (Castro) "Tony" Bats: Both   Throws: Right   Born 08/06/62

1987 SEASON AND MAJOR-LEAGUE CAREER BATTING TOTALS

	G	AB	H	2B	3B	HR	TB	R	RBI	TBB	IBB	SO	HP	SH	SF	SB	CS	SB%	GDP	AVG	OBP	SLG
87 TOR	146	578	186	29	8	5	246	90	67	51	3	48	5	4	4	32	12	.73	14	.322	.379	.426
5 YEARS	573	2096	634	99	31	20	855	286	204	140	5	158	12	19	12	75	38	.66	38	.302	.348	.408

	1987 SEASON											FOUR YEAR TOTALS (1984 – 1987)										
	Ave.	OBP	SLG	AB	H	2B	3B	HR	RBI	BB	SO	Ave.	OBP	SLG	AB	H	2B	3B	HR	RBI	BB	SO
Totals	.322	.379	.426	578	186	29	8	5	67	51	48	.303	.348	.409	2063	625	98	30	20	202	138	156
vs. Left	.297	.367	.380	192	57	8	1	2	16	21	18	.296	.354	.407	668	198	35	9	7	67	59	60
vs. Right	.334	.385	.448	386	129	21	7	3	51	30	30	.306	.345	.409	1395	427	63	21	13	135	79	96
at Home	.301	.363	.395	299	90	15	5	1	42	27	16	.302	.350	.411	998	301	54	17	7	97	69	60
on Road	.344	.397	.459	279	96	14	3	4	25	24	32	.304	.346	.407	1065	324	44	13	13	105	69	96
vs. Groundball	.313	.355	.410	288	90	19	3	1	41	19	18	.299	.343	.397	975	292	52	11	7	110	62	57
vs. Flyball	.331	.402	.441	290	96	10	5	4	26	32	30	.306	.352	.420	1088	333	46	19	13	92	76	99
vs. Finesse	.314	.351	.418	325	102	15	5	3	33	18	20	.308	.343	.424	1152	355	57	20	12	105	58	77
vs. Power	.332	.414	.435	253	84	14	3	2	34	33	28	.296	.354	.390	911	270	41	10	8	97	80	79
on Grass	.329	.379	.444	207	68	9	3	3	18	16	24	.297	.335	.390	817	243	30	8	10	74	46	78
on Artificial Turf	.318	.380	.415	371	118	20	5	2	49	35	24	.307	.356	.421	1246	382	68	22	10	128	92	78
Day Games	.293	.366	.374	198	58	6	2	2	23	23	16	.293	.340	.387	726	213	33	7	7	70	50	46
Night Games	.337	.386	.453	380	128	23	6	3	44	28	32	.308	.352	.420	1337	412	65	23	13	132	88	110
April	.232	.293	.317	82	19	0	2	1	6	7	6	.253	.296	.322	233	59	5	4	1	15	14	19
May	.353	.441	.471	102	36	7	1	1	14	16	11	.296	.361	.398	304	90	16	3	3	32	31	25
June	.343	.419	.537	108	37	11	2	2	15	14	9	.345	.396	.513	357	123	26	8	6	46	30	20
July	.310	.344	.371	116	36	5	1	0	11	6	15	.277	.314	.363	386	107	19	4	2	36	21	34
August	.375	.427	.489	88	33	3	2	1	8	5	3	.343	.383	.481	385	132	19	8	6	45	22	26
Sept/Oct	.305	.326	.341	82	25	3	0	0	13	3	4	.286	.320	.349	398	114	13	3	2	28	20	32
Bases Empty	.321	.375	.429	368	118	13	6	5	5	30	35	.305	.348	.409	1288	393	58	20	12	12	82	105
Leadoff	.269	.345	.341	208	56	8	2	1	1	23	25	.292	.337	.400	650	190	36	8	6	6	43	56
Not Leadoff	.387	.417	.544	160	62	5	4	4	4	7	10	.318	.358	.418	638	203	22	12	6	6	39	49
Runners On	.324	.387	.419	210	68	16	2	0	62	21	13	.299	.347	.408	775	232	40	10	8	190	56	51
First Base Only	.237	.307	.300	80	19	5	0	0	3	8	2	.278	.311	.397	335	93	11	4	7	22	16	13
Scoring Position	.377	.433	.492	130	49	11	2	0	59	13	11	.316	.374	.416	440	139	29	6	1	168	40	38
Late Innings, Close	.349	.396	.477	86	30	6	1	1	15	8	7	.324	.366	.462	346	112	18	9	4	51	24	29

RBI/Opportunities

	1987		Four Year	
Scoring Position	57 / 179	(32%)	161 / 600	(27%)
Scoring Position, 2 Out	24 / 73	(33%)	72 / 263	(27%)
On Third, Less than 2 Out	18 / 37	(49%)	53 / 116	(46%)
RBI in close games / RBI Total	37 / 67	(55%)	121 / 202	(60%)

Brian Fisher
Pittsburgh Pirates

Brian Fisher came to the Pirates in the Rick Rhoden trade. He was a reliever with the Yankees, and started the season in the bullpen for the Bucs. But a combination of problems in the starting staff and Fisher's ineffectiveness in the bullpen led Jim Leyland to move Fisher into the starting rotation. Leyland had hinted all through spring training that he would like to do that, so when Fisher struggled, it was no surprise. Fisher had been a starter in the minor leagues in the Braves organization; the Yankees moved him to the bullpen in 1985 when they acquired him for Rick Cerone.

Fisher always looked more like a starter than a reliever to me. His motion reminded me more of Tom Seaver than Goose Gossage, a full, deliberate motion. While his fastball is respectable, it definitely isn't in the Lee Smith category. Pirate pitching coach Ray Miller worked with Fisher to develop a changeup, and Fisher seemed to settle into his role as a starter and seemed to want to stay there.

He had an up and down season. If Fisher could have had 30 starts against the Cubs, he would have been a Cy Young winner. He got 2 of his 3 shutouts this season against the Cubs. His major problems were lack of control and loss of concentration with runners on base. Fisher would give up a couple of walks, and then *BOOM!* three-run homer.

But when he was on, he pitched quite well, and had the stamina to go all the way. After Reuschel's departure, Fisher was the team leader in complete games, innings pitched, and shutouts.

Fisher seems to be following in the Pirate tradition of being a good-hitting pitcher, knocking a couple of dingers this year. He's a big guy, at 6'4", 210, and despite his lack of experience as a hitter, he seems capable of doing something with pitchers' mistakes.

If you're in a rotisserie league, Fisher is the type of pitcher you learn to appreciate. He finished the season at 11–9, with 4.52 ERA in 185.1 innings pitched. Hardly Cy Young numbers, but a pitcher can have a long career as a number-three starter putting up numbers like that consistently. Fisher also looks like a workhorse of a pitcher. Rotisserie leaguers appreciate pitchers who go out there every 5 days.

Fisher is one of three players labeled "untouchable" by Syd Thrift, along with Mike Dunne and Doug Drabek. He will probably be the Pirates' number three starter this season, unless Dunne succumbs to sophomore jinx. If Fisher can master his pitches a little better, and maintain his concentration with runners on, look for Fisher to have a good year this year.

Sherri M. Nichols

Fisher, Brian Kevin   Bats: Right   Throws: Right   Born 03/18/62

1987 SEASON AND MAJOR-LEAGUE CAREER PITCHING TOTALS

	G	GS	CG	GF	IP	BFP	H	R	ER	HR	SH	SF	HB	TBB	IBB	SO	WP	Bk	W	L	Pct	ShO	Sv	ERA
87 PIT	37	26	6	1	185	792	185	99	93	27	6	5	4	72	7	117	3	3	11	9	.550	3	0	4.52
3 YEARS	154	26	6	50	380	1607	367	192	172	45	14	9	5	138	12	269	8	3	24	18	.571	3	20	4.07

1987: Finesse, Flyball   1986: Power, Flyball   1985: Power, Flyball

			1987 SEASON												FOUR YEAR TOTALS (1984 – 1987)								
	G	IP	H	BB	SO	SB	CS	W	L	S	ERA		G	IP	H	BB	SO	SB	CS	W	L	S	ERA
Totals	37	185.0	185	72	117	29	14	11	9	0	4.52		154	380.0	367	138	269	53	19	24	18	20	4.07
at Home	19	82.1	108	28	48	10	5	4	5	0	5.79		81	180.2	211	59	124	21	9	9	11	10	4.88
on Road	18	102.2	77	44	69	19	9	7	4	0	3.51		73	199.1	156	79	145	32	10	15	7	10	3.34
on Grass	13	63.2	59	27	46	6	4	5	3	0	4.10		56	135.1	133	54	101	9	6	6	7	8	4.12
on Artificial Turf	24	121.1	126	45	71	23	10	6	6	0	4.75		98	244.2	234	84	168	44	13	18	11	12	4.05
Day Games	9	46.0	35	24	28	10	4	4	2	0	3.72		107	210.2	185	86	155	29	9	15	11	16	3.63
Night Games	28	139.0	150	48	89	19	10	7	7	0	4.79		47	169.1	182	52	114	24	10	9	7	4	4.62
April	8	11.2	13	6	12	1	1	0	0	0	7.71		19	28.1	29	14	23	4	1	0	1	3	5.40
May	6	29.1	31	15	18	5	2	2	1	0	3.68		24	61.0	63	26	39	7	2	5	2	1	3.98
June	6	33.0	46	14	22	7	3	2	3	0	5.73		29	73.1	81	33	50	12	5	5	8	2	4.66
July	6	34.1	31	10	18	3	2	2	2	0	3.93		25	67.1	60	19	42	10	2	2	2	2	3.07
August	5	36.1	32	12	18	7	3	1	2	0	4.71		31	79.0	77	22	59	13	5	6	3	7	4.44
Sept/Oct	6	40.1	32	15	29	6	3	4	1	0	3.57		26	71.0	57	24	56	7	4	6	2	5	3.55

vs. Opponent Batters	Ave.	OBP	SLG	AB	H	2B	3B	HR	RBI	BB	SO		Ave.	OBP	SLG	AB	H	2B	3B	HR	RBI	BB	SO
Totals	.262	.332	.458	705	185	39	9	27	87	72	117		.255	.321	.408	1441	367	60	13	45	196	138	269
vs. Left	.267	.351	.440	375	100	24	7	9	44	50	55		.268	.351	.415	699	187	34	9	17	88	91	121
vs. Right	.258	.309	.479	330	85	15	2	18	43	22	62		.243	.290	.402	742	180	26	4	28	108	47	148
Bases Empty	.269	.342	.459	416	112	19	3	18	18	42	68		.257	.321	.404	798	205	28	4	27	27	71	163
Leadoff	.290	.359	.500	176	51	9	2	8	8	17	25		.270	.332	.429	333	90	10	2	13	13	29	60
Not Leadoff	.254	.330	.429	240	61	10	1	10	10	25	43		.247	.312	.385	465	115	18	2	14	14	42	103
Runners On Base	.253	.318	.457	289	73	20	6	9	69	30	49		.252	.320	.414	643	162	32	9	18	169	67	106
First Base Only	.294	.358	.505	109	32	11	3	2	11	11	15		.263	.316	.397	247	65	18	3	3	17	19	37
Scoring Position	.228	.294	.428	180	41	9	3	7	58	19	34		.245	.323	.424	396	97	14	6	15	152	48	69
Late Innings, Close	.275	.373	.471	51	14	2	1	2	9	7	8		.247	.332	.387	364	90	13	4	10	63	45	77

RBI/Opportunities

Scoring Position	44 / 231 (19%)	119 / 541 (22%)
Scoring Position, 2 Out	7 / 87 (8%)	36 / 233 (15%)
On Third, Less than 2 Out	19 / 39 (49%)	47 / 90 (52%)
RBI in close games / RBI Total	57 / 87 (66%)	134 / 196 (68%)

Carlton Fisk
Chicago White Sox

Carlton Fisk has now played seven seasons for the White Sox, but the relationship continues to be an uncomfortable one. The problem is not between Fisk and his teammates—he has long been a respected club leader and may well be the most admired player on the team. Nor is there a problem between Fisk and the fans—Pudge was a Chicago hero from day one, when he hit a dramatic homer to beat his former team in a battle of Sox. The problem is solely between Fisk and the club management. How can I put this? They don't think he's very good.

In 1985, Pudge had one of his greatest seasons. At age 37, he caught 130 games, belted a career high 37 homers, drove in 107 runs for another career high, and even stole 17 bases. His reward for this performance was a ticket out of town—at least, that's what the White Sox had in mind. With Hawk Harrelson calling the shots, a trade was worked out to send Fisk to (who else?) the Yankees for Don Baylor. Ultimately the deal fell through, so Fisk stayed with the Sox . . . but not as a catcher. Like it or not, he was made the club's left fielder, and his old job was given to the immortal Joel Skinner. This experiment lasted about a month. When May came, Fisk was back behind the plate. Pudge hit only 14 homers—the Hawk had done Fisk another favor by moving home plate farther away from the fences—and his average tumbled to .221. People were saying he was through. The White Sox seemed to think so, too, and thought they had another replacement ready in Ron Karkovice.

But Carlton Fisk is a proud man, and he wasn't going to let the '86 season be his epitaph. (He wasn't going to let Harrelson have that satisfaction, either.) Pudge had always kept himself in superb condition, but over the winter he worked harder than ever to get himself in shape. In '87 it all paid off. Not that the Sox made it easy for him. The season began with Karkovice catching; Fisk was the DH. As usual, that plan didn't last long. Karkovice couldn't hit his weight—he barely hit Eddie Gaedel's weight—and before April was out, Pudge was behind the plate again. And this time he gave the pretenders—and the club's management—something to think about. With a strong second half, Fisk raised his batting average 35 points over '86, belted 23 homers (18 of them on the road—Comiskey's still killing him), and, as always, handled the Sox pitching staff superbly. There was a flap at mid-season when the Sox banned beer in the clubhouse and Fisk threatened to sneak some in, but that's just Fisk and the Sox. The more they goad him, the better he seems to play. They are helping him along to the Hall of Fame election they won't think he will deserve.

Don Zminda

Fisk, Carlton Ernest "Carlton" or "Pudge"　　　　Bats: Right　　Throws: Right　　　Born 12/26/47

1987 SEASON AND MAJOR-LEAGUE CAREER BATTING TOTALS

	G	AB	H	2B	3B	HR	TB	R	RBI	TBB	IBB	SO	HP	SH	SF	SB	CS	SB%	GDP	AVG	OBP	SLG
87 CHA	135	454	116	22	1	23	209	68	71	39	8	72	8	1	6	1	4	.20	9	.256	.321	.460
18 YEARS	1962	6975	1883	338	43	304	3219	1071	1048	658	71	1078	119	24	66	116	53	.69	150	.270	.340	.462

	1987 SEASON											FOUR YEAR TOTALS (1984 – 1987)										
	Ave.	OBP	SLG	AB	H	2B	3B	HR	RBI	BB	SO	Ave.	OBP	SLG	AB	H	2B	3B	HR	RBI	BB	SO
Totals	.256	.321	.460	454	116	22	1	23	71	39	72	.237	.300	.439	1813	429	76	3	95	284	139	305
vs. Left	.236	.305	.451	182	43	10	1	9	27	17	26	.238	.297	.436	663	158	33	1	32	98	52	106
vs. Right	.268	.332	.467	272	73	12	0	14	44	22	46	.236	.302	.441	1150	271	43	2	63	186	87	199
at Home	.266	.328	.394	218	58	13	0	5	24	19	36	.225	.287	.406	916	206	39	2	41	126	72	157
on Road	.246	.316	.521	236	58	9	1	18	47	20	36	.249	.314	.473	897	223	37	1	54	158	67	148
vs. Groundball	.223	.291	.417	211	47	11	0	10	32	20	34	.233	.301	.409	850	198	34	1	38	136	71	144
vs. Flyball	.284	.348	.498	243	69	11	1	13	39	19	38	.240	.300	.465	963	231	42	2	57	148	68	161
vs. Finesse	.240	.317	.443	246	59	12	1	12	33	22	30	.242	.306	.461	1036	251	40	2	61	171	76	145
vs. Power	.274	.328	.481	208	57	10	0	11	38	17	42	.229	.294	.409	777	178	36	1	34	113	63	160
on Grass	.280	.338	.506	393	110	21	1	22	65	32	63	.236	.298	.443	1542	364	64	3	83	241	119	265
on Artificial Turf	.098	.222	.164	61	6	1	0	1	6	7	9	.240	.312	.417	271	65	12	0	12	43	20	40
Day Games	.239	.295	.415	142	34	4	0	7	15	9	31	.226	.304	.422	486	110	17	0	26	75	47	83
Night Games	.263	.333	.481	312	82	18	1	16	56	30	41	.240	.299	.445	1327	319	59	3	69	209	92	222
April	.268	.369	.375	56	15	1	1	1	8	8	7	.241	.310	.427	232	56	11	1	10	34	22	39
May	.149	.256	.284	67	10	3	0	2	8	7	18	.212	.288	.383	316	67	10	1	14	52	31	65
June	.207	.245	.379	87	18	3	0	4	11	3	16	.211	.259	.378	299	63	8	0	14	45	18	59
July	.309	.343	.532	94	29	3	0	6	17	5	12	.233	.285	.482	301	70	10	1	21	47	22	47
August	.339	.385	.661	59	20	4	0	5	11	5	11	.262	.298	.501	363	95	18	0	23	57	19	61
Sept/Oct	.264	.349	.516	91	24	8	0	5	16	11	8	.258	.321	.450	302	78	19	0	13	49	27	34
Bases Empty	.274	.338	.486	259	71	16	0	13	13	22	28	.231	.279	.441	1016	235	43	1	56	56	64	167
Leadoff	.248	.309	.425	113	28	8	0	4	4	8	15	.218	.266	.425	409	89	17	1	22	22	25	72
Not Leadoff	.295	.360	.534	146	43	8	0	9	9	14	13	.241	.287	.451	607	146	26	0	34	34	39	95
Runners On	.231	.300	.426	195	45	6	1	10	58	17	44	.243	.310	.437	797	194	33	2	39	228	75	138
First Base Only	.207	.258	.483	87	18	3	0	7	16	4	16	.228	.272	.436	360	82	12	0	21	48	20	55
Scoring Position	.250	.331	.380	108	27	3	1	3	42	13	28	.256	.339	.437	437	112	21	1	18	180	55	83
Late Innings, Close	.253	.344	.418	79	20	1	0	4	13	10	21	.262	.322	.456	305	80	10	2	15	54	26	63

RBI/Opportunities

	1987	Four Year
Scoring Position	38 / 158 (24%)	144 / 623 (23%)
Scoring Position, 2 Out	14 / 70 (20%)	53 / 268 (20%)
On Third, Less than 2 Out	17 / 29 (59%)	59 / 133 (44%)
RBI in close games / RBI Total	54 / 71 (76%)	204 / 284 (72%)

Mike Fitzgerald
Montreal Expos

For the first time since he came to the Expos in the Gary Carter trade three seasons ago, Mike Fitzgerald managed to play most of a season without missing time to injuries. After spending the first two weeks of the season on the DL with a hand still hurting from a 1986 injury, Fitzgerald settled in and finally proved he can get a full season out of his body.

Fitzgerald didn't actually play that much more than he has in the past—he spent the season platooning with Jeff Reed, despite the fact that after playing parts of three seasons in both the AL and NL, Reed hasn't proven he can hit major league pitching with any consistency. Fitzgerald didn't show much offensively himself—after hitting .282 in 73 games in 1986, he fell to .240 last year, and showed no power. He drove in 36 runs, which is about the same number he drives in every year, no matter how many at bats he gets. His biggest problems, though, came in the field. He had the second worst fielding percentage (.981) among all catchers with more than 100 games played, and his 12 errors tied him with Reed, again second from the bottom. (The worst in both categories was Benito Santiago, a rookie with a great arm, who figures to get better.) Above all, Fitzgerald was brutal at throwing out runners.

In the past, Fitzgerald benefitted from a reputation as being a smart catcher, a student of the game who was a winner despite not having above average skills. In 1985 and '86 the Expos were a combined 31 games above .500 in games Fitzgerald started, and 29 below with everyone else. Nice numbers, but I think they said a lot more about Sal Butera and Dann Bilardello than they did about Fitzgerald. This past season Fitzgerald was only slightly above .500, and had a poorer winning percentage than Reed. All season Montreal seemed to be winning despite its catching, never because of it.

Every year since the Carter deal the Expos have traded for a catcher, but always one to back-up, not replace, Fitzgerald, and they haven't said or done anything yet this winter to indicate they've lost any confidence in him. He's proved he can at least hit righties well enough to be an offensive asset, but if opponents can continue to run at will, as they did in 1987, Montreal won't get any closer to the top than they are now—especially with smart running teams like St. Louis and New York ahead of them. Despite all the talent Montreal picked up in trading Carter, it left a big hole in an important spot that has yet to be filled. The coming season may be Fitzgerald's last shot to prove he can do it.

Michael Cassin

Fitzgerald, Michael Roy "Mike" Bats: Right Throws: Right Born 03/28/64

1987 SEASON AND MAJOR-LEAGUE CAREER BATTING TOTALS

	G	AB	H	2B	3B	HR	TB	R	RBI	TBB	IBB	SO	HP	SH	SF	SB	CS	SB%	GDP	AVG	OBP	SLG
87 MON	107	287	69	11	0	3	89	32	36	42	7	54	1	3	1	3	4	.43	10	.240	.338	.310
5 YEARS	408	1171	278	46	3	17	381	98	142	134	33	220	5	13	12	12	9	.57	39	.237	.315	.325

	1987 SEASON											FOUR YEAR TOTALS (1984 – 1987)										
	Ave.	OBP	SLG	AB	H	2B	3B	HR	RBI	BB	SO	Ave.	OBP	SLG	AB	H	2B	3B	HR	RBI	BB	SO
Totals	.240	.338	.310	287	69	11	0	3	36	42	54	.240	.317	.327	1151	276	46	3	16	140	131	214
vs. Left	.213	.324	.291	127	27	4	0	2	14	20	30	.230	.320	.297	431	99	14	0	5	39	57	81
vs. Right	.262	.350	.325	160	42	7	0	1	22	22	24	.246	.315	.344	720	177	32	3	11	101	74	133
at Home	.253	.363	.325	154	39	8	0	1	26	26	25	.222	.299	.295	600	133	17	3	7	65	66	118
on Road	.226	.309	.293	133	30	3	0	2	10	16	29	.260	.338	.361	551	143	29	0	9	75	65	96
vs. Groundball	.238	.293	.278	151	36	6	0	0	18	12	26	.240	.312	.297	576	138	19	1	4	68	61	95
vs. Flyball	.243	.383	.346	136	33	5	0	3	18	30	28	.240	.323	.357	575	138	27	2	12	72	70	119
vs. Finesse	.204	.285	.240	167	34	6	0	0	15	19	26	.249	.310	.311	659	164	25	2	4	80	61	100
vs. Power	.292	.407	.408	120	35	5	0	3	21	23	28	.228	.326	.348	492	112	21	1	12	60	70	114
on Grass	.273	.349	.338	77	21	2	0	1	7	9	18	.259	.317	.362	459	119	21	1	8	58	39	84
on Artificial Turf	.229	.335	.300	210	48	9	0	2	29	33	36	.227	.317	.303	692	157	25	2	8	82	92	130
Day Games	.300	.364	.356	90	27	5	0	0	12	9	20	.267	.332	.357	367	98	20	2	3	45	36	67
Night Games	.213	.328	.289	197	42	6	0	3	24	33	34	.227	.310	.313	784	178	26	1	13	95	95	147
April	.267	.313	.333	15	4	1	0	0	1	1	3	.256	.350	.367	90	23	4	0	2	11	13	15
May	.194	.286	.269	67	13	2	0	1	6	9	16	.213	.301	.300	253	54	5	1	5	31	32	44
June	.268	.359	.411	56	15	2	0	2	13	8	6	.250	.337	.361	252	63	8	1	6	35	33	47
July	.318	.434	.341	44	14	1	0	0	7	9	4	.261	.327	.351	245	64	13	0	3	35	24	40
August	.227	.333	.250	44	10	1	0	0	4	7	12	.226	.290	.277	177	40	7	1	0	18	16	42
Sept/Oct	.213	.314	.279	61	13	4	0	0	5	8	13	.239	.311	.306	134	32	9	0	0	10	13	26
Bases Empty	.243	.321	.318	148	36	5	0	2	2	17	25	.229	.279	.321	654	150	20	2	12	12	45	134
Leadoff	.268	.333	.352	71	19	3	0	1	1	7	12	.260	.311	.346	269	70	9	1	4	4	20	50
Not Leadoff	.221	.310	.286	77	17	2	0	1	1	10	13	.208	.256	.304	385	80	11	1	8	8	25	84
Runners On	.237	.355	.302	139	33	6	0	1	34	25	29	.254	.364	.334	497	126	26	1	4	128	86	80
First Base Only	.192	.300	.250	52	10	3	0	0	2	8	9	.222	.279	.296	216	48	11	1	1	9	17	23
Scoring Position	.264	.387	.333	87	23	3	0	1	32	17	20	.278	.420	.363	281	78	15	0	3	119	69	57
Late Innings, Close	.233	.340	.279	43	10	2	0	0	5	7	7	.212	.290	.293	208	44	8	0	3	22	23	46

RBI/Opportunities

Scoring Position	28 / 133 (21%)	109 / 443 (25%)	
Scoring Position, 2 Out	10 / 68 (15%)	39 / 198 (20%)	
On Third, Less than 2 Out	12 / 20 (60%)	51 / 91 (56%)	
RBI in close games / RBI Total	24 / 36 (67%)	92 / 140 (66%)	

Tim Flannery
San Diego Padres

Actors often find themselves repeatedly cast in the same kinds of roles. Directors, casting people, and the like have seen Dabney Coleman play a nasty sleazeball so often and so well that they can't see him in another type of role. They're afraid to take a chance on casting him in another part. Sometimes they're right, sometimes not. Since the public sees him solely in these roles, they identify him as a nasty sleazeball. This is called type casting.

The same is true in baseball. At some point in his career, it was decided that Tim Flannery didn't have the necessary skills to play every day; that his greatest value would be as a utility role player. Flannery was intelligent enough to see that, like it or not, he'd have to adapt to this role in order to have a major league career. He made certain he was always ready to play at a moment's notice. He developed the "team" skills that increase a substitute's value: advancing runners, bunting, fielding multiple positions and "taking one for the team."

With the Padres' inadequate efforts to replace Alan Wiggins, Tim began recent seasons on the bench, only to finish as the team's starter at second. Interestingly, Flannery's statistics indicate that the more he plays, the more productive he is. His career easily separates into two categories: those years with more than 350 at bats and those with fewer than 300. Below is a capsule look at his performance:

	AB	H	BA	BB	OBA
more than 350 AB	1131	311	.275	142	.364
300 AB or less	1042	245	.235	98	.307

1988 will be Tim's tenth season as a Padre. He's long been the most popular player with the fans because of his hustle and enthusiasm. A pesky hitter, he will do anything he can to start or prolong a rally, and he's no slouch on defense. While not blessed with the range of some others, he's sure-handed, has a quick, accurate release and turns the double play well. Tim always gives 100 percent effort.

Last year Tim suffered a serious leg injury, which clearly hampered him when he tried to return to action. As one would expect, he probably returned too soon. One can't help wondering what Flannery's career and reputation would have been if he'd had the chance to play every day for the past six or seven years.

Bruce Erricson

Flannery, Timothy Earl "Tim" Bats: Left Throws: Right Born 09/29/57

1987 SEASON AND MAJOR-LEAGUE CAREER BATTING TOTALS

	G	AB	H	2B	3B	HR	TB	R	RBI	TBB	IBB	SO	HP	SH	SF	SB	CS	SB%	GDP	AVG	OBP	SLG
87 SD	106	276	63	5	1	0	70	23	20	42	4	30	2	4	2	2	4	.33	6	.228	.332	.254
9 YEARS	820	2173	556	67	21	9	692	230	182	240	34	241	28	26	21	17	20	.46	36	.256	.335	.318

	1987 SEASON										FOUR YEAR TOTALS (1984 – 1987)									
	Ave.	OBP	SLG	AB	H	2B	3B	HR	RBI	BB	SO	Ave.	OBP	SLG	AB	H	2B	3B	HR	RBI	BB	SO
Totals	.228	.332	.254	276	63	5	1	0	20	42	30	.267	.366	.327	1156	309	33	9	6	98	166	147
vs. Left	.244	.311	.268	41	10	1	0	0	2	4	4	.177	.244	.245	147	26	5	1	1	6	12	25
vs. Right	.226	.336	.251	235	53	4	1	0	18	38	26	.280	.383	.339	1009	283	28	8	5	92	154	122
at Home	.246	.361	.270	122	30	3	0	0	10	21	9	.276	.385	.333	529	146	12	3	4	47	84	65
on Road	.214	.309	.240	154	33	2	1	0	10	21	21	.260	.350	.322	627	163	21	6	2	51	82	82
vs. Groundball	.231	.322	.254	130	30	3	0	0	10	17	9	.262	.359	.304	565	148	14	2	2	46	79	63
vs. Flyball	.226	.341	.253	146	33	2	1	0	10	25	21	.272	.373	.349	591	161	19	7	4	52	87	84
vs. Finesse	.222	.321	.239	117	26	2	0	0	12	18	11	.287	.370	.348	609	175	19	6	2	58	76	56
vs. Power	.233	.341	.264	159	37	3	1	0	8	24	19	.245	.363	.303	547	134	14	3	4	40	90	91
on Grass	.241	.349	.266	199	48	3	1	0	15	32	18	.277	.376	.336	833	231	19	6	6	73	118	91
on Artificial Turf	.195	.287	.221	77	15	2	0	0	5	10	12	.241	.341	.303	323	78	14	3	0	25	48	56
Day Games	.202	.324	.234	94	19	1	1	0	6	17	8	.257	.357	.344	404	104	14	6	3	33	57	46
Night Games	.242	.336	.264	182	44	4	0	0	14	25	22	.273	.372	.318	752	205	19	3	3	65	109	101
April	.143	.333	.190	21	3	1	0	0	0	5	0	.252	.341	.328	119	30	7	1	0	5	15	9
May	.313	.353	.500	16	5	1	1	0	2	1	2	.282	.367	.423	156	44	8	4	2	19	21	19
June	.262	.347	.262	84	22	0	0	0	5	11	2	.275	.366	.360	222	61	2	4	3	25	32	14
July	.226	.311	.264	53	12	2	0	0	5	7	9	.276	.368	.308	214	59	7	0	0	15	32	30
August	.302	.413	.317	63	19	1	0	0	6	12	10	.305	.392	.342	243	74	6	0	1	20	35	41
Sept/Oct	.051	.191	.051	39	2	0	0	0	2	6	7	.203	.311	.218	202	41	3	0	0	14	31	34
Bases Empty	.178	.302	.195	169	30	3	0	0	0	28	21	.245	.351	.295	748	183	20	3	4	4	121	97
Leadoff	.153	.306	.203	59	9	3	0	0	0	12	7	.220	.337	.289	363	80	13	3	2	2	63	46
Not Leadoff	.191	.299	.191	110	21	0	0	0	0	16	14	.268	.365	.301	385	103	7	0	2	2	58	51
Runners On	.308	.382	.346	107	33	2	1	0	20	14	9	.309	.376	.385	408	126	13	6	2	94	45	50
First Base Only	.286	.362	.286	42	12	0	0	0	0	5	7	.312	.376	.396	154	48	8	1	1	6	16	20
Scoring Position	.323	.395	.385	65	21	2	1	0	20	9	2	.307	.375	.378	254	78	5	5	1	88	29	30
Late Innings, Close	.143	.276	.163	49	7	1	0	0	3	9	6	.209	.293	.258	244	51	7	1	1	14	29	39

RBI/Opportunities

Scoring Position	20 / 87	(23%)		84 / 352	(24%)	
Scoring Position, 2 Out	12 / 50	(24%)		46 / 198	(23%)	
On Third, Less than 2 Out	5 / 11	(45%)		28 / 54	(52%)	
RBI in close games / RBI Total	11 / 20	(55%)		62 / 98	(63%)	

Scott Fletcher
Texas Rangers

If you were limited to the Rangers' roster and had to match the word "intense" with one player, there is one name that immediately jumps to the fore, Scott Fletcher. A lot of observers wondered if he could keep that intensity as a regular during the seemingly endless baseball season. He quieted those critics in 1986, but those doubters are back again claiming that his constant tension finally broke a spring in August.

1987	AB	HITS	B.A.	2B/3B/HR	SLUG%	O.B.A.
APRIL-JULY	391	122	.312	20/ 4/ 4	.414	.373
AUG-OCT	197	47	.239	8/ 0/ 1	.299	.333

It was a long season: 668 plate appearances, 156 games—155 at shortstop, second only to that marvelous mechanical man in Baltimore. But his late season slippage may be traceable to a bad right elbow which bothered him all season in the field: He made a lot of extra errors, most on bad throws. I think it bothered him as a hitter toward the end. He seemed to have trouble driving the ball to the opposite field like he has done so consistently in the past. That may be why this was his first season in a long while that he had a significant platoon difference.

I've always admired Scooter as an excellent situational hitter, and he kept up his reputation in 1987. He hit well over .300 with men on base and specifically with men in scoring position. Over the last five years he has had over 450 at-bats with men in scoring position and sports a .317 average in that situation.

In 1987, Scott set a career high in walks with 61, and I wondered if he also tended to distribute his walks in situations where they would be more valuable. Well, yes he does. When a walk is as good as a single (bases empty) he retains more of his overall walk average than the average non-pitcher in that situation.

The Rangers have a pretty good grasp of Fletcher's abilities and deserved to be lauded for rescuing him from being a career back-up. However, they do have one blind spot: They think he can steal a base. In 1987 he made a career high 25 steal attempts, and there is nothing in his recent history to inspire such confidence.

Scooter started off his career stealing 16 bases in his first 21 attempts, but he was 5 for 10 in 1985 and 12 for 23 in 1986. Combined, that's one steal over .500 when you generally need a 63 to 65 percent success rate just to break even. And how did he do in those 25 attempts in 1987? One steal over .500, 13–12. Actually, I still think Fletcher can steal a base productively when he is allowed to chose his spots carefully. He just isn't the type of runner who can steal a base at will, whether his own or the manager's.

Craig R. Wright

Fletcher, Scott Brian   Bats: Right   Throws: Right   Born 07/30/58

1987 SEASON AND MAJOR-LEAGUE CAREER BATTING TOTALS

	G	AB	H	2B	3B	HR	TB	R	RBI	TBB	IBB	SO	HP	SH	SF	SB	CS	SB%	GDP	AVG	OBP	SLG
87 TEX	156	588	169	28	4	5	220	82	63	61	3	66	5	12	2	13	12	.52	14	.287	.358	.374
7 YEARS	715	2207	595	103	18	16	782	300	212	224	5	249	19	49	10	46	33	.58	46	.270	.341	.354

	1987 SEASON										FOUR YEAR TOTALS (1984 – 1987)									
	Ave.	OBP	SLG	AB	H	2B	3B	HR	RBI	BB	SO	Ave.	OBP	SLG	AB	H	2B	3B	HR	RBI	BB	SO
Totals	.287	.358	.374	588	169	28	4	5	63	61	66	.277	.347	.356	1875	519	83	13	13	179	189	218
vs. Left	.318	.388	.409	220	70	9	1	3	23	24	18	.287	.363	.374	728	209	31	4	8	64	86	72
vs. Right	.269	.341	.353	368	99	19	3	2	40	37	48	.270	.337	.344	1147	310	52	9	5	115	103	146
at Home	.341	.413	.463	287	98	17	3	4	37	31	25	.299	.372	.391	909	272	41	9	8	103	96	92
on Road	.236	.305	.289	301	71	11	1	1	26	30	41	.256	.324	.323	966	247	42	4	5	76	93	126
vs. Groundball	.333	.397	.431	297	99	15	4	2	43	29	32	.287	.352	.357	858	246	37	7	3	83	74	101
vs. Flyball	.241	.319	.316	291	70	13	0	3	20	32	34	.268	.343	.355	1017	273	46	6	10	96	115	117
vs. Finesse	.308	.357	.396	338	104	15	3	3	38	24	37	.288	.341	.365	1095	315	46	9	7	101	81	112
vs. Power	.260	.360	.344	250	65	13	1	2	25	37	29	.262	.355	.342	780	204	37	4	6	78	108	106
on Grass	.315	.383	.413	489	154	25	4	5	58	50	50	.286	.352	.368	1553	444	70	12	11	158	149	180
on Artificial Turf	.152	.234	.182	99	15	3	0	0	5	11	16	.233	.322	.298	322	75	13	1	2	21	40	38
Day Games	.320	.378	.434	122	39	7	2	1	17	12	18	.283	.354	.374	441	125	23	4	3	40	44	61
Night Games	.279	.353	.358	466	130	21	2	4	46	49	48	.275	.345	.350	1434	394	60	9	10	139	145	157
April	.360	.407	.467	75	27	3	1	1	12	5	9	.293	.370	.371	229	67	6	3	2	28	27	33
May	.291	.330	.369	103	30	3	1	1	10	6	11	.255	.325	.322	329	84	11	4	1	32	34	39
June	.300	.376	.464	110	33	8	2	2	12	13	15	.291	.359	.392	306	89	15	5	2	28	32	39
July	.311	.388	.369	103	32	6	0	0	12	13	10	.307	.357	.399	348	107	23	0	3	32	27	28
August	.247	.321	.289	97	24	4	0	0	7	9	13	.262	.322	.321	321	84	10	0	3	30	27	42
Sept/Oct	.230	.336	.300	100	23	4	0	1	10	15	8	.257	.340	.333	342	88	18	1	2	29	42	37
Bases Empty	.264	.346	.355	352	93	16	2	4	4	41	43	.262	.331	.346	1169	306	51	9	10	10	118	135
Leadoff	.229	.339	.330	109	25	2	0	3	3	17	10	.244	.323	.338	414	101	16	1	7	7	47	41
Not Leadoff	.280	.349	.366	243	68	14	2	1	1	24	33	.272	.336	.351	755	205	35	8	3	3	71	94
Runners On	.322	.377	.403	236	76	12	2	1	59	20	23	.302	.366	.371	706	213	32	4	3	169	71	83
First Base Only	.301	.345	.417	103	31	5	2	1	7	5	6	.274	.324	.355	310	85	13	3	2	12	21	30
Scoring Position	.338	.400	.391	133	45	7	0	0	52	15	17	.323	.397	.384	396	128	19	1	1	157	50	53
Late Innings, Close	.247	.352	.303	89	22	5	0	0	16	14	12	.242	.309	.280	264	64	10	0	0	35	25	43

RBI/Opportunities

Scoring Position	52 / 195	(27%)		153 / 570	(27%)
Scoring Position, 2 Out	27 / 98	(28%)		61 / 252	(24%)
On Third, Less than 2 Out	16 / 30	(53%)		59 / 108	(55%)
RBI in close games / RBI Total	43 / 63	(68%)		127 / 179	(71%)

Curt Ford
St. Louis Cardinals

Reserve outfielder Curt Ford was a big boost for the Cardinals in 1987. Ford's rookie season was spent as a back-up and platoon right fielder with Andy Van Slyke. His numbers were not overwhelming offensively, but Ford was popular due to some clutch hitting and some spectacular running catches in the outfield.

Van Slyke was traded in spring training in a major deal with Pittsburgh, not to open a spot for Ford, but to insert some power. The right field job was handed over to rookie Jim Lindeman, who was supposed to provide the power to protect Clark. However, the oft-injured Lindeman did not play as much as Ford.

Ford became a big contributor to the Cardinal offense, particularly in the first half of the season. At the All-Star break Ford was hitting a solid .323. Against Dennis Fischer in Montreal on June 27, Ford hit two of his three home runs, a two run shot in the third inning and a leadoff homer in the fifth. A broken right hand put Ford on the disabled list and his hitting suffered upon his return, as the hand bothered him the rest of the season, causing Ford to finish the year with a .285 overall average. Defensively, Ford finished with a very respectable .981 fielding average.

Ford has shown he can be a very good outfielder in the majors. It seems obvious he can hit—in addition to his fine stats in '87, his minor league batting record was very solid— and he has speed as well. But at the age of 27, he may be considered expendable by St. Louis and develop faster where he can get the chance for more playing time as a regular. Teams needing help in the outfield and needing a good hitter should be calling Dal Maxvill. The Redbirds will have to repeat the experiment with Lindeman in the lineup, as his '87 season was plagued with hamstring and back injuries and was not an indicator of his future.

Younger outfielders in the organization may figure more prominently in the future. John Morris is the best pinch hitter on the team except possibly Oquendo and is the player Whitey uses most in double switch situations. Lance Johnson and minor leaguer Alex Cole could fill the void if Ford is traded, and it looks like David Green may be trying for a comeback.

Rollie Loewen

Ford, Curtis Glenn "Curt"   Bats: Left   Throws: Right   Born 10/11/60

1987 SEASON AND MAJOR-LEAGUE CAREER BATTING TOTALS

	G	AB	H	2B	3B	HR	TB	R	RBI	TBB	IBB	SO	HP	SH	SF	SB	CS	SB%	GDP	AVG	OBP	SLG
87 STL	89	228	65	9	5	3	93	32	26	14	0	32	1	1	3	11	8	.58	5	.285	.325	.408
3 YEARS	185	454	124	26	7	5	179	64	58	41	2	62	1	2	5	25	13	.66	6	.273	.331	.394

	1987 SEASON											FOUR YEAR TOTALS (1984 – 1987)									
	Ave.	OBP	SLG	AB	H	2B	3B	HR	RBI	BB	SO	Ave.	OBP	SLG	AB	H	2B	3B	HR	RBI	BB	SO
Totals	.285	.325	.408	228	65	9	5	3	26	14	32	.273	.331	.394	454	124	26	7	5	58	41	62
vs. Left	.286	.348	.333	21	6	1	0	0	2	2	5	.240	.309	.300	50	12	3	0	0	6	5	12
vs. Right	.285	.323	.415	207	59	8	5	3	24	12	27	.277	.334	.406	404	112	23	7	5	52	36	50
at Home	.279	.316	.385	104	29	4	2	1	14	6	15	.286	.346	.408	206	59	16	3	1	34	20	28
on Road	.290	.333	.427	124	36	5	3	2	12	8	17	.262	.319	.383	248	65	10	4	4	24	21	34
vs. Groundball	.202	.241	.284	109	22	3	3	0	7	6	20	.208	.259	.288	212	44	11	3	0	18	15	36
vs. Flyball	.361	.400	.521	119	43	6	2	3	19	8	12	.331	.392	.488	242	80	15	4	5	40	26	26
vs. Finesse	.295	.350	.446	112	33	4	2	3	11	9	6	.291	.338	.419	258	75	15	3	4	31	19	20
vs. Power	.276	.301	.371	116	32	5	3	0	15	5	26	.250	.323	.362	196	49	11	4	1	27	22	42
on Grass	.276	.323	.368	87	24	2	3	0	7	6	11	.225	.270	.290	138	31	3	3	0	10	9	20
on Artificial Turf	.291	.327	.433	141	41	7	2	3	19	8	21	.294	.357	.440	316	93	23	4	5	48	32	42
Day Games	.239	.289	.352	71	17	4	2	0	4	5	8	.226	.299	.336	137	31	11	2	0	12	15	12
Night Games	.306	.341	.433	157	48	5	3	3	22	9	24	.293	.346	.420	317	93	15	5	5	46	26	50
April	.409	.480	.591	22	9	2	1	0	4	3	3	.409	.480	.591	22	9	2	1	0	4	3	3
May	.319	.347	.507	69	22	4	3	1	8	3	11	.319	.347	.507	69	22	4	3	1	8	3	11
June	.326	.348	.512	43	14	2	0	2	7	2	4	.309	.358	.495	97	30	7	1	3	11	8	11
July	.231	.292	.277	65	15	1	1	0	6	5	8	.256	.312	.318	129	33	6	1	0	17	10	16
August	.188	.222	.188	16	3	0	0	0	1	1	3	.202	.262	.287	94	19	3	1	1	13	8	13
Sept/Oct	.154	.154	.154	13	2	0	0	0	0	0	3	.256	.385	.349	43	11	4	0	0	5	9	8
Bases Empty	.273	.321	.383	128	35	4	2	2	2	8	19	.253	.319	.363	237	60	11	3	3	3	22	37
Leadoff	.302	.353	.413	63	19	2	1	1	1	4	8	.274	.331	.385	117	32	5	1	2	2	9	17
Not Leadoff	.246	.290	.354	65	16	2	1	1	1	4	11	.233	.308	.342	120	28	6	2	1	1	13	20
Runners On	.300	.330	.440	100	30	5	3	1	24	6	13	.295	.347	.429	217	64	15	4	2	55	19	25
First Base Only	.286	.342	.400	35	10	2	1	0	1	3	5	.288	.333	.425	73	21	3	2	1	4	5	6
Scoring Position	.308	.324	.462	65	20	3	2	1	23	3	8	.299	.354	.431	144	43	12	2	1	51	14	19
Late Innings, Close	.291	.344	.345	55	16	3	0	0	7	5	7	.327	.410	.426	101	33	8	1	0	13	15	12

RBI/Opportunities

Scoring Position	22 / 84	(26%)		49 / 190	(26%)	
Scoring Position, 2 Out	6 / 36	(17%)		17 / 86	(20%)	
On Third, Less than 2 Out	9 / 15	(60%)		16 / 32	(50%)	
RBI in close games / RBI Total	14 / 26	(54%)		36 / 58	(62%)	

Bob Forsch
St. Louis Cardinals

Pitcher run support is a statistic which can explain a lot of the variations in year-to-year performances of starting pitchers. Yet it's usually looked at simply as runs per game. This doesn't always tell the story, however. Sometimes it's necessary to break down run support further to get the full story. Runs per game can be too easily inflated by a few high scoring games.

In 1986, when Bob Forsch posted a 14–10 overall record, he actually pitched better than his record indicates. Though his run support per game of 4.30 was the highest on the team, it was inflated by a few blowouts in the Cardinals' favor. There were actually seventeen times in which the Cards scored three runs or less for their veteran hurler. His won-loss record was much more impressive given this fact.

1987 was the other side of the coin. Bob didn't pitch all that well, allowing over four and a half runs per nine innings. Yet he managed to post an 11–7 record. How did he do this? Once again his run support provides a lot of the answers. Forsch was again the best supported of all Cardinal pitchers with ten or more starts, but whereas he led the team with 4.30 runs in '86, in '87 his team-leading figure was 5.63. Almost six runs a game! And this time there were only eight times in his 30 starts in which he received three runs or less. Forsch didn't win any of them, nor did the Cardinals. In the 22 starts where he did get more than three

runs of support, the Cardinals were 16–6. Forsch lost games, in fact, where he was given eight and six runs to work with.

The fact is, Forsch wasn't really getting 4.30 runs per game in 1986. Most of the time he was getting considerably less, but a few times he got a good deal more, inflating his run support. His record in comparison to his run support suffered because of this. In 1987, on the other hand, he actually was getting close to 5.63 runs per game most of the time. And despite pitching poorly at times he posted a won-lost record that was more impressive than his pitching performance. The '87 runs per game figure was an accurate measure; the '86 figure was not.

1987 was an unusual season for Forsch in another sense. Throughout his career he has had a definite and consistently substantial home park advantage. In the eighties he has a winning percentage of over .600 at home, under .500 on the road. But in 1987 he was 8–3 in away games with a 4.19 ERA as opposed to 3–4 and 4.54 at home. Busch Stadium is the perfect park for a pitcher with Forsch's abilities, but last season he was a better pitcher on the road.

Forsch remains an excellent hitter. He hit .298 in 1987 and slugged two homeruns. And if you go back and look at the scoresheets you'll see that a number of his hits were key ones.

Russ Eagle

Forsch, Robert Herbert "Bob" Bats: Right Throws: Right Born 01/13/50

1987 SEASON AND MAJOR-LEAGUE CAREER PITCHING TOTALS

	G	GS	CG	GF	IP	BFP	H	R	ER	HR	SH	SF	HB	TBB	IBB	SO	WP	Bk	W	L	Pct	ShO	Sv	ERA
87 STL	33	30	2	1	179	755	189	90	86	15	7	6	4	45	4	89	2	1	11	7	.611	1	0	4.32
14 YEARS	425	389	66	11	2550	10625	2491	1178	1040	196	90	88	41	742	69	1039	86	10	154	123	.556	18	3	3.67

1987: Finesse, Flyball **1986: Finesse, Flyball** **1985: Finesse, Flyball** **1984: Finesse, Groundball**

1987 SEASON

	G	IP	H	BB	SO	SB	CS	W	L	S	ERA
Totals	33	179.0	189	45	89	11	7	11	7	0	4.32
at Home	15	69.1	72	24	49	6	4	3	4	0	4.54
on Road	18	109.2	117	21	40	5	3	8	3	0	4.19
on Grass	11	63.0	68	16	36	2	1	5	3	0	4.00
on Artificial Turf	22	116.0	121	29	53	9	6	6	4	0	4.50
Day Games	10	63.2	67	14	26	2	1	5	2	0	4.10
Night Games	23	115.1	122	31	63	9	6	6	5	0	4.45
April	4	22.1	27	4	11	0	0	2	1	0	4.43
May	5	28.0	40	6	9	5	1	2	0	0	5.79
June	5	29.2	35	7	16	1	1	2	2	0	5.46
July	7	40.0	30	14	14	1	1	3	0	0	2.92
August	6	30.1	30	10	15	3	3	1	1	0	3.86
Sept/Oct	6	28.2	27	4	24	1	1	1	3	0	4.08

FOUR YEAR TOTALS (1984 – 1987)

	G	IP	H	BB	SO	SB	CS	W	L	S	ERA
Totals	116	597.1	596	179	262	36	19	36	28	2	3.96
at Home	57	288.2	277	81	126	17	12	17	14	0	3.62
on Road	59	308.2	319	98	136	19	7	19	14	2	4.26
on Grass	44	208.1	215	73	94	13	5	13	11	2	4.45
on Artificial Turf	72	389.0	381	106	168	23	14	23	17	0	3.70
Day Games	32	174.0	173	58	79	10	3	11	9	2	3.88
Night Games	84	423.1	423	121	183	26	16	25	19	0	4.00
April	17	100.2	102	26	45	4	2	5	5	0	3.67
May	20	99.1	118	37	35	10	2	8	5	0	4.71
June	15	85.2	76	33	46	6	3	4	5	1	3.78
July	18	84.1	85	24	28	3	1	7	2	1	2.88
August	21	106.0	92	25	44	6	8	6	4	0	3.65
Sept/Oct	25	121.1	123	34	64	7	3	6	7	0	4.75

vs. Opponent Batters	Ave.	OBP	SLG	AB	H	2B	3B	HR	RBI	BB	SO
Totals	.273	.318	.410	693	189	38	6	15	75	45	89
vs. Left	.268	.316	.369	369	99	19	3	4	33	27	44
vs. Right	.278	.321	.457	324	90	19	3	11	42	18	45
Bases Empty	.254	.298	.380	426	108	25	4	7	7	25	61
Leadoff	.273	.304	.404	183	50	13	1	3	3	8	28
Not Leadoff	.239	.294	.362	243	58	12	3	4	4	17	33
Runners On Base	.303	.349	.457	267	81	13	2	8	68	20	28
First Base Only	.333	.361	.518	114	38	4	1	5	13	4	12
Scoring Position	.281	.341	.412	153	43	9	1	3	55	16	16
Late Innings, Close	.231	.333	.308	26	6	0	1	0	3	4	6

vs. Opponent Batters	Ave.	OBP	SLG	AB	H	2B	3B	HR	RBI	BB	SO
Totals	.262	.317	.395	2271	596	108	20	51	229	179	262
vs. Left	.263	.326	.374	1097	289	53	10	16	92	103	115
vs. Right	.261	.308	.415	1174	307	55	10	35	137	76	147
Bases Empty	.252	.296	.396	1435	362	73	14	35	35	88	176
Leadoff	.250	.283	.411	604	151	32	7	17	17	28	72
Not Leadoff	.254	.306	.385	831	211	41	7	18	18	60	104
Runners On Base	.280	.350	.394	836	234	35	6	16	194	91	86
First Base Only	.261	.318	.360	372	97	10	3	7	24	30	39
Scoring Position	.295	.374	.420	464	137	25	3	9	170	61	47
Late Innings, Close	.266	.344	.427	143	38	3	1	6	14	17	14

RBI/Opportunities

Scoring Position	48 / 197	(24%)
Scoring Position, 2 Out	18 / 91	(20%)
On Third, Less than 2 Out	19 / 36	(53%)
RBI in close games / RBI Total	54 / 75	(72%)

151 / 631	(24%)
49 / 270	(18%)
59 / 123	(48%)
163 / 229	(71%)

John Franco
Cincinnati Reds

John Franco was so impressive in short relief in 1986 that no one planned on missing Ted Power when he was moved to the starting rotation. As it turned out, Franco was dominating enough to surpass Jesse Orosco as the best left-handed relief pitcher in the National League.

Pete Rose was particularly stingy in using John in 1987. He appeared in 68 games and threw a grand total of 82 innings for an average of less than 1.3 innings per appearance. Because of the strong bullpen the Reds had in '87, Pete could afford to save his best for last. A typical Reds relief effort would go something like this: Frank Williams keeps the Reds ahead through the seventh inning; Rob Murphy then pitches the eighth, with Franco coming on in the ninth for the save. Franco got 32 saves on the year. He earned the saves in 68 appearances. The only other reliever in the National League with a higher percentage of saves/appearance was Steve Bedrosian. The 32 saves were also John's career best in that department. If the Reds combine the 1st half offensive performance and the second half performance of the starting pitchers over the course of an entire season, Franco will have a shot at a 40-save season.

Last year was a funny year for Cincinnati. There were times when, because the Reds would either get so far ahead, or so far behind their opponents, that it was pointless for Pete to send in Franco. He went 5, 6 or 7 days without getting into a game. Then Franco would take 2 or 3 appearances to get back into the swing of things. Meanwhile Reds' opponents would get the best of him during those brief periods of time.

Franco has all the right things going for him. He has great stuff, he's only 27 years old, he plays for one of the best offensive teams in baseball, and he has great setup men. Unfortunately the Reds didn't win enough games last year for John to get a real shot at 40 saves. It is unfortunate that this is the milestone by which relievers are judged, because there were many who were excellent in 1987, but did not come close to 40 saves.

Franco cannot be considered the key point to the Reds ballclub, but he is definitely a main ingredient in moving the Reds up the ladder and lifting them from division contenders to division winners. His outstanding performance must have the Dodgers muttering in their sleep; L.A., a club with a chronic short relief problem, traded Franco to the Reds for the immortal Rafael Landestoy back in '83.

Doug White

Franco, John Anthony "Johnny" Bats: Left Throws: Left Born 08/23/61

1987 SEASON AND MAJOR-LEAGUE CAREER PITCHING TOTALS

	G	GS	CG	GF	IP	BFP	H	R	ER	HR	SH	SF	HB	TBB	IBB	SO	WP	Bk	W	L	Pct	ShO	Sv	ERA
87 CIN	68	0	0	60	82	344	76	26	23	6	5	2	0	27	6	61	1	0	8	5	.615	0	32	2.52
4 YEARS	263	0	0	175	361	1515	323	121	103	21	28	10	5	147	30	261	11	2	32	16	.667	0	77	2.57

1987: Power, Groundball 1986: Power, Groundball 1985: Power, Groundball 1984: Power, Groundball

1987 SEASON

	G	IP	H	BB	SO	SB	CS	W	L	S	ERA
Totals	68	81.2	76	27	61	4	2	8	5	32	2.53
at Home	33	37.0	44	12	25	1	2	4	2	16	4.14
on Road	35	44.2	32	15	36	3	0	4	3	16	1.21
on Grass	25	28.2	20	12	26	1	1	2	1	12	1.57
on Artificial Turf	43	53.0	56	15	35	3	1	6	4	20	3.06
Day Games	20	27.0	19	12	20	3	0	2	2	11	1.33
Night Games	48	54.2	57	15	41	1	2	6	3	21	3.13
April	8	8.0	0	0	3	0	0	1	0	3	0.00
May	11	11.1	11	3	10	0	0	1	1	6	1.59
June	14	17.1	14	7	10	2	1	3	1	6	0.52
July	10	14.1	12	6	9	0	0	2	1	3	4.40
August	13	17.1	29	5	16	1	1	0	2	6	5.19
Sept/Oct	12	13.1	10	6	13	1	0	1	0	8	2.03

FOUR YEAR TOTALS (1984 – 1987)

	G	IP	H	BB	SO	SB	CS	W	L	S	ERA
Totals	263	361.0	323	147	261	19	21	32	16	77	2.57
at Home	138	196.1	175	70	127	11	11	17	6	40	2.52
on Road	125	164.2	148	77	134	8	10	15	10	37	2.62
on Grass	85	105.0	91	42	75	4	8	8	5	27	2.91
on Artificial Turf	178	256.0	232	105	186	15	13	24	11	50	2.43
Day Games	74	94.1	82	42	77	6	6	9	7	24	2.86
Night Games	189	266.2	241	105	184	13	15	23	9	53	2.46
April	24	30.2	21	15	18	1	1	1	1	6	2.05
May	43	60.2	58	32	53	3	3	5	2	14	2.82
June	52	70.2	59	26	41	3	4	7	4	13	1.91
July	42	63.2	45	23	46	2	5	9	1	8	2.12
August	49	73.2	77	25	51	6	3	5	2	16	2.57
Sept/Oct	53	61.2	63	26	52	4	5	5	6	20	3.79

vs. Opponent Batters — 1987 Season

vs. Opponent Batters	Ave.	OBP	SLG	AB	H	2B	3B	HR	RBI	BB	SO
Totals	.245	.304	.345	310	76	13	0	6	31	27	61
vs. Left	.239	.280	.283	46	11	2	0	0	7	3	11
vs. Right	.246	.308	.356	264	65	11	0	6	24	24	50
Bases Empty	.235	.274	.365	170	40	7	0	5	5	9	32
Leadoff	.278	.297	.500	72	20	4	0	4	4	2	12
Not Leadoff	.204	.257	.265	98	20	3	0	1	1	7	20
Runners On Base	.257	.338	.321	140	36	6	0	1	26	18	29
First Base Only	.339	.350	.441	59	20	3	0	1	4	1	9
Scoring Position	.198	.330	.235	81	16	3	0	0	22	17	20
Late Innings, Close	.245	.321	.324	216	53	8	0	3	24	25	41

vs. Opponent Batters — Four Year Totals

vs. Opponent Batters	Ave.	OBP	SLG	AB	H	2B	3B	HR	RBI	BB	SO
Totals	.244	.319	.332	1324	323	43	5	21	149	147	261
vs. Left	.212	.263	.258	283	60	5	1	2	35	20	53
vs. Right	.253	.334	.352	1041	263	38	4	19	114	127	208
Bases Empty	.241	.305	.335	711	171	23	4	12	12	66	134
Leadoff	.252	.305	.374	305	77	9	2	8	8	23	40
Not Leadoff	.232	.305	.305	406	94	14	2	4	4	43	94
Runners On Base	.248	.335	.328	613	152	20	1	9	137	81	127
First Base Only	.278	.309	.376	245	68	6	0	6	16	11	43
Scoring Position	.228	.350	.296	368	84	14	1	3	121	70	84
Late Innings, Close	.239	.315	.323	907	217	26	4	14	105	101	187

RBI/Opportunities

	1987		Four Year	
Scoring Position	21 / 124	(17%)	111 / 567	(20%)
Scoring Position, 2 Out	14 / 68	(21%)	53 / 287	(18%)
On Third, Less than 2 Out	6 / 23	(26%)	43 / 104	(41%)
RBI in close games / RBI Total	24 / 31	(77%)	110 / 149	(74%)

Julio Franco
Cleveland Indians

Easily the worst event in the Indians' disastrous 1987 was the elbow injury that Julio Franco suffered in mid-May. It not only ruined what could have been a brilliant season—it may very well have ended Franco's career both at short and in Cleveland.

Offensively, it was a fine one as is. As predicted in last year's *Stat Book*, Julio made major gains in his average, walks and steals (32 for 41). But it could have been better; a healthy Franco might have increased his power markedly, too.

When injured, Franco was hitting .301 and slugging .441. Even though he spent 17 games as the DH (which he loathes) and missed 20 more, Julio hit .326 for the rest of 1987. But he complained that he couldn't swing the bat hard anymore and hc wasn't kidding. Julio slugged .423 after the injury. If you simply project his extra-base hits out from the time of the injury, you can add four more doubles, another triple and three more homers to his stats. Had he increased his power with his average, he would have been an awesome hitter last year.

But the offensive damage is the least of the problem. Julio's rifle arm has always let him play extremely deep, maximizing his range. When forced to move in closer, his fielding skill disappeared. His range factor fell from 4.51 to 3.98; his DPs per 162 games fell from 98 to 77. In 111 games played, that's 59 fewer plays and 11 less DPs—70 outs. You can imagine how badly that hurt the Cleveland staff.

To make matters worse, the doctors don't know what caused the injury—they think it may be due to a flaw in his throwing motion. Management now hopes that rest is the answer. If not, they plan to try to revamp his motion. If all else fails, Franco, like Robin Yount, may be forced to switch to another position in 1988.

This leads us to the key problem. Since 1983, many Cleveland coaches, managers and executives have either worked with Franco on his mechanics, talked about moving him to another spot or trading him. They've done it so often that Julio now bristles at the implied criticism of his fielding; late in 1987, he laid down the law. Either I play shortstop, he said, or I don't play at all.

What should they do? Should Cleveland keep Julio and hope that the injury isn't serious—or, if it is, that he will eventually agree to move to another position? Or should they trade him immediately—before his value plummets?

Count me with group "A." Franco has every right to feel ill-used and there is every reason on earth to wait. Only when the medical evidence is final . . . Only when Julio stubbornly refuses to move . . . Only then would I trade a 26-year-old who hits as brilliantly as Julio Franco does.

Geoff Beckman

Franco, Julio Cesar | **Bats: Right** **Throws: Right** **Born 08/23/61**

1987 SEASON AND MAJOR-LEAGUE CAREER BATTING TOTALS

	G	AB	H	2B	3B	HR	TB	R	RBI	TBB	IBB	SO	HP	SH	SF	SB	CS	SB%	GDP	AVG	OBP	SLG
87 CLE	128	495	158	24	3	8	212	86	52	57	2	56	3	0	5	32	9	.78	23	.319	.389	.428
6 YEARS	762	2977	873	134	25	35	1162	416	378	215	8	318	15	5	35	106	49	.68	122	.293	.340	.390

	1987 SEASON											FOUR YEAR TOTALS (1984 – 1987)										
	Ave.	OBP	SLG	AB	H	2B	3B	HR	RBI	BB	SO	Ave.	OBP	SLG	AB	H	2B	3B	HR	RBI	BB	SO
Totals	.319	.389	.428	495	158	24	3	8	52	57	56	.298	.348	.392	2388	712	108	17	27	295	186	263
vs. Left	.308	.389	.492	130	40	10	1	4	12	18	21	.316	.368	.466	678	214	43	4	17	87	59	77
vs. Right	.323	.389	.405	365	118	14	2	4	40	39	35	.291	.340	.362	1710	498	65	13	10	208	127	186
at Home	.310	.383	.421	242	75	12	0	5	26	28	24	.302	.352	.392	1169	353	54	6	13	152	91	109
on Road	.328	.395	.435	253	83	12	3	3	26	29	32	.295	.344	.391	1219	359	54	11	14	143	95	154
vs. Groundball	.288	.380	.352	250	72	8	1	2	29	37	27	.294	.348	.368	1168	343	43	7	10	131	96	131
vs. Flyball	.351	.399	.506	245	86	16	2	6	23	20	29	.302	.348	.414	1220	369	65	10	17	164	90	132
vs. Finesse	.314	.367	.447	255	80	11	1	7	30	21	24	.309	.348	.405	1342	415	60	7	18	158	79	125
vs. Power	.325	.411	.408	240	78	13	2	1	22	36	32	.284	.348	.375	1046	297	48	10	9	137	107	138
on Grass	.304	.376	.392	431	131	21	1	5	42	49	49	.300	.352	.395	2045	613	97	14	23	256	165	217
on Artificial Turf	.422	.479	.672	64	27	3	2	3	10	8	7	.289	.327	.373	343	99	11	3	4	39	21	46
Day Games	.258	.327	.315	178	46	7	0	1	14	16	22	.291	.346	.377	815	237	34	3	10	100	66	110
Night Games	.353	.423	.492	317	112	17	3	7	38	41	34	.302	.349	.399	1573	475	74	14	17	195	120	153
April	.326	.400	.472	89	29	7	0	2	12	11	10	.307	.384	.439	303	93	23	1	5	50	38	37
May	.333	.429	.434	99	33	5	1	1	10	17	13	.260	.316	.340	427	111	14	4	4	38	35	63
June	.282	.318	.369	103	29	2	2	1	12	6	9	.284	.329	.351	402	114	15	3	2	41	28	44
July	.333	.444	.511	45	15	2	0	2	5	9	4	.311	.359	.389	373	116	15	1	4	46	28	26
August	.346	.418	.444	81	28	5	0	1	4	8	14	.325	.362	.431	459	149	23	1	8	59	25	54
Sept/Oct	.308	.349	.385	78	24	3	0	1	9	6	6	.304	.352	.408	424	129	18	7	4	61	32	39
Bases Empty	.350	.408	.463	283	99	14	3	4	4	28	31	.301	.347	.394	1320	397	64	10	13	13	94	156
Leadoff	.382	.406	.461	102	39	8	0	0	0	4	8	.320	.352	.395	438	140	23	2	2	2	22	48
Not Leadoff	.331	.410	.464	181	60	6	3	4	4	24	23	.291	.345	.393	882	257	41	8	11	11	72	108
Runners On	.278	.365	.382	212	59	10	0	4	48	29	25	.295	.351	.389	1068	315	44	7	14	282	92	107
First Base Only	.321	.418	.393	84	27	6	0	0	3	13	7	.291	.339	.375	419	122	17	0	6	22	29	36
Scoring Position	.250	.331	.375	128	32	4	0	4	45	16	18	.297	.359	.398	649	193	27	7	8	260	63	71
Late Innings, Close	.435	.494	.609	69	30	6	0	2	9	9	6	.281	.334	.386	342	96	13	4	5	50	28	29

RBI/Opportunities

Scoring Position	39 / 177 (22%)	238 / 876 (27%)
Scoring Position, 2 Out	15 / 64 (23%)	80 / 354 (23%)
On Third, Less than 2 Out	17 / 40 (43%)	115 / 203 (57%)
RBI in close games / RBI Total	40 / 52 (77%)	196 / 295 (66%)

Gary Gaetti
Minnesota Twins

Gary Gaetti is the best third baseman in the American League, but few people have bothered to notice. In New York City, a baseball player hits 25 home runs and the media reports his every word. In Minnesota you hit 30 homers and generally don't say any more about it. People get put away for talking to empty rooms.

Gary Gaetti has been the Rodney Dangerfield of ballplayers— no respect, except in Minnesota where they call him "The 'G' Man." At one time it was simply for the alliteration of his name, but now they've added another "G" for the "Great Gary Gaetti."

The World Series has started to change the range of his exposure. Some folks from St. Louis are just now catching on to the fact he did not spring forth from a cabbage patch with 31 homers and 109 RBIs. Heck, he had 34 homers and 108 RBIs the year before. Yeah, that was in the major leagues, not the Pacific Coast League. In the last three years, he has 101 doubles, 85 home runs, 280 RBIs, 27 stolen bases, and a .264 average. His isolated power last season was .228, comparable to Don Mattingly's .232, and his secondary average broke the .300 barrier (.308).

Defensively, Gaetti's raw range factor in 1987 was a conservative eighth in the American League, but his past statistics have been strong, and there are probably mitigating circumstances that account for that showing. Gary certainly did not look any different in the field. He was still diving after balls and coming up with accurate throws; he still snared the rockets down the line and nailed batters by a step or two. Gaetti pulled off both of those specialties in the Series against the lightning quick Cardinals and impressed the nation. He didn't have to impress the AL managers and coaches who had already voted him a second consecutive Gold Glove award.

Here in the off-season, there was a question of whether he would remain in Minnesota. He is righthanded, which means that in the Rubber Dome he doesn't often hit the Hefty-bag wall in right field and settle for a double. Yet, surprisingly, he is one Twin who does not have a history of strong home field advantage in the dome. That might have been a factor in his considering his free agency options.

Happily for the Twins, however, Gaetti opted to remain in Minnesota, though he didn't lack for options—the Cardinals, having just lost Jack Clark, apparently wanted him pretty badly. When push came to shove, Gaetti showed a refreshing kind of loyalty; he seemed unable to leave the guys (Hrbek, Brunansky, Viola, *et al*) with whom he'd first suffered, then shared a sweet triumph. Whether other triumphs lie ahead remains to be seen, but the Twins—and their fans—are sure glad he's sticking around.

Darren E. Peterson and Craig R. Wright

Gaetti, Gary Joseph Bats: Right Throws: Right Born 08/19/58

1987 SEASON AND MAJOR-LEAGUE CAREER BATTING TOTALS

	G	AB	H	2B	3B	HR	TB	R	RBI	TBB	IBB	SO	HP	SH	SF	SB	CS	SB%	GDP	AVG	OBP	SLG
87 MIN	154	584	150	36	2	31	283	95	109	37	7	92	3	1	3	10	7	.59	25	.257	.303	.485
7 YEARS	944	3446	878	185	14	138	1505	456	510	261	19	604	27	12	36	55	37	.60	102	.255	.309	.437

	1987 SEASON											FOUR YEAR TOTALS (1984 – 1987)										
	Ave.	OBP	SLG	AB	H	2B	3B	HR	RBI	BB	SO	Ave.	OBP	SLG	AB	H	2B	3B	HR	RBI	BB	SO
Totals	.257	.303	.485	584	150	36	2	31	109	37	92	.263	.317	.441	2329	613	130	7	90	346	170	370
vs. Left	.235	.287	.422	166	39	6	2	7	27	12	29	.253	.314	.420	671	170	28	3	26	88	58	105
vs. Right	.266	.309	.510	418	111	30	0	24	82	25	63	.267	.318	.449	1658	443	102	4	64	258	112	265
at Home	.306	.352	.575	301	92	23	2	18	57	20	47	.275	.326	.466	1171	322	74	6	46	181	83	198
on Road	.205	.250	.389	283	58	13	0	13	52	17	45	.251	.308	.415	1158	291	56	1	44	165	87	172
vs. Groundball	.256	.303	.453	289	74	15	0	14	56	20	41	.255	.309	.398	1131	288	52	1	36	164	86	169
vs. Flyball	.258	.303	.515	295	76	21	2	17	53	17	51	.271	.324	.482	1198	325	78	6	54	182	84	201
vs. Finesse	.294	.334	.577	293	86	19	2	20	71	18	32	.286	.337	.486	1249	357	77	4	55	207	91	163
vs. Power	.220	.272	.392	291	64	17	0	11	38	19	60	.237	.294	.389	1080	256	53	3	35	139	79	207
on Grass	.219	.269	.393	219	48	11	0	9	42	15	35	.270	.329	.443	891	241	46	0	36	134	71	127
on Artificial Turf	.279	.323	.540	365	102	25	2	22	67	22	57	.259	.310	.439	1438	372	84	7	54	212	99	243
Day Games	.267	.308	.508	187	50	9	0	12	35	11	31	.264	.324	.406	709	187	38	0	21	92	57	115
Night Games	.252	.301	.474	397	100	27	2	19	74	26	61	.263	.314	.456	1620	426	92	7	69	254	113	255
April	.210	.264	.494	81	17	3	1	6	17	6	15	.271	.335	.458	321	87	22	1	12	50	31	52
May	.315	.353	.537	108	34	6	0	6	17	7	21	.283	.349	.505	392	111	20	2	21	66	40	72
June	.253	.326	.418	79	20	4	0	3	13	9	11	.227	.289	.384	352	80	23	1	10	45	31	59
July	.218	.255	.465	101	22	7	0	6	19	5	15	.256	.288	.424	406	104	22	2	14	59	18	61
August	.287	.325	.583	108	31	9	1	7	30	4	17	.273	.320	.457	418	114	24	1	17	75	27	66
Sept/Oct	.243	.287	.393	107	26	7	0	3	13	6	13	.266	.303	.418	440	117	19	0	16	51	23	60
Bases Empty	.239	.282	.488	301	72	16	1	19	19	16	50	.260	.309	.438	1296	337	73	5	49	49	89	201
Leadoff	.219	.281	.500	128	28	9	0	9	9	9	16	.242	.287	.432	521	126	30	3	21	21	31	71
Not Leadoff	.254	.283	.480	173	44	7	1	10	10	7	34	.272	.323	.441	775	211	43	2	28	28	58	130
Runners On	.276	.325	.481	283	78	20	1	12	90	21	42	.267	.320	.445	1033	276	57	2	41	297	81	169
First Base Only	.237	.275	.386	114	27	5	0	4	8	6	16	.261	.301	.423	437	114	18	1	17	40	25	68
Scoring Position	.302	.356	.544	169	51	15	1	8	82	15	26	.272	.334	.461	596	162	39	1	24	257	56	101
Late Innings, Close	.231	.302	.449	78	18	5	0	4	9	7	19	.237	.318	.386	334	79	20	0	10	34	39	56

RBI/Opportunities

Scoring Position	64 / 221 (29%)	204 / 798 (26%)
Scoring Position, 2 Out	33 / 106 (31%)	84 / 366 (23%)
On Third, Less than 2 Out	18 / 41 (44%)	71 / 142 (50%)
RBI in close games / RBI Total	67 / 109 (61%)	213 / 346 (62%)

Greg Gagne
Minnesota Twins

As the bandwagon became more crowded last summer, a lot of Minnesotans were taking back all the bad things that they'd been saying about Greg Gagne for the past few years. A year ago the typical fan—if he had any reaction at all to Greg Gagne—would remark about the erratic arm, the lack of range, and the general lack of offense. Then he'd close with a few remarks about his "good speed and clean lifestyle."

Greg had basically been a throw-in in the Ron Davis for Roy Smalley deal, and the front office was happy to have him making any contribution at all—especially if he could do it for less than a hundred grand a year (he was paid $115,000 in '87). And he wasn't likely to embarrass the organization in any incidents off the field such as the one his former DP partner Tim Teufel was involved in down in Houston (ironically, Teufel had a squeaky clean rep when he was with the Twins).

But as the '87 campaign wore on and the Twins continued to hold first place, the fans weren't the only ones who began to see Gagne in a different light. Near midseason, the normally sensible Tom Kelly took leave of his senses and proclaimed Tony Fernandez and Greg Gagne the two best shortstops in the league. The comment would not bear repeating had it been uttered by Sparky Anderson or Chuck Tanner. TK had apparently forgotten which league Ripken and Trammell were in.

Offensively, the numbers pale beside Trammell, Ripken, Fernandez, and Franco. They aren't even that close to Dale Sveum's or Rey Quinones'. If you place Quinones' numbers—offensively and defensively next to Gagne's, it'd be hard to pick between them.

Defensively Guillen, Griffin, Fernandez, Ripken, and Trammell all have better range factors than Greg (4.17). Greg does have a strong arm, but his throws keep Hrbek loose around the bag (one irksome Gagne quality is his habit of smiling at everybody in sight after making an error). Hell, when Roy Smalley was the same age, he began a three-year streak of leading the league in assists. And Roy routinely handled more than 5 chances per game in those days. In the decade since, Twins fans have apparently forgotten what a good shortstop is. They sure are excited about this "hard-nosed, hustling, clean-living, shortstop." In short, Gagne is a classic example of a decent ballplayer getting more than his share of attention while his team rolls on toward its improbable dream.

Jim Rogde

Gagne, Gregory Carpenter "Greg" Bats: Right Throws: Right Born 11/12/61

1987 SEASON AND MAJOR-LEAGUE CAREER BATTING TOTALS

	G	AB	H	2B	3B	HR	TB	R	RBI	TBB	IBB	SO	HP	SH	SF	SB	CS	SB%	GDP	AVG	OBP	SLG
87 MIN	137	437	116	28	7	10	188	68	40	25	0	84	4	10	2	6	6	.50	3	.265	.310	.430
5 YEARS	419	1230	303	66	16	24	473	170	120	75	0	255	13	26	10	28	20	.58	12	.246	.294	.385

	1987 SEASON											FOUR YEAR TOTALS (1984 – 1987)									
	Ave.	OBP	SLG	AB	H	2B	3B	HR	RBI	BB	SO	Ave.	OBP	SLG	AB	H	2B	3B	HR	RBI	BB	SO
Totals	.265	.310	.430	437	116	28	7	10	40	25	84	.250	.299	.390	1202	300	65	16	24	117	75	249
vs. Left	.266	.294	.367	128	34	7	3	0	10	6	28	.247	.279	.391	381	94	22	6	7	39	19	88
vs. Right	.265	.316	.456	309	82	21	4	10	30	19	56	.251	.308	.390	821	206	43	10	17	78	56	161
at Home	.241	.303	.434	212	51	10	5	7	22	18	45	.238	.298	.412	592	141	30	11	17	66	47	119
on Road	.289	.316	.427	225	65	18	2	3	18	7	39	.261	.299	.369	610	159	35	5	7	51	28	130
vs. Groundball	.310	.352	.481	239	74	16	5	5	23	15	34	.248	.303	.366	588	146	27	9	8	53	40	98
vs. Flyball	.212	.259	.369	198	42	12	2	5	17	10	50	.251	.295	.414	614	154	38	7	16	64	35	151
vs. Finesse	.272	.311	.451	206	56	15	5	4	20	11	30	.248	.295	.416	646	160	42	11	15	71	36	107
vs. Power	.260	.309	.411	231	60	13	2	6	20	14	54	.252	.303	.360	556	140	23	5	9	46	39	142
on Grass	.269	.298	.421	171	46	13	2	3	12	5	30	.253	.294	.379	459	116	27	5	7	34	22	99
on Artificial Turf	.263	.317	.436	266	70	15	5	7	28	20	54	.248	.302	.397	743	184	38	11	17	83	53	150
Day Games	.235	.303	.379	132	31	7	0	4	9	12	26	.232	.292	.347	366	85	15	3	7	30	26	76
Night Games	.279	.313	.452	305	85	21	7	6	31	13	58	.257	.302	.409	836	215	50	13	17	87	49	173
April	.280	.315	.520	50	14	3	0	3	7	2	12	.267	.311	.417	180	48	11	2	4	18	11	37
May	.157	.232	.235	51	8	2	1	0	4	5	8	.254	.319	.379	169	43	9	3	2	13	16	32
June	.287	.337	.500	80	23	9	1	2	11	6	18	.238	.283	.368	223	53	13	2	4	25	14	51
July	.312	.338	.416	77	24	6	1	0	4	3	14	.245	.283	.358	212	52	15	3	1	16	11	40
August	.284	.289	.443	88	25	3	4	1	7	1	18	.264	.291	.443	174	46	9	5	4	24	7	42
Sept/Oct	.242	.324	.429	91	22	5	0	4	7	8	14	.238	.293	.389	244	58	8	1	9	21	16	47
Bases Empty	.275	.322	.460	265	73	19	3	8	8	14	48	.248	.297	.407	705	175	40	9	18	18	45	144
Leadoff	.295	.347	.455	88	26	6	1	2	2	6	15	.243	.299	.395	263	64	16	3	6	6	20	47
Not Leadoff	.266	.309	.463	177	47	13	2	6	6	8	33	.251	.296	.414	442	111	24	6	12	12	25	97
Runners On	.250	.292	.384	172	43	9	4	2	32	11	36	.252	.293	.366	497	125	25	7	6	99	30	105
First Base Only	.258	.290	.371	89	23	3	2	1	5	4	21	.232	.260	.305	233	54	7	2	2	10	9	49
Scoring Position	.241	.293	.398	83	20	6	2	1	27	7	15	.269	.321	.420	264	71	18	5	4	89	21	56
Late Innings, Close	.208	.269	.375	48	10	3	1	1	1	4	10	.232	.312	.333	138	32	9	1	1	12	16	34

RBI/Opportunities

Scoring Position	24 / 117 (21%)	78 / 358 (22%)
Scoring Position, 2 Out	10 / 50 (20%)	31 / 163 (19%)
On Third, Less than 2 Out	9 / 18 (50%)	25 / 58 (43%)
RBI in close games / RBI Total	21 / 40 (53%)	64 / 117 (55%)

Andres Galarraga
Montreal Expos

1987 became the season 1986 should have been for Andres Galarraga. Handed the first baseman's job before the '86 season, Galarraga had a bad spring and began the season platooning with Jason Thompson, then found his stroke early in the season and won back an everyday spot in the lineup. Galarraga was hitting for average, and leading all NL rookies with 8 homers and 25 RBIs early in July when first a knee, then a rib cage injury put him on the DL for two months. Returning September 4, Galarraga hit .327 with 16 RBIs for the rest of the year. He was able to keep up the pace for the entire 1987 season, batting .305 (seventh in the NL) with 90 RBIs, finishing second in the league with 40 doubles, and playing Gold Glove level defense.

Galarraga was famous in the minors, and in his home country of Venezuela, for tape measure homers, and he hit two monster shots during his one month with the Expos in 1985. Since then, power has given way to average. In his last two minor league seasons Galarraga had a HR% of 5.3 and batted in the .270's, while in the majors he's had a HR% of 2.6 and has become a .300 hitter. Despite cutting down his swing, Galarraga is still striking out a lot—127 times last year, against 41 walks. Most of his problems come against righthanders. There's a large gap in his average right vs. left, and although the difference in strikeout ratios is not that large, it's against the better righties that he most often seems overmatched. Montreal needs a solid left-handed hitter; the addition of one would help Galarraga more than anyone else in the lineup.

One knock against Galarraga in '86 was a lack of clutch hitting; all of his strikeouts seemed to come with one out and a man on third. Last season he learned to show more patience in RBI and late-game situations. One of the emotional high points of Montreal's season was his 2-out homer in the bottom of the 13th to beat the Cards on August 5; the night before, he had keyed a rally which overcame a 5–0 deficit. The two big victories over St. Louis gave the Expos the confidence they needed to remain in the race till the last weekend of the season.

Galarraga has yet to prove he can cut back the strikeouts, hit for power, and bat .300 in the same season, but there's no doubt the potential is there, and he's shown the willingness to do the hard work that was required to become a good fielder. Look for Galarraga to become the league's best allround first baseman in the near future, especially if the Expos find that lefty hitter.

Michael Cassin

Galarraga, Andres Jose

Bats: Right   **Throws: Right**   Born 06/18/61

1987 SEASON AND MAJOR-LEAGUE CAREER BATTING TOTALS

	G	AB	H	2B	3B	HR	TB	R	RBI	TBB	IBB	SO	HP	SH	SF	SB	CS	SB%	GDP	AVG	OBP	SLG
87 MON	147	551	168	40	3	13	253	72	90	41	13	127	10	0	4	7	10	.41	11	.305	.361	.459
3 YEARS	276	947	269	54	3	25	404	120	136	74	18	224	14	1	5	14	17	.45	19	.284	.343	.427

	1987 SEASON											FOUR YEAR TOTALS (1984 – 1987)										
	Ave.	OBP	SLG	AB	H	2B	3B	HR	RBI	BB	SO	Ave.	OBP	SLG	AB	H	2B	3B	HR	RBI	BB	SO
Totals	.305	.361	.459	551	168	40	3	13	90	41	127	.284	.343	.427	947	269	54	3	25	136	74	224
vs. Left	.321	.383	.539	165	53	15	0	7	28	17	34	.309	.371	.474	327	101	21	0	11	43	33	65
vs. Right	.298	.352	.425	386	115	25	3	6	62	24	93	.271	.328	.402	620	168	33	3	14	93	41	159
at Home	.314	.385	.492	264	83	24	1	7	48	24	59	.293	.359	.440	461	135	33	1	11	70	40	110
on Road	.296	.339	.429	287	85	16	2	6	42	17	68	.276	.328	.414	486	134	21	2	14	66	34	114
vs. Groundball	.309	.369	.438	256	79	13	1	6	38	21	52	.287	.349	.411	450	129	21	1	11	61	38	102
vs. Flyball	.302	.355	.478	295	89	27	2	7	52	20	75	.282	.338	.441	497	140	33	2	14	75	36	122
vs. Finesse	.326	.375	.473	319	104	24	1	7	53	21	56	.302	.357	.426	530	160	31	1	11	71	38	107
vs. Power	.276	.342	.440	232	64	16	2	6	37	20	71	.261	.326	.427	417	109	23	2	14	65	36	117
on Grass	.288	.344	.403	139	40	7	0	3	19	11	36	.263	.324	.384	255	67	10	0	7	34	21	61
on Artificial Turf	.311	.367	.478	412	128	33	3	10	71	30	91	.292	.350	.442	692	202	44	3	18	102	53	163
Day Games	.335	.393	.490	155	52	15	0	3	21	13	31	.303	.374	.457	317	96	19	0	10	39	32	70
Night Games	.293	.349	.447	396	116	25	3	10	69	28	96	.275	.327	.411	630	173	35	3	15	97	42	154
April	.319	.367	.458	72	23	7	0	1	15	3	13	.354	.422	.540	113	40	9	0	4	23	11	22
May	.371	.447	.562	89	33	8	0	3	21	13	18	.287	.359	.433	164	47	9	0	5	28	19	36
June	.340	.410	.574	94	32	11	1	3	18	8	22	.298	.359	.492	181	54	15	1	6	29	14	41
July	.266	.310	.392	79	21	5	1	1	11	3	19	.240	.277	.344	96	23	5	1	1	11	3	27
August	.291	.336	.398	103	30	3	1	2	11	6	22	.269	.320	.361	119	32	3	1	2	11	8	24
Sept/Oct	.254	.304	.386	114	29	6	0	3	14	8	33	.266	.314	.391	274	73	13	0	7	34	19	74
Bases Empty	.270	.308	.408	289	78	15	2	7	7	13	59	.260	.306	.406	508	132	25	2	15	15	31	117
Leadoff	.327	.367	.478	113	37	6	1	3	3	7	22	.311	.366	.495	206	64	12	1	8	8	18	52
Not Leadoff	.233	.270	.364	176	41	9	1	4	4	6	37	.225	.264	.344	302	68	13	1	7	7	13	65
Runners On	.344	.415	.515	262	90	25	1	6	83	28	68	.312	.379	.451	439	137	29	1	10	121	43	107
First Base Only	.362	.402	.610	105	38	14	0	4	14	6	19	.333	.362	.520	177	59	15	0	6	18	7	34
Scoring Position	.331	.423	.452	157	52	11	1	2	69	22	49	.298	.390	.405	262	78	14	1	4	103	36	73
Late Innings, Close	.234	.302	.390	77	18	4	1	2	11	6	21	.245	.319	.411	163	40	10	1	5	20	16	41

RBI/Opportunities

	1987		Four Year
Scoring Position	63 / 221	(29%)	93 / 364 (26%)
Scoring Position, 2 Out	25 / 97	(26%)	46 / 176 (26%)
On Third, Less than 2 Out	20 / 44	(45%)	24 / 65 (37%)
RBI in close games / RBI Total	53 / 90	(59%)	84 / 136 (62%)

Jim Gantner
Milwaukee Brewers

Jim Gantner is coming to the end of the line—and coming to it much, much faster than most people in Milwaukee want to admit. His isolated power (slugging percentage minus batting average) was .098—in a typical year, that would be in the bottom 20 in the league among players with 200+ at-bats. Gantner walked 19 times in 294 plate appearances. His secondary average (the sum of extra bases on hits, walks and steals divided by at-bats) was .192—and a .192 secondary average is as bad as a .192 batting average.

Did someone just say "It doesn't matter what a second baseman hits"? Well, even if that were true (which it isn't), it does matter if a second baseman can field, right? In 1987, there were 18 men who played 50 or more games at second base in the American League. Gantner's range factor was better than only four other men. He's even slipped in the area that used to be his bread and butter; Gantner was tenth in the league in double plays per game in 1987.

Gantner has escaped criticism for one reason: He has good numbers in the most popular offensive and defensive categories. Gantner's batting average was .272 in 1987; his .984 fielding percentage was the sixth best in the AL. The two things that you can say for Jim Gantner at this particular point in his career—the he makes good contact and has soft hands—are assets that almost any politician has.

Which, to be fair, is completely unfair. There's nothing the matter with Gantner other than the scourge of all ballplayers—age. He's 35 now, coming off an injury-plagued year. Father Time has nibbled away his reflexes just enough to take away his defensive prowess—the only thing that has kept him playing. Barring an injury, he'll never be a regular again; if he doesn't start shagging some fly balls to increase his value as a utility player, he won't be around a year from now.

Since I seem to be writing his eulogy, I should say that Gantner's been a joy to watch over the years. There are some players who behave like prototype Milwaukee Brewers—he's definitely one of them. The Brewers probably agree; he's one of three players from the '82 AL champs still here. Jim is on my list of top ten guys I'd like to buy a beer and a bratwurst—with special County Stadium Sauce, of course.

My fondest memory of Gantner was in the fifth game of the '82 playoff series against California. He barrelled into home with the eventual winning run on a two-run double by Cecil Cooper. At home plate, Charlie Moore, who scored in front of him, picked him up by the shoulders and shook him like a rag doll. That shining image was the single greatest moment in Milwaukee Brewers' history.

Scott Segrin

Gantner, James Elmer "Jim" Bats: Left Throws: Right Born 01/05/54

1987 SEASON AND MAJOR-LEAGUE CAREER BATTING TOTALS

	G	AB	H	2B	3B	HR	TB	R	RBI	TBB	IBB	SO	HP	SH	SF	SB	CS	SB%	GDP	AVG	OBP	SLG
87 MIL	81	265	72	14	0	4	98	37	30	19	2	22	5	4	1	6	2	.75	7	.272	.331	.370
12 YEARS	1201	4136	1138	169	23	44	1485	487	397	260	30	348	34	66	39	69	53	.57	84	.275	.320	.359

	1987 SEASON											FOUR YEAR TOTALS (1984 – 1987)										
	Ave.	OBP	SLG	AB	H	2B	3B	HR	RBI	BB	SO	Ave.	OBP	SLG	AB	H	2B	3B	HR	RBI	BB	SO
Totals	.272	.331	.370	265	72	14	0	4	30	19	22	.271	.312	.350	1898	514	81	6	19	168	108	165
vs. Left	.233	.280	.279	86	20	4	0	0	9	4	9	.270	.314	.306	582	157	19	1	0	48	32	51
vs. Right	.291	.355	.413	179	52	10	0	4	21	15	13	.271	.312	.369	1316	357	62	5	19	120	76	114
at Home	.298	.370	.347	121	36	6	0	0	11	11	12	.268	.311	.342	925	248	38	3	8	88	57	80
on Road	.250	.297	.389	144	36	8	0	4	19	8	10	.273	.314	.358	973	266	43	3	11	80	51	85
vs. Groundball	.301	.369	.385	143	43	9	0	1	16	13	10	.263	.308	.328	928	244	37	1	7	97	57	63
vs. Flyball	.238	.285	.352	122	29	5	0	3	14	6	12	.278	.316	.371	970	270	44	5	12	71	51	102
vs. Finesse	.283	.324	.362	127	36	7	0	1	10	8	7	.273	.305	.352	1077	294	42	2	13	97	50	81
vs. Power	.261	.338	.377	138	36	7	0	3	20	11	15	.268	.322	.347	821	220	39	4	6	71	58	84
on Grass	.269	.339	.352	216	58	12	0	2	20	18	18	.262	.306	.338	1581	415	65	5	15	139	97	136
on Artificial Turf	.286	.294	.449	49	14	2	0	2	10	1	4	.312	.344	.407	317	99	16	1	4	29	11	29
Day Games	.264	.327	.385	91	24	8	0	1	8	7	11	.267	.309	.346	569	152	28	1	5	56	34	52
Night Games	.276	.333	.362	174	48	6	0	3	22	12	11	.272	.314	.351	1329	362	53	5	14	112	74	113
April	.288	.365	.409	66	19	5	0	1	7	6	8	.270	.325	.363	256	69	12	3	2	26	19	25
May	.275	.333	.412	80	22	5	0	2	8	7	5	.275	.315	.374	342	94	17	1	5	29	20	26
June	.267	.326	.326	86	23	2	0	1	12	6	5	.276	.317	.347	398	110	13	0	5	46	22	27
July	.250	.273	.313	32	8	2	0	0	3	0	3	.278	.322	.339	327	91	14	0	2	25	20	26
August	.000	.000	.000	0	0	0	0	0	0	0	0	.285	.316	.381	270	77	17	0	3	19	12	25
Sept/Oct	.000	.000	.000	1	0	0	0	0	0	0	1	.239	.275	.298	305	73	8	2	2	23	15	36
Bases Empty	.312	.370	.404	141	44	10	0	1	1	10	9	.282	.318	.367	1105	312	55	3	11	11	55	84
Leadoff	.368	.419	.474	57	21	3	0	1	1	4	2	.286	.318	.364	423	121	19	1	4	4	19	25
Not Leadoff	.274	.337	.357	84	23	7	0	0	0	6	7	.280	.318	.370	682	191	36	2	7	7	36	59
Runners On	.226	.287	.331	124	28	4	0	3	29	9	13	.255	.303	.325	793	202	26	3	8	157	53	81
First Base Only	.196	.196	.304	56	11	3	0	1	5	0	2	.272	.294	.360	367	100	16	2	4	18	11	27
Scoring Position	.250	.350	.353	68	17	1	0	2	24	9	11	.239	.310	.296	426	102	10	1	4	139	42	54
Late Innings, Close	.277	.340	.447	47	13	2	0	2	9	4	6	.284	.341	.362	334	95	9	1	5	29	28	35

RBI/Opportunities

Scoring Position	22 / 95 (23%)	133 / 588 (23%)
Scoring Position, 2 Out	9 / 55 (16%)	43 / 285 (15%)
On Third, Less than 2 Out	6 / 10 (60%)	63 / 107 (59%)
RBI in close games / RBI Total	19 / 30 (63%)	108 / 168 (64%)

Gene Garber
Atlanta Braves/Kansas City Royals

When people talk about the best relief pitchers, Gene Garber is rarely mentioned. Therefore, it would surprise many to find him prominently featured in the list of top pitchers in saves and appearances. Eighteen saves in 1987 gave him 212 for his career and seventh place on the all time list, despite never leading a league in the category. Garber's 905 career games rank him as the ninth most active pitcher in major league history.

Durability is clearly the secret to Garber's success. Since 1973, he has appeared in relief at least 35 times each year and has collected eleven or more saves in ten different seasons. Although he turned forty during the off-season, Garber has been able to maintain his consistency even in the last few years.

Garber's whirling pitching motion confuses the batters; it is very difficult to pick up the ball upon release. This delivery accounts for his neutrality against righthanded and left-handed hitters. It also helps explain why he is so effective as a short reliever. The less he is seen by a team, the more difficult it is for an opposing batter to comprehend his side-arm delivery. Likewise, by pitching for only an inning in each game, Garber is available for use in consecutive games without risking injury.

Garber started slowly in 1987, although he recorded two of the Braves first three victories and had two wins and a save in his first three games. He was getting the ball up in the strike zone, a dangerous problem for a pitcher without an overpowering fastball. By the end of April, his ERA had ballooned to 6.92 and he had allowed nearly two baserunners per inning pitched. Such early season difficulties are typical of Garber, but as the weather gets warmer so does Garber. May and July have usually been his best months and 1987 was no different. From May 1 through the first week of August, Garber had a 2.59 ERA, five wins, and eight saves in 31 games. A mediocre performance in August including no saves prompted his trade to the Royals on August 31 for minor league catcher Terry Bell.

In spite of disappointing performances in his first two outings for the Royals, Garber turned in a fine September. In his last eleven appearances of the season, Garber allowed only one earned run and no walks in 11.2 innings while collecting eight saves. He gave the team something they had lacked all year—an effective finisher.

In 1988, Garber will have to battle Ted Power, Bud Black, and Dan Quisenberry to be the Royals' bullpen ace. This situation is nothing new to Garber; he has always had to fight for important relief roles. If he is to be the main stopper for the Royals, Garber will need to avoid his usual flat April. Considering his past, he will probably find a way to rise to the top.

Marc Bowman

Garber, Henry Eugene "Gene"

Bats: Right **Throws: Right** **Born 11/13/47**

1987 SEASON AND MAJOR-LEAGUE CAREER PITCHING TOTALS

	G	GS	CG	GF	IP	BFP	H	R	ER	HR	SH	SF	HB	TBB	IBB	SO	WP	Bk	W	L	Pct	ShO	Sv	ERA
87 ATL-KC	62	0	0	55	83	375	100	44	38	8	8	3	2	29	10	51	4	0	8	10	.444	0	18	4.12
18 YEARS	905	9	4	590	1476	6188	1435	639	547	119	92	45	35	432	153	920	30	8	96	109	.468	0	212	3.34

1987: Finesse, Groundball **1986: Finesse, Groundball** **1985: Finesse, Groundball** **1984: Finesse, Groundball**

1987 SEASON

	G	IP	H	BB	SO	SB	CS	W	L	S	ERA
Totals	62	83.2	100	29	51	18	3	8	10	17	4.09
at Home	32	49.1	60	16	31	13	1	7	3	6	4.01
on Road	30	34.1	40	13	20	5	2	1	7	11	4.19
on Grass	31	40.1	45	13	25	9	2	4	5	7	2.90
on Artificial Turf	31	43.1	55	16	26	9	1	4	5	10	5.19
Day Games	40	59.0	71	22	39	13	2	8	6	9	3.97
Night Games	22	24.2	29	7	12	5	1	0	4	8	4.38
April	10	13.0	20	5	4	0	0	3	2	2	6.92
May	12	15.0	11	7	12	3	1	4	1	3	2.40
June	9	15.1	17	5	11	3	0	1	3	3	2.93
July	8	14.0	16	5	16	5	1	0	1	2	3.21
August	10	12.0	23	6	5	5	0	0	3	0	7.50
Sept/Oct	13	14.1	13	1	3	2	1	0	0	7	2.51

FOUR YEAR TOTALS (1984 – 1987)

	G	IP	H	BB	SO	SB	CS	W	L	S	ERA
Totals	244	365.0	377	98	228	48	14	22	27	53	3.33
at Home	130	198.0	227	48	125	30	6	16	13	19	3.73
on Road	114	167.0	150	50	103	18	8	6	14	34	2.86
on Grass	90	138.1	149	31	92	18	4	6	10	20	3.32
on Artificial Turf	154	226.2	228	67	136	30	10	16	17	33	3.34
Day Games	179	275.0	298	73	180	36	9	18	20	34	3.37
Night Games	65	90.0	79	25	48	12	5	4	7	19	3.20
April	28	36.2	45	13	18	6	0	5	3	4	5.15
May	44	67.1	69	13	44	9	4	5	2	6	3.21
June	31	53.1	61	19	35	8	5	4	6	9	3.21
July	37	59.2	48	16	45	10	2	0	2	8	1.81
August	55	78.2	85	22	46	9	1	6	9	10	4.00
Sept/Oct	49	69.1	69	15	40	6	2	2	5	16	3.12

vs. Opponent Batters	Ave.	OBP	SLG	AB	H	2B	3B	HR	RBI	BB	SO
Totals	.300	.357	.438	333	100	18	2	8	51	29	51
vs. Left	.275	.339	.386	153	42	8	0	3	21	14	28
vs. Right	.322	.372	.483	180	58	10	2	5	30	15	23
Bases Empty	.340	.383	.528	144	49	13	1	4	4	9	22
Leadoff	.348	.375	.551	69	24	6	1	2	2	2	12
Not Leadoff	.333	.390	.507	75	25	7	0	2	2	7	10
Runners On Base	.270	.338	.370	189	51	5	1	4	47	20	29
First Base Only	.385	.385	.500	52	20	3	0	1	4	0	4
Scoring Position	.226	.323	.321	137	31	2	1	3	43	20	25
Late Innings, Close	.296	.359	.404	230	68	11	1	4	34	23	38

	Ave.	OBP	SLG	AB	H	2B	3B	HR	RBI	BB	SO
	.268	.316	.373	1401	376	63	3	26	179	98	228
	.255	.307	.353	679	173	32	1	11	78	50	112
	.281	.326	.392	722	203	31	2	15	101	48	116
	.274	.302	.384	742	203	33	2	15	15	29	117
	.261	.282	.354	314	82	15	1	4	4	8	52
	.283	.316	.407	428	121	18	1	11	11	21	65
	.263	.332	.361	659	173	30	1	11	164	69	111
	.276	.306	.387	225	62	13	0	4	15	10	34
	.256	.344	.348	434	111	17	1	7	149	59	77
	.272	.328	.371	731	199	29	2	13	101	61	108

RBI/Opportunities

Scoring Position	38 / 198	(19%)
Scoring Position, 2 Out	21 / 100	(21%)
On Third, Less than 2 Out	11 / 30	(37%)
RBI in close games / RBI Total	34 / 51	(67%)

	136 / 610	(22%)
	64 / 304	(21%)
	43 / 100	(43%)
	103 / 179	(58%)

Scott Garrelts
San Francisco Giants

A freak injury to Scott on September 13 cost him a trip to trivia heaven. As it was, he finished the year with 127 Ks and a ratio of 10.7 strikeouts per nine innings, the best strikeout total for a reliever in the majors, and the fifth-best Ks-per-9 innings rate, behind Nolan Ryan, Randy Myers, Joe Price and Dave Smith. Only Ryan and Garrelts threw more than 100 innings. Three times Giant relievers have whiffed 100 batters in a season; Scott has two of those seasons in the last three years. The missed trivia opportunity? Had Scott not missed 22 games, and rehabilitated the last 10 games, he most likely would have become the second pure relief pitcher in history to finish in the top 10 in strikeouts. (Those of you who don't enjoy research, the only reliever to do so was the "Monster," Dick Radatz.)

Garrelts is on the verge of being recognized as one of the top 5 relievers in the major leagues. If the Rules Committee's decision to re-establish the strike zone (knees to the letters) is enforced as stringently as the rules against doctoring the ball, then Scott's 92-MPH split-finger will complement his 95-MPH fastball to the tune of 30+ saves. The nearly impossible-to-catch split-finger contributed mightily to Scott's 55 walks in 106 innings; what kept him at the forefront of closers was opponents' minuscule .191 batting average in 1987. Garrelts' split-finger has to be seen to be believed; frequently, no one, not the hitter or the catcher, can see it. On the evening of May 25, Garrelts came in to face the Mets with a 2–1 lead and the bases loaded with no outs in the top of the ninth. Scott struck out the side on 10 pitches, none clocked under 91-MPH. Unfortunately for Scott, two of his split-finger pitches were so vicious that Bob Brenly never saw, let alone got a glove on them.

Two wild pitches, each producing a swinging strikeout for the first two outs of the inning. Two runs scored. Giants lose, 3–2. In the inimitable words of Roger Craig, "Don't get your dauber down."

It's kind of amazing how Scott has been bounced back and forth between the rotation and the bullpen. In his minor league career, Scott made only 4 relief appearances in 6 seasons. Then, in 1985, he became a full-time relief pitcher under Jim Davenport. He totaled 9 wins and 13 saves for a 62–100 club, the only club in franchise history to lose 100 games. Through his first 50 appearances in 1985 his ERA was an astonishing 0.99, and did not give up a run between May 29 and June 30. He was the Giants' sole representative in the All-Star Game. In 1986, he started the year in the rotation, and did not return to the pen until July 6. Nevertheless, he led the staff in saves with ten, and had the ninth best ERA in the league with a 3.11 mark. With win plus save totals of 22, 23 and 23 over the last three years, it's a good bet that Scott will share closer duties with Don Robinson as the Giants' bullpen mainstays over the next several years.

Michael Duca and Victor Hester

Garrelts, Scott William Bats: Right Throws: Right Born 10/30/61

1987 SEASON AND MAJOR-LEAGUE CAREER PITCHING TOTALS

	G	GS	CG	GF	IP	BFP	H	R	ER	HR	SH	SF	HB	TBB	IBB	SO	WP	Bk	W	L	Pct	ShO	Sv	ERA
87 SF	64	0	0	43	106	428	70	41	38	10	7	2	0	55	4	127	5	1	11	7	.611	0	12	3.23
6 YEARS	218	26	3	120	467	1970	371	190	165	39	31	14	8	242	32	410	28	4	37	27	.578	1	35	3.18

1987: Power, Groundball   1986: Power, Groundball   1985: Power, Groundball   1984: Power, Flyball

	1987 SEASON											FOUR YEAR TOTALS (1984 – 1987)										
	G	IP	H	BB	SO	SB	CS	W	L	S	ERA	G	IP	H	BB	SO	SB	CS	W	L	S	ERA
Totals	64	106.0	70	55	127	10	6	11	7	12	3.14	212	428.1	335	221	390	63	18	35	25	35	3.15
at Home	28	42.0	29	18	51	3	4	5	3	4	3.86	104	218.1	158	98	191	30	11	22	12	15	2.76
on Road	36	64.0	41	37	76	7	2	6	4	8	2.67	108	210.0	177	123	199	33	7	13	13	20	3.60
on Grass	25	40.2	28	27	46	4	3	6	3	3	2.43	107	221.0	167	116	191	40	9	23	11	12	2.65
on Artificial Turf	39	65.1	42	28	81	6	3	5	4	9	3.58	105	207.1	168	105	199	23	9	12	14	23	3.73
Day Games	44	73.0	44	37	84	3	5	9	5	8	3.08	163	341.1	258	170	293	46	14	31	19	25	3.08
Night Games	20	33.0	26	18	43	7	1	2	2	4	3.27	49	87.0	77	51	97	17	4	4	6	10	3.52
April	11	19.2	14	14	22	1	1	3	2	4	4.12	27	71.1	54	32	50	8	3	6	4	5	3.03
May	10	21.1	15	9	30	2	4	2	1	2	1.69	35	95.2	77	54	92	19	9	7	7	5	3.10
June	14	19.1	13	9	25	0	0	1	2	3	3.72	41	89.2	71	38	74	8	1	2	4	4	3.01
July	12	19.2	12	7	26	2	1	3	2	3	3.66	35	56.1	41	23	63	4	2	9	3	7	4.31
August	11	17.0	13	8	20	4	0	2	0	0	2.12	34	52.2	43	33	54	7	2	7	2	9	2.22
Sept/Oct	6	9.0	3	8	4	1	0	0	0	0	4.00	40	62.2	49	41	57	17	1	4	5	5	3.45

vs. Opponent Batters	Ave.	OBP	SLG	AB	H	2B	3B	HR	RBI	BB	SO	Ave.	OBP	SLG	AB	H	2B	3B	HR	RBI	BB	SO
Totals	.192	.297	.310	364	70	7	3	10	45	55	127	.218	.316	.321	1535	335	39	7	35	179	221	390
vs. Left	.180	.283	.284	194	35	2	3	4	21	28	67	.231	.330	.313	770	178	15	6	12	86	114	165
vs. Right	.206	.313	.341	170	35	5	0	6	24	27	60	.205	.302	.329	765	157	24	1	23	93	107	225
Bases Empty	.185	.288	.275	200	37	3	3	3	3	29	74	.212	.295	.309	865	183	24	6	16	16	103	212
Leadoff	.215	.347	.304	79	17	2	1	1	1	16	23	.239	.326	.335	364	87	13	2	6	6	47	72
Not Leadoff	.165	.246	.256	121	20	1	2	2	2	13	51	.192	.273	.289	501	96	11	4	10	10	56	140
Runners On Base	.201	.307	.354	164	33	4	0	7	42	26	53	.227	.342	.337	670	152	15	1	19	163	118	178
First Base Only	.197	.240	.366	71	14	0	0	4	8	4	21	.232	.293	.331	254	59	4	0	7	15	22	61
Scoring Position	.204	.350	.344	93	19	4	0	3	34	22	32	.224	.368	.341	416	93	11	1	12	148	96	117
Late Innings, Close	.196	.300	.309	265	52	6	3	6	32	40	93	.210	.317	.287	710	149	17	4	10	78	112	210

RBI/Opportunities

	1987		Four Year
Scoring Position	27 / 148 (18%)		124 / 670 (19%)
Scoring Position, 2 Out	10 / 70 (14%)		42 / 306 (14%)
On Third, Less than 2 Out	7 / 25 (28%)		50 / 119 (42%)
RBI in close games / RBI Total	32 / 45 (71%)		126 / 179 (70%)

Kirk Gibson
Detroit Tigers

Kirk Gibson has to be one of the most intense players in baseball. His desire to win is astonishing; he is undoubtedly the emotional leader of this team. He missed the first 24 games of 1987 due to a pulled muscle; Detroit was 9–15 in those games. His return began the surge that put the Tigers into the playoffs; Detroit was 80–43 (.650) in the games that he started and 18–21 (.462) in games that he didn't.

Aside from his "intangibles," Gibson is also a heck of a ballplayer—in the batter's box or on the bases. In his career, he has created 6.48 runs per 27 outs and 100.2 runs per 162 games; his lifetime offensive winning percentage is .672. There are Hall of Fame outfielders with lower numbers. Gibson has excellent speed, a commodity lacking on the Tigers, and has uses it to steal bases with a 76 percent success rate. He's a fairly intelligent baserunner who rarely runs Detroit out of innings.

Gibson has done all this in a park that is not helping his stats. For some unknown reason, Tiger Stadium is becoming more and more of a pitcher's park. Since 1983, Detroit has scored and allowed 3,631 runs at home and 3,888 on the road. That's a 7 percent drop—making Detroit only a slightly better hitter's park than County Stadium in Milwaukee. 1987 is the fourth year in the last six that Kirk has hit better on the road than he has in Tiger Stadium—it is quite possible that he would be an even better hitter if he played in almost any other park.

That concludes the good news—the bad news is defense. Although Kirk is a fine athlete, he's a terrible outfielder. He's not a good judge of fly balls (his range factors are consistently low) and his arm is neither strong nor accurate. After years of gnashing their teeth, Detroit finally moved Gibson from right to left in 1987. The move helped them only in the sense that it was easier to find a rightfielder than a leftfielder. Neither Kirk's bat or glove were affected by the switch; it did nothing at all for the Detroit defense.

That fact, coupled with his injury problems, suggests that Gibson might possibly be better off moving to first base or DH. The problem is that Detroit has a dearth of power-hitting outfielders and too many 1B/DHs on their roster now. The switch would also make Gibson a comparatively less valuable player. The easier your defensive position, the higher your production—especially RBI production—has to be. While Gibson is a good hitter, his best RBI total is 97, in 1985. His intense desire to get his teammates home induces him to swing at the first half-decent pitch that he sees with men in scoring position, reducing his effectiveness. Giving him a role that would increase the pressure on him to succeed could well make Gibson pressure himself into a bad year.

Jim Shaarda

Gibson, Kirk Harold

Bats: Left   Throws: Left   Born 05/28/57

1987 SEASON AND MAJOR-LEAGUE CAREER BATTING TOTALS

	G	AB	H	2B	3B	HR	TB	R	RBI	TBB	IBB	SO	HP	SH	SF	SB	CS	SB%	GDP	AVG	OBP	SLG
87 DET	128	487	135	25	3	24	238	95	79	71	8	117	5	1	4	26	7	.79	5	.277	.372	.489
9 YEARS	893	3210	885	140	35	150	1545	528	499	380	40	713	33	16	33	166	51	.76	35	.276	.355	.481

	1987 SEASON											FOUR YEAR TOTALS (1984 – 1987)										
	Ave.	OBP	SLG	AB	H	2B	3B	HR	RBI	BB	SO	Ave.	OBP	SLG	AB	H	2B	3B	HR	RBI	BB	SO
Totals	.277	.372	.489	487	135	25	3	24	79	71	117	.279	.367	.505	2040	570	96	20	108	353	273	464
vs. Left	.268	.374	.385	179	48	9	0	4	21	28	50	.253	.342	.423	681	172	29	3	27	101	82	193
vs. Right	.282	.371	.549	308	87	16	3	20	58	43	67	.293	.380	.546	1359	398	67	17	81	252	191	271
at Home	.242	.350	.471	240	58	9	2	14	44	37	57	.278	.365	.519	1004	279	46	11	58	190	134	223
on Road	.312	.394	.506	247	77	16	1	10	35	34	60	.281	.370	.491	1036	291	50	9	50	163	139	241
vs. Groundball	.272	.360	.467	276	75	15	3	11	42	36	58	.295	.379	.513	973	287	40	14	48	173	127	200
vs. Flyball	.284	.388	.517	211	60	10	0	13	37	35	59	.265	.357	.498	1067	283	56	6	60	180	146	264
vs. Finesse	.248	.333	.484	246	61	13	3	13	36	30	49	.277	.357	.520	1123	311	53	14	64	187	129	220
vs. Power	.307	.410	.494	241	74	12	0	11	43	41	68	.282	.381	.486	917	259	43	6	44	166	144	244
on Grass	.280	.378	.510	404	113	21	3	22	69	62	90	.289	.380	.519	1724	499	82	17	93	300	242	382
on Artificial Turf	.265	.340	.386	83	22	4	0	2	10	9	27	.225	.294	.430	316	71	14	3	15	53	31	82
Day Games	.258	.349	.437	151	39	6	0	7	25	19	36	.281	.354	.500	638	179	32	6	32	115	67	135
Night Games	.286	.382	.512	336	96	19	3	17	54	52	81	.279	.374	.507	1402	391	64	14	76	238	206	329
April	.000	.000	.000	0	0	0	0	0	0	0	0	.279	.374	.486	179	50	7	3	8	30	27	39
May	.281	.385	.517	89	25	4	1	5	14	13	20	.290	.365	.529	255	74	14	4	13	41	28	55
June	.312	.392	.523	109	34	9	1	4	20	14	24	.289	.370	.546	412	119	21	5	25	85	53	90
July	.209	.274	.419	86	18	3	0	5	13	7	23	.265	.353	.475	373	99	16	1	20	66	50	97
August	.296	.412	.469	98	29	5	0	4	19	19	29	.278	.375	.467	435	121	18	5	18	60	67	101
Sept/Oct	.276	.379	.505	105	29	4	1	6	13	18	21	.277	.356	.526	386	107	20	2	24	71	48	82
Bases Empty	.267	.354	.511	266	71	19	2	14	14	33	73	.268	.350	.498	1104	296	52	11	60	60	137	265
Leadoff	.277	.333	.543	94	26	5	1	6	6	8	27	.281	.358	.501	349	98	14	6	17	17	42	77
Not Leadoff	.262	.365	.494	172	45	14	1	8	8	25	46	.262	.347	.497	755	198	38	5	43	43	95	188
Runners On	.290	.392	.462	221	64	6	1	10	65	38	44	.293	.382	.513	936	274	44	9	48	293	136	199
First Base Only	.308	.411	.462	91	28	2	0	4	8	14	25	.302	.377	.489	407	123	18	2	18	45	47	84
Scoring Position	.277	.380	.462	130	36	4	1	6	57	24	19	.285	.386	.531	529	151	26	7	30	248	89	115
Late Innings, Close	.283	.419	.500	60	17	4	0	3	11	13	21	.258	.363	.471	291	75	10	2	16	49	47	82

RBI/Opportunities

	1987		FOUR YEAR	
Scoring Position	46 / 180	(26%)	192 / 753	(25%)
Scoring Position, 2 Out	14 / 64	(22%)	59 / 293	(20%)
On Third, Less than 2 Out	18 / 34	(53%)	77 / 160	(48%)
RBI in close games / RBI Total	48 / 79	(61%)	216 / 353	(61%)

Dwight Gooden
New York Mets

The useful lesson of the Dwight Gooden story is that the age of the hero is not over. When Dwight Gooden was on the top of the world two years ago, we read and heard constantly about what a level-headed, mature young man he was, what a great set of values he had and how he represented so much that was good about the youth of America. Looking backward, it is painfully obvious that Dwight never was what we tried to make him out to be. He was exceptional in that he could throw so hard and in that he could throw the ball where he wanted it to go and in that he learned so quickly; and because he had those qualities people who didn't really know him or understand him imputed to him qualities of character equal to his preternatural skills. The lesson we have learned is not that he is a bum but that he is a human being, and thus despite all we have read over the last twenty years about the lack of heroes in American society, about this being the age of the anti-hero, the fact remains that as a nation we desperately wanted Dwight Gooden to be a hero. We wanted him to represent our values.

Gooden's record through four seasons remains about as good as you can find for a pitcher's first four years. With 99 decisions he has 74 wins. Through 100 career decisions Tom Seaver had 64 wins, Steve Carlton had 52 wins, Jim Palmer had 68 and Catfish Hunter had 46. They were all older than Gooden is when they got to 100 decisions. Who was the last pitcher to win 75 of his first 100 decisions? I don't know if it has ever been done before. Given the high strike in 1988 and a clean start, Gooden may be as good as he has ever been.

Dwight continues to have more trouble than one would expect winning in day games. All power pitchers are less effective in day games, but not usually this much less effective.

Some Met fans will tell you that Gooden should shoulder the blame for the Mets' failure to repeat, which is simply a part of the same syndrome. You can't be thinking that way, guys; it's a loser's logic. The Cardinals lost John Tudor for a lot longer than the Mets lost Gooden, but they still won. Gooden last year was off by a game and a half (from 17–6 to 15–7); Darling was off by 2 and a half (from 15–6 to 12–8), Fernandez off by three games. Orosco and McDowell were way off, as were several non-pitchers. The critical blow was not any of these but the loss of Bobby Ojeda. Why then was it Gooden's fault? Because Gooden was supposed to be a hero, and turned out to be a human being.

Bill James

Gooden, Dwight Eugene Bats: Right Throws: Right Born 11/16/64

1987 SEASON AND MAJOR-LEAGUE CAREER PITCHING TOTALS

	G	GS	CG	GF	IP	BFP	H	R	ER	HR	SH	SF	HB	TBB	IBB	SO	WP	Bk	W	L	Pct	ShO	Sv	ERA
87 NYN	25	25	7	0	180	730	162	68	64	11	5	5	2	53	2	148	1	1	15	7	.682	3	0	3.20
4 YEARS	124	124	42	0	925	3694	718	283	253	48	24	17	10	275	11	892	14	14	73	26	.737	16	0	2.46

1987: Power, Groundball   1986: Power, Groundball   1985: Power, Flyball   1984: Power, Flyball

1987 SEASON

	G	IP	H	BB	SO	SB	CS	W	L	S	ERA
Totals	25	179.2	162	53	148	24	8	15	7	0	3.21
at Home	14	95.0	85	34	73	12	6	8	5	0	3.41
on Road	11	84.2	77	19	75	12	2	7	2	0	2.98
on Grass	10	57.2	69	15	46	12	4	4	4	0	5.15
on Artificial Turf	15	122.0	93	38	102	12	4	11	3	0	2.29
Day Games	19	135.0	122	41	106	16	7	12	5	0	3.13
Night Games	6	44.2	40	12	42	8	1	3	2	0	3.43
April	0	0.0	0	0	0	0	0	0	0	0	0.00
May	0	0.0	0	0	0	0	0	0	0	0	0.00
June	6	46.2	35	16	43	4	4	5	1	0	2.12
July	6	43.2	43	10	24	5	1	3	2	0	3.30
August	6	41.2	40	15	32	5	1	4	1	0	3.24
Sept/Oct	7	47.2	44	12	49	10	2	3	3	0	4.15

FOUR YEAR TOTALS (1984 – 1987)

	G	IP	H	BB	SO	SB	CS	W	L	S	ERA
Totals	124	924.1	718	275	892	126	31	73	26	0	2.45
at Home	64	480.1	343	148	474	54	19	42	12	0	2.15
on Road	60	444.0	375	127	418	72	12	31	14	0	2.80
on Grass	44	291.1	277	87	255	47	14	19	15	0	3.74
on Artificial Turf	80	633.0	441	188	637	79	17	54	11	0	1.88
Day Games	92	689.1	526	206	681	76	22	57	18	0	2.32
Night Games	32	235.0	192	69	211	50	9	16	8	0	2.83
April	14	102.1	66	26	92	14	4	8	2	0	1.67
May	16	112.1	91	33	132	7	3	9	6	0	2.88
June	24	188.1	141	69	160	39	9	14	4	0	2.34
July	21	150.1	125	49	125	16	2	12	4	0	2.81
August	24	173.1	157	44	172	19	3	15	4	0	2.96
Sept/Oct	25	197.2	138	54	211	31	10	15	6	0	2.05

vs. Opponent Batters — 1987

	Ave.	OBP	SLG	AB	H	2B	3B	HR	RBI	BB	SO
Totals	.244	.299	.344	665	162	26	4	11	61	53	148
vs. Left	.240	.305	.320	366	88	14	0	5	30	35	76
vs. Right	.247	.292	.375	299	74	12	4	6	31	18	72
Bases Empty	.253	.312	.367	392	99	17	2	8	8	33	91
Leadoff	.266	.322	.379	169	45	5	1	4	4	13	34
Not Leadoff	.242	.305	.359	223	54	12	1	4	4	20	57
Runners On Base	.231	.281	.311	273	63	9	2	3	53	20	57
First Base Only	.248	.268	.385	109	27	6	0	3	8	3	20
Scoring Position	.220	.289	.262	164	36	3	2	0	45	17	37
Late Innings, Close	.250	.319	.381	84	21	3	1	2	9	8	19

vs. Opponent Batters — Four Year Totals

	Ave.	OBP	SLG	AB	H	2B	3B	HR	RBI	BB	SO
Totals	.213	.273	.300	3367	718	109	19	48	252	275	892
vs. Left	.217	.280	.291	1897	412	61	11	19	127	165	440
vs. Right	.208	.264	.311	1470	306	48	8	29	125	110	452
Bases Empty	.218	.279	.315	2034	443	76	13	32	32	172	527
Leadoff	.219	.284	.333	857	188	24	8	19	19	77	210
Not Leadoff	.217	.275	.302	1177	255	52	5	13	13	95	317
Runners On Base	.206	.263	.276	1333	275	33	6	16	220	103	365
First Base Only	.228	.261	.307	589	134	19	2	8	25	27	138
Scoring Position	.190	.264	.251	744	141	14	4	8	195	76	227
Late Innings, Close	.221	.281	.292	497	110	12	1	7	30	41	146

RBI/Opportunities

	1987		Four Year
Scoring Position	43 / 211 (20%)		181 / 991 (18%)
Scoring Position, 2 Out	18 / 93 (19%)		64 / 431 (15%)
On Third, Less than 2 Out	16 / 32 (50%)		80 / 187 (43%)
RBI in close games / RBI Total	43 / 61 (70%)		185 / 252 (73%)

Rich Gossage
San Diego Padres

The "Daddy Goose" certainly made the most of a lousy season both personally and in a team capacity. Gossage began the year with tendonitis (and, to the amazement of many, the Padres), and consequently didn't make his first appearance until May 5. Combine that with a team that won only 12 of its first 51 games, and you can understand why Rich wasn't among the league leaders in saves.

The first 6 games in which the Goose appeared after escaping the disabled list were utter disasters for Gossage. The fearsome countenance and blazing fastball (one *Sports Illustrated* writer once said Gossage could throw a marshmallow through a locomotive) were undergoing spring training under competition; he pitched (?) a grand total of 5 and 2/3 innings and allowed 5 earned runs, for a whopping ERA of 8.04. But, once he recovered his form, he had a very Goose-like year.

Through July 2 Gossage had 17 appearances, but the Padres were floundering like no NL team had in memory (if you remember the '62 Mets you are really utilizing your memory in some questionable ways). But the Padres improved to 49–43 over their last 92 games and the Goose managed to get involved in 23 of those.

All in all, Gossage rebounded well from a dismal 1986 season. To begin with, he lowered his ERA from a ghastly 4.45 to a very respectable 3.12. You might figure he walked fewer and struck out more, right? Wrong, gopherball breath! He allowed 0.5 more walks per 9 innings than in '86 (3.3 in '87, 2.8 in '86) and he struck out over 1 less hitter per 9 innings (8.8 in '86 and 7.6 in '87). But he allowed 1.5 fewer hits per 9 innings last year than he did in 1986 (8.1 vs. 9.6). This was important to Goose.

The only other times he had allowed more hits than innings pitched was in 1973 and 1974 with the White Sox. Coincidentally, those were the only other years (aside from his rookie year) in which he had an ERA that climbed above the 3.94 mark.

One needs to consider a couple of factors in determining the effectiveness of Rich Gossage in 1988. Number 1 is his age—he will turn 37 on July 5. That is quite old for a hard thrower such as Gossage, but he still has a 60-foot fastball, and he may have a few good years left in his right arm.

Second, how good are his new club, the Cubs, going to be? Chicago finished poorly in '87, and had a woefully weak pitching staff. They could be better, but more likely will struggle to stay out of last place. For Goose, that could mean few opportunities for saves. Nevertheless, Gossage's experience in finishing out close games will be a steadying influence on the rest of the club; he might help the maturation process of Calvin Schiraldi, whether Schiraldi works out of the bullpen or not. However the Cubs perform, Gossage figures to help them.

Doug White

Gossage, Richard Michael "Rich"

Bats: Right   Throws: Right   Born 07/05/51

1987 SEASON AND MAJOR-LEAGUE CAREER PITCHING TOTALS

	G	GS	CG	GF	IP	BFP	H	R	ER	HR	SH	SF	HB	TBB	IBB	SO	WP	Bk	W	L	Pct	ShO	Sv	ERA
87 SD	40	0	0	30	52	217	47	18	18	4	2	3	0	19	6	44	2	0	5	4	.556	0	11	3.12
16 YEARS	765	37	16	558	1534	6334	1243	549	491	93	94	58	34	611	73	1319	48	3	106	93	.533	0	289	2.88

1987: Power, Flyball   1986: Power, Flyball   1985: Finesse, Flyball   1984: Power, Flyball

1987 SEASON

	G	IP	H	BB	SO	SB	CS	W	L	S	ERA
Totals	40	52.0	47	19	44	3	2	5	4	11	3.12
at Home	21	25.1	21	6	22	0	0	3	1	7	3.20
on Road	19	26.2	26	13	22	3	2	2	3	4	3.04
on Grass	13	14.0	10	7	12	1	0	2	2	5	3.21
on Artificial Turf	27	38.0	37	12	32	2	2	3	2	6	3.08
Day Games	29	35.2	30	15	31	1	1	3	2	10	3.79
Night Games	11	16.1	17	4	13	2	1	2	2	1	1.65
April	0	0.0	0	0	0	0	0	0	0	0	0.00
May	11	11.1	11	6	11	1	1	0	0	2	3.97
June	6	10.1	7	2	10	0	0	0	0	4	0.00
July	10	11.1	14	6	11	2	1	2	3	1	3.97
August	8	11.1	11	0	6	0	0	2	0	4	3.18
Sept/Oct	5	7.2	4	5	6	0	0	1	1	0	4.70

vs. Opponent Batters	Ave.	OBP	SLG	AB	H	2B	3B	HR	RBI	BB	SO
Totals	.244	.307	.383	193	47	13	1	4	26	19	44
vs. Left	.240	.336	.380	100	24	8	0	2	16	16	21
vs. Right	.247	.271	.387	93	23	5	1	2	10	3	23
Bases Empty	.248	.282	.371	105	26	7	0	2	2	5	27
Leadoff	.186	.239	.209	43	8	1	0	0	0	3	13
Not Leadoff	.290	.313	.484	62	18	6	0	2	2	2	14
Runners On Base	.239	.333	.398	88	21	6	1	2	24	14	17
First Base Only	.323	.382	.581	31	10	2	0	2	6	3	5
Scoring Position	.193	.310	.298	57	11	4	1	0	18	11	12
Late Innings, Close	.226	.301	.358	137	31	9	0	3	19	16	33

FOUR YEAR TOTALS (1984 – 1987)

	G	IP	H	BB	SO	SB	CS	W	L	S	ERA
	197	298.0	255	92	243	25	8	25	20	83	2.99
	102	149.2	125	35	118	11	3	17	8	44	2.65
	95	148.1	130	57	125	14	5	8	12	39	3.34
	64	93.2	86	29	76	11	2	6	6	30	2.98
	133	204.1	169	63	167	14	6	19	14	53	3.00
	150	230.1	189	71	186	20	6	19	12	67	3.01
	47	67.2	66	21	57	5	2	6	8	16	2.93
	27	41.1	29	10	32	1	2	3	1	15	2.40
	40	57.2	59	18	48	6	2	2	4	19	3.90
	34	57.2	39	22	43	3	0	2	1	15	2.18
	40	61.0	52	18	53	9	3	7	6	16	2.51
	29	35.2	36	5	29	3	0	5	4	13	4.29
	27	44.2	40	19	38	3	1	6	4	5	3.02

	Ave.	OBP	SLG	AB	H	2B	3B	HR	RBI	BB	SO
	.232	.291	.332	1097	255	38	7	19	138	92	243
	.248	.322	.365	545	135	21	5	11	77	61	106
	.217	.259	.299	552	120	17	2	8	61	31	137
	.212	.265	.287	595	126	18	3	7	7	43	148
	.189	.255	.248	238	45	3	1	3	3	21	67
	.227	.272	.314	357	81	15	2	4	4	22	81
	.257	.321	.384	502	129	20	4	12	131	49	95
	.283	.324	.425	212	60	9	0	7	17	13	28
	.238	.319	.355	290	69	11	4	5	114	36	67
	.229	.289	.325	878	201	30	3	16	115	76	197

RBI/Opportunities

Scoring Position	16 / 89 (18%)	100 / 430 (23%)
Scoring Position, 2 Out	11 / 48 (23%)	54 / 216 (25%)
On Third, Less than 2 Out	5 / 12 (42%)	33 / 75 (44%)
RBI in close games / RBI Total	20 / 26 (77%)	116 / 138 (84%)

113

Mike Greenwell
Boston Red Sox

A little knowledge can be a dangerous thing. Ask, for example, any "sabermetrician" about a typical Boston hitter and you will be told three things. First, he is devastating at home. Next, he's mediocre—or at least much less effective—on the road. Finally, because he spends most of his time at home lofting flies onto Fenway's inviting left field wall, he's thoroughly dismal on artificial surfaces. Take his offensive stats with a box of salt until proven differently, they shrewdly advise, because of the "park effect" of that little phone booth on Yawkey Way.

Needless to say, when any Boston rookie explodes onto the scene, the "experts" are skeptical. "Is he for real?" they ask. "How well would he perform without Fenway's help?" they wonder. Well, the wits are half right. Fenway is an excellent place to hit. Many batters do have their best games within its cozy walls. But Mike Greenwell is as much of a real thing as Coca-Cola—maybe, since there is only one Greenwell, more so.

Mike's 1987 home/road splits could have been produced by a Xerox machine. At home, he batted .327, slugged .571 and his on-base percentage was .387. On the road, he hit .328, slugged .569 and his OB% was .385. He drove in 44 runs in 62 games at home and 45 in 63 games on the road.

Greenwell is lethal on turf. His lifetime average on synthetic fodder is .449; his lifetime slugging percentage is .872.

Though, to give the experts their due, perhaps he performs so well because he does not take advantage of the Green Monster. In 239 career at-bats in Fenway Park, Greenwell is still looking for his first homer over the left field wall; he has hit only five doubles off of it.

For the first 117 games of 1987, Mike was used strictly as a platoon player; he started 63 of the 84 games where Boston faced a righthander and none of their 33 games against lefties. Obviously this means that he has a major weakness against lefties, right?

Wrong. Before he received his first start against a lefty on August 17, Greenwell was 14–35 (.400) against lefties in his career; six hits had been for extra bases. His career average against lefties is now .398—he has struck out only six times against them.

Due to this unfortunate delay, Mike missed qualifying for official status among the leaders by 46 plate appearances and finishing in impressive spots. Of AL players with at least 400 PA, he finished ninth in batting and tenth in slugging. He drove in one run for every 5.12 plate appearances; the only major leaguers with lower ratios were MVPs Andre Dawson (4.83) and George Bell (4.98). But, since Mike is only 24, he has plenty of time left to compile equally good figures and gain the acclaim that he deserves during the rest of his career.

Chuck Waseleski

Greenwell, Michael Lewis "Mike"　　　　Bats: Left　　Throws: Right　　Born 07/18/63

1987 SEASON AND MAJOR-LEAGUE CAREER BATTING TOTALS

	G	AB	H	2B	3B	HR	TB	R	RBI	TBB	IBB	SO	HP	SH	SF	SB	CS	SB%	GDP	AVG	OBP	SLG
87 BOS	125	412	135	31	6	19	235	71	89	35	1	40	6	0	3	5	4	.56	7	.328	.386	.570
3 YEARS	173	478	156	34	6	23	271	82	101	43	2	51	6	0	3	6	4	.60	8	.326	.387	.567

	1987 SEASON											TWO YEAR TOTALS (1986 – 1987)										
	Ave.	OBP	SLG	AB	H	2B	3B	HR	RBI	BB	SO	Ave.	OBP	SLG	AB	H	2B	3B	HR	RBI	BB	SO
Totals	.328	.386	.570	412	135	31	6	19	89	35	40	.327	.387	.555	447	146	33	6	19	93	40	47
vs. Left	.378	.420	.514	74	28	5	1	1	13	4	6	.377	.417	.519	77	29	6	1	1	13	4	6
vs. Right	.317	.379	.583	338	107	26	5	18	76	31	34	.316	.381	.562	370	117	27	5	18	80	36	41
at Home	.327	.387	.571	217	71	19	5	8	44	19	16	.332	.391	.563	229	76	19	5	8	46	20	18
on Road	.328	.385	.569	195	64	12	1	11	45	16	24	.321	.383	.546	218	70	14	1	11	47	20	29
vs. Groundball	.355	.401	.630	211	75	11	4	13	48	16	19	.360	.408	.622	222	80	11	4	13	48	18	20
vs. Flyball	.299	.371	.507	201	60	20	2	6	41	19	21	.293	.367	.489	225	66	22	2	6	45	22	27
vs. Finesse	.350	.397	.650	206	72	18	4	12	45	14	11	.352	.402	.635	219	77	18	4	12	46	16	14
vs. Power	.306	.375	.490	206	63	13	2	7	44	21	29	.303	.374	.478	228	69	15	2	7	47	24	33
on Grass	.305	.368	.517	354	108	26	5	13	70	32	35	.304	.368	.507	381	116	28	5	13	73	35	42
on Artificial Turf	.466	.500	.897	58	27	5	1	6	19	3	5	.455	.500	.833	66	30	5	1	6	20	5	5
Day Games	.355	.385	.637	124	44	13	5	4	22	5	14	.355	.385	.637	124	44	13	5	4	22	5	14
Night Games	.316	.387	.542	288	91	18	1	15	67	30	26	.316	.388	.523	323	102	20	1	15	71	35	33
April	.316	.350	.737	19	6	2	0	2	5	0	2	.316	.350	.737	19	6	2	0	2	5	0	2
May	.246	.306	.439	57	14	5	0	2	17	4	5	.246	.306	.439	57	14	5	0	2	17	4	5
June	.350	.394	.683	60	21	5	0	5	17	3	8	.350	.394	.683	60	21	5	0	5	17	3	8
July	.338	.398	.550	80	27	8	0	3	10	7	7	.329	.396	.537	82	27	8	0	3	10	8	7
August	.359	.468	.615	78	28	3	4	3	17	15	7	.347	.453	.571	98	34	5	4	3	19	18	11
Sept/Oct	.331	.357	.534	118	39	8	2	4	23	6	11	.336	.364	.519	131	44	8	2	4	25	7	14
Bases Empty	.287	.362	.545	178	51	13	3	9	9	18	17	.292	.370	.533	195	57	14	3	9	9	21	23
Leadoff	.314	.392	.629	70	22	7	0	5	5	9	9	.333	.416	.628	78	26	8	0	5	5	11	12
Not Leadoff	.269	.342	.491	108	29	6	3	4	4	9	8	.265	.338	.470	117	31	6	3	4	4	10	11
Runners On	.359	.405	.590	234	84	18	3	10	80	17	23	.353	.401	.571	252	89	19	3	10	84	19	24
First Base Only	.422	.447	.667	90	38	8	1	4	10	2	4	.417	.440	.646	96	40	8	1	4	10	2	4
Scoring Position	.319	.380	.542	144	46	10	2	6	70	15	19	.314	.379	.526	156	49	11	2	6	74	17	20
Late Innings, Close	.366	.416	.803	71	26	9	2	6	23	5	10	.366	.416	.803	142	52	18	4	12	46	10	20

RBI/Opportunities

Scoring Position	56 / 198	(28%)		60 / 215	(28%)	
Scoring Position, 2 Out	27 / 98	(28%)		29 / 110	(26%)	
On Third, Less than 2 Out	14 / 26	(54%)		15 / 27	(56%)	
RBI in close games / RBI Total	52 / 89	(58%)		104 / 93	(112%)	

114

Ken Griffey
Atlanta Braves

One could make a case that Ken Griffey was the key to the Atlanta offense in 1987. In June Griffey was hitting in the .360 range and doing a fine job following Dale Murphy in the Atlanta lineup. At that time the Braves were actually leading the league in runs scored but injuries soon took Ken out of the lineup. The Braves offense unraveled in the second half, ending up in the middle of the pack despite playing in one of the best hitters' parks in baseball.

Ken Griffey and Gary Roenicke combined to form an ideal platoon combination in 1987. Neither player is up to playing every day any longer, but together they produced 32 doubles, 23 home runs, and 89 RBIs. Throw in 78 walks and 90 runs scored and you have a decent left fielder. Griffey produced bigger numbers, with 14 HR, 39 extra base hits, 64 RBI, and a .286 average, but don't overlook Roenicke, who performed as though he were still working for the Earl of Baltimore—his 6% home run rate was over twice that of the league as a whole, substantially above Griffey's 3.5%; his RBI/AB was half again the league average, and was higher than Griffey's.

Naturally, Chuck Tanner doesn't want to stick with success like that; he plans to send Griffey/Roenicke to the bench in 1988. Chuck decided Dion James couldn't handle CF defensively, even though he led the league's outfielders in fielding average, and had a Range Factor of 2.12, which put him in the upper half of the league's center fielders. Tanner will move James to LF and Albert Hall or Terry Blocker will play CF. Trading Hall's offensive production for the platoon will not help matters, but the Braves don't have enough talent to plug gaps internally without creating new holes. One solution would be to install the platoon at first base, where Gerald Perry put up fine stats for a middle infielder—at a power position he is clearly inadequate. But Chuck Tanner is in love with Perry's 42 stolen bases so he'll probably stay with Gerald at first base. The Braves will likely be a terrible team with a great bench—Simmons, Griffey, and Roenicke would all be more valuable on a contender than on this team.

Although Ken has lost his speed, he has compensated with increased power and improved strike zone judgement. Although Ken's lifetime HR percentage is 2.0, it has been 2.3 or above 4 of the last 5 years. He makes contact and should be an effective pinch hitter as he closes out a fine career. Griffey should end up with 2000 career hits and a lifetime .300 average. The only question is if he can hang on long enough to still be playing when his son, Ken Jr., makes the majors. The Mariners made Ken Jr. the number-one pick in the 1987 draft and he may outdo dad before he is done.

Greg Gajus

Griffey, George Kenneth "Ken"   Bats: Left   Throws: Left   Born 04/10/50

1987 SEASON AND MAJOR-LEAGUE CAREER BATTING TOTALS

	G	AB	H	2B	3B	HR	TB	R	RBI	TBB	IBB	SO	HP	SH	SF	SB	CS	SB%	GDP	AVG	OBP	SLG
87 ATL	122	399	114	24	1	14	182	65	64	46	11	54	1	1	4	4	7	.36	12	.286	.358	.456
15 YEARS	1800	6525	1953	339	74	135	2845	1048	771	646	45	804	11	31	49	193	77	.71	96	.299	.361	.436

1987 SEASON

	Ave.	OBP	SLG	AB	H	2B	3B	HR	RBI	BB	SO
Totals	.286	.358	.456	399	114	24	1	14	64	46	54
vs. Left	.253	.298	.345	87	22	2	0	2	11	6	9
vs. Right	.295	.374	.487	312	92	22	1	12	53	40	45
at Home	.291	.355	.475	223	65	15	1	8	39	24	30
on Road	.278	.362	.432	176	49	9	0	6	25	22	24
vs. Groundball	.304	.375	.462	158	48	11	1	4	23	18	19
vs. Flyball	.274	.347	.452	241	66	13	0	10	41	28	35
vs. Finesse	.299	.385	.459	194	58	11	1	6	28	29	21
vs. Power	.273	.330	.454	205	56	13	0	8	36	17	33
on Grass	.281	.356	.423	324	91	20	1	8	51	39	43
on Artificial Turf	.307	.366	.600	75	23	4	0	6	13	7	11
Day Games	.352	.436	.535	142	50	15	1	3	27	20	12
Night Games	.249	.314	.412	257	64	9	0	11	37	26	42
April	.355	.431	.613	62	22	4	0	4	14	9	9
May	.340	.382	.600	50	17	5	1	2	13	3	3
June	.280	.333	.462	93	26	5	0	4	12	8	15
July	.208	.295	.299	77	16	1	0	2	11	10	11
August	.268	.381	.394	71	19	3	0	2	7	13	8
Sept/Oct	.304	.347	.435	46	14	6	0	0	7	3	8
Bases Empty	.325	.384	.560	209	68	8	1	13	13	19	27
Leadoff	.304	.354	.478	92	28	1	0	5	5	7	14
Not Leadoff	.342	.408	.624	117	40	7	1	8	8	12	13
Runners On	.242	.330	.342	190	46	16	0	1	51	27	27
First Base Only	.227	.293	.347	75	17	9	0	0	6	7	12
Scoring Position	.252	.353	.339	115	29	7	0	1	45	20	15
Late Innings, Close	.238	.264	.345	84	20	6	0	1	11	3	12

FOUR YEAR TOTALS (1984 – 1987)

	Ave.	OBP	SLG	AB	H	2B	3B	HR	RBI	BB	SO
Totals	.286	.340	.441	1726	493	94	9	52	246	151	204
vs. Left	.256	.291	.373	437	112	25	1	8	60	22	53
vs. Right	.296	.357	.464	1289	381	69	8	44	186	129	151
at Home	.293	.350	.476	871	255	51	5	33	133	79	106
on Road	.278	.330	.405	855	238	43	4	19	113	72	98
vs. Groundball	.266	.323	.391	819	218	42	3	18	101	70	89
vs. Flyball	.303	.356	.486	907	275	52	6	34	145	81	115
vs. Finesse	.283	.339	.433	929	263	53	4	26	123	83	83
vs. Power	.289	.342	.450	797	230	41	5	26	123	68	121
on Grass	.286	.343	.438	1420	406	78	6	42	206	130	167
on Artificial Turf	.284	.327	.454	306	87	16	3	10	40	21	37
Day Games	.311	.379	.486	566	176	44	5	15	86	62	64
Night Games	.273	.321	.419	1160	317	50	4	37	160	89	140
April	.300	.365	.440	257	77	14	2	6	38	27	20
May	.262	.312	.419	229	60	13	1	7	37	16	30
June	.291	.347	.446	285	83	15	1	9	35	25	31
July	.273	.330	.417	326	89	12	1	11	48	28	44
August	.289	.341	.455	332	96	16	3	11	50	26	39
Sept/Oct	.296	.359	.465	297	88	24	1	8	38	29	40
Bases Empty	.303	.349	.481	938	284	44	6	37	37	65	112
Leadoff	.319	.355	.478	379	121	12	3	14	14	21	40
Not Leadoff	.292	.344	.483	559	163	32	3	23	23	44	72
Runners On	.265	.336	.393	788	209	50	3	15	209	86	92
First Base Only	.273	.314	.401	319	87	29	0	4	17	19	33
Scoring Position	.260	.350	.388	469	122	21	3	11	192	67	59
Late Innings, Close	.289	.337	.407	332	96	15	0	8	47	24	38

RBI/Opportunities

Scoring Position	41 / 170 (24%)	165 / 663 (25%)	
Scoring Position, 2 Out	10 / 72 (14%)	49 / 285 (17%)	
On Third, Less than 2 Out	19 / 36 (53%)	69 / 118 (58%)	
RBI in close games / RBI Total	43 / 64 (67%)	142 / 246 (58%)	

Alfredo Griffin
Oakland Athletics

One of my favorite Italian dishes is Fettucini "Alfredo Griffin," who used to be the shortstop of the Oakland Athletics and will now join "Pasta-King" Lasorda and his merry meatballs.

There are many people who feel Griffin is a terrible player, an error-prone, slap-hitting, basepath maniac. As a loyal Oakland fan I commonly disputed those petty bourgeois propagandist fallacies, but my vision is clearing with his move to Dodge City. I distinctly do not bleed "Dodger blue."

Think about it; one can argue theoretically that Griffin is a valuable player—I've done it for three years, myself—but there isn't a man or woman on God's green earth who has been able to prove it. When you try, you keep coming up with the conclusion that he is costing you games.

Consider Griffin the hitter. He'll give you a decent average for a shortstop, but when examined closely it turns into a bunch of loose change, mostly singles and singles run into doubles. He walks about once a paycheck—when he isn't swinging at pick-off throws to first base. He's a good bunter, when he doesn't try to stretch it into a double. Griffin is what they call an exciting runner, not to be confused with a smart runner. One of my favorite ideas would be to have a Late Night "AlfredoCam," and have Griffin run the basepaths.

Defensively, Griffin is a slightly different story. There's no doubt he has the basic talents for the job. He has great range, a good arm, and he's accurate when he remembers to aim the ball. He makes some of the most dramatic plays you could ever ask for, but on a routine grounder he often boots it, offers us that engaging smile of his, and promises to make up for it later with some aggressive baserunning.

Now how can you not like a player like that? One way is to watch him play for your hometown nine for three years. But he's finally done his bit to help the A's. They traded Bill Caudill for Griffin and Dave Collins; they ship Griffin and Jay Howell in exchange for Bob Welch. That's a quality starter (impossible to find these days) for a blown-out stopper, a set-up man turned reliever and Fettucini. Now there's a deal! Way to go Alfredo!

I know what the Dodgers are saying: "We obtained a whirlwind shortstop who is gonna fill an infield hole the size of Mount St. Helens." Hey, I'm glad you're happy. You stole Tim Belcher last August in a late-season rage, and you once wanted to trade Alejandro Pena for Rickey Henderson. Enjoy Griffin. He has leadership skills—yeah, that's the ticket—he has heart! As long as he's in Dodgerland, and not in Oakland, pass the garlic bread!

Darren Peterson

Griffin, Alfredo Claudino   Bats: Both   Throws: Right   Born 03/06/57

1987 SEASON AND MAJOR-LEAGUE CAREER BATTING TOTALS

	G	AB	H	2B	3B	HR	TB	R	RBI	TBB	IBB	SO	HP	SH	SF	SB	CS	SB%	GDP	AVG	OBP	SLG
87 OAK	144	494	130	23	5	3	172	69	60	28	2	41	4	10	3	26	13	.67	9	.263	.306	.348
12 YEARS	1372	4902	1263	183	68	22	1648	570	396	222	12	431	20	94	38	161	114	.59	61	.258	.290	.336

	1987 SEASON											FOUR YEAR TOTALS (1984 – 1987)										
	Ave.	OBP	SLG	AB	H	2B	3B	HR	RBI	BB	SO	Ave.	OBP	SLG	AB	H	2B	3B	HR	RBI	BB	SO
Totals	.263	.306	.348	494	130	23	5	3	60	28	41	.267	.295	.338	2120	566	72	20	13	205	87	176
vs. Left	.245	.292	.309	188	46	7	1	1	19	11	13	.266	.291	.324	710	189	20	6	3	59	24	53
vs. Right	.275	.315	.373	306	84	16	4	2	41	17	28	.267	.298	.345	1410	377	52	14	10	146	63	123
at Home	.236	.278	.318	233	55	9	2	2	29	12	22	.250	.277	.304	1029	257	28	8	4	99	40	91
on Road	.287	.331	.375	261	75	14	3	1	31	16	19	.283	.313	.370	1091	309	44	12	9	106	47	85
vs. Groundball	.285	.325	.390	246	70	16	2	2	29	13	16	.275	.306	.350	1018	280	38	7	8	103	47	71
vs. Flyball	.242	.288	.306	248	60	7	3	1	31	15	25	.260	.286	.328	1102	286	34	13	5	102	40	105
vs. Finesse	.294	.336	.349	238	70	7	3	0	38	13	11	.259	.283	.313	1174	304	31	10	4	108	40	76
vs. Power	.234	.278	.348	256	60	16	2	3	22	15	30	.277	.311	.370	946	262	41	10	9	97	47	100
on Grass	.258	.303	.333	411	106	19	3	2	49	24	38	.272	.305	.343	1593	433	58	13	10	167	75	140
on Artificial Turf	.289	.322	.422	83	24	4	2	1	11	4	3	.252	.267	.323	527	133	14	7	3	38	12	36
Day Games	.286	.313	.380	192	55	11	2	1	22	8	12	.271	.291	.348	797	216	27	11	4	90	28	60
Night Games	.248	.302	.328	302	75	12	3	2	38	20	29	.265	.298	.333	1323	350	45	9	9	115	59	116
April	.256	.264	.360	86	22	4	1	1	10	1	7	.258	.292	.323	310	80	12	1	2	26	15	23
May	.293	.363	.378	82	24	5	1	0	9	8	5	.285	.319	.362	340	97	14	3	2	47	16	28
June	.247	.310	.286	77	19	3	0	0	5	6	6	.283	.323	.361	357	101	11	4	3	33	20	28
July	.278	.327	.320	97	27	4	0	0	8	6	10	.242	.275	.304	359	87	10	3	2	32	15	30
August	.262	.301	.430	107	28	6	3	2	20	6	8	.257	.282	.336	405	104	13	5	3	39	14	33
Sept/Oct	.222	.234	.244	45	10	1	0	0	8	1	5	.278	.291	.344	349	97	12	4	1	28	7	34
Bases Empty	.219	.276	.294	279	61	13	4	0	0	20	25	.254	.291	.320	1234	313	48	8	6	6	63	107
Leadoff	.172	.268	.222	99	17	3	1	0	0	12	9	.236	.285	.295	539	127	19	2	3	3	36	44
Not Leadoff	.244	.280	.333	180	44	10	3	0	0	8	16	.268	.296	.340	695	186	29	6	3	3	27	63
Runners On	.321	.346	.419	215	69	10	1	3	60	8	16	.286	.305	.363	886	253	24	12	7	199	24	69
First Base Only	.373	.381	.482	83	31	3	0	2	6	0	6	.313	.320	.397	368	115	11	4	4	15	3	31
Scoring Position	.288	.326	.379	132	38	7	1	1	54	8	10	.266	.295	.340	518	138	13	8	3	184	21	38
Late Innings, Close	.314	.333	.372	86	27	5	0	0	14	3	8	.251	.275	.319	351	88	10	4	2	40	12	33

RBI/Opportunities

	1987 SEASON		FOUR YEAR TOTALS	
Scoring Position	51 / 174	(29%)	174 / 685	(25%)
Scoring Position, 2 Out	25 / 81	(31%)	69 / 310	(22%)
On Third, Less than 2 Out	18 / 37	(49%)	76 / 142	(54%)
RBI in close games / RBI Total	41 / 60	(68%)	135 / 205	(66%)

Kevin Gross
Philadelphia Phillies

When baseball historians get around to recounting 1987 as the "Year of the Cheater" in major league baseball, prominent among the cases cited will be that of Phillies right-handed pitcher Kevin Gross. Gross was slapped with a ten-day suspension last season for allegedly scuffing the baseball in a game August 10 against the Cubs. Gross denied any wrongdoing, but the existence of some sandpaper on the heel of his glove, along with the revelation that his glove was "loaded" with a "sticky substance," was too much for NL president Bart Giamatti to ignore.

Gross probably set himself up for all of this during July when, after a game against Houston, Gross recounted what he claimed was evidence that the Astros Mike Scott had been scuffing game balls.

"A few of the balls he used were still in the game in my half of the inning," Gross was quoted as saying in *The Sporting News*. "So, I used them, and I was amazed at some of the pitches I was able to throw. They haven't done anything to him in two years, and it gets frustrating to worry about it all the time. So if I pitch in the same game as him, I'm going to let him scuff the ball, and then I'll use it."

One day after Gross was ejected from the game against the Cubs, it was revealed that he had conducted a pitching seminar at a baseball camp at Swarthmore College in which he was said to have explained the finer technique of baseball scuffing, while maintaining that he didn't use a scuff pitch himself.

All of this "to scuff or not to scuff" wasn't very helpful to Gross in real competition. He had dropped his prior seven decisions before the scuffing incident, and ended the season 9–16 with a 4.35 ERA. He allowed more than one hit per inning, and walked nearly four men per game.

In fairness, Gross did pitch early in the season with a herniated disc in his back, something about which he reminded Phillies management when club president Bill Giles said he would not pay Gross for the ten days of his suspension. That would have cost Gross more than $23,000. With the players' union threatening to ask for a citation for breach of contract if the Phillies did withhold that amount, Giles backed down, and Gross was paid.

It will be interesting to see if Gross is still with the Phillies on opening day.

Tom Henry

Gross, Kevin Frank

Bats: Right   **Throws: Right**   Born 08/08/61

1987 SEASON AND MAJOR-LEAGUE CAREER PITCHING TOTALS

	G	GS	CG	GF	IP	BFP	H	R	ER	HR	SH	SF	HB	TBB	IBB	SO	WP	Bk	W	L	Pct	ShO	Sv	ERA
87 PHI	34	33	3	1	201	878	205	107	97	26	8	6	10	87	7	110	3	7	9	16	.360	1	0	4.34
5 YEARS	170	131	18	10	874	3775	879	420	380	86	34	20	33	341	22	565	15	13	48	52	.480	6	1	3.91

1987: Finesse, Flyball   1986: Finesse, Flyball   1985: Power, Flyball   1984: Power, Groundball

1987 SEASON

	G	IP	H	BB	SO	SB	CS	W	L	S	ERA
Totals	34	200.2	205	87	110	36	12	9	16	0	4.35
at Home	20	119.1	110	51	66	24	9	5	11	0	3.85
on Road	14	81.1	95	36	44	12	3	4	5	0	5.09
on Grass	13	76.1	84	30	50	11	5	3	5	0	3.77
on Artificial Turf	21	124.1	121	57	60	25	7	6	11	0	4.71
Day Games	8	41.1	59	12	24	6	0	1	4	0	6.97
Night Games	26	159.1	146	75	86	30	12	8	12	0	3.67
April	4	22.0	21	9	11	6	0	0	3	0	3.68
May	5	33.2	35	12	17	6	3	3	1	0	3.48
June	6	38.0	40	16	20	9	2	3	3	0	5.21
July	6	35.2	36	18	12	3	1	0	2	0	4.29
August	7	36.2	43	15	24	8	2	2	3	0	4.91
Sept/Oct	6	34.2	30	17	26	4	4	1	4	0	4.15

vs. Opponent Batters	Ave.	OBP	SLG	AB	H	2B	3B	HR	RBI	BB	SO
Totals	.267	.347	.428	768	205	30	8	26	96	87	110
vs. Left	.276	.368	.429	427	118	19	5	12	56	58	52
vs. Right	.255	.320	.428	341	87	11	3	14	40	29	58
Bases Empty	.286	.377	.502	412	118	14	3	23	23	52	59
Leadoff	.289	.393	.506	180	52	11	2	8	8	25	27
Not Leadoff	.284	.364	.500	232	66	3	1	15	15	27	32
Runners On Base	.244	.312	.343	356	87	16	5	3	73	35	51
First Base Only	.229	.262	.320	153	35	5	3	1	7	7	22
Scoring Position	.256	.345	.360	203	52	11	2	2	66	28	29
Late Innings, Close	.269	.345	.500	52	14	3	0	3	7	6	8

FOUR YEAR TOTALS (1984 – 1987)

	G	IP	H	BB	SO	SB	CS	W	L	S	ERA
Totals	153	777.0	779	306	499	108	38	44	46	1	3.96
at Home	82	421.0	403	154	293	56	22	25	26	0	3.63
on Road	71	356.0	376	152	206	52	16	19	20	1	4.35
on Grass	59	293.2	294	116	206	38	18	16	18	1	4.08
on Artificial Turf	94	483.1	485	190	293	70	20	28	28	0	3.89
Day Games	38	184.2	228	75	119	23	7	9	14	0	5.65
Night Games	115	592.1	551	231	380	85	31	35	32	1	3.43
April	22	79.2	73	30	48	11	3	8	8	0	3.39
May	27	119.0	128	40	70	15	7	8	7	0	3.86
June	24	153.1	154	53	99	26	7	11	6	0	3.82
July	25	145.0	144	59	66	15	7	6	9	0	4.16
August	27	138.2	148	60	103	21	8	10	6	0	4.02
Sept/Oct	28	141.1	132	64	113	20	6	6	10	1	4.27

vs. Opponent Batters	Ave.	OBP	SLG	AB	H	2B	3B	HR	RBI	BB	SO
Totals	.262	.333	.400	2968	779	119	35	73	334	306	499
vs. Left	.267	.350	.411	1631	435	74	24	38	179	206	267
vs. Right	.257	.311	.386	1337	344	45	11	35	155	100	232
Bases Empty	.265	.335	.430	1674	444	67	17	58	58	167	286
Leadoff	.258	.331	.438	728	188	34	8	27	27	73	118
Not Leadoff	.271	.338	.423	946	256	33	9	31	31	94	168
Runners On Base	.259	.331	.362	1294	335	52	18	15	276	139	213
First Base Only	.245	.300	.348	535	131	21	8	6	27	42	76
Scoring Position	.269	.351	.372	759	204	31	10	9	249	97	137
Late Innings, Close	.302	.375	.425	301	91	14	4	5	34	35	48

RBI/Opportunities

Scoring Position	61 / 272 (22%)	226 / 1025 (22%)
Scoring Position, 2 Out	18 / 122 (15%)	83 / 488 (17%)
On Third, Less than 2 Out	25 / 52 (48%)	90 / 176 (51%)
RBI in close games / RBI Total	73 / 96 (76%)	243 / 334 (73%)

Kelly Gruber
Toronto Blue Jays

In the spring of 1987, Toronto virtually handed Kelly Gruber the regular third baseman's job. Their reason for ending the successful platoon combo of Rance Mulliniks and Garth Iorg was that Gruber could match their production and had superior power and speed. They were mistaken. Mulliniorg won the starting job back; by winter, Toronto was actively looking for a proven regular to replace the aging combo.

Toronto can hardly be blamed for the attempt; history certainly seemed to be on their side. As they had done with Willie Upshaw, Manny Lee, Jose Nunez and George Bell, Toronto obtained Gruber in the minor league draft. In the minors, Kelly had demonstrated an ability to hit for average (.296 at age 19), hit for power (21 homers in AAA in both 1984 and 1985; lcd his league in slugging in 1984) and run (21 steals in 1984). He's a converted shortstop who has led his leagues in several defensive categories; he seemed to be an exceptional young talent.

In some ways, Gruber did establish himself as a major leaguer. His glove impressed Toronto enough that he started the 1987 season as both the regular third baseman and backup shortstop. As the season progressed, he also played second base and the outfield. He was used fairly often as a pinch-runner and stole 12 bases in 14 tries. He is certainly a valuable utility player.

But Gruber did not show that he was a major league regular; there is some doubt about whether he ever will be one. In April, Mulliniks was moved to DH; Iorg went to the bench. On May 3, with Gruber hitting .148 and Fred McGriff and Cecil Fielder flourishing at the DH spot, Mulliniks began spending more time at third base. Playing more as a platoon player seemed to help Kelly—by May 31, his average was up to .286—but it was all downhill from there. By July 5, his average was down to .270. On August 2, it was .257. On August 30, he was at .243. As Kelly's average shrunk, his playing time declined; he had less than 100 at-bats after Aug. 2.

Fortunately for Kelly, he did show enough to earn himself another chance. Despite his .235 average, he slugged .396; his power was everything that was advertised. Though his chances per game figure was very low, that was because he played 45 of his 119 games at third as a defensive replacement. It's likely that he'll replace Iorg as the righty half of a productive platoon combo at third base—were his average to rise, he might even reclaim the regular's job.

But Gruber is 26 and at a crossroads in his career; the 1988 season will be "make or break" for him. He is useful and versatile enough to deserve a place as a spare part on any roster; but, unless he has a very strong 1988, he will never be anything more.

Dave Easby and Tony Formo

Gruber, Kelly Wayne   Bats: Right   Throws: Right   Born 02/26/62

1987 SEASON AND MAJOR-LEAGUE CAREER BATTING TOTALS

	G	AB	H	2B	3B	HR	TB	R	RBI	TBB	IBB	SO	HP	SH	SF	SB	CS	SB%	GDP	AVG	OBP	SLG
87 TOR	138	341	80	14	3	12	136	50	36	17	2	70	7	1	2	12	2	.86	11	.235	.283	.399
4 YEARS	245	513	112	18	4	18	192	71	54	22	2	105	7	3	4	14	7	.67	16	.218	.258	.374

	1987 SEASON											FOUR YEAR TOTALS (1984 – 1987)										
	Ave.	OBP	SLG	AB	H	2B	3B	HR	RBI	BB	SO	Ave.	OBP	SLG	AB	H	2B	3B	HR	RBI	BB	SO
Totals	.235	.283	.396	341	80	13	3	12	36	17	70	.218	.258	.372	513	112	17	4	18	54	22	105
vs. Left	.230	.289	.395	152	35	7	3	4	16	12	35	.217	.260	.363	226	49	9	3	6	22	13	50
vs. Right	.238	.279	.397	189	45	6	0	8	20	5	35	.220	.257	.380	287	63	8	1	12	32	9	55
at Home	.222	.283	.396	144	32	6	2	5	19	10	29	.204	.258	.378	230	47	7	3	9	33	15	51
on Road	.244	.284	.396	197	48	7	1	7	17	7	41	.230	.259	.367	283	65	10	1	9	21	7	54
vs. Groundball	.222	.262	.386	176	39	8	3	5	16	7	28	.215	.246	.402	246	53	10	3	10	29	8	38
vs. Flyball	.248	.306	.406	165	41	5	0	7	20	10	42	.221	.269	.345	267	59	7	1	8	25	14	67
vs. Finesse	.246	.287	.438	203	50	7	1	10	23	8	29	.235	.269	.405	289	68	9	2	12	32	10	44
vs. Power	.217	.278	.333	138	30	6	2	2	13	9	41	.196	.245	.330	224	44	8	2	6	22	12	61
on Grass	.237	.279	.360	139	33	5	0	4	12	6	31	.225	.252	.342	222	50	8	0	6	16	6	43
on Artificial Turf	.233	.286	.421	202	47	8	3	8	24	11	39	.213	.263	.395	291	62	9	4	12	38	16	62
Day Games	.183	.252	.304	115	21	3	1	3	10	7	23	.167	.216	.285	186	31	5	1	5	16	8	40
Night Games	.261	.300	.442	226	59	10	2	9	26	10	47	.248	.282	.422	327	81	12	3	13	38	14	65
April	.160	.222	.160	25	4	0	0	0	1	1	2	.214	.250	.357	42	9	0	0	2	4	1	9
May	.325	.365	.512	80	26	6	0	3	6	4	13	.255	.299	.409	110	28	6	1	3	6	6	18
June	.276	.321	.447	76	21	4	0	3	10	4	22	.247	.291	.423	97	24	5	0	4	13	5	26
July	.188	.206	.344	64	12	0	2	2	6	0	13	.160	.177	.293	75	12	0	2	2	7	0	17
August	.206	.239	.382	68	14	3	0	3	11	2	11	.223	.255	.383	94	21	3	0	4	13	3	13
Sept/Oct	.107	.286	.286	28	3	0	1	1	2	6	9	.189	.252	.337	95	18	3	1	3	11	7	22
Bases Empty	.224	.264	.420	205	46	6	2	10	10	6	44	.201	.239	.374	294	59	9	3	12	12	10	64
Leadoff	.225	.262	.450	80	18	4	1	4	4	3	19	.191	.233	.355	110	21	4	1	4	5	5	25
Not Leadoff	.224	.265	.400	125	28	2	1	6	6	3	25	.207	.244	.386	184	38	5	2	8	8	5	39
Runners On	.250	.311	.360	136	34	7	1	2	26	11	26	.242	.285	.370	219	53	8	1	6	42	12	41
First Base Only	.233	.258	.400	60	14	2	1	2	6	1	7	.267	.290	.411	90	24	2	1	3	8	2	11
Scoring Position	.263	.348	.329	76	20	5	0	0	20	10	19	.225	.282	.341	129	29	6	0	3	34	10	30
Late Innings, Close	.315	.387	.630	54	17	2	0	5	10	6	13	.241	.304	.446	83	20	2	0	5	11	7	18

RBI/Opportunities

Scoring Position	20 / 106 (19%)	31 / 182 (17%)
Scoring Position, 2 Out	7 / 49 (14%)	10 / 86 (12%)
On Third, Less than 2 Out	9 / 24 (38%)	14 / 36 (39%)
RBI in close games / RBI Total	20 / 36 (56%)	28 / 54 (52%)

Mark Gubicza
Kansas City Royals

Mark Gubicza is not, and probably never will be, an outstanding pitcher, and the Royals have acknowledged that fact by dangling him as trade bait three times. In the spring of '86 he was all set to go to San Francisco for Chili Davis when there developed a snag over the throw-in. The Giants wanted AA farmhand Van Snider, the Royals said take either Pat Sheridan or Darryl Motley. The collapse of this deal over basically nothing (Snider barely hit .200 in AAA last year, and Sheridan and Motley you know about) turned out a boon for the Royals, as a Chili Davis in '86 would have meant no Danny Tartabull in '87. The interesting aspect of the Tartabull deal is that the Royals would have surely parted with Gubicza to get him; it was the Mariners who insisted on Scott Bankhead, apparently because of his excellent strikeout to walk ratio. I assume it was the same story this past winter: The Reds had a choice between Gubicza and Danny Jackson for Stillwell, and again Gubicza was passed over; it'll be interesting to see if two major league teams in a row have guessed wrong (although in fairness, it's too soon to write off Bankhead).

Mark Gubicza's nickname (assuming it's not "Trade Bait") should be "Gimme a Light", because, as with just asking for a light, you never know what you're going to get. On his good days, with his fast ball and slider in gear, he can be as dominant as any pitcher in the league. his bad days tend to be just as bad—6 or 7 walks by the fourth inning, a couple of gappers on 3–1 pitches, and an early shower. And yet, in his way, he's remarkably consistent: In each of his four years in the majors, he's walked three batters for every four struck out, like clockwork. In three of those four years he's posted an ERA of 4.05, 4.06, and 3.98. His win totals read 10, 14, 12, and 13. But he showed some signs of breaking the mold in '87; his remarkably consistent innings pitched for the first three years (189, 177.33, 180.67) suddenly gave way to an unexpected 241.2, including ten complete games, as opposed to a previous high of four.

Could these increased innings pitched and complete games be the harbinger of a breakthrough year for Gubicza? I'm inclined to doubt it; his ERA, best ever in '86, was back up to almost four in '87. Unless he can figure out how to do something about his strikeout to walk ratio, I don't think he'll ever excel. He'll just continue as a model of inconsistent consistency. One thing is certain: After the '88 season, as after all recent seasons, the Royals will be desperate for offensive help at some position. Saberhagen, Leibrandt, and Bannister will probably be considered untouchable, and unless Bud Black has an unexpectedly vintage year, he lacks value. Most likely to be dangled as trade bait for '89? Need you ask?

Mike Kopf

Gubicza, Mark Steven

Bats: Right   Throws: Right   Born 08/14/62

1987 SEASON AND MAJOR-LEAGUE CAREER PITCHING TOTALS

	G	GS	CG	GF	IP	BFP	H	R	ER	HR	SH	SF	HB	TBB	IBB	SO	WP	Bk	W	L	Pct	ShO	Sv	ERA
87 KC	35	35	10	0	242	1036	231	114	107	18	6	11	6	120	3	166	14	1	13	18	.419	2	0	3.98
4 YEARS	128	116	17	2	789	3361	718	369	345	53	15	34	21	356	5	494	44	2	49	48	.505	6	0	3.94

1987: Power, Groundball   1986: Power, Groundball   1985: Power, Groundball   1984: Power, Groundball

1987 SEASON

	G	IP	H	BB	SO	SB	CS	W	L	S	ERA
Totals	35	241.2	231	120	166	23	15	13	18	0	3.95
at Home	17	122.1	118	53	71	15	6	7	10	0	3.75
on Road	18	119.1	113	67	95	8	9	6	8	0	4.22
on Grass	10	63.0	65	36	42	3	4	4	4	0	5.14
on Artificial Turf	25	178.2	166	84	124	20	11	9	14	0	3.58
Day Games	15	100.0	94	58	73	7	7	5	7	0	4.41
Night Games	20	141.2	137	62	93	16	8	8	11	0	3.68
April	4	24.2	23	12	11	3	1	1	3	0	4.74
May	6	35.2	36	21	23	2	2	2	2	0	4.29
June	6	45.2	37	25	32	4	1	3	3	0	3.94
July	6	43.1	45	16	31	6	3	2	2	0	2.70
August	6	40.1	43	26	27	4	2	1	5	0	6.02
Sept/Oct	7	52.0	47	20	42	4	6	4	3	0	2.94

vs. Opponent Batters	Ave.	OBP	SLG	AB	H	2B	3B	HR	RBI	BB	SO
Totals	.259	.347	.384	893	231	38	10	18	90	120	166
vs. Left	.260	.350	.385	512	133	20	7	10	57	72	83
vs. Right	.257	.342	.383	381	98	18	3	8	33	48	83
Bases Empty	.271	.356	.390	513	139	28	6	7	7	65	93
Leadoff	.268	.357	.371	224	60	16	2	1	1	30	39
Not Leadoff	.273	.356	.405	289	79	12	4	6	6	35	54
Runners On Base	.242	.334	.376	380	92	10	4	11	83	55	73
First Base Only	.288	.374	.405	153	44	4	1	4	13	20	24
Scoring Position	.211	.309	.357	227	48	6	3	7	70	35	49
Late Innings, Close	.329	.400	.457	70	23	3	0	2	7	9	15

FOUR YEAR TOTALS (1984 – 1987)

	G	IP	H	BB	SO	SB	CS	W	L	S	ERA
Totals	128	788.2	718	356	494	75	37	49	48	0	3.93
at Home	71	460.0	397	182	276	51	17	30	27	0	3.27
on Road	57	328.2	321	174	218	24	20	19	21	0	4.87
on Grass	33	196.0	179	101	126	14	12	12	12	0	4.32
on Artificial Turf	95	592.2	539	255	368	61	25	37	36	0	3.80
Day Games	42	245.2	234	133	161	18	17	16	15	0	4.65
Night Games	86	543.0	484	223	333	57	20	33	33	0	3.61
April	12	72.1	66	34	37	11	3	1	9	0	4.35
May	22	129.1	123	60	84	15	4	8	7	0	4.38
June	22	141.0	105	77	96	7	6	11	7	0	3.32
July	22	124.1	119	42	80	17	8	7	5	0	3.26
August	24	149.2	149	71	92	11	5	9	11	0	4.93
Sept/Oct	26	172.0	156	72	105	14	11	13	9	0	3.56

vs. Opponent Batters	Ave.	OBP	SLG	AB	H	2B	3B	HR	RBI	BB	SO
Totals	.245	.326	.361	2935	718	130	26	53	315	356	494
vs. Left	.251	.337	.373	1606	403	66	17	32	171	210	253
vs. Right	.237	.313	.346	1329	315	64	9	21	144	146	241
Bases Empty	.242	.325	.364	1683	407	89	13	30	30	204	273
Leadoff	.255	.333	.372	737	188	43	5	11	11	85	104
Not Leadoff	.232	.319	.357	946	219	46	8	19	19	119	169
Runners On Base	.248	.329	.357	1252	311	41	13	23	285	152	221
First Base Only	.251	.319	.349	522	131	19	7	6	31	51	80
Scoring Position	.247	.335	.363	730	180	22	6	17	254	101	141
Late Innings, Close	.276	.374	.412	221	61	10	1	6	19	35	47

RBI/Opportunities

Scoring Position	59 / 319 (18%)	223 / 1001 (22%)
Scoring Position, 2 Out	22 / 152 (14%)	76 / 441 (17%)
On Third, Less than 2 Out	25 / 57 (44%)	98 / 183 (54%)
RBI in close games / RBI Total	62 / 90 (69%)	223 / 315 (71%)

Pedro Guerrero
Los Angeles Dodgers

Last season, Pedro Guerrero returned to the form that made him one of the most feared hitters in the National League; he also exorcised baserunning ghosts that haunted him since he tore up a knee with an ill-considered slide during spring training 1986. That slide and injury forced him to miss nearly all of 1986 (he played in only 31 games), and helped contribute to the team's slide into mediocrity. The team's mediocrity continued in 1987, but Guerrero was outstanding.

"Impact player" is a popular term today, and Guerrero was truly that in 1987. His dominance of a game can be measured by his 27 homers, a number of which were shots that seemed to rocket from his bat into the stands. These can leave an opponent shell-shocked.

Guerrero's dominance can also be seen in his ability to generate multiple hits and multiple runs in a game. Overall, Guerrero had 56 multiple hit games en route to 184 hits for the season, second in overall hits in the NL only to league batting champ Tony Gwynn. These multiple hit performances consisted of two 4-hit games, 12 3-hit games, and 42 2-hit games. He can also dominate weeks and months at a time. He had an excellent May (.381, 37 for 97 with 9 homers and 22 RBIs), and he had two 11-game hitting streaks. He finished the season hitting in 17 straight and 25 of his last 27 (41 for 99 for a .414 average). This surge brought him to .338 for the year, also second in the NL behind Gwynn.

It was Guerrero's career best average. His 89 RBIs were not (he's driven in over 100 several times), but that can partly be blamed on the poor offense surrounding Guerrero much of the year. Nevertheless, when Guerrero gets hot, he's devastating and can drive in runs in bunches. He had 10 3-RBI games in 1987 and 9 2-RBI games. Some other pertinent numbers for Guerrero include: a .539 slugging percentage (eighth best in the NL), and a .416 on base percentage (fifth best in the league).

Perhaps the most encouraging numbers for the Dodgers and Guerrero in 1987 were these—he stole 9 bases in 16 attempts and didn't once foul up his knee. Also, he played in 152 of the Dodgers games. Only Steve Sax played in more games for the Dodgers. Now if only the Dodgers can get some lineup help around Guerrero. A healthy Mike Marshall, for example, might make it harder to pitch around Guerrero, who had 74 walks, 18 of them intentional. The biggest of those was issued by the Giants in an April game at Candlestick. They walked Guerrero in the 10th inning to pitch to a faltering Marshall. Marshall promptly homered and then nearly triggered a riot by gesturing angrily at the San Francisco bench as he rounded the bases. As the year progressed, however, Marshall missed 58 games, and Guerrero often had no punch following his potent bat.

Dean Hill

Guerrero, Pedro Bats: Right Throws: Right Born 06/29/56

1987 SEASON AND MAJOR-LEAGUE CAREER BATTING TOTALS

	G	AB	H	2B	3B	HR	TB	R	RBI	TBB	IBB	SO	HP	SH	SF	SB	CS	SB%	GDP	AVG	OBP	SLG
87 LA	152	545	184	25	2	27	294	89	89	74	18	85	4	0	7	9	7	.56	16	.338	.416	.539
10 YEARS	977	3387	1049	162	23	166	1755	537	550	392	74	578	21	9	34	84	41	.67	70	.310	.381	.518

	1987 SEASON											TWO YEAR TOTALS (1986 – 1987)										
	Ave.	OBP	SLG	AB	H	2B	3B	HR	RBI	BB	SO	Ave.	OBP	SLG	AB	H	2B	3B	HR	RBI	BB	SO
Totals	.338	.416	.539	545	184	25	2	27	89	74	85	.328	.403	.540	606	199	28	2	32	99	76	104
vs. Left	.365	.451	.575	167	61	7	2	8	26	27	21	.362	.438	.582	196	71	9	2	10	30	27	32
vs. Right	.325	.400	.524	378	123	18	0	19	63	47	64	.312	.387	.520	410	128	19	0	22	69	49	72
at Home	.324	.397	.495	275	89	11	0	12	43	34	44	.315	.387	.483	298	94	11	0	13	48	35	51
on Road	.352	.434	.585	270	95	14	2	15	46	40	41	.341	.419	.594	308	105	17	2	19	51	41	53
vs. Groundball	.318	.401	.441	261	83	8	0	8	36	36	43	.312	.392	.443	282	88	10	0	9	38	36	49
vs. Flyball	.356	.430	.630	284	101	17	2	19	53	38	42	.343	.414	.623	324	111	18	2	23	61	40	55
vs. Finesse	.334	.390	.541	320	107	18	0	16	50	29	36	.328	.381	.526	348	114	18	0	17	52	30	43
vs. Power	.342	.449	.538	225	77	7	2	11	39	45	49	.329	.431	.558	258	85	10	2	15	47	46	61
on Grass	.333	.414	.528	415	138	16	1	21	69	56	69	.325	.403	.534	461	150	19	1	25	78	57	82
on Artificial Turf	.354	.421	.577	130	46	9	1	6	20	18	16	.338	.405	.559	145	49	9	1	7	21	19	22
Day Games	.341	.405	.616	164	56	9	0	12	32	18	20	.341	.405	.616	164	56	9	0	12	32	18	20
Night Games	.336	.420	.507	381	128	16	2	15	57	56	65	.324	.403	.511	442	143	19	2	20	67	58	84
April	.333	.410	.653	72	24	4	2	5	18	9	13	.333	.410	.653	72	24	4	2	5	18	9	13
May	.381	.426	.701	97	37	4	0	9	22	9	20	.381	.426	.701	97	37	4	0	9	22	9	20
June	.238	.325	.317	101	24	2	0	2	8	13	19	.238	.325	.317	101	24	2	0	2	8	13	19
July	.415	.520	.683	82	34	4	0	6	16	19	12	.415	.520	.683	82	34	4	0	6	16	19	12
August	.255	.317	.340	94	24	5	0	1	5	8	12	.238	.297	.317	101	24	5	0	1	5	8	16
Sept/Oct	.414	.500	.596	99	41	6	0	4	20	16	9	.366	.439	.601	153	56	9	0	9	30	18	24
Bases Empty	.338	.412	.560	302	102	15	2	16	16	36	46	.340	.410	.578	332	113	18	2	19	19	37	54
Leadoff	.297	.391	.532	111	33	7	2	5	5	16	19	.315	.397	.605	124	39	8	2	8	8	16	25
Not Leadoff	.361	.425	.576	191	69	8	0	11	11	20	27	.356	.417	.563	208	74	10	0	11	11	21	29
Runners On	.337	.421	.514	243	82	10	0	11	73	38	39	.314	.396	.493	274	86	10	0	13	80	39	50
First Base Only	.331	.368	.492	118	39	7	0	4	10	6	18	.315	.360	.465	127	40	7	0	4	10	7	22
Scoring Position	.344	.461	.536	125	43	3	0	7	63	32	21	.313	.422	.517	147	46	3	0	9	70	32	28
Late Innings, Close	.272	.412	.420	81	22	6	0	2	11	20	14	.272	.412	.420	162	44	12	0	4	22	40	28

RBI/Opportunities

	1987			Two Year		
Scoring Position	51 / 181	(28%)		55 / 206	(27%)	
Scoring Position, 2 Out	15 / 69	(22%)		15 / 81	(19%)	
On Third, Less than 2 Out	25 / 44	(57%)		27 / 48	(56%)	
RBI in close games / RBI Total	62 / 89	(70%)		124 / 99	(125%)	

Ron Guidry
New York Yankees

Ron Guidry didn't get to have very much of a season in 1987. His year began badly when management's stupidity and his own stubbornness allowed $50,000 to keep him from re-signing before the deadline. Ron had to wait until May to be a Yankee again; by the time he got into a major league game, it was May 24. He waited until June 9 to break into the rotation; by September 6 (due to a slight tear in his rotator cuff), his year was over.

In between the late start and the early finish, Guidry didn't pitch that badly, but he finished with a losing record for the second consecutive year. His ERA was second only to Charles Hudson among Yankee starters and wasn't all that bad in these days of inflated run totals; he allowed only two unearned runs. He allowed fewer hits than innings pitched, fanned 7.34 men per nine innings and walked only 2.91.

Why Ron didn't have a winning season is fairly obvious to anyone who looks at the support he received. In 1987, Yankee batters scored 4.90 runs per game, but they didn't distribute it equally. Dennis Rasmussen (9–7, 4.75) got 6.35 R/G to work with. Tommy John (13–6, 4.03) got 5.56. Hudson (11–7, 3.61) got 5.53. Ron (5–8, 3.67) got 3.37 runs per start; the only Yankee starter with less than 4.00. Using Bill James's Pythagorean projection method, he won just about the number of games that he should have won, so we can say that he was just the victim of bad luck. It's awfully hard to win games when your teammates don't score any runs; it's the second straight season that Guidry has been victimized by his offense.

There's an old saying about power pitchers that goes "Get to them early or you won't get to them at all"; Ron certainly fit the pattern this year. In the first inning of his 17 starts, he struck out 15 men, but allowed 27 hits, 21 runs, 14 walks and seven homers, for a whopping 11.12 ERA. In the 93.1 other innings he pitched as a starter, he got 74 whiffs, allowed 76 hits, 28 runs (one unearned), 23 walks and seven homers. His ERA was 2.41.

If Ron can recover from his shoulder surgery, 1988 should be a perfect year for him to rebound. Billy Martin always improves the offense; his run support should be up. Moreover, Ron seems to enjoy playing for Martin and has always pitched well for him. His record with Martin as manager is 102–33 (.756); he's gone 61–47 (.565) with others at the helm. Guidry has won 20 games only three times in his career; Billy has been around for part of the year in every case. The only problem is that both Guidry and Billy don't seem to realize that the innings he piles up in those good years are largely to blame for the bad ones. Or, at least, Ron doesn't seem to realize it—and Billy consistently refuses to believe it.

Craig Christmann

Guidry, Ronald Ames "Ron"   Bats: Left   Throws: Left   Born 08/28/50

1987 SEASON AND MAJOR-LEAGUE CAREER PITCHING TOTALS

	G	GS	CG	GF	IP	BFP	H	R	ER	HR	SH	SF	HB	TBB	IBB	SO	WP	Bk	W	L	Pct	ShO	Sv	ERA
87 NYA	22	17	2	2	118	493	111	50	48	14	4	2	1	38	3	96	3	1	5	8	.385	0	0	3.66
13 YEARS	356	313	95	23	2337	9555	2141	925	848	219	69	64	11	618	21	1746	54	6	168	88	.656	26	4	3.27

1987: Power, Flyball   1986: Finesse, Flyball   1985: Finesse, Flyball   1984: Finesse, Flyball

	1987 SEASON											FOUR YEAR TOTALS (1984 – 1987)										
	G	IP	H	BB	SO	SB	CS	W	L	S	ERA	G	IP	H	BB	SO	SB	CS	W	L	S	ERA
Totals	22	117.2	111	38	96	14	5	5	8	0	3.67	115	764.2	779	162	506	51	31	46	37	0	3.81
at Home	12	59.1	49	17	50	8	3	2	4	0	2.58	62	419.0	416	73	285	26	22	29	16	0	3.26
on Road	10	58.1	62	21	46	6	2	3	4	0	4.78	53	345.2	363	89	221	25	9	17	21	0	4.50
on Grass	8	38.1	33	10	33	7	1	2	1	0	2.35	39	254.2	233	59	175	20	10	19	9	0	3.18
on Artificial Turf	14	79.1	78	28	63	7	4	3	7	0	4.31	76	510.0	546	103	331	31	21	27	28	0	4.15
Day Games	19	95.0	91	33	76	13	4	4	7	0	3.79	101	673.1	690	143	451	49	29	41	32	0	3.73
Night Games	3	22.2	20	5	20	1	1	1	1	0	3.18	14	91.1	89	19	55	2	2	5	5	0	4.53
April	0	0.0	0	0	0	0	0	0	0	0	0.00	15	106.0	103	24	65	7	5	5	5	0	3.48
May	4	6.1	7	1	6	2	0	0	1	0	2.84	22	134.1	126	24	86	13	6	7	7	0	3.55
June	6	29.2	30	7	24	2	1	1	2	0	3.03	23	144.1	161	27	92	10	3	8	7	0	3.80
July	6	42.1	37	12	35	5	2	2	1	0	2.34	19	137.1	131	32	86	9	6	10	5	0	3.34
August	5	32.2	33	15	31	4	2	1	4	0	5.79	19	130.0	137	30	107	8	5	6	8	0	4.22
Sept/Oct	1	6.2	4	3	0	1	0	1	0	0	5.40	17	112.2	121	25	70	4	6	10	5	0	4.63

vs. Opponent Batters	Ave.	OBP	SLG	AB	H	2B	3B	HR	RBI	BB	SO	Ave.	OBP	SLG	AB	H	2B	3B	HR	RBI	BB	SO
Totals	.248	.307	.417	448	111	26	4	14	47	38	96	.263	.301	.420	2966	779	138	24	94	315	162	506
vs. Left	.305	.367	.463	82	25	4	0	3	6	7	18	.258	.293	.395	534	138	16	3	17	50	25	99
vs. Right	.235	.293	.407	366	86	22	4	11	41	31	78	.264	.303	.426	2432	641	122	21	77	265	137	407
Bases Empty	.250	.318	.438	272	68	14	2	11	11	27	52	.262	.303	.420	1791	470	70	16	60	60	103	306
Leadoff	.196	.262	.366	112	22	5	1	4	4	10	19	.273	.310	.431	751	205	30	7	25	25	40	117
Not Leadoff	.287	.356	.488	160	46	9	1	7	7	17	33	.255	.297	.412	1040	265	40	9	35	35	63	189
Runners On Base	.244	.289	.386	176	43	12	2	3	36	11	44	.263	.298	.421	1175	309	68	8	34	255	59	200
First Base Only	.219	.260	.342	73	16	3	0	2	4	3	21	.278	.302	.436	551	153	33	3	16	42	18	91
Scoring Position	.262	.310	.417	103	27	9	2	1	32	8	23	.250	.295	.409	624	156	35	5	18	213	41	109
Late Innings, Close	.333	.378	.571	42	14	2	1	2	5	3	6	.310	.343	.469	303	94	15	3	9	35	15	45

RBI/Opportunities

Scoring Position	26 / 130 (20%)	181 / 788 (23%)
Scoring Position, 2 Out	14 / 72 (19%)	76 / 364 (21%)
On Third, Less than 2 Out	6 / 14 (43%)	63 / 120 (53%)
RBI in close games / RBI Total	30 / 47 (64%)	229 / 315 (73%)

Ozzie Guillen
Chicago White Sox

"Ozzie Guillen . . . batting leadoff!"

Yes, sabermetricians, things like this can happen, even in your golden age. It wasn't Chuck Tanner who pulled this move, either, or Ralph Houk (Ralph wouldn't have done it anyway; Ozzie's not a second baseman). It was Jim Fregosi, a man evidently in control of his senses. Fregosi chose Ozzie Guillen, who in his greatest season drew 22 walks and had an on base average of .303, to be his leadoff batter against righthanders.

And it worked. It worked brilliantly, in fact.

Guillen started 55 games as the White Sox leadoff hitter. The Sox were 33–22 in those games, a .600 winning percentage; with other leadoff men they played .411. The Sox averaged 5.49 runs per game with Guillen hitting first; with the other guys they averaged 4.17. In those 55 games Guillen batted .347 (83 for 239). "Old Eagle Eye" drew only eleven walks, but that was half his season total, and anyway, his on-base percentage was a fine .373; my hero, Gary Redus, had only a .357 OBA when he led off.

Ozzie hit thirteen doubles in the 55 games—he had only nine more in all his other games—and stole thirteen bases as well. To put an exclamation point on the whole thing, he scored 42 runs in those 55 games; that would project to 124 runs for a full season schedule.

Now, it's true that all those games were against right-handers, and Ozzie has hit much better against righties in his career. It's also true that a lot of the games came late in the year, when the Sox were playing very well, but heck, when your leadoff man is batting .347, that by itself is going to help you play well. More fundamentally, it's very, very true that this is the sort of thing that defies rational explanation. But it shows, pretty clearly, that playing your hunches still has its place in this game. When Fregosi put Guillen in the leadoff spot, the Sox were playing terribly; the man was desperate, so he took a chance. When the idea worked, he stayed with it, and it didn't matter if you or I or whoever thought it was a dumb move that went against all the percentages. I suppose one difference between a good manager and a bad one is that the good one will go against the grain sometimes; the trick is knowing that it's a long shot, and that once it stops working it's not likely to work again for a long while.

I personally think Fregosi is a good manager; my guess is that he would have yanked Guillen from the leadoff spot as soon as he started to cool off. But Ozzie never did. Who knows? Maybe he never will.

I can't wait to see the headline next spring: "KARKOVICE TO BAT CLEANUP."

Don Zminda

Guillen, Oswaldo Jose (Barrios) "Ozzie"　　　　Bats: Left　　Throws: Right　　Born 01/20/64

1987 SEASON AND MAJOR-LEAGUE CAREER BATTING TOTALS

	G	AB	H	2B	3B	HR	TB	R	RBI	TBB	IBB	SO	HP	SH	SF	SB	CS	SB%	GDP	AVG	OBP	SLG
87 CHA	149	560	156	22	7	2	198	64	51	22	2	52	1	13	8	25	8	.76	10	.279	.303	.354
3 YEARS	458	1598	427	62	20	5	544	193	131	46	4	140	3	33	14	40	16	.71	29	.267	.287	.340

	1987 SEASON											FOUR YEAR TOTALS (1984 – 1987)									
	Ave.	OBP	SLG	AB	H	2B	3B	HR	RBI	BB	SO	Ave.	OBP	SLG	AB	H	2B	3B	HR	RBI	BB	SO
Totals	.279	.303	.354	560	156	22	7	2	51	22	52	.267	.287	.340	1598	427	62	20	5	131	46	140
vs. Left	.201	.227	.238	164	33	4	1	0	10	6	18	.226	.249	.264	421	95	9	2	1	29	13	48
vs. Right	.311	.334	.402	396	123	18	6	2	41	16	34	.282	.300	.368	1177	332	53	18	4	102	33	92
at Home	.316	.352	.409	269	85	11	4	2	32	17	20	.283	.305	.363	785	222	27	12	4	75	29	60
on Road	.244	.256	.302	291	71	11	3	0	19	5	32	.252	.268	.319	813	205	35	8	1	56	17	80
vs. Groundball	.322	.348	.412	289	93	13	5	1	24	15	20	.286	.309	.355	768	220	25	11	2	60	28	54
vs. Flyball	.232	.253	.292	271	63	9	2	1	27	7	32	.249	.265	.327	830	207	37	9	3	71	18	86
vs. Finesse	.281	.304	.369	306	86	14	5	1	30	12	22	.265	.284	.348	923	245	40	12	4	69	25	66
vs. Power	.276	.301	.335	254	70	8	2	1	21	10	30	.270	.291	.330	675	182	22	8	1	62	21	74
on Grass	.288	.312	.362	489	141	20	5	2	47	19	46	.272	.293	.347	1369	372	55	18	4	115	43	123
on Artificial Turf	.211	.240	.296	71	15	2	2	0	4	3	6	.240	.248	.301	229	55	7	2	1	16	3	17
Day Games	.306	.319	.363	157	48	5	2	0	11	4	11	.274	.292	.341	449	123	18	6	0	34	13	34
Night Games	.268	.297	.350	403	108	17	5	2	40	18	41	.265	.284	.340	1149	304	44	14	5	97	33	106
April	.317	.386	.413	63	20	4	1	0	2	7	6	.282	.330	.353	170	48	8	2	0	12	12	11
May	.299	.344	.391	87	26	1	2	1	7	5	11	.242	.270	.308	260	63	3	4	2	17	9	24
June	.250	.262	.310	100	25	4	1	0	8	2	5	.244	.260	.309	262	64	10	2	1	24	6	21
July	.290	.292	.327	107	31	4	0	0	11	2	10	.297	.310	.375	283	84	18	2	0	29	7	23
August	.301	.316	.381	113	34	5	2	0	8	3	11	.290	.303	.355	307	89	11	3	1	20	6	28
Sept/Oct	.222	.242	.322	90	20	4	1	1	15	3	9	.250	.262	.342	316	79	12	7	1	29	6	33
Bases Empty	.291	.317	.374	350	102	15	7	0	0	12	37	.258	.280	.333	965	249	35	14	3	3	28	99
Leadoff	.329	.360	.402	164	54	8	2	0	0	8	19	.275	.300	.332	422	116	16	4	0	0	15	51
Not Leadoff	.258	.277	.349	186	48	7	5	0	0	4	18	.245	.264	.333	543	133	19	10	3	3	13	48
Runners On	.257	.281	.319	210	54	7	0	2	51	10	15	.281	.297	.352	633	178	27	6	2	128	18	41
First Base Only	.213	.213	.292	89	19	4	0	1	2	0	6	.255	.260	.324	275	70	16	0	1	3	2	19
Scoring Position	.289	.324	.339	121	35	3	0	1	49	10	9	.302	.325	.374	358	108	11	6	1	125	16	22
Late Innings, Close	.278	.301	.351	97	27	2	1	1	8	3	10	.296	.318	.358	274	81	5	3	2	23	9	24

RBI/Opportunities

Scoring Position	48 / 167 (29%)	120 / 470 (26%)
Scoring Position, 2 Out	13 / 70 (19%)	46 / 219 (21%)
On Third, Less than 2 Out	27 / 41 (66%)	50 / 92 (54%)
RBI in close games / RBI Total	30 / 51 (59%)	78 / 131 (60%)

Bill Gullickson
Cincinnati Reds/New York Yankees

William Lee Gullickson continued his enigmatic ways in 1987. His overall 14–13 record placed him on a stately level of consistency with Jack Morris, as the only two pitchers who have 12+ victories and a winning percentage in every one of the last 5 seasons. (Lower the Win requirement to 10 per year, and John Tudor could join the club.) Bill Gullickson has been one of the most durable and consistent pitchers of the decade. Since 1982, Bill has been good for at least 29 starts a year (matched only by Hough, Morris, Rhoden, Ryan, Stieb, Sutton, Valenzuela, and Welch). In 1987, however, Gullickson had his ups and downs on the way to this lofty plateau.

At the end of April, Bill looked invincible. He was off to a 3–0 start, with a 1.47 ERA and a phenomenal Hits Plus Walks per Inning Ratio of 0.75. At this time, Eric Davis was hitting around .400, Kal Daniels and Dave Parker led the league in HR, and even Bo Diaz was atop the NL in RBI. John Franco had not yet given up a run. Every indication was that Gullickson would finally have his 20-win season, and the Reds would go to the World Series. But as the record shows, things came unglued.

The undoing of Gullickson's 1987 involved excessive generosity with the long ball: 40 HR for the year in total. It is not true that Bill was actually competing with Sprint and MCI for market share, but it is understandable that such rumors got started. From early May until he left the Reds in August, Gullickson gave up .061 HR per AB, which by coincidence is exactly the lifetime average of Henry Aaron. Someone who knows StratOMatic could explain this better than I can, but it is intuitively obvious that you cannot be a great pitcher if every hitter on the other team (including their pitcher and shortstop) is Henry Aaron.

To give credit where due, Gullickson did, in fact, produce a fine first half in 1987, standing 9–5 at the All-Star break. Considering his 10–6 mark in the second half of 1986, it could be argued that Bill has just as much 20-win potential now as he did several years ago. His physical abilities remain essentially intact, and he has 8 years of major league experience working the corners, spotting his fastball, and throwing his breaking stuff from behind in the count.

When Gullickson was traded for Dennis Rasmussen, there was considerable reaction among Yankee fans that George had thrown away another great young talent in exchange for a washed-up has-been. People who think this way are probably unaware that Old Bill and Young Dennis are only 8 weeks apart in age. The big difference is that Gullickson had become a major league success at age 21. In 1980 for Montreal, he went 10–5 with a 3.00 ERA, struck out 18 in one game, and was named Rookie Pitcher of the Year, while Rasmussen was toiling in Salinas to produce 4 wins and a 5.45 ERA. In 1988 Rasmussen will be toiling for the Reds, but Gullickson will be working in the Japanese league. Is this what's known as a "trade deficit"?

John C. Benson

Gullickson, William Lee "Bill"   Bats: Right   Throws: Right   Born 02/20/59

1987 SEASON AND MAJOR-LEAGUE CAREER PITCHING TOTALS

	G	GS	CG	GF	IP	BFP	H	R	ER	HR	SH	SF	HB	TBB	IBB	SO	WP	Bk	W	L	Pct	ShO	Sv	ERA
87 CIN-NYA	35	35	4	0	213	896	218	128	115	40	8	8	3	50	7	117	4	1	14	13	.519	1	0	4.86
9 YEARS	248	242	41	2	1644	6805	1612	725	660	152	61	52	21	398	45	916	36	6	101	86	.540	9	0	3.61

1987: Finesse, Flyball   1986: Finesse, Flyball   1985: Finesse, Flyball   1984: Finesse, Flyball

1987 SEASON

	G	IP	H	BB	SO	SB	CS	W	L	S	ERA
Totals	35	213.0	218	50	117	24	8	14	13	0	4.86
at Home	19	115.1	122	25	65	14	2	9	6	0	5.31
on Road	16	97.2	96	25	52	10	6	5	7	0	4.33
on Grass	15	94.2	99	20	54	8	4	9	6	0	4.94
on Artificial Turf	20	118.1	119	30	63	16	4	5	7	0	4.79
Day Games	15	91.1	87	22	49	8	6	6	6	0	4.83
Night Games	20	121.2	131	28	68	16	2	8	7	0	4.88
April	5	33.2	26	4	18	1	2	3	1	0	2.41
May	6	39.2	40	7	28	6	2	4	1	0	4.54
June	6	29.0	39	8	14	4	1	0	3	0	7.76
July	5	33.2	33	11	14	4	0	3	2	0	3.74
August	6	36.1	39	11	17	4	2	1	4	0	5.45
Sept/Oct	7	40.2	41	9	26	5	1	3	2	0	5.53

FOUR YEAR TOTALS (1984 – 1987)

	G	IP	H	BB	SO	SB	CS	W	L	S	ERA
Totals	133	865.2	880	194	406	88	35	55	46	0	3.83
at Home	68	460.2	446	95	232	39	13	35	17	0	3.52
on Road	65	405.0	434	99	174	49	22	20	29	0	4.20
on Grass	48	302.0	317	68	136	34	13	25	14	0	4.08
on Artificial Turf	85	563.2	563	126	270	54	22	30	32	0	3.70
Day Games	44	266.0	288	62	122	27	14	13	19	0	4.57
Night Games	89	599.2	592	132	284	61	21	42	27	0	3.50
April	17	101.1	102	27	41	10	9	6	7	0	4.00
May	24	154.1	158	33	76	24	8	12	9	0	4.02
June	18	114.0	122	23	47	9	3	5	5	0	4.11
July	22	153.2	148	39	71	12	4	10	6	0	3.22
August	25	180.0	162	30	93	13	6	13	8	0	2.70
Sept/Oct	27	162.1	188	42	78	20	5	9	11	0	5.21

vs. Opponent Batters	Ave.	OBP	SLG	AB	H	2B	3B	HR	RBI	BB	SO
Totals	.264	.305	.473	827	218	43	5	40	114	50	117
vs. Left	.269	.314	.494	439	118	23	2	24	61	30	45
vs. Right	.258	.294	.448	388	100	20	3	16	53	20	72
Bases Empty	.253	.295	.469	529	134	21	3	29	29	30	83
Leadoff	.261	.294	.412	211	55	9	1	7	7	10	30
Not Leadoff	.248	.295	.506	318	79	12	2	22	22	20	53
Runners On Base	.282	.323	.480	298	84	22	2	11	85	20	34
First Base Only	.286	.325	.462	119	34	7	1	4	12	7	11
Scoring Position	.279	.322	.492	179	50	15	1	7	73	13	23
Late Innings, Close	.306	.342	.444	36	11	2	0	1	3	2	4

vs. Opponent Batters	Ave.	OBP	SLG	AB	H	2B	3B	HR	RBI	BB	SO
Totals	.266	.306	.418	3314	880	163	22	99	371	194	406
vs. Left	.270	.318	.422	1735	469	85	14	50	175	123	174
vs. Right	.260	.292	.413	1579	411	78	8	49	196	71	232
Bases Empty	.259	.297	.419	2070	537	97	12	70	70	109	273
Leadoff	.271	.309	.413	850	230	39	5	24	24	47	97
Not Leadoff	.252	.288	.424	1220	307	58	7	46	46	62	176
Runners On Base	.276	.321	.415	1244	343	66	10	29	301	85	133
First Base Only	.301	.328	.439	522	157	25	4	13	41	21	53
Scoring Position	.258	.317	.398	722	186	41	6	16	260	64	80
Late Innings, Close	.241	.292	.316	307	74	12	1	3	16	22	30

RBI/Opportunities

Scoring Position	62 / 222	(28%)
Scoring Position, 2 Out	22 / 109	(20%)
On Third, Less than 2 Out	24 / 35	(69%)
RBI in close games / RBI Total	63 / 114	(55%)

	226 / 929	(24%)
	81 / 431	(19%)
	100 / 164	(61%)
	252 / 371	(68%)

Jose Guzman
Texas Rangers

On August 20, Guzman had his best start of the year as he beat Chicago 5–1 in a complete game three-hitter. Although Jose was scheduled to get 4 days of rest and start again on the 25th, he was brought in as a reliever on the 23rd and threw two innings, allowing one run. He then went on to make his scheduled start on the 25th and was bombed. He allowed 5 runs in 5 2/3 innings, and it could have been worse as he allowed 14 base-runners including 7 walks.

While the Rangers did not routinely use such odd rest patterns, they did it more often than anyone else. They led the majors in starts that occurred with less than three days' rest since the pitchers last appearance. (Nine, which is about three times the average; no other team had more than 5.)

The results were pretty horrible:

W–L	IP	H	R	ER	W	K	ERA
1–3	41.3	51	36	30	44	34	6.53

The only other time they did this with Guzman, he allowed 9 walks in 6 1/3 innings. Other than those two starts on very short rest, he never walked more than 5 men in any other start. Needless to say, that bit of Ranger innovation is destined for the scrap pile.

That horrendous start on August 25 is worth mentioning in another regard. It was Guzman's only bad start in his last 11 outings. In the other 10 starts he never allowed more than 4 runs or more hits than innings pitched.

LAST 11 STARTS MINUS AUGUST 25TH

W–L	IP	H	R	ER	W	K	ERA
5–3	65	47	25	23	28	8	3.18

Now history says that it is best to be cautious about projecting strong finishes into future performance. In Jose's case there is more reason to be optimistic. He may be getting control of his congenital back problem which has plagued him off and on throughout his professional career. It was a major factor in his incredibly awful start in 1987.

The shock of seeing his career severely threatened shook Guzman out of a rather immature attitude toward his back trouble. He's always had instructions for nutrition and exercise that would help keep his back problems in check, but he tended to follow the prescribed programs only to the point where he would be feeling better. This season seems to have convinced Jose that he needs to stay consistently with the programs for prevention purposes rather than just recovery. The hope is that if Guzman does what he should to control his back problem, he could pitch with the quality and consistency he showed at the end of 1987.

Craig R. Wright

Guzman, Jose Alberto (Mirabal) Bats: Right Throws: Right Born 04/09/63

1987 SEASON AND MAJOR-LEAGUE CAREER PITCHING TOTALS

	G	GS	CG	GF	IP	BFP	H	R	ER	HR	SH	SF	HB	TBB	IBB	SO	WP	Bk	W	L	Pct	ShO	Sv	ERA
87 TEX	37	30	6	1	208	880	196	115	108	30	6	8	3	82	0	143	6	5	14	14	.500	0	0	4.67
3 YEARS	71	64	8	1	413	1777	422	229	205	56	13	12	9	156	3	254	10	5	26	31	.456	0	0	4.47

1987: Power, Groundball   1986: Finesse, Groundball   1985: Power, Flyball

1987 SEASON

	G	IP	H	BB	SO	SB	CS	W	L	S	ERA
Totals	37	208.1	196	82	143	32	3	14	14	0	4.67
at Home	21	108.1	105	39	68	16	1	9	9	0	4.98
on Road	16	100.0	91	43	75	16	2	5	5	0	4.32
on Grass	4	23.0	28	6	16	1	1	0	2	0	4.70
on Artificial Turf	33	185.1	168	76	127	31	2	14	12	0	4.66
Day Games	32	182.2	172	71	121	25	3	13	12	0	4.53
Night Games	5	25.2	24	11	22	7	0	1	2	0	5.61
April	4	18.0	18	5	7	1	1	1	1	0	5.50
May	6	26.1	41	12	18	3	2	1	4	0	8.54
June	6	36.1	26	4	29	0	0	4	1	0	2.48
July	6	38.1	40	12	21	10	0	2	4	0	5.40
August	8	33.1	27	26	24	12	0	2	1	0	4.59
Sept/Oct	7	56.0	44	23	44	6	0	4	3	0	3.54

vs. Opponent Batters	Ave.	OBP	SLG	AB	H	2B	3B	HR	RBI	BB	SO
Totals	.251	.322	.420	781	196	40	1	30	99	82	143
vs. Left	.240	.300	.363	408	98	17	0	11	49	34	72
vs. Right	.263	.344	.483	373	98	23	1	19	50	48	71
Bases Empty	.229	.310	.389	476	109	28	0	16	16	54	93
Leadoff	.210	.279	.320	200	42	10	0	4	4	18	44
Not Leadoff	.243	.332	.438	276	67	18	0	12	12	36	49
Runners On Base	.285	.339	.469	305	87	12	1	14	83	28	50
First Base Only	.313	.353	.563	128	40	9	1	7	15	8	17
Scoring Position	.266	.330	.401	177	47	3	0	7	68	20	33
Late Innings, Close	.250	.291	.404	52	13	3	1	1	3	3	9

FOUR YEAR TOTALS (1984 – 1987)

	G	IP	H	BB	SO	SB	CS	W	L	S	ERA
Totals	71	413.1	422	156	254	53	8	26	31	0	4.46
at Home	41	234.1	240	83	141	27	6	18	16	0	4.11
on Road	30	179.0	182	73	113	26	2	8	15	0	4.93
on Grass	11	60.1	74	21	44	10	1	1	7	0	5.37
on Artificial Turf	60	353.0	348	135	210	43	7	25	24	0	4.31
Day Games	62	364.2	372	140	220	45	8	24	27	0	4.32
Night Games	9	48.2	50	16	34	8	0	2	4	0	5.55
April	9	45.2	55	12	20	5	2	2	5	0	5.52
May	11	59.0	74	24	37	5	3	4	5	0	5.03
June	12	78.2	70	19	53	6	1	7	4	0	3.55
July	11	67.0	72	25	39	15	1	3	6	0	4.57
August	12	53.0	54	34	31	12	1	3	3	0	5.60
Sept/Oct	16	110.0	97	42	74	10	0	7	8	0	3.76

vs. Opponent Batters	Ave.	OBP	SLG	AB	H	2B	3B	HR	RBI	BB	SO
Totals	.266	.331	.423	1587	422	80	1	56	188	156	254
vs. Left	.270	.327	.414	853	230	45	0	26	101	72	128
vs. Right	.262	.336	.435	734	192	35	1	30	87	84	126
Bases Empty	.258	.321	.409	962	248	52	0	31	31	87	164
Leadoff	.231	.295	.362	403	93	20	0	11	11	36	76
Not Leadoff	.277	.339	.442	559	155	32	0	20	20	51	88
Runners On Base	.278	.347	.446	625	174	28	1	25	157	69	90
First Base Only	.323	.379	.549	266	86	19	1	13	31	24	31
Scoring Position	.245	.324	.370	359	88	9	0	12	126	45	59
Late Innings, Close	.280	.347	.411	107	30	6	1	2	8	11	14

RBI/Opportunities

Scoring Position	57 / 237 (24%)	106 / 488 (22%)
Scoring Position, 2 Out	17 / 105 (16%)	32 / 211 (15%)
On Third, Less than 2 Out	23 / 41 (56%)	45 / 90 (50%)
RBI in close games / RBI Total	62 / 99 (63%)	125 / 188 (66%)

Tony Gwynn
San Diego Padres

Tony Gwynn just keeps getting better. He's been making magic with his bat long enough that most of you are probably thinking in terms of a possible Hall of Fame career. Although we can argue for a long time about standards for entry, Tony probably needs at least 2800 hits to have a decent shot. According to the Favorite Toy method, Tony has about a 30 percent shot at 2800 hits, and, to reach 3000, he will need to perform at a level seldom reached in baseball history. Tony needs 2012 more hits, which is 10 years of production at the sustained level of his last three seasons, and basically means Tony will need to average 200 hits per year during his thirties. Pete Rose did that (202.5), and so did Ty Cobb (209). It also means that Tony will need to average 200 hits per year for 13 consecutive years. Pete Rose averaged 200+ hits per year from 1965 to 1980, 16 years. Cobb never made it to 14. Tony's as good a pure hitter as there is in the National League, but that's a hell of a mountain to climb.

In 1987, Tony set personal highs for runs, hits, doubles, triples, walks, BA, steals, SB%, total bases, and slugging average. Many of these also set team standards. To top it off, he won his second consecutive Gold Glove.

Gwynn had his off-field problems last year—he filed bankruptcy when his agent's investment program return fell well below the Mendoza line. Tony refused to discuss this, feeling it wasn't important to his performance between the white lines.

As good as 1987 was, it brought out his most glaring weakness—RBI's. Tony's .370 BA was a truly marvelous season—the eighth best batting average in the past 50 years. However, he achieved a singular honor—no other player in the modern era has hit .370 or better and failed to drive in at least 60 runs (playing in at least 100 games). In 1974 Rod Carew came close, driving in 55 runs while hitting .364, but Rod hit leadoff. Only Wee Willie Keeler in 1898 (.379, 44 RBI) and John McGraw in 1899 (.391, 33 RBI, 399 AB) come close, and they each played in 25 percent fewer games. With his OBA of .447, perhaps Tony will find a home in the leadoff spot this year.

Gwynn had a quest to steal more bases than his previous major league high of 37. Gwynn stole 56 in 1987, second to Vince Coleman's 109. He was first in hits (218), second in triples (13), and OBA (.447). He scored a career-high 119 runs, and tallied 82 walks, 25 intentional.

As stated above, Tony has a tough row to hoe for 3,000 hits—but, in this inflated era, it would be absolutely criminal for anyone to downgrade his talents and accomplishments if he winds up with 2,500—this is, unquestionably, one of the finest pure hitters of our lifetime; a joy to watch on the field, a bright and personable guy off the field. Congratulations to Dennis Brctz, who owns an autographed rookie card of Tony's.

J. Michael Duca, Brigg Hewitt and Bruce Erricson

Gwynn, Anthony Keith "Tony"

Bats: Left Throws: Left Born 05/09/60

1987 SEASON AND MAJOR-LEAGUE CAREER BATTING TOTALS

	G	AB	H	2B	3B	HR	TB	R	RBI	TBB	IBB	SO	HP	SH	SF	SB	CS	SB%	GDP	AVG	OBP	SLG
87 SD	157	589	218	36	13	7	301	119	54	82	26	35	3	2	4	56	12	.82	13	.370	.447	.511
6 YEARS	769	2953	988	143	39	34	1311	471	284	275	59	163	10	19	13	155	57	.73	79	.335	.392	.444

	1987 SEASON											FOUR YEAR TOTALS (1984 – 1987)										
	Ave.	OBP	SLG	AB	H	2B	3B	HR	RBI	BB	SO	Ave.	OBP	SLG	AB	H	2B	3B	HR	RBI	BB	SO
Totals	.370	.447	.511	589	218	36	13	7	54	82	35	.341	.400	.457	2459	839	119	35	32	230	238	126
vs. Left	.361	.433	.470	249	90	12	3	3	20	30	10	.324	.387	.431	891	289	34	11	13	82	87	48
vs. Right	.376	.457	.541	340	128	24	10	4	34	52	25	.351	.408	.472	1568	550	85	24	19	148	151	78
at Home	.390	.473	.574	282	110	15	11	5	25	44	19	.357	.413	.492	1218	435	57	25	19	111	114	68
on Road	.352	.423	.453	307	108	21	2	2	29	38	16	.326	.388	.423	1241	404	62	10	13	119	124	58
vs. Groundball	.357	.435	.529	272	97	15	10	4	26	36	20	.332	.389	.448	1243	413	57	21	15	111	111	54
vs. Flyball	.382	.458	.495	317	121	21	3	3	28	46	15	.350	.412	.466	1216	426	62	14	17	119	127	72
vs. Finesse	.390	.439	.546	313	122	23	7	4	28	27	14	.347	.393	.468	1352	469	76	17	18	119	97	46
vs. Power	.348	.455	.471	276	96	13	6	3	26	55	21	.334	.409	.444	1107	370	43	18	14	111	141	80
on Grass	.374	.452	.529	425	159	24	12	6	40	58	26	.344	.401	.464	1811	623	86	30	24	165	166	97
on Artificial Turf	.360	.435	.463	164	59	12	1	1	14	24	9	.333	.399	.437	648	216	33	5	8	65	72	29
Day Games	.333	.425	.476	189	63	12	3	3	17	29	13	.319	.390	.431	777	248	37	7	12	83	91	41
Night Games	.387	.458	.527	400	155	24	10	4	37	53	22	.351	.405	.469	1682	591	82	28	20	147	147	85
April	.333	.381	.467	90	30	4	1	2	7	7	6	.347	.398	.503	334	116	21	5	7	26	28	22
May	.337	.447	.484	95	32	9	1	1	7	17	5	.312	.400	.427	382	119	18	7	4	31	54	21
June	.473	.524	.667	93	44	5	5	1	16	11	3	.375	.426	.526	443	166	24	11	7	58	40	17
July	.292	.381	.396	96	28	5	1	1	9	15	9	.327	.367	.422	419	137	18	2	6	46	28	27
August	.402	.466	.556	117	47	9	3	1	10	13	7	.350	.400	.443	449	157	22	4	4	33	37	18
Sept/Oct	.378	.475	.490	98	37	4	2	1	5	19	5	.333	.403	.426	432	144	16	6	4	36	51	21
Bases Empty	.391	.447	.536	358	140	19	6	7	7	34	28	.337	.382	.459	1500	506	79	20	21	21	106	84
Leadoff	.348	.397	.474	135	47	4	2	3	3	10	12	.359	.396	.479	493	177	25	8	6	6	29	26
Not Leadoff	.417	.476	.574	223	93	15	4	4	4	24	16	.327	.375	.449	1007	329	54	12	15	15	77	58
Runners On	.338	.447	.472	231	78	17	7	0	47	48	7	.347	.425	.455	959	333	40	15	11	209	132	42
First Base Only	.381	.414	.571	105	40	10	5	0	8	6	1	.365	.404	.483	466	170	21	8	6	29	31	14
Scoring Position	.302	.468	.389	126	38	7	2	0	39	42	6	.331	.442	.428	493	163	19	7	5	180	101	28
Late Innings, Close	.341	.438	.466	88	30	6	1	1	7	16	10	.340	.423	.461	406	138	18	5	7	47	59	30

RBI/Opportunities

Scoring Position	36 / 196 (18%)	164 / 691 (24%)
Scoring Position, 2 Out	12 / 89 (13%)	63 / 306 (21%)
On Third, Less than 2 Out	18 / 34 (53%)	59 / 111 (53%)
RBI in close games / RBI Total	47 / 54 (87%)	161 / 230 (70%)

Mel Hall
Cleveland Indians

I have mixed feelings about simulation leagues. They help you look at players and teams more closely; that's good. But they can make you think that it's easy to run a baseball team. That's not so; at times, it can get downright tricky. Take, for example, Mel Hall. Everyone has an opinion about what to do with Mel. Each side can support their views. Let's run down the options; decide for yourself:

PLAY HIM EVERY DAY: Hall got the "can't hit left-ies" rap at age 22, by going 8–70 (.114) with no extra base hits and nine walks in his rookie season. Until 1987, he never had more than 26 ABs in a year against them again. Since (a) Hall can hit, (b) he hit lefties when given a chance in 1987 and (c) many other good players have had bad splits at age 22 (*e.g.,* Jesse Barfield hit .223 vs. righties at age 22 and never hit over .250 until age 25), he deserves a chance to play full-time.

PLATOON HIM: Mel's platoon partner (Carmen Castillo) has slugged .439 or better for the last five years. He has outslugged Mel in three of the four seasons that they have been teammates. Cleveland is getting more out of the combo than they would by making Hall a regular.

TRADE HIM: Hall is clearly not better than either Joe Carter or Cory Snyder. Also, Castillo hits the few righties he faces almost as well as lefties. Carmen has never had even 220 ABs in a year; if given 600, he might do as well as or better than Mel. Given the presence of Dave (.340 with 30 homers in AAA in '87) Clark, Hall should be traded.

KEEP HIM: Even if all of the above is true (and Snyder and Castillo have by no means proven to be superior to Mel), Hall and Clark are the only lefty power bats that Cleveland has. Only eight teams since 1969 (1981 included) won a pennant without having at least two lefty or switch hitters who reached double figures in homers in the lineup.

DH HIM: Excluding 1983 (when he played center field), Hall's lifetime range factor is 2.02; below average for a left fielder. Carter, Snyder and Clark all have better defensive stats, so Mel should DH.

DON'T DH HIM: Mel calls the DH job an unwarranted slur on his glove. That affects his hitting; through 1986, he'd hit .231 as the DH. He also worked very hard on his fielding in 1987 and improved his range factor to a creditable 2.16.

Not as easy as you thought, huh? Sure he can play; there are reasons why he should play left field for Cleveland. But he's 27, still hasn't had two straight good years (note his wretched OB% this year) and he's running out of time to prove himself. If Mel can't put it all together fast, I think that, like Mike Davis has just done, he'll end up leaving town via free agency with no regrets on either side.

Geoff Beckman

Hall, Melvin "Mel"

Bats: Left   Throws: Left   Born 09/16/60

1987 SEASON AND MAJOR-LEAGUE CAREER BATTING TOTALS

	G	AB	H	2B	3B	HR	TB	R	RBI	TBB	IBB	SO	HP	SH	SF	SB	CS	SB%	GDP	AVG	OBP	SLG
87 CLE	142	485	136	21	1	18	213	57	76	20	6	68	1	0	2	5	4	.56	7	.280	.309	.439
7 YEARS	582	1901	534	106	14	65	863	267	279	156	29	345	10	1	16	20	16	.56	26	.281	.336	.454

	1987 SEASON											FOUR YEAR TOTALS (1984 – 1987)									
	Ave.	OBP	SLG	AB	H	2B	3B	HR	RBI	BB	SO	Ave.	OBP	SLG	AB	H	2B	3B	HR	RBI	BB	SO
Totals	.280	.309	.439	485	136	21	1	18	76	20	68	.283	.334	.451	1400	396	80	7	47	217	109	223
vs. Left	.364	.417	.515	33	12	2	0	1	6	3	8	.214	.328	.296	98	21	5	0	1	10	17	26
vs. Right	.274	.301	.434	452	124	19	1	17	70	17	60	.288	.335	.462	1302	375	75	7	46	207	92	197
at Home	.288	.319	.441	222	64	10	0	8	39	10	25	.286	.333	.452	664	190	37	2	23	106	48	90
on Road	.274	.301	.437	263	72	11	1	10	37	10	43	.280	.335	.450	736	206	43	5	24	111	61	133
vs. Groundball	.318	.349	.539	267	85	12	1	15	50	12	31	.301	.349	.472	722	217	40	3	26	107	55	115
vs. Flyball	.234	.260	.317	218	51	9	0	3	26	8	37	.264	.318	.428	678	179	40	4	21	110	54	108
vs. Finesse	.308	.336	.515	237	73	14	1	11	40	10	25	.298	.340	.476	783	233	51	4	27	114	51	105
vs. Power	.254	.284	.367	248	63	7	0	7	36	10	43	.264	.327	.418	617	163	29	3	20	103	58	118
on Grass	.279	.300	.438	416	116	18	0	16	66	13	54	.281	.325	.446	1167	328	64	3	41	181	78	180
on Artificial Turf	.290	.359	.449	69	20	3	1	2	10	7	14	.292	.377	.472	233	68	16	4	6	36	31	43
Day Games	.297	.337	.539	165	49	10	0	10	29	11	29	.322	.374	.551	506	163	43	2	23	86	44	78
Night Games	.272	.294	.387	320	87	11	1	8	47	9	39	.261	.311	.394	894	233	37	5	24	131	65	145
April	.224	.274	.379	58	13	0	0	3	9	4	12	.251	.307	.392	199	50	10	0	6	33	16	37
May	.261	.270	.409	88	23	1	0	4	9	1	17	.273	.314	.481	231	63	15	3	9	28	14	41
June	.225	.262	.338	80	18	4	1	1	10	4	12	.307	.372	.516	244	75	14	2	11	46	25	37
July	.304	.321	.430	79	24	4	0	2	7	2	3	.264	.318	.413	242	64	10	1	8	34	19	39
August	.333	.359	.453	75	25	6	0	1	14	3	13	.303	.353	.410	234	71	14	1	3	33	18	37
Sept/Oct	.314	.351	.571	105	33	6	0	7	27	6	11	.292	.337	.480	250	73	17	0	10	43	17	32
Bases Empty	.287	.310	.476	275	79	13	0	13	13	8	38	.287	.331	.460	766	220	39	3	29	29	49	127
Leadoff	.269	.291	.508	130	35	4	0	9	9	4	19	.293	.322	.491	324	95	21	2	13	13	14	52
Not Leadoff	.303	.327	.448	145	44	9	0	4	4	4	19	.283	.337	.437	442	125	18	1	16	16	35	75
Runners On	.271	.308	.390	210	57	8	1	5	63	12	30	.278	.339	.440	634	176	41	4	18	188	60	96
First Base Only	.244	.261	.384	86	21	3	0	3	8	2	14	.261	.303	.433	261	68	13	1	10	27	16	50
Scoring Position	.290	.338	.395	124	36	5	1	2	55	10	16	.290	.363	.445	373	108	28	3	8	161	44	46
Late Innings, Close	.280	.299	.453	75	21	4	0	3	7	2	8	.296	.350	.495	206	61	14	0	9	35	17	24

RBI/Opportunities

	1987		Four Year	
Scoring Position	49 / 165	(30%)	139 / 498	(28%)
Scoring Position, 2 Out	15 / 77	(19%)	54 / 224	(24%)
On Third, Less than 2 Out	18 / 30	(60%)	46 / 89	(52%)
RBI in close games / RBI Total	49 / 76	(64%)	139 / 217	(64%)

Atlee Hammaker
San Francisco Giants

Loyalty is a strange concept, especially in modern sports.

It is pretty well known that ballplayers have a short life span— the "average" major leaguer's career in the big time is less than six years. Atlee Hammaker has spent six seasons as a member of the Giants' organization. In 1982, his first year, he worked 175 innings; he hasn't worked as many since then. In the intervening years Hammaker has spent as much time on the DL as many players spend in the ML. His 7 trips to the disabled list have totaled 462 days, or close to three full seasons.

Hammaker had a terrific season in 1983, leading the league in ERA (the first Giant to do so since Juan Marichal) and making the All-Star team. He earned notoriety in that game by becoming (and, to this day, remaining) the only pitcher in All-Star history to serve up a grand slam homer. Ah, gophers . . . like injuries, they've always plagued Hammaker. When he returned to the Giants last year after missing all of 1986, Atlee's home run rate was the highest of any San Francisco pitcher who threw 50+ innings. Nevertheless, he finished in the league's top 10 in ERA with 3.48. Then, there was the post-season. Even after Atlee tried to sneak a high fastball past Jim Lindeman in Game 3 of the LCS, Roger Craig demonstrated extreme loyalty by giving Atlee (road record: 13–28) the ball for Game 7 of the LCS.

Atlee left that game with a 7.88 ERA for the LCS, and the dubious distinction of having surrendered the only 2 homers the Cardinals managed to hit. Most Giant fans were very apprehensive when Atlee took the mound—Kelly Downs had not appeared in the LCS, Mike Krukow had pitched a masterful game in Game 4. In spite of it all, though, most Giant fans felt it was appropriate for Craig to show this kind of confidence in Atlee, who had performed well enough to be a serious candidate for Comeback Player of the Year. Although only 10–10, the Giants scored only 15 runs in Atlee's last 9 losses. The Giants had entered the year not expecting much of anything from Atlee, who had pitched only 1 spring training game in 1986. He missed the rest of the season due to his second rotator cuff surgery.

So, after sticking with a 39–39 pitcher through 6 years and 5 lengthy stints on the DL, after giving him the ball in Game 7, the Giants reaped the return on their invested loyalty—Hammaker declared free agency, and declined arbitration. Although finally signed within the final few hours, a bad taste must remain from the negotiations, as Al Rosen was quoted as saying he raised his final offer for "dear Atlee, he of the high fastball to Jim Lindeman and the high slider to Jose Oquendo. I raised the offer because I love him. I just watched the highlight film again and threw up." In spite of it all, Atlee will start 1988 as a major member of last year's best pitching staff in the Major Leagues.

Michael Duca

Hammaker, Charlton Atlee "Atlee"

Bats: Both   **Throws: Left**   **Born 01/24/58**

1987 SEASON AND MAJOR-LEAGUE CAREER PITCHING TOTALS

	G	GS	CG	GF	IP	BFP	H	R	ER	HR	SH	SF	HB	TBB	IBB	SO	WP	Bk	W	L	Pct	ShO	Sv	ERA
87 SF	31	27	2	1	168	706	159	73	67	22	3	3	3	57	10	107	8	7	10	10	.500	0	0	3.59
6 YEARS	128	118	15	3	758	3147	732	331	293	68	38	20	8	185	37	471	20	20	40	42	.488	5	0	3.48

1987: Finesse, Groundball

	1987 SEASON											TWO YEAR TOTALS (1986 – 1987)										
	G	IP	H	BB	SO	SB	CS	W	L	S	ERA	G	IP	H	BB	SO	SB	CS	W	L	S	ERA
Totals	31	168.0	159	57	107	26	8	10	10	0	3.59	31	168.0	159	57	107	26	8	10	10	0	3.59
at Home	16	102.1	80	32	53	13	6	9	2	0	2.73	16	102.1	80	32	53	13	6	9	2	0	2.73
on Road	15	65.2	79	25	54	13	2	1	8	0	4.93	15	65.2	79	25	54	13	2	1	8	0	4.93
on Grass	19	103.2	97	38	65	20	3	6	6	0	3.73	19	103.2	97	38	65	20	3	6	6	0	3.73
on Artificial Turf	12	64.1	62	19	42	6	5	4	4	0	3.36	12	64.1	62	19	42	6	5	4	4	0	3.36
Day Games	22	126.1	121	39	74	19	7	9	7	0	3.56	22	126.1	121	39	74	19	7	9	7	0	3.56
Night Games	9	41.2	38	18	33	7	1	1	3	0	3.67	9	41.2	38	18	33	7	1	1	3	0	3.67
April	0	0.0	0	0	0	0	0	0	0	0	0.00	0	0.0	0	0	0	0	0	0	0	0	0.00
May	7	29.0	24	8	18	3	2	2	1	0	1.86	7	29.0	24	8	18	3	2	2	1	0	1.86
June	6	36.0	32	12	27	6	1	2	4	0	4.25	6	36.0	32	12	27	6	1	2	4	0	4.25
July	6	37.0	41	16	19	6	2	2	3	0	3.65	6	37.0	41	16	19	6	2	2	3	0	3.65
August	6	36.0	30	12	23	4	1	3	1	0	3.25	6	36.0	30	12	23	4	1	3	1	0	3.25
Sept/Oct	6	30.0	32	9	20	7	2	1	1	0	4.80	6	30.0	32	9	20	7	2	1	1	0	4.80

vs. Opponent Batters	Ave.	OBP	SLG	AB	H	2B	3B	HR	RBI	BB	SO	Ave.	OBP	SLG	AB	H	2B	3B	HR	RBI	BB	SO
Totals	.248	.312	.386	640	159	22	0	22	66	57	107	.248	.312	.386	640	159	22	0	22	66	57	107
vs. Left	.168	.258	.215	107	18	2	0	1	3	11	24	.168	.258	.215	107	18	2	0	1	3	11	24
vs. Right	.265	.322	.420	533	141	20	0	21	63	46	83	.265	.322	.420	533	141	20	0	21	63	46	83
Bases Empty	.235	.291	.379	388	91	14	0	14	14	31	58	.235	.291	.379	388	91	14	0	14	14	31	58
Leadoff	.247	.303	.426	162	40	5	0	8	8	13	25	.247	.303	.426	162	40	5	0	8	8	13	25
Not Leadoff	.226	.283	.345	226	51	9	0	6	6	18	33	.226	.283	.345	226	51	9	0	6	6	18	33
Runners On Base	.270	.342	.397	252	68	8	0	8	52	26	49	.270	.342	.397	252	68	8	0	8	52	26	49
First Base Only	.343	.383	.491	108	37	4	0	4	10	6	14	.343	.383	.491	108	37	4	0	4	10	6	14
Scoring Position	.215	.314	.326	144	31	4	0	4	42	20	35	.215	.314	.326	144	31	4	0	4	42	20	35
Late Innings, Close	.282	.341	.385	39	11	1	0	1	3	4	8	.282	.341	.385	78	22	2	0	2	6	8	16

RBI/Opportunities

Scoring Position	36 / 199 (18%)	36 / 199 (18%)
Scoring Position, 2 Out	16 / 95 (17%)	32 / 190 (17%)
On Third, Less than 2 Out	8 / 34 (24%)	16 / 68 (24%)
RBI in close games / RBI Total	50 / 66 (76%)	100 / 66 (152%)

Mickey Hatcher
Los Angeles Dodgers

In the dark days since Jack Clark ended the Dodgers reign among baseball's elite, no weakness has been more glaring in Los Angeles than third base. With a couple of exceptions, the position has been a revolving door for 30 years—with Ron Cey's departure, it's back to "situation normal." Due partly to his age, partly to his .190 BA, partly to his .265 OBA, and partly to his .912 Fielding Average (whew, somebody open a window!), the Dodgers gave up on Bill Madlock and gave some of their minor league suspects a chance. When no one seemed able to play the position at the major league level, the Dodgers went on a talent hunt where they find most of their third basemen—their outfield.

Sure enough, there was Mickey Hatcher. Originally a Dodger, Hatcher was traded by LA as part of the Ken Landreaux deal with Minnesota. He showed good promise in the minors, alternating between third and the outfield while leading the PCL in hitting. As a major leaguer, however, he had credit for just 47 games at third entering the 1987 season, out of 762 career games. He didn't have too tough an act to follow, though, and his .929 fielding average was an improvement on Madlock. So was his Range Factor of 2.59—surprisingly enough, Hatcher's RF ranked in the middle of all NL third basemen who handled 100 or more chances.

Hatcher is one of those players who loves the game. If the owners ever go bankrupt (look out for low flying pigs) Hatcher would play for expenses. His on-field showmanship and clubhouse morale-boosting all make him a crowd favorite even in LA, where 60 percent of the fans think the game is played with a 24" red, white, blue, green and yellow ball. Hatcher is a joy to watch, and would be an asset even if he didn't hit—he seems to have inherited Jay Johnstone's role on this club.

Mickey's offense was more than adequate. He was third on the team with a .282 average and had 27 extra base hits in only 287 at bats. He walked once more than he struck out last season, which meant Lasorda was able to hit and run more because of Hatcher's bat control. However, Hatcher did have to go out and play the field. He did it enthusiastically, but Mickey is no threat to win a Gold Glove.

Hatcher isn't a youngster—he will be 33 on opening day. He's not so old he can't contribute to a winning team, but his ability to handle a position change into the infield at this stage in his career is questionable. His biggest value to the team is as a morale booster, pinch hitter and reserve outfielder. With all the injuries the Dodgers had, Hatcher could get 300 at bats in that role.

Carmen Corica

Hatcher, Michael Vaughn "Mickey" Bats: Right Throws: Right Born 03/15/55

1987 SEASON AND MAJOR-LEAGUE CAREER BATTING TOTALS

	G	AB	H	2B	3B	HR	TB	R	RBI	TBB	IBB	SO	HP	SH	SF	SB	CS	SB%	GDP	AVG	OBP	SLG
87 LA	101	287	81	19	1	7	123	27	42	20	4	19	1	3	3	2	3	.40	6	.282	.328	.429
9 YEARS	863	2830	796	152	17	35	1087	296	312	138	14	201	9	20	23	10	13	.43	91	.281	.314	.384

	1987 SEASON											FOUR YEAR TOTALS (1984 – 1987)									
	Ave.	OBP	SLG	AB	H	2B	3B	HR	RBI	BB	SO	Ave.	OBP	SLG	AB	H	2B	3B	HR	RBI	BB	SO
Totals	.282	.328	.429	287	81	19	1	7	42	20	19	.288	.325	.391	1624	468	95	9	18	192	92	102
vs. Left	.328	.384	.528	125	41	13	0	4	21	12	6	.326	.368	.461	573	187	43	2	10	79	42	31
vs. Right	.247	.283	.352	162	40	6	1	3	21	8	13	.267	.301	.353	1051	281	52	7	8	113	50	71
at Home	.255	.301	.401	137	35	8	0	4	22	8	8	.294	.329	.418	823	242	58	7	10	100	42	52
on Road	.307	.352	.453	150	46	11	1	3	20	12	11	.282	.321	.363	801	226	37	2	8	92	50	50
vs. Groundball	.312	.333	.411	141	44	11	0	1	26	5	7	.310	.337	.401	773	240	50	4	4	116	35	37
vs. Flyball	.253	.323	.445	146	37	8	1	6	16	15	12	.268	.314	.382	851	228	45	5	14	76	57	65
vs. Finesse	.277	.324	.440	159	44	9	1	5	21	10	7	.294	.329	.397	897	264	44	6	12	94	48	48
vs. Power	.289	.333	.414	128	37	10	0	2	21	10	12	.281	.320	.384	727	204	51	3	6	98	44	54
on Grass	.249	.296	.378	209	52	12	0	5	32	14	15	.260	.305	.343	722	188	31	1	9	90	48	47
on Artificial Turf	.372	.412	.564	78	29	7	1	2	10	6	4	.310	.341	.429	902	280	64	8	9	102	44	55
Day Games	.337	.381	.494	89	30	6	1	2	12	7	4	.322	.357	.432	518	167	28	4	7	61	28	33
Night Games	.258	.304	.399	198	51	13	0	5	30	13	15	.272	.310	.372	1106	301	67	5	11	131	64	69
April	.188	.263	.313	16	3	2	0	0	2	2	5	.246	.264	.345	232	57	13	2	2	26	6	16
May	.340	.354	.553	47	16	4	0	2	5	1	0	.323	.356	.430	300	97	18	1	4	32	15	18
June	.283	.313	.350	60	17	4	0	0	7	3	2	.279	.324	.341	308	86	17	1	0	28	21	19
July	.390	.419	.622	82	32	5	1	4	16	3	3	.301	.339	.438	256	77	13	2	6	34	14	18
August	.162	.266	.250	68	11	3	0	1	10	10	6	.272	.329	.382	301	82	22	1	3	45	26	19
Sept/Oct	.143	.200	.214	14	2	1	0	0	2	1	3	.304	.333	.414	227	69	12	2	3	27	10	12
Bases Empty	.274	.299	.417	168	46	12	0	4	4	6	11	.273	.307	.369	917	250	54	5	8	8	45	59
Leadoff	.295	.313	.449	78	23	6	0	2	2	2	6	.280	.303	.404	332	93	21	4	4	4	11	23
Not Leadoff	.256	.287	.389	90	23	6	0	2	2	4	5	.268	.309	.349	585	157	33	1	4	4	34	36
Runners On	.294	.365	.445	119	35	7	1	3	38	14	8	.308	.351	.420	707	218	41	4	10	184	47	43
First Base Only	.304	.373	.609	46	14	3	1	3	9	5	2	.315	.341	.438	308	97	16	2	6	18	12	16
Scoring Position	.288	.360	.342	73	21	4	0	0	29	9	6	.303	.358	.406	399	121	25	2	4	166	35	27
Late Innings, Close	.196	.255	.255	51	10	0	0	1	2	4	8	.253	.301	.339	233	59	8	0	4	32	16	20

RBI/Opportunities

	1987		FOUR YEAR
Scoring Position	28 / 104	(27%)	153 / 528 (29%)
Scoring Position, 2 Out	12 / 55	(22%)	64 / 260 (25%)
On Third, Less than 2 Out	8 / 14	(57%)	58 / 101 (57%)
RBI in close games / RBI Total	29 / 42	(69%)	113 / 192 (59%)

Billy Hatcher
Houston Astros

Billy Hatcher began the 1987 season knowing he had a job in the Astro outfield. He responded aggressively. He batted a solid .296. With only 150 more at bats than in 1986, he nearly doubled his runs scored, doubles, home runs, runs batted in and walk totals. His strikeout totals did not double, so he was able to improve on his walk-to-strikeout ratio from 1986. However, he does need to work on getting more walks (he got only 42 in 1987), developing some patience without losing his aggressiveness. Hatcher was the first Astro since Cesar Cedeno in '77 to steal over 50 bases, finishing with 53. He only got caught 9 times, which compares favorably with Vince Coleman in terms of success rate (Hatcher—86%, Coleman—83%).

The middle of August was a critical time for the Astros. They won ten of eleven games and were one-half game out of first on August 24. Hatcher played a big part in this winning streak, batting .500, scoring 15 runs and driving in 11. Hatcher went into a slump over the next eight games, while the 'Stros went into the dumpster, losing 7 of 8. It was at this time that the Giants stretched their lead, and the Astros began to drop out of contention.

On September 1 Hatcher was caught using a corked bat, and he was subsequently suspended for 10 days. Hatcher claimed he was using relief pitcher Dave Smith's batting practice bat. Since Dave only stepped into the batter's box 3 times all season, it takes quite a stretch of credi-bility to accept that Smith would even own a corked bat, let alone for it to find its way into the bat rack, and then into Billy's hands, all by accident. Perhaps this is why Hatcher (to his credit) didn't moan about the penalty, but took it like a gentleman. The Astros split the 8 games Billy missed; however, the suspension seemed to have an effect on Hatcher. Batting .312 when suspended, Billy hit only .203 after his return, scoring 9 runs, driving in 6, and stealing but 4 bases in his final 20 games. The Astros were 6+ out the day Hatcher returned; they finished a distant 14 games behind.

Welford McCaffrey

Baseball is the stuff of dreams, and hopes. None of us likes to think of the darker side of things, which is why one of the most poignant quotes to emerge from baseball is that of the ragamuffin waif who said "Say it ain't so, Joe" to Shoeless Joe Jackson on the courthouse steps.

My esteemed colleague suggests that the psychological effect of Billy Hatcher's suspension led to his dismal performance as a hitter at the end of 1987. The bottom line is that Billy was caught cheating, and I believe some consideration should be given to the possibility that his hitting stats went into the dumpster because he was using ordinary, legal equipment after the incident. We should know more in '88.

Michael Duca

Hatcher, William Augustus "Billy" Bats: Right Throws: Right Born 10/04/60

1987 SEASON AND MAJOR-LEAGUE CAREER BATTING TOTALS

	G	AB	H	2B	3B	HR	TB	R	RBI	TBB	IBB	SO	HP	SH	SF	SB	CS	SB%	GDP	AVG	OBP	SLG
87 HOU	141	564	167	28	3	11	234	96	63	42	1	70	9	7	5	53	9	.85	11	.296	.352	.415
4 YEARS	329	1155	316	55	8	19	444	176	109	73	3	134	17	15	8	95	27	.78	23	.274	.324	.384

	1987 SEASON											FOUR YEAR TOTALS (1984 – 1987)									
	Ave.	OBP	SLG	AB	H	2B	3B	HR	RBI	BB	SO	Ave.	OBP	SLG	AB	H	2B	3B	HR	RBI	BB	SO
Totals	.296	.352	.415	564	167	28	3	11	63	42	70	.274	.324	.384	1155	316	55	8	19	109	73	134
vs. Left	.277	.335	.406	202	56	12	1	4	28	17	29	.276	.324	.384	453	125	18	5	7	50	32	53
vs. Right	.307	.361	.420	362	111	16	2	7	35	25	41	.272	.324	.385	702	191	37	3	12	59	41	81
at Home	.305	.358	.382	259	79	11	0	3	27	20	43	.271	.318	.356	590	160	23	3	7	53	34	74
on Road	.289	.346	.443	305	88	17	3	8	36	22	27	.276	.331	.414	565	156	32	5	12	56	39	60
vs. Groundball	.299	.381	.394	264	79	10	3	3	30	29	32	.271	.339	.374	553	150	21	6	8	55	47	66
vs. Flyball	.293	.324	.433	300	88	18	0	8	33	13	38	.276	.309	.394	602	166	34	2	11	54	26	68
vs. Finesse	.285	.326	.376	298	85	12	0	5	32	16	24	.266	.312	.358	636	169	27	1	10	57	35	55
vs. Power	.308	.379	.459	266	82	16	3	6	31	26	46	.283	.339	.416	519	147	28	7	9	52	38	79
on Grass	.275	.340	.423	189	52	8	1	6	21	15	17	.253	.310	.386	430	109	16	4	11	46	30	43
on Artificial Turf	.307	.358	.411	375	115	20	2	5	42	27	53	.286	.332	.383	725	207	39	4	8	63	43	91
Day Games	.326	.377	.508	193	63	12	1	7	36	14	18	.291	.335	.451	461	134	30	4	12	56	25	42
Night Games	.280	.338	.367	371	104	16	2	4	27	28	52	.262	.317	.340	694	182	25	4	7	53	48	92
April	.391	.424	.598	87	34	7	1	3	12	4	11	.351	.383	.509	114	40	7	1	3	12	5	19
May	.282	.350	.350	103	29	5	1	0	11	11	13	.290	.348	.359	145	42	8	1	0	14	13	17
June	.292	.360	.434	113	33	4	0	4	12	11	21	.274	.320	.406	234	64	11	1	6	21	15	36
July	.236	.311	.309	55	13	1	0	1	4	4	7	.246	.287	.327	171	42	11	0	1	11	8	19
August	.333	.385	.492	120	40	8	1	3	18	8	9	.329	.379	.476	210	69	12	2	5	29	15	17
Sept/Oct	.209	.250	.244	86	18	3	0	0	6	4	9	.210	.257	.295	281	59	6	3	4	22	17	26
Bases Empty	.287	.342	.394	373	107	20	1	6	6	22	45	.278	.325	.394	747	208	40	5	12	12	43	88
Leadoff	.295	.371	.380	166	49	11	0	1	1	17	20	.281	.343	.366	331	93	18	2	2	2	28	42
Not Leadoff	.280	.317	.406	207	58	9	1	5	5	5	25	.276	.311	.416	416	115	22	3	10	10	15	46
Runners On	.314	.370	.455	191	60	8	2	5	57	20	25	.265	.312	.368	408	108	15	3	7	97	30	46
First Base Only	.304	.345	.443	79	24	2	0	3	8	5	11	.263	.296	.357	171	45	4	0	4	10	8	21
Scoring Position	.321	.386	.464	112	36	6	2	2	49	15	14	.266	.322	.376	237	63	11	3	3	87	22	25
Late Innings, Close	.333	.400	.500	90	30	8	2	1	16	9	14	.301	.356	.443	176	53	12	2	3	29	14	26

RBI/Opportunities

Scoring Position	41 / 163 (25%)	76 / 345 (22%)
Scoring Position, 2 Out	19 / 80 (24%)	33 / 155 (21%)
On Third, Less than 2 Out	15 / 30 (50%)	29 / 62 (47%)
RBI in close games / RBI Total	37 / 63 (59%)	64 / 109 (59%)

Von Hayes
Philadelphia Phillies

Did opponents pitch around Von Hayes in 1987? Not very likely, since he often hit in front of Mike Schmidt. Was he emulating Jason Thompson (watching pitches go past until reaching either ball four or called strike three)? No, his strikeouts were unchanged from 1986. A huge jump in walks is an ominous sign for players in the twilight of their careers—just ask Toby Harrah or Pete Rose. But Von Hayes is in his prime, and in other respects 1987 fits well with his previous seasonal progression. The season, then, must indicate simply that Hayes has become a disciplined, patient hitter with exceptional bat control and strike zone judgment.

Is there a precedent for Von's leap from 74 walks (11 percent of plate appearances) in 1986 to 121 (18 percent of appearances) in 1987? If so, what pattern did that player's future years take? Examining the careers of contemporary players and of some of the greats of the game, I found only one good match. At the age of 28, this player hit 17 homeruns and walked in 11 percent of his appearances; the next year he hit a career-best 23 homers and drew 100 bases on balls (16 percent of plate appearances), but lost a hefty chunk from his batting average. The year after that, he walked even more (20 percent), regained over half of his batting average loss, and recorded the highest on-base percentage of his career. That player was Mickey Cochrane, 1931–1933. Cochrane continued to draw bases on balls during the rest of his injury-shortened career.

1987 was the second straight star-quality season turned

in by Von. He reached his current productive level when he stopped copying his idol Ted Williams and reverted to his high school batting stance. With feet spread wide and bat held flat, it's strongly reminiscent of former Phil Garry Maddox. As in 1986, Hayes started slowly. On June 2, he was hitting just .224, but had walked 44 times in 45 games. In the next six weeks, though, he batted .385 (with 27 more walks) to reach .308 at the All-Star break. Until a swoon in the last couple of weeks, his average stayed in the .290-.300 range the rest of the season.

While his fielding has improved, Von remains an outfielder stuck at first base. Defense at first base is notoriously difficult to measure, but I can report that Hayes averaged 0.60 assists per game started, far behind Hernandez (0.99) and Bream (0.97) but ahead of Esasky (0.43) and Durham (0.50). Don't make too much of this, however, because Darrell Evans led the majors with 1.02 assists per start.

After two consecutive great years, tall, dark, and handsome bachelor Von Hayes should be one of the most popular people in sports-crazy Philadelphia. Though he has outlasted the unfair "Five-for-One" label, he's never caught the fancy of the fans. Apparently, Philadelphians prefer style and flash to professionalism, thoughtfulness, and dignity in their heroes. Hence, Hayes, Mike Schmidt, and even Julius Erving inspire less devotion than the likes of Glenn Wilson, hockey's Broad Street Bullies, and football coach/buffoon Buddy Ryan.

Neal Traven

Hayes, Von Francis

Bats: Left   Throws: Right   Born 08/31/58

1987 SEASON AND MAJOR-LEAGUE CAREER BATTING TOTALS

	G	AB	H	2B	3B	HR	TB	R	RBI	TBB	IBB	SO	HP	SH	SF	SB	CS	SB%	GDP	AVG	OBP	SLG
87 PHI	158	556	154	36	5	21	263	84	84	121	12	77	0	0	4	16	7	.70	12	.277	.404	.473
7 YEARS	937	3284	907	181	27	90	1412	483	450	407	42	465	10	15	20	169	66	.72	65	.276	.356	.430

1987 SEASON

	Ave.	OBP	SLG	AB	H	2B	3B	HR	RBI	BB	SO
Totals	.277	.404	.474	555	154	36	5	21	84	121	77
vs. Left	.234	.361	.347	167	39	8	1	3	21	35	31
vs. Right	.296	.422	.528	388	115	28	4	18	63	86	46
at Home	.253	.401	.477	277	70	14	3	14	51	71	30
on Road	.302	.407	.471	278	84	22	2	7	33	50	47
vs. Groundball	.300	.429	.495	277	83	19	4	9	45	65	39
vs. Flyball	.255	.378	.453	278	71	17	1	12	39	56	38
vs. Finesse	.277	.399	.466	292	81	19	3	10	40	62	29
vs. Power	.278	.409	.483	263	73	17	2	11	44	59	48
on Grass	.275	.383	.394	142	39	9	1	2	14	25	24
on Artificial Turf	.278	.411	.501	413	115	27	4	19	70	96	53
Day Games	.298	.372	.528	178	53	16	2	7	25	21	17
Night Games	.268	.417	.448	377	101	20	3	14	59	100	60
April	.246	.417	.338	65	16	3	0	1	9	19	12
May	.240	.410	.373	75	18	0	2	2	12	23	16
June	.333	.442	.667	87	29	12	1	5	14	17	5
July	.340	.463	.701	97	33	9	1	8	21	24	14
August	.298	.433	.456	114	34	7	1	3	17	27	14
Sept/Oct	.205	.271	.299	117	24	5	0	2	11	11	16
Bases Empty	.259	.384	.440	309	80	15	1	13	13	63	50
Leadoff	.330	.435	.526	97	32	4	0	5	5	18	10
Not Leadoff	.226	.362	.401	212	48	11	1	8	8	45	40
Runners On	.301	.427	.516	246	74	21	4	8	71	58	27
First Base Only	.367	.447	.667	90	33	13	1	4	13	13	8
Scoring Position	.263	.417	.429	156	41	8	3	4	58	45	19
Late Innings, Close	.284	.418	.455	88	25	6	0	3	12	21	13

FOUR YEAR TOTALS (1984 – 1987)

	Ave.	OBP	SLG	AB	H	2B	3B	HR	RBI	BB	SO
Totals	.285	.369	.450	2296	654	139	17	69	319	315	337
vs. Left	.232	.310	.337	630	146	26	2	12	83	73	118
vs. Right	.305	.391	.493	1666	508	113	15	57	236	242	219
at Home	.287	.380	.487	1115	320	58	12	47	183	170	147
on Road	.283	.359	.416	1181	334	81	5	22	136	145	190
vs. Groundball	.279	.366	.424	1112	310	63	9	27	155	156	174
vs. Flyball	.291	.372	.475	1184	344	76	8	42	164	159	163
vs. Finesse	.284	.362	.440	1229	349	68	11	34	169	155	159
vs. Power	.286	.377	.462	1067	305	71	6	35	150	160	178
on Grass	.285	.356	.416	627	179	42	2	12	67	71	98
on Artificial Turf	.285	.374	.463	1669	475	97	15	57	252	244	239
Day Games	.280	.354	.453	739	207	49	5	23	99	87	109
Night Games	.287	.376	.449	1557	447	90	12	46	220	228	228
April	.281	.385	.407	253	71	14	3	4	37	43	35
May	.290	.393	.432	338	98	20	2	8	44	59	67
June	.288	.386	.464	351	101	27	1	11	55	56	50
July	.288	.376	.540	396	114	24	5	22	70	57	58
August	.320	.393	.479	472	151	31	4	12	64	57	68
Sept/Oct	.245	.306	.374	486	119	23	2	12	49	43	59
Bases Empty	.275	.355	.457	1289	355	84	9	44	44	158	218
Leadoff	.318	.388	.541	444	141	30	6	19	19	51	50
Not Leadoff	.253	.337	.413	845	214	54	3	25	25	107	168
Runners On	.297	.390	.442	1007	299	55	8	25	275	157	119
First Base Only	.315	.367	.486	381	120	24	1	13	37	31	41
Scoring Position	.286	.403	.415	626	179	31	7	12	238	126	78
Late Innings, Close	.271	.352	.410	398	108	19	0	12	50	50	64

RBI/Opportunities

Scoring Position	49 / 226 (22%)	210 / 865 (24%)
Scoring Position, 2 Out	18 / 89 (20%)	76 / 361 (21%)
On Third, Less than 2 Out	19 / 36 (53%)	83 / 148 (56%)
RBI in close games / RBI Total	48 / 84 (57%)	203 / 319 (64%)

Neal Heaton
Montreal Expos

Montreal Expos manager Buck Rodgers was worried going into the 1987 season. Tim Raines was not going to return to the Montreal lineup until May 1, and Andre Dawson was a Chicago Cub. If that wasn't enough to keep him awake at night, he also had to worry about the fact that he didn't have a pitching staff. Even Jeff Reardon, the man who had saved 162 games for the Expos, including a total of 76 in the previous two seasons, was gone.

That Montreal finished third in the National League East with a 91–71 mark, and never did get their pitching straightened away, is nothing short of remarkable.

No fewer than 21 people took a turn on the mound for the Expos last season, including those well-known fireballers Tim Wallach and Vance Law. Some actually performed pretty well for an entire season. Others, like Neal Heaton, who came to Montreal in the trade that sent Reardon to Minnesota, were half season success stories. Fortunately for the Expos, about the time Heaton broke down, Pascual Perez and Dennis Martinez had arrived on the scene to pick up the slack.

Heaton gave an All-Star performance in the first two months of 1987, toting along the rest of the Expo staff with him. Without his performance, Montreal would have been in the lower reaches of the NL East. By June 4, he was 7–2 with a 3.84 ERA, attaining heights of success he had never known in a 39–56 career. He won three more times before the All-Star break despite getting hit hard, portending a difficult second half. After the break, he went 2–6 and was seldom used by Rodgers late in the season. Nevertheless, he was Montreal's biggest winner with 13.

A left-hander, Heaton may be getting ready to move into the prime of his career at the age of 28. His control improved dramatically in 1987 (just 37 walks in 193.1 innings), and after going a combined 16–32 the previous two seasons with Cleveland and the Twins, he might be ready now to fulfill the potential the New York Mets saw in him when they made him the first player selected in the January 1979 phase of the free agent draft. Heaton did not sign a contract with the Mets, waiting until 1981 when Cleveland made him a second round pick. Of continuing concern, however, is that Heaton has never once, in a six year career, had a season in which he allowed less than one hit per inning. Last year he allowed 207 in 193.1 innings, and that mark was compiled in a league in which the pitchers still hit. He also has yet to finish a season with an ERA below 4.00.

Tom Henry

Heaton, Neal

Bats: Left   **Throws: Left**   **Born 03/03/60**

1987 SEASON AND MAJOR-LEAGUE CAREER PITCHING TOTALS

	G	GS	CG	GF	IP	BFP	H	R	ER	HR	SH	SF	HB	TBB	IBB	SO	WP	Bk	W	L	Pct	ShO	Sv	ERA
87 MON	32	32	3	0	193	807	207	103	97	25	5	5	3	37	3	105	2	5	13	10	.565	1	0	4.52
6 YEARS	186	148	21	25	978	4237	1072	552	502	103	28	35	13	333	28	441	16	8	52	66	.441	6	8	4.62

1987: Finesse, Flyball   1986: Finesse, Flyball   1985: Finesse, Flyball   1984: Finesse, Flyball

1987 SEASON

	G	IP	H	BB	SO	SB	CS	W	L	S	ERA
Totals	32	193.1	207	37	105	23	11	13	10	0	4.52
at Home	17	109.1	112	18	60	7	7	7	4	0	3.87
on Road	15	84.0	95	19	45	16	4	6	6	0	5.36
on Grass	9	59.2	60	12	34	6	4	3	1	0	4.22
on Artificial Turf	23	133.2	147	25	71	17	7	10	9	0	4.65
Day Games	7	40.0	47	11	23	7	3	3	2	0	5.63
Night Games	25	153.1	160	26	82	16	8	10	8	0	4.23
April	4	28.0	23	5	17	5	0	3	1	0	4.18
May	6	43.1	37	7	24	4	1	3	1	0	3.95
June	6	36.2	41	7	20	4	2	4	1	0	4.91
July	5	32.1	32	4	18	1	5	2	1	0	3.06
August	6	30.2	50	4	18	6	2	0	2	0	6.16
Sept/Oct	5	22.1	24	10	8	3	1	1	4	0	5.24

vs. Opponent Batters	Ave.	OBP	SLG	AB	H	2B	3B	HR	RBI	BB	SO
Totals	.274	.308	.426	756	207	34	3	25	90	37	105
vs. Left	.244	.266	.415	123	30	7	1	4	15	4	24
vs. Right	.280	.316	.428	633	177	27	2	21	75	33	81
Bases Empty	.256	.285	.377	488	125	24	1	11	11	18	68
Leadoff	.232	.248	.338	198	46	4	1	5	5	3	23
Not Leadoff	.272	.310	.403	290	79	20	0	6	6	15	45
Runners On Base	.306	.348	.515	268	82	10	2	14	79	19	37
First Base Only	.304	.328	.530	115	35	6	1	6	17	3	13
Scoring Position	.307	.362	.503	153	47	4	1	8	62	16	24
Late Innings, Close	.348	.400	.435	46	16	4	0	0	7	3	9

FOUR YEAR TOTALS (1984 – 1987)

	G	IP	H	BB	SO	SB	CS	W	L	S	ERA
Totals	139	798.1	883	273	352	76	40	41	57	1	4.68
at Home	69	433.2	458	129	198	30	25	24	24	1	3.86
on Road	70	364.2	425	144	154	46	15	17	33	0	5.65
on Grass	45	265.0	283	92	109	26	11	14	14	0	4.18
on Artificial Turf	94	533.1	600	181	243	50	29	27	43	1	4.93
Day Games	91	505.0	579	192	206	43	27	26	39	0	4.90
Night Games	48	293.1	304	81	146	33	13	15	18	1	4.30
April	18	110.2	110	42	43	11	2	6	5	0	3.66
May	24	150.1	143	51	65	13	11	8	9	0	4.37
June	24	130.1	144	43	50	13	6	8	10	1	5.04
July	25	140.0	147	51	70	13	8	7	12	0	4.50
August	24	140.1	187	35	72	15	9	5	9	0	4.94
Sept/Oct	24	126.2	152	51	52	11	4	7	12	0	5.47

vs. Opponent Batters	Ave.	OBP	SLG	AB	H	2B	3B	HR	RBI	BB	SO
Totals	.283	.341	.434	3120	883	163	18	91	396	273	352
vs. Left	.277	.327	.439	570	158	35	6	15	79	43	79
vs. Right	.284	.344	.433	2550	725	128	12	76	317	230	273
Bases Empty	.287	.338	.428	1821	522	89	11	49	49	139	213
Leadoff	.285	.334	.438	786	224	38	8	22	22	57	89
Not Leadoff	.288	.341	.421	1035	298	51	3	27	27	82	124
Runners On Base	.278	.345	.443	1299	361	74	7	42	347	134	139
First Base Only	.270	.320	.416	608	164	37	2	16	56	44	63
Scoring Position	.285	.365	.466	691	197	37	5	26	291	90	76
Late Innings, Close	.311	.373	.477	193	60	15	1	5	23	18	25

RBI/Opportunities

	1987			Four Year		
Scoring Position	51 /	195	(26%)	247 /	930	(27%)
Scoring Position, 2 Out	10 /	79	(13%)	85 /	415	(20%)
On Third, Less than 2 Out	24 /	40	(60%)	99 /	182	(54%)
RBI in close games / RBI Total	66 /	90	(73%)	281 /	396	(71%)

Rickey Henderson
New York Yankees

Even though Rickey Henderson is a superstar, his personality takes a lot of heat from the fans and media. When, as in 1987, he's not producing superstar numbers, everyone lines up to take their shots. Rickey was given a major share of the blame for the Yankees' offensive demise; the 67 games he missed this year was the main evidence against him.

Exhibit B was his performance when he was able to take the field. Rickey didn't play particularly well when his "hammy" (as he calls his hamstring) was bothering him; many people thought that he was dogging it.

Exhibit C was his RBI total; Rickey's lowest since 1981. Though a lot of that was due to the number of games he missed and you could argue that RBIs aren't his job, it was a fair cop. Though he did draw walks at an amazing rate (Henderson's OB% actually rose from .423 to .427 with men on second and third), a walk is not as good as a hit in that situation; Rickey hit only .203 with men in scoring position this year.

The bottom line, however, is the numbers. Had Henderson gotten to 502 plate appearances, he would have been third in the AL in OB%. There aren't many leadoff men who can do that—especially while slugging .497. It's too bad that the Yankees didn't put him on the disabled list sooner—so more people understood that it was a serious injury—but they thought that a gimpy Henderson was better

than no Henderson at all. Given his stats, you can see why.

Another reason for Rickey's low RBI total was the timing of his homers; of the four that he *didn't* hit with the bases empty, each came with only one man on. He did, however, get games started with a bang in 1987—of the 10 homers he hit leading off innings, six came in the first frame.

The scouting report on Henderson is that he's a first ball hitter; 1987 demonstrated that clearly. He hit five of his 17 homers and had 12 of his 37 RBIs on the first pitch; almost 30 percent of his taters and ribbies in only 33 of his 358 at-bats. Three other counts saw him crush the ball, too. On 1–1 counts, he hit .516 with three homers in 31 ABs. On 2–1 counts, he hit .353 with four homers in 34 ABs. On 3–2, he hit .327 with three homers in 49 ABs. Oddly, he didn't fare very well on three supposedly good hitter's counts: His combined BA on 1–0, 2–0 and 3–1 counts was only .191, with one homer and five RBIs in 63 ABs. Finally, he wasn't a bad 2-strike hitter; he hit .272 in those situations.

One bit of good news was that, for the first time since joining the Yankees, Henderson found the Bronx to his liking. He hit .317 with 10 homers and a .590 SL% at home; his totals were .269, 7, .421 on the road. In the previous two years, Rickey hit .267 in Yankee Stadium (.307 on the road) with a sharp decrease in power.

Craig Christmann

Henderson, Rickey Henley Bats: Right Throws: Left Born 07/21/58

1987 SEASON AND MAJOR-LEAGUE CAREER BATTING TOTALS

	G	AB	H	2B	3B	HR	TB	R	RBI	TBB	IBB	SO	HP	SH	SF	SB	CS	SB%	GDP	AVG	OBP	SLG
87 NYA	95	358	104	17	3	17	178	78	37	80	1	52	2	0	0	41	8	.84	10	.291	.423	.497
9 YEARS	1182	4429	1286	205	42	120	1935	940	454	788	25	614	27	16	23	701	174	.80	70	.290	.399	.437

1987 SEASON

	Ave.	OBP	SLG	AB	H	2B	3B	HR	RBI	BB	SO
Totals	.291	.423	.497	358	104	17	3	17	37	80	52
vs. Left	.314	.445	.585	118	37	7	2	7	12	28	14
vs. Right	.279	.412	.454	240	67	10	1	10	25	52	38
at Home	.317	.453	.590	161	51	8	3	10	20	39	25
on Road	.269	.397	.421	197	53	9	0	7	17	41	27
vs. Groundball	.251	.362	.369	179	45	4	1	5	12	30	21
vs. Flyball	.330	.478	.626	179	59	13	2	12	25	50	31
vs. Finesse	.303	.411	.486	185	56	8	1	8	13	33	19
vs. Power	.277	.434	.509	173	48	9	2	9	24	47	33
on Grass	.291	.429	.522	289	84	13	3	16	34	68	42
on Artificial Turf	.290	.395	.391	69	20	4	0	1	3	12	10
Day Games	.357	.458	.550	129	46	7	0	6	14	22	14
Night Games	.253	.404	.467	229	58	10	3	11	23	58	38
April	.382	.512	.750	68	26	3	2	6	12	18	7
May	.290	.398	.480	100	29	7	0	4	6	17	14
June	.182	.357	.182	11	2	0	0	0	0	3	3
July	.253	.392	.316	79	20	2	0	1	7	17	10
August	.000	.000	.000	0	0	0	0	0	0	0	0
Sept/Oct	.270	.416	.520	100	27	5	1	6	12	25	18
Bases Empty	.314	.423	.556	239	75	13	3	13	13	43	33
Leadoff	.316	.408	.625	136	43	6	3	10	10	20	14
Not Leadoff	.311	.441	.466	103	32	7	0	3	3	23	19
Runners On	.244	.423	.378	119	29	4	0	4	24	37	19
First Base Only	.291	.418	.545	55	16	2	0	4	9	12	5
Scoring Position	.203	.427	.234	64	13	2	0	0	15	25	14
Late Innings, Close	.408	.540	.633	49	20	5	0	2	9	14	10

FOUR YEAR TOTALS (1984 – 1987)

	Ave.	OBP	SLG	AB	H	2B	3B	HR	RBI	BB	SO
Totals	.289	.397	.484	2015	583	103	17	85	241	354	279
vs. Left	.296	.418	.530	675	200	42	7	34	73	143	94
vs. Right	.286	.386	.460	1340	383	61	10	51	168	211	185
at Home	.280	.395	.473	933	261	48	9	38	105	174	132
on Road	.298	.399	.494	1082	322	55	8	47	136	180	147
vs. Groundball	.291	.389	.466	1014	295	45	8	39	124	157	135
vs. Flyball	.288	.404	.501	1001	288	58	9	46	117	197	144
vs. Finesse	.285	.376	.454	1162	331	60	4	43	116	165	136
vs. Power	.295	.424	.524	853	252	43	13	42	125	189	143
on Grass	.286	.395	.477	1688	482	85	14	70	204	300	232
on Artificial Turf	.309	.408	.520	327	101	18	3	15	37	54	47
Day Games	.291	.405	.464	632	184	33	2	24	70	119	89
Night Games	.289	.393	.493	1383	399	70	15	61	171	235	190
April	.283	.387	.476	269	76	10	3	12	38	46	38
May	.293	.393	.484	382	112	23	4	14	40	62	57
June	.358	.435	.582	352	126	22	3	17	50	48	46
July	.284	.411	.466	320	91	20	1	12	41	68	35
August	.248	.335	.431	290	72	13	2	13	34	38	41
Sept/Oct	.264	.401	.455	402	106	18	4	17	38	92	62
Bases Empty	.289	.391	.497	1319	381	75	14	57	57	220	191
Leadoff	.282	.384	.511	826	233	45	12	40	40	135	112
Not Leadoff	.300	.404	.473	493	148	30	2	17	17	85	79
Runners On	.290	.405	.460	696	202	28	3	28	184	134	88
First Base Only	.355	.444	.584	279	99	15	2	15	41	45	24
Scoring Position	.247	.379	.376	417	103	13	1	13	143	89	64
Late Innings, Close	.340	.444	.560	300	102	18	3	14	48	56	39

RBI/Opportunities

Scoring Position	15 / 104 (14%)	124 / 613 (20%)
Scoring Position, 2 Out	4 / 41 (10%)	46 / 284 (16%)
On Third, Less than 2 Out	7 / 24 (29%)	46 / 107 (43%)
RBI in close games / RBI Total	25 / 37 (68%)	149 / 241 (62%)

Tom Henke
Toronto Blue Jays

For the second consecutive season, a member of the Toronto bullpen had a better year than the Cy Young award winner and was curiously neglected in the voting. In 1986, it was Mark Eichhorn; in 1987, Tom Henke.

You can make a very good case for Henke as the AL's most dominant pitcher in 1987. Henke allowed fewer hits per nine innings than Roger Clemens (5.94/7.92), walked fewer men (2.39/2.65) struck out far more (12.26/8.18) had a much better strikeout to walk ratio (5.12/3.08) and had a lower ERA (2.49/2.97). The one category where Clemens is ahead is winning percentage; despite his league-leading 34 saves, Henke's 0–6 record must have hurt him badly with the voters.

Which is unfair; Henke's record was a tribute to his effectiveness. The only times that he wasn't used to protect leads in the late innings of close games were when he got some work to keep him sharp after not pitching for a few days. Other bullpen stoppers got an occasional win by losing a lead and having his teammates come back to win it; Henke usually came in and closed things off. When he didn't, his offense didn't give him enough help to pick up the occasional vultured win that could have meant well- deserved recognition.

Not only did Henke's 1987 compare favorably with Clemens, it also looks pretty good in comparison with seasons that have resulted in other pitchers getting MVP and/or Cy Young Awards:

PLAYER	YEAR	W-L	SV	ERA	IP	H/9IP	W/9IP	K/9IP	K/W
Henke	1987	0-6	34	2.49	94.	5.94	2.39	12.26	5.12
Bedrosian	87	5-3	40	2.83	89.	7.99	2.83	7.48	2.64
Hernandez	84	9-3	32	1.92	140.	6.16	2.31	7.18	3.11
Fingers	81	6-3	28	1.04	78.	6.35	1.50	7.04	4.69
Sutter	79	6-6	37	2.23	101.	5.97	2.85	9.80	3.44
Lyle	77	13-5	26	2.17	137.	8.61	2.17	4.47	2.06
Marshall	74	15-12	21	2.42	208.	8.26	2.42	6.19	2.55
Konstanty	50	16-7	22	2.66	152.	6.39	2.96	3.32	1.12

This isn't an exhaustive comparison of best seasons by relievers; other men may have had better years without winning an award. But it is certainly a fair cross section of good years. Compared with this set of distinguished seasons by award-winning pitchers, Henke was the most difficult to hit, by far the best strikeout pitcher and had the fourth-best control. His problem was that he was so good that he didn't blow enough leads to win any games.

Tony Formo

Henke, Thomas Anthony "Tom"

Bats: Right   **Throws: Right**   **Born 12/21/57**

1987 SEASON AND MAJOR-LEAGUE CAREER PITCHING TOTALS

	G	GS	CG	GF	IP	BFP	H	R	ER	HR	SH	SF	HB	TBB	IBB	SO	WP	Bk	W	L	Pct	ShO	Sv	ERA
87 TOR	72	0	0	62	94	363	62	27	26	10	3	5	0	25	3	128	5	0	0	6	.000	0	34	2.49
6 YEARS	204	0	0	159	285	1159	220	107	97	21	9	17	3	97	13	339	10	3	15	15	.500	0	77	3.06

1987: Power, Flyball   1986: Power, Flyball   1985: Power, Flyball   1984: Power, Flyball

1987 SEASON

	G	IP	H	BB	SO	SB	CS	W	L	S	ERA
Totals	72	94.0	62	25	128	9	2	0	6	34	2.49
at Home	37	50.0	28	11	67	0	2	0	2	17	1.62
on Road	35	44.0	34	14	61	9	0	0	4	17	3.48
on Grass	26	32.0	20	9	50	2	0	0	0	10	1.69
on Artificial Turf	46	62.0	42	16	78	7	2	0	6	24	2.90
Day Games	28	35.0	25	8	51	8	0	0	3	15	2.83
Night Games	44	59.0	37	17	77	1	2	0	3	19	2.29
April	12	11.1	7	2	13	0	0	0	0	4	0.00
May	10	14.2	6	4	21	1	0	0	1	4	1.84
June	12	15.2	17	8	26	2	1	0	2	5	6.32
July	14	19.1	8	5	24	1	0	0	1	10	1.86
August	13	18.0	12	4	23	3	1	0	1	7	2.00
Sept/Oct	11	15.0	12	2	21	2	0	0	1	4	2.40

vs. Opponent Batters	Ave.	OBP	SLG	AB	H	2B	3B	HR	RBI	BB	SO
Totals	.187	.242	.329	331	62	13	2	10	45	25	128
vs. Left	.171	.225	.287	164	28	8	1	3	17	12	59
vs. Right	.204	.258	.371	167	34	5	1	7	28	13	69
Bases Empty	.178	.215	.272	191	34	7	1	3	3	9	76
Leadoff	.189	.231	.297	74	14	2	0	2	2	4	29
Not Leadoff	.171	.205	.256	117	20	5	1	1	1	5	47
Runners On Base	.200	.275	.407	140	28	6	1	7	42	16	52
First Base Only	.200	.245	.300	50	10	2	0	1	2	3	19
Scoring Position	.200	.290	.467	90	18	4	1	6	40	13	33
Late Innings, Close	.184	.253	.325	228	42	9	1	7	35	22	86

FOUR YEAR TOTALS (1984 – 1987)

	G	IP	H	BB	SO	SB	CS	W	L	S	ERA
Totals	188	253.2	190	85	313	21	6	13	15	76	3.16
at Home	98	127.2	92	37	142	9	4	6	6	36	2.68
on Road	90	126.0	98	48	171	12	2	7	9	40	3.64
on Grass	62	82.0	67	30	102	10	2	7	4	16	3.18
on Artificial Turf	126	171.2	123	55	211	11	4	6	11	60	3.15
Day Games	85	111.1	88	39	141	12	2	6	5	35	3.23
Night Games	103	142.1	102	46	172	9	4	7	10	41	3.10
April	23	23.0	17	14	27	1	1	2	1	7	5.09
May	21	32.0	18	13	48	3	0	2	3	5	3.09
June	25	34.2	33	16	45	3	1	2	2	11	4.15
July	28	40.0	17	15	47	5	1	3	1	15	2.03
August	41	61.1	46	12	71	3	2	3	2	19	2.05
Sept/Oct	50	62.2	59	15	75	6	1	1	6	19	3.73

vs. Opponent Batters	Ave.	OBP	SLG	AB	H	2B	3B	HR	RBI	BB	SO
Totals	.207	.274	.319	916	190	36	3	20	121	85	313
vs. Left	.215	.288	.326	479	103	18	1	11	58	50	159
vs. Right	.199	.257	.311	437	87	18	2	9	63	35	154
Bases Empty	.189	.238	.272	493	93	18	1	7	7	32	178
Leadoff	.198	.256	.271	192	38	5	0	3	3	15	64
Not Leadoff	.183	.226	.272	301	55	13	1	4	4	17	114
Runners On Base	.229	.313	.374	423	97	18	2	13	114	53	135
First Base Only	.235	.282	.386	166	39	10	0	5	13	11	48
Scoring Position	.226	.330	.366	257	58	8	2	8	101	42	87
Late Innings, Close	.203	.275	.324	596	121	22	1	16	88	60	213

RBI/Opportunities

Scoring Position	32 / 135 (24%)	88 / 395 (22%)
Scoring Position, 2 Out	19 / 81 (23%)	45 / 206 (22%)
On Third, Less than 2 Out	7 / 19 (37%)	32 / 75 (43%)
RBI in close games / RBI Total	35 / 45 (78%)	90 / 121 (74%)

Mike Henneman
Detroit Tigers

If you like analogies, the story of Mike Henneman's 1987 is remarkably brief: He arrived in Detroit with as little fanfare as Willie Hernandez did in 1984, pitched like Mark Eichhorn did in 1986, was worked like Hernandez and may end up like either one in 1988.

In May, Detroit had an 11–18 record. The offense was scoring 4.21 runs per game; twelfth in the American League. The pitching, however, was second in the league in ERA. Had Willie Hernandez not been hurt, Henneman quite probably wouldn't have gotten his chance as early as he did.

Which, considering his past, is somewhat surprising. Anyone who saw Henneman pitch this year probably concluded that he was a journeyman minor leaguer who, like Eichhorn, had adopted his sidearm style as a last resort. Nothing could be further from the truth. Though Henneman, like Eichhorn, was 25 in his rookie season, he'd spent only three seasons in the minors, was not a converted starter and had genuinely impressive seasons in both AA and AAA under his belt. Though he had always had control problems, and allowed about a hit an inning, he allowed about one homer for every ten innings pitched and had ERAs of 2.43 and 2.95.

What *was* surprising was Mike's control. Once he arrived, he showed an amazing ability to throw his sinking fastball and changeup for strikes. He went 15.2 innings before he allowed his first walk. As King and Hernandez became steadily less effective, manager Sparky Anderson began using Mike as his long reliever, setup man, closer and even mopup man. Whatever Detroit needed, Mike was ready, willing and usually able to do.

Given the number of hats that Henneman was asked to wear in 1987, his final stats were very impressive. His ERA and 2.50–1 strikeout to walk ratio were the best of any Tiger reliever, and second only to Doyle Alexander on the team. He tied for the team lead in appearances, finished third in saves and, though he never started a game, was fourth in wins. He led all nonstarters in innings pitched; he allowed 10.9 baserunners per nine innings, third best on the staff. He was easily Detroit's most consistent reliever in 1987 and arguably the third best pitcher behind Morris and Alexander.

What is worrisome is Henneman's future. He pitched more innings in 1987 than he ever had before and seemed to tire by September. Like Eichhorn, his rookie season was so much better than anything in his past that it's hard to imagine him ever repeating it. Outside Tiger Stadium's friendly confines, he did not pitch well at all. Finally, Sparky Anderson has worked relievers beyond their tolerance in a year and paid the price down the road. Hopefully, Mike will not follow Hernandez down the "road to nowhere" in 1988—but there is certainly a chance that he will.

Jim Shaarda and Geoff Beckman

Henneman, Michael Alan "Mike"

Bats: Right   Throws: Right   Born 12/11/61

1987 SEASON AND MAJOR-LEAGUE CAREER PITCHING TOTALS

	G	GS	CG	GF	IP	BFP	H	R	ER	HR	SH	SF	HB	TBB	IBB	SO	WP	Bk	W	L	Pct	ShO	Sv	ERA
87 DET	55	0	0	28	97	399	86	36	32	8	2	2	3	30	5	75	7	0	11	3	.786	0	7	2.97
1 YEAR	55	0	0	28	97	399	86	36	32	8	2	2	3	30	5	75	7	0	11	3	.786	0	7	2.97

1987: Power, Groundball

	1987 SEASON											FOUR YEAR TOTALS (1984 – 1987)										
	G	IP	H	BB	SO	SB	CS	W	L	S	ERA	G	IP	H	BB	SO	SB	CS	W	L	S	ERA
Totals	55	96.2	86	30	75	2	3	11	3	7	2.98	55	96.2	86	30	75	2	3	11	3	7	2.98
at Home	24	49.0	30	7	41	1	2	7	0	4	1.65	24	49.0	30	7	41	1	2	7	0	4	1.65
on Road	31	47.2	56	23	34	1	1	4	3	3	4.34	31	47.2	56	23	34	1	1	4	3	3	4.34
on Grass	17	28.0	27	10	22	2	1	5	1	1	3.21	17	28.0	27	10	22	2	1	5	1	1	3.21
on Artificial Turf	38	68.2	59	20	53	0	2	6	2	6	2.88	38	68.2	59	20	53	0	2	6	2	6	2.88
Day Games	45	81.2	72	25	62	1	3	10	2	4	2.87	45	81.2	72	25	62	1	3	10	2	4	2.87
Night Games	10	15.0	14	5	13	1	0	1	1	3	3.60	10	15.0	14	5	13	1	0	1	1	3	3.60
April	0	0.0	0	0	0	0	0	0	0	0	0.00	0	0.0	0	0	0	0	0	0	0	0	0.00
May	9	15.2	9	0	14	0	1	2	0	1	1.15	9	15.2	9	0	14	0	1	2	0	1	1.15
June	12	15.1	18	8	8	0	0	1	0	0	4.11	12	15.1	18	8	8	0	0	1	0	0	4.11
July	9	22.0	18	6	18	0	0	5	1	1	2.05	9	22.0	18	6	18	0	0	5	1	1	2.05
August	11	21.0	21	6	17	0	2	1	0	2	2.14	11	21.0	21	6	17	0	2	1	0	2	2.14
Sept/Oct	14	22.2	20	10	18	2	0	2	2	3	5.16	14	22.2	20	10	18	2	0	2	2	3	5.16

vs. Opponent Batters	Ave.	OBP	SLG	AB	H	2B	3B	HR	RBI	BB	SO	Ave.	OBP	SLG	AB	H	2B	3B	HR	RBI	BB	SO
Totals	.238	.300	.351	362	86	13	2	8	39	30	75	.238	.300	.351	362	86	13	2	8	39	30	75
vs. Left	.238	.325	.407	172	41	7	2	6	20	20	29	.238	.325	.407	172	41	7	2	6	20	20	29
vs. Right	.237	.276	.300	190	45	6	0	2	19	10	46	.237	.276	.300	190	45	6	0	2	19	10	46
Bases Empty	.263	.315	.409	186	49	8	2	5	5	12	38	.263	.315	.409	186	49	8	2	5	5	12	38
Leadoff	.247	.301	.455	77	19	5	1	3	3	5	13	.247	.301	.455	77	19	5	1	3	3	5	13
Not Leadoff	.275	.325	.376	109	30	3	1	2	2	7	25	.275	.325	.376	109	30	3	1	2	2	7	25
Runners On Base	.210	.284	.290	176	37	5	0	3	34	18	37	.210	.284	.290	176	37	5	0	3	34	18	37
First Base Only	.247	.295	.329	73	18	3	0	1	5	5	12	.247	.295	.329	73	18	3	0	1	5	5	12
Scoring Position	.184	.277	.262	103	19	2	0	2	29	13	25	.184	.277	.262	103	19	2	0	2	29	13	25
Late Innings, Close	.176	.246	.272	125	22	4	1	2	11	10	27	.176	.246	.272	125	22	4	1	2	11	10	27

RBI/Opportunities

Scoring Position	26 / 146 (18%)	26 / 146 (18%)
Scoring Position, 2 Out	12 / 81 (15%)	12 / 81 (15%)
On Third, Less than 2 Out	10 / 29 (34%)	10 / 29 (34%)
RBI in close games / RBI Total	13 / 39 (33%)	13 / 39 (33%)

Keith Hernandez
New York Mets

After three very solid and consistent years in a row, Keith Hernandez turned in a slightly off year in 1987. In spite of the fact that the Mets' 1–2 punch turned out to be little more than a jab, Hernandez managed to keep his RBI and runs totals near his career average (his career high 18 home runs helped). The three most telling areas where his performance slacked off were his average (20 points off his last three seasons and his lowest in 10 years), strikeouts (a career high 104) and errors (10, with 7 coming in the last two months of the season).

Most of the errors seemed to reflect poor concentration (Keith actually had a routine throw drop out of his glove this past season) rather than the loss of a "step." And while Hernandez may well bounce back to hit .300 in 1988, his strikeout total is more troublesome and would also appear to be an issue of concentration. Hernandez turned 34 at the end of the '87 season. The Mets will keep his age in mind at contract renewal time, but I doubt that his '87 stats had much to do with his age. He's bounced back from subpar years before.

The monthly breakdowns below point to another important deviation from previous seasons. For the past few seasons you could count on Hernandez to put up subpar numbers in June and awesome numbers in September. This year June was typical but, unfortunately for the Mets, September was not. After averaging .352 the last three Septembers, Hernandez hit just .222 during the crucial September drive when the Mets were chasing the very catchable and Clark-less Cards. Remarkably, though he sat out several games with the flu, he had 17 RBI and scored 13 runs that month, but this was still a disappointment after a hot August that saw him hit 5 HRs, 10 doubles, score 20 runs and get 27 RBI.

When Hernandez was part of winning clubs in the past he was credited with an impact that went beyond his stats, a combination of drive and leadership, let's say. It seems reasonable that when his teams has a realistic shot at capturing the division but falls short he must also shoulder a share of the blame. While other Mets also share the burden of the September opportunity missed in 1987 (Howard Johnson and Gary Carter also had particularly disappointing Septembers), Keith Hernandez could have made the difference by himself had he managed his typical September. No one knows that better than Hernandez himself.

Andy Finn

Hernandez, Keith Bats: Left Throws: Left Born 10/20/53

1987 SEASON AND MAJOR-LEAGUE CAREER BATTING TOTALS

	G	AB	H	2B	3B	HR	TB	R	RBI	TBB	IBB	SO	HP	SH	SF	SB	CS	SB%	GDP	AVG	OBP	SLG
87 NYN	154	587	170	28	2	18	256	87	89	81	8	104	4	0	4	0	2	.00	15	.290	.377	.436
14 YEARS	1875	6677	2010	400	60	146	2968	1056	989	998	121	899	28	10	67	96	59	.62	144	.301	.391	.445

1987 SEASON

	Ave.	OBP	SLG	AB	H	2B	3B	HR	RBI	BB	SO
Totals	.290	.377	.436	587	170	28	2	18	89	81	104
vs. Left	.254	.343	.373	252	64	10	1	6	31	32	51
vs. Right	.316	.403	.484	335	106	18	1	12	58	49	53
at Home	.288	.386	.406	281	81	13	1	6	38	42	52
on Road	.291	.369	.464	306	89	15	1	12	51	39	52
vs. Groundball	.299	.383	.440	234	70	10	1	7	30	30	52
vs. Flyball	.283	.373	.433	353	100	18	1	11	59	51	52
vs. Finesse	.288	.363	.415	323	93	17	0	8	47	39	50
vs. Power	.292	.394	.462	264	77	11	2	10	42	42	54
on Grass	.290	.375	.430	414	120	17	1	13	63	54	79
on Artificial Turf	.289	.383	.451	173	50	11	1	5	26	27	25
Day Games	.329	.393	.477	216	71	14	0	6	34	22	34
Night Games	.267	.368	.412	371	99	14	2	12	55	59	70
April	.297	.391	.514	74	22	4	0	4	12	11	13
May	.340	.411	.420	100	34	3	1	1	7	12	21
June	.253	.315	.465	99	25	4	1	5	17	8	17
July	.310	.421	.360	100	31	5	0	0	9	20	13
August	.299	.387	.477	107	32	10	0	3	21	14	21
Sept/Oct	.243	.339	.402	107	26	2	0	5	23	16	19
Bases Empty	.281	.355	.442	303	85	14	1	11	11	33	59
Leadoff	.261	.333	.402	92	24	1	0	4	4	10	20
Not Leadoff	.289	.364	.460	211	61	13	1	7	7	23	39
Runners On	.299	.399	.430	284	85	14	1	7	78	48	45
First Base Only	.369	.444	.450	111	41	4	1	1	7	15	17
Scoring Position	.254	.373	.416	173	44	10	0	6	71	33	28
Late Innings, Close	.270	.360	.340	100	27	1	0	2	11	13	21

FOUR YEAR TOTALS (1984 – 1987)

	Ave.	OBP	SLG	AB	H	2B	3B	HR	RBI	BB	SO
Totals	.305	.396	.440	2281	695	127	7	56	357	349	321
vs. Left	.293	.369	.394	926	271	42	2	16	117	109	134
vs. Right	.313	.413	.472	1355	424	85	5	40	240	240	187
at Home	.311	.408	.436	1073	334	50	3	26	172	177	153
on Road	.299	.385	.444	1208	361	77	4	30	185	172	168
vs. Groundball	.316	.402	.441	1056	334	55	4	23	162	151	151
vs. Flyball	.295	.390	.439	1225	361	72	3	33	195	198	170
vs. Finesse	.312	.392	.433	1275	398	72	2	26	187	172	146
vs. Power	.295	.401	.449	1006	297	55	5	30	170	177	175
on Grass	.309	.399	.444	1581	488	77	4	43	260	243	233
on Artificial Turf	.296	.388	.431	700	207	50	3	13	97	106	88
Day Games	.319	.395	.459	837	267	52	1	21	135	105	107
Night Games	.296	.396	.429	1444	428	75	6	35	222	244	214
April	.300	.382	.411	287	86	17	0	5	36	38	30
May	.318	.404	.438	365	116	15	1	9	49	53	50
June	.261	.344	.403	395	103	19	2	11	51	49	60
July	.311	.436	.461	386	120	24	2	10	70	86	52
August	.314	.405	.451	437	137	33	0	9	80	66	74
Sept/Oct	.324	.405	.467	411	133	19	2	12	71	57	55
Bases Empty	.291	.372	.409	1224	356	58	3	27	27	157	192
Leadoff	.302	.363	.407	410	124	17	1	8	8	39	58
Not Leadoff	.285	.377	.410	814	232	41	2	19	19	118	134
Runners On	.321	.425	.476	1057	339	69	4	29	330	192	129
First Base Only	.360	.418	.504	405	146	26	1	10	41	40	40
Scoring Position	.296	.428	.459	652	193	43	3	19	289	152	89
Late Innings, Close	.295	.400	.385	397	117	16	1	6	53	69	62

RBI/Opportunities

	1987	Four Year
Scoring Position	60 / 231 (26%)	251 / 931 (27%)
Scoring Position, 2 Out	12 / 85 (14%)	65 / 335 (19%)
On Third, Less than 2 Out	27 / 43 (63%)	114 / 192 (59%)
Late close games / RBI Total	66 / 89 (74%)	273 / 357 (76%)

Tom Herr
St. Louis Cardinals

Mike Shannon, Cardinal broadcaster, has called Herr the "guts" of the ball club. That is about as good a description as can be made. Herr has consistently been in the upper echelon among National League second basemen in assists, double plays, and fielding percentage since becoming the regular second baseman in 1981. As the third place batter, Herr has the ability and knowledge of the strike zone to take pitches and allow Vince Coleman and Ozzie Smith the opportunity to steal, getting into scoring position. Herr led the Cardinals with 12 sacrifice flies and ranked sixth in the National league with 14 game winning RBI.

Herr hit two home runs, both right-handed, during the season. The first, however, was one of the most dramatic home runs hit in Busch Stadium. The Cardinals were playing the "hated" New York Mets April 18 before 50,000 fans on K-Mart seat cushion night. With the score tied and the bases loaded in the 10th inning, Herr hit a shot off Jesse Orosco for a grandslam home run. The place went nuts! As Herr circled the bases, thousands of K-Mart cushions came flying from the stands during a thunderous ovation as the fans celebrated the come-from-behind victory. The excitement carried over to the next afternoon as the Cardinals went on to sweep the three game series.

Teamed with the acrobatic Ozzie Smith, the Cardinal double play combination is one of the best in baseball. Herr played second base in 137 games in 1987 and turned 103 double plays. With runners on the corners, the Redbirds played for the double play which killed rallies or ended innings without the runner from third scoring. Herzog and the pitching staff have a lot of confidence the d.p. can be turned. Herr's pivot around second is quick and his throws are accurate, attested by his error total of only seven. Cardinal first basemen in '87 did not build their reputations saving errant throws.

Offensively, Herr had a fairly typical season, although he went on the 15-day disabled list in April. At the All-Star break Herr was hitting at a .270 clip and finished the season with an overall .263 average. Herr's worst hitting slump was a 14 for 94 streak (.149) followed by his best hitting streak of 26 for 70 (.371). Herr's biggest increases over the '86 season were in runs and RBI totals, with an increase from 48 runs to 73 runs scored and jumping from 61 to 83 RBI's. The only figure not in the norm was triples. It was the first time since Herr became a regular he did not hit any triples.

Rollie Loewen

Herr, Thomas Mitchell "Tom" — Bats: Both   Throws: Right   Born 04/04/56

1987 SEASON AND MAJOR-LEAGUE CAREER BATTING TOTALS

	G	AB	H	2B	3B	HR	TB	R	RBI	TBB	IBB	SO	HP	SH	SF	SB	CS	SB%	GDP	AVG	OBP	SLG
87 STL	141	510	134	29	0	2	169	73	83	68	3	62	3	4	12	19	4	.83	12	.263	.346	.331
9 YEARS	1014	3672	1008	179	31	18	1303	494	432	427	32	384	17	43	47	149	51	.75	66	.275	.349	.355

1987 SEASON

	Ave.	OBP	SLG	AB	H	2B	3B	HR	RBI	BB	SO
Totals	.263	.346	.331	510	134	29	0	2	83	68	62
vs. Left	.298	.386	.398	191	57	13	0	2	35	29	16
vs. Right	.241	.322	.292	319	77	16	0	0	48	39	46
at Home	.280	.368	.341	246	69	12	0	1	36	34	25
on Road	.246	.325	.322	264	65	17	0	1	47	34	37
vs. Groundball	.260	.348	.306	242	63	11	0	0	32	32	31
vs. Flyball	.265	.344	.354	268	71	18	0	2	51	36	31
vs. Finesse	.261	.328	.314	287	75	15	0	0	43	32	28
vs. Power	.265	.367	.354	223	59	14	0	2	40	36	34
on Grass	.223	.307	.264	121	27	5	0	0	21	16	16
on Artificial Turf	.275	.358	.352	389	107	24	0	2	62	52	46
Day Games	.310	.412	.386	171	53	13	0	0	27	31	19
Night Games	.239	.311	.304	339	81	16	0	2	56	37	43
April	.288	.393	.481	52	15	7	0	1	15	8	5
May	.293	.379	.310	58	17	1	0	0	2	7	12
June	.308	.393	.356	104	32	5	0	0	17	15	11
July	.200	.288	.263	95	19	6	0	0	15	13	11
August	.337	.380	.463	95	32	9	0	1	20	9	11
Sept/Oct	.179	.280	.189	106	19	1	0	0	14	16	12
Bases Empty	.250	.332	.299	244	61	12	0	0	0	29	28
Leadoff	.256	.322	.305	82	21	4	0	0	0	8	7
Not Leadoff	.247	.337	.296	162	40	8	0	0	0	21	21
Runners On	.274	.357	.361	266	73	17	0	2	83	39	34
First Base Only	.283	.339	.368	106	30	6	0	1	8	7	13
Scoring Position	.269	.368	.356	160	43	11	0	1	75	32	21
Late Innings, Close	.306	.367	.388	85	26	4	0	1	22	9	14

FOUR YEAR TOTALS (1984 – 1987)

	Ave.	OBP	SLG	AB	H	2B	3B	HR	RBI	BB	SO
	.274	.351	.358	2223	609	120	9	16	303	270	248
	.296	.367	.389	800	237	44	3	8	105	89	65
	.261	.342	.340	1423	372	76	6	8	198	181	183
	.279	.359	.356	1072	299	52	5	7	155	134	104
	.269	.344	.359	1151	310	68	4	9	148	136	144
	.296	.369	.370	1081	320	61	5	3	148	125	103
	.253	.334	.346	1142	289	59	4	13	155	145	145
	.285	.348	.368	1244	354	73	5	7	162	122	105
	.260	.355	.344	979	255	47	4	9	141	148	143
	.258	.329	.353	592	153	32	3	6	72	66	77
	.280	.359	.359	1631	456	88	6	10	231	204	171
	.278	.363	.361	776	216	45	2	5	94	103	95
	.272	.345	.356	1447	393	75	7	11	209	167	153
	.281	.385	.369	260	73	15	1	2	37	43	28
	.267	.333	.335	352	94	12	0	4	43	34	62
	.308	.378	.402	413	127	26	2	3	55	47	49
	.237	.311	.285	376	89	18	0	0	44	42	36
	.285	.355	.389	414	118	27	5	2	63	47	37
	.265	.353	.360	408	108	22	1	5	61	57	36
	.255	.336	.332	1208	308	62	2	9	9	146	
	.230	.323	.296	395	91	20	0	2	2	54	
	.267	.342	.349	813	217	42	2	7	7	92	
	.297	.370	.388	1015	301	58	7	7	294	124	
	.325	.373	.438	388	126	29	3	3	29	28	
	.279	.369	.357	627	175	29	4	4	265	96	
	.259	.326	.331	375	97	12	0	5	59	3	

RBI/Opportunities

Scoring Position	71 / 244	(29%)
Scoring Position, 2 Out	23 / 83	(28%)
On Third, Less than 2 Out	38 / 59	(64%)
RBI in close games / RBI Total	55 / 83	(66%)

	251 / 896	(28%)
	78 / 332	(23%)
	121 / 214	(57%)
	195 / 303	(64%)

Orel Hershiser
Los Angeles Dodgers

Quiz time!! Who were the two best pitchers in the National League over the last four years? Dwight Gooden was easy; even taking into account the time he lost last season, Gooden has been the best starter in the national League over the past four years.

But the second best starter in the National League over that period makes good Hot Stove League fodder. My candidate for the runner-up spot is Orel Hershiser IV.

In his four years in the big leagues he has won 60 games and lost only 41. His career winning percentage is .594—over the same time the Dodgers have played only .475 ball in games Hershiser hasn't started. Take away Valenzuela's 50 wins and 38 losses from the team and the Dodgers drop to a deadly .448 winning percentage without their best two starters. That averages out to 72–90. Yecch.

Hershiser's lifetime ERA is 2.91, outstanding even in the pitchers' park the Dodgers call home. Throughout his four years in the majors he has had one very consistent idiosyncrasy. He is a much better pitcher at home than on the road. At home in '87 his ERA was 2.42; on the road it was 3.70. At home he struck out 7 batters per game; on the road it dropped to under 6. At home his strikeout to walk ratio was 3.25 to 1; on the road it was 2.02 to 1.

The numbers have been very consistent over the years. His career ERA is a full run higher on the road. Knowing these numbers, or, maybe because he didn't know these numbers—*Buy This BOOK, Tommy!*—Lasorda made Hershiser his opening day starter on the road in '87. The game was in the Astrodome against the 1986 Cy Young winner. At first it looked like a good choice because over the past two years Hershiser had

a 2.49 ERA in the Dome . . . but, consider that Fernando Valenzuela has an ERA of 1.08 on the fake Texas Turf. When he was asked why he made the decision to start Hershiser over Fernando, Lasorda answered that he wanted to spread the opening day starts around the staff. Well, the Dodgers did finish fourth, so I guess Leo wasn't totally right about nice guys. Wake up and smell the coffee (espresso?), Tom. Learn to juggle your rotation so that Hershiser gets as many starts as possible at home, and as few as possible away. A few hundred miles north, the Giants have two pitchers who *love* Candlestick, and LaCoss and Hammaker get more home starts than road starts. It's not such a radical idea.

How did Orel stack up against some of the best NL pitchers going into the 1987 season, you ask? Here are the numbers:

	Opposition		
	BA	OBA	SLG
Hershiser	.224	.287	.303
Valenzuela	.223	.293	.341
Scott	.230	.299	.322
Darling	.237	.314	.349
Ryan	.216	.298	.321
Tudor	.232	.276	.343
Gooden	.206	.267	.289

Only Gooden has been better in all three categories.

No doubt, Hershiser is one of the best pitchers in the National League. At home, he may be one of the best pitchers in baseball.

Carmen Corica

Hershiser, Orel Leonard
Bats: Right   Throws: Right   Born 09/16/58

1987 SEASON AND MAJOR-LEAGUE CAREER PITCHING TOTALS

	G	GS	CG	GF	IP	BFP	H	R	ER	HR	SH	SF	HB	TBB	IBB	SO	WP	Bk	W	L	Pct	ShO	Sv	ERA
87 LA	37	35	10	2	265	1093	247	105	90	17	8	2	9	74	5	190	11	2	16	16	.500	1	1	3.06
5 YEARS	161	124	35	17	934	3842	806	360	302	48	30	15	24	284	29	655	37	6	60	41	.594	11	4	2.91

1987: Finesse, Groundball   1986: Finesse, Groundball   1985: Finesse, Groundball   1984: Power, Groundball

1987 SEASON

	G	IP	H	BB	SO	SB	CS	W	L	S	ERA
Totals	37	265.0	247	74	190	12	10	16	16	1	3.06
at Home	17	133.2	119	32	104	8	6	9	6	0	2.42
on Road	20	131.1	128	42	86	4	4	7	10	1	3.70
on Grass	11	78.1	77	18	54	4	2	5	4	0	3.22
on Artificial Turf	26	186.2	170	56	136	8	8	11	12	1	2.99
Day Games	25	189.1	176	47	134	9	8	12	9	0	2.71
Night Games	12	75.2	71	27	56	3	2	4	7	1	3.93
April	6	45.0	46	16	32	3	1	2	3	0	3.00
May	6	37.1	39	7	28	5	2	2	3	1	3.62
June	6	50.0	38	11	42	0	0	5	1	0	0.90
July	6	36.1	31	12	24	2	3	2	2	0	2.97
August	6	45.2	41	15	34	1	2	2	3	0	2.96
Sept/Oct	7	50.2	52	13	30	1	2	3	4	0	4.97

vs. Opponent Batters	Ave.	OBP	SLG	AB	H	2B	3B	HR	RBI	BB	SO
Totals	.247	.304	.352	1000	247	40	7	17	89	74	190
vs. Left	.270	.329	.383	592	160	27	5	10	53	49	92
vs. Right	.213	.268	.306	408	87	13	2	7	36	25	98
Bases Empty	.242	.296	.352	603	146	25	4	11	11	41	114
Leadoff	.240	.296	.335	254	61	11	2	3	3	18	49
Not Leadoff	.244	.296	.364	349	85	14	2	8	8	23	65
Runners On Base	.254	.317	.353	397	101	15	3	6	78	33	76
First Base Only	.289	.323	.422	180	52	11	2	3	9	9	21
Scoring Position	.226	.312	.295	217	49	4	1	3	69	24	55
Late Innings, Close	.301	.378	.444	153	46	7	3	3	18	18	23

FOUR YEAR TOTALS (1984 – 1987)

	G	IP	H	BB	SO	SB	CS	W	L	S	ERA
Totals	153	925.2	799	278	650	76	33	60	41	3	2.91
at Home	78	496.2	401	141	363	45	18	35	16	0	2.43
on Road	75	429.0	398	137	287	31	15	25	25	3	3.46
on Grass	58	327.0	294	92	215	34	10	16	13	1	3.08
on Artificial Turf	95	598.2	505	186	435	42	23	44	28	2	2.81
Day Games	109	683.2	574	190	478	54	22	47	25	1	2.69
Night Games	44	242.0	225	88	172	22	11	13	16	2	3.53
April	25	119.0	109	45	83	8	5	9	5	0	2.65
May	26	138.1	126	44	124	18	6	7	5	1	2.86
June	27	154.1	139	43	108	13	5	10	7	2	3.27
July	23	152.0	113	47	122	17	4	13	6	0	2.55
August	24	163.0	145	50	103	12	7	7	9	0	2.93
Sept/Oct	28	199.0	167	49	110	8	6	14	9	0	3.08

vs. Opponent Batters	Ave.	OBP	SLG	AB	H	2B	3B	HR	RBI	BB	SO
Totals	.231	.290	.317	3459	799	121	18	47	307	278	650
vs. Left	.249	.308	.337	1878	467	78	11	22	171	159	296
vs. Right	.210	.268	.293	1581	332	43	7	25	136	119	354
Bases Empty	.227	.275	.315	2107	479	75	11	29	29	134	396
Leadoff	.235	.284	.327	888	209	33	3	14	14	58	160
Not Leadoff	.221	.269	.306	1219	270	42	8	15	15	76	236
Runners On Base	.237	.312	.321	1352	320	46	7	18	278	144	254
First Base Only	.255	.296	.350	589	150	26	3	8	25	35	80
Scoring Position	.223	.322	.299	763	170	20	4	10	253	109	174
Late Innings, Close	.244	.323	.361	427	104	13	5	9	47	49	79

RBI/Opportunities

Scoring Position	63 / 298 (21%)	232 / 1074 (22%)
Scoring Position, 2 Out	17 / 123 (14%)	90 / 486 (19%)
On Third, Less than 2 Out	34 / 66 (52%)	96 / 201 (48%)
RBI in close games / RBI Total	72 / 89 (81%)	225 / 307 (73%)

Ted Higuera
Milwaukee Brewers

What a wonderful, unappreciated pitcher Teddy Higuera is. I call him wonderful, because he's won 53 games, lost 29 and rolled up a 3.50 ERA in three years in the majors. I call him unappreciated because I think he's the third-best left-handed starter in baseball—behind only Jimmy Key and John Tudor—and I doubt that many people would agree with me. If you look at the evidence, it's very hard to put him any lower. There are nine basic skills for a pitcher; Higuera is below average in only two.

STAMINA: Higuera has averaged 240.2 innings in his career and 12 complete games. He's good for about 7.1 innings per start.

STUFF: Though Higuera isn't that hard a thrower—his fastball is only in the high 80's and his slider doesn't sizzle—his pitches move around. He's allowed only 8.07 hits per nine innings in his career.

CONTACT: Higuera changes speeds very well—his straight change might be his best pitch—and fools a lot of batters because of it. He's averaged 7.15 strikeouts per nine innings.

CONTROL: Teddy throws strikes. He's walked 2.79 men per nine innings in his career.

BASESTEALING: Teodoro has a compact delivery and an excellent pickoff move. He's one of the toughest men to run on in the American League.

DOUBLE PLAYS: The big problem area. Higuera's ground/air ratio and DP support figures are always exceptionally low.

HOMERS: Teddy's raw figures (.90 homers per nine innings) are very good, but that's largely because Milwaukee is death to power hitters. He's vulnerable to the longball on the road and wouldn't be as effective a pitcher in almost any other park.

PERFORMANCE: The single best indicator of a pitcher's quality is his ERA; Higuera has had one of the ten best in the AL for the last two years.

ABILITY TO WIN: Though Higuera has never been badly hurt by his offense (like Key and Danny Jackson), he's never been exceptionally well-supported, either. His lifetime winning percentage is slightly better than projected—and .646 speaks for itself.

One thing that may surprise you—in one of two ways—is Teddy's age. He's no spring chicken, but he's not *that* much older than compatriot Fernando Valenzuela. Teddy turned 29 in 1987; Fernando turned 27. Had he not had a late start, I think Teddy would have had better career stats.

Finally: For some reason, the national media has become unnecessarily genteel about nicknames recently. Joe Medwick is now known as "Ducky"— when in fact he was called "Ducky-Wucky" during his career. The same thing seems to apply to Higuera. Forget what you read—or what it says at the top of the page—the man answers to "Teddy."

Geoff Beckman

Higuera, Teodoro Valenzuela (Ted)   Bats: Both   Throws: Left   Born 11/09/58

1987 SEASON AND MAJOR-LEAGUE CAREER PITCHING TOTALS

	G	GS	CG	GF	IP	BFP	H	R	ER	HR	SH	SF	HB	TBB	IBB	SO	WP	Bk	W	L	Pct	ShO	Sv	ERA
87 MIL	35	35	14	0	262	1084	236	120	112	24	6	9	2	87	2	240	4	2	18	10	.643	3	0	3.85
3 YEARS	101	99	36	2	722	2989	648	309	281	72	18	30	8	224	7	574	11	5	53	29	.646	9	0	3.50

1987: Power, Flyball   1986: Power, Flyball   1985: Finesse, Flyball

1987 SEASON												FOUR YEAR TOTALS (1984 – 1987)											
	G	IP	H	BB	SO	SB	CS	W	L	S	ERA		G	IP	H	BB	SO	SB	CS	W	L	S	ERA
Totals	35	261.1	236	87	240	20	9	18	10	0	3.86		101	722.0	648	224	574	43	27	53	29	0	3.50
at Home	19	149.1	134	44	146	9	3	12	4	0	3.50		50	369.2	326	112	307	22	11	29	11	0	3.36
on Road	16	112.0	102	43	94	11	6	6	6	0	4.34		51	352.1	322	112	267	21	16	24	18	0	3.65
on Grass	11	73.2	73	27	66	1	1	6	3	0	4.40		33	218.0	195	82	167	6	6	16	10	0	3.72
on Artificial Turf	24	187.2	163	60	174	19	8	12	7	0	3.64		68	504.0	453	142	407	37	21	37	19	0	3.41
Day Games	30	225.1	210	75	212	18	7	16	9	0	3.91		84	605.0	548	192	485	37	22	44	24	0	3.50
Night Games	5	36.0	26	12	28	2	2	2	1	0	3.25		17	117.0	100	32	89	6	5	9	5	0	3.46
April	5	35.2	33	14	34	3	2	4	0	0	3.28		12	89.1	75	31	76	5	3	7	2	0	3.22
May	6	41.0	46	11	47	2	1	0	5	0	6.59		18	121.1	110	40	112	5	3	6	10	0	4.23
June	6	37.0	47	14	35	3	1	2	2	0	6.08		18	107.0	114	33	86	6	5	7	6	0	4.79
July	6	45.1	51	13	36	8	2	4	1	0	3.77		17	120.0	118	34	91	10	5	11	3	0	3.75
August	5	44.0	23	14	39	1	0	3	1	0	1.64		17	131.2	117	35	96	10	3	11	2	0	2.60
Sept/Oct	7	58.1	36	21	49	3	3	5	1	0	2.62		19	152.2	114	51	113	7	8	11	6	0	2.77

vs. Opponent Batters	Ave.	OBP	SLG	AB	H	2B	3B	HR	RBI	BB	SO		Ave.	OBP	SLG	AB	H	2B	3B	HR	RBI	BB	SO
Totals	.241	.301	.368	981	236	47	3	24	110	87	240		.239	.297	.373	2710	648	122	13	72	270	224	574
vs. Left	.281	.311	.400	160	45	7	0	4	19	7	39		.255	.294	.387	439	112	21	2	11	45	24	103
vs. Right	.233	.300	.362	821	191	40	3	20	91	80	201		.236	.297	.371	2271	536	101	11	61	225	200	471
Bases Empty	.223	.291	.358	579	129	20	2	18	18	54	161		.235	.296	.381	1649	387	65	10	52	52	142	361
Leadoff	.227	.302	.347	242	55	6	1	7	7	25	67		.231	.293	.380	687	159	23	5	23	23	59	145
Not Leadoff	.220	.283	.365	337	74	14	1	11	11	29	94		.237	.298	.381	962	228	42	5	29	29	83	216
Runners On Base	.266	.316	.383	402	107	27	1	6	92	33	79		.246	.298	.362	1061	261	57	3	20	218	82	213
First Base Only	.227	.285	.348	198	45	9	0	5	13	16	41		.232	.273	.320	544	126	22	1	8	24	31	99
Scoring Position	.304	.345	.417	204	62	18	1	1	79	17	38		.261	.323	.406	517	135	35	2	12	194	51	114
Late Innings, Close	.190	.241	.286	147	28	3	1	3	12	10	32		.230	.283	.304	404	93	6	3	6	29	30	82

RBI/Opportunities

Scoring Position	75 / 275 (27%)	172 / 701 (25%)
Scoring Position, 2 Out	26 / 124 (21%)	57 / 318 (18%)
On Third, Less than 2 Out	29 / 49 (59%)	73 / 124 (59%)
RBI in close games / RBI Total	71 / 110 (65%)	184 / 270 (68%)

Donnie Hill
Chicago White Sox

A year ago Donnie Hill was acquired by the White Sox and immediately handed the second base job. All he was expected to do was erase the memory of Julio Cruz. Considering what Julio's last season had been like (209 at bats, 2 extra base hits), there seemed no way Hill could fail.

Never underestimate the hand baseball can deal you. In April Hill batted .190, but there were signs of hope as more than half his 11 hits were for extra bases, and he played errorless ball in the field.

In May we abandoned hope. Hill hit .091, and all three of his hits were singles. Even worse, he suddenly became allergic to ground balls. A routine two-hopper would be hit two steps to Donnie's right, and he would stand there pounding his glove like he never even saw it. White Sox fans are a hardened bunch, but even they began to wonder: was that Donnie Hill they were seeing, or Donny Osmond?

Well, there was a vision problem, all right, but it wasn't on the part of the fans. It turned out that Hill was suffering from conjuctivitis. This was a new disease for most of us—I thought at first it might be an irrational fear of conjunctions—but what it meant was that Hill's eyes were allergic to his contact lenses. Wearing glasses seemed to distort Donnie's depth perception, so there was nothing for Hill to do but go on the disabled list until a new, non-irritating set

of lenses could be found. Eventually a set was located, and Hill returned to the lineup. He still didn't dazzle anyone, but he did make us forget Julio Cruz. From June 1 on, Hill batted .263—he hit .368 in August—and wound up the season with a career-high nine homers. Toward the end of the year he was playing every day, holding down third against lefties (while Fred Manrique played second) and second base against righties (as Steve Lyons handled third). It was a makeshift arrangement at best; neither Manrique nor Lyons hit well enough to give much hope for the future, and Hill's work at third was, in a word, Hobsonian. His fielding average at the hot corner was less than .900.

As 1988 begins the White Sox seem intent on phasing Hill out. He appears likely to see some work at second when a righthander is pitching—Manrique, who hit well against southpaws in '87, will probably continue in that role. Where the Sox' lack of confidence in Hill is really reflected is in their decision to try Ken Williams at third. And then there is the selection of second baseman Santiago Garcia in the minor league draft. Garcia was last seen in August of '87, flailing away at a teammate with his bat. If only Garcia—or Hill, or Manrique, or *someone*—could attack pitches with such relish!

Don Zminda

Hill, Donald Earl "Don"   Bats: Both   Throws: Right   Born 11/20/60

1987 SEASON AND MAJOR-LEAGUE CAREER BATTING TOTALS

	G	AB	H	2B	3B	HR	TB	R	RBI	TBB	IBB	SO	HP	SH	SF	SB	CS	SB%	GDP	AVG	OBP	SLG
87 CHA	111	410	98	14	6	9	151	57	46	30	1	35	1	4	4	1	0	1.00	11	.239	.290	.368
5 YEARS	468	1474	388	56	10	20	524	180	154	85	4	139	1	33	12	17	8	.68	33	.263	.302	.355

	1987 SEASON											FOUR YEAR TOTALS (1984 – 1987)									
	Ave.	OBP	SLG	AB	H	2B	3B	HR	RBI	BB	SO	Ave.	OBP	SLG	AB	H	2B	3B	HR	RBI	BB	SO
Totals	.239	.290	.368	410	98	14	6	9	46	30	35	.263	.304	.356	1316	346	49	10	18	139	81	119
vs. Left	.262	.319	.400	130	34	3	0	5	14	12	13	.253	.302	.340	403	102	15	1	6	36	30	42
vs. Right	.229	.276	.354	280	64	11	6	4	32	18	22	.267	.305	.364	913	244	34	9	12	103	51	77
at Home	.254	.303	.363	201	51	11	4	1	19	14	11	.262	.303	.332	642	168	28	7	1	52	39	56
on Road	.225	.278	.373	209	47	3	2	8	27	16	24	.264	.305	.380	674	178	21	3	17	87	42	63
vs. Groundball	.271	.329	.357	207	56	8	2	2	19	18	16	.290	.329	.357	638	185	25	3	4	66	39	55
vs. Flyball	.207	.249	.379	203	42	6	4	7	27	12	19	.237	.280	.355	678	161	24	7	14	73	42	64
vs. Finesse	.239	.274	.362	218	52	7	4	4	18	11	17	.275	.301	.371	735	202	24	7	11	66	29	61
vs. Power	.240	.307	.375	192	46	7	2	5	28	19	18	.248	.307	.337	581	144	25	3	7	73	52	58
on Grass	.248	.299	.374	326	81	13	5	6	36	24	23	.258	.300	.334	1075	277	39	8	9	104	67	94
on Artificial Turf	.202	.253	.345	84	17	1	1	3	10	6	12	.286	.322	.456	241	69	10	2	9	35	14	25
Day Games	.242	.281	.392	120	29	3	0	5	14	7	8	.295	.336	.389	468	138	16	2	8	54	31	35
Night Games	.238	.293	.359	290	69	11	6	4	32	23	27	.245	.286	.338	848	208	33	8	10	85	50	84
April	.190	.277	.379	58	11	3	1	2	7	7	8	.222	.273	.358	212	47	7	2	6	24	15	17
May	.091	.184	.091	33	3	0	0	0	3	4	4	.244	.284	.279	172	42	3	0	1	17	10	20
June	.260	.302	.380	50	13	4	1	0	3	3	1	.257	.311	.325	191	49	9	2	0	13	15	15
July	.205	.234	.330	88	18	1	2	2	8	4	6	.253	.277	.341	249	63	9	2	3	24	9	18
August	.368	.419	.596	57	21	4	0	3	14	4	6	.323	.367	.445	263	85	18	1	4	38	17	24
Sept/Oct	.258	.301	.355	124	32	2	2	2	11	8	10	.262	.306	.354	229	60	3	3	4	23	15	25
Bases Empty	.233	.282	.364	236	55	7	3	6	6	15	20	.250	.293	.341	739	185	27	5	10	10	44	72
Leadoff	.266	.296	.340	94	25	4	0	1	1	4	7	.265	.310	.355	287	76	12	1	4	4	19	21
Not Leadoff	.211	.273	.380	142	30	3	3	5	5	11	13	.241	.282	.332	452	109	15	4	6	6	25	51
Runners On	.247	.301	.374	174	43	7	3	3	40	15	15	.279	.320	.376	577	161	22	5	8	129	37	47
First Base Only	.254	.277	.365	63	16	4	0	1	4	2	5	.272	.297	.368	228	62	11	1	3	11	8	17
Scoring Position	.243	.313	.378	111	27	3	3	2	36	13	10	.284	.335	.381	349	99	11	4	5	118	29	30
Late Innings, Close	.300	.364	.467	60	18	1	0	3	11	6	4	.291	.347	.398	196	57	4	1	5	19	17	12

RBI/Opportunities

Scoring Position	33 / 147 (22%)	108 / 456 (24%)
Scoring Position, 2 Out	13 / 65 (20%)	47 / 194 (24%)
On Third, Less than 2 Out	11 / 20 (55%)	39 / 74 (53%)
RBI in close games / RBI Total	30 / 46 (65%)	73 / 139 (53%)

Guy Hoffman
Cincinnati Reds

If he had any sense, Guy Hoffman would have been out of professional baseball by now. The southpaw made his major league debut with the White Sox in 1979 as an unimpressive long reliever. Over the next seven years, he struggled to get back to the big leagues and stay there, pitching for parts of three seasons with both Chicago clubs. His career statistics were eight wins and seven losses in 90 games over 8 seasons, yet he refused to quit.

In the spring of 1987, his persistence finally paid off. The Cubs traded him to Cincinnati where, through an amazing series of unrelated events, he won a job in the starting rotation. In search of a fifth starter, the Reds saw Mario Soto delayed by recurring shoulder problems, lost prospect Norm Charlton when he broke a finger, and found rookie Pat Pacillo simply not ready for the big leagues. Rose kept both Hoffman and righty Bill Landrum for the trip north; one would start and the other serve in long relief. By the luck of the draw, a lefty was needed when the spot in the rotation came up for the first time.

Once given the opportunity, Hoffman held on to the ball. He got off to a quick 7–1 start and was one of the few signs of hope on the Reds dismal starting staff. An elbow injury in mid-August hampered his effectiveness down the stretch. Hoffman was forced to pitch in pain because, even in his injured state, he was better than anyone else the Reds had.

Interestingly, Guy posted some decent numbers without out consistent benefit of the Reds' big bangers in the lineup—of his twenty-two starts, Hoffman worked nine with at least two of the Reds' big five (Davis, Parker, Bell, Daniels and Diaz) out of the lineup; further, he drew the second game of a twin bill twice, and pitched the final game before the All-Star break, when Davis, Daniels, Parker and Bell all used a day of sick leave.

Hoffman is a classic finesse pitcher. Although he doesn't strike out a lot of hitters, his strikeout to walk ratio is nearly 2 to 1; further, he hasn't allowed a lot of homers over the years.

At present, it is unclear whether the Reds consider Hoffman as a part of their future plans or merely as a stop gap in a transitional stage for their pitching staff. A full scale house cleaning in the Reds pitching department saw the departure of Ted Power and Bill Gullickson and the addition of Danny Jackson, Dennis Rasmussen, and Jose Rijo. That Hoffman is still on the roster would seem to indicate that he will return, perhaps as a long reliever. Still, one is struck by the similarities between Guy and another well-traveled lefty, Chris Welsh. Like Hoffman, Welsh surprised everyone by making the Red staff in '86. He got off to a hot start, then was hampered by arm injuries and wound' up 6–9. Welsh ended up being released during the off-season.

Sean Lahman and Bob Bailey

Hoffman, Guy Alan   Bats: Left   Throws: Left   Born 07/09/56

1987 SEASON AND MAJOR-LEAGUE CAREER PITCHING TOTALS

	G	GS	CG	GF	IP	BFP	H	R	ER	HR	SH	SF	HB	TBB	IBB	SO	WP	Bk	W	L	Pct	ShO	Sv	ERA
87 CIN	36	22	0	2	159	669	160	83	77	20	8	5	4	49	5	87	3	1	9	10	.474	0	0	4.36
5 YEARS	126	31	1	29	317	1361	334	155	147	28	16	10	7	120	19	178	12	3	17	17	.500	0	3	4.17

1987: Finesse, Groundball   1986: Finesse, Flyball

		1987 SEASON											FOUR YEAR TOTALS (1984 – 1987)										
	G	IP	H	BB	SO	SB	CS	W	L	S	ERA		G	IP	H	BB	SO	SB	CS	W	L	S	ERA
Totals	36	159.0	160	49	87	9	5	9	10	0	4.36		68	243.0	252	78	134	12	15	15	12	0	4.19
at Home	20	81.0	80	24	41	1	2	5	5	0	4.44		34	129.2	130	35	73	2	7	9	5	0	4.03
on Road	16	78.0	80	25	46	8	3	4	5	0	4.27		34	113.1	122	43	61	10	8	6	7	0	4.37
on Grass	13	60.0	67	13	33	4	2	0	4	0	4.50		32	118.1	126	28	71	5	9	5	4	0	3.80
on Artificial Turf	23	99.0	93	36	54	5	3	9	6	0	4.27		36	124.2	126	50	63	7	6	10	8	0	4.55
Day Games	9	49.1	56	15	29	3	2	2	4	0	4.20		29	110.2	123	35	65	4	8	6	5	0	3.98
Night Games	27	109.2	104	34	58	6	3	7	6	0	4.43		39	132.1	129	43	69	8	7	9	7	0	4.35
April	4	17.1	16	3	5	1	1	1	1	0	2.08		5	24.1	22	4	10	1	2	1	1	0	2.22
May	8	17.2	20	6	9	2	1	1	0	0	3.06		14	40.0	49	14	20	3	4	2	1	0	4.72
June	8	33.2	31	9	26	3	1	4	1	0	4.28		17	59.0	60	17	41	5	4	6	2	0	3.81
July	6	33.1	40	8	14	0	0	1	4	0	5.94		10	42.2	51	13	18	0	1	2	4	0	5.91
August	5	27.2	28	12	9	0	1	1	3	0	4.88		5	27.2	28	12	9	0	1	1	3	0	4.88
Sept/Oct	5	29.1	25	11	24	3	1	1	1	0	4.30		17	49.1	42	18	36	3	3	3	1	0	3.28

vs. Opponent Batters	Ave.	OBP	SLG	AB	H	2B	3B	HR	RBI	BB	SO		Ave.	OBP	SLG	AB	H	2B	3B	HR	RBI	BB	SO
Totals	.266	.323	.449	602	160	40	5	20	78	49	87		.274	.331	.435	921	252	61	5	26	120	78	134
vs. Left	.307	.388	.446	101	31	8	0	2	10	13	17		.283	.378	.392	166	47	12	0	2	19	25	28
vs. Right	.257	.309	.449	501	129	32	5	18	68	36	70		.272	.320	.445	755	205	49	5	24	101	53	106
Bases Empty	.255	.306	.396	369	94	18	2	10	10	26	57		.266	.315	.400	545	145	30	2	13	13	38	87
Leadoff	.267	.325	.440	150	40	7	2	5	5	12	20		.289	.344	.436	225	65	14	2	5	5	18	32
Not Leadoff	.247	.292	.365	219	54	11	0	5	5	14	37		.250	.294	.375	320	80	16	0	8	8	20	55
Runners On Base	.283	.348	.532	233	66	22	3	10	68	23	30		.285	.354	.487	376	107	31	3	13	107	40	47
First Base Only	.279	.322	.541	111	31	12	1	5	16	6	14		.273	.309	.477	172	47	15	1	6	20	8	18
Scoring Position	.287	.370	.525	122	35	10	2	5	52	17	16		.294	.387	.495	204	60	16	2	7	87	32	29
Late Innings, Close	.241	.241	.448	29	7	3	0	1	2	0	6		.279	.290	.382	68	19	4	0	1	4	1	11

RBI/Opportunities

Scoring Position	44 / 184 (24%)		75 / 303 (25%)
Scoring Position, 2 Out	18 / 75 (24%)		32 / 132 (24%)
On Third, Less than 2 Out	16 / 42 (38%)		24 / 62 (39%)
RBI in close games / RBI Total	52 / 78 (67%)		71 / 120 (59%)

Ricky Horton
St. Louis Cardinals

Ricky Horton is possibly the most underrated pitcher in baseball—he's even been underrated by his old team, the Cardinals. He's also been murderously unlucky, which is, of course, how you get to be underrated.

Horton came up in 1984, and went 8–4 as a starter late in the season, picking up another win in relief. But Kurt Kepshire turned in an even more spectacular half-season, and the Cards traded for John Tudor, who is the same type of pitcher as Horton, so Ricky got lost in the shuffle. In 1985, he had a perfectly good year as a reliever, but that was the year of the Committee, when Jeff Lahti and Ken Dayley turned in career years, and Todd Worrell came up late as the strikeout ace Whitey Herzog so loves. Ricky started '86 in the rotation, due to injuries, and did just fine. He gave up 1 run in 7 innings to open the season, but was pitching against Dwight Gooden, so he got no decision. Next he gave up 2 in 7 2/3, and lost. Then he had another good 6 innings, but was roughed up in the 7th, losing again. So he wasn't 3–0 or 2–1 when he had his first bad game. He was promptly benched and then he got hurt.

When he came back, Horton was the best reliever in the game. His ERA in relief in 1986 was 0.65 (that's "zero"), which makes even Dave Righetti look bad. He even went 3–0 in 5 spot starts. That, and a slow April by Worrell, got Horton some work early in 1987, and he took full advantage, trashing the league, particularly the Mets. He had 5 saves by May, with an ERA in the ones. Then he pitched in a game while sick with the flu. He was hammered for a bunch of runs and never fully recovered; the second half of 1987 is by far Horton's worst half-season in the majors. So, of course, that was the post-season wherein the Cardinals had the small pitching staff and could have used some innings from him.

With the Cards, Ricky was bottled up behind Tudor, Greg Mathews, and Joe Magrane for the left-handed junkball spots in the Cardinal rotation. That meant there was no serious chance he would be a rotation starter. He was also bottled up behind Worrell for the ace reliever job, and Ken Dayley throws hard, so Ricky was behind him, too. But Ricky Horton's career record as a starter is 14–8, and he put in a full year (spread over 1986–1987) as a world-class relief ace. The Cardinals valued him enough to pay him $400,000 per year, but apparently not enough to keep him; they have traded him to the White Sox in order to obtain a pitcher (Jose DeLeon) who might not even be as good. As a Cardinal fan, this kills me to say, but watch for Horton to win 20 or save 30, and for his new team to suddenly make a quantum leap in the pennant race.

Brock J. Hanke

Horton, Ricky Neal   Bats: Left   Throws: Left   Born 07/30/59

1987 SEASON AND MAJOR-LEAGUE CAREER PITCHING TOTALS

	G	GS	CG	GF	IP	BFP	H	R	ER	HR	SH	SF	HB	TBB	IBB	SO	WP	Bk	W	L	Pct	ShO	Sv	ERA
87 STL	67	6	0	24	125	533	127	58	53	15	6	3	0	42	10	55	3	4	8	3	.727	0	7	3.82
4 YEARS	195	36	2	53	441	1839	428	166	155	41	20	12	5	141	32	239	12	12	24	12	.667	1	12	3.16

1987: Finesse, Groundball   1986: Finesse, Groundball   1985: Power, Groundball   1984: Finesse, Flyball

	1987 SEASON											FOUR YEAR TOTALS (1984 – 1987)										
	G	IP	H	BB	SO	SB	CS	W	L	S	ERA	G	IP	H	BB	SO	SB	CS	W	L	S	ERA
Totals	67	125.1	127	42	55	2	4	8	3	7	3.88	195	441.0	428	141	239	16	15	24	12	12	3.18
at Home	35	58.2	56	16	25	0	1	4	1	3	3.22	95	201.1	192	59	107	5	7	11	3	6	2.86
on Road	32	66.2	71	26	30	2	3	4	2	4	4.45	100	239.2	236	82	132	11	8	13	9	6	3.45
on Grass	21	40.2	37	13	14	0	1	2	1	2	2.88	72	158.2	150	58	79	4	6	7	4	3	2.72
on Artificial Turf	46	84.2	90	29	41	2	3	6	2	5	4.36	123	282.1	278	83	160	12	9	17	8	9	3.44
Day Games	13	26.2	28	15	11	0	2	1	1	2	4.72	48	114.1	98	44	67	3	5	4	3	4	3.15
Night Games	54	98.2	99	27	44	2	2	7	2	5	3.65	147	326.2	330	97	172	13	10	20	9	8	3.20
April	10	16.0	12	3	15	0	0	0	0	4	1.13	28	59.2	49	17	43	1	0	0	3	4	2.72
May	13	19.0	17	5	5	0	1	2	0	1	3.32	35	54.1	42	17	29	2	1	3	1	2	1.82
June	12	20.2	24	6	7	1	1	1	0	2	4.79	29	62.2	59	23	37	4	5	5	1	2	3.16
July	8	31.1	33	14	11	0	1	2	1	0	4.60	32	87.0	97	31	45	4	5	3	2	2	3.72
August	12	19.2	20	8	7	0	1	1	1	0	4.12	34	78.2	86	25	41	2	1	7	3	2	4.46
Sept/Oct	12	18.2	21	6	10	1	0	2	1	0	4.34	37	98.2	95	28	44	3	3	6	2	0	2.74

vs. Opponent Batters	Ave.	OBP	SLG	AB	H	2B	3B	HR	RBI	BB	SO	Ave.	OBP	SLG	AB	H	2B	3B	HR	RBI	BB	SO
Totals	.264	.321	.443	481	127	25	8	15	68	42	55	.258	.315	.397	1660	428	80	14	41	184	141	239
vs. Left	.225	.288	.333	120	27	6	2	1	11	11	21	.225	.277	.290	427	96	12	2	4	43	31	81
vs. Right	.277	.332	.479	361	100	19	6	14	57	31	34	.269	.329	.434	1233	332	68	12	37	141	110	158
Bases Empty	.269	.319	.455	275	74	12	3	11	11	20	26	.252	.300	.405	989	249	45	7	31	31	68	138
Leadoff	.289	.314	.500	114	33	4	1	6	6	4	12	.264	.304	.420	405	107	16	4	13	13	23	53
Not Leadoff	.255	.322	.422	161	41	8	2	5	5	16	14	.243	.297	.396	584	142	29	3	18	18	45	85
Runners On Base	.257	.325	.427	206	53	13	5	4	57	22	29	.267	.337	.385	671	179	35	7	10	153	73	101
First Base Only	.307	.333	.587	75	23	6	3	3	13	3	13	.278	.321	.433	270	75	15	3	7	24	17	43
Scoring Position	.229	.320	.336	131	30	7	2	1	44	19	16	.259	.348	.352	401	104	20	4	3	129	56	58
Late Innings, Close	.262	.331	.421	126	33	1	2	5	20	13	16	.235	.313	.333	336	79	7	4	6	33	38	53

RBI/Opportunities

Scoring Position	39 / 170 (23%)	119 / 559 (21%)
Scoring Position, 2 Out	12 / 83 (14%)	43 / 262 (16%)
On Third, Less than 2 Out	18 / 29 (62%)	51 / 99 (52%)
RBI in close games / RBI Total	41 / 68 (60%)	104 / 184 (57%)

Charlie Hough
Texas Rangers

Burt Hawkins, the official scorer at Arlington Stadium, was severely criticized by catcher Geno Petralli for calling too many passed balls on what he felt should be wild pitches. His comments made it to the local papers and were eventually carried nationally. Truth is, the passed ball rate in Ranger road games was nearly identical to Hawkins' scoring. The official scorers have done a surprisingly good job of standardizing the passed ball call, far better than they do with the much more common error call. Yet it is also obvious that their standard needs to be changed when a knuckleball is involved.

The idea is that a passed ball allows a runner to advance on a pitch that should have been caught by the catcher; it is supposed to be the responsibility of the catcher. It goes in the catcher's defensive record, and the pitcher is not charged an earned run for runs scoring as a result of a passed ball. It is ridiculous, then, that knuckleballers commonly have a much higher association with passed balls than the worst defensive catcher in the league.

The Rangers set a major league record with 73 passed balls in 1987; 65 of them came with Charlie Hough on the mound. They used a three-man catching corps where each caught between 400–500 innings. All three had reasonable passed ball rates with the other pitchers and laughable ratios with Hough. Don Slaught was the *best,* and he still averaged a passed ball every five innings with Charlie. The overall passed ball rate with the other Ranger pitchers was one every 145 innings.

Having watched Hough work for years, let me suggest this new standard for passed balls on knuckleballs. First, forget whether it was a strike or not. Call it a passed ball only if the pitch gets away after striking the catcher's glove *in* the pocket. I know that sounds silly, but most of your passed ball knucklers that glance off the outer edges of the glove have moved so sharply and suddenly, that it is not fair to rule that they should have been caught. This is fairer to the catchers and dumps the responsibility for the extra runs back on the true guilty party, the knuckleball pitcher.

Why did Hough throw a record number of passed balls in 1987? I'm convinced a mechanical change had him throwing a sharper breaking knuckleball from the stretch position than from the wind-up. The in-game change was not only hard for the catchers to adjust to, it gave fits to the hitters. With men on base compared to bases empty, the opposing hitters hit 28 points less, their power was cut about a third, and they struck out 36 percent more. They also had a lot of trouble getting out of the way as Hough better than doubled his career-high in hit batsmen, and they were about three times more frequent from the stretch position than the wind-up.

Craig R. Wright

Hough, Charles Oliver "Charlie" Bats: Right Throws: Right Born 01/05/48

1987 SEASON AND MAJOR-LEAGUE CAREER PITCHING TOTALS

	G	GS	CG	GF	IP	BFP	H	R	ER	HR	SH	SF	HB	TBB	IBB	SO	WP	Bk	W	L	Pct	ShO	Sv	ERA
87 TEX	40	40	13	0	285	1231	238	159	120	36	5	14	19	124	1	223	12	9	18	13	.581	0	0	3.79
18 YEARS	649	233	78	239	2453	10358	2076	1122	974	234	77	63	109	1042	36	1606	123	17	149	128	.538	10	61	3.57

1987: Power, Flyball   1986: Finesse, Flyball   1985: Finesse, Groundball   1984: Finesse, Groundball

1987 SEASON

	G	IP	H	BB	SO	SB	CS	W	L	S	ERA
Totals	40	285.1	238	124	223	36	12	18	13	0	3.79
at Home	22	153.1	139	65	138	26	8	11	8	0	4.40
on Road	18	132.0	99	59	85	10	4	7	5	0	3.07
on Grass	10	68.0	60	33	50	10	3	1	3	0	3.57
on Artificial Turf	30	217.1	178	91	173	26	9	17	10	0	3.85
Day Games	33	233.2	192	98	192	32	11	17	10	0	3.62
Night Games	7	51.2	46	26	31	4	1	1	3	0	4.53
April	5	32.2	30	13	24	4	2	1	1	0	4.41
May	6	43.2	41	15	31	5	1	4	0	0	3.50
June	7	48.2	33	29	24	6	1	3	2	0	3.51
July	7	47.2	46	23	50	8	5	3	4	0	5.29
August	7	53.2	41	24	49	7	4	3	3	0	3.52
Sept/Oct	8	59.0	47	20	45	6	4	4	3	0	2.90

vs. Opponent Batters	Ave.	OBP	SLG	AB	H	2B	3B	HR	RBI	BB	SO
Totals	.222	.311	.372	1070	238	42	5	36	125	124	223
vs. Left	.239	.336	.375	510	122	14	2	17	65	71	93
vs. Right	.207	.288	.370	560	116	28	3	19	60	53	130
Bases Empty	.234	.314	.410	649	152	29	5	25	25	69	119
Leadoff	.244	.312	.402	271	66	12	2	9	9	24	49
Not Leadoff	.228	.315	.415	378	86	17	3	16	16	45	70
Runners On Base	.204	.307	.314	421	86	13	0	11	100	55	104
First Base Only	.228	.282	.348	158	36	7	0	4	9	11	28
Scoring Position	.190	.319	.293	263	50	6	0	7	91	44	76
Late Innings, Close	.213	.281	.394	127	27	5	0	6	14	9	30

FOUR YEAR TOTALS (1984 – 1987)

	G	IP	H	BB	SO	SB	CS	W	L	S	ERA
Totals	143	1032.0	884	390	674	91	31	65	53	0	3.66
at Home	69	503.0	446	181	352	52	16	35	24	0	3.74
on Road	74	529.0	438	209	322	39	15	30	29	0	3.57
on Grass	31	226.0	192	95	132	19	9	9	11	0	3.54
on Artificial Turf	112	806.0	692	295	542	72	22	56	42	0	3.70
Day Games	116	832.1	707	307	565	80	26	55	42	0	3.63
Night Games	27	199.2	177	83	109	11	5	10	11	0	3.79
April	16	102.1	92	46	68	10	3	3	4	0	4.31
May	24	163.2	155	53	98	13	1	13	9	0	4.07
June	26	207.0	146	81	121	13	8	12	9	0	2.52
July	23	172.1	143	72	132	13	4	12	10	0	3.97
August	27	192.2	176	79	129	20	7	14	10	0	4.11
Sept/Oct	27	194.0	172	59	126	22	8	11	11	0	3.48

vs. Opponent Batters	Ave.	OBP	SLG	AB	H	2B	3B	HR	RBI	BB	SO
Totals	.229	.302	.373	3856	884	160	22	117	431	390	674
vs. Left	.238	.311	.370	1982	471	68	15	55	235	208	327
vs. Right	.220	.293	.376	1874	413	92	7	62	196	182	347
Bases Empty	.227	.289	.381	2405	547	104	16	78	78	204	406
Leadoff	.228	.277	.381	997	227	43	7	32	32	65	164
Not Leadoff	.227	.298	.381	1408	320	61	9	46	46	139	242
Runners On Base	.232	.322	.360	1451	337	56	6	39	353	186	268
First Base Only	.233	.301	.358	579	135	27	3	13	36	55	79
Scoring Position	.232	.336	.361	872	202	29	3	26	317	131	189
Late Innings, Close	.215	.276	.317	511	110	18	2	10	45	40	98

RBI/Opportunities

	1987 SEASON	FOUR YEAR TOTALS
Scoring Position	81 / 392 (21%)	276 / 1219 (23%)
Scoring Position, 2 Out	38 / 196 (19%)	110 / 564 (20%)
On Third, Less than 2 Out	36 / 70 (51%)	110 / 215 (51%)
RBI in close games / RBI Total	81 / 125 (65%)	285 / 431 (66%)

Jack Howell
California Angels

On September 5, 1987, Jack Howell homered off New York Yankee reliever Dave Righetti. That was Howell's first and only homer off a left-handed pitcher in 1987. Howell got only 9 hits all season in 73 at bats against lefties (.123). It was a rather remarkable and entertaining homer; when Howell connected, the bat split in two, the barrel landed in the infield, Howell was left with the handle in his hands, and the ball carried well into the right field seats.

Fortunately, this crazy memory can be backed up. If I'm lying, I'm buying. The game was nationally televised and NBC announcers Vin Scully and Joe Garagiola marveled that they'd never seen anything like it before.

The incident is worth dwelling upon because it accents something about Howell that often doesn't come through—he is a very strong boy. Oddly, of those 9 hits off lefties, only three were singles; 3 went for doubles, 2 for triples, and 1 for the remarkable homer.

Besides his strength, he's got talent in the field and he's got bulldog determination to succeed. Strangely enough the Angels were able to sign this kid as a free agent from the University of Arizona in 1983. Somehow he was overlooked in the draft, and the Angels came up with a gem.

Yet in both 1986 and 1987, the Angels were hard-pressed to find a spot for Howell. In 1986, the Angels sent him back to Edmonton before opening day because Doug DeCinces was still the anchor at third base. He was recalled in late May and stuck the rest of the '86 season, getting into 63 games as a part-time player.

Last season, the Angels felt they couldn't hold him back any longer. DeCinces was still at third, but left field opened up with the departure of Reggie Jackson, which let Brian Downing slide into the full-time DH spot. So, Howell became the starting left fielder—at least most of the time. Manager Gene Mauch saw fit throughout the season to frequently sit Howell against left handers, hence the limited number of at-bats against them. Mauch also used Howell in right field and at second base occasionally, and he got into games at his natural position of third base when DeCinces was being rested or out with an injury.

Then in late September, the Angels cut DeCinces free and gave Howell the third base job permanently. In the minors he got very good marks for his defense at third, and the Angels figure he'll be there for many years.

Howell's 1987 numbers taken as a whole aren't all that impressive, but they occurred in a context that saw him out of his natural position much of the season and with only irregular use against lefties. Overall, he hit just .249. But he had 23 homers, and he drove in a total of 64 runs in 138 games. Off righthanders, he hit a respectable .269. I expect he will do much more in 1988 when he settles in full time at his natural position.

Dean Hill

Howell, Jack Robert   Bats: Left   Throws: Right   Born 08/18/61

1987 SEASON AND MAJOR-LEAGUE CAREER BATTING TOTALS

	G	AB	H	2B	3B	HR	TB	R	RBI	TBB	IBB	SO	HP	SH	SF	SB	CS	SB%	GDP	AVG	OBP	SLG
87 CAL	138	449	110	18	5	23	207	64	64	57	4	118	2	1	2	4	3	.57	7	.245	.331	.461
3 YEARS	244	737	178	36	7	32	324	109	103	92	6	179	2	8	5	7	4	.64	9	.242	.325	.440

	1987 SEASON											FOUR YEAR TOTALS (1984 – 1987)									
	Ave.	OBP	SLG	AB	H	2B	3B	HR	RBI	BB	SO	Ave.	OBP	SLG	AB	H	2B	3B	HR	RBI	BB	SO
Totals	.245	.331	.461	449	110	18	5	23	64	57	118	.242	.325	.440	737	178	36	7	32	103	92	179
vs. Left	.123	.200	.260	73	9	3	2	1	12	7	25	.153	.220	.299	137	21	6	4	2	22	12	39
vs. Right	.269	.356	.500	376	101	15	3	22	52	50	93	.262	.348	.472	600	157	30	3	30	81	80	140
at Home	.270	.344	.526	230	62	8	3	15	40	26	56	.243	.325	.456	366	89	16	4	18	57	45	87
on Road	.219	.319	.393	219	48	10	2	8	24	31	62	.240	.325	.423	371	89	20	3	14	46	47	92
vs. Groundball	.253	.352	.441	229	58	8	4	9	35	35	56	.272	.360	.469	335	91	17	5	13	51	47	73
vs. Flyball	.236	.309	.482	220	52	10	1	14	29	22	62	.216	.296	.415	402	87	19	2	19	52	45	106
vs. Finesse	.257	.335	.486	214	55	9	2	12	32	24	48	.229	.304	.421	380	87	19	3	16	51	41	79
vs. Power	.234	.328	.438	235	55	9	3	11	32	33	70	.255	.347	.459	357	91	17	4	16	52	51	100
on Grass	.247	.338	.486	368	91	13	3	23	61	50	90	.234	.326	.436	608	142	26	5	29	90	83	143
on Artificial Turf	.235	.300	.346	81	19	5	2	0	3	7	28	.279	.324	.457	129	36	10	2	3	13	9	36
Day Games	.200	.307	.417	120	24	5	0	7	15	17	38	.216	.306	.367	218	47	10	1	7	25	27	63
Night Games	.261	.341	.477	329	86	13	5	16	49	40	80	.252	.333	.470	519	131	26	6	25	78	65	116
April	.303	.385	.545	66	20	4	0	4	10	10	17	.303	.385	.545	66	20	4	0	4	10	10	17
May	.233	.291	.548	73	17	3	1	6	9	6	21	.187	.269	.430	107	20	3	1	7	11	12	33
June	.244	.361	.402	82	20	5	1	2	13	15	17	.248	.340	.419	129	32	10	3	2	21	18	22
July	.224	.337	.382	76	17	1	1	3	12	13	16	.236	.331	.386	127	30	2	1	5	17	18	28
August	.246	.307	.377	69	17	4	1	1	3	5	23	.269	.331	.475	160	43	10	1	7	19	14	45
Sept/Oct	.229	.304	.518	83	19	1	1	7	17	8	24	.223	.320	.426	148	33	7	1	7	25	20	34
Bases Empty	.245	.325	.466	253	62	13	2	13	13	30	67	.233	.310	.427	433	101	21	3	19	19	48	102
Leadoff	.245	.353	.412	102	25	5	0	4	4	17	19	.250	.344	.452	168	42	8	1	8	8	24	31
Not Leadoff	.245	.305	.503	151	37	8	2	9	9	13	48	.223	.287	.411	265	59	13	2	11	11	24	71
Runners On	.245	.339	.454	196	48	5	3	10	51	27	51	.253	.349	.457	304	77	15	4	13	84	44	77
First Base Only	.346	.430	.617	81	28	3	2	5	13	12	19	.312	.390	.560	125	39	7	3	6	16	16	29
Scoring Position	.174	.276	.339	115	20	2	1	5	38	15	32	.212	.322	.385	179	38	8	1	7	68	28	48
Late Innings, Close	.260	.345	.468	77	20	5	1	3	8	10	24	.219	.286	.398	128	28	6	1	5	11	12	40

RBI/Opportunities

Scoring Position	27 / 156 (17%)	52 / 251 (21%)
Scoring Position, 2 Out	9 / 58 (16%)	17 / 104 (16%)
On Third, Less than 2 Out	11 / 31 (35%)	20 / 45 (44%)
RBI in close games / RBI Total	44 / 64 (69%)	67 / 103 (65%)

Kent Hrbek
Minnesota Twins

Each of the three milestone games during the Twins 1987 season ended with the ball securely enveloped by the big glove of Minnesota native Kent Hrbek. Nothing could have been more appropriate. The West was won when Steve Lombardozzi speared a Gino Petralli line drive and threw to Hrbek doubling Oddibe McDowell off base. This set off the most emotional of the Twins clubhouse celebrations. Tiger hopes were dashed in the ALCS following a Matt Nokes grounder to Jeff Reardon who gingerly tossed the ball to the big target at first base. And the World Series was wrapped up after Gary Gaetti fielded a Willie McGee ground ball and sharply delivered the final throw of an extraordinary season to Hrbek.

To complete the symmetry, Hrbek was actually the senior Twin on the World Champion squad in terms of service in Minnesota. The 1987 team was assembled block by block beginning with Kent Hrbek as the foundation in August of 1981.

While his role has not diminished and he no longer is the club's most valuable player, he is still capable of winning back that title. He arrived in the major leagues as a high average hitter with good power. A batting title seemed imminent. By 1987, thirty to forty additional pounds and a change in hitting philosophy turned the left-handed hitter into a feared slugger. He also began to draw more walks as he battled the pitcher more for a ball he could knock out of the park.

All of this had a cost. His average dropped; his platoon difference widened, and his bulk limited him a bit on the base paths and in the field. Last year, Kent had the fewest plate appearances of any of his major league seasons and left handers were winning so many of the battles that Tom Kelly sometimes removed him from the lineup against southpaws.

There are reasons to suspect his troubles will not continue. The sight of the big guy doubled over trying to catch his breath after legging out a double makes one believe he has reached a point where he will now take his physical conditioning a bit more seriously in the future. To be fair, Hrbek played the last half of the season with a severe muscle pull. More important, a simple readjustment of his batting style could easily send him back to holding his own against all lefties while he continues to pound righties. He has so much hitting talent to work with, it's hard not to predict improvements.

The World Series marked the return of Hrbek to a portion of the national spotlight, but half a year too late. Tired of being snubbed and overshadowed by Murray and Mattingly in selection to the All-Star squad, he vowed to never play in any future All-Star games. Let's hope that will not prevent him from earning the honor.

Bill Jensen

Hrbek, Kent Alan   Bats: Left   Throws: Right   Born 05/21/60

1987 SEASON AND MAJOR-LEAGUE CAREER BATTING TOTALS

	G	AB	H	2B	3B	HR	TB	R	RBI	TBB	IBB	SO	HP	SH	SF	SB	CS	SB%	GDP	AVG	OBP	SLG
87 MIN	143	477	136	20	1	34	260	85	90	84	12	60	0	0	5	5	2	.71	13	.285	.389	.545
7 YEARS	904	3293	951	176	16	151	1612	490	564	403	66	475	16	2	33	16	13	.55	86	.289	.366	.490

	1987 SEASON											FOUR YEAR TOTALS (1984 – 1987)									
	Ave.	OBP	SLG	AB	H	2B	3B	HR	RBI	BB	SO	Ave.	OBP	SLG	AB	H	2B	3B	HR	RBI	BB	SO
Totals	.285	.389	.544	478	136	20	1	34	90	84	60	.285	.368	.494	2180	622	109	7	111	381	287	315
vs. Left	.225	.290	.370	138	31	2	0	6	21	14	23	.264	.332	.416	675	178	23	1	26	107	67	125
vs. Right	.309	.426	.615	340	105	18	1	28	69	70	37	.295	.384	.530	1505	444	86	6	85	274	220	190
at Home	.295	.413	.594	234	69	8	1	20	51	48	30	.311	.394	.548	1111	345	61	7	63	234	153	164
on Road	.275	.364	.496	244	67	12	0	14	39	36	30	.259	.342	.439	1069	277	48	0	48	147	134	151
vs. Groundball	.283	.401	.558	233	66	11	1	17	44	47	29	.288	.376	.500	1069	308	55	3	55	189	148	152
vs. Flyball	.286	.377	.531	245	70	9	0	17	46	37	31	.283	.361	.490	1111	314	54	4	56	192	139	163
vs. Finesse	.293	.404	.540	239	70	9	1	16	51	46	27	.296	.376	.503	1188	352	65	3	58	197	152	147
vs. Power	.276	.373	.548	239	66	11	0	18	39	38	33	.272	.360	.485	992	270	44	4	53	184	135	168
on Grass	.298	.387	.545	198	59	10	0	13	35	30	26	.261	.339	.454	807	211	38	0	39	116	95	116
on Artificial Turf	.275	.390	.543	280	77	10	1	21	55	54	34	.299	.385	.509	1373	411	71	7	72	265	192	199
Day Games	.284	.385	.539	141	40	6	0	10	27	25	24	.285	.361	.505	664	189	37	2	35	121	82	94
Night Games	.285	.390	.546	337	96	14	1	24	63	59	36	.286	.372	.490	1516	433	72	5	76	260	205	221
April	.257	.360	.365	74	19	2	0	2	13	12	11	.271	.377	.420	317	86	15	1	10	47	54	40
May	.273	.369	.557	88	24	1	0	8	16	14	12	.276	.350	.499	355	98	16	0	21	68	41	48
June	.286	.355	.667	84	24	2	0	10	20	9	11	.330	.397	.578	358	118	19	2	22	69	40	52
July	.266	.396	.456	79	21	3	0	4	11	17	11	.259	.344	.501	355	92	14	0	24	74	46	52
August	.326	.438	.696	92	30	8	1	8	21	19	8	.296	.377	.499	409	121	18	1	21	64	54	60
Sept/Oct	.295	.408	.459	61	18	4	0	2	9	13	7	.277	.361	.464	386	107	27	3	13	59	52	63
Bases Empty	.270	.361	.536	252	68	11	1	18	18	36	31	.275	.347	.482	1167	321	64	3	57	57	128	175
Leadoff	.268	.354	.473	112	30	3	1	6	6	15	13	.284	.349	.517	443	126	24	2	25	25	44	54
Not Leadoff	.271	.366	.586	140	38	8	0	12	12	21	18	.269	.345	.460	724	195	40	1	32	32	84	121
Runners On	.301	.417	.553	226	68	9	0	16	72	48	29	.297	.391	.509	1013	301	45	4	54	324	159	140
First Base Only	.366	.450	.688	112	41	6	0	10	22	17	12	.317	.383	.561	467	148	17	2	31	75	50	62
Scoring Position	.237	.389	.421	114	27	3	0	6	50	31	17	.280	.398	.465	546	153	28	2	23	249	109	78
Late Innings, Close	.329	.391	.618	76	25	4	0	6	16	9	6	.276	.370	.407	322	89	12	0	10	46	49	47

RBI/Opportunities

Scoring Position	41 / 172 (24%)	210 / 759 (28%)
Scoring Position, 2 Out	12 / 81 (15%)	59 / 305 (19%)
On Third, Less than 2 Out	20 / 38 (53%)	94 / 166 (57%)
RBI in close games / RBI Total	61 / 90 (68%)	250 / 381 (66%)

Glenn Hubbard
Atlanta Braves

Glenn Hubbard appears to be a generation too late. His performance level is that of an average second baseman from the 1950's, when they regularly hit .242 with little power. Offense was a rare commodity among middle infielders then. Hubbard's mastery of the fundamentals and ability to get on base are also indicative of players of that era. If it were not for his facial hair he would seem to have stepped directly out of a 1956 baseball card.

1987 was a career year for Hubbard. He had career highs in BA (.264), hits (117), doubles (33), walks (77), and OBA (.378). His .381 slugging average and 69 runs scored are the second highest totals of his career; meanwhile, he only struck out 57 times. This offensive display did not adversely affect his fielding. All in all, this was by far Hubbard's finest season.

Starting out like a house afire, Hubbard was hitting .313 with 17 doubles, 27 RBI, and .458 slugging average on July 1st. Then his hitting began to drop off at about the same time the rest of the Braves hitters went on vacation. Finally, Hubbard went into a devastating slump. He hit .190 (16 for 84) with four runs batted in and isolated power of .060, while his OBA dipped to .292 during a four week stretch from mid-August to mid-September. This resulted in Ronnie Gant's insertion as regular second baseman. Hubbard was barely heard from again, with only 26 AB in Atlanta's final 25 games.

Marc Bowman

The Braves won't have Glenn Hubbard to kick around anymore. Hub escaped the insanity of Atlanta management by declaring free agency.

The 30-year-old second baseman made the Atlanta front office look silly when he posted career highs in batting average and doubles despite rumors that he'd be traded. He had his usual high on-base average, and was decent on defense, leading all second basemen in the senior circuit in assists, double plays, and total chances per game.

Damaso Garcia was the projected starting second sacker prior to the 1987 season, but an injury kept him out the entire year. Meanwhile, Hub goes on and has a career year. And throughout the season, the announcers kept talking about how the Braves were going to ship Hubbard out when Garcia came back, which he never did.

Late in the season Ronnie Gant (another Damaso Garcia no-walk type) was given the job. In yet another burst of brilliance, however, Smiling Chuck decided "if you play second, you should hit second," and put the rookie there, in spite of Hubbard's OBA, third only to Dion James and Dale Murphy.

Baseball America asked Chuck Tanner where the Braves would have been without Zane Smith. Tanner's answer—"In the International League." Funny. The way the Braves played in 1987 I thought I was watching minor league ball. If they keep letting what little quality they have escape, they may as well join the IL.

Stacy Kaneshiro

Hubbard, Glenn Dee

Bats: Right **Throws: Right** **Born 09/25/57**

1987 SEASON AND MAJOR-LEAGUE CAREER BATTING TOTALS

	G	AB	H	2B	3B	HR	TB	R	RBI	TBB	IBB	SO	HP	SH	SF	SB	CS	SB%	GDP	AVG	OBP	SLG
87 ATL	141	443	117	33	2	5	169	69	38	77	17	57	6	4	3	1	1	.50	11	.264	.378	.381
10 YEARS	1196	4016	983	196	20	64	1411	498	403	487	53	570	30	59	35	32	33	.49	71	.245	.328	.351

1987 SEASON

	Ave.	OBP	SLG	AB	H	2B	3B	HR	RBI	BB	SO
Totals	.264	.378	.381	443	117	33	2	5	38	77	57
vs. Left	.288	.419	.433	104	30	9	0	2	12	24	12
vs. Right	.257	.365	.366	339	87	24	2	3	26	53	45
at Home	.252	.383	.365	222	56	12	2	3	19	45	32
on Road	.276	.373	.398	221	61	21	0	2	19	32	25
vs. Groundball	.282	.382	.388	206	58	12	2	2	25	32	24
vs. Flyball	.249	.375	.376	237	59	21	0	3	13	45	33
vs. Finesse	.262	.366	.398	244	64	19	1	4	27	37	26
vs. Power	.266	.393	.362	199	53	14	1	1	11	40	31
on Grass	.269	.397	.385	312	84	20	2	4	24	63	40
on Artificial Turf	.252	.329	.374	131	33	13	0	1	14	14	17
Day Games	.262	.353	.348	164	43	9	1	1	9	21	18
Night Games	.265	.392	.401	279	74	24	1	4	29	56	39
April	.323	.476	.431	65	21	7	0	0	9	17	6
May	.305	.394	.488	82	25	6	0	3	11	12	12
June	.293	.465	.453	75	22	5	2	1	7	23	10
July	.250	.333	.364	88	22	7	0	1	4	10	8
August	.233	.324	.322	90	21	8	0	0	5	12	12
Sept/Oct	.140	.196	.140	43	6	0	0	0	2	3	9
Bases Empty	.256	.344	.391	266	68	23	2	3	3	34	29
Leadoff	.284	.386	.413	109	31	11	0	1	1	18	10
Not Leadoff	.236	.314	.376	157	37	12	2	2	2	16	19
Runners On	.277	.423	.367	177	49	10	0	2	35	43	28
First Base Only	.281	.390	.393	89	25	4	0	2	4	13	11
Scoring Position	.273	.451	.341	88	24	6	0	0	31	30	17
Late Innings, Close	.257	.321	.338	74	19	3	0	1	4	6	10

FOUR YEAR TOTALS (1984 – 1987)

	Ave.	OBP	SLG	AB	H	2B	3B	HR	RBI	BB	SO
Totals	.241	.343	.345	1687	406	97	5	23	156	253	246
vs. Left	.238	.354	.335	495	118	28	1	6	45	91	71
vs. Right	.242	.338	.349	1192	288	69	4	17	111	162	175
at Home	.251	.359	.359	846	212	43	5	13	86	141	121
on Road	.231	.326	.331	841	194	54	0	10	70	112	125
vs. Groundball	.252	.350	.339	809	204	40	3	8	80	119	110
vs. Flyball	.230	.337	.351	878	202	57	2	15	76	134	136
vs. Finesse	.249	.338	.361	953	237	56	3	15	87	123	113
vs. Power	.230	.349	.324	734	169	41	2	8	69	130	133
on Grass	.249	.355	.353	1237	308	65	5	18	116	195	179
on Artificial Turf	.218	.309	.322	450	98	32	0	5	40	58	67
Day Games	.215	.303	.317	606	130	32	3	8	54	73	80
Night Games	.255	.364	.361	1081	276	65	2	15	102	180	166
April	.276	.407	.385	221	61	15	0	3	22	47	26
May	.259	.332	.407	332	86	25	0	8	44	36	47
June	.242	.390	.356	298	72	15	2	5	32	71	41
July	.241	.338	.364	291	70	22	1	4	30	42	39
August	.208	.291	.266	308	64	13	1	1	18	36	51
Sept/Oct	.224	.287	.287	237	53	7	1	2	10	21	42
Bases Empty	.243	.324	.354	991	241	61	5	13	13	117	129
Leadoff	.265	.356	.384	404	107	28	1	6	6	57	44
Not Leadoff	.228	.302	.334	587	134	33	4	7	7	60	85
Runners On	.237	.364	.332	696	165	36	0	10	143	136	117
First Base Only	.234	.319	.330	321	75	13	0	6	15	37	50
Scoring Position	.240	.397	.333	375	90	23	0	4	128	99	67
Late Innings, Close	.211	.306	.295	261	55	13	0	3	15	35	38

RBI/Opportunities

Scoring Position	29 / 152 (19%)
Scoring Position, 2 Out	11 / 74 (15%)
On Third, Less than 2 Out	13 / 24 (54%)
RBI in close games / RBI Total	27 / 38 (71%)

	113 / 594 (19%)
	39 / 274 (14%)
	47 / 112 (42%)
	88 / 156 (56%)

Bruce Hurst

Boston Red Sox

On August 14, Bruce Hurst beat the Texas Rangers, raising his record to 14–6 and lowering his ERA to 3.76. At the time, his name was being mentioned more often than Roger Clemens's as a serious contender for the Cy Young Award—giving new hope to second bananas everywhere.

But Clemens is still the AL's premier pitcher and Johnny Carson, not Ed McMahon, is still hosting NBC's *Tonight* show. What happened? Carson started dating again and decided that he'd need the money if he hoped to support two wives. Hurst won only one of his last eight decisions; his ERA in that period was 6.93. His reputation as a .500 pitcher, which seemingly had been buried in 1986, came howling out of the grave.

There was a great deal of speculation over the cause of Hurst's late-season ineffectiveness. Several sportswriters questioned his stamina. They noted that Hurst was eighth in the AL in innings pitched this year—that his 238.2 IP were nine more innings than he'd ever pitched in a year. His 5–1 September record and strong playoff showing in 1986, they said, happened only because he'd missed seven weeks in mid-season with a groin injury; his arm had been atypically fresh down the stretch.

Others blamed the bullpen. In 1987, Hurst tied Bret Saberhagen for second place in complete games. Four of those completions came in games where the final scores were 14–3, 11–2, 9–3 and 7–1. Some wags speculated that he'd done this out of necessity—that Boston relievers were capable of letting leads of even that magnitude slip away.

Some theorists noted that Rich Gedman, Bruce's favorite catcher, missed the second half of the season. Hurst was 6–2 in games where Gedman was his battery partner; with other catchers, he was 9–11. His ERA was 2.51 with Gedman catching, 5.35 with John Marzano, 5.40 with Danny Sheaffer and 5.49 with Marc Sullivan.

Once 1987 ended, however, the reason for the collapse filtered out—Bruce caught mononucleosis during the year. That would more than explain both his overall stats for his last eight starts and the in-game pattern (start strong and then die) during that period. In the first two innings of his starts after August 15, Hurst's ERA was 3.94; from the third inning on, it was 8.45.

In the last few years, Hurst has acquired a reputation as one of the rare southpaws who has learned to pitch in Fenway, but can't handle life on the road; his 1987 W-L split attached the label even more firmly to his head. Yes, it is an impressive split—but then why are his ERA splits nowhere near as pronounced? The disparity is more likely due to the uneven offensive support that he received. Boston scored 6.29 runs per nine innings for him in Fenway, and only 3.77 R/9IP on the road.

Chuck Waseleski

Hurst, Bruce Vee | Bats: Left   Throws: Left | Born 03/24/58

1987 SEASON AND MAJOR-LEAGUE CAREER PITCHING TOTALS

	G	GS	CG	GF	IP	BFP	H	R	ER	HR	SH	SF	HB	TBB	IBB	SO	WP	Bk	W	L	Pct	ShO	Sv	ERA
87 BOS	33	33	15	0	239	1001	239	124	117	35	5	8	1	76	5	190	3	1	15	13	.536	3	0	4.41
8 YEARS	204	185	47	5	1242	5342	1347	649	598	152	24	34	22	414	23	877	25	10	70	67	.511	12	0	4.33

1987: Power, Groundball   1986: Power, Flyball   1985: Power, Groundball   1984: Power, Flyball

1987 SEASON

	G	IP	H	BB	SO	SB	CS	W	L	S	ERA
Totals	33	238.2	239	76	190	18	7	15	13	0	4.41
at Home	18	136.0	137	37	113	6	4	12	4	0	4.30
on Road	15	102.2	102	39	77	12	3	3	9	0	4.56
on Grass	12	94.0	83	31	71	5	2	7	4	0	3.54
on Artificial Turf	21	144.2	156	45	119	13	5	8	9	0	4.98
Day Games	28	206.0	205	65	166	14	7	14	11	0	4.41
Night Games	5	32.2	34	11	24	4	0	1	2	0	4.41
April	5	32.1	31	12	21	7	2	2	3	0	4.45
May	6	47.2	33	11	43	1	0	3	1	0	2.27
June	6	48.1	51	14	33	1	3	4	1	0	3.54
July	5	36.0	42	10	33	1	1	2	1	0	6.00
August	6	47.1	44	15	42	3	0	3	3	0	3.99
Sept/Oct	5	27.0	38	14	18	5	1	1	4	0	8.33

FOUR YEAR TOTALS (1984 – 1987)

	G	IP	H	BB	SO	SB	CS	W	L	S	ERA
Totals	126	860.1	883	284	682	43	40	51	46	0	4.03
at Home	65	452.2	467	138	369	18	19	32	21	0	4.04
on Road	61	407.2	416	146	313	25	21	19	25	0	4.02
on Grass	43	290.2	298	87	206	16	7	18	15	0	4.09
on Artificial Turf	83	569.2	585	197	476	27	33	33	31	0	3.98
Day Games	110	756.2	784	245	605	35	34	48	40	0	4.01
Night Games	16	103.2	99	39	77	8	6	3	6	0	4.08
April	20	130.2	131	47	99	10	9	7	8	0	3.79
May	22	156.2	143	44	135	8	9	10	7	0	2.93
June	18	116.1	127	35	77	7	4	8	5	0	4.18
July	18	128.0	127	37	103	4	3	8	5	0	4.29
August	24	172.1	177	62	138	7	4	9	9	0	4.33
Sept/Oct	24	156.1	178	59	130	7	11	9	12	0	4.66

vs. Opponent Batters — 1987 Season

vs. Opponent Batters	Ave.	OBP	SLG	AB	H	2B	3B	HR	RBI	BB	SO
Totals	.262	.317	.432	911	239	44	3	35	110	76	190
vs. Left	.256	.345	.430	121	31	9	0	4	19	16	30
vs. Right	.263	.313	.433	790	208	35	3	31	91	60	160
Bases Empty	.257	.320	.426	552	142	21	3	22	22	51	124
Leadoff	.264	.320	.437	231	61	7	0	11	11	19	52
Not Leadoff	.252	.320	.417	321	81	14	3	11	11	32	72
Runners On Base	.270	.313	.443	359	97	23	0	13	88	25	66
First Base Only	.244	.269	.438	201	49	12	0	9	22	6	32
Scoring Position	.304	.362	.449	158	48	11	0	4	66	19	34
Late Innings, Close	.320	.369	.580	100	32	6	1	6	17	8	15

vs. Opponent Batters — Four Year Totals

	Ave.	OBP	SLG	AB	H	2B	3B	HR	RBI	BB	SO
Totals	.266	.323	.426	3318	883	177	13	109	361	284	682
vs. Left	.261	.323	.405	513	134	32	0	14	59	46	111
vs. Right	.267	.324	.430	2805	749	145	13	95	302	238	571
Bases Empty	.267	.330	.435	1933	516	89	10	72	72	183	387
Leadoff	.274	.336	.447	821	225	37	3	33	33	76	151
Not Leadoff	.262	.326	.426	1112	291	52	7	39	39	107	236
Runners On Base	.265	.314	.413	1385	367	88	3	37	289	101	295
First Base Only	.280	.320	.437	707	198	45	3	20	56	41	128
Scoring Position	.249	.307	.388	678	169	43	0	17	233	60	167
Late Innings, Close	.295	.345	.482	336	99	24	3	11	37	26	52

RBI/Opportunities

	1987	Four Year
Scoring Position	56 / 224 (25%)	200 / 906 (22%)
Scoring Position, 2 Out	18 / 90 (20%)	85 / 409 (21%)
On Third, Less than 2 Out	25 / 46 (54%)	73 / 165 (44%)
RBI in close games / RBI Total	76 / 110 (69%)	264 / 361 (73%)

Pete Incaviglia
Texas Rangers

Alright, with the constant comparisons to Dave Winfield and Bob Horner as recent players who made it without a day of minor league action, let it be noted that Incaviglia had a better second year than Winfield, but not as good as Horner who had actually had his "career" year in his sophomore season.

Except for some minor injuries cutting slightly into his playing time, Pete was untouched by a sophomore slump. Where last year he hit over .255 in only one month, in 1987 he hit .280 or higher in 3 of the 6 monthly periods. Overall, he hit 21 points higher (.271) and raised his slugging percentage 36 points to just under .500 (.497). He surprised many of his critics by continuing to improve while striking out at a prodigious rate; 29.8 percent of his PA were strikeouts, which is nearly identical to his 30.5 percent in 1986.

Pete continues to show an alarming platoon difference. After a .226–.306 split in 1986, he followed it up with a .232–.341 difference. At that rate he's going to have to hit over .300 overall just to get his average against righties up to .250. His platoon difference has helped create an image of him as a good clean-up hitter. When batting fourth (which he did about 60 percent of the time) he hit over .300 and slugged close to .550. But Valentine shifted him wisely in and out of the clean-up spot according to the opposing pitcher. Pete hit only .163 in the fifth spot, where he was often dropped with tough righthanders on the mound.

Incaviglia still has a ways to go before he is a competent situational hitter. He hit over 20 points lower with men on base; 30 points lower with men in scoring position. His home run rate declined about 19 percent with men on. The good news is that all three differences are an improvement over his rookie year. That's natural enough. Working with situational statistics since the 1970's, I've become convinced that situational hitting is largely a learned skill, and experience is a good teacher.

Last year I wrote, "He's a lot better than the .250 average of his rookie year." Well, I think he's also a lot better than his .271 average in his sophomore year. In fact, I can envision him hitting .300—but not while striking out in 30 percent of his plate appearances. He'll need to get it down to about 20 percent, which still means he can strikeout 120 times.

My biggest concern over Incaviglia is that he will be one of those players who constantly have to battle minor injuries every year. His style of play is meant for a different body, say, that of a rhino. His headfirst slides on defense and on the bases seem to detour through the ground rather than over it. Banged up shoulders, wrists, fingers, ankles, and pulled leg muscles have plagued his first two seasons. I'm not questioning his ability to play with pain; he's played through most of these injuries, but it is not a trend you would wish on any player.

Craig R. Wright

Incaviglia, Peter Joseph "Pete" Bats: Right Throws: Right Born 04/02/64

1987 SEASON AND MAJOR-LEAGUE CAREER BATTING TOTALS

	G	AB	H	2B	3B	HR	TB	R	RBI	TBB	IBB	SO	HP	SH	SF	SB	CS	SB%	GDP	AVG	OBP	SLG
87 TEX	139	509	138	26	4	27	253	85	80	48	1	168	1	0	5	9	3	.75	8	.271	.332	.497
2 YEARS	292	1049	273	47	6	57	503	167	168	103	3	353	5	0	12	12	5	.71	17	.260	.326	.480

	1987 SEASON											FOUR YEAR TOTALS (1984 – 1987)										
	Ave.	OBP	SLG	AB	H	2B	3B	HR	RBI	BB	SO	Ave.	OBP	SLG	AB	H	2B	3B	HR	RBI	BB	SO
Totals	.271	.332	.497	509	138	26	4	27	80	48	168	.260	.326	.480	1049	273	47	6	57	168	103	353
vs. Left	.341	.407	.632	182	62	12	1	13	37	21	54	.325	.391	.617	342	111	19	3	25	68	39	109
vs. Right	.232	.290	.422	327	76	14	3	14	43	27	114	.229	.294	.413	707	162	28	3	32	100	64	244
at Home	.259	.336	.451	255	66	12	2	11	40	30	85	.274	.344	.491	530	145	25	3	28	89	57	179
on Road	.283	.328	.543	254	72	14	2	16	40	18	83	.247	.306	.468	519	128	22	3	29	79	46	174
vs. Groundball	.287	.323	.505	275	79	16	4	12	42	16	83	.266	.319	.488	508	135	28	5	25	86	41	159
vs. Flyball	.252	.342	.487	234	59	10	0	15	38	32	85	.255	.332	.471	541	138	19	1	32	82	62	194
vs. Finesse	.303	.347	.589	297	90	16	3	21	56	20	79	.273	.328	.524	626	171	30	5	39	101	52	172
vs. Power	.226	.313	.368	212	48	10	1	6	24	28	89	.241	.323	.414	423	102	17	1	18	67	51	181
on Grass	.270	.335	.487	423	114	22	2	22	69	43	136	.264	.332	.485	884	233	41	4	49	150	91	290
on Artificial Turf	.279	.319	.547	86	24	4	2	5	11	5	32	.242	.292	.448	165	40	6	2	8	18	12	63
Day Games	.318	.393	.673	107	34	4	2	10	26	14	35	.274	.335	.548	219	60	9	3	15	41	21	74
Night Games	.259	.315	.450	402	104	22	2	17	54	34	133	.257	.324	.461	830	213	38	3	42	127	82	279
April	.324	.390	.662	74	24	1	0	8	19	8	23	.248	.318	.518	137	34	4	0	11	27	14	44
May	.289	.360	.474	97	28	7	1	3	11	12	31	.321	.380	.571	184	59	13	3	9	30	19	62
June	.216	.259	.451	102	22	5	2	5	14	5	39	.235	.299	.434	196	46	8	2	9	30	17	73
July	.269	.378	.484	93	25	8	0	4	15	17	28	.259	.341	.444	189	49	11	0	8	30	24	59
August	.280	.305	.500	100	28	2	1	6	16	4	30	.251	.306	.422	199	50	5	1	9	25	16	63
Sept/Oct	.256	.283	.395	43	11	3	0	1	5	2	17	.243	.304	.514	144	35	6	0	11	26	13	52
Bases Empty	.282	.352	.534	277	78	18	2	16	16	29	92	.275	.338	.519	553	152	32	2	33	33	52	186
Leadoff	.299	.368	.438	137	41	7	0	4	4	14	40	.281	.338	.447	253	71	15	0	9	9	21	78
Not Leadoff	.264	.335	.629	140	37	11	2	12	12	15	52	.270	.338	.580	300	81	17	2	24	24	31	108
Runners On	.259	.309	.453	232	60	8	2	11	64	19	76	.244	.312	.435	496	121	15	4	24	135	51	167
First Base Only	.263	.288	.456	114	30	5	1	5	14	4	33	.244	.295	.406	234	57	7	2	9	25	17	71
Scoring Position	.254	.326	.449	118	30	3	1	6	50	15	43	.244	.326	.462	262	64	8	2	15	110	34	96
Late Innings, Close	.243	.313	.500	70	17	6	0	4	11	8	27	.264	.345	.493	144	38	9	0	8	27	19	52

RBI/Opportunities

Scoring Position	41 / 169 (24%)	86 / 375 (23%)
Scoring Position, 2 Out	14 / 79 (18%)	33 / 181 (18%)
On Third, Less than 2 Out	20 / 38 (53%)	38 / 79 (48%)
RBI in close games / RBI Total	47 / 80 (59%)	111 / 168 (66%)

Garth Iorg
Toronto Blue Jays

That Garth Iorg, based on his playing time, warrants an essay in this book goes a very long way toward explaining how Toronto managed to lose the American League East in 1987. In 1987, Iorg crossbred Steve Balboni's batting average with Cory Snyder's strike zone judgement, Alfredo Griffin's power and Steve Sax's defense; the result was baseball's answer to the Frankenstein monster—a walking abomination that turned on the men who unleashed it on the world.

To be fair, the blame for Iorg's 1987 falls squarely on Toronto's shoulders. There's definitely a place for Garth Iorg on a world series champion, but the place is utility infielder. The man entered 1987 as a career .265 hitter with a .297 on-base percentage and .356 slugging percentage. In 2,140 major league at-bats, he had a whopping total of 218 runs created—3.53 runs created per 27 outs. Only once in his career (1985) has he managed to bring his OB% above .307 or his SL% over .376— and that was only as a platoon player. As Earl Weaver says, you never ask a player to do something that he's not capable of doing; that's exactly what the Blue Jays did to Iorg. No reasonable person should be surprised by anything that he did or did not do in 1987.

Some random notes on his unforgettable season:

1. Though Iorg's fielding percentage was the second highest of the four regular Toronto second basemen, both his range factor and double plays per game turned were the lowest of the lot. Iorg (3.67) made almost half a play less than either Manny Lee (4.14) or Mike Sharperson (4.16) and *almost a play and a half less* than Nelson Liriano (5.14). Iorg turned 58 DPs per 162 games, Sharperson turned 81, Lee turned 96 and Liriano turned 123.

2. He actually started a game at DH. The Blue Jays naturally (and deservedly) lost it.

3. On July 20, Iorg hit two homers (10 percent of his career total) in a game. I'll tell you that it's the same date that man first walked on the moon and let you insert your own punchline.

4. While I'm not surprised by the final results, I am surprised by how he arrived there. His platoon splits in 1987 are the opposite of his stats in his career to date.

5. He pinch-hit for Lloyd Moseby on September 7 against Dan Plesac. While I was tearing my hair out, he doubled down the left field line, sparking a three-run rally that won the game.

6. Maybe that last point is no surprise. It's spooky how, year after year, Iorg excels in "clutch" situations. If you believe that clutch hitters exist, Garth Iorg should be your patron saint.

Gord Fitzgerald

Iorg, Garth Ray Bats: Right Throws: Right Born 10/12/54

1987 SEASON AND MAJOR-LEAGUE CAREER BATTING TOTALS

	G	AB	H	2B	3B	HR	TB	R	RBI	TBB	IBB	SO	HP	SH	SF	SB	CS	SB%	GDP	AVG	OBP	SLG
87 TOR	122	310	65	11	0	4	88	35	30	21	0	52	2	6	3	2	2	.50	8	.210	.262	.284
9 YEARS	931	2450	633	125	16	20	850	251	238	114	9	298	11	21	19	23	17	.57	55	.258	.292	.347

	1987 SEASON											FOUR YEAR TOTALS (1984 – 1987)									
	Ave.	OBP	SLG	AB	H	2B	3B	HR	RBI	BB	SO	Ave.	OBP	SLG	AB	H	2B	3B	HR	RBI	BB	SO
Totals	.210	.262	.284	310	65	11	0	4	30	21	52	.253	.294	.352	1172	296	62	5	15	136	68	141
vs. Left	.181	.238	.225	138	25	3	0	1	14	11	18	.263	.306	.376	684	180	39	4	10	91	43	60
vs. Right	.233	.281	.331	172	40	8	0	3	16	10	34	.238	.277	.320	488	116	23	1	5	45	25	81
at Home	.209	.267	.264	148	31	5	0	1	15	10	26	.261	.300	.364	568	148	29	3	8	70	29	72
on Road	.210	.257	.302	162	34	6	0	3	15	11	26	.245	.289	.341	604	148	33	2	7	66	39	69
vs. Groundball	.241	.311	.286	133	32	6	0	0	15	13	19	.267	.323	.331	483	129	21	2	2	59	38	51
vs. Flyball	.186	.223	.282	177	33	5	0	4	15	8	33	.242	.273	.367	689	167	41	3	13	77	30	90
vs. Finesse	.186	.249	.217	161	30	5	0	0	10	13	20	.248	.288	.333	625	155	31	2	6	62	35	61
vs. Power	.235	.277	.356	149	35	6	0	4	20	8	32	.258	.301	.375	547	141	31	3	9	74	33	80
on Grass	.219	.266	.336	128	28	6	0	3	11	9	22	.253	.294	.357	459	116	28	1	6	50	29	56
on Artificial Turf	.203	.259	.247	182	37	5	0	1	19	12	30	.252	.294	.349	713	180	34	4	9	86	39	85
Day Games	.196	.239	.284	102	20	6	0	1	9	6	19	.237	.280	.351	410	97	24	1	7	44	25	56
Night Games	.216	.273	.284	208	45	5	0	3	21	15	33	.261	.302	.353	762	199	38	4	8	92	43	85
April	.087	.214	.087	23	2	0	0	0	1	3	2	.205	.261	.260	127	26	2	1	1	13	9	14
May	.167	.216	.167	48	8	0	0	0	4	3	8	.277	.321	.306	173	48	5	0	0	8	11	19
June	.292	.314	.308	65	19	1	0	0	6	3	5	.273	.298	.364	198	54	9	0	3	28	8	20
July	.291	.349	.468	79	23	5	0	3	14	6	15	.237	.301	.348	207	49	12	1	3	25	18	27
August	.154	.214	.244	78	12	4	0	1	5	6	14	.229	.275	.336	280	64	15	3	3	39	18	33
Sept/Oct	.059	.059	.118	17	1	1	0	0	0	0	8	.294	.309	.476	187	55	19	0	5	23	4	28
Bases Empty	.206	.245	.297	175	36	7	0	3	3	7	35	.235	.267	.333	625	147	33	2	8	8	25	85
Leadoff	.176	.200	.265	68	12	3	0	1	1	0	17	.230	.257	.337	252	58	14	2	3	3	7	31
Not Leadoff	.224	.272	.318	107	24	4	0	2	2	7	18	.239	.274	.330	373	89	19	0	5	5	18	54
Runners On	.215	.283	.267	135	29	4	0	1	27	14	17	.272	.324	.375	547	149	29	3	7	128	43	56
First Base Only	.140	.197	.175	57	8	2	0	0	0	4	9	.242	.281	.317	240	58	13	1	1	9	13	26
Scoring Position	.269	.341	.333	78	21	2	0	1	27	10	8	.296	.356	.420	307	91	16	2	6	119	30	30
Late Innings, Close	.268	.313	.321	56	15	3	0	0	10	5	7	.303	.348	.404	208	63	11	2	2	30	16	21

RBI/Opportunities

Scoring Position	26 / 106 (25%)	105 / 420 (25%)
Scoring Position, 2 Out	13 / 48 (27%)	52 / 195 (27%)
On Third, Less than 2 Out	10 / 21 (48%)	30 / 66 (45%)
RBI in close games / RBI Total	19 / 30 (63%)	91 / 136 (67%)

Bo Jackson
Kansas City Royals

I'm sure you're all sick and tired of Bo Jackson stories, but you're going to have to endure one more theory as to why what happened, happened. The Royals thought they had it all figured out. Here's a great athlete who's willing to forsake immediate millions in football in favor of a less instantly rewarding but longer-term career. So they sign Bo, and after a token stint in the minors he's in the bigs, confounding the non-believers with power hitting that, by the end of June, has him leading the team in homers and RBIs.

But the Royals behaved as though they never totally believed in their good fortune, or in Bo's opting to forsake quick megabucks.

The decision not to farm him out in '87, which looked great early on, could only have been justified at the time as a football prophylaxis. The lineup, after all, had been set—switching Seitzer to first and Balboni to DH to make way for Bo in left (which was even a new position for him)—this was totally unanticipated. The combination of Bo's torrid start and Brett's scheduled injury made it all look like, momentarily, a work of managerial genius.

What everyone left out of the equation, unfortunately, was the mind of Bo Jackson—the mind of a longtime superstar. He was used to nothing but spectacular success—in football. But even during the baseball days of wine and roses, in April and May, there were plenty of 0-for-4 games. He had probably never gone the equivalent of 0-for-4 in his football life. So the same results that would certainly not have shaken the confidence of, say Pete Incaviglia, nonetheless shook the confidence of Bo Jackson. This drooping confidence, combined with the millions of football dollars still being waved under his nose, produced the result that has surely irrevocably compromised his baseball career.

One question remains. Assuming that he had indeed burned his bridges, and purged football completely from his mind, could he have become the baseball superstar many predicted, or at least hoped? I'm inclined to doubt it. All the athletic ability in the world can't compensate for not playing the trade in earnest—ask the various football players who have attempted a career in professional boxing. Sure, Bo played baseball—as a hobby. Auburn is a football factory; if he had been serious about baseball he could have attended a combination football-baseball factory like Arizona State—that's what Reggie Jackson did. But Bo was training for a football career. Do you think even Babe Ruth could have practiced for another career and still become the Bambino? Maybe Bo could have had a good baseball career; the power is unquestionably there, and he might have learned to utilize his speed to a degree. But I don't see how he could have ever matriculated with the highest of honors—he simply skipped or slept through too many of the basic classes.

Mike Kopf

Jackson, Vincent Edward "Bo" Bats: Right Throws: Right Born 11/30/62

1987 SEASON AND MAJOR-LEAGUE CAREER BATTING TOTALS

	G	AB	H	2B	3B	HR	TB	R	RBI	TBB	IBB	SO	HP	SH	SF	SB	CS	SB%	GDP	AVG	OBP	SLG
87 KC	116	396	93	17	2	22	180	46	53	30	0	158	5	1	2	10	4	.71	3	.235	.296	.455
2 YEARS	141	478	110	19	3	24	207	55	62	37	0	192	7	1	2	13	5	.72	4	.230	.294	.433

	1987 SEASON											FOUR YEAR TOTALS (1984 – 1987)										
	Ave.	OBP	SLG	AB	H	2B	3B	HR	RBI	BB	SO	Ave.	OBP	SLG	AB	H	2B	3B	HR	RBI	BB	SO
Totals	.235	.296	.455	396	93	17	2	22	53	30	158	.230	.297	.433	478	110	19	3	24	62	37	192
vs. Left	.248	.315	.496	113	28	5	1	7	13	10	46	.224	.293	.448	134	30	5	2	7	14	12	58
vs. Right	.230	.288	.438	283	65	12	1	15	40	20	112	.233	.294	.427	344	80	14	1	17	48	25	134
at Home	.284	.344	.579	197	56	14	1	14	39	18	59	.278	.336	.531	241	67	14	1	15	43	19	76
on Road	.186	.247	.332	199	37	3	1	8	14	12	99	.181	.251	.333	237	43	5	2	9	19	18	116
vs. Groundball	.284	.335	.534	208	59	9	2	13	34	12	72	.285	.338	.520	246	70	10	3	14	39	15	84
vs. Flyball	.181	.254	.367	188	34	8	0	9	19	18	86	.172	.248	.341	232	40	9	0	10	23	22	108
vs. Finesse	.248	.299	.450	218	54	10	2	10	26	15	76	.259	.321	.459	266	69	11	3	12	35	21	89
vs. Power	.219	.291	.461	178	39	7	0	12	27	15	82	.193	.261	.401	212	41	8	0	12	27	16	103
on Grass	.178	.246	.306	157	28	3	1	5	10	11	79	.179	.250	.313	199	32	4	1	6	12	14	87
on Artificial Turf	.272	.328	.552	239	65	14	1	17	43	19	79	.261	.320	.505	299	78	15	2	18	50	23	105
Day Games	.258	.314	.419	93	24	6	0	3	8	7	33	.258	.314	.419	93	24	6	0	3	8	7	33
Night Games	.228	.290	.465	303	69	11	2	19	45	23	125	.223	.289	.436	385	86	13	3	21	54	30	159
April	.324	.378	.574	68	22	5	0	4	15	6	25	.324	.378	.574	68	22	5	0	4	15	6	25
May	.216	.289	.432	88	19	2	1	5	14	8	34	.216	.289	.432	88	19	2	1	5	14	8	34
June	.284	.341	.580	81	23	3	0	7	12	5	33	.284	.341	.580	81	23	3	0	7	12	5	33
July	.222	.287	.422	90	20	4	1	4	7	8	39	.222	.287	.422	90	20	4	1	4	7	8	39
August	.149	.200	.255	47	7	2	0	1	2	2	22	.149	.200	.255	47	7	2	0	1	2	2	22
Sept/Oct	.091	.130	.273	22	2	1	0	1	3	1	5	.183	.254	.317	104	19	3	1	3	12	8	39
Bases Empty	.258	.326	.530	217	56	9	1	16	16	18	83	.241	.306	.477	266	64	10	1	17	17	21	102
Leadoff	.250	.333	.545	88	22	2	0	8	8	10	32	.238	.322	.514	105	25	2	0	9	9	12	37
Not Leadoff	.264	.321	.519	129	34	7	1	8	8	8	51	.242	.295	.453	161	39	8	1	8	8	9	65
Runners On	.207	.258	.363	179	37	8	1	6	37	12	75	.217	.279	.377	212	46	9	2	7	45	16	90
First Base Only	.224	.262	.395	76	17	4	0	3	7	4	33	.228	.276	.402	92	21	4	0	4	9	6	39
Scoring Position	.194	.254	.340	103	20	4	1	3	30	8	42	.208	.281	.358	120	25	5	2	3	36	10	51
Late Innings, Close	.214	.308	.339	56	12	1	0	2	5	7	27	.214	.308	.339	112	24	2	0	4	10	14	54

RBI/Opportunities

Scoring Position	24 / 136 (18%)	29 / 160 (18%)
Scoring Position, 2 Out	15 / 63 (24%)	18 / 72 (25%)
On Third, Less than 2 Out	7 / 21 (33%)	8 / 23 (35%)
RBI in close games / RBI Total	19 / 53 (36%)	38 / 62 (61%)

Danny Jackson
Kansas City Royals

Danny Jackson turns 26 in 1988, and people are still waiting for him to become a great pitcher. "I *love* to watch Danny Jackson pitch," wrote Bill James in the 1986 *Baseball Abstract,* and it's easy to see why— when Jackson's on, he's overpowering. As James pointed out, Jackson is basically a two-pitch pitcher (fastball, slider), but both pitches are outstanding, and when he's got them working the opposition has little chance. "Whenever I see Danny pitch," Bill wrote, "I can tell in the first inning whether he's going to win."

Jackson had it together a lot more during 1985 than his 14–12 record would indicate. His run support of 3.78 runs per start was the fifth worst in the American League. This lack of support continued to plague him in the World Series; though Jackson's record was 1–1, his ERA was 1.69, and in the fifth game he performed the rare feat of striking out the side on nine pitches.

Such things tend to balance out with time, but Jackson faced the same problem in 1986. He had an excellent 3.20 ERA but a 11–12 record. This time his teammates averaged only 2.93 runs in his starts, the worst offensive support in the majors.

After those two solid seasons, the Royals had every reason to think that Danny would have a big year in 1987.

Kansas City showed its confidence by naming Jackson as their opening day starter. But they say, "Bad luck comes in threes," and Jackson wound up at 9–18. Although Danny wasn't as sharp as in the past, his 4.02 ERA was still a lot better than the league average of 4.46. What threatened to make him a 20-game loser was that for the third straight year, his teammates went into a slump whenever Danny took the mound. The Royals scored a pathetic 3.35 runs a game for Jackson; almost a run and a half less than they scored for their other starters (4.70).

In all honesty, though, lack of support was only one of Danny's problems. If it's true, as Bill says, that you can tell in the first inning when Jackson's going to win, you can also tell early when he's going to get shelled. In 1987 it happened all too often. Jackson failed to last five innings in eight of his 34 starts, and that's way too many early knockouts. The Royals couldn't be blamed for thinking that Jackson had regressed: the KO's were one sign, and the increased walks (from 79 to 109) were another. Danny is now a Red, and he must be drooling about all the runs that Kal Daniels and Eric Davis are going to score for him. Despite his past difficulties, I'll confidently make this prediction: Danny Jackson will finally be a big winner in 1988.

Don Zminda

Jackson, Danny Lynn **Bats: Right** **Throws: Left** **Born 01/05/62**

1987 SEASON AND MAJOR-LEAGUE CAREER PITCHING TOTALS

	G	GS	CG	GF	IP	BFP	H	R	ER	HR	SH	SF	HB	TBB	IBB	SO	WP	Bk	W	L	Pct	ShO	Sv	ERA
87 KC	36	34	11	1	224	981	219	115	100	11	8	7	7	109	1	152	5	0	9	18	.333	2	0	4.02
5 YEARS	119	107	20	7	713	3088	715	345	292	36	27	15	22	305	4	430	19	4	37	49	.430	6	1	3.69

1987: Power, Groundball   **1986: Power, Groundball**   **1985: Finesse, Groundball**   **1984: Power, Groundball**

	\multicolumn{11}{c}{1987 SEASON}											\multicolumn{11}{c}{FOUR YEAR TOTALS (1984 – 1987)}										
	G	IP	H	BB	SO	SB	CS	W	L	S	ERA	G	IP	H	BB	SO	SB	CS	W	L	S	ERA
Totals	36	224.0	219	109	152	16	9	9	18	0	4.02	115	693.2	689	299	421	33	31	36	48	1	3.65
at Home	19	121.1	117	57	86	7	2	6	9	0	4.30	56	336.2	332	140	197	12	8	20	20	1	3.50
on Road	17	102.2	102	52	66	9	7	3	9	0	3.68	59	357.0	357	159	224	21	23	16	28	0	3.78
on Grass	12	64.2	67	39	51	5	4	1	7	0	4.45	34	180.2	188	91	131	6	13	6	14	1	4.38
on Artificial Turf	24	159.1	152	70	101	11	5	8	11	0	3.84	81	513.0	501	208	290	27	18	30	34	0	3.39
Day Games	13	83.0	76	37	58	4	7	3	7	0	2.93	46	283.0	282	124	183	15	20	14	19	0	3.43
Night Games	23	141.0	143	72	94	12	2	6	11	0	4.66	69	410.2	407	175	238	18	11	22	29	1	3.79
April	5	31.0	33	18	13	1	2	0	4	0	4.35	15	82.2	80	48	36	3	6	1	6	0	3.16
May	6	40.0	33	17	46	3	2	2	2	0	3.15	22	123.2	136	55	92	7	4	7	8	0	4.22
June	6	35.1	40	23	24	6	2	2	4	0	5.35	17	105.2	111	52	64	6	7	7	10	0	4.17
July	7	31.2	30	9	20	1	1	0	3	0	3.69	18	98.2	88	32	63	4	3	6	6	1	3.19
August	6	48.1	38	19	31	3	1	3	3	0	3.35	17	117.2	111	40	84	5	5	8	8	0	3.59
Sept/Oct	6	37.2	45	23	18	2	1	2	2	0	4.54	26	165.1	163	72	82	8	6	7	10	0	3.43

vs. Opponent Batters	Ave.	OBP	SLG	AB	H	2B	3B	HR	RBI	BB	SO	Ave.	OBP	SLG	AB	H	2B	3B	HR	RBI	BB	SO
Totals	.258	.345	.364	849	219	37	10	11	99	109	152	.261	.337	.365	2637	689	128	28	35	284	299	421
vs. Left	.277	.328	.346	159	44	8	0	1	21	13	45	.272	.340	.370	514	140	23	6	5	55	54	115
vs. Right	.254	.348	.368	690	175	29	10	10	78	96	107	.259	.337	.364	2123	549	89	22	30	229	245	306
Bases Empty	.252	.345	.345	461	116	21	5	4	4	64	84	.254	.337	.354	1454	370	58	16	18	18	179	245
Leadoff	.256	.350	.348	207	53	12	2	1	1	29	38	.245	.333	.345	641	157	27	8	7	7	84	103
Not Leadoff	.248	.341	.343	254	63	9	3	3	3	35	46	.262	.340	.360	813	213	31	8	11	11	95	142
Runners On Base	.265	.344	.387	388	103	16	5	7	95	45	68	.270	.338	.379	1183	319	54	12	17	266	120	176
First Base Only	.264	.351	.393	163	43	8	2	3	11	20	25	.282	.345	.396	515	145	22	5	9	30	48	66
Scoring Position	.267	.338	.382	225	60	8	3	4	84	25	43	.260	.332	.365	668	174	32	7	8	236	72	110
Late Innings, Close	.198	.250	.292	96	19	3	0	2	9	7	21	.258	.324	.369	314	81	14	3	5	32	31	49

RBI/Opportunities

Scoring Position	75 / 316 (24%)	214 / 907 (24%)
Scoring Position, 2 Out	26 / 145 (18%)	77 / 396 (19%)
On Third, Less than 2 Out	32 / 55 (58%)	82 / 166 (49%)
RBI in close games / RBI Total	77 / 99 (78%)	214 / 284 (75%)

Reggie Jackson
Oakland Athletics

When Reggie's Hall of Fame election comes up, some will argue he could not have accomplished what he did without the benefits of the DH rule. The truth is, the DH rule badly hampered his career, sending it into an early decline and almost certainly shortening it for a man who wanted to play as long as he could contribute. For whatever reasons—mingling with the fans, keeping his head in the game, you name it—Reggie consistently hit like a Hall of Famer when his teams let him play in the field.

His last season was no exception. As a DH he batted .179, .241 as a pinch-hitter, and a cool .400 (22 for 55) for his few games in the field. Jackson began being used extensively as a DH in 1983 when he was 37. As a frame of reference, Mike Schmidt turned 37 in his MVP year of 1986. Over the next five seasons (1983–87), 73 percent of Reggie's at bats came as a DH, 27 percent as a position player. Overall, he batted a disappointing .227. As a DH he hit .210, but when they let him play in the field, he hit .272 with excellent power. He had 580 at bats as a non-DH, about a season's worth for a full-time player. In those 580 at-bats Reggie hit 34 doubles and 32 homers, with 101 RBI and a .503 slugging average—in other words, he hit like Reggie Jackson.

In 1985, the only season of his last five where he played the majority of his games in the field (81 in the outfield, 52 as the DH), Reggie hit only .196 and slugged .387 as a DH; in his non-DH games he hit .284 and slugged .545.

Reggie did hit well as a DH in the early years of the rule when it was used just to give him an occasional breather. But in 10 of his last 11 seasons, Jackson hit better—usually much, much better—when he played in the field. His career average as a DH is .227 with a .407 SLUG%. As a non-DH during the years the rule was in effect (since 1973), Jackson batted .279 and slugged .525.

While it is true that Reggie was not a good fielder late in his career, he was not taken out of the outfield because his bat couldn't carry the weight of his aging glove. His managers took away his glove because the DH rule gave them an option to keep Jackson in the lineup and have a better defensive player in the outfield. Mauch's decision in 1983–86 was that Brian Downing was a better outfielder than Jackson, and even then, Reggie was good enough to play about a third of his games in the outfield.

What no one realized is that option was converting a Hall of Fame slugger into a below average hitter and driving him out of the game. Reggie's earned a place in the Hall, but without the DH rule he might have arrived in Cooperstown with a career average in the .270s and with 600 career homers.

Craig R. Wright and Don Zminda

Jackson, Reginald Martinez "Reggie" Bats: Left   Throws: Left   Born 05/18/46

1987 SEASON AND MAJOR-LEAGUE CAREER BATTING TOTALS

	G	AB	H	2B	3B	HR	TB	R	RBI	TBB	IBB	SO	HP	SH	SF	SB	CS	SB%	GDP	AVG	OBP	SLG
87 OAK	115	336	74	14	1	15	135	42	43	33	0	97	4	0	1	2	1	.67	3	.220	.297	.402
21 YEARS	2820	9864	2584	463	49	563	4834	1551	1702	1375	164	2597	96	13	68	228	115	.66	183	.262	.356	.490

	1987 SEASON											FOUR YEAR TOTALS (1984 – 1987)										
	Ave.	OBP	SLG	AB	H	2B	3B	HR	RBI	BB	SO	Ave.	OBP	SLG	AB	H	2B	3B	HR	RBI	BB	SO
Totals	.217	.294	.399	336	73	14	1	15	43	33	97	.234	.335	.426	1740	407	70	5	85	267	258	490
vs. Left	.292	.333	.521	48	14	5	0	2	8	2	15	.233	.319	.405	378	88	17	0	16	61	44	125
vs. Right	.205	.288	.378	288	59	9	1	13	35	31	82	.234	.340	.432	1362	319	53	5	69	206	214	365
at Home	.212	.297	.388	165	35	8	0	7	24	17	57	.229	.336	.442	831	190	29	2	48	148	131	244
on Road	.222	.291	.409	171	38	6	1	8	19	16	40	.239	.335	.413	909	217	41	3	37	119	127	246
vs. Groundball	.219	.274	.372	196	43	9	0	7	21	13	61	.245	.340	.429	864	212	37	4	38	128	122	240
vs. Flyball	.214	.321	.436	140	30	5	1	8	22	20	36	.223	.331	.424	876	195	33	1	47	139	136	250
vs. Finesse	.225	.295	.406	160	36	6	1	7	16	16	37	.248	.337	.442	991	246	44	2	48	146	131	237
vs. Power	.210	.293	.392	176	37	8	0	8	27	17	60	.215	.333	.406	749	161	26	3	37	121	127	253
on Grass	.216	.298	.404	287	62	12	0	14	38	30	84	.233	.335	.430	1474	343	57	3	76	233	220	415
on Artificial Turf	.224	.269	.367	49	11	2	1	1	5	3	13	.241	.336	.406	266	64	13	2	9	34	38	75
Day Games	.241	.333	.414	116	28	6	1	4	17	13	37	.240	.345	.446	496	119	27	3	23	80	75	136
Night Games	.205	.273	.391	220	45	8	0	11	26	20	60	.232	.331	.419	1244	288	43	2	62	187	183	354
April	.230	.321	.459	74	17	3	1	4	11	9	20	.273	.346	.518	278	76	13	2	17	52	30	73
May	.148	.235	.180	61	9	2	0	0	1	7	14	.202	.309	.354	263	53	10	0	10	26	41	78
June	.236	.309	.514	72	17	2	0	6	18	7	17	.270	.386	.444	304	82	14	0	13	53	57	83
July	.184	.215	.395	76	14	4	0	4	6	3	30	.229	.322	.439	319	73	15	2	16	40	44	99
August	.243	.349	.378	37	9	2	0	1	4	4	12	.201	.304	.334	293	59	10	1	9	39	41	79
Sept/Oct	.438	.526	.500	16	7	1	0	0	3	3	4	.226	.332	.466	283	64	8	0	20	57	45	78
Bases Empty	.223	.302	.363	193	43	10	1	5	5	20	60	.217	.314	.378	920	200	39	2	35	35	128	272
Leadoff	.305	.374	.439	82	25	5	0	2	2	8	20	.231	.332	.371	385	89	12	0	14	14	57	99
Not Leadoff	.162	.250	.306	111	18	5	1	3	3	12	40	.207	.301	.383	535	111	27	2	21	21	71	173
Runners On	.210	.283	.448	143	30	4	0	10	38	13	37	.252	.356	.480	820	207	31	3	50	232	130	218
First Base Only	.283	.358	.683	60	17	3	0	7	15	7	15	.284	.355	.553	380	108	16	1	28	63	42	107
Scoring Position	.157	.228	.277	83	13	1	0	3	23	6	22	.225	.356	.418	440	99	15	2	22	169	88	111
Late Innings, Close	.200	.243	.371	70	14	3	0	3	6	4	20	.192	.299	.282	291	56	8	0	6	23	44	95

RBI/Opportunities

Scoring Position	20 / 112 (18%)	127 / 637 (20%)
Scoring Position, 2 Out	7 / 63 (11%)	50 / 319 (16%)
On Third, Less than 2 Out	7 / 20 (35%)	36 / 113 (32%)
RBI in close games / RBI Total	22 / 43 (51%)	173 / 267 (65%)

Brook Jacoby
Cleveland Indians

I rarely make flat statements, but I'll make one here: Save for Spike Owen, Brook Jacoby has the best name in baseball. His first name (which, by the way, is *not* a nickname) is perfect for a third baseman; his surname is short, firm and unflashy—just like a hot corner man should be.

OK, I'll make one more: Offensively, Jacoby is the most underrated third sacker around. He's one of four men (Boggs, Gaetti, Schmidt) that you can bet on to have a good year every year. He's the youngest (just turned 28) and has played the fewest major league games. You really have to wonder how much better he'd be now if he hadn't been stuck behind Bob Horner and reached the majors sooner.

Just one more: Nobody works harder—or more successfully—to improve than Brook. His average jumps each year: .264, .274, .288, .300. His slugging percentage keeps rising: .369, .426, .441, .541. His on-base percentage has climbed steadily: .314, .324, .350, .387. For the icing, after three years of rising strikeout totals (73, 120, 137), Brook fanned only 73 times in 1987. Though it's hard to see him getting much better, I don't think his 1987 is a fluke at all; in fact, I even predicted it in this space last year.

Last one: Jacoby is one of the most overrated defensive players in baseball. Though his range factor was fourth in the AL (80+ games or more at third), he also tied for the league lead in errors. The former stat is unusually high for him; the latter isn't. Brook missed leading the AL in errors by one in 1986. He was third in 1985. Of the 13 men with 80+ games at third in the AL in 1987, only four turned DPs less often than Brook; given Cleveland's pitching, we may safely assume that he didn't want for opportunities. Brook has made more DPs than errors in a season only twice in his career. He's not Floyd Rayford—but then Bill Mazeroski's preview doesn't keep telling me that Honey Bear is a defensive whiz.

By the way, Jacoby's godawful RBI total comes courtesy of the Indian lineup in 1987. Brook usually hit sixth, seventh or eighth, behind the likes of Mel Hall (.309 OB%), Joe Carter (.304), Carmen Castillo (.296) and Cory Snyder (.273). He led off a ton of innings and never had many men on base when he wasn't; how many runs are you supposed to drive in under those circumstances? And, unlike a certain Royal who shall remain nameless because you're probably as sick of hearing about the jerk as I am, not once did Jacoby complain that the batting order was hurting his stats.

Though I like Jake, 23-year-old Eddie Williams was voted the best defensive third baseman in the American Association by *Baseball America* this year and is also a very talented hitter. Expect him to push Jacoby over to first base this spring.

Geoff Beckman

Jacoby, Brook Wallace Bats: Right Throws: Right Born 11/23/59

1987 SEASON AND MAJOR-LEAGUE CAREER BATTING TOTALS

	G	AB	H	2B	3B	HR	TB	R	RBI	TBB	IBB	SO	HP	SH	SF	SB	CS	SB%	GDP	AVG	OBP	SLG
87 CLE	155	540	162	26	4	32	292	73	69	75	2	73	3	0	2	2	3	.40	19	.300	.387	.541
6 YEARS	615	2186	614	101	14	76	971	292	277	211	10	407	6	5	17	9	9	.50	65	.281	.343	.444

	1987 SEASON											FOUR YEAR TOTALS (1984 – 1987)										
	Ave.	OBP	SLG	AB	H	2B	3B	HR	RBI	BB	SO	Ave.	OBP	SLG	AB	H	2B	3B	HR	RBI	BB	SO
Totals	.300	.387	.541	540	162	26	4	32	69	75	73	.282	.345	.447	2168	612	101	14	76	276	211	404
vs. Left	.261	.382	.444	142	37	9	1	5	8	28	20	.278	.357	.439	627	174	27	4	22	71	79	105
vs. Right	.314	.389	.575	398	125	17	3	27	61	47	53	.284	.340	.450	1541	438	74	10	54	205	132	299
at Home	.279	.366	.564	280	78	13	2	21	39	38	40	.270	.337	.446	1079	291	50	7	42	146	111	202
on Road	.323	.410	.515	260	84	13	2	11	30	37	33	.295	.353	.448	1089	321	51	7	34	130	100	202
vs. Groundball	.277	.371	.517	271	75	10	2	17	38	38	32	.271	.335	.430	1069	290	50	6	36	136	103	185
vs. Flyball	.323	.404	.565	269	87	16	2	15	31	37	41	.293	.355	.463	1099	322	51	8	40	140	108	219
vs. Finesse	.317	.388	.502	271	86	12	1	12	33	29	20	.308	.361	.475	1180	363	58	8	41	149	99	161
vs. Power	.283	.386	.580	269	76	14	3	20	36	46	53	.252	.326	.414	988	249	43	6	35	127	112	243
on Grass	.294	.384	.543	449	132	20	4	28	54	65	62	.277	.342	.443	1836	508	81	13	66	238	184	345
on Artificial Turf	.330	.402	.527	91	30	6	0	4	15	10	11	.313	.365	.470	332	104	20	1	10	38	27	59
Day Games	.265	.363	.514	185	49	15	2	9	23	27	25	.269	.330	.450	736	198	38	4	29	99	68	148
Night Games	.318	.400	.555	355	113	11	2	23	46	48	48	.289	.353	.446	1432	414	63	10	47	177	143	256
April	.237	.341	.408	76	18	4	0	3	8	11	9	.249	.329	.389	285	71	14	1	8	32	33	48
May	.232	.321	.333	99	23	2	1	2	6	13	21	.261	.326	.382	395	103	13	1	11	45	38	85
June	.276	.357	.632	87	24	5	1	8	17	9	10	.273	.329	.467	396	108	19	2	18	58	31	70
July	.361	.415	.680	97	35	5	1	8	12	9	13	.285	.350	.449	379	108	19	2	13	48	38	73
August	.316	.441	.505	95	30	9	0	3	9	22	12	.308	.384	.451	377	116	19	4	9	41	47	69
Sept/Oct	.372	.439	.686	86	32	1	1	8	17	11	8	.315	.360	.542	336	106	17	4	17	52	24	59
Bases Empty	.318	.390	.642	321	102	17	3	27	27	37	42	.277	.334	.462	1204	334	53	8	51	51	101	227
Leadoff	.325	.388	.667	126	41	11	1	10	10	13	16	.300	.347	.505	483	145	24	3	23	23	35	80
Not Leadoff	.313	.391	.626	195	61	6	2	17	17	24	26	.262	.325	.433	721	189	29	5	28	28	66	147
Runners On	.274	.383	.393	219	60	9	1	5	42	38	31	.288	.362	.428	964	278	48	6	25	225	110	177
First Base Only	.340	.413	.515	97	33	6	1	3	11	11	12	.325	.370	.462	446	145	22	3	11	34	31	70
Scoring Position	.221	.362	.295	122	27	3	0	2	31	27	19	.257	.355	.400	518	133	26	3	14	191	79	107
Late Innings, Close	.282	.330	.518	85	24	1	2	5	9	5	12	.285	.327	.426	340	97	7	4	11	34	20	61

RBI/Opportunities

	1987		Four Year	
Scoring Position	29 / 175	(17%)	165 / 718	(23%)
Scoring Position, 2 Out	9 / 85	(11%)	60 / 335	(18%)
On Third, Less than 2 Out	6 / 27	(22%)	59 / 131	(45%)
RBI in close games / RBI Total	41 / 69	(59%)	163 / 276	(59%)

Chris James
Philadelphia Phillies

It looks like the Phillies have finally found themselves a left fielder in the young Texan, Chris James. After trying an assortment of has beens, never was'es, and might be's, it looks like they've come upon an up-and-coming star in the making.

1987 was an up-and-down year for James. He started as a center fielder, platooning with Milt Thompson, and was later relegated to the bench, backing up Mike Easler, Thompson, and Glenn Wilson. The last step for him was being sent down to Maine, to learn how to play third base. After a week or so, his luck began to change, as Easler returned to the Yankees, and James returned to the Phils. Placed in the lineup, he swung a hot bat, hitting well over .300, and going through fences to catch anything hit near him. He then hit an extended slump in September and the Phillies looked at another left fielder, Keith Hughes. After Hughes' .236 average against right-handed pitching, James should be in the Phillie lineup for years to come.

James, in little more than a half season, piled up some excellent statistics. His 43 extra hits placed him fifth on the Phillies, and his slugging pct. of .528 would have placed him with the league leaders, if he had enough at bats. His average of .293 placed him second on the team. In 115 games, he had only 2 errors, and played left field quite capably. After seeing the recent left fielders the Phillies sent out there, he looked like a Gold Glover.

If there is any knock on James, it is the same knock that any young ballplayer would have against him. He must learn to be patient and wait for his pitch. The Phillies can live with his strikeouts, but to be a star, he must learn that a walk is almost as good as a hit, especially in that Phillie lineup. He stole 3 bases in 1987, but he seems to have lost some of the speed he displayed in 1986. It looks like the leg injury he suffered in 1986 has slowed him down now.

Chris was bounced up and down in the batting order for the Phillies, without any ill effects. His run totals would have been considerably higher if the eighth hitters on the Phils would ever knock in any runs. Still, 54 runs scored is a pretty decent amount, considering his playing time.

In 1988, James should benefit from a year of experience under his belt. If he is left alone and allowed to mature as an everyday player, he could easily turn into a 30-HR, 100-RBI man—the ideal #3 hitter.

Walter DeSoi

James, Donald Christopher "Chris"   Bats: Right   Throws: Right   Born 10/04/62

1987 SEASON AND MAJOR-LEAGUE CAREER BATTING TOTALS

	G	AB	H	2B	3B	HR	TB	R	RBI	TBB	IBB	SO	HP	SH	SF	SB	CS	SB%	GDP	AVG	OBP	SLG
87 PHI	115	358	105	20	6	17	188	48	54	27	0	67	2	1	3	3	1	.75	4	.293	.344	.525
2 YEARS	131	404	118	23	6	18	207	53	59	28	0	80	2	2	3	3	1	.75	5	.292	.339	.512

	1987 SEASON											FOUR YEAR TOTALS (1984 – 1987)										
	Ave.	OBP	SLG	AB	H	2B	3B	HR	RBI	BB	SO	Ave.	OBP	SLG	AB	H	2B	3B	HR	RBI	BB	SO
Totals	.293	.344	.525	358	105	20	6	17	54	27	67	.292	.339	.512	404	118	23	6	18	59	28	80
vs. Left	.282	.327	.570	149	42	10	3	9	26	11	26	.275	.319	.550	171	47	11	3	10	28	12	30
vs. Right	.301	.355	.493	209	63	10	3	8	28	16	41	.305	.353	.485	233	71	12	3	8	31	16	50
at Home	.302	.366	.552	172	52	10	3	9	31	18	33	.304	.362	.536	194	59	12	3	9	33	18	40
on Road	.285	.322	.500	186	53	10	3	8	23	9	34	.281	.317	.490	210	59	11	3	9	26	10	40
vs. Groundball	.272	.312	.418	184	50	10	1	5	27	11	32	.276	.313	.429	217	60	13	1	6	31	12	42
vs. Flyball	.316	.377	.638	174	55	10	5	12	27	16	35	.310	.368	.610	187	58	10	5	12	28	16	38
vs. Finesse	.296	.340	.546	196	58	11	4	10	29	11	31	.301	.343	.543	219	66	12	4	11	32	12	36
vs. Power	.290	.348	.500	162	47	9	2	7	25	16	36	.281	.333	.476	185	52	11	2	7	27	16	44
on Grass	.235	.247	.506	85	20	2	0	7	14	2	17	.244	.255	.511	90	22	3	0	7	14	2	18
on Artificial Turf	.311	.372	.531	273	85	18	6	10	40	25	50	.306	.362	.513	314	96	20	6	11	45	26	62
Day Games	.318	.371	.580	88	28	3	1	6	11	8	24	.318	.371	.580	88	28	3	1	6	11	8	24
Night Games	.285	.334	.507	270	77	17	5	11	43	19	43	.285	.329	.494	316	90	20	5	12	48	20	56
April	.259	.333	.370	27	7	1	1	0	0	3	10	.250	.325	.417	36	9	1	1	1	2	4	13
May	.250	.294	.313	16	4	1	0	0	1	1	3	.278	.316	.333	18	5	1	0	0	1	1	3
June	.339	.377	.714	56	19	3	0	6	15	3	11	.339	.377	.714	56	19	3	0	6	15	3	11
July	.352	.380	.625	88	31	8	2	4	11	3	13	.352	.380	.625	88	31	8	2	4	11	3	13
August	.265	.330	.559	102	27	5	2	7	19	10	20	.265	.330	.559	102	27	5	2	7	19	10	20
Sept/Oct	.246	.308	.304	69	17	2	1	0	8	7	10	.260	.301	.327	104	27	5	1	0	11	7	20
Bases Empty	.330	.380	.575	200	66	13	3	10	10	14	32	.324	.369	.551	225	73	15	3	10	10	14	40
Leadoff	.342	.385	.493	73	25	5	0	2	2	4	13	.341	.376	.477	88	30	6	0	2	2	4	17
Not Leadoff	.323	.377	.622	127	41	8	3	8	8	10	19	.314	.365	.599	137	43	9	3	8	8	10	23
Runners On	.247	.299	.462	158	39	7	3	7	44	13	35	.251	.301	.464	179	45	8	3	8	49	14	40
First Base Only	.259	.333	.370	54	14	1	1	1	3	6	12	.267	.333	.383	60	16	2	1	1	3	6	13
Scoring Position	.240	.281	.510	104	25	6	2	6	41	7	23	.244	.285	.504	119	29	6	2	7	46	8	27
Late Innings, Close	.302	.373	.396	53	16	0	1	1	5	6	9	.302	.373	.396	106	32	0	2	2	10	12	18

RBI/Opportunities

	1987		FOUR YEAR	
Scoring Position	32 / 125	(26%)	36 / 144	(25%)
Scoring Position, 2 Out	9 / 53	(17%)	12 / 65	(18%)
On Third, Less than 2 Out	11 / 17	(65%)	11 / 18	(61%)
RBI in close games / RBI Total	34 / 54	(63%)	68 / 59	(115%)

Dion James
Atlanta Braves

In leafing though back issues of the *Baseball Abstract* I found these rather interesting comments by Bill James in the 1985 *Abstract:* "Strengths: hitting for average, speed, defense. Weaknesses: none proven. Looks real good to me . . . probably the Brewers' center fielder this year." Well, the Brewers, renowned for their ability to evaluate young talent, let this one get away.

So here's the question: How come nobody knew Dion James had such a fine season in 1987? One hundred and fifty or so games on national cable, and still mostly anonymous. The most notoriety achieved by Dion during the 1987 season occurred early in the year, in New York. On national television, and, soon, on *This Week in Baseball,* Dion hit a fly ball double which struck and killed a pigeon who mistakenly thought those things only happened in the American League.

James' 1987 should make most NL leadoff hitters green with envy. The evidence: 23 more doubles, 7 more homers, the same number of walks, half as many strikeouts, 23 point higher batting average, 34 point higher OBA than—Vince Coleman. Coleman had his best offensive season, and is generally considered the prototype leadoff hitter of the '80's. Of course, Dion did have 129 fewer at bats than Vince. Only the Reds' Kal Daniels and the Astros' Gerald Young truly compared with James in 1987.

James walked more than he struck out (70–63), an excellent trait for a leadoff man. The 37 doubles led his team and ranked fourth in the league. Six triples and 10 SB show some speed, although 10 of 18 basestealing as a leadoff hitter is not impressive. However, I agree with the analysts who question the value of the stolen base. James' on-base percentage surpassed his competitors, and I want a leadoff man on base as much as possible. Factor in 53 extra base hits and only 1 error, and you have a star.

James roared out of the gate to peak at .366 (.464 OBA) with 11 doubles and 20 runs scored by May 4. The oxygen must have been a bit thin up there, though, as Dion hibernated from then through May 30 (13 for 69). A nine game stretch from July 28 through August 6 more than compensated (20 for 40, 7 runs scored, 3 doubles, 2 homers, 8 RBIs). Then James proved he belonged with the NL elite by hitting .377 (40 for 106) with 11 doubles from August 28 to the season's end. A fine .294 mark ended at a sparkling .312. Although, in one of his typical bursts of creative managing, Chuck Tanner has decided that Dion can not handle the rigors of center field in Atlanta (even with its ground ball pitching staff), the raw stats just don't support his decision to move James to left field. He led all National League outfielders with a .996 fielding average, and his range factor of 2.12 ranked in the upper half of center fielders in the league. Considering that Atlanta finished second in the league in fielding and last in pitching, Tanner's time would be much better spent not tinkering with the one part of the club that isn't really broken—there's so many other targets of opportunity in Atlanta.

Robert L. Jones

James, Dion

Bats: Left **Throws: Left** **Born 11/09/62**

1987 SEASON AND MAJOR-LEAGUE CAREER BATTING TOTALS

	G	AB	H	2B	3B	HR	TB	R	RBI	TBB	IBB	SO	HP	SH	SF	SB	CS	SB%	GDP	AVG	OBP	SLG
87 ATL	134	494	154	37	6	10	233	80	61	70	2	63	2	5	3	10	8	.56	8	.312	.397	.472
4 YEARS	291	950	281	57	11	11	393	138	95	110	3	112	5	11	6	21	18	.54	15	.296	.370	.414

	1987 SEASON											TWO YEAR TOTALS (1986 – 1987)										
	Ave.	OBP	SLG	AB	H	2B	3B	HR	RBI	BB	SO	Ave.	OBP	SLG	AB	H	2B	3B	HR	RBI	BB	SO
Totals	.312	.397	.472	494	154	37	6	10	61	70	63	.312	.398	.472	494	154	37	6	10	61	70	63
vs. Left	.303	.442	.438	89	27	7	1	1	14	22	14	.303	.442	.438	89	27	7	1	1	14	22	14
vs. Right	.314	.386	.479	405	127	30	5	9	47	48	49	.314	.386	.479	405	127	30	5	9	47	48	49
at Home	.376	.466	.561	237	89	21	4	5	35	39	20	.376	.466	.561	237	89	21	4	5	35	39	20
on Road	.253	.331	.389	257	65	16	2	5	26	31	43	.253	.331	.389	257	65	16	2	5	26	31	43
vs. Groundball	.265	.349	.436	211	56	16	4	4	23	25	29	.265	.349	.436	211	56	16	4	4	23	25	29
vs. Flyball	.346	.432	.498	283	98	21	2	6	38	45	34	.346	.432	.498	283	98	21	2	6	38	45	34
vs. Finesse	.351	.439	.524	248	87	23	4	4	29	39	23	.351	.439	.524	248	87	23	4	4	29	39	23
vs. Power	.272	.354	.419	246	67	14	2	6	32	31	40	.272	.354	.419	246	67	14	2	6	32	31	40
on Grass	.328	.410	.509	381	125	29	5	10	53	53	49	.328	.410	.509	381	125	29	5	10	53	53	49
on Artificial Turf	.257	.354	.345	113	29	8	1	0	8	17	14	.257	.354	.345	113	29	8	1	0	8	17	14
Day Games	.275	.366	.427	178	49	15	0	4	15	26	26	.275	.366	.427	178	49	15	0	4	15	26	26
Night Games	.332	.415	.497	316	105	22	6	6	46	44	37	.332	.415	.497	316	105	22	6	6	46	44	37
April	.324	.440	.473	74	24	8	0	1	8	15	16	.324	.440	.473	74	24	8	0	1	8	15	16
May	.250	.349	.435	92	23	7	2	2	11	14	15	.250	.349	.435	92	23	7	2	2	11	14	15
June	.293	.404	.427	75	22	4	0	2	6	14	10	.293	.404	.427	75	22	4	0	2	6	14	10
July	.354	.475	.538	65	23	2	2	2	9	15	4	.354	.475	.538	65	23	2	2	2	9	15	4
August	.286	.309	.484	91	26	5	2	3	17	4	10	.286	.309	.484	91	26	5	2	3	17	4	10
Sept/Oct	.371	.425	.485	97	36	11	0	0	10	8	8	.371	.425	.485	97	36	11	0	0	10	8	8
Bases Empty	.308	.387	.458	321	99	24	3	6	6	40	37	.308	.387	.458	321	99	24	3	6	6	40	37
Leadoff	.342	.411	.546	196	67	18	2	6	6	22	26	.342	.411	.546	196	67	18	2	6	6	22	26
Not Leadoff	.256	.350	.320	125	32	6	1	0	0	18	11	.256	.350	.320	125	32	6	1	0	0	18	11
Runners On	.318	.415	.497	173	55	13	3	4	55	30	26	.318	.415	.497	173	55	13	3	4	55	30	26
First Base Only	.322	.420	.458	59	19	5	0	1	4	10	7	.322	.420	.458	59	19	5	0	1	4	10	7
Scoring Position	.316	.413	.518	114	36	8	3	3	51	20	19	.316	.413	.518	114	36	8	3	3	51	20	19
Late Innings, Close	.250	.337	.310	84	21	2	0	1	8	10	13	.250	.337	.310	168	42	4	0	2	16	20	26

RBI/Opportunities

	1987				Two Year		
Scoring Position	42 / 162	(26%)			42 / 162	(26%)	
Scoring Position, 2 Out	15 / 63	(24%)			15 / 63	(24%)	
On Third, Less than 2 Out	17 / 33	(52%)			17 / 33	(52%)	
RBI in close games / RBI Total	37 / 61	(61%)			74 / 61	(121%)	

Stan Jefferson
San Diego Padres

Patience, gentlemen, patience.

Entering the '84 season, the Padres' future had arrived. Thanks to trades, minor league development and free agents, San Diego finally fielded a competitive nine. Youth such as Gwynn, McReynolds, Dravecky, Show and Wiggins had major league experience, while Kennedy, Templeton, Garvey, Gossage and Nettles lent veteran experience and leadership to the team.

Then the worst possible thing happened: *SUCCESS!*

A decent Padre team won in a weak division and miraculously reached the World Series. Overnight, future expectations soared. What happened next? Management scrapped their game plan for player development. Within 3 years, the team was buried in the cellar.

One problem concerned Alan Wiggins' drug problem, which rendered him unplayable due to team policy. Management decided that the best solution to the second base situation was to find a "Wiggins clone." The result was the premature promotion (and possible ruin) of two good prospects, Bip Roberts and Joey Cora. When the Padres finally realized that their leadoff man didn't *have to* play second base, they obtained Jefferson. They planned to give him a chance in '87, and then make decisions on other outfield prospects (Mack, Abner, Byers, etc.). But Stan didn't really get a full opportunity.

His spring was abbreviated by wrist and leg injuries and a beaning. Newspaper reports stated that Bowa felt Jefferson didn't "want to play," but after several confrontations between the two, Larry apparently changed his mind. Stan played little during the team's dismal start, returning in time to help them start winning. Soon after, a rotator cuff injury was diagnosed, affecting his play the rest of the season. He finished the year in a dismal slump—in September and October, in 81 AB, Stan finished last in the league in Average (.111), Slugging (.185), and On-Base Average (.198).

During the season he made some baserunning errors, struck out often, and his on-base percentage was subpar. His stolen base rate (76 percent) was good and he showed some power. His speed helped give San Diego one of the fastest outfields in baseball.

His initial experience as a major league leadoff man was remarkably similar to that of Wiggins. Dick Williams stuck with Alan, who improved greatly. Jefferson shows more offensive potential in several categories and merits a *healthy* look in '88. If Bowa keeps Gwynn batting first, Stan will surely be sacrificed, and if the Padres dump him, some team may get a hell of a leadoff batter for 10 or 15 years.

Bruce Ericson

Jefferson, Stanley "Stan" Bats: Both   Throws: Right   Born 12/04/62

1987 SEASON AND MAJOR-LEAGUE CAREER BATTING TOTALS

	G	AB	H	2B	3B	HR	TB	R	RBI	TBB	IBB	SO	HP	SH	SF	SB	CS	SB%	GDP	AVG	OBP	SLG
87 SD	116	422	97	8	7	8	143	59	29	39	2	92	2	3	3	34	11	.76	6	.230	.296	.339
2 YEARS	130	446	102	9	7	9	152	65	32	41	2	100	3	3	3	34	11	.76	7	.229	.296	.341

	1987 SEASON											FOUR YEAR TOTALS (1984 – 1987)									
	Ave.	OBP	SLG	AB	H	2B	3B	HR	RBI	BB	SO	Ave.	OBP	SLG	AB	H	2B	3B	HR	RBI	BB	SO
Totals	.230	.296	.339	422	97	8	7	8	29	39	92	.229	.298	.341	446	102	9	7	9	32	41	100
vs. Left	.240	.310	.273	154	37	2	0	1	4	15	30	.250	.322	.287	164	41	3	0	1	4	16	32
vs. Right	.224	.288	.377	268	60	6	7	7	25	24	62	.216	.281	.372	282	61	6	7	8	28	25	68
at Home	.211	.298	.333	213	45	5	3	5	17	25	59	.214	.301	.342	234	50	6	3	6	20	27	66
on Road	.249	.295	.344	209	52	3	4	3	12	14	33	.245	.291	.340	212	52	3	4	3	12	14	34
vs. Groundball	.269	.319	.386	197	53	5	3	4	15	15	35	.264	.319	.389	208	55	5	3	5	18	17	37
vs. Flyball	.196	.277	.298	225	44	3	4	4	14	24	57	.197	.277	.298	238	47	4	4	4	14	24	63
vs. Finesse	.258	.308	.416	209	54	2	5	7	15	15	31	.254	.307	.420	224	57	3	5	8	18	17	34
vs. Power	.202	.285	.263	213	43	6	2	1	14	24	61	.203	.285	.261	222	45	6	2	1	14	24	66
on Grass	.220	.295	.353	309	68	8	6	7	26	32	75	.221	.297	.358	330	73	9	6	8	29	34	82
on Artificial Turf	.257	.300	.301	113	29	0	1	1	3	7	17	.250	.293	.293	116	29	0	1	1	3	7	18
Day Games	.220	.327	.299	127	28	2	1	2	9	20	36	.220	.327	.299	127	28	2	1	2	9	20	36
Night Games	.234	.282	.356	295	69	6	6	6	20	19	56	.232	.283	.357	319	74	7	6	7	23	21	64
April	.286	.318	.381	21	6	0	1	0	2	1	1	.286	.318	.381	21	6	0	1	0	2	1	1
May	.239	.366	.373	67	16	2	2	1	5	13	17	.239	.366	.373	67	16	2	2	1	5	13	17
June	.193	.266	.228	57	11	2	0	0	1	6	22	.193	.266	.228	57	11	2	0	0	1	6	22
July	.296	.352	.407	81	24	1	1	2	7	7	19	.296	.352	.407	81	24	1	1	2	7	7	19
August	.270	.294	.426	115	31	2	2	4	7	4	20	.270	.294	.426	115	31	2	2	4	7	4	20
Sept/Oct	.111	.198	.185	81	9	1	1	1	7	8	13	.133	.220	.229	105	14	2	1	2	10	10	21
Bases Empty	.262	.327	.384	279	73	6	5	6	6	25	70	.262	.325	.383	290	76	7	5	6	6	25	75
Leadoff	.264	.316	.384	159	42	2	4	3	3	11	39	.268	.317	.387	168	45	3	4	3	3	11	43
Not Leadoff	.258	.341	.383	120	31	4	1	3	3	14	31	.254	.336	.377	122	31	4	1	3	3	14	32
Runners On	.168	.237	.252	143	24	2	2	2	23	14	22	.167	.244	.263	156	26	2	2	3	26	16	25
First Base Only	.204	.250	.306	49	10	0	1	1	3	3	9	.185	.228	.278	54	10	0	1	1	3	3	11
Scoring Position	.149	.231	.223	94	14	2	1	1	20	11	13	.157	.252	.255	102	16	2	1	2	23	13	14
Late Innings, Close	.119	.189	.164	67	8	0	0	1	3	6	21	.119	.189	.164	134	16	0	0	2	6	12	42

RBI/Opportunities

	1987 SEASON	FOUR YEAR TOTALS
Scoring Position	18 / 131 (14%)	19 / 144 (13%)
Scoring Position, 2 Out	7 / 72 (10%)	8 / 77 (10%)
On Third, Less than 2 Out	8 / 14 (57%)	8 / 17 (47%)
RBI in close games / RBI Total	18 / 29 (62%)	36 / 32 (113%)

Steve Jeltz
Philadelphia Phillies

In spring training, Steve Jeltz was ticketed as the Phillies' shortstop for 1987; his change to switch-hitting for the '86 season had helped his hitting somewhat, but not very much—his average for the season was just .219. However, his fielding abilities were such that it was thought that his weak hitting could be tolerated, especially since the rest of the batting order looked to be so potent.

Unfortunately for Jeltz and the Phils, the rest of the team got off to such a bad start in the hitting department that Jeltz's even worse hitting success got management's attention early on. Since Steve was hitting only .153 near the end of May, Luis Aguayo was given some starts, and Jeltz was riding the bench. In June, Jeltz was sent up to Maine to "work on his problem." Down there, he did hit much better, and he was called up again in July. He resumed the regular shortstop job shortly thereafter, and his hitting did improve, as he hit about .250 for the rest of the year, ending up with a .231 season average. But the average doesn't tell the whole story. Although he had fair success in working walks, he had trouble with men on base, with only 12 RBIs for the season in about 300 ABs, the lowest total in the league. His fielding was reasonably steady, and occasionally spectacular, but late in the year rumors got around that

management felt that he was not making the big play in critical situations.

Since the big problem for all the Phillies all year long was their failure at bat and on the mound in critical games and situations, Jeltz fit right in. 1988 will be a critical year for Steve Jeltz, determining whether he has what it takes to be a major league shortstop. Oddly enough, this may depend to a large extent on how well his teammates hit, and thus take some of the pressure off Jeltz. Then he'll just have to field well, and chip in with an occasional hit.

J. R. Hambleton

A few amazing statistics on Jeltz's power (or lack of it). He had only 15 extra base hits in almost 300 at bats. He doesn't even have warning track power. When he does get one into the gap, he has a triple, because they play him so shallow. Here's amazing stat #2: he had more errors than RBI, 14 to 12. He also has very little speed for a shortstop, as witnessed by his one stolen base in three attempts, and only 37 runs scored.

Sad to say for the Phillies, though, he is the best of the crop in the entire organization.

Walter De Soi

Jeltz, Larry Steven "Steve" Bats: Both   Throws: Right   Born 05/28/59

1987 SEASON AND MAJOR-LEAGUE CAREER BATTING TOTALS

	G	AB	H	2B	3B	HR	TB	R	RBI	TBB	IBB	SO	HP	SH	SF	SB	CS	SB%	GDP	AVG	OBP	SLG
87 PHI	114	293	68	9	6	0	89	37	12	39	4	54	1	4	0	1	2	.33	13	.232	.324	.304
5 YEARS	389	1004	216	24	13	1	269	105	68	138	18	219	2	14	4	10	7	.59	33	.215	.310	.268

	1987 SEASON											FOUR YEAR TOTALS (1984 – 1987)										
	Ave.	OBP	SLG	AB	H	2B	3B	HR	RBI	BB	SO	Ave.	OBP	SLG	AB	H	2B	3B	HR	RBI	BB	SO
Totals	.231	.323	.303	294	68	9	6	0	12	39	54	.216	.311	.267	997	215	24	12	1	67	137	217
vs. Left	.175	.258	.262	80	14	3	2	0	7	9	16	.203	.300	.259	301	61	8	3	1	25	42	70
vs. Right	.252	.347	.318	214	54	6	4	0	5	30	38	.221	.315	.270	696	154	16	9	0	42	95	147
at Home	.209	.303	.270	163	34	4	3	0	9	22	33	.208	.292	.269	524	109	16	8	0	43	64	118
on Road	.260	.349	.344	131	34	5	3	0	3	17	21	.224	.330	.264	473	106	8	4	1	24	73	99
vs. Groundball	.255	.358	.335	161	41	3	5	0	10	25	35	.223	.320	.272	503	112	9	8	0	35	71	115
vs. Flyball	.203	.279	.263	133	27	6	1	0	2	14	19	.209	.301	.261	494	103	15	4	1	32	66	102
vs. Finesse	.256	.339	.345	168	43	5	5	0	8	21	20	.220	.300	.275	546	120	13	7	1	29	62	85
vs. Power	.198	.303	.246	126	25	4	1	0	4	18	34	.211	.323	.257	451	95	11	5	0	38	75	132
on Grass	.262	.366	.338	80	21	4	1	0	2	12	15	.214	.309	.246	248	53	6	1	0	13	32	47
on Artificial Turf	.220	.307	.290	214	47	5	5	0	10	27	39	.216	.311	.274	749	162	18	11	1	54	105	170
Day Games	.263	.385	.395	76	20	4	3	0	6	14	14	.239	.350	.324	284	68	9	6	1	31	48	64
Night Games	.220	.300	.271	218	48	5	3	0	6	25	40	.206	.294	.244	713	147	15	6	0	36	89	153
April	.136	.208	.136	44	6	0	0	0	1	4	12	.204	.297	.230	152	31	0	2	0	11	20	38
May	.167	.400	.167	18	3	0	0	0	0	7	2	.189	.309	.220	127	24	4	0	0	7	22	30
June	.220	.291	.280	50	11	1	1	0	3	5	8	.213	.327	.251	183	39	5	1	0	15	31	33
July	.233	.303	.367	30	7	2	1	0	2	3	4	.221	.331	.286	140	31	5	2	0	9	23	36
August	.289	.373	.371	97	28	4	2	0	4	12	15	.249	.322	.324	185	46	6	4	0	8	19	34
Sept/Oct	.236	.333	.345	55	13	2	2	0	2	8	13	.210	.284	.271	210	44	4	3	1	17	22	46
Bases Empty	.279	.364	.345	165	46	3	4	0	0	22	28	.225	.311	.264	564	127	11	4	1	1	70	121
Leadoff	.304	.415	.406	69	21	3	2	0	0	13	10	.244	.344	.298	225	55	5	2	1	1	34	41
Not Leadoff	.260	.324	.302	96	25	0	2	0	0	9	18	.212	.288	.242	339	72	6	2	0	0	36	80
Runners On	.171	.272	.248	129	22	6	2	0	12	17	26	.203	.311	.270	433	88	13	8	0	66	67	96
First Base Only	.250	.318	.367	60	15	5	1	0	1	5	10	.221	.305	.279	190	42	7	2	0	4	22	40
Scoring Position	.101	.235	.145	69	7	1	1	0	11	12	16	.189	.316	.263	243	46	6	6	0	62	45	56
Late Innings, Close	.222	.349	.361	36	8	1	2	0	2	6	9	.211	.344	.271	133	28	2	3	0	10	26	27

RBI/Opportunities

Scoring Position	9 / 89	(10%)	54 / 339	(16%)
Scoring Position, 2 Out	2 / 44	(5%)	25 / 173	(14%)
On Third, Less than 2 Out	5 / 14	(36%)	19 / 44	(43%)
RBI in close games / RBI Total	6 / 12	(50%)	39 / 67	(58%)

Tommy John
New York Yankees

On May 18, 1987, Tommy John pitched six scoreless innings in a 2–1 win against Oakland. Four days later, he turned 44. In 1987, he pitched more innings than he had since 1983. He was second on the team in wins. He led New York in innings pitched (though mostly because he was the only Yankee starter who wasn't injured, traded or sent to AAA). His 4.03 ERA was 43 points below the league average. He did allow 10.2 hits per nine innings, but he was only taken deep 12 times. The Yankees must have been overjoyed to get that kind of performance from a pitcher who was supposed to be a college coach in 1987.

That being said, a lot of John's 13–6 record—and the 22–11 record that New York had in his starts—can be attributed to the great support that he got from his offense. The Yankees scored 5.56 runs per start for John—over half a run better than their 4.90 seasonal average. When he pitched well, they made sure that he won; when he pitched badly and left early, they were able to take him off the hook.

Take, for example, his April 8 against the Tigers: 3.2 innings, five runs. New York came back to score six and give him a no-decision. On May 8, facing the Twins, he lasted 1.2 innings and gave up four runs; the Yankees scored 11 in the game. On July 7, again facing the Twins, he was facing a 7–0 loss until the lineup scored seven runs in the seventh to get him out of the books. They added five more runs in the eighth and won.

The truly amazing game in this string came on June 26. T.J. allowed eight runs in 1.1 innings. Against Boston. With Roger Clemens on the mound. New York scored eight runs against the Rocket Man—11 in the inning—and went on to win in extra innings.

To be fair, there were a few games where New York didn't score many runs and John pitched well and won; there were even a few where he took a tough loss. But, as you can see, he could easily have been 13–10; with the kind of support that Ron Guidry got, he would have been 7–12.

The 13 victories that Tommy posted in 1987 give him a total of 273; 27 wins away from a guaranteed ticket to Cooperstown. He's going to have a real struggle to get there; he'd need at least two more seasons like this one before he retires. Since 1987 was the first season in four years that John has been healthy, the first time in five years that he's hit double-digits in wins and it's highly unlikely (unless Jack Clark actually plays 162 games) that he'll get as much run support again, I don't expect it to happen again. Bill James's Favorite Toy agrees with me; it assesses his chances of winning 300 at 0 percent. Tommy John had an amazing sort of year in 1987; the Yankees would have been in real trouble without him. But I don't think he's got a prayer of reaching 300 career wins.

Craig Christmann

John, Thomas Edward "Tommy"   Bats: Right   Throws: Left   Born 05/22/43

1987 SEASON AND MAJOR-LEAGUE CAREER PITCHING TOTALS

	G	GS	CG	GF	IP	BFP	H	R	ER	HR	SH	SF	HB	TBB	IBB	SO	WP	Bk	W	L	Pct	ShO	Sv	ERA
87 NYA	33	33	3	0	188	802	212	95	84	12	12	1	6	47	7	63	9	0	13	6	.684	1	0	4.02
24 YEARS	715	658	162	20	4468	18626	4475	1876	1620	285	187	92	89	1191	96	2146	179	11	277	216	.562	46	4	3.26

1987: Finesse, Groundball   1986: Finesse, Groundball

1987 SEASON

	G	IP	H	BB	SO	SB	CS	W	L	S	ERA
Totals	33	187.2	212	47	63	17	6	13	6	0	4.03
at Home	16	90.1	108	25	29	7	5	6	3	0	4.38
on Road	17	97.1	104	22	34	10	1	7	3	0	3.70
on Grass	13	76.1	77	13	28	10	0	5	3	0	3.66
on Artificial Turf	20	111.1	135	34	35	7	6	8	3	0	4.28
Day Games	28	157.2	183	37	57	16	6	11	6	0	4.40
Night Games	5	30.0	29	10	6	1	0	2	0	0	2.10
April	3	17.2	12	5	7	3	0	1	0	0	2.55
May	6	32.0	41	4	10	2	1	4	1	0	4.22
June	5	26.0	35	7	6	3	0	2	2	0	6.58
July	6	40.2	36	10	15	6	0	3	0	0	2.43
August	6	29.2	31	9	10	3	1	2	1	0	3.94
Sept/Oct	7	41.2	57	12	15	0	4	1	2	0	4.54

TWO YEAR TOTALS (1986 – 1987)

	G	IP	H	BB	SO	SB	CS	W	L	S	ERA
Totals	46	258.1	285	62	91	23	10	18	9	0	3.73
at Home	25	131.0	154	35	43	11	7	8	5	0	4.19
on Road	21	127.1	131	27	48	12	3	10	4	0	3.25
on Grass	13	76.1	77	13	28	10	0	5	3	0	3.66
on Artificial Turf	33	182.0	208	49	63	13	10	13	6	0	3.76
Day Games	39	213.1	243	50	80	22	10	15	8	0	4.05
Night Games	7	45.0	42	12	11	1	0	3	1	0	2.20
April	3	17.2	12	5	7	3	0	1	0	0	2.55
May	11	54.1	60	11	15	5	1	6	1	0	3.64
June	8	41.0	55	9	13	4	2	3	3	0	5.93
July	6	40.2	36	10	15	6	0	3	0	0	2.43
August	11	63.0	65	15	26	5	3	4	3	0	3.00
Sept/Oct	7	41.2	57	12	15	0	4	1	2	0	4.54

vs. Opponent Batters	Ave.	OBP	SLG	AB	H	2B	3B	HR	RBI	BB	SO
Totals	.288	.335	.387	736	212	31	3	12	77	47	63
vs. Left	.203	.258	.260	123	25	4	0	1	12	8	18
vs. Right	.305	.351	.413	613	187	27	3	11	65	39	45
Bases Empty	.291	.326	.401	429	125	19	2	8	8	19	35
Leadoff	.288	.323	.466	191	55	9	2	7	7	9	18
Not Leadoff	.294	.328	.349	238	70	10	0	1	1	10	17
Runners On Base	.283	.348	.368	307	87	12	1	4	69	28	28
First Base Only	.315	.346	.425	127	40	6	1	2	6	6	8
Scoring Position	.261	.350	.328	180	47	6	0	2	63	22	20
Late Innings, Close	.343	.361	.400	35	12	2	0	0	1	1	0

vs. Opponent Batters	Ave.	OBP	SLG	AB	H	2B	3B	HR	RBI	BB	SO
Totals	.285	.330	.389	1001	285	38	3	20	102	62	91
vs. Left	.224	.283	.321	165	37	7	0	3	21	12	22
vs. Right	.297	.340	.402	836	248	31	3	17	81	50	69
Bases Empty	.301	.336	.409	584	176	23	2	12	12	25	48
Leadoff	.309	.342	.448	259	80	11	2	7	7	10	22
Not Leadoff	.295	.330	.378	325	96	12	0	5	5	15	26
Runners On Base	.261	.323	.360	417	109	15	1	8	90	37	43
First Base Only	.295	.328	.410	183	54	7	1	4	11	9	14
Scoring Position	.235	.320	.321	234	55	8	0	4	79	28	29
Late Innings, Close	.343	.361	.400	70	24	4	0	0	2	2	0

RBI/Opportunities

Scoring Position	59 / 246 (24%)
Scoring Position, 2 Out	19 / 105 (18%)
On Third, Less than 2 Out	22 / 48 (46%)
RBI in close games / RBI Total	56 / 77 (73%)

	71 / 319 (22%)
	38 / 210 (18%)
	44 / 96 (46%)
	112 / 102 (110%)

Howard Johnson
New York Mets

On July 1, 1987, New York City's AM country music station WHN became WFAN 24-hour sports radio. While providing a great service (which Jim Lampley compares to nuclear disarmament), it also raises the expectations of the fans to ridiculous proportions. This interesting phenomena occurs when otherwise rational people call talk shows and demand outrageous performance from athletes. On June 30, Howard Johnson was a ballplayer having a very good season in his first real opportunity at an everyday role. On July 1, he was having his one and only "career year" and he should be traded while the trading was good.

Johnson was obviously helped by the incredible shrinking strike zone and stubborn pitchers who *still* think they can throw a fastball by him. But in 1987 he had 550 at bats (only 55 less than '85 and '86 combined) and he put very good numbers on the board. He had said that if he got 500 at bats he would prove he could hit, and he did. He stole 32 bases, improved his walk to strikeout ratio, had a marked improvement from the right side of the plate and is *not* the horror at third base he is made out to be.

This is not to say HoJo is a great ballplayer or even to say that he will repeat his fine season in 1988 or beyond. But give the guy a break. This wasn't a serious aberration from the norm, this was a player who got his shot and made the most of it. But because he was tabbed as a platoon player with a big mouth he has mountains of public opinion to overcome. What does it take to overcome this? I suppose 17 years of Jose Cruz' stats.

Will Johnson repeat 1987 or will the polls ring true? He just turned 27, and he's learned to hit left-handed pitching. He seems to have trouble with the balls hit right at him (much like Mike Pagliarulo) but makes up for a lot of them with a very strong arm. On the bad side, if Davey Johnson is truly finished in New York the new manager may very well want more defense; or the Mets may need a place to put Greg Jeffries, the minor league phenom; or maybe I'm just wrong. Maybe Howard Johnson is just a one-season wonder and will be out of baseball in five years with an unimpressive resume. But if you were a team that has 80 third baseman in 26 years, would you get rid of the one who had the best season because amateur general managers call radio stations and tell you to?

Joe Nunziatta III

Johnson, Howard Michael   Bats: Both   Throws: Right   Born 11/29/60

1987 SEASON AND MAJOR-LEAGUE CAREER BATTING TOTALS

	G	AB	H	2B	3B	HR	TB	R	RBI	TBB	IBB	SO	HP	SH	SF	SB	CS	SB%	GDP	AVG	OBP	SLG
87 NYN	157	554	147	22	1	36	279	93	99	83	18	113	5	0	3	32	10	.76	8	.265	.364	.504
6 YEARS	568	1739	446	73	6	76	759	238	253	211	38	362	9	7	9	63	25	.72	26	.256	.338	.436

1987 SEASON

	Ave.	OBP	SLG	AB	H	2B	3B	HR	RBI	BB	SO
Totals	.265	.364	.504	554	147	22	1	36	99	83	113
vs. Left	.289	.376	.552	194	56	6	0	15	41	26	39
vs. Right	.253	.358	.478	360	91	16	1	21	58	57	74
at Home	.262	.364	.450	271	71	10	1	13	40	42	62
on Road	.269	.365	.555	283	76	12	0	23	59	41	51
vs. Groundball	.272	.382	.526	228	62	5	1	17	38	40	43
vs. Flyball	.261	.351	.488	326	85	17	0	19	61	43	70
vs. Finesse	.294	.385	.599	299	88	13	0	26	59	42	51
vs. Power	.231	.341	.392	255	59	9	1	10	40	41	62
on Grass	.282	.384	.495	380	107	16	1	21	62	61	78
on Artificial Turf	.230	.320	.523	174	40	6	0	15	37	22	35
Day Games	.308	.403	.535	198	61	12	0	11	33	32	37
Night Games	.242	.342	.486	356	86	10	1	25	66	51	76
April	.238	.347	.397	63	15	1	0	3	12	11	16
May	.227	.310	.443	88	20	4	0	5	13	10	26
June	.323	.393	.583	96	31	4	0	7	16	9	16
July	.293	.366	.616	99	29	2	0	10	21	11	17
August	.301	.440	.624	93	28	4	1	8	24	23	21
Sept/Oct	.209	.326	.348	115	24	7	0	3	13	19	17
Bases Empty	.232	.330	.467	306	71	9	0	21	21	42	63
Leadoff	.216	.291	.478	134	29	5	0	10	10	14	26
Not Leadoff	.244	.360	.459	172	42	4	0	11	11	28	37
Runners On	.306	.405	.548	248	76	13	1	15	78	41	50
First Base Only	.339	.373	.580	112	38	7	1	6	16	6	20
Scoring Position	.279	.426	.522	136	38	6	0	9	62	35	30
Late Innings, Close	.363	.450	.659	91	33	6	0	7	24	16	19

FOUR YEAR TOTALS (1984 – 1987)

	Ave.	OBP	SLG	AB	H	2B	3B	HR	RBI	BB	SO
Totals	.252	.335	.441	1518	383	68	6	69	234	187	322
vs. Left	.241	.321	.441	415	100	13	2	22	65	48	96
vs. Right	.257	.341	.442	1103	283	55	4	47	169	139	226
at Home	.238	.333	.398	731	174	30	3	27	104	102	158
on Road	.266	.338	.482	787	209	38	3	42	130	85	164
vs. Groundball	.251	.334	.444	676	170	23	4	33	106	82	135
vs. Flyball	.253	.336	.439	842	213	45	2	36	128	105	187
vs. Finesse	.253	.328	.439	798	202	37	0	37	113	87	145
vs. Power	.251	.343	.444	720	181	31	6	32	121	100	177
on Grass	.251	.340	.434	1101	276	46	6	48	168	148	229
on Artificial Turf	.257	.321	.460	417	107	22	0	21	66	39	93
Day Games	.262	.355	.435	543	142	27	2	21	78	81	110
Night Games	.247	.324	.445	975	241	41	4	48	156	106	212
April	.234	.333	.351	171	40	5	0	5	24	26	41
May	.219	.310	.366	224	49	10	1	7	34	29	56
June	.295	.361	.508	244	72	10	0	14	35	23	54
July	.267	.327	.503	322	86	16	0	20	59	28	61
August	.248	.363	.457	282	70	11	3	14	39	51	62
Sept/Oct	.240	.317	.411	275	66	16	2	9	43	30	48
Bases Empty	.241	.314	.425	837	202	34	3	38	38	85	167
Leadoff	.215	.279	.398	339	73	15	1	15	15	30	67
Not Leadoff	.259	.336	.444	498	129	19	2	23	23	55	100
Runners On	.266	.362	.461	681	181	34	3	31	196	102	155
First Base Only	.274	.320	.445	317	87	12	3	12	32	21	70
Scoring Position	.258	.393	.475	364	94	22	0	19	164	81	85
Late Innings, Close	.261	.337	.493	280	73	12	1	17	50	33	69

RBI/Opportunities

	1987			FOUR YEAR		
Scoring Position	45 / 213	(21%)		127 / 567	(22%)	
Scoring Position, 2 Out	20 / 109	(18%)		59 / 283	(21%)	
On Third, Less than 2 Out	15 / 41	(37%)		44 / 99	(44%)	
RBI in close games / RBI Total	62 / 99	(63%)		152 / 234	(65%)	

Wally Joyner
California Angels

When the California Angels opened spring training in 1987, manager Gene Mauch was often asked whether he feared his young first baseman would suffer the "sophomore jinx." It was Mauch's contention that he would not because Wally Joyner was one of those special players who would not forget how hard he worked to achieve the success he had as a rookie; it's the players who forget who suffer in their second seasons. Wally didn't forget.

Mauch proved a good prophet as Joyner even improved from his great rookie season. He hit five points less (.285 down from .290), but he jumped his runs scored from 82 to 100, his RBIs from 100 to 117, and his homers climbed from 22 to 34, including 4 in October, tying a major league record. We should not have been surprised by the jump in power. Remember he had physical problems in the second half last year and only one homer after the All-Star game.

In 1987, only 8 players scored 100 or more runs while also driving in 100 or more, joining AL MVP George Bell, Dwight Evans, Alan Trammell, Dale Murphy, Darryl Strawberry, Eric Davis and Juan Samuel. Very fast company.

Among major league first basemen, Joyner hit more homers and drove in more runs than such stars as Don Mattingly and Eddie Murray. Among major league first basemen, only Mark McGwire drove in more runs than Joyner's 118.

Joyner also became one of only 10 players in history to drive in 100 or more runs in his first two seasons in the majors. The others are Al Simmons, Glenn Wright, Tony Lazzeri, Pinky Whitney, Dale Alexander, Joe DiMaggio, Ted Williams, Ray Jablonski, and Joyner's rookie shadow, Jose Canseco (117 in '86 and 113 in '87).

Unlike 1986, Joyner sustained his production throughout the season. There was no tail-spin after the All-Star break. Joyner, in fact, was one of the few Angels not apparently afflicted by the team's overall second-half collapse. Another pleasant sign of growth was Joyner showing major improvement in his ability to hit lefthanders. In 1986, Joyner hit lefties at a .234 clip in 192 at-bats, versus .317 against righthanders. In 1987, Joyner raised his average against lefties to .284, nicely balanced against his .287 versus righthanders.

It will be interesting to see if Joyner can sustain the kind of production he's generated his first two seasons, particularly in homers. For a long time no one saw him as having much power potential until he tore up the winter league just before his rookie year. Although it was late coming, it sure appears to be here to stay.

The chemistry on the Angels has changed dramatically in Joyner's first two years. Reggie Jackson went after Wally's first year and now Doug DeCinces is gone too. Joyner may soon end up the leader of this club—not a bad choice.

Dean Hill

Joyner, Wallace Keith "Wally" Bats: Left Throws: Left Born 05/16/62

1987 SEASON AND MAJOR-LEAGUE CAREER BATTING TOTALS

	G	AB	H	2B	3B	HR	TB	R	RBI	TBB	IBB	SO	HP	SH	SF	SB	CS	SB%	GDP	AVG	OBP	SLG
87 CAL	149	564	161	33	1	34	298	100	117	72	12	64	5	2	10	8	2	.80	14	.285	.366	.528
2 YEARS	303	1157	333	60	4	56	569	182	217	129	20	122	7	12	22	13	4	.76	25	.288	.357	.492

	1987 SEASON											FOUR YEAR TOTALS (1984 – 1987)										
	Ave.	OBP	SLG	AB	H	2B	3B	HR	RBI	BB	SO	Ave.	OBP	SLG	AB	H	2B	3B	HR	RBI	BB	SO
Totals	.285	.366	.528	564	161	33	1	34	117	72	65	.288	.357	.492	1157	333	60	4	56	217	129	123
vs. Left	.284	.347	.478	201	57	15	0	8	39	20	25	.260	.319	.417	393	102	18	1	14	63	34	49
vs. Right	.287	.376	.556	363	104	18	1	26	78	52	40	.302	.375	.530	764	231	42	3	42	154	95	74
at Home	.261	.336	.505	307	80	16	1	19	57	37	39	.270	.342	.469	601	162	26	2	30	97	70	66
on Road	.315	.399	.556	257	81	17	0	15	60	35	26	.308	.373	.516	556	171	34	2	26	120	59	57
vs. Groundball	.259	.339	.456	274	71	15	0	13	45	32	30	.280	.349	.456	542	152	27	1	22	90	59	56
vs. Flyball	.310	.390	.597	290	90	18	1	21	72	40	35	.294	.363	.524	615	181	33	3	34	127	70	67
vs. Finesse	.266	.359	.502	267	71	15	0	16	53	38	24	.285	.354	.478	621	177	34	1	28	111	70	50
vs. Power	.303	.372	.552	297	90	18	1	18	64	34	41	.291	.360	.507	536	156	26	3	28	106	59	73
on Grass	.270	.352	.516	471	127	24	1	30	96	61	55	.282	.351	.481	991	279	46	4	48	180	109	102
on Artificial Turf	.366	.431	.591	93	34	9	0	4	21	11	10	.325	.391	.554	166	54	14	0	8	37	20	21
Day Games	.281	.366	.665	167	47	13	0	17	43	21	28	.305	.372	.589	341	104	25	0	24	71	34	46
Night Games	.287	.365	.471	397	114	20	1	17	74	51	37	.281	.350	.451	816	229	35	4	32	146	95	77
April	.297	.350	.505	91	27	4	0	5	19	9	6	.315	.362	.551	178	56	9	0	11	35	15	14
May	.265	.344	.530	83	22	4	0	6	16	9	10	.275	.336	.549	193	53	5	0	16	41	17	25
June	.293	.408	.576	99	29	7	0	7	29	22	15	.295	.378	.515	200	59	12	1	10	46	29	24
July	.293	.365	.547	75	22	5	1	4	17	8	5	.328	.392	.514	183	60	10	3	6	33	19	16
August	.289	.369	.515	97	28	7	0	5	16	13	11	.260	.342	.418	196	51	13	0	6	31	25	20
Sept/Oct	.277	.351	.504	119	33	6	0	7	20	11	18	.261	.345	.415	207	54	11	0	7	31	24	24
Bases Empty	.264	.331	.512	299	79	11	0	21	21	27	32	.264	.321	.475	617	163	26	1	34	34	49	65
Leadoff	.263	.328	.526	114	30	6	0	8	8	10	11	.259	.316	.477	216	56	8	0	13	13	17	24
Not Leadoff	.265	.333	.503	185	49	5	0	13	13	17	21	.267	.324	.474	401	107	18	1	21	21	32	41
Runners On	.309	.401	.547	265	82	22	1	13	96	45	33	.315	.399	.511	540	170	34	3	22	183	80	58
First Base Only	.276	.356	.457	105	29	7	0	4	11	13	14	.318	.388	.536	220	70	13	1	11	29	25	20
Scoring Position	.331	.426	.606	160	53	15	1	9	85	32	19	.313	.406	.494	320	100	21	2	11	154	55	38
Late Innings, Close	.186	.282	.304	102	19	6	0	2	14	13	8	.245	.335	.388	188	46	11	2	4	26	25	18

RBI/Opportunities

Scoring Position	70 / 234 (30%)	134 / 463 (29%)
Scoring Position, 2 Out	14 / 78 (18%)	43 / 180 (24%)
On Third, Less than 2 Out	35 / 53 (66%)	58 / 93 (62%)
RBI in close games / RBI Total	70 / 117 (60%)	131 / 217 (60%)

Terry Kennedy
Baltimore Orioles

Terry Kennedy enjoyed a very unusual season in 1987. Very few men in recent history have gotten so much acclaim while needing so many qualifiers attached to his year.

Take, for example, the All-Star voting. Terry didn't exactly have overwhelming numbers (13, 42, .257) at the break. But then Lance Parrish was floundering in Philly, Rich Gedman was going belly-up (no pun intended) in Boston and Matt Nokes was a write-in. With his competition either falling victim (in some manner) to free agency or unlisted, the fans correctly chose Kennedy as the best catcher listed on the ballot.

Or look at the trade. On one level, Baltimore made out like bandits; both Kennedy and Mark Williamson outplayed Storm Davis, while Rick Dempsey had a disastrous season in Cleveland. On another, it didn't really improve Baltimore. Kennedy's on-base percentage in 1987 was 10 points lower than Dempsey's was in 1986 (.299/.309). His slugging percentage beat Dempsey's 1986 figure by six points (.385/.379). Dempsey scored more runs and grounded into fewer double plays per at-bat. Since Kennedy held the same level of performance despite getting over 200 more plate appearances than Dempsey did in 1986, he clearly had a better year—but it wasn't as far ahead as his RBI totals and batting average might lead you to believe.

None of this is meant as a slur on Terry's accomplishments. He caught in 142 games and was the starting catcher in 135. Both marks led the league and set team records—far more than Baltimore had hoped for.

In fact, it may have been more than they should have asked for. Terry's offense has been sliding ever since 1982; the constant in that slide has been his awful Augusts. Through 1986, Terry's lifetime batting average is .234 in the dog days and .280 in the other five months; as you can see below, 1987 was no exception. Catching is a hot, sweaty, exhausting job at best and the Baltimore humidity won't help Terry hold up any better than San Diego's near-perfect climate did.

Another point: Kennedy is 31, and listed at 6'4", 230. In the last seven years, Terry has caught more games (934) than anyone but Gary Carter (940); given what happened to Carter in 1987, the durability derby is one race that the Orioles should not try to win.

Defensively, Kennedy was reasonably competent. Though he led the AL in assists (58; fewest ever for a leader), 107 of the 140 runners (76.4 percent) who tried to steal succeeded. On the bright side, he had the second-fewest passed balls (4) and the third-highest fielding percentage in the AL. Though the hope that having the same face behind the mask every day would help Baltimore's shaky staff proved to be false, no one is blaming Terry for the staff's complete collapse in 1987.

Greg Pryor and Sean Bramble

Kennedy, Terrence Edward "Terry" Bats: Left   Throws: Right   Born 06/04/56

1987 SEASON AND MAJOR-LEAGUE CAREER BATTING TOTALS

	G	AB	H	2B	3B	HR	TB	R	RBI	TBB	IBB	SO	HP	SH	SF	SB	CS	SB%	GDP	AVG	OBP	SLG
87 BAL	143	512	128	13	1	18	197	51	62	35	6	112	1	1	0	1	0	1.00	13	.250	.299	.385
10 YEARS	1105	3885	1044	190	11	100	1556	398	539	273	68	677	14	14	32	4	10	.29	95	.269	.317	.401

	1987 SEASON											FOUR YEAR TOTALS (1984 – 1987)										
	Ave.	OBP	SLG	AB	H	2B	3B	HR	RBI	BB	SO	Ave.	OBP	SLG	AB	H	2B	3B	HR	RBI	BB	SO
Totals	.250	.299	.385	512	128	13	1	18	62	35	112	.253	.301	.377	2006	508	78	4	54	250	136	387
vs. Left	.219	.255	.339	183	40	4	0	6	23	8	51	.222	.254	.343	586	130	21	1	16	76	23	158
vs. Right	.267	.323	.410	329	88	9	1	12	39	27	61	.266	.320	.391	1420	378	57	3	38	174	113	229
at Home	.213	.279	.383	240	51	6	1	11	27	22	59	.239	.291	.381	1005	240	38	3	33	129	73	204
on Road	.283	.318	.386	272	77	7	0	7	35	13	53	.268	.311	.373	1001	268	40	1	21	121	63	183
vs. Groundball	.281	.324	.400	270	76	9	1	7	38	17	41	.275	.326	.394	1044	287	45	2	25	132	77	163
vs. Flyball	.215	.272	.368	242	52	4	0	11	24	18	71	.230	.274	.359	962	221	33	2	29	118	59	224
vs. Finesse	.281	.312	.462	249	70	10	1	11	36	10	42	.278	.315	.421	1096	305	56	2	32	141	58	163
vs. Power	.221	.288	.312	263	58	3	0	7	26	25	70	.223	.285	.324	910	203	22	2	22	109	78	224
on Grass	.241	.291	.385	436	105	10	1	17	55	31	100	.248	.297	.378	1552	385	55	3	47	196	108	310
on Artificial Turf	.303	.346	.382	76	23	3	0	1	7	4	12	.271	.314	.372	454	123	23	1	7	54	28	77
Day Games	.286	.346	.378	119	34	2	0	3	12	10	22	.241	.289	.341	572	138	19	1	12	74	37	107
Night Games	.239	.285	.387	393	94	11	1	15	50	25	90	.258	.306	.391	1434	370	59	3	42	176	99	280
April	.284	.338	.405	74	21	3	0	2	9	6	15	.225	.287	.356	289	65	9	1	9	37	25	48
May	.265	.306	.412	102	27	3	0	4	11	5	20	.280	.326	.420	350	98	16	0	11	62	23	59
June	.258	.301	.505	97	25	3	0	7	17	6	21	.271	.319	.432	377	102	18	2	13	49	27	76
July	.260	.341	.301	73	19	1	1	0	6	9	13	.255	.305	.359	337	86	15	1	6	31	24	64
August	.227	.292	.352	88	20	2	0	3	11	8	21	.212	.257	.292	349	74	10	0	6	31	21	73
Sept/Oct	.205	.215	.295	78	16	1	0	2	8	1	22	.273	.309	.395	304	83	10	0	9	40	16	67
Bases Empty	.259	.292	.401	294	76	6	0	12	12	13	68	.250	.285	.378	1129	282	39	2	34	34	55	212
Leadoff	.305	.344	.492	118	36	1	0	7	7	7	22	.241	.279	.360	469	113	9	1	15	15	25	80
Not Leadoff	.227	.257	.341	176	40	5	0	5	5	6	46	.256	.289	.391	660	169	30	1	19	19	30	132
Runners On	.239	.308	.362	218	52	7	1	6	50	22	44	.258	.320	.375	877	226	39	2	20	216	81	175
First Base Only	.228	.276	.370	92	21	4	0	3	6	6	13	.255	.293	.356	357	91	15	0	7	19	19	62
Scoring Position	.246	.331	.357	126	31	3	1	3	44	16	31	.260	.338	.388	520	135	24	2	13	197	62	113
Late Innings, Close	.243	.341	.527	74	18	1	1	6	12	11	17	.263	.338	.389	357	94	13	1	10	39	40	71

RBI/Opportunities

Scoring Position	38 / 176	(22%)	171 / 700	(24%)
Scoring Position, 2 Out	21 / 88	(24%)	70 / 336	(21%)
On Third, Less than 2 Out	8 / 23	(35%)	55 / 126	(44%)
RBI in close games / RBI Total	42 / 62	(68%)	175 / 250	(70%)

Jimmy Key
Toronto Blue Jays

It may seem odd to say that Jimmy Key was a hard-luck pitcher this year, but let's look at his 1987 month by month; decide for yourself:

APRIL: Key made five starts, going 4–1 with a 3.03 ERA. Though Toronto scored 27 runs (5.40 runs per game) in his starts, 18 came in two games. In his only loss, Toronto was shut out.

MAY: Key went 2–2 with a 3.96 ERA in seven starts. He didn't pitch well in either loss, but he had quality starts in two no-decisions. He won neither because Toronto scored only 27 runs (3.88 R/G) in his starts.

JUNE: Key went 2–2 with a 1.55 ERA in seven starts. He took two losses and a no-decision due to gross non-support; Toronto scored only 18 runs (3.60 R/G) in his starts. Jesse Barfield lost a fly ball in the sun, resulting in an RBI triple in a 2–1 loss. Kelly Gruber committed two errors, allowing two unearned runs to score in a 3–2 loss. In Key's only no-decision (a quality start), the bullpen blew a 3–2 lead.

JULY: In seven starts, Key was 4–1 with a 2.87 ERA. Toronto went on a comparative offensive tear, scoring 29 runs (4.14 R/G). Jimmy's only loss was a complete game, 2–1 loss. In one no-decision, he left with the score tied 1–1 in the eighth; the other was a quality start.

AUGUST: Key started only four games (losing a start to arm trouble) and went 3–0 with a 3.21 ERA. For once,

Key was extremely well-supported; the Toronto offense scored 26 runs (6.50 R/G) in his starts. His one no-decision was—you guessed it—a quality start.

SEPTEMBER: Back to normal again: seven starts, 2–1, 2.26 ERA. Of the 39 runs (5.57 R/G) that Toronto scored for Key this month, 20 came in two games. Key made quality starts in two of the four no-decisions and allowed two runs in five innings in the other two.

OCTOBER: A fitting climax—one start, eight innings, one earned run (a wind-blown homer that George Bell could have caught), a 1.12 ERA and a 1–0 loss that clinched the pennant for Detroit on the last day of 1987.

Twenty-seven of Key's 36 starts were quality starts; he might have had more, but Jimy Williams used the hook early when he began using Key on short rest in September. Jimmy lasted less than five innings once. Only twice did he allow five or more earned runs in a game; he allowed two or less 25 times. Toronto scored only 161 runs (4.47 R/G) in his starts; they averaged 5.22 in 1987. Almost 25 percent of those runs (38) came in four starts; eliminate those games and his run support falls to 3.84 R/G—almost a run and a half below his team's average.

In 1987, Boston scored 181 runs (5.03 R/G) in Roger Clemens's 36 starts. Though I respect Clemens, I do think that those 20 extra runs are the reason that he—and not Key—won the Cy Young award in 1987.

Dave Easby

Key, James Edward "Jimmy"   Bats: Right   Throws: Left   Born 04/22/61

1987 SEASON AND MAJOR-LEAGUE CAREER PITCHING TOTALS

	G	GS	CG	GF	IP	BFP	H	R	ER	HR	SH	SF	HB	TBB	IBB	SO	WP	Bk	W	L	Pct	ShO	Sv	ERA
87 TOR	36	36	8	0	261	1033	210	93	80	24	11	3	2	66	6	161	8	5	17	8	.680	1	0	2.76
4 YEARS	170	103	15	24	768	3133	690	305	275	78	32	15	8	222	16	431	20	7	49	30	.620	3	10	3.22

1987: Finesse, Groundball   **1986: Finesse, Groundball**   **1985: Finesse, Groundball**   **1984: Power, Groundball**

	1987 SEASON											FOUR YEAR TOTALS (1984 – 1987)										
	G	IP	H	BB	SO	SB	CS	W	L	S	ERA	G	IP	H	BB	SO	SB	CS	W	L	S	ERA
Totals	36	261.0	210	66	161	4	10	17	8	0	2.76	170	767.2	690	222	431	26	23	49	30	10	3.21
at Home	21	156.2	107	37	100	2	7	10	4	0	2.36	88	425.2	375	117	238	14	14	28	18	3	3.19
on Road	15	104.1	103	29	61	2	3	7	4	0	3.36	82	342.0	315	105	193	12	9	21	12	7	3.26
on Grass	16	115.0	82	35	71	2	3	7	4	0	2.58	58	294.0	248	85	168	10	6	19	13	1	3.15
on Artificial Turf	20	146.0	128	31	90	2	7	10	4	0	2.90	112	473.2	442	137	263	16	17	30	17	9	3.25
Day Games	12	85.0	82	27	50	2	3	5	3	0	3.28	66	290.1	258	93	169	11	9	18	11	5	2.98
Night Games	24	176.0	128	39	111	2	7	12	5	0	2.51	104	477.1	432	129	262	15	14	31	19	5	3.38
April	5	35.2	25	16	15	0	1	4	1	0	3.03	20	79.2	72	32	39	1	3	6	5	1	4.63
May	7	47.2	46	7	35	0	2	2	2	0	3.97	33	122.0	110	39	73	6	3	8	5	3	4.06
June	5	40.2	23	9	26	1	3	2	2	0	1.55	29	141.1	111	37	89	6	5	8	6	0	2.04
July	7	53.1	38	14	40	0	2	4	1	0	2.87	29	146.2	141	40	86	0	6	10	4	0	3.56
August	4	28.0	26	5	17	0	1	3	0	0	3.21	27	117.2	119	27	62	6	3	9	6	3	3.52
Sept/Oct	8	55.2	52	15	28	3	1	2	2	0	2.10	32	160.1	137	47	82	7	3	8	4	3	2.41

vs. Opponent Batters	Ave.	OBP	SLG	AB	H	2B	3B	HR	RBI	BB	SO	Ave.	OBP	SLG	AB	H	2B	3B	HR	RBI	BB	SO
Totals	.221	.272	.344	951	210	29	8	24	85	66	161	.242	.296	.382	2856	690	130	18	78	285	222	431
vs. Left	.248	.290	.382	157	39	5	2	4	13	9	35	.247	.300	.352	599	148	20	5	11	55	45	131
vs. Right	.215	.268	.336	794	171	24	6	20	72	57	126	.240	.296	.389	2257	542	110	13	67	230	177	300
Bases Empty	.198	.248	.309	621	123	15	3	16	16	39	105	.236	.286	.364	1777	420	76	11	43	43	121	273
Leadoff	.209	.242	.271	258	54	8	1	2	2	10	41	.247	.284	.383	749	185	35	5	19	19	38	106
Not Leadoff	.190	.252	.336	363	69	7	2	14	14	29	64	.229	.287	.350	1028	235	41	6	24	24	83	167
Runners On Base	.264	.317	.409	330	87	14	5	8	69	27	56	.250	.314	.411	1079	270	54	7	35	242	101	158
First Base Only	.282	.325	.455	156	44	6	3	5	17	10	28	.260	.302	.455	503	131	26	3	22	60	30	73
Scoring Position	.247	.309	.368	174	43	8	2	3	52	17	28	.241	.323	.372	576	139	28	4	13	182	71	85
Late Innings, Close	.250	.330	.448	96	24	0	2	5	13	11	20	.271	.339	.408	424	115	13	3	13	60	43	65

RBI/Opportunities

Scoring Position	44 / 222 (20%)	155 / 760 (20%)	
Scoring Position, 2 Out	14 / 101 (14%)	61 / 336 (18%)	
On Third, Less than 2 Out	19 / 30 (63%)	59 / 123 (48%)	
RBI in close games / RBI Total	75 / 85 (88%)	218 / 285 (76%)	

Mike Kingery
Seattle Mariners

I remember well a Friday evening, September 19, 1986. The Mariners' season had ended 142 days earlier on a cool spring evening in Fenway Park, but, as we do every weekend the Mariners are at home, we drove 150 miles to Seattle for the three games against KC. This trip was easier than the rest because the highly touted Bo Jackson was with his team and I was anxious to see the kid play baseball. I left Seattle on Sunday somewhat impressed with Bo's abilities, but actually more intrigued with two other lesser known KC rookies: Kevin Seitzer and Mike Kingery.

As we all know, Seitzer became a first year sensation and would have nabbed the Rookie of the Year honors if it hadn't been for the slugger from Oakland. Bo Jackson . . . well, you know what happened to Bo, and if he continues his baseball career, it will be at Omaha in the shadow of Gary Thurman. And Mike Kingery? He got a return plane ticket to Seattle and a full year in the majors platooning in right field.

Kevin and Bo made the headlines. Mike didn't. The only time Kingery got ink was when he was mentioned as the third player in the controversial Tartabull deal. However, the lefty turned in a very productive year for his new team and all those local skeptics seemed to be pleased with Mike's performance.

His defense in the outfield is above average and it didn't take long before the opposition realized that it wasn't wise to test his arm for accuracy. "Crazy Legs" Kingery isn't what you would call poetry in motion, but he's fast enough on the basepaths to keep the opposing pitchers guessing. He doesn't hit left-handed pitching exceptionally well, but against righties he's just fine with a .292 average. In just 354 AB, he drove in 52, hit 9 homers, 4 triples and 25 doubles. Fairly productive for a platoon player.

But Kingery's greatest contribution to the '87 Mariners was his clutch hitting. You know, the numbers nobody sees except in books like this one. He hit .312 with runners in scoring position, .364 in scoring position with 2 out, .341 leading off an inning and .333 as the leadoff hitter. His averages in these crucial situations were consistently better than the run producers on the team. He was only 2 for 9 coming off the bench, but that double and homer produced more runs (5) than any other Mariner pinch-hitter.

To make room for Glenn Wilson, Kingery will move from right to left field and continue in his platoon role. Mike will probably never make headline news, but I'm sure he'll get his share of asterisks in Dick Williams' famous notebook.

Merrianna McCully

Kingery, Michael Scott "Mike"   Bats: Left   Throws: Left   Born 03/29/61

1987 SEASON AND MAJOR-LEAGUE CAREER BATTING TOTALS

	G	AB	H	2B	3B	HR	TB	R	RBI	TBB	IBB	SO	HP	SH	SF	SB	CS	SB%	GDP	AVG	OBP	SLG
87 SEA	120	354	99	25	4	9	159	38	52	27	0	43	2	1	6	7	9	.44	4	.280	.329	.449
2 YEARS	182	563	153	33	9	12	240	63	66	39	2	73	2	1	8	14	12	.54	8	.272	.317	.426

	1987 SEASON											FOUR YEAR TOTALS (1984 – 1987)									
	Ave.	OBP	SLG	AB	H	2B	3B	HR	RBI	BB	SO	Ave.	OBP	SLG	AB	H	2B	3B	HR	RBI	BB	SO
Totals	.280	.329	.449	354	99	25	4	9	52	27	43	.272	.317	.426	563	153	33	9	12	66	39	73
vs. Left	.179	.200	.282	39	7	1	0	1	1	1	8	.130	.164	.188	69	9	1	0	1	3	3	16
vs. Right	.292	.344	.470	315	92	24	4	8	51	26	35	.291	.338	.460	494	144	32	9	11	63	36	57
at Home	.305	.349	.523	174	53	17	3	5	26	12	22	.294	.333	.474	289	85	22	6	6	32	18	34
on Road	.256	.310	.378	180	46	8	1	4	26	15	21	.248	.300	.376	274	68	11	3	6	34	21	39
vs. Groundball	.268	.330	.402	194	52	12	1	4	22	17	20	.271	.329	.418	292	79	17	4	6	30	25	37
vs. Flyball	.294	.328	.506	160	47	13	3	5	30	10	23	.273	.303	.435	271	74	16	5	6	36	14	36
vs. Finesse	.286	.340	.451	182	52	12	3	4	27	15	19	.266	.317	.415	301	80	15	6	6	35	23	40
vs. Power	.273	.317	.448	172	47	13	1	5	25	12	24	.279	.317	.439	262	73	18	3	6	31	16	33
on Grass	.250	.308	.379	140	35	6	0	4	25	12	18	.251	.307	.386	207	52	9	2	5	30	17	28
on Artificial Turf	.299	.343	.495	214	64	19	4	5	27	15	25	.284	.323	.449	356	101	24	7	7	36	22	45
Day Games	.228	.288	.333	114	26	3	0	3	14	9	18	.256	.310	.363	160	41	4	2	3	18	12	24
Night Games	.304	.348	.504	240	73	22	4	6	38	18	25	.278	.320	.452	403	112	29	7	9	48	27	49
April	.254	.290	.356	59	15	1	1	1	7	3	7	.254	.290	.356	59	15	1	1	1	7	3	7
May	.316	.311	.561	57	18	4	2	2	16	1	5	.316	.311	.561	57	18	4	2	2	16	1	5
June	.167	.294	.286	42	7	0	1	1	4	6	10	.167	.294	.286	42	7	0	1	1	4	6	10
July	.286	.355	.482	56	16	5	0	2	8	6	11	.283	.341	.449	127	36	8	2	3	12	11	18
August	.321	.357	.551	78	25	9	0	3	12	5	5	.265	.299	.432	155	41	12	1	4	14	8	20
Sept/Oct	.290	.348	.387	62	18	6	0	0	5	6	5	.293	.343	.415	123	36	8	2	1	13	10	13
Bases Empty	.266	.320	.429	203	54	16	1	5	5	14	27	.263	.311	.431	327	86	22	6	7	7	21	47
Leadoff	.341	.385	.553	85	29	9	0	3	3	5	10	.304	.356	.552	125	38	11	4	4	4	9	19
Not Leadoff	.212	.273	.339	118	25	7	1	2	2	9	17	.238	.284	.356	202	48	11	2	3	3	12	28
Runners On	.298	.341	.477	151	45	9	3	4	47	13	16	.284	.327	.419	236	67	11	3	5	59	18	26
First Base Only	.276	.300	.448	58	16	5	1	1	5	2	6	.323	.350	.469	96	31	6	1	2	7	4	12
Scoring Position	.312	.364	.495	93	29	4	2	3	42	11	10	.257	.313	.386	140	36	5	2	3	52	14	14
Late Innings, Close	.250	.333	.450	40	10	3	1	1	8	5	4	.234	.289	.416	77	18	5	3	1	8	6	12

RBI/Opportunities

	1987		Four Year	
Scoring Position	35 / 131	(27%)	45 / 185	(24%)
Scoring Position, 2 Out	15 / 61	(25%)	17 / 85	(20%)
On Third, Less than 2 Out	14 / 22	(64%)	20 / 31	(65%)
RBI in close games / RBI Total	35 / 52	(67%)	44 / 66	(67%)

Bob Knepper
Houston Astros

If you happen to be searching for likely nominees to be the National League's Comeback Player of the Year in 1988, you might want to start and end with the Astros' Bob Knepper. Everything fell apart for this lefthander last year. Things got so bad that he actually ended up working out of the Astros' tattered bullpen, searching for the form that had helped him to win 47 games for Houston in the previous three seasons.

While Mike Scott got all the headlines, and Dave Smith and Charlie Kerfeld kept things interesting in the bullpen during the Astros' Western Division championship season in 1986, Knepper quietly put up some of the best numbers of his career, going 17–12 with a 3.14 ERA and tossing a league best five shutouts. Actually, the Astros probably should have known that Knepper was due for a fall. The only other time Knepper had won 17 games in a season was back in 1978 when he was still with the San Francisco Giants. He also lead the league in shutouts that season with six. He followed that performance with an awful 1979 season in which he won just nine games. A 9–16 season in 1980 precipitated his trade to Houston; Knepper went 9–5 in 1981, winning the Comeback Player of the Year Award with a career best 2.18 ERA.

Bob's 1987 collapse was complete. After combining with two others to shut-out Montreal in his first start, Knepper was consistently shelled. He was 3–10 by the All-Star break with an earned run average over 6.00. He was rapped for 226 hits in just under 178 innings of work. Even though the Astros play half their games in the best pitchers' park on the planet, 26 of those hits were homers. Another 54 baserunners reached on walks, and when all of it was added up, Knepper was 8–17 with a career-worst 5.27 earned run average.

Knepper let the team down when they needed him most. During June and July, when the Reds and Giants were beating each others' brains out (the Giants won 8 of 13 between June 8 and August 9), Knepper compiled a 2–7 record, preventing the Astros from catching up.

The once pitching-rich Astros have to count on a return to form by Knepper in 1988. The rest of the rotation is only so-so, and there doesn't appear to be any immediate help coming along the way. Mike Scott demonstrated last year that he can still be beaten, Nolan Ryan's arm simply isn't up to the strain for more than six innings at a time, and Danny Darwin is a journeyman. Knepper and young Jim Deshaies, who suffered through a difficult sophomore year, have to be counted on to fill some of the holes.

1988 should be make or break time for Bob. He will turn 34 in May, and has never strung two good seasons together. This will be his eighth year in the dome, and his *only* year with an ERA under 3.00 was 1981, his first.

Tom Henry and Doug White

Knepper, Robert Wesley "Bob"

Bats: Left   Throws: Left   Born 05/25/54

1987 SEASON AND MAJOR-LEAGUE CAREER PITCHING TOTALS

	G	GS	CG	GF	IP	BFP	H	R	ER	HR	SH	SF	HB	TBB	IBB	SO	WP	Bk	W	L	Pct	ShO	Sv	ERA
87 HOU	33	31	1	1	178	792	226	118	104	26	7	4	4	54	3	76	4	0	8	17	.320	0	0	5.26
12 YEARS	371	353	74	7	2324	9814	2335	1062	923	192	112	60	41	696	66	1282	48	4	122	135	.475	27	1	3.57

1987: Finesse, Groundball   1986: Finesse, Groundball   1985: Finesse, Groundball   1984: Finesse, Groundball

1987 SEASON / FOUR YEAR TOTALS (1984 – 1987)

	G	IP	H	BB	SO	SB	CS	W	L	S	ERA	G	IP	H	BB	SO	SB	CS	W	L	S	ERA
Totals	33	177.2	226	54	77	16	6	8	17	0	5.27	145	910.1	934	225	491	51	40	55	52	0	3.67
at Home	16	98.1	111	21	44	7	3	5	7	0	4.30	74	491.2	490	93	267	28	23	29	25	0	3.44
on Road	17	79.1	115	33	33	9	3	3	10	0	6.47	71	418.2	444	132	224	23	17	26	27	0	3.96
on Grass	10	51.0	70	18	27	4	1	1	8	0	6.35	43	249.1	268	69	147	14	4	16	17	0	4.08
on Artificial Turf	23	126.2	156	36	50	12	5	7	9	0	4.83	102	661.0	666	156	344	37	36	39	35	0	3.53
Day Games	11	42.0	69	23	17	6	1	2	6	0	7.29	42	244.0	254	73	125	16	7	15	15	0	3.80
Night Games	22	135.2	157	31	60	10	5	6	11	0	4.64	103	666.1	680	152	366	35	33	40	37	0	3.62
April	6	28.1	40	8	15	5	3	1	2	0	6.04	20	125.2	117	31	73	9	8	8	5	0	3.01
May	5	21.0	27	6	8	1	0	1	3	0	6.43	24	150.1	145	46	81	3	8	12	7	0	3.29
June	5	26.0	38	4	11	2	1	1	3	0	7.27	25	159.1	179	33	79	10	10	8	14	0	4.46
July	6	33.2	43	11	15	2	0	1	4	0	4.81	25	154.2	156	31	90	6	3	6	9	0	3.38
August	6	41.1	44	10	16	2	1	3	2	0	4.14	25	171.2	167	38	87	7	5	12	8	0	3.46
Sept/Oct	5	27.1	34	15	12	4	1	1	3	0	3.95	26	148.2	170	46	81	16	6	9	9	0	4.36

vs. Opponent Batters	Ave.	OBP	SLG	AB	H	2B	3B	HR	RBI	BB	SO	Ave.	OBP	SLG	AB	H	2B	3B	HR	RBI	BB	SO
Totals	.313	.362	.503	722	226	37	11	26	105	54	77	.267	.311	.411	3504	934	169	31	92	374	225	491
vs. Left	.277	.310	.412	119	33	3	2	3	13	5	19	.256	.284	.393	496	127	22	5	12	45	19	111
vs. Right	.320	.372	.521	603	193	34	9	23	92	49	58	.268	.315	.414	3008	807	147	26	80	329	206	380
Bases Empty	.300	.345	.506	417	125	22	5	18	18	27	47	.264	.299	.408	2137	564	101	15	59	59	104	315
Leadoff	.266	.301	.441	177	47	9	2	6	6	9	23	.269	.306	.395	892	240	40	6	20	20	47	124
Not Leadoff	.325	.377	.554	240	78	13	3	12	12	18	24	.260	.294	.418	1245	324	61	9	39	39	57	191
Runners On Base	.331	.383	.498	305	101	15	6	8	87	27	30	.271	.330	.416	1367	370	68	16	33	315	121	176
First Base Only	.393	.422	.607	122	48	7	5	3	15	6	12	.289	.317	.444	613	177	30	10	15	51	25	74
Scoring Position	.290	.360	.426	183	53	8	1	5	72	21	18	.256	.340	.394	754	193	38	6	18	264	96	102
Late Innings, Close	.306	.370	.388	49	15	2	1	0	5	5	3	.261	.318	.356	261	68	10	3	3	18	22	30

RBI/Opportunities

Scoring Position	61 / 244 (25%)	226 / 1038 (22%)
Scoring Position, 2 Out	35 / 119 (29%)	99 / 489 (20%)
On Third, Less than 2 Out	21 / 47 (45%)	82 / 193 (42%)
RBI in close games / RBI Total	78 / 105 (74%)	265 / 374 (71%)

Ray Knight
Baltimore Orioles

Poor Ray Knight. After being the World Series MVP in 1986, he miscalculated, and turned down a one-year, $800,000 deal. When the Mets withdrew their offer and the other owners colluded, he had to swallow his pride and take the one offer that he received—to play for the last-place Baltimore Orioles. The Orioles offered his pride one balm, by giving him the two-year deal that he wanted, but the total amount of the contract was almost the same amount of the Mets' offer.

1987 turned out worse than most people expected. Ray doesn't play for the money—he and wife (pro golfer Nancy Lopez) don't need more bucks—so much as he plays for the competition and recognition. He got neither. The Orioles lost more games in 1987 than they had since 1955; Ray didn't play especially well in the process. The Mets, meanwhile, got a 30–30 season from Ray's replacement (Howard Johnson) and had another strong year; Ray's memory died easily in New York.

Ray generally comes out of spring training ready to rock and roll and swings a hot bat through May. Through 1986, his career average was .294 before June 1 and .271 after it. Last year, his bat was glowing in the dark in April, but the fade began a little sooner. But even with a less-than-prosperous May, he still hit 32 points higher in the first two months than he did for the remainder of the year. As he usually does, he didn't add much power or on-base ability to that package.

There were two areas where Ray lived up to expectations. First, he helped solidify what had been a porous defensive infield. Ray led all AL third basemen in range factor, was fourth in double plays per game and sixth in fielding percentage. In 1986, Orioles third sackers made 40 errors; in 1987, they made only 23.

Secondly, Knight bought the Orioles some time. Baltimore is salivating over a 22-year-old named Craig Worthington; he should be ready before the 1988 season is complete. Billy Ripken's surprising performance in the second half and rookie Pete Stanicek's apparent readiness for prime time (a .274 average with eight steals in 30 games) make the infield a crowded place. Ray was unhappy about the writing on the dugout wall (*i.e.,* the lineup card)—more and more often, as the season ended, he was asked to DH, fill in for a gimpy Eddie Murray at first base or, worst of all, sit a few out.

1988 will probably be Ray's last season anywhere, and it's unlikely that he'll see much playing time during it. He could still be a useful replacement part for a contender, but a team like the Orioles—who are trying to get on the AL East merry-go-round—need to play men with a future. Sadly, Ray Knight's future is behind him.

Greg Pryor

Knight, Charles Ray "Ray"

Bats: Right   Throws: Right   Born 12/28/52

1987 SEASON AND MAJOR-LEAGUE CAREER BATTING TOTALS

	G	AB	H	2B	3B	HR	TB	R	RBI	TBB	IBB	SO	HP	SH	SF	SB	CS	SB%	GDP	AVG	OBP	SLG
87 BAL	150	563	144	24	0	14	210	46	65	39	3	90	6	0	1	0	0	.00	16	.256	.310	.373
12 YEARS	1390	4530	1246	254	25	81	1793	456	562	323	43	549	33	20	58	13	24	.35	157	.275	.324	.396

	1987 SEASON											FOUR YEAR TOTALS (1984 – 1987)										
	Ave.	OBP	SLG	AB	H	2B	3B	HR	RBI	BB	SO	Ave.	OBP	SLG	AB	H	2B	3B	HR	RBI	BB	SO
Totals	.256	.310	.373	563	144	24	0	14	65	39	90	.258	.306	.364	1691	436	74	2	34	212	113	228
vs. Left	.218	.293	.354	206	45	4	0	8	24	21	34	.279	.320	.436	709	198	34	1	25	102	43	89
vs. Right	.277	.321	.384	357	99	20	0	6	41	18	56	.242	.297	.313	982	238	40	1	9	110	70	139
at Home	.274	.319	.411	270	74	13	0	8	32	16	42	.258	.308	.391	814	210	41	2	21	114	57	119
on Road	.239	.302	.338	293	70	11	0	6	33	23	48	.258	.305	.340	877	226	33	0	13	98	56	109
vs. Groundball	.281	.339	.394	292	82	15	0	6	31	24	43	.257	.311	.360	848	218	46	1	13	98	63	106
vs. Flyball	.229	.279	.351	271	62	9	0	8	34	15	47	.259	.302	.369	843	218	28	1	21	114	50	122
vs. Finesse	.261	.322	.391	261	68	10	0	8	31	22	35	.255	.303	.364	906	231	40	1	19	97	59	100
vs. Power	.252	.300	.358	302	76	14	0	6	34	17	55	.261	.310	.364	785	205	34	1	15	115	54	128
on Grass	.258	.312	.383	481	124	18	0	14	57	32	72	.259	.311	.376	1164	302	48	2	28	148	80	155
on Artificial Turf	.244	.303	.317	82	20	6	0	0	8	7	18	.254	.296	.338	527	134	26	0	6	64	33	73
Day Games	.257	.336	.360	136	35	5	0	3	20	15	24	.261	.311	.364	486	127	20	0	10	64	34	57
Night Games	.255	.302	.377	427	109	19	0	11	45	24	66	.256	.304	.364	1205	309	54	2	24	148	79	171
April	.338	.427	.493	71	24	5	0	2	14	9	8	.287	.347	.454	216	62	12	0	8	36	18	21
May	.235	.292	.378	98	23	5	0	3	12	7	14	.260	.316	.395	281	73	20	0	6	34	22	38
June	.269	.298	.389	108	29	4	0	3	8	5	18	.245	.279	.338	364	89	11	1	7	36	18	55
July	.247	.295	.303	89	22	2	0	1	9	6	12	.227	.286	.306	229	52	7	1	3	31	19	37
August	.230	.280	.350	100	23	6	0	2	11	6	17	.263	.305	.335	278	73	11	0	3	38	16	31
Sept/Oct	.237	.295	.351	97	23	2	0	3	11	6	21	.269	.316	.375	323	87	13	0	7	37	20	46
Bases Empty	.229	.288	.322	301	69	10	0	6	6	20	48	.237	.286	.333	939	223	38	2	16	16	59	135
Leadoff	.217	.252	.311	106	23	1	0	3	3	3	21	.234	.272	.335	346	81	12	1	7	7	16	44
Not Leadoff	.236	.307	.328	195	46	9	0	3	3	17	27	.239	.294	.332	593	142	26	1	9	9	43	91
Runners On	.286	.336	.431	262	75	14	0	8	59	19	42	.283	.332	.403	752	213	36	0	18	196	54	93
First Base Only	.302	.331	.457	116	35	6	0	4	10	5	19	.265	.294	.396	336	89	17	0	9	26	14	36
Scoring Position	.274	.340	.411	146	40	8	0	4	49	14	23	.298	.360	.409	416	124	19	0	9	170	40	57
Late Innings, Close	.329	.376	.424	85	28	2	0	2	16	6	9	.265	.300	.374	294	78	12	1	6	36	14	38

RBI/Opportunities

Scoring Position	43 / 199 (22%)	150 / 568 (26%)
Scoring Position, 2 Out	23 / 96 (24%)	60 / 244 (25%)
On Third, Less than 2 Out	8 / 35 (23%)	56 / 124 (45%)
RBI in close games / RBI Total	40 / 65 (62%)	115 / 212 (54%)

John Kruk
San Diego Padres

John Kruk very quietly had an outstanding season in 1987. He finished fourth in the National League in batting with a .313 average, sixth in on-base percentage at .406, had a slugging percentage of .488, and drove in 91 runs in 447 at-bats. As a pinch hitter he was excellent, going 6 for 12 with 1 home run and 5 RBIs.

Kruk began the season as the Padre left fielder and started 29 games there, hitting .337. The Padres were only 5–24 in those games, however, and he was moved to first base. While playing first, John hit only .301, but he drove in 71 runs and hit with more power. The Padres were 43–51 with him at first. With all the young outfielders the Padres have, they are better off with Kruk at first.

He had 22 multi-RBI games in 1987, including 6 games with 3 or more RBI, one with 5, and one with 7. His 20 homers were a surprise because he never hit more than 11 in the minor leagues. His 18 stolen bases were also a surprise as he never showed much speed in the minors.

He doesn't get the publicity he deserves because he plays in San Diego and the Padres aren't a very good team. In New York, Rafael Santana is praised as an All-Star shortstop and Al Leiter is going to be the next great Yankee southpaw; when the Twins won the pennant, Steve Lombardozzi suddenly became a great second baseman. But John Kruk, the Barney Rubble look-alike, has Rodney Dangerfield's disease. Even Tony Gwynn, who has consistently been near the top of the NL batting race the past few years, doesn't get the recognition he deserves. If Kruk played on the Yankees he would be touted as the best young player in baseball; instead, he is one of the best-kept secrets.

Dennis Bronstein

On April 25 of last year, Padre General Manager Jack McKeon, when talking about John Kruk, was quoted as saying "Everyone says he can hit. Well, some guys are OK in the first or second spot. But, he's had too many chances with runners on base." This shows remarkable stupidity on the part of a respected baseball executive. Of course, at that time, Steve Garvey was the starting first baseman, Larry Bowa was splitting left field between Carmelo Martinez and John Kruk, the Padre offense was moribund, and the team was the laughing stock of the National League.

On May 3, Bowa faced the fact that the Padre offense could no longer carry Garvey, and benched him. A month later, Kruk became the regular first baseman. The Padres then began to play decent ball, threatening until the last week of the season to get out the cellar.

Kruk was third on the Padres in terms of Runs Created per 27 outs (behind Gwynn and Randy Ready). Rather than trying to find people who fill roles in the lineup (speed leading off, bat control batting second, high average third, power fourth), it seems to me that the Padres would be better off stuffing the lineup with people who create runs.

David Bradley

Kruk, John Martin   Bats: Left   Throws: Left   Born 02/09/61

1987 SEASON AND MAJOR-LEAGUE CAREER BATTING TOTALS

	G	AB	H	2B	3B	HR	TB	R	RBI	TBB	IBB	SO	HP	SH	SF	SB	CS	SB%	GDP	AVG	OBP	SLG
87 SD	138	447	140	14	2	20	218	72	91	73	15	93	0	3	4	18	10	.64	6	.313	.406	.488
2 YEARS	260	725	226	30	4	24	336	105	129	118	15	151	0	5	6	20	14	.59	17	.312	.405	.463

	1987 SEASON											FOUR YEAR TOTALS (1984 – 1987)										
	Ave.	OBP	SLG	AB	H	2B	3B	HR	RBI	BB	SO	Ave.	OBP	SLG	AB	H	2B	3B	HR	RBI	BB	SO
Totals	.313	.406	.488	447	140	14	2	20	91	73	93	.312	.405	.463	725	226	30	4	24	129	118	151
vs. Left	.255	.329	.380	137	35	3	1	4	28	16	38	.273	.356	.366	216	59	6	1	4	40	29	58
vs. Right	.339	.439	.535	310	105	11	1	16	63	57	55	.328	.425	.505	509	167	24	3	20	89	89	93
at Home	.298	.416	.437	215	64	6	0	8	38	45	51	.302	.414	.440	318	96	17	0	9	50	62	76
on Road	.328	.397	.534	232	76	8	2	12	53	28	42	.319	.398	.482	407	130	13	4	15	79	56	75
vs. Groundball	.309	.413	.435	191	59	3	0	7	38	36	41	.283	.385	.383	339	96	10	0	8	55	59	76
vs. Flyball	.316	.401	.527	256	81	11	2	13	53	37	52	.337	.424	.534	386	130	20	4	16	74	59	75
vs. Finesse	.319	.409	.473	226	72	10	2	7	43	36	38	.320	.400	.452	394	126	21	2	9	63	55	66
vs. Power	.308	.404	.502	221	68	4	0	13	48	37	55	.302	.412	.477	331	100	9	2	15	66	63	85
on Grass	.302	.401	.457	328	99	6	0	15	65	56	71	.299	.392	.439	515	154	18	0	18	89	82	115
on Artificial Turf	.345	.423	.571	119	41	8	2	5	26	17	22	.343	.437	.524	210	72	12	4	6	40	36	36
Day Games	.272	.385	.434	136	37	4	0	6	22	25	28	.302	.396	.445	245	74	11	0	8	34	38	48
Night Games	.331	.416	.511	311	103	10	2	14	69	48	65	.317	.410	.473	480	152	19	4	16	95	80	103
April	.262	.404	.452	42	11	2	0	2	3	10	8	.246	.350	.391	69	17	4	0	2	4	11	16
May	.405	.506	.581	74	30	4	0	3	16	15	17	.402	.496	.577	97	39	5	0	4	20	18	21
June	.315	.432	.384	73	23	0	1	1	14	15	18	.309	.435	.372	94	29	1	1	1	19	21	21
July	.329	.402	.566	76	25	3	0	5	16	10	10	.333	.405	.523	111	37	6	0	5	19	14	17
August	.320	.382	.588	97	31	3	1	7	30	11	19	.314	.405	.537	188	59	11	2	9	40	30	38
Sept/Oct	.235	.327	.329	85	20	2	0	2	12	12	21	.271	.361	.355	166	45	3	1	3	27	24	38
Bases Empty	.321	.407	.467	240	77	5	0	10	10	35	41	.292	.387	.426	394	115	15	1	12	12	61	77
Leadoff	.284	.366	.405	116	33	2	0	4	4	15	16	.276	.363	.371	170	47	4	0	4	4	23	26
Not Leadoff	.355	.444	.524	124	44	3	0	6	6	20	25	.304	.405	.469	224	68	11	1	8	8	38	51
Runners On	.304	.406	.512	207	63	9	2	10	81	38	52	.335	.429	.508	331	111	15	3	12	117	57	74
First Base Only	.254	.329	.451	71	18	1	2	3	9	8	13	.352	.428	.549	122	43	5	2	5	14	16	21
Scoring Position	.331	.441	.544	136	45	8	0	7	72	30	34	.325	.429	.483	209	68	10	1	7	103	41	53
Late Innings, Close	.372	.465	.512	86	32	3	0	3	18	15	17	.348	.438	.442	138	48	4	0	3	26	22	30

RBI/Opportunities

	1987		Four Year	
Scoring Position	60 / 207	(29%)	89 / 308	(29%)
Scoring Position, 2 Out	26 / 92	(28%)	44 / 136	(32%)
On Third, Less than 2 Out	20 / 42	(48%)	28 / 59	(47%)
RBI in close games / RBI Total	67 / 91	(74%)	95 / 129	(74%)

Mike LaCoss
San Francisco Giants

Every time the pundits are convinced that Mike La-Coss is history, this well-traveled and enigmatic right-hander becomes reminiscent of Lazarus. He has now produced two unlikely comebacks in two consecutive years.

Mike's first return from the Land of Ex-Players came in 1986. After washing out with Kansas City and Omaha in a futile 1985, LaCoss joined the Giants organization, just before spring training, and proceeded to compile a 9–3 record and 2.76 ERA before the All-Star break. Even Roger Craig must have been a little surprised. But then the remainder of 1986 (1–10, 4.91) made it look like the first half had been just so much borrowed time.

LaCoss arrived at spring training, 1987, once again classified as unlikely to succeed. The *Scouting Report* was doubtful that Mike could have a starting role, and even questioned whether he was good enough to remain in the major leagues. The Giants were indeed able to find him a spot on their 1987 roster, but as the season wore on, it looked more and more like the doubtful critics had been correct all along. By mid-year, LaCoss had a 4.48 ERA, and opposing hitters had been smacking him around at a .300 clip. Mike had staggered to a 7–5 W-L mark; being with a winning club did no harm to his record. LaCoss had made some appearances out of the bull pen, and there were questions about how he could help the Giants, if at all, in the second half.

Once again, Mike LaCoss leaped off the scrap heap and all but silenced his critics. From the All-Star break on, he remained a winning pitcher, and he obviously deserved it. Mike's second half numbers included a 2.87 ERA and an excellent hits plus walks per inning ratio of 1.18 (compared to a dreadful 1.70 in the first half). He contributed two complete games and ended up with 13 Wins, the most by anyone in a Giants uniform. (Rick Reuschel also won 13 games, but of course most of these came with Pittsburgh.) From August 1, when the Giants were 3 games behind the Reds, until September 19, the Giants went 7–2 against Cincinnati, effectively ending the pennant race. LaCoss went 4–0 against his former teammates during that 6-week stretch. All factors considered, Mike LaCoss was one of the superior starting pitchers in the National League in the second half of 1987. There is certainly nothing in his numbers that would raise any doubts about his ability to perform at the major league level in 1988.

Mike will be 32 in May. No one would argue that he still possesses all the ability that earned him his 1979 All-Star Game appearance. He may even be washed up, finally. But if the experts write him off before he 1988 season begins, be prepared for another surprise. He obviously reacts strongly to reports of his demise.

John C. Benson

LaCoss, Michael James "Mike" Bats: Right Throws: Right Born 05/30/56

1987 SEASON AND MAJOR-LEAGUE CAREER PITCHING TOTALS

	G	GS	CG	GF	IP	BFP	H	R	ER	HR	SH	SF	HB	TBB	IBB	SO	WP	Bk	W	L	Pct	ShO	Sv	ERA
87 SF	39	26	2	4	171	728	184	78	70	16	9	3	2	63	12	79	6	1	13	10	.565	1	0	3.68
10 YEARS	320	189	23	39	1350	5810	1408	692	606	82	71	34	19	550	77	566	45	15	74	77	.490	8	6	4.04

1987: Finesse, Groundball   1986: Finesse, Groundball   1985: Power, Groundball   1984: Power, Groundball

		1987 SEASON											FOUR YEAR TOTALS (1984 – 1987)										
	G	IP	H	BB	SO	SB	CS	W	L	S	ERA		G	IP	H	BB	SO	SB	CS	W	L	S	ERA
Totals	39	171.0	184	63	79	17	4	13	10	0	3.68		136	548.0	544	217	277	63	29	31	29	4	3.83
at Home	20	100.1	100	37	52	7	2	7	8	0	3.23		67	300.0	269	116	156	31	10	18	14	3	3.33
on Road	19	70.2	84	26	27	10	2	6	2	0	4.33		69	248.0	275	101	121	32	19	13	15	1	4.43
on Grass	16	69.1	72	27	28	8	2	7	3	0	2.86		50	202.1	205	91	90	21	13	13	13	0	4.31
on Artificial Turf	23	101.2	112	36	51	9	2	6	7	0	4.25		86	345.2	339	126	187	42	16	18	16	4	3.54
Day Games	28	118.2	128	49	57	12	2	7	9	0	3.72		81	324.0	323	128	159	34	14	17	21	0	4.00
Night Games	11	52.1	56	14	22	5	2	6	1	0	3.61		55	224.0	221	89	118	29	15	14	8	4	3.58
April	6	17.1	20	10	5	2	0	1	1	0	5.19		22	44.2	41	20	19	5	1	2	1	0	4.23
May	7	29.2	33	7	21	4	0	4	1	0	3.34		23	100.2	93	31	57	13	2	9	2	1	2.86
June	7	25.0	33	13	9	4	1	1	2	0	6.12		30	111.1	110	51	53	8	10	6	4	3	3.88
July	7	24.2	36	13	12	2	1	2	2	0	3.28		24	106.1	107	43	58	12	7	6	7	0	3.72
August	6	44.2	31	9	19	2	0	3	2	0	2.22		19	100.2	103	36	50	13	4	5	8	0	4.47
Sept/Oct	6	29.2	31	11	13	3	2	2	2	0	3.64		18	84.1	90	36	40	12	5	3	7	0	4.06

vs. Opponent Batters	Ave.	OBP	SLG	AB	H	2B	3B	HR	RBI	BB	SO		Ave.	OBP	SLG	AB	H	2B	3B	HR	RBI	BB	SO
Totals	.283	.346	.419	651	184	29	6	16	74	63	79		.264	.334	.368	2063	544	77	17	35	246	217	277
vs. Left	.304	.373	.468	365	111	19	4	11	46	41	41		.259	.338	.363	1104	286	38	13	17	126	133	140
vs. Right	.255	.312	.357	286	73	10	2	5	28	22	38		.269	.329	.374	959	258	39	4	18	120	84	137
Bases Empty	.292	.342	.427	377	110	18	3	9	9	28	46		.249	.306	.338	1208	301	41	9	16	16	97	170
Leadoff	.329	.385	.473	167	55	9	0	5	5	15	21		.284	.343	.370	522	148	17	2	8	8	47	68
Not Leadoff	.262	.308	.390	210	55	9	3	4	4	13	25		.223	.277	.313	686	153	24	7	8	8	50	102
Runners On Base	.270	.351	.409	274	74	11	3	7	65	35	33		.284	.372	.412	855	243	36	8	19	230	120	107
First Base Only	.308	.368	.449	107	33	5	2	2	7	10	11		.274	.343	.389	332	91	11	3	7	23	35	38
Scoring Position	.246	.342	.383	167	41	6	1	5	58	25	22		.291	.389	.426	523	152	25	5	12	207	85	69
Late Innings, Close	.296	.427	.549	71	21	4	1	4	15	17	8		.230	.335	.354	226	52	12	2	4	26	36	31

RBI/Opportunities

	1987			Four Year
Scoring Position	47 / 229	(21%)		178 / 739 (24%)
Scoring Position, 2 Out	20 / 96	(21%)		75 / 310 (24%)
On Third, Less than 2 Out	18 / 43	(42%)		63 / 142 (44%)
RBI in close games / RBI Total	51 / 74	(69%)		151 / 246 (61%)

Mark Langston
Seattle Mariners

He is touted by his peers as being one of the best, if not the best, left-handed starter in baseball, but little is known about Mark Langston. He's been hidden in obscurity in Seattle, where late-breaking box scores never make east coast press deadlines or ESPN highlight films. His only claim to fame was an AP wire photo of him dancing during a 1985 rain delay in Kansas City. As the story goes, a few KC fans saw Mark break dancing in the dugout. After some prodding by the crowd, a fellow pitcher called the booth requesting a selection of tunes and Langston proceeded to entertain in the rain.

Since then he's been an All-Star, had three AL strikeout crowns, the third best winning record in 1987, and a Gold Glove. Yet Mark's notoriety is still nil. As Vin Scully pointed out during the 1987 All-Star game, many seem to think that Roger Clemens is the American League king of the strikeout pitch, but in reality it's Langston. As the "never lost for words" Scully watched Langston pitch the strongest two innings of the All-Star game, it was amusing listening to the master of baseball prose search for stats to best describe the performance of someone he obviously knew little about, but was very impressed with. After stammering through two innings, he finally summed it up in typical Vin Scully fashion, "He's a *dandy!*"

Anyone who has followed Mark's career knows he is capable of being a consistent 20-game winner, and Langston came within one game of reaching that plateau in 1987. He is a power pitcher with a bag full of pitches. When he has control of those pitches, he is unbeatable and in '87 his control and concentration improved dramatically. The secret to his strikeout success was best described by Norm Hitzges, a Texas Ranger announcer: "I don't know of a guy (Langston) in the American League that's harder to hit once he gets well ahead of you, 'cause he's got, he's really got 5 different pitches. And you sit there waiting for him to throw you that blistering fast ball, and if he throws you anything else around the strike zone, he can really tie you up!"

Besides the strong left arm, Mark has a few other attributes. He is a fierce battler, fields the ball well, and is a pitching horse. In 1987, 6.08 IP was the major league average for a starter. There were only five starters with 200 or more IP who averaged 7.50 IP per start or better. They were Clemens, Morris, Saberhagen, Alexander, and Langston.

The biggest rap against Mark has been his lack of control and consistency. But his game seems to be coming together now. His walks per 9 innings dropped to 3.77 from the previous year's 4.63, and well below his career average of 5.08. Langston's personalized license plates reflect his number one priority. They read: NO WALKS. In actuality, he should be sporting Roger Clemens' personalized plates which read SUPER K.

Merrianna McCully

Langston, Mark Edward

Bats: Right   Throws: Left   **Born 08/20/60**

1987 SEASON AND MAJOR-LEAGUE CAREER PITCHING TOTALS

	G	GS	CG	GF	IP	BFP	H	R	ER	HR	SH	SF	HB	TBB	IBB	SO	WP	Bk	W	L	Pct	ShO	Sv	ERA
87 SEA	35	35	14	0	272	1152	242	132	116	30	12	6	5	114	0	262	9	2	19	13	.594	3	0	3.84
4 YEARS	131	128	30	1	863	3751	786	458	407	98	33	23	19	446	8	783	26	10	55	51	.519	5	0	4.24

1987: Power, Flyball   1986: Power, Flyball   1985: Power, Groundball   1984: Power, Flyball

1987 SEASON

	G	IP	H	BB	SO	SB	CS	W	L	S	ERA
Totals	35	271.2	242	114	262	26	10	19	13	0	3.84
at Home	16	126.0	111	52	126	12	4	7	8	0	4.29
on Road	19	145.2	131	62	136	14	6	12	5	0	3.46
on Grass	12	86.2	75	43	87	9	6	6	5	0	4.26
on Artificial Turf	23	185.0	167	71	175	17	4	13	8	0	3.65
Day Games	15	116.0	102	48	104	9	3	11	2	0	3.34
Night Games	20	155.2	140	66	158	17	7	8	11	0	4.22
April	5	39.1	35	15	36	5	3	3	2	0	3.66
May	6	50.0	43	19	53	3	2	3	2	0	4.14
June	6	49.2	39	18	48	3	1	4	2	0	4.17
July	5	37.0	36	14	29	4	1	1	3	0	5.35
August	6	46.1	41	23	41	4	1	4	1	0	2.14
Sept/Oct	7	49.1	48	25	55	7	2	4	3	0	3.83

vs. Opponent Batters	Ave.	OBP	SLG	AB	H	2B	3B	HR	RBI	BB	SO
Totals	.238	.317	.383	1015	242	45	6	30	118	114	262
vs. Left	.197	.265	.293	147	29	2	0	4	14	14	42
vs. Right	.245	.325	.399	868	213	43	6	26	104	100	220
Bases Empty	.225	.321	.367	564	127	22	2	18	18	78	148
Leadoff	.245	.329	.438	249	61	14	2	10	10	30	60
Not Leadoff	.210	.316	.311	315	66	8	0	8	8	48	88
Runners On Base	.255	.310	.404	451	115	23	4	12	100	36	114
First Base Only	.228	.278	.374	219	50	11	3	5	15	13	56
Scoring Position	.280	.340	.431	232	65	12	1	7	85	23	58
Late Innings, Close	.277	.313	.383	94	26	4	0	2	9	5	21

FOUR YEAR TOTALS (1984 – 1987)

	G	IP	H	BB	SO	SB	CS	W	L	S	ERA
Totals	131	862.2	786	446	783	64	32	55	51	0	4.25
at Home	62	424.1	367	208	421	35	15	26	23	0	4.22
on Road	69	438.1	419	238	362	29	17	29	28	0	4.23
on Grass	40	253.2	243	138	235	22	12	16	17	0	4.47
on Artificial Turf	91	609.0	543	308	548	42	20	39	34	0	4.14
Day Games	54	340.1	334	189	282	18	11	24	21	0	4.23
Night Games	77	522.1	452	257	501	46	21	31	30	0	4.24
April	19	123.2	116	69	84	10	6	8	8	0	4.22
May	23	154.2	151	77	123	7	5	9	9	0	4.42
June	20	132.0	108	54	134	9	5	12	6	0	3.61
July	18	117.0	98	54	116	7	6	5	8	0	4.46
August	25	169.0	147	100	148	10	5	12	9	0	3.89
Sept/Oct	26	166.1	166	92	178	21	5	9	11	0	4.82

vs. Opponent Batters	Ave.	OBP	SLG	AB	H	2B	3B	HR	RBI	BB	SO
Totals	.243	.336	.398	3230	786	154	25	98	395	446	783
vs. Left	.195	.282	.310	529	103	18	2	13	53	65	153
vs. Right	.253	.346	.415	2701	683	136	23	85	342	381	630
Bases Empty	.230	.334	.391	1810	416	81	14	61	61	282	470
Leadoff	.223	.326	.380	786	175	37	6	25	25	119	188
Not Leadoff	.235	.341	.399	1024	241	44	8	36	36	163	282
Runners On Base	.261	.337	.406	1420	370	73	11	37	334	164	313
First Base Only	.248	.317	.379	628	156	29	4	15	40	61	142
Scoring Position	.270	.353	.427	792	214	44	7	22	294	103	171
Late Innings, Close	.273	.362	.395	311	85	18	1	6	31	43	63

RBI/Opportunities

Scoring Position	70 / 305 (23%)	246 / 1072 (23%)
Scoring Position, 2 Out	28 / 137 (20%)	94 / 475 (20%)
On Third, Less than 2 Out	18 / 51 (35%)	87 / 191 (46%)
RBI in close games / RBI Total	66 / 118 (56%)	266 / 395 (67%)

Carney Lansford
Oakland Athletics

Despite Carney Lansford's mild-mannered appearance, he is all business on the field. Although he is known to be active in his religion, he refrains from using his baseball position to proselytize. And no one can accuse him of being unaggressive or meek on the field. On the contrary, Carney does have a temper and occasionally has had to be peeled off of an opposing pitcher after he or a teammate has been the victim of a high hard one. He also has a reputation for having to be dragged away from bench-clearing brawls.

Lansford has probably been the most reliable quality player on the team over the last five years. He is almost certainly the best high-average hitter to ever to wear an Oakland uniform. He is one of only five players here to hit .300 in a full season. In the last couple of years, Carney has sacrificed his average somewhat to provide more power and production.

He was the only Athletic hitter to play in September like he expected (and wanted) to win the division. At times, Carney literally seemed to carry the A's offense by himself. Probably the most significant change in his style was becoming a more patient hitter and looking for a pitch he could drive. He drew 60 walks, which was easily a career high, as well as second on the team to McGwire. His .366 on-base average was his highest since he was the batting champion back in 1981.

Carney's lack of range at third keeps him from being a legitimate candidate for the Gold Glove Award, but he is almost perfect on balls he can get to and has a strong and accurate arm.

In spite of turning 30 in 1987, Lansford is one of the A's most effective baserunners, and he seems to be improving every year. He had among the best SB% on the team this year (77 percent) and his 27 steals were a new career high.

The A's have turned down several tempting trade offers for sorely needed starting pitching to keep Carney on the team. Few people familiar with the organization would argue with that decision, especially when there isn't another decent third baseman in the organization. Mark McGwire was a third baseman, but he wasn't very good defensively and is now firmly anchored at first base.

Carney's determination and dedication to his team and the fans makes his presence essential to the future of the A's. With Murphy and Jackson gone, Carney can fill the leadership void by virtue of his sterling professionalism and is a natural choice to be the next team Captain.

Susan Nelson

Lansford, Carney Ray — Bats: Right — Throws: Right — Born 02/07/57

1987 SEASON AND MAJOR-LEAGUE CAREER BATTING TOTALS

	G	AB	H	2B	3B	HR	TB	R	RBI	TBB	IBB	SO	HP	SH	SF	SB	CS	SB%	GDP	AVG	OBP	SLG
87 OAK	151	554	160	27	4	19	252	89	76	60	11	44	9	5	3	27	8	.77	9	.289	.366	.455
10 YEARS	1290	5032	1467	239	34	132	2170	723	639	379	35	568	35	38	57	135	65	.68	104	.292	.342	.431

	1987 SEASON											FOUR YEAR TOTALS (1984 – 1987)										
	Ave.	OBP	SLG	AB	H	2B	3B	HR	RBI	BB	SO	Ave.	OBP	SLG	AB	H	2B	3B	HR	RBI	BB	SO
Totals	.289	.366	.455	554	160	27	4	19	76	60	44	.288	.340	.436	2143	618	92	15	65	268	157	184
vs. Left	.280	.352	.440	175	49	4	0	8	22	17	16	.296	.345	.437	695	206	25	5	21	63	50	58
vs. Right	.293	.372	.462	379	111	23	4	11	54	43	28	.285	.337	.436	1448	412	67	10	44	205	107	126
at Home	.288	.371	.469	271	78	16	3	9	31	31	25	.310	.358	.473	1054	327	57	8	33	144	76	82
on Road	.290	.361	.442	283	82	11	1	10	45	29	19	.267	.323	.400	1089	291	35	7	32	124	81	102
vs. Groundball	.256	.328	.381	281	72	11	3	6	30	23	19	.280	.329	.416	1060	297	42	9	28	129	71	78
vs. Flyball	.322	.403	.531	273	88	16	1	13	46	37	25	.296	.350	.456	1083	321	50	6	37	139	86	106
vs. Finesse	.270	.353	.442	274	74	12	1	11	36	31	20	.300	.336	.454	1229	369	52	7	41	151	64	75
vs. Power	.307	.379	.468	280	86	15	3	8	40	29	24	.272	.344	.412	914	249	40	8	24	117	93	109
on Grass	.286	.363	.448	458	131	24	4	14	57	49	35	.293	.343	.445	1794	526	81	12	56	226	127	148
on Artificial Turf	.302	.380	.490	96	29	3	0	5	19	11	9	.264	.326	.390	349	92	11	3	9	42	30	36
Day Games	.305	.396	.490	200	61	12	2	7	27	25	14	.306	.364	.481	813	249	35	7	31	110	69	61
Night Games	.280	.348	.435	354	99	15	2	12	49	35	30	.277	.325	.409	1330	369	57	8	34	158	88	123
April	.296	.396	.432	81	24	3	1	2	12	12	12	.268	.331	.354	339	91	9	4	4	42	30	35
May	.189	.286	.270	74	14	3	0	1	4	10	7	.266	.327	.450	353	94	15	1	16	41	32	36
June	.326	.426	.554	92	30	9	0	4	15	13	8	.286	.344	.425	409	117	21	0	12	47	33	34
July	.323	.376	.475	99	32	2	2	3	11	8	6	.294	.328	.423	381	112	15	5	8	43	19	31
August	.340	.388	.585	106	36	5	0	7	22	8	6	.323	.359	.538	331	107	14	3	17	53	18	28
Sept/Oct	.235	.310	.363	102	24	5	1	2	12	9	5	.294	.347	.433	330	97	18	2	8	42	25	20
Bases Empty	.284	.356	.448	324	92	18	1	11	11	28	17	.279	.324	.426	1260	352	55	8	38	38	76	98
Leadoff	.311	.349	.571	119	37	7	0	8	8	6	6	.282	.312	.452	458	129	19	1	19	19	19	33
Not Leadoff	.268	.359	.376	205	55	11	1	3	3	22	11	.278	.331	.411	802	223	36	7	19	19	57	65
Runners On	.296	.380	.465	230	68	9	3	8	65	32	27	.301	.360	.451	883	266	37	7	27	230	81	86
First Base Only	.257	.310	.343	105	27	3	0	2	5	7	13	.322	.351	.455	385	124	19	1	10	24	16	38
Scoring Position	.328	.431	.568	125	41	6	3	6	60	25	14	.285	.366	.448	498	142	18	6	17	206	65	48
Late Innings, Close	.218	.320	.322	87	19	3	0	2	10	12	9	.244	.312	.393	336	82	9	4	11	53	32	45

RBI/Opportunities

Scoring Position	45 / 180 (25%)	172 / 687 (25%)
Scoring Position, 2 Out	19 / 73 (26%)	71 / 309 (23%)
On Third, Less than 2 Out	12 / 32 (38%)	63 / 130 (48%)
RBI in close games / RBI Total	52 / 76 (68%)	179 / 268 (67%)

Barry Larkin
Cincinnati Reds

Larkin or Stillwell? That was the question the Reds faced last year. The situation was reminiscent of 1978 when the Padres first brought Ozzie up. Bill Almon was doing a fine job, but Smith was obviously a better shortstop. The Padres never really knew what to do with Almon. The Reds did have the sense to try Stillwell at second. Supposedly, Larkin can't play second, though I've never heard why.

Well, the Reds made their decision—Larkin over Stillwell. They didn't go wrong. The trade-offs are about even—Larkin is a year older, but he's also a little bigger, which should give him more durability. Stillwell seems to have better range and a stronger arm, although his range factor was 3.75 to Barry's 4.42, but Larkin is definitely a better offensive player, and a hometown boy.

Unlike the Padres, who traded Almon after the 1979 season for next to nothing (31-year-old Dave Cash, who retired after the 1980 season), the Reds got an outstanding talent for Stillwell, Danny Jackson, who should give them the rotation anchor they've been seeking.

The key to the trade, through, was Jeff Treadway, the Nashville second baseman, who performed well when brought up at the end of the season. He should be a strong candidate for Rookie of the Year. Since Larkin can't play second, and the Royals, who really wanted Stillwell badly, were willing to part with Jackson in exchange for him, what else could the Reds do?

Treadway and Larkin are similar types of hitters, but the shortstop is about a half step ahead. In 1986 at Denver the two played together and performed excellently; they had Major League Equivalent averages of .299 (Treadway) and .302 (Larkin), with good on-base and slugging figures.

Barry wasn't hitting that well before he was hurt turning a double play in April, and he came back slowly when he returned (despite having an off year with the bat, Barry was fourth among NL shortstops in Runs Created/Game). I think his slow start was due to the intense competition he faced in spring training; he peaked too early. I believe Larkin, like Eric Davis last spring, will respond very favorably to not needing to compete for his job this year.

Larkin may win some Gold Gloves and Silver Sluggers later in his career. In addition to having a good Range Factor, which should improve as he learns the hitters, he looks good out there and his bat and team should be good enough to attract attention. After Ozzie retires he'll be among the best of the league.

The Reds look very strong up the middle for the next 5–6 years: this season Larkin is 24, Treadway 25, Davis 26, and their best minor league catcher, Joe Oliver, who could make the team this spring, is 23.

Tom Locker

Larkin, Barry Louis

Bats: Right Throws: Right Born 04/28/64

1987 SEASON AND MAJOR-LEAGUE CAREER BATTING TOTALS

	G	AB	H	2B	3B	HR	TB	R	RBI	TBB	IBB	SO	HP	SH	SF	SB	CS	SB%	GDP	AVG	OBP	SLG
87 CIN	125	439	107	16	2	12	163	64	43	36	3	52	5	5	3	21	6	.78	8	.244	.306	.371
2 YEARS	166	598	152	20	5	15	227	91	62	45	4	73	5	5	4	29	6	.83	10	.254	.310	.380

1987 SEASON / FOUR YEAR TOTALS (1984 – 1987)

	Ave.	OBP	SLG	AB	H	2B	3B	HR	RBI	BB	SO	Ave.	OBP	SLG	AB	H	2B	3B	HR	RBI	BB	SO
Totals	.244	.306	.371	439	107	16	2	12	43	36	52	.254	.310	.380	598	152	20	5	15	62	45	73
vs. Left	.275	.349	.450	131	36	4	2	5	16	14	12	.293	.358	.459	181	53	5	2	7	24	18	12
vs. Right	.231	.288	.338	308	71	12	0	7	27	22	40	.237	.288	.345	417	99	15	3	8	38	27	61
at Home	.237	.306	.349	241	57	9	0	6	27	24	32	.248	.307	.378	323	80	11	2	9	38	28	40
on Road	.253	.307	.399	198	50	7	2	6	16	12	20	.262	.313	.382	275	72	9	3	6	24	17	33
vs. Groundball	.229	.291	.338	201	46	5	1	5	17	16	25	.253	.304	.354	277	70	6	2	6	24	19	32
vs. Flyball	.256	.319	.399	238	61	11	1	7	26	20	27	.255	.314	.402	321	82	14	3	9	38	26	41
vs. Finesse	.221	.286	.342	222	49	10	1	5	20	19	21	.232	.286	.349	298	69	12	1	7	25	22	31
vs. Power	.267	.328	.401	217	58	6	1	7	23	17	31	.277	.333	.410	300	83	8	4	8	37	23	42
on Grass	.271	.339	.458	107	29	3	1	5	9	8	12	.294	.357	.438	153	45	5	1	5	16	12	19
on Artificial Turf	.235	.296	.343	332	78	13	1	7	34	28	40	.240	.293	.360	445	107	15	4	10	46	33	54
Day Games	.274	.355	.411	146	40	8	0	4	13	17	22	.299	.371	.437	197	59	10	1	5	23	21	31
Night Games	.229	.281	.352	293	67	8	2	8	30	19	30	.232	.278	.352	401	93	10	4	10	39	24	42
April	.313	.389	.500	16	5	0	0	1	3	2	4	.313	.389	.500	16	5	0	0	1	3	2	4
May	.193	.247	.349	83	16	4	0	3	7	4	7	.193	.247	.349	83	16	4	0	3	7	4	7
June	.184	.286	.388	49	9	4	0	2	8	7	7	.184	.286	.388	49	9	4	0	2	8	7	7
July	.278	.346	.361	97	27	3	1	1	5	7	12	.278	.346	.361	97	27	3	1	1	5	7	12
August	.240	.267	.281	96	23	1	0	1	4	4	10	.242	.273	.306	157	38	2	1	2	9	7	20
Sept/Oct	.276	.348	.459	98	27	4	1	4	16	12	12	.291	.347	.449	196	57	7	3	6	30	18	23
Bases Empty	.211	.271	.320	256	54	8	1	6	6	19	39	.216	.267	.322	357	77	10	2	8	8	23	52
Leadoff	.255	.327	.431	102	26	3	0	5	5	10	18	.250	.314	.387	160	40	4	0	6	6	14	23
Not Leadoff	.182	.232	.247	154	28	5	1	1	1	9	21	.188	.227	.269	197	37	6	2	2	2	9	29
Runners On	.290	.354	.443	183	53	8	1	6	37	17	13	.311	.372	.465	241	75	10	3	7	54	22	21
First Base Only	.350	.409	.463	80	28	4	1	3	7	7	4	.367	.426	.480	98	36	4	2	1	4	9	7
Scoring Position	.243	.314	.427	103	25	4	0	5	34	10	9	.273	.335	.455	143	39	6	1	6	50	13	14
Late Innings, Close	.282	.329	.338	71	20	1	0	1	4	5	8	.326	.360	.379	95	31	2	0	1	7	5	8

RBI/Opportunities

	1987		Four Year	
Scoring Position	28 / 147	(19%)	43 / 202	(21%)
Scoring Position, 2 Out	7 / 59	(12%)	14 / 88	(16%)
On Third, Less than 2 Out	11 / 27	(41%)	18 / 40	(45%)
RBI in close games / RBI Total	25 / 43	(58%)	36 / 62	(58%)

Tim Laudner
Minnesota Twins

You may recall the 1982 Topps Rookie All-Star Team. Acquisition of the players named to that team would place you on the way to a pennant in 1988. The team featured an infield of Kent Hrbek-1b, Steve Sax-2b, Ryne Sandberg-3b, Cal Ripken-ss, and an outfield with Tom Brunansky, Chili Davis, and Willie McGee. This being the '80s, you could complain about the lousy pitching (Ed Vande Berg and Bill Laskey). Nevertheless, except for the battery, your lineup would be filled by players with major league All-Star game experience. This assemblage of high-priced talent would also have Tim Laudner behind the plate.

Tim Laudner's career has not been without recognition or notable performances. He was the 1981 Southern League MVP after hitting 42 home runs in Orlando. A product of the Twins' farm system, he homered in his first two major league games. Thus encouraged, former Twins owner Calvin Griffith traded Butch Wynegar and installed Laudner as the regular catcher in 1982. His power has produced some memorable moments capped by his three RBIs in game two of the World Series.

What Laudner is as a hitter is pretty clear; Bill James characterized him as "a big guy with a huge swing, but he connects often enough to justify the gamble." Last season Laudner averaged a home run every 18 AB, which was second only to Matt Nokes among AL catchers. And he needed every one of them as he hit only .191—which was abnormally low even for Laudner.

Tim has bad knees and isn't very mobile or quick as a catcher although he has a good throwing arm. He doesn't throw out a lot of runners, but neither does any other Twin catcher.

1982 was the only major league season in which Laudner had more than 300 AB. Until 1987, it was also the last season that Laudner was the team's number one catcher. In '83 and '84, Billy Gardner was convinced that Tim was a defensive liability and taught Dave Engle to catch. In '85 and '86, the left-handed hitting Mark Salas took over many of Laudner's duties. Tom Kelly (Laudner's Orlando manager) began 1987 by stating the Twins were in search of a defensive specialist who could help lower the pitching staff's ERA. Dissatisfaction with Laudner's pitch selection was no secret. Bob Boone was a free agent, but the Twins opted for Tom Nieto.

Nieto and Salas played a great deal during the first third of the season. An injury to Nieto in May and the trade of Salas in June returned Tim to an everyday spot. In all fairness, the staff ERA actually dropped some when Laudner took over the bulk of the catching. He isn't likely to ever reach the All-Star status of his Topps teammates, but if the Twins can find a left-handed hitting catcher who could spell Laudner against hard throwing righties, he is capable of helping the club.

Bill Jensen

Laudner, Timothy Jon "Tim"   Bats: Right   Throws: Right   Born 06/07/58

1987 SEASON AND MAJOR-LEAGUE CAREER BATTING TOTALS

	G	AB	H	2B	3B	HR	TB	R	RBI	TBB	IBB	SO	HP	SH	SF	SB	CS	SB%	GDP	AVG	OBP	SLG
87 MIN	113	288	55	7	1	16	112	30	43	23	0	80	1	3	2	1	0	1.00	4	.191	.252	.389
7 YEARS	517	1424	311	68	3	58	559	159	182	129	3	399	7	11	9	2	3	.40	23	.218	.285	.393

	1987 SEASON											FOUR YEAR TOTALS (1984 – 1987)										
	Ave.	OBP	SLG	AB	H	2B	3B	HR	RBI	BB	SO	Ave.	OBP	SLG	AB	H	2B	3B	HR	RBI	BB	SO
Totals	.190	.252	.388	289	55	7	1	16	43	23	79	.215	.279	.403	908	195	38	2	43	126	77	258
vs. Left	.192	.279	.444	99	19	2	1	7	19	12	22	.250	.335	.488	420	105	21	2	25	64	50	99
vs. Right	.189	.236	.358	190	36	5	0	9	24	11	57	.184	.228	.330	488	90	17	0	18	62	27	159
at Home	.172	.247	.344	151	26	3	1	7	16	14	41	.221	.296	.447	421	93	21	1	24	63	40	120
on Road	.210	.257	.435	138	29	4	0	9	27	9	38	.209	.264	.366	487	102	17	1	19	63	37	138
vs. Groundball	.196	.268	.405	148	29	2	1	9	22	14	34	.227	.285	.430	440	100	16	2	23	60	33	117
vs. Flyball	.184	.233	.369	141	26	5	0	7	21	9	45	.203	.273	.378	468	95	22	0	20	66	44	141
vs. Finesse	.184	.247	.336	152	28	3	1	6	20	13	30	.222	.283	.391	504	112	20	1	21	67	41	119
vs. Power	.197	.257	.445	137	27	4	0	10	23	10	49	.205	.274	.418	404	83	18	1	22	59	36	139
on Grass	.218	.263	.445	110	24	4	0	7	23	7	30	.208	.265	.360	375	78	15	0	14	51	30	106
on Artificial Turf	.173	.245	.352	179	31	3	1	9	20	16	49	.220	.288	.433	533	117	23	2	29	75	47	152
Day Games	.179	.255	.476	84	15	4	0	7	19	9	31	.195	.258	.376	266	52	15	0	11	35	21	90
Night Games	.195	.250	.351	205	40	3	1	9	24	14	48	.223	.288	.414	642	143	23	2	32	91	56	168
April	.091	.167	.364	11	1	0	0	1	2	1	5	.180	.226	.390	100	18	3	0	6	15	6	33
May	.180	.219	.344	61	11	1	0	3	12	3	14	.222	.293	.418	158	35	7	0	8	28	16	42
June	.188	.264	.458	48	9	1	0	4	10	5	13	.209	.295	.452	115	24	4	0	8	21	14	36
July	.233	.313	.483	60	14	1	1	4	8	7	16	.232	.279	.432	155	36	5	1	8	21	10	43
August	.177	.257	.371	62	11	3	0	3	8	6	21	.222	.286	.381	194	43	8	1	7	24	17	55
Sept/Oct	.191	.208	.277	47	9	1	0	1	3	1	10	.210	.265	.366	186	39	11	0	6	17	14	49
Bases Empty	.171	.216	.326	175	30	4	1	7	7	9	49	.219	.278	.425	485	106	18	2	26	26	39	133
Leadoff	.189	.250	.432	74	14	4	1	4	4	5	14	.224	.286	.425	174	39	7	2	8	8	14	38
Not Leadoff	.158	.190	.248	101	16	0	0	3	3	4	35	.215	.274	.424	311	67	11	0	18	18	25	95
Runners On	.219	.302	.482	114	25	3	0	9	36	14	30	.210	.275	.378	423	89	20	0	17	100	38	125
First Base Only	.208	.255	.438	48	10	2	0	3	6	3	13	.213	.251	.397	174	37	8	0	8	20	9	49
Scoring Position	.227	.333	.515	66	15	1	0	6	30	11	17	.209	.290	.365	249	52	12	0	9	80	29	76
Late Innings, Close	.171	.244	.341	41	7	1	0	2	5	4	14	.163	.239	.302	129	21	6	0	4	13	13	45

RBI/Opportunities

Scoring Position	22 / 94	(23%)	66 / 340	(19%)	
Scoring Position, 2 Out	4 / 36	(11%)	24 / 157	(15%)	
On Third, Less than 2 Out	9 / 16	(56%)	23 / 60	(38%)	
RBI in close games / RBI Total	26 / 43	(60%)	71 / 126	(56%)	

Mike LaValliere
Pittsburgh Pirates

Just before the start of the 1987 season, Syd Thrift traded Tony Pena to St. Louis for a package that included a short, stocky catcher with a lifetime batting average of .221. This catcher, upon his arrival in Pittsburgh, proclaimed to the local media that he was going to make us forget about what's-his-name. For one season at least, Mike LaValliere did just that.

In a town accustomed to good defense at catcher, LaValliere impressed with his defensive exploits. He won his first Gold Glove in 1987, and it was a well-deserved honor. The Gold Glove for catching typically goes to the catcher who best shuts down the running game, which LaValliere did quite well. Only 6 percent of the time did a runner on first attempt to steal second and succeed, compared with the league average of 9 percent. The interesting facet of this is that LaValliere doesn't have the exceptionally strong arm of a Tony Pena; he's so effective because he's the fastest in the league at getting rid of the ball. He is noticeably quicker than other catchers I watched.

LaValliere did more defensively than just stop base stealers. He only allowed 2 passed balls all season (compared with Pena's total of 16 the year before). He seemed to be good at handling pitchers. It's always difficult to how good someone is at such a subjective and ill-defined thing as "handling pitchers," but it was certainly the case that Leyland seemed more satisfied with LaValliere's game-calling than he had been the year before with Pena's.

LaValliere also had a good season offensively last year, beyond all expectations. He hit .300 for the season with a more than respectable .377 on base percentage. He had reasonable doubles power. On the other hand, he showed no home run power, hitting only one for the year. He also has no speed, going 3 for 8 in the stolen base department. In fact, his lack of speed coupled with his short, stocky frame gave him the nickname of "Smoky," because he reminded people of former Pirate catcher Smoky Burgess.

LaValliere had intended to work on learning to switch-hit in the Instructional League this winter, but a knee injury early in the off-season put that idea on hold. He probably will give it a try again next winter, if not before.

It's still questionable as to whether Lavalliere can maintain last year's offense. If LaValliere's offense returns to its previous levels, it will be interesting to see what Jim Leyland does about catcher. LaValliere is clearly his best defensive catcher, but Leyland hasn't shown much willingness to sacrifice offense for defense. There are two catchers in the Pirates' system (Mackey Sasser and Tom Prince) who had good seasons last year in the minors and who might be ready to step in should LaValliere stumble. As a fan, I hope that doesn't happen; I really enjoy watching LaValliere behind the plate.

Sherri Nichols

LaValliere, Michael Eugene "Mike" Bats: Left Throws: Right Born 08/18/60

1987 SEASON AND MAJOR-LEAGUE CAREER BATTING TOTALS

	G	AB	H	2B	3B	HR	TB	R	RBI	TBB	IBB	SO	HP	SH	SF	SB	CS	SB%	GDP	AVG	OBP	SLG
87 PIT	121	340	102	19	0	1	124	33	36	43	9	32	1	3	3	0	0	.00	4	.300	.377	.365
4 YEARS	249	684	178	30	2	4	224	53	72	88	14	74	2	13	6	0	1	.00	13	.260	.344	.327

	1987 SEASON											FOUR YEAR TOTALS (1984 – 1987)										
	Ave.	OBP	SLG	AB	H	2B	3B	HR	RBI	BB	SO	Ave.	OBP	SLG	AB	H	2B	3B	HR	RBI	BB	SO
Totals	.300	.377	.365	340	102	19	0	1	36	43	32	.260	.344	.327	684	178	30	2	4	72	88	74
vs. Left	.221	.302	.273	77	17	4	0	0	6	9	13	.213	.289	.294	136	29	8	0	1	16	15	26
vs. Right	.323	.399	.392	263	85	15	0	1	30	34	19	.272	.357	.336	548	149	22	2	3	56	73	48
at Home	.305	.378	.368	174	53	8	0	1	21	21	16	.256	.341	.314	347	89	12	1	2	39	46	36
on Road	.295	.377	.361	166	49	11	0	0	15	22	16	.264	.346	.341	337	89	18	1	2	33	42	38
vs. Groundball	.355	.432	.420	169	60	11	0	0	15	23	17	.283	.371	.337	350	99	14	1	1	31	48	38
vs. Flyball	.246	.323	.310	171	42	8	0	1	21	20	15	.237	.315	.317	334	79	16	1	3	41	40	36
vs. Finesse	.281	.356	.315	178	50	6	0	0	15	21	11	.260	.339	.307	384	100	12	0	2	41	46	32
vs. Power	.321	.400	.420	162	52	13	0	1	21	22	21	.260	.349	.353	300	78	18	2	2	31	42	42
on Grass	.274	.361	.333	84	23	5	0	0	7	12	10	.258	.351	.325	151	39	8	1	0	15	22	19
on Artificial Turf	.309	.383	.375	256	79	14	0	1	29	31	22	.261	.342	.328	533	139	22	1	4	57	66	55
Day Games	.283	.379	.349	106	30	7	0	0	8	17	9	.250	.338	.307	228	57	11	1	0	24	32	27
Night Games	.308	.376	.372	234	72	12	0	1	28	26	23	.265	.346	.338	456	121	19	1	4	48	56	47
April	.343	.452	.429	35	12	3	0	0	3	7	4	.247	.360	.294	85	21	4	0	0	9	15	11
May	.286	.359	.329	70	20	3	0	0	8	8	8	.278	.356	.311	90	25	3	0	0	10	11	10
June	.274	.387	.339	62	17	4	0	0	7	11	7	.286	.386	.378	119	34	6	1	1	16	19	14
July	.213	.290	.262	61	13	3	0	0	5	7	5	.197	.288	.238	122	24	5	0	0	11	16	11
August	.397	.451	.524	63	25	5	0	1	8	7	4	.280	.347	.409	132	37	9	1	2	13	14	11
Sept/Oct	.306	.346	.327	49	15	1	0	0	5	3	4	.272	.336	.316	136	37	3	0	1	13	13	17
Bases Empty	.308	.344	.384	198	61	12	0	1	1	10	20	.262	.317	.334	389	102	18	2	2	2	30	44
Leadoff	.280	.325	.360	75	21	6	0	0	0	4	8	.271	.335	.375	144	39	8	2	1	1	13	14
Not Leadoff	.325	.357	.398	123	40	6	0	1	1	6	12	.257	.305	.310	245	63	10	0	1	1	17	30
Runners On	.289	.416	.338	142	41	7	0	0	35	33	12	.258	.376	.319	295	76	12	0	2	70	58	30
First Base Only	.286	.397	.327	49	14	2	0	0	2	9	1	.236	.336	.283	106	25	2	0	1	4	16	7
Scoring Position	.290	.425	.344	93	27	5	0	0	33	24	11	.270	.397	.339	189	51	10	0	1	66	42	23
Late Innings, Close	.314	.364	.373	51	16	3	0	0	3	4	5	.265	.328	.368	117	31	7	1	1	11	11	16

RBI/Opportunities

	1987		Four Year	
Scoring Position	31 / 136	(23%)	62 / 276	(22%)
Scoring Position, 2 Out	12 / 66	(18%)	26 / 135	(19%)
On Third, Less than 2 Out	12 / 20	(60%)	25 / 44	(57%)
RBI in close games / RBI Total	20 / 36	(56%)	44 / 72	(61%)

Vance Law
Montreal Expos

Vance Law is the kind of player who could really help the Cubs, except they have no place to play him. Perhaps Law will add the outfield to his jack-of-all-trades resumé. He could platoon in left field with Jerry Mumphrey or Rafael Palmeiro, and take over for Keith Moreland at third as a late-inning defensive replacement.

For some reason, it seems we should expect more than that from him. He rebounded from a poor 1986 to knock out 119 hits in 133 games in 1987, all while the Expos shuffled him from position to position. He showed flashes of power with 12 home runs, and he had 27 doubles.

He's an all round good player who has gotten the reputation of being less than a starter. Partly that's because of his 1986 season, when he was beset by personal problems and batted just .225, and partly because of how the Expos handled him.

Certainly White Sox fans will remember him for the stability he provided at third, stability the Sox have lacked since they traded him after the 1984 season. Law also played a lot of shortstop for the Sox; he was a semi-regular there in 1982, playing 85 games at the position and not disgracing himself. When he went to Montreal he was given still another position, second base, and was competent enough to be the nominal regular for three seasons. The Expos never seemed content with Vance, however. They continually moved him in and out of the lineup and had him fill in at other positions. Vance even volunteered to pitch a few times in blowout games (of course his father, Vern, won the Cy Young Award in 1960). Not surprisingly, he did a good job.

So he's obviously versatile, but it's a case of a player's versatility hurting him in the eyes of his bosses. Baseball men speak with great fondness about "everyday players." One gets the feeling that they appreciate a player they can pencil in automatically because it's one less thing to think about.

The question, then, about Vance Law is why hasn't he been treated that way? The Cubs haven't got a regular slot for him, and that's a shame. He can be counted on for 100-plus hits with decent pop in his bat. He has averaged 110 hits a season over the last six years. By way of comparison, 476 players went to the plate last season in the National League. Only 80, 17 percent, managed 100 or more hits.

Law carries a good on-base average (.347 last season) and provides steady play in the field. Here's hoping the Cubs give him a chance to fulfill his potential.

Mike O'Donnell

Law, Vance Aaron

Bats: Right   Throws: Right   Born 10/01/56

1987 SEASON AND MAJOR-LEAGUE CAREER BATTING TOTALS

	G	AB	H	2B	3B	HR	TB	R	RBI	TBB	IBB	SO	HP	SH	SF	SB	CS	SB%	GDP	AVG	OBP	SLG
87 MON	133	436	119	27	1	12	184	52	56	51	5	62	0	2	3	8	5	.62	8	.273	.347	.422
8 YEARS	857	2704	685	135	20	53	1019	331	313	297	10	423	6	33	26	31	20	.61	62	.253	.326	.377

	1987 SEASON											FOUR YEAR TOTALS (1984 – 1987)										
	Ave.	OBP	SLG	AB	H	2B	3B	HR	RBI	BB	SO	Ave.	OBP	SLG	AB	H	2B	3B	HR	RBI	BB	SO
Totals	.273	.347	.422	436	119	27	1	12	57	51	62	.256	.334	.393	1796	459	92	11	44	212	215	299
vs. Left	.288	.384	.412	153	44	10	0	3	18	24	21	.256	.339	.409	626	160	34	1	20	71	79	90
vs. Right	.265	.326	.428	283	75	17	1	9	39	27	41	.256	.331	.384	1170	299	58	10	24	141	136	209
at Home	.268	.339	.397	209	56	18	0	3	31	24	29	.265	.349	.414	871	231	54	5	22	121	115	139
on Road	.278	.354	.445	227	63	9	1	9	26	27	33	.246	.319	.372	925	228	38	6	22	91	100	160
vs. Groundball	.293	.354	.410	205	60	10	1	4	28	20	30	.266	.335	.389	841	224	41	7	16	102	90	134
vs. Flyball	.255	.341	.433	231	59	17	0	8	29	31	32	.246	.333	.396	955	235	51	4	28	110	125	165
vs. Finesse	.268	.316	.447	246	66	17	0	9	32	17	29	.250	.307	.387	1045	261	52	5	27	120	86	156
vs. Power	.279	.383	.389	190	53	10	1	3	25	34	33	.264	.369	.401	751	198	40	6	17	92	129	143
on Grass	.263	.346	.331	118	31	2	0	2	14	15	18	.250	.308	.391	759	190	29	3	24	91	67	127
on Artificial Turf	.277	.347	.456	318	88	25	1	10	43	36	44	.259	.352	.393	1037	269	63	8	20	121	148	172
Day Games	.284	.338	.426	141	40	8	0	4	18	12	21	.257	.334	.406	608	156	34	3	17	78	74	109
Night Games	.268	.351	.420	295	79	19	1	8	39	39	41	.255	.334	.386	1188	303	58	8	27	134	141	190
April	.274	.316	.493	73	20	4	0	4	9	5	13	.240	.304	.372	258	62	13	0	7	24	24	52
May	.312	.423	.430	93	29	8	0	1	14	18	16	.247	.333	.364	324	80	17	0	7	36	42	60
June	.250	.329	.344	64	16	3	0	1	9	8	7	.246	.332	.401	342	84	15	4	10	45	45	67
July	.372	.437	.679	78	29	10	1	4	10	9	7	.283	.364	.457	304	86	21	4	8	38	39	36
August	.189	.256	.243	74	14	1	0	1	8	7	11	.248	.310	.349	318	79	11	3	5	33	29	42
Sept/Oct	.204	.259	.278	54	11	1	0	1	7	4	8	.272	.364	.416	250	68	15	0	7	36	36	42
Bases Empty	.279	.331	.459	244	68	15	1	9	9	19	36	.249	.317	.393	1038	258	51	6	29	29	104	173
Leadoff	.250	.280	.448	96	24	7	0	4	4	4	13	.245	.291	.394	371	91	15	2	12	12	24	67
Not Leadoff	.297	.362	.466	148	44	8	1	5	5	15	23	.250	.331	.393	667	167	36	4	17	17	80	106
Runners On	.266	.366	.375	192	51	12	0	3	48	32	26	.265	.358	.392	758	201	41	5	15	183	111	126
First Base Only	.250	.299	.361	72	18	5	0	1	3	5	9	.287	.346	.453	300	86	21	1	9	28	27	43
Scoring Position	.275	.400	.383	120	33	7	0	2	45	27	17	.251	.365	.352	458	115	20	4	6	155	84	83
Late Innings, Close	.297	.366	.473	74	22	5	1	2	12	8	6	.279	.355	.409	308	86	15	5	5	38	36	45

RBI/Opportunities

Scoring Position	42 / 181 (23%)	143 / 660 (22%)
Scoring Position, 2 Out	17 / 94 (18%)	57 / 289 (20%)
On Third, Less than 2 Out	17 / 31 (55%)	54 / 118 (46%)
RBI in close games / RBI Total	33 / 57 (58%)	140 / 212 (66%)

Charlie Leibrandt
Kansas City Royals

Charlie Leibrandt is the kind of pitcher that everyone seems to admire. You know, the kind of guy who doesn't seem to have great "stuff" but goes out there and wins anyway. He doesn't overpower hitters, but rather uses outstanding control to keep the runners off base.

Have you ever noticed how folks tend to see such pitchers as being more intelligent and gutsy than power pitchers? You take a quality control pitcher like Leibrandt and you automatically start hearing words like "smart," "doesn't give an inch," and "uses his talent to the fullest." On the other hand, we tend to assume that a wild power pitcher is all talent, no brains, and if he doesn't win, he's a bum. Get a control pitcher who can't quite cut it, and we tend to excuse him as not being able to overcome his obvious lack of talent.

Now think about that. Do power pitchers walk more because they are stupid? Do we really think not walking batters is so smart that it never occurred to power pitchers? Did you ever notice that a pitcher like Sandy Koufax, who had both great power and great control, was never referred to as a "smart" pitcher? Why is it smart for guys like Charlie Leibrandt to not walk batters, but not smart for someone like Koufax?

It's an odd set of prejudices, and probably should be reworked. Let's face it, to be a good major league pitcher you have to do something right. Usually you have either outstanding stuff or outstanding stuff. Sometimes you have both and go to the Hall of Fame; sometimes you have neither and end up in Elmira. But I don't see how we can assume so easily that which talent(s) a pitcher has is a function of intelligence. What about those power pitchers where the coach finds a mechanical flaw, and a slight correction zeros in his pitches on home plate? Do we say he must have stopped off at the drugstore and bought some "smart" pills?

Maybe throwing strikes is just as much a talent as the ability to throw hard. I suspect we see control pitchers as being smart and hard working because the talent of throwing strikes is simply not as obvious as the talent to throw hard. A power pitcher doesn't have more talent, just a different kind of talent, and if we realize that, we can stop looking for the "extra" that seemingly makes the "less" talented control pitcher successful.

Here's to a Charlie Leibrandt, not only a good pitcher, but a talented one.

Kent Kirchstein

Leibrandt, Charles Louis "Charlie"

Bats: Right   Throws: Left   Born 10/04/56

1987 SEASON AND MAJOR-LEAGUE CAREER PITCHING TOTALS

	G	GS	CG	GF	IP	BFP	H	R	ER	HR	SH	SF	HB	TBB	IBB	SO	WP	Bk	W	L	Pct	ShO	Sv	ERA
87 KC	35	35	8	0	240	1015	235	104	91	23	5	5	1	74	2	151	9	3	16	11	.593	3	0	3.41
8 YEARS	208	167	30	14	1169	4976	1214	533	480	88	56	29	14	362	22	526	27	15	74	55	.574	10	2	3.70

1987: Finesse, Groundball   1986: Finesse, Flyball   1985: Finesse, Groundball   1984: Finesse, Groundball

	1987 SEASON											FOUR YEAR TOTALS (1984 – 1987)										
	G	IP	H	BB	SO	SB	CS	W	L	S	ERA	G	IP	H	BB	SO	SB	CS	W	L	S	ERA
Totals	35	240.0	235	74	151	16	7	16	11	0	3.41	126	852.2	854	243	420	42	28	58	38	0	3.43
at Home	16	112.2	102	34	68	7	2	8	4	0	3.28	58	387.2	400	99	178	18	18	27	16	0	3.39
on Road	19	127.1	133	40	83	9	5	8	7	0	3.53	68	465.0	454	144	242	24	10	31	22	0	3.46
on Grass	7	37.0	44	15	22	2	0	3	2	0	4.38	29	197.1	198	52	84	14	7	16	8	0	3.06
on Artificial Turf	28	203.0	191	59	129	14	7	13	9	0	3.24	97	655.1	656	191	336	28	21	42	30	0	3.54
Day Games	13	89.1	96	27	58	7	4	7	4	0	3.43	49	327.2	331	104	164	18	7	22	16	0	3.65
Night Games	22	150.2	139	47	93	9	3	9	7	0	3.40	77	525.0	523	139	256	24	21	36	22	0	3.29
April	5	30.1	33	12	21	4	0	3	1	0	2.37	14	97.0	87	33	49	4	3	10	1	0	2.51
May	5	40.0	31	5	28	0	1	3	2	0	2.47	16	117.0	103	31	50	8	5	5	8	0	3.31
June	7	49.2	49	14	28	3	2	2	3	0	3.08	24	163.2	169	47	83	6	7	9	10	0	3.46
July	5	36.0	29	12	23	2	1	2	2	0	3.00	23	148.2	154	43	61	6	4	10	6	0	3.63
August	6	44.1	49	13	27	5	2	3	1	0	3.45	24	165.1	169	44	90	10	2	11	7	0	3.43
Sept/Oct	7	39.2	44	18	24	2	1	3	2	0	5.90	25	161.0	172	45	87	8	7	13	6	0	3.86

vs. Opponent Batters	Ave.	OBP	SLG	AB	H	2B	3B	HR	RBI	BB	SO	Ave.	OBP	SLG	AB	H	2B	3B	HR	RBI	BB	SO
Totals	.253	.307	.392	929	235	50	5	23	89	74	151	.260	.311	.383	3287	854	162	18	69	321	243	420
vs. Left	.232	.273	.310	155	36	4	1	2	12	9	23	.262	.306	.353	645	169	20	3	11	65	41	90
vs. Right	.257	.314	.408	774	199	46	4	21	77	65	128	.259	.312	.390	2642	685	142	15	58	256	202	330
Bases Empty	.257	.297	.425	567	146	36	4	17	17	32	95	.266	.307	.398	1969	524	105	10	45	45	116	250
Leadoff	.262	.291	.451	237	62	15	3	8	8	10	33	.264	.299	.393	842	222	43	6	18	42	79
Not Leadoff	.255	.301	.406	330	84	21	1	9	9	22	62	.268	.313	.402	1127	302	62	4	27	27	74	171
Runners On Base	.246	.322	.340	362	89	14	1	6	72	42	56	.250	.316	.360	1318	330	57	8	24	276	127	170
First Base Only	.309	.364	.409	149	46	9	0	2	5	13	24	.276	.326	.401	583	161	32	1	13	34	43	81
Scoring Position	.202	.294	.291	213	43	5	1	4	67	29	32	.230	.308	.328	735	169	25	7	11	242	84	89
Late Innings, Close	.202	.294	.348	89	18	5	1	2	6	12	14	.246	.315	.382	293	72	14	4	6	25	30	42

RBI/Opportunities

Scoring Position	61 / 295 (21%)	222 / 1011 (22%)
Scoring Position, 2 Out	22 / 143 (15%)	77 / 488 (16%)
On Third, Less than 2 Out	29 / 51 (57%)	99 / 178 (56%)
RBI in close games / RBI Total	59 / 89 (66%)	232 / 321 (72%)

Chet Lemon
Detroit Tigers

Chet Lemon has been a very good player in his big-league career. Since 1976, he has been one of the best center fielders in the AL; although he has never won a Gold Glove award, he almost certainly deserved a couple of them, most recently in 1984. Lemon set AL records in 1977 for most putouts by an outfielder with 512; he also holds the AL record for most years by an outfielder with 400 or more putouts with 5.

Lemon came to Detroit in the off-season of 1981–82. He suffered through a poor first year in his new home. One of the reasons seemed to be that he was moved from center field to right field by Sparky Anderson so that Kirk Gibson could play center. This must have been especially galling for Chet, since Gibson, a terrible outfielder and a young player, was displacing Lemon when he was an established star at his position. In 1983, Chet was back in center where he belonged; Gibson was back in right, although he didn't belong there either.

Chet didn't do any better offensively in 1983, but in the Tigers' magical 1984, he excelled, upping his BA and SA by over 30 points and playing brilliantly in the field. In 1985, he slumped like most of the Tigers; in 1986, he hit rock bottom in Detroit.

After 1984, the Tigers signed Lemon to a very long-term, guaranteed contract: He is theirs until the end of the 1992 season, for somewhat less than a million bucks a year.

As Chet struggled through 1986 along with the Tigers, the fans became increasingly vocal about their dislike for him. After all, he had a couple of nagging injuries, so he must have been dogging it, right? After all, why bust your butt when you are guaranteed a fat salary regardless of how you do, right? Wrong, dead wrong. The ironic part of this was that Lemon had gotten himself in trouble over his career in Detroit by playing over his injuries, hurting his performance and frequently re-injuring himself. Chet has always played full-speed-ahead baseball—he slides headfirst into first base on close plays there. How stupid to assume that he had become a loafer just because his paycheck was guaranteed!

Last season proved all these doubters wrong. Lemon, with the same cushy contract, played regularly and well. He has slowed down a couple steps on defense, but that is easily understandable due to his age. If anything, he tries too hard in the field to get to balls that he can't catch, watching hits skid by his sliding body instead of playing them safely on the hop.

In 1992 when his contract expires, Chet will be 37. He may be playing even then, or he may be just another memory of days gone by. Whichever, don't let anyone with his 25-cent analysis tell you that Lemon gave up because he had it made, and don't let anyone with an ax to grind tell you how it was all free agency's fault.

Gary Gillette

Lemon, Chester Earl "Chet"

Bats: Right   Throws: Right   Born 02/12/55

1987 SEASON AND MAJOR-LEAGUE CAREER BATTING TOTALS

	G	AB	H	2B	3B	HR	TB	R	RBI	TBB	IBB	SO	HP	SH	SF	SB	CS	SB%	GDP	AVG	OBP	SLG
87 DET	146	470	130	30	3	20	226	75	75	70	1	82	8	0	5	0	0	.00	17	.277	.376	.481
13 YEARS	1612	5620	1559	332	51	186	2551	822	741	596	34	827	132	45	47	53	67	.44	141	.277	.358	.454

	1987 SEASON											FOUR YEAR TOTALS (1984 – 1987)									
	Ave.	OBP	SLG	AB	H	2B	3B	HR	RBI	BB	SO	Ave.	OBP	SLG	AB	H	2B	3B	HR	RBI	BB	SO
Totals	.277	.376	.481	470	130	30	3	20	75	70	82	.271	.349	.458	1899	514	113	16	70	272	205	311
vs. Left	.272	.382	.494	180	49	14	1	8	24	32	26	.318	.390	.552	689	219	53	6	32	108	82	105
vs. Right	.279	.372	.472	290	81	16	2	12	51	38	56	.244	.326	.404	1210	295	60	10	38	164	123	206
at Home	.260	.379	.471	223	58	17	0	10	34	40	44	.266	.350	.458	912	243	51	5	38	130	104	146
on Road	.291	.373	.490	247	72	13	3	10	41	30	38	.275	.349	.457	987	271	62	11	32	142	101	165
vs. Groundball	.289	.381	.435	246	71	17	2	5	31	35	40	.289	.367	.466	902	261	55	10	28	126	97	147
vs. Flyball	.263	.371	.531	224	59	13	1	15	44	35	42	.254	.333	.450	997	253	58	6	42	146	108	164
vs. Finesse	.295	.366	.493	268	79	21	1	10	38	30	34	.288	.353	.475	1092	314	76	9	37	147	95	148
vs. Power	.252	.388	.465	202	51	9	2	10	37	40	48	.248	.345	.434	807	200	37	7	33	125	110	163
on Grass	.276	.382	.481	399	110	25	3	17	61	65	70	.269	.347	.456	1621	436	91	13	62	228	171	259
on Artificial Turf	.282	.338	.479	71	20	5	0	3	14	5	12	.281	.364	.468	278	78	22	3	8	44	34	52
Day Games	.291	.384	.624	141	41	12	1	11	27	17	30	.266	.337	.491	613	163	35	5	31	100	54	110
Night Games	.271	.373	.419	329	89	18	2	9	48	53	52	.273	.355	.442	1286	351	78	11	39	172	151	201
April	.180	.354	.361	61	11	3	1	2	6	15	9	.258	.339	.446	267	69	20	3	8	35	31	35
May	.279	.415	.488	43	12	3	0	2	8	9	9	.309	.390	.482	272	84	14	3	9	45	35	48
June	.287	.360	.540	87	25	7	0	5	21	10	14	.257	.313	.457	304	78	24	2	11	46	25	42
July	.297	.388	.486	74	22	2	0	4	13	10	14	.277	.343	.398	329	91	18	2	6	31	32	60
August	.380	.426	.630	92	35	11	0	4	15	6	18	.271	.323	.472	343	93	18	0	17	56	25	62
Sept/Oct	.221	.341	.372	113	25	4	2	3	12	20	18	.258	.354	.487	384	99	19	6	19	59	57	64
Bases Empty	.261	.364	.466	253	66	12	2	12	12	38	51	.265	.335	.462	1026	272	65	10	39	39	105	172
Leadoff	.257	.325	.422	109	28	6	0	4	4	9	19	.281	.335	.481	430	121	33	1	17	17	33	66
Not Leadoff	.264	.391	.500	144	38	6	2	8	8	29	32	.253	.335	.448	596	151	32	9	22	22	72	106
Runners On	.295	.390	.498	217	64	18	1	8	63	32	31	.277	.353	.452	873	242	48	6	31	233	100	139
First Base Only	.260	.343	.417	96	25	7	1	2	6	9	13	.274	.325	.423	409	112	22	3	11	33	28	59
Scoring Position	.322	.424	.562	121	39	11	0	6	57	23	18	.280	.376	.478	464	130	26	3	20	200	72	80
Late Innings, Close	.206	.286	.349	63	13	4	1	1	8	7	14	.251	.331	.385	299	75	15	2	7	37	36	49

RBI/Opportunities

Scoring Position	47 / 178	(26%)	162 / 671	(24%)
Scoring Position, 2 Out	14 / 74	(19%)	69 / 326	(21%)
On Third, Less than 2 Out	18 / 46	(39%)	56 / 126	(44%)
RBI in close games / RBI Total	31 / 75	(41%)	140 / 272	(51%)

Jeffrey Leonard
San Francisco Giants

I am occasionally dumbfounded at what upsets people. A caller to a local radio show recently suggested (seriously) that the umpires should put a stopwatch on hitters who have just homered, with the idea being that anyone who takes longer than 25 seconds to round the bases would be called out. Now, I like a briskly played game as well as the next fan, but, if you want to speed up games, you might as well order all relief pitchers to run in from the bullpen like Craig Lefferts does. Jeffrey has always had what the players call a "Cadillac" home run trot. Even serious Giant fans did not realize that "one flap down" was a significant change for Jeffrey. It doesn't seem to me that this behavior is deserving of any more attention, or uproar, than starting a game (or an inning) with a somersault or backflip. And, I honestly wonder if anyone would have batted an eye if it had been Jack Clark, or Will Clark. How come Jeffrey Leonard, Dave Parker, and Vic Power are "showboats," while Mickey Hatcher and Joe Charbonneau are "eccentric"? I was born at night, folks, but I wasn't born last night.

So who is this stone-faced man that Roger Craig describes as "the heart and soul" of his team? Leonard played over a month in 1986 with a severely injured wrist, because Craig said "an 0-for-4 Jeffrey Leonard is still going to play for me, because of the intensity he drags out of his teammates." Leonard was viewed as the key to the advent of the Al Rosen/Roger Craig era. Jeffrey was known to wear his cap backwards during batting practice, and brought his hard-ass attitude into the clubhouse and dugout. When Leonard heard Craig wouldn't tolerate anyone out of uniform, his reaction was "Well, I guess I'm gone." Instead, he discovered in Roger Craig a competitor as intense as himself, who brought a totally positive attitude to the ballpark and tolerated no negativity at all.

It must have made a difference. Going into 1986, Jeffrey needed to be jump started around Memorial Day each year. Under Roger Craig, he has hit .354 and .329 in April, .381 and .315 in May. He led the National League in hitting for 21 days in 1987, hitting .374 as of May 27. Although he wound up hitting .280, he was again hampered by injuries in the second half, with a hamstring pull and a nagging wrist injury.

Leonard's LCS was so outstanding that he became one of the few members of a losing sports team to be honored as MVP (.417 BA, .500 OBA, .917 SLG). He took the award with typical Jeffrey Leonard class—'I'd trade the award, and the $50,000 bonus in my contract, for a ticket to Minnesota. I'm sure this will mean something after I retire, but we still have a job to do." Division champions rarely repeat, but, with Jeffrey kicking tail and taking names, the Giants will not find it easy to get complacent.

J. Michael Duca

Leonard, Jeffrey "Jeff" Bats: Right Throws: Right Born 09/22/55

1987 SEASON AND MAJOR-LEAGUE CAREER BATTING TOTALS

	G	AB	H	2B	3B	HR	TB	R	RBI	TBB	IBB	SO	HP	SH	SF	SB	CS	SB%	GDP	AVG	OBP	SLG
87 SF	131	503	141	29	4	19	235	70	63	21	6	68	2	0	5	16	7	.70	17	.280	.309	.467
11 YEARS	993	3467	949	156	35	100	1475	449	491	242	31	686	12	7	33	136	49	.74	99	.274	.320	.425

1987 SEASON

	Ave.	OBP	SLG	AB	H	2B	3B	HR	RBI	BB	SO
Totals	.280	.309	.467	503	141	29	4	19	64	21	68
vs. Left	.283	.306	.462	145	41	11	0	5	16	6	17
vs. Right	.279	.310	.469	358	100	18	4	14	48	15	51
at Home	.280	.311	.471	225	63	14	1	9	27	11	37
on Road	.281	.307	.464	278	78	15	3	10	37	10	31
vs. Groundball	.320	.337	.525	244	78	16	2	10	34	6	27
vs. Flyball	.243	.283	.413	259	63	13	2	9	30	15	41
vs. Finesse	.272	.300	.480	246	67	17	2	10	32	9	25
vs. Power	.288	.317	.455	257	74	12	2	9	32	12	43
on Grass	.277	.309	.463	365	101	21	1	15	43	17	51
on Artificial Turf	.290	.308	.478	138	40	8	3	4	21	4	17
Day Games	.303	.329	.472	218	66	12	2	7	27	10	38
Night Games	.263	.293	.463	285	75	17	2	12	37	11	30
April	.354	.391	.634	82	29	6	1	5	16	5	10
May	.381	.403	.743	113	43	14	3	7	17	4	13
June	.196	.223	.289	97	19	3	0	2	7	3	15
July	.225	.279	.343	102	23	6	0	2	9	8	18
August	.267	.273	.307	75	20	0	0	1	11	1	11
Sept/Oct	.206	.206	.382	34	7	0	0	2	4	0	1
Bases Empty	.297	.316	.530	283	84	21	3	13	13	8	36
Leadoff	.316	.333	.570	79	25	6	1	4	4	2	6
Not Leadoff	.289	.310	.515	204	59	15	2	9	9	6	30
Runners On	.259	.300	.386	220	57	8	1	6	51	13	32
First Base Only	.276	.300	.425	87	24	5	1	2	7	2	9
Scoring Position	.248	.300	.361	133	33	3	0	4	44	11	23
Late Innings, Close	.284	.330	.432	88	25	3	2	2	10	7	11

FOUR YEAR TOTALS (1984 – 1987)

	Ave.	OBP	SLG	AB	H	2B	3B	HR	RBI	BB	SO
Totals	.275	.315	.436	1865	513	88	12	63	254	109	360
vs. Left	.313	.339	.527	571	179	32	3	28	85	24	66
vs. Right	.258	.305	.396	1294	334	56	9	35	169	85	294
at Home	.282	.322	.444	891	251	37	6	32	113	53	191
on Road	.269	.309	.429	974	262	51	6	31	141	56	169
vs. Groundball	.312	.345	.461	861	269	46	5	24	124	42	122
vs. Flyball	.243	.289	.415	1004	244	42	7	39	130	67	238
vs. Finesse	.281	.315	.458	1026	288	50	6	40	144	50	167
vs. Power	.268	.315	.410	839	225	38	6	23	110	59	193
on Grass	.278	.318	.448	1394	388	60	7	54	200	82	281
on Artificial Turf	.265	.305	.403	471	125	28	5	9	54	27	79
Day Games	.293	.329	.463	882	258	42	6	32	122	50	190
Night Games	.259	.302	.413	983	255	46	6	31	132	59	170
April	.277	.328	.473	311	86	16	3	13	48	24	64
May	.312	.354	.500	362	113	24	4	12	47	23	68
June	.254	.295	.406	429	109	15	4	14	51	25	89
July	.269	.312	.412	364	98	19	0	11	43	23	66
August	.301	.328	.473	239	72	9	1	10	45	10	45
Sept/Oct	.219	.238	.306	160	35	5	0	3	20	4	28
Bases Empty	.280	.311	.458	974	273	54	7	35	35	44	177
Leadoff	.292	.313	.488	373	109	20	4	15	15	11	62
Not Leadoff	.273	.311	.439	601	164	34	3	20	20	33	115
Runners On	.269	.319	.413	891	240	34	5	28	219	65	183
First Base Only	.301	.336	.443	359	108	17	2	10	30	18	53
Scoring Position	.248	.308	.393	532	132	17	3	18	189	47	130
Late Innings, Close	.254	.309	.395	339	86	13	4	9	37	28	76

RBI/Opportunities

Scoring Position	38 / 167 (23%)	155 / 678 (23%)
Scoring Position, 2 Out	12 / 62 (19%)	55 / 291 (19%)
On Third, Less than 2 Out	20 / 40 (50%)	64 / 131 (49%)
RBI in close games / RBI Total	50 / 64 (78%)	189 / 254 (74%)

Steve Lombardozzi
Minnesota Twins

One of Manager Tom Kelly's few public displays of emotion came in the top of the ninth inning of the sixth game of the World Series. With the Twins leading 11–5 and the Cardinals down to their last out, Tom Herr grounded the ball through the hole to right field. It should have been a routine out, but Steve Lombardozzi had moved to cover second base when Vince Coleman broke from first base on the pitch. A glance into the dugout quickly made it clear this was not the intended plan. Standing capless in the dugout, Kelly glowered out at Lombo with that mixture of disbelief and anger common to hard-nosed managers.

While one dumb play was unlikely to prevent a Twins victory, Jeff Reardon would have to throw more pitches than necessary with a seventh game in the offing. Although the play was never made an issue after the game, another sign of the skipper's unhappiness was the insertion of Al Newman at second base for the final innings of the deciding game.

A glance at Lombardozzi's offensive statistics indicate why such mistakes might bring a lasting and angry response. Steve simply must provide solid defensive play to justify his starting role. Except for his walk totals, his offensive numbers in 1987 were similar to his '86 figures. Given his young age, there had been hope for improvement.

He did have his moments in '87, though. A ninth inning three-run homer in Seattle ignited an exciting Twins victory. His three-run homer at Texas in September helped win the pennant, and he had some timely hits in the Series. With his defense and strike zone judgment, he should be able to get by with a .260 BA.

Earlier in the year there were already signs that Lombardozzi was not one of Kelly's favorite players. Much of the reduction in Lombo's playing time came when the manager attempted to institute a platoon system in the middle infield. Newman was unable to win a full-time job at second, but he continued to make regular appearances as Kelly kept the bench active.

Lombardozzi made it to the majors on the strength of his defense. In 1985 the Twins grew dissatisfied with the fielding of Tim Teufel and his inability to turn the double play to their satisfaction—the Twins' pitching staff has a knack of forcing recognition of these deficiencies. Lombo, called up in late August of '85, hit well enough in September to encourage an off-season trade of Teufel. Because he has good range and makes a quick pivot on the DP, his defense at second base has kept him in the lineup, but the feeling lingers that he has to do more or 1988 may be his last in a Twins uniform.

Bill Jensen

Lombardozzi, Stephen Paul "Steve"

Bats: Right   Throws: Right   Born 04/26/60

1987 SEASON AND MAJOR-LEAGUE CAREER BATTING TOTALS

	G	AB	H	2B	3B	HR	TB	R	RBI	TBB	IBB	SO	HP	SH	SF	SB	CS	SB%	GDP	AVG	OBP	SLG
87 MIN	136	432	103	19	3	8	152	51	38	33	1	66	4	9	1	5	1	.83	10	.238	.298	.352
3 YEARS	320	939	226	43	9	16	335	114	77	91	3	148	5	22	2	11	4	.73	18	.241	.311	.357

1987 SEASON

	Ave.	OBP	SLG	AB	H	2B	3B	HR	RBI	BB	SO
Totals	.238	.298	.352	432	103	19	3	8	38	33	66
vs. Left	.288	.333	.417	139	40	10	1	2	10	9	17
vs. Right	.215	.281	.321	293	63	9	2	6	28	24	49
at Home	.211	.272	.315	213	45	9	2	3	15	18	29
on Road	.265	.324	.388	219	58	10	1	5	23	15	37
vs. Groundball	.258	.297	.382	217	56	12	3	3	20	12	23
vs. Flyball	.219	.299	.321	215	47	7	0	5	18	21	43
vs. Finesse	.294	.340	.443	221	65	12	3	5	25	15	18
vs. Power	.180	.254	.256	211	38	7	0	3	13	18	48
on Grass	.267	.328	.382	165	44	5	1	4	18	11	29
on Artificial Turf	.221	.279	.333	267	59	14	2	4	20	22	37
Day Games	.252	.321	.370	127	32	8	2	1	8	10	22
Night Games	.233	.288	.344	305	71	11	1	7	30	23	44
April	.245	.362	.347	49	12	2	0	1	3	9	11
May	.303	.347	.404	89	27	3	0	2	5	6	5
June	.145	.192	.174	69	10	2	0	0	1	2	8
July	.250	.286	.425	80	20	5	3	1	10	3	9
August	.241	.322	.380	79	19	5	0	2	13	9	18
Sept/Oct	.227	.271	.348	66	15	2	0	2	6	4	15
Bases Empty	.235	.295	.342	272	64	14	0	5	5	20	40
Leadoff	.283	.325	.416	113	32	6	0	3	3	7	23
Not Leadoff	.201	.274	.289	159	32	8	0	2	2	13	17
Runners On	.244	.303	.369	160	39	5	3	3	33	13	26
First Base Only	.215	.261	.215	65	14	0	0	0	2	4	11
Scoring Position	.263	.330	.474	95	25	5	3	3	31	9	15
Late Innings, Close	.245	.373	.388	49	12	1	0	2	8	9	6

FOUR YEAR TOTALS (1984 – 1987)

	Ave.	OBP	SLG	AB	H	2B	3B	HR	RBI	BB	SO
Totals	.241	.311	.357	939	226	43	9	16	77	91	148
vs. Left	.257	.319	.386	280	72	19	1	5	27	25	36
vs. Right	.234	.307	.344	659	154	24	8	11	50	66	112
at Home	.243	.314	.375	477	116	26	5	9	42	49	69
on Road	.238	.307	.338	462	110	17	4	7	35	42	79
vs. Groundball	.262	.323	.386	451	118	23	6	7	33	40	54
vs. Flyball	.221	.299	.330	488	108	20	3	9	44	51	94
vs. Finesse	.280	.341	.429	510	143	27	8	11	56	46	53
vs. Power	.193	.275	.270	429	83	16	1	5	21	45	95
on Grass	.239	.310	.342	348	83	10	4	6	30	32	63
on Artificial Turf	.242	.311	.365	591	143	33	5	10	47	59	85
Day Games	.232	.300	.343	280	65	16	3	3	19	24	47
Night Games	.244	.315	.363	659	161	27	6	13	58	67	101
April	.235	.318	.347	98	23	5	0	2	7	12	21
May	.280	.356	.470	168	47	7	2	7	21	20	19
June	.241	.308	.319	166	40	7	3	0	5	14	18
July	.219	.276	.364	151	33	10	3	2	12	11	24
August	.201	.286	.280	164	33	7	0	2	16	19	33
Sept/Oct	.260	.314	.354	192	50	7	1	3	16	15	33
Bases Empty	.243	.299	.359	585	142	30	4	10	10	44	84
Leadoff	.273	.313	.427	253	69	14	2	7	7	15	42
Not Leadoff	.220	.288	.307	332	73	16	2	3	3	29	42
Runners On	.237	.328	.353	354	84	13	5	6	67	47	64
First Base Only	.242	.294	.282	149	36	2	2	0	5	11	23
Scoring Position	.234	.350	.405	205	48	11	3	6	62	36	41
Late Innings, Close	.264	.347	.391	110	29	3	1	3	13	13	15

RBI/Opportunities

Scoring Position	25 / 128 (20%)	49 / 288 (17%)
Scoring Position, 2 Out	14 / 59 (24%)	29 / 144 (20%)
On Third, Less than 2 Out	6 / 17 (35%)	9 / 37 (24%)
RBI in close games / RBI Total	24 / 38 (63%)	47 / 77 (61%)

Fred Lynn
Baltimore Orioles

Is there tragedy in Fred Lynn's career? I think so—but probably not the same one that most people do. I don't grieve over the thought that Lynn's injuries will keep him out of the Hall of Fame, for two reasons.

Reason one is that Lynn is a "fair-good" shot to make it. In his 1986 *Abstract*, Bill James introduced a "Hall of Fame Projection System," a point-count system of career achievements based on past voting trends. If you get 100 or more points in a career, you either have been or will be elected to the Hall of Fame; 90–99 gives you a strong chance; 80–89 means that you'd better have some serious intangibles. Currently Lynn has 83 points, giving him (I'd guess) a 40 percent chance of election so far.

Also, unless Lynn completely collapses, he should end his career with 300 homers (he has 264) and 2000 hits (1732 so far), which would push his career total up to 90, increasing the chance to probably 55 percent.

Finally, Fred's injuries—which are currently working against him on the field—will eventually work for him with the voters. These people are usually very kind to injury-prone stars; Lynn is an easy case to make. The man was an MVP, a batting champ, a nine-time All-Star, four-time Gold Glove winner, averaged .290 with 25 homers and 75 walks . . . gee, what *would* he have done if he'd stayed healthy?

The other reason I don't grieve for Lynn is that he doesn't deserve it. A Jack Clark or Chris Brown—who tries his best but just can't stay healthy—is one thing; a guy who spends his career running into walls and breaking up double plays in blowouts is another. Durability entails making certain sacrifices; players who have long careers because they never do suicidal things usually get a rap for not hustling because of it. Lynn prefers the "Fragile Fred" nickname to the sort of treatment that teammate Eddie Murray has received; that's his choice.

Now what I do think is a tragedy is that Lynn never had a chance to play for Gene Mauch or Earl Weaver earlier in his career. Looking at the number of players on the contending Boston teams who had injuries eat holes in their careers (Lynn, Rick Burleson, Bill Campbell, Carlton Fisk, Jim Willoughby, Jerry Remy, Butch Hobson), you really have to believe that bad management was to blame for some of them. I mean, someone could have told them that it's better to give 85 percent in 150 games than it is to give 100 percent in 120 games; it seems clear that nobody ever did. I think that Weaver, Mauch or half a dozen other managers would have tried to do that—and probably could have succeeded. Lynn doesn't seem unintelligent; it just looks like he's never learned the facts of life. As a result, he'll never win another MVP award—unless, of course, you happen to have his card in your table-top league this year.

Geoff Beckman

Lynn, Fredric Michael "Fred"

Bats: Left   Throws: Left   Born 02/03/52

1987 SEASON AND MAJOR-LEAGUE CAREER BATTING TOTALS

	G	AB	H	2B	3B	HR	TB	R	RBI	TBB	IBB	SO	HP	SH	SF	SB	CS	SB%	GDP	AVG	OBP	SLG
87 BAL	111	396	100	24	0	23	193	49	60	39	6	72	1	0	2	3	7	.30	8	.253	.320	.487
14 YEARS	1648	5985	1732	360	40	264	2964	955	986	755	73	919	27	23	72	67	51	.57	134	.289	.368	.495

	1987 SEASON											FOUR YEAR TOTALS (1984 – 1987)									
	Ave.	OBP	SLG	AB	H	2B	3B	HR	RBI	BB	SO	Ave.	OBP	SLG	AB	H	2B	3B	HR	RBI	BB	SO
Totals	.253	.320	.487	396	100	24	0	23	60	39	72	.268	.350	.476	1758	472	77	6	92	274	222	329
vs. Left	.224	.297	.400	125	28	7	0	5	11	13	28	.238	.322	.424	509	121	25	2	22	76	61	125
vs. Right	.266	.330	.528	271	72	17	0	18	49	26	44	.281	.361	.497	1249	351	52	4	70	198	161	204
at Home	.241	.290	.461	191	46	9	0	11	28	14	30	.259	.338	.492	847	219	34	1	54	147	102	163
on Road	.263	.346	.512	205	54	15	0	12	32	25	42	.278	.361	.461	911	253	43	5	38	127	120	166
vs. Groundball	.280	.330	.495	214	60	13	0	11	35	16	38	.300	.381	.523	923	277	47	3	51	150	121	157
vs. Flyball	.220	.307	.478	182	40	11	0	12	25	23	34	.234	.315	.424	835	195	30	3	41	124	101	172
vs. Finesse	.282	.343	.500	188	53	14	0	9	25	17	25	.287	.358	.493	971	279	43	5	49	143	108	132
vs. Power	.226	.299	.476	208	47	10	0	14	35	22	47	.245	.341	.455	787	193	34	1	43	131	114	197
on Grass	.251	.321	.501	351	88	19	0	23	58	36	64	.268	.351	.478	1456	390	60	3	80	233	186	274
on Artificial Turf	.267	.313	.378	45	12	5	0	0	2	3	8	.272	.347	.467	302	82	17	3	12	41	36	55
Day Games	.229	.314	.486	105	24	6	0	7	20	12	23	.271	.362	.515	458	124	20	1	30	81	66	97
Night Games	.261	.322	.488	291	76	18	0	16	40	27	49	.268	.345	.462	1300	348	57	5	62	193	156	232
April	.208	.311	.312	77	16	5	0	1	5	11	14	.280	.366	.412	311	87	15	1	8	29	42	49
May	.316	.396	.620	79	25	3	0	7	17	11	14	.291	.373	.512	326	95	10	1	20	59	43	56
June	.228	.299	.405	79	18	2	0	4	13	8	13	.223	.296	.403	273	61	5	1	14	42	28	54
July	.263	.282	.579	38	10	6	0	2	7	1	5	.282	.332	.539	308	87	21	2	18	54	23	65
August	.294	.333	.647	68	20	3	0	7	13	4	20	.271	.386	.487	306	83	13	1	17	50	57	67
Sept/Oct	.200	.254	.400	55	11	5	0	2	5	4	6	.252	.335	.500	234	59	13	0	15	40	29	38
Bases Empty	.250	.297	.479	240	60	16	0	13	13	15	38	.266	.336	.470	986	262	50	5	47	47	104	189
Leadoff	.230	.267	.430	100	23	5	0	5	5	5	13	.232	.303	.395	357	83	14	1	14	14	36	57
Not Leadoff	.264	.318	.514	140	37	11	0	8	8	10	25	.285	.355	.512	629	179	36	4	33	33	68	132
Runners On	.256	.352	.500	156	40	8	0	10	47	24	34	.272	.368	.484	772	210	27	1	45	227	118	140
First Base Only	.260	.308	.411	73	19	5	0	2	5	5	11	.287	.362	.455	376	108	16	1	15	36	44	60
Scoring Position	.253	.385	.578	83	21	3	0	8	42	19	23	.258	.373	.513	396	102	11	0	30	191	74	80
Late Innings, Close	.247	.310	.442	77	19	3	0	4	12	6	18	.258	.359	.455	279	72	11	1	14	41	43	64

RBI/Opportunities

Scoring Position	26 / 125 (21%)	136 / 564 (24%)
Scoring Position, 2 Out	7 / 48 (15%)	37 / 230 (16%)
On Third, Less than 2 Out	13 / 29 (45%)	69 / 121 (57%)
RBI in close games / RBI Total	53 / 60 (88%)	183 / 274 (67%)

Bill Madlock
Los Angeles Dodgers/Detroit Tigers

The fascinating thing about history is that it truly does repeat. In 1984, the Detroit Tigers, who needed some lefty punch, signed veteran free agent Ruppert Jones. Jones hit .284 and slugged .516 in a platoon role; Detroit won the AL East. In 1987, the Detroit Tigers, who needed some righty punch, signed veteran free agent Bill Madlock. Madlock hit .279 and slugged .450 in a part-time role; Detroit won the AL East. It was the third time in his career that Madlock had joined a team in mid-season and helped win them a division title.

Though you could argue either way about Rupe, I'm sure that without Madlock Detroit would never have beaten Toronto. Until the Mad Dog arrived, Alan Trammell and Chet Lemon were the only two Tiger righties with any amount of sock in their bats. To make matters worse, almost all of the Tigers have major problems against lefties—they either lose their power (Kirk Gibson), their average (Darrell Evans) or both (Lou Whitaker). The imbalance was deadly; opposing lefties were clobbering Detroit.

Madlock was signed on June 4; at the time, Detroit was 5–10 (.333 record; #12 in the AL) and scoring 3.93 runs per game (#13 in the AL) against southpaw starters. After he arrived, they were 17–19 (.472) and scored 6.64 R/G. While Madlock is obviously not responsible for all of that improvement, he definitely played a part in it. His slugging percentage was the fourth best on the team (Herndon, Trammell, Lemon); he created 5.03 runs per 27 outs, sixth best on the team (Herndon, Trammell, Lemon, Dwight Lowry, Mike Heath).

If you've already looked at Madlock's platoon breakdowns, you may be wondering about my sanity or the proofreading. No, I'm not crazy and that is no misprint—Bill did hit better against righties; there are two reasons why. The first is that Madlock's body began to wear down in mid-August; he played very little in the last ten games of the season. When he did play, it was generally against lefties; he simply didn't do the job. The second reason? The man has a .305 career average and has won four batting titles; you can't do that unless you can hit righties.

Despite Madlock's production, his future in Motown is cloudy. Though Detroit would like to re-sign Madlock, they're unwilling to pay a 37-year-old first baseman/DH a high salary. Given their team platoon splits in batting average (.262; .276 vs. righties), on-base percentage (.337/.355) and slugging percentage (.417/.466), I think that they need Madlock—or someone like him—very badly in 1988. If (as they did with Jones after '84) Detroit decides to economize here, then (as happened in 1985), I think that they will pay for it on the field in 1988.

Steve Lysogorski

Madlock, Bill · **Bats: Right** **Throws: Right** **Born 01/12/51**

1987 SEASON AND MAJOR-LEAGUE CAREER BATTING TOTALS

	G	AB	H	2B	3B	HR	TB	R	RBI	TBB	IBB	SO	HP	SH	SF	SB	CS	SB%	GDP	AVG	OBP	SLG
87 LA-DET	108	387	102	18	0	17	171	61	57	34	1	50	11	9	4	4	3	.57	14	.264	.337	.442
15 YEARS	1806	6594	2008	348	34	163	2913	920	860	605	121	510	68	36	69	174	90	.66	190	.305	.365	.442

	1987 SEASON											FOUR YEAR TOTALS (1984 – 1987)										
	Ave.	OBP	SLG	AB	H	2B	3B	HR	RBI	BB	SO	Ave.	OBP	SLG	AB	H	2B	3B	HR	RBI	BB	SO
Totals	.264	.338	.443	386	102	18	0	17	57	34	50	.268	.331	.393	1681	451	78	1	43	217	141	175
vs. Left	.267	.323	.465	172	46	10	0	8	28	13	26	.282	.345	.439	586	165	32	0	20	86	57	62
vs. Right	.262	.350	.425	214	56	8	0	9	29	21	24	.261	.323	.368	1095	286	46	1	23	131	84	113
at Home	.261	.322	.433	180	47	7	0	8	28	14	22	.273	.341	.388	812	222	36	0	19	111	78	87
on Road	.267	.352	.451	206	55	11	0	9	29	20	28	.264	.321	.397	869	229	42	1	24	106	63	88
vs. Groundball	.279	.347	.429	219	61	9	0	8	28	20	25	.279	.341	.383	827	231	30	1	18	93	69	87
vs. Flyball	.246	.326	.461	167	41	9	0	9	29	14	25	.258	.321	.402	854	220	48	0	25	124	72	88
vs. Finesse	.284	.322	.442	190	54	6	0	8	32	10	14	.278	.317	.387	969	269	41	1	21	123	53	84
vs. Power	.245	.352	.444	196	48	12	0	9	25	24	36	.256	.348	.400	712	182	37	0	22	94	88	91
on Grass	.272	.326	.456	309	84	15	0	14	50	21	37	.277	.333	.410	903	250	36	0	28	115	68	84
on Artificial Turf	.234	.379	.390	77	18	3	0	3	7	13	13	.258	.328	.373	778	201	42	1	15	102	73	91
Day Games	.272	.362	.580	81	22	4	0	7	14	9	11	.292	.341	.434	489	143	18	0	17	65	33	52
Night Games	.262	.331	.407	305	80	14	0	10	43	25	39	.258	.327	.376	1192	308	60	1	26	152	108	123
April	.143	.250	.143	7	1	0	0	0	1	1	2	.192	.235	.254	177	34	8	0	1	16	10	16
May	.189	.271	.377	53	10	1	0	3	6	5	3	.257	.316	.343	303	78	11	0	5	27	25	34
June	.301	.344	.542	83	25	2	0	6	13	3	7	.268	.322	.428	355	95	16	1	13	41	26	30
July	.297	.416	.500	64	19	1	0	4	10	10	12	.273	.343	.410	300	82	14	0	9	44	29	33
August	.355	.451	.553	76	27	9	0	2	13	10	7	.316	.391	.475	263	83	15	0	9	47	29	24
Sept/Oct	.194	.227	.301	103	20	5	0	2	14	5	19	.279	.329	.392	283	79	14	0	6	42	22	38
Bases Empty	.244	.305	.438	217	53	12	0	10	10	18	28	.257	.304	.383	945	243	45	1	24	24	62	101
Leadoff	.367	.433	.650	60	22	5	0	4	4	7	7	.298	.349	.455	319	95	17	0	11	11	25	30
Not Leadoff	.197	.254	.357	157	31	7	0	6	6	11	21	.236	.280	.347	626	148	28	1	13	13	37	71
Runners On	.290	.377	.450	169	49	6	0	7	47	16	22	.283	.358	.405	736	208	33	0	19	193	79	74
First Base Only	.338	.407	.623	77	26	4	0	6	14	5	8	.283	.341	.479	315	89	17	0	15	37	24	30
Scoring Position	.250	.354	.304	92	23	2	0	1	33	11	14	.283	.370	.349	421	119	16	0	4	156	55	44
Late Innings, Close	.311	.380	.489	45	14	2	0	2	6	5	6	.246	.310	.336	289	71	11	0	5	35	27	28

RBI/Opportunities

Scoring Position	32 / 135 (24%)	150 / 588 (26%)
Scoring Position, 2 Out	14 / 57 (25%)	43 / 235 (18%)
On Third, Less than 2 Out	15 / 31 (48%)	73 / 127 (57%)
RBI in close games / RBI Total	37 / 57 (65%)	156 / 217 (72%)

Rick Mahler
Atlanta Braves

Rick Mahler turned 34 in 1987, and that, more than his performance the past two years, will be his biggest obstacle to overcome in 1988. With the Braves being as pitching rich as they are, Mahler will undoubtedly get a shot to go for a record fourth opening day shutout. But if he continues to perform at '86 and '87 levels, he may need to look for a new occupation.

When Rick is on, he is an ideal type of pitcher for Fulton County Stadium. He keeps the ball down, doesn't surrender home runs, and gets a large number of double plays. But unfortunately for the Braves, Mahler has not been on since 1985. After a 1986 campaign that had to be one of the worst seasons ever for a full season rotation starter, Mahler was again named #1 starter by Chuck Tanner. On Opening Night Mahler turned in a brilliant two hit shutout against the Phillies, his first and last good outing in 1987.

The two statistics that seem to jump off the page at you are walks and hits allowed. In 1984 Mahler had a year that would fall somewhere in the "above average to good" category (13–10, 3.12 ERA). That year he threw 222 innings and allowed but 62 walks, an average of 1 walk every 3.58 innings. In 1985 that average was 1 walk every 3.37 innings and in 1986 he gave the opposition a free base runner every 2.50 innings. 1987 continued the downward slide in the walk department, when he walked a batter once every 2.32 innings. Chances are that these numbers are a result of a re-

alization by the opposition that patience at the plate will result in walks. The other major problem that plagued Mahler in 1987 was his tendency to give up hits. He allowed 212 hits in only 197 innings. A quick look through the 15 best NL pitchers in terms of ERA shows only one case where the pitcher allowed more hits than innings pitched.

Finally, even Mr. Positive, Chuck Tanner, tossed in the towel and banished Mahler to the bullpen, where, in long relief, he turned in a 2–1 record with a 4.15 ERA in 26 innings. This doesn't look like much of a haven for an older player with Mahler's salary. One of the many Braves problems with their pitching is that they have a number of pitchers with similar characteristics to Mahler. Zane Smith, Jeff Dedmon, Gene Garber, and Charlie Puleo are all pitchers who try to keep the ball down, don't strike out many people, and rely on their defense. Building your staff for your ball park is a good idea but the Braves have carried it to an extreme. The Braves defense is above average at only two positions (2B and RF) and adding a strikeout pitcher just for variety would probably help the staff. The Braves staff was last in the majors in strikeouts in 1987.

Despite his troubles, Rick Mahler has endured with quiet dignity. He is a player that one hopes will do well— but given his age and the youth movement he is likely to be phased out in 1988.

Greg Gajus and Doug White

Mahler, Richard Keith "Ricky" Bats: Right Throws: Right Born 08/05/53

1987 SEASON AND MAJOR-LEAGUE CAREER PITCHING TOTALS

	G	GS	CG	GF	IP	BFP	H	R	ER	HR	SH	SF	HB	TBB	IBB	SO	WP	Bk	W	L	Pct	ShO	Sv	ERA
87 ATL	39	28	3	1	197	849	212	118	109	24	9	3	2	85	8	95	5	2	8	13	.381	1	0	4.98
9 YEARS	255	182	31	18	1281	5448	1344	630	573	113	57	35	12	446	46	624	28	9	69	72	.489	6	2	4.03

1987: Finesse, Groundball   1986: Finesse, Groundball   1985: Finesse, Groundball   1984: Finesse, Groundball

	1987 SEASON											FOUR YEAR TOTALS (1984 – 1987)										
	G	IP	H	BB	SO	SB	CS	W	L	S	ERA	G	IP	H	BB	SO	SB	CS	W	L	S	ERA
Totals	39	196.2	212	85	95	9	14	8	13	0	4.99	155	923.0	976	321	445	60	43	52	56	0	4.08
at Home	22	114.0	112	43	53	3	6	6	6	0	4.18	76	460.1	477	153	209	26	18	27	23	0	3.97
on Road	17	82.2	100	42	42	6	8	2	7	0	6.10	79	462.2	499	168	236	34	25	25	33	0	4.16
on Grass	14	74.2	83	39	33	4	8	1	3	0	5.30	52	305.0	340	114	135	23	18	15	18	0	4.40
on Artificial Turf	25	122.0	129	46	62	5	6	7	10	0	4.80	103	618.0	636	207	310	37	25	37	38	0	3.92
Day Games	31	157.1	160	63	74	5	9	7	8	0	4.46	114	688.2	708	239	319	41	32	38	38	0	3.75
Night Games	8	39.1	52	22	21	4	5	1	5	0	7.09	41	234.1	268	82	126	19	11	14	18	0	5.03
April	6	39.0	35	17	23	1	5	2	2	0	3.46	24	121.1	115	39	52	4	9	8	6	0	3.12
May	7	44.1	54	24	18	3	3	0	4	0	6.29	28	169.2	183	72	78	17	7	9	10	0	4.40
June	6	35.0	34	13	19	2	1	2	2	0	5.91	25	172.2	172	58	83	10	6	14	6	0	3.81
July	6	37.0	43	15	20	1	3	2	3	0	3.65	25	154.0	179	59	84	10	6	7	13	0	4.38
August	6	25.0	32	9	12	1	1	1	2	0	6.48	26	150.0	175	51	66	13	8	6	12	0	4.92
Sept/Oct	8	16.1	14	7	3	1	1	1	2	0	3.86	27	155.1	152	42	82	6	7	8	9	0	3.65

vs. Opponent Batters	Ave.	OBP	SLG	AB	H	2B	3B	HR	RBI	BB	SO	Ave.	OBP	SLG	AB	H	2B	3B	HR	RBI	BB	SO
Totals	.283	.356	.437	750	212	34	5	24	107	85	95	.276	.336	.405	3536	976	148	25	86	413	321	445
vs. Left	.313	.389	.467	403	126	25	2	11	54	51	47	.295	.356	.431	1927	568	95	18	44	232	183	219
vs. Right	.248	.316	.403	347	86	9	3	13	53	34	48	.254	.313	.374	1609	408	53	7	42	181	138	226
Bases Empty	.270	.332	.424	441	119	18	1	16	16	40	57	.269	.316	.403	2128	572	91	13	56	56	146	270
Leadoff	.308	.369	.470	185	57	10	1	6	6	17	26	.267	.316	.409	889	237	34	9	25	25	63	111
Not Leadoff	.242	.305	.391	256	62	8	0	10	10	23	31	.270	.316	.398	1239	335	57	4	31	31	83	159
Runners On Base	.301	.388	.456	309	93	16	4	8	91	45	38	.287	.365	.408	1408	404	57	12	30	357	175	175
First Base Only	.283	.364	.449	127	36	11	2	2	10	15	12	.304	.361	.420	595	181	33	3	10	38	52	48
Scoring Position	.313	.405	.462	182	57	5	2	6	81	30	26	.274	.368	.400	813	223	24	9	20	319	123	127
Late Innings, Close	.347	.434	.542	72	25	5	0	3	14	11	7	.305	.387	.425	315	96	11	0	9	36	42	32

RBI/Opportunities

Scoring Position	71 / 252 (28%)	275 / 1132 (24%)
Scoring Position, 2 Out	29 / 107 (27%)	109 / 534 (20%)
On Third, Less than 2 Out	21 / 48 (44%)	102 / 199 (51%)
RBI in close games / RBI Total	83 / 107 (78%)	297 / 413 (72%)

Candy Maldonado
San Francisco Giants

Candy Maldonado was traded in December 1985, for Alex Treviso, and the deal is turning out to be more and more of a steal for the Giants. He has endeared himself to Giants players and fans, living up to his nickname of the "Candyman."

In 1986, Maldonado had an amazing year. He hit .252, 27 points higher than 1985, and led the Giants with 18 homers and 88 RBIs, the latter among the top 10 in the NL, while spending the first four-plus months of the season as a pinch hitter, setting team records for pinch hits and pinch homers in the process.

In 1987, Maldonado was hitting .332 and was among the league leaders in many offensive categories, until on June 27 he broke his finger chasing down a foul ball in the terribly narrow Candlestick foul territory. His 7-week stint on the DL cost him a berth in the All-Star Game, and may well have cost him a shot at the league's MVP award. At the time of the injury Candy was fourth in the league in batting average, seventh in runs scored, second in hits, second in doubles, ninth in RBIs, and second in GWRBIs. The Giants went 17–19 without him in the lineup, and were 5 games out, equal to their biggest deficit of the year, when he returned August 7. From that day to the end of the season, the Giants posted a 36–17 record (.679), gaining 11 games on the Reds and 15+ on the Astros. Although Candy had a very slow August, in September, he had 25 RBIs in his final 29 games. Candy tied a major league record with 3 sac flies in a game at Shea August 29. He also hit for the cycle (only the fourth SF Giant to do so) May 4 in St. Louis, in one of the all-time comebacks for the Giant team, who spotted the Cards 7 runs in St. Louis, then put 10 runs on the board in the final 5 innings.

Candy's defense improved significantly during the season, and he led Giant outfielders with 7 assists. Candy has a very strong arm; however, neither he nor any other person in the park knows quite where the ball will head when it's released. Unfortunately for Candy and the Giants, his greatest defensive lapses of the year occurred in the playoffs, and may have cost the Giants a shot at the world championship, although all the defense in the world wouldn't compensate for 0 runs scored in the last 22 innings of LCS play.

Candy was remarkably consistent versus lefthanders (.295, 1 HR every 14 AB) and righthanders (.290, 1 HR every 14.1 AB). However, his home/away and grass/turf breakdowns show definite preferences. At home he averaged a home run every 16.3 AB and an RBI every 5.1; on the road these marks fell to 1 in 35.7 and 1 in 5.4. On natural grass he homered every 19.7 AB and a drove in a run every 4.8; on turf his averages dipped to 1 HR every 35.7 AB and an RBI every 7.1. Interestingly in each case the lower BA produced better offensive stats—there is more to hitting than batting average. Maldonado equalled or surpassed his career totals in virtually every category in 1986; in 1987, he improved on every offensive stat except doubles (28 to 31), in 15 fewer games than 1986. A normalized year, based on 1987 performance, shows:

.292 607 AB, 177 Hits, 28 HR, 38 2B, 6 3B, 121 RBI

The Giants would be happy to see a full year line like that in 1988, or any other year, from Candy.

J. Michael Duca

Maldonado, Candido (Guadarrama) "Candy" Bats: Right Throws: Right Born 09/05/60

1987 SEASON AND MAJOR-LEAGUE CAREER BATTING TOTALS

	G	AB	H	2B	3B	HR	TB	R	RBI	TBB	IBB	SO	HP	SH	SF	SB	CS	SB%	GDP	AVG	OBP	SLG
87 SF	118	442	129	28	4	20	225	69	85	34	4	78	6	0	7	8	8	.50	9	.292	.346	.509
7 YEARS	547	1392	360	81	9	49	606	168	223	98	13	245	10	4	15	13	16	.45	31	.259	.309	.435

1987 SEASON / FOUR YEAR TOTALS (1984 – 1987)

	Ave.	OBP	SLG	AB	H	2B	3B	HR	RBI	BB	SO	Ave.	OBP	SLG	AB	H	2B	3B	HR	RBI	BB	SO
Totals	.292	.346	.509	442	129	28	4	20	85	34	78	.264	.314	.447	1314	347	80	8	48	217	92	224
vs. Left	.295	.371	.515	132	39	9	1	6	21	17	21	.269	.320	.442	631	170	38	4	21	94	50	96
vs. Right	.290	.334	.506	310	90	19	3	14	64	17	57	.259	.308	.451	683	177	42	4	27	123	42	128
at Home	.241	.288	.474	228	55	9	1	14	45	14	44	.234	.278	.398	645	151	33	2	23	106	38	122
on Road	.346	.406	.547	214	74	19	3	6	40	20	34	.293	.347	.493	669	196	47	6	25	111	54	102
vs. Groundball	.294	.352	.492	187	55	9	2	8	37	16	32	.279	.326	.462	602	168	33	4	23	105	41	99
vs. Flyball	.290	.341	.522	255	74	19	2	12	48	18	46	.251	.304	.434	712	179	47	4	25	112	51	125
vs. Finesse	.266	.324	.464	222	59	13	2	9	39	17	34	.264	.306	.451	708	187	44	5	26	119	41	99
vs. Power	.318	.367	.555	220	70	15	2	11	46	17	44	.264	.322	.442	606	160	36	3	22	98	51	125
on Grass	.278	.328	.493	335	93	15	3	17	70	25	61	.265	.310	.450	955	253	53	5	38	171	61	171
on Artificial Turf	.336	.400	.561	107	36	13	1	3	15	9	17	.262	.325	.437	359	94	27	3	10	46	31	53
Day Games	.348	.385	.522	184	64	16	2	4	42	13	30	.281	.327	.446	549	154	35	4	16	103	38	95
Night Games	.252	.317	.500	258	65	12	2	16	43	21	48	.252	.304	.447	765	193	45	4	32	114	54	129
April	.326	.378	.483	89	29	8	0	2	13	8	15	.317	.354	.477	199	63	12	1	6	26	12	33
May	.313	.376	.576	99	31	7	2	5	19	6	16	.243	.301	.431	255	62	17	2	9	37	17	38
June	.360	.394	.607	89	32	7	0	5	16	4	14	.305	.350	.500	200	61	16	1	7	31	13	30
July	.000	.000	.000	0	0	0	0	0	0	0	0	.256	.326	.368	117	30	4	0	3	19	12	21
August	.187	.253	.413	75	14	3	1	4	16	7	19	.203	.266	.420	231	47	9	1	13	44	20	42
Sept/Oct	.256	.317	.444	90	23	3	1	4	21	9	14	.269	.307	.455	312	84	22	3	10	60	18	60
Bases Empty	.298	.355	.551	225	67	13	1	14	14	18	41	.246	.290	.432	706	174	36	1	31	31	41	123
Leadoff	.313	.378	.583	115	36	7	0	8	8	10	17	.241	.279	.432	324	78	14	0	16	16	15	60
Not Leadoff	.282	.331	.518	110	31	6	1	6	6	8	24	.251	.299	.432	382	96	22	1	15	15	26	63
Runners On	.286	.336	.465	217	62	15	3	6	71	16	37	.285	.340	.464	608	173	44	7	17	186	51	101
First Base Only	.265	.299	.434	83	22	6	1	2	11	2	15	.273	.302	.429	245	67	14	3	6	24	8	43
Scoring Position	.299	.357	.485	134	40	9	2	4	60	14	22	.292	.364	.488	363	106	30	4	11	162	43	58
Late Innings, Close	.338	.369	.550	80	27	8	0	3	16	3	9	.292	.329	.520	271	79	18	1	14	53	14	44

RBI/Opportunities

	1987		Four Year	
Scoring Position	54 / 180	(30%)	137 / 506	(27%)
Scoring Position, 2 Out	18 / 78	(23%)	50 / 232	(22%)
On Third, Less than 2 Out	20 / 37	(54%)	50 / 97	(52%)
RBI in close games / RBI Total	56 / 85	(66%)	146 / 217	(67%)

Fred Manrique
Chicago White Sox

Fred Manrique is a classic example of a "he'll do" player. Many teams, usually the mediocre ones, have holes in their lineup or pitching staff which they fill with players like Manrique. In the "He'll Do Theory", a team picks up a not-very-talented or over-the-hill player to play a position or two in hopes of marking time till a real ballplayer comes along. They're fillers until they find someone better or until a hot prospect is ready."

With some of these teams, nobody better ever seems to come along, and the hot prospect never quite makes it out of AAA. Take the 1987 White Sox— please! Now there is a team so in love with the "he'll do" concept that they mass produce them. They are the General Motors of mediocrity. Tim Hulett was replaced by Steve Lyons, and before that there was Wayne Tolleson. Fred Manrique replaced (and later platooned with) Donnie Hill. Bill Long replaced Joel Davis. Scott Nielsen and Dave LaPoint replaced the immortal Neil Allen. Ray Searage replaced Joel McKeon. The White Sox have had such players littering their roster for what seems like forever, and the supply from their farm system seems endless. You'd think they would eventually produce a real prospect just by accident. No wonder the White Sox have won only one league pennant and one division title in the past 68 years.

Not that Fred Manrique is a bad ballplayer, mind you. He is an excellent defensive player who hits lefties with a little power, and he did just fine when Donnie Hill was struggling to hit .200. But Fred struggles against righties and it's a right-handed world. That leaves him with enough ability that he could help a few select clubs as a starter and nearly everyone as a role player. He belongs on what Bill James referred to in his 1987 *Abstract* as the "Ken Phelps All-Star Team." It's made up of players who might help a team if given a chance.

The White Sox seem to be shaky on this concept. It was never Bill's intent that a team should try for a whole club of Phelpses and Manriques. Bill's guess was that the Ken Phelps All-Stars would win 70–80 games. The problem is the White Sox are loaded with players of Manrique's caliber; they are choking to death on Manriques. The White Sox have won between 70 and 80 games 10 times since 1971. If not for the division title in 1983, the White Sox story for the past 17 seasons has been one of relentless mediocrity, a team that passes from season to season and from decade to decade, going nowhere and content to be just another nameless, faceless fifth-place collection of blahs.

Andrew Berman

Manrique, Fred Eloi (Reyes) Bats: Right Throws: Right Born 11/05/61

1987 SEASON AND MAJOR-LEAGUE CAREER BATTING TOTALS

	G	AB	H	2B	3B	HR	TB	R	RBI	TBB	IBB	SO	HP	SH	SF	SB	CS	SB%	GDP	AVG	OBP	SLG
87 CHA	115	298	77	13	3	4	108	30	29	19	1	69	1	9	3	5	3	.63	4	.258	.302	.362
5 YEARS	161	365	91	14	4	6	131	38	33	21	1	86	2	9	3	6	4	.60	6	.249	.292	.359

1987 SEASON

	Ave.	OBP	SLG	AB	H	2B	3B	HR	RBI	BB	SO
Totals	.258	.302	.362	298	77	13	3	4	29	19	69
vs. Left	.299	.361	.451	144	43	10	3	2	9	13	34
vs. Right	.221	.245	.279	154	34	3	0	2	20	6	35
at Home	.305	.359	.440	141	43	7	3	2	19	13	29
on Road	.217	.248	.293	157	34	6	0	2	10	6	40
vs. Groundball	.248	.294	.329	149	37	4	1	2	23	10	27
vs. Flyball	.268	.310	.396	149	40	9	2	2	6	9	42
vs. Finesse	.244	.281	.344	160	39	7	3	1	15	8	27
vs. Power	.275	.327	.384	138	38	6	0	3	14	11	42
on Grass	.276	.324	.372	250	69	12	3	2	24	18	57
on Artificial Turf	.167	.184	.313	48	8	1	0	2	5	1	12
Day Games	.272	.322	.370	81	22	2	0	2	10	6	9
Night Games	.253	.295	.359	217	55	11	3	2	19	13	60
April	.462	.533	.538	13	6	1	0	0	1	2	2
May	.175	.172	.228	57	10	3	0	0	4	0	15
June	.194	.219	.290	31	6	0	0	1	2	1	7
July	.407	.484	.519	27	11	3	0	0	3	4	6
August	.300	.345	.480	100	30	5	2	3	15	8	26
Sept/Oct	.200	.253	.243	70	14	1	1	0	4	4	13
Bases Empty	.256	.280	.361	180	46	7	3	2	2	5	44
Leadoff	.188	.200	.328	64	12	1	1	2	2	1	22
Not Leadoff	.293	.322	.379	116	34	6	2	0	0	4	22
Runners On	.263	.333	.364	118	31	6	0	2	27	14	25
First Base Only	.231	.273	.269	52	12	2	0	0	0	3	11
Scoring Position	.288	.375	.439	66	19	4	0	2	27	11	14
Late Innings, Close	.227	.227	.273	44	10	0	1	0	1	0	12

TWO YEAR TOTALS (1986 – 1987)

	Ave.	OBP	SLG	AB	H	2B	3B	HR	RBI	BB	SO
Totals	.254	.298	.362	315	80	13	3	5	30	20	70
vs. Left	.286	.347	.441	161	46	10	3	3	10	14	35
vs. Right	.221	.245	.279	154	34	3	0	2	20	6	35
at Home	.291	.344	.419	148	43	7	3	2	19	13	30
on Road	.222	.256	.311	167	37	6	0	3	11	7	40
vs. Groundball	.248	.293	.327	153	38	4	1	2	23	10	27
vs. Flyball	.259	.302	.395	162	42	9	2	3	7	10	43
vs. Finesse	.240	.279	.333	171	41	7	3	1	15	9	27
vs. Power	.271	.321	.396	144	39	6	0	4	15	11	43
on Grass	.276	.323	.370	257	71	12	3	2	24	18	57
on Artificial Turf	.155	.183	.328	58	9	1	0	3	6	2	13
Day Games	.272	.322	.370	81	22	2	0	2	10	6	9
Night Games	.248	.290	.359	234	58	11	3	3	20	14	61
April	.462	.533	.538	13	6	1	0	0	1	2	2
May	.175	.172	.228	57	10	3	0	0	4	0	15
June	.194	.219	.290	31	6	0	0	1	2	1	7
July	.407	.484	.519	27	11	3	0	0	3	4	6
August	.300	.345	.480	100	30	5	2	3	15	8	26
Sept/Oct	.195	.247	.264	87	17	1	1	1	5	5	14
Bases Empty	.249	.275	.363	193	48	7	3	3	3	6	45
Leadoff	.174	.197	.304	69	12	1	1	2	2	2	22
Not Leadoff	.290	.318	.395	124	36	6	2	1	1	4	23
Runners On	.262	.331	.361	122	32	6	0	2	27	14	25
First Base Only	.222	.263	.259	54	12	2	0	0	0	3	11
Scoring Position	.294	.378	.441	68	20	4	0	2	27	11	14
Late Innings, Close	.227	.227	.273	88	20	0	2	0	2	0	24

RBI/Opportunities

Scoring Position	24 / 101	(24%)	24 / 103	(23%)
Scoring Position, 2 Out	12 / 49	(24%)	12 / 50	(24%)
On Third, Less than 2 Out	10 / 16	(63%)	10 / 17	(59%)
RBI in close games / RBI Total	15 / 29	(52%)	30 / 30	(100%)

181

Mike Marshall
Los Angeles Dodgers

Mike Marshall's 1987 season was very much a snapshot of his career. Marshall played well during the rare times he was healthy, but the number and variety of his 1987 injuries must have set some sort of perverse medical record. Mike missed games for a bad back, a pulled thigh muscle, a finger injury, food poisoning, stomach flu, a bruised shin, and a sprained wrist. About the only thing he didn't suffer was a recurrence of a previous Marshall malady, Morton's Toe. Isn't that where your foot gets stuck in a frozen pie?

Rightly or wrongly, Mike Marshall has become one of the few white players to be accused of malingering. In '87 the charge led to a feud between Marshall and the Dodgers' finest offensive player, Pedro Guerrero. Whether the charges are fair or not is hard to say; since Guerrero is 31 and still hasn't learned how to slide, he may not be the most credible witness. At any case, Marshall appears to be one of those players who may never put together a full season. When he is healthy, though, Mike is still a fine offensive player.

Marshall's primary value is his power and RBIs. Last year, however, he rarely had people on base to advance. The Dodgers' team OBA was a laughable .309, last in the league by a wide margin (Houston was next at .318; the league average was .328). When one remembers that Guerrero could drive home only 89 runs despite a splendid season, Marshall's figures begin to look a lot better. In point of fact Marshall averaged an RBI for every 5.94 plate appearances; Guerrero averaged one for every 7.08.

Aside from his brittleness, Marshall's major weakness continues to be lack of patience. He walked only 18 times last year and has never drawn more than 43 walks in a season. At times he appears so anxious to drive in runs (and, presumably, to prove his worth), that he will swing at anything. Unlike Guerrero, who has learned to become a selective hitter, Mike has shown no development in this area.

The Dodgers have shopped Marshall and it may be best for Mike to get out of Los Angeles. Despite the fact that he has never quite put it all together, Marshall remains an intriguing talent. One suspects that, given good health and a fresh start in a new city, he might finally begin to realize some of his vast potential.

But while the move might be good for Marshall, it might not be good for the Dodgers. If Mike's back (his major recurring medical problem) is okay, it may not be wise to trade him. Marshall will be 28 in 1988, in the prime of his career. When healthy he combines a high average and good power, an uncommon combination. Given his injury history, the Dodgers are unlikely to get an equitable talent package for a player of his caliber. One might consider an off-season conditioning program before simply giving up.

Greg Gajus and Don Zminda

Marshall, Michael Allen "Mike"　　　　Bats: Right　　Throws: Right　　Born 01/12/60

1987 SEASON AND MAJOR-LEAGUE CAREER BATTING TOTALS

	G	AB	H	2B	3B	HR	TB	R	RBI	TBB	IBB	SO	HP	SH	SF	SB	CS	SB%	GDP	AVG	OBP	SLG
87 LA	104	402	118	19	0	16	185	45	72	18	2	79	4	0	4	0	5	.00	13	.294	.327	.460
7 YEARS	679	2330	634	107	3	106	1065	292	360	179	22	553	21	3	17	20	25	.44	48	.272	.327	.457

	1987 SEASON											FOUR YEAR TOTALS (1984 – 1987)										
	Ave.	OBP	SLG	AB	H	2B	3B	HR	RBI	BB	SO	Ave.	OBP	SLG	AB	H	2B	3B	HR	RBI	BB	SO
Totals	.294	.327	.460	402	118	19	0	16	72	18	79	.272	.322	.466	1745	474	84	2	84	285	122	399
vs. Left	.280	.313	.464	125	35	8	0	5	18	5	20	.274	.345	.492	569	156	34	0	30	94	62	129
vs. Right	.300	.333	.458	277	83	11	0	11	54	13	59	.270	.311	.454	1176	318	50	2	54	191	60	270
at Home	.284	.327	.404	183	52	7	0	5	24	10	34	.274	.321	.472	877	240	40	1	44	143	58	194
on Road	.301	.328	.507	219	66	12	0	11	48	8	45	.270	.324	.461	868	234	44	1	40	142	64	205
vs. Groundball	.340	.350	.550	209	71	11	0	11	50	5	41	.294	.344	.481	798	235	39	1	36	142	58	181
vs. Flyball	.244	.303	.363	193	47	8	0	5	22	13	38	.252	.304	.454	947	239	45	1	48	143	64	218
vs. Finesse	.321	.343	.517	240	77	14	0	11	43	8	34	.285	.326	.478	1006	287	54	1	46	154	56	193
vs. Power	.253	.305	.377	162	41	5	0	5	29	10	45	.253	.318	.451	739	187	30	1	38	131	66	206
on Grass	.286	.325	.439	301	86	13	0	11	53	15	59	.275	.323	.467	1327	365	55	1	66	222	85	294
on Artificial Turf	.317	.333	.525	101	32	6	0	5	19	3	20	.261	.321	.464	418	109	29	1	18	63	37	105
Day Games	.273	.314	.469	128	35	4	0	7	27	7	23	.268	.316	.474	548	147	17	0	32	100	35	106
Night Games	.303	.333	.456	274	83	15	0	9	45	11	56	.273	.325	.463	1197	327	67	2	52	185	87	293
April	.292	.338	.458	72	21	3	0	3	15	3	21	.270	.317	.487	337	91	13	0	20	62	21	86
May	.133	.161	.133	30	4	0	0	0	3	1	5	.253	.327	.456	237	60	12	0	12	42	26	53
June	.370	.402	.609	92	34	7	0	5	16	5	17	.303	.361	.497	330	100	16	0	16	45	30	80
July	.237	.266	.408	76	18	4	0	3	10	2	18	.240	.279	.438	258	62	15	0	12	37	13	57
August	.371	.371	.629	35	13	3	0	2	12	0	2	.240	.281	.382	283	68	13	0	9	39	16	61
Sept/Oct	.289	.330	.402	97	28	2	0	3	16	7	16	.310	.343	.523	300	93	15	2	15	60	16	62
Bases Empty	.255	.292	.375	192	49	5	0	6	6	8	46	.255	.296	.445	922	235	38	1	45	45	52	226
Leadoff	.297	.333	.473	91	27	1	0	5	5	4	21	.267	.309	.464	405	108	11	0	23	23	24	88
Not Leadoff	.218	.255	.287	101	22	4	0	1	1	4	25	.246	.286	.429	517	127	27	1	22	22	28	138
Runners On	.329	.358	.538	210	69	14	0	10	66	10	33	.290	.346	.491	823	239	46	1	39	240	70	173
First Base Only	.333	.363	.517	87	29	4	0	4	9	3	14	.301	.335	.491	352	106	19	0	16	39	17	77
Scoring Position	.325	.356	.553	123	40	10	0	6	57	7	19	.282	.353	.490	471	133	27	1	23	201	53	96
Late Innings, Close	.224	.258	.362	58	13	2	0	2	15	2	19	.245	.286	.386	290	71	8	0	11	47	16	66

RBI/Opportunities

	1987 SEASON	FOUR YEAR TOTALS
Scoring Position	47 / 153 (31%)	162 / 618 (26%)
Scoring Position, 2 Out	19 / 72 (26%)	66 / 283 (23%)
On Third, Less than 2 Out	12 / 29 (41%)	56 / 119 (47%)
RBI in close games / RBI Total	47 / 72 (65%)	204 / 285 (72%)

Carmelo Martinez
San Diego Padres

What will they do with Carmelo *this* year?

The Padres obtained Martinez from the Cubs prior to the '84 season to add more power to their lineup. Dick Williams put him in left field, feeling that his bat would offset his defensive failings. The gamble paid off. The chubby Puerto Rican enjoyed a productive rookie year, hitting .250 with 13 homers and 66 RBIs. Although an alien in the outfield, he worked hard and was among the league leaders in assists.

The next year he improved offensively (.253, 21 HR, 72 RBI) but the team stopped winning and Padre fans found his glovework less forgivable. In '86, Steve Boros couldn't decide where to play him. With Garvey and Kruk playing full time, "Mallow" batted only 244 times and suffered through a dismal, frustrating year. Last season he got another chance, surprising everyone by hitting .273 and driving in 70 runs.

Carmelo is a quality hitter who, if allowed to play everyday at first base, should hit 25 to 30 homers and drive in 90 to 100 runs. For a young power hitter he is very patient at the plate; his walk totals are always high. He has worked on his tendency to overswing in clutch situations, and has learned to hit to the opposite field. An amiable man who has weathered cruel treatment from Padre fans, he is a good first baseman.

The Cubs traded Martinez because they had Leon Durham. A glance at the two men's records since 1984 is enlightening. (1986 is excluded, as Martinez played so sparingly.) Durham has a decided advantage in the home run, slugging and speed categories. However, Leon hits the vast majority of his round-trippers in Wrigley Field. If the Cubs had swapped Durham and kept Martinez, the numbers might easily be reversed. While Leon's batting average is 21 points higher, his on-base percentage is nearly identical. He also drove in only 26 more runs while hitting nearly half again as many homers. "Mallow" is three years younger. Did Chicago keep the wrong man?

It wouldn't surprise me to see Carmelo traded. San Diego needs to make some decisions about several talented young outfielders, and Kruk seems secure at first base. Martinez has been lost in the shuffle before, and if he stays with the Padres, it could happen again to him. Only 27, Martinez should produce a lot of offense for some team for the next 6 to 10 years.

	AB	R	H	2B	3B	HR	RBI	BA	BB	SB	OBA	SLG
Durham	1454	14	405	84	7	71	234	.279	184	25	.360	.492
Martinez	1449	87	374	77	5	49	208	.258	225	6	.358	.420

Bruce Erricson

Martinez, Carmelo (Salgado)   Bats: Right   Throws: Right   Born 07/28/60

1987 SEASON AND MAJOR-LEAGUE CAREER BATTING TOTALS

	G	AB	H	2B	3B	HR	TB	R	RBI	TBB	IBB	SO	HP	SH	SF	SB	CS	SB%	GDP	AVG	OBP	SLG
87 SD	139	447	122	21	2	15	192	59	70	70	5	82	3	1	4	5	5	.50	11	.273	.372	.430
5 YEARS	580	1782	455	90	5	64	747	223	249	264	15	311	11	4	21	7	13	.35	40	.255	.351	.419

	1987 SEASON											FOUR YEAR TOTALS (1984 – 1987)										
	Ave.	OBP	SLG	AB	H	2B	3B	HR	RBI	BB	SO	Ave.	OBP	SLG	AB	H	2B	3B	HR	RBI	BB	SO
Totals	.273	.372	.430	447	122	21	2	15	70	70	82	.255	.354	.415	1693	432	87	5	58	233	260	292
vs. Left	.272	.395	.478	184	50	11	0	9	32	37	30	.266	.387	.461	621	165	41	1	26	92	125	98
vs. Right	.274	.355	.395	263	72	10	2	6	38	33	52	.249	.334	.389	1072	267	46	4	32	141	135	194
at Home	.282	.390	.468	216	61	8	1	10	42	37	40	.256	.368	.439	825	211	34	3	37	135	146	148
on Road	.264	.355	.394	231	61	13	1	5	28	33	42	.255	.341	.393	868	221	53	2	21	98	114	144
vs. Groundball	.327	.419	.492	199	65	14	2	5	36	32	28	.267	.371	.424	846	226	52	3	25	118	139	135
vs. Flyball	.230	.334	.379	248	57	7	0	10	34	38	54	.243	.338	.406	847	206	35	2	33	115	121	157
vs. Finesse	.246	.347	.417	228	56	8	2	9	31	36	36	.250	.350	.412	871	218	41	1	30	122	131	138
vs. Power	.301	.398	.443	219	66	13	0	6	39	34	46	.260	.359	.418	822	214	46	0	28	111	129	154
on Grass	.285	.383	.483	323	92	15	2	15	62	50	58	.266	.368	.446	1241	330	61	5	51	195	202	213
on Artificial Turf	.242	.345	.290	124	30	6	0	0	8	20	24	.226	.315	.330	452	102	26	0	7	38	58	79
Day Games	.259	.383	.469	143	37	9	0	7	30	29	25	.269	.378	.450	542	146	27	1	23	84	97	82
Night Games	.280	.367	.411	304	85	12	2	8	40	41	57	.248	.343	.399	1151	286	60	4	35	149	163	210
April	.200	.257	.338	65	13	4	1	1	7	5	13	.247	.335	.416	219	54	11	1	8	27	29	45
May	.299	.419	.429	77	23	1	0	3	14	14	14	.266	.360	.433	293	78	14	1	11	41	41	57
June	.306	.443	.613	62	19	4	0	5	19	16	10	.276	.377	.464	323	89	19	0	14	54	53	52
July	.280	.385	.427	75	21	5	0	2	13	14	15	.222	.333	.371	275	61	15	1	8	37	47	46
August	.218	.315	.256	78	17	1	1	0	5	10	11	.228	.328	.336	250	57	11	2	4	28	36	39
Sept/Oct	.322	.392	.522	90	29	6	0	4	12	11	19	.279	.379	.447	333	93	17	0	13	46	54	53
Bases Empty	.234	.324	.417	218	51	7	0	11	11	28	43	.230	.337	.394	903	208	39	2	35	35	144	165
Leadoff	.255	.324	.520	98	25	2	0	8	8	9	18	.228	.327	.421	373	85	14	2	18	18	54	66
Not Leadoff	.217	.324	.333	120	26	5	0	3	3	19	25	.232	.344	.375	530	123	25	0	17	17	90	99
Runners On	.310	.415	.441	229	71	14	2	4	59	42	39	.284	.375	.439	790	224	48	3	23	198	116	127
First Base Only	.320	.382	.470	100	32	8	2	1	7	9	16	.322	.381	.500	342	110	27	2	10	31	32	40
Scoring Position	.302	.437	.419	129	39	6	0	3	52	33	23	.254	.371	.393	448	114	21	1	13	167	84	87
Late Innings, Close	.216	.293	.270	74	16	4	0	0	9	8	17	.239	.324	.343	335	80	17	0	6	46	42	65

RBI/Opportunities

Scoring Position	44 / 198 (22%)	141 / 651 (22%)
Scoring Position, 2 Out	11 / 92 (12%)	40 / 292 (14%)
On Third, Less than 2 Out	26 / 47 (55%)	69 / 142 (49%)
RBI in close games / RBI Total	50 / 70 (71%)	154 / 233 (66%)

Dave Martinez
Chicago Cubs

For Dave Martinez, 1987 was a year of survival. He was the only member of the Cubs' outfield "youth movement"—a movement that also included Rafael Palmeiro and the not-so-youthful Chico Walker—to stick with the ball club throughout the year. Martinez started the season struggling, but finished it with a bang. He also provided the Cubs with a decent center fielder, one who was able to cover the turf of the other ballparks as well as the grass in Wrigley Field.

Success didn't come easily for Martinez. A left-handed hitter, he opened the season platooning in center with Bob Dernier. But while Dernier got off to a blazing start, Martinez hit around .200 for the first six weeks. Since Dave had hit only .139 in his '86 debut, manager Gene Michael must have been tempted to go with Denier full time. Fortunately, Michael was well aware of Dernier's chronic problems against righties. And while he wasn't hitting, Martinez's fielding was excellent. He provided better range in center field than any other Cub outfielder in recent years. So he played, at least against righties.

Then an injury to another Cub player gave Dave his big break. When Ryne Sandberg hurt his ankle, Michael moved Martinez from his usual eighth spot in the batting order to leadoff. And just like the big jump in the batting lineup, Dave's batting average soared to new heights. By August Martinez was flirting with 300. When Sandberg returned, the Cubs didn't tamper with success. Martinez stayed as the leadoff man against righties, and ended up hitting .292. He also showed an ability to get on base, drawing 57 walks and posting an on-base percentage of .372. It was quite a comeback after such a terrible start.

Dave has added excitement to the Cubs with his hitting and his defense, but more might be hoped for in the way of stealing bases. Despite exceptional speed, Martinez had only 24 stolen base attempts, being successful 16 times. Since the Cubs lack team speed, they need for Martinez, who is one of their best runners, to become more aggressive in this respect, as he probably will after he settles in as a regular.

Dave Martinez survived 1987, and began to bloom. Since Dernier has signed with the Phillies, Martinez should have the starting job in center field won. However, the Cubs' front office has indicated that he should and will be platooned again. Why don't they give him a chance to play every day?

Vincent Vrotny

Martinez, David "Dave" Bats: Left Throws: Left Born 09/26/64

1987 SEASON AND MAJOR-LEAGUE CAREER BATTING TOTALS

	G	AB	H	2B	3B	HR	TB	R	RBI	TBB	IBB	SO	HP	SH	SF	SB	CS	SB%	GDP	AVG	OBP	SLG
87 CHN	142	459	134	18	8	8	192	70	36	57	4	96	2	1	1	16	8	.67	4	.292	.372	.418
2 YEARS	195	567	149	19	9	9	213	83	43	63	4	118	3	1	2	20	10	.67	5	.263	.339	.376

	1987 SEASON											FOUR YEAR TOTALS (1984 – 1987)										
	Ave.	OBP	SLG	AB	H	2B	3B	HR	RBI	BB	SO	Ave.	OBP	SLG	AB	H	2B	3B	HR	RBI	BB	SO
Totals	.292	.372	.418	459	134	18	8	8	36	57	96	.263	.339	.376	567	149	19	9	9	43	63	118
vs. Left	.261	.320	.391	23	6	0	0	1	1	2	8	.242	.286	.333	33	8	0	0	1	1	2	12
vs. Right	.294	.374	.420	436	128	18	8	7	35	55	88	.264	.342	.378	534	141	19	9	8	42	61	106
at Home	.281	.366	.433	231	65	10	5	5	17	30	42	.249	.328	.384	297	74	10	6	6	20	33	57
on Road	.303	.377	.404	228	69	8	3	3	19	27	54	.278	.350	.367	270	75	9	3	3	23	30	61
vs. Groundball	.347	.405	.465	202	70	10	4	2	18	20	32	.300	.356	.403	253	76	10	5	2	19	21	40
vs. Flyball	.249	.347	.381	257	64	8	4	6	18	37	64	.232	.325	.354	314	73	9	4	7	24	42	78
vs. Finesse	.275	.356	.384	258	71	12	5	2	13	32	44	.250	.327	.356	320	80	13	6	3	17	35	56
vs. Power	.313	.392	.463	201	63	6	3	6	23	25	52	.279	.354	.401	247	69	6	3	6	26	28	62
on Grass	.288	.373	.420	326	94	13	6	6	23	43	67	.254	.333	.372	406	103	13	7	7	26	46	86
on Artificial Turf	.301	.369	.414	133	40	5	2	2	13	14	29	.286	.354	.385	161	46	6	2	2	17	17	32
Day Games	.277	.366	.412	289	80	10	7	5	23	40	54	.241	.322	.358	377	91	10	8	6	28	44	73
Night Games	.318	.383	.429	170	54	8	1	3	13	17	42	.305	.371	.411	190	58	9	1	3	15	19	45
April	.240	.356	.340	50	12	0	1	1	7	9	5	.240	.356	.340	50	12	0	1	1	7	9	5
May	.271	.373	.300	70	19	2	0	0	4	12	11	.271	.373	.300	70	19	2	0	0	4	12	11
June	.360	.450	.535	86	31	6	3	1	5	13	9	.311	.393	.445	119	37	7	3	1	7	15	13
July	.324	.385	.507	71	23	2	1	3	6	6	14	.243	.297	.398	103	25	2	1	4	9	7	25
August	.265	.327	.439	98	26	6	1	3	9	9	28	.260	.321	.430	100	26	6	1	3	9	9	28
Sept/Oct	.274	.337	.345	84	23	2	2	0	5	8	29	.240	.301	.304	125	30	2	3	0	7	11	36
Bases Empty	.300	.373	.453	300	90	13	6	7	7	33	55	.264	.334	.405	363	96	13	7	8	8	36	69
Leadoff	.291	.355	.444	151	44	7	2	4	4	14	29	.264	.327	.390	182	48	7	2	4	4	16	35
Not Leadoff	.309	.391	.463	149	46	6	4	3	3	19	26	.265	.342	.420	181	48	6	5	4	4	20	34
Runners On	.277	.370	.352	159	44	5	2	1	29	24	41	.260	.345	.324	204	53	6	2	1	35	27	49
First Base Only	.277	.319	.338	65	18	1	0	1	2	4	17	.264	.304	.310	87	23	1	0	1	2	5	19
Scoring Position	.277	.400	.362	94	26	4	2	0	27	20	24	.256	.371	.333	117	30	5	2	0	33	22	30
Late Innings, Close	.324	.403	.426	68	22	2	1	1	5	9	16	.291	.365	.395	86	25	2	2	1	5	10	18

RBI/Opportunities

Scoring Position	26 / 132 (20%)	31 / 166 (19%)
Scoring Position, 2 Out	11 / 73 (15%)	12 / 83 (14%)
On Third, Less than 2 Out	6 / 15 (40%)	10 / 24 (42%)
RBI in close games / RBI Total	24 / 36 (67%)	28 / 43 (65%)

Dennis Martinez
Montreal Expos

One of the most heartwarming stories to come out of the 1987 season was the return to form of Dennis Martinez. After several years of fighting a major alcohol abuse problem and a variety of baseball related injuries, Martinez—to the astonishment of people in baseball—became one of the better pitchers in the National League over the second half of the season.

Though never a big star on an Oriole staff that included Jim Palmer, Mike Flanagan and Scott McGregor, Martinez was a consistently good hurler in the late seventies and early eighties. Dennis won between 14 and 16 games five times between 1977 and 1982, led the American League in starts, innings pitched and complete games in '79 and tied for the league lead in wins in 1981. But then came troubled times. After he'd posted ERAs above 5.00 for three straight seasons, the Orioles concluded that Martinez was finished. Demoted to Rochester of the International League early in 1986, he soon found himself traded to the pitching poor Expos. Montreal was hoping to catch lightning in a bottle, but Dennis could only compile a 3–6 record and a 4.59 ERA in 98 innings. After a performance like that, no one could have expected that Martinez would be the ace of the Montreal staff a year later.

The Expos certainly didn't. Martinez was a free agent after the '86 season and, like Tim Raines, returned to the Montreal organization on May 1. After a so-so conditioning stint in the minors—he pitched briefly in Class A, then was 3–2 at AAA Indianapolis with a 4.46 ERA—Dennis returned to Montreal. The Expos, shorthanded because of a decimating series of injuries in the starting rotation, gave Martinez the ball more because he was there than because they had any real expectations. "We brought in anyone who could throw a ball," manager Buck Rodgers said.

What they got in return was a gutty 11–4 record, a 3.30 earned run average, and someone who could go out and pitch a steady seven innings almost every time out.

After a no-decision in his first start, Martinez tossed a three-hit shut-out at the New York Mets on June 15. In fact, the Expos won eleven of Martinez' first twelve starts.

Put together with another substance abuse rehab project, former Atlanta star Pascual Perez, who was 7–0, the Expos got a combined 18–4 record out of two pitchers that the rest of major league baseball thought were washed up. The Expos remained in the pennant chase until the last weeks of the season because they had one of the steadiest starting rotations in the league over the second half of the season—thanks to two remarkable comebacks.

Tom Henry

Martinez, Jose Dennis (Emilia) "Dennis"   Bats: Right   Throws: Right   Born 05/14/55

1987 SEASON AND MAJOR-LEAGUE CAREER PITCHING TOTALS

	G	GS	CG	GF	IP	BFP	H	R	ER	HR	SH	SF	HB	TBB	IBB	SO	WP	Bk	W	L	Pct	ShO	Sv	ERA
87 MON	22	22	2	0	145	599	133	59	53	9	4	3	6	40	2	84	4	2	11	4	.733	1	0	3.29
12 YEARS	360	280	72	38	2019	8559	2058	1010	923	207	58	68	48	651	30	1005	56	10	122	103	.542	12	5	4.11

1987: Finesse, Flyball   1986: Finesse, Groundball   1985: Finesse, Flyball   1984: Finesse, Flyball

	1987 SEASON											FOUR YEAR TOTALS (1984 – 1987)										
	G	IP	H	BB	SO	SB	CS	W	L	S	ERA	G	IP	H	BB	SO	SB	CS	W	L	S	ERA
Totals	22	144.2	133	40	84	18	3	11	4	0	3.30	112	571.0	595	170	294	67	12	33	30	0	4.56
at Home	11	81.0	64	23	47	5	3	6	1	0	2.44	54	281.1	293	85	159	34	7	15	17	0	4.70
on Road	11	63.2	69	17	37	13	0	5	3	0	4.38	58	289.2	302	85	135	33	5	18	13	0	4.44
on Grass	0	0.0	0	0	0	0	0	0	0	0	0.00	29	140.1	154	40	69	22	3	6	10	0	4.49
on Artificial Turf	22	144.2	133	40	84	18	3	11	4	0	3.30	83	430.2	441	130	225	45	9	27	20	0	4.60
Day Games	5	32.0	30	5	17	5	0	3	1	0	2.53	71	324.0	351	99	150	40	3	17	20	0	5.03
Night Games	17	112.2	103	35	67	13	3	8	3	0	3.51	41	247.0	244	71	144	27	9	16	10	0	3.97
April	0	0.0	0	0	0	0	0	0	0	0	0.00	13	36.2	39	11	16	3	0	2	1	0	4.17
May	0	0.0	0	0	0	0	0	0	0	0	0.00	12	40.1	52	18	16	5	2	3	4	0	6.25
June	5	34.2	29	9	23	8	0	3	0	0	2.86	19	100.2	96	35	45	16	1	5	4	0	4.02
July	5	30.1	31	9	15	2	0	3	1	0	4.45	21	121.1	132	28	76	13	3	7	7	0	5.27
August	6	42.1	43	14	22	6	3	1	2	0	3.19	22	134.1	131	34	63	16	3	8	6	0	3.62
Sept/Oct	6	37.1	30	8	24	2	0	4	1	0	2.89	25	137.2	145	44	78	14	3	8	8	0	4.90

vs. Opponent Batters	Ave.	OBP	SLG	AB	H	2B	3B	HR	RBI	BB	SO	Ave.	OBP	SLG	AB	H	2B	3B	HR	RBI	BB	SO
Totals	.244	.301	.355	546	133	28	3	9	52	40	84	.269	.323	.433	2209	595	113	12	75	278	170	294
vs. Left	.236	.292	.340	347	82	19	1	5	38	28	55	.248	.310	.399	1241	308	62	7	37	147	112	178
vs. Right	.256	.317	.382	199	51	9	2	4	14	12	29	.296	.340	.477	968	287	51	5	38	131	58	116
Bases Empty	.237	.289	.353	329	78	17	3	5	5	22	42	.262	.307	.421	1369	359	66	11	43	43	87	182
Leadoff	.266	.325	.403	139	37	6	2	3	3	11	12	.265	.300	.429	567	150	32	5	17	17	28	73
Not Leadoff	.216	.262	.316	190	41	11	1	2	2	11	30	.261	.312	.415	802	209	34	6	26	26	59	109
Runners On Base	.253	.318	.359	217	55	11	0	4	47	18	42	.281	.347	.454	840	236	47	1	32	235	83	112
First Base Only	.250	.315	.357	84	21	6	0	1	5	6	8	.272	.327	.435	345	94	23	0	11	32	26	28
Scoring Position	.256	.320	.361	133	34	5	0	3	42	12	34	.287	.361	.467	495	142	24	1	21	203	57	84
Late Innings, Close	.171	.209	.220	41	7	2	0	0	2	2	8	.250	.303	.378	172	43	9	2	3	17	13	21

RBI/Opportunities

Scoring Position	38 / 168 (23%)	170 / 671 (25%)
Scoring Position, 2 Out	22 / 86 (26%)	84 / 319 (26%)
On Third, Less than 2 Out	11 / 28 (39%)	56 / 119 (47%)
RBI in close games / RBI Total	37 / 52 (71%)	177 / 278 (64%)

Don Mattingly

New York Yankees

1987 was an amazing year for this amazing player. A series of back and wrist injuries kept Don Mattingly out of 20 games; as a result, he failed to get 200 hits for the first time in three years. He did not lead the American League in doubles for the first time since 1983—nor, for that matter, in any offensive category. He also didn't cross the .300 line until June 1.

But it certainly wasn't a wasted year. Even with almost 100 fewer at-bats, Don's homer, RBI and runs scored totals were very close to his 1986 numbers. He tied Dale Long's record of homering in eight consecutive games; breaking Babe Ruth's record of 10 consecutive games with an extra base hit in the process. He set a single-game record for put-outs by a first baseman (naturally during a Tommy John start). Finally, he set a major league record by hitting six grand slams in a season.

Odd as it may seem in retrospect, many writers and fans were wondering what was wrong with Mattingly early in the year. The more logical question is "What was wrong with the writers and fans?" Don's average shouldn't have been a major surprise (he'd hit .327 before June 1 and .344 after it from '84–86) and his diminished power (one homer for every 32 ABs) should have been taken for granted. Don has always hit over half of his homers in the last two months of the season; 1987 (one homer for every 15.7 ABs after

6/1) was no exception.

When 1987 began, Mattingly had hit exactly 0 grand slams in the pros; his lifetime average with the bases loaded was .255 (12–47) with one extra base hit. This year, Don publicly vowed to bring his production up; he did a fair job of it. His 1987 line: 19 AB, 9 hits, 1 double, 6 homers, 33 RBIs, 2 sac flies, a .474 batting average and 1.474 slugging percentage. Take that, Pat Tabler.

Opposing managers often try to get a fresh arm into the game against Mattingly; in 1987, that wasn't a very good idea. New pitchers were brought into games during innings to face Don 25 times; he had 11 hits, with a double, three homers and 20 RBIs—a .440 BA and an .840 SL%. The results were even worse when, as was usually the case, the pitcher was a lefty. Don went 9–19 (.474) with all the extra-base hits (1.000 SL%) and 17 RBIs against southpaws. The moral: The saying "Any portsider in a storm" should be ignored when Mattingly is up.

The frustrating points about Mattingly's 1987 were that (a) injuries to Rickey Henderson and Willie Randolph cut into what could have been a slew of RBIs and (b) he works for a man who doesn't appreciate him. When George Steinbrenner accused Mattingly of not being a team player, you had to wonder what manner of demons were inhabiting his mind.

Craig Christmann and Marisa B. Lo

Mattingly, Donald Arthur "Don"   **Bats: Left**   **Throws: Left**   **Born 04/20/62**

1987 SEASON AND MAJOR-LEAGUE CAREER BATTING TOTALS

	G	AB	H	2B	3B	HR	TB	R	RBI	TBB	IBB	SO	HP	SH	SF	SB	CS	SB%	GDP	AVG	OBP	SLG
87 NYA	141	569	186	38	2	30	318	93	115	51	13	38	1	0	8	1	4	.20	16	.327	.378	.559
6 YEARS	713	2792	923	198	13	123	1516	442	516	222	50	179	6	13	45	4	7	.36	73	.331	.376	.543

	1987 SEASON											FOUR YEAR TOTALS (1984 – 1987)										
	Ave.	OBP	SLG	AB	H	2B	3B	HR	RBI	BB	SO	Ave.	OBP	SLG	AB	H	2B	3B	HR	RBI	BB	SO
Totals	.327	.378	.559	569	186	38	2	30	115	51	38	.337	.381	.560	2501	842	183	9	119	483	201	147
vs. Left	.302	.355	.523	199	60	9	1	11	49	16	15	.318	.362	.531	890	283	67	3	39	188	66	56
vs. Right	.341	.391	.578	370	126	29	1	19	66	35	23	.347	.392	.575	1611	559	116	6	80	295	135	91
at Home	.336	.384	.572	283	95	14	1	17	56	24	25	.332	.375	.569	1203	399	77	2	68	252	95	75
on Road	.318	.373	.545	286	91	24	1	13	59	27	13	.341	.387	.552	1298	443	106	7	51	231	106	72
vs. Groundball	.329	.370	.548	292	96	24	2	12	53	22	15	.340	.377	.562	1247	424	92	7	57	227	83	61
vs. Flyball	.325	.387	.570	277	90	14	0	18	62	29	23	.333	.385	.557	1254	418	91	2	62	256	118	86
vs. Finesse	.300	.352	.510	290	87	22	0	13	53	25	13	.325	.364	.530	1362	442	97	3	59	224	95	64
vs. Power	.355	.406	.609	279	99	16	2	17	62	26	25	.351	.401	.595	1139	400	86	6	60	259	106	83
on Grass	.323	.374	.553	474	153	30	2	25	89	41	32	.334	.380	.552	2098	700	147	6	100	403	172	123
on Artificial Turf	.347	.402	.589	95	33	8	0	5	26	10	6	.352	.390	.598	403	142	36	3	19	80	29	24
Day Games	.333	.379	.529	210	70	12	1	9	39	17	16	.337	.384	.554	836	282	61	3	38	145	69	47
Night Games	.323	.378	.577	359	116	26	1	21	76	34	22	.336	.380	.563	1665	560	122	6	81	338	132	100
April	.265	.337	.494	83	22	9	2	2	18	10	9	.289	.348	.443	305	88	29	3	4	57	29	18
May	.321	.409	.477	109	35	5	0	4	16	17	4	.341	.402	.556	428	146	27	1	21	81	44	24
June	.410	.465	.590	39	16	1	0	2	11	4	3	.333	.378	.505	378	126	21	1	14	64	27	23
July	.374	.415	.758	99	37	8	0	10	24	7	6	.343	.388	.612	423	145	38	2	24	83	31	27
August	.306	.345	.541	111	34	8	0	6	17	7	3	.351	.398	.600	453	159	30	1	27	82	36	18
Sept/Oct	.328	.353	.523	128	42	7	0	6	29	6	13	.346	.385	.593	514	178	38	1	29	116	34	37
Bases Empty	.317	.361	.528	290	92	20	1	13	13	20	16	.338	.373	.567	1314	444	96	8	63	63	74	85
Leadoff	.302	.362	.453	86	26	1	0	4	4	8	5	.345	.373	.593	423	146	29	2	24	24	19	24
Not Leadoff	.324	.361	.559	204	66	19	1	9	9	12	11	.334	.373	.554	891	298	67	6	39	39	55	61
Runners On	.337	.395	.591	279	94	18	1	17	102	31	22	.335	.398	.552	1187	398	87	1	56	420	127	62
First Base Only	.354	.396	.515	130	46	7	1	4	11	9	8	.336	.371	.536	548	184	39	1	23	63	31	23
Scoring Position	.322	.394	.658	149	48	11	0	13	91	22	14	.335	.418	.565	639	214	48	0	33	357	96	39
Late Innings, Close	.234	.348	.377	77	18	3	1	2	13	14	7	.328	.398	.512	381	125	18	2	16	77	45	15

RBI/Opportunities

Scoring Position	67 / 213 (31%)	292 / 919 (32%)
Scoring Position, 2 Out	20 / 96 (21%)	89 / 362 (25%)
On Third, Less than 2 Out	28 / 48 (58%)	130 / 204 (64%)
RBI in close games / RBI Total	72 / 115 (63%)	332 / 483 (69%)

Lance McCullers
San Diego Padres

In this space last year, I said that Lance McCullers would have to develop something else beside his fastball in 1987 if he hoped to keep succeeding. Apparently he didn't read the piece. Or maybe he just ignored it; neither manager Larry Bowa nor pitching coach Galen Cisco could get him to listen to reason in 1987, either.

The cost of this failure to communicate is that almost all of Lance's stats went sour this year. The good news is that his strikeout to walk ratio rose to a fine 2.14-1. But he allowed a hit and a half more per nine innings (8.39; up from 6.82), he allowed homers more often, his ERA rose almost a run—and 1987 is the second straight year that all of those stats have risen. Though Lance saved 11 more games in 1987, he nailed only 16 of his 28 save chances and didn't save a game for over a month. For the second straight year, "Baby Goose" finished the year playing second fiddle to the parent model.

The basic problem is that Lance is a 23-year-old kid. He simply fell in love with his fastball this spring and decided to just blow everyone away in 1987. He had a strong April; had San Diego won any games, he might have even have saved a few.

But then, as it usually does, reality set in. I can understand why Lance dotes on his heater—95 percent of the men on the planet can't throw as hard as he can—but there are very few major league regulars who can't hit a fastball, no matter how quickly or how much it moves. Especially if they know it's coming. In a six-game stretch in early May, Lance allowed seven hits (one a homer), three walks and seven earned runs in 6.1 innings, raising his ERA to 5.71. He spent the rest of 1987 bringing it down.

To make matters worse, Bowa couldn't afford (and didn't need) to give Lance any breaks. With his job hanging by a thread in mid-May, patience with a young player—no matter how talented—was an unaffordable luxury. Bowa had other options (Rich Gossage and Craig Lefferts), so he used them. When the Chris Brown trade brought a fling of new arms onto the roster, Bowa spent the rest of 1987 trying them out at Lance's expense. McCullers needed to overwhelm in order to get more work; he just didn't do it.

Lance's 1987 wasn't a total disaster. Despite what must have been an overwhelming temptation, Bowa wisely refused to yank him out of the bullpen and throw him into the rotation; Lance doesn't have to wonder what his role is. McCullers didn't pitch badly; he doesn't have to wonder if he has enough talent. He's still young; he doesn't have to wonder if he's running out of chances. But, if he doesn't become less of a thrower and more of a pitcher in 1988, I'll have to wonder if he's ever going to fulfill even half of the potential that he has.

Geoff Beckman

McCullers, Lance Graye Bats: Both Throws: Right Born 03/08/64

1987 SEASON AND MAJOR-LEAGUE CAREER PITCHING TOTALS

	G	GS	CG	GF	IP	BFP	H	R	ER	HR	SH	SF	HB	TBB	IBB	SO	WP	Bk	W	L	Pct	ShO	Sv	ERA
87 SD	78	0	0	41	123	540	115	60	51	11	6	2	2	59	11	126	5	1	8	10	.444	0	16	3.73
3 YEARS	169	7	0	81	294	1232	241	121	102	26	21	5	7	133	23	245	10	5	18	22	.450	0	26	3.12

1987: Power, Flyball   1986: Power, Flyball   1985: Power, Flyball

1987 SEASON

	G	IP	H	BB	SO	SB	CS	W	L	S	ERA
Totals	78	124.0	116	59	126	15	9	8	10	16	3.77
at Home	39	63.2	54	33	77	9	3	6	5	8	3.11
on Road	39	60.1	62	26	49	6	6	2	5	8	4.48
on Grass	25	42.0	38	21	39	3	4	2	4	7	3.21
on Artificial Turf	53	82.0	78	38	87	12	5	6	6	9	4.06
Day Games	55	88.0	82	43	98	11	5	7	8	10	3.48
Night Games	23	36.0	34	16	28	4	4	1	2	6	4.50
April	10	12.2	16	7	17	1	1	2	2	2	5.68
May	14	18.0	18	13	14	3	0	0	1	4	4.00
June	11	25.1	23	8	25	3	2	2	2	4	4.26
July	13	23.2	20	15	24	3	4	2	1	1	4.94
August	15	23.1	19	7	26	1	0	1	1	3	2.70
Sept/Oct	15	21.0	20	9	20	4	2	1	3	3	1.71

vs. Opponent Batters	Ave.	OBP	SLG	AB	H	2B	3B	HR	RBI	BB	SO
Totals	.246	.331	.378	471	116	27	1	11	61	59	126
vs. Left	.226	.340	.301	239	54	12	0	2	25	42	66
vs. Right	.267	.321	.457	232	62	15	1	9	36	17	60
Bases Empty	.247	.311	.396	235	58	15	1	6	6	22	51
Leadoff	.232	.276	.374	99	23	6	1	2	2	6	22
Not Leadoff	.257	.336	.412	136	35	9	0	4	4	16	29
Runners On Base	.246	.350	.360	236	58	12	0	5	55	37	75
First Base Only	.296	.367	.479	71	21	4	0	3	9	8	24
Scoring Position	.224	.343	.309	165	37	8	0	2	46	29	51
Late Innings, Close	.248	.347	.391	266	66	15	1	7	33	40	69

FOUR YEAR TOTALS (1984 – 1987)

	G	IP	H	BB	SO	SB	CS	W	L	S	ERA
Totals	169	295.0	242	133	245	32	20	18	22	26	3.14
at Home	82	147.1	118	64	140	19	9	11	8	13	2.81
on Road	87	147.2	124	69	105	13	11	7	14	13	3.47
on Grass	48	82.2	71	47	70	5	10	5	9	10	3.16
on Artificial Turf	121	212.1	171	86	175	27	10	13	13	16	3.14
Day Games	123	213.2	181	104	192	26	14	15	17	17	3.07
Night Games	46	81.1	61	29	53	6	6	3	5	9	3.32
April	17	20.2	23	9	24	3	2	3	3	2	4.35
May	29	34.1	24	22	24	5	0	0	1	4	2.36
June	26	51.2	44	17	44	5	4	5	3	4	3.31
July	18	54.2	46	30	44	8	5	3	4	1	4.12
August	35	69.2	52	23	56	2	4	3	3	8	2.58
Sept/Oct	44	64.0	53	32	53	9	5	4	8	7	2.81

vs. Opponent Batters	Ave.	OBP	SLG	AB	H	2B	3B	HR	RBI	BB	SO
Totals	.227	.313	.351	1066	242	50	2	26	130	133	245
vs. Left	.251	.359	.353	521	131	24	1	9	61	88	101
vs. Right	.204	.266	.349	545	111	26	1	17	69	45	144
Bases Empty	.235	.303	.362	583	137	28	2	14	14	57	116
Leadoff	.225	.287	.321	240	54	12	1	3	3	21	45
Not Leadoff	.242	.314	.391	343	83	16	1	11	11	36	71
Runners On Base	.217	.325	.337	483	105	22	0	12	116	76	129
First Base Only	.220	.281	.372	164	36	7	0	6	17	14	46
Scoring Position	.216	.345	.320	319	69	15	0	6	99	62	83
Late Innings, Close	.235	.340	.361	527	124	25	1	13	67	83	125

RBI/Opportunities

Scoring Position	41 / 249 (16%)	84 / 493 (17%)
Scoring Position, 2 Out	19 / 124 (15%)	39 / 242 (16%)
On Third, Less than 2 Out	12 / 46 (26%)	29 / 84 (35%)
RBI in close games / RBI Total	38 / 61 (62%)	83 / 130 (64%)

Oddibe McDowell
Texas Rangers

When Oddibe returned from his adventure with the butter knife, he eventually hit a hot streak which brought his average up to .270 by mid-June. At that point he was the best all round offensive player on the Rangers' roster. Then he met a diabolical tennis court and came away with a severe ankle sprain that knocked him out of the lineup and into a long slump.

His second half was bad enough to set off a lot of trade talk among the media and fans, and there were indications that the front office was considering it. I thought such talk was unrealistic for two reasons. First, the Rangers are desperate for left-handed bats. They tear up lefty pitchers, .278 team average with a 5.37 run-rate, but are mediocre or worse versus righties. No one, not O'Brien, not Sierra, nor any other Ranger player, banged out more extra-base hits per at-bat against righties than Little Mac did. And this was a bad year! The second reason you don't trade McDowell is the simple principle that you don't sell low. It seems obvious his future value is greater than his present market value.

Maybe it isn't so obvious. Very few people noticed the progress that Oddibe did make in 1987. There is no denying the obvious statistic of his batting average which dropped from .266 to .241, but he also slightly improved his home run rate, jumped his double-triple rate over 36%, set a career high in walk average, and was caught stealing only twice in 26 attempts—making him the most efficient base-stealer in either league (those with 20 steals or more). Let's be honest, Oddibe is never going to be the kind of player whose value is reflected in his batting average; his strength is in his broad offensive base with pluses in power, walks, and speed on the bases.

1987 was McDowell's worst year in the field, continuing a trend since his arrival in the majors. In 1984, with the US Olympic team, and then in 1985 with the Rangers, Oddibe seemed comfortable playing a shallower center field. Each year, however, the Rangers ask him to back up. The idea makes sense; he comes in well, so put him out where everything will be in front of him. That way he may catch the occasional looping two-bagger-to-be and prevent the liners from going for extra bases. The results haven't been as sensible. Frankly, Little Mac's a bit wall-shy. Slowing down and finding the wall interferes with his judgment, and he's now playing too deep to snare the line drives he used to pick off so well. The idea of playing shallow would also de-emphasize Oddibe's arm which is better suited to throws at 300 feet rather than 400 feet. I'd let the opposition have a few more cheap doubles if it returned McDowell's defensive form to that of 1985 when he averaged 2.7 put-outs per game compared to 1987's abysmal 2.1.

Allen Sheffield

McDowell, Oddibe Bats: Left   Throws: Left   Born 08/25/62

1987 SEASON AND MAJOR-LEAGUE CAREER BATTING TOTALS

	G	AB	H	2B	3B	HR	TB	R	RBI	TBB	IBB	SO	HP	SH	SF	SB	CS	SB%	GDP	AVG	OBP	SLG
87 TEX	128	407	98	26	4	14	174	65	52	51	0	99	0	3	2	24	2	.92	8	.241	.324	.428
3 YEARS	393	1385	347	64	16	50	593	233	143	152	7	296	4	11	6	82	24	.77	26	.251	.325	.428

	1987 SEASON											FOUR YEAR TOTALS (1984 – 1987)									
	Ave.	OBP	SLG	AB	H	2B	3B	HR	RBI	BB	SO	Ave.	OBP	SLG	AB	H	2B	3B	HR	RBI	BB	SO
Totals	.241	.324	.428	407	98	26	4	14	52	51	99	.251	.325	.428	1385	347	64	16	50	143	152	296
vs. Left	.225	.371	.352	71	16	3	0	2	13	17	16	.230	.320	.376	322	74	13	5	8	32	41	82
vs. Right	.244	.313	.443	336	82	23	4	12	39	34	83	.257	.327	.444	1063	273	51	11	42	111	111	214
at Home	.250	.315	.413	196	49	11	3	5	23	19	46	.267	.328	.440	689	184	28	11	23	74	61	143
on Road	.232	.332	.441	211	49	15	1	9	29	32	53	.234	.323	.417	696	163	36	5	27	69	91	153
vs. Groundball	.248	.296	.466	206	51	13	1	10	30	15	46	.260	.319	.445	704	183	37	6	27	75	61	131
vs. Flyball	.234	.350	.388	201	47	13	3	4	22	36	53	.241	.332	.411	681	164	27	10	23	68	91	165
vs. Finesse	.264	.323	.476	227	60	18	3	8	33	20	42	.276	.331	.494	800	221	43	13	35	87	65	123
vs. Power	.211	.325	.367	180	38	8	1	6	19	31	57	.215	.318	.338	585	126	21	3	15	56	87	173
on Grass	.224	.294	.367	335	75	21	3	7	37	34	82	.242	.315	.398	1161	281	49	12	36	114	121	245
on Artificial Turf	.319	.449	.708	72	23	5	1	7	15	17	17	.295	.377	.585	224	66	15	4	14	29	31	51
Day Games	.229	.318	.365	96	22	7	0	2	9	13	25	.254	.339	.437	284	72	18	2	10	25	37	57
Night Games	.244	.326	.447	311	76	19	4	12	43	38	74	.250	.322	.426	1101	275	46	14	40	118	115	239
April	.184	.295	.316	38	7	2	0	1	4	6	8	.241	.354	.426	108	26	8	0	4	11	19	20
May	.177	.316	.290	62	11	4	0	1	5	13	17	.207	.286	.319	213	44	10	1	4	23	24	47
June	.358	.445	.663	95	34	9	1	6	21	15	27	.303	.370	.540	300	91	17	6	14	40	32	65
July	.278	.286	.556	54	15	5	2	2	8	1	8	.257	.301	.475	261	67	11	5	12	29	17	60
August	.152	.212	.253	79	12	5	0	1	5	6	20	.231	.306	.373	268	62	15	1	7	16	29	60
Sept/Oct	.241	.326	.392	79	19	1	1	3	9	10	19	.243	.331	.396	235	57	3	3	9	24	31	44
Bases Empty	.251	.325	.456	239	60	15	2	10	10	26	54	.253	.323	.457	889	225	42	11	39	39	92	184
Leadoff	.255	.339	.471	102	26	10	0	4	4	13	20	.254	.325	.470	492	125	27	8	21	21	52	100
Not Leadoff	.248	.313	.445	137	34	5	2	6	6	13	34	.252	.320	.441	397	100	15	3	18	18	40	84
Runners On	.226	.323	.387	168	38	11	2	4	42	25	45	.246	.326	.377	496	122	22	5	11	104	60	112
First Base Only	.169	.229	.299	77	13	2	1	2	6	6	21	.232	.286	.339	224	52	7	1	5	16	17	38
Scoring Position	.275	.393	.462	91	25	9	1	2	36	19	24	.257	.356	.408	272	70	15	4	6	88	43	74
Late Innings, Close	.246	.395	.344	61	15	1	1	1	10	15	8	.248	.360	.405	210	52	5	2	8	28	37	40

RBI/Opportunities

	1987		Four Year	
Scoring Position	29 / 132	(22%)	74 / 377	(20%)
Scoring Position, 2 Out	12 / 60	(20%)	30 / 177	(17%)
On Third, Less than 2 Out	11 / 26	(42%)	25 / 69	(36%)
RBI in close games / RBI Total	35 / 52	(67%)	88 / 143	(62%)

Roger McDowell
New York Mets

I was at Larry's house, talking about our tabletop baseball league. It was the opening game of the crucial Met—Cardinal series in September. After the Mets had what was felt to be a safe lead, my friend's wife had come home from work. She had turned the game off to watch something else. Larry had turned the game back on just as I went to the bathroom. I came out. He said "You won't believe it; they lost."

As I watched the replay over and over, I tried to convince myself that the pitch was a good pitch. I tried to convince myself that Pendleton had just gotten a hold of one of McDowell's sharp sinkers and mashed it. No such luck. It was a mediocre pitch over the heart of the plate and Pendleton did what he should have. Boom.

As the ball sailed over Mookie's head, so sailed away the season. I got into my car and drove home. All the way home the Mets' post-game talk show host was fielding the distraught callers as best he could. The image of that homer is still crystal clear.

The Mets' management spent many hours at the winter meetings trying to get a right-handed reliever who could come in, throw some smoke and punch out the hitters. This is what the rumored Bob Welch deal was all about. You didn't hear much about the need for this when Roger's hits to innings pitched ratio was .84/1.00 in '86.

This year it soared to 1.07/1.00 and indeed at times Roger couldn't get anyone out. On a radio talk show, he admitted to confusion about the speed of his delivery during the season. This problem with his delivery results from Roger's rushed recovery from a hernia.

In McDowell's first 14 appearances of 1987, his ERA was 5.92. He developed a hernia just as spring training came to a close (scant days before we got the good news about Dwight's substance abuse problem) and the team was without him for the first 32 games. If you can assume that your other closer (the dearly departed Jesse Orosco) is at the top of his game, the injury is no real problem. However, Jesse was terrible on several occasions and even when Roger came back his stuff wasn't up to last year's standards. It appeared he had needed more time on the DL and hadn't gotten it because of the bonfire blazing away in the bullpen. His ERA after the first 14 games was 3.50, and he wound up with 25 saves. Despite the Pendleton homer and some other bad moments, his performance gave hope he can regain his '86 form in 1988.

Gary Klug

McDowell, Roger Alan

Bats: Right   Throws: Right   Born 12/21/60

1987 SEASON AND MAJOR-LEAGUE CAREER PITCHING TOTALS

	G	GS	CG	GF	IP	BFP	H	R	ER	HR	SH	SF	HB	TBB	IBB	SO	WP	Bk	W	L	Pct	ShO	Sv	ERA
87 NYN	56	0	0	45	89	384	95	41	41	7	5	5	2	28	4	32	3	1	7	5	.583	0	25	4.15
3 YEARS	193	2	0	133	344	1424	310	132	124	20	18	10	6	107	17	167	12	6	27	19	.587	0	64	3.24

1987: Finesse, Groundball   1986: Finesse, Groundball   1985: Finesse, Groundball

1987 SEASON / FOUR YEAR TOTALS (1984 – 1987)

	G	IP	H	BB	SO	SB	CS	W	L	S	ERA	G	IP	H	BB	SO	SB	CS	W	L	S	ERA
Totals	56	89.0	95	28	32	3	1	7	5	24	4.15	193	344.1	310	107	167	26	12	27	19	63	3.24
at Home	28	52.0	50	12	19	2	1	5	3	12	4.50	93	182.2	148	52	85	10	6	17	9	31	2.66
on Road	28	37.0	45	16	13	1	0	2	2	12	3.65	100	161.2	162	55	82	16	6	10	10	32	3.90
on Grass	24	35.1	45	11	9	2	0	3	4	10	5.86	82	154.0	144	45	78	12	6	12	11	27	4.09
on Artificial Turf	32	53.2	50	17	23	1	1	4	1	14	3.02	111	190.1	166	62	89	14	6	15	8	36	2.55
Day Games	41	68.1	77	18	25	2	1	6	4	17	4.74	140	257.2	231	70	125	17	6	22	13	46	3.11
Night Games	15	20.2	18	10	7	1	0	1	1	7	3.63	53	86.2	79	37	42	9	6	5	6	17	3.63
April	0	0.0	0	0	0	0	0	0	0	0	0.00	15	26.0	25	9	22	4	2	4	0	1	3.46
May	9	17.1	20	4	10	1	0	2	1	3	4.15	31	68.0	59	18	38	3	2	6	2	9	3.04
June	14	19.0	27	7	7	0	0	2	2	5	5.68	32	60.1	59	26	30	2	2	6	4	8	3.13
July	10	19.0	17	1	5	2	0	1	0	6	1.42	33	60.2	54	12	28	5	1	2	6	14	2.37
August	13	19.0	16	4	3	0	0	2	2	7	4.74	42	64.2	49	12	21	5	2	7	5	19	3.62
Sept/Oct	10	14.2	15	12	7	0	1	0	0	3	4.91	40	64.2	64	30	28	7	3	2	2	12	3.90

vs. Opponent Batters	Ave.	OBP	SLG	AB	H	2B	3B	HR	RBI	BB	SO	Ave.	OBP	SLG	AB	H	2B	3B	HR	RBI	BB	SO
Totals	.276	.330	.366	344	95	10	0	7	52	28	32	.242	.300	.328	1283	310	43	4	20	140	107	167
vs. Left	.243	.311	.320	169	41	4	0	3	18	16	19	.241	.313	.336	622	150	24	4	9	69	64	68
vs. Right	.309	.349	.411	175	54	6	0	4	34	12	13	.242	.288	.321	661	160	19	0	11	71	43	99
Bases Empty	.269	.328	.394	160	43	5	0	5	5	14	10	.228	.285	.296	709	162	22	1	8	8	56	95
Leadoff	.342	.368	.548	73	25	3	0	4	4	3	2	.248	.303	.330	303	75	10	0	5	5	24	30
Not Leadoff	.207	.296	.264	87	18	2	0	1	1	11	8	.214	.272	.271	406	87	12	1	3	3	32	65
Runners On Base	.283	.332	.342	184	52	5	0	2	47	14	22	.258	.318	.368	574	148	21	3	12	132	51	72
First Base Only	.247	.286	.301	73	18	1	0	1	2	3	7	.241	.270	.327	257	62	7	0	5	14	9	25
Scoring Position	.306	.359	.369	111	34	4	0	1	45	11	15	.271	.353	.401	317	86	14	3	7	118	42	47
Late Innings, Close	.272	.316	.377	228	62	6	0	6	41	16	19	.246	.305	.342	801	197	24	4	15	101	69	97

RBI/Opportunities

Scoring Position	43 / 156 (28%)	104 / 453 (23%)
Scoring Position, 2 Out	24 / 75 (32%)	42 / 204 (21%)
On Third, Less than 2 Out	11 / 25 (44%)	40 / 81 (49%)
RBI in close games / RBI Total	41 / 52 (79%)	111 / 140 (79%)

Andy McGaffigan
Montreal Expos

Before the 1987 season Andy McGaffigan had established a reputation as a valuable starter-reliever. No more than a handful of major league pitchers have been consistently effective in this role—Juan Berenguer and Ron Robinson come quickly to mind—and McGaffigan, though better coming out of the bullpen, had been as good a swingman as anyone. Andy was at his best in '86; while starting 14 games and relieving in 34 more, he compiled a 10–5 record with a 2.65 ERA.

McGaffigan might have expected more of the same in '87, but with the departure of Jeff Reardon, he was asked to finish games for the first time in his career. He proved he could handle this job as well; sharing the Expo closer's role with Tim Burke and several others, McGaffigan recorded 12 saves and posted a 2.39 ERA, easily the lowest of his career. He was a real workhouse, appearing in 69 games (another career best) and logging 120.1 innings in relief. Only Mark Eichhorn, Lance McCullers and Jeff D. Robinson had more bullpen innings than McGaffigan, and no one did as well in combining durability with effectiveness.

McGaffigan has several things going for him. He's obviously capable of handling a heavy workload; he's a hard thrower with an excellent strikeout ratio; he doesn't walk an excessive amount of hitters; and he gives up very few home run balls. And, of course, he's versatile. The Expos seem well stocked with starters for '88, and Burke appears to have established himself as the number-one closer, so McGaffigan is slated for middle relief. He figures to do well in that job, or almost any other he's asked to perform.

About the only thing McGaffigan doesn't handle well, in fact, is a bat. He's not just a bad hitter; he's one of the worst hitters to ever play in major league competition. With the lumber, 1987 was your typical Andy McGaffigan season—0 for 17 with 12 strikeouts. McGaffigan has now recorded only 5 hits in 120 career at bats, making his lifetime BA an awe-inspiring .042. According to Pete Palmer, Andy now ranks second-to-last among all players with at least 100 lifetime at bats; only the great Ron Herbel, at .029, is ahead of (or behind) him. Catching Herbel won't be easy. Not only does his work as a reliever mean that McGaffigan gets a limited number of at bats; even one cheap single, maybe a bad call by a Giant scorer trying to protect Herbel's reputation, would set him back for several years. As it stands, McGaffigan needs to go 0 for his next 56 at bats to slink down to .028. The pressure will be intense; after all, Joe DiMaggio needed only a hit a game, while Andy needs out after out after out. Then there's the national media, who are bound to be sticking microphones in his face and asking, "Were you trying to make an out on that one?" It'll be a struggle, but we'll be pulling for you, Andy.

Don Zminda

McGaffigan, Andrew Joseph "Andy" Bats: Right Throws: Right Born 10/25/56

1987 SEASON AND MAJOR-LEAGUE CAREER PITCHING TOTALS

	G	GS	CG	GF	IP	BFP	H	R	ER	HR	SH	SF	HB	TBB	IBB	SO	WP	Bk	W	L	Pct	ShO	Sv	ERA
87 MON	69	0	0	30	120	500	105	38	32	5	5	3	3	42	7	100	6	0	5	2	.714	0	12	2.40
7 YEARS	211	51	3	61	575	2378	508	226	206	40	27	13	9	193	26	443	22	14	25	25	.500	1	17	3.22

1987: Power, Flyball   1986: Power, Groundball   1985: Power, Flyball   1984: Power, Groundball

1987 SEASON / FOUR YEAR TOTALS (1984 – 1987)

	G	IP	H	BB	SO	SB	CS	W	L	S	ERA		G	IP	H	BB	SO	SB	CS	W	L	S	ERA
Totals	69	119.2	105	42	100	18	2	5	2	13	2.41		162	425.2	367	150	344	54	11	21	16	16	2.96
at Home	36	56.1	58	19	47	7	0	3	0	4	3.04		82	211.0	184	69	165	29	4	10	7	6	3.03
on Road	33	63.1	47	23	53	11	2	2	2	9	1.85		80	214.2	183	81	179	25	7	11	9	10	2.89
on Grass	19	26.2	23	9	25	5	0	1	1	5	2.36		55	150.1	132	50	132	18	6	8	8	6	3.29
on Artificial Turf	50	93.0	82	33	75	13	2	4	1	8	2.42		107	275.1	235	100	212	36	5	13	8	10	2.78
Day Games	16	32.0	21	9	34	6	1	1	1	5	1.13		44	114.2	104	38	97	13	5	4	8	6	3.53
Night Games	53	87.2	84	33	66	12	1	4	1	8	2.87		118	311.0	263	112	247	41	6	17	8	10	2.75
April	8	14.0	9	4	13	3	0	0	0	4	0.64		17	43.0	31	19	36	5	1	2	0	4	2.72
May	12	20.1	23	5	22	6	0	0	0	3	3.10		27	63.1	57	25	48	9	0	4	4	4	2.56
June	12	19.1	16	7	12	1	0	0	1	1	3.26		23	54.2	48	18	40	5	2	2	4	1	3.62
July	11	13.2	15	3	9	1	0	2	1	1	2.63		21	50.0	50	11	41	4	1	2	2	1	2.70
August	12	25.0	21	12	22	3	2	2	0	1	1.80		35	108.2	95	42	88	12	6	6	5	2	3.31
Sept/Oct	14	27.1	21	11	22	4	0	1	0	3	2.63		39	106.0	86	35	91	19	1	5	1	4	2.72

vs. Opponent Batters	Ave.	OBP	SLG	AB	H	2B	3B	HR	RBI	BB	SO		Ave.	OBP	SLG	AB	H	2B	3B	HR	RBI	BB	SO
Totals	.234	.302	.319	448	105	17	3	5	38	42	100		.234	.301	.334	1571	367	69	11	22	145	150	344
vs. Left	.266	.338	.386	241	64	13	2	4	23	26	52		.243	.323	.333	834	203	36	6	9	69	98	175
vs. Right	.198	.259	.242	207	41	4	1	1	15	16	48		.223	.275	.334	737	164	33	5	13	76	52	169
Bases Empty	.262	.321	.369	244	64	10	2	4	4	20	51		.242	.301	.350	909	220	42	7	14	14	76	190
Leadoff	.259	.292	.352	108	28	4	0	2	2	5	28		.256	.311	.372	390	100	15	0	10	10	31	82
Not Leadoff	.265	.342	.382	136	36	6	2	2	2	15	23		.231	.294	.333	519	120	27	7	4	4	45	108
Runners On Base	.201	.281	.260	204	41	7	1	1	34	22	49		.222	.301	.311	662	147	27	4	8	131	74	154
First Base Only	.146	.213	.220	82	12	3	0	1	3	6	17		.199	.257	.296	267	53	13	2	3	11	20	55
Scoring Position	.238	.324	.287	122	29	4	1	0	31	16	32		.238	.329	.322	395	94	14	2	5	120	54	99
Late Innings, Close	.200	.286	.293	150	30	8	0	2	11	18	38		.216	.300	.310	310	67	18	1	3	25	37	70

RBI/Opportunities

Scoring Position	30 / 182 (16%)	108 / 562 (19%)
Scoring Position, 2 Out	10 / 88 (11%)	47 / 270 (17%)
On Third, Less than 2 Out	15 / 33 (45%)	39 / 92 (42%)
RBI in close games / RBI Total	19 / 38 (50%)	97 / 145 (67%)

Willie McGee
St Louis Cardinals

Willie McGee is one of baseball's unique players. He has some definite weaknesses in his game offensively, but he has still managed to accomplish a great deal since he came to the Cardinals in a little publicized trade during the 1981 World Series. I can't think of any other active player who's had season totals in his career exceeding, in various years, 100 runs scored, 200 hits, 100 RBIs, 35 doubles, 15 triples, and 50 stolen bases, won a batting title and an MVP award, been awarded several Gold Gloves, and played on a World Championship team. McGee may not be Dale Murphy, but for Bob Sykes he ain't bad.

One thing that Willie is not is a good baserunner. It's not really fair to judge him on his 1987 season because it was obvious that he was not comfortable with his knee following surgery, but the fact is, despite his speed, Willie has always had trouble navigating the basepaths. During the 1982 NLCS he turned an easy inside-the-park homer into a triple by coming into third with his head down and not watching his coach. In Game 7 of the '87 NLCS he overran second base after a double and was tagged out. These instances stand out because they occurred in postseason play, but if you watch many Cardinal games you know that they are not out of the ordinary for Willie. In fact he was tagged out following two of his triples last season after overrunning or oversliding third base, and there were at least two others

where he did the same thing and the umpire gave him a break. And Willie won't let the umpire miss a close call. If he thinks he's out he gets up and heads for the dugout without waiting for the call. He's been tagged out several times in his career after doing this.

If we're going to talk about McGee's bad baserunning, however, we have to give him credit for improving as a base stealer in '87. Whether it was the knee injury or something else, Willie did a much better job of picking his spots to run. The result was an 80 percent success rate, 16 for 20, that was a big improvement over his 19 for 35 performance of 1986. McGee was a poor base stealer when he first came to the majors, but he had made himself into a pretty good one, stealing 138 bases in 1983–85 with an 80 percent success rate. Then came his knee problems, and though he'll probably never be a base stealing force again, he can still be successful at it if he approaches it the way he did in '87.

Among McGee's personal highlights in '87: Hit .365 and slugged .538 versus the Giants, including 11 RBIs . . . Collected 21 hits and drove home 14 runners against the Cubbies, hitting .412 and slugging .706 . . . Against Pittsburgh, Willie collected 24 base hits, nine of them for extra bases . . . Was also bad news in Atlanta, against whom he managed to drive home 15 runners with only 12 hits.

Russ Eagle

McGee, Willie Dean Bats: Both Throws: Right Born 11/02/58

1987 SEASON AND MAJOR-LEAGUE CAREER BATTING TOTALS

	G	AB	H	2B	3B	HR	TB	R	RBI	TBB	IBB	SO	HP	SH	SF	SB	CS	SB%	GDP	AVG	OBP	SLG
87 STL	153	620	177	37	11	11	269	76	105	24	5	90	2	1	5	16	4	.80	24	.285	.312	.434
6 YEARS	844	3323	983	138	63	43	1376	455	416	162	20	494	6	5	21	197	66	.75	64	.296	.328	.414

	1987 SEASON											FOUR YEAR TOTALS (1984 – 1987)										
	Ave.	OBP	SLG	AB	H	2B	3B	HR	RBI	BB	SO	Ave.	OBP	SLG	AB	H	2B	3B	HR	RBI	BB	SO
Totals	.285	.312	.434	620	177	37	11	11	105	24	90	.298	.333	.429	2300	686	104	47	34	285	124	338
vs. Left	.288	.309	.500	208	60	16	5	6	42	8	35	.289	.322	.476	781	226	39	19	23	116	40	157
vs. Right	.284	.313	.400	412	117	21	6	5	63	16	55	.303	.339	.404	1519	460	65	28	11	169	84	181
at Home	.297	.316	.457	300	89	20	5	6	53	10	45	.309	.337	.447	1110	343	51	24	18	127	51	167
on Road	.275	.308	.412	320	88	17	6	5	52	14	45	.288	.329	.412	1190	343	53	23	16	158	73	171
vs. Groundball	.258	.288	.351	279	72	14	3	2	43	11	41	.284	.322	.388	1122	319	50	24	6	125	64	153
vs. Flyball	.308	.331	.501	341	105	23	8	9	62	13	49	.312	.343	.468	1178	367	54	23	28	160	60	185
vs. Finesse	.322	.342	.441	338	109	21	5	3	59	10	34	.308	.341	.432	1282	395	67	28	12	149	68	150
vs. Power	.241	.276	.426	282	68	16	6	8	46	14	56	.286	.323	.424	1018	291	37	19	22	136	56	188
on Grass	.268	.316	.414	157	42	7	2	4	26	10	26	.285	.328	.408	613	175	32	8	9	81	38	84
on Artificial Turf	.292	.310	.441	463	135	30	9	7	79	14	64	.303	.335	.436	1687	511	72	39	25	204	86	254
Day Games	.303	.332	.412	211	64	9	4	2	36	8	30	.317	.351	.461	823	261	32	22	14	107	42	113
Night Games	.276	.301	.445	409	113	28	7	9	69	16	60	.288	.323	.411	1477	425	72	25	20	178	82	225
April	.295	.333	.426	61	18	3	1	1	13	4	9	.271	.309	.374	262	71	3	6	4	34	15	46
May	.248	.278	.385	109	27	4	1	3	25	3	20	.274	.318	.393	420	115	15	10	5	60	26	67
June	.337	.352	.485	101	34	6	3	1	18	3	13	.299	.333	.411	418	125	18	10	3	53	22	60
July	.325	.347	.496	117	38	9	1	3	19	4	20	.326	.352	.513	347	113	24	7	9	42	14	50
August	.264	.292	.384	125	33	8	2	1	19	5	12	.327	.362	.462	364	119	17	7	6	52	20	46
Sept/Oct	.252	.281	.430	107	27	7	3	2	11	5	16	.292	.328	.419	489	143	27	7	7	44	27	69
Bases Empty	.275	.294	.403	298	82	20	6	2	2	8	43	.303	.328	.426	1297	393	60	27	15	15	49	192
Leadoff	.261	.285	.353	119	31	9	1	0	0	4	15	.298	.324	.410	503	150	25	11	3	3	19	71
Not Leadoff	.285	.301	.436	179	51	11	5	2	2	4	28	.306	.331	.436	794	243	35	16	12	12	30	121
Runners On	.295	.328	.463	322	95	17	5	9	103	16	47	.292	.341	.433	1003	293	44	20	19	270	75	146
First Base Only	.391	.412	.627	110	43	7	2	5	15	4	16	.295	.336	.432	359	106	13	6	8	26	22	50
Scoring Position	.245	.286	.377	212	52	10	3	4	88	12	31	.290	.344	.433	644	187	31	14	11	244	53	96
Late Innings, Close	.254	.292	.368	114	29	9	2	0	17	5	24	.256	.304	.369	379	97	17	7	4	57	25	73

RBI/Opportunities

	1987		FOUR YEAR	
Scoring Position	77 / 279	(28%)	220 / 834	(26%)
Scoring Position, 2 Out	23 / 132	(17%)	76 / 372	(20%)
On Third, Less than 2 Out	35 / 56	(63%)	90 / 164	(55%)
RBI in close games / RBI Total	77 / 105	(73%)	191 / 285	(67%)

Mark McGwire
Oakland Athletics

No baseball fan in America missed what Mark McGwire did to the rookie home run record in 1987. Most people, however, are less familiar with his other unprecedented offensive accomplishment for a rookie. His .618 slugging percentage broke the record for an American League rookie, passing Ted Williams' mark of .609 set in 1939. It was the highest ever in either league among rookies playing in 120 games or more.

McGwire joined George Bell as the first major leaguers since 1980 to exceed a .600 slugging percentage in a full season. He also was the only player in the American League to have over half his hits go for extra bases in 1987.

McGwire set or broke two other less publicized, but still impressive, records. He became the first rookie and fourteenth major leaguer to get five home runs in two consecutive games, and he tied a major league record by scoring in nine consecutive plate appearances.

Of Mark's 49 home runs, 28 were hit on the road—seven in Tiger stadium alone—which suggests he would have easily hit 50 if he had an easier home park than the Coliseum. Seventeen were hit on the first pitch, and 20 were leading off innings. He had seven multiple home run games, and the A's record when he hit the long ball was 23–18.

McGwire caused a bit of a stir and some disappointment among the fans when he left the team in Chicago on the last day of the season to be with his wife, who was about to give birth to their first child. That cost him a shot at 50 home runs and the A's a chance at second place. However, family priorities are a refreshing change from the interests of some other excellent athletes but flawed human beings.

There is a tremendous focus on winning it all in modern sports, but that is not always the bottom line with every fan, particularly baseball fans. Sure, many fans don't consider a baseball season worthwhile unless their team is in a pennant race until the bitter end. However, as a follower of an average team with limited resources to compete for big-money players, I often think that the progress of the season is more enjoyable in retrospect than the final standings. I think it would have been a lot of fun to have been a Milwaukee fan with the variety of experiences they went through in 1987. I could see it as preferable to a season ticket in the Metro-Dumb or to be disappointed again by the underachieving Blue Jays.

Likewise, the pleasure of watching a Rickey Henderson, Jose Canseco, or Mark McGwire start out and grow during the first five years of their careers can be more satisfying than ticker tape parades and champagne (or Diet Pepsi) in the locker room. That's one thing the fans in the major markets will miss even if their clubs eventually nab these types of players.

Susan Nelson

McGwire, Mark David

Bats: Right   **Throws: Right**   **Born 10/01/63**

1987 SEASON AND MAJOR-LEAGUE CAREER BATTING TOTALS

	G	AB	H	2B	3B	HR	TB	R	RBI	TBB	IBB	SO	HP	SH	SF	SB	CS	SB%	GDP	AVG	OBP	SLG
87 OAK	151	557	161	28	4	49	344	97	118	71	8	131	5	0	8	1	1	.50	6	.289	.370	.618
2 YEARS	169	610	171	29	4	52	364	107	127	75	8	149	6	0	8	1	2	.33	6	.280	.361	.597

	1987 SEASON											FOUR YEAR TOTALS (1984 – 1987)										
	Ave.	OBP	SLG	AB	H	2B	3B	HR	RBI	BB	SO	Ave.	OBP	SLG	AB	H	2B	3B	HR	RBI	BB	SO
Totals	.289	.370	.618	557	161	28	4	49	118	71	131	.280	.361	.597	610	171	29	4	52	127	75	149
vs. Left	.287	.400	.626	171	49	10	0	16	38	35	40	.280	.388	.594	207	58	11	0	18	45	38	50
vs. Right	.290	.355	.614	386	112	18	4	33	80	36	91	.280	.345	.598	403	113	18	4	34	82	37	99
at Home	.277	.366	.572	278	77	15	2	21	49	38	67	.268	.358	.552	299	80	15	2	22	53	41	75
on Road	.301	.373	.663	279	84	13	2	28	69	33	64	.293	.363	.640	311	91	14	2	30	74	34	74
vs. Groundball	.347	.405	.670	291	101	16	3	24	56	28	48	.348	.406	.659	305	106	17	3	24	60	29	51
vs. Flyball	.226	.333	.560	266	60	12	1	25	62	43	83	.213	.317	.534	305	65	12	1	28	67	46	98
vs. Finesse	.340	.415	.772	285	97	21	3	32	73	36	48	.319	.394	.714	329	105	22	3	34	81	39	62
vs. Power	.235	.323	.456	272	64	7	1	17	45	35	83	.235	.322	.459	281	66	7	1	18	46	36	87
on Grass	.288	.366	.619	486	140	25	2	44	105	59	115	.280	.355	.600	533	149	26	2	47	113	62	132
on Artificial Turf	.296	.395	.606	71	21	3	2	5	13	12	16	.286	.394	.571	77	22	3	2	5	14	13	17
Day Games	.297	.382	.668	202	60	5	2	22	44	26	44	.297	.382	.668	202	60	5	2	22	44	26	44
Night Games	.285	.363	.589	355	101	23	2	27	74	45	87	.272	.350	.561	408	111	24	2	30	83	49	105
April	.250	.361	.519	52	13	2	0	4	12	9	16	.250	.361	.519	52	13	2	0	4	12	9	16
May	.275	.391	.813	91	25	0	2	15	24	18	20	.275	.391	.813	91	25	0	2	15	24	18	20
June	.304	.363	.647	102	31	6	1	9	20	10	19	.304	.363	.647	102	31	6	1	9	20	10	19
July	.314	.360	.618	102	32	4	0	9	27	4	25	.314	.360	.618	102	32	4	0	9	27	4	25
August	.212	.316	.374	99	21	5	1	3	12	15	28	.208	.303	.392	125	26	6	1	5	16	17	36
Sept/Oct	.351	.419	.694	111	39	11	0	9	23	15	23	.319	.390	.616	138	44	11	0	10	28	17	33
Bases Empty	.279	.359	.635	315	88	14	1	32	32	37	75	.264	.345	.603	348	92	14	1	34	34	41	87
Leadoff	.303	.365	.775	142	43	7	0	20	20	14	37	.301	.367	.778	153	46	7	0	22	22	16	40
Not Leadoff	.260	.354	.520	173	45	7	1	12	12	23	38	.236	.329	.467	195	46	7	1	12	12	25	47
Runners On	.302	.383	.595	242	73	14	3	17	86	34	56	.302	.380	.588	262	79	15	3	18	93	34	62
First Base Only	.317	.367	.693	101	32	9	1	9	23	7	19	.302	.351	.660	106	32	9	1	9	23	7	21
Scoring Position	.291	.393	.525	141	41	5	2	8	63	27	37	.301	.397	.538	156	47	6	2	9	70	27	41
Late Innings, Close	.276	.323	.529	87	24	2	1	6	10	5	22	.276	.323	.529	174	48	4	2	12	20	10	44

RBI/Opportunities

Scoring Position	47 / 201 (23%)	53 / 219 (24%)
Scoring Position, 2 Out	20 / 98 (20%)	24 / 108 (22%)
On Third, Less than 2 Out	19 / 40 (48%)	20 / 42 (48%)
RBI in close games / RBI Total	66 / 118 (56%)	132 / 127 (104%)

Mark McLemore
California Angels

Last spring, Mark McLemore seized the chance to move from "second baseman of the future" to "second baseman of today" with the California Angels. For at least two seasons McLemore had been viewed as one of the team's top prospects, and the second base job was now open thanks to Bobby Grich's retirement shortly after the 1986 season.

But, by late summer, McLemore's slumping bat had prompted the Angels to look elsewhere, at least temporarily, for second base help. The Angels subsequently obtained Johnny Ray, a proven big league hitter, from Pittsburgh on August 29 and optioned McLemore to the minors for a couple of days, recalling him after September 1.

This doesn't mean the Angels have given up on McLemore, who is just 23. The plan is to move Ray to the outfield and give Mark another shot at second base, for there is some very visible talent here. A switch-hitter with great speed, McLemore had been a consistent hitter in five minor league seasons. He has shown exceptional baserunning skills and received raves for his defensive play. *Baseball America*'s annual "best tools" survey named him the Pacific Coast League's best defensive second baseman in 1986. This background, coupled with McLemore's fine spring in 1987 (25 for 83, .301), may have caused the Angels

to rush him to fill the shoes of their former All-Star and veteran leader, Bobby Grich.

McLemore did have a good April (20 for 76, .263), but then began to falter at the plate. He hit .209 in May, .212 in June, and .198 in July. In prior years, when the rest of the lineup was being productive, the Angels might have been able to carry McLemore's offensive dead weight. But in 1987 there were too many lineup holes, too many non-productive positions already for the team to do this.

Although Johnny Ray responded well to his new environment, hitting .346 in 30 games with the Angels, the Angels did not overlook that McLemore also finished the season strongly, hitting .295 (28 for 95) in his final 37 games. That final stretch was highlighted by 4 RBIs in a 4 for 4 performance against Cleveland.

Although a liability at the plate, McLemore was very impressive on the base paths. Despite playing in only 138 games with an on-base percentage of just .310, he stole 25 bases. He was caught only 8 times for an impressive 76 percent success rate. Defensively, as well, McLemore showed flashes of brilliance. Overall, in the AL in 1987, only Harold Reynolds, Frank White, Marty Barrett, and Lou Whitaker fielded more balls cleanly at second base.

Dean Hill

McLemore, Mark Tremell **Bats: Both** **Throws: Right** **Born 10/04/64**

1987 SEASON AND MAJOR-LEAGUE CAREER BATTING TOTALS

	G	AB	H	2B	3B	HR	TB	R	RBI	TBB	IBB	SO	HP	SH	SF	SB	CS	SB%	GDP	AVG	OBP	SLG
87 CAL	138	433	102	13	3	3	130	61	41	48	0	72	0	15	3	25	8	.76	7	.236	.310	.300
2 YEARS	143	437	102	13	3	3	130	61	41	49	0	74	0	16	3	25	9	.74	7	.233	.309	.297

	1987 SEASON											TWO YEAR TOTALS (1986 – 1987)										
	Ave.	OBP	SLG	AB	H	2B	3B	HR	RBI	BB	SO	Ave.	OBP	SLG	AB	H	2B	3B	HR	RBI	BB	SO
Totals	.236	.310	.300	433	102	13	3	3	41	48	72	.233	.309	.297	437	102	13	3	3	41	49	74
vs. Left	.222	.293	.294	126	28	4	1	1	10	13	12	.222	.293	.294	126	28	4	1	1	10	13	12
vs. Right	.241	.317	.303	307	74	9	2	2	31	35	60	.238	.315	.299	311	74	9	2	2	31	36	62
at Home	.235	.315	.319	213	50	7	1	3	24	26	32	.234	.317	.318	214	50	7	1	3	24	27	33
on Road	.236	.305	.282	220	52	6	2	0	17	22	40	.233	.301	.278	223	52	6	2	0	17	22	41
vs. Groundball	.243	.316	.307	202	49	8	1	1	17	22	37	.239	.311	.302	205	49	8	1	1	17	22	38
vs. Flyball	.229	.305	.294	231	53	5	2	2	24	26	35	.228	.307	.293	232	53	5	2	2	24	27	36
vs. Finesse	.246	.316	.294	211	52	7	0	1	15	22	31	.245	.318	.292	212	52	7	0	1	15	23	32
vs. Power	.225	.304	.306	222	50	6	3	2	26	26	41	.222	.300	.302	225	50	6	3	2	26	26	42
on Grass	.234	.306	.300	363	85	11	2	3	36	39	59	.234	.307	.299	364	85	11	2	3	36	40	60
on Artificial Turf	.243	.329	.300	70	17	2	1	0	5	9	13	.233	.317	.288	73	17	2	1	0	5	9	14
Day Games	.241	.294	.348	141	34	5	2	2	13	11	25	.241	.294	.348	141	34	5	2	2	13	11	25
Night Games	.233	.317	.277	292	68	8	1	1	28	37	47	.230	.315	.274	296	68	8	1	1	28	38	49
April	.263	.364	.303	76	20	3	0	0	7	12	13	.263	.364	.303	76	20	3	0	0	7	12	13
May	.209	.280	.275	91	19	4	1	0	5	9	14	.209	.280	.275	91	19	4	1	0	5	9	14
June	.212	.287	.259	85	18	2	1	0	6	9	20	.212	.287	.259	85	18	2	1	0	6	9	20
July	.198	.242	.256	86	17	2	0	1	10	6	12	.198	.242	.256	86	17	2	0	1	10	6	12
August	.278	.360	.392	79	22	1	1	2	8	10	12	.278	.360	.392	79	22	1	1	2	8	10	12
Sept/Oct	.375	.444	.438	16	6	1	0	0	5	2	1	.300	.391	.350	20	6	1	0	0	5	3	3
Bases Empty	.233	.290	.287	240	56	5	1	2	2	19	37	.230	.289	.284	243	56	5	1	2	2	20	38
Leadoff	.240	.315	.280	100	24	1	0	1	1	11	14	.235	.310	.275	102	24	1	0	1	1	11	14
Not Leadoff	.229	.270	.293	140	32	4	1	1	1	8	23	.227	.273	.291	141	32	4	1	1	1	9	24
Runners On	.238	.333	.316	193	46	8	2	1	39	29	35	.237	.332	.314	194	46	8	2	1	39	29	36
First Base Only	.253	.364	.360	75	19	3	1	1	4	13	8	.250	.360	.355	76	19	3	1	1	4	13	9
Scoring Position	.229	.314	.288	118	27	5	1	0	35	16	27	.229	.314	.288	118	27	5	1	0	35	16	27
Late Innings, Close	.351	.438	.416	77	27	0	1	1	11	12	11	.351	.438	.416	154	54	0	2	2	22	24	22

RBI/Opportunities

Scoring Position	34 / 166	(20%)			34 / 166	(20%)	
Scoring Position, 2 Out	14 / 93	(15%)			14 / 93	(15%)	
On Third, Less than 2 Out	12 / 22	(55%)			12 / 22	(55%)	
RBI in close games / RBI Total	32 / 41	(78%)			64 / 41	(156%)	

Kevin McReynolds
New York Mets

I live in the media center of the known universe, the advertising mecca where Reggie Jackson had a candy bar named after him. Kevin McReynolds arrives here and what do we hear? Nothing. McReynolds is quiet. He is the most soft-spoken athlete I can remember in a long time. He makes Mark Bavaro sound like Sparky Anderson. On a team where all summer it seemed the clothesline couldn't hold all the dirty laundry, the only thing I can remember Kevin saying was "Hi Mom, don't worry, they're takin' good care of me here in New York."

As for Kevin's on the field performance, you must understand we have been watching George Foster play left field for years. George had a habit of treating line drives as if they were live grenades (Ooh, here comes one . . . let's see, I hope it doesn't go into the corncr. Oh darn, there it goes . . . I'll just have to trot after it. There, now I've picked it up; let's turn around and see where the runner is . . .).

I'm not saying that McReynolds is the reincarnation of Joe Jackson but he covers his ground. His ability to go to his right to get a single, pick up the ball on the run, and fire to second is just something to see. The Met left fielders haven't exactly been defensive gems, you know. Why, for many long years the position has been filled by the likes of Dave Kingman, Steve Henderson, George Theodore and Foster.

All in all a fine defensive left fielder, Kevin played center field for the Padres but the weight he carries in his thighs hampers him at that position. In left he combines his natural athletic ability with less ground to cover.

As for his offense, a batting average of .276, 29 homers and 95 RBIs is exactly what the Mets thought they would get when they traded for him. One of the New York writers felt he chokes withMets in scoring position, but I couldn't find much fault with Kevin at the plate.

The Mets' TV broadcasters talk a great deal about McReynolds' short, compact swing. He likes the ball from the middle of the plate on in and had trouble last year with the outside slider which he often tried to pull. When he was slumping he would see that pitch a great deal more than he would care to.

One result of that short swing is line drive homers over the auxiliary scoreboard at Shea. Those balls land in the Loge, and whenever Kevin would get "locked in" the ball would jump off his bat and in a flash become a souvenir for some lucky Loge fan. His home runs have less arc and get out of the park quicker than any other Met. Kevin is a talented player.

Gerry Klug

McReynolds, Walter Kevin "Kevin"   Bats: Right   Throws: Right   Born 10/16/59

1987 SEASON AND MAJOR-LEAGUE CAREER BATTING TOTALS

	G	AB	H	2B	3B	HR	TB	R	RBI	TBB	IBB	SO	HP	SH	SF	SB	CS	SB%	GDP	AVG	OBP	SLG
87 NYN	151	590	163	32	5	29	292	86	95	39	5	70	1	1	8	14	1	.93	13	.276	.318	.495
5 YEARS	647	2379	633	116	22	94	1075	319	355	194	26	332	5	11	33	31	14	.69	54	.266	.319	.452

	1987 SEASON											FOUR YEAR TOTALS (1984 – 1987)									
	Ave.	OBP	SLG	AB	H	2B	3B	HR	RBI	BB	SO	Ave.	OBP	SLG	AB	H	2B	3B	HR	RBI	BB	SO
Totals	.276	.318	.495	590	163	32	5	29	95	39	70	.269	.321	.459	2239	602	113	21	90	341	182	303
vs. Left	.290	.325	.534	221	64	14	2	12	36	11	25	.290	.349	.505	747	217	40	9	34	123	70	85
vs. Right	.268	.314	.472	369	99	18	3	17	59	28	45	.258	.307	.436	1492	385	73	12	56	218	112	218
at Home	.275	.324	.503	298	82	12	1	18	51	22	37	.276	.331	.470	1102	304	48	11	48	167	97	164
on Road	.277	.312	.486	292	81	20	4	11	44	17	33	.262	.311	.448	1137	298	65	10	42	174	85	139
vs. Groundball	.268	.314	.485	235	63	13	1	12	38	18	27	.281	.334	.488	1094	307	52	8	53	184	94	125
vs. Flyball	.282	.321	.501	355	100	19	4	17	57	21	43	.258	.308	.431	1145	295	61	13	37	157	88	178
vs. Finesse	.285	.330	.465	312	89	18	4	10	39	23	26	.300	.345	.487	1215	365	63	13	46	181	89	111
vs. Power	.266	.304	.529	278	74	14	1	19	56	16	44	.231	.294	.425	1024	237	50	8	44	160	93	192
on Grass	.272	.312	.491	426	116	23	2	22	68	27	49	.266	.319	.455	1644	437	77	15	68	245	137	238
on Artificial Turf	.287	.333	.506	164	47	9	3	7	27	12	21	.277	.327	.469	595	165	36	6	22	96	45	65
Day Games	.242	.276	.419	215	52	10	2	8	34	11	29	.248	.300	.434	761	189	32	8	31	120	59	116
Night Games	.296	.341	.539	375	111	22	3	21	61	28	41	.279	.332	.472	1478	413	81	13	59	221	123	187
April	.311	.377	.590	61	19	2	0	5	10	7	11	.279	.341	.484	283	79	12	2	14	44	27	47
May	.235	.291	.373	102	24	8	0	2	12	8	9	.276	.330	.475	381	105	21	2	17	67	31	49
June	.313	.346	.596	99	31	7	0	7	19	6	8	.268	.315	.457	396	106	21	6	14	54	28	46
July	.298	.333	.538	104	31	6	2	5	22	6	13	.247	.314	.430	365	90	22	3	13	56	36	49
August	.264	.297	.418	110	29	3	1	4	14	6	17	.277	.324	.454	372	103	14	2	16	58	27	50
Sept/Oct	.254	.292	.500	114	29	6	2	6	18	6	12	.269	.320	.457	442	119	23	6	16	62	33	62
Bases Empty	.325	.360	.572	311	101	21	1	18	18	16	27	.267	.312	.468	1224	327	60	12	54	54	79	155
Leadoff	.391	.432	.618	110	43	8	1	5	5	7	8	.291	.333	.501	477	139	22	9	20	20	29	51
Not Leadoff	.289	.319	.547	201	58	13	0	13	13	9	19	.252	.299	.447	747	188	38	3	34	34	50	104
Runners On	.222	.274	.409	279	62	11	4	11	77	23	43	.271	.336	.447	1015	275	53	9	36	287	103	148
First Base Only	.240	.298	.427	96	23	3	0	5	10	8	15	.274	.318	.440	405	111	22	3	13	36	26	50
Scoring Position	.213	.262	.399	183	39	8	4	6	67	15	28	.269	.347	.452	610	164	31	6	23	251	77	98
Late Innings, Close	.228	.286	.277	101	23	2	0	1	13	9	9	.235	.289	.367	425	100	16	2	12	61	33	72

RBI/Opportunities

Scoring Position	53 / 238 (22%)	206 / 846 (24%)
Scoring Position, 2 Out	25 / 100 (25%)	85 / 358 (24%)
On Third, Less than 2 Out	17 / 40 (43%)	79 / 152 (52%)
RBI in close games / RBI Total	63 / 95 (66%)	238 / 341 (70%)

Kevin Mitchell
San Diego Padres/San Francisco Giants

On opening day 1988, the Giants' starting infield should be Will Clark, 24, at first; Robby Thompson, 25, at second; José Uribe, 28, at short, and Kevin Mitchell, 26, at third. The acquisition of Brett Butler has likely installed Kevin at third base for the foreseeable future; otherwise, there was talk of moving him to center field. Kevin is a much better third baseman than anyone in San Francisco thought when Chris Brown was traded for him: His Range Factor of 2.75 trailed only Moreland (2.85), Wallach (2.94), Schmidt (3.00) and Pendleton (3.24) among all players who patrolled the hot corner at least 50 games last year. During his time as a Giant, Kevin made some spectacular plays, but there were three things about him that most surprised San Francisco fans and management:

1) He has a very strong and accurate arm.

2) From July 4 he hit 15 homers as a Giant, equalling his best full season in baseball

3) He wears short-sleeved shirts at Candlestick. At night. Every night.

When Kevin joined the Giants, about all San Francisco fans knew about him was:

a) He had finished third in Rookie of the Year balloting behind Todd Worrell and Robby Thompson, but, being from New York during the Mets' championship year, he *must* have been a creation of the media, not a true talent, because

b) he had just been traded for the second time in 5 months,

and must be a troublemaker, because

c) the story was out that he didn't like San Diego; even though it was his home town, it was too "tame"—Kevin's idea of relaxation was to go out and get in a good fight (he reputedly has scars across his back and chest from chain-whippings received as a youthful gang member), and

d) he'd never amount to more than a utility player, since he had performed at 6 positions in his short rookie season alone.

July 4. Foggy, rainy day at Wrigley. Les Lancaster on the mound. Wind blowing in. Kevin's first two at-bats as a Giant result in two home runs, both into the wind, one out on Waveland Avenue. His first 4-RBI day.

By August, Kevin became an offensive force, going 32-for-84 (.381) during the month, with 5 HR and 11 RBIs. He did two things Giant third basemen of the recent past had not done—he played every day, nearly needing to be arm wrestled out of the lineup when hurt, and he caught everything that came near him. Chris Brown had done one of those things, Joel Youngblood the other, but neither had done both. As a Giant, Mitchell slugged .530, trailing only Will Clark. Though it was only a half-season, that .530 trailed only Mike Schmidt's .548 among third basemen.

As October rolled around, Kevin acquired his second year of post-season experience, not bad for a sophomore. The Giants have a young (all well under 30), post-season experienced, intact infield. No other National League team can say that.

Michael Duca

Mitchell, Kevin Darrell

Bats: Right　　**Throws: Right**　　**Born 01/13/62**

1987 SEASON AND MAJOR-LEAGUE CAREER BATTING TOTALS

	G	AB	H	2B	3B	HR	TB	R	RBI	TBB	IBB	SO	HP	SH	SF	SB	CS	SB%	GDP	AVG	OBP	SLG
87 SD-SF	131	464	130	20	2	22	220	68	70	48	4	88	2	0	1	9	6	.60	10	.280	.350	.474
3 YEARS	246	806	224	42	4	34	376	119	114	81	4	152	3	1	2	12	10	.55	16	.278	.345	.467

1987 SEASON / FOUR YEAR TOTALS (1984 – 1987)

	Ave.	OBP	SLG	AB	H	2B	3B	HR	RBI	BB	SO	Ave.	OBP	SLG	AB	H	2B	3B	HR	RBI	BB	SO
Totals	.280	.350	.474	464	130	20	2	22	70	48	88	.278	.346	.467	806	224	42	4	34	114	82	152
vs. Left	.338	.418	.647	139	47	11	1	10	24	19	20	.319	.382	.557	345	110	27	2	17	51	35	51
vs. Right	.255	.319	.400	325	83	9	1	12	46	29	68	.247	.320	.399	461	114	15	2	17	63	47	101
at Home	.291	.360	.476	227	66	11	2	9	35	23	43	.294	.361	.473	395	116	26	3	13	60	41	75
on Road	.270	.340	.473	237	64	9	0	13	35	25	45	.263	.331	.460	411	108	16	1	21	54	41	77
vs. Groundball	.244	.299	.387	217	53	5	1	8	32	17	43	.265	.323	.421	385	102	17	2	13	52	32	67
vs. Flyball	.312	.391	.551	247	77	15	1	14	38	31	45	.290	.366	.508	421	122	25	2	21	62	50	85
vs. Finesse	.265	.309	.449	234	62	8	1	11	31	13	41	.270	.316	.461	419	113	22	2	18	50	26	65
vs. Power	.296	.387	.500	230	68	12	1	11	39	35	47	.287	.376	.473	387	111	20	2	16	64	56	87
on Grass	.293	.372	.478	335	98	16	2	14	51	41	63	.287	.361	.464	575	165	33	3	21	82	66	113
on Artificial Turf	.248	.287	.465	129	32	4	0	8	19	7	25	.255	.306	.472	231	59	9	1	13	32	16	39
Day Games	.308	.389	.524	185	57	11	1	9	30	24	31	.293	.363	.505	321	94	21	1	15	50	35	55
Night Games	.262	.322	.441	279	73	9	1	13	40	24	57	.268	.335	.441	485	130	21	3	19	64	47	97
April	.269	.313	.423	78	21	4	1	2	9	5	16	.297	.336	.475	101	30	7	1	3	13	6	19
May	.192	.288	.250	52	10	0	0	1	7	7	10	.226	.294	.312	93	21	2	0	2	11	9	19
June	.255	.344	.418	55	14	3	0	2	7	8	10	.345	.425	.560	116	40	13	0	4	19	17	18
July	.268	.324	.526	97	26	7	0	6	16	8	19	.258	.320	.515	163	42	9	0	11	23	15	31
August	.381	.429	.607	84	32	2	1	5	11	6	14	.290	.355	.485	169	49	6	3	7	19	16	37
Sept/Oct	.276	.372	.500	98	27	4	0	6	20	14	19	.256	.337	.415	164	42	5	0	7	29	19	28
Bases Empty	.247	.320	.442	251	62	12	2	11	11	25	48	.254	.319	.443	449	114	23	4	18	18	41	77
Leadoff	.282	.344	.529	85	24	4	1	5	5	8	20	.255	.312	.471	157	40	6	2	8	8	13	32
Not Leadoff	.229	.308	.398	166	38	8	1	6	6	17	28	.253	.323	.428	292	74	17	2	10	10	28	45
Runners On	.319	.384	.512	213	68	8	0	11	59	23	40	.308	.378	.496	357	110	19	0	16	96	41	75
First Base Only	.344	.359	.489	90	31	4	0	3	6	2	12	.343	.379	.489	137	47	5	0	5	11	8	21
Scoring Position	.301	.400	.528	123	37	4	0	8	53	21	28	.286	.378	.500	220	63	14	0	11	85	33	54
Late Innings, Close	.215	.279	.304	79	17	1	0	2	13	7	18	.245	.291	.381	139	34	4	0	5	21	9	30

RBI/Opportunities

	1987 Season	Four Year Totals
Scoring Position	40 / 172 (23%)	68 / 302 (23%)
Scoring Position, 2 Out	21 / 81 (26%)	36 / 139 (26%)
On Third, Less than 2 Out	8 / 23 (35%)	16 / 50 (32%)
RBI in close games / RBI Total	51 / 70 (73%)	78 / 114 (68%)

Dale Mohorcic
Texas Rangers

I remember last summer when Mohorcic was in his first week with the Rangers and some players started talking about their service time in the majors, which determines their rights to arbitration and free agency as well as pension benefits. When asked what his service time was, the 30-year-old rookie said, "Counting today? Three days."

Dale was never drafted; he entered professional baseball by signing as a 22-year-old free agent with an independent club. Toronto purchased his contract at the end of that first season but released him a year later. Pittsburgh signed him and he languished in their minors for 6 years until he signed as a free agent with Texas in 1985. By 1986 he was the Rangers' best reliever and he did it again in 1987.

Perseverance and a remarkably durable arm allowed him to hang around long enough to develop an out pitch, a steady sinker backed by consistent location down in the strike zone. In both seasons he has given up fewer home runs per inning than the league average, but what his sinker really stops are the doubles and triples. When a batter tries to pull a sinker, he tends to hit the ball on the ground, not in the air, so the outfielders can lean to the middle and close off the alleys with Mohorcic on the mound.

Of course, groundballs don't usually go for extra-bases, anyway, and the Rangers' two best defensive infielders play the corners. In 1987 the opposing batters had only 9 doubles and 1 triple in 361 at-bats versus Mohorcic. That's less than half the normal frequency for an average pitcher.

Last year, he was the hardest working reliever in the American League relative to his time on the major league roster. He nearly did it again in 1987; he was fourth in the league with 74 appearances despite being disabled part of the season with internal bleeding. When he went on the disabled list in mid-August, he was tied with Mark Eichhorn for the league lead in appearances, and Toronto had played 3 more games than Texas. "Horse" was on target for 91 appearances and 126 innings.

For a reliever to work that frequently, he has to make a lot of appearances without a day off between appearances. Thirty times in 74 appearances the Horse was pitching without a day off. California's whole bullpen didn't make 30 appearances with 0 days rest (27).

Strangely enough, Mohorcic really doesn't pitch well on short rest. In both 1986 and 1987 it was his worst rest pattern. Overall, his career difference is:

	G	IP	H-AVG	R-AVG	ERA	W-AVG	K-AVG
0 DAYS REST	58	70.3	9.60	3.71	3.33	2.18	3.97
OTHER	75	108.0	8.25	2.50	2.42	1.42	3.83

Craig R. Wright

Mohorcic, Dale Robert

Bats: Left   Throws: Left   Born 01/25/56

1987 SEASON AND MAJOR-LEAGUE CAREER PITCHING TOTALS

	G	GS	CG	GF	IP	BFP	H	R	ER	HR	SH	SF	HB	TBB	IBB	SO	WP	Bk	W	L	Pct	ShO	Sv	ERA
87 TEX	74	0	0	54	99	390	88	34	33	11	7	2	2	19	6	48	3	4	7	6	.538	0	16	3.00
2 YEARS	132	0	0	74	178	715	174	59	55	16	8	2	3	34	12	77	4	4	9	10	.474	0	23	2.78

1987: Finesse, Groundball   1986: Finesse, Groundball

1987 SEASON

	G	IP	H	BB	SO	SB	CS	W	L	S	ERA
Totals	74	99.1	88	19	48	6	2	7	6	16	2.99
at Home	40	51.0	47	8	25	1	1	4	3	7	3.53
on Road	34	48.1	41	11	23	5	1	3	3	9	2.42
on Grass	14	22.1	18	5	13	3	1	2	1	2	1.21
on Artificial Turf	60	77.0	70	14	35	3	1	5	5	14	3.51
Day Games	64	83.0	74	12	40	3	2	6	5	14	3.14
Night Games	10	16.1	14	7	8	3	0	1	1	2	2.20
April	11	16.1	13	5	8	2	1	1	1	2	3.31
May	15	27.1	22	5	11	2	0	3	1	2	2.63
June	15	21.0	12	3	13	2	0	1	0	7	1.29
July	15	17.0	18	4	9	0	0	1	0	4	4.24
August	8	7.1	6	0	1	0	0	0	2	1	3.68
Sept/Oct	10	10.1	17	2	6	0	1	1	2	0	4.35

vs. Opponent Batters	Ave.	OBP	SLG	AB	H	2B	3B	HR	RBI	BB	SO
Totals	.245	.285	.368	359	88	9	1	11	54	19	48
vs. Left	.298	.335	.444	151	45	7	0	5	25	8	16
vs. Right	.207	.249	.313	208	43	2	1	6	29	11	32
Bases Empty	.270	.302	.379	174	47	5	1	4	4	6	25
Leadoff	.261	.292	.362	69	18	1	0	2	2	2	11
Not Leadoff	.276	.309	.390	105	29	4	1	2	2	4	14
Runners On Base	.222	.270	.357	185	41	4	0	7	50	13	23
First Base Only	.156	.177	.299	77	12	2	0	3	8	2	9
Scoring Position	.269	.331	.398	108	29	2	0	4	42	11	14
Late Innings, Close	.295	.333	.483	176	52	7	1	8	37	11	20

FOUR YEAR TOTALS (1984 – 1987)

	G	IP	H	BB	SO	SB	CS	W	L	S	ERA
Totals	132	178.1	174	34	77	9	7	9	10	23	2.78
at Home	67	91.1	86	15	40	3	4	6	3	9	2.66
on Road	65	87.0	88	19	37	6	3	3	7	14	2.90
on Grass	22	29.1	26	5	18	3	1	2	2	3	2.15
on Artificial Turf	110	149.0	148	29	59	6	6	7	8	20	2.90
Day Games	110	148.2	141	23	66	6	7	8	7	21	2.72
Night Games	22	29.2	33	11	11	3	0	1	3	2	3.03
April	11	16.1	13	5	8	2	1	1	1	2	3.31
May	16	28.0	23	6	11	2	0	3	1	2	2.57
June	26	38.0	32	8	16	2	0	2	0	7	1.42
July	27	33.1	33	5	13	1	3	1	0	5	3.24
August	27	29.2	29	2	12	1	1	1	3	5	2.73
Sept/Oct	25	33.0	44	8	17	1	2	1	5	2	3.82

vs. Opponent Batters	Ave.	OBP	SLG	AB	H	2B	3B	HR	RBI	BB	SO
Totals	.261	.298	.370	667	174	23	1	16	87	34	77
vs. Left	.292	.339	.405	274	80	13	0	6	34	19	27
vs. Right	.239	.268	.346	393	94	10	1	10	53	15	50
Bases Empty	.280	.307	.386	329	92	9	1	8	8	11	41
Leadoff	.303	.328	.417	132	40	3	0	4	4	4	19
Not Leadoff	.264	.293	.365	197	52	6	1	4	4	7	22
Runners On Base	.243	.289	.355	338	82	14	0	8	79	23	36
First Base Only	.227	.243	.376	141	32	9	0	4	12	3	16
Scoring Position	.254	.320	.340	197	50	5	0	4	67	20	20
Late Innings, Close	.282	.317	.414	309	87	12	1	9	48	17	36

RBI/Opportunities

	1987	Four Year
Scoring Position	34 / 153 (22%)	59 / 279 (21%)
Scoring Position, 2 Out	9 / 58 (16%)	20 / 118 (17%)
On Third, Less than 2 Out	13 / 33 (39%)	22 / 57 (39%)
RBI in close games / RBI Total	41 / 54 (76%)	65 / 87 (75%)

Paul Molitor
Milwaukee Brewers

The Milwaukee Brewers had a lot of big moments in 1987—they won their first 13 games, had their first no-hit game and finished third in the AL East—but the biggest was Paul Molitor's 39-game hitting streak; the longest one of the decade.

Molitor also had what was perhaps the best single season ever by a Brewer. He didn't have as much power as Cecil Cooper did in 1980 and Robin Yount's 1982 was a marvelous year . . . but he was second in the league in batting and on-base percentage, fourth in stolen bases, fifth in slugging percentage and led everyone in runs scored and doubles, despite missing 44 games due to an injury.

Speaking of injuries—what was all of that garbage about Molitor's streak deserving an asterisk because he was a designated hitter? How on earth did being a DH lengthen his streak? The pinheads who argued that not playing the field kept him more physically fit managed to ignore the fact that not playing the field had its drawbacks—until he got a hit, he had to sit on the bench and stew in his own juices. This isn't springboard diving—there aren't any degrees of difficulty. Either you do something or you don't—Molitor did.

Another related question: Why is Tom Trebelhorn insisting on playing Molitor in the field in 1988? He's a born DH. Well, not a born DH, but he's sure a prototype now.

He's not a particularly outstanding fielder and he's so consistently injury-prone that you cringe every time he puts on a glove. Maybe it's just coincidence that Molitor had his best season ever when he didn't bang himself up day after day by diving for balls—but it's sure an odd one if it is. Since Molitor has shown that he can adjust to sitting on the bench while he's waiting to hit and the DH has been a sore spot for Milwaukee ever since the inception of the rule, why not just ask Paul to do only what he does best?

Molitor's chances of repeating his 1987 seem fairly strong because of his plate discipline. When a player hits for a very high average, he can expect pitchers to throw him fewer strikes the next year; if he doesn't lay off the borderline pitches and take more walks, his average will drop—the Cleveland Indians demonstrated that neatly this year. But, since Molitor would have drawn about 90 walks if he'd stayed healthy, he should be able to keep his average above .320 in 1988.

On the night that Molitor's streak was snapped, he was on deck when Rick Manning got the game winning hit in extra innings—when he did, the Brewer fans actually booed. It's just as well that Manning's contract ran out this year—being the man who both helped stop Molitor's streak and ended Gorman Thomas' reign made him Public Enemy #1 in Milwaukee in 1987.

Scott Segrin and Kent Kirchstein

Molitor, Paul Leo

Bats: Right   Throws: Right   Born 08/22/56

1987 SEASON AND MAJOR-LEAGUE CAREER BATTING TOTALS

	G	AB	H	2B	3B	HR	TB	R	RBI	TBB	IBB	SO	HP	SH	SF	SB	CS	SB%	GDP	AVG	OBP	SLG
87 MIL	118	465	164	41	5	16	263	114	75	69	2	67	2	5	1	45	10	.82	4	.353	.438	.566
10 YEARS	1128	4604	1367	241	50	95	1993	790	465	433	25	582	18	55	35	276	77	.78	73	.297	.357	.433

1987 SEASON

	Ave.	OBP	SLG	AB	H	2B	3B	HR	RBI	BB	SO
Totals	.353	.438	.566	465	164	41	5	16	75	69	67
vs. Left	.331	.426	.476	145	48	12	0	3	13	23	15
vs. Right	.363	.443	.606	320	116	29	5	13	62	46	52
at Home	.394	.470	.610	231	91	21	4	7	38	33	35
on Road	.312	.406	.521	234	73	20	1	9	37	36	32
vs. Groundball	.340	.433	.545	235	80	21	3	7	31	37	25
vs. Flyball	.365	.443	.587	230	84	20	2	9	44	32	42
vs. Finesse	.340	.411	.541	259	88	22	3	8	45	30	30
vs. Power	.369	.469	.597	206	76	19	2	8	30	39	37
on Grass	.376	.455	.599	404	152	35	5	15	71	57	57
on Artificial Turf	.197	.329	.344	61	12	6	0	1	4	12	10
Day Games	.352	.451	.594	128	45	12	2	5	18	23	16
Night Games	.353	.432	.555	337	119	29	3	11	57	46	51
April	.395	.462	.642	81	32	9	1	3	15	10	7
May	.217	.308	.217	23	5	0	0	0	3	3	5
June	.255	.333	.412	51	13	5	0	1	6	6	9
July	.415	.472	.708	65	27	6	2	3	17	7	9
August	.381	.479	.602	118	45	12	1	4	16	21	16
Sept/Oct	.331	.430	.535	127	42	9	1	5	18	22	17
Bases Empty	.314	.406	.502	299	94	24	4	8	8	46	42
Leadoff	.338	.421	.544	160	54	11	2	6	6	23	21
Not Leadoff	.288	.389	.453	139	40	13	2	2	2	23	21
Runners On	.422	.495	.681	166	70	17	1	8	67	23	25
First Base Only	.379	.455	.638	58	22	4	1	3	9	8	8
Scoring Position	.444	.516	.704	108	48	13	0	5	58	15	17
Late Innings, Close	.425	.488	.685	73	31	5	1	4	17	9	15

FOUR YEAR TOTALS (1984 – 1987)

	Ave.	OBP	SLG	AB	H	2B	3B	HR	RBI	BB	SO
	.307	.374	.456	1524	468	94	14	35	184	165	236
	.310	.379	.442	448	139	26	3	9	43	48	58
	.306	.372	.462	1076	329	68	11	26	141	117	178
	.337	.398	.503	722	243	46	10	18	104	75	103
	.281	.353	.414	802	225	48	4	17	80	90	133
	.308	.376	.449	740	228	48	7	14	74	78	98
	.306	.372	.463	784	240	46	7	21	110	87	138
	.308	.362	.456	871	268	51	9	20	100	73	118
	.306	.389	.456	653	200	43	5	15	84	92	118
	.323	.388	.479	1297	419	83	13	31	172	140	190
	.216	.292	.326	227	49	11	1	4	12	25	46
	.285	.360	.415	467	133	28	3	9	47	56	78
	.317	.380	.474	1057	335	66	11	26	137	109	158
	.316	.396	.452	263	83	20	2	4	36	35	44
	.277	.356	.413	155	43	5	2	4	20	19	21
	.310	.379	.503	171	53	13	1	6	21	19	30
	.309	.358	.448	259	80	17	2	5	30	20	30
	.315	.389	.474	289	91	18	2	8	40	34	48
	.305	.368	.447	387	118	21	5	8	37	38	63
	.288	.349	.438	1004	289	62	10	23	23	95	160
	.306	.363	.467	578	177	31	7	16	16	52	87
	.263	.330	.399	426	112	31	3	7	7	43	73
	.344	.423	.490	520	179	32	4	12	161	70	76
	.315	.378	.452	197	62	11	2	4	17	20	20
	.362	.449	.514	323	117	21	2	8	144	50	56
	.361	.411	.557	244	88	17	2	9	40	21	41

RBI/Opportunities

Scoring Position	47 / 141	(33%)		126 / 443	(28%)
Scoring Position, 2 Out	17 / 64	(27%)		57 / 215	(27%)
On Third, Less than 2 Out	16 / 29	(55%)		39 / 76	(51%)
RBI in close games / RBI Total	47 / 75	(63%)		110 / 184	(60%)

Mike Moore
Seattle Mariners

Mike Moore is a baseball curiosity. There's no doubt about his ability; he was the first player chosen in the 1981 draft, and though he's had only one winning season in the majors, scouts still say that he has all the tools. After some early struggles Moore put it all together in 1985, going 17–10 with a 3.46 ERA. But two years later he was 9–19, leading the league in losses, with a 4.71 ERA.

Even with a collective record of 20–32 for the last two years, he's still considered the number-two starter on the Mariner team behind Mark Langston. He's also coveted by many other teams and has been the subject of trade rumors for the last two years, but it looks like the snakebit Moore will be pitching from the Kingdome mound again in 1988.

After watching Moore for the last two years, I get the feeling that he needs to find some confidence. It looks like the Mariner management is doing its best to help Mike accomplish this by relentlessly handing him the ball every five days. Nonetheless it seems to me that an air of a defeatism exhumes from Moore, not in his words, but in his actions on the mound. Unfortunately, that feeling seems to be reflected in the fielding behind him. It's almost like the rest of the team comes on the field fretting about what stupid move they'll make to cause Moore another loss. Of the 41 starting pitchers to pitch 200 or more innings, Moore was third in percentage of unearned runs with 16.55 percent (23 runs). This could be used as a factor in Moore's defense, but it's hardly an excuse when his ERA was third highest in this same group of pitchers. It becomes even less of a factor when you consider that nearly a fourth (24.53%–39 UER) of Charlie Hough's runs were unearned, and he ended the season 18–13.

It's the wins that make Moore's role in the Mariner rotation curious. In comparing the records of the top five pitchers on every team, the five Mariner starters had the third-best winning record in the majors. The third, fourth, and fifth starters had the fifth-most wins. Moore's record of 9–19 put him in the fifth spot in the rotation based on wins/losses. Only Joe Magrane (9–7) matched that many wins in the fifth spot on any major league team. Let's hope that next year Moore can better justify his place as the number-two starter. The patience of the Mariner management must be wearing thin.

Merrianna McCully

Moore, Michael Wayne "Mike"   Bats: Right   Throws: Right   Born 11/26/59

1987 SEASON AND MAJOR-LEAGUE CAREER PITCHING TOTALS

	G	GS	CG	GF	IP	BFP	H	R	ER	HR	SH	SF	HB	TBB	IBB	SO	WP	Bk	W	L	Pct	ShO	Sv	ERA
87 SEA	33	33	12	0	231	1020	268	145	121	29	9	8	0	84	3	115	4	2	9	19	.321	0	0	4.71
6 YEARS	190	185	47	3	1228	5325	1302	679	613	122	35	37	26	472	25	755	38	8	57	81	.413	6	1	4.49

1987: Finesse, Groundball   1986: Finesse, Groundball   1985: Finesse, Groundball   1984: Power, Groundball

1987 SEASON

	G	IP	H	BB	SO	SB	CS	W	L	S	ERA
Totals	33	231.0	268	84	115	8	5	9	19	0	4.68
at Home	15	109.1	116	36	58	4	4	4	8	0	4.12
on Road	18	121.2	152	48	57	4	1	5	11	0	5.25
on Grass	6	37.0	54	14	21	2	0	1	5	0	6.08
on Artificial Turf	27	194.0	214	70	94	6	5	8	14	0	4.45
Day Games	14	96.1	118	36	45	3	1	5	8	0	5.04
Night Games	19	134.2	150	48	70	5	4	4	11	0	4.48
April	5	34.0	36	17	16	2	0	1	3	0	4.76
May	5	30.2	39	18	14	2	2	1	3	0	5.28
June	5	29.1	40	7	19	1	0	1	3	0	5.83
July	5	33.1	42	13	14	1	0	0	4	0	5.94
August	7	58.1	62	14	32	1	2	3	4	0	3.39
Sept/Oct	6	45.1	49	15	20	1	1	3	2	0	4.37

vs. Opponent Batters	Ave.	OBP	SLG	AB	H	2B	3B	HR	RBI	BB	SO
Totals	.292	.348	.460	919	268	54	7	29	123	84	115
vs. Left	.298	.353	.463	547	163	33	6	15	70	49	58
vs. Right	.282	.341	.457	372	105	21	1	14	53	35	57
Bases Empty	.287	.344	.483	516	148	34	5	19	19	45	69
Leadoff	.317	.362	.555	227	72	22	1	10	10	16	22
Not Leadoff	.263	.330	.426	289	76	12	4	9	9	29	47
Runners On Base	.298	.353	.432	403	120	20	2	10	104	39	46
First Base Only	.292	.329	.447	161	47	7	0	6	16	9	23
Scoring Position	.302	.368	.421	242	73	13	2	4	88	30	23
Late Innings, Close	.236	.327	.393	89	21	5	0	3	7	12	14

FOUR YEAR TOTALS (1984 – 1987)

	G	IP	H	BB	SO	SB	CS	W	L	S	ERA
Totals	140	956.0	1013	333	574	46	34	44	59	1	4.32
at Home	70	490.0	516	175	314	23	17	25	25	1	3.99
on Road	70	466.0	497	158	260	23	17	19	34	0	4.69
on Grass	39	264.1	286	77	174	11	6	12	20	0	4.15
on Artificial Turf	101	691.2	727	256	400	35	28	32	39	1	4.40
Day Games	52	344.1	369	116	199	15	15	15	24	0	4.60
Night Games	88	611.2	644	217	375	31	19	29	35	1	4.16
April	21	145.0	152	64	82	8	6	5	8	0	4.03
May	20	126.0	127	56	79	9	4	5	11	0	4.50
June	21	126.2	147	42	74	5	4	6	6	0	5.26
July	24	164.0	180	46	82	2	7	7	13	0	4.66
August	27	196.0	196	60	125	10	7	9	11	1	3.58
Sept/Oct	27	198.1	211	65	132	12	6	12	10	0	4.31

vs. Opponent Batters	Ave.	OBP	SLG	AB	H	2B	3B	HR	RBI	BB	SO
Totals	.273	.332	.410	3711	1013	185	25	91	436	333	574
vs. Left	.275	.343	.405	2067	569	100	18	44	227	216	275
vs. Right	.270	.318	.416	1644	444	85	7	47	209	117	299
Bases Empty	.260	.321	.399	2162	563	112	17	51	51	192	358
Leadoff	.270	.321	.424	933	252	52	7	26	26	70	133
Not Leadoff	.253	.321	.379	1229	311	60	10	25	25	122	225
Runners On Base	.291	.348	.425	1549	450	73	8	40	385	141	216
First Base Only	.310	.346	.474	677	210	31	4	24	59	37	97
Scoring Position	.275	.350	.388	872	240	42	4	16	326	104	119
Late Innings, Close	.269	.340	.391	386	104	20	3	7	40	41	61

RBI/Opportunities

Scoring Position	80 / 314 (25%)
Scoring Position, 2 Out	27 / 125 (22%)
On Third, Less than 2 Out	36 / 58 (62%)
RBI in close games / RBI Total	84 / 123 (68%)

	294 / 1185 (25%)
	112 / 511 (22%)
	126 / 235 (54%)
	313 / 436 (72%)

Keith Moreland
Chicago Cubs

Ah, the switch to third base. To allow the entrance of NL MVP Andre Dawson in right, it was perfectly timed. As an effort to improve the Cubs offensively and defensively at third, the experiment must be considered an unqualified success. But wait—hold the enthusiasm—we're only talking about improving over Ron Cey here. The Cubs figured that a typical Moreland year at the plate would be enough. They got it. Moreland got his hands on more balls than Cey did at third (notice I didn't say fielded cleanly), thereby committing a league-leading 28 errors. In sum, the defense cannot be considered significantly worse than in 1986. All in all, you gotta hand it to Gene Michael and Dallas Green for the switch.

By year's end, 1987 was a Moreland-like season. Keith's seasonal averages for 1982 through 1986 (all Chicago years) were 15 HRs, 81 RBIs, and .285 average. In '87 Keith showed uncharacteristic power (a career high 27 homers) with a consequent decline in batting average, resulting in very similar overall production.

Let us ponder a more subtle question: Did the switch to third affect Moreland? I heard a number of interviews early in the season in which Keith denied it, at times vehemently. I'm sorry, Keith, but the cold, hard numbers tell a different story. Through April 30, Moreland had a .164

average with only one homer and 8 RBIs; through May 28, the dismal start was far from over. The ledger: .188, 3 HRs, 15 RBIs. That's 45 games played with stats that most shortstops would be embarrassed about. (Aside: To this amateur observer it seemed Keith was playing quite adequate defense through the slump; the errors seemed to increase when he began to hit better.) On May 30, Moreland went 3 for 5 with two runs and one ribbie to ignite a rally that carried him to the season's end. From then on, he hit .298 with 24 HRs and 73 RBIs. Vintage Moreland stuff there. Those numbers are quite similar to Dawson's for that same period. If only he walked a little more. He seemed to be swinging harder and more often than in other years. To atone for errors, maybe?

Keith Moreland did warm up to his new assignment as 1987 wore on. But the Cubs, needing relief pitching and perhaps concerned about Moreland's defensive problems, have traded him to San Diego to obtain Goose Gossage. As a Padre Moreland will be playing for ex-teammate Larry Bowa, the sort of manager who admires an aggressive player. Exactly how Bowa will use Moreland was not clear as we went to press—will he be at third, replacing Chris Brown, or go back to the outfield?—but Keith figures to see plenty of action in 1988.

Robert L. Jones

Moreland, Bobby Keith "Keith"

Bats: Right   Throws: Right   Born 05/02/54

1987 SEASON AND MAJOR-LEAGUE CAREER BATTING TOTALS

	G	AB	H	2B	3B	HR	TB	R	RBI	TBB	IBB	SO	HP	SH	SF	SB	CS	SB%	GDP	AVG	OBP	SLG
87 CHN	153	563	150	29	1	27	262	63	88	39	4	66	0	3	9	3	3	.50	15	.266	.309	.465
10 YEARS	1040	3645	1030	171	14	110	1559	426	565	334	45	419	11	16	56	23	28	.45	102	.283	.340	.428

	1987 SEASON											FOUR YEAR TOTALS (1984 – 1987)									
	Ave.	OBP	SLG	AB	H	2B	3B	HR	RBI	BB	SO	Ave.	OBP	SLG	AB	H	2B	3B	HR	RBI	BB	SO
Totals	.266	.309	.465	563	150	29	1	27	88	39	66	.281	.335	.428	2231	627	106	7	69	353	194	243
vs. Left	.295	.362	.451	122	36	10	0	3	17	15	15	.305	.384	.468	555	169	31	3	18	77	77	55
vs. Right	.259	.294	.469	441	114	19	1	24	71	24	51	.273	.318	.414	1676	458	75	4	51	276	117	188
at Home	.290	.338	.548	272	79	11	1	19	55	22	29	.298	.355	.491	1113	332	54	4	51	213	101	114
on Road	.244	.282	.388	291	71	18	0	8	33	17	37	.264	.316	.364	1118	295	52	3	18	140	93	129
vs. Groundball	.252	.291	.421	242	61	6	1	11	34	14	28	.278	.335	.402	1016	282	35	5	27	154	92	100
vs. Flyball	.277	.323	.498	321	89	23	0	16	54	25	38	.284	.335	.449	1215	345	71	2	42	199	102	143
vs. Finesse	.280	.321	.469	322	90	17	1	14	54	24	33	.293	.339	.429	1278	374	58	4	36	209	97	123
vs. Power	.249	.293	.461	241	60	12	0	13	34	15	33	.265	.330	.426	953	253	48	3	33	144	97	120
on Grass	.287	.335	.510	390	112	16	1	23	68	31	41	.292	.351	.458	1571	459	71	5	60	263	149	177
on Artificial Turf	.220	.250	.364	173	38	13	0	4	20	8	25	.255	.296	.355	660	168	35	2	9	90	45	66
Day Games	.281	.327	.507	359	101	16	1	21	64	27	38	.291	.347	.465	1481	431	74	5	58	264	131	150
Night Games	.240	.277	.392	204	49	13	0	6	24	12	28	.261	.312	.353	750	196	32	2	11	89	63	93
April	.164	.192	.233	73	12	2	0	1	8	3	9	.247	.304	.332	259	64	10	0	4	35	22	29
May	.229	.283	.324	105	24	4	0	2	8	8	8	.265	.342	.370	332	88	11	0	8	41	39	28
June	.280	.302	.607	107	30	5	0	10	31	5	15	.285	.343	.494	407	116	21	2	20	80	38	50
July	.349	.404	.605	86	30	2	1	6	13	8	14	.290	.351	.444	372	108	17	2	12	58	35	55
August	.245	.313	.431	102	25	7	0	4	14	11	10	.290	.333	.434	435	126	25	1	12	68	29	43
Sept/Oct	.322	.347	.556	90	29	9	0	4	14	4	10	.293	.341	.446	426	125	22	2	13	71	31	38
Bases Empty	.269	.305	.471	312	84	16	1	15	15	16	38	.281	.331	.427	1172	329	54	2	38	38	89	130
Leadoff	.269	.290	.425	134	36	6	0	5	5	4	16	.289	.331	.437	540	156	26	0	18	18	34	52
Not Leadoff	.270	.316	.506	178	48	10	1	10	10	12	22	.274	.332	.419	632	173	28	2	20	20	55	78
Runners On	.263	.314	.458	251	66	13	0	12	73	23	28	.281	.344	.428	1059	298	52	5	31	315	105	113
First Base Only	.308	.378	.570	107	33	7	0	7	19	12	11	.284	.340	.445	398	113	18	2	14	41	34	41
Scoring Position	.229	.268	.375	144	33	6	0	5	54	11	17	.280	.345	.418	661	185	34	3	17	274	71	72
Late Innings, Close	.224	.272	.329	76	17	2	0	2	4	5	11	.286	.356	.431	360	103	19	0	11	61	39	42

RBI/Opportunities

Scoring Position	47 / 198 (24%)	241 / 900 (27%)
Scoring Position, 2 Out	17 / 96 (18%)	94 / 443 (21%)
On Third, Less than 2 Out	22 / 39 (56%)	95 / 166 (57%)
RBI in close games / RBI Total	47 / 88 (53%)	244 / 353 (69%)

Mike Morgan
Seattle Mariners

Mikey, Mikey, quite capricious, how does your ball game go? With inconsistency and fickle fate, and cheap hits all in a row. When he's good, he's very very good, but when he's bad, he's horrid.

And just how inconsistent is Mike Morgan you ask? So unpredictable that the Mariners joined the list of clubs that have thrown in the towel. After three years of waiting for Morgan to fulfill all his predicted potential, he was traded to Baltimore, the fifth major league team to take on the challenge of this mystifying hurler.

1987 was not a year of being consistently mediocre for Mike. It was a year of extreme highs and extreme lows. It was a year that you can easily divide in half by number of runs given up. In 16 of his 31 starts, Mike gave up 3 or less earned runs. In those games his line reads: 123.67 IP, 13 quality starts, 12 wins, 3 losses and 1 no-decision that the club went on to win. His ERA was 2.26 and he pitched an average of 7.729 innings per start. Wow!

On the flip side of this chameleon pitcher, we have 15 games in which he gave up 4 or more earned runs. In these disasters, he pitched 79.67 innings, won none and lost 14 with 1 no decision that the club went on to lose. His ERA was 8.47 and he averaged 5.311 IP per start. Yuk!

Mike came out of spring training as the "New Mike Morgan." he was the prize graduate of the Mariner positive thinking seminars conducted to instill confidence and a win-

ning attitude on a team that had never experienced a winning season. All of his outings in spring training, except one, reflected a new and exciting confidence in his performance on the mound.

Then the season started. He lost his first three games, going only 15 innings and giving up 18 runs, and Williams sent him to the pen. The gutsy Morgan spent a long evening talking to his pitching coach Billy Connors and it was suggested that he approach Williams and ask for another chance. He did and was granted a second opportunity. In the next 12 games, Mike went 94.1 innings, won 6 and lost 5 with 1 no decision. Eight of the games were quality starts and his ERA was a respectable 3.53. The rest of the year was the same story. A roller coaster ride.

There was one team that only saw the best of Morgan. Mike faced the Baltimore Orioles 3 times. He was 2 and 1 in those games, threw 25 innings, and allowed 4 runs for a 1.44 ERA. The most inspiring of those encounters was a 12–zip complete game shutout with 7 hits and no walks.

Dick Williams said that Baltimore probably picked up Morgan just to keep him out of their hair. That's not the way I see it, and I'm sure that's not the way Baltimore views the acquisition either. Just keep in mind how long it took Mike Scott to become a pitcher. It's possible the Mariners gave up on Mike Morgan one year too early.

Merrianna McCully

Morgan, Michael Thomas "Mike"   **Bats: Right**   **Throws: Right**   **Born 10/08/59**

1987 SEASON AND MAJOR-LEAGUE CAREER PITCHING TOTALS

	G	GS	CG	GF	IP	BFP	H	R	ER	HR	SH	SF	HB	TBB	IBB	SO	WP	Bk	W	L	Pct	ShO	Sv	ERA
87 SEA	34	31	8	2	207	898	245	117	107	25	8	5	5	53	3	85	11	0	12	17	.414	2	0	4.65
7 YEARS	135	109	22	8	713	3169	835	419	384	80	22	17	14	290	11	313	36	1	33	62	.347	3	1	4.85

1987: Finesse, Groundball   **1986: Finesse, Groundball**   **1985: Power, Groundball**

1987 SEASON

	G	IP	H	BB	SO	SB	CS	W	L	S	ERA
Totals	34	207.0	245	53	85	15	12	12	17	0	4.70
at Home	18	127.2	148	24	55	9	6	7	10	0	4.86
on Road	16	79.1	97	29	30	6	6	5	7	0	4.42
on Grass	9	57.2	62	16	24	1	4	3	3	0	3.59
on Artificial Turf	25	149.1	183	37	61	14	8	9	14	0	5.12
Day Games	11	60.0	69	22	26	3	5	4	4	0	3.45
Night Games	23	147.0	176	31	59	12	7	8	13	0	5.20
April	6	25.2	32	4	11	1	2	1	3	0	7.36
May	6	50.0	44	10	26	4	3	4	2	0	2.88
June	5	36.1	46	9	14	1	1	1	3	0	3.47
July	6	25.0	32	12	6	3	0	2	3	0	6.84
August	6	37.0	47	8	15	1	3	2	4	0	4.86
Sept/Oct	5	33.0	44	10	13	5	3	2	2	0	4.91

vs. Opponent Batters	Ave.	OBP	SLG	AB	H	2B	3B	HR	RBI	BB	SO
Totals	.296	.340	.455	827	245	42	7	25	104	53	85
vs. Left	.302	.345	.468	447	135	25	5	13	55	31	49
vs. Right	.289	.335	.439	380	110	17	2	12	49	22	36
Bases Empty	.310	.359	.487	458	142	21	6	16	16	33	51
Leadoff	.312	.366	.467	199	62	9	2	6	6	16	13
Not Leadoff	.309	.354	.502	259	80	12	4	10	10	17	38
Runners On Base	.279	.317	.415	369	103	21	1	9	88	20	34
First Base Only	.327	.340	.481	156	51	9	0	5	13	2	14
Scoring Position	.244	.303	.366	213	52	12	1	4	75	18	20
Late Innings, Close	.273	.333	.455	22	6	1	0	1	3	2	2

FOUR YEAR TOTALS (1984 – 1987)

	G	IP	H	BB	SO	SB	CS	W	L	S	ERA
Totals	73	429.1	499	144	203	32	22	24	35	1	4.72
at Home	37	233.0	273	70	121	21	10	12	20	0	5.10
on Road	36	196.1	226	74	82	11	12	12	15	1	4.26
on Grass	18	109.1	117	44	57	4	5	6	9	0	4.12
on Artificial Turf	55	320.0	382	100	146	28	17	18	26	1	4.92
Day Games	25	138.1	150	50	66	5	8	7	11	1	3.84
Night Games	48	291.0	349	94	137	27	14	17	24	0	5.13
April	14	58.2	64	22	23	2	3	3	6	1	5.37
May	12	79.2	86	30	46	5	4	6	6	0	4.29
June	11	72.1	88	19	33	5	5	3	4	0	3.48
July	12	61.2	82	26	16	7	1	5	6	0	6.13
August	12	78.2	87	23	47	5	5	3	8	0	4.58
Sept/Oct	12	78.1	92	24	38	8	4	4	5	0	4.83

vs. Opponent Batters	Ave.	OBP	SLG	AB	H	2B	3B	HR	RBI	BB	SO
Totals	.292	.348	.443	1706	499	86	9	51	205	144	203
vs. Left	.291	.349	.433	906	264	44	6	24	107	82	106
vs. Right	.294	.348	.455	800	235	42	3	27	98	62	97
Bases Empty	.305	.362	.480	939	286	49	7	34	34	82	115
Leadoff	.285	.355	.447	407	116	15	3	15	15	43	43
Not Leadoff	.320	.367	.506	532	170	34	4	19	19	39	72
Runners On Base	.278	.332	.398	767	213	37	2	17	171	62	88
First Base Only	.308	.348	.441	331	102	15	1	9	26	19	32
Scoring Position	.255	.321	.365	436	111	22	1	8	145	43	56
Late Innings, Close	.387	.439	.507	75	29	3	0	2	9	7	9

RBI/Opportunities

Scoring Position	67 / 274 (24%)	130 / 562 (23%)
Scoring Position, 2 Out	23 / 116 (20%)	50 / 260 (19%)
On Third, Less than 2 Out	26 / 57 (46%)	45 / 91 (49%)
RBI in close games / RBI Total	61 / 104 (59%)	127 / 205 (62%)

Jack Morris
Detroit Tigers

If there is any pitcher in baseball who is a worthwhile bet in the free agent market, Jack Morris is that pitcher. If you take the average of Morris's stats from 1979 (the first year he went into the rotation) through 1987, you'd get 248.1 innings, 219 hits, an 18–11 record and a 3.52 ERA. He has failed to pitch 200 innings only twice in that span—by a combined total of 4.1 innings—and has never spent a day on the disabled list in his professional career.

In 1987, Morris's stats were amazingly similar to his average year; that only serves to illustrate what a consistent pitcher Morris has been. That his name was even mentioned as a Cy Young award candidate during what was, for him, an average year shows what a truly great pitcher he has been throughout his career.

Morris hasn't yet won a Cy Young award for several reasons. First, because he's durable, Morris will almost always stay in a game long enough to get either a win or a loss; since 1979, he's made 301 starts and gotten the decision in 228 games (75.7 percent). In order to post a typical "Cy Young" record in 26+ decisions a year, you really have to have an awesome year. Morris has only had three seasons ('79, '81, '86) like that; each time someone else had a better season that year.

His workload, naturally, also keeps his ERA from being impressively low. Morris has been in the top ten in four of the last five years—but if you're going to win that award, you almost have to win the title.

Also, in every year, Jack has a streak where he can't throw a strike and can't buy a win. He's allowed 3.2 walks per nine innings over the last nine years. He's led the league in wild pitches four times—in 1987, with an unbelievable total of 24. During those streaks, he also gives up a lot of gopher balls; he's allowed 79 in the last two years. Again, it's tough to win an award when you pitch awfully for a month or so.

With more consistent support, 1987 could have been a Cy Young year for Jack. He didn't pitch particularly well in April or May, but the Tiger offense was equal to the task. Detroit scored 5.90 runs per game in his first ten starts; Jack was 6–2 on May 30. In June, they scored 6.28 R/G; that, coupled with Morris's blazing June, gave him an 11–3 record.

After that, Detroit tailed off. Morris had 3.80 R/G to work with in July, 4.80 in August and 3.50 after September 1. Though he pitched better in the last three months (3.22 ERA) than he did in the first three (3.58), he was only 7–8. Detroit wound up scoring fewer runs in Morris's starts (5.18) than they did on the season (5.53); the spotty offense meant that Morris projected to win one more game than he actually did. The moral of this story: It takes more than just great pitching to win games.

Jim Shaarda, Steve Lysogorski and Geoff Beckman

Morris, John Scott "Jack" Bats: Right   Throws: Right   Born 05/16/55

1987 SEASON AND MAJOR-LEAGUE CAREER PITCHING TOTALS

	G	GS	CG	GF	IP	BFP	H	R	ER	HR	SH	SF	HB	TBB	IBB	SO	WP	Bk	W	L	Pct	ShO	Sv	ERA
87 DET	34	34	13	0	266	1101	227	111	100	39	6	5	1	93	7	208	24	1	18	11	.621	0	0	3.38
11 YEARS	336	314	123	10	2388	9932	2122	1021	942	252	73	70	24	847	65	1535	116	9	162	105	.607	19	0	3.55

1987: Power, Flyball   1986: Power, Flyball   1985: Power, Flyball   1984: Power, Groundball

1987 SEASON

	G	IP	H	BB	SO	SB	CS	W	L	S	ERA
Totals	34	266.0	227	93	208	31	9	18	11	0	3.32
at Home	20	157.1	127	38	120	13	6	8	7	0	3.15
on Road	14	108.2	100	55	88	18	3	10	4	0	3.56
on Grass	9	70.2	60	19	58	9	4	4	2	0	2.93
on Artificial Turf	25	195.1	167	74	150	22	5	14	9	0	3.46
Day Games	30	234.0	193	82	178	27	6	15	10	0	3.35
Night Games	4	32.0	34	11	30	4	3	3	1	0	2.81
April	5	42.0	37	17	28	6	0	3	2	0	3.00
May	5	33.0	32	6	27	4	5	3	0	0	4.91
June	6	48.1	34	18	37	5	2	5	1	0	2.79
July	5	39.0	38	8	24	2	0	1	2	0	3.69
August	5	42.1	29	14	41	2	1	3	2	0	2.98
Sept/Oct	8	61.1	57	30	51	12	1	3	4	0	3.08

FOUR YEAR TOTALS (1984 – 1987)

	G	IP	H	BB	SO	SB	CS	W	L	S	ERA
Totals	139	1030.1	889	372	770	90	33	74	41	0	3.36
at Home	71	514.0	449	170	361	41	20	34	22	0	3.50
on Road	68	516.1	440	202	409	49	13	40	19	0	3.21
on Grass	41	311.2	262	101	225	24	10	22	10	0	3.32
on Artificial Turf	98	718.2	627	271	545	66	23	52	31	0	3.39
Day Games	116	849.0	739	320	611	73	27	61	36	0	3.52
Night Games	23	181.1	150	52	159	17	6	13	5	0	2.63
April	21	169.0	138	58	120	14	3	14	6	0	3.04
May	23	165.2	127	65	143	15	14	12	6	0	2.82
June	23	168.0	163	57	112	14	6	13	5	0	4.29
July	21	158.1	147	45	118	9	6	10	7	0	2.79
August	24	164.1	145	66	122	12	2	12	8	0	4.27
Sept/Oct	27	205.0	169	81	155	26	2	13	9	0	3.07

vs. Opponent Batters

vs. Opponent Batters	Ave.	OBP	SLG	AB	H	2B	3B	HR	RBI	BB	SO
Totals	.228	.293	.391	996	227	29	8	39	98	93	208
vs. Left	.236	.313	.441	533	126	17	4	28	68	61	94
vs. Right	.218	.269	.333	463	101	12	4	11	30	32	114
Bases Empty	.229	.284	.403	633	145	21	4	27	27	49	138
Leadoff	.195	.272	.346	246	48	9	2	8	8	26	60
Not Leadoff	.251	.293	.439	387	97	12	2	19	19	23	78
Runners On Base	.226	.308	.369	363	82	8	4	12	71	44	70
First Base Only	.288	.343	.503	153	44	4	4	7	21	12	22
Scoring Position	.181	.283	.271	210	38	4	0	5	50	32	48
Late Innings, Close	.248	.304	.432	125	31	5	0	6	15	10	25

vs. Opponent Batters	Ave.	OBP	SLG	AB	H	2B	3B	HR	RBI	BB	SO
Totals	.230	.298	.372	3858	889	130	29	120	376	372	770
vs. Left	.231	.305	.377	2070	479	69	19	65	222	219	396
vs. Right	.229	.290	.367	1788	410	61	10	55	154	153	374
Bases Empty	.230	.297	.386	2356	542	93	16	81	81	225	485
Leadoff	.224	.284	.390	977	219	36	9	36	36	81	189
Not Leadoff	.234	.307	.384	1379	323	57	7	45	45	144	296
Runners On Base	.231	.299	.351	1502	347	37	13	39	295	147	285
First Base Only	.253	.296	.376	699	177	17	6	19	51	41	113
Scoring Position	.212	.302	.329	803	170	20	7	20	244	106	172
Late Innings, Close	.249	.316	.407	462	115	17	1	18	51	45	84

RBI/Opportunities

Scoring Position	45 / 284 (16%)	208 / 1074 (19%)
Scoring Position, 2 Out	9 / 130 (7%)	60 / 491 (12%)
On Third, Less than 2 Out	22 / 50 (44%)	93 / 192 (48%)
RBI in close games / RBI Total	66 / 98 (67%)	280 / 376 (74%)

Jim Morrison
Pittsburgh Pirates

Jim Morrison had his season in the sun in 1986, playing regularly for only the second time in his career. In 1987, it was back to his usual role as a part-time player. Morrison started the season as the regular third baseman, but it turned out that he was only keeping the position warm for Bobby Bonilla, who took over the job when he started hitting like he had in spring training. Morrison's offense had dropped off a little, but the ultimate reason for his losing his job was to make room for Bonilla.

As the season moved along, and the pennant races drew tighter, it became clear that contenders were willing to deal, so Thrift took advantage of this to ship Morrison to Detroit for Darnell Coles. The Tigers had given up on Coles, who was hitting .181 for them with 5 out-of-the-park shots, 4 with his bat and 1 with his arm. Morrison clearly didn't fit into the Pirates' plans, and was the type of veteran that's good to have around for a stretch drive. He can hit with power and play a passable third base, and in a pinch can play short or second without too much damage.

Morrison should still be effective as a role player for the Tigers. He has usually continued to hit fairly well even when seeing limited action. Morrison is prone to slumps, however, when he starts trying to pull everything. When he's going well, you will see him taking pitches the other way, and in the last couple of years, he's discovered that he can hit home runs to the opposite field as well.

Coles had become a head case in Detroit; when a player has gone that badly for a team, something is needed to break up the pattern of failure. The Tigers traded a young but unpredictable talent for an older, not as talented player that they had a good idea of what he was going to give them. The Tigers unfortunately seem to have a lot of older players, and not much in the farm system, but this trade was still not a completely unreasonable move for them to make. From the Pirates' standpoint, the trade was perfectly reasonable. The Pirates didn't have room to play Morrison everyday, and weren't in a position where they needed a player like Morrison on their bench. The Pirates needed young, talented players, and were willing to take a chance on Coles developing into a good player. There's no doubt that Coles has the tools to be a very good player; the question is, can he turn himself around? Even if he doesn't, the Pirates didn't give up much in Morrison to find out.

Sherri M. Nichols

Morrison, James Forrest "Jim" Bats: Right Throws: Right Born 09/23/52

1987 SEASON AND MAJOR-LEAGUE CAREER BATTING TOTALS

	G	AB	H	2B	3B	HR	TB	R	RBI	TBB	IBB	SO	HP	SH	SF	SB	CS	SB%	GDP	AVG	OBP	SLG
87 PIT-DET	130	465	116	23	2	13	182	56	65	29	3	83	2	1	7	10	6	.63	10	.249	.292	.391
11 YEARS	1014	3209	846	163	16	110	1371	358	416	203	14	494	25	43	36	50	34	.60	73	.264	.309	.427

	1987 SEASON											FOUR YEAR TOTALS (1984 – 1987)									
	Ave.	OBP	SLG	AB	H	2B	3B	HR	RBI	BB	SO	Ave.	OBP	SLG	AB	H	2B	3B	HR	RBI	BB	SO
Totals	.249	.292	.391	465	116	23	2	13	65	29	83	.266	.312	.428	1550	412	83	8	51	220	104	267
vs. Left	.274	.343	.426	190	52	9	1	6	28	22	31	.276	.330	.423	608	168	32	3	17	78	54	88
vs. Right	.233	.254	.367	275	64	14	1	7	37	7	52	.259	.299	.432	942	244	51	5	34	142	50	179
at Home	.264	.314	.426	216	57	12	1	7	28	15	37	.278	.331	.449	762	212	42	5	26	103	57	123
on Road	.237	.273	.361	249	59	11	1	6	37	14	46	.254	.293	.409	788	200	41	3	25	117	47	144
vs. Groundball	.247	.282	.379	235	58	13	0	6	35	13	39	.267	.318	.409	723	193	40	3	19	102	57	130
vs. Flyball	.252	.303	.404	230	58	10	2	7	30	16	44	.265	.306	.445	827	219	43	5	32	118	47	137
vs. Finesse	.252	.287	.402	246	62	11	1	8	34	13	36	.265	.302	.427	869	230	44	5	29	111	49	127
vs. Power	.247	.298	.379	219	54	12	1	5	31	16	47	.267	.323	.430	681	182	39	3	22	109	55	140
on Grass	.235	.280	.350	183	43	6	0	5	26	12	38	.264	.305	.429	443	117	21	2	16	66	27	86
on Artificial Turf	.259	.300	.418	282	73	17	2	8	39	17	45	.266	.315	.428	1107	295	62	6	35	154	77	181
Day Games	.220	.281	.365	159	35	6	1	5	25	15	34	.285	.330	.473	522	149	29	3	21	89	35	84
Night Games	.265	.298	.405	306	81	17	1	8	40	14	49	.256	.302	.406	1028	263	54	5	30	131	69	183
April	.333	.395	.583	72	24	6	0	4	14	8	8	.287	.349	.453	150	43	7	0	6	18	15	27
May	.217	.220	.340	106	23	8	1	1	13	0	24	.238	.283	.366	273	65	11	3	6	33	17	62
June	.245	.321	.372	94	23	6	0	2	11	11	14	.225	.276	.366	276	62	17	2	6	38	20	49
July	.281	.343	.391	64	18	1	0	2	7	6	10	.291	.349	.453	247	72	13	0	9	37	22	32
August	.226	.242	.398	93	21	2	1	4	15	3	19	.246	.273	.418	285	70	15	2	10	41	12	42
Sept/Oct	.194	.237	.194	36	7	0	0	0	5	1	8	.313	.352	.514	319	100	20	1	14	53	18	55
Bases Empty	.242	.285	.403	248	60	14	1	8	8	14	44	.255	.303	.432	842	215	52	2	31	31	56	151
Leadoff	.263	.305	.374	99	26	5	0	2	2	5	16	.287	.327	.484	349	100	22	1	15	15	20	53
Not Leadoff	.228	.272	.423	149	34	9	1	6	6	9	28	.233	.285	.396	493	115	30	1	16	16	36	98
Runners On	.258	.300	.378	217	56	9	1	5	57	15	39	.278	.322	.424	708	197	31	6	20	189	48	116
First Base Only	.284	.330	.443	88	25	3	1	3	9	6	12	.286	.320	.447	304	87	13	3	10	30	15	40
Scoring Position	.240	.281	.333	129	31	6	0	2	48	9	27	.272	.324	.406	404	110	18	3	10	159	33	76
Late Innings, Close	.208	.287	.347	72	15	2	1	2	8	6	17	.235	.292	.391	289	68	10	4	9	36	21	61

RBI/Opportunities

	1987	Four Year
Scoring Position	43 / 174 (25%)	139 / 547 (25%)
Scoring Position, 2 Out	15 / 83 (18%)	54 / 251 (22%)
On Third, Less than 2 Out	23 / 38 (61%)	61 / 119 (51%)
RBI in close games / RBI Total	42 / 65 (65%)	136 / 220 (62%)

Lloyd Moseby
Toronto Blue Jays

It's hard to star when you're surrounded by supernovas. In 1986, there was a 40-homer eruption to Lloyd Moseby's left. This year, there was a 49-homer explosion on his right. There's an All-Star shortstop, some Cy Young candidates and an awfully good catcher directly in front of him. If he turns around, he can wave to the best bullpen in baseball.

How good is Moseby? In 1987, he batted .282; three points below Wally Joyner. He hit 26 homers; three less than Alvin Davis. He had 96 RBIs; Eddie Murray had 91. He stole 39 bases; Phil Bradley beat him by one. True, all four men have advantages over Moseby in some other area—but then none of them can play center field for a major league team.

Aside from his teammates, Moseby's major problem stems from the type of changes that he's made in his game over the last few years. In 1983, he hit .315; he hasn't come close to .300 since. To the general public—who turn a blind eye toward everything but a player's batting average—he's been declining badly. But if you look more carefully at his performance, he hasn't slipped that much at all.

Moseby walked 51 times in 1983, giving him a .376 on-base percentage. He's averaged 72 walks since; his OB%s have been .368, .345, .329 and .358.

Moseby hit 18 homers in 1983 and slugged .499. He's averaged 21 since; his SL%s are .470, .426, .418 and .473.

Moseby had 81 RBIs in 1983. Despite leading off or batting second a lot of late, he's had 92, 82, 70 and 96 ribbies in the last four years.

Moseby stole 27 bases in 35 tries (77.1 percent) and grounded into a double play every 53.9 at-bats in 1983. He's averaged 37 steals, been safe 77.8 percent of the time and grounded into one DP every 62 at-bats since then.

Here are some other Moseby tidbits that you probably don't know. In 1983, Moseby had 604 plate appearances; he's had 688, 670, 668 and 670 in the last four years. He's always very high in the league in defensive innings played. He's one of only six men who plays in an open-air turf park—on turf that is, by popular acclaim, the second-worst in the majors. When Dale Murphy moved to right, Lloyd (who's 6'3" and 200 pounds) became the largest center-fielder in baseball. He's probably the biggest player in the majors who bats first or second. Finally, his range factor has dropped for the last three years—this year to tenth in the AL.

Moseby is a wonderful athlete, but there are limits to everything. He might benefit if Toronto would do any of the following: cut down on his playing time, bat him lower in the order, get him out of center field, install new turf or get the dome built. Or, better yet, maybe they could give him a hardship discharge to a team where the competition for the limelight isn't quite as fierce.

Geoff Beckman, Dave Easby and Darren Peterson

Moseby, Lloyd Anthony

Bats: Left   Throws: Right   Born 11/05/59

1987 SEASON AND MAJOR-LEAGUE CAREER BATTING TOTALS

	G	AB	H	2B	3B	HR	TB	R	RBI	TBB	IBB	SO	HP	SH	SF	SB	CS	SB%	GDP	AVG	OBP	SLG
87 TOR	155	592	167	27	4	26	280	106	96	70	4	124	2	3	3	39	7	.85	11	.282	.358	.473
8 YEARS	1129	4150	1095	200	50	128	1779	619	566	421	34	821	38	30	36	200	71	.74	73	.264	.335	.429

	1987 SEASON											FOUR YEAR TOTALS (1984 – 1987)										
	Ave.	OBP	SLG	AB	H	2B	3B	HR	RBI	BB	SO	Ave.	OBP	SLG	AB	H	2B	3B	HR	RBI	BB	SO
Totals	.282	.358	.473	592	167	27	4	26	96	70	124	.269	.350	.447	2357	633	109	31	83	344	288	459
vs. Left	.278	.362	.419	198	55	9	2	5	26	25	45	.254	.326	.390	830	211	35	9	20	100	80	178
vs. Right	.284	.357	.500	394	112	18	2	21	70	45	79	.276	.363	.477	1527	422	74	22	63	244	208	281
at Home	.292	.371	.503	298	87	12	3	15	49	37	66	.274	.360	.478	1148	314	54	20	47	189	150	229
on Road	.272	.345	.442	294	80	15	1	11	47	33	58	.264	.341	.417	1209	319	55	11	36	155	138	230
vs. Groundball	.302	.370	.514	288	87	19	3	12	54	31	59	.279	.356	.467	1109	309	52	17	41	171	132	198
vs. Flyball	.263	.348	.434	304	80	8	1	14	42	39	65	.260	.345	.429	1248	324	57	14	42	173	156	261
vs. Finesse	.298	.351	.481	339	101	15	4	13	50	27	59	.287	.358	.472	1353	388	64	21	48	182	146	211
vs. Power	.261	.368	.462	253	66	12	0	13	46	43	65	.244	.340	.413	1004	245	45	10	35	162	142	248
on Grass	.279	.350	.432	229	64	12	1	7	35	25	43	.261	.344	.407	916	239	40	8	26	112	113	171
on Artificial Turf	.284	.363	.499	363	103	15	3	19	61	45	81	.273	.354	.472	1441	394	69	23	57	232	175	288
Day Games	.280	.348	.469	211	59	7	0	11	30	21	40	.276	.358	.455	838	231	30	9	34	116	100	151
Night Games	.283	.364	.475	381	108	20	4	15	66	49	84	.265	.346	.442	1519	402	79	22	49	228	188	308
April	.238	.281	.357	84	20	4	0	2	10	5	22	.270	.341	.442	326	88	14	3	12	45	35	64
May	.271	.307	.479	96	26	5	0	5	17	4	25	.279	.348	.474	405	113	23	7	14	58	42	79
June	.284	.397	.520	102	29	2	2	6	22	19	20	.272	.371	.470	423	115	18	9	16	64	67	87
July	.220	.388	.418	91	20	4	1	4	14	25	22	.226	.323	.377	385	87	16	6	10	53	55	82
August	.306	.333	.480	98	30	2	0	5	15	5	15	.291	.357	.469	409	119	16	3	17	64	43	67
Sept/Oct	.347	.407	.545	121	42	10	1	4	18	12	20	.271	.346	.443	409	111	22	3	14	60	46	80
Bases Empty	.288	.373	.457	326	94	18	2	11	11	42	76	.258	.341	.416	1357	350	61	15	41	41	168	280
Leadoff	.264	.328	.396	106	28	8	0	2	2	10	19	.257	.330	.410	478	123	21	5	14	14	52	92
Not Leadoff	.300	.394	.486	220	66	10	2	9	9	32	57	.258	.346	.419	879	227	40	10	27	27	116	188
Runners On	.274	.340	.492	266	73	9	2	15	85	28	48	.283	.359	.489	1000	283	48	16	42	303	120	179
First Base Only	.217	.259	.425	106	23	1	0	7	14	6	19	.295	.344	.514	420	124	21	4	21	54	31	63
Scoring Position	.313	.389	.538	160	50	8	2	8	71	22	29	.274	.369	.471	580	159	27	12	21	249	89	116
Late Innings, Close	.234	.333	.415	94	22	5	0	4	13	14	26	.253	.340	.409	372	94	17	4	11	52	49	82

RBI/Opportunities

Scoring Position	56 / 221 (25%)	213 / 814 (26%)
Scoring Position, 2 Out	17 / 90 (19%)	54 / 304 (18%)
On Third, Less than 2 Out	21 / 37 (57%)	95 / 168 (57%)
RBI in close games / RBI Total	58 / 96 (60%)	215 / 344 (63%)

Jamie Moyer
Chicago Cubs

1987 was Jamie Moyer's first full season with the Chicago Cubs. Over the course of the season, he could best be described as, "inconsistently less than average." He did throw an occasional two-hitter (once, anyway) and he even managed to pitch past the seventh inning a few times. His usual outing, however, was laced with sporadic control.

Over the course of the season Moyer walked 4.34 batters per nine innings, a dangerously high ratio for a pitcher working in Wrigley Field. The numerous pitches he threw were reflected in his inability to complete games (one in 33 starts) and in the fact that he averaged only 5.95 innings per start. I use the word "sporadic" in describing his control because there were many games where he sailed along fine until, in one inning, he would walk a batter, balk him to second, hit the next guy, and completely lose his finesse.

Cub announcers Steve Stone, Lou Boudreau, DeWayne Staats, and Holy Harry Caray often attributed Jamie's wildness to his fear of the home run. This would surely explain his tendency not to throw strikes. The trouble with that theory, though, is that Jamie Moyer led the Cub staff by allowing 28 gopher balls, and was only surpassed by Rick Sutcliffe in striking out the opposition. He also walked more men per inning on the road (.511) than he did in homer haven Wrigley Field (.452).

Another factor as to why Jamie couldn't finish his games was beyond Jamie's control. The Cub offense rarely scored enough runs for him. They contributed an average of 3.8 runs with Moyer as their pitcher, whereas teammate Sutcliffe benefitted from Cub production averaging 5.3 runs per stint. With not enough offense behind Moyer, percentage-minded manager Gene Michael found the need to pinch-hit for him in the later innings.

Moyer did have some positive qualities. He led the Cubs in pitching against left-handed batters. That group of hitters only mustered a .220 batting average against him. It's unfortunate for him that lefties represented only 14.6 percent of the batters he faced. He also was second, among the "usual" starters on the staff, in lowest percentage of "stolen bases against" (.658); Lester Lancaster's was lower (.550).

As mentioned above, Moyer does have finesse. With future experience, one can expect him to be one of the more prominent deliverers in the league. His need is not to lose his fear of the home run, but to establish his prowess as a controlled pitcher. Perhaps the absence of ex-Cub pitching coach Herm Starrette will be the key to Jamie Moyer's self-discovery.

Paul Adler

Moyer, Jamie   Bats: Left   Throws: Left   Born 11/18/62

1987 SEASON AND MAJOR-LEAGUE CAREER PITCHING TOTALS

	G	GS	CG	GF	IP	BFP	H	R	ER	HR	SH	SF	HB	TBB	IBB	SO	WP	Bk	W	L	Pct	ShO	Sv	ERA
87 CHN	35	33	1	1	201	899	210	127	114	28	14	7	5	97	9	147	11	2	12	15	.444	0	0	5.10
2 YEARS	51	49	2	1	288	1294	317	179	163	38	17	10	8	139	10	192	14	5	19	19	.500	1	0	5.09

1987: Power, Groundball   1986: Finesse, Groundball

1987 SEASON

	G	IP	H	BB	SO	SB	CS	W	L	S	ERA
Totals	35	201.0	210	97	147	25	12	12	15	0	5.06
at Home	18	108.1	106	49	81	12	8	5	7	0	4.82
on Road	17	92.2	104	48	66	13	4	7	8	0	5.44
on Grass	24	138.0	143	63	99	16	9	8	9	0	4.83
on Artificial Turf	11	63.0	67	34	48	9	3	4	6	0	5.71
Day Games	23	136.1	141	62	98	18	12	6	10	0	5.35
Night Games	12	64.2	69	35	49	7	0	6	5	0	4.59
April	5	26.2	23	11	30	2	2	2	1	0	3.38
May	6	32.0	28	20	15	4	2	3	2	0	3.94
June	6	42.0	39	20	27	6	0	3	2	0	4.71
July	6	35.1	38	17	29	8	5	1	2	0	4.84
August	5	29.0	35	18	16	2	2	1	4	0	9.00
Sept/Oct	7	36.0	47	11	30	3	1	2	4	0	5.00

vs. Opponent Batters	Ave.	OBP	SLG	AB	H	2B	3B	HR	RBI	BB	SO
Totals	.271	.353	.428	776	210	28	5	28	117	97	147
vs. Left	.222	.336	.398	108	24	2	1	5	12	18	15
vs. Right	.278	.355	.433	668	186	26	4	23	105	79	132
Bases Empty	.274	.348	.414	435	119	15	2	14	14	48	96
Leadoff	.293	.367	.452	188	55	5	2	7	7	21	42
Not Leadoff	.259	.335	.385	247	64	10	0	7	7	27	54
Runners On Base	.267	.357	.446	341	91	13	3	14	103	49	51
First Base Only	.229	.292	.389	157	36	2	1	7	15	14	24
Scoring Position	.299	.406	.495	184	55	11	2	7	88	35	27
Late Innings, Close	.313	.421	.575	80	25	4	1	5	15	14	4

FOUR YEAR TOTALS (1984 – 1987)

	G	IP	H	BB	SO	SB	CS	W	L	S	ERA
Totals	51	288.1	317	139	192	35	17	19	19	0	5.06
at Home	28	167.1	180	82	109	17	11	9	8	0	4.84
on Road	23	121.0	137	57	83	18	6	10	11	0	5.43
on Grass	34	197.0	217	96	127	21	12	12	10	0	4.84
on Artificial Turf	17	91.1	100	43	65	14	5	7	9	0	5.62
Day Games	35	203.2	225	99	131	24	15	11	12	0	5.17
Night Games	16	84.2	92	40	61	11	2	8	7	0	4.89
April	5	26.2	23	11	30	2	2	2	1	0	3.38
May	6	32.0	28	20	15	4	2	3	2	0	3.94
June	8	51.0	54	24	32	10	0	4	3	0	5.65
July	10	58.1	60	26	45	10	6	3	3	0	4.17
August	10	55.1	64	31	29	4	2	3	6	0	7.48
Sept/Oct	12	65.0	88	27	41	5	5	4	4	0	4.71

vs. Opponent Batters	Ave.	OBP	SLG	AB	H	2B	3B	HR	RBI	BB	SO
Totals	.283	.363	.435	1120	317	46	5	38	160	139	192
vs. Left	.242	.356	.443	149	36	7	1	7	19	26	21
vs. Right	.289	.364	.434	971	281	39	4	31	141	113	171
Bases Empty	.284	.361	.425	609	173	25	2	19	19	71	122
Leadoff	.310	.372	.474	274	85	8	2	11	11	26	55
Not Leadoff	.263	.352	.385	335	88	17	0	8	8	45	67
Runners On Base	.282	.365	.446	511	144	21	3	19	141	68	70
First Base Only	.284	.351	.455	225	64	8	1	8	18	23	31
Scoring Position	.280	.375	.455	286	80	13	2	11	123	45	39
Late Innings, Close	.287	.384	.509	108	31	4	1	6	20	16	9

RBI/Opportunities

Scoring Position	72 / 269 (27%)	100 / 405 (25%)
Scoring Position, 2 Out	34 / 141 (24%)	42 / 192 (22%)
On Third, Less than 2 Out	21 / 34 (62%)	34 / 65 (52%)
RBI in close games / RBI Total	89 / 117 (76%)	118 / 160 (74%)

Jerry Mumphrey
Chicago Cubs

When the Cubs broke spring training last April, Jerry Mumphrey probably thought that his life would be easy. His role would be that of left-handed pinch hitter, with an occasional game in the outfield. But with the spring training fallout of the can't miss prospect Rafael Palmeiro, and the early season fadeout of Chico Walker, Mumphrey was asked to play nearly every day in Gene Michael's platoon system.

Jerry took full advantage of the opportunity he was given. He appeared in 118 ballgames and had over 300 at bats. He ended up hitting .333. Not too shabby; among all National League players with 300+ AB, only Tony Gwynn, Pedro Guerrero and Kal Daniels had higher batting averages. Jerry really didn't hit for much power, belting only 13 home runs with 44 RBI. He played an adequate defensive left field, but he seemed to have lost a few steps and did not display the best arm in the world. At times Jerry seemed lost and confused in the outfield. He just filled in a very weak point in the Cub lineup doing the best job that he could, allowing time for the youngsters to develop in the minor leagues.

When Palmeiro came up to the senior circuit in Au-gust, Jerry once again was sent to the bench to become a full time pinch hitter. The prolonged periods of rest really seemed to benefit Jerry, as he did not appear to tire. He also seemed to provide a calming force and be a teacher for the young outfielders, using his many years of experience in the National League to help the young outfielders, Dave Martinez and Palmeiro, learn how to play the hitters.

Jerry provided the same leadership and experience that Manny Trillo did for the infield. His insight and calming influence in the clubhouse seemed evident in the younger players. Maybe the Cubs will be able to use Jerry in the role that he seemed to fill the best in 1987, that of the switch-hitting pinch hitter who hits better from the left hand side, and an occasional left fielder. Even if he cannot end the game with one swing of the bat as well as some pinch hitters, Jerry is able to come off the bench cold and get on base in order to start off a rally. He is a smart baserunner who has lost his speed but will not kill you with stupid baserunning mistakes.

Jerry Mumphrey is a good man to have on the bench. May the Cubs find that he is able to produce once again in 1988.

Vincent Vrotny

Mumphrey, Jerry Wayne Bats: Both   Throws: Right   Born 09/09/52

1987 SEASON AND MAJOR-LEAGUE CAREER BATTING TOTALS

	G	AB	H	2B	3B	HR	TB	R	RBI	TBB	IBB	SO	HP	SH	SF	SB	CS	SB%	GDP	AVG	OBP	SLG
87 CHN	118	309	103	19	2	13	165	41	44	35	6	47	0	1	1	1	1	.50	5	.333	.400	.534
14 YEARS	1522	4927	1433	215	55	70	1968	657	566	471	47	672	4	29	41	174	80	.69	105	.291	.351	.399

1987 SEASON

	Ave.	OBP	SLG	AB	H	2B	3B	HR	RBI	BB	SO
Totals	.333	.400	.534	309	103	19	2	13	44	35	47
vs. Left	.143	.250	.286	7	1	1	0	0	0	1	1
vs. Right	.338	.404	.540	302	102	18	2	13	44	34	46
at Home	.288	.366	.487	156	45	8	1	7	23	19	23
on Road	.379	.435	.582	153	58	11	1	6	21	16	24
vs. Groundball	.316	.390	.500	136	43	8	1	5	22	17	18
vs. Flyball	.347	.408	.561	173	60	11	1	8	22	18	29
vs. Finesse	.360	.425	.629	178	64	14	2	10	31	21	19
vs. Power	.298	.366	.405	131	39	5	0	3	13	14	28
on Grass	.318	.390	.498	223	71	14	1	8	30	27	31
on Artificial Turf	.372	.426	.628	86	32	5	1	5	14	8	16
Day Games	.294	.374	.471	204	60	10	1	8	30	26	35
Night Games	.410	.452	.657	105	43	9	1	5	14	9	12
April	.429	.600	.857	7	3	0	0	1	4	3	0
May	.377	.421	.493	69	26	5	0	1	10	6	10
June	.271	.346	.443	70	19	3	0	3	10	8	13
July	.298	.365	.526	57	17	1	0	4	7	6	9
August	.355	.412	.629	62	22	6	1	3	6	6	8
Sept/Oct	.364	.440	.568	44	16	4	1	1	7	6	7
Bases Empty	.371	.421	.629	175	65	13	1	10	10	15	23
Leadoff	.328	.368	.547	64	21	2	0	4	4	4	4
Not Leadoff	.396	.451	.676	111	44	11	1	6	6	11	19
Runners On	.284	.374	.410	134	38	6	1	3	34	20	24
First Base Only	.259	.306	.431	58	15	4	0	2	6	4	13
Scoring Position	.303	.419	.395	76	23	2	1	1	28	16	11
Late Innings, Close	.347	.439	.612	49	17	2	1	3	14	8	5

FOUR YEAR TOTALS (1984 – 1987)

Ave.	OBP	SLG	AB	H	2B	3B	HR	RBI	BB	SO
.298	.356	.422	1586	472	75	9	35	220	154	228
.234	.308	.274	376	88	15	0	0	40	43	56
.317	.372	.469	1210	384	60	9	35	180	111	172
.311	.379	.444	761	237	39	7	16	111	84	106
.285	.336	.402	825	235	36	2	19	109	70	122
.305	.361	.436	730	223	38	6	15	118	68	89
.291	.353	.411	856	249	37	3	20	102	86	139
.311	.368	.466	874	272	42	6	27	125	82	90
.281	.343	.369	712	200	33	3	8	95	72	138
.310	.368	.450	751	233	31	4	22	103	72	110
.286	.346	.398	835	239	44	5	13	117	82	118
.300	.368	.443	601	180	26	3	18	92	69	90
.296	.349	.410	985	292	49	6	17	128	85	138
.289	.361	.385	187	54	6	3	2	27	21	24
.299	.371	.405	294	88	14	1	5	39	34	33
.273	.331	.385	286	78	11	0	7	39	25	47
.314	.379	.438	299	94	12	2	7	35	31	49
.301	.355	.464	319	96	21	2	9	47	27	50
.308	.359	.448	201	62	11	1	5	33	16	25
.298	.344	.426	857	255	48	4	18	18	60	119
.308	.347	.414	367	113	16	1	7	7	22	37
.290	.341	.435	490	142	32	3	11	11	38	82
.298	.377	.418	729	217	27	5	17	202	94	109
.299	.352	.440	291	87	12	1	9	24	24	39
.297	.393	.404	438	130	15	4	8	178	70	70
.286	.363	.374	297	85	9	1	5	51	36	50

RBI/Opportunities

Scoring Position	25 / 109 (23%)	161 / 604 (27%)
Scoring Position, 2 Out	9 / 54 (17%)	57 / 271 (21%)
On Third, Less than 2 Out	9 / 17 (53%)	71 / 119 (60%)
RBI in close games / RBI Total	33 / 44 (75%)	148 / 220 (67%)

Dale Murphy
Atlanta Braves

The 1987 National League MVP ballot provided clear evidence that despite prodding from sabermetricians, the writers who voted still are not aware of the walk column. Dale Murphy and Andre Dawson were two extremely well-matched award candidates. Both players had career years with 40+ homers and 100+ RBIs, played a superb RF after years in CF, and kept bad "Superstation" teams afloat. Murphy was buried in the voting (he finished 11th with 34 points) despite having higher batting, on base, slugging and secondary averages than Andre. Dawson had five more HR and 32 more RBIs (in 55 more AB); Murphy had 25 more runs scored and 83(!) more walks than Dawson. Murphy accounted for approximately 19 percent of the Braves offense, Dawson approximately 15 percent of the Cubs runs. I'm not saying that Murphy should have been the MVP (Tony Gwynn had a better year than both of them), but the award shouldn't have gone to the league's fourth best right fielder either.

Dale passed the 300 HR mark in 1987 and we can start to put his career accomplishments in historical perspective. Under the Bill James Hall of Fame Prediction System in the 1986 *Abstract*, Murphy has already accumulated 108 points, which would probably rank as the sixth greatest ever

(see the *Historical Baseball Abstract*) in terms of career value. Would anyone who saw Murphy as an awkward reserve catcher in the late '70s believe that this is the same player?

There was some sentiment in Atlanta for using Murphy to make a Gary Carter type trade—a superstar for help at three or four positions. While the Carter trade was a qualified success for the Expos most of these trades haven't worked. The similar trades of Tom Seaver, Ricky Henderson, and Frank Robinson set their teams back years. Such trades are usually grounded in economics, which is not a problem in Atlanta given the importance of the Braves to Turner Broadcasting. The Braves' record of evaluating talent is so abysmal in the '80s that I wouldn't expect them to get equitable talent for a Rick Mahler, much less a Dale Murphy. The trade rumors subsided after Dale signed a new three-year contract in November.

Murphy is widely known as one of the classiest players in the game, but he seems destined to be another Ernie Banks. The Braves are only starting to rebuild and don't seem likely to contend for the next few years. Murphy may be an elder statesman before he gets another chance to savor the magic of 1982.

Greg Gajus

Murphy, Dale Bryan Bats: Right Throws: Right Born 03/12/56

1987 SEASON AND MAJOR-LEAGUE CAREER BATTING TOTALS

	G	AB	H	2B	3B	HR	TB	R	RBI	TBB	IBB	SO	HP	SH	SF	SB	CS	SB%	GDP	AVG	OBP	SLG
87 ATL	159	566	167	27	1	44	328	115	105	115	29	136	7	0	5	16	6	.73	11	.295	.417	.580
12 YEARS	1519	5583	1555	241	33	310	2792	928	927	732	115	1230	23	6	38	145	58	.71	121	.279	.362	.500

	1987 SEASON											FOUR YEAR TOTALS (1984 – 1987)									
	Ave.	OBP	SLG	AB	H	2B	3B	HR	RBI	BB	SO	Ave.	OBP	SLG	AB	H	2B	3B	HR	RBI	BB	SO
Totals	.295	.417	.580	566	167	27	1	44	105	115	136	.288	.381	.535	2403	691	120	18	146	399	360	552
vs. Left	.320	.512	.653	150	48	8	0	14	30	60	32	.311	.436	.586	695	216	33	7	48	119	157	148
vs. Right	.286	.376	.553	416	119	19	1	30	75	55	104	.278	.356	.514	1708	475	87	11	98	280	203	404
at Home	.346	.493	.673	269	93	11	1	25	61	77	52	.301	.410	.562	1175	354	55	7	79	206	212	240
on Road	.249	.338	.495	297	74	16	0	19	44	38	84	.274	.352	.509	1228	337	65	11	67	193	148	312
vs. Groundball	.299	.405	.558	251	75	11	0	18	50	45	61	.285	.379	.495	1102	314	50	4	58	185	165	253
vs. Flyball	.292	.426	.597	315	92	16	1	26	55	70	75	.290	.383	.568	1301	377	70	14	88	214	195	299
vs. Finesse	.329	.424	.619	307	101	21	1	22	56	50	67	.304	.378	.554	1373	418	80	14	78	230	162	269
vs. Power	.255	.409	.533	259	66	6	0	22	49	65	69	.265	.386	.510	1030	273	40	4	68	169	198	283
on Grass	.314	.445	.628	411	129	16	1	37	88	94	94	.295	.394	.549	1769	522	79	13	115	300	282	378
on Artificial Turf	.245	.337	.452	155	38	11	0	7	17	21	42	.267	.345	.494	634	169	41	5	31	99	78	174
Day Games	.332	.447	.678	199	66	10	1	19	42	42	49	.303	.399	.559	789	239	38	4	52	130	125	177
Night Games	.275	.401	.526	367	101	17	0	25	63	73	87	.280	.372	.523	1614	452	82	14	94	269	235	375
April	.325	.404	.542	83	27	7	1	3	10	11	23	.316	.405	.633	297	94	22	3	22	61	44	69
May	.320	.492	.691	97	31	3	0	11	20	33	25	.291	.397	.529	416	121	16	1	27	62	73	93
June	.309	.427	.670	97	30	5	0	10	23	19	21	.272	.382	.493	416	113	19	2	23	62	73	103
July	.209	.321	.363	91	19	2	0	4	13	15	18	.253	.349	.494	387	98	18	3	23	62	57	97
August	.327	.410	.614	101	33	5	0	8	18	15	27	.316	.392	.587	424	134	25	3	28	75	54	96
Sept/Oct	.278	.425	.577	97	27	5	0	8	21	22	22	.283	.368	.501	463	131	20	6	23	77	59	94
Bases Empty	.322	.412	.629	307	99	17	1	25	25	46	68	.292	.370	.533	1331	388	72	14	74	74	165	294
Leadoff	.325	.384	.605	157	51	11	0	11	11	15	38	.314	.382	.567	545	171	33	6	31	31	60	119
Not Leadoff	.320	.440	.653	150	48	6	1	14	14	31	30	.276	.362	.510	786	217	39	8	43	43	105	175
Runners On	.263	.422	.521	259	68	10	0	19	80	69	68	.283	.394	.536	1072	303	48	4	72	325	195	258
First Base Only	.286	.353	.486	105	30	6	0	5	13	11	23	.288	.349	.516	473	136	22	1	28	67	45	93
Scoring Position	.247	.457	.545	154	38	4	0	14	67	58	45	.279	.425	.553	599	167	26	3	44	258	150	165
Late Innings, Close	.205	.345	.386	88	18	4	0	4	11	19	30	.278	.396	.527	400	111	22	3	24	73	79	107

RBI/Opportunities

Scoring Position	48 / 256 (19%)	191 / 869 (22%)
Scoring Position, 2 Out	18 / 124 (15%)	81 / 388 (21%)
On Third, Less than 2 Out	19 / 42 (45%)	67 / 162 (41%)
RBI in close games / RBI Total	73 / 105 (70%)	286 / 399 (72%)

Eddie Murray
Baltimore Orioles

In 1986, Eddie Murray went on the disabled list for the first time in ten seasons, missed 24 games and saw his homer and RBI totals plummet—even allowing for the missed games. Baltimore was outraged to learn that Murray was human. Fans booed him. The media questioned both his heart and his skill. Owner Edward Bennett Williams publicly said that Murray wasn't worth his paycheck. When Murray responded by requesting a trade, the howls of outrage grew even louder. Baltimore finished in last place.

Things didn't improve much in 1987. Murray hit 30 homers again, but his average was a career-low .277; his 91 RBIs were down from his past marks, His comment that baseball was "just a job" alienated many. The Orioles had their second consecutive losing season—the first time that has happened since 1958–59.

Is Murray to blame for the losing? In his two "off" years Eddie averaged .289 with 24 homers and 88 RBIs. On the basis of those numbers, the Orioles' problems can't all be laid at Murray's locker.

Many of the problems with Murray are imaginary. He has always shunned interviews and never made excuses. His play was solid—never flashy—and his strength was his consistency. When the Orioles were winning, people called him a steady, quiet player. With his team losing and injuries affecting his play, the words "surly" and "lazy" have been substituted.

Other problems are Murray's own doing. Like many quiet players, he does not play the "image game" well. In the winter of 1986, Murray finally admitted something that had been obvious for months—the wrist injury had affected his power. Had he said that during the season, he might have taken much less abuse.

In 1987, Eddie's baseball card bore a photograph of him wearing glasses; questions about his eyesight were raised. Murray insisted that he had no vision problems; anyone who watched him misplay balls that he had fielded easily in the past had to wonder about his capacity for either self-delusion or vanity.

There have been mistakes on both sides. Murray carried sunflower seeds in his back pocket and snacked between pitches in 1987 and never spoke save to complain. Williams's remarks, however, were unfair—as was the alleged warning (Don't use Murray as your role model) that management gave to the younger Orioles.

One mistake that—luckily—hasn't been made yet is a trade. Though Murray is 31 and his best seasons are probably behind him, he is still an exceptional player; the sort that you rebuild a team around. If Baltimore finds more talent to surround Eddie with, the losing will stop; if everyone lets Murray alone, he should continue to excel in 1988.

Chris Williams and Mark Prysant

Murray, Eddie Clarence

Bats: Both   **Throws: Right**   Born 02/24/56

1987 SEASON AND MAJOR-LEAGUE CAREER BATTING TOTALS

	G	AB	H	2B	3B	HR	TB	R	RBI	TBB	IBB	SO	HP	SH	SF	SB	CS	SB%	GDP	AVG	OBP	SLG
87 BAL	160	618	171	28	3	30	295	89	91	73	6	80	0	0	3	1	2	.33	15	.277	.352	.477
11 YEARS	1659	6242	1850	324	23	305	3135	973	1106	782	123	849	15	2	68	56	22	.72	148	.296	.372	.502

	1987 SEASON										FOUR YEAR TOTALS (1984 – 1987)									
	Ave.	OBP	SLG	AB	H	2B	3B	HR	RBI	BB	SO	Ave.	OBP	SLG	AB	H	2B	3B	HR	RBI	BB	SO
Totals	.277	.352	.477	618	171	28	3	30	91	73	80	.296	.385	.494	2284	675	116	8	107	409	342	284
vs. Left	.271	.336	.475	221	60	10	1	11	35	22	33	.280	.367	.473	710	199	37	2	32	117	96	94
vs. Right	.280	.360	.479	397	111	18	2	19	56	51	47	.302	.393	.503	1574	476	79	6	75	292	246	190
at Home	.263	.347	.433	300	79	9	0	14	37	39	45	.298	.392	.498	1116	333	49	3	56	204	174	129
on Road	.289	.356	.519	318	92	19	3	16	54	34	35	.293	.377	.490	1168	342	67	5	51	205	168	155
vs. Groundball	.274	.346	.462	329	90	18	1	14	48	38	37	.292	.377	.476	1121	327	60	3	47	195	158	136
vs. Flyball	.280	.358	.495	289	81	10	2	16	43	35	43	.299	.392	.511	1163	348	56	5	60	214	184	148
vs. Finesse	.275	.342	.458	306	84	17	0	13	41	32	30	.286	.364	.461	1227	351	64	2	49	205	155	134
vs. Power	.279	.361	.497	312	87	11	3	17	50	41	50	.307	.408	.532	1057	324	52	6	58	204	187	150
on Grass	.267	.345	.458	524	140	22	0	26	76	64	71	.295	.385	.496	1952	575	99	3	96	354	298	245
on Artificial Turf	.330	.388	.585	94	31	6	3	4	15	9	9	.301	.381	.482	332	100	17	5	11	55	44	39
Day Games	.253	.313	.377	162	41	8	0	4	18	15	22	.286	.375	.463	669	191	31	2	28	113	98	90
Night Games	.285	.365	.513	456	130	20	3	26	73	58	58	.300	.389	.507	1615	484	85	6	79	296	244	194
April	.181	.255	.301	83	15	5	1	1	13	9	12	.247	.338	.419	291	72	9	1	13	61	41	43
May	.343	.410	.713	108	37	5	1	11	27	13	8	.337	.432	.578	389	131	22	3	22	93	66	40
June	.257	.308	.376	109	28	7	0	2	4	8	18	.273	.353	.438	411	112	23	0	15	53	51	55
July	.276	.377	.663	98	27	3	1	11	28	16	10	.290	.384	.573	328	95	16	1	25	75	50	40
August	.321	.390	.425	106	34	2	0	3	11	12	17	.342	.425	.505	398	136	16	2	15	70	58	47
Sept/Oct	.263	.349	.368	114	30	6	0	2	8	15	15	.276	.378	.454	467	129	30	1	17	57	76	59
Bases Empty	.279	.337	.470	330	92	14	2	15	15	29	39	.274	.362	.442	1200	329	49	3	49	49	165	150
Leadoff	.271	.331	.484	155	42	8	2	7	7	14	11	.274	.364	.443	585	160	26	2	23	23	83	64
Not Leadoff	.286	.342	.457	175	50	6	0	8	8	15	28	.275	.360	.442	615	169	23	1	26	26	82	86
Runners On	.274	.367	.486	288	79	14	1	15	76	44	41	.319	.414	.551	1084	346	67	5	58	360	177	134
First Base Only	.263	.325	.480	152	40	9	0	8	18	14	13	.307	.373	.506	544	167	34	1	24	61	57	51
Scoring Position	.287	.408	.493	136	39	5	1	7	58	30	28	.331	.451	.596	540	179	33	4	34	299	120	83
Late Innings, Close	.255	.320	.404	94	24	5	0	3	13	9	15	.315	.409	.586	336	106	20	1	23	85	53	44

RBI/Opportunities

	1987		Four Year	
Scoring Position	47 / 199	(24%)	235 / 812	(29%)
Scoring Position, 2 Out	15 / 95	(16%)	80 / 364	(22%)
On Third, Less than 2 Out	16 / 29	(55%)	92 / 154	(60%)
RBI in close games / RBI Total	67 / 91	(74%)	294 / 409	(72%)

Juan Nieves
Milwaukee Brewers

Most people agree that any pitcher who throws a no-hitter—no matter what his stats look like—has shown signs that he has real talent. Rather than cite this hoary cliché, I've decided to use some statistics to show how likely it is that Juan Nieves was a better pitcher than he seemed to be in 1987.

In 1987, Nieves pitched 195.2 innings (587 outs) and allowed 199 hits. If you divide 199 into 587, the result—.339, or 33.9 percent—is his chance of allowing a hit before getting an out. To make things simpler, let's say that he had a 66.1 percent chance of getting an out before allowing a hit, OK?

The rules of probability say that the chance that an event will always occur in a given number of trials can be figured by raising the chance of the event to the power of the number of trials. If, like most people, you didn't understand that, let me use a simple example:

Let's say that you flip a coin; you have a 50 percent chance of getting heads. If you flip it twice, the chance that you'll get two heads is 25 percent (.5 × .5). Your chances of getting three heads on three flips is 12.5 percent (.5 times .5 times .5). With me so far?

Back to Nieves. His chance of getting two batters out before allowing a hit was 43.7 percent (.661 × .661) in 1987. His chance of getting three outs—i.e., pitching a hit-less inning—was 28.8 percent (.661 × .661 × .661). To save space, I'll just tell you that his chance of getting 27 outs in 1987 before allowing a hit was .001371 percent—that the odds were 71,575–1 against his pitching a no-hitter in 1987. In other words, if you assume that Nieves's 1987 was his true level of ability, his no-hitter was a major fluke.

But look what happens to the odds if you assume that Nieves's 1987 stats were even a small fluke—that some of the hits that he allowed were due to inexperience, poor defensive support or just bad luck. Had Nieves allowed just three less hits, his hits per nine innings figure wouldn't have changed much—it would have fallen from 9.15 to 9.02. It would have reduced the odds against a no-hitter to 58,136–1. If he'd allowed just ten less hits—8.69 H/9IP—the odds fall to 36,005–1. What do you think is more likely—that Nieves threw a no-hitter due to exceptional good luck or that he allowed a few more hits than a pitcher with his talent would normally allow due to some other factor?

The answer is pretty obvious if you've seen Nieves pitch. He has stretches where he gets behind the hitter and has to come in with his "rising" fastball; the resulting line drive is usually not caught by the Milwaukee defense. If he develops more consistent control, he'll improve greatly—since he's just turned 23, I think that he will. I wouldn't be at all surprised to see Nieves win 17–20 games in 1988.

Geoff Beckman

Nieves, Juan Manuel (Cruz)   Bats: Left   Throws: Left   Born 01/05/65

1987 SEASON AND MAJOR-LEAGUE CAREER PITCHING TOTALS

	G	GS	CG	GF	IP	BFP	H	R	ER	HR	SH	SF	HB	TBB	IBB	SO	WP	Bk	W	L	Pct	ShO	Sv	ERA
87 MIL	34	33	3	0	196	867	199	112	106	24	3	7	2	100	5	163	4	0	14	8	.636	1	0	4.87
2 YEARS	69	66	7	0	381	1701	423	236	207	41	6	12	3	177	5	279	7	1	25	20	.556	4	0	4.89

1987: Power, Flyball   **1986: Power, Flyball**

1987 SEASON

	G	IP	H	BB	SO	SB	CS	W	L	S	ERA
Totals	34	195.1	199	100	163	19	11	14	8	0	4.88
at Home	11	63.2	72	38	61	5	5	4	4	0	6.22
on Road	23	131.2	127	62	102	14	6	10	4	0	4.24
on Grass	8	48.2	44	29	45	5	3	5	1	0	4.07
on Artificial Turf	26	146.2	155	71	118	14	8	9	7	0	5.15
Day Games	27	154.1	159	84	128	14	10	12	6	0	5.13
Night Games	7	41.0	40	16	35	5	1	2	2	0	3.95
April	4	24.0	21	13	12	2	1	2	0	0	4.88
May	6	36.0	31	19	28	5	1	2	2	0	3.75
June	6	29.0	30	22	29	2	4	1	3	0	5.90
July	6	29.2	36	14	20	3	2	2	1	0	7.58
August	6	38.2	46	16	38	4	1	4	0	0	4.66
Sept/Oct	6	38.0	35	16	36	3	2	3	2	0	3.32

FOUR YEAR TOTALS (1984 – 1987)

	G	IP	H	BB	SO	SB	CS	W	L	S	ERA
Totals	69	380.0	423	177	279	27	24	25	20	0	4.90
at Home	28	141.2	177	76	110	10	11	8	10	0	6.29
on Road	41	238.1	246	101	169	17	13	17	10	0	4.08
on Grass	17	103.1	99	52	80	5	7	8	2	0	3.92
on Artificial Turf	52	276.2	324	125	199	22	17	17	18	0	5.27
Day Games	58	317.0	356	156	227	22	22	21	17	0	5.03
Night Games	11	63.0	67	21	52	5	2	4	3	0	4.29
April	8	47.1	44	26	31	2	5	2	1	0	4.75
May	13	78.0	80	39	48	5	2	7	2	0	4.27
June	11	60.2	64	30	44	6	6	2	4	0	4.60
July	12	66.2	71	35	50	5	6	6	3	0	5.13
August	11	57.2	85	21	49	4	1	4	3	0	6.55
Sept/Oct	14	69.2	79	26	57	5	4	4	7	0	4.39

vs. Opponent Batters	Ave.	OBP	SLG	AB	H	2B	3B	HR	RBI	BB	SO
Totals	.264	.348	.420	754	199	42	2	24	92	100	163
vs. Left	.187	.308	.293	123	23	4	0	3	18	22	40
vs. Right	.279	.357	.445	631	176	38	2	21	74	78	123
Bases Empty	.258	.348	.422	427	110	25	0	15	15	58	90
Leadoff	.249	.346	.420	181	45	10	0	7	7	26	36
Not Leadoff	.264	.349	.423	246	65	15	0	8	8	32	54
Runners On Base	.272	.349	.419	327	89	17	2	9	77	42	73
First Base Only	.285	.380	.438	144	41	9	2	3	10	22	32
Scoring Position	.262	.325	.404	183	48	8	0	6	67	20	41
Late Innings, Close	.200	.300	.400	35	7	2	1	1	4	5	7

Ave.	OBP	SLG	AB	H	2B	3B	HR	RBI	BB	SO
.282	.356	.419	1502	423	78	3	41	191	177	279
.255	.346	.353	255	65	11	1	4	29	36	70
.287	.359	.433	1247	358	67	2	37	162	141	209
.268	.348	.412	831	223	45	1	24	24	101	159
.271	.362	.430	358	97	22	1	11	11	50	65
.266	.338	.397	473	126	23	0	13	13	51	94
.298	.366	.429	671	200	33	2	17	167	76	120
.301	.378	.424	302	91	12	2	7	18	37	53
.295	.357	.434	369	109	21	0	10	149	39	67
.243	.314	.374	107	26	3	1	3	10	11	20

RBI/Opportunities

Scoring Position	55 / 240 (23%)	128 / 482 (27%)
Scoring Position, 2 Out	20 / 104 (19%)	55 / 221 (25%)
On Third, Less than 2 Out	21 / 42 (50%)	40 / 74 (54%)
RBI in close games / RBI Total	58 / 92 (63%)	130 / 191 (68%)

Matt Nokes
Detroit Tigers

One of the most overlooked post-season honors (probably because I'm the one who gives it) is the "Don Mattingly Award," which goes to the player with the most unexpected power stats in a year. In 1987, despite strong competition from Wade Boggs, the honor went to Matt Nokes. Nokes, who batted .282 and slugged .444 in his minor league career, bettered his batting average by seven points and his slugging percentage by 92 points in his rookie season. Given a difficult task—replace an All-Star and fan favorite—Matt came through with flying colors. 1987 marked his first appearance in a mid-season classic—very likely the first of many.

Nokes owes at least part of his success to manager Sparky Anderson's uncharacteristically intelligent conduct this year. Not once did Anderson claim that Nokes would make Johnny Bench and Lance Parrish look sick; instead, he said that Matt would platoon at catcher with Mike Heath. The plan was to both protect Nokes from lefties (who, as you can see below, tie him in knots) and reduce the amount of pressure to a bare minimum; it worked like a charm. Heath hit .350 in April and .329 in May before falling apart; by then Nokes was firmly entrenched in the majors.

Another unusually shrewd decision also avoided a potential crisis. Nokes had trouble with both his footwork and his release this year; he's not agile behind the plate and doesn't get rid of the ball quickly. As a result, the Detroit staff threw 22 more wild pitches, allowed 31 more steals and caught nine fewer men in 1987. Some of that decline is only natural; anyone would look bad compared to Lance Parrish. But, since Detroit's 72 WPs missed leading the majors by only two and opposing runners succeeded on 73.8 percent of their steal attempts, it's also true that Nokes's fielding simply needs work.

Left unchecked, the problem might have mushroomed to the point where it could have slowed Nokes's development. But, thankfully, it wasn't allowed to. Through July 2, Detroit had played 75 games; Nokes had played in 64 of them. But he caught only 39 games in that span—and, fairly often, played only part of the game behind the plate. That seems to have helped Matt; when he caught 70 of the final 87 games, his offense tapered off somewhat.

The defensive problems are the reason that some members of the Detroit organization feel that Matt would be better off at first base or DH. I disagree. It is far easier to teach a 30-homer player good defensive habits than to teach a defensive catcher to hit 30 homers. With coaching and a lot of hard work, Matt could certainly become adequate defensively—that would make him one of the best catchers in the league.

Jim Shaarda

Nokes, Matthew Dodge "Matt"

Bats: Left   Throws: Right   Born 10/31/63

1987 SEASON AND MAJOR-LEAGUE CAREER BATTING TOTALS

	G	AB	H	2B	3B	HR	TB	R	RBI	TBB	IBB	SO	HP	SH	SF	SB	CS	SB%	GDP	AVG	OBP	SLG
87 DET	135	461	133	14	2	32	247	69	87	35	2	70	6	3	3	2	1	.67	13	.289	.345	.536
3 YEARS	161	538	152	17	2	35	278	74	94	37	3	80	7	3	3	2	1	.67	16	.283	.335	.517

1987 SEASON

	Ave.	OBP	SLG	AB	H	2B	3B	HR	RBI	BB	SO
Totals	.289	.345	.536	461	133	14	2	32	87	36	70
vs. Left	.207	.278	.356	87	18	1	0	4	12	9	23
vs. Right	.307	.360	.578	374	115	13	2	28	75	27	47
at Home	.308	.374	.542	214	66	4	2	14	36	19	39
on Road	.271	.318	.530	247	67	10	0	18	51	17	31
vs. Groundball	.264	.314	.483	261	69	8	2	15	39	20	39
vs. Flyball	.320	.383	.605	200	64	6	0	17	48	16	31
vs. Finesse	.291	.338	.547	247	72	10	1	17	46	14	27
vs. Power	.285	.351	.523	214	61	4	1	15	41	22	43
on Grass	.309	.365	.568	398	123	12	2	29	71	32	60
on Artificial Turf	.159	.209	.333	63	10	2	0	3	16	4	10
Day Games	.268	.314	.570	142	38	7	0	12	33	9	20
Night Games	.298	.358	.520	319	95	7	2	20	54	27	50
April	.310	.359	.552	58	18	2	0	4	14	5	10
May	.300	.360	.512	80	24	2	0	5	16	8	12
June	.341	.393	.659	82	28	3	1	7	15	6	13
July	.265	.315	.574	68	18	3	0	6	11	3	11
August	.207	.258	.354	82	17	3	0	3	15	5	9
Sept/Oct	.308	.376	.571	91	28	1	1	7	16	9	15
Bases Empty	.287	.366	.616	216	62	7	2	20	20	23	24
Leadoff	.341	.394	.703	91	31	6	0	9	9	5	9
Not Leadoff	.248	.347	.552	125	31	1	2	11	11	18	15
Runners On	.290	.324	.465	245	71	7	0	12	67	13	46
First Base Only	.366	.385	.594	101	37	2	0	7	16	3	21
Scoring Position	.236	.285	.375	144	34	5	0	5	51	10	25
Late Innings, Close	.250	.292	.471	68	17	0	0	5	16	4	13

TWO YEAR TOTALS (1986 – 1987)

	Ave.	OBP	SLG	AB	H	2B	3B	HR	RBI	BB	SO
	.291	.347	.534	485	141	15	2	33	89	37	71
	.205	.276	.352	88	18	1	0	4	12	9	23
	.310	.361	.574	397	123	14	2	29	77	28	48
	.303	.367	.534	221	67	5	2	14	36	19	40
	.280	.326	.534	264	74	10	0	19	53	18	31
	.268	.316	.480	269	72	8	2	15	40	20	40
	.319	.381	.602	216	69	7	0	18	49	17	31
	.296	.339	.536	267	79	11	1	17	47	14	28
	.284	.352	.532	218	62	4	1	16	42	23	43
	.310	.365	.564	422	131	13	2	30	73	33	61
	.159	.209	.333	63	10	2	0	3	16	4	10
	.268	.314	.570	142	38	7	0	12	33	9	20
	.300	.358	.519	343	103	8	2	21	56	28	51
	.310	.359	.552	58	18	2	0	4	14	5	10
	.300	.360	.512	80	24	2	0	5	16	8	12
	.341	.393	.659	82	28	3	1	7	15	6	13
	.265	.315	.574	68	18	3	0	6	11	3	11
	.207	.258	.354	82	17	3	0	3	15	5	9
	.313	.373	.557	115	36	2	1	8	18	10	16
	.293	.367	.620	229	67	8	2	21	21	23	24
	.364	.411	.737	99	36	7	0	10	10	5	9
	.238	.336	.531	130	31	1	2	11	11	18	15
	.289	.325	.457	256	74	7	0	12	68	14	47
	.358	.375	.569	109	39	2	0	7	16	3	22
	.238	.290	.374	147	35	5	0	5	52	11	25
	.250	.292	.471	136	34	0	0	10	32	8	26

RBI/Opportunities

Scoring Position	40 / 192 (21%)	41 / 196 (21%)
Scoring Position, 2 Out	20 / 87 (23%)	20 / 89 (22%)
On Third, Less than 2 Out	14 / 33 (42%)	15 / 34 (44%)
RBI in close games / RBI Total	62 / 87 (71%)	124 / 89 (139%)

Ken Oberkfell
Atlanta Braves

Buddy Bell of the Reds was declared the fielding champion of National League third basemen with a .979 average, 93 putouts and 241 assists in 142 games.

Ken Oberkfell of the Braves also had a .979 fielding average with 76 putouts and 248 assists, but in 126 games. One more thing: Oberkfell took part in 20 double plays; Buddy Bell was in on 17. Oberkfell, in other words, was one of the more solid fielders in the league. His problem was one of perception, when anyone perceived him at all.

He is more of a second baseman as a hitter, and the Braves would like him to play there—if they could replace him at third.

He came up with the Cardinals as a second baseman. In his first four seasons, he played 241 games at second, 37 at third and two at shortstop.

Last season, according to the rankings used by the major leagues to determine free-agent status, Oberkfell was sixth-best among NL third basemen. Mike Schmidt, Bell, Tim Wallach, Terry Pendleton and Keith Moreland ranked ahead of him. Denny Walling, Howard Johnson, Chris Brown and Kevin Mitchell ranked behind him. Those players, minus Walling and Brown, were the only National League players to put in 100 or more games at third base.

The rankings, a combination of league rankings in several offensive and defensive categories, are somewhat deceptive. Oberkfell does well in the fielding categories, and his .280 batting average was better than Johnson's and Moreland's, and equal to Mitchell's. But Oberkfell came in last among these regular third basemen in slugging average; his .362 trailed Pendleton's next-lowest of .412. Of this group, only Moreland (.309) had a lower on-base average than Oberkfell (.342).

Ask any manager whom they would prefer at third, Oberkfell or Howard Johnson, and the answer would probably be unanimous: the guy who hit all those homers, Johnson. National League teams are easily dissatisfied with their third basemen, mostly because the standard has been so high for the last 10 years or so. Schmidt has been so steady with his combination of power and fielding that he has made it look too easy. And when a team has had to sacrifice something in a third baseman, the glove work went. That's why Moreland has lasted at third for the Cubs.

Only eight players put in 100 or more games at third, an indication of this dissatisfaction. Oberkfell, a decent player, suffered from it.

Braves manager Chuck Tanner used Oberkfell in a variety of double shifts, often moving him to second with another player going to third. Graig Nettles played 40 games at third, Rafael Ramirez 12, Paul Runge 10 and Ted Simmons (yes, the old catcher) played 2.

Dissatisfied or not, good third basemen are hard to find. Don't look for the Braves to replace Oberkfell any time soon.

Mike O'Donnell

Oberkfell, Kenneth Ray "Ken"

Bats: Left   Throws: Right   Born 05/04/56

1987 SEASON AND MAJOR-LEAGUE CAREER BATTING TOTALS

	G	AB	H	2B	3B	HR	TB	R	RBI	TBB	IBB	SO	HP	SH	SF	SB	CS	SB%	GDP	AVG	OBP	SLG
87 ATL	135	508	142	29	2	3	184	59	48	48	5	29	2	5	3	3	3	.50	13	.280	.342	.362
11 YEARS	1194	3931	1112	198	38	23	1455	467	351	462	54	282	18	34	28	57	39	.59	96	.283	.359	.370

	1987 SEASON										FOUR YEAR TOTALS (1984 – 1987)									
	Ave.	OBP	SLG	AB	H	2B	3B	HR	RBI	BB	SO	Ave.	OBP	SLG	AB	H	2B	3B	HR	RBI	BB	SO
Totals	.280	.342	.362	508	142	29	2	3	48	48	29	.273	.354	.358	1747	477	91	11	12	152	213	134
vs. Left	.310	.349	.415	142	44	11	2	0	17	8	10	.264	.329	.342	447	118	21	4	2	51	41	49
vs. Right	.268	.340	.342	366	98	18	0	3	31	40	19	.276	.362	.364	1300	359	70	7	10	101	172	85
at Home	.293	.363	.382	259	76	15	1	2	29	29	13	.282	.365	.370	898	253	44	7	7	89	116	57
on Road	.265	.320	.341	249	66	14	1	1	19	19	16	.264	.341	.346	849	224	47	4	5	63	97	77
vs. Groundball	.252	.315	.312	218	55	7	0	2	19	19	11	.257	.323	.323	818	210	32	5	4	66	79	52
vs. Flyball	.300	.362	.400	290	87	22	2	1	29	29	18	.287	.379	.390	929	267	59	6	8	86	134	82
vs. Finesse	.263	.317	.351	259	68	12	1	3	20	21	11	.279	.348	.374	973	271	53	8	8	75	104	59
vs. Power	.297	.368	.373	249	74	17	1	0	28	27	18	.266	.360	.339	774	206	38	3	4	77	109	75
on Grass	.282	.349	.360	358	101	17	1	3	36	37	19	.281	.363	.368	1215	341	60	8	10	107	156	86
on Artificial Turf	.273	.325	.367	150	41	12	1	0	12	11	10	.256	.331	.336	532	136	31	3	2	45	57	48
Day Games	.317	.391	.402	189	60	13	0	1	20	23	7	.286	.368	.366	590	169	34	2	3	52	77	44
Night Games	.257	.312	.339	319	82	16	2	2	28	25	22	.266	.346	.354	1157	308	57	9	9	100	136	90
April	.329	.417	.370	73	24	3	0	0	6	11	3	.297	.374	.358	212	63	11	1	0	20	26	12
May	.325	.367	.453	117	38	13	1	0	10	9	6	.317	.380	.403	315	100	20	2	1	22	33	21
June	.250	.324	.350	60	15	4	1	0	9	6	2	.288	.353	.414	333	96	21	3	5	38	33	18
July	.229	.280	.329	70	16	4	0	1	7	5	0	.250	.331	.336	304	76	16	2	2	30	37	29
August	.271	.327	.323	96	26	2	0	1	9	7	7	.264	.363	.350	303	80	13	2	3	25	46	27
Sept/Oct	.250	.324	.315	92	23	3	0	1	7	10	11	.221	.314	.275	280	62	10	1	1	17	38	27
Bases Empty	.290	.339	.377	297	86	18	1	2	2	20	15	.275	.345	.356	1025	282	57	4	6	6	108	81
Leadoff	.295	.319	.384	112	33	8	1	0	0	4	5	.255	.311	.327	392	100	23	1	1	1	32	22
Not Leadoff	.286	.350	.373	185	53	10	0	2	2	16	10	.288	.366	.374	633	182	34	3	5	5	76	59
Runners On	.265	.347	.341	211	56	11	1	1	46	28	14	.270	.361	.361	722	195	34	7	6	146	105	53
First Base Only	.296	.374	.383	81	24	4	0	1	5	10	3	.298	.351	.367	319	95	16	0	2	8	26	19
Scoring Position	.246	.331	.315	130	32	7	1	0	41	18	11	.248	.369	.357	403	100	18	7	4	138	79	34
Late Innings, Close	.274	.349	.356	73	20	6	0	0	6	9	6	.242	.342	.300	293	71	14	0	1	21	45	22

RBI/Opportunities

	1987		FOUR YEAR	
Scoring Position	40 / 179	(22%)	127 / 589	(22%)
Scoring Position, 2 Out	17 / 85	(20%)	57 / 286	(20%)
On Third, Less than 2 Out	17 / 30	(57%)	43 / 85	(51%)
RBI in close games / RBI Total	31 / 48	(65%)	99 / 152	(65%)

Pete O'Brien
Texas Rangers

It isn't too often that you see a hitter put together back-to-back seasons as similar as O'Brien's 1986–87 seasons.

	AB	H	BA	2B	3B	HR	SLUG%	RUNS	RBI
1986	551	160	.290	23	3	23	.468	86	90
1987	569	163	.286	26	1	23	.457	84	88

There was a big drop in his walk column from a career-high 87 walks to just 59 in almost exactly the same number of plate appearances. This turn in his hitting style may have been a reaction to his success in hitting more aggressively against LHP in 1986. Remember, this is an extremely thoughtful hitter who has a history of experimentation. Incidentally, he kept his aggressive style against LHP in 1987 and did not do nearly as well as in 1986 (.247 average, .339 SLUG%, and .294 OBA).

O'Brien's consistency actually has held over a four-year period. His batting average has never been below .267 or higher than .290, his homers have ranged from 18 to 23, and his RBI's from 80 to 92. Yet he is subject to some of the longest in-season slumps I have ever seen. They usually last over 100 at-bats, and every year a segment of the fans becomes alarmed and wonders if he will ever recover.

In 1984, he missed a chance at his first super year (targeted for .300 with over 20 homers) when he fell into a deep slump and hit under .250 with just 2 homers in his last 112 at-bats. In 1985 he got off to a terrible start. In his first 117 at-bats he hit only .171 with just 5 extra-base hits. In 1986 he reversed himself and was blazing out of the gates. On May 4 he was still hitting over .400 and slugging over .700, but he immediately went into a lengthy slump where he hit only .206 and had only one homer in 107 at-bats.

In 1987 O'Brien again made fans panic with a slump right at the beginning of the year. On May 11, five weeks into the season, he was hitting .214 with just 4 homers in 98 at-bats. He then threw in a new twist by losing his home run stroke for half a season. At the All-Star break he had 19 dingers and was on target for a total of 36. In the remaining 76 games he had only 4 homers.

Most field observers suggest that it is his constant experimentation and tinkering with his swing and hitting strategy that sets off these legendary in-season slumps. For example, Bobby Valentine traces O'Brien's early slump in '87 to Pete's experimenting too much towards the end of spring training, and when the opening bell rang, he simply couldn't find his normal stroke. But it's a hell of a lot better than hitting .237 from beginning to end.

Craig R. Wright

O'Brien, Peter Michael "Pete"   Bats: Right   Throws: Right   Born 02/09/58

1987 SEASON AND MAJOR-LEAGUE CAREER BATTING TOTALS

	G	AB	H	2B	3B	HR	TB	R	RBI	TBB	IBB	SO	HP	SH	SF	SB	CS	SB%	GDP	AVG	OBP	SLG
87 TEX	159	569	163	26	1	23	260	84	88	59	6	61	0	0	10	0	4	.00	9	.286	.348	.457
6 YEARS	790	2804	765	137	15	98	1226	362	416	332	31	300	2	7	32	18	27	.40	69	.273	.347	.437

1987 SEASON

	Ave.	OBP	SLG	AB	H	2B	3B	HR	RBI	BB	SO
Totals	.286	.348	.457	569	163	26	1	23	88	59	61
vs. Left	.247	.294	.339	186	46	8	0	3	20	13	30
vs. Right	.305	.373	.514	383	117	18	1	20	68	46	31
at Home	.272	.341	.426	265	72	14	0	9	43	32	28
on Road	.299	.354	.484	304	91	12	1	14	45	27	33
vs. Groundball	.270	.333	.427	281	76	8	0	12	43	29	25
vs. Flyball	.302	.362	.486	288	87	18	1	11	45	30	36
vs. Finesse	.274	.315	.401	339	93	17	1	8	43	23	29
vs. Power	.304	.393	.539	230	70	9	0	15	45	36	32
on Grass	.284	.347	.443	469	133	22	1	17	68	51	45
on Artificial Turf	.300	.352	.520	100	30	4	0	6	20	8	16
Day Games	.255	.331	.343	137	35	4	1	2	15	17	16
Night Games	.296	.353	.493	432	128	22	0	21	73	42	45
April	.194	.273	.343	67	13	4	0	2	8	8	8
May	.273	.333	.556	99	27	1	0	9	21	9	10
June	.350	.400	.573	103	36	5	0	6	22	10	9
July	.293	.350	.457	92	27	6	0	3	10	9	8
August	.327	.388	.394	104	34	5	1	0	15	11	9
Sept/Oct	.250	.319	.385	104	26	5	0	3	12	12	17
Bases Empty	.269	.328	.450	320	86	13	0	15	15	28	31
Leadoff	.280	.331	.462	132	37	6	0	6	6	10	11
Not Leadoff	.261	.325	.441	188	49	7	0	9	9	18	20
Runners On	.309	.372	.466	249	77	13	1	8	73	31	30
First Base Only	.363	.430	.510	102	37	9	0	2	10	12	14
Scoring Position	.272	.335	.435	147	40	4	1	6	63	19	16
Late Innings, Close	.295	.370	.568	88	26	3	0	7	16	11	7

FOUR YEAR TOTALS (1984 – 1987)

	Ave.	OBP	SLG	AB	H	2B	3B	HR	RBI	BB	SO
Totals	.282	.356	.456	2213	625	109	9	86	350	268	231
vs. Left	.249	.314	.345	670	167	31	0	11	85	66	104
vs. Right	.297	.374	.505	1543	458	78	9	75	265	202	127
at Home	.287	.360	.455	1069	307	62	0	39	185	132	111
on Road	.278	.352	.458	1144	318	47	9	47	165	136	120
vs. Groundball	.282	.353	.443	1097	309	45	6	40	158	129	100
vs. Flyball	.283	.359	.470	1116	316	64	3	46	192	139	131
vs. Finesse	.278	.334	.454	1314	365	65	5	52	204	121	109
vs. Power	.289	.386	.461	899	260	44	4	34	146	147	122
on Grass	.285	.359	.452	1840	524	93	4	69	291	227	187
on Artificial Turf	.271	.340	.477	373	101	16	5	17	59	41	44
Day Games	.269	.347	.383	480	129	17	4	10	61	61	51
Night Games	.286	.358	.477	1733	496	92	5	76	289	207	180
April	.257	.340	.467	261	67	15	2	12	44	34	27
May	.262	.317	.416	389	102	19	1	13	52	31	37
June	.313	.395	.497	384	120	21	1	16	67	54	40
July	.277	.341	.459	401	111	17	1	18	65	40	44
August	.309	.372	.483	418	129	23	4	14	71	43	41
Sept/Oct	.267	.378	.414	360	96	14	0	13	51	66	42
Bases Empty	.276	.343	.455	1211	334	54	2	53	53	124	131
Leadoff	.264	.321	.433	432	114	20	1	17	17	36	44
Not Leadoff	.282	.355	.467	779	220	34	1	36	36	88	87
Runners On	.290	.376	.458	1002	291	55	7	33	297	144	100
First Base Only	.289	.354	.452	454	131	26	3	14	45	46	39
Scoring Position	.292	.393	.464	548	160	29	4	19	252	98	61
Late Innings, Close	.276	.363	.435	359	99	15	0	14	44	50	39

RBI/Opportunities

	1987		Four Year	
Scoring Position	55 / 195	(28%)	207 / 767	(27%)
Scoring Position, 2 Out	22 / 100	(22%)	67 / 334	(20%)
On Third, Less than 2 Out	18 / 30	(60%)	78 / 135	(58%)
RBI in close games / RBI Total	60 / 88	(68%)	229 / 350	(65%)

Steve Ontiveros
Oakland Athletics

Steve Ontiveros is the perfect example of the recent products of the A's minor league system. His occasional flashes of brilliance are overwhelmed by his more frequent mental and physical eccentricities.

By some quirk of fate, Ontiveros had a great June and was named American League Pitcher of the Month. However, outside of that month, Steve was little better than inconsistent. What follows is a breakdown of Steve's numbers before, during, and after his most effective period:

	G	IP	ER	W	L	SV	HR	BB	K	ERA
Apr–May	12	23.1	13	0	1	1	3	10	25	5.01
June	5	27.1	2	5	0	0	1	6	23	0.66
July–Oct	18	100.1	53	5	7	0	15	34	51	4.75

You can find similar inconsistency between his rookie season and 1986. After a brilliant second half in his rookie season in '85, he pitched poorly in his sophomore season. His troubles were related to a sore arm, and there has been some talk that Steve's arm was hurting in 1987 as well. They say he tried to keep it hidden from the team, which LaRussa did not appreciate.

Steve is a bit of an oddball who quickly picks up loose threads to weave a new way of doing things. Fortunately, his crazier ideas don't last long. He once decided that driving golf balls the morning before a start was the reason he had a good outing; he felt it helped his concentration. From then on, he vowed, he would follow the same routine before every game. Of course, his next start was poor, and we never heard another word about golf.

Ontiveros seems better suited to starting rather than relief work. He was 8–5 as a starter with a 3.90 ERA, and that'll get you by in the American League. He does lack somewhat in stamina, averaging only 5.2 innings per start, but given the A's strength in middle relief, that was acceptable. With Eckersley, Lavelle, Nelson, and Plunk around, his chances of returning to the bullpen are slight.

Steve may also end up as trade bait. It would be tempting to give him more time to get over his mental and physical fidgets and settle down to being a professional pitcher. However, with the sudden house-cleaning mood that seems to have struck the organization and the fact that Steve's role on the team may be limited by his durability, they may try to move him while his value is reasonably high.

Susan Nelson

Ontiveros, Steven "Steve" Bats: Right Throws: Right Born 03/05/61

1987 SEASON AND MAJOR-LEAGUE CAREER PITCHING TOTALS

	G	GS	CG	GF	IP	BFP	H	R	ER	HR	SH	SF	HB	TBB	IBB	SO	WP	Bk	W	L	Pct	ShO	Sv	ERA
87 OAK	35	22	2	6	151	645	141	78	67	19	6	2	4	50	3	97	4	1	10	8	.556	1	1	3.99
3 YEARS	120	22	2	51	299	1234	258	135	121	33	9	10	7	94	8	187	9	1	13	13	.500	1	19	3.64

1987: Finesse, Groundball   1986: Power, Flyball   1985: Finesse, Groundball

1987 SEASON

	G	IP	H	BB	SO	SB	CS	W	L	S	ERA
Totals	35	150.2	141	50	97	12	3	10	8	1	4.00
at Home	16	79.2	75	26	53	7	3	5	4	0	3.50
on Road	19	71.0	66	24	44	5	0	5	4	1	4.56
on Grass	10	54.2	50	15	28	4	1	2	4	0	4.94
on Artificial Turf	25	96.0	91	35	69	8	2	8	4	1	3.47
Day Games	30	124.2	125	40	78	10	3	8	7	0	4.11
Night Games	5	26.0	16	10	19	2	0	2	1	1	3.46
April	2	2.1	2	1	0	1	0	0	0	0	0.00
May	10	21.0	22	9	23	1	0	0	1	1	5.14
June	5	27.1	14	6	23	3	0	5	0	0	0.66
July	6	35.0	37	12	16	3	1	0	4	0	4.11
August	5	29.1	30	10	20	2	0	2	1	0	6.14
Sept/Oct	7	35.2	36	12	15	2	2	3	2	0	4.29

vs. Opponent Batters	Ave.	OBP	SLG	AB	H	2B	3B	HR	RBI	BB	SO
Totals	.242	.305	.381	583	141	20	2	19	62	50	97
vs. Left	.241	.323	.400	290	70	11	1	11	33	34	57
vs. Right	.242	.287	.362	293	71	9	1	8	29	16	40
Bases Empty	.231	.296	.380	355	82	13	2	12	12	30	60
Leadoff	.218	.281	.354	147	32	6	1	4	4	13	28
Not Leadoff	.240	.307	.399	208	50	7	1	8	8	17	32
Runners On Base	.259	.319	.382	228	59	7	0	7	50	20	37
First Base Only	.311	.349	.466	103	32	4	0	4	10	6	10
Scoring Position	.216	.296	.312	125	27	3	0	3	40	14	27
Late Innings, Close	.286	.382	.416	77	22	4	0	2	9	9	18

FOUR YEAR TOTALS (1984 – 1987)

	G	IP	H	BB	SO	SB	CS	W	L	S	ERA
Totals	120	298.0	258	94	187	20	5	13	13	19	3.65
at Home	61	162.2	126	49	103	11	5	7	9	9	3.04
on Road	59	135.1	132	45	84	9	0	6	4	10	4.39
on Grass	43	108.1	87	30	57	6	1	4	6	9	4.07
on Artificial Turf	77	189.2	171	64	130	14	4	9	7	10	3.42
Day Games	100	249.1	224	78	160	18	5	10	12	13	3.68
Night Games	20	48.2	34	16	27	2	0	3	1	6	3.51
April	12	18.2	16	6	10	1	0	0	0	1	2.41
May	21	42.0	49	18	37	2	0	1	3	3	6.21
June	22	59.2	34	13	46	7	2	5	0	3	1.21
July	24	65.2	57	17	33	5	1	1	5	6	3.43
August	16	51.1	41	20	30	3	0	2	1	5	3.86
Sept/Oct	25	60.2	61	20	31	2	2	4	4	1	4.75

	Ave.	OBP	SLG	AB	H	2B	3B	HR	RBI	BB	SO
Totals	.232	.293	.364	1114	258	41	4	33	122	94	187
vs. Left	.250	.326	.387	556	139	24	2	16	69	62	94
vs. Right	.213	.259	.342	558	119	17	2	17	53	32	93
Bases Empty	.233	.294	.393	634	148	26	3	23	23	51	108
Leadoff	.241	.306	.428	257	62	13	1	11	11	24	44
Not Leadoff	.228	.285	.369	377	86	13	2	12	12	27	64
Runners On Base	.229	.293	.327	480	110	15	1	10	99	43	79
First Base Only	.247	.286	.363	215	53	8	1	5	15	12	25
Scoring Position	.215	.298	.298	265	57	7	0	5	84	31	54
Late Innings, Close	.215	.290	.329	353	76	14	1	8	39	34	65

RBI/Opportunities

	1987		Four Year	
Scoring Position	34 / 172	(20%)	74 / 377	(20%)
Scoring Position, 2 Out	13 / 87	(15%)	33 / 190	(17%)
On Third, Less than 2 Out	13 / 24	(54%)	26 / 56	(46%)
RBI in close games / RBI Total	42 / 62	(68%)	78 / 122	(64%)

Spike Owen
Boston Red Sox

Spike Owen remains the secret shortstop in the American League. He has fielded indoors; he has fielded outdoors. His glove has worked on the West Coast; he has vacuumed up ground balls on the East Coast. He led AL shortstops in range factor in 1985 and 1986 and is usually among the league leaders in double plays. But, after five years, Owen is perceived by the fans as a generic, disposable non-Dominican shortstop.

There are two reasons for this. Spike does not do many spectacular acrobatics. He does not run out from under his cap after every ground ball and popup. Instead, he is usually waiting in the right place when the ball leaves the bat; he is a master of the "atom ball."

Or he was, until 1987. After years of excellence, Owen finished eleventh among the 14 regular shortstops in double plays per game and dead last in range factor. Since Boston has a home-grown Owen clone (whose name doesn't rhyme—it's Jody Reed) whom they like better than Spike, Mr. Owen may either be fighting for his job or introducing himself to new teammates in 1988.

A first glance at Spike's offensive numbers does tend to leave one with a poor impression. But if you look at all the stats, some useful skills start to show up. Spike Owen's 1987 fits comfortably into the pattern established in his first four years. He matched his best batting average (with very little help from his home park) and set a new high in OB%. His power figures remain consistent with past performance. Owen has above-average speed, but cannot steal bases effectively. He is always able to hit a lot of triples, but he's never reached the 70 percent success mark in his stolen base attempts.

Owen's left/right breakdowns have fluctuated from year to year; his big platoon differential in 1987 was a new development. Perhaps that was why Boston failed to take effective advantage of it this year. Other Boston shortstops went a combined 16–93 (.172) against lefties and 68–227 (.300) against righties this year.

The strongest component of Spike's offense is his bat control. He is a fine bunter and has a low strikeout rate. His forte is moving runners from first base with no outs. He advanced 60 percent in 1987, an outstanding figure that he has matched before in his career. As a bonus, Spike's batting average rose over 60 points with runners in scoring position.

So here you have a superb defensive player with good bunting skills and great bat control: Even if no one else thinks too much of Spike, Gene Mauch must be in love.

Fred Percival

Owen, Spike Dee   Bats: Both   Throws: Right   Born 04/19/61

1987 SEASON AND MAJOR-LEAGUE CAREER BATTING TOTALS

	G	AB	H	2B	3B	HR	TB	R	RBI	TBB	IBB	SO	HP	SH	SF	SB	CS	SB%	GDP	AVG	OBP	SLG
87 BOS	132	437	113	17	7	2	150	50	48	53	2	43	1	9	4	11	8	.58	9	.259	.337	.343
5 YEARS	636	2153	516	80	31	14	700	261	194	208	3	228	8	37	14	52	31	.63	34	.240	.307	.325

	1987 SEASON											FOUR YEAR TOTALS (1984 – 1987)									
	Ave.	OBP	SLG	AB	H	2B	3B	HR	RBI	BB	SO	Ave.	OBP	SLG	AB	H	2B	3B	HR	RBI	BB	SO
Totals	.256	.335	.341	437	112	17	7	2	48	53	43	.246	.315	.334	1847	455	69	28	12	173	183	184
vs. Left	.321	.393	.455	134	43	8	2	2	19	16	14	.270	.335	.380	503	136	26	7	5	56	46	56
vs. Right	.228	.310	.290	303	69	9	5	0	29	37	29	.237	.307	.316	1344	319	43	21	7	117	137	128
at Home	.263	.341	.371	224	59	8	5	2	28	28	21	.251	.321	.350	954	239	38	18	7	93	99	103
on Road	.249	.329	.310	213	53	9	2	0	20	25	22	.242	.308	.316	893	216	31	10	5	80	84	81
vs. Groundball	.217	.301	.279	226	49	10	2	0	21	27	24	.224	.292	.305	869	195	30	14	4	81	81	84
vs. Flyball	.299	.372	.408	211	63	7	5	2	27	26	19	.266	.335	.359	978	260	39	14	8	92	102	100
vs. Finesse	.260	.339	.349	215	56	11	4	0	21	25	16	.240	.292	.321	1029	247	38	18	3	95	77	85
vs. Power	.252	.332	.333	222	56	6	3	2	27	28	27	.254	.342	.350	818	208	31	10	9	78	106	99
on Grass	.257	.335	.344	381	98	13	7	2	42	46	35	.244	.320	.325	962	235	32	14	6	93	109	89
on Artificial Turf	.250	.338	.321	56	14	4	0	0	6	7	8	.249	.308	.342	885	220	37	14	6	80	74	95
Day Games	.209	.292	.297	158	33	3	4	1	21	19	20	.255	.320	.338	530	135	18	7	4	52	53	57
Night Games	.283	.360	.366	279	79	14	3	1	27	34	23	.243	.312	.332	1317	320	51	21	8	121	130	127
April	.139	.225	.194	36	5	2	0	0	2	4	5	.212	.278	.268	231	49	9	2	0	9	21	23
May	.257	.350	.371	35	9	2	1	0	3	5	4	.254	.336	.399	268	68	13	10	2	25	33	35
June	.273	.348	.404	99	27	7	3	0	12	12	7	.289	.347	.416	377	109	21	9	3	46	34	29
July	.278	.330	.342	79	22	1	2	0	11	7	3	.279	.332	.349	315	88	13	3	1	34	26	26
August	.234	.324	.287	94	22	2	0	1	11	13	13	.192	.268	.227	344	66	6	0	2	31	36	38
Sept/Oct	.287	.374	.372	94	27	3	1	1	9	12	11	.240	.315	.327	312	75	7	4	4	28	33	33
Bases Empty	.239	.323	.291	251	60	8	1	1	1	30	28	.235	.303	.307	1077	253	39	9	7	7	105	117
Leadoff	.240	.303	.290	100	24	5	0	0	0	8	9	.233	.301	.302	437	102	18	3	2	2	41	43
Not Leadoff	.238	.335	.291	151	36	3	1	1	1	22	19	.236	.305	.311	640	151	21	6	5	5	64	74
Runners On	.280	.352	.409	186	52	9	6	1	47	23	15	.262	.329	.370	770	202	30	19	5	166	78	67
First Base Only	.229	.297	.373	83	19	3	3	1	6	8	7	.254	.313	.380	342	87	17	10	2	23	29	23
Scoring Position	.320	.393	.437	103	33	6	3	0	41	15	8	.269	.341	.362	428	115	13	9	3	143	49	44
Late Innings, Close	.203	.271	.281	64	13	0	1	1	5	6	3	.201	.279	.257	284	57	7	3	1	18	31	32

RBI/Opportunities

	1987		Four Year
Scoring Position	39 / 147 (27%)		134 / 602 (22%)
Scoring Position, 2 Out	11 / 58 (19%)		48 / 278 (17%)
On Third, Less than 2 Out	18 / 30 (60%)		60 / 111 (54%)
RBI in close games / RBI Total	24 / 48 (50%)		103 / 173 (60%)

Mike Pagliarulo
New York Yankees

In 1987, Mike Pagliarulo had the same type of year that he's had throughout his career. First, he had a terrible start. Then he completely turned it around and played great ball for two months. But in August, he began slowing down again—in September, he stopped hitting for average and lost almost all of his power. The result was a season that, though it seemed certain to be better than his past, was no different.

Compare Mike's last two seasons and you'll see almost identical stats. In 18 more at-bats this year, he had two more hits, two more doubles, four more homers, seven more runs scored, sixteen more RBIs and one less walk. He hit .234 in 1987; his career BA is .237. He slugged .479 in 1987, his career SL% is .462. His 1987 on-base percentage was .305; his lifetime figure is .310. When your most recent season matches up so closely with your career totals, it's usually an indication that you aren't going to get any better than you are right now.

Another sign of progress, or lack of it, is a player's batting splits. If you do something in your most recent year that you've never been able to do before, there's at least a chance that you'll keep improving. But if you compare Mike's monthly records for 1987 to those in his career, you can see that the pattern hasn't changed much. To be fair, he's had injuries in both 1986 (hamstring) and 1987 (elbow) which may explain the late-season slumps. But, as Jack Clark has shown, a history of late-season injuries can be as bad as a history of late season slumps.

Mike continues to struggle in Yankee Stadium. A typical player will hit 15–20 points better in his home park, with a corresponding increase in power. Pagliarulo loses about 15–30 points at home; he's hit half of his career homers and 65 percent of his doubles on the road.

The two bright spots to Pags's 1987 are his defense and platoon splits. He was the fifth-best defensive third baseman in the AL this year; a tribute to his work ethic. Mike, a career .193 hitter (.271 OB%, .291 SL%) vs. southpaws at the beginning of 1987, had his best year against lefties in 1987; unfortunately, he tailed off badly against righties. If his stats against righties were to snap back, he'd be about a .250 hitter with .500 SL% and an average OB%—in other words, a very fine ballplayer.

Having Billy Martin around in 1988 could be either a blessing or a curse for Pagliarulo. Martin has always been able to help sluggers with low averages improve; he may be able to do that with Mike this year. On the other hand, Billy isn't likely to be as patient as Lou Piniella was. Mike will be 28 in 1988 and, on the whole, shows no signs of improving. If Mike doesn't improve, Martin may decide that the best thing to do with him is to make him a platoon player in 1988.

Daniel Stone and Arnie Braunstein

Pagliarulo, Michael Timothy "Mike"   Bats: Right   Throws: Right   Born 03/15/60

1987 SEASON AND MAJOR-LEAGUE CAREER BATTING TOTALS

	G	AB	H	2B	3B	HR	TB	R	RBI	TBB	IBB	SO	HP	SH	SF	SB	CS	SB%	GDP	AVG	OBP	SLG
87 NYA	150	522	122	26	3	32	250	76	87	53	9	111	2	2	3	1	3	.25	9	.234	.305	.479
4 YEARS	504	1607	381	81	11	86	742	226	254	167	23	363	10	6	11	5	4	.56	30	.237	.311	.462

	1987 SEASON											FOUR YEAR TOTALS (1984 – 1987)										
	Ave.	OBP	SLG	AB	H	2B	3B	HR	RBI	BB	SO	Ave.	OBP	SLG	AB	H	2B	3B	HR	RBI	BB	SO
Totals	.234	.305	.479	522	122	26	3	32	87	53	111	.237	.311	.462	1607	381	81	11	86	254	167	363
vs. Left	.230	.283	.355	152	35	7	0	4	20	11	43	.207	.276	.318	396	82	18	1	8	46	34	123
vs. Right	.235	.314	.530	370	87	19	3	28	67	42	68	.247	.322	.509	1211	299	63	10	78	208	133	240
at Home	.214	.308	.473	243	52	10	1	17	48	32	56	.231	.317	.451	769	178	28	6	43	126	92	186
on Road	.251	.302	.484	279	70	16	2	15	39	21	55	.242	.305	.471	838	203	53	5	43	128	75	177
vs. Groundball	.236	.299	.440	275	65	20	0	12	41	25	59	.232	.304	.422	815	189	41	3	36	120	85	178
vs. Flyball	.231	.312	.522	247	57	6	3	20	46	28	52	.242	.318	.503	792	192	40	8	50	134	82	185
vs. Finesse	.246	.308	.492	264	65	10	2	17	39	23	48	.257	.314	.497	878	226	42	6	52	137	71	185
vs. Power	.221	.302	.465	258	57	16	1	15	48	30	63	.213	.307	.420	729	155	39	5	34	117	96	178
on Grass	.232	.305	.478	435	101	20	3	27	74	45	87	.237	.312	.463	1355	321	67	10	73	213	143	298
on Artificial Turf	.241	.305	.483	87	21	6	0	5	13	8	24	.238	.303	.456	252	60	14	1	13	41	24	65
Day Games	.238	.323	.405	168	40	7	0	7	21	21	33	.219	.302	.407	538	118	16	2	27	76	62	124
Night Games	.232	.296	.514	354	82	19	3	25	66	32	78	.246	.315	.489	1069	263	65	9	59	178	105	239
April	.162	.260	.235	68	11	2	0	1	7	8	13	.200	.316	.350	160	32	9	0	5	19	26	36
May	.233	.317	.489	90	21	4	2	5	13	10	17	.211	.298	.436	218	46	9	2	12	37	26	48
June	.283	.352	.533	92	26	5	0	6	18	11	25	.271	.340	.517	269	73	18	0	16	42	29	62
July	.273	.380	.636	77	21	4	0	8	17	14	15	.293	.348	.578	287	84	15	2	21	56	25	53
August	.229	.250	.543	105	24	6	0	9	16	3	23	.240	.302	.529	329	79	14	6	23	55	29	75
Sept/Oct	.211	.268	.389	90	19	5	1	3	16	7	18	.195	.263	.326	344	67	16	1	9	45	32	89
Bases Empty	.221	.284	.456	307	68	12	3	18	18	26	59	.227	.290	.446	893	203	39	9	46	46	78	195
Leadoff	.218	.297	.435	124	27	5	2	6	6	13	18	.218	.294	.446	363	79	12	4	21	21	38	73
Not Leadoff	.224	.276	.470	183	41	7	1	12	12	13	41	.234	.288	.445	530	124	27	5	25	25	40	122
Runners On	.251	.333	.512	215	54	14	0	14	69	27	52	.249	.332	.482	714	178	42	2	40	208	89	168
First Base Only	.277	.333	.628	94	26	9	0	8	18	8	21	.254	.304	.510	343	87	23	1	21	50	25	75
Scoring Position	.231	.333	.421	121	28	5	0	6	51	19	31	.245	.355	.456	371	91	19	1	19	158	64	93
Late Innings, Close	.152	.227	.354	79	12	1	0	5	14	8	15	.209	.291	.397	239	50	6	0	13	39	28	61

RBI/Opportunities

Scoring Position	41 / 177 (23%)	127 / 542 (23%)
Scoring Position, 2 Out	10 / 78 (13%)	38 / 236 (16%)
On Third, Less than 2 Out	21 / 35 (60%)	54 / 107 (50%)
RBI in close games / RBI Total	50 / 87 (57%)	150 / 254 (59%)

Rafael Palmeiro
Chicago Cubs

Rafael Palmeiro hit 14 home runs and 15 doubles in 81 games last year, causing Cubs fans to work themselves into a fine lather about this young phenom.

They should ask themselves why Palmeiro played in only 81 games. In part, he had only himself to blame. He was one of those sure things in spring training—several publications tabbed him the number-one prospect in baseball—but played himself into a trip to Des Moines.

When Palmeiro finally came up to the big-league club, management didn't quite know what to do with him. Palmeiro is a lefty swinger and thrower whose natural position is left field. But the Cubs already had a solid left-handed stick there in Jerry Mumphrey—Mumphrey was on his way to a .333 season, in fact. Palmeiro can also play first, but the Cubs had a left-handed hitter there as well in Leon Durham. Palmeiro didn't field well enough to play center (Dave Martinez, another lefty swinger, was there, anyway) and even he wasn't phenomenal enough to move Andre Dawson out of right, so for the rest of the season he shuttled between first (18 games) and left (45), not really claiming either position, even on a platoon basis. He also pinch hit 31 times.

Mumphrey has signed with the club and the much-maligned and under-appreciated Durham has not been traded. The question is, will Palmeiro have the competitive fire to beat out one of those established players this spring?

Of course, a more decisive team than the Cubs would make room for Palmeiro. He's young and he can hit, and unlike Durham, he does about the same outside of Wrigley Field as in. He hit nine of his homers on the road, where he batted .278 compared to .273 at home. He hit well at night (.283, 8 home runs), and the Cubs can always use a few nighthawks.

His slugging average was a healthy .543. He also was a patient hitter; with 20 walks, he had an on-base average of .336.

His weakness may be left-handed pitching, but the Cubs gave him only 26 at-bats against lefties last season. He had three hits against them.

Ideally, the Cubs would simply give him a job. He's at the stage now where the only way to pass final judgment on his abilities is by seeing him on the field day after day.

The best outfield for the Cubs would have Palmeiro in left, Dave Martinez in center and Andre Dawson in right. How the Cubs handle Palmeiro will be an interesting test of the team's new leadership.

Mike O'Donnell

Palmeiro, Rafael (Corrales)   Bats: Left   Throws: Left   Born 09/24/64

1987 SEASON AND MAJOR-LEAGUE CAREER BATTING TOTALS

	G	AB	H	2B	3B	HR	TB	R	RBI	TBB	IBB	SO	HP	SH	SF	SB	CS	SB%	GDP	AVG	OBP	SLG
87 CHN	84	221	61	15	1	14	120	32	30	20	1	26	1	0	2	2	2	.50	4	.276	.336	.543
2 YEARS	106	294	79	19	1	17	151	41	42	24	1	32	2	0	2	3	3	.50	8	.269	.326	.514

1987 SEASON

	Ave.	OBP	SLG	AB	H	2B	3B	HR	RBI	BB	SO
Totals	.276	.336	.543	221	61	15	1	14	30	20	26
vs. Left	.115	.226	.231	26	3	0	0	1	3	4	3
vs. Right	.297	.352	.585	195	58	15	1	13	27	16	23
at Home	.273	.333	.500	88	24	3	1	5	13	9	12
on Road	.278	.338	.571	133	37	12	0	9	17	11	14
vs. Groundball	.270	.333	.520	100	27	7	0	6	14	10	13
vs. Flyball	.281	.338	.562	121	34	8	1	8	16	10	13
vs. Finesse	.287	.328	.557	122	35	7	1	8	15	8	11
vs. Power	.263	.345	.525	99	26	8	0	6	15	12	15
on Grass	.239	.304	.437	142	34	5	1	7	19	14	18
on Artificial Turf	.342	.395	.734	79	27	10	0	7	11	6	8
Day Games	.270	.333	.504	115	31	7	1	6	15	11	15
Night Games	.283	.339	.585	106	30	8	0	8	15	9	11
April	.000	.000	.000	0	0	0	0	0	0	0	0
May	.000	.000	.000	0	0	0	0	0	0	0	0
June	.265	.350	.559	34	9	2	1	2	7	5	2
July	.282	.300	.462	39	11	1	0	2	4	1	3
August	.278	.307	.569	72	20	6	0	5	10	3	11
Sept/Oct	.276	.371	.553	76	21	6	0	5	9	11	10
Bases Empty	.299	.341	.591	127	38	10	0	9	9	7	19
Leadoff	.306	.333	.714	49	15	5	0	5	5	2	7
Not Leadoff	.295	.345	.513	78	23	5	0	4	4	5	12
Runners On	.245	.330	.479	94	23	5	1	5	21	13	7
First Base Only	.292	.358	.563	48	14	2	1	3	7	5	1
Scoring Position	.196	.304	.391	46	9	3	0	2	14	8	6
Late Innings, Close	.333	.395	.487	39	13	3	0	1	4	4	9

FOUR YEAR TOTALS (1984 – 1987)

	Ave.	OBP	SLG	AB	H	2B	3B	HR	RBI	BB	SO
	.269	.328	.514	294	79	19	1	17	42	24	32
	.118	.205	.235	34	4	1	0	1	3	4	3
	.288	.343	.550	260	75	18	1	16	39	20	29
	.254	.314	.452	126	32	5	1	6	20	11	16
	.280	.335	.560	168	47	14	0	11	22	13	16
	.248	.310	.454	141	35	8	0	7	19	12	16
	.288	.341	.569	153	44	11	1	10	23	12	16
	.283	.317	.526	173	49	10	1	10	24	8	15
	.248	.338	.496	121	30	9	0	7	18	16	17
	.235	.300	.428	187	44	7	1	9	28	17	23
	.327	.374	.664	107	35	12	0	8	14	7	9
	.270	.333	.504	115	31	7	1	6	15	11	15
	.268	.321	.520	179	48	12	0	11	27	13	17
	.000	.000	.000	0	0	0	0	0	0	0	0
	.000	.000	.000	0	0	0	0	0	0	0	0
	.265	.350	.559	34	9	2	1	2	7	5	2
	.282	.300	.462	39	11	1	0	2	4	1	3
	.278	.307	.569	72	20	6	0	5	10	3	11
	.262	.335	.490	149	39	10	0	8	21	15	16
	.296	.345	.549	162	48	11	0	10	10	11	21
	.296	.345	.722	54	16	5	0	6	6	4	7
	.296	.345	.463	108	32	6	0	4	4	7	14
	.235	.304	.470	132	31	8	1	7	32	13	11
	.263	.333	.491	57	15	2	1	3	7	5	1
	.213	.282	.453	75	16	6	0	4	25	8	10
	.333	.395	.487	78	26	6	0	2	8	8	18

RBI/Opportunities

Scoring Position	11 / 63 (17%)	18 / 93 (19%)
Scoring Position, 2 Out	4 / 28 (14%)	6 / 40 (15%)
On Third, Less than 2 Out	5 / 9 (56%)	6 / 14 (43%)
RBI in close games / RBI Total	21 / 30 (70%)	42 / 42 (100%)

Dave Parker
Cincinnati Reds

They say a picture is worth a thousand words. So is a name—Steve Garvey. Yes, Dave Parker has become a Garvey clone. He always had a tendency to "Garvitis," his strengths, including BA, HR and RBI, and his weaknesses, OBP, GIDP and defense, are almost exactly the same as Steve's. But now it looks as though he's been infected by the dread disease. The first sign that "Garvitis" will be fatal is a drop in BA without a corresponding increase in OBA. Are you listening, Dave Parker?

"Adventures in Right Field, the Saga Continues," starring Dave Parker, did boffo box office last season. Despite an excellent range factor, 2.12, he cost the Reds runs; only Glenn Wilson had more errors (11 to Parker's 10) and Wilson played 12 more games. Although there was nothing new or innovative, à la Lonnie Smith, in Parker's abuse of his position, he was consistently amusing. Missing cutoff men, throwing to the wrong base, "snapping" the glove a millisecond before the ball arrived, giving up on balls he could catch, all continued to be a part of his repertoire last season.

Dave slipped substantially at the end of last season, his average dropping from near .300 to .253 at season's end. His knees seemed to be bothering him a lot, plus he was getting pushed from behind by several of the Reds' youngsters. Nick Esasky, Paul O'Neill and Tracy Jones all had better OW% than Parker; O'Neill and Jones pinch hit frequently and were platooned, yet were still able to deliver Range Factors in the vicinity of Parker's.

The grass in the American League should help Dave's knees considerably. However, although he hits about 10 points higher on grass (his SLG drops), he's always hit a lot of pop fouls. In Pittsburgh and Cincy these drifted out of play; Oakland's foul territory is huge. I look for this to take 10–15 points off his BA.

Tom Locker

It may seem like a strange statement to make for a man who drove in 97 runs, but a game by game review gives support to the assertion that Dave Parker assembled his HR and RBI totals with savage, short outbursts followed by lengthy periods of hibernation:

April 26	vs. Houston	2 for 5,	2 HR, 5 RBI
July 23	vs. Montreal	3 for 5,	1 HR, 6 RBI
July 29	vs. San Diego	3 for 4,	1 HR, 6 RBI
Sept 15	vs. Atlanta	5 for 5,	2 HR, 8 RBI

Remove those 4 games, 3 against sub-.500 ball clubs, and you don't just eliminate one quarter of his power and RBIs, you get the following line:

.239 BA 20 HR 72 RBI 570 AB 136 hits

Those stats, normalized, compare with such AL luminaries as Henry Cotto, Doug DeCinces, and Kelly Gruber in Batting Average, RBI per At-Bat, and HR per At-Bat.

Bob Bailey

Parker, David Gene "Dave"　　　　Bats: Left　　Throws: Right　　Born 06/09/51

1987 SEASON AND MAJOR-LEAGUE CAREER BATTING TOTALS

	G	AB	H	2B	3B	HR	TB	R	RBI	TBB	IBB	SO	HP	SH	SF	SB	CS	SB%	GDP	AVG	OBP	SLG
87 CIN	153	589	149	28	0	26	255	77	97	44	13	104	8	0	6	7	3	.70	14	.253	.311	.433
15 YEARS	1932	7316	2173	425	69	273	3555	1055	1190	539	141	1176	48	1	59	147	102	.59	158	.297	.347	.486

	1987 SEASON											FOUR YEAR TOTALS (1984 – 1987)										
	Ave.	OBP	SLG	AB	H	2B	3B	HR	RBI	BB	SO	Ave.	OBP	SLG	AB	H	2B	3B	HR	RBI	BB	SO
Totals	.253	.311	.433	589	149	28	0	26	97	44	104	.281	.334	.469	2468	694	129	7	107	433	193	399
vs. Left	.239	.285	.410	205	49	11	0	8	43	9	45	.277	.305	.441	845	234	41	4	30	168	30	164
vs. Right	.260	.324	.445	384	100	17	0	18	54	35	59	.283	.348	.484	1623	460	88	3	77	265	163	235
at Home	.282	.339	.478	291	82	15	0	14	53	23	38	.291	.344	.495	1215	354	70	3	57	228	102	177
on Road	.225	.284	.389	298	67	13	0	12	44	21	66	.271	.324	.445	1253	340	59	4	50	205	91	222
vs. Groundball	.285	.348	.535	260	74	11	0	18	53	24	38	.282	.333	.465	1204	340	58	3	52	231	93	175
vs. Flyball	.228	.280	.353	329	75	17	0	8	44	20	66	.280	.335	.473	1264	354	71	4	55	202	100	224
vs. Finesse	.239	.292	.406	318	76	14	0	13	47	21	41	.277	.323	.463	1366	378	70	1	61	229	93	176
vs. Power	.269	.332	.465	271	73	14	0	13	50	23	63	.287	.346	.476	1102	316	59	6	46	204	100	223
on Grass	.208	.262	.376	173	36	8	0	7	24	12	37	.274	.327	.454	738	202	32	1	33	115	55	131
on Artificial Turf	.272	.331	.457	416	113	20	0	19	73	32	67	.284	.337	.476	1730	492	97	6	74	318	138	268
Day Games	.189	.242	.373	201	38	7	0	10	29	13	41	.261	.322	.464	804	210	42	2	39	151	73	139
Night Games	.286	.346	.464	388	111	21	0	16	68	31	63	.291	.340	.472	1664	484	87	5	68	282	120	260
April	.298	.333	.606	94	28	5	0	8	18	5	22	.284	.320	.460	324	92	18	0	13	46	17	54
May	.284	.357	.451	102	29	5	0	4	14	10	23	.318	.372	.523	415	132	26	1	19	78	34	63
June	.229	.296	.429	105	24	3	0	6	20	8	17	.264	.335	.451	432	114	18	0	21	76	44	65
July	.240	.296	.385	104	25	6	0	3	22	7	16	.260	.313	.459	407	106	20	2	19	78	30	67
August	.219	.276	.302	96	21	5	0	1	8	6	13	.248	.303	.399	439	109	21	3	13	60	33	77
Sept/Oct	.250	.306	.432	88	22	4	0	4	15	8	13	.313	.361	.521	451	141	26	1	22	95	35	73
Bases Empty	.228	.273	.383	311	71	15	0	11	11	16	54	.249	.291	.413	1276	318	71	3	44	44	72	219
Leadoff	.273	.302	.455	143	39	8	0	6	6	5	23	.307	.332	.550	482	148	35	2	26	26	17	69
Not Leadoff	.190	.249	.321	168	32	7	0	5	5	11	31	.214	.267	.330	794	170	36	1	18	18	55	150
Runners On	.281	.350	.489	278	78	13	0	15	86	28	50	.315	.379	.529	1192	376	58	4	63	389	121	180
First Base Only	.336	.364	.602	113	38	3	0	9	20	5	9	.325	.352	.538	526	171	26	1	28	68	22	62
Scoring Position	.242	.342	.412	165	40	10	0	6	66	23	41	.308	.398	.523	666	205	32	3	35	321	99	118
Late Innings, Close	.233	.268	.322	90	21	2	0	2	9	4	25	.271	.338	.452	425	115	25	2	16	67	43	88

RBI/Opportunities

Scoring Position	51 / 236 (22%)	257 / 914 (28%)	
Scoring Position, 2 Out	8 / 95 (8%)	86 / 380 (23%)	
On Third, Less than 2 Out	23 / 46 (50%)	102 / 190 (54%)	
RBI in close games / RBI Total	61 / 97 (63%)	299 / 433 (69%)	

Lance Parrish
Philadelphia Phillies

Lance Parrish suffered through a disappointing and difficult season in 1987. One of the biggest questions that begged to be answered when the Phillies signed Parrish as a free agent in March was whether his chronic back difficulties would allow him to catch a full slate of games. Lance laid those fears to rest by appearing in 130 contests—that was the good news. The bad news was that his offensive performance was below par, and the anticipated defensive improvement the Phillies so desperately needed behind the plate never really materialized.

Lance just did not seem to look good at or behind the plate, especially in the first half of the season. A good deal of this probably had to do with the fact that he was rusty. Parrish missed the second half of the 1986 season, and then became embroiled in very long and protracted contract negotiations that delayed his arrival in spring training. The on-again, off-again nature of the contract talks may have also had a negative psychological impact on his early season performance. Lance seemed awkward, lunging at many balls outside of the strike zone.

He had a high number of passed balls. A newspaper story that quoted Parrish as expressing reservations about ever signing with the Phillies added more pressure and triggered fan resentment; he had become a target of the Philadelphia boo-birds.

Parrish's performance did improve over the second half of the season (aside from hitting better, he threw out more baserunners). Despite his overall disappointing 1987 (his .399 slugging percentage was the second lowest of his career), the fact remains that Lance is a key player in the Phillies' 1988 plans. Darren Daulton's return from injury in 1987 did nothing to indicate that he was ready to win the starting catching position, nor does John Russell fit that bill. The Phillies are hoping that there is truth to the theory that it takes a player who is switching leagues a year to adjust, because if they have any aspirations of a pennant drive in 1988, a Lance Parrish performance circa second-half 1987 is imperative.

Other random observations about Parrish: The Phillies seemed to have cornered the market the last several years on the world's slowest running catchers (Bob Boone, Bo Diaz, Ozzie Virgil), and Lance slogs with the best of them. He hits into an awful lot of double plays, his specialty being banging the ball as hard as he can to the shortstop. The fact that Mike Schmidt and Von Hayes (with their high on-base percentages) are batting in front of him gives him plenty of opportunities. It is interesting to note his similarities with Glenn Wilson: Both arrived from the Tigers, had poor first years, and are very popular with their teammates. They also had similar 1987 seasons (low slugging percentage, on-base percentage, and secondary average). Now that Wilson has been traded, maybe Parrish will not feel the need to emulate his buddy.

Tom Forsaith

Parrish, Lance Michael Bats: Right Throws: Right Born 06/15/56

1987 SEASON AND MAJOR-LEAGUE CAREER BATTING TOTALS

	G	AB	H	2B	3B	HR	TB	R	RBI	TBB	IBB	SO	HP	SH	SF	SB	CS	SB%	GDP	AVG	OBP	SLG
87 PHI	130	466	114	21	0	17	186	42	67	47	2	104	1	1	3	0	1	.00	23	.245	.313	.399
11 YEARS	1276	4739	1237	222	23	229	2192	619	767	381	39	951	20	14	38	22	31	.42	139	.261	.316	.463

	1987 SEASON											FOUR YEAR TOTALS (1984 – 1987)									
	Ave.	OBP	SLG	AB	H	2B	3B	HR	RBI	BB	SO	Ave.	OBP	SLG	AB	H	2B	3B	HR	RBI	BB	SO
Totals	.245	.313	.399	466	114	21	0	17	67	47	104	.253	.313	.449	1920	485	70	4	100	325	167	397
vs. Left	.304	.391	.464	138	42	4	0	6	16	21	30	.282	.357	.490	620	175	21	3	34	99	76	109
vs. Right	.220	.278	.372	328	72	17	0	11	51	26	74	.238	.291	.430	1300	310	49	1	66	226	91	288
at Home	.252	.322	.389	234	59	17	0	5	34	24	59	.264	.329	.435	931	246	42	3	37	149	88	188
on Road	.237	.305	.409	232	55	4	0	12	33	23	45	.242	.297	.463	989	239	28	1	63	176	79	209
vs. Groundball	.259	.337	.427	239	62	10	0	10	42	28	50	.264	.322	.447	903	238	33	2	43	159	76	185
vs. Flyball	.229	.287	.370	227	52	11	0	7	25	19	54	.243	.306	.451	1017	247	37	2	57	166	91	212
vs. Finesse	.281	.341	.455	242	68	12	0	10	33	23	44	.271	.328	.483	1065	289	40	1	61	191	89	185
vs. Power	.205	.284	.339	224	46	9	0	7	34	24	60	.229	.294	.408	855	196	30	3	39	134	78	212
on Grass	.246	.341	.404	114	28	3	0	5	16	17	24	.264	.326	.478	1320	348	44	4	77	239	121	244
on Artificial Turf	.244	.304	.398	352	86	18	0	12	51	30	80	.228	.284	.387	600	137	26	0	23	86	46	153
Day Games	.195	.259	.398	123	24	1	0	8	19	11	28	.221	.279	.383	583	129	19	0	25	84	46	134
Night Games	.262	.332	.399	343	90	20	0	9	48	36	76	.266	.328	.479	1337	356	51	4	75	241	121	263
April	.188	.257	.328	64	12	0	0	3	13	6	18	.210	.266	.359	276	58	5	0	12	51	21	59
May	.257	.329	.351	74	19	4	0	1	8	8	13	.297	.351	.490	353	105	13	2	17	57	29	76
June	.205	.247	.359	78	16	3	0	3	10	4	18	.261	.311	.454	399	104	17	0	20	67	29	76
July	.262	.306	.387	80	21	4	0	2	11	5	16	.217	.280	.398	309	67	8	0	16	45	27	60
August	.290	.389	.527	93	27	7	0	5	15	15	16	.269	.353	.565	308	83	18	2	23	66	40	62
Sept/Oct	.247	.322	.403	77	19	3	0	3	10	9	23	.247	.300	.411	275	68	9	0	12	39	21	64
Bases Empty	.230	.317	.339	230	53	7	0	6	6	28	50	.248	.309	.449	969	240	35	2	52	52	85	201
Leadoff	.177	.262	.250	96	17	4	0	1	1	11	22	.208	.269	.376	452	94	20	1	18	18	38	97
Not Leadoff	.269	.355	.403	134	36	3	0	5	5	17	28	.282	.343	.513	517	146	15	1	34	34	47	104
Runners On	.258	.310	.458	236	61	14	0	11	61	19	54	.258	.316	.450	951	245	35	2	48	273	82	196
First Base Only	.282	.357	.485	103	29	9	0	4	15	12	20	.275	.324	.510	386	106	17	1	24	64	28	66
Scoring Position	.241	.273	.436	133	32	5	0	7	46	7	34	.246	.310	.409	565	139	18	1	24	209	54	130
Late Innings, Close	.214	.290	.369	84	18	1	0	4	11	9	21	.235	.309	.400	310	73	6	0	15	48	33	71

RBI/Opportunities

Scoring Position	34 / 165 (21%)	166 / 754 (22%)
Scoring Position, 2 Out	15 / 85 (18%)	68 / 344 (20%)
On Third, Less than 2 Out	10 / 21 (48%)	59 / 133 (44%)
RBI in close games / RBI Total	40 / 67 (60%)	210 / 325 (65%)

Larry Parrish
Texas Rangers

Performing as a designated hitter is not the walk in the park that some folks think it is. Logically, it seems that any player should be able to quickly adjust to hitting in the DH role. But, for unknown reasons, there have been many talented players who never were able to adjust to the role (See the Reggie Jackson player essay in this book). A few years back, after the 1984 season, I was afraid that Larry Parrish might be one of those whose career would start to die if he were put in that role.

The Rangers first considered having Larry DH more back in 1983, but he detested the idea and hit only .244 in 45 at-bats in the role. In 1984 the plan became a little more firm and Parrish DH'ed about 40 percent of the time. He had a fine year and was named the Rangers' "Player of the Year," but he clearly won the award more for his hitting as a right fielder than a DH.

1984	AB	HITS	B.A.	2B/3B/HR	SLUG%	O.B.A.
DH	243	64	.263	12/ 1/ 5	.383	.317
OTHER	370	111	.300	30/ 0/17	.519	.351

Yet Parrish went on from there to become an outstanding DH, performing better in that role than any other in each of the last three years.

1985-87	AB	HITS	B.A.	2B/3B/HR	SLUG%	O.B.A.
DH	900	248	.276	45/ 2/51	.500	.391
OTHER	464	115	.248	10/ 1/26	.443	.324

Okay, so how did Larry Parrish become an accomplished DH when others, like Reggie Jackson, continued to struggle in the role despite extensive experience? I believe it was solely a matter of attitude and commitment. Reggie Jackson would say in his declining years that he accepted the DH role, but he knew in his heart he still could get by in the outfield. He could still run, throw and catch the ball, just not with the efficiency of his younger days. He hedged on his commitment to being a DH, and he continued to express interest in playing at least occasionally in the field right through his final season.

Not so for Larry Parrish who, in 1985, had a severe knee injury turn him forcefully to the DH role. He still has to wear a very serious looking brace, and since the injury he has been able to play exactly one inning in the outfield. He wasn't much of a third baseman when he had two good knees, and he knew he didn't have the skills or durability to go back to third base on anything other than an occasional basis. Unlike most players, Larry knew with a sense of certainty that he was now a DH.

Fate took away his sense of choice and made Larry Parrish commit to the DH, and that, I believe made all the difference.

Craig R. Wright

Parrish, Larry Alton   Bats: Right   Throws: Right   Born 10/10/53

1987 SEASON AND MAJOR-LEAGUE CAREER BATTING TOTALS

	G	AB	H	2B	3B	HR	TB	R	RBI	TBB	IBB	SO	HP	SH	SF	SB	CS	SB%	GDP	AVG	OBP	SLG
87 TEX	152	557	149	22	1	32	269	79	100	49	7	154	3	0	4	3	1	.75	10	.268	.328	.483
14 YEARS	1771	6386	1701	346	32	242	2837	818	940	501	77	1248	39	31	52	30	35	.46	179	.266	.321	.444

	1987 SEASON											FOUR YEAR TOTALS (1984 – 1987)										
	Ave.	OBP	SLG	AB	H	2B	3B	HR	RBI	BB	SO	Ave.	OBP	SLG	AB	H	2B	3B	HR	RBI	BB	SO
Totals	.268	.328	.483	557	149	22	1	32	100	49	154	.272	.333	.475	1980	538	97	4	99	346	176	461
vs. Left	.268	.346	.516	190	51	5	0	14	35	22	60	.274	.349	.530	592	162	27	1	41	114	69	144
vs. Right	.267	.318	.466	367	98	17	1	18	65	27	94	.271	.325	.451	1388	376	70	3	58	232	107	317
at Home	.264	.335	.477	277	73	11	0	16	46	29	69	.275	.340	.478	1000	275	52	2	49	179	96	223
on Road	.271	.320	.489	280	76	11	1	16	54	20	85	.268	.325	.471	980	263	45	2	50	167	80	238
vs. Groundball	.303	.352	.522	274	83	15	0	15	57	20	57	.298	.349	.493	967	288	56	2	43	174	76	186
vs. Flyball	.233	.305	.445	283	66	7	1	17	43	29	97	.247	.317	.457	1013	250	41	2	56	172	100	275
vs. Finesse	.269	.324	.481	320	86	14	0	18	51	27	78	.274	.327	.485	1137	311	60	2	59	202	92	219
vs. Power	.266	.333	.485	237	63	8	1	14	49	22	76	.269	.339	.460	843	227	37	2	40	144	84	242
on Grass	.269	.326	.498	484	130	22	1	29	88	41	133	.270	.332	.480	1690	457	87	3	87	297	151	388
on Artificial Turf	.260	.341	.384	73	19	0	0	3	12	8	21	.279	.337	.445	290	81	10	1	12	49	25	73
Day Games	.252	.294	.462	119	30	5	1	6	16	7	37	.265	.312	.466	423	112	20	1	21	67	30	88
Night Games	.272	.337	.489	438	119	17	0	26	84	42	117	.274	.338	.477	1557	426	77	3	78	279	146	373
April	.225	.267	.408	71	16	1	0	4	5	3	22	.273	.322	.454	293	80	9	1	14	45	20	66
May	.393	.450	.708	89	35	7	0	7	35	10	16	.274	.342	.480	325	89	19	0	16	71	34	72
June	.245	.304	.510	102	25	6	0	7	15	9	32	.267	.330	.522	356	95	19	0	24	68	34	88
July	.225	.300	.427	89	20	3	0	5	16	10	20	.271	.333	.493	306	83	19	2	15	52	29	60
August	.245	.317	.415	94	23	4	0	4	11	10	30	.287	.334	.474	310	89	19	0	13	50	22	75
Sept/Oct	.268	.320	.429	112	30	1	1	5	18	7	34	.262	.328	.428	390	102	12	1	17	60	37	100
Bases Empty	.217	.273	.391	299	65	11	1	13	13	22	90	.247	.300	.446	1052	260	47	3	52	52	78	260
Leadoff	.222	.278	.393	117	26	3	1	5	5	8	30	.240	.293	.434	479	115	23	2	22	22	35	111
Not Leadoff	.214	.270	.390	182	39	8	0	8	8	14	60	.253	.305	.455	573	145	24	1	30	30	43	149
Runners On	.326	.388	.589	258	84	11	0	19	87	27	64	.300	.366	.508	928	278	50	1	47	294	98	201
First Base Only	.285	.338	.447	123	35	5	0	5	14	10	35	.267	.323	.436	420	112	20	0	17	45	35	91
Scoring Position	.363	.430	.719	135	49	6	0	14	73	17	29	.327	.400	.567	508	166	30	1	30	249	63	110
Late Innings, Close	.241	.298	.356	87	21	1	0	3	13	6	26	.249	.324	.430	309	77	14	0	14	53	33	91

RBI/Opportunities

Scoring Position	52 / 175 (30%)	198 / 677 (29%)
Scoring Position, 2 Out	24 / 89 (27%)	72 / 287 (25%)
On Third, Less than 2 Out	15 / 29 (52%)	75 / 142 (53%)
RBI in close games / RBI Total	48 / 100 (48%)	207 / 346 (60%)

Dan Pasqua

New York Yankees

1987 was a lost season for Dan Pasqua. His strong finish in 1986 had won at least part of the left field job this year; when he cemented the job by having a fine spring training, he appeared ready to be a solid regular. The Yankees never gave him that chance in the regular season. He started slowly and was then shipped to AAA for the third straight year.

Manager Lou Piniella never exactly gave up on Pasqua, but he sure didn't let Dan work things out by playing, either. One week, Dan would be playing semi-regularly; the next he'd be sitting on the bench in the next; neither for any particular reason. Piniella was trying to find a platoon combination or a regular who could win games—it was a combination that he never found.

Part of the problem may have been that Piniella and Pasqua are almost mirror images of each other. Lou was a contact hitter; Dan swings like a lumberjack. Lou drew very few walks; Pasqua is a patient hitter. Lou was a singles hitter; Pasqua has a lot of power. Finally, Lou never struck out much—Pasqua does so at a fearful rate. Perhaps Lou, finding it hard to relate to this type of player, just wasn't willing to give him the chance that he might have given to a player more like himself. . . . Gary Ward is a far more similar player to Piniella than Pasqua; he got a career's worth of chances in 1987.

A contributing factor was Pasqua's problems against lefties. He's a career .182 hitter against southpaws; in 1987, he didn't get a hit against one until June. Since New York didn't have the patience to play Dan very much, they certainly weren't going to let him adapt to lefties; since they see a lot of lefties, it cut into his playing time even more.

But the key problem was simply that New York had other options in 1987. Pasqua was not the only Yankee who had a bad start in 1987; third baseman Mike Pagliarulo was even worse in April and May. On June 1, Pags was batting .203, slugging .380 and had an on-base percentage of .292; Dan's figures were .198, .362 and .333. After that point, Pags hit .247, slugged .522 and had a .312 OB%; Dan hit .252, slugged .455 and had a .310 OB%. The major difference between the two is that New York gave Mike some 400 more plate appearances after 6/1; Dan got about 230.

If Pasqua had gotten 500 at-bats in 1987, I believe that he would have hit 30 homers, walked 70 times and had 80 RBIs. I think he could do that in any year he gets that chance; it's a shame that the Yankees have never been willing to find out if he could produce those kinds of numbers. That being so, a trade was probably best for Dan's future. The White Sox should be willing to allow him to prove himself; they shouldn't be facing much pennant pressure in 1988.

Craig Christmann

Pasqua, Daniel Anthony "Dan"

Bats: Left Throws: Left Born 10/17/61

1987 SEASON AND MAJOR-LEAGUE CAREER BATTING TOTALS

	G	AB	H	2B	3B	HR	TB	R	RBI	TBB	IBB	SO	HP	SH	SF	SB	CS	SB%	GDP	AVG	OBP	SLG
87 NYA	113	318	74	7	1	17	134	42	42	40	3	99	1	2	1	0	2	.00	7	.233	.319	.421
3 YEARS	275	746	187	27	2	42	344	103	112	103	10	215	5	3	3	2	2	.50	12	.251	.344	.461

	1987 SEASON											FOUR YEAR TOTALS (1984 – 1987)										
	Ave.	OBP	SLG	AB	H	2B	3B	HR	RBI	BB	SO	Ave.	OBP	SLG	AB	H	2B	3B	HR	RBI	BB	SO
Totals	.233	.319	.421	318	74	7	1	17	42	40	99	.251	.344	.461	746	187	27	2	42	112	103	215
vs. Left	.164	.246	.200	55	9	2	0	0	3	6	19	.182	.272	.298	121	22	5	0	3	15	13	42
vs. Right	.247	.334	.468	263	65	5	1	17	39	34	80	.264	.358	.493	625	165	22	2	39	97	90	173
at Home	.277	.372	.411	141	39	1	0	6	13	21	43	.261	.362	.473	368	96	12	0	22	53	58	99
on Road	.198	.276	.429	177	35	6	1	11	29	19	56	.241	.326	.450	378	91	15	2	20	59	45	116
vs. Groundball	.247	.325	.433	178	44	7	1	8	23	20	60	.261	.347	.454	399	104	16	2	19	57	51	118
vs. Flyball	.214	.313	.407	140	30	0	0	9	19	20	39	.239	.341	.470	347	83	11	0	23	55	52	97
vs. Finesse	.261	.361	.479	165	43	4	1	10	21	25	48	.271	.354	.504	395	107	15	1	25	57	50	109
vs. Power	.203	.272	.359	153	31	3	0	7	21	15	51	.228	.333	.413	351	80	12	1	17	55	53	106
on Grass	.234	.325	.396	273	64	5	0	13	34	36	84	.242	.342	.435	620	150	19	1	33	88	92	180
on Artificial Turf	.222	.286	.578	45	10	2	1	4	8	4	15	.294	.357	.587	126	37	8	1	9	24	11	35
Day Games	.237	.342	.443	97	23	2	0	6	16	15	29	.262	.350	.480	271	71	14	0	15	41	36	72
Night Games	.231	.309	.412	221	51	5	1	11	26	25	70	.244	.341	.451	475	116	13	2	27	71	67	143
April	.130	.241	.217	46	6	1	0	1	4	7	18	.130	.241	.217	46	6	1	0	1	4	7	18
May	.243	.391	.457	70	17	0	0	5	11	16	20	.257	.409	.533	105	27	2	0	9	18	26	31
June	.208	.323	.358	53	11	2	0	2	8	9	23	.218	.312	.323	124	27	4	0	3	13	17	41
July	.160	.160	.440	25	4	2	1	1	3	0	6	.273	.333	.576	99	27	5	2	7	18	9	22
August	.284	.314	.478	67	19	1	0	4	10	3	18	.278	.355	.485	194	54	7	0	11	29	23	51
Sept/Oct	.298	.355	.526	57	17	1	0	4	6	5	14	.258	.337	.489	178	46	8	0	11	30	21	52
Bases Empty	.250	.308	.439	180	45	5	1	9	9	15	55	.256	.322	.478	410	105	14	1	25	25	40	109
Leadoff	.260	.299	.493	73	19	2	0	5	5	4	19	.268	.317	.542	168	45	4	0	14	14	12	45
Not Leadoff	.243	.314	.402	107	26	3	1	4	4	11	36	.248	.326	.434	242	60	10	1	11	11	28	64
Runners On	.210	.333	.399	138	29	2	0	8	33	25	44	.244	.364	.440	336	82	13	1	17	87	63	106
First Base Only	.226	.333	.387	62	14	1	0	3	6	9	16	.265	.383	.437	151	40	6	1	6	13	28	42
Scoring Position	.197	.333	.408	76	15	1	0	5	27	16	28	.227	.348	.443	185	42	7	0	11	74	35	64
Late Innings, Close	.235	.333	.412	51	12	1	1	2	9	8	14	.204	.355	.381	113	23	3	1	5	21	27	34

RBI/Opportunities

Scoring Position	21 / 106 (20%)	57 / 254 (22%)
Scoring Position, 2 Out	3 / 39 (8%)	19 / 107 (18%)
On Third, Less than 2 Out	10 / 23 (43%)	21 / 42 (50%)
RBI in close games / RBI Total	27 / 42 (64%)	64 / 112 (57%)

Tony Pena
St. Louis Cardinals

Cardinal fans have suffered through a lot of disappointment during the 1980's with regard to their starting catchers. It seems that every time the team makes a move to acquire a starting catcher, the player's career hits a low point. Hopefully Tony Pena's new glasses, by correcting his eyesight, will correct this problem in 1988.

The eighties began with the immensely popular Ted Simmons behind the plate in St. Louis. Simmons was an excellent hitter who probably should have been made a first baseman early in his career, and while Cardinal fans had no complaint with Simmons, the team never won so much as a division title while he was there. When Whitey Herzog arrive and replaced Simmons with Darrell Porter, the move was not popular. When Porter hit just .224 and .231 during his first two seasons as a Cardinal, the move became very unpopular. Actually, although Porter's best years were indeed behind him, he wasn't that bad. He was a big improvement defensively over Simmons, and with his walks and power he made a modest contribution to the offense. And his postseason performance in '82 at least temporarily won him fan support in St. Louis.

Porter was followed in 1986 by Mike Heath. Heath was a disaster and was gone before season's end. And the Cardinals began spring training in '87 with the catching position being one of their big question marks, a question they thought they had answered a few days before the season began when they acquired Pena from Pittsburgh. Tony then broke a finger in the third game of the season and didn't return until late May. Unfortunately, he didn't bring his bat with him.

Pena was actually a better hitter during his injury-shortened first half. At midseason he was hitting .260 and had an OBA of .333. Then he hit .198 in July, .165 in August and .179 in September/October. This was the exact opposite of the pattern Tony had seemed to follow at Pittsburgh, where he was usually a slow starter and one of the league's top hitters during the season's second half. During the final week of the season he was fitted with a pair of glasses, and during the NLCS and World Series he looked like a totally different hitter. The Cardinals are banking on these glasses, as they have signed Pena to a new two-year deal worth over one million dollars per year.

An interesting (?) piece of trivia on the Cardinal teams of the past two seasons: St. Louis stole 262 bases in 1986 and 248 in 1987. Which players produced the team's first stolen bases during each of these two seasons? The answers: Mike Heath in '86 and Tony Pena in '87. This trend doesn't go back any further though. In 1985 it was Joaquin Andujar.

Russ Eagle

Pena, Antonio Francisco (Padilla) "Tony"　　　　Bats: Right　　Throws: Right　　Born 06/04/57

1987 SEASON AND MAJOR-LEAGUE CAREER BATTING TOTALS

	G	AB	H	2B	3B	HR	TB	R	RBI	TBB	IBB	SO	HP	SH	SF	SB	CS	SB%	GDP	AVG	OBP	SLG
87 STL	116	384	82	13	4	5	118	40	44	36	9	54	1	2	2	6	1	.86	19	.214	.281	.307
8 YEARS	917	3256	903	153	19	68	1298	347	384	210	37	426	11	24	15	48	42	.53	108	.277	.322	.399

	1987 SEASON											FOUR YEAR TOTALS (1984 – 1987)										
	Ave.	OBP	SLG	AB	H	2B	3B	HR	RBI	BB	SO	Ave.	OBP	SLG	AB	H	2B	3B	HR	RBI	BB	SO
Totals	.214	.281	.307	384	82	13	4	5	44	36	54	.262	.316	.380	1986	521	93	10	40	233	154	269
vs. Left	.226	.280	.321	137	31	4	0	3	17	11	15	.288	.340	.418	612	176	28	2	16	68	49	67
vs. Right	.206	.282	.300	247	51	9	4	2	27	25	39	.251	.305	.362	1374	345	65	8	24	165	105	202
at Home	.225	.274	.310	187	42	7	3	1	21	13	25	.265	.321	.370	986	261	45	7	15	113	82	112
on Road	.203	.288	.305	197	40	6	1	4	23	23	29	.260	.310	.389	1000	260	48	3	25	120	72	157
vs. Groundball	.201	.242	.291	199	40	5	2	3	27	11	24	.275	.325	.391	955	263	44	6	18	119	68	113
vs. Flyball	.227	.321	.324	185	42	8	2	2	17	25	30	.250	.308	.370	1031	258	49	4	22	114	86	156
vs. Finesse	.226	.293	.322	208	47	11	0	3	23	19	27	.259	.304	.372	1162	301	57	4	22	121	74	133
vs. Power	.199	.268	.290	176	35	2	4	2	21	17	27	.267	.332	.391	824	220	36	6	18	112	80	136
on Grass	.167	.257	.211	90	15	2	1	0	8	11	18	.235	.291	.339	510	120	21	1	10	53	39	88
on Artificial Turf	.228	.289	.337	294	67	11	3	5	36	25	36	.272	.325	.394	1476	401	72	9	30	180	115	181
Day Games	.217	.284	.302	106	23	4	1	1	9	10	17	.267	.330	.364	580	155	25	2	9	65	54	79
Night Games	.212	.280	.309	278	59	9	3	4	35	26	37	.260	.310	.386	1406	366	68	8	31	168	100	190
April	.100	.308	.100	10	1	0	0	0	0	2	3	.259	.333	.395	205	53	10	0	6	16	22	31
May	.286	.333	.393	28	8	1	1	0	7	2	5	.247	.281	.368	288	71	11	3	6	42	14	47
June	.292	.337	.385	96	28	4	1	1	12	7	7	.280	.326	.398	397	111	22	2	7	46	28	54
July	.198	.283	.284	81	16	3	2	0	7	10	12	.275	.337	.377	363	100	15	2	6	33	34	42
August	.165	.253	.271	85	14	3	0	2	7	10	7	.255	.312	.365	364	93	15	2	7	48	30	47
Sept/Oct	.179	.225	.274	84	15	2	0	2	11	5	20	.252	.301	.377	369	93	20	1	8	48	26	48
Bases Empty	.216	.275	.288	222	48	7	3	1	1	17	38	.264	.318	.389	1099	290	54	7	23	23	87	158
Leadoff	.215	.263	.301	93	20	3	1	1	1	5	15	.277	.323	.410	458	127	25	3	10	10	30	66
Not Leadoff	.217	.284	.279	129	28	4	2	0	0	12	23	.254	.315	.373	641	163	29	4	13	13	57	92
Runners On	.210	.290	.333	162	34	6	1	4	43	19	16	.260	.312	.369	887	231	39	3	17	210	67	111
First Base Only	.214	.257	.343	70	15	3	0	2	5	4	7	.269	.300	.378	357	96	16	1	7	23	16	39
Scoring Position	.207	.312	.326	92	19	3	1	2	38	15	9	.255	.319	.362	530	135	23	2	10	187	51	72
Late Innings, Close	.207	.270	.305	82	17	3	1	1	4	6	13	.246	.301	.332	410	101	18	1	5	40	31	55

RBI/Opportunities

Scoring Position	32 / 129 (25%)	163 / 708 (23%)
Scoring Position, 2 Out	7 / 49 (14%)	54 / 303 (18%)
On Third, Less than 2 Out	19 / 35 (54%)	63 / 132 (48%)
RBI in close games / RBI Total	28 / 44 (64%)	160 / 233 (69%)

Terry Pendleton
St. Louis Cardinals

Whitey Herzog is often praised, by various individuals and publications, as being among the best judges of talent in baseball today. His handling of Terry Pendleton is more evidence in his corner. There are managers who would have given up on Pendleton during the past two seasons, but Whitey stayed with him, and in 1987 the Cardinals and Herzog reaped the benefits of this patience.

After an impressive rookie campaign in 1984, Pendleton turned in back-to-back poor seasons. He didn't hit for average, and he didn't draw many walks. But he played spectacular defense and hustled constantly, qualities that Herzog likes in a player. He showed up early for spring training in '87 to work on his hitting, and like Vince Coleman, turned himself from an offensive liability to one of the team's strengths.

Pendleton's improvement at the plate was similar to Coleman's. The key in both cases was becoming more patient. Prior to last season, Pendleton's career high in walks was 37. He nearly doubled that with 70 in '87. His patience made him a much better hitter, not only in terms of average but power as well. Pendleton's twelve home runs were one of the bigger surprises of the season, and his 45 extra base hits were easily the most in his career.

Going into the final month of the season it looked as though Pendleton was going to join Clark and McGee in giving the Cardinals three 100-RBI men. Terry had 86 ribbies entering September but had his only bad month of the season, hitting .219 with 10 RBIs the rest of the way. But two of those RBIs were the biggest ones of the season, not only for the Cardinals but for the New York Mets as well.

On September 11 the Cardinals began a three-game series at New York. They were slumping terribly, having just been swept by Montreal, and their lead was down to a game and a half over the Mets. With two outs in the ninth inning they trailed by three runs in the first game of the series. They were one out away from having their lead cut to only half a game. But after an RBI single by Willie McGee, Pendleton hit a Roger McDowell pitch over the center field wall to tie the game. The Cards went on to win the game, take two out of three in the series, and they left New York with their lead back at two and a half games. The Mets never got closer than a game and a half from that point on. It was, without a doubt, the biggest hit by anyone in a Cardinal uniform since Jack Clark's pennant-winning homer at Los Angeles in 1985.

Russ Eagle

Pendleton, Terry Lee   Bats: Both   Throws: Right   Born 07/16/60

1987 SEASON AND MAJOR-LEAGUE CAREER BATTING TOTALS

	G	AB	H	2B	3B	HR	TB	R	RBI	TBB	IBB	SO	HP	SH	SF	SB	CS	SB%	GDP	AVG	OBP	SLG
87 STL	159	583	167	29	4	12	240	82	96	70	6	74	2	3	9	19	12	.61	18	.286	.360	.412
4 YEARS	534	1982	524	87	15	19	698	231	257	157	23	240	3	12	24	80	35	.70	55	.264	.316	.352

	1987 SEASON											FOUR YEAR TOTALS (1984 – 1987)										
	Ave.	OBP	SLG	AB	H	2B	3B	HR	RBI	BB	SO	Ave.	OBP	SLG	AB	H	2B	3B	HR	RBI	BB	SO
Totals	.286	.360	.412	583	167	29	4	12	96	70	75	.264	.316	.352	1982	524	87	15	19	257	157	241
vs. Left	.337	.386	.447	208	70	9	1	4	38	18	19	.281	.321	.371	676	190	33	5	6	93	44	64
vs. Right	.259	.346	.392	375	97	20	3	8	58	52	56	.256	.313	.342	1306	334	54	10	13	164	113	177
at Home	.266	.331	.375	293	78	15	1	5	44	28	33	.265	.314	.358	992	263	48	10	8	125	73	107
on Road	.307	.388	.448	290	89	14	3	7	52	42	42	.264	.318	.346	990	261	39	5	11	132	84	134
vs. Groundball	.305	.384	.495	275	84	17	1	11	56	35	35	.285	.334	.387	967	276	49	5	13	140	72	109
vs. Flyball	.269	.338	.338	308	83	12	3	1	40	35	40	.244	.299	.319	1015	248	38	10	6	117	85	132
vs. Finesse	.281	.358	.385	299	84	12	2	5	49	37	27	.256	.297	.325	1082	277	40	7	7	128	67	100
vs. Power	.292	.362	.440	284	83	17	2	7	47	33	48	.274	.337	.384	900	247	47	8	12	129	90	141
on Grass	.316	.381	.481	158	50	8	0	6	28	19	28	.258	.315	.340	480	124	15	0	8	62	43	71
on Artificial Turf	.275	.352	.386	425	117	21	4	6	68	51	47	.266	.316	.356	1502	400	72	15	11	195	114	170
Day Games	.310	.367	.486	216	67	15	1	7	45	21	23	.283	.332	.379	709	201	34	2	10	98	53	87
Night Games	.272	.356	.368	367	100	14	3	5	51	49	52	.254	.307	.337	1273	323	53	13	9	159	104	154
April	.309	.333	.420	81	25	6	0	1	8	3	7	.249	.303	.326	221	55	11	0	2	18	17	38
May	.330	.397	.408	103	34	5	0	1	20	14	10	.281	.337	.349	295	83	17	0	1	48	27	30
June	.283	.374	.394	99	28	2	0	3	15	14	16	.222	.282	.299	261	58	8	0	4	29	21	36
July	.307	.383	.475	101	31	6	1	3	18	12	16	.294	.343	.378	333	98	14	1	4	42	24	41
August	.277	.391	.468	94	26	6	3	2	25	19	10	.247	.314	.366	413	102	17	7	6	68	41	47
Sept/Oct	.219	.272	.314	105	23	4	0	2	10	8	16	.279	.318	.366	459	128	20	7	2	52	27	49
Bases Empty	.256	.328	.354	308	79	13	1	5	5	33	39	.256	.302	.336	1045	267	47	5	9	9	69	129
Leadoff	.269	.365	.403	119	32	8	1	2	2	18	13	.276	.321	.369	406	112	21	4	3	3	27	50
Not Leadoff	.249	.304	.323	189	47	5	0	3	3	15	26	.243	.289	.315	639	155	26	1	6	6	42	79
Runners On	.320	.393	.476	275	88	16	3	7	91	37	36	.274	.335	.370	937	257	40	10	10	248	88	112
First Base Only	.321	.374	.528	106	34	7	0	5	10	9	14	.269	.311	.363	342	92	14	0	6	16	21	35
Scoring Position	.320	.404	.444	169	54	9	3	2	81	28	22	.277	.348	.375	595	165	26	10	4	232	67	77
Late Innings, Close	.287	.368	.515	101	29	7	2	4	17	12	23	.265	.329	.391	358	95	22	4	5	38	33	62

RBI/Opportunities

Scoring Position	73 / 247 (30%)	212 / 811 (26%)
Scoring Position, 2 Out	32 / 100 (32%)	82 / 332 (25%)
On Third, Less than 2 Out	29 / 51 (57%)	86 / 153 (56%)
RBI in close games / RBI Total	61 / 96 (64%)	159 / 257 (62%)

Gerald Perry
Atlanta Braves

Gerald Perry is one of the most exciting players in the majors. He can turn a routine single into a double, steal a base, or make the easiest defensive play into a memorable experience. Although he is 27 years old, he only has about two full seasons of major league experience; he is still learning to play the game. 1987 was Perry's first full season in the majors; therefore, his season's statistics are all "career highs."

It took nearly the entire season before Chuck Tanner realized that Gerald Perry wasn't a No. 3 hitter. Perry, originally an outfielder, doesn't draw enough walks (on-base average .329) to justify batting that high in the order. Dion James, this season's projected left fielder, will probably bat third, which he did in September of 1987.

Perry didn't win a regular job until late June. Through May 21, he was hitting .211, slugging .303, with 2 HR and 15 RBI. As his playing time increased, so did his performance—in a 36-game stretch from the end of June until mid-August, Perry hit .328, with 6 HR, 19 RBI, and 16 SB.

Perry can be an outfielder's worst nightmare due to his repeated attempts to take an extra base. His most common tactic is to round a base "too far," inducing the fielder to throw behind him. Then, Perry will utilize his exceptional speed to go to the next base. He will often succeed, but will occasionally be caught by an outfielder with a good arm. He needs to learn which outfielders' arms can be exploited and which cannot.

His basestealing was extraordinary through July 30, as he was 24 of 29 (83 percent success rate). He stole three bases in one game against Nolan Ryan. However, something happened to Perry in the second half of the season. Maybe he got bored of the mediocre play of the team, but, after August 1, Perry was 16 of 26 as a basestealer. Three of his 10 CS after August 1 were at third base, and another at home.

His 42 SB eclipsed Brett Butler's 1983 team record 39. However, either he or Chuck Tanner needs to pay attention to the fact that Dale Murphy was at the plate on many of those steals—frequently leading to an intentional walk for Murphy (who led the league with 29), rather than a big inning.

Gerald came close to winning a Granite Glove for his efforts at first this year. Some of his mistakes are due to poor mechanics, others due to his incorrect choices of plays, such as going for the lead runner (and getting no one) instead of the sure out at first. Several of his 14 errors were on ground balls hit directly at him; experience should be a good teacher, if Gerald is an apt pupil. Gerald's fielding average finished ahead of only Sid Bream and Jack Clark among first basemen who handled at least 1000 chances.

Perry hit with good extra base power. However, he must draw more walks to preserve his place in the lineup, or else he must significantly improve on his total of 12 home runs.

Marc Bowman and Stacy Kaneshiro

Perry, Gerald June Bats: Left Throws: Right Born 10/30/60

1987 SEASON AND MAJOR-LEAGUE CAREER BATTING TOTALS

	G	AB	H	2B	3B	HR	TB	R	RBI	TBB	IBB	SO	HP	SH	SF	SB	CS	SB%	GDP	AVG	OBP	SLG
87 ATL	142	533	144	35	2	12	219	77	74	48	1	63	1	3	5	42	16	.72	18	.270	.329	.411
5 YEARS	430	1227	320	56	4	25	459	162	151	145	8	137	3	6	15	66	35	.65	39	.261	.337	.374

1987 SEASON

	Ave.	OBP	SLG	AB	H	2B	3B	HR	RBI	BB	SO
Totals	.270	.329	.411	533	144	35	2	12	74	48	63
vs. Left	.256	.321	.480	125	32	11	1	5	17	11	21
vs. Right	.275	.331	.390	408	112	24	1	7	57	37	42
at Home	.259	.331	.369	255	66	20	1	2	32	28	23
on Road	.281	.327	.450	278	78	15	1	10	42	20	40
vs. Groundball	.274	.320	.413	230	63	15	1	5	30	15	32
vs. Flyball	.267	.335	.409	303	81	20	1	7	44	33	31
vs. Finesse	.280	.325	.425	268	75	21	0	6	36	19	26
vs. Power	.260	.332	.396	265	69	14	2	6	38	29	37
on Grass	.273	.332	.404	403	110	28	2	7	50	37	46
on Artificial Turf	.262	.319	.431	130	34	7	0	5	24	11	17
Day Games	.271	.329	.427	199	54	11	1	6	30	17	25
Night Games	.269	.329	.401	334	90	24	1	6	44	31	38
April	.210	.254	.290	62	13	2	0	1	7	4	10
May	.241	.305	.345	87	21	3	0	2	16	8	12
June	.272	.348	.407	81	22	6	1	1	11	10	10
July	.342	.390	.447	76	26	5	0	1	9	6	9
August	.290	.342	.533	107	31	9	1	5	15	9	12
Sept/Oct	.258	.321	.392	120	31	10	0	2	16	11	10
Bases Empty	.261	.321	.390	287	75	20	1	5	5	25	37
Leadoff	.245	.297	.340	94	23	4	1	1	1	7	9
Not Leadoff	.269	.332	.415	193	52	16	0	4	4	18	28
Runners On	.280	.338	.435	246	69	15	1	7	69	23	26
First Base Only	.270	.336	.440	100	27	6	1	3	9	10	14
Scoring Position	.288	.339	.432	146	42	9	0	4	60	13	12
Late Innings, Close	.333	.380	.452	84	28	7	0	1	14	7	16

TWO YEAR TOTALS (1986 – 1987)

	Ave.	OBP	SLG	AB	H	2B	3B	HR	RBI	BB	SO
Totals	.270	.328	.408	603	163	37	2	14	85	56	67
vs. Left	.273	.340	.516	128	35	11	1	6	19	12	21
vs. Right	.269	.328	.379	475	128	26	1	8	66	44	46
at Home	.258	.328	.376	287	74	20	1	4	39	31	24
on Road	.282	.332	.437	316	89	17	1	10	46	25	43
vs. Groundball	.273	.324	.414	256	70	16	1	6	36	19	34
vs. Flyball	.268	.335	.403	347	93	21	1	8	49	37	33
vs. Finesse	.283	.331	.422	315	89	23	0	7	43	24	29
vs. Power	.257	.329	.392	288	74	14	2	7	42	32	38
on Grass	.274	.336	.407	452	124	29	2	9	59	44	48
on Artificial Turf	.258	.313	.411	151	39	8	0	5	26	12	19
Day Games	.271	.329	.427	199	54	11	1	6	30	17	25
Night Games	.270	.331	.399	404	109	26	1	8	55	39	42
April	.210	.254	.290	62	13	2	0	1	7	4	10
May	.243	.304	.339	115	28	5	0	2	20	10	12
June	.282	.372	.417	103	29	6	1	2	13	16	11
July	.342	.390	.447	76	26	5	0	1	9	6	9
August	.290	.342	.533	107	31	9	1	5	15	9	12
Sept/Oct	.257	.312	.393	140	36	10	0	3	21	11	13
Bases Empty	.265	.320	.386	332	88	20	1	6	6	27	40
Leadoff	.239	.288	.342	117	28	4	1	2	2	8	10
Not Leadoff	.279	.338	.409	215	60	16	0	4	4	19	30
Runners On	.277	.342	.435	271	75	17	1	8	79	29	27
First Base Only	.266	.333	.422	109	29	6	1	3	9	11	14
Scoring Position	.284	.348	.444	162	46	11	0	5	70	18	13
Late Innings, Close	.333	.380	.452	168	56	14	0	2	28	14	32

RBI/Opportunities

Scoring Position	53 / 186	(28%)
Scoring Position, 2 Out	17 / 66	(26%)
On Third, Less than 2 Out	22 / 46	(48%)
RBI in close games / RBI Total	55 / 74	(74%)

	62 / 214	(29%)
	22 / 80	(28%)
	25 / 51	(49%)
	110 / 85	(129%)

Gary Pettis
California Angels

Fast, graceful, acrobatic. These all describe the gifts Gary Pettis brings to his outfield play. And these are the gifts he can bring to the Detroit Tigers in 1988. After a dismal 1987, the Angels traded Pettis to Detroit for pitcher Dan Petry.

The tragedy of 1987 is that it held such promise for Pettis. He was coming off his best season ever, followed by a sparkling '86 AL Championship Series against Boston. He'd just won a Gold Glove, his second in just three seasons.

He started 1987 as if it would be his best yet, 17 hits in his first 54 at-bats (.315). But it was downhill from there, and at an alarmingly consistent rate. He hit .253 for April, .221 for May, .195 for June, .159 in July, and .095 in August before the Angels finally optioned him to Edmonton. He was recalled September 1, and finished 10 for 40 (.250), but it was too little, too late. The emergence of Devon White as an outfielder with nearly comparable defensive skills, as well as power and more consistency at the plate, combined with the signing of free agent Chili Davis in the off-season to make Pettis totally expendable.

It's Pettis' glove that remains his saving grace and his hope for a major league future. He was the top vote getter in Gold Glove voting among AL outfielders in both '85 and '86. He led in putouts in '86 with 462. He probably would have won a third award in 1987 if he had played more regularly.

After a dismal rookie season at the plate, it looked like Pettis had developed into an acceptable offensive player for a man with his defensive skills. In fact, he seemed to be improving each season. He was hitting in the mid-.250s, his RBI and run totals continued to improve, and he drew an increasing number of walks each year. He also was one of the AL's best base stealers his first three seasons with 48, 56, and 50. That was enough to make him the club's career leader in steals before 1987 began.

But 1987 was a nightmare for Pettis and the Angels. Overall, he hit just .208 and scored just 49 runs after leading the team with 93 in 1986. His 17 RBIs were a career low for a full season, and he stole just 24 bases, although his success rate was excellent at 83 percent.

Perhaps Pettis' downfall was caused most by his inability to reduce his strikeouts despite putting in many hours of work with team hitting instructors. He'd averaged 124 Ks per season going into 1987, and he fanned 124 times in just 394 at-bats in 1987. Only guys who can muscle the ball out of the park regularly can get away with that. Pettis had exactly one homer in '87 (an inside-the-park homer), and he's never had more than 5 in a season.

Dean Hill

Pettis, Gary George
Bats: Both   Throws: Right   Born 04/03/58

1987 SEASON AND MAJOR-LEAGUE CAREER BATTING TOTALS

	G	AB	H	2B	3B	HR	TB	R	RBI	TBB	IBB	SO	HP	SH	SF	SB	CS	SB%	GDP	AVG	OBP	SLG
87 CAL	133	394	82	13	2	1	102	49	17	52	0	124	1	1	0	24	5	.83	8	.208	.302	.259
6 YEARS	584	1863	451	59	23	13	595	296	143	250	3	513	4	31	8	186	47	.80	25	.242	.332	.319

	1987 SEASON											FOUR YEAR TOTALS (1984 – 1987)										
	Ave.	OBP	SLG	AB	H	2B	3B	HR	RBI	BB	SO	Ave.	OBP	SLG	AB	H	2B	3B	HR	RBI	BB	SO
Totals	.208	.302	.259	394	82	13	2	1	17	52	124	.240	.332	.310	1773	425	57	20	9	136	245	496
vs. Left	.172	.248	.250	128	22	5	1	1	4	13	28	.248	.321	.317	577	143	19	6	3	45	63	123
vs. Right	.226	.327	.263	266	60	8	1	0	13	39	96	.236	.337	.306	1196	282	38	14	6	91	182	373
at Home	.221	.300	.284	204	45	8	1	1	12	23	63	.232	.323	.293	819	190	23	9	3	64	111	227
on Road	.195	.305	.232	190	37	5	1	0	5	29	61	.246	.340	.324	954	235	34	11	6	72	134	269
vs. Groundball	.167	.245	.195	174	29	3	1	0	5	18	56	.230	.318	.312	833	192	25	11	7	64	106	228
vs. Flyball	.241	.345	.309	220	53	10	1	1	12	34	68	.248	.345	.307	940	233	32	9	2	72	139	268
vs. Finesse	.225	.289	.290	200	45	8	1	1	9	17	57	.250	.328	.324	987	247	37	9	6	64	112	251
vs. Power	.191	.314	.227	194	37	5	1	0	8	35	67	.226	.337	.291	786	178	20	11	3	72	133	245
on Grass	.223	.316	.276	337	75	11	2	1	17	46	105	.243	.334	.312	1472	357	43	16	9	120	204	404
on Artificial Turf	.123	.219	.158	57	7	2	0	0	0	6	19	.226	.323	.299	301	68	14	4	0	16	41	92
Day Games	.202	.275	.264	129	26	5	0	1	7	13	37	.262	.345	.351	519	136	20	7	4	51	68	133
Night Games	.211	.315	.257	265	56	8	2	0	10	39	87	.230	.327	.293	1254	289	37	13	5	85	177	363
April	.253	.309	.368	87	22	7	0	1	4	6	23	.247	.335	.343	324	80	15	5	2	21	42	86
May	.221	.295	.253	95	21	3	0	0	4	10	30	.213	.292	.269	305	65	7	2	2	23	34	89
June	.195	.347	.244	82	16	2	1	0	2	19	24	.250	.351	.310	352	88	9	3	2	20	55	105
July	.159	.266	.188	69	11	0	1	0	2	10	31	.231	.326	.285	242	56	6	2	1	21	34	75
August	.095	.208	.143	21	2	1	0	0	2	3	7	.220	.324	.269	268	59	9	2	0	18	41	70
Sept/Oct	.250	.318	.250	40	10	0	0	0	3	4	9	.273	.361	.376	282	77	11	6	2	33	39	71
Bases Empty	.229	.316	.292	236	54	10	1	1	1	29	71	.238	.327	.303	1131	269	40	11	4	4	148	316
Leadoff	.234	.333	.327	107	25	7	0	1	1	16	33	.239	.339	.309	599	143	21	6	3	3	91	169
Not Leadoff	.225	.301	.264	129	29	3	1	0	0	13	38	.237	.312	.297	532	126	19	5	1	1	57	147
Runners On	.177	.282	.209	158	28	3	1	0	16	23	53	.243	.342	.321	642	156	17	9	5	132	97	180
First Base Only	.233	.324	.283	60	14	1	1	0	1	8	19	.224	.323	.270	259	58	4	4	0	5	38	64
Scoring Position	.143	.257	.163	98	14	2	0	0	15	15	34	.256	.355	.355	383	98	13	5	5	127	59	116
Late Innings, Close	.262	.324	.292	65	17	2	0	0	4	6	22	.236	.322	.289	242	57	7	3	0	18	31	72

RBI/Opportunities

Scoring Position	15 / 131 (11%)	114 / 542 (21%)
Scoring Position, 2 Out	2 / 49 (4%)	50 / 258 (19%)
On Third, Less than 2 Out	8 / 22 (36%)	46 / 95 (48%)
RBI in close games / RBI Total	10 / 17 (59%)	84 / 136 (62%)

Ken Phelps
Seattle Mariners

In the off-season of 1986–87 there was a lot of noise coming out of Seattle. Surprise, it wasn't just Phil Bradley's annual grumbling; a lot of that noise was coming from Ken Phelps' corner. Ken Phelps? I wasn't even sure he could talk and almost sure, given his history of no respect, that no reporter would listen.

It goes to show you what a little success can do to you. Having found his voice, Phelps lashed out at the Tartabull trade, at the Mariners' tight purse strings during arbitration, and was very critical of the Mariners in a pre-season magazine article. Ken was quoted as saying, "I'd welcome a trade. We've seen a lot of good players come and go in this organization, and it makes everybody look around and say, 'Well, I could be next.' If a player's salary gets too high, he becomes very expendable."

That was rather stunning considering that Phelps had a reputation of quietly doing a good job even when management was seriously screwing up his own career. You have to wonder if a lot of those harsh words weren't frustrated feelings built up over those years of abuse. You have to remember this is a guy who couldn't catch a break until Dick Williams entered his career a few months before his thirty-second birthday. Now Williams didn't do a damn thing to make Phelps a productive player other than to just stick him in there every day against RHP. Project his 1983–85 performance—before Williams—into 600 PA and you get the numbers shown below.

And he was doing that hitting in the #6–8 slot while being shuffled in and out of the lineup in a haphazard fashion that gave him little more than 200 PAs a year. Ken probably needed to get a few things off his chest once he got the chance to prove himself and showed that he belonged.

By April, Phelps had quieted down again. He even apologized and said he was wrong about the Tartabull trade. He wasn't, but we understood that he was really saying he was wrong to publicly pop off the way he had.

Some folks wondered if Phelps would continue to produce being used so much more; maybe his past managers were just carefully matching him up to his best advantage. Under Williams, Phelps has solidly laid that theory to rest. Playing about 70 percent of the time his performance has improved considerably:

	AB	B.A.	2B/3B/HR	BB	SLUG%	OBA	R	RBI
1986-87	676	.233	29/ 5/51	168	.492	.353	137	132
600 PA Projection	469	.253	20/ 3/35	117	.537	.408	95	92

It's been a quiet winter for Phelps. Rather than talk of being traded, he's looking for a two-year contract with the Mariners. If there's any justice, they'll throw in a little extra. They owe him.

Merrianna McCully and Craig R. Wright

Phelps, Kenneth Allen "Ken" Bats: Left Throws: Left Born 08/06/54

1987 SEASON AND MAJOR-LEAGUE CAREER BATTING TOTALS

	G	AB	H	2B	3B	HR	TB	R	RBI	TBB	IBB	SO	HP	SH	SF	SB	CS	SB%	GDP	AVG	OBP	SLG
87 SEA	120	332	86	13	1	27	182	68	68	80	5	75	8	0	4	1	1	.50	7	.259	.410	.548
8 YEARS	491	1243	300	45	7	91	632	218	224	267	18	320	20	1	14	8	7	.53	13	.241	.380	.508

	1987 SEASON											FOUR YEAR TOTALS (1984 – 1987)										
	Ave.	OBP	SLG	AB	H	2B	3B	HR	RBI	BB	SO	Ave.	OBP	SLG	AB	H	2B	3B	HR	RBI	BB	SO
Totals	.259	.410	.548	332	86	13	1	27	68	80	75	.245	.394	.525	1081	265	41	5	84	207	253	277
vs. Left	.270	.451	.622	37	10	4	0	3	8	11	8	.226	.373	.411	146	33	10	1	5	28	28	39
vs. Right	.258	.405	.539	295	76	9	1	24	60	69	67	.248	.397	.543	935	232	31	4	79	179	225	238
at Home	.232	.394	.555	164	38	6	1	15	36	42	34	.252	.396	.564	555	140	21	4	48	118	126	136
on Road	.286	.427	.542	168	48	7	0	12	32	38	41	.238	.391	.485	526	125	20	1	36	89	127	141
vs. Groundball	.284	.409	.582	194	55	7	0	17	42	39	43	.255	.392	.538	550	140	16	1	46	111	121	126
vs. Flyball	.225	.412	.500	138	31	6	1	10	26	41	32	.235	.395	.512	531	125	25	4	38	96	132	151
vs. Finesse	.270	.419	.546	174	47	7	1	13	33	42	32	.269	.401	.583	609	164	25	2	54	128	129	125
vs. Power	.247	.401	.551	158	39	6	0	14	35	38	43	.214	.385	.451	472	101	16	3	30	79	124	152
on Grass	.279	.405	.535	129	36	6	0	9	24	25	32	.220	.373	.447	418	92	11	0	28	59	97	115
on Artificial Turf	.246	.414	.557	203	50	7	1	18	44	55	43	.261	.407	.575	663	173	30	5	56	148	156	162
Day Games	.299	.415	.639	97	29	6	0	9	16	18	21	.250	.380	.549	284	71	13	0	24	47	56	67
Night Games	.243	.408	.511	235	57	7	1	18	52	62	54	.243	.398	.517	797	194	28	5	60	160	197	210
April	.328	.452	.707	58	19	1	0	7	18	14	15	.280	.416	.660	100	28	2	0	12	26	24	30
May	.258	.390	.636	66	17	4	0	7	15	15	14	.238	.379	.622	164	39	4	1	19	39	38	44
June	.182	.348	.182	55	10	0	0	0	3	11	9	.222	.369	.425	207	46	9	0	11	31	45	46
July	.222	.333	.361	36	8	2	0	1	4	4	13	.259	.412	.530	185	48	11	0	13	35	46	48
August	.283	.473	.736	53	15	4	1	6	15	19	9	.241	.379	.491	232	56	9	2	15	39	51	57
Sept/Oct	.266	.429	.578	64	17	2	0	6	13	17	15	.249	.404	.518	193	48	6	2	14	37	49	52
Bases Empty	.263	.383	.575	179	47	8	0	16	16	29	39	.249	.359	.531	590	147	23	1	47	47	95	141
Leadoff	.253	.367	.614	83	21	3	0	9	9	13	17	.232	.348	.494	259	60	11	0	19	19	44	68
Not Leadoff	.271	.397	.542	96	26	5	0	7	7	16	22	.263	.368	.559	331	87	12	1	28	28	51	73
Runners On	.255	.438	.516	153	39	5	1	11	52	51	36	.240	.424	.519	491	118	18	4	37	160	158	136
First Base Only	.279	.437	.632	68	19	1	1	7	15	19	15	.252	.414	.541	218	55	5	2	18	39	60	54
Scoring Position	.235	.439	.424	85	20	4	0	4	37	32	21	.231	.432	.502	273	63	13	2	19	121	98	82
Late Innings, Close	.156	.372	.281	32	5	1	0	1	4	11	13	.200	.380	.445	155	31	2	0	12	25	45	48

RBI/Opportunities

Scoring Position	30 / 140 (21%)	88 / 447 (20%)
Scoring Position, 2 Out	12 / 74 (16%)	27 / 216 (13%)
On Third, Less than 2 Out	11 / 29 (38%)	35 / 86 (41%)
RBI in close games / RBI Total	32 / 68 (47%)	128 / 207 (62%)

Tony Phillips
Oakland Athletics

Tony Phillips is a fine athlete with skills to get on base and score runs. Phillips first reached the majors with Oakland in 1982, playing more at shortstop than second base for the Athletics until Alfredo Griffin arrived in 1985. The A's have selected Phillips (repeatedly) as their regular second baseman and leadoff batter in recent seasons, only to see their plans dashed by a plague of injuries. In 1985 he broke his foot—twice. In 1986 he suffered a season-ending leg injury in August, and in 1987 a July arm injury did him in.

Bill James' Favorite Toy model of established major league performance shows a big difference between what we can expect in a typical year from Phillips as compared to his counterpart, Tony Bernazard. Also included for comparison is a theoretical full year (524 AB) from Phillips:

	Avg	AB	R	H	HR	RBI	SB	E
Phillips actual	.250	363	53	91	7	43	9	12
Bernazard actual	.272	524	78	143	15	59	14	17
Phillips theoretical	.250	524	77	131	10	62	13	17

Conclusions are obvious: (1) Phillips' injuries over the past three years have had a significant, negative impact on his output, and (2) If Phillips could play a full year, every year, he would have numbers very similar to Bernazard.

This last statement has an ironic context; if Phillips could play a full year, every year, there would not be any analysis here comparing him to Tony Bernazard.

In July of 1987 when Phillips suffered his latest annual calamity, the A's were a contending team with no time to experiment. They promptly acquired Bernazard, who helped the A's somewhat and helped himself immensely. During the 30 games between his acquisition and Phillips' return to the active roster, Bernazard hit .385 with 20 runs scored and 15 RBI. Phillips, in comparison, did little to help himself when he finally did return. His second half numbers amounted to a paltry .188 average in 85 AB.

Tony may have reached his peak in the spring of 1986 when he attracted national attention by hitting over .340 through most of May and leading the league in runs scored. The runs continued coming until his August injury. Arguably, he could have scored 100 with a full season. The A's have decided not to re-sign Bernazard, but Phillips will get new competition from free agent signee Glenn Hubbard. We may yet see the fine major league season that Phillips seems innately capable of producing, but in 1988 Tony will probably have a platoon or utility role. Phillips should be useful in such a capacity, but not the outstanding player he could easily be if he could remain healthy.

John C. Benson

Phillips, Keith Anthony "Tony"   Bats: Both   Throws: Right   Born 04/25/59

1987 SEASON AND MAJOR-LEAGUE CAREER BATTING TOTALS

	G	AB	H	2B	3B	HR	TB	R	RBI	TBB	IBB	SO	HP	SH	SF	SB	CS	SB%	GDP	AVG	OBP	SLG
87 OAK	111	379	91	20	0	10	141	48	46	57	1	76	0	2	3	7	6	.54	9	.240	.337	.372
6 YEARS	613	1925	488	84	15	27	683	274	195	248	3	374	7	37	15	53	32	.62	22	.254	.338	.355

	1987 SEASON										FOUR YEAR TOTALS (1984 – 1987)									
	Ave.	OBP	SLG	AB	H	2B	3B	HR	RBI	BB	SO	Ave.	OBP	SLG	AB	H	2B	3B	HR	RBI	BB	SO
Totals	.240	.337	.372	379	91	20	0	10	46	57	76	.258	.343	.369	1432	369	70	10	23	152	188	278
vs. Left	.289	.403	.383	128	37	3	0	3	16	25	17	.313	.396	.427	473	148	21	3	9	58	67	58
vs. Right	.215	.302	.367	251	54	17	0	7	30	32	59	.230	.315	.340	959	221	49	7	14	94	121	220
at Home	.251	.351	.383	175	44	8	0	5	19	28	40	.241	.331	.350	688	166	33	3	12	78	94	141
on Road	.230	.325	.363	204	47	12	0	5	27	29	36	.273	.353	.386	744	203	37	7	11	74	94	137
vs. Groundball	.206	.302	.314	194	40	12	0	3	15	27	47	.241	.324	.337	692	167	35	5	7	63	85	141
vs. Flyball	.276	.373	.432	185	51	8	0	7	31	30	29	.273	.360	.399	740	202	35	5	16	89	103	137
vs. Finesse	.251	.333	.369	187	47	10	0	4	21	24	40	.263	.334	.369	776	204	41	4	11	71	87	132
vs. Power	.229	.341	.375	192	44	10	0	6	25	33	36	.252	.352	.369	656	165	29	6	12	81	101	146
on Grass	.248	.342	.385	314	78	16	0	9	43	46	63	.258	.341	.368	1214	313	59	6	21	137	157	233
on Artificial Turf	.200	.316	.308	65	13	4	0	1	3	11	13	.257	.351	.372	218	56	11	4	2	15	31	45
Day Games	.192	.285	.232	125	24	5	0	0	7	17	24	.239	.325	.333	507	121	21	6	5	53	67	103
Night Games	.264	.363	.441	254	67	15	0	10	39	40	52	.268	.352	.388	925	248	49	4	18	99	121	175
April	.266	.396	.392	79	21	4	0	2	6	17	11	.287	.401	.371	178	51	9	0	2	11	34	32
May	.235	.323	.376	85	20	6	0	2	9	11	21	.278	.349	.390	277	77	12	2	5	30	30	49
June	.247	.348	.412	97	24	4	0	4	16	15	17	.212	.304	.294	293	62	8	2	4	29	39	55
July	.303	.378	.394	33	10	3	0	0	4	4	9	.284	.381	.410	229	65	18	1	3	29	36	41
August	.182	.357	.273	11	2	1	0	0	0	3	3	.225	.327	.320	178	40	8	3	1	13	27	39
Sept/Oct	.189	.250	.297	74	14	2	0	2	11	7	15	.267	.318	.422	277	74	15	2	8	40	22	62
Bases Empty	.212	.309	.301	236	50	9	0	4	4	33	52	.241	.325	.341	910	219	37	6	14	14	113	181
Leadoff	.189	.280	.242	95	18	5	0	0	0	12	16	.239	.329	.330	427	102	19	1	6	6	57	77
Not Leadoff	.227	.327	.340	141	32	4	0	4	4	21	36	.242	.321	.350	483	117	18	5	8	8	56	104
Runners On	.287	.382	.490	143	41	11	0	6	42	24	24	.287	.375	.418	522	150	33	4	9	138	75	97
First Base Only	.302	.413	.587	63	19	6	0	4	11	12	14	.284	.366	.418	208	59	14	1	4	15	27	37
Scoring Position	.275	.358	.412	80	22	5	0	2	31	12	10	.290	.381	.417	314	91	19	3	5	123	48	60
Late Innings, Close	.242	.342	.530	66	16	4	0	5	18	11	14	.281	.387	.447	228	64	16	2	6	35	41	46

RBI/Opportunities

	1987		Four Year	
Scoring Position	25 / 104	(24%)	106 / 433	(24%)
Scoring Position, 2 Out	9 / 49	(18%)	39 / 194	(20%)
On Third, Less than 2 Out	10 / 16	(63%)	36 / 70	(51%)
RBI in close games / RBI Total	32 / 46	(70%)	91 / 152	(60%)

Dan Plesac
Milwaukee Brewers

Dan Plesac, who was drafted in the first round in '83, is one of five Milwaukee #1 draft picks on the team. The others are Yount ('73), Molitor ('77), Sveum ('82) and Surhoff ('85). They're not simply on the team—they *are* the team.

On the strength of Dan's 1986, Milwaukee made him their closer this year. His stats are a good illustration of what happens when a quality pitcher moves from setup man to closer. Despite having six more appearances, he pitched fewer innings this year. Since he entered more games when Milwaukee had the lead in 1987, he lost about the same number of games as he did in 1986, but had fewer wins and more saves. Since he didn't have to worry about pacing himself, he could fire the ball more—his hits per innings dropped and his strikeouts per nine innings rose. Finally, since a closer stays in the game come what may (unlike a setup man, who gets yanked when trouble strikes), other Milwaukee relievers didn't get a chance to allow the men that Plesac did put on to score. Result: Even though he had a slump (which was due to an injury) toward the end of 1987, Dan's ERA dropped.

The injury caused Dan several kinds of trouble in 1987; it will be interesting to see how he bounces back from it in 1988. Aside from hurting his September stats, it earned him a spot in manager Tom Trebelhorn's doghouse. When Dan got hurt, he tried to come back too soon, got shelled and then reinjured his arm. Trebelhorn gave him a good chewing out and put him on the bench for another two weeks. That gave Chuck Crim and Dave Stapleton a chance to shine. The competition for ace reliever could be much more intense in 1988 than you might think.

It may even push Plesac into the rotation, which would not be as odd a move as it sounds. Dan was a starter in the minors and was slated to be the fifth starter when he hit the majors in 1986. But in April, while the schedule was still light, he was sent to the bullpen to get his feet wet. He did so well there that he never left. With starters at such a premium—especially the left-handed variety—Milwaukee may decide to make the switch if they feel that Crim can carry the closer's load. Since Plesac has been successful as a starter, and seems to have the physical ability for the job, I think it would be the right decision to make. Why settle for 100 innings and 25 saves when you can get 250 innings and 15 wins?

But if Milwaukee does it, they should do it before Dan gets too comfortable in the bullpen. It wouldn't be an easy transition for him; he's already developed a reliever's mentality that would be tough to shake. And even if he can handle another switch, you really shouldn't keep such a talented pitcher wondering what his role is any longer than you have to.

Scott Segrin

Plesac, Daniel Thomas "Dan" Bats: Left Throws: Left Born 02/04/62

1987 SEASON AND MAJOR-LEAGUE CAREER PITCHING TOTALS

	G	GS	CG	GF	IP	BFP	H	R	ER	HR	SH	SF	HB	TBB	IBB	SO	WP	Bk	W	L	Pct	ShO	Sv	ERA
87 MIL	57	0	0	47	79	325	63	30	23	8	1	2	3	23	1	89	6	0	5	6	.455	0	23	2.62
2 YEARS	108	0	0	80	170	702	144	64	53	13	7	7	3	52	2	164	10	0	15	13	.536	0	37	2.81

1987: Power, Flyball   1986: Power, Flyball

1987 SEASON

	G	IP	H	BB	SO	SB	CS	W	L	S	ERA
Totals	57	79.1	63	23	89	4	2	5	6	23	2.61
at Home	27	35.1	30	6	43	3	1	2	2	9	3.31
on Road	30	44.0	33	17	46	1	1	3	4	14	2.05
on Grass	23	28.2	20	7	39	0	1	1	2	10	2.20
on Artificial Turf	34	50.2	43	16	50	4	1	4	4	13	2.84
Day Games	48	68.2	52	20	80	4	2	5	4	18	2.75
Night Games	9	10.2	11	3	9	0	0	0	2	5	1.69
April	10	13.2	7	3	14	0	0	0	0	7	0.66
May	9	9.1	8	5	13	2	0	0	0	4	0.96
June	13	19.0	12	5	26	0	1	4	0	5	1.89
July	11	18.1	18	7	18	2	1	1	4	4	4.91
August	8	13.1	7	1	14	0	0	0	0	2	1.35
Sept/Oct	6	5.2	11	2	4	0	0	0	2	1	7.94

vs. Opponent Batters	Ave.	OBP	SLG	AB	H	2B	3B	HR	RBI	BB	SO
Totals	.213	.275	.318	296	63	7	0	8	44	23	89
vs. Left	.145	.226	.291	55	8	2	0	2	7	6	19
vs. Right	.228	.286	.324	241	55	5	0	6	37	17	70
Bases Empty	.176	.241	.216	153	27	3	0	1	1	11	48
Leadoff	.153	.219	.254	59	9	3	0	1	1	4	20
Not Leadoff	.191	.255	.191	94	18	0	0	0	0	7	28
Runners On Base	.252	.310	.427	143	36	4	0	7	43	12	41
First Base Only	.234	.300	.391	64	15	1	0	3	6	6	23
Scoring Position	.266	.318	.456	79	21	3	0	4	37	6	18
Late Innings, Close	.241	.308	.370	216	52	7	0	7	40	19	60

FOUR YEAR TOTALS (1984 – 1987)

	G	IP	H	BB	SO	SB	CS	W	L	S	ERA
Totals	108	170.1	144	52	164	10	6	15	13	37	2.80
at Home	53	85.2	80	23	86	9	2	8	5	15	3.47
on Road	55	84.2	64	29	78	1	4	7	8	22	2.13
on Grass	39	58.1	47	17	62	5	3	3	3	15	2.78
on Artificial Turf	69	112.0	97	35	102	5	3	12	10	22	2.81
Day Games	93	148.2	123	46	146	10	6	14	10	30	3.03
Night Games	15	21.2	21	6	18	0	0	1	3	7	1.25
April	15	23.1	13	6	22	1	1	1	1	7	2.31
May	16	26.2	25	10	26	2	1	2	2	7	2.36
June	23	31.0	22	10	35	0	1	5	2	9	2.03
July	18	31.0	31	12	26	7	1	2	5	6	4.35
August	19	33.2	23	7	34	0	0	4	0	3	1.60
Sept/Oct	17	24.2	30	7	21	0	2	1	3	5	4.38

vs. Opponent Batters	Ave.	OBP	SLG	AB	H	2B	3B	HR	RBI	BB	SO
Totals	.227	.288	.330	634	144	18	4	13	82	52	164
vs. Left	.215	.291	.333	135	29	5	1	3	20	15	36
vs. Right	.230	.287	.329	499	115	13	3	10	62	37	128
Bases Empty	.216	.274	.287	324	70	10	2	3	3	24	88
Leadoff	.221	.264	.324	136	30	6	1	2	2	7	32
Not Leadoff	.213	.282	.261	188	40	4	1	1	1	17	56
Runners On Base	.239	.302	.374	310	74	8	2	10	79	28	76
First Base Only	.238	.298	.369	130	31	3	1	4	10	11	31
Scoring Position	.239	.305	.378	180	43	5	1	6	69	17	45
Late Innings, Close	.242	.308	.360	422	102	16	2	10	65	38	106

RBI/Opportunities

Scoring Position	27 / 114 (24%)	56 / 262 (21%)
Scoring Position, 2 Out	13 / 57 (23%)	21 / 132 (16%)
On Third, Less than 2 Out	8 / 21 (38%)	21 / 49 (43%)
RBI in close games / RBI Total	40 / 44 (91%)	66 / 82 (80%)

Luis Polonia
Oakland Athletics

Luis Polonia had not really been considered much of a prospect until spring training in 1987. He had done well in AAA in 1986 and was slated to play another full season at Tacoma because he was still young and the A's had a surplus of outfielders at the major league level. All those plans changed after Luis had an impressive spring training and an early-season collision put both Mike Davis and Dwayne Murphy out of action.

Luis opened some eyes with his penchant for slashing doubles and triples into the gaps and his all-out style of play. Extra base hits don't come easy in this ballpark and have been a rare commodity since the glory days of the early seventies. For three months, Oakland fans had the pleasure of seeing Luis play every day, and he took full advantage of the opportunity. Although he slumped later in the year and was benched for a while, he recovered strongly enough to finish third on the team after McGwire and Lansford in batting. He certainly eased the pain of losing Mike Davis to free agency, and now the A's say they have no interest in signing Murphy. It looks like Polonia's replacement job has become permanent. His ten triples (second in the league) were the most for an Oakland player since Phil Gar-

ner hit 12 in 1976. The 22-year-old also led the team in stolen bases despite appearing in only 125 games. His SB% of 78 percent was very respectable, as well.

Luis is an enthusiastic but very green defensive player. He doesn't seem to judge the distance of line drives very well and does not get a good jump on the ball. An upcoming shift to right could help, and with his speed, work ethic, and the security of a guaranteed position, he should only get better.

Because of his size, 5' 8", 155 pounds, Polonia was not considered much of an amateur prospect. The A's organization acquired him almost as a second thought. He speaks English quite well, having taught himself as a child in anticipation of playing baseball here. As he tells it, he talked the A's into signing him to their rookie team for Latin American players by offering to double as interpreter.

Luis is confident—some would say cocky—but sweet natured and outgoing. He has been observed singing along with the National Anthem before games, and projects an aura of being very much his own man and comfortable with himself.

Susan Nelson

Polonia, Luis Andrew (Almonte)

Bats: Both   Throws: Left   Born 10/12/64

1987 SEASON AND MAJOR-LEAGUE CAREER BATTING TOTALS

	G	AB	H	2B	3B	HR	TB	R	RBI	TBB	IBB	SO	HP	SH	SF	SB	CS	SB%	GDP	AVG	OBP	SLG
87 OAK	125	435	125	16	10	4	173	78	49	32	1	64	0	1	1	29	7	.81	4	.287	.335	.398
1 YEAR	125	435	125	16	10	4	173	78	49	32	1	64	0	1	1	29	7	.81	4	.287	.335	.398

1987 SEASON

	Ave.	OBP	SLG	AB	H	2B	3B	HR	RBI	BB	SO
Totals	.287	.335	.398	435	125	16	10	4	49	32	64
vs. Left	.236	.292	.326	89	21	2	3	0	8	7	17
vs. Right	.301	.347	.416	346	104	14	7	4	41	25	47
at Home	.258	.312	.364	217	56	12	4	1	22	17	31
on Road	.317	.359	.431	218	69	4	6	3	27	15	33
vs. Groundball	.243	.269	.348	230	56	8	5	2	24	8	33
vs. Flyball	.337	.404	.454	205	69	8	5	2	25	24	31
vs. Finesse	.253	.298	.346	237	60	7	6	1	28	15	31
vs. Power	.328	.380	.460	198	65	9	4	3	21	17	33
on Grass	.292	.343	.386	373	109	15	7	2	42	29	53
on Artificial Turf	.258	.288	.468	62	16	1	3	2	7	3	11
Day Games	.242	.293	.314	153	37	9	1	0	11	11	30
Night Games	.312	.359	.443	282	88	7	9	4	38	21	34
April	.208	.296	.417	24	5	0	1	1	3	3	2
May	.407	.453	.610	59	24	4	1	2	10	5	13
June	.289	.347	.344	90	26	3	1	0	8	8	9
July	.324	.336	.414	111	36	6	2	0	16	2	15
August	.186	.183	.329	70	13	2	4	0	7	0	14
Sept/Oct	.259	.368	.333	81	21	1	1	1	5	14	11
Bases Empty	.258	.324	.367	264	68	7	8	2	2	26	47
Leadoff	.256	.322	.354	164	42	4	3	2	2	16	30
Not Leadoff	.260	.327	.390	100	26	3	5	0	0	10	17
Runners On	.333	.354	.444	171	57	9	2	2	47	6	17
First Base Only	.328	.349	.475	61	20	3	0	2	5	2	3
Scoring Position	.336	.357	.427	110	37	6	2	0	42	4	14
Late Innings, Close	.300	.323	.367	60	18	2	1	0	7	2	13

FOUR YEAR TOTALS (1984 – 1987)

	Ave.	OBP	SLG	AB	H	2B	3B	HR	RBI	BB	SO
Totals	.287	.335	.398	435	125	16	10	4	49	32	64
vs. Left	.236	.292	.326	89	21	2	3	0	8	7	17
vs. Right	.301	.347	.416	346	104	14	7	4	41	25	47
at Home	.258	.312	.364	217	56	12	4	1	22	17	31
on Road	.317	.359	.431	218	69	4	6	3	27	15	33
vs. Groundball	.243	.269	.348	230	56	8	5	2	24	8	33
vs. Flyball	.337	.404	.454	205	69	8	5	2	25	24	31
vs. Finesse	.253	.298	.346	237	60	7	6	1	28	15	31
vs. Power	.328	.380	.460	198	65	9	4	3	21	17	33
on Grass	.292	.343	.386	373	109	15	7	2	42	29	53
on Artificial Turf	.258	.288	.468	62	16	1	3	2	7	3	11
Day Games	.242	.293	.314	153	37	9	1	0	11	11	30
Night Games	.312	.359	.443	282	88	7	9	4	38	21	34
April	.208	.296	.417	24	5	0	1	1	3	3	2
May	.407	.453	.610	59	24	4	1	2	10	5	13
June	.289	.347	.344	90	26	3	1	0	8	8	9
July	.324	.336	.414	111	36	6	2	0	16	2	15
August	.186	.183	.329	70	13	2	4	0	7	0	14
Sept/Oct	.259	.368	.333	81	21	1	1	1	5	14	11
Bases Empty	.258	.324	.367	264	68	7	8	2	2	26	47
Leadoff	.256	.322	.354	164	42	4	3	2	2	16	30
Not Leadoff	.260	.327	.390	100	26	3	5	0	0	10	17
Runners On	.333	.354	.444	171	57	9	2	2	47	6	17
First Base Only	.328	.349	.475	61	20	3	0	2	5	2	3
Scoring Position	.336	.357	.427	110	37	6	2	0	42	4	14
Late Innings, Close	.300	.323	.367	60	18	2	1	0	7	2	13

RBI/Opportunities

Scoring Position	42 / 135	(31%)
Scoring Position, 2 Out	16 / 61	(26%)
On Third, Less than 2 Out	14 / 29	(48%)
RBI in close games / RBI Total	30 / 49	(61%)

	42 / 135	(31%)
	16 / 61	(26%)
	14 / 29	(48%)
	30 / 49	(61%)

Ted Power
Cincinnati Reds

Ted Power pitched himself off the Reds in late August and September of last year. Over his last eight starts he went 0–6 with a 5.20 earned run average. Until August 25 he was the ace of the Reds' disappointing staff, with a 10–7 record. He didn't miss a start all year, chalked up one complete-game shutout, and left four other games without having yielded an earned run.

Power pitched more innings (204) than any other Reds' pitcher in 1987, an impressive feat considering 1987 was his first year as a full time starter in the NL. As the Reds' bullpen closer in 1985 he'd battled a propensity for bases on balls. By 1987, starting every fifth day, Power had won that battle, striking out just about two hitters for each that he walked. But he gave up home runs in bundles, 28 in 204 innings. (Home runs were contagious on the Cincinnati staff. The top four starters, Power, Tom Browning, Bill Gullickson and Guy Hoffman, served up 108 in 710 2/3 innings, or 1.6 every 9 innings.)

After San Francisco acquired Rick Reuschel from the Pirates for their pennant push, the Reds also began to cast about for pitching help. Supposedly the Yankees had agreed in late August to take Power for Dennis Rasmussen; then, the Reds' owner, marvelous Marge Schott, vetoed trading Ted because of his "high civic profile" in Cincinnati, so the Reds substituted Bill Gullickson. Power had his last "qual-ity" start of the season on August 25 when he gave up just four hits in a 1–0 loss in Pittsburgh. Talk about not trading a guy at the peak of his value!

When the Reds finally did trade Power, it was along with Kurt Stillwell to Kansas City for pitcher Danny Jackson and an infielder of marginal value, Angel Salazar. In other words, in August, New York would have accepted Ted Power even-up for Dennis Rasmussen; by the end of the season all Power would bring by himself was Salazar. (The Cincinnati papers led local fans to believe that the Royals were offering Jackson straight up for Stillwell off and on throughout 1987, and that the Reds wouldn't make the deal, choosing to hold onto their young talent at least during the season. Of course, in retrospect, Rasmussen for Gullickson wasn't too bad for the Reds, since Wild Bill decided to earn his Ph.D. in sushi-making this winter.)

The Reds expect a lot from Jackson, but they gave up quite a bit: 204 innings in Power's arm and a young every-day shortstop. Giving up Power throws their rotation a little out of whack. It will feature at least three lefties for sure (Jackson, Browning, Rasmussen) and maybe a fourth (Guy Hoffman).

Sometimes what really counts is not just who you trade away and receive in return, but when.

Mike Marrero

Power, Ted Henry   Bats: Right   Throws: Right   Born 01/31/55

1987 SEASON AND MAJOR-LEAGUE CAREER PITCHING TOTALS

	G	GS	CG	GF	IP	BFP	H	R	ER	HR	SH	SF	HB	TBB	IBB	SO	WP	Bk	W	L	Pct	ShO	Sv	ERA
87 CIN	34	34	2	0	204	887	213	115	102	28	8	7	3	71	7	133	3	2	10	13	.435	1	0	4.50
7 YEARS	298	56	3	141	681	2928	660	333	299	61	40	34	7	293	40	430	16	6	44	42	.512	1	41	3.95

1987: Finesse, Flyball   **1986: Power, Flyball**   **1985: Power, Flyball**   **1984: Power, Flyball**

1987 SEASON

	G	IP	H	BB	SO	SB	CS	W	L	S	ERA
Totals	34	204.0	213	71	133	20	6	10	13	0	4.50
at Home	16	85.0	98	35	56	7	1	3	5	0	5.72
on Road	18	119.0	115	36	77	13	5	7	8	0	3.63
on Grass	11	73.1	66	19	53	4	3	4	4	0	4.30
on Artificial Turf	23	130.2	147	52	80	16	3	6	9	0	4.61
Day Games	10	67.1	62	23	43	3	3	5	3	0	3.61
Night Games	24	136.2	151	48	90	17	3	5	10	0	4.94
April	5	28.0	26	9	16	1	1	2	0	0	3.54
May	6	41.0	38	14	31	3	1	2	2	0	3.95
June	5	35.0	38	8	21	2	0	2	1	0	3.86
July	6	31.1	38	9	22	7	1	2	2	0	6.03
August	6	35.2	33	15	22	4	2	2	4	0	4.04
Sept/Oct	6	33.0	40	16	21	3	1	0	4	0	5.73

vs. Opponent Batters	Ave.	OBP	SLG	AB	H	2B	3B	HR	RBI	BB	SO
Totals	.267	.327	.439	798	213	49	2	28	108	71	133
vs. Left	.285	.347	.440	425	121	29	2	11	56	44	71
vs. Right	.247	.302	.437	373	92	20	0	17	52	27	62
Bases Empty	.267	.322	.446	457	122	30	2	16	16	35	69
Leadoff	.263	.319	.407	194	51	14	1	4	4	16	28
Not Leadoff	.270	.324	.475	263	71	16	1	12	12	19	41
Runners On Base	.267	.332	.428	341	91	19	0	12	92	36	64
First Base Only	.255	.338	.416	137	35	7	0	5	14	16	24
Scoring Position	.275	.329	.436	204	56	12	0	7	78	20	40
Late Innings, Close	.289	.373	.356	45	13	3	0	0	0	5	5

FOUR YEAR TOTALS (1984 – 1987)

	G	IP	H	BB	SO	SB	CS	W	L	S	ERA
Totals	232	521.2	486	214	351	43	19	37	32	39	3.66
at Home	125	256.2	259	106	170	20	9	17	15	20	4.00
on Road	107	265.0	227	108	181	23	10	20	17	19	3.36
on Grass	78	176.1	157	76	122	8	9	12	8	14	3.93
on Artificial Turf	154	345.1	329	138	229	35	10	25	24	25	3.54
Day Games	60	154.1	136	70	100	6	7	13	9	11	3.67
Night Games	172	367.1	350	144	251	37	12	24	23	28	3.68
April	32	60.2	66	28	39	3	2	3	3	3	4.15
May	40	90.2	67	34	70	9	4	5	3	7	2.98
June	39	83.0	85	36	52	4	0	6	8	7	4.01
July	38	78.1	73	29	47	9	1	5	3	6	3.91
August	39	81.1	82	39	57	13	5	7	7	2	4.32
Sept/Oct	44	127.2	113	48	86	5	7	11	8	14	3.17

vs. Opponent Batters	Ave.	OBP	SLG	AB	H	2B	3B	HR	RBI	BB	SO
Totals	.250	.324	.377	1946	486	92	7	47	254	214	351
vs. Left	.268	.351	.405	954	256	53	7	21	127	125	162
vs. Right	.232	.297	.350	992	230	39	0	26	127	89	189
Bases Empty	.248	.312	.371	1045	259	51	3	24	24	96	173
Leadoff	.268	.328	.379	456	122	28	1	7	7	41	69
Not Leadoff	.233	.300	.365	589	137	23	2	17	17	55	104
Runners On Base	.252	.337	.383	901	227	41	4	23	230	118	178
First Base Only	.257	.329	.399	346	89	14	1	11	28	36	62
Scoring Position	.249	.342	.373	555	138	27	3	12	202	82	116
Late Innings, Close	.268	.358	.372	530	142	22	3	9	74	73	82

RBI/Opportunities

	1987	Four Year
Scoring Position	68 / 257 (26%)	179 / 818 (22%)
Scoring Position, 2 Out	27 / 117 (23%)	72 / 360 (20%)
On Third, Less than 2 Out	22 / 36 (61%)	66 / 149 (44%)
RBI in close games / RBI Total	84 / 108 (78%)	172 / 254 (68%)

Jim Presley
Seattle Mariners

Remember all those major league strikeout records set by the Mariners in 1986? Most Ks by a club in a 9-inning game, most Ks by both clubs in a 9-inning game, most Ks by a club in 2 consecutive games, and, of course, the most Ks by an AL team in a year. Remember all that? I do, and it was the best thing that could have happened to the Mariners!

Yeah, it's true, the "Rocket" did the Mariners a favor. All that negative notoriety on that cool April night in Fenway was the last straw and the M's went shopping for a new manager. Now call this sour grapes if you want, but any strikeout pitcher who was on top of his game that night would have gotten the record. Just think what damage Langston could have done to his own teammates!

One complete season later, under Dick Williams, the M's have gone from being the worst free swingers to being nearly the best. In 1987, only 2 clubs in the majors had fewer Ks than the Ms. The Mariners SO/AB ratio improved by a whopping 33.27 percent. Only Montreal came remotely close to the M's "swing" in strikeout stats. Why? Because no one was left of that 4/29/86 lineup except Ken Phelps, Phil Bradley, and Jim Presley.

In 1987, Presley's SO/AB ratio improved, but only by 2.26 percent. His strikeouts are tolerated because Jim is a power hitter and the Ks are a normal part of being a slugger. However, Presley's offensive production dropped off somewhat in a year that the Mariners set all kinds of offensive club records.

Things didn't go well for Pres from the onset of spring training where he was a contract holdout. It didn't last long, but it seemed to take a toll on the talented third baseman. Shortly thereafter, a bout with food poisoning or a stomach disorder, put Presley in the hospital. After that, he just never seemed to fully recover and ended the year with a set of disappointing stats compared to his past record.

There have been trade rumors spurred by the fact that Pres has high market value and there is a talented youngster breathing down his neck. Edgar Martinez not only fields exceptionally well, but has Wade Boggs' discipline at the plate. Hey, we're talking 356 BB versus 201 SO in 1,851 minor league AB and a .372 BA in his 43 major league AB.

Trouble is, the Mariners are short in right-handed HR pop and really can't afford to deal away Presley's power stats from that side of the plate. For the first time in two years, Presley doesn't have a lock on third base and the competition for the spot in spring training should be intense. One possible solution that Williams has suggested is playing Pres at third against righties, and against lefties, playing Martinez at third and Presley as the DH. That would keep Presley's bat in the order while giving his understudy opportunity to steal the show.

Merrianna McCully

Presley, James Arthur "Jim"   Bats: Right   Throws: Right   Born 10/23/61

1987 SEASON AND MAJOR-LEAGUE CAREER BATTING TOTALS

	G	AB	H	2B	3B	HR	TB	R	RBI	TBB	IBB	SO	HP	SH	SF	SB	CS	SB%	GDP	AVG	OBP	SLG
87 SEA	152	575	142	23	6	24	249	78	88	38	1	157	4	1	4	2	0	1.00	15	.247	.296	.433
4 YEARS	532	2012	519	101	12	89	911	259	315	120	14	492	10	5	19	5	7	.42	66	.258	.300	.453

	1987 SEASON											FOUR YEAR TOTALS (1984 – 1987)										
	Ave.	OBP	SLG	AB	H	2B	3B	HR	RBI	BB	SO	Ave.	OBP	SLG	AB	H	2B	3B	HR	RBI	BB	SO
Totals	.247	.296	.433	575	142	23	6	24	88	38	157	.258	.300	.453	2013	519	101	12	89	315	120	492
vs. Left	.268	.310	.426	190	51	13	1	5	23	12	41	.289	.332	.474	589	170	34	3	23	85	39	132
vs. Right	.236	.289	.436	385	91	10	5	19	65	26	116	.245	.287	.444	1424	349	67	9	66	230	81	360
at Home	.257	.295	.455	288	74	16	4	11	43	13	80	.269	.312	.473	1029	277	64	7	44	159	59	245
on Road	.237	.297	.411	287	68	7	2	13	45	25	77	.246	.288	.431	984	242	37	5	45	156	61	247
vs. Groundball	.260	.313	.422	296	77	14	2	10	46	19	66	.258	.307	.418	944	244	50	4	31	144	61	215
vs. Flyball	.233	.279	.444	279	65	9	4	14	42	19	91	.257	.294	.483	1069	275	51	8	58	171	59	277
vs. Finesse	.256	.296	.449	305	78	15	1	14	55	16	65	.255	.292	.442	1124	287	64	4	46	170	57	222
vs. Power	.237	.297	.415	270	64	8	5	10	33	22	92	.261	.311	.466	889	232	37	8	43	145	63	270
on Grass	.258	.317	.443	221	57	6	1	11	39	19	59	.243	.286	.432	760	185	26	3	37	124	47	188
on Artificial Turf	.240	.283	.427	354	85	17	5	13	49	19	98	.267	.309	.465	1253	334	75	9	52	191	73	304
Day Games	.239	.314	.387	142	34	5	2	4	19	14	45	.269	.321	.486	484	130	23	5	24	86	34	121
Night Games	.249	.290	.448	433	108	18	4	20	69	24	112	.254	.293	.442	1529	389	78	7	65	229	86	371
April	.261	.309	.443	88	23	2	1	4	16	4	22	.227	.281	.416	238	54	7	1	12	38	16	64
May	.277	.321	.525	101	28	3	2	6	21	7	34	.293	.323	.507	304	89	19	2	14	51	14	79
June	.240	.277	.423	104	25	3	2	4	13	5	32	.292	.340	.566	332	97	20	4	21	62	24	83
July	.233	.247	.333	90	21	3	0	2	6	1	25	.249	.279	.403	385	96	16	2	13	40	15	100
August	.229	.288	.459	109	25	8	1	5	18	9	27	.238	.280	.407	361	86	22	3	11	55	21	79
Sept/Oct	.241	.337	.398	83	20	4	0	3	14	12	17	.247	.300	.427	393	97	17	0	18	69	30	87
Bases Empty	.244	.287	.403	308	75	10	3	11	11	18	83	.257	.291	.445	1088	280	51	6	47	47	50	264
Leadoff	.210	.260	.412	119	25	2	2	6	6	7	34	.254	.279	.458	448	114	20	4	21	21	14	93
Not Leadoff	.265	.305	.397	189	50	8	1	5	5	11	49	.259	.299	.436	640	166	31	2	26	26	36	171
Runners On	.251	.306	.468	267	67	13	3	13	77	20	74	.258	.311	.462	925	239	50	6	42	268	70	228
First Base Only	.221	.264	.452	104	23	4	1	6	13	5	35	.233	.270	.428	416	97	16	1	21	49	20	99
Scoring Position	.270	.332	.479	163	44	9	2	7	64	15	39	.279	.343	.489	509	142	34	5	21	219	50	129
Late Innings, Close	.250	.313	.513	76	19	1	2	5	13	7	21	.244	.302	.449	287	70	10	2	15	46	24	76

RBI/Opportunities

Scoring Position	53 / 212 (25%)	182 / 685 (27%)
Scoring Position, 2 Out	28 / 106 (26%)	83 / 329 (25%)
On Third, Less than 2 Out	12 / 34 (35%)	53 / 122 (43%)
RBI in close games / RBI Total	59 / 88 (67%)	193 / 315 (61%)

Kirby Puckett
Minnesota Twins

The 1987 season, capped by the Twins' World Series victory, has given casual baseball fans and non-fans everywhere a chance to see one of my favorite players and one of the sport's most exciting young stars, Kirby Puckett. Even if you can forget Puckett's Gold Glove skills as an outfielder and his immense skills at the plate, you can't ignore the enthusiasm and joy he seems to bring to a game. They can be worth the price of admission, and are, for me, what the game is—or should be—about.

Sure, Puckett was a known figure before 1987, thanks to his explosion as a power and high-average hitter in 1986, just his third in the majors. But Kirby's 1986 stats were so different from what he'd done his first two seasons, some feared he might be a fluke. I mean, who was that guy masquerading as Kirby Puckett? Where was the guy who hit .296 in 1984 and .288 in 1985 with a paltry 4 homers in those first 189 games? Could this be the same person who hit .328 in 1986 with 31 homers, 96 RBIs and 119 runs scored? Had to be, no way of mistaking his body type.

Last season showed that Puckett's development into one of the game's premier hitters has apparently been completed. His .332 average was fourth best in the AL. He also hit 28 homers, scored 96 runs and drove in a career-high 99.

Whenever you looked at a top ten batting list, Puckett was always above .300, but 1987 had some sharp differences from his past performances. In prior years, Puckett was a pretty consistent hitter throughout a season. His "worst" month tended to be July, but a .280 lifetime average (through the first three years, anyway) in July isn't bad. This season, there was a stretch through July where he couldn't seem to buy a hit. Between July 7 and Aug. 2, Puckett managed just 18 hits in 85 at bats (.212, 120 points below his season average).

With that kind of slump buried in the middle of his season, his highs had to run off the chart. He hit .424 (42 for 99) between June 8 and July 5 with 20 runs scored in that three-week period, and he also caught fire for the pennant race. From August 3 to the end of the season, Puckett hit .352 with 12 homers in 219 at-bats.

Then, after a poor play-off series against Detroit, Puckett climaxed a good Series with six hits in his final eight at-bats in Games 6 and 7. In a city where they sell Teddy Bears in the image of Kirby Puckett and carve Halloween pumpkins in an image known as Kirby Pumpkin, it was an ideal finish for the ideal player.

Dean Hill

Puckett, Kirby   Bats: Right   Throws: Right   Born 03/14/61

1987 SEASON AND MAJOR-LEAGUE CAREER BATTING TOTALS

	G	AB	H	2B	3B	HR	TB	R	RBI	TBB	IBB	SO	HP	SH	SF	SB	CS	SB%	GDP	AVG	OBP	SLG
87 MIN	157	624	207	32	5	28	333	96	99	32	7	91	6	0	6	12	7	.63	16	.332	.367	.534
4 YEARS	607	2552	794	110	29	63	1151	358	300	123	12	346	21	11	11	67	38	.64	50	.311	.347	.451

	1987 SEASON											FOUR YEAR TOTALS (1984 – 1987)										
	Ave.	OBP	SLG	AB	H	2B	3B	HR	RBI	BB	SO	Ave.	OBP	SLG	AB	H	2B	3B	HR	RBI	BB	SO
Totals	.332	.367	.534	624	207	32	5	28	99	32	91	.311	.347	.451	2552	794	110	29	63	299	123	346
vs. Left	.339	.377	.627	177	60	10	4	11	32	11	24	.335	.366	.509	741	248	38	14	21	93	35	92
vs. Right	.329	.363	.497	447	147	22	1	17	67	21	67	.301	.339	.427	1811	546	72	15	42	206	88	254
at Home	.301	.343	.537	309	93	15	2	18	59	19	44	.330	.369	.485	1283	424	62	17	34	166	68	173
on Road	.362	.390	.530	315	114	17	3	10	40	13	47	.292	.323	.417	1269	370	48	12	29	133	55	173
vs. Groundball	.346	.379	.564	321	111	23	1	15	51	16	32	.310	.349	.454	1241	385	56	16	30	141	67	139
vs. Flyball	.317	.354	.502	303	96	9	4	13	48	16	59	.312	.344	.449	1311	409	54	13	33	158	56	207
vs. Finesse	.335	.375	.519	310	104	15	0	14	53	17	31	.306	.341	.446	1391	425	61	16	34	153	62	144
vs. Power	.328	.358	.548	314	103	17	5	14	46	15	60	.318	.353	.457	1161	369	49	13	29	146	61	202
on Grass	.336	.365	.452	241	81	11	1	5	28	10	41	.295	.324	.408	963	284	38	7	19	102	41	141
on Artificial Turf	.329	.368	.585	383	126	21	4	23	71	22	50	.321	.360	.477	1589	510	72	22	44	197	82	205
Day Games	.377	.400	.618	199	75	11	2	11	34	7	36	.314	.353	.446	757	238	36	5	18	89	36	112
Night Games	.311	.352	.494	425	132	21	3	17	65	25	55	.310	.344	.453	1795	556	74	24	45	210	87	234
April	.354	.407	.622	82	29	2	1	6	15	6	13	.360	.391	.602	264	95	11	4	15	48	12	32
May	.322	.345	.461	115	37	4	0	4	22	4	17	.323	.355	.454	421	136	14	4	11	61	21	54
June	.382	.423	.627	102	39	9	2	4	11	8	17	.312	.338	.420	452	141	22	6	5	32	18	48
July	.245	.295	.357	98	24	3	1	2	12	6	13	.272	.313	.400	437	119	19	5	9	46	25	66
August	.339	.361	.563	112	38	10	0	5	17	4	17	.317	.354	.450	464	147	22	5	10	49	27	72
Sept/Oct	.348	.374	.583	115	40	4	1	7	22	4	14	.304	.331	.442	514	156	22	5	13	63	20	74
Bases Empty	.344	.379	.579	340	117	16	2	20	20	14	46	.304	.335	.437	1603	487	70	13	39	39	70	213
Leadoff	.434	.462	.628	113	49	7	0	5	5	4	11	.317	.349	.423	874	277	33	6	16	16	41	98
Not Leadoff	.300	.338	.555	227	68	9	2	15	15	10	35	.288	.318	.453	729	210	37	7	23	23	29	115
Runners On	.317	.353	.479	284	90	16	3	8	79	18	45	.323	.358	.475	949	307	40	16	24	260	53	133
First Base Only	.347	.382	.581	124	43	10	2	5	16	6	17	.347	.379	.503	392	136	16	6	11	31	19	41
Scoring Position	.294	.331	.400	160	47	6	1	3	65	12	28	.307	.343	.456	557	171	24	10	13	229	34	92
Late Innings, Close	.299	.341	.636	77	23	4	2	6	14	5	10	.297	.335	.459	333	99	6	6	12	49	19	51

RBI/Opportunities

	1987 Season		Four Year Totals	
Scoring Position	59 / 203	(29%)	199 / 701	(28%)
Scoring Position, 2 Out	14 / 71	(20%)	80 / 288	(28%)
On Third, Less than 2 Out	30 / 53	(57%)	73 / 140	(52%)
RBI in close games / RBI Total	72 / 99	(73%)	196 / 299	(66%)

Rey Quinones
Seattle Mariners

That big Boston/Seattle trade made during the pennant race of 1986 was not at all popular in Seattle. After all, the M's traded away lifetime Mariner veterans Dave Henderson and Spike Owen. Spike was considered the nicest guy in Seattle sports next to Seahawk wide receiver Steve Largent. The fans were upset and the press, for the most part, ripped the trade apart. One enraged sportswriter wrote that Lou Gorman (Boston's GM) must have rolled over and had a cigarette after he completed the trade. The Mariners had again traded away the farm! Two local stars, deemed good enough to help take the Red Sox to the Series, were traded for four absolute unknowns.

The Mariners, as usual, patiently explained that it was the young Boston shortstop, Rey Quinones, they were after; everyone would understand the move when they saw Quinones field his position. They further explained that Ted Williams was very high on the 22-year-old's hitting potential. Williams said Rey's swing was so sweet that no one should tamper with it.

Yeah, sure! There he was. Skinny, awkward, and moping around like a kid that just lost his puppy! Sweet swing all right! Finished the season with a .189 batting avg. in 122 at bats. He played his position OK, and there were flickers of brilliance, but for the most part, the fans were not convinced.

If the Seattle fans were disenchanted, just think how Rey felt. One day he was the starting SS on a well known club on its way to the Series. What a thrill for a rookie! Then you're told, "Sorry kid, we love ya, but we feel that we need a veteran SS to take us to the promised land, so clean out your locker. Here's your plane ticket to Seattle." *Seattle . . . last place Seattle!* You bet Rey was disappointed.

Apparently the youngster found his lost puppy over the winter. Rey Quinones emerged from spring training happy and looking like the fellow that Ted Williams had profiled. He was hitting the ball hard and with authority to all fields. He was moving runners and somehow stopping balls that Seattle fans had grown accustomed to seeing scoot through the infield. He was consistent and productive even after the mid-season death of his father—his average hovered around .280 for the entire year. Rey surprised everyone with his display of power in the form of 12 homers and his productive 56 RBIs batting in the number eight position.

Quinones has some faults. He misses signs and occasionally makes a foolish play, but the general feeling, in Seattle, is that he can only get better.

Meanwhile, on the east coast, the BoSox were hurting for someone to fill the void between second and third, and Lou Gorman was checking out his pants pockets. Seems that the Mariners had picked them clean of one talented shortstop during that lusty, one night "quick fix" affair the year before.

Merrianna McCully

Quinones, Rey Francisco (Santiago)

Bats: Right   Throws: Right   Born 11/11/63

1987 SEASON AND MAJOR-LEAGUE CAREER BATTING TOTALS

	G	AB	H	2B	3B	HR	TB	R	RBI	TBB	IBB	SO	HP	SH	SF	SB	CS	SB%	GDP	AVG	OBP	SLG
87 SEA	135	478	132	18	2	12	190	55	56	26	0	71	4	6	3	1	3	.25	14	.276	.317	.397
2 YEARS	233	790	200	34	3	14	282	87	78	50	0	128	7	11	5	5	6	.45	21	.253	.302	.357

	1987 SEASON											FOUR YEAR TOTALS (1984 – 1987)										
	Ave.	OBP	SLG	AB	H	2B	3B	HR	RBI	BB	SO	Ave.	OBP	SLG	AB	H	2B	3B	HR	RBI	BB	SO
Totals	.276	.317	.397	478	132	18	2	12	56	26	71	.253	.302	.357	790	200	34	3	14	78	50	128
vs. Left	.290	.345	.443	131	38	6	1	4	18	10	19	.256	.314	.368	234	60	12	1	4	25	18	41
vs. Right	.271	.306	.380	347	94	12	1	8	38	16	52	.252	.296	.353	556	140	22	2	10	53	32	87
at Home	.330	.372	.466	221	73	7	1	7	34	12	25	.290	.336	.417	379	110	19	1	9	46	23	50
on Road	.230	.268	.339	257	59	11	1	5	22	14	46	.219	.270	.302	411	90	15	2	5	32	27	78
vs. Groundball	.249	.298	.339	245	61	6	2	4	26	15	30	.242	.295	.325	385	93	13	2	5	35	26	54
vs. Flyball	.305	.337	.459	233	71	12	0	8	30	11	41	.264	.308	.388	405	107	21	1	9	43	24	74
vs. Finesse	.277	.303	.419	253	70	11	2	7	28	7	26	.247	.284	.373	445	110	25	2	9	44	20	57
vs. Power	.276	.332	.373	225	62	7	0	5	28	19	45	.261	.324	.336	345	90	9	1	5	34	30	71
on Grass	.241	.280	.344	195	47	8	0	4	17	11	34	.246	.301	.343	399	98	19	1	6	37	30	71
on Artificial Turf	.300	.342	.435	283	85	10	2	8	39	15	37	.261	.302	.371	391	102	15	2	8	41	20	57
Day Games	.261	.295	.415	142	37	8	1	4	15	6	23	.246	.301	.382	228	56	14	1	5	19	15	34
Night Games	.283	.326	.390	336	95	10	1	8	41	20	48	.256	.302	.347	562	144	20	2	9	59	35	94
April	.296	.318	.407	81	24	3	0	2	8	3	10	.296	.318	.407	81	24	3	0	2	8	3	10
May	.262	.323	.429	84	22	2	0	4	11	8	14	.248	.348	.380	121	30	4	0	4	15	19	21
June	.245	.273	.340	53	13	2	0	1	6	2	8	.225	.250	.317	120	27	3	1	2	13	4	15
July	.318	.358	.477	88	28	5	0	3	15	5	12	.304	.343	.456	158	48	12	0	4	19	9	22
August	.242	.273	.274	95	23	3	0	0	4	3	15	.224	.262	.263	152	34	6	0	0	6	7	25
Sept/Oct	.286	.345	.455	77	22	3	2	2	12	5	12	.234	.280	.335	158	37	6	2	2	17	8	35
Bases Empty	.251	.283	.385	291	73	13	1	8	8	10	50	.233	.281	.338	464	108	20	1	9	9	28	82
Leadoff	.272	.311	.464	125	34	7	1	5	5	7	26	.252	.299	.381	210	53	10	1	5	5	14	43
Not Leadoff	.235	.262	.325	166	39	6	0	3	3	3	24	.217	.266	.303	254	55	10	0	4	4	14	39
Runners On	.316	.367	.417	187	59	5	1	4	48	16	21	.282	.327	.383	326	92	14	2	5	69	22	46
First Base Only	.333	.367	.467	75	25	4	0	2	6	4	14	.289	.324	.407	135	39	7	0	3	10	7	27
Scoring Position	.304	.367	.384	112	34	1	1	2	42	12	7	.277	.329	.366	191	53	7	2	2	59	15	19
Late Innings, Close	.338	.384	.600	65	22	0	1	5	18	6	13	.241	.300	.407	108	26	1	1	5	18	10	26

RBI/Opportunities

Scoring Position	38 / 151 (25%)	55 / 255 (22%)
Scoring Position, 2 Out	19 / 85 (22%)	25 / 140 (18%)
On Third, Less than 2 Out	11 / 19 (58%)	19 / 37 (51%)
RBI in close games / RBI Total	35 / 56 (63%)	46 / 78 (59%)

Jamie Quirk
Kansas City Royals

This isn't the kind of player you expect to see with a player essay in the *GABSB*. This is the kind of guy who gets sold for Gerry Ako and cash (August 1978), released and named a coach (March 1984), sold outright (September 1984), and released again (October 1984). Then here he is, at age 32, catching regularly for the Royals. He was sixth in the league in games caught, ahead of Terry Steinbach, Tim Laudner, B. J. Surhoff, and Don Slaught.

Of course, it wasn't meant to happen that way. Ed Hearn was supposed to be the everyday catcher till his shoulder blew out right at the start of the year. It would be hard to see where the club suffered from the change. Quirk wasn't a plus player at the position, mainly due to his bat, but he was better than Sundberg in 1986:

	B.A.	SLUG%	OBA.	RBI per 100 AB
Sundberg '86	.212	.322	.303	9.8
Quirk '87	.236	.345	.307	11.2.

The pitching staff certainly didn't seem to suffer with Quirk taking over the number one role:

	W–L	ERA	% BELOW LEAGUE ERA
1986	76–86	3.82	8.2%
1987	83–79	3.86	13.5%

The Royals were not as successful in stopping the running game, but the Royals' other catchers were the likely culprits (Owen, Macfarlane, Hearn, and Madison). Quirk was the Royals' best at gunning down runners even when Sundberg was still around (1985–86, gunned down 25 of 47, 53 percent).

I've always been fascinated by converted catchers. Such a change late in a player's career rarely pays off. Converted catchers usually struggle defensively for two or three years; some, like Mike Heath, never learn the intricacies of the role. Others, like Bob Boone, eventually turn into super catchers.

Jamie Quirk was a late conversion. He never caught a professional game until his eighth season as a pro. He had been drafted as a shortstop and ended up primarily as a third baseman, a very good one, I might add. In 1975 he led the American Association third basemen in assists, double plays, and fielding percentage. He wasn't much of a hitter, though, and Kansas City had a third baseman, who was a pretty good hitter, Quirk's drinking buddy, George Brett.

If you find yourself at age 27 with a career average of .228, and your best asset is simply the fact you throw right-handed and hit left, you go ask the manager if he would like to have a left-handed hitting catcher around. The answer is, invariably, yes. And, oh, did they suffer with him for three years. Steals were up about 60 percent when Quirk went behind the plate; his average Catcher ERA was literally a full run above the other catchers in 273 innings from 1980–82. But he eventually became an excellent defensive catcher, and this marginal talent now has a good shot at a 15-season career in the majors.

Craig R. Wright

Quirk, James Patrick "Jamie" Bats: Left Throws: Right Born 10/22/54

1987 SEASON AND MAJOR-LEAGUE CAREER BATTING TOTALS

	G	AB	H	2B	3B	HR	TB	R	RBI	TBB	IBB	SO	HP	SH	SF	SB	CS	SB%	GDP	AVG	OBP	SLG
87 KC	109	296	70	17	0	5	102	24	33	28	1	56	4	2	4	1	0	1.00	8	.236	.307	.345
13 YEARS	643	1484	356	75	4	28	523	124	158	91	10	284	11	7	13	4	6	.40	39	.240	.286	.352

1987 SEASON

	Ave.	OBP	SLG	AB	H	2B	3B	HR	RBI	BB	SO
Totals	.236	.307	.345	296	70	17	0	5	33	28	56
vs. Left	.235	.316	.294	17	4	1	0	0	1	1	4
vs. Right	.237	.307	.348	279	66	16	0	5	32	27	52
at Home	.218	.279	.293	147	32	11	0	0	11	14	24
on Road	.255	.335	.396	149	38	6	0	5	22	14	32
vs. Groundball	.252	.317	.362	163	41	12	0	2	19	13	29
vs. Flyball	.218	.296	.323	133	29	5	0	3	14	15	27
vs. Finesse	.283	.355	.446	166	47	12	0	5	19	17	22
vs. Power	.177	.247	.215	130	23	5	0	0	14	11	34
on Grass	.281	.379	.430	114	32	5	0	4	21	14	24
on Artificial Turf	.209	.260	.291	182	38	12	0	1	12	14	32
Day Games	.194	.246	.306	62	12	4	0	1	12	5	12
Night Games	.248	.323	.355	234	58	13	0	4	21	23	44
April	.095	.286	.190	21	2	2	0	0	4	5	1
May	.308	.393	.346	52	16	2	0	0	2	7	4
June	.217	.217	.348	69	15	3	0	2	5	0	12
July	.188	.278	.250	16	3	1	0	0	0	1	3
August	.348	.429	.530	66	23	6	0	2	16	9	17
Sept/Oct	.153	.215	.236	72	11	3	0	1	6	6	19
Bases Empty	.206	.278	.294	180	37	7	0	3	3	16	36
Leadoff	.164	.263	.299	67	11	3	0	2	2	8	13
Not Leadoff	.230	.287	.292	113	26	4	0	1	1	8	23
Runners On	.284	.351	.422	116	33	10	0	2	30	12	20
First Base Only	.298	.355	.368	57	17	4	0	0	1	3	12
Scoring Position	.271	.347	.475	59	16	6	0	2	29	9	8
Late Innings, Close	.364	.391	.500	44	16	6	0	0	5	1	7

FOUR YEAR TOTALS (1984 – 1987)

	Ave.	OBP	SLG	AB	H	2B	3B	HR	RBI	BB	SO
Totals	.233	.294	.362	575	134	30	1	14	65	47	108
vs. Left	.182	.229	.212	33	6	1	0	0	2	1	10
vs. Right	.236	.298	.371	542	128	29	1	14	63	46	98
at Home	.228	.289	.362	298	68	20	1	6	28	26	51
on Road	.238	.299	.361	277	66	10	0	8	37	21	57
vs. Groundball	.247	.303	.361	316	78	18	0	6	39	23	55
vs. Flyball	.216	.282	.363	259	56	12	1	8	26	24	53
vs. Finesse	.275	.330	.427	335	92	22	1	9	39	27	51
vs. Power	.175	.244	.271	240	42	8	0	5	26	20	57
on Grass	.263	.341	.414	198	52	6	0	8	35	20	41
on Artificial Turf	.218	.268	.334	377	82	24	1	6	30	27	67
Day Games	.225	.269	.324	142	32	8	0	2	20	9	24
Night Games	.236	.302	.374	433	102	22	1	12	45	38	84
April	.133	.270	.300	30	4	2	0	1	6	5	2
May	.284	.379	.346	81	23	5	0	0	2	12	9
June	.204	.225	.324	108	22	4	0	3	6	3	21
July	.188	.250	.229	48	9	2	0	0	4	3	11
August	.290	.363	.450	100	29	7	0	3	23	11	26
Sept/Oct	.226	.270	.385	208	47	10	1	7	24	13	39
Bases Empty	.210	.268	.318	343	72	16	0	7	7	25	67
Leadoff	.222	.286	.333	135	30	9	0	2	2	11	26
Not Leadoff	.202	.256	.308	208	42	7	0	5	5	14	41
Runners On	.267	.331	.427	232	62	14	1	7	58	22	41
First Base Only	.301	.342	.416	113	34	7	0	2	7	5	24
Scoring Position	.235	.321	.437	119	28	7	1	5	51	17	17
Late Innings, Close	.292	.333	.425	113	33	12	0	1	13	6	17

RBI/Opportunities

Scoring Position	22 / 82 (27%)	40 / 166 (24%)
Scoring Position, 2 Out	10 / 46 (22%)	12 / 88 (14%)
On Third, Less than 2 Out	8 / 11 (73%)	20 / 27 (74%)
RBI in close games / RBI Total	19 / 33 (58%)	45 / 65 (69%)

Dan Quisenberry
Kansas City Royals

It didn't show in the stats he rang up that year, but the decline of Dan Quisenberry began in 1985, when it suddenly seemed impossible for him to get left-handed batters out. Remember the monster controversy over the second game of the '85 Series, when Howser refused to pull Leibrandt until it was too late? Howser was too discreet to say so, but he just didn't trust Quiz to face the left-handed hitting Van Slyke. And it was *déjà vu* in the sixth game. First Howser passes up the chance to break a scoreless tie in the bottom of the seventh by pinch hitting for Leibrandt. Then, with Charley obviously weakening in the top of the eighth, Howser stays in the dugout while Harper singles in the first run and Smith walks to load the bases. One more hit and the Cardinals blow the game open and win the Series. Howser has the most desperate situation of his career, Quiz gets the ground ball he needs, and continues to hold the fort until Dane Iorg's heroics. Two days later, in the euphoria of ultimate victory, I doubt if one Royals fan in ten could have told who the winning pitcher of the sixth game was, who in fact managed to lock the barn door before the horse could be totally absconded with. It was the greatest performance of Quisenberry's illustrious career and he got no credit for it.

But life is unfair, and if no one noticed that Quiz saved the Series, everyone noticed in '86 and '87 when he started taking his lumps—lefthanders resumed eating him alive. The sudden hostility of fans in '87 made me furious. I know baseball is a game of "what have you done for me lately?", but couldn't people have retained a fleeting memory of the good times, and remarked merely, "he hasn't got it anymore"? Apparently not. All I heard was that he was a bum who'd let that lifetime contract go to his head.

Well, I don't believe the money ruined him, and frankly, I'm not convinced that he's ruined at all. When I look at last year's stats I still see a pitcher with an ERA under three who doesn't walk people. Every point raised in last year's *GABSB* Quisenberry comment still holds: If there's no place for him as a closer, why not long or middle relief, why not even try him as a starter? You'd think the Royals would cast about for some way to get a return on their sizable investment.

Then again, maybe I just can't bring myself to face reality—perhaps it is all over for Quiz. We'll probably find out for certain this year. If it is the end of the line, he'll leave as the greatest reliever in Royals history, and a rich man to boot. But I'll always remember him as the man who got Willie McGee when the Royals were hanging by their fingernails. Truly a clutch performance. I never would have thought it a last hurrah.

Mike Kopf

Quisenberry, Daniel Raymond "Dan" Bats: Right Throws: Right Born 02/07/53

1987 SEASON AND MAJOR-LEAGUE CAREER PITCHING TOTALS

	G	GS	CG	GF	IP	BFP	H	R	ER	HR	SH	SF	HB	TBB	IBB	SO	WP	Bk	W	L	Pct	ShO	Sv	ERA
87 KC	47	0	0	39	49	215	58	15	15	3	1	1	1	10	3	17	0	0	4	1	.800	0	8	2.76
9 YEARS	553	0	0	490	894	3615	887	282	251	52	43	34	7	134	56	312	3	0	51	43	.543	0	237	2.53

1987: Finesse, Groundball   1986: Finesse, Groundball   1985: Finesse, Groundball   1984: Finesse, Groundball

1987 SEASON											FOUR YEAR TOTALS (1984 – 1987)										
	G	IP	H	BB	SO	SB	CS	W	L	S	ERA	G	IP	H	BB	SO	SB	CS	W	L	S	ERA
Totals	47	49.1	58	10	17	4	2	4	0	8	2.74	265	389.0	413	62	148	20	12	21	19	101	2.59
at Home	23	27.1	23	4	11	1	1	4	0	3	0.99	134	197.2	197	29	76	5	8	15	7	49	2.19
on Road	24	22.0	35	6	6	3	1	0	0	5	4.91	131	191.1	216	33	72	15	4	6	12	52	3.01
on Grass	11	13.2	11	6	5	2	0	1	0	1	1.98	69	100.2	106	24	38	5	5	6	5	23	2.77
on Artificial Turf	36	35.2	47	4	12	2	2	3	0	7	3.03	196	288.1	307	38	110	15	7	15	14	78	2.53
Day Games	20	19.2	32	6	5	3	1	0	0	3	5.49	106	157.0	184	29	61	14	3	4	11	40	3.04
Night Games	27	29.2	26	4	12	1	1	4	0	5	0.91	159	232.0	229	33	87	6	9	17	8	61	2.29
April	6	6.2	7	2	4	0	0	1	0	0	0.00	32	48.0	49	7	22	2	1	4	3	12	1.69
May	12	14.1	16	1	3	1	0	1	0	6	2.51	48	72.0	67	10	26	2	3	3	3	19	2.75
June	10	6.2	7	0	4	0	0	0	0	1	4.05	46	62.1	65	9	21	2	2	2	1	18	2.17
July	8	10.2	9	4	4	1	1	2	0	0	1.69	48	69.0	86	14	25	5	3	3	5	18	3.26
August	7	7.1	12	3	2	2	1	0	0	1	4.91	45	68.0	67	14	27	5	3	4	4	18	2.51
Sept/Oct	4	3.2	7	0	0	0	0	0	0	0	4.91	46	69.2	79	8	27	4	0	6	3	16	2.84

vs. Opponent Batters	Ave.	OBP	SLG	AB	H	2B	3B	HR	RBI	BB	SO	Ave.	OBP	SLG	AB	H	2B	3B	HR	RBI	BB	SO
Totals	.287	.322	.421	202	58	14	2	3	37	10	17	.273	.301	.366	1515	413	56	8	23	188	62	148
vs. Left	.320	.364	.466	103	33	7	1	2	21	7	11	.298	.338	.403	794	237	37	5	12	93	47	59
vs. Right	.253	.279	.374	99	25	7	1	1	16	3	6	.244	.260	.325	721	176	19	3	11	95	15	89
Bases Empty	.227	.265	.289	97	22	4	1	0	0	4	10	.261	.278	.349	800	209	24	5	12	12	18	72
Leadoff	.158	.179	.184	38	6	1	0	0	0	1	5	.239	.253	.347	326	78	11	3	6	6	6	25
Not Leadoff	.271	.317	.356	59	16	3	1	0	0	3	5	.276	.296	.350	474	131	13	2	6	6	12	47
Runners On Base	.343	.375	.543	105	36	10	1	3	37	6	7	.285	.326	.385	715	204	32	3	11	176	44	76
First Base Only	.324	.324	.595	37	12	1	0	3	6	0	1	.290	.295	.405	279	81	10	2	6	17	2	19
Scoring Position	.353	.400	.515	68	24	9	1	0	31	6	6	.282	.344	.372	436	123	22	1	5	159	42	57
Late Innings, Close	.330	.358	.495	91	30	7	1	2	25	3	5	.276	.307	.361	927	256	33	5	12	141	40	102

RBI/Opportunities

Scoring Position	29 / 93	(31%)	147 / 615	(24%)
Scoring Position, 2 Out	15 / 55	(27%)	73 / 304	(24%)
On Third, Less than 2 Out	7 / 16	(44%)	47 / 106	(44%)
RBI in close games / RBI Total	25 / 37	(68%)	141 / 188	(75%)

Tim Raines
Montreal Expos

A number of players who were never known for reaching the fences became home run hitters in 1987. Tim Raines was one, but in his case it seemed more of a deliberate decision than any accident of balls, cork, or humidity. His 18 homers (in 139 games) topped his previous high by 7, and was second on the team to Tim Wallach. Raines always did have more power than he was given credit for. This was his sixth straight season with 30 or more doubles, and he's never had less than 8 triples in a year. His speed, obviously, is a major factor, but being a straight-away hitter, Raines' extra base hits are much more often long drives to the gap, not grounders down the line.

The long ball hitting started early. After being forced to sit out spring training and the season's first 21 games, Raines hit the first pitch he saw for a triple. He won that first game with a grand slam in the 10th inning; in fact he had 3 game winning home runs in his first 4 games. And he stayed hot, hitting close to .400 for the month of May, before settling in to finish at .330, third in the league, while scoring a league-leading 123 runs.

Raines is a .300 hitter no matter how you break down his stats; batting right or left, home or away, grass or turf, first half or second half, even month by month—he's virtu-ally slump-proof. During one season or another in his career, Raines has led the league in doubles, runs scored, stolen bases, batting average, or outfield assists. Despite his ill-fated stab at free agency, Raines has adjusted well to playing in Montreal—it has always been a good doubles and triples park, and the addition of the roof this season helped visibility, meaning swinging for the fences made more sense than it had in the past.

The only downside in Raines' season was a drop from 70 to 50 in stolen bases. Surprisingly, Raines stole more than 30 bases in the first half, when he was batting third in the lineup, then hardly ran at all in the second half while leading off. As he improved his other offensive skills over the years, stealing has seemed to have become less important to Raines. It's hard to gage if this has hurt the Expos, since he still picks his spots well, and he's always shown a reluctance to risk taking the bat out of a hot hitter's hand. This year, Wallach, Andres Galarraga, and Mitch Webster were all hitting well enough to drive him in anyway.

More than anyone, Raines is the reason Montreal has been a better team than has been expected over the past few years. He's the best player in the National League.

Michael Cassin

Raines, Timothy "Tim"

Bats: Both   Throws: Right   Born 09/16/59

1987 SEASON AND MAJOR-LEAGUE CAREER BATTING TOTALS

	G	AB	H	2B	3B	HR	TB	R	RBI	TBB	IBB	SO	HP	SH	SF	SB	CS	SB%	GDP	AVG	OBP	SLG
87 MON	139	530	175	34	8	18	279	123	68	90	26	52	4	0	3	50	5	.91	9	.330	.429	.526
9 YEARS	1021	3902	1203	214	63	66	1741	727	382	559	78	428	17	16	21	511	74	.87	56	.308	.395	.446

1987 SEASON

	Ave.	OBP	SLG	AB	H	2B	3B	HR	RBI	BB	SO
Totals	.330	.429	.526	530	175	34	8	18	68	90	52
vs. Left	.394	.468	.612	165	65	13	4	5	23	21	19
vs. Right	.301	.412	.488	365	110	21	4	13	45	69	33
at Home	.337	.437	.525	276	93	15	5	9	32	49	29
on Road	.323	.420	.528	254	82	19	3	9	36	41	23
vs. Groundball	.321	.418	.494	249	80	16	3	7	24	40	28
vs. Flyball	.338	.438	.555	281	95	18	5	11	44	50	24
vs. Finesse	.344	.427	.557	323	111	17	5	14	44	45	28
vs. Power	.309	.431	.478	207	64	17	3	4	24	45	24
on Grass	.340	.439	.556	144	49	12	2	5	21	25	14
on Artificial Turf	.326	.425	.516	386	126	22	6	13	47	65	38
Day Games	.338	.447	.554	130	44	10	3	4	16	27	14
Night Games	.327	.423	.517	400	131	24	5	14	52	63	38
April	.000	.000	.000	0	0	0	0	0	0	0	0
May	.349	.444	.566	106	37	9	1	4	18	17	14
June	.388	.462	.553	103	40	8	0	3	18	14	7
July	.267	.349	.422	90	24	5	0	3	8	13	8
August	.322	.418	.600	115	37	6	4	6	17	18	15
Sept/Oct	.319	.459	.474	116	37	6	3	2	7	28	8
Bases Empty	.334	.410	.540	335	112	22	7	11	11	39	27
Leadoff	.357	.431	.578	154	55	9	5	5	5	17	10
Not Leadoff	.315	.392	.508	181	57	13	2	6	6	22	17
Runners On	.323	.458	.503	195	63	12	1	7	57	51	25
First Base Only	.303	.376	.579	76	23	7	1	4	11	9	8
Scoring Position	.336	.500	.454	119	40	5	0	3	46	42	17
Late Innings, Close	.358	.494	.657	67	24	4	2	4	15	19	7

FOUR YEAR TOTALS (1984 – 1987)

	Ave.	OBP	SLG	AB	H	2B	3B	HR	RBI	BB	SO
Totals	.323	.409	.477	2307	745	137	40	46	231	336	241
vs. Left	.321	.390	.484	717	230	39	12	18	87	81	76
vs. Right	.324	.418	.474	1590	515	98	28	28	144	255	165
at Home	.322	.414	.468	1141	367	62	24	19	110	176	119
on Road	.324	.405	.485	1166	378	75	16	27	121	160	122
vs. Groundball	.324	.406	.476	1098	356	67	20	20	107	150	108
vs. Flyball	.322	.413	.477	1209	389	70	20	26	124	186	133
vs. Finesse	.322	.400	.470	1355	436	66	18	33	150	172	123
vs. Power	.325	.423	.486	952	309	71	22	13	81	164	118
on Grass	.334	.423	.499	623	208	42	5	17	76	98	70
on Artificial Turf	.319	.404	.469	1684	537	95	35	29	155	238	171
Day Games	.340	.432	.501	767	261	43	19	14	79	128	82
Night Games	.314	.398	.465	1540	484	94	21	32	152	208	159
April	.300	.385	.443	237	71	16	3	4	20	33	23
May	.304	.404	.479	378	115	19	7	11	49	62	50
June	.347	.413	.491	403	140	28	3	8	51	45	41
July	.305	.382	.441	406	124	20	7	7	29	52	40
August	.337	.431	.503	433	146	29	8	9	47	70	38
Sept/Oct	.331	.428	.487	450	149	25	12	7	35	74	49
Bases Empty	.328	.402	.494	1505	494	103	31	28	28	183	144
Leadoff	.326	.394	.488	789	257	49	20	13	13	86	77
Not Leadoff	.331	.412	.500	716	237	54	11	15	15	97	67
Runners On	.313	.422	.445	802	251	34	9	18	203	153	97
First Base Only	.343	.388	.518	338	116	19	5	10	31	25	35
Scoring Position	.291	.442	.392	464	135	15	4	8	172	128	62
Late Innings, Close	.339	.437	.483	389	132	22	5	8	44	68	43

RBI/Opportunities

Scoring Position	40 / 184 (22%)	157 / 699 (22%)
Scoring Position, 2 Out	11 / 70 (16%)	54 / 300 (18%)
On Third, Less than 2 Out	13 / 29 (45%)	57 / 119 (48%)
RBI in close games / RBI Total	39 / 68 (57%)	144 / 231 (62%)

Willie Randolph
New York Yankees

If Willie Randolph's 1986 caused any concern about his future (especially in pinstripes), his 1987 put it to rest. Willie set a new high in batting average and tied his personal highs in homers and RBIs. His 1987 on-base percentage was the second-best of his career; fourth in the American League. His 96 runs scored were three off his best year. He also had the best strikeout to walk ratio of his career. He led New York in runs scored and walks. It was the best year of his career.

Defensively, the news was even better. In 1986, Willie committed a career-high 20 errors, most of any AL second baseman. During the off-season, the Yankees made two moves designed to correct that: installing a completely new infield surface in Yankee Stadium and using one man as their primary shortstop. Whether it was due to better bounces or familiarity with his keystone partner, Randolph's fielding improved dramatically. He was third in the league in range factor, sixth in fielding percentage and second in double plays per game in 1987.

Randolph could have produced some truly overwhelming statistics in 1987 had he played a full season. Unfortunately, he played in only 120 games—20 fewer than he did in 1986. In early July, Willie tore the cartilage in his knee. The surgery that was required caused him to miss both the All-Star game and 26 regular-season games and also damaged his statistics. Willie was hitting .309, with a .416 OB%

and .420 SL% before the injury; he hit .295, with a .408 OB% and .402 SL% after it.

The injury was even more damaging to his team. New York had a 55–34 record (.618) when Randolph went on the DL on July 15, and was in first place by three games. The Yankees lost 15 of the 26 games that he missed and were in third place, 2.5 games out, when he returned. It's doubtful that losing their captain for a month cost New York the pennant—but it is no coincidence that his injury started the slide to fourth place.

You can, however, argue that New York should have been better prepared for the injury than they were. Since 1982, Randolph has missed 178 games—just under 30 a year. By comparison, Dave Winfield (the only other Yankee regular who has been with the team since 1982) has missed only 74 games—22 of those coming in 1982. While this is probably more a comment on the relative demands of the two positions—few players ever run into the right fielder in order to break up double plays—it's not an impressive record even for a second baseman. Since Willie is 33, New York ought to try to develop either a substitute or potential replacement in 1988.

But maybe they aren't to blame. In every area, Willie Randolph is one of the best second basemen in baseball; finding a replacement for him when he retires will be much easier to say than it will be to do.

Daniel Stone and Marisa B. Lo

Randolph, Willie Larry   Bats: Right   Throws: Right   Born 07/06/54

1987 SEASON AND MAJOR-LEAGUE CAREER BATTING TOTALS

	G	AB	H	2B	3B	HR	TB	R	RBI	TBB	IBB	SO	HP	SH	SF	SB	CS	SB%	GDP	AVG	OBP	SLG
87 NYA	120	449	137	24	2	7	186	96	67	82	1	25	2	5	5	11	1	.92	15	.305	.411	.414
13 YEARS	1614	5960	1648	240	57	46	2140	993	518	957	28	479	26	68	50	244	78	.76	164	.277	.376	.359

	1987 SEASON											FOUR YEAR TOTALS (1984 – 1987)										
	Ave.	OBP	SLG	AB	H	2B	3B	HR	RBI	BB	SO	Ave.	OBP	SLG	AB	H	2B	3B	HR	RBI	BB	SO
Totals	.305	.411	.414	449	137	24	2	7	67	82	25	.286	.390	.364	2002	572	84	8	19	188	347	155
vs. Left	.331	.467	.459	133	44	8	0	3	22	34	7	.322	.423	.430	686	221	36	4	10	56	121	39
vs. Right	.294	.385	.396	316	93	16	2	4	45	48	18	.267	.373	.330	1316	351	48	4	9	132	226	116
at Home	.292	.395	.399	253	74	14	2	3	32	44	12	.285	.401	.369	993	283	42	7	9	93	195	69
on Road	.321	.430	.434	196	63	10	0	4	35	38	13	.286	.379	.360	1009	289	42	1	10	95	152	86
vs. Groundball	.319	.420	.407	216	69	8	1	3	27	37	12	.289	.398	.350	957	277	36	2	6	77	172	71
vs. Flyball	.292	.402	.421	233	68	16	1	4	40	45	13	.282	.383	.377	1045	295	48	6	13	111	175	84
vs. Finesse	.282	.379	.376	234	66	13	0	3	29	36	12	.276	.365	.356	1112	307	44	3	13	98	154	68
vs. Power	.330	.444	.456	215	71	11	2	4	38	46	13	.298	.419	.374	890	265	40	5	6	90	193	87
on Grass	.294	.400	.402	398	117	21	2	6	58	72	23	.287	.394	.368	1708	491	72	7	17	161	304	133
on Artificial Turf	.392	.492	.510	51	20	3	0	1	9	10	2	.276	.366	.344	294	81	12	1	2	27	43	22
Day Games	.305	.408	.430	151	46	11	1	2	22	26	8	.282	.395	.370	613	173	28	4	6	56	113	49
Night Games	.305	.412	.406	298	91	13	1	5	45	56	17	.287	.388	.361	1389	399	56	4	13	132	234	106
April	.280	.407	.333	75	21	4	0	0	9	15	3	.286	.401	.343	280	80	13	0	1	21	53	24
May	.299	.386	.449	107	32	5	1	3	22	16	6	.305	.416	.390	397	121	14	4	4	46	77	29
June	.371	.487	.515	97	36	9	1	1	15	22	9	.275	.378	.360	400	110	23	1	3	40	66	42
July	.237	.326	.263	38	9	1	0	0	1	5	1	.290	.373	.349	324	94	11	1	2	30	43	13
August	.200	.238	.200	20	4	0	0	0	0	1	2	.250	.346	.315	292	73	9	2	2	16	43	24
Sept/Oct	.313	.423	.438	112	35	5	0	3	20	23	4	.304	.423	.417	309	94	14	0	7	35	65	23
Bases Empty	.290	.396	.359	262	76	10	1	2	2	45	16	.290	.396	.369	1226	355	50	7	11	215	96
Leadoff	.286	.387	.374	91	26	6	1	0	0	15	6	.311	.417	.395	527	164	22	5	4	4	96	32
Not Leadoff	.292	.401	.351	171	50	4	0	2	2	30	10	.273	.380	.349	699	191	28	2	7	7	119	64
Runners On	.326	.430	.492	187	61	14	1	5	65	37	9	.280	.383	.357	776	217	34	1	8	177	132	59
First Base Only	.342	.422	.507	73	25	6	0	2	6	10	3	.311	.383	.395	309	96	14	0	4	14	36	20
Scoring Position	.316	.435	.482	114	36	8	1	3	59	27	6	.259	.383	.332	467	121	20	1	4	163	96	39
Late Innings, Close	.397	.519	.460	63	25	4	0	0	12	16	4	.308	.405	.363	325	100	13	1	1	35	53	29

RBI/Opportunities

Scoring Position	53 / 185 (29%)	154 / 708 (22%)
Scoring Position, 2 Out	18 / 79 (23%)	49 / 310 (16%)
On Third, Less than 2 Out	23 / 39 (59%)	70 / 141 (50%)
RBI in close games / RBI Total	36 / 67 (54%)	107 / 188 (57%)

Shane Rawley
Philadelphia Phillies

Shane Rawley, the Phillies' ace lefty, was well on his way to a 20-win season for 1987, but ran into a September swoon, as did his ballclub. He finished at 17–11, which was good enough to place him second in wins in the NL. (Needless to say, it wasn't a banner year for pitching.) His other pitching statistics weren't too overpowering, either. His ERA was 4.39, which didn't even lead his own team. He can't be considered a strikeout pitcher either, with 123 Ks in 229.2 innings, and 86 walks.

But how does a pitcher with these other average numbers still manage to win 17 games then? The answer is consistency. Rawley goes out on the mound and gives you the same effort, day in and day out. He's not overpowering, but he has the knowledge of pitching that few other pitchers possess. If the Phillies go out and get him 5 runs, he'll give up 4 in 7 innings and get the win. With more offensive help he wins big. He was seventh in the league in innings pitched, and led the league in starts, with 36. He averaged a little over 6.2 innings per start. The Phillies' workhorse bullpen was always ready to bail him out, and Rawley only finished 4 games, one a shutout. He also gave up 23 home runs, just about 1 every 10 innings.

The problem with the Phillies, though, is that they expect Rawley to win every time out. He should be expected to win about 15 games, and exceeded that last year—his only season with over 15 wins. The Phillies always have promising young pitchers—they should put them next to Rawley's locker and hope that they absorb some of his knowledge of the game. If Don Carman or Kevin Gross take in some of his information, either one of them could develop into a big winner. But perhaps the Phillies' answer is getting a proven starter. They bungled last year's chances by letting Jack Morris slip by them. They had another chance again this year, but history repeated itself.

1988 should be another solid year for Rawley. He's only 32 and his best years look like they're ahead of him. If he has any weakness as a pitcher, it is his performance in day games. It looks like he is at his best at night, with shadows deceiving his pitches. He should be a vital part of the Phillies' starting rotation for many years to come, and if his experience does eventually rub off on the rest of the staff, it will be a plus for Lee Elia's team of the future.

Walter DeSoi

Rawley, Shane William

Bats: Right   Throws: Left   Born 07/27/55

1987 SEASON AND MAJOR-LEAGUE CAREER PITCHING TOTALS

	G	GS	CG	GF	IP	BFP	H	R	ER	HR	SH	SF	HB	TBB	IBB	SO	WP	Bk	W	L	Pct	ShO	Sv	ERA
87 PHI	36	36	4	0	230	1005	250	118	112	23	10	9	5	86	8	123	3	2	17	11	.607	1	0	4.38
10 YEARS	410	173	36	138	1528	6551	1547	717	660	107	78	51	24	596	56	836	46	6	98	90	.521	6	40	3.89

1987: Finesse, Flyball   1986: Finesse, Flyball   1985: Finesse, Groundball   1984: Finesse, Groundball

	1987 SEASON											FOUR YEAR TOTALS (1984 – 1987)										
	G	IP	H	BB	SO	SB	CS	W	L	S	ERA	G	IP	H	BB	SO	SB	CS	W	L	S	ERA
Totals	36	229.2	250	86	123	26	12	17	11	0	4.39	124	748.1	767	271	384	77	33	53	35	0	3.93
at Home	16	111.0	124	35	56	12	4	8	4	0	4.38	64	381.1	393	149	198	43	19	27	19	0	3.94
on Road	20	118.2	126	51	67	14	8	9	7	0	4.40	60	367.0	374	122	186	34	14	26	16	0	3.92
on Grass	10	57.1	76	18	31	12	3	3	3	0	5.49	38	204.0	260	68	107	28	10	8	16	0	5.34
on Artificial Turf	26	172.1	174	68	92	14	9	14	8	0	4.02	86	544.1	507	203	277	49	23	45	19	0	3.41
Day Games	9	57.0	59	27	38	7	4	4	4	0	3.47	35	197.1	200	78	116	16	9	10	10	0	4.15
Night Games	27	172.2	191	59	85	19	8	13	7	0	4.69	89	551.0	567	193	268	61	24	43	25	0	3.84
April	5	29.2	35	18	11	4	2	1	1	0	3.64	17	105.2	102	46	41	8	5	7	4	0	3.15
May	6	41.1	42	11	24	5	2	5	1	0	2.83	21	119.0	130	44	67	17	6	10	8	0	4.01
June	5	32.1	44	8	16	3	2	2	3	0	5.85	24	119.1	126	41	62	11	5	8	6	0	3.92
July	6	39.1	39	13	23	4	1	5	0	0	3.66	24	151.2	158	55	93	18	7	11	6	0	3.92
August	7	51.1	51	15	27	8	2	4	1	0	3.33	19	140.1	122	42	69	10	4	12	1	0	2.82
Sept/Oct	7	35.2	39	21	22	2	3	0	5	0	7.82	19	112.1	129	43	52	13	6	5	10	0	6.01

vs. Opponent Batters	Ave.	OBP	SLG	AB	H	2B	3B	HR	RBI	BB	SO	Ave.	OBP	SLG	AB	H	2B	3B	HR	RBI	BB	SO
Totals	.279	.343	.428	895	250	56	4	23	105	86	123	.265	.329	.394	2890	767	156	11	65	301	271	384
vs. Left	.286	.353	.457	105	30	9	0	3	15	11	11	.263	.328	.393	369	97	22	1	8	46	36	53
vs. Right	.278	.341	.424	790	220	47	4	20	90	75	112	.266	.329	.395	2521	670	134	10	57	255	235	331
Bases Empty	.287	.348	.429	506	145	32	2	12	12	44	69	.267	.324	.395	1699	453	82	8	40	40	140	223
Leadoff	.299	.360	.466	221	66	14	1	7	7	19	27	.268	.320	.415	728	195	29	3	24	24	54	98
Not Leadoff	.277	.340	.400	285	79	18	1	5	5	25	42	.266	.327	.380	971	258	53	5	16	16	86	125
Runners On Base	.270	.336	.427	389	105	24	2	11	93	42	54	.264	.335	.394	1191	314	74	3	25	261	131	161
First Base Only	.325	.371	.494	166	54	13	0	5	15	12	19	.301	.343	.448	525	158	39	1	12	41	34	60
Scoring Position	.229	.312	.377	223	51	11	2	6	78	30	35	.234	.329	.351	666	156	35	2	13	220	97	101
Late Innings, Close	.337	.391	.554	83	28	1	1	5	17	8	12	.258	.310	.402	256	66	8	1	9	25	20	38

RBI/Opportunities

Scoring Position	67 / 316 (21%)	191 / 922 (21%)
Scoring Position, 2 Out	28 / 150 (19%)	73 / 444 (16%)
On Third, Less than 2 Out	27 / 56 (48%)	74 / 147 (50%)
RBI in close games / RBI Total	78 / 105 (74%)	215 / 301 (71%)

236

Johnny Ray
Pittsburgh Pirates/California Angels

You should be careful what you ask for. Johnny Ray told Pirate GM Syd Thrift that he was unhappy and wanted to be traded, and Ray was gone within the week, leaving the second base job to Jose Lind, who hadn't played in a single major league game. Ray was reportedly unhappy because, with Lind being given a shot, it didn't look like Ray was going to have enough appearances to meet some of his incentive clauses. It's a little hard to evaluate this trade; at least on the surface, it doesn't look like the Pirates got very much for Ray; one of the players, Bill Merrifield, was not on the Pirates 40-man roster this winter, but was not claimed in the waiver draft.

I'm somewhat pessimistic about Johnny Ray's future as a regular. He seems to have lost more of his already limited range, and he doesn't really have a major league arm. At the plate, he never seemed to get into a groove last year, and that really hurt the Pirate offense. Batting Ray third and Sid Bream fourth was a deadly combination; they helped boost opponents' double-play totals. It took the trading of Ray to get him out of the number 3 spot and to get Andy Van Slyke in there.

It may be time to consider platooning Ray. With the exception of a couple of seasons, he has consistently hit for better average and more power from the left side. For Ray to be successful, he needs to hit at least .300. He doesn't walk very much or have much home run power. He may develop more power as he ages; that would make him a more valuable hitter than the slow doubles hitter he is now.

The Angels are reportedly considering moving Ray to left field. I think that would be a big mistake, as Ray would be a slow outfielder with no arm. Even with the weak arm, third base would seem to be a more reasonable place to put him. He has always been a sure-handed infielder; if he got to the ball, he usually made the play. Of course, if his offense bounces back, and he develops more power, you could live with him in the outfield, with Devon White and Chili Davis to help cover some of his territory. I assume that the reason for moving Ray to the outfield is twofold; one, to give Mark McLemore a chance at second, and two, to move Brian Downing to the DH spot to extend his career.

Despite all the negative things I've said about Ray, I do like him. He's a nice guy who has spent most of his career with a bad team. He's the type of guy who builds a house for his parents and puts his younger brothers and sisters through school when he makes it. It's a shame that, having survived the lean years with Pittsburgh, he's not going to be around for the better years to come.

Sherri M. Nichols

Ray, John Cornelius "Johnny"

Bats: Both Throws: Right Born 03/01/57

1987 SEASON AND MAJOR-LEAGUE CAREER BATTING TOTALS

	G	AB	H	2B	3B	HR	TB	R	RBI	TBB	IBB	SO	HP	SH	SF	SB	CS	SB%	GDP	AVG	OBP	SLG
87 PIT-CAL	153	599	173	30	3	5	224	64	69	44	4	46	0	1	6	4	2	.67	22	.289	.334	.374
7 YEARS	961	3652	1053	213	26	37	1429	430	406	262	32	217	8	32	33	68	42	.62	92	.288	.335	.391

1987 SEASON

	Ave.	OBP	SLG	AB	H	2B	3B	HR	RBI	BB	SO
Totals	.289	.333	.374	599	173	30	3	5	69	43	46
vs. Left	.265	.315	.328	238	63	9	0	2	20	18	20
vs. Right	.305	.345	.404	361	110	21	3	3	49	25	26
at Home	.302	.353	.404	275	83	11	1	5	41	24	22
on Road	.278	.316	.349	324	90	19	2	0	28	19	24
vs. Groundball	.321	.371	.411	280	90	17	1	2	32	24	22
vs. Flyball	.260	.299	.342	319	83	13	2	3	37	19	24
vs. Finesse	.303	.338	.391	307	93	12	3	3	40	18	22
vs. Power	.274	.328	.356	292	80	18	0	2	29	25	24
on Grass	.288	.318	.349	229	66	14	0	0	22	11	18
on Artificial Turf	.289	.342	.389	370	107	16	3	5	47	32	28
Day Games	.299	.345	.396	187	56	9	0	3	27	13	14
Night Games	.284	.328	.364	412	117	21	3	2	42	30	32
April	.256	.318	.397	78	20	2	0	3	14	7	6
May	.257	.297	.330	109	28	6	1	0	14	7	12
June	.271	.310	.346	107	29	3	1	1	12	7	9
July	.289	.366	.349	83	24	5	0	0	6	10	4
August	.317	.368	.413	104	33	5	1	1	10	9	5
Sept/Oct	.331	.344	.407	118	39	9	0	0	13	10	10
Bases Empty	.286	.326	.356	315	90	14	1	2	2	19	22
Leadoff	.248	.282	.295	105	26	5	0	0	0	5	3
Not Leadoff	.305	.348	.386	210	64	9	1	2	2	14	19
Runners On	.292	.341	.394	284	83	16	2	3	67	24	24
First Base Only	.308	.351	.439	107	33	6	1	2	7	7	7
Scoring Position	.282	.335	.367	177	50	10	1	1	60	17	17
Late Innings, Close	.297	.339	.465	101	30	9	1	2	14	7	9

FOUR YEAR TOTALS (1984 – 1987)

	Ave.	OBP	SLG	AB	H	2B	3B	HR	RBI	BB	SO
Totals	.294	.344	.394	2327	683	134	12	25	284	184	148
vs. Left	.268	.317	.335	731	196	35	1	4	71	53	60
vs. Right	.305	.356	.420	1596	487	99	11	21	213	131	88
at Home	.283	.341	.380	1125	318	63	4	13	139	102	79
on Road	.304	.346	.406	1202	365	71	8	12	145	82	69
vs. Groundball	.309	.357	.401	1102	341	64	5	9	137	86	61
vs. Flyball	.279	.332	.387	1225	342	70	7	16	147	98	87
vs. Finesse	.303	.345	.397	1278	387	66	8	13	154	86	64
vs. Power	.282	.342	.389	1049	296	68	4	12	130	98	84
on Grass	.305	.347	.392	673	205	38	3	5	83	45	45
on Artificial Turf	.289	.342	.394	1654	478	96	9	20	201	139	103
Day Games	.313	.369	.428	713	223	47	4	9	110	66	46
Night Games	.285	.332	.379	1614	460	87	8	16	174	118	102
April	.312	.359	.416	298	93	17	1	4	46	22	14
May	.297	.352	.393	384	114	25	3	2	40	34	36
June	.241	.285	.324	410	99	19	3	3	48	26	33
July	.289	.347	.372	339	98	17	1	3	24	30	23
August	.314	.360	.418	421	132	25	2	5	52	31	17
Sept/Oct	.309	.364	.434	475	147	31	2	8	74	41	25
Bases Empty	.292	.338	.388	1311	383	69	6	15	15	91	72
Leadoff	.291	.327	.386	461	134	22	2	6	6	25	15
Not Leadoff	.293	.344	.389	850	249	47	4	9	9	66	57
Runners On	.295	.352	.401	1016	300	65	6	10	269	93	76
First Base Only	.292	.333	.386	383	112	21	3	3	21	23	25
Scoring Position	.297	.364	.409	633	188	44	3	7	248	70	51
Late Innings, Close	.268	.333	.391	437	117	28	4	6	53	43	36

RBI/Opportunities

Scoring Position	56 / 232	(24%)
Scoring Position, 2 Out	21 / 92	(23%)
On Third, Less than 2 Out	18 / 45	(40%)
RBI in close games / RBI Total	48 / 69	(70%)

	226 / 833	(27%)
	79 / 316	(25%)
	86 / 167	(51%)
	204 / 284	(72%)

Randy Ready
San Diego Padres

There are certain players who, despite outstanding minor league credentials, have to wait years before getting a real opportunity in the major leagues. For years Tom Paciorek languished in AAA and on the Dodger bench, before getting his chance in his thirties. Jack Perconte performed well in his only shot, but soon slid back into baseball purgatory. Gerald Perry finally got his shot in 1987, and performed beyond most expectations.

On June 12, 1986, Randy Ready was traded from Milwaukee to San Diego for minor leaguer Tim Pyznarski, the 1986 PCL Player of the Year. He brought with him a .190 batting average and a Hall-of-Fame collection of pine time. He got into one game for the Padres before a life-threatening brain injury struck down his wife. The Padres graciously gave Randy paid time off to spend the remainder of the season with his wife Doreen. Randy played in 10 games at Las Vegas near the end of the season.

Larry Bowa must have seen something he liked, because even though Randy was the "fifth wheel" in the Padre infield coming out of Yuma, 1987 proved to be his best opportunity ever. At age 26, Randy had impressive minor league stats—in 524 games he hit .343 with two batting titles, 319 RBI, and a slugging average of .535. His major league totals showed a .240 batting average and .371 slugging after 121 games over 3+ years. Last year, Randy more than doubled his career totals for games, runs, hits, doubles, tripled his home run total, and hit .309 with a slugging average of .520. He collected 67 walks, scored 69 runs, only struck out 44 times, gave great effort on a club not noted for great effort, stole 7 out of 10 bases, and finished second to Tony Gwynn in runs created per 27 outs at 8.7. The only thing Randy did *not* accomplish was winning a position—he put in 51 games at second, 52 games at third, and 16 games in the outfield. He seems to be stuck with the "utility man" label.

There is a ray of hope, however—Larry Bowa says that Ready is the "odds-on" favorite for the second base spot next year. Of course, this is the same Larry Bowa who decided to keep, and then publish, a diary of the 1987 Padre season (Misery loves company? All yours for just $15.95 . . .). However, Ready seemed to perform very well under trying circumstances last year (he often didn't know he was playing third until moments before game time, compliments of Padre third baseman Chris ("D.L.") Brown and his "gamer" attitude). In September, Randy went on a tear—he was seventh in the league in hitting with a .337 BA, tied for the league lead in homers with 8, and had the second highest slugging average in the NL. Perhaps 1988 will be the year Randy finally plays more than 6 consecutive games.

Bruce Erricson, Brigg Hewitt and David Bradley

Ready, Randy Max Bats: Right Throws: Right Born 01/08/60

1987 SEASON AND MAJOR-LEAGUE CAREER BATTING TOTALS

	G	AB	H	2B	3B	HR	TB	R	RBI	TBB	IBB	SO	HP	SH	SF	SB	CS	SB%	GDP	AVG	OBP	SLG
87 SD	124	350	108	26	6	12	182	69	54	67	2	44	3	2	1	7	3	.70	7	.309	.423	.520
5 YEARS	245	773	209	48	14	18	339	127	98	110	3	98	4	8	3	9	4	.69	18	.270	.363	.439

	1987 SEASON											TWO YEAR TOTALS (1986 – 1987)										
	Ave.	OBP	SLG	AB	H	2B	3B	HR	RBI	BB	SO	Ave.	OBP	SLG	AB	H	2B	3B	HR	RBI	BB	SO
Totals	.309	.423	.520	350	108	26	6	12	54	67	44	.285	.394	.472	432	123	30	6	13	58	76	54
vs. Left	.331	.473	.566	175	58	15	4	6	26	46	18	.310	.444	.519	210	65	18	4	6	28	50	23
vs. Right	.286	.367	.474	175	50	11	2	6	28	21	26	.261	.343	.428	222	58	12	2	7	30	26	31
at Home	.339	.443	.579	171	58	12	4	7	34	30	20	.308	.411	.512	211	65	14	4	7	37	35	22
on Road	.279	.404	.464	179	50	14	2	5	20	37	24	.262	.379	.434	221	58	16	2	6	21	41	32
vs. Groundball	.337	.434	.536	166	56	13	4	4	23	28	17	.308	.404	.502	201	62	16	4	5	25	32	24
vs. Flyball	.283	.413	.505	184	52	13	2	8	31	39	27	.264	.386	.446	231	61	14	2	8	33	44	30
vs. Finesse	.291	.409	.447	179	52	7	3	5	25	33	17	.266	.374	.401	237	63	11	3	5	26	38	25
vs. Power	.327	.437	.596	171	56	19	3	7	29	34	27	.308	.419	.559	195	60	19	3	8	32	38	29
on Grass	.335	.433	.559	254	85	20	5	9	42	42	31	.303	.396	.498	317	96	22	5	10	46	47	39
on Artificial Turf	.240	.398	.417	96	23	6	1	3	12	25	13	.235	.390	.400	115	27	8	1	3	12	29	15
Day Games	.339	.450	.613	124	42	10	3	6	22	24	19	.339	.450	.613	124	42	10	3	6	22	24	19
Night Games	.292	.408	.469	226	66	16	3	6	32	43	25	.263	.372	.416	308	81	20	3	7	36	52	35
April	.250	.357	.458	24	6	5	0	0	3	4	4	.192	.276	.288	52	10	5	0	0	4	6	6
May	.273	.385	.382	55	15	4	1	0	6	10	4	.243	.339	.359	103	25	7	1	1	8	15	11
June	.377	.448	.468	77	29	4	0	1	12	10	9	.361	.442	.458	83	30	5	0	1	13	12	10
July	.254	.392	.441	59	15	3	1	2	9	14	10	.254	.392	.441	59	15	3	1	2	9	14	10
August	.286	.435	.571	49	14	5	3	1	8	11	7	.286	.435	.571	49	14	5	3	1	8	11	7
Sept/Oct	.337	.457	.698	86	29	5	1	8	16	18	10	.337	.457	.698	86	29	5	1	8	16	18	10
Bases Empty	.280	.409	.518	193	54	14	4	8	8	40	27	.269	.396	.487	238	64	17	4	9	9	48	32
Leadoff	.266	.383	.481	79	21	4	2	3	3	15	8	.240	.360	.438	96	23	6	2	3	3	18	12
Not Leadoff	.289	.426	.544	114	33	10	2	5	5	25	19	.289	.420	.521	142	41	11	2	6	6	30	20
Runners On	.344	.441	.522	157	54	12	2	4	46	27	17	.304	.393	.454	194	59	13	2	4	49	28	22
First Base Only	.375	.467	.672	64	24	5	1	4	13	10	6	.325	.404	.566	83	27	6	1	4	14	10	9
Scoring Position	.323	.423	.419	93	30	7	1	0	33	17	11	.288	.385	.369	111	32	7	1	0	35	18	13
Late Innings, Close	.214	.389	.304	56	12	2	0	1	7	15	10	.214	.389	.304	112	24	4	0	2	14	30	20

RBI/Opportunities

Scoring Position	31 / 129 (24%)	33 / 150 (22%)
Scoring Position, 2 Out	15 / 60 (25%)	17 / 72 (24%)
On Third, Less than 2 Out	10 / 21 (48%)	10 / 22 (45%)
RBI in close games / RBI Total	29 / 54 (54%)	58 / 58 (100%)

238

Jeff Reardon
Minnesota Twins

Did Jeff Reardon really have a good season, or was a mediocre year hidden in the hoopla of a pennant race and ultimately a World Championship?

Twins' fans could be forgiven if during the course of the 1987 season they suffered from a gloomy sense of *déjà vu*. Jeff Reardon, V.P. Andy MacPhail's celebrated off season acquisition, seemed destined to earn his own niche in the Ron Davis wing of the Twins Fantastic Finish Hall of Fame. The credentials:

—April 19 and 25: In a preview of coming events, Jeff gave up 5 runs and 5 walks in 4 innings while protecting Twins' leads against the Angels.

—May 8: A 7–5 Twins' lead in the bottom of the ninth evaporates after Reardon allows 4 walks and 2 home runs, one a grand slam, for an 11–7 loss.

—May 12: The Terminator enters the game in the bottom of the 8th and gives up a grand slam to Fred Lynn to tie the game. In the 9th, two singles followed by a Larry Sheets' homer seals the Twins' fate.

—May 16: Bill Buckner's three-run ninth inning shot insures a Red Sox win.

—May 17: Reardon participates in a Twins' pitching collapse during a 7-run Boston rally in the 8th. He is credited with a bases loaded walk and two singles. Twins win in spite of this nonsense after Gaetti, Brunansky, and Hrbek homer in the 9th and 10th.

—June 2: Buckner's two-run single in the bottom of the 9th hands the beleaguered reliever his 4th loss.

—June 27: Reardon's third pitch of the 8th inning quickly departs as a grand slam for Mike Stanley and is followed two batters later by a Curtis Wilkerson home run(!) in a 7–2 Rangers' victory. Well, you get the picture.

There is a rather disturbing and uncanny resemblance between Ron Davis's 1984 stats and Reardon's 1987 numbers.

	ERA	G	GF	SV	IP	H	R	ER	HR
Davis	4.42	64	57	29	83	79	44	42	11
Reardon	4.48	63	58	31	80.3	70	41	40	14

One of the tests faced by Tom Kelly last season was what do when Reardon failed. A manager, particularly a rookie manager, is frequently under pressure from the front office to make a high-priced player justify the expense. Kelly responded in outstanding fashion. Without assigning Reardon to the bench, he made good use of Frazier, Atherton, and Berenguer in keeping the team on track. Reardon responded with some fine outings and never developed the type of arm trouble he experienced in Montreal (although he was held out of several save situations toward the end of the season).

Is Jeff just a rich man's Ron Davis? There are some strong arguments for this assessment. But when Reardon takes the mound in the ninth inning of a close game and assumes that haughty, ace-reliever glare you have a distinctly different feel than when Davis was out there.

Bill Jensen

Reardon, Jeffrey James "Jeff"

Bats: Right **Throws: Right** **Born 10/01/55**

1987 SEASON AND MAJOR-LEAGUE CAREER PITCHING TOTALS

	G	GS	CG	GF	IP	BFP	H	R	ER	HR	SH	SF	HB	TBB	IBB	SO	WP	Bk	W	L	Pct	ShO	Sv	ERA
87 MIN	63	0	0	58	80	337	70	41	40	14	1	3	3	28	4	83	2	0	8	8	.500	0	31	4.50
9 YEARS	519	0	0	398	747	3106	621	267	247	68	45	20	13	274	52	620	17	0	50	54	.481	0	193	2.98

1987: Power, Flyball   1986: Finesse, Flyball   1985: Power, Flyball   1984: Power, Flyball

1987 SEASON

	G	IP	H	BB	SO	SB	CS	W	L	S	ERA
Totals	63	80.1	70	28	84	8	0	8	8	31	4.48
at Home	33	44.0	36	14	47	5	0	5	2	19	3.48
on Road	30	36.1	34	14	37	3	0	3	6	12	5.70
on Grass	23	31.2	22	11	32	2	0	2	2	12	3.13
on Artificial Turf	40	48.2	48	17	52	6	0	6	6	19	5.36
Day Games	22	30.1	25	13	35	3	0	3	4	10	5.93
Night Games	41	50.0	45	15	49	5	0	5	4	21	3.60
April	7	8.2	11	5	3	0	0	1	1	4	7.27
May	12	14.2	16	10	19	2	0	1	2	6	7.36
June	12	15.0	15	2	18	2	0	2	1	6	4.20
July	10	12.2	11	2	13	1	0	1	1	6	2.13
August	10	13.0	9	6	14	2	0	1	2	3	5.54
Sept/Oct	12	16.1	8	3	17	1	0	2	1	6	1.65

FOUR YEAR TOTALS (1984 – 1987)

	G	IP	H	BB	SO	SB	CS	W	L	S	ERA
	256	344.0	291	117	297	34	6	24	32	130	3.61
	126	171.1	157	63	152	20	4	16	18	64	3.83
	130	172.2	134	54	145	14	2	8	14	66	3.39
	95	128.2	106	47	105	8	4	10	11	44	3.36
	161	215.1	185	70	192	26	2	14	21	86	3.76
	71	98.2	79	32	83	6	1	6	8	36	4.01
	185	245.1	212	85	214	28	5	18	24	94	3.45
	32	51.0	42	22	34	5	1	4	4	15	3.18
	51	72.0	51	22	70	9	1	7	3	28	2.13
	45	61.0	55	17	59	6	0	4	6	24	3.98
	37	41.1	53	13	32	6	3	1	6	17	5.44
	44	57.1	42	31	45	5	1	3	9	22	4.87
	47	61.1	48	12	57	3	0	5	4	24	2.93

vs. Opponent Batters

vs. Opponent Batters	Ave.	OBP	SLG	AB	H	2B	3B	HR	RBI	BB	SO
Totals	.232	.301	.417	302	70	14	0	14	59	28	84
vs. Left	.301	.364	.532	156	47	9	0	9	40	16	30
vs. Right	.158	.231	.295	146	23	5	0	5	19	12	54
Bases Empty	.213	.284	.344	160	34	9	0	4	4	15	43
Leadoff	.133	.200	.217	60	8	2	0	1	1	4	21
Not Leadoff	.260	.333	.420	100	26	7	0	3	3	11	22
Runners On Base	.254	.319	.500	142	36	5	0	10	55	13	41
First Base Only	.200	.231	.400	50	10	4	0	2	4	2	15
Scoring Position	.283	.361	.554	92	26	1	0	8	51	11	26
Late Innings, Close	.258	.325	.445	229	59	10	0	11	53	22	66

	Ave.	OBP	SLG	AB	H	2B	3B	HR	RBI	BB	SO
	.228	.294	.358	1276	291	44	4	38	169	117	297
	.258	.332	.396	667	172	22	2	22	108	75	121
	.195	.250	.317	609	119	22	2	16	61	42	176
	.226	.280	.351	695	157	25	1	20	20	51	149
	.185	.240	.293	276	51	7	1	7	7	19	63
	.253	.306	.389	419	106	18	0	13	13	32	86
	.231	.310	.367	581	134	19	3	18	149	66	148
	.229	.282	.380	205	47	8	1	7	18	15	50
	.231	.324	.359	376	87	11	2	11	131	51	98
	.236	.304	.365	998	236	30	4	30	148	95	237

RBI/Opportunities

Scoring Position	36 / 143 (25%)
Scoring Position, 2 Out	22 / 77 (29%)
On Third, Less than 2 Out	10 / 30 (33%)
RBI in close games / RBI Total	53 / 59 (90%)

	107 / 545 (20%)
	46 / 277 (17%)
	34 / 88 (39%)
	148 / 169 (88%)

Gary Redus
Chicago White Sox

Like another Gary—Hart—Gary Redus runs into trouble once that first dazzling impression has worn off. When he came up to the majors at the end of the 1982 season, Redus was considered one the jewels of the Reds' farm system. What else could you think of a guy who'd broken into baseball with a .462 batting average and 100 runs scored in 68 games? The next spring Redus won a regular job but soon found he couldn't hold it. From '83 to'85, Gary got into 349 games, an average of 116 a year. He stole bases and scored runs at an impressive rate, averaging 63 steals and 97 runs per 162 games. But his batting average was only .251, and, according to one distinguished publication and a folk-hero manager, most of his outs were flyouts.

I take it Gary Redus has hit more flyballs to left than anyone in the history of baseball. That seems to be a serious crime in Cincinnati, and sooner than you could say John Denny, Redus was a Phillie. Not for long. Redus was Philadelphia's left fielder on opening day of 1986, but by the end of April he was on the disabled list. By the time he returned the Phils had discovered what a nice young man Jeff Stone was. Eventually Gary got into 90 games, stealing 25 bases, scoring 62 runs and hitting 11 home runs. For a full season, that projects to 45 steals, 112 runs and 20 homers. No matter; with his .247 average and a zillion more flyouts, Redus was considered a disappointment. It was on to the White Sox, in exchange for Joe (Radar Arm) Cowley.

I was impressed watching Redus play in 1987, but I didn't have too much company. Gary's batting average was his lowest yet (.236); even so, it was a typical Gary Redus year. Despite a painful hamstring injury, he scored 78 runs, stole 52 bases, hit 12 homers and drew 69 walks in 127 games. Not to belabor the point, but over a full year that would be 99 runs, 66 steals, 15 homers, and 88 walks. His secondary average, an excellent measure of the offensive skills not shown in batting averages, was .411, an outstanding figure for anyone, but just normal for Redus.

In the field he was a real surprise to me, showing excellent range and judgment (he played the left field wall in Fenway like a veteran), and a fine throwing arm as well. He led all Sox outfielders with 12 assists; he seemed popular with his teammates.

Yet all year long I kept reading about what a lousy year he was having. I could understand this if it came from some less-than-astute sportswriter, but the Sox front office seemed to believe it as well. They traded for Dan Pasqua after the season, and if Redus figures in their plans for 1988, it's news to me. For the crimes of being less durable than average, a flyball hitter, and concentrating his offensive value outside the traditional measure of batting average, he seems destined yet again for another uniform change.

Don Zminda

Redus, Gary Eugene

Bats: Right   Throws: Right   Born 11/01/56

1987 SEASON AND MAJOR-LEAGUE CAREER BATTING TOTALS

	G	AB	H	2B	3B	HR	TB	R	RBI	TBB	IBB	SO	HP	SH	SF	SB	CS	SB%	GDP	AVG	OBP	SLG
87 CHA	130	475	112	26	6	12	186	78	48	69	0	90	0	3	7	52	11	.83	7	.236	.328	.392
6 YEARS	589	1991	488	106	28	54	812	362	189	288	13	423	8	11	17	223	57	.80	19	.245	.340	.408

	1987 SEASON											FOUR YEAR TOTALS (1984 – 1987)										
	Ave.	OBP	SLG	AB	H	2B	3B	HR	RBI	BB	SO	Ave.	OBP	SLG	AB	H	2B	3B	HR	RBI	BB	SO
Totals	.236	.328	.392	475	112	26	6	12	48	69	90	.246	.341	.401	1455	358	83	17	36	131	212	291
vs. Left	.269	.372	.473	201	54	14	3	7	20	35	27	.260	.377	.410	607	158	36	8	13	50	115	109
vs. Right	.212	.295	.332	274	58	12	3	5	28	34	63	.236	.314	.394	848	200	47	9	23	81	97	182
at Home	.244	.331	.374	238	58	13	3	4	30	34	41	.267	.362	.438	749	200	48	10	20	82	114	145
on Road	.228	.326	.409	237	54	13	3	8	18	35	49	.224	.318	.361	706	158	35	7	16	49	98	146
vs. Groundball	.255	.342	.410	239	61	16	3	5	28	33	40	.252	.338	.395	737	186	38	8	17	62	94	123
vs. Flyball	.216	.315	.373	236	51	10	3	7	20	36	50	.240	.344	.407	718	172	45	9	19	69	118	168
vs. Finesse	.237	.307	.401	274	65	16	4	7	26	29	50	.257	.341	.430	824	212	51	11	23	75	104	130
vs. Power	.234	.355	.378	201	47	10	2	5	22	40	40	.231	.340	.363	631	146	32	6	13	56	108	161
on Grass	.235	.325	.367	395	93	21	5	7	40	56	71	.229	.321	.358	645	148	36	7	11	63	91	124
on Artificial Turf	.237	.344	.512	80	19	5	1	5	8	13	19	.259	.357	.435	810	210	47	10	25	68	121	167
Day Games	.233	.315	.404	146	34	6	2	5	14	19	32	.240	.332	.422	488	117	28	8	15	40	68	104
Night Games	.237	.334	.386	329	78	20	4	7	34	50	58	.249	.346	.390	967	241	55	9	21	91	144	187
April	.205	.333	.288	73	15	4	1	0	4	14	19	.258	.373	.363	190	49	13	2	1	12	35	40
May	.253	.345	.463	95	24	4	2	4	11	14	21	.296	.360	.478	226	67	11	3	8	20	23	53
June	.196	.288	.353	51	10	2	0	2	4	7	12	.211	.333	.368	204	43	13	2	5	20	38	37
July	.250	.322	.375	80	20	3	2	1	5	9	15	.240	.321	.396	288	69	18	3	7	22	35	56
August	.253	.346	.429	91	23	8	1	2	13	14	11	.244	.339	.427	307	75	16	5	10	33	45	51
Sept/Oct	.235	.316	.400	85	20	5	0	3	11	11	12	.229	.327	.358	240	55	12	2	5	24	36	54
Bases Empty	.240	.332	.428	304	73	18	6	9	9	42	49	.248	.340	.414	975	242	57	15	25	25	136	187
Leadoff	.299	.390	.507	134	40	14	1	4	4	20	18	.249	.339	.412	527	131	36	4	14	14	72	91
Not Leadoff	.194	.286	.365	170	33	4	5	5	5	22	31	.248	.342	.417	448	111	21	11	11	11	64	96
Runners On	.228	.322	.327	171	39	8	0	3	39	27	41	.242	.341	.373	480	116	26	2	11	106	76	104
First Base Only	.189	.302	.216	74	14	2	0	0	1	12	18	.237	.350	.311	190	45	8	0	2	6	33	34
Scoring Position	.258	.336	.412	97	25	6	0	3	38	15	23	.245	.335	.414	290	71	18	2	9	100	43	70
Late Innings, Close	.300	.383	.429	70	21	3	0	2	6	10	15	.233	.335	.343	245	57	10	1	5	23	38	61

RBI/Opportunities

Scoring Position	33 / 140 (24%)	88 / 414 (21%)	
Scoring Position, 2 Out	14 / 63 (22%)	43 / 216 (20%)	
On Third, Less than 2 Out	13 / 26 (50%)	26 / 59 (44%)	
RBI in close games / RBI Total	24 / 48 (50%)	79 / 131 (60%)	

Rick Reuschel
Pittsburgh Pirates/San Francisco Giants

The lowest moment of the season for the Pirates was probably the weekend after Reuschel was traded to the Giants. There had been so many trades and rumors of trades, and now Reuschel, who had been the best pitcher on the staff all summer and who had stated a desire to remain in Pittsburgh, was gone. The Bucs lost three straight to Atlanta, before coming back to Pittsburgh for a Syd Thrift pep talk and a 27–11 finish. Reuschel, in the meantime, packed his bags and helped the Giants wrap up the western division. The joke was that Thrift's plan to get the Pirates into the playoffs was to send them there one at a time: Reuschel with the Giants, Morrison with the Tigers, Pena with the Cardinals.

The Giants acquisition of Reuschel had an extra effect on the pennant race in that it meant that the Reds were not able to obtain him. Reportedly, Reuschel vetoed a trade to Cincinnati because of the way the Reds treated him in 1985 when he was attempting his comeback. The fact that the Pirates had given him a chance and had rewarded him handsomely with one of the few multi-year contracts the new owners have signed was a major factor in Reuschel's desire to stay in Pittsburgh.

Reuschel rebounded from last season's off-year with a pretty good season. He finished with 13 victories, and perhaps should have had more; early in the season, he took leads into the 8th and 9th innings, only to see the Pirate bullpen give away the lead. Some of Don Robinson's 11 victories really should have been Reuschel's.

It was a lot of fun to watch Reuschel pitch. He's very much the professional, always concentrating, never forgetting the little things. He holds runners on base, and fields his position very well, winning his second Gold Glove in three years. He hits reasonably well for a pitcher, and moves very well for a big man. He's pretty consistent; if he can get through the first couple of innings (when his sinkerball doesn't sink as well), he'll usually give you seven or eight innings.

Reuschel is only 25 victories away from 200 victories, and would like a shot at reaching that plateau. The Giants just signed him to a contract extension through 1989, so he should have a reasonable shot at the 200 victory plateau, if he stays healthy. When Reuschel left Pittsburgh, there were rumors that he was having arm trouble.

Even if the arm trouble is just a myth, the Pirates probably did the right thing in trading Reuschel. Veteran starting pitchers that can help a team win a pennant race were in short supply, and the Pirates were able to obtain much-needed bullpen help. I'll miss seeing Reuschel pitch, but he helped the Pirates more by what he could fetch in trade than by what he could do on the mound.

Sherri M. Nichols

Reuschel, Rickey Eugene "Rick" Bats: Right Throws: Right Born 05/16/49

1987 SEASON AND MAJOR-LEAGUE CAREER PITCHING TOTALS

	G	GS	CG	GF	IP	BFP	H	R	ER	HR	SH	SF	HB	TBB	IBB	SO	WP	Bk	W	L	Pct	ShO	Sv	ERA
87 PIT-SF	34	33	12	0	227	920	207	91	78	13	8	8	8	42	3	107	7	0	13	9	.591	4	0	3.09
15 YEARS	470	447	93	14	2999	12584	3032	1286	1134	184	140	94	79	801	95	1759	83	10	175	164	.516	24	4	3.40

1987: Finesse, Flyball   1986: Finesse, Groundball   1985: Finesse, Groundball   1984: Finesse, Groundball

1987 SEASON												FOUR YEAR TOTALS (1984 – 1987)											
	G	IP	H	BB	SO	SB	CS	W	L	S	ERA	G	IP	H	BB	SO	SB	CS	W	L	S	ERA
Totals	34	226.2	207	42	107	5	9	13	9	0	3.10	119	728.2	715	174	413	33	31	41	38	1	3.38
at Home	17	108.0	99	17	47	3	2	7	4	0	3.42	62	379.2	365	90	211	21	13	29	16	0	3.32
on Road	17	118.2	108	25	60	2	7	6	5	0	2.81	57	349.0	350	84	202	12	18	12	22	1	3.48
on Grass	11	75.1	64	15	37	0	5	3	3	0	3.11	46	286.0	286	65	152	8	12	13	13	0	3.52
on Artificial Turf	23	151.1	143	27	70	5	4	10	6	0	3.09	73	442.2	429	109	261	25	19	28	25	1	3.31
Day Games	14	89.2	71	18	46	0	4	5	5	0	3.11	46	260.2	270	67	147	5	9	12	13	0	4.11
Night Games	20	137.0	136	24	61	5	5	8	4	0	3.09	73	468.0	445	107	266	28	22	29	25	1	2.98
April	4	25.2	22	10	15	2	2	0	1	0	2.81	10	58.2	63	22	28	2	2	2	3	0	3.68
May	6	43.0	41	10	22	2	4	3	1	0	1.67	17	121.0	114	27	56	3	6	7	4	0	2.45
June	6	47.0	35	11	21	0	2	3	2	0	2.68	25	158.2	162	45	87	8	9	10	9	0	3.97
July	5	36.2	32	3	16	0	1	2	1	0	2.45	22	123.1	132	32	74	9	3	7	9	0	4.01
August	6	31.2	43	2	14	1	0	1	2	0	5.68	22	129.0	138	27	79	7	8	6	9	0	3.49
Sept/Oct	7	42.2	34	6	19	0	0	4	2	0	3.80	23	138.0	106	21	89	4	3	9	4	1	2.80

vs. Opponent Batters	Ave.	OBP	SLG	AB	H	2B	3B	HR	RBI	BB	SO	Ave.	OBP	SLG	AB	H	2B	3B	HR	RBI	BB	SO
Totals	.242	.282	.350	854	207	33	10	13	81	42	107	.258	.303	.370	2771	714	129	21	47	286	174	413
vs. Left	.258	.295	.393	484	125	26	9	7	41	23	39	.273	.321	.392	1452	397	80	16	20	140	101	143
vs. Right	.222	.265	.295	370	82	7	1	6	40	19	68	.240	.282	.346	1319	317	49	5	27	146	73	270
Bases Empty	.234	.276	.340	517	121	18	8	7	7	23	74	.250	.289	.365	1655	414	74	16	28	28	84	259
Leadoff	.268	.303	.395	220	59	8	4	4	4	7	32	.274	.310	.408	704	193	36	8	14	14	33	92
Not Leadoff	.209	.256	.300	297	62	10	4	3	3	16	42	.232	.274	.333	951	221	38	8	14	14	51	167
Runners On Base	.255	.290	.365	337	86	15	2	6	74	19	33	.269	.322	.378	1116	300	55	5	19	258	90	154
First Base Only	.264	.291	.390	159	42	12	1	2	9	6	17	.286	.317	.424	486	139	28	3	11	37	22	66
Scoring Position	.247	.290	.343	178	44	3	1	4	65	13	16	.256	.325	.343	630	161	27	2	8	221	68	88
Late Innings, Close	.202	.269	.310	84	17	3	0	2	7	6	14	.267	.326	.395	266	71	16	0	6	29	22	38

RBI/Opportunities

Scoring Position	58 / 229 (25%)	205 / 863 (24%)	
Scoring Position, 2 Out	15 / 94 (16%)	67 / 363 (18%)	
On Third, Less than 2 Out	30 / 49 (61%)	94 / 170 (55%)	
RBI in close games / RBI Total	63 / 81 (78%)	211 / 286 (74%)	

Craig Reynolds
Houston Astros

It is time to give this guy some credit. Craig Reynolds just goes on and on. Not a season goes by in which the Houston Astros are not touting someone to be their new shortstop of the decade, or at least their new shortstop of the season who will give some phenom more time to develop. And yet, at the end of every season, there is Craig Reynolds having played in more than 100 games, getting 300–400 at-bats, hitting around .260 and playing solid, if unspectacular defense.

Name all of the people in major league baseball who have been playing shortstop since 1975, Reynolds' first season. Alfredo Griffin didn't play his first major league game until 1976. Alan Trammell came on to the scene one year later, and Ozzie arrived in 1978. Robin Yount? He hasn't played shortstop in three years. Dave Concepcion of the Reds is the only active player in the major leagues who has played shortstop every year since then, and even he was the shortstop of last resort in 1987, the Reds using Barry Larkin and Kurt Stillwell instead. Concepcion played a lot of second base last season, and did time at first and third as well, but only played two games at shortstop last year.

Now, try naming all of the shortstops with whom Reynolds has had to compete for a starting job. Larry Milbourne, Mike Fischlin, Jimmy Sexton, Julio Gonzalez, Bert Pena and Dickie Thon all fit that category. And in 1988, his competition will come from Rafael Ramirez, obtained in an off-season deal with Atlanta. Ramirez, of course, is best known as the guy who leads National League shortstops in errors season after season. By 1989, the competition could come from youngster Chuck Jackson, a third baseman by trade, whom the Astros started to work out at shortstop in the instructional league last fall.

The downside for Reynolds is that he is 35 now, and his production has been slipping. He doesn't have nearly the range as he once did in the field and, while he hit .253 last season, he drove in just 28 runs in 375 at-bats. Measured differently, general managers and agents like to site a statistic called the "run production average" (RPA) of players during arbitration hearings. The figure is derived by taking the sum of the number of runs scored, plus RBIs, minus home runs, and dividing it all by the total number of plate appearances. Reynolds had the lowest figure in the major leagues last season at .142. Garry Pettis of California had the worst mark in the American League at .145. By contrast, Cincinnati's Eric Davis had the best mark in baseball, .326.

Tom Henry

Reynolds, Gordon Craig "Craig"

Bats: Left   Throws: Right   Born 12/27/52

1987 SEASON AND MAJOR-LEAGUE CAREER BATTING TOTALS

	G	AB	H	2B	3B	HR	TB	R	RBI	TBB	IBB	SO	HP	SH	SF	SB	CS	SB%	GDP	AVG	OBP	SLG
87 HOU	135	374	95	17	3	4	130	35	28	30	8	44	0	4	8	5	1	.83	4	.254	.303	.348
13 YEARS	1312	4116	1063	132	65	39	1442	444	349	200	27	365	9	118	37	54	32	.63	46	.258	.292	.350

	1987 SEASON											FOUR YEAR TOTALS (1984 – 1987)										
	Ave.	OBP	SLG	AB	H	2B	3B	HR	RBI	BB	SO	Ave.	OBP	SLG	AB	H	2B	3B	HR	RBI	BB	SO
Totals	.253	.303	.347	375	95	17	3	4	28	30	44	.259	.290	.364	1594	413	57	25	20	161	76	158
vs. Left	.140	.196	.140	43	6	0	0	0	0	3	10	.218	.247	.277	289	63	7	2	2	12	11	55
vs. Right	.268	.317	.373	332	89	17	3	4	28	27	34	.268	.299	.383	1305	350	50	23	18	149	65	103
at Home	.259	.316	.323	189	49	8	2	0	10	17	19	.265	.300	.354	775	205	26	14	5	71	43	76
on Road	.247	.291	.371	186	46	9	1	4	18	13	25	.254	.280	.374	819	208	31	11	15	90	33	82
vs. Groundball	.265	.317	.406	170	45	9	3	3	18	14	17	.274	.304	.402	729	200	26	17	11	92	35	68
vs. Flyball	.244	.292	.298	205	50	8	0	1	10	16	27	.246	.277	.332	865	213	31	8	9	69	41	90
vs. Finesse	.259	.310	.376	197	51	9	1	4	17	16	18	.267	.299	.383	845	226	28	14	14	90	43	66
vs. Power	.247	.296	.315	178	44	8	2	0	11	14	26	.250	.279	.342	749	187	29	11	6	71	33	92
on Grass	.262	.303	.402	122	32	5	0	4	15	8	17	.260	.288	.382	484	126	20	3	11	69	21	48
on Artificial Turf	.249	.304	.320	253	63	12	3	0	13	22	27	.259	.290	.356	1110	287	37	22	9	92	55	110
Day Games	.230	.254	.292	113	26	4	0	1	6	4	15	.275	.300	.389	393	108	15	3	8	44	16	37
Night Games	.263	.323	.370	262	69	13	3	3	22	26	29	.254	.286	.356	1201	305	42	22	12	117	60	121
April	.298	.370	.362	47	14	3	0	0	3	6	6	.314	.364	.484	159	50	9	0	6	26	13	13
May	.283	.320	.391	46	13	3	1	0	7	3	3	.274	.301	.365	274	75	11	7	0	26	11	29
June	.303	.319	.439	66	20	3	0	2	7	2	6	.275	.296	.398	284	78	7	5	6	32	9	33
July	.203	.274	.257	74	15	4	0	0	3	8	10	.225	.270	.305	315	71	10	3	3	23	20	32
August	.279	.338	.426	61	17	1	1	2	5	6	6	.285	.311	.394	284	81	13	3	4	26	11	21
Sept/Oct	.198	.241	.259	81	16	3	1	0	3	5	13	.209	.241	.295	278	58	7	7	1	28	12	30
Bases Empty	.289	.333	.393	211	61	12	2	2	2	14	21	.248	.277	.348	903	224	32	11	12	12	36	88
Leadoff	.289	.341	.395	76	22	3	1	1	1	6	7	.261	.283	.365	329	86	11	4	5	5	10	34
Not Leadoff	.289	.329	.393	135	39	9	1	1	1	8	14	.240	.273	.338	574	138	21	7	7	7	26	54
Runners On	.207	.267	.287	164	34	5	1	2	26	16	23	.274	.310	.385	691	189	25	14	8	149	40	70
First Base Only	.291	.317	.392	79	23	3	1	1	4	3	11	.298	.317	.415	325	97	10	8	4	21	9	32
Scoring Position	.129	.229	.188	85	11	2	0	1	22	13	12	.251	.304	.358	366	92	15	6	4	128	31	38
Late Innings, Close	.239	.292	.299	67	16	1	0	1	3	5	10	.245	.283	.324	278	68	8	1	4	23	15	26

RBI/Opportunities

	1987		Four Year
Scoring Position	20 / 124	(16%)	116 / 492 (24%)
Scoring Position, 2 Out	5 / 64	(8%)	44 / 231 (19%)
On Third, Less than 2 Out	13 / 20	(65%)	48 / 87 (55%)
RBI in close games / RBI Total	21 / 28	(75%)	116 / 161 (72%)

Harold Reynolds
Seattle Mariners

I love predictions. They signal the beginning of the baseball season. I start prowling the news stands late in January looking for anything that says "Baseball" on it. All those experts. They're so smart. Or are they! Here's what Earl Weaver had to say about the Mariner infield last spring. "The infield is a big minus, because we're looking at only one premier player: third baseman Jim Presley. I doubt whether Rey Quinones can develop at shortstop . . . or if Harold Reynolds can at second."

Maybe the reason why Dick Williams is so successful is that he has an eye for talent and the patience to let it develop. Now that doesn't sound like the old grump we've heard so much about, does it? Well, it's true. His tolerance with Quinones, and especially Reynolds, has rewarded Mariner fans with the most exciting double play combination in the American League.

Dick Williams proclaimed Harold Reynolds as his most valuable player of 1987. Why Harold and not Langston? I would assume because of the effort and improvement in Harold's play. What a year the second sacker had; he played in the All-Star game, was named to *Baseball America*'s AL All-Star team, and won the league's stolen base crown. By year's end, some were predicting that Reynolds would eventually be the successor to Frank White as the best second baseman in the AL.

Major League success didn't come easy, and Harold came awfully close to calling it quits after some hard times in Seattle. In 1985, Reynolds was called up to replace Jack Perconte. It was an extremely unpopular move and eventually caused the departure of Hal Keller, the Mariners' GM. Reynolds also suffered. He was the target of boos from a normally sedate Mariner following. It affected the sensitive Reynolds, and the career .300 minor leaguer failed miserably at the plate. Soon he was tagged "good glove, no bat."

In the spring of '86, second base was up for grabs between Reynolds, Perconte , and Danny Tartabull. Perconte had the best spring, but was released. Harold was showcased for the Giants, but they decided to stick with their own rookie, Robbie Thompson. Tartabull was awarded the job and Harold went to Calgary again.

1986 was also the year of the strikeout for the M's and that prompted a change in managers. Enter Dick Williams. Soon thereafter, Tartabull got sick and Reynolds was called up. He's played second ever since. Again, Reynolds was not successful at the plate. Batting leadoff most of the time, he ended the year with a pitiful .222 average.

In 1987, Williams moved him to the number 9 position. Harold gained confidence in the less demanding role. The rest is history. Feeling comfortable with his assignment in the batting order, Reynolds ended the season with impressive offensive stats and continued to thrill Mariner fans with his range and fielding abilities.

1988 will present Reynolds with some new challenges. Williams has announced that Harold will probably be returning to the top of the order.

Merrianna McCully

Reynolds, Harold Craig

Bats: Both   **Throws: Right**   **Born 10/26/60**

1987 SEASON AND MAJOR-LEAGUE CAREER BATTING TOTALS

	G	AB	H	2B	3B	HR	TB	R	RBI	TBB	IBB	SO	HP	SH	SF	SB	CS	SB%	GDP	AVG	OBP	SLG
87 SEA	160	530	146	31	8	1	196	73	35	39	0	34	2	8	5	60	20	.75	7	.275	.325	.370
5 YEARS	383	1148	275	57	14	2	366	145	66	87	0	100	6	20	6	94	37	.72	14	.240	.295	.319

	1987 SEASON										FOUR YEAR TOTALS (1984 – 1987)									
	Ave.	OBP	SLG	AB	H	2B	3B	HR	RBI	BB	SO	Ave.	OBP	SLG	AB	H	2B	3B	HR	RBI	BB	SO
Totals	.275	.325	.370	530	146	31	8	1	35	39	34	.242	.299	.320	1089	263	53	13	2	65	85	91
vs. Left	.278	.320	.370	162	45	8	2	1	12	10	14	.239	.295	.314	318	76	14	2	2	21	23	32
vs. Right	.274	.327	.370	368	101	23	6	0	23	29	20	.243	.300	.322	771	187	39	11	0	44	62	59
at Home	.233	.296	.319	257	60	11	4	1	11	22	15	.223	.290	.314	542	121	25	9	2	27	48	43
on Road	.315	.353	.418	273	86	20	4	0	24	17	19	.260	.308	.325	547	142	28	4	0	38	37	48
vs. Groundball	.264	.317	.344	276	73	14	4	0	20	21	19	.256	.312	.330	540	138	28	6	0	34	42	46
vs. Flyball	.287	.333	.398	254	73	17	4	1	15	18	15	.228	.286	.310	549	125	25	7	2	31	43	45
vs. Finesse	.268	.295	.356	298	80	15	4	1	21	12	14	.239	.280	.317	641	153	30	7	2	42	36	48
vs. Power	.284	.360	.388	232	66	16	4	0	14	27	20	.246	.323	.324	448	110	23	6	0	23	49	43
on Grass	.320	.366	.422	206	66	15	3	0	21	16	11	.247	.300	.309	421	104	20	3	0	27	32	37
on Artificial Turf	.247	.298	.336	324	80	16	5	1	14	23	23	.238	.298	.326	668	159	33	10	2	38	53	54
Day Games	.273	.320	.410	139	38	9	5	0	10	10	13	.246	.316	.340	285	70	15	6	0	20	29	35
Night Games	.276	.326	.355	391	108	22	3	1	25	29	21	.240	.292	.312	804	193	38	7	2	45	56	56
April	.293	.325	.387	75	22	5	1	0	5	4	6	.225	.292	.304	102	23	6	1	0	5	10	9
May	.284	.326	.352	88	25	4	1	0	7	6	3	.263	.307	.342	152	40	10	1	0	12	10	11
June	.235	.311	.321	81	19	5	1	0	3	8	6	.225	.278	.283	191	43	9	1	0	6	13	18
July	.262	.333	.412	80	21	5	2	1	9	8	7	.230	.303	.323	226	52	10	4	1	22	23	18
August	.340	.385	.480	100	34	10	2	0	4	8	4	.246	.304	.332	199	49	13	2	0	7	17	13
Sept/Oct	.236	.268	.274	106	25	2	1	0	7	5	8	.256	.293	.329	219	56	5	4	1	13	12	22
Bases Empty	.286	.344	.396	318	91	20	6	1	1	27	24	.249	.311	.338	659	164	35	9	2	2	58	58
Leadoff	.262	.329	.346	130	34	9	1	0	0	12	10	.240	.308	.321	296	71	16	4	0	0	28	31
Not Leadoff	.303	.355	.431	188	57	11	5	1	1	15	14	.256	.313	.353	363	93	19	5	2	2	30	27
Runners On	.259	.296	.330	212	55	11	2	0	34	12	10	.230	.274	.291	430	99	18	4	0	63	27	33
First Base Only	.277	.311	.376	101	28	8	1	0	2	5	4	.243	.278	.307	202	49	11	1	0	3	10	17
Scoring Position	.243	.282	.288	111	27	3	1	0	32	7	6	.219	.271	.276	228	50	7	3	0	60	17	16
Late Innings, Close	.267	.317	.347	75	20	4	1	0	5	6	6	.215	.287	.285	144	31	6	2	0	6	15	15

RBI/Opportunities

Scoring Position	32 / 148 (22%)	59 / 320 (18%)
Scoring Position, 2 Out	10 / 62 (16%)	22 / 155 (14%)
On Third, Less than 2 Out	15 / 29 (52%)	23 / 53 (43%)
RBI in close games / RBI Total	18 / 35 (51%)	33 / 65 (51%)

R. J. Reynolds
Pittsburgh Pirates

R. J. Reynolds is what you call an "average" National League batter. Look at this comparison of his 1987 season to the National League as a whole, proportioned to Reynolds' 369 at-bats plus walks:

	Reynolds	League
At-Bats	335	336
Runs	49	44
Hits	87	87
Doubles	24	16
Triples	1	2
Home Runs	7	9
Walks	34	33
Strikeouts	80	59
Total Bases	134	135
Batting Average	.260	.261
On-Base Percentage	.323	.327
Slugging Percentage	.400	.403

(Note: Reynolds' "Runs" is the average of his Runs Scored and RBIs. The discrepancy in the League's Batting Average is due to round-off error. The League has just over 335.5 At-Bats and just under 87.5 Hits.)

This is about as good a match as you'll find anywhere, and it makes Reynolds a benchmark for evaluating the Pittsburgh Pirates as they try to turn themselves into a contender. Contenders, you see, have average hitters on their benches, while weaker teams have to start them. Pittsburgh played Reynolds half-time and finished at about .500. For the Pirates to get any better and still start Reynolds, they'd have to come up with a superstar somewhere else to help carry the lineup. They'd have to be a team whose lineup was infield-driven, a team like the Tigers. Reynolds might well keep a starting job on the Tigers and have them still contend. He wouldn't bat very high, but if you have Alan Trammell and Lou Whitaker, you can afford to bat R. J. Reynolds seventh. The Pirates, however, just traded their only real hitter in the infield, and can't get away with this plan. They have to find outfielders who can play a bigger role in the lineup.

To contend, Jim Leyland has to make a decision in the outfield, a decision which will shape his lineup. Barry Bonds and Andy Van Slyke are going to play. One other spot remains. Leyland can play John "Ghost of Eddie Yost" Cangelosi and bat him leadoff. Cangelosi gets on base as much as anyone, and can run, but he has no power at all. Leyland can play Mike Diaz and bat him in a power spot. Diaz doesn't walk nor hit for average. Whichever one he plays will not give him the strength of the other, but will play a real, defined role in the batting order. But, if Leyland tries to put off the decision by playing Reynolds, who has more power than Cangelosi and gets on base more than Diaz, he's going to end up with an undefined batting order with kid infielders in key batting roles. the Pirates need better than that to contend in the NL East, and that's R. J. Reynolds' curse. He can play major league baseball, but he's just too average for the team he's on.

Brock J. Hanke

Reynolds, Robert James "R.J."   Bats: Both   Throws: Right   Born 04/19/59

1987 SEASON AND MAJOR-LEAGUE CAREER BATTING TOTALS

	G	AB	H	2B	3B	HR	TB	R	RBI	TBB	IBB	SO	HP	SH	SF	SB	CS	SB%	GDP	AVG	OBP	SLG
87 PIT	117	335	87	24	1	7	134	47	51	34	8	80	0	0	6	14	1	.93	5	.260	.323	.400
5 YEARS	436	1369	365	81	12	23	539	182	176	113	14	256	4	15	15	60	20	.75	28	.267	.321	.394

	1987 SEASON										FOUR YEAR TOTALS (1984 – 1987)									
	Ave.	OBP	SLG	AB	H	2B	3B	HR	RBI	BB	SO	Ave.	OBP	SLG	AB	H	2B	3B	HR	RBI	BB	SO
Totals	.260	.323	.400	335	87	24	1	7	51	34	80	.268	.323	.396	1314	352	81	12	21	165	110	245
vs. Left	.351	.391	.386	57	20	2	0	0	10	5	2	.272	.309	.353	346	94	17	4	1	43	20	41
vs. Right	.241	.309	.403	278	67	22	1	7	41	29	78	.267	.328	.411	968	258	64	8	20	122	90	204
at Home	.267	.318	.401	172	46	15	1	2	23	15	40	.273	.332	.417	640	175	48	7	10	82	58	121
on Road	.252	.328	.399	163	41	9	0	5	28	19	40	.263	.315	.375	674	177	33	5	11	83	52	124
vs. Groundball	.255	.320	.418	165	42	10	1	5	23	16	38	.295	.348	.432	590	174	35	8	10	78	49	91
vs. Flyball	.265	.325	.382	170	45	14	0	2	28	18	42	.246	.304	.366	724	178	46	4	11	87	61	154
vs. Finesse	.278	.360	.457	151	42	12	0	5	23	20	24	.268	.318	.396	705	189	36	6	14	94	51	91
vs. Power	.245	.291	.353	184	45	12	1	2	28	14	56	.268	.329	.396	609	163	45	6	7	71	59	154
on Grass	.229	.302	.385	96	22	3	0	4	15	10	28	.270	.322	.374	522	141	23	2	9	66	40	109
on Artificial Turf	.272	.331	.406	239	65	21	1	3	36	24	52	.266	.324	.410	792	211	58	10	12	99	70	136
Day Games	.288	.319	.459	111	32	8	1	3	20	6	28	.259	.293	.363	421	109	21	4	5	57	22	86
Night Games	.246	.324	.371	224	55	16	0	4	31	28	52	.272	.337	.411	893	243	60	8	16	108	88	159
April	.393	.414	.536	28	11	4	0	0	2	1	2	.315	.356	.486	111	35	13	0	2	11	7	19
May	.290	.355	.449	69	20	6	1	1	11	7	16	.290	.345	.414	297	86	22	3	3	34	25	52
June	.316	.395	.500	76	24	5	0	3	14	10	16	.282	.351	.425	294	83	17	2	7	41	31	55
July	.071	.156	.089	56	4	1	0	0	2	6	20	.224	.288	.328	192	43	9	1	3	23	18	40
August	.222	.278	.349	63	14	5	0	1	13	6	13	.203	.255	.297	172	35	9	2	1	23	13	34
Sept/Oct	.326	.375	.535	43	14	3	0	2	9	4	13	.282	.325	.419	248	70	11	4	5	33	16	45
Bases Empty	.254	.310	.382	173	44	13	0	3	3	14	38	.265	.320	.391	752	199	50	6	11	11	61	127
Leadoff	.303	.329	.447	76	23	5	0	2	2	3	16	.286	.339	.438	308	88	20	3	7	7	25	46
Not Leadoff	.216	.296	.330	97	21	8	0	1	1	11	22	.250	.306	.358	444	111	30	3	4	4	36	81
Runners On	.265	.335	.420	162	43	11	1	4	48	20	42	.272	.327	.402	562	153	31	6	10	154	49	118
First Base Only	.313	.353	.625	64	20	6	1	4	11	4	17	.294	.329	.479	211	62	12	3	7	23	11	43
Scoring Position	.235	.325	.286	98	23	5	0	0	37	16	25	.259	.327	.356	351	91	19	3	3	131	38	75
Late Innings, Close	.263	.348	.351	57	15	2	0	1	14	9	17	.247	.302	.354	263	65	16	3	2	34	22	65

RBI/Opportunities

Scoring Position	35 / 141 (25%)	120 / 475 (25%)
Scoring Position, 2 Out	11 / 67 (16%)	46 / 215 (21%)
On Third, Less than 2 Out	15 / 25 (60%)	48 / 86 (56%)
RBI in close games / RBI Total	36 / 51 (71%)	111 / 165 (67%)

Rick Rhoden
New York Yankees

When the Yankees traded for Rick Rhoden after the 1986 season, they expected to get a workhorse who would solidify their rotation. After all, the thinking went, Rick had pitched at least 213 innings for the last five years. That mindset helps explain why his 1987 was something of a disappointment to management.

Though Rick did lead the team in victories (also matching his personal high), he started only 29 games and pitched only 181.2 innings. He was hit on the shoulder by a Harold Reynolds line drive on August 18; that affected his performance (he never went more than five innings in any start for the rest of the year) and forced him to miss the last three weeks of the season. Had that not happened, New York's second half would have been considerably less dismal than it turned out to be.

One reason why is that New York was scheduled to play 14 of their last 20 games at home; Rhoden has an unusual ability to succeed in his home park. He was 29–10 (13–14 away) with Los Angeles, 48–37 (31–36 away) with Pittsburgh and 10–3 (6–7 away) with New York. Or should I say "downright weird"—from '84 to '86, he had a 3.13 ERA on plastic and a 3.79 ERA on grass; he more than turned that around this year.

But when he was healthy, Rhoden lived up to expectations. With a shaky rotation (which the Yankees' usually was), you need one pitcher who can give the long and middle relievers a day off. Rick averaged over six innings per start, tops on the club. But, though he reached the eighth inning nine times—more than any other Yankee—he didn't lead the team in complete games.

Not that the bullpen gave Rhoden anything to complain about. Dave Righetti recorded saves in half of Rick's 16 wins; the rest of the pen added four saves. They were 12-for-12 in save chances in Rhoden's wins. If the offense had done their jobs as well, he might have had a chance at 20 wins. Though the Yankees scored 4.90 runs per game, they scored only 4.36 in Rhoden's starts.

Rhoden's reputation for making baseballs do funny things, coupled with the umpires' increased vigilance this year, may have caused him some problems in 1987. In midseason, opposing managers began paying very close attention to Rick and were constantly haranguing the umpires to search him. They never actually caught him in the act, but they did rattle him; on a few occasions, his game fell apart right after he was searched. I don't know if he quit messing with the ball for fear of being caught or if the interruption just broke his concentration—but, whatever it was, opponents should keep it up as often as possible. At least in 1987, Rhoden wasn't the same pitcher after a visit from the men in blue.

Craig Christmann

Rhoden, Richard Alan "Rick"

Bats: Right   Throws: Right   Born 05/16/53

1987 SEASON AND MAJOR-LEAGUE CAREER PITCHING TOTALS

	G	GS	CG	GF	IP	BFP	H	R	ER	HR	SH	SF	HB	TBB	IBB	SO	WP	Bk	W	L	Pct	ShO	Sv	ERA
87 NYA	30	29	4	1	182	764	184	84	78	22	6	7	3	61	5	107	9	1	16	10	.615	0	0	3.86
14 YEARS	363	333	64	12	2299	9621	2292	987	896	171	86	55	28	704	50	1284	77	23	137	107	.561	16	1	3.51

1987: Finesse, Groundball   1986: Finesse, Groundball   1985: Finesse, Groundball   1984: Finesse, Groundball

	1987 SEASON											FOUR YEAR TOTALS (1984 – 1987)										
	G	IP	H	BB	SO	SB	CS	W	L	S	ERA	G	IP	H	BB	SO	SB	CS	W	L	S	ERA
Totals	30	181.2	184	61	107	14	12	16	10	0	3.86	132	887.0	865	268	530	62	52	55	46	0	3.40
at Home	15	93.0	90	28	50	3	10	10	3	0	3.29	70	480.1	459	140	279	29	34	34	21	0	3.02
on Road	15	88.2	94	33	57	11	2	6	7	0	4.47	62	406.2	406	128	251	33	18	21	25	0	3.85
on Grass	8	39.1	39	16	27	4	2	3	4	0	4.35	39	254.0	241	80	151	20	15	16	13	0	3.19
on Artificial Turf	22	142.1	145	45	80	10	10	13	6	0	3.73	93	633.0	624	188	379	42	37	39	33	0	3.50
Day Games	23	145.1	127	44	87	7	11	16	5	0	3.16	49	318.2	295	99	197	16	19	23	17	0	3.50
Night Games	7	36.1	57	17	20	7	1	0	5	0	6.69	83	568.1	570	169	333	46	33	32	29	0	3.36
April	4	25.0	24	9	16	3	4	2	2	0	3.60	18	113.1	124	36	64	8	12	7	8	0	3.73
May	6	40.1	40	11	25	5	2	4	1	0	4.02	22	152.0	150	48	74	10	6	10	6	0	3.14
June	6	36.2	30	12	19	1	3	3	2	0	3.68	23	156.1	141	39	101	8	11	11	7	0	3.17
July	6	36.2	36	16	22	2	3	4	1	0	2.45	24	160.2	154	58	101	8	14	9	11	0	2.91
August	6	34.0	43	12	23	2	0	2	3	0	4.50	23	163.0	157	47	113	13	6	12	6	0	3.31
Sept/Oct	2	9.0	11	1	2	1	0	1	1	0	8.00	22	141.2	139	40	77	15	6	6	8	0	4.38

vs. Opponent Batters	Ave.	OBP	SLG	AB	H	2B	3B	HR	RBI	BB	SO	Ave.	OBP	SLG	AB	H	2B	3B	HR	RBI	BB	SO
Totals	.268	.327	.419	687	184	30	4	22	74	61	107	.257	.312	.380	3360	865	159	21	70	321	268	530
vs. Left	.275	.342	.455	363	100	17	3	14	47	37	47	.263	.322	.367	1788	471	75	13	28	163	154	230
vs. Right	.259	.311	.380	324	84	13	1	8	27	24	60	.251	.301	.394	1572	394	84	8	42	158	114	300
Bases Empty	.274	.329	.432	424	116	20	4	13	13	34	61	.262	.307	.393	2063	541	102	12	48	48	133	303
Leadoff	.256	.311	.415	176	45	7	3	5	5	13	28	.271	.308	.431	873	237	44	7	27	27	45	117
Not Leadoff	.286	.342	.444	248	71	13	1	8	8	21	33	.255	.307	.366	1190	304	58	5	21	21	88	186
Runners On Base	.259	.324	.399	263	68	10	0	9	61	27	46	.250	.320	.359	1297	324	57	9	22	273	135	227
First Base Only	.310	.328	.483	116	36	5	0	5	12	3	18	.260	.302	.354	554	144	17	4	9	28	33	77
Scoring Position	.218	.322	.333	147	32	5	0	4	49	24	28	.242	.333	.362	743	180	40	5	13	245	102	150
Late Innings, Close	.163	.196	.327	49	8	2	0	2	2	2	7	.266	.325	.368	323	86	14	2	5	21	28	55

RBI/Opportunities

Scoring Position	41 / 205	(20%)	214 / 995	(22%)
Scoring Position, 2 Out	15 / 98	(15%)	91 / 492	(18%)
On Third, Less than 2 Out	17 / 34	(50%)	68 / 148	(46%)
RBI in close games / RBI Total	47 / 74	(64%)	227 / 321	(71%)

Jim Rice
Boston Red Sox

Boston fans who were expecting to enjoy the "new look" Jim Rice of 1986 last season instead found themselves watching the old model from '84–'85. Gone were the short stroke and the hits up the gaps; gone were the long, low doubles and the singles to right. Back was the big swing, and with it came Jim's old specialty, the double play ball.

There have been calls for Mr. Rice to change his uniform number to 643 for greater scoring convenience—and with good reason. He has, to date, 293 career GIDPs; 18 less than Carl Yastrzemski's American League record for most in a career. He is a strong bet to break Hank Aaron's record for career GIDPs (328) during the '88 campaign and a mortal lock to do so before his career ends. In 1987 he exceeded his '86 twofer total (19) by three, with only two thirds the plate appearances; he finished third in the AL to Gary Gaetti (25) and Julio Franco (23).

Accompanying the jump in DPs was a loss in power, particularly against lefties. He slugged 180 points less against them in 1987. For the third time in the last four years, he had more GIDPs than home runs. The line drives of 1986 were one and two hoppers to an infielder in 1987. His HR frequency was the same as in '86, but his doubles rate was off by one third.

Rice was hurt for much of 1987, so some of the drop in performance can be blamed on his sore elbow. But I believe that there was another factor involved. During spring training he had perceived that the team was going nowhere in 1987; after the thrills of '86, this was an unexciting prospectus. It was a long season for the Red Sox, and it was a long season for Jim Rice. Boston's dismal road record reflects the disinterest of the team as a whole; in Rice's case, indifference caused a return to some old bad habits.

What will it take to get Rice more interested in the 1988 season? One possible motivator is the prospect of competition; another is that 1988 is the last year of his current contract. Since there are plenty of quality young outfielders in the Boston system, Jim will likely receive only one more opportunity to contribute as the regular left fielder; only some excellent work with the lumber will forestall his demotion to platoon DH. Pride alone may spur Rice to a return to past glories next year.

If that is not enough, there is fiscal necessity; management will be unlikely to pick up Jim's option for 1989 if he does not tear up the league this year. Do you replace baseball's highest-paid player of 1987 with someone who makes one tenth the wage? It'll be an easy decision if there is no increase in production from Mr. Rice in 1988.

Fred Percival

Rice, James Edward "Jim"   Bats: Right   Throws: Right   Born 03/08/53

1987 SEASON AND MAJOR-LEAGUE CAREER BATTING TOTALS

	G	AB	H	2B	3B	HR	TB	R	RBI	TBB	IBB	SO	HP	SH	SF	SB	CS	SB%	GDP	AVG	OBP	SLG
87 BOS	108	404	112	14	0	13	165	66	62	45	3	77	7	0	3	1	1	.50	22	.277	.357	.408
14 YEARS	1898	7531	2275	345	74	364	3860	1171	1351	609	75	1295	60	5	83	56	33	.63	293	.302	.355	.513

	1987 SEASON											FOUR YEAR TOTALS (1984 – 1987)										
	Ave.	OBP	SLG	AB	H	2B	3B	HR	RBI	BB	SO	Ave.	OBP	SLG	AB	H	2B	3B	HR	RBI	BB	SO
Totals	.277	.357	.408	404	112	14	0	13	62	45	77	.294	.353	.468	2225	655	98	12	88	397	202	332
vs. Left	.285	.371	.398	123	35	2	0	4	16	16	19	.308	.386	.496	595	183	30	2	26	104	78	70
vs. Right	.274	.351	.413	281	77	12	0	9	46	29	58	.290	.340	.458	1630	472	68	10	62	293	124	262
at Home	.305	.391	.447	190	58	6	0	7	32	24	36	.320	.373	.510	1106	354	59	8	45	215	95	164
on Road	.252	.326	.374	214	54	8	0	6	30	21	41	.269	.333	.426	1119	301	39	4	43	182	107	168
vs. Groundball	.279	.351	.363	201	56	8	0	3	34	19	37	.297	.352	.435	1084	322	43	7	31	180	91	145
vs. Flyball	.276	.364	.453	203	56	6	0	10	28	26	40	.292	.354	.499	1141	333	55	5	57	217	111	187
vs. Finesse	.277	.342	.381	202	56	6	0	5	32	18	34	.288	.340	.462	1248	360	51	5	52	213	98	144
vs. Power	.277	.372	.436	202	56	8	0	8	30	27	43	.302	.369	.475	977	295	47	7	36	184	104	188
on Grass	.297	.374	.439	330	98	14	0	11	57	36	63	.301	.357	.486	1872	563	85	12	79	358	166	274
on Artificial Turf	.189	.282	.270	74	14	0	0	2	5	9	14	.261	.330	.374	353	92	13	0	9	39	36	58
Day Games	.245	.298	.342	155	38	6	0	3	19	9	35	.283	.335	.460	735	208	31	3	31	125	56	112
Night Games	.297	.392	.450	249	74	8	0	10	43	36	42	.300	.361	.472	1490	447	67	9	57	272	146	220
April	.214	.329	.400	70	15	4	0	3	4	8	16	.239	.315	.395	306	73	13	1	11	45	30	43
May	.328	.403	.397	58	19	4	0	0	10	8	10	.304	.354	.457	381	116	17	1	13	67	30	60
June	.272	.342	.369	103	28	4	0	2	20	10	21	.325	.379	.518	434	141	30	3	16	85	37	70
July	.376	.414	.559	93	35	2	0	5	15	6	17	.291	.336	.433	402	117	9	3	14	60	27	58
August	.188	.289	.281	32	6	0	0	1	6	4	7	.261	.337	.418	364	95	13	1	14	61	41	61
Sept/Oct	.188	.322	.313	48	9	0	0	2	7	9	6	.334	.401	.577	338	113	16	3	20	79	37	40
Bases Empty	.280	.358	.455	189	53	6	0	9	9	21	37	.281	.336	.458	1045	294	45	4	44	44	84	154
Leadoff	.280	.363	.420	100	28	2	0	4	4	12	18	.279	.337	.448	466	130	22	0	19	19	40	62
Not Leadoff	.281	.354	.494	89	25	4	0	5	5	9	19	.283	.335	.466	579	164	23	4	25	25	44	92
Runners On	.274	.356	.367	215	59	8	0	4	53	24	40	.306	.371	.476	1180	361	53	8	44	353	118	178
First Base Only	.275	.333	.385	91	25	4	0	2	5	6	13	.285	.323	.451	501	143	23	3	18	43	26	64
Scoring Position	.274	.372	.355	124	34	4	0	2	48	18	27	.321	.403	.495	679	218	30	5	26	310	92	114
Late Innings, Close	.265	.342	.324	68	18	1	0	1	9	7	14	.257	.328	.429	331	85	13	1	14	59	34	57

RBI/Opportunities

Scoring Position	43 / 174 (25%)	267 / 951 (28%)
Scoring Position, 2 Out	14 / 81 (17%)	83 / 369 (22%)
On Third, Less than 2 Out	17 / 31 (55%)	112 / 208 (54%)
RBI in close games / RBI Total	44 / 62 (71%)	273 / 397 (69%)

Dave Righetti
New York Yankees

Dave Righetti has now spent four full seasons as the Yankee stopper, but the debate over whether he should start or relieve rages on, both among Yankee fans and—with Billy Martin back—maybe Yankee management, too. Given his off-season, what are his chances to return to the rotation in 1988? Probably quite slim, for two reasons.

When a reliever's ERA goes from 2.45 to 3.51, it's usually logical to conclude that his ability to strand inherited runners decreased right along with it. That was true with Righetti, but to a much smaller degree than you'd suspect. In 1986, Dave stranded 39 of the 48 runners (81.2 percent) that he inherited; in 1987, he stranded 28 of 39 (71.2 percent). The 10 percent drop looks larger on paper than it is on the field—had Righetti stranded runners as often in 1987 as he did in 1986, he would have stranded only three more men. The pitcher most badly hurt by Righetti's ineffectiveness was Dave himself.

The second reason that Righetti is likely to remain a reliever is the perception that the ace reliever is more valuable than the ace starter—which seems to have taken hold on virtually every winning team. Since 1982, the 24 division champions have had a total of six 20-game winners as opposed to nine 30-game savers. In that period, the only world champion to have a 20-game winner on their roster was the 1985 Royals; four of the six champs have had a 30-save man. If anything, the perception that the relief ace is more valuable seems to be increasing. In the last two years, Roger Clemens has been the only 20-game winner on a division champ; Dave Smith, Todd Worrell and Jeff Reardon have all saved 30 for division winners. In 1987, there were two 20-game winners and seven 30-game savers.

The only argument for moving Righetti to the rotation would be his declining effectiveness. It's an argument which can be made. Righetti, many observers claim, has lost something off his pitches. That appears to be true. Righetti allowed exactly nine hits per nine innings pitched in 1987—almost a hit more than he has in any other year in the bullpen. Until last year, his strikeout per nine innings pitched stats had been declining sharply—from 8.41 to 7.74 to 7.00 to 7.29. His walks per nine innings skyrocketed last year—to 4.17—and his strikeout to walk ratio was easily the worst of his career.

On the other hand, Righetti has never saved less than 29 games in a season—and he's four saves away from second place on the Yankees' all-time save list. He's won the stomach acid award in each of the last two seasons; New York is 89–11 when he's pitched in save situations over the past two years. He's gotten the job done and is awfully young (just turned 29) to be burned out. New York needs all the help it can get in the rotation—but they need Righetti in the bullpen even more.

Michael Cassin

Righetti, David Allan "Dave"   Bats: Left   Throws: Left   Born 11/28/58

1987 SEASON AND MAJOR-LEAGUE CAREER PITCHING TOTALS

	G	GS	CG	GF	IP	BFP	H	R	ER	HR	SH	SF	HB	TBB	IBB	SO	WP	Bk	W	L	Pct	ShO	Sv	ERA
87 NYA	60	0	0	54	95	419	95	45	37	9	6	5	2	44	4	77	1	3	8	6	.571	0	31	3.51
8 YEARS	354	76	13	238	927	3899	792	357	315	49	40	28	12	384	27	776	29	12	66	50	.569	2	138	3.06

1987: Power, Groundball   1986: Power, Groundball   1985: Power, Flyball   1984: Power, Groundball

1987 SEASON

	G	IP	H	BB	SO	SB	CS	W	L	S	ERA
Totals	60	95.0	95	44	77	1	2	8	6	31	3.51
at Home	32	48.1	39	17	38	0	2	5	2	17	2.79
on Road	28	46.2	56	27	39	1	0	3	4	14	4.24
on Grass	20	29.0	22	14	21	0	1	3	1	10	2.48
on Artificial Turf	40	66.0	73	30	56	1	1	5	5	21	3.95
Day Games	51	77.1	78	32	61	0	2	7	5	26	3.61
Night Games	9	17.2	17	12	16	1	0	1	1	5	3.06
April	11	15.1	14	12	10	0	1	2	1	6	4.70
May	9	15.0	14	4	16	0	0	1	0	6	3.60
June	10	19.1	25	6	17	0	0	2	3	3	4.66
July	10	15.1	14	9	9	0	0	1	0	4	1.76
August	9	13.1	10	9	7	0	0	0	0	6	2.03
Sept/Oct	11	16.2	18	4	18	1	1	2	2	6	3.78

FOUR YEAR TOTALS (1984 – 1987)

	G	IP	H	BB	SO	SB	CS	W	L	S	ERA
Totals	272	405.0	358	161	342	20	11	33	27	137	2.73
at Home	133	204.1	163	66	187	12	6	22	9	68	2.20
on Road	139	200.2	195	95	155	8	5	11	18	69	3.27
on Grass	88	128.1	108	58	109	6	5	15	8	40	2.24
on Artificial Turf	184	276.2	250	103	233	14	6	18	19	97	2.96
Day Games	230	344.1	299	136	293	16	11	30	23	113	2.77
Night Games	42	60.2	59	25	49	4	0	3	4	24	2.52
April	38	58.1	56	34	41	2	5	6	3	18	3.39
May	44	66.0	48	18	61	3	1	5	4	22	1.91
June	44	61.0	67	34	54	6	1	6	7	14	4.87
July	44	69.0	55	24	55	1	1	5	3	23	1.83
August	49	74.0	53	30	57	3	1	6	4	26	1.46
Sept/Oct	53	76.2	79	21	74	5	2	5	6	34	3.29

vs. Opponent Batters	Ave.	OBP	SLG	AB	H	2B	3B	HR	RBI	BB	SO
Totals	.262	.341	.362	362	95	9	0	9	55	44	77
vs. Left	.271	.324	.396	96	26	3	0	3	17	9	19
vs. Right	.259	.348	.350	266	69	6	0	6	38	35	58
Bases Empty	.242	.322	.335	161	39	3	0	4	4	17	37
Leadoff	.299	.373	.448	67	20	1	0	3	3	7	20
Not Leadoff	.202	.286	.255	94	19	2	0	1	1	10	17
Runners On Base	.279	.356	.383	201	56	6	0	5	51	27	40
First Base Only	.256	.337	.366	82	21	3	0	2	4	10	18
Scoring Position	.294	.369	.395	119	35	3	0	3	47	17	22
Late Innings, Close	.257	.341	.346	280	72	4	0	7	48	38	62

	Ave.	OBP	SLG	AB	H	2B	3B	HR	RBI	BB	SO
Totals	.238	.312	.319	1504	358	49	2	23	188	161	342
vs. Left	.233	.323	.324	352	82	14	0	6	52	48	88
vs. Right	.240	.308	.318	1152	276	35	2	17	136	113	254
Bases Empty	.222	.288	.297	717	159	21	0	11	11	65	174
Leadoff	.241	.305	.354	294	71	9	0	8	8	26	75
Not Leadoff	.208	.276	.258	423	88	12	0	3	3	39	99
Runners On Base	.253	.332	.339	787	199	28	2	12	177	96	168
First Base Only	.248	.318	.328	311	77	10	0	5	12	32	69
Scoring Position	.256	.341	.347	476	122	18	2	7	165	64	99
Late Innings, Close	.242	.318	.320	1174	284	36	1	18	165	133	267

RBI/Opportunities

Scoring Position	43 / 164 (26%)	147 / 679 (22%)
Scoring Position, 2 Out	20 / 88 (23%)	64 / 334 (19%)
On Third, Less than 2 Out	15 / 23 (65%)	52 / 110 (47%)
RBI in close games / RBI Total	48 / 55 (87%)	173 / 188 (92%)

Earnest Riles
Milwaukee Brewers

1987 was an important year for Earnest Riles—1988 is a critical one. At age 27, he is working on what will probably be the last chance that he ever has to be a major league regular.

After Riles's good rookie season in 1985—he hit .286, slugged .377 and had a .339 on-base percentage—1986 was a nightmare. He had big drops in most of the significant offensive categories and a pathetically low range factor at shortstop.

Things didn't improve last year. An off-season accident (he severed a tendon in his index finger) caused Riles to miss all of spring training and most of the first half of 1987. As you can see from the stats, it took him quite a while to play himself into shape; even after he did, the results weren't remarkable. Riles batted .264, slugged .352 and had a .338 OB% after the All-Star break. They're improvements, but still not particularly good numbers—even for a shortstop.

To make matters worse, Riles is no longer a shortstop. His injury, coupled with a spring training injury to prospect Edgar Diaz, forced Milwaukee to use third baseman Dale Sveum at short. Sveum hit extremely well; while he didn't play good defense, he fielded better than Riles had in either of his two years. By the time that Earnest was ready to return to the lineup, the only open position was third base.

Riles won the job—but largely because Milwaukee decided to keep Paul Molitor off the playing field. Earnest certainly didn't impress anyone with his glove. Of the 16 men with 50 or more games played at third base in 1987, 12 had higher range factors than Riles did. Though he was tenth in double plays per game, Riles had the second-lowest fielding percentage in the league. Riles's defensive stats in the majors have to be the part of his game that is most mystifying—not once has he even come close to approaching the outstanding figures that he had in the minors.

In conclusion, the report card for Riles's 1987 isn't good. His batting average crept up nine points over 1986 and his OB% rose eight points, but his SL% was down another six points. Neither his OB% nor SL% are acceptable, his fielding was below average and he added no speed (3–7 in steal attempts). He's not a good shortstop; at third base—a power hitter's position—he is a very large hole in the Milwaukee lineup.

Even giving the finger injury maximum credit for Riles's problems in 1987, he has still had two disappointing seasons in a row and seems to be playing only for lack of alternatives. Baseball history is littered with the corpses of players who never got the job done after a first big year; if Milwaukee finds a credible third base candidate or if Riles doesn't perform well in 1988, he'll be added to that list.

Tom Henry

Riles, Earnest "Ernie" Bats: Left Throws: Right Born 10/02/60

1987 SEASON AND MAJOR-LEAGUE CAREER BATTING TOTALS

	G	AB	H	2B	3B	HR	TB	R	RBI	TBB	IBB	SO	HP	SH	SF	SB	CS	SB%	GDP	AVG	OBP	SLG
87 MIL	83	276	72	11	1	4	97	38	38	30	1	47	1	3	6	3	4	.43	6	.261	.329	.351
3 YEARS	344	1248	332	47	10	18	453	161	130	120	1	181	4	15	12	12	13	.48	36	.266	.329	.363

	1987 SEASON											FOUR YEAR TOTALS (1984 – 1987)										
	Ave.	OBP	SLG	AB	H	2B	3B	HR	RBI	BB	SO	Ave.	OBP	SLG	AB	H	2B	3B	HR	RBI	BB	SO
Totals	.261	.329	.351	276	72	11	1	4	38	30	47	.266	.329	.363	1248	332	47	10	18	130	120	181
vs. Left	.175	.250	.228	57	10	3	0	0	5	6	18	.217	.285	.294	313	68	7	4	3	29	28	64
vs. Right	.283	.349	.384	219	62	8	1	4	33	24	29	.282	.344	.386	935	264	40	6	15	101	92	117
at Home	.286	.365	.376	133	38	7	1	1	17	19	22	.293	.359	.379	605	177	25	6	5	59	66	82
on Road	.238	.293	.329	143	34	4	0	3	21	11	25	.241	.301	.348	643	155	22	4	13	71	54	99
vs. Groundball	.247	.297	.323	158	39	4	1	2	29	13	21	.269	.331	.351	632	170	21	5	7	73	60	84
vs. Flyball	.280	.370	.390	118	33	7	0	2	9	17	26	.263	.328	.375	616	162	26	5	11	57	60	97
vs. Finesse	.272	.318	.380	158	43	5	0	4	25	13	20	.294	.340	.403	695	204	31	6	11	79	54	83
vs. Power	.246	.343	.314	118	29	6	1	0	13	17	27	.231	.316	.313	553	128	16	4	7	51	66	98
on Grass	.270	.333	.369	244	66	10	1	4	34	25	43	.269	.332	.369	1057	284	40	9	16	111	101	160
on Artificial Turf	.188	.297	.219	32	6	1	0	0	4	5	4	.251	.318	.330	191	48	7	1	2	19	19	21
Day Games	.301	.326	.446	83	25	7	1	1	14	5	12	.264	.322	.372	398	105	16	3	7	43	36	51
Night Games	.244	.330	.311	193	47	4	0	3	24	25	35	.267	.333	.359	850	227	31	7	11	87	84	130
April	.000	.000	.000	0	0	0	0	0	0	0	0	.214	.257	.329	70	15	0	1	2	8	4	16
May	.000	.000	.000	0	0	0	0	0	0	0	0	.305	.351	.411	141	43	6	0	3	18	10	16
June	.125	.125	.125	8	1	0	0	0	0	0	3	.249	.326	.347	193	48	7	3	2	17	22	26
July	.242	.325	.354	99	24	5	0	2	15	13	15	.258	.333	.360	275	71	12	2	4	28	32	39
August	.308	.341	.372	78	24	2	0	1	16	4	11	.302	.346	.392	265	80	6	3	4	37	18	35
Sept/Oct	.253	.340	.352	91	23	4	1	1	7	13	18	.247	.321	.336	304	75	16	1	3	22	34	49
Bases Empty	.254	.342	.394	142	36	9	1	3	3	19	28	.261	.325	.360	694	181	34	7	7	7	66	113
Leadoff	.204	.259	.296	54	11	3	1	0	0	4	10	.269	.320	.351	279	75	17	3	0	0	21	37
Not Leadoff	.284	.388	.455	88	25	6	0	3	3	15	18	.255	.328	.366	415	106	17	4	7	7	45	76
Runners On	.269	.316	.306	134	36	2	0	1	35	11	19	.273	.335	.366	554	151	13	3	11	123	54	68
First Base Only	.246	.283	.263	57	14	1	0	0	0	3	8	.302	.360	.404	245	74	11	1	4	13	22	24
Scoring Position	.286	.337	.338	77	22	1	0	1	35	8	11	.249	.316	.337	309	77	2	2	7	110	32	44
Late Innings, Close	.308	.321	.404	52	16	3	1	0	8	1	6	.268	.319	.338	213	57	7	1	2	25	16	27

RBI/Opportunities

	1987			Four Year		
Scoring Position	33 /	112	(29%)	96 /	423	(23%)
Scoring Position, 2 Out	19 /	58	(33%)	48 /	203	(24%)
On Third, Less than 2 Out	12 /	20	(60%)	34 /	71	(48%)
RBI in close games / RBI Total	28 /	38	(74%)	89 /	130	(68%)

Billy Ripken
Baltimore Orioles

What more could the Orioles have expected from Billy Ripken? After arriving in July, he hit .308 and played the best defense of any Baltimore second baseman since Bobby Grich. OK, it was a hollow .308—his secondary average (extra bases on hits, walks and stolen bases divided by at-bats) was only .171—but it wasn't bad for a 22-year-old.

Especially for a 22-year-old with his past. The real question about Ripken is "How did he manage to impress the Oriole management enough to get promoted to the majors so quickly when he seemed so thoroughly overmatched by minor league pitching?" Take a look at the record.

After hitting .223 in a season and a half in the rookies leagues, Ripken was promoted anyway. We'll pass that; even marginal prospects get at least one shot in A ball. In 1984, Ripken hit .230, slugged .296 and had a .295 on-base percentage. Would you have dropped him back down or kept him there for another season?

Baltimore did neither. Ripken started 1985 in AA, hit badly and was sent down to A ball again, where he hit only a bit better than he did the year before. His combined totals: .219 BA, .264 SL%. In 1986, he spent a full year in AA, hitting .268, slugging .345 and boasting a .296 OB%; he grounded into the most double plays in the Southern League to boot. I didn't think that he'd be a good AAA player in 1987—but, three months and a *Sports Illustrated*

cover later, he was hitting .300 in the majors.

Within a week of his arrival, it became clear why Billy was promoted—he's a defensive wizard with a capital "W." Eighteen AL second basemen played 50+ games in 1987; Billy had the fifth-best range factor (5.09), and was tops in both fielding percentage (.990) and double plays per 162 games (148). He played errorless ball in his first 25 games. To the Baltimore staff—who weren't getting good defensive support and, frankly, needed all the support that they could get—Ripken was a godsend. Baltimore went 28–29 (.491) with him in the lineup; they were 39–66 (.371) without him. The icing was his hustle and enthusiasm, which won over even the crustiest skeptics; I wouldn't be surprised if they had the same effect on the Oriole management while he was in the minors.

Unfortunately, Billy doesn't seem to have much room to improve. He'll probably lose a number of points on his average in 1988. He's not as big as his brother; I don't think he'll get into double-digits in homers. Without a power surge, he'll have to walk more, but he walked about as often in the majors as he ever did in the minors. Finally, a late-season ankle injury may damage his defensive value.

But he's only 22—he's got time to improve. And, as his career to date shows, Baltimore will give him every opportunity to do it.

Ken McKusick

Ripken, William Oliver "Billy"
Bats: Right   Throws: Right   Born 12/16/64

1987 SEASON AND MAJOR-LEAGUE CAREER BATTING TOTALS

	G	AB	H	2B	3B	HR	TB	R	RBI	TBB	IBB	SO	HP	SH	SF	SB	CS	SB%	GDP	AVG	OBP	SLG
87 BAL	58	234	72	9	0	2	87	27	20	21	0	23	0	1	1	4	1	.80	3	.308	.363	.372
1 YEAR	58	234	72	9	0	2	87	27	20	21	0	23	0	1	1	4	1	.80	3	.308	.363	.372

	1987 SEASON											FOUR YEAR TOTALS (1984 – 1987)										
	Ave.	OBP	SLG	AB	H	2B	3B	HR	RBI	BB	SO	Ave.	OBP	SLG	AB	H	2B	3B	HR	RBI	BB	SO
Totals	.308	.363	.372	234	72	9	0	2	20	21	23	.308	.363	.372	234	72	9	0	2	20	21	23
vs. Left	.348	.392	.427	89	31	4	0	1	8	7	7	.348	.392	.427	89	31	4	0	1	8	7	7
vs. Right	.283	.346	.338	145	41	5	0	1	12	14	16	.283	.346	.338	145	41	5	0	1	12	14	16
at Home	.287	.322	.313	115	33	3	0	0	6	6	14	.287	.322	.313	115	33	3	0	0	6	6	14
on Road	.328	.400	.429	119	39	6	0	2	14	15	9	.328	.400	.429	119	39	6	0	2	14	15	9
vs. Groundball	.282	.341	.323	124	35	2	0	1	11	11	12	.282	.341	.323	124	35	2	0	1	11	11	12
vs. Flyball	.336	.388	.427	110	37	7	0	1	9	10	11	.336	.388	.427	110	37	7	0	1	9	10	11
vs. Finesse	.261	.315	.339	115	30	3	0	2	9	9	10	.261	.315	.339	115	30	3	0	2	9	9	10
vs. Power	.353	.409	.403	119	42	6	0	0	11	12	13	.353	.409	.403	119	42	6	0	0	11	12	13
on Grass	.299	.358	.335	197	59	7	0	0	10	18	20	.299	.358	.335	197	59	7	0	0	10	18	20
on Artificial Turf	.351	.390	.568	37	13	2	0	2	10	3	3	.351	.390	.568	37	13	2	0	2	10	3	3
Day Games	.220	.235	.280	50	11	0	0	1	7	1	6	.220	.235	.280	50	11	0	0	1	7	1	6
Night Games	.332	.395	.397	184	61	9	0	1	13	20	17	.332	.395	.397	184	61	9	0	1	13	20	17
April	.000	.000	.000	0	0	0	0	0	0	0	0	.000	.000	.000	0	0	0	0	0	0	0	0
May	.000	.000	.000	0	0	0	0	0	0	0	0	.000	.000	.000	0	0	0	0	0	0	0	0
June	.000	.000	.000	0	0	0	0	0	0	0	0	.000	.000	.000	0	0	0	0	0	0	0	0
July	.268	.333	.352	71	19	3	0	1	6	7	6	.268	.333	.352	71	19	3	0	1	6	7	6
August	.350	.389	.410	117	41	4	0	1	12	8	16	.350	.389	.410	117	41	4	0	1	12	8	16
Sept/Oct	.261	.346	.304	46	12	2	0	0	2	6	1	.261	.346	.304	46	12	2	0	0	2	6	1
Bases Empty	.297	.366	.348	138	41	7	0	0	0	15	17	.297	.366	.348	138	41	7	0	0	0	15	17
Leadoff	.277	.333	.319	47	13	2	0	0	0	4	3	.277	.333	.319	47	13	2	0	0	0	4	3
Not Leadoff	.308	.382	.363	91	28	5	0	0	0	11	14	.308	.382	.363	91	28	5	0	0	0	11	14
Runners On	.323	.359	.406	96	31	2	0	2	20	6	6	.323	.359	.406	96	31	2	0	2	20	6	6
First Base Only	.333	.357	.370	54	18	2	0	0	2	2	1	.333	.357	.370	54	18	2	0	0	2	2	1
Scoring Position	.310	.362	.452	42	13	0	0	2	18	4	5	.310	.362	.452	42	13	0	0	2	18	4	5
Late Innings, Close	.207	.233	.207	29	6	0	0	0	0	1	4	.207	.233	.207	29	6	0	0	0	0	1	4

RBI/Opportunities

Scoring Position	14 / 59 (24%)	14 / 59 (24%)
Scoring Position, 2 Out	7 / 26 (27%)	7 / 26 (27%)
On Third, Less than 2 Out	4 / 8 (50%)	4 / 8 (50%)
RBI in close games / RBI Total	13 / 20 (65%)	13 / 20 (65%)

Cal Ripken
Baltimore Orioles

One of the hardest lessons to learn is "Always be fair—even if it hurts to do it". That's something that, in Cal Ripken, Jr.'s case, people don't seem willing to do. Local opinion of his strcak has plummeted to the point where people often call Ripken's desire to play in every game a selfish whim that is damaging either himself, his team or both. Frankly, I think that stinks.

In the past, the case that people (myself included) have made against Cal's streak hinges on defense. Since his record-setting defensive season in 1984, his range factors have been falling consistently: from 5.43 in 1984 to 4.72 in 1985 to 4.45 in 1986. His bat has been mostly unaffected, the party line admitted, but his drop in range clearly indicates that Ripken would benefit from more rest.

In 1987, however, Ripken should have effectively stymied the critics. His range factor for 1987 was 4.44—about equal to his 1986 mark; fourth best in the American League. He turned 103 double plays per 162 games; second best in the AL. His .973 fielding percentage was the second best in his career and sixth among AL regular shortstops.

But, unluckily for Cal, 1987 was also his worst offensive season of his career. Though his power and walk totals were as good as always, his batting average fell 37 points from his career mark; the fifth straight year that it has fallen.

Which, of course, people have latched onto. I've seen many fans say that, though Cal has stabilized his defense at a very high level, his offensive decline can obviously be traced to the streak—so he clearly needs to be rested. And that, folks, is where I draw the line.

Could Ripken use more rest? Most players do benefit from 5–10 games off a year. Do I think that the streak is the cause of the decline? Maybe. Can it be proven? Absolutely not. Players have offensive drops that are just as great every year: Jesse Barfield, Joe Carter and Jim Rice, to name three. The difference between those cases and this one is that Ripken's streak is a lightning rod for any and all problems.

If you think that Ripken's streak explains his 1987 stats, I suggest that you examine the careers of anyone with a long streak; Lou Gehrig's 1929 and Billy Williams's 1966 in particular. No, Ripken has never matched his .318 average of 1983—but, since he's hit .300 only two other times in a ten-year professional career, I find that rather unsurprising. I think he's proven that he's a .275–.285 hitter; I think that he'll snap back to that level next year, no matter how much or little he plays. Given the Orioles' 1987 centerfielder and second baseman, you'd think that people would appreciate Cal Ripken a lot more than they do.

Geoff Beckman

Ripken, Calvin Edwin Jr. "Cal"   Bats: Right   Throws: Right   Born 08/24/60

1987 SEASON AND MAJOR-LEAGUE CAREER BATTING TOTALS

	G	AB	H	2B	3B	HR	TB	R	RBI	TBB	IBB	SO	HP	SH	SF	SB	CS	SB%	GDP	AVG	OBP	SLG
87 BAL	162	624	157	28	3	27	272	97	98	81	0	77	1	0	11	3	5	.38	19	.252	.333	.436
7 YEARS	992	3834	1084	211	23	160	1821	626	570	394	10	494	11	2	38	14	18	.44	130	.283	.348	.475

	1987 SEASON											FOUR YEAR TOTALS (1984 – 1987)										
	Ave.	OBP	SLG	AB	H	2B	3B	HR	RBI	BB	SO	Ave.	OBP	SLG	AB	H	2B	3B	HR	RBI	BB	SO
Totals	.252	.333	.436	624	157	28	3	27	98	81	77	.280	.352	.469	2534	710	132	16	105	375	289	294
vs. Left	.243	.311	.433	210	51	15	2	7	24	23	18	.291	.363	.514	735	214	56	6	32	99	86	59
vs. Right	.256	.344	.437	414	106	13	1	20	74	58	59	.276	.348	.451	1799	496	76	10	73	276	203	235
at Home	.248	.313	.465	310	77	12	2	17	50	31	32	.272	.349	.472	1219	332	57	6	58	184	145	145
on Road	.255	.352	.408	314	80	16	1	10	48	50	45	.287	.356	.467	1315	378	75	10	47	191	144	149
vs. Groundball	.312	.397	.533	330	103	21	2	16	63	50	33	.301	.373	.496	1222	368	61	9	53	202	145	126
vs. Flyball	.184	.259	.327	294	54	7	1	11	35	31	44	.261	.333	.444	1312	342	71	7	52	173	144	168
vs. Finesse	.266	.330	.428	320	85	17	1	11	37	31	31	.285	.352	.472	1374	391	72	9	56	185	142	130
vs. Power	.237	.337	.444	304	72	11	2	16	61	50	46	.275	.353	.466	1160	319	60	7	49	190	147	164
on Grass	.243	.320	.424	531	129	20	2	24	85	64	66	.273	.347	.456	2138	583	105	14	86	310	250	253
on Artificial Turf	.301	.409	.505	93	28	8	1	3	13	17	11	.321	.381	.543	396	127	27	2	19	65	39	41
Day Games	.285	.378	.515	165	47	8	0	10	32	26	21	.292	.366	.492	746	218	37	5	34	126	90	97
Night Games	.240	.317	.407	459	110	20	3	17	66	55	56	.275	.347	.460	1788	492	95	11	71	249	199	197
April	.341	.423	.659	82	28	6	1	6	23	13	11	.303	.389	.558	317	96	18	3	19	68	46	41
May	.250	.320	.500	116	29	6	1	7	18	12	21	.266	.338	.501	421	112	26	5	21	64	46	70
June	.270	.339	.414	111	30	4	0	4	12	12	11	.278	.349	.400	428	119	20	1	10	44	47	43
July	.214	.333	.316	98	21	4	0	2	15	17	12	.310	.388	.519	426	132	23	3	20	75	54	44
August	.211	.280	.367	109	23	3	1	4	16	12	11	.265	.334	.420	445	118	21	3	14	60	48	44
Sept/Oct	.241	.325	.398	108	26	5	0	4	14	15	11	.268	.330	.447	497	133	24	1	21	64	48	52
Bases Empty	.240	.331	.384	341	82	13	3	10	10	45	41	.278	.349	.464	1370	381	67	8	57	57	148	162
Leadoff	.260	.331	.407	123	32	4	1	4	4	12	16	.326	.371	.542	485	158	29	2	24	24	34	55
Not Leadoff	.229	.331	.372	218	50	9	2	6	6	33	25	.252	.337	.420	885	223	38	6	33	33	114	107
Runners On	.265	.336	.498	283	75	15	0	17	88	36	36	.283	.357	.476	1164	329	65	8	48	318	141	132
First Base Only	.248	.306	.383	133	33	9	0	3	7	11	16	.270	.323	.452	549	148	36	5	18	48	43	59
Scoring Position	.280	.360	.600	150	42	6	0	14	81	25	20	.294	.385	.498	615	181	29	3	30	270	98	73
Late Innings, Close	.226	.263	.323	93	21	1	1	2	11	5	15	.307	.363	.497	384	118	18	2	17	66	34	52

RBI/Opportunities

Scoring Position	60 / 217 (28%)	222 / 856 (26%)
Scoring Position, 2 Out	21 / 95 (22%)	61 / 348 (18%)
On Third, Less than 2 Out	26 / 43 (60%)	97 / 167 (58%)
RBI in close games / RBI Total	70 / 98 (71%)	255 / 375 (68%)

Jeff Robinson
Pittsburgh Pirates

Give the Pittsburgh Pirates credit. It looks like they may have pulled off another deal that makes sense for the future of the franchise.

Frankly, I was puzzled when San Francisco sent 26-year-old Jeff Robinson and young reliever Scott Medvin to the Pirates for 38-year-old Rick Reuschel. Sure, Reuschel still had a few pitches left in him, and nobody was dazzled by the Giants' starting rotation, but the Reds were self-destructing by the time the deal was made, and nobody else in the National League Western Division was making a run at first place, so what was the point?

It may have been that San Francisco had obtained reliever Don Robinson from Pittsburgh a few weeks earlier, and that Scott Garrelts was ready to return from the disabled list, but San Francisco's short-term gain is likely to become Pittsburgh's long-term return on investment. Robinson, for some reason, was strangely unappreciated in San Francisco. Maybe it was the way he broke in, as a starter, in 1984; Jeff went 7-15, with a 4.56 ERA. Maybe it was his low save total, though that had more to do with the way he was being used than anything.

Whatever the thinking was, the Pirates now have a reliever who has quietly put up some pretty impressive numbers the past two seasons, and who can be counted on to do the same thing for several years to come. There are at least two right-handed relievers in the National League who have been highly effective for two years now, but whose names don't yet cause people to forget Rollie Fingers. Jeff Robinson is one of them, and Frank Williams of Cincinnati is the other. What they have in common is that both were on the San Francisco roster in 1986. Robinson went 6-3 with eight saves in 64 outings, and posted a 3.36 ERA. Williams was 3-1 with one save in 36 games, and racked up a microscopic 1.20 ERA. Williams was traded to the Reds after the 1986 season and appeared in 85 games last season, playing an integral role in giving Cincinnati the best bullpen in baseball, although he was credited with only two saves. Robinson was dealt to Pittsburgh in August, and before his season was over, had appeared in 81 games, compiling an 8-9 mark. He saved 14 games and had a 2.85 earned run average.

A mid-season slump may have had something to do with the Giants seeking pennant insurance in the form of Don Robinson. Jeff Robinson also has been prone to periods of wildness. He walked 54 batters in 123.1 innings last year, but only six in 26.2 innings with the Pirates. If he can harness his control, Robinson has a chance to emerge as the Pirates stopper in 1988.

Tom Henry

Robinson, Jeffrey Daniel "Jeff" Bats: Right Throws: Right Born 12/13/60

1987 SEASON AND MAJOR-LEAGUE CAREER PITCHING TOTALS

	G	GS	CG	GF	IP	BFP	H	R	ER	HR	SH	SF	HB	TBB	IBB	SO	WP	Bk	W	L	Pct	ShO	Sv	ERA
87 SF-PIT	81	0	0	40	124	495	89	43	39	11	10	4	1	54	11	101	5	2	8	9	.471	0	14	2.83
4 YEARS	187	34	1	62	412	1734	392	199	172	33	16	16	9	148	23	301	24	4	21	27	.438	1	22	3.76

1987: Power, Groundball **1986: Power, Groundball** **1985: Power, Groundball** **1984: Finesse, Groundball**

1987 SEASON

	G	IP	H	BB	SO	SB	CS	W	L	S	ERA
Totals	80	123.1	88	52	100	6	11	8	8	14	2.77
at Home	41	60.2	44	23	51	3	5	4	3	6	2.37
on Road	39	62.2	44	29	49	3	6	4	5	8	3.16
on Grass	28	38.2	34	17	30	2	5	3	4	6	3.26
on Artificial Turf	52	84.2	54	35	70	4	6	5	4	8	2.55
Day Games	50	75.2	58	31	68	3	6	5	4	9	3.09
Night Games	30	47.2	30	21	32	3	5	3	4	5	2.27
April	12	19.1	10	5	17	0	1	2	0	4	1.86
May	12	20.1	21	14	16	0	3	1	4	3	4.43
June	14	20.2	13	12	13	1	3	2	1	1	2.61
July	15	24.0	14	13	20	2	1	1	0	2	1.88
August	12	15.1	16	3	16	1	1	1	2	0	5.28
Sept/Oct	15	23.2	14	5	18	2	2	1	1	4	1.52

vs. Opponent Batters	Ave.	OBP	SLG	AB	H	2B	3B	HR	RBI	BB	SO
Totals	.208	.294	.336	423	88	21	0	11	41	52	100
vs. Left	.236	.321	.373	233	55	14	0	6	23	29	54
vs. Right	.174	.260	.289	190	33	7	0	5	18	23	46
Bases Empty	.209	.278	.349	249	52	14	0	7	7	24	60
Leadoff	.267	.333	.465	101	27	8	0	4	4	10	24
Not Leadoff	.169	.241	.270	148	25	6	0	3	3	14	36
Runners On Base	.207	.314	.316	174	36	7	0	4	34	28	40
First Base Only	.305	.359	.441	59	18	2	0	2	5	5	11
Scoring Position	.157	.294	.252	115	18	5	0	2	29	23	29
Late Innings, Close	.206	.290	.328	253	52	10	0	7	19	30	60

FOUR YEAR TOTALS (1984 – 1987)

	G	IP	H	BB	SO	SB	CS	W	L	S	ERA
Totals	186	411.2	391	146	300	36	20	21	26	22	3.74
at Home	90	196.2	186	63	156	12	7	10	8	11	3.29
on Road	96	215.0	205	83	144	24	13	11	18	11	4.14
on Grass	80	183.1	193	67	129	15	7	8	12	10	4.22
on Artificial Turf	106	228.1	198	79	171	21	13	13	14	12	3.35
Day Games	130	284.2	281	95	212	19	12	15	14	15	3.70
Night Games	56	127.0	110	51	88	17	8	6	12	7	3.83
April	26	63.1	46	26	57	7	1	6	3	5	2.70
May	29	65.0	68	24	52	3	3	2	7	6	4.29
June	33	74.0	74	25	54	6	5	5	6	2	4.01
July	32	70.1	61	29	48	3	3	4	3	3	3.45
August	30	63.1	69	18	37	7	2	3	3	0	4.97
Sept/Oct	36	75.2	73	24	52	10	6	1	4	6	3.09

vs. Opponent Batters	Ave.	OBP	SLG	AB	H	2B	3B	HR	RBI	BB	SO
Totals	.254	.318	.370	1542	391	66	7	33	174	146	300
vs. Left	.282	.349	.424	804	227	42	6	20	92	83	133
vs. Right	.222	.283	.310	738	164	24	1	13	82	63	167
Bases Empty	.239	.295	.355	904	216	40	4	19	19	72	174
Leadoff	.260	.303	.381	388	101	23	0	8	8	24	66
Not Leadoff	.223	.289	.335	516	115	17	4	11	11	48	108
Runners On Base	.274	.349	.390	638	175	26	3	14	155	74	126
First Base Only	.306	.346	.407	248	76	11	1	4	12	15	44
Scoring Position	.254	.350	.379	390	99	15	2	10	143	59	82
Late Innings, Close	.223	.287	.340	435	97	13	1	12	38	39	104

RBI/Opportunities

	1987			Four Year		
Scoring Position	26 / 176	(15%)		123 / 574	(21%)	
Scoring Position, 2 Out	7 / 81	(9%)		45 / 238	(19%)	
On Third, Less than 2 Out	11 / 26	(42%)		52 / 115	(45%)	
RBI in close games / RBI Total	24 / 41	(59%)		109 / 174	(63%)	

251

Bruce Ruffin
Philadelphia Phillies

Bruce Ruffin sure makes a person believe in the sophomore jinx. After a year like he had in 1986 (9–4, 2.46 ERA) one might have expected bigger and better things out of Bruce in 1987. The Phillies obviously did; Ruffin's poise on the mound in '86—after only a brief minor league apprenticeship—made more than one Philadelphia observer describe him a "young Steve Carlton."

Unfortunately, Ruffin spent much of last year pitching like the '87 Steve Carlton. His problems were numerous, beginning with a terrible start, but in general they revolved around the fact that Bruce was simply allowing too many hits. In '86 he'd simply destroyed left-handed hitters, holding them to a .138 batting average. That average nearly doubled last year (to .269). Meanwhile righties, who'd fared pretty well against Bruce in '86, did even better the second time around.

In plain truth, the Phillies may have overestimated Ruffin's potential. Rather than being a young Carlton, Ruffin is more like a young Tommy John—he's a finesse pitcher who gets a lot of groundball outs but gives up a large amount of hits and doesn't strike out very many batters. Nothing wrong with that, but a pitcher of this type is much more likely to have an ERA of 4.35, as Bruce did in '87, than 2.46. It's also true, that, as Bill James has noted, pitchers from the Tommy John school tend to be very team-dependant; that is, their record tends to be disproportionately good for a winning team and disproportionately bad for a struggling team . . . like the '87 Phillies, for example.

An examination of Bruce's record without the '86 expectations helps put it in better perspective. If you look at other starting pitchers who had ERAs around the 4.35 mark, you come up with some surprising results. For example, fellow Philly Shane Rawley had an ERA of 4.39, yet his record was a good 17–11. Scott Sanderson had a 4.29 ERA and an 8–9 record. Guy Hoffman's record was 8–9 but he had a 4.37 ERA. Mike Deshaies went 11–6 with a 4.62 ERA. Bryn Smith was 10–9 with a 4.37 ERA. Neal Heaton's ERA was 4.52 but he had a 13–10 record. Ron Darling was 12–8 with a 4.29 ERA. Bob Forsch's numbers were 11–7, 4.32. None of these pitchers had great years, and none bring to mind the '72-vintage Carlton. Yet there's some pretty decent workmen there.

Coming out of a big-time college program (Texas) and being very mature for his age, Ruffin started his career with an advantage over most young pitchers. That advantage tended to dissipate as the hitters learned that he simply doesn't throw very hard. Which is not to say he won't be a successful pitcher. If he truly does emulate Tommy John, he'll be very successful indeed. Don't give up on him yet, Philadelphia.

Doug White and Don Zminda

Ruffin, Bruce Wayne

Bats: Left   Throws: Left   Born 10/04/63

1987 SEASON AND MAJOR-LEAGUE CAREER PITCHING TOTALS

	G	GS	CG	GF	IP	BFP	H	R	ER	HR	SH	SF	HB	TBB	IBB	SO	WP	Bk	W	L	Pct	ShO	Sv	ERA
87 PHI	35	35	3	0	205	884	236	118	99	17	8	10	2	73	4	93	6	0	11	14	.440	1	0	4.35
2 YEARS	56	56	9	0	351	1484	374	171	139	23	10	14	3	117	10	163	6	1	20	18	.526	1	0	3.56

1987: Finesse, Groundball   1986: Finesse, Groundball

	1987 SEASON										FOUR YEAR TOTALS (1984 – 1987)									
	G	IP	H	BB	SO	SB	CS	W	L	S	ERA	G	IP	H	BB	SO	SB	CS	W	L	S	ERA
Totals	35	204.2	236	73	93	18	11	11	14	0	4.35	56	351.0	374	117	163	34	17	20	18	0	3.56
at Home	15	87.2	106	35	43	8	4	7	3	0	5.13	27	175.1	188	60	79	13	7	13	5	0	3.64
on Road	20	117.0	130	38	50	10	7	4	11	0	3.77	29	175.2	186	57	84	21	10	7	13	0	3.48
on Grass	11	67.1	72	21	34	5	6	3	4	0	3.48	18	116.0	115	34	59	10	6	5	5	0	2.72
on Artificial Turf	24	137.1	164	52	59	13	5	8	10	0	4.78	38	235.0	259	83	104	24	11	15	13	0	3.98
Day Games	11	63.0	72	21	32	3	5	1	6	0	3.86	16	100.0	102	29	50	8	5	4	7	0	2.88
Night Games	24	141.2	164	52	61	15	6	10	8	0	4.57	40	251.0	272	88	113	26	12	16	11	0	3.84
April	4	24.0	32	11	16	3	2	1	1	0	5.25	4	24.0	32	11	16	3	2	1	1	0	5.25
May	6	28.0	37	11	17	3	0	2	3	0	7.39	6	28.0	37	11	17	3	0	2	3	0	7.39
June	6	33.1	40	9	16	3	2	1	2	0	3.24	7	39.2	47	10	21	4	2	1	2	0	3.40
July	6	44.2	40	12	11	0	2	5	1	0	1.81	12	89.2	82	26	29	2	5	8	3	0	2.41
August	6	35.1	39	18	19	8	1	0	4	0	5.86	12	78.2	74	28	43	14	6	5	5	0	3.43
Sept/Oct	7	39.1	48	12	14	1	5	1	3	0	4.12	15	91.0	102	31	37	8	4	3	4	0	3.26

vs. Opponent Batters	Ave.	OBP	SLG	AB	H	2B	3B	HR	RBI	BB	SO	Ave.	OBP	SLG	AB	H	2B	3B	HR	RBI	BB	SO
Totals	.299	.355	.425	790	236	35	7	17	103	73	93	.279	.336	.393	1339	374	65	9	23	147	117	163
vs. Left	.269	.333	.351	134	36	3	1	2	12	13	21	.220	.289	.313	214	47	4	2	4	21	21	45
vs. Right	.305	.360	.441	656	200	32	6	15	91	60	72	.291	.345	.408	1125	327	61	7	19	126	96	118
Bases Empty	.313	.365	.450	453	142	18	7	10	10	36	46	.288	.340	.405	778	224	34	9	13	13	61	91
Leadoff	.316	.389	.446	193	61	8	4	3	3	22	21	.272	.338	.374	334	91	14	4	4	4	32	35
Not Leadoff	.312	.347	.454	260	81	10	3	7	7	14	25	.300	.342	.428	444	133	20	5	9	9	29	56
Runners On Base	.279	.343	.392	337	94	17	0	7	93	37	47	.267	.330	.376	561	150	31	0	10	134	56	72
First Base Only	.245	.318	.346	159	39	7	0	3	9	17	19	.257	.319	.360	261	67	15	0	4	15	24	32
Scoring Position	.309	.364	.433	178	55	10	0	4	84	20	28	.277	.338	.390	300	83	16	0	6	119	32	40
Late Innings, Close	.313	.340	.479	48	15	2	0	2	4	2	6	.295	.331	.429	112	33	6	0	3	15	6	12

RBI/Opportunities

Scoring Position	75 / 241 (31%)	106 / 398 (27%)
Scoring Position, 2 Out	23 / 95 (24%)	32 / 167 (19%)
On Third, Less than 2 Out	38 / 51 (75%)	54 / 82 (66%)
RBI in close games / RBI Total	73 / 103 (71%)	107 / 147 (73%)

Nolan Ryan
Houston Astros

In 1986 Nolan Ryan developed arm problems and was limited in his number of pitches per outing to a hundred. At the start of the '87 season he was again limited to a hundred pitches, but even then many were worried he would not last the season. He did make it through the season, however, and pitched better than even an average Ryan year though he only had an 8–16 record to show for it.

The Ryan Express roared through the league in 1987. On September 4, he struck out Mike LaValliere for his 209th K of the year; that set a record for strikeouts in a season by a 40-year-old player. He ended the season with 270 strikeouts, another record with his 11th year of 200 or more. On September 9 he struck out 16 Giants in 7 innings, his highest single-game National League total. He struck out 11.46 per nine innings. And, the Express is more under control, striking out three for every one he walked. He has been issuing fewer free passes; three of his best years in terms of walks have been 1984, 1985 and 1987. This was also the third best year of his career in ERA, as he posted a 2.76. An incredible year for a pitcher many thought would not make it through the year.

Will his strikeout records and no-hitters be enough to get him to Cooperstown, or does he need 300 wins to compensate for his barely .500 record? Was he responsible for his miserable 8–16 record? Does last year help explain why his lifetime won-lost percentage is only .519, while his life-time ERA is a very respectable 3.13 over 21 years?

In 1987, the Astros gave Ryan precious little support. The Astros scored 2.47 runs a game while Ryan pitched (Ryan gave up 2.21 runs a game). They scored 4.21 runs a game for every other Astro pitcher, almost 2 runs a game better. They batted at a paltry .232 clip in Ryan's games, .258 for the rest of the staff. Ryan pitched well in 24 of his 34 starts (a well-pitched game is defined here as an ERA of 3.00 or less for the game). In only 5 of those 24 games did he get more than 3 runs while he was the pitcher of record, and suffered 17 losses or no-decisions. Only once all year did he have a bad outing and have the team score a pile of runs to win the game for him, and that was his first start of the season.

As the season wore on, the 'Stros recognized their lack of support. Lanier juggled lineups (he would later joke that he gave Ryan the lineup card whenever he pitched so Ryan would be responsible for the outcome), and his teammates tried harder. Perhaps too hard; in any event, they didn't produce on offense.

Ryan only missed one start during the year (he sprained an ankle during the All-Star break), and was allowed to raise his number of pitches thrown to 150 by the end of the year. Ryan has signed a one-year contract with Houston for 1988. This year, there is little question about the soundness of his arm.

Welford McCaffrey

Ryan, Lynn Nolan "Nolan"　　　　　Bats: Right　　Throws: Right　　Born 01/31/47

1987 SEASON AND MAJOR-LEAGUE CAREER PITCHING TOTALS

	G	GS	CG	GF	IP	BFP	H	R	ER	HR	SH	SF	HB	TBB	IBB	SO	WP	Bk	W	L	Pct	ShO	Sv	ERA
87 HOU	34	34	0	0	212	873	154	75	65	14	9	1	4	87	2	270	10	2	8	16	.333	0	0	2.76
21 YEARS	645	611	203	13	4327	18190	3144	1718	1505	242	172	110	117	2355	67	4547	219	24	261	242	.519	54	3	3.13

1987: Power, Flyball　　　1986: Power, Flyball　　　1985: Power, Groundball　　　1984: Power, Flyball

1987 SEASON

	G	IP	H	BB	SO	SB	CS	W	L	S	ERA
Totals	34	211.2	154	87	270	45	7	8	16	0	2.76
at Home	17	114.0	79	38	154	18	2	5	7	0	2.21
on Road	17	97.2	75	49	116	27	5	3	9	0	3.41
on Grass	12	63.1	53	30	82	13	3	2	7	0	3.84
on Artificial Turf	22	148.1	101	57	188	32	4	6	9	0	2.31
Day Games	13	74.0	58	35	86	19	3	3	6	0	3.65
Night Games	21	137.2	96	52	184	26	4	5	10	0	2.29
April	4	25.2	17	10	36	6	2	1	2	0	2.45
May	6	38.1	23	17	45	6	0	1	2	0	2.82
June	6	32.2	35	8	43	8	1	2	4	0	4.68
July	5	26.2	19	18	29	9	1	0	5	0	2.36
August	6	37.2	21	13	51	6	1	1	1	0	2.15
Sept/Oct	7	50.2	39	21	66	10	2	3	2	0	2.31

FOUR YEAR TOTALS (1984 – 1987)

	G	IP	H	BB	SO	SB	CS	W	L	S	ERA
Totals	129	805.1	621	333	870	139	33	42	47	0	3.25
at Home	66	436.2	299	162	474	71	11	26	19	0	2.58
on Road	63	368.2	322	171	396	68	22	16	28	0	4.03
on Grass	35	200.0	157	92	236	32	10	12	9	0	3.19
on Artificial Turf	94	605.1	464	241	634	107	23	30	38	0	3.26
Day Games	38	224.2	202	86	226	36	10	11	15	0	4.01
Night Games	91	580.2	419	247	644	103	23	31	32	0	2.96
April	20	126.0	100	42	126	21	9	7	8	0	3.86
May	24	161.0	109	67	171	24	8	9	6	0	2.40
June	16	96.0	93	34	101	21	5	7	7	0	3.75
July	23	136.0	102	70	154	30	1	4	15	0	3.90
August	23	147.0	112	62	163	23	7	7	6	0	3.43
Sept/Oct	23	139.1	105	58	155	20	3	8	5	0	2.52

vs. Opponent Batters	Ave.	OBP	SLG	AB	H	2B	3B	HR	RBI	BB	SO
Totals	.200	.284	.292	771	154	23	3	14	65	87	270
vs. Left	.211	.300	.289	402	85	7	3	6	31	51	133
vs. Right	.187	.266	.295	369	69	16	0	8	34	36	137
Bases Empty	.190	.277	.269	468	89	12	2	7	7	52	176
Leadoff	.191	.265	.236	199	38	3	0	2	2	19	74
Not Leadoff	.190	.285	.294	269	51	9	2	5	5	33	102
Runners On Base	.215	.295	.327	303	65	11	1	7	58	35	94
First Base Only	.257	.322	.438	105	27	5	1	4	9	10	25
Scoring Position	.192	.281	.268	198	38	6	0	3	49	25	69
Late Innings, Close	.155	.246	.172	58	9	1	0	0	3	7	29

vs. Opponent Batters	Ave.	OBP	SLG	AB	H	2B	3B	HR	RBI	BB	SO
Totals	.211	.292	.313	2938	621	105	19	52	293	333	870
vs. Left	.211	.299	.294	1465	309	42	11	19	131	184	422
vs. Right	.212	.286	.333	1473	312	63	8	33	162	149	448
Bases Empty	.199	.277	.282	1762	351	54	13	22	22	185	542
Leadoff	.218	.300	.308	744	162	25	6	10	10	86	213
Not Leadoff	.186	.260	.263	1018	189	29	7	12	12	99	329
Runners On Base	.230	.315	.360	1176	270	51	6	30	271	148	328
First Base Only	.243	.298	.404	445	108	25	4	13	42	35	98
Scoring Position	.222	.325	.332	731	162	26	2	17	229	113	230
Late Innings, Close	.209	.269	.319	282	59	8	1	7	32	23	82

RBI/Opportunities

Scoring Position	45 / 268	(17%)
Scoring Position, 2 Out	24 / 128	(19%)
On Third, Less than 2 Out	13 / 48	(27%)
RBI in close games / RBI Total	51 / 65	(78%)

	198 / 1028	(19%)
	80 / 447	(18%)
	79 / 205	(39%)
	236 / 293	(81%)

Bret Saberhagen
Kansas City Royals

Very few fans and researchers know what it is like to put yourself on the line making predictions about ballplayers, knowing that your professional reputation, your livelihood, rides on your accuracy. In the baseball business you are battling for the slightest edge and often have to act on a 55–45 hunch, that is you have a 55 percent chance of being right—but you also have a 45 percent chance of being wrong. Bret Saberhagen has grown to be a favorite of mine because he has consistently left me on the 55 percent side of some tough calls.

After Saberhagen's Cy Young year, the topic was what to expect from him in 1986. Most predicted that such a young pitcher could be counted on only to get better. From my studies of workloads of young pitchers, I cited his youth and his slight frame and noted that it would not be unusual for such a pitcher to have an off-year after such a sudden jump in his workload, but there should be no lasting damage.

When Saberhagen had a rough year in 1986 and experienced some shoulder trouble, I stood by my previous analysis and said that the effect should not be a lasting one, that I expected him to bounce back quite well in 1987.

Well, he did, especially in the first half, but I was alarmed at how hard Manager Billy Gardner was working Bret. At the end of June, Saberhagen's season began it's deep dive:

	W–L	CG	ST	IP	H AVG	ERA	W AVG	K AVG	BATTERS PER START
Thru June	13–2	9	15	124.1	6.93	2.17	1.88	5.70	33.1
After June	5–8	3	18	132.1	10.20	4.49	1.84	5.71	31.9

It's hard to explain why there should be a major difference between his Cy Young year of 235 innings with 29.8 batters per start and his 1987 season of 256.2 innings and 32.4 BPS. I guess the easiest point to make is that the extra innings and batters came when Saberhagen was likely to be the most fatigued, and that is dangerous for a player his age (only 23 in '87), his style, and with his physical build. In his case, 32.4 BPS in 257 innings is serious.

Specifically because of the 1987 season and the likelihood he will continue to have at least regular use, I place the odds very high, around 80 percent, that he will not have the lengthy career once envisioned for him, that he will show a premature aging process in his effectiveness. That's down the road. For 1988 the most likely scenario is an off-year similar to 1986 in effectiveness, but with more durability. He has distinctly raised his chances of disabling arm trouble, but not to a point where it approaches 50 percent. That's my professional opinion. It pains me to predict problems for any player, not to mention a bright talent like Bret. It's my desire that someday my research can be used to effectively help protect whole generations of pitchers.

Craig R. Wright

Saberhagen, Bret William
Bats: Right   Throws: Right   Born 04/13/64

1987 SEASON AND MAJOR-LEAGUE CAREER PITCHING TOTALS

	G	GS	CG	GF	IP	BFP	H	R	ER	HR	SH	SF	HB	TBB	IBB	SO	WP	Bk	W	L	Pct	ShO	Sv	ERA
87 KC	33	33	15	0	257	1048	246	99	96	27	8	5	6	53	2	163	6	1	18	10	.643	4	0	3.36
4 YEARS	133	108	31	13	806	3265	760	326	304	74	28	20	11	156	8	506	15	6	55	39	.585	8	1	3.39

1987: Finesse, Groundball   1986: Finesse, Groundball   1985: Finesse, Flyball   1984: Finesse, Groundball

1987 SEASON

	G	IP	H	BB	SO	SB	CS	W	L	S	ERA
Totals	33	256.2	246	53	163	10	9	18	11	0	3.37
at Home	18	138.0	138	20	90	9	5	11	4	0	3.59
on Road	15	118.2	108	33	73	1	4	7	7	0	3.11
on Grass	7	54.1	44	13	46	1	3	4	0	0	2.65
on Artificial Turf	26	202.1	202	40	117	9	6	14	11	0	3.56
Day Games	11	86.2	82	19	49	0	4	5	6	0	3.22
Night Games	22	170.0	164	34	114	10	5	13	5	0	3.44
April	4	33.2	22	6	14	0	1	4	0	0	1.34
May	6	47.0	45	10	36	4	1	5	1	0	3.06
June	5	43.2	29	10	29	3	0	4	1	0	1.85
July	6	43.0	51	4	25	1	3	2	5	0	5.23
August	5	33.1	42	9	24	0	2	1	1	0	5.67
Sept/Oct	7	56.0	57	14	35	2	2	2	3	0	3.21

vs. Opponent Batters	Ave.	OBP	SLG	AB	H	2B	3B	HR	RBI	BB	SO
Totals	.252	.294	.400	975	246	49	7	27	90	53	163
vs. Left	.242	.290	.391	512	124	30	2	14	45	34	103
vs. Right	.263	.298	.410	463	122	19	5	13	45	19	60
Bases Empty	.263	.298	.423	612	161	29	6	19	19	26	106
Leadoff	.277	.297	.465	256	71	12	3	10	10	6	47
Not Leadoff	.253	.298	.393	356	90	17	3	9	9	20	59
Runners On Base	.234	.287	.361	363	85	20	1	8	71	27	57
First Base Only	.232	.288	.354	164	38	11	0	3	11	11	22
Scoring Position	.236	.286	.367	199	47	9	1	5	60	16	35
Late Innings, Close	.269	.296	.444	108	29	5	1	4	11	4	17

FOUR YEAR TOTALS (1984 – 1987)

	G	IP	H	BB	SO	SB	CS	W	L	S	ERA
Totals	133	805.2	760	156	506	45	30	55	40	1	3.40
at Home	64	420.1	389	68	257	26	15	27	17	1	3.10
on Road	69	385.1	371	88	249	19	15	28	23	0	3.71
on Grass	33	172.0	144	44	114	12	7	11	10	0	3.61
on Artificial Turf	100	633.2	616	112	392	33	23	44	30	1	3.32
Day Games	56	324.0	301	66	209	15	10	24	18	0	3.44
Night Games	77	481.2	459	90	297	30	20	31	22	1	3.34
April	18	108.0	94	20	44	8	3	8	5	0	2.75
May	22	153.0	152	33	95	7	2	10	8	0	3.53
June	23	147.2	127	34	90	9	4	8	9	0	3.05
July	25	149.0	139	16	101	7	5	11	8	1	3.56
August	19	90.0	96	21	64	4	5	8	2	0	4.80
Sept/Oct	26	158.0	152	32	112	10	11	10	8	0	3.08

vs. Opponent Batters	Ave.	OBP	SLG	AB	H	2B	3B	HR	RBI	BB	SO
Totals	.249	.287	.381	3049	760	126	27	74	294	156	506
vs. Left	.247	.289	.390	1670	412	67	17	46	170	99	309
vs. Right	.252	.284	.371	1379	348	59	10	28	124	57	197
Bases Empty	.253	.286	.381	1907	483	68	16	48	48	84	328
Leadoff	.262	.293	.393	789	207	27	8	20	20	33	138
Not Leadoff	.247	.282	.373	1118	276	41	8	28	28	51	190
Runners On Base	.243	.287	.381	1142	277	58	11	26	246	72	178
First Base Only	.228	.262	.361	548	125	22	6	13	42	23	81
Scoring Position	.256	.310	.399	594	152	36	5	13	204	49	97
Late Innings, Close	.225	.263	.362	334	75	6	2	12	25	17	51

RBI/Opportunities

Scoring Position	54 / 247	(22%)	182 / 751	(24%)
Scoring Position, 2 Out	19 / 125	(15%)	62 / 345	(18%)
On Third, Less than 2 Out	17 / 34	(50%)	74 / 126	(59%)
RBI in close games / RBI Total	67 / 90	(74%)	213 / 294	(72%)

Angel Salazar
Kansas City

I think it's time to let Bill Virdon off the hook for this one. Many thought he rushed Ironside (because he never walks, that's why) Salazar, and maybe he did, but no more than the Mets rushed Jose Oquendo, and we all know what he's doing now. Given the same much-needed change of scenery, Salazar has still proven unable to cut the mustard. For a moment, it looked like it might prove otherwise. When Buddy Biancalana again proved himself unequal to the task early in '87, Salazar was handed shortstop on a platter, and (it must be acknowledged) defensively he was terrific. Indeed, after an early series with the Angels, Gene Mauch was quoted to the effect that Salazar's play was the most dominant defensive performance he had seen since the heyday of Mark Belanger.

The trouble was, defense is all he and Belanger had in common; he couldn't begin to carry the Gold Glover's bat. I know that sounds absurd, as Belanger has the reputation as an all-time great field, no-hit shortstop. That's a little unfair, because in his best years he posted averages of .287, .270, and .266, and he always managed to draw at least 40 walks, sometimes considerably more. Ironside, on the other hand . . . well, his bat was so dead that the umpires started checking it for embalming fluid instead of cork. Go through this book and I'm sure you'll find other players whose BA and OBP are deplorably similar, and you might discover one or two whose BA and SA are horrifyingly synonymous,

but I'll wager that no one but Salazar offers virtually matching BA, OBP, and SA. He's truly unique. I frankly doubt that the greatest defensive shortstop of all time could play for long with those numbers, not even for the '27 Yankees. Certainly not for the already anemic '87 Royals.

Eventually, reluctantly, the Royals pulled the plug. Biancalana had already been shipped to Houston, so they fell back on Mariners and Mets cast-off Ross Jones, who at least produced a batting average, but nothing else. Finally, George Brett's former caddy, Bill Pecota, showed unexpected offensive strength in various fill-in roles, and was inserted out of desperation, although no one considers shortstop his natural position. The end result, of course, was the trade for Kurt Stillwell, which could have—and from the Royals retrospective point of view definitely should have—happened after the '86 season. It's doubtful that any unproven player will enter '88 with more job security than Stillwell—there's simply no one else. No one questions his defensive credentials, and if he can hit .250 with some semblance of normal OBP and SA, he'll look like Tony Fernandez by comparison to what's gone before. As for Ironside, all I can say is that Pete Rose better hope Barry Larkin stays healthy, because two automatic outs at the bottom of the lineup might slow down even the most irresistible offensive juggernaut. Don't say you weren't warned, Skip.

Mike Kopf

Salazar, Argenis Antonio "Angel"

Bats: Right   Throws: Right   Born 11/04/61

1987 SEASON AND MAJOR-LEAGUE CAREER BATTING TOTALS

	G	AB	H	2B	3B	HR	TB	R	RBI	TBB	IBB	SO	HP	SH	SF	SB	CS	SB%	GDP	AVG	OBP	SLG
87 KC	116	317	65	7	0	2	78	24	21	6	0	46	0	8	1	4	4	.50	6	.205	.219	.246
4 YEARS	349	826	173	32	5	2	221	65	58	18	0	139	3	18	4	6	6	.50	12	.209	.228	.268

	1987 SEASON										FOUR YEAR TOTALS (1984 – 1987)									
	Ave.	OBP	SLG	AB	H	2B	3B	HR	RBI	BB	SO	Ave.	OBP	SLG	AB	H	2B	3B	HR	RBI	BB	SO
Totals	.205	.219	.246	317	65	7	0	2	21	6	46	.209	.228	.266	789	165	31	4	2	57	17	130
vs. Left	.198	.207	.286	91	18	2	0	2	7	1	15	.260	.269	.347	242	63	13	1	2	22	3	32
vs. Right	.208	.224	.230	226	47	5	0	0	14	5	31	.186	.210	.230	547	102	18	3	0	35	14	98
at Home	.182	.200	.227	132	24	3	0	1	10	3	12	.204	.221	.257	339	69	11	2	1	26	5	43
on Road	.222	.233	.259	185	41	4	0	1	11	3	34	.213	.233	.273	450	96	20	2	1	31	12	87
vs. Groundball	.207	.215	.272	169	35	5	0	2	11	2	23	.205	.221	.258	380	78	12	1	2	22	7	55
vs. Flyball	.203	.224	.216	148	30	2	0	0	10	4	23	.213	.235	.274	409	87	19	3	0	35	10	75
vs. Finesse	.212	.215	.254	189	40	5	0	1	15	1	22	.221	.232	.277	470	104	21	1	1	35	5	64
vs. Power	.195	.226	.234	128	25	2	0	1	6	5	24	.191	.222	.251	319	61	10	3	1	22	12	66
on Grass	.232	.241	.268	138	32	2	0	1	10	2	21	.215	.232	.263	331	71	11	1	1	21	8	57
on Artificial Turf	.184	.202	.229	179	33	5	0	1	11	4	25	.205	.225	.269	458	94	20	3	1	36	9	73
Day Games	.212	.218	.235	85	18	2	0	0	6	1	18	.171	.183	.220	246	42	6	3	0	22	3	53
Night Games	.203	.219	.250	232	47	5	0	2	15	5	28	.227	.248	.287	543	123	25	1	2	35	14	77
April	.295	.289	.364	44	13	3	0	0	3	0	3	.214	.233	.292	154	33	8	2	0	10	4	23
May	.223	.231	.301	103	23	2	0	2	12	1	15	.227	.242	.289	211	48	7	0	2	21	4	31
June	.143	.152	.154	91	13	1	0	0	1	1	13	.171	.175	.212	170	29	5	1	0	6	1	28
July	.203	.244	.216	74	15	1	0	0	5	4	13	.192	.223	.238	151	29	7	0	0	8	6	29
August	1.000	1.000	1.000	1	1	0	0	0	0	0	0	.281	.293	.368	5	7	16	3	1	0	7	19
Sept/Oct	.000	.000	.000	4	0	0	0	0	0	0	2	.217	.234	.239	46	10	1	0	0	5	1	10
Bases Empty	.209	.225	.257	187	39	6	0	1	1	4	28	.202	.221	.261	460	93	22	1	1	1	11	72
Leadoff	.174	.183	.228	92	16	5	0	0	0	1	10	.189	.204	.250	212	40	13	0	0	0	4	26
Not Leadoff	.242	.265	.284	95	23	1	0	1	1	3	18	.214	.235	.270	248	53	9	1	1	1	7	46
Runners On	.200	.211	.231	130	26	1	0	1	20	2	18	.219	.232	.274	329	72	9	3	1	56	6	58
First Base Only	.151	.167	.151	53	8	0	0	0	0	1	6	.180	.191	.201	139	25	1	1	0	2	2	25
Scoring Position	.234	.241	.286	77	18	1	0	1	20	1	12	.247	.262	.326	190	47	8	2	1	54	4	33
Late Innings, Close	.158	.158	.184	38	6	1	0	0	0	0	10	.191	.191	.213	89	17	2	0	0	3	0	17

RBI/Opportunities

Scoring Position	19 / 96 (20%)	50 / 246 (20%)
Scoring Position, 2 Out	7 / 50 (14%)	18 / 119 (15%)
On Third, Less than 2 Out	7 / 14 (50%)	21 / 36 (58%)
RBI in close games / RBI Total	12 / 21 (57%)	32 / 57 (56%)

Juan Samuel
Philadelphia Phillies

The most important development in Samuel's 1987 season was that he finally (finally!) made some pitchers throw him strikes to get him out. His 60 walks represented nearly double his previous lifetime best. By laying off some of the unhittable pitches that he has chased in the past, Samuel had far more opportunities to hit strikes. The result of this was not a .300 batting average, as many of the media had predicted might happen, but rather a noticeable increase in power. For Samuel this meant hitting 20 or more home runs for the first time, a career-high 28.

The Philadelphia media has made much ado about Samuel's "Quadruple Doubles." This accomplishment is defined as "a batter producing double figures for the season in doubles, triples, home runs, and stolen bases." Samuel apparently is the first major leaguer to perform this feat in each of his first four major league seasons. However, this "statistic" strikes me as even more artificial than, say, the 30–30 club. After all, I bet it is much more common to get a Quadruple Double than it is to have only a "Triple Double" in triples, home runs, stolen bases, and *not* doubles! In fact, how many full-time major leaguers do not hit 10 doubles in a season? So, unlike basketball's single game "Triple Double," the components in this feat are not each notable accomplishments in themselves. Therefore, to carry the silly argument to its next level, why not create a "Quintuple Double" and add another easy to achieve feat, like 10 walks in the season? (Don't worry, Samuel would still have qualified!)

Much more impressive to me than his Quadruple Double is the fact that in 1987 Samuel became only the third second baseman to produce at least 80 long hits in a season. The two previous second sackers to accomplish this feat were Charley Gehringer, who did it in 1936 when he hit 60 doubles, and Rogers Hornsby, who did it five times. For comparison, when Ryne Sandberg had his "all everything" season in 1984, he had 74 long hits. Although 80 long hits is an impressive and rare feat, long hits are not exactly the media's favorite statistic, so this Samuel accomplishment was buried under his well-publicized "failure" to join the somewhat artificial but popular "30–30" club.

Samuel seems to have a good attitude and has worked hard on his fielding. He is a noticeably improved fielder over his rookie and sophomore seasons. Many experts have advocated moving him to the outfield, but he is no longer a big liability at second base. It is clearly to the Phillies' advantage to have such a productive player in the middle infield, so as to leave the outfield spots to those with high offensive capabilities and "easier to place" defensive skills.

Dan Heisman

Samuel, Juan Milton

Bats: Right   Throws: Right   Born 12/09/60

1987 SEASON AND MAJOR-LEAGUE CAREER BATTING TOTALS

	G	AB	H	2B	3B	HR	TB	R	RBI	TBB	IBB	SO	HP	SH	SF	SB	CS	SB%	GDP	AVG	OBP	SLG
87 PHI	160	655	178	37	15	28	329	113	100	60	5	162	5	0	6	35	15	.70	12	.272	.335	.502
5 YEARS	644	2675	719	141	61	80	1222	423	326	151	13	629	27	3	20	205	65	.76	35	.269	.312	.457

	1987 SEASON											FOUR YEAR TOTALS (1984 – 1987)										
	Ave.	OBP	SLG	AB	H	2B	3B	HR	RBI	BB	SO	Ave.	OBP	SLG	AB	H	2B	3B	HR	RBI	BB	SO
Totals	.272	.335	.502	655	178	37	15	28	100	60	162	.269	.312	.457	2610	701	140	59	78	321	147	612
vs. Left	.249	.344	.492	181	45	9	4	9	25	25	47	.255	.296	.427	750	191	41	14	20	84	41	178
vs. Right	.281	.331	.506	474	133	28	11	19	75	35	115	.274	.318	.469	1860	510	99	45	58	237	106	434
at Home	.287	.367	.559	320	92	22	10	15	55	40	73	.263	.317	.464	1264	332	68	32	41	159	91	299
on Road	.257	.302	.448	335	86	15	5	13	45	20	89	.274	.307	.450	1346	369	72	27	37	162	56	313
vs. Groundball	.256	.318	.432	336	86	15	7	10	45	28	82	.266	.313	.429	1239	330	61	28	28	133	70	285
vs. Flyball	.288	.352	.577	319	92	22	8	18	55	32	80	.271	.311	.483	1371	371	79	31	50	188	77	327
vs. Finesse	.278	.316	.503	356	99	21	7	15	52	17	77	.276	.307	.464	1471	406	82	34	42	178	54	291
vs. Power	.264	.355	.502	299	79	16	8	13	48	43	85	.259	.317	.449	1139	295	58	25	36	143	93	321
on Grass	.244	.298	.413	172	42	4	2	7	23	11	48	.280	.317	.461	690	193	29	12	24	88	30	171
on Artificial Turf	.282	.348	.534	483	136	33	13	21	77	49	114	.265	.310	.456	1920	508	111	47	54	233	117	441
Day Games	.292	.364	.531	192	56	12	5	8	28	22	48	.281	.328	.517	814	229	48	21	34	115	54	180
Night Games	.263	.322	.490	463	122	25	10	20	72	38	114	.263	.304	.430	1796	472	92	38	44	206	93	432
April	.272	.333	.444	81	22	7	2	1	9	8	24	.284	.331	.418	261	74	14	6	3	22	19	65
May	.267	.316	.533	105	28	5	1	7	22	8	16	.266	.302	.442	428	114	20	8	13	53	22	93
June	.262	.336	.467	107	28	4	3	4	14	11	23	.279	.318	.471	480	134	28	11	14	64	26	106
July	.278	.375	.574	108	30	4	2	8	22	16	33	.272	.323	.502	438	119	21	13	18	66	32	113
August	.280	.357	.480	125	35	9	5	2	17	15	33	.264	.301	.461	492	130	30	11	15	70	26	116
Sept/Oct	.271	.288	.504	129	35	8	2	6	16	2	33	.254	.287	.434	511	130	27	10	15	46	22	119
Bases Empty	.248	.320	.468	404	100	24	7	17	17	39	106	.263	.307	.436	1586	417	89	30	42	42	96	388
Leadoff	.271	.342	.532	203	55	16	5	9	9	19	53	.259	.309	.437	760	197	46	16	19	19	52	179
Not Leadoff	.224	.297	.403	201	45	8	2	8	8	20	53	.266	.304	.436	826	220	43	14	23	23	44	209
Runners On	.311	.358	.558	251	78	13	8	11	83	21	56	.277	.311	.489	1024	284	51	29	36	279	51	224
First Base Only	.287	.340	.425	87	25	4	1	2	5	6	22	.280	.306	.455	393	110	21	9	10	32	14	88
Scoring Position	.323	.368	.628	164	53	9	7	9	78	15	34	.276	.313	.510	631	174	30	20	26	247	37	136
Late Innings, Close	.272	.387	.467	92	25	5	2	3	16	18	28	.256	.315	.423	407	104	17	6	13	55	36	114

RBI/Opportunities

	1987		Four Year	
Scoring Position	65 / 210	(31%)	206 / 804	(26%)
Scoring Position, 2 Out	25 / 98	(26%)	87 / 379	(23%)
On Third, Less than 2 Out	24 / 38	(63%)	66 / 125	(53%)
RBI in close games / RBI Total	64 / 100	(64%)	205 / 321	(64%)

Ryne Sandberg
Chicago Cubs

After a sub-par 1986 season (sub-par for him, anyway; good for most other second baseman), Ryne Sandberg got off to a great start in 1987. By June 13 he was hitting .286 with 17 doubles and 11 home runs (only 3 fewer homers than all of 1986), with an on base percentage of .375 and a slugging percentage of .509. But on that fateful day Ryne hurt his ankle running to first base and did not return to the lineup until after the All-Star break. At first his replacement, Paul Noce, did just fine, hitting over .300 and fielding brilliantly. In his limited time at second Noce even out-ranged Ryno, with 5.95 chances per nine innings to Sandberg's 5.33. (This may not be an illusion; Noce also had a higher range factor at short than Dunston.) Eventually, Noce's offense faded, proving what we knew all along. That is, Paul Noce is no Ryne Sandberg.

Neither, apparently, was Ryne Sandberg after his injury. His defense did not suffer at all; his range factor and fielding percentage were almost identical pre- and postinjury, leading to another well deserved Gold Glove. However, Ryno's offense slipped noticeably after his return. He hit .301 for the remainder of the season, but it was a fairly empty .301. Despite having more at bats after the injury than before it, Ryno had only 8 doubles and 5 home runs

after returning to the lineup, for a .388 slugging percentage. Good for mere mortals, but inadequate by Ryne Sandberg standards. In addition, 14 of Ryno's 21 stolen bases came before the mishap in St. Louis. He seemed more hesitant on the base paths the latter part of the season, perhaps fearful of a re-occurrence of his injury. Then again, the entire Cub team's base stealing tailed off dramatically after the first two months, although Sandberg and Dunston being sidelined at the same time surely had something to do with it.

Often when a player suffers a serious injury, he becomes more susceptible to injury than in previous years. Even so, I would be surprised to see that happen with Ryne Sandberg. He doesn't play out of control. Compared to most second basemen, Ryno doesn't make a lot of spectacular diving plays. He simply makes most of the plays, fielding second base in much the same fashion that Joe DiMaggio played center field. Sandberg rarely takes reckless chances on the base paths; he is an aggressive, but smart base runner. He has good habits and keeps himself in excellent physical condition. Ryno will only be 29 in 1988; he is still in his prime. We should see a return to top form for Ryne Sandberg in 1988.

Pat McCormick

Sandberg, Ryne Dee   Bats: Right   Throws: Right   Born 09/18/59

1987 SEASON AND MAJOR-LEAGUE CAREER BATTING TOTALS

	G	AB	H	2B	3B	HR	TB	R	RBI	TBB	IBB	SO	HP	SH	SF	SB	CS	SB%	GDP	AVG	OBP	SLG
87 CHN	132	523	154	25	2	16	231	81	59	59	4	79	2	1	2	21	2	.91	11	.294	.367	.442
7 YEARS	922	3669	1056	178	41	90	1586	575	404	301	24	526	13	25	26	210	54	.80	54	.288	.342	.432

	1987 SEASON											FOUR YEAR TOTALS (1984 – 1987)									
	Ave.	OBP	SLG	AB	H	2B	3B	HR	RBI	BB	SO	Ave.	OBP	SLG	AB	H	2B	3B	HR	RBI	BB	SO
Totals	.294	.367	.442	523	154	25	2	16	59	59	79	.300	.357	.471	2395	718	120	32	75	302	214	356
vs. Left	.307	.412	.439	114	35	9	0	2	13	21	16	.302	.364	.455	587	177	32	8	14	61	59	74
vs. Right	.291	.353	.443	409	119	16	2	14	46	38	63	.299	.354	.476	1808	541	88	24	61	241	155	282
at Home	.300	.357	.463	257	77	14	2	8	33	23	39	.310	.368	.512	1184	367	65	21	44	165	112	182
on Road	.289	.376	.421	266	77	11	0	8	26	36	40	.290	.345	.430	1211	351	55	11	31	137	102	174
vs. Groundball	.269	.361	.363	212	57	5	0	5	24	30	33	.302	.365	.465	1077	325	53	15	31	137	108	152
vs. Flyball	.312	.371	.495	311	97	20	2	11	35	29	46	.298	.350	.475	1318	393	67	17	44	165	106	204
vs. Finesse	.294	.356	.451	306	90	11	2	11	34	29	37	.302	.351	.475	1382	418	58	18	48	182	104	177
vs. Power	.295	.382	.429	217	64	14	0	5	25	30	42	.296	.364	.465	1013	300	62	14	27	120	110	179
on Grass	.294	.357	.456	377	111	18	2	13	48	37	56	.305	.361	.497	1702	519	86	26	63	229	155	254
on Artificial Turf	.295	.391	.404	146	43	7	0	3	11	22	23	.287	.345	.405	693	199	34	6	12	73	59	102
Day Games	.319	.386	.482	332	106	17	2	11	39	36	46	.306	.365	.491	1580	484	85	25	52	202	148	226
Night Games	.251	.335	.372	191	48	8	0	5	20	23	33	.287	.340	.432	815	234	35	7	23	100	66	130
April	.270	.379	.405	74	20	7	0	1	7	12	10	.243	.312	.395	309	75	20	3	7	33	30	43
May	.280	.361	.551	118	33	6	1	8	18	15	21	.323	.385	.522	439	142	25	7	16	59	44	71
June	.333	.404	.571	42	14	4	0	2	8	5	4	.318	.358	.538	368	117	19	7	16	53	23	45
July	.344	.379	.426	61	21	2	0	1	4	4	6	.312	.362	.488	375	117	15	6	13	45	30	55
August	.325	.385	.410	117	38	1	0	3	14	11	18	.308	.360	.442	455	140	17	1	14	51	37	67
Sept/Oct	.252	.325	.342	111	28	5	1	1	8	12	20	.283	.355	.432	449	127	24	8	9	61	50	75
Bases Empty	.299	.368	.487	308	92	18	2	12	12	34	46	.302	.353	.489	1395	421	78	18	49	49	110	206
Leadoff	.302	.347	.483	116	35	9	0	4	4	8	19	.311	.350	.561	444	138	33	6	22	22	27	72
Not Leadoff	.297	.381	.490	192	57	9	2	8	8	26	27	.298	.354	.455	951	283	45	12	27	27	83	134
Runners On	.288	.365	.377	215	62	7	0	4	47	25	33	.297	.364	.445	1000	297	42	14	26	253	104	150
First Base Only	.372	.419	.477	86	32	3	0	2	5	6	10	.321	.363	.487	421	135	20	4	14	40	27	51
Scoring Position	.233	.331	.310	129	30	4	0	2	42	19	23	.280	.364	.415	579	162	22	10	12	213	77	99
Late Innings, Close	.287	.380	.350	80	23	2	0	1	14	12	14	.299	.360	.463	365	109	12	9	10	60	35	59

RBI/Opportunities

Scoring Position	39 / 178 (22%)	192 / 780 (25%)
Scoring Position, 2 Out	20 / 85 (24%)	73 / 339 (22%)
On Third, Less than 2 Out	12 / 29 (41%)	66 / 123 (54%)
RBI in close games / RBI Total	37 / 59 (63%)	195 / 302 (65%)

Scott Sanderson
Chicago Cubs

Scott Sanderson has become the Bob Horner of the Cub pitching staff. In 1984, his first year with the Cubs, Scott went 8–5 with a 3.14 ERA despite missing more than a month with back problems. In 1985 he had a 3.12 ERA in only 121 innings, although because of poor support he was 5–6. We all sat around and said, "Just wait until Sanderson gets in a full season. He'll win 15 easy." Well, we're still waiting. In his four years with the Cubs, Scott has qualified for the ERA title only once (1986), and then only by 7.2 innings. He just keeps getting injured. Cub fans have gotten used to this; in the notes section of a 1987 scoresheet I wrote, "Sanderson hurt? Gee, that's unusual."

More to the point, however, seeing Scott for four years makes us wonder if he is anything more than an average pitcher. The last two years he has had losing records and ERAs over 4.00. He usually gets off to a good start, hits a mid-season slump, then finishes the year well enough to save his job. His 1984–86 3-year breakdowns confirm this impression. From April to September–October of 1984–86 Scott's ERAs were 2.74, 3.20, 3.43, 3.42, 5.78 and 2.32 (!). In 1986 his season ERA was 4.19, but his September-October ERA was 3.26. In 1987 Scott was 4–6, 4.56 at the end of July; from August on, he was 4–3, 3.92, practically assuring himself of a 1988 roster spot. Then again, the competition on the Cubs staff isn't exactly stellar.

Scotty has the basic tools to be a good pitcher. He has a good fastball and a fine curve. When he mixes the two effectively, he usually has a good outing. His difficulties come when he falls in love with his slow curve and keeps throwing it until it gets belted all over the ballpark. Another problem is that he holds onto the ball interminably between pitches, especially with runners on base. When he finally gets around to delivering the ball, he does it from an excruciatingly slow windup. He probably puts the fielders to sleep; certainly he exasperates Harry Caray, fans who want their dinners and the "No Lights at Wrigley" crowd when he drags a 3:05 game into the sunset. (One advantage of this used to be that when Lee Smith time rolled around, it was too dark for the hitters to see. But of course Smith has now departed.)

In the last two seasons Scott has spent part of his time in middle relief, and has done pretty well. Maybe that's his niche; I don't know. For now it looks as though the Cubs have in Scott Sanderson a mediocre, injury-prone pitcher.

Pat McCormick

Sanderson, Scott Douglas

Bats: Right   Throws: Right   Born 07/22/56

1987 SEASON AND MAJOR-LEAGUE CAREER PITCHING TOTALS

	G	GS	CG	GF	IP	BFP	H	R	ER	HR	SH	SF	HB	TBB	IBB	SO	WP	Bk	W	L	Pct	ShO	Sv	ERA
87 CHN	32	22	0	5	145	631	156	72	69	23	4	5	3	50	5	106	1	0	8	9	.471	0	2	4.28
10 YEARS	261	229	30	12	1459	6029	1399	623	566	145	60	50	18	378	28	989	22	7	86	78	.524	9	5	3.49

1987: Power, Flyball   1986: Finesse, Flyball   1985: Finesse, Flyball   1984: Finesse, Flyball

1987 SEASON

	G	IP	H	BB	SO	SB	CS	W	L	S	ERA
Totals	32	144.2	156	50	106	16	5	8	9	2	4.29
at Home	13	58.0	67	22	50	5	3	3	4	1	4.97
on Road	19	86.2	89	28	56	11	2	5	5	1	3.84
on Grass	20	88.1	97	33	66	9	5	5	6	1	4.18
on Artificial Turf	12	56.1	59	17	40	7	0	3	3	1	4.47
Day Games	24	107.2	107	35	86	6	3	7	5	2	3.85
Night Games	8	37.0	49	15	20	10	2	1	4	0	5.59
April	1	5.1	6	2	3	2	0	1	0	0	3.38
May	7	42.1	40	11	33	1	1	2	1	0	4.25
June	4	14.1	29	5	16	2	2	0	3	0	7.53
July	9	21.0	16	8	15	0	1	1	2	2	3.43
August	5	27.2	29	11	20	4	0	3	1	0	2.93
Sept/Oct	6	34.0	36	13	19	7	1	1	2	0	4.76

vs. Opponent Batters	Ave.	OBP	SLG	AB	H	2B	3B	HR	RBI	BB	SO
Totals	.274	.333	.469	569	156	26	8	23	65	50	106
vs. Left	.294	.366	.482	326	96	15	5	12	34	37	46
vs. Right	.247	.287	.453	243	60	11	3	11	31	13	60
Bases Empty	.291	.338	.506	340	99	17	4	16	16	22	60
Leadoff	.255	.309	.447	141	36	5	2	6	6	11	28
Not Leadoff	.317	.358	.548	199	63	12	2	10	10	11	32
Runners On Base	.249	.327	.415	229	57	9	4	7	49	28	46
First Base Only	.260	.302	.430	100	26	3	1	4	10	5	22
Scoring Position	.240	.344	.403	129	31	6	3	3	39	23	24
Late Innings, Close	.230	.314	.410	61	14	0	1	3	7	7	12

FOUR YEAR TOTALS (1984 – 1987)

	G	IP	H	BB	SO	SB	CS	W	L	S	ERA
Totals	112	576.0	561	138	386	41	30	30	31	3	3.73
at Home	52	275.1	254	72	201	19	12	16	14	1	3.66
on Road	60	300.2	307	66	185	22	18	14	17	2	3.77
on Grass	70	363.0	336	93	262	25	19	20	18	1	3.55
on Artificial Turf	42	213.0	225	45	124	16	11	10	13	2	4.01
Day Games	82	434.0	410	103	312	24	22	25	21	2	3.44
Night Games	30	142.0	151	35	74	17	8	5	10	1	4.63
April	12	77.2	68	14	45	5	5	6	3	0	2.78
May	24	138.0	129	32	96	4	5	7	2	0	3.52
June	13	74.2	74	19	59	2	4	1	8	0	4.22
July	23	97.1	88	24	70	6	10	6	6	2	3.42
August	19	104.0	120	29	65	12	5	5	8	0	5.02
Sept/Oct	21	84.1	82	20	51	12	1	5	4	1	3.31

vs. Opponent Batters	Ave.	OBP	SLG	AB	H	2B	3B	HR	RBI	BB	SO
Totals	.257	.301	.414	2186	561	106	26	62	228	138	386
vs. Left	.259	.311	.426	1222	316	60	17	37	119	93	182
vs. Right	.254	.288	.398	964	245	46	9	25	109	45	204
Bases Empty	.259	.299	.424	1365	354	70	16	41	41	76	243
Leadoff	.254	.289	.405	568	144	30	7	14	14	28	85
Not Leadoff	.263	.307	.438	797	210	40	9	27	27	48	158
Runners On Base	.252	.304	.397	821	207	36	10	21	187	62	143
First Base Only	.266	.297	.409	364	97	16	3	10	30	15	53
Scoring Position	.241	.308	.387	457	110	20	7	11	157	47	90
Late Innings, Close	.233	.287	.350	180	42	1	1	6	15	13	28

RBI/Opportunities

Scoring Position	32 / 182 (18%)	132 / 593 (22%)
Scoring Position, 2 Out	7 / 82 (9%)	39 / 268 (15%)
On Third, Less than 2 Out	18 / 37 (49%)	67 / 122 (55%)
RBI in close games / RBI Total	43 / 65 (66%)	171 / 228 (75%)

Rafael Santana
New York Mets

Rafael Santana's asset to a club is his defense. He has a reliable glove, and has hovered around the middle of the pack in adjusted Range Factor for the past few years. He is what is known as a "steady" shortstop. You know, one who "makes all the plays." This is by no means a quality to be overlooked, especially in the Met infield of the past few years where the abilities of Wally Backman, Tim Teufel and Howard Johnson have been, shall we say, somewhat inconsistent.

Raffy's main fielding problem is lack of range to his right. His arm isn't as strong as he would like, so plays in the hole pose a special problem. As if to tease the weak-hearted Met fans, Santana likes to arc the ball across the diamond and just catch the runner by a half-step. Very amusing. I prefer what I remember of Jose Oquendo's throws—heat seeking missiles that burnt a hole in Hernandez' glove.

His prowess with the bat (and I use prowess with great caution) has improved in the past season. Much was made during the winter meetings of his RBIs in 1987 (44). He was fourth in the NL among shortstops, following Smith (75), Brooks (72) and Templeton (48). I am tempted to say that the other eight must have been run over by a truck, but it is true.

Yankee fans should not rejoice at his RBI output, how-ever. The rest of the league became aware that the Met pitchers were generally ineffective and were being pinch-hit for early. With Lee Mazzilli the likely on-deck batter, who would you rather pitch to, Raffy or Lee?

Ah, the fond memories of spring training scenes. Fade in to countless hours of Bill Robinson working with Raffy in the batting cage, soft-tossing balls to him and watching Raffy's bat—swoosh!—come crashing down and—thwack!—the ball rocketing into the netting. Fade to black. Fade in countless scenes of Davey popping antacids and sending Dave Magadan up to hit for Santana whenever he could. Robinson will now be able to spend more time teaching Gary Carter to adjust to old age.

On December 11, Raffy was traded to the Yankees. This may not make the earth move in Peoria, but here in the Big Apple it is the first trade on the major league level between the two NY teams since the infamous Ray Burris deal in 1977. Much of this has to do with the normal skittishness to make a blunder with a cross-town rival, but more has to do with George Steinbrenner's paranoia. After this deal had been consummated, both Lou Piniella and Joe McIlvane were seemingly jumping for joy, as if a cure from some dread disease had been found or detente had been reached. Ah, we New Yorkers find joy in such small things.

Gerry Klug

Santana, Rafael Francisco (de la Cruz)

Bats: Right   Throws: Right   Born 01/31/58

1987 SEASON AND MAJOR-LEAGUE CAREER BATTING TOTALS

	G	AB	H	2B	3B	HR	TB	R	RBI	TBB	IBB	SO	HP	SH	SF	SB	CS	SB%	GDP	AVG	OBP	SLG
87 NYN	139	439	112	21	2	5	152	41	44	29	10	57	1	0	1	1	1	.50	11	.255	.302	.346
5 YEARS	513	1528	379	62	4	8	473	135	115	105	34	173	4	6	6	2	5	.29	43	.248	.297	.310

	1987 SEASON											FOUR YEAR TOTALS (1984 – 1987)										
	Ave.	OBP	SLG	AB	H	2B	3B	HR	RBI	BB	SO	Ave.	OBP	SLG	AB	H	2B	3B	HR	RBI	BB	SO
Totals	.255	.302	.346	439	112	21	2	5	44	29	57	.248	.296	.310	1514	376	62	4	8	113	103	171
vs. Left	.262	.322	.363	168	44	6	1	3	20	14	16	.266	.327	.332	576	153	19	2	5	45	52	59
vs. Right	.251	.289	.336	271	68	15	1	2	24	15	41	.238	.277	.297	938	223	43	2	3	68	51	112
at Home	.244	.297	.330	221	54	13	0	2	21	17	31	.234	.285	.293	731	171	32	1	3	54	53	88
on Road	.266	.307	.362	218	58	8	2	3	23	12	26	.262	.307	.327	783	205	30	3	5	59	50	83
vs. Groundball	.275	.340	.357	171	47	8	0	2	15	16	20	.253	.306	.317	679	172	27	2	4	51	50	75
vs. Flyball	.243	.277	.340	268	65	13	2	3	29	13	37	.244	.289	.305	835	204	35	2	4	62	53	96
vs. Finesse	.263	.293	.347	236	62	12	1	2	26	9	22	.251	.288	.312	837	210	37	1	4	66	42	82
vs. Power	.246	.313	.345	203	50	9	1	3	18	20	35	.245	.306	.309	677	166	25	3	4	47	61	89
on Grass	.255	.305	.347	314	80	18	1	3	34	23	39	.245	.292	.310	1057	259	50	2	5	83	70	119
on Artificial Turf	.256	.295	.344	125	32	3	1	2	10	6	18	.256	.306	.311	457	117	12	2	3	30	33	52
Day Games	.269	.310	.379	145	39	11	1	1	17	8	13	.227	.274	.287	560	127	24	2	2	45	36	53
Night Games	.248	.298	.330	294	73	10	1	4	27	21	44	.261	.309	.324	954	249	38	2	6	68	67	118
April	.197	.246	.262	61	12	1	0	1	3	4	9	.184	.244	.245	163	30	4	0	2	10	13	23
May	.333	.367	.439	57	19	3	0	1	7	3	10	.246	.278	.302	179	44	7	0	1	10	8	27
June	.257	.333	.400	70	18	2	1	2	13	8	10	.253	.312	.318	233	59	7	1	2	28	20	20
July	.294	.318	.388	85	25	8	0	0	6	3	8	.266	.304	.314	290	77	14	0	0	13	16	29
August	.259	.291	.383	81	21	5	1	1	10	4	10	.286	.316	.365	353	101	20	1	2	30	16	37
Sept/Oct	.200	.269	.224	85	17	2	0	0	5	7	10	.220	.294	.277	296	65	10	2	1	22	30	35
Bases Empty	.235	.267	.315	251	59	11	0	3	3	10	35	.251	.289	.311	883	222	37	2	4	4	46	113
Leadoff	.232	.262	.323	99	23	6	0	1	1	4	12	.258	.295	.326	368	95	18	2	1	1	19	37
Not Leadoff	.237	.270	.309	152	36	5	0	2	2	6	23	.247	.285	.301	515	127	19	0	3	3	27	76
Runners On	.282	.346	.388	188	53	10	2	2	41	19	22	.244	.306	.309	631	154	25	2	4	109	57	58
First Base Only	.338	.372	.432	74	25	4	0	1	3	4	7	.283	.308	.393	269	76	9	0	3	8	10	17
Scoring Position	.246	.331	.360	114	28	6	2	1	38	15	15	.215	.305	.279	362	78	16	2	1	101	47	41
Late Innings, Close	.153	.194	.220	59	9	2	1	0	7	3	10	.214	.263	.251	243	52	7	1	0	12	16	38

RBI/Opportunities

Scoring Position	33 / 159 (21%)	95 / 494 (19%)	
Scoring Position, 2 Out	15 / 76 (20%)	35 / 247 (14%)	
On Third, Less than 2 Out	11 / 26 (42%)	42 / 89 (47%)	
RBI in close games / RBI Total	24 / 44 (55%)	72 / 113 (64%)	

Benito Santiago
San Diego Padres

After the '86 season, Padre management decided that Benito Santiago was ready for the major leagues. Rather than have the 21-year-old rookie learn from the bench, they traded Terry Kennedy and handed the job to the youngster.

Initially, it appeared the Pads had again pushed a promising ballplayer along too quickly. Despite flashes of brilliance, Benito began producing passed balls and errors at a record rate. By June 8 he had committed 14 errors. His hitting soon began to suffer, and friction erupted between members of the pitching staff and their rookie receiver; rumors surfaced that there were racially based tensions at work, too.

Larry Bowa took action. He benched Santiago for three days and held meetings with his catcher and pitchers. Bowa then returned Benito to the lineup, making it clear that he was the starting catcher. Results: the passed balls and errors occurred much less frequently, fewer runners stole successfully, Benito's batting improved and, not coincidentally, the team started winning.

Santiago went on to have a superlative rookie season. He finished the year by setting a record for consecutive game hitting for a rookie and was a far better catcher at season's end, earning the NL Rookie of the Year award in a runaway.

His hitting is more impressive when compared to other catchers' first full seasons. In recent history, NL receivers' "first full" statistics show that only Ted Simmons, Gary Carter, Tony Pena and Ozzie Virgil approached Benito's totals. Of this group, all but Carter had at least 74 major league games and much bench time under their belts when their full-season chance came. Even Johnny Bench didn't enjoy a more productive initiation.

Benito's future looks bright. He's exciting to watch and will throw to any base at anytime. Like many Dominican hitters, he's a free swinger with a poor strikeout to walk ratio (112 to 16!). While one would expect his overall production to lessen in '88, with proper coaching and additional experience, he may soon become the best all-round backstop in the league. The only question is whether his slight build (6'1", 175 lbs.) can withstand the day-to-day pounding of his profession.

	AGE	AB	R	H	2B	3B	HR	RBI	AVG	SB	BB	OBA	SA
Santiago	21	546	64	164	33	2	18	79	.300	21	16	.324	.467
Bench	21	564	67	155	40	2	15	82	.275	1	31	.313	.433
Simmons	21	510	64	155	32	4	7	77	.304	1	36	.347	.424
Carter	21	503	58	136	20	1	17	68	.270	5	72	.360	.416
Pena	24	497	53	147	28	4	11	63	.296	2	17	.323	.435
Virgil	27	456	61	119	21	2	18	68	.261	1	45	.331	.434

Bruce Erricson

Santiago, Benito (Rivera)

Bats: Right   Throws: Right   Born 09/03/65

1987 SEASON AND MAJOR-LEAGUE CAREER BATTING TOTALS

	G	AB	H	2B	3B	HR	TB	R	RBI	TBB	IBB	SO	HP	SH	SF	SB	CS	SB%	GDP	AVG	OBP	SLG
87 SD	146	546	164	33	2	18	255	64	79	16	2	112	5	1	4	21	12	.64	12	.300	.324	.467
2 YEARS	163	608	182	35	2	21	284	74	85	18	2	124	5	1	5	21	13	.62	12	.299	.322	.467

1987 SEASON

	Ave.	OBP	SLG	AB	H	2B	3B	HR	RBI	BB	SO
Totals	.300	.324	.467	546	164	33	2	18	79	16	112
vs. Left	.341	.363	.577	182	62	17	1	8	29	6	32
vs. Right	.280	.304	.412	364	102	16	1	10	50	10	80
at Home	.281	.307	.471	274	77	17	1	11	45	10	50
on Road	.320	.342	.463	272	87	16	1	7	34	6	62
vs. Groundball	.319	.342	.473	260	83	16	0	8	41	7	47
vs. Flyball	.283	.308	.462	286	81	17	2	10	38	9	65
vs. Finesse	.294	.311	.449	272	80	19	1	7	30	5	44
vs. Power	.307	.337	.485	274	84	14	1	11	49	11	68
on Grass	.284	.308	.442	394	112	21	1	13	54	11	84
on Artificial Turf	.342	.365	.533	152	52	12	1	5	25	5	28
Day Games	.297	.324	.418	165	49	9	1	3	18	7	30
Night Games	.302	.324	.488	381	115	24	1	15	61	9	82
April	.282	.291	.474	78	22	4	1	3	7	1	16
May	.280	.306	.355	93	26	1	0	2	9	2	23
June	.247	.291	.342	73	18	4	0	1	10	4	20
July	.301	.337	.458	83	25	7	0	2	15	4	20
August	.330	.357	.566	106	35	7	0	6	25	5	13
Sept/Oct	.336	.342	.549	113	38	10	1	4	13	0	20
Bases Empty	.293	.317	.438	290	85	19	1	7	7	6	72
Leadoff	.293	.304	.358	123	36	8	0	0	0	1	34
Not Leadoff	.293	.326	.497	167	49	11	1	7	7	5	38
Runners On	.309	.332	.500	256	79	14	1	11	72	10	40
First Base Only	.322	.333	.521	121	39	3	0	7	16	1	14
Scoring Position	.296	.331	.481	135	40	11	1	4	56	9	26
Late Innings, Close	.396	.408	.564	101	40	6	1	3	18	2	22

TWO YEAR TOTALS (1986 – 1987)

	Ave.	OBP	SLG	AB	H	2B	3B	HR	RBI	BB	SO
Totals	.299	.322	.467	608	182	35	2	21	85	18	124
vs. Left	.343	.364	.583	204	70	17	1	10	34	7	35
vs. Right	.277	.301	.408	404	112	18	1	11	51	11	89
at Home	.279	.306	.478	301	84	19	1	13	48	12	55
on Road	.319	.339	.456	307	98	16	1	8	37	6	69
vs. Groundball	.315	.338	.466	292	92	17	0	9	44	8	52
vs. Flyball	.285	.308	.468	316	90	18	2	12	41	10	72
vs. Finesse	.297	.312	.448	306	91	20	1	8	33	5	47
vs. Power	.301	.332	.487	302	91	15	1	13	52	13	77
on Grass	.283	.308	.445	434	123	23	1	15	59	13	90
on Artificial Turf	.339	.359	.523	174	59	12	1	6	26	5	34
Day Games	.297	.324	.418	165	49	9	1	3	18	7	30
Night Games	.300	.322	.485	443	133	26	1	18	67	11	94
April	.282	.291	.474	78	22	4	1	3	7	1	16
May	.280	.306	.355	93	26	1	0	2	9	2	23
June	.247	.291	.342	73	18	4	0	1	10	4	20
July	.301	.337	.458	83	25	7	0	2	15	4	20
August	.330	.357	.566	106	35	7	0	6	25	5	13
Sept/Oct	.320	.330	.520	175	56	12	1	7	19	2	32
Bases Empty	.300	.320	.459	327	98	20	1	10	10	6	80
Leadoff	.312	.322	.418	141	44	9	0	2	2	1	37
Not Leadoff	.290	.320	.489	186	54	11	1	8	8	5	43
Runners On	.299	.324	.477	281	84	15	1	11	75	12	44
First Base Only	.331	.341	.528	127	42	4	0	7	16	1	14
Scoring Position	.273	.312	.435	154	42	11	1	4	59	11	30
Late Innings, Close	.396	.408	.564	202	80	12	2	6	36	4	44

RBI/Opportunities

Scoring Position	49 / 183	(27%)
Scoring Position, 2 Out	24 / 89	(27%)
On Third, Less than 2 Out	17 / 32	(53%)
RBI in close games / RBI Total	47 / 79	(59%)

52 / 207	(25%)
25 / 100	(25%)
18 / 38	(47%)
94 / 85	(111%)

Steve Sax
Los Angeles Dodgers

Steve Sax has been notorious for years for his inconsistent defense at second base, but after 1987 his offensive consistency is becoming almost as notable. Speculating on what Sax might do at the plate is like speculating in the stock market. Sax has hit as high as .332 and as low as .243, had as few as 8 and as many as 43 doubles, and slugged from .304 to .441. His superb 1986 season is completely out of character with the rest of his career—his 1987 totals were much closer to his career norms. Sax hit in the .260 range for most of the year, finishing strongly to raise his final average to .280.

Sax is a player who does not fit easily into a clearly defined offensive role. His fine base-stealing abilities tempt the Dodgers to use him at the top of the lineup, but he has never been a particularly patient hitter. If he hits .332 like in 1986 he can lead off but when he hits a more normal .270–.280 he might as well bat eighth. Sax's stats are badly hurt by Dodger Stadium as he is a much better hitter on ersatz lawn. Perhaps the Dodgers should consider batting Sax at the top of the lineup on foreign plastic and at the bottom of the lineup on domestic grass.

The acquisition of John Shelby has apparently ended the speculation about the Dodgers moving Sax to center field.

Greg Gajus

The failure to lure Gary Gaetti from the World Champions has Tommy Lasagna (apparently seriously) considering moving Steve to third base to plug that void in 1988.

Sax clearly does not produce power numbers acceptable for a corner infielder, particularly with the non-existent Dodger attack (365 fewer total bases than the Giants in 1987), and, as flaky as his throwing arm once was, his fielding average in 1987 was better than Juan Samuel, Johnny Ray, and Ron Oester, and only .003 behind Ryne Sandberg, and his range factor trailed only Sandberg and Samuel among starters, and that only by 2 chances per month. However, the Dodger "brass" seem bound and determined to force Mariano Duncan to prove that he can not handle *any* major league defensive assignments, so they want to remove the .982 fielding half of the fifth best DP combo in the NL, to give the .930 half his job. And they said blacks don't have the "necessities" to manage at the big league level? You can run, but you can't hide, Mariano. I give this experiment (rated "R"—unsuitable for viewers under 17) until May 1, at the outside. It may not even come "north" from Vero Beach, if we're all lucky.

Michael Duca

Sax, Stephen Louis "Steve"

Bats: Right   **Throws: Right**   **Born 01/29/60**

1987 SEASON AND MAJOR-LEAGUE CAREER BATTING TOTALS

	G	AB	H	2B	3B	HR	TB	R	RBI	TBB	IBB	SO	HP	SH	SF	SB	CS	SB%	GDP	AVG	OBP	SLG
87 LA	157	610	171	22	7	6	225	84	46	44	5	61	3	5	1	37	11	.77	13	.280	.331	.369
7 YEARS	931	3680	1043	140	31	25	1320	504	276	318	30	355	13	35	12	248	114	.69	70	.283	.342	.359

	1987 SEASON											FOUR YEAR TOTALS (1984 – 1987)										
	Ave.	OBP	SLG	AB	H	2B	3B	HR	RBI	BB	SO	Ave.	OBP	SLG	AB	H	2B	3B	HR	RBI	BB	SO
Totals	.280	.331	.369	610	171	22	7	6	47	44	61	.285	.344	.361	2300	655	96	19	14	180	204	215
vs. Left	.278	.330	.376	205	57	10	2	2	15	15	14	.280	.340	.375	781	219	46	5	6	60	72	57
vs. Right	.281	.332	.365	405	114	12	5	4	32	29	47	.287	.347	.354	1519	436	50	14	8	120	132	158
at Home	.260	.310	.325	289	75	9	2	2	16	19	28	.264	.327	.323	1103	291	40	5	5	69	101	100
on Road	.299	.351	.408	321	96	13	5	4	31	25	33	.304	.360	.397	1197	364	56	14	9	111	103	115
vs. Groundball	.269	.314	.305	275	74	8	1	0	18	17	31	.271	.332	.321	1009	273	37	4	2	74	87	96
vs. Flyball	.290	.345	.421	335	97	14	6	6	29	27	30	.296	.354	.393	1291	382	59	15	12	106	117	119
vs. Finesse	.261	.308	.348	330	86	14	3	3	21	22	27	.286	.334	.352	1299	372	52	9	5	85	91	97
vs. Power	.304	.359	.393	280	85	8	4	3	26	22	34	.283	.357	.374	1001	283	44	10	9	95	113	118
on Grass	.280	.331	.355	439	123	13	4	4	30	31	45	.272	.336	.339	1648	448	56	12	10	116	157	157
on Artificial Turf	.281	.333	.404	171	48	9	3	2	17	13	16	.317	.365	.419	652	207	40	7	4	64	47	58
Day Games	.233	.266	.312	189	44	7	1	2	16	9	21	.274	.336	.348	715	196	30	4	5	66	67	58
Night Games	.302	.359	.394	421	127	15	6	4	31	35	40	.290	.348	.367	1585	459	66	15	9	114	137	157
April	.198	.263	.264	91	18	4	1	0	4	7	10	.278	.347	.355	248	69	11	1	2	17	25	21
May	.321	.368	.453	106	34	4	2	2	7	8	16	.284	.340	.393	387	110	19	4	5	30	33	48
June	.266	.322	.321	109	29	3	0	1	14	9	10	.252	.321	.306	405	102	11	4	1	33	41	39
July	.247	.272	.286	77	19	1	1	0	4	3	5	.284	.332	.344	363	103	12	2	2	29	27	33
August	.279	.328	.360	111	31	7	1	0	5	7	10	.262	.305	.322	432	113	24	1	0	25	26	45
Sept/Oct	.345	.402	.483	116	40	3	2	3	13	10	10	.340	.407	.437	465	158	19	7	4	46	52	29
Bases Empty	.289	.334	.387	401	116	14	5	5	5	24	37	.287	.337	.366	1542	442	68	12	10	10	114	135
Leadoff	.289	.326	.404	218	63	7	3	4	4	11	21	.282	.331	.364	871	246	41	6	6	6	62	75
Not Leadoff	.290	.343	.366	183	53	7	2	1	1	13	16	.292	.345	.368	671	196	27	6	4	4	52	60
Runners On	.263	.326	.335	209	55	8	2	1	42	20	24	.281	.357	.352	758	213	28	7	4	170	90	80
First Base Only	.253	.314	.316	79	20	2	0	1	3	7	6	.261	.314	.318	299	78	8	0	3	8	23	27
Scoring Position	.269	.333	.346	130	35	6	2	0	39	13	18	.294	.383	.375	459	135	20	7	1	162	67	53
Late Innings, Close	.360	.423	.500	100	36	6	1	2	14	11	11	.332	.391	.436	376	125	18	3	5	38	36	36

RBI/Opportunities

Scoring Position	38 / 173 (22%)	155 / 653 (24%)
Scoring Position, 2 Out	18 / 80 (23%)	68 / 321 (21%)
On Third, Less than 2 Out	14 / 32 (44%)	49 / 105 (47%)
RBI in close games / RBI Total	32 / 47 (68%)	121 / 180 (67%)

Calvin Schiraldi
Boston Red Sox

Ever notice how much Calvin Schiraldi resembles a certain horror writer who swears allegiance to the Red Sox? The dark, shaggy brow and the brooding expression certainly invite comparisons to Stephen King. The likeness was more than just physical in 1987; there was an eerie similarity in both men's work as well. Harmless objects—like the Boston bullpen telephone—took on a threatening demeanor. Shivers went up the hapless Boston fan's spine as each man performed his duties. And, often enough, another Boston lead suffered a grisly fate . . . just like in the books.

Schiraldi's Boston short story had a happy beginning. He was the bullpen savior of the club in the last half of 1986. He had his ERA under 1.50, with nine saves and four wins in 25 appearances. But a sinister pattern was developing. Schiraldi's July ERA was 0.71, rising to 1.33 in August and 2.00 in September. October should not be discussed in polite company; it set the pattern for his 1987.

The lurking horror was unleashed when word got around that Schiraldi had trouble throwing his breaking ball for strikes, particularly to left-handed batters. Calvin has a decent heater, but he couldn't get it past enough of the batters who were waiting for it. In 1987 he had the highest walk rate on the team; not a good statistic for a short reliever, who usually runs out of bases to put people on very quickly. That is just what happened during the year. First,

a threatening situation became a crisis. Then Calvin would get behind on the count, send number one down the chute and it would be lights out for the Red Sox.

To be fair, Schiraldi was effective against right-handed batters. No Boston pitcher allowed righties a lower batting average, on-base percentage or slugging percentage in 1987. But then Calvin did not look or act like a typical closer last year. When he was on the mound, he always wore a frightened expression and sweated in torrents; a pitcher who gives hitters the impression that he wishes he were somewhere else will not intimidate anybody. Schiraldi had obviously lost his confidence after the 1986 World Series; nothing he did in 1987 helped restore it.

In 1988, Calvin has a chance to take a fresh mental grip on the baseball—out in the sunshine and away from those dark corners of the past. Perhaps the Cubs will use him as a spot man against righties; if so, he has a good chance to succeed. Perhaps they will try him as a starter; he certainly showed signs (7 IP, 3 hits, 0 runs, 11 strikeouts in his only start of 1987) of being able to succeed there. But if Chicago insists on using Schiraldi as a stopper and he is unable to solve his problems, the right-field bleacher fans in the Friendly Confines will have to ice down their arms between his appearances.

Fred Percival

Schiraldi, Calvin Drew   **Bats: Right   Throws: Right   Born 06/16/62**

1987 SEASON AND MAJOR-LEAGUE CAREER PITCHING TOTALS

	G	GS	CG	GF	IP	BFP	H	R	ER	HR	SH	SF	HB	TBB	IBB	SO	WP	Bk	W	L	Pct	ShO	Sv	ERA
87 BOS	62	1	0	52	84	361	75	45	41	15	5	2	1	40	5	93	5	2	8	5	.615	0	6	4.39
4 YEARS	102	8	0	75	178	770	174	93	86	27	7	3	5	76	7	185	8	3	14	10	.583	0	15	4.35

1987: Power, Flyball   1986: Power, Flyball   1985: Power, Flyball   1984: Power, Groundball

1987 SEASON / FOUR YEAR TOTALS (1984 – 1987)

	G	IP	H	BB	SO	SB	CS	W	L	S	ERA		G	IP	H	BB	SO	SB	CS	W	L	S	ERA
Totals	62	83.2	76	40	93	13	4	8	5	6	4.41		102	178.1	175	76	185	25	6	14	10	15	4.34
at Home	29	44.0	34	21	39	7	2	4	0	5	3.27		44	73.2	73	27	69	13	2	7	2	7	3.67
on Road	33	39.2	42	19	54	6	2	4	5	1	5.67		58	104.2	102	49	116	12	4	7	8	8	4.82
on Grass	20	30.1	27	16	37	6	1	2	2	2	4.75		37	69.1	68	30	79	12	2	5	3	5	4.02
on Artificial Turf	42	53.1	49	24	56	7	3	6	3	4	4.22		65	109.0	107	46	106	13	4	9	7	10	4.54
Day Games	52	64.1	56	38	62	10	2	6	3	5	4.34		79	127.2	117	60	121	17	4	11	6	11	3.60
Night Games	10	19.1	20	2	31	3	2	2	2	1	4.66		23	50.2	58	16	64	8	2	3	4	4	6.22
April	8	8.0	9	11	9	1	0	0	2	0	9.00		10	14.2	18	13	11	1	0	1	2	2	7.98
May	8	11.0	9	6	14	0	1	2	1	0	4.09		10	18.0	15	13	22	0	2	2	1	0	4.00
June	14	18.2	13	5	13	5	0	2	1	3	1.93		19	30.2	39	7	23	9	0	3	2	3	6.16
July	10	11.0	13	5	15	3	1	2	1	0	8.18		14	23.2	23	11	27	5	2	2	1	0	4.18
August	10	14.0	16	7	21	1	1	2	0	0	5.79		22	34.1	27	10	45	2	1	4	1	6	3.15
Sept/Oct	12	21.0	16	6	21	3	1	0	0	1	2.14		27	57.0	53	22	57	8	1	2	3	4	3.32

vs. Opponent Batters	Ave.	OBP	SLG	AB	H	2B	3B	HR	RBI	BB	SO		Ave.	OBP	SLG	AB	H	2B	3B	HR	RBI	BB	SO
Totals	.242	.328	.424	314	76	12	0	15	56	40	93		.257	.332	.429	680	175	28	4	27	106	76	185
vs. Left	.287	.395	.517	143	41	6	0	9	35	27	32		.268	.355	.462	325	87	10	1	17	57	45	70
vs. Right	.205	.265	.345	171	35	6	0	6	21	13	61		.248	.310	.400	355	88	18	3	10	49	31	115
Bases Empty	.231	.337	.301	143	33	4	0	2	2	22	39		.259	.337	.376	340	88	12	2	8	8	39	84
Leadoff	.186	.273	.186	59	11	0	0	0	0	7	18		.259	.325	.399	143	37	2	0	6	6	14	32
Not Leadoff	.262	.380	.381	84	22	4	0	2	2	15	21		.259	.345	.360	197	51	10	2	2	2	25	52
Runners On Base	.251	.319	.526	171	43	8	0	13	54	18	54		.256	.327	.482	340	87	16	2	19	98	37	101
First Base Only	.229	.289	.529	70	16	3	0	6	13	6	22		.248	.313	.496	137	34	7	0	9	20	13	38
Scoring Position	.267	.339	.525	101	27	5	0	7	41	12	32		.261	.336	.473	203	53	9	2	10	78	24	63
Late Innings, Close	.215	.320	.396	149	32	3	0	8	28	23	46		.212	.300	.394	231	49	6	0	12	38	29	74

RBI/Opportunities

Scoring Position	30 / 131 (23%)	60 / 269 (22%)
Scoring Position, 2 Out	14 / 67 (21%)	25 / 128 (20%)
On Third, Less than 2 Out	6 / 21 (29%)	19 / 45 (42%)
RBI in close games / RBI Total	28 / 56 (50%)	50 / 106 (47%)

Dave Schmidt
Baltimore Orioles

In 1987, Dave Schmidt became a victim of his success. Assigned to long relief in spring, he had (thanks to Baltimore's weak rotation) no shortage of chances to demonstrate his prowess. Dave's command of his sinker made him so effective that, by May, manager Cal Ripken tried him as a closer. The experiment bombed (7.73 ERA in three outings), so Ripken wisely abandoned it. On the strength of both his control (8 walks in 44 innings) and the lineup's offensive prowess in May, Schmidt was 6–1 with a 2.86 ERA after his first 20 games.

At that point, the Baltimore rotation was in such a shambles that Ripken simply couldn't resist the urge to let his best pitcher try to stabilize it. It was an understandable impulse, but one that involved a great deal of risk.

When 1987 began, Dave had a total of 14 career starts. His career stats in that role (3–9, 4.67) were unimpressive when compared to his relief totals (20–19, 2.76). Eight of those starts, moreover, were for the 1982 Rangers, who bore an uncanny likeness to the '87 Orioles. With the Texas staff floundering, Schmidt (who was 3–1 with a 2.23 ERA as a reliever that year) had also been inserted into the rotation. The result: a 1–5 record, a 4.60 ERA and an elbow injury that required surgery and ended his 1982 a month early.

Ripken took the risk anyway—in the short term, it paid off spectacularly. In the next five weeks, Schmidt went 4–1 in 10 starts, with a 2.59 ERA, pitching three-hit and two-hit shutouts. But, by July 26, Dave had pitched more innings than he had in any season since 1982; right about then, his elbow began to give way. Schmidt missed a start, tried to come back and looked thoroughly awful in his next four starts, surrendering 32 hits and 18 earned runs in 19.2 innings. By August 23, he was on the sidelines; by early September he'd already had elbow surgery.

The striking thing about Schmidt's 1987 is its similarity to Don Aase's 1986. First, the Orioles signed a veteran reliever who, in limited playing time, had enjoyed a solid career. Then, when he got off to a strong start, Baltimore decided to use him to fill a glaring need. Both times, there was evidence to suggest that the switch was a gamble—that the player's arm would never be able to stand the strain of his new role. Each time the Orioles chose to disregard it—and then watched the player literally fall apart at the seams. In each case, the player had by far the best season of his career—but entered the following season wondering if he still had a career. One might claim that the Orioles have merely been unlucky—but it seems far more likely that their luck is the direct result of some very ill-conceived designs.

Tim Mulligan and Sean Bramble

Schmidt, David Joseph "Dave"   Bats: Right   Throws: Right   Born 04/22/57

1987 SEASON AND MAJOR-LEAGUE CAREER PITCHING TOTALS

	G	GS	CG	GF	IP	BFP	H	R	ER	HR	SH	SF	HB	TBB	IBB	SO	WP	Bk	W	L	Pct	ShO	Sv	ERA
87 BAL	35	14	2	7	124	515	128	57	52	13	0	1	1	26	2	70	2	0	10	5	.667	2	1	3.77
7 YEARS	256	28	3	142	560	2343	563	236	206	41	20	13	13	145	35	340	20	2	33	33	.500	3	35	3.31

1987: Finesse, Groundball   1986: Finesse, Groundball   1985: Finesse, Groundball   1984: Power, Groundball

	1987 SEASON											FOUR YEAR TOTALS (1984 – 1987)										
	G	IP	H	BB	SO	SB	CS	W	L	S	ERA	G	IP	H	BB	SO	SB	CS	W	L	S	ERA
Totals	35	123.2	128	26	70	16	3	10	5	1	3.78	178	372.0	372	95	229	38	8	26	23	26	3.27
at Home	18	79.2	78	15	51	11	2	4	2	1	3.39	92	212.0	201	46	133	25	4	14	10	18	3.14
on Road	17	44.0	50	11	19	5	1	6	3	0	4.50	86	160.0	171	49	96	13	4	12	13	8	3.49
on Grass	13	56.0	33	6	33	3	2	5	1	1	1.61	42	99.0	73	15	64	5	3	7	4	3	2.18
on Artificial Turf	22	67.2	95	20	37	13	1	5	4	0	5.59	136	273.0	299	80	165	33	5	19	19	23	3.69
Day Games	29	104.1	104	22	61	15	3	9	3	1	3.45	149	312.1	301	74	194	33	8	23	19	22	3.14
Night Games	6	19.1	24	4	9	1	0	1	2	0	5.59	29	59.2	71	21	35	5	0	3	4	4	4.07
April	8	19.0	14	4	9	2	0	2	1	1	2.84	26	52.2	48	9	35	7	2	3	2	2	3.59
May	10	21.2	21	3	11	6	1	4	0	0	1.66	30	58.1	63	16	29	14	2	5	5	2	3.09
June	8	33.1	37	7	21	1	1	2	1	0	4.05	32	83.2	79	17	58	3	2	6	2	3	2.90
July	6	33.2	30	8	22	3	0	2	0	0	3.21	37	75.0	62	21	46	4	0	3	3	10	2.40
August	3	16.0	26	4	7	4	1	0	3	0	8.44	32	57.1	71	15	36	7	2	5	7	7	4.08
Sept/Oct	0	0.0	0	0	0	0	0	0	0	0	0.00	21	45.0	49	17	25	3	0	4	4	2	4.40

vs. Opponent Batters	Ave.	OBP	SLG	AB	H	2B	3B	HR	RBI	BB	SO	Ave.	OBP	SLG	AB	H	2B	3B	HR	RBI	BB	SO
Totals	.263	.301	.411	487	128	21	6	13	57	26	70	.259	.305	.390	1435	372	58	17	32	170	95	229
vs. Left	.313	.358	.484	217	68	12	2	7	33	15	29	.269	.324	.411	681	183	31	12	14	87	56	105
vs. Right	.222	.254	.352	270	60	9	4	6	24	11	41	.251	.288	.371	754	189	27	5	18	83	39	124
Bases Empty	.264	.302	.407	280	74	12	2	8	8	14	39	.266	.302	.425	789	210	37	8	24	24	39	117
Leadoff	.205	.231	.359	117	24	6	0	4	4	4	13	.234	.256	.362	334	78	16	3	7	7	10	46
Not Leadoff	.307	.351	.442	163	50	6	2	4	4	10	26	.290	.334	.470	455	132	21	5	17	17	29	71
Runners On Base	.261	.300	.415	207	54	9	4	5	49	12	31	.251	.310	.348	646	162	21	9	8	146	56	112
First Base Only	.298	.330	.452	84	25	5	1	2	6	4	16	.263	.296	.345	232	61	9	2	2	8	11	46
Scoring Position	.236	.280	.390	123	29	4	3	3	43	8	15	.244	.317	.350	414	101	12	7	6	138	45	66
Late Innings, Close	.320	.354	.453	75	24	5	1	1	8	4	6	.278	.328	.369	425	118	17	2	6	51	32	64

RBI/Opportunities

Scoring Position	37 / 153 (24%)	125 / 554 (23%)
Scoring Position, 2 Out	14 / 69 (20%)	56 / 261 (21%)
On Third, Less than 2 Out	17 / 28 (61%)	46 / 102 (45%)
RBI in close games / RBI Total	39 / 57 (68%)	97 / 170 (57%)

Mike Schmidt
Philadelphia Phillies

In 1987 Michael Jack Schmidt turned in a season essentially identical to his 1986 MVP year. It's a measure of his greatness that no one noticed. The National League player whose numbers were most similar to Schmidt's finished a close fourth in the 1987 MVP balloting while Mike was way back at fourteenth—a career year for Tim Wallach is merely an average one for Mike Schmidt.

Schmidt appeared to be heading toward a spectacular year, reaching 13 homers and 36 RBIs before suffering a rib injury on May 21. He eventually made a rare visit to the disabled list, and ended up playing fewer games than in any full season since 1978. While he recorded the second 3-homer game of his career soon after returning, Mike suffered through an extended homer drought, socking just one in the next three weeks. Clearly, the injury curtailed his power for much of the year, yet he never once used it as an excuse. Instead, Schmidt spent the summer stroking singles (90 of them, the second highest number in his career), knocking in runs, and maintaining his batting average. Only in strike-shortened 1981 did Schmidt exceed 1987's .293 clip.

In the field, Schmidt played almost exclusively at third base. Though not as exceptional as in 1986, he remains one of the premier defensive third basemen in baseball. Only Pendleton and Ray Knight (?!) exceeded his range factor of 3.02 successful chances per start (Wallach wasn't far behind at 2.80).

As Bill James has demonstrated, the typical baseball player turns in his peak performances in his late twenties. Later in his career, batting average drops; the player compensates with better power and strike zone judgment, drawing an increasing number of walks. The player often moves to a less demanding fielding position. Schmidt defies this stereotype in many respects. His four best seasonal batting averages have been recorded since his thirtieth birthday (his career average is up to .270). Oddly, he appears to have become a less patient hitter, as both strikeouts and walks have declined in the last couple of years. The first base experiment is over—Schmidt started there just eight times, while his erstwhile backup Rick Schu had 21 starts at first. In fact, Schmidt made three appearances at shortstop in 1987.

Schmidt is the finest player ever to grace the red pinstripes of the Phillies. He's also an intelligent, thoughtful gentleman who wears the mantle of his greatness with quiet dignity. To top it off, he shares my wife's birthday! What more could I ask of the guy?

Mike says he'll retire at the completion of his new two-year contract, and I believe him. He'll pass Foxx, Mantle, and probably Reggie in 1988, and has a decent shot at 600 homers and fourth on the all-time list before he's through. A certain Hall of Famer, Mike Schmidt is undoubtedly the best third baseman in the history of the game.

Neal Traven

Schmidt, Michael Jack "Mike"   Bats: Right   Throws: Right   Born 09/27/49

1987 SEASON AND MAJOR-LEAGUE CAREER BATTING TOTALS

	G	AB	H	2B	3B	HR	TB	R	RBI	TBB	IBB	SO	HP	SH	SF	SB	CS	SB%	GDP	AVG	OBP	SLG
87 PHI	147	522	153	28	0	35	286	88	113	83	15	80	2	0	6	2	1	.67	17	.293	.388	.548
16 YEARS	2254	7814	2107	380	57	530	4191	1435	1505	1437	187	1824	73	16	99	171	91	.65	139	.270	.384	.536

	1987 SEASON											FOUR YEAR TOTALS (1984 – 1987)										
	Ave.	OBP	SLG	AB	H	2B	3B	HR	RBI	BB	SO	Ave.	OBP	SLG	AB	H	2B	3B	HR	RBI	BB	SO
Totals	.293	.388	.548	522	153	28	0	35	113	83	80	.284	.384	.541	2151	611	111	9	141	431	351	397
vs. Left	.331	.442	.556	133	44	9	0	7	27	28	11	.306	.423	.557	575	176	34	1	36	104	117	95
vs. Right	.280	.368	.545	389	109	19	0	28	86	55	69	.276	.369	.535	1576	435	77	8	105	327	234	302
at Home	.342	.433	.585	260	89	18	0	15	67	43	38	.298	.399	.555	1018	303	61	3	65	224	173	179
on Road	.244	.343	.511	262	64	10	0	20	46	40	42	.272	.371	.528	1133	308	50	6	76	207	178	218
vs. Groundball	.272	.350	.493	272	74	12	0	16	56	34	35	.278	.373	.507	1013	282	50	1	60	202	153	174
vs. Flyball	.316	.427	.608	250	79	16	0	19	57	49	45	.289	.394	.570	1138	329	61	8	81	229	198	223
vs. Finesse	.311	.378	.604	283	88	14	0	23	69	32	45	.290	.367	.550	1216	353	55	6	83	246	146	191
vs. Power	.272	.399	.481	239	65	14	0	12	44	51	35	.276	.404	.528	935	258	56	3	58	185	205	206
on Grass	.258	.338	.422	128	33	6	0	5	15	15	15	.275	.371	.496	571	157	24	3	32	95	86	108
on Artificial Turf	.305	.404	.589	394	120	22	0	30	98	68	65	.287	.389	.557	1580	454	87	6	109	336	265	289
Day Games	.280	.421	.503	143	40	5	0	9	28	35	25	.298	.400	.562	694	207	35	2	48	143	118	138
Night Games	.298	.374	.565	379	113	23	0	26	85	48	55	.277	.376	.531	1457	404	76	7	93	288	233	259
April	.284	.410	.552	67	19	0	0	6	19	15	12	.280	.376	.493	282	79	9	0	17	63	44	54
May	.286	.311	.629	70	20	3	0	7	17	3	18	.261	.356	.512	326	85	16	0	22	63	49	75
June	.300	.402	.543	70	21	5	0	4	12	11	10	.300	.385	.523	363	109	24	3	17	60	49	58
July	.305	.433	.526	95	29	6	0	5	21	23	11	.264	.372	.499	375	99	14	1	24	73	66	66
August	.327	.434	.566	113	37	9	0	6	22	21	12	.310	.408	.608	400	124	31	2	28	86	73	60
Sept/Oct	.252	.314	.495	107	27	5	0	7	22	10	17	.284	.389	.585	405	115	17	3	33	86	70	84
Bases Empty	.290	.387	.548	252	73	11	0	18	18	40	40	.283	.372	.565	1107	313	60	3	82	82	157	203
Leadoff	.291	.388	.496	127	37	5	0	7	7	20	19	.289	.365	.585	506	146	28	1	40	40	61	90
Not Leadoff	.288	.386	.600	125	36	6	0	11	11	20	21	.278	.377	.547	601	167	32	2	42	42	96	113
Runners On	.296	.389	.548	270	80	17	0	17	95	43	40	.285	.396	.515	1044	298	51	6	59	349	194	194
First Base Only	.279	.370	.523	111	31	3	0	8	18	15	14	.274	.344	.489	409	112	18	2	22	56	43	61
Scoring Position	.308	.402	.566	159	49	14	0	9	77	28	26	.293	.426	.532	635	186	33	4	37	293	151	133
Late Innings, Close	.295	.415	.545	88	26	4	0	6	17	18	13	.304	.420	.560	359	109	15	4	23	69	72	72

RBI/Opportunities

Scoring Position	59 / 222	(27%)	228 / 922	(25%)
Scoring Position, 2 Out	27 / 113	(24%)	91 / 432	(21%)
On Third, Less than 2 Out	20 / 36	(56%)	84 / 175	(48%)
RBI in close games / RBI Total	83 / 113	(73%)	305 / 431	(71%)

Dick Schofield
California Angels

My father, a St. Louis Cardinal fan for nearly forty years, used to take me to Busch Memorial Stadium during the late sixties where we saw Dick's father, "Ducky" Schofield, play as a utility infielder. Now that I live in California, it is special to me to have a chance to watch the younger Schofield mature into a fine everyday player.

During his first three years in the major leagues Schofield was the consummate "all-field, no-hit" player. His average dredged near .200 with virtually no home run or RBI capability. Many scouts felt that Schofield was a potential .270-hitter who was rushed to the majors so fast that he was unable to apprentice the art of hitting along the way. This seems to be a plausible explanation given Schofield's back-to-back increase in offensive production during '86 and '87.

In the last two seasons Schofield has raised his average well above the Mendoza-line to the .250 level, doubling his homer and RBI totals in addition to a sharp reduction in strikeouts. Had it not been for a mid-season injury that shelved him for nearly a month, Schofield would have enjoyed even better numbers in '87.

Despite his recent rise, there still appears to be room for improvement. Schofield lacks discipline at the plate and tries to pull every ball into left. If he could drive an occasional ball to the right side, he might reach that .270 average envisioned by some scouts. It might also help if he took a month's vacation during June; his career average for that month is now .195.

The one area of Schofield's game that has never been questioned is his defensive prowess. He is a steady shortstop, positions himself well, and can give you a spectacular play occasionally; in 1987 he made only 9 errors and led the league with a .984 fielding percentage. While not possessing the range of Ozzie Smith or Tony Fernandez, Schofield fields every ball he can reach and charges the ball with vengeance, an art that seems to be vanishing with the advent of faster fields and artificial turf.

Schofield always surprises people with his speed. He doesn't have the classic look or form of a sprinter, but the results are pretty much the same. He is an opportunistic baserunner, and was successful on 19 of 22 stolen base attempts in '87 and 23 for 28 the year before. He's a good candidate for 30 steals if he can jump his on-base percentage a bit.

Although there is a question of how well he will recover from the shoulder separation that knocked him out of 26 games at the end of the season, it appears that with his trend of steady improvement, the maligned early years of Schofield's career should remain a distant memory.

Gary Schultz

Schofield, Richard Craig "Dick"

Bats: Right   Throws: Right   Born 11/21/62

1987 SEASON AND MAJOR-LEAGUE CAREER BATTING TOTALS

	G	AB	H	2B	3B	HR	TB	R	RBI	TBB	IBB	SO	HP	SH	SF	SB	CS	SB%	GDP	AVG	OBP	SLG
87 CAL	134	479	120	17	3	9	170	52	46	37	0	63	2	10	3	19	3	.86	4	.251	.305	.355
5 YEARS	581	1829	418	65	15	37	624	212	169	159	2	275	22	45	15	58	14	.81	29	.229	.296	.341

	1987 SEASON										FOUR YEAR TOTALS (1984 – 1987)									
	Ave.	OBP	SLG	AB	H	2B	3B	HR	RBI	BB	SO	Ave.	OBP	SLG	AB	H	2B	3B	HR	RBI	BB	SO
Totals	.251	.305	.355	479	120	17	3	9	46	37	63	.229	.296	.339	1775	407	63	15	34	165	153	267
vs. Left	.267	.324	.379	161	43	8	2	2	13	14	13	.255	.330	.368	612	156	26	8	9	45	64	82
vs. Right	.242	.296	.343	318	77	9	1	7	33	23	50	.216	.278	.324	1163	251	37	7	25	120	89	185
at Home	.257	.310	.335	257	66	6	1	4	25	21	34	.219	.287	.313	883	193	23	6	16	82	78	143
on Road	.243	.300	.378	222	54	11	2	5	21	16	29	.240	.305	.365	892	214	40	9	18	83	75	124
vs. Groundball	.274	.337	.365	230	63	6	3	3	18	21	28	.242	.306	.337	846	205	27	7	13	69	68	108
vs. Flyball	.229	.275	.345	249	57	11	0	6	28	16	35	.217	.286	.341	929	202	36	8	21	96	85	159
vs. Finesse	.274	.313	.461	230	63	10	3	9	29	13	25	.237	.293	.369	979	232	37	13	22	92	68	127
vs. Power	.229	.298	.257	249	57	7	0	0	17	24	38	.220	.299	.303	796	175	26	2	12	73	85	140
on Grass	.239	.295	.331	402	96	12	2	7	37	31	56	.226	.293	.331	1502	339	48	13	28	139	131	230
on Artificial Turf	.312	.361	.481	77	24	5	1	2	9	6	7	.249	.309	.385	273	68	15	2	6	26	22	37
Day Games	.261	.333	.440	134	35	8	2	4	16	14	20	.251	.319	.388	498	125	23	9	9	52	47	78
Night Games	.246	.294	.322	345	85	9	1	5	30	23	43	.221	.287	.320	1277	282	40	6	25	113	106	189
April	.256	.311	.341	82	21	1	0	2	10	6	13	.240	.294	.402	271	65	9	1	11	35	20	41
May	.186	.224	.304	102	19	4	1	2	9	5	13	.201	.251	.310	313	63	13	3	5	28	21	58
June	.216	.283	.340	97	21	3	0	3	14	8	11	.195	.269	.284	328	64	10	2	5	29	32	49
July	.364	.442	.455	44	16	1	0	1	4	7	3	.242	.332	.354	198	48	5	1	5	17	27	21
August	.317	.362	.460	63	20	6	0	1	7	5	9	.254	.304	.379	311	79	15	3	6	37	23	48
Sept/Oct	.253	.299	.319	91	23	2	2	0	2	6	14	.249	.307	.325	354	88	11	5	2	19	30	50
Bases Empty	.250	.311	.359	284	71	10	3	5	5	25	35	.242	.294	.351	1042	252	36	9	20	20	77	145
Leadoff	.278	.325	.409	115	32	2	2	3	3	8	12	.246	.301	.366	415	102	12	4	10	10	33	56
Not Leadoff	.231	.301	.325	169	39	8	1	2	2	17	23	.239	.289	.341	627	150	24	5	10	10	44	89
Runners On	.251	.297	.349	195	49	7	0	4	41	12	28	.211	.286	.322	733	155	27	6	14	145	76	122
First Base Only	.238	.297	.274	84	20	3	0	0	1	6	9	.204	.266	.291	323	66	12	2	4	13	26	44
Scoring Position	.261	.298	.405	111	29	4	0	4	40	6	19	.217	.302	.346	410	89	15	4	10	132	50	78
Late Innings, Close	.176	.213	.189	74	13	1	0	0	2	3	10	.205	.258	.303	244	50	7	1	5	21	17	35

RBI/Opportunities

	1987	Four Year
Scoring Position	34 / 147 (23%)	110 / 583 (19%)
Scoring Position, 2 Out	15 / 71 (21%)	44 / 274 (16%)
On Third, Less than 2 Out	14 / 28 (50%)	40 / 93 (43%)
RBI in close games / RBI Total	23 / 46 (50%)	90 / 165 (55%)

Mike Scioscia
Los Angeles Dodgers

The 1987 season had something of a twist in it for Mike Scoscia. The Dodger catcher is known for his aggressive plate blocking and getting hurt occasionally during these collisions. In 1987, Scoscia appeared in a career-high 142 games. Yet his only serious injury came June 1 when he fractured the middle finger of his left hand during batting practice.

Otherwise, Scoscia was the mainstay of the Dodger lineup. Defensively, Scoscia is one of the National League's better catchers. He's got a strong arm and was tied for second among NL catchers in assists with 80. He's also generally considered to be a good handler of pitchers.

Offensively, Scoscia had a, well, a typical Scoscia season. He hit .265, scored 44 runs, hit 6 homers, and drove in 38 runs. He also walked 55 times and struck out just 23 times in 461 at bats. He even stole 7 bases in 11 attempts. He entered the '87 season as a lifetime .264 hitter who generally drives in between 30–40 runs in a full season, and he hits 5–7 homers a season and never more than 7. He's only struck out more than 30 times once during his 8-year career (31 in 1982), and his 55 walks are down from his 62 in '86 and his career-high 77 in '85, the last year the team won the NL West title. That year he also set a personal high in RBIs with 53, as well as a career-high 47 runs scored.

Yes, in 1987 he was typically Mike Scioscia. But is a typical Mike Scioscia something good to have?

In 1987, 22 catchers appeared in 100 or more games and 16 of them had more homers than Scoscia did, 13 scored more runs than Scoscia did, and 16 had more RBIs than Mike did. In fact, 12 of them had more RBIs than Scoscia's career best. Of the 12 catchers in the NL who appeared in 100 or more games, 8 had more homers, 9 had more RBIs, and 7 scored more runs. Many Dodger fans I know, feel Mike is one of baseball's best and least-appreciated catchers. I'm not sure I agree.

I can appreciate his defensive skills, and I like watching him play. But unless the Dodgers can improve their woeful offense or get Scioscia to change his hitting style and become more aggressive at the probable cost of more strike-outs, I'm not sure they can afford to get as little production out of the catching position as they do with Scioscia producing typical Scoscia seasons.

Dean Hill

Scioscia, Michael Lorri "Mike" Bats: Left Throws: Right Born 11/27/58

1987 SEASON AND MAJOR-LEAGUE CAREER BATTING TOTALS

	G	AB	H	2B	3B	HR	TB	R	RBI	TBB	IBB	SO	HP	SH	SF	SB	CS	SB%	GDP	AVG	OBP	SLG
87 LA	142	461	122	26	1	6	168	44	38	55	9	23	1	4	2	7	4	.64	13	.265	.343	.364
8 YEARS	807	2429	641	117	7	32	868	225	237	343	54	153	12	36	22	18	13	.58	63	.264	.355	.357

	1987 SEASON											FOUR YEAR TOTALS (1984 – 1987)										
	Ave.	OBP	SLG	AB	H	2B	3B	HR	RBI	BB	SO	Ave.	OBP	SLG	AB	H	2B	3B	HR	RBI	BB	SO
Totals	.265	.343	.364	461	122	26	1	6	38	55	23	.272	.369	.376	1605	436	88	5	23	155	246	93
vs. Left	.275	.358	.351	131	36	8	1	0	10	16	11	.242	.334	.316	364	88	16	1	3	26	50	27
vs. Right	.261	.337	.370	330	86	18	0	6	28	39	12	.280	.379	.393	1241	348	72	4	20	129	196	66
at Home	.260	.345	.315	219	57	6	0	2	16	29	5	.272	.377	.333	735	200	30	0	5	67	124	38
on Road	.269	.341	.409	242	65	20	1	4	22	26	18	.271	.363	.411	870	236	58	5	18	88	122	55
vs. Groundball	.275	.357	.348	204	56	12	0	1	14	26	7	.283	.380	.366	704	199	36	1	7	64	108	31
vs. Flyball	.257	.332	.377	257	66	14	1	5	24	29	16	.263	.361	.383	901	237	52	4	16	91	138	62
vs. Finesse	.286	.344	.373	255	73	13	0	3	21	22	12	.292	.385	.395	889	260	54	2	11	98	133	37
vs. Power	.238	.342	.354	206	49	13	1	3	17	33	11	.246	.350	.352	716	176	34	3	12	57	113	56
on Grass	.280	.362	.369	336	94	18	0	4	26	44	13	.287	.388	.394	1164	334	64	2	19	110	191	66
on Artificial Turf	.224	.290	.352	125	28	8	1	2	12	11	10	.231	.319	.327	441	102	24	3	4	45	55	27
Day Games	.284	.364	.381	134	38	7	0	2	16	18	6	.275	.376	.369	509	140	27	3	5	44	82	30
Night Games	.257	.334	.358	327	84	19	1	4	22	37	17	.270	.366	.379	1096	296	61	2	18	111	164	63
April	.321	.411	.462	78	25	5	0	2	9	12	5	.300	.412	.408	233	70	11	1	4	28	44	21
May	.259	.344	.329	85	22	3	0	1	5	11	3	.246	.329	.340	268	66	11	1	4	18	33	14
June	.150	.244	.175	40	6	1	0	0	1	5	3	.263	.384	.325	194	51	9	0	1	23	38	9
July	.227	.280	.373	75	17	8	0	1	6	6	4	.298	.381	.404	225	67	18	0	2	28	31	12
August	.315	.374	.438	89	28	6	1	1	9	9	3	.281	.387	.419	303	85	20	2	6	28	53	18
Sept/Oct	.255	.346	.319	94	24	3	0	1	8	12	5	.254	.337	.356	382	97	19	1	6	30	47	19
Bases Empty	.270	.349	.412	274	74	19	1	6	6	32	15	.259	.352	.387	945	245	54	5	19	19	135	60
Leadoff	.263	.318	.414	99	26	6	0	3	3	8	3	.248	.347	.411	355	88	17	1	13	13	54	21
Not Leadoff	.274	.365	.411	175	48	13	1	3	3	24	12	.266	.356	.373	590	157	37	4	6	6	81	39
Runners On	.257	.335	.294	187	48	7	0	0	32	23	8	.289	.391	.359	660	191	34	0	4	136	111	33
First Base Only	.250	.268	.300	80	20	4	0	0	1	2	2	.321	.389	.401	299	96	18	0	2	9	33	11
Scoring Position	.262	.377	.290	107	28	3	0	0	31	21	6	.263	.392	.324	361	95	16	0	2	127	78	22
Late Innings, Close	.233	.305	.360	86	20	5	0	2	9	9	7	.229	.330	.315	292	67	14	1	3	23	44	24

RBI/Opportunities

	1987	Four Year
Scoring Position	31 / 150 (21%)	119 / 538 (22%)
Scoring Position, 2 Out	11 / 74 (15%)	50 / 252 (20%)
On Third, Less than 2 Out	12 / 22 (55%)	43 / 92 (47%)
RBI in close games / RBI Total	22 / 38 (58%)	99 / 155 (64%)

Mike Scott
Houston Astros

If Mike Scott's performance seemed disappointing in 1987, it was mostly because of the expectations he'd built. Starting with his pennant-clinching no-hitter against the Giants, the Scott of late '86 had seemed unbeatable. After he'd twice overpowered the Mets in the playoffs, Scott was being held in the same regard as Sandy Koufax and Bob Gibson had once been; his aura of invincibility was so great that the sixth game of the playoffs was played, and watched, as if it were the seventh—everyone assumed that if Houston won, Scott was a lock the next day.

That was a tough act to follow, but Mike began '87 like it wouldn't be a problem. In June he was leading the league in ERA, and through July 9, entering his last start before the All Star break, Scott was 10–4, 2.47; in the Year of the Hitter, he still couldn't be hit. But then a funny thing happened. For the rest of the year Scott was quite ordinary, going 6–9 with a 4.10 ERA. He still won 16 games and finished seventh in the ERA race, but the aura had left him. Mike Scott was good, but no longer invincible.

Scott's second-half performance begs the question of whether he fell victim to the great scuffball controversy. The evidence is a little confusing. In late April, A. Bartlett Giamatti, who probably spent his Yale career looking up students' sleeves for notes, announced a crackdown on naughty pitchers and hitters. Scott was a specific target, but continual checking seemed to have no effect on him; Scott was never disciplined, and he kept right on winning. To Giamatti's discomfort, the opposition began growing cynical. Typical was the July diatribe by—ahem—Kevin Gross, in which Gross stated he had picked up balls scuffed by Scott and used them in his own half-inning, with "amazing" results. Gross added that he was going to repeat this trick whenever the two pitchers hooked up.

Shortly thereafter, both Joe Niekro and Gross were caught and suspended . . . and right about that time, Scott stopped looking like Cy Young. Coincidence? Well, maybe. Strangely enough, Scott was still looking unbeatable at home. From July 28 to September 16, he was 4–0, 1.69 in the Dome; during the same period he was 0–6, 7.94 on the road. Bob Brenly of the Giants surmised that Scott was afraid to doctor pitches away from home, and that's a possibility; it's hard to see in the Astrodome, the home team keeps used balls in their dugout ballbag, and maybe the umps just never noticed what he was doing. But Scott had shown the same tendency (overpowering at home, lousy on the road) back in '85, when they weren't checking him. Maybe when he leaves Houston, they need to remind him to pack his sandpaper. Was that his secret in '86?

Don Zminda

Scott, Michael Warren "Mike"   Bats: Right   Throws: Right   Born 04/26/55

1987 SEASON AND MAJOR-LEAGUE CAREER PITCHING TOTALS

	G	GS	CG	GF	IP	BFP	H	R	ER	HR	SH	SF	HB	TBB	IBB	SO	WP	Bk	W	L	Pct	ShO	Sv	ERA
87 HOU	36	36	8	0	248	1010	199	94	89	21	8	3	4	79	6	233	10	2	16	13	.552	3	0	3.23
9 YEARS	248	221	24	12	1408	5866	1311	635	566	102	70	49	20	442	28	983	30	15	81	75	.519	13	3	3.62

1987: Power, Flyball   1986: Power, Flyball   1985: Finesse, Flyball   1984: Finesse, Groundball

1987 SEASON	G	IP	H	BB	SO	SB	CS	W	L	S	ERA	FOUR YEAR TOTALS (1984 – 1987)	G	IP	H	BB	SO	SB	CS	W	L	S	ERA
Totals	36	247.2	199	79	233	39	7	16	13	0	3.20		140	898.2	754	274	759	123	36	57	42	0	3.17
at Home	17	123.0	87	35	131	13	3	10	3	0	2.20		68	473.0	353	114	409	52	18	35	18	0	2.47
on Road	19	124.2	112	44	102	26	4	6	10	0	4.26		72	425.2	401	160	350	71	18	22	24	0	3.97
on Grass	11	72.0	58	38	56	12	1	5	5	0	4.88		34	201.1	189	87	177	37	9	13	11	0	4.74
on Artificial Turf	25	175.2	141	41	177	27	6	11	8	0	2.56		106	697.1	565	187	582	86	27	44	31	0	2.72
Day Games	10	58.2	66	24	46	15	1	1	8	0	6.29		41	231.2	230	86	185	36	11	8	18	0	4.43
Night Games	26	189.0	133	55	187	24	6	15	5	0	2.29		99	667.0	524	188	574	87	25	49	24	0	2.75
April	6	44.0	31	8	49	3	1	3	1	0	2.05		22	134.0	116	40	113	14	4	8	5	0	3.09
May	6	36.1	22	17	33	8	1	2	2	0	2.97		24	141.1	123	55	135	24	8	5	7	0	3.63
June	6	45.0	26	10	53	7	0	4	1	0	2.40		24	172.0	124	37	140	24	7	13	6	0	2.35
July	5	31.2	36	17	34	9	3	2	3	0	4.26		23	145.0	128	46	125	18	7	9	10	0	3.23
August	6	44.2	47	11	34	5	1	2	3	0	4.03		21	145.0	128	45	107	21	4	11	9	0	3.10
Sept/Oct	7	46.0	37	16	30	7	1	3	3	0	3.91		26	161.1	135	51	139	22	6	11	5	0	3.79

vs. Opponent Batters	Ave.	OBP	SLG	AB	H	2B	3B	HR	RBI	BB	SO		Ave.	OBP	SLG	AB	H	2B	3B	HR	RBI	BB	SO
Totals	.217	.281	.331	916	199	33	4	21	88	79	233		.227	.286	.338	3328	754	131	23	65	313	274	759
vs. Left	.234	.301	.335	508	119	16	4	9	48	47	99		.234	.299	.326	1743	408	66	17	20	143	161	304
vs. Right	.196	.257	.326	408	80	17	0	12	40	32	134		.218	.271	.352	1585	346	65	6	45	170	113	455
Bases Empty	.191	.242	.307	587	112	20	3	14	14	38	150		.211	.262	.324	2104	443	83	15	42	42	145	451
Leadoff	.209	.231	.352	244	51	6	1	9	9	7	59		.217	.264	.352	870	189	27	6	26	26	55	183
Not Leadoff	.178	.250	.274	343	61	14	2	5	5	31	91		.206	.261	.305	1234	254	56	9	16	16	90	268
Runners On Base	.264	.347	.374	329	87	13	1	7	74	41	83		.254	.325	.363	1224	311	48	8	23	271	129	308
First Base Only	.310	.366	.487	113	35	8	0	4	10	10	19		.283	.335	.413	477	135	24	4	10	33	37	88
Scoring Position	.241	.337	.315	216	52	5	1	3	64	31	64		.236	.320	.331	747	176	24	4	13	238	92	220
Late Innings, Close	.261	.289	.337	92	24	4	0	1	9	4	28		.214	.282	.316	294	63	13	1	5	22	28	69

RBI/Opportunities

Scoring Position	57 / 301 (19%)	213 / 1003 (21%)	
Scoring Position, 2 Out	22 / 141 (16%)	71 / 449 (16%)	
On Third, Less than 2 Out	22 / 51 (43%)	99 / 186 (53%)	
RBI in close games / RBI Total	58 / 88 (66%)	222 / 313 (71%)	

Bob Sebra
Montreal Expos

"I know there is a major league pitcher in there."

With that statement, Expos manager Buck Rodgers announced that Bob Sebra would be his pitching "project" for the 1988 season. Rodgers and pitching coach Larry Bearnarth spent most of the 1987 season working with a number of other "projects," and they parlayed those efforts into a contending club, one that only dropped out of the pennant chase in the last week of the season. Dennis Martinez, Pascual Perez, Bryn Smith, Neal Heaton, Joe Hesketh and even Charlie Lea were on the project list last season, while the second year righthander Sebra had to fend for himself.

Consistency was his biggest problem. "Sometimes he looks great for a stretch, and then he reverts back to being a high school pitcher. He gets too emotional," Rodgers said last September. "You're about to give up on him, and then you see those flashes. He's got a great major league arm, and he's got major league insides—the guts," he said.

Sebra was the pitcher of the future that the Expos obtained when they finally decided that Pete Incaviglia was serious about not signing with Montreal, and traded him to Texas. Sebra and infielder Jimmy Anderson moved north of the border in that November 1985 deal. Sebra immediately displayed the promise that Montreal had hoped for, lighting up the AAA American Association by going 9–2 for Indianapolis. Called up to Montreal in the middle of the

1986 season, he put together a 5–5 mark in 17 games, and sported a good 3.55 earned run average. He allowed less than a hit per inning, and walked just 25 in 91.1 innings.

But 1987 was a completely different story. Sebra started slowly and never did get untracked. While people like Heaton, Martinez and Perez were taking turns carrying the Expos starting rotation, Sebra struggled, threatened with the loss of his starting spot almost weekly. When his record fell to 3–8, even his spot on the roster was at risk.

He never did return to the minors, but was moved to the bullpen for a time. He ended the season having made 27 starts in 36 appearances, and his 6–15 won-loss record easily was the worst on the staff. His ERA of 4.41 also left something to be desired.

There were some pluses in an otherwise trying season. Sebra's four complete games led the Montreal staff, as did his 156 strikeouts (in only 177.2 innings).

Rodgers certainly would like to have a more settled starting staff in 1988 than he had in 1987, and he will need one if the Expos expect to contend this season. Montreal won eight more games last year than they should have using the Pythagorean theory formula, leading one to believe that if Montreal is to avoid a significant fall in 1988, Sebra is going to have to contribute more than he did a year ago.

Tom Henry

Sebra, Robert Bush "Bob"　　　　　　　　Bats: Right　　Throws: Right　　Born 12/11/61

1987 SEASON AND MAJOR-LEAGUE CAREER PITCHING TOTALS

	G	GS	CG	GF	IP	BFP	H	R	ER	HR	SH	SF	HB	TBB	IBB	SO	WP	Bk	W	L	Pct	ShO	Sv	ERA
87 MON	36	27	4	3	177	765	184	99	87	15	12	7	3	67	0	156	8	2	6	15	.286	1	0	4.42
3 YEARS	60	44	7	7	288	1244	292	155	140	28	15	12	7	106	4	235	10	5	11	22	.333	2	0	4.38

1987: Power, Flyball　　　　1986: Finesse, Flyball　　　　1985: Power, Flyball

	1987 SEASON											FOUR YEAR TOTALS (1984 – 1987)										
	G	IP	H	BB	SO	SB	CS	W	L	S	ERA	G	IP	H	BB	SO	SB	CS	W	L	S	ERA
Totals	36	177.2	184	67	156	36	7	6	15	0	4.41	60	289.1	292	106	235	54	10	11	22	0	4.35
at Home	17	88.0	84	32	95	19	5	2	7	0	4.30	29	146.2	137	51	134	26	6	4	10	0	4.17
on Road	19	89.2	100	35	61	17	2	4	8	0	4.52	31	142.2	155	55	101	28	4	7	12	0	4.54
on Grass	13	72.2	79	35	56	15	4	3	7	0	5.20	20	101.2	108	49	74	24	4	3	8	0	5.13
on Artificial Turf	23	105.0	105	32	100	21	3	3	8	0	3.86	40	187.2	184	57	161	30	6	8	14	0	3.93
Day Games	10	46.1	51	21	30	9	2	2	3	0	5.44	19	82.2	90	35	59	12	3	4	6	0	5.44
Night Games	26	131.1	133	46	126	27	5	4	12	0	4.04	41	206.2	202	71	176	42	7	7	16	0	3.92
April	4	23.1	25	12	15	5	0	1	3	0	3.86	4	23.1	25	12	15	5	0	1	3	0	3.86
May	6	31.1	33	17	29	6	1	2	2	0	4.60	6	31.1	33	17	29	6	1	2	2	0	4.60
June	6	27.1	29	4	32	6	1	1	3	0	4.61	7	32.1	34	8	33	9	1	1	3	0	4.45
July	6	42.2	32	11	35	6	0	2	2	0	2.32	13	60.2	55	22	51	7	0	3	5	0	4.30
August	6	34.1	41	12	28	10	2	0	4	0	4.98	12	75.1	82	19	54	19	4	2	5	0	4.30
Sept/Oct	8	18.2	24	11	17	3	3	0	1	0	8.20	18	66.1	63	28	53	8	4	2	4	0	4.48

vs. Opponent Batters	Ave.	OBP	SLG	AB	H	2B	3B	HR	RBI	BB	SO	Ave.	OBP	SLG	AB	H	2B	3B	HR	RBI	BB	SO
Totals	.272	.337	.410	676	184	42	3	15	91	67	156	.264	.329	.409	1104	292	63	6	28	142	106	235
vs. Left	.260	.329	.398	377	98	24	2	8	45	39	82	.262	.338	.422	614	161	36	4	18	75	70	122
vs. Right	.288	.347	.425	299	86	18	1	7	46	28	74	.267	.317	.392	490	131	27	2	10	67	36	113
Bases Empty	.251	.315	.376	391	98	22	0	9	9	34	94	.251	.310	.375	653	164	37	1	14	14	53	144
Leadoff	.284	.335	.462	169	48	12	0	6	6	11	39	.267	.316	.444	277	74	20	1	9	9	18	55
Not Leadoff	.225	.301	.311	222	50	10	0	3	3	23	55	.239	.306	.324	376	90	17	0	5	5	35	89
Runners On Base	.302	.366	.456	285	86	20	3	6	82	33	62	.284	.354	.457	451	128	26	5	14	128	53	91
First Base Only	.394	.447	.670	94	37	12	1	4	17	9	14	.359	.410	.627	153	55	16	2	7	25	13	23
Scoring Position	.257	.329	.351	191	49	8	2	2	65	24	48	.245	.328	.369	298	73	10	3	7	103	40	68
Late Innings, Close	.189	.211	.270	37	7	0	0	1	4	1	8	.189	.250	.311	74	14	3	0	2	8	6	14

RBI/Opportunities

	1987		FOUR YEAR
Scoring Position	59 / 254	(23%)	88 / 402 (22%)
Scoring Position, 2 Out	23 / 115	(20%)	33 / 185 (18%)
On Third, Less than 2 Out	23 / 41	(56%)	37 / 60 (62%)
RBI in close games / RBI Total	60 / 91	(66%)	97 / 142 (68%)

Kevin Seitzer
Kansas City Royals

After the Clint Hurdle fiasco of the late '70s, maybe the Royals just did not want to burden anyone with being a phenom. No, that's not right; never was there a more highly touted phenom than Bo Jackson (and again, look what happened). I guess it just shows that they don't know who their real phenoms are—Mark Gubicza was in the rotation ahead of Bret Saberhagen. All of which is a way of saying that the Royals didn't realize how good Kevin Seitzer really was.

Kevin Seitzer just plain tore up the league. He hit all year, against all kinds of pitching, to all fields, and drew walks. He was a sensation and he was 25 years old. A late bloomer? No, he tore the cover off the ball at every stop in the minors. And yet, in mid-'86, with the Royals pennant chances evaporating, and with the offense in the doldrums, they reached down to Omaha for help and brought up—Mike Kingery. Don't get me wrong, Kingery did well, and had they not showcased him late, they might not have Danny Tartabull today (if the Mariners had demanded Seitzer instead of Kingery, would the Royals have listened?). But the fact remains, Seitzer was ready, and he proved it in September when he finally got the call. It's been said that he had no position, but since coming to the bigs,

he's filled three: left field throughout spring training before the emergence of Bo, first base when the season started, and then third when Brett was injured, and he did not disgrace himself at any of them. He did lead the team in errors, and his range is not the greatest; he's no potential Gold Glover, but neither is there any reason to think that he won't improve with experience.

Did you know that Seitzer bats with his hands separated about an inch? Is anyone else in the majors doing that? If not, who was the last? I had always heard that such a grip inhibited power hitting, yet Seitzer was good for 15 homers, and I wouldn't be surprised to see more than that in '88. I was always counseled against hand separation in Little League; I wonder what big league instructors think of it. Anyway, now that he's on top, will we see other players—at all levels—begin to emulate him? I confess to knowing nothing about hitting strokes, but a slight hand separation sure seems like something that might help the likes of Gary Pettis. I suppose I just want the fun of getting in on the ground floor of a rediscovered trend. I'm hoping the next Royals star has a Gene Woodling batting stance. Now that would be worthy of emulation.

Mike Kopf

Seitzer, Kevin Lee

Bats: Right   **Throws: Right**   **Born 03/26/62**

1987 SEASON AND MAJOR-LEAGUE CAREER BATTING TOTALS

	G	AB	H	2B	3B	HR	TB	R	RBI	TBB	IBB	SO	HP	SH	SF	SB	CS	SB%	GDP	AVG	OBP	SLG
87 KC	161	641	207	33	8	15	301	105	83	80	0	85	2	1	1	12	7	.63	18	.323	.399	.470
2 YEARS	189	737	238	37	9	17	344	121	94	99	0	99	3	1	1	12	7	.63	18	.323	.405	.467

	1987 SEASON										FOUR YEAR TOTALS (1984 – 1987)									
	Ave.	OBP	SLG	AB	H	2B	3B	HR	RBI	BB	SO	Ave.	OBP	SLG	AB	H	2B	3B	HR	RBI	BB	SO
Totals	.323	.399	.470	641	207	33	8	15	84	80	85	.323	.405	.467	737	238	37	9	17	95	99	99
vs. Left	.309	.386	.434	175	54	6	5	2	13	22	20	.306	.396	.435	193	59	6	5	3	15	29	22
vs. Right	.328	.404	.483	466	153	27	3	13	71	58	65	.329	.408	.478	544	179	31	4	14	80	70	77
at Home	.335	.413	.511	319	107	21	7	7	48	42	33	.351	.432	.529	367	129	25	8	8	56	51	39
on Road	.311	.386	.429	322	100	12	1	8	36	38	52	.295	.378	.405	370	109	12	1	9	39	48	60
vs. Groundball	.328	.399	.461	332	109	17	3	7	49	37	39	.327	.407	.453	373	122	18	4	7	56	47	44
vs. Flyball	.317	.399	.479	309	98	16	5	8	35	43	46	.319	.403	.481	364	116	19	5	10	39	52	55
vs. Finesse	.302	.376	.420	371	112	16	5	6	45	44	37	.310	.386	.427	436	135	18	6	7	53	53	44
vs. Power	.352	.430	.537	270	95	17	3	9	39	36	48	.342	.431	.525	301	103	19	3	10	42	46	55
on Grass	.320	.404	.436	241	77	8	1	6	29	32	36	.298	.388	.404	265	79	8	1	6	29	37	42
on Artificial Turf	.325	.396	.490	400	130	25	7	9	55	48	49	.337	.414	.502	472	159	29	8	11	66	62	57
Day Games	.371	.451	.570	151	56	7	4	5	26	22	20	.371	.451	.570	151	56	7	4	5	26	22	20
Night Games	.308	.383	.439	490	151	26	4	10	58	58	65	.311	.392	.440	586	182	30	5	12	69	77	79
April	.382	.453	.592	76	29	3	5	1	12	10	7	.382	.453	.592	76	29	3	5	1	12	10	7
May	.267	.388	.337	101	27	4	0	1	11	19	17	.267	.388	.337	101	27	4	0	1	11	19	17
June	.281	.333	.360	114	32	3	0	2	9	9	16	.281	.333	.360	114	32	3	0	2	9	9	16
July	.346	.402	.551	107	37	13	0	3	16	10	14	.346	.402	.551	107	37	13	0	3	16	10	14
August	.395	.467	.605	119	47	5	1	6	21	15	14	.395	.467	.605	119	47	5	1	6	21	15	14
Sept/Oct	.282	.366	.403	124	35	5	2	2	15	17	17	.300	.399	.423	220	66	9	3	4	26	36	31
Bases Empty	.334	.405	.469	377	126	19	4	8	8	43	45	.336	.408	.471	435	146	22	5	9	9	51	51
Leadoff	.312	.371	.449	138	43	5	1	4	4	12	21	.340	.402	.484	153	52	5	1	5	5	15	21
Not Leadoff	.347	.424	.481	239	83	14	3	4	4	31	24	.333	.411	.465	282	94	17	4	4	4	36	30
Runners On	.307	.391	.470	264	81	14	4	7	76	37	40	.305	.401	.460	302	92	15	4	8	86	48	48
First Base Only	.300	.349	.475	120	36	4	1	5	15	9	16	.291	.340	.448	134	39	4	1	5	15	10	20
Scoring Position	.313	.422	.465	144	45	10	3	2	61	28	24	.315	.442	.470	168	53	11	3	3	71	38	28
Late Innings, Close	.337	.396	.419	86	29	7	0	0	19	9	10	.337	.396	.419	172	58	14	0	0	38	18	20

RBI/Opportunities

Scoring Position	53 / 200 (27%)	62 / 238 (26%)
Scoring Position, 2 Out	22 / 75 (29%)	22 / 86 (26%)
On Third, Less than 2 Out	18 / 36 (50%)	23 / 47 (49%)
RBI in close games / RBI Total	47 / 84 (56%)	94 / 95 (99%)

Larry Sheets
Baltimore Orioles

At the end of the 1987 season, the Baltimore media chose Larry Sheets as the "Most Valuable Oriole." It was a good choice—but picking him as Baltimore's "Comeback Player of the Year" would have been more apt. Sheets had to hurdle a number of obstacles on his way to a very solid 1987.

First there was the flap about his defense. To be fair, it's a very real issue. Larry can hit, but that's about all he can do. He has very little speed and lacks good baseball instincts. His 1.89 range factor wasn't the worst figure in the American League in 1987, but it was in that general area. He may be the worst defensive outfielder in recent Oriole history—and, when you remember that Benny Ayala, Dan Ford, Carlos Lopez and Andres Mora have played out there lately, that's saying a lot.

But, even so, Sheets entered 1987 as a .271 hitter with a .471 slugging percentage. The decision to play Ken Gerhart (whose offensive potential is limited) in left field and John Shelby (one of the worst offensive players in the AL in 1986) in right, forcing Sheets to fight half of the Oriole roster for playing time as the DH, was indefensible. Yet that, for half of April, was just what Baltimore did.

The next problem Sheets faced was his .136 lifetime average against lefties. The Orioles decided, based on 44 at-bats, that Larry was a platoon player. Despite his overwhelming start, it was not until May—with nine of the 16 Baltimore hitters at or below the Mendoza line—that he began to face southpaws. When he did, he destroyed them.

There are still more battles ahead for Sheets. It would be best if Larry could move to DH and concentrate solely on hitting, but that could be said about almost all the Oriole hitters. Sheets played 124 games in the field in 1987 and will probably play even more there in 1988; he'll need to keep his defensive lapses from affecting his hitting.

Next, manager Cal Ripken puts a very high value on double plays—he expects his defense to turn them and his offense to avoid them. That, and Larry's lack of speed, was the reason that Sheets often batted eighth early in 1987 and hit seventh against lefties even as late as September. Given Sheets's RBI totals, it was a poor move on Ripken's part, but Larry will have to hit his way up into the top of the order next year anyway.

A third problem is his walk totals—which, for a player with his power, are unacceptable. If opposing pitchers are more careful about what they throw and Larry is not more selective about what he swings, his stats could plummet next year.

But it's quite possible that Larry will master each challenge. Though he's 28, he has, for various reasons, played less than 1000 professional games so far. He may well continue to develop in 1988.

Jason Kupferberg, Ken McKusick and Mark Prysant

Sheets, Larry Kent　　　Bats: Left　　Throws: Right　　Born 12/06/59

1987 SEASON AND MAJOR-LEAGUE CAREER BATTING TOTALS																					
	G	AB	H	2B	3B	HR	TB	R	RBI	TBB	IBB	SO	HP	SH	SF	SB	CS	SB%	GDP	AVG	OBP	SLG
87 BAL	135	469	148	23	0	31	264	74	94	31	1	67	3	0	5	1	1	.50	16	.316	.358	.563
4 YEARS	368	1151	333	49	1	67	585	162	206	81	6	178	7	2	8	3	2	.60	47	.289	.338	.508

	1987 SEASON											FOUR YEAR TOTALS (1984 – 1987)									
	Ave.	OBP	SLG	AB	H	2B	3B	HR	RBI	BB	SO	Ave.	OBP	SLG	AB	H	2B	3B	HR	RBI	BB	SO
Totals	.315	.358	.562	470	148	23	0	31	94	31	67	.289	.338	.508	1152	333	49	1	67	206	81	178
vs. Left	.303	.348	.538	145	44	4	0	10	29	8	22	.265	.319	.471	189	50	6	0	11	37	14	36
vs. Right	.320	.363	.572	325	104	19	0	21	65	23	45	.294	.341	.515	963	283	43	1	56	169	67	142
at Home	.322	.371	.624	242	78	10	0	21	57	20	29	.297	.345	.521	599	178	26	0	36	116	43	89
on Road	.307	.344	.496	228	70	13	0	10	37	11	38	.280	.329	.494	553	155	23	1	31	90	38	89
vs. Groundball	.313	.347	.511	272	85	12	0	14	52	13	38	.285	.331	.467	613	175	25	1	28	99	38	100
vs. Flyball	.318	.373	.631	198	63	11	0	17	42	18	29	.293	.345	.555	539	158	24	0	39	107	43	78
vs. Finesse	.287	.317	.506	237	68	10	0	14	42	11	35	.294	.327	.518	670	197	25	1	41	113	31	96
vs. Power	.343	.398	.618	233	80	13	0	17	52	20	32	.282	.352	.494	482	136	24	0	26	93	50	82
on Grass	.316	.358	.573	412	130	19	0	29	82	26	59	.290	.338	.509	1008	292	42	1	59	183	70	155
on Artificial Turf	.310	.359	.483	58	18	4	0	2	12	5	8	.285	.338	.500	144	41	7	0	8	23	11	23
Day Games	.278	.331	.508	126	35	8	0	7	21	10	23	.276	.322	.498	323	89	18	0	18	54	22	58
Night Games	.328	.369	.581	344	113	15	0	24	73	21	44	.294	.344	.511	829	244	31	1	49	152	59	120
April	.357	.424	.393	28	10	1	0	0	5	3	5	.323	.377	.510	96	31	4	1	4	17	8	10
May	.346	.379	.753	81	28	3	0	10	22	5	13	.333	.373	.652	210	70	10	0	19	51	14	36
June	.269	.329	.487	78	21	5	0	4	18	6	8	.261	.324	.427	218	57	9	0	9	44	19	29
July	.295	.325	.474	78	23	5	0	3	12	4	12	.253	.303	.395	162	41	8	0	5	19	12	24
August	.330	.376	.660	94	31	4	0	9	20	7	14	.296	.342	.616	216	64	9	0	20	46	15	39
Sept/Oct	.315	.353	.495	111	35	5	0	5	17	6	15	.280	.317	.436	250	70	9	0	10	29	13	40
Bases Empty	.330	.384	.582	261	86	12	0	18	18	22	33	.286	.336	.480	629	180	29	0	31	31	46	104
Leadoff	.336	.375	.504	113	38	4	0	5	5	6	15	.312	.351	.478	253	79	12	0	10	10	14	39
Not Leadoff	.324	.390	.642	148	48	8	0	13	13	16	18	.269	.326	.481	376	101	17	0	21	21	32	65
Runners On	.297	.326	.536	209	62	11	0	13	76	9	34	.293	.337	.541	523	153	20	1	36	175	35	74
First Base Only	.273	.328	.555	110	30	7	0	8	20	7	15	.279	.324	.544	272	76	9	0	21	47	16	33
Scoring Position	.323	.324	.515	99	32	4	0	5	56	2	19	.307	.350	.538	251	77	11	1	15	128	19	41
Late Innings, Close	.299	.333	.481	77	23	2	0	4	15	4	14	.236	.291	.407	182	43	4	0	9	27	14	41

RBI/Opportunities		
Scoring Position	48 / 132 (36%)	106 / 341 (31%)
Scoring Position, 2 Out	19 / 63 (30%)	38 / 149 (26%)
On Third, Less than 2 Out	19 / 32 (59%)	43 / 70 (61%)
RBI in close games / RBI Total	50 / 94 (53%)	117 / 206 (57%)

John Shelby
Baltimore Orioles/Los Angeles Dodgers

Since the Dodgers realized that Ken Landreaux wasn't even their centerfielder of the past, let alone the future, they have looked high and low for a replacement. At the beginning of the 1987 season they gave the job to Mike Ramsey (a move that even shocked Ramsey, who thought he was going down—in a way, he was, but with the ship), but Ramsey's inexperience showed and he lost his job a month into the season. So, the Dodgers turned to the trade market in their search for a centerfielder, and came up with John Shelby, who couldn't start for a woeful Baltimore team in center field.

Before he left the Orioles Shelby showed flashes of brilliance but was very inconsistent from season to season. His batting average fluctuated by more than 40 points each year. 1987 followed the pattern again but, to the Dodgers' benefit, this was an "up" year. Shelby's average climbed 49 points over his 1986 season.

The starting job in the Dodger outfield was John's from the first day. It was hoped that his power and experience would finally surface and the Dodgers could have a solid outfield in Guerrero, Marshall and Shelby. The 1987 results weren't exactly what they had hoped for.

1987 was Shelby's best year as a major leaguer. A lifetime .240 hitter going into the season, John raised his *career* batting average 10 points by hitting .277. It was also his best power year. He brought 30 lifetime homers from the American League, but he hit 21 in 1987; added to his 26 doubles

he became one of the power threats in the Dodger lineup. Shelby drew only 31 bases on balls in 1987, and by September the "book" was out— Shelby isn't a very selective hitter. When NL pitchers stopped giving John good pitches to hit, he tried futilely to hit bad ones. As a result, his power dropped significantly, as he hit but 3 homers after August 31.

Defensively, Shelby can be a standout. He is blessed with an outstanding arm. In five seasons in the minors he twice led his league in assists. Major league runners have been reluctant to test his arm. He also possesses decent speed, and gets a pretty good jump on balls. Last year he had his second best season on the basepaths when he stole 16, and several of his catches should help the Dodger highlight film exceed 5 minutes this year.

When the '88 season starts Shelby will be 30 years old. Unless he's a late bloomer his best years are history. The Dodgers can count on him to be a good defensive centerfielder and adequate at the plate (hmmmmm—sounds like a "young" Ken Landreaux). He seems best suited as a fourth outfielder, however, or a platoon player. If the Dodgers are to climb back into contention, Shelby can help by coming off the bench and giving their often injured regulars ("Iron Mike" Marshall in particular) a rest. If he continues as the regular centerfielder he will also have to continue to improve with age. Of course, all things are possible in Hollywood, right?

Carmen Corica

Shelby, John T. Bats: Both Throws: Right Born 02/23/58

1987 SEASON AND MAJOR-LEAGUE CAREER BATTING TOTALS

	G	AB	H	2B	3B	HR	TB	R	RBI	TBB	IBB	SO	HP	SH	SF	SB	CS	SB%	GDP	AVG	OBP	SLG
87 BAL-LA	141	508	138	26	0	22	230	65	72	32	2	110	1	2	9	16	7	.70	9	.272	.311	.453
7 YEARS	632	1862	463	76	13	52	721	253	207	95	4	370	3	24	11	68	21	.76	22	.249	.285	.387

1987 SEASON

	Ave.	OBP	SLG	AB	H	2B	3B	HR	RBI	BB	SO
Totals	.272	.311	.453	508	138	26	0	22	72	32	110
vs. Left	.320	.353	.571	175	56	11	0	11	33	11	38
vs. Right	.246	.289	.390	333	82	15	0	11	39	21	72
at Home	.235	.276	.358	260	61	8	0	8	34	16	57
on Road	.310	.348	.552	248	77	18	0	14	38	16	53
vs. Groundball	.282	.315	.450	238	67	10	0	10	31	13	49
vs. Flyball	.263	.307	.456	270	71	16	0	12	41	19	61
vs. Finesse	.267	.305	.458	288	77	16	0	13	38	16	52
vs. Power	.277	.318	.445	220	61	10	0	9	34	16	58
on Grass	.263	.307	.441	376	99	16	0	17	58	26	84
on Artificial Turf	.295	.321	.485	132	39	10	0	5	14	6	26
Day Games	.295	.331	.494	166	49	9	0	8	25	11	40
Night Games	.260	.301	.433	342	89	17	0	14	47	21	70
April	.160	.192	.280	25	4	0	0	1	2	1	10
May	.256	.304	.419	43	11	1	0	2	5	3	10
June	.237	.276	.465	114	27	8	0	6	18	7	20
July	.250	.292	.385	104	26	5	0	3	12	7	24
August	.327	.355	.558	113	37	5	0	7	16	6	23
Sept/Oct	.303	.347	.450	109	33	7	0	3	19	8	23
Bases Empty	.275	.328	.464	280	77	14	0	13	13	21	49
Leadoff	.260	.304	.417	96	25	6	0	3	3	5	15
Not Leadoff	.283	.340	.489	184	52	8	0	10	10	16	34
Runners On	.268	.290	.439	228	61	12	0	9	59	11	61
First Base Only	.275	.288	.490	102	28	4	0	6	13	2	19
Scoring Position	.262	.292	.397	126	33	8	0	3	46	9	42
Late Innings, Close	.188	.250	.306	85	16	4	0	2	12	7	23

FOUR YEAR TOTALS (1984 – 1987)

	Ave.	OBP	SLG	AB	H	2B	3B	HR	RBI	BB	SO
Totals	.245	.282	.391	1500	368	58	11	46	178	77	300
vs. Left	.257	.291	.428	549	141	24	2	22	65	27	107
vs. Right	.239	.276	.369	951	227	34	9	24	113	50	193
at Home	.216	.251	.328	732	158	23	1	19	76	35	151
on Road	.273	.311	.451	768	210	35	10	27	102	42	149
vs. Groundball	.245	.278	.386	682	167	19	7	21	83	33	128
vs. Flyball	.246	.284	.395	818	201	39	4	25	95	44	172
vs. Finesse	.251	.286	.390	794	199	33	6	22	95	37	123
vs. Power	.239	.277	.391	706	169	25	5	24	83	40	177
on Grass	.243	.280	.383	1240	301	46	7	38	154	65	253
on Artificial Turf	.258	.291	.427	260	67	12	4	8	24	12	47
Day Games	.271	.302	.437	517	140	27	4	17	72	25	99
Night Games	.232	.271	.366	983	228	31	7	29	106	52	201
April	.188	.234	.268	149	28	5	2	1	7	9	35
May	.233	.268	.380	150	35	3	2	5	16	7	28
June	.239	.272	.413	293	70	12	0	13	41	14	54
July	.198	.235	.319	273	54	9	3	6	33	14	60
August	.290	.328	.449	272	79	12	2	9	30	16	54
Sept/Oct	.281	.313	.438	363	102	17	2	12	51	17	69
Bases Empty	.236	.277	.376	874	206	26	5	29	29	49	167
Leadoff	.242	.274	.375	392	95	10	3	12	12	16	66
Not Leadoff	.230	.280	.378	482	111	16	2	17	17	33	101
Runners On	.259	.287	.411	626	162	32	6	17	149	28	133
First Base Only	.259	.282	.453	278	72	10	4	12	32	9	53
Scoring Position	.259	.290	.376	348	90	22	2	5	117	19	80
Late Innings, Close	.192	.240	.289	266	51	11	3	3	25	17	58

RBI/Opportunities

Scoring Position	41 / 170	(24%)
Scoring Position, 2 Out	22 / 86	(26%)
On Third, Less than 2 Out	13 / 29	(45%)
RBI in close games / RBI Total	44 / 72	(61%)

108 / 470	(23%)
60 / 233	(26%)
28 / 76	(37%)
111 / 178	(62%)

Pat Sheridan
Detroit Tigers

When, in 1985, the Detroit Tigers fell from 104 wins to 85 wins, manager Sparky Anderson concluded that the problem was that the team lacked speed and defense; in 1986, the Tigers acquired Dave Collins to meet those needs. Collins became one of the worst regulars in the majors that year, scoring only 44 runs despite leading off for most of the year. In 1987, the job of losing games as Detroit's "speedy gloveman" fell to Pat Sheridan.

What does Sheridan have going for him? Aside from his glove, not much. He's a .261 lifetime hitter with a .312 on-base percentage and .372 slugging percentage who strikes out about twice as often as he walks, homers almost every month and has stolen 69 bases in 96 tries (71.8 percent).

In the first half of 1987, Sheridan hit .274, stole a few bases, and looked graceful afield. Every other aspect of his game was a complete zero. Pat had a strikeout to walk ratio near 3 to 1, the fewest extra base hits per at-bat of any Tiger and, at one point, was solely responsible for an astounding 40 percent (10 of 25), of the team's caught-stealing total.

After the break, Sheridan improved his secondary stats markedly. His K/W ratio dropped to about 2 to 1, he hit a few doubles, and greatly improved his basestealing percentage. But his average was only .224; he was thus summarily benched in favor of late season call-up Scott Lusader, which was appropriate. Though, all things consid-

ered, Sheridan's second half was not significantly worse than his first half, he was one of the worst major league regulars of 1987.

Why did he play? There are numerous reasons. Pat's low salary makes him attractive to the thrifty Tigers. He, like Collins, Cesar Geronimo and Tom Brookens, is a light-hitting defensive whiz—just the kind of player that his manager was and (as a result) likes to play. But his greatest asset is that Sheridan knows how to "get along."

Contrary to popular belief, Anderson is a very dictatorial manager who insists on a docile clubhouse. In 1986, for example, he announced that he planned to platoon Darrell Evans (the reigning AL home run king and the Tigers' MVP for 1985); when Evans put up an understandable and rather mild protest, Anderson frostily threatened to trade him. The only reason that Evans stayed in Detroit is that, unlike Jason Thompson, Ron LeFlore, Steve Kemp and Glenn Wilson, he quickly realized that Sparky would prefer to trade him—whether or not there was an adequate replacement handy—and meekly accepted his fate.

Given Gary Pettis's past behavior and Anderson's notorious impatience with rookies like Lusader, there is a very solid chance that Sheridan will not only make the team, but reclaim a starting role. If so, he will almost certainly be one of the worst major league regulars of 1988.

Daniel Z. Douthat and Jim McDonald

Sheridan, Patrick Arthur "Pat"   Bats: Left   Throws: Right   Born 12/04/57

1987 SEASON AND MAJOR-LEAGUE CAREER BATTING TOTALS

	G	AB	H	2B	3B	HR	TB	R	RBI	TBB	IBB	SO	HP	SH	SF	SB	CS	SB%	GDP	AVG	OBP	SLG
87 DET	141	421	109	19	3	6	152	57	49	44	4	90	1	2	5	18	13	.58	7	.259	.327	.361
6 YEARS	567	1678	438	73	12	30	625	223	174	149	13	341	4	16	11	69	27	.72	23	.261	.321	.372

	1987 SEASON											FOUR YEAR TOTALS (1984 – 1987)										
	Ave.	OBP	SLG	AB	H	2B	3B	HR	RBI	BB	SO	Ave.	OBP	SLG	AB	H	2B	3B	HR	RBI	BB	SO
Totals	.259	.327	.361	421	109	19	3	6	49	44	90	.259	.324	.371	1344	348	61	10	23	138	130	276
vs. Left	.195	.250	.234	77	15	3	0	0	6	5	24	.194	.245	.257	175	34	6	1	1	11	10	56
vs. Right	.273	.344	.390	344	94	16	3	6	43	39	66	.269	.335	.388	1169	314	55	9	22	127	120	220
at Home	.278	.324	.396	187	52	11	1	3	26	15	45	.262	.321	.386	629	165	37	4	11	70	57	130
on Road	.244	.330	.333	234	57	8	2	3	23	29	45	.256	.326	.357	715	183	24	6	12	68	73	146
vs. Groundball	.284	.354	.409	225	64	9	2	5	31	27	49	.257	.319	.365	650	167	24	5	12	75	61	130
vs. Flyball	.230	.294	.306	196	45	10	1	1	18	17	41	.261	.329	.376	694	181	37	5	11	63	69	146
vs. Finesse	.277	.324	.396	235	65	9	2	5	24	16	38	.276	.331	.411	790	218	37	8	18	90	65	130
vs. Power	.237	.330	.317	186	44	10	1	1	25	28	52	.235	.314	.312	554	130	24	2	5	48	65	146
on Grass	.261	.317	.363	375	98	16	2	6	45	32	82	.261	.322	.365	827	216	34	5	14	89	76	183
on Artificial Turf	.239	.397	.348	46	11	3	1	0	4	12	8	.255	.327	.379	517	132	27	5	9	49	54	93
Day Games	.308	.383	.399	143	44	7	0	2	11	17	27	.286	.353	.411	406	116	15	3	10	48	42	84
Night Games	.234	.298	.342	278	65	12	3	4	38	27	63	.247	.311	.353	938	232	46	7	13	90	88	192
April	.284	.324	.313	67	19	0	1	0	5	4	7	.268	.325	.347	213	57	6	4	1	16	18	29
May	.306	.351	.435	85	26	3	1	2	15	6	24	.252	.312	.401	274	69	10	2	9	36	24	65
June	.286	.371	.390	77	22	5	0	1	10	11	18	.296	.354	.437	247	73	15	1	6	26	23	48
July	.236	.295	.292	72	17	4	0	0	3	6	16	.250	.296	.311	228	57	10	2	0	16	15	44
August	.274	.349	.493	73	20	5	1	3	11	9	17	.268	.357	.389	198	53	10	1	4	23	28	43
Sept/Oct	.106	.232	.149	47	5	2	0	0	5	8	8	.212	.295	.315	184	39	10	0	3	21	22	47
Bases Empty	.249	.329	.356	225	56	8	2	4	4	26	45	.260	.326	.376	758	197	29	7	15	15	73	148
Leadoff	.259	.333	.407	108	28	3	2	3	3	11	20	.215	.280	.330	288	62	6	3	7	7	25	56
Not Leadoff	.239	.326	.308	117	28	5	0	1	1	15	25	.287	.353	.404	470	135	23	4	8	8	48	92
Runners On	.270	.324	.367	196	53	11	1	2	45	18	45	.258	.321	.363	586	151	32	3	8	123	57	128
First Base Only	.237	.265	.363	80	19	5	1	1	5	3	18	.250	.287	.388	232	58	17	3	3	18	12	42
Scoring Position	.293	.360	.371	116	34	6	0	1	40	15	27	.263	.342	.347	354	93	15	0	5	105	45	86
Late Innings, Close	.200	.262	.291	55	11	2	0	1	4	4	7	.246	.311	.337	199	49	9	3	1	13	18	38

RBI/Opportunities

Scoring Position	37 / 170 (22%)	95 / 505 (19%)
Scoring Position, 2 Out	19 / 89 (21%)	43 / 240 (18%)
On Third, Less than 2 Out	13 / 31 (42%)	35 / 90 (39%)
RBI in close games / RBI Total	24 / 49 (49%)	90 / 138 (65%)

Eric Show
San Diego Padres

The sole surviving member of the San Diego Padre chapter of the John Birch Society is a complex individual. Eric is very intelligent, knowledgeable in physics, and enjoys playing his guitar. He is prone to displays of temper when things aren't going well for him. Last season he had run-ins with Tony Gwynn and Benito Santiago, and made national headlines when he beaned Andre Dawson. The latter incident (terrifying to watch) was caused by a pitch that "got away," made to a batter who is notorious for crowding the plate and diving into pitches. Show (rhymes with now) is not a headhunter. Immediately after the incident, he apologized to all parties. His apology was sincere and without qualification. However, the Chicago press and Dawson himself seemed determined to turn the accident into an excuse for war. The notion of a Padre-Cub death match was more than a little amusing—one presumes that both teams would swing and miss a lot—but it was averted when Show conveniently missed his turn the next time the two clubs got together.

Rather than being the kind of pitcher who stirs such response, Eric is considered too soft in San Diego. He's renowned for giving up a lot of home runs and for blowing big leads. He seems to do his best in close games. There's been talk of trading the righthander (the Giants turned him down and held out for Dravecky), but it's hard to understand why. For six years he's been a quality starter for a generally poor team. 1987 was his first losing season. From 1982 through '86 he had the highest winning percentage (.587, 61–43) among NL pitchers who were starters all 5 years. During that same period, his ERA was 0.02 from fourth place.

Last season was a roller coaster year for Eric. His first win, in April, was a shutout. His second win didn't come until mid-June. From early June to early July he was 3–2 and had reduced his ERA from 4.30 to 3.62. From then to late August he was 2–6 and his ERA grew to 4.35. Then, in his last 7 games he was 2–1 and lowered his ERA to 3.84.

Despite the inconsistency Show was easily the best Padre starter in '87. He allowed only 8.2 hits per 9 innings and spun 3 shutouts. Early in the season there was concern that he hadn't fully recovered from the arm injury he sustained in '86. However, he came around in June and finished the year in strong fashion. Eric has the ability to be a 20-game winner under the right circumstances; since he's never won more than 15, that's unlikely, but he remains a steady hurler who can be depended on for quality work. Look for him to be tough in 1988.

Bruce Erricson

Show, Eric Vaughn Bats: Right Throws: Right Born 05/19/56

1987 SEASON AND MAJOR-LEAGUE CAREER PITCHING TOTALS

	G	GS	CG	GF	IP	BFP	H	R	ER	HR	SH	SF	HB	TBB	IBB	SO	WP	Bk	W	L	Pct	ShO	Sv	ERA
87 SD	34	34	5	0	206	887	188	99	88	26	9	5	9	85	7	117	6	5	8	16	.333	3	0	3.84
7 YEARS	222	170	21	17	1156	4855	1019	484	436	119	69	25	34	460	31	686	25	11	70	62	.530	10	6	3.39

1987: Finesse, Flyball   1986: Power, Flyball   1985: Finesse, Flyball   1984: Finesse, Flyball

1987 SEASON

	G	IP	H	BB	SO	SB	CS	W	L	S	ERA
Totals	34	206.1	188	85	117	16	5	8	16	0	3.84
at Home	18	112.0	83	49	71	9	1	5	6	0	2.73
on Road	16	94.1	105	36	46	7	4	3	10	0	5.15
on Grass	15	88.2	81	37	51	7	1	4	7	0	3.45
on Artificial Turf	19	117.2	107	48	66	9	4	4	9	0	4.13
Day Games	27	170.2	129	70	99	10	4	8	10	0	3.16
Night Games	7	35.2	59	15	18	6	1	0	6	0	7.07
April	5	33.1	22	9	19	2	0	1	1	0	3.24
May	7	42.0	37	17	26	4	0	0	6	0	5.14
June	5	27.2	23	11	10	1	3	2	2	0	2.93
July	6	33.1	36	12	18	2	2	2	3	0	4.32
August	6	37.2	37	24	21	4	0	1	3	0	4.78
Sept/Oct	5	32.1	33	12	23	3	0	2	1	0	1.95

FOUR YEAR TOTALS (1984 – 1987)

	G	IP	H	BB	SO	SB	CS	W	L	S	ERA
Totals	125	782.1	684	330	456	54	41	44	41	0	3.34
at Home	63	387.2	322	168	253	24	22	22	19	0	3.20
on Road	62	394.2	362	162	203	30	19	22	22	0	3.49
on Grass	41	260.0	244	109	145	18	11	14	15	0	3.60
on Artificial Turf	84	522.1	440	221	311	36	30	30	26	0	3.22
Day Games	93	575.2	495	243	353	36	29	35	29	0	3.47
Night Games	32	206.2	189	87	103	18	12	9	12	0	3.00
April	19	129.2	92	42	81	8	5	6	5	0	2.78
May	25	158.0	133	77	108	18	6	8	10	0	3.70
June	22	133.0	115	70	68	4	13	9	8	0	3.72
July	19	113.1	111	46	68	8	7	7	6	0	3.41
August	23	134.1	123	56	62	9	5	8	7	0	3.48
Sept/Oct	17	114.0	110	39	69	7	5	6	5	0	2.84

vs. Opponent Batters	Ave.	OBP	SLG	AB	H	2B	3B	HR	RBI	BB	SO
Totals	.242	.322	.404	778	188	40	4	26	89	85	117
vs. Left	.246	.328	.399	426	105	23	3	12	41	53	67
vs. Right	.236	.314	.409	352	83	17	1	14	48	32	50
Bases Empty	.248	.308	.432	491	122	23	2	21	21	37	74
Leadoff	.257	.312	.381	202	52	11	1	4	4	16	28
Not Leadoff	.242	.305	.467	289	70	12	1	17	17	21	46
Runners On Base	.230	.343	.355	287	66	17	2	5	68	48	43
First Base Only	.209	.341	.291	110	23	6	0	1	5	19	16
Scoring Position	.243	.344	.395	177	43	11	2	4	63	29	27
Late Innings, Close	.227	.292	.386	44	10	1	0	2	3	3	9

	Ave.	OBP	SLG	AB	H	2B	3B	HR	RBI	BB	SO
Totals	.237	.317	.372	2881	684	113	14	82	282	330	456
vs. Left	.265	.352	.401	1538	407	67	11	40	144	208	191
vs. Right	.206	.276	.339	1343	277	46	3	42	138	122	265
Bases Empty	.248	.320	.397	1765	438	74	7	58	58	181	275
Leadoff	.250	.312	.403	745	186	32	5	24	24	68	114
Not Leadoff	.247	.325	.392	1020	252	42	2	34	34	113	161
Runners On Base	.220	.313	.332	1116	246	39	7	24	224	149	181
First Base Only	.226	.309	.348	500	113	15	2	14	36	57	75
Scoring Position	.216	.317	.320	616	133	24	5	10	188	92	106
Late Innings, Close	.251	.328	.399	243	61	5	2	9	17	27	32

RBI/Opportunities

Scoring Position	54 / 245 (22%)	169 / 847 (20%)	
Scoring Position, 2 Out	17 / 115 (15%)	56 / 421 (13%)	
On Third, Less than 2 Out	19 / 39 (49%)	70 / 125 (56%)	
RBI in close games / RBI Total	65 / 89 (73%)	221 / 282 (78%)	

Ruben Sierra
Texas Rangers

Jose Rijo and Ruben Sierra are two very young ball-players with several similarities. They are both extremely talented; both were rushed to the majors very early in their careers, and both had their share of problems starting out. There the comparison ends as Sierra has left Rijo in the realm of potential and begun a march toward stardom.

Ruben is a complete blend of natural talent, and the Rangers are hoping over time to develop him into your Dale Murphy-type of outfielder. Pshaw, you say. Take a look at last season's stats: more home runs than Pete Incaviglia, Cal Ripken, George Brett, and Jesse Barfield. More RBIs than Danny Tartabull, Alvin Davis, and Robin Yount. His isolated power is .207, comparable to Alan Trammell at .208. His secondary average is .292, well above average. He doesn't walk much, but his home of Puerto Rico is close enough to the Dominican Republic to explain that; you don't get off the island and into the majors by drawing walks. All in all, a good year of development for Ruben Sierra, and remember, we are talking about a 22-year-old kid here.

The Texas Rangers are hoping that twenty years from now Gary Ward will be the answer to an oft-asked trivia question along the lines of Wally Pipp and Lou Gehrig, *i.e.,* who did Ruben Sierra replace in the Rangers' outfield? That isn't a slap against Ward, mind you; he performed well for the Rangers. What may elevate Ward to trivia status is the raw potential of Ruben to be a true "franchise" player. Ruben is one of those rare players who can very nearly do it all. He runs very well, has a good glove, makes consistent, hard contact at the plate, and has amazing power. His home runs aren't sky-high fly balls, either; they are more of the sizzling liner, lighting bolt variety.

Defensively, Sierra has all the skills, he just needs time and patience. Scouts have said he runs like a jaguar and throws like John Elway. In 1987 his raw range factor was in the upper half of right fielders, and he had 17 assists to tie Jesse Barfield for the league lead. He did make 11 errors, but he wasn't dropping fly balls; he just tended to over-charge some hits and occasionally threw too aggressively.

If there is a concern about Sierra's development, it is that he is painfully young and impressionable. This is his first experience with a real media blitz, and he could run into trouble reading his own press releases. One too many comparisons to Roberto Clemente could sink his natural talent.

Wes Osborn and Darren E. Peterson

Sierra, Ruben Angel (Garcia)

Bats: Both   Throws: Right   Born 10/06/65

1987 SEASON AND MAJOR-LEAGUE CAREER BATTING TOTALS

	G	AB	H	2B	3B	HR	TB	R	RBI	TBB	IBB	SO	HP	SH	SF	SB	CS	SB%	GDP	AVG	OBP	SLG
87 TEX	158	643	169	35	4	30	302	97	109	39	4	114	2	0	12	16	11	.59	18	.263	.302	.470
2 YEARS	271	1025	270	48	14	46	484	147	164	61	7	179	3	1	17	23	19	.55	26	.263	.302	.472

	1987 SEASON											FOUR YEAR TOTALS (1984 – 1987)									
	Ave.	OBP	SLG	AB	H	2B	3B	HR	RBI	BB	SO	Ave.	OBP	SLG	AB	H	2B	3B	HR	RBI	BB	SO
Totals	.263	.302	.470	643	169	35	4	30	109	39	114	.263	.302	.472	1025	270	48	14	46	164	61	179
vs. Left	.249	.267	.456	237	59	11	1	12	35	8	32	.250	.267	.449	336	84	15	2	16	50	12	43
vs. Right	.271	.321	.478	406	110	24	3	18	74	31	82	.270	.319	.483	689	186	33	12	30	114	49	136
at Home	.276	.323	.502	315	87	18	4	15	64	21	54	.263	.299	.487	487	128	20	10	23	95	26	92
on Road	.250	.282	.439	328	82	17	0	15	45	18	60	.264	.304	.459	538	142	28	4	23	69	35	87
vs. Groundball	.258	.306	.425	322	83	16	1	12	46	24	58	.252	.298	.428	484	122	22	6	17	67	34	81
vs. Flyball	.268	.297	.514	321	86	19	3	18	63	15	56	.274	.306	.512	541	148	26	8	29	97	27	98
vs. Finesse	.272	.305	.486	356	97	19	3	17	54	18	56	.270	.302	.488	574	155	24	10	27	83	29	86
vs. Power	.251	.297	.449	287	72	16	1	13	55	21	58	.255	.301	.452	451	115	24	4	19	81	32	93
on Grass	.263	.301	.474	536	141	30	4	25	97	32	93	.258	.296	.461	833	215	37	12	36	139	48	146
on Artificial Turf	.262	.304	.449	107	28	5	0	5	12	7	21	.286	.329	.521	192	55	11	2	10	25	13	33
Day Games	.246	.293	.387	142	35	6	1	4	24	11	32	.238	.281	.407	214	51	8	2	8	36	15	39
Night Games	.267	.304	.493	501	134	29	3	26	85	28	82	.270	.308	.490	811	219	40	12	38	128	46	140
April	.214	.263	.400	70	15	2	1	3	15	4	15	.214	.263	.400	70	15	2	1	3	15	4	15
May	.287	.342	.463	108	31	5	1	4	16	10	25	.287	.342	.463	108	31	5	1	4	16	10	25
June	.276	.336	.431	116	32	9	0	3	11	10	16	.236	.282	.396	225	53	13	1	7	18	14	41
July	.297	.317	.619	118	35	10	2	8	28	4	20	.278	.312	.580	176	49	11	6	10	36	9	28
August	.254	.287	.525	118	30	5	0	9	24	7	22	.287	.326	.550	209	60	11	4	12	41	14	34
Sept/Oct	.230	.250	.345	113	26	4	0	3	15	4	16	.262	.288	.422	237	62	6	1	10	38	10	36
Bases Empty	.260	.309	.440	327	85	12	1	15	15	22	59	.254	.294	.457	540	137	21	7	25	25	30	98
Leadoff	.259	.298	.380	108	28	4	0	3	3	6	14	.243	.278	.360	189	46	8	1	4	4	9	26
Not Leadoff	.260	.314	.470	219	57	8	1	12	12	16	45	.259	.303	.510	351	91	13	6	21	21	21	72
Runners On	.266	.295	.500	316	84	23	3	15	94	17	55	.274	.312	.489	485	133	27	7	21	139	31	81
First Base Only	.305	.346	.539	128	39	11	2	5	14	8	15	.323	.371	.528	195	63	15	2	7	19	15	25
Scoring Position	.239	.262	.473	188	45	12	1	10	80	9	40	.241	.273	.462	290	70	12	5	14	120	16	56
Late Innings, Close	.227	.262	.392	97	22	2	1	4	16	5	17	.271	.298	.482	170	46	7	4	7	24	7	30

RBI/Opportunities

	1987		FOUR YEAR
Scoring Position	63 / 246	(26%)	97 / 381 (25%)
Scoring Position, 2 Out	21 / 103	(20%)	35 / 169 (21%)
On Third, Less than 2 Out	28 / 52	(54%)	41 / 77 (53%)
RBI in close games / RBI Total	74 / 109	(68%)	108 / 164 (66%)

Roy Smalley
Minnesota Twins

Baseball analysis is often criticized for taking the spirit out of the game in the same way the pleasantly ephemeral quality is removed from a captured and mounted butterfly. Systematic study by number-touting villains supposedly reduces the game to lifelessness in the name of knowledge. Rest assured, though, that we are not approaching that feared state any time soon. One way we know this is true is by looking at the career of Roy Smalley.

Smalley demonstrates how far baseball has come and how far there is yet to go in recognizing even the most obvious of a player's talents. During his first stint with the Twins (1977–1982), he was an under-appreciated shortstop who in several ways was the prototype for the Yount-Ripken power hitting infielder. A problem with being a prototype is that frequently people look for reasons why you will not succeed rather than examining what you do well. As a fielder, Smalley had the most noticeable of problems. In '77,'78, and '79, he committed a total of 87 errors, establishing a reputation which plagues him yet today. Nowadays any number of analysts would have pointed to his range (in '77 he led the league in chances per game) and his hitting ability (good power and on-base percentage) and submit that Smalley's value far exceeded the negatives of the high error totals. The voices for a rational argument were not in place a decade ago, or at least not where they could be heard.

Acquired by the Yankees in 1982, Smalley's experience as a shortstop, encouraged New York to turn him into a utility infielder. With a back injury seriously curtailing his ability to play shortstop and with Graig Nettles at third, Roy never fit into the Yankees. Sentenced to serve time next with the White Sox, Roy played most frequently at third base. By then he was no longer much of a fielder. A look at his numbers would have suggested Chicago try him at DH. But LaRussa had a team of designated hitters and endured Smalley in the field until they sent him packing.

In 1985, the Twins were in need of a DH and a shortstop. In an amazing and ironic way, the team that didn't want him at shortstop when he could field, acquired him to play the position when all the evidence clearly indicated he was no longer up to the task. Returned to his old position, Roy hit better than any Twins' DH and played worse than any of the team's shortstops. Finally, in 1986, a few years after he should have, Smalley was used primarily as a DH. He turned in a credible performance, but in his mid-30's his talents were slipping with age.

All this is neither a way of saying that Smalley has been unpredictable nor that baseball men don't know what they are looking for; it's a way of saying that the butterfly still has a lot of life in it.

Bill Jensen

Smalley, Roy Frederick Jr.

Bats: Both   Throws: Right   Born 10/25/52

1987 SEASON AND MAJOR-LEAGUE CAREER BATTING TOTALS

	G	AB	H	2B	3B	HR	TB	R	RBI	TBB	IBB	SO	HP	SH	SF	SB	CS	SB%	GDP	AVG	OBP	SLG
87 MIN	110	309	85	16	1	8	127	32	34	36	1	52	1	0	1	2	0	1.00	7	.275	.352	.411
13 YEARS	1653	5657	1454	244	25	163	2237	745	694	771	47	908	14	98	54	27	34	.44	121	.257	.345	.395

1987 SEASON

	Ave.	OBP	SLG	AB	H	2B	3B	HR	RBI	BB	SO
Totals	.275	.352	.411	309	85	16	1	8	34	36	52
vs. Left	.250	.280	.375	24	6	0	0	1	6	1	4
vs. Right	.277	.357	.414	285	79	16	1	7	28	35	48
at Home	.271	.342	.436	140	38	8	0	5	17	14	26
on Road	.278	.359	.391	169	47	8	1	3	17	22	26
vs. Groundball	.307	.372	.423	163	50	8	1	3	18	17	26
vs. Flyball	.240	.329	.397	146	35	8	0	5	16	19	26
vs. Finesse	.264	.340	.389	144	38	4	1	4	19	17	25
vs. Power	.285	.362	.430	165	47	12	0	4	15	19	27
on Grass	.277	.363	.394	137	38	7	0	3	17	19	21
on Artificial Turf	.273	.342	.424	172	47	9	1	5	17	17	31
Day Games	.277	.365	.422	83	23	3	0	3	15	12	17
Night Games	.274	.347	.407	226	62	13	1	5	19	24	35
April	.274	.313	.516	62	17	7	1	2	8	4	9
May	.298	.377	.340	47	14	2	0	0	2	5	9
June	.382	.440	.579	76	29	6	0	3	16	8	7
July	.167	.250	.185	54	9	1	0	0	4	6	12
August	.194	.356	.444	36	7	0	0	3	3	9	8
Sept/Oct	.265	.342	.265	34	9	0	0	0	1	4	7
Bases Empty	.299	.368	.435	184	55	8	1	5	5	19	31
Leadoff	.328	.384	.493	67	22	3	1	2	2	6	7
Not Leadoff	.282	.359	.402	117	33	5	0	3	3	13	24
Runners On	.240	.329	.376	125	30	8	0	3	29	17	21
First Base Only	.254	.313	.390	59	15	5	0	1	5	5	6
Scoring Position	.227	.342	.364	66	15	3	0	2	24	12	15
Late Innings, Close	.259	.306	.310	58	15	3	0	0	6	4	10

FOUR YEAR TOTALS (1984 – 1987)

	Ave.	OBP	SLG	AB	H	2B	3B	HR	RBI	BB	SO
Totals	.247	.335	.403	1500	371	68	6	51	175	201	262
vs. Left	.181	.274	.295	237	43	12	0	5	27	31	45
vs. Right	.260	.347	.423	1263	328	56	6	46	148	170	217
at Home	.251	.342	.424	736	185	34	3	29	97	101	132
on Road	.243	.329	.382	764	186	34	3	22	78	100	130
vs. Groundball	.275	.357	.426	748	206	38	3	23	96	96	119
vs. Flyball	.219	.314	.379	752	165	30	3	28	79	105	143
vs. Finesse	.260	.345	.420	803	209	41	3	27	89	105	126
vs. Power	.232	.324	.383	697	162	27	3	24	86	96	136
on Grass	.241	.326	.381	751	181	29	2	24	86	99	133
on Artificial Turf	.254	.344	.425	749	190	39	4	27	89	102	129
Day Games	.237	.332	.362	439	104	17	1	12	50	64	88
Night Games	.252	.337	.419	1061	267	51	5	39	125	137	174
April	.279	.356	.454	240	67	20	2	6	30	29	35
May	.287	.370	.461	258	74	12	0	11	29	33	43
June	.274	.338	.479	292	80	15	3	13	45	28	47
July	.211	.327	.324	256	54	11	0	6	28	44	50
August	.192	.287	.363	240	46	3	1	12	22	32	49
Sept/Oct	.234	.341	.308	214	50	7	0	3	21	35	38
Bases Empty	.246	.325	.428	866	213	33	4	39	39	101	143
Leadoff	.269	.338	.462	353	95	15	1	17	17	37	45
Not Leadoff	.230	.317	.405	513	118	18	3	22	22	64	98
Runners On	.249	.351	.368	634	158	35	2	12	136	100	119
First Base Only	.267	.322	.409	296	79	19	1	7	26	24	37
Scoring Position	.234	.373	.331	338	79	16	1	5	110	76	82
Late Innings, Close	.199	.289	.281	267	53	11	1	3	34	34	56

RBI/Opportunities

	1987		Four Year	
Scoring Position	19 / 91	(21%)	95 / 485	(20%)
Scoring Position, 2 Out	10 / 49	(20%)	41 / 241	(17%)
On Third, Less than 2 Out	4 / 12	(33%)	32 / 72	(44%)
RBI in close games / RBI Total	21 / 34	(62%)	108 / 175	(62%)

Dave Smith
Houston Astros

It is often said that every modern team *has* to have a stopper in the bullpen. But how common is it to have one? And just as important, how common is it to have one that you can count on year after year? Let's use these criteria: 1. The man must save at least 20 games. 2. The man must save at least two fifths of his games pitched. 3. The man must pitch no more than twice as many innings as he does games. That means he must only be used in the late innings. In 1987, the National League had 6 pitchers who met those standards: Steve Bedrosian, John Franco, Lee Smith, Roger McDowell, Todd Worrell and Dave Smith. Of the 6, Dave Smith has been meeting those criteria for more years (3) than anyone other than his namesake Lee. With the Cub ace traded to the American League, that leaves Dave as the senior stopper in the NL.

That position is certainly not consistent with Dave Smith's reputation. He is usually regarded as just another good reliever, largely because he doesn't pitch very many innings. In the three years in question, Dave has pitched 79.1, 56 and 60 innings. None of the other 5 has met the criteria while pitching fewer than 80. In fact, in a bit of poking around, I couldn't find anyone else ever who had met the criteria in fewer than 80 innings. In 1986, Smith actually saved half as many games as innings pitched (33 in 56), which is also unmatched as far as I could find.

Dave has noticed this about himself. Last year, he was complaining to the national press about not getting enough work. At the time, his ERA was just above 0.50, which is beyond the outstanding and into the ridiculous, and he felt that this entitled him to at least as much action as the rest of the stoppers were getting—and, of course, as much reputation. After all, Dave was in his contract year. It's hard to argue with an ERA like that, but Dave Smith may be well advised to be cautious. Remember, he is the senior NL stopper, with 3 whole years of consistency. It's apparently quite hard to do that job year in and year out, and there's been a suspicious correlation between large numbers of innings pitched and the ruination of pitchers' arms. Bruce Sutter, for example, pitched a career-high 122.2 innings in 1985, the year before he went to Atlanta and his arm fell off.

Most of the people who meet the stopper criteria pitch between 80 and 100 innings per year. Dave Smith is significantly under that, at about 50 to 70, but then, he's also been consistent. Six is half of 12, and that means that only half the NL teams have stoppers at all. If I had one of them, and he was being exceptionally consistent, I'd be truly reluctant to change his usage formula. Dave Smith has finally received a good money contract, and his best plan might just be to take his 60 innings and keep the good work up for as many years as possible.

Brock J. Hanke

Smith, David Stanley "Dave"   Bats: Right   Throws: Right   Born 01/21/55

1987 SEASON AND MAJOR-LEAGUE CAREER PITCHING TOTALS

	G	GS	CG	GF	IP	BFP	H	R	ER	HR	SH	SF	HB	TBB	IBB	SO	WP	Bk	W	L	Pct	ShO	Sv	ERA
87 HOU	50	0	0	44	60	240	39	13	11	0	3	1	1	21	8	73	2	2	2	3	.400	0	24	1.65
8 YEARS	411	1	0	275	586	2418	492	190	164	22	36	15	10	202	38	410	19	10	40	32	.556	0	124	2.52

1987: Power, Groundball   1986: Power, Flyball   1985: Finesse, Flyball   1984: Finesse, Groundball

1987 SEASON / FOUR YEAR TOTALS (1984 – 1987)

	G	IP	H	BB	SO	SB	CS	W	L	S	ERA	G	IP	H	BB	SO	SB	CS	W	L	S	ERA
Totals	50	60.0	39	21	73	8	0	2	3	24	1.65	221	272.2	207	80	204	26	4	20	19	89	2.21
at Home	28	36.2	22	14	44	7	0	1	2	13	1.47	119	149.1	116	40	117	14	2	16	9	45	2.17
on Road	22	23.1	17	7	29	1	0	1	1	11	1.93	102	123.1	91	40	87	12	2	4	10	44	2.26
on Grass	14	16.0	13	5	21	1	0	1	0	8	0.00	54	60.2	44	24	45	6	1	3	6	25	1.93
on Artificial Turf	36	44.0	26	16	52	7	0	1	3	16	2.25	167	212.0	163	56	159	20	3	17	13	64	2.29
Day Games	14	13.2	14	5	13	1	0	1	1	7	2.63	62	74.2	62	29	48	9	2	3	8	28	2.89
Night Games	36	46.1	25	16	60	7	0	1	2	17	1.36	159	198.0	145	51	156	17	2	17	11	61	1.95
April	7	7.1	3	0	9	0	0	0	0	5	0.00	33	40.2	29	3	33	2	1	3	1	15	0.89
May	8	10.2	2	2	15	0	0	0	0	3	0.00	37	44.1	31	13	32	3	0	2	4	12	2.23
June	11	15.2	6	7	22	2	0	0	0	6	1.15	39	51.1	23	22	52	4	2	0	4	19	1.75
July	8	8.1	8	4	13	0	0	2	0	4	2.16	32	42.0	38	15	27	5	1	6	2	10	3.21
August	7	9.0	6	4	10	2	0	0	0	4	2.00	36	45.0	36	14	37	4	0	5	2	17	2.40
Sept/Oct	9	9.0	14	4	4	4	0	0	3	2	5.00	44	49.1	50	13	23	8	0	4	6	16	2.74

vs. Opponent Batters	Ave.	OBP	SLG	AB	H	2B	3B	HR	RBI	BB	SO	Ave.	OBP	SLG	AB	H	2B	3B	HR	RBI	BB	SO
Totals	.182	.257	.229	214	39	6	2	0	25	21	73	.211	.271	.286	982	207	23	6	13	99	80	204
vs. Left	.204	.297	.239	113	23	2	1	0	11	15	25	.191	.261	.249	461	88	9	3	4	42	44	75
vs. Right	.158	.211	.218	101	16	4	1	0	14	6	48	.228	.279	.319	521	119	14	3	9	57	36	129
Bases Empty	.164	.211	.224	116	19	3	2	0	0	7	42	.207	.266	.277	512	106	10	4	6	6	41	116
Leadoff	.191	.240	.277	47	9	0	2	0	0	3	13	.218	.297	.320	206	45	3	3	4	4	23	35
Not Leadoff	.145	.192	.188	69	10	3	0	0	0	4	29	.199	.244	.248	306	61	7	1	2	2	18	81
Runners On Base	.204	.307	.235	98	20	3	0	0	25	14	31	.215	.276	.296	470	101	13	2	7	93	39	88
First Base Only	.194	.242	.226	31	6	1	0	0	1	2	5	.253	.278	.322	174	44	5	2	1	7	6	28
Scoring Position	.209	.333	.239	67	14	2	0	0	24	12	26	.193	.275	.280	296	57	8	0	6	86	33	60
Late Innings, Close	.196	.269	.241	158	31	3	2	0	23	15	49	.224	.284	.310	686	154	16	5	11	84	56	129

RBI/Opportunities

Scoring Position	24 / 104 (23%)	76 / 405 (19%)
Scoring Position, 2 Out	7 / 50 (14%)	25 / 194 (13%)
On Third, Less than 2 Out	10 / 19 (53%)	32 / 68 (47%)
RBI in close games / RBI Total	23 / 25 (92%)	85 / 99 (86%)

Lee Smith
Chicago Cubs

"It's the bottom of the ninth, the Cubs are ahead, and Lee Smith is coming in to pitch." In 1987, these words made Cub fans cringe, hide their eyes, or go to the refrigerator to get a beer, because the game could be going on for a while. Lee Smith should be considered one of the best relief pitchers of the 1980s. However, last season Smith did not pitch as well as his numbers indicate, and his years of effectiveness may be behind him.

Smith began the year by trying to develop a new pitch, the slider. He fell in love with his new toy and used this pitch almost exclusively during the first part of the season; whether that was the reason or not, he was noticeably less effective than in previous years. Smith also had all sorts of ailments, including a sore arm, a bad back, and aching knees. It seemed as though Lee had disappeared at the end of the season due to his ailments. He was pitching for a last place team, so even though he saved 36 games, most of Smith's saves were early in the year when the Cubs were playing well. He tailed off, like the rest of the ball club, during the last two months of the season. The late inning stopper is supposed to be able to halt his team's slide by saving a few games and giving the team some confidence. But Smith did not provide the needed confidence for the Cubs in 1987.

Lee appeared in 62 ballgames for the Cubs during the 1987 season. He saved 36, accounting for almost half of the Cub wins. He also lost 10 games, which is 12 percent of the games that the Cubs lost. This is not a good statistic for a late inning reliever to have. You figure that once in a while that a closer will lose a ball game for you; that is the nature of his job. But when a late inning reliever is the loser in 12 percent of his team's defeats, you have to wonder about his effectiveness. Smith also blew 12 save opportunities during the 1987 season. If Lee would have been able to save at least half of the games he lost, the Cubs would have ended up in fourth place. Not a division winner, but better than ending up in the basement.

A late inning reliever is supposed to keep runners off the basepaths, because if he allows runners, that means the runners who were on base when he came into the game probably scored. Lee allowed 106 base runners to reach base in 84 innings pitched, an average of 1.26 per inning. That's a huge figure especially when he only pitches in one or two innings a game. No wonder he lost ten games; he could not do his job keeping opponents off the bases.

A change of scenery may be the best thing to happen to Lee. I hope that the Red Sox fans will discover the old Lee Smith. I hope that the 1987 Lee Smith does not show up in Fenway.

Vincent Vrotny

Smith, Lee Arthur Bats: Right Throws: Right Born 12/04/57

1987 SEASON AND MAJOR-LEAGUE CAREER PITCHING TOTALS

	G	GS	CG	GF	IP	BFP	H	R	ER	HR	SH	SF	HB	TBB	IBB	SO	WP	Bk	W	L	Pct	ShO	Sv	ERA
87 CHN	62	0	0	55	84	360	84	30	29	4	4	0	0	32	5	96	4	0	4	10	.286	0	36	3.11
8 YEARS	458	6	0	342	682	2827	591	240	221	38	41	19	6	264	61	644	34	4	40	51	.440	0	180	2.92

1987: Power, Groundball   1986: Power, Flyball   1985: Power, Flyball   1984: Power, Flyball

1987 SEASON

	G	IP	H	BB	SO	SB	CS	W	L	S	ERA
Totals	62	84.0	84	32	96	13	4	4	10	36	3.11
at Home	28	38.1	47	8	43	2	3	3	5	16	3.76
on Road	34	45.2	37	24	53	11	1	1	5	20	2.56
on Grass	36	49.0	56	13	58	3	3	3	6	21	3.67
on Artificial Turf	26	35.0	28	19	38	10	1	1	4	15	2.31
Day Games	41	56.1	61	15	60	5	3	3	7	25	2.88
Night Games	21	27.2	23	17	36	8	1	1	3	11	3.58
April	8	11.0	10	5	19	2	1	0	2	4	2.45
May	14	20.2	12	2	21	3	0	1	1	9	1.74
June	13	14.1	22	6	17	1	0	1	2	7	5.02
July	6	9.2	8	1	9	0	1	0	1	5	1.86
August	13	18.1	19	13	17	7	1	2	1	7	1.47
Sept/Oct	8	10.0	13	5	13	0	1	0	3	4	8.10

vs. Opponent Batters	Ave.	OBP	SLG	AB	H	2B	3B	HR	RBI	BB	SO
Totals	.259	.326	.358	324	84	18	1	4	38	32	96
vs. Left	.266	.356	.384	177	47	12	0	3	19	25	47
vs. Right	.252	.286	.327	147	37	6	1	1	19	7	49
Bases Empty	.266	.311	.409	154	41	10	0	4	4	10	41
Leadoff	.231	.275	.431	65	15	7	0	2	2	4	11
Not Leadoff	.292	.337	.393	89	26	3	0	2	2	6	30
Runners On Base	.253	.339	.312	170	43	8	1	0	34	22	55
First Base Only	.254	.323	.271	59	15	1	0	0	0	6	22
Scoring Position	.252	.346	.333	111	28	7	1	0	34	16	33
Late Innings, Close	.270	.339	.367	259	70	14	1	3	35	27	75

FOUR YEAR TOTALS (1984 – 1987)

	G	IP	H	BB	SO	SB	CS	W	L	S	ERA
Totals	262	373.0	338	141	387	50	17	29	30	133	3.23
at Home	138	202.1	196	62	213	26	11	17	14	67	3.65
on Road	124	170.2	142	79	174	24	6	12	16	66	2.74
on Grass	180	259.0	247	90	272	33	14	24	20	85	3.72
on Artificial Turf	82	114.0	91	51	115	17	3	5	10	48	2.13
Day Games	192	276.1	257	91	277	31	13	23	21	97	3.32
Night Games	70	96.2	81	50	110	19	4	6	9	36	2.98
April	29	41.2	37	19	56	3	3	2	5	15	2.81
May	48	75.1	61	23	73	11	2	7	4	26	2.99
June	51	68.1	60	36	69	8	5	4	8	21	3.56
July	45	69.2	54	23	78	5	2	5	4	27	2.84
August	47	65.1	65	20	55	15	3	9	4	22	2.34
Sept/Oct	42	52.2	61	20	56	8	2	2	5	22	5.13

vs. Opponent Batters	Ave.	OBP	SLG	AB	H	2B	3B	HR	RBI	BB	SO
Totals	.244	.313	.355	1388	338	59	9	26	168	141	387
vs. Left	.257	.345	.369	759	195	38	4	13	95	102	195
vs. Right	.227	.272	.339	629	143	21	5	13	73	39	192
Bases Empty	.259	.314	.385	691	179	32	2	17	17	55	194
Leadoff	.264	.313	.438	292	77	17	2	10	10	21	68
Not Leadoff	.256	.314	.346	399	102	15	0	7	7	34	126
Runners On Base	.228	.313	.326	697	159	27	7	9	151	86	193
First Base Only	.263	.325	.370	243	64	10	2	4	16	22	58
Scoring Position	.209	.307	.302	454	95	17	5	5	135	64	135
Late Innings, Close	.243	.314	.360	1101	268	48	7	22	150	114	307

RBI/Opportunities

Scoring Position	30 / 151 (20%)	116 / 636 (18%)
Scoring Position, 2 Out	13 / 75 (17%)	42 / 283 (15%)
On Third, Less than 2 Out	9 / 20 (45%)	44 / 106 (42%)
RBI in close games / RBI Total	35 / 38 (92%)	150 / 168 (89%)

Ozzie Smith
St. Louis Cardinals

Ozzie Smith had a tremendous season in 1987, and might have been the National League's Most Valuable Player had he not been on the same team as Jack Clark. Of course Clark probably would have been the MVP had he not been injured. As it turned out Smith and Clark split the vote, finishing second and third, respectively, and Andre Dawson, himself a deserving recipient, won the award.

The fact that Ozzie finished second in the voting is a tribute to the man and his work habits. The Cardinals were widely criticized only a few years ago for paying two million dollars a year to a "defensive specialist." But in 1987 that defensive specialist hit over .300, scored over 100 runs, drove in 75 runs while batting in the number two spot in the lineup, stole 43 bases while being caught only nine times, walked 89 times for a .392 on-base average, and missed a chance on the last day of the season to lead the National League in doubles. His secondary average for the season was an even .300. No one can ever accuse Smith of taking the money and running. Each season since he signed his contract, or each season since he became a Cardinal for that matter, he has improved his game offensively. And through it all he has remained a spectacular defensive shortstop.

Ozzie just missed a couple of records in 1987. He made his tenth error of the season on September 29, with only six games left in the season. The National League record for fewest errors by a shortstop is 9, held by Larry Bowa. Ozzie also had a shot at the modern day mark for most RBIs without hitting a home run. The record is 76; Smith finished with 75.

Smith blamed his slow start at the plate last season on having to adjust to hitting in the number-two spot, behind Vince Coleman. Once he settled in, however, he had a remarkably consistent year, as is evidenced by his monthly batting statistics. From May to September his lowest monthly batting average was .294. Smith's favorite opponent in '87 was Montreal. Against the Expos he collected 27 hits, drove home eleven runs, and stole seven bases, compiling a .397 average and .485 slugging mark. Smith hit over .400 against Atlanta, Cincinnati and Los Angeles, and he slugged over .500 against each of these three teams.

Whitey Herzog's acquisition of Ozzie for Garry Templeton has turned out to be one of his best deals. Cardinal fans weren't that sorry to see Templeton go, of course, given the circumstances. But the fact is that most people felt at the time that the Padres had gotten the better end of the deal. After all, if you go back to about 1979, you will see that Templeton was the league's premier offensive shortstop while Smith was a .211 hitter. Now the situation is basically reversed. The Cardinals definitely got the better end of this one, getting Templeton's best years as well as Ozzie's.

Russ Eagle

Smith, Osborne Earl "Ozzie"   Bats: Both   Throws: Right   Born 12/26/54

1987 SEASON AND MAJOR-LEAGUE CAREER BATTING TOTALS

	G	AB	H	2B	3B	HR	TB	R	RBI	TBB	IBB	SO	HP	SH	SF	SB	CS	SB%	GDP	AVG	OBP	SLG
87 STL	158	600	182	40	4	0	230	104	75	89	3	36	1	12	4	43	9	.83	9	.303	.392	.383
10 YEARS	1475	5339	1351	219	42	13	1693	687	449	617	60	341	22	137	28	346	89	.80	98	.253	.331	.317

1987 SEASON

	Ave.	OBP	SLG	AB	H	2B	3B	HR	RBI	BB	SO
Totals	.303	.392	.383	600	182	40	4	0	75	89	36
vs. Left	.250	.346	.318	220	55	15	0	0	30	33	12
vs. Right	.334	.419	.421	380	127	25	4	0	45	56	24
at Home	.287	.375	.371	286	82	20	2	0	36	41	16
on Road	.318	.408	.395	314	100	20	2	0	39	48	20
vs. Groundball	.296	.375	.366	284	84	20	0	0	28	37	15
vs. Flyball	.310	.407	.399	316	98	20	4	0	47	52	21
vs. Finesse	.310	.391	.381	323	100	21	1	0	38	44	19
vs. Power	.296	.393	.386	277	82	19	3	0	37	45	17
on Grass	.317	.399	.402	164	52	12	1	0	23	23	11
on Artificial Turf	.298	.389	.376	436	130	28	3	0	52	66	25
Day Games	.286	.363	.357	199	57	12	1	0	34	25	12
Night Games	.312	.406	.397	401	125	28	3	0	41	64	24
April	.185	.308	.215	65	12	2	0	0	6	12	5
May	.343	.445	.434	99	34	9	0	0	17	19	5
June	.308	.380	.393	107	33	7	1	0	19	13	4
July	.294	.390	.373	102	30	6	1	0	13	15	7
August	.316	.397	.404	114	36	8	1	0	13	16	5
Sept/Oct	.327	.402	.416	113	37	8	1	0	7	14	10
Bases Empty	.300	.397	.371	340	102	24	0	0	0	55	20
Leadoff	.358	.469	.433	120	43	9	0	0	0	25	4
Not Leadoff	.268	.356	.336	220	59	15	0	0	0	30	16
Runners On	.308	.385	.400	260	80	16	4	0	75	34	16
First Base Only	.329	.394	.447	85	28	6	2	0	7	8	4
Scoring Position	.297	.380	.377	175	52	10	2	0	68	26	12
Late Innings, Close	.294	.397	.353	102	30	6	0	0	19	18	3

FOUR YEAR TOTALS (1984 – 1987)

	Ave.	OBP	SLG	AB	H	2B	3B	HR	RBI	BB	SO
Totals	.281	.369	.356	2063	580	101	16	7	227	289	107
vs. Left	.278	.381	.372	702	195	43	1	7	75	119	39
vs. Right	.283	.363	.348	1361	385	58	15	0	152	170	68
at Home	.282	.373	.358	974	275	53	6	3	109	139	51
on Road	.280	.366	.354	1089	305	48	10	4	118	150	56
vs. Groundball	.296	.373	.364	1010	299	56	5	1	108	125	44
vs. Flyball	.267	.366	.348	1053	281	45	11	6	119	164	63
vs. Finesse	.289	.366	.368	1145	331	59	8	5	118	137	54
vs. Power	.271	.373	.341	918	249	42	8	2	109	152	53
on Grass	.282	.360	.357	571	161	30	5	1	65	71	28
on Artificial Turf	.281	.373	.355	1492	419	71	11	6	162	218	79
Day Games	.293	.372	.373	726	213	39	5	3	93	93	35
Night Games	.274	.368	.346	1337	367	62	11	4	134	196	72
April	.224	.331	.293	259	58	8	2	2	25	42	15
May	.290	.380	.378	362	105	27	1	1	43	53	15
June	.295	.370	.354	387	114	16	2	1	44	47	19
July	.282	.354	.373	308	87	17	4	1	35	33	12
August	.258	.345	.318	337	87	16	2	0	31	45	19
Sept/Oct	.315	.413	.395	410	129	17	5	2	49	69	27
Bases Empty	.274	.358	.348	1197	328	66	5	4	4	157	67
Leadoff	.315	.416	.399	429	135	29	2	1	1	74	17
Not Leadoff	.251	.324	.319	768	193	37	3	3	3	83	50
Runners On	.291	.384	.367	866	252	35	11	3	223	132	40
First Base Only	.312	.361	.404	314	98	17	6	0	17	23	10
Scoring Position	.279	.395	.346	552	154	18	5	3	206	109	30
Late Innings, Close	.279	.376	.363	366	102	15	5	2	47	58	18

RBI/Opportunities

	1987		1984–1987	
Scoring Position	65 / 246	(26%)	196 / 821	(24%)
Scoring Position, 2 Out	23 / 106	(22%)	61 / 349	(17%)
On Third, Less than 2 Out	25 / 44	(57%)	89 / 161	(55%)
RBI in close games / RBI Total	52 / 75	(69%)	152 / 227	(67%)

Zane Smith
Atlanta Braves

For the third consecutive year, pre-season forecasters are saying of Zane Smith: "This impressive young hurler is finally ready to emerge as one of baseball's great starting pitchers." Such predictions are relatively common. Fine young arms always inspire optimism, but rarely produce the desired results. Zane Smith may be the rare exception, the one who actually blossoms. We can say with some certainty that 1988 will be the year that decides the question: Is Zane Smith an outstanding pitcher, or just another journeyman?

In 1987 Zane showed some significant and measurable improvement. His 15–10 won-lost record was so good, within context, that it actually overstates his accomplishments for the year. The Braves' next best starters, David Palmer and Rick Mahler, produced only 8 wins each. Zane Smith is not the only case of a good pitcher on a bad staff, but nowhere else in the major leagues can you find anyone who came so close to winning as many games as his team's second and third best pitchers combined. Zane was good in 1987, but not that good.

The main source of improvement was Smith's control. Before 1987, he averaged 4.78 walks per 9 innings. His '87 average was 3.38, and after the All-Star break it was 3.24. Those one or two baserunners per game were a significant

factor with a team that played 49 one-run games during the year. While keeping the ball over the plate, Zane also kept it in the park rather effectively. His indicated ERA, based on BB and HR, was only 2.95 last year.

One of the most encouraging numbers from Zane's 1987 campaign was his ratio of hits plus walks per inning. His career ratio through 1986 was 1.50 H+BB per IP. Frankly, that is a bad number. You cannot stay in the majors with a ratio that high, unless you are young, with good stuff, and appear likely to improve soon. Zane did improve. In 1987, his ratio dropped to 1.39, which is marginally acceptable. After the All-Star break, his ratio was a highly respectable 1.30, not quite star quality, but showing definite improvement and promise for the future.

Smith's ERA showed little change from '86 to '87. But the League as a whole deteriorated considerably in the ERA category, so Zane did well just to hold his numbers steady. It is becoming increasingly obvious why so many teams over the past three to four years have expressed an interest in trading for Zane Smith. Even with a team as bad as the Atlanta Braves, there is a good possibility that Zane will perform with sufficient excellence in 1988 to attract national attention.

John C. Benson

Smith, Zane William

Bats: Left **Throws: Left** **Born 12/28/60**

1987 SEASON AND MAJOR-LEAGUE CAREER PITCHING TOTALS

	G	GS	CG	GF	IP	BFP	H	R	ER	HR	SH	SF	HB	TBB	IBB	SO	WP	Bk	W	L	Pct	ShO	Sv	ERA
87 ATL	36	36	9	0	242	1035	245	130	110	19	12	5	5	91	6	130	5	1	15	10	.600	3	0	4.09
4 YEARS	119	89	14	5	614	2642	605	316	269	32	42	12	13	289	19	370	15	1	33	36	.478	6	1	3.94

1987: Finesse, Groundball 1986: Power, Groundball 1985: Power, Groundball 1984: Power, Groundball

1987 SEASON / FOUR YEAR TOTALS (1984 – 1987)

	G	IP	H	BB	SO	SB	CS	W	L	S	ERA	G	IP	H	BB	SO	SB	CS	W	L	S	ERA
Totals	36	242.0	245	91	130	32	4	15	10	0	4.09	119	613.2	605	289	370	89	27	33	36	1	3.95
at Home	18	110.2	136	46	60	14	1	6	6	0	5.69	62	317.0	340	150	200	38	11	15	18	1	4.43
on Road	18	131.1	109	45	70	18	3	9	4	0	2.74	57	296.2	265	139	170	51	16	18	18	0	3.40
on Grass	14	87.1	94	36	52	17	1	4	7	0	4.95	36	195.2	203	93	122	34	7	9	16	0	4.28
on Artificial Turf	22	154.2	151	55	78	15	3	11	3	0	3.61	83	418.0	402	196	248	55	20	24	20	1	3.79
Day Games	26	173.0	180	61	90	18	3	11	8	0	4.32	86	454.1	457	205	267	54	21	25	27	1	4.10
Night Games	10	69.0	65	30	40	14	1	4	2	0	3.52	33	159.1	148	84	103	35	6	8	9	0	3.50
April	6	41.2	43	10	25	4	0	2	1	0	3.02	20	93.1	81	30	61	9	0	5	4	0	2.89
May	7	44.1	51	24	26	5	1	3	2	0	5.08	23	109.2	116	59	80	18	4	6	7	0	4.35
June	6	40.0	38	13	23	10	1	3	1	0	4.05	19	117.0	118	55	69	25	6	7	5	0	3.38
July	5	30.1	31	12	13	1	0	1	2	0	4.75	17	103.0	93	49	63	9	7	4	7	0	4.02
August	6	46.2	39	17	22	4	1	5	1	0	3.28	11	75.1	75	37	32	5	5	5	5	0	4.42
Sept/Oct	6	39.0	43	15	21	8	1	1	3	0	4.62	29	115.1	122	59	65	23	5	6	8	1	4.60

vs. Opponent Batters	Ave.	OBP	SLG	AB	H	2B	3B	HR	RBI	BB	SO	Ave.	OBP	SLG	AB	H	2B	3B	HR	RBI	BB	SO
Totals	.266	.333	.377	922	245	40	3	19	115	91	130	.265	.348	.372	2286	605	119	15	32	276	289	370
vs. Left	.257	.310	.314	105	27	3	0	1	12	8	22	.250	.300	.316	320	80	13	1	2	34	23	83
vs. Right	.267	.336	.386	817	218	37	3	18	103	83	108	.267	.355	.381	1966	525	106	14	30	242	266	287
Bases Empty	.258	.324	.345	530	137	22	3	6	6	48	76	.264	.347	.361	1255	331	66	10	12	12	158	192
Leadoff	.223	.304	.308	224	50	7	0	4	4	23	28	.254	.334	.357	560	142	28	3	8	8	65	80
Not Leadoff	.284	.338	.373	306	87	15	3	2	2	25	48	.272	.358	.364	695	189	38	7	4	4	93	112
Runners On Base	.276	.346	.421	392	108	18	0	13	109	43	54	.266	.348	.385	1031	274	53	5	20	264	131	178
First Base Only	.267	.315	.417	187	50	7	0	7	20	13	20	.256	.310	.366	429	110	15	1	10	31	33	56
Scoring Position	.283	.372	.424	205	58	11	0	6	89	30	34	.272	.373	.399	602	164	38	4	10	233	98	122
Late Innings, Close	.309	.338	.441	68	21	3	0	2	9	2	6	.264	.354	.343	201	53	10	0	2	22	27	31

RBI/Opportunities

Scoring Position	77 / 280 (28%)	209 / 840 (25%)
Scoring Position, 2 Out	30 / 135 (22%)	78 / 379 (21%)
On Third, Less than 2 Out	24 / 44 (55%)	73 / 145 (50%)
RBI in close games / RBI Total	83 / 115 (72%)	189 / 276 (68%)

Cory Snyder
Cleveland Indians

When a player has as bad a year as Cory Snyder just did (and his 1987 would fit real nicely into Dave Kingman's career, which is my benchmark for lousy), there's no point to analysis. So, rather than mention that he had the worst K/W ratio of any AL player with 100 whiffs (worse than even the Royals' dedicated hobbyist), I'll discuss what may have caused it and make a few points about what to look for in 1988.

COMMON SENSE: When pitchers notice that you slug .500 and strike out 769 percent as often as you walk, they may decide to see what happens if they stop throwing strikes. If you keep swinging, they'll throw even less strikes.

STUBBORNNESS: That line of reasoning did not go unvocalized in 1987; the advice Cory received ranged from "Nail the #*&%#@ bat to your %$@*&&% shoulder!!" to "Maybe you and Joe Cowley should work out together." He ignored it all—he just kept saying that he'd hit his way out of it if people would only leave him alone. It took several months before he realized that it just wasn't going to happen.

INEXPERIENCE: Which, in a way, made things even worse. Snyder is not terribly likely to win membership in Mensa; his concept of patience at the plate was "I won't swing at anything this time." When word got around, teams started getting called third strikes on belt-high fastballs; that got him to start swinging wildly again. I've seen canaries in blenders that looked more poised than Cory did last year; by September, he couldn't even beat up on lefties anymore.

SHORTSTOP: Snyder's bat died around the time that Cleveland made the brilliant decision to carry 11 pitchers and no utility infielder, meaning that Cory had to play short any time that either Julio Franco or Tony Bernazard took a rest. He fielded .918 and hit in the low .200's in those games; the only people to benefit from this innovative strategy were rotisserie leaguers. Come to think of it, his offense tailed off in 1986 at about the same time he started playing short. . . .

The one bright spot to Snyder's 1987 was his defense. He tied for third in the AL in assists and, for someone who'd never played the outfield until 1986, had an impressive range factor. You've got to think that he'll only get better with the glove in time.

And at bat? I think Cory can hit .260; with his power, he'd have to draw about 65 walks to be productive. He'll do that in 1988 because he'll have to. Cleveland has scads of outfielders; they don't have to be patient with him and they say that they won't be. If Snyder is hitting .230 in May, his playing time will drop like a rock. Since not playing drives Cory crazy, it will probably be the spur that goads him into becoming more patient—and thus more productive—next year.

Geoff Beckman

Snyder, James Cory "Cory"   Bats: Right   Throws: Right   Born 11/11/62

1987 SEASON AND MAJOR-LEAGUE CAREER BATTING TOTALS

	G	AB	H	2B	3B	HR	TB	R	RBI	TBB	IBB	SO	HP	SH	SF	SB	CS	SB%	GDP	AVG	OBP	SLG
87 CLE	157	577	136	24	2	33	263	74	82	31	4	166	1	0	6	5	1	.83	3	.236	.273	.456
2 YEARS	260	993	249	45	3	57	471	132	151	47	4	289	1	1	6	7	4	.64	11	.251	.284	.474

	1987 SEASON											FOUR YEAR TOTALS (1984 – 1987)										
	Ave.	OBP	SLG	AB	H	2B	3B	HR	RBI	BB	SO	Ave.	OBP	SLG	AB	H	2B	3B	HR	RBI	BB	SO
Totals	.236	.273	.456	577	136	24	2	33	82	31	166	.251	.284	.474	993	249	45	3	57	151	47	289
vs. Left	.221	.271	.399	163	36	12	1	5	19	12	55	.263	.296	.477	281	74	19	1	13	42	14	86
vs. Right	.242	.274	.478	414	100	12	1	28	63	19	111	.246	.279	.473	712	175	26	2	44	109	33	203
at Home	.214	.255	.442	276	59	12	0	17	42	17	76	.240	.276	.478	462	111	21	1	29	74	25	136
on Road	.256	.290	.468	301	77	12	2	16	40	14	90	.260	.290	.471	531	138	24	2	28	77	22	153
vs. Groundball	.281	.320	.548	299	84	13	2	21	47	18	74	.293	.326	.540	491	144	24	2	31	81	25	124
vs. Flyball	.187	.223	.356	278	52	11	0	12	35	13	92	.209	.242	.410	502	105	21	1	26	70	22	165
vs. Finesse	.247	.272	.414	295	73	11	1	12	37	11	70	.263	.286	.478	525	138	25	2	28	78	18	127
vs. Power	.223	.275	.500	282	63	13	1	21	45	20	96	.237	.281	.470	468	111	20	1	29	73	29	162
on Grass	.236	.270	.457	488	115	22	1	28	66	25	129	.255	.288	.486	821	209	36	2	50	123	41	227
on Artificial Turf	.236	.289	.449	89	21	2	1	5	16	6	37	.233	.261	.419	172	40	9	1	7	28	6	62
Day Games	.202	.236	.399	208	42	7	2	10	22	10	55	.226	.258	.438	340	77	11	2	19	43	15	105
Night Games	.255	.294	.488	369	94	17	0	23	60	21	111	.263	.297	.493	653	172	34	1	38	108	32	184
April	.267	.300	.523	86	23	5	1	5	11	4	24	.267	.300	.523	86	23	5	1	5	11	4	24
May	.167	.190	.344	96	16	2	0	5	14	3	33	.167	.190	.344	96	16	2	0	5	14	3	33
June	.265	.315	.398	83	22	2	0	3	11	7	25	.269	.303	.497	145	39	7	1	8	22	8	45
July	.269	.295	.593	108	29	8	0	9	25	4	28	.274	.302	.528	197	54	11	0	13	37	8	51
August	.234	.288	.523	107	25	5	1	8	15	9	29	.251	.290	.498	239	60	9	1	16	34	14	64
Sept/Oct	.216	.252	.330	97	21	2	0	3	6	4	27	.248	.281	.426	230	57	11	0	10	33	10	72
Bases Empty	.249	.279	.496	345	86	12	2	23	23	14	99	.257	.287	.497	571	147	23	3	36	36	24	160
Leadoff	.306	.333	.599	147	45	7	0	12	12	6	38	.293	.326	.524	246	72	10	1	15	15	12	60
Not Leadoff	.207	.238	.419	198	41	5	2	11	11	8	61	.231	.258	.477	325	75	13	2	21	21	12	100
Runners On	.216	.266	.397	232	50	12	0	10	59	17	67	.242	.279	.443	422	102	22	0	21	115	23	129
First Base Only	.250	.301	.500	96	24	3	0	7	14	6	25	.270	.302	.540	174	47	8	0	13	26	7	48
Scoring Position	.191	.242	.324	136	26	9	0	3	45	11	42	.222	.263	.375	248	55	14	0	8	89	16	81
Late Innings, Close	.292	.304	.652	89	26	5	0	9	23	2	23	.280	.301	.560	150	42	9	0	11	32	5	39

RBI/Opportunities

	1987		Four Year	
Scoring Position	37 / 181	(20%)	74 / 313	(24%)
Scoring Position, 2 Out	16 / 94	(17%)	31 / 153	(20%)
On Third, Less than 2 Out	12 / 28	(43%)	25 / 53	(47%)
RBI in close games / RBI Total	52 / 82	(63%)	93 / 151	(62%)

Bob Stanley
Boston Red Sox

In January, Bob Stanley fell on ice outside his home, cutting his hand on some broken glass. He underwent lengthy surgery afterwards, and the prognosis for his pitching is uncertain.

"Steamer" had an awful year in 1987, as the stats and the Fenway boo-birds will attest. After losing his job as Bo-Sox bullpen ace during the '86 pennant race, he was put into the starting rotation for 1987 for the first time since 1980. He couldn't hold onto that job, either, and was eventually relegated to mop-up work.

Barring a comeback, the most vivid memory most baseball fans will hold of Steamer is that "wild" pitch in Game Six of the 1986 Series (which was clearly a passed ball). That's too bad, for Bob could have been a pioneer.

In 1982, Houk used Stanley early and often: Stanley set an AL record with 168.1 IP in relief in only 48 games with 14 saves. Houk made big Bob the ace in 1983, and Stanley relieved in 64 games, notching 33 saves. In '84, Stanley slumped, getting only 22 saves in 57 games. In '85, he pitched better in limited use, his season being shortened by surgery.

What were the reasons for his decline, and were they related to how he was used? I believe that because of the way he pitched, Bob should never have been used in short relief, even when he was getting batters out effectively enough to be an ace reliever. The primary reason is this: Bob Stanley has never been a classic short reliever, certainly not in the modern mold of a Goose or a Bruce. Stanley has always been a finesse pitcher who induces grounders; his best pitches are a sinker and a palm ball. He has never had an especially good H/IP ratio, even in good years he allowed a hit or more per inning. He survived on his good control and his sinker, getting grounders and keeping the batters from hitting homers.

Now, if you had to choose the perfect relief situation for this guy, what would it be? It certainly wouldn't be with runners in scoring position in the late innings of a close game, for in that situation you'd want a power pitcher, who's more likely to get a strikeout than give up a hit. No, the best situation would be starting an inning, where the singles Bob would give up are no worse than walks, and where his low-homer, low-walk propensities would prevent the big inning. Medium to long relief in a close game (but not necessarily a game in which you were ahead) would be a much more effective usage for Stanley than as a closer.

Why doesn't some enterprising manager try using good pitchers, who are well-suited for medium and long relief but not for short relief, in their better roles instead of trying to shove them into a role they are not equipped to handle well? Hell, I don't know. Ask Ralph Houk and John McNamara.

Gary Gillette

Stanley, Robert William "Bob"

Bats: Right   Throws: Right   Born 11/10/54

1987 SEASON AND MAJOR-LEAGUE CAREER PITCHING TOTALS

	G	GS	CG	GF	IP	BFP	H	R	ER	HR	SH	SF	HB	TBB	IBB	SO	WP	Bk	W	L	Pct	ShO	Sv	ERA
87 BOS	34	20	4	5	153	676	198	96	85	17	13	4	1	42	7	67	3	0	4	15	.211	1	0	5.00
11 YEARS	537	85	21	323	1527	6463	1666	702	611	103	70	45	33	416	78	604	16	1	104	91	.533	7	123	3.60

1987: Finesse, Groundball   1986: Finesse, Groundball   1985: Finesse, Groundball   1984: Finesse, Groundball

1987 SEASON

	G	IP	H	BB	SO	SB	CS	W	L	S	ERA
Totals	34	152.2	198	42	67	6	8	4	15	0	5.01
at Home	15	73.2	85	14	30	2	4	3	5	0	4.28
on Road	19	79.0	113	28	37	4	4	1	10	0	5.70
on Grass	13	62.1	86	17	24	5	0	2	8	0	5.49
on Artificial Turf	21	90.1	112	25	43	1	8	2	7	0	4.68
Day Games	29	135.0	163	36	59	5	8	4	12	0	4.53
Night Games	5	17.2	35	6	8	1	0	0	3	0	8.66
April	5	33.1	40	9	11	1	1	2	3	0	4.05
May	6	39.1	48	8	14	0	2	0	4	0	5.26
June	7	26.0	39	7	12	1	2	1	1	0	5.19
July	5	6.2	10	1	5	0	0	0	2	0	8.10
August	5	32.2	42	10	18	4	1	1	3	0	4.68
Sept/Oct	6	14.2	19	7	7	0	2	0	2	0	5.52

vs. Opponent Batters	Ave.	OBP	SLG	AB	H	2B	3B	HR	RBI	BB	SO
Totals	.321	.363	.468	616	198	33	3	17	88	42	67
vs. Left	.358	.413	.522	299	107	21	2	8	37	29	28
vs. Right	.287	.314	.416	317	91	12	1	9	51	13	39
Bases Empty	.354	.392	.503	322	114	20	2	8	4	20	38
Leadoff	.415	.445	.599	147	61	13	1	4	4	8	16
Not Leadoff	.303	.348	.423	175	53	7	1	4	4	12	22
Runners On Base	.286	.333	.429	294	84	13	1	9	80	22	29
First Base Only	.280	.313	.424	125	35	7	1	3	10	5	8
Scoring Position	.290	.347	.432	169	49	6	0	6	70	17	21
Late Innings, Close	.382	.435	.539	76	29	6	0	2	13	8	7

FOUR YEAR TOTALS (1984 – 1987)

	G	IP	H	BB	SO	SB	CS	W	L	S	ERA
Totals	205	429.1	496	117	219	14	15	25	37	48	4.09
at Home	99	212.0	250	50	106	5	10	14	16	22	4.46
on Road	106	217.1	246	67	113	9	5	11	21	26	3.73
on Grass	72	152.1	178	36	68	6	4	8	14	15	4.37
on Artificial Turf	133	277.0	318	81	151	8	11	17	23	33	3.93
Day Games	174	369.2	411	101	191	11	14	22	28	42	4.02
Night Games	31	59.2	85	16	28	3	1	3	9	6	4.53
April	30	88.0	85	17	39	1	3	3	8	8	3.07
May	38	86.2	99	23	37	2	4	3	7	14	4.57
June	40	80.0	91	24	41	2	2	8	4	12	4.39
July	33	51.1	49	18	36	1	2	6	5	6	3.16
August	38	84.1	124	24	43	6	2	3	10	3	5.12
Sept/Oct	26	39.0	48	11	23	2	2	2	3	5	3.69

vs. Opponent Batters	Ave.	OBP	SLG	AB	H	2B	3B	HR	RBI	BB	SO
Totals	.292	.337	.424	1698	496	78	10	42	261	117	219
vs. Left	.306	.370	.441	832	255	44	4	20	129	85	93
vs. Right	.278	.304	.408	866	241	34	6	22	132	32	126
Bases Empty	.281	.316	.411	872	245	43	5	20	20	44	134
Leadoff	.318	.353	.499	371	118	25	3	12	12	20	51
Not Leadoff	.253	.288	.345	501	127	18	2	8	8	24	83
Runners On Base	.304	.360	.438	826	251	35	5	22	241	73	85
First Base Only	.318	.348	.449	305	97	15	2	7	23	13	21
Scoring Position	.296	.366	.432	521	154	20	3	15	218	60	64
Late Innings, Close	.272	.329	.400	705	192	30	3	18	121	60	99

RBI/Opportunities

Scoring Position	60 / 213 (28%)	190 / 737 (26%)
Scoring Position, 2 Out	23 / 92 (25%)	64 / 301 (21%)
On Third, Less than 2 Out	29 / 39 (74%)	87 / 152 (57%)
RBI in close games / RBI Total	70 / 88 (80%)	198 / 261 (76%)

Mike Stanley
Texas Rangers

Mike Stanley's climb to the majors has been a remarkable combination of talent and circumstance. The Rangers' drafted him in the sixteenth round of the 1985 June draft. Stints at three clubs that first summer produced a combined .319 average and won him the starting job at Tulsa in 1986. Stanley's hot start combined with injuries to Don Slaught and Darrell Porter to get him promoted to the big club in late June, barely a year after he was first drafted. It was a brief stay, but it helped solidify his future as a Ranger in 1987.

The only setback Mike had in his development was when Joe Ferguson managed him in winter ball and inexplicably played Stanley at first base. The Rangers wanted Stanley to work on his catching, and this incident is believed to have been a factor in the eventual firing of Ferguson from the Ranger coaching staff. Mike had to begin 1987 at AAA, but a .335 average with 13 homers and 54 RBIs in just 46 games put him back in the majors.

With Texas he was slowed by injury and illness (chicken pox) and hit only .273, but he also drove in a run every 5.8 at-bats, the second best ratio on the club. With Slaught's trade he is sure to be the starting catcher in 1988.

Dic Humphrey

I like Stanley a lot as a hitter, but I'd like him even more if the Rangers weren't locking him into being a catcher. It strikes me as a dangerous gamble to take a talented hitter and play him at such a demanding position unless it is obviously his natural position.

Stanley has a long history of *not* hitting as well as a catcher. It was true in AA, in AAA, and in the major leagues. With Texas he has hit over .300 as a third baseman, as a left fielder, as a DH, as a pinch-hitter, and pretty close to it as a first baseman (.292). We're only talking about a total of 65 at-bats, but as a non-catcher he is hitting .354, which is exactly 100 points higher than he has hit as a catcher. The difference in his slugging was close to 300 points, .631 to .343.

As a defensive catcher Mike was the Rangers' worst in throwing out base stealers (5 for 77, honest), the worst in passed balls both with and without Hough, and the worst in "Catcher ERA" by over half an earned run. Catching is probably the most coachable of all positions, and Stanley is raw enough that there are plenty of easy improvements that could be made, but the Rangers may be painting themselves into a dangerous corner.

It seems like all the circumstances dictate the Rangers must move in this direction, but it wasn't so long ago that other options could have been explored that would have made Stanley's presence a clear positive instead of a potential weak link in their 1988 campaign.

Craig R. Wright

Stanley, Robert Michael "Mike"

Bats: Right   Throws: Right   Born 05/25/63

1987 SEASON AND MAJOR-LEAGUE CAREER BATTING TOTALS

	G	AB	H	2B	3B	HR	TB	R	RBI	TBB	IBB	SO	HP	SH	SF	SB	CS	SB%	GDP	AVG	OBP	SLG
87 TEX	78	216	59	8	1	6	87	34	37	31	0	48	1	1	4	3	0	1.00	6	.273	.361	.403
2 YEARS	93	246	69	11	1	7	103	38	38	34	0	55	1	1	4	4	0	1.00	6	.280	.365	.419

	1987 SEASON											FOUR YEAR TOTALS (1984 – 1987)										
	Ave.	OBP	SLG	AB	H	2B	3B	HR	RBI	BB	SO	Ave.	OBP	SLG	AB	H	2B	3B	HR	RBI	BB	SO
Totals	.273	.361	.403	216	59	8	1	6	37	31	48	.279	.364	.417	247	69	11	1	7	38	34	55
vs. Left	.283	.354	.404	99	28	6	0	2	13	11	20	.308	.371	.453	117	36	8	0	3	14	12	23
vs. Right	.265	.367	.402	117	31	2	1	4	24	20	28	.254	.357	.385	130	33	3	1	4	24	22	32
at Home	.321	.402	.459	109	35	6	0	3	23	15	21	.308	.388	.433	120	37	6	0	3	23	16	22
on Road	.224	.320	.346	107	24	2	1	3	14	16	27	.252	.340	.402	127	32	5	1	4	15	18	33
vs. Groundball	.294	.383	.392	102	30	2	1	2	13	16	20	.315	.402	.417	108	34	3	1	2	13	17	21
vs. Flyball	.254	.341	.412	114	29	6	0	4	24	15	28	.252	.333	.417	139	35	8	0	5	25	17	34
vs. Finesse	.304	.379	.384	125	38	4	0	2	12	16	18	.303	.378	.380	142	43	5	0	2	12	18	21
vs. Power	.231	.336	.429	91	21	4	1	4	25	15	30	.248	.344	.467	105	26	6	1	5	26	16	34
on Grass	.290	.371	.432	176	51	7	0	6	36	24	35	.280	.361	.413	189	53	7	0	6	36	25	37
on Artificial Turf	.200	.319	.275	40	8	1	1	0	1	7	13	.276	.373	.431	58	16	4	1	1	2	9	18
Day Games	.353	.455	.618	34	12	0	0	3	9	8	10	.353	.455	.618	34	12	0	0	3	9	8	10
Night Games	.258	.341	.363	182	47	8	1	3	28	23	38	.268	.347	.385	213	57	11	1	4	29	26	45
April	.000	.000	.000	0	0	0	0	0	0	0	0	.000	.000	.000	0	0	0	0	0	0	0	0
May	.000	.000	.000	0	0	0	0	0	0	0	0	.000	.000	.000	0	0	0	0	0	0	0	0
June	.324	.385	.408	71	23	0	0	2	10	7	14	.310	.363	.393	84	26	1	0	2	10	7	17
July	.288	.419	.492	59	17	6	0	2	16	13	13	.288	.419	.492	59	17	6	0	2	16	13	13
August	.233	.310	.383	60	14	1	1	2	10	8	16	.233	.310	.383	60	14	1	1	2	10	8	16
Sept/Oct	.192	.276	.231	26	5	1	0	0	1	3	5	.273	.360	.409	44	12	3	0	1	2	6	9
Bases Empty	.256	.331	.359	117	30	3	0	3	3	12	26	.263	.331	.387	137	36	5	0	4	4	13	30
Leadoff	.255	.314	.362	47	12	2	0	1	1	4	10	.259	.322	.352	54	14	2	0	1	1	5	10
Not Leadoff	.257	.342	.357	70	18	1	0	2	2	8	16	.265	.337	.410	83	22	3	0	3	3	8	20
Runners On	.293	.393	.455	99	29	5	1	3	34	19	22	.300	.400	.455	110	33	6	1	3	34	21	25
First Base Only	.289	.347	.422	45	13	3	0	1	3	4	13	.327	.397	.462	52	17	4	0	1	3	6	14
Scoring Position	.296	.425	.481	54	16	2	1	2	31	15	9	.276	.403	.448	58	16	2	1	2	31	15	11
Late Innings, Close	.409	.462	.682	22	9	1	1	1	8	3	5	.409	.462	.682	44	18	2	2	2	16	6	10

RBI/Opportunities

Scoring Position	25 / 86	(29%)		25 / 90	(28%)
Scoring Position, 2 Out	9 / 38	(24%)		9 / 40	(23%)
On Third, Less than 2 Out	11 / 17	(65%)		11 / 17	(65%)
RBI in close games / RBI Total	23 / 37	(62%)		46 / 38	(121%)

282

Terry Steinbach
Oakland Athletics

The A's have gone through the past few seasons with precious little pitching, and catching at the major league level hasn't been one of their real bright spots, either. So, it was no real surprise that this club, which once traded a manager for a catcher (Chuck Tanner for Manny Sanguillen), has made do with Mickey Tettleton in about half their games in 1985–86 even though he had a career B.A. of .233 with 55 RBI in 498 career at-bats entering 1987.

Then this past spring, the A's gave Terry Steinbach, the Most Valuable Player in the Southern League, a good long look. Terry was just one of the seemingly millions of rookies the A's had around, including Luis Polonia, Dave Otto, Stan Javier, Rob Nelson, Mark McGwire, Walt Weiss, and Greg Cadaret.

Terry made the squad, and came north as part of a catching tandem with Tettleton. The scuttlebutt on Steinbach was that he had a great stick, but his defense was questionable. So, of course, he went out and hit .224 in April. Tony LaRussa stuck by his young receiver, however, and Terry eventually started 96 games for the A's, and hit about .300 from May through August. He finished at .284, trailing only Matt Nokes and B. J. Surhoff among backstops who appeared in 80 games.

As it turned out, the original report was probably correct—9 catchers finished above Steinbach in fielding average. In assists per game, which correlates highly with opposition caught stealing, Terry ranked in the middle of the pack, eighth in the league at .37 per game.

But he can hit. He put together a .316 average with men on base, and hit .250 with men in scoring position. What was particularly surprising was that LaRussa generally hit him in the 6 through 8 slots; in fact, only once did Terry hit higher than sixth in the order. Yet Terry produced more big hits than just about any Athletic. Twenty of his 56 RBIs tied the game or put the A's ahead. Only Canseco had more (38), but Jose also had a lot more total RBIs (113) to trail Steinbach .336 to .357 in ratio of significant RBIs.

Steinbach, a third baseman just three years ago, may not be totally adjusted to catching yet. He hit especially well in the games he didn't catch. As a pinch hitter he was 4 for 7, and as a designated hitter he was 8 for 25 (.320) with a slugging percentage of .600.

It will be interesting to see what the future holds for Terry—the A's went out and signed Ron Hassey in the off-season, and *Baseball America* lists the A's top position player prospect as Scott Hemond, another catcher. But the A's show no interest in shifting Steinbach, and he looks like he can, with a little more experience, settle into the position defensively.

J. Michael Duca

Steinbach, Terry Lee Bats: Right Throws: Right Born 03/02/62

1987 SEASON AND MAJOR-LEAGUE CAREER BATTING TOTALS

	G	AB	H	2B	3B	HR	TB	R	RBI	TBB	IBB	SO	HP	SH	SF	SB	CS	SB%	GDP	AVG	OBP	SLG
87 OAK	122	391	111	16	3	16	181	66	56	32	2	66	9	3	3	1	2	.33	10	.284	.349	.463
2 YEARS	128	406	116	16	3	18	192	69	60	33	2	66	9	3	3	1	2	.33	10	.286	.350	.473

1987 SEASON

	Ave.	OBP	SLG	AB	H	2B	3B	HR	RBI	BB	SO
Totals	.284	.349	.463	391	111	16	3	16	56	32	66
vs. Left	.292	.359	.504	137	40	8	3	5	15	12	22
vs. Right	.280	.344	.441	254	71	8	0	11	41	20	44
at Home	.234	.308	.360	175	41	4	0	6	22	17	24
on Road	.324	.384	.546	216	70	12	3	10	34	15	42
vs. Groundball	.288	.366	.444	198	57	8	1	7	26	21	32
vs. Flyball	.280	.332	.482	193	54	8	2	9	30	11	34
vs. Finesse	.278	.356	.429	205	57	5	1	8	22	21	21
vs. Power	.290	.342	.500	186	54	11	2	8	34	11	45
on Grass	.295	.358	.491	332	98	13	2	16	51	28	55
on Artificial Turf	.220	.303	.305	59	13	3	1	0	5	4	11
Day Games	.350	.410	.504	123	43	7	0	4	18	10	18
Night Games	.254	.321	.444	268	68	9	3	12	38	22	48
April	.224	.304	.429	49	11	2	1	2	9	6	10
May	.404	.472	.617	47	19	2	1	2	9	5	5
June	.230	.319	.361	61	14	2	0	2	6	8	10
July	.293	.310	.549	82	24	7	1	4	12	2	15
August	.299	.356	.403	77	23	2	0	2	12	4	14
Sept/Oct	.267	.360	.440	75	20	1	0	4	8	7	12
Bases Empty	.259	.335	.432	220	57	6	1	10	10	20	36
Leadoff	.282	.358	.447	85	24	5	0	3	3	7	14
Not Leadoff	.244	.320	.422	135	33	1	1	7	7	13	22
Runners On	.316	.368	.503	171	54	10	2	6	46	12	30
First Base Only	.386	.407	.639	83	32	5	2	4	12	3	14
Scoring Position	.250	.337	.375	88	22	5	0	2	34	9	16
Late Innings, Close	.282	.346	.423	71	20	1	0	3	10	7	14

FOUR YEAR TOTALS (1984 – 1987)

	Ave.	OBP	SLG	AB	H	2B	3B	HR	RBI	BB	SO
Totals	.286	.350	.473	406	116	16	3	18	60	33	66
vs. Left	.301	.365	.545	143	43	8	3	7	19	12	22
vs. Right	.278	.342	.433	263	73	8	0	11	41	21	44
at Home	.235	.310	.358	179	42	4	0	6	22	18	24
on Road	.326	.383	.564	227	74	12	3	12	38	15	42
vs. Groundball	.291	.368	.447	199	58	8	1	7	26	21	32
vs. Flyball	.280	.332	.498	207	58	8	2	11	34	12	34
vs. Finesse	.280	.355	.439	214	60	5	1	9	23	21	21
vs. Power	.292	.344	.510	192	56	11	2	9	37	12	45
on Grass	.297	.359	.503	344	102	13	2	18	55	29	55
on Artificial Turf	.226	.304	.306	62	14	3	1	0	5	4	11
Day Games	.350	.410	.504	123	43	7	0	4	18	10	18
Night Games	.258	.324	.459	283	73	9	3	14	42	23	48
April	.224	.304	.429	49	11	2	1	2	9	6	10
May	.404	.472	.617	47	19	2	1	2	9	5	5
June	.230	.319	.361	61	14	2	0	2	6	8	10
July	.293	.310	.549	82	24	7	1	4	12	2	15
August	.299	.356	.403	77	23	2	0	2	12	4	14
Sept/Oct	.278	.363	.489	90	25	1	0	6	12	8	12
Bases Empty	.257	.332	.435	230	59	6	1	11	11	21	36
Leadoff	.289	.360	.478	90	26	5	0	4	4	7	14
Not Leadoff	.236	.314	.407	140	33	1	1	7	7	14	22
Runners On	.324	.374	.523	176	57	10	2	7	49	12	30
First Base Only	.388	.409	.635	85	33	5	2	4	12	3	14
Scoring Position	.264	.346	.418	91	24	5	0	3	37	9	16
Late Innings, Close	.282	.346	.423	142	40	2	0	6	20	14	28

RBI/Opportunities

Scoring Position	29 / 124 (23%)	30 / 127 (24%)
Scoring Position, 2 Out	11 / 61 (18%)	12 / 63 (19%)
On Third, Less than 2 Out	11 / 21 (52%)	11 / 21 (52%)
RBI in close games / RBI Total	36 / 56 (64%)	72 / 60 (120%)

Dave Stewart
Oakland Athletics

Several articles in national publications have justified not choosing Dave Stewart for the Cy Young Award because it took him five tries to win his twentieth game in September. But Dave's accomplishments in 1987 should not be so easily dismissed. His determination and concentration were contagious, and he often inspired the sometimes lethargic A's to have a winning attitude in spite of themselves. Besides, any man who can win twenty games with the 1987 Athletics has really worked his tail off.

Dave was among the top pitchers in the league in several important categories: tied for first in victories and games started, sixth in strikeouts, ninth in ERA, and seventh in innings pitched. Certainly his durability was valued by the A's. He was the only starting pitcher the A's could count on the entire year, their only starter not to miss a turn in the rotation. He failed to reach the sixth inning only five times in 37 games. He was the first Oakland pitcher to pitch over 260 innings since Rick Langford completed 28 games in 1980, and he was the first to exceed 200 strikeouts since Vida Blue fanned 301 in 1971.

Time after time Stewart kept the A's from sinking into an extended losing streak. Twelve of his twenty victories followed losses. He, more than any other Oakland player is responsible for the A's never having a losing streak longer than 5 games.

Stewart was used most often after four days rest, where his record was 13–9. But he did all right in his seven starts on three days rest, as he went 4–2. Dave accomplished all this while averaging less run support per start than the other Oakland pitchers, 4.7 compared to 5.1. In the four games between his nineteenth and twentieth victories, they scored an average of only three runs.

Dave prefers pitching in day games, and the hotter the better. His 1987 record during July and August was 9–2 with an ERA of 3.21. His ERA in other months was 3.95, and August has traditionally been the best month of his career. He sometimes has trouble getting loose in cool weather, and when that happens he can't control his breaking pitches and his fastball becomes fair game.

Dave's value to this organization goes beyond the ballpark. He spends countless hours performing community work in his hometown and has become a very visible public relations asset to the team. Although people outside the Bay Area continue to make jokes about Dave's past, he's done well by this community in the present, and he has earned our respect both on and off the field.

Susan Nelson

Stewart, David Keith "Dave"   Bats: Right   Throws: Right   Born 02/19/57

1987 SEASON AND MAJOR-LEAGUE CAREER PITCHING TOTALS

	G	GS	CG	GF	IP	BFP	H	R	ER	HR	SH	SF	HB	TBB	IBB	SO	WP	Bk	W	L	Pct	ShO	Sv	ERA
87 OAK	37	37	8	0	261	1103	224	121	107	24	7	5	6	105	2	205	11	0	20	13	.606	1	0	3.69
8 YEARS	284	109	17	87	1025	4404	955	488	444	102	46	31	21	415	33	689	50	4	59	53	.527	2	19	3.90

1987: Power, Flyball   1986: Power, Flyball   1985: Power, Flyball   1984: Power, Flyball

1987 SEASON

	G	IP	H	BB	SO	SB	CS	W	L	S	ERA
Totals	37	261.1	224	105	205	32	9	20	13	0	3.65
at Home	18	133.0	105	53	109	15	6	11	6	0	2.84
on Road	19	128.1	119	52	96	17	3	9	7	0	4.56
on Grass	12	84.1	73	25	79	7	4	7	5	0	2.77
on Artificial Turf	25	177.0	151	80	126	25	5	13	8	0	4.12
Day Games	32	230.1	197	91	178	31	8	17	11	0	3.36
Night Games	5	31.0	27	14	27	1	1	3	2	0	6.10
April	5	35.0	34	20	27	4	3	3	2	0	4.11
May	5	34.1	27	14	30	4	1	3	2	0	3.93
June	6	38.2	29	14	34	8	1	3	3	0	3.72
July	6	45.1	34	19	36	8	0	4	0	0	2.58
August	7	50.0	46	15	44	1	2	5	2	0	3.78
Sept/Oct	8	58.0	54	23	34	7	2	2	4	0	4.03

FOUR YEAR TOTALS (1984 – 1987)

	G	IP	H	BB	SO	SB	CS	W	L	S	ERA
Totals	152	701.0	660	302	501	81	23	36	38	4	4.24
at Home	81	386.2	355	160	291	50	12	19	20	1	3.93
on Road	71	314.1	305	142	210	31	11	17	18	3	4.64
on Grass	48	235.0	207	99	184	25	9	14	15	1	3.37
on Artificial Turf	104	466.0	453	203	317	56	14	22	23	3	4.67
Day Games	122	594.2	552	255	423	73	18	31	32	4	4.09
Night Games	30	106.1	108	47	78	8	5	5	6	0	5.16
April	23	81.1	88	46	60	12	3	3	10	2	5.64
May	22	83.0	78	34	60	8	4	6	3	1	4.23
June	29	119.1	106	48	81	16	2	4	6	1	4.37
July	27	118.0	103	57	79	15	1	8	3	0	4.19
August	24	141.1	129	49	113	9	7	9	5	0	3.69
Sept/Oct	27	158.0	156	68	108	21	6	6	11	0	3.99

vs. Opponent Batters	Ave.	OBP	SLG	AB	H	2B	3B	HR	RBI	BB	SO
Totals	.229	.306	.357	980	224	48	3	24	104	105	205
vs. Left	.233	.314	.357	554	129	26	2	13	53	67	119
vs. Right	.223	.294	.357	426	95	22	1	11	51	38	86
Bases Empty	.227	.296	.363	595	135	27	3	16	16	56	127
Leadoff	.221	.289	.398	249	55	13	2	9	9	23	51
Not Leadoff	.231	.300	.338	346	80	14	1	7	7	33	76
Runners On Base	.231	.321	.348	385	89	21	0	8	88	49	78
First Base Only	.240	.339	.409	154	37	11	0	5	17	22	24
Scoring Position	.225	.308	.307	231	52	10	0	3	71	27	54
Late Innings, Close	.240	.330	.400	100	24	4	0	4	12	14	20

vs. Opponent Batters	Ave.	OBP	SLG	AB	H	2B	3B	HR	RBI	BB	SO
Totals	.247	.324	.395	2676	660	126	17	79	316	302	501
vs. Left	.256	.342	.401	1415	362	65	10	40	167	188	255
vs. Right	.236	.302	.389	1261	298	61	7	39	149	114	246
Bases Empty	.249	.314	.409	1582	394	74	13	51	51	147	303
Leadoff	.239	.300	.399	664	159	29	7	21	21	56	119
Not Leadoff	.256	.324	.416	918	235	45	6	30	30	91	184
Runners On Base	.243	.338	.375	1094	266	52	4	28	265	155	198
First Base Only	.273	.374	.411	411	112	22	1	11	36	66	54
Scoring Position	.225	.315	.353	683	154	30	3	17	229	89	144
Late Innings, Close	.232	.325	.368	323	75	12	1	10	35	45	49

RBI/Opportunities

Scoring Position	61 / 303 (20%)	192 / 915 (21%)
Scoring Position, 2 Out	22 / 138 (16%)	64 / 415 (15%)
On Third, Less than 2 Out	25 / 45 (56%)	77 / 157 (49%)
RBI in close games / RBI Total	69 / 104 (66%)	189 / 316 (60%)

Dave Stieb
Toronto Blue Jays

A graph of Dave Stieb's career since 1985 bears a striking resemblance to a daily graph of last October's Dow Jones Industrial Averages. Innings pitched are down from 265 to 205 to 185. Strikeouts have dropped from 167 to 127 to 115. ERA is up from 2.48 to 4.74 to 4.09.

To be fair, 1987 was a much better year for Stieb than 1986. He allowed 75 fewer hits in only 20 less innings. He cut 65 points off his ERA in a year where the league average rose 28. He allowed 13 fewer homers in a year where taters were springing up everywhere. But Dave never looked like the pitcher that he was only three years ago, either. What he *did* look like was a man who once averaged 270 innings pitched, 7.2 innings per start and 13 complete games for four straight years ('82–'85). There are an awful lot of fastball/slider pitchers who have broken down under much less strain. Dave has to hurl 225 innings in 1988 in order to guarantee his contract for '89–'91; that doesn't look too likely at his present rate.

What will he have to do to get those extra 40 innings? First, he'll have to reduce the walks. In 1985, Dave walked 3.26 men per nine innings. In 1986, he walked 3.82. Last year, he walked 4.23. The rising figures suggest that even Dave realizes that he's lost something off his pitches. He used to just fire the ball in there (in 1982, he walked only 2.34 men per game); now he's nibbling more and more. While the drops in hits and homers made up for it this year, walking one man every two innings is not a habit that you want to get into.

Then he'll have to learn how to pitch in the daytime. From 1984–86, Stieb was 27–20 with a 2.92 ERA under the lights and 10–13 with a 3.89 ERA when the sun was shining. In 1987, his breakdowns were *really* like night and day: 2–3, 6.60 during the day; 11–6, 3.28 at night.

He'll also have to stay healthy. Dave's slider induces periodic bouts of tendinitis, which renders his arm sliderless. Since he looks like he'll have to make the transition from power pitcher to finesse pitcher, it might help if he begins working on another pitch that's easier on his arm.

Finally, he has to grow up. Stieb has spent his career glowering at teammates who make errors, snarling at umpires who won't give him a close pitch, growling about lack of support and having tantrums when he makes a mistake. When he had the ability to blow everyone away, it was merely an exasperating sidelight—now, when his success depends both on good support and a cool head in a tight situation, it's self-indulgent, self-destructive behavior. There are people in Toronto who feel that, like Steve Rogers in his glory days with the Expos, Stieb's behavior affects the people around him—that no one breaks their necks to make him look good. It may not be true—but a new attitude certainly wouldn't hurt Stieb, either.

Mike FitzGerald, Tony Formo and Darren Peterson

Stieb, David Andrew "Dave"   Bats: Right   Throws: Right   Born 07/22/57

1987 SEASON AND MAJOR-LEAGUE CAREER PITCHING TOTALS

	G	GS	CG	GF	IP	BFP	H	R	ER	HR	SH	SF	HB	TBB	IBB	SO	WP	Bk	W	L	Pct	ShO	Sv	ERA
87 TOR	33	31	3	1	185	789	164	92	84	16	5	5	7	87	4	115	4	0	13	9	.591	1	0	4.09
9 YEARS	292	285	88	3	2044	8523	1837	865	774	167	70	51	82	718	30	1184	35	8	115	101	.532	22	1	3.41

1987: Power, Flyball   1986: Power, Groundball   1985: Power, Groundball   1984: Power, Flyball

1987 SEASON

	G	IP	H	BB	SO	SB	CS	W	L	S	ERA
Totals	33	185.0	164	87	115	12	13	13	9	0	4.09
at Home	14	77.2	70	40	51	4	6	5	4	0	4.98
on Road	19	107.1	94	47	64	8	7	8	5	0	3.44
on Grass	10	45.0	46	23	34	1	3	2	3	0	6.60
on Artificial Turf	23	140.0	118	64	81	11	10	11	6	0	3.28
Day Games	15	82.1	77	37	55	5	7	6	4	0	3.28
Night Games	18	102.2	87	50	60	7	6	7	5	0	4.73
April	4	19.0	25	12	16	3	5	0	2	0	6.63
May	6	33.0	33	16	15	3	2	3	1	0	4.09
June	5	27.0	24	16	12	2	0	3	2	0	4.00
July	5	38.0	26	10	25	3	2	3	0	0	2.61
August	6	43.1	34	12	33	1	4	4	2	0	3.32
Sept/Oct	7	24.2	22	21	14	0	0	0	2	0	5.84

vs. Opponent Batters	Ave.	OBP	SLG	AB	H	2B	3B	HR	RBI	BB	SO
Totals	.239	.329	.377	685	164	38	4	16	80	87	115
vs. Left	.242	.338	.390	364	88	20	2	10	47	53	57
vs. Right	.237	.319	.361	321	76	18	2	6	33	34	58
Bases Empty	.217	.311	.370	405	88	24	1	12	12	53	74
Leadoff	.225	.320	.428	173	39	14	0	7	7	23	28
Not Leadoff	.211	.304	.328	232	49	10	1	5	5	30	46
Runners On Base	.271	.355	.386	280	76	14	3	4	68	34	41
First Base Only	.254	.343	.356	118	30	4	1	2	7	13	15
Scoring Position	.284	.363	.407	162	46	10	2	2	61	21	26
Late Innings, Close	.056	.105	.056	36	2	0	0	0	1	2	9

FOUR YEAR TOTALS (1984 – 1987)

	G	IP	H	BB	SO	SB	CS	W	L	S	ERA
Totals	141	922.0	824	358	607	45	41	50	42	1	3.41
at Home	65	437.0	415	165	279	23	24	27	19	0	3.54
on Road	76	485.0	409	193	328	22	17	23	23	1	3.28
on Grass	47	283.0	288	105	189	10	13	12	16	1	4.29
on Artificial Turf	94	639.0	536	253	418	35	28	38	26	0	2.99
Day Games	57	361.0	316	157	244	18	14	16	17	0	3.44
Night Games	84	561.0	508	201	363	27	27	34	25	1	3.37
April	19	114.2	114	50	72	5	8	5	7	0	4.08
May	24	163.2	135	68	113	7	11	11	6	0	3.24
June	23	157.1	140	60	91	8	2	8	8	0	3.20
July	23	150.0	123	49	86	11	9	10	4	1	2.70
August	25	173.0	145	53	128	4	7	9	6	0	3.43
Sept/Oct	27	163.1	167	78	117	10	4	7	11	0	3.91

vs. Opponent Batters	Ave.	OBP	SLG	AB	H	2B	3B	HR	RBI	BB	SO
Totals	.240	.313	.371	3428	824	150	20	86	345	358	607
vs. Left	.244	.322	.378	1850	451	79	13	48	196	214	276
vs. Right	.236	.302	.362	1578	373	71	7	38	149	144	331
Bases Empty	.232	.309	.377	2003	465	88	13	59	59	222	349
Leadoff	.243	.319	.406	857	208	43	9	29	29	95	147
Not Leadoff	.224	.302	.356	1146	257	45	8	30	30	127	202
Runners On Base	.252	.318	.362	1425	359	62	7	27	286	136	258
First Base Only	.264	.326	.386	671	177	30	2	16	45	59	108
Scoring Position	.241	.311	.341	754	182	32	5	11	241	77	150
Late Innings, Close	.275	.339	.433	363	100	19	1	12	45	35	62

RBI/Opportunities

Scoring Position	57 / 223 (26%)	212 / 1004 (21%)
Scoring Position, 2 Out	21 / 99 (21%)	82 / 458 (18%)
On Third, Less than 2 Out	21 / 43 (49%)	76 / 174 (44%)
RBI in close games / RBI Total	54 / 80 (68%)	272 / 345 (79%)

Kurt Stillwell
Cincinnati Reds

The battle to replace Davey Concepcion at shortstop left one casualty: Kurt Stillwell. As a 20-year-old rookie in 1986, the switch-hitter struggled at the plate and in the field. By season's end he had lost the shortstop job to former Olympian Barry Larkin. Stillwell played winter ball and entered the 1987 spring camp with hopes of regaining his starting job, but he just made the roster as the fifth infielder.

A knee injury to Larkin in the first week of the season gave Stillwell another chance to prove himself. Despite playing well in the field and hitting over .300, Stillwell drew pine time when Larkin returned from the DL. Not long after, Buddy Bell pulled a hamstring and Kurt was forced into action. He acquitted himself well, despite no previous experience playing third base at any level of organized baseball. When Bell returned to health, Stillwell returned to his field-level seat. Next, a terrible knee injury ended Ron Oester's season, and Stillwell learned another new position at the major league level. By September, he lost this job to Jeff Treadway. If the season had just been a bit longer, maybe Pete would have let Kurt lose the first base job, too.

The Reds' mishandling of this prospect was unusual and confusing. He arrived in the major leagues as the heir apparent to Concepcion, but over the next two years became no more than a utility infielder. With less than 250 games in the minors, the Reds had enough faith in Stillwell to give him a shot at taking over for one of the best shortstops in recent history, but after 674 big league at bats, they decided he wasn't good enough to crack their lineup.

Stillwell's play can't be considered disappointing by any stretch of the imagination. Sure, he struggled early, but he was only three years out of Thousand Oaks High School when he was thrust into the spotlight. He was unfortunate enough to be forced to mature rapidly at a time when the Reds had an abundance of quality young players pushing for playing time. Larkin and Treadway are both older than Stillwell and had more post high school experience. The Reds realized Stillwell was too good to waste on the bench and traded him to help bolster their woeful starting staff, arguably the worst in the National League (removing the stats of the pure relief pitchers left a starting and double-duty staff ERA of 4.62, the equal of the worst staff in the league).

Danny Jackson should give Cincinnati a lot of innings; only 8 NL pitchers threw more innings than Jackson, although his innings will obviously drop in the DH-less league. Meanwhile, Kurt Stillwell will now ply his trade in front of Bill James; soon, all America will know about him.

Sean Lahman

Stillwell, Kurt Andrew   Bats: Both   Throws: Right   Born 06/04/65

1987 SEASON AND MAJOR-LEAGUE CAREER BATTING TOTALS

	G	AB	H	2B	3B	HR	TB	R	RBI	TBB	IBB	SO	HP	SH	SF	SB	CS	SB%	GDP	AVG	OBP	SLG
87 CIN	131	395	102	20	7	4	148	54	33	32	2	50	2	2	2	4	6	.40	5	.258	.316	.375
2 YEARS	235	674	166	26	8	4	220	85	59	62	3	97	4	6	2	10	8	.56	10	.246	.313	.326

	1987 SEASON											FOUR YEAR TOTALS (1984 – 1987)										
	Ave.	OBP	SLG	AB	H	2B	3B	HR	RBI	BB	SO	Ave.	OBP	SLG	AB	H	2B	3B	HR	RBI	BB	SO
Totals	.258	.316	.375	395	102	20	7	4	33	32	50	.246	.313	.326	674	166	26	8	4	59	62	97
vs. Left	.227	.286	.289	97	22	2	2	0	9	6	16	.235	.324	.284	183	43	5	2	0	16	22	30
vs. Right	.268	.325	.403	298	80	18	5	4	24	26	34	.251	.308	.342	491	123	21	6	4	43	40	67
at Home	.260	.323	.433	150	39	9	4	3	12	14	22	.239	.310	.339	301	72	13	4	3	24	29	51
on Road	.257	.311	.339	245	63	11	3	1	21	18	28	.252	.315	.316	373	94	13	4	1	35	33	46
vs. Groundball	.275	.317	.370	189	52	11	2	1	14	11	23	.260	.321	.336	339	88	17	3	1	28	29	46
vs. Flyball	.243	.314	.379	206	50	9	5	3	19	21	27	.233	.305	.316	335	78	9	5	3	31	33	51
vs. Finesse	.269	.332	.423	208	56	11	6	3	17	20	22	.254	.325	.360	342	87	15	6	3	24	36	51
vs. Power	.246	.297	.321	187	46	9	1	1	16	12	28	.238	.300	.292	332	79	11	2	1	35	26	46
on Grass	.225	.294	.318	129	29	7	1	1	11	11	16	.219	.292	.276	228	50	8	1	1	20	22	28
on Artificial Turf	.274	.326	.402	266	73	13	6	3	22	21	34	.260	.323	.352	446	116	18	7	3	39	40	69
Day Games	.223	.303	.354	130	29	4	2	3	12	15	17	.216	.305	.293	232	50	5	2	3	20	29	42
Night Games	.275	.322	.385	265	73	16	5	1	21	17	33	.262	.317	.344	442	116	21	6	1	39	33	55
April	.314	.377	.486	70	22	4	1	2	13	6	8	.308	.370	.440	91	28	4	1	2	14	8	14
May	.288	.360	.318	66	19	2	0	0	4	7	7	.240	.339	.288	104	25	3	1	0	7	15	17
June	.211	.237	.316	76	16	3	1	1	7	3	11	.185	.234	.252	119	22	3	1	1	8	8	22
July	.250	.274	.367	60	15	3	2	0	2	2	7	.243	.282	.324	111	27	5	2	0	9	6	15
August	.225	.310	.360	89	20	5	2	1	5	11	12	.241	.322	.329	158	38	7	2	1	11	19	18
Sept/Oct	.294	.351	.441	34	10	3	1	0	2	3	5	.286	.330	.352	91	26	4	1	0	10	6	11
Bases Empty	.231	.291	.319	238	55	8	5	1	1	19	25	.224	.295	.286	398	89	12	5	1	1	39	56
Leadoff	.250	.333	.338	80	20	4	0	1	1	10	6	.204	.288	.263	152	31	6	0	1	1	18	24
Not Leadoff	.222	.268	.310	158	35	4	5	0	0	9	19	.236	.299	.301	246	58	6	5	0	0	21	32
Runners On	.299	.353	.459	157	47	12	2	3	32	13	25	.279	.334	.384	276	77	14	3	3	58	23	41
First Base Only	.338	.373	.577	71	24	7	2	2	8	4	9	.277	.314	.438	112	31	8	2	2	8	6	16
Scoring Position	.267	.337	.360	86	23	5	0	1	24	9	16	.280	.348	.348	164	46	6	1	1	50	17	25
Late Innings, Close	.250	.303	.309	68	17	2	1	0	8	6	10	.223	.273	.273	121	27	4	1	0	16	9	22

RBI/Opportunities

Scoring Position	22 / 117 (19%)	47 / 226 (21%)
Scoring Position, 2 Out	10 / 52 (19%)	23 / 106 (22%)
On Third, Less than 2 Out	6 / 15 (40%)	12 / 35 (34%)
RBI in close games / RBI Total	18 / 33 (55%)	36 / 59 (61%)

Les Straker
Minnesota Twins

Beginning in April as the fifth starter behind Bert Blyleven, Frank Viola, Mark Portugal, and Mike Smithson, Les Straker finished the year with three post-season starts. Used prudently, the 28-year-old Venezuelan right-hander accumulated only 154 1/3 innings in 31 games.

Last spring, attempting to minimize the effect on his bullpen of having two inexperienced starters pitching back-to-back, Tom Kelly placed Smithson (a potential inning eater) between Portugal and Straker—a reasonable move that upset future minor leaguer Smithson. Lester was also matched up with early season off-days in order to maintain a regular schedule for Blyleven and Viola. When Portugal and Smithson moved on to the AAA Portland Beavers, they were replaced by an over-age Steve Carlton, an over-used Juan Berenguer, an over-equipped Joe Niekro, and an over-matched group of minor leaguers. Through it all, Straker persisted, and Kelly stayed true to a five-man rotation.

This devotion to a five-man carousel, including several less than adequate pitchers, was almost certainly influenced by Kelly's experience as the third base coach for the '84 Twins. Billy Gardner's late season four-man rotation brought the team's three best pitchers (Viola, Smithson, and Butcher) to a late season pennant race with tired arms. The collapse reached legendary proportions in the final series at Cleveland and left an indelible impression on everyone involved. Kelly avoided that scenario and had his three best starters available for a strong October showing.

Kelly pulled it off by taking advantage of playing in the AL West. Treating his team's leads as an opportunity to keep his best two starters rested, he battled mediocrity with mediocrity. Because he did not live in fear of falling out of the race and because he recognized the opportunity this presented, Kelly received the ultimate dividend.

Kelly was tentative about placing Straker on the pitching merry-go-round and watched him closely for signs of motion sickness. Les rarely went beyond six innings and was occasionally pulled from the starting rotation. Some excellent games during the stretch drive eventually established him as the Twins #3 starter.

Whether Kelly can develop young pitchers will probably determine the length of his managerial tenure. Much of the Twins future success depends on how some of the much publicized young arms in the organization's minor league system perform on their arrival in the majors. The care taken with Straker (not young; but, a rookie nevertheless) created the impression that he may be able to work well with more talented newcomers. Unfortunately, from a group that included Joe Klink, Mark Portugal, Roy Smith, and Allan Anderson, Kelly was unable match his performance with Straker. To be sure, even moderate success with one of five such pitchers was encouraging.

Bill Jensen

Straker, Lester Paul (Bolnalda) "Les" Bats: Right Throws: Right Born 10/10/59

1987 SEASON AND MAJOR-LEAGUE CAREER PITCHING TOTALS

	G	GS	CG	GF	IP	BFP	H	R	ER	HR	SH	SF	HB	TBB	IBB	SO	WP	Bk	W	L	Pct	ShO	Sv	ERA
87 MIN	31	26	1	1	154	656	150	79	75	24	6	6	2	59	6	76	2	5	8	10	.444	0	0	4.38
1 YEAR	31	26	1	1	154	656	150	79	75	24	6	6	2	59	6	76	2	5	8	10	.444	0	0	4.38

1987: Finesse, Groundball

	1987 SEASON											FOUR YEAR TOTALS (1984 – 1987)										
	G	IP	H	BB	SO	SB	CS	W	L	S	ERA	G	IP	H	BB	SO	SB	CS	W	L	S	ERA
Totals	31	154.1	150	59	76	20	10	8	10	0	4.37	31	154.1	150	59	76	20	10	8	10	0	4.37
at Home	13	67.2	67	22	39	9	1	6	3	0	4.12	13	67.2	67	22	39	9	1	6	3	0	4.12
on Road	18	86.2	83	37	37	11	9	2	7	0	4.57	18	86.2	83	37	37	11	9	2	7	0	4.57
on Grass	9	40.1	45	14	20	3	3	1	2	0	5.13	9	40.1	45	14	20	3	3	1	2	0	5.13
on Artificial Turf	22	114.0	105	45	56	17	7	7	8	0	4.11	22	114.0	105	45	56	17	7	7	8	0	4.11
Day Games	12	69.1	61	27	30	6	5	2	6	0	3.89	12	69.1	61	27	30	6	5	2	6	0	3.89
Night Games	19	85.0	89	32	46	14	5	6	4	0	4.76	19	85.0	89	32	46	14	5	6	4	0	4.76
April	3	13.0	9	7	9	4	1	1	0	0	2.08	3	13.0	9	7	9	4	1	1	0	0	2.08
May	5	24.1	24	14	13	3	2	1	2	0	4.81	5	24.1	24	14	13	3	2	1	2	0	4.81
June	7	30.0	33	8	14	3	2	1	3	0	4.20	7	30.0	33	8	14	3	2	1	3	0	4.20
July	5	27.1	26	11	13	3	2	2	1	0	4.94	5	27.1	26	11	13	3	2	2	1	0	4.94
August	5	28.1	29	10	9	3	1	1	3	0	5.40	5	28.1	29	10	9	3	1	1	3	0	5.40
Sept/Oct	6	31.1	29	9	18	4	2	2	1	0	3.73	6	31.1	29	9	18	4	2	2	1	0	3.73

vs. Opponent Batters	Ave.	OBP	SLG	AB	H	2B	3B	HR	RBI	BB	SO	Ave.	OBP	SLG	AB	H	2B	3B	HR	RBI	BB	SO
Totals	.257	.325	.443	583	150	22	7	24	64	59	76	.257	.325	.443	583	150	22	7	24	64	59	76
vs. Left	.265	.338	.489	321	85	12	6	16	40	36	45	.265	.338	.489	321	85	12	6	16	40	36	45
vs. Right	.248	.308	.385	262	65	10	1	8	24	23	31	.248	.308	.385	262	65	10	1	8	24	23	31
Bases Empty	.272	.336	.456	364	99	13	6	14	14	34	45	.272	.336	.456	364	99	13	6	14	14	34	45
Leadoff	.265	.331	.411	151	40	7	0	5	5	15	16	.265	.331	.411	151	40	7	0	5	5	15	16
Not Leadoff	.277	.339	.488	213	59	6	6	9	9	19	29	.277	.339	.488	213	59	6	6	9	9	19	29
Runners On Base	.233	.307	.420	219	51	9	1	10	50	25	31	.233	.307	.420	219	51	9	1	10	50	25	31
First Base Only	.250	.324	.410	100	25	4	0	4	9	10	12	.250	.324	.410	100	25	4	0	4	9	10	12
Scoring Position	.218	.293	.429	119	26	5	1	6	41	15	19	.218	.293	.429	119	26	5	1	6	41	15	19
Late Innings, Close	.421	.452	.974	38	16	2	2	5	10	3	2	.421	.452	.974	38	16	2	2	5	10	3	2

RBI/Opportunities

Scoring Position	32 / 160 (20%)	32 / 160 (20%)
Scoring Position, 2 Out	10 / 66 (15%)	10 / 66 (15%)
On Third, Less than 2 Out	12 / 29 (41%)	12 / 29 (41%)
RBI in close games / RBI Total	50 / 64 (78%)	50 / 64 (78%)

Darryl Strawberry
New York Mets

Darryl Strawberry had a great year in 1987. Thirty-nine homeruns, 104 runs batted in, 36 stolen bases, a slugging percentage of .583 and 97 walks add up to a great year. Combine this with a new aggressiveness on the base paths, an outstanding throwing arm and new-found maturity and you have the makings of immense but realistic expectations.

Strawberry (a great "ballplayer-type" name) has always been weighted down with obnoxious predictions for his future greatness. But now, after five years in the major leagues, at 26 years old, we can reasonably assess what Darryl might do over the rest of his career.

He decreased his strikeouts per at-bat by 7 percent in 1987, a direct result of laying off bad pitches. He did not swing at the low, outside curve as much as in previous years and it caused a predictable ripple effect. He established career heights in all major categories. Since ballplayers do not "unlearn" the strike zone, it is not unreasonable to assume Strawberry will maintain or improve his current level of production for several years.

Thirty-six stolen bases grew from a green light from the manager and very thoughtful, bold base running. Strawberry has always had the speed to steal thirty bases and take the extra base, but he never really knew *how*. Something clicked this year, something along the lines of, "Hey, I'm *fast*—I can take these bases." And it certainly is a joy to watch a ballplayer go from first to third in just a few long strides.,

Darryl is not Dave Winfield in the field, but he certainly is a very good rightfielder. He plays too deep, but for some reason all Met outfielders play too deep. Darryl uses deep positioning as a safety valve against the fear of balls getting by him. Only a concerted effort by Darryl and his coaches will give him the confidence to play shallow, which will allow him to realize his potential as a fielder. In the meantime, his wondrous athletic ability and the howitzer connected to his left shoulder will have to do.

Most important, the growing up process, in which a great athlete becomes a great baseball player, has taken hold with Strawberry. It may have been Dwight's troubles. It may have been Davey Johnson correctly treating him like a 14-year-old when he overslept in Chicago. It may have been Lee Mazzilli lambasting him after he "called in sick" for a key July game versus St. Louis. Whatever "it" was, it showed Strawberry his importance to the Mets. In the second half of the season he played hurt, carried the team from his long overdue cleanup slot and he emerged as a leader on the field.

Here's hoping that Darryl Strawberry can live up to the expectations he has created for himself. Not the expectations of others.

Joe Nunziata III

Strawberry, Darryl Eugene

Bats: Left   Throws: Left   Born 03/02/62

1987 SEASON AND MAJOR-LEAGUE CAREER BATTING TOTALS

	G	AB	H	2B	3B	HR	TB	R	RBI	TBB	IBB	SO	HP	SH	SF	SB	CS	SB%	GDP	AVG	OBP	SLG
87 NYN	154	532	151	32	5	39	310	108	104	97	13	122	7	0	4	36	12	.75	4	.284	.398	.583
5 YEARS	670	2342	622	116	25	147	1229	400	447	364	59	618	18	1	22	136	49	.74	30	.266	.366	.525

	1987 SEASON										FOUR YEAR TOTALS (1984 – 1987)									
	Ave.	OBP	SLG	AB	H	2B	3B	HR	RBI	BB	SO	Ave.	OBP	SLG	AB	H	2B	3B	HR	RBI	BB	SO
Totals	.283	.398	.582	533	151	32	5	39	104	97	122	.267	.372	.527	1923	514	101	18	121	373	317	491
vs. Left	.248	.330	.517	230	57	10	2	16	49	25	58	.234	.314	.438	740	173	25	6	38	127	81	214
vs. Right	.310	.446	.630	303	94	22	3	23	55	72	64	.288	.406	.583	1183	341	76	12	83	246	236	277
at Home	.322	.418	.629	264	85	17	2	20	56	40	57	.266	.363	.514	905	241	51	7	53	177	137	230
on Road	.245	.380	.535	269	66	15	3	19	48	57	65	.268	.379	.539	1018	273	50	11	68	196	180	261
vs. Groundball	.300	.416	.551	207	62	14	1	12	32	40	44	.271	.377	.482	882	239	48	9	40	142	147	209
vs. Flyball	.273	.387	.601	326	89	18	4	27	72	57	78	.264	.368	.566	1041	275	53	9	81	231	170	282
vs. Finesse	.302	.419	.629	291	88	15	4	24	63	56	51	.288	.390	.553	1037	299	63	11	63	198	171	204
vs. Power	.260	.373	.525	242	63	17	1	15	41	41	71	.243	.351	.498	886	215	38	7	58	175	146	287
on Grass	.299	.408	.597	375	112	20	4	28	71	66	80	.271	.372	.514	1314	356	69	11	76	250	209	335
on Artificial Turf	.247	.375	.544	158	39	12	1	11	33	31	42	.259	.371	.557	609	158	32	7	45	123	108	156
Day Games	.271	.404	.552	181	49	11	2	12	32	39	37	.266	.367	.521	703	187	35	6	44	141	108	165
Night Games	.290	.395	.597	352	102	21	3	27	72	58	85	.268	.374	.531	1220	327	66	12	77	232	209	326
April	.303	.369	.618	76	23	7	1	5	17	8	14	.294	.370	.571	282	83	19	1	19	55	34	61
May	.259	.422	.635	85	22	2	0	10	16	24	24	.233	.351	.437	270	63	12	2	13	35	49	71
June	.241	.358	.532	79	19	6	1	5	15	13	18	.264	.389	.515	235	62	16	2	13	41	47	56
July	.292	.432	.483	89	26	4	2	3	10	21	21	.280	.383	.545	382	107	20	6	23	79	63	104
August	.276	.379	.571	98	27	3	1	8	18	15	25	.239	.355	.453	364	87	12	3	20	63	64	100
Sept/Oct	.321	.416	.642	106	34	10	0	8	28	16	20	.287	.384	.618	390	112	22	4	33	100	60	99
Bases Empty	.260	.356	.493	296	77	15	3	16	16	39	71	.240	.334	.484	1019	245	53	9	59	59	138	268
Leadoff	.244	.328	.500	160	39	9	1	10	10	17	39	.229	.322	.502	476	109	23	7	31	31	62	113
Not Leadoff	.279	.387	.485	136	38	6	2	6	6	22	32	.250	.345	.468	543	136	30	2	28	28	76	155
Runners On	.312	.447	.692	237	74	17	2	23	88	58	51	.298	.414	.576	904	269	48	9	62	314	179	223
First Base Only	.370	.471	.770	100	37	8	1	10	23	18	21	.324	.391	.621	398	129	27	5	27	68	43	82
Scoring Position	.270	.431	.635	137	37	9	1	13	65	40	30	.277	.429	.542	506	140	21	4	35	246	136	141
Late Innings, Close	.202	.340	.333	84	17	2	0	3	5	17	22	.237	.352	.426	329	78	12	1	16	49	58	100

RBI/Opportunities

Scoring Position	44 / 204 (22%)	188 / 776 (24%)	
Scoring Position, 2 Out	16 / 97 (16%)	74 / 393 (19%)	
On Third, Less than 2 Out	11 / 26 (42%)	64 / 131 (49%)	
RBI in close games / RBI Total	69 / 104 (66%)	243 / 373 (65%)	

Franklin Stubbs
Los Angeles Dodgers

Whenever I see Franklin Stubbs, I am always reminded of a character from *The Twilight Zone* named Franklin that was haunted by visions of a slot machine that pursued him, uttering his name in a deep, harsh, mechanical sound punctuated by the clinks of ringing coins, "Frank-linnnn . . . Frank-linnnn." If Stubbs does not raise his offensive production soon, he too will be haunted by visions of the wealth that could have been his.

Franklin Stubbs is at a critical moment in his career. He turned twenty seven and after receiving significant playing time in both 1986 and 1987, he has not demonstrated the abilities that would earn him a full-time job. Unless he can significantly improve his average, he just does not hit well enough to justify playing him at either first base or left field, his two positions.

Stubbs does have other offensive abilities that together with a reasonable batting average, say .270 to .280, would make him an asset to the offense-starved Dodgers. He walks about once for every ten at-bats and has some power, being capable of hitting 20 to 25 home runs over a full season. However, he's no Gorman Thomas whose eye and power are so good that he can support his weak average. He steals some bases at a high percentage of success (17 out of 19 over the last two seasons). The full package with a good average would resemble Andy Van Slyke, the kind of player that can really help a team but often gets ignored because he has many good skills but no outstanding skills. The big difference is that Van Slyke is an excellent fielder, while Stubbs is average to above-average at both left field and first.

But no one plays leftfielders or first basemen for their gloves. The key to improving Stubbs' performance would seem to lie on the road. He hits better in Dodger Stadium, one of the toughest places to hit in the National League, than on the road. He also fits the pattern of a player trying too hard to hit home runs; he strikes out a lot and hits very few doubles. His minor league record does not encourage optimism about his ability to overcome his limitations and break through to a higher level of performance. Although he moved through the Dodger system quickly, he never had a dominant offensive season in the minors. If he fails to show any significant improvement in the first months of 1988, one of the slew of other Dodger outfield prospects (Gonzalez, Devereaux, Chris Gwynn) seems likely to replace Stubbs and leave him haunted with visions of what could have been. Frank-linnnn . . . Frank-linnn . . .

Jim Morrow

Stubbs, Franklin Lee

Bats: Left **Throws: Left** **Born 10/21/60**

1987 SEASON AND MAJOR-LEAGUE CAREER BATTING TOTALS

	G	AB	H	2B	3B	HR	TB	R	RBI	TBB	IBB	SO	HP	SH	SF	SB	CS	SB%	GDP	AVG	OBP	SLG
87 LA	129	386	90	16	3	16	160	48	52	31	9	85	1	3	2	8	1	.89	7	.233	.290	.415
4 YEARS	358	1032	229	29	7	47	413	125	129	92	23	258	3	10	5	17	4	.81	16	.222	.286	.400

	1987 SEASON											FOUR YEAR TOTALS (1984 – 1987)										
	Ave.	OBP	SLG	AB	H	2B	3B	HR	RBI	BB	SO	Ave.	OBP	SLG	AB	H	2B	3B	HR	RBI	BB	SO
Totals	.233	.290	.415	386	90	16	3	16	52	31	85	.222	.286	.400	1032	229	29	7	47	129	92	258
vs. Left	.186	.205	.186	86	16	0	0	0	5	1	22	.204	.224	.283	230	47	3	0	5	17	5	50
vs. Right	.247	.313	.480	300	74	16	3	16	47	30	63	.227	.303	.434	802	182	26	7	42	112	87	208
at Home	.167	.221	.287	209	35	7	0	6	21	14	49	.213	.277	.373	520	111	13	2	22	63	47	131
on Road	.311	.371	.565	177	55	9	3	10	31	17	36	.230	.295	.428	512	118	16	5	25	66	45	127
vs. Groundball	.248	.307	.455	165	41	8	1	8	24	13	32	.262	.317	.479	474	124	14	4	27	72	37	97
vs. Flyball	.222	.278	.385	221	49	8	2	8	28	18	53	.188	.261	.333	558	105	15	3	20	57	55	161
vs. Finesse	.213	.256	.376	202	43	11	2	6	24	11	28	.232	.285	.405	556	129	22	4	22	75	41	109
vs. Power	.255	.327	.457	184	47	5	1	10	28	20	57	.210	.287	.395	476	100	7	3	25	54	51	149
on Grass	.205	.268	.380	297	61	11	1	13	39	25	69	.208	.273	.377	777	162	20	3	35	96	70	201
on Artificial Turf	.326	.368	.528	89	29	5	2	3	13	6	16	.263	.326	.471	255	67	9	4	12	33	22	57
Day Games	.264	.322	.462	106	28	5	2	4	12	9	24	.237	.302	.425	320	76	10	4	14	37	30	71
Night Games	.221	.279	.396	280	62	11	1	12	40	22	61	.215	.279	.389	712	153	19	3	33	92	62	187
April	.301	.348	.602	83	25	4	0	7	17	6	24	.234	.288	.490	145	34	4	0	11	27	11	52
May	.277	.326	.361	83	23	4	0	1	6	6	18	.263	.324	.432	190	50	7	2	7	21	17	50
June	.203	.268	.378	74	15	4	0	3	13	7	15	.249	.325	.469	209	52	7	0	13	34	24	40
July	.221	.294	.455	77	17	2	2	4	8	7	10	.225	.284	.424	231	52	5	4	11	25	18	46
August	.034	.094	.069	29	1	1	0	0	1	2	8	.114	.173	.171	123	14	1	0	2	3	9	37
Sept/Oct	.225	.279	.375	40	9	1	1	1	7	3	10	.201	.272	.321	134	27	5	1	3	19	13	33
Bases Empty	.194	.247	.352	227	44	8	2	8	8	15	55	.211	.255	.385	592	125	14	4	27	27	34	136
Leadoff	.190	.261	.357	84	16	3	1	3	3	7	18	.241	.279	.427	232	56	6	2	11	11	11	41
Not Leadoff	.196	.238	.350	143	28	5	1	5	5	8	37	.192	.240	.358	360	69	8	2	16	16	23	95
Runners On	.289	.350	.503	159	46	8	1	8	44	16	30	.236	.324	.420	440	104	15	3	20	102	58	122
First Base Only	.303	.361	.485	66	20	3	0	3	7	6	8	.275	.327	.451	182	50	5	0	9	19	14	44
Scoring Position	.280	.343	.516	93	26	5	1	5	37	10	22	.209	.322	.399	258	54	10	3	11	83	44	78
Late Innings, Close	.175	.278	.349	63	11	2	0	3	8	9	21	.201	.318	.367	169	34	3	2	7	20	29	53

RBI/Opportunities

	1987			Four Year		
Scoring Position	28 /	124	(23%)	65 /	357	(18%)
Scoring Position, 2 Out	13 /	61	(21%)	28 /	172	(16%)
On Third, Less than 2 Out	7 /	20	(35%)	20 /	54	(37%)
RBI in close games / RBI Total	41 /	52	(79%)	93 /	129	(72%)

B. J. Surhoff
Milwaukee Brewers

When was the last time that there's been a more wonderful crop of rookie catchers? You can't help but think that there is a future superstar in the group of Nokes, Steinbach, Santiago and Surhoff. And not a moment too soon.

If you compare their 1987 stats, you might think that Surhoff is the runt of the litter. But, ten years from now, you'll see that he turned out to be the cream of the crop. First of all, he's the second youngest of the lot—a year younger than Nokes, and two years younger than Steinbach. Secondly, he's much, much greener. Entering 1987, Nokes had 604 professional games already under his belt. Santiago had 470. Steinbach had 469. Surhoff had 192. Reason #3: The more often a player walks, the longer and better his career will be. Santiago walked once every 34 at-bats. Nokes drew a walk every 13 ABs. Steinbach got a free pass for every 12 ABs. Surhoff walked once for every 11. Finally, though this isn't very scientific, B.J. is the closest I have ever seen to a "can't miss" player. The last rookie that I had similar feelings about—that I was sure you could build a team around some day—turned out to be Paul Molitor.

One of the things that somebody will have to look into 20 years down the road is the effect that playing on an Olympic team has on a player. It seems pretty tough to faze these guys; Surhoff is no exception to that rule. In '87, he'd deliver the clutch two-out hit or move the runner from first to third with the consistency that most veterans would envy. Despite playing in only 115 games, he led the Brewers in sacrifice flies in 1987. In his first at-bat in a game, he'd line a double to deep right center; next time up, he'd whistle an inside curve ball three feet over the third baseman's head and right down the line. The next night he'd throw out Gary Pettis, who was trying to steal second base with the lead run. A few days later, he'd talk a rookie pitcher out of a tough jam—the next game, he'd get a pinch hit in the top of the seventh and then play three flawless innings at third base. Every time I looked up, Surhoff was doing things to help the Brewers win ball games; every time I opened the newspaper, someone else was getting credit for it. He's fast replacing Robin Yount as my favorite major league player to watch.

If B.J. has a weakness it would be his defense. But then he played a lot of shortstop in college; he's really still learning to catch. But he has very quick hands and a rocket—he might turn himself into one of the better receivers in the league in a few years.

And, just to prove that I'm not biased, there's one thing that Surhoff can't do. He stole 11 bases in 21 tries for an atrocious 52.4 percent success rate; someone should nail his foot to first base next year.

Scott Segrin

Surhoff, William James "B.J."

Bats: Left   Throws: Right   Born 08/04/64

1987 SEASON AND MAJOR-LEAGUE CAREER BATTING TOTALS

	G	AB	H	2B	3B	HR	TB	R	RBI	TBB	IBB	SO	HP	SH	SF	SB	CS	SB%	GDP	AVG	OBP	SLG
87 MIL	115	395	118	22	3	7	167	50	68	36	1	30	0	5	9	11	10	.52	13	.299	.350	.423
1 YEAR	115	395	118	22	3	7	167	50	68	36	1	30	0	5	9	11	10	.52	13	.299	.350	.423

1987 SEASON

	Ave.	OBP	SLG	AB	H	2B	3B	HR	RBI	BB	SO
Totals	.299	.350	.423	395	118	22	3	7	68	36	30
vs. Left	.318	.379	.424	85	27	3	0	2	17	9	6
vs. Right	.294	.342	.423	310	91	19	3	5	51	27	24
at Home	.314	.355	.464	194	61	10	2	5	41	15	13
on Road	.284	.345	.383	201	57	12	1	2	27	21	17
vs. Groundball	.299	.323	.433	231	69	10	3	5	37	11	20
vs. Flyball	.299	.385	.409	164	49	12	0	2	31	25	10
vs. Finesse	.317	.353	.467	199	63	11	2	5	33	13	9
vs. Power	.281	.347	.378	196	55	11	1	2	35	23	21
on Grass	.306	.358	.426	350	107	20	2	6	64	33	25
on Artificial Turf	.244	.286	.400	45	11	2	1	1	4	3	5
Day Games	.265	.331	.379	132	35	4	1	3	23	14	15
Night Games	.316	.360	.445	263	83	18	2	4	45	22	15
April	.256	.327	.442	43	11	2	0	2	8	5	6
May	.250	.245	.292	48	12	2	0	0	7	0	6
June	.351	.402	.581	74	26	6	1	3	17	7	5
July	.288	.316	.438	73	21	4	2	1	11	4	3
August	.306	.407	.333	72	22	2	0	0	9	13	5
Sept/Oct	.306	.347	.412	85	26	6	0	1	16	7	5
Bases Empty	.270	.329	.386	215	58	12	2	3	3	19	16
Leadoff	.263	.300	.434	76	20	5	1	2	2	4	5
Not Leadoff	.273	.344	.360	139	38	7	1	1	1	15	11
Runners On	.333	.374	.467	180	60	10	1	4	65	17	14
First Base Only	.342	.375	.474	76	26	7	0	1	7	4	6
Scoring Position	.327	.373	.462	104	34	3	1	3	58	13	8
Late Innings, Close	.306	.381	.431	72	22	3	0	2	19	10	7

FOUR YEAR TOTALS (1984 – 1987)

	Ave.	OBP	SLG	AB	H	2B	3B	HR	RBI	BB	SO
	.299	.350	.423	395	118	22	3	7	68	36	30
	.318	.379	.424	85	27	3	0	2	17	9	6
	.294	.342	.423	310	91	19	3	5	51	27	24
	.314	.355	.464	194	61	10	2	5	41	15	13
	.284	.345	.383	201	57	12	1	2	27	21	17
	.299	.323	.433	231	69	10	3	5	37	11	20
	.299	.385	.409	164	49	12	0	2	31	25	10
	.317	.353	.467	199	63	11	2	5	33	13	9
	.281	.347	.378	196	55	11	1	2	35	23	21
	.306	.358	.426	350	107	20	2	6	64	33	25
	.244	.286	.400	45	11	2	1	1	4	3	5
	.265	.331	.379	132	35	4	1	3	23	14	15
	.316	.360	.445	263	83	18	2	4	45	22	15
	.256	.327	.442	43	11	2	0	2	8	5	6
	.250	.245	.292	48	12	2	0	0	7	0	6
	.351	.402	.581	74	26	6	1	3	17	7	5
	.288	.316	.438	73	21	4	2	1	11	4	3
	.306	.407	.333	72	22	2	0	0	9	13	5
	.306	.347	.412	85	26	6	0	1	16	7	5
	.270	.329	.386	215	58	12	2	3	3	19	16
	.263	.300	.434	76	20	5	1	2	2	4	5
	.273	.344	.360	139	38	7	1	1	1	15	11
	.333	.374	.467	180	60	10	1	4	65	17	14
	.342	.375	.474	76	26	7	0	1	7	4	6
	.327	.373	.462	104	34	3	1	3	58	13	8
	.306	.381	.431	72	22	3	0	2	19	10	7

RBI/Opportunities

Scoring Position	50 / 156 (32%)	50 / 156 (32%)
Scoring Position, 2 Out	22 / 70 (31%)	22 / 70 (31%)
On Third, Less than 2 Out	18 / 29 (62%)	18 / 29 (62%)
RBI in close games / RBI Total	39 / 68 (57%)	39 / 68 (57%)

Rick Sutcliffe
Chicago Cubs

As a 17-game winner with the Cleveland Indians in 1983, Rick Sutcliffe's ratio of walks per 9 innings pitched, 3.77, indicated less than razor-sharp control. Early 1984 saw the same pattern as Sut averaged 4.39 BB/9IP with Cleveland. Upon being traded to the Chicago Cubs that June, Rick stated that because of the talent of the team now behind him he could just wing the ball in there and let 'em hit it. His statistics bore out his words; during his spectacular 16–1 Cy Young season Sut's BB/9IP ratio declined to 2.33. Despite nagging injuries in 1985, Rick kept his walks down to a respectable 3.05 per game. Then came 1986. Sutcliffe's record fell to 5–14, his ERA rose to 4.64 and his BB/9IP jumped to 4.89. Injuries that took away his good fastball were cited as the primary reason.

Perhaps this is so, but I can't help thinking that the deplorable state of the Cub outfield had something to do with the decline. By 1986 the Cub outfield had more gaps than Nixon's White House tapes. As a flyball pitcher, Sutcliffe became wary of getting the ball into the strike zone, because balls hit to the outfield had a nasty habit of falling in safely. As a result, the big redhead pitched more tentatively than he had before. His walks increased; good control being vital to a Wrigley Field pitcher's success, Rick's record suffered.

In 1987 Rick still had not recovered his good fastball.

At first, he pitched as he had in the previous year, walking seven in less than three innings on Opening Day. Gradually, however, the addition of Andre Dawson and Dave Martinez to the everyday Cub outfield bolstered Rick's confidence. His BB/9IP steadily decreased: 5.58 in April, 4.36 in May, 4.28 in June. By July Sutcliffe was in vintage 1984 form:

	W–L	K/BB	B/9IP	ERA
1984	16–1	3.97	2.33	2.69
July 1987	5–0	3.45	2.23	2.50

In August, the injury bug hit again, and Rick's numbers declined to 1986 form: 0–2, 5.82 ERA, 5.29 BB/9IP. He got enough back in September to hold his BB/9IP to 3.06 and fashion a 3.40 ERA, although with the general collapse of the team he was only 3–4 in this period. Even so, Rick Sutcliffe just missed another Cy Young award in 1987. His 3.68 ERA just missed being in the league's top 10, no mean feat for a Wrigley field pitcher. Overall, Sutcliffe's 1987 performance was good enough to prove to Cub fans that he can still pitch. Look for a fine 1988 season from the Red Baron.

Pat McCormick

Sutcliffe, Richard Lee "Rick"   Bats: Left   Throws: Right   Born 06/21/56

1987 SEASON AND MAJOR-LEAGUE CAREER PITCHING TOTALS

	G	GS	CG	GF	IP	BFP	H	R	ER	HR	SH	SF	HB	TBB	IBB	SO	WP	Bk	W	L	Pct	ShO	Sv	ERA
87 CHN	34	34	6	0	237	1012	223	106	97	24	9	8	4	106	14	174	9	4	18	10	.643	1	0	3.68
11 YEARS	285	225	47	29	1653	7033	1551	775	702	140	59	49	27	705	45	1108	59	23	104	78	.571	13	6	3.82

1987: Power, Groundball   **1986: Power, Flyball**   **1985: Power, Flyball**   **1984: Power, Flyball**

1987 SEASON

	G	IP	H	BB	SO	SB	CS	W	L	S	ERA
Totals	34	237.0	223	106	174	35	7	18	10	0	3.68
at Home	18	123.1	114	63	95	18	4	10	5	0	3.50
on Road	16	113.2	109	43	79	17	3	8	5	0	3.88
on Grass	21	142.0	136	71	109	22	5	10	7	0	3.93
on Artificial Turf	13	95.0	87	35	65	13	2	8	3	0	3.32
Day Games	25	175.1	158	82	131	26	6	15	6	0	3.29
Night Games	9	61.2	65	24	43	9	1	3	4	0	4.82
April	5	30.2	25	19	21	4	0	3	2	0	4.11
May	6	43.1	30	21	34	7	3	4	0	0	2.08
June	6	40.0	37	19	29	5	2	3	2	0	4.72
July	5	36.0	39	9	31	5	0	5	0	0	2.50
August	5	34.0	43	20	22	8	1	0	2	0	5.82
Sept/Oct	7	53.0	49	18	37	6	1	3	4	0	3.40

vs. Opponent Batters	Ave.	OBP	SLG	AB	H	2B	3B	HR	RBI	BB	SO
Totals	.252	.332	.402	884	223	42	9	24	93	106	174
vs. Left	.262	.357	.420	500	131	30	5	13	46	72	99
vs. Right	.240	.299	.378	384	92	12	4	11	47	34	75
Bases Empty	.244	.313	.401	544	133	24	5	17	17	52	109
Leadoff	.247	.313	.414	227	56	10	5	6	6	22	49
Not Leadoff	.243	.312	.391	317	77	14	0	11	11	30	60
Runners On Base	.265	.361	.403	340	90	18	4	7	76	54	65
First Base Only	.300	.359	.471	140	42	8	2	4	11	11	26
Scoring Position	.240	.363	.355	200	48	10	2	3	65	43	39
Late Innings, Close	.288	.404	.425	73	21	5	1	1	9	14	15

FOUR YEAR TOTALS (1984 – 1987)

	G	IP	H	BB	SO	SB	CS	W	L	S	ERA
Totals	117	788.1	742	331	611	92	32	51	38	0	3.79
at Home	57	386.2	362	180	300	41	20	27	15	0	3.68
on Road	60	401.2	380	151	311	51	12	24	23	0	3.92
on Grass	75	494.1	467	210	397	55	22	30	24	0	3.86
on Artificial Turf	42	294.0	275	121	214	37	10	21	14	0	3.70
Day Games	86	581.1	540	254	434	63	27	40	24	0	3.58
Night Games	31	207.0	202	77	177	29	5	11	14	0	4.43
April	22	151.2	134	69	103	15	7	10	8	0	3.15
May	21	138.0	129	60	105	19	7	8	8	0	4.11
June	23	161.0	142	73	124	20	6	9	10	0	3.75
July	15	97.2	99	37	79	10	0	11	1	0	3.32
August	17	112.0	120	53	87	16	4	6	4	0	4.58
Sept/Oct	19	128.0	118	39	113	12	8	7	7	0	4.01

vs. Opponent Batters	Ave.	OBP	SLG	AB	H	2B	3B	HR	RBI	BB	SO
Totals	.250	.325	.385	2971	742	131	31	70	313	331	611
vs. Left	.255	.333	.390	1634	417	85	18	33	153	188	346
vs. Right	.243	.315	.380	1337	325	46	13	37	160	143	265
Bases Empty	.241	.304	.372	1791	432	74	20	40	40	159	375
Leadoff	.262	.318	.404	762	200	36	15	14	14	62	162
Not Leadoff	.225	.293	.348	1029	232	38	5	26	26	97	213
Runners On Base	.263	.355	.406	1180	310	57	11	30	273	172	236
First Base Only	.277	.324	.416	512	142	25	5	12	35	33	86
Scoring Position	.251	.377	.398	668	168	32	6	18	238	139	150
Late Innings, Close	.268	.345	.402	276	74	14	4	5	29	32	53

RBI/Opportunities

	1987		1984–1987
Scoring Position	57 / 296 (19%)		201 / 968 (21%)
Scoring Position, 2 Out	27 / 150 (18%)		85 / 482 (18%)
On Third, Less than 2 Out	19 / 51 (37%)		67 / 159 (42%)
RBI in close games / RBI Total	66 / 93 (71%)		225 / 313 (72%)

Don Sutton
California Angels

It is time for the annual ritual. Every year, we review Don Sutton's career, noting that his lifetime totals are awesome. We say that his performance last year was better than anyone could reasonably expect from such an old hurler, and we emphasize the fact that he seems to retain excellent control and unparalleled mound smarts. Finally we speculate that he might be able to have one more productive season. Here goes this year's version. . . .

The clock *is* winding down on the seemingly ageless Don Sutton; it's just a lot slower than for your average player. But then, Hall of Famers are far from average. Symbolic of the gradual, almost imperceptible erosion of his skills, Sutton's record of 21 consecutive years with 100 or more strikeouts came to an end in 1987; he had only 99 Ks—tsk, tsk. One phantom checked swing, or a missed ball four on a 3–2 count, would have been like one tick of the clock in a 22-year continuum.

Sutton failed to win his usual 15 games in 1987, compiling a record of "only" 11–11. That was, of course, the second highest number of wins on a beleaguered Angels staff, and .500 is a good percentage if your team is 75–87 for the year and has the worst hitting in the league. There was considerable evidence that Sutton had much of his old skill intact in 1987. His ratio of hits plus walks per inning was an admirable 1.25 for the full year, and an outstanding 1.20 after the All-Star break. Many "good" starting pitchers survive with ratios in excess of 1.30. Sutton in 1987 was particularly effective at avoiding the base on balls, averaging just 1.92 walks per 9 innings, second only to Bret Saberhagen (1.85) among AL pitchers with 150 or more innings pitched.

Unfortunately, there was also evidence that Sutton has lost some of his skill in keeping the longball from creating too many big innings. His 1987 ERA of 4.70 was the highest of his career. He's always been home run prone, but his 38 roundtrippers in less than 200 innings was clearly overdoing it. Sutton's ERA was 5.53 after the All-Star break, including a disastrous 7.58 in September–October, fifth worst in the American League.

Sutton is going to spring training in 1988 with a new contract from the Dodgers, who lost 89 games last year. It should all look familiar to Don: Vero Beach, the palm trees in the outfield, the Dodger clubhouse, the Dodger uniform. It should look a lot like 20 years ago when, in 1968, he helped the Dodgers recover from an 89-loss season. Of course, they only recovered three wins to go 76–86. This time Sutton will be 43 years old in April, and the clock is ticking.

John C. Benson

Sutton, Donald Howard "Don"   Bats: Right   Throws: Right   Born 04/02/45

1987 SEASON AND MAJOR-LEAGUE CAREER PITCHING TOTALS

	G	GS	CG	GF	IP	BFP	H	R	ER	HR	SH	SF	HB	TBB	IBB	SO	WP	Bk	W	L	Pct	ShO	Sv	ERA
87 CAL	35	34	1	0	192	795	199	101	100	38	2	5	7	41	0	99	7	0	11	11	.500	0	0	4.69
22 YEARS	758	740	178	12	5195	21251	4601	2060	1876	465	201	122	81	1313	96	3530	110	17	321	250	.562	58	5	3.25

1987: Finesse, Flyball   1986: Finesse, Flyball   1985: Finesse, Flyball   1984: Finesse, Flyball

	1987 SEASON											FOUR YEAR TOTALS (1984 – 1987)										
	G	IP	H	BB	SO	SB	CS	W	L	S	ERA	G	IP	H	BB	SO	SB	CS	W	L	S	ERA
Totals	35	191.2	199	41	99	11	9	11	10	0	4.70	136	837.1	836	200	465	62	25	55	43	0	3.99
at Home	16	94.2	92	23	56	7	7	3	5	0	4.28	72	463.1	442	109	260	26	18	28	23	0	3.67
on Road	19	97.0	107	18	43	4	2	8	5	0	5.10	64	374.0	394	91	205	36	7	27	20	0	4.40
on Grass	9	44.1	54	7	25	4	1	4	3	0	5.48	40	255.1	258	60	136	20	6	19	10	0	3.74
on Artificial Turf	26	147.1	145	34	74	7	8	7	7	0	4.46	96	582.0	578	140	329	42	19	36	33	0	4.11
Day Games	29	160.1	156	33	84	9	7	9	8	0	4.72	110	687.2	656	160	376	41	21	45	33	0	3.80
Night Games	6	31.1	43	8	15	2	2	2	2	0	4.60	26	149.2	180	40	89	21	4	10	10	0	4.87
April	5	27.2	33	6	12	3	6	1	3	0	4.23	18	100.2	119	40	54	8	7	5	9	0	5.54
May	6	33.2	39	11	15	4	1	1	2	0	5.35	22	130.2	153	30	74	12	3	5	9	0	5.10
June	6	35.1	38	2	20	3	0	3	2	0	3.06	24	164.1	138	25	98	10	6	13	6	0	2.85
July	5	27.2	19	8	15	0	1	2	1	0	4.88	22	138.2	134	31	77	10	3	12	5	0	3.57
August	6	37.2	31	9	19	1	1	2	1	0	3.58	24	158.2	143	33	88	11	3	11	6	0	3.35
Sept/Oct	7	29.2	39	5	18	0	0	2	1	0	7.58	26	144.1	149	41	74	11	3	9	8	0	4.36

vs. Opponent Batters	Ave.	OBP	SLG	AB	H	2B	3B	HR	RBI	BB	SO	Ave.	OBP	SLG	AB	H	2B	3B	HR	RBI	BB	SO
Totals	.269	.311	.458	740	199	24	1	38	95	41	99	.257	.301	.411	3254	836	131	9	118	366	200	465
vs. Left	.233	.286	.398	369	86	11	1	16	38	24	46	.247	.301	.385	1659	410	62	5	52	180	124	247
vs. Right	.305	.338	.518	371	113	13	0	22	57	17	53	.267	.301	.439	1595	426	69	4	66	186	76	218
Bases Empty	.256	.305	.419	465	119	11	1	21	21	30	63	.246	.289	.396	2041	503	80	6	71	71	120	298
Leadoff	.291	.327	.487	189	55	5	1	10	10	9	29	.252	.286	.407	833	210	30	3	31	31	39	124
Not Leadoff	.232	.291	.373	276	64	6	0	11	11	21	34	.243	.291	.388	1208	293	50	3	40	40	81	174
Runners On Base	.291	.322	.524	275	80	13	0	17	74	11	36	.275	.320	.438	1213	333	51	3	47	295	80	167
First Base Only	.326	.350	.530	132	43	9	0	6	15	4	11	.304	.333	.459	593	180	30	1	20	57	25	74
Scoring Position	.259	.297	.517	143	37	4	0	11	59	7	25	.247	.309	.418	620	153	21	2	27	238	55	93
Late Innings, Close	.207	.207	.552	29	6	1	0	3	4	0	5	.293	.316	.519	181	53	6	1	11	21	6	19

RBI/Opportunities

Scoring Position	43 / 187 (23%)	191 / 791 (24%)
Scoring Position, 2 Out	11 / 73 (15%)	73 / 390 (19%)
On Third, Less than 2 Out	16 / 35 (46%)	68 / 121 (56%)
RBI in close games / RBI Total	79 / 95 (83%)	262 / 366 (72%)

Dale Sveum
Milwaukee Brewers

Q: What do Dale do in a pool in Alabama? A: Dale Sveum. Actually, it's surprising how well the broadcasters pronounce his name; I expected them to butcher it to death.

In 1986, Rene Lachemann, in his infinite wisdom, proclaimed that Sveum could be the Brewers' third baseman for the next 10 years. At the time, Sveum had about 25 major league at-bats. However, there may have been some foresight on Lachemann's part. Partly on performance, partly because he had a lot to improve on, Sveum was, without doubt, the most improved Brewer in 1987. Though he still thinks that *Ball Four* is just a book title and it was the year of the homer, 25 homers and 95 RBIs are pretty impressive for a shortstop who was 23 during the 1987 season.

There was a lot of talk about how much Sveum's defense improved this year, which both is and isn't true. When someone fields .865 at third base in one year and doesn't embarrass himself at shortstop the next year, you can say that he's come a long way. But his defense is still much closer to what Hubie Brooks would consider a good season than to what Ozzie Smith would consider a poor one; he was tenth among regular (80+ games played) shortstops in the AL in range factor in 1987. The real reason for the "improvement" was that Dale had become a good hitter. If he doesn't keep hitting well enough to justify his glove, it won't take people long to realize that he isn't that good of a fielder at all.

If he does keep hitting, it will be a major surprise. Before 1987, Dale had hit a total of 30 homers in 2,106 at-bats in pro ball. His best slugging percentage was .489, mostly because he hit .329 that year. Though young players usually develop power as they mature, you do have to wonder whether a guy who hit .248 with 20 doubles, five triples and seven homers in 520 at-bats in the Pacific Coast League is really this good.

But who knows? If Paul Molitor hadn't been hurt in 1986, Dale probably wouldn't have made the team. But he did and he played well enough to earn another look. Tom Trebelhorn didn't decide to keep Sveum until Edgar Diaz got hurt in spring training this year. But he had to; now Dale will have to slump his way out of the majors. The kid is a battler; maybe he'll keep winning his fights in 1988.

Remember those bubble blowing contests they used to have—the ones that Kurt Bevacqua would always win? If Sveum keeps playing, they're going to make a comeback; Dale will win every year. If they have performance categories, he'll win Most Acrobatic (for the one he blew this year while diving head-long for a grounder) and Best by a Mustachioed Player. If chewing bubble gum and playing baseball at the same time is an indication of intelligence, then this is the guy I want on my College Bowl team.

Scott Segrin

Sveum, Dale Curtis

Bats: Both   Throws: Right   Born 11/23/63

1987 SEASON AND MAJOR-LEAGUE CAREER BATTING TOTALS

	G	AB	H	2B	3B	HR	TB	R	RBI	TBB	IBB	SO	HP	SH	SF	SB	CS	SB%	GDP	AVG	OBP	SLG
87 MIL	153	535	135	27	3	25	243	86	95	40	4	133	1	5	5	2	6	.25	11	.252	.303	.454
2 YEARS	244	852	213	40	5	32	359	121	130	72	4	196	2	10	6	6	9	.40	18	.250	.308	.421

	1987 SEASON											FOUR YEAR TOTALS (1984 – 1987)										
	Ave.	OBP	SLG	AB	H	2B	3B	HR	RBI	BB	SO	Ave.	OBP	SLG	AB	H	2B	3B	HR	RBI	BB	SO
Totals	.252	.303	.454	535	135	27	3	25	95	40	133	.250	.308	.421	852	213	40	5	32	130	72	196
vs. Left	.286	.338	.535	185	53	11	1	11	34	16	46	.281	.348	.502	281	79	19	2	13	46	30	61
vs. Right	.234	.284	.411	350	82	16	2	14	61	24	87	.235	.287	.382	571	134	21	3	19	84	42	135
at Home	.261	.314	.436	257	67	14	2	9	37	20	68	.248	.315	.401	416	103	21	2	13	54	40	97
on Road	.245	.292	.471	278	68	13	1	16	58	20	65	.252	.301	.440	436	110	19	3	19	76	32	99
vs. Groundball	.245	.284	.438	290	71	16	2	12	48	15	69	.240	.293	.400	445	107	23	3	14	68	32	94
vs. Flyball	.261	.324	.473	245	64	11	1	13	47	25	64	.260	.324	.445	407	106	17	2	18	62	40	102
vs. Finesse	.223	.279	.396	273	61	14	3	9	35	21	57	.226	.288	.385	465	105	22	5	14	52	41	92
vs. Power	.282	.329	.515	262	74	13	0	16	60	19	76	.279	.332	.465	387	108	18	0	18	78	31	104
on Grass	.261	.318	.482	452	118	25	3	23	86	39	112	.253	.316	.439	708	179	34	4	30	112	66	164
on Artificial Turf	.205	.214	.301	83	17	2	0	2	9	1	21	.236	.267	.333	144	34	6	1	2	18	6	32
Day Games	.199	.269	.361	166	33	6	3	5	16	15	45	.222	.292	.352	270	60	8	3	7	28	26	67
Night Games	.276	.318	.496	369	102	21	0	20	79	25	88	.263	.315	.454	582	153	32	2	25	102	46	129
April	.276	.337	.434	76	21	6	0	2	14	7	22	.276	.337	.434	76	21	6	0	2	14	7	22
May	.200	.214	.325	80	16	1	0	3	9	2	28	.283	.307	.428	145	41	7	1	4	21	6	42
June	.217	.267	.361	83	18	6	0	2	13	6	21	.206	.254	.322	180	37	9	0	4	21	12	37
July	.259	.337	.556	81	21	3	0	7	20	9	15	.277	.363	.489	137	38	5	0	8	27	18	29
August	.260	.324	.510	100	26	6	2	5	22	10	20	.239	.314	.458	142	34	7	3	6	23	16	25
Sept/Oct	.287	.322	.504	115	33	5	1	6	17	6	27	.244	.297	.430	172	42	6	1	8	24	13	41
Bases Empty	.234	.288	.385	291	68	9	1	11	11	21	79	.234	.291	.374	470	110	11	2	17	17	37	115
Leadoff	.235	.289	.409	132	31	3	1	6	6	9	36	.224	.277	.380	205	46	3	1	9	9	14	53
Not Leadoff	.233	.287	.365	159	37	6	0	5	5	12	43	.242	.302	.370	265	64	8	1	8	8	23	62
Runners On	.275	.321	.537	244	67	18	2	14	84	19	54	.270	.327	.479	382	103	29	3	15	113	35	81
First Base Only	.258	.287	.495	97	25	6	1	5	11	4	20	.247	.300	.443	158	39	9	2	6	15	12	33
Scoring Position	.286	.341	.565	147	42	12	1	9	73	15	34	.286	.345	.504	224	64	20	1	9	98	23	48
Late Innings, Close	.267	.302	.545	101	27	7	0	7	21	5	22	.266	.307	.455	154	41	8	0	7	27	9	31

RBI/Opportunities

Scoring Position	56 / 200	(28%)	78 / 304	(26%)
Scoring Position, 2 Out	27 / 98	(28%)	41 / 150	(27%)
On Third, Less than 2 Out	17 / 31	(55%)	22 / 46	(48%)
RBI in close games / RBI Total	63 / 95	(66%)	84 / 130	(65%)

Greg Swindell
Cleveland Indians

Greg Swindell enters 1988 as a major question mark—a victim of a severe elbow injury who (depending on the source) either may miss part of the season or will miss all of it. Yonder hangs a tale about the value of statistical analysis.

An issue of the late, lamented *Bill James Baseball Abstract Newsletter* included a study of the top-50 picks in the amateur draft. One finding: Hitters chosen in the first ten picks are strong bets to become stars; *pitchers* drafted in the first ten picks almost never pan out. In the first 17 years of the draft (1965–81), 57 pitchers were among the top ten picks. Only 15 ever went on to win or save ten games in a season. The best of the bunch were Joe Coleman, J. R. Richard and Jon Matlack. In that period, over a dozen hitters chosen in the top ten became stars.

Why the disparity? Apparently because there are a limited number of pitches in an arm. Pitchers get chosen in the top ten because they look polished; since they usually gain polish by throwing a tremendous number of innings at a very young age, they are good bets to get hurt. Most star hurlers in the majors (*e.g.,* Dave Stieb) often became pitchers relatively late in their school days and, for that reason, were drafted lower. In fact, the only top-ten pitcher to ever win a Cy Young Award—Dwight Gooden—was a third baseman until his senior year in high school.

The research supports a famous cliché. Virtually every star pitcher (Gaylord Perry, Bob Feller, Warren Spahn and Tom Seaver, to name the ones I know) who writes a *How To Pitch* book warns young players not to be too anxious to begin pitching. While I normally assume that most baseball nuggets of wisdom are pyrite until proven otherwise, apparently there's gold in this one.

Just ask Swindell. By late 1986—after throwing less than 80 innings in pro ball—he was already complaining that his elbow was really sore and that he was looking forward to resting it over the winter. By the 80-inning mark in 1987, his readings on the radar gun had gone from 93+ to sub-90 and he was being shelled regularly. By 100, he was on the DL.

Indian fans like to note that another fireballer from the University of Texas (Roger Clemens) stormed through the minors, looked great in his rookie season, went down with a sore arm in his second year and won the Cy Young in his third year. Maybe history will repeat; I hope so. Greg has a good curve, a super change, fine control and a veteran's knowledge of how to set batters up. When healthy, he glided through games, often retiring a dozen or more men in a row. If healthy, he is a 70–30 bet to win 15–20 games and lead the league in strikeouts in 1988; it would be a dirty shame if his arm miseries prevent him from ever reaching those marks.

Geoff Beckman

Swindell, Forrest Gregory "Greg"

Bats: Right Throws: Left Born 01/02/65

1987 SEASON AND MAJOR-LEAGUE CAREER PITCHING TOTALS

	G	GS	CG	GF	IP	BFP	H	R	ER	HR	SH	SF	HB	TBB	IBB	SO	WP	Bk	W	L	Pct	ShO	Sv	ERA
87 CLE	16	15	4	0	102	441	112	62	58	18	4	3	1	37	1	97	0	1	3	8	.273	1	0	5.12
2 YEARS	25	24	5	0	164	696	169	97	87	27	7	4	2	52	1	143	3	3	8	10	.444	1	0	4.77

1987: Power, Flyball   1986: Finesse, Flyball

1987 SEASON

	G	IP	H	BB	SO	SB	CS	W	L	S	ERA
Totals	16	102.1	112	37	97	5	9	3	8	0	5.10
at Home	6	47.1	46	15	44	3	3	2	3	0	3.80
on Road	10	55.0	66	22	53	2	6	1	5	0	6.22
on Grass	7	52.2	63	13	57	2	5	3	4	0	4.10
on Artificial Turf	9	49.2	49	24	40	3	4	0	4	0	6.16
Day Games	13	88.1	93	31	85	4	8	3	6	0	4.28
Night Games	3	14.0	19	6	12	1	1	0	2	0	10.29
April	6	34.0	29	11	29	1	2	1	3	0	4.76
May	6	47.1	57	15	51	1	6	2	2	0	3.61
June	4	21.0	26	11	17	3	1	0	3	0	9.00
July	0	0.0	0	0	0	0	0	0	0	0	0.00
August	0	0.0	0	0	0	0	0	0	0	0	0.00
Sept/Oct	0	0.0	0	0	0	0	0	0	0	0	0.00

vs. Opponent Batters	Ave.	OBP	SLG	AB	H	2B	3B	HR	RBI	BB	SO
Totals	.283	.343	.467	396	112	17	1	18	57	37	97
vs. Left	.309	.333	.574	68	21	6	0	4	17	3	13
vs. Right	.277	.345	.445	328	91	11	1	14	40	34	84
Bases Empty	.268	.333	.417	235	63	8	0	9	9	23	64
Leadoff	.258	.321	.381	97	25	3	0	3	3	9	21
Not Leadoff	.275	.342	.442	138	38	5	0	6	6	14	43
Runners On Base	.304	.358	.540	161	49	9	1	9	48	14	33
First Base Only	.343	.387	.529	70	24	2	1	3	8	4	16
Scoring Position	.275	.337	.549	91	25	7	0	6	40	10	17
Late Innings, Close	.315	.403	.481	54	17	3	0	2	9	8	12

FOUR YEAR TOTALS (1984 – 1987)

	G	IP	H	BB	SO	SB	CS	W	L	S	ERA
Totals	25	164.0	169	52	143	8	13	8	10	0	4.77
at Home	11	80.1	78	23	65	4	4	5	4	0	3.92
on Road	14	83.2	91	29	78	4	9	3	6	0	5.59
on Grass	7	52.2	63	13	57	2	5	3	4	0	4.10
on Artificial Turf	18	111.1	106	39	86	6	8	5	6	0	5.09
Day Games	20	135.1	135	43	116	6	11	8	7	0	4.26
Night Games	5	28.2	34	9	27	2	2	0	3	0	7.22
April	6	34.0	29	11	29	1	2	1	3	0	4.76
May	6	47.1	57	15	51	1	6	2	2	0	3.61
June	4	21.0	26	11	17	3	1	0	3	0	9.00
July	0	0.0	0	0	0	0	0	0	0	0	0.00
August	2	11.0	12	4	7	0	0	0	1	0	4.91
Sept/Oct	7	50.2	45	11	39	3	4	5	1	0	4.09

vs. Opponent Batters	Ave.	OBP	SLG	AB	H	2B	3B	HR	RBI	BB	SO
Totals	.268	.324	.439	631	169	25	1	27	84	52	143
vs. Left	.266	.293	.468	94	25	7	0	4	19	4	16
vs. Right	.268	.329	.434	537	144	18	1	23	65	48	127
Bases Empty	.254	.311	.407	386	98	14	0	15	15	32	93
Leadoff	.256	.308	.387	160	41	6	0	5	5	12	30
Not Leadoff	.252	.313	.420	226	57	8	0	10	10	20	63
Runners On Base	.290	.343	.490	245	71	11	1	12	69	20	50
First Base Only	.301	.345	.456	103	31	2	1	4	10	5	18
Scoring Position	.282	.342	.514	142	40	9	0	8	59	15	32
Late Innings, Close	.315	.403	.481	108	34	6	0	4	18	16	24

RBI/Opportunities

	1987			Four Year		
Scoring Position	29 /	126	(23%)	45 /	185	(24%)
Scoring Position, 2 Out	18 /	63	(29%)	36 /	126	(29%)
On Third, Less than 2 Out	6 /	17	(35%)	12 /	34	(35%)
RBI in close games / RBI Total	40 /	57	(70%)	80 /	84	(95%)

Pat Tabler
Cleveland Indians

It happens every spring. I write a piece that says "Pat Tabler is one of the worst first basemen in baseball"; people tell me that I've sold him short. Since 1987 was Tabler's best year ever, I don't expect any of this to matter . . . but I'm a stubborn cuss; I'm going to say it again:

In 1987, Tabler hit fewer homers (11) than any regular first baseman in the majors. It was his career high.

The best way to measure power is by subtracting a player's batting average from his slugging percentage (known as "isolated power"). Tabler's IP in 1987 was .132. That was (save for 100 at-bats in 1981) also a career best and also the lowest figure in the group.

Tabler drew one walk for every 10.8 ABs in 1987—his best ratio since 1984. Only seven regulars walked less often.

Tabler's secondary average (extra bases on hits, walks and steals divided by at-bats) was .224—very near his career best. That would be an acceptable figure only for a shortstop; again, it's the lowest number of any regular.

Tabler had the third-lowest fielding percentage among major league regulars and tied two men for the American League lead in errors.

Tabler's sole plus—his batting average—is inadequate compensation for his many weaknesses.

Let's suppose that we replace Tabler with an average first baseman. Let's assume that the replacement hits .260 (a generous estimate; only four regulars didn't bat .260 in 1987). That translates to 144 hits in 553 ABs. Tabler collected 170 hits. That's, at most, 26 hits gained.

Now here's what you lose. The average first baseman in 1987 hit 14 more homers and drew 20 more walks per 553 at-bats than Pat Tabler did. Would you, assuming that your name is not Ken Harrelson, willingly make that trade-off? I didn't think so.

Folks, it's very simple. Tabler is not as good as Don Mattingly. Or Eddie Murray. Or Dwight Evans. Or Wally Joyner. Or Greg Walker. Or Darrell Evans. Or George Brett, Kent Hrbek, Mark McGwire, Alvin Davis or Pete O'Brien. Would you bench Jack Clark for Pat Tabler? Glenn Davis? Andres Galarraga? Keith Hernandez? Von Hayes? John Kruk? Will Clark? If you agree that each man named is a better player, then you have just placed Pat Tabler in the bottom third of all major league first basemen; I submit that any worker who finishes in the bottom third of a ranking of his peers is, *by definition,* one of the worst at his profession. You couldn't ask for a better bench player, but it should be a felony to play Tabler at first base day after day. Do I make myself clear? I hope so; I'd hate to have to do this again next year.

Geoff Beckman

Tabler, Patrick Sean "Pat" Bats: Right Throws: Right Born 02/02/58

1987 SEASON AND MAJOR-LEAGUE CAREER BATTING TOTALS

	G	AB	H	2B	3B	HR	TB	R	RBI	TBB	IBB	SO	HP	SH	SF	SB	CS	SB%	GDP	AVG	OBP	SLG
87 CLE	151	553	170	34	3	11	243	66	86	51	6	84	6	3	5	5	2	.71	6	.307	.369	.439
7 YEARS	726	2519	736	132	19	40	1026	316	338	229	14	385	16	10	21	13	15	.46	73	.292	.352	.407

1987 SEASON

	Ave.	OBP	SLG	AB	H	2B	3B	HR	RBI	BB	SO
Totals	.307	.369	.439	553	170	34	3	11	86	51	85
vs. Left	.366	.412	.564	172	63	14	1	6	35	13	12
vs. Right	.281	.350	.383	381	107	20	2	5	51	38	73
at Home	.333	.394	.481	285	95	21	3	5	47	27	38
on Road	.280	.342	.396	268	75	13	0	6	39	24	47
vs. Groundball	.305	.377	.437	279	85	14	1	7	41	30	40
vs. Flyball	.310	.361	.442	274	85	20	2	4	45	21	45
vs. Finesse	.316	.357	.450	282	89	15	1	7	41	16	36
vs. Power	.299	.381	.428	271	81	19	2	4	45	35	49
on Grass	.319	.376	.463	477	152	33	3	10	80	41	73
on Artificial Turf	.237	.330	.289	76	18	1	0	1	6	10	12
Day Games	.302	.378	.411	192	58	9	0	4	34	22	35
Night Games	.310	.364	.454	361	112	25	3	7	52	29	50
April	.338	.404	.550	80	27	8	0	3	14	7	16
May	.330	.348	.495	109	36	9	0	3	20	3	12
June	.260	.339	.354	96	25	6	0	1	12	11	14
July	.356	.463	.478	90	32	4	2	1	8	16	15
August	.328	.382	.474	116	38	6	1	3	27	11	17
Sept/Oct	.194	.227	.210	62	12	1	0	0	5	3	11
Bases Empty	.261	.317	.420	283	74	21	3	6	6	21	43
Leadoff	.222	.252	.333	99	22	7	2	0	0	4	15
Not Leadoff	.283	.350	.467	184	52	14	1	6	6	17	28
Runners On	.356	.421	.459	270	96	13	0	5	80	30	42
First Base Only	.312	.353	.376	109	34	4	0	1	2	4	17
Scoring Position	.385	.461	.516	161	62	9	0	4	78	26	25
Late Innings, Close	.293	.372	.378	82	24	1	0	2	9	10	16

FOUR YEAR TOTALS (1984 – 1987)

	Ave.	OBP	SLG	AB	H	2B	3B	HR	RBI	BB	SO
Totals	.301	.355	.416	1903	572	102	11	32	261	154	278
vs. Left	.324	.381	.460	635	206	38	3	14	94	60	65
vs. Right	.289	.342	.394	1268	366	64	8	18	167	94	213
at Home	.336	.389	.466	953	320	54	5	20	156	81	120
on Road	.265	.320	.366	950	252	48	6	12	105	73	158
vs. Groundball	.293	.347	.388	923	270	38	4	14	106	73	134
vs. Flyball	.308	.362	.443	980	302	64	7	18	155	81	144
vs. Finesse	.312	.350	.429	1067	333	61	5	18	141	60	136
vs. Power	.286	.361	.400	836	239	41	6	14	120	94	142
on Grass	.315	.368	.434	1640	516	93	8	29	239	134	234
on Artificial Turf	.213	.275	.304	263	56	9	3	3	22	20	44
Day Games	.302	.361	.402	646	195	33	4	8	83	57	105
Night Games	.300	.352	.423	1257	377	69	7	24	178	97	173
April	.336	.399	.493	286	96	25	1	6	39	28	39
May	.283	.327	.383	368	104	19	3	4	50	24	54
June	.266	.320	.336	271	72	8	1	3	36	21	39
July	.300	.358	.428	297	89	13	2	7	37	25	47
August	.327	.385	.448	413	135	22	2	8	64	40	65
Sept/Oct	.284	.323	.399	268	76	15	2	4	35	16	34
Bases Empty	.280	.330	.395	1015	284	60	6	15	15	74	156
Leadoff	.289	.323	.371	380	110	22	3	1	1	19	55
Not Leadoff	.274	.334	.409	635	174	38	3	14	14	55	101
Runners On	.324	.381	.440	888	288	42	5	17	246	80	122
First Base Only	.302	.348	.399	371	112	17	2	5	15	23	47
Scoring Position	.340	.403	.470	517	176	25	3	12	231	57	75
Late Innings, Close	.281	.352	.411	285	80	7	3	8	43	31	49

RBI/Opportunities

	1987	Four Year
Scoring Position	72 / 231 (31%)	210 / 701 (30%)
Scoring Position, 2 Out	37 / 104 (36%)	79 / 314 (25%)
On Third, Less than 2 Out	21 / 35 (60%)	78 / 123 (63%)
RBI in close games / RBI Total	49 / 86 (57%)	164 / 261 (63%)

Frank Tanana
Detroit Tigers

The 1987 season was a microcosm of Frank Tanana's career. In 1973, as a 19-year-old with an outstanding fastball, Tanana quickly showed himself to be one of the premier lefthanders in the league. After five years and 73 complete games, his arm gave out. Denied the quick and easy way of retiring hitters (*i.e.,* blowing them away), he struggled to become a complete pitcher, learning to fool hitters with various off-speed pitches. He spent several mediocre seasons making the adjustment. Finally, at age 30 (an age when finesse pitchers with losing records tend to run out of chances), he began pitching well again—first in Texas and then in Detroit. It's possible that it happened just in time to save his career.

In 1987, Tanana started off brilliantly; he had a 13–7 record and a 3.54 ERA on August 11. With Jack Morris having trouble winning games and Walt Terrell only a game over .500, he was the staff ace during Detroit's midsummer rise from pretender to contender. Then, in back-to-back games, Tanana was forced from the game due to weather. On August 16, 130-degree heat caused him to leave in the sixth; five days later, he was ineffective after a long rain delay. What effect these games actually had on him is unknown, but he struggled badly after that. The Tigers were scoring runs in bunches, and often took him off the hook after he left the game; even so, Tanana was 0–3 with an horrible 9.33 ERA. In the final six games of the year, with De-

troit 2+ games back and desperately needing some wins to save the season, Tanana responded with a 1-run, 8-inning performance over Baltimore; on the final day of the year, his complete-game shutout over Toronto gave Detroit the divisional title. Like his career overall, he began to pitch well again just in the nick of time.

Despite Tanana's roller coaster year, his future with Detroit seems secure. He's a quality pitcher—the only quality lefty on the Tiger staff. He's also exactly the sort of pitcher who should do well at Tiger Stadium. He rarely walks anyone, which keeps the 8.89 hits that he allows every nine innings from advancing any runners. He doesn't allow a great many homers (1.11 per nine innings; slightly less than the league average) to begin with; the long power alleys at Michigan and Trumbull turn about half of the long drives that he does surrender into outs. Though he's not very effective in shutting off the running game, he does serve up a lot of ground balls; the tall infield grass slows them just enough to give Messrs. Whitaker, Trammell, etc., ample double play opportunities. And he is very successful in Tiger Stadium.

Another of Tanana's assets may be his experience; his assistance could be valuable to some of the Tigers' younger pitchers like Robinson and King as they assume their roles in Detroit's future.

Jim Shaarda

Tanana, Frank Daryl

Bats: Left   Throws: Left   Born 07/03/53

1987 SEASON AND MAJOR-LEAGUE CAREER PITCHING TOTALS

	G	GS	CG	GF	IP	BFP	H	R	ER	HR	SH	SF	HB	TBB	IBB	SO	WP	Bk	W	L	Pct	ShO	Sv	ERA
87 DET	34	34	5	0	219	924	216	106	95	27	8	11	5	56	5	146	6	0	15	10	.600	3	0	3.90
15 YEARS	442	426	128	6	2976	12437	2812	1286	1136	301	118	74	90	828	68	2071	79	22	174	163	.516	31	0	3.44

1987: Finesse, Flyball   **1986: Finesse, Flyball**   **1985: Power, Groundball**   **1984: Finesse, Groundball**

1987 SEASON

	G	IP	H	BB	SO	SB	CS	W	L	S	ERA
Totals	34	218.2	216	56	146	23	6	15	10	0	3.91
at Home	16	109.0	94	25	75	11	2	10	5	0	3.06
on Road	18	109.2	122	31	71	12	4	5	5	0	4.76
on Grass	9	61.2	58	19	49	8	1	4	2	0	3.65
on Artificial Turf	25	157.0	158	37	97	15	5	11	8	0	4.01
Day Games	28	180.0	177	45	129	22	5	14	9	0	3.85
Night Games	6	38.2	39	11	17	1	1	1	1	0	4.19
April	4	28.0	16	9	17	2	0	2	1	0	2.57
May	6	36.1	43	11	25	7	2	2	2	0	4.71
June	5	41.1	28	12	25	2	1	3	1	0	2.40
July	6	41.0	42	9	26	3	0	3	3	0	4.17
August	7	41.1	56	8	30	5	2	3	2	0	5.23
Sept/Oct	6	30.2	31	7	23	4	1	2	1	0	4.11

FOUR YEAR TOTALS (1984 – 1987)

	G	IP	H	BB	SO	SB	CS	W	L	S	ERA
Totals	134	868.1	866	259	566	62	21	54	48	0	3.87
at Home	69	443.0	436	125	285	27	11	32	27	0	3.88
on Road	65	425.1	430	134	281	35	10	22	21	0	3.85
on Grass	37	219.1	230	76	156	25	5	14	14	0	4.35
on Artificial Turf	97	649.0	636	183	410	37	16	40	34	0	3.69
Day Games	116	759.1	741	224	501	55	15	51	40	0	3.70
Night Games	18	109.0	125	35	65	7	6	3	8	0	5.04
April	18	109.2	108	41	66	6	2	7	7	0	4.19
May	22	136.2	137	39	91	15	3	7	9	0	4.21
June	22	159.2	138	56	91	12	7	11	6	0	3.21
July	22	146.0	149	46	106	9	2	8	9	0	3.76
August	25	161.0	179	33	98	8	3	11	8	0	4.14
Sept/Oct	25	155.1	155	44	114	12	4	10	9	0	3.82

vs. Opponent Batters	Ave.	OBP	SLG	AB	H	2B	3B	HR	RBI	BB	SO
Totals	.256	.302	.410	844	216	37	6	27	94	56	146
vs. Left	.234	.295	.365	137	32	4	1	4	11	11	31
vs. Right	.260	.304	.419	707	184	33	5	23	83	45	115
Bases Empty	.248	.294	.438	512	127	24	5	21	21	30	90
Leadoff	.264	.319	.415	212	56	10	2	6	6	15	36
Not Leadoff	.237	.275	.453	300	71	14	3	15	15	15	54
Runners On Base	.268	.315	.367	332	89	13	1	6	73	26	56
First Base Only	.285	.309	.396	144	41	7	0	3	9	5	19
Scoring Position	.255	.320	.346	188	48	6	1	3	64	21	37
Late Innings, Close	.253	.269	.320	75	19	3	1	0	3	2	12

	Ave.	OBP	SLG	AB	H	2B	3B	HR	RBI	BB	SO
Totals	.257	.310	.416	3365	866	151	29	108	380	259	566
vs. Left	.259	.308	.413	583	151	30	6	16	59	40	118
vs. Right	.257	.311	.416	2782	715	121	23	92	321	219	448
Bases Empty	.252	.296	.421	2064	521	96	18	72	72	125	348
Leadoff	.251	.287	.393	857	215	40	5	24	24	41	140
Not Leadoff	.254	.303	.441	1207	306	56	13	48	48	84	208
Runners On Base	.265	.332	.407	1301	345	55	11	36	308	134	218
First Base Only	.287	.321	.448	578	166	29	5	18	50	29	79
Scoring Position	.248	.340	.375	723	179	26	6	18	258	105	139
Late Innings, Close	.275	.333	.424	236	65	10	2	7	26	21	32

RBI/Opportunities

Scoring Position	59 / 250 (24%)	220 / 1003 (22%)
Scoring Position, 2 Out	21 / 112 (19%)	82 / 471 (17%)
On Third, Less than 2 Out	25 / 44 (57%)	99 / 190 (52%)
RBI in close games / RBI Total	66 / 94 (70%)	257 / 380 (68%)

Danny Tartabull
Kansas City Royals

What's the big difference between Tartabull and George Bell in 1987? Their averages are nearly identical, break them down by at-bat and park factor and their power is pretty close. There are no noticeable differences in their speed or defensive values, and Danny walks about twice as much. The big difference is Bell played for an awesome offensive team that scored 845 runs to KC's 715.

I'm not big on runs scored and RBIs. What I use is a little program that adjusts for park factors and converts performance into run values. This is how it interpreted their 1987 seasons:

	B.A.	SLUG%	OBA	Run Value	OUTS	Runs per 27 Outs Expended
Tartabull	.308	.555	.390	121	425	7.69
Bell	.308	.586	.352	118	449	7.10

It should have been fairly obvious that Tartabull was going to be, and now is, one heck of a player. Look, he was a minor league batting champion at age 18, a very rare accomplishment. From 1983 to 1985 he hit .301 in Chattanooga, .304 in Salt Lake City, .300 in 20 at-bats in Seattle, .300 at Calgary, and .328 in 61 at-bats at Seattle. That suggests to me he should have been in Seattle long before 1986.

His whole career seems to be a long line of "Three Stooges" management decisions. When he was with the Reds they didn't think he could cut it at third base, so they moved him to second base. When Seattle got him they thought he couldn't make it at second base, so they moved him to shortstop.

After a couple years of that nonsense, Dick Williams showed up and said, "No, no, guys, the defensive spectrum moves in the other direction." A month into his seventh professional season, playing as a rookie in the major leagues, they finally sent Tartabull to the outfield.

I'm sure it wasn't the easiest way for Danny to break in, but he still clobbered the ball at the plate. And, for some reason this seemed to surprise Seattle. They had downplayed his 40 homers at Calgary because the PCL was a hitter's league and Calgary was its best home run park. But what happens when you put a powerful player in such a situation? He hits more homers than anyone else. What did Tartabull do? He hit more homers than anyone else. Heck, in his previous September call-ups in the majors he hit a homer every 27 at-bats and an extra-base hit every 8 at-bats.

The Mariners slipped another gear when they shipped him to Kansas City for pitching. Repeat after me, all you table-top GMs, *"Don't trade a star position player for pitching."* Why? Because pitchers are too volatile in their health and patterns of effectiveness. A star position player gives a more solid return, something you can plan on and build your team around. You can bet that is what Kansas City is doing.

Craig R. Wright

Tartabull, Danilo (Mora) "Dan"

Bats: Right   Throws: Right   Born 10/30/62

1987 SEASON AND MAJOR-LEAGUE CAREER BATTING TOTALS

	G	AB	H	2B	3B	HR	TB	R	RBI	TBB	IBB	SO	HP	SH	SF	SB	CS	SB%	GDP	AVG	OBP	SLG
87 KC	158	582	180	27	3	34	315	95	101	79	2	136	1	0	5	9	4	.69	14	.309	.390	.541
4 YEARS	324	1174	344	60	10	62	610	182	211	150	4	310	3	2	9	14	12	.54	25	.293	.372	.520

	1987 SEASON											FOUR YEAR TOTALS (1984 – 1987)										
	Ave.	OBP	SLG	AB	H	2B	3B	HR	RBI	BB	SO	Ave.	OBP	SLG	AB	H	2B	3B	HR	RBI	BB	SO
Totals	.309	.390	.541	582	180	27	3	34	101	79	136	.293	.372	.520	1174	344	60	10	62	211	150	310
vs. Left	.289	.389	.503	149	43	7	2	7	23	25	39	.301	.393	.497	302	91	20	3	11	45	47	80
vs. Right	.316	.390	.554	433	137	20	1	27	78	54	97	.290	.364	.528	872	253	40	7	51	166	103	230
at Home	.291	.381	.511	282	82	13	2	15	43	42	57	.284	.365	.507	580	165	30	6	29	95	73	146
on Road	.327	.398	.570	300	98	14	1	19	58	37	79	.301	.379	.532	594	179	30	4	33	116	77	164
vs. Groundball	.331	.407	.545	299	99	14	1	16	46	38	52	.306	.375	.522	588	180	35	4	28	92	65	133
vs. Flyball	.286	.372	.537	283	81	13	2	18	55	41	84	.280	.369	.517	586	164	25	6	34	119	85	177
vs. Finesse	.323	.388	.500	322	104	14	2	13	52	36	56	.315	.384	.531	661	208	34	8	31	123	75	131
vs. Power	.292	.391	.592	260	76	13	1	21	49	43	80	.265	.358	.505	513	136	26	2	31	88	75	179
on Grass	.326	.395	.549	233	76	10	0	14	44	27	65	.303	.380	.523	449	136	21	3	24	90	58	131
on Artificial Turf	.298	.387	.536	349	104	17	3	20	57	52	71	.287	.367	.517	725	208	39	7	38	121	92	179
Day Games	.287	.356	.476	143	41	3	0	8	25	16	34	.269	.350	.516	279	75	11	2	18	54	35	79
Night Games	.317	.400	.563	439	139	24	3	26	76	63	102	.301	.379	.521	895	269	49	8	44	157	115	231
April	.289	.337	.355	76	22	2	0	1	5	5	17	.264	.344	.410	144	38	6	0	5	21	17	45
May	.318	.384	.534	88	28	1	0	6	17	10	16	.299	.366	.549	144	43	3	3	9	26	16	36
June	.340	.417	.532	94	32	4	1	4	15	13	20	.326	.399	.516	184	60	9	1	8	28	23	40
July	.214	.310	.378	98	21	5	1	3	9	14	24	.254	.321	.437	197	50	8	2	8	34	20	50
August	.297	.388	.604	111	33	7	0	9	27	17	34	.267	.352	.564	202	54	12	0	16	46	27	67
Sept/Oct	.383	.474	.757	115	44	8	1	11	28	20	25	.327	.417	.584	303	99	22	4	16	56	47	72
Bases Empty	.316	.402	.565	294	93	15	2	18	18	41	71	.284	.366	.489	613	174	32	5	28	28	78	159
Leadoff	.301	.367	.581	136	41	7	2	9	9	14	27	.272	.345	.504	276	75	14	4	14	14	31	65
Not Leadoff	.329	.430	.551	158	52	8	0	9	9	27	44	.294	.382	.478	337	99	18	1	14	14	47	94
Runners On	.302	.378	.517	288	87	12	1	16	83	38	65	.303	.379	.553	561	170	28	5	34	183	72	151
First Base Only	.328	.389	.571	119	39	5	0	8	16	12	24	.314	.387	.574	242	76	13	1	16	38	29	63
Scoring Position	.284	.370	.479	169	48	7	1	8	67	26	41	.295	.373	.536	319	94	15	4	18	145	43	88
Late Innings, Close	.300	.356	.550	80	24	5	0	5	16	7	18	.298	.359	.492	181	54	10	2	7	33	17	57

RBI/Opportunities

	1987			Four Year		
Scoring Position	53 / 228	(23%)		109 / 438	(25%)	
Scoring Position, 2 Out	15 / 101	(15%)		39 / 209	(19%)	
On Third, Less than 2 Out	26 / 49	(53%)		44 / 85	(52%)	
RBI in close games / RBI Total	75 / 101	(74%)		151 / 211	(72%)	

Walt Terrell
Detroit Tigers

The best way to show the amount of respect that Walt Terrell gets is to retell a story from mid-1985. With his team lodged snugly in the bowels of the AL East and allowing runs at a ferocious pace, Cleveland manager Pat Corrales was asked why the Indians hadn't tried to obtain Terrell over the past winter. "Because we didn't want him," that noted judge of pitching replied. "We've got five guys in our rotation with more talent."

And so it goes . . . when talk turns to Terrell, even Tony Kubek starts sounding like Bill James. People will point out that he gets great support, that he's dogmeat on the road, that he allows half a zillion hits and that his strikeout to walk ratio bites the hairy wazoo. Even Sparky Anderson hates Walt—the highest praise that he can muster is that Terrell is the best #3 starter in baseball.

And I just don't understand why. No, you wouldn't want Terrell to be your staff ace (unless you're a Cleveland fan) and Ray Charles couldn't confuse him with Jack Morris, but he isn't Jack Lazorko, either. In 158 starts, he's won 66 games and posted a .545 lifetime winning percentage.

Terrell's support has never been awful, but he's never gotten barrels of runs, either. Terrell has had 703 runs scored for him in his career. That's 4.45 a game—about average. He's allowed 514 runs in 1060.2 innings; 4.36 runs per nine innings. That projects to a .509 lifetime record; Terrell is making good use of his support.

His home park? Well, there you do have a case. Though Terrell never benefited from Shea, Tiger Stadium is the main reason that he wins baseball games. Aside from what it does to his stats, his teammates pound on opposing pitchers in his starts—in the last two years, they've scored 5.64 R/G in his starts at home, and 4.57 on the road.

But be realistic, folks. If you've read the comments in this book carefully for the last two years, you should be beginning to get the idea that winning records don't just happen. Put a journeyman in a park that helps him, give him a defense, good support and a bullpen and he'll win 20 games. Put a star in a bad park with no defense, no offense and no bullpen behind him and he won't break .500. If Roger Clemens, Dwight Gooden or Jimmy Key pitched for the 1988 Cubs, we'd all be wondering what happened to them (makes you wonder what Al Nipper will do there, doesn't it?).

Terrell is a durable groundball pitcher who gets a lot of double plays and cuts down the running game; that offsets his poor control and ability to allow hits and would make him a winner on almost any team. If he stays healthy and in Detroit, he has a shot at 125 lifetime wins. He's not a pennant-winning pitcher . . . but if you can find someone who'll go 10 games over .500, Walt will help him win a pennant for you.

Geoff Beckman

Terrell, Charles Walter "Walt"   **Bats: Left**   **Throws: Right**   **Born 05/11/58**

1987 SEASON AND MAJOR-LEAGUE CAREER PITCHING TOTALS

	G	GS	CG	GF	IP	BFP	H	R	ER	HR	SH	SF	HB	TBB	IBB	SO	WP	Bk	W	L	Pct	ShO	Sv	ERA
87 DET	35	35	10	0	245	1057	254	123	110	30	3	10	3	94	7	143	8	0	17	10	.630	1	0	4.04
6 YEARS	160	158	31	2	1061	4542	1051	514	463	94	37	33	16	436	27	547	30	1	66	55	.545	9	0	3.93

1987: Finesse, Groundball   1986: Finesse, Groundball   1985: Power, Groundball   1984: Finesse, Groundball

1987 SEASON	G	IP	H	BB	SO	SB	CS	W	L	S	ERA	FOUR YEAR TOTALS (1984–1987)	G	IP	H	BB	SO	SB	CS	W	L	S	ERA
Totals	35	244.2	254	94	143	8	5	17	10	0	4.05		136	906.0	906	367	480	25	32	58	44	0	3.98
at Home	17	138.1	118	45	79	2	2	13	2	0	2.47		67	475.2	421	172	253	10	14	35	14	0	3.14
on Road	18	106.1	136	49	64	6	3	4	8	0	6.09		69	430.1	485	195	227	15	18	23	30	0	4.94
on Grass	8	51.1	63	22	34	2	1	5	2	0	4.38		40	255.2	273	104	150	10	13	13	13	0	4.37
on Artificial Turf	27	193.1	191	72	109	6	4	12	8	0	3.96		96	650.1	633	263	330	15	19	45	31	0	3.83
Day Games	29	210.1	211	74	122	5	3	16	7	0	3.72		108	733.2	714	285	379	18	21	49	32	0	3.83
Night Games	6	34.1	43	20	21	3	2	1	3	0	6.03		28	172.1	192	82	101	7	11	9	12	0	4.70
April	4	29.1	34	9	14	2	1	1	3	0	3.07		18	115.2	128	42	49	4	4	8	5	0	4.05
May	6	46.0	38	22	36	2	0	3	2	0	3.33		24	163.0	155	65	104	4	6	11	8	0	3.59
June	5	29.2	31	14	20	0	0	2	2	0	4.85		21	135.2	133	67	62	1	6	8	10	0	3.98
July	7	46.0	53	16	23	1	1	2	1	0	5.09		24	165.2	143	65	99	5	5	8	7	0	3.97
August	6	43.1	45	18	25	3	1	3	2	0	4.36		24	171.0	173	72	91	7	7	10	8	0	4.21
Sept/Oct	7	50.1	53	15	25	0	2	6	0	0	3.58		25	155.0	174	56	75	4	4	13	6	0	4.18

vs. Opponent Batters	Ave.	OBP	SLG	AB	H	2B	3B	HR	RBI	BB	SO		Ave.	OBP	SLG	AB	H	2B	3B	HR	RBI	BB	SO
Totals	.268	.333	.424	948	254	50	4	30	109	94	143		.263	.333	.395	3448	906	160	20	85	385	367	480
vs. Left	.256	.326	.418	476	122	26	3	15	57	49	69		.254	.325	.370	1792	455	90	11	32	179	190	211
vs. Right	.280	.340	.430	472	132	24	1	15	52	45	74		.272	.342	.421	1656	451	70	9	53	206	177	269
Bases Empty	.276	.334	.431	561	155	28	1	19	19	47	79		.256	.330	.392	1969	505	86	8	55	55	215	297
Leadoff	.265	.316	.487	238	63	12	1	13	13	17	35		.254	.326	.392	858	218	36	5	24	24	91	122
Not Leadoff	.285	.347	.390	323	92	16	0	6	6	30	44		.258	.333	.392	1111	287	50	3	31	31	124	175
Runners On Base	.256	.331	.413	387	99	22	3	11	90	47	64		.271	.338	.398	1479	401	74	12	30	330	152	183
First Base Only	.261	.338	.431	188	49	9	1	7	19	21	26		.285	.340	.427	737	210	39	6	18	59	61	68
Scoring Position	.251	.325	.397	199	50	13	2	4	71	26	38		.257	.335	.369	742	191	35	6	12	271	91	115
Late Innings, Close	.299	.358	.495	107	32	6	3	5	16	11	11		.281	.346	.447	331	93	13	3	12	42	34	34

RBI/Opportunities

Scoring Position	63 / 277 (23%)	240 / 1009 (24%)
Scoring Position, 2 Out	16 / 118 (14%)	79 / 444 (18%)
On Third, Less than 2 Out	33 / 60 (55%)	102 / 191 (53%)
RBI in close games / RBI Total	70 / 109 (64%)	272 / 385 (71%)

Tim Teufel

New York Mets

Tim Teufel had an outstanding 1987 season at the plate. Everything off his bat was a line drive. Most of the credit for his improved hitting was given to his new batting stance, dubbed "The Teufel Shuffle." When he steps into the batter's box, he wiggles his rear end. I don't know if this had any effect, but you can't argue with the results.

Teufel got off to a fast start while his platoon partner Wally Backman struggled, raising the question of whether or not Teufel should play every day. A look at their final stats shows that Teufel was clearly much better at the plate. In the same number of at-bats (Backman had 1 more), Teufel hit 58 points higher (.308 to .250), had an OBA 89 points higher (.396 to .307), and slugged a whopping 258 points higher (.545 to .287). Teufel had 43 extra base hits to Backman's 8, scored 12 more runs(55 to 43), and drove in 38 more runs (61 to 23). The main reason why I thought Teufel should have played every day is their different approaches to hitting. Backman would go up to bat trying to bunt his way on while Teufel would go up and try to drive the ball. As for the platoon differential, Teufel hits righties just as well as he hits lefties.

Defensively Teufel leaves something to be desired. Although he has improved he will never be mistaken for Ryne Sandberg or Lou Whitaker. He is solid with his glove but his range is limited. Those of you who don't see him play too often and only remember his error in game 1 of the '86 World Series might disagree, but I see him play every day. He does have good hands. Most of his errors come on ground balls up the middle. Having Keith Hernandez with his outstanding range playing first base allows Teufel to play closer to second base enabling him to get to more of the balls up the middle. If he can keep his offense up the Mets can live with his defense.

Teufel came up with the Twins at the end of 1983 and showed promise as he hit .308 and slugged .538 in 21 games. In 1984 he played regularly for the only time in his career, 157 games, as the Twins second baseman. He hit .262 with 76 walks, 30 doubles, and 14 homers. Defensively he led the league in assists. In 1985 he did much of the same in 138 games hitting .260 with 10 homers. After the season he was traded to the Mets for Billy Beane. In 1986 he platooned with Wally Backman and helped the Mets win the World Series. He struggled during the first part of the year but came around at the end and finished with a .287 average. If 1987 was representative of Teufel's ability, he is a valuable player. If 1987 was a career year he is still a good utility player.

Dennis Bronstein

Teufel, Timothy Shawn "Tim" Bats: Right Throws: Right Born 07/07/58

1987 SEASON AND MAJOR-LEAGUE CAREER BATTING TOTALS

	G	AB	H	2B	3B	HR	TB	R	RBI	TBB	IBB	SO	HP	SH	SF	SB	CS	SB%	GDP	AVG	OBP	SLG
87 NYN	97	299	92	29	0	14	163	55	61	44	2	53	2	3	2	3	2	.60	7	.308	.398	.545
5 YEARS	506	1658	447	110	8	45	708	235	209	202	13	246	8	17	13	9	9	.50	46	.270	.349	.427

1987 SEASON / FOUR YEAR TOTALS (1984 – 1987)

	Ave.	OBP	SLG	AB	H	2B	3B	HR	RBI	BB	SO	Ave.	OBP	SLG	AB	H	2B	3B	HR	RBI	BB	SO
Totals	.308	.396	.545	299	92	29	0	14	61	43	53	.268	.350	.422	1580	423	103	7	42	203	199	238
vs. Left	.321	.412	.563	190	61	22	0	8	35	30	27	.270	.356	.419	689	186	48	2	17	80	95	83
vs. Right	.284	.368	.514	109	31	7	0	6	26	13	26	.266	.345	.423	891	237	55	5	25	123	104	155
at Home	.326	.419	.538	132	43	16	0	4	19	22	18	.264	.340	.419	783	207	50	4	21	107	92	119
on Road	.293	.377	.551	167	49	13	0	10	42	21	35	.271	.359	.424	797	216	53	3	21	96	107	119
vs. Groundball	.287	.362	.483	143	41	13	0	5	29	17	30	.258	.338	.398	791	204	48	0	21	103	96	124
vs. Flyball	.327	.426	.603	156	51	16	0	9	32	26	23	.278	.362	.445	789	219	55	7	21	100	103	114
vs. Finesse	.353	.424	.628	156	55	16	0	9	33	19	22	.277	.344	.448	869	241	60	2	28	115	89	102
vs. Power	.259	.367	.455	143	37	13	0	5	28	24	31	.256	.357	.390	711	182	43	5	14	88	110	136
on Grass	.285	.367	.490	200	57	17	0	8	33	27	34	.265	.354	.401	765	203	52	2	16	85	108	124
on Artificial Turf	.354	.453	.657	99	35	12	0	6	28	16	19	.270	.346	.440	815	220	51	5	26	118	91	114
Day Games	.303	.397	.590	122	37	14	0	7	25	18	20	.276	.359	.463	525	145	37	2	19	84	69	78
Night Games	.311	.395	.514	177	55	15	0	7	36	25	33	.264	.346	.401	1055	278	66	5	23	119	130	160
April	.387	.472	.484	31	12	3	0	0	5	5	8	.270	.354	.387	230	62	15	0	4	37	30	34
May	.316	.438	.526	38	12	5	0	1	6	9	7	.280	.364	.415	275	77	12	2	7	37	37	47
June	.270	.341	.595	37	10	3	0	3	11	3	10	.267	.335	.453	258	69	25	1	7	34	25	32
July	.370	.435	.722	54	20	7	0	4	12	6	8	.280	.367	.420	250	70	15	1	6	31	34	34
August	.348	.455	.609	46	16	6	0	2	10	9	6	.291	.388	.464	265	77	17	1	9	25	42	40
Sept/Oct	.237	.317	.419	93	22	5	0	4	17	11	14	.225	.297	.391	302	68	19	2	9	39	31	51
Bases Empty	.325	.411	.529	157	51	14	0	6	6	21	27	.254	.338	.413	862	219	52	5	25	25	107	141
Leadoff	.373	.429	.647	51	19	5	0	3	3	4	6	.288	.353	.498	299	86	22	1	13	13	29	34
Not Leadoff	.302	.403	.472	106	32	9	0	3	3	17	21	.236	.330	.368	563	133	30	4	12	12	78	107
Runners On	.289	.380	.563	142	41	15	0	8	55	22	26	.284	.365	.432	718	204	51	2	17	178	92	97
First Base Only	.128	.196	.234	47	6	2	0	1	4	4	5	.305	.347	.444	311	95	23	1	6	21	20	33
Scoring Position	.368	.461	.726	95	35	13	0	7	51	18	21	.268	.376	.423	407	109	28	1	11	157	72	64
Late Innings, Close	.286	.426	.469	49	14	3	0	2	9	12	5	.253	.361	.379	261	66	12	0	7	36	44	40

RBI/Opportunities

	1987 Season			Four Year Totals		
Scoring Position	39 / 135	(29%)		137 / 582	(24%)	
Scoring Position, 2 Out	15 / 57	(26%)		46 / 227	(20%)	
On Third, Less than 2 Out	10 / 21	(48%)		56 / 112	(50%)	
RBI in close games / RBI Total	35 / 61	(57%)		127 / 203	(63%)	

Bobby Thigpen
Chicago White Sox

The Bobby Thigpen saga is not only the story of a young pitcher; it's the story of how a losing team operates. When the White Sox brought up Thigpen in late 1986, the situation was ideal for him. Not only was the club going nowhere on its way to a 90-loss season, the late inning relief man, Bob James, was injured. With nothing to lose, the Sox tried Thigpen in the role of closer. The results were beyond anyone's expectations. In fourteen appearances Thigpen compiled a 2–0 record, seven saves and a 1.77 ERA. He held opposing batters to a .205 average and was especially tough on lefty swingers (.170 BA, one extra base hit).

After such a debut, Thigpen might have expected that he'd won the closer's role for 1987. But when the season started the late-inning job went to James, who'd been injured, overweight and ineffective in '86. Thigpen was the setup man. To be fair, there was some logic to this; James had been brilliant in 1985, and there was the chance he would return to form with time to heal. But when the season began and James started getting pounded on a regular basis, Thigpen still wasn't given a shot at the top slot. This is the White Sox we're talking about: Hey, why trust Bobby Thigpen when you've got someone like Jimmy Winn?

Though he generally pitched well in middle relief, Thigpen's reward was a ticket to the minors—it seemed that he'd often had difficulty with the first batter he faced, and the Sox concluded from this that he was better off learning to be a starter. Never mind that Thigpen had been a starter during a stint at AA Birmingham with harrowing results (8–11, 4.68). Bobby dutifully reported to Hawaii and, as a starter, spent a couple of months getting sand kicked in his face. On the mainland, the White Sox weren't doing much better when they had a brainstorm—why don't we bring back Thigpen and try him in late relief?

What a great idea! Thigpen responded just as he had in '86— brilliantly. In August he had five saves and a 1.89 ERA. In September–October he was even better, with four wins, nine saves and a 1.93 ERA in sixteen appearances. He ended up with the Rolaids Relief Man of the Month award, the first time a Sox player had won anything since Joe Cowley was named Kelloggs Frosted "Flake of the Month" back in '86. The evidence seems clear: Thigpen is born to close. The Sox might have suspected this in 1985, when he turned in a 1.72 ERA and 74 strikeouts in 52 innings at Niagara Falls. They might have suspected it in the spring of '86, when *Baseball America* named him the top relief prospect in the minor leagues. They might have suspected it in September of '86, when he was pitching so splendidly for the big club. Who knows, they might even be suspecting it now.

Don Zminda

Thigpen, Robert Thomas "Bobby" Bats: Right Throws: Right Born 07/17/63

1987 SEASON AND MAJOR-LEAGUE CAREER PITCHING TOTALS

	G	GS	CG	GF	IP	BFP	H	R	ER	HR	SH	SF	HB	TBB	IBB	SO	WP	Bk	W	L	Pct	ShO	Sv	ERA
87 CHA	51	0	0	37	89	369	86	30	27	10	6	0	3	24	5	52	0	0	7	5	.583	0	16	2.73
2 YEARS	71	0	0	51	125	511	112	37	34	11	7	1	4	36	5	72	0	0	9	5	.643	0	23	2.45

1987: Finesse, Flyball   1986: Finesse, Flyball

1987 SEASON

	G	IP	H	BB	SO	SB	CS	W	L	S	ERA
Totals	51	89.2	86	24	52	3	3	7	5	16	2.71
at Home	30	55.1	57	12	38	1	2	4	2	10	2.77
on Road	21	34.1	29	12	14	2	1	3	3	6	2.62
on Grass	16	26.0	29	12	15	1	2	2	2	3	3.12
on Artificial Turf	35	63.2	57	12	37	2	1	5	3	13	2.54
Day Games	44	72.1	73	18	48	2	3	6	5	13	3.36
Night Games	7	17.1	13	6	4	1	0	1	0	3	0.00
April	9	19.0	20	6	6	0	0	0	1	1	3.79
May	8	14.2	13	5	6	0	2	2	1	0	3.07
June	0	0.0	0	0	0	0	0	0	0	0	0.00
July	7	9.0	14	1	7	0	0	1	0	1	4.00
August	11	19.0	16	3	15	3	0	0	2	5	1.89
Sept/Oct	16	28.0	23	9	18	0	1	4	1	9	1.93

vs. Opponent Batters	Ave.	OBP	SLG	AB	H	2B	3B	HR	RBI	BB	SO
Totals	.256	.311	.372	336	86	7	1	10	40	24	52
vs. Left	.277	.340	.367	177	49	4	0	4	16	16	25
vs. Right	.233	.278	.377	159	37	3	1	6	24	8	27
Bases Empty	.281	.316	.416	178	50	4	1	6	6	8	27
Leadoff	.347	.380	.547	75	26	4	1	3	3	4	8
Not Leadoff	.233	.269	.320	103	24	0	0	3	3	4	19
Runners On Base	.228	.307	.323	158	36	3	0	4	34	16	25
First Base Only	.232	.293	.319	69	16	0	0	2	4	5	10
Scoring Position	.225	.317	.326	89	20	3	0	2	30	11	15
Late Innings, Close	.238	.295	.348	210	50	5	0	6	23	16	31

FOUR YEAR TOTALS (1984 – 1987)

	G	IP	H	BB	SO	SB	CS	W	L	S	ERA
Totals	71	125.1	112	36	72	5	3	9	5	23	2.44
at Home	40	72.0	67	17	48	1	2	5	2	15	2.38
on Road	31	53.1	45	19	24	4	1	4	3	8	2.53
on Grass	22	38.0	38	17	22	2	2	2	2	6	2.61
on Artificial Turf	49	87.1	74	19	50	3	1	7	3	17	2.37
Day Games	59	100.2	95	30	64	3	3	7	5	18	2.95
Night Games	12	24.2	17	6	8	2	0	2	0	5	0.36
April	9	19.0	20	6	6	0	0	0	1	1	3.79
May	8	14.2	13	5	6	0	2	2	1	0	3.07
June	0	0.0	0	0	0	0	0	0	0	0	0.00
July	7	9.0	14	1	7	0	0	1	0	1	4.00
August	21	38.1	28	14	25	4	0	0	2	8	1.41
Sept/Oct	26	44.1	37	10	28	1	1	6	1	13	2.23

vs. Opponent Batters	Ave.	OBP	SLG	AB	H	2B	3B	HR	RBI	BB	SO
Totals	.242	.301	.343	463	112	10	2	11	52	36	72
vs. Left	.252	.320	.326	230	58	5	0	4	20	22	33
vs. Right	.232	.281	.361	233	54	5	2	7	32	14	39
Bases Empty	.255	.296	.379	243	62	7	1	7	7	13	37
Leadoff	.314	.346	.500	102	32	5	1	4	4	5	13
Not Leadoff	.213	.260	.291	141	30	2	0	3	3	8	24
Runners On Base	.227	.306	.305	220	50	3	1	4	45	23	35
First Base Only	.233	.303	.300	90	21	0	0	2	4	8	13
Scoring Position	.223	.308	.308	130	29	3	1	2	41	15	22
Late Innings, Close	.229	.276	.334	293	67	8	1	7	32	18	44

RBI/Opportunities

	1987			Four Year		
Scoring Position	24 /	124	(19%)	35 /	179	(20%)
Scoring Position, 2 Out	11 /	64	(17%)	14 /	87	(16%)
On Third, Less than 2 Out	4 /	19	(21%)	8 /	32	(25%)
RBI in close games / RBI Total	28 /	40	(70%)	37 /	52	(71%)

Andres Thomas
Atlanta Braves

Everyone (except perhaps Chuck Tanner) knows that Andres Thomas is currently an awful offensive ballplayer. Thomas combines a low batting average, pathetic OB%, limited power, terrible strike zone judgment, and poor base stealing stats into one package that had the worst offensive won/loss percentage in the league (.242) among players with 300 or more at bats.

Despite his stats I find it hard to blame Thomas for his shortcomings. I do find it easy to blame Chuck Tanner for giving Thomas offensive roles he clearly cannot handle. In 1987, Tanner used Thomas almost exclusively in the #2 and #6 slots in the lineup. Would you use a player with a .268 OBA in the #2 position? Anybody, including Ozzie Virgil, would have been a better choice.

Chuck finally came to his senses in mid-season and installed Ken Oberkfell in the #2 slot. However, instead of dropping Thomas to the bottom of the order he put him in the #6 slot. Who would you bat sixth, a player with a .312 SLG PCT (Thomas) or one with a .471 SLG PCT (Virgil)? With Thomas batting sixth, the Braves #5 hitters (usually Griffey or Roenicke) stopped seeing hittable pitches in key situations. Chuck Tanner used Glen Hubbard in the eighth spot the entire year (.264 BA .378 OBA .381 SLG) instead of Thomas and the only reason I can think of is that Hub just doesn't look very athletic.

Thomas replaced Rafael Ramirez as the Braves shortstop in 1986 and one would be hard pressed to name two more similar players. They have identical weaknesses (offense) and strengths (they sure look good at times). After Thomas and Ramirez went down with injuries in 1987, Jeff Blauser was given a trial at SS. Blauser, who had been impressive in spring training, provided steadier defense and a little offense. The Braves apparently consider Blauser a prospect, judging from the buildup they've given him; he is, in fact, a former number one-draft choice. Be that as it may, there is little evidence to suggest Blauser will hit consistently at the major league level.

Despite his poor play so far in his career, I wouldn't write off Andres Thomas just yet. Going into the 1988 season he is only 24 years old, still young enough to raise the level of his play. Another Latin shortstop started his career with many of the same characteristics (low average, OBA, and SLG) as Thomas before blossoming at age 25. That shortstop turned out to be one of the best ever—Dave Concepcion.

Greg Gajus

Thomas, Andres Perez Bats: Right Throws: Right Born 11/10/63

1987 SEASON AND MAJOR-LEAGUE CAREER BATTING TOTALS

	G	AB	H	2B	3B	HR	TB	R	RBI	TBB	IBB	SO	HP	SH	SF	SB	CS	SB%	GDP	AVG	OBP	SLG
87 ATL	82	324	75	11	0	5	101	29	39	14	0	50	2	3	0	6	5	.55	7	.231	.268	.312
3 YEARS	199	665	161	28	2	11	226	61	73	22	2	101	2	6	2	10	11	.48	22	.242	.268	.340

	1987 SEASON											FOUR YEAR TOTALS (1984 – 1987)										
	Ave.	OBP	SLG	AB	H	2B	3B	HR	RBI	BB	SO	Ave.	OBP	SLG	AB	H	2B	3B	HR	RBI	BB	SO
Totals	.231	.268	.312	324	75	11	0	5	39	14	50	.242	.268	.340	665	161	28	2	11	73	22	101
vs. Left	.229	.260	.302	96	22	4	0	1	9	3	8	.251	.266	.350	243	61	13	1	3	21	4	25
vs. Right	.232	.271	.316	228	53	7	0	4	30	11	42	.237	.269	.334	422	100	15	1	8	52	18	76
at Home	.259	.283	.351	174	45	4	0	4	22	5	29	.234	.261	.317	312	73	9	1	5	33	11	45
on Road	.200	.250	.267	150	30	7	0	1	17	9	21	.249	.274	.360	353	88	19	1	6	40	11	56
vs. Groundball	.250	.286	.286	140	35	5	0	0	18	7	21	.272	.300	.376	287	78	14	2	4	36	12	42
vs. Flyball	.217	.254	.332	184	40	6	0	5	21	7	29	.220	.243	.312	378	83	14	0	7	37	10	59
vs. Finesse	.255	.281	.352	165	42	7	0	3	22	5	21	.254	.270	.368	342	87	17	2	6	41	7	41
vs. Power	.208	.254	.270	159	33	4	0	2	17	9	29	.229	.265	.310	323	74	11	0	5	32	15	60
on Grass	.248	.280	.350	246	61	10	0	5	32	9	38	.233	.259	.308	481	112	16	1	6	51	16	72
on Artificial Turf	.179	.229	.192	78	14	1	0	0	7	5	12	.266	.289	.424	184	49	12	1	5	22	6	29
Day Games	.209	.229	.270	115	24	4	0	1	10	2	16	.226	.245	.312	221	50	14	1	1	23	5	35
Night Games	.244	.288	.335	209	51	7	0	4	29	12	34	.250	.279	.354	444	111	14	1	10	50	17	66
April	.244	.311	.415	41	10	4	0	1	6	3	6	.255	.317	.418	55	14	6	0	1	8	4	6
May	.200	.233	.243	70	14	3	0	0	6	3	13	.256	.286	.347	121	31	8	0	1	11	5	21
June	.273	.341	.390	77	21	0	0	3	10	7	10	.271	.312	.429	133	36	1	1	6	16	7	15
July	.215	.222	.252	107	23	4	0	0	11	1	17	.258	.274	.360	186	48	11	1	2	22	4	32
August	.241	.241	.345	29	7	0	0	1	6	0	4	.184	.195	.237	76	14	1	0	1	9	1	14
Sept/Oct	.000	.000	.000	0	0	0	0	0	0	0	0	.191	.200	.202	94	18	1	0	0	7	1	13
Bases Empty	.211	.251	.277	166	35	5	0	2	2	8	29	.231	.256	.333	351	81	14	2	6	6	11	63
Leadoff	.237	.274	.254	59	14	1	0	0	0	3	12	.244	.262	.331	127	31	5	0	2	2	3	23
Not Leadoff	.196	.239	.290	107	21	4	0	2	2	5	17	.223	.253	.335	224	50	9	2	4	4	8	40
Runners On	.253	.285	.348	158	40	6	0	3	37	6	21	.255	.282	.347	314	80	14	0	5	67	11	38
First Base Only	.250	.262	.375	64	16	2	0	2	4	1	10	.273	.278	.364	132	36	3	0	3	7	1	16
Scoring Position	.255	.300	.330	94	24	4	0	1	33	5	11	.242	.285	.335	182	44	11	0	2	60	10	22
Late Innings, Close	.167	.231	.167	48	8	0	0	0	3	4	10	.213	.274	.269	108	23	3	0	1	10	9	18

RBI/Opportunities

Scoring Position	30 / 126 (24%)		54 / 251	(22%)	
Scoring Position, 2 Out	20 / 64 (31%)		34 / 119	(29%)	
On Third, Less than 2 Out	7 / 18 (39%)		14 / 42	(33%)	
RBI in close games / RBI Total	24 / 39 (62%)		43 / 73	(59%)	

Milt Thompson
Philadelphia Phillies

On June 30, new Philadelphia manager Lee Elia declared "I'm a Stoney guy." With Milt Thompson down to .255 after a fast start, Jeff Stone would become the Phils' regular center fielder upon returning from the disabled list (he bruised his hand when hit by a pitch). The next day, Stone was sent on injury rehab to AAA Maine to pick up some playing time in center; his expected return date was July 5. But Stone didn't hit his weight and looked uncomfortable in the field, so the Phils decided to extend his visit to Old Orchard Beach. By July 11, Elia indicated that Thompson would stay in the lineup even after Stone's recall, and by the All-Star break it was suggested that Stone might not even be called up after his rehab. Stone was eventually recalled on July 20, languishing on the Phils' bench for the rest of the season.

But this isn't supposed to be a report on the star-crossed career of Jeff Stone. Between Elia's Stoney statement and the All-Star break, Thompson cemented his place as the Phils' starting center fielder by batting .333. And that was just the beginning—Milt hit a ringing .344 in the second half and finished with the ninth best average in the league. Only five National Leaguers stole more bases. All in all, he finally established himself as a solid major league ballplayer.

At least, that's what the Phillies hope.

I'm not convinced. Until he proves that he can hit left-handed pitching, Thompson remains at best a platoon player. He hit 40 points higher against southpaws than in the previous three years, and still only got to .214. Spending half the season hitting behind Juan Samuel, Milt knocked in just 43 runs. Samuel and Schmidt both scored more runs than he did, with Hayes close behind. He struck out twice as often as he walked.

Much of the Phils' 1987 offensive weakness resulted from the presence of Samuel and Thompson, who combined for almost 250 whiffs, at the top of the batting order. The Bradley trade should correct that in 1988. In my opinion, they should go against righties with Bradley leading off, followed by Hayes. I think Samuel has matured enough to hit third, where he might finally ring up that monster year we've been waiting for. Then come Schmidt, James, Parrish, Thompson, and the shortstop. Facing lefties, move Hayes to center and bat first baseman Schu in Milt's spot. Bob Dernier needn't place a big order with Hillerich & Bradsby.

Thompson turned in decent defensive statistics in center field. His 2.90 range factor based on games started trailed only the remarkable Gary Pettis, Eric Davis, and Brett Butler among CFs (thanks to Howard Ahlskog of the *APBA Journal* for info on games started by position). Yet he didn't look all that good out there, consistently breaking the wrong way on flyballs—raw speed can make up for an awful lot of little mistakes.

Neal Traven

Thompson, Milton Bernard "Milt"   Bats: Left   Throws: Right   Born 01/05/59

1987 SEASON AND MAJOR-LEAGUE CAREER BATTING TOTALS

	G	AB	H	2B	3B	HR	TB	R	RBI	TBB	IBB	SO	HP	SH	SF	SB	CS	SB%	GDP	AVG	OBP	SLG
87 PHI	150	527	159	26	9	7	224	86	43	42	2	87	0	3	3	46	10	.82	5	.302	.351	.425
4 YEARS	344	1107	319	41	12	15	429	157	76	86	4	196	4	9	5	88	20	.81	11	.288	.340	.388

	1987 SEASON											FOUR YEAR TOTALS (1984 – 1987)										
	Ave.	OBP	SLG	AB	H	2B	3B	HR	RBI	BB	SO	Ave.	OBP	SLG	AB	H	2B	3B	HR	RBI	BB	SO
Totals	.302	.351	.425	527	159	26	9	7	43	42	87	.288	.340	.388	1107	319	41	12	15	76	86	196
vs. Left	.214	.283	.250	84	18	3	0	0	2	8	14	.194	.244	.218	165	32	4	0	0	5	11	32
vs. Right	.318	.365	.458	443	141	23	9	7	41	34	73	.305	.357	.417	942	287	37	12	15	71	75	164
at Home	.330	.382	.474	270	89	16	7	3	24	24	48	.311	.363	.431	562	175	26	10	7	41	45	104
on Road	.272	.319	.374	257	70	10	2	4	19	18	39	.264	.317	.343	545	144	15	2	8	35	41	92
vs. Groundball	.278	.327	.370	273	76	8	4	3	18	20	52	.268	.318	.342	555	149	16	5	5	34	39	104
vs. Flyball	.327	.378	.484	254	83	18	5	4	25	22	35	.308	.363	.433	552	170	25	7	10	42	47	92
vs. Finesse	.321	.364	.489	280	90	17	6	6	33	20	38	.306	.346	.425	572	175	25	8	9	53	35	85
vs. Power	.279	.337	.352	247	69	9	3	1	10	22	49	.269	.334	.348	535	144	16	4	6	23	51	111
on Grass	.252	.295	.344	131	33	6	0	2	6	8	19	.282	.325	.362	436	123	16	2	5	21	24	72
on Artificial Turf	.318	.370	.452	396	126	20	9	5	37	34	68	.292	.350	.404	671	196	25	10	10	55	62	124
Day Games	.302	.337	.432	162	49	7	1	4	14	9	25	.270	.318	.361	352	95	10	2	6	26	25	68
Night Games	.301	.357	.422	365	110	19	8	3	29	33	62	.297	.350	.400	755	224	31	10	9	50	61	128
April	.314	.351	.386	70	22	3	1	0	3	4	10	.258	.305	.326	132	34	4	1	1	7	9	23
May	.210	.297	.324	105	22	3	3	1	6	13	14	.204	.271	.296	186	38	5	3	2	10	17	31
June	.266	.301	.392	79	21	5	1	1	4	4	18	.270	.311	.400	100	27	5	1	2	8	6	21
July	.408	.452	.684	76	31	6	3	3	9	7	10	.383	.415	.591	115	44	7	4	3	10	7	20
August	.417	.425	.546	108	45	6	1	2	17	3	15	.367	.377	.471	221	81	11	3	2	25	5	42
Sept/Oct	.202	.290	.236	89	18	3	0	0	4	11	20	.269	.347	.337	353	95	9	0	5	16	42	59
Bases Empty	.296	.341	.416	351	104	19	4	5	5	24	58	.281	.328	.388	740	208	31	6	12	12	52	131
Leadoff	.305	.344	.403	154	47	6	0	3	3	9	23	.296	.335	.388	358	106	13	1	6	6	21	60
Not Leadoff	.289	.340	.426	197	57	13	4	2	2	15	35	.267	.322	.387	382	102	18	5	6	6	31	71
Runners On	.313	.371	.443	176	55	7	5	2	38	18	29	.302	.359	.387	367	111	10	6	3	64	34	65
First Base Only	.373	.420	.533	75	28	2	2	2	6	6	11	.340	.386	.453	159	54	3	3	3	9	12	22
Scoring Position	.267	.336	.376	101	27	5	3	0	32	12	18	.274	.339	.337	208	57	7	3	0	55	22	43
Late Innings, Close	.313	.352	.458	83	26	2	2	2	7	5	20	.314	.364	.418	194	61	7	2	3	15	15	44

RBI/Opportunities

Scoring Position	29 / 132	(22%)		52 / 278	(19%)
Scoring Position, 2 Out	10 / 71	(14%)		18 / 139	(13%)
On Third, Less than 2 Out	13 / 17	(76%)		24 / 35	(69%)
RBI in close games / RBI Total	35 / 43	(81%)		61 / 76	(80%)

Robby Thompson
San Francisco Giants

Robby Thompson is quite a story. This fine, gritty young infielder from Florida was scouted and signed by Don Zimmer's son Tom. Robby was very selective, having been drafted by Oakland and Seattle before finally signing with San Francisco.

A look at his bio shows he was married in 1984, and that his children were born in 1982 and 1986, and that he made the jump from AA to the Bigs in 1986. What it doesn't tell you is that Robby and his wife adopted their niece, Kristeena Marie, when both her parents (Brenda's sister and her husband) were victims of a fatal traffic accident in 1985. Sudden families are always difficult, but they are especially so on an AA salary. However, the good news was that Thompson made the major league roster, and, even with the minimum salary, experienced a 500 percent raise. He then went on to win every Rookie of the Year award except the Baseball Writers' of America.

Robby suffered no sophomore jinx in performance, but he did start the season with an identical back injury to Joe Montana's. Having the benefit of care from Montana's physician, he played through the pain, helping the Giants set a franchise record for double plays with a ML-leading 193. He is a fine clutch hitter, hitting .333 (28 for 84) with men in scoring position, and .452 (19 for 42) with MISP and two out. He has good power, with 37.3 percent extra-base hit percentage. Only two second basemen in the league exceeded that—Juan Samuel (44.9 percent), and, surprise, Tim Teufel (46.7 percent!). Thompson's OBA of .338 exceeded Samuel's and trailed Teufel's .398. (Teufel is an interesting case—he was 8 for 18 as a pinch-hitter, but with only 2 extra-base hits. As a starter, he had 41 EBH out of 84 hits.) Such well-known second basemen as Sandberg (27.9 percent EBH), Doran (23.7 percent), Herr (23.1 percent) and Sax (20.5 percent) trailed such lesser-knowns as Glenn Hubbard (34.2 percent), Vance Law (33.6 percent), and Kurt Stillwell (30.2 percent).

Thompson was consistent at home and on the road (.263, 7, 23 home, .260, 3, 21 away), but dramatically improved on turf over 1986 (.250 vs. .214). In 1986 he hit lefties 21 points higher; in 1987, 69 points higher (.310 vs. .241). While the Giants experienced great success with Robby hitting leadoff (24–11), expect to see Brett Butler start 154 or more games there in 1988. Thompson should slide back to the #2 slot, where his franchise-record 18 sacrifices in 1986 may be extended. Thompson is Roger Craig's favorite practitioner of the suicide squeeze; Butler's career 3.7 percent doubles rate suggests at least 24 two-base hits. With Butler's career 69 percent stolen base percentage, he should be on third with no outs at least a half-dozen times in 1988. Third basemen of the National League, beware.

It will be interesting to see the figures at the end of the season for the Giants' keystone combination. Although they are mostly renowned for their defense, they also constitute one of the premier offensive duos in the league. Taking On-base Average, Extra-Base Hit Percentage, Slugging Average and Batting Average, the Mets have the best offensive duo, finishing first or second in each category. The Giants were third in each category; since no other team was so consistently high, overall the Giants rank as having the second best keystone combination on offense in the league.

Michael Duca

Thompson, Robert Randall "Rob" Bats: Right Throws: Right Born 05/10/62

1987 SEASON AND MAJOR-LEAGUE CAREER BATTING TOTALS

	G	AB	H	2B	3B	HR	TB	R	RBI	TBB	IBB	SO	HP	SH	SF	SB	CS	SB%	GDP	AVG	OBP	SLG
87 SF	132	420	110	26	5	10	176	62	44	40	3	91	8	6	0	16	11	.59	8	.262	.338	.419
2 YEARS	281	969	259	53	8	17	379	135	91	82	3	203	13	24	1	28	26	.52	19	.267	.332	.391

1987 SEASON

	Ave.	OBP	SLG	AB	H	2B	3B	HR	RBI	BB	SO
Totals	.262	.338	.419	420	110	26	5	10	44	40	91
vs. Left	.310	.382	.465	129	40	7	2	3	16	10	18
vs. Right	.241	.318	.399	291	70	19	3	7	28	30	73
at Home	.263	.346	.449	205	54	11	3	7	23	20	40
on Road	.260	.329	.391	215	56	15	2	3	21	20	51
vs. Groundball	.264	.340	.423	182	48	13	2	4	21	18	34
vs. Flyball	.261	.336	.416	238	62	13	3	6	23	22	57
vs. Finesse	.241	.335	.406	212	51	11	3	6	21	23	45
vs. Power	.284	.341	.433	208	59	15	2	4	23	17	46
on Grass	.266	.343	.427	316	84	18	3	9	37	31	64
on Artificial Turf	.250	.322	.394	104	26	8	2	1	7	9	27
Day Games	.320	.383	.489	178	57	11	2	5	23	14	35
Night Games	.219	.305	.368	242	53	15	3	5	21	26	56
April	.208	.311	.358	53	11	2	0	2	8	7	14
May	.378	.417	.600	45	17	4	0	2	8	2	11
June	.224	.290	.388	85	19	5	0	3	6	7	20
July	.218	.265	.333	78	17	2	2	1	10	5	15
August	.303	.367	.424	99	30	10	1	0	6	9	20
Sept/Oct	.267	.405	.483	60	16	3	2	2	6	10	11
Bases Empty	.250	.324	.415	284	71	21	4	6	6	28	67
Leadoff	.230	.305	.399	148	34	13	3	2	2	14	29
Not Leadoff	.272	.344	.434	136	37	8	1	4	4	14	38
Runners On	.287	.366	.426	136	39	5	1	4	38	12	24
First Base Only	.212	.268	.346	52	11	2	1	1	4	3	10
Scoring Position	.333	.423	.476	84	28	3	0	3	34	9	14
Late Innings, Close	.217	.325	.348	69	15	6	0	1	9	10	16

FOUR YEAR TOTALS (1984 – 1987)

	Ave.	OBP	SLG	AB	H	2B	3B	HR	RBI	BB	SO
Totals	.267	.332	.391	969	259	53	8	17	91	82	203
vs. Left	.296	.361	.434	297	88	17	3	6	31	24	51
vs. Right	.254	.320	.372	672	171	36	5	11	60	58	152
at Home	.280	.356	.435	460	129	28	5	11	51	46	83
on Road	.255	.310	.352	509	130	25	3	6	40	36	120
vs. Groundball	.269	.339	.391	450	121	26	4	7	44	42	90
vs. Flyball	.266	.326	.391	519	138	27	4	10	47	40	113
vs. Finesse	.288	.351	.426	524	151	29	5	11	51	43	97
vs. Power	.243	.311	.351	445	108	24	3	6	40	39	106
on Grass	.281	.353	.422	711	200	40	6	16	76	69	139
on Artificial Turf	.229	.273	.306	258	59	13	2	1	15	13	64
Day Games	.300	.364	.440	420	126	25	5	8	48	35	80
Night Games	.242	.308	.353	549	133	28	3	9	43	47	123
April	.229	.322	.328	131	30	7	0	2	16	17	31
May	.331	.375	.496	127	42	9	0	4	16	8	26
June	.235	.293	.344	183	43	8	0	4	15	14	35
July	.251	.301	.374	171	43	7	4	2	17	12	42
August	.285	.332	.393	214	61	15	1	2	14	14	40
Sept/Oct	.280	.372	.434	143	40	7	3	3	13	17	29
Bases Empty	.267	.322	.401	621	166	40	5	11	11	47	144
Leadoff	.260	.327	.419	258	67	20	3	5	5	24	50
Not Leadoff	.273	.318	.388	363	99	20	2	6	6	23	94
Runners On	.267	.343	.374	348	93	13	3	6	80	35	59
First Base Only	.243	.289	.364	140	34	7	2	2	9	8	20
Scoring Position	.284	.377	.380	208	59	6	1	4	71	27	39
Late Innings, Close	.262	.331	.354	164	43	9	0	2	17	16	35

RBI/Opportunities

	1987		Four Year	
Scoring Position	28 / 117	(24%)	62 / 297	(21%)
Scoring Position, 2 Out	20 / 56	(36%)	31 / 127	(24%)
On Third, Less than 2 Out	5 / 22	(23%)	22 / 58	(38%)
RBI in close games / RBI Total	19 / 44	(43%)	53 / 91	(58%)

Wayne Tolleson
New York Yankees

On May 27, Wayne Tolleson doubled. On July 20, he knocked in a run. They turned out to be the last extra base hit and RBI that he would get in the 1987 season. While the Yankees didn't expect Wayne to lead the league in total bases or RBIs, his failure to contribute anything but infrequent singles made him a costly luxury for New York in 1987.

Or maybe the Yankees did expect him to do one or the other; when they chose to make Wayne their regular shortstop this season, they couldn't have been thinking very clearly. Focusing solely on Tolleson's 1986—when he set career highs in games played (141), at-bats (475), doubles (16), walks (52) and RBIs (43) and tied career-bests in triples (5) and homers (3)— management decided that he had The Right Stuff for the job. More sensible minds might have guessed that trying to turn a 30-year-old spare part into a regular at the game's most demanding position wouldn't work. It didn't; that error in judgment really hurt the Yankees in 1987.

Tolleson had a strong start offensively and his steady, though unspectacular, play in the field helped solidify the Yankee infield. But after May, it was all downhill. Wayne hit .187 from June 1 on, with no power—literally—and 23 walks in over 200 plate appearances.

If you weren't a Yankee fan, it was amusing to watch what defenses would do when Tolleson batted in the second half. When he batted lefty, the leftfielder would set up about 150 feet behind third base and 20–25 feet from the foul line (the reverse when he batted righty). That effectively ended any chance that Wayne had of blooping one down the line—which was the only way he had of hitting for extra bases. When he tried to pull the ball, it only made things worse—his slump deepened as he began striking out. Wayne fanned 72 times in 349 ABs in 1987; when you have absolutely no power, you simply must make contact more often than that.

To cap off his season, Tolleson's right shoulder began giving him problems. His arm, which wasn't strong enough for shortstop to begin with, turned into linguini *al dente*; limiting his range to the point where he went from marginal plus to huge minus defensively. With his bat gone and his glove rapidly going, the Yankees were finally forced to take action—in early August, Tolleson came out of the lineup so that he could recover. He never did—he had to have surgery on his shoulder over the winter and remains a question mark for 1988.

It would be nice to think that the Yankees have learned something from this debacle, but it's doubtful. George Steinbrenner has no patience and could never tolerate the mistakes that young shortstops invariably make; as a result, New York will be forced to employ veteran retreads like Tolleson and Rafael Santana for a very long time.

Craig Christmann and Arnie Braunstein

Tolleson, Jimmy Wayne "Wayne" Bats: Both   Throws: Right   Born 11/22/55

1987 SEASON AND MAJOR-LEAGUE CAREER BATTING TOTALS

	G	AB	H	2B	3B	HR	TB	R	RBI	TBB	IBB	SO	HP	SH	SF	SB	CS	SB%	GDP	AVG	OBP	SLG
87 NYA	121	349	77	4	0	1	84	48	22	43	0	72	0	6	0	5	3	.63	3	.221	.306	.241
7 YEARS	689	2049	510	52	14	8	614	265	115	189	0	328	7	47	9	101	40	.72	36	.249	.313	.300

	1987 SEASON											FOUR YEAR TOTALS (1984 – 1987)										
	Ave.	OBP	SLG	AB	H	2B	3B	HR	RBI	BB	SO	Ave.	OBP	SLG	AB	H	2B	3B	HR	RBI	BB	SO
Totals	.221	.306	.241	349	77	4	0	1	22	43	72	.253	.320	.305	1485	376	38	12	5	92	143	241
vs. Left	.198	.315	.208	106	21	1	0	0	5	18	31	.256	.330	.328	472	121	13	6	3	33	52	93
vs. Right	.230	.302	.255	243	56	3	0	1	17	25	41	.252	.314	.294	1013	255	25	6	2	59	91	148
at Home	.211	.314	.230	152	32	3	0	0	10	23	31	.264	.331	.316	740	195	20	8	1	52	75	109
on Road	.228	.300	.249	197	45	1	0	1	12	20	41	.243	.308	.294	745	181	18	4	4	40	68	132
vs. Groundball	.209	.276	.231	182	38	1	0	1	7	17	35	.236	.304	.282	709	167	19	4	2	37	68	114
vs. Flyball	.234	.337	.251	167	39	3	0	0	15	26	37	.269	.334	.326	776	209	19	8	3	55	75	127
vs. Finesse	.211	.266	.243	185	39	3	0	1	11	14	36	.258	.310	.309	818	211	18	6	4	47	62	122
vs. Power	.232	.347	.238	164	38	1	0	0	11	29	36	.247	.330	.300	667	165	20	6	1	45	81	119
on Grass	.221	.307	.231	290	64	3	0	0	17	36	60	.260	.328	.310	1259	327	32	11	3	80	127	194
on Artificial Turf	.220	.303	.288	59	13	1	0	1	5	7	12	.217	.272	.279	226	49	6	1	2	12	16	47
Day Games	.279	.360	.297	111	31	2	0	0	9	14	20	.272	.338	.327	419	114	13	2	2	38	43	67
Night Games	.193	.281	.214	238	46	2	0	1	13	29	52	.246	.312	.296	1066	262	25	10	3	54	100	174
April	.348	.403	.394	66	23	3	0	0	3	6	11	.302	.377	.378	225	68	10	2	1	19	27	29
May	.200	.301	.244	90	18	1	0	1	9	13	19	.234	.307	.275	291	68	4	1	2	16	31	57
June	.212	.309	.212	85	18	0	0	0	6	12	16	.216	.296	.261	291	63	8	1	1	13	33	42
July	.197	.265	.197	76	15	0	0	0	4	7	17	.278	.346	.304	230	64	3	0	1	21	24	38
August	.091	.231	.091	22	2	0	0	0	0	4	6	.250	.292	.323	220	55	6	5	0	10	13	39
Sept/Oct	.100	.182	.100	10	1	0	0	0	0	1	3	.254	.300	.311	228	58	7	3	0	13	15	36
Bases Empty	.199	.285	.227	216	43	3	0	1	1	26	46	.259	.325	.309	900	233	23	8	2	2	88	155
Leadoff	.188	.289	.188	85	16	0	0	0	0	12	21	.247	.327	.296	372	92	5	5	1	1	44	68
Not Leadoff	.206	.283	.252	131	27	3	0	1	1	14	25	.267	.323	.318	528	141	18	3	1	1	44	87
Runners On	.256	.340	.263	133	34	1	0	0	21	17	26	.244	.309	.299	585	143	15	4	3	90	55	86
First Base Only	.224	.286	.224	58	13	0	0	0	0	5	11	.254	.300	.301	272	69	6	2	1	6	18	39
Scoring Position	.280	.379	.293	75	21	1	0	0	21	12	15	.236	.317	.297	313	74	9	2	2	84	37	47
Late Innings, Close	.286	.375	.347	49	14	0	0	1	5	7	10	.273	.346	.347	245	67	3	3	3	17	27	40

RBI/Opportunities

Scoring Position	21 / 110	(19%)		78 / 457	(17%)	
Scoring Position, 2 Out	6 / 48	(13%)		29 / 213	(14%)	
On Third, Less than 2 Out	9 / 20	(45%)		28 / 63	(44%)	
RBI in close games / RBI Total	11 / 22	(50%)		59 / 92	(64%)	

Alan Trammell
Detroit Tigers

When Tigers manager Sparky Anderson announced that he planned to use Alan Trammell in the clean-up spot in 1987, a lot of people in Motown were ready to fit him for sleeveless pajamas. Trammell, people reminded him, had never hit more than 21 homers or batted in 75 runs in his career and hadn't hit .300 since 1984; per 600 at-bats, he'd averaged 12 homers and 65 RBIs. "The only way that this will pay off," one writer said, "is if Trammell has the best season of his life."

He did. Trammell set career highs in runs, hits, homers, RBIs, total bases, batting average, and on-base, slugging and stolen base percentages. With the exception of the runs scored figure (two better than his previous personal best), none of his previous bests were anywhere close to his 1987 figures. He had 137 runs created; second only to Wade Boggs. Trammell didn't just "return to form"—he went far, far beyond it.

How did he do it? Good question. Normally when someone has a sharp jump in production, you can see a reason in his splits—he's never hit lefties before, had his best year ever at home or something like that. In this case, Alan simply added about 50 points of batting average with a proportional increase in power to every split.

The only theory that holds up at all is a look at his 1986. Beginning in July, Alan went on a tear and hasn't stopped since. Was it because, after a year and a half of bat-

tling injuries of all kinds, he was finally healthy? That might be. 1984 was Trammell's best year until now; when he got hurt in 1985, both his hitting and fielding began to decline. A good deal of his range returned in 1987; he was sixth in the league in range factor and third in double plays per game in 1987. Though Alan isn't the Gold Glover that he once was, he's one of the better defensive shortstops in the league again. Maybe his bat also needed time to recover—it's as good an explanation as any.

Finally: Anyone who believes that George Bell was the AL MVP in 1987 is sadly mistaken. There's no basis whatsoever for the contention.

On offense, Bell's SL% is 54 points better than Trammell's; Alan's OB% is 52 points above George's. That's a push. Bell, however, made 36 more outs. As a result, Trammell created both more runs (137–125) and more runs per 27 outs (8.94–7.54). He was a better hitter than Bell was in 1987.

Defense? Bell had a range factor that you'd expect from King Kong Bundy; he was one of the worst leftfielders in the league. And get this— Trammell made 19 errors in 1987; Bell made 11.

Even ignoring (as you should) the minor gap in performance in the last week, it's not a difficult question to answer. Alan Trammell was, by any standard you want to use, the AL's Most Valuable Player in 1987.

Geoff Beckman and Steve Lysogorski

Trammell, Alan Stuart

Bats: Right **Throws: Right** **Born 02/21/58**

1987 SEASON AND MAJOR-LEAGUE CAREER BATTING TOTALS

	G	AB	H	2B	3B	HR	TB	R	RBI	TBB	IBB	SO	HP	SH	SF	SB	CS	SB%	GDP	AVG	OBP	SLG
87 DET	151	597	205	34	3	28	329	109	105	60	8	47	3	2	6	21	2	.91	11	.343	.402	.551
11 YEARS	1440	5228	1505	248	45	118	2197	811	609	548	24	566	21	102	49	170	80	.68	83	.288	.355	.420

1987 SEASON

	Ave.	OBP	SLG	AB	H	2B	3B	HR	RBI	BB	SO
Totals	.343	.402	.551	597	205	34	3	28	105	60	47
vs. Left	.360	.419	.575	214	77	11	1	11	48	24	19
vs. Right	.334	.393	.538	383	128	23	2	17	57	36	28
at Home	.348	.404	.534	296	103	16	0	13	53	27	20
on Road	.339	.401	.568	301	102	18	3	15	52	33	27
vs. Groundball	.362	.414	.570	307	111	15	2	15	50	29	20
vs. Flyball	.324	.390	.531	290	94	19	1	13	55	31	27
vs. Finesse	.348	.389	.531	305	106	17	3	11	57	23	16
vs. Power	.339	.416	.572	292	99	17	0	17	48	37	31
on Grass	.352	.407	.561	506	178	29	1	25	94	49	39
on Artificial Turf	.297	.375	.495	91	27	5	2	3	11	11	8
Day Games	.371	.446	.566	175	65	11	1	7	30	23	14
Night Games	.332	.384	.545	422	140	23	2	21	75	37	33
April	.333	.358	.431	51	17	2	0	1	8	2	3
May	.330	.375	.456	103	34	4	0	3	14	7	10
June	.376	.438	.716	109	41	8	1	9	21	12	13
July	.266	.320	.372	94	25	4	0	2	18	8	9
August	.310	.377	.540	113	35	6	1	6	24	12	4
Sept/Oct	.417	.490	.677	127	53	10	1	7	20	19	8
Bases Empty	.365	.417	.612	299	109	18	1	18	18	25	22
Leadoff	.394	.433	.621	132	52	7	1	7	7	9	5
Not Leadoff	.341	.405	.605	167	57	11	0	11	11	16	17
Runners On	.322	.388	.490	298	96	16	2	10	87	35	25
First Base Only	.368	.410	.561	114	42	6	2	4	13	8	3
Scoring Position	.293	.376	.446	184	54	10	0	6	74	27	22
Late Innings, Close	.410	.452	.639	83	34	4	0	5	22	8	8

FOUR YEAR TOTALS (1984 – 1987)

	Ave.	OBP	SLG	AB	H	2B	3B	HR	RBI	BB	SO
Totals	.298	.361	.467	2331	694	122	22	76	306	229	238
vs. Left	.304	.378	.500	800	243	45	8	32	110	95	72
vs. Right	.295	.352	.449	1531	451	77	14	44	196	134	166
at Home	.301	.369	.452	1134	341	53	7	35	152	119	113
on Road	.295	.353	.480	1197	353	69	15	41	154	110	125
vs. Groundball	.320	.378	.494	1089	349	61	13	34	151	102	103
vs. Flyball	.278	.346	.443	1242	345	61	9	42	155	127	135
vs. Finesse	.299	.348	.477	1293	386	62	17	45	176	98	109
vs. Power	.297	.376	.454	1038	308	60	5	31	130	131	129
on Grass	.294	.360	.459	1953	574	97	17	64	254	201	197
on Artificial Turf	.317	.364	.505	378	120	25	5	12	52	28	41
Day Games	.296	.364	.467	734	217	44	8	22	96	75	75
Night Games	.299	.360	.466	1597	477	78	14	54	210	154	163
April	.322	.384	.537	270	87	16	6	10	42	27	24
May	.286	.339	.409	399	114	20	1	9	41	32	41
June	.291	.342	.449	454	132	22	4	14	57	35	47
July	.258	.338	.387	326	84	17	2	7	39	40	38
August	.299	.359	.494	478	143	21	6	20	74	44	52
Sept/Oct	.332	.406	.530	404	134	26	3	16	53	51	36
Bases Empty	.302	.356	.489	1303	393	67	15	49	49	108	130
Leadoff	.326	.364	.550	438	143	23	6	21	21	26	30
Not Leadoff	.289	.352	.458	865	250	44	9	28	28	82	100
Runners On	.293	.366	.439	1028	301	55	7	27	257	121	108
First Base Only	.312	.363	.477	449	140	27	4	13	40	36	40
Scoring Position	.278	.368	.409	579	161	28	3	14	217	85	68
Late Innings, Close	.300	.370	.408	343	103	13	0	8	57	39	35

RBI/Opportunities

Scoring Position	62 / 252 (25%)	193 / 809 (24%)	
Scoring Position, 2 Out	20 / 96 (21%)	90 / 364 (25%)	
On Third, Less than 2 Out	27 / 51 (53%)	70 / 139 (50%)	
RBI in close games / RBI Total	65 / 105 (62%)	188 / 306 (61%)	

John Tudor

St. Louis Cardinals

The freak accident that cost John Tudor almost four months of his 1987 season may have been a blessing in disguise for the Cardinals. Although Tudor was 2–1 at the time, it wasn't because he was pitching well; his ERA was over six. There were rumors that the arm injury that had caused him to miss the end of the '86 season was still bothering him, and his performance didn't do anything to dispel those rumors. The time off waiting for his knee to heal may have been what his arm needed as well, and indeed he threw much better when he returned.

Tudor's return, in fact, was one of the keys to the Cardinals' holding off the Mets and Montreal and winning the National League East. Tudor pitched thirteen games after he came off the disabled list, and the Cardinals won twelve of them. For the season they were twelve games over .500 when Tudor started and only sixteen games over .500 with all other starting pitchers. Considering the way John was throwing early in the year it's doubtful he would have been this successful without the time off. So maybe Cardinal fans should say a word of thanks to Barry Lyons.

Since the bottom line is winning and losing, 1987 was a successful year for Tudor. He was 10–2 and the Cards were 14–2 in his starts. From a statistical standpoint, however, it was his worst year as a Cardinal, as is evidenced by the chart below:

PER NINE INNINGS	1985	1986	1987
HITS	6.84	8.10	9.38
WALKS	1.60	2.18	3.00
RUNS	2.25	3.32	4.03
HR	0.46	0.90	1.03
ERA	1.93	2.92	3.84

Of course when you start off with a season like Tudor had in 1985 you can get a good deal worse and still be a pretty good pitcher. It's doubtful that his ERA will continue to jump by a run per year in 1988.

Tudor also continues to pitch much better at Busch Stadium than he does on the road. Although his home and away records were identical last season, his ERA at Busch was over two runs a game better than it was on the road. As a Cardinal, he is now 28–5 at Busch, 16–12 elsewhere.

1987 was the second time in three years that Tudor has had and opportunity to win a World Series for his team, and he pitched poorly both times. Before he starts getting a reputation for "not winning the big one," however, two things should be remembered. First of all, in both series he had already won one game, both times with outstanding games, and secondly, he was pitching on short rest both times. I'm sure Whitey would be willing to try his luck a third time.

Russ Eagle

Tudor, John Thomas

Bats: Left **Throws: Left** **Born 02/02/54**

1987 SEASON AND MAJOR-LEAGUE CAREER PITCHING TOTALS

	G	GS	CG	GF	IP	BFP	H	R	ER	HR	SH	SF	HB	TBB	IBB	SO	WP	Bk	W	L	Pct	ShO	Sv	ERA
87 STL	16	16	0	0	96	405	100	43	41	11	3	2	1	32	1	54	1	0	10	2	.833	0	0	3.84
9 YEARS	220	208	44	4	1439	5937	1351	587	528	135	48	39	26	398	21	829	18	7	95	60	.613	14	1	3.30

1987: Finesse, Flyball   1986: Finesse, Flyball   1985: Finesse, Flyball   1984: Finesse, Flyball

		1987 SEASON											FOUR YEAR TOTALS (1984 – 1987)										
	G	IP	H	BB	SO	SB	CS	W	L	S	ERA	G	IP	H	BB	SO	SB	CS	W	L	S	ERA
Totals	16	96.0	100	32	54	4	5	10	2	0	3.84	114	802.0	706	190	447	36	37	56	28	0	2.78
at Home	8	50.0	48	15	29	1	3	5	1	0	2.88	58	430.2	357	88	231	12	22	34	10	0	2.24
on Road	8	46.0	52	17	25	3	2	5	1	0	4.89	56	371.1	349	102	216	24	15	22	18	0	3.42
on Grass	6	35.2	34	16	17	2	1	3	2	0	4.29	42	305.1	243	80	160	14	16	22	10	0	2.68
on Artificial Turf	10	60.1	66	16	37	2	4	7	0	0	3.58	72	496.2	463	110	287	22	21	34	18	0	2.83
Day Games	3	15.2	19	7	9	1	1	2	0	0	4.60	29	196.2	176	54	120	14	6	11	11	0	2.97
Night Games	13	80.1	81	25	45	3	4	8	2	0	3.70	85	605.1	530	136	327	22	31	45	17	0	2.72
April	3	16.1	26	7	8	2	0	2	1	0	6.06	17	115.2	106	37	55	11	4	6	6	0	3.11
May	0	0.0	0	0	0	0	0	0	0	0	0.00	17	120.1	109	31	51	8	5	4	7	0	3.52
June	0	0.0	0	0	0	0	0	0	0	0	0.00	18	133.1	97	26	72	1	2	9	5	0	2.23
July	0	0.0	0	0	0	0	0	0	0	0	0.00	16	118.2	113	17	64	3	6	10	4	0	2.73
August	7	42.0	38	16	19	0	3	3	1	0	3.43	24	163.0	154	49	101	5	14	12	3	0	2.93
Sept/Oct	6	37.2	36	9	27	2	2	5	0	0	3.35	22	151.0	127	30	104	8	6	15	3	0	2.32

vs. Opponent Batters	Ave.	OBP	SLG	AB	H	2B	3B	HR	RBI	BB	SO	Ave.	OBP	SLG	AB	H	2B	3B	HR	RBI	BB	SO
Totals	.272	.331	.455	367	100	26	4	11	41	32	54	.237	.282	.357	2983	706	129	16	66	239	190	447
vs. Left	.246	.310	.446	65	16	5	1	2	8	6	18	.215	.258	.316	469	101	19	2	8	34	27	128
vs. Right	.278	.335	.457	302	84	21	3	9	33	26	36	.241	.287	.365	2514	605	110	14	58	205	163	319
Bases Empty	.298	.342	.502	225	67	17	4	7	7	15	32	.232	.269	.358	1945	452	86	13	44	44	98	282
Leadoff	.302	.323	.500	96	29	7	3	2	2	3	15	.241	.275	.384	792	191	42	7	19	19	37	106
Not Leadoff	.295	.355	.504	129	38	10	1	5	5	12	17	.226	.265	.340	1153	261	44	6	25	25	61	176
Runners On Base	.232	.315	.380	142	33	9	0	4	34	17	22	.245	.306	.355	1038	254	43	3	22	195	92	165
First Base Only	.190	.261	.349	63	12	4	0	2	6	5	12	.262	.302	.374	470	123	24	1	9	24	26	69
Scoring Position	.266	.355	.405	79	21	5	0	2	28	12	10	.231	.310	.340	568	131	19	2	13	171	66	96
Late Innings, Close	.375	.444	.563	16	6	3	0	0	3	2	2	.274	.322	.384	336	92	14	1	7	33	24	34

RBI/Opportunities

Scoring Position	25 / 109 (23%)	149 / 758 (20%)
Scoring Position, 2 Out	11 / 49 (22%)	54 / 352 (15%)
On Third, Less than 2 Out	10 / 19 (53%)	63 / 133 (47%)
RBI in close games / RBI Total	32 / 41 (78%)	192 / 239 (80%)

Willie Upshaw
Toronto Blue Jays

For the second year in a row, Willie Upshaw had the best stolen base (10) to homers (15) ratio among American League starting first basemen, though his dominance in this stat fell off from 1986 (23–9). This often-overlooked stat indicates that either the Blue Jays know something about baseball that nobody else does or that something is wrong in Toronto. To put it another way: During the 1987 stretch run, Toronto's first baseman was batting eighth and their shortstop was batting third.

Why? It's certainly not for lack of alternatives. In 1987, Toronto platooned Fred McGriff and Cecil Fielder at DH, and they hit a combined .270 with 29 homers, a .380 on-base percentage and a .548 slugging percentage. Both men can play first; had they played there in 1987, Toronto would have needed only to find a regular (or a platoon combo) who could hit .244 with 15 homers, 58 RBIs and 58 walks in 577 plate appearances to break even on the deal. Between Rick Leach, Juan Beniquez, Upshaw (against righties), any one of the outfielders at Syracuse or a veteran DH from another club, you'd think that they could have managed to do that.

So how has Upshaw managed to keep his job? There are five reasons:

1. HIS PAST. In 1983, Upshaw hit .306 with 27 homers and 104 RBIs and, at 27, appeared to be on his way to a fine career. Even though he has never hit more than 19 homers or better than .278 again—and those numbers have been falling for the last four years—people are reluctant to give up on him.

2. HIS STARTS. If Dave Winfield is "Mr. May," then Upshaw is "Mr. March and April." He always whaps the stuffing out of grapefruit league pitching and comes out of the gate strong; each year, that convinces management that he's finally regained his form. By the time he descends into sub-mediocrity, Toronto is reluctant to make changes in the middle of a pennant race.

3. HIS PERSONALITY. Willie is a nice guy and a hard worker, who is very popular with his teammates, coaches, the media and even the fans. Unlike some of his more talented teammates, he never cries about anything. Nobody likes to tell a nice guy that he can't play baseball.

4. HIS FIELDING. Though he's not Keith Hernandez, Willie has good range and soft hands; he turns the 3–6–3 DP as well as anyone. McGriff is unproven; Fielder is the antithesis of his name.

5. HIS SALARY. Upshaw signed a long term deal when he was putting up big numbers; he made a reported $900,000 in 1987. It's hard to trade a man with that contract and even harder to eat it.

Since Willie is now 31, one would hope that Toronto will lose patience with him in 1988; there is no reason in the world to keep playing him.

Dave Easby and Tony Formo

Upshaw, Willie Clay

Bats: Left Throws: Left Born 04/27/57

1987 SEASON AND MAJOR-LEAGUE CAREER BATTING TOTALS

	G	AB	H	2B	3B	HR	TB	R	RBI	TBB	IBB	SO	HP	SH	SF	SB	CS	SB%	GDP	AVG	OBP	SLG
87 TOR	150	512	125	22	4	15	200	68	58	58	4	78	3	3	1	10	11	.48	7	.244	.324	.391
9 YEARS	1115	3710	982	177	42	112	1579	538	478	390	46	576	21	27	24	76	50	.60	50	.265	.336	.426

1987 SEASON

	Ave.	OBP	SLG	AB	H	2B	3B	HR	RBI	BB	SO
Totals	.244	.324	.391	512	125	22	4	15	58	58	78
vs. Left	.208	.305	.319	144	30	6	2	2	18	19	30
vs. Right	.258	.332	.418	368	95	16	2	13	40	39	48
at Home	.225	.319	.369	236	53	9	2	7	25	32	36
on Road	.261	.329	.409	276	72	13	2	8	33	26	42
vs. Groundball	.251	.339	.425	247	62	13	0	10	31	33	31
vs. Flyball	.238	.310	.358	265	63	9	4	5	27	25	47
vs. Finesse	.238	.300	.379	290	69	11	3	8	25	26	36
vs. Power	.252	.354	.405	222	56	11	1	7	33	32	42
on Grass	.242	.329	.401	207	50	8	2	7	25	25	31
on Artificial Turf	.246	.321	.384	305	75	14	2	8	33	33	47
Day Games	.258	.361	.436	163	42	6	1	7	19	27	26
Night Games	.238	.305	.370	349	83	16	3	8	39	31	52
April	.267	.353	.520	75	20	3	2	4	12	10	10
May	.284	.344	.420	88	25	6	0	2	10	8	13
June	.250	.299	.460	100	25	7	1	4	14	6	13
July	.225	.313	.296	71	16	2	0	1	6	8	19
August	.194	.279	.258	93	18	1	1	1	8	10	14
Sept/Oct	.247	.363	.388	85	21	3	0	3	8	16	9
Bases Empty	.237	.304	.367	300	71	11	2	8	8	28	46
Leadoff	.182	.250	.291	110	20	3	0	3	3	10	16
Not Leadoff	.268	.335	.411	190	51	8	2	5	5	18	30
Runners On	.255	.351	.425	212	54	11	2	7	50	30	32
First Base Only	.245	.330	.436	94	23	4	1	4	10	10	11
Scoring Position	.263	.367	.415	118	31	7	1	3	40	20	21
Late Innings, Close	.260	.387	.338	77	20	2	2	0	4	15	14

FOUR YEAR TOTALS (1984 – 1987)

	Ave.	OBP	SLG	AB	H	2B	3B	HR	RBI	BB	SO
Totals	.262	.338	.417	2155	565	112	24	58	266	239	322
vs. Left	.245	.305	.392	693	170	31	13	15	97	55	131
vs. Right	.270	.353	.429	1462	395	81	11	43	169	184	191
at Home	.263	.346	.421	1010	266	65	14	22	131	128	163
on Road	.261	.331	.414	1145	299	47	10	36	135	111	159
vs. Groundball	.271	.350	.422	1026	278	56	12	25	126	120	127
vs. Flyball	.254	.328	.413	1129	287	56	12	33	140	119	195
vs. Finesse	.261	.318	.401	1228	321	68	13	26	136	99	150
vs. Power	.263	.363	.438	927	244	44	11	32	130	140	172
on Grass	.252	.330	.406	880	222	32	5	31	106	94	122
on Artificial Turf	.269	.344	.425	1275	343	80	19	27	160	145	200
Day Games	.245	.333	.395	750	184	41	7	19	79	99	127
Night Games	.271	.341	.429	1405	381	71	17	39	187	140	195
April	.302	.389	.563	288	87	20	5	15	51	41	40
May	.261	.331	.373	375	98	17	5	5	45	39	55
June	.249	.332	.417	405	101	21	4	13	57	49	69
July	.278	.341	.436	374	104	21	7	8	47	35	59
August	.244	.307	.377	385	94	20	2	9	36	34	55
Sept/Oct	.247	.330	.366	328	81	13	1	8	30	41	44
Bases Empty	.260	.329	.414	1180	307	58	8	36	36	120	173
Leadoff	.251	.309	.392	474	119	21	2	14	14	40	66
Not Leadoff	.266	.342	.429	706	188	37	6	22	22	80	107
Runners On	.265	.345	.421	975	258	54	16	22	230	119	149
First Base Only	.286	.340	.472	392	112	25	6	12	36	30	55
Scoring Position	.250	.349	.386	583	146	29	10	10	194	89	94
Late Innings, Close	.247	.344	.384	352	87	12	6	8	35	51	64

RBI/Opportunities

Scoring Position	34 / 165 (21%)	173 / 778 (22%)
Scoring Position, 2 Out	15 / 80 (19%)	71 / 378 (19%)
On Third, Less than 2 Out	10 / 25 (40%)	64 / 131 (49%)
RBI in close games / RBI Total	34 / 58 (59%)	173 / 266 (65%)

José Uribe
San Francisco Giants

Ooooo—Ree Bay. Oooooo—Ree Bay.

Giant fans sure enjoyed watching the two best short-stops in the National League go after each other in the LCS. José outhit Ozzie, and each committed only one error in the LCS. José participated in more DP's, but, coming from San Pedro de Macorís, his OBA was lower than the Wizard's, because it is not macho to take a walk.

Last year I wrote that Uribe's batting eye couldn't find the big "E" on the eye chart and that he would need to raise his average 10–15 points to remain a starter. In the off-season, José went back to the Dominican Republic, where his brother-in-law would toss kernels of corn at him for 2 hours a day. José hit them with a bat, to sharpen his stroke and batting eye. He came to the Cactus League and tore it up, hitting .469 to lead the league. Then, in the fifth game of the season, he tore up something else—his hamstring. He tried 2 comebacks too soon, and didn't fully return to the lineup until July 4. At that point in time, Roger Craig had fielded his opening day infield together for exactly 22 innings. José hit well in the 2nd half, finishing at .291, with an extra-base hit percentage of 28.9. His OBA of .343 and SLG of .424 weren't shabby for shortstops, either. Only Ozzie finished significantly ahead of him in either category, with an OBA of .392. No regular shortstop outslugged Uribe. Last year, José was the toughest to double up in the

National League, with 2 GIDPs total, 1 per 226 AB. This year, the competition got tough—Will Clark's ratio was 1 per 264.5 AB, Gerald Young's, 1 per 274 at bats—but, José came through again, with a phenomenal 1 every 309 at bats—he has grounded into only 3 DPs in two years!

This year's area for improvement, José, is artificial turf. With your speed, you should be able to adjust your swing and hit better than .229.

What Uribe has always done well is turn the DP. His fielding is very important in the Giants' scheme of things. At home the pitchers have the confidence to throw inside with the wind and high grass at the 'Stick. With the successful use of the split-finger to induce ground balls, the Giants' infielders and especially the shortstop must field well. Uribe's injury could have spelled doom, but the play of Chris Speier and Matt Williams kept the Giants going. The key was Matt Williams. His college reputation was as a good power hitter but somewhat erratic at shortstop. Williams concentrated on making the plays in the field while he suffered at the plate with a steady diet of breaking balls. The Giants maintained their double-play continuity. For the Giants to remain contenders they must receive excellent play at short and second. Uribe's strength is still his glove work, and if he hits .265, the Giants will keep grooming Williams for third base and not rush Tony Perezchica.

Victor Hester, M. Duca

Uribe, Jose Altagracia Gonzalez

Bats: Both   **Throws: Right**   **Born 01/21/59**

1987 SEASON AND MAJOR-LEAGUE CAREER BATTING TOTALS

	G	AB	H	2B	3B	HR	TB	R	RBI	TBB	IBB	SO	HP	SH	SF	SB	CS	SB%	GDP	AVG	OBP	SLG
87 SF	95	309	90	16	5	5	131	44	30	24	9	35	1	5	1	12	2	.86	1	.291	.343	.424
4 YEARS	407	1257	308	51	10	11	412	140	102	115	36	170	3	14	1	43	15	.74	9	.245	.310	.328

	1987 SEASON											FOUR YEAR TOTALS (1984 – 1987)										
	Ave.	OBP	SLG	AB	H	2B	3B	HR	RBI	BB	SO	Ave.	OBP	SLG	AB	H	2B	3B	HR	RBI	BB	SO
Totals	.291	.343	.424	309	90	16	5	5	30	24	35	.245	.310	.328	1257	308	51	10	11	102	115	170
vs. Left	.260	.311	.406	96	25	5	0	3	13	6	10	.226	.284	.333	372	84	19	0	7	42	28	63
vs. Right	.305	.358	.432	213	65	11	5	2	17	18	25	.253	.320	.325	885	224	32	10	4	60	87	107
at Home	.316	.346	.503	155	49	11	3	4	18	7	16	.242	.312	.340	632	153	31	5	7	48	63	75
on Road	.266	.341	.344	154	41	5	2	1	12	17	19	.248	.307	.315	625	155	20	5	4	54	52	95
vs. Groundball	.302	.353	.413	126	38	8	3	0	12	9	9	.254	.317	.337	552	140	26	4	4	53	50	70
vs. Flyball	.284	.337	.432	183	52	8	2	5	18	15	26	.238	.304	.321	705	168	25	6	7	49	65	100
vs. Finesse	.317	.362	.470	164	52	8	4	3	19	12	16	.252	.299	.341	721	182	30	8	6	59	47	79
vs. Power	.262	.323	.372	145	38	8	1	2	11	12	19	.235	.323	.310	536	126	21	2	5	43	68	91
on Grass	.324	.361	.500	204	66	14	5	4	23	11	21	.254	.319	.344	912	232	42	8	8	77	85	114
on Artificial Turf	.229	.311	.276	105	24	2	0	1	7	13	14	.220	.284	.284	345	76	9	2	3	25	30	56
Day Games	.368	.407	.552	125	46	9	4	2	18	9	10	.257	.318	.339	623	160	30	6	3	55	55	74
Night Games	.239	.300	.337	184	44	7	1	3	12	15	25	.233	.302	.317	634	148	21	4	8	47	60	96
April	.333	.368	.444	18	6	2	0	0	1	1	4	.262	.302	.320	122	32	7	0	0	7	7	18
May	.310	.355	.414	29	9	0	0	1	3	2	2	.243	.298	.322	202	49	8	1	2	20	16	29
June	.000	.000	.000	0	0	0	0	0	0	0	0	.201	.260	.280	189	38	6	3	1	11	15	18
July	.259	.326	.358	81	21	5	0	1	5	8	12	.247	.322	.328	235	58	10	0	3	17	26	31
August	.264	.323	.379	87	23	6	2	0	9	8	10	.239	.300	.315	238	57	12	3	0	19	21	39
Sept/Oct	.330	.370	.521	94	31	3	3	3	12	5	7	.273	.348	.380	271	74	8	3	5	28	30	35
Bases Empty	.281	.314	.389	185	52	8	3	2	2	9	23	.229	.285	.306	742	170	24	6	7	7	58	108
Leadoff	.325	.358	.494	77	25	6	2	1	1	4	8	.229	.297	.313	310	71	11	3	3	3	30	38
Not Leadoff	.250	.283	.315	108	27	2	1	1	1	5	15	.229	.276	.301	432	99	13	3	4	4	28	70
Runners On	.306	.383	.476	124	38	8	2	3	28	15	12	.268	.341	.359	515	138	27	4	4	95	57	62
First Base Only	.396	.429	.717	53	21	4	2	3	9	2	5	.262	.275	.378	225	59	8	3	4	14	3	21
Scoring Position	.239	.353	.296	71	17	4	0	0	19	13	7	.272	.386	.345	290	79	19	1	0	81	54	41
Late Innings, Close	.309	.377	.418	55	17	3	0	1	3	6	8	.239	.325	.319	213	51	9	1	2	12	27	26

RBI/Opportunities

Scoring Position	19 / 101 (19%)	78 / 418 (19%)
Scoring Position, 2 Out	6 / 53 (11%)	33 / 212 (16%)
On Third, Less than 2 Out	7 / 15 (47%)	23 / 67 (34%)
RBI in close games / RBI Total	19 / 30 (63%)	63 / 102 (62%)

Fernando Valenzuela
Los Angeles Dodgers

For most pitchers, it might be satisfying to be one of only six in the league who won at least 14 games while finishing the season with an ERA under 4.00. That might be particularly gratifying in a year when balls were flying out of the park in record numbers. And it might be especially gratifying to have done it for a lousy team, a team that finished 73–89.

Fernando Valenzuela had just such a season in 1987, and because he is Fernando, it must be considered a lousy season. After all, in 1986, Valenzuela won 21 games for the first time in his career, and he did it for a mediocre Dodger team that finished that season 73–89. He also finished '86 with a 3.14 ERA, and in 269.1 innings he'd given up just 224 hits and 85 walks.

What was different for Fernando in 1987?

It's true that the Dodgers were equally bad both seasons, and in 1986, the team was missing its most potent offensive weapon, Pedro Guerrero. Guerrero was back in '87 as devastating as ever. Yet the '87 Dodgers scored 3 fewer runs than the '86 edition.

No one was sure what contributed to Valenzuela's slide into mere mortality. Some speculated he'd thrown too many screwballs over his career, and some thought the 269.1 innings he'd thrown in 1986—including a major league leading 20 complete games—caught up with him in '87. Also, in '87, he was victimized by a Dodger bullpen that at times was so bad that a tiring and struggling Fernando was a better choice for manager Tom Lasorda than a fresh reliever. The Dodger offense, meanwhile, wasn't scoring nearly enough when he was pitching poorly and hardly scoring at all when he pitched well.

Valenzuela also contributed to his own problems in '87. He gave up 254 hits in 251 innings, and he walked a personal high (and team record) 124 batters. Through part of July, all of August, and most of September, his ERA was over 4.00. His final ERA of 3.98 was the highest of his career, as were the 25 homers he gave up, the 111 earned runs, the 254 hits, and the 14 wild pitches.

But despite this, Valenzuela finished on an upbeat note. He won five of his last eight decisions to finish 14–14 and had an ERA of 3.05 during that stretch. And overall, his 12 complete games tied him for best in the league with Rick Reuschel of the Pirates and Giants, and 14 wins were eighth best in the league. His 190 strikeouts were fourth best in the NL, and he was third in innings pitched. He even had a homer, seventh in his career, and 8 RBI.

Yes, it might have been a good season for many pitchers, but not when the name is Fernando Valenzuela.

Dean Hill

Valenzuela, Fernando (Anguamea)   Bats: Left   Throws: Left   Born 11/01/60

1987 SEASON AND MAJOR-LEAGUE CAREER PITCHING TOTALS

	G	GS	CG	GF	IP	BFP	H	R	ER	HR	SH	SF	HB	TBB	IBB	SO	WP	Bk	W	L	Pct	ShO	Sv	ERA
87 LA	34	34	12	0	251	1116	254	120	111	25	18	2	4	124	4	190	14	1	14	14	.500	1	0	3.98
8 YEARS	244	234	96	4	1805	7479	1549	709	618	111	113	35	14	664	44	1464	68	5	113	82	.579	27	1	3.08

1987: Power, Flyball   1986: Power, Groundball   1985: Power, Groundball   1984: Power, Groundball

	1987 SEASON											FOUR YEAR TOTALS (1984 – 1987)										
	G	IP	H	BB	SO	SB	CS	W	L	S	ERA	G	IP	H	BB	SO	SB	CS	W	L	S	ERA
Totals	34	251.0	254	124	190	19	9	14	14	0	3.98	137	1053.2	909	416	880	79	48	64	52	0	3.13
at Home	15	121.0	116	59	83	9	3	6	7	0	3.50	65	520.0	432	181	427	31	24	30	23	0	2.68
on Road	19	130.0	138	65	107	10	6	8	7	0	4.43	72	533.2	477	235	453	48	24	34	29	0	3.58
on Grass	10	72.0	85	29	52	6	2	2	4	0	4.75	43	321.2	298	115	277	32	13	16	19	0	3.78
on Artificial Turf	24	179.0	169	95	138	13	7	12	10	0	3.67	94	732.0	611	301	603	47	35	48	33	0	2.85
Day Games	26	203.0	193	97	155	12	7	13	8	0	3.46	101	787.0	667	301	662	51	37	49	36	0	2.92
Night Games	8	48.0	61	27	35	7	2	1	6	0	6.19	36	266.2	242	115	218	28	11	15	16	0	3.78
April	5	37.0	38	12	36	2	3	3	1	0	2.92	21	163.0	135	46	141	6	13	11	7	0	2.10
May	5	38.0	40	18	28	4	1	2	1	0	4.26	22	174.2	145	75	151	16	8	11	8	0	2.99
June	6	43.0	40	17	28	6	1	2	3	0	3.77	23	168.2	165	72	141	17	7	10	11	0	3.84
July	6	37.1	46	21	24	0	1	2	3	0	5.79	23	169.2	140	63	136	10	4	12	8	0	3.18
August	6	46.1	43	34	45	6	2	2	4	0	4.27	23	182.2	158	84	165	15	10	10	11	0	3.60
Sept/Oct	6	49.1	47	22	29	1	1	3	2	0	3.10	25	195.0	166	76	146	15	6	10	7	0	3.05

vs. Opponent Batters	Ave.	OBP	SLG	AB	H	2B	3B	HR	RBI	BB	SO	Ave.	OBP	SLG	AB	H	2B	3B	HR	RBI	BB	SO
Totals	.262	.348	.401	968	254	49	5	25	108	124	190	.233	.307	.336	3904	909	160	14	71	368	416	880
vs. Left	.228	.283	.377	167	38	9	2	4	12	13	43	.240	.294	.349	730	175	36	4	12	62	56	169
vs. Right	.270	.361	.406	801	216	40	3	21	96	111	147	.231	.310	.332	3174	734	124	10	59	306	360	711
Bases Empty	.270	.367	.415	489	132	23	3	14	14	73	102	.217	.294	.315	2273	494	94	6	39	39	244	568
Leadoff	.240	.339	.344	221	53	6	1	5	5	33	52	.210	.278	.292	977	205	38	3	12	12	92	245
Not Leadoff	.295	.390	.474	268	79	17	2	9	9	40	50	.223	.306	.333	1296	289	56	3	27	27	152	323
Runners On Base	.255	.328	.386	479	122	26	2	11	94	51	88	.254	.326	.364	1631	415	66	8	32	329	172	312
First Base Only	.315	.369	.535	200	63	19	2	7	22	16	34	.284	.325	.434	698	198	42	6	17	55	42	118
Scoring Position	.211	.300	.280	279	59	7	0	4	72	35	54	.233	.326	.311	933	217	24	2	15	274	130	194
Late Innings, Close	.218	.302	.296	142	31	6	1	1	8	17	27	.221	.295	.285	594	131	21	1	5	54	63	122

RBI/Opportunities

Scoring Position	65 / 389 (17%)		247 / 1287 (19%)
Scoring Position, 2 Out	30 / 182 (16%)		98 / 604 (16%)
On Third, Less than 2 Out	23 / 74 (31%)		99 / 228 (43%)
RBI in close games / RBI Total	75 / 108 (69%)		272 / 368 (74%)

David Valle
Seattle Mariners

David Valle was one of those born-again prospects. The Mariners were pretty excited to make him their second-round pick in the 1978 June draft. But he was only 17 years old and his climb to the majors was long and rocky. By age 22 he had gone from prospect to suspect. In his last two seasons he had hit .209 at Salt Lake City and .239 at Chattanooga. But he started to pick up the pace, had a good year at Calgary in 1986 and sparkled in his September call-up.

During that nine-year journey the Mariners placed a lot of emphasis on getting a good defensive catcher. First they went out and got Bob Kearney because they liked the way he shut down the running game. Then they wanted Steve Yeager because they felt he was such an excellent handler of pitchers. We fans should have picked up on the fact that the press releases didn't do a lot of talking about their bats—which I suppose was appropriate since their bats themselves were rather mute.

David was a welcome change. He not only has a decent bat for a catcher, but his defensive work is also highly praised. For some, David's 1987 season was a bit of a disappointment. He had made all those "rookie to watch" lists, and with the trade of Danny Tartabull, manager Dick Williams was hoping that Valle would replace some of the lost right-handed power. Valle came close to that, averaging a homer every 27 at-bats versus Tartabull's one per 20 at-bats in his rookie year. But Valle also hit just .255 and had an on-base average of just .292. He ended up with 325 at-bats as he was platooned a lot with the left-handed hitting Scott Bradley. Still, the Mariners would have been thrilled to get such a contribution out of Valle just a couple years ago. It's hard to imagine them being too disappointed with what they got.

Actually, the Mariners had to be pleased with the production they got from their catching tandem. If you combine the top two catchers on each team, they come out a strong challenging fifth.

Per 550 AT-BATS	Runs	B.A.	2B/3B/HR	RBI
Schroeder and Surhoff	72	.312	29/ 3/18	94
Nokes and Heath	77	.286	23/ 2/30	90
Fisk and Karkovice	77	.226	22/ 1/26	80
Steinbach and Tettleto	78	.252	17/ 3/22	75
Valle and Bradley	61	.267	26/ 3/14	79

Williams has declared Valle his starting catcher for 1988, but it's only logical that Bradley will see considerable action again. What Dave has to watch out for is his reputed short fuse setting off a counter explosion from his manager. Dick doesn't tolerate too many incidents of players slamming down bats when they should be running out pop flies and routine grounders.

Craig R. Wright and Merrianna McCully

Valle, David "Dave"

Bats: Right   **Throws: Right**   **Born 10/30/60**

1987 SEASON AND MAJOR-LEAGUE CAREER BATTING TOTALS

	G	AB	H	2B	3B	HR	TB	R	RBI	TBB	IBB	SO	HP	SH	SF	SB	CS	SB%	GDP	AVG	OBP	SLG
87 SEA	95	324	83	16	3	12	141	40	53	15	2	46	3	0	4	2	0	1.00	13	.256	.292	.435
4 YEARS	161	474	120	21	3	18	201	56	76	24	2	75	4	1	4	2	0	1.00	16	.253	.292	.424

	1987 SEASON											TWO YEAR TOTALS (1986 – 1987)									
	Ave.	OBP	SLG	AB	H	2B	3B	HR	RBI	BB	SO	Ave.	OBP	SLG	AB	H	2B	3B	HR	RBI	BB	SO
Totals	.255	.292	.434	325	83	16	3	12	53	15	46	.267	.312	.468	378	101	19	3	17	68	22	53
vs. Left	.304	.340	.554	148	45	10	3	7	33	9	18	.306	.348	.565	170	52	11	3	9	39	12	22
vs. Right	.215	.251	.333	177	38	6	0	5	20	6	28	.236	.279	.389	208	49	8	0	8	29	10	31
at Home	.243	.285	.431	181	44	10	0	8	28	8	23	.256	.309	.474	215	55	11	0	12	40	14	29
on Road	.271	.301	.438	144	39	6	3	4	25	7	23	.282	.312	.460	163	46	8	3	5	28	8	24
vs. Groundball	.259	.305	.395	162	42	7	3	3	20	8	22	.261	.313	.417	180	47	7	3	5	24	11	25
vs. Flyball	.252	.279	.472	163	41	9	0	9	33	7	24	.273	.308	.515	198	54	12	0	12	44	11	28
vs. Finesse	.261	.296	.455	176	46	6	2	8	27	8	21	.277	.317	.484	213	59	7	2	11	36	12	27
vs. Power	.248	.287	.409	149	37	10	1	4	26	7	25	.255	.302	.448	165	42	12	1	6	32	10	26
on Grass	.288	.319	.468	111	32	6	1	4	21	6	14	.305	.336	.500	128	39	8	1	5	24	7	15
on Artificial Turf	.238	.278	.416	214	51	10	2	8	32	9	32	.248	.297	.452	250	62	11	2	12	44	15	38
Day Games	.200	.228	.387	75	15	3	1	3	11	3	15	.200	.228	.387	75	15	3	1	3	11	3	15
Night Games	.272	.311	.448	250	68	13	2	9	42	12	31	.284	.330	.488	303	86	16	2	14	57	19	38
April	.250	.294	.563	32	8	1	0	3	5	2	6	.250	.294	.563	32	8	1	0	3	5	2	6
May	.326	.354	.535	43	14	3	0	2	16	2	4	.326	.354	.535	43	14	3	0	2	16	2	4
June	.333	.391	.667	42	14	5	3	1	8	4	5	.321	.419	.660	53	17	6	3	2	10	9	7
July	.210	.242	.468	62	13	4	0	4	9	3	7	.215	.246	.462	65	14	4	0	4	9	3	9
August	.276	.286	.382	76	21	2	0	2	8	0	7	.276	.286	.382	76	21	2	0	2	8	0	7
Sept/Oct	.186	.240	.200	70	13	1	0	0	7	4	17	.248	.293	.385	109	27	3	0	4	20	6	20
Bases Empty	.223	.253	.430	179	40	12	2	7	7	6	26	.238	.280	.456	206	49	14	2	9	9	11	31
Leadoff	.242	.265	.455	66	16	5	0	3	3	2	8	.291	.341	.570	79	23	7	0	5	5	6	10
Not Leadoff	.212	.246	.416	113	24	7	2	4	4	4	18	.205	.241	.386	127	26	7	2	4	4	5	21
Runners On	.295	.338	.438	146	43	4	1	5	46	9	20	.302	.346	.483	172	52	5	1	8	59	11	22
First Base Only	.250	.311	.304	56	14	0	0	1	2	4	6	.265	.315	.353	68	18	0	0	2	4	4	8
Scoring Position	.322	.354	.522	90	29	4	1	4	44	5	14	.327	.365	.567	104	34	5	1	6	55	7	14
Late Innings, Close	.226	.241	.415	53	12	1	0	3	7	1	6	.226	.241	.415	106	24	2	0	6	14	2	12

RBI/Opportunities

Scoring Position	38 / 121 (31%)	45 / 141 (32%)	
Scoring Position, 2 Out	18 / 58 (31%)	21 / 66 (32%)	
On Third, Less than 2 Out	12 / 22 (55%)	13 / 26 (50%)	
RBI in close games / RBI Total	27 / 53 (51%)	54 / 68 (79%)	

Andy Van Slyke
Pittsburgh Pirates

In 1987, Andy Van Slyke parlayed his first opportunity for full-time play into his best season ever. He posted improvements in all of his offensive stats, highlighted by 21 HR and 93 runs scored. Andy was among the top center-fielders offensively in 1987.

In 1986, Andy was playing in Busch Stadium, a good park for line drive hitting and for hitting for average. That seemed to be fine with him, as he always hit better at home than on the road, but it did hurt him in one critical respect: It severely curtailed his power hitting. Moving to Three Rivers Stadium in 1987, he was able to continue to play in a turf park where his speed would be valuable (indeed, in 1987 Andy stole 13 more bases than in 1986, while being caught exactly the same number of times that he had been in 1986); at the same time he moved to a park in which the HR could be a significant part of a player's offensive attack. And indeed, in 1987 Andy hit 61 percent more HR than in 1986, while using only 35 percent more AB.

The other big improvement in Andy's performance came in batting average, where he jumped from .270 to .293. It seems unlikely that the park change was responsible for this, and Pirate fans can hope that, as Andy moves through his prime years,he has simply improved his play.

The only troubling part about Andy's season is something that seemed to be characteristic of the Pirate hitters last year; namely, that his impressive increase in batting average was accompanied by a decrease in his walk frequency, with the result that his on base percentage only increased by .015, from .344 to .359. If Andy can get his walk frequency back up without losing too much off of his batting average, it would seem obvious that he should be the Pirate leadoff hitter. Even with his current numbers, he seems best suited to the job. His excellent base stealing, and the fact that he is the Pirate with the best track record for getting on base, and the fact that he is the least likely of the good Pirate hitters to develop into a power hitter all project him into the role. The problem for the Pirates is that, with their power problems it will be difficult to place their hitter with the highest 1987 slugging percentage first in the batting order.

Andy is only 27 going into the 1988 season, and considering that he's never really had an off-season, and that he seems to be developing as a hitter, it's likely that he is one player that the Pirates can count on to produce for them over the next several years as they try to become a championship team. Andy is a solid, dependable player; he is one piece of the puzzle solved for the Pirates.

Peter Palmieri

Van Slyke, Andrew James "Andy" Bats: Left Throws: Right Born 12/21/60

1987 SEASON AND MAJOR-LEAGUE CAREER BATTING TOTALS

	G	AB	H	2B	3B	HR	TB	R	RBI	TBB	IBB	SO	HP	SH	SF	SB	CS	SB%	GDP	AVG	OBP	SLG
87 PIT	157	564	165	36	11	21	286	93	82	56	4	122	4	3	3	34	8	.81	6	.293	.359	.507
5 YEARS	678	2076	557	115	33	62	924	298	286	259	29	396	8	7	12	138	34	.80	24	.268	.350	.445

	1987 SEASON											FOUR YEAR TOTALS (1984 – 1987)										
	Ave.	OBP	SLG	AB	H	2B	3B	HR	RBI	BB	SO	Ave.	OBP	SLG	AB	H	2B	3B	HR	RBI	BB	SO
Totals	.293	.359	.507	564	165	36	11	21	82	56	122	.269	.349	.449	1767	476	100	28	54	248	213	331
vs. Left	.231	.292	.358	229	53	10	5	3	26	18	56	.213	.280	.336	441	94	20	11	4	52	40	106
vs. Right	.334	.403	.609	335	112	26	6	18	56	38	66	.288	.371	.487	1326	382	80	17	50	196	173	225
at Home	.273	.353	.475	278	76	15	4	11	46	35	56	.272	.362	.453	859	234	48	16	25	135	122	154
on Road	.311	.365	.538	286	89	21	7	10	36	21	66	.267	.336	.446	908	242	52	12	29	113	91	177
vs. Groundball	.306	.371	.502	245	75	8	2	12	44	25	43	.272	.352	.426	809	220	39	7	24	117	98	130
vs. Flyball	.282	.349	.511	319	90	28	9	9	38	31	79	.267	.346	.469	958	256	61	21	30	131	115	201
vs. Finesse	.302	.371	.481	295	89	21	4	8	33	29	47	.283	.358	.471	945	267	64	15	28	115	108	133
vs. Power	.283	.346	.535	269	76	15	7	13	49	27	75	.254	.338	.425	822	209	36	13	26	133	105	198
on Grass	.289	.346	.550	149	43	8	5	7	21	13	32	.268	.336	.452	482	129	24	7	17	58	50	95
on Artificial Turf	.294	.363	.492	415	122	28	6	14	61	43	90	.270	.353	.448	1285	347	76	21	37	190	163	236
Day Games	.331	.395	.580	157	52	12	6	5	24	18	31	.270	.353	.445	611	165	38	9	17	86	81	98
Night Games	.278	.344	.479	407	113	24	5	16	58	38	91	.269	.346	.452	1156	311	62	19	37	162	132	233
April	.269	.371	.404	52	14	3	2	0	8	8	11	.268	.373	.371	194	52	11	3	1	22	32	37
May	.244	.284	.427	82	20	3	0	4	12	5	22	.262	.337	.462	260	68	12	2	12	46	30	45
June	.330	.402	.650	100	33	7	2	7	19	11	21	.265	.349	.455	325	86	20	6	10	42	41	67
July	.269	.345	.471	104	28	8	2	3	12	12	24	.238	.329	.409	286	68	13	6	8	35	39	59
August	.325	.373	.547	117	38	9	1	5	19	9	21	.293	.354	.502	317	93	24	3	12	50	30	51
Sept/Oct	.294	.366	.477	109	32	6	4	2	12	11	23	.283	.354	.462	385	109	20	8	11	53	41	72
Bases Empty	.296	.358	.514	331	98	23	8	11	11	30	72	.265	.332	.442	975	258	55	17	28	28	97	182
Leadoff	.340	.370	.592	103	35	10	2	4	4	5	19	.292	.339	.533	383	112	29	6	17	17	27	61
Not Leadoff	.276	.353	.478	228	63	13	6	7	7	25	53	.247	.328	.383	592	146	26	11	11	11	70	121
Runners On	.288	.360	.498	233	67	13	3	10	71	26	50	.275	.368	.458	792	218	45	11	26	220	116	149
First Base Only	.247	.326	.429	77	19	5	0	3	7	8	16	.271	.336	.452	314	85	21	3	10	29	30	48
Scoring Position	.308	.376	.532	156	48	8	3	7	64	18	34	.278	.387	.462	478	133	24	8	16	191	86	101
Late Innings, Close	.333	.347	.677	93	31	6	1	8	29	3	23	.268	.351	.455	310	83	16	3	12	53	41	72

RBI/Opportunities

Scoring Position	54 / 212 (25%)	167 / 689 (24%)
Scoring Position, 2 Out	24 / 96 (25%)	62 / 311 (20%)
On Third, Less than 2 Out	13 / 42 (31%)	63 / 138 (46%)
RBI in close games / RBI Total	60 / 82 (73%)	160 / 248 (65%)

Frank Viola
Minnesota Twins

Two reasons for Frank Viola's 1987 success are his killer change-up and four days rest. Frank's change-up, generally credited to former Twins' pitching coach Johnny Podres, has taken several seasons to develop. In '86 the pitch helped increase his strikeout totals, a trend that continued in 1987 when he ended the regular season with 197 Ks. Another encouraging sign is that, while establishing the lowest ERA of his career, he also decreased his walks from the previous season. Confidence in and control of the change-up were major contributors to his success. He also established an ability to either win with that pitch as his out-pitch or win while relying on his fastball and curve, depending on which was working best.

In the three previous years, under Billy Gardner and Ray Miller, Frank Viola typically received a lot of work in April and May, frequently pitching on three days rest and accumulating quite a few innings. This early work load seemed to create difficulties for him each June that were only alleviated by periods of rest and off-rotation starts. Then, his tired arm rejuvenated, Frank would finish the season strongly. Perhaps Tom Kelly's most important decision of the year involved putting Viola on a regular schedule in a five-man rotation. During the three previous seasons, Viola's lowest ERA (3.98) was produced on 4 days rest. Such

starts accounted for 50 percent of his games. His highest ERA (4.12) came in games following three days rest. In '87 these trends continued, but Kelly limited him to just 3 starts on three days rest as opposed to 7 starts in '84 and '86 and 10 starts in '85.

A look at the innings pitched totals for the last four years shows that Kelly did not reduce the number of innings pitched by his ace. More important, he reduced the number of innings pitched when it can be assumed that the pitcher's arm is tired. Frank's number of complete games fell not only through the use of an obviously more effective bullpen, but also by not letting Frank throw too many pitches in a game. Like Blyleven, Viola liked to finish what he started. Kelly simply asserted control of how long a man was going to pitch and was able to convince him that it was for the good of the team. This practice continued in the seventh game of the World Series. TV viewers were treated to the sight of Tom Kelly huddled with Viola in the dugout as the rookie manager explained his reasons for inserting Reardon in the top of the ninth.

A World Championship ring on your finger can be mighty convincing evidence of the intelligence of Kelly's method and of his powers of persuasion.

Bill Jensen

Viola, Frank John Bats: Left Throws: Left Born 12/07/56

1987 SEASON AND MAJOR-LEAGUE CAREER PITCHING TOTALS

	G	GS	CG	GF	IP	BFP	H	R	ER	HR	SH	SF	HB	TBB	IBB	SO	WP	Bk	W	L	Pct	ShO	Sv	ERA
87 MIN	36	36	7	0	252	1037	230	91	81	29	7	3	6	66	1	197	1	1	17	10	.630	1	0	2.89
6 YEARS	201	200	40	0	1343	5688	1368	682	611	176	24	20	23	420	14	883	35	7	80	74	.519	7	0	4.09

1987: Finesse, Flyball   1986: Power, Flyball   1985: Finesse, Flyball   1984: Finesse, Flyball

1987 SEASON

	G	IP	H	BB	SO	SB	CS	W	L	S	ERA
Totals	36	251.2	230	66	197	6	7	17	10	0	2.90
at Home	19	137.0	129	33	113	1	4	11	3	0	2.69
on Road	17	114.2	101	33	84	5	3	6	7	0	3.14
on Grass	8	53.2	50	9	34	1	2	4	1	0	2.85
on Artificial Turf	28	198.0	180	57	163	5	5	13	9	0	2.91
Day Games	13	88.2	78	23	58	3	3	5	5	0	2.74
Night Games	23	163.0	152	43	139	3	4	12	5	0	2.98
April	5	33.0	30	16	27	1	1	1	3	0	3.55
May	6	40.2	37	9	27	0	2	2	2	0	4.43
June	6	41.1	40	4	28	2	2	3	1	0	1.96
July	6	48.0	36	10	44	3	1	5	0	0	1.88
August	7	45.2	50	14	34	0	1	3	2	0	3.94
Sept/Oct	6	43.0	37	13	37	0	0	3	2	0	1.88

vs. Opponent Batters	Ave.	OBP	SLG	AB	H	2B	3B	HR	RBI	BB	SO
Totals	.241	.293	.378	955	230	44	0	29	84	66	197
vs. Left	.252	.312	.384	159	40	6	0	5	17	12	33
vs. Right	.239	.289	.377	796	190	38	0	24	67	54	164
Bases Empty	.246	.297	.384	589	145	27	0	18	18	38	117
Leadoff	.240	.292	.398	246	59	12	0	9	9	16	46
Not Leadoff	.251	.302	.373	343	86	15	0	9	9	22	71
Runners On Base	.232	.286	.369	366	85	17	0	11	66	28	80
First Base Only	.250	.315	.400	180	45	9	0	6	14	16	34
Scoring Position	.215	.259	.339	186	40	8	0	5	52	12	46
Late Innings, Close	.250	.286	.317	120	30	5	0	1	7	4	15

FOUR YEAR TOTALS (1984 – 1987)

	G	IP	H	BB	SO	SB	CS	W	L	S	ERA
Totals	144	1005.2	974	290	672	31	40	69	49	0	3.67
at Home	67	490.1	479	127	350	11	21	34	17	0	3.36
on Road	77	515.1	495	163	322	20	19	35	32	0	3.96
on Grass	42	293.0	285	76	183	8	10	17	16	0	3.81
on Artificial Turf	102	712.2	689	214	489	23	30	52	33	0	3.60
Day Games	61	410.2	383	127	246	16	14	30	23	0	3.68
Night Games	83	595.0	591	163	426	15	26	39	26	0	3.66
April	21	152.0	138	53	97	4	6	8	9	0	3.49
May	24	155.1	164	49	96	4	7	9	10	0	4.64
June	22	153.0	151	37	107	11	9	13	6	0	3.35
July	24	177.1	157	52	114	7	6	13	7	0	3.40
August	25	172.0	182	48	99	1	6	11	8	0	3.77
Sept/Oct	28	196.0	182	51	159	4	6	15	9	0	3.44

vs. Opponent Batters	Ave.	OBP	SLG	AB	H	2B	3B	HR	RBI	BB	SO
Totals	.253	.306	.401	3856	974	177	17	120	405	290	672
vs. Left	.270	.317	.411	689	186	31	3	20	80	45	112
vs. Right	.249	.303	.398	3167	788	146	14	100	325	245	560
Bases Empty	.248	.302	.392	2348	582	105	12	70	70	178	422
Leadoff	.249	.299	.409	982	245	41	4	36	36	68	175
Not Leadoff	.247	.304	.380	1366	337	64	8	34	34	110	247
Runners On Base	.260	.311	.414	1508	392	72	5	50	335	112	250
First Base Only	.251	.300	.401	768	193	41	1	24	64	52	114
Scoring Position	.269	.323	.427	740	199	31	4	26	271	60	136
Late Innings, Close	.260	.306	.384	362	94	15	3	8	41	22	50

RBI/Opportunities

Scoring Position	43 / 232 (19%)	225 / 942 (24%)
Scoring Position, 2 Out	15 / 112 (13%)	95 / 434 (22%)
On Third, Less than 2 Out	12 / 29 (41%)	72 / 144 (50%)
RBI in close games / RBI Total	67 / 84 (80%)	282 / 405 (70%)

Ozzie Virgil
Atlanta Braves

Since discovering sabermetrics and Bill James' approaches to baseball analysis, I've tried very hard not to allow bold media statements to influence me without first checking them out for accuracy. How did I get misled here? It seems like I heard people say that Virgil would provide solid defense and lots of power for the Braves. OK, 42 homers in two years isn't bad, but lots of guys could do that. I'd watched Bruce Benedict show flashes of defensive excellence, but "steadiness only" was a better description for his defense. Somehow I thought Virgil was the equal of (if not superior to) Benedict.

So I looked into the 1987 *Baseball Abstract* for defensive tidbits on Ozzie Virgil. Well, first of all, in 1986, the team ERA with Virgil catching was lower than when Benedict or Simmons caught. OK, but other factors can feed into that (which pitchers he caught, day/night games, bullpen runs allowed, etc). Then I noticed 1.28 Opponents' Stolen Bases per game started by Virgil. I looked up his career stats to see if he was as bad as that seemed. No catcher who had started more than 136 games in his career through 1986 (Virgil had started 407) had a poorer ratio of opponents' stolen bases per game started than Ozzie's 1.09. No media person told me his attack on would-be base thieves was so impotent. Didn't anyone notice? This guy is on national cable TV now, and, if anything, he's worse than he was with Philadelphia. Guess the Phillies saw the Braves coming on

this one.

The value of the stolen base will long be argued, but it is, to a certain extent, a measure of a catcher's skills. Of course, how well a pitching staff holds runners on, and whether management allows a catcher to call his own pitchouts, also have a major effect, as does the issue of whether your staff is primarily power or finesse pitchers.

Virgil produced a personal high of 27 HRs and 72 RBIs in 1987 for the Braves. Through June 20 he'd belted 20 homers for a 45 HR/90 RBI pace. He was briefly tied with Andre Dawson for the league lead in homers. Then the summer heat (or reality) got to him—June 21 through July 19, 0 homers; 1 on July 20, then no more until August 11, then no more until August 23. This early success (which sort of mirrored the rest of the league) had an unfortunate effect on Ozzie's swing—his walks fell from 1 per 5.7 AB in 1986 to 1 per 9.1 in 1987. His singles actually fell (despite the increase in average) from 1 every 6.4 AB to 1 every 6.6 AB from '86 to '87. Odd how Fulton County Stadium does that to hitters.

With as many holes as the Braves have to fill for 1988, I suppose Virgil's homers (at 1987's pace) counterbalance his defense acceptably for another year or so, but a look into the Braves' farm system shows no prospects on the horizon. A trade is the only likely solution in the medium to long range.

Bob Jones

Virgil, Osvaldo Jose Jr. "Ozzie"

Bats: Right   Throws: Right   Born 12/07/56

1987 SEASON AND MAJOR-LEAGUE CAREER BATTING TOTALS

	G	AB	H	2B	3B	HR	TB	R	RBI	TBB	IBB	SO	HP	SH	SF	SB	CS	SB%	GDP	AVG	OBP	SLG
87 ATL	123	429	106	13	1	27	202	57	72	47	4	81	7	2	1	0	1	.00	18	.247	.331	.471
8 YEARS	620	1922	465	73	6	88	814	233	274	222	20	393	24	6	11	2	5	.29	71	.242	.326	.424

	1987 SEASON											FOUR YEAR TOTALS (1984 – 1987)									
	Ave.	OBP	SLG	AB	H	2B	3B	HR	RBI	BB	SO	Ave.	OBP	SLG	AB	H	2B	3B	HR	RBI	BB	SO
Totals	.247	.331	.471	429	106	13	1	27	72	47	81	.246	.333	.430	1670	410	59	6	79	243	204	330
vs. Left	.218	.328	.427	110	24	2	0	7	18	16	20	.242	.340	.406	458	111	14	2	19	62	68	67
vs. Right	.257	.331	.486	319	82	11	1	20	54	31	61	.247	.330	.439	1212	299	45	4	60	181	136	263
at Home	.258	.354	.516	213	55	8	1	15	44	29	38	.267	.352	.465	824	220	37	6	38	129	102	171
on Road	.236	.307	.426	216	51	5	0	12	28	18	43	.225	.314	.396	846	190	22	0	41	114	102	159
vs. Groundball	.278	.366	.540	187	52	7	0	14	34	23	29	.238	.331	.407	730	174	20	5	31	99	94	136
vs. Flyball	.223	.303	.417	242	54	6	1	13	38	24	52	.251	.335	.448	940	236	39	1	48	144	110	194
vs. Finesse	.259	.321	.502	243	63	6	1	17	41	16	32	.251	.325	.473	943	237	39	1	56	152	90	137
vs. Power	.231	.342	.430	186	43	7	0	10	31	31	49	.238	.344	.374	727	173	20	5	23	91	114	193
on Grass	.252	.340	.455	310	78	10	1	17	55	37	54	.233	.329	.417	823	192	23	1	42	130	108	161
on Artificial Turf	.235	.305	.513	119	28	3	0	10	17	10	27	.257	.337	.443	847	218	36	5	37	113	96	169
Day Games	.259	.322	.453	139	36	3	0	8	22	10	29	.256	.324	.460	528	135	20	2	28	84	45	105
Night Games	.241	.334	.479	290	70	10	1	19	50	37	52	.241	.337	.416	1142	275	39	4	51	159	159	225
April	.231	.333	.442	52	12	2	0	3	6	4	14	.257	.328	.456	171	44	7	0	9	28	14	34
May	.250	.364	.726	84	21	1	0	13	19	14	21	.252	.345	.523	333	84	10	1	26	53	46	74
June	.247	.291	.432	81	20	3	0	4	16	4	12	.270	.339	.474	304	82	11	0	17	50	31	54
July	.167	.275	.267	60	10	3	0	1	3	8	8	.216	.308	.345	278	60	14	2	6	28	36	46
August	.316	.358	.513	76	24	4	1	3	15	5	13	.260	.353	.465	288	75	13	2	14	47	41	58
Sept/Oct	.250	.348	.368	76	19	0	0	3	13	12	13	.220	.303	.311	296	65	4	1	7	37	36	64
Bases Empty	.247	.335	.532	235	58	7	0	20	20	28	51	.249	.323	.451	912	227	34	3	48	48	97	188
Leadoff	.191	.321	.393	89	17	3	0	5	5	15	17	.245	.326	.445	364	89	18	2	17	17	42	55
Not Leadoff	.281	.344	.616	146	41	4	0	15	15	13	34	.252	.321	.454	548	138	16	1	31	31	55	133
Runners On	.247	.326	.397	194	48	6	1	7	52	19	30	.241	.338	.405	758	183	25	3	31	195	107	142
First Base Only	.229	.308	.457	70	16	4	0	4	9	7	8	.239	.300	.468	310	74	12	1	19	41	66	53
Scoring Position	.258	.336	.363	124	32	2	1	3	43	12	22	.243	.362	.362	448	109	13	2	12	154	81	89
Late Innings, Close	.208	.287	.375	72	15	0	0	4	14	8	14	.231	.329	.330	303	70	4	1	8	45	44	76

RBI/Opportunities

Scoring Position	37 / 169 (22%)	133 / 648 (21%)	
Scoring Position, 2 Out	11 / 77 (14%)	50 / 296 (17%)	
On Third, Less than 2 Out	15 / 36 (42%)	53 / 120 (44%)	
RBI in close games / RBI Total	44 / 72 (61%)	157 / 243 (65%)	

Greg Walker
Chicago White Sox

Always a hard worker, Greg Walker continues to improve his game. Going into the 1987 season, Greg had shown two major weaknesses as a hitter: a lack of discipline at the plate and an inability to hit lefthanders. In his typically quiet way, Walker made significant progress in both areas. Greg almost doubled his previous career high in walks last year, jumping from 44 to a club-high 75. Given that the White Sox are a team which idolizes Benny Goodman (Swing Swing Swing), the improvement is especially noteworthy. Walker's progress against lefties was just as impressive. Prior to '87 Greg had totaled only 8 homers in his career against southpaws versus 65 against righties; last year the numbers were 13 vs. lefties (in 209 at bats), 14 vs. righties (357 AB).

With that sort of progress, Walker's total figures (27 HR, 94 RBI, .256 BA) have to be a disappointment. There are some extenuating circumstances, however. In the past Walker had always been a fast starter; in '84–'86 he hit .296 in April, with a .548 SA. Last year, though, he hit exactly .100 (7 for 70). Greg's not the complaining sort, but it's quite possible he was still recovering from the broken right hand he'd suffered the previous August; he'd also broken his right wrist earlier in 1986. From May 1 of '87 on, Walker hit .278, with a .368 OBA and .496 slugging; I believe those figures more accurately represent his improvement.

It's also true that Walker is hampered somewhat by his home ballpark. Since the Hawk moved home plate back before the '86 season, Comiskey has been tough on sluggers, depressing the homer rate by nearly 20 percent. Walker has fared better than most, belting 18 homers in Chicago during '86–'87, 22 on the road. With a better hitter's home park, Greg would have easily topped 30 homers in '87.

Defensively Walker has worked hard to become an adequate fielder. Pop flies, once an adventure for Greg, are no longer a problem. He remains weak on the 3–6–3 double play, however; Greg usually chooses to step on the bag first, then throw to second for a tag play, which is definitely doing it the hard way. But it's better than starting off throwing the ball into left field. He's not really an asset defensively, but he's hardly a liability, either.

Despite some good offensive numbers, Greg Walker probably ranks in the middle of American League first basemen. You'd have to place him below Mattingly, McGwire, Joyner, Hrbek, and the Evans boys, and about on a par with guys like Pete O'Brien, Alvin Davis and the Eddie Murray '87 model. That's not bad company, but Walker wants to be even better. The gains he made in 1987 should help him get there.

Don Zminda

Walker, Gregory Lee "Greg"   Bats: Left   Throws: Right   Born 10/06/59

1987 SEASON AND MAJOR-LEAGUE CAREER BATTING TOTALS

	G	AB	H	2B	3B	HR	TB	R	RBI	TBB	IBB	SO	HP	SH	SF	SB	CS	SB%	GDP	AVG	OBP	SLG
87 CHA	157	566	145	33	2	27	263	85	94	75	7	112	5	1	5	2	1	.67	12	.256	.346	.465
6 YEARS	663	2215	598	128	18	100	1062	296	374	213	23	382	13	1	17	18	11	.62	44	.270	.335	.479

	1987 SEASON											FOUR YEAR TOTALS (1984 – 1987)									
	Ave.	OBP	SLG	AB	H	2B	3B	HR	RBI	BB	SO	Ave.	OBP	SLG	AB	H	2B	3B	HR	RBI	BB	SO
Totals	.256	.346	.465	566	145	33	2	27	94	75	112	.269	.335	.481	1891	508	110	14	88	312	184	322
vs. Left	.238	.324	.467	210	50	9	0	13	43	22	50	.228	.298	.399	566	129	32	1	21	88	51	122
vs. Right	.267	.358	.463	356	95	24	2	14	51	53	62	.286	.350	.516	1325	379	78	13	67	224	133	200
at Home	.249	.352	.443	273	68	15	1	12	50	43	43	.275	.351	.507	934	257	58	12	45	165	107	161
on Road	.263	.339	.485	293	77	18	1	15	44	32	69	.262	.318	.456	957	251	52	2	43	147	77	161
vs. Groundball	.262	.342	.462	290	76	15	2	13	53	36	56	.279	.348	.507	896	250	53	8	45	155	94	142
vs. Flyball	.250	.349	.467	276	69	18	0	14	41	39	56	.259	.323	.458	995	258	57	6	43	157	90	180
vs. Finesse	.239	.321	.435	301	72	18	1	13	38	34	45	.269	.329	.513	1071	288	61	7	62	181	91	150
vs. Power	.275	.373	.498	265	73	15	1	14	56	41	67	.268	.342	.440	820	220	49	7	26	131	93	172
on Grass	.262	.352	.484	477	125	26	1	26	87	65	89	.269	.338	.486	1595	429	91	12	77	277	163	274
on Artificial Turf	.225	.310	.360	89	20	7	1	1	7	10	23	.267	.318	.456	296	79	19	2	11	35	21	48
Day Games	.242	.328	.439	157	38	10	0	7	17	19	33	.266	.328	.482	533	142	31	6	24	69	48	89
Night Games	.262	.352	.474	409	107	23	2	20	77	56	79	.270	.337	.481	1358	366	79	8	64	243	136	233
April	.100	.182	.243	70	7	2	1	2	9	7	22	.229	.288	.444	205	47	12	4	8	29	17	44
May	.313	.367	.594	96	30	7	1	6	18	10	18	.304	.359	.525	299	91	18	3	14	44	27	58
June	.258	.385	.562	89	23	6	0	7	16	16	16	.244	.321	.503	360	88	22	1	23	76	38	56
July	.244	.340	.422	90	22	4	0	4	12	12	19	.256	.323	.420	383	98	19	4	12	53	37	58
August	.275	.375	.461	102	28	7	0	4	15	17	16	.266	.338	.481	297	79	20	1	14	48	33	50
Sept/Oct	.294	.368	.454	119	35	7	0	4	24	13	21	.303	.363	.510	347	105	19	1	17	62	32	56
Bases Empty	.243	.322	.430	309	75	16	0	14	14	33	56	.260	.314	.451	1030	268	57	7	42	42	78	181
Leadoff	.270	.377	.423	111	30	8	0	3	3	17	20	.279	.337	.481	445	124	32	5	16	16	37	85
Not Leadoff	.227	.288	.434	198	45	8	0	11	11	16	36	.246	.297	.429	585	144	25	2	26	26	41	96
Runners On	.272	.373	.506	257	70	17	2	13	80	42	56	.279	.357	.517	861	240	53	7	46	270	106	141
First Base Only	.312	.395	.661	109	34	9	1	9	21	13	24	.285	.344	.526	382	109	26	3	20	50	32	65
Scoring Position	.243	.357	.392	148	36	8	1	4	59	29	32	.273	.367	.509	479	131	27	4	26	220	74	76
Late Innings, Close	.259	.384	.444	81	21	6	0	3	16	15	15	.259	.326	.450	278	72	15	1	12	54	26	53

RBI/Opportunities

Scoring Position	50 / 211 (24%)	171 / 659 (26%)
Scoring Position, 2 Out	23 / 106 (22%)	67 / 322 (21%)
On Third, Less than 2 Out	17 / 33 (52%)	54 / 105 (51%)
RBI in close games / RBI Total	54 / 94 (57%)	220 / 312 (71%)

Tim Wallach
Montreal Expos

Over the past three season, the Expos have dealt away clean-up hitters Gary Carter and Al Oliver, and at the start of the 1987 campaign, Andre Dawson departed via free agency. With each of these moves, Tim Wallach hoped to land in the clean-up slot in the batting order. However, it took an early season injury to Hubie Brooks to give Wallach the opportunity. He responded by holding on to the slot for the rest of the season, batting .298 with 26 home runs and 123 RBIs, and a major league leading 42 doubles.

Wallach broke the team RBI record by 10 despite batting only .284 with men in scoring position. It is interesting to note that in 1983, Dawson set the team RBI standard despite batting significantly lower with men in scoring position than his .299 season average. That is a strong indication that the batting average with men in scoring position must be taken with a grain of salt. It is, as batting average is, a very hollow stat. One of the reasons that Wallach led the majors with 97 baserunners driven in, was that he doubled in the ridiculous total of 29 runs.

Through the interpretation of a future-runs table designed for 1987, which takes into account the league average of 9.03 runs per game, Wallach measures out at +37.92 runs, which is an MVP calibre season and second on the club to Tim Raines' +53.15 figure. (Which, of course, begs a question we seem to ask every year: What happened to Raines in the MVP voting?) What is most surprising is Wallach's rating when Raines batted in the third position, and when he didn't. Wallach was +29.39 runs in the 81 games in which Raines batted third. In the other 81 games, Wallach was only +8.53 runs. To say that Wallach benefitted from the fact that Raines was on base in front of him is the logical conclusion. However, Raines scored the incredible total of 69 runs in the 81 games that he spent in the number three slot. A player of Raines' abilities could expect to score a total of about 55 to 60 runs when batting third. Since he scored so many more, one has to give Wallach credit for many of the rest.

Wallach turned 30 at the end of the '87 season, so he should still be in his prime. His career thus far has been riddled with slumps and injuries; given that, it's risky to expect a repeat of '87 from him. But he was a productive player prior to this, and remains outstanding on defense. Even if he returns to his previous level, he'll still be a good one.

Brent MacInnes

Wallach, Timothy Charles "Tim" Bats: Right Throws: Right Born 09/14/57

1987 SEASON AND MAJOR-LEAGUE CAREER BATTING TOTALS

	G	AB	H	2B	3B	HR	TB	R	RBI	TBB	IBB	SO	HP	SH	SF	SB	CS	SB%	GDP	AVG	OBP	SLG
87 MON	153	593	177	42	4	26	305	89	123	37	5	98	7	0	7	9	5	.64	6	.298	.343	.514
8 YEARS	992	3624	948	198	19	136	1592	427	529	276	41	570	43	5	30	35	33	.51	78	.262	.319	.439

	1987 SEASON											FOUR YEAR TOTALS (1984 – 1987)									
	Ave.	OBP	SLG	AB	H	2B	3B	HR	RBI	BB	SO	Ave.	OBP	SLG	AB	H	2B	3B	HR	RBI	BB	SO
Totals	.300	.345	.516	593	178	42	4	26	124	37	98	.261	.319	.442	2224	581	125	12	84	348	169	350
vs. Left	.311	.356	.447	161	50	17	1	1	26	11	28	.263	.323	.426	619	163	47	3	16	90	54	85
vs. Right	.296	.340	.542	432	128	25	3	25	98	26	70	.260	.317	.447	1605	418	78	9	68	258	115	265
at Home	.300	.349	.552	290	87	26	4	13	64	19	45	.261	.326	.426	1071	279	63	9	32	166	93	167
on Road	.300	.340	.482	303	91	16	0	13	60	18	53	.262	.312	.456	1153	302	62	3	52	182	76	183
vs. Groundball	.310	.354	.505	277	86	16	1	12	70	19	47	.263	.326	.433	1052	277	47	3	42	183	90	164
vs. Flyball	.291	.336	.525	316	92	26	3	14	54	18	51	.259	.313	.449	1172	304	78	9	42	165	79	186
vs. Finesse	.301	.344	.556	349	105	27	4	18	81	22	47	.274	.320	.462	1305	357	79	10	49	208	79	183
vs. Power	.299	.346	.459	244	73	15	0	8	43	15	51	.244	.317	.412	919	224	46	2	35	140	90	167
on Grass	.312	.349	.500	154	48	5	0	8	31	8	29	.259	.313	.473	613	159	28	2	33	97	43	108
on Artificial Turf	.296	.343	.522	439	130	37	4	18	93	29	69	.262	.321	.430	1611	422	97	10	51	251	126	242
Day Games	.298	.318	.494	168	50	12	0	7	30	5	26	.267	.318	.460	768	205	43	3	33	118	51	123
Night Games	.301	.355	.525	425	128	30	4	19	94	32	72	.258	.319	.432	1456	376	82	9	51	230	118	227
April	.271	.302	.390	59	16	4	0	1	10	3	9	.305	.352	.496	282	86	19	1	11	54	21	37
May	.308	.346	.504	117	36	8	0	5	29	5	19	.273	.313	.453	411	112	28	2	14	62	22	59
June	.301	.368	.573	103	31	13	0	5	26	11	13	.278	.350	.480	367	102	28	2	14	63	41	55
July	.333	.373	.604	96	32	7	2	5	21	5	15	.247	.299	.441	392	97	19	3	17	66	28	71
August	.330	.373	.580	100	33	5	1	6	23	7	15	.258	.306	.414	403	104	15	3	14	62	28	60
Sept/Oct	.254	.296	.415	118	30	5	1	4	15	6	27	.217	.276	.379	369	80	16	1	14	41	29	68
Bases Empty	.310	.334	.544	294	91	17	2	16	16	9	54	.256	.295	.433	1217	311	60	9	46	46	67	207
Leadoff	.343	.361	.573	143	49	8	2	7	7	2	30	.299	.335	.515	515	154	32	5	23	23	26	82
Not Leadoff	.278	.310	.517	151	42	9	0	9	9	7	24	.224	.266	.373	702	157	28	4	23	23	41	125
Runners On	.291	.354	.488	299	87	25	2	10	108	28	44	.268	.336	.452	1007	270	65	3	38	302	102	143
First Base Only	.307	.371	.534	88	27	7	2	3	13	8	13	.282	.317	.463	369	104	21	2	14	43	18	53
Scoring Position	.284	.347	.469	211	60	18	0	7	95	20	31	.260	.347	.445	638	166	44	1	24	259	84	90
Late Innings, Close	.375	.398	.688	80	30	4	0	7	25	3	16	.261	.326	.437	375	98	15	0	17	60	36	64

RBI/Opportunities

Scoring Position	80 / 277 (29%)	213 / 867 (25%)
Scoring Position, 2 Out	34 / 135 (25%)	87 / 407 (21%)
On Third, Less than 2 Out	26 / 54 (48%)	72 / 157 (46%)
RBI in close games / RBI Total	93 / 124 (75%)	260 / 348 (75%)

Denny Walling
Houston Astros

In 1987, Denny Walling completed ten years of continuous service with the Houston Astros. He may be the only player, other than pitchers and catchers, to have achieved this milestone of longevity on one team without ever achieving 400 at-bats in a single season. Obviously, for a player to compile this type of record, he must have value to his team, but he must also have one or more significant limitations to prevent him from becoming a full-time regular.

Walling's greatest value is his versatility. He bats left and throws right—a good combination for a utility player. He is a reliable pinch-hitter (.533, second only to Ken Griffey in the league among players with at least 15 AB, on 8 for 15 with 2 doubles and 2 GWRBI, a meaningless figure in many cases, but certainly of value as a pinch-hitting stat), and he can play several defensive positions. He has adequate speed and power and has delivered some big hits—notably a game-winning eleventh inning hit for a 1–0 victory over the Dodgers in the 1981 strike year playoffs, and a home run that broke a 0–0 tie in Mike Scott's division-clinching no-hitter over the Giants in 1986. He has a .280 average over his eleven seasons with Houston and has been the most difficult Astro to strike out over the last five years—fanning less than once every ten at bats.

Why, then, has Walling been unable to win a full-time position as a regular player? One supposition might be that he is a defensive liability. However, this is clearly not the case. He has mastered three positions—outfield, first base, and third base—and with his quick hands and rifle arm, he is above average at each one. Another guess might be that he is injury prone. However, he has spent only one two-week stint on the disabled list since joining the Astros.

The answer is partially in the numbers. Walling hits right-handed pitchers much better than he hits lefties. In the 1984–1986 period he batted .298 against righthanders but only .230 against lefties. With the Astros array of switch-hitters, his services are not needed when a lefthander is on the hill. Walling is also a noted fastball hitter. Veteran Astro observer and former coach Buddy Hancken once noted "Walling is a great fastball hitter, but throw him a curve and he will hit the nicest little ground ball to second base you have ever seen." However, the figures do not completely support Walling's prowess as a fastball hitter. In the 1984–1986 period, he batted .322 against finesse pitchers but only .248 against power pitchers.

Walling appears to have no chance of a 400 at bat season with Houston now that another switch-hitter, Ken Caminiti, has arrived to play third base. However, if the Astros regain their status as a contender, look for Walling to play an important role in key situations.

Bill Gilbert

Walling, Dennis Martin　　　　Bats: Left　　Throws: Right　　Born 04/17/54

1987 SEASON AND MAJOR-LEAGUE CAREER BATTING TOTALS

	G	AB	H	2B	3B	HR	TB	R	RBI	TBB	IBB	SO	HP	SH	SF	SB	CS	SB%	GDP	AVG	OBP	SLG
87 HOU	110	325	92	21	4	5	136	45	33	39	1	37	0	2	4	5	1	.83	9	.283	.356	.418
13 YEARS	1013	2458	686	116	28	46	996	332	327	266	24	256	2	4	23	42	18	.70	45	.279	.347	.405

	1987 SEASON											FOUR YEAR TOTALS (1984 – 1987)										
	Ave.	OBP	SLG	AB	H	2B	3B	HR	RBI	BB	SO	Ave.	OBP	SLG	AB	H	2B	3B	HR	RBI	BB	SO
Totals	.283	.356	.418	325	92	21	4	5	33	39	37	.287	.343	.427	1301	374	75	11	28	167	116	122
vs. Left	.200	.222	.314	35	7	1	0	1	3	1	10	.224	.267	.265	170	38	4	0	1	18	10	33
vs. Right	.293	.370	.431	290	85	20	4	4	30	38	27	.297	.354	.451	1131	336	71	11	27	149	106	89
at Home	.288	.364	.372	156	45	7	0	2	19	19	18	.293	.344	.405	649	190	36	5	9	84	54	58
on Road	.278	.349	.462	169	47	14	4	3	14	20	19	.282	.342	.448	652	184	39	6	19	83	62	64
vs. Groundball	.325	.391	.481	154	50	13	1	3	21	18	18	.304	.356	.418	622	189	38	3	9	78	53	53
vs. Flyball	.246	.325	.363	171	42	8	3	2	12	21	19	.272	.331	.434	679	185	37	8	19	89	63	69
vs. Finesse	.266	.320	.395	177	47	10	2	3	18	16	11	.308	.351	.446	718	221	38	8	15	106	53	36
vs. Power	.304	.398	.446	148	45	11	2	2	15	23	26	.262	.333	.403	583	153	37	3	13	61	63	86
on Grass	.255	.365	.429	98	25	7	2	2	7	17	10	.286	.352	.447	385	110	20	3	12	50	40	35
on Artificial Turf	.295	.352	.414	227	67	14	2	3	26	22	27	.288	.339	.418	916	264	55	8	16	117	76	87
Day Games	.240	.315	.333	96	23	7	1	0	7	12	7	.291	.348	.446	327	95	25	1	8	44	31	25
Night Games	.301	.374	.454	229	69	14	3	5	26	27	30	.286	.341	.420	974	279	50	10	20	123	85	97
April	.273	.294	.394	33	9	1	0	1	2	1	2	.320	.366	.431	153	49	8	0	3	17	11	10
May	.339	.371	.446	56	19	6	0	0	4	4	11	.294	.327	.402	204	60	17	1	1	22	11	25
June	.246	.347	.400	65	16	2	1	2	8	10	6	.226	.316	.357	199	45	7	2	5	23	26	16
July	.311	.388	.486	74	23	7	3	0	7	10	7	.282	.357	.430	284	80	18	3	6	39	34	30
August	.250	.306	.318	44	11	3	0	0	4	4	5	.311	.348	.461	254	79	12	4	6	36	15	22
Sept/Oct	.264	.381	.415	53	14	2	0	2	8	10	6	.295	.354	.469	207	61	13	1	7	30	19	19
Bases Empty	.328	.400	.460	174	57	14	3	1	1	21	19	.299	.344	.433	713	213	51	6	11	11	49	64
Leadoff	.339	.381	.441	59	20	6	0	0	0	4	8	.291	.321	.445	254	74	20	2	5	5	11	30
Not Leadoff	.322	.409	.470	115	37	8	3	1	1	17	11	.303	.356	.427	459	139	31	4	6	6	38	34
Runners On	.232	.306	.371	151	35	7	1	4	32	18	18	.274	.346	.418	588	161	24	5	17	156	67	58
First Base Only	.250	.333	.446	56	14	5	0	2	6	7	5	.289	.332	.453	232	67	12	1	8	22	15	15
Scoring Position	.221	.291	.326	95	21	2	1	2	26	11	13	.264	.354	.396	356	94	12	4	9	134	52	43
Late Innings, Close	.316	.422	.368	38	12	2	0	0	3	7	7	.253	.336	.339	233	59	8	0	4	23	29	31

RBI/Opportunities

Scoring Position	23 / 125 (18%)	118 / 482 (24%)	
Scoring Position, 2 Out	9 / 57 (16%)	42 / 199 (21%)	
On Third, Less than 2 Out	9 / 21 (43%)	49 / 98 (50%)	
RBI in close games / RBI Total	20 / 33 (61%)	106 / 167 (63%)	

Gary Ward
New York Yankees

The Yankees signed Gary Ward last winter because they correctly believed, after going 23–33 against southpaws in 1986, that they needed help against lefthanders. By May 31, they were accepting congratulations for their brilliance—Ward was hitting .299 and on pace for 115 RBIs in 1987. Right about then, things began to go sour; from June 1 through the end of the season, Ward hit only .222. He had 37 RBIs after two months; he drove in 41 in the next four.

What happened is pretty easy to see from the stats. Ward had always been a good hitter with men in scoring position in his career, hitting .310 in that situation from '84–'86. He began 1987 in an even higher gear; his high RBI count was due to his ability to get hits with men on base. In April and May, he hit .364 (20–55) with men in scoring position. Though he tailed off a bit in June and July, hitting .311 (14–45), he was still a bit above his normal level. But from August on, he went 6–39 (.154), driving in only eight runners from second or third in the last ten weeks. With Rickey Henderson and Willie Randolph out with injuries, the Yankees really needed the heart of their offense to convert on their opportunities; Ward just wasn't there when New York needed him late in the season.

Why it happened is another question. The problem was that Ward's power began steadily disappearing as the season progressed. In the first two months, he hit seven homers (one every 25.3 at-bats), smacked 12 doubles and had a .486 slugging percentage. From June to October, he hit only nine homers (one every 39 ABs), 10 doubles and one triple, for a .332 slugging percentage. That's not quite what you like to see in the heart of your batting order, so New York tried using Gary in the first or second spots. His .291 on-base percentage didn't make him a very attractive candidate for that job, either.

Why did Ward's power disappear? I don't know—no, let me put it this way . . . I know the reason that his power disappeared, but I don't know why. Despite his size (6'2", 207), Gary has always done most of his hitting to the opposite field; when he was doing well, most of his power was to right field. Of his 19 extra-base hits in April and May, 12 went to right, four went to center and only three were pulled; six of his seven homers went the other way and the other went to center. From June through the end of the season, he began trying to pull everything—that's when his slump started. Of his 20 EBHs in the last four months, 10 (including three homers) went to left, four (including two homers) went to center and only six (four of them homers) went to right. Gary had been prospering by hitting the ball the other way; when, for who knows what reason, he began behaving like Don Baylor, his game fell completely apart.

Craig Christmann

Ward, Gary Lamell Bats: Right Throws: Right Born 12/06/53

1987 SEASON AND MAJOR-LEAGUE CAREER BATTING TOTALS

	G	AB	H	2B	3B	HR	TB	R	RBI	TBB	IBB	SO	HP	SH	SF	SB	CS	SB%	GDP	AVG	OBP	SLG
87 NYA	146	529	131	22	1	16	203	65	78	33	2	101	1	2	4	9	1	.90	20	.248	.291	.384
9 YEARS	977	3647	1031	166	37	108	1595	509	497	273	22	625	10	7	28	80	26	.75	121	.283	.332	.437

	1987 SEASON											FOUR YEAR TOTALS (1984 – 1987)										
	Ave.	OBP	SLG	AB	H	2B	3B	HR	RBI	BB	SO	Ave.	OBP	SLG	AB	H	2B	3B	HR	RBI	BB	SO
Totals	.248	.291	.384	529	131	22	1	16	78	33	101	.281	.332	.420	2104	592	86	17	57	278	158	365
vs. Left	.281	.322	.378	196	55	7	0	4	33	12	28	.290	.345	.442	677	196	32	7	19	106	58	100
vs. Right	.228	.273	.387	333	76	15	1	12	45	21	73	.278	.325	.409	1427	396	54	10	38	172	100	265
at Home	.282	.320	.402	259	73	10	0	7	44	15	47	.307	.355	.449	1022	314	46	9	27	154	76	170
on Road	.215	.263	.367	270	58	12	1	9	34	18	54	.257	.309	.392	1082	278	40	8	30	124	82	195
vs. Groundball	.244	.282	.391	271	66	10	0	10	45	15	48	.301	.345	.442	1028	309	49	6	28	151	68	148
vs. Flyball	.252	.300	.376	258	65	12	1	6	33	18	53	.263	.319	.399	1076	283	37	11	29	127	90	217
vs. Finesse	.251	.288	.378	275	69	14	0	7	41	15	38	.299	.343	.434	1210	362	52	9	31	161	81	162
vs. Power	.244	.295	.390	254	62	8	1	9	37	18	63	.257	.316	.400	894	230	34	8	26	117	77	203
on Grass	.249	.287	.379	454	113	17	0	14	71	25	92	.278	.327	.411	1783	496	71	12	47	237	128	325
on Artificial Turf	.240	.313	.413	75	18	5	1	2	7	8	9	.299	.359	.470	321	96	15	5	10	41	30	40
Day Games	.258	.305	.376	194	50	9	1	4	32	14	46	.244	.303	.335	508	124	17	1	9	55	44	101
Night Games	.242	.283	.388	335	81	13	0	12	46	19	55	.293	.341	.447	1596	468	69	16	48	223	114	264
April	.308	.341	.449	78	24	8	0	1	17	4	10	.270	.327	.375	285	77	13	1	5	40	24	45
May	.293	.358	.515	99	29	4	0	6	20	9	19	.259	.326	.400	390	101	17	1	12	52	38	62
June	.216	.239	.315	111	24	2	0	3	20	4	24	.270	.305	.378	415	112	16	4	7	59	22	71
July	.205	.284	.295	78	16	1	0	2	7	9	17	.261	.314	.374	326	85	10	3	7	31	26	65
August	.174	.182	.279	86	15	3	0	2	7	1	18	.300	.337	.492	370	111	16	5	15	56	21	66
Sept/Oct	.299	.349	.455	77	23	4	1	2	7	6	13	.333	.386	.500	318	106	14	3	11	40	27	56
Bases Empty	.214	.261	.358	285	61	9	1	10	10	18	62	.268	.316	.397	1219	327	41	10	32	32	85	220
Leadoff	.244	.286	.403	119	29	4	0	5	5	7	24	.309	.349	.459	499	154	24	6	13	13	31	74
Not Leadoff	.193	.243	.325	166	32	5	1	5	5	11	38	.240	.293	.354	720	173	17	4	19	19	54	146
Runners On	.287	.326	.414	244	70	13	0	6	68	15	39	.299	.352	.451	885	265	45	7	25	246	73	145
First Base Only	.288	.315	.462	104	30	6	0	4	11	4	14	.294	.321	.451	384	113	15	3	13	39	15	46
Scoring Position	.286	.333	.379	140	40	7	0	2	57	11	25	.303	.374	.451	501	152	30	4	12	207	58	99
Late Innings, Close	.268	.308	.479	71	19	3	0	4	13	4	16	.277	.331	.413	329	91	12	3	9	41	27	63

RBI/Opportunities

	1987		FOUR YEAR
Scoring Position	53 / 196 (27%)		178 / 675 (26%)
Scoring Position, 2 Out	22 / 100 (22%)		74 / 311 (24%)
On Third, Less than 2 Out	18 / 29 (62%)		51 / 107 (48%)
RBI in close games / RBI Total	47 / 78 (60%)		191 / 278 (69%)

Mitch Webster
Montreal Expos

When the Expos upset the pre-season predictions by staying in the NL East race until the end of the year, the most frequently asked question was what would have happened if Andre Dawson had still been with the team. If you're willing to concede that Dawson would not and could not have done in Montreal what he did in Chicago, you don't have to ask: Moved from centerfield to replace Dawson in right, Mitch Webster put up numbers comparable to what Dawson did in his last three seasons with the Expos. Webster's and Dawson's stats were in the same general range in batting average, extra base hits, and runs created. Batting second, Webster couldn't match Dawson in RBIs, but he was on base often enough to score 101 runs, and combined with Tim Raines to help Tim Wallach to by far the best RBI totals of his career.

Webster continued his patterns of hitting better for average from the right side, and hitting for power only on the road. Never a home run hitter until he reached the majors (he hit only two in his first three years as a pro), he hit two homers in a game for the second time in his career, and hit his first ever grand slam in an important game against the Mets. With a smooth, level swing, and the ability to hit to all fields from both sides of the plate, Webster has all the tools to be a fine player. But he seemed to come from nowhere to be an above average major league ballplayer. After an only fair minor league career, Webster, in less than three full seasons with Montreal, is already showing signs of long term consistency. He's a .280 hitter who'll hive you 45–55 extra base hits a year, is willing to take a walk, has good speed on the bases and in the field, and won't take you out of a game with a mental mistake. The 1987 cliché of choice, a player who "stays within himself," is exactly what you get with Webster.

There's no reason to think Webster will change his game, or put up numbers very different from what he has over the past two seasons any time in the near future. The Expos are now talking of finding a new shortstop and moving Hubie Brooks to right, sending Webster back to center. If Brooks can make the adjustment, or if Herm Winningham finally becomes the ballplayer he should be, the Expos outfield can be as good as it was supposed to have become in the early years of Dawson—Cromartie —Valentine. In any case, Webster will be a part of it.

Michael Cassin

Webster, Mitchell Dean "Mitch" Bats: Both Throws: Left Born 05/16/59

1987 SEASON AND MAJOR-LEAGUE CAREER BATTING TOTALS

	G	AB	H	2B	3B	HR	TB	R	RBI	TBB	IBB	SO	HP	SH	SF	SB	CS	SB%	GDP	AVG	OBP	SLG
87 MON	156	588	165	30	8	15	256	101	63	70	5	95	6	8	4	33	10	.77	6	.281	.361	.435
5 YEARS	422	1410	397	71	24	34	618	233	146	149	12	214	10	12	10	84	35	.71	19	.282	.352	.438

	1987 SEASON											FOUR YEAR TOTALS (1984 – 1987)										
	Ave.	OBP	SLG	AB	H	2B	3B	HR	RBI	BB	SO	Ave.	OBP	SLG	AB	H	2B	3B	HR	RBI	BB	SO
Totals	.281	.361	.435	588	165	30	8	15	63	70	95	.283	.355	.441	1376	390	69	23	34	142	147	206
vs. Left	.289	.347	.458	201	58	11	1	7	26	17	29	.314	.361	.502	490	154	30	4	18	65	34	67
vs. Right	.276	.367	.424	387	107	19	7	8	37	53	66	.266	.351	.407	886	236	39	19	16	77	113	139
at Home	.267	.353	.439	285	76	14	4	9	34	36	43	.263	.335	.421	649	171	32	14	14	70	69	87
on Road	.294	.368	.432	303	89	16	4	6	29	34	52	.301	.372	.459	727	219	37	9	20	72	78	119
vs. Groundball	.295	.374	.462	288	85	16	4	8	31	34	38	.311	.378	.479	652	203	38	10	17	66	69	75
vs. Flyball	.267	.348	.410	300	80	14	4	7	32	36	57	.258	.334	.407	724	187	31	13	17	76	78	131
vs. Finesse	.281	.352	.416	356	100	12	3	10	34	37	53	.290	.354	.430	814	236	29	11	21	77	79	103
vs. Power	.280	.374	.466	232	65	18	5	5	29	33	42	.274	.355	.457	562	154	40	12	13	65	68	103
on Grass	.297	.379	.424	158	47	10	2	2	18	21	25	.324	.391	.468	370	120	22	2	9	41	39	60
on Artificial Turf	.274	.354	.440	430	118	20	6	13	45	49	70	.268	.341	.431	1006	270	47	21	25	101	108	146
Day Games	.294	.368	.486	177	52	11	4	5	19	19	28	.293	.361	.483	451	132	26	9	14	58	47	67
Night Games	.275	.358	.414	411	113	19	4	10	44	51	67	.279	.351	.421	925	258	43	14	20	84	100	139
April	.286	.368	.403	77	22	4	1	1	7	8	11	.267	.335	.390	146	39	10	1	2	14	13	24
May	.302	.368	.415	106	32	9	0	1	12	11	14	.301	.381	.425	186	56	14	0	3	21	24	20
June	.296	.378	.449	98	29	5	2	2	9	13	12	.270	.360	.423	222	60	12	5	4	17	31	26
July	.286	.320	.473	91	26	4	2	3	11	3	11	.287	.324	.459	244	70	11	5	7	26	12	36
August	.257	.394	.426	101	26	3	1	4	9	24	21	.279	.365	.422	251	70	9	6	5	23	35	36
Sept/Oct	.261	.333	.443	115	30	5	2	4	15	11	26	.291	.356	.486	327	95	13	6	13	41	32	64
Bases Empty	.278	.353	.435	338	94	14	6	9	9	34	56	.285	.348	.461	801	228	40	16	23	23	73	124
Leadoff	.267	.340	.433	90	24	5	2	2	2	8	11	.311	.366	.496	254	79	17	3	8	8	20	31
Not Leadoff	.282	.357	.435	248	70	9	4	7	7	26	45	.272	.340	.444	547	149	23	13	15	15	53	93
Runners On	.284	.371	.436	250	71	16	2	6	54	36	39	.282	.362	.414	575	162	29	7	11	119	74	82
First Base Only	.279	.353	.402	122	34	9	0	2	7	14	19	.295	.350	.410	271	80	16	3	3	15	23	39
Scoring Position	.289	.387	.469	128	37	7	2	4	47	22	20	.270	.372	.418	304	82	13	4	8	104	51	43
Late Innings, Close	.289	.360	.434	76	22	5	0	2	9	9	16	.242	.316	.369	236	57	10	1	6	29	26	34

RBI/Opportunities

Scoring Position	38 / 178	(21%)	90 / 422	(21%)
Scoring Position, 2 Out	14 / 72	(19%)	36 / 182	(20%)
On Third, Less than 2 Out	12 / 30	(40%)	31 / 67	(46%)
RBI in close games / RBI Total	29 / 63	(46%)	82 / 142	(58%)

Bill Wegman
Milwaukee Brewers

I probably shouldn't say it—but since I'd never forgive myself if I kept quiet and it happened, I will: I suspect that Bill Wegman will become one of the best starters in the AL in 1988.

Why? Well, Wegman was an effective pitcher in the minors. His ERAs were (in order) 4.17, 2.81, 1.30, 2.45 and 4.02. In each year, he was younger than the average player in his league.

He did it by doing three things. He's tough to run against. He gets a high number of ground balls. Most importantly, he allows very few walks; in the minors, he allowed (in order) 4.82, 1.90, 2.17, 2.26 and 2.49 walks per nine innings. Two things are important about that:

First, Wegman's best ERAs in the minors came in the same years when he walked the fewest men. Even though he always allowed about a hit an inning and had problems with homers, he pitched effectively that way.

Secondly, Bill has been able to achieve those same performance levels in the majors. Wegman walked 1.95 men per nine innings in 1986 and 2.12 in 1987. He has allowed more than a hit an inning and 30+ homers in both 1986 and 1987. In other words, he's done the same things that made him a good pitcher in the minors—but, for some reason, he isn't getting results.

What's the reason? Bad support. The 1986 Brewers couldn't field— they were #11 in double plays, #12 in errors and their defensive efficiency record (a stat, created by Bill James, that measures a team's ability to turn balls put into play into outs) was .684—third worst in the AL. Milwaukee scored 4.14 runs per game (also #12 in the AL); they scored 4.03 for Bill. In 11 of his 32 starts, they scored two runs or less.

Put it together: A pitcher who wins by getting batters to put the ball in play, while not walking anyone and getting the double play, plays for a team that can't catch anything, doesn't turn the DP and gives him no support. Bill's 1986 (5–12; 5.13) seems reasonable in that context.

Now look at his 1987. Milwaukee was again #12 in the AL in errors; their DER dropped to a woeful .676. But they were third in double plays turned. Though Wegman allowed hits, walks and homers about as often as he did in 1986, his ERA dropped almost a run.

Though Wegman got better support (5.50 R/G) in 1987, it was of the "feast or famine" variety. In his 32 starts, Milwaukee scored 0–3 runs 13 times and 8+ runs nine times.

An August arm injury cost Wegman four starts and affected his September stats.

If the Brewers put a good defense behind Wegman and give him 4–5 runs a game in 65 percent of his starts in 1988, I think that both his ERA and record will be vastly improved. If so, you read it here first.

Geoff Beckman

Wegman, William Edward "Bill"   Bats: Right   Throws: Right   Born 12/19/62

1987 SEASON AND MAJOR-LEAGUE CAREER PITCHING TOTALS

	G	GS	CG	GF	IP	BFP	H	R	ER	HR	SH	SF	HB	TBB	IBB	SO	WP	Bk	W	L	Pct	ShO	Sv	ERA
87 MIL	34	33	7	0	225	934	229	113	106	31	4	6	6	53	2	102	0	2	12	11	.522	0	0	4.24
3 YEARS	72	68	9	1	441	1843	463	241	226	66	8	12	13	99	4	190	5	5	19	23	.452	0	0	4.61

1987: Finesse, Flyball   **1986: Finesse, Flyball**   **1985: Finesse, Groundball**

1987 SEASON

	G	IP	H	BB	SO	SB	CS	W	L	S	ERA
Totals	34	225.0	229	53	101	20	8	12	11	0	4.24
at Home	20	142.2	134	26	67	9	6	7	5	0	3.66
on Road	14	82.1	95	27	34	11	2	5	6	0	5.25
on Grass	13	89.2	94	21	37	11	4	6	3	0	3.71
on Artificial Turf	21	135.1	135	32	64	9	4	6	8	0	4.59
Day Games	28	187.0	190	39	87	16	7	9	8	0	4.09
Night Games	6	38.0	39	14	14	4	1	3	3	0	4.97
April	5	34.0	30	11	15	4	2	2	1	0	3.18
May	5	36.0	35	7	18	3	2	1	4	0	5.25
June	7	43.2	51	12	18	1	2	3	2	0	4.53
July	6	47.0	47	3	20	5	1	2	2	0	2.87
August	4	21.0	27	4	14	2	0	0	1	0	6.43
Sept/Oct	7	43.1	39	16	16	5	1	4	1	0	4.36

FOUR YEAR TOTALS (1984 – 1987)

	G	IP	H	BB	SO	SB	CS	W	L	S	ERA
Totals	72	441.0	463	99	189	29	18	19	23	0	4.61
at Home	41	265.0	267	43	122	16	11	10	10	0	4.25
on Road	31	176.0	196	56	67	13	7	9	13	0	5.16
on Grass	22	142.0	155	26	63	14	8	6	6	0	3.99
on Artificial Turf	50	299.0	308	73	126	15	10	13	17	0	4.91
Day Games	62	380.2	397	82	164	25	15	15	17	0	4.56
Night Games	10	60.1	66	17	25	4	3	4	6	0	4.92
April	9	58.1	56	19	21	6	3	2	2	0	3.55
May	12	81.1	88	17	36	4	7	1	8	0	5.09
June	12	77.1	85	16	36	2	2	5	3	0	5.00
July	11	74.2	75	9	28	5	1	3	5	0	3.86
August	11	64.0	72	11	35	3	4	1	2	0	5.06
Sept/Oct	17	85.1	87	27	33	9	1	7	3	0	4.85

vs. Opponent Batters — 1987 Season

	Ave.	OBP	SLG	AB	H	2B	3B	HR	RBI	BB	SO
Totals	.265	.310	.425	865	229	40	3	31	98	53	101
vs. Left	.257	.308	.420	467	120	22	3	16	51	33	54
vs. Right	.274	.311	.432	398	109	18	0	15	47	20	47
Bases Empty	.267	.314	.415	540	144	25	2	17	17	33	55
Leadoff	.276	.322	.457	221	61	10	0	10	10	14	23
Not Leadoff	.260	.308	.386	319	83	15	2	7	7	19	32
Runners On Base	.262	.303	.443	325	85	15	1	14	81	20	46
First Base Only	.268	.325	.438	153	41	6	1	6	14	12	17
Scoring Position	.256	.283	.448	172	44	9	0	8	67	8	29
Late Innings, Close	.307	.354	.427	75	23	4	1	1	7	6	7

vs. Opponent Batters — Four Year Totals

	Ave.	OBP	SLG	AB	H	2B	3B	HR	RBI	BB	SO
Totals	.271	.312	.442	1711	463	80	8	66	209	99	189
vs. Left	.264	.312	.436	939	248	42	4	37	112	64	100
vs. Right	.278	.311	.451	772	215	38	4	29	97	35	89
Bases Empty	.264	.307	.434	1063	281	47	5	41	41	62	110
Leadoff	.273	.314	.470	436	119	18	1	22	22	25	43
Not Leadoff	.258	.303	.408	627	162	29	4	19	19	37	67
Runners On Base	.281	.319	.457	648	182	33	3	25	168	37	79
First Base Only	.271	.318	.441	306	83	14	1	12	28	20	33
Scoring Position	.289	.320	.471	342	99	19	2	13	140	17	46
Late Innings, Close	.296	.336	.451	142	42	9	2	3	12	9	14

RBI/Opportunities

	1987 Season	Four Year Totals
Scoring Position	55 / 203 (27%)	119 / 409 (29%)
Scoring Position, 2 Out	19 / 96 (20%)	49 / 196 (25%)
On Third, Less than 2 Out	18 / 26 (69%)	39 / 58 (67%)
RBI in close games / RBI Total	81 / 98 (83%)	170 / 209 (81%)

Bob Welch
Los Angeles Dodgers

One of the most important truths about baseball is that media images distort peoples' impressions of player's careers. Consider Bob Welch, to be specific, in comparison to Fernando Valenzuela. Pitching for the same team, over much the same years (Welch's career is 2 years longer), they have the following records:

	Valenzuela	Welch
Innings Pitched	1806	1820
ERA	3.08	3.14
Wins	113	115
Losses	82	86
W–L Percentage	.579	.572

Yes, Fernando strikes out more batters (not that many, it's about 200 for the career), but he also walks more. All in all, it's a pretty close match, but you'd think that Welch pitched in the Mexican League for all the press he gets. It's not just the press, either. Valenzuela has been given more innings to pitch than Welch every year except 1980, when Fernando came up late and only got 18, and 1987, when Welch pitched exactly 1 more inning than Fernando, despite posting an ERA 2/3 of a run better.

Now the Dodgers have traded Bob Welch, and it's hard to see why. Last year, he was as good a starter as they had (his ERA was higher than Orel Hershiser's, but his Won-Lost Percentage was better). On top of that, the famed Dodger pitching well may finally have run dry. Shawn Hillegas looked promising last year, but he's only won four major league games. Tim Belcher is a prospect, also, but one has to wonder why the A's were willing to deal him for Rick Honeycutt. In addition L.A. has the aptly named Timothy Leary, whose 1987 went like this: Tune Up (on the sidelines), Turn On (your fastball), Drop Out (of the rotation). It's an iffy situation, to say the least, and one has to ask whether the Dodgers, who don't figure to score a lot of runs, really had a starting pitcher to trade.

But Bob Welch has a no-impact name, has never won more than 16 games (which is what happens if you don't get full time work), doesn't hit well and didn't have his best season at the start of his career. Even his big moment, striking out Reggie Jackson in the '78 Series, was quickly forgotten when Reggie took him deep the next time around (and the Dodgers blew the Series). Welch played for a team with a lot of high-profile pitchers, and his reputation has been that of just another one of the guys. The fourth man in the rotation. The fact that he's pitched a lot better than that hasn't been able to overcome the media image.

Brock J. Hanke and Don Zminda

Welch, Robert Lynn "Bob" Bats: Right   Throws: Right   Born 11/03/56

1987 SEASON AND MAJOR-LEAGUE CAREER PITCHING TOTALS

	G	GS	CG	GF	IP	BFP	H	R	ER	HR	SH	SF	HB	TBB	IBB	SO	WP	Bk	W	L	Pct	ShO	Sv	ERA
87 LA	35	35	6	0	252	1027	204	94	90	21	10	6	4	86	6	196	4	4	15	9	.625	4	0	3.21
10 YEARS	292	267	47	16	1821	7525	1631	702	635	133	77	50	37	565	42	1292	37	25	115	86	.572	23	8	3.14

1987: Power, Flyball   1986: Finesse, Flyball   1985: Finesse, Flyball   1984: Power, Flyball

1987 SEASON											FOUR YEAR TOTALS (1984 – 1987)										
	G	IP	H	BB	SO	SB	CS	W	L	S	ERA	G	IP	H	BB	SO	SB	CS	W	L	S	ERA
Totals	35	251.2	204	86	196	20	17	15	9	0	3.22	122	833.1	763	234	601	69	41	49	39	0	3.18
at Home	19	136.0	113	35	105	8	11	7	6	0	3.24	64	453.0	425	109	327	36	26	27	21	0	3.04
on Road	16	115.2	91	51	91	12	6	8	3	0	3.19	58	380.1	338	125	274	33	15	22	18	0	3.34
on Grass	11	82.2	66	25	56	6	4	6	1	0	2.72	41	275.0	261	79	190	24	11	16	12	0	3.47
on Artificial Turf	24	169.0	138	61	140	14	13	9	8	0	3.46	81	558.1	502	155	411	45	30	33	27	0	3.01
Day Games	28	206.2	162	59	158	14	16	13	7	0	2.87	94	662.2	601	171	481	53	34	41	26	0	2.96
Night Games	7	45.0	42	27	38	6	1	2	2	0	4.80	28	170.2	162	63	120	16	7	8	13	0	4.01
April	5	36.1	25	12	27	3	2	3	1	0	2.23	16	119.0	97	37	84	7	6	8	5	0	1.82
May	5	35.2	32	12	32	3	0	3	1	0	3.53	15	92.0	103	27	76	9	0	5	6	0	4.99
June	6	43.0	40	18	33	4	5	2	2	0	4.60	23	143.2	159	48	94	16	8	5	8	0	4.51
July	6	43.0	37	14	34	2	2	1	2	0	3.35	22	151.2	125	36	112	7	8	9	8	0	2.73
August	7	47.2	38	20	37	4	6	2	3	0	2.64	24	166.1	141	52	126	13	10	10	8	0	2.81
Sept/Oct	6	46.0	32	10	33	4	2	4	0	0	2.93	22	160.2	138	34	109	17	9	12	4	0	2.74

vs. Opponent Batters	Ave.	OBP	SLG	AB	H	2B	3B	HR	RBI	BB	SO	Ave.	OBP	SLG	AB	H	2B	3B	HR	RBI	BB	SO
Totals	.221	.289	.342	921	204	40	4	21	81	86	196	.242	.295	.360	3150	763	136	25	62	277	234	601
vs. Left	.236	.301	.345	533	126	22	3	10	39	50	100	.241	.294	.342	1663	401	69	16	22	123	126	275
vs. Right	.201	.273	.338	388	78	18	1	11	42	36	96	.243	.296	.381	1487	362	67	9	40	154	108	326
Bases Empty	.207	.265	.310	604	125	24	4	10	10	45	130	.243	.282	.366	1942	471	83	17	41	41	104	359
Leadoff	.191	.232	.289	246	47	7	1	5	5	13	49	.246	.287	.366	809	199	30	5	19	19	47	132
Not Leadoff	.218	.288	.324	358	78	17	3	5	5	32	81	.240	.278	.366	1133	272	53	12	22	22	57	227
Runners On Base	.249	.332	.404	317	79	16	0	11	71	41	66	.242	.314	.351	1208	292	53	8	21	236	130	242
First Base Only	.262	.338	.468	141	37	5	0	8	17	16	24	.260	.320	.398	488	127	21	2	14	39	43	86
Scoring Position	.239	.327	.352	176	42	11	0	3	54	25	42	.229	.311	.319	720	165	32	6	7	197	87	156
Late Innings, Close	.271	.330	.344	96	26	4	0	1	10	9	9	.252	.295	.388	325	82	13	2	9	35	20	42

RBI/Opportunities

Scoring Position	48 / 251 (19%)	180 / 959 (19%)
Scoring Position, 2 Out	18 / 123 (15%)	73 / 446 (16%)
On Third, Less than 2 Out	19 / 37 (51%)	71 / 154 (46%)
RBI in close games / RBI Total	65 / 81 (80%)	222 / 277 (80%)

Lou Whitaker
Detroit Tigers

Lou Whitaker is one of two veteran middle infielders for the AL Eastern Champion Detroit Tigers. One of the two led the Tigers' charge in 1987 to the title, turning in a Most Valuable Player-type performance; the other turned in a ho-hum year. So, who is the MVP and who is the journeyman? Every serious baseball fan knows the answers, of course, the former is Alan Trammell and the latter is Lou Whitaker.

The point of this exercise is to compare these two players. While a current comparison is made at a time most favorable to Trammell, the similarities of these two players on the field prior to last season is enlightening.

Whitaker is about nine months older than Trammell. They both came up to the Tigers in September 1977 and have stayed in the bigs with Detroit ever since; they are now the longest-playing second base-shortstop combination in major league history. Neither has ever played a big-league game at another position, although Sparky made an aborted attempt to move Lou to third base in spring training 1985 (to allow the late, great, Chris Pittaro to play second for Detroit!).

At the start of the 1987 season, this was the career scoreboard for the two: Whitaker had played in four All-Star games, had been selected to *The Sporting News'* *(TSN)* post-season All-Star team twice, had three Gold Glove awards, had three Silver Slugger awards, and had one Rookie of the Year award; Trammell had played in two All-Star games (and was named to another), had four Gold Glove awards, and had one *TSN* Comeback Player of the The Year award, and one World Series MVP award. Their career statistics were eerily similar, see Table 1 below.

Whitaker had led the league in the following categories: Games (once), Assists at 2B (twice), Fielding Average (once), Total Chances (once) and Double Plays (once); Trammell had led the league only in Sacrifice Hits (twice). Which would you have picked as the better player?

Well, 1987 has come and gone. Keep this in mind, however—the same manager that had the perspicacity (or the blind luck) to bat Trammell at cleanup in '87 has said that Lou Whitaker is the best hitter on the team, and that he could lead the league in hitting any time he wanted to. Whitaker has been treated much more harshly by the fans and the press in Detroit than Trammell has. When Lou played badly, it's said he isn't trying or doesn't care; when Alan played badly, it's said that he's trying as hard as he can. This double standard is not fair. Trammell will never have another year like 1987; Whitaker is just as capable as Trammell of catching lightning in a bottle for a full season.

Gary Gillette

TABLE 1

	G	AB	R	H	2B	3B	HR	RBI	TBB	SO	SB	BA	OBA	SA
Whitaker	1283	4705	724	1320	202	49	93	522	576	575	95	.281	.357	.404
Trammell	1289	4631	702	1300	214	42	90	504	468	519	149	.281	.349	.403

Whitaker, Louis Rodman "Lou"

Bats: Left **Throws: Right** **Born 05/12/57**

1987 SEASON AND MAJOR-LEAGUE CAREER BATTING TOTALS

	G	AB	H	2B	3B	HR	TB	R	RBI	TBB	IBB	SO	HP	SH	SF	SB	CS	SB%	GDP	AVG	OBP	SLG
87 DET	149	604	160	38	6	16	258	110	59	71	2	108	1	4	4	13	5	.72	5	.265	.341	.427
11 YEARS	1432	5309	1480	240	55	109	2157	834	581	647	38	683	7	64	51	108	61	.64	87	.279	.355	.406

	1987 SEASON										FOUR YEAR TOTALS (1984 – 1987)									
	Ave.	OBP	SLG	AB	H	2B	3B	HR	RBI	BB	SO	Ave.	OBP	SLG	AB	H	2B	3B	HR	RBI	BB	SO
Totals	.265	.341	.427	604	160	38	6	16	59	71	108	.275	.350	.432	2355	648	118	21	70	261	276	297
vs. Left	.217	.279	.327	226	49	9	2	4	21	19	47	.223	.293	.321	708	158	24	6	11	73	70	135
vs. Right	.294	.376	.487	378	111	29	4	12	38	52	61	.298	.374	.480	1647	490	94	15	59	188	206	162
at Home	.261	.341	.435	283	74	17	1	10	28	34	50	.269	.347	.429	1145	308	54	9	37	136	141	145
on Road	.268	.342	.421	321	86	21	5	6	31	37	58	.281	.352	.436	1210	340	64	12	33	125	135	152
vs. Groundball	.274	.353	.442	328	90	22	3	9	38	40	48	.279	.352	.455	1160	324	73	10	37	136	130	134
vs. Flyball	.254	.327	.409	276	70	16	3	7	21	31	60	.271	.348	.410	1195	324	45	11	33	125	146	163
vs. Finesse	.259	.331	.425	332	86	19	3	10	32	35	51	.272	.337	.429	1341	365	65	11	41	141	132	140
vs. Power	.272	.354	.430	272	74	19	3	6	27	36	57	.279	.366	.437	1014	283	53	10	29	120	144	157
on Grass	.263	.345	.427	506	133	31	5	14	54	64	90	.272	.347	.424	1980	538	93	17	58	224	235	246
on Artificial Turf	.276	.321	.429	98	27	7	1	2	5	7	18	.293	.363	.477	375	110	25	4	12	37	41	51
Day Games	.276	.341	.481	185	51	13	2	7	19	18	37	.264	.342	.421	717	189	33	4	24	83	88	98
Night Games	.260	.341	.403	419	109	25	4	9	40	53	71	.280	.353	.437	1638	459	85	17	46	178	188	199
April	.250	.333	.333	72	18	3	0	1	5	9	14	.299	.367	.427	281	84	14	2	6	25	30	35
May	.277	.346	.543	94	26	4	0	7	13	10	20	.291	.365	.463	395	115	18	1	16	46	46	47
June	.264	.331	.377	106	28	5	2	1	7	11	19	.276	.351	.430	435	120	18	5	13	47	51	56
July	.250	.343	.375	88	22	5	0	2	12	13	14	.289	.357	.450	398	115	23	4	11	40	43	50
August	.284	.361	.500	116	33	12	2	3	14	14	20	.263	.351	.443	438	115	27	5	14	62	60	54
Sept/Oct	.258	.331	.406	128	33	9	2	2	8	14	21	.243	.319	.380	408	99	18	4	10	41	46	55
Bases Empty	.297	.374	.465	391	116	27	6	9	9	47	68	.276	.347	.423	1517	418	83	15	37	37	164	190
Leadoff	.335	.406	.508	242	81	19	4	5	5	28	43	.290	.361	.447	915	265	49	10	25	25	102	108
Not Leadoff	.235	.321	.396	149	35	8	2	4	4	19	25	.254	.324	.387	602	153	34	5	12	12	62	82
Runners On	.207	.282	.357	213	44	11	0	7	50	24	40	.274	.358	.449	838	230	35	6	33	224	112	107
First Base Only	.270	.343	.416	89	24	4	0	3	9	10	20	.332	.386	.545	374	124	19	2	19	46	33	43
Scoring Position	.161	.239	.315	124	20	7	0	4	41	14	20	.228	.338	.371	464	106	16	4	14	178	79	64
Late Innings, Close	.293	.333	.463	82	24	6	1	2	5	5	19	.298	.387	.442	339	101	17	1	10	44	49	56

RBI/Opportunities

Scoring Position	35 / 170 (21%)	155 / 669 (23%)
Scoring Position, 2 Out	9 / 85 (11%)	67 / 334 (20%)
On Third, Less than 2 Out	19 / 35 (54%)	63 / 119 (53%)
RBI in close games / RBI Total	29 / 59 (49%)	159 / 261 (61%)

Devon White
California Angels

One of the many awards that fills baseball's off-season is the Rawlings Gold Glove awards. Traditionally, the Gold Glove selections cause a certain amount of outrage, and usually there is a case or two where a selection is highly questionable. Perhaps the greatest injustice in recent years came in the selection of the outfielders for the AL Gold Glove team in 1987.

The Gold Glove winners in the AL outfield were Kirby Puckett, Jesse Barfield, and Dave Winfield. While both Puckett and Barfield probably belong, Winfield was a horrible choice given the exclusion of perhaps the best defensive outfielder in the league, Devon White.

Player	PCT	G	PO	A	E	DP	RF
Puckett	.986	147	341	8	5	2	2.37
Barfield	.992	158	341	17	3	4	2.27
Winfield	.989	145	253	6	3	1	1.79
White	.980	159	424	16	9	3	2.77

White led the American League in outfield putouts, a record that belongs almost exclusively to centerfielders as more balls are hit to center than either to right or left field, yet Devon played the vast majority of his games in right field. Prior to White, the last primary rightfielder to lead a major league in put-outs was Dave Parker in 1977. The last American Leaguer was Wally Moses in 1945. Devon also came up with 16 assists, one behind the league coleaders, Barfield and Sierra.

Some may argue that White's Gold Glove slight was simply because he was a rookie, but there is precedent for rookies receiving Gold Glove awards—Fred Lynn won a Gold Glove in his rookie year. Just this year Pittsburgh catcher Mike LaValliere won a Gold Glove in his first full season, although not technically a rookie. It's not as if the voters didn't have any advance notice of White's fielding prowess. In spring training, White was being billed as a better defensive outfielder than teammate Gary Pettis, the only outfielder to repeat on the 1985–86 AL Gold Glove squads.

Winfield's award over White was a classic example of the voters' perceptions overriding obvious realities. Winfield had won six previous Gold Gloves, and it was easy to give the award to a proven veteran even he has lost a step or two over the years. It's hard to listen to the professionals calling the voting for the All-Star game a sham when they can make a choice like this.

Offensively, Devon White reminds me of a Willie Wilson with power. On August 17, White hit a grand slam against Oakland to become the first rookie to join the 20-homer/20-steal club since Mitchell Page in 1977. If he could balance out the strikeout to walk ratio (he set a record for switch-hitters with 138 Ks), he could make a great #3 hitter.

Unfortunately, with the trading of Pettis to Detroit, I'm afraid the switch-hitting Jamaican will be placed into the leadoff role, essentially negating his power.

Darren E. Peterson and Craig R. Wright

White, Devon Markes

Bats: Both   Throws: Right   Born 12/29/62

1987 SEASON AND MAJOR-LEAGUE CAREER BATTING TOTALS

	G	AB	H	2B	3B	HR	TB	R	RBI	TBB	IBB	SO	HP	SH	SF	SB	CS	SB%	GDP	AVG	OBP	SLG
87 CAL	159	639	168	33	5	24	283	103	87	39	2	135	2	14	2	32	11	.74	8	.263	.306	.443
3 YEARS	209	697	181	34	6	25	302	118	90	46	2	146	3	14	2	41	12	.77	8	.260	.307	.433

	1987 SEASON											TWO YEAR TOTALS (1986 – 1987)										
	Ave.	OBP	SLG	AB	H	2B	3B	HR	RBI	BB	SO	Ave.	OBP	SLG	AB	H	2B	3B	HR	RBI	BB	SO
Totals	.263	.306	.443	639	168	33	5	24	87	39	135	.261	.308	.436	690	180	34	6	25	90	45	143
vs. Left	.246	.296	.477	199	49	9	2	11	26	13	36	.250	.299	.463	216	54	9	2	11	26	14	38
vs. Right	.270	.311	.427	440	119	24	3	13	61	26	99	.266	.311	.424	474	126	25	4	14	64	31	105
at Home	.248	.293	.417	314	78	14	3	11	39	19	67	.245	.291	.409	335	82	14	4	11	40	21	71
on Road	.277	.320	.468	325	90	19	2	13	48	20	68	.276	.323	.462	355	98	20	2	14	50	24	72
vs. Groundball	.253	.294	.420	312	79	15	2	11	41	18	72	.256	.299	.430	328	84	15	3	12	44	20	75
vs. Flyball	.272	.318	.465	327	89	18	3	13	46	21	63	.265	.315	.442	362	96	19	3	13	46	25	68
vs. Finesse	.289	.332	.487	304	88	18	3	12	46	20	56	.288	.333	.483	333	96	18	4	13	49	23	58
vs. Power	.239	.283	.403	335	80	15	2	12	41	19	79	.235	.283	.392	357	84	16	2	12	41	22	85
on Grass	.267	.308	.449	528	141	26	5	20	74	30	112	.265	.308	.445	569	151	27	6	21	76	34	117
on Artificial Turf	.243	.300	.414	111	27	7	0	4	13	9	23	.240	.303	.397	121	29	7	0	4	14	11	26
Day Games	.240	.293	.401	192	46	9	2	6	25	14	37	.240	.293	.401	192	46	9	2	6	25	14	37
Night Games	.273	.312	.461	447	122	24	3	18	62	25	98	.269	.313	.450	498	134	25	4	19	65	31	106
April	.280	.343	.591	93	26	4	2	7	14	8	18	.280	.343	.591	93	26	4	2	7	14	8	18
May	.257	.270	.358	109	28	6	1	1	8	2	23	.257	.270	.358	109	28	6	1	1	8	2	23
June	.336	.385	.617	107	36	7	1	7	22	8	25	.336	.385	.617	107	36	7	1	7	22	8	25
July	.263	.288	.430	114	30	7	0	4	22	4	26	.263	.288	.430	114	30	7	0	4	22	4	26
August	.185	.246	.306	108	20	5	1	2	13	9	26	.185	.246	.306	108	20	5	1	2	13	9	26
Sept/Oct	.259	.310	.380	108	28	4	0	3	8	8	17	.252	.312	.371	159	40	5	1	4	11	14	25
Bases Empty	.274	.317	.481	347	95	21	3	15	15	22	72	.270	.315	.468	385	104	22	3	16	16	25	77
Leadoff	.286	.324	.457	105	30	7	1	3	3	6	21	.293	.326	.463	123	36	7	1	4	4	6	23
Not Leadoff	.269	.314	.492	242	65	14	2	12	12	16	51	.260	.310	.469	262	68	15	2	12	12	19	54
Runners On	.250	.294	.397	292	73	12	2	9	72	17	63	.249	.298	.397	305	76	12	3	9	74	20	66
First Base Only	.245	.278	.391	110	27	5	1	3	7	4	23	.254	.292	.412	114	29	5	2	3	8	5	23
Scoring Position	.253	.303	.401	182	46	7	1	6	65	13	40	.246	.301	.387	191	47	7	1	6	66	15	43
Late Innings, Close	.246	.288	.475	118	29	6	0	7	24	6	29	.246	.288	.475	236	58	12	0	14	48	12	58

RBI/Opportunities

Scoring Position	55 / 223 (25%)	56 / 237 (24%)
Scoring Position, 2 Out	22 / 107 (21%)	22 / 115 (19%)
On Third, Less than 2 Out	18 / 33 (55%)	19 / 35 (54%)
RBI in close games / RBI Total	56 / 87 (64%)	112 / 90 (124%)

Frank White
Kansas City Royals

Frank White had yet another good season in 1987. However, for the first time since the mid-1970s, his offensive output did not increase. While there was no dramatic drop-off in his performance, some of White's numbers did show a slight downturn from previous seasons. A poor start followed by a fine second half left White with a mixed bag of pluses and minuses.

White's .245 batting average was his lowest in ten years and his .400 slugging average was his lowest since 1981. His 17 homers were down from 22 in each of the previous two seasons. Likewise, his 32 doubles were fewer than his 37 in 1986. White's isolated power of .155 was down considerably from his career best of .193 in 1986.

However, White still managed to drive in 78 runs, his second best career total. That is probably a result of both White hitting better with runners on base and the Royals having more baserunners in 1987. Also, his batting eye continued to improve. While he still struck out 86 times last year (similar to his 88 Ks in 1986 and 86 in 1985), White drew 51 walks—easily the best total of his career. This marked the first time since 1975 that his strikeouts-to-walks ratio was less than 2 to 1.

White's slow start left him with a .222 average and five homers through June 11. Minor knee problems (astroturf?) during part of the year prompted his taking an occasional day off during the hottest part of the summer, especially day games at home. This appeared to pay off later when, as in past seasons, White finished strongly. He batted .275 with eight homers, 15 doubles, and 30 runs batted in, and slugging .485 from August 7 to the end of the season.

White's defensive play continues to sparkle. By winning his eighth Gold Glove in 1987, he is tied with Bill Mazeroski for the most ever by a second baseman. White made only two errors in 92 games from mid-May until the end of August, and he finished the year with an excellent .987 fielding average and a good range factor of 5.12. Even at age 37, he still turns the double play well. White may have lost a half-step, but he makes up for it with excellent positioning prior to the pitch. It will be interesting to see if he can hold off Harold Reynolds and all the other challengers to win that ninth Gold Glove in '88.

Although 1987 did not hurt White's chances of being considered for the Hall of Fame, it didn't help a lot, either. In previous years, White has said that he will retire after the 1988 season. If he does retire, he will likely be going out while still near the top of his game.

Marc Bowman

White, Frank

Bats: Right   Throws: Right   Born 09/04/50

1987 SEASON AND MAJOR-LEAGUE CAREER BATTING TOTALS

	G	AB	H	2B	3B	HR	TB	R	RBI	TBB	IBB	SO	HP	SH	SF	SB	CS	SB%	GDP	AVG	OBP	SLG
87 KC	154	563	138	32	2	17	225	67	78	51	5	86	2	4	4	1	3	.25	16	.245	.308	.400
15 YEARS	1957	6663	1721	346	55	148	2621	810	771	351	24	884	21	89	53	167	78	.68	126	.258	.295	.393

	1987 SEASON											FOUR YEAR TOTALS (1984 – 1987)										
	Ave.	OBP	SLG	AB	H	2B	3B	HR	RBI	BB	SO	Ave.	OBP	SLG	AB	H	2B	3B	HR	RBI	BB	SO
Totals	.245	.308	.400	563	138	32	2	17	78	51	86	.259	.306	.430	2171	562	116	11	78	287	149	332
vs. Left	.284	.352	.453	148	42	10	0	5	22	15	18	.272	.324	.438	591	161	28	2	22	77	46	71
vs. Right	.231	.292	.381	415	96	22	2	12	56	36	68	.254	.300	.427	1580	401	88	9	56	210	103	261
at Home	.273	.355	.418	256	70	19	0	6	40	33	33	.264	.317	.424	1070	282	63	5	33	158	83	140
on Road	.221	.267	.384	307	68	13	2	11	38	18	53	.254	.296	.436	1101	280	53	6	45	129	66	192
vs. Groundball	.254	.307	.420	283	72	19	2	8	44	22	36	.272	.314	.439	1022	278	63	6	32	130	61	141
vs. Flyball	.236	.309	.379	280	66	13	0	9	34	29	50	.247	.300	.422	1149	284	53	5	46	157	88	191
vs. Finesse	.247	.304	.384	320	79	16	2	8	39	26	35	.264	.307	.439	1229	324	63	6	47	147	74	159
vs. Power	.243	.314	.420	243	59	16	0	9	39	25	51	.253	.306	.418	942	238	53	5	31	140	75	173
on Grass	.227	.277	.405	242	55	11	1	10	31	16	38	.243	.285	.431	864	210	37	4	39	106	51	154
on Artificial Turf	.259	.331	.396	321	83	21	1	7	47	35	48	.269	.320	.430	1307	352	79	7	39	181	98	178
Day Games	.244	.309	.386	127	31	6	0	4	13	11	15	.262	.311	.438	543	142	34	4	18	61	39	93
Night Games	.245	.308	.404	436	107	26	2	13	65	40	71	.258	.305	.428	1628	420	82	7	60	226	110	239
April	.205	.293	.315	73	15	2	0	2	10	9	8	.243	.287	.408	272	66	14	2	9	35	17	42
May	.247	.320	.430	93	23	8	0	3	14	10	15	.263	.315	.449	392	103	26	1	15	55	30	57
June	.255	.302	.340	94	24	3	1	1	15	8	18	.253	.292	.347	352	89	9	3	6	40	21	50
July	.226	.301	.333	93	21	4	0	2	8	10	17	.235	.299	.432	324	76	13	0	17	49	30	53
August	.278	.333	.500	108	30	9	0	5	19	8	15	.278	.323	.464	418	116	28	1	16	64	27	66
Sept/Oct	.245	.294	.441	102	25	6	1	4	12	6	13	.271	.313	.462	413	112	26	4	15	44	24	64
Bases Empty	.224	.284	.385	299	67	13	1	11	11	24	49	.244	.288	.437	1221	298	61	5	55	55	75	188
Leadoff	.220	.277	.378	127	28	5	0	5	5	10	18	.252	.293	.419	523	132	25	1	20	20	30	80
Not Leadoff	.227	.289	.390	172	39	8	1	6	6	14	31	.238	.285	.451	698	166	36	4	35	35	45	108
Runners On	.269	.334	.417	264	71	19	1	6	67	27	37	.278	.329	.421	950	264	55	6	23	232	74	144
First Base Only	.286	.342	.410	105	30	5	1	2	6	8	13	.298	.334	.431	392	117	18	2	10	25	20	61
Scoring Position	.258	.330	.421	159	41	14	0	4	61	19	24	.263	.326	.414	558	147	37	4	13	207	54	83
Late Innings, Close	.164	.263	.284	67	11	2	0	2	6	9	9	.248	.301	.419	339	84	13	0	15	50	26	49

RBI/Opportunities

Scoring Position	49 / 219 (22%)	173 / 740 (23%)
Scoring Position, 2 Out	20 / 111 (18%)	69 / 362 (19%)
On Third, Less than 2 Out	18 / 38 (47%)	62 / 119 (52%)
RBI in close games / RBI Total	56 / 78 (72%)	196 / 287 (68%)

Ed Whitson
San Diego Padres

For over a decade we've been waiting for Ed Whitson to fulfill everyone's expectations. Four times his ERA has been below 3.30, but only once has he won over 11 games. He's pitched above .500 just thrice (once with a 4–2 record). He's often described as having a lot of "stuff" (exactly what is stuff?) and can be overpowering. He's had a couple of outstanding half-seasons, but has lacked the consistency to produce an outstanding year. His best season was '84 with the pennant-winning Padres (14–8, 3.24) when Dick Williams' tendency to go to his (tremendous) bullpen early and often may have cost him some victories. Whitson's career probably reached its zenith when he won the pivotal third game of the playoffs that year. In the World Series it was a different story. He was knocked out in the first inning of his only start, leaving him with a lifetime Series ERA of 40.50. Since then Ed's career has taken a disastrous turn.

Whitson's calamitous stay with the Yankees (are you listening, Jack Clark?) has been well documented. In 1987 many considered him San Diego's most effective starter early on because he was victorious in many of the pathetically few San Diego wins. By August 3 his record was 10–7. He failed to win another game. His winning percentage had been misleading and his poor performance caught up to him late in the year. Below is a brief comparison of Whitson's and Show's seasons.

Only once did Whitson bring his ERA below 4.50.

Show kept his below Whitson's all-season and finished 0.89 lower than his teammate.

	Whitson			Show		
	W–L	ERA	HR	W–L	ERA	HR
4/27	2–2	5.48	10	1–1	3.24	5
5/11	4–4	4.79	14	1–3	4.66	12
6/1	5–6	5.09	16	1–7	4.30	13
7/6	8–7	4.47	20	4–9	3.62	14
8/3	10–7	4.76	25	5–12	4.03	18
9/7	10–10	4.70	32	6–16	4.20	24
END	10–13	4.73	36	8–16	3.84	26

Eddie Lee's biggest problem was the home run. His strike out to walk ratio was better than 2 to 1, and he allowed slightly fewer than 3 walks per nine innings. His WHIP's (walks and hits divided by innings pitched, for you non-Rotisserie Leaguers) were 1.27, better than the league average. But, while Show normally surrenders a lot of homers (averaging 20 per year), Whitson, who only once yielded over 19, gave up 36. If he'd cut that figure to his previous high of 23, his ERA would have been significantly improved, and he very likely would have been a winning pitcher. If he can reduce his homer outlay, Ed should once again become an effective pitcher. He may even have that exceptional season we've been waiting for; but, certainly, he should be a $3 mainstay of hundreds of Rotisserie Staffs.

Bruce Erricson

Whitson, Eddie Lee

Bats: Right   Throws: Right   Born 05/19/55

1987 SEASON AND MAJOR-LEAGUE CAREER PITCHING TOTALS

	G	GS	CG	GF	IP	BFP	H	R	ER	HR	SH	SF	HB	TBB	IBB	SO	WP	Bk	W	L	Pct	ShO	Sv	ERA
87 SD	36	34	3	0	206	858	197	113	108	36	4	2	3	64	3	135	2	1	10	13	.435	1	0	4.72
11 YEARS	340	223	19	48	1502	6464	1532	755	681	146	61	53	22	541	36	864	25	8	79	86	.479	7	8	4.08

1987: Finesse, Flyball   1986: Power, Flyball   1985: Finesse, Flyball   1984: Finesse, Flyball

1987 SEASON

	G	IP	H	BB	SO	SB	CS	W	L	S	ERA
Totals	36	205.1	197	64	135	20	6	10	13	0	4.73
at Home	19	107.0	101	36	75	9	4	5	7	0	4.96
on Road	17	98.1	96	28	60	11	2	5	6	0	4.48
on Grass	13	73.0	73	18	40	4	1	5	4	0	4.81
on Artificial Turf	23	132.1	124	46	95	16	5	5	9	0	4.69
Day Games	30	167.0	163	52	107	13	5	7	12	0	5.12
Night Games	6	38.1	34	12	28	7	1	3	1	0	3.05
April	5	27.1	23	10	21	2	2	3	2	0	4.94
May	7	41.2	40	18	29	8	2	2	4	0	5.18
June	5	33.2	27	11	20	1	0	3	1	0	3.48
July	6	37.1	43	11	22	5	0	2	0	0	5.30
August	5	27.2	25	6	13	2	0	0	2	0	4.55
Sept/Oct	8	37.2	39	8	30	2	2	0	4	0	4.78

vs. Opponent Batters	Ave.	OBP	SLG	AB	H	2B	3B	HR	RBI	BB	SO
Totals	.251	.309	.443	784	197	28	7	36	102	64	135
vs. Left	.283	.349	.440	427	121	15	5	14	47	41	64
vs. Right	.213	.261	.445	357	76	13	2	22	55	23	71
Bases Empty	.236	.309	.405	491	116	13	2	22	22	50	82
Leadoff	.238	.316	.446	193	46	4	0	12	12	21	30
Not Leadoff	.235	.305	.379	298	70	9	2	10	10	29	52
Runners On Base	.276	.310	.505	293	81	15	5	14	80	14	53
First Base Only	.267	.296	.514	146	39	8	2	8	20	6	27
Scoring Position	.286	.323	.497	147	42	7	3	6	60	8	26
Late Innings, Close	.350	.381	.667	60	21	1	0	6	13	3	13

FOUR YEAR TOTALS (1984 – 1987)

	G	IP	H	BB	SO	SB	CS	W	L	S	ERA
Totals	128	665.2	718	209	400	55	22	40	38	0	4.60
at Home	62	337.1	352	96	205	26	14	21	18	0	4.24
on Road	66	328.1	366	113	195	29	8	19	20	0	4.96
on Grass	38	188.1	223	40	120	12	3	10	14	0	5.26
on Artificial Turf	90	477.1	495	169	280	43	19	30	24	0	4.34
Day Games	100	515.1	563	162	304	37	17	31	32	0	4.63
Night Games	28	150.1	155	47	96	18	5	9	6	0	4.49
April	19	93.2	95	36	52	6	3	7	8	0	4.32
May	19	94.2	110	38	66	14	6	7	7	0	5.80
June	20	105.0	108	32	61	4	3	10	4	0	3.77
July	23	134.1	137	37	67	13	3	10	4	0	3.89
August	22	122.1	141	34	73	10	1	3	8	0	5.59
Sept/Oct	25	115.2	127	32	81	8	6	3	7	0	4.36

vs. Opponent Batters	Ave.	OBP	SLG	AB	H	2B	3B	HR	RBI	BB	SO
Totals	.276	.330	.434	2601	718	112	24	84	330	209	400
vs. Left	.284	.343	.432	1405	399	59	13	41	168	124	191
vs. Right	.267	.315	.437	1196	319	53	11	43	162	85	209
Bases Empty	.264	.324	.408	1518	400	59	10	47	47	134	234
Leadoff	.276	.331	.437	646	178	26	6	22	22	53	91
Not Leadoff	.255	.319	.388	872	222	33	4	25	25	81	143
Runners On Base	.294	.339	.471	1083	318	53	14	37	283	75	166
First Base Only	.308	.342	.515	517	159	23	6	24	64	27	80
Scoring Position	.281	.337	.431	566	159	30	8	13	219	48	86
Late Innings, Close	.281	.333	.489	139	39	5	0	8	19	11	24

RBI/Opportunities

Scoring Position	49 / 176 (28%)	195 / 721 (27%)
Scoring Position, 2 Out	27 / 84 (32%)	68 / 316 (22%)
On Third, Less than 2 Out	15 / 34 (44%)	82 / 149 (55%)
RBI in close games / RBI Total	86 / 102 (84%)	233 / 330 (71%)

Ernie Whitt
Toronto Blue Jays

More than any other player in their history, Ernie Whitt personifies the Toronto Blue Jays. He's been with Toronto since day one. From '76–'79, both he and his team stumbled about (Ernie in the minors; Toronto in the AL East basement), learning their respective trades. In 1980–81, Ernie made the majors and Toronto stopped losing 100 games . . . but the locals were beginning to wonder if either would ever play good baseball. In 1982, they did—Ernie slugged .440 with a .317 OB%; Toronto tied the mighty Indians for sixth. Since then, Ernie's OB%s have been between .323 and .346, his SL%s between .425 and .459 and Toronto has won between 86 and 99 games. Of all the men chosen in the expansion drafts, Ernie has now played more games with the team who chose him than anyone except Jim Fregosi.

Ernie has progressed in the old-fashioned way—hard work. He's learned to use his ungainly, off-balance swing to his advantage lately. Like a cricket player, Ernie simply sweeps at the ball—that lets him cream low pitches. Unlike cricketers (who need to use the entire field), Whitt consistently puts his extra-base hits into a very small area. His doubles and homers are usually within 30 feet of the right field foul pole; last year he hit more than one directly off the pole.

Whitt's intelligence served him well this year. Whitt began 1987 at the bottom of the order, where his job was to score whatever men he could with extra base hits. Accordingly, he hit .255 and slugged .421, giving him an "isolated power" figure (SL% minus BA) of .166. When Jesse Barfield went into a tailspin, Ernie began batting third, ahead of George Bell. Knowing that he'd get better pitches to hit and that he could leave the power hitting to Bell, Ernie cut down on his swing a bit. His IP dropped to .153—but his average rose to .375. Since he had almost 200 at-bats in both situations, those percentages are meaningful.

Whitt's injury probably cost Toronto first place, for two reasons. First, Ernie (a Michigan native) always hits the Tigers hard. In his career against the Tigers through 1987, he's hit 19 homers with 60 RBIs in only 301 total ABs; from '84 to '86, he hit .276 with 5 homers and 13 RBIs in only 58 ABs in Tiger Stadium.

Second, Ernie is the team leader. He is generally the one who faces the media after painful losses (while others hide in the trainer's room) and always the one who rallies the team. After an eight-game losing streak in early July, he called a "players only" team meeting; Toronto won seven of their next eight games. Finally, though he could have taken the season off after his rib injury on September 29 (as many "stars" will do), Ernie traveled with the team and died with them. His fire—and his tireless charity work—make Whitt easily the most popular Blue Jay.

Dave Easby, Gord Fitzgerald, Mike FitzGerald
and Susan Nelson

Whitt, Leo Ernest "Ernie" Bats: Left Throws: Right Born 06/13/52

1987 SEASON AND MAJOR-LEAGUE CAREER BATTING TOTALS

	G	AB	H	2B	3B	HR	TB	R	RBI	TBB	IBB	SO	HP	SH	SF	SB	CS	SB%	GDP	AVG	OBP	SLG
87 TOR	135	446	120	24	1	19	203	57	75	44	4	50	1	0	3	0	1	.00	17	.269	.334	.455
11 YEARS	970	2749	691	131	12	105	1161	323	398	292	36	361	3	17	28	13	18	.42	70	.251	.321	.422

1987 SEASON / FOUR YEAR TOTALS (1984 – 1987)

	Ave.	OBP	SLG	AB	H	2B	3B	HR	RBI	BB	SO	Ave.	OBP	SLG	AB	H	2B	3B	HR	RBI	BB	SO
Totals	.269	.334	.455	446	120	24	1	19	75	44	50	.256	.327	.445	1568	402	76	6	69	241	169	197
vs. Left	.238	.314	.286	63	15	3	0	0	8	6	15	.248	.321	.362	210	52	7	1	5	23	21	55
vs. Right	.274	.337	.483	383	105	21	1	19	67	38	35	.258	.329	.457	1358	350	69	5	64	218	148	142
at Home	.262	.339	.481	214	56	12	1	11	43	25	29	.247	.335	.441	744	184	44	5	30	118	99	102
on Road	.276	.329	.431	232	64	12	0	8	32	19	21	.265	.320	.448	824	218	32	1	39	123	70	95
vs. Groundball	.307	.358	.516	225	69	14	0	11	45	18	23	.280	.344	.459	796	223	39	2	33	134	79	82
vs. Flyball	.231	.311	.394	221	51	10	1	8	30	26	27	.232	.310	.430	772	179	37	4	36	107	90	115
vs. Finesse	.269	.322	.479	238	64	11	0	13	44	19	19	.263	.325	.464	879	231	48	3	41	135	84	86
vs. Power	.269	.348	.428	208	56	13	1	6	31	25	31	.248	.330	.419	689	171	28	3	28	106	85	111
on Grass	.254	.304	.362	177	45	7	0	4	21	13	16	.261	.316	.442	647	169	21	0	32	96	54	75
on Artificial Turf	.279	.353	.517	269	75	17	1	15	54	31	34	.253	.335	.446	921	233	55	6	37	145	115	122
Day Games	.278	.344	.444	169	47	8	1	6	22	16	19	.267	.337	.434	535	143	27	4	18	81	56	69
Night Games	.264	.328	.462	277	73	16	0	13	53	28	31	.251	.323	.450	1033	259	49	2	51	160	113	128
April	.265	.367	.388	49	13	3	0	1	7	9	3	.223	.319	.363	157	35	10	0	4	18	23	16
May	.265	.315	.434	83	22	8	0	2	9	6	7	.257	.317	.442	269	69	17	0	11	44	24	26
June	.212	.278	.348	66	14	3	0	2	12	6	12	.271	.342	.479	240	65	15	1	11	42	26	24
July	.286	.342	.443	70	20	2	0	3	11	6	14	.263	.334	.432	278	73	8	3	11	39	30	41
August	.344	.402	.516	93	32	5	1	3	16	8	7	.288	.348	.489	319	92	18	2	14	52	28	47
Sept/Oct	.224	.295	.541	85	19	3	0	8	20	9	7	.223	.308	.426	305	68	8	0	18	46	38	43
Bases Empty	.274	.333	.444	234	64	13	0	9	9	20	26	.250	.309	.446	841	210	47	2	38	38	71	106
Leadoff	.293	.309	.500	92	27	7	0	4	4	2	11	.255	.299	.452	330	84	21	1	14	14	21	37
Not Leadoff	.261	.348	.408	142	37	6	0	5	5	18	15	.247	.315	.442	511	126	26	1	24	24	50	69
Runners On	.264	.335	.467	212	56	11	1	10	66	24	24	.264	.350	.443	727	192	29	4	31	203	98	91
First Base Only	.250	.313	.432	88	22	4	0	4	10	8	8	.299	.355	.503	304	91	11	3	15	40	26	35
Scoring Position	.274	.350	.492	124	34	7	1	6	56	16	16	.239	.347	.400	423	101	18	1	16	163	72	56
Late Innings, Close	.222	.301	.306	72	16	6	0	0	12	9	10	.263	.333	.387	274	72	14	1	6	41	30	31

RBI/Opportunities

Scoring Position	45 / 166 (27%)		132 / 586 (23%)
Scoring Position, 2 Out	20 / 84 (24%)		40 / 265 (15%)
On Third, Less than 2 Out	15 / 27 (56%)		57 / 108 (53%)
RBI in close games / RBI Total	40 / 75 (53%)		150 / 241 (62%)

Bill Wilkinson
Seattle Mariners

During game three of the 1987 ALCS, Bob Costas noted that, "To find a good left-handed reliever . . . you've got a better chance of finding Amelia Earhart!"

Well, Amelia was sighted flying low and fast in the vicinity of the Kingdome pitching mound this past season. She returned out of nowhere as a 5'10" left-handed relief pitcher that local announcers call the "Colorado Kid" and visiting broadcasters call the "Blade." His teammates simply call him "Wilky."

The undersized pitcher has been in the Mariner system since Seattle gambled their fourth round pick on him in the 1983 June draft. No one had envisioned him as a reliever before 1987. In his 74 minor league appearances, only one was in a relief role. Prior to last season, his only major league experience was two starts in 1985.

After the 1986 season, the Mariners made another one of those controversial deals. For the second year in a row, and probably the last, they outfitted the Dodgers with a left-handed reliever. The M's then went on a minor buying binge trying to fill the vacated spot on their pitching staff. They picked up Tony Ferriera and Stan Clarke for $50,000 each in the minor league free agent draft. They, along with Bill Wilkinson, were invited to spring training where the job of left-handed reliever was put up for grabs.

Wilkinson was the long shot. Not only was the relief role foreign to him, but he was coming off a poor year at Calgary where he was 8–8 with a 4.78 ERA. But Wilkinson made an impression with his deadly aim and several strong spring outings. He made the club, but Dick Williams was reluctant to use him early in the year. That changed drastically by the end of the year when Williams was clearly using him as his stopper. He had saves in his last three appearances of 1987, and 4 in his last 6. He earned that promotion with a truly super mid-season streak. From June 16 to August 12, he gave up only 2 earned runs and 12 hits in 26.7 innings (0.68 ERA). In one stretch he allowed only 2 of 29 inherited runners to score.

Other than both being lefties, there isn't a lot of similarity between Mark Langston and Wilkinson in physique or style, but their statistics seemed cloned from each other. Which one averaged 8.67 strikeouts per nine innings and which one averaged 8.62 Ks? Which averaged 8.0 hits per 9 innings and which was 7.2? Which was tagged for a homer every 9.1 innings and which did it every 9.5? Who had the 3.84 ERA and who had the 3.66? (Bill's numbers are the second group.) That should give you an idea of the "stuff" this kid seems to have.

With performance like that, it was surprising to see the Mariners reportedly offering Dave Righetti more money than any other team other than the Yankees. Must have been they were going to make him a starter: The bullpen job is taken.

Merrianna McCully

Wilkinson, William Carl "Bill" Bats: Right   Throws: Left   Born 08/10/64

1987 SEASON AND MAJOR-LEAGUE CAREER PITCHING TOTALS

	G	GS	CG	GF	IP	BFP	H	R	ER	HR	SH	SF	HB	TBB	IBB	SO	WP	Bk	W	L	Pct	ShO	Sv	ERA
87 SEA	56	0	0	29	76	303	61	33	31	8	2	6	0	21	1	73	0	0	3	4	.429	0	10	3.67
2 YEARS	58	2	0	29	82	333	69	42	40	10	2	6	0	27	2	78	0	0	3	6	.333	0	10	4.39

1987: Power, Groundball

	1987 SEASON											TWO YEAR TOTALS (1986 – 1987)										
	G	IP	H	BB	SO	SB	CS	W	L	S	ERA	G	IP	H	BB	SO	SB	CS	W	L	S	ERA
Totals	56	76.1	61	21	73	5	1	3	3	10	3.66	56	76.1	61	21	73	5	1	3	3	10	3.66
at Home	27	38.0	40	10	36	3	1	3	2	3	5.21	27	38.0	40	10	36	3	1	3	2	3	5.21
on Road	29	38.1	21	11	37	2	0	0	1	7	2.11	29	38.1	21	11	37	2	0	0	1	7	2.11
on Grass	13	18.0	11	3	13	1	1	1	0	1	2.50	13	18.0	11	3	13	1	1	1	0	1	2.50
on Artificial Turf	43	58.1	50	18	60	4	0	2	3	9	4.01	43	58.1	50	18	60	4	0	2	3	9	4.01
Day Games	22	27.2	15	10	29	1	0	0	1	5	2.60	22	27.2	15	10	29	1	0	0	1	5	2.60
Night Games	34	48.2	46	11	44	4	1	3	2	5	4.25	34	48.2	46	11	44	4	1	3	2	5	4.25
April	5	6.0	5	1	4	1	0	0	0	0	1.50	5	6.0	5	1	4	1	0	0	0	0	1.50
May	13	13.0	19	5	8	2	0	0	0	1	8.31	13	13.0	19	5	8	2	0	0	0	1	8.31
June	7	10.1	5	3	9	0	0	1	1	3	4.35	7	10.1	5	3	9	0	0	1	1	3	4.35
July	8	15.1	10	4	16	0	0	1	0	0	1.17	8	15.1	10	4	16	0	0	1	0	0	1.17
August	8	16.2	9	2	15	1	1	0	1	2	2.70	8	16.2	9	2	15	1	1	0	1	2	2.70
Sept/Oct	15	15.0	13	6	21	1	0	1	1	4	3.60	15	15.0	13	6	21	1	0	1	1	4	3.60

vs. Opponent Batters	Ave.	OBP	SLG	AB	H	2B	3B	HR	RBI	BB	SO	Ave.	OBP	SLG	AB	H	2B	3B	HR	RBI	BB	SO
Totals	.223	.272	.350	274	61	9	1	8	37	21	73	.223	.272	.350	274	61	9	1	8	37	21	73
vs. Left	.192	.243	.394	104	20	3	0	6	18	7	29	.192	.243	.394	104	20	3	0	6	18	7	29
vs. Right	.241	.289	.324	170	41	6	1	2	19	14	44	.241	.289	.324	170	41	6	1	2	19	14	44
Bases Empty	.174	.242	.333	144	25	3	1	6	6	13	39	.174	.242	.333	144	25	3	1	6	6	13	39
Leadoff	.218	.271	.527	55	12	3	1	4	4	4	14	.218	.271	.527	55	12	3	1	4	4	4	14
Not Leadoff	.146	.224	.213	89	13	0	0	2	2	9	25	.146	.224	.213	89	13	0	0	2	2	9	25
Runners On Base	.277	.306	.369	130	36	6	0	2	31	8	34	.277	.306	.369	130	36	6	0	2	31	8	34
First Base Only	.304	.328	.375	56	17	1	0	1	2	2	17	.304	.328	.375	56	17	1	0	1	2	2	17
Scoring Position	.257	.291	.365	74	19	5	0	1	29	6	17	.257	.291	.365	74	19	5	0	1	29	6	17
Late Innings, Close	.202	.256	.311	119	24	4	0	3	13	9	37	.202	.256	.311	238	48	8	0	6	26	18	74

RBI/Opportunities

Scoring Position	26 / 99 (26%)		26 / 99 (26%)	
Scoring Position, 2 Out	10 / 41 (24%)		20 / 82 (24%)	
On Third, Less than 2 Out	11 / 21 (52%)		22 / 42 (52%)	
RBI in close games / RBI Total	18 / 37 (49%)		36 / 37 (97%)	

Kenny Williams
Chicago White Sox

I remember Kenny Williams' recent spring training performances for two reasons: 1) he always hit at least one inside-the-park home run, and 2) he would be among the last cut. Like corruption in politics, it's a Chicago tradition to mega-hype certain players during pre-season who rarely, if ever, amount to anything. Williams was one of those mega-hyped players who just could not make it. (The rap on him was that he couldn't hit a breaking pitch if his life depended on it.)

Yet Williams was called up in June, and he did a credible enough job to remain in center field for the rest of the season. It was scary at first; he and Ivan Calderon collided at least twice in the outfield in June. But the situation improved quickly. According to Don Zminda in the *Chicago Baseball Report,* Williams would have had 450 putouts in a full season. And given the Sox offensive woes, his .281 batting average, third best on the club, was welcome relief.

It would be nice to say that Williams will be the Sox centerfielder for years to come. Unfortunately, the 1988 season could be a disaster for Williams for several reasons. He drew just 10 walks in 391 at-bats, and he struck out 83 times. Few players last very long with numbers like that, particularly when they are not power hitters. Unless he

shows a lot more patience, he is likely to struggle at the plate next year. There is also some evidence that his .281 average was a hollow figure. Williams's weaknesses is that he had a terrible time hitting in the clutch. According to the *Chicago Baseball Report,* he hit just .207 (12 for 58) and struck out 20 times, among the worst clutch totals on the team. In clutch situations with men in scoring position, he was worse, .125 (just 3 for 24) and struck out 13 times. These situational weaknesses could be chalked up to inexperience or random chance, but I have my doubts. My impression was that his impatience at the plate was allowing the pitchers to manipulate him whenever they needed to be most careful.

The most disturbing news about the future plans for Kenny is an experiment at third base. Doesn't he have enough other things to work on without trying to make such a difficult transition? If Williams falters next year, it will be a major disappointment for this fan. Even with the Sox wallowing in the basement for much of the summer, Williams was an exciting player to watch— reminiscent of another Williams (No-neck, not Billy) who was so popular in Chicago.

Andrew Berman

Williams, Kenneth Royal "Ken"   Bats: Right   Throws: Right   Born 04/06/64

1987 SEASON AND MAJOR-LEAGUE CAREER BATTING TOTALS

	G	AB	H	2B	3B	HR	TB	R	RBI	TBB	IBB	SO	HP	SH	SF	SB	CS	SB%	GDP	AVG	OBP	SLG
87 CHA	116	391	110	18	2	11	165	48	50	10	0	83	9	3	1	21	10	.68	5	.281	.314	.422
2 YEARS	131	422	114	18	2	12	172	50	51	11	0	94	10	3	1	22	11	.67	6	.270	.304	.408

	1987 SEASON											TWO YEAR TOTALS (1986 – 1987)										
	Ave.	OBP	SLG	AB	H	2B	3B	HR	RBI	BB	SO	Ave.	OBP	SLG	AB	H	2B	3B	HR	RBI	BB	SO
Totals	.281	.314	.422	391	110	18	2	11	50	10	83	.270	.306	.408	422	114	18	2	12	51	11	94
vs. Left	.296	.319	.503	159	47	7	1	8	22	3	39	.274	.303	.468	186	51	7	1	9	23	4	50
vs. Right	.272	.310	.366	232	63	11	1	3	28	7	44	.267	.305	.360	236	63	11	1	3	28	7	44
at Home	.326	.358	.466	193	63	13	1	4	27	6	37	.328	.362	.480	198	65	13	1	5	28	7	39
on Road	.237	.271	.379	198	47	5	1	7	23	4	46	.219	.252	.344	224	49	5	1	7	23	4	55
vs. Groundball	.308	.340	.465	198	61	9	2	6	29	5	35	.307	.338	.460	202	62	9	2	6	29	5	35
vs. Flyball	.254	.287	.378	193	49	9	0	5	21	5	48	.236	.273	.359	220	52	9	0	6	22	6	59
vs. Finesse	.261	.298	.411	207	54	9	2	6	32	6	33	.256	.296	.405	227	58	9	2	7	33	7	41
vs. Power	.304	.332	.435	184	56	9	0	5	18	4	50	.287	.314	.410	195	56	9	0	5	18	4	53
on Grass	.290	.319	.438	345	100	17	2	10	49	8	75	.286	.316	.437	357	102	17	2	11	50	9	81
on Artificial Turf	.217	.280	.304	46	10	1	0	1	1	2	8	.185	.243	.246	65	12	1	0	1	1	2	13
Day Games	.318	.350	.473	110	35	4	2	3	15	4	26	.318	.350	.473	110	35	4	2	3	15	4	26
Night Games	.267	.299	.402	281	75	14	0	8	35	6	57	.253	.287	.385	312	79	14	0	9	36	7	68
April	.000	.000	.000	0	0	0	0	0	0	0	0	.000	.000	.000	0	0	0	0	0	0	0	0
May	.281	.324	.438	32	9	2	0	1	3	0	5	.281	.324	.438	32	9	2	0	1	3	0	5
June	.321	.354	.474	78	25	6	0	2	12	2	17	.321	.354	.474	78	25	6	0	2	12	2	17
July	.217	.258	.349	83	18	3	1	2	12	3	18	.217	.258	.349	83	18	3	1	2	12	3	18
August	.340	.354	.489	94	32	5	0	3	14	1	14	.340	.354	.489	94	32	5	0	3	14	1	14
Sept/Oct	.250	.291	.375	104	26	2	1	3	9	4	29	.222	.266	.341	135	30	2	1	4	10	5	40
Bases Empty	.285	.311	.411	214	61	9	0	6	6	3	37	.268	.298	.396	235	63	9	0	7	7	4	45
Leadoff	.189	.211	.351	74	14	3	0	3	3	1	11	.195	.224	.378	82	16	3	0	4	4	1	13
Not Leadoff	.336	.363	.443	140	47	6	0	3	3	2	26	.307	.338	.405	153	47	6	0	3	3	3	32
Runners On	.277	.317	.435	177	49	9	2	5	44	7	46	.273	.312	.422	187	51	9	2	5	44	7	49
First Base Only	.287	.313	.512	80	23	4	1	4	11	1	16	.291	.315	.500	86	25	4	1	4	11	1	17
Scoring Position	.268	.321	.371	97	26	5	1	1	33	6	30	.257	.309	.356	101	26	5	1	1	33	6	32
Late Innings, Close	.207	.254	.310	58	12	3	0	1	5	2	20	.207	.254	.310	116	24	6	0	2	10	4	40

RBI/Opportunities

Scoring Position	31 / 123 (25%)	31 / 127 (24%)
Scoring Position, 2 Out	15 / 65 (23%)	15 / 65 (23%)
On Third, Less than 2 Out	9 / 19 (47%)	9 / 20 (45%)
RBI in close games / RBI Total	20 / 50 (40%)	40 / 51 (78%)

Mark Williamson
Baltimore Orioles

An apparent afterthought in the Terry Kennedy trade, Mark Williamson may be the player who evens Baltimore's score with San Diego for the appalling Alan Wiggins deal. The Padres inflicted Wiggins, his multi-million dollar contract and numerous associated headaches on Baltimore in June of 1985; it wasn't until August 1987 that the Orioles were able to completely rid themselves of him.

Williamson, however, was a small glimmer of light that was faintly evident in a season that was as dark as the Baltimore Harbor Tunnel during a power outage. When the team ERA soars into the stratospheric 5.00 range, pitchers who keep their ERAs hovering around 4.00 are valuable property.

If you toss out Don Aase's eight innings, Mark had the second-best ERA (3.77) on the Oriole staff. He was fourth on the team in wins and tops in winning percentage. Pretty impressive stats for a player that the team didn't expect to take north with them when spring training ended—not to mention a rookie. Despite being named the "Rolaids Relief Pitcher of the Year" in the Pacific Coast League in 1986 (10–3, 3.36, 16 saves), the Padres didn't even invite him up for the proverbial cup of coffee in 1986.

That probably affected his performance, too. Williamson had stretches of near-brilliance followed by periods where he was rocked hard. He tended to pitch in streaks—either great or awful—and the Orioles, try as they might, never knew which Williamson to expect. That is just what you'd expect from a man with less than 400 innings of minor league experience. Exclusively a reliever, Mark needed five years to accumulate those innings; his 125 innings in 1987 were more than he's ever pitched in the pros before. Though he's 28, he's still learning his craft.

Another thing that seemed to affect Mark in 1987 was intentional walks. He issued 15 this year (tops in the majors) and didn't pitch well after throwing four deliberate wide ones in a game. Maybe that's because he's a control pitcher and the idea of putting anyone on base by choice bugged him. Maybe it was just that he likes to nibble and he couldn't risk it with no margin for error. In any case, it might be nice to see how he does without the handicap in 1988.

If Mark improves even marginally in 1988, he'll be of significant value to the struggling Oriole staff. He compares remarkably well to staff "ace" Dave Schmidt: one more inning pitched, two more runs (four more earned), six less hits, one less homer and only two more unintentional walks. Schmidt is no Jimmy Key, but Key ain't in the Baltimore Beauty Pageant. Since beauty is in the eye of the beholder and the Baltimore judges don't have a whole lot to behold anymore, Mark Williamson is as good a bet to walk down the runway in 1988 as anyone else on the club.

Greg Pryor

Williamson, Mark Alan Bats: Right Throws: Right Born 07/21/59

1987 SEASON AND MAJOR-LEAGUE CAREER PITCHING TOTALS

	G	GS	CG	GF	IP	BFP	H	R	ER	HR	SH	SF	HB	TBB	IBB	SO	WP	Bk	W	L	Pct	ShO	Sv	ERA
87 BAL	61	2	0	36	125	520	122	59	56	12	5	3	3	41	15	73	3	0	8	9	.471	0	3	4.03
1 YEAR	61	2	0	36	125	520	122	59	56	12	5	3	3	41	15	73	3	0	8	9	.471	0	3	4.03

1987: Finesse, Groundball

	1987 SEASON											FOUR YEAR TOTALS (1984 – 1987)											
	G	IP	H	BB	SO	SB	CS	W	L	S	ERA	G	IP	H	BB	SO	SB	CS	W	L	S	ERA
Totals	61	125.0	122	41	73	14	6	8	9	3	4.03	61	125.0	122	41	73	14	6	8	9	3	4.03
at Home	34	61.0	60	21	30	7	3	5	5	2	4.43	34	61.0	60	21	30	7	3	5	5	2	4.43
on Road	27	64.0	62	20	43	7	3	3	4	1	3.66	27	64.0	62	20	43	7	3	3	4	1	3.66
on Grass	15	22.2	27	13	17	5	1	1	3	1	5.56	15	22.2	27	13	17	5	1	1	3	1	5.56
on Artificial Turf	46	102.1	95	28	56	9	5	7	6	2	3.69	46	102.1	95	28	56	9	5	7	6	2	3.69
Day Games	52	106.0	105	38	63	11	6	8	9	3	4.58	52	106.0	105	38	63	11	6	8	9	3	4.58
Night Games	9	19.0	17	3	10	3	0	0	0	0	0.95	9	19.0	17	3	10	3	0	0	0	0	0.95
April	8	14.0	14	10	9	2	0	1	2	1	6.43	8	14.0	14	10	9	2	0	1	2	1	6.43
May	11	22.1	18	9	15	3	0	1	1	1	3.22	11	22.1	18	9	15	3	0	1	1	1	3.22
June	9	29.1	37	6	15	5	2	0	3	0	5.22	9	29.1	37	6	15	5	2	0	3	0	5.22
July	9	16.2	13	4	9	0	1	3	1	1	2.16	9	16.2	13	4	9	0	1	3	1	1	2.16
August	12	24.0	21	5	16	3	2	3	2	0	3.00	12	24.0	21	5	16	3	2	3	2	0	3.00
Sept/Oct	12	18.2	19	7	9	1	1	0	0	0	4.34	12	18.2	19	7	9	1	1	0	0	0	4.34

vs. Opponent Batters	Ave.	OBP	SLG	AB	H	2B	3B	HR	RBI	BB	SO	Ave.	OBP	SLG	AB	H	2B	3B	HR	RBI	BB	SO
Totals	.261	.322	.387	468	122	17	3	12	69	41	73	.261	.322	.387	468	122	17	3	12	69	41	73
vs. Left	.271	.338	.395	210	57	7	2	5	32	20	33	.271	.338	.395	210	57	7	2	5	32	20	33
vs. Right	.252	.310	.380	258	65	10	1	7	37	21	40	.252	.310	.380	258	65	10	1	7	37	21	40
Bases Empty	.243	.290	.388	255	62	10	3	7	7	14	50	.243	.290	.388	255	62	10	3	7	7	14	50
Leadoff	.190	.243	.260	100	19	7	0	0	0	7	20	.190	.243	.260	100	19	7	0	0	0	7	20
Not Leadoff	.277	.321	.471	155	43	3	3	7	7	7	30	.277	.321	.471	155	43	3	3	7	7	7	30
Runners On Base	.282	.358	.385	213	60	7	0	5	62	27	23	.282	.358	.385	213	60	7	0	5	62	27	23
First Base Only	.295	.304	.372	78	23	3	0	1	5	1	9	.295	.304	.372	78	23	3	0	1	5	1	9
Scoring Position	.274	.384	.393	135	37	4	0	4	57	26	14	.274	.384	.393	135	37	4	0	4	57	26	14
Late Innings, Close	.340	.417	.494	162	55	8	1	5	34	21	17	.340	.417	.494	162	55	8	1	5	34	21	17

RBI/Opportunities

Scoring Position	51 / 212 (24%)	51 / 212 (24%)
Scoring Position, 2 Out	25 / 101 (25%)	25 / 101 (25%)
On Third, Less than 2 Out	20 / 40 (50%)	20 / 40 (50%)
RBI in close games / RBI Total	49 / 69 (71%)	49 / 69 (71%)

Glenn Wilson
Philadelphia Phillies

Glenn Wilson had a very ineffective offensive season in 1987. Wilson's package of an abysmally low secondary average (.190), combined with a poor on-base percentage and slugging percentage, added up to a player who was putting a drain on the Phillies' offense. His trade to the Seattle Mariners for outfielder Phil Bradley should provide the Phillies with the leadoff hitter they so badly need. Glenn made several positive contributions in his four seasons with the Phillies, but he never developed the consistency to be an outstanding major league ballplayer.

Wilson's biggest asset as a baseball player is his throwing arm. His aggressive style in right field makes him a very interesting and exciting outfielder to observe. His arm is very strong and is usually quite accurate. One of his favorite plays is to throw behind runners on the basepaths to try and catch them off-guard. In addition to that, he often tries to throw batters out at first base on sharply hit balls to right field. His eighteen assists led all major league outfielders. Wilson's actual fielding skills are not tremendous—he also led National League outfielders with 11 errors, and his range is probably just better than average. Nevertheless, his all-out style plus terrific arm make defense his forte.

Glenn had had the reputation of being a good RBI man, with his 102 RBI in 1985 being his best performance. This 1985 performance spawned a Phillies television commercial casting Wilson as "Glenn-Bo," complete with camouflage and baseball bats strapped to his body. Glenn was being promoted as the new big gun in the Phillies' offense. Because the commercial was so ridiculously bad, it caught everybody's attention, and it turned Wilson into something of a folk hero as well as a media/fan darling. But after that 1985 campaign, his production continued to slip, with the 54 RBI he produced in 1987 being a far cry from what was expected.

The inconsistency that Wilson displayed in 1987 is typical of his career thus far. He had a pretty good first part of the season, but then began tailing off, never really to recover. By the end of the season, the Phillies were giving rookie Keith Hughes a good deal of playing time in right field, thus fueling trade speculation. Glenn's .381 slugging percentage was the second lowest of the Phillies' normal starting eight. Add to that his typically low on-base percentage, and you have production (or lack thereof) that is hard to accept when it is coming from your rightfielder. It will be interesting to see what type of effect Dick Williams will have on Wilson in Seattle; maybe he will be able to prod a more consistent, productive year out of Glenn in 1988.

Tom Forsaith

Wilson, Glenn Dwight

Bats: Right   Throws: Right   Born 12/22/58

1987 SEASON AND MAJOR-LEAGUE CAREER BATTING TOTALS

	G	AB	H	2B	3B	HR	TB	R	RBI	TBB	IBB	SO	HP	SH	SF	SB	CS	SB%	GDP	AVG	OBP	SLG
87 PHI	154	569	150	21	2	14	217	55	54	38	2	82	1	0	6	3	6	.33	18	.264	.308	.381
6 YEARS	830	2927	786	151	21	72	1195	320	370	172	6	476	9	4	29	25	16	.61	86	.269	.308	.408

1987 SEASON

	Ave.	OBP	SLG	AB	H	2B	3B	HR	RBI	BB	SO
Totals	.264	.308	.381	569	150	21	2	14	54	38	82
vs. Left	.271	.307	.355	155	42	7	0	2	12	9	15
vs. Right	.261	.308	.391	414	108	14	2	12	42	29	67
at Home	.252	.315	.342	278	70	8	1	5	28	28	37
on Road	.275	.300	.419	291	80	13	1	9	26	10	45
vs. Groundball	.271	.315	.384	310	84	9	1	8	27	20	43
vs. Flyball	.255	.299	.378	259	66	12	1	6	27	18	39
vs. Finesse	.265	.305	.403	298	79	13	2	8	30	17	32
vs. Power	.262	.311	.358	271	71	8	0	6	24	21	50
on Grass	.291	.319	.443	158	46	9	0	5	13	6	26
on Artificial Turf	.253	.304	.358	411	104	12	2	9	41	32	56
Day Games	.283	.330	.339	180	51	5	1	1	17	13	31
Night Games	.254	.298	.401	389	99	16	1	13	37	25	51
April	.246	.290	.415	65	16	0	1	3	5	4	9
May	.263	.297	.463	95	25	5	1	4	13	5	15
June	.340	.372	.472	106	36	5	0	3	11	6	15
July	.233	.292	.320	103	24	3	0	2	10	9	13
August	.225	.282	.261	111	25	4	0	0	10	9	15
Sept/Oct	.270	.309	.382	89	24	4	0	2	5	5	15
Bases Empty	.281	.329	.439	303	85	11	2	11	11	21	43
Leadoff	.316	.350	.441	136	43	6	1	3	3	7	19
Not Leadoff	.251	.313	.437	167	42	5	1	8	8	14	24
Runners On	.244	.284	.316	266	65	10	0	3	43	17	39
First Base Only	.248	.300	.364	121	30	5	0	3	8	9	15
Scoring Position	.241	.270	.276	145	35	5	0	0	35	8	24
Late Innings, Close	.273	.345	.364	99	27	3	0	2	9	11	15

FOUR YEAR TOTALS (1984 – 1987)

	Ave.	OBP	SLG	AB	H	2B	3B	HR	RBI	BB	SO
Totals	.265	.307	.401	2102	557	111	14	49	271	132	346
vs. Left	.259	.300	.395	636	165	41	0	15	77	39	84
vs. Right	.267	.310	.404	1466	392	70	14	34	194	93	262
at Home	.276	.326	.417	1024	283	56	8	24	148	79	155
on Road	.254	.288	.386	1078	274	55	6	25	123	53	191
vs. Groundball	.276	.314	.386	1022	282	46	6	18	124	59	147
vs. Flyball	.255	.300	.416	1080	275	65	8	31	147	73	199
vs. Finesse	.265	.300	.410	1130	300	55	12	28	154	59	156
vs. Power	.264	.315	.391	972	257	56	2	21	117	73	190
on Grass	.251	.282	.378	566	142	28	4	12	57	23	103
on Artificial Turf	.270	.316	.410	1536	415	83	10	37	214	109	243
Day Games	.256	.301	.385	672	172	31	4	16	83	46	116
Night Games	.269	.310	.408	1430	385	80	10	33	188	86	230
April	.232	.286	.382	267	62	9	5	7	35	20	43
May	.246	.281	.385	358	88	19	2	9	47	18	68
June	.296	.332	.475	375	111	27	2	12	59	21	66
July	.241	.299	.357	373	90	14	1	9	41	31	49
August	.267	.314	.384	375	100	19	2	7	47	26	58
Sept/Oct	.299	.330	.418	354	106	23	2	5	42	16	62
Bases Empty	.271	.319	.408	1123	304	65	7	25	25	78	184
Leadoff	.295	.341	.425	475	140	30	4	8		33	76
Not Leadoff	.253	.303	.395	648	164	35	3	17	17	45	108
Runners On	.258	.295	.393	979	253	46	7	24	246	54	162
First Base Only	.245	.279	.373	424	104	20	2	10	30	20	64
Scoring Position	.268	.308	.409	555	149	26	5	14	216	34	98
Late Innings, Close	.280	.334	.399	371	104	20	0	8	41	30	72

RBI/Opportunities

	1987		Four Year	
Scoring Position	35 / 180	(19%)	180 / 731	(25%)
Scoring Position, 2 Out	15 / 91	(16%)	64 / 343	(19%)
On Third, Less than 2 Out	13 / 26	(50%)	70 / 126	(56%)
RBI in close games / RBI Total	34 / 54	(63%)	189 / 271	(70%)

Willie Wilson
Kansas City Royals

Oh, he made us such promises. After nine years in the league, Willie Wilson suddenly had a vision, not unlike Saul of Tarsus on the road to Damascus, of what it takes to be an outstanding leadoff man. So he repented of his past heresy, and swore that from now on, he would be positively Hendersonic in his pursuit of bases on balls. And lo, in spring training it came to pass that he walked with some consistency. If he didn't seem exactly like a born-again Willie Wilson, he did seem at least the image of a new, improved leadoff man, one who would help rejuvenate an offense that was wretched in '86.

Came the regular season, though, and it was the same old story. Willie just went up and hacked away, most of the time futilely. It was especially deplorable since: a) Kevin Seitzer was following him to the plate; and, b) when Wilson did reach base, he was running judiciously; his stolen base game really did revive. He simply was not on base often enough for it to have a significant influence.

In last year's *GABSB* I wrote that Wilson was "still terrific defensively." I am now prepared to recant. There was a bit of controversy stirred up in KC when he was passed over for the Gold Glove, although for once in his life, Wilson neglected to mouth off. But two political cartoonists, of all people, jumped into the act, one showing Wilson being awarded a "Gold Snub," the other comparing the leagues bestowal of the Gold Glove on Frank White with its presentation of the middle finger to Wilson. Pure Homerism of the most distasteful sort, for if I heard the radio broadcasters say it once I heard it a hundred times, "Willie got a late break on that ball." Sure he can still run them down, but that instant of indecision is beginning to cost the Royals. No way is he Gold Glove material any longer.

Willie's biggest contribution in '87 was leading the cacophony of abuse heaped upon Bo Jackson and management after Bo signed for his multi-million dollar hobby. Wilson, and everyone else, was entitled to a certain level of resentment—Bo was unquestionably the recipient of special treatment from co-owner Neville Chamberlain Fogelman. But Wilson was more than resentful; his fury knew no bounds, and was, frankly, irrational.

So the organization gave Bo a break he hadn't earned; they did the same thing in '84 when they handed a lifetime contract to a convicted felon who coincidentally played center field. It's odd, but with Wilson and the Royals, the usual player-management relationship is reversed; it's Willie who quickly forgets the good times and screams "What have you done for me lately?" while the Royals maintain a discreet silence, not that they have much choice, the folly of lifetime contracts being what it is. But one day soon—perhaps very soon—Wilson will find himself a .240 hitter with a .270 OBP, and, lifetime contract or not, the Royals' discreet silence will come to a deafening halt.

Mike Kopf

Wilson, Willie James Bats: Both Throws: Right Born 07/09/55

1987 SEASON AND MAJOR-LEAGUE CAREER BATTING TOTALS

	G	AB	H	2B	3B	HR	TB	R	RBI	TBB	IBB	SO	HP	SH	SF	SB	CS	SB%	GDP	AVG	OBP	SLG
87 KC	146	610	170	18	15	4	230	97	30	32	2	88	6	4	1	59	11	.84	9	.279	.320	.377
12 YEARS	1413	5518	1627	194	112	34	2147	872	387	281	21	749	49	42	16	529	100	.84	49	.295	.334	.389

	1987 SEASON											FOUR YEAR TOTALS (1984 – 1987)										
	Ave.	OBP	SLG	AB	H	2B	3B	HR	RBI	BB	SO	Ave.	OBP	SLG	AB	H	2B	3B	HR	RBI	BB	SO
Totals	.279	.320	.377	610	170	18	15	4	30	32	88	.281	.324	.385	2387	671	87	52	19	161	130	335
vs. Left	.241	.270	.312	170	41	5	2	1	11	7	35	.296	.325	.399	676	200	29	10	7	48	30	110
vs. Right	.293	.340	.402	440	129	13	13	3	19	25	53	.275	.323	.379	1711	471	58	42	12	113	100	225
at Home	.296	.334	.399	321	95	13	10	0	18	17	40	.284	.331	.394	1192	339	40	35	7	84	71	150
on Road	.260	.305	.353	289	75	5	5	4	12	15	48	.278	.316	.376	1195	332	47	17	12	77	59	185
vs. Groundball	.303	.336	.421	323	98	13	8	3	19	15	43	.296	.336	.401	1154	342	47	25	8	80	62	146
vs. Flyball	.251	.303	.328	287	72	5	7	1	11	17	45	.267	.312	.370	1233	329	40	27	11	81	68	189
vs. Finesse	.281	.309	.390	359	101	12	9	3	24	12	46	.286	.323	.397	1387	397	54	32	12	96	68	157
vs. Power	.275	.336	.359	251	69	6	6	1	6	20	42	.274	.324	.368	1000	274	33	20	7	65	62	178
on Grass	.252	.304	.341	214	54	4	3	3	10	13	36	.279	.319	.378	896	250	37	14	8	55	47	141
on Artificial Turf	.293	.329	.396	396	116	14	12	1	20	19	52	.282	.326	.389	1491	421	50	38	11	106	83	194
Day Games	.230	.278	.322	152	35	6	4	0	5	9	30	.268	.309	.389	574	154	21	12	8	43	31	91
Night Games	.295	.335	.395	458	135	12	11	4	25	23	58	.285	.328	.384	1813	517	66	40	11	118	99	244
April	.234	.272	.312	77	18	2	2	0	3	2	8	.260	.293	.353	235	61	5	7	1	17	9	35
May	.354	.400	.494	79	28	2	3	1	3	4	11	.282	.325	.405	373	105	14	7	6	22	22	51
June	.269	.287	.345	119	32	3	0	2	3	3	18	.279	.323	.373	448	125	15	9	3	25	29	64
July	.272	.306	.427	103	28	4	6	0	4	5	17	.289	.327	.404	460	133	17	12	4	32	26	57
August	.271	.345	.346	107	29	3	1	1	5	11	16	.289	.328	.379	454	131	13	11	2	35	26	66
Sept/Oct	.280	.321	.360	125	35	4	3	0	12	7	18	.278	.309	.384	417	116	23	6	3	30	18	62
Bases Empty	.282	.322	.382	411	116	9	10	4	4	21	64	.276	.313	.382	1562	431	52	36	14	14	82	233
Leadoff	.303	.349	.399	238	72	3	7	2	2	15	38	.274	.317	.385	859	235	26	23	8	8	53	129
Not Leadoff	.254	.283	.358	173	44	6	3	2	2	6	26	.279	.308	.378	703	196	26	13	6	6	29	104
Runners On	.271	.318	.367	199	54	9	5	0	26	11	24	.291	.332	.390	825	240	35	16	5	147	48	102
First Base Only	.294	.327	.353	102	30	4	1	0	1	3	10	.301	.330	.392	375	113	16	6	2	11	14	44
Scoring Position	.247	.308	.381	97	24	5	4	0	25	8	14	.282	.333	.389	450	127	19	10	3	136	34	58
Late Innings, Close	.358	.395	.519	81	29	5	4	0	6	4	10	.305	.340	.390	354	108	12	9	0	34	18	49

RBI/Opportunities

	1987 SEASON	FOUR YEAR TOTALS
Scoring Position	24 / 121 (20%)	125 / 551 (23%)
Scoring Position, 2 Out	10 / 69 (14%)	43 / 275 (16%)
On Third, Less than 2 Out	7 / 15 (47%)	55 / 92 (60%)
RBI in close games / RBI Total	18 / 30 (60%)	108 / 161 (67%)

Dave Winfield
New York Yankees

No matter what Dave Winfield does, it won't matter. Until he hits the game-winning homer in the bottom of the ninth inning of the seventh game of the World Series, he'll be known in New York as "Mr. May"—an overpaid underachiever who's taught the Yankees how to lose.

1987, unfortunately, did nothing to shatter this perception. While both Don Mattingly (slow start, injury) and Rickey Henderson (injury) were not contributing, Winfield carried New York almost singlehandedly into first place. He had a torrid May, had 25 RBIs in one 22-game stretch and had two 12-game hitting streaks. He was batting .295 with 20 homers and 68 RBIs at the All-Star break. Even George Steinbrenner finally had to admit that Winfield was playing brilliantly.

Then, in the second half . . . pffft. While Toronto and Detroit were rolling past, Winfield hit almost forty points lower, with only seven homers and 29 RBIs. If you're thinking that maybe the injuries to Henderson and Randolph cut down on Dave's chances with men in scoring position, think again. Winfield had only sixteen extra-base hits—just three more than Mattingly had during his eight-game homer streak—after the break. Luckily for Dave, Steinbrenner was focusing his attention on Lou Piniella and Mark Salas by that time.

Whether the nickname is fair or not, one thing is true—Winfield is not the world's most consistent ballplayer. Here are his first half/second half batting splits as a Yankee:

HALF	1981	1982	1983	1984	1985	1986	1987
FIRST	.324	.295	.250	.370	.297	.222	.293
SECOND	.258	.267	.316	.313	.251	.301	.254

This sort of wide disparity—the average differential is 56 points— may explain why Winfield has never gotten as much acclaim as he deserves. If you go to see him, there's a 50 percent chance that he's not playing his best ball; if he isn't being Mr. May, he's being Mr. August.

But, despite that, there's no doubt that Winfield is a great player— he may not be consistent from month to month, but he is consistent year to year. Excepting the strike year, he's had 90+ RBIs in 11 of the last 12 years. He's a lifetime .285 hitter who's fallen below .275 only once in that span. He's hit 332 career homers, despite playing in two unfriendly home parks. He remains one of the best fielders in the game—both with glove and his arm—and always hits well in clutch situations. It's a shame that most of his fame stems from his big contract.

Michael Cassin

Winfield, David Mark "Dave"   Bats: Right   Throws: Right   Born 10/03/51

1987 SEASON AND MAJOR-LEAGUE CAREER BATTING TOTALS

	G	AB	H	2B	3B	HR	TB	R	RBI	TBB	IBB	SO	HP	SH	SF	SB	CS	SB%	GDP	AVG	OBP	SLG
87 NYA	156	575	158	22	1	27	263	83	97	76	5	96	0	1	3	5	6	.45	20	.275	.358	.457
15 YEARS	2120	7862	2241	375	72	332	3756	1218	1331	867	136	1136	18	14	74	200	82	.71	225	.285	.354	.478

	1987 SEASON											FOUR YEAR TOTALS (1984 – 1987)										
	Ave.	OBP	SLG	AB	H	2B	3B	HR	RBI	BB	SO	Ave.	OBP	SLG	AB	H	2B	3B	HR	RBI	BB	SO
Totals	.275	.358	.457	575	158	22	1	27	97	76	96	.288	.356	.476	2340	673	121	16	96	415	258	369
vs. Left	.345	.449	.621	177	61	10	0	13	36	35	26	.291	.387	.520	759	221	38	8	40	142	125	100
vs. Right	.244	.314	.384	398	97	12	1	14	61	41	70	.286	.340	.455	1581	452	83	8	56	273	133	269
at Home	.283	.374	.450	269	76	12	0	11	42	41	39	.292	.369	.485	1106	323	58	7	47	210	139	154
on Road	.268	.343	.464	306	82	10	1	16	55	35	57	.284	.345	.468	1234	350	63	9	49	205	119	215
vs. Groundball	.270	.360	.374	289	78	12	0	6	41	42	47	.283	.357	.426	1156	327	59	8	30	182	136	190
vs. Flyball	.280	.355	.542	286	80	10	1	21	56	34	49	.292	.356	.525	1184	346	62	8	66	233	122	179
vs. Finesse	.279	.333	.462	312	87	10	1	15	47	26	45	.292	.346	.460	1286	376	62	8	46	205	109	173
vs. Power	.270	.384	.452	263	71	12	0	12	50	50	51	.282	.368	.495	1054	297	59	8	50	210	149	196
on Grass	.277	.364	.464	481	133	19	1	23	78	68	76	.290	.361	.486	1977	573	104	14	85	361	228	299
on Artificial Turf	.266	.324	.426	94	25	3	0	4	19	8	20	.275	.331	.424	363	100	17	2	11	54	30	70
Day Games	.296	.373	.398	196	58	5	0	5	29	26	29	.306	.372	.489	759	232	31	6	32	137	84	112
Night Games	.264	.350	.488	379	100	17	1	22	68	50	67	.279	.348	.470	1581	441	90	10	64	278	174	257
April	.342	.478	.534	73	25	2	0	4	15	19	11	.292	.399	.458	253	74	11	2	9	34	45	41
May	.250	.322	.510	104	26	4	1	7	21	21	21	.254	.318	.473	414	105	23	4	20	76	39	66
June	.314	.397	.578	102	32	6	0	7	25	14	14	.337	.395	.533	409	138	22	2	18	82	39	61
July	.236	.317	.371	89	21	3	0	3	12	11	18	.290	.359	.488	369	107	21	2	16	69	40	55
August	.245	.321	.340	94	23	3	0	2	11	11	12	.286	.365	.457	420	120	18	3	16	72	53	64
Sept/Oct	.274	.331	.416	113	31	4	0	4	13	10	20	.272	.330	.446	475	129	26	3	17	82	42	82
Bases Empty	.237	.319	.434	316	75	9	1	17	17	38	57	.273	.337	.457	1176	321	66	3	48	48	114	204
Leadoff	.237	.303	.432	139	33	3	0	8	8	13	23	.296	.357	.472	496	147	30	0	19	19	47	83
Not Leadoff	.237	.332	.435	177	42	6	1	9	9	25	34	.256	.323	.446	680	174	36	3	29	29	67	121
Runners On	.320	.403	.486	259	83	13	0	10	80	38	39	.302	.378	.496	1164	352	55	13	48	367	144	165
First Base Only	.269	.352	.398	108	29	5	0	3	8	14	22	.271	.334	.454	498	135	22	6	19	50	47	64
Scoring Position	.358	.438	.550	151	54	8	0	7	72	24	17	.326	.410	.527	666	217	33	7	29	317	97	101
Late Innings, Close	.264	.340	.471	87	23	3	0	5	20	10	11	.269	.332	.437	364	98	14	1	15	62	34	64

RBI/Opportunities

	1987		FOUR YEAR	
Scoring Position	61 / 206	(30%)	270 / 908	(30%)
Scoring Position, 2 Out	28 / 96	(29%)	97 / 394	(25%)
On Third, Less than 2 Out	18 / 46	(39%)	107 / 197	(54%)
RBI in close games / RBI Total	61 / 97	(63%)	262 / 415	(63%)

Bobby Witt
Texas Rangers

Lordy, this guy throws a lot of pitches! He must lead the league in 30-pitch innings, and 40-pitch innings, and 50-pitch innings, if you get my drift. That, of course, is the central reason it took Witt so long to get his first complete game. Let the record show that in the final start of the 1987 season, the 56th start of his major league career, Bobby Witt went the distance for the first time. It was a 9-inning four-hitter (8-walker), for a 2–1 victory over Minnesota.

Even though he walked more batters per inning in 1987 than in 1986, I thought he showed better command of his pitches than in his rookie season. You have to understand that his fastball can be so overpowering that a lot of hitters have adopted a strategy of just waiting him out in hopes of getting him down in the count where they can either draw a walk or catch him letting up to throw a strike. Certainly there was improvement despite the higher walk rate.

	IP	H-AVG	R-AVG	ERA	W-AVG	K-AVG
1986	157.2	7.42	5.94	5.48	8.16	9.93
1987	143.0	7.17	5.16	4.91	8.81	10.07

It's easy to stay enthusiastic about his future. He's been in the majors way ahead of the development of his pitching; remember he had only 35 minor league innings to buffer his jump from college to the majors. There are three solid reasons to look towards 1988 as a possible breakthrough year for Witt. For one, he should be healthier. In 1987 Witt started off plagued by some shoulder trouble which was traced back to his involvement in a faulty off-season conditioning program rather than going with what was recommended by the Rangers. Whatever the cause, from July 22 on, he was able to take his regular turn in the rotation.

Consistent health will also mean more consistent use in 1988, and, like most pitchers with control trouble, Witt has better control and is more effective with regular use.

1987	IP	H-AVG	R-AVG	ERA	W-AVG	K-AVG
4 days rest	74.1	7.14	4.96	4.60	8.11	10.05
Other	68.1	7.11	5.40	5.27	9.48	10.14

But what Witt should really look forward to in 1988 is the umpires operating under a directive to call more high strikes. Is there a pitcher anywhere in the majors who could benefit more from the new strike zone definition? Well, maybe teammate Mitch Williams, or perhaps even Edwin Correa. Hmm, is there a pitching staff better suited to benefit from the new ruling than the Texas Rangers? Isn't Ranger GM Tom Grieve on the rules committee? No need to ask which way he voted.

Craig R. Wright

Witt, Robert Andrew "Bobby"

Bats: Right   Throws: Right   Born 05/11/64

1987 SEASON AND MAJOR-LEAGUE CAREER PITCHING TOTALS

	G	GS	CG	GF	IP	BFP	H	R	ER	HR	SH	SF	HB	TBB	IBB	SO	WP	Bk	W	L	Pct	ShO	Sv	ERA
87 TEX	26	25	1	0	143	673	114	82	78	10	5	5	3	140	1	160	7	2	8	10	.444	0	0	4.91
2 YEARS	57	56	1	0	301	1414	244	186	174	28	8	14	6	283	3	334	29	5	19	19	.500	0	0	5.20

1987: Power, Flyball   1986: Power, Flyball

1987 SEASON												FOUR YEAR TOTALS (1984 – 1987)											
	G	IP	H	BB	SO	SB	CS	W	L	S	ERA		G	IP	H	BB	SO	SB	CS	W	L	S	ERA
Totals	26	143.0	114	140	160	44	2	8	10	0	4.91		57	300.2	244	283	334	88	6	19	19	0	5.21
at Home	13	81.0	61	76	89	23	2	4	3	0	3.89		29	171.0	130	145	183	43	4	10	6	0	3.95
on Road	13	62.0	53	64	71	21	0	4	7	0	6.24		28	129.2	114	138	151	45	2	9	13	0	6.87
on Grass	8	37.2	29	39	40	13	0	3	2	0	5.02		16	80.1	58	85	106	27	1	6	5	0	5.49
on Artificial Turf	18	105.1	85	101	120	31	2	5	8	0	4.87		41	220.1	186	198	228	61	5	13	14	0	5.11
Day Games	22	124.2	101	124	144	39	2	7	8	0	4.69		50	265.0	219	255	299	79	5	17	16	0	5.16
Night Games	4	18.1	13	16	16	5	0	1	2	0	6.38		7	35.2	25	28	35	9	1	2	3	0	5.55
April	3	16.1	12	20	22	4	0	0	1	0	4.41		7	37.2	23	44	49	10	1	2	1	0	4.06
May	4	17.0	14	18	19	6	1	1	2	0	6.35		10	45.2	39	47	33	12	3	1	6	0	7.09
June	2	13.0	3	12	11	5	0	2	0	0	2.08		8	44.0	34	39	48	14	1	4	2	0	5.11
July	5	27.0	21	21	27	8	0	1	2	0	4.00		9	44.0	36	39	48	14	0	2	5	0	5.73
August	6	36.2	29	39	48	9	0	3	2	0	4.66		11	62.1	52	61	82	17	0	5	2	0	4.33
Sept/Oct	6	33.0	35	30	33	12	1	1	3	0	6.55		12	67.0	60	53	74	21	1	5	3	0	5.10

vs. Opponent Batters	Ave.	OBP	SLG	AB	H	2B	3B	HR	RBI	BB	SO		Ave.	OBP	SLG	AB	H	2B	3B	HR	RBI	BB	SO
Totals	.219	.385	.325	520	114	21	2	10	62	140	160		.221	.380	.348	1103	244	52	2	28	150	283	334
vs. Left	.229	.387	.332	292	67	10	1	6	36	74	74		.239	.399	.358	606	145	31	1	13	85	160	155
vs. Right	.206	.382	.316	228	47	11	1	4	26	66	86		.199	.357	.336	497	99	21	1	15	65	123	179
Bases Empty	.209	.420	.318	239	50	11	0	5	5	86	80		.213	.391	.344	541	115	26	0	15	15	157	164
Leadoff	.217	.427	.374	115	25	6	0	4	4	42	42		.234	.417	.395	248	58	10	0	10	10	78	82
Not Leadoff	.202	.414	.266	124	25	5	0	1	1	44	38		.195	.367	.300	293	57	16	0	5	5	79	82
Runners On Base	.228	.351	.331	281	64	10	2	5	57	54	80		.230	.370	.352	562	129	26	2	13	135	126	170
First Base Only	.260	.379	.404	104	27	4	1	3	9	20	24		.254	.371	.416	209	53	8	1	8	22	39	57
Scoring Position	.209	.335	.288	177	37	6	1	2	48	34	56		.215	.369	.314	353	76	18	1	5	113	87	113
Late Innings, Close	.211	.423	.263	38	8	2	0	0	0	13	12		.276	.425	.345	58	16	4	0	0	2	14	16

RBI/Opportunities

	1987		Four Year
Scoring Position	42 / 247	(17%)	99 / 537 (18%)
Scoring Position, 2 Out	7 / 108	(6%)	30 / 253 (12%)
On Third, Less than 2 Out	21 / 38	(55%)	41 / 79 (52%)
RBI in close games / RBI Total	47 / 62	(76%)	110 / 150 (73%)

Mike Witt
California Angels

At the age of 27, Witt stands at the crossroads: The question is whether he will have a Hall of Fame career or just a good career. He has now firmly laid the foundation upon which a great career could be built. His 87 wins compares reasonably well with the totals of the most recent 300-game winners in the majors at the same age:

PITCHER	CAREER WINS AT AGE 27
Don Sutton	102
Tom Seaver	95
Steve Carlton	94
Mike Witt	87
Phil Niekro	6

Despite four straight seasons of 15 or more wins, Mike has not always been a picture of consistency, nor a pitcher of consistency for that matter. When hot, Witt is probably the best pitcher in baseball. He has a Blylevenish curveball, a more than respectable fastball, and he changes speeds well. But he's also had a history of pitching poorly when he doesn't have everything just right. Cutting down or learning to pitch better in his cold streaks could help him become the dominant pitcher of his era.

In that sense, 1987 was an encouraging year. Unlike 1986 when Witt had number of hot streaks, this last season was mostly a struggle. He gave up more hits than innings pitched, his walks were up, and he gave up a lot of home runs. Yet he managed to salvage a number of games in which he likely would have fallen apart just two years ago, and ultimately turned a bad year into a productive one where he was arguably one of the top fifteen starters in the league. He somehow ended up winning 16 games while pitching for a last place club.

Was Witt's off-season simply that—an off-season—or was there a physical problem that may threaten his future effectiveness? It would be hard to build a case for the injury theory. He was remarkably durable, 36 starts, 247 innings. He sent 192 batters back to the bench with their bats in hand, and that, too, does not sound like a pitcher who was hurting.

I basically go along with the simple "off-season" theory. When Witt is going well he is a deadly combination of being both a power pitcher and a groundball pitcher. In 1987 it seems he simply got the ball up in the strike zone a bit more than he should. Too many homers and not enough grounders. I expect he'll get back on track next year.

Kent Kirchstein

Witt, Michael Atwater "Mike" — Bats: Right   Throws: Right   Born 07/20/60

1987 SEASON AND MAJOR-LEAGUE CAREER PITCHING TOTALS

	G	GS	CG	GF	IP	BFP	H	R	ER	HR	SH	SF	HB	TBB	IBB	SO	WP	Bk	W	L	Pct	ShO	Sv	ERA
87 CAL	36	36	10	0	247	1065	252	128	110	34	6	6	4	84	4	192	6	0	16	14	.533	0	0	4.01
7 YEARS	237	205	53	18	1476	6203	1398	668	590	126	36	39	40	508	28	1013	48	3	87	73	.544	8	5	3.60

1987: Power, Groundball   1986: Power, Groundball   1985: Power, Groundball   1984: Power, Groundball

1987 SEASON

	G	IP	H	BB	SO	SB	CS	W	L	S	ERA
Totals	36	247.0	252	84	192	7	5	16	14	0	4.01
at Home	19	137.2	128	48	98	5	2	9	8	0	4.05
on Road	17	109.1	124	36	94	2	3	7	6	0	3.95
on Grass	11	76.2	77	28	76	4	1	6	5	0	3.99
on Artificial Turf	25	170.1	175	56	116	3	4	10	9	0	4.02
Day Games	31	208.1	208	73	169	6	4	15	11	0	4.06
Night Games	5	38.2	44	11	23	1	1	1	3	0	3.72
April	5	33.0	29	11	31	4	1	2	2	0	5.18
May	6	36.2	38	21	29	1	1	3	2	0	3.93
June	6	45.0	31	15	40	0	1	4	1	0	1.60
July	6	37.1	47	8	34	0	1	4	1	0	4.34
August	6	40.0	46	17	19	0	1	2	3	0	4.72
Sept/Oct	7	55.0	61	12	39	2	0	1	5	0	4.58

FOUR YEAR TOTALS (1984 – 1987)

	G	IP	H	BB	SO	SB	CS	W	L	S	ERA
Totals	139	1012.2	925	339	776	47	39	64	44	0	3.46
at Home	69	521.2	444	171	392	17	21	36	23	0	3.17
on Road	70	491.0	481	168	384	30	18	28	21	0	3.74
on Grass	42	300.0	272	113	251	13	11	21	15	0	4.11
on Artificial Turf	97	712.2	653	226	525	34	28	43	29	0	3.18
Day Games	119	865.2	776	305	664	39	32	58	38	0	3.40
Night Games	20	147.0	149	34	112	8	7	6	6	0	3.73
April	21	148.0	124	57	115	10	5	8	7	0	3.77
May	21	142.2	147	70	104	7	6	7	11	0	4.10
June	24	185.2	158	57	157	8	7	15	6	0	2.57
July	23	176.0	162	52	143	5	9	13	3	0	3.12
August	22	162.0	146	52	106	5	6	12	6	0	2.94
Sept/Oct	28	198.1	188	51	151	12	6	9	11	0	4.31

vs. Opponent Batters — 1987

	Ave.	OBP	SLG	AB	H	2B	3B	HR	RBI	BB	SO
Totals	.261	.321	.435	965	252	48	9	34	115	84	192
vs. Left	.272	.338	.463	525	143	26	4	22	65	52	90
vs. Right	.248	.300	.402	440	109	22	5	12	50	32	102
Bases Empty	.272	.327	.440	552	150	32	8	15	15	42	108
Leadoff	.319	.372	.496	238	76	11	5	7	7	20	34
Not Leadoff	.236	.292	.398	314	74	21	3	8	8	22	74
Runners On Base	.247	.314	.429	413	102	16	1	19	100	42	84
First Base Only	.251	.300	.467	199	50	4	0	13	27	13	41
Scoring Position	.243	.325	.393	214	52	12	1	6	73	29	43
Late Innings, Close	.255	.339	.400	110	28	2	1	4	11	14	17

vs. Opponent Batters — Four Year Totals

	Ave.	OBP	SLG	AB	H	2B	3B	HR	RBI	BB	SO
Totals	.242	.304	.372	3819	925	160	25	95	387	339	776
vs. Left	.251	.313	.385	2165	544	90	14	57	219	193	382
vs. Right	.230	.293	.355	1654	381	70	11	38	168	146	394
Bases Empty	.241	.298	.361	2294	552	94	17	49	49	186	494
Leadoff	.248	.307	.367	971	241	30	8	23	23	83	192
Not Leadoff	.235	.292	.356	1323	311	64	9	26	26	103	302
Runners On Base	.245	.313	.389	1525	373	66	8	46	338	153	282
First Base Only	.244	.294	.396	742	181	33	4	24	67	52	131
Scoring Position	.245	.329	.382	783	192	33	4	22	271	101	151
Late Innings, Close	.225	.306	.351	484	109	12	2	15	48	56	86

RBI/Opportunities

	1987		Four Year	
Scoring Position	61 / 281	(22%)	228 / 1057	(22%)
Scoring Position, 2 Out	24 / 128	(19%)	93 / 475	(20%)
On Third, Less than 2 Out	20 / 52	(38%)	83 / 189	(44%)
RBI in close games / RBI Total	79 / 115	(69%)	268 / 387	(69%)

Todd Worrell
St. Louis Cardinals

Todd Worrell was the Cardinal's #1 pick in the 1982 summer draft. He was voted to the *Sporting News* College Baseball All-America team that same year. In the Cardinals' dreadful 1986 season, Todd was named Rookie Pitcher of the Year and Fireman of the Year by the *Sporting News,* Rookie of the Year by the BBWAA and was the National League's Rolaids Relief Man. He established a record (36) for the most saves by a rookie and led the league in that department as well as in intentional walks. Surprisingly, without the recognition, in 1987 he was better. Statistically speaking his numbers were remarkably similar to his rookie year but his most notable improvement was in strikeouts. As effective a reliever as Whitey Herzog could hope for, Todd was continually protecting small leads and getting the needed strikeout with runners in scoring position. Worrell's strikeout to walk ratio of 2.7 to 1 (4 to 1 not counting intentional walks) was up from 1.8 to 1 in 1986. In 1987 he struck out 8.75 men per nine innings, allowing only 8.18 hits. Todd got 33 saves out of 47 chances (third best in the NL), and few pitchers were subject to the pressure he was under. He is calm under pressure and challenges hitters, frequently working the count full. More than once he struck out the side when duty called.

Every Cardinal pitcher was used to comfortable leads during the first part of the season, but during the dog days when the Cards were only playing .500 baseball, Todd was outstanding. From the first of August his record was 4–0 with 12 saves in 27 appearances while his ERA levelled off from 3.64 to 2.66. The fact that his team competed in 14 post-season games is a sign of his effectiveness. Good management helps a pitcher to excel also. Todd has a very clever manager. If Todd's numbers weren't as good as Bedrosian's or Smith's it's only because Herzog has more depth in the bullpen. If Todd were with the Cubs he'd have seen more action than Three Finger Brown.

Tracy Thibeau

Two years of evidence seems to indicate that Todd Worrell may be one of those players who is a habitual slow starter. He was so bad during some parts of April and May last season that the radio call-in shows on KMOX in St. Louis were flooded with callers suggesting, or demanding in a few cases, that Worrell be optioned to Louisville to iron out his pitching problems.

Unlike '86, when his ERA was under two runs a game in both April and May despite control problems (15 walks in 16 IP), Todd was really getting rocked early last year. His ERA was over five in April, over six in May. Control problems still had a lot to do with it, as Worrell couldn't seem to get anything over but his fastball. But once Todd got straightened out, he was spectacular.

Russ Eagle

Worrell, Todd Roland

Bats: Right   Throws: Right   Born 06/28/59

1987 SEASON AND MAJOR-LEAGUE CAREER PITCHING TOTALS

	G	GS	CG	GF	IP	BFP	H	R	ER	HR	SH	SF	HB	TBB	IBB	SO	WP	Bk	W	L	Pct	ShO	Sv	ERA
87 STL	75	0	0	54	95	395	86	29	28	8	4	2	0	34	11	92	1	0	8	6	.571	0	33	2.65
3 YEARS	166	0	0	125	221	913	189	65	59	19	11	10	1	82	29	182	4	0	20	16	.556	0	74	2.40

1987: Power, Flyball   1986: Power, Flyball   1985: Power, Flyball

1987 SEASON

	G	IP	H	BB	SO	SB	CS	W	L	S	ERA
Totals	76	94.2	86	34	92	11	2	8	6	33	2.66
at Home	37	44.1	39	12	38	4	2	5	3	12	3.25
on Road	39	50.1	47	22	54	7	0	3	3	21	2.15
on Grass	24	28.2	21	11	35	3	0	0	1	14	1.57
on Artificial Turf	52	66.0	65	23	57	8	2	8	5	19	3.14
Day Games	21	25.0	26	8	31	5	0	1	3	12	3.24
Night Games	55	69.2	60	26	61	6	2	7	3	21	2.45
April	6	5.0	5	5	4	0	1	0	0	3	5.40
May	16	13.2	21	4	11	3	1	0	2	8	6.59
June	13	20.1	12	6	22	2	0	3	1	5	0.89
July	13	15.1	19	5	19	5	0	1	3	5	4.11
August	16	22.2	19	8	16	1	0	3	0	6	0.79
Sept/Oct	12	17.2	10	6	20	0	0	1	0	6	2.04

FOUR YEAR TOTALS (1984 – 1987)

	G	IP	H	BB	SO	SB	CS	W	L	S	ERA
Totals	167	220.0	189	82	182	21	8	20	16	74	2.41
at Home	85	111.1	91	33	81	9	6	13	8	32	2.59
on Road	82	108.2	98	49	101	12	2	7	8	42	2.24
on Grass	59	76.0	61	41	70	6	1	4	6	30	2.13
on Artificial Turf	108	144.0	128	41	112	15	7	16	10	44	2.56
Day Games	44	55.2	54	19	55	8	1	3	6	22	3.07
Night Games	123	164.1	135	63	127	13	7	17	10	52	2.19
April	15	21.2	16	20	11	3	1	1	1	6	2.08
May	27	30.2	36	7	20	4	3	2	4	11	3.82
June	30	42.1	31	19	46	4	2	5	6	12	1.49
July	25	30.2	26	9	29	6	0	2	3	13	2.64
August	30	39.0	38	11	23	1	1	5	1	14	1.85
Sept/Oct	40	55.2	42	16	53	3	1	5	1	18	2.75

vs. Opponent Batters — 1987 Season

	Ave.	OBP	SLG	AB	H	2B	3B	HR	RBI	BB	SO
Totals	.242	.307	.366	355	86	14	3	8	43	34	92
vs. Left	.234	.335	.317	145	34	3	0	3	15	23	43
vs. Right	.248	.285	.400	210	52	11	3	5	28	11	49
Bases Empty	.291	.343	.473	165	48	9	3	5	5	13	41
Leadoff	.286	.342	.457	70	20	2	2	2	2	6	13
Not Leadoff	.295	.343	.484	95	28	7	1	3	3	7	28
Runners On Base	.200	.277	.274	190	38	5	0	3	38	21	51
First Base Only	.195	.244	.247	77	15	4	0	0	3	5	21
Scoring Position	.204	.298	.292	113	23	1	0	3	35	16	30
Late Innings, Close	.235	.308	.372	285	67	12	3	7	40	31	78

vs. Opponent Batters — Four Year Totals

	Ave.	OBP	SLG	AB	H	2B	3B	HR	RBI	BB	SO
Totals	.234	.303	.363	809	189	36	6	19	94	82	182
vs. Left	.246	.337	.381	357	88	11	2	11	41	50	86
vs. Right	.223	.275	.350	452	101	25	4	8	53	32	96
Bases Empty	.280	.333	.458	382	107	24	4	11	11	30	80
Leadoff	.304	.360	.503	161	49	10	2	6	6	14	23
Not Leadoff	.262	.312	.425	221	58	17	2	5	5	16	57
Runners On Base	.192	.279	.279	427	82	9	2	8	83	52	102
First Base Only	.196	.236	.261	153	30	4	0	2	7	8	33
Scoring Position	.190	.300	.288	274	52	5	2	6	76	44	69
Late Innings, Close	.230	.303	.356	644	148	26	5	15	85	68	149

RBI/Opportunities

	1987 Season	Four Year Totals
Scoring Position	29 / 166 (17%)	63 / 402 (16%)
Scoring Position, 2 Out	17 / 95 (18%)	27 / 205 (13%)
On Third, Less than 2 Out	5 / 26 (19%)	20 / 68 (29%)
RBI in close games / RBI Total	40 / 43 (93%)	87 / 94 (93%)

Rich Yett
Cleveland Indians

"Doo-doo-doo-doo . . . doo-doo-doo-doo . . . Submitted for your approval: 21-year-old Rich Yett. In his first International League season, his ERA is the eighth best; over one run lower than Zane Smith's or John Cerutti's are. Two men have more strikeouts, two pitch more complete games. It is merely a matter of time, Mr. Yett believes, before he leaves AAA. And leave it he shall—but only to enter . . . The Twilight Zone."

Rod Serling never said that—but if he were still living, he might have. Four years later—years spent in those bastions of great pitching, Minnesota and Cleveland—Rich Yett has a grand total of 15 starts (nine of which his teams have won) under his belt. Is he a major league starter, you ask? I don't know; I'd sorta kinda like to find out.

But I *do* know that Yett won't make anyone forget Tom Henke—or even Tom Buskey. 1987 is the second straight year that Cleveland has looked at Rich's 94-MPH heater, his hard (mostly to control) slider and split-finger, and they decided that he could solve their bullpen problems. If he can, he hasn't done it so far. Rich is 5–7, with two saves, a 5.50 ERA and 101 hits and 61 walks allowed in 103 career innings pitched in relief.

The problem, as you can see, is control. Whenever Rich pitches, he'll have an inning where he can't get anything but his fastball over the plate; when that happens, it's only a matter of time until someone takes him deep. One inning later, he's slicing corners and breaking bats. If your starter does that (Kirk McCaskill and Danny Jackson do it a lot), you still have a good shot at winning; if your stopper does it, you're meat. If Rich makes it in the majors, it must be as a starter.

Can he make it? If you look at his starting stats (3–5, 4.89, 80 hits and 37 walks in 73 innings), you won't be impressed—but you should put a very large asterisk beside those totals.

In his first four starts of '87, Yett had allowed 23 hits and 8 walks in 18.1 IP—but he was 1–0 with a 2.94 ERA. Unfortunately he twisted his ankle fielding a bunt in that fourth start. That, for power pitchers, is a major injury. In order to throw hard, you must push off the mound with all your strength and absorb all of the energy with your legs. If your ankle is sore, you can't push off hard; since every pitch you throw is like a hammer-blow to your legs, your legs just get worse and worse. Rich missed a start, allowed no earned runs in nine innings next time and then reinjured the ankle. Despite the injury, he tried to keep pitching; as his September stats show, he shouldn't have.

"His destination in 1988, 15 wins. His goals—30 starts and healthy legs—are well-marked. The course between Rich Yett and success seems clear—barring further detour to . . . the Twilight Zone. . . . "

Geoff Beckman

Yett, Richard Martin "Rich"

Bats: Right   Throws: Right   Born 10/06/62

1987 SEASON AND MAJOR-LEAGUE CAREER PITCHING TOTALS

	G	GS	CG	GF	IP	BFP	H	R	ER	HR	SH	SF	HB	TBB	IBB	SO	WP	Bk	W	L	Pct	ShO	Sv	ERA
87 CLE	37	11	2	13	98	432	96	63	57	21	4	2	3	49	3	59	9	0	3	9	.250	0	1	5.23
3 YEARS	77	15	3	30	177	787	181	112	103	31	6	6	4	88	7	109	18	0	8	12	.400	1	2	5.24

1987: Power, Groundball   1986: Power, Flyball   1985: Power, Flyball

1987 SEASON

	G	IP	H	BB	SO	SB	CS	W	L	S	ERA
Totals	37	97.2	96	49	59	3	8	3	9	1	5.25
at Home	17	41.2	38	19	28	2	4	2	1	0	4.97
on Road	20	56.0	58	30	31	1	4	1	8	1	5.46
on Grass	13	43.1	30	17	20	1	4	2	2	0	3.32
on Artificial Turf	24	54.1	66	32	39	2	4	1	7	1	6.79
Day Games	30	81.0	78	43	50	3	7	3	6	0	5.22
Night Games	7	16.2	18	6	9	0	1	0	3	1	5.40
April	9	18.1	10	6	16	0	2	1	0	0	2.95
May	10	12.0	10	9	7	0	1	0	3	1	8.25
June	8	17.0	22	9	13	1	0	0	2	0	7.41
July	0	0.0	0	0	0	0	0	0	0	0	0.00
August	4	25.0	18	9	14	1	2	2	0	0	0.72
Sept/Oct	6	25.1	36	16	9	1	3	0	4	0	8.53

vs. Opponent Batters	Ave.	OBP	SLG	AB	H	2B	3B	HR	RBI	BB	SO
Totals	.257	.347	.488	373	96	17	3	21	54	49	59
vs. Left	.244	.337	.381	176	43	7	1	5	22	24	29
vs. Right	.269	.356	.584	197	53	10	2	16	32	25	30
Bases Empty	.263	.349	.479	213	56	12	2	10	10	26	28
Leadoff	.333	.394	.611	90	30	3	2	6	6	9	12
Not Leadoff	.211	.317	.382	123	26	9	0	4	4	17	16
Runners On Base	.250	.344	.500	160	40	5	1	11	44	23	31
First Base Only	.276	.329	.605	76	21	1	0	8	16	5	13
Scoring Position	.226	.356	.405	84	19	4	1	3	28	18	18
Late Innings, Close	.220	.339	.360	50	11	1	0	2	7	9	10

FOUR YEAR TOTALS (1984 – 1987)

	G	IP	H	BB	SO	SB	CS	W	L	S	ERA
	77	176.2	181	88	109	6	13	8	12	2	5.25
	38	81.0	86	37	60	2	9	5	2	0	5.22
	39	95.2	95	51	49	4	4	3	10	2	5.27
	23	53.2	39	25	28	1	4	2	1	1	4.02
	54	123.0	142	63	81	5	9	6	10	1	5.78
	64	153.1	156	77	97	5	12	8	9	1	5.11
	13	23.1	25	11	12	1	1	0	3	1	6.17
	13	23.1	17	8	19	1	2	1	0	1	3.86
	21	27.1	26	16	19	1	2	2	3	1	5.93
	15	27.2	34	15	22	1	3	1	2	0	6.18
	6	18.1	20	7	10	1	1	1	1	0	6.38
	10	38.0	36	17	19	1	3	2	1	0	3.55
	12	42.0	48	25	20	1	3	1	5	0	6.00

	Ave.	OBP	SLG	AB	H	2B	3B	HR	RBI	BB	SO
	.265	.351	.460	682	181	32	4	31	105	88	109
	.255	.338	.380	345	88	15	2	8	43	43	52
	.276	.364	.543	337	93	17	2	23	62	45	57
	.250	.327	.434	392	98	18	3	16	16	43	60
	.269	.345	.487	156	42	4	3	8	8	18	21
	.237	.316	.398	236	56	14	0	8	8	25	39
	.286	.382	.497	290	83	14	1	15	89	45	49
	.289	.341	.547	128	37	3	0	10	21	9	21
	.284	.410	.457	162	46	11	1	5	68	36	28
	.252	.353	.427	103	26	3	0	5	21	16	20

RBI/Opportunities

Scoring Position	23 / 121 (19%)
Scoring Position, 2 Out	8 / 64 (13%)
On Third, Less than 2 Out	11 / 21 (52%)
RBI in close games / RBI Total	30 / 54 (56%)

	57 / 249 (23%)
	24 / 128 (19%)
	23 / 47 (49%)
	52 / 105 (50%)

Curt Young
Oakland Athletics

The Oakland A's have been looking for an anchor for their rotation ever since Vida stopped being True Blue and became a Giant. A whole bunch of folks have been auditioned for the spot, including Moose ("Ouch!") Haas, Joaquin ("Youneverknow") Andujar, Rick Langford, and a cast of thousands. Finally, in 1987, they found their man. Nope, not Dave Stewart; although Stew is now 29–18 as an Athletic, in the six previous seasons, he was 30–35 with an ERA of 4.00. The real anchor to this staff also gets my vote as the most overlooked pitcher in the league—not Mark Langston, but Curt Young.

Young has produced good seasons back to back, and with 198 IP in 1986, 203 IP in 1987. In 1986, he faced 4.17 batters per inning, among the best in the AL. In 1987, he improved that to 4.08, second only to Jimmy Key's amazing 3.96 figure. Curt did this by ranking fifteenth in hits per inning (8.60) among the 28 AL hurlers with 200+ innings. His control (1.95 walks per nine innings) very nearly led the league among the 200-inning pitchers, but Floyd Bannister snuck past him with a 1.93 mark.

Actually, Young's winning percentage as an Athletic over the last 2 years is almost exactly the same as Stewart's (.619 versus .617). Young's .650 winning percentage in 1987 (13–7) trailed only Key and Clemens. He increased his complete games to 6 this year, and his ERA of 4.08 is decep-tively high and traceable to a mid-season injury. He strained the bicep on his pitching arm in June, went on the DL for 21 days, and was feeling the effects of the injury even when he returned. At the All-Star break he was 9–5, averaging only 7.4 hits per 9 innings, with an ERA of 3.49. His first 7 starts after the injury he actually managed a winning record (2–1), but had a 7.82 ERA in 35.2 innings. By September he was back to top form with a 2.74 ERA in 7 games.

Young did a great job of keeping the A's in the game when he started. Although Stewart was one of only two 20-game winners in baseball, the team played .538 in Stewart's starts. It was .214 in Rijo's games, .500 for Ontiveros, .538 for Andujar, and only Storm Davis at .600 was close to Young's .613 record for his starts.

There aren't a whole lot of good southpaws in the American League—only 10 pitched 200 or more innings in 1987. Only 7 have averaged 200+ innings for two years. Only Key has faced fewer batters per inning during that period than Young (4.0 vs. 4.1). Only Teddy Higuera (.644) and Key (.620) had a better W–L percentage. A lot of the off-season fanfare in Oakland has been over the strength of the Oakland offense with the addition of Dave Parker. But you can't get to the World Series without good front-line pitching, and A's fans feel pretty good with a big three of Welch, Stewart, and Young.

J. Michael Duca

Young, Curtis Allen "Curt" Bats: Right Throws: Left Born 04/16/60

1987 SEASON AND MAJOR-LEAGUE CAREER PITCHING TOTALS

	G	GS	CG	GF	IP	BFP	H	R	ER	HR	SH	SF	HB	TBB	IBB	SO	WP	Bk	W	L	Pct	ShO	Sv	ERA
87 OAK	31	31	6	0	203	828	194	102	92	38	6	4	3	44	0	124	2	1	13	7	.650	0	0	4.08
5 YEARS	107	84	13	5	565	2393	562	298	270	82	15	18	20	159	1	305	14	3	35	25	.583	3	0	4.30

1987: Finesse, Flyball   1986: Finesse, Flyball   1985: Finesse, Flyball   1984: Finesse, Flyball

1987 SEASON

	G	IP	H	BB	SO	SB	CS	W	L	S	ERA
Totals	31	203.0	194	44	124	9	9	13	7	0	4.08
at Home	13	90.2	78	20	59	4	6	5	3	0	3.67
on Road	18	112.1	116	24	65	5	3	8	4	0	4.41
on Grass	13	83.1	85	20	49	4	3	6	2	0	4.32
on Artificial Turf	18	119.2	109	24	75	5	6	7	5	0	3.91
Day Games	26	172.2	161	37	98	7	8	12	5	0	3.86
Night Games	5	30.1	33	7	26	2	1	1	2	0	5.34
April	5	38.2	30	9	26	2	4	3	1	0	2.79
May	6	46.1	37	10	22	2	3	3	2	0	2.53
June	6	36.1	33	6	24	0	0	3	2	0	5.45
July	2	9.1	11	2	9	0	1	1	0	0	5.79
August	6	34.1	46	5	17	0	1	1	2	0	7.34
Sept/Oct	6	38.0	37	12	26	5	0	2	0	0	2.61

FOUR YEAR TOTALS (1984 – 1987)

	G	IP	H	BB	SO	SB	CS	W	L	S	ERA
	99	555.2	545	154	300	27	23	35	24	0	4.10
	48	292.0	255	82	155	15	14	17	10	0	3.61
	51	263.2	290	72	145	12	9	18	14	0	4.68
	40	218.0	213	69	120	10	5	14	10	0	4.13
	59	337.2	332	85	180	17	18	21	14	0	4.10
	82	479.2	463	125	248	22	22	30	19	0	3.88
	17	76.0	82	29	52	5	1	5	5	0	5.57
	9	57.0	56	19	35	3	5	3	3	0	5.21
	11	81.0	68	16	40	4	4	6	3	0	2.56
	13	84.1	72	23	51	5	1	6	6	0	4.48
	19	88.2	89	31	47	4	5	5	2	0	3.45
	21	106.1	125	25	57	2	3	7	6	0	5.16
	26	138.1	135	40	70	9	5	8	4	0	3.97

vs. Opponent Batters

	Ave.	OBP	SLG	AB	H	2B	3B	HR	RBI	BB	SO
Totals	.252	.293	.453	771	194	35	3	38	96	44	124
vs. Left	.218	.243	.361	147	32	6	0	5	13	3	19
vs. Right	.260	.304	.474	624	162	29	3	33	83	41	105
Bases Empty	.247	.294	.435	494	122	20	2	23	23	31	86
Leadoff	.228	.283	.411	197	45	9	0	9	9	13	32
Not Leadoff	.259	.302	.451	297	77	11	2	14	14	18	54
Runners On Base	.260	.292	.484	277	72	15	1	15	73	13	38
First Base Only	.250	.280	.507	144	36	4	0	11	23	6	19
Scoring Position	.271	.303	.459	133	36	11	1	4	50	7	19
Late Innings, Close	.262	.324	.410	61	16	0	0	3	10	5	6

	Ave.	OBP	SLG	AB	H	2B	3B	HR	RBI	BB	SO
	.255	.305	.427	2137	545	106	9	81	259	154	300
	.225	.263	.318	431	97	13	0	9	43	20	62
	.263	.316	.454	1706	448	93	9	72	216	134	238
	.248	.297	.413	1306	324	62	6	47	47	88	190
	.257	.299	.449	544	140	31	2	23	23	30	68
	.241	.295	.387	762	184	31	4	24	24	58	122
	.266	.319	.449	831	221	44	3	34	212	66	110
	.272	.324	.453	382	104	16	1	17	45	29	46
	.261	.316	.445	449	117	28	2	17	167	37	64
	.219	.269	.329	155	34	5	0	4	15	10	16

RBI/Opportunities

Scoring Position	43 / 166	(26%)
Scoring Position, 2 Out	11 / 70	(16%)
On Third, Less than 2 Out	19 / 30	(63%)
RBI in close games / RBI Total	65 / 96	(68%)

	140 / 596	(23%)
	47 / 263	(18%)
	60 / 104	(58%)
	180 / 259	(69%)

Gerald Young
Houston Astros

See if you can spot the similarities in these three trades:

Sept. 3, 1982—The Astros trade pitcher Don Sutton to the Brewers for pitchers Mike Madden and Frank DiPino, and outfielder Kevin Bass, a player with nine major league at-bats.

Aug. 31, 1984—The Astros trade third baseman Ray Knight to the Mets for infielder Manny Lee, a player to be named and outfielder Gerald Young, a Class AA player with no major league experience.

Dec. 16, 1984—The Astros trade outfielder Jerry Mumphrey to the Cubs for a player to be named and outfielder Billy Hatcher, a player with 172 major league at-bats.

These trades are the kind every baseball executive talks about, but only a few consistently make. In each, the Astros gave up a player in his thirties with good (but diminishing) trade value, for young players, and those young players have contributed. Al Rosen, now general manager of the Giants, made the first two trades. Dick Wagner, now a member of the commissioner's staff, made the last.

In this retooling, the Astros gave up three players who will average 38 years old this season. In return, they got a new outfield.

Young is the latest to display major league ability. He led the Astros in batting average (.321) and stole 26 bases in less than half a season. More than that, he proved himself well-suited to the Astros' game plan. He hits for average and is very fast. With Young in center, Hatcher was able to move to left, a position more in keeping with his offensive abilities. And Young is a switch-hitter; that, too, fits the Astros' mold. They ended the season with eight switch-hitters on their roster, the most in the National League. The Expos were second with 7, followed by the Cardinals (6); Mets, Pirates and Cubs (5); Reds, Dodgers, Padres and Giants (3, if the Giants count Atlee Hammaker); and the Braves and Phillies (2).

That the Astros and Cardinals should rank high in using switch-hitters is not surprising. Before he became manager of the Astros, Hal Lanier was a coach for Whitey Herzog in St. Louis. The feeling here is that using switch-hitters is a matter of personal preference to some degree, and that the success of the Cardinals and Astros has brought switch-hitting back into fashion. After the 1984 season, 43 switch-hitters were listed in the official National League averages; after the 1987 season, 53 were listed (some were not on a major league roster at the end of the season).

The Cardinals used five of their six switch-hitters as regulars; the Astros, with Ashby, Bass, Doran, Caminiti and Young, could match that total next season. Even if they don't, Young figures to get extensive playing time. Though he seems unlikely to hit .321 again—in the minors he never batted higher than .280 over a full season—Young is a player of obvious talent and potential.

Mike O'Donnell

Young, Gerald Anthony

Bats: Both Throws: Right Born 10/22/64

1987 SEASON AND MAJOR-LEAGUE CAREER BATTING TOTALS

	G	AB	H	2B	3B	HR	TB	R	RBI	TBB	IBB	SO	HP	SH	SF	SB	CS	SB%	GDP	AVG	OBP	SLG
87 HOU	71	274	88	9	2	1	104	44	15	26	0	27	1	0	2	26	9	.74	1	.321	.380	.380
1 YEAR	71	274	88	9	2	1	104	44	15	26	0	27	1	0	2	26	9	.74	1	.321	.380	.380

	1987 SEASON											FOUR YEAR TOTALS (1984 – 1987)										
	Ave.	OBP	SLG	AB	H	2B	3B	HR	RBI	BB	SO	Ave.	OBP	SLG	AB	H	2B	3B	HR	RBI	BB	SO
Totals	.321	.380	.380	274	88	9	2	1	15	26	27	.321	.380	.380	274	88	9	2	1	15	26	27
vs. Left	.390	.425	.467	105	41	5	0	1	7	6	12	.390	.425	.467	105	41	5	0	1	7	6	12
vs. Right	.278	.353	.325	169	47	4	2	0	8	20	15	.278	.353	.325	169	47	4	2	0	8	20	15
at Home	.359	.423	.441	145	52	8	2	0	8	16	14	.359	.423	.441	145	52	8	2	0	8	16	14
on Road	.279	.329	.310	129	36	1	0	1	7	10	13	.279	.329	.310	129	36	1	0	1	7	10	13
vs. Groundball	.352	.424	.445	128	45	7	1	1	6	15	13	.352	.424	.445	128	45	7	1	1	6	15	13
vs. Flyball	.295	.340	.322	146	43	2	1	0	9	11	14	.295	.340	.322	146	43	2	1	0	9	11	14
vs. Finesse	.333	.403	.404	156	52	6	1	1	8	18	15	.333	.403	.404	156	52	6	1	1	8	18	15
vs. Power	.305	.346	.347	118	36	3	1	0	7	8	12	.305	.346	.347	118	36	3	1	0	7	8	12
on Grass	.308	.357	.341	91	28	0	0	1	3	7	9	.308	.357	.341	91	28	0	0	1	3	7	9
on Artificial Turf	.328	.390	.399	183	60	9	2	0	12	19	18	.328	.390	.399	183	60	9	2	0	12	19	18
Day Games	.350	.416	.412	80	28	2	0	1	3	8	6	.350	.416	.412	80	28	2	0	1	3	8	6
Night Games	.309	.364	.366	194	60	7	2	0	12	18	21	.309	.364	.366	194	60	7	2	0	12	18	21
April	.000	.000	.000	0	0	0	0	0	0	0	0	.000	.000	.000	0	0	0	0	0	0	0	0
May	.000	.000	.000	0	0	0	0	0	0	0	0	.000	.000	.000	0	0	0	0	0	0	0	0
June	.000	.000	.000	0	0	0	0	0	0	0	0	.000	.000	.000	0	0	0	0	0	0	0	0
July	.262	.306	.308	65	17	3	0	0	6	5	6	.262	.306	.308	65	17	3	0	0	6	5	6
August	.289	.357	.351	114	33	3	2	0	4	11	11	.289	.357	.351	114	33	3	2	0	4	11	11
Sept/Oct	.400	.457	.463	95	38	3	0	1	5	10	10	.400	.457	.463	95	38	3	0	1	5	10	10
Bases Empty	.311	.366	.372	196	61	7	1	1	1	16	18	.311	.366	.372	196	61	7	1	1	1	16	18
Leadoff	.319	.383	.362	116	37	3	1	0	0	11	13	.319	.383	.362	116	37	3	1	0	0	11	13
Not Leadoff	.300	.341	.387	80	24	4	0	1	1	5	5	.300	.341	.387	80	24	4	0	1	1	5	5
Runners On	.346	.411	.397	78	27	2	1	0	14	10	9	.346	.411	.397	78	27	2	1	0	14	10	9
First Base Only	.371	.405	.457	35	13	1	1	0	1	2	6	.371	.405	.457	35	13	1	1	0	1	2	6
Scoring Position	.326	.415	.349	43	14	1	0	0	13	8	3	.326	.415	.349	43	14	1	0	0	13	8	3
Late Innings, Close	.340	.397	.415	53	18	4	0	0	4	5	6	.340	.397	.415	53	18	4	0	0	4	5	6

RBI/Opportunities

Scoring Position	13 / 64 (20%)	13 / 64 (20%)
Scoring Position, 2 Out	5 / 33 (15%)	5 / 33 (15%)
On Third, Less than 2 Out	8 / 12 (67%)	8 / 12 (67%)
RBI in close games / RBI Total	11 / 15 (73%)	11 / 15 (73%)

Matt Young
Los Angeles Dodgers

Matt Young can number himself among two of the less successful groups of the 1980's, promising young Mariner starting pitchers and Dodger relief aces. Of course, the most notable event in Young's career has been his shift from the former group to the latter. However, the change in role and then scenery shortly thereafter did not greatly improve Young's success on the mound, leading to his trade back to the American League.

What's confusing about Young is that he has been effective for good stretches as both a starter and a reliever, only to slip back again. When he came up to Seattle as a starter in '83, it looked for certain that the M's had uncovered a gem, as Matt won 11 games for a bad ball club and turned in an excellent 3.27 ERA. His effectiveness slipped badly the next two seasons, however, and in '85 he was a 19-game loser. As Merrianna McCully noted here last year, one of Young's problems was that he seemed to psyche himself out by worrying too much about his upcoming starts. Hence the switch to the bullpen, which at first was a complete success; over a two-month period in June and July of '86, Matt racked up eight saves, with a sub-2.00 ERA. His mental problems, if that's what they were, seemed to be solved. Used as a reliever, he had less time to think and

seemed to rely more on his natural stuff, which is excellent.

But then he began to struggle again. Matt got hammered during the latter stages of '86, and he was no bargain last year, either. In '87, he seemed far from ideally suited for the life of a relief ace. He did allow very few home runs, but he countered that by yielding way too many hits. And he had decent control, but control is a more valuable skill for a starter than a reliever. All in all, it wasn't pretty. Part of the problem may be that Young has usually had trouble with right-handed hitters, and as a closer was often forced to face the opponents' best righty pinch hitters. Whatever the case, he didn't have the Dodgers forgetting Ron Perranoski. (Heck, he probably had them pining for Ed Vande Berg.)

Now it's on to Oakland, and it's hard to say how the A's are going to use him. One possible role for Young might be as a middle reliever, especially in games in which he comes in for a kayoed righty starter. Used this way, Young would face a higher proportion of lefties, which should increase his effectiveness. His role would be to hold the other team close in the hope the Athletics could catch up—shades of Bob Stanley under Ralph Houk. Middle relief is not a glamorous job, but it beats driving trucks for a living.

Jim Morrow and Don Zminda

Young, Matthew John "Matt"   Bats: Left   Throws: Left   Born 08/09/58

1987 SEASON AND MAJOR-LEAGUE CAREER PITCHING TOTALS

	G	GS	CG	GF	IP	BFP	H	R	ER	HR	SH	SF	HB	TBB	IBB	SO	WP	Bk	W	L	Pct	ShO	Sv	ERA
87 LA	47	0	0	31	54	234	62	30	27	3	1	1	0	17	5	42	3	0	5	8	.385	0	11	4.50
5 YEARS	204	94	12	65	693	3018	731	382	336	63	17	20	23	275	15	463	23	6	42	56	.429	4	25	4.36

1987: Power, Groundball   1986: Power, Groundball   1985: Power, Groundball   1984: Power, Groundball

	1987 SEASON											FOUR YEAR TOTALS (1984 – 1987)										
	G	IP	H	BB	SO	SB	CS	W	L	S	ERA	G	IP	H	BB	SO	SB	CS	W	L	S	ERA
Totals	47	54.2	62	18	43	3	1	5	8	11	4.45	171	490.0	553	197	334	26	25	31	41	25	4.85
at Home	23	30.1	27	6	23	1	1	4	2	6	2.08	90	291.2	288	105	213	12	11	23	16	14	3.76
on Road	24	24.1	35	12	20	2	0	1	6	5	7.40	81	198.1	265	92	121	14	14	8	25	11	6.44
on Grass	14	18.2	24	5	16	1	0	2	1	5	3.86	37	93.2	116	36	62	6	5	6	9	8	4.71
on Artificial Turf	33	36.0	38	13	27	2	1	3	7	6	4.75	134	396.1	437	161	272	20	20	25	32	17	4.88
Day Games	32	38.0	36	10	31	2	1	5	4	9	2.37	73	161.0	202	73	102	13	9	11	18	13	5.93
Night Games	15	16.2	26	8	12	1	0	0	4	2	9.18	98	329.0	351	124	232	13	16	20	23	12	4.29
April	9	8.1	13	4	5	1	1	0	3	1	9.72	24	77.0	93	43	49	6	4	5	10	1	6.43
May	9	9.0	11	4	16	0	0	1	2	3	5.00	33	90.2	100	37	63	3	3	8	6	5	3.87
June	7	10.1	6	2	8	0	0	2	0	2	1.74	31	84.2	95	34	55	6	5	8	7	6	5.63
July	9	15.2	18	5	7	1	0	2	1	2	4.02	28	77.0	95	28	56	3	4	2	4	7	5.03
August	11	10.2	12	3	6	1	0	0	1	3	1.69	29	52.1	51	16	41	5	4	2	5	6	3.96
Sept/Oct	2	0.2	2	0	1	0	0	0	1	0	27.00	26	108.1	119	39	70	3	5	6	9	0	4.24

vs. Opponent Batters	Ave.	OBP	SLG	AB	H	2B	3B	HR	RBI	BB	SO	Ave.	OBP	SLG	AB	H	2B	3B	HR	RBI	BB	SO
Totals	.287	.340	.380	216	62	11	0	3	37	18	43	.286	.352	.415	1931	553	86	12	46	273	197	334
vs. Left	.231	.275	.308	65	15	2	0	1	9	4	12	.243	.310	.317	420	102	12	2	5	45	41	100
vs. Right	.311	.367	.411	151	47	9	0	2	28	14	31	.298	.364	.442	1511	451	74	10	41	228	156	234
Bases Empty	.253	.284	.330	91	23	4	0	1	1	4	19	.274	.336	.411	1005	275	46	7	26	26	94	163
Leadoff	.310	.356	.381	42	13	3	0	0	0	3	10	.291	.348	.400	447	130	22	3	7	7	39	61
Not Leadoff	.204	.220	.286	49	10	1	0	1	1	1	9	.260	.326	.419	558	145	24	4	19	19	55	102
Runners On Base	.312	.379	.416	125	39	7	0	2	36	14	24	.300	.370	.419	926	278	40	5	20	247	103	171
First Base Only	.429	.444	.600	35	15	3	0	1	3	1	6	.295	.343	.389	380	112	16	1	6	14	28	66
Scoring Position	.267	.356	.344	90	24	4	0	1	33	13	18	.304	.387	.440	546	166	24	4	14	233	75	105
Late Innings, Close	.317	.359	.387	142	45	7	0	1	26	10	30	.297	.349	.387	444	132	21	2	5	65	36	84

RBI/Opportunities

Scoring Position	29 / 132 (22%)	200 / 785 (25%)
Scoring Position, 2 Out	7 / 50 (14%)	78 / 364 (21%)
On Third, Less than 2 Out	14 / 37 (38%)	77 / 156 (49%)
RBI in close games / RBI Total	26 / 37 (70%)	179 / 273 (66%)

Mike Young
Baltimore Orioles

Oriole fans have a reputation as some of the most knowledgeable ones in the country; one wonders why so few of them participate in the local talk shows. The abuse that Eddie Murray takes is the most flagrant example of yahooism, but Mike Young's case runs a close second. Tragically, the fans' views about Young seem to mirror the Baltimore management's.

Earl Weaver was responsible for Mike's meteoric rise and at fault for his stunning fall. In August 1985 Mike set a team record for most RBIs in a month; he spent August 1986 in Rochester. Why was a player in his prime (26) sent to AAA after hitting 28 homers and slugging .513 the year before? Maybe Earl will explain it to everyone in his next book.

During spring training in 1987, Mike injured his thumb, was out until May and then had to play himself into shape. Manager Cal Ripken made sure that it didn't happen quickly by benching Mike several times for future stars Lee Lacy and Jim Dwyer. Once Young went into a slump, though, Ripken immediately made him a regular. End result: another wasted year.

Will Young ever match his 1985 level of performance? Between 1987 and 1986, 68 other players both qualified for the batting title (*i.e.,* had 502 plate appearances in a season) and slugged .500 or better. 44 of those men have repeated that level of performance in another season. Twenty others have slugged at least .470 or better. Thus, Mike is almost certain to repeat his 1985 at some point in his career.

The four exceptions to the rule (Ron Kittle, Gary Ward, Leon Roberts and Willie McGee) are very different players save for one thing: each has poor strike zone judgement. If you combine their career walk totals and prorate them into 600 at-bats, they project to draw 43 walks. Mike would average 75; as you can see from his May stats, he's quite willing to let a pitch go by. Why should Young be an exception to the rule when he is not like the other exceptions? Very simply, he shouldn't be.

Actually, Mike's May stats may be the key reason that he's unpopular with the fans and, apparently, Ripken. In his 42 PAs that month, he failed to put the ball into play 21 times. Hitters who don't make contact often— either because they walk a lot, strike out a lot or both—seem to irritate the majority of fans (who worship high batting averages at the expense of everything else) and managers (who counsel hitters to "get your cuts"). That's especially true if the hitter is slumping; he'll usually be told that he won't get any hits if he doesn't swing. You'll notice that the less Mike walked in a month, the more he played.

In 1987, Brooks Robinson said, "You just have to put Mike Young in left field and cross your fingers"; Baltimore should do just that in 1988.

Ken McKusick

Young, Michael Darren "Mike"

Bats: Both   **Throws: Right**   **Born 03/20/60**

1987 SEASON AND MAJOR-LEAGUE CAREER BATTING TOTALS

	G	AB	H	2B	3B	HR	TB	R	RBI	TBB	IBB	SO	HP	SH	SF	SB	CS	SB%	GDP	AVG	OBP	SLG
87 BAL	110	363	87	10	1	16	147	46	39	46	2	91	2	0	1	10	7	.59	7	.240	.328	.405
6 YEARS	520	1621	410	66	6	70	698	227	216	203	11	404	17	9	7	21	15	.58	35	.253	.341	.431

1987 SEASON / FOUR YEAR TOTALS (1984 – 1987)

	Ave.	OBP	SLG	AB	H	2B	3B	HR	RBI	BB	SO	Ave.	OBP	SLG	AB	H	2B	3B	HR	RBI	BB	SO
Totals	.240	.328	.405	363	87	10	1	16	39	46	91	.255	.344	.435	1583	404	64	5	70	214	201	395
vs. Left	.236	.341	.354	144	34	2	0	5	14	21	37	.254	.335	.415	568	144	19	2	23	67	63	124
vs. Right	.242	.318	.438	219	53	8	1	11	25	25	54	.256	.349	.445	1015	260	45	3	47	147	138	271
at Home	.237	.327	.442	190	45	4	1	11	26	24	43	.264	.360	.470	760	201	32	2	40	107	107	179
on Road	.243	.328	.364	173	42	6	0	5	13	22	48	.247	.328	.402	823	203	32	3	30	107	94	216
vs. Groundball	.224	.320	.393	201	45	5	1	9	22	28	45	.242	.332	.435	794	192	31	4	38	107	102	191
vs. Flyball	.259	.337	.420	162	42	5	0	7	17	18	46	.269	.355	.435	789	212	33	1	32	107	99	204
vs. Finesse	.251	.319	.422	187	47	3	1	9	19	18	33	.275	.355	.464	821	226	41	3	36	110	95	173
vs. Power	.227	.337	.386	176	40	7	0	7	20	28	58	.234	.332	.403	762	178	23	2	34	104	106	222
on Grass	.242	.333	.415	318	77	8	1	15	37	42	82	.259	.348	.443	1358	352	49	3	65	191	173	327
on Artificial Turf	.222	.286	.333	45	10	2	0	1	2	4	9	.231	.321	.382	225	52	15	2	5	23	28	68
Day Games	.278	.360	.418	79	22	5	0	2	9	10	15	.234	.317	.381	457	107	23	1	14	47	54	115
Night Games	.229	.319	.401	284	65	5	1	14	30	36	76	.264	.354	.456	1126	297	41	4	56	167	147	280
April	.000	.000	.000	0	0	0	0	0	0	0	0	.243	.364	.351	111	27	6	0	2	11	21	30
May	.242	.405	.424	33	8	0	0	2	3	9	12	.250	.366	.404	208	52	14	0	6	24	38	56
June	.287	.365	.475	101	29	2	1	5	15	12	21	.257	.331	.428	292	75	7	2	13	43	32	76
July	.216	.293	.432	74	16	1	0	5	10	8	15	.235	.304	.431	281	66	10	3	13	33	28	76
August	.220	.312	.293	82	18	3	0	1	4	10	23	.269	.371	.534	264	71	13	0	19	52	42	58
Sept/Oct	.219	.287	.397	73	16	4	0	3	7	7	20	.265	.328	.417	427	113	14	0	17	51	40	99
Bases Empty	.245	.329	.399	208	51	6	1	8	8	24	51	.246	.325	.428	879	216	31	3	41	41	101	222
Leadoff	.223	.310	.291	103	23	1	0	2	2	11	25	.249	.316	.432	377	94	9	0	20	20	35	88
Not Leadoff	.267	.347	.505	105	28	5	1	6	6	13	26	.243	.331	.424	502	122	22	3	21	21	66	134
Runners On	.232	.326	.413	155	36	4	0	8	31	22	40	.267	.358	.443	704	188	33	2	29	173	100	173
First Base Only	.310	.389	.500	84	26	1	0	5	10	11	22	.295	.384	.480	319	94	15	1	14	31	46	70
Scoring Position	.141	.253	.310	71	10	3	0	3	21	11	18	.244	.336	.413	385	94	18	1	15	142	54	103
Late Innings, Close	.290	.362	.516	62	18	2	0	4	9	7	16	.244	.347	.435	262	64	11	0	13	46	41	73

RBI/Opportunities

Scoring Position	17 / 95 (18%)	117 / 540 (22%)
Scoring Position, 2 Out	4 / 47 (9%)	46 / 267 (17%)
On Third, Less than 2 Out	6 / 10 (60%)	37 / 72 (51%)
RBI in close games / RBI Total	22 / 39 (56%)	136 / 214 (64%)

Robin Yount
Milwaukee Brewers

Was there anyone in baseball who deserved to have a better 1987 than Robin Yount did? After two exasperating years, laden with injuries, rehabilitations, power dropoffs and numerous other aggravations, Yount finally got himself back on track last year.

The major step that Yount made in 1987 was in hitting the longball. His batting average stayed right where it was; his on-base percentage was down four points. But his slugging percentage rose 29 points in 1987— even when you account for the league-wide power surge, it was up. That, I assume, is because, as Scott Segrin mentioned in this space last year, Yount was able to do his workouts in the winter of 1986. Since he had to lay off for two years and has only been working out for one, I wouldn't be surprised if he brings up his power even more in 1988.

One thing that didn't change in 1987 was Yount's inconsistent power—most of his homers came in two big bunches. Unlike most players—who have tears where they hit for both average and power—Yount has never really done that. His average is usually pretty consistent; some months he just adds a passel of extra bases to his quota of hits.

Defensively, there were some surprises in Yount's 1987. Robin's stolen 185 bases in his career at a 70.3 percent success rate; had he played for managers who liked to run, he might have over 400 steals by now. He averages a little less than seven triples a year and grounds into a double play once every 52.5 at-bats. The point is that he's fast—not in Bo (zo) Jackson's claws, but he can move. When he was a shortstop, I thought that he was without question the best in the AL at snarfing up pop flies and line drives. He had a howitzer for an arm, too.

Given all that, you'd figure that Yount would have numbers very close to the best in the AL. You'd be right in one respect. Robin's range factor was 2.57—fifth in the AL. But his five assists is awfully low— and not due to the injury, either. Yount had fewer assists per 162 games than he had in either 1985 or 1986. Most puzzling of all, he committed five errors—I wouldn't have expected that at all. Maybe he'll improve with experience. But even if he doesn't, who cares? He's an above-average fielder who hits very well—I'll take that package any day.

Open letter to Tom Trebelhorn: Would you please explain why a .353 hitter led off, a 100-RBI man hit second and were followed by a .269 hitter, a guy with a .371 OB% and only 13 homers and a 28-homer man with a better OB% than the #3 man for most of 1987? Friend, if you put your two best hitters a few spots lower in the lineup, you might find that you score even more runs in 1988—and, if you win the division a few years down the road, you might even get Robin Yount another MVP award.

Geoff Beckman

Yount, Robin R Bats: Right Throws: Right Born 09/16/55

1987 SEASON AND MAJOR-LEAGUE CAREER BATTING TOTALS

	G	AB	H	2B	3B	HR	TB	R	RBI	TBB	IBB	SO	HP	SH	SF	SB	CS	SB%	GDP	AVG	OBP	SLG
87 MIL	158	635	198	25	9	21	304	99	103	76	10	94	1	6	5	19	9	.68	9	.312	.384	.479
14 YEARS	1969	7672	2217	405	91	174	3326	1142	930	611	48	874	21	85	77	185	78	.70	146	.289	.340	.434

	1987 SEASON											FOUR YEAR TOTALS (1984 – 1987)										
	Ave.	OBP	SLG	AB	H	2B	3B	HR	RBI	BB	SO	Ave.	OBP	SLG	AB	H	2B	3B	HR	RBI	BB	SO
Totals	.311	.383	.478	634	197	25	9	21	103	76	94	.301	.370	.454	2246	675	109	26	61	297	254	289
vs. Left	.268	.333	.366	194	52	9	2	2	22	20	28	.283	.358	.412	672	190	29	8	14	82	83	90
vs. Right	.330	.404	.527	440	145	16	7	19	81	56	66	.308	.375	.471	1574	485	80	18	47	215	171	199
at Home	.354	.422	.550	311	110	13	6	12	62	37	47	.319	.385	.496	1116	356	58	17	35	172	120	142
on Road	.269	.345	.409	323	87	12	3	9	41	39	47	.282	.356	.412	1130	319	51	9	26	125	134	147
vs. Groundball	.357	.434	.520	333	119	14	2	12	54	45	44	.332	.412	.487	1079	358	58	7	32	149	148	125
vs. Flyball	.259	.324	.432	301	78	11	7	9	49	31	50	.272	.330	.422	1167	317	51	19	29	148	106	164
vs. Finesse	.309	.361	.469	350	108	16	5	10	53	29	37	.306	.364	.464	1270	388	69	18	32	171	120	119
vs. Power	.313	.407	.489	284	89	9	4	11	50	47	57	.294	.377	.441	976	287	40	8	29	126	134	170
on Grass	.319	.392	.498	530	169	21	7	20	94	66	76	.304	.374	.458	1925	586	86	21	56	262	218	244
on Artificial Turf	.269	.333	.375	104	28	4	2	1	9	10	18	.277	.346	.427	321	89	23	5	5	35	36	45
Day Games	.343	.381	.572	201	69	8	4	10	41	14	36	.302	.361	.489	716	216	38	9	26	100	69	94
Night Games	.296	.384	.434	433	128	17	5	11	62	62	58	.300	.374	.437	1530	459	71	17	35	197	185	195
April	.279	.354	.407	86	24	3	1	2	16	10	13	.294	.368	.398	309	91	12	4	4	35	36	37
May	.293	.371	.500	92	27	5	1	4	6	12	21	.331	.389	.509	344	114	16	3	13	44	33	50
June	.320	.391	.474	97	31	4	1	3	17	12	16	.294	.373	.427	398	117	28	2	7	49	51	55
July	.360	.422	.614	114	41	5	3	6	23	12	19	.303	.376	.481	416	126	22	8	12	61	48	55
August	.296	.362	.365	115	34	3	1	1	15	13	8	.281	.363	.407	430	121	18	3	10	53	56	43
Sept/Oct	.308	.388	.492	130	40	5	2	5	26	17	17	.304	.359	.504	349	106	13	6	15	55	30	49
Bases Empty	.258	.326	.391	345	89	11	4	9	9	35	54	.278	.342	.419	1274	354	60	15	30	30	124	168
Leadoff	.254	.318	.339	118	30	6	2	0	0	11	22	.265	.324	.389	486	129	26	8	6	6	42	63
Not Leadoff	.260	.331	.419	227	59	5	2	9	9	24	32	.286	.353	.438	788	225	34	7	24	24	82	105
Runners On	.374	.446	.581	289	108	14	5	12	94	41	40	.330	.408	.499	972	321	49	11	31	267	130	121
First Base Only	.471	.518	.696	102	48	3	1	6	14	9	9	.365	.416	.590	427	156	20	5	22	54	36	37
Scoring Position	.321	.411	.519	187	60	11	4	6	80	32	31	.303	.402	.428	545	165	29	6	9	213	94	84
Late Innings, Close	.281	.363	.323	96	27	1	0	1	14	14	18	.304	.389	.418	335	102	14	0	8	44	48	44

RBI/Opportunities

	1987	Four Year
Scoring Position	70 / 248 (28%)	193 / 755 (26%)
Scoring Position, 2 Out	31 / 112 (28%)	67 / 316 (21%)
On Third, Less than 2 Out	18 / 33 (55%)	76 / 139 (55%)
RBI in close games / RBI Total	70 / 103 (68%)	200 / 297 (67%)

Abner, Shawn Wesley

Bats: Right Throws: Right Born 06/17/66

1987 SEASON AND MAJOR-LEAGUE CAREER BATTING TOTALS

	G	AB	H	2B	3B	HR	TB	R	RBI	TBB	IBB	SO	HP	SH	SF	SB	CS	SB%	GDP	AVG	OBP	SLG
87 SD	16	47	13	3	1	2	24	5	7	2	0	8	0	0	0	1	0	1.00	0	.277	.306	.511
1 YEAR	16	47	13	3	1	2	24	5	7	2	0	8	0	0	0	1	0	1.00	0	.277	.306	.511

	1987 SEASON											FOUR YEAR TOTALS (1984 – 1987)										
	AVG	OBP	SLG	AB	H	2B	3B	HR	RBI	BB	SO	AVG	OBP	SLG	AB	H	2B	3B	HR	RBI	BB	SO
Totals	.277	.306	.511	47	13	3	1	2	7	2	8	.277	.306	.511	47	13	3	1	2	7	2	8
vs. Left	.231	.259	.346	26	6	1	1	0	2	1	4	.231	.259	.346	26	6	1	1	0	2	1	4
vs. Right	.333	.364	.714	21	7	2	0	2	5	1	4	.333	.364	.714	21	7	2	0	2	5	1	4
At Home	.321	.345	.500	28	9	2	0	1	4	1	5	.321	.345	.500	28	9	2	0	1	4	1	5
On Road	.211	.250	.526	19	4	1	1	1	3	1	3	.211	.250	.526	19	4	1	1	1	3	1	3

Acker, James Justin "Jim"

Bats: Right Throws: Right Born 09/24/58

1987 SEASON AND MAJOR-LEAGUE CAREER PITCHING TOTALS

	G	GS	CG	GF	IP	BFP	H	R	ER	HR	SH	SF	HB	TBB	IBB	SO	WP	Bk	W	L	Pct	ShO	Sv	ERA
87 ATL	68	0	0	41	115	491	109	57	53	11	3	3	4	51	4	68	1	0	4	9	.308	0	14	4.15
5 YEARS	243	27	0	93	526	2260	540	264	235	41	21	17	24	205	15	256	14	1	24	29	.453	0	26	4.02

1987: Finesse, Groundball   1986: Finesse, Groundball   1985: Power, Groundball   1984: Finesse, Groundball

	1987 SEASON										FOUR YEAR TOTALS (1984 – 1987)									
	G	IP	H	BB	SO	SB	CS	W	L	S	ERA	G	IP	H	BB	SO	SB	CS	W	L	S	ERA
Totals	68	114.1	109	51	68	13	3	4	9	14	4.17	205	427.2	437	167	212	38	18	19	28	25	3.96
At Home	34	60.0	56	25	35	7	2	4	1	7	4.50	97	216.0	201	77	108	23	10	10	8	12	3.83
On Road	34	54.1	53	26	33	6	1	0	8	7	3.81	108	211.2	236	90	104	15	8	9	20	13	4.08
vs. Opposing Batters	AVG	OBP	SLG	AB	H	2B	3B	HR	RBI	BB	SO	AVG	OBP	SLG	AB	H	2B	3B	HR	RBI	BB	SO
Totals	.253	.336	.384	430	109	21	1	11	65	51	68	.270	.340	.387	1616	437	69	9	34	219	167	212
vs. Left	.238	.317	.329	231	55	12	0	3	35	27	31	.280	.353	.385	838	235	34	6	14	120	94	87
vs. Right	.271	.358	.447	199	54	9	1	8	30	24	37	.260	.326	.389	778	202	35	3	20	99	73	125

Agosto, Juan Roberto (Gonzalez)

Bats: Left Throws: Left Born 02/23/58

1987 SEASON AND MAJOR-LEAGUE CAREER PITCHING TOTALS

	G	GS	CG	GF	IP	BFP	H	R	ER	HR	SH	SF	HB	TBB	IBB	SO	WP	Bk	W	L	Pct	ShO	Sv	ERA
87 HOU	27	0	0	13	27	118	26	12	8	1	3	0	0	10	1	6	1	0	1	1	.500	0	2	2.67
7 YEARS	198	1	0	71	217	947	227	116	101	10	18	8	10	96	10	116	5	0	10	11	.476	0	18	4.19

1987: Finesse, Groundball   1986: Power, Groundball

	1987 SEASON										TWO YEAR TOTALS (1986 – 1987)									
	G	IP	H	BB	SO	SB	CS	W	L	S	ERA	G	IP	H	BB	SO	SB	CS	W	L	S	ERA
Totals	27	27.1	26	10	6	4	0	1	1	2	2.63	53	52.1	75	28	18	8	1	2	5	3	5.50
At Home	13	15.2	12	5	2	1	0	1	0	2	1.15	26	30.0	37	14	10	3	1	1	1	3	3.90
On Road	14	11.2	14	5	4	3	0	0	1	0	4.63	27	22.1	38	14	8	5	0	1	4	0	7.66
vs. Opposing Batters	AVG	OBP	SLG	AB	H	2B	3B	HR	RBI	BB	SO	AVG	OBP	SLG	AB	H	2B	3B	HR	RBI	BB	SO
Totals	.248	.313	.324	105	26	3	1	1	14	10	6	.339	.418	.425	221	75	9	2	2	40	28	18
vs. Left	.214	.313	.214	28	6	0	0	0	5	4	3	.279	.395	.279	68	19	0	0	0	10	12	11
vs. Right	.260	.313	.364	77	20	3	1	1	9	6	3	.366	.429	.490	153	56	9	2	2	30	16	7

Aguayo, Luis (Muriel)

Bats: Right Throws: Right Born 03/13/59

1987 SEASON AND MAJOR-LEAGUE CAREER BATTING TOTALS

	G	AB	H	2B	3B	HR	TB	R	RBI	TBB	IBB	SO	HP	SH	SF	SB	CS	SB%	GDP	AVG	OBP	SLG
87 PHI	94	209	43	9	1	12	90	25	21	15	1	56	5	3	2	0	0	.00	5	.206	.273	.431
8 YEARS	422	770	184	32	9	30	324	114	88	67	9	151	17	10	8	5	3	.63	17	.239	.311	.421

	1987 SEASON											FOUR YEAR TOTALS (1984 – 1987)										
	AVG	OBP	SLG	AB	H	2B	3B	HR	RBI	BB	SO	AVG	OBP	SLG	AB	H	2B	3B	HR	RBI	BB	SO
Totals	.206	.273	.431	209	43	9	1	12	21	15	56	.237	.312	.428	579	137	26	5	25	66	53	124
vs. Left	.276	.304	.645	76	21	5	1	7	11	2	18	.228	.307	.411	241	55	10	2	10	23	23	44
vs. Right	.165	.257	.308	133	22	4	0	5	10	13	38	.243	.316	.441	338	82	16	3	15	43	30	80
At Home	.207	.245	.435	92	19	4	1	5	10	3	21	.247	.325	.459	283	70	15	3	13	37	25	61
On Road	.205	.293	.427	117	24	5	0	7	11	12	35	.226	.300	.399	296	67	11	2	12	29	28	63

Aguilera, Richard Warren "Rick"

Bats: Right   Throws: Right   Born 12/31/61

1987 SEASON AND MAJOR-LEAGUE CAREER PITCHING TOTALS

	G	GS	CG	GF	IP	BFP	H	R	ER	HR	SH	SF	HB	TBB	IBB	SO	WP	Bk	W	L	Pct	ShO	Sv	ERA
87 NYN	18	17	1	0	115	494	124	53	46	12	7	2	3	33	2	77	9	0	11	3	.786	0	0	3.60
3 YEARS	67	56	5	3	379	1606	387	172	151	35	20	11	12	106	5	255	19	5	31	17	.646	0	0	3.59

1987: Finesse, Groundball   1986: Finesse, Groundball   1985: Finesse, Flyball

	1987 SEASON											FOUR YEAR TOTALS (1984 – 1987)									
	G	IP	H	BB	SO	SB	CS	W	L	S	ERA	G	IP	H	BB	SO	SB	CS	W	L	S	ERA
Totals	18	115.0	124	33	77	6	0	11	3	0	3.60	67	379.0	387	106	255	24	14	31	17	0	3.59
At Home	10	68.1	71	19	48	3	0	6	2	0	3.82	32	182.1	177	48	135	9	4	14	6	0	3.36
On Road	8	46.2	53	14	29	3	0	5	1	0	3.28	35	196.2	210	58	120	15	10	17	11	0	3.80
vs. Opposing Batters	AVG	OBP	SLG	AB	H	2B	3B	HR	RBI	BB	SO	AVG	OBP	SLG	AB	H	2B	3B	HR	RBI	BB	SO
Totals	.276	.329	.421	449	124	23	3	12	45	33	77	.266	.316	.407	1457	387	79	11	35	153	106	255
vs. Left	.299	.358	.443	221	66	8	3	6	21	19	31	.277	.335	.409	714	198	41	7	13	70	60	103
vs. Right	.254	.299	.399	228	58	15	0	6	24	14	46	.254	.298	.405	743	189	38	4	22	83	46	152

Akerfelds, Darrel Wayne

Bats: Right   Throws: Right   Born 06/12/62

1987 SEASON AND MAJOR-LEAGUE CAREER PITCHING TOTALS

	G	GS	CG	GF	IP	BFP	H	R	ER	HR	SH	SF	HB	TBB	IBB	SO	WP	Bk	W	L	Pct	ShO	Sv	ERA
87 CLE	16	13	1	0	75	347	84	60	56	18	2	4	7	38	1	42	7	0	2	6	.250	0	0	6.72
2 YEARS	18	13	1	2	80	373	91	65	60	20	2	4	7	41	2	47	9	0	2	6	.250	0	0	6.75

1987: Power, Flyball   1986: Power, Flyball

	1987 SEASON											FOUR YEAR TOTALS (1984 – 1987)									
	G	IP	H	BB	SO	SB	CS	W	L	S	ERA	G	IP	H	BB	SO	SB	CS	W	L	S	ERA
Totals	16	74.2	84	38	42	11	2	2	6	0	6.75	18	80.0	91	41	47	11	2	2	6	0	6.75
At Home	7	30.2	39	13	15	2	2	0	1	0	7.63	8	32.1	41	14	17	2	2	0	1	0	7.52
On Road	9	44.0	45	25	27	9	0	2	5	0	6.14	10	47.2	50	27	30	9	0	2	5	0	6.23
vs. Opposing Batters	AVG	OBP	SLG	AB	H	2B	3B	HR	RBI	BB	SO	AVG	OBP	SLG	AB	H	2B	3B	HR	RBI	BB	SO
Totals	.284	.374	.530	296	84	13	3	18	48	38	42	.285	.375	.536	319	91	14	3	20	56	41	47
vs. Left	.300	.383	.613	150	45	5	3	12	34	18	21	.288	.370	.590	156	45	5	3	12	34	18	24
vs. Right	.267	.365	.445	146	39	8	0	6	14	20	21	.282	.379	.485	163	46	9	0	8	22	23	23

Aldrich, Jay Robert

Bats: Right   Throws: Right   Born 04/14/61

1987 SEASON AND MAJOR-LEAGUE CAREER PITCHING TOTALS

	G	GS	CG	GF	IP	BFP	H	R	ER	HR	SH	SF	HB	TBB	IBB	SO	WP	Bk	W	L	Pct	ShO	Sv	ERA
87 MIL	31	0	0	9	58	253	71	33	32	8	3	3	2	13	3	22	1	1	3	1	.750	0	0	4.97
1 YEAR	31	0	0	9	58	253	71	33	32	8	3	3	2	13	3	22	1	1	3	1	.750	0	0	4.97

1987: Finesse, Groundball

	1987 SEASON											FOUR YEAR TOTALS (1984 – 1987)									
	G	IP	H	BB	SO	SB	CS	W	L	S	ERA	G	IP	H	BB	SO	SB	CS	W	L	S	ERA
Totals	31	58.1	71	13	22	2	3	3	1	0	4.94	31	58.1	71	13	22	2	3	3	1	0	4.94
At Home	18	30.1	43	8	14	0	2	3	1	0	6.23	18	30.1	43	8	14	0	2	3	1	0	6.23
On Road	13	28.0	28	5	8	2	1	0	0	0	3.54	13	28.0	28	5	8	2	1	0	0	0	3.54
vs. Opposing Batters	AVG	OBP	SLG	AB	H	2B	3B	HR	RBI	BB	SO	AVG	OBP	SLG	AB	H	2B	3B	HR	RBI	BB	SO
Totals	.306	.344	.461	232	71	8	2	8	41	13	22	.306	.344	.461	232	71	8	2	8	41	13	22
vs. Left	.282	.336	.464	110	31	1	2	5	19	9	10	.282	.336	.464	110	31	1	2	5	19	9	10
vs. Right	.328	.352	.459	122	40	7	0	3	22	4	12	.328	.352	.459	122	40	7	0	3	22	4	12

Allen, Neil Patrick

Bats: Right   Throws: Right   Born 01/24/58

1987 SEASON AND MAJOR-LEAGUE CAREER PITCHING TOTALS

	G	GS	CG	GF	IP	BFP	H	R	ER	HR	SH	SF	HB	TBB	IBB	SO	WP	Bk	W	L	Pct	ShO	Sv	ERA
87 CHA-NYA	23	11	0	6	75	342	97	52	49	8	4	2	2	36	1	42	1	0	0	8	.000	0	0	5.88
9 YEARS	390	57	7	211	869	3727	856	408	371	58	47	30	7	380	61	550	37	3	53	66	.445	5	75	3.84

1987: Finesse, Groundball   1986: Finesse, Groundball   1985: Power, Flyball   1984: Finesse, Groundball

	1987 SEASON											FOUR YEAR TOTALS (1984 – 1987)									
	G	IP	H	BB	SO	SB	CS	W	L	S	ERA	G	IP	H	BB	SO	SB	CS	W	L	S	ERA
Totals	23	74.1	97	36	42	5	5	0	8	0	5.93	142	364.2	361	153	191	14	21	18	20	6	4.22
At Home	12	45.2	59	20	19	0	2	0	5	0	4.93	65	175.1	160	66	93	3	7	10	6	4	3.80
On Road	11	28.2	38	16	23	5	3	0	3	0	7.53	77	189.1	201	87	98	11	14	8	14	2	4.61
vs. Opposing Batters	AVG	OBP	SLG	AB	H	2B	3B	HR	RBI	BB	SO	AVG	OBP	SLG	AB	H	2B	3B	HR	RBI	BB	SO
Totals	.326	.399	.477	298	97	15	3	8	53	36	42	.262	.337	.376	1376	361	62	8	26	183	153	191
vs. Left	.303	.368	.485	165	50	7	1	7	25	17	23	.250	.326	.373	659	165	28	4	15	76	74	95
vs. Right	.353	.436	.466	133	47	8	2	1	28	19	19	.273	.346	.378	717	196	34	4	11	107	79	96

344

Almon, William Francis "Bill"

Bats: Right   Throws: Right   Born 11/21/52

1987 SEASON AND MAJOR-LEAGUE CAREER BATTING TOTALS

	G	AB	H	2B	3B	HR	TB	R	RBI	TBB	IBB	SO	HP	SH	SF	SB	CS	SB%	GDP	AVG	OBP	SLG
87 PIT-NYN	68	74	17	4	0	0	21	13	5	9	0	21	0	0	0	1	0	1.00	0	.230	.313	.284
14 YEARS	1216	3304	843	136	25	36	1137	389	295	247	24	625	6	42	29	128	60	.68	53	.255	.306	.344

1987 SEASON	AVG	OBP	SLG	AB	H	2B	3B	HR	RBI	BB	SO
Totals	.230	.313	.284	74	17	4	0	0	5	9	21
vs. Left	.205	.271	.250	44	9	2	0	0	2	4	11
vs. Right	.267	.371	.333	30	8	2	0	0	3	5	10
At Home	.300	.400	.300	30	9	0	0	0	3	5	8
On Road	.182	.250	.273	44	8	4	0	0	2	4	13

FOUR YEAR TOTALS (1984 – 1987)	AVG	OBP	SLG	AB	H	2B	3B	HR	RBI	BB	SO
	.239	.304	.381	725	173	39	2	20	76	72	162
	.242	.312	.388	433	105	23	2	12	31	44	89
	.233	.294	.370	292	68	16	0	8	45	28	73
	.263	.338	.419	372	98	22	0	12	46	44	76
	.212	.268	.340	353	75	17	2	8	30	28	86

Andersen, Larry Eugene

Bats: Right   Throws: Right   Born 05/06/53

1987 SEASON AND MAJOR-LEAGUE CAREER PITCHING TOTALS

	G	GS	CG	GF	IP	BFP	H	R	ER	HR	SH	SF	HB	TBB	IBB	SO	WP	Bk	W	L	Pct	ShO	Sv	ERA
87 HOU	67	0	0	31	102	440	95	46	39	7	7	4	2	41	10	94	1	0	9	5	.643	0	5	3.44
10 YEARS	356	1	0	136	555	2352	556	263	226	43	31	24	12	183	37	345	11	3	21	20	.512	0	19	3.66

1987: Power, Groundball   1986: Finesse, Groundball   1985: Power, Groundball   1984: Finesse, Groundball

1987 SEASON	G	IP	H	BB	SO	SB	CS	W	L	S	ERA
Totals	67	101.2	95	41	94	8	1	9	5	5	3.45
At Home	33	52.2	47	20	52	4	1	4	4	1	2.56
On Road	34	49.0	48	21	42	4	0	5	1	4	4.41

vs. Opposing Batters	AVG	OBP	SLG	AB	H	2B	3B	HR	RBI	BB	SO
Totals	.247	.319	.366	385	95	19	3	7	42	41	94
vs. Left	.232	.324	.342	190	44	12	0	3	22	26	41
vs. Right	.262	.315	.390	195	51	7	3	4	20	15	53

FOUR YEAR TOTALS (1984 – 1987)	G	IP	H	BB	SO	SB	CS	W	L	S	ERA
	236	342.2	341	118	240	40	17	17	16	13	3.23
	114	169.0	153	53	119	18	9	10	6	5	2.66
	122	173.2	188	65	121	22	8	7	10	8	3.83

	AVG	OBP	SLG	AB	H	2B	3B	HR	RBI	BB	SO
	.264	.325	.369	1294	341	57	11	19	168	118	240
	.272	.351	.375	603	164	27	4	9	80	74	100
	.256	.301	.363	691	177	30	7	10	88	44	140

Andujar, Joaquin

Bats: Both   Throws: Right   Born 12/21/52

1987 SEASON AND MAJOR-LEAGUE CAREER PITCHING TOTALS

	G	GS	CG	GF	IP	BFP	H	R	ER	HR	SH	SF	HB	TBB	IBB	SO	WP	Bk	W	L	Pct	ShO	Sv	ERA
87 OAK	13	13	1	0	61	265	63	43	41	11	1	1	3	26	0	32	0	1	3	5	.375	0	0	6.05
12 YEARS	382	295	68	33	2075	8657	1922	912	822	146	93	51	46	710	60	997	33	30	125	113	.525	19	9	3.57

1987: Finesse, Groundball   1986: Finesse, Groundball   1985: Finesse, Flyball   1984: Finesse, Flyball

1987 SEASON	G	IP	H	BB	SO	SB	CS	W	L	S	ERA
Totals	13	60.2	63	26	32	5	1	3	5	0	6.08
At Home	9	40.1	40	20	24	5	0	1	4	0	6.02
On Road	4	20.1	23	6	8	0	1	2	1	0	6.20

vs. Opposing Batters	AVG	OBP	SLG	AB	H	2B	3B	HR	RBI	BB	SO
Totals	.269	.348	.449	234	63	7	1	11	38	26	32
vs. Left	.267	.356	.397	116	31	4	1	3	17	16	15
vs. Right	.271	.341	.500	118	32	3	0	8	21	10	17

FOUR YEAR TOTALS (1984 – 1987)	G	IP	H	BB	SO	SB	CS	W	L	S	ERA
	115	747.0	685	234	363	75	19	56	38	1	3.67
	62	411.2	369	131	215	44	11	26	28	1	3.74
	53	335.1	316	103	148	31	8	30	10	0	3.62

	AVG	OBP	SLG	AB	H	2B	3B	HR	RBI	BB	SO
	.246	.305	.371	2789	685	109	17	69	290	234	363
	.265	.330	.393	1383	366	60	8	34	147	136	143
	.227	.279	.349	1406	319	49	9	35	143	98	220

Armas, Antonio Rafael (Machado) "Tony"

Bats: Right   Throws: Right   Born 07/02/53

1987 SEASON AND MAJOR-LEAGUE CAREER BATTING TOTALS

	G	AB	H	2B	3B	HR	TB	R	RBI	TBB	IBB	SO	HP	SH	SF	SB	CS	SB%	GDP	AVG	OBP	SLG
87 CAL	28	81	16	3	1	3	30	8	9	1	0	11	0	1	1	1	0	1.00	3	.198	.205	.370
12 YEARS	1252	4594	1150	177	36	227	2080	550	736	231	35	1066	15	10	48	17	17	.50	134	.250	.286	.453

1987 SEASON	AVG	OBP	SLG	AB	H	2B	3B	HR	RBI	BB	SO
Totals	.198	.205	.370	81	16	3	1	3	9	1	11
vs. Left	.216	.216	.412	51	11	2	1	2	7	0	5
vs. Right	.167	.188	.300	30	5	1	0	1	2	1	6
At Home	.176	.171	.324	34	6	2	0	1	4	0	3
On Road	.213	.229	.404	47	10	1	1	2	5	1	8

FOUR YEAR TOTALS (1984 – 1987)	AVG	OBP	SLG	AB	H	2B	3B	HR	RBI	BB	SO
	.262	.296	.484	1530	401	70	15	80	254	75	334
	.281	.320	.472	470	132	27	6	17	64	29	76
	.254	.285	.490	1060	269	43	9	63	190	46	258
	.279	.321	.507	732	204	39	7	38	141	46	130
	.247	.272	.464	798	197	31	8	42	113	29	204

Arnold, Tony Dale
Bats: Right   Throws: Right   Born 05/03/59

1987 SEASON AND MAJOR-LEAGUE CAREER PITCHING TOTALS

	G	GS	CG	GF	IP	BFP	H	R	ER	HR	SH	SF	HB	TBB	IBB	SO	WP	Bk	W	L	Pct	ShO	Sv	ERA
87 BAL	27	0	0	10	53	239	71	35	34	8	4	1	2	17	5	18	1	0	0	0	.000	0	0	5.77
2 YEARS	38	0	0	13	78	343	96	50	44	8	7	1	2	28	8	25	1	0	0	2	.000	0	0	5.08

1987: Finesse, Groundball   1986: Finesse, Flyball

	1987 SEASON											FOUR YEAR TOTALS (1984 – 1987)										
	G	IP	H	BB	SO	SB	CS	W	L	S	ERA	G	IP	H	BB	SO	SB	CS	W	L	S	ERA
Totals	27	53.0	71	17	18	4	2	0	0	0	5.77	38	78.1	96	28	25	5	5	0	2	0	5.06
At Home	13	29.1	34	10	7	1	2	0	0	0	5.22	20	47.0	46	18	14	2	4	0	1	0	3.83
On Road	14	23.2	37	7	11	3	0	0	0	0	6.46	18	31.1	50	10	11	3	1	0	1	0	6.89

vs. Opposing Batters	AVG	OBP	SLG	AB	H	2B	3B	HR	RBI	BB	SO	AVG	OBP	SLG	AB	H	2B	3B	HR	RBI	BB	SO
Totals	.330	.383	.544	215	71	18	2	8	40	17	18	.315	.375	.485	305	96	22	3	8	48	28	25
vs. Left	.351	.407	.714	77	27	9	2	5	20	8	6	.304	.367	.574	115	35	10	3	5	24	12	8
vs. Right	.319	.369	.449	138	44	9	0	3	20	9	12	.321	.380	.432	190	61	12	0	3	24	16	17

Assenmacher, Paul Andre
Bats: Left   Throws: Left   Born 12/10/60

1987 SEASON AND MAJOR-LEAGUE CAREER PITCHING TOTALS

	G	GS	CG	GF	IP	BFP	H	R	ER	HR	SH	SF	HB	TBB	IBB	SO	WP	Bk	W	L	Pct	ShO	Sv	ERA
87 ATL	52	0	0	10	55	251	58	41	31	8	2	1	1	24	4	39	0	0	1	1	.500	0	2	5.07
2 YEARS	113	0	0	37	123	538	119	64	50	13	9	2	1	50	8	95	2	3	8	4	.667	0	9	3.66

1987: Power, Flyball   1986: Power, Groundball

	1987 SEASON											FOUR YEAR TOTALS (1984 – 1987)										
	G	IP	H	BB	SO	SB	CS	W	L	S	ERA	G	IP	H	BB	SO	SB	CS	W	L	S	ERA
Totals	52	54.2	58	24	39	2	0	1	1	2	5.10	113	123.0	119	50	95	6	3	8	4	9	3.66
At Home	22	26.1	32	6	17	1	0	0	0	2	5.47	53	65.1	56	17	52	4	2	4	1	7	2.89
On Road	30	28.1	26	18	22	1	0	1	1	0	4.76	60	57.2	63	33	43	2	1	4	3	2	4.53

vs. Opposing Batters	AVG	OBP	SLG	AB	H	2B	3B	HR	RBI	BB	SO	AVG	OBP	SLG	AB	H	2B	3B	HR	RBI	BB	SO
Totals	.260	.333	.448	223	58	14	2	8	43	24	39	.250	.322	.387	476	119	18	4	13	70	50	95
vs. Left	.177	.261	.253	79	14	3	0	1	8	8	17	.225	.307	.306	160	36	5	1	2	17	18	36
vs. Right	.306	.373	.556	144	44	11	2	7	35	16	22	.263	.330	.427	316	83	13	3	11	53	32	59

Atherton, Keith Rowe
Bats: Right   Throws: Right   Born 02/19/59

1987 SEASON AND MAJOR-LEAGUE CAREER PITCHING TOTALS

	G	GS	CG	GF	IP	BFP	H	R	ER	HR	SH	SF	HB	TBB	IBB	SO	WP	Bk	W	L	Pct	ShO	Sv	ERA
87 MIN	59	0	0	29	79	348	81	46	40	10	2	3	4	30	4	51	1	0	7	5	.583	0	2	4.56
5 YEARS	261	0	0	131	453	1944	433	217	205	58	17	24	8	180	28	293	9	1	26	33	.441	0	21	4.07

1987: Finesse, Flyball   1986: Power, Flyball   1985: Power, Flyball   1984: Power, Flyball

	1987 SEASON											FOUR YEAR TOTALS (1984 – 1987)										
	G	IP	H	BB	SO	SB	CS	W	L	S	ERA	G	IP	H	BB	SO	SB	CS	W	L	S	ERA
Totals	59	79.1	81	30	51	8	1	7	5	2	4.54	232	385.0	380	157	253	30	15	24	28	17	4.30
At Home	28	37.1	32	13	26	6	0	5	1	1	2.89	118	197.2	173	83	141	17	6	15	8	10	3.60
On Road	31	42.0	49	17	25	2	1	2	4	1	6.00	114	187.1	207	74	112	13	9	9	20	7	5.04

vs. Opposing Batters	AVG	OBP	SLG	AB	H	2B	3B	HR	RBI	BB	SO	AVG	OBP	SLG	AB	H	2B	3B	HR	RBI	BB	SO
Totals	.262	.332	.424	309	81	14	3	10	51	30	51	.259	.331	.426	1469	380	71	11	51	220	157	253
vs. Left	.265	.339	.444	162	43	7	2	6	25	17	28	.281	.368	.462	676	190	31	5	27	96	92	104
vs. Right	.259	.325	.401	147	38	7	1	4	26	13	23	.240	.299	.396	793	190	40	6	24	124	65	149

Bailey, John Mark "Mark"
Bats: Both   Throws: Right   Born 11/04/61

1987 SEASON AND MAJOR-LEAGUE CAREER BATTING TOTALS

	G	AB	H	2B	3B	HR	TB	R	RBI	TBB	IBB	SO	HP	SH	SF	SB	CS	SB%	GDP	AVG	OBP	SLG
87 HOU	35	64	13	1	0	0	14	5	3	10	0	21	0	1	0	1	0	1.00	3	.203	.311	.219
4 YEARS	314	893	201	36	1	23	308	99	97	158	23	207	3	3	5	2	4	.33	33	.225	.342	.345

	1987 SEASON											FOUR YEAR TOTALS (1984 – 1987)									
	AVG	OBP	SLG	AB	H	2B	3B	HR	RBI	BB	SO	AVG	OBP	SLG	AB	H	2B	3B	HR	RBI	BB	SO
Totals	.203	.311	.219	64	13	1	0	0	3	10	21	.225	.342	.345	893	201	36	1	23	97	158	207
vs. Left	.214	.333	.250	28	6	1	0	0	2	5	7	.239	.352	.347	331	79	15	0	7	36	57	63
vs. Right| .194	.293	.194	36	7	0	0	0	1	5	14	.217	.336	.343	562	122	21	1	16	61	101	144
At Home	.269	.406	.308	26	7	1	0	0	1	6	9	.249	.363	.381	441	110	22	0	12	52	79	102
On Road	.158	.238	.158	38	6	0	0	0	2	4	12	.201	.322	.310	452	91	14	1	11	45	79	105

Balboni, Stephen Charles "Steve"
Bats: Right   Throws: Right   Born 01/16/57

1987 SEASON AND MAJOR-LEAGUE CAREER BATTING TOTALS

	G	AB	H	2B	3B	HR	TB	R	RBI	TBB	IBB	SO	HP	SH	SF	SB	CS	SB%	GDP	AVG	OBP	SLG
87 KC	121	386	80	11	1	24	165	44	60	34	1	97	2	0	3	0	0	.00	11	.207	.273	.427
7 YEARS	614	2136	492	92	8	124	972	248	336	189	12	609	12	0	17	1	1	.50	45	.230	.294	.455

	1987 SEASON												FOUR YEAR TOTALS (1984 – 1987)									
	AVG	OBP	SLG	AB	H	2B	3B	HR	RBI	BB	SO		AVG	OBP	SLG	AB	H	2B	3B	HR	RBI	BB	SO
Totals	.207	.273	.427	386	80	11	1	24	60	34	97		.232	.297	.465	1937	450	87	6	117	312	174	548
vs. Left	.194	.265	.379	103	20	1	0	6	10	10	27		.242	.333	.477	553	134	22	0	36	79	75	165
vs. Right	.212	.276	.445	283	60	10	1	18	50	24	70		.228	.283	.460	1384	316	65	6	81	233	99	383
At Home	.189	.255	.347	190	36	6	0	8	22	16	49		.219	.280	.424	963	211	54	4	45	142	79	262
On Road	.224	.290	.505	196	44	5	1	16	38	18	48		.245	.315	.505	974	239	33	2	72	170	95	286

Ballard, Jeffrey Scott "Jeff"
Bats: Left   Throws: Left   Born 08/13/63

1987 SEASON AND MAJOR-LEAGUE CAREER PITCHING TOTALS

	G	GS	CG	GF	IP	BFP	H	R	ER	HR	SH	SF	HB	TBB	IBB	SO	WP	Bk	W	L	Pct	ShO	Sv	ERA
87 BAL	14	14	0	0	70	327	100	60	51	15	0	1	0	35	1	27	0	1	2	8	.200	0	0	6.56
1 YEAR	14	14	0	0	70	327	100	60	51	15	0	1	0	35	1	27	0	1	2	8	.200	0	0	6.56

1987: Finesse, Groundball

	1987 SEASON											FOUR YEAR TOTALS (1984 – 1987)										
	G	IP	H	BB	SO	SB	CS	W	L	S	ERA		G	IP	H	BB	SO	SB	CS	W	L	S	ERA
Totals	14	69.2	100	35	27	9	7	2	8	0	6.59		14	69.2	100	35	27	9	7	2	8	0	6.59
At Home	9	41.1	61	25	15	8	4	0	7	0	7.62		9	41.1	61	25	15	8	4	0	7	0	7.62
On Road	5	28.1	39	10	12	1	3	2	1	0	5.08		5	28.1	39	10	12	1	3	2	1	0	5.08
vs. Opposing Batters	AVG	OBP	SLG	AB	H	2B	3B	HR	RBI	BB	SO		AVG	OBP	SLG	AB	H	2B	3B	HR	RBI	BB	SO
Totals	.344	.413	.560	291	100	18	0	15	51	35	27		.344	.413	.560	291	100	18	0	15	51	35	27
vs. Left	.385	.478	.615	39	15	3	0	2	7	7	5		.385	.478	.615	39	15	3	0	2	7	7	5
vs. Right	.337	.402	.552	252	85	15	0	13	44	28	22		.337	.402	.552	252	85	15	0	13	44	28	22

Baller, Jay Scot
Bats: Right   Throws: Right   Born 10/06/60

1987 SEASON AND MAJOR-LEAGUE CAREER PITCHING TOTALS

	G	GS	CG	GF	IP	BFP	H	R	ER	HR	SH	SF	HB	TBB	IBB	SO	WP	Bk	W	L	Pct	ShO	Sv	ERA
87 CHN	23	0	0	9	29	139	38	22	22	4	2	0	0	20	2	27	5	2	0	1	.000	0	0	6.83
4 YEARS	83	5	0	30	143	645	155	84	77	20	11	0	4	67	13	107	9	7	4	8	.333	0	6	4.85

1987: Power, Flyball   1986: Power, Flyball   1985: Finesse, Flyball

	1987 SEASON											FOUR YEAR TOTALS (1984 – 1987)										
	G	IP	H	BB	SO	SB	CS	W	L	S	ERA		G	IP	H	BB	SO	SB	CS	W	L	S	ERA
Totals	23	29.1	38	20	27	2	0	0	1	0	6.75		79	135.0	148	65	100	11	6	4	8	6	4.93
At Home	9	11.0	15	7	9	1	0	0	1	0	6.55		34	53.2	68	23	47	4	2	3	4	2	5.70
On Road	14	18.1	23	13	18	1	0	0	0	0	6.87		45	81.1	80	42	53	7	4	1	4	4	4.43
vs. Opposing Batters	AVG	OBP	SLG	AB	H	2B	3B	HR	RBI	BB	SO		AVG	OBP	SLG	AB	H	2B	3B	HR	RBI	BB	SO
Totals	.325	.423	.496	117	38	6	1	4	23	20	27		.280	.359	.485	528	148	37	7	19	81	65	100
vs. Left	.415	.492	.698	53	22	4	1	3	14	8	9		.292	.372	.459	281	82	19	5	6	34	36	43
vs. Right	.250	.368	.328	64	16	2	0	1	9	12	18		.267	.344	.514	247	66	18	2	13	47	29	57

Bando, Christopher Michael "Chris"
Bats: Both   Throws: Right   Born 02/04/56

1987 SEASON AND MAJOR-LEAGUE CAREER BATTING TOTALS

	G	AB	H	2B	3B	HR	TB	R	RBI	TBB	IBB	SO	HP	SH	SF	SB	CS	SB%	GDP	AVG	OBP	SLG
87 CLE	89	211	46	9	0	5	70	20	16	12	0	28	0	6	0	0	0	.00	6	.218	.260	.332
7 YEARS	464	1210	282	45	2	26	409	128	133	130	6	184	1	24	14	1	5	.17	40	.233	.305	.338

	1987 SEASON												FOUR YEAR TOTALS (1984 – 1987)									
	AVG	OBP	SLG	AB	H	2B	3B	HR	RBI	BB	SO		AVG	OBP	SLG	AB	H	2B	3B	HR	RBI	BB	SO
Totals	.218	.260	.332	211	46	9	0	5	16	12	28		.235	.305	.343	858	202	33	1	19	96	89	133
vs. Left	.176	.208	.176	51	9	0	0	0	0	2	6		.246	.284	.331	305	75	9	1	5	31	17	37
vs. Right	.231	.276	.381	160	37	9	0	5	16	10	22		.230	.316	.349	553	127	24	0	14	65	72	96
At Home	.233	.275	.320	103	24	3	0	2	7	6	12		.249	.313	.351	413	103	16	1	8	50	41	59
On Road	.204	.246	.343	108	22	6	0	3	9	6	16		.222	.298	.335	445	99	17	0	11	46	48	74

Bankhead, Michael Scott "Scott"

Bats: Right **Throws: Right** **Born 07/31/63**

1987 SEASON AND MAJOR-LEAGUE CAREER PITCHING TOTALS

	G	GS	CG	GF	IP	BFP	H	R	ER	HR	SH	SF	HB	TBB	IBB	SO	WP	Bk	W	L	Pct	ShO	Sv	ERA
87 SEA	27	25	2	1	149	642	168	96	90	35	3	6	3	37	0	95	2	2	9	8	.529	0	0	5.44
2 YEARS	51	42	2	3	270	1159	289	162	152	49	8	11	6	74	7	189	3	2	17	17	.500	0	0	5.07

1987: Finesse, Flyball   1986: Power, Flyball

	1987 SEASON											FOUR YEAR TOTALS (1984 – 1987)										
	G	IP	H	BB	SO	SB	CS	W	L	S	ERA	G	IP	H	BB	SO	SB	CS	W	L	S	ERA
Totals	27	149.1	167	37	95	9	5	9	8	0	5.42	51	270.1	288	74	189	18	9	17	17	0	5.06
At Home	12	72.2	73	17	51	5	3	5	3	0	4.58	26	136.1	140	36	98	11	5	9	9	0	5.15
On Road	15	76.2	94	20	44	4	2	4	5	0	6.22	25	134.0	148	38	91	7	4	8	8	0	4.97

vs. Opposing Batters	AVG	OBP	SLG	AB	H	2B	3B	HR	RBI	BB	SO	AVG	OBP	SLG	AB	H	2B	3B	HR	RBI	BB	SO
Totals	.282	.324	.528	593	167	29	6	35	91	37	95	.272	.319	.479	1060	288	53	10	49	147	74	189
vs. Left	.296	.330	.503	328	97	20	6	12	47	17	45	.271	.314	.463	601	163	28	9	23	86	38	99
vs. Right	.264	.317	.558	265	70	9	0	23	44	20	50	.272	.326	.501	459	125	25	1	26	61	36	90

Barker, Leonard Harold "Len"

Bats: Right **Throws: Right** **Born 07/07/55**

1987 SEASON AND MAJOR-LEAGUE CAREER PITCHING TOTALS

	G	GS	CG	GF	IP	BFP	H	R	ER	HR	SH	SF	HB	TBB	IBB	SO	WP	Bk	W	L	Pct	ShO	Sv	ERA
87 MIL	11	11	0	0	44	198	54	27	26	6	1	0	2	17	1	22	0	0	2	1	.667	0	0	5.32
11 YEARS	248	194	35	26	1323	5674	1289	695	639	96	65	41	21	513	20	975	65	2	74	76	.493	7	5	4.35

1987: Finesse, Groundball

	1987 SEASON											TWO YEAR TOTALS (1986 – 1987)										
	G	IP	H	BB	SO	SB	CS	W	L	S	ERA	G	IP	H	BB	SO	SB	CS	W	L	S	ERA
Totals	11	43.2	54	17	22	3	3	2	1	0	5.36	11	43.2	54	17	22	3	3	2	1	0	5.36
At Home	6	22.2	25	10	11	0	3	2	1	0	4.37	6	22.2	25	10	11	0	3	2	1	0	4.37
On Road	5	21.0	29	7	11	3	0	0	0	0	6.43	5	21.0	29	7	11	3	0	0	0	0	6.43

vs. Opposing Batters	AVG	OBP	SLG	AB	H	2B	3B	HR	RBI	BB	SO	AVG	OBP	SLG	AB	H	2B	3B	HR	RBI	BB	SO
Totals	.303	.371	.478	178	54	9	2	6	24	17	22	.303	.371	.478	178	54	9	2	6	24	17	22
vs. Left	.360	.433	.558	86	31	7	2	2	15	9	10	.360	.433	.558	86	31	7	2	2	15	9	10
vs. Right	.250	.310	.402	92	23	2	0	4	9	8	12	.250	.310	.402	92	23	2	0	4	9	8	12

Bean, William Daro "Bill"

Bats: Left **Throws: Left** **Born 03/29/62**

1987 SEASON AND MAJOR-LEAGUE CAREER BATTING TOTALS

	G	AB	H	2B	3B	HR	TB	R	RBI	TBB	IBB	SO	HP	SH	SF	SB	CS	SB%	GDP	AVG	OBP	SLG
87 DET	26	66	17	2	0	0	19	6	4	5	0	11	0	0	0	1	1	.50	1	.258	.310	.288
1 YEAR	26	66	17	2	0	0	19	6	4	5	0	11	0	0	0	1	1	.50	1	.258	.310	.288

	1987 SEASON										FOUR YEAR TOTALS (1984 – 1987)									
	AVG	OBP	SLG	AB	H	2B	3B	HR	RBI	BB	SO	AVG	OBP	SLG	AB	H	2B	3B	HR	RBI	BB	SO
Totals	.258	.310	.288	66	17	2	0	0	4	5	11	.258	.310	.288	66	17	2	0	0	4	5	11
vs. Left	.000	.000	.000	0	0	0	0	0	0	0	0	.000	.000	.000	0	0	0	0	0	0	0	0
vs. Right	.258	.310	.288	66	17	2	0	0	4	5	11	.258	.310	.288	66	17	2	0	0	4	5	11
At Home	.364	.400	.424	33	12	2	0	0	3	2	7	.364	.400	.424	33	12	2	0	0	3	2	7
On Road	.152	.222	.152	33	5	0	0	0	1	3	4	.152	.222	.152	33	5	0	0	0	1	3	4

Bell, Jay Stuart

Bats: Right **Throws: Right** **Born 12/11/65**

1987 SEASON AND MAJOR-LEAGUE CAREER BATTING TOTALS

	G	AB	H	2B	3B	HR	TB	R	RBI	TBB	IBB	SO	HP	SH	SF	SB	CS	SB%	GDP	AVG	OBP	SLG
87 CLE	38	125	27	9	1	2	44	14	13	8	0	31	1	3	0	2	0	1.00	0	.216	.269	.352
2 YEARS	43	139	32	11	1	3	54	17	17	10	0	34	1	3	0	2	0	1.00	0	.230	.287	.388

	1987 SEASON										FOUR YEAR TOTALS (1984 – 1987)									
	AVG	OBP	SLG	AB	H	2B	3B	HR	RBI	BB	SO	AVG	OBP	SLG	AB	H	2B	3B	HR	RBI	BB	SO
Totals	.216	.269	.352	125	27	9	1	2	13	8	31	.230	.287	.388	139	32	11	1	3	17	10	34
vs. Left	.289	.357	.500	38	11	3	1	1	6	4	8	.319	.396	.532	47	15	5	1	1	9	6	9
vs. Right	.184	.228	.287	87	16	6	0	1	7	4	23	.185	.227	.315	92	17	6	0	2	8	4	25
At Home	.222	.300	.381	63	14	5	1	1	4	7	13	.224	.307	.388	67	15	6	1	1	5	8	14
On Road	.210	.234	.323	62	13	4	0	1	9	1	18	.236	.267	.389	72	17	5	0	2	12	2	20

Belliard, Rafael Leonidas
Bats: Right   Throws: Right   Born 10/24/61

1987 SEASON AND MAJOR-LEAGUE CAREER BATTING TOTALS

	G	AB	H	2B	3B	HR	TB	R	RBI	TBB	IBB	SO	HP	SH	SF	SB	CS	SB%	GDP	AVG	OBP	SLG
87 PIT	81	203	42	4	3	1	55	26	15	20	6	2	5	3	2	15	1	.83	4	.207	.286	.271
6 YEARS	248	557	124	9	5	1	146	67	47	46	12	86	6	13	2	22	4	.85	12	.223	.288	.262

1987 SEASON	AVG	OBP	SLG	AB	H	2B	3B	HR	RBI	BB	SO
Totals	.207	.289	.271	203	42	4	3	1	15	21	25
vs. Left	.213	.314	.293	75	16	2	2	0	2	9	10
vs. Right	.203	.275	.258	128	26	2	1	1	13	12	15
At Home	.187	.299	.220	91	17	1	1	0	6	12	11
On Road	.223	.281	.313	112	25	3	2	1	9	9	14

FOUR YEAR TOTALS (1984 – 1987)	AVG	OBP	SLG	AB	H	2B	3B	HR	RBI	BB	SO
	.222	.289	.262	554	123	9	5	1	47	47	85
vs. Left	.227	.296	.256	203	46	2	2	0	13	18	28
vs. Right	.219	.285	.265	351	77	7	3	1	34	29	57
At Home	.198	.277	.225	262	52	3	2	0	23	24	33
On Road	.243	.300	.295	292	71	6	3	1	24	23	52

Benedict, Bruce Edwin
Bats: Right   Throws: Right   Born 08/18/55

1987 SEASON AND MAJOR-LEAGUE CAREER BATTING TOTALS

	G	AB	H	2B	3B	HR	TB	R	RBI	TBB	IBB	SO	HP	SH	SF	SB	CS	SB%	GDP	AVG	OBP	SLG
87 ATL	37	95	14	1	0	1	18	4	5	17	0	15	0	2	0	0	1	.00	2	.147	.277	.189
10 YEARS	826	2482	608	88	6	17	759	191	235	286	47	207	12	42	19	12	18	.40	73	.245	.324	.306

1987 SEASON	AVG	OBP	SLG	AB	H	2B	3B	HR	RBI	BB	SO
Totals	.147	.277	.189	95	14	1	0	1	5	17	15
vs. Left	.103	.188	.138	29	3	1	0	0	0	3	3
vs. Right	.167	.313	.212	66	11	0	0	1	5	14	12
At Home	.180	.293	.260	50	9	1	0	1	3	8	7
On Road	.111	.259	.111	45	5	0	0	0	2	9	8

FOUR YEAR TOTALS (1984 – 1987)	AVG	OBP	SLG	AB	H	2B	3B	HR	RBI	BB	SO
	.208	.291	.266	763	159	25	2	5	63	88	62
vs. Left	.220	.306	.314	223	49	11	2	2	19	26	8
vs. Right	.204	.285	.246	540	110	14	0	3	44	62	54
At Home	.234	.314	.301	402	94	18	0	3	35	45	28
On Road	.180	.266	.227	361	65	7	2	2	28	43	34

Beniquez, Juan Jose (Torres)
Bats: Right   Throws: Right   Born 05/13/50

1987 SEASON AND MAJOR-LEAGUE CAREER BATTING TOTALS

	G	AB	H	2B	3B	HR	TB	R	RBI	TBB	IBB	SO	HP	SH	SF	SB	CS	SB%	GDP	AVG	OBP	SLG
87 KC-TOR	96	255	64	12	1	8	102	20	47	16	1	39	2	2	3	0	0	.00	12	.251	.297	.400
16 YEARS	1473	4593	1257	188	30	78	1739	601	468	341	11	545	31	86	31	104	76	.58	141	.274	.326	.379

1987 SEASON	AVG	OBP	SLG	AB	H	2B	3B	HR	RBI	BB	SO
Totals	.251	.297	.400	255	64	12	1	8	47	16	39
vs. Left	.267	.306	.491	116	31	8	0	6	26	6	16
vs. Right	.237	.289	.324	139	33	4	1	2	21	10	23
At Home	.232	.279	.357	112	26	6	1	2	21	7	16
On Road	.266	.312	.434	143	38	6	0	6	26	9	23

FOUR YEAR TOTALS (1984 – 1987)	AVG	OBP	SLG	AB	H	2B	3B	HR	RBI	BB	SO
	.302	.355	.418	1363	411	57	6	30	164	108	177
vs. Left	.337	.385	.492	581	196	28	4	18	77	43	52
vs. Right	.275	.334	.363	782	215	29	2	12	87	65	125
At Home	.321	.373	.444	683	219	25	4	17	90	56	82
On Road	.282	.338	.393	680	192	32	2	13	74	52	95

Benzinger, Todd Eric
Bats: Both   Throws: Right   Born 02/11/63

1987 SEASON AND MAJOR-LEAGUE CAREER BATTING TOTALS

	G	AB	H	2B	3B	HR	TB	R	RBI	TBB	IBB	SO	HP	SH	SF	SB	CS	SB%	GDP	AVG	OBP	SLG
87 BOS	73	223	62	11	1	8	99	36	43	22	3	41	2	3	3	5	4	.56	5	.278	.344	.444
1 YEAR	73	223	62	11	1	8	99	36	43	22	3	41	2	3	3	5	4	.56	5	.278	.344	.444

1987 SEASON	AVG	OBP	SLG	AB	H	2B	3B	HR	RBI	BB	SO
Totals	.278	.344	.444	223	62	11	1	8	43	22	41
vs. Left	.325	.371	.450	80	26	4	0	2	18	7	12
vs. Right	.252	.329	.441	143	36	7	1	6	25	15	29
At Home	.311	.390	.528	106	33	6	1	5	21	14	18
On Road	.248	.299	.368	117	29	5	0	3	22	8	23

FOUR YEAR TOTALS (1984 – 1987)	AVG	OBP	SLG	AB	H	2B	3B	HR	RBI	BB	SO
	.278	.344	.444	223	62	11	1	8	43	22	41
vs. Left	.325	.371	.450	80	26	4	0	2	18	7	12
vs. Right	.252	.329	.441	143	36	7	1	6	25	15	29
At Home	.311	.390	.528	106	33	6	1	5	21	14	18
On Road	.248	.299	.368	117	29	5	0	3	22	8	23

Berenguer, Juan Bautista

Bats: Right   Throws: Right   Born 11/30/54

1987 SEASON AND MAJOR-LEAGUE CAREER PITCHING TOTALS

	G	GS	CG	GF	IP	BFP	H	R	ER	HR	SH	SF	HB	TBB	IBB	SO	WP	Bk	W	L	Pct	ShO	Sv	ERA
87 MIN	47	6	0	13	112	473	100	51	49	10	2	4	0	47	7	110	6	0	8	1	.889	0	4	3.94
10 YEARS	230	92	5	55	757	3257	659	375	336	74	11	26	21	382	22	608	26	8	38	42	.475	2	9	3.99

1987: Power, Flyball   1986: Power, Flyball   1985: Power, Flyball   1984: Power, Flyball

1987 SEASON

	G	IP	H	BB	SO	SB	CS	W	L	S	ERA
Totals	47	112.0	100	47	110	9	3	8	1	4	3.94
At Home	23	62.1	46	19	56	4	1	5	0	1	2.31
On Road	24	49.2	54	28	54	5	2	3	1	3	5.98
vs. Opposing Batters	AVG	OBP	SLG	AB	H	2B	3B	HR	RBI	BB	SO
Totals	.238	.312	.374	420	100	23	2	10	54	47	110
vs. Left	.278	.360	.462	223	62	15	1	8	38	29	50
vs. Right	.193	.257	.274	197	38	8	1	2	16	18	60

FOUR YEAR TOTALS (1984 – 1987)

	G	IP	H	BB	SO	SB	CS	W	L	S	ERA
Totals	155	448.2	406	218	382	36	23	26	20	8	3.89
At Home	77	241.2	215	109	206	19	11	15	11	4	3.87
On Road	78	207.0	191	109	176	17	12	11	9	4	3.96
	AVG	OBP	SLG	AB	H	2B	3B	HR	RBI	BB	SO
Totals	.241	.328	.367	1682	406	74	9	40	203	218	382
vs. Left	.262	.355	.405	903	237	41	5	26	104	130	190
vs. Right	.217	.295	.323	779	169	33	4	14	99	88	192

Bergman, David Bruce "Dave"

Bats: Left   Throws: Left   Born 06/06/53

1987 SEASON AND MAJOR-LEAGUE CAREER BATTING TOTALS

	G	AB	H	2B	3B	HR	TB	R	RBI	TBB	IBB	SO	HP	SH	SF	SB	CS	SB%	GDP	AVG	OBP	SLG
87 DET	91	172	47	7	3	6	78	25	22	30	4	23	1	1	3	0	1	.00	1	.273	.379	.453
12 YEARS	823	1425	357	50	13	32	529	176	152	210	25	193	5	13	16	13	6	.68	30	.251	.345	.371

1987 SEASON

	AVG	OBP	SLG	AB	H	2B	3B	HR	RBI	BB	SO
Totals	.273	.379	.453	172	47	7	3	6	22	30	23
vs. Left	.263	.263	.263	19	5	0	0	0	2	0	4
vs. Right	.275	.390	.477	153	42	7	3	6	20	30	19
At Home	.306	.394	.482	85	26	3	0	4	10	13	15
On Road	.241	.364	.425	87	21	4	3	2	12	17	8

FOUR YEAR TOTALS (1984 – 1987)

	AVG	OBP	SLG	AB	H	2B	3B	HR	RBI	BB	SO
Totals	.247	.336	.376	713	176	23	9	17	82	97	94
vs. Left	.236	.300	.291	55	13	1	1	0	4	5	7
vs. Right	.248	.339	.383	658	163	22	8	17	78	92	87
At Home	.238	.331	.375	357	85	9	5	10	47	52	47
On Road	.256	.341	.376	356	91	14	4	7	35	45	47

Berra, Dale Anthony

Bats: Right   Throws: Right   Born 12/13/56

1987 SEASON AND MAJOR-LEAGUE CAREER BATTING TOTALS

	G	AB	H	2B	3B	HR	TB	R	RBI	TBB	IBB	SO	HP	SH	SF	SB	CS	SB%	GDP	AVG	OBP	SLG
87 HOU	19	45	8	3	0	0	11	3	2	8	3	12	0	0	1	0	0	.00	0	.178	.296	.244
11 YEARS	853	2553	603	109	9	49	877	236	278	210	57	422	12	33	27	32	17	.65	54	.236	.294	.344

1987 SEASON

	AVG	OBP	SLG	AB	H	2B	3B	HR	RBI	BB	SO
Totals	.178	.296	.244	45	8	3	0	0	2	8	12
vs. Left	.159	.255	.205	44	7	2	0	0	1	6	12
vs. Right	1.000	1.000	2.000	1	1	1	0	0	1	2	0
At Home	.160	.313	.200	25	4	1	0	0	2	6	8
On Road	.200	.273	.300	20	4	2	0	0	0	2	4

FOUR YEAR TOTALS (1984 – 1987)

	AVG	OBP	SLG	AB	H	2B	3B	HR	RBI	BB	SO
Totals	.222	.278	.319	712	158	31	1	12	75	58	124
vs. Left	.244	.306	.378	320	78	17	1	8	30	29	50
vs. Right	.204	.256	.270	392	80	14	0	4	45	29	74
At Home	.243	.299	.371	342	83	12	1	10	41	29	55
On Road	.203	.259	.270	370	75	19	0	2	34	29	69

Biancalana, Roland Americo "Buddy"

Bats: Both   Throws: Right   Born 02/02/60

1987 SEASON AND MAJOR-LEAGUE CAREER BATTING TOTALS

	G	AB	H	2B	3B	HR	TB	R	RBI	TBB	IBB	SO	HP	SH	SF	SB	CS	SB%	GDP	AVG	OBP	SLG
87 KC-HOU	55	71	11	1	0	1	15	5	7	2	0	22	0	1	0	0	0	.00	1	.155	.178	.211
6 YEARS	311	550	113	16	7	6	161	70	30	41	0	157	0	15	0	8	7	.53	8	.205	.261	.293

1987 SEASON

	AVG	OBP	SLG	AB	H	2B	3B	HR	RBI	BB	SO
Totals	.155	.178	.211	71	11	1	0	1	7	2	22
vs. Left	.118	.143	.206	34	4	0	0	1	5	1	12
vs. Right	.189	.211	.216	37	7	1	0	0	2	1	10
At Home	.154	.175	.256	39	6	1	0	1	7	1	9
On Road	.156	.182	.156	32	5	0	0	0	0	1	13

FOUR YEAR TOTALS (1984 – 1987)

	AVG	OBP	SLG	AB	H	2B	3B	HR	RBI	BB	SO
Totals	.205	.260	.291	533	109	16	6	6	30	40	150
vs. Left	.202	.250	.258	124	25	2	1	1	9	8	29
vs. Right	.205	.263	.301	409	84	14	5	5	21	32	121
At Home	.217	.290	.313	281	61	11	5	2	21	29	71
On Road	.190	.224	.266	252	48	5	1	4	9	11	79

Bielecki, Michael Joseph "Mike"
Bats: Right Throws: Right Born 07/31/59

1987 SEASON AND MAJOR-LEAGUE CAREER PITCHING TOTALS

	G	GS	CG	GF	IP	BFP	H	R	ER	HR	SH	SF	HB	TBB	IBB	SO	WP	Bk	W	L	Pct	ShO	Sv	ERA
87 PIT	8	8	2	0	46	192	43	25	24	6	5	2	1	12	0	25	3	0	2	3	.400	0	0	4.70
4 YEARS	55	42	2	2	245	1087	241	138	124	21	17	8	4	126	4	131	11	7	10	17	.370	0	0	4.56

1987: Finesse, Groundball   1986: Power, Groundball   1985: Power, Flyball   1984: Finesse, Groundball

	1987 SEASON											FOUR YEAR TOTALS (1984 – 1987)											
	G	IP	H	BB	SO	SB	CS	W	L	S	ERA	G	IP	H	BB	SO	SB	CS	W	L	S	ERA
Totals	8	45.0	43	12	25	6	2	2	3	0	4.80	55	243.2	241	126	131	24	14	10	17	0	4.58
At Home	4	26.2	22	4	11	2	1	2	0	0	3.71	25	128.1	125	66	68	11	7	5	8	0	4.77
On Road	4	18.1	21	8	14	4	1	0	3	0	6.38	30	115.1	116	60	63	13	7	5	9	0	4.37

	AVG	OBP	SLG	AB	H	2B	3B	HR	RBI	BB	SO	AVG	OBP	SLG	AB	H	2B	3B	HR	RBI	BB	SO
vs. Opposing Batters																						
Totals	.250	.299	.448	172	43	12	2	6	22	12	25	.259	.347	.402	932	241	47	12	21	113	126	131
vs. Left	.250	.302	.438	96	24	9	0	3	12	7	10	.255	.328	.409	521	133	29	6	13	66	56	52
vs. Right	.250	.296	.461	76	19	3	2	3	10	5	15	.263	.370	.394	411	108	18	6	8	47	70	79

Birkbeck, Michael Lawrence "Mike"
Bats: Right Throws: Right Born 03/10/61

1987 SEASON AND MAJOR-LEAGUE CAREER PITCHING TOTALS

	G	GS	CG	GF	IP	BFP	H	R	ER	HR	SH	SF	HB	TBB	IBB	SO	WP	Bk	W	L	Pct	ShO	Sv	ERA
87 MIL	10	10	1	0	45	210	63	33	31	8	1	2	0	19	0	25	2	0	1	4	.200	0	0	6.20
2 YEARS	17	14	1	2	67	307	87	45	42	8	1	2	0	31	0	38	3	0	2	5	.286	0	0	5.64

1987: Finesse, Groundball   1986: Power, Groundball

	1987 SEASON											FOUR YEAR TOTALS (1984 – 1987)											
	G	IP	H	BB	SO	SB	CS	W	L	S	ERA	G	IP	H	BB	SO	SB	CS	W	L	S	ERA
Totals	10	45.0	63	19	25	6	4	1	4	0	6.20	17	67.0	87	31	38	9	5	2	5	0	5.64
At Home	6	27.1	34	12	19	2	2	1	2	0	5.27	8	36.2	42	16	22	2	3	2	2	0	4.42
On Road	4	17.2	29	7	6	4	2	0	2	0	7.64	9	30.1	45	15	16	7	2	0	3	0	7.12

	AVG	OBP	SLG	AB	H	2B	3B	HR	RBI	BB	SO	AVG	OBP	SLG	AB	H	2B	3B	HR	RBI	BB	SO
vs. Opposing Batters																						
Totals	.335	.392	.532	188	63	11	1	8	28	19	25	.319	.386	.462	273	87	13	1	8	35	31	38
vs. Left	.267	.323	.367	90	24	3	0	2	7	8	11	.258	.336	.326	132	34	3	0	2	11	16	14
vs. Right	.398	.455	.684	98	39	8	1	6	21	11	14	.376	.433	.589	141	53	10	1	6	24	15	24

Black, Harry Ralston "Buddy"
Bats: Left Throws: Left Born 06/30/57

1987 SEASON AND MAJOR-LEAGUE CAREER PITCHING TOTALS

	G	GS	CG	GF	IP	BFP	H	R	ER	HR	SH	SF	HB	TBB	IBB	SO	WP	Bk	W	L	Pct	ShO	Sv	ERA
87 KC	29	18	0	4	122	520	126	63	49	16	1	3	5	35	2	61	6	0	8	6	.571	0	1	3.61
7 YEARS	201	128	16	32	956	4018	921	445	393	98	27	20	29	281	21	489	28	12	54	56	.491	3	10	3.70

1987: Finesse, Groundball   1986: Finesse, Flyball   1985: Finesse, Groundball   1984: Finesse, Groundball

	1987 SEASON											FOUR YEAR TOTALS (1984 – 1987)											
	G	IP	H	BB	SO	SB	CS	W	L	S	ERA	G	IP	H	BB	SO	SB	CS	W	L	S	ERA
Totals	29	122.1	126	35	61	16	2	8	6	1	3.60	153	706.0	668	201	391	46	25	40	43	10	3.56
At Home	14	63.1	57	10	33	11	0	5	1	1	3.13	79	379.2	345	97	203	30	14	24	17	6	3.20
On Road	15	59.0	69	25	28	5	2	3	5	0	4.12	74	326.1	323	104	188	16	11	16	26	4	3.97

	AVG	OBP	SLG	AB	H	2B	3B	HR	RBI	BB	SO	AVG	OBP	SLG	AB	H	2B	3B	HR	RBI	BB	SO
vs. Opposing Batters																						
Totals	.266	.321	.432	474	126	19	6	16	56	35	61	.248	.301	.381	2693	668	112	20	69	284	201	391
vs. Left	.233	.280	.397	116	27	5	1	4	15	8	19	.230	.279	.342	634	146	20	6	13	63	43	99
vs. Right	.277	.334	.444	358	99	14	5	12	41	27	42	.254	.308	.393	2059	522	92	14	56	221	158	292

Blauser, Jeffrey Michael "Jeff"
Bats: Right Throws: Right Born 11/08/65

1987 SEASON AND MAJOR-LEAGUE CAREER BATTING TOTALS

	G	AB	H	2B	3B	HR	TB	R	RBI	TBB	IBB	SO	HP	SH	SF	SB	CS	SB%	GDP	AVG	OBP	SLG
87 ATL	51	165	40	6	3	2	58	11	15	18	1	34	3	1	0	7	3	.70	4	.242	.328	.352
1 YEAR	51	165	40	6	3	2	58	11	15	18	1	34	3	1	0	7	3	.70	4	.242	.328	.352

	1987 SEASON											FOUR YEAR TOTALS (1984 – 1987)											
	AVG	OBP	SLG	AB	H	2B	3B	HR	RBI	BB	SO	AVG	OBP	SLG	AB	H	2B	3B	HR	RBI	BB	SO
Totals	.242	.328	.352	165	40	6	3	2	15	18	34	.242	.328	.352	165	40	6	3	2	15	18	34
vs. Left	.277	.346	.511	47	13	1	2	2	9	5	8	.277	.346	.511	47	13	1	2	2	9	5	8
vs. Right	.229	.321	.288	118	27	5	1	0	6	13	26	.229	.321	.288	118	27	5	1	0	6	13	26
At Home	.295	.382	.462	78	23	4	3	1	8	10	13	.295	.382	.462	78	23	4	3	1	8	10	13
On Road	.195	.278	.253	87	17	2	0	1	7	8	21	.195	.278	.253	87	17	2	0	1	7	8	21

Bochy, Bruce Douglas

Bats: Right   Throws: Right   Born 04/16/55

1987 SEASON AND MAJOR-LEAGUE CAREER BATTING TOTALS

	G	AB	H	2B	3B	HR	TB	R	RBI	TBB	IBB	SO	HP	SH	SF	SB	CS	SB%	GDP	AVG	OBP	SLG
87 SD	38	75	12	3	0	2	21	8	11	11	1	21	0	0	1	0	1	.00	3	.160	.264	.280
9 YEARS	358	802	192	37	2	26	311	75	93	67	14	177	2	4	6	1	2	.33	25	.239	.298	.388

	1987 SEASON										FOUR YEAR TOTALS (1984 – 1987)									
	AVG	OBP	SLG	AB	H	2B	3B	HR	RBI	BB	SO	AVG	OBP	SLG	AB	H	2B	3B	HR	RBI	BB	SO
Totals	.160	.264	.280	75	12	3	0	2	11	11	21	.234	.292	.433	406	95	19	1	20	61	34	95
vs. Left	.139	.262	.194	36	5	2	0	0	2	6	13	.232	.288	.459	246	57	12	1	14	37	20	54
vs. Right	.179	.267	.359	39	7	1	0	2	9	5	8	.237	.297	.394	160	38	7	0	6	24	14	41
At Home	.125	.317	.219	32	4	0	0	1	4	9	12	.215	.301	.454	163	35	6	0	11	26	20	45
On Road	.186	.217	.326	43	8	3	0	1	7	2	9	.247	.286	.420	243	60	13	1	9	35	14	50

Bolton, Thomas Edward "Tom"

Bats: Left   Throws: Left   Born 05/06/62

1987 SEASON AND MAJOR-LEAGUE CAREER PITCHING TOTALS

	G	GS	CG	GF	IP	BFP	H	R	ER	HR	SH	SF	HB	TBB	IBB	SO	WP	Bk	W	L	Pct	ShO	Sv	ERA
87 BOS	29	0	0	5	62	287	83	33	30	5	3	3	2	27	2	49	3	0	1	0	1.000	0	0	4.35
1 YEAR	29	0	0	5	62	287	83	33	30	5	3	3	2	27	2	49	3	0	1	0	1.000	0	0	4.35

1987: Power, Groundball

	1987 SEASON										FOUR YEAR TOTALS (1984 – 1987)									
	G	IP	H	BB	SO	SB	CS	W	L	S	ERA	G	IP	H	BB	SO	SB	CS	W	L	S	ERA
Totals	29	61.2	83	27	49	4	3	1	0	0	4.38	29	61.2	83	27	49	4	3	1	0	0	4.38
At Home	12	26.2	44	13	21	3	0	1	0	0	6.75	12	26.2	44	13	21	3	0	1	0	0	6.75
On Road	17	35.0	39	14	28	1	3	0	0	0	2.57	17	35.0	39	14	28	1	3	0	0	0	2.57
vs. Opposing Batters	AVG	OBP	SLG	AB	H	2B	3B	HR	RBI	BB	SO	AVG	OBP	SLG	AB	H	2B	3B	HR	RBI	BB	SO
Totals	.329	.394	.440	252	83	11	1	5	39	27	49	.329	.394	.440	252	83	11	1	5	39	27	49
vs. Left	.333	.418	.427	96	32	4	1	1	19	13	21	.333	.418	.427	96	32	4	1	1	19	13	21
vs. Right	.327	.379	.449	156	51	7	0	4	20	14	28	.327	.379	.449	156	51	7	0	4	20	14	28

Bonilla, Juan Guillermo

Bats: Right   Throws: Right   Born 02/12/56

1987 SEASON AND MAJOR-LEAGUE CAREER BATTING TOTALS

	G	AB	H	2B	3B	HR	TB	R	RBI	TBB	IBB	SO	HP	SH	SF	SB	CS	SB%	GDP	AVG	OBP	SLG
87 NYA	23	55	14	3	0	1	20	6	3	5	0	6	0	3	0	0	0	.00	2	.255	.317	.364
6 YEARS	429	1462	375	50	9	7	464	145	101	116	16	108	9	22	7	7	10	.41	44	.256	.314	.317

	1987 SEASON										FOUR YEAR TOTALS (1984 – 1987)									
	AVG	OBP	SLG	AB	H	2B	3B	HR	RBI	BB	SO	AVG	OBP	SLG	AB	H	2B	3B	HR	RBI	BB	SO
Totals	.255	.317	.364	55	14	3	0	1	3	5	6	.239	.304	.301	355	85	14	1	2	23	30	30
vs. Left	.385	.448	.577	26	10	2	0	1	2	3	3	.255	.314	.348	141	36	7	0	2	11	12	13
vs. Right	.138	.194	.172	29	4	1	0	0	1	2	3	.229	.298	.271	214	49	7	1	0	12	18	17
At Home	.296	.321	.444	27	8	1	0	1	2	1	3	.205	.273	.255	161	33	5	0	1	9	13	15
On Road	.214	.313	.286	28	6	2	0	0	1	4	3	.268	.330	.340	194	52	9	1	1	14	17	15

Booker, Gregory Scott "Greg"

Bats: Right   Throws: Right   Born 06/22/60

1987 SEASON AND MAJOR-LEAGUE CAREER PITCHING TOTALS

	G	GS	CG	GF	IP	BFP	H	R	ER	HR	SH	SF	HB	TBB	IBB	SO	WP	Bk	W	L	Pct	ShO	Sv	ERA
87 SD	44	0	0	16	68	288	62	29	24	5	2	1	3	30	1	17	1	1	1	1	.500	0	1	3.18
5 YEARS	108	2	0	42	170	757	177	88	74	14	10	5	4	87	9	64	12	1	3	4	.429	0	1	3.92

1987: Finesse, Groundball   1986: Finesse, Flyball

	1987 SEASON										TWO YEAR TOTALS (1986 – 1987)									
	G	IP	H	BB	SO	SB	CS	W	L	S	ERA	G	IP	H	BB	SO	SB	CS	W	L	S	ERA
Totals	44	68.2	62	30	17	13	1	1	1	1	3.15	53	79.2	72	34	24	15	1	2	1	1	2.94
At Home	21	40.1	42	13	10	8	1	1	0	1	3.35	25	45.1	47	15	14	9	1	1	0	1	3.38
On Road	23	28.1	20	17	7	5	0	0	1	0	2.86	28	34.1	25	19	10	6	0	1	1	0	2.36
vs. Opposing Batters	AVG	OBP	SLG	AB	H	2B	3B	HR	RBI	BB	SO	AVG	OBP	SLG	AB	H	2B	3B	HR	RBI	BB	SO
Totals	.246	.332	.325	252	62	5	0	5	24	30	17	.244	.327	.332	295	72	9	1	5	28	34	24
vs. Left	.309	.424	.409	110	34	2	0	3	10	21	3	.287	.395	.388	129	37	4	0	3	12	22	6
vs. Right	.197	.253	.261	142	28	3	0	2	14	9	14	.211	.271	.289	166	35	5	1	2	16	12	18

Booker, Roderick Stewart "Rod"

Bats: Left   Throws: Right   Born 09/04/58

1987 SEASON AND MAJOR-LEAGUE CAREER BATTING TOTALS

	G	AB	H	2B	3B	HR	TB	R	RBI	TBB	IBB	SO	HP	SH	SF	SB	CS	SB%	GDP	AVG	OBP	SLG
87 STL	44	47	13	1	1	0	16	9	8	7	1	7	0	2	0	2	0	1.00	0	.277	.370	.340
1 YEAR	44	47	13	1	1	0	16	9	8	7	1	7	0	2	0	2	0	1.00	0	.277	.370	.340

	1987 SEASON											FOUR YEAR TOTALS (1984 – 1987)										
	AVG	OBP	SLG	AB	H	2B	3B	HR	RBI	BB	SO	AVG	OBP	SLG	AB	H	2B	3B	HR	RBI	BB	SO
Totals	.277	.370	.340	47	13	1	1	0	8	7	7	.277	.370	.340	47	13	1	1	0	8	7	7
vs. Left	.286	.375	.286	7	2	0	0	0	0	1	2	.286	.375	.286	7	2	0	0	0	0	1	2
vs. Right	.275	.370	.350	40	11	1	1	0	8	6	5	.275	.370	.350	40	11	1	1	0	8	6	5
At Home	.333	.444	.367	30	10	1	0	0	7	6	4	.333	.444	.367	30	10	1	0	0	7	6	4
On Road	.176	.222	.294	17	3	0	1	0	1	1	3	.176	.222	.294	17	3	0	1	0	1	1	3

Bordi, Richard Albert "Rich"

Bats: Right   Throws: Right   Born 04/18/59

1987 SEASON AND MAJOR-LEAGUE CAREER PITCHING TOTALS

	G	GS	CG	GF	IP	BFP	H	R	ER	HR	SH	SF	HB	TBB	IBB	SO	WP	Bk	W	L	Pct	ShO	Sv	ERA
87 NYA	16	1	0	6	33	149	42	28	28	7	1	0	0	12	0	23	0	1	3	1	.750	0	0	7.64
8 YEARS	171	15	0	59	363	1572	377	190	175	42	12	9	6	116	14	241	2	1	20	19	.513	0	10	4.34

1987: Power, Flyball   1986: Power, Flyball   1985: Finesse, Flyball   1984: Finesse, Groundball

	1987 SEASON										FOUR YEAR TOTALS (1984 – 1987)										
	G	IP	H	BB	SO	SB	CS	W	L	S	ERA	G	IP	H	BB	SO	SB	CS	W	L	S	ERA
Totals	16	33.0	42	12	23	4	2	3	1	0	7.64	150	321.1	320	102	211	36	10	20	15	9	4.15
At Home	9	23.2	27	9	15	2	2	2	1	0	6.85	84	206.0	191	57	121	18	8	13	9	7	3.41
On Road	7	9.1	15	3	8	2	0	1	0	0	9.64	66	115.1	129	45	90	18	2	7	6	2	5.46
vs. Opposing Batters	AVG	OBP	SLG	AB	H	2B	3B	HR	RBI	BB	SO	AVG	OBP	SLG	AB	H	2B	3B	HR	RBI	BB	SO
Totals	.309	.365	.529	136	42	5	2	7	29	12	23	.256	.313	.393	1248	320	43	10	36	171	102	211
vs. Left	.308	.375	.385	65	20	2	0	1	7	7	9	.290	.354	.429	559	162	20	5	16	76	56	77
vs. Right	.310	.355	.662	71	22	3	2	6	22	5	14	.229	.278	.364	689	158	23	5	20	95	46	134

Bosio, Christopher Louis "Chris"

Bats: Right   Throws: Right   Born 04/03/63

1987 SEASON AND MAJOR-LEAGUE CAREER PITCHING TOTALS

	G	GS	CG	GF	IP	BFP	H	R	ER	HR	SH	SF	HB	TBB	IBB	SO	WP	Bk	W	L	Pct	ShO	Sv	ERA
87 MIL	46	19	2	11	170	734	187	102	99	18	3	3	1	50	3	150	14	2	11	8	.579	1	2	5.24
2 YEARS	56	23	2	11	205	888	228	129	126	27	4	3	1	63	3	179	16	3	11	12	.478	1	2	5.53

1987: Power, Groundball   1986: Power, Groundball

	1987 SEASON										FOUR YEAR TOTALS (1984 – 1987)										
	G	IP	H	BB	SO	SB	CS	W	L	S	ERA	G	IP	H	BB	SO	SB	CS	W	L	S	ERA
Totals	46	170.1	187	50	150	20	2	11	8	2	5.23	56	205.0	228	63	179	26	3	11	12	2	5.53
At Home	19	73.2	84	20	73	7	0	4	4	0	6.23	24	93.0	104	28	85	9	1	4	6	0	6.19
On Road	27	96.2	103	30	77	13	2	7	4	2	4.47	32	112.0	124	35	94	17	2	7	6	2	4.98
vs. Opposing Batters	AVG	OBP	SLG	AB	H	2B	3B	HR	RBI	BB	SO	AVG	OBP	SLG	AB	H	2B	3B	HR	RBI	BB	SO
Totals	.276	.326	.415	677	187	32	4	18	90	50	150	.279	.330	.442	817	228	42	5	27	119	63	179
vs. Left	.264	.322	.424	356	94	18	3	11	42	30	79	.274	.331	.462	424	116	24	4	16	59	36	87
vs. Right	.290	.329	.405	321	93	14	1	7	48	20	71	.285	.329	.420	393	112	18	1	11	60	27	92

Bosley, Thaddis "Thad"

Bats: Left   Throws: Left   Born 09/17/56

1987 SEASON AND MAJOR-LEAGUE CAREER BATTING TOTALS

	G	AB	H	2B	3B	HR	TB	R	RBI	TBB	IBB	SO	HP	SH	SF	SB	CS	SB%	GDP	AVG	OBP	SLG
87 KC	80	140	39	6	1	1	50	13	16	9	2	26	0	1	2	0	0	.00	2	.279	.318	.357
11 YEARS	667	1416	392	43	12	18	513	165	137	128	13	239	1	13	11	43	23	.65	28	.277	.335	.362

	1987 SEASON											FOUR YEAR TOTALS (1984 – 1987)										
	AVG	OBP	SLG	AB	H	2B	3B	HR	RBI	BB	SO	AVG	OBP	SLG	AB	H	2B	3B	HR	RBI	BB	SO
Totals	.279	.318	.357	140	39	6	1	1	16	9	26	.297	.365	.418	538	160	18	7	11	66	60	101
vs. Left	.357	.400	.429	14	5	1	0	0	2	1	5	.379	.455	.448	29	11	2	0	0	6	4	11
vs. Right	.270	.309	.349	126	34	5	1	1	14	8	21	.293	.360	.417	509	149	16	7	11	60	56	90
At Home	.348	.400	.457	46	16	3	1	0	4	4	9	.350	.430	.467	257	90	12	3	4	38	38	42
On Road	.245	.277	.309	94	23	3	0	1	12	5	17	.249	.302	.374	281	70	6	4	7	28	22	59

Boston, Daryl Lamont
Bats: Left   Throws: Left   Born 01/04/63

1987 SEASON AND MAJOR-LEAGUE CAREER BATTING TOTALS

	G	AB	H	2B	3B	HR	TB	R	RBI	TBB	IBB	SO	HP	SH	SF	SB	CS	SB%	GDP	AVG	OBP	SLG
87 CHA	103	337	87	21	2	10	142	51	29	25	2	68	0	4	3	12	6	.67	5	.258	.307	.421
4 YEARS	289	851	207	48	7	18	323	108	69	64	6	165	0	8	5	35	17	.67	12	.243	.295	.380

1987 SEASON	AVG	OBP	SLG	AB	H	2B	3B	HR	RBI	BB	SO
Totals	.258	.307	.421	337	87	21	2	10	29	25	68
vs. Left	.305	.311	.373	59	18	4	0	0	5	1	17
vs. Right	.248	.306	.432	278	69	17	2	10	24	24	51
At Home	.321	.365	.488	168	54	9	2	5	17	12	37
On Road	.195	.250	.355	169	33	12	0	5	12	13	31

FOUR YEAR TOTALS (1984 – 1987)	AVG	OBP	SLG	AB	H	2B	3B	HR	RBI	BB	SO
Totals	.243	.295	.380	851	207	48	7	18	69	64	165
vs. Left	.234	.283	.319	141	33	7	1	1	10	10	36
vs. Right	.245	.297	.392	710	174	41	6	17	59	54	129
At Home	.267	.321	.395	405	108	21	5	7	31	34	79
On Road	.222	.270	.365	446	99	27	2	11	38	30	86

Bradley, Scott William
Bats: Left   Throws: Right   Born 03/22/60

1987 SEASON AND MAJOR-LEAGUE CAREER BATTING TOTALS

	G	AB	H	2B	3B	HR	TB	R	RBI	TBB	IBB	SO	HP	SH	SF	SB	CS	SB%	GDP	AVG	OBP	SLG
87 SEA	102	342	95	15	1	5	127	34	43	15	1	18	3	2	4	0	1	.00	13	.278	.310	.371
4 YEARS	207	632	175	26	5	10	241	61	74	30	5	31	8	4	6	1	3	.25	28	.277	.315	.381

1987 SEASON	AVG	OBP	SLG	AB	H	2B	3B	HR	RBI	BB	SO
Totals	.278	.310	.371	342	95	15	1	5	43	15	18
vs. Left	.259	.273	.352	54	14	2	0	1	9	1	3
vs. Right	.281	.317	.375	288	81	13	1	4	34	14	15
At Home	.290	.329	.448	145	42	6	1	5	24	9	4
On Road	.269	.297	.315	197	53	9	0	0	19	6	14

FOUR YEAR TOTALS (1984 – 1987)	AVG	OBP	SLG	AB	H	2B	3B	HR	RBI	BB	SO
Totals	.277	.315	.381	632	175	26	5	10	74	30	31
vs. Left	.225	.244	.325	80	18	3	1	1	9	1	6
vs. Right	.284	.325	.389	552	157	23	4	9	65	29	25
At Home	.307	.355	.467	287	88	13	3	9	42	20	10
On Road	.252	.281	.310	345	87	13	2	1	32	10	21

Brower, Robert Richard "Bob"
Bats: Right   Throws: Right   Born 01/10/60

1987 SEASON AND MAJOR-LEAGUE CAREER BATTING TOTALS

	G	AB	H	2B	3B	HR	TB	R	RBI	TBB	IBB	SO	HP	SH	SF	SB	CS	SB%	GDP	AVG	OBP	SLG
87 TEX	127	303	79	10	3	14	137	63	46	36	0	66	0	9	1	15	9	.63	2	.261	.338	.452
2 YEARS	148	312	80	11	3	14	139	66	46	36	0	69	0	9	1	16	11	.59	2	.256	.332	.446

1987 SEASON	AVG	OBP	SLG	AB	H	2B	3B	HR	RBI	BB	SO
Totals	.261	.338	.452	303	79	10	3	14	46	36	66
vs. Left	.273	.355	.466	176	48	8	1	8	21	23	39
vs. Right	.244	.314	.433	127	31	2	2	6	25	13	27
At Home	.297	.363	.503	155	46	7	2	7	20	16	40
On Road	.223	.314	.399	148	33	3	1	7	26	20	26

FOUR YEAR TOTALS (1984 – 1987)	AVG	OBP	SLG	AB	H	2B	3B	HR	RBI	BB	SO
Totals	.256	.332	.446	312	80	11	3	14	46	36	69
vs. Left	.269	.350	.462	182	49	9	1	8	21	23	41
vs. Right	.238	.308	.423	130	31	2	2	6	25	13	28
At Home	.286	.350	.484	161	46	7	2	7	20	16	42
On Road	.225	.314	.404	151	34	4	1	7	26	20	27

Brumley, Anthony Michael "Mike"
Bats: Both   Throws: Right   Born 04/09/63

1987 SEASON AND MAJOR-LEAGUE CAREER BATTING TOTALS

	G	AB	H	2B	3B	HR	TB	R	RBI	TBB	IBB	SO	HP	SH	SF	SB	CS	SB%	GDP	AVG	OBP	SLG
87 CHN	39	104	21	2	2	1	30	8	9	10	1	30	1	1	1	7	1	.88	2	.202	.276	.288
1 YEAR	39	104	21	2	2	1	30	8	9	10	1	30	1	1	1	7	1	.88	2	.202	.276	.288

1987 SEASON	AVG	OBP	SLG	AB	H	2B	3B	HR	RBI	BB	SO
Totals	.200	.276	.286	105	21	2	2	1	9	10	30
vs. Left	.222	.333	.222	18	4	0	0	0	2	3	5
vs. Right	.195	.263	.299	87	17	2	2	1	7	7	25
At Home	.186	.262	.220	59	11	0	1	0	5	5	18
On Road	.217	.294	.370	46	10	2	1	1	4	5	12

FOUR YEAR TOTALS (1984 – 1987)	AVG	OBP	SLG	AB	H	2B	3B	HR	RBI	BB	SO
Totals	.200	.276	.286	105	21	2	2	1	9	10	30
vs. Left	.222	.333	.222	18	4	0	0	0	2	3	5
vs. Right	.195	.263	.299	87	17	2	2	1	7	7	25
At Home	.186	.262	.220	59	11	0	1	0	5	5	18
On Road	.217	.294	.370	46	10	2	1	1	4	5	12

Bryant, Ralph Wendell

Bats: Left   Throws: Right   Born 05/20/61

1987 SEASON AND MAJOR-LEAGUE CAREER BATTING TOTALS

	G	AB	H	2B	3B	HR	TB	R	RBI	TBB	IBB	SO	HP	SH	SF	SB	CS	SB%	GDP	AVG	OBP	SLG
87 LA	46	69	17	2	1	2	27	7	10	10	2	24	1	0	1	2	1	.67	0	.246	.346	.391
3 YEARS	79	150	38	6	3	8	74	22	24	15	2	51	2	0	2	2	2	.50	1	.253	.325	.493

	1987 SEASON										TWO YEAR TOTALS (1986 – 1987)									
	AVG	OBP	SLG	AB	H	2B	3B	HR	RBI	BB	SO	AVG	OBP	SLG	AB	H	2B	3B	HR	RBI	BB	SO
Totals	.246	.346	.391	69	17	2	1	2	10	10	24	.250	.327	.500	144	36	6	3	8	23	15	49
vs. Left	.000	.000	.000	2	0	0	0	0	0	0	1	.000	.000	.000	6	0	0	0	0	0	0	1
vs. Right	.254	.354	.403	67	17	2	1	2	10	10	23	.261	.338	.522	138	36	6	3	8	23	15	48
At Home	.250	.306	.281	32	8	1	0	0	4	3	13	.224	.266	.345	58	13	2	1	1	8	4	24
On Road	.243	.378	.486	37	9	1	1	2	6	7	11	.267	.364	.605	86	23	4	2	7	15	11	25

Burleson, Richard Paul "Rick"

Bats: Right   Throws: Right   Born 04/29/51

1987 SEASON AND MAJOR-LEAGUE CAREER BATTING TOTALS

	G	AB	H	2B	3B	HR	TB	R	RBI	TBB	IBB	SO	HP	SH	SF	SB	CS	SB%	GDP	AVG	OBP	SLG
87 BAL	62	206	43	14	1	2	65	26	14	17	0	30	3	6	0	0	2	.00	7	.209	.279	.316
13 YEARS	1346	5139	1401	256	23	50	1853	656	449	420	11	477	28	84	46	72	68	.51	138	.273	.328	.361

	1987 SEASON										FOUR YEAR TOTALS (1984 – 1987)									
	AVG	OBP	SLG	AB	H	2B	3B	HR	RBI	BB	SO	AVG	OBP	SLG	AB	H	2B	3B	HR	RBI	BB	SO
Totals	.209	.279	.316	206	43	14	1	2	14	17	30	.249	.326	.356	481	120	28	1	7	43	51	64
vs. Left	.195	.279	.299	77	15	6	1	0	5	8	13	.229	.312	.342	231	53	12	1	4	22	27	34
vs. Right	.217	.279	.326	129	28	8	0	2	9	9	17	.268	.339	.368	250	67	16	0	3	21	24	30
At Home	.218	.283	.373	110	24	9	1	2	8	8	16	.237	.315	.371	232	55	17	1	4	19	25	33
On Road	.198	.274	.250	96	19	5	0	0	6	9	14	.261	.336	.341	249	65	11	0	3	24	26	31

Butera, Salvatore Philip "Sal"

Bats: Right   Throws: Right   Born 09/25/51

1987 SEASON AND MAJOR-LEAGUE CAREER BATTING TOTALS

	G	AB	H	2B	3B	HR	TB	R	RBI	TBB	IBB	SO	HP	SH	SF	SB	CS	SB%	GDP	AVG	OBP	SLG
87 CIN-MIN	56	122	21	5	0	2	32	8	14	8	0	22	0	2	2	0	0	.00	7	.172	.220	.262
8 YEARS	336	741	168	22	2	7	215	60	70	85	4	76	3	13	7	0	0	.00	31	.227	.306	.290

	1987 SEASON										FOUR YEAR TOTALS (1984 – 1987)									
	AVG	OBP	SLG	AB	H	2B	3B	HR	RBI	BB	SO	AVG	OBP	SLG	AB	H	2B	3B	HR	RBI	BB	SO
Totals	.172	.220	.262	122	21	5	0	2	14	8	22	.201	.286	.299	358	72	12	1	7	42	43	44
vs. Left	.308	.308	.308	26	8	0	0	0	2	0	3	.283	.350	.387	106	30	3	1	2	10	11	6
vs. Right	.135	.198	.250	96	13	5	0	2	12	8	19	.167	.260	.262	252	42	9	0	5	32	32	38
At Home	.283	.292	.391	46	13	2	0	1	8	1	8	.207	.267	.274	164	34	6	1	1	19	14	20
On Road	.105	.179	.184	76	8	3	0	1	6	7	14	.196	.301	.320	194	38	6	0	6	23	29	24

Cadaret, Gregory James "Greg"

Bats: Left   Throws: Left   Born 02/27/62

1987 SEASON AND MAJOR-LEAGUE CAREER PITCHING TOTALS

	G	GS	CG	GF	IP	BFP	H	R	ER	HR	SH	SF	HB	TBB	IBB	SO	WP	Bk	W	L	Pct	ShO	Sv	ERA
87 OAK	29	0	0	7	40	176	37	22	20	6	2	2	1	24	1	30	1	0	6	2	.750	0	0	4.50
1 YEAR	29	0	0	7	40	176	37	22	20	6	2	2	1	24	1	30	1	0	6	2	.750	0	0	4.50

1987: Power, Groundball

	1987 SEASON										FOUR YEAR TOTALS (1984 – 1987)									
	G	IP	H	BB	SO	SB	CS	W	L	S	ERA	G	IP	H	BB	SO	SB	CS	W	L	S	ERA
Totals	29	39.2	37	24	30	0	1	6	2	0	4.54	29	39.2	37	24	30	0	1	6	2	0	4.54
At Home	13	20.0	9	7	19	0	1	3	1	0	1.80	13	20.0	9	7	19	0	1	3	1	0	1.80
On Road	16	19.2	28	17	11	0	0	3	1	0	7.32	16	19.2	28	17	11	0	0	3	1	0	7.32
vs. Opposing Batters	AVG	OBP	SLG	AB	H	2B	3B	HR	RBI	BB	SO	AVG	OBP	SLG	AB	H	2B	3B	HR	RBI	BB	SO
Totals	.252	.356	.401	147	37	4	0	6	23	24	30	.252	.356	.401	147	37	4	0	6	23	24	30
vs. Left	.231	.333	.323	65	15	0	0	2	5	9	13	.231	.333	.323	65	15	0	0	2	5	9	13
vs. Right	.268	.374	.463	82	22	4	0	4	18	15	17	.268	.374	.463	82	22	4	0	4	18	15	17

Calhoun, Jeffrey Wilton "Jeff"

Bats: Left   Throws: Left   Born 04/11/58

1987 SEASON AND MAJOR-LEAGUE CAREER PITCHING TOTALS

	G	GS	CG	GF	IP	BFP	H	R	ER	HR	SH	SF	HB	TBB	IBB	SO	WP	Bk	W	L	Pct	ShO	Sv	ERA
87 PHI	42	0	0	15	43	183	25	13	7	1	5	2	1	26	8	31	2	0	3	1	.750	0	1	1.47
4 YEARS	115	0	0	45	149	615	114	53	38	6	11	4	1	64	15	103	10	1	6	7	.462	0	5	2.30

1987: Power, Flyball   1986: Finesse, Flyball

1987 SEASON

	G	IP	H	BB	SO	SB	CS	W	L	S	ERA
Totals	42	42.2	25	26	31	1	0	3	1	1	1.48
At Home	21	26.2	9	8	19	0	0	3	0	1	0.00
On Road	21	16.0	16	18	12	1	0	0	1	0	3.94

vs. Opposing Batters	AVG	OBP	SLG	AB	H	2B	3B	HR	RBI	BB	SO
Totals	.168	.292	.255	149	25	8	1	1	14	26	31
vs. Left	.250	.349	.404	52	13	5	0	1	9	8	6
vs. Right	.124	.261	.175	97	12	3	1	0	5	18	25

TWO YEAR TOTALS (1986 – 1987)

	G	IP	H	BB	SO	SB	CS	W	L	S	ERA
	62	69.1	53	38	45	4	2	4	1	1	2.34
	33	45.0	26	14	29	3	1	4	0	1	1.20
	29	24.1	27	24	16	1	1	0	1	0	4.44

AVG	OBP	SLG	AB	H	2B	3B	HR	RBI	BB	SO
.209	.312	.335	254	53	14	3	4	32	38	45
.244	.347	.366	82	20	7	0	1	10	13	11
.192	.294	.320	172	33	7	3	3	22	25	34

Camacho, Ernest Carlos "Ernie"

Bats: Right   Throws: Right   Born 02/01/56

1987 SEASON AND MAJOR-LEAGUE CAREER PITCHING TOTALS

	G	GS	CG	GF	IP	BFP	H	R	ER	HR	SH	SF	HB	TBB	IBB	SO	WP	Bk	W	L	Pct	ShO	Sv	ERA
87 CLE	15	0	0	10	14	69	21	14	14	1	1	0	3	5	1	9	4	0	0	1	.000	0	1	9.00
7 YEARS	153	3	0	102	213	942	216	99	94	11	14	14	8	96	13	117	15	5	7	17	.292	0	44	3.97

1987: Finesse, Groundball   1986: Power, Groundball   1985: Power, Flyball   1984: Finesse, Groundball

1987 SEASON

	G	IP	H	BB	SO	SB	CS	W	L	S	ERA
Totals	15	13.2	21	5	9	2	0	0	1	1	9.22
At Home	4	4.2	5	3	2	1	0	0	1	0	5.79
On Road	11	9.0	16	2	7	1	0	0	0	1	11.00

vs. Opposing Batters	AVG	OBP	SLG	AB	H	2B	3B	HR	RBI	BB	SO
Totals	.350	.426	.517	60	21	5	1	1	20	5	9
vs. Left	.391	.462	.609	23	9	3	1	0	8	2	3
vs. Right	.324	.405	.459	37	12	2	0	1	12	3	6

FOUR YEAR TOTALS (1984 – 1987)

	G	IP	H	BB	SO	SB	CS	W	L	S	ERA
	137	174.1	168	74	95	18	1	7	15	44	3.61
	66	85.2	88	39	46	11	1	3	6	20	3.99
	71	88.2	80	35	49	7	0	4	9	24	3.25

AVG	OBP	SLG	AB	H	2B	3B	HR	RBI	BB	SO
.256	.334	.332	656	168	22	2	8	101	74	95
.292	.374	.394	315	92	13	2	5	50	40	42
.223	.297	.276	341	76	9	0	3	51	34	53

Caminiti, Kenneth Gene "Ken"

Bats: Both   Throws: Right   Born 04/21/63

1987 SEASON AND MAJOR-LEAGUE CAREER BATTING TOTALS

	G	AB	H	2B	3B	HR	TB	R	RBI	TBB	IBB	SO	HP	SH	SF	SB	CS	SB%	GDP	AVG	OBP	SLG
87 HOU	63	203	50	7	1	3	68	10	23	12	1	44	0	2	1	0	0	.00	6	.246	.287	.335
1 YEAR	63	203	50	7	1	3	68	10	23	12	1	44	0	2	1	0	0	.00	6	.246	.287	.335

1987 SEASON

	AVG	OBP	SLG	AB	H	2B	3B	HR	RBI	BB	SO
Totals	.246	.287	.335	203	50	7	1	3	23	12	44
vs. Left	.310	.349	.430	100	31	6	0	2	13	6	19
vs. Right	.184	.227	.243	103	19	1	1	1	10	6	25
At Home	.267	.313	.389	90	24	3	1	2	12	6	20
On Road	.230	.267	.292	113	26	4	0	1	11	6	24

FOUR YEAR TOTALS (1984 – 1987)

	AVG	OBP	SLG	AB	H	2B	3B	HR	RBI	BB	SO
	.246	.287	.335	203	50	7	1	3	23	12	44
	.310	.349	.430	100	31	6	0	2	13	6	19
	.184	.227	.243	103	19	1	1	1	10	6	25
	.267	.313	.389	90	24	3	1	2	12	6	20
	.230	.267	.292	113	26	4	0	1	11	6	24

Campbell, Michael Thomas "Mike"

Bats: Right   Throws: Right   Born 02/17/54

1987 SEASON AND MAJOR-LEAGUE CAREER PITCHING TOTALS

	G	GS	CG	GF	IP	BFP	H	R	ER	HR	SH	SF	HB	TBB	IBB	SO	WP	Bk	W	L	Pct	ShO	Sv	ERA
87 SEA	9	9	1	0	49	215	41	29	26	9	2	3	2	25	2	35	1	1	1	4	.200	0	0	4.78
1 YEAR	9	9	1	0	49	215	41	29	26	9	2	3	2	25	2	35	1	1	1	4	.200	0	0	4.78

1987: Power, Flyball

1987 SEASON

	G	IP	H	BB	SO	SB	CS	W	L	S	ERA
Totals	9	49.1	41	25	35	6	2	1	4	0	4.74
At Home	7	38.1	32	19	28	4	2	1	2	0	5.17
On Road	2	11.0	9	6	7	2	0	0	2	0	3.27

vs. Opposing Batters	AVG	OBP	SLG	AB	H	2B	3B	HR	RBI	BB	SO
Totals	.224	.319	.399	183	41	5	0	9	25	25	35
vs. Left	.248	.344	.419	105	26	3	0	5	16	17	20
vs. Right	.192	.284	.372	78	15	2	0	4	9	8	15

FOUR YEAR TOTALS (1984 – 1987)

	G	IP	H	BB	SO	SB	CS	W	L	S	ERA
	9	49.1	41	25	35	6	2	1	4	0	4.74
	7	38.1	32	19	28	4	2	1	2	0	5.17
	2	11.0	9	6	7	2	0	0	2	0	3.27

AVG	OBP	SLG	AB	H	2B	3B	HR	RBI	BB	SO
.224	.319	.399	183	41	5	0	9	25	25	35
.248	.344	.419	105	26	3	0	5	16	17	20
.192	.284	.372	78	15	2	0	4	9	8	15

Cangelosi, John Anthony

Bats: Both **Throws: Left** **Born 03/10/63**

1987 SEASON AND MAJOR-LEAGUE CAREER BATTING TOTALS

	G	AB	H	2B	3B	HR	TB	R	RBI	TBB	IBB	SO	HP	SH	SF	SB	CS	SB%	GDP	AVG	OBP	SLG
87 PIT	104	182	50	8	3	4	76	44	18	46	1	33	3	1	1	21	6	.78	3	.275	.427	.418
3 YEARS	246	622	153	24	6	6	207	111	50	117	1	95	11	8	4	71	23	.76	8	.246	.373	.333

	1987 SEASON											FOUR YEAR TOTALS (1984 – 1987)									
	AVG	OBP	SLG	AB	H	2B	3B	HR	RBI	BB	SO	AVG	OBP	SLG	AB	H	2B	3B	HR	RBI	BB	SO
Totals	.275	.427	.418	182	50	8	3	4	18	46	33	.246	.373	.333	622	153	24	6	6	50	117	95
vs. Left	.282	.400	.485	103	29	7	1	4	15	19	15	.245	.374	.405	237	58	16	2	6	26	45	36
vs. Right	.266	.458	.329	79	21	1	2	0	3	27	18	.247	.372	.288	385	95	8	4	0	24	72	59
At Home	.294	.411	.431	102	30	4	2	2	13	20	21	.255	.391	.353	306	78	11	5	3	28	62	49
On Road	.250	.444	.400	80	20	4	1	2	5	26	12	.237	.354	.313	316	75	13	1	3	22	55	46

Carlton, Steven Norman "Steve"

Bats: Left **Throws: Left** **Born 12/22/44**

1987 SEASON AND MAJOR-LEAGUE CAREER PITCHING TOTALS

	G	GS	CG	GF	IP	BFP	H	R	ER	HR	SH	SF	HB	TBB	IBB	SO	WP	Bk	W	L	Pct	ShO	Sv	ERA
87 CLE-MIN	32	21	3	5	152	693	165	111	97	24	7	4	4	86	4	91	7	5	6	14	.300	0	1	5.74
23 YEARS	737	708	254	12	5207	21629	4652	2111	1846	409	235	122	53	1828	149	4131	183	88	329	243	.575	55	2	3.19

1987: Power, Flyball   1986: Power, Flyball   1985: Power, Flyball   1984: Power, Flyball

	1987 SEASON											FOUR YEAR TOTALS (1984 – 1987)									
	G	IP	H	BB	SO	SB	CS	W	L	S	ERA	G	IP	H	BB	SO	SB	CS	W	L	S	ERA
Totals	32	152.0	165	86	91	12	5	6	14	1	5.74	113	649.1	659	304	422	62	28	29	43	1	4.46
At Home	15	84.1	85	39	52	7	5	3	7	0	5.02	53	326.1	312	143	216	33	11	13	19	0	4.16
On Road	17	67.2	80	47	39	5	0	3	7	1	6.65	60	323.0	347	161	206	29	17	16	24	1	4.74

	AVG	OBP	SLG	AB	H	2B	3B	HR	RBI	BB	SO	AVG	OBP	SLG	AB	H	2B	3B	HR	RBI	BB	SO
vs. Opposing Batters																						
Totals	.279	.372	.461	592	165	28	4	24	95	86	91	.264	.345	.409	2492	659	121	16	69	326	304	422
vs. Left	.262	.344	.383	107	28	5	1	2	10	13	18	.246	.315	.350	357	88	14	4	5	43	35	70
vs. Right	.282	.378	.478	485	137	23	3	22	85	73	73	.267	.350	.419	2135	571	107	12	64	283	269	352

Carman, Donald Wayne "Don"

Bats: Left **Throws: Left** **Born 08/14/59**

1987 SEASON AND MAJOR-LEAGUE CAREER PITCHING TOTALS

	G	GS	CG	GF	IP	BFP	H	R	ER	HR	SH	SF	HB	TBB	IBB	SO	WP	Bk	W	L	Pct	ShO	Sv	ERA
87 PHI	35	35	3	0	211	886	194	110	99	34	11	5	5	69	7	125	3	1	13	11	.542	2	0	4.22
5 YEARS	168	49	5	56	445	1837	373	194	175	53	21	13	10	165	25	326	13	3	32	21	.604	3	9	3.54

1987: Finesse, Flyball   1986: Power, Flyball   1985: Power, Flyball   1984: Power, Flyball

	1987 SEASON											FOUR YEAR TOTALS (1984 – 1987)									
	G	IP	H	BB	SO	SB	CS	W	L	S	ERA	G	IP	H	BB	SO	SB	CS	W	L	S	ERA
Totals	35	211.0	194	69	125	23	10	13	11	0	4.22	167	445.0	373	165	326	55	27	32	21	8	3.54
At Home	17	101.0	92	30	69	10	3	6	7	0	4.72	80	219.2	180	78	175	23	13	18	9	5	3.77
On Road	18	110.0	102	39	56	13	7	7	4	0	3.76	87	225.1	193	87	151	32	14	14	12	3	3.32

	AVG	OBP	SLG	AB	H	2B	3B	HR	RBI	BB	SO	AVG	OBP	SLG	AB	H	2B	3B	HR	RBI	BB	SO
vs. Opposing Batters																						
Totals	.244	.306	.431	796	194	37	5	34	92	69	125	.230	.302	.382	1625	373	68	10	53	178	165	326
vs. Left	.312	.364	.468	109	34	8	0	3	11	6	14	.254	.302	.386	303	77	15	2	7	35	18	58
vs. Right	.233	.297	.425	687	160	29	5	31	81	63	111	.224	.301	.380	1322	296	53	8	46	143	147	268

Castillo, Juan (Bryan)

Bats: Both **Throws: Right** **Born 01/25/62**

1987 SEASON AND MAJOR-LEAGUE CAREER BATTING TOTALS

	G	AB	H	2B	3B	HR	TB	R	RBI	TBB	IBB	SO	HP	SH	SF	SB	CS	SB%	GDP	AVG	OBP	SLG
87 MIL	116	321	72	11	4	3	100	44	28	33	0	76	3	14	1	15	7	.68	1	.224	.302	.312
2 YEARS	142	375	81	11	5	3	111	50	33	38	0	88	4	16	1	16	8	.67	3	.216	.294	.296

	1987 SEASON											FOUR YEAR TOTALS (1984 – 1987)									
	AVG	OBP	SLG	AB	H	2B	3B	HR	RBI	BB	SO	AVG	OBP	SLG	AB	H	2B	3B	HR	RBI	BB	SO
Totals	.225	.302	.313	320	72	11	4	3	28	33	76	.217	.296	.297	374	81	11	5	3	33	38	88
vs. Left	.219	.229	.299	137	30	4	2	1	7	2	28	.213	.226	.284	155	33	4	2	1	9	2	32
vs. Right	.230	.349	.322	183	42	7	2	2	21	31	48	.219	.336	.306	219	48	7	3	2	24	36	56
At Home	.262	.330	.378	164	43	6	2	3	16	16	35	.256	.327	.364	195	50	6	3	3	21	19	42
On Road	.186	.273	.244	156	29	5	2	0	12	17	41	.173	.259	.223	179	31	5	2	0	12	19	46

Castillo, Monte Carmelo "Carmelo"

Bats: Right   Throws: Right   Born 06/08/58

1987 SEASON AND MAJOR-LEAGUE CAREER BATTING TOTALS

	G	AB	H	2B	3B	HR	TB	R	RBI	TBB	IBB	SO	HP	SH	SF	SB	CS	SB%	GDP	AVG	OBP	SLG
87 CLE	89	220	55	17	0	11	105	27	31	16	0	52	0	1	4	1	1	.50	0	.250	.296	.477
6 YEARS	398	976	247	46	4	43	430	144	138	67	2	195	9	3	8	8	6	.57	24	.253	.305	.441

	1987 SEASON											FOUR YEAR TOTALS (1984 – 1987)									
	AVG	OBP	SLG	AB	H	2B	3B	HR	RBI	BB	SO	AVG	OBP	SLG	AB	H	2B	3B	HR	RBI	BB	SO
Totals	.250	.296	.477	220	55	17	0	11	31	16	52	.259	.309	.461	820	212	40	3	40	124	57	172
vs. Left	.266	.336	.516	124	33	10	0	7	21	14	29	.261	.318	.489	501	131	24	3	28	79	41	106
vs. Right	.229	.240	.427	96	22	7	0	4	10	2	23	.254	.294	.417	319	81	16	0	12	45	16	66
At Home	.314	.368	.619	118	37	12	0	8	21	12	28	.297	.345	.545	407	121	26	3	23	75	31	82
On Road	.176	.206	.314	102	18	5	0	3	10	4	24	.220	.273	.378	413	91	14	0	17	49	26	90

Cerutti, John Joseph

Bats: Left   Throws: Left   Born 04/28/60

1987 SEASON AND MAJOR-LEAGUE CAREER PITCHING TOTALS

	G	GS	CG	GF	IP	BFP	H	R	ER	HR	SH	SF	HB	TBB	IBB	SO	WP	Bk	W	L	Pct	ShO	Sv	ERA
87 TOR	44	21	2	6	151	638	144	75	74	30	3	2	1	59	5	92	5	1	11	4	.733	0	0	4.41
3 YEARS	82	42	4	10	303	1290	304	155	145	56	7	7	3	110	7	186	15	1	20	10	.667	1	1	4.31

1987: Finesse, Flyball   1986: Finesse, Flyball   1985: Power, Flyball

	1987 SEASON											FOUR YEAR TOTALS (1984 – 1987)										
	G	IP	H	BB	SO	SB	CS	W	L	S	ERA	G	IP	H	BB	SO	SB	CS	W	L	S	ERA
Totals	44	151.1	144	59	92	8	5	11	4	0	4.40	82	303.1	304	110	186	14	13	20	10	1	4.30
At Home	23	67.2	66	34	41	7	1	3	2	0	5.99	40	131.0	137	52	87	9	5	5	5	0	5.50
On Road	21	83.2	78	25	51	1	4	8	2	0	3.12	42	172.1	167	58	99	5	8	15	5	1	3.39

vs. Opposing Batters	AVG	OBP	SLG	AB	H	2B	3B	HR	RBI	BB	SO	AVG	OBP	SLG	AB	H	2B	3B	HR	RBI	BB	SO
Totals	.251	.321	.476	573	144	27	6	30	69	59	92	.261	.325	.467	1163	304	53	9	56	149	110	186
vs. Left	.246	.308	.440	134	33	6	1	6	19	12	26	.259	.310	.449	274	71	10	3	12	38	20	52
vs. Right	.253	.325	.487	439	111	21	5	24	50	47	66	.262	.330	.472	889	233	43	6	44	111	90	134

Cey, Ronald Charles "Ron"

Bats: Right   Throws: Right   Born 02/15/48

1987 SEASON AND MAJOR-LEAGUE CAREER BATTING TOTALS

	G	AB	H	2B	3B	HR	TB	R	RBI	TBB	IBB	SO	HP	SH	SF	SB	CS	SB%	GDP	AVG	OBP	SLG
87 OAK	45	104	23	6	0	4	41	12	11	22	1	32	1	0	1	0	0	.00	4	.221	.359	.394
17 YEARS	2073	7162	1868	328	21	316	3186	977	1139	1012	117	1235	62	26	82	24	29	.45	185	.261	.354	.445

	1987 SEASON											FOUR YEAR TOTALS (1984 – 1987)									
	AVG	OBP	SLG	AB	H	2B	3B	HR	RBI	BB	SO	AVG	OBP	SLG	AB	H	2B	3B	HR	RBI	BB	SO
Totals	.221	.359	.394	104	23	6	0	4	11	22	32	.242	.335	.438	1365	330	72	2	64	207	185	312
vs. Left	.237	.372	.421	76	18	5	0	3	9	16	26	.254	.371	.500	410	104	26	0	25	70	73	99
vs. Right	.179	.324	.321	28	5	1	0	1	2	6	6	.237	.319	.412	955	226	46	2	39	137	112	213
At Home	.203	.345	.362	69	14	2	0	3	5	15	16	.242	.344	.443	693	168	35	1	34	115	105	166
On Road	.257	.386	.457	35	9	4	0	1	6	7	16	.241	.326	.433	672	162	37	1	30	92	80	146

Childress, Rodney Osborne "Rocky"

Bats: Right   Throws: Right   Born 02/18/62

1987 SEASON AND MAJOR-LEAGUE CAREER PITCHING TOTALS

	G	GS	CG	GF	IP	BFP	H	R	ER	HR	SH	SF	HB	TBB	IBB	SO	WP	Bk	W	L	Pct	ShO	Sv	ERA
87 HOU	32	0	0	12	48	201	46	17	16	4	3	3	0	18	6	26	0	0	1	2	.333	0	0	3.00
3 YEARS	50	1	0	15	84	364	95	43	41	7	5	5	0	28	9	41	1	0	1	3	.250	0	0	4.39

1987: Finesse, Groundball   1986: Finesse, Flyball

	1987 SEASON											TWO YEAR TOTALS (1986 – 1987)										
	G	IP	H	BB	SO	SB	CS	W	L	S	ERA	G	IP	H	BB	SO	SB	CS	W	L	S	ERA
Totals	32	48.1	46	18	26	3	1	1	2	0	2.98	34	51.0	50	19	27	4	1	1	2	0	3.18
At Home	13	19.0	20	8	8	0	0	1	1	0	2.84	13	19.0	20	8	8	0	0	1	1	0	2.84
On Road	19	29.1	26	10	18	3	1	0	1	0	3.07	21	32.0	30	11	19	4	1	0	1	0	3.38

vs. Opposing Batters	AVG	OBP	SLG	AB	H	2B	3B	HR	RBI	BB	SO	AVG	OBP	SLG	AB	H	2B	3B	HR	RBI	BB	SO
Totals	.260	.323	.384	177	46	6	2	4	25	18	26	.266	.329	.394	188	50	8	2	4	27	19	27
vs. Left	.306	.375	.506	85	26	4	2	3	13	10	10	.315	.379	.511	92	29	5	2	3	14	10	10
vs. Right	.217	.275	.272	92	20	2	0	1	12	8	16	.219	.280	.281	96	21	3	0	1	13	9	17

Christensen, John Lawrence

Bats: Right   Throws: Right   Born 09/05/60

1987 SEASON AND MAJOR-LEAGUE CAREER BATTING TOTALS

	G	AB	H	2B	3B	HR	TB	R	RBI	TBB	IBB	SO	HP	SH	SF	SB	CS	SB%	GDP	AVG	OBP	SLG
87 SEA	53	132	32	6	1	2	46	19	12	12	0	28	0	2	0	2	0	1.00		.242	.306	.348
3 YEARS	109	256	56	12	2	5	87	31	28	32	1	53	0	3	1	3	3	.50	6	.219	.304	.340

	1987 SEASON											TWO YEAR TOTALS (1986 – 1987)										
	AVG	OBP	SLG	AB	H	2B	3B	HR	RBI	BB	SO	AVG	OBP	SLG	AB	H	2B	3B	HR	RBI	BB	SO
Totals	.242	.306	.348	132	32	6	1	2	12	12	28	.242	.303	.348	132	32	6	1	2	12	12	28
vs. Left	.229	.302	.352	105	24	5	1	2	10	11	17	.229	.302	.352	105	24	5	1	2	10	11	17
vs. Right	.296	.321	.333	27	8	1	0	0	2	1	11	.296	.321	.333	27	8	1	0	0	2	1	11
At Home	.246	.325	.391	69	17	4	0	2	9	8	13	.246	.325	.391	69	17	4	0	2	9	8	13
On Road	.238	.284	.302	63	15	2	1	0	3	4	15	.238	.284	.302	63	15	2	1	0	3	4	15

Clark, David Earl "Dave"

Bats: Left   Throws: Right   Born 09/03/62

1987 SEASON AND MAJOR-LEAGUE CAREER BATTING TOTALS

	G	AB	H	2B	3B	HR	TB	R	RBI	TBB	IBB	SO	HP	SH	SF	SB	CS	SB%	GDP	AVG	OBP	SLG
87 CLE	29	87	18	5	0	3	32	11	12	2	0	24	0	0	0	1	0	1.00	4	.207	.225	.368
2 YEARS	47	145	34	6	0	6	58	21	21	9	0	35	0	2	1	2	0	1.00	5	.234	.277	.400

	1987 SEASON											FOUR YEAR TOTALS (1984 – 1987)										
	AVG	OBP	SLG	AB	H	2B	3B	HR	RBI	BB	SO	AVG	OBP	SLG	AB	H	2B	3B	HR	RBI	BB	SO
Totals	.207	.225	.368	87	18	5	0	3	12	2	24	.234	.276	.400	145	34	6	0	6	21	9	35
vs. Left	.000	.000	.000	6	0	0	0	0	0	0	3	.267	.313	.333	15	4	1	0	1	1	1	6
vs. Right	.222	.241	.395	81	18	5	0	3	12	2	21	.231	.273	.408	130	30	5	0	6	20	8	29
At Home	.200	.220	.275	40	8	0	0	1	5	1	10	.255	.296	.373	51	13	0	0	2	6	3	11
On Road	.213	.229	.447	47	10	5	0	2	7	1	14	.223	.267	.415	94	21	6	0	4	15	6	24

Clarke, Stanley Martin "Stan"

Bats: Left   Throws: Left   Born 08/09/60

1987 SEASON AND MAJOR-LEAGUE CAREER PITCHING TOTALS

	G	GS	CG	GF	IP	BFP	H	R	ER	HR	SH	SF	HB	TBB	IBB	SO	WP	Bk	W	L	Pct	ShO	Sv	ERA
87 SEA	22	0	0	9	23	107	31	14	14	7	1	3	0	10	1	13	3	0	2	2	.500	0	0	5.48
4 YEARS	46	0	0	22	51	231	62	33	33	14	5	5	0	27	2	31	3	3	3	4	.429	0	0	5.82

1987: Finesse, Flyball   1986: Power, Flyball

	1987 SEASON										TWO YEAR TOTALS (1986 – 1987)									
	G	IP	H	BB	SO	SB	CS	W	L	S	ERA	G	IP	H	BB	SO	SB	CS	W	L	S	ERA
Totals	22	23.1	31	10	13	1	1	2	2	0	5.40	32	36.0	49	20	22	2	2	2	3	0	6.75
At Home	8	9.1	16	3	5	0	0	0	0	0	7.71	14	16.2	30	7	9	1	1	0	0	0	10.26
On Road	14	14.0	15	7	8	1	1	2	2	0	3.86	18	19.1	19	13	13	1	1	2	3	0	3.72

vs. Opposing Batters	AVG	OBP	SLG	AB	H	2B	3B	HR	RBI	BB	SO	AVG	OBP	SLG	AB	H	2B	3B	HR	RBI	BB	SO
Totals	.333	.387	.591	93	31	3	0	7	24	10	13	.348	.418	.610	141	49	4	0	11	38	20	22
vs. Left	.341	.396	.659	41	14	1	0	4	16	5	10	.397	.439	.690	58	23	2	0	5	20	6	15
vs. Right	.327	.379	.538	52	17	2	0	3	8	5	3	.313	.404	.554	83	26	2	0	6	18	14	7

Clear, Mark Alan

Bats: Right   Throws: Right   Born 05/27/56

1987 SEASON AND MAJOR-LEAGUE CAREER PITCHING TOTALS

	G	GS	CG	GF	IP	BFP	H	R	ER	HR	SH	SF	HB	TBB	IBB	SO	WP	Bk	W	L	Pct	ShO	Sv	ERA
87 MIL	58	1	0	37	78	360	70	46	39	9	2	5	5	55	3	81	3	0	8	5	.615	0	6	4.50
9 YEARS	452	1	0	321	768	3446	646	378	330	56	35	36	33	524	45	772	47	4	70	49	.588	0	83	3.87

1987: Power, Flyball   1986: Power, Groundball   1985: Power, Flyball   1984: Power, Flyball

	1987 SEASON										FOUR YEAR TOTALS (1984 – 1987)									
	G	IP	H	BB	SO	SB	CS	W	L	S	ERA	G	IP	H	BB	SO	SB	CS	W	L	S	ERA
Totals	58	78.2	70	55	81	9	5	8	5	6	4.46	205	275.0	215	211	297	47	10	22	16	33	3.57
At Home	26	38.0	35	19	40	4	1	4	1	3	4.50	96	135.0	100	80	153	23	5	13	4	15	3.07
On Road	32	40.2	35	36	41	5	4	4	4	3	4.43	109	140.0	115	131	144	24	5	9	12	18	4.11

vs. Opposing Batters	AVG	OBP	SLG	AB	H	2B	3B	HR	RBI	BB	SO	AVG	OBP	SLG	AB	H	2B	3B	HR	RBI	BB	SO
Totals	.238	.363	.401	294	70	15	3	9	47	55	81	.216	.355	.312	995	215	37	5	16	147	211	297
vs. Left	.250	.394	.464	140	35	9	3	5	30	32	37	.207	.379	.292	459	95	15	3	6	72	126	143
vs. Right	.227	.333	.344	154	35	6	0	4	17	23	44	.224	.332	.328	536	120	22	2	10	75	85	154

Clements, Patrick Brian "Pat"

Bats: Right   Throws: Left   Born 02/02/62

1987 SEASON AND MAJOR-LEAGUE CAREER PITCHING TOTALS

	G	GS	CG	GF	IP	BFP	H	R	ER	HR	SH	SF	HB	TBB	IBB	SO	WP	Bk	W	L	Pct	ShO	Sv	ERA
87 NYA	55	0	0	20	80	347	91	45	44	4	6	4	3	30	2	36	8	2	3	3	.500	0	7	4.95
3 YEARS	188	0	0	58	237	1003	230	102	100	11	19	9	7	102	13	103	13	2	8	9	.471	0	12	3.80

1987: Finesse, Groundball   1986: Finesse, Groundball   1985: Finesse, Groundball

	1987 SEASON										
	G	IP	H	BB	SO	SB	CS	W	L	S	ERA
Totals	55	79.1	91	30	36	2	1	3	3	7	4.99
At Home	27	41.1	47	11	21	1	0	1	1	5	3.48
On Road	28	38.0	44	19	15	1	1	2	2	2	6.63

vs. Opposing Batters	AVG	OBP	SLG	AB	H	2B	3B	HR	RBI	BB	SO
Totals	.298	.363	.397	305	91	18	0	4	50	30	36
vs. Left	.173	.264	.259	81	14	4	0	1	13	8	19
vs. Right	.344	.398	.446	224	77	14	0	3	37	22	17

	FOUR YEAR TOTALS (1984 – 1987)										
	G	IP	H	BB	SO	SB	CS	W	L	S	ERA
	188	236.2	230	102	103	11	5	8	9	12	3.80

	AVG	OBP	SLG	AB	H	2B	3B	HR	RBI	BB	SO
	.266	.344	.356	868	231	43	1	11	114	102	103
	.239	.338	.341	276	66	13	0	5	46	39	47
	.279	.347	.363	592	165	30	1	6	68	63	56

Coles, Darnell

Bats: Right   Throws: Right   Born 06/02/62

1987 SEASON AND MAJOR-LEAGUE CAREER BATTING TOTALS

	G	AB	H	2B	3B	HR	TB	R	RBI	TBB	IBB	SO	HP	SH	SF	SB	CS	SB%	GDP	AVG	OBP	SLG
87 DET-PIT	93	268	54	13	1	10	99	34	39	34	3	43	3	5	3	1	4	.20	4	.201	.295	.369
5 YEARS	337	1083	259	57	4	32	420	133	142	112	6	182	12	16	13	9	11	.45	25	.239	.314	.388

	1987 SEASON									
	AVG	OBP	SLG	AB	H	2B	3B	HR	RBI	BB	SO
Totals	.201	.295	.369	268	54	13	1	10	39	34	43
vs. Left	.201	.306	.409	154	31	8	0	8	25	22	21
vs. Right	.202	.281	.316	114	23	5	1	2	14	12	22
At Home	.234	.327	.454	141	33	7	0	8	27	19	22
On Road	.165	.259	.276	127	21	6	1	2	12	15	21

	FOUR YEAR TOTALS (1984 – 1987)									
	AVG	OBP	SLG	AB	H	2B	3B	HR	RBI	BB	SO
	.235	.312	.387	991	233	50	4	31	136	105	170
	.224	.311	.364	393	88	19	0	12	54	50	53
	.242	.313	.403	598	145	31	4	19	82	55	117
	.255	.331	.420	483	123	20	0	20	80	55	89
	.217	.294	.356	508	110	30	4	11	56	50	81

Collins, David S "Dave"

Bats: Both   Throws: Left   Born 10/20/52

1987 SEASON AND MAJOR-LEAGUE CAREER BATTING TOTALS

	G	AB	H	2B	3B	HR	TB	R	RBI	TBB	IBB	SO	HP	SH	SF	SB	CS	SB%	GDP	AVG	OBP	SLG
87 CIN	57	85	25	5	0	0	30	19	5	11	0	12	2	2	0	9	0	1.00	1	.294	.388	.353
13 YEARS	1425	4569	1256	176	50	32	1628	631	349	433	14	606	36	59	29	378	135	.74	55	.275	.340	.356

	1987 SEASON									
	AVG	OBP	SLG	AB	H	2B	3B	HR	RBI	BB	SO
Totals	.294	.388	.353	85	25	5	0	0	5	11	12
vs. Left	.321	.424	.393	28	9	2	0	0	2	5	4
vs. Right	.281	.369	.333	57	16	3	0	0	3	6	8
At Home	.239	.300	.283	46	11	2	0	0	4	4	6
On Road	.359	.479	.436	39	14	3	0	0	1	7	6

	FOUR YEAR TOTALS (1984 – 1987)									
	AVG	OBP	SLG	AB	H	2B	3B	HR	RBI	BB	SO
	.279	.342	.374	1324	369	63	21	7	104	117	139
	.262	.307	.360	286	75	16	3	2	33	17	27
	.283	.351	.378	1038	294	47	18	5	71	100	112
	.263	.330	.368	642	169	30	14	3	46	60	70
	.293	.353	.380	682	200	33	7	4	58	57	69

Comstock, Keith Martin

Bats: Left   Throws: Left   Born 12/23/55

1987 SEASON AND MAJOR-LEAGUE CAREER PITCHING TOTALS

	G	GS	CG	GF	IP	BFP	H	R	ER	HR	SH	SF	HB	TBB	IBB	SO	WP	Bk	W	L	Pct	ShO	Sv	ERA
87 SF-SD	41	0	0	15	57	244	52	30	29	5	3	4	0	31	5	59	6	1	2	1	.667	0	1	4.58
2 YEARS	45	0	0	17	63	272	58	36	35	7	4	4	0	35	5	61	6	1	2	1	.667	0	1	5.00

1987: Power, Flyball

	1987 SEASON									
	G	IP	H	BB	SO	SB	CS	W	L	S	ERA
Totals	42	56.2	52	31	59	3	2	2	1	1	4.61
At Home	21	30.1	25	15	35	1	1	0	1	1	3.86
On Road	21	26.1	27	16	24	2	1	2	0	0	5.47

vs. Opposing Batters	AVG	OBP	SLG	AB	H	2B	3B	HR	RBI	BB	SO
Totals	.252	.344	.364	206	52	6	1	5	30	31	59
vs. Left	.290	.351	.377	69	20	3	0	1	13	7	14
vs. Right	.234	.341	.358	137	32	3	1	4	17	24	45

	TWO YEAR TOTALS (1986 – 1987)									
	G	IP	H	BB	SO	SB	CS	W	L	S	ERA
	42	56.2	52	31	59	3	2	2	1	1	4.61
	21	30.1	25	15	35	1	1	0	1	1	3.86
	21	26.1	27	16	24	2	1	2	0	0	5.47

	AVG	OBP	SLG	AB	H	2B	3B	HR	RBI	BB	SO
	.252	.344	.364	206	52	6	1	5	30	31	59
	.290	.351	.377	69	20	3	0	1	13	7	14
	.234	.341	.358	137	32	3	1	4	17	24	45

Concepcion, David Ismael (Benitez) "Dave"

Bats: Right **Throws: Right** **Born 06/17/48**

1987 SEASON AND MAJOR-LEAGUE CAREER BATTING TOTALS

	G	AB	H	2B	3B	HR	TB	R	RBI	TBB	IBB	SO	HP	SH	SF	SB	CS	SB%	GDP	AVG	OBP	SLG
87 CIN	104	279	89	15	0	1	107	32	33	28	5	24	0	1	3	4	3	.57	10	.319	.377	.384
18 YEARS	2404	8526	2287	380	48	101	3066	982	942	718	88	1163	21	73	86	318	107	.75	262	.268	.324	.360

	1987 SEASON											FOUR YEAR TOTALS (1984 – 1987)									
	AVG	OBP	SLG	AB	H	2B	3B	HR	RBI	BB	SO	AVG	OBP	SLG	AB	H	2B	3B	HR	RBI	BB	SO
Totals	.319	.377	.384	279	89	15	0	1	33	28	24	.262	.323	.338	1681	441	73	5	15	169	156	206
vs. Left	.340	.392	.420	150	51	9	0	1	17	14	11	.298	.359	.403	598	178	36	0	9	54	61	59
vs. Right	.295	.361	.341	129	38	6	0	0	16	14	13	.243	.302	.303	1083	263	37	5	6	115	95	147
At Home	.316	.361	.406	133	42	9	0	1	14	10	7	.261	.325	.339	824	215	41	4	5	86	80	95
On Road	.322	.392	.363	146	47	6	0	0	19	18	17	.264	.320	.338	857	226	32	1	10	83	76	111

Cone, David Brian "Dave"

Bats: Left **Throws: Right** **Born 01/02/63**

1987 SEASON AND MAJOR-LEAGUE CAREER PITCHING TOTALS

	G	GS	CG	GF	IP	BFP	H	R	ER	HR	SH	SF	HB	TBB	IBB	SO	WP	Bk	W	L	Pct	ShO	Sv	ERA
87 NYA	21	13	1	0	99	420	87	46	41	11	4	3	5	44	1	68	2	4	5	6	.455	1	3	3.73
2 YEARS	32	13	1	5	122	528	116	60	55	13	4	3	6	57	2	89	5	4	5	6	.455	1	3	4.06

1987: Power, Flyball **1986: Power, Flyball**

	1987 SEASON										FOUR YEAR TOTALS (1984 – 1987)									
	G	IP	H	BB	SO	SB	CS	W	L	S	ERA	G	IP	H	BB	SO	SB	CS	W	L	S	ERA
Totals	21	99.1	87	44	68	9	11	5	6	1	3.71	32	122.0	116	57	89	10	13	5	6	1	4.06
At Home	9	45.2	46	22	30	4	7	3	3	0	3.94	15	56.0	61	30	36	4	8	3	3	0	4.50
On Road	12	53.2	41	22	38	5	4	2	3	1	3.52	17	66.0	55	27	53	6	5	2	3	1	3.68
vs. Opposing Batters	AVG	OBP	SLG	AB	H	2B	3B	HR	RBI	BB	SO	AVG	OBP	SLG	AB	H	2B	3B	HR	RBI	BB	SO
Totals	.239	.327	.387	364	87	15	3	11	40	44	68	.253	.342	.406	458	116	21	5	13	58	57	89
vs. Left	.233	.338	.376	189	44	8	2	5	19	28	26	.268	.370	.434	235	63	12	3	7	34	35	33
vs. Right	.246	.314	.400	175	43	7	1	6	21	16	42	.238	.310	.377	223	53	9	2	6	24	22	56

Conroy, Timothy James "Tim"

Bats: Left **Throws: Left** **Born 04/03/60**

1987 SEASON AND MAJOR-LEAGUE CAREER PITCHING TOTALS

	G	GS	CG	GF	IP	BFP	H	R	ER	HR	SH	SF	HB	TBB	IBB	SO	WP	Bk	W	L	Pct	ShO	Sv	ERA
87 STL	10	9	0	0	41	188	48	26	25	0	3	2	1	25	3	22	2	0	3	2	.600	0	0	5.49
7 YEARS	135	71	5	21	466	2081	438	279	244	47	8	23	10	284	13	307	31	2	18	32	.360	1	0	4.71

1987: Power, Flyball **1986: Power, Flyball** **1985: Finesse, Flyball** **1984: Power, Flyball**

	1987 SEASON										FOUR YEAR TOTALS (1984 – 1987)									
	G	IP	H	BB	SO	SB	CS	W	L	S	ERA	G	IP	H	BB	SO	SB	CS	W	L	S	ERA
Totals	10	40.2	48	25	22	6	2	3	2	0	5.53	89	274.1	274	159	178	31	10	9	20	0	5.18
At Home	6	19.0	23	14	10	4	1	1	1	0	7.11	49	154.2	153	87	90	19	7	4	12	0	5.12
On Road	4	21.2	25	11	12	2	1	2	1	0	4.15	40	119.2	121	72	88	12	3	5	8	0	5.26
vs. Opposing Batters	AVG	OBP	SLG	AB	H	2B	3B	HR	RBI	BB	SO	AVG	OBP	SLG	AB	H	2B	3B	HR	RBI	BB	SO
Totals	.306	.400	.395	157	48	12	1	0	17	25	22	.263	.360	.419	1042	274	58	9	29	140	159	178
vs. Left	.313	.389	.375	32	10	2	0	0	3	4	6	.230	.337	.354	243	56	8	5	4	24	39	48
vs. Right	.304	.403	.400	125	38	10	1	0	14	21	16	.273	.368	.439	799	218	50	4	25	116	120	130

Cook, Michael Horace "Mike"

Bats: Right **Throws: Right** **Born 08/14/63**

1987 SEASON AND MAJOR-LEAGUE CAREER PITCHING TOTALS

	G	GS	CG	GF	IP	BFP	H	R	ER	HR	SH	SF	HB	TBB	IBB	SO	WP	Bk	W	L	Pct	ShO	Sv	ERA
87 CAL	16	1	0	6	34	148	34	21	21	7	1	0	0	18	0	27	3	1	1	2	.333	0	0	5.56
2 YEARS	21	2	0	7	43	194	47	33	30	10	1	0	0	25	1	33	3	1	1	4	.200	0	0	6.28

1987: Power, Flyball **1986: Power, Flyball**

	1987 SEASON										FOUR YEAR TOTALS (1984 – 1987)									
	G	IP	H	BB	SO	SB	CS	W	L	S	ERA	G	IP	H	BB	SO	SB	CS	W	L	S	ERA
Totals	16	34.1	34	18	27	4	3	1	2	0	5.50	21	43.0	47	25	33	4	3	1	4	0	6.28
At Home	7	17.1	19	10	12	3	2	1	1	0	6.23	9	20.1	24	14	13	3	2	1	2	0	7.08
On Road	9	17.0	15	8	15	1	1	0	1	0	4.76	12	22.2	23	11	20	1	1	0	2	0	5.56
vs. Opposing Batters	AVG	OBP	SLG	AB	H	2B	3B	HR	RBI	BB	SO	AVG	OBP	SLG	AB	H	2B	3B	HR	RBI	BB	SO
Totals	.264	.354	.465	129	34	5	0	7	22	18	27	.280	.373	.500	168	47	7	0	10	31	25	33
vs. Left	.321	.397	.589	56	18	3	0	4	15	7	7	.316	.400	.519	79	25	4	0	4	19	11	11
vs. Right	.219	.321	.370	73	16	2	0	3	7	11	20	.247	.350	.483	89	22	3	0	6	12	14	22

Cooper, Cecil Celester

Bats: Left **Throws: Left** **Born 12/20/49**

1987 SEASON AND MAJOR-LEAGUE CAREER BATTING TOTALS

	G	AB	H	2B	3B	HR	TB	R	RBI	TBB	IBB	SO	HP	SH	SF	SB	CS	SB%	GDP	AVG	OBP	SLG
87 MIL	63	250	62	13	0	6	93	25	36	17	2	51	0	0	3	1	1	.50	4	.248	.293	.372
17 YEARS	1896	7349	2192	415	47	241	3424	1012	1125	448	79	911	17	46	79	89	49	.64	150	.298	.337	.466

	1987 SEASON											FOUR YEAR TOTALS (1984 – 1987)									
	AVG	OBP	SLG	AB	H	2B	3B	HR	RBI	BB	SO	AVG	OBP	SLG	AB	H	2B	3B	HR	RBI	BB	SO
Totals	.248	.293	.372	250	62	13	0	6	36	17	51	.273	.311	.403	2026	553	104	12	45	277	115	274
vs. Left	.259	.308	.358	81	21	5	0	1	13	7	19	.298	.342	.413	642	191	31	5	11	107	43	101
vs. Right	.243	.285	.379	169	41	8	0	5	23	10	32	.262	.296	.398	1384	362	73	7	34	170	72	173
At Home	.296	.342	.463	108	32	6	0	4	22	8	18	.271	.312	.393	944	256	46	6	19	129	58	135
On Road	.211	.255	.303	142	30	7	0	2	14	9	33	.274	.310	.411	1082	297	58	6	26	148	57	139

Cora, Jose Manuel (Amaro) "Joey"

Bats: Both **Throws: Right** **Born 05/14/65**

1987 SEASON AND MAJOR-LEAGUE CAREER BATTING TOTALS

	G	AB	H	2B	3B	HR	TB	R	RBI	TBB	IBB	SO	HP	SH	SF	SB	CS	SB%	GDP	AVG	OBP	SLG
87 SD	77	241	57	7	2	0	68	23	13	28	1	26	1	5	1	15	11	.58	4	.237	.317	.282
1 YEAR	77	241	57	7	2	0	68	23	13	28	1	26	1	5	1	15	11	.58	4	.237	.317	.282

	1987 SEASON											FOUR YEAR TOTALS (1984 – 1987)									
	AVG	OBP	SLG	AB	H	2B	3B	HR	RBI	BB	SO	AVG	OBP	SLG	AB	H	2B	3B	HR	RBI	BB	SO
Totals	.237	.317	.282	241	57	7	2	0	13	28	26	.237	.317	.282	241	57	7	2	0	13	28	26
vs. Left	.245	.308	.286	98	24	2	1	0	4	9	10	.245	.308	.286	98	24	2	1	0	4	9	10
vs. Right	.231	.323	.280	143	33	5	1	0	9	19	16	.231	.323	.280	143	33	5	1	0	9	19	16
At Home	.207	.310	.225	111	23	2	0	0	4	16	14	.207	.310	.225	111	23	2	0	0	4	16	14
On Road	.262	.324	.331	130	34	5	2	0	9	12	12	.262	.324	.331	130	34	5	2	0	9	12	12

Correa, Edwin Josue (Andino) "Ed"

Bats: Right **Throws: Right** **Born 04/29/66**

1987 SEASON AND MAJOR-LEAGUE CAREER PITCHING TOTALS

	G	GS	CG	GF	IP	BFP	H	R	ER	HR	SH	SF	HB	TBB	IBB	SO	WP	Bk	W	L	Pct	ShO	Sv	ERA
87 TEX	15	15	0	0	70	339	83	63	59	17	1	2	4	52	2	61	9	0	3	5	.375	0	0	7.59
3 YEARS	52	48	4	3	282	1276	261	174	162	34	5	5	7	189	4	260	29	2	16	19	.457	2	0	5.17

1987: Power, Flyball   **1986: Power, Groundball**   **1985: Power, Flyball**

	1987 SEASON										FOUR YEAR TOTALS (1984 – 1987)								
	G	IP	H	BB	SO	SB	CS	W	L	S	ERA	G	IP	H	BB	SO	SB	CS	W	L	S	ERA
Totals	15	70.0	83	52	61	19	3	3	5	0	7.59	52	282.2	261	189	260	54	12	16	19	0	5.16
At Home	6	29.2	39	16	30	9	1	2	1	0	8.49	22	120.2	110	64	127	22	5	9	7	0	5.07
On Road	9	40.1	44	36	31	10	2	1	4	0	6.92	30	162.0	151	125	133	32	7	7	12	0	5.22

vs. Opposing Batters	AVG	OBP	SLG	AB	H	2B	3B	HR	RBI	BB	SO	AVG	OBP	SLG	AB	H	2B	3B	HR	RBI	BB	SO
Totals	.297	.412	.552	279	83	16	2	17	55	52	61	.244	.359	.390	1069	261	48	3	34	144	189	260
vs. Left	.243	.350	.404	136	33	5	1	5	17	22	30	.230	.335	.325	547	126	21	2	9	53	86	121
vs. Right	.350	.469	.692	143	50	11	1	12	38	30	31	.259	.383	.458	522	135	27	1	25	91	103	139

Cotto, Henry

Bats: Right **Throws: Right** **Born 01/05/61**

1987 SEASON AND MAJOR-LEAGUE CAREER BATTING TOTALS

	G	AB	H	2B	3B	HR	TB	R	RBI	TBB	IBB	SO	HP	SH	SF	SB	CS	SB%	GDP	AVG	OBP	SLG
87 NYA	68	149	35	10	0	5	60	21	20	6	0	35	1	0	0	4	2	.67	7	.235	.269	.403
4 YEARS	242	431	109	19	0	7	149	60	40	21	2	87	2	4	1	17	6	.74	12	.253	.290	.346

	1987 SEASON											TWO YEAR TOTALS (1986 – 1987)									
	AVG	OBP	SLG	AB	H	2B	3B	HR	RBI	BB	SO	AVG	OBP	SLG	AB	H	2B	3B	HR	RBI	BB	SO
Totals	.233	.268	.400	150	35	10	0	5	20	6	35	.226	.256	.361	230	52	13	0	6	26	8	52
vs. Left	.198	.226	.321	81	16	4	0	2	12	3	18	.196	.217	.283	138	27	6	0	2	15	4	29
vs. Right	.275	.315	.493	69	19	6	0	3	8	3	17	.272	.309	.478	92	25	7	0	4	11	4	23
At Home	.250	.283	.500	88	22	7	0	5	17	4	20	.240	.261	.426	129	31	9	0	5	20	4	28
On Road	.210	.246	.258	62	13	3	0	0	3	2	15	.208	.245	.277	101	21	4	0	1	6	4	24

Crawford, Steven Ray "Steve"

Bats: Right   Throws: Right   Born 04/29/58

1987 SEASON AND MAJOR-LEAGUE CAREER PITCHING TOTALS

	G	GS	CG	GF	IP	BFP	H	R	ER	HR	SH	SF	HB	TBB	IBB	SO	WP	Bk	W	L	Pct	ShO	Sv	ERA
87 BOS	29	0	0	7	73	324	91	48	43	13	0	0	2	32	2	43	2	0	5	4	.556	0	0	5.30
7 YEARS	173	16	2	74	382	1674	456	210	176	42	13	13	6	126	24	195	13	0	19	16	.543	0	17	4.15

1987: Finesse, Groundball   1986: Finesse, Flyball   1985: Finesse, Groundball   1984: Finesse, Groundball

1987 SEASON	G	IP	H	BB	SO	SB	CS	W	L	S	ERA
Totals	29	72.2	90	32	43	2	1	5	4	0	5.33
At Home	14	37.2	43	14	21	0	1	5	1	0	4.54
On Road	15	35.0	47	18	22	2	0	0	3	0	6.17

FOUR YEAR TOTALS (1984 – 1987)	G	IP	H	BB	SO	SB	CS	W	L	S	ERA
Totals	148	283.0	331	100	154	9	8	16	11	17	4.10
At Home	80	140.1	169	51	83	4	7	11	3	10	4.43
On Road	68	142.2	162	49	71	5	1	5	8	7	3.79

vs. Opposing Batters	AVG	OBP	SLG	AB	H	2B	3B	HR	RBI	BB	SO
Totals	.310	.383	.517	290	90	19	1	13	56	32	43
vs. Left	.333	.405	.538	132	44	9	0	6	21	16	17
vs. Right	.291	.364	.500	158	46	10	1	7	35	16	26

	AVG	OBP	SLG	AB	H	2B	3B	HR	RBI	BB	SO
Totals	.298	.357	.441	1112	331	62	5	29	185	100	154
vs. Left	.319	.391	.464	524	167	35	1	13	88	62	60
vs. Right	.279	.325	.420	588	164	27	4	16	97	38	94

Crews, Stanley Timothy "Tim"

Bats: Right   Throws: Right   Born 04/03/61

1987 SEASON AND MAJOR-LEAGUE CAREER PITCHING TOTALS

	G	GS	CG	GF	IP	BFP	H	R	ER	HR	SH	SF	HB	TBB	IBB	SO	WP	Bk	W	L	Pct	ShO	Sv	ERA
87 LA	20	0	0	7	29	124	30	9	8	2	1	1	2	8	1	20	0	0	1	1	.500	0	3	2.48
1 YEAR	20	0	0	7	29	124	30	9	8	2	1	1	2	8	1	20	0	0	1	1	.500	0	3	2.48

1987: Finesse, Flyball

1987 SEASON	G	IP	H	BB	SO	SB	CS	W	L	S	ERA
Totals	20	29.0	30	7	20	0	0	1	1	3	2.48
At Home	10	13.0	16	3	9	0	0	1	1	1	3.46
On Road	10	16.0	14	4	11	0	0	0	0	2	1.69

FOUR YEAR TOTALS (1984 – 1987)	G	IP	H	BB	SO	SB	CS	W	L	S	ERA
Totals	20	29.0	30	7	20	0	0	1	1	3	2.48
At Home	10	13.0	16	3	9	0	0	1	1	1	3.46
On Road	10	16.0	14	4	11	0	0	0	0	2	1.69

vs. Opposing Batters	AVG	OBP	SLG	AB	H	2B	3B	HR	RBI	BB	SO
Totals	.268	.320	.384	112	30	7	0	2	14	7	20
vs. Left	.211	.246	.351	57	12	2	0	2	8	3	8
vs. Right	.327	.393	.418	55	18	5	0	0	6	4	12

	AVG	OBP	SLG	AB	H	2B	3B	HR	RBI	BB	SO
Totals	.268	.320	.384	112	30	7	0	2	14	7	20
vs. Left	.211	.246	.351	57	12	2	0	2	8	3	8
vs. Right	.327	.393	.418	55	18	5	0	0	6	4	12

Crim, Charles Robert "Chuck"

Bats: Right   Throws: Right   Born 07/23/61

1987 SEASON AND MAJOR-LEAGUE CAREER PITCHING TOTALS

	G	GS	CG	GF	IP	BFP	H	R	ER	HR	SH	SF	HB	TBB	IBB	SO	WP	Bk	W	L	Pct	ShO	Sv	ERA
87 MIL	53	5	0	18	130	549	133	60	53	15	6	1	3	39	5	56	2	1	6	8	.429	0	12	3.67
1 YEAR	53	5	0	18	130	549	133	60	53	15	6	1	3	39	5	56	2	1	6	8	.429	0	12	3.67

1987: Finesse, Groundball

1987 SEASON	G	IP	H	BB	SO	SB	CS	W	L	S	ERA
Totals	53	130.0	133	39	56	8	4	6	8	12	3.67
At Home	28	67.2	71	21	31	6	2	4	4	7	3.19
On Road	25	62.1	62	18	25	2	2	2	4	5	4.19

FOUR YEAR TOTALS (1984 – 1987)	G	IP	H	BB	SO	SB	CS	W	L	S	ERA
Totals	53	130.0	133	39	56	8	4	6	8	12	3.67
At Home	28	67.2	71	21	31	6	2	4	4	7	3.19
On Road	25	62.1	62	18	25	2	2	2	4	5	4.19

vs. Opposing Batters	AVG	OBP	SLG	AB	H	2B	3B	HR	RBI	BB	SO
Totals	.266	.322	.390	500	133	15	1	15	61	39	56
vs. Left	.286	.357	.436	227	65	7	0	9	30	24	27
vs. Right	.249	.292	.352	273	68	8	1	6	31	15	29

	AVG	OBP	SLG	AB	H	2B	3B	HR	RBI	BB	SO
Totals	.266	.322	.390	500	133	15	1	15	61	39	56
vs. Left	.286	.357	.436	227	65	7	0	9	30	24	27
vs. Right	.249	.292	.352	273	68	8	1	6	31	15	29

Cruz, Jose (Dilan)

Bats: Left   Throws: Left   Born 12/02/54

1987 SEASON AND MAJOR-LEAGUE CAREER BATTING TOTALS

	G	AB	H	2B	3B	HR	TB	R	RBI	TBB	IBB	SO	HP	SH	SF	SB	CS	SB%	GDP	AVG	OBP	SLG
87 HOU	126	365	88	17	4	11	146	47	38	36	3	65	0	1	3	4	1	.80	4	.241	.307	.400
18 YEARS	2315	7837	2235	389	94	164	3304	1027	1070	890	141	1023	7	27	82	317	135	.70	117	.285	.355	.422

1987 SEASON	AVG	OBP	SLG	AB	H	2B	3B	HR	RBI	BB	SO
Totals	.241	.307	.397	365	88	16	4	11	38	36	65
vs. Left	.227	.270	.359	128	29	3	1	4	13	8	25
vs. Right	.249	.326	.418	237	59	13	3	7	25	28	40
At Home	.267	.320	.439	180	48	9	2	6	22	15	31
On Road	.216	.295	.357	185	40	7	2	5	16	21	34

FOUR YEAR TOTALS (1984 – 1987)	AVG	OBP	SLG	AB	H	2B	3B	HR	RBI	BB	SO
Totals	.287	.352	.426	1988	571	100	25	42	284	207	292
vs. Left	.276	.320	.400	765	211	26	12	15	121	53	127
vs. Right	.294	.370	.442	1223	360	74	13	27	163	154	165
At Home	.289	.358	.402	966	279	47	13	12	131	110	137
On Road	.286	.345	.449	1022	292	53	12	30	153	97	155

Daulton, Darren Arthur

Bats: Left   Throws: Right   Born 01/03/62

1987 SEASON AND MAJOR-LEAGUE CAREER BATTING TOTALS

	G	AB	H	2B	3B	HR	TB	R	RBI	TBB	IBB	SO	HP	SH	SF	SB	CS	SB%	GDP	AVG	OBP	SLG
87 PHI	53	129	25	6	0	3	40	10	13	16	1	37	0	4	1	0	0	.00	0	.194	.281	.310
4 YEARS	140	373	78	13	1	15	138	43	45	71	4	116	1	6	3	5	3	.63	2	.209	.335	.370

	1987 SEASON										FOUR YEAR TOTALS (1984 – 1987)									
	AVG	OBP	SLG	AB	H	2B	3B	HR	RBI	BB	SO	AVG	OBP	SLG	AB	H	2B	3B	HR	RBI	BB	SO
Totals	.194	.281	.310	129	25	6	0	3	13	16	37	.208	.333	.370	370	77	13	1	15	45	70	115
vs. Left	.125	.222	.250	8	1	1	0	0	1	1	3	.162	.295	.216	37	6	2	0	0	1	7	18
vs. Right	.198	.285	.314	121	24	5	0	3	12	15	34	.213	.338	.387	333	71	11	1	15	44	63	97
At Home	.259	.355	.389	54	14	4	0	1	7	8	15	.229	.379	.380	166	38	8	1	5	20	39	47
On Road	.147	.226	.253	75	11	2	0	2	6	8	22	.191	.294	.363	204	39	5	0	10	25	31	68

Davidson, John Mark "Mark"

Bats: Right   Throws: Right   Born 02/15/61

1987 SEASON AND MAJOR-LEAGUE CAREER BATTING TOTALS

	G	AB	H	2B	3B	HR	TB	R	RBI	TBB	IBB	SO	HP	SH	SF	SB	CS	SB%	GDP	AVG	OBP	SLG
87 MIN	102	150	40	4	1	1	49	32	14	13	1	26	0	4	2	9	2	.82	4	.267	.321	.327
2 YEARS	138	218	48	7	1	1	60	37	16	19	1	48	0	7	2	11	5	.69	5	.220	.280	.275

	1987 SEASON										FOUR YEAR TOTALS (1984 – 1987)									
	AVG	OBP	SLG	AB	H	2B	3B	HR	RBI	BB	SO	AVG	OBP	SLG	AB	H	2B	3B	HR	RBI	BB	SO
Totals	.267	.321	.327	150	40	4	1	1	14	13	26	.220	.280	.275	218	48	7	1	1	16	19	48
vs. Left	.243	.310	.291	103	25	3	1	0	8	10	18	.218	.279	.275	142	31	6	1	0	8	12	30
vs. Right	.319	.346	.404	47	15	1	0	1	6	3	8	.224	.282	.276	76	17	1	0	1	8	7	18
At Home	.256	.315	.305	82	21	2	1	0	7	7	14	.215	.291	.264	121	26	4	1	0	8	13	24
On Road	.279	.329	.353	68	19	2	0	1	7	6	12	.227	.267	.289	97	22	3	0	1	8	6	24

Davis, George Earl "Storm"

Bats: Right   Throws: Right   Born 12/26/61

1987 SEASON AND MAJOR-LEAGUE CAREER PITCHING TOTALS

	G	GS	CG	GF	IP	BFP	H	R	ER	HR	SH	SF	HB	TBB	IBB	SO	WP	Bk	W	L	Pct	ShO	Sv	ERA
87 SD-OAK	26	15	0	5	93	420	98	61	54	8	2	3	2	47	6	65	9	1	3	8	.273	0	0	5.23
6 YEARS	180	136	27	17	948	3993	917	439	401	64	24	27	10	329	27	551	31	6	57	48	.543	4	1	3.81

1987: Power, Groundball   1986: Finesse, Groundball   1985: Finesse, Flyball   1984: Finesse, Groundball

	1987 SEASON										FOUR YEAR TOTALS (1984 – 1987)									
	G	IP	H	BB	SO	SB	CS	W	L	S	ERA	G	IP	H	BB	SO	SB	CS	W	L	S	ERA
Totals	25	91.0	95	47	63	14	7	3	8	0	5.34	116	645.0	638	237	357	58	30	36	37	1	3.92
At Home	9	46.1	46	20	36	7	4	2	4	0	4.47	56	338.1	341	117	208	26	15	20	22	1	3.75
On Road	16	44.2	49	27	27	7	3	1	4	0	6.25	60	306.2	297	120	149	32	15	16	15	0	4.14

vs. Opposing Batters	AVG	OBP	SLG	AB	H	2B	3B	HR	RBI	BB	SO	AVG	OBP	SLG	AB	H	2B	3B	HR	RBI	BB	SO
Totals	.266	.352	.412	357	95	16	6	8	53	47	63	.259	.324	.368	2464	638	107	18	42	269	237	357
vs. Left	.297	.384	.421	195	58	7	4	3	27	28	29	.271	.352	.392	1260	342	61	11	23	145	157	198
vs. Right	.228	.314	.401	162	37	9	2	5	26	19	34	.246	.293	.343	1204	296	46	7	19	124	80	159

Davis, Joel Clark

Bats: Left   Throws: Right   Born 01/30/65

1987 SEASON AND MAJOR-LEAGUE CAREER PITCHING TOTALS

	G	GS	CG	GF	IP	BFP	H	R	ER	HR	SH	SF	HB	TBB	IBB	SO	WP	Bk	W	L	Pct	ShO	Sv	ERA
87 CHA	13	9	1	1	55	243	56	35	35	7	1	1	0	29	1	25	1	0	1	5	.167	0	0	5.73
3 YEARS	44	39	3	1	231	1018	242	133	123	22	5	5	2	106	1	116	6	1	8	13	.381	0	0	4.79

1987: Finesse, Groundball   1986: Finesse, Groundball   1985: Finesse, Groundball

	1987 SEASON										FOUR YEAR TOTALS (1984 – 1987)									
	G	IP	H	BB	SO	SB	CS	W	L	S	ERA	G	IP	H	BB	SO	SB	CS	W	L	S	ERA
Totals	13	55.0	56	29	25	1	2	1	5	0	5.73	44	231.2	242	106	116	16	8	8	13	0	4.78
At Home	6	29.1	33	17	13	1	0	1	2	0	6.14	21	115.2	121	56	60	3	5	5	5	0	4.59
On Road	7	25.2	23	12	12	0	2	0	3	0	5.26	23	116.0	121	50	56	13	3	3	8	0	4.97

vs. Opposing Batters	AVG	OBP	SLG	AB	H	2B	3B	HR	RBI	BB	SO	AVG	OBP	SLG	AB	H	2B	3B	HR	RBI	BB	SO
Totals	.264	.351	.434	212	56	9	3	7	34	29	25	.269	.346	.416	900	242	38	14	22	112	106	116
vs. Left	.269	.356	.471	104	28	4	1	5	18	14	13	.286	.364	.448	475	136	21	7	14	61	58	58
vs. Right	.259	.347	.398	108	28	5	2	2	16	15	12	.249	.325	.379	425	106	17	7	8	51	48	58

Davis, John Kirk

Bats: Right Throws: Right Born 01/05/63

1987 SEASON AND MAJOR-LEAGUE CAREER PITCHING TOTALS

	G	GS	CG	GF	IP	BFP	H	R	ER	HR	SH	SF	HB	TBB	IBB	SO	WP	Bk	W	L	Pct	ShO	Sv	ERA
87 KC	27	0	0	12	44	181	29	13	11	0	0	4	2	26	4	24	2	0	5	2	.714	0	2	2.25
1 YEAR	27	0	0	12	44	181	29	13	11	0	0	4	2	26	4	24	2	0	5	2	.714	0	2	2.25

1987: Power, Groundball

1987 SEASON	G	IP	H	BB	SO	SB	CS	W	L	S	ERA
Totals	27	43.2	29	26	24	6	2	5	2	2	2.27
At Home	11	19.2	15	10	9	4	1	2	1	0	1.83
On Road	16	24.0	14	16	15	2	1	3	1	2	2.63

vs. Opposing Batters	AVG	OBP	SLG	AB	H	2B	3B	HR	RBI	BB	SO
Totals	.193	.315	.247	150	29	6	1	0	17	26	24
vs. Left	.242	.358	.288	66	16	3	0	0	8	13	11
vs. Right	.155	.280	.214	84	13	3	1	0	9	13	13

FOUR YEAR TOTALS (1984 – 1987)	G	IP	H	BB	SO	SB	CS	W	L	S	ERA
Totals	27	43.2	29	26	24	6	2	5	2	2	2.27
At Home	11	19.2	15	10	9	4	1	2	1	0	1.83
On Road	16	24.0	14	16	15	2	1	3	1	2	2.63

vs. Opposing Batters	AVG	OBP	SLG	AB	H	2B	3B	HR	RBI	BB	SO
Totals	.193	.315	.247	150	29	6	1	0	17	26	24
vs. Left	.242	.358	.288	66	16	3	0	0	8	13	11
vs. Right	.155	.280	.214	84	13	3	1	0	9	13	13

Davis, Mark William

Bats: Left Throws: Left Born 10/19/60

1987 SEASON AND MAJOR-LEAGUE CAREER PITCHING TOTALS

	G	GS	CG	GF	IP	BFP	H	R	ER	HR	SH	SF	HB	TBB	IBB	SO	WP	Bk	W	L	Pct	ShO	Sv	ERA
87 SF-SD	63	11	1	18	133	566	123	64	59	14	7	2	6	59	8	98	6	2	9	8	.529	0	2	3.99
7 YEARS	284	71	4	82	667	2832	622	349	318	79	39	26	18	267	38	560	32	9	31	52	.373	2	13	4.29

1987: Power, Flyball   1986: Power, Flyball   1985: Power, Flyball   1984: Power, Flyball

1987 SEASON	G	IP	H	BB	SO	SB	CS	W	L	S	ERA
Totals	64	134.2	126	59	100	9	8	9	8	2	3.94
At Home	33	65.0	53	27	53	3	3	4	4	1	2.91
On Road	31	69.2	73	32	47	6	5	5	4	1	4.91

vs. Opposing Batters	AVG	OBP	SLG	AB	H	2B	3B	HR	RBI	BB	SO
Totals	.251	.336	.389	501	126	21	3	14	59	59	100
vs. Left	.222	.300	.342	117	26	5	0	3	15	11	22
vs. Right	.260	.347	.404	384	100	16	3	11	44	48	78

FOUR YEAR TOTALS (1984 – 1987)	G	IP	H	BB	SO	SB	CS	W	L	S	ERA
Totals	254	508.0	479	188	445	39	24	24	44	13	4.18
At Home	119	250.1	232	88	223	15	14	14	23	6	3.77
On Road	135	257.2	247	100	222	24	10	10	21	7	4.58

vs. Opposing Batters	AVG	OBP	SLG	AB	H	2B	3B	HR	RBI	BB	SO
Totals	.253	.322	.398	1891	479	81	9	58	248	188	445
vs. Left	.194	.255	.299	458	89	14	2	10	53	35	131
vs. Right	.272	.344	.429	1433	390	67	7	48	195	153	314

Davis, Ronald Gene "Ron"

Bats: Right Throws: Right Born 08/06/55

1987 SEASON AND MAJOR-LEAGUE CAREER PITCHING TOTALS

	G	GS	CG	GF	IP	BFP	H	R	ER	HR	SH	SF	HB	TBB	IBB	SO	WP	Bk	W	L	Pct	ShO	Sv	ERA
87 CHN-LA	25	0	0	8	36	169	50	27	24	8	0	2	1	18	3	32	3	2	0	0	.000	0	0	6.00
10 YEARS	472	0	0	336	729	3145	720	351	327	78	34	34	21	294	56	582	39	8	46	52	.469	0	130	4.04

1987: Power, Groundball   1986: Power, Flyball   1985: Power, Groundball   1984: Power, Flyball

1987 SEASON	G	IP	H	BB	SO	SB	CS	W	L	S	ERA
Totals	25	36.0	50	18	32	1	3	0	0	0	6.00
At Home	13	16.1	30	7	11	1	0	0	0	0	9.92
On Road	12	19.2	20	11	21	0	3	0	0	0	2.75

vs. Opposing Batters	AVG	OBP	SLG	AB	H	2B	3B	HR	RBI	BB	SO
Totals	.338	.408	.561	148	50	7	1	8	30	18	32
vs. Left	.366	.425	.648	71	26	3	1	5	15	7	13
vs. Right	.312	.393	.481	77	24	4	0	3	15	11	19

FOUR YEAR TOTALS (1984 – 1987)	G	IP	H	BB	SO	SB	CS	W	L	S	ERA
Totals	199	242.1	270	126	218	24	5	11	25	56	5.46
At Home	98	121.0	140	60	115	13	1	9	5	28	5.13
On Road	101	121.1	130	66	103	11	4	2	20	28	5.79

vs. Opposing Batters	AVG	OBP	SLG	AB	H	2B	3B	HR	RBI	BB	SO
Totals	.285	.369	.463	948	270	41	10	36	192	126	218
vs. Left	.292	.387	.495	463	135	17	7	21	101	72	99
vs. Right	.278	.350	.433	485	135	24	3	15	91	54	119

Dawley, William Chester "Bill"

Bats: Right Throws: Right Born 02/06/58

1987 SEASON AND MAJOR-LEAGUE CAREER PITCHING TOTALS

	G	GS	CG	GF	IP	BFP	H	R	ER	HR	SH	SF	HB	TBB	IBB	SO	WP	Bk	W	L	Pct	ShO	Sv	ERA
87 STL	60	0	0	17	97	406	93	51	48	15	6	2	1	38	11	65	4	1	5	8	.385	0	2	4.45
5 YEARS	263	0	0	123	454	1864	393	174	162	46	38	15	3	160	34	286	14	2	27	28	.491	0	25	3.21

1987: Power, Flyball   1986: Finesse, Flyball   1985: Power, Flyball   1984: Finesse, Flyball

1987 SEASON	G	IP	H	BB	SO	SB	CS	W	L	S	ERA
Totals	60	96.2	93	38	65	6	5	5	8	2	4.47
At Home	32	56.0	57	23	34	3	2	4	6	1	4.82
On Road	28	40.2	36	15	31	3	3	1	2	1	3.98

vs. Opposing Batters	AVG	OBP	SLG	AB	H	2B	3B	HR	RBI	BB	SO
Totals	.259	.330	.457	359	93	22	2	15	56	38	65
vs. Left	.256	.360	.380	129	33	7	0	3	16	21	14
vs. Right	.261	.312	.500	230	60	15	2	12	40	17	51

FOUR YEAR TOTALS (1984 – 1987)	G	IP	H	BB	SO	SB	CS	W	L	S	ERA
Totals	215	373.1	342	138	226	20	13	21	22	11	3.30
At Home	110	197.0	174	71	124	13	4	9	12	6	3.43
On Road	105	176.1	168	67	102	7	9	12	10	5	3.16

vs. Opposing Batters	AVG	OBP	SLG	AB	H	2B	3B	HR	RBI	BB	SO
Totals	.249	.318	.384	1371	342	60	7	37	185	138	226
vs. Left	.266	.346	.397	564	150	27	4	13	78	69	66
vs. Right	.238	.298	.375	807	192	33	3	24	107	69	160

Dayett, Brian Kelly

Bats: Right   Throws: Right   Born 01/22/57

1987 SEASON AND MAJOR-LEAGUE CAREER BATTING TOTALS

	G	AB	H	2B	3B	HR	TB	R	RBI	TBB	IBB	SO	HP	SH	SF	SB	CS	SB%	GDP	AVG	OBP	SLG
87 CHN	97	177	49	14	1	5	80	20	25	20	0	37	0	0	1	0	0	.00	3	.277	.348	.452
5 YEARS	218	426	110	26	2	14	182	45	68	37	0	71	2	1	6	0	1	.00	9	.258	.316	.427

	1987 SEASON											TWO YEAR TOTALS (1986 – 1987)									
	AVG	OBP	SLG	AB	H	2B	3B	HR	RBI	BB	SO	AVG	OBP	SLG	AB	H	2B	3B	HR	RBI	BB	SO
Totals	.277	.348	.452	177	49	14	1	5	25	20	37	.275	.338	.467	244	67	18	1	9	36	26	47
vs. Left	.331	.391	.540	124	41	11	0	5	19	13	19	.315	.366	.521	146	46	12	0	6	23	13	22
vs. Right	.151	.250	.245	53	8	3	1	0	6	7	18	.214	.301	.388	98	21	6	1	3	13	13	25
At Home	.228	.330	.392	79	18	8	1	1	12	12	16	.262	.345	.485	103	27	9	1	4	18	14	20
On Road	.316	.364	.500	98	31	6	0	4	13	8	21	.284	.335	.454	141	40	9	0	5	18	12	27

Dayley, Kenneth Grant "Ken"

Bats: Left   Throws: Left   Born 02/25/59

1987 SEASON AND MAJOR-LEAGUE CAREER PITCHING TOTALS

	G	GS	CG	GF	IP	BFP	H	R	ER	HR	SH	SF	HB	TBB	IBB	SO	WP	Bk	W	L	Pct	ShO	Sv	ERA
87 STL	53	0	0	29	61	260	52	21	18	2	2	1	2	33	8	63	5	0	9	5	.643	0	4	2.66
6 YEARS	192	33	0	76	365	1574	382	190	159	32	24	12	6	137	25	272	14	0	23	31	.426	0	20	3.92

1987: Power, Flyball   1986: Power, Groundball   1985: Power, Groundball   1984: Finesse, Flyball

	1987 SEASON											FOUR YEAR TOTALS (1984 – 1987)									
	G	IP	H	BB	SO	SB	CS	W	L	S	ERA	G	IP	H	BB	SO	SB	CS	W	L	S	ERA
Totals	53	61.0	52	33	63	5	2	9	5	4	2.66	148	188.2	203	73	168	12	3	13	17	20	3.48
At Home	26	25.2	33	13	26	3	2	3	1	1	4.56	76	98.1	116	31	82	6	2	6	8	10	3.57
On Road	27	35.1	19	20	37	2	0	6	4	3	1.27	72	90.1	87	42	86	6	1	7	9	10	3.39
vs. Opposing Batters	AVG	OBP	SLG	AB	H	2B	3B	HR	RBI	BB	SO	AVG	OBP	SLG	AB	H	2B	3B	HR	RBI	BB	SO
Totals	.234	.337	.338	222	52	9	4	2	28	33	63	.278	.345	.396	730	203	37	8	11	108	73	168
vs. Left	.247	.337	.301	73	18	2	1	0	5	9	26	.294	.355	.369	214	63	9	2	1	28	19	57
vs. Right	.228	.337	.356	149	34	7	3	2	23	24	37	.271	.341	.407	516	140	28	6	10	80	54	111

Dempsey, John Rikard "Rick"

Bats: Right   Throws: Right   Born 09/13/49

1987 SEASON AND MAJOR-LEAGUE CAREER BATTING TOTALS

	G	AB	H	2B	3B	HR	TB	R	RBI	TBB	IBB	SO	HP	SH	SF	SB	CS	SB%	GDP	AVG	OBP	SLG
87 CLE	60	141	25	10	0	1	38	16	9	23	0	29	1	4	1	0	0	.00	4	.177	.295	.270
19 YEARS	1479	4090	964	193	12	79	1418	454	389	489	9	605	17	61	33	17	17	.50	106	.236	.318	.347

	1987 SEASON											FOUR YEAR TOTALS (1984 – 1987)									
	AVG	OBP	SLG	AB	H	2B	3B	HR	RBI	BB	SO	AVG	OBP	SLG	AB	H	2B	3B	HR	RBI	BB	SO
Totals	.177	.295	.270	141	25	10	0	1	9	23	29	.225	.319	.370	1161	261	55	1	37	124	158	252
vs. Left	.167	.286	.333	42	7	4	0	1	4	7	5	.277	.374	.483	422	117	28	1	19	65	66	78
vs. Right	.182	.299	.242	99	18	6	0	0	5	16	24	.195	.287	.304	739	144	27	0	18	59	92	174
At Home	.169	.250	.282	71	12	5	0	1	4	8	17	.219	.320	.360	553	121	24	0	18	61	81	130
On Road	.186	.337	.257	70	13	5	0	0	5	15	12	.230	.318	.378	608	140	31	1	19	63	77	122

Dernier, Robert Eugene "Bob"

Bats: Right   Throws: Right   Born 01/05/57

1987 SEASON AND MAJOR-LEAGUE CAREER BATTING TOTALS

	G	AB	H	2B	3B	HR	TB	R	RBI	TBB	IBB	SO	HP	SH	SF	SB	CS	SB%	GDP	AVG	OBP	SLG
87 CHN	93	199	63	4	4	8	99	38	21	19	0	19	1	1	0	16	7	.70	4	.317	.379	.497
8 YEARS	729	2130	554	84	15	21	731	329	129	199	2	254	7	32	5	201	54	.79	31	.260	.325	.343

	1987 SEASON											FOUR YEAR TOTALS (1984 – 1987)									
	AVG	OBP	SLG	AB	H	2B	3B	HR	RBI	BB	SO	AVG	OBP	SLG	AB	H	2B	3B	HR	RBI	BB	SO
Totals	.317	.379	.497	199	63	4	4	8	21	19	19	.264	.330	.355	1528	404	64	13	16	92	144	164
vs. Left	.340	.408	.553	141	48	3	3	7	16	15	12	.300	.370	.423	487	146	21	6	9	44	53	38
vs. Right	.259	.306	.362	58	15	1	1	1	5	4	7	.248	.310	.323	1041	258	43	7	7	48	91	126
At Home	.313	.364	.475	99	31	2	1	4	9	8	9	.286	.344	.385	740	212	34	6	9	45	63	67
On Road	.320	.393	.520	100	32	2	3	4	12	11	10	.244	.317	.326	788	192	30	7	7	47	81	97

Deshaies, James Joseph "Jim"

Bats: Left   Throws: Left   Born 06/23/60

1987 SEASON AND MAJOR-LEAGUE CAREER PITCHING TOTALS

	G	GS	CG	GF	IP	BFP	H	R	ER	HR	SH	SF	HB	TBB	IBB	SO	WP	Bk	W	L	Pct	ShO	Sv	ERA
87 HOU	26	25	1	0	152	648	149	81	78	22	9	3	0	57	7	104	4	5	11	6	.647	0	0	4.62
4 YEARS	56	53	2	0	306	1297	288	148	139	39	13	7	2	123	9	239	4	12	23	12	.657	1	0	4.09

1987: Power, Flyball   1986: Power, Flyball   1985: Finesse, Flyball   1984: Power, Flyball

	1987 SEASON											FOUR YEAR TOTALS (1984 – 1987)										
	G	IP	H	BB	SO	SB	CS	W	L	S	ERA	G	IP	H	BB	SO	SB	CS	W	L	S	ERA
Totals	26	152.0	149	57	104	18	14	11	6	0	4.62	56	306.0	288	123	239	31	23	23	12	0	4.09
At Home	11	75.1	59	18	53	8	4	6	0	0	2.75	28	165.2	139	51	128	18	9	12	4	0	3.21
On Road	15	76.2	90	39	51	10	10	5	6	0	6.46	28	140.1	149	72	111	13	14	11	8	0	5.13

vs. Opposing Batters	AVG	OBP	SLG	AB	H	2B	3B	HR	RBI	BB	SO	AVG	OBP	SLG	AB	H	2B	3B	HR	RBI	BB	SO
Totals	.257	.322	.427	579	149	26	3	22	69	57	104	.250	.322	.408	1152	288	55	5	39	126	123	239
vs. Left	.263	.345	.404	99	26	8	0	2	7	13	15	.265	.345	.440	200	53	13	2	6	17	25	37
vs. Right	.256	.317	.431	480	123	18	3	20	62	44	89	.247	.317	.401	952	235	42	3	33	109	98	202

Devereaux, Michael "Mike"

Bats: Right   Throws: Right   Born 04/10/63

1987 SEASON AND MAJOR-LEAGUE CAREER BATTING TOTALS

	G	AB	H	2B	3B	HR	TB	R	RBI	TBB	IBB	SO	HP	SH	SF	SB	CS	SB%	GDP	AVG	OBP	SLG
87 LA	19	54	12	3	0	0	15	7	4	3	0	10	0	1	0	3	1	.75	0	.222	.263	.278
1 YEAR	19	54	12	3	0	0	15	7	4	3	0	10	0	1	0	3	1	.75	0	.222	.263	.278

	1987 SEASON											FOUR YEAR TOTALS (1984 – 1987)										
	AVG	OBP	SLG	AB	H	2B	3B	HR	RBI	BB	SO	AVG	OBP	SLG	AB	H	2B	3B	HR	RBI	BB	SO
Totals	.222	.263	.278	54	12	3	0	0	4	3	10	.222	.263	.278	54	12	3	0	0	4	3	10
vs. Left	.211	.250	.263	38	8	2	0	0	2	2	7	.211	.250	.263	38	8	2	0	0	2	2	7
vs. Right	.250	.294	.313	16	4	1	0	0	2	1	3	.250	.294	.313	16	4	1	0	0	2	1	3
At Home	.296	.345	.296	27	8	0	0	0	2	2	5	.296	.345	.296	27	8	0	0	0	2	2	5
On Road	.148	.179	.259	27	4	3	0	0	2	1	5	.148	.179	.259	27	4	3	0	0	2	1	5

Diaz, Michael Anthony "Mike"

Bats: Right   Throws: Right   Born 04/15/60

1987 SEASON AND MAJOR-LEAGUE CAREER BATTING TOTALS

	G	AB	H	2B	3B	HR	TB	R	RBI	TBB	IBB	SO	HP	SH	SF	SB	CS	SB%	GDP	AVG	OBP	SLG
87 PIT	103	241	58	8	2	16	118	28	48	31	3	42	3	0	7	1	0	1.00	6	.241	.326	.490
3 YEARS	206	457	116	18	2	28	222	52	85	50	3	85	5	0	10	1	1	.50	11	.254	.328	.486

	1987 SEASON											FOUR YEAR TOTALS (1984 – 1987)										
	AVG	OBP	SLG	AB	H	2B	3B	HR	RBI	BB	SO	AVG	OBP	SLG	AB	H	2B	3B	HR	RBI	BB	SO
Totals	.241	.326	.490	241	58	8	2	16	48	31	42	.253	.328	.487	450	114	17	2	28	84	50	85
vs. Left	.256	.350	.565	168	43	6	2	14	29	24	26	.261	.340	.542	299	78	11	2	23	48	35	58
vs. Right	.205	.271	.315	73	15	2	0	2	19	7	16	.238	.305	.377	151	36	6	0	5	36	15	27
At Home	.231	.317	.521	121	28	4	2	9	28	17	18	.241	.310	.500	216	52	7	2	15	46	23	39
On Road	.250	.336	.458	120	30	4	0	7	20	14	24	.265	.344	.474	234	62	10	0	13	38	27	46

DiPino, Frank Michael

Bats: Left   Throws: Left   Born 10/22/56

1987 SEASON AND MAJOR-LEAGUE CAREER PITCHING TOTALS

	G	GS	CG	GF	IP	BFP	H	R	ER	HR	SH	SF	HB	TBB	IBB	SO	WP	Bk	W	L	Pct	ShO	Sv	ERA
87 CHN	69	0	0	20	80	343	75	31	28	7	6	4	1	34	2	61	5	0	3	3	.500	0	4	3.15
7 YEARS	302	6	0	153	412	1757	376	193	169	31	27	17	7	177	31	340	18	2	18	32	.360	0	47	3.69

1987: Power, Groundball   1986: Power, Groundball   1985: Power, Flyball   1984: Power, Groundball

	1987 SEASON											FOUR YEAR TOTALS (1984 – 1987)										
	G	IP	H	BB	SO	SB	CS	W	L	S	ERA	G	IP	H	BB	SO	SB	CS	W	L	S	ERA
Totals	69	79.2	75	34	61	4	5	3	3	3	3.16	241	311.1	292	143	245	22	14	13	26	26	3.73
At Home	36	43.1	33	21	40	2	2	3	2	2	2.70	122	155.2	140	71	122	16	3	10	14	11	3.70
On Road	33	36.1	42	13	21	2	3	0	1	1	3.72	119	155.2	152	72	123	6	11	3	12	15	3.76

vs. Opposing Batters	AVG	OBP	SLG	AB	H	2B	3B	HR	RBI	BB	SO	AVG	OBP	SLG	AB	H	2B	3B	HR	RBI	BB	SO
Totals	.252	.326	.366	298	75	11	1	7	40	34	61	.251	.333	.370	1162	292	48	3	28	167	143	245
vs. Left	.245	.284	.340	94	23	3	0	2	16	5	23	.235	.300	.330	324	76	10	0	7	52	30	71
vs. Right	.255	.345	.377	204	52	8	1	5	24	29	38	.258	.345	.385	838	216	38	3	21	115	113	174

Dodson, Patrick Neal "Pat"
Bats: Left **Throws: Left** **Born 10/11/59**

1987 SEASON AND MAJOR-LEAGUE CAREER BATTING TOTALS

	G	AB	H	2B	3B	HR	TB	R	RBI	TBB	IBB	SO	HP	SH	SF	SB	CS	SB%	GDP	AVG	OBP	SLG
87 BOS	26	42	7	3	0	2	16	4	6	8	1	13	0	0	2	0	0	.00	0	.167	.288	.381
2 YEARS	35	54	12	5	0	3	26	7	9	11	1	16	0	0	2	0	0	.00	0	.222	.343	.481

	1987 SEASON										FOUR YEAR TOTALS (1984 – 1987)									
	AVG	OBP	SLG	AB	H	2B	3B	HR	RBI	BB	SO	AVG	OBP	SLG	AB	H	2B	3B	HR	RBI	BB	SO
Totals	.167	.288	.381	42	7	3	0	2	6	8	13	.222	.343	.481	54	12	5	0	3	9	11	16
vs. Left	.167	.286	.417	12	2	0	0	1	3	2	7	.167	.286	.417	12	2	0	0	1	3	2	7
vs. Right	.167	.289	.367	30	5	3	0	1	3	6	6	.238	.358	.500	42	10	5	0	2	6	9	9
At Home	.158	.227	.368	19	3	1	0	1	2	2	5	.233	.333	.433	30	7	3	0	1	4	5	8
On Road	.174	.333	.391	23	4	2	0	1	4	6	8	.208	.355	.542	24	5	2	0	2	5	6	8

Dowell, Kenneth Allen "Ken"
Bats: Right **Throws: Right** **Born 01/19/61**

1987 SEASON AND MAJOR-LEAGUE CAREER BATTING TOTALS

	G	AB	H	2B	3B	HR	TB	R	RBI	TBB	IBB	SO	HP	SH	SF	SB	CS	SB%	GDP	AVG	OBP	SLG
87 PHI	15	39	5	0	0	0	5	4	1	2	0	5	0	1	0	0	0	.00	1	.128	.171	.128
1 YEAR	15	39	5	0	0	0	5	4	1	2	0	5	0	1	0	0	0	.00	1	.128	.171	.128

	1987 SEASON										FOUR YEAR TOTALS (1984 – 1987)									
	AVG	OBP	SLG	AB	H	2B	3B	HR	RBI	BB	SO	AVG	OBP	SLG	AB	H	2B	3B	HR	RBI	BB	SO
Totals	.128	.171	.128	39	5	0	0	0	1	2	5	.128	.171	.128	39	5	0	0	0	1	2	5
vs. Left	.200	.200	.200	10	2	0	0	0	0	0	1	.200	.200	.200	10	2	0	0	0	0	0	1
vs. Right	.103	.161	.103	29	3	0	0	0	1	2	4	.103	.161	.103	29	3	0	0	0	1	2	4
At Home	.105	.105	.105	19	2	0	0	0	0	0	3	.105	.105	.105	19	2	0	0	0	0	0	3
On Road	.150	.227	.150	20	3	0	0	0	1	2	2	.150	.227	.150	20	3	0	0	0	1	2	2

Downs, Kelly Robert
Bats: Right **Throws: Right** **Born 10/25/60**

1987 SEASON AND MAJOR-LEAGUE CAREER PITCHING TOTALS

	G	GS	CG	GF	IP	BFP	H	R	ER	HR	SH	SF	HB	TBB	IBB	SO	WP	Bk	W	L	Pct	ShO	Sv	ERA
87 SF	41	28	4	4	186	797	185	83	75	14	7	1	4	67	11	137	12	4	12	9	.571	3	1	3.63
2 YEARS	55	42	5	4	274	1169	263	112	102	19	11	5	7	97	18	201	15	6	16	13	.552	3	1	3.35

1987: Power, Groundball   1986: Power, Groundball

	1987 SEASON											FOUR YEAR TOTALS (1984 – 1987)									
	G	IP	H	BB	SO	SB	CS	W	L	S	ERA	G	IP	H	BB	SO	SB	CS	W	L	S	ERA
Totals	41	186.0	186	67	137	18	9	12	9	1	3.68	55	274.1	264	97	201	25	10	16	13	1	3.38
At Home	20	85.1	78	31	68	8	2	5	5	1	3.59	26	123.1	110	45	94	9	3	7	7	1	3.65
On Road	21	100.2	108	36	69	10	7	7	4	0	3.75	29	151.0	154	52	107	16	7	9	6	0	3.16

vs. Opposing Batters	AVG	OBP	SLG	AB	H	2B	3B	HR	RBI	BB	SO	AVG	OBP	SLG	AB	H	2B	3B	HR	RBI	BB	SO
Totals	.259	.325	.366	718	186	33	1	14	73	67	137	.252	.318	.353	1049	264	45	2	19	99	97	201
vs. Left	.281	.342	.373	424	119	22	1	5	40	38	75	.265	.331	.358	593	157	30	2	7	49	56	106
vs. Right	.228	.302	.357	294	67	11	0	9	33	29	62	.235	.300	.346	456	107	15	0	12	50	41	95

Driessen, Daniel "Dan"
Bats: Left **Throws: Right** **Born 07/29/51**

1987 SEASON AND MAJOR-LEAGUE CAREER BATTING TOTALS

	G	AB	H	2B	3B	HR	TB	R	RBI	TBB	IBB	SO	HP	SH	SF	SB	CS	SB%	GDP	AVG	OBP	SLG
87 STL	24	60	14	2	0	1	19	5	11	7	1	8	0	0	1	0	0	.00	2	.233	.309	.317
15 YEARS	1732	5479	1464	282	23	153	2251	746	763	761	100	719	28	11	65	154	63	.71	128	.267	.356	.411

	1987 SEASON										TWO YEAR TOTALS (1986 – 1987)									
	AVG	OBP	SLG	AB	H	2B	3B	HR	RBI	BB	SO	AVG	OBP	SLG	AB	H	2B	3B	HR	RBI	BB	SO
Totals	.233	.309	.317	60	14	2	0	1	11	7	8	.240	.331	.350	100	24	5	0	2	14	16	14
vs. Left	.250	.222	.250	8	2	0	0	0	2	0	1	.261	.333	.348	23	6	2	0	0	2	3	3
vs. Right	.231	.322	.327	52	12	2	0	1	9	7	7	.234	.344	.351	77	18	3	0	2	12	13	11
At Home	.286	.316	.314	35	10	1	0	0	6	2	5	.300	.368	.420	50	15	3	0	1	7	6	7
On Road	.160	.300	.320	25	4	1	0	1	5	5	3	.180	.317	.280	50	9	2	0	1	7	10	7

Ducey, Robert Thomas "Bob"

Bats: Left   Throws: Right   Born 05/24/65

1987 SEASON AND MAJOR-LEAGUE CAREER BATTING TOTALS

	G	AB	H	2B	3B	HR	TB	R	RBI	TBB	IBB	SO	HP	SH	SF	SB	CS	SB%	GDP	AVG	OBP	SLG
87 TOR	34	48	9	1	0	1	13	12	6	8	0	10	0	0	1	2	0	1.00	0	.188	.298	.271
1 YEAR	34	48	9	1	0	1	13	12	6	8	0	10	0	0	1	2	0	1.00	0	.188	.298	.271

1987 SEASON											FOUR YEAR TOTALS (1984 – 1987)									
	AVG	OBP	SLG	AB	H	2B	3B	HR	RBI	BB	SO	AVG	OBP	SLG	AB	H	2B	3B	HR	RBI	BB	SO
Totals	.188	.298	.271	48	9	1	0	1	6	8	10	.188	.298	.271	48	9	1	0	1	6	8	10
vs. Left	.176	.300	.353	17	3	0	0	1	4	3	5	.176	.300	.353	17	3	0	0	1	4	3	5
vs. Right	.194	.297	.226	31	6	1	0	0	2	5	5	.194	.297	.226	31	6	1	0	0	2	5	5
At Home	.222	.318	.389	18	4	0	0	1	6	3	2	.222	.318	.389	18	4	0	0	1	6	3	2
On Road	.167	.286	.200	30	5	1	0	0	0	5	8	.167	.286	.200	30	5	1	0	0	0	5	8

Dwyer, James Edward "Jim"

Bats: Left   Throws: Left   Born 01/03/50

1987 SEASON AND MAJOR-LEAGUE CAREER BATTING TOTALS

	G	AB	H	2B	3B	HR	TB	R	RBI	TBB	IBB	SO	HP	SH	SF	SB	CS	SB%	GDP	AVG	OBP	SLG
87 BAL	92	241	66	7	1	15	120	54	33	37	4	57	1	1	1	4	1	.80	4	.274	.371	.498
15 YEARS	1135	2369	609	102	17	71	958	358	301	336	28	352	11	26	30	24	15	.62	40	.257	.348	.404

1987 SEASON											FOUR YEAR TOTALS (1984 – 1987)									
	AVG	OBP	SLG	AB	H	2B	3B	HR	RBI	BB	SO	AVG	OBP	SLG	AB	H	2B	3B	HR	RBI	BB	SO
Totals	.274	.371	.498	241	66	7	1	15	33	37	57	.257	.352	.439	795	204	37	6	32	121	120	143
vs. Left	.308	.308	.538	13	4	0	0	1	2	0	4	.240	.240	.400	25	6	1	0	1	2	0	7
vs. Right	.272	.375	.496	228	62	7	1	14	31	37	53	.257	.355	.440	770	198	36	6	31	119	120	136
At Home	.238	.375	.381	84	20	3	0	3	9	19	20	.225	.343	.361	360	81	15	2	10	56	66	62
On Road	.293	.369	.561	157	46	4	1	12	24	18	37	.283	.360	.503	435	123	22	4	22	65	54	81

Easler, Michael Anthony "Mike"

Bats: Left   Throws: Right   Born 11/29/50

1987 SEASON AND MAJOR-LEAGUE CAREER BATTING TOTALS

	G	AB	H	2B	3B	HR	TB	R	RBI	TBB	IBB	SO	HP	SH	SF	SB	CS	SB%	GDP	AVG	OBP	SLG
87 PHI-NYA	98	277	78	10	0	5	103	20	31	20	0	52	1	0	3	1	1	.50	5	.282	.329	.372
14 YEARS	1151	3677	1078	189	25	118	1671	465	522	321	46	696	17	6	40	20	26	.43	85	.293	.349	.454

1987 SEASON											FOUR YEAR TOTALS (1984 – 1987)									
	AVG	OBP	SLG	AB	H	2B	3B	HR	RBI	BB	SO	AVG	OBP	SLG	AB	H	2B	3B	HR	RBI	BB	SO
Totals	.282	.329	.372	277	78	10	0	5	31	20	52	.291	.351	.448	1936	563	96	11	62	274	180	402
vs. Left	.167	.279	.167	36	6	0	0	0	5	5	14	.245	.301	.358	494	121	20	3	10	52	38	151
vs. Right	.299	.337	.402	241	72	10	0	5	26	15	38	.307	.367	.479	1442	442	76	8	52	222	142	251
At Home	.314	.362	.415	159	50	7	0	3	19	12	29	.308	.367	.472	964	297	57	7	29	144	92	212
On Road	.237	.283	.314	118	28	3	0	2	12	8	23	.274	.334	.424	972	266	39	4	33	130	88	190

Easley, Kenneth Logan "Logan"

Bats: Right   Throws: Right   Born 11/04/61

1987 SEASON AND MAJOR-LEAGUE CAREER PITCHING TOTALS

	G	GS	CG	GF	IP	BFP	H	R	ER	HR	SH	SF	HB	TBB	IBB	SO	WP	Bk	W	L	Pct	ShO	Sv	ERA
87 PIT	17	0	0	7	26	118	23	17	16	5	3	2	1	17	4	21	2	1	1	1	.500	0	1	5.54
1 YEAR	17	0	0	7	26	118	23	17	16	5	3	2	1	17	4	21	2	1	1	1	.500	0	1	5.54

1987: Power, Groundball

1987 SEASON											FOUR YEAR TOTALS (1984 – 1987)									
	G	IP	H	BB	SO	SB	CS	W	L	S	ERA	G	IP	H	BB	SO	SB	CS	W	L	S	ERA
Totals	17	26.2	23	17	21	2	3	1	1	1	5.40	17	26.2	23	17	21	2	3	1	1	1	5.40
At Home	11	16.2	12	9	17	2	1	1	0	1	4.86	11	16.2	12	9	17	2	1	1	0	1	4.86
On Road	6	10.0	11	8	4	0	2	0	1	0	6.30	6	10.0	11	8	4	0	2	0	1	0	6.30

vs. Opposing Batters	AVG	OBP	SLG	AB	H	2B	3B	HR	RBI	BB	SO	AVG	OBP	SLG	AB	H	2B	3B	HR	RBI	BB	SO
Totals	.240	.357	.448	96	23	5	0	5	22	17	21	.240	.357	.448	96	23	5	0	5	22	17	21
vs. Left	.186	.321	.302	43	8	2	0	1	7	9	12	.186	.321	.302	43	8	2	0	1	7	9	12
vs. Right	.283	.387	.566	53	15	3	0	4	15	8	9	.283	.387	.566	53	15	3	0	4	15	8	9

Easterly, James Morris "Jamie"

Bats: Both   Throws: Left   Born 02/17/53

1987 SEASON AND MAJOR-LEAGUE CAREER PITCHING TOTALS

	G	GS	CG	GF	IP	BFP	H	R	ER	HR	SH	SF	HB	TBB	IBB	SO	WP	Bk	W	L	Pct	ShO	Sv	ERA
87 CLE	16	0	0	1	32	137	26	17	16	4	2	2	1	13	1	22	5	0	1	1	.500	0	0	4.50
13 YEARS	321	36	0	105	614	2744	663	360	314	48	33	30	17	319	30	350	38	2	23	33	.411	0	14	4.60

1987: Power, Flyball   1986: Power, Groundball

	1987 SEASON											TWO YEAR TOTALS (1986 – 1987)										
	G	IP	H	BB	SO	SB	CS	W	L	S	ERA	G	IP	H	BB	SO	SB	CS	W	L	S	ERA
Totals	16	31.2	26	13	22	4	0	1	1	0	4.55	29	49.1	53	25	31	4	0	1	3	0	5.66
At Home	10	21.1	19	9	15	3	0	1	1	0	4.64	15	25.1	33	12	17	3	0	1	2	0	6.75
On Road	6	10.1	7	4	7	1	0	0	0	0	4.35	14	24.0	20	13	14	1	0	0	1	0	4.50
vs. Opposing Batters	AVG	OBP	SLG	AB	H	2B	3B	HR	RBI	BB	SO	AVG	OBP	SLG	AB	H	2B	3B	HR	RBI	BB	SO
Totals	.218	.296	.353	119	26	4	0	4	20	13	22	.275	.354	.430	193	53	9	0	7	43	25	31
vs. Left	.170	.264	.340	47	8	2	0	2	6	5	11	.260	.326	.416	77	20	3	0	3	17	7	15
vs. Right	.250	.317	.361	72	18	2	0	2	14	8	11	.284	.372	.440	116	33	6	0	4	26	18	16

Eisenreich, James Michael "Jim"

Bats: Left   Throws: Left   Born 04/18/59

1987 SEASON AND MAJOR-LEAGUE CAREER BATTING TOTALS

	G	AB	H	2B	3B	HR	TB	R	RBI	TBB	IBB	SO	HP	SH	SF	SB	CS	SB%	GDP	AVG	OBP	SLG
87 KC	44	105	25	8	2	4	49	10	21	7	2	13	0	0	3	1	1	.50	2	.238	.278	.467
4 YEARS	92	243	64	16	2	6	102	22	33	21	3	31	1	0	5	3	1	.75	4	.263	.319	.420

	1987 SEASON											TWO YEAR TOTALS (1986 – 1987)										
	AVG	OBP	SLG	AB	H	2B	3B	HR	RBI	BB	SO	AVG	OBP	SLG	AB	H	2B	3B	HR	RBI	BB	SO
Totals	.238	.278	.467	105	25	8	2	4	21	7	13	.238	.274	.467	105	25	8	2	4	21	7	13
vs. Left	.000	.000	.000	3	0	0	0	0	0	0	0	.000	.000	.000	3	0	0	0	0	0	0	0
vs. Right	.245	.286	.480	102	25	8	2	4	21	7	13	.245	.286	.480	102	25	8	2	4	21	7	13
At Home	.302	.350	.660	53	16	6	2	3	13	5	6	.302	.350	.660	53	16	6	2	3	13	5	6
On Road	.173	.200	.269	52	9	2	0	1	8	2	7	.173	.200	.269	52	9	2	0	1	8	2	7

Engle, Ralph David "Dave"

Bats: Right   Throws: Right   Born 11/30/56

1987 SEASON AND MAJOR-LEAGUE CAREER BATTING TOTALS

	G	AB	H	2B	3B	HR	TB	R	RBI	TBB	IBB	SO	HP	SH	SF	SB	CS	SB%	GDP	AVG	OBP	SLG
87 MON	59	84	19	4	0	1	26	7	14	6	1	11	0	0	0	1	0	1.00	5	.226	.278	.310
7 YEARS	533	1541	409	82	13	29	604	192	172	111	7	172	3	3	14	5	5	.50	56	.265	.313	.392

	1987 SEASON										TWO YEAR TOTALS (1986 – 1987)										
	AVG	OBP	SLG	AB	H	2B	3B	HR	RBI	BB	SO	AVG	OBP	SLG	AB	H	2B	3B	HR	RBI	BB	SO
Totals	.226	.278	.310	84	19	4	0	1	14	6	11	.241	.284	.324	170	41	11	0	1	18	13	24
vs. Left	.239	.271	.348	46	11	2	0	1	11	2	7	.244	.290	.341	123	30	9	0	1	13	8	19
vs. Right	.211	.286	.263	38	8	2	0	0	3	4	4	.234	.308	.277	47	11	2	0	0	5	5	5
At Home	.295	.340	.432	44	13	3	0	1	12	3	3	.225	.296	.315	89	20	5	0	1	14	9	9
On Road	.150	.209	.175	40	6	1	0	0	2	3	8	.259	.294	.333	81	21	6	0	0	4	4	15

Farr, Steven Michael "Steve"

Bats: Right   Throws: Right   Born 12/12/56

1987 SEASON AND MAJOR-LEAGUE CAREER PITCHING TOTALS

	G	GS	CG	GF	IP	BFP	H	R	ER	HR	SH	SF	HB	TBB	IBB	SO	WP	Bk	W	L	Pct	ShO	Sv	ERA
87 KC	47	0	0	19	91	408	97	47	42	9	0	3	2	44	4	88	2	0	4	3	.571	0	1	4.15
4 YEARS	150	19	0	61	354	1503	327	162	152	35	6	10	13	149	19	290	10	3	17	19	.472	0	11	3.86

1987: Power, Flyball   1986: Power, Flyball   1985: Power, Flyball   1984: Power, Groundball

	1987 SEASON											FOUR YEAR TOTALS (1984 – 1987)										
	G	IP	H	BB	SO	SB	CS	W	L	S	ERA	G	IP	H	BB	SO	SB	CS	W	L	S	ERA
Totals	47	91.0	97	44	88	18	7	4	3	1	4.15	150	354.0	327	149	290	31	23	17	19	11	3.84
At Home	24	45.1	45	30	43	6	1	2	1	1	4.37	80	196.1	179	91	164	16	11	12	7	6	3.71
On Road	23	45.2	52	14	45	12	6	2	2	0	3.94	70	157.2	148	58	126	15	12	5	12	5	4.05
vs. Opposing Batters	AVG	OBP	SLG	AB	H	2B	3B	HR	RBI	BB	SO	AVG	OBP	SLG	AB	H	2B	3B	HR	RBI	BB	SO
Totals	.271	.351	.416	358	97	19	3	9	59	44	88	.247	.323	.381	1324	327	54	9	35	175	149	290
vs. Left	.274	.369	.432	146	40	7	2	4	22	22	34	.239	.331	.372	637	152	23	7	16	80	88	117
vs. Right	.269	.339	.406	212	57	12	1	5	37	22	54	.255	.316	.389	687	175	31	2	19	95	61	173

Farrell, John Edward

Bats: Right Throws: Right Born 08/04/62

1987 SEASON AND MAJOR-LEAGUE CAREER PITCHING TOTALS

	G	GS	CG	GF	IP	BFP	H	R	ER	HR	SH	SF	HB	TBB	IBB	SO	WP	Bk	W	L	Pct	ShO	Sv	ERA
87 CLE	10	9	1	1	69	297	68	29	26	7	3	1	5	22	1	28	1	1	5	1	.833	0	0	3.39
1 YEAR	10	9	1	1	69	297	68	29	26	7	3	1	5	22	1	28	1	1	5	1	.833	0	0	3.39

1987: Finesse, Flyball

	G	IP	H	BB	SO	SB	CS	W	L	S	ERA
1987 SEASON											
Totals	10	69.0	68	22	28	2	3	5	1	0	3.39
At Home	4	22.2	28	7	5	0	1	2	1	0	5.16
On Road	6	46.1	40	15	23	2	2	3	0	0	2.53

vs. Opposing Batters	AVG	OBP	SLG	AB	H	2B	3B	HR	RBI	BB	SO
Totals	.255	.323	.401	267	68	14	2	7	25	22	28
vs. Left	.270	.360	.426	141	38	9	2	3	14	19	12
vs. Right	.238	.278	.373	126	30	5	0	4	11	3	16

	G	IP	H	BB	SO	SB	CS	W	L	S	ERA
FOUR YEAR TOTALS (1984 – 1987)											
	10	69.0	68	22	28	2	3	5	1	0	3.39
	4	22.2	28	7	5	0	1	2	1	0	5.16
	6	46.1	40	15	23	2	2	3	0	0	2.53

	AVG	OBP	SLG	AB	H	2B	3B	HR	RBI	BB	SO
	.255	.323	.401	267	68	14	2	7	25	22	28
	.270	.360	.426	141	38	9	2	3	14	19	12
	.238	.278	.373	126	30	5	0	4	11	3	16

Felder, Michael Otis "Mike"

Bats: Both Throws: Right Born 11/18/62

1987 SEASON AND MAJOR-LEAGUE CAREER BATTING TOTALS

	G	AB	H	2B	3B	HR	TB	R	RBI	TBB	IBB	SO	HP	SH	SF	SB	CS	SB%	GDP	AVG	OBP	SLG
87 MIL	108	289	77	5	7	2	102	48	31	28	0	23	0	9	2	34	8	.81	3	.266	.329	.353
3 YEARS	167	500	125	8	11	3	164	80	44	46	1	45	0	11	7	54	11	.83	7	.250	.309	.328

	AVG	OBP	SLG	AB	H	2B	3B	HR	RBI	BB	SO
1987 SEASON											
Totals	.269	.331	.355	290	78	5	7	2	31	28	23
vs. Left	.316	.385	.379	95	30	2	2	0	10	12	6
vs. Right	.246	.303	.344	195	48	3	5	2	21	16	17
At Home	.302	.399	.421	126	38	2	5	1	19	21	9
On Road	.244	.273	.305	164	40	3	2	1	12	7	14

	AVG	OBP	SLG	AB	H	2B	3B	HR	RBI	BB	SO
FOUR YEAR TOTALS (1984 – 1987)											
	.251	.310	.329	501	126	8	11	3	44	46	45
	.311	.363	.373	161	50	2	4	0	13	15	10
	.224	.285	.309	340	76	6	7	3	31	31	35
	.280	.365	.386	246	69	4	8	2	27	34	18
	.224	.254	.275	255	57	4	3	1	17	12	27

Fermin, Felix Jose

Bats: Right Throws: Right Born 10/09/63

1987 SEASON AND MAJOR-LEAGUE CAREER BATTING TOTALS

	G	AB	H	2B	3B	HR	TB	R	RBI	TBB	IBB	SO	HP	SH	SF	SB	CS	SB%	GDP	AVG	OBP	SLG
87 PIT	23	68	17	0	0	0	17	6	4	4	1	9	1	2	0	0	0	.00	3	.250	.301	.250
1 YEAR	23	68	17	0	0	0	17	6	4	4	1	9	1	2	0	0	0	.00	3	.250	.301	.250

	AVG	OBP	SLG	AB	H	2B	3B	HR	RBI	BB	SO
1987 SEASON											
Totals	.250	.301	.250	68	17	0	0	0	4	4	9
vs. Left	.171	.237	.171	35	6	0	0	0	0	3	6
vs. Right	.333	.371	.333	33	11	0	0	0	4	1	3
At Home	.286	.348	.286	42	12	0	0	0	1	3	1
On Road	.192	.222	.192	26	5	0	0	0	3	1	8

	AVG	OBP	SLG	AB	H	2B	3B	HR	RBI	BB	SO
FOUR YEAR TOTALS (1984 – 1987)											
	.250	.301	.250	68	17	0	0	0	4	4	9
	.171	.237	.171	35	6	0	0	0	0	3	6
	.333	.371	.333	33	11	0	0	0	4	1	3
	.286	.348	.286	42	12	0	0	0	1	3	1
	.192	.222	.192	26	5	0	0	0	3	1	8

Fielder, Cecil Grant

Bats: Right Throws: Right Born 09/21/63

1987 SEASON AND MAJOR-LEAGUE CAREER BATTING TOTALS

	G	AB	H	2B	3B	HR	TB	R	RBI	TBB	IBB	SO	HP	SH	SF	SB	CS	SB%	GDP	AVG	OBP	SLG
87 TOR	82	175	47	7	1	14	98	30	32	20	2	48	1	0	1	0	1	.00	6	.269	.345	.560
3 YEARS	146	332	83	13	1	22	164	43	61	32	2	91	2	0	2	0	1	.00	11	.250	.318	.494

	AVG	OBP	SLG	AB	H	2B	3B	HR	RBI	BB	SO
1987 SEASON											
Totals	.269	.345	.560	175	47	7	1	14	32	20	48
vs. Left	.268	.343	.582	153	41	7	1	13	30	17	40
vs. Right	.273	.360	.409	22	6	0	0	1	2	3	8
At Home	.344	.422	.756	90	31	5	1	10	21	11	24
On Road	.188	.263	.353	85	16	2	0	4	11	9	24

	AVG	OBP	SLG	AB	H	2B	3B	HR	RBI	BB	SO
TWO YEAR TOTALS (1986 – 1987)											
	.233	.308	.484	258	60	9	1	18	45	26	75
	.244	.319	.497	193	47	8	1	13	33	21	56
	.200	.268	.446	65	13	1	0	5	12	5	19
	.289	.362	.614	114	33	5	1	10	23	12	35
	.188	.262	.382	144	27	4	0	8	22	14	40

Finley, Charles Edward "Chuck"

Bats: Left Throws: Left Born 11/26/62

1987 SEASON AND MAJOR-LEAGUE CAREER PITCHING TOTALS

	G	GS	CG	GF	IP	BFP	H	R	ER	HR	SH	SF	HB	TBB	IBB	SO	WP	Bk	W	L	Pct	ShO	Sv	ERA
87 CAL	35	3	0	17	91	405	102	54	47	7	2	2	3	43	3	63	4	3	2	7	.222	0	0	4.65
2 YEARS	60	3	0	24	137	603	142	71	64	9	6	2	4	66	4	100	6	3	5	8	.385	0	0	4.20

1987: Power, Groundball   1986: Power, Groundball

	1987 SEASON											FOUR YEAR TOTALS (1984 – 1987)										
	G	IP	H	BB	SO	SB	CS	W	L	S	ERA	G	IP	H	BB	SO	SB	CS	W	L	S	ERA
Totals	35	90.2	102	43	63	1	5	2	7	0	4.67	60	137.0	142	66	100	5	8	5	8	0	4.20
At Home	16	41.1	45	19	36	0	2	2	4	0	5.23	30	67.1	67	35	54	2	4	3	4	0	4.95
On Road	19	49.1	57	24	27	1	3	0	3	0	4.20	30	69.2	75	31	46	3	4	2	4	0	3.49
vs. Opposing Batters	AVG	OBP	SLG	AB	H	2B	3B	HR	RBI	BB	SO	AVG	OBP	SLG	AB	H	2B	3B	HR	RBI	BB	SO
Totals	.287	.367	.411	355	102	23	0	7	49	43	63	.270	.354	.377	525	142	29	0	9	72	66	100
vs. Left	.263	.303	.361	133	35	10	0	1	19	8	29	.265	.322	.341	211	56	13	0	1	30	18	39
vs. Right	.302	.402	.441	222	67	13	0	6	30	35	34	.274	.374	.401	314	86	16	0	8	42	48	61

Flanagan, Michael Kendall "Mike"

Bats: Left Throws: Left Born 12/16/51

1987 SEASON AND MAJOR-LEAGUE CAREER PITCHING TOTALS

	G	GS	CG	GF	IP	BFP	H	R	ER	HR	SH	SF	HB	TBB	IBB	SO	WP	Bk	W	L	Pct	ShO	Sv	ERA
87 BAL-TOR	23	23	4	0	144	619	148	72	65	12	6	1	0	51	4	93	3	0	6	8	.429	0	0	4.06
13 YEARS	351	334	98	10	2234	9377	2238	1038	957	206	81	59	22	707	33	1268	71	6	142	111	.561	17	1	3.86

1987: Finesse, Flyball   1986: Finesse, Groundball   1985: Finesse, Groundball   1984: Finesse, Groundball

	1987 SEASON											FOUR YEAR TOTALS (1984 – 1987)										
	G	IP	H	BB	SO	SB	CS	W	L	S	ERA	G	IP	H	BB	SO	SB	CS	W	L	S	ERA
Totals	23	144.0	148	51	93	9	3	6	8	0	4.06	101	628.2	641	226	346	33	16	30	37	0	4.07
At Home	12	81.1	82	26	58	6	2	5	3	0	3.32	48	294.2	293	108	164	15	7	20	11	0	3.60
On Road	11	62.2	66	25	35	3	1	1	5	0	5.03	53	334.0	348	118	182	18	9	10	26	0	4.47
vs. Opposing Batters	AVG	OBP	SLG	AB	H	2B	3B	HR	RBI	BB	SO	AVG	OBP	SLG	AB	H	2B	3B	HR	RBI	BB	SO
Totals	.264	.325	.409	560	148	39	3	12	52	51	93	.265	.328	.408	2415	641	125	12	65	270	226	346
vs. Left	.250	.312	.270	100	25	2	0	0	6	9	16	.240	.294	.314	442	106	17	2	4	46	34	81
vs. Right	.267	.327	.439	460	123	37	3	12	46	42	77	.271	.335	.429	1973	535	108	10	61	224	192	265

Foley, Thomas Michael "Tom"

Bats: Left Throws: Right Born 09/09/59

1987 SEASON AND MAJOR-LEAGUE CAREER BATTING TOTALS

	G	AB	H	2B	3B	HR	TB	R	RBI	TBB	IBB	SO	HP	SH	SF	SB	CS	SB%	GDP	AVG	OBP	SLG
87 MON	106	280	82	18	3	5	121	35	28	11	0	40	1	1	0	6	10	.38	6	.293	.322	.432
5 YEARS	472	1168	302	58	11	14	424	118	110	97	23	164	1	6	6	22	18	.55	15	.259	.314	.363

	1987 SEASON										FOUR YEAR TOTALS (1984 – 1987)									
	AVG	OBP	SLG	AB	H	2B	3B	HR	RBI	BB	SO	AVG	OBP	SLG	AB	H	2B	3B	HR	RBI	BB	SO
Totals	.293	.322	.432	280	82	18	3	5	28	11	40	.264	.316	.372	1070	282	54	10	14	101	84	147
vs. Left	.227	.227	.273	22	5	1	0	0	0	0	5	.237	.282	.250	152	36	2	0	0	8	10	31
vs. Right	.298	.330	.446	258	77	17	3	5	28	11	35	.268	.322	.392	918	246	52	10	14	93	74	116
At Home	.314	.346	.479	121	38	7	2	3	8	5	21	.284	.346	.414	476	135	26	6	8	43	47	62
On Road	.277	.303	.396	159	44	11	1	2	20	6	19	.247	.291	.338	594	147	28	4	6	58	37	85

Francona, Terry Jon

Bats: Left Throws: Left Born 04/22/59

1987 SEASON AND MAJOR-LEAGUE CAREER BATTING TOTALS

	G	AB	H	2B	3B	HR	TB	R	RBI	TBB	IBB	SO	HP	SH	SF	SB	CS	SB%	GDP	AVG	OBP	SLG
87 CIN	102	207	47	5	0	3	61	16	12	10	1	12	1	1	0	2	0	1.00	5	.227	.266	.295
7 YEARS	553	1282	354	56	5	12	456	112	108	52	11	81	5	12	6	10	11	.48	22	.276	.306	.356

	1987 SEASON										FOUR YEAR TOTALS (1984 – 1987)									
	AVG	OBP	SLG	AB	H	2B	3B	HR	RBI	BB	SO	AVG	OBP	SLG	AB	H	2B	3B	HR	RBI	BB	SO
Totals	.227	.266	.295	207	47	5	0	3	12	10	12	.275	.304	.362	826	227	42	3	8	69	33	45
vs. Left	.053	.143	.053	19	1	0	0	0	1	2	2	.290	.316	.323	93	27	3	0	0	12	4	12
vs. Right	.245	.279	.319	188	46	5	0	3	11	8	10	.273	.303	.367	733	200	39	3	8	57	29	33
At Home	.227	.261	.291	110	25	1	0	2	9	5	8	.268	.302	.358	377	101	19	3	3	29	18	26
On Road	.227	.272	.299	97	22	4	0	1	3	5	4	.281	.306	.365	449	126	23	0	5	40	15	19

Fraser, William Patrick "Willie"

Bats: Right   Throws: Right   Born 05/26/64

1987 SEASON AND MAJOR-LEAGUE CAREER PITCHING TOTALS

	G	GS	CG	GF	IP	BFP	H	R	ER	HR	SH	SF	HB	TBB	IBB	SO	WP	Bk	W	L	Pct	ShO	Sv	ERA
87 CAL	36	23	5	6	177	744	160	85	77	26	5	4	6	63	3	106	12	1	10	10	.500	1	1	3.92
2 YEARS	37	24	5	6	181	764	166	89	81	26	6	5	6	64	3	108	12	1	10	10	.500	1	1	4.03

1987: Finesse, Flyball   1986: Finesse, Groundball

1987 SEASON

	G	IP	H	BB	SO	SB	CS	W	L	S	ERA
Totals	36	176.1	160	63	106	16	4	10	10	1	3.93
At Home	14	72.1	64	34	48	9	2	2	6	1	4.48
On Road	22	104.0	96	29	58	7	2	8	4	0	3.55

vs. Opposing Batters	AVG	OBP	SLG	AB	H	2B	3B	HR	RBI	BB	SO
Totals	.240	.309	.414	667	160	34	2	26	82	63	106
vs. Left	.250	.331	.423	324	81	16	2	12	41	37	44
vs. Right	.230	.289	.405	343	79	18	0	14	41	26	62

FOUR YEAR TOTALS (1984 – 1987)

	G	IP	H	BB	SO	SB	CS	W	L	S	ERA
Totals	37	180.2	166	64	108	16	4	10	10	1	4.04
At Home	14	72.1	64	34	48	9	2	2	6	1	4.48
On Road	23	108.1	102	30	60	7	2	8	4	0	3.74

vs. Opposing Batters	AVG	OBP	SLG	AB	H	2B	3B	HR	RBI	BB	SO
Totals	.243	.311	.417	684	166	35	3	26	85	64	108
vs. Left	.254	.335	.431	327	83	16	3	12	41	38	45
vs. Right	.232	.288	.403	357	83	19	0	14	44	26	63

Frazier, George Allen

Bats: Right   Throws: Right   Born 11/13/54

1987 SEASON AND MAJOR-LEAGUE CAREER PITCHING TOTALS

	G	GS	CG	GF	IP	BFP	H	R	ER	HR	SH	SF	HB	TBB	IBB	SO	WP	Bk	W	L	Pct	ShO	Sv	ERA
87 MIN	54	0	0	26	81	363	77	49	45	9	1	10	2	51	4	58	6	1	5	5	.500	0	2	5.00
10 YEARS	415	0	0	193	676	2942	653	349	315	54	34	39	16	313	48	449	26	3	35	43	.449	0	29	4.19

1987: Power, Flyball   1986: Power, Flyball   1985: Power, Groundball   1984: Power, Flyball

1987 SEASON

	G	IP	H	BB	SO	SB	CS	W	L	S	ERA
Totals	54	81.1	77	51	58	15	6	5	5	2	4.98
At Home	25	39.0	34	20	28	9	1	4	1	2	4.15
On Road	29	42.1	43	31	30	6	5	1	4	0	5.74

vs. Opposing Batters	AVG	OBP	SLG	AB	H	2B	3B	HR	RBI	BB	SO
Totals	.257	.358	.397	300	77	15	0	9	54	51	58
vs. Left	.247	.343	.400	170	42	11	0	5	29	26	32
vs. Right	.269	.377	.392	130	35	4	0	4	25	25	26

FOUR YEAR TOTALS (1984 – 1987)

	G	IP	H	BB	SO	SB	CS	W	L	S	ERA
Totals	214	343.2	349	193	252	50	24	24	23	14	4.95
At Home	110	179.2	172	84	137	26	9	15	8	9	4.66
On Road	104	164.0	177	109	115	24	15	9	15	5	5.32

vs. Opposing Batters	AVG	OBP	SLG	AB	H	2B	3B	HR	RBI	BB	SO
Totals	.266	.359	.404	1310	349	66	6	34	215	193	252
vs. Left	.265	.360	.398	656	174	33	6	14	101	98	108
vs. Right	.268	.358	.410	654	175	33	0	20	114	95	144

Frobel, Douglas Steven "Doug"

Bats: Left   Throws: Right   Born 06/06/59

1987 SEASON AND MAJOR-LEAGUE CAREER BATTING TOTALS

	G	AB	H	2B	3B	HR	TB	R	RBI	TBB	IBB	SO	HP	SH	SF	SB	CS	SB%	GDP	AVG	OBP	SLG
87 CLE	29	40	4	0	0	2	10	5	5	5	1	13	0	0	1	0	0	.00	1	.100	.196	.250
5 YEARS	268	542	109	21	4	20	198	70	58	55	8	155	2	6	2	13	10	.57	14	.201	.276	.365

1987 SEASON

	AVG	OBP	SLG	AB	H	2B	3B	HR	RBI	BB	SO
Totals	.100	.196	.250	40	4	0	0	2	5	5	13
vs. Left	.000	.000	.000	0	0	0	0	0	0	0	0
vs. Right	.100	.196	.250	40	4	0	0	2	5	5	13
At Home	.111	.242	.333	27	3	0	0	2	5	5	10
On Road	.077	.077	.077	13	1	0	0	0	0	0	3

TWO YEAR TOTALS (1986 – 1987)

	AVG	OBP	SLG	AB	H	2B	3B	HR	RBI	BB	SO
Totals	.100	.224	.250	40	4	0	0	2	5	5	13
vs. Left	.000	.000	.000	0	0	0	0	0	0	0	0
vs. Right	.100	.196	.250	40	4	0	0	2	5	5	13
At Home	.111	.242	.333	27	3	0	0	2	5	5	10
On Road	.077	.077	.077	13	1	0	0	0	0	0	3

Gainey, Telmanch "Ty"

Bats: Left   Throws: Right   Born 12/25/60

1987 SEASON AND MAJOR-LEAGUE CAREER BATTING TOTALS

	G	AB	H	2B	3B	HR	TB	R	RBI	TBB	IBB	SO	HP	SH	SF	SB	CS	SB%	GDP	AVG	OBP	SLG
87 HOU	18	24	3	0	0	0	3	1	1	2	0	9	0	0	0	1	0	1.00	0	.125	.192	.125
3 YEARS	57	111	24	3	1	1	32	12	7	10	0	37	2	1	0	4	1	.80	0	.216	.293	.288

1987 SEASON

	AVG	OBP	SLG	AB	H	2B	3B	HR	RBI	BB	SO
Totals	.125	.192	.125	24	3	0	0	0	1	2	9
vs. Left	.000	.200	.000	4	0	0	0	0	0	1	1
vs. Right	.150	.190	.150	20	3	0	0	0	1	1	8
At Home	.067	.125	.067	15	1	0	0	0	0	1	7
On Road	.222	.300	.222	9	2	0	0	0	1	1	2

TWO YEAR TOTALS (1986 – 1987)

	AVG	OBP	SLG	AB	H	2B	3B	HR	RBI	BB	SO
Totals	.243	.333	.351	74	18	3	1	1	7	8	28
vs. Left	.111	.333	.111	9	1	0	0	0	0	3	3
vs. Right	.262	.314	.385	65	17	3	1	1	7	5	25
At Home	.206	.289	.206	34	7	0	0	0	2	4	14
On Road	.275	.341	.475	40	11	3	1	1	5	4	14

Gallagher, David Thomas "Dave"

Bats: Right　Throws: Right　Born 09/20/60

1987 SEASON AND MAJOR-LEAGUE CAREER BATTING TOTALS

	G	AB	H	2B	3B	HR	TB	R	RBI	TBB	IBB	SO	HP	SH	SF	SB	CS	SB%	GDP	AVG	OBP	SLG
87 CLE	15	36	4	1	1	0	7	2	1	2	0	5	0	1	0	2	0	1.00	1	.111	.158	.194
1 YEAR	15	36	4	1	1	0	7	2	1	2	0	5	0	1	0	2	0	1.00	1	.111	.158	.194

	1987 SEASON											FOUR YEAR TOTALS (1984 – 1987)										
	AVG	OBP	SLG	AB	H	2B	3B	HR	RBI	BB	SO	AVG	OBP	SLG	AB	H	2B	3B	HR	RBI	BB	SO
Totals	.111	.158	.194	36	4	1	1	0	1	2	5	.111	.158	.194	36	4	1	1	0	1	2	5
vs. Left	.067	.125	.067	15	1	0	0	0	0	1	2	.067	.125	.067	15	1	0	0	0	0	1	2
vs. Right	.143	.182	.286	21	3	1	1	0	1	1	3	.143	.182	.286	21	3	1	1	0	1	1	3
At Home	.120	.185	.200	25	3	0	1	0	1	2	4	.120	.185	.200	25	3	0	1	0	1	2	4
On Road	.091	.091	.182	11	1	1	0	0	0	0	1	.091	.091	.182	11	1	1	0	0	0	0	1

Gallego, Michael Anthony–Mike"

Bats: Right　Throws: Right　Born 10/31/60

1987 SEASON AND MAJOR-LEAGUE CAREER BATTING TOTALS

	G	AB	H	2B	3B	HR	TB	R	RBI	TBB	IBB	SO	HP	SH	SF	SB	CS	SB%	GDP	AVG	OBP	SLG
87 OAK	72	124	31	6	0	2	43	18	14	12	0	21	1	5	1	0	1	.00	5	.250	.319	.347
3 YEARS	168	238	57	13	1	3	81	33	27	25	0	41	2	9	2	1	4	.20	7	.239	.315	.340

	1987 SEASON											TWO YEAR TOTALS (1986 – 1987)										
	AVG	OBP	SLG	AB	H	2B	3B	HR	RBI	BB	SO	AVG	OBP	SLG	AB	H	2B	3B	HR	RBI	BB	SO
Totals	.250	.319	.347	124	31	6	0	2	14	12	21	.255	.315	.342	161	41	8	0	2	18	13	27
vs. Left	.300	.348	.467	60	18	4	0	2	7	5	12	.308	.345	.462	78	24	6	0	2	11	5	15
vs. Right	.203	.292	.234	64	13	2	0	0	7	7	9	.205	.283	.229	83	17	2	0	0	7	8	12
At Home	.247	.309	.329	73	18	6	0	0	9	6	13	.235	.290	.296	98	23	6	0	0	9	7	18
On Road	.255	.333	.373	51	13	0	0	2	5	6	8	.286	.348	.413	63	18	2	0	2	9	6	9

Gant, Ronald Edwin "Ron"

Bats: Right　Throws: Right　Born 03/02/65

1987 SEASON AND MAJOR-LEAGUE CAREER BATTING TOTALS

	G	AB	H	2B	3B	HR	TB	R	RBI	TBB	IBB	SO	HP	SH	SF	SB	CS	SB%	GDP	AVG	OBP	SLG
87 ATL	21	83	22	4	0	2	32	9	9	1	0	11	0	1	1	4	2	.67	3	.265	.271	.386
1 YEAR	21	83	22	4	0	2	32	9	9	1	0	11	0	1	1	4	2	.67	3	.265	.271	.386

	1987 SEASON											FOUR YEAR TOTALS (1984 – 1987)										
	AVG	OBP	SLG	AB	H	2B	3B	HR	RBI	BB	SO	AVG	OBP	SLG	AB	H	2B	3B	HR	RBI	BB	SO
Totals	.265	.271	.386	83	22	4	0	2	9	1	11	.265	.271	.386	83	22	4	0	2	9	1	11
vs. Left	.208	.240	.208	24	5	0	0	0	3	1	3	.208	.240	.208	24	5	0	0	0	3	1	3
vs. Right	.288	.283	.458	59	17	4	0	2	6	0	8	.288	.283	.458	59	17	4	0	2	6	0	8
At Home	.289	.308	.395	38	11	1	0	1	3	1	4	.289	.308	.395	38	11	1	0	1	3	1	4
On Road	.244	.239	.378	45	11	3	0	1	6	0	7	.244	.239	.378	45	11	3	0	1	6	0	7

Garcia, Leonardo Antonio "Leo"

Bats: Left　Throws: Left　Born 11/06/62

1987 SEASON AND MAJOR-LEAGUE CAREER BATTING TOTALS

	G	AB	H	2B	3B	HR	TB	R	RBI	TBB	IBB	SO	HP	SH	SF	SB	CS	SB%	GDP	AVG	OBP	SLG
87 CIN	31	30	6	0	0	1	9	8	2	4	0	8	0	0	1	3	1	.75	0	.200	.286	.300
1 YEAR	31	30	6	0	0	1	9	8	2	4	0	8	0	0	1	3	1	.75	0	.200	.286	.300

	1987 SEASON											FOUR YEAR TOTALS (1984 – 1987)										
	AVG	OBP	SLG	AB	H	2B	3B	HR	RBI	BB	SO	AVG	OBP	SLG	AB	H	2B	3B	HR	RBI	BB	SO
Totals	.200	.286	.300	30	6	0	0	1	2	4	8	.200	.286	.300	30	6	0	0	1	2	4	8
vs. Left	.200	.200	.200	5	1	0	0	0	0	0	1	.200	.200	.200	5	1	0	0	0	0	0	1
vs. Right	.200	.300	.320	25	5	0	0	1	2	4	7	.200	.300	.320	25	5	0	0	1	2	4	7
At Home	.125	.167	.125	16	2	0	0	0	1	1	4	.125	.167	.125	16	2	0	0	0	1	1	4
On Road	.286	.412	.500	14	4	0	0	1	1	3	4	.286	.412	.500	14	4	0	0	1	1	3	4

Gardner, Wesley Brian "Wes"

Bats: Right   Throws: Right   Born 04/29/61

1987 SEASON AND MAJOR-LEAGUE CAREER PITCHING TOTALS

	G	GS	CG	GF	IP	BFP	H	R	ER	HR	SH	SF	HB	TBB	IBB	SO	WP	Bk	W	L	Pct	ShO	Sv	ERA
87 BOS	49	1	0	29	90	401	98	55	54	17	4	2	2	42	7	70	4	0	3	6	.333	0	10	5.40
4 YEARS	80	1	0	49	128	582	151	89	80	18	9	5	2	58	11	101	6	0	4	9	.308	0	11	5.63

1987: Power, Flyball   1986: Finesse, Flyball

1987 SEASON

	G	IP	H	BB	SO	SB	CS	W	L	S	ERA
Totals	49	89.2	98	42	70	0	1	3	6	11	5.42
At Home	24	49.1	51	15	34	0	1	2	1	8	3.10
On Road	25	40.1	47	27	36	0	0	1	5	3	8.26

vs. Opposing Batters	AVG	OBP	SLG	AB	H	2B	3B	HR	RBI	BB	SO
Totals	.279	.358	.493	351	98	24	0	17	57	42	70
vs. Left	.315	.414	.549	162	51	14	0	8	30	28	29
vs. Right	.249	.306	.444	189	47	10	0	9	27	14	41

TWO YEAR TOTALS (1986 – 1987)

	G	IP	H	BB	SO	SB	CS	W	L	S	ERA
	50	90.2	99	42	71	0	1	3	6	11	5.46
	24	49.1	51	15	34	0	1	2	1	8	3.10
	26	41.1	48	27	37	0	0	1	5	3	8.27

	AVG	OBP	SLG	AB	H	2B	3B	HR	RBI	BB	SO
	.280	.357	.497	354	99	24	1	17	58	42	71
	.315	.410	.558	165	52	14	1	8	31	28	30
	.249	.306	.444	189	47	10	0	9	27	14	41

Garner, Philip Mason "Phil"

Bats: Right   Throws: Right   Born 04/30/49

1987 SEASON AND MAJOR-LEAGUE CAREER BATTING TOTALS

	G	AB	H	2B	3B	HR	TB	R	RBI	TBB	IBB	SO	HP	SH	SF	SB	CS	SB%	GDP	AVG	OBP	SLG
87 HOU-LA	113	238	49	9	0	5	73	29	23	28	8	44	0	5	4	6	1	.86	5	.206	.285	.307
15 YEARS	1845	6123	1592	299	82	109	2382	780	737	563	74	839	34	67	59	225	104	.68	131	.260	.323	.389

1987 SEASON

	AVG	OBP	SLG	AB	H	2B	3B	HR	RBI	BB	SO
Totals	.206	.285	.307	238	49	9	0	5	23	28	44
vs. Left	.231	.311	.357	143	33	6	0	4	16	18	23
vs. Right	.168	.245	.232	95	16	3	0	1	7	10	21
At Home	.198	.291	.225	111	22	3	0	0	6	15	17
On Road	.213	.280	.378	127	27	6	0	5	17	13	27

FOUR YEAR TOTALS (1984 – 1987)

	AVG	OBP	SLG	AB	H	2B	3B	HR	RBI	BB	SO
	.259	.325	.384	1388	360	63	19	24	160	135	224
	.281	.346	.419	732	206	36	13	13	91	77	99
	.235	.300	.345	656	154	27	6	11	69	58	125
	.274	.341	.364	689	189	29	9	5	71	70	97
	.245	.308	.403	699	171	34	10	19	89	65	127

Garvey, Steven Patrick "Steve"

Bats: Right   Throws: Right   Born 12/22/48

1987 SEASON AND MAJOR-LEAGUE CAREER BATTING TOTALS

	G	AB	H	2B	3B	HR	TB	R	RBI	TBB	IBB	SO	HP	SH	SF	SB	CS	SB%	GDP	AVG	OBP	SLG
87 SD	27	76	16	2	0	1	21	5	9	1	0	10	1	0	0	0	0	.00	3	.211	.231	.276
19 YEARS	2332	8835	2599	440	43	272	3941	1143	1308	479	113	1003	29	33	90	83	62	.57	251	.294	.329	.446

1987 SEASON

	AVG	OBP	SLG	AB	H	2B	3B	HR	RBI	BB	SO
Totals	.211	.221	.276	76	16	2	0	1	9	0	10
vs. Left	.258	.258	.387	31	8	1	0	1	4	0	4
vs. Right	.178	.196	.200	45	8	1	0	0	5	0	6
At Home	.242	.265	.273	33	8	1	0	0	2	0	4
On Road	.186	.186	.279	43	8	1	0	1	7	0	6

FOUR YEAR TOTALS (1984 – 1987)

	AVG	OBP	SLG	AB	H	2B	3B	HR	RBI	BB	SO
	.272	.301	.399	1904	517	85	8	47	257	82	213
	.289	.326	.468	619	179	34	1	25	87	36	61
	.263	.289	.365	1285	338	51	7	22	170	46	152
	.269	.305	.407	927	249	42	4	26	128	50	110
	.274	.297	.391	977	268	43	4	21	129	32	103

Gedman, Richard Leo "Rich"

Bats: Left   Throws: Right   Born 09/26/59

1987 SEASON AND MAJOR-LEAGUE CAREER BATTING TOTALS

	G	AB	H	2B	3B	HR	TB	R	RBI	TBB	IBB	SO	HP	SH	SF	SB	CS	SB%	GDP	AVG	OBP	SLG
87 BOS	52	151	31	8	0	1	42	11	13	10	2	24	0	1	3	0	0	.00	2	.205	.250	.278
8 YEARS	708	2282	614	141	12	70	989	255	301	160	43	346	12	15	18	3	2	.60	61	.269	.318	.433

1987 SEASON

	AVG	OBP	SLG	AB	H	2B	3B	HR	RBI	BB	SO
Totals	.205	.250	.278	151	31	8	0	1	13	10	24
vs. Left	.286	.297	.400	35	10	1	0	1	7	1	7
vs. Right	.181	.236	.241	116	21	7	0	0	6	9	17
At Home	.222	.255	.333	90	20	7	0	1	10	5	8
On Road	.180	.242	.197	61	11	1	0	0	3	5	16

FOUR YEAR TOTALS (1984 – 1987)

	AVG	OBP	SLG	AB	H	2B	3B	HR	RBI	BB	SO
	.268	.323	.453	1560	418	93	9	59	230	126	236
	.230	.274	.359	343	79	13	2	9	57	19	67
	.279	.337	.479	1217	339	80	7	50	173	107	169
	.284	.333	.473	790	224	54	6	28	130	61	114
	.252	.312	.431	770	194	39	3	31	100	65	122

Gerhart, Harold Kenneth "Ken"

Bats: Right   Throws: Right   Born 05/19/61

1987 SEASON AND MAJOR-LEAGUE CAREER BATTING TOTALS

	G	AB	H	2B	3B	HR	TB	R	RBI	TBB	IBB	SO	HP	SH	SF	SB	CS	SB%	GDP	AVG	OBP	SLG
87 BAL	92	284	69	10	2	14	125	41	34	17	0	53	1	6	2	9	2	.82	7	.243	.286	.440
2 YEARS	112	353	85	12	2	15	146	45	41	21	0	71	1	6	4	9	3	.75	8	.241	.282	.414

	1987 SEASON											FOUR YEAR TOTALS (1984 – 1987)										
	AVG	OBP	SLG	AB	H	2B	3B	HR	RBI	BB	SO	AVG	OBP	SLG	AB	H	2B	3B	HR	RBI	BB	SO
Totals	.243	.286	.440	284	69	10	2	14	34	17	53	.241	.281	.414	353	85	12	2	15	41	21	71
vs. Left	.240	.272	.364	129	31	4	0	4	10	6	24	.223	.253	.344	157	35	4	0	5	15	7	34
vs. Right	.245	.298	.503	155	38	6	2	10	24	11	29	.255	.305	.469	196	50	8	2	10	26	14	37
At Home	.216	.264	.373	134	29	6	0	5	12	8	24	.212	.249	.358	165	35	6	0	6	17	8	30
On Road	.267	.306	.500	150	40	4	2	9	22	9	29	.266	.312	.463	188	50	6	2	9	24	13	41

Gideon, Byron Brett

Bats: Right   Throws: Right   Born 08/08/63

1987 SEASON AND MAJOR-LEAGUE CAREER PITCHING TOTALS

	G	GS	CG	GF	IP	BFP	H	R	ER	HR	SH	SF	HB	TBB	IBB	SO	WP	Bk	W	L	Pct	ShO	Sv	ERA
87 PIT	29	0	0	17	37	153	34	22	19	6	2	0	1	10	3	31	2	0	1	5	.167	0	3	4.62
1 YEAR	29	0	0	17	37	153	34	22	19	6	2	0	1	10	3	31	2	0	1	5	.167	0	3	4.62

1987: Power, Flyball

	1987 SEASON											FOUR YEAR TOTALS (1984 – 1987)										
	G	IP	H	BB	SO	SB	CS	W	L	S	ERA	G	IP	H	BB	SO	SB	CS	W	L	S	ERA
Totals	29	37.0	34	10	31	10	1	1	5	3	4.62	29	37.0	34	10	31	10	1	1	5	3	4.62
At Home	16	22.0	18	7	19	3	0	1	3	2	4.09	16	22.0	18	7	19	3	0	1	3	2	4.09
On Road	13	15.0	16	3	12	7	1	0	2	1	5.40	13	15.0	16	3	12	7	1	0	2	1	5.40
vs. Opposing Batters	AVG	OBP	SLG	AB	H	2B	3B	HR	RBI	BB	SO	AVG	OBP	SLG	AB	H	2B	3B	HR	RBI	BB	SO
Totals	.243	.298	.393	140	34	3	0	6	17	10	31	.243	.298	.393	140	34	3	0	6	17	10	31
vs. Left	.333	.391	.571	63	21	3	0	4	13	6	6	.333	.391	.571	63	21	3	0	4	13	6	6
vs. Right	.169	.220	.247	77	13	0	0	2	4	4	25	.169	.220	.247	77	13	0	0	2	4	4	25

Gladden, Clinton Daniel "Dan"

Bats: Both   Throws: Right   Born 07/07/57

1987 SEASON AND MAJOR-LEAGUE CAREER BATTING TOTALS

	G	AB	H	2B	3B	HR	TB	R	RBI	TBB	IBB	SO	HP	SH	SF	SB	CS	SB%	GDP	AVG	OBP	SLG
87 MIN	121	438	109	21	2	8	158	69	38	38	2	72	3	1	2	25	9	.74	8	.249	.312	.361
5 YEARS	469	1696	462	71	13	24	631	265	148	155	8	257	17	27	6	119	53	.69	29	.272	.338	.372

	1987 SEASON											FOUR YEAR TOTALS (1984 – 1987)										
	AVG	OBP	SLG	AB	H	2B	3B	HR	RBI	BB	SO	AVG	OBP	SLG	AB	H	2B	3B	HR	RBI	BB	SO
Totals	.249	.312	.361	438	109	21	2	8	38	38	72	.274	.341	.375	1633	448	69	13	23	139	150	246
vs. Left	.258	.307	.362	163	42	11	0	2	13	11	19	.281	.354	.366	513	144	25	2	5	32	55	73
vs. Right	.244	.315	.360	275	67	10	2	6	25	27	53	.271	.334	.379	1120	304	44	11	18	107	95	173
At Home	.271	.342	.404	203	55	11	2	4	15	21	23	.280	.357	.390	789	221	30	6	15	67	86	113
On Road	.230	.285	.323	235	54	10	0	4	23	17	49	.269	.325	.360	844	227	39	7	8	72	64	133

Glavine, Thomas Michael "Tom"

Bats: Left   Throws: Left   Born 03/25/66

1987 SEASON AND MAJOR-LEAGUE CAREER PITCHING TOTALS

	G	GS	CG	GF	IP	BFP	H	R	ER	HR	SH	SF	HB	TBB	IBB	SO	WP	Bk	W	L	Pct	ShO	Sv	ERA
87 ATL	9	9	0	0	50	238	55	34	31	5	2	3	3	33	4	20	1	1	2	4	.333	0	0	5.58
1 YEAR	9	9	0	0	50	238	55	34	31	5	2	3	3	33	4	20	1	1	2	4	.333	0	0	5.58

1987: Power, Groundball

	1987 SEASON											FOUR YEAR TOTALS (1984 – 1987)										
	G	IP	H	BB	SO	SB	CS	W	L	S	ERA	G	IP	H	BB	SO	SB	CS	W	L	S	ERA
Totals	9	50.1	55	33	20	4	4	2	4	0	5.54	9	50.1	55	33	20	4	4	2	4	0	5.54
At Home	4	24.1	25	12	11	0	3	2	2	0	5.55	4	24.1	25	12	11	0	3	2	2	0	5.55
On Road	5	26.0	30	21	9	4	1	0	2	0	5.54	5	26.0	30	21	9	4	1	0	2	0	5.54
vs. Opposing Batters	AVG	OBP	SLG	AB	H	2B	3B	HR	RBI	BB	SO	AVG	OBP	SLG	AB	H	2B	3B	HR	RBI	BB	SO
Totals	.279	.386	.421	197	55	11	1	5	31	33	20	.279	.386	.421	197	55	11	1	5	31	33	20
vs. Left	.259	.375	.333	27	7	2	0	0	5	4	1	.259	.375	.333	27	7	2	0	0	5	4	1
vs. Right	.282	.387	.435	170	48	9	1	5	26	29	19	.282	.387	.435	170	48	9	1	5	26	29	19

Gleaton, Jerry Don

Bats: Left   Throws: Left   Born 09/14/57

1987 SEASON AND MAJOR-LEAGUE CAREER PITCHING TOTALS

	G	GS	CG	GF	IP	BFP	H	R	ER	HR	SH	SF	HB	TBB	IBB	SO	WP	Bk	W	L	Pct	ShO	Sv	ERA
87 KC	48	0	0	22	51	210	38	28	24	4	3	3	0	28	3	44	4	1	4	4	.500	0	5	4.24
7 YEARS	123	16	1	42	206	894	210	125	111	22	11	15	5	93	8	106	15	1	10	14	.417	0	8	4.85

1987: Power, Flyball

1987 SEASON	G	IP	H	BB	SO	SB	CS	W	L	S	ERA
Totals	48	50.2	38	28	44	2	4	4	4	5	4.44
At Home	26	25.1	15	16	22	0	2	0	2	5	4.26
On Road	22	25.1	23	12	22	2	2	4	2	0	4.62

vs. Opposing Batters	AVG	OBP	SLG	AB	H	2B	3B	HR	RBI	BB	SO
Totals	.215	.319	.322	177	38	5	1	4	25	28	44
vs. Left	.197	.275	.295	61	12	3	0	1	8	7	16
vs. Right	.224	.341	.336	116	26	2	1	3	17	21	28

TWO YEAR TOTALS (1986 – 1987)	G	IP	H	BB	SO	SB	CS	W	L	S	ERA
	48	50.2	38	28	44	2	4	4	4	5	4.44
	26	25.1	15	16	22	0	2	0	2	5	4.26
	22	25.1	23	12	22	2	2	4	2	0	4.62

	AVG	OBP	SLG	AB	H	2B	3B	HR	RBI	BB	SO
	.215	.319	.322	177	38	5	1	4	25	28	44
	.197	.275	.295	61	12	3	0	1	8	7	16
	.224	.341	.336	116	26	2	1	3	17	21	28

Gonzales, Rene Adrian

Bats: Right   Throws: Right   Born 09/03/61

1987 SEASON AND MAJOR-LEAGUE CAREER BATTING TOTALS

	G	AB	H	2B	3B	HR	TB	R	RBI	TBB	IBB	SO	HP	SH	SF	SB	CS	SB%	GDP	AVG	OBP	SLG
87 BAL	37	60	16	2	1	1	23	14	7	3	0	11	0	2	0	1	0	1.00	2	.267	.302	.383
3 YEARS	77	116	26	3	1	1	34	20	9	7	0	22	1	2	0	1	2	.33	2	.224	.274	.293

1987 SEASON	AVG	OBP	SLG	AB	H	2B	3B	HR	RBI	BB	SO
Totals	.267	.302	.383	60	16	2	1	1	7	3	11
vs. Left	.250	.289	.333	36	9	1	1	0	3	2	3
vs. Right	.292	.320	.458	24	7	1	0	1	4	1	8
At Home	.310	.356	.476	42	13	2	1	1	6	3	6
On Road	.167	.167	.167	18	3	0	0	0	1	0	5

TWO YEAR TOTALS (1986 – 1987)	AVG	OBP	SLG	AB	H	2B	3B	HR	RBI	BB	SO
	.221	.272	.302	86	19	2	1	1	7	5	18
	.212	.255	.269	52	11	1	1	0	3	3	8
	.235	.278	.353	34	8	1	0	1	4	2	10
	.294	.357	.431	51	15	2	1	1	6	5	9
	.114	.114	.114	35	4	0	0	0	1	0	9

Gonzalez, Jose Rafael (Gutierrez)

Bats: Right   Throws: Right   Born 11/23/64

1987 SEASON AND MAJOR-LEAGUE CAREER BATTING TOTALS

	G	AB	H	2B	3B	HR	TB	R	RBI	TBB	IBB	SO	HP	SH	SF	SB	CS	SB%	GDP	AVG	OBP	SLG
87 LA	19	16	3	2	0	0	5	2	1	1	0	2	0	0	1	5	0	1.00		.188	.222	.313
3 YEARS	99	120	26	9	1	2	43	23	7	9	0	34	0	2	1	10	4	.71	1	.217	.269	.358

1987 SEASON	AVG	OBP	SLG	AB	H	2B	3B	HR	RBI	BB	SO
Totals	.188	.222	.313	16	3	2	0	0	1	1	2
vs. Left	.300	.300	.500	10	3	2	0	0	0	0	1
vs. Right	.000	.125	.000	6	0	0	0	0	1	1	1
At Home	.143	.143	.286	7	1	1	0	0	0	0	1
On Road	.222	.273	.333	9	2	1	0	0	1	1	1

TWO YEAR TOTALS (1986 – 1987)	AVG	OBP	SLG	AB	H	2B	3B	HR	RBI	BB	SO
	.211	.263	.349	109	23	7	1	2	7	8	31
	.265	.306	.441	68	18	6	0	2	5	4	17
	.122	.196	.195	41	5	1	1	0	2	4	14
	.204	.278	.327	49	10	3	0	1	1	5	10
	.217	.250	.367	60	13	4	1	1	6	3	21

Gordon, Donald Thomas "Don"

Bats: Right   Throws: Right   Born 10/10/59

1987 SEASON AND MAJOR-LEAGUE CAREER PITCHING TOTALS

	G	GS	CG	GF	IP	BFP	H	R	ER	HR	SH	SF	HB	TBB	IBB	SO	WP	Bk	W	L	Pct	ShO	Sv	ERA
87 TOR-CLE	26	0	0	9	51	228	57	36	23	5	1	2	4	15	3	23	0	0	0	3	.000	0	1	4.06
2 YEARS	40	0	0	15	73	330	85	56	40	6	2	4	5	23	4	36	0	0	0	4	.000	0	2	4.93

1987: Finesse, Groundball   1986: Finesse, Groundball

1987 SEASON	G	IP	H	BB	SO	SB	CS	W	L	S	ERA
Totals	26	50.2	57	15	23	3	2	0	3	1	4.09
At Home	14	31.2	34	12	16	1	2	0	1	1	2.56
On Road	12	19.0	23	3	7	2	0	0	2	0	6.63

vs. Opposing Batters	AVG	OBP	SLG	AB	H	2B	3B	HR	RBI	BB	SO
Totals	.277	.335	.437	206	57	14	2	5	37	15	23
vs. Left	.258	.316	.404	89	23	8	1	1	15	7	12
vs. Right	.291	.349	.462	117	34	6	1	4	22	8	11

FOUR YEAR TOTALS (1984 – 1987)	G	IP	H	BB	SO	SB	CS	W	L	S	ERA
	40	72.1	85	23	36	3	4	0	4	2	4.98
	22	45.0	51	15	27	1	4	0	2	1	3.40
	18	27.1	34	8	9	2	0	0	2	1	7.57

	AVG	OBP	SLG	AB	H	2B	3B	HR	RBI	BB	SO
	.287	.345	.426	296	85	19	2	6	55	23	36
	.275	.338	.420	131	36	11	1	2	26	13	17
	.297	.350	.430	165	49	8	1	4	29	10	19

Gott, James William "Jim"

Bats: Right   Throws: Right   Born 08/03/59

1987 SEASON AND MAJOR-LEAGUE CAREER PITCHING TOTALS

	G	GS	CG	GF	IP	BFP	H	R	ER	HR	SH	SF	HB	TBB	IBB	SO	WP	Bk	W	L	Pct	ShO	Sv	ERA
87 SF-PIT	55	3	0	30	87	382	81	43	33	4	2	1	2	40	7	90	5	0	1	2	.333	0	13	3.41
6 YEARS	189	96	10	50	671	2917	663	361	317	51	23	17	14	287	20	453	20	3	29	42	.408	3	16	4.25

1987: Power, Groundball   1986: Power, Groundball

	1987 SEASON											TWO YEAR TOTALS (1986 – 1987)										
	G	IP	H	BB	SO	SB	CS	W	L	S	ERA	G	IP	H	BB	SO	SB	CS	W	L	S	ERA
Totals	55	87.1	81	40	90	9	6	1	2	13	3.40	64	100.1	97	53	99	9	6	1	2	14	3.95
At Home	25	40.0	34	18	44	2	3	0	1	8	3.15	30	47.0	43	23	50	2	3	0	1	8	3.64
On Road	30	47.1	47	22	46	7	3	1	1	5	3.61	34	53.1	54	30	49	7	3	1	1	6	4.22

vs. Opposing Batters	AVG	OBP	SLG	AB	H	2B	3B	HR	RBI	BB	SO	AVG	OBP	SLG	AB	H	2B	3B	HR	RBI	BB	SO
Totals	.240	.324	.315	337	81	9	2	4	43	40	90	.250	.342	.320	388	97	11	2	4	50	53	99
vs. Left	.286	.396	.416	161	46	5	2	4	23	29	47	.295	.405	.416	190	56	7	2	4	28	35	52
vs. Right	.199	.250	.222	176	35	4	0	0	20	11	43	.207	.275	.227	198	41	4	0	0	22	18	47

Grant, Mark Andrew

Bats: Right   Throws: Right   Born 10/24/63

1987 SEASON AND MAJOR-LEAGUE CAREER PITCHING TOTALS

	G	GS	CG	GF	IP	BFP	H	R	ER	HR	SH	SF	HB	TBB	IBB	SO	WP	Bk	W	L	Pct	ShO	Sv	ERA
87 SF-SD	33	25	2	2	163	720	170	88	77	22	15	1	1	73	8	90	8	3	7	9	.438	1	1	4.25
3 YEARS	48	36	2	6	227	990	232	132	119	28	17	4	2	97	8	127	11	4	8	14	.364	1	2	4.72

1987: Finesse, Flyball   1986: Finesse, Flyball

	1987 SEASON											TWO YEAR TOTALS (1986 – 1987)										
	G	IP	H	BB	SO	SB	CS	W	L	S	ERA	G	IP	H	BB	SO	SB	CS	W	L	S	ERA
Totals	33	163.1	170	73	90	7	7	7	9	1	4.24	37	173.1	176	78	95	7	8	7	10	1	4.21
At Home	16	93.2	87	35	52	3	5	4	5	0	3.94	18	95.2	89	38	53	3	5	4	5	0	4.05
On Road	17	69.2	83	38	38	4	2	3	4	1	4.65	19	77.2	87	40	42	4	3	3	5	1	4.40

vs. Opposing Batters	AVG	OBP	SLG	AB	H	2B	3B	HR	RBI	BB	SO	AVG	OBP	SLG	AB	H	2B	3B	HR	RBI	BB	SO
Totals	.270	.346	.433	630	170	33	2	22	78	73	90	.265	.343	.420	664	176	33	2	22	82	78	95
vs. Left	.259	.344	.379	367	95	21	1	7	29	48	47	.252	.333	.365	389	98	21	1	7	30	48	50
vs. Right	.285	.349	.510	263	75	12	1	15	49	25	43	.284	.356	.498	275	78	12	1	15	52	30	45

Griffin, Michael Leroy "Mike"

Bats: Right   Throws: Right   Born 06/26/57

1987 SEASON AND MAJOR-LEAGUE CAREER PITCHING TOTALS

	G	GS	CG	GF	IP	BFP	H	R	ER	HR	SH	SF	HB	TBB	IBB	SO	WP	Bk	W	L	Pct	ShO	Sv	ERA
87 BAL	23	6	1	6	74	331	78	/39	36	9	2	3	3	33	3	42	1	1	3	5	.375	0	1	4.38
5 YEARS	64	24	1	15	198	887	225	109	98	19	9	7	4	70	5	100	6	3	7	15	.318	0	3	4.45

1987: Finesse, Flyball

	1987 SEASON											TWO YEAR TOTALS (1986 – 1987)										
	G	IP	H	BB	SO	SB	CS	W	L	S	ERA	G	IP	H	BB	SO	SB	CS	W	L	S	ERA
Totals	23	74.1	78	33	42	3	2	3	5	1	4.36	23	74.1	78	33	42	3	2	3	5	1	4.36
At Home	12	43.1	42	18	29	0	2	2	2	0	3.95	12	43.1	42	18	29	0	2	2	2	0	3.95
On Road	11	31.0	36	15	13	3	0	1	3	1	4.94	11	31.0	36	15	13	3	0	1	3	1	4.94

vs. Opposing Batters	AVG	OBP	SLG	AB	H	2B	3B	HR	RBI	BB	SO	AVG	OBP	SLG	AB	H	2B	3B	HR	RBI	BB	SO
Totals	.269	.347	.445	290	78	16	4	9	39	33	42	.269	.347	.445	290	78	16	4	9	39	33	42
vs. Left	.267	.347	.467	150	40	11	2	5	19	18	17	.267	.347	.467	150	40	11	2	5	19	18	17
vs. Right	.271	.346	.421	140	38	5	2	4	20	15	25	.271	.346	.421	140	38	5	2	4	20	15	25

Gross, Gregory Eugene "Greg"

Bats: Left   Throws: Left   Born 08/01/52

1987 SEASON AND MAJOR-LEAGUE CAREER BATTING TOTALS

	G	AB	H	2B	3B	HR	TB	R	RBI	TBB	IBB	SO	HP	SH	SF	SB	CS	SB%	GDP	AVG	OBP	SLG
87 PHI	114	133	38	4	1	1	47	14	12	25	4	12	1	1	3	0	0	.00	2	.286	.395	.353
15 YEARS	1651	3537	1031	129	46	7	1273	437	299	496	48	241	6	39	38	39	44	.47	84	.291	.376	.360

	1987 SEASON											TWO YEAR TOTALS (1986 – 1987)										
	AVG	OBP	SLG	AB	H	2B	3B	HR	RBI	BB	SO	AVG	OBP	SLG	AB	H	2B	3B	HR	RBI	BB	SO
Totals	.286	.395	.353	133	38	4	1	1	12	25	12	.269	.386	.329	234	63	9	1	1	20	46	23
vs. Left	.300	.364	.300	10	3	0	0	0	0	1	1	.214	.313	.214	28	6	0	0	0	1	4	4
vs. Right	.285	.397	.358	123	35	4	1	1	12	24	11	.277	.398	.345	206	57	9	1	1	19	42	19
At Home	.316	.420	.386	57	18	2	1	0	4	11	4	.310	.423	.390	100	31	6	1	0	10	21	11
On Road	.263	.376	.329	76	20	2	0	1	8	14	8	.239	.362	.284	134	32	3	0	1	10	25	12

Grubb, John Maywood

Bats: Left   Throws: Right   Born 08/04/48

1987 SEASON AND MAJOR-LEAGUE CAREER BATTING TOTALS

	G	AB	H	2B	3B	HR	TB	R	RBI	TBB	IBB	SO	HP	SH	SF	SB	CS	SB%	GDP	AVG	OBP	SLG
87 DET	59	114	23	6	0	2	35	9	13	15	0	16	0	0	2	0	0	.00	4	.202	.290	.307
16 YEARS	1424	4154	1153	207	29	99	1715	553	475	566	41	558	36	32	35	27	33	.45	74	.278	.366	.413

		1987 SEASON											FOUR YEAR TOTALS (1984 – 1987)									
	AVG	OBP	SLG	AB	H	2B	3B	HR	RBI	BB	SO	AVG	OBP	SLG	AB	H	2B	3B	HR	RBI	BB	SO
Totals	.202	.290	.307	114	23	6	0	2	13	15	16	.272	.368	.453	655	178	31	2	28	106	101	105
vs. Left	.000	.000	.000	4	0	0	0	0	0	0	1	.200	.259	.280	25	5	2	0	0	2	2	7
vs. Right	.209	.299	.318	110	23	6	0	2	13	15	15	.275	.372	.460	630	173	29	2	28	104	99	98
At Home	.255	.357	.447	47	12	3	0	2	6	8	4	.282	.375	.459	344	97	12	2	15	56	51	47
On Road	.164	.240	.209	67	11	3	0	0	7	7	12	.260	.361	.447	311	81	19	0	13	50	50	58

Guante, Cecilio (Magallane)

Bats: Right   Throws: Right   Born 02/02/60

1987 SEASON AND MAJOR-LEAGUE CAREER PITCHING TOTALS

	G	GS	CG	GF	IP	BFP	H	R	ER	HR	SH	SF	HB	TBB	IBB	SO	WP	Bk	W	L	Pct	ShO	Sv	ERA
87 NYA	23	0	0	9	44	195	42	30	28	8	0	4	1	20	0	46	3	0	3	2	.600	0	1	5.73
6 YEARS	224	0	0	99	399	1680	341	169	149	33	16	18	15	156	20	339	13	2	16	19	.457	0	21	3.36

1987: Power, Flyball   1986: Power, Flyball   1985: Power, Flyball   1984: Power, Flyball

		1987 SEASON									FOUR YEAR TOTALS (1984 – 1987)									
	G	IP	H	BB	SO	SB	CS	W	L	S	ERA	G	IP	H	BB	SO	SB	CS	W	L	S	ERA
Totals	23	44.1	42	20	46	6	3	3	2	1	5.68	165	272.2	223	105	231	24	18	14	13	12	3.37
At Home	11	30.2	23	14	35	5	3	3	0	1	4.11	81	145.0	106	52	126	11	9	7	1	7	2.92
On Road	12	13.2	19	6	11	1	0	0	2	0	9.22	84	127.2	117	53	105	13	9	7	12	5	3.88
vs. Opposing Batters	AVG	OBP	SLG	AB	H	2B	3B	HR	RBI	BB	SO	AVG	OBP	SLG	AB	H	2B	3B	HR	RBI	BB	SO
Totals	.247	.323	.441	170	42	9	0	8	28	20	46	.224	.298	.373	995	223	49	9	27	119	105	231
vs. Left	.237	.337	.447	76	18	4	0	4	14	12	15	.248	.340	.407	408	101	20	6	11	47	58	73
vs. Right	.255	.311	.436	94	24	5	0	4	14	8	31	.208	.266	.349	587	122	29	3	16	72	47	158

Guetterman, Arthur Lee "Lee"

Bats: Left   Throws: Left   Born 11/22/58

1987 SEASON AND MAJOR-LEAGUE CAREER PITCHING TOTALS

	G	GS	CG	GF	IP	BFP	H	R	ER	HR	SH	SF	HB	TBB	IBB	SO	WP	Bk	W	L	Pct	ShO	Sv	ERA
87 SEA	25	17	2	3	113	483	117	60	48	13	2	5	2	35	2	42	3	0	11	4	.733	1	0	3.82
3 YEARS	69	21	3	12	193	858	234	129	112	20	5	10	6	67	5	82	6	0	11	8	.579	1	0	5.22

1987: Finesse, Groundball   1986: Finesse, Groundball

		1987 SEASON									FOUR YEAR TOTALS (1984 – 1987)									
	G	IP	H	BB	SO	SB	CS	W	L	S	ERA	G	IP	H	BB	SO	SB	CS	W	L	S	ERA
Totals	25	113.1	117	35	42	13	2	11	4	0	3.81	69	193.2	234	67	82	17	5	11	8	0	5.20
At Home	11	54.1	56	19	23	4	1	6	0	0	3.64	36	97.0	121	36	44	7	1	6	3	0	5.66
On Road	14	59.0	61	16	19	9	1	5	4	0	3.97	33	96.2	113	31	38	10	4	5	5	0	4.75
vs. Opposing Batters	AVG	OBP	SLG	AB	H	2B	3B	HR	RBI	BB	SO	AVG	OBP	SLG	AB	H	2B	3B	HR	RBI	BB	SO
Totals	.267	.320	.419	439	117	22	3	13	51	35	42	.304	.359	.449	769	234	39	6	20	112	67	82
vs. Left	.167	.228	.222	72	12	4	0	0	6	6	7	.268	.327	.369	179	48	8	2	2	26	16	19
vs. Right	.286	.338	.458	367	105	18	3	13	45	29	35	.315	.369	.473	590	186	31	4	18	86	51	63

Gwynn, Christopher Karlton "Chris"

Bats: Left   Throws: Left   Born 10/13/64

1987 SEASON AND MAJOR-LEAGUE CAREER BATTING TOTALS

	G	AB	H	2B	3B	HR	TB	R	RBI	TBB	IBB	SO	HP	SH	SF	SB	CS	SB%	GDP	AVG	OBP	SLG
87 LA	17	32	7	1	0	0	8	2	2	1	0	7	0	1	0	0	0	.00	0	.219	.242	.250
1 YEAR	17	32	7	1	0	0	8	2	2	1	0	7	0	1	0	0	0	.00	0	.219	.242	.250

		1987 SEASON											FOUR YEAR TOTALS (1984 – 1987)									
	AVG	OBP	SLG	AB	H	2B	3B	HR	RBI	BB	SO	AVG	OBP	SLG	AB	H	2B	3B	HR	RBI	BB	SO
Totals	.219	.242	.250	32	7	1	0	0	2	1	7	.219	.242	.250	32	7	1	0	0	2	1	7
vs. Left	.250	.250	.250	4	1	0	0	0	1	0	2	.250	.250	.250	4	1	0	0	0	1	0	2
vs. Right	.214	.241	.250	28	6	1	0	0	1	1	5	.214	.241	.250	28	6	1	0	0	1	1	5
At Home	.083	.083	.083	12	1	0	0	0	0	0	1	.083	.083	.083	12	1	0	0	0	0	0	1
On Road	.300	.333	.350	20	6	1	0	0	2	1	6	.300	.333	.350	20	6	1	0	0	2	1	6

Haas, Bryan Edmund "Moose"

Bats: Right   Throws: Right   Born 04/22/56

1987 SEASON AND MAJOR-LEAGUE CAREER PITCHING TOTALS

	G	GS	CG	GF	IP	BFP	H	R	ER	HR	SH	SF	HB	TBB	IBB	SO	WP	Bk	W	L	Pct	ShO	Sv	ERA
87 OAK	9	9	0	0	41	181	57	29	26	7	1	1	0	13	0	1	2	2	.500	0	0	5.71
12 YEARS	266	252	56	8	1655	6928	1717	806	738	162	39	65	10	436	36	853	40	4	100	83	.546	8	2	4.01

1987: Finesse, Groundball   1986: Finesse, Flyball

1987 SEASON	G	IP	H	BB	SO	SB	CS	W	L	S	ERA
Totals	9	40.2	57	9	13	2	3	2	2	0	5.75
At Home	5	20.0	33	5	7	2	2	1	2	0	5.85
On Road	4	20.2	24	4	6	0	1	1	0	0	5.66

vs. Opposing Batters	AVG	OBP	SLG	AB	H	2B	3B	HR	RBI	BB	SO
Totals	.335	.367	.541	170	57	12	1	7	25	9	13
vs. Left	.307	.336	.446	101	31	5	0	3	15	5	7
vs. Right	.377	.411	.681	69	26	7	1	4	10	4	6

TWO YEAR TOTALS (1986 – 1987)	G	IP	H	BB	SO	SB	CS	W	L	S	ERA
Totals	21	113.0	115	28	53	7	5	9	4	0	3.82
At Home	9	45.1	57	15	26	3	3	3	3	0	3.97
On Road	12	67.2	58	13	27	4	2	6	1	0	3.72

	AVG	OBP	SLG	AB	H	2B	3B	HR	RBI	BB	SO
Totals	.264	.308	.404	436	115	26	1	11	46	28	53
vs. Left	.294	.344	.416	221	65	9	0	6	25	18	19
vs. Right	.233	.269	.391	215	50	17	1	5	21	10	34

Habyan, John Gabriel

Bats: Right   Throws: Right   Born 01/29/64

1987 SEASON AND MAJOR-LEAGUE CAREER PITCHING TOTALS

	G	GS	CG	GF	IP	BFP	H	R	ER	HR	SH	SF	HB	TBB	IBB	SO	WP	Bk	W	L	Pct	ShO	Sv	ERA
87 BAL	27	13	0	4	116	493	110	67	62	20	4	4	2	40	1	64	3	0	6	7	.462	0	1	4.81
3 YEARS	35	18	0	6	145	622	137	85	75	23	6	5	2	58	3	80	4	0	8	10	.444	0	1	4.66

1987: Finesse, Flyball   1986: Finesse, Flyball

1987 SEASON	G	IP	H	BB	SO	SB	CS	W	L	S	ERA
Totals	27	116.1	110	40	64	13	3	6	7	1	4.80
At Home	12	57.0	63	14	26	6	2	3	5	0	6.00
On Road	15	59.1	47	26	38	7	1	3	2	1	3.64

vs. Opposing Batters	AVG	OBP	SLG	AB	H	2B	3B	HR	RBI	BB	SO
Totals	.248	.311	.447	443	110	18	5	20	54	40	64
vs. Left	.254	.318	.441	256	65	11	5	9	21	24	29
vs. Right	.241	.301	.455	187	45	7	0	11	33	16	35

TWO YEAR TOTALS (1986 – 1987)	G	IP	H	BB	SO	SB	CS	W	L	S	ERA
Totals	33	142.2	134	58	78	17	5	7	10	1	4.73
At Home	15	77.0	80	22	36	9	4	4	5	0	5.38
On Road	18	65.2	54	36	42	8	1	3	5	1	3.97

	AVG	OBP	SLG	AB	H	2B	3B	HR	RBI	BB	SO
Totals	.249	.321	.442	539	134	23	6	23	68	58	78
vs. Left	.258	.332	.433	298	77	13	6	9	27	33	34
vs. Right	.237	.307	.452	241	57	10	0	14	41	25	44

Hairston, Jerry Wayne

Bats: Both   Throws: Right   Born 02/16/52

1987 SEASON AND MAJOR-LEAGUE CAREER BATTING TOTALS

	G	AB	H	2B	3B	HR	TB	R	RBI	TBB	IBB	SO	HP	SH	SF	SB	CS	SB%	GDP	AVG	OBP	SLG
87 CHA	66	126	29	8	0	5	52	14	20	25	2	25	1	1	2	0	0	.00	4	.230	.357	.413
12 YEARS	854	1694	437	91	6	30	630	216	205	282	18	240	8	13	21	4	5	.44	35	.258	.363	.372

1987 SEASON	AVG	OBP	SLG	AB	H	2B	3B	HR	RBI	BB	SO
Totals	.230	.357	.413	126	29	8	0	5	20	25	25
vs. Left	.254	.375	.441	59	15	5	0	2	9	11	13
vs. Right	.209	.341	.388	67	14	3	0	3	11	14	12
At Home	.259	.421	.431	58	15	4	0	2	11	16	8
On Road	.206	.295	.397	68	14	4	0	3	9	9	17

FOUR YEAR TOTALS (1984 – 1987)	AVG	OBP	SLG	AB	H	2B	3B	HR	RBI	BB	SO
Totals	.255	.362	.393	718	183	44	2	17	85	121	98
vs. Left	.257	.357	.414	191	49	12	0	6	27	28	37
vs. Right	.254	.364	.385	527	134	32	2	11	58	93	61
At Home	.279	.401	.428	348	97	26	1	8	49	72	45
On Road	.232	.323	.359	370	86	18	1	9	36	49	53

Hall, Albert

Bats: Both   Throws: Right   Born 03/07/59

1987 SEASON AND MAJOR-LEAGUE CAREER BATTING TOTALS

	G	AB	H	2B	3B	HR	TB	R	RBI	TBB	IBB	SO	HP	SH	SF	SB	CS	SB%	GDP	AVG	OBP	SLG
87 ATL	92	292	83	20	4	3	120	54	24	38	3	36	2	4	1	33	10	.77	5	.284	.369	.411
7 YEARS	270	541	139	28	6	4	191	94	37	65	4	75	2	8	1	49	19	.72	10	.257	.338	.353

1987 SEASON	AVG	OBP	SLG	AB	H	2B	3B	HR	RBI	BB	SO
Totals	.284	.369	.411	292	83	20	4	3	24	38	36
vs. Left	.287	.358	.377	122	35	8	0	1	9	13	16
vs. Right	.282	.378	.435	170	48	12	4	2	15	25	20
At Home	.294	.401	.441	136	40	7	2	3	13	23	19
On Road	.276	.339	.385	156	43	13	2	0	11	15	17

TWO YEAR TOTALS (1986 – 1987)	AVG	OBP	SLG	AB	H	2B	3B	HR	RBI	BB	SO
Totals	.278	.361	.392	342	95	22	4	3	25	43	42
vs. Left	.284	.353	.366	134	38	8	0	1	9	14	17
vs. Right	.274	.366	.409	208	57	14	4	2	16	29	25
At Home	.281	.380	.404	178	50	9	2	3	14	27	24
On Road	.274	.339	.378	164	45	13	2	0	11	16	18

Hall, Andrew Clark "Drew"

Bats: Left   Throws: Left   Born 03/27/63

1987 SEASON AND MAJOR-LEAGUE CAREER PITCHING TOTALS

	G	GS	CG	GF	IP	BFP	H	R	ER	HR	SH	SF	HB	TBB	IBB	SO	WP	Bk	W	L	Pct	ShO	Sv	ERA
87 CHN	21	0	0	7	33	147	40	31	25	4	1	2	0	14	0	20	1	0	1	1	.500	0	0	6.82
2 YEARS	26	4	1	8	57	248	64	43	37	7	2	2	0	24	0	41	1	0	2	3	.400	0	1	5.84

1987: Finesse, Flyball   1986: Power, Groundball

	1987 SEASON											FOUR YEAR TOTALS (1984 – 1987)										
	G	IP	H	BB	SO	SB	CS	W	L	S	ERA	G	IP	H	BB	SO	SB	CS	W	L	S	ERA
Totals	21	33.0	40	14	20	2	3	1	1	0	6.82	26	56.2	64	24	41	2	4	2	3	1	5.88
At Home	13	19.1	25	11	12	0	1	0	0	0	7.91	16	36.1	39	16	27	0	2	1	0	1	4.95
On Road	8	13.2	15	3	8	2	2	1	1	0	5.27	10	20.1	25	8	14	2	2	1	3	0	7.52
vs. Opposing Batters	AVG	OBP	SLG	AB	H	2B	3B	HR	RBI	BB	SO	AVG	OBP	SLG	AB	H	2B	3B	HR	RBI	BB	SO
Totals	.308	.370	.462	130	40	6	1	4	31	14	20	.291	.358	.441	220	64	10	1	7	40	24	41
vs. Left	.270	.289	.378	37	10	2	1	0	9	1	4	.298	.333	.526	57	17	5	1	2	13	3	9
vs. Right	.323	.398	.495	93	30	4	0	4	22	13	16	.288	.366	.411	163	47	5	0	5	27	21	32

Hamilton, Jeffrey Robert "Jeff"

Bats: Right   Throws: Right   Born 03/19/64

1987 SEASON AND MAJOR-LEAGUE CAREER BATTING TOTALS

	G	AB	H	2B	3B	HR	TB	R	RBI	TBB	IBB	SO	HP	SH	SF	SB	CS	SB%	GDP	AVG	OBP	SLG
87 LA	35	83	18	3	0	0	21	5	1	7	2	22	1	0	0	0	1	.00	0	.217	.286	.253
2 YEARS	106	230	51	8	0	5	74	27	20	9	3	65	1	0	2	0	1	.00	3	.222	.252	.322

	1987 SEASON											FOUR YEAR TOTALS (1984 – 1987)										
	AVG	OBP	SLG	AB	H	2B	3B	HR	RBI	BB	SO	AVG	OBP	SLG	AB	H	2B	3B	HR	RBI	BB	SO
Totals	.217	.286	.253	83	18	3	0	0	1	7	22	.222	.252	.322	230	51	8	0	5	20	9	65
vs. Left	.250	.314	.250	32	8	0	0	0	1	3	8	.264	.293	.333	87	23	3	0	1	9	4	19
vs. Right	.196	.268	.255	51	10	3	0	0	0	4	14	.196	.227	.315	143	28	5	0	4	11	5	46
At Home	.241	.305	.278	54	13	2	0	0	0	4	12	.264	.292	.368	125	33	7	0	2	11	4	34
On Road	.172	.250	.207	29	5	1	0	0	1	3	10	.171	.205	.267	105	18	1	0	3	9	5	31

Harper, Terry Joe

Bats: Right   Throws: Right   Born 08/19/55

1987 SEASON AND MAJOR-LEAGUE CAREER BATTING TOTALS

	G	AB	H	2B	3B	HR	TB	R	RBI	TBB	IBB	SO	HP	SH	SF	SB	CS	SB%	GDP	AVG	OBP	SLG
87 DET-PIT	67	130	32	6	0	4	50	12	17	16	1	19	0	1	0	1	1	.50	8	.246	.329	.385
8 YEARS	540	1467	371	55	5	36	544	147	180	144	7	248	8	4	9	37	28	.57	52	.253	.321	.371

	1987 SEASON											FOUR YEAR TOTALS (1984 – 1987)										
	AVG	OBP	SLG	AB	H	2B	3B	HR	RBI	BB	SO	AVG	OBP	SLG	AB	H	2B	3B	HR	RBI	BB	SO
Totals	.246	.329	.385	130	32	6	0	4	17	16	19	.249	.315	.379	989	246	36	3	29	127	93	155
vs. Left	.254	.338	.398	118	30	5	0	4	16	15	15	.237	.299	.373	464	110	19	1	14	59	42	63
vs. Right	.167	.231	.250	12	2	1	0	0	1	1	4	.259	.329	.385	525	136	17	2	15	68	51	92
At Home	.185	.284	.308	65	12	2	0	2	12	9	12	.269	.340	.410	468	126	22	1	14	69	47	78
On Road	.308	.375	.462	65	20	4	0	2	5	7	7	.230	.293	.351	521	120	14	2	15	58	46	77

Harris, Greg Allen

Bats: Both   Throws: Right   Born 11/02/55

1987 SEASON AND MAJOR-LEAGUE CAREER PITCHING TOTALS

	G	GS	CG	GF	IP	BFP	H	R	ER	HR	SH	SF	HB	TBB	IBB	SO	WP	Bk	W	L	Pct	ShO	Sv	ERA
87 TEX	42	19	0	14	141	629	157	92	76	18	7	3	4	56	3	106	4	2	5	10	.333	0	0	4.85
7 YEARS	258	44	1	137	581	2474	535	280	243	60	25	18	19	234	18	479	16	8	27	35	.435	0	36	3.76

1987: Power, Groundball   1986: Power, Flyball   1985: Power, Groundball   1984: Power, Flyball

	1987 SEASON											FOUR YEAR TOTALS (1984 – 1987)										
	G	IP	H	BB	SO	SB	CS	W	L	S	ERA	G	IP	H	BB	SO	SB	CS	W	L	S	ERA
Totals	42	140.2	157	56	106	15	4	5	10	0	4.86	207	419.1	372	166	357	36	14	22	24	34	3.37
At Home	22	81.1	84	27	61	7	2	3	2	0	4.65	101	219.1	194	65	177	17	6	16	9	16	3.41
On Road	20	59.1	73	29	45	8	2	2	8	0	5.16	106	200.0	178	101	180	19	8	6	15	18	3.33
vs. Opposing Batters	AVG	OBP	SLG	AB	H	2B	3B	HR	RBI	BB	SO	AVG	OBP	SLG	AB	H	2B	3B	HR	RBI	BB	SO
Totals	.280	.348	.439	560	157	29	3	18	78	56	106	.239	.313	.375	1558	372	72	10	40	189	166	357
vs. Left	.256	.319	.363	270	69	15	1	4	31	26	50	.228	.304	.347	741	169	29	7	15	85	82	157
vs. Right	.303	.375	.510	290	88	14	2	14	47	30	56	.248	.321	.400	817	203	43	3	25	104	84	200

Hart, Michael Lawrence "Mike"

Bats: Left Throws: Left Born 02/12/58

1987 SEASON AND MAJOR-LEAGUE CAREER BATTING TOTALS

	G	AB	H	2B	3B	HR	TB	R	RBI	TBB	IBB	SO	HP	SH	SF	SB	CS	SB%	GDP	AVG	OBP	SLG
87 BAL	34	76	12	2	0	4	26	7	12	6	0	19	0	2	1	1	4	.20	1	.158	.217	.342
2 YEARS	47	105	17	2	0	4	31	7	17	7	0	21	0	2	2	1	5	.17	1	.162	.211	.295

	1987 SEASON										FOUR YEAR TOTALS (1984 – 1987)									
	AVG	OBP	SLG	AB	H	2B	3B	HR	RBI	BB	SO	AVG	OBP	SLG	AB	H	2B	3B	HR	RBI	BB	SO
Totals	.158	.217	.342	76	12	2	0	4	12	6	19	.158	.214	.342	76	12	2	0	4	12	6	19
vs. Left	.083	.185	.208	24	2	0	0	1	2	3	8	.083	.185	.208	24	2	0	0	1	2	3	8
vs. Right	.192	.232	.404	52	10	2	0	3	10	3	11	.192	.232	.404	52	10	2	0	3	10	3	11
At Home	.143	.210	.286	56	8	2	0	2	8	5	12	.143	.210	.286	56	8	2	0	2	8	5	12
On Road	.200	.238	.500	20	4	0	0	2	4	1	7	.200	.238	.500	20	4	0	0	2	4	1	7

Hassey, Ronald William "Ron"

Bats: Left Throws: Right Born 02/27/53

1987 SEASON AND MAJOR-LEAGUE CAREER BATTING TOTALS

	G	AB	H	2B	3B	HR	TB	R	RBI	TBB	IBB	SO	HP	SH	SF	SB	CS	SB%	GDP	AVG	OBP	SLG
87 CHA	49	145	31	9	0	3	49	15	12	17	2	11	2	0	1	0	0	.00	9	.214	.303	.338
10 YEARS	842	2476	689	130	7	53	992	264	334	291	24	246	15	15	25	10	9	.53	84	.278	.354	.401

	1987 SEASON										FOUR YEAR TOTALS (1984 – 1987)									
	AVG	OBP	SLG	AB	H	2B	3B	HR	RBI	BB	SO	AVG	OBP	SLG	AB	H	2B	3B	HR	RBI	BB	SO
Totals	.214	.303	.338	145	31	9	0	3	12	17	11	.288	.366	.440	935	269	55	3	27	127	110	91
vs. Left	.000	.200	.000	16	0	0	0	0	0	3	2	.216	.288	.249	185	40	6	0	0	13	17	25
vs. Right	.240	.317	.380	129	31	9	0	3	12	14	9	.305	.385	.487	750	229	49	3	27	114	93	66
At Home	.200	.268	.293	75	15	4	0	1	6	7	5	.294	.382	.428	442	130	27	1	10	58	60	44
On Road	.229	.337	.386	70	16	5	0	2	6	10	6	.282	.351	.450	493	139	28	2	17	69	50	47

Havens, Bradley David "Brad"

Bats: Left Throws: Left Born 11/17/59

1987 SEASON AND MAJOR-LEAGUE CAREER PITCHING TOTALS

	G	GS	CG	GF	IP	BFP	H	R	ER	HR	SH	SF	HB	TBB	IBB	SO	WP	Bk	W	L	Pct	ShO	Sv	ERA
87 LA	31	1	0	10	35	157	30	18	17	2	1	0	1	23	11	23	3	3	0	0	.000	0	1	4.37
6 YEARS	148	60	6	34	487	2115	501	289	271	62	15	15	2	204	24	311	19	5	21	32	.396	2	5	5.01

1987: Power, Flyball 1986: Power, Flyball 1985: Power, Flyball

	1987 SEASON									FOUR YEAR TOTALS (1984 – 1987)								
	G	IP	H	BB	SO	SB	CS	W	L	S	ERA	G	IP	H	BB	SO	SB	CS	W	L	S	ERA
Totals	31	35.0	30	23	23	3	0	0	0	1	4.37	85	120.1	114	62	99	11	5	3	4	2	5.01
At Home	16	14.1	15	11	8	1	0	0	0	0	4.40	47	61.2	66	33	54	5	2	1	2	0	5.11
On Road	15	20.2	15	12	15	2	0	0	0	1	4.35	38	58.2	48	29	45	6	3	2	2	2	4.91

	vs. Opposing Batters											FOUR YEAR TOTALS (1984 – 1987)								
	AVG	OBP	SLG	AB	H	2B	3B	HR	RBI	BB	SO	AVG	OBP	SLG	AB	H	2B	3B	HR	RBI	BB	SO
Totals	.227	.346	.326	132	30	7	0	2	21	23	23	.253	.345	.411	450	114	26	3	13	77	62	99
vs. Left	.327	.400	.408	49	16	4	0	0	14	5	7	.251	.333	.368	171	43	9	1	3	31	20	37
vs. Right	.169	.317	.277	83	14	3	0	2	7	18	16	.254	.352	.437	279	71	17	2	10	46	42	62

Hawkins, Melton Andrew "Andy"

Bats: Right Throws: Right Born 01/21/60

1987 SEASON AND MAJOR-LEAGUE CAREER PITCHING TOTALS

	G	GS	CG	GF	IP	BFP	H	R	ER	HR	SH	SF	HB	TBB	IBB	SO	WP	Bk	W	L	Pct	ShO	Sv	ERA
87 SD	24	20	0	2	118	516	131	71	66	16	5	3	2	49	2	51	2	3	3	10	.231	0	0	5.03
6 YEARS	166	139	15	14	886	3806	893	443	390	83	51	34	20	336	26	398	18	14	46	47	.495	5	0	3.96

1987: Finesse, Flyball 1986: Finesse, Flyball 1985: Finesse, Flyball 1984: Power, Flyball

	1987 SEASON									FOUR YEAR TOTALS (1984 – 1987)								
	G	IP	H	BB	SO	SB	CS	W	L	S	ERA	G	IP	H	BB	SO	SB	CS	W	L	S	ERA
Totals	24	117.2	131	49	51	5	7	3	10	0	5.05	130	701.2	721	261	314	54	27	39	35	0	4.13
At Home	12	58.1	72	20	30	0	5	1	5	0	5.55	68	384.1	395	124	163	24	14	22	18	0	3.70
On Road	12	59.1	59	29	21	5	2	2	5	0	4.55	62	317.1	326	137	151	30	13	17	17	0	4.62

	vs. Opposing Batters											FOUR YEAR TOTALS (1984 – 1987)								
	AVG	OBP	SLG	AB	H	2B	3B	HR	RBI	BB	SO	AVG	OBP	SLG	AB	H	2B	3B	HR	RBI	BB	SO
Totals	.287	.356	.468	457	131	31	2	16	63	49	51	.268	.333	.409	2689	721	135	15	71	316	261	314
vs. Left	.336	.415	.515	229	77	20	0	7	33	33	17	.300	.374	.452	1315	394	77	6	37	161	157	138
vs. Right	.237	.293	.421	228	54	11	2	9	30	16	34	.238	.293	.368	1374	327	58	9	34	155	104	176

Heath, Michael Thomas "Mike"

Bats: Right **Throws: Right** **Born 02/05/55**

1987 SEASON AND MAJOR-LEAGUE CAREER BATTING TOTALS

	G	AB	H	2B	3B	HR	TB	R	RBI	TBB	IBB	SO	HP	SH	SF	SB	CS	SB%	GDP	AVG	OBP	SLG
87 DET	93	270	76	16	0	8	116	34	33	21	0	42	3	1	1	1	5	.17	5	.281	.339	.430
10 YEARS	946	3088	774	129	20	63	1132	350	358	210	17	416	12	33	24	39	33	.54	81	.251	.299	.367

	1987 SEASON											FOUR YEAR TOTALS (1984 – 1987)									
	AVG	OBP	SLG	AB	H	2B	3B	HR	RBI	BB	SO	AVG	OBP	SLG	AB	H	2B	3B	HR	RBI	BB	SO
Totals	.281	.339	.430	270	76	16	0	8	33	21	42	.251	.306	.398	1469	368	66	12	42	188	116	230
vs. Left	.302	.356	.465	159	48	11	0	5	18	12	15	.284	.336	.459	658	187	40	6	21	93	53	92
vs. Right	.252	.314	.378	111	28	5	0	3	15	9	27	.223	.281	.348	811	181	26	6	21	95	63	138
At Home	.297	.352	.531	145	43	10	0	8	21	12	23	.257	.309	.433	723	186	31	6	28	96	54	107
On Road	.264	.324	.312	125	33	6	0	0	12	9	19	.244	.303	.363	746	182	35	6	14	92	62	123

Heathcock, Ronald Jeffrey "Jeff"

Bats: Right **Throws: Right** **Born 11/18/59**

1987 SEASON AND MAJOR-LEAGUE CAREER PITCHING TOTALS

	G	GS	CG	GF	IP	BFP	H	R	ER	HR	SH	SF	HB	TBB	IBB	SO	WP	Bk	W	L	Pct	ShO	Sv	ERA
87 HOU	19	2	0	2	43	174	44	15	15	4	2	3	1	9	1	15	1	1	4	2	.667	0	1	3.14
3 YEARS	39	12	1	9	127	511	113	54	46	14	4	5	3	26	1	52	3	2	9	4	.692	0	3	3.26

1987: Finesse, Flyball

	1987 SEASON										TWO YEAR TOTALS (1986 – 1987)									
	G	IP	H	BB	SO	SB	CS	W	L	S	ERA	G	IP	H	BB	SO	SB	CS	W	L	S	ERA
Totals	19	42.2	44	9	15	3	1	4	2	1	3.16	19	42.2	44	9	15	3	1	4	2	1	3.16
At Home	10	24.1	27	2	9	3	0	2	1	1	2.59	10	24.1	27	2	9	3	0	2	1	1	2.59
On Road	9	18.1	17	7	6	0	1	2	1	0	3.93	9	18.1	17	7	6	0	1	2	1	0	3.93

vs. Opposing Batters	AVG	OBP	SLG	AB	H	2B	3B	HR	RBI	BB	SO	AVG	OBP	SLG	AB	H	2B	3B	HR	RBI	BB	SO
Totals	.277	.314	.440	159	44	6	4	4	16	9	15	.277	.314	.440	159	44	6	4	4	16	9	15
vs. Left	.373	.402	.560	75	28	5	3	1	7	4	1	.373	.402	.560	75	28	5	3	1	7	4	1
vs. Right	.190	.233	.333	84	16	1	1	3	9	5	14	.190	.233	.333	84	16	1	1	3	9	5	14

Heep, Daniel William "Danny"

Bats: Left **Throws: Left** **Born 07/03/57**

1987 SEASON AND MAJOR-LEAGUE CAREER BATTING TOTALS

	G	AB	H	2B	3B	HR	TB	R	RBI	TBB	IBB	SO	HP	SH	SF	SB	CS	SB%	GDP	AVG	OBP	SLG
87 LA	60	98	16	4	0	0	20	7	9	8	0	10	0	1	0	1	0	1.00	6	.163	.226	.204
9 YEARS	620	1411	354	75	5	25	514	151	158	161	21	185	6	3	22	10	12	.45	43	.251	.326	.364

	1987 SEASON											FOUR YEAR TOTALS (1984 – 1987)									
	AVG	OBP	SLG	AB	H	2B	3B	HR	RBI	BB	SO	AVG	OBP	SLG	AB	H	2B	3B	HR	RBI	BB	SO
Totals	.163	.226	.204	98	16	4	0	0	9	8	10	.253	.330	.364	763	193	38	4	13	96	91	90
vs. Left	.143	.250	.143	7	1	0	0	0	0	1	1	.233	.349	.279	86	20	4	0	0	14	15	16
vs. Right	.165	.224	.209	91	15	4	0	0	9	7	9	.256	.328	.375	677	173	34	4	13	82	76	74
At Home	.136	.208	.136	44	6	0	0	0	3	4	4	.266	.351	.364	357	95	13	2	6	41	46	39
On Road	.185	.241	.259	54	10	4	0	0	6	4	6	.241	.312	.365	406	98	25	2	7	55	45	51

Henderson, David Lee "Dave"

Bats: Right **Throws: Right** **Born 07/21/58**

1987 SEASON AND MAJOR-LEAGUE CAREER BATTING TOTALS

	G	AB	H	2B	3B	HR	TB	R	RBI	TBB	IBB	SO	HP	SH	SF	SB	CS	SB%	GDP	AVG	OBP	SLG
87 BOS-SF	90	205	48	12	0	8	84	32	26	30	0	53	0	1	2	3	1	.75	3	.234	.329	.410
7 YEARS	780	2379	603	129	12	88	1020	317	300	216	12	507	9	10	14	29	19	.60	38	.253	.316	.429

	1987 SEASON											FOUR YEAR TOTALS (1984 – 1987)									
	AVG	OBP	SLG	AB	H	2B	3B	HR	RBI	BB	SO	AVG	OBP	SLG	AB	H	2B	3B	HR	RBI	BB	SO
Totals	.234	.329	.410	205	48	12	0	8	26	30	53	.256	.322	.429	1445	370	85	6	51	184	136	323
vs. Left	.272	.366	.506	81	22	7	0	4	10	12	20	.279	.341	.475	448	125	30	2	18	64	39	77
vs. Right	.210	.306	.347	124	26	5	0	4	16	18	33	.246	.313	.408	997	245	55	4	33	120	97	246
At Home	.231	.329	.405	121	28	9	0	4	16	18	30	.272	.340	.462	768	209	46	5	30	110	75	158
On Road	.238	.330	.417	84	20	3	0	4	10	12	23	.238	.301	.391	677	161	39	1	21	74	61	165

Henderson, Stephen Curtis "Steve"

Bats: Right **Throws: Right** **Born 11/18/52**

1987 SEASON AND MAJOR-LEAGUE CAREER BATTING TOTALS

	G	AB	H	2B	3B	HR	TB	R	RBI	TBB	IBB	SO	HP	SH	SF	SB	CS	SB%	GDP	AVG	OBP	SLG
87 OAK	46	114	33	7	0	3	49	14	9	12	1	19	0	0	0	0	0	.00	7	.289	.357	.430
11 YEARS	1043	3438	966	160	49	68	1428	455	423	379	31	663	13	11	22	78	57	.58	107	.281	.353	.415

		1987 SEASON									TWO YEAR TOTALS (1986 – 1987)									
	AVG	OBP	SLG	AB	H	2B	3B	HR	RBI	BB	SO	AVG	OBP	SLG	AB	H	2B	3B	HR	RBI	BB	SO
Totals	.289	.357	.430	114	33	7	0	3	9	12	19	.250	.308	.371	140	35	8	0	3	12	12	24
vs. Left	.311	.374	.467	90	28	5	0	3	9	9	9	.280	.333	.421	107	30	6	0	3	12	9	12
vs. Right	.208	.296	.292	24	5	2	0	0	0	3	10	.152	.222	.212	33	5	2	0	0	0	3	12
At Home	.179	.238	.282	39	7	1	0	1	3	3	9	.191	.240	.298	47	9	2	0	1	5	3	11
On Road	.347	.417	.507	75	26	6	0	2	6	9	10	.280	.340	.409	93	26	6	0	2	7	9	13

Hendrick, George Andrew

Bats: Right **Throws: Right** **Born 10/18/49**

1987 SEASON AND MAJOR-LEAGUE CAREER BATTING TOTALS

	G	AB	H	2B	3B	HR	TB	R	RBI	TBB	IBB	SO	HP	SH	SF	SB	CS	SB%	GDP	AVG	OBP	SLG
87 CAL	65	162	39	10	0	5	64	14	25	14	1	18	0	0	0	0	0	.00	8	.241	.301	.395
17 YEARS	1979	7002	1949	342	27	264	3137	929	1092	560	76	993	21	20	83	59	46	.56	209	.278	.330	.448

		1987 SEASON									FOUR YEAR TOTALS (1984 – 1987)									
	AVG	OBP	SLG	AB	H	2B	3B	HR	RBI	BB	SO	AVG	OBP	SLG	AB	H	2B	3B	HR	RBI	BB	SO
Totals	.241	.301	.395	162	39	10	0	5	25	14	18	.255	.308	.396	1183	302	67	2	32	172	94	184
vs. Left	.232	.294	.384	125	29	7	0	4	20	11	14	.256	.313	.409	575	147	35	1	17	84	51	69
vs. Right	.270	.325	.432	37	10	3	0	1	5	3	4	.255	.304	.385	608	155	32	1	15	88	43	115
At Home	.174	.240	.290	69	12	5	0	1	2	6	9	.245	.301	.363	593	145	37	0	11	79	49	91
On Road	.290	.347	.473	93	27	5	0	4	23	8	9	.266	.316	.431	590	157	30	2	21	93	45	93

Hernandez, Guillermo (Villanueva) "Willie"

Bats: Left **Throws: Left** **Born 11/14/55**

1987 SEASON AND MAJOR-LEAGUE CAREER PITCHING TOTALS

	G	GS	CG	GF	IP	BFP	H	R	ER	HR	SH	SF	HB	TBB	IBB	SO	WP	Bk	W	L	Pct	ShO	Sv	ERA
87 DET	45	0	0	31	49	217	53	27	20	8	2	3	0	20	7	30	1	0	3	4	.429	0	8	3.67
11 YEARS	649	11	0	356	947	3941	866	386	349	85	58	33	20	302	71	699	34	6	62	56	.525	0	122	3.32

1987: Finesse, Flyball **1986: Power, Flyball** **1985: Finesse, Flyball** **1984: Power, Flyball**

		1987 SEASON									FOUR YEAR TOTALS (1984 – 1987)									
	G	IP	H	BB	SO	SB	CS	W	L	S	ERA	G	IP	H	BB	SO	SB	CS	W	L	S	ERA
Totals	45	49.0	53	20	30	2	1	3	4	8	3.67	263	384.2	318	91	295	18	9	28	24	95	2.74
At Home	16	17.0	21	4	8	1	1	2	2	1	4.76	125	184.1	150	41	149	14	5	17	11	41	2.78
On Road	29	32.0	32	16	22	1	0	1	2	7	3.09	138	200.1	168	50	146	4	4	11	13	54	2.70
vs. Opposing Batters	AVG	OBP	SLG	AB	H	2B	3B	HR	RBI	BB	SO	AVG	OBP	SLG	AB	H	2B	3B	HR	RBI	BB	SO
Totals	.276	.340	.469	192	53	7	3	8	35	20	30	.223	.269	.349	1425	318	47	6	40	169	91	295
vs. Left	.232	.276	.377	69	16	2	1	2	13	5	10	.190	.219	.251	411	78	11	1	4	40	16	82
vs. Right	.301	.374	.520	123	37	5	2	6	22	15	20	.237	.289	.389	1014	240	36	5	36	129	75	213

Herndon, Larry Darnell

Bats: Right **Throws: Right** **Born 11/03/53**

1987 SEASON AND MAJOR-LEAGUE CAREER BATTING TOTALS

	G	AB	H	2B	3B	HR	TB	R	RBI	TBB	IBB	SO	HP	SH	SF	SB	CS	SB%	GDP	AVG	OBP	SLG
87 DET	89	225	73	13	2	9	117	32	47	23	0	35	0	0	6	1	0	1.00	12	.324	.378	.520
13 YEARS	1461	4703	1295	181	76	103	1937	589	530	330	24	756	15	32	35	92	56	.62	117	.275	.323	.412

		1987 SEASON									FOUR YEAR TOTALS (1984 – 1987)									
	AVG	OBP	SLG	AB	H	2B	3B	HR	RBI	BB	SO	AVG	OBP	SLG	AB	H	2B	3B	HR	RBI	BB	SO
Totals	.324	.378	.520	225	73	13	2	9	47	23	35	.269	.325	.412	1357	365	56	15	36	164	115	217
vs. Left	.373	.426	.593	177	66	11	2	8	40	20	24	.297	.359	.469	744	221	31	11	25	112	76	100
vs. Right	.146	.192	.250	48	7	2	0	1	7	3	11	.235	.282	.343	613	144	25	4	11	52	39	117
At Home	.313	.372	.583	115	36	6	2	7	27	12	15	.279	.332	.441	667	186	25	10	21	82	55	97
On Road	.336	.384	.455	110	37	7	0	2	20	11	20	.259	.317	.384	690	179	31	5	15	82	60	120

Hesketh, Joseph Thomas "Joe"

Bats: Right   Throws: Left   Born 02/15/59

1987 SEASON AND MAJOR-LEAGUE CAREER PITCHING TOTALS

	G	GS	CG	GF	IP	BFP	H	R	ER	HR	SH	SF	HB	TBB	IBB	SO	WP	Bk	W	L	Pct	ShO	Sv	ERA
87 MON	18	0	0	3	29	128	23	12	10	2	2	0	2	15	3	31	1	0	0	0	.000	0	1	3.10
4 YEARS	69	45	3	5	312	1290	278	122	108	25	14	6	4	106	12	243	9	9	18	12	.600	2	2	3.12

1987: Power, Groundball   1986: Power, Flyball   1985: Power, Flyball   1984: Power, Flyball

1987 SEASON	G	IP	H	BB	SO	SB	CS	W	L	S	ERA
Totals	18	28.2	23	15	31	1	0	0	0	1	3.14
At Home	7	11.1	8	11	8	1	0	0	0	0	3.18
On Road	11	17.1	15	4	23	0	0	0	0	1	3.12

vs. Opposing Batters	AVG	OBP	SLG	AB	H	2B	3B	HR	RBI	BB	SO
Totals	.211	.317	.303	109	23	4	0	2	9	15	31
vs. Left	.237	.341	.342	38	9	1	0	1	4	4	11
vs. Right	.197	.305	.282	71	14	3	0	1	5	11	20

FOUR YEAR TOTALS (1984 – 1987)	G	IP	H	BB	SO	SB	CS	W	L	S	ERA
Totals	69	311.2	278	106	243	29	11	18	12	2	3.12
At Home	33	156.1	150	52	130	13	3	10	6	0	3.22
On Road	36	155.1	128	54	113	16	8	8	6	2	3.01

vs. Opposing Batters	AVG	OBP	SLG	AB	H	2B	3B	HR	RBI	BB	SO
Totals	.240	.305	.368	1159	278	63	5	25	108	106	243
vs. Left	.217	.287	.276	203	44	4	1	2	18	18	48
vs. Right	.245	.308	.387	956	234	59	4	23	90	88	195

Hillegas, Shawn Patrick

Bats: Right   Throws: Right   Born 08/21/64

1987 SEASON AND MAJOR-LEAGUE CAREER PITCHING TOTALS

	G	GS	CG	GF	IP	BFP	H	R	ER	HR	SH	SF	HB	TBB	IBB	SO	WP	Bk	W	L	Pct	ShO	Sv	ERA
87 LA	12	10	0	1	58	252	52	27	23	5	4	1	0	31	0	51	4	0	4	3	.571	0	0	3.57
1 YEAR	12	10	0	1	58	252	52	27	23	5	4	1	0	31	0	51	4	0	4	3	.571	0	0	3.57

1987: Power, Flyball

1987 SEASON	G	IP	H	BB	SO	SB	CS	W	L	S	ERA
Totals	12	58.0	52	31	51	9	3	4	3	0	3.57
At Home	5	28.0	33	12	20	6	2	1	2	0	4.50
On Road	7	30.0	19	19	31	3	1	3	1	0	2.70

vs. Opposing Batters	AVG	OBP	SLG	AB	H	2B	3B	HR	RBI	BB	SO
Totals	.241	.335	.343	216	52	5	1	5	24	31	51
vs. Left	.275	.398	.404	109	30	3	1	3	17	23	27
vs. Right	.206	.261	.280	107	22	2	0	2	7	8	24

FOUR YEAR TOTALS (1984 – 1987)	G	IP	H	BB	SO	SB	CS	W	L	S	ERA
Totals	12	58.0	52	31	51	9	3	4	3	0	3.57
At Home	5	28.0	33	12	20	6	2	1	2	0	4.50
On Road	7	30.0	19	19	31	3	1	3	1	0	2.70

vs. Opposing Batters	AVG	OBP	SLG	AB	H	2B	3B	HR	RBI	BB	SO
Totals	.241	.335	.343	216	52	5	1	5	24	31	51
vs. Left	.275	.398	.404	109	30	3	1	3	17	23	27
vs. Right	.206	.261	.280	107	22	2	0	2	7	8	24

Hinzo, Thomas Lee "Tommy"

Bats: Both   Throws: Right   Born 06/18/64

1987 SEASON AND MAJOR-LEAGUE CAREER BATTING TOTALS

	G	AB	H	2B	3B	HR	TB	R	RBI	TBB	IBB	SO	HP	SH	SF	SB	CS	SB%	GDP	AVG	OBP	SLG
87 CLE	67	257	68	9	3	3	92	31	21	10	0	47	2	10	1	9	4	.69	6	.265	.296	.358
1 YEAR	67	257	68	9	3	3	92	31	21	10	0	47	2	10	1	9	4	.69	6	.265	.296	.358

1987 SEASON	AVG	OBP	SLG	AB	H	2B	3B	HR	RBI	BB	SO
Totals	.261	.292	.352	261	68	9	3	3	20	10	47
vs. Left	.391	.443	.547	64	25	4	0	2	8	5	5
vs. Right	.218	.240	.289	197	43	5	3	1	12	5	42
At Home	.225	.268	.358	120	27	5	1	3	7	6	25
On Road	.291	.313	.348	141	41	4	2	0	13	4	22

FOUR YEAR TOTALS (1984 – 1987)	AVG	OBP	SLG	AB	H	2B	3B	HR	RBI	BB	SO
Totals	.261	.292	.352	261	68	9	3	3	20	10	47
vs. Left	.391	.443	.547	64	25	4	0	2	8	5	5
vs. Right	.218	.240	.289	197	43	5	3	1	12	5	42
At Home	.225	.268	.358	120	27	5	1	3	7	6	25
On Road	.291	.313	.348	141	41	4	2	0	13	4	22

Hoffman, Glenn Edward

Bats: Right   Throws: Right   Born 07/07/58

1987 SEASON AND MAJOR-LEAGUE CAREER BATTING TOTALS

	G	AB	H	2B	3B	HR	TB	R	RBI	TBB	IBB	SO	HP	SH	SF	SB	CS	SB%	GDP	AVG	OBP	SLG
87 BOS-LA	61	187	40	8	0	0	48	15	16	10	1	32	4	5	0	0	1	.00	6	.214	.269	.257
8 YEARS	718	2059	502	103	9	22	689	238	207	133	9	296	19	46	14	5	14	.26	51	.244	.294	.335

1987 SEASON	AVG	OBP	SLG	AB	H	2B	3B	HR	RBI	BB	SO
Totals	.214	.269	.257	187	40	8	0	0	16	10	32
vs. Left	.183	.246	.233	60	11	3	0	0	5	2	11
vs. Right	.228	.279	.268	127	29	5	0	0	11	8	21
At Home	.240	.269	.293	75	18	4	0	0	6	3	8
On Road	.196	.268	.232	112	22	4	0	0	10	7	24

TWO YEAR TOTALS (1986 – 1987)	AVG	OBP	SLG	AB	H	2B	3B	HR	RBI	BB	SO
Totals	.214	.280	.262	210	45	10	0	0	17	12	35
vs. Left	.180	.250	.230	61	11	3	0	0	6	3	12
vs. Right	.228	.277	.275	149	34	7	0	0	11	9	23
At Home	.242	.274	.308	91	22	6	0	0	6	4	10
On Road	.193	.265	.227	119	23	4	0	0	11	8	25

385

Holton, Brian John
Bats: Right   Throws: Right   Born 11/29/59

1987 SEASON AND MAJOR-LEAGUE CAREER PITCHING TOTALS

	G	GS	CG	GF	IP	BFP	H	R	ER	HR	SH	SF	HB	TBB	IBB	SO	WP	Bk	W	L	Pct	ShO	Sv	ERA
87 LA	53	1	0	26	83	360	87	39	36	11	2	3	0	32	11	58	0	4	3	2	.600	0	2	3.90
3 YEARS	68	4	0	30	111	487	124	59	52	12	4	4	1	39	13	83	2	4	6	6	.500	0	2	4.22

1987: Power, Flyball   1986: Power, Groundball

1987 SEASON

	G	IP	H	BB	SO	SB	CS	W	L	S	ERA
Totals	53	83.0	87	32	57	11	4	3	2	2	3.90
At Home	24	39.2	39	16	27	3	1	2	0	0	2.50
On Road	29	43.1	48	16	30	8	3	1	2	2	5.19

vs. Opposing Batters	AVG	OBP	SLG	AB	H	2B	3B	HR	RBI	BB	SO
Totals	.269	.333	.427	323	87	14	2	11	44	32	57
vs. Left	.274	.363	.395	157	43	7	0	4	13	22	15
vs. Right	.265	.303	.458	166	44	7	2	7	31	10	42

TWO YEAR TOTALS (1986 – 1987)

	G	IP	H	BB	SO	SB	CS	W	L	S	ERA
Totals	65	107.1	115	38	81	16	4	5	5	2	4.02
At Home	29	49.0	52	19	38	4	1	3	1	0	2.94
On Road	36	58.1	63	19	43	12	3	2	4	2	4.94

vs. Opposing Batters	AVG	OBP	SLG	AB	H	2B	3B	HR	RBI	BB	SO
Totals	.274	.334	.425	419	115	23	2	12	56	38	81
vs. Left	.293	.371	.429	198	58	12	0	5	21	25	23
vs. Right	.258	.300	.421	221	57	11	2	7	35	13	58

Honeycutt, Frederick Wayne "Rick"
Bats: Left   Throws: Left   Born 06/29/54

1987 SEASON AND MAJOR-LEAGUE CAREER PITCHING TOTALS

	G	GS	CG	GF	IP	BFP	H	R	ER	HR	SH	SF	HB	TBB	IBB	SO	WP	Bk	W	L	Pct	ShO	Sv	ERA
87 LA-OAK	34	24	1	1	140	631	158	91	73	13	1	3	4	54	4	102	5	1	3	16	.158	1	0	4.69
11 YEARS	309	268	47	13	1703	7237	1776	841	726	152	63	49	36	507	58	751	31	10	90	121	.427	11	1	3.84

1987: Power, Groundball   1986: Finesse, Groundball   1985: Finesse, Groundball   1984: Finesse, Groundball

1987 SEASON

	G	IP	H	BB	SO	SB	CS	W	L	S	ERA
Totals	34	139.2	158	54	102	9	8	3	16	0	4.70
At Home	15	77.2	87	23	54	5	6	2	9	0	4.29
On Road	19	62.0	71	31	48	4	2	1	7	0	5.23

vs. Opposing Batters	AVG	OBP	SLG	AB	H	2B	3B	HR	RBI	BB	SO
Totals	.278	.343	.425	569	158	37	4	13	71	54	102
vs. Left	.193	.244	.307	114	22	3	2	2	14	7	22
vs. Right	.299	.367	.455	455	136	34	2	11	57	47	80

FOUR YEAR TOTALS (1984 – 1987)

	G	IP	H	BB	SO	SB	CS	W	L	S	ERA
Totals	126	636.1	643	199	344	43	33	32	46	1	3.51
At Home	63	351.0	342	87	184	18	17	19	21	0	2.92
On Road	63	285.1	301	112	160	25	16	13	25	1	4.23

vs. Opposing Batters	AVG	OBP	SLG	AB	H	2B	3B	HR	RBI	BB	SO
Totals	.261	.317	.378	2466	643	133	15	42	241	199	344
vs. Left	.204	.239	.299	431	88	16	5	5	52	19	83
vs. Right	.273	.332	.395	2035	555	117	10	37	189	180	261

Horn, Samuel Lee "Sam"
Bats: Left   Throws: Left   Born 11/02/63

1987 SEASON AND MAJOR-LEAGUE CAREER BATTING TOTALS

	G	AB	H	2B	3B	HR	TB	R	RBI	TBB	IBB	SO	HP	SH	SF	SB	CS	SB%	GDP	AVG	OBP	SLG
87 BOS	46	158	44	7	0	14	93	31	34	17	0	55	2	0	0	0	1	.00	5	.278	.356	.589
1 YEAR	46	158	44	7	0	14	93	31	34	17	0	55	2	0	0	0	1	.00	5	.278	.356	.589

1987 SEASON

	AVG	OBP	SLG	AB	H	2B	3B	HR	RBI	BB	SO
Totals	.278	.356	.589	158	44	7	0	14	34	17	55
vs. Left	.276	.382	.655	29	8	2	0	3	9	4	15
vs. Right	.279	.350	.574	129	36	5	0	11	25	13	40
At Home	.306	.383	.597	72	22	3	0	6	18	8	22
On Road	.256	.333	.581	86	22	4	0	8	16	9	33

FOUR YEAR TOTALS (1984 – 1987)

	AVG	OBP	SLG	AB	H	2B	3B	HR	RBI	BB	SO
Totals	.278	.356	.589	158	44	7	0	14	34	17	55
vs. Left	.276	.382	.655	29	8	2	0	3	9	4	15
vs. Right	.279	.350	.574	129	36	5	0	11	25	13	40
At Home	.306	.383	.597	72	22	3	0	6	18	8	22
On Road	.256	.333	.581	86	22	4	0	8	16	9	33

Howe, Steven Roy "Steve"
Bats: Left   Throws: Left   Born 03/10/58

1987 SEASON AND MAJOR-LEAGUE CAREER PITCHING TOTALS

	G	GS	CG	GF	IP	BFP	H	R	ER	HR	SH	SF	HB	TBB	IBB	SO	WP	Bk	W	L	Pct	ShO	Sv	ERA
87 TEX	24	0	0	15	31	131	33	15	15	2	2	0	3	8	1	19	2	1	3	3	.500	0	1	4.35
6 YEARS	268	0	0	169	379	1582	367	140	114	13	31	18	7	89	40	212	10	1	29	31	.483	0	60	2.71

1987: Finesse, Groundball

1987 SEASON

	G	IP	H	BB	SO	SB	CS	W	L	S	ERA
Totals	24	31.1	33	8	19	2	2	3	3	1	4.31
At Home	12	16.1	14	4	10	2	2	2	0	0	2.76
On Road	12	15.0	19	4	9	0	0	1	3	1	6.00

vs. Opposing Batters	AVG	OBP	SLG	AB	H	2B	3B	HR	RBI	BB	SO
Totals	.280	.341	.398	118	33	6	1	2	15	8	19
vs. Left	.200	.282	.314	35	7	2	1	0	2	2	6
vs. Right	.313	.367	.434	83	26	4	0	2	13	6	13

TWO YEAR TOTALS (1986 – 1987)

	G	IP	H	BB	SO	SB	CS	W	L	S	ERA
Totals	24	31.1	33	8	19	2	2	3	3	1	4.31
At Home	12	16.1	14	4	10	2	2	2	0	0	2.76
On Road	12	15.0	19	4	9	0	0	1	3	1	6.00

vs. Opposing Batters	AVG	OBP	SLG	AB	H	2B	3B	HR	RBI	BB	SO
Totals	.280	.341	.398	118	33	6	1	2	15	8	19
vs. Left	.200	.282	.314	35	7	2	1	0	2	2	6
vs. Right	.313	.367	.434	83	26	4	0	2	13	6	13

Howell, Jay Canfield
Bats: Right **Throws: Right** **Born 11/26/55**

1987 SEASON AND MAJOR-LEAGUE CAREER PITCHING TOTALS

	G	GS	CG	GF	IP	BFP	H	R	ER	HR	SH	SF	HB	TBB	IBB	SO	WP	Bk	W	L	Pct	ShO	Sv	ERA
87 OAK	36	0	0	27	44	200	48	30	29	6	3	2	1	21	1	35	4	0	3	4	.429	0	16	5.93
8 YEARS	238	21	2	146	434	1892	447	214	201	30	14	19	9	167	13	347	19	2	29	30	.492	0	68	4.17

1987: Power, Groundball   1986: Power, Groundball   1985: Power, Flyball   1984: Power, Groundball

1987 SEASON

	G	IP	H	BB	SO	SB	CS	W	L	S	ERA
Totals	36	44.2	48	21	35	4	2	3	4	16	5.84
At Home	16	19.2	16	7	21	2	0	1	1	8	5.03
On Road	20	25.0	32	14	14	2	2	2	3	.8	6.48

vs. Opposing Batters	AVG	OBP	SLG	AB	H	2B	3B	HR	RBI	BB	SO
Totals	.276	.354	.471	174	48	10	3	6	31	21	35
vs. Left	.253	.340	.373	83	21	5	1	1	10	10	15
vs. Right	.297	.365	.560	91	27	5	2	5	21	11	20

FOUR YEAR TOTALS (1984 – 1987)

	G	IP	H	BB	SO	SB	CS	W	L	S	ERA
Totals	198	299.2	285	109	254	17	8	24	22	68	3.30
At Home	100	160.1	148	48	138	11	1	18	9	35	2.75
On Road	98	139.1	137	61	116	6	7	6	13	33	4.00

	AVG	OBP	SLG	AB	H	2B	3B	HR	RBI	BB	SO
Totals	.251	.316	.349	1137	285	45	5	19	135	109	254
vs. Left	.256	.333	.342	562	144	26	2	6	58	64	116
vs. Right	.245	.299	.357	575	141	19	3	13	77	45	138

Howell, Kenneth "Ken"
Bats: Right **Throws: Right** **Born 11/28/60**

1987 SEASON AND MAJOR-LEAGUE CAREER PITCHING TOTALS

	G	GS	CG	GF	IP	BFP	H	R	ER	HR	SH	SF	HB	TBB	IBB	SO	WP	Bk	W	L	Pct	ShO	Sv	ERA
87 LA	40	2	0	17	55	239	54	32	30	7	6	0	0	29	2	60	5	1	3	4	.429	0	1	4.91
4 YEARS	190	3	0	103	290	1239	257	142	127	23	20	7	4	136	18	303	13	3	18	28	.391	0	31	3.94

1987: Power, Groundball   1986: Power, Flyball   1985: Power, Flyball   1984: Power, Flyball

1987 SEASON

	G	IP	H	BB	SO	SB	CS	W	L	S	ERA
Totals	40	54.2	54	29	60	4	2	3	4	1	4.94
At Home	17	21.0	16	8	23	2	0	1	0	1	4.29
On Road	23	33.2	38	21	37	2	2	2	4	0	5.35

vs. Opposing Batters	AVG	OBP	SLG	AB	H	2B	3B	HR	RBI	BB	SO
Totals	.265	.356	.446	204	54	12	2	7	27	29	60
vs. Left	.271	.381	.375	96	26	5	1	1	7	17	25
vs. Right	.259	.333	.509	108	28	7	1	6	20	12	35

FOUR YEAR TOTALS (1984 – 1987)

	G	IP	H	BB	SO	SB	CS	W	L	S	ERA
Totals	190	289.2	257	136	303	25	16	18	28	31	3.91
At Home	98	146.2	122	59	141	15	11	9	14	15	3.74
On Road	92	143.0	135	77	162	10	5	9	14	16	4.15

	AVG	OBP	SLG	AB	H	2B	3B	HR	RBI	BB	SO
Totals	.240	.325	.352	1072	257	41	5	23	135	136	303
vs. Left	.245	.343	.326	531	130	20	4	5	51	79	128
vs. Right	.235	.308	.377	541	127	21	1	18	84	57	175

Hudson, Charles Lynn
Bats: Both **Throws: Right** **Born 03/16/59**

1987 SEASON AND MAJOR-LEAGUE CAREER PITCHING TOTALS

	G	GS	CG	GF	IP	BFP	H	R	ER	HR	SH	SF	HB	TBB	IBB	SO	WP	Bk	W	L	Pct	ShO	Sv	ERA
87 NYA	35	16	6	7	155	641	137	63	62	19	2	6	3	57	1	100	5	0	11	7	.611	2	0	3.60
5 YEARS	162	121	13	16	835	3561	829	416	363	87	30	25	6	294	19	499	16	12	43	49	.467	3	0	3.91

1987: Finesse, Flyball   1986: Finesse, Flyball   1985: Power, Flyball   1984: Finesse, Flyball

1987 SEASON

	G	IP	H	BB	SO	SB	CS	W	L	S	ERA
Totals	35	154.2	137	57	100	7	7	11	7	0	3.61
At Home	16	72.2	66	27	48	2	4	4	4	0	4.09
On Road	19	82.0	71	30	52	5	3	7	3	0	3.18

vs. Opposing Batters	AVG	OBP	SLG	AB	H	2B	3B	HR	RBI	BB	SO
Totals	.240	.308	.392	572	137	20	5	19	60	57	100
vs. Left	.269	.354	.426	249	67	10	4	7	34	36	35
vs. Right	.217	.270	.365	323	70	10	1	12	26	21	65

FOUR YEAR TOTALS (1984 – 1987)

	G	IP	H	BB	SO	SB	CS	W	L	S	ERA
Totals	136	665.1	671	241	398	74	19	35	41	0	4.04
At Home	65	308.2	328	99	191	29	9	13	21	0	4.34
On Road	71	356.2	343	142	207	45	10	22	20	0	3.81

	AVG	OBP	SLG	AB	H	2B	3B	HR	RBI	BB	SO
Totals	.261	.325	.407	2567	671	109	21	74	303	241	398
vs. Left	.278	.350	.418	1307	363	59	14	32	164	148	169
vs. Right	.244	.298	.395	1260	308	50	7	42	139	93	229

Hughes, Keith Wills
Bats: Left **Throws: Left** **Born 09/12/63**

1987 SEASON AND MAJOR-LEAGUE CAREER BATTING TOTALS

	G	AB	H	2B	3B	HR	TB	R	RBI	TBB	IBB	SO	HP	SH	SF	SB	CS	SB%	GDP	AVG	OBP	SLG
87 NYA-PHI	41	80	20	2	0	0	22	8	10	7	0	13	1	0	0	0	0	.00	1	.250	.318	.275
1 YEAR	41	80	20	2	0	0	22	8	10	7	0	13	1	0	0	0	0	.00	1	.250	.318	.275

1987 SEASON

	AVG	OBP	SLG	AB	H	2B	3B	HR	RBI	BB	SO
Totals	.250	.318	.275	80	20	2	0	0	10	7	13
vs. Left	.750	.750	.750	4	3	0	0	0	0	0	0
vs. Right	.224	.298	.250	76	17	2	0	0	10	7	13
At Home	.226	.294	.258	31	7	1	0	0	2	3	5
On Road	.265	.333	.286	49	13	1	0	0	8	4	8

FOUR YEAR TOTALS (1984 – 1987)

	AVG	OBP	SLG	AB	H	2B	3B	HR	RBI	BB	SO
Totals	.250	.318	.275	80	20	2	0	0	10	7	13
vs. Left	.750	.750	.750	4	3	0	0	0	0	0	0
vs. Right	.224	.298	.250	76	17	2	0	0	10	7	13
At Home	.226	.294	.258	31	7	1	0	0	2	3	5
On Road	.265	.333	.286	49	13	1	0	0	8	4	8

Huismann, Mark Lawrence

Bats: Right   Throws: Right   Born 05/11/58

1987 SEASON AND MAJOR-LEAGUE CAREER PITCHING TOTALS

	G	GS	CG	GF	IP	BFP	H	R	ER	HR	SH	SF	HB	TBB	IBB	SO	WP	Bk	W	L	Pct	ShO	Sv	ERA
87 SEA-CLE	26	0	0	11	50	212	48	32	28	7	4	3	2	12	0	38	3	0	2	3	.400	0	2	5.04
5 YEARS	132	1	0	64	272	1149	273	141	127	35	9	14	4	78	6	193	15	1	11	11	.500	0	10	4.20

1987: Power, Flyball   1986: Finesse, Groundball   1985: Finesse, Groundball   1984: Power, Groundball

1987 SEASON	G	IP	H	BB	SO	SB	CS	W	L	S	ERA
Totals	26	50.0	48	12	38	5	1	2	3	2	5.04
At Home	14	25.0	18	7	14	1	1	1	1	2	3.60
On Road	12	25.0	30	5	24	4	0	1	2	0	6.48

vs. Opposing Batters	AVG	OBP	SLG	AB	H	2B	3B	HR	RBI	BB	SO
Totals	.251	.298	.435	191	48	12	1	7	38	12	38
vs. Left	.270	.290	.472	89	24	7	1	3	15	2	12
vs. Right	.235	.304	.402	102	24	5	0	4	23	10	26

FOUR YEAR TOTALS (1984 – 1987)	G	IP	H	BB	SO	SB	CS	W	L	S	ERA
	119	241.0	244	61	173	19	6	9	10	10	4.03
	65	135.1	126	34	94	10	5	6	5	5	3.39
	54	105.2	118	27	79	9	1	3	5	5	4.85

	AVG	OBP	SLG	AB	H	2B	3B	HR	RBI	BB	SO
	.263	.309	.432	929	244	43	6	34	134	61	173
	.295	.336	.456	458	135	22	5	14	61	28	51
	.231	.282	.408	471	109	21	1	20	73	33	122

Hulett, Timothy Craig "Tim"

Bats: Right   Throws: Right   Born 01/12/60

1987 SEASON AND MAJOR-LEAGUE CAREER BATTING TOTALS

	G	AB	H	2B	3B	HR	TB	R	RBI	TBB	IBB	SO	HP	SH	SF	SB	CS	SB%	GDP	AVG	OBP	SLG
87 CHA	68	240	52	10	0	7	83	20	28	10	1	41	0	5	2	0	2	.00	6	.217	.246	.346
5 YEARS	373	1167	279	45	9	29	429	126	109	62	2	217	5	15	9	12	7	.63	25	.239	.278	.368

1987 SEASON	AVG	OBP	SLG	AB	H	2B	3B	HR	RBI	BB	SO
Totals	.217	.246	.346	240	52	10	0	7	28	10	41
vs. Left	.247	.265	.432	81	20	3	0	4	11	2	13
vs. Right	.201	.237	.302	159	32	7	0	3	17	8	28
At Home	.161	.188	.268	112	18	3	0	3	10	4	21
On Road	.266	.296	.414	128	34	7	0	4	18	6	20

FOUR YEAR TOTALS (1984 – 1987)	AVG	OBP	SLG	AB	H	2B	3B	HR	RBI	BB	SO
	.239	.279	.368	1162	278	45	9	29	109	62	217
	.266	.311	.433	436	116	16	6	15	43	30	77
	.223	.259	.329	726	162	29	3	14	66	32	140
	.231	.276	.351	572	132	19	7	12	45	35	111
	.247	.281	.385	590	146	26	2	17	64	27	106

Hume, Thomas Hubert "Tom"

Bats: Right   Throws: Right   Born 03/29/53

1987 SEASON AND MAJOR-LEAGUE CAREER PITCHING TOTALS

	G	GS	CG	GF	IP	BFP	H	R	ER	HR	SH	SF	HB	TBB	IBB	SO	WP	Bk	W	L	Pct	ShO	Sv	ERA
87 PHI-CIN	49	6	0	5	84	379	89	54	50	10	8	4	5	43	5	33	3	0	2	4	.333	0	0	5.36
11 YEARS	543	55	5	267	1086	4645	1106	521	465	88	63	43	24	384	86	536	26	2	57	71	.445	0	92	3.85

1987: Finesse, Flyball   1986: Finesse, Groundball   1985: Power, Groundball   1984: Finesse, Groundball

1987 SEASON	G	IP	H	BB	SO	SB	CS	W	L	S	ERA
Totals	49	84.0	89	43	33	8	2	2	4	0	5.36
At Home	24	54.2	58	24	22	7	2	2	2	0	4.61
On Road	25	29.1	31	19	11	1	0	2	2	0	6.75

vs. Opposing Batters	AVG	OBP	SLG	AB	H	2B	3B	HR	RBI	BB	SO
Totals	.278	.369	.450	320	89	19	3	10	53	43	33
vs. Left	.336	.433	.487	152	51	10	2	3	25	26	10
vs. Right	.226	.309	.417	168	38	9	1	7	28	17	23

FOUR YEAR TOTALS (1984 – 1987)	G	IP	H	BB	SO	SB	CS	W	L	S	ERA
	207	371.2	385	153	193	69	12	13	23	10	4.33
	98	197.0	201	80	100	37	9	7	7	2	4.02
	109	174.2	184	73	93	32	3	6	16	8	4.69

	AVG	OBP	SLG	AB	H	2B	3B	HR	RBI	BB	SO
	.271	.343	.414	1422	385	64	16	36	214	153	193
	.289	.385	.430	647	187	26	10	15	92	101	67
	.255	.305	.401	775	198	38	6	21	122	52	126

Innis, Jeffrey David "Jeff"

Bats: Right   Throws: Right   Born 07/05/62

1987 SEASON AND MAJOR-LEAGUE CAREER PITCHING TOTALS

	G	GS	CG	GF	IP	BFP	H	R	ER	HR	SH	SF	HB	TBB	IBB	SO	WP	Bk	W	L	Pct	ShO	Sv	ERA
87 NYN	17	1	0	8	26	109	29	9	9	5	0	0	1	4	1	28	1	1	0	1	.000	0	0	3.12
1 YEAR	17	1	0	8	26	109	29	9	9	5	0	0	1	4	1	28	1	1	0	1	.000	0	0	3.12

1987: Power, Groundball

1987 SEASON	G	IP	H	BB	SO	SB	CS	W	L	S	ERA
Totals	17	25.2	29	4	28	4	1	0	1	0	3.16
At Home	7	8.1	9	3	10	1	0	0	1	0	1.08
On Road	10	17.1	20	1	18	3	1	0	0	0	4.15

vs. Opposing Batters	AVG	OBP	SLG	AB	H	2B	3B	HR	RBI	BB	SO
Totals	.279	.312	.462	104	29	4	0	5	9	4	28
vs. Left	.378	.410	.676	37	14	2	0	3	5	2	3
vs. Right	.224	.257	.343	67	15	2	0	2	4	2	25

FOUR YEAR TOTALS (1984 – 1987)	G	IP	H	BB	SO	SB	CS	W	L	S	ERA
	17	25.2	29	4	28	4	1	0	1	0	3.16
	7	8.1	9	3	10	1	0	0	1	0	1.08
	10	17.1	20	1	18	3	1	0	0	0	4.15

	AVG	OBP	SLG	AB	H	2B	3B	HR	RBI	BB	SO
	.279	.312	.462	104	29	4	0	5	9	4	28
	.378	.410	.676	37	14	2	0	3	5	2	3
	.224	.257	.343	67	15	2	0	2	4	2	25

Jackson, Charles Leo "Chuck"

Bats: Right   Throws: Right   Born 03/19/63

1987 SEASON AND MAJOR-LEAGUE CAREER BATTING TOTALS

	G	AB	H	2B	3B	HR	TB	R	RBI	TBB	IBB	SO	HP	SH	SF	SB	CS	SB%	GDP	AVG	OBP	SLG
87 HOU	35	71	15	3	0	1	21	3	6	7	0	19	0	3	0	1	1	.50	1	.211	.282	.296
1 YEAR	35	71	15	3	0	1	21	3	6	7	0	19	0	3	0	1	1	.50	1	.211	.282	.296

	1987 SEASON											FOUR YEAR TOTALS (1984 – 1987)										
	AVG	OBP	SLG	AB	H	2B	3B	HR	RBI	BB	SO	AVG	OBP	SLG	AB	H	2B	3B	HR	RBI	BB	SO
Totals	.211	.282	.296	71	15	3	0	1	6	7	19	.211	.282	.296	71	15	3	0	1	6	7	19
vs. Left	.206	.325	.353	34	7	2	0	1	3	6	8	.206	.325	.353	34	7	2	0	1	3	6	8
vs. Right	.216	.237	.243	37	8	1	0	0	3	1	11	.216	.237	.243	37	8	1	0	0	3	1	11
At Home	.222	.286	.244	45	10	1	0	0	4	4	11	.222	.286	.244	45	10	1	0	0	4	4	11
On Road	.192	.276	.385	26	5	2	0	1	2	3	8	.192	.276	.385	26	5	2	0	1	2	3	8

Jackson, Michael Ray

Bats: Right   Throws: Right   Born 12/22/64

1987 SEASON AND MAJOR-LEAGUE CAREER PITCHING TOTALS

	G	GS	CG	GF	IP	BFP	H	R	ER	HR	SH	SF	HB	TBB	IBB	SO	WP	Bk	W	L	Pct	ShO	Sv	ERA
87 PHI	55	7	0	8	109	468	88	55	51	16	3	4	3	56	6	93	6	8	3	10	.231	0	1	4.21
2 YEARS	64	7	0	12	122	522	100	60	56	18	3	4	5	60	7	96	6	8	3	10	.231	0	1	4.13

1987: Power, Flyball   1986: Finesse, Flyball

	1987 SEASON											FOUR YEAR TOTALS (1984 – 1987)										
	G	IP	H	BB	SO	SB	CS	W	L	S	ERA	G	IP	H	BB	SO	SB	CS	W	L	S	ERA
Totals	55	109.1	88	56	93	22	3	3	10	1	4.20	64	122.2	100	60	96	22	4	3	10	1	4.11
At Home	25	55.0	28	28	48	15	0	2	3	1	2.13	30	63.0	33	30	50	15	0	2	3	1	2.43
On Road	30	54.1	60	28	45	7	3	1	7	0	6.29	34	59.2	67	30	46	7	4	1	7	0	5.88
vs. Opposing Batters	AVG	OBP	SLG	AB	H	2B	3B	HR	RBI	BB	SO	AVG	OBP	SLG	AB	H	2B	3B	HR	RBI	BB	SO
Totals	.218	.316	.377	403	88	14	1	16	52	56	93	.222	.318	.381	451	100	16	1	18	60	60	96
vs. Left	.263	.397	.405	190	50	7	1	6	26	40	31	.270	.398	.400	215	58	8	1	6	29	42	32
vs. Right	.178	.236	.352	213	38	7	0	10	26	16	62	.178	.236	.364	236	42	8	0	12	31	18	64

James, Robert Harvey "Bob"

Bats: Right   Throws: Right   Born 08/15/58

1987 SEASON AND MAJOR-LEAGUE CAREER PITCHING TOTALS

	G	GS	CG	GF	IP	BFP	H	R	ER	HR	SH	SF	HB	TBB	IBB	SO	WP	Bk	W	L	Pct	ShO	Sv	ERA
87 CHA	43	0	0	32	54	238	54	32	28	10	4	2	4	17	6	34	3	0	4	6	.400	0	10	4.67
8 YEARS	279	2	0	194	407	1755	377	194	172	39	27	21	17	157	24	340	24	7	24	26	.480	0	73	3.80

1987: Finesse, Flyball   1986: Finesse, Flyball   1985: Power, Flyball   1984: Power, Flyball

	1987 SEASON											FOUR YEAR TOTALS (1984 – 1987)										
	G	IP	H	BB	SO	SB	CS	W	L	S	ERA	G	IP	H	BB	SO	SB	CS	W	L	S	ERA
Totals	43	54.2	54	17	34	7	2	4	6	10	4.61	223	319.0	297	108	245	36	5	23	23	66	3.58
At Home	22	31.2	31	10	21	4	2	3	2	4	4.55	113	171.0	161	62	135	18	5	14	10	34	3.68
On Road	21	23.0	23	7	13	3	0	1	4	6	4.70	110	148.0	136	46	110	18	0	9	13	32	3.47
vs. Opposing Batters	AVG	OBP	SLG	AB	H	2B	3B	HR	RBI	BB	SO	AVG	OBP	SLG	AB	H	2B	3B	HR	RBI	BB	SO
Totals	.255	.319	.472	212	54	6	5	10	36	17	34	.246	.310	.383	1206	297	58	10	29	180	108	245
vs. Left	.283	.330	.554	92	26	3	2	6	16	7	13	.254	.326	.392	586	149	26	5	15	82	63	122
vs. Right	.233	.311	.408	120	28	3	3	4	20	10	21	.239	.294	.374	620	148	32	5	14	98	45	123

Javier, Stanley Julian Antonio (de Javier)

Bats: Both   Throws: Right   Born 01/09/65

1987 SEASON AND MAJOR-LEAGUE CAREER BATTING TOTALS

	G	AB	H	2B	3B	HR	TB	R	RBI	TBB	IBB	SO	HP	SH	SF	SB	CS	SB%	GDP	AVG	OBP	SLG
87 OAK	81	151	28	3	1	2	39	22	9	19	3	33	0	6	0	3	2	.60	2	.185	.276	.258
3 YEARS	147	272	52	11	1	2	71	36	17	35	3	61	1	6	0	11	2	.85	4	.191	.286	.261

	1987 SEASON											FOUR YEAR TOTALS (1984 – 1987)										
	AVG	OBP	SLG	AB	H	2B	3B	HR	RBI	BB	SO	AVG	OBP	SLG	AB	H	2B	3B	HR	RBI	BB	SO
Totals	.185	.276	.258	151	28	3	1	2	9	19	33	.191	.286	.261	272	52	11	1	2	17	35	61
vs. Left	.165	.253	.212	85	14	1	0	1	2	10	17	.157	.244	.214	140	22	5	0	1	6	15	27
vs. Right	.212	.307	.318	66	14	2	1	1	7	9	16	.227	.329	.311	132	30	6	1	1	11	20	34
At Home	.264	.354	.345	87	23	2	1	1	6	12	15	.235	.349	.302	149	35	5	1	1	11	25	30
On Road	.078	.169	.141	64	5	1	0	1	3	7	18	.138	.203	.211	123	17	6	0	1	6	10	31

Johnson, Joseph Richard "Joe"

Bats: Right   Throws: Right   Born 10/30/61

1987 SEASON AND MAJOR-LEAGUE CAREER PITCHING TOTALS

	G	GS	CG	GF	IP	BFP	H	R	ER	HR	SH	SF	HB	TBB	IBB	SO	WP	Bk	W	L	Pct	ShO	Sv	ERA
87 TOR	14	14	0	0	67	289	77	44	38	10	2	1	2	18	0	27	3	0	3	5	.375	0	0	5.10
3 YEARS	62	58	3	1	328	1414	367	185	163	30	13	9	10	99	10	149	8	1	20	18	.526	0	0	4.47

1987: Finesse, Groundball   1986: Finesse, Flyball   1985: Finesse, Flyball

1987 SEASON	G	IP	H	BB	SO	SB	CS	W	L	S	ERA
Totals	14	66.2	77	18	27	5	3	3	5	0	5.13
At Home	9	44.0	50	13	16	2	3	1	4	0	4.30
On Road	5	22.2	27	5	11	3	0	2	1	0	6.75

vs. Opposing Batters	AVG	OBP	SLG	AB	H	2B	3B	HR	RBI	BB	SO
Totals	.289	.338	.489	266	77	19	2	10	39	18	27
vs. Left	.265	.303	.435	147	39	11	1	4	12	8	16
vs. Right	.319	.379	.555	119	38	8	1	6	27	10	11

FOUR YEAR TOTALS (1984 – 1987)	G	IP	H	BB	SO	SB	CS	W	L	S	ERA
	62	327.1	367	99	149	21	12	20	18	0	4.48
	32	163.1	185	40	70	6	7	8	11	0	4.30
	30	164.0	182	59	79	15	5	12	7	0	4.66

	AVG	OBP	SLG	AB	H	2B	3B	HR	RBI	BB	SO
	.286	.338	.420	1283	367	64	9	30	161	99	149
	.290	.344	.426	680	197	35	5	16	77	56	94
	.282	.331	.413	603	170	29	4	14	84	43	55

Johnson, Kenneth Lance "Lance"

Bats: Left   Throws: Left   Born 07/06/63

1987 SEASON AND MAJOR-LEAGUE CAREER BATTING TOTALS

	G	AB	H	2B	3B	HR	TB	R	RBI	TBB	IBB	SO	HP	SH	SF	SB	CS	SB%	GDP	AVG	OBP	SLG
87 STL	33	59	13	2	1	0	17	4	7	4	1	6	0	0	0	6	1	.86	2	.220	.270	.288
1 YEAR	33	59	13	2	1	0	17	4	7	4	1	6	0	0	0	6	1	.86	2	.220	.270	.288

1987 SEASON	AVG	OBP	SLG	AB	H	2B	3B	HR	RBI	BB	SO
Totals	.220	.270	.288	59	13	2	1	0	7	4	6
vs. Left	.167	.167	.167	6	1	0	0	0	0	0	1
vs. Right	.226	.281	.302	53	12	2	1	0	7	4	5
At Home	.262	.295	.333	42	11	1	1	0	6	2	5
On Road	.118	.211	.176	17	2	1	0	0	1	2	1

FOUR YEAR TOTALS (1984 – 1987)	AVG	OBP	SLG	AB	H	2B	3B	HR	RBI	BB	SO
	.220	.270	.288	59	13	2	1	0	7	4	6
	.167	.167	.167	6	1	0	0	0	0	0	1
	.226	.281	.302	53	12	2	1	0	7	4	5
	.262	.295	.333	42	11	1	1	0	6	2	5
	.118	.211	.176	17	2	1	0	0	1	2	1

Johnson, Wallace Darnell

Bats: Both   Throws: Right   Born 12/25/56

1987 SEASON AND MAJOR-LEAGUE CAREER BATTING TOTALS

	G	AB	H	2B	3B	HR	TB	R	RBI	TBB	IBB	SO	HP	SH	SF	SB	CS	SB%	GDP	AVG	OBP	SLG
87 MON	75	85	21	5	0	1	29	7	14	7	0	6	0	0	2	5	0	1.00	0	.247	.298	.341
6 YEARS	210	312	77	8	4	2	99	30	34	26	1	25	0	0	2	17	5	.77	3	.247	.303	.317

1987 SEASON	AVG	OBP	SLG	AB	H	2B	3B	HR	RBI	BB	SO
Totals	.244	.298	.337	86	21	5	0	1	14	7	6
vs. Left	.400	.400	.400	5	2	0	0	0	0	0	0
vs. Right	.235	.292	.333	81	19	5	0	1	14	7	6
At Home	.227	.327	.250	44	10	1	0	0	7	7	4
On Road	.262	.262	.429	42	11	4	0	1	7	0	2

FOUR YEAR TOTALS (1984 – 1987)	AVG	OBP	SLG	AB	H	2B	3B	HR	RBI	BB	SO
	.262	.315	.329	237	62	8	1	2	28	19	19
	.260	.327	.280	50	13	1	0	0	4	5	7
	.262	.312	.342	187	49	7	1	2	24	14	12
	.265	.341	.325	117	31	2	1	1	14	14	11
	.258	.288	.333	120	31	6	0	1	14	5	8

Jones, Barry Louis

Bats: Right   Throws: Right   Born 02/15/63

1987 SEASON AND MAJOR-LEAGUE CAREER PITCHING TOTALS

	G	GS	CG	GF	IP	BFP	H	R	ER	HR	SH	SF	HB	TBB	IBB	SO	WP	Bk	W	L	Pct	ShO	Sv	ERA
87 PIT	32	0	0	10	43	203	55	34	27	6	3	2	0	23	6	28	3	0	2	4	.333	0	1	5.65
2 YEARS	58	0	0	20	80	362	84	50	39	9	5	3	0	44	8	57	5	0	5	8	.385	0	4	4.39

1987: Power, Groundball   1986: Power, Groundball

1987 SEASON	G	IP	H	BB	SO	SB	CS	W	L	S	ERA
Totals	32	43.2	55	23	28	2	4	2	4	1	5.77
At Home	18	25.1	30	11	12	1	3	2	1	0	4.97
On Road	14	18.1	25	12	16	1	1	0	3	1	6.87

vs. Opposing Batters	AVG	OBP	SLG	AB	H	2B	3B	HR	RBI	BB	SO
Totals	.314	.390	.497	175	55	10	2	6	33	23	28
vs. Left	.289	.368	.398	83	24	4	1	1	15	11	9
vs. Right	.337	.410	.587	92	31	6	1	5	18	12	19

FOUR YEAR TOTALS (1984 – 1987)	G	IP	H	BB	SO	SB	CS	W	L	S	ERA
	58	81.0	84	44	57	7	4	5	8	4	4.44
	33	47.0	48	25	25	5	3	3	3	1	3.83
	25	34.0	36	19	32	2	1	2	5	3	5.29

	AVG	OBP	SLG	AB	H	2B	3B	HR	RBI	BB	SO
	.271	.360	.432	310	84	15	4	9	51	44	57
	.273	.350	.403	139	38	5	2	3	25	17	18
	.269	.367	.456	171	46	10	2	6	26	27	39

Jones, Douglas Reid "Doug"

Bats: Right Throws: Right Born 06/24/57

1987 SEASON AND MAJOR-LEAGUE CAREER PITCHING TOTALS

	G	GS	CG	GF	IP	BFP	H	R	ER	HR	SH	SF	HB	TBB	IBB	SO	WP	Bk	W	L	Pct	ShO	Sv	ERA
87 CLE	49	0	0	29	91	400	101	45	32	4	5	5	6	24	5	87	0	0	6	5	.545	0	8	3.16
3 YEARS	64	0	0	36	112	493	124	53	40	5	6	6	7	31	6	100	0	0	7	5	.583	0	9	3.21

1987: Power, Groundball   1986: Finesse, Groundball

1987 SEASON	G	IP	H	BB	SO	SB	CS	W	L	S	ERA
Totals	49	91.1	101	24	87	3	0	6	5	8	3.15
At Home	28	52.2	63	14	51	0	0	5	1	0	3.76
On Road	21	38.2	38	10	36	3	0	1	4	8	2.33

vs. Opposing Batters	AVG	OBP	SLG	AB	H	2B	3B	HR	RBI	BB	SO
Totals	.280	.331	.352	361	101	14	0	4	62	24	87
vs. Left	.267	.309	.316	187	50	6	0	1	28	12	40
vs. Right	.293	.354	.391	174	51	8	0	3	34	12	47

TWO YEAR TOTALS (1986 – 1987)	G	IP	H	BB	SO	SB	CS	W	L	S	ERA
Totals	60	109.1	119	30	99	3	0	7	5	9	3.05
At Home	33	60.0	72	16	55	0	0	5	1	1	3.60
On Road	27	49.1	47	14	44	3	0	2	4	8	2.37

	AVG	OBP	SLG	AB	H	2B	3B	HR	RBI	BB	SO
Totals	.276	.329	.341	431	119	16	0	4	69	30	99
vs. Left	.268	.310	.314	220	59	7	0	1	34	14	41
vs. Right	.284	.349	.370	211	60	9	0	3	35	16	58

Jones, James Condia "Jimmy"

Bats: Right Throws: Right Born 04/20/64

1987 SEASON AND MAJOR-LEAGUE CAREER PITCHING TOTALS

	G	GS	CG	GF	IP	BFP	H	R	ER	HR	SH	SF	HB	TBB	IBB	SO	WP	Bk	W	L	Pct	ShO	Sv	ERA
87 SD	30	22	2	4	146	639	154	85	67	14	5	5	5	54	2	51	3	2	9	7	.563	1	0	4.13
2 YEARS	33	25	3	4	164	704	164	91	72	15	6	5	5	57	2	66	3	2	11	7	.611	2	0	3.95

1987: Finesse, Groundball   1986: Finesse, Flyball

1987 SEASON	G	IP	H	BB	SO	SB	CS	W	L	S	ERA
Totals	30	145.2	154	54	51	12	2	9	7	0	4.14
At Home	17	77.0	80	26	29	8	1	4	5	0	3.62
On Road	13	68.2	74	28	22	4	1	5	2	0	4.72

vs. Opposing Batters	AVG	OBP	SLG	AB	H	2B	3B	HR	RBI	BB	SO
Totals	.270	.336	.386	570	154	20	2	14	73	54	51
vs. Left	.268	.338	.366	306	82	12	0	6	37	32	27
vs. Right	.273	.333	.409	264	72	8	2	8	36	22	24

FOUR YEAR TOTALS (1984 – 1987)	G	IP	H	BB	SO	SB	CS	W	L	S	ERA
Totals	33	163.2	164	57	66	13	2	11	7	0	3.96
At Home	19	86.0	89	29	39	9	1	5	5	0	3.77
On Road	14	77.2	75	28	27	4	1	6	2	0	4.17

	AVG	OBP	SLG	AB	H	2B	3B	HR	RBI	BB	SO
Totals	.260	.324	.374	631	164	21	3	15	78	57	66
vs. Left	.258	.325	.361	349	90	13	1	7	40	34	37
vs. Right	.262	.323	.390	282	74	8	2	8	38	23	29

Jones, Ross A.

Bats: Right Throws: Right Born 01/14/60

1987 SEASON AND MAJOR-LEAGUE CAREER BATTING TOTALS

	G	AB	H	2B	3B	HR	TB	R	RBI	TBB	IBB	SO	HP	SH	SF	SB	CS	SB%	GDP	AVG	OBP	SLG
87 KC	39	114	29	4	2	0	37	10	10	5	0	15	1	1	3	1	0	1.00	5	.254	.285	.325
3 YEARS	67	145	32	5	2	0	41	12	11	8	0	23	1	1	3	1	1	.50	5	.221	.261	.283

1987 SEASON	AVG	OBP	SLG	AB	H	2B	3B	HR	RBI	BB	SO
Totals	.254	.285	.325	114	29	4	2	0	10	5	15
vs. Left	.333	.359	.417	36	12	1	1	0	4	2	1
vs. Right	.218	.250	.282	78	17	3	1	0	6	3	14
At Home	.313	.342	.433	67	21	4	2	0	6	3	10
On Road	.170	.200	.170	47	8	0	0	0	4	2	5

TWO YEAR TOTALS (1986 – 1987)	AVG	OBP	SLG	AB	H	2B	3B	HR	RBI	BB	SO
Totals	.230	.257	.289	135	31	4	2	0	10	5	19
vs. Left	.310	.333	.381	42	13	1	1	0	4	2	2
vs. Right	.194	.222	.247	93	18	3	1	0	6	3	17
At Home	.301	.329	.411	73	22	4	2	0	6	3	10
On Road	.145	.169	.145	62	9	0	0	0	4	2	9

Jones, Ruppert Sanderson

Bats: Left Throws: Left Born 03/12/55

1987 SEASON AND MAJOR-LEAGUE CAREER BATTING TOTALS

	G	AB	H	2B	3B	HR	TB	R	RBI	TBB	IBB	SO	HP	SH	SF	SB	CS	SB%	GDP	AVG	OBP	SLG
87 CAL	85	192	47	8	2	8	83	25	28	20	2	38	0	1	0	2	1	.67	4	.245	.316	.432
12 YEARS	1331	4415	1103	215	38	147	1835	643	579	534	38	817	12	43	34	143	84	.63	87	.250	.330	.416

1987 SEASON	AVG	OBP	SLG	AB	H	2B	3B	HR	RBI	BB	SO
Totals	.245	.316	.432	192	47	8	2	8	28	20	38
vs. Left	.357	.400	.643	14	5	1	0	1	5	1	1
vs. Right	.236	.310	.416	178	42	7	2	7	23	19	37
At Home	.259	.323	.400	85	22	1	1	3	8	8	16
On Road	.234	.311	.458	107	25	7	1	5	20	12	22

FOUR YEAR TOTALS (1984 – 1987)	AVG	OBP	SLG	AB	H	2B	3B	HR	RBI	BB	SO
Totals	.242	.333	.451	1189	288	58	8	58	181	162	254
vs. Left	.200	.285	.400	115	23	6	1	5	24	14	27
vs. Right	.247	.339	.456	1074	265	52	7	53	157	148	227
At Home	.257	.360	.476	552	142	28	3	29	84	88	121
On Road	.229	.309	.429	637	146	30	5	29	97	74	133

Jones, Tracy Donald
Bats: Right   Throws: Right   Born 03/31/61

1987 SEASON AND MAJOR-LEAGUE CAREER BATTING TOTALS

	G	AB	H	2B	3B	HR	TB	R	RBI	TBB	IBB	SO	HP	SH	SF	SB	CS	SB%	GDP	AVG	OBP	SLG
87 CIN	117	359	104	17	3	10	157	53	44	23	0	40	3	0	5	31	8	.79	10	.290	.333	.437
2 YEARS	163	445	134	20	3	12	196	69	54	32	1	45	3	0	6	38	9	.81	12	.301	.348	.440

	1987 SEASON											FOUR YEAR TOTALS (1984 – 1987)									
	AVG	OBP	SLG	AB	H	2B	3B	HR	RBI	BB	SO	AVG	OBP	SLG	AB	H	2B	3B	HR	RBI	BB	SO
Totals	.290	.333	.437	359	104	17	3	10	44	23	40	.301	.347	.440	445	134	20	3	12	54	32	45
vs. Left	.349	.405	.521	169	59	10	2	5	21	17	17	.341	.394	.500	232	79	12	2	7	26	22	21
vs. Right	.237	.265	.363	190	45	7	1	5	23	6	23	.258	.295	.376	213	55	8	1	5	28	10	24
At Home	.300	.364	.456	160	48	9	2	4	13	14	10	.301	.372	.451	193	58	10	2	5	17	20	13
On Road	.281	.308	.422	199	56	8	1	6	31	9	30	.302	.328	.433	252	76	10	1	7	37	12	32

Karkovice, Ronald Joseph "Ron"
Bats: Right   Throws: Right   Born 08/08/63

1987 SEASON AND MAJOR-LEAGUE CAREER BATTING TOTALS

	G	AB	H	2B	3B	HR	TB	R	RBI	TBB	IBB	SO	HP	SH	SF	SB	CS	SB%	GDP	AVG	OBP	SLG
87 CHA	39	85	6	0	0	2	12	7	7	7	0	40	2	1	0	3	0	1.00	2	.071	.160	.141
2 YEARS	76	182	30	7	0	6	55	20	20	16	0	77	3	2	1	4	0	1.00	5	.165	.243	.302

	1987 SEASON											FOUR YEAR TOTALS (1984 – 1987)									
	AVG	OBP	SLG	AB	H	2B	3B	HR	RBI	BB	SO	AVG	OBP	SLG	AB	H	2B	3B	HR	RBI	BB	SO
Totals	.071	.160	.141	85	6	0	0	2	7	7	40	.165	.245	.302	182	30	7	0	6	20	16	77
vs. Left	.048	.111	.119	42	2	0	0	1	5	3	21	.152	.212	.304	79	12	3	0	3	11	6	35
vs. Right	.093	.204	.163	43	4	0	0	1	2	4	19	.175	.265	.301	103	18	4	0	3	9	10	42
At Home	.081	.128	.162	37	3	0	0	1	2	2	18	.153	.189	.271	85	13	4	0	2	8	4	36
On Road	.063	.182	.125	48	3	0	0	1	5	5	22	.175	.286	.330	97	17	3	0	4	12	12	41

Kearney, Robert Henry "Bob"
Bats: Right   Throws: Right   Born 10/03/56

1987 SEASON AND MAJOR-LEAGUE CAREER BATTING TOTALS

	G	AB	H	2B	3B	HR	TB	R	RBI	TBB	IBB	SO	HP	SH	SF	SB	CS	SB%	GDP	AVG	OBP	SLG
87 SEA	24	47	8	4	1	0	14	5	1	1	0	9	0	3	0	0	0	.00	0	.170	.188	.298
8 YEARS	479	1356	316	66	3	27	469	131	133	67	3	235	12	30	9	9	12	.43	32	.233	.274	.346

	1987 SEASON											FOUR YEAR TOTALS (1984 – 1987)									
	AVG	OBP	SLG	AB	H	2B	3B	HR	RBI	BB	SO	AVG	OBP	SLG	AB	H	2B	3B	HR	RBI	BB	SO
Totals	.170	.188	.298	47	8	4	1	0	1	1	9	.231	.265	.347	987	228	51	3	19	96	42	175
vs. Left	.171	.194	.314	35	6	3	1	0	1	1	6	.201	.234	.334	338	68	19	1	8	26	13	55
vs. Right	.167	.167	.250	12	2	1	0	0	0	0	3	.247	.281	.353	649	160	32	2	11	70	29	120
At Home	.167	.194	.300	30	5	2	1	0	1	1	8	.261	.298	.404	495	129	31	2	12	59	25	88
On Road	.176	.176	.294	17	3	2	0	0	0	0	1	.201	.231	.289	492	99	20	1	7	37	17	87

Keedy, Charles Patrick "Pat"
Bats: Right   Throws: Right   Born 01/10/58

1987 SEASON AND MAJOR-LEAGUE CAREER BATTING TOTALS

	G	AB	H	2B	3B	HR	TB	R	RBI	TBB	IBB	SO	HP	SH	SF	SB	CS	SB%	GDP	AVG	OBP	SLG
87 CHA	17	41	7	1	0	2	14	6	2	2	0	14	0	1	0	1	0	1.00	0	.171	.209	.341
2 YEARS	20	45	9	2	0	3	20	7	3	2	0	14	0	1	0	1	1	.50	0	.200	.234	.444

	1987 SEASON											TWO YEAR TOTALS (1986 – 1987)									
	AVG	OBP	SLG	AB	H	2B	3B	HR	RBI	BB	SO	AVG	OBP	SLG	AB	H	2B	3B	HR	RBI	BB	SO
Totals	.171	.209	.341	41	7	1	0	2	2	2	14	.171	.209	.341	41	7	1	0	2	2	2	14
vs. Left	.138	.167	.276	29	4	1	0	1	1	1	12	.138	.167	.276	29	4	1	0	1	1	1	12
vs. Right	.250	.308	.500	12	3	0	0	1	1	1	2	.250	.308	.500	12	3	0	0	1	1	1	2
At Home	.087	.125	.087	23	2	0	0	0	0	1	8	.087	.125	.087	23	2	0	0	0	0	1	8
On Road	.278	.316	.667	18	5	1	0	2	2	1	6	.278	.316	.667	18	5	1	0	2	2	1	6

Kelly, Roberto Conrado (Gray) "Bobby"

Bats: Right   Throws: Right   Born 10/01/64

1987 SEASON AND MAJOR-LEAGUE CAREER BATTING TOTALS

	G	AB	H	2B	3B	HR	TB	R	RBI	TBB	IBB	SO	HP	SH	SF	SB	CS	SB%	GDP	AVG	OBP	SLG
87 NYA	23	52	14	3	0	1	20	12	7	5	0	15	0	1	1	9	3	.75	0	.269	.328	.385
1 YEAR	23	52	14	3	0	1	20	12	7	5	0	15	0	1	1	9	3	.75	0	.269	.328	.385

	1987 SEASON										FOUR YEAR TOTALS (1984 – 1987)									
	AVG	OBP	SLG	AB	H	2B	3B	HR	RBI	BB	SO	AVG	OBP	SLG	AB	H	2B	3B	HR	RBI	BB	SO
Totals	.269	.328	.385	52	14	3	0	1	7	5	15	.269	.328	.385	52	14	3	0	1	7	5	15
vs. Left	.242	.333	.424	33	8	3	0	1	5	5	10	.242	.333	.424	33	8	3	0	1	5	5	10
vs. Right	.316	.316	.316	19	6	0	0	0	2	0	5	.316	.316	.316	19	6	0	0	0	2	0	5
At Home	.207	.303	.241	29	6	1	0	0	2	4	10	.207	.303	.241	29	6	1	0	0	2	4	10
On Road	.348	.360	.565	23	8	2	0	1	5	1	5	.348	.360	.565	23	8	2	0	1	5	1	5

Kerfeld, Charles Patrick "Charlie"

Bats: Right   Throws: Right   Born 09/28/63

1987 SEASON AND MAJOR-LEAGUE CAREER PITCHING TOTALS

	G	GS	CG	GF	IP	BFP	H	R	ER	HR	SH	SF	HB	TBB	IBB	SO	WP	Bk	W	L	Pct	ShO	Sv	ERA
87 HOU	21	0	0	11	30	137	34	22	22	3	4	1	1	21	2	17	0	0	0	2	.000	0	0	6.60
3 YEARS	93	6	0	42	168	720	149	76	70	10	11	11	3	88	7	124	8	2	15	6	.714	0	7	3.75

1987: Power, Groundball   1986: Power, Groundball   1985: Power, Groundball

	1987 SEASON										FOUR YEAR TOTALS (1984 – 1987)									
	G	IP	H	BB	SO	SB	CS	W	L	S	ERA	G	IP	H	BB	SO	SB	CS	W	L	S	ERA
Totals	21	29.2	34	21	17	6	1	0	2	1	6.67	93	167.2	149	88	124	25	2	15	6	8	3.70
At Home	11	15.2	17	12	10	3	0	0	1	1	7.47	45	85.2	73	40	63	12	1	8	2	5	3.47
On Road	10	14.0	17	9	7	3	1	0	1	0	5.79	48	82.0	76	48	61	13	1	7	4	3	3.95

vs. Opposing Batters	AVG	OBP	SLG	AB	H	2B	3B	HR	RBI	BB	SO	AVG	OBP	SLG	AB	H	2B	3B	HR	RBI	BB	SO
Totals	.309	.421	.482	110	34	8	1	3	21	21	17	.245	.341	.336	607	149	19	3	10	77	88	124
vs. Left	.333	.509	.641	39	13	3	0	3	11	14	2	.277	.392	.428	264	73	12	2	8	38	50	40
vs. Right	.296	.359	.394	71	21	5	1	0	10	7	15	.222	.299	.265	343	76	7	1	2	39	38	84

Kiefer, Steven George "Steve"

Bats: Right   Throws: Right   Born 10/18/60

1987 SEASON AND MAJOR-LEAGUE CAREER BATTING TOTALS

	G	AB	H	2B	3B	HR	TB	R	RBI	TBB	IBB	SO	HP	SH	SF	SB	CS	SB%	GDP	AVG	OBP	SLG
87 MIL	28	99	20	4	0	5	39	17	17	7	0	28	1	1	2	0	0	.00	3	.202	.257	.394
4 YEARS	93	211	40	6	3	6	70	32	29	10	0	60	1	5	5	2	1	.67	4	.190	.225	.332

	1987 SEASON										TWO YEAR TOTALS (1986 – 1987)									
	AVG	OBP	SLG	AB	H	2B	3B	HR	RBI	BB	SO	AVG	OBP	SLG	AB	H	2B	3B	HR	RBI	BB	SO
Totals	.202	.257	.394	99	20	4	0	5	17	7	28	.190	.237	.371	105	20	4	0	5	17	7	32
vs. Left	.209	.261	.512	43	9	1	0	4	11	3	18	.184	.231	.449	49	9	1	0	4	11	3	22
vs. Right	.196	.254	.304	56	11	3	0	1	6	4	10	.196	.254	.304	56	11	3	0	1	6	4	10
At Home	.200	.273	.414	70	14	3	0	4	13	6	18	.200	.273	.414	70	14	3	0	4	13	6	18
On Road	.207	.219	.345	29	6	1	0	1	4	1	10	.171	.184	.286	35	6	1	0	1	4	1	14

Kilgus, Paul Nelson

Bats: Left   Throws: Left   Born 02/02/62

1987 SEASON AND MAJOR-LEAGUE CAREER PITCHING TOTALS

	G	GS	CG	GF	IP	BFP	H	R	ER	HR	SH	SF	HB	TBB	IBB	SO	WP	Bk	W	L	Pct	ShO	Sv	ERA
87 TEX	25	12	0	2	89	385	95	45	41	14	2	0	2	31	2	42	0	0	2	7	.222	0	0	4.15
1 YEAR	25	12	0	2	89	385	95	45	41	14	2	0	2	31	2	42	0	0	2	7	.222	0	0	4.15

1987: Finesse, Groundball

	1987 SEASON										FOUR YEAR TOTALS (1984 – 1987)									
	G	IP	H	BB	SO	SB	CS	W	L	S	ERA	G	IP	H	BB	SO	SB	CS	W	L	S	ERA
Totals	25	89.1	95	31	42	2	6	2	7	0	4.13	25	89.1	95	31	42	2	6	2	7	0	4.13
At Home	10	34.2	36	11	17	0	4	0	4	0	4.67	10	34.2	36	11	17	0	4	0	4	0	4.67
On Road	15	54.2	59	20	25	2	2	2	3	0	3.79	15	54.2	59	20	25	2	2	2	3	0	3.79

vs. Opposing Batters	AVG	OBP	SLG	AB	H	2B	3B	HR	RBI	BB	SO	AVG	OBP	SLG	AB	H	2B	3B	HR	RBI	BB	SO
Totals	.271	.334	.454	350	95	20	1	14	41	31	42	.271	.334	.454	350	95	20	1	14	41	31	42
vs. Left	.250	.313	.539	76	19	4	0	6	14	7	11	.250	.313	.539	76	19	4	0	6	14	7	11
vs. Right	.277	.340	.431	274	76	16	1	8	27	24	31	.277	.340	.431	274	76	16	1	8	27	24	31

King, Eric Steven

Bats: Right **Throws: Right** **Born 04/10/64**

1987 SEASON AND MAJOR-LEAGUE CAREER PITCHING TOTALS

	G	GS	CG	GF	IP	BFP	H	R	ER	HR	SH	SF	HB	TBB	IBB	SO	WP	Bk	W	L	Pct	ShO	Sv	ERA
87 DET	55	4	0	26	116	513	111	67	63	15	3	3	4	60	10	89	5	1	6	9	.400	0	9	4.89
2 YEARS	88	20	3	35	254	1092	219	121	117	26	9	4	12	123	13	168	9	4	17	13	.567	1	12	4.15

1987: Power, Flyball   1986: Finesse, Groundball

1987 SEASON	G	IP	H	BB	SO	SB	CS	W	L	S	ERA
Totals	55	116.0	111	60	89	12	3	6	9	9	4.89
At Home	26	56.0	62	30	39	5	2	2	4	2	5.95
On Road	29	60.0	49	30	50	7	1	4	5	7	3.90
vs. Opposing Batters	AVG	OBP	SLG	AB	H	2B	3B	HR	RBI	BB	SO
Totals	.250	.342	.392	444	111	16	1	15	60	60	89
vs. Left	.239	.331	.357	230	55	10	1	5	25	31	47
vs. Right	.262	.355	.430	214	56	6	0	10	35	29	42

FOUR YEAR TOTALS (1984 – 1987)	G	IP	H	BB	SO	SB	CS	W	L	S	ERA
	88	254.1	219	123	168	20	8	17	13	12	4.14
	40	123.2	98	55	72	8	6	8	4	3	3.78
	48	130.2	121	68	96	12	2	9	9	9	4.48
	AVG	OBP	SLG	AB	H	2B	3B	HR	RBI	BB	SO
	.232	.322	.359	945	219	40	1	26	110	123	168
	.239	.324	.374	476	114	23	1	13	54	59	82
	.224	.320	.343	469	105	17	0	13	56	64	86

Kinnunen, Michael John "Mike"

Bats: Left **Throws: Left** **Born 04/01/58**

1987 SEASON AND MAJOR-LEAGUE CAREER PITCHING TOTALS

	G	GS	CG	GF	IP	BFP	H	R	ER	HR	SH	SF	HB	TBB	IBB	SO	WP	Bk	W	L	Pct	ShO	Sv	ERA
87 BAL	18	0	0	4	20	97	27	14	11	3	0	1	0	16	1	14	1	0	0	0	.000	0	0	4.95
3 YEARS	48	0	0	18	52	240	64	38	30	5	0	3	1	30	2	23	4	0	0	0	.000	0	0	5.19

1987: Power, Groundball   1986: Finesse, Flyball

1987 SEASON	G	IP	H	BB	SO	SB	CS	W	L	S	ERA
Totals	18	20.0	27	16	14	1	2	0	0	0	4.95
At Home	9	9.1	10	11	5	1	0	0	0	0	3.86
On Road	9	10.2	17	5	9	0	2	0	0	0	5.91
vs. Opposing Batters	AVG	OBP	SLG	AB	H	2B	3B	HR	RBI	BB	SO
Totals	.338	.443	.500	80	27	4	0	3	17	16	14
vs. Left	.290	.410	.419	31	9	1	0	1	8	7	3
vs. Right	.367	.466	.551	49	18	3	0	2	9	9	11

TWO YEAR TOTALS (1986 – 1987)	G	IP	H	BB	SO	SB	CS	W	L	S	ERA
	27	27.0	35	21	15	2	3	0	0	0	5.33
	13	12.0	14	12	5	2	1	0	0	0	3.75
	14	15.0	21	9	10	0	2	0	0	0	6.60
	AVG	OBP	SLG	AB	H	2B	3B	HR	RBI	BB	SO
	.330	.438	.491	106	35	5	0	4	23	21	15
	.318	.456	.432	44	14	2	0	1	11	12	3
	.339	.423	.532	62	21	3	0	3	12	9	12

Kipper, Robert Wayne "Bob"

Bats: Right **Throws: Left** **Born 07/08/64**

1987 SEASON AND MAJOR-LEAGUE CAREER PITCHING TOTALS

	G	GS	CG	GF	IP	BFP	H	R	ER	HR	SH	SF	HB	TBB	IBB	SO	WP	Bk	W	L	Pct	ShO	Sv	ERA
87 PIT	24	20	1	0	111	493	117	74	73	25	4	3	2	52	4	83	5	0	5	9	.357	1	0	5.92
3 YEARS	51	44	1	2	253	1113	268	158	146	47	8	9	4	96	7	177	8	3	12	20	.375	1	0	5.19

1987: Power, Flyball   1986: Finesse, Flyball   1985: Finesse, Flyball

1987 SEASON	G	IP	H	BB	SO	SB	CS	W	L	S	ERA
Totals	24	110.2	117	52	83	17	6	5	9	0	5.94
At Home	13	64.2	67	32	53	8	4	2	5	0	5.57
On Road	11	46.0	50	20	30	9	2	3	4	0	6.46
vs. Opposing Batters	AVG	OBP	SLG	AB	H	2B	3B	HR	RBI	BB	SO
Totals	.271	.350	.516	432	117	25	3	25	70	52	83
vs. Left	.203	.241	.241	79	16	3	0	0	7	3	16
vs. Right	.286	.372	.578	353	101	22	3	25	63	49	67

FOUR YEAR TOTALS (1984 – 1987)	G	IP	H	BB	SO	SB	CS	W	L	S	ERA
	51	252.2	268	96	177	36	14	12	20	0	5.20
	25	132.2	145	54	99	18	9	4	12	0	5.49
	26	120.0	123	42	78	18	5	8	8	0	4.88
	AVG	OBP	SLG	AB	H	2B	3B	HR	RBI	BB	SO
	.269	.334	.481	995	268	56	7	47	144	96	177
	.244	.271	.305	164	40	8	1	0	17	5	31
	.274	.346	.516	831	228	48	6	47	127	91	146

Kittle, Ronald Dale "Ron"

Bats: Right **Throws: Right** **Born 01/05/58**

1987 SEASON AND MAJOR-LEAGUE CAREER BATTING TOTALS

	G	AB	H	2B	3B	HR	TB	R	RBI	TBB	IBB	SO	HP	SH	SF	SB	CS	SB%	GDP	AVG	OBP	SLG
87 NYA	59	159	44	5	0	12	85	21	28	10	1	36	1	0	3	0	1	.00	4	.277	.318	.535
6 YEARS	595	1929	452	66	3	127	905	259	327	167	16	537	23	0	20	16	15	.52	43	.234	.300	.469

1987 SEASON	AVG	OBP	SLG	AB	H	2B	3B	HR	RBI	BB	SO
Totals	.277	.318	.535	159	44	5	0	12	28	10	36
vs. Left	.309	.368	.553	94	29	5	0	6	19	9	19
vs. Right	.231	.239	.508	65	15	0	0	6	9	1	17
At Home	.288	.337	.603	73	21	2	0	7	16	7	16
On Road	.267	.300	.477	86	23	3	0	5	12	3	20

FOUR YEAR TOTALS (1984 – 1987)	AVG	OBP	SLG	AB	H	2B	3B	HR	RBI	BB	SO
	.227	.295	.457	1380	313	45	0	91	220	125	375
	.232	.313	.443	600	139	22	0	35	95	69	155
	.223	.280	.468	780	174	23	0	56	125	56	220
	.223	.295	.445	681	152	25	0	42	105	70	180
	.230	.295	.469	699	161	20	0	49	115	55	195

Knudson, Mark Richard

Bats: Right   Throws: Right   Born 10/28/60

1987 SEASON AND MAJOR-LEAGUE CAREER PITCHING TOTALS

	G	GS	CG	GF	IP	BFP	H	R	ER	HR	SH	SF	HB	TBB	IBB	SO	WP	Bk	W	L	Pct	ShO	Sv	ERA
87 MIL	15	8	1	3	62	288	88	46	37	7	3	5	0	14	1	26	1	0	4	4	.500	0	0	5.37
3 YEARS	30	18	1	5	134	614	179	95	83	19	7	5	1	37	7	59	3	0	5	12	.294	0	0	5.57

1987: Finesse, Flyball   1986: Finesse, Flyball

1987 SEASON												TWO YEAR TOTALS (1986 – 1987)										
	G	IP	H	BB	SO	SB	CS	W	L	S	ERA	G	IP	H	BB	SO	SB	CS	W	L	S	ERA
Totals	15	62.0	88	14	26	3	1	4	4	0	5.37	28	122.1	158	34	55	13	4	5	10	0	5.30
At Home	9	29.0	55	8	12	0	1	3	3	0	7.45	15	56.2	91	16	23	7	1	4	4	0	6.99
On Road	6	33.0	33	6	14	3	0	1	1	0	3.55	13	65.2	67	18	32	6	3	1	6	0	3.84

vs. Opposing Batters	AVG	OBP	SLG	AB	H	2B	3B	HR	RBI	BB	SO	AVG	OBP	SLG	AB	H	2B	3B	HR	RBI	BB	SO
Totals	.331	.358	.444	266	88	9	0	7	39	14	26	.307	.348	.460	515	158	20	1	19	75	34	55
vs. Left	.324	.359	.453	139	45	6	0	4	25	10	17	.296	.344	.432	257	76	12	1	7	39	20	28
vs. Right	.339	.356	.433	127	43	3	0	3	14	4	9	.318	.352	.488	258	82	8	0	12	36	14	27

Krukow, Michael Edward "Mike"

Bats: Right   Throws: Right   Born 01/21/52

1987 SEASON AND MAJOR-LEAGUE CAREER PITCHING TOTALS

	G	GS	CG	GF	IP	BFP	H	R	ER	HR	SH	SF	HB	TBB	IBB	SO	WP	Bk	W	L	Pct	ShO	Sv	ERA
87 SF	30	28	3	0	163	699	182	98	87	24	10	8	2	46	6	104	3	3	5	6	.455	0	0	4.80
12 YEARS	341	327	40	4	2022	8699	2040	998	878	178	91	66	41	718	78	1385	66	19	113	110	.507	10	1	3.91

1987: Finesse, Flyball   1986: Finesse, Flyball   1985: Power, Flyball   1984: Power, Flyball

1987 SEASON												FOUR YEAR TOTALS (1984 – 1987)										
	G	IP	H	BB	SO	SB	CS	W	L	S	ERA	G	IP	H	BB	SO	SB	CS	W	L	S	ERA
Totals	30	163.0	182	46	104	13	10	5	6	0	4.86	127	802.0	796	228	573	87	27	44	38	1	3.87
At Home	16	86.2	89	24	58	7	5	1	3	0	4.36	64	433.2	397	110	317	35	17	25	16	0	3.07
On Road	14	76.1	93	22	46	6	5	4	3	0	5.42	63	368.1	399	118	256	52	10	19	22	1	4.79

vs. Opposing Batters	AVG	OBP	SLG	AB	H	2B	3B	HR	RBI	BB	SO	AVG	OBP	SLG	AB	H	2B	3B	HR	RBI	BB	SO
Totals	.288	.334	.463	633	182	31	4	24	88	46	104	.257	.308	.403	3093	796	141	22	89	341	228	573
vs. Left	.313	.371	.486	348	109	15	3	13	51	34	50	.278	.337	.434	1661	462	81	14	50	200	149	285
vs. Right	.256	.286	.435	285	73	16	1	11	37	12	54	.233	.273	.368	1432	334	60	8	39	141	79	288

Kunkel, Jeffrey William "Jeff"

Bats: Right   Throws: Right   Born 03/25/62

1987 SEASON AND MAJOR-LEAGUE CAREER BATTING TOTALS

	G	AB	H	2B	3B	HR	TB	R	RBI	TBB	IBB	SO	HP	SH	SF	SB	CS	SB%	GDP	AVG	OBP	SLG
87 TEX	15	32	7	0	0	1	10	1	2	0	0	10	1	1	0	0	1	.00	0	.219	.242	.313
4 YEARS	75	191	40	2	3	5	63	18	11	2	0	50	2	4	2	4	4	.50	2	.209	.223	.330

1987 SEASON											TWO YEAR TOTALS (1986 – 1987)									
	AVG	OBP	SLG	AB	H	2B	3B	HR	RBI	BB	SO	AVG	OBP	SLG	AB	H	2B	3B	HR	RBI	BB	SO
Totals	.219	.242	.313	32	7	0	0	1	2	0	10	.222	.245	.356	45	10	0	0	2	4	0	12
vs. Left	.217	.250	.348	23	5	0	0	1	1	0	8	.222	.250	.333	27	6	0	0	1	2	0	9
vs. Right	.222	.222	.222	9	2	0	0	0	1	0	2	.222	.222	.389	18	4	0	0	1	2	0	3
At Home	.182	.182	.182	11	2	0	0	0	0	0	3	.211	.211	.368	19	4	0	0	1	1	0	5
On Road	.238	.273	.381	21	5	0	0	1	2	0	7	.231	.259	.346	26	6	0	0	1	3	0	7

Lacy, Leondaus "Leon"

Bats: Right   Throws: Right   Born 04/10/49

1987 SEASON AND MAJOR-LEAGUE CAREER BATTING TOTALS

	G	AB	H	2B	3B	HR	TB	R	RBI	TBB	IBB	SO	HP	SH	SF	SB	CS	SB%	GDP	AVG	OBP	SLG
87 BAL	87	258	63	13	3	7	103	35	28	32	0	49	0	2	1	3	2	.60	5	.244	.326	.399
16 YEARS	1523	4549	1303	207	42	91	1867	650	458	372	26	657	9	41	33	185	86	.68	86	.286	.339	.410

1987 SEASON											FOUR YEAR TOTALS (1984 – 1987)									
	AVG	OBP	SLG	AB	H	2B	3B	HR	RBI	BB	SO	AVG	OBP	SLG	AB	H	2B	3B	HR	RBI	BB	SO
Totals	.244	.326	.399	258	63	13	3	7	28	32	49	.292	.343	.417	1715	500	79	10	39	193	140	276
vs. Left	.237	.306	.404	156	37	10	2	4	20	16	24	.295	.354	.459	647	191	33	5	21	74	58	80
vs. Right	.255	.356	.392	102	26	3	1	3	8	16	25	.289	.337	.392	1068	309	46	5	18	119	82	196
At Home	.231	.318	.346	130	30	7	1	2	8	17	32	.302	.356	.417	848	256	44	3	16	87	73	156
On Road	.258	.336	.453	128	33	6	2	5	20	15	17	.281	.331	.418	867	244	35	7	23	106	67	120

Laga, Michael Russell "Mike"

Bats: Left   Throws: Left   Born 06/14/60

1987 SEASON AND MAJOR-LEAGUE CAREER BATTING TOTALS

	G	AB	H	2B	3B	HR	TB	R	RBI	TBB	IBB	SO	HP	SH	SF	SB	CS	SB%	GDP	AVG	OBP	SLG
87 STL	17	29	4	1	0	1	8	4	4	2	1	7	0	0	2	0	0	.00	1	.138	.182	.276
6 YEARS	107	276	62	16	0	12	114	29	40	18	3	81	1	0	2	1	0	1.00	5	.225	.273	.413

	1987 SEASON											TWO YEAR TOTALS (1986 – 1987)										
	AVG	OBP	SLG	AB	H	2B	3B	HR	RBI	BB	SO	AVG	OBP	SLG	AB	H	2B	3B	HR	RBI	BB	SO
Totals	.138	.182	.276	29	4	1	0	1	4	2	7	.192	.272	.417	120	23	6	0	7	20	12	38
vs. Left	.143	.143	.286	7	1	1	0	0	1	0	2	.222	.222	.667	9	2	1	0	1	2	0	2
vs. Right	.136	.192	.273	22	3	0	0	1	3	2	5	.189	.270	.396	111	21	5	0	6	18	12	36
At Home	.071	.067	.071	14	1	0	0	0	1	0	4	.182	.267	.379	66	12	4	0	3	10	8	22
On Road	.200	.278	.467	15	3	1	0	1	3	2	3	.204	.267	.463	54	11	2	0	4	10	4	16

Lake, Steven Michael "Steve"

Bats: Right   Throws: Right   Born 03/14/57

1987 SEASON AND MAJOR-LEAGUE CAREER BATTING TOTALS

	G	AB	H	2B	3B	HR	TB	R	RBI	TBB	IBB	SO	HP	SH	SF	SB	CS	SB%	GDP	AVG	OBP	SLG
87 STL	74	179	45	7	2	2	62	19	19	10	4	18	0	5	1	0	0	.00	2	.251	.289	.346
5 YEARS	231	505	117	19	3	8	166	45	58	18	8	59	3	11	3	1	0	1.00	12	.232	.261	.329

	1987 SEASON											TWO YEAR TOTALS (1986 – 1987)										
	AVG	OBP	SLG	AB	H	2B	3B	HR	RBI	BB	SO	AVG	OBP	SLG	AB	H	2B	3B	HR	RBI	BB	SO
Totals	.251	.289	.346	179	45	7	2	2	19	10	18	.263	.302	.364	247	65	9	2	4	33	13	25
vs. Left	.308	.337	.423	78	24	3	0	2	10	4	7	.302	.331	.437	126	38	5	0	4	19	6	9
vs. Right	.208	.252	.287	101	21	4	2	0	9	6	11	.223	.266	.289	121	27	4	2	0	14	7	16
At Home	.253	.278	.333	87	22	4	0	1	10	3	7	.252	.291	.315	111	28	4	0	1	14	6	12
On Road	.250	.300	.359	92	23	3	2	1	9	7	11	.272	.306	.404	136	37	5	2	3	19	7	13

Lamp, Dennis Patrick

Bats: Right   Throws: Right   Born 09/23/52

1987 SEASON AND MAJOR-LEAGUE CAREER PITCHING TOTALS

	G	GS	CG	GF	IP	BFP	H	R	ER	HR	SH	SF	HB	TBB	IBB	SO	WP	Bk	W	L	Pct	ShO	Sv	ERA
87 OAK	36	5	0	10	57	262	76	38	32	5	3	3	1	22	3	36	4	0	1	3	.250	0	0	5.05
11 YEARS	432	162	21	126	1411	6047	1540	708	619	94	75	27	25	433	58	626	35	4	75	79	.487	7	33	3.95

1987: Finesse, Groundball   1986: Finesse, Groundball   1985: Finesse, Groundball   1984: Power, Groundball

	1987 SEASON										FOUR YEAR TOTALS (1984 – 1987)									
	G	IP	H	BB	SO	SB	CS	W	L	S	ERA	G	IP	H	BB	SO	SB	CS	W	L	S	ERA
Totals	36	56.2	76	22	36	9	2	1	3	0	5.08	185	320.1	362	110	179	35	4	22	17	13	4.35
At Home	14	26.0	29	10	17	4	1	0	1	0	4.15	82	154.2	168	54	91	15	2	11	7	8	3.90
On Road	22	30.2	47	12	19	5	1	1	2	0	5.87	103	165.2	194	56	88	20	2	11	10	5	4.78
vs. Opposing Batters	AVG	OBP	SLG	AB	H	2B	3B	HR	RBI	BB	SO	AVG	OBP	SLG	AB	H	2B	3B	HR	RBI	BB	SO
Totals	.326	.382	.455	233	76	13	1	5	40	22	36	.287	.344	.389	1261	362	39	6	26	186	110	178
vs. Left	.316	.405	.379	95	30	3	0	1	15	15	16	.295	.370	.364	539	159	12	2	7	74	65	62
vs. Right	.333	.365	.507	138	46	10	1	4	25	7	20	.281	.323	.409	722	203	27	4	19	112	45	116

Lancaster, Lester Wayne

Bats: Right   Throws: Right   Born 04/21/62

1987 SEASON AND MAJOR-LEAGUE CAREER PITCHING TOTALS

	G	GS	CG	GF	IP	BFP	H	R	ER	HR	SH	SF	HB	TBB	IBB	SO	WP	Bk	W	L	Pct	ShO	Sv	ERA
87 CHN	27	18	0	4	132	578	138	76	72	14	5	6	1	51	5	78	7	8	8	3	.727	0	0	4.91
1 YEAR	27	18	0	4	132	578	138	76	72	14	5	6	1	51	5	78	7	8	8	3	.727	0	0	4.91

1987: Finesse, Flyball

	1987 SEASON										FOUR YEAR TOTALS (1984 – 1987)									
	G	IP	H	BB	SO	SB	CS	W	L	S	ERA	G	IP	H	BB	SO	SB	CS	W	L	S	ERA
Totals	27	132.1	138	51	78	11	7	8	3	0	4.90	27	132.1	138	51	78	11	7	8	3	0	4.90
At Home	14	69.2	69	28	37	7	4	6	2	0	4.78	14	69.2	69	28	37	7	4	6	2	0	4.78
On Road	13	62.2	69	23	41	4	3	2	1	0	5.03	13	62.2	69	23	41	4	3	2	1	0	5.03
vs. Opposing Batters	AVG	OBP	SLG	AB	H	2B	3B	HR	RBI	BB	SO	AVG	OBP	SLG	AB	H	2B	3B	HR	RBI	BB	SO
Totals	.268	.332	.406	515	138	27	1	14	61	51	78	.268	.332	.406	515	138	27	1	14	61	51	78
vs. Left	.321	.382	.485	262	84	17	1	8	36	28	31	.321	.382	.485	262	84	17	1	8	36	28	31
vs. Right	.213	.278	.324	253	54	10	0	6	25	23	47	.213	.278	.324	253	54	10	0	6	25	23	47

Landreaux, Kenneth Francis "Ken"

Bats: Left   Throws: Right   Born 12/22/54

1987 SEASON AND MAJOR-LEAGUE CAREER BATTING TOTALS

	G	AB	H	2B	3B	HR	TB	R	RBI	TBB	IBB	SO	HP	SH	SF	SB	CS	SB%	GDP	AVG	OBP	SLG
87 LA	115	182	37	4	0	6	59	17	23	16	2	28	1	3	2	5	3	.63	4	.203	.269	.324
11 YEARS	1264	4101	1099	180	45	91	1642	522	479	299	33	421	19	39	45	145	60	.71	78	.268	.317	.400

	AVG	OBP	SLG	AB	H	2B	3B	HR	RBI	BB	SO		AVG	OBP	SLG	AB	H	2B	3B	HR	RBI	BB	SO
				1987 SEASON												**FOUR YEAR TOTALS (1984 – 1987)**								
Totals	.203	.269	.324	182	37	4	0	6	23	16	28		.253	.301	.376	1385	350	54	9	33	149	100	139
vs. Left	.200	.238	.250	20	4	1	0	0	2	1	4		.238	.303	.337	181	43	9	0	3	25	16	28
vs. Right	.204	.272	.333	162	33	3	0	6	21	15	24		.255	.300	.382	1204	307	45	9	30	124	84	111
At Home	.297	.343	.462	91	27	3	0	4	14	6	11		.253	.309	.347	672	170	25	1	12	69	57	64
On Road	.110	.196	.187	91	10	1	0	2	9	10	17		.252	.294	.404	713	180	29	8	21	80	43	75

Landrum, Terry Lee "Tito"

Bats: Right   Throws: Right   Born 10/25/54

1987 SEASON AND MAJOR-LEAGUE CAREER BATTING TOTALS

	G	AB	H	2B	3B	HR	TB	R	RBI	TBB	IBB	SO	HP	SH	SF	SB	CS	SB%	GDP	AVG	OBP	SLG
87 STL-LA	81	117	26	4	0	1	33	13	10	10	2	30	1	1	0	2	2	.50	1	.222	.289	.282
8 YEARS	594	971	245	40	11	13	346	118	109	81	6	190	5	12	10	17	18	.49	24	.252	.310	.356

	AVG	OBP	SLG	AB	H	2B	3B	HR	RBI	BB	SO		AVG	OBP	SLG	AB	H	2B	3B	HR	RBI	BB	SO
				1987 SEASON												**FOUR YEAR TOTALS (1984 – 1987)**								
Totals	.222	.289	.282	117	26	4	0	1	10	10	30		.245	.305	.346	656	161	28	4	10	74	57	128
vs. Left	.230	.287	.276	87	20	4	0	0	7	6	23		.236	.302	.339	513	121	23	3	8	64	49	100
vs. Right	.200	.294	.300	30	6	0	0	1	3	4	7		.280	.318	.371	143	40	5	1	2	10	8	28
At Home	.203	.254	.288	59	12	2	0	1	4	3	12		.260	.320	.394	312	81	15	3	7	46	28	52
On Road	.241	.323	.276	58	14	2	0	0	6	7	18		.233	.291	.302	344	80	13	1	3	28	29	76

Landrum, Thomas William "Bill"

Bats: Right   Throws: Right   Born 08/17/57

1987 SEASON AND MAJOR-LEAGUE CAREER PITCHING TOTALS

	G	GS	CG	GF	IP	BFP	H	R	ER	HR	SH	SF	HB	TBB	IBB	SO	WP	Bk	W	L	Pct	ShO	Sv	ERA
87 CIN	44	2	0	14	65	276	68	35	34	3	7	2	0	34	6	42	4	1	3	2	.600	0	2	4.71
2 YEARS	54	2	0	18	78	341	91	46	44	3	8	3	0	38	6	56	4	1	3	2	.600	0	2	5.08

1987: Power, Groundball   1986: Power, Flyball

	G	IP	H	BB	SO	SB	CS	W	L	S	ERA		G	IP	H	BB	SO	SB	CS	W	L	S	ERA
					1987 SEASON												**FOUR YEAR TOTALS (1984 – 1987)**							
Totals	44	65.1	68	34	42	7	7	3	2	2	4.68		54	78.2	91	38	56	9	7	3	2	2	5.03
At Home	25	36.2	40	16	25	3	2	2	0	1	4.91		29	42.2	54	18	30	3	2	2	0	1	5.70
On Road	19	28.2	28	18	17	4	5	1	2	1	4.40		25	36.0	37	20	26	6	5	1	2	1	4.25
vs. Opposing Batters	AVG	OBP	SLG	AB	H	2B	3B	HR	RBI	BB	SO		AVG	OBP	SLG	AB	H	2B	3B	HR	RBI	BB	SO
Totals	.292	.379	.403	233	68	11	3	3	37	34	42		.312	.387	.414	292	91	15	3	3	46	38	56
vs. Left	.270	.381	.380	100	27	3	1	2	10	18	15		.270	.363	.365	126	34	4	1	2	15	19	19
vs. Right	.308	.377	.421	133	41	8	2	1	27	16	27		.343	.406	.452	166	57	11	2	1	31	19	37

LaPoint, David Jeffrey "Dave"

Bats: Left   Throws: Left   Born 07/29/59

1987 SEASON AND MAJOR-LEAGUE CAREER PITCHING TOTALS

	G	GS	CG	GF	IP	BFP	H	R	ER	HR	SH	SF	HB	TBB	IBB	SO	WP	Bk	W	L	Pct	ShO	Sv	ERA
87 STL-CHA	20	14	2	3	99	420	95	41	39	11	1	0	1	36	0	51	4	1	7	4	.636	1	0	3.55
8 YEARS	211	145	7	17	998	4329	1057	494	435	80	54	28	11	394	37	583	47	16	53	53	.500	3	1	3.92

1987: Finesse, Groundball   1986: Finesse, Groundball   1985: Finesse, Groundball   1984: Power, Groundball

	G	IP	H	BB	SO	SB	CS	W	L	S	ERA		G	IP	H	BB	SO	SB	CS	W	L	S	ERA
					1987 SEASON												**FOUR YEAR TOTALS (1984 – 1987)**							
Totals	20	98.2	95	36	51	5	5	7	4	0	3.56		124	627.1	667	243	380	52	29	30	41	0	3.99
At Home	11	59.1	63	26	31	5	2	5	1	0	3.79		59	326.0	330	132	198	28	18	16	14	0	3.51
On Road	9	39.1	32	10	20	0	3	2	3	0	3.20		65	301.1	337	111	182	24	11	14	27	0	4.51
vs. Opposing Batters	AVG	OBP	SLG	AB	H	2B	3B	HR	RBI	BB	SO		AVG	OBP	SLG	AB	H	2B	3B	HR	RBI	BB	SO
Totals	.249	.315	.382	382	95	16	1	11	33	36	51		.273	.339	.402	2440	667	95	24	57	274	243	380
vs. Left	.262	.326	.310	42	11	2	0	0	2	4	6		.270	.314	.363	397	107	10	3	7	31	26	47
vs. Right	.247	.314	.391	340	84	14	1	11	31	32	45		.274	.344	.410	2043	560	85	21	50	243	217	333

Larkin, Eugene Thomas "Gene"

Bats: Both   Throws: Right   Born 10/24/62

1987 SEASON AND MAJOR-LEAGUE CAREER BATTING TOTALS

	G	AB	H	2B	3B	HR	TB	R	RBI	TBB	IBB	SO	HP	SH	SF	SB	CS	SB%	GDP	AVG	OBP	SLG
87 MIN	85	233	62	11	2	4	89	23	28	25	3	31	2	0	2	1	4	.20	4	.266	.340	.382
1 YEAR	85	233	62	11	2	4	89	23	28	25	3	31	2	0	2	1	4	.20	4	.266	.340	.382

	1987 SEASON											FOUR YEAR TOTALS (1984 – 1987)										
	AVG	OBP	SLG	AB	H	2B	3B	HR	RBI	BB	SO	AVG	OBP	SLG	AB	H	2B	3B	HR	RBI	BB	SO
Totals	.266	.340	.382	233	62	11	2	4	28	25	31	.266	.340	.382	233	62	11	2	4	28	25	31
vs. Left	.286	.375	.377	77	22	2	1	1	9	11	11	.286	.375	.377	77	22	2	1	1	9	11	11
vs. Right	.256	.322	.385	156	40	9	1	3	19	14	20	.256	.322	.385	156	40	9	1	3	19	14	20
At Home	.295	.367	.384	112	33	6	2	0	13	13	13	.295	.367	.384	112	33	6	2	0	13	13	13
On Road	.240	.313	.380	121	29	5	0	4	15	12	18	.240	.313	.380	121	29	5	0	4	15	12	18

Lavelle, Gary Robert

Bats: Both   Throws: Left   Born 01/03/49

1987 SEASON AND MAJOR-LEAGUE CAREER PITCHING TOTALS

	G	GS	CG	GF	IP	BFP	H	R	ER	HR	SH	SF	HB	TBB	IBB	SO	WP	Bk	W	L	Pct	ShO	Sv	ERA
87 TOR-OAK	29	0	0	11	32	157	40	24	21	2	3	2	0	22	1	23	1	1	2	3	.400	0	1	5.91
13 YEARS	745	3	0	399	1086	4604	1004	413	353	51	81	36	13	440	126	769	19	18	80	77	.510	0	136	2.93

1987: Power, Groundball

	1987 SEASON											TWO YEAR TOTALS (1986 – 1987)										
	G	IP	H	BB	SO	SB	CS	W	L	S	ERA	G	IP	H	BB	SO	SB	CS	W	L	S	ERA
Totals	29	32.0	40	22	23	1	0	2	3	1	5.91	29	32.0	40	22	23	1	0	2	3	1	5.91
At Home	13	17.1	17	6	13	0	0	1	1	1	1.56	13	17.1	17	6	13	0	0	1	1	1	1.56
On Road	16	14.2	23	16	10	1	0	1	2	0	11.05	16	14.2	23	16	10	1	0	1	2	0	11.05
vs. Opposing Batters	AVG	OBP	SLG	AB	H	2B	3B	HR	RBI	BB	SO	AVG	OBP	SLG	AB	H	2B	3B	HR	RBI	BB	SO
Totals	.308	.403	.454	130	40	9	2	2	26	22	23	.308	.403	.454	130	40	9	2	2	26	22	23
vs. Left	.239	.333	.370	46	11	3	0	1	13	7	14	.239	.333	.370	46	11	3	0	1	13	7	14
vs. Right	.345	.440	.500	84	29	6	2	1	13	15	9	.345	.440	.500	84	29	6	2	1	13	15	9

Lawless, Thomas James "Tom"

Bats: Right   Throws: Right   Born 12/19/56

1987 SEASON AND MAJOR-LEAGUE CAREER BATTING TOTALS

	G	AB	H	2B	3B	HR	TB	R	RBI	TBB	IBB	SO	HP	SH	SF	SB	CS	SB%	GDP	AVG	OBP	SLG
87 STL	19	25	2	1	0	0	3	5	0	3	0	5	0	1	0	2	0	1.00	1	.080	.179	.120
5 YEARS	215	384	83	14	1	1	102	48	17	27	1	63	0	7	1	35	10	.78	10	.216	.267	.266

	1987 SEASON											TWO YEAR TOTALS (1986 – 1987)										
	AVG	OBP	SLG	AB	H	2B	3B	HR	RBI	BB	SO	AVG	OBP	SLG	AB	H	2B	3B	HR	RBI	BB	SO
Totals	.080	.179	.120	25	2	1	0	0	0	3	5	.203	.254	.234	64	13	2	0	0	3	5	13
vs. Left	.067	.125	.133	15	1	1	0	0	0	1	4	.256	.298	.302	43	11	2	0	0	3	3	11
vs. Right	.100	.250	.100	10	1	0	0	0	0	2	1	.095	.174	.095	21	2	0	0	0	0	2	2
At Home	.077	.077	.154	13	1	1	0	0	0	0	2	.125	.152	.156	32	4	1	0	0	0	1	8
On Road	.083	.267	.083	12	1	0	0	0	0	3	3	.281	.351	.313	32	9	1	0	0	3	4	5

Lazorko, Jack Thomas

Bats: Right   Throws: Right   Born 03/30/56

1987 SEASON AND MAJOR-LEAGUE CAREER PITCHING TOTALS

	G	GS	CG	GF	IP	BFP	H	R	ER	HR	SH	SF	HB	TBB	IBB	SO	WP	Bk	W	L	Pct	ShO	Sv	ERA
87 CAL	26	11	2	5	118	487	108	68	60	20	2	3	2	44	5	55	3	1	5	6	.455	0	0	4.58
4 YEARS	59	12	2	14	185	785	176	100	90	28	4	4	6	78	9	89	3	1	5	7	.417	0	2	4.38

1987: Finesse, Flyball   1986: Finesse, Groundball

	1987 SEASON											TWO YEAR TOTALS (1986 – 1987)										
	G	IP	H	BB	SO	SB	CS	W	L	S	ERA	G	IP	H	BB	SO	SB	CS	W	L	S	ERA
Totals	26	117.2	108	44	55	6	10	5	6	0	4.59	29	124.1	116	48	58	6	10	5	6	0	4.56
At Home	13	66.0	65	30	34	2	6	4	3	0	6.27	15	69.2	72	33	35	2	6	4	3	0	6.33
On Road	13	51.2	43	14	21	4	4	1	3	0	2.44	14	54.2	44	15	23	4	4	1	3	0	2.30
vs. Opposing Batters	AVG	OBP	SLG	AB	H	2B	3B	HR	RBI	BB	SO	AVG	OBP	SLG	AB	H	2B	3B	HR	RBI	BB	SO
Totals	.248	.318	.439	435	108	17	3	20	63	44	55	.251	.322	.435	462	116	19	3	20	67	48	58
vs. Left	.289	.369	.553	190	55	8	3	12	32	25	7	.298	.382	.561	198	59	10	3	12	34	28	7
vs. Right	.216	.277	.351	245	53	9	0	8	31	19	48	.216	.275	.341	264	57	9	0	8	33	20	51

Leach, Richard Max "Rick"

Bats: Left   Throws: Left   Born 05/04/57

1987 SEASON AND MAJOR-LEAGUE CAREER BATTING TOTALS

	G	AB	H	2B	3B	HR	TB	R	RBI	TBB	IBB	SO	HP	SH	SF	SB	CS	SB%	GDP	AVG	OBP	SLG
87 TOR	98	195	55	13	1	3	79	26	25	25	2	25	3	0	1	0	1	.00	3	.282	.371	.405
7 YEARS	524	1107	289	60	8	15	410	128	121	105	10	137	4	5	12	6	4	.60	25	.261	.324	.370

1987 SEASON	AVG	OBP	SLG	AB	H	2B	3B	HR	RBI	BB	SO
Totals	.282	.371	.405	195	55	13	1	3	24	25	25
vs. Left	.375	.500	.563	16	6	3	0	0	3	4	6
vs. Right	.274	.358	.391	179	49	10	1	3	21	21	19
At Home	.264	.357	.436	110	29	8	1	3	13	14	13
On Road	.306	.388	.365	85	26	5	0	0	11	11	12

FOUR YEAR TOTALS (1984 – 1987)	AVG	OBP	SLG	AB	H	2B	3B	HR	RBI	BB	SO
Totals	.285	.341	.404	564	161	33	5	8	71	49	72
vs. Left	.255	.314	.319	47	12	3	0	0	5	4	10
vs. Right	.288	.343	.412	517	149	30	5	8	66	45	62
At Home	.272	.320	.414	309	84	17	3	7	37	21	37
On Road	.302	.364	.392	255	77	16	2	1	34	28	35

Leach, Terry Hester

Bats: Right   Throws: Right   Born 03/13/54

1987 SEASON AND MAJOR-LEAGUE CAREER PITCHING TOTALS

	G	GS	CG	GF	IP	BFP	H	R	ER	HR	SH	SF	HB	TBB	IBB	SO	WP	Bk	W	L	Pct	ShO	Sv	ERA
87 NYN	44	12	1	7	131	542	132	54	47	14	8	1	1	29	5	61	0	1	11	1	.917	1	0	3.23
5 YEARS	114	18	3	27	274	1131	258	109	98	21	18	4	2	76	14	141	0	1	17	7	.708	3	4	3.22

1987: Finesse, Groundball   1986: Power, Flyball

1987 SEASON	G	IP	H	BB	SO	SB	CS	W	L	S	ERA
Totals	44	131.0	132	29	61	18	8	11	1	0	3.23
At Home	21	40.2	52	8	21	9	3	3	0	0	4.65
On Road	23	90.1	80	21	40	9	5	8	1	0	2.59

vs. Opposing Batters	AVG	OBP	SLG	AB	H	2B	3B	HR	RBI	BB	SO
Totals	.262	.303	.403	504	132	27	1	14	49	29	61
vs. Left	.272	.317	.424	243	66	17	1	6	24	16	20
vs. Right	.253	.290	.383	261	66	10	0	8	25	13	41

TWO YEAR TOTALS (1986 – 1987)	G	IP	H	BB	SO	SB	CS	W	L	S	ERA
Totals	50	137.2	138	32	65	18	8	11	1	0	3.20
At Home	23	42.1	52	10	22	9	3	3	0	0	4.46
On Road	27	95.1	86	22	43	9	5	8	1	0	2.64

vs. Opposing Batters	AVG	OBP	SLG	AB	H	2B	3B	HR	RBI	BB	SO
Totals	.260	.303	.394	531	138	27	1	14	51	32	65
vs. Left	.272	.317	.417	254	69	17	1	6	25	17	22
vs. Right	.249	.289	.372	277	69	10	0	8	26	15	43

Leary, Timothy James "Tim"

Bats: Right   Throws: Right   Born 12/23/58

1987 SEASON AND MAJOR-LEAGUE CAREER PITCHING TOTALS

	G	GS	CG	GF	IP	BFP	H	R	ER	HR	SH	SF	HB	TBB	IBB	SO	WP	Bk	W	L	Pct	ShO	Sv	ERA
87 LA	39	12	0	11	108	469	121	62	57	15	6	1	2	36	5	61	3	1	3	11	.214	0	1	4.75
6 YEARS	100	57	4	16	396	1729	453	215	188	42	14	10	12	120	12	241	14	5	20	31	.392	2	1	4.27

1987: Finesse, Flyball   1986: Finesse, Groundball   1985: Power, Groundball   1984: Finesse, Groundball

1987 SEASON	G	IP	H	BB	SO	SB	CS	W	L	S	ERA
Totals	39	107.2	121	36	61	12	4	3	11	1	4.76
At Home	20	55.1	60	17	29	6	3	2	5	0	4.55
On Road	19	52.1	61	19	32	6	1	1	6	1	4.99

vs. Opposing Batters	AVG	OBP	SLG	AB	H	2B	3B	HR	RBI	BB	SO
Totals	.285	.343	.460	424	121	23	3	15	60	36	61
vs. Left	.289	.344	.451	204	59	12	3	5	28	16	18
vs. Right	.282	.343	.468	220	62	11	0	10	32	20	43

FOUR YEAR TOTALS (1984 – 1987)	G	IP	H	BB	SO	SB	CS	W	L	S	ERA
Totals	97	383.0	438	115	229	39	18	19	30	1	4.32
At Home	49	195.2	218	55	107	21	11	10	16	0	4.37
On Road	48	187.1	220	60	122	18	7	9	14	1	4.28

vs. Opposing Batters	AVG	OBP	SLG	AB	H	2B	3B	HR	RBI	BB	SO
Totals	.288	.339	.429	1520	438	68	10	42	180	115	229
vs. Left	.294	.356	.435	752	221	35	4	21	86	72	87
vs. Right	.283	.321	.423	768	217	33	6	21	94	43	142

Lee, Manuel Lora

Bats: Both   Throws: Right   Born 06/17/65

1987 SEASON AND MAJOR-LEAGUE CAREER BATTING TOTALS

	G	AB	H	2B	3B	HR	TB	R	RBI	TBB	IBB	SO	HP	SH	SF	SB	CS	SB%	GDP	AVG	OBP	SLG
87 TOR	56	121	31	2	3	1	42	14	11	6	0	13	0	1	1	2	0	1.00	1	.256	.289	.347
3 YEARS	155	239	55	2	4	2	71	31	18	12	0	32	0	4	2	3	5	.38	8	.230	.265	.297

1987 SEASON	AVG	OBP	SLG	AB	H	2B	3B	HR	RBI	BB	SO
Totals	.256	.289	.347	121	31	2	3	1	11	6	13
vs. Left	.313	.340	.438	48	15	0	0	0	6	2	4
vs. Right	.219	.256	.288	73	16	2	0	1	5	4	9
At Home	.200	.269	.233	60	12	0	1	0	5	6	9
On Road	.311	.311	.459	61	19	2	2	1	6	0	4

TWO YEAR TOTALS (1986 – 1987)	AVG	OBP	SLG	AB	H	2B	3B	HR	RBI	BB	SO
Totals	.236	.269	.317	199	47	2	4	2	18	10	23
vs. Left	.299	.329	.418	67	20	0	4	0	8	3	6
vs. Right	.205	.241	.265	132	27	2	0	2	10	7	17
At Home	.218	.266	.287	101	22	0	2	1	10	7	13
On Road	.255	.275	.347	98	25	2	2	1	8	3	10

Lefferts, Craig Lindsey

Bats: Left　**Throws: Left**　**Born 09/29/57**

1987 SEASON AND MAJOR-LEAGUE CAREER PITCHING TOTALS

	G	GS	CG	GF	IP	BFP	H	R	ER	HR	SH	SF	HB	TBB	IBB	SO	WP	Bk	W	L	Pct	ShO	Sv	ERA
87 SD-SF	77	0	0	22	98	416	92	47	42	13	6	2	2	33	11	57	6	3	5	5	.500	0	6	3.86
5 YEARS	338	5	0	121	484	1994	433	186	166	44	33	14	6	160	30	293	13	6	27	27	.500	0	23	3.09

1987: Finesse, Flyball　**1986: Power, Flyball**　**1985: Finesse, Flyball**　**1984: Finesse, Flyball**

1987 SEASON

	G	IP	H	BB	SO	SB	CS	W	L	S	ERA
Totals	77	99.0	92	33	57	4	3	5	5	6	3.82
At Home	37	46.0	34	14	29	1	1	4	1	3	2.93
On Road	40	53.0	58	19	28	3	2	1	4	3	4.58

vs. Opposing Batters	AVG	OBP	SLG	AB	H	2B	3B	HR	RBI	BB	SO
Totals	.247	.310	.410	373	92	18	2	13	52	33	57
vs. Left	.228	.264	.412	114	26	4	1	5	24	5	25
vs. Right	.255	.329	.409	259	66	14	1	8	28	28	32

FOUR YEAR TOTALS (1984 – 1987)

	G	IP	H	BB	SO	SB	CS	W	L	S	ERA
Totals	282	395.2	353	131	233	31	17	24	23	22	3.07
At Home	139	200.1	156	56	134	18	9	18	9	10	2.47
On Road	143	195.1	197	75	99	13	8	6	14	12	3.69

vs. Opposing Batters	AVG	OBP	SLG	AB	H	2B	3B	HR	RBI	BB	SO
Totals	.243	.306	.364	1452	353	68	7	31	164	131	233
vs. Left	.211	.265	.303	379	80	12	1	7	47	27	84
vs. Right	.254	.321	.385	1073	273	56	6	24	117	104	149

Leiper, David Paul "Dave"

Bats: Left　**Throws: Left**　**Born 06/18/62**

1987 SEASON AND MAJOR-LEAGUE CAREER PITCHING TOTALS

	G	GS	CG	GF	IP	BFP	H	R	ER	HR	SH	SF	HB	TBB	IBB	SO	WP	Bk	W	L	Pct	ShO	Sv	ERA
87 OAK-SD	57	0	0	7	68	291	65	36	30	8	4	4	1	23	0	43	3	1	3	1	.750	0	2	3.97
3 YEARS	98	0	0	18	107	466	105	60	54	13	6	7	3	46	4	61	6	1	6	3	.667	0	3	4.54

1987: Finesse, Groundball　**1986: Power, Flyball**

1987 SEASON

	G	IP	H	BB	SO	SB	CS	W	L	S	ERA
Totals	57	67.2	65	23	43	5	4	3	1	2	3.99
At Home	28	38.0	25	11	25	3	3	1	0	0	2.13
On Road	29	29.2	40	12	18	2	1	2	1	2	6.37

vs. Opposing Batters	AVG	OBP	SLG	AB	H	2B	3B	HR	RBI	BB	SO
Totals	.251	.310	.398	259	65	8	3	8	45	23	43
vs. Left	.196	.262	.330	112	22	3	0	4	17	10	20
vs. Right	.293	.348	.449	147	43	5	3	4	28	13	23

FOUR YEAR TOTALS (1984 – 1987)

	G	IP	H	BB	SO	SB	CS	W	L	S	ERA
Totals	98	106.1	105	46	61	7	7	6	3	3	4.57
At Home	50	54.0	47	21	32	4	4	3	2	0	3.83
On Road	48	52.1	58	25	29	3	3	3	1	3	5.33

vs. Opposing Batters	AVG	OBP	SLG	AB	H	2B	3B	HR	RBI	BB	SO
Totals	.260	.334	.421	404	105	16	5	13	76	46	61
vs. Left	.206	.291	.345	165	34	5	0	6	34	20	31
vs. Right	.297	.365	.473	239	71	11	5	7	42	26	30

LeMaster, Johnnie Lee

Bats: Right　**Throws: Right**　**Born 06/19/54**

1987 SEASON AND MAJOR-LEAGUE CAREER BATTING TOTALS

	G	AB	H	2B	3B	HR	TB	R	RBI	TBB	IBB	SO	HP	SH	SF	SB	CS	SB%	GDP	AVG	OBP	SLG
87 OAK	20	24	2	0	0	0	2	3	1	1	0	4	0	0	0	0	1	.00	0	.083	.120	.083
12 YEARS	1039	3191	709	109	19	22	922	320	229	241	37	564	7	57	19	94	51	.65	52	.222	.277	.289

1987 SEASON

	AVG	OBP	SLG	AB	H	2B	3B	HR	RBI	BB	SO
Totals	.083	.120	.083	24	2	0	0	0	1	1	4
vs. Left	.091	.091	.091	11	1	0	0	0	1	0	1
vs. Right	.077	.143	.077	13	1	0	0	0	0	1	3
At Home	.063	.118	.063	16	1	0	0	0	0	1	3
On Road	.125	.125	.125	8	1	0	0	0	1	0	1

TWO YEAR TOTALS (1986 – 1987)

	AVG	OBP	SLG	AB	H	2B	3B	HR	RBI	BB	SO
Totals	.083	.103	.083	24	2	0	0	0	1	1	4
vs. Left	.091	.091	.091	11	1	0	0	0	1	0	1
vs. Right	.077	.143	.077	13	1	0	0	0	0	1	3
At Home	.063	.118	.063	16	1	0	0	0	0	1	3
On Road	.125	.125	.125	8	1	0	0	0	1	0	1

Lind, Jose (Salgado)

Bats: Right　**Throws: Right**　**Born 05/01/64**

1987 SEASON AND MAJOR-LEAGUE CAREER BATTING TOTALS

	G	AB	H	2B	3B	HR	TB	R	RBI	TBB	IBB	SO	HP	SH	SF	SB	CS	SB%	GDP	AVG	OBP	SLG
87 PIT	35	143	46	8	4	0	62	21	11	8	1	12	0	6	0	2	1	.67	5	.322	.358	.434
1 YEAR	35	143	46	8	4	0	62	21	11	8	1	12	0	6	0	2	1	.67	5	.322	.358	.434

1987 SEASON

	AVG	OBP	SLG	AB	H	2B	3B	HR	RBI	BB	SO
Totals	.322	.358	.434	143	46	8	4	0	11	8	12
vs. Left	.342	.368	.507	73	25	6	3	0	6	3	4
vs. Right	.300	.347	.357	70	21	2	1	0	5	5	8
At Home	.313	.353	.425	80	25	5	2	0	7	5	4
On Road	.333	.364	.444	63	21	3	2	0	4	3	8

FOUR YEAR TOTALS (1984 – 1987)

	AVG	OBP	SLG	AB	H	2B	3B	HR	RBI	BB	SO
Totals	.322	.358	.434	143	46	8	4	0	11	8	12
vs. Left	.342	.368	.507	73	25	6	3	0	6	3	4
vs. Right	.300	.347	.357	70	21	2	1	0	5	5	8
At Home	.313	.353	.425	80	25	5	2	0	7	5	4
On Road	.333	.364	.444	63	21	3	2	0	4	3	8

Lindeman, James William "Jim"

Bats: Right   Throws: Right   Born 01/10/62

1987 SEASON AND MAJOR-LEAGUE CAREER BATTING TOTALS

	G	AB	H	2B	3B	HR	TB	R	RBI	TBB	IBB	SO	HP	SH	SF	SB	CS	SB%	GDP	AVG	OBP	SLG
87 STL	75	207	43	13	0	8	80	20	28	11	0	56	3	2	4	3	1	.75	4	.208	.253	.386
2 YEARS	94	262	57	14	0	9	98	27	34	13	0	66	3	2	5	4	2	.67	6	.218	.258	.374

1987 SEASON	AVG	OBP	SLG	AB	H	2B	3B	HR	RBI	BB	SO
Totals	.208	.253	.386	207	43	13	0	8	28	11	56
vs. Left	.208	.252	.366	101	21	4	0	4	13	7	27
vs. Right	.208	.254	.406	106	22	9	0	4	15	4	29
At Home	.196	.233	.313	112	22	7	0	2	15	5	33
On Road	.221	.276	.474	95	21	6	0	6	13	6	23

FOUR YEAR TOTALS (1984 – 1987)	AVG	OBP	SLG	AB	H	2B	3B	HR	RBI	BB	SO
Totals	.218	.257	.374	262	57	14	0	9	34	13	66
vs. Left	.229	.268	.371	140	32	5	0	5	18	9	34
vs. Right	.205	.246	.377	122	25	9	0	4	16	4	32
At Home	.189	.227	.288	132	25	7	0	2	16	6	37
On Road	.246	.289	.462	130	32	7	0	7	18	7	29

Liriano, Nelson Arturo (Bonilla)

Bats: Both   Throws: Right   Born 06/03/64

1987 SEASON AND MAJOR-LEAGUE CAREER BATTING TOTALS

	G	AB	H	2B	3B	HR	TB	R	RBI	TBB	IBB	SO	HP	SH	SF	SB	CS	SB%	GDP	AVG	OBP	SLG
87 TOR	37	158	38	6	2	2	54	29	10	16	2	22	0	2	0	13	2	.87	3	.241	.310	.342
1 YEAR	37	158	38	6	2	2	54	29	10	16	2	22	0	2	0	13	2	.87	3	.241	.310	.342

1987 SEASON	AVG	OBP	SLG	AB	H	2B	3B	HR	RBI	BB	SO
Totals	.241	.310	.342	158	38	6	2	2	10	16	22
vs. Left	.167	.222	.310	42	7	0	0	2	7	3	6
vs. Right	.267	.341	.353	116	31	6	2	0	3	13	16
At Home	.263	.324	.384	99	26	5	2	1	6	9	15
On Road	.203	.288	.271	59	12	1	0	1	4	7	7

FOUR YEAR TOTALS (1984 – 1987)	AVG	OBP	SLG	AB	H	2B	3B	HR	RBI	BB	SO
Totals	.241	.310	.342	158	38	6	2	2	10	16	22
vs. Left	.167	.222	.310	42	7	0	0	2	7	3	6
vs. Right	.267	.341	.353	116	31	6	2	0	3	13	16
At Home	.263	.324	.384	99	26	5	2	1	6	9	15
On Road	.203	.288	.271	59	12	1	0	1	4	7	7

Long, William Douglas "Bill"

Bats: Right   Throws: Right   Born 02/29/60

1987 SEASON AND MAJOR-LEAGUE CAREER PITCHING TOTALS

	G	GS	CG	GF	IP	BFP	H	R	ER	HR	SH	SF	HB	TBB	IBB	SO	WP	Bk	W	L	Pct	ShO	Sv	ERA
87 CHA	29	23	5	2	169	699	179	85	82	20	6	3	3	28	1	72	0	1	8	8	.500	2	1	4.37
2 YEARS	33	26	5	3	183	770	204	102	98	24	7	4	3	33	3	85	1	1	8	9	.471	2	1	4.82

1987: Finesse, Groundball

1987 SEASON	G	IP	H	BB	SO	SB	CS	W	L	S	ERA
Totals	29	169.0	179	28	72	8	4	8	8	1	4.37
At Home	14	68.1	78	13	28	2	1	2	5	1	5.14
On Road	15	100.2	101	15	44	6	3	6	3	0	3.84

vs. Opposing Batters	AVG	OBP	SLG	AB	H	2B	3B	HR	RBI	BB	SO
Totals	.272	.303	.434	659	179	37	5	20	80	28	72
vs. Left	.279	.307	.439	344	96	17	4	10	45	13	39
vs. Right	.263	.298	.429	315	83	20	1	10	35	15	33

TWO YEAR TOTALS (1986 – 1987)	G	IP	H	BB	SO	SB	CS	W	L	S	ERA
Totals	29	169.0	179	28	72	8	4	8	8	1	4.37
At Home	14	68.1	78	13	28	2	1	2	5	1	5.14
On Road	15	100.2	101	15	44	6	3	6	3	0	3.84

	AVG	OBP	SLG	AB	H	2B	3B	HR	RBI	BB	SO
Totals	.272	.303	.434	659	179	37	5	20	80	28	72
vs. Left	.279	.307	.439	344	96	17	4	10	45	13	39
vs. Right	.263	.298	.429	315	83	20	1	10	35	15	33

Lopes, David Earl "Davey"

Bats: Right   Throws: Right   Born 05/03/46

1987 SEASON AND MAJOR-LEAGUE CAREER BATTING TOTALS

	G	AB	H	2B	3B	HR	TB	R	RBI	TBB	IBB	SO	HP	SH	SF	SB	CS	SB%	GDP	AVG	OBP	SLG
87 HOU	47	43	10	2	0	1	15	4	6	13	2	8	0	0	0	2	1	.67	0	.233	.411	.349
16 YEARS	1812	6354	1671	232	50	155	2468	1023	614	833	38	852	31	74	48	557	114	.83	126	.263	.349	.388

1987 SEASON	AVG	OBP	SLG	AB	H	2B	3B	HR	RBI	BB	SO
Totals	.233	.411	.349	43	10	2	0	1	6	13	8
vs. Left	.205	.404	.333	39	8	2	0	1	5	13	7
vs. Right	.500	.500	.500	4	2	0	0	0	1	0	1
At Home	.200	.333	.280	25	5	2	0	0	1	5	5
On Road	.278	.500	.444	18	5	0	0	1	5	8	3

FOUR YEAR TOTALS (1984 – 1987)	AVG	OBP	SLG	AB	H	2B	3B	HR	RBI	BB	SO
Totals	.270	.374	.424	820	221	35	4	28	121	139	111
vs. Left	.253	.372	.442	344	87	18	1	15	55	67	45
vs. Right	.282	.376	.412	476	134	17	3	13	66	72	66
At Home	.277	.383	.459	386	107	18	2	16	60	68	53
On Road	.263	.367	.394	434	114	17	2	12	61	71	58

Lopez, Aurelio Alejandro (Rios)

Bats: Right   Throws: Right   Born 10/05/48

1987 SEASON AND MAJOR-LEAGUE CAREER PITCHING TOTALS

	G	GS	CG	GF	IP	BFP	H	R	ER	HR	SH	SF	HB	TBB	IBB	SO	WP	Bk	W	L	Pct	ShO	Sv	ERA
87 HOU	26	0	0	5	38	164	39	22	19	6	5	2	2	12	0	21	1	0	2	1	.667	0	1	4.50
11 YEARS	459	9	0	281	910	3818	785	392	360	102	45	43	15	367	39	635	34	4	62	36	.633	0	93	3.56

1987: Finesse, Flyball   1986: Finesse, Flyball   1985: Power, Flyball   1984: Power, Flyball

	1987 SEASON											FOUR YEAR TOTALS (1984 – 1987)											
	G	IP	H	BB	SO	SB	CS	W	L	S	ERA		G	IP	H	BB	SO	SB	CS	W	L	S	ERA
Totals	26	37.2	39	12	21	5	2	2	1	1	4.54		193	339.2	294	130	212	33	15	18	12	27	3.71
At Home	15	21.0	16	4	10	3	1	2	0	1	2.14		103	185.0	163	59	103	19	9	9	5	12	3.79
On Road	11	16.2	23	8	11	2	1	0	1	0	7.56		90	154.2	131	71	109	14	6	9	7	15	3.61
vs. Opposing Batters	AVG	OBP	SLG	AB	H	2B	3B	HR	RBI	BB	SO		AVG	OBP	SLG	AB	H	2B	3B	HR	RBI	BB	SO
Totals	.273	.333	.455	143	39	6	1	6	29	12	21		.235	.307	.385	1253	294	45	7	43	189	130	212
vs. Left	.292	.370	.415	65	19	2	0	2	12	6	10		.227	.311	.359	618	140	18	2	20	89	74	109
vs. Right	.256	.302	.487	78	20	4	1	4	17	6	11		.243	.303	.409	635	154	27	5	23	100	56	103

Loynd, Michael Wallace "Mike"

Bats: Right   Throws: Right   Born 03/26/64

1987 SEASON AND MAJOR-LEAGUE CAREER PITCHING TOTALS

	G	GS	CG	GF	IP	BFP	H	R	ER	HR	SH	SF	HB	TBB	IBB	SO	WP	Bk	W	L	Pct	ShO	Sv	ERA
87 TEX	26	8	0	6	69	328	82	53	47	14	1	2	1	38	0	48	4	0	1	5	.167	0	1	6.13
2 YEARS	35	16	0	7	111	521	131	83	72	18	2	4	3	57	1	81	6	0	3	7	.300	0	2	5.84

1987: Power, Flyball   1986: Power, Groundball

	1987 SEASON											FOUR YEAR TOTALS (1984 – 1987)											
	G	IP	H	BB	SO	SB	CS	W	L	S	ERA		G	IP	H	BB	SO	SB	CS	W	L	S	ERA
Totals	26	69.1	82	38	48	16	4	1	5	1	6.10		35	111.1	131	57	81	23	9	3	7	2	5.82
At Home	14	46.0	54	28	32	11	1	1	3	0	6.26		20	78.1	86	39	59	16	5	3	4	1	5.63
On Road	12	23.1	28	10	16	5	3	0	2	1	5.79		15	33.0	45	18	22	7	4	0	3	1	6.27
vs. Opposing Batters	AVG	OBP	SLG	AB	H	2B	3B	HR	RBI	BB	SO		AVG	OBP	SLG	AB	H	2B	3B	HR	RBI	BB	SO
Totals	.287	.370	.486	286	82	13	1	14	53	38	48		.288	.368	.462	455	131	21	2	18	77	57	81
vs. Left	.313	.392	.522	134	42	4	0	8	24	17	16		.299	.372	.467	214	64	10	1	8	31	24	28
vs. Right	.263	.351	.454	152	40	9	1	6	29	21	32		.278	.365	.456	241	67	11	1	10	46	33	53

Lucas, Gary Paul

Bats: Left   Throws: Left   Born 11/08/54

1987 SEASON AND MAJOR-LEAGUE CAREER PITCHING TOTALS

	G	GS	CG	GF	IP	BFP	H	R	ER	HR	SH	SF	HB	TBB	IBB	SO	WP	Bk	W	L	Pct	ShO	Sv	ERA
87 CAL	48	0	0	21	74	320	66	41	30	7	7	2	2	35	5	44	3	1	1	5	.167	0	3	3.65
8 YEARS	409	18	0	206	669	2795	618	274	224	41	51	27	7	227	65	410	24	5	29	44	.397	0	63	3.01

1987: Power, Groundball   1986: Finesse, Flyball   1985: Finesse, Flyball   1984: Power, Groundball

	1987 SEASON											FOUR YEAR TOTALS (1984 – 1987)											
	G	IP	H	BB	SO	SB	CS	W	L	S	ERA		G	IP	H	BB	SO	SB	CS	W	L	S	ERA
Totals	48	74.1	66	36	44	4	0	1	5	3	3.63		179	240.2	228	86	148	24	5	11	11	15	3.22
At Home	26	45.1	30	17	27	1	0	1	2	1	2.58		91	142.1	111	41	86	10	4	7	3	7	2.28
On Road	22	29.0	36	19	17	3	0	0	3	2	5.28		88	98.1	117	45	62	14	1	4	8	8	4.58
vs. Opposing Batters	AVG	OBP	SLG	AB	H	2B	3B	HR	RBI	BB	SO		AVG	OBP	SLG	AB	H	2B	3B	HR	RBI	BB	SO
Totals	.241	.329	.365	274	66	11	1	7	43	36	44		.252	.317	.365	905	228	40	4	18	113	86	148
vs. Left	.281	.383	.448	96	27	5	1	3	19	17	16		.276	.342	.393	308	85	16	1	6	44	32	57
vs. Right	.219	.298	.320	178	39	6	0	4	24	19	28		.240	.304	.350	597	143	24	3	12	69	54	91

Lusader, Scott Edward

Bats: Left   Throws: Left   Born 09/30/64

1987 SEASON AND MAJOR-LEAGUE CAREER BATTING TOTALS

	G	AB	H	2B	3B	HR	TB	R	RBI	TBB	IBB	SO	HP	SH	SF	SB	CS	SB%	GDP	AVG	OBP	SLG
87 DET	23	47	15	3	1	1	23	8	8	5	1	7	0	1	1	1	0	1.00	0	.319	.377	.489
1 YEAR	23	47	15	3	1	1	23	8	8	5	1	7	0	1	1	1	0	1.00	0	.319	.377	.489

	1987 SEASON										FOUR YEAR TOTALS (1984 – 1987)									
	AVG	OBP	SLG	AB	H	2B	3B	HR	RBI	BB	SO	AVG	OBP	SLG	AB	H	2B	3B	HR	RBI	BB	SO
Totals	.319	.377	.489	47	15	3	1	1	8	5	7	.319	.377	.489	47	15	3	1	1	8	5	7
vs. Left	.250	.250	.375	8	2	1	0	0	0	0	1	.250	.250	.375	8	2	1	0	0	0	0	1
vs. Right	.333	.400	.513	39	13	2	1	1	8	5	6	.333	.400	.513	39	13	2	1	1	8	5	6
At Home	.303	.368	.424	33	10	1	0	1	6	4	5	.303	.368	.424	33	10	1	0	1	6	4	5
On Road	.357	.400	.643	14	5	2	1	0	2	1	2	.357	.400	.643	14	5	2	1	0	2	1	2

Lynch, Edward Francis "Ed"

Bats: Right   Throws: Right   Born 02/25/56

1987 SEASON AND MAJOR-LEAGUE CAREER PITCHING TOTALS

	G	GS	CG	GF	IP	BFP	H	R	ER	HR	SH	SF	HB	TBB	IBB	SO	WP	Bk	W	L	Pct	ShO	Sv	ERA
87 CHN	58	8	0	19	110	498	130	74	66	17	6	1	2	48	7	80	1	0	2	9	.182	0	4	5.40
8 YEARS	248	119	8	49	940	4003	1050	470	418	89	42	27	14	229	33	396	10	6	47	54	.465	2	8	4.00

1987: Power, Flyball   1986: Finesse, Flyball   1985: Finesse, Flyball   1984: Finesse, Flyball

1987 SEASON

	G	IP	H	BB	SO	SB	CS	W	L	S	ERA
Totals	58	110.2	130	48	80	4	7	2	9	4	5.37
At Home	29	55.2	67	22	41	3	4	0	3	3	4.53
On Road	29	55.0	63	26	39	1	3	2	6	1	6.22

vs. Opposing Batters	AVG	OBP	SLG	AB	H	2B	3B	HR	RBI	BB	SO
Totals	.295	.366	.488	441	130	20	7	17	79	48	80
vs. Left	.330	.408	.534	206	68	10	7	6	37	26	30
vs. Right	.264	.328	.447	235	62	10	0	11	42	22	50

FOUR YEAR TOTALS (1984 – 1987)

	G	IP	H	BB	SO	SB	CS	W	L	S	ERA
	153	527.0	594	122	265	12	23	28	30	6	4.15
	77	281.0	321	55	139	6	14	16	15	5	3.84
	76	246.0	273	67	126	6	9	12	15	1	4.46

	AVG	OBP	SLG	AB	H	2B	3B	HR	RBI	BB	SO
	.285	.325	.438	2081	594	102	18	60	273	122	265
	.310	.350	.478	1069	331	54	15	32	136	66	105
	.260	.299	.396	1012	263	48	3	28	137	56	160

Lyons, Barry Stephen

Bats: Right   Throws: Right   Born 06/03/60

1987 SEASON AND MAJOR-LEAGUE CAREER BATTING TOTALS

	G	AB	H	2B	3B	HR	TB	R	RBI	TBB	IBB	SO	HP	SH	SF	SB	CS	SB%	GDP	AVG	OBP	SLG
87 NYN	53	130	33	4	1	4	51	15	24	8	1	24	2	0	3	0	0	.00	1	.254	.301	.392
2 YEARS	59	139	33	4	1	4	51	16	26	9	2	26	2	0	3	0	0	.00	1	.237	.288	.367

1987 SEASON

	AVG	OBP	SLG	AB	H	2B	3B	HR	RBI	BB	SO
Totals	.254	.301	.392	130	33	4	1	4	24	8	24
vs. Left	.250	.318	.350	40	10	1	0	1	3	4	7
vs. Right	.256	.293	.411	90	23	3	1	3	21	4	17
At Home	.259	.343	.500	58	15	2	0	4	13	6	11
On Road	.250	.263	.306	72	18	2	1	0	11	2	13

FOUR YEAR TOTALS (1984 – 1987)

	AVG	OBP	SLG	AB	H	2B	3B	HR	RBI	BB	SO
	.237	.288	.367	139	33	4	1	4	26	9	26
	.222	.300	.311	45	10	1	0	1	4	5	9
	.245	.282	.394	94	23	3	1	3	22	4	17
	.242	.333	.468	62	15	2	0	4	14	7	12
	.234	.247	.286	77	18	2	1	0	12	2	14

Lyons, Stephen John "Steve"

Bats: Left   Throws: Right   Born 06/03/60

1987 SEASON AND MAJOR-LEAGUE CAREER BATTING TOTALS

	G	AB	H	2B	3B	HR	TB	R	RBI	TBB	IBB	SO	HP	SH	SF	SB	CS	SB%	GDP	AVG	OBP	SLG
87 CHA	76	193	54	11	1	1	70	26	19	12	0	37	0	4	1	3	1	.75	4	.280	.320	.363
3 YEARS	310	811	208	34	7	7	277	108	69	63	2	148	2	10	8	19	16	.54	10	.256	.309	.342

1987 SEASON

	AVG	OBP	SLG	AB	H	2B	3B	HR	RBI	BB	SO
Totals	.280	.320	.363	193	54	11	1	1	19	12	37
vs. Left	.320	.320	.360	25	8	1	0	0	2	0	6
vs. Right	.274	.320	.363	168	46	10	1	1	17	12	31
At Home	.280	.316	.336	107	30	6	0	0	12	6	23
On Road	.279	.326	.395	86	24	5	1	1	7	6	14

FOUR YEAR TOTALS (1984 – 1987)

	AVG	OBP	SLG	AB	H	2B	3B	HR	RBI	BB	SO
	.256	.309	.342	811	208	34	7	7	69	63	148
	.272	.313	.360	125	34	2	3	1	12	8	31
	.254	.308	.338	686	174	32	4	6	57	55	117
	.264	.319	.358	424	112	17	4	5	44	35	74
	.248	.298	.323	387	96	17	3	2	25	28	74

Mack, Shane Lee

Bats: Right   Throws: Right   Born 12/07/63

1987 SEASON AND MAJOR-LEAGUE CAREER BATTING TOTALS

	G	AB	H	2B	3B	HR	TB	R	RBI	TBB	IBB	SO	HP	SH	SF	SB	CS	SB%	GDP	AVG	OBP	SLG
87 SD	105	238	57	11	3	4	86	28	25	18	0	47	3	6	2	4	6	.40	11	.239	.299	.361
1 YEAR	105	238	57	11	3	4	86	28	25	18	0	47	3	6	2	4	6	.40	11	.239	.299	.361

1987 SEASON

	AVG	OBP	SLG	AB	H	2B	3B	HR	RBI	BB	SO
Totals	.239	.299	.361	238	57	11	3	4	25	18	47
vs. Left	.265	.313	.417	132	35	4	2	4	20	7	24
vs. Right	.208	.282	.292	106	22	7	1	0	5	11	23
At Home	.225	.293	.396	111	25	7	3	2	15	10	26
On Road	.252	.304	.331	127	32	4	0	2	10	8	21

FOUR YEAR TOTALS (1984 – 1987)

	AVG	OBP	SLG	AB	H	2B	3B	HR	RBI	BB	SO
	.239	.299	.361	238	57	11	3	4	25	18	47
	.265	.313	.417	132	35	4	2	4	20	7	24
	.208	.282	.292	106	22	7	1	0	5	11	23
	.225	.293	.396	111	25	7	3	2	15	10	26
	.252	.304	.331	127	32	4	0	2	10	8	21

Maddux, Gregory Alan "Greg"

Bats: Right　　Throws: Right　　Born 04/14/66

1987 SEASON AND MAJOR-LEAGUE CAREER PITCHING TOTALS

	G	GS	CG	GF	IP	BFP	H	R	ER	HR	SH	SF	HB	TBB	IBB	SO	WP	Bk	W	L	Pct	ShO	Sv	ERA
87 CHN	30	27	1	2	156	701	181	111	97	17	7	1	4	74	13	101	4	7	6	14	.300	1	0	5.60
2 YEARS	36	32	2	3	187	845	225	131	116	20	8	1	5	85	15	121	6	7	8	18	.308	1	0	5.58

1987: Power, Groundball　　　1986: Finesse, Groundball

	1987 SEASON											FOUR YEAR TOTALS (1984 – 1987)										
	G	IP	H	BB	SO	SB	CS	W	L	S	ERA	G	IP	H	BB	SO	SB	CS	W	L	S	ERA
Totals	30	155.2	181	74	101	33	9	6	14	0	5.61	36	186.2	225	85	121	37	10	8	18	0	5.59
At Home	14	79.1	84	34	63	13	5	1	6	0	4.65	16	83.2	94	37	65	14	6	1	8	0	5.16
On Road	16	76.1	97	40	38	20	4	5	8	0	6.60	20	103.0	131	48	56	23	4	7	10	0	5.94

vs. Opposing Batters	AVG	OBP	SLG	AB	H	2B	3B	HR	RBI	BB	SO	AVG	OBP	SLG	AB	H	2B	3B	HR	RBI	BB	SO
Totals	.294	.373	.452	615	181	36	5	17	99	74	101	.302	.376	.457	746	225	44	6	20	115	85	121
vs. Left	.326	.408	.494	334	109	26	3	8	57	46	47	.326	.407	.486	387	126	29	3	9	63	52	53
vs. Right	.256	.331	.402	281	72	10	2	9	42	28	54	.276	.343	.426	359	99	15	3	11	52	33	68

Magadan, David Joseph "Dave"

Bats: Left　　Throws: Right　　Born 09/30/62

1987 SEASON AND MAJOR-LEAGUE CAREER BATTING TOTALS

	G	AB	H	2B	3B	HR	TB	R	RBI	TBB	IBB	SO	HP	SH	SF	SB	CS	SB%	GDP	AVG	OBP	SLG
87 NYN	85	192	61	13	1	3	85	21	24	22	2	22	0	1	1	0	0	.00	5	.318	.386	.443
2 YEARS	95	210	69	13	1	3	93	24	27	25	2	23	0	1	1	0	0	.00	6	.329	.398	.443

	1987 SEASON										FOUR YEAR TOTALS (1984 – 1987)									
	AVG	OBP	SLG	AB	H	2B	3B	HR	RBI	BB	SO	AVG	OBP	SLG	AB	H	2B	3B	HR	RBI	BB	SO
Totals	.318	.386	.443	192	61	13	1	3	24	22	22	.329	.398	.443	210	69	13	1	3	27	25	23
vs. Left	.438	.481	.625	48	21	3	0	2	14	5	4	.412	.456	.588	51	21	3	0	2	14	5	4
vs. Right	.278	.354	.382	144	40	10	1	1	10	17	18	.302	.380	.396	159	48	10	1	1	13	20	19
At Home	.382	.451	.539	89	34	8	0	2	16	12	10	.396	.467	.528	106	42	8	0	2	19	15	10
On Road	.262	.327	.359	103	27	5	1	1	8	10	12	.260	.325	.356	104	27	5	1	1	8	10	13

Magrane, Joseph David "Joe"

Bats: Right　　Throws: Left　　Born 07/02/64

1987 SEASON AND MAJOR-LEAGUE CAREER PITCHING TOTALS

	G	GS	CG	GF	IP	BFP	H	R	ER	HR	SH	SF	HB	TBB	IBB	SO	WP	Bk	W	L	Pct	ShO	Sv	ERA
87 STL	27	26	4	0	170	722	157	75	67	9	9	3	10	60	6	101	9	7	9	7	.563	2	0	3.55
1 YEAR	27	26	4	0	170	722	157	75	67	9	9	3	10	60	6	101	9	7	9	7	.563	2	0	3.55

1987: Finesse, Groundball

	1987 SEASON											FOUR YEAR TOTALS (1984 – 1987)										
	G	IP	H	BB	SO	SB	CS	W	L	S	ERA	G	IP	H	BB	SO	SB	CS	W	L	S	ERA
Totals	27	170.1	157	60	101	17	3	9	7	0	3.54	27	170.1	157	60	101	17	3	9	7	0	3.54
At Home	13	86.1	81	30	50	12	0	5	2	0	2.81	13	86.1	81	30	50	12	0	5	2	0	2.81
On Road	14	84.0	76	30	51	5	3	4	5	0	4.29	14	84.0	76	30	51	5	3	4	5	0	4.29

vs. Opposing Batters	AVG	OBP	SLG	AB	H	2B	3B	HR	RBI	BB	SO	AVG	OBP	SLG	AB	H	2B	3B	HR	RBI	BB	SO
Totals	.245	.318	.337	641	157	28	2	9	63	60	101	.245	.318	.337	641	157	28	2	9	63	60	101
vs. Left	.226	.301	.312	93	21	3	1	1	8	9	21	.226	.301	.312	93	21	3	1	1	8	9	21
vs. Right	.248	.321	.341	548	136	25	1	8	55	51	80	.248	.321	.341	548	136	25	1	8	55	51	80

Manning, Richard Eugene "Rick"

Bats: Left　　Throws: Right　　Born 09/02/54

1987 SEASON AND MAJOR-LEAGUE CAREER BATTING TOTALS

	G	AB	H	2B	3B	HR	TB	R	RBI	TBB	IBB	SO	HP	SH	SF	SB	CS	SB%	GDP	AVG	OBP	SLG
87 MIL	97	114	26	7	1	0	35	21	13	12	0	18	0	2	1	4	0	1.00	3	.228	.299	.307
13 YEARS	1555	5248	1349	189	43	56	1792	664	458	471	33	616	9	61	43	168	78	.68	104	.257	.317	.341

	1987 SEASON										FOUR YEAR TOTALS (1984 – 1987)									
	AVG	OBP	SLG	AB	H	2B	3B	HR	RBI	BB	SO	AVG	OBP	SLG	AB	H	2B	3B	HR	RBI	BB	SO
Totals	.228	.299	.307	114	26	7	1	0	13	12	18	.240	.301	.358	876	210	33	10	17	89	77	89
vs. Left	.333	.348	.429	21	7	2	0	0	4	1	3	.224	.270	.335	170	38	5	1	4	27	12	24
vs. Right	.204	.288	.280	93	19	5	1	0	9	11	15	.244	.308	.364	706	172	28	9	13	62	65	65
At Home	.238	.333	.310	42	10	3	0	0	6	6	7	.234	.297	.345	380	89	14	5	6	34	34	37
On Road	.222	.278	.306	72	16	4	1	0	9	6	11	.244	.304	.369	496	121	19	5	11	55	43	52

Martinez, Edgar

Bats: Right   Throws: Right   Born 01/02/63

1987 SEASON AND MAJOR-LEAGUE CAREER BATTING TOTALS

	G	AB	H	2B	3B	HR	TB	R	RBI	TBB	IBB	SO	HP	SH	SF	SB	CS	SB%	GDP	AVG	OBP	SLG
87 SEA	13	43	16	5	2	0	25	6	5	2	0	5	1	0	0	0	0	.00	0	.372	.413	.581
1 YEAR	13	43	16	5	2	0	25	6	5	2	0	5	1	0	0	0	0	.00	0	.372	.413	.581

1987 SEASON												FOUR YEAR TOTALS (1984 – 1987)										
	AVG	OBP	SLG	AB	H	2B	3B	HR	RBI	BB	SO	AVG	OBP	SLG	AB	H	2B	3B	HR	RBI	BB	SO
Totals	.372	.413	.581	43	16	5	2	0	5	2	5	.372	.413	.581	43	16	5	2	0	5	2	5
vs. Left	.214	.313	.286	14	3	1	0	0	0	1	2	.214	.313	.286	14	3	1	0	0	0	1	2
vs. Right	.448	.467	.724	29	13	4	2	0	5	1	3	.448	.467	.724	29	13	4	2	0	5	1	3
At Home	.308	.400	.615	13	4	2	1	0	1	1	1	.308	.400	.615	13	4	2	1	0	1	1	1
On Road	.400	.419	.567	30	12	3	1	0	4	1	4	.400	.419	.567	30	12	3	1	0	4	1	4

Marzano, John Robert

Bats: Right   Throws: Right   Born 02/14/63

1987 SEASON AND MAJOR-LEAGUE CAREER BATTING TOTALS

	G	AB	H	2B	3B	HR	TB	R	RBI	TBB	IBB	SO	HP	SH	SF	SB	CS	SB%	GDP	AVG	OBP	SLG
87 BOS	52	168	41	11	0	5	67	20	24	7	0	41	3	2	2	0	1	.00	3	.244	.283	.399
1 YEAR	52	168	41	11	0	5	67	20	24	7	0	41	3	2	2	0	1	.00	3	.244	.283	.399

1987 SEASON												FOUR YEAR TOTALS (1984 – 1987)										
	AVG	OBP	SLG	AB	H	2B	3B	HR	RBI	BB	SO	AVG	OBP	SLG	AB	H	2B	3B	HR	RBI	BB	SO
Totals	.244	.283	.399	168	41	11	0	5	24	7	41	.244	.283	.399	168	41	11	0	5	24	7	41
vs. Left	.209	.271	.279	43	9	3	0	0	3	3	13	.209	.271	.279	43	9	3	0	0	3	3	13
vs. Right	.256	.288	.440	125	32	8	0	5	21	4	28	.256	.288	.440	125	32	8	0	5	21	4	28
At Home	.273	.309	.477	88	24	6	0	4	14	2	25	.273	.309	.477	88	24	6	0	4	14	2	25
On Road	.213	.256	.313	80	17	5	0	1	10	5	16	.213	.256	.313	80	17	5	0	1	10	5	16

Mason, Michael Paul "Mike"

Bats: Left   Throws: Left   Born 11/21/58

1987 SEASON AND MAJOR-LEAGUE CAREER PITCHING TOTALS

	G	GS	CG	GF	IP	BFP	H	R	ER	HR	SH	SF	HB	TBB	IBB	SO	WP	Bk	W	L	Pct	ShO	Sv	ERA
87 TEX-CHN	25	10	0	3	67	315	80	45	42	10	4	4	5	45	2	49	2	0	4	3	.571	0	0	5.64
6 YEARS	135	90	7	14	599	2598	617	327	297	64	20	26	11	240	14	356	17	3	29	38	.433	2	0	4.46

1987: Power, Flyball   1986: Power, Groundball   1985: Finesse, Flyball   1984: Finesse, Groundball

1987 SEASON											FOUR YEAR TOTALS (1984 – 1987)										
	G	IP	H	BB	SO	SB	CS	W	L	S	ERA	G	IP	H	BB	SO	SB	CS	W	L	S	ERA
Totals	25	67.0	80	45	49	9	1	4	3	0	5.64	126	565.1	586	225	339	48	15	28	34	0	4.39
At Home	10	29.0	35	29	23	5	1	1	1	0	6.52	58	270.1	286	114	188	23	6	13	14	0	4.59
On Road	15	38.0	45	16	26	4	0	3	2	0	4.97	68	295.0	300	111	151	25	9	15	20	0	4.24

vs. Opposing Batters	AVG	OBP	SLG	AB	H	2B	3B	HR	RBI	BB	SO	AVG	OBP	SLG	AB	H	2B	3B	HR	RBI	BB	SO
Totals	.311	.418	.490	257	80	14	1	10	47	45	49	.270	.339	.411	2174	586	96	14	61	270	225	339
vs. Left	.340	.446	.604	53	18	2	0	4	15	9	10	.275	.351	.403	447	123	19	1	12	59	51	63
vs. Right	.304	.411	.461	204	62	12	1	6	32	36	39	.268	.336	.413	1727	463	77	13	49	211	174	276

Mathews, Gregory Inman "Greg"

Bats: Both   Throws: Left   Born 05/17/63

1987 SEASON AND MAJOR-LEAGUE CAREER PITCHING TOTALS

	G	GS	CG	GF	IP	BFP	H	R	ER	HR	SH	SF	HB	TBB	IBB	SO	WP	Bk	W	L	Pct	ShO	Sv	ERA
87 STL	32	32	2	0	198	822	184	87	82	17	9	2	0	71	5	108	7	2	11	11	.500	1	0	3.73
2 YEARS	55	54	3	1	343	1413	323	148	141	32	16	3	2	115	8	175	12	8	22	19	.537	1	0	3.70

1987: Finesse, Flyball   1986: Finesse, Flyball

1987 SEASON											FOUR YEAR TOTALS (1984 – 1987)										
	G	IP	H	BB	SO	SB	CS	W	L	S	ERA	G	IP	H	BB	SO	SB	CS	W	L	S	ERA
Totals	32	197.2	184	71	108	13	7	11	11	0	3.73	55	343.0	323	115	175	20	15	22	19	0	3.70
At Home	17	102.1	99	33	55	6	3	6	7	0	4.05	25	156.0	144	46	79	8	4	11	9	0	3.75
On Road	15	95.1	85	38	53	7	4	5	4	0	3.40	30	187.0	179	69	96	12	11	11	10	0	3.66

vs. Opposing Batters	AVG	OBP	SLG	AB	H	2B	3B	HR	RBI	BB	SO	AVG	OBP	SLG	AB	H	2B	3B	HR	RBI	BB	SO
Totals	.249	.314	.385	740	184	44	3	17	70	71	108	.253	.314	.394	1277	323	76	4	32	124	115	175
vs. Left	.240	.321	.336	125	30	6	0	2	15	15	14	.242	.311	.356	219	53	11	1	4	23	22	27
vs. Right	.250	.312	.395	615	154	38	3	15	55	56	94	.255	.315	.402	1058	270	65	3	28	101	93	148

Matthews, Gary Nathaniel

Bats: Right   Throws: Right   Born 07/05/50

1987 SEASON AND MAJOR-LEAGUE CAREER BATTING TOTALS

	G	AB	H	2B	3B	HR	TB	R	RBI	TBB	IBB	SO	HP	SH	SF	SB	CS	SB%	GDP	AVG	OBP	SLG
87 CHN-SEA	89	161	39	4	0	3	52	13	23	19	1	33	0	0	1	0	1	.00	7	.242	.320	.323
16 YEARS	2033	7147	2011	319	51	234	3134	1083	978	940	46	1125	21	19	62	183	74	.71	179	.281	.364	.439

	1987 SEASON										FOUR YEAR TOTALS (1984 – 1987)									
	AVG	OBP	SLG	AB	H	2B	3B	HR	RBI	BB	SO	AVG	OBP	SLG	AB	H	2B	3B	HR	RBI	BB	SO
Totals	.242	.320	.323	161	39	4	0	3	23	19	33	.264	.375	.424	1320	348	53	3	51	191	241	253
vs. Left	.244	.333	.305	82	20	2	0	1	9	11	16	.298	.390	.455	413	123	15	1	16	59	65	57
vs. Right	.241	.307	.342	79	19	2	0	2	14	8	17	.248	.369	.410	907	225	38	2	35	132	176	196
At Home	.250	.329	.391	64	16	3	0	2	14	8	17	.272	.384	.463	614	167	24	3	29	106	113	131
On Road	.237	.315	.278	97	23	1	0	1	9	11	16	.256	.368	.391	706	181	29	0	22	85	128	122

Matuszek, Leonard James "Len"

Bats: Left   Throws: Right   Born 09/27/54

1987 SEASON AND MAJOR-LEAGUE CAREER BATTING TOTALS

	G	AB	H	2B	3B	HR	TB	R	RBI	TBB	IBB	SO	HP	SH	SF	SB	CS	SB%	GDP	AVG	OBP	SLG
87 LA	16	15	1	0	0	0	1	0	0	1	0	4	0	0	0	0	0	.00	0	.067	.125	.067
7 YEARS	379	820	192	40	5	30	332	113	119	88	9	168	7	3	14	8	10	.44	19	.234	.309	.405

	1987 SEASON										FOUR YEAR TOTALS (1984 – 1987)									
	AVG	OBP	SLG	AB	H	2B	3B	HR	RBI	BB	SO	AVG	OBP	SLG	AB	H	2B	3B	HR	RBI	BB	SO
Totals	.067	.125	.067	15	1	0	0	0	0	1	4	.245	.331	.434	539	132	26	2	24	84	69	119
vs. Left	.000	.000	.000	1	0	0	0	0	0	0	0	.161	.217	.196	56	9	2	0	0	3	3	17
vs. Right	.071	.133	.071	14	1	0	0	0	0	1	4	.255	.345	.462	483	123	24	2	24	81	66	102
At Home	.000	.000	.000	6	0	0	0	0	0	0	2	.257	.352	.433	245	63	7	0	12	43	36	47
On Road	.111	.200	.111	9	1	0	0	0	0	1	2	.235	.313	.435	294	69	19	2	12	41	33	72

Mazzilli, Lee Louis

Bats: Both   Throws: Right   Born 03/25/55

1987 SEASON AND MAJOR-LEAGUE CAREER BATTING TOTALS

	G	AB	H	2B	3B	HR	TB	R	RBI	TBB	IBB	SO	HP	SH	SF	SB	CS	SB%	GDP	AVG	OBP	SLG
87 NYN	88	124	38	8	1	3	57	26	24	21	3	14	0	0	3	5	3	.63	3	.306	.399	.460
12 YEARS	1331	3882	1025	184	24	87	1518	540	430	596	40	576	17	12	29	188	89	.68	58	.264	.362	.391

	1987 SEASON										FOUR YEAR TOTALS (1984 – 1987)									
	AVG	OBP	SLG	AB	H	2B	3B	HR	RBI	BB	SO	AVG	OBP	SLG	AB	H	2B	3B	HR	RBI	BB	SO
Totals	.306	.399	.460	124	38	8	1	3	24	21	14	.260	.380	.368	658	171	32	3	11	69	128	109
vs. Left	.341	.420	.477	44	15	0	0	2	12	6	3	.261	.354	.341	138	36	2	0	3	22	20	26
vs. Right	.287	.388	.450	80	23	8	1	1	12	15	11	.260	.387	.375	520	135	30	3	8	47	108	83
At Home	.429	.514	.679	56	24	5	0	3	17	13	5	.297	.414	.425	313	93	17	1	7	41	66	52
On Road	.206	.289	.279	68	14	3	1	0	7	8	9	.226	.349	.316	345	78	15	2	4	28	62	57

McCaskill, Kirk Edward

Bats: Right   Throws: Right   Born 04/09/61

1987 SEASON AND MAJOR-LEAGUE CAREER PITCHING TOTALS

	G	GS	CG	GF	IP	BFP	H	R	ER	HR	SH	SF	HB	TBB	IBB	SO	WP	Bk	W	L	Pct	ShO	Sv	ERA
87 CAL	14	13	1	0	75	334	84	52	47	14	3	1	2	34	0	56	1	0	4	6	.400	1	0	5.64
3 YEARS	78	75	17	1	511	2154	480	255	238	56	11	11	11	190	2	360	16	2	33	28	.541	4	0	4.19

1987: Power, Flyball   1986: Power, Flyball   1985: Finesse, Groundball

	1987 SEASON										FOUR YEAR TOTALS (1984 – 1987)								
	G	IP	H	BB	SO	SB	CS	W	L	S	ERA	G	IP	H	BB	SO	SB	CS	W	L	S	ERA
Totals	14	74.2	84	34	56	1	5	4	6	0	5.67	78	510.2	480	190	360	14	18	33	28	0	4.18
At Home	5	28.2	31	12	19	0	1	1	1	0	5.02	35	238.2	212	75	157	6	8	14	10	0	3.85
On Road	9	46.0	53	22	37	1	4	3	5	0	6.07	43	272.0	268	115	203	8	10	19	18	0	4.50

vs. Opposing Batters	AVG	OBP	SLG	AB	H	2B	3B	HR	RBI	BB	SO	AVG	OBP	SLG	AB	H	2B	3B	HR	RBI	BB	SO
Totals	.286	.363	.463	294	84	10	0	14	45	34	56	.249	.316	.385	1931	480	74	11	56	225	190	360
vs. Left	.314	.382	.532	156	49	7	0	9	26	16	21	.263	.332	.406	1066	280	46	7	31	122	110	165
vs. Right	.254	.342	.384	138	35	3	0	5	19	18	35	.231	.297	.360	865	200	28	4	25	103	80	195

McClendon, Lloyd Glenn

Bats: Right   Throws: Right   Born 01/11/59

1987 SEASON AND MAJOR-LEAGUE CAREER BATTING TOTALS

	G	AB	H	2B	3B	HR	TB	R	RBI	TBB	IBB	SO	HP	SH	SF	SB	CS	SB%	GDP	AVG	OBP	SLG
87 CIN	45	72	15	5	0	2	26	8	13	4	0	15	0	0	1	1	0	1.00	1	.208	.247	.361
1 YEAR	45	72	15	5	0	2	26	8	13	4	0	15	0	0	1	1	0	1.00	1	.208	.247	.361

	1987 SEASON											FOUR YEAR TOTALS (1984 – 1987)										
	AVG	OBP	SLG	AB	H	2B	3B	HR	RBI	BB	SO	AVG	OBP	SLG	AB	H	2B	3B	HR	RBI	BB	SO
Totals	.208	.247	.361	72	15	5	0	2	13	4	15	.208	.247	.361	72	15	5	0	2	13	4	15
vs. Left	.184	.200	.342	38	7	3	0	1	5	1	11	.184	.200	.342	38	7	3	0	1	5	1	11
vs. Right	.235	.297	.382	34	8	2	0	1	8	3	4	.235	.297	.382	34	8	2	0	1	8	3	4
At Home	.152	.194	.182	33	5	1	0	0	4	2	4	.152	.194	.182	33	5	1	0	0	4	2	4
On Road	.256	.293	.513	39	10	4	0	2	9	2	11	.256	.293	.513	39	10	4	0	2	9	2	11

McClure, Robert Craig "Bob"

Bats: Right   Throws: Left   Born 04/29/52

1987 SEASON AND MAJOR-LEAGUE CAREER PITCHING TOTALS

	G	GS	CG	GF	IP	BFP	H	R	ER	HR	SH	SF	HB	TBB	IBB	SO	WP	Bk	W	L	Pct	ShO	Sv	ERA
87 MON	52	0	0	16	52	222	47	30	20	8	5	2	0	20	3	33	0	1	6	1	.857	0	5	3.46
13 YEARS	476	73	12	164	977	4225	942	468	416	86	41	38	27	428	31	590	23	23	54	49	.524	1	46	3.83

1987: Finesse, Flyball   1986: Power, Groundball   1985: Power, Flyball   1984: Finesse, Flyball

	1987 SEASON											FOUR YEAR TOTALS (1984 – 1987)										
	G	IP	H	BB	SO	SB	CS	W	L	S	ERA	G	IP	H	BB	SO	SB	CS	W	L	S	ERA
Totals	52	52.2	47	20	33	3	2	6	1	5	3.42	194	357.0	363	135	211	14	13	18	16	15	3.96
At Home	29	30.2	29	14	22	1	2	4	0	3	3.23	95	184.0	194	67	111	9	10	13	6	6	3.82
On Road	23	22.0	18	6	11	2	0	2	1	2	3.68	99	173.0	169	68	100	5	3	5	10	9	4.11
vs. Opposing Batters	AVG	OBP	SLG	AB	H	2B	3B	HR	RBI	BB	SO	AVG	OBP	SLG	AB	H	2B	3B	HR	RBI	BB	SO
Totals	.241	.309	.431	195	47	9	2	8	29	20	33	.267	.332	.402	1365	364	64	14	31	187	135	211
vs. Left	.175	.230	.363	80	14	4	1	3	7	6	17	.221	.286	.347	389	86	13	6	8	52	36	82
vs. Right	.287	.362	.478	115	33	5	1	5	22	14	16	.285	.350	.424	976	278	51	8	23	135	99	129

McGregor, Scott Houston

Bats: Both   Throws: Left   Born 01/18/54

1987 SEASON AND MAJOR-LEAGUE CAREER PITCHING TOTALS

	G	GS	CG	GF	IP	BFP	H	R	ER	HR	SH	SF	HB	TBB	IBB	SO	WP	Bk	W	L	Pct	ShO	Sv	ERA
87 BAL	26	15	1	4	85	393	112	69	63	15	6	5	3	35	1	39	3	4	2	7	.222	1	0	6.67
12 YEARS	352	305	83	24	2123	8900	2218	1013	932	232	76	73	26	511	26	894	28	12	138	105	.568	23	5	3.95

1987: Finesse, Flyball   1986: Finesse, Flyball   1985: Finesse, Flyball   1984: Finesse, Flyball

	1987 SEASON											FOUR YEAR TOTALS (1984 – 1987)										
	G	IP	H	BB	SO	SB	CS	W	L	S	ERA	G	IP	H	BB	SO	SB	CS	W	L	S	ERA
Totals	26	85.1	112	35	39	8	9	2	7	0	6.64	125	688.2	770	211	287	48	28	42	48	0	4.70
At Home	15	42.0	57	19	26	6	5	0	5	0	6.43	64	353.1	385	101	160	24	12	24	23	0	4.08
On Road	11	43.1	55	16	13	2	4	2	2	0	6.85	61	335.1	385	110	127	24	16	18	25	0	5.37
vs. Opposing Batters	AVG	OBP	SLG	AB	H	2B	3B	HR	RBI	BB	SO	AVG	OBP	SLG	AB	H	2B	3B	HR	RBI	BB	SO
Totals	.326	.388	.509	344	112	14	2	15	61	35	39	.284	.335	.451	2715	770	116	16	102	341	211	287
vs. Left	.242	.324	.339	62	15	0	0	2	11	7	8	.243	.282	.441	564	137	21	2	29	79	30	69
vs. Right	.344	.403	.546	282	97	14	2	13	50	28	31	.294	.349	.453	2151	633	95	14	73	262	181	218

McGriff, Frederick Stanley "Fred"

Bats: Left   Throws: Left   Born 10/31/63

1987 SEASON AND MAJOR-LEAGUE CAREER BATTING TOTALS

	G	AB	H	2B	3B	HR	TB	R	RBI	TBB	IBB	SO	HP	SH	SF	SB	CS	SB%	GDP	AVG	OBP	SLG
87 TOR	107	295	73	16	0	20	149	58	43	60	4	104	1	0	0	3	2	.60	3	.247	.376	.505
2 YEARS	110	300	74	16	0	20	150	59	43	60	4	106	1	0	0	3	2	.60	3	.247	.374	.500

	1987 SEASON											FOUR YEAR TOTALS (1984 – 1987)										
	AVG	OBP	SLG	AB	H	2B	3B	HR	RBI	BB	SO	AVG	OBP	SLG	AB	H	2B	3B	HR	RBI	BB	SO
Totals	.247	.376	.505	295	73	16	0	20	43	60	104	.247	.374	.500	300	74	16	0	20	43	60	106
vs. Left	.154	.241	.346	26	4	2	0	1	1	3	14	.154	.241	.346	26	4	2	0	1	1	3	14
vs. Right	.257	.388	.520	269	69	14	0	19	42	57	90	.255	.386	.515	274	70	14	0	19	42	57	92
At Home	.223	.368	.453	139	31	11	0	7	19	31	52	.229	.372	.457	140	32	11	0	7	19	31	52
On Road	.269	.384	.551	156	42	5	0	13	24	29	52	.262	.376	.538	160	42	5	0	13	24	29	54

McGriff, Terence Roy "Terry"

Bats: Right   Throws: Right   Born 09/23/63

1987 SEASON AND MAJOR-LEAGUE CAREER BATTING TOTALS

	G	AB	H	2B	3B	HR	TB	R	RBI	TBB	IBB	SO	HP	SH	SF	SB	CS	SB%	GDP	AVG	OBP	SLG
87 CIN	34	89	20	3	0	2	29	6	11	8	0	17	0	0	0	0	0	.00	3	.225	.289	.326
1 YEAR	34	89	20	3	0	2	29	6	11	8	0	17	0	0	0	0	0	.00	3	.225	.289	.326

	1987 SEASON										FOUR YEAR TOTALS (1984 – 1987)									
	AVG	OBP	SLG	AB	H	2B	3B	HR	RBI	BB	SO	AVG	OBP	SLG	AB	H	2B	3B	HR	RBI	BB	SO
Totals	.225	.289	.326	89	20	3	0	2	11	8	17	.225	.289	.326	89	20	3	0	2	11	8	17
vs. Left	.235	.350	.294	17	4	1	0	0	0	3	4	.235	.350	.294	17	4	1	0	0	0	3	4
vs. Right	.222	.273	.333	72	16	2	0	2	11	5	13	.222	.273	.333	72	16	2	0	2	11	5	13
At Home	.333	.389	.455	33	11	1	0	1	5	3	6	.333	.389	.455	33	11	1	0	1	5	3	6
On Road	.161	.230	.250	56	9	2	0	1	6	5	11	.161	.230	.250	56	9	2	0	1	6	5	11

McRae, Harold Abraham "Hal"

Bats: Right   Throws: Right   Born 07/10/45

1987 SEASON AND MAJOR-LEAGUE CAREER BATTING TOTALS

	G	AB	H	2B	3B	HR	TB	R	RBI	TBB	IBB	SO	HP	SH	SF	SB	CS	SB%	GDP	AVG	OBP	SLG
87 KC	18	32	10	3	0	1	16	5	9	5	1	1	0	0	0	0	0	.00	1	.313	.405	.500
19 YEARS	2084	7218	2091	484	66	191	3280	940	1097	648	69	779	79	28	85	109	78	.58	186	.290	.351	.454

	1987 SEASON										FOUR YEAR TOTALS (1984 – 1987)									
	AVG	OBP	SLG	AB	H	2B	3B	HR	RBI	BB	SO	AVG	OBP	SLG	AB	H	2B	3B	HR	RBI	BB	SO
Totals	.313	.405	.500	32	10	3	0	1	9	5	1	.273	.341	.413	947	259	49	4	25	158	101	132
vs. Left	.438	.571	.750	16	7	2	0	1	6	5	0	.284	.362	.462	476	135	30	2	17	84	63	60
vs. Right	.188	.188	.250	16	3	1	0	0	3	0	1	.263	.318	.363	471	124	19	2	8	74	38	72
At Home	.227	.320	.455	22	5	2	0	1	6	3	0	.282	.350	.423	485	137	29	3	11	90	53	62
On Road	.500	.583	.600	10	5	1	0	0	3	2	1	.264	.331	.403	462	122	20	1	14	68	48	70

Meacham, Robert Andrew "Bob"

Bats: Both   Throws: Right   Born 08/25/60

1987 SEASON AND MAJOR-LEAGUE CAREER BATTING TOTALS

	G	AB	H	2B	3B	HR	TB	R	RBI	TBB	IBB	SO	HP	SH	SF	SB	CS	SB%	GDP	AVG	OBP	SLG
87 NYA	77	203	55	11	1	5	83	28	21	19	0	33	6	3	1	6	5	.55	2	.271	.349	.409
5 YEARS	410	1256	299	49	8	8	388	184	107	126	1	254	18	44	13	51	23	.69	17	.238	.314	.309

	1987 SEASON										FOUR YEAR TOTALS (1984 – 1987)									
	AVG	OBP	SLG	AB	H	2B	3B	HR	RBI	BB	SO	AVG	OBP	SLG	AB	H	2B	3B	HR	RBI	BB	SO
Totals	.271	.349	.409	203	55	11	1	5	21	19	33	.238	.314	.310	1205	287	47	8	8	103	122	244
vs. Left	.306	.379	.459	85	26	4	0	3	14	10	16	.255	.328	.333	439	112	17	4	3	42	45	91
vs. Right	.246	.328	.373	118	29	7	1	2	7	9	17	.228	.306	.298	766	175	30	4	5	61	77	153
At Home	.280	.352	.409	93	26	6	0	2	10	7	14	.242	.314	.316	582	141	23	4	4	47	57	125
On Road	.264	.347	.409	110	29	5	1	3	11	12	19	.234	.314	.305	623	146	24	4	4	56	65	119

Meads, David Donald "Dave"

Bats: Left   Throws: Left   Born 01/07/64

1987 SEASON AND MAJOR-LEAGUE CAREER PITCHING TOTALS

	G	GS	CG	GF	IP	BFP	H	R	ER	HR	SH	SF	HB	TBB	IBB	SO	WP	Bk	W	L	Pct	ShO	Sv	ERA
87 HOU	45	0	0	21	49	209	60	31	30	8	2	3	1	16	2	32	1	0	5	3	.625	0	0	5.51
1 YEAR	45	0	0	21	49	209	60	31	30	8	2	3	1	16	2	32	1	0	5	3	.625	0	0	5.51

1987: Finesse, Flyball

	1987 SEASON										FOUR YEAR TOTALS (1984 – 1987)									
	G	IP	H	BB	SO	SB	CS	W	L	S	ERA	G	IP	H	BB	SO	SB	CS	W	L	S	ERA
Totals	45	48.2	60	16	32	4	1	5	3	0	5.55	45	48.2	60	16	32	4	1	5	3	0	5.55
At Home	20	22.0	22	3	13	2	1	5	0	0	3.27	20	22.0	22	3	13	2	1	5	0	0	3.27
On Road	25	26.2	38	13	19	2	0	0	3	0	7.43	25	26.2	38	13	19	2	0	0	3	0	7.43

	AVG	OBP	SLG	AB	H	2B	3B	HR	RBI	BB	SO	AVG	OBP	SLG	AB	H	2B	3B	HR	RBI	BB	SO
vs. Opposing Batters																						
Totals	.321	.372	.535	187	60	8	4	8	30	16	32	.321	.372	.535	187	60	8	4	8	30	16	32
vs. Left	.268	.317	.411	56	15	2	0	2	7	4	11	.268	.317	.411	56	15	2	0	2	7	4	11
vs. Right	.344	.395	.588	131	45	6	4	6	23	12	21	.344	.395	.588	131	45	6	4	6	23	12	21

Melvin, Robert Paul "Bob"

Bats: Right Throws: Right Born 10/28/61

1987 SEASON AND MAJOR-LEAGUE CAREER BATTING TOTALS

	G	AB	H	2B	3B	HR	TB	R	RBI	TBB	IBB	SO	HP	SH	SF	SB	CS	SB%	GDP	AVG	OBP	SLG
87 SF	84	246	49	8	0	11	90	31	31	17	3	44	0	0	2	0	4	.00	7	.199	.249	.366
3 YEARS	214	596	127	26	3	16	207	65	60	35	4	134	0	5	5	3	6	.33	15	.213	.255	.347

	1987 SEASON										FOUR YEAR TOTALS (1984 – 1987)									
	AVG	OBP	SLG	AB	H	2B	3B	HR	RBI	BB	SO	AVG	OBP	SLG	AB	H	2B	3B	HR	RBI	BB	SO
Totals	.199	.249	.366	246	49	8	0	11	31	17	44	.213	.255	.347	596	127	26	3	16	60	35	134
vs. Left	.242	.272	.414	99	24	2	0	5	16	4	8	.274	.313	.432	241	66	12	1	8	29	14	36
vs. Right	.170	.235	.333	147	25	6	0	6	15	13	36	.172	.216	.290	355	61	14	2	8	31	21	98
At Home	.175	.221	.360	114	20	3	0	6	16	7	15	.199	.229	.337	267	53	13	0	8	27	11	51
On Road	.220	.273	.371	132	29	5	0	5	15	10	29	.225	.275	.356	329	74	13	3	8	33	24	83

Mercado, Orlando (Rodriguez)

Bats: Right Throws: Right Born 11/07/61

1987 SEASON AND MAJOR-LEAGUE CAREER BATTING TOTALS

	G	AB	H	2B	3B	HR	TB	R	RBI	TBB	IBB	SO	HP	SH	SF	SB	CS	SB%	GDP	AVG	OBP	SLG
87 DET-LA	17	27	6	1	0	0	7	3	2	3	0	1	0	0	0	0	0	.00	0	.222	.300	.259
5 YEARS	168	402	84	16	4	3	117	26	36	27	0	58	3	4	4	3	3	.50	9	.209	.261	.291

	1987 SEASON										FOUR YEAR TOTALS (1984 – 1987)									
	AVG	OBP	SLG	AB	H	2B	3B	HR	RBI	BB	SO	AVG	OBP	SLG	AB	H	2B	3B	HR	RBI	BB	SO
Totals	.222	.300	.259	27	6	1	0	0	2	3	1	.227	.277	.285	207	47	5	2	1	14	13	26
vs. Left	.238	.333	.286	21	5	1	0	0	2	3	0	.225	.309	.282	71	16	1	0	1	4	9	6
vs. Right	.167	.167	.167	6	1	0	0	0	0	0	1	.228	.259	.287	136	31	4	2	0	10	4	20
At Home	.154	.214	.154	13	2	0	0	0	0	1	0	.255	.300	.343	102	26	2	2	1	9	7	12
On Road	.286	.375	.357	14	4	1	0	0	2	2	1	.200	.254	.229	105	21	3	0	0	5	6	14

Miller, Darrell Keith

Bats: Right Throws: Right Born 02/26/59

1987 SEASON AND MAJOR-LEAGUE CAREER BATTING TOTALS

	G	AB	H	2B	3B	HR	TB	R	RBI	TBB	IBB	SO	HP	SH	SF	SB	CS	SB%	GDP	AVG	OBP	SLG
87 CAL	53	108	26	5	0	4	43	14	16	9	0	13	2	2	3	1	0	1.00	5	.241	.303	.398
4 YEARS	154	254	64	9	2	6	95	33	28	18	0	40	3	2	4	1	1	.50	8	.252	.305	.374

	1987 SEASON										TWO YEAR TOTALS (1986 – 1987)									
	AVG	OBP	SLG	AB	H	2B	3B	HR	RBI	BB	SO	AVG	OBP	SLG	AB	H	2B	3B	HR	RBI	BB	SO
Totals	.241	.303	.398	108	26	5	0	4	16	9	13	.236	.296	.364	165	39	7	1	4	20	13	21
vs. Left	.255	.311	.400	55	14	2	0	2	8	4	8	.232	.292	.358	95	22	4	1	2	11	8	14
vs. Right	.226	.295	.396	53	12	3	0	2	8	5	5	.243	.295	.371	70	17	3	0	2	9	5	7
At Home	.297	.352	.484	64	19	3	0	3	11	5	5	.273	.320	.409	88	24	3	0	3	13	6	9
On Road	.159	.235	.273	44	7	2	0	1	5	4	8	.195	.264	.312	77	15	4	1	1	7	7	12

Miller, Keith Alan

Bats: Right Throws: Right Born 06/12/63

1987 SEASON AND MAJOR-LEAGUE CAREER BATTING TOTALS

	G	AB	H	2B	3B	HR	TB	R	RBI	TBB	IBB	SO	HP	SH	SF	SB	CS	SB%	GDP	AVG	OBP	SLG
87 NYN	25	51	19	2	2	0	25	14	1	2	0	6	1	3	0	8	1	.89	1	.373	.407	.490
1 YEAR	25	51	19	2	2	0	25	14	1	2	0	6	1	3	0	8	1	.89	1	.373	.407	.490

	1987 SEASON										FOUR YEAR TOTALS (1984 – 1987)									
	AVG	OBP	SLG	AB	H	2B	3B	HR	RBI	BB	SO	AVG	OBP	SLG	AB	H	2B	3B	HR	RBI	BB	SO
Totals	.373	.407	.490	51	19	2	2	0	1	2	6	.373	.407	.490	51	19	2	2	0	1	2	6
vs. Left	.476	.476	.667	21	10	0	2	0	1	0	1	.476	.476	.667	21	10	0	2	0	1	0	1
vs. Right	.300	.364	.367	30	9	2	0	0	0	2	5	.300	.364	.367	30	9	2	0	0	0	2	5
At Home	.292	.292	.375	24	7	0	1	0	0	0	2	.292	.292	.375	24	7	0	1	0	0	0	2
On Road	.444	.500	.593	27	12	2	1	0	1	2	4	.444	.500	.593	27	12	2	1	0	1	2	4

Milner, Eddie James
Bats: Left   Throws: Left   Born 05/21/55

1987 SEASON AND MAJOR-LEAGUE CAREER BATTING TOTALS

	G	AB	H	2B	3B	HR	TB	R	RBI	TBB	IBB	SO	HP	SH	SF	SB	CS	SB%	GDP	AVG	OBP	SLG
87 SF	101	214	54	14	0	4	80	38	19	24	3	33	0	1	0	10	9	.53	2	.252	.328	.374
8 YEARS	781	2344	598	110	28	42	890	373	193	282	14	271	6	22	9	143	70	.67	28	.255	.335	.380

1987 SEASON	AVG	OBP	SLG	AB	H	2B	3B	HR	RBI	BB	SO
Totals	.252	.328	.374	214	54	14	0	4	19	24	33
vs. Left	.156	.229	.156	32	5	0	0	0	0	3	12
vs. Right	.269	.345	.412	182	49	14	0	4	19	21	21
At Home	.236	.317	.400	110	26	6	0	4	8	13	13
On Road	.269	.339	.346	104	28	8	0	0	11	11	20

FOUR YEAR TOTALS (1984 – 1987)	AVG	OBP	SLG	AB	H	2B	3B	HR	RBI	BB	SO
Totals	.250	.330	.379	1427	357	63	17	29	128	172	170
vs. Left	.210	.298	.262	214	45	6	1	1	13	27	45
vs. Right	.257	.337	.400	1213	312	57	16	28	115	145	125
At Home	.261	.344	.409	689	180	32	8	18	65	89	77
On Road	.240	.318	.351	738	177	31	9	11	63	83	93

Minton, Gregory Brian "Greg"
Bats: Both   Throws: Right   Born 07/29/51

1987 SEASON AND MAJOR-LEAGUE CAREER PITCHING TOTALS

	G	GS	CG	GF	IP	BFP	H	R	ER	HR	SH	SF	HB	TBB	IBB	SO	WP	Bk	W	L	Pct	ShO	Sv	ERA
87 SF-CAL	56	0	0	29	99	418	101	37	35	6	6	2	2	39	7	44	3	0	6	4	.600	0	11	3.18
13 YEARS	593	7	0	362	947	4045	928	389	338	37	68	31	10	405	116	387	49	8	50	56	.472	0	135	3.21

1987: Finesse, Groundball   1986: Finesse, Groundball   1985: Finesse, Groundball   1984: Finesse, Groundball

1987 SEASON	G	IP	H	BB	SO	SB	CS	W	L	S	ERA
Totals	56	99.1	101	39	44	3	1	6	5	11	3.17
At Home	22	46.1	49	18	19	1	1	3	2	4	3.11
On Road	34	53.0	52	21	25	2	0	3	3	7	3.23

vs. Opposing Batters	AVG	OBP	SLG	AB	H	2B	3B	HR	RBI	BB	SO
Totals	.274	.345	.369	369	101	15	1	6	44	39	44
vs. Left	.282	.353	.376	170	48	5	1	3	23	19	15
vs. Right	.266	.338	.362	199	53	10	0	3	21	20	29

FOUR YEAR TOTALS (1984 – 1987)	G	IP	H	BB	SO	SB	CS	W	L	S	ERA
Totals	246	389.0	392	184	163	43	17	19	22	39	3.59
At Home	107	174.2	174	68	69	17	7	9	9	17	3.45
On Road	139	214.1	218	116	94	26	10	10	13	22	3.70

vs. Opposing Batters	AVG	OBP	SLG	AB	H	2B	3B	HR	RBI	BB	SO
Totals	.267	.349	.361	1466	392	53	9	22	204	184	163
vs. Left	.290	.381	.386	651	189	25	5	9	101	96	52
vs. Right	.249	.323	.341	815	203	28	4	13	103	88	111

Mirabella, Paul Thomas
Bats: Left   Throws: Left   Born 03/20/54

1987 SEASON AND MAJOR-LEAGUE CAREER PITCHING TOTALS

	G	GS	CG	GF	IP	BFP	H	R	ER	HR	SH	SF	HB	TBB	IBB	SO	WP	Bk	W	L	Pct	ShO	Sv	ERA
87 MIL	29	0	0	9	29	133	30	20	16	0	2	3	0	16	3	14	2	0	2	1	.667	0	2	4.97
10 YEARS	203	31	3	56	366	1654	398	226	197	30	22	17	10	184	19	191	15	1	13	25	.342	1	9	4.84

1987: Finesse, Groundball   1986: Power, Groundball

1987 SEASON	G	IP	H	BB	SO	SB	CS	W	L	S	ERA
Totals	29	29.1	30	16	14	0	1	2	1	2	4.91
At Home	14	12.2	17	6	8	0	1	0	1	2	3.55
On Road	15	16.2	13	10	6	0	0	2	0	0	5.94

vs. Opposing Batters	AVG	OBP	SLG	AB	H	2B	3B	HR	RBI	BB	SO
Totals	.265	.348	.354	113	30	6	2	0	29	16	14
vs. Left	.289	.382	.378	45	13	2	1	0	17	8	7
vs. Right	.250	.325	.338	68	17	4	1	0	12	8	7

TWO YEAR TOTALS (1986 – 1987)	G	IP	H	BB	SO	SB	CS	W	L	S	ERA
Totals	37	35.2	43	19	20	1	1	2	1	2	5.55
At Home	19	15.1	24	7	10	1	1	0	1	2	4.70
On Road	18	20.1	19	12	10	0	0	2	0	0	6.20

vs. Opposing Batters	AVG	OBP	SLG	AB	H	2B	3B	HR	RBI	BB	SO
Totals	.299	.373	.417	144	43	8	3	1	40	19	20
vs. Left	.278	.379	.389	54	15	2	2	0	21	10	11
vs. Right	.311	.370	.433	90	28	6	1	1	19	9	9

Mitchell, John Kyle
Bats: Right   Throws: Right   Born 08/11/65

1987 SEASON AND MAJOR-LEAGUE CAREER PITCHING TOTALS

	G	GS	CG	GF	IP	BFP	H	R	ER	HR	SH	SF	HB	TBB	IBB	SO	WP	Bk	W	L	Pct	ShO	Sv	ERA
87 NYN	20	19	1	0	112	493	124	64	51	6	6	5	2	36	3	57	7	1	3	6	.333	0	0	4.10
2 YEARS	24	20	1	1	122	533	134	68	55	7	6	5	2	40	3	59	9	1	3	7	.300	0	0	4.06

1987: Finesse, Groundball   1986: Finesse, Groundball

1987 SEASON	G	IP	H	BB	SO	SB	CS	W	L	S	ERA
Totals	20	111.2	124	36	57	8	7	3	6	0	4.11
At Home	11	68.1	71	26	36	1	5	3	1	0	3.95
On Road	9	43.1	53	10	21	7	2	0	5	0	4.36

vs. Opposing Batters	AVG	OBP	SLG	AB	H	2B	3B	HR	RBI	BB	SO
Totals	.279	.333	.365	444	124	18	1	6	55	36	57
vs. Left	.292	.354	.358	243	71	8	1	2	25	24	24
vs. Right	.264	.306	.373	201	53	10	0	4	30	12	33

FOUR YEAR TOTALS (1984 – 1987)	G	IP	H	BB	SO	SB	CS	W	L	S	ERA
Totals	24	121.2	134	40	59	8	9	3	7	0	4.07
At Home	14	77.1	80	30	37	1	7	3	2	0	3.96
On Road	10	44.1	54	10	22	7	2	0	5	0	4.26

vs. Opposing Batters	AVG	OBP	SLG	AB	H	2B	3B	HR	RBI	BB	SO
Totals	.279	.334	.369	480	134	20	1	7	59	40	59
vs. Left	.287	.351	.349	258	74	8	1	2	25	26	24
vs. Right	.270	.314	.392	222	60	12	0	5	34	14	35

Moore, Charles William "Charlie"

Bats: Right   Throws: Right   Born 06/21/53

1987 SEASON AND MAJOR-LEAGUE CAREER BATTING TOTALS

	G	AB	H	2B	3B	HR	TB	R	RBI	TBB	IBB	SO	HP	SH	SF	SB	CS	SB%	GDP	AVG	OBP	SLG
87 TOR	51	107	23	10	1	1	38	15	7	13	0	12	1	4	0	0	0	.00	2	.215	.306	.355
15 YEARS	1334	4033	1052	187	43	36	1433	456	408	346	12	470	11	71	21	51	57	.47	104	.261	.319	.355

	1987 SEASON										FOUR YEAR TOTALS (1984 – 1987)								
	AVG	OBP	SLG	AB	H	2B	3B	HR	RBI	BB	SO	AVG	OBP	SLG	AB	H	2B	3B	HR	RBI	BB	SO
Totals	.215	.306	.355	107	23	10	1	1	7	13	12	.238	.295	.327	879	209	42	9	6	94	71	129
vs. Left	.231	.320	.363	91	21	10	1	0	4	12	9	.260	.322	.369	396	103	22	6	3	43	36	44
vs. Right	.125	.222	.313	16	2	0	0	1	3	1	3	.219	.273	.292	483	106	20	3	3	51	35	85
At Home	.224	.333	.429	49	11	7	0	1	2	8	5	.264	.314	.380	439	116	27	6	4	48	32	61
On Road	.207	.281	.293	58	12	3	1	0	5	5	7	.211	.277	.273	440	93	15	3	2	46	39	68

Morris, John Daniel

Bats: Left   Throws: Left   Born 02/23/61

1987 SEASON AND MAJOR-LEAGUE CAREER BATTING TOTALS

	G	AB	H	2B	3B	HR	TB	R	RBI	TBB	IBB	SO	HP	SH	SF	SB	CS	SB%	GDP	AVG	OBP	SLG
87 STL	101	157	41	6	4	3	64	22	23	11	4	22	1	1	0	5	2	.71	2	.261	.314	.408
2 YEARS	140	257	65	6	5	4	93	30	37	18	6	37	1	1	1	11	4	.73	4	.253	.303	.362

	1987 SEASON										FOUR YEAR TOTALS (1984 – 1987)								
	AVG	OBP	SLG	AB	H	2B	3B	HR	RBI	BB	SO	AVG	OBP	SLG	AB	H	2B	3B	HR	RBI	BB	SO
Totals	.261	.314	.408	157	41	6	4	3	23	11	22	.253	.303	.362	257	65	6	5	4	37	18	37
vs. Left	.200	.200	.250	20	4	1	0	0	3	0	4	.303	.324	.333	33	10	1	0	0	8	1	6
vs. Right	.270	.329	.431	137	37	5	4	3	20	11	18	.246	.300	.366	224	55	5	5	4	29	17	31
At Home	.232	.293	.435	69	16	3	4	1	10	6	10	.231	.297	.389	108	25	3	4	2	15	10	17
On Road	.284	.330	.386	88	25	3	0	2	13	5	12	.268	.308	.342	149	40	3	1	2	22	8	20

Moses, John William

Bats: Both   Throws: Left   Born 08/09/57

1987 SEASON AND MAJOR-LEAGUE CAREER BATTING TOTALS

	G	AB	H	2B	3B	HR	TB	R	RBI	TBB	IBB	SO	HP	SH	SF	SB	CS	SB%	GDP	AVG	OBP	SLG
87 SEA	116	390	96	16	4	3	129	58	38	29	2	49	3	8	3	23	15	.61	6	.246	.301	.331
6 YEARS	386	1060	263	42	10	7	346	147	86	83	5	152	5	15	7	70	41	.63	20	.248	.304	.326

	1987 SEASON										FOUR YEAR TOTALS (1984 – 1987)								
	AVG	OBP	SLG	AB	H	2B	3B	HR	RBI	BB	SO	AVG	OBP	SLG	AB	H	2B	3B	HR	RBI	BB	SO
Totals	.246	.301	.331	390	96	16	4	3	38	29	49	.251	.304	.326	886	222	33	8	6	77	67	127
vs. Left	.209	.277	.256	129	27	3	0	1	8	11	11	.242	.311	.319	260	63	9	1	3	16	25	28
vs. Right	.264	.313	.368	261	69	13	4	2	30	18	38	.254	.301	.329	626	159	24	7	3	61	42	99
At Home	.220	.286	.294	214	47	8	1	2	15	17	26	.227	.294	.309	475	108	17	5	4	35	41	64
On Road	.278	.319	.375	176	49	8	3	1	23	12	23	.277	.316	.345	411	114	16	3	2	42	26	63

Mulliniks, Steven Rance "Rance"

Bats: Left   Throws: Right   Born 01/15/56

1987 SEASON AND MAJOR-LEAGUE CAREER BATTING TOTALS

	G	AB	H	2B	3B	HR	TB	R	RBI	TBB	IBB	SO	HP	SH	SF	SB	CS	SB%	GDP	AVG	OBP	SLG
87 TOR	124	332	103	28	1	11	166	37	44	34	1	55	0	3	3	1	1	.50	10	.310	.371	.500
11 YEARS	946	2620	717	178	13	54	1083	332	318	303	15	395	7	19	23	12	11	.52	71	.274	.348	.413

	1987 SEASON										FOUR YEAR TOTALS (1984 – 1987)								
	AVG	OBP	SLG	AB	H	2B	3B	HR	RBI	BB	SO	AVG	OBP	SLG	AB	H	2B	3B	HR	RBI	BB	SO
Totals	.310	.371	.500	332	103	28	1	11	44	34	55	.297	.369	.452	1389	412	97	7	35	188	164	213
vs. Left	.389	.450	.667	18	7	2	0	1	2	2	4	.284	.377	.403	67	19	5	0	1	4	10	14
vs. Right	.306	.367	.490	314	96	26	1	10	42	32	51	.297	.368	.455	1322	393	92	7	34	184	154	199
At Home	.315	.364	.531	162	51	15	1	6	23	13	32	.303	.376	.469	671	203	56	4	16	94	80	111
On Road	.306	.378	.471	170	52	13	0	5	21	21	23	.291	.362	.436	718	209	41	3	19	94	84	102

Murphy, Dwayne Keith
Bats: Left   Throws: Right   Born 03/18/55

1987 SEASON AND MAJOR-LEAGUE CAREER BATTING TOTALS

	G	AB	H	2B	3B	HR	TB	R	RBI	TBB	IBB	SO	HP	SH	SF	SB	CS	SB%	GDP	AVG	OBP	SLG
87 OAK	82	219	51	7	0	8	82	39	35	58	2	61	0	3	4	4	4	.50	5	.233	.388	.374
10 YEARS	1213	4047	999	129	20	153	1627	614	563	694	35	883	18	82	45	99	59	.63	90	.247	.356	.402

	1987 SEASON											FOUR YEAR TOTALS (1984 – 1987)										
	AVG	OBP	SLG	AB	H	2B	3B	HR	RBI	BB	SO	AVG	OBP	SLG	AB	H	2B	3B	HR	RBI	BB	SO
Totals	.233	.388	.374	219	51	7	0	8	36	58	61	.245	.353	.418	1630	399	56	8	70	222	273	375
vs. Left	.182	.304	.288	66	12	1	0	2	6	12	22	.218	.305	.359	518	113	11	4	18	60	66	135
vs. Right	.255	.421	.412	153	39	6	0	6	30	46	39	.257	.375	.445	1112	286	45	4	52	162	207	240
At Home	.178	.339	.297	101	18	6	0	2	13	25	27	.225	.345	.363	782	176	28	4	24	86	143	174
On Road	.280	.429	.441	118	33	1	0	6	23	33	34	.263	.361	.468	848	223	28	4	46	136	130	201

Murphy, Robert Albert "Rob"
Bats: Left   Throws: Left   Born 05/26/60

1987 SEASON AND MAJOR-LEAGUE CAREER PITCHING TOTALS

	G	GS	CG	GF	IP	BFP	H	R	ER	HR	SH	SF	HB	TBB	IBB	SO	WP	Bk	W	L	Pct	ShO	Sv	ERA
87 CIN	87	0	0	21	101	415	91	37	34	7	1	2	0	32	5	99	1	0	8	5	.615	0	3	3.03
3 YEARS	123	0	0	35	154	622	119	43	40	8	4	5	0	55	7	136	6	0	14	5	.737	0	4	2.34

1987: Power, Flyball   1986: Power, Groundball   1985: Power, Flyball

	1987 SEASON										FOUR YEAR TOTALS (1984 – 1987)									
	G	IP	H	BB	SO	SB	CS	W	L	S	ERA	G	IP	H	BB	SO	SB	CS	W	L	S	ERA
Totals	87	100.2	91	32	99	10	3	8	5	3	3.04	123	154.0	119	55	136	12	4	14	5	4	2.34
At Home	48	55.0	57	17	54	4	2	5	3	1	3.93	67	83.2	72	31	72	5	2	7	3	2	3.01
On Road	39	45.2	34	15	45	6	1	3	2	2	1.97	56	70.1	47	24	64	7	2	7	2	2	1.54
vs. Opposing Batters	AVG	OBP	SLG	AB	H	2B	3B	HR	RBI	BB	SO	AVG	OBP	SLG	AB	H	2B	3B	HR	RBI	BB	SO
Totals	.239	.297	.355	380	91	17	3	7	38	32	99	.213	.283	.306	558	119	22	3	8	50	55	136
vs. Left	.240	.292	.314	121	29	6	0	1	10	9	33	.208	.265	.268	168	35	7	0	1	13	13	46
vs. Right	.239	.299	.375	259	62	11	3	6	28	23	66	.215	.290	.323	390	84	15	3	7	37	42	90

Musselman, Jeffrey Joseph "Jeff"
Bats: Left   Throws: Left   Born 06/21/63

1987 SEASON AND MAJOR-LEAGUE CAREER PITCHING TOTALS

	G	GS	CG	GF	IP	BFP	H	R	ER	HR	SH	SF	HB	TBB	IBB	SO	WP	Bk	W	L	Pct	ShO	Sv	ERA
87 TOR	68	1	0	14	89	381	75	43	41	7	7	1	3	54	12	54	5	3	12	5	.706	0	3	4.15
2 YEARS	74	1	0	14	94	410	83	50	47	8	7	1	3	59	13	58	5	3	12	5	.706	0	3	4.50

1987: Power, Groundball   1986: Power, Groundball

	1987 SEASON										FOUR YEAR TOTALS (1984 – 1987)									
	G	IP	H	BB	SO	SB	CS	W	L	S	ERA	G	IP	H	BB	SO	SB	CS	W	L	S	ERA
Totals	68	89.0	75	54	54	7	2	12	5	3	4.15	74	94.2	83	59	58	9	3	12	5	3	4.47
At Home	32	40.2	29	27	23	3	1	10	2	0	4.20	34	42.2	31	30	24	5	1	10	2	0	5.06
On Road	36	48.1	46	27	31	4	1	2	3	3	4.10	40	52.0	52	29	34	4	2	2	3	3	3.98
vs. Opposing Batters	AVG	OBP	SLG	AB	H	2B	3B	HR	RBI	BB	SO	AVG	OBP	SLG	AB	H	2B	3B	HR	RBI	BB	SO
Totals	.237	.352	.372	317	75	18	2	7	39	54	54	.243	.359	.384	341	83	18	3	8	48	59	58
vs. Left	.156	.244	.248	109	17	4	0	2	8	11	23	.172	.261	.254	122	21	4	0	2	11	13	26
vs. Right	.279	.405	.438	208	58	14	2	5	31	43	31	.283	.410	.457	219	62	14	3	6	37	46	32

Myers, Randall Kirk "Randy"
Bats: Left   Throws: Left   Born 09/19/62

1987 SEASON AND MAJOR-LEAGUE CAREER PITCHING TOTALS

	G	GS	CG	GF	IP	BFP	H	R	ER	HR	SH	SF	HB	TBB	IBB	SO	WP	Bk	W	L	Pct	ShO	Sv	ERA
87 NYN	54	0	0	18	75	314	61	36	33	6	7	6	0	30	5	92	3	0	3	6	.333	0	6	3.96
3 YEARS	65	0	0	24	88	374	72	41	38	7	7	6	1	40	6	107	3	0	3	6	.333	0	6	3.89

1987: Power, Flyball   1986: Power, Flyball

	1987 SEASON										TWO YEAR TOTALS (1986 – 1987)									
	G	IP	H	BB	SO	SB	CS	W	L	S	ERA	G	IP	H	BB	SO	SB	CS	W	L	S	ERA
Totals	54	74.2	61	30	92	5	2	3	6	6	3.98	64	85.1	72	39	105	5	2	3	6	6	4.01
At Home	27	34.2	30	12	46	2	1	1	0	3	4.41	31	39.2	33	18	52	2	1	1	0	3	4.54
On Road	27	40.0	31	18	46	3	1	2	6	3	3.60	33	45.2	39	21	53	3	1	2	6	3	3.55
vs. Opposing Batters	AVG	OBP	SLG	AB	H	2B	3B	HR	RBI	BB	SO	AVG	OBP	SLG	AB	H	2B	3B	HR	RBI	BB	SO
Totals	.224	.296	.342	272	61	10	2	6	29	30	92	.229	.311	.346	315	72	12	2	7	34	39	105
vs. Left	.173	.244	.296	81	14	3	2	1	6	8	36	.167	.262	.278	90	15	3	2	1	6	12	38
vs. Right	.246	.318	.361	191	47	7	0	5	23	22	56	.253	.331	.373	225	57	9	0	6	28	27	67

Nelson, Robert Augustus "Rob"
Bats: Left   Throws: Left   Born 05/17/64

1987 SEASON AND MAJOR-LEAGUE CAREER BATTING TOTALS

	G	AB	H	2B	3B	HR	TB	R	RBI	TBB	IBB	SO	HP	SH	SF	SB	CS	SB%	GDP	AVG	OBP	SLG
87 OAK-SD	17	35	5	1	0	0	6	1	1	1	0	20	0	1	0	0	0	.00	0	.143	.167	.171
2 YEARS	22	44	7	2	0	0	9	2	1	2	0	24	0	1	0	0	0	.00	0	.159	.196	.205

	1987 SEASON											FOUR YEAR TOTALS (1984 – 1987)										
	AVG	OBP	SLG	AB	H	2B	3B	HR	RBI	BB	SO	AVG	OBP	SLG	AB	H	2B	3B	HR	RBI	BB	SO
Totals	.143	.167	.171	35	5	1	0	0	1	1	20	.159	.196	.205	44	7	2	0	0	1	2	24
vs. Left	.667	.667	.667	3	2	0	0	0	0	0	1	.667	.667	.667	3	2	0	0	0	0	0	1
vs. Right	.094	.121	.125	32	3	1	0	0	1	1	19	.122	.163	.171	41	5	2	0	0	1	2	23
At Home	.250	.250	.313	16	4	1	0	0	1	0	7	.222	.263	.278	18	4	1	0	0	1	1	9
On Road	.053	.100	.053	19	1	0	0	0	0	1	13	.115	.148	.154	26	3	1	0	0	0	1	15

Nelson, Wayland Eugene "Gene"
Bats: Right   Throws: Right   Born 12/03/60

1987 SEASON AND MAJOR-LEAGUE CAREER PITCHING TOTALS

	G	GS	CG	GF	IP	BFP	H	R	ER	HR	SH	SF	HB	TBB	IBB	SO	WP	Bk	W	L	Pct	ShO	Sv	ERA
87 OAK	54	6	0	15	124	530	120	58	54	12	3	5	5	35	0	94	7	0	6	5	.545	0	3	3.92
7 YEARS	214	65	6	60	654	2842	665	345	321	78	26	14	20	264	13	399	32	4	34	39	.466	1	12	4.42

1987: Finesse, Flyball   1986: Finesse, Flyball   1985: Power, Groundball   1984: Finesse, Groundball

	1987 SEASON											FOUR YEAR TOTALS (1984 – 1987)										
	G	IP	H	BB	SO	SB	CS	W	L	S	ERA	G	IP	H	BB	SO	SB	CS	W	L	S	ERA
Totals	54	123.2	120	35	94	5	3	6	5	3	3.93	174	458.2	454	160	301	21	19	25	26	12	4.08
At Home	26	69.2	60	20	58	3	3	4	2	1	3.36	85	230.1	216	85	162	9	11	15	12	3	3.71
On Road	28	54.0	60	15	36	2	0	2	3	2	4.67	89	228.1	238	75	139	12	8	10	14	9	4.49
vs. Opposing Batters	AVG	OBP	SLG	AB	H	2B	3B	HR	RBI	BB	SO	AVG	OBP	SLG	AB	H	2B	3B	HR	RBI	BB	SO
Totals	.249	.304	.411	482	120	28	7	12	64	35	94	.258	.321	.425	1758	454	96	22	51	224	160	301
vs. Left	.259	.300	.393	239	62	12	4	4	32	15	43	.258	.317	.407	857	221	48	10	20	100	76	138
vs. Right	.239	.307	.428	243	58	16	3	8	32	20	51	.259	.325	.442	901	233	48	12	31	124	84	163

Nettles, Graig
Bats: Left   Throws: Right   Born 08/20/44

1987 SEASON AND MAJOR-LEAGUE CAREER BATTING TOTALS

	G	AB	H	2B	3B	HR	TB	R	RBI	TBB	IBB	SO	HP	SH	SF	SB	CS	SB%	GDP	AVG	OBP	SLG
87 ATL	112	177	37	8	1	5	62	16	33	22	4	25	0	0	2	1	0	1.00	6	.209	.294	.350
21 YEARS	2620	8893	2209	324	28	389	3756	1188	1300	1079	92	1190	50	12	88	32	36	.47	193	.248	.330	.422

	1987 SEASON											FOUR YEAR TOTALS (1984 – 1987)										
	AVG	OBP	SLG	AB	H	2B	3B	HR	RBI	BB	SO	AVG	OBP	SLG	AB	H	2B	3B	HR	RBI	BB	SO
Totals	.209	.294	.350	177	37	8	1	5	33	22	25	.234	.328	.398	1366	319	51	3	56	214	193	201
vs. Left	.229	.291	.313	48	11	2	1	0	7	5	7	.185	.258	.327	275	51	13	1	8	37	24	47
vs. Right	.202	.295	.364	129	26	6	0	5	26	17	18	.246	.345	.416	1091	268	38	2	48	177	169	154
At Home	.232	.330	.378	82	19	4	1	2	23	13	10	.242	.346	.427	660	160	24	1	32	132	105	102
On Road	.189	.260	.326	95	18	4	0	3	10	9	15	.225	.312	.371	706	159	27	2	24	82	88	99

Newman, Albert Dwayne "Al"
Bats: Both   Throws: Right   Born 06/30/60

1987 SEASON AND MAJOR-LEAGUE CAREER BATTING TOTALS

	G	AB	H	2B	3B	HR	TB	R	RBI	TBB	IBB	SO	HP	SH	SF	SB	CS	SB%	GDP	AVG	OBP	SLG
87 MIN	110	307	68	15	5	0	93	44	29	34	0	27	0	7	1	15	11	.58	5	.221	.298	.303
3 YEARS	230	521	110	19	5	1	142	74	38	58	2	51	0	11	3	28	23	.55	9	.211	.289	.273

	1987 SEASON											FOUR YEAR TOTALS (1984 – 1987)										
	AVG	OBP	SLG	AB	H	2B	3B	HR	RBI	BB	SO	AVG	OBP	SLG	AB	H	2B	3B	HR	RBI	BB	SO
Totals	.221	.298	.303	307	68	15	5	0	29	34	27	.211	.289	.273	521	110	19	5	1	38	58	51
vs. Left	.319	.407	.489	94	30	10	3	0	11	14	12	.285	.377	.431	144	41	12	3	1	14	22	20
vs. Right	.178	.248	.221	213	38	5	2	0	18	20	15	.183	.253	.212	377	69	7	2	0	24	36	31
At Home	.235	.339	.327	153	36	8	3	0	20	24	15	.213	.312	.273	253	54	9	3	0	26	37	30
On Road	.208	.255	.279	154	32	7	2	0	9	10	12	.209	.266	.272	268	56	10	2	1	12	21	21

Nichols, Thomas Reid "Reid"

Bats: Right Throws: Right Born 08/05/58

	G	AB	H	2B	3B	HR	TB	R	RBI	TBB	IBB	SO	HP	SH	SF	SB	CS	SB%	GDP	AVG	OBP	SLG
1987 SEASON AND MAJOR-LEAGUE CAREER BATTING TOTALS																						
87 MON	77	147	39	8	2	4	63	22	20	14	1	13	1	0	2	2	1	.67	4	.265	.329	.429
8 YEARS	540	1160	308	63	8	22	453	156	131	99	6	149	9	16	10	27	21	.56	16	.266	.326	.391

1987 SEASON	AVG	OBP	SLG	AB	H	2B	3B	HR	RBI	BB	SO
Totals	.265	.329	.429	147	39	8	2	4	20	14	13
vs. Left	.278	.342	.451	133	37	7	2	4	20	13	9
vs. Right	.143	.200	.214	14	2	1	0	0	0	1	4
At Home	.293	.354	.507	75	22	3	2	3	12	7	6
On Road	.236	.305	.347	72	17	5	0	1	8	7	7

FOUR YEAR TOTALS (1984 – 1987)	AVG	OBP	SLG	AB	H	2B	3B	HR	RBI	BB	SO
Totals	.250	.318	.357	557	139	25	4	9	70	54	71
vs. Left	.266	.328	.380	418	111	21	3	7	55	40	50
vs. Right	.201	.288	.288	139	28	4	1	2	15	14	21
At Home	.279	.346	.421	290	81	15	4	6	49	28	36
On Road	.217	.288	.288	267	58	10	0	3	21	26	35

Niedenfuer, Thomas Edward "Tom"

Bats: Right Throws: Right Born 08/13/59

	G	GS	CG	GF	IP	BFP	H	R	ER	HR	SH	SF	HB	TBB	IBB	SO	WP	Bk	W	L	Pct	ShO	Sv	ERA
1987 SEASON AND MAJOR-LEAGUE CAREER PITCHING TOTALS																								
87 LA-BAL	60	0	0	47	68	303	68	37	34	12	0	4	2	31	4	47	3	0	4	5	.444	0	14	4.50
7 YEARS	355	0	0	208	492	2038	430	173	164	42	26	19	10	167	52	387	8	1	33	33	.500	0	77	3.00

1987: Power, Flyball 1986: Power, Flyball 1985: Power, Flyball 1984: Power, Flyball

1987 SEASON	G	IP	H	BB	SO	SB	CS	W	L	S	ERA
Totals	60	69.0	68	31	47	8	4	4	5	14	4.43
At Home	31	35.0	36	13	21	4	0	3	0	7	3.86
On Road	29	34.0	32	18	26	4	4	1	5	7	5.03
vs. Opposing Batters	AVG	OBP	SLG	AB	H	2B	3B	HR	RBI	BB	SO
Totals	.257	.334	.445	265	68	10	2	12	47	31	47
vs. Left	.292	.372	.547	137	40	6	1	9	25	18	19
vs. Right	.219	.295	.336	128	28	4	1	3	22	13	28

FOUR YEAR TOTALS (1984 – 1987)	G	IP	H	BB	SO	SB	CS	W	L	S	ERA
Totals	217	302.2	279	107	249	26	18	19	25	55	3.30
At Home	114	165.2	157	36	133	16	8	10	9	31	3.04
On Road	103	137.0	122	71	116	10	10	9	16	24	3.68
vs. Opposing Batters	AVG	OBP	SLG	AB	H	2B	3B	HR	RBI	BB	SO
Totals	.247	.312	.384	1131	279	49	5	32	152	107	249
vs. Left	.266	.345	.441	590	157	31	3	22	81	72	119
vs. Right	.226	.274	.322	541	122	18	2	10	71	35	130

Niekro, Joseph Franklin "Joe"

Bats: Right Throws: Right Born 11/07/44

	G	GS	CG	GF	IP	BFP	H	R	ER	HR	SH	SF	HB	TBB	IBB	SO	WP	Bk	W	L	Pct	ShO	Sv	ERA
1987 SEASON AND MAJOR-LEAGUE CAREER PITCHING TOTALS																								
87 NYA-MIN	27	26	1	0	147	655	155	101	87	15	2	5	10	64	0	84	13	0	7	13	.350	0	0	5.33
21 YEARS	697	498	107	91	3573	15107	3450	1607	1418	274	126	112	65	1253	71	1740	170	5	220	203	.520	29	16	3.57

1987: Finesse, Groundball 1986: Finesse, Flyball 1985: Finesse, Flyball 1984: Finesse, Groundball

1987 SEASON	G	IP	H	BB	SO	SB	CS	W	L	S	ERA
Totals	27	147.0	155	64	84	32	6	7	13	0	5.33
At Home	9	54.0	54	26	28	12	1	4	4	0	4.50
On Road	18	93.0	101	38	56	20	5	3	9	0	5.81
vs. Opposing Batters	AVG	OBP	SLG	AB	H	2B	3B	HR	RBI	BB	SO
Totals	.270	.351	.420	574	155	33	4	15	79	64	84
vs. Left	.288	.367	.484	306	88	23	2	11	45	38	41
vs. Right	.250	.332	.347	268	67	10	2	4	34	26	43

FOUR YEAR TOTALS (1984 – 1987)	G	IP	H	BB	SO	SB	CS	W	L	S	ERA
Totals	125	746.1	728	323	391	136	30	43	48	0	4.03
At Home	59	350.0	343	170	184	58	18	18	22	0	3.88
On Road	66	396.1	385	153	207	78	12	25	26	0	4.18
vs. Opposing Batters	AVG	OBP	SLG	AB	H	2B	3B	HR	RBI	BB	SO
Totals	.255	.332	.380	2853	728	119	14	70	318	323	391
vs. Left	.271	.359	.405	1417	384	65	7	37	145	195	162
vs. Right	.240	.305	.356	1436	344	54	7	33	173	128	229

Niekro, Philip Henry "Phil"

Bats: Right Throws: Right Born 04/01/39

	G	GS	CG	GF	IP	BFP	H	R	ER	HR	SH	SF	HB	TBB	IBB	SO	WP	Bk	W	L	Pct	ShO	Sv	ERA
1987 SEASON AND MAJOR-LEAGUE CAREER PITCHING TOTALS																								
87 TOR-CLE-AT	L 26	26	2	0	139	637	163	99	97	22	2	5	4	66	1	64	10	3	7	13	.350	0	0	6.28
24 YEARS	864	716	245	83	5404	22678	5044	2337	2012	482	219	102	123	1809	86	3342	226	42	318	274	.537	45	29	3.35

1987: Finesse, Flyball 1986: Finesse, Flyball 1985: Finesse, Flyball 1984: Finesse, Flyball

1987 SEASON	G	IP	H	BB	SO	SB	CS	W	L	S	ERA
Totals	26	138.2	163	66	64	12	8	7	13	0	6.30
At Home	11	55.0	76	32	19	5	2	2	6	0	8.18
On Road	15	83.2	87	34	45	7	6	5	7	0	5.06
vs. Opposing Batters	AVG	OBP	SLG	AB	H	2B	3B	HR	RBI	BB	SO
Totals	.291	.367	.489	560	163	33	6	22	82	66	64
vs. Left	.324	.401	.513	312	101	18	4	11	46	39	28
vs. Right	.250	.324	.460	248	62	15	2	11	36	27	36

FOUR YEAR TOTALS (1984 – 1987)	G	IP	H	BB	SO	SB	CS	W	L	S	ERA
Totals	125	784.2	826	357	430	56	31	50	44	0	4.27
At Home	61	366.1	389	178	191	24	15	24	20	0	4.45
On Road	64	418.1	437	179	239	32	16	26	24	0	4.11
vs. Opposing Batters	AVG	OBP	SLG	AB	H	2B	3B	HR	RBI	BB	SO
Totals	.271	.347	.421	3051	826	145	21	90	361	357	430
vs. Left	.279	.360	.427	1651	460	69	16	48	210	208	186
vs. Right	.261	.332	.413	1400	366	76	5	42	151	149	244

Nielson, Jeffrey Scott "Scott"
Bats: Right   Throws: Right   Born 12/18/58

1987 SEASON AND MAJOR-LEAGUE CAREER PITCHING TOTALS

	G	GS	CG	GF	IP	BFP	H	R	ER	HR	SH	SF	HB	TBB	IBB	SO	WP	Bk	W	L	Pct	ShO	Sv	ERA
87 CHA	19	7	1	7	66	299	83	48	46	9	1	2	1	25	1	23	2	0	3	5	.375	1	2	6.27
2 YEARS	29	16	3	8	122	534	149	77	71	21	1	2	3	37	1	43	2	0	7	9	.438	3	2	5.24

1987: Finesse, Groundball   1986: Finesse, Groundball

1987 SEASON	G	IP	H	BB	SO	SB	CS	W	L	S	ERA
Totals	19	66.1	83	25	23	11	2	3	5	2	6.24
At Home	10	36.1	45	13	11	3	2	2	3	0	6.94
On Road	9	30.0	38	12	12	8	0	1	2	2	5.40

vs. Opposing Batters	AVG	OBP	SLG	AB	H	2B	3B	HR	RBI	BB	SO
Totals	.307	.366	.456	270	83	9	2	9	55	25	23
vs. Left	.292	.338	.408	120	35	4	2	2	16	9	9
vs. Right	.320	.387	.493	150	48	5	0	7	39	16	14

FOUR YEAR TOTALS (1984 – 1987)	G	IP	H	BB	SO	SB	CS	W	L	S	ERA
Totals	29	122.1	149	37	43	14	3	7	9	2	5.22
At Home	14	57.0	77	14	18	5	2	3	6	0	6.79
On Road	15	65.1	72	23	25	9	1	4	3	2	3.86

	AVG	OBP	SLG	AB	H	2B	3B	HR	RBI	BB	SO
Totals	.303	.355	.479	491	149	19	2	21	82	37	43
vs. Left	.307	.356	.455	231	71	6	2	8	31	18	15
vs. Right	.300	.353	.500	260	78	13	0	13	51	19	28

Nieto, Thomas Andrew "Tom"
Bats: Right   Throws: Right   Born 10/27/60

1987 SEASON AND MAJOR-LEAGUE CAREER BATTING TOTALS

	G	AB	H	2B	3B	HR	TB	R	RBI	TBB	IBB	SO	HP	SH	SF	SB	CS	SB%	GDP	AVG	OBP	SLG
87 MIN	41	105	21	7	1	1	33	7	12	8	0	24	3	5	0	0	0	.00	1	.200	.276	.314
4 YEARS	199	509	115	24	4	5	162	34	65	45	11	100	7	11	2	0	3	.00	16	.226	.297	.318

1987 SEASON	AVG	OBP	SLG	AB	H	2B	3B	HR	RBI	BB	SO
Totals	.200	.276	.314	105	21	7	1	1	12	8	24
vs. Left	.279	.295	.442	43	12	4	0	1	6	1	9
vs. Right	.145	.264	.226	62	9	3	1	0	6	7	15
At Home	.203	.288	.288	59	12	3	1	0	2	4	17
On Road	.196	.260	.348	46	9	4	0	1	10	4	7

TWO YEAR TOTALS (1986 – 1987)	AVG	OBP	SLG	AB	H	2B	3B	HR	RBI	BB	SO
Totals	.200	.289	.318	170	34	10	2	2	19	14	45
vs. Left	.229	.280	.343	70	16	5	0	1	9	5	20
vs. Right	.180	.274	.300	100	18	5	2	1	10	9	25
At Home	.191	.276	.287	94	18	4	1	1	5	8	29
On Road	.211	.277	.355	76	16	6	1	1	14	6	16

Nipper, Albert Samuel "Al"
Bats: Right   Throws: Right   Born 04/02/59

1987 SEASON AND MAJOR-LEAGUE CAREER PITCHING TOTALS

	G	GS	CG	GF	IP	BFP	H	R	ER	HR	SH	SF	HB	TBB	IBB	SO	WP	Bk	W	L	Pct	ShO	Sv	ERA
87 BOS	30	30	6	0	174	777	196	115	105	30	8	9	7	62	1	89	5	0	11	12	.478	0	0	5.43
5 YEARS	113	107	21	4	694	3036	739	396	356	86	19	21	28	250	7	342	16	3	42	43	.494	0	0	4.62

1987: Finesse, Groundball   1986: Finesse, Groundball   1985: Power, Groundball   1984: Finesse, Groundball

1987 SEASON	G	IP	H	BB	SO	SB	CS	W	L	S	ERA
Totals	30	174.0	196	62	89	21	5	11	12	0	5.43
At Home	12	73.0	85	25	35	4	3	5	4	0	4.07
On Road	18	101.0	111	37	54	17	2	6	8	0	6.42

vs. Opposing Batters	AVG	OBP	SLG	AB	H	2B	3B	HR	RBI	BB	SO
Totals	.283	.344	.497	692	196	46	6	30	102	62	89
vs. Left	.267	.318	.471	374	100	20	4	16	53	28	43
vs. Right	.302	.374	.528	318	96	26	2	14	49	34	46

FOUR YEAR TOTALS (1984 – 1987)	G	IP	H	BB	SO	SB	CS	W	L	S	ERA
Totals	110	677.2	722	243	337	41	22	41	42	0	4.66
At Home	51	338.2	354	105	167	16	13	18	17	0	3.88
On Road	59	339.0	368	138	170	25	9	23	25	0	5.47

	AVG	OBP	SLG	AB	H	2B	3B	HR	RBI	BB	SO
Totals	.271	.333	.440	2661	722	156	18	86	347	243	337
vs. Left	.275	.340	.426	1410	388	76	13	37	178	138	167
vs. Right	.267	.325	.456	1251	334	80	5	49	169	105	170

Nixon, Otis Junior
Bats: Both   Throws: Right   Born 01/09/59

1987 SEASON AND MAJOR-LEAGUE CAREER BATTING TOTALS

	G	AB	H	2B	3B	HR	TB	R	RBI	TBB	IBB	SO	HP	SH	SF	SB	CS	SB%	GDP	AVG	OBP	SLG
87 CLE	19	17	1	0	0	0	1	2	1	3	0	4	0	0	0	2	3	.40	0	.059	.200	.059
5 YEARS	290	379	80	8	1	3	99	87	19	33	0	59	0	9	1	59	26	.69	5	.211	.274	.261

1987 SEASON	AVG	OBP	SLG	AB	H	2B	3B	HR	RBI	BB	SO
Totals	.059	.200	.059	17	1	0	0	0	1	3	4
vs. Left	.000	.333	.000	2	0	0	0	0	0	1	0
vs. Right	.067	.176	.067	15	1	0	0	0	1	2	4
At Home	.000	.250	.000	6	0	0	0	0	1	2	2
On Road	.091	.167	.091	11	1	0	0	0	0	1	2

TWO YEAR TOTALS (1986 – 1987)	AVG	OBP	SLG	AB	H	2B	3B	HR	RBI	BB	SO
Totals	.232	.326	.286	112	26	4	1	0	9	16	16
vs. Left	.256	.356	.308	39	10	2	0	0	3	6	5
vs. Right	.219	.313	.274	73	16	2	1	0	6	10	11
At Home	.137	.254	.157	51	7	1	0	0	2	8	7
On Road	.311	.391	.393	61	19	3	1	0	7	8	9

Nixon, Robert Donell "Donell"

Bats: Right   Throws: Right   Born 12/31/61

1987 SEASON AND MAJOR-LEAGUE CAREER BATTING TOTALS

	G	AB	H	2B	3B	HR	TB	R	RBI	TBB	IBB	SO	HP	SH	SF	SB	CS	SB%	GDP	AVG	OBP	SLG
87 SEA	46	132	33	4	0	3	46	17	12	13	0	28	2	4	0	21	7	.75	3	.250	.327	.348
1 YEAR	46	132	33	4	0	3	46	17	12	13	0	28	2	4	0	21	7	.75	3	.250	.327	.348

	1987 SEASON											FOUR YEAR TOTALS (1984 – 1987)										
	AVG	OBP	SLG	AB	H	2B	3B	HR	RBI	BB	SO	AVG	OBP	SLG	AB	H	2B	3B	HR	RBI	BB	SO
Totals	.250	.327	.348	132	33	4	0	3	12	13	28	.250	.327	.348	132	33	4	0	3	12	13	28
vs. Left	.262	.326	.333	42	11	0	0	1	4	3	11	.262	.326	.333	42	11	0	0	1	4	3	11
vs. Right	.244	.327	.356	90	22	4	0	2	8	10	17	.244	.327	.356	90	22	4	0	2	8	10	17
At Home	.288	.347	.424	66	19	3	0	2	4	6	16	.288	.347	.424	66	19	3	0	2	4	6	16
On Road	.212	.307	.273	66	14	1	0	1	8	7	12	.212	.307	.273	66	14	1	0	1	8	7	12

Noboa, Miliciades Arturo (Diaz) "Junior"

Bats: Right   Throws: Right   Born 11/10/64

1987 SEASON AND MAJOR-LEAGUE CAREER BATTING TOTALS

	G	AB	H	2B	3B	HR	TB	R	RBI	TBB	IBB	SO	HP	SH	SF	SB	CS	SB%	GDP	AVG	OBP	SLG
87 CLE	39	80	18	2	1	0	22	7	7	3	1	6	0	5	0	1	0	1.00	1	.225	.253	.275
2 YEARS	62	91	22	2	1	0	26	10	7	3	1	8	0	6	0	2	0	1.00	2	.242	.266	.286

	1987 SEASON											TWO YEAR TOTALS (1986 – 1987)										
	AVG	OBP	SLG	AB	H	2B	3B	HR	RBI	BB	SO	AVG	OBP	SLG	AB	H	2B	3B	HR	RBI	BB	SO
Totals	.237	.266	.289	76	18	2	1	0	7	3	6	.237	.266	.289	76	18	2	1	0	7	3	6
vs. Left	.250	.294	.250	32	8	0	0	0	3	2	3	.250	.294	.250	32	8	0	0	0	3	2	3
vs. Right	.227	.244	.318	44	10	2	1	0	4	1	3	.227	.244	.318	44	10	2	1	0	4	1	3
At Home	.280	.308	.340	50	14	1	1	0	6	2	1	.280	.308	.340	50	14	1	1	0	6	2	1
On Road	.154	.185	.192	26	4	1	0	0	1	1	5	.154	.185	.192	26	4	1	0	0	1	1	5

Noce, Paul David

Bats: Right   Throws: Right   Born 12/16/59

1987 SEASON AND MAJOR-LEAGUE CAREER BATTING TOTALS

	G	AB	H	2B	3B	HR	TB	R	RBI	TBB	IBB	SO	HP	SH	SF	SB	CS	SB%	GDP	AVG	OBP	SLG
87 CHN	70	180	41	9	2	3	63	17	14	6	1	49	2	4	0	5	3	.63	2	.228	.261	.350
1 YEAR	70	180	41	9	2	3	63	17	14	6	1	49	2	4	0	5	3	.63	2	.228	.261	.350

	1987 SEASON											FOUR YEAR TOTALS (1984 – 1987)										
	AVG	OBP	SLG	AB	H	2B	3B	HR	RBI	BB	SO	AVG	OBP	SLG	AB	H	2B	3B	HR	RBI	BB	SO
Totals	.228	.261	.350	180	41	9	2	3	14	6	49	.228	.261	.350	180	41	9	2	3	14	6	49
vs. Left	.148	.193	.148	54	8	0	0	0	3	3	18	.148	.193	.148	54	8	0	0	0	3	3	18
vs. Right	.262	.290	.437	126	33	9	2	3	11	3	31	.262	.290	.437	126	33	9	2	3	11	3	31
At Home	.234	.265	.415	94	22	6	1	3	8	2	25	.234	.265	.415	94	22	6	1	3	8	2	25
On Road	.221	.256	.279	86	19	3	1	0	6	4	24	.221	.256	.279	86	19	3	1	0	6	4	24

Noles, Dickie Ray

Bats: Right   Throws: Right   Born 11/19/56

1987 SEASON AND MAJOR-LEAGUE CAREER PITCHING TOTALS

	G	GS	CG	GF	IP	BFP	H	R	ER	HR	SH	SF	HB	TBB	IBB	SO	WP	Bk	W	L	Pct	ShO	Sv	ERA
87 CHN-DET	45	1	0	19	66	294	61	32	26	1	5	1	5	28	1	33	4	2	4	2	.667	0	4	3.55
9 YEARS	274	94	3	67	856	3756	896	479	426	64	40	28	34	338	27	454	23	16	36	50	.419	3	11	4.48

1987: Finesse, Groundball   1986: Power, Groundball   1985: Finesse, Groundball   1984: Power, Flyball

	1987 SEASON										FOUR YEAR TOTALS (1984 – 1987)									
	G	IP	H	BB	SO	SB	CS	W	L	S	ERA	G	IP	H	BB	SO	SB	CS	W	L	S	ERA
Totals	45	66.1	61	28	33	13	4	4	2	4	3.53	144	339.2	366	137	177	51	10	15	17	5	4.77
At Home	23	38.2	31	15	23	11	2	3	2	0	3.26	71	173.0	194	73	82	31	7	8	8	0	4.94
On Road	22	27.2	30	13	10	2	2	1	0	4	3.90	73	166.2	172	64	95	20	3	7	9	5	4.64

vs. Opposing Batters	AVG	OBP	SLG	AB	H	2B	3B	HR	RBI	BB	SO	AVG	OBP	SLG	AB	H	2B	3B	HR	RBI	BB	SO
Totals	.238	.324	.336	256	61	14	4	1	31	28	33	.274	.343	.401	1337	366	59	9	31	194	137	177
vs. Left	.285	.352	.408	130	37	9	2	1	19	14	15	.311	.383	.456	698	217	34	5	19	119	82	82
vs. Right	.190	.297	.262	126	24	5	2	0	12	14	18	.233	.299	.341	639	149	25	4	12	75	55	95

416

Nolte, Eric Carl

Bats: Left   Throws: Left   Born 04/28/64

1987 SEASON AND MAJOR-LEAGUE CAREER PITCHING TOTALS

	G	GS	CG	GF	IP	BFP	H	R	ER	HR	SH	SF	HB	TBB	IBB	SO	WP	Bk	W	L	Pct	ShO	Sv	ERA
87 SD	12	12	1	0	67	293	57	28	24	6	2	1	2	36	2	44	3	1	2	6	.250	0	0	3.22
1 YEAR	12	12	1	0	67	293	57	28	24	6	2	1	2	36	2	44	3	1	2	6	.250	0	0	3.22

1987: Power, Groundball

	1987 SEASON											FOUR YEAR TOTALS (1984 – 1987)										
	G	IP	H	BB	SO	SB	CS	W	L	S	ERA	G	IP	H	BB	SO	SB	CS	W	L	S	ERA
Totals	12	67.1	57	36	44	9	1	2	6	0	3.21	12	67.1	57	36	44	9	1	2	6	0	3.21
At Home	4	23.0	17	18	15	5	0	1	2	0	2.35	4	23.0	17	18	15	5	0	1	2	0	2.35
On Road	8	44.1	40	18	29	4	1	1	4	0	3.65	8	44.1	40	18	29	4	1	1	4	0	3.65

vs. Opposing Batters	AVG	OBP	SLG	AB	H	2B	3B	HR	RBI	BB	SO	AVG	OBP	SLG	AB	H	2B	3B	HR	RBI	BB	SO
Totals	.226	.326	.337	252	57	10	0	6	21	36	44	.226	.326	.337	252	57	10	0	6	21	36	44
vs. Left	.289	.372	.474	38	11	1	0	2	4	3	4	.289	.372	.474	38	11	1	0	2	4	3	4
vs. Right	.215	.319	.313	214	46	9	0	4	17	33	40	.215	.319	.313	214	46	9	0	4	17	33	40

Nunez, Edwin (Martinez) "Ed"

Bats: Right   Throws: Right   Born 05/27/63

1987 SEASON AND MAJOR-LEAGUE CAREER PITCHING TOTALS

	G	GS	CG	GF	IP	BFP	H	R	ER	HR	SH	SF	HB	TBB	IBB	SO	WP	Bk	W	L	Pct	ShO	Sv	ERA
87 SEA	48	0	0	40	47	198	45	20	20	7	3	4	1	18	3	34	2	0	3	4	.429	0	12	3.83
6 YEARS	191	11	0	126	299	1272	280	136	125	43	12	10	7	116	12	228	5	5	14	17	.452	0	35	3.76

1987: Power, Flyball   1986: Finesse, Flyball

	1987 SEASON											TWO YEAR TOTALS (1986 – 1987)										
	G	IP	H	BB	SO	SB	CS	W	L	S	ERA	G	IP	H	BB	SO	SB	CS	W	L	S	ERA
Totals	48	47.1	45	18	34	1	2	3	4	10	3.80	62	69.0	70	23	51	5	2	4	6	10	4.43
At Home	28	29.0	23	10	21	1	1	2	2	5	4.66	34	40.0	33	14	33	3	1	2	3	5	4.95
On Road	20	18.1	22	8	13	0	1	1	2	5	2.45	28	29.0	37	9	18	2	1	2	3	5	3.72

vs. Opposing Batters	AVG	OBP	SLG	AB	H	2B	3B	HR	RBI	BB	SO	AVG	OBP	SLG	AB	H	2B	3B	HR	RBI	BB	SO
Totals	.262	.328	.424	172	45	5	1	7	28	18	34	.269	.326	.450	260	70	9	1	12	45	23	51
vs. Left	.286	.343	.490	98	28	3	1	5	18	8	17	.264	.316	.457	140	37	4	1	7	23	10	24
vs. Right	.230	.310	.338	74	17	2	0	2	10	10	17	.275	.338	.442	120	33	5	0	5	22	13	27

Nunez, Jose (Jimenez)

Bats: Right   Throws: Right   Born 01/13/64

1987 SEASON AND MAJOR-LEAGUE CAREER PITCHING TOTALS

	G	GS	CG	GF	IP	BFP	H	R	ER	HR	SH	SF	HB	TBB	IBB	SO	WP	Bk	W	L	Pct	ShO	Sv	ERA
87 TOR	37	9	0	13	97	427	91	57	54	12	8	5	0	58	8	99	3	1	5	2	.714	0	0	5.01
1 YEAR	37	9	0	13	97	427	91	57	54	12	8	5	0	58	8	99	3	1	5	2	.714	0	0	5.01

1987: Power, Flyball

	1987 SEASON											FOUR YEAR TOTALS (1984 – 1987)										
	G	IP	H	BB	SO	SB	CS	W	L	S	ERA	G	IP	H	BB	SO	SB	CS	W	L	S	ERA
Totals	37	96.2	91	58	99	13	5	5	2	0	5.03	37	96.2	91	58	99	13	5	5	2	0	5.03
At Home	20	47.2	43	22	55	5	2	4	1	0	5.10	20	47.2	43	22	55	5	2	4	1	0	5.10
On Road	17	49.0	48	36	44	8	3	1	1	0	4.96	17	49.0	48	36	44	8	3	1	1	0	4.96

vs. Opposing Batters	AVG	OBP	SLG	AB	H	2B	3B	HR	RBI	BB	SO	AVG	OBP	SLG	AB	H	2B	3B	HR	RBI	BB	SO
Totals	.256	.356	.430	356	91	16	5	12	57	58	99	.256	.356	.430	356	91	16	5	12	57	58	99
vs. Left	.315	.409	.503	149	47	7	3	5	33	25	28	.315	.409	.503	149	47	7	3	5	33	25	28
vs. Right	.213	.317	.377	207	44	9	2	7	24	33	71	.213	.317	.377	207	44	9	2	7	24	33	71

O'Connor, Jack William

Bats: Left   Throws: Left   Born 06/02/58

1987 SEASON AND MAJOR-LEAGUE CAREER PITCHING TOTALS

	G	GS	CG	GF	IP	BFP	H	R	ER	HR	SH	SF	HB	TBB	IBB	SO	WP	Bk	W	L	Pct	ShO	Sv	ERA
87 BAL	29	0	0	7	46	202	46	23	22	5	1	3	0	23	4	33	3	0	1	1	.500	0	2	4.30
6 YEARS	129	28	6	37	319	1426	343	187	173	36	15	11	4	163	22	177	10	2	14	17	.452	1	2	4.88

1987: Power, Flyball

	1987 SEASON											TWO YEAR TOTALS (1986 – 1987)										
	G	IP	H	BB	SO	SB	CS	W	L	S	ERA	G	IP	H	BB	SO	SB	CS	W	L	S	ERA
Totals	29	46.0	46	23	33	4	0	1	1	2	4.30	29	46.0	46	23	33	4	0	1	1	2	4.30
At Home	19	35.0	32	16	21	4	0	1	0	1	3.34	19	35.0	32	16	21	4	0	1	0	1	3.34
On Road	10	11.0	14	7	12	0	0	0	1	1	7.36	10	11.0	14	7	12	0	0	0	1	1	7.36

vs. Opposing Batters	AVG	OBP	SLG	AB	H	2B	3B	HR	RBI	BB	SO	AVG	OBP	SLG	AB	H	2B	3B	HR	RBI	BB	SO
Totals	.263	.343	.417	175	46	12	0	5	32	23	33	.263	.343	.417	175	46	12	0	5	32	23	33
vs. Left	.240	.296	.520	50	12	5	0	3	8	4	10	.240	.296	.520	50	12	5	0	3	8	4	10
vs. Right	.272	.361	.376	125	34	7	0	2	24	19	23	.272	.361	.376	125	34	7	0	2	24	19	23

O'Malley, Thomas Patrick "Tom"

Bats: Left   Throws: Right   Born 12/25/60

1987 SEASON AND MAJOR-LEAGUE CAREER BATTING TOTALS

	G	AB	H	2B	3B	HR	TB	R	RBI	TBB	IBB	SO	HP	SH	SF	SB	CS	SB%	GDP	AVG	OBP	SLG
87 TEX	45	117	32	8	0	1	43	10	12	15	1	9	0	0	2	0	0	.00	7	.274	.351	.368
6 YEARS	361	1054	270	45	5	10	355	98	107	119	15	125	5	6	7	2	8	.20	36	.256	.332	.337

	1987 SEASON											FOUR YEAR TOTALS (1984 – 1987)										
	AVG	OBP	SLG	AB	H	2B	3B	HR	RBI	BB	SO	AVG	OBP	SLG	AB	H	2B	3B	HR	RBI	BB	SO
Totals	.274	.351	.368	117	32	8	0	1	12	15	9	.238	.303	.312	353	84	17	0	3	35	34	39
vs. Left	.167	.167	.167	6	1	0	0	0	0	0	2	.200	.250	.233	30	6	1	0	0	3	2	5
vs. Right	.279	.359	.378	111	31	8	0	1	12	15	7	.241	.307	.319	323	78	16	0	3	32	32	34
At Home	.194	.318	.250	36	7	2	0	0	3	7	3	.196	.266	.248	153	30	5	0	1	10	15	19
On Road	.309	.367	.420	81	25	6	0	1	9	8	6	.270	.330	.360	200	54	12	0	2	25	19	20

O'Neal, Randall Jeffrey "Randy"

Bats: Right   Throws: Right   Born 08/30/60

1987 SEASON AND MAJOR-LEAGUE CAREER PITCHING TOTALS

	G	GS	CG	GF	IP	BFP	H	R	ER	HR	SH	SF	HB	TBB	IBB	SO	WP	Bk	W	L	Pct	ShO	Sv	ERA
87 ATL-STL	17	11	0	2	66	300	81	42	39	12	2	2	2	26	3	37	10	0	4	2	.667	0	0	5.32
4 YEARS	86	37	2	19	302	1288	300	160	139	33	6	15	7	112	15	169	24	0	14	15	.483	0	3	4.14

1987: Finesse, Groundball   1986: Finesse, Groundball   1985: Finesse, Groundball   1984: Power, Groundball

	1987 SEASON										FOUR YEAR TOTALS (1984 – 1987)										
	G	IP	H	BB	SO	SB	CS	W	L	S	ERA	G	IP	H	BB	SO	SB	CS	W	L	S	ERA
Totals	17	65.2	81	26	37	4	5	4	2	0	5.35	86	301.1	300	112	169	12	14	14	15	3	4.15
At Home	9	38.2	41	10	23	3	1	2	1	0	3.96	42	135.0	134	46	77	7	3	6	7	2	3.73
On Road	8	27.0	40	16	14	1	4	2	1	0	7.33	44	166.1	166	66	92	5	11	8	8	1	4.49

vs. Opposing Batters	AVG	OBP	SLG	AB	H	2B	3B	HR	RBI	BB	SO	AVG	OBP	SLG	AB	H	2B	3B	HR	RBI	BB	SO
Totals	.302	.366	.496	268	81	12	2	12	36	26	37	.261	.328	.409	1148	300	59	6	33	138	112	169
vs. Left	.341	.419	.489	135	46	7	2	3	16	19	18	.254	.334	.391	583	148	26	3	16	66	71	73
vs. Right	.263	.308	.504	133	35	5	0	9	20	7	19	.269	.320	.428	565	152	33	3	17	72	41	96

O'Neill, Paul Andrew

Bats: Left   Throws: Left   Born 02/25/63

1987 SEASON AND MAJOR-LEAGUE CAREER BATTING TOTALS

	G	AB	H	2B	3B	HR	TB	R	RBI	TBB	IBB	SO	HP	SH	SF	SB	CS	SB%	GDP	AVG	OBP	SLG
87 CIN	84	160	41	14	1	7	78	24	28	18	1	29	0	0	0	2	1	.67	3	.256	.331	.488
3 YEARS	92	174	45	15	1	7	83	25	29	19	1	32	0	0	0	2	1	.67	3	.259	.332	.477

	1987 SEASON											TWO YEAR TOTALS (1986 – 1987)										
	AVG	OBP	SLG	AB	H	2B	3B	HR	RBI	BB	SO	AVG	OBP	SLG	AB	H	2B	3B	HR	RBI	BB	SO
Totals	.256	.331	.488	160	41	14	1	7	28	18	29	.253	.331	.481	162	41	14	1	7	28	19	30
vs. Left	.091	.167	.182	11	1	1	0	0	1	1	3	.091	.167	.182	11	1	1	0	0	1	1	3
vs. Right	.268	.343	.510	149	40	13	1	7	27	17	26	.265	.343	.503	151	40	13	1	7	27	18	27
At Home	.253	.347	.494	83	21	8	0	4	15	12	12	.247	.340	.482	85	21	8	0	4	15	12	13
On Road	.260	.313	.481	77	20	6	1	3	13	6	17	.260	.321	.481	77	20	6	1	3	13	7	17

Oester, Ronald John "Ron"

Bats: Both   Throws: Right   Born 05/05/56

1987 SEASON AND MAJOR-LEAGUE CAREER BATTING TOTALS

	G	AB	H	2B	3B	HR	TB	R	RBI	TBB	IBB	SO	HP	SH	SF	SB	CS	SB%	GDP	AVG	OBP	SLG
87 CIN	69	237	60	9	6	2	87	28	23	22	4	51	0	2	0	2	3	.40	8	.253	.317	.367
10 YEARS	1049	3605	955	158	32	41	1300	405	307	318	81	581	4	42	25	38	22	.63	103	.265	.323	.361

	1987 SEASON											FOUR YEAR TOTALS (1984 – 1987)										
	AVG	OBP	SLG	AB	H	2B	3B	HR	RBI	BB	SO	AVG	OBP	SLG	AB	H	2B	3B	HR	RBI	BB	SO
Totals	.253	.317	.367	237	60	9	6	2	23	22	51	.263	.323	.347	1839	484	84	14	14	139	166	297
vs. Left	.200	.262	.217	60	12	1	0	0	5	5	20	.228	.280	.281	508	116	19	1	2	27	37	97
vs. Right	.271	.335	.418	177	48	8	6	2	22	17	31	.276	.340	.372	1331	368	65	13	12	112	129	200
At Home	.232	.304	.296	125	29	4	2	0	10	13	25	.270	.332	.360	944	255	47	7	8	75	87	146
On Road	.277	.331	.446	112	31	5	4	2	13	9	26	.256	.314	.333	895	229	37	7	6	64	79	151

Ojeda, Robert Michael "Bobby"

Bats: Left   Throws: Left   Born 12/17/57

1987 SEASON AND MAJOR-LEAGUE CAREER PITCHING TOTALS

	G	GS	CG	GF	IP	BFP	H	R	ER	HR	SH	SF	HB	TBB	IBB	SO	WP	Bk	W	L	Pct	ShO	Sv	ERA
87 NYN	10	7	0	0	46	192	45	23	20	5	3	1	0	10	1	21	1	0	3	5	.375	0	0	3.91
8 YEARS	182	150	27	17	982	4149	964	458	418	84	40	26	12	347	20	594	14	5	65	49	.570	7	1	3.83

1987: Finesse, Flyball   1986: Finesse, Flyball   1985: Power, Flyball   1984: Power, Flyball

1987 SEASON

	G	IP	H	BB	SO	SB	CS	W	L	S	ERA
Totals	10	46.1	45	10	21	4	2	3	5	0	3.88
At Home	6	26.2	27	5	11	3	2	2	2	0	2.70
On Road	4	19.2	18	5	10	1	0	1	3	0	5.49

vs. Opposing Batters	AVG	OBP	SLG	AB	H	2B	3B	HR	RBI	BB	SO
Totals	.253	.291	.416	178	45	10	2	5	20	10	21
vs. Left	.244	.277	.444	45	11	2	2	1	4	2	5
vs. Right	.256	.296	.406	133	34	8	0	4	16	8	16

FOUR YEAR TOTALS (1984 – 1987)

	G	IP	H	BB	SO	SB	CS	W	L	S	ERA
Totals	114	638.0	607	206	408	49	37	42	33	1	3.50
At Home	57	323.1	316	97	223	19	18	19	16	0	3.62
On Road	57	314.2	291	109	185	30	19	23	17	1	3.35

	AVG	OBP	SLG	AB	H	2B	3B	HR	RBI	BB	SO
Totals	.252	.311	.369	2406	607	101	18	48	231	206	408
vs. Left	.241	.291	.339	439	106	17	4	6	34	31	93
vs. Right	.255	.315	.376	1967	501	84	14	42	197	175	315

Olwine, Edward R. "Ed"

Bats: Right   Throws: Left   Born 05/28/58

1987 SEASON AND MAJOR-LEAGUE CAREER PITCHING TOTALS

	G	GS	CG	GF	IP	BFP	H	R	ER	HR	SH	SF	HB	TBB	IBB	SO	WP	Bk	W	L	Pct	ShO	Sv	ERA
87 ATL	27	0	0	9	23	104	25	16	13	4	1	1	1	8	1	12	1	0	0	1	.000	0	1	5.09
2 YEARS	64	0	0	21	71	293	60	36	31	9	2	2	2	25	8	49	6	2	0	1	.000	0	2	3.93

1987: Finesse, Flyball   1986: Power, Groundball

1987 SEASON

	G	IP	H	BB	SO	SB	CS	W	L	S	ERA
Totals	27	23.1	25	8	12	1	0	0	1	1	5.01
At Home	13	12.0	14	5	8	1	0	0	0	1	6.00
On Road	14	11.1	11	3	4	0	0	0	1	0	3.97

vs. Opposing Batters	AVG	OBP	SLG	AB	H	2B	3B	HR	RBI	BB	SO
Totals	.269	.330	.452	93	25	3	1	4	15	8	12
vs. Left	.297	.333	.459	37	11	0	0	2	5	2	6
vs. Right	.250	.328	.446	56	14	3	1	2	10	6	6

FOUR YEAR TOTALS (1984 – 1987)

	G	IP	H	BB	SO	SB	CS	W	L	S	ERA
Totals	64	71.0	60	25	49	7	1	0	1	2	3.93
At Home	35	33.0	32	13	24	1	0	0	0	1	4.64
On Road	29	38.0	28	12	25	6	1	0	1	1	3.32

	AVG	OBP	SLG	AB	H	2B	3B	HR	RBI	BB	SO
Totals	.229	.298	.382	262	60	9	2	9	32	25	49
vs. Left	.217	.239	.358	106	23	3	0	4	12	3	24
vs. Right	.237	.333	.397	156	37	6	2	5	20	22	25

Oquendo, Jose Manuel (Contreras)

Bats: Both   Throws: Right   Born 07/04/63

1987 SEASON AND MAJOR-LEAGUE CAREER BATTING TOTALS

	G	AB	H	2B	3B	HR	TB	R	RBI	TBB	IBB	SO	HP	SH	SF	SB	CS	SB%	GDP	AVG	OBP	SLG
87 STL	116	248	71	9	0	1	83	43	24	54	6	29	0	6	4	4	4	.50	6	.286	.408	.335
4 YEARS	393	903	224	25	1	2	257	115	64	103	14	135	4	14	10	24	17	.59	21	.248	.325	.285

1987 SEASON

	AVG	OBP	SLG	AB	H	2B	3B	HR	RBI	BB	SO
Totals	.286	.408	.335	248	71	9	0	1	24	54	29
vs. Left	.277	.375	.339	112	31	4	0	1	12	20	11
vs. Right	.294	.435	.331	136	40	5	0	0	12	34	18
At Home	.297	.424	.342	111	33	5	0	0	10	26	16
On Road	.277	.395	.328	137	38	4	0	1	14	28	13

FOUR YEAR TOTALS (1984 – 1987)

	AVG	OBP	SLG	AB	H	2B	3B	HR	RBI	BB	SO
Totals	.268	.358	.308	575	154	18	1	1	47	84	75
vs. Left	.284	.363	.340	215	61	9	0	1	19	29	21
vs. Right	.258	.356	.289	360	93	9	1	0	28	55	54
At Home	.275	.361	.319	276	76	10	1	0	19	39	39
On Road	.261	.356	.298	299	78	8	0	1	28	45	36

Orosco, Jesse

Bats: Right   Throws: Left   Born 04/21/57

1987 SEASON AND MAJOR-LEAGUE CAREER PITCHING TOTALS

	G	GS	CG	GF	IP	BFP	H	R	ER	HR	SH	SF	HB	TBB	IBB	SO	WP	Bk	W	L	Pct	ShO	Sv	ERA
87 NYN	58	0	0	41	77	335	78	41	38	5	5	4	2	31	9	78	2	0	3	9	.250	0	16	4.44
8 YEARS	372	4	0	246	595	2465	480	207	181	40	25	18	12	240	36	506	13	6	47	47	.500	0	107	2.74

1987: Power, Flyball   1986: Power, Flyball   1985: Power, Flyball   1984: Power, Flyball

1987 SEASON

	G	IP	H	BB	SO	SB	CS	W	L	S	ERA
Totals	58	77.1	78	31	78	10	3	3	9	16	4.42
At Home	26	41.2	39	16	49	6	2	2	4	8	2.81
On Road	32	35.2	39	15	29	4	1	1	5	8	6.31

vs. Opposing Batters	AVG	OBP	SLG	AB	H	2B	3B	HR	RBI	BB	SO
Totals	.266	.336	.358	293	78	12	0	5	40	31	78
vs. Left	.230	.275	.243	74	17	1	0	0	3	5	21
vs. Right	.279	.356	.397	219	61	11	0	5	37	26	57

FOUR YEAR TOTALS (1984 – 1987)

	G	IP	H	BB	SO	SB	CS	W	L	S	ERA
Totals	230	324.1	266	134	293	31	4	29	27	85	3.00
At Home	103	156.1	148	62	151	12	2	14	15	37	3.22
On Road	127	168.0	118	72	142	19	2	15	12	48	2.79

	AVG	OBP	SLG	AB	H	2B	3B	HR	RBI	BB	SO
Totals	.222	.301	.319	1196	266	41	1	24	135	134	293
vs. Left	.199	.250	.221	276	55	3	0	1	21	19	78
vs. Right	.229	.315	.348	920	211	38	1	23	114	115	215

Orta, Jorge (Nunez)

Bats: Left　　**Throws: Right**　　**Born 11/26/50**

	G	AB	H	2B	3B	HR	TB	R	RBI	TBB	IBB	SO	HP	SH	SF	SB	CS	SB%	GDP	AVG	OBP	SLG
							1987 SEASON AND MAJOR-LEAGUE CAREER BATTING TOTALS															
87 KC	21	50	9	4	0	2	19	3	4	3	1	8	0	0	0	0	0	.00	0	.180	.226	.380
16 YEARS	1755	5829	1619	267	63	130	2402	733	745	500	46	715	29	33	67	79	60	.57	125	.278	.334	.412

	1987 SEASON										FOUR YEAR TOTALS (1984 – 1987)									
	AVG	OBP	SLG	AB	H	2B	3B	HR	RBI	BB	SO	AVG	OBP	SLG	AB	H	2B	3B	HR	RBI	BB	SO
Totals	.180	.226	.380	50	9	4	0	2	4	3	8	.277	.324	.419	1089	302	62	10	24	145	76	109
vs. Left	.000	.000	.000	0	0	0	0	0	0	0	0	.235	.291	.235	51	12	0	0	0	3	4	11
vs. Right	.180	.226	.380	50	9	4	0	2	4	3	8	.279	.326	.428	1038	290	62	10	24	142	72	98
At Home	.000	.000	.000	9	0	0	0	0	0	0	2	.275	.323	.411	535	147	36	5	9	70	39	50
On Road	.220	.273	.463	41	9	4	0	2	4	3	6	.280	.325	.426	554	155	26	5	15	75	37	59

Ortiz, Adalberto Colon "Junior"

Bats: Right　　**Throws: Right**　　**Born 10/24/59**

	G	AB	H	2B	3B	HR	TB	R	RBI	TBB	IBB	SO	HP	SH	SF	SB	CS	SB%	GDP	AVG	OBP	SLG
							1987 SEASON AND MAJOR-LEAGUE CAREER BATTING TOTALS															
87 PIT	75	192	52	8	1	1	65	16	22	15	1	23	0	5	1	0	2	.00	6	.271	.322	.339
6 YEARS	267	673	179	25	1	2	212	49	64	37	2	105	1	9	5	3	3	.50	15	.266	.303	.315

	1987 SEASON										FOUR YEAR TOTALS (1984 – 1987)									
	AVG	OBP	SLG	AB	H	2B	3B	HR	RBI	BB	SO	AVG	OBP	SLG	AB	H	2B	3B	HR	RBI	BB	SO
Totals	.271	.322	.339	192	52	8	1	1	22	15	23	.275	.319	.333	465	128	19	1	2	52	32	68
vs. Left	.275	.316	.325	160	44	8	0	0	16	10	17	.278	.322	.327	245	68	12	0	0	23	18	30
vs. Right	.250	.351	.406	32	8	0	1	1	6	5	6	.273	.315	.341	220	60	7	1	2	29	14	38
At Home	.271	.336	.323	96	26	3	1	0	15	10	13	.275	.319	.322	211	58	8	1	0	24	15	28
On Road	.271	.307	.354	96	26	5	0	1	7	5	10	.276	.319	.343	254	70	11	0	2	28	17	40

Owen, Lawrence Thomas "Larry"

Bats: Right　　**Throws: Right**　　**Born 04/25/58**

	G	AB	H	2B	3B	HR	TB	R	RBI	TBB	IBB	SO	HP	SH	SF	SB	CS	SB%	GDP	AVG	OBP	SLG
							1987 SEASON AND MAJOR-LEAGUE CAREER BATTING TOTALS															
87 KC	76	164	31	6	0	5	52	17	14	16	0	51	0	7	1	0	0	.00	5	.189	.260	.317
5 YEARS	134	271	51	10	0	7	82	25	27	25	3	75	0	9	2	0	1	.00	7	.188	.255	.303

	1987 SEASON										TWO YEAR TOTALS (1986 – 1987)									
	AVG	OBP	SLG	AB	H	2B	3B	HR	RBI	BB	SO	AVG	OBP	SLG	AB	H	2B	3B	HR	RBI	BB	SO
Totals	.189	.260	.317	164	31	6	0	5	14	16	51	.189	.258	.317	164	31	6	0	5	14	16	51
vs. Left	.226	.291	.419	93	21	3	0	5	11	9	23	.226	.291	.419	93	21	3	0	5	11	9	23
vs. Right	.141	.218	.183	71	10	3	0	0	3	7	28	.141	.218	.183	71	10	3	0	0	3	7	28
At Home	.189	.241	.311	74	14	3	0	2	8	5	19	.189	.241	.311	74	14	3	0	2	8	5	19
On Road	.189	.275	.322	90	17	3	0	3	6	11	32	.189	.275	.322	90	17	3	0	3	6	11	32

Pacillo, Patrick Michael "Pat"

Bats: Right　　**Throws: Right**　　**Born 07/23/63**

	G	GS	CG	GF	IP	BFP	H	R	ER	HR	SH	SF	HB	TBB	IBB	SO	WP	Bk	W	L	Pct	ShO	Sv	ERA
							1987 SEASON AND MAJOR-LEAGUE CAREER PITCHING TOTALS																	
87 CIN	12	7	0	2	40	176	41	30	27	7	2	2	1	19	0	23	3	0	3	3	.500	0	0	6.08
1 YEAR	12	7	0	2	40	176	41	30	27	7	2	2	1	19	0	23	3	0	3	3	.500	0	0	6.08

1987: Power, Flyball

	1987 SEASON										FOUR YEAR TOTALS (1984 – 1987)									
	G	IP	H	BB	SO	SB	CS	W	L	S	ERA	G	IP	H	BB	SO	SB	CS	W	L	S	ERA
Totals	12	39.2	41	19	23	4	1	3	3	0	6.13	12	39.2	41	19	23	4	1	3	3	0	6.13
At Home	7	26.2	21	9	18	1	0	2	2	0	4.05	7	26.2	21	9	18	1	0	2	2	0	4.05
On Road	5	13.0	20	10	5	3	1	1	1	0	10.38	5	13.0	20	10	5	3	1	1	1	0	10.38

vs. Opposing Batters	AVG	OBP	SLG	AB	H	2B	3B	HR	RBI	BB	SO	AVG	OBP	SLG	AB	H	2B	3B	HR	RBI	BB	SO
Totals	.270	.351	.480	152	41	7	2	7	27	19	23	.270	.351	.480	152	41	7	2	7	27	19	23
vs. Left	.258	.362	.461	89	23	4	1	4	16	14	12	.258	.362	.461	89	23	4	1	4	16	14	12
vs. Right	.286	.333	.508	63	18	3	1	3	11	5	11	.286	.333	.508	63	18	3	1	3	11	5	11

Paciorek, James Joseph "Jim"

Bats: Both   Throws: Right   Born 06/07/60

1987 SEASON AND MAJOR-LEAGUE CAREER BATTING TOTALS

	G	AB	H	2B	3B	HR	TB	R	RBI	TBB	IBB	SO	HP	SH	SF	SB	CS	SB%	GDP	AVG	OBP	SLG
87 MIL	48	101	23	5	0	2	34	16	10	12	0	20	0	0	3	1	0	1.00	3	.228	.302	.337
1 YEAR	48	101	23	5	0	2	34	16	10	12	0	20	0	0	3	1	0	1.00	3	.228	.302	.337

	1987 SEASON											FOUR YEAR TOTALS (1984 – 1987)										
	AVG	OBP	SLG	AB	H	2B	3B	HR	RBI	BB	SO	AVG	OBP	SLG	AB	H	2B	3B	HR	RBI	BB	SO
Totals	.228	.302	.337	101	23	5	0	2	10	12	20	.228	.302	.337	101	23	5	0	2	10	12	20
vs. Left	.221	.276	.353	68	15	3	0	2	7	6	13	.221	.276	.353	68	15	3	0	2	7	6	13
vs. Right	.242	.350	.303	33	8	2	0	0	3	6	7	.242	.350	.303	33	8	2	0	0	3	6	7
At Home	.250	.342	.375	32	8	1	0	1	2	5	6	.250	.342	.375	32	8	1	0	1	2	5	6
On Road	.217	.282	.319	69	15	4	0	1	8	7	14	.217	.282	.319	69	15	4	0	1	8	7	14

Paciorek, Thomas Marian "Tom"

Bats: Right   Throws: Right   Born 11/02/46

1987 SEASON AND MAJOR-LEAGUE CAREER BATTING TOTALS

	G	AB	H	2B	3B	HR	TB	R	RBI	TBB	IBB	SO	HP	SH	SF	SB	CS	SB%	GDP	AVG	OBP	SLG
87 TEX	27	60	17	3	0	3	29	6	12	1	0	19	1	1	1	0	1	.00	3	.283	.302	.483
18 YEARS	1392	4121	1162	232	30	86	1712	494	503	245	25	704	38	22	39	55	38	.59	92	.282	.325	.415

	1987 SEASON											FOUR YEAR TOTALS (1984 – 1987)										
	AVG	OBP	SLG	AB	H	2B	3B	HR	RBI	BB	SO	AVG	OBP	SLG	AB	H	2B	3B	HR	RBI	BB	SO
Totals	.283	.302	.483	60	17	3	0	3	12	1	19	.268	.307	.357	874	234	36	3	12	83	43	165
vs. Left	.244	.256	.512	41	10	2	0	3	11	0	13	.284	.318	.376	535	152	18	2	9	52	26	98
vs. Right	.368	.400	.421	19	7	1	0	0	1	1	6	.242	.290	.327	339	82	18	1	3	31	17	67
At Home	.293	.286	.488	41	12	2	0	2	6	0	12	.279	.320	.366	426	119	20	1	5	42	24	72
On Road	.263	.333	.474	19	5	1	0	1	6	1	7	.257	.295	.348	448	115	16	2	7	41	19	93

Pagnozzi, Thomas Alan "Tom"

Bats: Right   Throws: Right   Born 07/30/62

1987 SEASON AND MAJOR-LEAGUE CAREER BATTING TOTALS

	G	AB	H	2B	3B	HR	TB	R	RBI	TBB	IBB	SO	HP	SH	SF	SB	CS	SB%	GDP	AVG	OBP	SLG
87 STL	27	48	9	1	0	2	16	8	9	4	2	13	0	1	0	1	0	1.00	0	.188	.250	.333
1 YEAR	27	48	9	1	0	2	16	8	9	4	2	13	0	1	0	1	0	1.00	0	.188	.250	.333

	1987 SEASON											FOUR YEAR TOTALS (1984 – 1987)										
	AVG	OBP	SLG	AB	H	2B	3B	HR	RBI	BB	SO	AVG	OBP	SLG	AB	H	2B	3B	HR	RBI	BB	SO
Totals	.188	.250	.333	48	9	1	0	2	9	4	13	.188	.250	.333	48	9	1	0	2	9	4	13
vs. Left	.227	.320	.500	22	5	0	0	2	7	3	6	.227	.320	.500	22	5	0	0	2	7	3	6
vs. Right	.154	.185	.192	26	4	1	0	0	2	1	7	.154	.185	.192	26	4	1	0	0	2	1	7
At Home	.179	.281	.393	28	5	0	0	2	7	4	5	.179	.281	.393	28	5	0	0	2	7	4	5
On Road	.200	.200	.250	20	4	1	0	0	2	0	8	.200	.200	.250	20	4	1	0	0	2	0	8

Palmer, David William

Bats: Right   Throws: Right   Born 10/19/57

1987 SEASON AND MAJOR-LEAGUE CAREER PITCHING TOTALS

	G	GS	CG	GF	IP	BFP	H	R	ER	HR	SH	SF	HB	TBB	IBB	SO	WP	Bk	W	L	Pct	ShO	Sv	ERA
87 ATL	28	28	0	0	152	687	169	94	83	17	9	5	7	64	4	111	5	0	8	11	.421	0	0	4.91
8 YEARS	185	149	9	14	940	3990	882	429	377	69	36	22	21	375	31	651	32	5	57	47	.548	3	2	3.61

1987: Power, Groundball   1986: Power, Groundball   1985: Power, Groundball   1984: Power, Groundball

	1987 SEASON										FOUR YEAR TOTALS (1984 – 1987)									
	G	IP	H	BB	SO	SB	CS	W	L	S	ERA	G	IP	H	BB	SO	SB	CS	W	L	S	ERA
Totals	28	152.1	169	64	111	30	4	8	11	0	4.90	107	603.0	579	277	453	111	39	33	34	0	4.00
At Home	15	75.1	93	35	54	17	3	4	7	0	6.21	54	305.1	300	136	222	55	16	15	19	0	4.04
On Road	13	77.0	76	29	57	13	1	4	4	0	3.62	53	297.2	279	141	231	56	23	18	15	0	3.99

	vs. Opposing Batters																			
	AVG	OBP	SLG	AB	H	2B	3B	HR	RBI	BB	SO	AVG	OBP	SLG	AB	H	2B	3B	HR	RBI	BB	SO
Totals	.280	.353	.428	603	169	28	5	17	86	64	111	.254	.336	.361	2281	579	81	16	44	259	277	453
vs. Left	.288	.369	.448	330	95	18	4	9	41	41	65	.257	.347	.358	1213	312	49	11	17	111	16	258
vs. Right	.271	.334	.403	273	74	10	1	8	45	23	46	.250	.322	.365	1068	267	32	5	27	148	111	195

Pankovitz, James Franklin "Jim"

Bats: Right　　Throws: Right　　Born 08/06/55

1987 SEASON AND MAJOR-LEAGUE CAREER BATTING TOTALS

	G	AB	H	2B	3B	HR	TB	R	RBI	TBB	IBB	SO	HP	SH	SF	SB	CS	SB%	GDP	AVG	OBP	SLG
87 HOU	50	61	14	2	0	1	19	7	8	6	1	13	0	0	0	2	0	1.00	2	.230	.299	.311
4 YEARS	248	427	111	18	1	7	152	49	43	36	3	87	1	2	1	6	2	.75	10	.260	.318	.356

	1987 SEASON										FOUR YEAR TOTALS (1984 – 1987)									
	AVG	OBP	SLG	AB	H	2B	3B	HR	RBI	BB	SO	AVG	OBP	SLG	AB	H	2B	3B	HR	RBI	BB	SO
Totals	.230	.299	.311	61	14	2	0	1	8	6	13	.260	.318	.356	427	111	18	1	7	43	36	87
vs. Left	.271	.340	.375	48	13	2	0	1	6	5	10	.245	.295	.344	273	67	10	1	5	26	19	55
vs. Right	.077	.143	.077	13	1	0	0	0	2	1	3	.286	.358	.377	154	44	8	0	2	17	17	32
At Home	.222	.282	.222	36	8	0	0	0	5	3	7	.238	.309	.312	202	48	7	1	2	17	21	42
On Road	.240	.321	.440	25	6	2	0	1	3	3	6	.280	.326	.396	225	63	11	0	5	26	15	45

Parrett, Jeffrey Dale "Jeff"

Bats: Right　　Throws: Right　　Born 08/26/61

1987 SEASON AND MAJOR-LEAGUE CAREER PITCHING TOTALS

	G	GS	CG	GF	IP	BFP	H	R	ER	HR	SH	SF	HB	TBB	IBB	SO	WP	Bk	W	L	Pct	ShO	Sv	ERA
87 MON	45	0	0	26	62	267	53	33	29	8	5	1	0	30	4	56	6	1	7	6	.538	0	6	4.21
2 YEARS	57	0	0	32	82	358	72	44	40	11	5	2	0	43	4	77	8	1	7	7	.500	0	6	4.39

1987: Power, Flyball　　1986: Power, Flyball

	1987 SEASON											FOUR YEAR TOTALS (1984 – 1987)										
	G	IP	H	BB	SO	SB	CS	W	L	S	ERA	G	IP	H	BB	SO	SB	CS	W	L	S	ERA
Totals	45	62.0	53	30	56	13	1	7	6	6	4.21	57	82.1	72	43	77	17	1	7	7	6	4.37
At Home	22	36.2	26	17	32	7	0	3	4	4	3.93	27	48.2	36	25	43	8	0	3	5	4	4.25
On Road	23	25.1	27	13	24	6	1	4	2	2	4.62	30	33.2	36	18	34	9	1	4	2	2	4.54
vs. Opposing Batters	AVG	OBP	SLG	AB	H	2B	3B	HR	RBI	BB	SO	AVG	OBP	SLG	AB	H	2B	3B	HR	RBI	BB	SO
Totals	.229	.317	.385	231	53	10	1	8	32	30	56	.234	.326	.390	308	72	11	2	11	43	43	77
vs. Left	.245	.329	.403	139	34	7	0	5	19	18	29	.243	.335	.395	185	45	8	1	6	25	26	39
vs. Right	.207	.298	.359	92	19	3	1	3	13	12	27	.220	.312	.382	123	27	3	1	5	18	17	38

Parsons, Casey Robert

Bats: Left　　Throws: Right　　Born 04/14/54

1987 SEASON AND MAJOR-LEAGUE CAREER BATTING TOTALS

	G	AB	H	2B	3B	HR	TB	R	RBI	TBB	IBB	SO	HP	SH	SF	SB	CS	SB%	GDP	AVG	OBP	SLG
87 CLE	18	25	4	0	0	1	7	2	5	0	0	5	0	0	0	0	0	.00	2	.160	.160	.280
4 YEARS	63	53	10	1	0	2	17	9	10	3	1	11	2	2	1	0	0	.00	2	.189	.254	.321

	1987 SEASON										TWO YEAR TOTALS (1986 – 1987)									
	AVG	OBP	SLG	AB	H	2B	3B	HR	RBI	BB	SO	AVG	OBP	SLG	AB	H	2B	3B	HR	RBI	BB	SO
Totals	.160	.160	.280	25	4	0	0	1	5	0	5	.160	.160	.280	25	4	0	0	1	5	0	5
vs. Left	.000	.000	.000	0	0	0	0	0	0	0	0	.000	.000	.000	0	0	0	0	0	0	0	0
vs. Right	.160	.160	.280	25	4	0	0	1	5	0	5	.160	.160	.280	25	4	0	0	1	5	0	5
At Home	.364	.364	.636	11	4	0	0	1	5	0	1	.364	.364	.636	11	4	0	0	1	5	0	1
On Road	.000	.000	.000	14	0	0	0	0	0	0	4	.000	.000	.000	14	0	0	0	0	0	0	4

Patterson, Robert Chandler "Bob"

Bats: Right　　Throws: Right　　Born 05/16/59

1987 SEASON AND MAJOR-LEAGUE CAREER PITCHING TOTALS

	G	GS	CG	GF	IP	BFP	H	R	ER	HR	SH	SF	HB	TBB	IBB	SO	WP	Bk	W	L	Pct	ShO	Sv	ERA
87 PIT	15	7	0	2	43	201	49	34	32	5	6	3	1	22	4	27	1	0	1	4	.200	0	0	6.70
3 YEARS	29	12	0	6	83	386	111	65	63	7	7	4	1	30	6	48	1	2	3	7	.300	0	0	6.83

1987: Power, Flyball　　1986: Finesse, Flyball

	1987 SEASON											TWO YEAR TOTALS (1986 – 1987)										
	G	IP	H	BB	SO	SB	CS	W	L	S	ERA	G	IP	H	BB	SO	SB	CS	W	L	S	ERA
Totals	15	43.0	49	22	27	1	2	1	4	0	6.28	26	79.1	98	27	47	2	3	3	7	0	5.67
At Home	10	28.2	28	17	16	1	1	1	2	0	5.34	17	52.2	54	19	29	2	2	3	2	0	4.61
On Road	5	14.1	21	5	11	0	1	0	2	0	8.16	9	26.2	44	8	18	0	1	0	5	0	7.76
vs. Opposing Batters	AVG	OBP	SLG	AB	H	2B	3B	HR	RBI	BB	SO	AVG	OBP	SLG	AB	H	2B	3B	HR	RBI	BB	SO
Totals	.290	.371	.473	169	49	14	1	5	32	22	27	.305	.358	.449	321	98	27	2	5	51	27	47
vs. Left	.220	.319	.366	41	9	3	0	1	9	6	9	.242	.338	.387	62	15	6	0	1	11	9	14
vs. Right	.313	.388	.508	128	40	11	1	4	23	16	18	.320	.363	.463	259	83	21	2	4	40	18	33

Pecota, William Joseph "Bill"
Bats: Right   Throws: Right   Born 02/16/60

1987 SEASON AND MAJOR-LEAGUE CAREER BATTING TOTALS

	G	AB	H	2B	3B	HR	TB	R	RBI	TBB	IBB	SO	HP	SH	SF	SB	CS	SB%	GDP	AVG	OBP	SLG
87 KC	66	156	43	5	1	3	59	22	14	15	0	25	1	0	0	5	0	1.00	3	.276	.343	.378
2 YEARS	78	185	49	7	1	3	67	25	16	18	0	28	2	0	1	5	2	.71	4	.265	.335	.362

	1987 SEASON											FOUR YEAR TOTALS (1984 – 1987)										
	AVG	OBP	SLG	AB	H	2B	3B	HR	RBI	BB	SO	AVG	OBP	SLG	AB	H	2B	3B	HR	RBI	BB	SO
Totals	.276	.343	.378	156	43	5	1	3	14	15	25	.265	.337	.362	185	49	7	1	3	16	18	28
vs. Left	.286	.364	.429	49	14	1	0	2	8	6	9	.271	.333	.407	59	16	2	0	2	10	6	9
vs. Right	.271	.333	.355	107	29	4	1	1	6	9	16	.262	.336	.341	126	33	5	1	1	6	12	19
At Home	.250	.310	.300	80	20	2	1	0	9	7	8	.242	.314	.295	95	23	3	1	0	9	9	10
On Road	.303	.376	.461	76	23	3	0	3	5	8	17	.289	.356	.433	90	26	4	0	3	7	9	18

Pedrique, Alfredo Jose (Garcia) "Al"
Bats: Right   Throws: Right   Born 08/11/60

1987 SEASON AND MAJOR-LEAGUE CAREER BATTING TOTALS

	G	AB	H	2B	3B	HR	TB	R	RBI	TBB	IBB	SO	HP	SH	SF	SB	CS	SB%	GDP	AVG	OBP	SLG
87 NYN-PIT	93	252	74	10	1	1	89	24	27	19	4	29	3	6	1	5	4	.56	7	.294	.349	.353
1 YEAR	93	252	74	10	1	1	89	24	27	19	4	29	3	6	1	5	4	.56	7	.294	.349	.353

	1987 SEASON											FOUR YEAR TOTALS (1984 – 1987)										
	AVG	OBP	SLG	AB	H	2B	3B	HR	RBI	BB	SO	AVG	OBP	SLG	AB	H	2B	3B	HR	RBI	BB	SO
Totals	.294	.349	.357	252	74	11	1	1	27	19	29	.294	.349	.357	252	74	11	1	1	27	19	29
vs. Left	.296	.351	.326	135	40	4	0	0	10	11	12	.296	.351	.326	135	40	4	0	0	10	11	12
vs. Right	.291	.346	.393	117	34	7	1	1	17	8	17	.291	.346	.393	117	34	7	1	1	17	8	17
At Home	.308	.361	.346	133	41	5	0	0	12	9	14	.308	.361	.346	133	41	5	0	0	12	9	14
On Road	.277	.336	.370	119	33	6	1	1	15	10	15	.277	.336	.370	119	33	6	1	1	15	10	15

Pena, Adalberto (Rivera) "Bert"
Bats: Both   Throws: Right   Born 07/11/59

1987 SEASON AND MAJOR-LEAGUE CAREER BATTING TOTALS

	G	AB	H	2B	3B	HR	TB	R	RBI	TBB	IBB	SO	HP	SH	SF	SB	CS	SB%	GDP	AVG	OBP	SLG
87 HOU	21	46	7	0	0	0	7	5	0	2	0	7	1	0	0	0	0	.00	3	.152	.204	.152
6 YEARS	88	153	31	4	0	1	38	18	10	13	3	28	1	2	1	1	0	1.00	10	.203	.268	.248

	1987 SEASON											TWO YEAR TOTALS (1986 – 1987)										
	AVG	OBP	SLG	AB	H	2B	3B	HR	RBI	BB	SO	AVG	OBP	SLG	AB	H	2B	3B	HR	RBI	BB	SO
Totals	.152	.204	.152	46	7	0	0	0	0	2	7	.173	.250	.187	75	13	1	0	0	2	7	12
vs. Left	.162	.225	.162	37	6	0	0	0	0	2	5	.164	.246	.164	55	9	0	0	0	1	5	8
vs. Right	.111	.111	.111	9	1	0	0	0	0	0	2	.200	.273	.250	20	4	1	0	0	1	2	4
At Home	.182	.182	.182	22	4	0	0	0	0	0	3	.154	.241	.154	26	4	0	0	0	1	3	3
On Road	.125	.222	.125	24	3	0	0	0	0	2	4	.184	.259	.204	49	9	1	0	0	1	4	9

Pena, Alejandro (Vasquez)
Bats: Right   Throws: Right   Born 06/25/59

1987 SEASON AND MAJOR-LEAGUE CAREER PITCHING TOTALS

	G	GS	CG	GF	IP	BFP	H	R	ER	HR	SH	SF	HB	TBB	IBB	SO	WP	Bk	W	L	Pct	ShO	Sv	ERA
87 LA	37	7	0	17	87	377	82	41	34	9	5	6	2	37	5	76	0	1	2	7	.222	0	11	3.52
7 YEARS	168	72	12	45	598	2516	556	252	212	34	24	14	8	199	33	413	9	5	28	28	.500	7	15	3.19

1987: Power, Flyball   1986: Power, Flyball   1985: Power, Flyball   1984: Finesse, Groundball

	1987 SEASON											FOUR YEAR TOTALS (1984 – 1987)										
	G	IP	H	BB	SO	SB	CS	W	L	S	ERA	G	IP	H	BB	SO	SB	CS	W	L	S	ERA
Totals	37	87.1	82	37	76	11	2	2	7	11	3.50	91	361.0	349	116	259	37	20	15	16	12	3.27
At Home	20	53.2	47	16	46	9	1	0	4	6	2.52	45	183.0	156	52	121	22	11	8	10	7	2.51
On Road	17	33.2	35	21	30	2	1	2	3	5	5.08	46	178.0	193	64	138	15	9	7	6	5	4.04

vs. Opposing Batters	AVG	OBP	SLG	AB	H	2B	3B	HR	RBI	BB	SO	AVG	OBP	SLG	AB	H	2B	3B	HR	RBI	BB	SO
Totals	.251	.325	.382	327	82	14	1	9	38	37	76	.253	.311	.357	1377	349	63	5	23	131	116	259
vs. Left	.237	.320	.305	177	42	4	1	2	14	23	39	.257	.328	.354	704	181	28	5	10	53	76	122
vs. Right	.267	.331	.473	150	40	10	0	7	24	14	37	.250	.292	.360	673	168	35	0	13	78	40	137

Pena, Hipolito (Concepcion)

Bats: Left   Throws: Left   Born 01/30/64

1987 SEASON AND MAJOR-LEAGUE CAREER PITCHING TOTALS

	G	GS	CG	GF	IP	BFP	H	R	ER	HR	SH	SF	HB	TBB	IBB	SO	WP	Bk	W	L	Pct	ShO	Sv	ERA
87 PIT	16	1	0	2	26	115	16	14	13	2	2	0	0	26	3	16	0	2	0	3	.000	0	1	4.50
2 YEARS	26	2	0	5	34	153	23	24	21	5	2	0	1	29	4	22	0	2	0	6	.000	0	2	5.56

1987: Power, Groundball   1986: Power, Groundball

1987 SEASON	G	IP	H	BB	SO	SB	CS	W	L	S	ERA
Totals	16	25.2	16	26	16	6	1	0	3	1	4.56
At Home	11	14.0	5	11	9	4	1	0	1	1	2.57
On Road	5	11.2	11	15	7	2	0	0	2	0	6.94

vs. Opposing Batters	AVG	OBP	SLG	AB	H	2B	3B	HR	RBI	BB	SO
Totals	.182	.368	.318	88	16	6	0	2	8	26	16
vs. Left	.105	.320	.158	19	2	1	0	0	2	6	6
vs. Right	.203	.382	.362	69	14	5	0	2	6	20	10

FOUR YEAR TOTALS (1984 – 1987)	G	IP	H	BB	SO	SB	CS	W	L	S	ERA
	26	34.0	23	29	22	8	2	0	6	2	5.56
	15	18.2	8	11	12	5	1	0	1	2	2.41
	11	15.1	15	18	10	3	1	0	5	0	9.39

	AVG	OBP	SLG	AB	H	2B	3B	HR	RBI	BB	SO
	.189	.349	.369	122	23	7	0	5	14	29	22
	.100	.289	.233	30	3	1	0	1	3	7	10
	.217	.368	.413	92	20	6	0	4	11	22	12

Perez, Pascual Gross

Bats: Right   Throws: Right   Born 05/17/59

1987 SEASON AND MAJOR-LEAGUE CAREER PITCHING TOTALS

	G	GS	CG	GF	IP	BFP	H	R	ER	HR	SH	SF	HB	TBB	IBB	SO	WP	Bk	W	L	Pct	ShO	Sv	ERA
87 MON	10	10	2	0	70	273	52	21	18	5	3	1	1	16	1	58	1	1	7	0	1.000	0	0	2.31
7 YEARS	130	121	15	3	769	3243	780	368	323	70	38	17	14	228	33	486	21	10	43	41	.512	2	0	3.78

1987: Power, Groundball

1987 SEASON	G	IP	H	BB	SO	SB	CS	W	L	S	ERA
Totals	10	70.1	52	16	58	6	3	7	0	0	2.30
At Home	5	33.1	32	11	28	5	1	3	0	0	2.97
On Road	5	37.0	20	5	30	1	2	4	0	0	1.70

vs. Opposing Batters	AVG	OBP	SLG	AB	H	2B	3B	HR	RBI	BB	SO
Totals	.206	.256	.298	252	52	8	0	5	21	16	58
vs. Left	.226	.289	.295	146	33	4	0	2	10	12	32
vs. Right	.179	.207	.302	106	19	4	0	3	11	4	26

TWO YEAR TOTALS (1986 – 1987)	G	IP	H	BB	SO	SB	CS	W	L	S	ERA
	10	70.1	52	16	58	6	3	7	0	0	2.30
	5	33.1	32	11	28	5	1	3	0	0	2.97
	5	37.0	20	5	30	1	2	4	0	0	1.70

	AVG	OBP	SLG	AB	H	2B	3B	HR	RBI	BB	SO
	.206	.256	.298	252	52	8	0	5	21	16	58
	.226	.289	.295	146	33	4	0	2	10	12	32
	.179	.207	.302	106	19	4	0	3	11	4	26

Perry, William Patrick "Pat"

Bats: Left   Throws: Left   Born 02/04/59

1987 SEASON AND MAJOR-LEAGUE CAREER PITCHING TOTALS

	G	GS	CG	GF	IP	BFP	H	R	ER	HR	SH	SF	HB	TBB	IBB	SO	WP	Bk	W	L	Pct	ShO	Sv	ERA
87 STL-CIN	57	0	0	16	81	324	60	34	32	7	3	1	3	25	4	39	3	0	5	2	.714	0	2	3.56
3 YEARS	109	0	0	37	162	654	122	65	61	12	3	8	3	62	14	74	9	0	8	5	.615	0	4	3.39

1987: Finesse, Flyball   1986: Finesse, Flyball   1985: Finesse, Flyball

1987 SEASON	G	IP	H	BB	SO	SB	CS	W	L	S	ERA
Totals	57	81.0	60	25	38	6	1	5	2	2	3.56
At Home	30	43.1	29	12	20	3	1	3	1	1	3.12
On Road	27	37.2	31	13	18	3	0	2	1	1	4.06

vs. Opposing Batters	AVG	OBP	SLG	AB	H	2B	3B	HR	RBI	BB	SO
Totals	.205	.274	.342	292	60	15	2	7	31	25	38
vs. Left	.239	.268	.370	92	22	7	1	1	8	2	10
vs. Right	.190	.277	.330	200	38	8	1	6	23	23	28

FOUR YEAR TOTALS (1984 – 1987)	G	IP	H	BB	SO	SB	CS	W	L	S	ERA
	109	162.0	123	62	73	8	3	8	5	4	3.39
	50	73.1	65	26	35	4	3	3	2	1	4.17
	59	88.2	58	36	38	4	0	5	3	3	2.74

	AVG	OBP	SLG	AB	H	2B	3B	HR	RBI	BB	SO
	.212	.291	.337	579	123	26	5	12	64	62	73
	.246	.278	.357	171	42	9	2	2	14	6	17
	.199	.297	.328	408	81	17	3	10	50	56	56

Petralli, Eugene James "Gene"

Bats: Both   Throws: Right   Born 09/25/59

1987 SEASON AND MAJOR-LEAGUE CAREER BATTING TOTALS

	G	AB	H	2B	3B	HR	TB	R	RBI	TBB	IBB	SO	HP	SH	SF	SB	CS	SB%	GDP	AVG	OBP	SLG
87 TEX	101	202	61	11	2	7	97	28	31	27	2	29	2	0	1	0	2	.00	4	.302	.388	.480
6 YEARS	237	490	139	24	5	9	200	55	61	45	2	62	3	4	5	4	2	.67	16	.284	.344	.408

1987 SEASON	AVG	OBP	SLG	AB	H	2B	3B	HR	RBI	BB	SO
Totals	.302	.388	.480	202	61	11	2	7	31	27	29
vs. Left	.267	.353	.267	15	4	0	0	0	0	2	3
vs. Right	.305	.391	.497	187	57	11	2	7	31	25	26
At Home	.319	.423	.532	94	30	6	1	4	15	16	12
On Road	.287	.355	.435	108	31	5	1	3	16	11	17

FOUR YEAR TOTALS (1984 – 1987)	AVG	OBP	SLG	AB	H	2B	3B	HR	RBI	BB	SO
	.278	.339	.412	442	123	22	5	9	60	40	55
	.194	.242	.194	31	6	0	0	0	1	2	6
	.285	.346	.428	411	117	22	5	9	59	38	49
	.273	.362	.410	183	50	8	1	5	24	25	23
	.282	.321	.413	259	73	14	4	4	36	15	32

Petry, Daniel Joseph "Dan"
Bats: Right **Throws: Right** **Born 11/13/58**

1987 SEASON AND MAJOR-LEAGUE CAREER PITCHING TOTALS

	G	GS	CG	GF	IP	BFP	H	R	ER	HR	SH	SF	HB	TBB	IBB	SO	WP	Bk	W	L	Pct	ShO	Sv	ERA
87 DET	30	21	0	3	135	628	148	101	84	22	4	7	10	76	5	93	8	1	9	7	.563	0	0	5.60
9 YEARS	257	245	47	5	1639	6924	1528	776	683	164	49	39	37	648	56	866	58	5	107	81	.569	10	0	3.75

1987: Power, Groundball   1986: Finesse, Groundball   1985: Finesse, Groundball   1984: Finesse, Groundball

1987 SEASON

	G	IP	H	BB	SO	SB	CS	W	L	S	ERA
Totals	30	134.2	148	76	93	19	6	9	7	0	5.61
At Home	13	62.0	66	32	44	6	4	4	4	0	5.95
On Road	17	72.2	82	44	49	13	2	5	3	0	5.33

vs. Opposing Batters	AVG	OBP	SLG	AB	H	2B	3B	HR	RBI	BB	SO
Totals	.279	.375	.463	531	148	26	3	22	82	76	93
vs. Left	.272	.367	.433	254	69	13	2	8	40	39	41
vs. Right	.285	.383	.491	277	79	13	1	14	42	37	52

FOUR YEAR TOTALS (1984 – 1987)

	G	IP	H	BB	SO	SB	CS	W	L	S	ERA
	119	722.2	691	276	402	59	35	47	38	0	3.95
	60	377.2	344	139	216	28	23	22	24	0	3.88
	59	345.0	347	137	186	31	12	25	14	0	4.02

	AVG	OBP	SLG	AB	H	2B	3B	HR	RBI	BB	SO
Totals	.251	.321	.397	2753	691	128	14	82	316	276	402
vs. Left	.242	.318	.387	1472	356	58	10	45	166	164	207
vs. Right	.262	.324	.409	1281	335	70	4	37	150	112	195

Plunk, Eric Vaughn
Bats: Right **Throws: Right** **Born 09/03/63**

1987 SEASON AND MAJOR-LEAGUE CAREER PITCHING TOTALS

	G	GS	CG	GF	IP	BFP	H	R	ER	HR	SH	SF	HB	TBB	IBB	SO	WP	Bk	W	L	Pct	ShO	Sv	ERA
87 OAK	32	11	0	11	95	432	91	53	50	8	3	5	2	62	3	90	5	2	4	6	.400	0	2	4.74
2 YEARS	58	26	0	13	215	969	182	128	121	22	5	8	7	164	5	188	14	8	8	13	.381	0	2	5.07

1987: Power, Flyball   1986: Power, Flyball

1987 SEASON

	G	IP	H	BB	SO	SB	CS	W	L	S	ERA
Totals	32	95.0	91	62	90	12	4	4	6	2	4.74
At Home	16	46.1	41	36	43	6	3	2	3	2	4.86
On Road	16	48.2	50	26	47	6	1	2	3	0	4.62

vs. Opposing Batters	AVG	OBP	SLG	AB	H	2B	3B	HR	RBI	BB	SO
Totals	.253	.362	.368	359	91	17	0	8	49	62	90
vs. Left	.276	.371	.365	192	53	11	0	2	25	30	43
vs. Right	.228	.353	.371	167	38	6	0	6	24	32	47

FOUR YEAR TOTALS (1984 – 1987)

	G	IP	H	BB	SO	SB	CS	W	L	S	ERA
	58	215.1	182	164	188	29	11	8	13	2	5.06
	29	109.2	91	95	97	12	6	5	6	2	5.33
	29	105.2	91	69	91	17	5	3	7	0	4.77

	AVG	OBP	SLG	AB	H	2B	3B	HR	RBI	BB	SO
Totals	.232	.364	.353	784	182	29	0	22	105	164	188
vs. Left	.248	.374	.350	431	107	17	0	9	52	88	88
vs. Right	.212	.353	.357	353	75	12	0	13	53	76	100

Polidor, Gustavo Adolfo (Gonzalez) "Gus"
Bats: Right **Throws: Right** **Born 10/26/61**

1987 SEASON AND MAJOR-LEAGUE CAREER BATTING TOTALS

	G	AB	H	2B	3B	HR	TB	R	RBI	TBB	IBB	SO	HP	SH	SF	SB	CS	SB%	GDP	AVG	OBP	SLG
87 CAL	63	137	36	3	0	2	45	12	15	2	0	15	1	0	1	0	0	.00	3	.263	.277	.328
3 YEARS	71	157	42	4	0	2	52	14	16	3	0	15	1	0	1	0	0	.00	5	.268	.284	.331

1987 SEASON

	AVG	OBP	SLG	AB	H	2B	3B	HR	RBI	BB	SO
Totals	.263	.277	.328	137	36	3	0	2	15	2	15
vs. Left	.241	.267	.293	58	14	0	0	1	3	1	11
vs. Right	.278	.284	.354	79	22	3	0	1	12	1	4
At Home	.326	.347	.326	46	15	0	0	0	6	2	8
On Road	.231	.239	.330	91	21	3	0	2	9	0	7

TWO YEAR TOTALS (1986 – 1987)

	AVG	OBP	SLG	AB	H	2B	3B	HR	RBI	BB	SO
Totals	.263	.280	.327	156	41	4	0	2	16	3	15
vs. Left	.260	.289	.315	73	19	1	0	1	4	2	11
vs. Right	.265	.271	.337	83	22	3	0	1	12	1	4
At Home	.328	.344	.344	61	20	1	0	0	7	2	8
On Road	.221	.237	.316	95	21	3	0	2	9	1	7

Porter, Darrell Ray
Bats: Left **Throws: Right** **Born 01/17/52**

1987 SEASON AND MAJOR-LEAGUE CAREER BATTING TOTALS

	G	AB	H	2B	3B	HR	TB	R	RBI	TBB	IBB	SO	HP	SH	SF	SB	CS	SB%	GDP	AVG	OBP	SLG
87 TEX	85	130	31	3	0	7	55	19	21	30	4	43	2	0	1	0	0	.00	2	.238	.387	.423
17 YEARS	1782	5539	1369	237	48	188	2266	765	826	905	106	1025	45	18	63	39	37	.51	102	.247	.354	.409

1987 SEASON

	AVG	OBP	SLG	AB	H	2B	3B	HR	RBI	BB	SO
Totals	.238	.387	.423	130	31	3	0	7	20	30	43
vs. Left	.250	.250	.250	8	2	0	0	0	0	0	3
vs. Right	.238	.394	.434	122	29	3	0	7	20	30	40
At Home	.242	.415	.435	62	15	0	0	4	12	18	25
On Road	.235	.358	.412	68	16	3	0	3	8	12	18

FOUR YEAR TOTALS (1984 – 1987)

	AVG	OBP	SLG	AB	H	2B	3B	HR	RBI	BB	SO
Totals	.235	.344	.412	947	223	37	5	40	153	153	221
vs. Left	.246	.335	.437	142	35	5	2	6	36	20	34
vs. Right	.234	.346	.407	805	188	32	3	34	117	133	187
At Home	.249	.359	.429	434	108	18	3	18	80	73	112
On Road	.224	.331	.398	513	115	19	2	22	73	80	109

Portugal, Mark Steven

Bats: Right   Throws: Right   Born 10/30/62

1987 SEASON AND MAJOR-LEAGUE CAREER PITCHING TOTALS

	G	GS	CG	GF	IP	BFP	H	R	ER	HR	SH	SF	HB	TBB	IBB	SO	WP	Bk	W	L	Pct	ShO	Sv	ERA
87 MIN	13	7	0	3	44	204	58	40	38	13	0	1	1	24	1	28	2	0	1	3	.250	0	0	7.77
3 YEARS	46	26	3	10	181	790	194	112	107	26	5	6	2	88	2	107	8	1	8	16	.333	0	1	5.32

1987: Power, Groundball   1986: Power, Groundball   1985: Power, Groundball

1987 SEASON

	G	IP	H	BB	SO	SB	CS	W	L	S	ERA
Totals	13	44.0	58	24	28	12	1	1	3	0	7.77
At Home	6	18.1	35	13	15	9	1	0	2	0	11.29
On Road	7	25.2	23	11	13	3	0	1	1	0	5.26

vs. Opposing Batters	AVG	OBP	SLG	AB	H	2B	3B	HR	RBI	BB	SO
Totals	.326	.407	.607	178	58	11	0	13	36	24	28
vs. Left	.255	.339	.481	106	27	6	0	6	16	14	23
vs. Right	.431	.506	.792	72	31	5	0	7	20	10	5

FOUR YEAR TOTALS (1984 – 1987)

	G	IP	H	BB	SO	SB	CS	W	L	S	ERA
Totals	46	181.0	194	88	107	16	5	8	16	1	5.32
At Home	21	77.1	93	43	48	10	3	4	6	1	6.05
On Road	25	103.2	101	45	59	6	2	4	10	1	4.77

	AVG	OBP	SLG	AB	H	2B	3B	HR	RBI	BB	SO
Totals	.282	.363	.453	689	194	38	1	26	89	88	107
vs. Left	.246	.340	.401	362	89	21	1	11	44	52	66
vs. Right	.321	.390	.511	327	105	17	0	15	45	36	41

Powell, Alonzo Sidney

Bats: Right   Throws: Right   Born 12/12/64

1987 SEASON AND MAJOR-LEAGUE CAREER BATTING TOTALS

	G	AB	H	2B	3B	HR	TB	R	RBI	TBB	IBB	SO	HP	SH	SF	SB	CS	SB%	GDP	AVG	OBP	SLG
87 MON	14	41	8	3	0	0	11	3	4	5	0	17	0	0	0	0	0	.00	0	.195	.283	.268
1 YEAR	14	41	8	3	0	0	11	3	4	5	0	17	0	0	0	0	0	.00	0	.195	.283	.268

1987 SEASON

	AVG	OBP	SLG	AB	H	2B	3B	HR	RBI	BB	SO
Totals	.195	.283	.268	41	8	3	0	0	4	5	16
vs. Left	.353	.450	.471	17	6	2	0	0	1	3	5
vs. Right	.083	.154	.125	24	2	1	0	0	3	2	11
At Home	.125	.222	.125	8	1	0	0	0	2	1	3
On Road	.212	.297	.303	33	7	3	0	0	2	4	13

FOUR YEAR TOTALS (1984 – 1987)

	AVG	OBP	SLG	AB	H	2B	3B	HR	RBI	BB	SO
Totals	.195	.283	.268	41	8	3	0	0	4	5	16
vs. Left	.353	.450	.471	17	6	2	0	0	1	3	5
vs. Right	.083	.154	.125	24	2	1	0	0	3	2	11
At Home	.125	.222	.125	8	1	0	0	0	2	1	3
On Road	.212	.297	.303	33	7	3	0	0	2	4	13

Powell, Dennis Clay

Bats: Right   Throws: Left   Born 08/13/63

1987 SEASON AND MAJOR-LEAGUE CAREER PITCHING TOTALS

	G	GS	CG	GF	IP	BFP	H	R	ER	HR	SH	SF	HB	TBB	IBB	SO	WP	Bk	W	L	Pct	ShO	Sv	ERA
87 SEA	16	3	0	1	34	147	32	13	12	3	2	2	0	15	0	17	0	0	1	3	.250	0	0	3.18
3 YEARS	59	11	0	12	128	552	127	64	60	15	11	5	2	53	10	67	10	2	4	11	.267	0	1	4.22

1987: Finesse, Flyball   1986: Finesse, Groundball   1985: Power, Groundball

1987 SEASON

	G	IP	H	BB	SO	SB	CS	W	L	S	ERA
Totals	16	34.1	32	15	17	0	1	1	3	0	3.15
At Home	6	18.0	17	9	7	0	0	0	2	0	3.00
On Road	10	16.1	15	6	10	0	1	1	1	0	3.31

vs. Opposing Batters	AVG	OBP	SLG	AB	H	2B	3B	HR	RBI	BB	SO
Totals	.250	.324	.375	128	32	7	0	3	14	15	17
vs. Left	.233	.306	.279	43	10	2	0	0	4	5	7
vs. Right	.259	.333	.424	85	22	5	0	3	10	10	10

FOUR YEAR TOTALS (1984 – 1987)

	G	IP	H	BB	SO	SB	CS	W	L	S	ERA
Totals	59	129.0	127	53	67	4	8	4	11	1	4.19
At Home	22	44.2	52	19	21	0	0	0	5	0	5.04
On Road	37	84.1	75	34	46	4	8	4	6	1	3.74

	AVG	OBP	SLG	AB	H	2B	3B	HR	RBI	BB	SO
Totals	.264	.336	.401	481	127	21	0	15	61	53	67
vs. Left	.187	.252	.231	134	25	3	0	1	12	12	23
vs. Right	.294	.368	.467	347	102	18	0	14	49	41	44

Price, Joseph Walter "Joe"

Bats: Right   Throws: Left   Born 11/29/56

1987 SEASON AND MAJOR-LEAGUE CAREER PITCHING TOTALS

	G	GS	CG	GF	IP	BFP	H	R	ER	HR	SH	SF	HB	TBB	IBB	SO	WP	Bk	W	L	Pct	ShO	Sv	ERA
87 SF	20	0	0	5	35	137	19	10	10	5	0	0	1	13	2	42	1	0	2	2	.500	0	1	2.57
8 YEARS	246	75	10	45	696	2916	631	302	271	71	30	23	8	252	28	492	11	1	38	33	.535	1	9	3.50

1987: Power, Flyball   1986: Power, Flyball   1985: Power, Flyball   1984: Power, Flyball

1987 SEASON

	G	IP	H	BB	SO	SB	CS	W	L	S	ERA
Totals	20	35.0	19	13	42	3	1	2	2	1	2.57
At Home	7	11.2	8	3	14	0	1	0	0	0	3.09
On Road	13	23.1	11	10	28	3	0	2	2	1	2.31

vs. Opposing Batters	AVG	OBP	SLG	AB	H	2B	3B	HR	RBI	BB	SO
Totals	.154	.241	.301	123	19	3	0	5	9	13	42
vs. Left	.176	.200	.324	34	6	2	0	1	2	1	10
vs. Right	.146	.255	.292	89	13	1	0	4	7	12	32

FOUR YEAR TOTALS (1984 – 1987)

	G	IP	H	BB	SO	SB	CS	W	L	S	ERA
Totals	101	313.0	303	119	253	18	11	12	19	2	4.11
At Home	48	169.0	165	63	126	8	6	7	6	0	3.73
On Road	53	144.0	138	56	127	10	5	5	13	2	4.56

	AVG	OBP	SLG	AB	H	2B	3B	HR	RBI	BB	SO
Totals	.251	.318	.404	1209	303	55	7	39	155	119	253
vs. Left	.247	.295	.409	247	61	10	3	8	28	17	47
vs. Right	.252	.324	.403	962	242	45	4	31	127	102	206

Puhl, Terry Stephen

Bats: Left   Throws: Right   Born 07/08/56

1987 SEASON AND MAJOR-LEAGUE CAREER BATTING TOTALS

	G	AB	H	2B	3B	HR	TB	R	RBI	TBB	IBB	SO	HP	SH	SF	SB	CS	SB%	GDP	AVG	OBP	SLG
87 HOU	90	122	28	5	0	2	39	9	15	11	0	16	0	1	0	1	1	.50	3	.230	.293	.320
11 YEARS	1245	4208	1178	193	50	59	1648	588	378	417	42	429	23	51	32	185	85	.69	51	.280	.346	.392

1987 SEASON

	AVG	OBP	SLG	AB	H	2B	3B	HR	RBI	BB	SO
Totals	.230	.293	.320	122	28	5	0	2	15	11	16
vs. Left	.111	.200	.111	9	1	0	0	0	0	1	2
vs. Right	.239	.301	.336	113	27	5	0	2	15	10	14
At Home	.197	.250	.268	71	14	2	0	1	7	5	11
On Road	.275	.351	.392	51	14	3	0	1	8	6	5

FOUR YEAR TOTALS (1984 – 1987)

	AVG	OBP	SLG	AB	H	2B	3B	HR	RBI	BB	SO
Totals	.277	.347	.401	937	260	48	10	16	107	103	108
vs. Left	.268	.323	.339	239	64	10	2	1	29	20	38
vs. Right	.281	.355	.423	698	196	38	8	15	78	83	70
At Home	.278	.347	.377	485	135	21	6	5	53	52	49
On Road	.277	.348	.427	452	125	27	4	11	54	51	59

Puleo, Charles Michael "Charlie"

Bats: Right   Throws: Right   Born 02/07/55

1987 SEASON AND MAJOR-LEAGUE CAREER PITCHING TOTALS

	G	GS	CG	GF	IP	BFP	H	R	ER	HR	SH	SF	HB	TBB	IBB	SO	WP	Bk	W	L	Pct	ShO	Sv	ERA
87 ATL	35	16	1	2	123	524	122	63	58	11	7	9	0	40	0	99	0	1	6	8	.429	0	0	4.24
6 YEARS	112	72	3	14	497	2189	494	274	243	48	27	22	11	256	21	300	9	4	23	33	.411	1	1	4.40

1987: Power, Flyball   1986: Power, Flyball

1987 SEASON

	G	IP	H	BB	SO	SB	CS	W	L	S	ERA
Totals	35	123.1	122	40	99	24	4	6	8	0	4.23
At Home	17	55.2	52	16	48	9	2	4	2	0	3.88
On Road	18	67.2	70	24	51	15	2	2	6	0	4.52

vs. Opposing Batters	AVG	OBP	SLG	AB	H	2B	3B	HR	RBI	BB	SO
Totals	.262	.319	.391	466	122	21	3	11	59	40	99
vs. Left	.283	.348	.457	247	70	10	3	9	38	26	44
vs. Right	.237	.285	.315	219	52	11	0	2	21	14	55

TWO YEAR TOTALS (1986 – 1987)

	G	IP	H	BB	SO	SB	CS	W	L	S	ERA
Totals	40	147.2	135	52	117	24	5	7	10	0	4.02
At Home	19	68.2	57	20	62	9	3	5	3	0	3.54
On Road	21	79.0	78	32	55	15	2	2	7	0	4.44

	AVG	OBP	SLG	AB	H	2B	3B	HR	RBI	BB	SO
Totals	.246	.312	.380	548	135	22	3	15	68	52	117
vs. Left	.266	.341	.438	290	77	11	3	11	44	34	54
vs. Right	.225	.277	.314	258	58	11	0	4	24	18	63

Quinones, Luis Raul

Bats: Both   Throws: Right   Born 11/11/63

1987 SEASON AND MAJOR-LEAGUE CAREER BATTING TOTALS

	G	AB	H	2B	3B	HR	TB	R	RBI	TBB	IBB	SO	HP	SH	SF	SB	CS	SB%	GDP	AVG	OBP	SLG
87 CHN	49	101	22	6	0	0	28	12	8	10	0	16	0	0	0	0	0	.00	0	.218	.288	.277
3 YEARS	139	249	49	9	4	0	66	30	23	14	1	37	1	5	2	4	2	.67	1	.197	.241	.265

1987 SEASON

	AVG	OBP	SLG	AB	H	2B	3B	HR	RBI	BB	SO
Totals	.218	.288	.277	101	22	6	0	0	8	10	16
vs. Left	.133	.235	.133	15	2	0	0	0	1	2	6
vs. Right	.233	.298	.302	86	20	6	0	0	7	8	10
At Home	.294	.351	.412	34	10	4	0	0	3	3	4
On Road	.179	.257	.209	67	12	2	0	0	5	7	12

FOUR YEAR TOTALS (1984 – 1987)

	AVG	OBP	SLG	AB	H	2B	3B	HR	RBI	BB	SO
Totals	.198	.248	.261	207	41	7	3	0	19	13	33
vs. Left	.119	.174	.119	42	5	0	0	0	4	3	14
vs. Right	.218	.267	.297	165	36	7	3	0	15	10	19
At Home	.237	.271	.300	80	19	5	0	0	8	4	14
On Road	.173	.234	.236	127	22	2	3	0	11	9	19

Ramirez, Rafael Emilio (Peguero)

Bats: Right   Throws: Right   Born 02/18/59

1987 SEASON AND MAJOR-LEAGUE CAREER BATTING TOTALS

	G	AB	H	2B	3B	HR	TB	R	RBI	TBB	IBB	SO	HP	SH	SF	SB	CS	SB%	GDP	AVG	OBP	SLG
87 ATL	56	179	47	12	0	1	62	22	21	8	0	16	2	4	1	6	3	.67	3	.263	.300	.346
8 YEARS	927	3537	929	139	21	37	1221	387	301	173	17	386	16	52	23	93	64	.59	72	.263	.298	.345

1987 SEASON

	AVG	OBP	SLG	AB	H	2B	3B	HR	RBI	BB	SO
Totals	.263	.300	.346	179	47	12	0	1	21	8	16
vs. Left	.323	.353	.400	65	21	5	0	0	10	3	5
vs. Right	.228	.270	.316	114	26	7	0	1	11	5	11
At Home	.253	.300	.325	83	21	6	0	0	11	5	7
On Road	.271	.300	.365	96	26	6	0	1	10	3	9

FOUR YEAR TOTALS (1984 – 1987)

	AVG	OBP	SLG	AB	H	2B	3B	HR	RBI	BB	SO
Totals	.253	.282	.332	1834	464	79	9	16	160	75	210
vs. Left	.245	.277	.315	603	148	25	4	3	54	27	66
vs. Right	.257	.285	.340	1231	316	54	5	13	106	48	144
At Home	.262	.301	.340	860	225	39	5	6	81	48	91
On Road	.245	.266	.325	974	239	40	4	10	79	27	119

Ramos, Domingo Antonio (de Ramos)

Bats: Right   Throws: Right   Born 03/29/58

1987 SEASON AND MAJOR-LEAGUE CAREER BATTING TOTALS

	G	AB	H	2B	3B	HR	TB	R	RBI	TBB	IBB	SO	HP	SH	SF	SB	CS	SB%	GDP	AVG	OBP	SLG
87 SEA	42	103	32	6	0	2	44	9	11	3	0	12	1	2	0	0	1	.00	1	.311	.336	.427
8 YEARS	292	620	140	22	0	5	177	59	44	45	0	79	3	10	2	5	6	.45	20	.226	.281	.285

	1987 SEASON										TWO YEAR TOTALS (1986 – 1987)										
	AVG	OBP	SLG	AB	H	2B	3B	HR	RBI	BB	SO	AVG	OBP	SLG	AB	H	2B	3B	HR	RBI	BB	SO
Totals	.311	.336	.427	103	32	6	0	2	11	3	12	.248	.294	.317	202	50	8	0	2	16	11	25
vs. Left	.263	.300	.316	38	10	2	0	0	2	2	6	.241	.333	.293	58	14	3	0	0	3	8	9
vs. Right	.338	.358	.492	65	22	4	0	2	9	1	6	.250	.275	.326	144	36	5	0	2	13	3	16
At Home	.282	.320	.394	71	20	5	0	1	8	3	11	.246	.288	.331	118	29	7	0	1	11	6	16
On Road	.375	.375	.500	32	12	1	0	1	3	0	1	.250	.300	.298	84	21	1	0	1	5	5	9

Ramsey, Michael James "Mike"

Bats: Both   Throws: Left   07/08/60

1987 SEASON AND MAJOR-LEAGUE CAREER BATTING TOTALS

	G	AB	H	2B	3B	HR	TB	R	RBI	TBB	IBB	SO	HP	SH	SF	SB	CS	SB%	GDP	AVG	OBP	SLG
87 LA	48	125	29	4	2	0	37	18	12	10	0	32	0	2	1	2	4	.33	3	.232	.287	.296
1 YEAR	48	125	29	4	2	0	37	18	12	10	0	32	0	2	1	2	4	.33	3	.232	.287	.296

	1987 SEASON										FOUR YEAR TOTALS (1984 – 1987)										
	AVG	OBP	SLG	AB	H	2B	3B	HR	RBI	BB	SO	AVG	OBP	SLG	AB	H	2B	3B	HR	RBI	BB	SO
Totals	.232	.287	.296	125	29	4	2	0	12	10	32	.232	.287	.296	125	29	4	2	0	12	10	32
vs. Left	.194	.265	.323	31	6	2	1	0	3	3	3	.194	.265	.323	31	6	2	1	0	3	3	3
vs. Right	.245	.294	.287	94	23	2	1	0	9	7	29	.245	.294	.287	94	23	2	1	0	9	7	29
At Home	.236	.259	.255	55	13	1	0	0	5	2	10	.236	.259	.255	55	13	1	0	0	5	2	10
On Road	.229	.308	.329	70	16	3	2	0	7	8	22	.229	.308	.329	70	16	3	2	0	7	8	22

Rasmussen, Dennis Lee

Bats: Left   Throws: Left   Born 04/18/59

1987 SEASON AND MAJOR-LEAGUE CAREER PITCHING TOTALS

	G	GS	CG	GF	IP	BFP	H	R	ER	HR	SH	SF	HB	TBB	IBB	SO	WP	Bk	W	L	Pct	ShO	Sv	ERA
87 NYA-CIN	33	32	2	0	191	814	184	100	97	36	8	6	5	67	1	128	7	2	13	8	.619	0	0	4.57
5 YEARS	114	104	8	2	657	2736	578	331	307	91	13	23	12	251	2	445	24	5	43	25	.632	1	0	4.21

1987: Finesse, Flyball   1986: Finesse, Flyball   1985: Power, Flyball   1984: Power, Flyball

	1987 SEASON										FOUR YEAR TOTALS (1984 – 1987)										
	G	IP	H	BB	SO	SB	CS	W	L	S	ERA	G	IP	H	BB	SO	SB	CS	W	L	S	ERA
Totals	33	191.1	184	67	128	14	14	13	8	0	4.56	110	642.2	568	243	432	33	36	43	25	0	4.26
At Home	15	90.1	80	34	73	6	5	8	4	0	3.79	49	287.1	245	123	211	12	15	23	11	0	4.23
On Road	18	101.0	104	33	55	8	9	5	4	0	5.26	61	355.1	323	120	221	21	21	20	14	0	4.28

vs. Opposing Batters	AVG	OBP	SLG	AB	H	2B	3B	HR	RBI	BB	SO	AVG	OBP	SLG	AB	H	2B	3B	HR	RBI	BB	SO
Totals	.253	.318	.474	728	184	41	6	36	85	67	128	.238	.309	.412	2387	568	108	19	90	277	243	432
vs. Left	.283	.345	.491	106	30	5	1	5	15	10	22	.244	.306	.383	426	104	16	2	13	47	38	73
vs. Right	.248	.313	.471	622	154	36	5	31	70	57	106	.237	.310	.419	1961	464	92	17	77	230	205	359

Rayford, Floyd Kinnard

Bats: Right   Throws: Right   Born 07/27/57

1987 SEASON AND MAJOR-LEAGUE CAREER BATTING TOTALS

	G	AB	H	2B	3B	HR	TB	R	RBI	TBB	IBB	SO	HP	SH	SF	SB	CS	SB%	GDP	AVG	OBP	SLG
87 BAL	20	50	11	0	0	2	17	5	3	2	0	9	0	0	0	0	0	.00	2	.220	.250	.340
7 YEARS	390	1044	255	43	1	38	414	112	117	55	1	225	3	9	4	4	5	.44	28	.244	.283	.397

	1987 SEASON										FOUR YEAR TOTALS (1984 – 1987)										
	AVG	OBP	SLG	AB	H	2B	3B	HR	RBI	BB	SO	AVG	OBP	SLG	AB	H	2B	3B	HR	RBI	BB	SO
Totals	.220	.250	.340	50	11	0	0	2	3	2	9	.255	.289	.413	869	222	39	1	32	97	39	179
vs. Left	.229	.229	.400	35	8	0	0	2	3	0	6	.281	.311	.489	374	105	15	0	21	47	17	73
vs. Right	.200	.294	.200	15	3	0	0	0	0	2	3	.236	.272	.356	495	117	24	1	11	50	22	106
At Home	.217	.280	.348	23	5	0	0	1	2	2	6	.278	.317	.447	425	118	22	1	16	54	23	85
On Road	.222	.222	.333	27	6	0	0	1	1	0	3	.234	.261	.381	444	104	17	0	16	43	16	94

Reed, Jeffrey Scott "Jeff"

Bats: Left **Throws: Right** **Born 11/12/62**

1987 SEASON AND MAJOR-LEAGUE CAREER BATTING TOTALS

	G	AB	H	2B	3B	HR	TB	R	RBI	TBB	IBB	SO	HP	SH	SF	SB	CS	SB%	GDP	AVG	OBP	SLG
87 MON	75	207	44	11	0	1	58	15	21	12	1	20	1	4	4	0	1	.00	8	.213	.254	.280
4 YEARS	168	403	88	20	1	3	119	33	31	30	1	48	2	8	4	1	1	.50	10	.218	.273	.295

	1987 SEASON										FOUR YEAR TOTALS (1984 – 1987)									
	AVG	OBP	SLG	AB	H	2B	3B	HR	RBI	BB	SO	AVG	OBP	SLG	AB	H	2B	3B	HR	RBI	BB	SO
Totals	.213	.254	.280	207	44	11	0	1	21	12	20	.218	.273	.295	403	88	20	1	3	31	30	48
vs. Left	.258	.294	.387	31	8	4	0	0	7	2	4	.262	.304	.357	42	11	4	0	0	7	2	7
vs. Right	.205	.247	.261	176	36	7	0	1	14	10	16	.213	.270	.288	361	77	16	1	3	24	28	41
At Home	.163	.204	.233	86	14	3	0	1	9	5	9	.200	.262	.288	205	41	12	0	2	17	18	26
On Road	.248	.290	.314	121	30	8	0	0	12	7	11	.237	.285	.303	198	47	8	1	1	14	12	22

Reed, Jerry Maxwell

Bats: Right **Throws: Right** **Born 10/08/55**

1987 SEASON AND MAJOR-LEAGUE CAREER PITCHING TOTALS

	G	GS	CG	GF	IP	BFP	H	R	ER	HR	SH	SF	HB	TBB	IBB	SO	WP	Bk	W	L	Pct	ShO	Sv	ERA
87 SEA	39	1	0	17	82	340	79	32	31	7	2	1	3	24	3	51	1	0	1	2	.333	0	7	3.40
6 YEARS	107	11	0	45	240	1016	243	121	108	27	5	6	7	77	6	131	6	0	10	9	.526	0	15	4.05

1987: Finesse, Flyball **1986: Finesse, Flyball**

	1987 SEASON										TWO YEAR TOTALS (1986 – 1987)									
	G	IP	H	BB	SO	SB	CS	W	L	S	ERA	G	IP	H	BB	SO	SB	CS	W	L	S	ERA
Totals	38	78.1	78	24	49	13	2	1	2	6	3.56	49	113.0	116	37	65	16	3	5	2	6	3.42
At Home	19	37.2	37	12	33	7	0	1	1	2	3.11	25	60.1	58	20	45	7	1	4	1	2	2.69
On Road	19	40.2	41	12	16	6	2	0	1	4	3.98	24	52.2	58	17	20	9	2	1	1	4	4.27
vs. Opposing Batters	AVG	OBP	SLG	AB	H	2B	3B	HR	RBI	BB	SO	AVG	OBP	SLG	AB	H	2B	3B	HR	RBI	BB	SO
Totals	.260	.320	.373	300	78	11	1	7	35	24	49	.264	.325	.385	439	116	17	3	10	49	37	65
vs. Left	.271	.329	.368	133	36	4	0	3	16	11	18	.260	.313	.350	200	52	6	0	4	22	15	25
vs. Right	.251	.313	.377	167	42	7	1	4	19	13	31	.268	.335	.414	239	64	11	3	6	27	22	40

Reuss, Jerry

Bats: Left **Throws: Left** **Born 06/19/49**

1987 SEASON AND MAJOR-LEAGUE CAREER PITCHING TOTALS

	G	GS	CG	GF	IP	BFP	H	R	ER	HR	SH	SF	HB	TBB	IBB	SO	WP	Bk	W	L	Pct	ShO	Sv	ERA
87 LA-CIN-CAL	25	23	1	1	119	539	166	92	79	18	8	2	3	29	3	49	4	1	4	10	.286	1	0	5.97
19 YEARS	562	491	124	40	3338	14180	3372	1530	1330	210	206	71	52	1047	114	1793	102	19	198	173	.534	38	11	3.59

1987: Finesse, Groundball **1986: Finesse, Groundball** **1985: Finesse, Groundball** **1984: Finesse, Groundball**

	1987 SEASON										FOUR YEAR TOTALS (1984 – 1987)									
	G	IP	H	BB	SO	SB	CS	W	L	S	ERA	G	IP	H	BB	SO	SB	CS	W	L	S	ERA
Totals	25	119.0	166	29	49	2	3	4	10	0	5.97	108	504.2	574	135	206	26	20	25	33	2	4.24
At Home	16	76.2	105	18	30	2	3	2	6	0	5.05	55	274.2	311	64	104	18	12	13	16	0	3.80
On Road	9	42.1	61	11	19	0	0	2	4	0	7.65	53	230.0	263	71	102	8	8	12	17	2	4.77
vs. Opposing Batters	AVG	OBP	SLG	AB	H	2B	3B	HR	RBI	BB	SO	AVG	OBP	SLG	AB	H	2B	3B	HR	RBI	BB	SO
Totals	.334	.373	.511	497	166	22	6	18	78	29	49	.288	.333	.417	1995	574	83	15	48	226	135	206
vs. Left	.345	.371	.500	84	29	2	1	3	11	4	11	.288	.322	.401	312	90	8	3	7	37	16	40
vs. Right	.332	.373	.513	413	137	20	5	15	67	25	38	.288	.336	.419	1683	484	75	12	41	189	119	166

Reynolds, Ronn Dwayne

Bats: Right **Throws: Right** **Born 09/28/58**

1987 SEASON AND MAJOR-LEAGUE CAREER BATTING TOTALS

	G	AB	H	2B	3B	HR	TB	R	RBI	TBB	IBB	SO	HP	SH	SF	SB	CS	SB%	GDP	AVG	OBP	SLG
87 HOU	38	102	17	4	0	1	24	5	7	3	0	29	0	1	1	0	1	.00	3	.167	.189	.235
5 YEARS	135	341	66	11	0	4	89	21	20	17	1	90	1	3	3	0	1	.00	10	.194	.232	.261

	1987 SEASON										FOUR YEAR TOTALS (1984 – 1987)									
	AVG	OBP	SLG	AB	H	2B	3B	HR	RBI	BB	SO	AVG	OBP	SLG	AB	H	2B	3B	HR	RBI	BB	SO
Totals	.167	.189	.235	102	17	4	0	1	7	3	29	.196	.220	.277	271	53	10	0	4	18	8	77
vs. Left	.129	.182	.194	31	4	2	0	0	1	2	6	.212	.248	.346	104	22	5	0	3	8	5	27
vs. Right	.183	.192	.254	71	13	2	0	1	6	1	23	.186	.202	.234	167	31	5	0	1	10	3	50
At Home	.125	.140	.208	48	6	4	0	0	3	1	15	.211	.227	.301	123	26	8	0	1	11	2	37
On Road	.204	.232	.259	54	11	0	0	1	4	2	14	.182	.214	.257	148	27	2	0	3	7	6	40

Rijo, Jose Antonio (Abreu)

Bats: Right   Throws: Right   Born 05/13/65

1987 SEASON AND MAJOR-LEAGUE CAREER PITCHING TOTALS

	G	GS	CG	GF	IP	BFP	H	R	ER	HR	SH	SF	HB	TBB	IBB	SO	WP	Bk	W	L	Pct	ShO	Sv	ERA
87 OAK	21	14	1	3	82	394	106	67	54	10	0	3	2	41	1	67	5	2	2	7	.222	0	0	5.93
4 YEARS	96	54	5	21	402	1811	409	249	212	45	21	13	8	210	11	355	13	7	19	30	.388	0	3	4.75

1987: Power, Groundball   1986: Power, Flyball   1985: Power, Flyball   1984: Power, Flyball

	1987 SEASON											FOUR YEAR TOTALS (1984 – 1987)										
	G	IP	H	BB	SO	SB	CS	W	L	S	ERA	G	IP	H	BB	SO	SB	CS	W	L	S	ERA
Totals	21	82.1	106	41	67	7	3	2	7	0	5.90	96	402.0	409	210	355	45	16	19	30	3	4.75
At Home	10	41.1	51	18	39	4	3	2	3	0	4.35	40	174.2	167	95	161	19	11	8	10	1	4.07
On Road	11	41.0	55	23	28	3	0	0	4	0	7.46	56	227.1	242	115	194	26	5	11	20	2	5.27
vs. Opposing Batters	AVG	OBP	SLG	AB	H	2B	3B	HR	RBI	BB	SO	AVG	OBP	SLG	AB	H	2B	3B	HR	RBI	BB	SO
Totals	.305	.379	.455	347	106	16	3	10	52	41	67	.263	.350	.413	1558	409	74	13	45	215	210	355
vs. Left	.303	.387	.491	175	53	11	2	6	31	25	37	.274	.377	.448	796	218	43	9	26	132	132	174
vs. Right	.308	.370	.419	172	53	5	1	4	21	16	30	.251	.321	.377	762	191	31	4	19	83	78	181

Ritchie, Wallace Reid "Wally"

Bats: Left   Throws: Left   Born 07/12/65

1987 SEASON AND MAJOR-LEAGUE CAREER PITCHING TOTALS

	G	GS	CG	GF	IP	BFP	H	R	ER	HR	SH	SF	HB	TBB	IBB	SO	WP	Bk	W	L	Pct	ShO	Sv	ERA
87 PHI	49	0	0	13	62	273	60	27	26	8	5	2	1	29	11	45	2	3	3	2	.600	0	3	3.77
1 YEAR	49	0	0	13	62	273	60	27	26	8	5	2	1	29	11	45	2	3	3	2	.600	0	3	3.77

1987: Power, Flyball

	1987 SEASON											FOUR YEAR TOTALS (1984 – 1987)										
	G	IP	H	BB	SO	SB	CS	W	L	S	ERA	G	IP	H	BB	SO	SB	CS	W	L	S	ERA
Totals	49	62.0	60	29	45	8	0	3	2	3	3.77	49	62.0	60	29	45	8	0	3	2	3	3.77
At Home	25	33.1	38	19	27	4	0	1	1	2	5.13	25	33.1	38	19	27	4	0	1	1	2	5.13
On Road	24	28.2	22	10	18	4	0	2	1	1	2.20	24	28.2	22	10	18	4	0	2	1	1	2.20
vs. Opposing Batters	AVG	OBP	SLG	AB	H	2B	3B	HR	RBI	BB	SO	AVG	OBP	SLG	AB	H	2B	3B	HR	RBI	BB	SO
Totals	.254	.336	.428	236	60	11	3	8	28	29	45	.254	.336	.428	236	60	11	3	8	28	29	45
vs. Left	.318	.366	.515	66	21	1	3	2	9	5	13	.318	.366	.515	66	21	1	3	2	9	5	13
vs. Right	.229	.325	.394	170	39	10	0	6	19	24	32	.229	.325	.394	170	39	10	0	6	19	24	32

Rivera, Luis Antonio (Pedraza)

Bats: Right   Throws: Right   Born 01/03/64

1987 SEASON AND MAJOR-LEAGUE CAREER BATTING TOTALS

	G	AB	H	2B	3B	HR	TB	R	RBI	TBB	IBB	SO	HP	SH	SF	SB	CS	SB%	GDP	AVG	OBP	SLG
87 MON	18	32	5	2	0	0	7	0	1	1	0	8	0	0	0	0	0	.00	0	.156	.182	.219
2 YEARS	73	198	39	13	1	0	54	20	14	18	0	41	2	1	1	1	1	.50	1	.197	.269	.273

	1987 SEASON											FOUR YEAR TOTALS (1984 – 1987)										
	AVG	OBP	SLG	AB	H	2B	3B	HR	RBI	BB	SO	AVG	OBP	SLG	AB	H	2B	3B	HR	RBI	BB	SO
Totals	.156	.182	.219	32	5	2	0	0	1	1	8	.197	.269	.273	198	39	13	1	0	14	18	41
vs. Left	.227	.227	.318	22	5	2	0	0	1	0	4	.242	.293	.330	91	22	6	1	0	4	7	15
vs. Right	.000	.091	.000	10	0	0	0	0	0	1	4	.159	.250	.224	107	17	7	0	0	10	11	26
At Home	.111	.158	.167	18	2	1	0	0	1	1	5	.191	.256	.273	110	21	7	1	0	10	10	20
On Road	.214	.214	.286	14	3	1	0	0	0	0	3	.205	.286	.273	88	18	6	0	0	4	8	21

Robidoux, William Joseph "Billy"

Bats: Left   Throws: Right   Born 01/13/64

1987 SEASON AND MAJOR-LEAGUE CAREER BATTING TOTALS

	G	AB	H	2B	3B	HR	TB	R	RBI	TBB	IBB	SO	HP	SH	SF	SB	CS	SB%	GDP	AVG	OBP	SLG
87 MIL	23	62	12	0	0	0	12	9	4	8	1	17	0	0	0	0	1	.00	0	.194	.286	.194
3 YEARS	97	294	62	10	0	4	84	29	33	53	2	69	0	0	1	0	1	.00	9	.211	.330	.286

	1987 SEASON											FOUR YEAR TOTALS (1984 – 1987)										
	AVG	OBP	SLG	AB	H	2B	3B	HR	RBI	BB	SO	AVG	OBP	SLG	AB	H	2B	3B	HR	RBI	BB	SO
Totals	.194	.286	.194	62	12	0	0	0	4	8	17	.211	.330	.286	294	62	10	0	4	33	53	69
vs. Left	.286	.444	.286	7	2	0	0	0	1	2	3	.300	.410	.500	50	15	1	0	3	12	10	18
vs. Right	.182	.262	.182	55	10	0	0	0	3	6	14	.193	.314	.242	244	47	9	0	1	21	43	51
At Home	.148	.179	.148	27	4	0	0	0	2	1	9	.173	.300	.213	127	22	5	0	0	6	23	27
On Road	.229	.357	.229	35	8	0	0	0	2	7	8	.240	.354	.341	167	40	5	0	4	27	30	42

Robinson, Don Allen

Bats: Right   Throws: Right   Born 06/08/57

1987 SEASON AND MAJOR-LEAGUE CAREER PITCHING TOTALS

	G	GS	CG	GF	IP	BFP	H	R	ER	HR	SH	SF	HB	TBB	IBB	SO	WP	Bk	W	L	Pct	ShO	Sv	ERA
87 PIT-SF	67	0	0	54	108	460	105	42	41	7	7	3	0	40	6	79	7	1	11	7	.611	0	19	3.42
10 YEARS	368	126	22	157	1244	5292	1194	580	528	105	61	42	19	459	56	851	62	9	70	70	.500	3	50	3.82

1987: Power, Flyball   1986: Power, Flyball   1985: Power, Flyball   1984: Power, Flyball

	1987 SEASON											FOUR YEAR TOTALS (1984 – 1987)										
	G	IP	H	BB	SO	SB	CS	W	L	S	ERA	G	IP	H	BB	SO	SB	CS	W	L	S	ERA
Totals	68	109.0	106	42	80	7	6	11	8	19	3.47	213	395.2	361	160	308	30	18	24	29	46	3.41
At Home	35	48.1	48	19	33	3	2	6	2	12	3.72	102	185.0	175	65	156	14	7	15	9	23	3.31
On Road	33	60.2	58	23	47	4	4	5	6	7	3.26	111	210.2	186	95	152	16	11	9	20	23	3.50
vs. Opposing Batters	AVG	OBP	SLG	AB	H	2B	3B	HR	RBI	BB	SO	AVG	OBP	SLG	AB	H	2B	3B	HR	RBI	BB	SO
Totals	.257	.323	.378	413	106	23	3	7	52	42	80	.244	.317	.352	1480	361	76	6	24	171	160	308
vs. Left	.240	.319	.330	221	53	12	1	2	22	26	44	.227	.320	.302	679	154	32	2	5	58	94	143
vs. Right	.276	.329	.432	192	53	11	2	5	30	16	36	.258	.314	.395	801	207	44	4	19	113	66	165

Robinson, Jeffrey Mark "Jeff"

Bats: Right   Throws: Right   Born 12/13/60

1987 SEASON AND MAJOR-LEAGUE CAREER PITCHING TOTALS

	G	GS	CG	GF	IP	BFP	H	R	ER	HR	SH	SF	HB	TBB	IBB	SO	WP	Bk	W	L	Pct	ShO	Sv	ERA
87 DET	29	21	2	2	127	569	132	86	76	16	2	2	7	54	3	98	4	3	9	6	.600	1	0	5.39
1 YEAR	29	21	2	2	127	569	132	86	76	16	2	2	7	54	3	98	4	3	9	6	.600	1	0	5.39

1987: Power, Groundball

	1987 SEASON											FOUR YEAR TOTALS (1984 – 1987)										
	G	IP	H	BB	SO	SB	CS	W	L	S	ERA	G	IP	H	BB	SO	SB	CS	W	L	S	ERA
Totals	29	127.1	132	54	98	9	5	9	6	0	5.37	29	127.1	132	54	98	9	5	9	6	0	5.37
At Home	15	61.2	52	30	51	3	2	2	2	0	5.40	15	61.2	52	30	51	3	2	2	2	0	5.40
On Road	14	65.2	80	24	47	6	3	7	4	0	5.35	14	65.2	80	24	47	6	3	7	4	0	5.35
vs. Opposing Batters	AVG	OBP	SLG	AB	H	2B	3B	HR	RBI	BB	SO	AVG	OBP	SLG	AB	H	2B	3B	HR	RBI	BB	SO
Totals	.262	.340	.413	504	132	22	3	16	74	54	98	.262	.340	.413	504	132	22	3	16	74	54	98
vs. Left	.226	.310	.394	279	63	14	3	9	39	35	47	.226	.310	.394	279	63	14	3	9	39	35	47
vs. Right	.307	.378	.436	225	69	8	0	7	35	19	51	.307	.378	.436	225	69	8	0	7	35	19	51

Robinson, Ronald Dean "Ron"

Bats: Right   Throws: Right   Born 03/24/62

1987 SEASON AND MAJOR-LEAGUE CAREER PITCHING TOTALS

	G	GS	CG	GF	IP	BFP	H	R	ER	HR	SH	SF	HB	TBB	IBB	SO	WP	Bk	W	L	Pct	ShO	Sv	ERA
87 CIN	48	18	0	14	154	638	148	71	63	14	8	7	1	43	8	99	2	0	7	5	.583	0	4	3.68
4 YEARS	163	35	1	57	419	1744	400	186	165	38	16	15	4	131	22	316	8	2	25	17	.595	0	19	3.54

1987: Finesse, Flyball   1986: Power, Flyball   1985: Power, Flyball   1984: Finesse, Groundball

	1987 SEASON											FOUR YEAR TOTALS (1984 – 1987)										
	G	IP	H	BB	SO	SB	CS	W	L	S	ERA	G	IP	H	BB	SO	SB	CS	W	L	S	ERA
Totals	48	153.2	148	43	99	14	10	7	5	3	3.69	163	418.1	400	131	316	37	29	25	17	18	3.55
At Home	25	74.2	83	23	47	10	3	2	5	0	4.58	85	219.1	225	68	157	21	15	10	12	8	4.06
On Road	23	79.0	65	20	52	4	7	5	0	3	2.85	78	199.0	175	63	159	16	14	15	5	10	2.98
vs. Opposing Batters	AVG	OBP	SLG	AB	H	2B	3B	HR	RBI	BB	SO	AVG	OBP	SLG	AB	H	2B	3B	HR	RBI	BB	SO
Totals	.256	.305	.411	579	148	34	7	14	67	43	99	.253	.310	.395	1578	400	80	15	38	181	131	316
vs. Left	.292	.339	.456	274	80	20	5	5	40	22	30	.290	.355	.426	753	218	39	11	14	98	79	103
vs. Right	.223	.274	.370	305	68	14	2	9	27	21	69	.221	.267	.367	825	182	41	4	24	83	52	213

Rodriguez, Ricardo "Rick"

Bats: Right   Throws: Right   Born 09/21/60

1987 SEASON AND MAJOR-LEAGUE CAREER PITCHING TOTALS

	G	GS	CG	GF	IP	BFP	H	R	ER	HR	SH	SF	HB	TBB	IBB	SO	WP	Bk	W	L	Pct	ShO	Sv	ERA
87 OAK	15	0	0	11	24	112	32	8	8	1	1	0	1	15	1	9	0	0	1	0	1.000	0	0	3.00
2 YEARS	18	3	0	11	40	184	49	20	20	5	1	0	1	22	1	11	2	1	2	2	.500	0	0	4.50

1987: Finesse, Groundball   1986: Finesse, Flyball

	1987 SEASON											FOUR YEAR TOTALS (1984 – 1987)										
	G	IP	H	BB	SO	SB	CS	W	L	S	ERA	G	IP	H	BB	SO	SB	CS	W	L	S	ERA
Totals	15	24.1	32	15	9	0	4	1	0	0	2.96	18	40.2	49	22	11	1	4	2	2	0	4.43
At Home	8	12.2	13	7	5	0	3	0	0	0	2.13	10	26.1	27	11	6	1	3	1	1	0	3.42
On Road	7	11.2	19	8	4	0	1	1	0	0	3.86	8	14.1	22	11	5	0	1	1	1	0	6.28
vs. Opposing Batters	AVG	OBP	SLG	AB	H	2B	3B	HR	RBI	BB	SO	AVG	OBP	SLG	AB	H	2B	3B	HR	RBI	BB	SO
Totals	.337	.432	.442	95	32	1	3	1	10	15	9	.306	.393	.469	160	49	3	4	5	20	22	11
vs. Left	.385	.458	.462	52	20	0	2	0	4	7	3	.371	.440	.494	89	33	2	3	1	9	11	3
vs. Right	.279	.404	.419	43	12	1	1	1	6	8	6	.225	.337	.437	71	16	1	1	4	11	11	8

Roenicke, Gary Steven
Bats: Right   Throws: Right   Born 12/05/54

1987 SEASON AND MAJOR-LEAGUE CAREER BATTING TOTALS

	G	AB	H	2B	3B	HR	TB	R	RBI	TBB	IBB	SO	HP	SH	SF	SB	CS	SB%	GDP	AVG	OBP	SLG
87 ATL	67	151	33	8	0	9	68	25	28	32	0	23	1	0	3	0	0	.00	4	.219	.353	.450
11 YEARS	1015	2594	644	130	4	120	1142	356	403	398	16	413	41	23	26	16	20	.44	73	.248	.354	.440

1987 SEASON	AVG	OBP	SLG	AB	H	2B	3B	HR	RBI	BB	SO
Totals	.219	.353	.450	151	33	8	0	9	28	32	23
vs. Left	.205	.329	.453	117	24	5	0	8	25	22	16
vs. Right	.265	.432	.441	34	9	3	0	1	3	10	7
At Home	.288	.409	.671	73	21	4	0	8	20	15	10
On Road	.154	.303	.244	78	12	4	0	1	8	17	13

FOUR YEAR TOTALS (1984 – 1987)	AVG	OBP	SLG	AB	H	2B	3B	HR	RBI	BB	SO
Totals	.228	.353	.412	838	191	41	1	37	133	161	131
vs. Left	.231	.363	.434	549	127	25	1	28	101	113	82
vs. Right	.221	.334	.370	289	64	16	0	9	32	48	49
At Home	.255	.383	.493	408	104	16	0	27	80	83	62
On Road	.202	.325	.335	430	87	25	1	10	53	78	69

Roenicke, Ronald Jon "Ron"
Bats: Both   Throws: Left   Born 08/19/56

1987 SEASON AND MAJOR-LEAGUE CAREER BATTING TOTALS

	G	AB	H	2B	3B	HR	TB	R	RBI	TBB	IBB	SO	HP	SH	SF	SB	CS	SB%	GDP	AVG	OBP	SLG
87 PHI	63	78	13	3	1	1	21	9	4	14	1	15	0	0	0	1	0	1.00	2	.167	.293	.269
7 YEARS	513	1039	251	50	3	17	358	137	108	186	14	187	4	15	8	24	9	.73	16	.242	.357	.345

1987 SEASON	AVG	OBP	SLG	AB	H	2B	3B	HR	RBI	BB	SO
Totals	.167	.293	.269	78	13	3	1	1	4	14	15
vs. Left	.289	.357	.500	38	11	3	1	1	4	4	7
vs. Right	.050	.240	.050	40	2	0	0	0	0	10	8
At Home	.119	.260	.167	42	5	2	0	0	2	8	9
On Road	.222	.333	.389	36	8	1	1	1	2	6	6

FOUR YEAR TOTALS (1984 – 1987)	AVG	OBP	SLG	AB	H	2B	3B	HR	RBI	BB	SO
Totals	.239	.375	.362	506	121	26	3	10	61	112	99
vs. Left	.306	.412	.447	170	52	10	1	4	22	32	33
vs. Right	.205	.356	.318	336	69	16	2	6	39	80	66
At Home	.246	.400	.386	264	65	15	2	6	32	69	55
On Road	.231	.345	.335	242	56	11	1	4	29	43	44

Romero, Edgardo Ralph (Rivera) "Ed"
Bats: Right   Throws: Right   Born 12/09/57

1987 SEASON AND MAJOR-LEAGUE CAREER BATTING TOTALS

	G	AB	H	2B	3B	HR	TB	R	RBI	TBB	IBB	SO	HP	SH	SF	SB	CS	SB%	GDP	AVG	OBP	SLG
87 BOS	88	235	64	5	0	0	69	23	14	18	0	22	0	1	2	0	2	.00	9	.272	.322	.294
9 YEARS	599	1585	400	65	1	7	488	189	136	124	2	130	3	29	13	9	8	.53	43	.252	.306	.308

1987 SEASON	AVG	OBP	SLG	AB	H	2B	3B	HR	RBI	BB	SO
Totals	.272	.322	.294	235	64	5	0	0	14	18	22
vs. Left	.153	.225	.167	72	11	1	0	0	4	7	9
vs. Right	.325	.366	.350	163	53	4	0	0	10	11	13
At Home	.296	.353	.324	108	32	3	0	0	7	10	10
On Road	.252	.294	.268	127	32	2	0	0	7	8	12

FOUR YEAR TOTALS (1984 – 1987)	AVG	OBP	SLG	AB	H	2B	3B	HR	RBI	BB	SO
Totals	.247	.305	.294	1076	266	39	1	3	89	91	84
vs. Left	.212	.283	.267	397	84	19	0	1	26	40	29
vs. Right	.268	.318	.309	679	182	20	1	2	63	51	55
At Home	.244	.303	.304	536	131	21	1	3	38	45	38
On Road	.250	.308	.283	540	135	18	0	0	51	46	46

Royster, Jeron Kennis "Jerry"
Bats: Right   Throws: Right   Born 10/18/52

1987 SEASON AND MAJOR-LEAGUE CAREER BATTING TOTALS

	G	AB	H	2B	3B	HR	TB	R	RBI	TBB	IBB	SO	HP	SH	SF	SB	CS	SB%	GDP	AVG	OBP	SLG
87 CHA-NYA	73	196	52	13	0	7	86	26	27	23	1	32	1	3	2	4	2	.67	5	.265	.342	.439
15 YEARS	1360	4106	1031	162	33	40	1379	544	351	405	19	518	11	66	33	189	95	.67	88	.251	.318	.336

1987 SEASON	AVG	OBP	SLG	AB	H	2B	3B	HR	RBI	BB	SO
Totals	.265	.342	.439	196	52	13	0	7	27	23	32
vs. Left	.269	.325	.441	145	39	10	0	5	21	13	19
vs. Right	.255	.387	.431	51	13	3	0	2	6	10	13
At Home	.273	.349	.436	110	30	9	0	3	15	13	16
On Road	.256	.333	.442	86	22	4	0	4	12	10	16

FOUR YEAR TOTALS (1984 – 1987)	AVG	OBP	SLG	AB	H	2B	3B	HR	RBI	BB	SO
Totals	.253	.327	.375	929	235	51	4	18	105	103	149
vs. Left	.272	.344	.409	592	161	39	3	12	64	68	75
vs. Right	.220	.295	.315	337	74	12	1	6	41	35	74
At Home	.256	.327	.387	457	117	31	1	9	54	49	70
On Road	.250	.326	.362	472	118	20	3	9	51	54	79

Runge, Paul William

Bats: Right Throws: Right Born 05/21/58

1987 SEASON AND MAJOR-LEAGUE CAREER BATTING TOTALS

	G	AB	H	2B	3B	HR	TB	R	RBI	TBB	IBB	SO	HP	SH	SF	SB	CS	SB%	GDP	AVG	OBP	SLG
87 ATL	27	47	10	1	0	3	20	9	8	5	0	10	0	2	0	0	1	.00	1	.213	.288	.426
7 YEARS	131	269	64	8	1	4	86	32	19	40	0	54	0	10	1	5	5	.50	8	.238	.335	.320

	1987 SEASON											TWO YEAR TOTALS (1986 – 1987)										
	AVG	OBP	SLG	AB	H	2B	3B	HR	RBI	BB	SO	AVG	OBP	SLG	AB	H	2B	3B	HR	RBI	BB	SO
Totals	.213	.288	.426	47	10	1	0	3	8	5	10	.218	.302	.400	55	12	1	0	3	8	7	14
vs. Left	.269	.345	.538	26	7	1	0	2	7	3	3	.259	.355	.519	27	7	1	0	2	7	4	4
vs. Right	.143	.217	.286	21	3	0	0	1	1	2	7	.179	.258	.286	28	5	0	0	1	1	3	10
At Home	.250	.400	.450	20	5	1	0	1	4	5	6	.208	.387	.375	24	5	1	0	1	4	7	8
On Road	.185	.185	.407	27	5	0	0	2	4	0	4	.226	.226	.419	31	7	0	0	2	4	0	6

Russell, Jeffrey Lee "Jeff"

Bats: Right Throws: Right Born 09/02/61

1987 SEASON AND MAJOR-LEAGUE CAREER PITCHING TOTALS

	G	GS	CG	GF	IP	BFP	H	R	ER	HR	SH	SF	HB	TBB	IBB	SO	WP	Bk	W	L	Pct	ShO	Sv	ERA
87 TEX	52	2	0	12	97	442	109	56	48	9	0	5	2	52	5	56	6	1	5	4	.556	0	3	4.45
5 YEARS	145	55	6	22	491	2144	512	278	240	52	16	18	9	197	19	295	17	5	23	35	.397	2	5	4.40

1987: Power, Groundball   1986: Power, Groundball   1985: Power, Groundball   1984: Finesse, Flyball

	1987 SEASON										FOUR YEAR TOTALS (1984 – 1987)									
	G	IP	H	BB	SO	SB	CS	W	L	S	ERA	G	IP	H	BB	SO	SB	CS	W	L	S	ERA
Totals	52	97.1	109	52	56	13	3	5	4	3	4.44	135	423.0	454	175	255	50	17	19	30	5	4.62
At Home	25	41.0	52	27	17	8	3	1	2	2	5.71	62	190.1	219	77	110	29	10	9	9	3	4.96
On Road	27	56.1	57	25	39	5	0	4	2	1	3.51	73	232.2	235	98	145	21	7	10	21	2	4.33
vs. Opposing Batters	AVG	OBP	SLG	AB	H	2B	3B	HR	RBI	BB	SO	AVG	OBP	SLG	AB	H	2B	3B	HR	RBI	BB	SO
Totals	.285	.369	.418	383	109	22	1	9	64	52	56	.274	.343	.418	1655	454	85	9	45	236	175	255
vs. Left	.291	.362	.467	182	53	11	0	7	36	22	27	.293	.365	.454	769	225	49	3	23	121	90	115
vs. Right	.279	.374	.373	201	56	11	1	2	28	30	29	.258	.324	.387	886	229	36	6	22	115	85	140

Russell, John William

Bats: Right Throws: Right Born 01/05/61

1987 SEASON AND MAJOR-LEAGUE CAREER BATTING TOTALS

	G	AB	H	2B	3B	HR	TB	R	RBI	TBB	IBB	SO	HP	SH	SF	SB	CS	SB%	GDP	AVG	OBP	SLG
87 PHI	24	62	9	1	0	3	19	5	8	3	0	17	0	0	0	0	1	.00	4	.145	.185	.306
4 YEARS	237	692	160	42	3	27	289	73	102	58	4	225	3	1	7	2	3	.40	17	.231	.291	.418

	1987 SEASON										FOUR YEAR TOTALS (1984 – 1987)									
	AVG	OBP	SLG	AB	H	2B	3B	HR	RBI	BB	SO	AVG	OBP	SLG	AB	H	2B	3B	HR	RBI	BB	SO
Totals	.145	.185	.306	62	9	1	0	3	8	3	17	.231	.291	.418	692	160	42	3	27	102	58	225
vs. Left	.132	.154	.237	38	5	1	0	1	5	1	9	.231	.312	.401	294	68	21	1	9	38	33	87
vs. Right	.167	.231	.417	24	4	0	0	2	3	2	8	.231	.274	.430	398	92	21	2	18	64	25	138
At Home	.129	.182	.226	31	4	0	0	1	4	2	13	.277	.334	.496	365	101	26	3	16	65	32	121
On Road	.161	.188	.387	31	5	1	0	2	4	1	4	.180	.242	.330	327	59	16	0	11	37	26	104

Ryal, Mark Dwayne

Bats: Left Throws: Left Born 04/28/60

1987 SEASON AND MAJOR-LEAGUE CAREER BATTING TOTALS

	G	AB	H	2B	3B	HR	TB	R	RBI	TBB	IBB	SO	HP	SH	SF	SB	CS	SB%	GDP	AVG	OBP	SLG
87 CAL	58	100	20	6	0	5	41	7	18	3	1	15	0	1	0	0	0	.00	4	.200	.223	.410
4 YEARS	89	178	38	9	0	7	68	17	26	9	2	25	0	2	0	1	0	1.00	7	.213	.251	.382

	1987 SEASON										TWO YEAR TOTALS (1986 – 1987)									
	AVG	OBP	SLG	AB	H	2B	3B	HR	RBI	BB	SO	AVG	OBP	SLG	AB	H	2B	3B	HR	RBI	BB	SO
Totals	.200	.223	.410	100	20	6	0	5	18	3	15	.242	.270	.447	132	32	6	0	7	23	5	19
vs. Left	.000	.000	.000	3	0	0	0	0	1	0	2	.000	.250	.000	3	0	0	0	0	1	1	2
vs. Right	.206	.230	.423	97	20	6	0	5	17	3	13	.248	.271	.457	129	32	6	0	7	22	4	17
At Home	.186	.205	.419	43	8	1	0	3	9	1	6	.214	.241	.446	56	12	1	0	4	11	2	7
On Road	.211	.237	.404	57	12	5	0	2	9	2	9	.263	.291	.447	76	20	5	0	3	12	3	12

Sakata, Lenn Haruki
Bats: Right   Throws: Right   Born 06/08/53

1987 SEASON AND MAJOR-LEAGUE CAREER BATTING TOTALS

	G	AB	H	2B	3B	HR	TB	R	RBI	TBB	IBB	SO	HP	SH	SF	SB	CS	SB%	GDP	AVG	OBP	SLG
87 NYA	19	45	12	0	1	2	20	5	4	2	0	4	1	0	0	0	1	.00	2	.267	.313	.444
11 YEARS	565	1289	296	46	4	25	425	163	109	97	5	158	8	22	7	30	17	.64	33	.230	.286	.330

	1987 SEASON										TWO YEAR TOTALS (1986 – 1987)									
	AVG	OBP	SLG	AB	H	2B	3B	HR	RBI	BB	SO	AVG	OBP	SLG	AB	H	2B	3B	HR	RBI	BB	SO
Totals	.267	.313	.444	45	12	0	1	2	4	2	4	.304	.352	.430	79	24	2	1	2	9	5	10
vs. Left	.303	.343	.485	33	10	0	0	2	4	1	2	.283	.321	.415	53	15	1	0	2	8	2	5
vs. Right	.167	.231	.333	12	2	0	1	0	0	1	2	.346	.400	.462	26	9	1	1	0	1	3	5
At Home	.263	.333	.526	19	5	0	1	1	2	1	2	.348	.392	.500	46	16	2	1	1	7	3	7
On Road	.269	.296	.385	26	7	0	0	1	2	1	2	.242	.286	.333	33	8	0	0	1	2	2	3

Salas, Mark Bruce
Bats: Left   Throws: Right   Born 03/08/61

1987 SEASON AND MAJOR-LEAGUE CAREER BATTING TOTALS

	G	AB	H	2B	3B	HR	TB	R	RBI	TBB	IBB	SO	HP	SH	SF	SB	CS	SB%	GDP	AVG	OBP	SLG
87 MIN-NYA	72	160	40	6	0	6	64	21	21	15	1	23	3	1	2	0	1	.00	2	.250	.322	.400
4 YEARS	297	798	210	34	9	23	331	101	96	51	8	95	5	7	8	3	3	.50	17	.263	.309	.415

	1987 SEASON										FOUR YEAR TOTALS (1984 – 1987)									
	AVG	OBP	SLG	AB	H	2B	3B	HR	RBI	BB	SO	AVG	OBP	SLG	AB	H	2B	3B	HR	RBI	BB	SO
Totals	.250	.322	.400	160	40	6	0	6	21	15	23	.263	.309	.415	798	210	34	9	23	96	51	95
vs. Left	.200	.250	.200	15	3	0	0	0	1	1	4	.250	.323	.304	56	14	1	1	0	8	6	11
vs. Right	.255	.329	.421	145	37	6	0	6	20	14	19	.264	.308	.423	742	196	33	8	23	88	45	84
At Home	.235	.312	.395	81	19	4	0	3	10	7	14	.266	.312	.449	410	109	19	7	14	49	26	53
On Road	.266	.333	.405	79	21	2	0	3	11	8	9	.260	.305	.379	388	101	15	2	9	47	25	42

Salazar, Luis Ernesto (Garcia)
Bats: Right   Throws: Right   Born 05/19/56

1987 SEASON AND MAJOR-LEAGUE CAREER BATTING TOTALS

	G	AB	H	2B	3B	HR	TB	R	RBI	TBB	IBB	SO	HP	SH	SF	SB	CS	SB%	GDP	AVG	OBP	SLG
87 SD	84	189	48	5	0	3	62	13	17	14	2	30	0	1	2	3	3	.50	2	.254	.302	.328
8 YEARS	735	2325	613	84	24	42	871	245	249	98	26	388	6	33	17	106	42	.72	36	.264	.293	.375

	1987 SEASON										TWO YEAR TOTALS (1986 – 1987)									
	AVG	OBP	SLG	AB	H	2B	3B	HR	RBI	BB	SO	AVG	OBP	SLG	AB	H	2B	3B	HR	RBI	BB	SO
Totals	.254	.302	.328	189	48	5	0	3	17	14	30	.250	.294	.321	196	49	5	0	3	17	15	33
vs. Left	.258	.287	.361	97	25	4	0	2	7	4	18	.250	.284	.346	104	26	4	0	2	7	5	21
vs. Right	.250	.317	.293	92	23	1	0	1	10	10	12	.250	.317	.293	92	23	1	0	1	10	10	12
At Home	.284	.310	.326	95	27	1	0	1	7	4	16	.281	.307	.323	96	27	1	0	1	7	4	17
On Road	.223	.295	.330	94	21	4	0	2	10	10	14	.220	.295	.320	100	22	4	0	2	10	11	16

Sambito, Joseph Charles "Joe"
Bats: Left   Throws: Left   Born 06/28/52

1987 SEASON AND MAJOR-LEAGUE CAREER PITCHING TOTALS

	G	GS	CG	GF	IP	BFP	H	R	ER	HR	SH	SF	HB	TBB	IBB	SO	WP	Bk	W	L	Pct	ShO	Sv	ERA
87 BOS	47	0	0	16	38	171	46	29	29	8	2	0	0	16	3	35	3	0	2	6	.250	0	0	6.87
11 YEARS	461	5	1	274	630	2588	562	241	212	48	35	15	10	195	32	489	18	1	37	38	.493	1	84	3.03

1987: Power, Flyball   1986: Power, Flyball   1985: Power, Groundball   1984: Finesse, Flyball

	1987 SEASON										FOUR YEAR TOTALS (1984 – 1987)									
	G	IP	H	BB	SO	SB	CS	W	L	S	ERA	G	IP	H	BB	SO	SB	CS	W	L	S	ERA
Totals	47	37.2	46	16	35	0	2	2	6	0	6.93	140	140.2	160	56	94	9	5	4	6	12	5.37
At Home	18	17.1	32	6	15	0	1	2	2	0	8.31	67	78.2	90	24	46	4	3	2	2	6	4.58
On Road	29	20.1	14	10	20	0	1	0	4	0	5.75	73	62.0	70	32	48	5	2	1	4	6	6.39

vs. Opposing Batters	AVG	OBP	SLG	AB	H	2B	3B	HR	RBI	BB	SO	AVG	OBP	SLG	AB	H	2B	3B	HR	RBI	BB	SO
Totals	.299	.365	.532	154	46	8	2	8	28	16	35	.288	.353	.450	556	160	30	3	18	104	56	94
vs. Left	.231	.277	.385	78	18	4	1	2	10	5	23	.200	.277	.284	215	43	10	1	2	28	23	57
vs. Right	.368	.448	.684	76	28	4	1	6	18	11	12	.343	.401	.554	341	117	20	2	16	76	33	37

434

Schatzeder, Daniel Ernest "Dan"

Bats: Left   Throws: Left   Born 12/01/54

1987 SEASON AND MAJOR-LEAGUE CAREER PITCHING TOTALS

	G	GS	CG	GF	IP	BFP	H	R	ER	HR	SH	SF	HB	TBB	IBB	SO	WP	Bk	W	L	Pct	ShO	Sv	ERA
87 PHI-MIN	56	1	0	13	82	372	104	58	48	12	2	1	1	32	10	58	8	0	6	2	.750	0	0	5.27
11 YEARS	384	119	18	82	1158	4869	1082	531	477	117	51	36	18	410	51	642	47	4	64	61	.512	4	6	3.71

1987: Power, Flyball   1986: Finesse, Flyball   1985: Finesse, Flyball   1984: Finesse, Flyball

1987 SEASON

	G	IP	H	BB	SO	SB	CS	W	L	S	ERA
Totals	56	81.1	104	32	58	7	1	6	2	0	5.31
At Home	23	37.2	45	13	31	3	0	1	1	0	4.30
On Road	33	43.2	59	19	27	4	1	5	1	0	6.18

vs. Opposing Batters	AVG	OBP	SLG	AB	H	2B	3B	HR	RBI	BB	SO
Totals	.314	.370	.502	331	104	22	2	12	66	32	58
vs. Left	.305	.346	.432	118	36	9	0	2	18	7	23
vs. Right	.319	.383	.540	213	68	13	2	10	48	25	35

FOUR YEAR TOTALS (1984 – 1987)

	G	IP	H	BB	SO	SB	CS	W	L	S	ERA
(Totals)	171	410.0	398	134	258	39	10	22	19	2	3.60
(At Home)	85	227.2	200	64	155	22	2	13	8	1	2.65
(On Road)	86	182.1	198	70	103	17	8	9	11	1	4.84

	AVG	OBP	SLG	AB	H	2B	3B	HR	RBI	BB	SO
(Totals)	.256	.314	.409	1554	398	74	11	47	195	134	258
(vs. Left)	.263	.306	.342	380	100	19	1	3	45	23	73
(vs. Right)	.254	.317	.430	1174	298	55	10	44	150	111	185

Scherrer, William Joseph "Bill"

Bats: Left   Throws: Left   Born 01/20/58

1987 SEASON AND MAJOR-LEAGUE CAREER PITCHING TOTALS

	G	GS	CG	GF	IP	BFP	H	R	ER	HR	SH	SF	HB	TBB	IBB	SO	WP	Bk	W	L	Pct	ShO	Sv	ERA
87 CIN	23	0	0	10	33	151	43	17	16	3	1	3	0	16	4	24	2	0	1	1	.500	0	0	4.36
6 YEARS	216	2	0	80	300	1302	292	144	131	29	18	14	2	135	29	201	8	0	8	9	.471	0	11	3.93

1987: Power, Flyball   1986: Power, Groundball

1987 SEASON

	G	IP	H	BB	SO	SB	CS	W	L	S	ERA
Totals	23	33.1	43	16	24	10	1	1	1	0	4.32
At Home	12	21.0	25	6	15	1	1	1	0	0	2.57
On Road	11	12.1	18	10	9	9	0	0	1	0	7.30

vs. Opposing Batters	AVG	OBP	SLG	AB	H	2B	3B	HR	RBI	BB	SO
Totals	.328	.393	.489	131	43	6	3	3	20	16	24
vs. Left	.366	.422	.610	41	15	3	2	1	9	4	9
vs. Right	.311	.381	.433	90	28	3	1	2	11	12	15

TWO YEAR TOTALS (1986 – 1987)

	G	IP	H	BB	SO	SB	CS	W	L	S	ERA
(Totals)	36	54.1	62	38	40	10	1	1	2	0	5.47
(At Home)	18	34.1	37	17	24	1	1	1	1	0	3.67
(On Road)	18	20.0	25	21	16	9	0	0	1	0	8.55

	AVG	OBP	SLG	AB	H	2B	3B	HR	RBI	BB	SO
(Totals)	.297	.402	.469	209	62	12	3	6	37	38	40
(vs. Left)	.313	.410	.493	67	21	5	2	1	12	11	17
(vs. Right)	.289	.399	.458	142	41	7	1	5	25	27	23

Schroeder, Alfred William "Bill"

Bats: Right   Throws: Right   Born 09/07/58

1987 SEASON AND MAJOR-LEAGUE CAREER BATTING TOTALS

	G	AB	H	2B	3B	HR	TB	R	RBI	TBB	IBB	SO	HP	SH	SF	SB	CS	SB%	GDP	AVG	OBP	SLG
87 MIL	75	250	83	12	0	14	137	35	42	16	0	56	3	1	0	5	2	.71	3	.332	.379	.548
5 YEARS	276	944	243	42	1	46	425	121	118	48	3	253	14	11	5	6	5	.55	17	.257	.302	.450

1987 SEASON

	AVG	OBP	SLG	AB	H	2B	3B	HR	RBI	BB	SO
Totals	.332	.379	.548	250	83	12	0	14	42	16	56
vs. Left	.344	.368	.550	131	45	3	0	8	22	4	38
vs. Right	.319	.391	.546	119	38	9	0	6	20	12	18
At Home	.350	.386	.533	120	42	7	0	5	21	6	28
On Road	.315	.373	.562	130	41	5	0	9	21	10	28

FOUR YEAR TOTALS (1984 – 1987)

	AVG	OBP	SLG	AB	H	2B	3B	HR	RBI	BB	SO
(Totals)	.264	.308	.458	871	230	40	0	43	111	45	230
(vs. Left)	.300	.333	.523	327	98	10	0	21	50	15	96
(vs. Right)	.243	.294	.419	544	132	30	0	22	61	30	134
(At Home)	.256	.298	.406	446	114	19	0	16	45	19	120
(On Road)	.273	.319	.513	425	116	21	0	27	66	26	110

Schrom, Kenneth Marvin "Ken"

Bats: Right   Throws: Right   Born 11/23/54

1987 SEASON AND MAJOR-LEAGUE CAREER PITCHING TOTALS

	G	GS	CG	GF	IP	BFP	H	R	ER	HR	SH	SF	HB	TBB	IBB	SO	WP	Bk	W	L	Pct	ShO	Sv	ERA
87 CLE	32	29	4	0	154	695	185	126	111	29	9	6	3	57	1	61	4	2	6	13	.316	1	0	6.49
7 YEARS	176	137	22	12	900	3907	963	535	481	125	38	40	25	320	17	372	13	4	51	51	.500	3	1	4.81

1987: Finesse, Flyball   1986: Finesse, Flyball   1985: Finesse, Flyball   1984: Finesse, Flyball

1987 SEASON

	G	IP	H	BB	SO	SB	CS	W	L	S	ERA
Totals	32	153.2	185	57	61	12	6	6	13	0	6.50
At Home	19	96.2	127	36	44	8	5	3	8	0	6.70
On Road	13	57.0	58	21	17	4	1	3	5	0	6.16

vs. Opposing Batters	AVG	OBP	SLG	AB	H	2B	3B	HR	RBI	BB	SO
Totals	.298	.357	.508	620	185	37	3	29	110	57	61
vs. Left	.316	.363	.548	323	102	18	3	17	56	27	30
vs. Right	.279	.350	.465	297	83	19	0	12	54	30	31

FOUR YEAR TOTALS (1984 – 1987)

	G	IP	H	BB	SO	SB	CS	W	L	S	ERA
(Totals)	120	657.1	722	206	271	53	25	34	43	0	5.08
(At Home)	70	397.2	441	117	174	29	15	23	25	0	4.98
(On Road)	50	259.2	281	89	97	24	10	11	18	0	5.27

	AVG	OBP	SLG	AB	H	2B	3B	HR	RBI	BB	SO
(Totals)	.281	.334	.466	2573	722	140	10	106	354	206	271
(vs. Left)	.301	.354	.486	1394	419	68	8	58	190	117	127
(vs. Right)	.257	.311	.444	1179	303	72	2	48	164	89	144

Schu, Rick Spencer "Rich"

Bats: Right   Throws: Right   Born 01/26/62

1987 SEASON AND MAJOR-LEAGUE CAREER BATTING TOTALS

	G	AB	H	2B	3B	HR	TB	R	RBI	TBB	IBB	SO	HP	SH	SF	SB	CS	SB%	GDP	AVG	OBP	SLG
87 PHI	92	196	46	6	3	7	79	24	23	20	1	36	2	0	1	0	2	.00	1	.235	.311	.403
4 YEARS	313	849	216	39	9	24	345	122	77	82	5	164	6	4	4	10	10	.50	9	.254	.323	.406

1987 SEASON	AVG	OBP	SLG	AB	H	2B	3B	HR	RBI	BB	SO
Totals	.235	.311	.403	196	46	6	3	7	23	20	36
vs. Left	.265	.330	.471	102	27	4	1	5	12	10	14
vs. Right	.202	.290	.330	94	19	2	2	2	11	10	22
At Home	.250	.324	.470	100	25	3	2	5	14	10	19
On Road	.219	.296	.333	96	21	3	1	2	9	10	17

FOUR YEAR TOTALS (1984 – 1987)	AVG	OBP	SLG	AB	H	2B	3B	HR	RBI	BB	SO
Totals	.254	.323	.406	849	216	39	9	24	77	82	164
vs. Left	.278	.342	.483	352	98	20	5	14	34	33	57
vs. Right	.237	.310	.352	497	118	19	4	10	43	49	107
At Home	.263	.336	.416	392	103	21	6	9	38	43	73
On Road	.247	.312	.398	457	113	18	3	15	39	39	91

Searage, Raymond Mark "Ray"

Bats: Left   Throws: Left   Born 05/01/55

1987 SEASON AND MAJOR-LEAGUE CAREER PITCHING TOTALS

	G	GS	CG	GF	IP	BFP	H	R	ER	HR	SH	SF	HB	TBB	IBB	SO	WP	Bk	W	L	Pct	ShO	Sv	ERA
87 CHA	58	0	0	18	56	240	56	28	26	9	1	2	1	24	3	33	2	0	2	3	.400	0	2	4.18
5 YEARS	184	0	0	76	220	954	208	94	88	20	11	7	3	109	17	150	7	1	7	9	.438	0	11	3.60

1987: Finesse, Flyball   1986: Power, Flyball   1985: Power, Flyball   1984: Power, Flyball

1987 SEASON	G	IP	H	BB	SO	SB	CS	W	L	S	ERA
Totals	58	55.2	56	24	33	1	3	2	3	2	4.20
At Home	30	33.2	33	16	20	1	2	1	2	0	3.74
On Road	28	22.0	23	8	13	0	1	1	1	2	4.91

vs. Opposing Batters	AVG	OBP	SLG	AB	H	2B	3B	HR	RBI	BB	SO
Totals	.264	.339	.467	212	56	14	1	9	42	24	33
vs. Left	.306	.379	.518	85	26	7	1	3	19	9	12
vs. Right	.236	.313	.433	127	30	7	0	6	23	15	21

FOUR YEAR TOTALS (1984 – 1987)	G	IP	H	BB	SO	SB	CS	W	L	S	ERA
Totals	158	183.0	174	92	134	11	7	6	9	10	3.59
At Home	79	108.2	116	59	81	7	3	5	6	3	4.06
On Road	79	74.1	58	33	53	4	4	1	3	7	2.91

vs. Opposing Batters	AVG	OBP	SLG	AB	H	2B	3B	HR	RBI	BB	SO
Totals	.253	.341	.389	689	174	36	2	18	101	92	134
vs. Left	.260	.346	.391	235	61	15	2	4	40	30	54
vs. Right	.249	.338	.388	454	113	21	0	14	61	62	80

Sellers, Jeffrey Doyle "Jeff"

Bats: Right   Throws: Right   Born 05/11/64

1987 SEASON AND MAJOR-LEAGUE CAREER PITCHING TOTALS

	G	GS	CG	GF	IP	BFP	H	R	ER	HR	SH	SF	HB	TBB	IBB	SO	WP	Bk	W	L	Pct	ShO	Sv	ERA
87 BOS	25	22	4	0	140	620	161	85	82	10	8	8	3	61	0	99	2	0	7	8	.467	2	0	5.27
3 YEARS	43	39	6	0	244	1083	275	151	136	24	11	11	6	108	2	156	7	1	12	15	.444	2	0	5.02

1987: Power, Groundball   1986: Finesse, Flyball

1987 SEASON	G	IP	H	BB	SO	SB	CS	W	L	S	ERA
Totals	25	139.2	161	61	99	10	8	7	8	0	5.22
At Home	11	69.2	80	23	55	3	3	4	3	0	5.04
On Road	14	70.0	81	38	44	7	5	3	5	0	5.40

vs. Opposing Batters	AVG	OBP	SLG	AB	H	2B	3B	HR	RBI	BB	SO
Totals	.299	.368	.438	539	161	37	4	10	72	61	99
vs. Left	.304	.372	.436	289	88	20	3	4	46	33	42
vs. Right	.292	.364	.440	250	73	17	1	6	26	28	57

TWO YEAR TOTALS (1986 – 1987)	G	IP	H	BB	SO	SB	CS	W	L	S	ERA
Totals	39	221.2	251	101	150	15	11	10	15	0	5.12
At Home	19	118.1	132	43	83	6	4	6	7	0	4.94
On Road	20	103.1	119	58	67	9	7	4	8	0	5.31

vs. Opposing Batters	AVG	OBP	SLG	AB	H	2B	3B	HR	RBI	BB	SO
Totals	.293	.367	.442	857	251	49	5	23	116	101	150
vs. Left	.302	.373	.427	473	143	29	3	8	70	55	64
vs. Right	.281	.361	.461	384	108	20	2	15	46	46	86

Sharperson, Michael Tyrone "Mike"

Bats: Right   Throws: Right   Born 10/04/60

1987 SEASON AND MAJOR-LEAGUE CAREER BATTING TOTALS

	G	AB	H	2B	3B	HR	TB	R	RBI	TBB	IBB	SO	HP	SH	SF	SB	CS	SB%	GDP	AVG	OBP	SLG
87 TOR-LA	42	129	29	6	1	0	37	11	10	11	1	20	1	1	0	2	1	.67	3	.225	.291	.287
1 YEAR	42	129	29	6	1	0	37	11	10	11	1	20	1	1	0	2	1	.67	3	.225	.291	.287

1987 SEASON	AVG	OBP	SLG	AB	H	2B	3B	HR	RBI	BB	SO
Totals	.225	.291	.287	129	29	6	1	0	10	11	20
vs. Left	.243	.263	.243	37	9	0	0	0	2	1	5
vs. Right	.217	.301	.304	92	20	6	1	0	8	10	15
At Home	.241	.302	.328	58	14	3	1	0	6	5	9
On Road	.211	.282	.254	71	15	3	0	0	4	6	11

FOUR YEAR TOTALS (1984 – 1987)	AVG	OBP	SLG	AB	H	2B	3B	HR	RBI	BB	SO
Totals	.225	.291	.287	129	29	6	1	0	10	11	20
vs. Left	.243	.263	.243	37	9	0	0	0	2	1	5
vs. Right	.217	.301	.304	92	20	6	1	0	8	10	15
At Home	.241	.302	.328	58	14	3	1	0	6	5	9
On Road	.211	.282	.254	71	15	3	0	0	4	6	11

Sheaffer, Danny Todd

Bats: Right   Throws: Right   Born 08/02/61

1987 SEASON AND MAJOR-LEAGUE CAREER BATTING TOTALS

	G	AB	H	2B	3B	HR	TB	R	RBI	TBB	IBB	SO	HP	SH	SF	SB	CS	SB%	GDP	AVG	OBP	SLG
87 BOS	25	66	8	1	0	1	12	5	5	0	0	14	0	1	1	0	0	.00	2	.121	.119	.182
1 YEAR	25	66	8	1	0	1	12	5	5	0	0	14	0	1	1	0	0	.00	2	.121	.119	.182

1987 SEASON

	AVG	OBP	SLG	AB	H	2B	3B	HR	RBI	BB	SO
Totals	.121	.119	.182	66	8	1	0	1	5	0	14
vs. Left	.174	.174	.217	23	4	1	0	0	2	0	5
vs. Right	.093	.091	.163	43	4	0	0	1	3	0	9
At Home	.000	.000	.000	16	0	0	0	0	0	0	2
On Road	.160	.157	.240	50	8	1	0	1	5	0	12

FOUR YEAR TOTALS (1984 – 1987)

	AVG	OBP	SLG	AB	H	2B	3B	HR	RBI	BB	SO
	.121	.119	.182	66	8	1	0	1	5	0	14
	.174	.174	.217	23	4	1	0	0	2	0	5
	.093	.091	.163	43	4	0	0	1	3	0	9
	.000	.000	.000	16	0	0	0	0	0	0	2
	.160	.157	.240	50	8	1	0	1	5	0	12

Shields, Stephen Mack "Steve"

Bats: Right   Throws: Right   Born 11/30/58

1987 SEASON AND MAJOR-LEAGUE CAREER PITCHING TOTALS

	G	GS	CG	GF	IP	BFP	H	R	ER	HR	SH	SF	HB	TBB	IBB	SO	WP	Bk	W	L	Pct	ShO	Sv	ERA
87 SEA	20	0	0	10	30	144	43	25	22	7	0	3	0	12	1	22	3	0	2	0	1.000	0	3	6.60
3 YEARS	52	6	0	17	120	543	145	84	73	21	6	8	1	55	8	59	10	0	3	2	.600	0	3	5.48

1987: Power, Flyball   1986: Finesse, Groundball

1987 SEASON

	G	IP	H	BB	SO	SB	CS	W	L	S	ERA
Totals	20	30.0	43	12	22	4	0	2	0	3	6.90
At Home	8	14.0	21	4	13	2	0	1	0	1	7.07
On Road	12	16.0	22	8	9	2	0	1	0	2	6.75

vs. Opposing Batters	AVG	OBP	SLG	AB	H	2B	3B	HR	RBI	BB	SO
Totals	.333	.382	.589	129	43	8	2	7	32	12	22
vs. Left	.344	.368	.623	61	21	3	1	4	18	4	9
vs. Right	.324	.395	.559	68	22	5	1	3	14	8	13

TWO YEAR TOTALS (1986 – 1987)

	G	IP	H	BB	SO	SB	CS	W	L	S	ERA
	29	51.1	59	23	30	6	0	2	0	3	6.14
	14	29.1	33	12	20	4	0	1	0	1	6.14
	15	22.0	26	11	10	2	0	1	0	2	6.14

	AVG	OBP	SLG	AB	H	2B	3B	HR	RBI	BB	SO
	.289	.353	.549	204	59	11	3	12	47	23	30
	.293	.336	.535	99	29	4	1	6	27	9	13
	.286	.370	.562	105	30	7	2	6	20	14	17

Shipley, Craig Barry

Bats: Both   Throws: Right   Born 01/07/63

1987 SEASON AND MAJOR-LEAGUE CAREER BATTING TOTALS

	G	AB	H	2B	3B	HR	TB	R	RBI	TBB	IBB	SO	HP	SH	SF	SB	CS	SB%	GDP	AVG	OBP	SLG
87 LA	26	35	9	1	0	0	10	3	2	0	0	6	0	0	0	0	0	.00	2	.257	.257	.286
2 YEARS	38	62	12	2	0	0	14	6	6	2	1	11	1	1	0	0	0	.00	3	.194	.231	.226

1987 SEASON

	AVG	OBP	SLG	AB	H	2B	3B	HR	RBI	BB	SO
Totals	.257	.257	.286	35	9	1	0	0	2	0	6
vs. Left	.250	.250	.333	12	3	1	0	0	0	0	1
vs. Right	.261	.261	.261	23	6	0	0	0	2	0	5
At Home	.091	.091	.091	11	1	0	0	0	0	0	3
On Road	.333	.333	.375	24	8	1	0	0	2	0	3

FOUR YEAR TOTALS (1984 – 1987)

	AVG	OBP	SLG	AB	H	2B	3B	HR	RBI	BB	SO
	.194	.242	.226	62	12	2	0	0	6	2	11
	.185	.214	.222	27	5	1	0	0	3	1	1
	.200	.243	.229	35	7	1	0	0	3	1	10
	.111	.143	.111	27	3	0	0	0	2	0	6
	.257	.297	.314	35	9	2	0	0	4	2	5

Shirley, Robert Charles "Bob"

Bats: Right   Throws: Left   Born 06/25/54

1987 SEASON AND MAJOR-LEAGUE CAREER PITCHING TOTALS

	G	GS	CG	GF	IP	BFP	H	R	ER	HR	SH	SF	HB	TBB	IBB	SO	WP	Bk	W	L	Pct	ShO	Sv	ERA
87 NYA-KC	15	1	0	7	41	189	46	32	29	9	0	6	0	22	0	13	1	0	1	0	1.000	0	0	6.37
11 YEARS	434	162	16	105	1431	6106	1432	689	608	127	73	54	20	543	72	790	15	11	67	94	.416	2	18	3.82

1987: Finesse, Flyball   1986: Finesse, Flyball   1985: Finesse, Flyball   1984: Finesse, Flyball

1987 SEASON

	G	IP	H	BB	SO	SB	CS	W	L	S	ERA
Totals	15	41.1	46	22	13	1	1	1	0	0	6.31
At Home	7	20.0	28	11	6	1	1	1	0	0	9.45
On Road	8	21.1	18	11	7	0	0	0	0	0	3.38

vs. Opposing Batters	AVG	OBP	SLG	AB	H	2B	3B	HR	RBI	BB	SO
Totals	.286	.360	.516	161	46	6	2	9	37	22	13
vs. Left	.222	.240	.467	45	10	2	0	3	17	2	5
vs. Right	.310	.403	.534	116	36	4	2	6	20	20	8

FOUR YEAR TOTALS (1984 – 1987)

	G	IP	H	BB	SO	SB	CS	W	L	S	ERA
	143	370.0	376	126	180	11	18	9	12	5	3.96
	72	224.1	227	71	109	7	13	8	6	3	3.57
	71	145.2	149	55	71	4	5	1	6	2	4.57

	AVG	OBP	SLG	AB	H	2B	3B	HR	RBI	BB	SO
	.268	.327	.408	1403	376	59	16	35	184	126	180
	.223	.271	.328	412	92	12	5	7	51	28	87
	.287	.350	.441	991	284	47	11	28	133	98	93

Simmons, Nelson Bernard

Bats: Both   Throws: Right   Born 06/27/63

1987 SEASON AND MAJOR-LEAGUE CAREER BATTING TOTALS

	G	AB	H	2B	3B	HR	TB	R	RBI	TBB	IBB	SO	HP	SH	SF	SB	CS	SB%	GDP	AVG	OBP	SLG
87 BAL	16	49	13	1	1	1	19	3	4	3	0	8	0	0	2	0	1	.00	3	.265	.296	.388
3 YEARS	100	330	86	14	1	11	135	38	40	31	6	54	0	0	6	2	1	.67	9	.261	.319	.409

	1987 SEASON											TWO YEAR TOTALS (1986 – 1987)										
	AVG	OBP	SLG	AB	H	2B	3B	HR	RBI	BB	SO	AVG	OBP	SLG	AB	H	2B	3B	HR	RBI	BB	SO
Totals	.265	.296	.388	49	13	1	1	1	4	3	8	.265	.276	.388	49	13	1	1	1	4	3	8
vs. Left	.259	.267	.370	27	7	1	1	0	3	1	6	.259	.267	.370	27	7	1	1	0	3	1	6
vs. Right	.273	.333	.409	22	6	0	0	1	1	2	2	.273	.333	.409	22	6	0	0	1	1	2	2
At Home	.158	.227	.158	19	3	0	0	0	1	2	3	.158	.227	.158	19	3	0	0	0	1	2	3
On Road	.333	.344	.533	30	10	1	1	1	3	1	5	.333	.344	.533	30	10	1	1	1	3	1	5

Simmons, Ted Lyle

Bats: Both   Throws: Right   Born 08/09/49

1987 SEASON AND MAJOR-LEAGUE CAREER BATTING TOTALS

	G	AB	H	2B	3B	HR	TB	R	RBI	TBB	IBB	SO	HP	SH	SF	SB	CS	SB%	GDP	AVG	OBP	SLG
87 ATL	73	177	49	8	0	4	69	20	30	21	5	23	0	0	2	1	1	.50	4	.277	.350	.390
20 YEARS	2378	8573	2451	477	47	246	3760	1068	1378	840	186	685	39	11	99	21	33	.39	283	.286	.349	.439

	1987 SEASON											FOUR YEAR TOTALS (1984 – 1987)										
	AVG	OBP	SLG	AB	H	2B	3B	HR	RBI	BB	SO	AVG	OBP	SLG	AB	H	2B	3B	HR	RBI	BB	SO
Totals	.277	.350	.390	177	49	8	0	4	30	21	23	.252	.314	.360	1329	335	64	4	24	183	120	109
vs. Left	.264	.306	.440	91	24	7	0	3	20	6	16	.258	.312	.411	492	127	32	2	13	83	38	44
vs. Right	.291	.392	.337	86	25	1	0	1	10	15	7	.249	.315	.331	837	208	32	2	11	100	82	65
At Home	.278	.337	.367	79	22	4	0	1	20	8	7	.241	.298	.345	638	154	28	1	12	95	52	56
On Road	.276	.360	.408	98	27	4	0	3	10	13	16	.262	.329	.375	691	181	36	3	12	88	68	53

Sisk, Douglas Randall "Doug"

Bats: Right   Throws: Right   Born 09/26/57

1987 SEASON AND MAJOR-LEAGUE CAREER PITCHING TOTALS

	G	GS	CG	GF	IP	BFP	H	R	ER	HR	SH	SF	HB	TBB	IBB	SO	WP	Bk	W	L	Pct	ShO	Sv	ERA
87 NYN	55	0	0	17	78	339	83	38	30	5	5	2	3	22	4	37	2	0	3	1	.750	0	3	3.46
6 YEARS	263	0	0	128	413	1802	396	180	142	11	24	6	18	210	25	163	11	3	17	16	.515	0	33	3.09

1987: Finesse, Groundball   1986: Finesse, Groundball   1985: Finesse, Groundball   1984: Power, Groundball

	1987 SEASON										FOUR YEAR TOTALS (1984 – 1987)										
	G	IP	H	BB	SO	SB	CS	W	L	S	ERA	G	IP	H	BB	SO	SB	CS	W	L	S	ERA
Totals	55	78.0	83	22	37	6	1	3	1	3	3.46	188	299.1	303	147	126	17	14	12	11	21	3.46
At Home	25	35.2	43	11	17	0	1	0	0	2	3.79	91	142.0	143	67	60	6	4	2	5	10	3.11
On Road	30	42.1	40	11	20	6	0	3	1	1	3.19	97	157.1	160	80	66	11	10	10	6	11	3.78

vs. Opposing Batters	AVG	OBP	SLG	AB	H	2B	3B	HR	RBI	BB	SO	AVG	OBP	SLG	AB	H	2B	3B	HR	RBI	BB	SO
Totals	.269	.322	.377	308	83	12	3	5	44	22	37	.265	.350	.340	1142	303	46	6	9	146	147	126
vs. Left	.268	.325	.341	138	37	8	1	0	15	12	13	.258	.356	.331	516	133	25	2	3	61	79	41
vs. Right	.271	.321	.406	170	46	4	2	5	29	10	24	.272	.345	.347	626	170	21	4	6	85	68	85

Skinner, Joel Patrick

Bats: Right   Throws: Right   Born 02/21/61

1987 SEASON AND MAJOR-LEAGUE CAREER BATTING TOTALS

	G	AB	H	2B	3B	HR	TB	R	RBI	TBB	IBB	SO	HP	SH	SF	SB	CS	SB%	GDP	AVG	OBP	SLG
87 NYA	64	139	19	4	0	3	32	9	14	8	0	46	1	4	2	0	0	.00	9	.137	.187	.230
5 YEARS	249	589	127	19	2	9	177	47	60	36	0	162	2	7	5	2	4	.33	21	.216	.261	.301

	1987 SEASON											FOUR YEAR TOTALS (1984 – 1987)										
	AVG	OBP	SLG	AB	H	2B	3B	HR	RBI	BB	SO	AVG	OBP	SLG	AB	H	2B	3B	HR	RBI	BB	SO
Totals	.137	.187	.230	139	19	4	0	3	14	8	46	.215	.261	.301	578	124	19	2	9	59	36	161
vs. Left	.111	.167	.200	45	5	1	0	1	5	3	10	.206	.260	.253	233	48	5	0	2	21	17	54
vs. Right	.149	.196	.245	94	14	3	0	2	9	5	36	.220	.261	.333	345	76	14	2	7	38	19	107
At Home	.098	.164	.164	61	6	1	0	1	8	4	20	.193	.232	.261	280	54	8	1	3	27	13	81
On Road	.167	.205	.282	78	13	3	0	2	6	4	26	.235	.287	.339	298	70	11	1	6	32	23	80

Slaught, Donald Martin "Don"
Bats: Right   Throws: Right   Born 09/11/59

1987 SEASON AND MAJOR-LEAGUE CAREER BATTING TOTALS

	G	AB	H	2B	3B	HR	TB	R	RBI	TBB	IBB	SO	HP	SH	SF	SB	CS	SB%	GDP	AVG	OBP	SLG
87 TEX	95	237	53	15	2	8	96	25	16	24	3	51	1	4	0	0	3	.00	7	.224	.298	.405
6 YEARS	542	1694	458	95	15	36	691	181	175	100	8	245	14	19	12	11	10	.52	42	.270	.314	.408

1987 SEASON	AVG	OBP	SLG	AB	H	2B	3B	HR	RBI	BB	SO
Totals	.224	.298	.405	237	53	15	2	8	16	24	51
vs. Left	.237	.313	.459	135	32	8	2	6	11	14	28
vs. Right	.206	.277	.333	102	21	7	0	2	5	10	23
At Home	.256	.311	.432	125	32	5	1	5	8	9	21
On Road	.188	.283	.375	112	21	10	1	3	8	15	30

FOUR YEAR TOTALS (1984 – 1987)	AVG	OBP	SLG	AB	H	2B	3B	HR	RBI	BB	SO
Totals	.261	.308	.412	1303	340	76	11	33	139	80	206
vs. Left	.285	.332	.479	466	133	29	5	17	66	31	80
vs. Right	.247	.295	.375	837	207	47	6	16	73	49	126
At Home	.291	.338	.443	646	188	43	5	15	64	42	90
On Road	.231	.280	.382	657	152	33	6	18	75	38	116

Smiley, John Patrick
Bats: Left   Throws: Left   Born 03/17/65

1987 SEASON AND MAJOR-LEAGUE CAREER PITCHING TOTALS

	G	GS	CG	GF	IP	BFP	H	R	ER	HR	SH	SF	HB	TBB	IBB	SO	WP	Bk	W	L	Pct	ShO	Sv	ERA
87 PIT	63	0	0	19	75	336	69	49	48	7	0	3	0	50	8	58	5	1	5	5	.500	0	4	5.76
2 YEARS	75	0	0	21	87	378	73	55	53	9	0	3	0	54	8	67	5	1	6	5	.545	0	4	5.48

1987: Power, Groundball   1986: Power, Groundball

1987 SEASON	G	IP	H	BB	SO	SB	CS	W	L	S	ERA
Totals	63	75.0	69	50	58	4	1	5	5	4	5.76
At Home	34	48.2	27	30	36	3	1	5	3	2	2.77
On Road	29	26.1	42	20	22	1	0	0	2	2	11.28
vs. Opposing Batters	AVG	OBP	SLG	AB	H	2B	3B	HR	RBI	BB	SO
Totals	.244	.354	.389	283	69	16	2	7	44	50	58
vs. Left	.195	.287	.299	87	17	4	1	1	9	12	21
vs. Right	.265	.383	.429	196	52	12	1	6	35	38	37

FOUR YEAR TOTALS (1984 – 1987)	G	IP	H	BB	SO	SB	CS	W	L	S	ERA
	75	86.2	73	54	67	6	2	6	5	4	5.50
	40	55.0	28	32	41	4	1	5	3	2	2.62
	35	31.2	45	22	26	2	1	1	2	2	10.52
	AVG	OBP	SLG	AB	H	2B	3B	HR	RBI	BB	SO
	.227	.336	.374	321	73	16	2	9	47	54	67
	.190	.278	.280	100	19	4	1	1	9	13	26
	.244	.361	.416	221	54	12	1	8	38	41	41

Smith, Bryn Nelson
Bats: Right   Throws: Right   Born 08/11/55

1987 SEASON AND MAJOR-LEAGUE CAREER PITCHING TOTALS

	G	GS	CG	GF	IP	BFP	H	R	ER	HR	SH	SF	HB	TBB	IBB	SO	WP	Bk	W	L	Pct	ShO	Sv	ERA
87 MON	26	26	2	0	150	643	164	81	73	16	7	5	2	31	4	94	2	0	10	9	.526	0	0	4.38
7 YEARS	219	129	16	34	985	4115	954	437	377	77	52	20	17	255	31	587	21	9	59	50	.541	7	6	3.44

1987: Finesse, Groundball   1986: Finesse, Groundball   1985: Finesse, Groundball   1984: Finesse, Groundball

1987 SEASON	G	IP	H	BB	SO	SB	CS	W	L	S	ERA
Totals	26	150.1	164	31	94	19	3	10	9	0	4.37
At Home	14	82.0	89	23	58	10	3	6	3	0	4.50
On Road	12	68.1	75	8	36	9	0	4	6	0	4.21
vs. Opposing Batters	AVG	OBP	SLG	AB	H	2B	3B	HR	RBI	BB	SO
Totals	.274	.310	.410	598	164	25	4	16	72	31	94
vs. Left	.261	.294	.372	349	91	11	2	8	45	18	49
vs. Right	.293	.332	.462	249	73	14	2	8	27	13	45

FOUR YEAR TOTALS (1984 – 1987)	G	IP	H	BB	SO	SB	CS	W	L	S	ERA
	116	739.0	717	186	427	77	28	50	35	0	3.58
	57	374.2	346	104	239	32	16	26	16	0	3.31
	59	364.1	371	82	188	45	12	24	19	0	3.83
	AVG	OBP	SLG	AB	H	2B	3B	HR	RBI	BB	SO
	.252	.298	.373	2840	717	124	22	58	296	186	427
	.263	.311	.373	1539	405	66	14	25	162	108	207
	.240	.284	.373	1301	312	58	8	33	134	78	220

Smith, Lonnie
Bats: Right   Throws: Right   Born 12/22/55

1987 SEASON AND MAJOR-LEAGUE CAREER BATTING TOTALS

	G	AB	H	2B	3B	HR	TB	R	RBI	TBB	IBB	SO	HP	SH	SF	SB	CS	SB%	GDP	AVG	OBP	SLG
87 KC	48	167	42	7	1	3	60	26	8	24	0	31	4	0	2	9	4	.69	1	.251	.355	.359
10 YEARS	957	3315	957	173	38	44	1338	597	297	350	7	489	57	14	23	308	107	.74	50	.289	.364	.404

1987 SEASON	AVG	OBP	SLG	AB	H	2B	3B	HR	RBI	BB	SO
Totals	.251	.355	.359	167	42	7	1	3	8	24	31
vs. Left	.280	.390	.380	50	14	3	1	0	2	9	8
vs. Right	.239	.341	.350	117	28	4	0	3	6	15	23
At Home	.259	.365	.346	81	21	4	0	1	3	13	11
On Road	.244	.347	.372	86	21	3	1	2	5	11	20

FOUR YEAR TOTALS (1984 – 1987)	AVG	OBP	SLG	AB	H	2B	3B	HR	RBI	BB	SO
Totals	.263	.347	.369	1723	454	77	18	23	149	197	288
vs. Left	.280	.358	.395	532	149	29	7	6	42	66	81
vs. Right	.256	.342	.358	1191	305	48	11	17	107	131	207
At Home	.266	.360	.372	830	221	40	12	8	74	109	127
On Road	.261	.335	.366	893	233	37	6	15	75	88	161

Smithson, Billy Mike "Mike"

Bats: Left   Throws: Right   Born 01/21/55

1987 SEASON AND MAJOR-LEAGUE CAREER PITCHING TOTALS

	G	GS	CG	GF	IP	BFP	H	R	ER	HR	SH	SF	HB	TBB	IBB	SO	WP	Bk	W	L	Pct	ShO	Sv	ERA
87 MIN	21	20	0	0	109	494	126	76	72	17	1	5	9	38	3	53	4	2	4	7	.364	0	0	5.94
6 YEARS	169	167	39	1	1086	4668	1154	574	527	122	28	32	57	311	19	597	41	8	60	66	.476	5	0	4.37

1987: Finesse, Groundball   1986: Finesse, Groundball   1985: Finesse, Groundball   1984: Finesse, Flyball

1987 SEASON

	G	IP	H	BB	SO	SB	CS	W	L	S	ERA
Totals	21	109.0	126	38	53	22	1	4	7	0	5.94
At Home	9	49.2	52	18	20	9	0	2	1	0	4.71
On Road	12	59.1	74	20	33	13	1	2	6	0	6.98

vs. Opposing Batters	AVG	OBP	SLG	AB	H	2B	3B	HR	RBI	BB	SO
Totals	.286	.351	.469	441	126	24	3	17	71	38	53
vs. Left	.320	.371	.593	253	81	18	0	17	57	21	30
vs. Right	.239	.326	.303	188	45	6	3	0	14	17	23

FOUR YEAR TOTALS (1984 – 1987)

	G	IP	H	BB	SO	SB	CS	W	L	S	ERA
Totals	128	816.0	870	227	439	90	22	47	48	0	4.47
At Home	61	396.0	420	104	228	43	11	26	18	0	4.27
On Road	67	420.0	450	123	211	47	11	21	30	0	4.65

vs. Opposing Batters	AVG	OBP	SLG	AB	H	2B	3B	HR	RBI	BB	SO
Totals	.273	.322	.434	3192	870	162	22	103	385	227	439
vs. Left	.292	.339	.485	1888	551	110	13	76	268	135	218
vs. Right	.245	.298	.360	1304	319	52	9	27	117	92	221

Snell, Nathaniel "Nat"

Bats: Right   Throws: Right   Born 09/02/52

1987 SEASON AND MAJOR-LEAGUE CAREER PITCHING TOTALS

	G	GS	CG	GF	IP	BFP	H	R	ER	HR	SH	SF	HB	TBB	IBB	SO	WP	Bk	W	L	Pct	ShO	Sv	ERA
87 DET	22	2	0	12	39	168	39	20	17	5	2	1	0	19	3	19	4	0	1	2	.333	0	0	3.92
4 YEARS	104	2	0	48	219	919	216	102	80	19	9	6	2	72	12	96	7	0	7	6	.538	0	5	3.29

1987: Finesse, Groundball   1986: Finesse, Groundball   1985: Finesse, Groundball   1984: Power, Flyball

1987 SEASON

	G	IP	H	BB	SO	SB	CS	W	L	S	ERA
Totals	22	38.2	39	19	19	0	1	1	2	0	3.96
At Home	12	15.1	12	8	4	0	0	1	0	0	4.70
On Road	10	23.1	27	11	15	0	1	0	2	0	3.47

vs. Opposing Batters	AVG	OBP	SLG	AB	H	2B	3B	HR	RBI	BB	SO
Totals	.267	.349	.438	146	39	6	2	5	26	19	19
vs. Left	.281	.365	.563	64	18	4	1	4	15	9	1
vs. Right	.256	.337	.341	82	21	2	1	1	11	10	18

FOUR YEAR TOTALS (1984 – 1987)

	G	IP	H	BB	SO	SB	CS	W	L	S	ERA
Totals	104	219.0	216	72	96	3	7	7	6	5	3.29
At Home	55	113.1	107	31	47	1	5	4	0	2	2.86
On Road	49	105.2	109	41	49	2	2	3	6	3	3.75

vs. Opposing Batters	AVG	OBP	SLG	AB	H	2B	3B	HR	RBI	BB	SO
Totals	.260	.319	.383	830	216	35	5	19	114	72	96
vs. Left	.278	.335	.428	367	102	16	3	11	47	32	25
vs. Right	.246	.306	.348	463	114	19	2	8	67	40	71

Sorensen, Lary Alan

Bats: Right   Throws: Right   Born 10/04/55

1987 SEASON AND MAJOR-LEAGUE CAREER PITCHING TOTALS

	G	GS	CG	GF	IP	BFP	H	R	ER	HR	SH	SF	HB	TBB	IBB	SO	WP	Bk	W	L	Pct	ShO	Sv	ERA
87 MON	23	5	0	6	48	215	56	32	25	7	2	2	3	12	1	21	1	0	3	4	.429	0	1	4.69
10 YEARS	334	235	69	41	1719	7307	1936	881	791	146	62	54	31	399	49	560	31	20	93	103	.474	10	4	4.14

1987: Finesse, Groundball

1987 SEASON

	G	IP	H	BB	SO	SB	CS	W	L	S	ERA
Totals	23	47.2	56	12	21	2	1	3	4	1	4.72
At Home	10	19.1	36	5	14	1	0	1	4	0	10.24
On Road	13	28.1	20	7	7	1	1	2	0	1	0.95

vs. Opposing Batters	AVG	OBP	SLG	AB	H	2B	3B	HR	RBI	BB	SO
Totals	.286	.333	.459	196	56	11	1	7	32	12	21
vs. Left	.311	.373	.511	90	28	6	0	4	18	9	8
vs. Right	.264	.297	.415	106	28	5	1	3	14	3	13

TWO YEAR TOTALS (1986 – 1987)

	G	IP	H	BB	SO	SB	CS	W	L	S	ERA
Totals	23	47.2	56	12	21	2	1	3	4	1	4.72
At Home	10	19.1	36	5	14	1	0	1	4	0	10.24
On Road	13	28.1	20	7	7	1	1	2	0	1	0.95

vs. Opposing Batters	AVG	OBP	SLG	AB	H	2B	3B	HR	RBI	BB	SO
Totals	.286	.333	.459	196	56	11	1	7	32	12	21
vs. Left	.311	.373	.511	90	28	6	0	4	18	9	8
vs. Right	.264	.297	.415	106	28	5	1	3	14	3	13

Speier, Chris Edward

Bats: Right   Throws: Right   Born 06/28/50

1987 SEASON AND MAJOR-LEAGUE CAREER BATTING TOTALS

	G	AB	H	2B	3B	HR	TB	R	RBI	TBB	IBB	SO	HP	SH	SF	SB	CS	SB%	GDP	AVG	OBP	SLG
87 SF	111	317	79	13	0	11	125	39	39	42	5	51	3	1	1	4	7	.36	3	.249	.342	.394
17 YEARS	2150	6948	1713	289	49	109	2427	737	700	819	104	940	34	66	43	39	51	.43	174	.247	.327	.349

1987 SEASON

	AVG	OBP	SLG	AB	H	2B	3B	HR	RBI	BB	SO
Totals	.249	.342	.394	317	79	13	0	11	39	42	51
vs. Left	.272	.337	.424	92	25	2	0	4	13	9	15
vs. Right	.240	.344	.382	225	54	11	0	7	26	33	36
At Home	.226	.332	.365	159	36	4	0	6	17	24	28
On Road	.272	.352	.424	158	43	9	0	5	22	18	23

FOUR YEAR TOTALS (1984 – 1987)

	AVG	OBP	SLG	AB	H	2B	3B	HR	RBI	BB	SO
Totals	.239	.310	.373	848	203	39	1	24	95	84	144
vs. Left	.256	.315	.410	266	68	9	1	10	34	24	40
vs. Right	.232	.308	.356	582	135	30	0	14	61	60	104
At Home	.227	.306	.345	432	98	16	1	11	48	48	71
On Road	.252	.314	.401	416	105	23	0	13	47	36	73

Spilman, William Harry "Harry"

Bats: Left   Throws: Right   Born 07/18/54

1987 SEASON AND MAJOR-LEAGUE CAREER BATTING TOTALS

	G	AB	H	2B	3B	HR	TB	R	RBI	TBB	IBB	SO	HP	SH	SF	SB	CS	SB%	GDP	AVG	OBP	SLG
87 SF	83	90	24	5	0	1	32	5	14	9	0	20	0	0	2	1	1	.50	3	.267	.327	.356
10 YEARS	484	729	175	30	0	17	256	85	111	70	6	115	3	3	9	1	2	.33	15	.240	.306	.351

	1987 SEASON										TWO YEAR TOTALS (1986 – 1987)									
	AVG	OBP	SLG	AB	H	2B	3B	HR	RBI	BB	SO	AVG	OBP	SLG	AB	H	2B	3B	HR	RBI	BB	SO
Totals	.267	.327	.356	90	24	5	0	1	14	9	20	.270	.332	.408	233	63	14	0	6	44	24	41
vs. Left	.667	.750	.667	3	2	0	0	0	0	1	1	.429	.500	.571	7	3	1	0	0	0	1	3
vs. Right	.253	.309	.345	87	22	5	0	1	14	8	19	.265	.331	.403	226	60	13	0	6	44	23	38
At Home	.222	.317	.389	36	8	3	0	1	6	5	11	.286	.381	.440	84	24	7	0	2	17	13	15
On Road	.296	.333	.333	54	16	2	0	0	8	4	9	.262	.309	.389	149	39	7	0	4	27	11	26

St.Claire, Randy Anthony

Bats: Right   Throws: Right   Born 08/23/60

1987 SEASON AND MAJOR-LEAGUE CAREER PITCHING TOTALS

	G	GS	CG	GF	IP	BFP	H	R	ER	HR	SH	SF	HB	TBB	IBB	SO	WP	Bk	W	L	Pct	ShO	Sv	ERA
87 MON	44	0	0	24	67	282	64	31	30	9	1	3	1	20	4	43	4	0	3	3	.500	0	7	4.03
4 YEARS	101	0	0	44	163	690	157	72	69	14	8	6	3	54	13	93	6	0	10	6	.625	0	8	3.81

1987: Finesse, Flyball   1986: Power, Groundball

	1987 SEASON											TWO YEAR TOTALS (1986 – 1987)										
	G	IP	H	BB	SO	SB	CS	W	L	S	ERA	G	IP	H	BB	SO	SB	CS	W	L	S	ERA
Totals	44	67.0	64	20	43	10	0	3	3	7	4.03	55	86.0	77	26	64	11	0	5	3	8	3.66
At Home	19	31.1	30	9	26	6	0	2	3	2	5.17	24	40.1	38	14	36	7	0	3	3	2	4.91
On Road	25	35.2	34	11	17	4	0	1	0	5	3.03	31	45.2	39	12	28	4	0	2	0	6	2.56

vs. Opposing Batters	AVG	OBP	SLG	AB	H	2B	3B	HR	RBI	BB	SO	AVG	OBP	SLG	AB	H	2B	3B	HR	RBI	BB	SO
Totals	.250	.304	.395	256	64	6	2	9	37	20	43	.236	.292	.374	326	77	8	2	11	42	26	64
vs. Left	.280	.316	.376	125	35	2	2	2	12	8	20	.256	.298	.360	164	42	4	2	3	14	11	34
vs. Right	.221	.292	.412	131	29	4	0	7	25	12	23	.216	.287	.389	162	35	4	0	8	28	15	30

Stanicek, Peter Louis "Pete"

Bats: Both   Throws: Right   Born 04/16/63

1987 SEASON AND MAJOR-LEAGUE CAREER BATTING TOTALS

	G	AB	H	2B	3B	HR	TB	R	RBI	TBB	IBB	SO	HP	SH	SF	SB	CS	SB%	GDP	AVG	OBP	SLG
87 BAL	30	113	31	3	0	0	34	9	9	8	1	19	2	1	0	8	1	.89	2	.274	.333	.301
1 YEAR	30	113	31	3	0	0	34	9	9	8	1	19	2	1	0	8	1	.89	2	.274	.333	.301

	1987 SEASON										FOUR YEAR TOTALS (1984 – 1987)									
	AVG	OBP	SLG	AB	H	2B	3B	HR	RBI	BB	SO	AVG	OBP	SLG	AB	H	2B	3B	HR	RBI	BB	SO
Totals	.274	.333	.301	113	31	3	0	0	9	8	19	.274	.333	.301	113	31	3	0	0	9	8	19
vs. Left	.286	.314	.327	49	14	2	0	0	3	2	6	.286	.314	.327	49	14	2	0	0	3	2	6
vs. Right	.266	.347	.281	64	17	1	0	0	6	6	13	.266	.347	.281	64	17	1	0	0	6	6	13
At Home	.323	.382	.339	62	20	1	0	0	7	5	12	.323	.382	.339	62	20	1	0	0	7	5	12
On Road	.216	.273	.255	51	11	2	0	0	2	3	7	.216	.273	.255	51	11	2	0	0	2	3	7

Steels, James Earl "Jim"

Bats: Left   Throws: Left   Born 05/30/61

1987 SEASON AND MAJOR-LEAGUE CAREER BATTING TOTALS

	G	AB	H	2B	3B	HR	TB	R	RBI	TBB	IBB	SO	HP	SH	SF	SB	CS	SB%	GDP	AVG	OBP	SLG
87 SD	62	68	13	1	1	0	16	9	6	11	0	14	0	1	1	3	2	.60	2	.191	.300	.235
1 YEAR	62	68	13	1	1	0	16	9	6	11	0	14	0	1	1	3	2	.60	2	.191	.300	.235

	1987 SEASON										FOUR YEAR TOTALS (1984 – 1987)									
	AVG	OBP	SLG	AB	H	2B	3B	HR	RBI	BB	SO	AVG	OBP	SLG	AB	H	2B	3B	HR	RBI	BB	SO
Totals	.188	.309	.232	69	13	1	1	0	6	12	14	.188	.309	.232	69	13	1	1	0	6	12	14
vs. Left	.167	.286	.167	6	1	0	0	0	0	1	2	.167	.286	.167	6	1	0	0	0	0	1	2
vs. Right	.190	.311	.238	63	12	1	1	0	6	11	12	.190	.311	.238	63	12	1	1	0	6	11	12
At Home	.167	.189	.222	36	6	0	1	0	3	1	7	.167	.189	.222	36	6	0	1	0	3	1	7
On Road	.212	.409	.242	33	7	1	0	0	3	11	7	.212	.409	.242	33	7	1	0	0	3	11	7

Stefero, John Robert
Bats: Left   Throws: Right   Born 09/22/59

1987 SEASON AND MAJOR-LEAGUE CAREER BATTING TOTALS

	G	AB	H	2B	3B	HR	TB	R	RBI	TBB	IBB	SO	HP	SH	SF	SB	CS	SB%	GDP	AVG	OBP	SLG
87 MON	18	56	11	0	0	1	14	4	3	3	1	17	0	0	0	0	0	.00	2	.196	.237	.250
3 YEARS	79	187	44	3	0	3	56	20	20	22	1	44	0	0	1	0	1	.00	3	.235	.314	.299

	1987 SEASON											FOUR YEAR TOTALS (1984 – 1987)										
	AVG	OBP	SLG	AB	H	2B	3B	HR	RBI	BB	SO	AVG	OBP	SLG	AB	H	2B	3B	HR	RBI	BB	SO
Totals	.196	.237	.250	56	11	0	0	1	3	3	17	.222	.296	.284	176	39	2	0	3	16	19	42
vs. Left	.000	.000	.000	1	0	0	0	0	0	0	0	.143	.143	.143	7	1	0	0	0	0	0	1
vs. Right	.200	.241	.255	55	11	0	0	1	3	3	17	.225	.302	.290	169	38	2	0	3	16	19	41
At Home	.174	.208	.174	23	4	0	0	0	0	1	7	.194	.250	.269	93	18	1	0	2	9	7	21
On Road	.212	.257	.303	33	7	0	0	1	3	2	10	.253	.344	.301	83	21	1	0	1	7	12	21

Stewart, Samuel Lee "Sammy"
Bats: Right   Throws: Right   Born 10/28/54

1987 SEASON AND MAJOR-LEAGUE CAREER PITCHING TOTALS

	G	GS	CG	GF	IP	BFP	H	R	ER	HR	SH	SF	HB	TBB	IBB	SO	WP	Bk	W	L	Pct	ShO	Sv	ERA
87 CLE	25	0	0	16	27	130	25	22	17	4	0	1	1	21	1	25	2	0	4	2	.667	0	3	5.67
10 YEARS	359	25	4	181	957	4121	863	421	382	77	41	34	16	502	43	586	41	7	59	48	.551	1	45	3.59

1987: Power, Flyball   1986: Power, Flyball   1985: Power, Groundball   1984: Power, Flyball

	1987 SEASON											FOUR YEAR TOTALS (1984 – 1987)										
	G	IP	H	BB	SO	SB	CS	W	L	S	ERA	G	IP	H	BB	SO	SB	CS	W	L	S	ERA
Totals	25	27.0	25	21	25	4	0	4	2	3	5.67	168	313.1	287	182	205	25	11	20	14	25	3.82
At Home	16	17.0	18	14	18	0	0	4	1	1	6.35	89	178.1	147	113	128	5	8	13	5	13	3.18
On Road	9	10.0	7	7	7	4	0	0	1	2	4.50	79	135.0	140	69	77	20	3	7	9	12	4.67
vs. Opposing Batters	AVG	OBP	SLG	AB	H	2B	3B	HR	RBI	BB	SO	AVG	OBP	SLG	AB	H	2B	3B	HR	RBI	BB	SO
Totals	.234	.362	.374	107	25	3	0	4	18	21	25	.248	.350	.376	1159	287	40	5	33	182	182	205
vs. Left	.167	.322	.250	48	8	1	0	1	3	10	13	.255	.385	.362	517	132	21	2	10	67	108	85
vs. Right	.288	.394	.475	59	17	2	0	3	15	11	12	.241	.319	.388	642	155	19	3	23	115	74	120

Stoddard, Robert Lyle "Bob"
Bats: Right   Throws: Right   Born 03/08/57

1987 SEASON AND MAJOR-LEAGUE CAREER PITCHING TOTALS

	G	GS	CG	GF	IP	BFP	H	R	ER	HR	SH	SF	HB	TBB	IBB	SO	WP	Bk	W	L	Pct	ShO	Sv	ERA
87 KC	17	2	0	4	40	190	51	26	19	3	1	1	3	22	2	23	4	0	1	3	.250	0	1	4.28
7 YEARS	119	45	5	23	433	1844	437	222	194	56	15	10	14	160	6	223	23	5	18	27	.400	2	3	4.03

1987: Power, Groundball   1986: Power, Flyball

	1987 SEASON											TWO YEAR TOTALS (1986 – 1987)										
	G	IP	H	BB	SO	SB	CS	W	L	S	ERA	G	IP	H	BB	SO	SB	CS	W	L	S	ERA
Totals	17	40.0	51	22	23	4	2	1	3	1	4.28	35	63.1	71	33	40	7	2	2	3	2	3.55
At Home	10	19.0	27	10	15	2	2	0	1	1	4.74	18	32.0	38	17	26	4	2	0	1	0	3.66
On Road	7	21.0	24	12	8	2	0	1	2	0	3.86	17	31.1	33	16	14	3	0	2	2	0	3.45
vs. Opposing Batters	AVG	OBP	SLG	AB	H	2B	3B	HR	RBI	BB	SO	AVG	OBP	SLG	AB	H	2B	3B	HR	RBI	BB	SO
Totals	.313	.402	.429	163	51	6	2	3	21	22	23	.283	.372	.390	251	71	11	2	4	34	33	40
vs. Left	.254	.346	.352	71	18	2	1	1	9	10	9	.230	.328	.310	113	26	4	1	1	11	17	18
vs. Right	.359	.444	.489	92	33	4	1	2	12	12	14	.326	.409	.457	138	45	7	1	3	23	16	22

Stoddard, Timothy Paul "Tim"
Bats: Right   Throws: Right   Born 01/24/53

1987 SEASON AND MAJOR-LEAGUE CAREER PITCHING TOTALS

	G	GS	CG	GF	IP	BFP	H	R	ER	HR	SH	SF	HB	TBB	IBB	SO	WP	Bk	W	L	Pct	ShO	Sv	ERA
87 NYA	57	0	0	23	93	386	83	38	36	13	0	3	0	30	2	78	3	0	4	3	.571	0	8	3.48
11 YEARS	443	0	0	246	653	2814	593	295	274	66	35	22	8	322	43	537	30	2	39	33	.542	0	73	3.78

1987: Power, Flyball   1986: Power, Flyball   1985: Power, Flyball   1984: Power, Flyball

	1987 SEASON											FOUR YEAR TOTALS (1984 – 1987)										
	G	IP	H	BB	SO	SB	CS	W	L	S	ERA	G	IP	H	BB	SO	SB	CS	W	L	S	ERA
Totals	57	93.0	83	30	78	13	3	4	3	8	3.48	213	339.2	297	181	288	53	12	20	19	16	3.87
At Home	30	52.2	46	18	42	7	2	3	1	4	2.91	115	179.1	147	91	151	25	5	15	8	8	3.51
On Road	27	40.1	37	12	36	6	1	1	2	4	4.24	98	160.1	150	90	137	28	7	5	11	8	4.27
vs. Opposing Batters	AVG	OBP	SLG	AB	H	2B	3B	HR	RBI	BB	SO	AVG	OBP	SLG	AB	H	2B	3B	HR	RBI	BB	SO
Totals	.235	.293	.391	353	83	10	3	13	42	30	78	.237	.332	.382	1255	297	46	13	37	180	181	288
vs. Left	.276	.340	.448	145	40	5	1	6	18	14	18	.257	.363	.418	533	137	20	9	16	78	89	83
vs. Right	.207	.260	.351	208	43	5	2	7	24	16	60	.222	.308	.356	722	160	26	4	21	102	92	205

Stone, Jeffrey Glen "Jeff"

Bats: Left **Throws: Right** **Born 12/26/60**

1987 SEASON AND MAJOR-LEAGUE CAREER BATTING TOTALS

	G	AB	H	2B	3B	HR	TB	R	RBI	TBB	IBB	SO	HP	SH	SF	SB	CS	SB%	GDP	AVG	OBP	SLG
87 PHI	66	125	32	7	1	1	44	19	16	8	0	38	3	0	0	3	1	.75	2	.256	.316	.352
5 YEARS	296	827	241	21	16	11	327	116	64	52	0	167	10	5	2	68	17	.80	10	.291	.340	.395

	1987 SEASON										FOUR YEAR TOTALS (1984 – 1987)									
	AVG	OBP	SLG	AB	H	2B	3B	HR	RBI	BB	SO	AVG	OBP	SLG	AB	H	2B	3B	HR	RBI	BB	SO
Totals	.256	.316	.352	125	32	7	1	1	16	8	38	.289	.338	.389	823	238	21	14	11	61	52	166
vs. Left	.100	.308	.200	10	1	1	0	0	0	1	6	.304	.374	.424	125	38	5	2	2	5	11	28
vs. Right	.270	.317	.365	115	31	6	1	1	16	7	32	.287	.332	.383	698	200	16	12	9	56	41	138
At Home	.246	.303	.344	61	15	3	0	1	10	3	13	.314	.363	.430	423	133	9	8	8	39	29	76
On Road	.266	.329	.359	64	17	4	1	0	6	5	25	.262	.312	.345	400	105	12	6	3	22	23	90

Sullivan, Marc Cooper

Bats: Right **Throws: Right** **Born 07/25/58**

1987 SEASON AND MAJOR-LEAGUE CAREER BATTING TOTALS

	G	AB	H	2B	3B	HR	TB	R	RBI	TBB	IBB	SO	HP	SH	SF	SB	CS	SB%	GDP	AVG	OBP	SLG
87 BOS	60	160	27	5	0	2	38	11	10	4	0	43	2	6	1	0	0	.00	5	.169	.198	.237
5 YEARS	137	360	67	11	0	5	93	37	28	18	0	92	6	11	2	0	0	.00	6	.186	.236	.258

	1987 SEASON										FOUR YEAR TOTALS (1984 – 1987)									
	AVG	OBP	SLG	AB	H	2B	3B	HR	RBI	BB	SO	AVG	OBP	SLG	AB	H	2B	3B	HR	RBI	BB	SO
Totals	.169	.198	.237	160	27	5	0	2	10	4	43	.184	.234	.257	354	65	11	0	5	28	18	90
vs. Left	.250	.264	.308	52	13	3	0	0	1	1	13	.203	.265	.288	153	31	4	0	3	10	11	37
vs. Right	.130	.167	.204	108	14	2	0	2	9	3	30	.169	.210	.234	201	34	7	0	2	18	7	53
At Home	.147	.169	.213	75	11	2	0	1	4	1	20	.193	.234	.295	166	32	5	0	4	17	6	43
On Road	.188	.222	.259	85	16	3	0	1	6	3	23	.176	.234	.223	188	33	6	0	1	11	12	47

Sundberg, James Howard "Jim"

Bats: Right **Throws: Right** **Born 05/18/51**

1987 SEASON AND MAJOR-LEAGUE CAREER BATTING TOTALS

	G	AB	H	2B	3B	HR	TB	R	RBI	TBB	IBB	SO	HP	SH	SF	SB	CS	SB%	GDP	AVG	OBP	SLG
87 CHN	61	139	28	2	0	4	42	9	15	19	3	40	2	1	0	0	0	.00	3	.201	.306	.302
14 YEARS	1824	5729	1425	231	35	87	1987	587	594	663	31	894	22	105	36	20	37	.35	153	.249	.327	.347

	1987 SEASON										FOUR YEAR TOTALS (1984 – 1987)									
	AVG	OBP	SLG	AB	H	2B	3B	HR	RBI	BB	SO	AVG	OBP	SLG	AB	H	2B	3B	HR	RBI	BB	SO
Totals	.201	.306	.302	139	28	2	0	4	15	19	40	.234	.312	.358	1283	300	42	9	33	135	147	261
vs. Left	.261	.414	.435	23	6	1	0	1	6	6	7	.235	.316	.415	400	94	16	4	16	51	48	79
vs. Right	.190	.282	.276	116	22	1	0	3	9	13	33	.233	.311	.332	883	206	26	5	17	84	99	182
At Home	.206	.316	.309	68	14	1	0	2	8	10	20	.224	.293	.326	639	143	20	3	13	65	63	135
On Road	.197	.296	.296	71	14	1	0	2	7	9	20	.244	.331	.390	644	157	22	6	20	70	84	126

Taylor, Donald Clyde "Dorn"

Bats: Right **Throws: Right** **Born 08/11/58**

1987 SEASON AND MAJOR-LEAGUE CAREER PITCHING TOTALS

	G	GS	CG	GF	IP	BFP	H	R	ER	HR	SH	SF	HB	TBB	IBB	SO	WP	Bk	W	L	Pct	ShO	Sv	ERA
87 PIT	14	8	0	0	53	226	48	35	34	10	1	2	1	28	1	37	3	0	2	3	.400	0	0	5.77
1 YEAR	14	8	0	0	53	226	48	35	34	10	1	2	1	28	1	37	3	0	2	3	.400	0	0	5.77

1987: Power, Groundball

	1987 SEASON										FOUR YEAR TOTALS (1984 – 1987)									
	G	IP	H	BB	SO	SB	CS	W	L	S	ERA	G	IP	H	BB	SO	SB	CS	W	L	S	ERA
Totals	14	53.1	48	28	37	2	5	2	3	0	5.74	14	53.1	48	28	37	2	5	2	3	0	5.74
At Home	6	27.0	26	11	22	1	3	1	1	0	5.67	6	27.0	26	11	22	1	3	1	1	0	5.67
On Road	8	26.1	22	17	15	1	2	1	2	0	5.81	8	26.1	22	17	15	1	2	1	2	0	5.81
vs. Opposing Batters	AVG	OBP	SLG	AB	H	2B	3B	HR	RBI	BB	SO	AVG	OBP	SLG	AB	H	2B	3B	HR	RBI	BB	SO
Totals	.247	.342	.459	194	48	7	2	10	33	28	37	.247	.342	.459	194	48	7	2	10	33	28	37
vs. Left	.273	.365	.515	99	27	5	2	5	16	15	14	.273	.365	.515	99	27	5	2	5	16	15	14
vs. Right	.221	.318	.400	95	21	2	0	5	17	13	23	.221	.318	.400	95	21	2	0	5	17	13	23

Tettleton, Mickey Lee

Bats: Both   Throws: Right   Born 09/16/60

1987 SEASON AND MAJOR-LEAGUE CAREER BATTING TOTALS

	G	AB	H	2B	3B	HR	TB	R	RBI	TBB	IBB	SO	HP	SH	SF	SB	CS	SB%	GDP	AVG	OBP	SLG
87 OAK	82	211	41	3	0	8	68	19	26	30	0	65	0	5	2	1	1	.50	3	.194	.292	.322
4 YEARS	283	709	157	26	1	22	251	78	81	108	0	196	3	17	7	10	4	.71	15	.221	.324	.354

	1987 SEASON											FOUR YEAR TOTALS (1984 – 1987)										
	AVG	OBP	SLG	AB	H	2B	3B	HR	RBI	BB	SO	AVG	OBP	SLG	AB	H	2B	3B	HR	RBI	BB	SO
Totals	.194	.292	.322	211	41	3	0	8	26	30	65	.221	.323	.354	709	157	26	1	22	81	107	196
vs. Left	.214	.323	.310	84	18	2	0	2	7	14	19	.228	.331	.388	263	60	12	0	10	28	41	66
vs. Right	.181	.271	.331	127	23	1	0	6	19	16	46	.217	.318	.334	446	97	14	1	12	53	66	130
At Home	.219	.311	.381	105	23	2	0	5	14	15	35	.231	.335	.359	368	85	12	1	11	38	58	105
On Road	.170	.273	.264	106	18	1	0	3	12	15	30	.211	.310	.349	341	72	14	0	11	43	49	91

Tewksbury, Robert Alan "Bob"

Bats: Right   Throws: Right   Born 11/30/60

1987 SEASON AND MAJOR-LEAGUE CAREER PITCHING TOTALS

	G	GS	CG	GF	IP	BFP	H	R	ER	HR	SH	SF	HB	TBB	IBB	SO	WP	Bk	W	L	Pct	ShO	Sv	ERA
87 NYA-CHN	15	9	0	4	51	242	79	41	38	6	5	1	1	20	3	22	1	2	1	8	.111	0	0	6.71
2 YEARS	38	29	2	4	181	800	223	99	86	14	9	8	6	51	3	71	4	4	10	13	.435	0	0	4.28

1987: Power, Groundball   1986: Finesse, Groundball

	1987 SEASON											FOUR YEAR TOTALS (1984 – 1987)										
	G	IP	H	BB	SO	SB	CS	W	L	S	ERA	G	IP	H	BB	SO	SB	CS	W	L	S	ERA
Totals	15	51.1	79	20	22	1	1	1	8	0	6.84	38	181.2	223	51	71	2	4	10	13	0	4.31
At Home	6	26.1	38	9	13	0	1	1	3	0	5.47	16	86.0	102	22	35	0	3	5	4	0	3.45
On Road	9	25.0	41	11	9	1	0	0	5	0	8.28	22	95.2	121	29	36	2	1	5	9	0	5.08
vs. Opposing Batters	AVG	OBP	SLG	AB	H	2B	3B	HR	RBI	BB	SO	AVG	OBP	SLG	AB	H	2B	3B	HR	RBI	BB	SO
Totals	.367	.422	.502	215	79	11	0	6	35	20	22	.307	.353	.428	726	223	32	7	14	83	51	71
vs. Left	.367	.415	.468	109	40	8	0	1	8	9	8	.287	.327	.408	373	107	14	5	7	30	22	29
vs. Right	.368	.429	.538	106	39	3	0	5	27	11	14	.329	.380	.450	353	116	18	2	7	53	29	42

Thon, Richard William "Dickie"

Bats: Right   Throws: Right   Born 06/20/58

1987 SEASON AND MAJOR-LEAGUE CAREER BATTING TOTALS

	G	AB	H	2B	3B	HR	TB	R	RBI	TBB	IBB	SO	HP	SH	SF	SB	CS	SB%	GDP	AVG	OBP	SLG
87 HOU	32	66	14	1	0	1	18	6	3	16	3	13	0	1	0	3	0	1.00	1	.212	.366	.273
9 YEARS	681	2145	579	100	24	33	826	264	195	178	25	288	5	18	14	101	39	.72	38	.270	.325	.385

	1987 SEASON											FOUR YEAR TOTALS (1984 – 1987)										
	AVG	OBP	SLG	AB	H	2B	3B	HR	RBI	BB	SO	AVG	OBP	SLG	AB	H	2B	3B	HR	RBI	BB	SO
Totals	.212	.366	.273	66	14	1	0	1	3	16	13	.248	.318	.340	612	152	20	3	10	54	63	116
vs. Left	.196	.348	.250	56	11	0	0	1	2	13	10	.250	.327	.331	396	99	12	1	6	30	46	63
vs. Right	.300	.462	.400	10	3	1	0	0	1	3	3	.245	.302	.356	216	53	8	2	4	24	17	53
At Home	.176	.300	.206	34	6	1	0	0	0	6	3	.225	.295	.309	320	72	12	3	3	22	31	53
On Road	.250	.429	.344	32	8	0	0	1	3	10	10	.274	.344	.373	292	80	8	0	7	32	32	63

Thornton, Andre "Andy"

Bats: Right   Throws: Right   Born 08/13/49

1987 SEASON AND MAJOR-LEAGUE CAREER BATTING TOTALS

	G	AB	H	2B	3B	HR	TB	R	RBI	TBB	IBB	SO	HP	SH	SF	SB	CS	SB%	GDP	AVG	OBP	SLG
87 CLE	36	85	10	2	0	0	12	8	5	10	0	25	0	0	2	1	0	1.00	1	.118	.206	.141
14 YEARS	1565	5291	1342	244	22	253	2389	792	895	876	69	851	41	14	71	48	37	.56	129	.254	.360	.452

	1987 SEASON											FOUR YEAR TOTALS (1984 – 1987)										
	AVG	OBP	SLG	AB	H	2B	3B	HR	RBI	BB	SO	AVG	OBP	SLG	AB	H	2B	3B	HR	RBI	BB	SO
Totals	.118	.206	.141	85	10	2	0	0	5	10	25	.241	.330	.418	1534	370	55	0	72	258	213	246
vs. Left	.075	.150	.094	53	4	1	0	0	3	5	16	.241	.351	.420	486	117	15	0	24	77	85	75
vs. Right	.188	.297	.219	32	6	1	0	0	2	5	9	.241	.320	.417	1048	253	40	0	48	181	128	171
At Home	.163	.245	.186	43	7	1	0	0	4	5	11	.274	.357	.482	770	211	31	0	43	158	107	102
On Road	.071	.167	.095	42	3	1	0	0	1	5	14	.208	.303	.353	764	159	24	0	29	100	106	144

Thurman, Gary Montez

Bats: Right   Throws: Right   Born 11/12/64

1987 SEASON AND MAJOR-LEAGUE CAREER BATTING TOTALS

	G	AB	H	2B	3B	HR	TB	R	RBI	TBB	IBB	SO	HP	SH	SF	SB	CS	SB%	GDP	AVG	OBP	SLG
87 KC	27	81	24	2	0	0	26	12	5	8	0	20	0	1	0	7	2	.78	1	.296	.360	.321
1 YEAR	27	81	24	2	0	0	26	12	5	8	0	20	0	1	0	7	2	.78	1	.296	.360	.321

1987 SEASON	AVG	OBP	SLG	AB	H	2B	3B	HR	RBI	BB	SO	FOUR YEAR TOTALS (1984 – 1987)	AVG	OBP	SLG	AB	H	2B	3B	HR	RBI	BB	SO
Totals	.296	.360	.321	81	24	2	0	0	5	8	20		.296	.360	.321	81	24	2	0	0	5	8	20
vs. Left	.353	.421	.412	17	6	1	0	0	0	2	5		.353	.421	.412	17	6	1	0	0	0	2	5
vs. Right	.281	.343	.297	64	18	1	0	0	5	6	15		.281	.343	.297	64	18	1	0	0	5	6	15
At Home	.227	.277	.250	44	10	1	0	0	1	3	10		.227	.277	.250	44	10	1	0	0	1	3	10
On Road	.378	.452	.405	37	14	1	0	0	4	5	10		.378	.452	.405	37	14	1	0	0	4	5	10

Thurmond, Mark Anthony

Bats: Left   Throws: Left   Born 09/12/56

1987 SEASON AND MAJOR-LEAGUE CAREER PITCHING TOTALS

	G	GS	CG	GF	IP	BFP	H	R	ER	HR	SH	SF	HB	TBB	IBB	SO	WP	Bk	W	L	Pct	ShO	Sv	ERA
87 DET	48	0	0	23	62	280	83	32	29	5	1	4	0	24	4	21	4	0	0	1	.000	0	5	4.21
5 YEARS	179	89	6	35	617	2625	655	283	245	47	40	17	5	200	21	233	7	4	35	31	.530	3	10	3.57

1987: Finesse, Groundball   1986: Finesse, Groundball   1985: Finesse, Groundball   1984: Finesse, Groundball

1987 SEASON	G	IP	H	BB	SO	SB	CS	W	L	S	ERA	FOUR YEAR TOTALS (1984 – 1987)	G	IP	H	BB	SO	SB	CS	W	L	S	ERA
Totals	48	61.2	83	24	21	5	1	0	1	5	4.23		158	501.0	551	167	184	49	19	28	28	10	3.79
At Home	23	29.0	39	12	8	2	0	0	1	3	4.03		82	264.2	288	78	104	23	10	14	17	6	3.64
On Road	25	32.2	44	12	13	3	1	0	0	2	4.41		76	236.1	263	89	80	26	9	14	11	4	3.96
vs. Opposing Batters	AVG	OBP	SLG	AB	H	2B	3B	HR	RBI	BB	SO		AVG	OBP	SLG	AB	H	2B	3B	HR	RBI	BB	SO
Totals	.331	.384	.466	251	83	15	2	5	53	24	21		.283	.339	.394	1944	551	74	10	40	240	167	184
vs. Left	.273	.330	.364	88	24	5	0	1	19	9	10		.239	.298	.308	402	96	11	1	5	51	35	57
vs. Right	.362	.413	.521	163	59	10	2	4	34	15	11		.295	.350	.416	1542	455	63	9	35	189	132	127

Tibbs, Jay Lindsey

Bats: Right   Throws: Right   Born 01/04/62

1987 SEASON AND MAJOR-LEAGUE CAREER PITCHING TOTALS

	G	GS	CG	GF	IP	BFP	H	R	ER	HR	SH	SF	HB	TBB	IBB	SO	WP	Bk	W	L	Pct	ShO	Sv	ERA
87 MON	19	12	0	2	83	366	95	55	46	10	2	1	0	34	2	54	1	1	4	5	.444	0	0	4.99
4 YEARS	103	91	11	4	592	2494	579	296	257	40	31	13	3	220	16	309	22	4	27	32	.458	5	0	3.91

1987: Power, Groundball   1986: Finesse, Groundball   1985: Finesse, Groundball   1984: Finesse, Groundball

1987 SEASON	G	IP	H	BB	SO	SB	CS	W	L	S	ERA	FOUR YEAR TOTALS (1984 – 1987)	G	IP	H	BB	SO	SB	CS	W	L	S	ERA
Totals	19	82.2	95	34	54	7	4	4	5	0	5.01		103	591.2	579	220	309	33	27	27	32	0	3.91
At Home	8	34.2	37	14	23	4	3	2	2	0	4.15		52	310.2	286	108	161	13	12	14	16	0	3.59
On Road	11	48.0	58	20	31	3	1	2	3	0	5.63		51	281.0	293	112	148	20	15	13	16	0	4.26
vs. Opposing Batters	AVG	OBP	SLG	AB	H	2B	3B	HR	RBI	BB	SO		AVG	OBP	SLG	AB	H	2B	3B	HR	RBI	BB	SO
Totals	.289	.354	.450	329	95	19	2	10	48	34	54		.260	.327	.380	2226	579	104	21	40	242	220	309
vs. Left	.296	.372	.481	162	48	14	2	4	22	20	22		.273	.341	.397	1173	320	67	14	17	120	121	141
vs. Right	.281	.337	.419	167	47	5	0	6	26	14	32		.246	.311	.360	1053	259	37	7	23	122	99	168

Treadway, Hugh Jeffrey "Jeff"

Bats: Left   Throws: Right   Born 01/22/63

1987 SEASON AND MAJOR-LEAGUE CAREER BATTING TOTALS

	G	AB	H	2B	3B	HR	TB	R	RBI	TBB	IBB	SO	HP	SH	SF	SB	CS	SB%	GDP	AVG	OBP	SLG
87 CIN	23	84	28	4	0	2	38	9	4	2	0	6	1	3	0	1	0	1.00	1	.333	.356	.452
1 YEAR	23	84	28	4	0	2	38	9	4	2	0	6	1	3	0	1	0	1.00	1	.333	.356	.452

1987 SEASON	AVG	OBP	SLG	AB	H	2B	3B	HR	RBI	BB	SO	FOUR YEAR TOTALS (1984 – 1987)	AVG	OBP	SLG	AB	H	2B	3B	HR	RBI	BB	SO
Totals	.333	.356	.452	84	28	4	0	2	4	2	6		.333	.356	.452	84	28	4	0	2	4	2	6
vs. Left	.143	.250	.143	7	1	0	0	0	0	0	0		.143	.250	.143	7	1	0	0	0	0	0	0
vs. Right	.351	.367	.481	77	27	4	0	2	4	2	6		.351	.367	.481	77	27	4	0	2	4	2	6
At Home	.311	.326	.467	45	14	1	0	2	3	0	3		.311	.326	.467	45	14	1	0	2	3	0	3
On Road	.359	.390	.436	39	14	3	0	0	1	2	3		.359	.390	.436	39	14	3	0	0	1	2	3

Trevino, Alejandro (Castro) "Alex"

Bats: Right   Throws: Right   Born 08/26/57

1987 SEASON AND MAJOR-LEAGUE CAREER BATTING TOTALS

	G	AB	H	2B	3B	HR	TB	R	RBI	TBB	IBB	SO	HP	SH	SF	SB	CS	SB%	GDP	AVG	OBP	SLG
87 LA	72	144	32	7	1	3	50	16	16	6	2	28	4	1	1	1	0	1.00	7	.222	.271	.347
10 YEARS	744	2020	499	88	9	18	659	208	202	167	25	259	12	22	16	14	8	.64	65	.247	.306	.326

	1987 SEASON											FOUR YEAR TOTALS (1984 – 1987)										
	AVG	OBP	SLG	AB	H	2B	3B	HR	RBI	BB	SO	AVG	OBP	SLG	AB	H	2B	3B	HR	RBI	BB	SO
Totals	.222	.271	.347	144	32	7	1	3	16	6	28	.239	.304	.365	775	185	46	2	16	89	69	116
vs. Left	.222	.297	.370	81	18	4	1	2	12	6	17	.232	.306	.341	349	81	16	2	6	34	34	60
vs. Right	.222	.234	.317	63	14	3	0	1	4	0	11	.244	.303	.385	426	104	30	0	10	55	35	56
At Home	.187	.247	.293	75	14	0	1	2	7	5	9	.235	.294	.358	388	91	22	1	8	44	32	52
On Road	.261	.297	.406	69	18	7	0	1	9	1	19	.243	.315	.372	387	94	24	1	8	45	37	64

Trillo, Jesus Manuel Marcano "Manny"

Bats: Right   Throws: Right   Born 01/25/50

1987 SEASON AND MAJOR-LEAGUE CAREER BATTING TOTALS

	G	AB	H	2B	3B	HR	TB	R	RBI	TBB	IBB	SO	HP	SH	SF	SB	CS	SB%	GDP	AVG	OBP	SLG
87 CHN	108	214	63	8	0	8	95	27	26	25	0	37	0	4	1	0	3	.00	6	.294	.367	.444
15 YEARS	1687	5747	1513	234	33	60	1993	580	557	442	35	701	33	84	48	54	57	.49	141	.263	.317	.347

	1987 SEASON											FOUR YEAR TOTALS (1984 – 1987)										
	AVG	OBP	SLG	AB	H	2B	3B	HR	RBI	BB	SO	AVG	OBP	SLG	AB	H	2B	3B	HR	RBI	BB	SO
Totals	.294	.367	.444	214	63	8	0	8	26	25	37	.255	.315	.345	1218	311	55	3	16	106	106	157
vs. Left	.298	.362	.447	94	28	2	0	4	11	10	18	.261	.318	.345	383	100	14	0	6	31	32	56
vs. Right	.292	.370	.442	120	35	6	0	4	15	15	19	.253	.313	.345	835	211	41	3	10	75	74	101
At Home	.348	.416	.554	112	39	5	0	6	13	13	16	.253	.311	.362	580	147	30	0	11	53	48	75
On Road	.235	.313	.324	102	24	3	0	2	13	12	21	.257	.319	.329	638	164	25	3	5	53	58	82

Trout, Steven Russell "Steve"

Bats: Left   Throws: Left   Born 07/30/57

1987 SEASON AND MAJOR-LEAGUE CAREER PITCHING TOTALS

	G	GS	CG	GF	IP	BFP	H	R	ER	HR	SH	SF	HB	TBB	IBB	SO	WP	Bk	W	L	Pct	ShO	Sv	ERA
87 CHN-NYA	25	20	3	2	121	532	123	63	59	7	1	2	2	64	0	59	12	0	6	7	.462	2	0	4.39
10 YEARS	267	220	32	23	1415	6124	1536	711	626	81	71	38	28	530	44	625	45	9	80	82	.494	9	4	3.98

1987: Finesse, Groundball   1986: Finesse, Groundball   1985: Finesse, Groundball   1984: Finesse, Groundball

	1987 SEASON										FOUR YEAR TOTALS (1984 – 1987)									
	G	IP	H	BB	SO	SB	CS	W	L	S	ERA	G	IP	H	BB	SO	SB	CS	W	L	S	ERA
Totals	25	121.1	123	64	59	17	5	6	7	0	4.38	118	613.0	654	264	253	53	46	33	28	0	3.93
At Home	12	74.0	62	32	40	10	2	5	1	0	2.31	63	341.1	351	150	149	26	19	19	10	0	3.72
On Road	13	47.1	61	32	19	7	3	1	6	0	7.61	55	271.2	303	114	104	27	27	14	18	0	4.24

vs. Opposing Batters	AVG	OBP	SLG	AB	H	2B	3B	HR	RBI	BB	SO	AVG	OBP	SLG	AB	H	2B	3B	HR	RBI	BB	SO
Totals	.266	.356	.359	463	123	20	1	7	49	64	59	.281	.355	.366	2324	654	89	12	28	246	264	253
vs. Left	.283	.368	.417	60	17	5	0	1	6	6	9	.299	.361	.371	348	104	17	1	2	37	32	42
vs. Right	.263	.354	.350	403	106	15	1	6	43	58	50	.278	.354	.365	1976	550	72	11	26	209	232	211

Trujillo, Michael Andrew "Mike"

Bats: Right   Throws: Right   Born 01/12/60

1987 SEASON AND MAJOR-LEAGUE CAREER PITCHING TOTALS

	G	GS	CG	GF	IP	BFP	H	R	ER	HR	SH	SF	HB	TBB	IBB	SO	WP	Bk	W	L	Pct	ShO	Sv	ERA
87 SEA	28	7	0	6	66	284	70	46	45	12	1	2	2	26	0	36	6	1	4	4	.500	0	1	6.14
3 YEARS	69	18	2	18	197	860	221	118	107	24	5	5	5	70	4	78	8	1	11	10	.524	1	3	4.89

1987: Finesse, Groundball   1986: Finesse, Groundball

	1987 SEASON										TWO YEAR TOTALS (1986 – 1987)									
	G	IP	H	BB	SO	SB	CS	W	L	S	ERA	G	IP	H	BB	SO	SB	CS	W	L	S	ERA
Totals	28	65.2	70	26	36	3	5	4	5	1	6.17	42	112.2	109	47	59	5	6	7	7	2	4.95
At Home	15	37.1	36	15	26	1	4	2	3	0	6.03	23	68.1	61	29	37	2	5	5	3	0	4.74
On Road	13	28.1	34	11	10	2	1	2	2	1	6.35	19	44.1	48	18	22	3	1	2	4	2	5.28

vs. Opposing Batters	AVG	OBP	SLG	AB	H	2B	3B	HR	RBI	BB	SO	AVG	OBP	SLG	AB	H	2B	3B	HR	RBI	BB	SO
Totals	.277	.346	.466	253	70	12	0	12	44	26	36	.256	.331	.412	425	109	15	0	17	61	47	59
vs. Left	.283	.363	.442	120	34	4	0	5	18	15	19	.259	.356	.389	216	56	4	0	8	27	33	32
vs. Right	.271	.331	.489	133	36	8	0	7	26	11	17	.254	.304	.435	209	53	11	0	9	34	14	27

Tunnell, Byron Lee "Lee"

Bats: Right   Throws: Right   Born 10/30/60

1987 SEASON AND MAJOR-LEAGUE CAREER PITCHING TOTALS

	G	GS	CG	GF	IP	BFP	H	R	ER	HR	SH	SF	HB	TBB	IBB	SO	WP	Bk	W	L	Pct	ShO	Sv	ERA
87 STL	32	9	0	3	74	335	90	45	40	5	3	4	1	34	7	49	2	5	4	4	.500	0	0	4.86
5 YEARS	122	66	5	15	470	2023	481	248	219	38	13	13	6	194	20	273	22	12	21	28	.429	3	1	4.19

1987: Power, Groundball

1987 SEASON	G	IP	H	BB	SO	SB	CS	W	L	S	ERA
Totals	32	74.1	90	34	49	7	2	4	4	0	4.84
At Home	13	44.0	45	16	33	7	1	4	2	0	4.09
On Road	19	30.1	45	18	16	0	1	0	2	0	5.93
vs. Opposing Batters	AVG	OBP	SLG	AB	H	2B	3B	HR	RBI	BB	SO
Totals	.307	.377	.430	293	90	15	3	5	45	34	49
vs. Left	.254	.348	.328	134	34	8	1	0	9	20	26
vs. Right	.352	.401	.516	159	56	7	2	5	36	14	23

TWO YEAR TOTALS (1986 – 1987)	G	IP	H	BB	SO	SB	CS	W	L	S	ERA
Totals	32	74.1	90	34	49	7	2	4	4	0	4.84
At Home	13	44.0	45	16	33	7	1	4	2	0	4.09
On Road	19	30.1	45	18	16	0	1	0	2	0	5.93
	AVG	OBP	SLG	AB	H	2B	3B	HR	RBI	BB	SO
Totals	.307	.377	.430	293	90	15	3	5	45	34	49
vs. Left	.254	.348	.328	134	34	8	1	0	9	20	26
vs. Right	.352	.401	.516	159	56	7	2	5	36	14	23

Vande Berg, Edward John "Ed"

Bats: Right   Throws: Left   Born 10/26/58

1987 SEASON AND MAJOR-LEAGUE CAREER PITCHING TOTALS

	G	GS	CG	GF	IP	BFP	H	R	ER	HR	SH	SF	HB	TBB	IBB	SO	WP	Bk	W	L	Pct	ShO	Sv	ERA
87 CLE	55	0	0	18	72	321	96	42	41	9	0	5	0	21	2	40	5	0	1	0	1.000	0	0	5.13
6 YEARS	387	17	2	139	481	2103	528	233	209	50	19	22	5	189	31	296	22	5	23	26	.469	0	20	3.91

1987: Finesse, Groundball   1986: Power, Groundball   1985: Power, Groundball   1984: Power, Groundball

1987 SEASON	G	IP	H	BB	SO	SB	CS	W	L	S	ERA
Totals	55	72.1	96	21	40	2	3	1	0	0	5.10
At Home	28	40.1	56	11	21	2	0	1	0	0	6.25
On Road	27	32.0	40	10	19	0	3	0	3	0	3.66
vs. Opposing Batters	AVG	OBP	SLG	AB	H	2B	3B	HR	RBI	BB	SO
Totals	.325	.364	.468	295	96	11	2	9	56	21	40
vs. Left	.276	.319	.321	134	37	6	0	0	19	9	18
vs. Right	.366	.401	.590	161	59	5	2	9	37	12	22

FOUR YEAR TOTALS (1984 – 1987)	G	IP	H	BB	SO	SB	CS	W	L	S	ERA
Totals	241	341.2	415	135	187	15	16	12	18	10	4.32
At Home	119	163.2	211	66	91	7	7	6	9	5	4.84
On Road	122	178.0	204	69	96	8	9	6	9	5	3.89
	AVG	OBP	SLG	AB	H	2B	3B	HR	RBI	BB	SO
Totals	.304	.365	.452	1366	415	64	11	39	218	135	187
vs. Left	.257	.335	.340	444	114	17	4	4	60	53	61
vs. Right	.326	.380	.507	922	301	47	7	35	158	82	126

Walewander, James "Jim"

Bats: Both   Throws: Right   Born 05/02/62

1987 SEASON AND MAJOR-LEAGUE CAREER BATTING TOTALS

	G	AB	H	2B	3B	HR	TB	R	RBI	TBB	IBB	SO	HP	SH	SF	SB	CS	SB%	GDP	AVG	OBP	SLG
87 DET	53	54	13	3	1	1	21	24	4	7	0	6	0	2	0	2	1	.67	2	.241	.328	.389
1 YEAR	53	54	13	3	1	1	21	24	4	7	0	6	0	2	0	2	1	.67	2	.241	.328	.389

1987 SEASON	AVG	OBP	SLG	AB	H	2B	3B	HR	RBI	BB	SO
Totals	.241	.328	.389	54	13	3	1	1	4	7	6
vs. Left	.250	.368	.250	16	4	0	0	0	2	3	0
vs. Right	.237	.310	.447	38	9	3	1	1	2	4	6
At Home	.222	.323	.481	27	6	2	1	1	2	4	5
On Road	.259	.333	.296	27	7	1	0	0	2	3	1

FOUR YEAR TOTALS (1984 – 1987)	AVG	OBP	SLG	AB	H	2B	3B	HR	RBI	BB	SO
Totals	.241	.328	.389	54	13	3	1	1	4	7	6
vs. Left	.250	.368	.250	16	4	0	0	0	2	3	0
vs. Right	.237	.310	.447	38	9	3	1	1	2	4	6
At Home	.222	.323	.481	27	6	2	1	1	2	4	5
On Road	.259	.333	.296	27	7	1	0	0	2	3	1

Walk, Robert Vernon "Bob"

Bats: Right   Throws: Right   Born 11/26/56

1987 SEASON AND MAJOR-LEAGUE CAREER PITCHING TOTALS

	G	GS	CG	GF	IP	BFP	H	R	ER	HR	SH	SF	HB	TBB	IBB	SO	WP	Bk	W	L	Pct	ShO	Sv	ERA
87 PIT	39	12	1	6	117	498	107	52	43	11	6	2	3	51	2	78	7	3	8	2	.800	1	0	3.31
8 YEARS	166	101	8	15	691	2981	694	361	320	62	31	18	14	292	16	404	35	10	41	34	.547	4	2	4.17

1987: Power, Groundball   1986: Finesse, Groundball   1985: Power, Groundball   1984: Power, Flyball

1987 SEASON	G	IP	H	BB	SO	SB	CS	W	L	S	ERA
Totals	39	117.0	107	51	78	12	6	8	2	0	3.31
At Home	21	73.2	64	32	48	10	5	6	0	0	3.05
On Road	18	43.1	43	19	30	2	1	2	2	0	3.74
vs. Opposing Batters	AVG	OBP	SLG	AB	H	2B	3B	HR	RBI	BB	SO
Totals	.246	.328	.377	435	107	16	4	11	51	51	78
vs. Left	.253	.330	.378	233	59	11	3	4	24	26	35
vs. Right	.238	.326	.376	202	48	5	1	7	27	25	43

FOUR YEAR TOTALS (1984 – 1987)	G	IP	H	BB	SO	SB	CS	W	L	S	ERA
Totals	94	327.2	304	137	206	28	19	18	14	2	3.54
At Home	49	160.1	143	59	103	17	8	9	8	2	3.59
On Road	45	167.1	161	78	103	11	11	9	6	0	3.50
	AVG	OBP	SLG	AB	H	2B	3B	HR	RBI	BB	SO
Totals	.250	.327	.379	1215	304	45	12	29	141	137	206
vs. Left	.259	.338	.375	640	166	23	9	11	58	76	92
vs. Right	.240	.315	.383	575	138	22	3	18	83	61	114

Walker, Cleotha "Chico"

Bats: Both   Throws: Right   Born 11/25/57

1987 SEASON AND MAJOR-LEAGUE CAREER BATTING TOTALS

	G	AB	H	2B	3B	HR	TB	R	RBI	TBB	IBB	SO	HP	SH	SF	SB	CS	SB%	GDP	AVG	OBP	SLG
87 CHN	47	105	21	4	0	0	25	15	7	12	1	23	0	2	2	11	4	.73	1	.200	.277	.238
7 YEARS	128	299	70	7	4	2	91	47	23	29	2	61	1	3	5	30	12	.71	5	.234	.299	.304

	1987 SEASON											FOUR YEAR TOTALS (1984 – 1987)									
	AVG	OBP	SLG	AB	H	2B	3B	HR	RBI	BB	SO	AVG	OBP	SLG	AB	H	2B	3B	HR	RBI	BB	SO
Totals	.200	.277	.238	105	21	4	0	0	7	12	23	.227	.293	.291	220	50	7	2	1	15	22	49
vs. Left	.167	.286	.167	12	2	0	0	0	1	2	3	.226	.294	.258	31	7	1	0	0	1	3	7
vs. Right	.204	.276	.247	93	19	4	0	0	6	10	20	.228	.292	.296	189	43	6	2	1	14	19	42
At Home	.153	.224	.169	59	9	1	0	0	4	6	14	.202	.280	.248	109	22	3	1	0	8	13	24
On Road	.261	.346	.326	46	12	3	0	0	3	6	9	.252	.306	.333	111	28	4	1	1	7	9	25

Walter, Gene Winston

Bats: Left   Throws: Left   Born 11/22/60

1987 SEASON AND MAJOR-LEAGUE CAREER PITCHING TOTALS

	G	GS	CG	GF	IP	BFP	H	R	ER	HR	SH	SF	HB	TBB	IBB	SO	WP	Bk	W	L	Pct	ShO	Sv	ERA
87 NYN	21	0	0	6	20	89	18	10	7	0	1	1	1	13	3	11	1	0	1	2	.333	0	0	3.15
3 YEARS	93	0	0	32	140	597	119	63	54	8	6	5	5	70	11	113	7	0	3	6	.333	0	4	3.47

1987: Power, Groundball   1986: Power, Groundball   1985: Power, Groundball

	1987 SEASON											FOUR YEAR TOTALS (1984 – 1987)									
	G	IP	H	BB	SO	SB	CS	W	L	S	ERA	G	IP	H	BB	SO	SB	CS	W	L	S	ERA
Totals	21	19.2	18	13	11	3	0	1	2	0	3.20	93	139.2	119	70	113	14	6	3	6	4	3.48
At Home	11	11.0	7	5	7	1	0	1	0	0	1.64	46	75.2	57	35	56	9	5	2	2	3	2.62
On Road	10	8.2	11	8	4	2	0	0	2	0	5.19	47	64.0	62	35	57	5	1	1	4	1	4.50

vs. Opposing Batters	AVG	OBP	SLG	AB	H	2B	3B	HR	RBI	BB	SO	AVG	OBP	SLG	AB	H	2B	3B	HR	RBI	BB	SO
Totals	.240	.360	.347	75	18	3	1	1	11	13	11	.232	.326	.330	512	119	20	3	8	62	70	113
vs. Left	.310	.429	.552	29	9	2	1	1	8	5	6	.188	.312	.263	133	25	5	1	1	18	23	44
vs. Right	.196	.315	.217	46	9	1	0	0	3	8	5	.248	.331	.354	379	94	15	2	7	44	47	69

Washington, Claudell

Bats: Left   Throws: Left   Born 08/31/54

1987 SEASON AND MAJOR-LEAGUE CAREER BATTING TOTALS

	G	AB	H	2B	3B	HR	TB	R	RBI	TBB	IBB	SO	HP	SH	SF	SB	CS	SB%	GDP	AVG	OBP	SLG
87 NYA	102	312	87	17	0	9	131	42	44	27	2	54	0	0	0	10	1	.91	3	.279	.336	.420
14 YEARS	1631	5800	1611	292	61	139	2442	804	709	413	71	1083	32	22	45	280	122	.70	125	.278	.327	.421

	1987 SEASON											FOUR YEAR TOTALS (1984 – 1987)									
	AVG	OBP	SLG	AB	H	2B	3B	HR	RBI	BB	SO	AVG	OBP	SLG	AB	H	2B	3B	HR	RBI	BB	SO
Totals	.279	.336	.420	312	87	17	0	9	44	27	54	.275	.345	.447	1398	385	68	8	52	178	147	257
vs. Left	.361	.435	.475	61	22	4	0	1	3	8	12	.286	.353	.415	287	82	18	2	5	29	31	60
vs. Right	.259	.311	.406	251	65	13	0	8	41	19	42	.273	.343	.455	1111	303	50	6	47	149	116	197
At Home	.299	.361	.451	144	43	7	0	5	21	14	20	.280	.345	.457	700	196	32	4	28	93	69	110
On Road	.262	.315	.393	168	44	10	0	4	23	13	34	.271	.344	.437	698	189	36	4	24	85	78	147

Washington, Ronald "Ron"

Bats: Right   Throws: Right   Born 04/29/52

1987 SEASON AND MAJOR-LEAGUE CAREER BATTING TOTALS

	G	AB	H	2B	3B	HR	TB	R	RBI	TBB	IBB	SO	HP	SH	SF	SB	CS	SB%	GDP	AVG	OBP	SLG
87 BAL	26	79	16	3	1	1	24	7	6	1	0	15	0	1	0	0	1	.00	2	.203	.213	.304
8 YEARS	488	1356	356	50	20	18	500	159	125	56	1	227	4	13	12	25	15	.63	29	.263	.291	.369

	1987 SEASON											TWO YEAR TOTALS (1986 – 1987)									
	AVG	OBP	SLG	AB	H	2B	3B	HR	RBI	BB	SO	AVG	OBP	SLG	AB	H	2B	3B	HR	RBI	BB	SO
Totals	.203	.213	.304	79	16	3	1	1	6	1	15	.229	.238	.379	153	35	6	1	5	17	4	36
vs. Left	.163	.163	.256	43	7	1	0	1	3	0	8	.194	.208	.323	93	18	3	0	3	6	2	24
vs. Right	.250	.270	.361	36	9	2	1	0	3	1	7	.283	.302	.467	60	17	3	1	2	11	2	12
At Home	.182	.200	.250	44	8	1	1	0	2	1	10	.270	.293	.461	89	24	3	1	4	11	3	22
On Road	.229	.229	.371	35	8	2	0	1	4	0	5	.172	.179	.266	64	11	3	0	1	6	1	14

Wasinger, Mark Thomas

Bats: Right   Throws: Right   Born 08/04/61

1987 SEASON AND MAJOR-LEAGUE CAREER BATTING TOTALS

	G	AB	H	2B	3B	HR	TB	R	RBI	TBB	IBB	SO	HP	SH	SF	SB	CS	SB%	GDP	AVG	OBP	SLG
87 SF	44	80	22	3	0	1	28	16	3	8	0	14	0	2	0	2	0	1.00	3	.275	.341	.350
2 YEARS	47	88	22	3	0	1	28	16	4	8	0	16	0	3	0	2	0	1.00	3	.250	.313	.318

	1987 SEASON										FOUR YEAR TOTALS (1984 – 1987)									
	AVG	OBP	SLG	AB	H	2B	3B	HR	RBI	BB	SO	AVG	OBP	SLG	AB	H	2B	3B	HR	RBI	BB	SO
Totals	.275	.341	.350	80	22	3	0	1	3	8	14	.250	.313	.318	88	22	3	0	1	4	8	16
vs. Left	.281	.361	.438	32	9	2	0	1	1	4	7	.231	.302	.359	39	9	2	0	1	2	4	8
vs. Right	.271	.327	.292	48	13	1	0	0	2	4	7	.265	.321	.286	49	13	1	0	0	2	4	8
At Home	.381	.422	.524	42	16	3	0	1	1	3	5	.381	.422	.524	42	16	3	0	1	1	3	5
On Road	.158	.256	.158	38	6	0	0	0	2	5	9	.130	.216	.130	46	6	0	0	0	3	5	11

Weiss, Walter William "Walt"

Bats: Both   Throws: Right   Born 11/28/63

1987 SEASON AND MAJOR-LEAGUE CAREER BATTING TOTALS

	G	AB	H	2B	3B	HR	TB	R	RBI	TBB	IBB	SO	HP	SH	SF	SB	CS	SB%	GDP	AVG	OBP	SLG
87 OAK	16	26	12	4	0	0	16	3	1	2	0	2	0	1	0	1	2	.33	0	.462	.500	.615
1 YEAR	16	26	12	4	0	0	16	3	1	2	0	2	0	1	0	1	2	.33	0	.462	.500	.615

	1987 SEASON										FOUR YEAR TOTALS (1984 – 1987)									
	AVG	OBP	SLG	AB	H	2B	3B	HR	RBI	BB	SO	AVG	OBP	SLG	AB	H	2B	3B	HR	RBI	BB	SO
Totals	.462	.500	.615	26	12	4	0	0	1	2	2	.462	.500	.615	26	12	4	0	0	1	2	2
vs. Left	.300	.300	.400	10	3	1	0	0	0	0	1	.300	.300	.400	10	3	1	0	0	0	0	1
vs. Right	.563	.611	.750	16	9	3	0	0	1	2	1	.563	.611	.750	16	9	3	0	0	1	2	1
At Home	.500	.563	.643	14	7	2	0	0	1	2	2	.500	.563	.643	14	7	2	0	0	1	2	2
On Road	.417	.417	.583	12	5	2	0	0	0	0	0	.417	.417	.583	12	5	2	0	0	0	0	0

Wells, David Lee "Dave"

Bats: Left   Throws: Left

1987 SEASON AND MAJOR-LEAGUE CAREER PITCHING TOTALS

	G	GS	CG	GF	IP	BFP	H	R	ER	HR	SH	SF	HB	TBB	IBB	SO	WP	Bk	W	L	Pct	ShO	Sv	ERA
87 TOR	18	2	0	6	29	132	37	14	13	0	1	0	0	12	0	32	4	0	4	3	.571	0	1	4.03
1 YEAR	18	2	0	6	29	132	37	14	13	0	1	0	0	12	0	32	4	0	4	3	.571	0	1	4.03

1987: Power, Groundball

	1987 SEASON										FOUR YEAR TOTALS (1984 – 1987)									
	G	IP	H	BB	SO	SB	CS	W	L	S	ERA	G	IP	H	BB	SO	SB	CS	W	L	S	ERA
Totals	18	29.2	37	12	32	1	4	4	3	1	3.94	18	29.2	37	12	32	1	4	4	3	1	3.94
At Home	10	13.1	17	6	10	0	2	2	1	0	3.38	10	13.1	17	6	10	0	2	2	1	0	3.38
On Road	8	16.1	20	6	22	1	2	2	2	1	4.41	8	16.1	20	6	22	1	2	2	2	1	4.41

vs. Opposing Batters	AVG	OBP	SLG	AB	H	2B	3B	HR	RBI	BB	SO	AVG	OBP	SLG	AB	H	2B	3B	HR	RBI	BB	SO
Totals	.311	.374	.370	119	37	7	0	0	13	12	32	.311	.374	.370	119	37	7	0	0	13	12	32
vs. Left	.318	.375	.318	44	14	0	0	0	4	4	5	.318	.375	.318	44	14	0	0	0	4	4	5
vs. Right	.307	.373	.400	75	23	7	0	0	9	8	27	.307	.373	.400	75	23	7	0	0	9	8	27

Wiggins, Alan Anthony "Al"

Bats: Both   Throws: Right   Born 02/17/58

1987 SEASON AND MAJOR-LEAGUE CAREER BATTING TOTALS

	G	AB	H	2B	3B	HR	TB	R	RBI	TBB	IBB	SO	HP	SH	SF	SB	CS	SB%	GDP	AVG	OBP	SLG
87 BAL	85	306	71	4	2	1	82	37	15	28	0	34	1	6	1	20	7	.74	6	.232	.298	.268
7 YEARS	631	2247	581	61	19	5	695	346	118	235	4	193	8	54	9	242	68	.78	18	.259	.330	.309

	1987 SEASON										FOUR YEAR TOTALS (1984 – 1987)									
	AVG	OBP	SLG	AB	H	2B	3B	HR	RBI	BB	SO	AVG	OBP	SLG	AB	H	2B	3B	HR	RBI	BB	SO
Totals	.232	.298	.268	306	71	4	2	1	15	28	34	.252	.324	.305	1476	372	38	14	4	81	156	131
vs. Left	.231	.268	.246	130	30	2	0	0	6	6	15	.283	.344	.354	508	144	25	1	3	25	46	39
vs. Right	.233	.318	.284	176	41	2	2	1	9	22	19	.236	.314	.279	968	228	13	13	1	56	110	92
At Home	.231	.286	.248	117	27	2	0	0	5	9	13	.246	.324	.304	711	175	22	5	3	35	81	57
On Road	.233	.305	.280	189	44	2	2	1	10	19	21	.258	.325	.306	765	197	16	9	1	46	75	74

Wilkerson, Curtis Vernon "Curt"

Bats: Both   Throws: Right   Born 04/26/61

1987 SEASON AND MAJOR-LEAGUE CAREER BATTING TOTALS

	G	AB	H	2B	3B	HR	TB	R	RBI	TBB	IBB	SO	HP	SH	SF	SB	CS	SB%	GDP	AVG	OBP	SLG
87 TEX	85	138	37	5	3	2	54	28	14	6	0	16	2	0	0	6	3	.67	2	.268	.308	.391
5 YEARS	493	1253	307	38	13	3	380	144	78	63	0	198	9	18	6	44	27	.62	18	.245	.285	.303

	1987 SEASON										FOUR YEAR TOTALS (1984 – 1987)									
	AVG	OBP	SLG	AB	H	2B	3B	HR	RBI	BB	SO	AVG	OBP	SLG	AB	H	2B	3B	HR	RBI	BB	SO
Totals	.268	.308	.391	138	37	5	3	2	14	6	16	.247	.287	.305	1218	301	38	12	3	77	61	193
vs. Left	.286	.286	.476	21	6	1	0	1	2	0	1	.233	.302	.296	270	63	10	2	1	16	25	43
vs. Right	.265	.312	.376	117	31	4	3	1	12	6	15	.251	.282	.308	948	238	28	10	2	61	36	150
At Home	.269	.300	.373	67	18	2	1	1	5	2	7	.244	.284	.292	582	142	15	5	1	35	28	87
On Road	.268	.316	.408	71	19	3	2	1	9	4	9	.250	.289	.318	636	159	23	7	2	42	33	106

Williams, Edward Laquan "Eddie"

Bats: Right   Throws: Right   Born 11/01/64

1987 SEASON AND MAJOR-LEAGUE CAREER BATTING TOTALS

	G	AB	H	2B	3B	HR	TB	R	RBI	TBB	IBB	SO	HP	SH	SF	SB	CS	SB%	GDP	AVG	OBP	SLG
87 CLE	22	64	11	4	0	1	18	9	4	9	0	19	1	0	1	0	0	.00	2	.172	.280	.281
2 YEARS	27	71	12	4	0	1	19	11	5	9	0	22	1	0	1	0	0	.00	2	.169	.268	.268

	1987 SEASON										FOUR YEAR TOTALS (1984 – 1987)									
	AVG	OBP	SLG	AB	H	2B	3B	HR	RBI	BB	SO	AVG	OBP	SLG	AB	H	2B	3B	HR	RBI	BB	SO
Totals	.172	.280	.281	64	11	4	0	1	4	9	19	.169	.268	.268	71	12	4	0	1	5	9	22
vs. Left	.250	.400	.333	12	3	1	0	0	0	3	3	.222	.333	.278	18	4	1	0	0	1	3	5
vs. Right	.154	.250	.269	52	8	3	0	1	4	6	16	.151	.246	.264	53	8	3	0	1	4	6	17
At Home	.278	.409	.389	18	5	2	0	0	1	4	5	.286	.400	.381	21	6	2	0	0	2	4	6
On Road	.130	.226	.239	46	6	2	0	1	3	5	14	.120	.211	.220	50	6	2	0	1	3	5	16

Williams, Frank Lee

Bats: Right   Throws: Right   Born 02/13/58

1987 SEASON AND MAJOR-LEAGUE CAREER PITCHING TOTALS

	G	GS	CG	GF	IP	BFP	H	R	ER	HR	SH	SF	HB	TBB	IBB	SO	WP	Bk	W	L	Pct	ShO	Sv	ERA
87 CIN	85	0	0	19	106	446	101	37	27	5	5	3	2	39	9	60	4	0	4	0	1.000	0	2	2.29
4 YEARS	231	1	1	61	337	1412	289	133	110	12	21	10	15	146	26	238	16	6	18	9	.667	1	6	2.94

1987: Finesse, Groundball   1986: Finesse, Groundball   1985: Power, Groundball   1984: Power, Groundball

	1987 SEASON										FOUR YEAR TOTALS (1984 – 1987)									
	G	IP	H	BB	SO	SB	CS	W	L	S	ERA	G	IP	H	BB	SO	SB	CS	W	L	S	ERA
Totals	85	105.1	101	39	60	8	8	4	0	2	2.31	231	337.0	289	146	238	31	26	18	9	6	2.91
At Home	43	59.2	55	17	37	3	3	0	0	1	1.51	116	175.1	128	73	132	11	11	5	4	3	2.16
On Road	42	45.2	46	22	23	5	5	4	0	1	3.35	115	161.2	161	73	106	20	15	13	5	3	3.79

vs. Opposing Batters	AVG	OBP	SLG	AB	H	2B	3B	HR	RBI	BB	SO	AVG	OBP	SLG	AB	H	2B	3B	HR	RBI	BB	SO
Totals	.254	.322	.360	397	101	23	2	5	48	39	60	.237	.319	.315	1220	289	49	5	12	147	146	238
vs. Left	.235	.319	.271	166	39	4	1	0	9	21	25	.280	.369	.359	532	149	25	4	3	55	76	79
vs. Right	.268	.324	.424	231	62	19	1	5	39	18	35	.203	.278	.281	688	140	24	1	9	92	70	159

Williams, Matthew Derrick "Matt"

Bats: Right   Throws: Right   11/28/65

1987 SEASON AND MAJOR-LEAGUE CAREER BATTING TOTALS

	G	AB	H	2B	3B	HR	TB	R	RBI	TBB	IBB	SO	HP	SH	SF	SB	CS	SB%	GDP	AVG	OBP	SLG
87 SF	84	245	46	9	2	8	83	28	21	16	4	68	1	3	1	4	3	.57	5	.188	.240	.339
1 YEAR	84	245	46	9	2	8	83	28	21	16	4	68	1	3	1	4	3	.57	5	.188	.240	.339

	1987 SEASON										FOUR YEAR TOTALS (1984 – 1987)									
	AVG	OBP	SLG	AB	H	2B	3B	HR	RBI	BB	SO	AVG	OBP	SLG	AB	H	2B	3B	HR	RBI	BB	SO
Totals	.188	.240	.339	245	46	9	2	8	21	16	68	.188	.240	.339	245	46	9	2	8	21	16	68
vs. Left	.192	.241	.385	78	15	1	1	4	7	5	19	.192	.241	.385	78	15	1	1	4	7	5	19
vs. Right	.186	.239	.317	167	31	8	1	4	14	11	49	.186	.239	.317	167	31	8	1	4	14	11	49
At Home	.179	.227	.357	112	20	5	0	5	9	7	31	.179	.227	.357	112	20	5	0	5	9	7	31
On Road	.195	.250	.323	133	26	4	2	3	12	9	37	.195	.250	.323	133	26	4	2	3	12	9	37

Williams, Mitchell Steven "Mitch"

Bats: Left   Throws: Left   Born 11/17/64

1987 SEASON AND MAJOR-LEAGUE CAREER PITCHING TOTALS

	G	GS	CG	GF	IP	BFP	H	R	ER	HR	SH	SF	HB	TBB	IBB	SO	WP	Bk	W	L	Pct	ShO	Sv	ERA
87 TEX	85	1	0	32	109	469	63	47	39	9	4	3	7	94	7	129	4	2	8	6	.571	0	6	3.22
2 YEARS	165	1	0	70	207	904	132	86	78	17	5	6	18	173	15	219	9	7	16	12	.571	0	14	3.39

1987: Power, Flyball   1986: Power, Flyball

1987 SEASON	G	IP	H	BB	SO	SB	CS	W	L	S	ERA
Totals	85	108.2	63	94	129	6	11	8	6	6	3.23
At Home	41	57.0	34	50	67	2	6	6	2	1	2.84
On Road	44	51.2	29	44	62	4	5	2	4	5	3.66

vs. Opposing Batters	AVG	OBP	SLG	AB	H	2B	3B	HR	RBI	BB	SO
Totals	.175	.353	.280	361	63	7	2	9	50	94	129
vs. Left	.146	.305	.244	123	18	3	0	3	17	24	50
vs. Right	.189	.376	.298	238	45	4	2	6	33	70	79

FOUR YEAR TOTALS (1984 – 1987)	G	IP	H	BB	SO	SB	CS	W	L	S	ERA
Totals	165	206.2	132	173	219	14	16	16	12	14	3.40
At Home	80	109.0	72	87	111	4	7	9	5	6	3.14
On Road	85	97.2	60	86	108	10	9	7	7	8	3.69

vs. Opposing Batters	AVG	OBP	SLG	AB	H	2B	3B	HR	RBI	BB	SO
Totals	.188	.352	.304	703	132	21	5	17	93	173	219
vs. Left	.174	.309	.282	241	42	8	0	6	32	43	79
vs. Right	.195	.373	.316	462	90	13	5	11	61	130	140

Williams, Reginald Dewayne "Reggie"

Bats: Right   Throws: Right   Born 08/29/60

1987 SEASON AND MAJOR-LEAGUE CAREER BATTING TOTALS

	G	AB	H	2B	3B	HR	TB	R	RBI	TBB	IBB	SO	HP	SH	SF	SB	CS	SB%	GDP	AVG	OBP	SLG
87 LA	39	36	4	0	0	0	4	6	4	5	0	9	0	0	1	1	1	.50	2	.111	.214	.111
3 YEARS	189	348	91	14	2	4	121	45	36	28	9	70	2	9	2	11	4	.73	10	.261	.318	.348

1987 SEASON	AVG	OBP	SLG	AB	H	2B	3B	HR	RBI	BB	SO
Totals	.111	.214	.111	36	4	0	0	0	4	5	9
vs. Left	.129	.229	.129	31	4	0	0	0	3	4	6
vs. Right	.000	.143	.000	5	0	0	0	0	1	1	3
At Home	.231	.353	.231	13	3	0	0	0	4	3	3
On Road	.043	.120	.043	23	1	0	0	0	0	2	6

FOUR YEAR TOTALS (1984 – 1987)	AVG	OBP	SLG	AB	H	2B	3B	HR	RBI	BB	SO
Totals	.261	.318	.348	348	91	14	2	4	36	28	70
vs. Left	.267	.332	.345	206	55	9	2	1	16	19	37
vs. Right	.254	.299	.352	142	36	5	0	3	20	9	33
At Home	.272	.332	.343	169	46	7	1	1	16	15	32
On Road	.251	.306	.352	179	45	7	1	3	20	13	38

Wilson, William Hayward "Mookie"

Bats: Both   Throws: Right   Born 02/09/56

1987 SEASON AND MAJOR-LEAGUE CAREER BATTING TOTALS

	G	AB	H	2B	3B	HR	TB	R	RBI	TBB	IBB	SO	HP	SH	SF	SB	CS	SB%	GDP	AVG	OBP	SLG
87 NYN	124	385	115	19	7	9	175	58	34	35	8	85	2	2	1	21	6	.78	2	.299	.359	.455
8 YEARS	924	3400	949	143	56	49	1351	509	283	203	31	582	13	10	9	259	82	.76	35	.279	.321	.397

1987 SEASON	AVG	OBP	SLG	AB	H	2B	3B	HR	RBI	BB	SO
Totals	.299	.359	.455	385	115	19	7	9	34	35	85
vs. Left	.271	.329	.404	225	61	13	4	3	13	19	46
vs. Right	.338	.401	.525	160	54	6	3	6	21	16	39
At Home	.267	.337	.415	176	47	7	2	5	16	18	42
On Road	.325	.379	.488	209	68	12	5	4	18	17	43

FOUR YEAR TOTALS (1984 – 1987)	AVG	OBP	SLG	AB	H	2B	3B	HR	RBI	BB	SO
Totals	.284	.333	.427	1690	480	80	30	34	159	121	299
vs. Left	.282	.333	.433	769	217	40	17	14	69	59	135
vs. Right	.286	.333	.422	921	263	40	13	20	90	62	164
At Home	.288	.341	.431	810	233	42	10	18	80	65	143
On Road	.281	.326	.424	880	247	38	20	16	79	56	156

Winn, James Francis "Jim"

Bats: Right   Throws: Right   Born 09/23/59

1987 SEASON AND MAJOR-LEAGUE CAREER PITCHING TOTALS

	G	GS	CG	GF	IP	BFP	H	R	ER	HR	SH	SF	HB	TBB	IBB	SO	WP	Bk	W	L	Pct	ShO	Sv	ERA
87 CHA	56	0	0	24	94	422	95	54	50	10	4	0	6	62	5	44	4	0	4	6	.400	0	6	4.79
5 YEARS	152	10	0	57	288	1257	288	160	146	27	10	4	10	146	15	150	21	4	11	17	.393	0	10	4.56

1987: Power, Groundball   1986: Power, Groundball   1985: Finesse, Groundball   1984: Power, Groundball

1987 SEASON	G	IP	H	BB	SO	SB	CS	W	L	S	ERA
Totals	56	93.1	95	62	44	9	3	4	6	6	4.82
At Home	28	46.0	50	37	28	6	1	2	1	5	5.67
On Road	28	47.1	45	25	16	3	2	2	5	1	3.99

vs. Opposing Batters	AVG	OBP	SLG	AB	H	2B	3B	HR	RBI	BB	SO
Totals	.271	.390	.397	350	95	12	1	10	57	62	44
vs. Left	.263	.401	.336	152	40	5	0	2	19	35	10
vs. Right	.278	.381	.444	198	55	7	1	8	38	27	34

FOUR YEAR TOTALS (1984 – 1987)	G	IP	H	BB	SO	SB	CS	W	L	S	ERA
Totals	145	275.2	276	140	147	33	8	11	17	10	4.47
At Home	69	126.0	128	68	82	14	4	4	3	5	4.86
On Road	76	149.2	148	72	65	19	4	7	14	5	4.15

vs. Opposing Batters	AVG	OBP	SLG	AB	H	2B	3B	HR	RBI	BB	SO
Totals	.265	.355	.373	1042	276	34	2	25	137	140	147
vs. Left	.275	.371	.377	459	126	14	0	11	55	70	54
vs. Right	.257	.343	.370	583	150	20	2	14	82	70	93

Winningham, Herman Son "Herm"

Bats: Left   Throws: Right   Born 12/01/61

1987 SEASON AND MAJOR-LEAGUE CAREER BATTING TOTALS

	G	AB	H	2B	3B	HR	TB	R	RBI	TBB	IBB	SO	HP	SH	SF	SB	CS	SB%	GDP	AVG	OBP	SLG
87 MON	137	347	83	20	3	4	121	34	41	34	7	68	0	1	4	29	10	.74	10	.239	.304	.349
4 YEARS	366	871	208	33	12	11	298	92	78	81	13	198	0	3	8	63	27	.70	15	.239	.301	.342

1987 SEASON	AVG	OBP	SLG	AB	H	2B	3B	HR	RBI	BB	SO
Totals	.239	.304	.349	347	83	20	3	4	41	34	68
vs. Left	.333	.382	.433	30	10	3	0	0	4	3	9
vs. Right	.230	.296	.341	317	73	17	3	4	37	31	59
At Home	.272	.332	.367	180	49	9	1	2	27	16	38
On Road	.204	.275	.329	167	34	11	2	2	14	18	30

FOUR YEAR TOTALS (1984 – 1987)	AVG	OBP	SLG	AB	H	2B	3B	HR	RBI	BB	SO
Totals	.239	.301	.342	871	208	33	12	11	78	81	198
vs. Left	.288	.313	.375	104	30	3	0	2	11	5	34
vs. Right	.232	.300	.338	767	178	30	12	9	67	76	164
At Home	.220	.299	.300	440	97	12	7	3	43	50	105
On Road	.258	.303	.385	431	111	21	5	8	35	31	93

Woodson, Tracy Michael

Bats: Right   Throws: Right   Born 10/05/62

1987 SEASON AND MAJOR-LEAGUE CAREER BATTING TOTALS

	G	AB	H	2B	3B	HR	TB	R	RBI	TBB	IBB	SO	HP	SH	SF	SB	CS	SB%	GDP	AVG	OBP	SLG
87 LA	53	136	31	8	1	1	44	14	11	9	2	21	2	0	1	1	1	.50	2	.228	.284	.324
1 YEAR	53	136	31	8	1	1	44	14	11	9	2	21	2	0	1	1	1	.50	2	.228	.284	.324

1987 SEASON	AVG	OBP	SLG	AB	H	2B	3B	HR	RBI	BB	SO
Totals	.226	.282	.321	137	31	8	1	1	11	9	21
vs. Left	.225	.273	.300	40	9	3	0	0	2	2	7
vs. Right	.227	.286	.330	97	22	5	1	1	9	7	14
At Home	.185	.214	.333	54	10	5	0	1	6	2	4
On Road	.253	.323	.313	83	21	3	1	0	5	7	17

FOUR YEAR TOTALS (1984 – 1987)	AVG	OBP	SLG	AB	H	2B	3B	HR	RBI	BB	SO
Totals	.226	.282	.321	137	31	8	1	1	11	9	21
vs. Left	.225	.273	.300	40	9	3	0	0	2	2	7
vs. Right	.227	.286	.330	97	22	5	1	1	9	7	14
At Home	.185	.214	.333	54	10	5	0	1	6	2	4
On Road	.253	.323	.313	83	21	3	1	0	5	7	17

Wynegar, Harold Delano "Butch"

Bats: Both   Throws: Right   Born 03/14/56

1987 SEASON AND MAJOR-LEAGUE CAREER BATTING TOTALS

	G	AB	H	2B	3B	HR	TB	R	RBI	TBB	IBB	SO	HP	SH	SF	SB	CS	SB%	GDP	AVG	OBP	SLG
87 CAL	31	92	19	2	0	0	21	4	5	9	0	13	0	1	0	0	0	.00	2	.207	.277	.228
12 YEARS	1274	4275	1088	172	14	64	1480	490	498	618	40	421	17	58	34	10	13	.43	117	.255	.349	.346

1987 SEASON	AVG	OBP	SLG	AB	H	2B	3B	HR	RBI	BB	SO
Totals	.207	.277	.228	92	19	2	0	0	5	9	13
vs. Left	.280	.333	.320	25	7	1	0	0		2	3
vs. Right	.179	.257	.194	67	12	1	0	0	4	7	10
At Home	.163	.217	.163	43	7	0	0	0	1	3	5
On Road	.245	.327	.286	49	12	2	0	0	4	6	8

FOUR YEAR TOTALS (1984 – 1987)	AVG	OBP	SLG	AB	H	2B	3B	HR	RBI	BB	SO
Totals	.237	.342	.326	1037	246	34	2	18	111	168	112
vs. Left	.251	.354	.386	370	93	19	2	9	48	60	49
vs. Right	.229	.336	.292	667	153	15	0	9	63	108	63
At Home	.232	.335	.316	531	123	17	2	8	48	84	52
On Road	.243	.350	.336	506	123	17	0	10	63	84	60

Wynne, Marvell

Bats: Left   Throws: Left   Born 12/17/59

1987 SEASON AND MAJOR-LEAGUE CAREER BATTING TOTALS

	G	AB	H	2B	3B	HR	TB	R	RBI	TBB	IBB	SO	HP	SH	SF	SB	CS	SB%	GDP	AVG	OBP	SLG
87 SD	98	188	47	8	2	2	65	17	24	20	1	37	0	4	1	11	6	.65	5	.250	.321	.346
5 YEARS	595	1832	455	73	20	18	622	215	144	133	5	263	5	24	7	68	51	.57	29	.248	.300	.340

1987 SEASON	AVG	OBP	SLG	AB	H	2B	3B	HR	RBI	BB	SO
Totals	.250	.321	.346	188	47	8	2	2	24	20	37
vs. Left	.231	.318	.256	39	9	1	0	0	2	5	15
vs. Right	.255	.321	.369	149	38	7	2	2	22	15	22
At Home	.162	.230	.300	80	13	1	2	2	13	7	17
On Road	.315	.385	.380	108	34	7	0	0	11	13	20

FOUR YEAR TOTALS (1984 – 1987)	AVG	OBP	SLG	AB	H	2B	3B	HR	RBI	BB	SO
Totals	.250	.295	.336	1466	366	57	18	11	118	95	211
vs. Left	.241	.296	.319	386	93	11	5	3	25	30	75
vs. Right	.253	.295	.342	1080	273	46	13	8	93	65	136
At Home	.261	.304	.367	725	189	33	10	8	70	45	106
On Road	.239	.287	.305	741	177	24	8	3	48	50	105

Youmans, Floyd Everett
Bats: Right   Throws: Right   Born 05/11/64

1987 SEASON AND MAJOR-LEAGUE CAREER PITCHING TOTALS

	G	GS	CG	GF	IP	BFP	H	R	ER	HR	SH	SF	HB	TBB	IBB	SO	WP	Bk	W	L	Pct	ShO	Sv	ERA
87 MON	23	23	3	0	116	505	112	63	60	13	6	5	1	47	2	94	3	1	9	8	.529	3	0	4.66
3 YEARS	70	67	9	3	412	1741	314	183	167	30	14	14	6	214	7	350	18	2	26	23	.531	5	0	3.65

1987: Power, Flyball   1986: Power, Flyball   1985: Power, Flyball

1987 SEASON

	G	IP	H	BB	SO	SB	CS	W	L	S	ERA
Totals	23	116.1	112	47	94	32	3	9	8	0	4.64
At Home	10	52.2	55	25	43	18	1	4	3	0	4.78
On Road	13	63.2	57	22	51	14	2	5	5	0	4.52

vs. Opposing Batters	AVG	OBP	SLG	AB	H	2B	3B	HR	RBI	BB	SO
Totals	.251	.321	.415	446	112	28	3	13	58	47	94
vs. Left	.284	.364	.447	257	73	20	2	6	38	33	38
vs. Right	.206	.259	.370	189	39	8	1	7	20	14	56

FOUR YEAR TOTALS (1984 – 1987)

	G	IP	H	BB	SO	SB	CS	W	L	S	ERA
Totals	70	412.1	314	214	350	109	11	26	23	0	3.62
At Home	32	199.1	148	112	176	58	4	10	14	0	4.02
On Road	38	213.0	166	102	174	51	7	16	9	0	3.30

	AVG	OBP	SLG	AB	H	2B	3B	HR	RBI	BB	SO
Totals	.210	.309	.329	1492	314	65	11	30	165	214	350
vs. Left	.222	.331	.336	855	190	38	7	15	96	139	180
vs. Right	.195	.279	.320	637	124	27	4	15	69	75	170

Youngblood, Joel Randolph
Bats: Right   Throws: Right   Born 08/28/51

1987 SEASON AND MAJOR-LEAGUE CAREER BATTING TOTALS

	G	AB	H	2B	3B	HR	TB	R	RBI	TBB	IBB	SO	HP	SH	SF	SB	CS	SB%	GDP	AVG	OBP	SLG
87 SF	69	91	23	3	0	3	35	9	11	5	0	13	1	0	1	1	1	.50	3	.253	.296	.385
12 YEARS	1249	3418	913	171	23	77	1361	428	393	309	28	551	33	16	29	59	53	.53	69	.267	.331	.398

1987 SEASON

	AVG	OBP	SLG	AB	H	2B	3B	HR	RBI	BB	SO
Totals	.253	.296	.385	91	23	3	0	3	11	5	13
vs. Left	.169	.231	.288	59	10	1	0	2	5	4	9
vs. Right	.406	.424	.563	32	13	2	0	1	6	1	4
At Home	.286	.318	.500	42	12	3	0	2	6	2	7
On Road	.224	.278	.286	49	11	0	0	1	5	3	6

FOUR YEAR TOTALS (1984 – 1987)

	AVG	OBP	SLG	AB	H	2B	3B	HR	RBI	BB	SO
Totals	.258	.330	.367	974	251	38	1	22	114	101	170
vs. Left	.250	.318	.340	344	86	13	0	6	31	33	57
vs. Right	.262	.337	.381	630	165	25	1	16	83	68	113
At Home	.247	.323	.348	469	116	20	0	9	54	52	87
On Road	.267	.337	.384	505	135	18	1	13	60	49	83

II

THE TEAMS

AMERICAN LEAGUE
HITTING

	Ave.	OBP	SLG	AB	H	2B	3B	HR	RBI	BB	SO
				1987 SEASON							
Totals	.265	.333	.425	77826	20617	3665	461	2634	10479	7813	13442
vs. Left	.265	.333	.422	24986	6625	1178	140	821	3299	2508	4386
vs. Right	.265	.334	.427	52840	13992	2487	321	1813	7180	5305	9056
at Home	.270	.341	.436	38017	10260	1850	266	1309	5284	4021	6380
on Road	.260	.326	.415	39809	10357	1815	195	1325	5195	3792	7062
vs. Groundball	.273	.339	.426	39534	10807	1909	244	1219	5333	3844	6168
vs. Flyball	.256	.327	.424	38292	9810	1756	217	1415	5146	3969	7274
vs. Finesse	.272	.330	.438	40632	11065	1922	272	1418	5411	3404	5599
vs. Power	.257	.337	.412	37194	9552	1743	189	1216	5068	4409	7843
on Grass	.267	.335	.425	55738	14862	2557	282	1904	7632	5646	9626
on Artificial Turf	.261	.328	.426	22088	5755	1108	179	730	2847	2167	3816
Day Games	.263	.333	.428	23899	6295	1163	145	824	3151	2430	4277
Night Games	.266	.333	.424	53927	14322	2502	316	1810	7328	5383	9165
April	.256	.333	.409	9952	2551	468	66	308	1299	1106	1755
May	.260	.330	.429	12769	3326	556	67	487	1702	1302	2284
June	.267	.336	.436	13188	3519	633	84	476	1868	1335	2289
July	.268	.330	.429	12921	3458	606	82	440	1750	1200	2166
August	.270	.337	.434	13979	3772	712	74	477	1945	1389	2414
Sept/Oct	.266	.333	.413	15017	3991	690	88	446	1915	1481	2534
Bases Empty	.260	.326	.424	44112	11487	2048	269	1538	1538	4036	7641
Leadoff	.266	.328	.435	18546	4928	908	100	676	676	1613	3075
Not Leadoff	.257	.325	.416	25566	6559	1140	169	862	862	2423	4566
Runners On	.271	.343	.428	33714	9130	1617	192	1096	8941	3777	5801
First Base Only	.277	.334	.440	14303	3964	686	73	497	1307	1120	2243
Scoring Position	.266	.349	.419	19411	5166	931	119	599	7634	2657	3558
Late Innings, Close	.262	.335	.405	11749	3074	480	65	357	1619	1287	2199

RBI/Opportunities		
Scoring Position	6485 / 27034	(24%)
Scoring Position, 2 Out	2514 / 12325	(20%)
On Third, Less than 2 Out	2448 / 4929	(50%)
RBI in close games / RBI Total	6350 / 10479	(61%)

I hate to add to the pile of stories about increased offense this year, but I have to. You see, I have a theory about what caused it, too. But mine—unlike many others—is supported by hard evidence.

In the last few years, I've read many pieces about the weather's effect on baseball. Many people, both independent scientific researchers and the baseball analysis community, feel that it has a major one. It is a proven fact that objects travel faster through warm air than they do through cold air. Hot weather would thus tend to help offense—especially power hitting. Since pitches will move more quickly and bats can be swung harder, balls put into play will be moving more quickly. These fast-moving balls will encounter less resistance in the warm air, and thus go even farther with their added velocity. This is what broadcasters routinely refer to as "carry." With me so far?

Here comes the tough part. The chart below lists the league average (pro-rated to 600 at-bats and rounded to the nearest whole number) for the AL in 1986 and at various points during 1987. The first line contains the final 1986 numbers. The next four lines show 1987 cumulative figures on each of four dates. The final line is for the entire '87 season. I think you will see that the weather has a strong impact on the data:

Date	R	H	D	T	HR	RBI	W	K	SB	CS	BA	OBP	SLG
1986	81	156	27	4	18	76	59	101	11	6	.262	.330	.408
5/3	83	153	28	3	19	77	66	106	15	7	.254	.331	.408
5/31	84	155	27	4	21	79	64	107	14	7	.259	.330	.425
7/14	85	157	28	4	21	82	62	105	13	6	.261	.333	.447
8/16	87	159	29	4	21	82	61	104	13	6	.265	.330	.430
1987	86	159	28	4	20	81	60	104	13	6	.265	.333	.425

I've been working regularly with baseball stats for five years; I have never seen a theory so clearly verified. If weight training or the lively ball explain the jump in offense, why do runs, hits, doubles, homers, RBIs and SLG each follow the temperature curve? Do the walk and strikeout stats support the idea that a small strike zone or inept pitching caused it?

1987 was, according to meteorologists, a much warmer year than 1986. It was hotter, the heat wave arrived sooner, and it stayed until September. Given the data, I think it is safe to say that the weather was the major cause of the offensive surge in 1987.

Geoff Beckman

AMERICAN LEAGUE
PITCHING

	1987 SEASON										
	G	IP	H	BB	SO	SB	CS	W	L	S	ERA
Totals	6185	20195.2	20617	7813	13442	1731	763	1134	1134	474	4.47
at Home	3055	10384.0	10357	3792	7062	843	398	624	510	225	4.30
on Road	3130	9811.2	10260	4021	6380	888	365	510	624	249	4.66
Day Games	1960	6223.0	6295	2430	4277	536	241	348	348	149	4.37
Night Games	4225	13972.2	14322	5383	9165	1195	522	786	786	325	4.52
on Grass	4441	14452.2	14862	5646	9626	1174	577	810	810	344	4.54
on Artificial Turf	1744	5743.0	5755	2167	3816	557	186	324	324	130	4.30
April	790	2611.2	2551	1106	1755	250	113	147	147	55	4.29
May	1038	3343.1	3326	1302	2284	274	149	187	187	83	4.43
June	1058	3403.2	3519	1335	2289	278	133	192	192	86	4.75
July	1018	3335.1	3458	1200	2166	291	94	187	187	77	4.54
August	1059	3592.1	3772	1389	2414	266	125	202	202	82	4.59
Sept/Oct	1222	3909.1	3991	1481	2534	372	149	219	219	91	4.22

vs. Opponent Batters	Ave.	OBP	SLG	AB	H	2B	3B	HR	RBI	BB	SO
Totals	.265	.333	.425	77826	20617	3665	461	2634	10479	7813	13442
vs. Left	.267	.338	.427	32358	8639	1554	211	1070	4448	3455	5299
vs. Right	.263	.330	.424	45468	11978	2111	250	1564	6031	4358	8143
Bases Empty	.260	.326	.424	44112	11487	2048	269	1538	1538	4036	7641
Leadoff	.266	.328	.435	18546	4928	908	100	676	676	1613	3075
Not Leadoff	.257	.325	.416	25566	6559	1140	169	862	862	2423	4566
Runners On Base	.271	.343	.428	33714	9130	1617	192	1096	8941	3777	5801
First Base Only	.277	.334	.440	14303	3964	686	73	497	1307	1120	2243
Scoring Position	.266	.349	.419	19411	5166	931	119	599	7634	2657	3558
Late Innings, Close	.262	.335	.405	11749	3074	480	65	357	1619	1287	2199

RBI/Opportunities					
Scoring Position			6485 / 27034	(24%)	
Scoring Position, 2 Out			2514 / 12325	(20%)	
On Third, Less than 2 Out			2448 / 4929	(50%)	
RBI in close games / RBI Total			6350 / 10479	(61%)	

I often forget that many people who don't pay as much attention to numbers as I do may not know what the standards for successful pitching are. For that reason I've devoted this space to a short course on six numbers that I use to evaluate pitchers, listed in descending order of value. Hopefully this will make some of the things said in the other essays more meaningful to you.

ERA: If I could know only one thing about a pitcher, this would be it. But there are two adjustments to make. First, league average ERA in the American League is usually .50 to .70 runs higher (due to the NL's Neanderthal ideas about the DH); remember that when someone crosses leagues. Second, my studies show that 10 percent of all runs scored are charged to a pitcher not in the game at the time the runs score. It's helpful to know that a 3.30 ERA for a reliever means the same thing as a 3.00 ERA for a starter.

H/9IP: Short for hits per nine innings pitched. With this and the following definitions, "game" is often substituted for "nine innings" (Hits per game). The AL average in 1987 was 9.19 (or 204 hits per 200 IP); like all the league figures, it's higher than normal this year. H/9IP is not always infallible (a single isn't as damaging as an extra base hit), but it's generally very accurate. Each hit allowed is worth about half a point of ERA.

W/9IP: The number of walks allowed is usually a conscious choice. A power pitcher, who throws harder, will generally allow more walks than average (AL: 3.48; 77 in 200 IP), but compensate by allowing fewer H/9IP and getting more K/9IP. A finesse pitcher will be just the reverse. Since you can win either way, you really have to view this stat in the context of the other ones.

K/9IP: The average is 5.99, or 132 per 200 IP. This stat has most of its value as an indicator of trouble. K/9IP stats are a reflection of how hard a pitcher throws. If his numbers are less than average, he'd better not walk anyone—because he'll allow a lot more hits. Anything under 5.00 and the odds are that he'll be in the minors very soon. By the way, the NL's average is usually .2–.4 higher than the AL's.

K/W: A simple way to balance the last two stats. If you're much below the average (1.72/1), you've got problems. If you put a lot of people on base without being able to get a key whiff when you need it, you obviously won't last very long.

HR/9IP: Very like the walk stat—the more taters you allow, the lower your H/9IP and the higher your K/9IP have to be if you hope to win. The average is 1.17 (or 26 per 200 IP).

How do you know what the appropriate trade-offs in each category are? Hey, you'll have to learn that yourself; either that or wait until next year's book.

Geoff Beckman

BALTIMORE ORIOLES
HITTING

	Ave.	OBP	SLG	AB	H	2B	3B	HR	RBI	BB	SO
				1987 SEASON							
Totals	.258	.322	.418	5577	1437	219	20	211	701	524	939
vs. Left	.243	.301	.386	2087	508	78	8	68	235	171	361
vs. Right	.266	.334	.436	3490	929	141	12	143	466	353	578
at Home	.250	.315	.414	2723	681	99	8	110	335	255	463
on Road	.265	.330	.422	2854	756	120	12	101	366	269	476
vs. Groundball	.274	.337	.428	2951	810	126	11	102	396	275	441
vs. Flyball	.239	.306	.406	2626	627	93	9	109	305	249	498
vs. Finesse	.263	.316	.420	2750	722	110	8	102	322	212	369
vs. Power	.253	.328	.416	2827	715	109	12	109	379	312	570
on Grass	.255	.321	.418	4716	1203	173	13	190	599	453	809
on Artificial Turf	.272	.327	.415	861	234	46	7	21	102	71	130
Day Games	.257	.323	.409	1480	380	64	3	52	193	145	249
Night Games	.258	.322	.421	4097	1057	155	17	159	508	379	690
April	.262	.338	.405	721	189	35	4	20	95	79	127
May	.270	.333	.491	997	269	35	6	58	149	96	156
June	.252	.313	.409	972	245	42	3	35	112	85	163
July	.253	.322	.409	882	223	31	4	33	119	90	130
August	.264	.325	.422	988	261	32	2	40	123	87	182
Sept/Oct	.246	.307	.365	1017	250	44	1	25	103	87	181
Bases Empty	.260	.323	.414	3188	830	125	9	116	116	280	528
Leadoff	.264	.319	.419	1347	356	50	6	49	49	101	212
Not Leadoff	.257	.326	.411	1841	474	75	3	67	67	179	316
Runners On	.254	.321	.422	2389	607	94	11	95	585	244	411
First Base Only	.252	.309	.413	1161	292	47	4	44	106	91	170
Scoring Position	.257	.332	.431	1228	315	47	7	51	479	153	241
Late Innings, Close	.256	.313	.408	862	221	26	3	33	119	70	157

RBI/Opportunities			
Scoring Position	392 / 1701	(23%)	
Scoring Position, 2 Out	151 / 775	(19%)	
On Third, Less than 2 Out	137 / 292	(47%)	
RBI in close games / RBI Total	471 / 701	(67%)	

The mighty have fallen with a sickening thud. The Orioles' 95 losses were the most for the team since 1955, when the roster featured players like Art Schallock and Jim Pyburn. It was no illusion, either—the '87 club finished with an incredible 11–54 record against the five teams above them in the AL East.

A reading of the team's rankings in the league batting statistics makes for a woeful tale: Batting Average, 12th; On Base Percentage, 13th; Runs, 13th; Total Bases, 10th (despite being 3rd in home runs). The dearth of Doubles (14th), Triples (13th) and Stolen Bases (14th) provides another lamentable insight: no team speed. This is partly evidenced by the Orioles' seemingly unending search for a decent leadoff hitter. Many were called, but the Birds couldn't get as much as a busy signal. Was there any good news? Not much. Terry Kennedy was named the AL All-Star Catcher, although pretty much by default. Larry Sheets emerged as more than a left-handed platoon slugger (.316, 31, 94). Clubhouse whiner and ne'er-do-well Alan Wiggins caught the bus out of town following a verbal and physical confrontation with manager Cal Senior. Another Ripken (just call me Bill) surprised a lot of people with his bat, glove and enthusiasm. Pete Stanicek showed some late foot. That's about it.

Cal Ripken Jr.'s batting average trailed off dramatically, but otherwise he was his usual productive self (.252, 27, 98 in '87; .291, 27, 94 over the previous five years). Fred Lynn hit 23 home runs for the fourth consecutive year. But he did it while playing in fewer games (111) than ever before and batted a less-than-scintillating .253. Although Eddie Murray continued to put up respectable numbers (.277, 30, 91), a comparison with his previous five years' average (.306, 28, 108) is not encouraging. Worse still, he made the rather startling public declaration that it might be time to move on; Baltimore was no longer an enjoyable place to play. The noted Oriole cohesiveness, chemistry, whatever you want to call it, was gone. The bench was disgruntled, overpaid, and underplayed. The farm system, in spite of finishing with a .547 winning percentage, was largely bankrupt. The Orioles haven't made a decent first round draft pick since the early part of the decade.

Owner Edward Bennett Williams looked around and said, "Enough!" Heads rolled. General Manager Hank Peters and Director of Minor Leagues and Scouting, Tom Giordano, were handed theirs. A former White Sox GM, Roland Hemond, is now running the Baltimore operation. Hemond's reputed to wheel and deal to an extent that would make even Trader Jack McKeon nervous. But there's nothing to trade and no place to hide. The dearth of tradeable talent makes it possible only to prove the validity of that computer cliché "Garbage In, Garbage Out". The team with the best record in the majors since 1969 has shot its bolt. No pitching, no prospects, and no hope. The AL East looks stronger than ever and the Orioles look to be D.O.A. in seventh place with 90 plus losses.

Greg Pryor

BALTIMORE ORIOLES
PITCHING

						1987 SEASON					
	G	IP	H	BB	SO	SB	CS	W	L	S	ERA
Totals	456	1439.2	1555	547	870	145	56	67	95	30	5.01
at Home	234	745.0	797	269	454	77	26	31	51	13	5.00
on Road	222	694.2	758	278	416	68	30	36	44	17	5.03
Day Games	127	382.1	381	147	234	49	18	19	24	10	4.38
Night Games	329	1057.1	1174	400	636	96	38	48	71	20	5.24
on Grass	393	1231.0	1332	474	749	128	54	57	81	27	5.04
on Artificial Turf	63	208.2	223	73	121	17	2	10	14	3	4.83
April	51	185.2	179	67	126	19	6	9	12	2	4.22
May	92	256.2	266	111	151	36	17	17	11	10	4.80
June	84	246.2	304	114	142	24	7	5	23	2	6.24
July	59	230.2	229	71	147	14	8	16	10	6	3.94
August	71	250.1	259	79	156	28	9	13	15	6	5.11
Sept/Oct	99	269.2	318	105	148	24	9	7	24	4	5.47

vs. Opponent Batters	Ave.	OBP	SLG	AB	H	2B	3B	HR	RBI	BB	SO
Totals	.277	.341	.464	5622	1555	290	44	226	829	547	870
vs. Left	.275	.340	.469	2190	602	110	23	90	326	214	306
vs. Right	.278	.342	.461	3432	953	180	21	136	503	333	564
Bases Empty	.271	.330	.471	3226	873	183	24	139	139	271	503
Leadoff	.281	.342	.494	1319	370	89	5	61	61	119	194
Not Leadoff	.264	.322	.456	1907	503	94	19	78	78	152	309
Runners On Base	.285	.356	.455	2396	682	107	20	87	690	276	367
First Base Only	.281	.331	.463	953	268	45	7	38	100	66	129
Scoring Position	.287	.371	.450	1443	414	62	13	49	590	210	238
Late Innings, Close	.282	.351	.435	816	230	34	5	27	122	87	127

RBI/Opportunities		
Scoring Position	505 / 1980	(26%)
Scoring Position, 2 Out	204 / 892	(23%)
On Third, Less than 2 Out	188 / 361	(52%)
RBI in close games / RBI Total	516 / 829	(62%)

The formerly pitching-rich Orioles have been reduced to the equivalent of sleeping on park benches—joining the Cleveland Indians as the new "homeless" of the American League. It wasn't just where they bedded down, but the contents of their miserable shopping bags that made it all seem so sad. Theirs is a pitching staff that, at mid-season, had 60 percent of the original starting rotation (Dixon, Flanagan and McGregor) pitching in AAA.

This is a pitching staff whose big winner notched ten victories. Even back in the salad days of 1954 and 1955, when the team collected 54 and 57 wins respectively, there were pitchers who garnered at least 12 wins. This is a staff that included such notables as Mike Kinnunen, Tony Arnold, and the immensely forgettable Doug Corbett (0–2, 7.83). And, of course, this rogues' gallery has to include Rotisserie Baseball's one-man disaster—Jeff Ballard (2–8, 6.59, 69.2 Innings Pitched, 100 Hits and 35 Walks Allowed for a H+W/IP ratio of 1.93).

Mike Boddicker, for the third straight year, faded badly in the second half. Scott McGregor was awful all year (2–7, 6.64). He has mercifully lobbed in his prayer book, chanted the magic mantra "Rotator Cuff," and will be seen no more. Eric Bell, heir apparent to McGregor's Finesse Pitcher title, approached adequacy on occasions but most often looked a bit lost—13 to be exact (10–13, 5.45). Mike Flanagan was traded to Toronto for hard-throwing Jose Mesa (1–3, 6.03). Dave Schmidt was the class act (10–5, 3.77). But gosh, whatta class!

After Don Aase, the Most Valuable Oriole in 1986,

turned up lame in April, the bullpen was reduced to providing only "comic relief." Mark Williamson (8–9, 4.03, 3 saves) and John Habyan (6–7, 4.80, 1 save) had their moments. But the fact that the stopper was Tom Niedenfuer (3–5, 4.99, 13 saves) says it all. Fireman Niedenfuer developed spontaneous combustion when he gave up back-to-back-to-back home runs in the ninth while trying to protect a three-run lead in Detroit. Old Buffalo Head fit in nicely with the other comedians.

Prospects for the future do not soar. There is no talent waiting in the wings. For that matter, there's very little talent in the wings they have. It is easy to predict that the team ERA will dip below 5 with the new strike zone. Other than that . . . The addition of Mike Morgan will provide a much needed work horse. Last year only Boddicker exceeded 165 innings. Unfortunately, Boddicker is due for a first half to match his last three second halves. Don Aase's not likely to return to form. Look for his name to top only alphabetical lists. Bell, Williamson, Habyan, Mesa and yes, even Ballard, are the pitchers of the future. This future is one that will prove to be a lot more exciting for opposing American league batters than it will for Oriole fans.

The similarities between the Orioles and the Dallas Cowboys are striking. Both have been consistent powers in their divisions, both were considered "class" organizations, but neither has drafted any productive talent for some time. Both teams have been re-cast as losers.

Greg Pryor

BOSTON RED SOX
HITTING

	Ave.	OBP	SLG	AB	H	2B	3B	HR	RBI	BB	SO
Totals	.278	.351	.430	5586	1553	273	26	174	802	606	825
vs. Left	.298	.364	.444	1583	471	75	5	49	244	160	224
vs. Right	.270	.346	.424	4003	1082	198	21	125	558	446	601
at Home	.294	.367	.459	2710	796	153	18	86	419	302	373
on Road	.263	.336	.402	2876	757	120	8	88	383	304	452
vs. Groundball	.283	.359	.428	2767	784	131	14	80	391	306	347
vs. Flyball	.273	.344	.432	2819	769	142	12	94	411	300	478
vs. Finesse	.295	.355	.464	2750	812	131	14	102	412	241	292
vs. Power	.261	.348	.396	2836	741	142	12	72	390	365	533
on Grass	.280	.356	.430	4716	1322	230	24	142	691	529	689
on Artificial Turf	.266	.328	.430	870	231	43	2	32	111	77	136
Day Games	.262	.334	.415	1930	506	88	13	60	251	197	298
Night Games	.286	.361	.438	3656	1047	185	13	114	551	409	527
April	.235	.317	.370	722	170	33	2	20	81	79	118
May	.251	.322	.400	891	224	43	1	29	126	87	131
June	.301	.384	.459	976	294	53	7	29	166	122	140
July	.304	.358	.469	942	286	47	5	33	126	82	125
August	.283	.365	.459	915	259	41	6	36	150	112	146
Sept/Oct	.281	.350	.410	1140	320	56	5	27	153	124	165
Bases Empty	.269	.333	.412	3102	834	150	9	92	92	276	456
Leadoff	.281	.343	.437	1319	371	65	0	47	47	114	191
Not Leadoff	.260	.326	.393	1783	463	85	9	45	45	162	265
Runners On	.289	.373	.452	2484	719	123	17	82	710	330	369
First Base Only	.293	.354	.461	1044	306	57	8	34	86	86	131
Scoring Position	.287	.385	.445	1440	413	66	9	48	624	244	238
Late Innings, Close	.247	.327	.360	858	212	30	5	19	111	98	138

RBI/Opportunities		
Scoring Position	526 / 2163	(24%)
Scoring Position, 2 Out	202 / 960	(21%)
On Third, Less than 2 Out	206 / 395	(52%)
RBI in close games / RBI Total	478 / 802	(60%)

Despite all the new faces in the batting order last year, Boston's bottom line—runs—came out exactly the same relative to the league as in 1986. The Sox ranked fourth in runs scored both years. American League runs were up 6 percent in '87; the same with the Red Sox. There was one significant difference: The '86 squad scored 16 more runs on the road than at home with one extra home game. This past year, despite two extra road games, home scoring was 30 runs higher. The Sox batted 30 percentage points higher at Fenway than elsewhere in '87; the '86 team hit a point lower at home. Check the home/road W-L splits for the significance of these figures. Here is a likely 1988 lineup:

Ellis Burks—The Sox feel that they have found a natural leadoff man. He can hit and he can scoot. He beats out bunts, steals bases and has shown some serious power. That's all true, but hey—his OBP was below the league average . . . a serious shortcoming when batting ahead of Wade Boggs.

Marty Barrett—A good BA, but again a disappointing OBP. Like Burks, he swings at too many pitches best left alone.

Wade Boggs—He led the majors in Runs Created; just imagine how many RBIs the man could collect if only the two guys batting ahead of him could get on base more often!

Dwight Evans—Fourth in AL Runs Created behind Wade, Trammell and Bell; he had his finest hitting year. Like Jack Clark, he combines the long ball with an OBP that is among his league's leaders.

Jim Rice/Sam Horn—Rice ended last year as a part-time DH, but is expected to see more action in '88 with a healed elbow. Horn was used mostly against RH pitching last year; hopes are that he can hit everybody this year. He had the highest home run rate on the team after his late arrival in '87.

Mike Greenwell—The most promising member of the Sox youth movement; can this guy hit! His RC/PA rate was about 20 percent better than the more-publicized Kevin Seitzer.

Todd Benzinger—Really developed for Boston last year; his 1987 AL stats were better than his 1986 IL figures. He'll be the fourth outfielder if Jim Rice returns to his old form.

Spike Owen—No liability on offense; around the league average in OBP. He's got no power, but can handle the bat to advance a runner.

John Marzano/Rich Gedman—Gedman's '87 season was so bad that he's the early favorite for Comeback of the Year in '88. The Beantowners hope he can, because John Marzano didn't show them much last year with a K rate near 25 percent and indifferent power.

The offensive key for this team is to have the top two hitters get on base more and stop making so many outs. The middle of the order is unsurpassed in run-producing ability, and will do the job if given the opportunity.

Fred Percival

BOSTON RED SOX
PITCHING

						1987 SEASON					
	G	IP	H	BB	SO	SB	CS	W	L	S	ERA
Totals	398	1436.0	1583	517	1034	107	57	78	84	17	4.78
at Home	184	736.0	797	223	514	43	30	50	30	13	4.37
on Road	214	700.0	786	294	520	64	27	28	54	4	5.21
Day Games	147	502.2	574	197	380	39	16	25	31	6	5.03
Night Games	251	933.1	1009	320	654	68	41	53	53	11	4.64
on Grass	335	1223.1	1346	434	879	88	50	68	69	15	4.75
on Artificial Turf	63	212.2	237	83	155	19	7	10	15	2	4.95
April	55	192.1	208	66	138	19	8	9	13	4	4.49
May	64	239.0	245	85	168	12	12	13	14	2	4.41
June	80	245.1	281	97	181	13	12	15	12	3	5.47
July	64	231.2	244	82	154	23	4	11	15	0	4.82
August	60	237.0	276	81	188	19	8	14	13	4	4.82
Sept/Oct	75	290.2	329	106	205	21	13	16	17	4	4.61

vs. Opponent Batters	Ave.	OBP	SLG	AB	H	2B	3B	HR	RBI	BB	SO
Totals	.282	.344	.450	5609	1583	313	30	190	784	517	1034
vs. Left	.287	.354	.447	2535	728	159	18	70	366	262	425
vs. Right	.278	.335	.453	3074	855	154	12	120	418	255	609
Bases Empty	.289	.348	.453	3084	890	169	20	99	99	265	578
Leadoff	.299	.355	.467	1329	398	73	7	45	45	107	245
Not Leadoff	.280	.343	.442	1755	492	96	13	54	54	158	333
Runners On Base	.274	.338	.448	2525	693	144	10	91	685	252	456
First Base Only	.284	.335	.449	1085	308	67	2	36	96	74	171
Scoring Position	.267	.341	.447	1440	385	77	8	55	589	178	285
Late Innings, Close	.292	.366	.473	807	236	35	6	33	122	96	167

RBI/Opportunities		
Scoring Position	485 / 1956	(25%)
Scoring Position, 2 Out	169 / 835	(20%)
On Third, Less than 2 Out	206 / 381	(54%)
RBI in close games / RBI Total	465 / 784	(59%)

Pitching carried the Red Sox in 1986 and a shortage of pitching sank them in 1987. Oil Can Boyd, #2 on the staff in Wins and IPs in '86 could not use his arm last year. Bob Stanley was brought out of the bullpen into the Can's spot in the rotation; Calvin Schiraldi would be the closer in the pen. Stanley would join Al Nipper, Jeff Sellers, Roger Clemens and Bruce Hurst in the rotation. The hope was that Clemens and Hurst would pick up where they left off in '86, Stanley could junkball his way through games, and that Nipper and Sellers would win once in a while. That was the plan, anyway. The reality of the season was harsh indeed.

Clemens missed spring training and didn't find his form until June. By then the Sox were out of contention, because only Hurst had been effective. But bad as the starters were, the bullpen was much, much worse. Only two pitchers, Schiraldi and Wes Gardner, recorded saves in 1987. They combined for 16, the lowest full-season total since the As' iron man, 94-complete-games 1980 season. The relief staff achieved a statistical rarity: They lost more games (24) than they saved, while demonstrating to fans that there was no such thing as a safe Red Sox lead. Naturally, manager John McNamara tended to leave his starters in long after they would normally have been pulled. It's no coincidence that the Sox led the league in complete games. Bruce Hurst finished 15, even though he was ill and ineffective the last two months of the season.

Some good things did happen with the staff last year. Roger Clemens showed that when in shape he can do whatever he wants to on a pitching mound. Jeff Sellers, the mop-up man in the starting rotation, finished very well. He had a 3.47 ERA in his last nine appearances, and a 3–3 won-lost record. The Red Sox scored just one run in each of the three games he lost. There was an 11-inning no-decision in there, too. The news got better after the season ended. It was revealed that Hurst's late-season collapse was due to mononucleosis and not a tired arm. Oil Can is throwing well and his arm is expected to rejoin the staff for this campaign. Now if manager Mac can just locate the Can's head . . . And of course there was THE TRADE.

Thanks to it, this coming season the starters have Lee Smith to hand the ball to. Last year he had more than twice the saves of the entire Boston bullpen. Look for fewer complete games, more rested starters and overall more effective pitching. The stopper in the pen will make everyone more confident; all the starters will work harder and better knowing that there is actually some help on call for a change. If Smith's knees and Boyd's arm both function for the entire season, it will be difficult to deny Boston the 1988 division title.

Fred Percival

CALIFORNIA ANGELS
HITTING

	1987 SEASON										
	Ave.	OBP	SLG	AB	H	2B	3B	HR	RBI	BB	SO
Totals	.252	.326	.400	5570	1405	256	26	172	709	590	926
vs. Left	.253	.325	.399	1785	452	83	11	52	223	189	259
vs. Right	.252	.326	.401	3785	953	173	15	120	486	401	667
at Home	.255	.330	.403	2743	700	114	14	88	342	300	447
on Road	.249	.322	.397	2827	705	142	12	84	367	290	479
vs. Groundball	.260	.333	.398	2678	695	125	13	73	335	285	444
vs. Flyball	.246	.319	.402	2892	710	131	13	99	374	305	482
vs. Finesse	.263	.327	.427	2705	712	130	13	96	363	246	383
vs. Power	.242	.325	.375	2865	693	126	13	76	346	344	543
on Grass	.250	.325	.395	4614	1153	197	21	144	584	494	758
on Artificial Turf	.264	.332	.424	956	252	59	5	28	125	96	168
Day Games	.253	.328	.436	1687	426	85	7	70	231	175	284
Night Games	.252	.325	.385	3883	979	171	19	102	478	415	642
April	.271	.350	.450	785	213	38	3	32	111	93	132
May	.225	.296	.368	893	201	36	4	28	91	88	169
June	.243	.339	.407	914	222	39	6	33	128	128	177
July	.249	.322	.379	914	228	42	5	22	130	98	150
August	.263	.324	.407	1012	266	56	3	28	120	89	154
Sept/Oct	.261	.326	.396	1052	275	45	5	29	129	94	144
Bases Empty	.246	.317	.402	3136	772	136	13	109	109	311	504
Leadoff	.253	.330	.420	1314	332	63	5	49	49	144	187
Not Leadoff	.241	.308	.389	1822	440	73	8	60	60	167	317
Runners On	.260	.337	.398	2434	633	120	13	63	600	279	422
First Base Only	.283	.348	.416	956	271	47	7	22	67	85	143
Scoring Position	.245	.330	.386	1478	362	73	6	41	533	194	279
Late Innings, Close	.249	.323	.372	972	242	39	3	25	123	103	177

RBI/Opportunities		
Scoring Position	453 / 2014	(22%)
Scoring Position, 2 Out	152 / 892	(17%)
On Third, Less than 2 Out	184 / 362	(51%)
RBI in close games / RBI Total	457 / 709	(64%)

The Angels were the worst-hitting AL team in 1987. Their .252 composite average was six points below the next-to-worst White Sox. Six points may not sound like much, but in this context (averages of averages, encompassing all players for an entire year) it is a huge difference. If you climb six points above Chicago, you pass half the league and arrive at respectability. Six points below them you live in a world of your own.

Considering that California came within one pitch of the World Series in 1986, we may well ask what happened to that Championship team. To keep the answer in perspective, we must first remember that while the '86 Angels were not exactly a lumber company, they did achieve mediocrity in most offensive categories and led the league in walks.

The walks declined sharply when Reggie Jackson took his patience and sentimentally small strike zone to Oakland. Among the individual contributors who remained with California, Gary Pettis led the decline with a spectacular swan dive from his career heights of 1986. All he did was drop his average 50 points, eliminate half of his stolen bases and runs, and lose 70 percent of his RBIs. His second half amounted to .164 with 13 runs scored. It is no surprise that he has since departed.

Doug DeCinces finally started to act his age, hitting .234. Jack Howell went .245 for the year, with a second half .223 effectively ruining an auspicious spring. Mark McLemore was a dubious short-term replacement for Bobby Grich but showed some promise; in the second half he improved from .218 to .271, but stopped stealing bases. In the miscellaneous losses category, Ruppert Jones and George Hendrick continued to age with less grace than a good Bordeaux.

On the positive side, newcomer Devon White showed marvelous speed and power, especially in the first half when he hit .286 with 17 HR, 53 RBI and 20 SB. Brian Downing remained a force at the plate, and Bob Boone and Dick Schofield contributed as much offense as anyone could reasonably expect. Wally Joyner blossomed at the plate, consolidating all his rookie accomplishments and establishing himself as one of the AL's premier sluggers. Joyner also earned a place in history as a living refutation of the Most Similar Rookie Method for predicting future performance (he was supposedly destined to go the way of Tom Tresh).

1988 will bring both good news and bad news. Chili Davis will provide six or eight times as much offense as Gary Pettis. Johnny Ray will hit .300 and contribute mightily in other categories as well. Joyner will surpass Kent Hrbek, Pete O'Brien and Eddie Murray as the first baseman most deserving comparison to Don Mattingly. On the downside, Devon White and Jack Howell will be prime candidates for the sophomore jinx. Overall, California's hitting will suffice to make them contenders only because they live in a division where 88 wins could be enough.

John C. Benson

CALIFORNIA ANGELS
PITCHING

						1987 SEASON					
	G	IP	H	BB	SO	SB	CS	W	L	S	ERA
Totals	406	1457.1	1481	505	941	72	56	75	87	36	4.38
at Home	200	756.0	732	269	496	39	32	38	43	16	4.33
on Road	206	701.1	749	236	445	33	24	37	44	20	4.44
Day Games	118	440.1	410	154	324	20	15	25	24	8	3.94
Night Games	288	1017.0	1071	351	617	52	41	50	63	28	4.58
on Grass	342	1222.1	1223	424	799	58	44	63	72	33	4.40
on Artificial Turf	64	235.0	258	81	142	14	12	12	15	3	4.29
April	59	208.1	202	84	159	18	16	12	11	5	4.45
May	66	232.2	248	97	145	12	7	9	17	4	4.91
June	55	249.0	219	64	171	9	11	17	11	8	3.18
July	75	238.2	243	76	150	7	6	15	11	10	4.37
August	73	265.1	271	94	154	6	9	13	16	6	4.34
Sept/Oct	78	263.1	298	90	162	20	7	9	21	3	5.06

vs. Opponent Batters	Ave.	OBP	SLG	AB	H	2B	3B	HR	RBI	BB	SO
Totals	.264	.327	.430	5600	1481	243	24	212	755	505	941
vs. Left	.270	.338	.443	2440	659	109	12	96	328	246	364
vs. Right	.260	.319	.420	3160	822	134	12	116	427	259	577
Bases Empty	.254	.316	.406	3245	823	127	17	111	111	275	524
Leadoff	.283	.336	.449	1354	383	57	9	50	50	100	190
Not Leadoff	.233	.301	.375	1891	440	70	8	61	61	175	334
Runners On Base	.279	.342	.463	2355	658	116	7	101	644	230	417
First Base Only	.284	.333	.469	1061	301	47	3	48	115	72	186
Scoring Position	.276	.349	.458	1294	357	69	4	53	529	158	231
Late Innings, Close	.258	.336	.391	897	231	34	4	26	111	104	163

RBI/Opportunities			
Scoring Position		436 / 1787	(24%)
Scoring Position, 2 Out		177 / 788	(22%)
On Third, Less than 2 Out		140 / 316	(44%)
RBI in close games / RBI Total		491 / 755	(65%)

More than any other team, the Angels are living proof that pitching is a fragile commodity, of which you can never have too much. In the spring of 1987 it looked like California pitchers would be a force for years to come. Kirk McCaskill, Mike Witt, John Candelaria, Don Sutton, Donnie Moore and Gary Lucas had all just completed outstanding seasons. The young arms of Chuck Finley, Willie Fraser, Ray Chadwick and Urbano Lugo held the promise of imminent excellence.

Quite surprisingly, the only real gem in the group that assembled at Palm Springs was an unlikely rookie named DeWayne Buice. When at first it appeared that California did not have a major league role for DeWayne, he summed up the situation with marvelous insight and perhaps a little prescience: "You must have the best staff in baseball if you don't need me on your roster." Buice was soon part of the team, a big part.

The Angels' mound corps simply disintegrated as the season unfolded. McCaskill made three brilliant starts in April, went on the DL, and never recovered. His second half "comeback" amounted to 50 innings of suffering, accurately described by his 6.89 ERA. Similarly, John Candelaria started 3–0 with a 1.33 ERA and climbed to 4–0, but was listed "Personal—21 Days" on June 19. After that he contributed little beyond mediocrity. Witt stood at 11–5 and 3.31 at the All-Star break, but fell to 5–9 in the second half, including a league-leading five losses in September. Moore had five saves by mid-May, and still had five in late October. Fraser earned a starting role and remained among the league's ERA leaders through mid-June. But the heat of summer transformed the rookie sensation into just another journeyman.

In June, Jerry Reuss came over and appeared initially to be a savior (3–0, 1.61). But he too succumbed to the "not-for-long-you-don't" syndrome. Reuss and Sutton wrapped up their seasons with September-October ERAs of 6.82 and 7.58, respectively. They earned the distinction of joining Witt in the little box under the caption "SEPT–OCT: WORST PITCHING" on the page of *USA Today* that reported final full-year stats for 1987.

The outlook for 1988 is generally grim. Reasonable expectations for excellence at this time a year ago have now been replaced by doubt. A team that has good pitching does not go out and trade for Dan Petry at the Winter Meetings. (If the Mets and Angels had any conversations in Dallas about pitching, it must have sounded like two geriatric patients comparing surgical scars.) Simply stated, the Angels staff in 1988 will need improvement from just about everyone. Even newcomers like Bryan Harvey, Mike Cook, and possibly Mike Fetters will have to make significant contributions for the Angels to be contenders.

John C. Benson

CHICAGO WHITE SOX
HITTING

	Ave.	OBP	SLG	AB	H	2B	3B	HR	RBI	BB	SO
						1987 SEASON					
Totals	.258	.319	.415	5538	1427	283	36	173	707	487	971
vs. Left	.250	.313	.424	1990	498	98	10	76	244	176	393
vs. Right	.262	.322	.411	3548	929	185	26	97	463	311	578
at Home	.274	.336	.425	2719	744	152	22	72	372	259	436
on Road	.242	.302	.406	2819	683	131	14	101	335	228	535
vs. Groundball	.270	.331	.426	2778	749	151	20	81	369	253	441
vs. Flyball	.246	.307	.405	2760	678	132	16	92	338	234	530
vs. Finesse	.262	.311	.431	3006	787	168	25	97	371	204	430
vs. Power	.253	.328	.397	2532	640	115	11	76	336	283	541
on Grass	.264	.325	.424	4718	1247	244	29	150	621	421	822
on Artificial Turf	.220	.280	.368	820	180	39	7	23	86	66	149
Day Games	.257	.321	.415	1577	405	80	7	52	180	148	284
Night Games	.258	.318	.416	3961	1022	203	29	121	527	339	687
April	.215	.294	.326	623	134	29	5	10	59	67	121
May	.247	.320	.424	889	220	42	5	35	113	90	182
June	.243	.302	.420	948	230	50	5	36	124	76	167
July	.273	.323	.421	953	260	40	7	29	123	73	155
August	.277	.337	.443	1028	285	62	6	32	141	94	174
Sept/Oct	.272	.325	.426	1097	298	60	8	31	147	87	172
Bases Empty	.260	.318	.422	3224	839	168	25	101	101	254	532
Leadoff	.270	.327	.425	1340	362	89	5	36	36	108	219
Not Leadoff	.253	.312	.420	1884	477	79	20	65	65	146	313
Runners On	.254	.319	.407	2314	588	115	11	72	606	233	439
First Base Only	.248	.298	.423	982	244	51	3	38	98	63	171
Scoring Position	.258	.333	.395	1332	344	64	8	34	508	170	268
Late Innings, Close	.259	.335	.384	864	224	40	4	20	98	97	173

RBI/Opportunities		
Scoring Position	449 / 1834	(24%)
Scoring Position, 2 Out	164 / 819	(20%)
On Third, Less than 2 Out	184 / 336	(55%)
RBI in close games / RBI Total	414 / 707	(59%)

Make no bones about it—hitting-wise, this is a bad ball club. Despite some improvement during the second half of 1987, the White Sox still wound up eleventh in the league in runs scored, thirteenth in team batting, fourteenth and last in on-base percentage, fourteenth as well in walks, and tenth in home runs. Even after September 1, when the Sox were 22–10, it was the pitching that carried the club; Chicago's September/October average of 4.8 runs a game was mediocre by '87 standards. And in fact, the situation is even worse than it seems at first.

Before the '86 season Ken Harrelson, in the great tradition of Second City comedy, was named the White Sox general manager. One of his first moves was to make Comiskey Park bigger by moving home plate back eight feet; the idea was to cut down on the number of cheap, "Marty Barrett," home runs. It worked, to that extent; over the last two years the Sox and their opponents have hit 19 percent fewer homers in Chicago than in enemy ballparks. But the decrease in fourbaggers was more than made up for by the extra singles, doubles and triples which dropped safely in the added acreage. In '87, run scoring by the Sox and their opponents was 9 percent higher in Comiskey than on the road, with batting averages a whopping 27 points higher (.272 to .245). In some ways the park is now similar to Astroturf parks like Royals and Busch Stadiums—home runs are down, but the wide open spaces reward hitters who find the gaps. Indeed,

speedy line-drive types Daryl Boston, Ozzie Guillen, Fred Manrique and Kenny Williams have done very well in the new, bigger ballpark. On the other hand, Pudge Fisk has found he likes the new dimensions about as much as he enjoys a clubhouse without beer.

Curiously, the White Sox have made neither of the expected responses to this situation; they haven't moved home plate back out again, and they haven't stocked up on line-drive hitters, either. The 681st trade between the Sox and Yankees was supposed to net Roberto Kelly, who fits the speed mold and also would have looked nifty in our St. Patrick's Day parade. Instead the Sox got Dan Pasqua, whose Yankee Stadium stroke seems much more suited for that other Chicago team; Pasqua also adds another left-handed bat to a club which has struggled against southpaws in recent years. In addition, Pasqua figures to take Gary Redus's job, and while Redus didn't really thrive at Comiskey (as everyone knows, he hits too many flyballs), he is an unappreciated offensive player with speed, run-scoring ability and the bonus of excellent range in the outfield. I do like Dan Pasqua, but it's hard to see how his replacing Redus is going to help the White Sox much overall.

Barring some earth-shattering developments, 1988 figures to be yet another season in which the Sox struggle for runs.

Don Zminda

CHICAGO WHITE SOX
PITCHING

1987 SEASON											
	G	IP	H	BB	SO	SB	CS	W	L	S	ERA
Totals	432	1447.2	1436	537	792	98	51	77	85	37	4.30
at Home	222	733.0	769	291	416	46	25	38	43	20	4.68
on Road	210	714.2	667	246	376	52	26	39	42	17	3.90
Day Games	124	407.0	386	151	215	20	15	21	24	10	4.18
Night Games	308	1040.2	1050	386	577	78	36	56	61	27	4.34
on Grass	370	1239.2	1229	465	686	74	44	67	71	33	4.29
on Artificial Turf	62	208.0	207	72	106	24	7	10	14	4	4.28
April	51	161.1	151	79	92	6	5	6	12	3	4.02
May	80	246.2	204	101	128	9	7	14	13	8	3.90
June	73	243.1	271	100	133	16	13	7	21	1	5.73
July	72	243.1	246	84	120	17	7	14	13	7	3.92
August	74	266.0	296	94	150	27	13	14	16	8	4.80
Sept/Oct	82	287.0	268	79	169	23	6	22	10	10	3.42

vs. Opponent Batters	Ave.	OBP	SLG	AB	H	2B	3B	HR	RBI	BB	SO
Totals	.259	.327	.416	5538	1436	226	38	189	723	537	792
vs. Left	.269	.342	.424	2316	623	92	16	78	308	255	312
vs. Right	.252	.316	.411	3222	813	134	22	111	415	282	480
Bases Empty	.246	.312	.409	3206	790	130	18	118	118	284	449
Leadoff	.253	.319	.401	1328	336	51	8	43	43	118	167
Not Leadoff	.242	.307	.414	1878	454	79	10	75	75	166	282
Runners On Base	.277	.348	.427	2332	646	96	20	71	605	253	343
First Base Only	.274	.332	.413	1029	282	40	5	31	79	85	149
Scoring Position	.279	.359	.437	1303	364	56	15	40	526	168	194
Late Innings, Close	.274	.340	.448	881	241	42	5	34	132	85	123

RBI/Opportunities		
Scoring Position	444 / 1809	(25%)
Scoring Position, 2 Out	176 / 852	(21%)
On Third, Less than 2 Out	161 / 322	(50%)
RBI in close games / RBI Total	450 / 723	(62%)

Growing up a White Sox fan in the fifties, I learned to accept certain things as givens. Despite a popgun attack, my heroes contended for the pennant every year; we unfailingly had a slick-fielding Venezuelan shortstop, but never a good third baseman; the Yankees were our bitter enemies and would remain so forever; and, most importantly, we always, *always* had a strong and deep pitching staff. More than three decades later, it's amazing how little has changed. Sad to say, we're no longer contenders, and since 1984 the Yankees have been our allies (and always were, of course; Eastasia was and is now our enemy), but otherwise it all still fits. Even the pitching part.

In 1986 the Sox overcame a woeful start to finish third in the American League in team ERA; despite injuries, curious personnel moves and a similar beginning in '87, the Sox still wound up fourth in the pitching derby. Wasn't it always this way? And won't it always be? Judging from the moves they've made, White Sox management seems to think so. After the surprisingly strong showing of the '86 mound staff, the club dealt away Joe Cowley, Gene Nelson and Bill Dawley, all of whom had pitched effectively, and simply released the talented Dave Schmidt, who they thought was asking for too much money. Cowley proved no great loss (to say the least), but for most of '87 the Sox struggled for the kind of middle relief that Schmidt, Nelson and Dawley had provided. Still, the staff weathered the storm and looked like the best mound corps in the league in September. So how does management respond this time, given the painful lesson of their '86 moves and the severe shortage of pitching talent throughout baseball? Why, by tempting fate again, of course.

Since the season ended the Sox have dealt away longtime starters Floyd Bannister and Richard Dotson, and at press time were shopping their third-best starter, Jose DeLeon. The club did get some pitching prospects in the Dotson and Bannister deals, but still, it's one whale of a gamble. As if those moves weren't daring enough, the Sox also fired the architect of the '86 and '87 staffs, pitching coach Dick Bosman. Now maybe Bosman wasn't a genius; maybe he was just lucky. But in a year and a half he had turned around the careers of Dotson, Bannister and DeLeon, had developed Bobby Thigpen into a reliable reliever, and had gotten good work from such unlikely hurlers as Steve Carlton, Neil Allen (for a while, anyway) and Dave LaPoint. Consider Carlton. With four other clubs in '86–'87, Lefty was 11–25, 5.81; in ten starts under Bosman he was 4–3, 3.69. Just a coincidence? I'm not so sure; I think Bosman had an awful lot to do with that. Now Bos is gone, along with Dotson, etc. I ought to be worried. But I'm not. Hey, these are the White Sox; we *always* have good pitching.

Don Zminda

CLEVELAND INDIANS
HITTING

	Ave.	OBP	SLG	AB	H	2B	3B	HR	RBI	BB	SO
					1987 SEASON						
Totals	.263	.324	.422	5607	1476	267	30	187	690	489	978
vs. Left	.265	.338	.420	1496	397	88	6	44	183	165	271
vs. Right	.262	.318	.422	4111	1079	179	24	143	507	324	707
at Home	.266	.330	.432	2759	735	139	18	94	345	259	450
on Road	.260	.318	.412	2848	741	128	12	93	345	230	528
vs. Groundball	.270	.334	.433	2841	766	130	19	99	376	261	436
vs. Flyball	.257	.313	.410	2766	710	137	11	88	314	228	542
vs. Finesse	.277	.326	.427	2798	774	125	15	89	349	196	380
vs. Power	.250	.321	.416	2809	702	142	15	98	341	293	598
on Grass	.264	.324	.423	4771	1259	231	25	159	588	417	805
on Artificial Turf	.260	.322	.415	836	217	36	5	28	102	72	173
Day Games	.240	.305	.402	1977	475	94	12	67	225	178	369
Night Games	.276	.334	.433	3630	1001	173	18	120	465	311	609
April	.239	.305	.408	750	179	42	2	27	87	69	140
May	.250	.314	.397	936	234	36	6	30	101	86	178
June	.258	.322	.411	853	220	34	8	27	110	75	140
July	.269	.326	.437	947	255	50	5	33	117	80	146
August	.278	.340	.425	1061	295	56	2	32	135	99	188
Sept/Oct	.276	.328	.443	1060	293	49	7	38	140	80	186
Bases Empty	.271	.327	.458	3207	868	164	23	130	130	252	543
Leadoff	.267	.315	.461	1357	362	73	7	59	59	93	219
Not Leadoff	.274	.335	.455	1850	506	91	16	71	71	159	324
Runners On	.253	.320	.373	2400	608	103	7	57	560	237	435
First Base Only	.274	.325	.409	985	270	48	2	27	71	67	162
Scoring Position	.239	.317	.348	1415	338	55	5	30	489	170	273
Late Innings, Close	.264	.320	.449	815	215	32	4	37	107	66	143

RBI/Opportunities		
Scoring Position	432 / 1942	(22%)
Scoring Position, 2 Out	158 / 873	(18%)
On Third, Less than 2 Out	159 / 342	(46%)
RBI in close games / RBI Total	433 / 690	(63%)

Good offenses do three things: draw walks, hit for average and hit for power. Forget the other stuff that people talk about—good baserunning, unselfishly advancing runners with outs, and clutch hitting are trivial in comparison. If you get people on base with free passes, move them around with some singles and pound them home with extra base hits, you'll outscore everyone else—even if your players run like William Conrad, think like Ayn Rand and bear down like the Toronto Blue Jays. If you can't do one of the three, you'll have trouble scoring unless you're very good at the other two. If you can only do one, then you'd better be ten miles ahead of everyone else if you expect to go anywhere at all. That last is just what Cleveland did in 1986—and what they couldn't do in 1987.

The 1986 Indians, to the naked eye, had a beautifully balanced offense: first in team batting average and slugging percentage; fifth in on-base percentage. But let's take a closer look. Cleveland's isolated power (SLG minus BA) was .156, sixth in the AL. They were *last* in isolated walks (OBP minus BA) with .053. They led the AL in runs scored with 841 because they hit gobs of singles; 89 more than anyone else in the league. Cleveland batted .284 in 1986, better than any team since the 1982 Royals. They were 13 points ahead of the #2 team and 22 points above the league average.

What's wrong with this picture? Very simple. Batting average is the least consistent of the three offensive skills. Players who walk don't suddenly lose their batting eyes. Players with power don't lose their muscles in a year. But the difference between a .300 hitter and a .250 hitter is just one extra hit a week. Building an offense around high averages is like paying off your debts by going on *Wheel of Fortune.* People have done it, but it's not something you want to count on. When the Royals' team BA fell 14 points to .271 in 1983, they scored 88 fewer runs. And that is just what happened to Cleveland. Both their 1987 isolated power (.159; 6th) and isolated walks (.061; tied for last) were almost identical to their 1986 figures. The sole reason that the Tribe scored 89 fewer runs than in '86 was the 21 point drop in team BA. Only Julio Franco, Brett Butler, Brook Jacoby and Andy Allanson hit for higher averages in 1987 than they did in 1986.

Do not expect improvement in the offense this year. Cleveland's team BA was an acceptable seventh and is likely to rise. Eight Indians hit .215 or less; six of them have been released. The lineup has at least an adequate power core. The team's ability to draw walks departed with Brett Butler. Unless this lack can be remedied an offensive improvement is possible but unlikely.

Geoff Beckman

CLEVELAND INDIANS
PITCHING

	1987 SEASON										
	G	IP	H	BB	SO	SB	CS	W	L	S	ERA
Totals	470	1422.2	1566	606	849	111	53	61	101	25	5.29
at Home	240	739.0	843	292	442	51	30	35	46	8	5.41
on Road	230	683.2	723	314	407	60	23	26	55	17	5.16
Day Games	153	510.1	598	187	328	37	25	20	38	9	5.18
Night Games	317	912.1	968	419	521	74	28	41	63	16	5.35
on Grass	405	1221.1	1354	523	740	91	46	53	85	20	5.35
on Artificial Turf	65	201.1	212	83	109	20	7	8	16	5	4.92
April	70	193.0	203	95	121	12	8	8	14	3	5.60
May	66	238.0	246	93	161	18	15	8	20	3	4.92
June	76	219.0	250	98	136	22	10	10	15	6	5.63
July	86	239.1	268	108	130	17	4	10	17	3	5.87
August	80	268.1	269	104	148	10	8	15	15	6	4.56
Sept/Oct	92	265.0	330	108	153	32	8	10	20	4	5.33

vs. Opponent Batters	Ave.	OBP	SLG	AB	H	2B	3B	HR	RBI	BB	SO
Totals	.278	.351	.455	5623	1566	271	31	219	901	606	849
vs. Left	.276	.346	.433	2390	660	114	18	75	361	252	322
vs. Right	.280	.354	.470	3233	906	157	13	144	540	354	527
Bases Empty	.273	.337	.459	3090	845	150	17	130	130	274	474
Leadoff	.281	.340	.465	1311	368	65	6	55	55	110	191
Not Leadoff	.268	.335	.455	1779	477	85	11	75	75	164	283
Runners On Base	.285	.366	.449	2533	721	121	14	89	771	332	375
First Base Only	.280	.349	.430	1028	288	46	6	32	88	96	147
Scoring Position	.288	.378	.462	1505	433	75	8	57	683	236	228
Late Innings, Close	.287	.370	.417	837	240	37	3	22	135	106	137

RBI/Opportunities		
Scoring Position	568 / 2194	(26%)
Scoring Position, 2 Out	222 / 1012	(22%)
On Third, Less than 2 Out	220 / 414	(53%)
RBI in close games / RBI Total	518 / 901	(57%)

Doesn't everyone enjoy the team capsules in *The Sporting News*? All fans must appreciate the relentlessly upbeat tone of the reporting, no matter how dreary the game results have been. A writer can't go too far wrong following this established formula . . . .

On September 19, Cleveland lost 3–1 to Minnesota. That third run tied the AL record for "Most runs allowed, 162-game season" (863), held by the '61 A's. Indians hurlers had labored all season to reach this total. Now with only 13 games left, the '62 Mets' major league mark of 948 seemed unreachable—especially since New York had done it in 161 games. But this pitching staff was equal to the challenge. Fueled by a late-season surge that saw them allow 56 runs in their last seven games, the Tribe allowed run #949 in the sixth inning of game 161.

The record was truly a team effort. Cleveland used 21 pitchers, only four short of the AL record for pitchers used in a season. Only two had ERAs under 4.00. Fifteen were over 5.00. Ten were over 5.50. The 1987 Indians were the first major league team without an eight-game winner since the 1899 Cleveland Spiders, the squad hailed as the worst of all time. This city's baseball tradition is an ancient one.

Experienced veteran leadership helped this tradition live. Nine Indians were 30 or older in 1987: Doug Jones, Jamie Easterly, Tom Candiotti, Sammy Stewart, Ken Schrom, Phil Niekro, Steve Carlton, Ernie Camacho and Mike Armstrong. Only six (John Farrell, Scott Bailes, Greg Swindell, Reggie Ritter, Tom Waddell, Jeff Kaiser) had

never pitched in a major league game for another team before joining the Tribe.

Cleveland displayed an impressive breadth of skills: last in wins, ERA, runs and earned runs allowed. The most wild pitches. Thirteenth in saves, hits, homers, walks and strikeouts. Near the leaders' totals for hit batsmen and balks. The three disappointing areas were complete games (6th), shutouts (tied for 7th) and games started (tied for 1st!).

A missed opportunity was "Most homers allowed, 162-game season." Cleveland (219) tried valiantly, but just could not keep pace with the '87 Orioles and their record-breaking 226. The ill-timed trading of Niekro and Carlton probably cost them the record; the inexplicable decision to use Frank Wills (the only Indian not to allow a homer) also hurt.

The '88 team will be hard-pressed to match this performance level. With Niekro and Carlton gone, Tom Seaver retired and Don Sutton signing with his childhood team, there is a serious shortage of over-40 starters. One doubts that Kaiser (16.20) and Waddell (14.29) can duplicate their '87 ERAs. Cleveland astutely kept Schrom on their 40-man roster this winter, but Pat Corrales (who induced arm injuries for Swindell, Bailes and Easterly) is history. Barring a blockbuster deal (they've spoken about trading for Steve Trout and Charlie Hudson), the Tribe's best hope for 1988 is that new pitching coach Mark Wiley can work the same miracles that he did with the 1987 Orioles.

Geoff Beckman

DETROIT TIGERS
HITTING

				1987 SEASON							
	Ave.	OBP	SLG	AB	H	2B	3B	HR	RBI	BB	SO
Totals	.272	.349	.451	5649	1535	274	32	225	840	654	913
vs. Left	.263	.338	.420	2023	533	98	6	69	290	226	347
vs. Right	.276	.355	.468	3626	1002	176	26	156	550	428	566
at Home	.270	.348	.460	2715	733	122	9	125	417	318	461
on Road	.273	.350	.443	2934	802	152	23	100	423	336	452
vs. Groundball	.278	.351	.447	2947	819	144	23	103	417	333	434
vs. Flyball	.265	.346	.455	2702	716	130	9	122	423	321	479
vs. Finesse	.271	.334	.452	3010	817	141	22	120	436	279	392
vs. Power	.272	.365	.449	2639	718	133	10	105	404	375	521
on Grass	.276	.352	.461	4789	1324	229	24	202	731	554	767
on Artificial Turf	.245	.329	.397	860	211	45	8	23	109	100	146
Day Games	.277	.355	.485	1773	492	92	9	86	274	203	296
Night Games	.269	.346	.436	3876	1043	182	23	139	566	451	617
April	.250	.335	.387	703	176	30	6	18	84	88	86
May	.277	.358	.455	925	256	38	2	41	143	114	162
June	.294	.364	.518	949	279	55	7	48	161	104	152
July	.254	.326	.420	871	221	31	0	38	125	89	154
August	.284	.362	.473	1051	298	69	8	38	173	124	174
Sept/Oct	.265	.343	.435	1150	305	51	9	42	154	135	185
Bases Empty	.271	.349	.463	3068	830	155	24	129	129	348	487
Leadoff	.293	.362	.497	1303	382	71	12	57	57	128	198
Not Leadoff	.254	.340	.437	1765	448	84	12	72	72	220	289
Runners On	.273	.348	.437	2581	705	119	8	96	711	306	426
First Base Only	.296	.358	.482	1094	324	46	5	49	118	94	178
Scoring Position	.256	.342	.404	1487	381	73	3	47	593	212	248
Late Innings, Close	.259	.331	.406	762	197	36	2	24	97	80	143

RBI/Opportunities		
Scoring Position	498 / 2127	(23%)
Scoring Position, 2 Out	192 / 967	(20%)
On Third, Less than 2 Out	200 / 422	(47%)
RBI in close games / RBI Total	461 / 840	(55%)

The most important fact relating to the Detroit offense in 1987 was that the team scored a total of 896 runs. That was 34 runs more than the next best mark in the AL, and 74 better than the best mark in the NL. OK, so you say, so what? Everyone knows that the Motowners play in a classic hitter's park. Wrong, wrong, wrong, let me say it again, wrong. All you sabermetric buckaroos (and doearoos?) who knew that Tiger Stadium has been a pitcher's park for the last few years move to the head of the line and take home a free Domino's pizza. (Those who failed the pop quiz must take home two Domino's pizzas.)

Yeah, I know you doubters want proof. So here it is: The Tigers and their opponents scored 772 combined runs in venerable Tiger Stadium last year in 81 games, but on the road the Cats and their hosts scored 848 runs combined in 81 games. All of this says that the Bengals' hitters are underrated and that their vaunted pitching staff has been overrated in recent seasons. These numbers are consistent with those from the 1982–86 period.

So just which Cats were the pride of the litter offensively, and just which ones were the offensive runts? The following review covers all the regulars and important part-timers. (The numbers in parentheses are Runs Created per Game followed by the player's ranking among AL regulars at his position. Thanks to Tom Locker for this data.)

Obviously, shortstop Alan Trammell had one hellacious year (8.87 RC/G, #1). Rookie surprise catcher-DH Matt Nokes also pounded more than a few Budweisers out

of the park (6.49, #1). Darrell Evans turned in a decent season for a first baseman and a remarkable season for a 40-year-old geezer (6.48, #8). Center fielder Chet Lemon rebounded well from his disastrous 1986 numbers (6.28, #5-Tie); left fielder Kirk Gibson produced well (by sabermetric standards) when healthy, although the fans got on his case for his relatively low RBI count (6.52, #4-Tie). DH Bill Madlock (5.41, #9) stepped out of the grave after coming over from the Dodgers and helped against left-handers; and Lou Whitaker continued to hit above par for second sackers but well below what the management and the fans expected of him (5.10, #2-Tie). In part-time roles, outfielder-DH Larry Herndon (7.63) killed lefties and catcher-utility man Mike Heath performed well (4.84).

On the other hand, Tom Brookens reclaimed his job at third base during the season, again getting straight A's for persistence and hustle and straight Fs for hitting (3.69, #14). Right fielder Pat Sheridan (3.98, #14), who became one of manager Sparky Anderson's pet reclamation projects, hit an empty .259 in a platoon role. DH John Grubb (2.89) and third baseman Darnell Coles (2.40) disappeared into a black hole, although Coles later reappeared in Pittsburgh. Coles' replacement, Jim Morrison (2.31), fared no better.

Just don't let any drunk in a bar tell you that the '87 Tigers did it mainly on the strength of their pitching.

Gary Gillette

DETROIT TIGERS
PITCHING

	G	IP	H	BB	SO	SB	CS	W	L	S	ERA
Totals	409	1456.0	1430	563	976	117	43	98	64	31	4.01
at Home	190	744.0	662	253	500	48	23	54	27	10	3.58
on Road	219	712.0	768	310	476	69	20	44	37	21	4.46
Day Games	138	464.1	454	182	307	37	15	34	16	8	3.92
Night Games	271	991.2	976	381	669	80	28	64	48	23	4.06
on Grass	342	1238.1	1195	479	822	96	35	85	52	22	3.98
on Artificial Turf	67	217.2	235	84	154	21	8	13	12	9	4.18
April	47	184.0	168	78	121	20	4	9	12	1	3.38
May	77	239.2	229	96	175	22	12	15	11	6	4.24
June	72	238.0	219	116	156	17	4	17	9	7	4.20
July	56	230.1	234	67	148	12	2	17	9	5	4.18
August	71	265.1	285	84	182	16	13	19	11	5	4.21
Sept/Oct	86	298.2	295	122	194	30	8	21	12	7	3.77

vs. Opponent Batters	Ave.	OBP	SLG	AB	H	2B	3B	HR	RBI	BB	SO
Totals	.256	.325	.407	5589	1430	232	36	180	690	563	976
vs. Left	.244	.324	.406	2480	605	109	19	85	317	295	404
vs. Right	.265	.326	.408	3109	825	123	17	95	373	268	572
Bases Empty	.249	.311	.401	3223	803	133	17	108	108	270	575
Leadoff	.243	.306	.400	1339	325	58	7	46	46	114	237
Not Leadoff	.254	.314	.403	1884	478	75	10	62	62	156	338
Runners On Base	.265	.344	.414	2366	627	99	19	72	582	293	401
First Base Only	.284	.341	.457	1032	293	47	9	38	106	84	142
Scoring Position	.250	.346	.381	1334	334	52	10	34	476	209	259
Late Innings, Close	.259	.331	.398	895	232	35	7	25	122	94	145

RBI/Opportunities

Scoring Position	413 / 1880	(22%)
Scoring Position, 2 Out	149 / 864	(17%)
On Third, Less than 2 Out	167 / 352	(47%)
RBI in close games / RBI Total	413 / 690	(60%)

The Tigers' pitching and defense allowed only 735 runs in 1987, good for third in the league. Most of the credit goes to the starters, whom manager Sparky Anderson relied upon to keep the relievers in the bullpen and off the mound. Detroit totaled only 31 saves even though the Tigers had the best record in baseball. To indicate how confused the situation was when the phone rang in the pen, Mike Henneman led the team in relief appearances, Eric King in saves and Willie Hernandez in games finished!

At the start of the year, Sparky designated Hernandez and King as his closers. Willie got shelled early and went on the DL twice, ending his reign as the Tigers' relief ace. King struggled all year long, was tried as a starter for a short while, and was eventually relegated to long relief. Mark Thurmond was used in short relief, long relief, and "no relief" situations. Henneman, the rookie sidearmer, was the best of the lot, gradually gaining Sparky's trust as a closer. After everyone else fell by the wayside, Mike was the ace until a few bad appearances during the September pennant race pushed him back into the pack.

The starters fared much better. Jack Morris had one of his best years, although you couldn't tell from his won-lost record. Morris had a poor second half record because he was the victim of poor support and bad luck. By avoiding his annual slump, Morris' ERA was more than one run better than the league average (3.38 vs. 4.46) for the first time in his career. Walt Terrell's normally big home/road differential became huge; he pitched brilliantly at home (17 GS, 13–2 W-L, 2.41 ERA) and abysmally on the road (18 GS, 4–8 W-L, 6.09 ERA). Frank Tanana echoed Terrell, going 10–5 with a 3.06 ERA at home and 5–5, 4.76, on the road. The fourth and fifth spots in the rotation were a problem all season long until the acquisition of Doyle Alexander. Sparky gave Jeff Robinson 21 starts and spoke very highly of him; however, with the rookie carrying an ERA well over 5.00 all summer, he was banished to a mop-up role when the pennant race heated up. Longtime stalwart Dan Petry struggled valiantly but futilely to return to form; he too was banished to long relief when the going got tough.

Enter Doyle Alexander, who might as well have been called Alexander the Great for his astonishing and brilliant performance (11 GS, 9–0 W-L, 88.1 IP, 63 H, 3 HR, 1.53 ERA) in Detroit. By allowing the Tigers to start only Alexander, Morris, Terrell and Tanana, the Alexander trade turned a struggling staff with two weak links (Petry and Robinson, who were killing them as starters and forcing them to call on their shaky bullpen early and often) into a nearly invincible rotation that saved the relievers from overexposure. The Detroit pitching staff has been given too much credit for the team's successes recently, but Tiger pitching was nonetheless effective.

Gary Gillette

KANSAS CITY ROYALS
HITTING

				1987 SEASON							
	Ave.	OBP	SLG	AB	H	2B	3B	HR	RBI	BB	SO
Totals	.262	.328	.412	5499	1443	239	40	168	677	523	1034
vs. Left	.263	.327	.416	1484	391	61	12	47	176	140	286
vs. Right	.262	.328	.411	4015	1052	178	28	121	501	383	748
at Home	.268	.335	.423	2686	720	141	28	73	352	274	427
on Road	.257	.320	.402	2813	723	98	12	95	325	249	607
vs. Groundball	.276	.336	.419	2829	782	130	18	79	356	247	466
vs. Flyball	.248	.319	.405	2670	661	109	22	89	321	276	568
vs. Finesse	.272	.328	.416	3078	836	135	24	87	371	259	440
vs. Power	.251	.326	.407	2421	607	104	16	81	306	264	594
on Grass	.262	.328	.404	2159	565	73	8	73	260	202	461
on Artificial Turf	.263	.327	.417	3340	878	166	32	95	417	321	573
Day Games	.268	.329	.416	1386	372	60	11	41	157	124	276
Night Games	.260	.327	.411	4113	1071	179	29	127	520	399	758
April	.262	.334	.394	627	164	27	7	14	76	67	101
May	.274	.334	.423	920	252	37	5	30	119	79	167
June	.251	.295	.381	942	236	35	2	28	96	57	173
July	.243	.309	.376	937	228	44	10	20	99	91	199
August	.282	.362	.462	1012	285	46	4	43	147	123	203
Sept/Oct	.262	.329	.425	1061	278	50	12	33	140	106	191
Bases Empty	.261	.326	.415	3094	807	118	23	104	104	280	598
Leadoff	.251	.305	.407	1324	332	40	10	49	49	97	255
Not Leadoff	.268	.342	.420	1770	475	78	13	55	55	183	343
Runners On	.264	.329	.409	2405	636	121	17	64	573	243	436
First Base Only	.270	.321	.411	1066	288	51	6	29	85	73	170
Scoring Position	.260	.336	.407	1339	348	70	11	35	488	170	266
Late Innings, Close	.261	.327	.392	762	199	34	6	18	91	74	154

RBI/Opportunities			
Scoring Position	411 / 1824	(23%)	
Scoring Position, 2 Out	164 / 863	(19%)	
On Third, Less than 2 Out	157 / 313	(50%)	
RBI in close games / RBI Total	407 / 677	(60%)	

Royals fans spent all season scratching their heads, trying to figure it out. They knew the offense had been pitiful in '86; that it needed significant improvement in '87 if contention was to be possible. So Kevin Seitzer, and then later Danny Tartabull, arrived and proceeded to excel beyond anyone's expectations. They were real offensive forces. Add in Bo Jackson's early offensive surge, and it would seem that the Royals should have become an offensive juggernaut. But Kansas City finished the year last in runs scored in the American League. How was that possible?

Easy. The rest of the offense not only conspired to negate the achievements of Tartabull and Seitzer, it effectively obliterated them. Willie Wilson was an unsatisfactory leadoff man. George Brett was injured early, had to learn a new position, and never really kicked into gear. Frank White, who had had his best offensive year in '86, began to show his age at the plate. Steve Balboni was a bust; forget about the revisionist opinion that points to his 24 homers in 387 appearances as proof that his only problem was not enough at-bats. Baloney. Manager Billy Gardner stayed with him, and stayed with him, and he did not produce. His 24 dingers were possibly the quietest power surge in Royals history.

There is worse. Jim Sundberg was a terrible offensive player in '86. Management knew they had to make a move and eventually traded for Ed Hearn, who promptly went rotator cuff-up. Unable or unwilling to deal again, Kansas City was left with the platoon combination of Larry Owen and Jamie Quirk. They provided an excellent offensive equivalent of Sunny's wretched '86 season. As for Angel Salazar, the numbers he threw up were enough to make one lust after Omar Moreno; it's likely he was the worst offensive player in the major leagues. The DH position was never settled. Balboni started out there. Juan Beniquez was inserted on occasion, and later Jim Eisenreich and Lonnie Smith had their chance. None excelled.

The outlook for '88 is just as poor. While Seitzer and Tartabull stay healthy there are no worries at third or in right. Every other offensive player is a question mark. White, Brett and Wilson are all old enough so that complete seasons are to be hoped for, not expected. Any substitution means a loss in scoring. Hearn's rehabilitation from his rotator surgery is uncertain. Even if he comes back, he is far from a proven major league hitter. Kurt Stillwell, if he hits .250 and draws some walks, will look like Ty Cobb in comparison to his predecessor. This is the one position at which offensive improvement is guaranteed. Bo Jackson? He'll probably show up to play, but this time he'll have to earn a spot on the roster. Gary Thurman is the likely starter in left. New manager John Wathan wants to run and is eager to utilize Gary's speed. He will need every MPH. The team is old, catcher is still a gaping hole, and it's hard for me to believe that 1987's worst AL offense is going to be much better in '88.

Mike Kopf

KANSAS CITY ROYALS
PITCHING

1987 SEASON											
	G	IP	H	BB	SO	SB	CS	W	L	S	ERA
Totals	387	1424.0	1424	548	923	124	64	83	79	25	3.87
at Home	195	730.0	718	260	462	69	24	46	35	12	3.90
on Road	192	694.0	706	288	461	55	40	37	44	13	3.85
Day Games	104	351.0	353	163	252	29	17	18	22	5	4.05
Night Games	283	1073.0	1071	385	671	95	47	65	57	20	3.82
on Grass	149	530.2	552	219	347	40	32	28	34	8	3.99
on Artificial Turf	238	893.1	872	329	576	84	32	55	45	17	3.81
April	45	165.1	176	66	94	12	5	9	10	1	3.86
May	65	242.0	216	77	188	14	9	18	9	10	3.16
June	60	239.1	228	99	167	29	12	12	16	1	4.10
July	65	241.2	259	81	148	20	13	10	18	2	4.02
August	72	256.0	275	115	159	25	10	16	13	3	4.50
Sept/Oct	80	279.2	270	110	167	24	15	18	13	8	3.60

vs. Opponent Batters	Ave.	OBP	SLG	AB	H	2B	3B	HR	RBI	BB	SO
Totals	.261	.330	.398	5450	1424	266	48	128	647	548	923
vs. Left	.260	.328	.388	2016	524	100	15	43	243	208	365
vs. Right	.262	.332	.404	3434	900	166	33	85	404	340	558
Bases Empty	.264	.329	.410	3062	808	165	31	73	73	279	522
Leadoff	.263	.318	.414	1319	347	78	14	31	31	100	211
Not Leadoff	.264	.337	.406	1743	461	87	17	42	42	179	311
Runners On Base	.258	.332	.384	2388	616	101	17	55	574	269	401
First Base Only	.273	.339	.398	971	265	43	6	22	69	88	149
Scoring Position	.248	.328	.374	1417	351	58	11	33	505	181	252
Late Innings, Close	.255	.323	.392	756	193	31	6	20	97	78	129

RBI/Opportunities		
Scoring Position	442 / 1947	(23%)
Scoring Position, 2 Out	179 / 940	(19%)
On Third, Less than 2 Out	164 / 332	(49%)
RBI in close games / RBI Total	387 / 647	(60%)

It seems that nothing can hold down Royal pitching for long. In 1983 Dennis Leonard destroyed his knee and Vida Blue became a drug abuser. Then in 1984 surprisingly good pitching helped Kansas City to an unexpected division title. In 1986 Bret Saberhagen went from Cy Young winner to Cy Dung stinker, Mark Gubicza and Bud Black fell out of the rotation, and Dan Quisenberry became just another reliever. The staff still led the League in ERA; it was the offense that dragged the team under. The 1987 campaign repeated this pattern. A highly regarded rookie (Scott Bankhead) was traded, the Cy Young designate (Danny Jackson) went into the tank, and Quisenberry disappeared. Yet pitching was still the team's strength. Part of it is luck (e.g., Bob Tufts for Charley Leibrandt), part of it is Royals Stadium, and part of it seems to be that the Royals have developed a nose for pitching talent not unlike that of the Twins for hitters.

The '87 season opened auspiciously for Kansas City when it became apparent that Saberhagen had returned to his '85 form. Also cause for encouragement was Mark Gubicza's start. His previous career stats had shown him as 0 for April. But the pluses were balanced by the puzzling failure of Jackson, the loss of confidence in Quisenberry, and the ineffectiveness of bullpen ace designate Steve Farr. Eventually John Davis was summoned from Omaha to be chairman of a committee, and later Gene Garber was ob-

tained as special assistant for the stretch drive. Of course by this time Saberhagen was struggling, and Gubicza had endured his usual ups and downs. A good generalization would be that the Royals' pitching staff was never in sync all season. But then neither were the Twins' or Cardinals' staffs.

What the future holds is an interesting question. Jackson was dispatched for a desperately needed shortstop plus Ted Power. Power can probably help in a swing role. The four-young-pitchers-for-Floyd Bannister deal looks on the surface like Vida Blue all over again, except that Bannister is not a burned-out hulk. Nor has he ever been a great pitcher. But if—and it may be a gigantic if—he can hold his '87 form (and 16–11 for the wretched Chisox is very good form indeed) Kansas City's already good-to-excellent rotation may be significantly improved. The departure of Davis to Chicago leaves the opportunity for Garber to resume his oft-interrupted role of ace reliever. A rehabilitated Farr and/or Quiz is waiting in the wings. It all sounds pretty iffy, and surely at least one of the above names will go belly up or blow out his arm. But history indicates that the Royals will pitch well. Of course, they pitched well in '86 and '87 and failed to win. The key to the coming season lies with the offense. And for that reason the Bannister trade may turn out to be not good or bad, but irrelevant.

Mike Kopf

MILWAUKEE BREWERS
HITTING

				1987 SEASON							
	Ave.	OBP	SLG	AB	H	2B	3B	HR	RBI	BB	SO
Totals	.276	.346	.428	5624	1552	272	46	163	832	598	1040
vs. Left	.274	.340	.410	1835	503	85	12	47	253	185	356
vs. Right	.277	.349	.436	3789	1049	187	34	116	579	413	684
at Home	.293	.362	.443	2729	800	134	29	72	426	292	506
on Road	.260	.331	.413	2895	752	138	17	91	406	306	534
vs. Groundball	.287	.351	.433	3044	873	147	25	83	463	297	513
vs. Flyball	.263	.340	.421	2580	679	125	21	80	369	301	527
vs. Finesse	.277	.335	.431	3019	835	139	28	90	432	263	472
vs. Power	.275	.358	.424	2605	717	133	18	73	400	335	568
on Grass	.284	.354	.438	4764	1351	236	41	140	738	511	876
on Artificial Turf	.234	.304	.367	860	201	36	5	23	94	87	164
Day Games	.281	.347	.451	1806	507	92	21	58	266	182	347
Night Games	.274	.346	.416	3818	1045	180	25	105	566	416	693
April	.295	.367	.481	738	218	40	5	29	130	81	136
May	.240	.302	.386	811	195	41	4	23	78	72	164
June	.275	.346	.407	943	259	43	8	22	141	101	176
July	.283	.348	.467	1005	284	47	12	38	170	99	177
August	.278	.358	.408	1024	285	48	8	23	157	126	172
Sept/Oct	.282	.351	.422	1103	311	53	9	28	156	119	215
Bases Empty	.258	.331	.401	3088	796	147	27	80	80	321	570
Leadoff	.265	.331	.421	1326	352	65	12	39	39	121	252
Not Leadoff	.252	.331	.385	1762	444	82	15	41	41	200	318
Runners On	.298	.364	.461	2536	756	125	19	83	752	277	470
First Base Only	.300	.345	.457	1010	303	44	8	33	91	63	167
Scoring Position	.297	.376	.463	1526	453	81	11	50	661	214	303
Late Innings, Close	.297	.366	.428	925	275	43	6	22	147	101	172

RBI/Opportunities							
Scoring Position	559 / 2106 (27%)
Scoring Position, 2 Out	240 / 1009 (24%)
On Third, Less than 2 Out	193 / 355 (54%)
RBI in close games / RBI Total	521 / 832 (63%)

Many of the cognoscenti have been saying that, based primarily on hitting prowess, Milwaukee should win the AL East in 1988. It is all very reminiscent of the Cleveland bandwagon that rolled through at this time last year. Sure enough, the Brewers were an offensive force in 1987, especially in the second half. After the All-Star break, this club amassed an awesome .288 average. They got the most hits and scored the most runs in major league ball, and while they were at it led their league in triples, stolen bases and RBIs.

Should we extrapolate last year's performance, and assume that '88 will pick up where '87 left off? That would be a mistake! Some Brewers simply played over their heads last season. Paul Molitor is very good, and in the past has been underrated. But he is definitely not a .350 hitter. Greg Brock may have benefited immensely from leaving Dodgertown and becoming an everyday player, but it is highly unlikely that a lifetime .233 platooner can be transformed into a .299 hitter at the age of 30 just by changing cities. Bill Schroeder, turning 30 this year, was a career .231 hitter before last season. Even in the minors, he seldom hit over .260; his .332 in 1987 was a fluke.

Some players like B. J. Surhoff (.333) and Glenn Braggs (.298) had second half '87 numbers that seem to reflect their true potential, and so we should expect excellent results from them in 1988 and beyond. But the whole Milwaukee lineup was feeding off its own success last year. Each individual performer, by exceeding his natural abilities, elevated his teammates as well. One man's fortuitous hit creates an extra run for the man in front of him, and an extra RBI for someone behind. When reality returns in 1988, it will affect the whole team, not just a few individuals. We saw plenty of streaky performances in 1987 based on this interrelatedness and its psychological effects.

Although they will not win the East, the Brewers will indeed be a fine hitting team in 1988. Surhoff could make people re-think the 1987 Rookie of the Year award. Brock will hit around .260, which would have pleased the Dodgers but will disappoint the Brewers. Paul Molitor may appear again at second base and give the club more offense than any other team will receive from that position. Rob Deer will hit .229 with 23 home runs; Dale Sveum will hopefully produce as many homers as errors. The young veteran Robin Yount will be excellent as usual, while the elderly phenom Brad Komminsk may actually amount to something and make people forget Billy Joe Robidoux (which they are eager to do).

Milwaukee will finish fourth, maybe third. This team's hitting is almost as good as what we saw in 1987. Unfortunately for them, they play in a division where the best pitching usually wins.

John C. Benson

MILWAUKEE BREWERS
PITCHING

	G	IP	H	BB	SO	SB	CS	W	L	S	ERA
1987 SEASON											
Totals	444	1464.0	1548	529	1038	119	58	91	71	45	4.62
at Home	220	740.0	810	241	552	47	32	48	33	21	4.74
on Road	224	724.0	738	288	486	72	26	43	38	24	4.50
Day Games	149	475.1	485	168	329	29	21	31	22	19	4.32
Night Games	295	988.2	1063	361	709	90	37	60	49	26	4.77
on Grass	377	1246.1	1336	447	902	96	50	80	57	38	4.63
on Artificial Turf	67	217.2	212	82	136	23	8	11	14	7	4.55
April	61	192.0	187	75	128	16	7	18	3	9	4.17
May	67	212.2	231	80	170	21	13	6	18	4	5.33
June	85	244.0	295	108	176	16	13	13	15	7	5.90
July	74	257.2	292	71	171	28	8	15	13	7	4.82
August	74	268.2	286	89	195	18	6	18	11	8	4.32
Sept/Oct	83	289.0	257	106	198	20	11	21	11	10	3.43

vs. Opponent Batters	Ave.	OBP	SLG	AB	H	2B	3B	HR	RBI	BB	SO
Totals	.271	.333	.415	5703	1548	264	25	169	770	529	1038
vs. Left	.272	.340	.424	2147	584	95	15	67	303	219	375
vs. Right	.271	.330	.410	3556	964	169	10	102	467	310	663
Bases Empty	.264	.325	.405	3182	840	137	11	97	97	271	586
Leadoff	.268	.329	.429	1345	360	67	3	48	48	118	254
Not Leadoff	.261	.322	.388	1837	480	70	8	49	49	153	332
Runners On Base	.281	.344	.428	2521	708	127	14	72	673	258	452
First Base Only	.284	.345	.436	1093	310	50	6	35	91	101	177
Scoring Position	.279	.343	.422	1428	398	77	8	37	582	157	275
Late Innings, Close	.241	.309	.345	989	238	29	7	20	112	96	195

RBI/Opportunities		
Scoring Position	502 / 1947	(26%)
Scoring Position, 2 Out	182 / 842	(22%)
On Third, Less than 2 Out	189 / 366	(52%)
RBI in close games / RBI Total	463 / 770	(60%)

The Brewers had the ninth-best team ERA in the league in 1987, an accurate measure of their pitching strength. Milwaukee was a shade worse than Seattle, virtually tied with 10th- and 11th-ranked Minnesota and Texas. Contrary to popular belief, the Brewers do not play in a "hitter's park." But the team's front office seems determined to emphasize hitting rather than pitching.

Aside from Ted Higuera, there is no star performer who can take the mound. Higuera and his numbers often seem out of place in Milwaukee. The club was 20 games over .500 last year, eight of those attributable to Ted, and most of the remainder due to Brewers hitting. He showed his phenomenal potential in a stretch from August to September when he was 5–0 with an 0.84 ERA; in 43 innings he yielded only 15 hits and 4 runs. In the second half of last season he avoided home runs better than any other AL hurler with 110 or more innings. After the All-Star break he gave up only six, for a ratio of 0.42 HRs per nine innings. Roger Clemens and Dwight Gooden were close. Higuera is a reminder that weak-pitching teams always seem to have one great hurler (Robin Roberts with the Phillies in the fifties, Mel Stottlemyre of the Nixon-era Yankees, for example).

Bill Wegman, Juan Nieves, Chris Bosio and company are a modest group of yeomen whose greatest strength is their youth. Bosio, who will turn 26 just before opening day, is the oldest of the group. Wegman, who will be 25 all season, is probably the best of the three right now. His strong point is control. Bill's limitation of walks to 0.23 per inning was fourth best among AL starters after Bret Saberhagen, Floyd Bannister and Curt Young. Unfortunately, Wegman gave up more than one hit per inning, many of them fair ball souvenirs. His skills are of the type that can deteriorate rapidly.

Juan Nieves has been highly touted. He has a 90 mph+ fastball and, when his concentration is intact, good mechanics. Despite his no-hitter and obvious youth (22) he still has a lot to prove at the major league level. Nieves will need better control, a sharper breaking ball, and that elusive quality called poise. Many great young throwers have failed to go far beyond mediocrity for lack of these three vital ingredients.

In the bullpen, Dan Plesac looked like an established star until physical problems made him stop pitching. He may come back strong in 1988, but that is nowhere near certain. Newcomer Chuck Crim filled in admirably last year. After the All-Star break he contributed 12 saves and a 2.89 ERA. If Plesac is not usable, Crim may be a savior.

The Brewers' pitching may improve slightly in 1988. Higuera may pitch great all year. Nieves may develop dramatically. Plesac may come back, or Crim may become a star. If all these things happen, the Brewers may actually become contenders. Otherwise, pitching will hold them back.

John C. Benson

MINNESOTA TWINS
HITTING

	Ave.	OBP	SLG	AB	H	2B	3B	HR	RBI	BB	SO
1987 SEASON											
Totals	.261	.328	.430	5443	1422	258	35	196	733	523	897
vs. Left	.266	.326	.428	1571	418	77	17	48	207	142	247
vs. Right	.259	.329	.430	3872	1004	181	18	148	526	381	650
at Home	.268	.341	.453	2678	717	129	25	106	377	287	442
on Road	.255	.316	.407	2765	705	129	10	90	356	236	455
vs. Groundball	.275	.339	.440	2721	748	138	20	90	371	259	377
vs. Flyball	.248	.317	.420	2722	674	120	15	106	362	264	520
vs. Finesse	.276	.338	.458	2642	729	128	22	103	402	239	318
vs. Power	.247	.319	.403	2801	693	130	13	93	331	284	579
on Grass	.256	.321	.410	2145	550	96	7	73	290	195	365
on Artificial Turf	.264	.333	.442	3298	872	162	28	123	443	328	532
Day Games	.265	.333	.439	1639	435	81	6	64	222	158	310
Night Games	.259	.326	.425	3804	987	177	29	132	511	365	587
April	.260	.326	.425	703	183	31	5	25	99	66	127
May	.267	.330	.431	949	253	37	4	37	136	89	149
June	.277	.346	.470	955	265	52	6	40	142	100	145
July	.240	.304	.394	896	215	42	9	26	102	82	126
August	.271	.337	.460	953	258	55	7	37	138	94	178
Sept/Oct	.251	.323	.395	987	248	41	4	31	116	92	172
Bases Empty	.258	.323	.429	3127	806	138	16	122	122	274	534
Leadoff	.269	.335	.445	1303	350	63	7	51	51	118	201
Not Leadoff	.250	.314	.418	1824	456	75	9	71	71	156	333
Runners On	.266	.336	.430	2316	616	120	19	74	611	249	363
First Base Only	.268	.321	.421	1018	273	47	8	31	90	78	142
Scoring Position	.264	.346	.437	1298	343	73	11	43	521	171	221
Late Innings, Close	.261	.335	.437	751	196	34	7	28	99	82	147

RBI/Opportunities

Scoring Position	441 / 1800 (25%)
Scoring Position, 2 Out	172 / 813 (21%)
On Third, Less than 2 Out	161 / 324 (50%)
RBI in close games / RBI Total	451 / 733 (62%)

1987 was indeed the year of the Minnesota Twins in baseball. After watching them compile a 1986 record of 71–91, most oddsmakers pegged the Twins as 125-to-1 or 150-to-1 long shots in 1987. And rightfully so, as on paper the 1987 team looked much like the 1986 failure. But something magical happened to these guys, turning an average ball club playing below expectations into an average ball club playing above expectations. The Big Four (Tom Brunansky, Gary Gaetti, Kent Hrbek, and Kirby Puckett) each had years consistent with their past, not that far above or below their personal averages. In fact, the unusual thing about all the regulars is that they don't have off years. They're almost *too* consistent. Hrbek and Brunansky did manage an extra 14 homers in 1987, despite having 134 fewer at-bats. Greg Gagne showed moderate improvement, both at bat and in the field, particularly in the second half of the season. But overall, the offense was rather mediocre in 1987, just like it was in 1986. True, the Twins scored an extra 45 runs in 1987, but the rest of the league scored an average of 48 runs more in 1987. So the 14-game improvement in the standings is certainly not due to Twins bats.

As for the Dome-field advantage, I don't believe it was just a matter of Twins fans making a lot of noise all year. The fact is, most early season games were played in front of 20,000 or fewer Minnesotans, and anyone who has listened to Garrison Keillor knows that Minnesotans are just too cautious for 20,000 of them to make that much noise. The noise that was present during the postseason games was new to the Twins, as well as the Tigers and Cardinals. No, there was something magical about the Twins in the Dome. They won 56 games there during the regular season, and then 6 in a row in the postseason. Of the 56 regular season wins, only 40 occurred without Minnesota batting in the ninth inning. The other 16 were won in their last at-bat. In these victories the Twins scored 24 runs from the ninth inning on while using only 51 outs.

I took their runs scored and runs allowed from each inning and simulated the 81 regular season home games on my computer several thousand times, and found they should have won only 49 games on the average, given their runs scored and runs allowed (The Pythagorean rule says only 47 wins based on runs scored per game, and 50 wins based on runs scored per inning). This mysterious 7-game advantage was the magic factor in winning the AL West. It could have been mere luck, or just tremendous clutch performances in a few key spots. Whatever it was, it turned an ordinary season into a World Championship. Look for baseball to start giving playoff home field advantages to the team with the best record, like other sports already do.

Dave Robinson

MINNESOTA TWINS
PITCHING

						1987 SEASON					
	G	IP	H	BB	SO	SB	CS	W	L	S	ERA
Totals	451	1427.1	1465	564	991	168	45	85	77	39	4.67
at Home	217	742.0	716	276	546	87	15	56	25	23	3.92
on Road	234	685.1	749	288	445	81	30	29	52	16	5.48
Day Games	148	431.1	459	174	328	62	18	27	22	14	4.88
Night Games	303	996.0	1006	390	663	106	27	58	55	25	4.57
on Grass	179	530.2	578	228	350	51	23	24	38	13	5.60
on Artificial Turf	272	896.2	887	336	641	117	22	61	39	26	4.12
April	52	184.1	179	73	128	31	5	12	9	5	4.10
May	79	248.1	258	101	172	27	5	14	14	7	5.29
June	84	246.2	257	108	192	29	13	17	11	10	4.56
July	72	235.2	248	87	168	32	8	13	14	7	4.93
August	77	243.2	263	102	149	17	4	13	15	3	5.06
Sept/Oct	87	268.2	260	93	182	32	10	16	14	7	3.99

vs. Opponent Batters	Ave.	OBP	SLG	AB	H	2B	3B	HR	RBI	BB	SO
Totals	.266	.337	.438	5514	1465	275	23	210	766	564	991
vs. Left	.276	.349	.486	2529	698	142	11	122	408	280	447
vs. Right	.257	.326	.398	2985	767	133	12	88	358	284	544
Bases Empty	.259	.332	.424	3121	809	141	12	116	116	311	560
Leadoff	.257	.325	.431	1303	335	63	2	53	53	120	235
Not Leadoff	.261	.336	.419	1818	474	78	10	63	63	191	325
Runners On Base	.274	.343	.457	2393	656	134	11	94	650	253	431
First Base Only	.285	.336	.462	1030	294	55	5	39	99	66	160
Scoring Position	.266	.348	.453	1363	362	79	6	55	551	187	271
Late Innings, Close	.257	.335	.402	865	222	46	4	24	126	98	175

RBI/Opportunities		
Scoring Position	451 / 1908	(24%)
Scoring Position, 2 Out	179 / 860	(21%)
On Third, Less than 2 Out	163 / 354	(46%)
RBI in close games / RBI Total	465 / 766	(61%)

The Twins' pitching went from bad to better between 1986 and 1987. The staff ERA dropped from 4.77 (the worst mark in the majors in 1986) to a more respectable 4.63 (5th from the bottom in the AL in 1987). The runs allowed went from 839 to 806. Factor in the increased scoring in the league, and this is a significant improvement. Toronto and Seattle were the only other two AL teams to post better marks in those categories in 1987 than they had the year before.

A big difference between Minnesota's pitching in 1986 and 1987 was the addition of Jeff Reardon and Juan Berenguer. Neither posted spectacular numbers by any means, but like the rest of the team, seemed to rise to the occasion at crucial times. Most of the holdovers from earlier seasons had years consistent with their past. The major exception was Frank Viola, who became a bona fide left-handed all-star, far surpassing expectations which had been diminishing each year. Bert had a very Blyleven-like year, leading the team in almost every category and finishing just over .500. However, he did walk more and strike out fewer, which is an indication he's becoming more of a nibbler with advancing age and HR totals.

The most notable item about the Twins' pitching was their Jekyl-and-Hyde performance at home and on the road. They outscored their opponents at home by a margin of 411 to 348, while being outscored on the road by 458 to 375. Overall, they were outscored by 806 to 786, making them the first team to make the World Series while being outscored during the regular season. At home, they often jumped ahead in the first inning, outscoring their opponents by a margin of 80 to 30 in that frame. They were unscored on in extra innings at home, winning all seven such games. (Hooray for Reardon!) But on the road, they were outscored both early and late, especially in the 9th innings, when they allowed a whopping .90 runs per inning. (Boo, Reardon!) It's been said that a team's record in close games is primarily a measure of their bullpen. The Twins were 20–5 in one-run decisions at home and 4–17 on the road. Uff da!

What do the Twins need to be a better team? I would place the main priority on getting some left-handed help for Frank Viola. They need someone who can get left-handed batters out, both at home and on the road. Only Frank could get lefties out consistently. Bert "Be Home" Blyleven held lefties to a lower batting average, but also surrendered 32 of his 46 HRs to them! Nobody in the bullpen had much luck against lefthanders. But this is a problem for a lot of teams nowadays, and I don't expect much improvement by next year, barring a major trade involving one or more of the everyday players. The tendency is to stand pat with a winning team. I don't look for the Twins to repeat as champions of anything. With the team they have, I would expect about a .500 record and hope for a lot more magic.

Dave Robinson

NEW YORK YANKEES
HITTING

	Ave.	OBP	SLG	AB	H	2B	3B	HR	RBI	BB	SO
Totals	.262	.336	.418	5512	1445	239	16	196	749	604	949
vs. Left	.276	.354	.421	1847	509	83	3	60	265	222	323
vs. Right	.255	.327	.416	3665	936	156	13	136	484	382	626
at Home	.269	.348	.427	2674	720	111	9	98	381	319	449
on Road	.255	.324	.409	2838	725	128	7	98	368	285	500
vs. Groundball	.261	.328	.392	2834	741	126	6	77	349	276	476
vs. Flyball	.263	.345	.446	2678	704	113	10	119	400	328	473
vs. Finesse	.259	.322	.413	2903	751	133	8	100	360	266	423
vs. Power	.266	.351	.423	2609	694	106	8	96	389	338	526
on Grass	.261	.336	.413	4649	1213	188	14	164	633	513	791
on Artificial Turf	.269	.338	.444	863	232	51	2	32	116	91	158
Day Games	.277	.348	.413	1903	527	88	6	53	254	199	311
Night Games	.254	.330	.421	3609	918	151	10	143	495	405	638
April	.267	.357	.412	701	187	37	4	19	106	98	115
May	.267	.351	.455	965	258	44	4	43	144	121	156
June	.269	.347	.413	955	257	37	2	32	147	111	182
July	.255	.334	.415	881	225	37	1	34	115	102	141
August	.240	.284	.396	949	228	38	1	36	99	57	162
Sept/Oct	.273	.344	.415	1061	290	46	4	32	138	115	193
Bases Empty	.252	.320	.407	3166	799	130	14	111	111	304	557
Leadoff	.246	.313	.404	1314	323	49	6	49	49	124	223
Not Leadoff	.257	.325	.410	1852	476	81	8	62	62	180	334
Runners On	.275	.356	.432	2346	646	109	2	85	638	300	392
First Base Only	.279	.342	.445	1024	286	48	1	40	95	94	161
Scoring Position	.272	.366	.422	1322	360	61	1	45	543	206	231
Late Innings, Close	.261	.351	.386	798	208	27	2	23	118	109	149

RBI/Opportunities

Scoring Position	461 / 1884	(24%)
Scoring Position, 2 Out	172 / 847	(20%)
On Third, Less than 2 Out	182 / 373	(49%)
RBI in close games / RBI Total	442 / 749	(59%)

The Yankee offense resembled two different characters last season, with the personalities splitting at the All-Star break. In the first half they were Godzilla, scoring 5.36 runs per game; after the break they turned into Bambi as the RPG average dropped to 4.26. That enormous fall-off contributed greatly to their losing second-half record. Key factors in the collapse were the injuries which took Willie Randolph and Rickey Henderson out of the lineup. With those players batting 1–2 the top third of the Yankee order is the best in baseball, and either one is well suited to hit in the leadoff spot. The loss of one hurt, but as long as one was available the lineup worked. When they both were missing at the same time, manager Lou Pinella was forced to go with either Claudell Washington or Henry Cotto in the #1 spot. I guess it made sense to Lou; they both run pretty well and play CF and isn't that the definition of a leadoff batter? To be perfectly fair to Pinella, he really didn't have many options. But Washington had an OBP of .336 and Cotto's was (yech!) .269. With those guys leading off, the Yankees had one foot in the grave in the first inning of every game.

While injuries played a large role in the death of the offense, the terminal illness suffered by Gary Ward's bat must also be blamed. Ward looked like he was on his way to a career year early in the season. He was hitting .299 with 37 RBI on June 1 and was on a pace to drive in 115 runs for the year. He became an integral part of the offense in the early going and Lou Pinella was counting on him heavily for the rest of way. But his bat went into a coma after the All-Star break, with 6 HRs, 7 doubles, a .219 BA and 17 RBIs in 61 games.

Another interesting turnaround for the Yankees was their performance against lefty pitching. In 1986 the club simply could not touch southpaws (23–33). While they didn't beat up on the breed in '87, at least they finished over .500 against them. Unfortunately, New York forgot how to beat the poor-to-mediocre righties. Pitchers like Al Nipper, Bill Long and Tom Candiotti owned them. The Bronx Bombers may be the only club in the American League happy to see Nip working for the Cubbies.

If for no other reason, new manager Billy Martin will make the Yankee offense better this year because Rickey Henderson will play much harder for him than he did for Pinella. As much as Rickey might deny it, there was tension between him and his manager last year. Unfortunately, increased output from Henderson isn't going to be enough to get Billy a pennant without more help. The names of Rafael Santana and Don Slaught are not exactly associated with ringing bats. If Steinbrenner doesn't come up with a bona fide offensive threat or two for GM Pinella to acquire it's going to be another long season in the Bronx.

Craig Christmann

NEW YORK YANKEES
PITCHING

	1987 SEASON										
	G	IP	H	BB	SO	SB	CS	W	L	S	ERA
Totals	440	1446.1	1475	542	900	114	64	89	73	47	4.39
at Home	216	741.0	723	254	471	45	36	51	30	27	3.86
on Road	224	705.1	752	288	429	69	28	38	43	20	4.95
Day Games	154	493.0	478	164	297	39	14	30	25	15	4.11
Night Games	286	953.1	997	378	603	75	50	59	48	32	4.53
on Grass	368	1235.0	1230	443	784	92	57	78	60	42	4.28
on Artificial Turf	72	211.1	245	99	116	22	7	11	13	5	5.03
April	53	184.0	170	77	115	10	9	14	7	7	3.91
May	72	251.0	243	84	147	24	11	17	11	8	3.91
June	83	252.2	257	76	165	15	11	17	11	7	4.45
July	72	237.0	247	90	155	24	10	15	11	6	4.06
August	76	245.2	269	112	164	22	9	11	17	9	5.02
Sept/Oct	84	276.0	289	103	154	19	14	15	16	10	4.83

vs. Opponent Batters	Ave.	OBP	SLG	AB	H	2B	3B	HR	RBI	BB	SO
Totals	.266	.332	.418	5551	1475	243	33	179	715	542	900
vs. Left	.265	.334	.414	1852	491	79	10	59	242	194	281
vs. Right	.266	.331	.420	3699	984	164	23	120	473	348	619
Bases Empty	.264	.328	.427	3170	837	130	22	114	114	285	495
Leadoff	.256	.319	.411	1326	339	53	9	45	45	115	209
Not Leadoff	.270	.335	.438	1844	498	77	13	69	69	170	286
Runners On Base	.268	.336	.407	2381	638	113	11	65	601	257	405
First Base Only	.268	.322	.427	1022	274	49	4	35	90	78	160
Scoring Position	.268	.346	.391	1359	364	64	7	30	511	179	245
Late Innings, Close	.266	.330	.402	788	210	25	2	26	109	78	135

RBI/Opportunities		
Scoring Position	445 / 1887	(24%)
Scoring Position, 2 Out	181 / 886	(20%)
On Third, Less than 2 Out	166 / 345	(48%)
RBI in close games / RBI Total	419 / 715	(59%)

The thing that really jumps off the page at you when you look at the New York pitching totals is the name with the most innings pitched next to it. Go ahead. Take a look; I'll wait for you. . . .

No, your eyes aren't playing tricks on you and it isn't a misprint. Tommy John pitched more innings than any other Yankee hurler in '87. Think about this for a moment: John turned 44 during the season. If not for personal conflicts, he'd still be coaching college baseball. At times when he shuffled out of the dugout, I was sure that he wasn't going to be able to finish the climb to the top of the mound. This pitcher was the iron man of the Yankee staff in '87. He averaged 5.67 innings per start. Don't get me wrong; I'm not knocking Tommy. He did more than anyone could have expected, and without him the Yankees would have been buried even deeper in the division. But the fact remains that a staff which had to lean this heavily on T.J. just wasn't doing its job.

The pitching started the year tolerably and then got worse. New York opponents scored 4.40 runs per game in the first half of the season and 5.01 after the All-Star break. Steve Trout certainly aided in the inflation of opponents' run totals. He was as confused a pitcher as you will ever see—he simply didn't know where the ball was going. One of the most interesting displays of the '87 season was the Trout-Mark Salas battery. Steve would throw the ball as hard as he could, somewhere. Meanwhile, Mark would play statue behind the plate while waiting to see where the pitch would finally come to rest. If they could have played together for an entire season there's no telling what WP and PB records would have been set.

It seems that George is going to keep trying pitchers from Chicago until either he gets it right or the apocalypse comes. Rich Dotson is the latest in a line that includes Rick Reuschel, Britt Burns and Steve Trout. If Dotson is healthy (and that's a huge IF), the club should have a better staff this year. At least it will be a more consistent one under new manager Billy Martin. The bullpen could be thin, so look for Billy to overwork Dotson and Rick Rhoden. The tender arms of Ron Guidry and John Candelaria must be aching in anticipation of the workouts Billy has planned for them.

Expect Ron Guidry to have a fine season if his shoulder surgery works out. Last year he was again the victim of non-support. His mates scored 3.37 runs per Guidry start while averaging 4.90 overall. That makes two years in a row without runs to work with. His luck is due to change, and he's always pitched well for Martin. Of course, he's also paid the price in the season following a Billyball summer.

Craig Christmann

OAKLAND ATHLETICS
HITTING

	Ave.	OBP	SLG	AB	H	2B	3B	HR	RBI	BB	SO
				1987 SEASON							
Totals	.260	.333	.428	5511	1431	263	33	199	762	593	1056
vs. Left	.264	.341	.435	1846	487	82	12	70	250	216	338
vs. Right	.258	.329	.424	3665	944	181	21	129	512	377	718
at Home	.251	.330	.412	2645	664	134	14	88	347	304	511
on Road	.268	.336	.442	2866	767	129	19	111	415	289	545
vs. Groundball	.261	.325	.418	2832	738	144	18	89	366	260	503
vs. Flyball	.259	.341	.437	2679	693	119	15	110	396	333	553
vs. Finesse	.272	.338	.450	2765	752	130	17	109	395	272	418
vs. Power	.247	.328	.406	2746	679	133	16	90	367	321	638
on Grass	.263	.335	.431	4637	1219	225	23	170	644	496	885
on Artificial Turf	.243	.320	.408	874	212	38	10	29	118	97	171
Day Games	.271	.345	.446	2061	558	116	9	76	294	223	380
Night Games	.253	.326	.417	3450	873	147	24	123	468	370	676
April	.246	.326	.408	768	189	37	6	25	105	89	176
May	.263	.347	.455	847	223	36	6	38	110	108	156
June	.265	.341	.452	926	245	42	3	42	140	105	159
July	.287	.331	.462	964	277	53	5	35	135	60	195
August	.250	.329	.405	965	241	46	10	28	147	110	185
Sept/Oct	.246	.324	.388	1041	256	49	3	31	125	121	185
Bases Empty	.243	.316	.409	3185	774	146	19	115	115	321	635
Leadoff	.260	.331	.439	1309	340	64	6	53	53	133	246
Not Leadoff	.231	.306	.388	1876	434	82	13	62	62	188	389
Runners On	.282	.355	.453	2326	657	117	14	84	647	272	421
First Base Only	.313	.368	.506	958	300	53	3	42	114	78	163
Scoring Position	.261	.346	.416	1368	357	64	11	42	533	194	258
Late Innings, Close	.263	.331	.421	886	233	41	3	31	129	90	185

RBI/Opportunities		
Scoring Position	450 / 1886	(24%)
Scoring Position, 2 Out	187 / 868	(22%)
On Third, Less than 2 Out	157 / 361	(43%)
RBI in close games / RBI Total	458 / 762	(60%)

Without Mark McGwire, nobody would really have paid much attention to the A's offensive accomplishments in 1987. Let's face it: If McGwire had not existed, Oakland would have been about as interesting as, well, Oakland. Thanks to the red-headed rookie, the A's offense did improve slightly over last year in relation to both the division and the league. They went from fourth to second in runs and fourth to first in home runs in the West. Although Carney Lansford, Terry Steinbach and Jose Canseco also did well, the rest of their outfield production after the All-Star break (and Mike Davis' altercation with a door in Boston) was disappointing. Likewise, their middle infield did not contribute much either at bat or on the field, especially after Tony Phillips went on the DL. And their bench was almost non-existent. Reggie Jackson did little except increase attendance by 360,000 and be the first and only Athletic to appear in the *National Enquirer* (the two are probably related).

The lack of improvement in stolen base success (69 percent in '87, 69.5 percent in '86) continues to cost the A's runs. Base stealing seems to be considered necessary in upholding the Rickey Henderson tradition. However, it would probably be better in the long view if the running philosophy depended more upon game circumstance and less upon living up to an obsolete reputation. The trade of team CS leader Alfredo Griffin will lead to a strengthening of this

weakness in 1988. The A's have obtained Dave Parker, who ought to be some improvement over the Jackson-Cey DH combination. Look for him to play some outfield with Davis gone and Dwayne Murphy not offered a contract. Expect to see Canseco moved to right, Luis Polonia to left, and Stan Javier in center when Parker is the DH.

Walt Weiss, first round draft pick in 1985, had a good year in AA and impressed team officials when he played well at short and hit some after being called up in September. Although the A's would have liked to keep him at AAA for one full year, the Major League job is his as of the Alfredo Griffin/Bob Welch trade. Weiss will be the next Alan Trammell and will be Oakland's third consecutive rookie-of-the-year. Defensive whizzes Glenn Hubbard and Mike Gallego will contend for playing time at second in light of the A's failure to offer contracts to the two Tonys, Phillips and Bernazard. Although either could be signed by spring training, the organization is not unhappy to lose their hefty salaries. Bernazard did not perform well offensively or defensively and Phillips' injuries were becoming all too frequent. Ron "Helmet Head" Hassey has been signed, so Mickey Tettleton and his anemic bat are probably history. With the club's lack of outfield depth, AA draftee Doug Jennings could win a roster spot, depending on how he does in spring training.

Susan Nelson

OAKLAND ATHLETICS
PITCHING

					1987 SEASON						
	G	IP	H	BB	SO	SB	CS	W	L	S	ERA
Totals	490	1445.2	1442	531	1042	117	54	81	81	41	4.39
at Home	236	740.0	666	263	580	64	37	42	39	20	3.71
on Road	254	705.2	776	268	462	53	17	39	42	21	5.11
Day Games	189	548.2	535	183	418	42	20	33	28	18	4.08
Night Games	301	897.0	907	348	624	75	34	48	53	23	4.59
on Grass	408	1224.1	1202	434	882	101	49	70	66	34	4.20
on Artificial Turf	82	221.1	240	97	160	16	5	11	15	7	5.45
April	70	201.1	205	105	135	27	17	9	14	4	4.65
May	75	229.0	223	74	166	10	10	15	10	7	3.66
June	78	238.0	219	79	182	19	6	16	11	9	4.31
July	85	243.1	246	84	172	23	4	12	15	6	4.51
August	87	257.0	265	84	190	6	7	15	14	8	4.66
Sept/Oct	95	277.0	284	105	197	32	10	14	17	7	4.55

vs. Opponent Batters	Ave.	OBP	SLG	AB	H	2B	3B	HR	RBI	BB	SO
Totals	.258	.324	.412	5580	1442	262	34	176	739	531	1042
vs. Left	.258	.330	.391	2554	660	119	14	64	320	274	474
vs. Right	.258	.320	.430	3026	782	143	20	112	419	257	568
Bases Empty	.255	.318	.410	3168	809	149	22	99	99	272	596
Leadoff	.251	.316	.405	1324	332	61	7	43	43	121	234
Not Leadoff	.259	.320	.414	1844	477	88	15	56	56	151	362
Runners On Base	.262	.332	.415	2412	633	113	12	77	640	259	446
First Base Only	.271	.325	.449	1020	276	53	3	41	104	77	167
Scoring Position	.256	.337	.390	1392	357	60	9	36	536	182	279
Late Innings, Close	.247	.321	.396	884	218	37	4	29	126	94	181

	RBI/Opportunities		
Scoring Position	464 / 1946	(24%)	
Scoring Position, 2 Out	170 / 873	(19%)	
On Third, Less than 2 Out	191 / 348	(55%)	
RBI in close games / RBI Total	443 / 739	(60%)	

Relative to the league, Oakland's pitching was markedly improved over 1986 in most categories. Manager Tony LaRussa said before the season that he would not tolerate pitchers who did not throw strikes. Sure enough, the staff's K/BB ratio improved to almost 2–1, up from 3–2 in 1986 and almost 1–1 in 1985. They jumped from 13th to 5th in the league for BB allowed and from 8th to 3rd in strikeouts.

The A's had more saves than any other team in the division. Jay Howell and Dennis Eckersley became the first American League pitchers on the same team to each exceed 15 saves since the 1973 Chicago White Sox. Gene Nelson, until he ran out of gas in August, was as effective as Eckersley in middle relief. The relievers as a group, in fact, might be considered the A's greatest strength in 1987 and salvaged what could have been a disaster caused by the decimation of the starting staff.

There has been some gnashing of teeth among local sportswriters and team functionaries about the recently discovered fact that the A's turned the fewest double plays in the league. Actually, the A's have turned the fewest DPs in the AL for the last three years, not so much because of poor fielding but because their pitchers are a fly ball staff to the extreme. Of course, the proposed solution by Bay Area experts is to get a new SS and 2B posthaste, which has actually occurred as of this writing. There will be much consternation among these experts when Oakland ranks last again in 1988.

The starting rotation has already been overhauled for 1988. Jose Rijo went in the Dave Parker trade. Dave Stewart has established himself as numero uno. Bob Welch will be at least the number two starter, followed by Storm Davis, Curt Young, and Steve Ontiveros or Rick Honeycutt. Although the A's have depleted their stock of minor league pitching, (Darrel Akerfelds, Tim Belcher, Dave Leiper, Tim Birtsas, Jose Rijo and Wally Whitehurst gone within six months), they still have Bruce Tanner, who is coming off knee surgery but could be a factor later on. Desperate for left-handed relief, they have re-signed Gary Lavelle to hold clubhouse prayer meetings, which couldn't hurt, and traded for erratic but talented Matt Young.

As the Athletics' starting staff is beginning to look more promising, the big question mark now becomes the bullpen and whether it can repeat the good work of 1987. Jay Howell is gone, but the A's should have enough options remaining with Eckersley, Nelson, Young, and Eric Plunk. The organization has finally changed its philosophy from internal development to external acquisition when it realized, at least from the pitching standpoint, that nobody was being developed. This franchise is on the brink of either establishing itself or falling by the wayside. The winter's actions should result in 90 victories and a Division Championship in 1988. And yes, the A's will at last win a game in the Metrodome.

Susan Nelson

SEATTLE MARINERS
HITTING

	Ave.	OBP	SLG	AB	H	2B	3B	HR	RBI	BB	SO
1987 SEASON											
Totals	.272	.335	.428	5511	1499	282	48	161	717	500	863
vs. Left	.265	.324	.422	1742	462	96	12	51	220	149	272
vs. Right	.275	.340	.431	3769	1037	186	36	110	497	351	591
at Home	.273	.340	.459	2706	740	141	26	103	378	257	418
on Road	.271	.329	.399	2805	759	141	22	58	339	243	445
vs. Groundball	.271	.339	.410	2887	783	135	25	72	360	279	413
vs. Flyball	.273	.330	.448	2624	716	147	23	89	357	221	450
vs. Finesse	.275	.328	.436	2980	820	146	27	93	377	221	369
vs. Power	.268	.343	.419	2531	679	136	21	68	340	279	494
on Grass	.281	.337	.417	2172	611	116	14	50	289	183	338
on Artificial Turf	.266	.333	.436	3339	888	166	34	111	428	317	525
Day Games	.248	.312	.389	1448	359	73	13	35	173	130	262
Night Games	.281	.343	.442	4063	1140	209	35	126	544	370	601
April	.267	.337	.408	772	206	31	6	22	100	79	130
May	.282	.337	.438	900	254	42	13	24	127	78	157
June	.250	.319	.391	884	221	47	12	18	99	81	137
July	.280	.325	.455	885	248	47	6	32	114	56	133
August	.275	.344	.457	995	274	65	4	36	136	99	130
Sept/Oct	.275	.344	.416	1075	296	50	7	29	141	107	176
Bases Empty	.272	.328	.427	3151	858	170	30	86	86	239	499
Leadoff	.273	.331	.449	1324	362	81	11	43	43	106	200
Not Leadoff	.271	.327	.412	1827	496	89	19	43	43	133	299
Runners On	.272	.343	.430	2360	641	112	18	75	631	261	364
First Base Only	.282	.343	.466	923	260	48	7	36	92	82	132
Scoring Position	.265	.343	.406	1437	381	64	11	39	539	179	232
Late Innings, Close	.266	.340	.423	711	189	22	9	24	107	81	133

RBI/Opportunities		
Scoring Position	468 / 1956	(24%)
Scoring Position, 2 Out	185 / 894	(21%)
On Third, Less than 2 Out	175 / 346	(51%)
RBI in close games / RBI Total	419 / 717	(58%)

The Seattle Mariner offense in 1987 showed great improvement over 1986. The team consisted of and depended on speed rather than home runs, a drastic change from Mariner clubs past. The team batting average increased 19 points and was third best in the league. Team OBP and slugging were up. Total offensive production improved from 718 runs in 1986 to 760 runs in 1987.

Their doubles total was second only to Chicago's. They led the league in triples, but were last in home runs. There was still a 2 percent increase in Seattle dingers from '86, but the club lost ground on the league as a whole, which was up 15 percent. The team's most-utilized offensive weapon was the stolen base. The Mariners total of SBs was second to Milwaukee's. The Ms could easily have led the league, but for some reason the aggressive running game disappeared after the All-Star break. At that point they were 45–43, 3.5 games out with 102 SBs in 143 attempts. In their next 42 games they attempted only 41 steals and went 16–26 to drop out of contention. In September they went back to their aggressive ways and filched 40 bases in 51 attempts.

Individually, Harold Reynolds led the league in both SB and CS. The Mariner middle infield was one of the most productive in the league. Reynolds and Rey Quinones both had BAs above the league average. Harold supplied the speed and stolen bases while Rey provided some pop with a dozen home runs. The catching was handled by the solid platoon of Scott Bradley and Dave Valle, who together provided 31 doubles and 17 HRs.

It may appear on the surface that the Mariner offense will miss 1987 team batting champ Phil Bradley in 1988, but there are three reasons why they will not. First is the man they got for him, Glenn Wilson. While he won't contribute Phil's stolen bases or .300 career average, he will provide more home run power and better defense. Mickey Brantley will play the entire season and take up some of the slack. And finally, should Seattle ever allow Ken Phelps to play every day as the DH he will hit over 40 home runs. These three players will more than compensate the loss of Phil Bradley.

The rest of the offense in '88 will be pretty much as in '87. Last year's right field platoon of Mike Kingery and the various righthanders will move to left and most likely consist of Kingery and Dave Hengel, who hit 30 HRs in the PCL last year. Brantley will be in center and Wilson in right full time. The infield will be intact with Jim Presley, Quinones, Reynolds and Alvin Davis. The Scott Bradley-Valle catching platoon will remain. Scoring 800 runs should be no problem with Phelps and Brantley playing daily and the addition of Wilson and Hengel to the Mariner lineup. But will 800 runs be enough?

Steve Russell

SEATTLE MARINERS
PITCHING

1987 SEASON											
	G	IP	H	BB	SO	SB	CS	W	L	S	ERA
Totals	413	1430.2	1501	497	919	112	49	78	84	31	4.53
at Home	199	737.0	751	243	500	56	27	40	41	12	4.53
on Road	214	693.2	750	254	419	56	22	38	43	19	4.54
Day Games	107	384.2	394	138	253	30	15	22	22	7	4.23
Night Games	306	1046.0	1107	359	666	82	34	56	62	24	4.65
on Grass	161	534.0	580	191	324	37	17	34	28	16	4.53
on Artificial Turf	252	896.2	921	306	595	75	32	44	56	15	4.54
April	53	203.0	198	68	144	20	7	12	11	4	4.74
May	72	234.0	257	87	147	18	12	14	12	5	4.85
June	61	237.0	246	57	151	12	4	13	14	7	4.44
July	70	226.0	256	89	131	20	8	10	16	3	5.50
August	72	254.0	271	93	162	14	8	12	17	3	4.04
Sept/Oct	85	276.2	273	103	184	28	10	17	14	9	3.87

vs. Opponent Batters	Ave.	OBP	SLG	AB	H	2B	3B	HR	RBI	BB	SO
Totals	.271	.331	.439	5533	1501	263	34	199	758	497	919
vs. Left	.278	.333	.444	2336	650	112	19	79	331	200	346
vs. Right	.266	.330	.435	3197	851	151	15	120	427	297	573
Bases Empty	.263	.326	.439	3150	829	141	20	124	124	284	542
Leadoff	.282	.335	.496	1327	374	73	8	65	65	102	195
Not Leadoff	.250	.320	.397	1823	455	68	12	59	59	182	347
Runners On Base	.282	.337	.439	2383	672	122	14	75	634	213	377
First Base Only	.293	.337	.457	1028	301	53	4	36	97	58	159
Scoring Position	.274	.338	.426	1355	371	69	10	39	537	155	218
Late Innings, Close	.271	.332	.394	675	183	27	1	18	86	65	136

RBI/Opportunities		
Scoring Position	459 / 1825	(25%)
Scoring Position, 2 Out	162 / 801	(20%)
On Third, Less than 2 Out	177 / 334	(53%)
RBI in close games / RBI Total	433 / 758	(57%)

It was obvious at the end of the 1986 season that if the Mariners were going to go anywhere in 1987 the pitching staff would need to improve drastically. They had the second highest ERA (4.65) in the AL, and led the league in opposition baserunners. It was under these circumstances that Billy Connors was hired as pitching coach. He proved to be an excellent choice. Last year the Seattle ERA ranking improved to eighth, and the opposition baserunners total was seventh lowest, with 175 fewer than in '86. The Mariners can thank Mr. Connors for the individual improvements that changed these rankings.

Any discussion of the Mariner staff must start with lefthander Mark Langston. Mark won a club record 19 games while winning his third strikeout title in his four years in the league. His ERA dropped from 4.85 to 3.84. The rest of the starting rotation consisted of Mike Moore, Mike Morgan, Scott Bankhead and Lee Guetterman, with Mike Campbell contributing in September. Moore was having his second disappointing year in a row after winning 17 games in '85, but then something kicked in and his last 12 starts produced a 6–5 record and 3.76 ERA. Mike Moore can make or break the M's this season.

Morgan, depending on how you look at it, either was second on the team in wins or second in losses with 17. He was both, actually, but the fact is that he was 23–34 with a .291 opponent BA over the past two years. He won't be missed in '88. Bankhead was great in April (4–1, 2.94), but

suffered most of the rest of the year with a bad shoulder. Winter surgery has the club hoping that he'll contribute for the entire season this time. Guetterman was the surprise of the staff in the first half. Campbell was 15–2, 2.77 in Calgary and was voted the PCL MVP.

In the bullpen lefthander Bill Wilkinson emerged as the man manager Dick Williams counted on when the game was on the line. Jerry Reed ended the year as the #1 righthander out of the pen. Edwin Nunez had 10 saves at the All-Star break, but inexplicably pitched only 22 innings in the second half.

The picture for 1988 looks promising. Langston will be the ace, no question. Moore will get 35 starts, and will dominate if he pitches up to expectations. Lefty Steve Trout is very anxious to be reunited with coach Connors; they were together on the Cubs in '84. Letting Guetterman go for Trout was a wise move. A healthy Bankhead will be a winner, and Campbell should provide quality innings. Morgan is gone in a trade for Ken Dixon; no harm done, since nothing is expected from either. The pen will be in fine shape with the addition of Mike Jackson. He'll start in middle relief, but should end up as the RH stopper. Wilkinson will return as the LH closer. Reed, Nunez and Dennis Powell will support. Overall, the staff looks deep and should rank in the top third of the league.

Steve Russell

TEXAS RANGERS
HITTING

	Ave.	OBP	SLG	AB	H	2B	3B	HR	RBI	BB	SO
				1987 SEASON							
Totals	.266	.333	.430	5564	1478	264	35	194	771	567	1081
vs. Left	.277	.340	.454	1928	534	92	9	77	267	186	370
vs. Right	.260	.330	.418	3636	944	172	26	117	504	381	711
at Home	.279	.349	.443	2753	767	134	20	93	398	297	521
on Road	.253	.317	.418	2811	711	130	15	101	373	270	560
vs. Groundball	.272	.337	.426	2739	745	125	16	88	368	268	474
vs. Flyball	.259	.330	.435	2825	733	139	19	106	403	299	607
vs. Finesse	.280	.334	.451	3098	868	154	21	111	417	250	493
vs. Power	.247	.333	.404	2466	610	110	14	83	354	317	588
on Grass	.270	.336	.434	4679	1263	225	30	161	664	467	883
on Artificial Turf	.243	.321	.410	885	215	39	5	33	107	100	198
Day Games	.269	.348	.422	1253	337	57	12	37	176	156	269
Night Games	.265	.329	.433	4311	1141	207	23	157	595	411	812
April	.263	.337	.429	658	173	24	5	25	84	71	142
May	.254	.331	.424	917	233	43	4	35	133	108	187
June	.279	.342	.473	990	276	58	7	40	144	96	206
July	.286	.353	.471	921	263	56	8	33	150	101	152
August	.255	.314	.399	998	254	43	7	29	130	87	191
Sept/Oct	.258	.325	.392	1080	279	40	4	32	130	104	203
Bases Empty	.258	.326	.426	3158	816	146	16	117	117	300	624
Leadoff	.265	.332	.427	1325	351	61	5	48	48	126	239
Not Leadoff	.254	.321	.425	1833	465	85	11	69	69	174	385
Runners On	.275	.343	.436	2406	662	118	19	77	654	267	457
First Base Only	.272	.329	.427	1060	288	58	7	31	96	87	192
Scoring Position	.278	.353	.443	1346	374	60	12	46	558	180	265
Late Innings, Close	.256	.348	.393	844	216	31	5	25	125	119	156

RBI/Opportunities		
Scoring Position	474 / 1871	(25%)
Scoring Position, 2 Out	196 / 877	(22%)
On Third, Less than 2 Out	180 / 350	(51%)
RBI in close games / RBI Total	454 / 771	(59%)

In three seasons, manager Bobby Valentine and general manager Tom Grieve have built the Rangers into a formidable offensive force. Last year they led their division in runs and slugging percentage. They set six team offensive records, surpassing marks set only a year earlier. The dip in wins to 75 last year from 87 a year earlier occurred in spite of this performance.

1986's rookie sensations, Ruben Sierra and Pete Incaviglia, led the way in the 1987 scoring surge. Sierra was named the team's MVP, hitting 30 home runs and leading the team in RBIs, ABs, hits and total bases. Incaviglia blasted 27 home runs while raising his batting average 21 points. Veterans Pete O'Brien, Larry Parrish and Scott Fletcher had their expected fine seasons. O'Brien was the team leader in Runs Created, and Parrish led in home runs. Fletcher had a career best in hits. Rookies established themselves at three positions: second base (Jerry "The Governor" Browne), catcher (Mike Stanley), and outfield (Bob Brower). Browne had a good OBP with more walks than strikeouts, and he shared the leadoff slot with Brower from July on.

There was a prominent flaw in this picture of offensive dominance. The Rangers were the AL whiff kings. Texas was the only AL team with over 1000 strikeouts in both 1986 and 1987; their league-high rate was one SO per 5.15 at-bats (AL average 1:5.79). All indications for 1988 are that they'll make the kilo K club three years in a row. Their caught stealing figures are also alarming, but the baserunning is better than the numbers make it appear. Valentine usually sent runners from first base in two strike/two out situations. A lot of the caught stealings occurred in this circumstance, when the cost of losing the runner was low.

Oddibe McDowell and Steve Buechele disappointed. McDowell failed to produce leading off, and by July was hitting low in the order. The locally popular Buechele was reduced to a platoon with Tom O'Malley by August. This year Oddibe and Steve will be expected to turn their potential into reality on the field. The paltry offense from catcher Don Slaught spurred Valentine to use lumbermen Gino Petralli and Mike Stanley. It's doubtful if their hitting compensated for their defensive damage. Petralli even managed to set an AL season mark for passed balls during his turns behind the plate. Although, to be fair, it should be mentioned that he did handle all of Charlie Hough's games.

Bill James's Pythagorean theory applied to 1987 hitting statistics projected to 78 wins. The Rangers underachieved by three, winning only 75. It seemed like they won even fewer. While the victory fall-off was not surprising, the depth of it was. The decline has raised the question, faintly, as to whether the team will ever win a championship with its current direction. The Rangers are both young and basically set at every position; non-pitching rookies will not impact in 1988. The offense will be the strength of the team, but fans' patience with "potential" is growing thin. The time is very near when these youngsters will be expected to play championship baseball.

Dic Humphrey

TEXAS RANGERS
PITCHING

	1987 SEASON										
	G	IP	H	BB	SO	SB	CS	W	L	S	ERA
Totals	491	1444.1	1388	760	1103	205	55	75	87	27	4.63
at Home	248	749.0	723	386	584	113	32	43	38	10	4.64
on Road	243	695.1	665	374	519	92	23	32	49	17	4.62
Day Games	116	316.2	313	198	232	51	11	14	22	6	4.69
Night Games	375	1127.2	1075	562	871	154	44	61	65	21	4.61
on Grass	419	1228.1	1181	644	951	173	49	68	69	24	4.54
on Artificial Turf	72	216.0	207	116	152	32	6	7	18	3	5.13
April	61	174.1	165	95	134	27	6	8	11	2	4.65
May	90	235.1	261	131	195	34	11	11	16	3	5.32
June	81	254.2	231	121	173	37	6	16	12	10	4.31
July	87	240.0	228	116	177	35	4	14	13	5	4.39
August	88	257.0	252	166	227	35	10	12	17	4	5.08
Sept/Oct	84	283.0	251	131	197	37	18	14	18	3	4.13

vs. Opponent Batters	Ave.	OBP	SLG	AB	H	2B	3B	HR	RBI	BB	SO
Totals	.253	.347	.415	5487	1388	249	21	199	782	760	1103
vs. Left	.252	.344	.402	2468	621	102	6	86	350	334	469
vs. Right	.254	.350	.425	3019	767	147	15	113	432	426	634
Bases Empty	.254	.348	.424	3001	763	138	13	115	115	402	603
Leadoff	.246	.336	.398	1276	314	55	5	43	43	159	263
Not Leadoff	.260	.357	.443	1725	449	83	8	72	72	243	340
Runners On Base	.251	.346	.404	2486	625	111	8	84	667	358	500
First Base Only	.261	.329	.436	1008	263	46	5	40	98	99	175
Scoring Position	.245	.356	.382	1478	362	65	3	44	569	259	325
Late Innings, Close	.255	.343	.417	815	208	35	5	29	121	100	178

RBI/Opportunities				
Scoring Position		486 / 2142	(23%)	
Scoring Position, 2 Out		206 / 1008	(20%)	
On Third, Less than 2 Out		175 / 374	(47%)	
RBI in close games / RBI Total		473 / 782	(60%)	

The Rangers' 1987 pitching was horrible. It was so bad the team lost twelve more games than in '86, despite material offensive increases. The staff ERA ballooned to 4.63, and runs allowed increased by 106. Texas came back to win 18 games when behind after one inning. This was tops in the league, but occurred largely because the pitching staff presented 52 opportunities. The pitching set five club records for futility: Most Walks, Balks, Hit Batsmen, Earned Runs and Runs. The first three categories led the league. The walk total was 760, and only one other AL team issued even 600 passes. The Rangers won a meager nine games when scoring fewer than four runs.

Knuckleballer Charlie Hough was the only reliable starter. He posted career highs in wins, innings pitched and starts. The last two led the league. Three second year players of great promise—Bobby Witt, Jose Guzman and Edwin Correa—were counted on to join Hough in the rotation, but they doomed the season as collectively they threw over 100 fewer innings, won seven fewer games, and increased their combined ERA by over half a run.

Witt, the fastballing strikeout artist, is dominating when he finds the plate. He has led the American League in walks in both his big league seasons and is averaging a breathtaking 8.5 walks per nine innings pitched in his career. His 1.78 pitching ratio last year (baserunners/IP) was the worst in the majors. Injuries limited his playing time, but he had a couple of outstanding outings, including his first complete game in 56 starts on September 30.

Guzman and Correa went in opposite directions. After a spotty start Guzman finished strong and actually increased his wins and innings pitched. Correa is still trying to forget 1987 as he won only three games with a 7.59 ERA. His season ended in July with the discovery of a fractured bone in his shoulder, hopefully the cause of the awful pitching.

In the bullpen, Greg Harris flopped early, then Dale Mohorcic became the stopper and led Texas in saves. Many wondered why he was not the stopper from the beginning; as in 1986, he led the team in appearances and ERA. He is a big, hard thrower. Mohorcic's season essentially ended in August with a bleeding ulcer. He saved sixteen games in little more than half a season, and could save 25 to 30 this year. Other relievers include Mitch Williams, a lefthander with a marvelous arm who only occasionally finds the plate, and the inconsistent Jeff Russell.

A year ago the Minnesota Twins made a daring move and traded for a premier bullpen ace. The resulting World Championship speaks for itself. The Rangers are in a similar position now, with a great offense and promising starters. If a genuine closer is found, Texas will be a contender. More likely, the same cast as last year will pitch to the tune of 80–84 wins.

Dic Humphrey

TORONTO BLUE JAYS
HITTING

	Ave.	OBP	SLG	AB	H	2B	3B	HR	RBI	BB	SO
1987 SEASON											
Totals	.269	.336	.446	5635	1514	276	38	215	789	555	970
vs. Left	.261	.331	.434	1769	462	82	17	63	242	181	339
vs. Right	.272	.339	.451	3866	1052	194	21	152	547	374	631
at Home	.268	.341	.448	2777	743	147	26	101	395	298	476
on Road	.270	.332	.443	2858	771	129	12	114	394	257	494
vs. Groundball	.288	.350	.474	2686	774	157	16	103	416	245	403
vs. Flyball	.251	.324	.420	2949	740	119	22	112	373	310	567
vs. Finesse	.272	.328	.452	3128	850	152	28	119	404	256	420
vs. Power	.265	.346	.437	2507	664	124	10	96	385	299	550
on Grass	.263	.329	.431	2209	582	94	9	86	300	211	377
on Artificial Turf	.272	.341	.455	3426	932	182	29	129	489	344	593
Day Games	.261	.335	.435	1979	516	93	16	73	255	212	342
Night Games	.273	.337	.452	3656	998	183	22	142	534	343	628
April	.250	.331	.414	681	170	34	6	22	82	80	104
May	.273	.337	.446	929	254	46	3	36	132	86	170
June	.275	.339	.479	981	270	46	8	46	158	94	172
July	.265	.339	.429	923	245	39	5	34	125	97	183
August	.275	.336	.454	1028	283	55	6	39	149	88	175
Sept/Oct	.267	.336	.441	1093	292	56	10	38	143	110	166
Bases Empty	.267	.329	.445	3218	858	155	21	126	126	276	574
Leadoff	.263	.318	.435	1341	353	74	8	47	47	100	233
Not Leadoff	.269	.336	.452	1877	505	81	13	79	79	176	341
Runners On	.271	.346	.446	2417	656	121	17	89	663	279	396
First Base Only	.253	.312	.422	1022	259	41	4	41	98	79	161
Scoring Position	.285	.370	.464	1395	397	80	13	48	565	200	235
Late Innings, Close	.263	.346	.413	939	247	45	6	28	148	117	172

RBI/Opportunities		
Scoring Position	471 / 1926	(24%)
Scoring Position, 2 Out	179 / 868	(21%)
On Third, Less than 2 Out	173 / 358	(48%)
RBI in close games / RBI Total	484 / 789	(61%)

In 1987 the Toronto Blue Jays scored the third-highest number of runs in the American League and the most in their brief history. They trailed only Milwaukee and, unfortunately, Detroit.

As complete units, the biggest single difference between the Toronto and Detroit offenses was in their respective abilities to draw walks. The Tigers received 77 more bases on balls than the Jays did. However, unlike in recent years this difference was due more to Tiger excellence than a free-swinging performance by the Blue Jays. Indeed, the addition of Fred McGriff and Cecil Fielder as the DH tandem (80 BB in 550 PAs) was the primary reason that Toronto finally moved into the upper half of the AL in this important category. As the failure to take walks has been the most glaring weakness in Toronto's big hitters—as opposed to their lesser hitters, whose most glaring weaknesses are similar to those of Mario Mendoza—Jays fans can only hope that this is a sign of things to come.

Walks aside, Toronto's 845 runs would be sufficient to win the division nine times out of ten, given their pitching staff. And this was achieved despite platoon combinations at catcher and third base with inadequate right-handed elements; with a first baseman who was neither adept at reaching base (.321 OBP) nor hitting with power (.391 slugging); and with a combination of second basemen who combined to hit .218 (and a quiet .218 at that). Meanwhile the left-handed halves of those two platoons along with the SS, DH and OF positions provided production ranging from very good to MVP. What the Blue Jay offense most resembled was a beauty queen with Karl Malden's nose, Leon Spinks' teeth, and Fido's breath. From afar the combination is OK; get a little closer and the flaws are embarrassing. Add some key injuries and no amount of plastic surgery will repair the situation. Those of you who think the Jays choked in the final week should give your heads a shake. Removing Tony Fernandez and Ernie Whitt from this team transformed the offense from that beauty queen with a few flaws into the Elephant Man with nice hair.

At this writing nothing much has changed for 1988. Garth Iorg won't be back, so the inexplicable temptation to use him as a regular won't be there. Nelson Liriano will play at second base. While he's not the second coming of Lou Whitaker, he should be an improvement on last year's production. The holes at catcher and third base still exist, and Willie Upshaw is still on the roster. Upshaw may prevent Fielder and McGriff from getting some at-bats, which would not be a good thing. For the past two years the Jays have been admirably carried by about six players. These six were both as healthy and productive as one could realistically hope for. Methinks that can't last forever. Unless some action is taken to fill their gaping holes, the Blue Jays will be fortunate to score as many runs as they did last year.

Gord Fitzgerald

TORONTO BLUE JAYS
PITCHING

1987 SEASON											
	G	IP	H	BB	SO	SB	CS	W	L	S	ERA
Totals	498	1454.0	1323	567	1064	122	58	96	66	43	3.74
at Home	254	752.0	650	272	545	58	29	52	29	20	3.54
on Road	244	702.0	673	295	519	64	29	44	37	23	3.96
Day Games	186	515.1	475	224	380	52	21	29	28	14	4.09
Night Games	312	938.2	848	343	684	70	37	67	38	29	3.56
on Grass	193	547.1	524	241	411	49	27	35	28	19	3.95
on Artificial Turf	305	906.2	799	326	653	73	31	61	38	24	3.62
April	62	182.2	160	78	120	13	10	12	8	5	3.65
May	73	238.1	199	85	171	17	8	16	11	6	3.47
June	86	250.0	242	98	164	20	11	17	11	8	4.03
July	81	240.0	218	94	195	19	8	15	12	10	4.20
August	84	258.0	235	92	190	23	11	17	12	9	3.87
Sept/Oct	112	285.0	269	120	224	30	10	19	12	5	3.28

vs. Opponent Batters	Ave.	OBP	SLG	AB	H	2B	3B	HR	RBI	BB	SO
Totals	.244	.316	.395	5427	1323	268	40	158	620	567	1064
vs. Left	.254	.325	.401	2105	534	112	15	56	245	222	409
vs. Right	.238	.311	.392	3322	789	156	25	102	375	345	655
Bases Empty	.241	.308	.395	3184	768	155	25	95	95	293	634
Leadoff	.258	.315	.428	1346	347	65	10	48	48	110	250
Not Leadoff	.229	.302	.371	1838	421	90	15	47	47	183	384
Runners On Base	.247	.328	.395	2243	555	113	15	63	525	274	430
First Base Only	.256	.313	.403	943	241	45	8	26	75	76	172
Scoring Position	.242	.338	.390	1300	314	68	7	37	450	198	258
Late Innings, Close	.227	.313	.366	844	192	33	6	24	98	106	208

RBI/Opportunities		
Scoring Position	385 / 1826	(21%)
Scoring Position, 2 Out	158 / 872	(18%)
On Third, Less than 2 Out	141 / 330	(43%)
RBI in close games / RBI Total	414 / 620	(67%)

The Toronto Blue Jays had the best pitching staff in the Major Leagues in 1987. No rational person could dispute this statement. Opposing teams scored 655 runs against the Blue Jays; the only other American League team to permit fewer than 735 was Kansas City with 691 at spacious Royals Stadium. Toronto also allowed fewer runs than the National League leader, San Francisco. The last AL team to allow the fewest runs in the majors over the course of a season was the 1974 A's. The Jays held the opposition to two or fewer runs in a game 54 times, to three or fewer 84 times, and to four or fewer 101 times. This was accomplished in a league where the average of runs scored per team per game was 4.9!

How did they do it? With three good arms in the starting rotation and an outstanding bullpen. First the rotation. There is no pitcher in baseball I'd rather watch than Jimmy Key. In. Out. Up. Down. All the while changing speeds. The best lefty in the AL. Jim Clancy posted the seventh-best ERA of all pitchers with at least 162 innings. In light of the performances of these two, Dave Stieb's inconsistent season was sufficient for a third starter, especially in the minefield that was American League pitching in 1987. The Gang of Four (Joe Johnson, Jose Nunez, John Cerutti, and Mike Flanagan) that started the bulk of Toronto's other games averaged out as lousy.

Meanwhile, what seemed like an impossibility as recently as 1984 became a reality in 1987: The bullpen was

great. Jeff Musselman was added to the 1986 dynamic duo of Mark Eichhorn and Tom (Holy strikeouts, Batman!) Henke to form a terrific trio. Mark led the league in appearances, Tom was third and Jeff was fifth. It was often like watching a parade with manager Jimy Williams acting as Grand Marshall. Twenty-two times all three appeared in the same game, and 48 times Henke appeared in the same contest as one of the other two. Fortunately we're talking about three distinct types of pitchers: A right-handed sidewinder, a stylish lefty, and a right-handed rocket launcher. The launcher was the premier closer in the AL and yes, I do know what his W-L record was. That's what happens when you don't pad it with vulture victories.

The rotation may improve this season. The sixty starts that don't go to Key, Clancy and Stieb figure to go to Flanagan and Musselman. Mike proved that he's far from washed up by posting a 2.38 ERA in seven starts with the Blue Jay defense behind him. Jeff has followed the same path that Key took to the starting rotation, and his rookie season was more impressive than Jimmy's. John Cerutti will be the best eighth man on any staff and, if needed, will step into the rotation. Lefty Dave Wells, who was impressive after being recalled in September (24 IP, 1.50 ERA) will be given an opportunity to be this year's Musselman. This pitching staff is what will make Toronto a contender in 1988.

Gord Fitzgerald

NATIONAL LEAGUE
HITTING

	Ave.	OBP	SLG	AB	H	2B	3B	HR	RBI	BB	SO
				1987 SEASON							
Totals	.261	.328	.403	66286	17276	3125	435	1824	8238	6577	11657
vs. Left	.263	.332	.409	21554	5664	1062	132	605	2713	2207	3702
vs. Right	.260	.327	.401	44732	11612	2063	303	1219	5525	4370	7955
at Home	.265	.336	.412	32412	8599	1531	227	919	4247	3387	5515
on Road	.256	.321	.396	33874	8677	1594	208	905	3991	3190	6142
vs. Groundball	.265	.333	.396	30311	8034	1361	195	736	3776	3024	4994
vs. Flyball	.257	.325	.410	35975	9242	1764	240	1088	4462	3553	6663
vs. Finesse	.266	.326	.412	35479	9450	1700	240	999	4341	3042	5054
vs. Power	.254	.332	.393	30807	7826	1425	195	825	3897	3535	6603
on Grass	.260	.330	.405	32999	8585	1446	188	985	4092	3338	5895
on Artificial Turf	.261	.327	.402	33287	8691	1679	247	839	4146	3239	5762
Day Games	.265	.332	.418	24155	6407	1170	153	736	3064	2375	4230
Night Games	.258	.327	.395	42131	10869	1955	282	1088	5174	4202	7427
April	.258	.326	.403	8556	2204	424	53	238	1027	853	1591
May	.266	.336	.416	11162	2972	549	77	324	1475	1142	1982
June	.262	.328	.410	11239	2948	525	69	332	1450	1089	1983
July	.263	.329	.407	10822	2849	507	77	298	1307	1048	1841
August	.264	.332	.405	11889	3135	556	83	318	1478	1205	1974
Sept/Oct	.251	.320	.382	12618	3168	564	76	314	1501	1240	2286
Bases Empty	.256	.319	.399	37852	9685	1725	247	1067	1067	3299	6705
Leadoff	.264	.324	.414	16021	4237	763	105	472	472	1335	2696
Not Leadoff	.250	.315	.388	21831	5448	962	142	595	595	1964	4009
Runners On	.267	.341	.409	28434	7591	1400	188	757	7171	3278	4952
First Base Only	.281	.333	.433	11372	3198	602	69	329	973	828	1761
Scoring Position	.257	.346	.393	17062	4393	798	119	428	6198	2450	3191
Late Innings, Close	.260	.336	.388	10971	2852	491	56	266	1421	1247	2143

RBI/Opportunities		
Scoring Position	5328 / 23782	(22%)
Scoring Position, 2 Out	2080 / 10969	(19%)
On Third, Less than 2 Out	2000 / 4242	(47%)
RBI in close games / RBI Total	5337 / 8238	(65%)

In the year of the home run, a sequential offense aided by only 94 homers led the National League in runs scored for most of the season. The Cardinal offense was finally overtaken by the Mets, but not until the division title had been settled. The Redbirds had five men with at least 68 walks, and five who drove in at least 70 baserunners. New York put the same number of people on base as Saint Louis, but hit 98 more home runs. Despite the fact that the Cards stole 89 more bases, the Mets should still have outscored them by more than 25 runs. The Mets had three players combine for 104 HRs, but their offense gelled too late.

The Reds and Giants both tallied 783 runs. San Francisco had nine men in double figures for home runs; Cincinnati had eight. Atlanta scored 747 runs as they became even more dependent on Dale Murphy. He had 35 more runs and 31 more RBIs than anyone else on the club. Montreal, with 741 scores, got great years from Tims Raines and Wallach. The Expos ran a very efficient sequential offense.

Pittsburgh scored 723 runs without a true offensive star. The Cubs scored only 720 runs despite a league-best 209 home runs. Philadelphia staggered out of the gate offensively because Von Hayes was not driving in any runs and Lance Parrish wasn't hitting anything. The slow start limited the Phils' run total to 702. San Diego had four .300 hitters and 6 under .250 as they scored only 668 times. The aging Astros slumped to 11th in runs scored. LA's tawdry tally total was 635. Ten of the sixteen Dodgers with over 100 ABs hit less than .250.

The Mets shape up as the 1988 offensive power in the East. Recall that the Cards had a very strong sequential offense in 1985 that fell apart in 1986. Pendleton and Ozzie make this attack more balanced, but it was very dependent Jack Clark, and Clark is gone. Look for a decline this year. The team to watch is Philadelphia, who should gain from the addition of Phil Bradley and the acclimation of Parrish. Montreal will dip; too many players are coming off of career seasons. Pittsburgh needs a Grade-A hitting year from Van Slyke, Bonilla or Bonds. Chicago needs a leadoff man.

In the West, the Reds' fate is in the bats of their young outfield. If Eric Davis can play a full season, the Reds should easily lead the division in runs. San Francisco, another team lacking star quality, won't match last year's 205 homers. Will Clark and Candy Maldonado must have huge years in order for the Giants to match their '87 runs total. San Diego could improve as its youngsters mature. Los Angeles has a lot of men who could have big years, but their acquisition of Alfredo Griffin tells us where they are headed. Atlanta and Houston will be lucky to match last year's respective totals.

Brent MacInnes

NATIONAL LEAGUE
PITCHING

	1987 SEASON											
	G	IP	H	BB	SO	SB	CS	W	L	S	ERA
Totals	5975	17379.0	17276	6577	11657	1852	729	971	971	495	4.09
at Home	2986	8933.1	8677	3190	6142	905	370	530	441	238	3.87
on Road	2989	8445.2	8599	3387	5515	947	359	441	530	257	4.32
Day Games	2190	6296.0	6412	2375	4230	654	279	352	352	186	4.15
Night Games	3785	11083.0	10869	4202	7427	1198	450	619	619	309	4.05
on Grass	2918	8658.2	8585	3338	5895	832	393	485	485	246	4.06
on Artificial Turf	3057	8720.1	8691	3239	5762	1020	336	486	486	249	4.11
April	785	2253.2	2204	853	1591	206	97	126	126	66	3.91
May	1012	2888.0	2972	1142	1982	334	136	162	162	93	4.45
June	983	2944.1	2948	1089	1983	337	113	166	166	81	4.25
July	931	2845.2	2849	1048	1841	260	122	158	158	75	3.99
August	1051	3117.2	3135	1205	1974	350	122	173	173	81	4.07
Sept/Oct	1213	3329.2	3168	1240	2286	365	139	186	186	99	3.84

vs. Opponent Batters	Ave.	OBP	SLG	AB	H	2B	3B	HR	RBI	BB	SO
Totals	.261	.328	.403	66286	17276	3125	435	1824	8238	6577	11657
vs. Left	.268	.341	.404	27658	7416	1353	227	648	3254	3049	4493
vs. Right	.255	.319	.403	38628	9860	1772	208	1176	4984	3528	7164
Bases Empty	.256	.319	.399	37852	9685	1725	247	1067	1067	3299	6705
Leadoff	.264	.324	.414	16021	4237	763	105	472	472	1335	2696
Not Leadoff	.250	.315	.388	21831	5448	962	142	595	595	1964	4009
Runners On Base	.267	.341	.409	28434	7591	1400	188	757	7171	3278	4952
First Base Only	.281	.333	.433	11372	3198	602	69	329	973	828	1761
Scoring Position	.257	.346	.393	17062	4393	798	119	428	6198	2450	3191
Late Innings, Close	.260	.336	.388	10971	2852	491	56	266	1421	1247	2143

RBI/Opportunities		
Scoring Position	5328 / 23782	(22%)
Scoring Position, 2 Out	2080 / 10969	(19%)
On Third, Less than 2 Out	2000 / 4242	(47%)
RBI in close games / RBI Total	5337 / 8238	(65%)

San Francisco led the league in pitching in the same way that they scored a lot of runs: They got significant contributions from a lot of players, namely Garrelts, Hammaker, Downs, LaCoss and Dravecky. All these guys had ERAs under 3.68. Los Angeles had the top three IP totals in Hershiser, Welch and Valenzuela. Fernando was badly overworked, and often threw over 150 pitches in a game. The Astros fell to third in ERA because of Bob Knepper's awful season.

The great Met pitching of 1986 dropped off mainly because Gooden missed two months and Ojeda missed most of the season. Journeyman Terry Leach turned in a great year, but he couldn't offset the ballooned ERAs of Darling, McDowell and Orosco. The Cardinals had their usual socialist pitching staff, with no one winning more than eleven games. Todd Worrell (33 saves and 2.66 ERA) was their key man. Montreal's staff finished sixth, aided by great relief from Burke and McGaffigan and a 27–5 record in games started by Perez and Martinez.

Philadelphia had the most balanced starting four in Carmen, Gross, Ruffin and Rawley. All had between 200 and 230 IP and between 33 and 36 starts. Their ERAs (4.22–4.39) were also consistent, but not in the neighborhood the Phillies wanted. Steve Bedrosian saved 40 games in only 89 innings of work. Despite good performances from the young Mike Dunne and the old Rick Reuschel, the Pirates still finished 8th in ERA. The Reds had the rare combination of the worst starting rotation and the best bullpen. The

Padres gave up the most home runs and had the fewest saves in a season highlighted by Lance McCullers' 126 Ks in 123 innings. With the exception of Lee Smith, Frank DiPino and NL victory leader Rick Sutcliffe, the Cubbies were unimpressive. Despite Zane Smith, Atlanta was worse.

This year the Mets will improve. New York has a healthy starting staff and Randy Myers in place of Jesse Orosco. Montreal has the depth to get better; the Phillies should also gain. Pittsburgh needs a supporting cast to go with the young arms of Dunne, Drabek and Fisher. The Cardinals were inconsistent last year and are an unknown quantity for 1988. Chicago should be helped by Al Nipper, but Calvin Schiraldi is not Lee Smith.

San Francisco will regress in the West as several pitchers, especially Hammaker, Downs and LaCoss, won't match last year's numbers. The Dodgers' bullpen will be better but Shawn Hillegas will have a hard time replacing Bob Welch. Cincinnati will be vastly improved as Danny Jackson, Dennis Rasmussen and Jose Rijo infuse some quality into a very bad rotation. San Diego improved as the season went on but must get some mileage out of Whitson and Hawkins to move up. Houston is in the same situation; #4 and #5 starters Knepper and Deshaies must contribute. Atlanta is in disarray. They should have signed Bob Horner and taught him to pitch.

Here are the three to watch on the mound this year: Danny Jackson, Don Carman and Floyd Youmans.

Brent MacInnes

ATLANTA BRAVES
HITTING

	Ave.	OBP	SLG	AB	H	2B	3B	HR	RBI	BB	SO
						**1987 SEASON**					
Totals	.258	.339	.403	5428	1401	284	24	152	696	641	834
vs. Left	.257	.347	.412	1577	405	87	7	48	223	215	240
vs. Right	.259	.335	.400	3851	996	197	17	104	473	426	594
at Home	.277	.367	.436	2668	739	143	17	82	391	371	373
on Road	.240	.310	.372	2760	662	141	7	70	305	270	461
vs. Groundball	.262	.338	.400	2417	634	124	11	62	312	264	364
vs. Flyball	.255	.340	.406	3011	767	160	13	90	384	377	470
vs. Finesse	.271	.342	.422	2856	775	166	11	81	363	293	362
vs. Power	.243	.335	.382	2572	626	118	13	71	333	348	472
on Grass	.262	.347	.408	3982	1042	194	21	115	534	507	600
on Artificial Turf	.248	.314	.391	1446	359	90	3	37	162	134	234
Day Games	.263	.341	.413	1946	511	100	6	60	248	227	290
Night Games	.256	.337	.398	3482	890	184	18	92	448	414	544
April	.269	.361	.405	707	190	46	1	16	86	94	127
May	.272	.354	.455	1012	275	59	6	38	163	130	155
June	.252	.342	.405	898	226	40	4	30	115	119	131
July	.239	.310	.352	867	207	42	4	16	87	88	115
August	.268	.334	.421	920	247	45	4	29	121	91	136
Sept/Oct	.250	.333	.378	1024	256	52	5	23	124	119	170
Bases Empty	.261	.332	.415	3061	799	161	17	92	92	308	457
Leadoff	.270	.336	.417	1313	355	76	7	34	34	124	196
Not Leadoff	.254	.329	.414	1748	444	85	10	58	58	184	261
Runners On	.254	.347	.388	2367	602	123	7	60	604	333	377
First Base Only	.250	.321	.389	929	232	50	2	25	72	91	149
Scoring Position	.257	.363	.388	1438	370	73	5	35	532	242	228
Late Innings, Close	.242	.325	.349	868	210	41	2	16	101	102	161

RBI/Opportunities		
Scoring Position	465 / 2084	(22%)
Scoring Position, 2 Out	179 / 940	(19%)
On Third, Less than 2 Out	182 / 382	(48%)
RBI in close games / RBI Total	446 / 696	(64%)

Despite an awful second half, the 1987 Braves improved tremendously over their pitiful 1986 offensive performance. Atlanta's runs scored were up a whopping 21 percent, much more than the league increase of 8 percent. The Braves also outperformed their runs created estimate (736) by 11 runs, which is amazing given how poorly suited they are for their home park and manager Chuck Tanner's novel ideas on lineup selection. Four regulars (Dale Murphy, Glenn Hubbard, Ozzie Virgil and the LF platoon) provided significantly better production over 1986. The addition of Dion James gave the club its best leadoff hitter since Brett Butler.

The Braves did two things well in 1987: They got on base and hit doubles. They tied for second in the league with the Mets for OBA and missed leading in walks by three. With the exception of Andres Thomas, every regular was willing to take a walk. The team's doubles total was third in the league as James, Gerald Perry and Hubbard all had more than thirty.

The obvious problem with the offense is that no one except Dale Murphy was driving in all those baserunners. The Braves had more LOB in 1987 than anyone except the Mets. Murph had 105 RBIs despite being continually pitched around; no one else had more than 74. Tokyo Bob Horner is despised in Atlanta, but he is exactly the type of player the Braves need to balance their offense. Murphy and Virgil were the only legitimate power threats, accounting for 47 percent of the team's HRs. The lineup is filled with contact hitters, easily leading the league in fewest strikeouts.

The Braves would probably improve offensively if they had a manager who had an idea of how to select a batting order. Tanner used Andres Thomas extensively in the #2 slot despite his .268 OBA. Chuck eventually moved him to #6, where his .312 SLG could cause maximum damage. There were obvious alternatives for both hitting positions with Hubbard (.378 OBA) and Virgil (.471 SLG). Tanner usually batted Perry third, where he compiled fine stats—for a middle infielder. His numbers were clearly inadequate for a first baseman.

Can the club improve in 1988? With this group of players it looks impossible. If Murphy has a better year than 1987 he'll be the obvious MVP. Hubbard's reward for his fine year was his release; his likely replacement has never played AAA. The LF platoon is being sent to the bench so that James can play in left—the new CF is unlikely to outproduce the platoon. Perry might improve, but he is 27. Few 27-year-olds significantly raise the level of their play. Like all teams in hitters' parks, Atlanta practically has to lead the league in runs scored in order to contend. Nearly everything had to go right last year for this offense to move all the way up to average, and every maneuver they are making for 1988 is working against further improvement. It looks like another long year for America's Team.

Greg Gajus

ATLANTA BRAVES
PITCHING

						1987 SEASON						
	G	IP	H	BB	SO	SB	CS	W	L	S	ERA	
Totals	485	1427.2	1529	587	837	185	54	69	92	32	4.63	
at Home	247	737.0	820	285	428	91	26	42	39	19	4.91	
on Road	238	690.2	709	302	409	94	28	27	53	13	4.34	
Day Games	185	503.1	579	211	271	68	22	20	36	8	4.88	
Night Games	300	924.1	951	376	566	117	32	49	56	24	4.50	
on Grass	357	1069.2	1141	414	608	123	43	56	63	23	4.61	
on Artificial Turf	128	358.0	388	173	229	62	11	13	29	9	4.70	
April	64	188.0	199	70	116	15	10	9	12	2	4.07	
May	90	263.0	293	108	155	34	11	16	12	10	4.72	
June	77	237.2	233	78	144	33	6	11	16	6	4.32	
July	70	227.2	239	88	137	26	9	9	17	4	4.43	
August	79	239.1	264	109	137	41	5	11	17	2	5.08	
Sept/Oct	105	272.0	301	134	148	36	13	13	18	8	5.00	

vs. Opponent Batters	Ave.	OBP	SLG	AB	H	2B	3B	HR	RBI	BB	SO
Totals	.276	.347	.421	5532	1529	253	30	163	793	587	837
vs. Left	.288	.362	.433	2323	668	111	14	66	325	271	340
vs. Right	.268	.337	.413	3209	861	142	16	97	468	316	497
Bases Empty	.266	.330	.409	3077	818	141	17	88	88	279	456
Leadoff	.278	.338	.435	1315	365	59	8	44	44	109	174
Not Leadoff	.257	.325	.389	1762	453	82	9	44	44	170	282
Runners On Base	.290	.367	.437	2455	711	112	13	75	705	308	381
First Base Only	.297	.360	.463	958	285	49	7	32	95	86	105
Scoring Position	.285	.371	.421	1497	426	63	6	43	610	222	276
Late Innings, Close	.308	.381	.465	802	247	50	2	24	133	92	113

RBI/Opportunities			
Scoring Position		523 / 2126	(25%)
Scoring Position, 2 Out		225 / 1013	(22%)
On Third, Less than 2 Out		176 / 361	(49%)
RBI in close games / RBI Total		506 / 793	(64%)

About the best thing that can be said about the Braves' pitching in 1987 is that it was a team effort. Starters, closers, and middle relief, both the rookies and the veterans, all shared the same stink. Atlanta was last in the league in ERA, saves, shutouts, hits and runs allowed, hit batters and strikeouts. The pitchers who produced this disaster were pretty much the same group who performed fairly well in 1986. But in 1987 they allowed 100 more hits and 46 more home runs.

The entire staff throws 83-mph fastballs, gets a lot of groundballs, allows a lot of hits, tries to keep the ball in the park, relies on the defense, and couldn't strike out Bo Jackson. When executed well, this is an ideal approach to pitching in Fulton County Stadium, but a little variety wouldn't hurt. The Braves got rid of the only two pitchers (Doyle Alexander and Dave Palmer) who deviated from the style. Also, the staff was relying on a defense that was, at best, below average. Second base and right field were the only two positions where there was quality leather. Notice the difference between Doyle Alexander (Braves) and Doyle Alexander (Tigers)?

One of the mysteries of baseball is why managers are so reluctant to give players a chance when things aren't working. While his hurlers were being shelled with regularity, Chuck Tanner refused to give chances to pitchers whose work merited an extended trial. Both Jeff Dedmon and Charlie Puleo pitched well in the limited opportunities they received, but with the Atlanta youth movement they will probably be bypassed again this year.

The Braves did make some progress in identifying their pitching problems. Rick Mahler was finally bumped from the rotation after a year and a half of disastrous hurling, and 40-year-old Gene Garber was dealt to Kansas City. The trade of Alexander and the signing of Palmer by the Phillies will leave an extremely young staff here in 1988.

Despite this near-total commitment to youth, the Braves pitching will improve this year; after all, it could hardly be worse. Dion James is moving from center field (where he was inadequate) to left, where he will be a defensive improvement over the Ken Griffey/Gary Roenicke platoon. James will be replaced in CF by Albert Hall or Terry Blocker—either would be an improvement defensively. The loss of Glenn Hubbard will hurt, but Ronnie Gant displayed good range in his limited September trial. Learning to pitch in a hitters' park is a difficult proposition (just ask the Cubs), but the Braves have several possible candidates. The best of the group, Derek Lilliquist, saw little action due to a late signing, but should be ready in 1988. If just two of the youngsters develop and Jim Acker evolves into a closer the Braves' pitching will be better than in 1987. And if they are extraordinarily lucky, Bruce (remember him?) Sutter will come back. . . .

Greg Gajus

CHICAGO CUBS
HITTING

	Ave.	OBP	SLG	AB	H	2B	3B	HR	RBI	BB	SO
				1987 SEASON							
Totals	.264	.326	.432	5584	1476	244	33	209	683	504	1064
vs. Left	.270	.335	.418	1283	346	54	5	42	150	126	245
vs. Right	.263	.323	.436	4301	1130	190	28	167	533	378	819
at Home	.272	.333	.457	2753	750	123	21	114	369	249	503
on Road	.256	.319	.408	2831	726	121	12	95	314	255	561
vs. Groundball	.269	.332	.412	2387	642	94	14	73	281	225	399
vs. Flyball	.261	.322	.447	3197	834	150	19	136	402	279	665
vs. Finesse	.275	.329	.449	3248	893	152	24	122	387	262	497
vs. Power	.250	.322	.408	2336	583	92	9	87	296	242	567
on Grass	.266	.329	.438	3900	1039	164	22	154	504	360	729
on Artificial Turf	.260	.319	.418	1684	437	80	11	55	179	144	335
Day Games	.268	.329	.447	3612	967	157	26	146	464	325	666
Night Games	.258	.321	.405	1972	509	87	7	63	219	179	398
April	.256	.323	.415	684	175	31	3	24	82	67	107
May	.260	.321	.432	1006	262	42	4	41	123	91	179
June	.273	.330	.440	985	269	46	8	34	127	81	187
July	.281	.341	.456	858	241	31	4	37	113	76	179
August	.275	.337	.470	1011	278	46	5	47	132	96	189
Sept/Oct	.241	.307	.380	1040	251	48	9	26	106	93	223
Bases Empty	.271	.327	.457	3215	872	148	23	134	134	257	635
Leadoff	.273	.320	.453	1350	368	70	6	54	54	90	243
Not Leadoff	.270	.333	.459	1865	504	78	17	80	80	167	392
Runners On	.255	.324	.399	2369	604	96	10	75	549	247	429
First Base Only	.277	.325	.448	1012	280	49	2	40	97	70	165
Scoring Position	.239	.323	.363	1357	324	47	8	35	452	177	264
Late Innings, Close	.280	.348	.433	842	236	27	3	32	115	88	172

RBI/Opportunities			
Scoring Position	392 / 1843	(21%)	
Scoring Position, 2 Out	149 / 852	(17%)	
On Third, Less than 2 Out	149 / 335	(44%)	
RBI in close games / RBI Total	430 / 683	(63%)	

One may wonder how a team that led the league in home runs could end up mired in the basement. Actually, it can be very easy. The Cubs scored 720 runs and allowed 801, which projects to a record of 72–89 (one game against Atlanta was not played). They were in reality four games better than that. However, using the basic runs created formula, Chicago should have scored 784 runs, which would project to 79–82. The question should be: Why did the Cubs underproduce runs by 8 percent?

The main force in the Chicago attack was Andre Dawson, for those of you summering in Antarctica. Not only did he hit a ton of homers, he gave the team and the fans a measure of hope that the Cubs could come from behind—a number of his home runs came late in close games. Despite well-publicized knee troubles, he managed to play in 153 games, which was important to a team platooning in the two other outfield slots. Those platoons, by the way, were very successful. CFs Dave Martinez and Bob Dernier combined for a .299 average and 32 SBs. LFs Jerry Mumphrey and Brian Dayett combined for a .312 average and 18 HRs (Rafael Palmeiro and his 6.3 HR% spent some time in left also). On a championship team these platoons would be widely hailed; on a last place team they are forgotten. Manager Gene Michael sure knew how to use his outfielders.

Look at this sequence: 15, 16, 16, 14, 12, 27. This is home run output as a regular over Keith Moreland's ca-reer—all with Wrigley Field as his home park. In the year of the "rabbit ball" and corked bats, few noticed this sudden and dramatic increase by the Cub third baseman. It is almost unheard of for a player to do this at age 33, and thus surprising that Moreland's bat was never checked.

The rest of the infield was fairly quiet. Ryne Sandberg rebounded from an off-year to .294, with 21/23 SB, and Shawon Dunston continued to deny his potential, but both missed a large part of the season due to injury. It was then that the slim chance the Cubs had in the race faded to nothing. Leon "Bull" Durham hit for power at home again while spending much more time than usual on the bench. Jody Davis turned in a very typical year, except for an RBI dropoff.

Why the low run production? The Cubs had the third-lowest base on balls total in the NL in 1987. They didn't get enough people on base because they didn't walk. When Chicago players did reach, they stole fewer bases than anyone and had a lower-than-average percentage, despite Sandberg and the centerfielders. The Cubbies struck out 10 percent more than an average team, so they weren't advancing their men on outs. But take heart, Cub fans—even if everything had gone right, you were still a good ten games behind the Cardinals.

John Stryker

CHICAGO CUBS
PITCHING

	G	IP	H	BB	SO	SB	CS	W	L	S	ERA
						1987 SEASON					
Totals	488	1434.2	1524	628	1024	169	69	76	85	47	4.56
at Home	241	736.1	758	322	548	83	38	40	40	22	4.35
on Road	247	698.1	766	306	476	86	31	36	45	25	4.79
Day Games	326	947.1	1016	419	689	109	48	48	57	28	4.58
Night Games	162	487.1	508	209	335	60	21	28	28	19	4.54
on Grass	337	1020.0	1070	445	745	116	49	54	59	33	4.53
on Artificial Turf	151	414.2	454	183	279	53	20	22	26	14	4.67
April	56	180.1	173	79	140	27	12	10	10	6	3.64
May	90	260.0	235	110	178	32	11	18	10	13	3.81
June	86	253.1	281	121	185	30	9	12	17	8	4.83
July	66	220.0	235	80	166	23	15	12	13	7	4.34
August	97	251.0	296	138	168	31	12	14	14	8	5.59
Sept/Oct	93	270.0	304	100	187	26	10	10	21	5	4.90

vs. Opponent Batters	Ave.	OBP	SLG	AB	H	2B	3B	HR	RBI	BB	SO
Totals	.275	.349	.425	5541	1524	267	43	159	761	628	1024
vs. Left	.297	.375	.466	2390	710	143	27	69	325	296	396
vs. Right	.258	.330	.394	3151	814	124	16	90	436	332	628
Bases Empty	.272	.341	.424	3040	828	151	21	89	89	303	601
Leadoff	.268	.334	.424	1308	350	66	14	37	37	124	248
Not Leadoff	.276	.347	.423	1732	478	85	7	52	52	179	353
Runners On Base	.278	.358	.426	2501	696	116	22	70	672	325	423
First Base Only	.284	.342	.444	987	280	49	5	33	90	82	164
Scoring Position	.275	.368	.415	1514	416	67	17	37	582	243	259
Late Innings, Close	.281	.364	.413	901	253	41	6	22	132	117	179

RBI/Opportunities		
Scoring Position	505 / 2140	(24%)
Scoring Position, 2 Out	186 / 985	(19%)
On Third, Less than 2 Out	189 / 375	(50%)
RBI in close games / RBI Total	454 / 761	(60%)

For the Chicago Cubs to be successful, they do not need the best pitching numbers in the league; Wrigley Field allows too many cheap runs for an ERA title to ever be a likelihood. But the club cannot afford the worst stats either, unless their offense is unquestionably the best in history. The 1987 Cubs ranked eleventh in ERA, and gave Atlanta a run for their money for last. Pitching doomed the North Siders.

Incredibly, this staff had one of the league's best pitchers. Rick Sutcliffe came within two votes of his second Cy Young Award (needless to say, no last place club has ever had both an MVP and a Cy Young Award winner). His ERA of 3.68 could best be described as "good for Wrigley," but he pitched through severe pain in a finger on his pitching hand in mid-season. He was outstanding when healthy, and again appears to be the staff ace the Cubs signed to a long-term contract after the 1984 season.

Other than Sutcliffe, the starting pitching was dreadful. Kids Jamie Moyer and Greg Maddux had decent first halves, then collapsed as the season progressed. Whether they can make it at this level is to be seen, but they still rate as promising. Les Lancaster benefited from some timely support (8–3, 4.90 ERA). Steve Trout pitched two shutouts; he thus proved he didn't belong and was promptly exiled to the Yankees, where he finally pitched like a Cub. Ed Lynch, Mike Mason, Bob Tewksbury, and even Dickie Noles(!) started also; manager Gene Michael was grasping at straws in a bad situation.

Chicago relief was adequate, as it has always been in the Lee Smith era. Lee had another fine season (36 saves for a last-place team), but was jeered unmercifully on the dozen or so occasions that he lost the lead. The callers to sports talk shows were vicious on those days; I wonder if they will miss him now that he is gone. While Dickie Noles and Frank DiPino had fine years in support of Smith, the rest of the long relief crew didn't. Most often it made no difference, as the young starters dug too deep of a hole to get out of. A key management decision for 1988 will be what role to assign to new acquisition Calvin Schiraldi.

The main theme of this staff: Lack of Control. The Cubs walked 15 percent more men than the league average, and you can't blame that on the park. Wrigley actually makes those walks more dangerous—free passes are a death sentence when the wind is blowing out. No man on this staff was innocent, though Sutcliffe and Smith could be excused because of their otherwise fine performances. With all the young arms there may be hope for education, but new general manager Jim Frey had better see that some learning takes place. Bad habits like these are hard to break. Bases on balls are the first step down the basement stairs.

John Stryker

CINCINNATI REDS
HITTING

	1987 SEASON										
	Ave.	OBP	SLG	AB	H	2B	3B	HR	RBI	BB	SO
Totals	.266	.329	.427	5561	1477	262	29	192	748	514	928
vs. Left	.268	.338	.425	1630	437	79	6	55	221	166	293
vs. Right	.265	.326	.427	3931	1040	183	23	137	527	348	635
at Home	.268	.335	.431	2729	732	135	13	94	378	267	409
on Road	.263	.324	.423	2832	745	127	16	98	370	247	519
vs. Groundball	.272	.339	.429	2524	686	114	16	84	362	253	377
vs. Flyball	.260	.321	.424	3037	791	148	13	108	386	261	551
vs. Finesse	.272	.331	.440	2873	781	141	16	103	378	248	390
vs. Power	.259	.328	.413	2688	696	121	13	89	370	266	538
on Grass	.254	.322	.423	1651	420	76	10	61	206	163	288
on Artificial Turf	.270	.332	.428	3910	1057	186	19	131	542	351	640
Day Games	.258	.325	.425	1987	512	94	8	74	250	191	339
Night Games	.270	.332	.428	3574	965	168	21	118	498	323	589
April	.283	.348	.484	761	215	41	8	32	123	75	144
May	.258	.319	.418	924	238	39	2	35	128	79	155
June	.252	.316	.435	912	230	52	5	35	124	83	168
July	.279	.331	.425	951	265	40	6	29	135	70	140
August	.245	.320	.367	964	236	36	2	26	102	105	152
Sept/Oct	.279	.344	.442	1049	293	54	6	35	136	102	169
Bases Empty	.256	.314	.405	3225	824	134	15	106	106	258	543
Leadoff	.272	.330	.436	1338	364	56	5	51	51	112	216
Not Leadoff	.244	.302	.383	1887	460	78	10	55	55	146	327
Runners On	.280	.350	.457	2336	653	128	14	86	642	256	385
First Base Only	.285	.330	.468	986	281	49	7	39	102	62	128
Scoring Position	.276	.364	.449	1350	372	79	7	47	540	194	257
Late Innings, Close	.251	.321	.370	891	224	40	3	20	122	90	179

RBI/Opportunities		
Scoring Position	445 / 1902	(23%)
Scoring Position, 2 Out	165 / 875	(19%)
On Third, Less than 2 Out	151 / 310	(49%)
RBI in close games / RBI Total	472 / 748	(63%)

The 1975 World Champion Reds are remembered as one of the great teams of all time. Compare some of their offensive statistics to those of the 1987 team:

	1975 Reds	1987 Reds
Batting Average	.271	.266
Stolen Bases	168	169
Home Runs	124	192

The numbers for the current Reds make their offense look much more effective than it really was. Despite hitting 68 more homers than the '75 Champs and having a comparable BA and SB figure, the Reds' 1987 edition scored 57 fewer runs. The reason is bases on balls. The Champs took a whopping 177 more walks (691–514). That is a difference of more than one baserunner a game! How about contemporary comparisons? The Atlanta Braves hit eight points lower as a team than the Reds, but their OBP was nine points higher because they outwalked Cincinnati 641–514. The Mets' BA/SB/HR figures were a match with those of the Reds. Yet New York took 78 more passes and scored 40 more runs. The Cardinals outscored the Reds despite a lower BA and 98 fewer home runs. By now you know why.

How does Cincinnati plan to address their poor OBP situation? No one knows, least of all manager Pete Rose, who has not even recognized that there is a problem. Lets go down his probable 1988 lineup against RHP:

Tracy Jones will lead off. He took one walk per 17 plate appearances (1:17). His OBP was just barely above the league average, making his leadoff qualifications questionable. Then comes Jeff Treadway(1:40+). The core of the lineup, Kal Daniels, Eric Davis and Buddy Bell, can't be faulted. Their OBPs were as good as their other numbers. The good news stops at the six hole and Nick Esasky (1:13), then gets worse with Bo Diaz (1:27). Barry Larkin finishes the lineup at 1:14.

The organization unloaded Dave Parker while he still had some value. However, the Reds missed the same opportunity with Bo Diaz. He slumped sickeningly after the All-Star game, and will never again put up good offensive numbers. Despite writing off Bo's bat, Cincinnati does figure to improve some offensively. Jones and Paul O'Neill each created more runs per plate appearance than Parker did last year. Rose finally did retire, and has committed to playing Esasky every day at first base. Maybe the team will even catch a break and get injury-free seasons out of DiMaggio and Williams—er, Davis and Daniels. All in all, the offense looks even better going into 1988 than it did going into 1987, when the Reds seemed a cinch to take the NL West. Rose now knows how good Davis and Daniels are; he can't give 600 at-bats to Parker anymore; Esasky will get a fair shot at first, and Buddy Bell figures to have at least one more productive year. Oh, and they released Terry Francona!

Mike Marrero & Roger Weber

CINCINNATI REDS
PITCHING

	G	IP	H	BB	SO	SB	CS	W	L	S	ERA
						1987 SEASON					
Totals	554	1452.1	1486	485	919	140	68	84	78	43	4.24
at Home	296	745.0	780	239	477	62	28	42	39	19	4.41
on Road	258	707.1	706	246	442	78	40	42	39	24	4.07
Day Games	195	523.0	512	149	353	39	23	32	26	14	4.04
Night Games	359	929.1	974	336	566	101	45	52	52	29	4.36
on Grass	154	416.1	417	166	252	40	29	24	24	14	4.06
on Artificial Turf	400	1036.0	1069	319	667	100	39	60	54	29	4.32
April	74	200.0	170	55	116	8	9	15	7	6	3.19
May	86	236.2	256	69	158	28	8	13	14	7	4.83
June	98	242.1	261	88	146	27	10	14	13	7	4.83
July	91	245.2	286	80	151	19	10	13	14	6	4.87
August	92	253.2	266	93	159	26	14	9	20	6	4.36
Sept/Oct	113	274.0	247	100	189	32	17	20	10	11	3.32

vs. Opponent Batters	Ave.	OBP	SLG	AB	H	2B	3B	HR	RBI	BB	SO
Totals	.267	.326	.429	5558	1486	311	39	170	721	485	919
vs. Left	.276	.341	.426	2007	553	116	16	51	249	205	298
vs. Right	.263	.317	.431	3551	933	195	23	119	472	280	621
Bases Empty	.262	.315	.427	3246	849	164	18	112	112	243	548
Leadoff	.275	.324	.445	1355	372	81	6	46	46	97	214
Not Leadoff	.252	.308	.414	1891	477	83	12	66	66	146	334
Runners On Base	.276	.341	.433	2312	637	147	21	58	609	242	371
First Base Only	.268	.310	.415	956	256	59	8	22	79	53	137
Scoring Position	.281	.361	.445	1356	381	88	13	36	530	189	234
Late Innings, Close	.260	.333	.378	835	217	40	4	17	93	93	143

RBI/Opportunities		
Scoring Position	462 / 1877	(25%)
Scoring Position, 2 Out	190 / 888	(21%)
On Third, Less than 2 Out	161 / 330	(49%)
RBI in close games / RBI Total	446 / 721	(62%)

If they could have figured out a way to begin their games in the seventh inning, the Cincinnati pitching staff would have been with the league leaders. John Franco, Rob Murphy and Frank Williams were the best in a remarkable pen that set a new major league record for number of appearances. But since all NL games start in the first inning, the Reds had to keep using their starters, and those guys were just terrible. Too often in 1987 the game was already lost by the seventh inning.

Mario Soto's arm problems did him in again in May. The Reds are not counting on him for 1988. Tom Browning pitched poorly early, and did not improve during a Nashville rehab stint. The big club had to recall him in midsummer, whereupon he reported to management that his arm had been bothering him in April. Then Cincinnati traded Bill Gullickson's gopher ball to the Yankees for Dennis Rasmussen's. Dennis pitched moderately well in his NL debut, but it says here that the hitters will begin to rip into him on his second time through the league this year.

A composite of the '87 Cincinnati staff would be a control pitcher who threw the ball over the plate and let 'em hit it. The Reds had the fewest wild pitches in the majors, tied for fewest hit batsmen, and only the Expos issued fewer walks. But they were among the league's worst in home runs and hits allowed.

GM Murray Cook got Danny Jackson for manager Pete Rose this winter. Pete loves southpaws, perhaps because he couldn't hit them. Jackson won 37 games for Kansas City in just over three seasons. Danny can expect much more offensive support from the Reds than he received from the Royals. December brought Jose "Blame It On" Rijo and Tim Birtsas from Oakland for Dave Parker. Birtsas looks like damaged goods. A story going around Cincinnati has it that, after the consummation of the trade, A's GM Sandy Alderson teased Mr. Cook. "Congratulations, Murray! You got two good arms. Problem is, they both belong to Rijo."

Indeed, the Reds aren't counting on either of these ex-A's for 1988. Cook has said, "We feel we are pretty well set with the addition of Jackson." Yet the Reds will lack for right-handed starting depth without Soto, particularly if sophomore Pat Pacillo can't improve on his miserable 1987. The only righty certain to pitch every fourth or fifth day is Ron Robinson. For the Reds' pitching to improve, Browning has to return to his form of '85–'86 and Jackson will have to pitch at the level Gullickson did in '86. The Reds still look one starter short of a decent rotation. Murray Cook to the contrary, Jose Rijo is this team's best bet to be that starter. However the rotation turns out, look for Cincinnati to overtake San Francisco this year.

Mike Marrero and Roger Weber

HOUSTON ASTROS
HITTING

	Ave.	OBP	SLG	AB	H	2B	3B	HR	RBI	BB	SO
1987 SEASON											
Totals	.253	.318	.373	5486	1386	237	28	122	603	526	936
vs. Left	.246	.314	.363	1990	489	81	9	45	207	193	363
vs. Right	.257	.321	.378	3496	897	156	19	77	396	333	573
at Home	.263	.332	.369	2717	714	113	11	51	306	281	479
on Road	.243	.305	.377	2769	672	124	17	71	297	245	457
vs. Groundball	.261	.334	.389	2529	661	113	16	59	306	271	401
vs. Flyball	.245	.304	.359	2957	725	124	12	63	297	255	535
vs. Finesse	.261	.318	.380	2852	745	121	15	63	314	236	407
vs. Power	.243	.319	.364	2634	641	116	13	59	289	290	529
on Grass	.244	.312	.378	1662	406	72	6	46	189	160	272
on Artificial Turf	.256	.321	.371	3824	980	165	22	76	414	366	664
Day Games	.241	.301	.361	1736	418	72	5	42	182	151	303
Night Games	.258	.326	.378	3750	968	165	23	80	421	375	633
April	.259	.311	.393	721	187	34	1	20	77	53	122
May	.262	.336	.386	901	236	50	7	16	108	102	145
June	.246	.315	.378	912	224	35	4	26	106	94	185
July	.250	.310	.371	900	225	41	7	18	89	78	132
August	.265	.333	.378	1000	265	41	6	20	117	101	167
Sept/Oct	.237	.303	.339	1052	249	36	3	22	106	98	185
Bases Empty	.253	.314	.372	3144	795	132	18	69	69	265	526
Leadoff	.268	.323	.399	1340	359	58	6	35	35	104	210
Not Leadoff	.242	.307	.353	1804	436	74	12	34	34	161	316
Runners On	.252	.323	.374	2342	591	105	10	53	534	261	410
First Base Only	.261	.313	.382	970	253	43	3	23	67	69	152
Scoring Position	.246	.330	.367	1372	338	62	7	30	467	192	258
Late Innings, Close	.271	.346	.381	984	267	46	4	18	123	114	170

RBI/Opportunities		
Scoring Position	399 / 1902	(21%)
Scoring Position, 2 Out	157 / 933	(17%)
On Third, Less than 2 Out	151 / 310	(49%)
RBI in close games / RBI Total	413 / 603	(68%)

Only three National League teams scored fewer runs in 1987 than they did in 1986, and the Astros were one of them. While their offense produced at just under the same rate as the previous year, the rest of the league blew right past them. The Astros dropped from 8th to 11th in scoring, ahead of only the Albuquerque West squad at Dodger Stadium; their total was 83 runs below the NL average. This made it two straight years of the Hal Lanier regime in which the run total has dropped. Oh yeah—the Astros also lost 20 more games than they did in '86.

The impotence of the Astros offense is evident when you examine the league LOB figures. Only the Dodgers put fewer men on base than Houston, but the Astros had the fifth-highest number left on. Sure, they were a successful base stealing team, but the SBs were irrelevant; they just meant that the baserunners were left standing on second instead of first. Talk about run support! Nolan Ryan, the National League's most effective starting pitcher in 1987, lost twice as many games as he won despite giving up only 2.2 runs per start.

Houston had platooned at shortstop and third base successfully in '86, and was hoping to do the same in '87. In addition, management wanted to platoon at catcher too, since switch-hitting Alan Ashby has a much better OBP when batting from the left side, and needed to be rested any-

way. It was no secret around the league that the Astros could not hit left-handed pitching last year. A big reason is that the righty halves of the infield platoons did poorly. Third baseman Phil Garner was shipped out and shortstop Dickie Thon, sadly, had to leave because he just could not see well. Then the club brought up players from Tucson so often it was ridiculous. All these guys did was demonstrate why they had not made the club in April. When the farmhand approach failed, Houston made a bold move and traded for late-night television star Buddy (.213 lifetime) Biancalana. Buddy contributed one hit to the cause. Finally, new GM Bill Wood got to work on the problem over the winter, and has brought in two new players. Too bad neither one is going to help the scoring. His RHB shortstop acquisition, Rafael Ramirez, has reverse platoon figures and can't hit lefties. His new RHB catcher, Marc Sullivan, has never been known to hit any type of pitching.

There is some right-handed hitting on the roster; for the club to prosper Billy Hatcher and Glenn Davis, along with switch hitters Bill Doran, Kevin Bass and Gerald Young will have to string some hits together. NL teams will be loading up the southpaws for Houston again this year, so these people will be the offensive key for the Astros in 1988.

Welford McCaffrey

494

HOUSTON ASTROS
PITCHING

						1987 SEASON						
	G	IP	H	BB	SO	SB	CS	W	L	S	ERA	
Totals	478	1441.1	1363	525	1138	199	52	76	86	34	3.84	
at Home	233	751.0	645	234	620	97	19	47	34	19	2.88	
on Road	245	690.1	718	291	518	102	33	29	52	15	4.90	
Day Games	157	451.1	447	187	349	58	20	21	31	12	4.75	
Night Games	321	990.0	919	338	789	141	32	55	55	22	3.44	
on Grass	157	412.2	448	183	311	67	18	17	31	9	5.19	
on Artificial Turf	321	1028.2	915	342	827	132	34	59	55	25	3.31	
April	65	189.2	170	62	181	18	10	12	9	6	3.46	
May	80	236.0	195	94	197	31	10	12	15	4	4.04	
June	75	245.2	229	77	205	30	5	16	11	7	3.92	
July	74	235.0	230	104	173	33	8	10	17	5	3.79	
August	89	261.0	271	74	184	35	6	15	14	7	3.76	
Sept/Oct	95	274.0	268	114	198	52	13	11	20	5	4.01	

vs. Opponent Batters	Ave.	OBP	SLG	AB	H	2B	3B	HR	RBI	BB	SO
Totals	.250	.317	.387	5451	1363	225	48	141	641	525	1138
vs. Left	.251	.328	.376	2255	567	87	23	49	241	250	443
vs. Right	.249	.310	.394	3196	796	138	25	92	400	275	695
Bases Empty	.235	.298	.373	3219	756	133	28	85	85	271	698
Leadoff	.222	.275	.338	1348	299	44	8	32	32	93	282
Not Leadoff	.244	.314	.398	1871	457	89	20	53	53	178	416
Runners On Base	.272	.344	.406	2232	607	92	20	56	556	254	440
First Base Only	.291	.340	.444	858	250	40	11	23	74	60	146
Scoring Position	.260	.346	.383	1374	357	52	9	33	482	194	294
Late Innings, Close	.246	.318	.351	870	214	39	8	12	104	87	202

	RBI/Opportunities	
Scoring Position	415 / 1893	(22%)
Scoring Position, 2 Out	190 / 917	(21%)
On Third, Less than 2 Out	148 / 331	(45%)
RBI in close games / RBI Total	422 / 641	(66%)

Pitching may not mean everything in baseball, but it sure means a lot to the Houston Astros. In 1986, despite tallying fewer runs than the National league average, Houston outscored its opponents by 85 runs. That '86 staff had the NL's lowest opposition runs total. But things didn't go quite as well for them last year. Opponents scored 109 more runs, almost double the league average scoring increase (56). However, this total was still low enough for the staff to place third in runs allowed.

Nolan Ryan had a super year. He had the National League's lowest ERA among starters who worked at least 75 innings. Nolan also claimed the league strikeout title. In fact, the only two pitchers to surpass 200 Ks in 1987 pitched for Houston. Mike Scott, of course, was the other. The opinion around the league was that Scott was bringing garnets to the diamond, as in garnet paper. Mike had a 4.45 ERA in his first six NL years. Foes are convinced that customized baseballs were the reason he cut that figure in half during his '86 Cy Young campaign. Mike continued that pace through June 21 last year, when he was 9–3, 2.10. The Astros were a half game out. But then he turned into the old Mike Scott for the rest of the year, winning only 7 more games out of 17 decisions. Was baseball's anti-scuff campaign the reason? Despite all the accusations, he has never been caught with a pocket workshop, so no one can say for sure.

The fifth man in the Houston rotation, Danny Darwin, pitched up to expectations. The same could not be said for the #3 and #4 men. Bob Knepper had his worst year ever. At times he looked like a batting practice pitcher. Jim Deshaies had arm problems starting in June and went on the disabled list in July. He did not pitch as well as his W-L record indicates, and was never consistent.

A non-starter also regressed. Charlie Kerfeld, the big man in middle relief for Houston in '86, was the big man only at his waistline in '87. But others in the pen did well. Larry Anderson was effective as set-up man for Dave Smith, the club's primo last out specialist (60 IP and 44 finishes in 50 appearances). Juan Agosto, Rocky Childress and Jeff Heathcock all did well in limited action, and provided at least hope for future middle relief.

The Astros must have outstanding pitching offsetting their weak offense to contend. There are three strong starters and two top relief men. However, there are two questions in the rotation and a shaky middle relief corps. Kerfeld's progress down on the fat farm, and the recoveries of Knepper and Deshaies will determine Houston's finish this year.

Welford McCaffrey

LOS ANGELES DODGERS
HITTING

	Ave.	OBP	SLG	AB	H	2B	3B	HR	RBI	BB	SO
						1987 SEASON					
Totals	.252	.309	.371	5517	1389	236	23	125	595	445	923
vs. Left	.265	.323	.389	1805	479	92	9	38	196	146	277
vs. Right	.245	.303	.362	3712	910	144	14	87	399	299	646
at Home	.240	.297	.337	2649	637	90	5	52	259	208	416
on Road	.262	.320	.402	2868	752	146	18	73	336	237	507
vs. Groundball	.258	.315	.360	2568	662	97	8	50	282	209	408
vs. Flyball	.247	.304	.380	2949	727	139	15	75	313	236	515
vs. Finesse	.250	.297	.371	3066	767	144	10	69	315	194	396
vs. Power	.254	.324	.370	2451	622	92	13	56	280	251	527
on Grass	.249	.309	.363	4021	1001	154	12	93	435	339	671
on Artificial Turf	.259	.308	.393	1496	388	82	11	32	160	106	252
Day Games	.255	.308	.387	1644	420	73	7	43	192	124	265
Night Games	.250	.310	.364	3873	969	163	16	82	403	321	658
April	.249	.312	.381	803	200	36	5	20	93	69	172
May	.256	.307	.386	868	222	33	4	24	89	63	150
June	.246	.303	.366	893	220	42	4	19	91	73	140
July	.256	.309	.404	884	226	37	5	28	99	68	132
August	.248	.300	.341	996	247	44	2	15	97	70	151
Sept/Oct	.255	.322	.355	1073	274	44	3	19	126	102	178
Bases Empty	.244	.300	.365	3229	789	139	12	75	75	238	527
Leadoff	.246	.298	.372	1364	335	58	8	33	33	95	215
Not Leadoff	.243	.301	.359	1865	454	81	4	42	42	143	312
Runners On	.262	.322	.380	2288	600	97	11	50	520	207	396
First Base Only	.278	.318	.423	972	270	47	5	28	80	52	136
Scoring Position	.251	.325	.348	1316	330	50	6	22	440	155	260
Late Innings, Close	.231	.307	.337	944	218	45	5	15	104	102	193

RBI/Opportunities				
Scoring Position		395 / 1798	(22%)	
Scoring Position, 2 Out		152 / 836	(18%)	
On Third, Less than 2 Out		150 / 338	(44%)	
RBI in close games / RBI Total		390 / 595	(66%)	

The Dodger organization, including management at all levels, is in a protracted slump. Los Angeles has had two consecutive years with 89 losses, losing records in three of four seasons, and considerable public embarrassment. Even the emergence of the Giants is a rub against the Dodgers. Not since the Yankee collapse of 1965–68 have we seen such a good organizational reputation so badly tarnished. At least LA will not fall as far as the old Yankees, partly because they never achieved such a high level of dominance, and because the current system of "balance" provides a safety net.

Hitting is their most obvious weakness. The Dodgers were the worst hitters in major league ball in 1987. In the National League, Los Angeles scored the fewest runs (only 77 percent of the Mets' output), hit the fewest doubles and triples, and had the fewest RBIs. They might sound like patient hitters, but they also had the fewest walks of any major league team—and, of course, the fewest total bases.

You might think they were emphasizing defense, loading up with good-field, no-hit players. But the Dodgers committed more errors than any other team in the majors. In summary, this is a bad team.

The club showed the same weaknesses in 1986. Many prognosticators had, in fact, reviewed LA's 1986 offense and predicted that 1987 would bring significant improvement. They were wrong. While the team batting average zoomed from .251 to .252, the output was down by three runs.

It is a mystery why the Dodgers did not improve in 1987. There are plenty of individual improvements to be noted. Pedro Guerrero came back with flying colors: he hit .338 with 89 runs, 27 HR and 89 RBI, compared to .246 with 7 runs, 5 HR and 10 RBI in 1986. Enos Cabell went away and took his anemic numbers with him. Greg Brock packed up his .234 average and 33 runs and tried AL pitching. John Shelby and Mickey Hatcher were among the new arrivals; each batted over .275. Mike Marshall improved from .233 with 53 RBI to .294, 72. Franklin Stubbs provided at least as much offense in '87 as he had in '86. Mike Scioscia improved in every offensive category. Steve Sax dropped off from his career year, but his .280 average is not the kind of number that hurts a team. Steve hit more home runs and made fewer errors in 1987 than he had in '86. But the rest of the team got much, much worse.

This club's best hope for 1988 is to improve their pitching. On offense they need a catcher who can drive in 39 runs, a first baseman and a shortstop who can hit over .235, and a third baseman who can reach double figures in HR. The Dodgers need people who can meet these minimums, because every other team in the league has players who perform above these marks.

John C. Benson

LOS ANGELES DODGERS
PITCHING

	1987 SEASON											
	G	IP	H	BB	SO	SB	CS	W	L	S	ERA
Totals	443	1455.0	1415	565	1097	120	61	73	89	32	3.72
at Home	215	752.0	715	245	555	64	33	40	41	14	3.21
on Road	228	703.0	700	320	542	56	28	33	48	18	4.26
Day Games	135	434.0	447	158	323	36	13	23	25	11	3.75
Night Games	308	1021.0	968	407	774	84	48	50	64	21	3.70
on Grass	316	1093.0	1032	390	813	86	46	62	58	25	3.37
on Artificial Turf	127	362.0	383	175	284	34	15	11	31	7	4.77
April	65	207.0	200	68	165	17	8	12	11	2	3.26
May	68	228.1	238	88	195	27	10	11	15	4	3.90
June	69	241.2	213	90	183	24	11	13	14	5	3.39
July	76	233.2	242	100	170	9	8	10	16	4	4.58
August	79	257.2	249	122	196	23	16	10	19	6	3.70
Sept/Oct	86	286.2	273	97	188	20	8	17	14	11	3.48

vs. Opponent Batters	Ave.	OBP	SLG	AB	H	2B	3B	HR	RBI	BB	SO
Totals	.255	.325	.382	5554	1415	263	27	130	625	565	1097
vs. Left	.256	.326	.370	2403	616	100	17	46	238	246	419
vs. Right	.254	.325	.392	3151	799	163	10	84	387	319	678
Bases Empty	.247	.311	.370	3170	783	144	18	70	70	283	633
Leadoff	.248	.308	.361	1343	333	57	7	27	27	114	258
Not Leadoff	.246	.313	.377	1827	450	87	11	43	43	169	375
Runners On Base	.265	.344	.398	2384	632	119	9	60	555	282	464
First Base Only	.292	.342	.453	981	286	63	4	29	83	71	169
Scoring Position	.247	.344	.360	1403	346	56	5	31	472	211	295
Late Innings, Close	.267	.342	.365	988	264	47	4	14	121	111	182

RBI/Opportunities	
Scoring Position	410 / 2006 (20%)
Scoring Position, 2 Out	156 / 926 (17%)
On Third, Less than 2 Out	167 / 380 (44%)
RBI in close games / RBI Total	407 / 625 (65%)

Dodger pitchers give us excellent evidence that fans, media and management should pay more attention to the pitching ratio statistic. Rotisserie enthusiasts are intimately familiar with this little number: (H + BB)/IP. In my opinion, it is a better, more meaningful statistic than ERA as a measure of pitching performance. Here are some questions that would take a long time to answer without using pitching ratio (PR):

Los Angeles has the second-best ERA in the National League in 1987. Their hitting and fielding statistics were virtually identical to those of 1986. So why, if their pitching improved, did they lose 89 games again? Well, the Dodger pitching did not improve; it deteriorated. The team PR was 1.32 in 1986 and 1.36 in 1987. That difference meant 153 extra baserunners in '87, almost one a game more. Although LA had the NL's 2nd-lowest ERA, they were only 7th in PR (not nearly good enough when you have the worst hitting and the worst fielding).

Fernando Valenzuela seemed to struggle some last season, but he has bounced back from minor problems before. Is Fernando still one of the premier pitchers in the game today? Unfortunately, he may be over the hill. His lifetime PR before 1987 was 1.18; his annual figures over the last six seasons never varied from this number by more than .15. But Fernando ballooned to 1.51 last year. He may be a journeyman hurler for a few more years, but starters who produce a season PR as high as 1.50 seldom return to good form. It is much easier to come back from a bad ERA.

How good are Tim Belcher, Tim Crews and Brad Havens? Belcher and Crews both had good ERAs (2.38 and 2.48 respectively), but Belcher's PR was a strong 1.09 while Crews had a middling 1.31. To the extent that 30 innings is a valid measure, look for Belcher to be excellent and Crews to be mediocre. Havens, with a PR of 1.50, did not show much promise.

So who was the best Dodger pitcher in 1987? Bob Welch was. Orel Hershiser was a close second. Welch's PR was 1.15, Hershiser's 1.21. In 1986 Welch had a PR of 1.20, while Orel was 1.29, so the 1987 outcome was consistent. How bad was Rick Honeycutt in 1987? He was horrible. His PR was 1.54, among the worst in baseball.

Will Jesse Orosco help the bullpen this year? Before 1987 he had an excellent lifetime figure of 1.18, and had been consistent over the years. But last season he exploded to 1.42, so there is a good possibility that Jesse has lost his effectiveness. Jay Howell, the other reliever in the A's/Mets trade, turned in PRs of 1.43 in '86 and 1.56 in '87, worse than Jesse's. The pitching ratios of these two relievers indicate that the Dodger bullpen has not been strengthened by the trade of the club's top starter.

John C. Benson

MONTREAL EXPOS
HITTING

	Ave.	OBP	SLG	AB	H	2B	3B	HR	RBI	BB	SO
				1987 SEASON							
Totals	.266	.328	.401	5529	1468	310	39	120	697	501	918
vs. Left	.286	.346	.430	1632	466	110	10	35	221	150	265
vs. Right	.257	.321	.389	3897	1002	200	29	85	476	351	653
at Home	.272	.339	.417	2724	742	163	23	62	375	266	430
on Road	.259	.317	.385	2805	726	147	16	58	322	235	488
vs. Groundball	.267	.326	.383	2603	694	133	18	45	310	219	394
vs. Flyball	.265	.331	.416	2926	774	177	21	75	387	282	524
vs. Finesse	.266	.320	.405	3230	859	173	22	77	400	245	441
vs. Power	.265	.340	.395	2299	609	137	17	43	297	256	477
on Grass	.268	.329	.390	1468	393	76	8	29	176	131	260
on Artificial Turf	.265	.328	.405	4061	1075	234	31	91	521	370	658
Day Games	.271	.328	.412	1632	443	106	11	34	193	131	271
Night Games	.263	.328	.396	3897	1025	204	28	86	504	370	647
April	.236	.302	.340	664	157	35	2	10	65	57	118
May	.290	.356	.432	982	285	64	6	21	143	97	169
June	.287	.351	.439	944	271	61	5	24	146	93	138
July	.273	.324	.429	875	239	57	8	21	102	64	138
August	.245	.315	.374	997	244	37	10	24	110	102	161
Sept/Oct	.255	.314	.379	1067	272	56	8	20	131	88	194
Bases Empty	.258	.311	.394	3176	819	166	25	72	72	231	514
Leadoff	.266	.310	.401	1361	362	67	12	31	31	78	214
Not Leadoff	.252	.313	.388	1815	457	99	13	41	41	153	300
Runners On	.276	.350	.410	2353	649	144	14	48	625	270	404
First Base Only	.272	.325	.406	908	247	63	4	17	66	65	144
Scoring Position	.278	.364	.412	1445	402	81	10	31	559	205	260
Late Innings, Close	.285	.347	.452	794	226	43	6	26	121	77	137

RBI/Opportunities							
Scoring Position				485 /	2009	(24%)	
Scoring Position, 2 Out				192 /	914	(21%)	
On Third, Less than 2 Out				171 /	363	(47%)	
RBI in close games / RBI Total				438 /	697	(63%)	

The 1987 Expos set a team record for runs scored with 741, but that was entirely a function of the increased offense in the league. Montreal finished 6th in runs scored, which is a fairly valid indication of how good the offense was. The most significant phenomenon was that Olympic Stadium, previously a haven for pitchers, produced runs at an 11 percent higher rate than Expos road games. Because the roof doesn't moderate the inside temperature (it varied between 43 and 91 degrees last season), the inflated offensive totals should level off in future years.

By virtually any formula, the Expo offense was very efficient. In this way it resembled the 1985 squad. When running a sequential offense (the Expos were 6th in runs scored but only 10th in home runs) you must have some players who drive in a lot of baserunners. In 1985 it was Hubie Brooks and Andre Dawson. This year, Tim Wallach led the league by driving in 97 runners. Andres Galarraga drove in 77 and Brooks, despite missing one quarter of the season, accounted for 58.

In terms of the batting order, Montreal got significant production from the #1 through #7 slots. For example, Tim Raines scored 69 runs in 81 games while batting third, which translates into 138 over a full season. Wallach scored 89 batting fourth and Galarraga tallied 72 batting #6. Somebody was obviously hitting behind each of these people.

There were a lot of individual surprises. Despite not playing until May 2nd, Raines turned in a season's worth of numbers. He reached base an incredible 276 times. The Expos were 10th in runs scored at the time of his return, but finished the year 6th. Wallach had his best season and Galarraga developed into an effective high-average line drive hitter. The Montreal bench, arguably the worst in baseball in '86, improved significantly last year. Tom Foley batted .293 and slugged .432; Reid Nichols, .265 and .429. Both Wallace Johnson and Dave Engle were effective pinch hitters, driving in 14 runs apiece in 85 and 84 respective at-bats.

The Expos' offense will have to decline in 1988. The three best hitters (Raines, Wallach and Galarraga) are all coming off their best seasons and will have a hard time repeating. Brooks has missed 120 games over the past two seasons and will have to learn a new position. Both these factors point to lower production. However, the main problem will be up the middle. Vance Law is now with the Cubs and Hubie is in right field. The new second baseman, Casey Candaele, had the same number of PAs as Law in '87, with 33 fewer RBIs. The Luis Rivera/Tom Foley platoon at short and the Jeff Reed/Mike Fitzgerald combo behind the plate finish up the offense, so the bottom of the Montreal batting order is not going to scare anybody.

Brent MacInnes

MONTREAL EXPOS
PITCHING

	1987 SEASON										
	G	IP	H	BB	SO	SB	CS	W	L	S	ERA
Totals	497	1450.1	1428	446	1012	202	46	91	71	51	3.92
at Home	248	744.0	733	242	544	94	29	48	33	20	3.94
on Road	249	706.1	695	204	468	108	17	43	38	31	3.90
Day Games	146	425.0	416	136	317	64	18	25	23	17	3.90
Night Games	351	1025.1	1012	310	695	138	28	66	48	34	3.93
on Grass	130	369.1	360	110	267	56	12	25	17	18	3.83
on Artificial Turf	367	1081.0	1068	336	745	146	34	66	54	33	3.95
April	63	172.0	177	57	107	28	2	8	12	7	4.55
May	89	249.1	255	77	191	35	5	17	11	10	4.01
June	87	244.0	276	72	163	36	10	15	12	7	4.94
July	62	236.0	200	58	151	23	7	18	8	5	2.78
August	93	266.0	264	90	176	41	12	15	14	9	3.76
Sept/Oct	103	283.0	256	92	224	39	10	18	14	13	3.69

vs. Opponent Batters	Ave.	OBP	SLG	AB	H	2B	3B	HR	RBI	BB	SO
Totals	.257	.312	.393	5566	1428	268	29	145	675	446	1012
vs. Left	.259	.320	.393	2749	713	147	17	62	335	247	473
vs. Right	.254	.305	.394	2817	715	121	12	83	340	199	539
Bases Empty	.245	.296	.370	3267	802	144	15	78	78	224	585
Leadoff	.247	.290	.381	1367	337	60	5	38	38	79	223
Not Leadoff	.245	.301	.363	1900	465	84	10	40	40	145	362
Runners On Base	.272	.334	.426	2299	626	124	14	67	597	222	427
First Base Only	.294	.340	.480	875	257	57	5	32	93	57	130
Scoring Position	.259	.331	.393	1424	369	67	9	35	504	165	297
Late Innings, Close	.220	.281	.320	823	181	37	0	15	86	70	170

RBI/Opportunities		
Scoring Position	437 / 1930	(23%)
Scoring Position, 2 Out	155 / 888	(17%)
On Third, Less than 2 Out	174 / 334	(52%)
RBI in close games / RBI Total	423 / 675	(63%)

Six was a big number for the Montreal staff in 1987. The six starters led a group that finished 6th in runs allowed and 6th in ERA. All six contributed, but in different forms and at different times. Neal Heaton started the season with strong run support. In June he had a league-leading 10 victories. But he failed to get a single one after July and finished with just 13 wins. Bob Sebra was second on the team in number of starts, but had only 6 wins to show for them. Bryn Smith won 10 and lost 9 after starting the season on the disabled list. Floyd Youmans, who alternated time between the DL and starting rotation, hung around long enough to win an NL Pitcher of the Month award in July. Next into the fray was Dennis Martinez, the Expos' most effective starter. Naturally, due to contract hassles he became a free agent who didn't get his first start until June 10. Finally, the amazing Pascual Perez was not promoted from Indianapolis until late August. He then went 7–0, with a 2.30 ERA.

The bullpen, which was supposed to fall apart without Jeff Reardon, was actually better than in 1986. Montreal's unmatched 12–1 extra-inning record illustrates the effectiveness of the firemen. Tim Burke and Andy McGaffigan were both excellent in short and middle relief. Bob McClure was effective from the left side. The only problem was manager Buck Rodgers' chosen stopper, Jeff Parrett, who blew numerous leads, including two key save opportunities in August.

The coming season should be a good one for the starting rotation. All six starters are signed, so contracts are not an obstacle. Floyd Youmans has something to prove because he is now 'rehabilitated" and he will qualify for arbitration after this season. Both Dennis Martinez and Pascual Perez will be available for the entire season. Bryn Smith has another one-year "produce or else" contract. Bob Sebra must win and do it early in the season in order to keep his starting slot. Neal Heaton is in the same situation as Sebra; Neal won only once in the last nine weeks of 1987. If Heaton fails, Joe Hesketh, who pitched well in relief late in the season, is available. Moreover, Montreal has arguably the two finest mound prospects in AA ball: Southern League ERA leader Brian Holman and 6'10" lefthander Randy Johnson. The only thing the Expos have to fear is that retreads Perez and Martinez may not hold up over a full season, but they have enough depth to take care of that contingency. Burke and McGaffigan will have a hard time repeating last year's relief heroics. But if (when) Rodgers finds out that Parrett can't handle the stopper role, Burke will take over. The team should be okay from the left side with McClure and Hesketh. Montreal appears to have the overall pitching quality required to contend once again.

Brent MacInnes

NEW YORK METS
HITTING

	Ave.	OBP	SLG	AB	H	2B	3B	HR	RBI	BB	SO
						1987 SEASON					
Totals	.268	.339	.434	5603	1499	287	34	192	771	592	1012
vs. Left	.263	.335	.433	2103	554	105	12	76	300	219	367
vs. Right	.270	.341	.434	3500	945	182	22	116	471	373	645
at Home	.278	.350	.440	2716	754	139	11	93	384	295	485
on Road	.258	.328	.428	2887	745	148	23	99	387	297	527
vs. Groundball	.273	.349	.428	2228	609	111	9	72	295	253	383
vs. Flyball	.264	.332	.437	3375	890	176	25	120	476	339	629
vs. Finesse	.275	.338	.439	3000	824	144	21	102	400	282	433
vs. Power	.259	.340	.428	2603	675	143	13	90	371	310	579
on Grass	.274	.344	.436	3910	1073	192	21	133	537	411	701
on Artificial Turf	.252	.326	.428	1693	426	95	13	59	234	181	311
Day Games	.280	.347	.447	2076	581	122	13	66	288	208	351
Night Games	.260	.334	.426	3527	918	165	21	126	483	384	661
April	.265	.336	.452	675	179	32	5	28	93	74	127
May	.268	.345	.436	924	248	51	7	30	106	105	187
June	.269	.331	.443	974	262	47	7	36	138	85	175
July	.281	.351	.433	939	264	49	5	28	124	102	160
August	.262	.342	.434	976	256	49	7	35	149	114	184
Sept/Oct	.260	.329	.413	1115	290	59	3	35	161	112	179
Bases Empty	.266	.329	.429	3145	836	158	17	107	107	275	571
Leadoff	.269	.328	.441	1328	357	77	8	45	45	109	236
Not Leadoff	.264	.329	.420	1817	479	81	9	62	62	166	335
Runners On	.270	.351	.440	2458	663	129	17	85	664	317	441
First Base Only	.296	.352	.459	948	281	51	5	31	88	78	152
Scoring Position	.253	.351	.428	1510	382	78	12	54	576	239	289
Late Innings, Close	.257	.347	.374	888	228	32	3	22	107	122	173

RBI/Opportunities		
Scoring Position	470 / 2108	(22%)
Scoring Position, 2 Out	182 / 957	(19%)
On Third, Less than 2 Out	163 / 351	(46%)
RBI in close games / RBI Total	481 / 771	(62%)

The New York Mets had the most fruitful offense in the National League for the second year in a row. The yield was up 40 runs with better efficiency; the '87 LOB count was lower than that of '86. Their power numbers expanded in proportion with the rest of the league, but their BA and OBP figures did not keep up with inflation due to a decrease in the base on balls total. The overall effect was a slight shift in offensive profile toward that of a free-swinging masher.

This is not to say that the Mets have metamorphosed into Orioles. There is speed in this lineup. The leadoff platoon of Lenny (Fastest White Guy in Baseball) Dykstra and Mookie Wilson doesn't spend a lot of time between bases. Manager Davey Johnson only wishes they could get on those bases more often, as the OBP of the #1 hitting spot was only adequate. Darryl Strawberry and Howard Johnson crafted the ballyhooed quad 30 (30 HRs and SBs each). But, while Strawberry has the build of a gazelle, HoJo and another slugger, Kevin McReynolds, look too meaty to be speedy. NL batteries and outfielders were frequently reminded that with these Mets looks are definitely deceiving.

New acquisition McReynolds was single-battedly responsible for the decrease in the team base on balls total. The two men he replaced—Danny Heep and Kevin Mitchell—totaled 63 walks against their 513 at-bats in 1986. Last year, McReynolds took 39 passes with 590 ABs. Despite 95 RBIs, his production has to be rated as disappointing. He was one of the two Mets who failed to deliver in the cleanup spot before Strawberry was installed there. The other dropout from the #4 slot was 1986's RBI honcho, Gary Carter. In 1986 Carter drove in 13.4 percent of New York's runs, but slumped to 10.1 percent last year.

Strawberry took over cleanup in midseason. It now looks like he'll be there for some time to come. Darryl was the league's pre-eminent offensive player in Sept.–Oct. He was in the top three in home runs, doubles, RBIs, runs, stolen bases and slugging percentage. Keith Hernandez set a career high for HRs with 18, but paid a price. His strikeout figure was his highest ever, and his OBP was his lowest in nine seasons. Tim Teufel was devastating against LH pitching. If he could only hit righties the man would be a sensation.

Finally a regular after five years of part-time play, Howard Johnson responded to his manager's confidence with his finest offensive year. His numbers look even better when you consider that he was batting ahead of the weak-hitting Rafael Santana.

The offensive combination that worked so well in 1987 will only improve with Kevin Elster boosting production at shortstop. Dave Magadan and Lee Mazzilli hold proven bats on the bench. If not on the squad, Keith Miller and Gregg Jeffries will be just a phone call away, and can contribute when needed. New York should hold off Cincinnati to lead the NL in offense for a third straight year in 1988.

Fred Percival

NEW YORK METS
PITCHING

	1987 SEASON										
	G	IP	H	BB	SO	SB	CS	W	L	S	ERA
Totals	471	1454.0	1406	510	1032	161	57	92	70	50	3.84
at Home	231	740.0	708	257	543	68	40	49	32	25	3.73
on Road	240	714.0	698	253	489	93	17	43	38	25	3.96
Day Games	187	524.1	559	178	361	66	29	28	30	19	4.38
Night Games	284	929.2	847	332	671	95	28	64	40	31	3.54
on Grass	329	1032.2	994	362	747	95	48	67	47	35	3.71
on Artificial Turf	142	421.1	412	148	285	66	9	25	23	15	4.17
April	59	177.2	186	74	133	22	7	11	9	8	4.56
May	88	241.0	257	96	180	33	20	13	14	7	3.88
June	73	247.1	229	86	176	24	9	16	12	6	3.64
July	70	240.2	242	68	125	32	7	16	11	10	3.96
August	83	261.0	250	96	190	22	7	18	11	9	3.97
Sept/Oct	98	286.1	242	90	228	28	7	18	13	10	3.33

vs. Opponent Batters	Ave.	OBP	SLG	AB	H	2B	3B	HR	RBI	BB	SO
Totals	.254	.318	.382	5535	1406	236	35	135	647	510	1032
vs. Left	.255	.322	.378	2418	617	107	21	49	251	234	393
vs. Right	.253	.316	.386	3117	789	129	14	86	396	276	639
Bases Empty	.259	.321	.394	3110	805	138	19	81	81	264	573
Leadoff	.268	.330	.407	1335	358	59	8	37	37	114	230
Not Leadoff	.252	.315	.383	1775	447	79	11	44	44	150	343
Runners On Base	.248	.315	.368	2425	601	98	16	54	566	246	459
First Base Only	.256	.309	.388	995	255	41	6	26	73	71	182
Scoring Position	.242	.319	.355	1430	346	57	10	28	493	175	277
Late Innings, Close	.265	.330	.373	997	264	30	3	24	131	98	195

RBI/Opportunities		
Scoring Position	436 / 1959	(22%)
Scoring Position, 2 Out	186 / 896	(21%)
On Third, Less than 2 Out	160 / 348	(46%)
RBI in close games / RBI Total	447 / 647	(69%)

Through wise drafting and outright theft in trades, the Mets have established a pitching staff that averaged 97 wins over the last four years, easily the best record in baseball. New York went into 1987 with what seemed like too many pitchers. But then Dwight Gooden, Roger McDowell, Bob Ojeda, David Cone, Rick Aguilera, Sid Fernandez and Ron Darling missed part or all of the season. In the end the old adage "You can never have too much pitching" was shown to be true again.

Gooden is the ace of this staff, and the paladin of the entire team. The Mets showed spirit and moved into contention last season only after he rejoined the club. Dwight relies on his curveball as his out pitch, rather than on his fastball. When he can get Lord Charles over, he dominates. When he does not, he struggles.

Darling got off to a disastrous start in 1987. He abandoned his well-developed curveball and relied too heavily on his splitter. While an effective pitch when he's ahead in the count, it draws few swings when he's behind. The latter was the case with almost every batter in the first half of the year.

The loss of Ojeda for the entire season was the difference between first and second place for New York in '87. Bob was the best and most consistent starter in the '86 Championship season. The fourth starter going into 1988 is Fernandez. He happened to be #1 just a year ago, while Gooden was away. But as was the case in '86, El Sid faltered in the second half. He stopped using his curveball and was pounded. He suffered a series of physical aggravations, probably weight-related. He must have a big year if he is to have a future on the staff. Aguilera and Cone will vie for the 5th starter's role. Cone has better stuff, but less experience.

Terry Leach, spot and swing man, kept the Mets on the map during Gooden's rehab. He had the hottest two months of his career right when New York needed his help. He's already returned to obscurity, but now he'll have something to recount to his grandchildren.

During the off-season New York replaced the oldest members of its bullpen structure. Jesse Orosco, Mets career save leader, and Doug Sisk, solid middle man, have departed. McDowell and Randy Myers are the new closing combination. Roger's greatest asset is his ability to pitch almost every day and in a variety of situations. His '87 work was not up to the standard he had set in 1986. He will not stay in his key position very long without an improvement. Myers started slowly last year, but by September he had written Orosco's ticket out of town.

The team's major trading goal in the off-season was to replenish their drained minor league pitching corps. This was accomplished in the various trades. Thus the Mets head into 1988 and try to see if, indeed, they have too much pitching.

Sunil Agarwal

PHILADELPHIA PHILLIES
HITTING

	Ave.	OBP	SLG	AB	H	2B	3B	HR	RBI	BB	SO
							1987 SEASON				
Totals	.254	.327	.410	5475	1390	248	51	169	662	587	1109
vs. Left	.250	.328	.417	1500	375	72	13	51	177	174	290
vs. Right	.255	.326	.408	3975	1015	176	38	118	485	413	819
at Home	.263	.343	.425	2706	711	136	32	80	367	331	537
on Road	.245	.311	.396	2769	679	112	19	89	295	256	572
vs. Groundball	.253	.325	.388	2853	723	108	28	73	345	299	574
vs. Flyball	.254	.329	.435	2622	667	140	23	96	317	288	535
vs. Finesse	.259	.318	.425	2929	760	135	31	96	353	248	495
vs. Power	.247	.336	.394	2546	630	113	20	73	309	339	614
on Grass	.241	.312	.380	1414	341	56	6	43	141	137	293
on Artificial Turf	.258	.332	.421	4061	1049	192	45	126	521	450	816
Day Games	.253	.329	.415	1638	414	70	15	55	195	186	343
Night Games	.254	.326	.409	3837	976	178	36	114	467	401	766
April	.232	.305	.353	671	156	20	5	17	73	71	153
May	.238	.317	.417	866	204	29	8	36	113	96	178
June	.269	.326	.439	933	251	50	8	31	113	76	181
July	.277	.357	.469	916	254	51	13	33	130	114	179
August	.279	.356	.429	1070	298	58	11	27	130	129	187
Sept/Oct	.221	.290	.344	1029	227	40	6	25	103	101	231
Bases Empty	.255	.328	.415	3099	791	135	25	103	103	319	628
Leadoff	.278	.347	.445	1316	366	65	10	45	45	133	247
Not Leadoff	.238	.314	.392	1783	425	70	15	58	58	186	381
Runners On	.252	.325	.405	2376	599	113	26	66	559	268	481
First Base Only	.277	.343	.435	939	260	47	7	29	82	91	165
Scoring Position	.236	.314	.386	1437	339	66	19	37	477	177	316
Late Innings, Close	.256	.355	.403	890	228	31	8	28	114	135	197

RBI/Opportunities		
Scoring Position	398 / 1903	(21%)
Scoring Position, 2 Out	155 / 886	(17%)
On Third, Less than 2 Out	141 / 290	(49%)
RBI in close games / RBI Total	434 / 662	(66%)

Second in runs, second in home runs, second in slugging percentage, second in OBP, second in the NL East. That was the tale of the Phillies in 1986.

PRELUDE

Pessimists pointed out that they finished farther behind the leader than any other second place team in history, but the Phils weren't even close to the worst runners-up of all time, the '83 Royals at 79–83. In 1986 Philadelphia finished in the top 25 percent for NL runs scored for the third season since 1983.

While it wasn't broken, president Bill Giles did tinker with the offense. He signed Lance Parrish to improve on John Russell's numbers. He couldn't resist picking up Mike Easler for recurrent doghouse occupant Charles Hudson. Injured Gary Redus was sacrificed for pitching help. The strategy was to go with a set lineup except for a little playing time for rookie outfielder Chris James against LHP. Von Hayes wouldn't have to worry about splitting time between first base and the outfield. Easler would give the lineup better left-right balance and, along with Parrish, better protection for Mike Schmidt. When the club opened the season, it was considered to be the most likely challenger to New York.

OPUS 1987

Well, the plan turned out like Bloom County's Opus, not an opus of one of the classical masters. Philadelphia's offense did not share in the National League's 7 percent surge in scoring. In fact, the Phils were down 37 runs, the only league member to register a double-digit drop. For a team with most of its stars in the lineup instead of on the mound, this was a collapse of startling dimensions. Mike Easler hit a ridiculously soft .282 and was turned back over to the AL. Lance Parrish didn't make anyone forget Russell. And Juan Samuel had a career season in 1987. He created more runs than any other major league second baseman, almost doubled his walk rate, yet still had a worse OBP than any other full-time leadoff man in the Division. Meanwhile Jeff Stone came to bat 125 times and stole three bases; shortstop Luis Aguayo hit 12 homers (tied for 2nd in the NL at his position) in 209 at-bats; Mike Schmidt matched his 1986 MVP numbers.

POSTLUDE

The Phillies have apparently decided that they were right in the winter of 1985 when Samuel was moved down in the order. They traded for Phil Bradley, and may have gotten their best leadoff man since Richie Ashburn. The price was the loss of Glenn Wilson from the seventh spot. The signs are good for Chris James and Milt Thompson to continue their hitting. The acquisition of Bob Dernier may finally let Hayes set aside his outfielder's glove. The offense will be back up at the top of the league as long as the bench stays where it belongs. Philadelphia is looking for shortstop help only a year after Tom Foley burned a hole in president Bill Giles' pocket. It doesn't look like the position can be improved much, but it is a good excuse to give Russell and/or Stone a fresh start elsewhere.

Clem Comly

PHILADELPHIA PHILLIES
PITCHING

		G	IP	H	BB	SO	SB	CS	W	L	S	ERA
						1987 SEASON						
Totals		551	1448.1	1453	587	877	184	60	80	82	48	4.19
at Home		273	748.0	726	286	470	106	26	43	38	23	4.09
on Road		278	700.1	727	301	407	78	34	37	44	25	4.29
Day Games		167	426.1	449	163	262	59	20	25	23	13	3.97
Night Games		384	1022.0	1004	424	615	125	40	55	59	35	4.28
on Grass		153	361.0	403	165	228	28	18	16	26	11	4.64
on Artificial Turf		398	1087.1	1050	422	649	156	42	64	56	37	4.04
April		71	178.1	181	94	108	26	4	7	13	3	4.34
May		82	231.0	225	87	146	28	10	15	11	10	4.13
June		94	240.1	267	89	142	34	10	13	15	10	4.94
July		84	242.1	246	83	122	23	8	18	9	11	3.64
August		104	283.0	279	118	166	45	11	15	15	8	3.91
Sept/Oct		116	273.1	255	116	193	28	17	12	19	6	4.25

vs. Opponent Batters	Ave.	OBP	SLG	AB	H	2B	3B	HR	RBI	BB	SO
Totals	.263	.335	.414	5526	1453	258	37	167	695	587	877
vs. Left	.283	.371	.429	1772	502	86	14	48	230	240	258
vs. Right	.253	.317	.406	3754	951	172	23	119	465	347	619
Bases Empty	.270	.334	.432	3103	838	142	24	104	104	279	496
Leadoff	.280	.351	.449	1307	366	69	13	42	42	134	202
Not Leadoff	.263	.321	.419	1796	472	73	11	62	62	145	294
Runners On Base	.254	.336	.390	2423	615	116	13	63	591	308	381
First Base Only	.279	.327	.421	982	274	56	4	25	73	66	123
Scoring Position	.237	.342	.370	1441	341	60	9	38	518	242	258
Late Innings, Close	.255	.325	.382	918	234	28	4	27	107	93	157

RBI/Opportunities		
Scoring Position	444 / 2076	(21%)
Scoring Position, 2 Out	156 / 943	(17%)
On Third, Less than 2 Out	194 / 407	(48%)
RBI in close games / RBI Total	439 / 695	(63%)

The most likely scenario for the Phillies to win the pennant race contains the 1961 Reds plot line. This calls for the club to have great hitting, plus the starting pitchers outperforming their past records, plus an excellent bullpen to win the close games, plus off years from the other contenders. Just how likely is this to happen?

Dave Palmer was gathered in over the winter to join Shane Rawley, Don Carman, Bruce Ruffin and Kevin Gross in the starting rotation. Rawley is the only one of this group who will not have to improve to be effective. As a wild card possibility, the Phils may have the next Marty Bystrom in the minors right now in the form of Starvin' Marvin Freeman. This guy looked great in 1986, then ate too well, then hurt his arm. But disappointment has been commonplace with this staff. A weird pattern on this team is that recently starters have had their ERAs rise with experience! Look at this chart:

	Year 1	Year 2	Year 3	Year 4
Bystrom	1.50	3.33	4.85	4.60
Carman	2.08	3.22	4.22	
Hudson	3.35	4.04	3.78	4.94
K. Gross	3.56	4.12	3.41	4.02
Ruffin	2.46	4.35		
Rawley	3.31	3.54	4.39	

I don't believe that the criticism of president Bill Giles & Co. for letting Dave "Smoke" Stewart get away is fair. They gave him a few appearances during the regular season and a full shot in spring training, but he did not pitch that well.

It is intriguing that the Phillies have had no success with home-grown relievers. Don Carman's sophomore year was so terrible that he was moved to the rotation. Mike Jackson lost 10 games in 55 appearances last year while Wally Ritchie had a pitching ratio of 1.44. But what this team has done (in a sometimes expensive manner) is to re-tread relievers from other teams. You all know about Steve Bedrosian. But in the '80's the Phils have also picked up former stoppers (led their teams in saves) Sparky Lyle, Bill Campbell and Tom Hume. And, of course, the amazing Kent Tekulve. At age 40 he led the National League in appearances for the umpty-umpth time last year. Tekulve, who needs 57 appearances to become the second pitcher to work in 1000 games, has gone from setup man to closer to setup man again in his career, all the while retaining his effectiveness. Former Astros farmhand Jeff Calhoun is the designated southpaw, completing one of the top four bullpens in the league.

For the winning scenario to be realized, Philadelphia will need as many arms in spring training as can be gathered. The best of that group will have to coalesce into a solid rotation, and then outperform their career records in 1988.

Clem Comly

PITTSBURGH PIRATES
HITTING

				1987 SEASON							
	Ave.	OBP	SLG	AB	H	2B	3B	HR	RBI	BB	SO
Totals	.264	.330	.403	5537	1464	283	45	131	684	535	914
vs. Left	.257	.322	.396	2425	624	112	22	60	283	226	379
vs. Right	.270	.336	.408	3112	840	171	23	71	401	309	535
at Home	.271	.339	.417	2744	744	138	24	71	378	280	426
on Road	.258	.321	.389	2793	720	145	21	60	306	255	488
vs. Groundball	.273	.339	.403	2590	706	131	17	58	313	258	414
vs. Flyball	.257	.322	.402	2947	758	152	28	73	371	277	500
vs. Finesse	.267	.327	.399	2947	786	148	18	69	347	259	394
vs. Power	.262	.332	.407	2590	678	135	27	62	337	276	520
on Grass	.258	.322	.396	1456	375	71	11	36	156	137	280
on Artificial Turf	.267	.332	.405	4081	1089	212	34	95	528	398	634
Day Games	.268	.333	.414	1756	470	86	18	45	213	173	289
Night Games	.263	.328	.398	3781	994	197	27	86	471	362	625
April	.259	.338	.418	648	168	36	8	17	79	77	100
May	.253	.315	.391	917	232	45	8	22	120	80	171
June	.258	.327	.394	1012	261	48	6	26	119	104	165
July	.245	.318	.359	895	219	37	4	19	86	92	155
August	.296	.353	.445	990	293	63	8	23	140	90	137
Sept/Oct	.271	.328	.408	1075	291	54	11	24	140	92	186
Bases Empty	.258	.315	.396	3140	809	156	26	75	75	249	508
Leadoff	.270	.326	.425	1337	361	73	10	38	38	104	205
Not Leadoff	.248	.307	.374	1803	448	83	16	37	37	145	303
Runners On	.273	.348	.412	2397	655	127	19	56	609	286	406
First Base Only	.293	.347	.449	949	278	60	5	26	85	71	142
Scoring Position	.260	.349	.388	1448	377	67	14	30	524	215	264
Late Innings, Close	.268	.338	.428	899	241	46	7	28	128	95	167

RBI/Opportunities		
Scoring Position	452 / 2032	(22%)
Scoring Position, 2 Out	184 / 927	(20%)
On Third, Less than 2 Out	186 / 400	(47%)
RBI in close games / RBI Total	455 / 684	(67%)

Well, the Buccos finally climbed out of the cellar in 1987; their victory output was up 25 percent. These guys are becoming fun to watch. They scratch, claw and battle, and appear to be hugely enjoying themselves. And, like any team effecting an all-out youth movement, they can sometimes drive you crazy. And all this excitement is accompanied by the lowest payroll in the majors. So they must be improving, no?

No, not necessarily. The Pirates' improvement was entirely offensive; the pitching remained 8th in the league. As the Cleveland Indians know, good pitching beats good hitting. The Bucs went 27–45 against the top four teams in their division last season, then took the Cubs 14 out of 18. Pittsburgh would still own the cellar if the W-L split with Chicago had been more realistic. Here is the lineup I'd like to see for 1988:

LF: Barry Bonds could be a legitimate 30-homer man, but he's got to work on the strikeouts. Like father, like son, I guess. 2B: I don't think Jose Lind's a .300 hitter. He shows good speed but very little power. CF: Andy Van Slyke is a solid, dependable hitter, seemingly good for 20 to 25 homers; a terrific baserunner. I think leaving St. Louis did him a world of good. 1B: Sid Bream's a productive player, but I always have this nagging feeling he should be doing more. He's subject to periodic power outages. He did handle lefties well, which had been a concern about him. 3B: Bobby

Bonilla may yet justify management's faith in his potential. He is still raw, but has a physique that makes me think he could bench-press Three Rivers Stadium. RF: GM Syd Bream wants Darnell Coles to play here full time. It would be a major blunder to replace the productive R. J. Reynolds. C: Mike LaValliere is great! He's such a terrific defensive catcher that he could hit .235 and still be allowed to play whenever he wished. SS: Al Pedrique believes he's a .290 hitter. The guy shows a lot of faith, since no one I know believes it. At least he keeps Rafael Belliard out of the lineup. BENCH: John Cangelosi is the best of this group, a real hustler with a great batting eye. Junior Ortiz is a good, solid backup catcher. Neither Terry Harper nor Mike Diaz excites me.

The Pirates must continue to sharply improve this year in order to compete with their division playmates. Will they? Not likely. There is no way that Pedrique and LaValliere will match their 1987 production. I doubt if Lind will, but he at least has a chance. While I have no problems with El Syd's master housecleaning—who really misses George Hendrick, Steve Kemp or John Candelaria?—I would think it prudent to keep some veterans to provide the power of example. They would provide stability during the roster turnover. This club is going to miss Jim Morrison and Johnny Ray.

Bill Thomas

PITTSBURGH PIRATES
PITCHING

1987 SEASON											
	G	IP	H	BB	SO	SB	CS	W	L	S	ERA
Totals	475	1445.0	1377	562	914	133	81	80	82	39	4.19
at Home	253	752.0	703	278	485	64	38	47	34	24	3.91
on Road	222	693.0	674	284	429	69	43	33	48	15	4.49
Day Games	141	451.1	432	166	305	37	27	28	23	12	3.95
Night Games	334	993.2	945	396	609	96	54	52	59	27	4.30
on Grass	118	360.2	335	140	241	26	24	19	23	9	4.17
on Artificial Turf	357	1084.1	1042	422	673	107	57	61	59	30	4.20
April	64	169.0	165	73	129	16	8	8	11	4	4.47
May	84	237.0	236	115	152	15	19	13	14	8	4.94
June	78	262.0	269	114	161	24	16	13	17	2	4.57
July	82	239.0	217	78	147	14	14	11	15	6	3.65
August	69	254.2	242	86	128	32	11	15	14	7	4.10
Sept/Oct	98	283.1	248	96	197	32	13	20	11	12	3.59

vs. Opponent Batters	Ave.	OBP	SLG	AB	H	2B	3B	HR	RBI	BB	SO
Totals	.253	.324	.407	5439	1377	257	44	164	699	562	914
vs. Left	.258	.330	.403	2577	666	127	30	62	302	273	364
vs. Right	.248	.318	.411	2862	711	130	14	102	397	289	550
Bases Empty	.245	.316	.391	3137	769	128	26	92	92	310	543
Leadoff	.272	.336	.432	1325	361	66	8	43	43	120	211
Not Leadoff	.225	.302	.360	1812	408	62	18	49	49	190	332
Runners On Base	.264	.333	.430	2302	608	129	18	72	607	252	371
First Base Only	.279	.332	.431	914	255	50	7	25	83	70	132
Scoring Position	.254	.334	.429	1388	353	79	11	47	524	182	239
Late Innings, Close	.259	.334	.380	900	233	41	4	20	124	101	177

RBI/Opportunities		
Scoring Position	430 / 1909	(23%)
Scoring Position, 2 Out	120 / 770	(16%)
On Third, Less than 2 Out	187 / 369	(51%)
RBI in close games / RBI Total	457 / 699	(65%)

"It was the best of times, it was the worst of times."—Charles Dickens
"It is always darkest just before the day dawneth."—Thomas Fuller
"The foundation must be laid in youth."—Havelock Ellis
"Who are those guys!?!"—Ray Miller

So it must have been with the Pittsburgh pitching coach as he steered his staff through the 1987 season. A total of 22 pitchers—easily two thirds of whom had not yet reached age 25—took the mound during the season. Miller and manager Jim Leyland must at varying times have felt like stockbrokers, summer camp counselors, faith healers, bus clerks, magicians and human doormats as they maneuvered this crew. In no particular order, the key figures in this procession:

Rick Reuschel, despite pitching well—and cruelly suffering at the hands of his bullpen—came to realize as the season progressed that he was a goner. He stylishly pleaded his case to end his career here, but GM Syd Thrift sent him to the Giants.

Don Robinson, without the durability to continue middle relief and spot roles, was assigned to be the right-handed stopper. He failed—losing, among others, eight or nine leads of Reuschel's. One can only imagine Mr. Reuschel's initial reaction to the news that Robinson too had been dispatched to the Giants.

Doug Drabek got off to a horrible start, got hurt, and then started putting it all together near the All-Star break.

Showing a good fastball, workable off-speed stuff and a lion's heart, he finished with an ERA under 4.00. He should be the second starter this year.

Brian Fisher had a winning year, but a high ERA. He's one of those guys who seems to throw nothing but 95-mph fastballs, so you have to wonder how long he'll last. He was seen to be using some new pitches as the season progressed, however. At least until the jury returns, he's the third starter.

Ahh! Mike Dunne. Whatever good things you've heard about him are all true. He's a sinker, slider pitcher; changes speeds and has poise that belies his age of 24. His future looks terrific as the ace of this staff.

Jeff Robinson and Jim Gott are the right-handed tandem in the bullpen. Their work at the end of '87 showed promise. Gott appears to have the better stuff, but Robinson has the advantages of youth and stamina, so he should get the bulk of the work.

There is a crowd of contenders for the fourth and fifth starting spots. Bob Kipper, Mike Bielecki, and Vicente Palacios are the best bets. Look for Bob Patterson, John Smiley and Bob Walk to fill out the bullpen.

Prognosis: A lot of wheat here, but more than a little chaff. If this club is to continue improving this year the pitching staff will have to account for somewhere near two thirds of it. The potential is there if Miller and Leyland can assemble all these pieces.

Bill Thomas

SAN DIEGO PADRES
HITTING

	Ave.	OBP	SLG	AB	H	2B	3B	HR	RBI	BB	SO
						1987 SEASON					
Totals	.260	.332	.378	5457	1419	209	48	113	621	577	992
vs. Left	.271	.343	.402	2040	552	88	15	50	233	221	351
vs. Right	.254	.325	.364	3417	867	121	33	63	388	356	641
at Home	.255	.333	.383	2627	669	96	31	60	318	304	505
on Road	.265	.330	.373	2830	750	113	17	53	303	273	487
vs. Groundball	.273	.341	.392	2537	692	102	25	50	315	259	421
vs. Flyball	.249	.324	.366	2920	727	107	23	63	306	318	571
vs. Finesse	.266	.326	.387	2719	722	104	29	56	302	241	397
vs. Power	.255	.337	.369	2738	697	105	19	57	319	336	595
on Grass	.260	.332	.382	3996	1038	141	40	89	471	423	749
on Artificial Turf	.261	.331	.368	1461	381	68	8	24	150	154	243
Day Games	.256	.331	.383	1867	478	72	12	47	220	207	335
Night Games	.262	.332	.375	3590	941	137	36	66	401	370	657
April	.235	.299	.342	757	178	33	6	12	62	66	127
May	.263	.348	.353	937	246	35	7	12	99	117	173
June	.272	.349	.378	903	246	31	8	16	117	110	181
July	.272	.339	.411	841	229	35	8	22	105	87	164
August	.272	.336	.404	973	265	35	12	23	125	91	158
Sept/Oct	.244	.316	.376	1046	255	40	7	28	113	106	189
Bases Empty	.254	.323	.363	3103	788	106	21	63	63	301	585
Leadoff	.241	.306	.347	1326	319	37	10	28	28	121	243
Not Leadoff	.264	.336	.374	1777	469	69	11	35	35	180	342
Runners On	.268	.343	.398	2354	631	103	27	50	558	276	407
First Base Only	.289	.329	.437	953	275	40	16	23	80	54	150
Scoring Position	.254	.351	.373	1401	356	63	11	27	478	222	257
Late Innings, Close	.250	.326	.333	921	230	33	4	12	105	104	189

RBI/Opportunities					
Scoring Position		423 / 2006	(21%)		
Scoring Position, 2 Out		193 / 994	(19%)		
On Third, Less than 2 Out		159 / 344	(46%)		
RBI in close games / RBI Total		421 / 621	(68%)		

The 1987 season was one Padres fans have not forgotten, although they certainly have tried. The year started dismally and had few high points. There was a streak in June through August where the Padres had the best record in the NL West, but Peter Ueberroth refused to disregard the earlier games in the final standings.

The talent seemed to be there, if perhaps a bit on the raw side. Benito Santiago, arguably the best arm behind the plate in the league, fired pickoff throws that sometimes went as far as 250 feet. Offensively, he thrilled the normally comatose crowds with his 34-game hitting streak. Twice he extended it in his last at-bat, and one of those was in extra innings.

Tony Gwynn won the batting title and a Gold Glove in right field. Third base was largely unoccupied. Kevin Mitchell slept through the first half of the season offensively and defensively. After a surprise mid-season trade Chris Brown limped through part of the second half in the same style. Carmelo Martinez and Stan Jefferson showed occasional signs of promise, with Martinez hitting in the .270's but ho-hum overall; Jefferson displayed fleetness, but had the worst September in the league. Garry Templeton continued to play a sometimes thrilling shortstop with arthritic knees and a bad back, but he seemed puzzled by the concept of hitting. A late-season change to glasses didn't help; maybe he's closing his eyes at the plate.

Pleasant surprises were John "Burger King" Kruk at first base and Randy Ready at third. Both topped .300 and played solid defense. John Kruk's likeness to his hero Pete Rose is remarkable—all hustle and little boy glee at playing big league ball.

The San Diego offense will explode in 1988. There is talent at almost every position and players who *can* hit. Kruk has shown the fans that a first baseman can be a hitter *and* have defensive range, something Steve Garvey had made them forget. Youngsters Shane Mack and Shawn Abner are full of potential. They had limited playing time in '87 but appear to have the right tools, if not enough seasoning. Randy Ready is a bluecollar-type player who deserves a starting position even if it means leaving Brown licking his many wounds on the bench. If Tempy's body holds out and he can somehow touch bat to ball, shortstop is a well-filled position. If not, Gary Green and Roberto Alomar are waiting in the wings; both unproven, but reportedly with potential.

Second base is a mystery. Longtime utility player Tim Flannery had a sluggish year and Joey Cora may or may not be prepared to handle the job or the bat. The Padres' off season is once again punctuated by cries of "We need a second baseman," a team motto for at least five years. Somehow, this position never gets filled.

All in all, San Diego has some wonderful diamond-in-the-rough talent with a core of proven players. Watch out, National League—these could be the kids to beat!

Katherine and Bruce Wayne

SAN DIEGO PADRES
PITCHING

						1987 SEASON					
	G	IP	H	BB	SO	SB	CS	W	L	S	ERA
Totals	497	1433.1	1403	602	897	127	51	65	97	33	4.28
at Home	248	738.0	677	300	514	63	24	37	44	18	3.78
on Road	249	695.1	726	302	383	64	27	28	53	15	4.81
Day Games	168	492.1	468	188	285	35	15	24	32	14	4.08
Night Games	329	941.0	935	414	612	92	36	41	65	19	4.39
on Grass	363	1068.1	999	424	685	81	38	51	69	24	4.04
on Artificial Turf	134	365.0	404	178	212	46	13	14	28	9	4.98
April	72	202.2	203	75	150	11	14	6	17	3	4.40
May	88	242.0	257	129	139	32	7	6	22	6	5.54
June	71	235.1	205	83	131	23	7	15	12	9	3.71
July	77	222.2	233	102	147	19	10	11	14	4	4.81
August	88	254.0	234	104	155	20	4	16	12	7	3.72
Sept/Oct	101	276.2	271	109	175	22	9	11	20	4	3.68

vs. Opponent Batters	Ave.	OBP	SLG	AB	H	2B	3B	HR	RBI	BB	SO
Totals	.256	.332	.409	5476	1403	253	30	175	703	602	897
vs. Left	.266	.350	.405	2530	674	128	15	64	294	322	375
vs. Right	.247	.317	.413	2946	729	125	15	111	409	280	522
Bases Empty	.254	.324	.408	3127	794	137	15	105	105	303	500
Leadoff	.263	.328	.425	1309	344	64	8	44	44	124	198
Not Leadoff	.248	.320	.396	1818	450	73	7	61	61	179	302
Runners On Base	.259	.343	.411	2349	609	116	15	70	598	299	397
First Base Only	.264	.332	.415	944	249	47	3	30	84	90	155
Scoring Position	.256	.350	.408	1405	360	69	12	40	514	209	242
Late Innings, Close	.258	.343	.425	840	217	45	4	29	106	108	189

	RBI/Opportunities	
Scoring Position	433 / 1961	(22%)
Scoring Position, 2 Out	185 / 930	(20%)
On Third, Less than 2 Out	149 / 331	(45%)
RBI in close games / RBI Total	447 / 703	(64%)

The best got away, but the promise remains. Dave Dravecky and Craig Lefferts were given a reprieve and sent to San Francisco and the division title, while Mark Grant, Mark Davis and Keith Comstock joined the ranks of the question mark. The 1987 staff was mired in mediocrity, yet can still hope for improvement. Eric Nolte vaulted from Class A ball to the majors and convinced most fans that the jump was justified. Jimmy Jones was given the time and the innings to develop as a starting pitcher and this season is looking to blend consistency with his acknowledged occasional brilliance.

Andy Hawkins, Eric Show and Ed Whitson should form the mainstay of a solid starting corps, but injuries and an inexplicable up-and-down attitude may continue to frustrate Padres fans and coaches alike. Grant showed obvious talent, although like his fellow pitchers he seemed unable to have two good games in a row. Davis was a calm, solid hurler, as effective pitching for the club as he was when throwing against them. He is not good enough to carry a team that is not hitting, however. Comstock, a well-traveled player who has spent time in Japan, is at this point a "maybe." It's hard to speculate about his next season, as he may not make the 24-man roster, but he certainly had some good moments in 1987. There are, however, many, many moments in a baseball season, and San Diego needs many more good moments from the starters than there were last year.

The bullpen could be solid if Goose Gossage recognizes the limitations of age and develops a change-up curve, and if Lance "Baby Goose" McCullers blasts through the bad luck and occasional lapses of concentration that proved so humbling to him in '87. The elder Goose had many outings that must have instilled thoughts of retirement. However, the off-season sometimes rejuvenates tired old arms, so there may be a year left for the flaming fastball, if used sparingly and mixed with a couple of other effective pitches.

All in all, nobody can predict how this staff will fare in '88. With a new pitching coach, perhaps some better luck, a lefty power pitcher and some offensive support, there can be hope for this crew. Best guess: Jones, Show and Nolte will lead the staff by mid-year, but Whitson, Hawkins and Gossage will bomb.

San Diego Jack Murphy Stadium is the third-best home run park in the National League. The front runners, in Chicago and Atlanta, get a lot more publicity, and have much bigger reputations. Well, the Padres pitching staff is trying to raise the Murph's low profile and improve its status. Their technique is simple; they lead the league in home runs allowed. 1987 marked the second year of their master plan, with Ed Whitson taking over the directorship from LaMarr Hoyt. When you read sports columns and listen to broadcast commentaries you'll find out whether it's working. If you hear something like, "Yeah—I hear they have to drag the warning track between innings out in San Diego . . ." you'll know that the campaign is succeeding.

Katherine and Bruce Wayne

SAN FRANCISCO GIANTS
HITTING

	Ave.	OBP	SLG	AB	H	2B	3B	HR	RBI	BB	SO
1987 SEASON											
Totals	.260	.324	.430	5608	1458	274	32	205	732	511	1094
vs. Left	.262	.319	.445	1673	439	85	10	67	224	133	317
vs. Right	.259	.326	.423	3935	1019	189	22	138	508	378	777
at Home	.259	.324	.447	2703	700	127	13	118	356	250	508
on Road	.261	.324	.414	2905	758	147	19	87	376	261	586
vs. Groundball	.262	.326	.407	2483	650	117	15	71	312	225	435
vs. Flyball	.259	.323	.448	3125	808	157	17	134	420	286	659
vs. Finesse	.264	.320	.444	2863	755	137	19	114	382	218	455
vs. Power	.256	.329	.415	2745	703	137	13	91	350	293	639
on Grass	.262	.327	.437	4079	1067	192	21	160	543	382	788
on Artificial Turf	.256	.318	.412	1529	391	82	11	45	189	129	306
Day Games	.275	.339	.450	2309	636	124	16	82	319	214	464
Night Games	.249	.314	.416	3299	822	150	16	123	413	297	630
April	.270	.330	.437	788	213	40	5	27	98	70	174
May	.278	.339	.462	926	257	59	8	32	128	77	170
June	.234	.284	.406	919	215	38	0	40	108	60	191
July	.254	.313	.404	966	245	45	5	30	120	81	174
August	.251	.317	.409	999	251	48	7	32	123	94	203
Sept/Oct	.274	.360	.462	1010	277	44	7	44	155	129	182
Bases Empty	.248	.309	.426	3305	818	162	20	129	129	273	675
Leadoff	.256	.313	.449	1355	347	68	10	58	58	107	256
Not Leadoff	.242	.305	.409	1950	471	94	10	71	71	166	419
Runners On	.278	.346	.436	2303	640	112	12	76	603	238	419
First Base Only	.289	.330	.449	889	257	47	7	27	82	45	140
Scoring Position	.271	.355	.428	1414	383	65	5	49	521	193	279
Late Innings, Close	.271	.338	.433	1031	279	61	5	32	142	102	200

RBI/Opportunities		
Scoring Position	441 / 1939	(23%)
Scoring Position, 2 Out	170 / 869	(20%)
On Third, Less than 2 Out	153 / 359	(43%)
RBI in close games / RBI Total	466 / 732	(64%)

What made the 1987 season such a success for the Giants? Only two years earlier they had lost 100 games. Clearly, the major answer is GM Al Rosen's well-publicized trades and player transactions. Here are my comments by position:

1ST BASE—Will Clark should hold down this position for a long time to come with his superb blend of power and a high BA. He handles left-handed pitching very well. He should become even better when he gains some maturity. He hasn't won any fan popularity contests in the Bay Area as yet, due to his asinine interviews.

2ND BASE—Robbie Thompson's 1986 Rookie of the Year campaign orchestrated by the Giants was bush league. Granted the man can field, but .270 singles hitters are a dime a dozen. Let me ask you this: How many other major league second basemen would you trade straight up for Thompson?

SHORTSTOP—The good news is that Jose Uribe is second only to the Wizard defensively in the NL. The bad news is that 1987 was Uribe's career year offensively.

3RD BASE—Replacing the chronically unavailable Chris Brown with Kevin Mitchell made a world of difference. Mitchell is full of raw talent, with great flexibility. The Giants also have Matt Williams lurking in the future as a possible third baseman. I would groom Williams for second base and give Thompson his walking papers when Matt is ready for the majors.

LEFTFIELD—I will never defend notorious loafers like Chris Brown or Mike Marshall (did I really hear that Marshall sat out because of warts?). However, Jeffrey (don't dare call him Jeff) Leonard lies at the opposite extreme. He might be great when healthy, but he really impairs the Giant offense when he insists on playing hurt.

CENTERFIELD—Al Rosen again demonstrated his faculty for building a winning team when he signed Brett Butler. On base percentage is one of the most underrated statistics in baseball. The great Indians offense of 1986 was set up by the ability of their top two hitters, Butler and Tony Bernazard, to get on base. Butler, a bona fide leadoff hitter, fills a void that the Giants have had since they lost Bobby Bonds.

RIGHTFIELD—Candy Maldonado was acquired after the 1985 season for Alex Trevino. Is Al Rosen a genius or what?

CATCHER—Bob Brenly is capable both with the glove and the bat, a nice combination that ranks him in the upper third of NL catchers.

BENCH—Chris Speier had a career year if there ever was one, but he still will be a big help; a brilliant procurement by Rosen. Harry Spilman is a valuable pinch hitter and utility man. The bench is deep with guys like Mike Aldrete, Joel Youngblood and Bob Melvin sitting on it.

I look for a drop in offensive output this year, mostly due to Uribe and Thompson returning to reality. The offense as a whole is not near the top of the league and will have a difficult time giving the pitching staff adequate support.

Ira Saltz

SAN FRANCISCO GIANTS
PITCHING

						1987 SEASON					
	G	IP	H	BB	SO	SB	CS	W	L	S	ERA
Totals	511	1471.0	1408	547	1038	132	81	90	72	38	3.70
at Home	240	743.0	658	252	517	57	43	46	35	16	3.45
on Road	271	728.0	750	295	521	75	38	44	37	22	3.96
Day Games	202	614.1	570	226	415	55	31	42	26	17	3.37
Night Games	309	856.2	839	321	623	77	50	48	46	21	3.94
on Grass	372	1084.1	1024	404	765	92	56	68	52	28	3.69
on Artificial Turf	139	386.2	384	143	273	40	25	22	20	10	3.72
April	67	210.1	202	79	139	10	9	16	7	10	3.38
May	79	231.1	253	94	180	23	19	11	15	5	4.79
June	90	240.1	237	102	183	30	15	11	16	5	4.19
July	91	254.0	239	108	193	22	14	14	13	7	3.44
August	83	268.0	237	71	175	16	12	18	11	5	3.12
Sept/Oct	101	267.0	240	93	168	31	12	20	10	6	3.40

vs. Opponent Batters	Ave.	OBP	SLG	AB	H	2B	3B	HR	RBI	BB	SO
Totals	.255	.323	.387	5518	1408	235	28	146	625	547	1038
vs. Left	.266	.339	.396	2409	641	101	20	57	278	265	442
vs. Right	.247	.311	.381	3109	767	134	8	89	347	282	596
Bases Empty	.251	.315	.381	3158	793	135	15	82	82	282	583
Leadoff	.275	.343	.439	1340	369	63	6	48	48	132	246
Not Leadoff	.233	.295	.339	1818	424	72	9	34	34	150	337
Runners On Base	.261	.334	.395	2360	615	100	13	64	543	265	455
First Base Only	.297	.341	.450	956	284	40	5	32	82	60	168
Scoring Position	.236	.330	.358	1404	331	60	8	32	461	205	287
Late Innings, Close	.243	.329	.404	1029	250	43	6	37	139	134	227

RBI/Opportunities			
Scoring Position	395 / 1944	(20%)	
Scoring Position, 2 Out	153 / 890	(17%)	
On Third, Less than 2 Out	137 / 332	(41%)	
RBI in close games / RBI Total	442 / 625	(71%)	

When I think of San Francisco pitching, I think of the split-fingered fastball. This club's staff was the National League ERA champ, allowing the fewest runs in the league last year while finishing third in strikeouts. The following is a short dissertation on the subject of the splitter, the pitch credited with the success of the team's pitchers.

The Giants led the world in turning double plays last year. Clearly, the number of ground balls that result from the splitter accounts for the high GDP total. Certainly the staff deserves more of the credit than Rob Thompson does. San Francisco had the second-highest wild pitch total in the league, also as a result of the ubiquity of the splitter. I remember a 1–0 game Scott Garrelts was brought in to save against the Mets. New York had loaded the bases with no outs. Garrelts struck out the side, but the Mets took the lead on two wild pitches, both splitters.

Overall, I think the pitch is vastly overrated. The only pitcher I can think of who has significantly risen in stature as a result of that pitch is Mike Scott. In my opinion (don't sue me, Mike) it is sandpaper which has bolstered Scott's career. The founder of the split-fingered fastball, Bruce Sutter, is still packing his arm in ice and hasn't thrown a pitch since . . . In fact, the man on the Giants staff who features the splitter the most prominently is Mike Krukow. Notice how dead his arm was last year? Did you notice the long list of disabled hurlers this year? Is it a coincidence that arm trouble for pitchers has risen as the splitter has spread? For example, Roger Craig popularized the pitch with Detroit in 1984. Have you noticed the physical problems that have plagued Dan Petry and Willie Hernandez since?

Yes, it is a tough pitch to hit, but if you hang a splitter, watch it sail over the fence. I attribute part of the significant rise in home runs to the popularity of this pitch, as well as the rise in strikeouts. No one can doubt that it is a double-edged sword in a pitcher's arsenal.

Enough about the split-fingered fastball. Let's run down the staff. GM Al Rosen acquired Dave Dravecky, Craig Lefferts, Don Robinson and Rick Reuschel during the season. Dravecky stabilized the staff in the second half, taking over the stopper role from the ineffective Krukow. The bullpen was full of ground ball pitchers like Garrelts, Jeff Robinson, and Greg Minton. Don Robinson provided the staff with a fireballer, a breed not recently associated with the Giants.

San Francisco is a good, solid team, but does not tower over its competition. I think the splitter will take a further toll in injuries to the pitching staff. Reuschel is an on-again, off-again pitcher, due for a bad year in '88. The combination means that this club will not repeat in 1988.

Ira Saltz

ST. LOUIS CARDINALS
HITTING

				1987 SEASON							
	Ave.	OBP	SLG	AB	H	2B	3B	HR	RBI	BB	SO
Totals	.263	.340	.378	5501	1449	251	49	94	746	644	933
vs. Left	.263	.342	.389	1896	498	97	14	38	278	238	315
vs. Right	.264	.339	.373	3605	951	154	35	56	468	406	618
at Home	.264	.335	.379	2676	707	128	26	42	366	285	444
on Road	.263	.345	.378	2825	742	123	23	52	380	359	489
vs. Groundball	.260	.335	.365	2592	675	117	18	39	343	289	424
vs. Flyball	.266	.344	.390	2909	774	134	31	55	403	355	509
vs. Finesse	.270	.341	.382	2896	783	135	24	47	400	316	387
vs. Power	.256	.338	.374	2605	666	116	25	47	346	328	546
on Grass	.267	.349	.374	1460	390	58	10	26	200	188	264
on Artificial Turf	.262	.336	.380	4041	1059	193	39	68	546	456	669
Day Games	.285	.362	.414	1952	557	94	16	42	300	238	314
Night Games	.251	.328	.358	3549	892	157	33	52	446	406	619
April	.275	.352	.412	677	186	40	4	15	96	80	120
May	.294	.366	.419	909	267	43	10	17	155	105	150
June	.286	.360	.391	954	273	35	10	15	146	111	141
July	.253	.344	.370	930	235	42	8	17	117	128	173
August	.257	.336	.381	993	255	54	9	17	132	122	149
Sept/Oct	.224	.289	.313	1038	233	37	8	13	100	98	200
Bases Empty	.248	.323	.350	3010	745	128	28	42	42	325	536
Leadoff	.266	.350	.377	1293	344	58	13	20	20	158	215
Not Leadoff	.234	.303	.330	1717	401	70	15	22	22	167	321
Runners On	.283	.359	.411	2491	704	123	21	52	704	319	397
First Base Only	.310	.367	.453	917	284	56	6	21	72	80	138
Scoring Position	.267	.355	.388	1574	420	67	15	31	632	239	259
Late Innings, Close	.260	.336	.367	1019	265	46	6	17	139	116	205

	RBI/Opportunities		
Scoring Position	563 /	2256	(25%)
Scoring Position, 2 Out	202 /	986	(20%)
On Third, Less than 2 Out	244 /	460	(53%)
RBI in close games / RBI Total	491 /	746	(66%)

From the opening day of the 1987 season right through the Series, manager Whitey Herzog could not make out a lineup without first visiting the trainer's room. The Cardinals totaled 324 days of players on the disabled list and the emergency leave list. This figure would be even higher if Jack Clark's September and October were included. During this period he was listed as active, but in reality unable to perform. Thus the key to the team's success was the strength of the bench and its assiduous use by Whitey. Steve Lake, Jose Oquendo, Curt Ford, Dan Driessen and John Morris all performed in much larger roles than originally planned, and Home Run Tom Lawless emerged from the bottom of the roster for post season action.

Vince Coleman raised his OBP dramatically in 1987, his most effective year. A reduction in strikeouts would make him a .300 hitter and push his on base figure to near .400. Tom Herr was #2 among NL second basemen in double plays. Herr's key role in the Cardinal attack was to make contact so Coleman could cover that last 90 feet to home plate.

Tony Pena is the most popular catcher here since Tim McCarver. But Pena's poor hitting prompted hitting coach Johnny Lewis to suggest an eye test. Sure enough, Tony needed glasses. They made the difference, for he hit over .300 with the specs on, compared with .214 overall. He'll be wearing contacts this year.

The sleeper on the St. Louis 40 man roster could be a former, forgotten-about Cardinal. David Green was dealt to the Giants in the Jack Clark deal. There he drank his way out of organized baseball. But the Redbirds gave him another chance at Louisville last year, and he hit .356 in 50 games there. He is now 27 and has all the tools to help the big club in 1988.

Outside of Clark, no Cardinal had a career year. Ozzie Smith broke .300 for the first time (.303), but his average has been climbing over the past three seasons. Terry Pendleton hit .324 in 67 games when he came up in 1984. Although he dropped in '85 and '86, his .286 average with 96 RBI's could be his median for the next few years.

Jim Lindeman and Bob Horner will be dropped into the Jack Clark power gap in '88. Jim's .208 '87 BA, and low AB and HR totals were due to a ruptured disc. It's a good thing Jim's back will be 100 percent this season, for he will be asked to carry a lot of the offense on it. Remember, his bat was the reason St. Louis felt able to trade Andy Van Slyke to get Tony Pena. Horner seems perfect as Clark's roster replacement, since he's another part-time RH power hitter. Willie McGee drove in over 100 runs for the first time last year, but even the three of these hitters together cannot compensate for Clark's loss. The Cardinals have no chance of repeating as NL East Champs.

Rollie Loewen

ST. LOUIS CARDINALS
PITCHING

	G	IP	H	BB	SO	SB	CS	W	L	S	ERA
1987 SEASON											
Totals	525	1466.0	1484	533	872	100	49	95	67	48	3.94
at Home	261	747.0	754	250	441	56	26	49	32	19	3.78
on Road	264	719.0	730	283	431	44	23	46	35	29	4.11
Day Games	181	503.1	517	194	300	28	13	36	20	21	3.90
Night Games	344	962.2	967	339	572	72	36	59	47	27	3.96
on Grass	132	370.2	362	135	233	22	12	26	16	17	3.71
on Artificial Turf	393	1095.1	1122	398	639	78	37	69	51	31	4.02
April	65	178.2	178	67	107	8	4	12	8	9	3.93
May	88	232.1	272	75	111	16	6	17	9	9	4.84
June	85	254.1	248	89	164	22	5	17	11	9	3.75
July	88	249.0	240	99	159	17	12	16	11	6	3.72
August	95	268.1	283	104	140	18	12	17	12	7	3.99
Sept/Oct	104	283.1	263	99	191	19	10	16	16	8	3.53

vs. Opponent Batters	Ave.	OBP	SLG	AB	H	2B	3B	HR	RBI	BB	SO
Totals	.265	.331	.404	5590	1484	299	45	129	653	533	872
vs. Left	.268	.340	.378	1825	489	100	13	25	186	200	292
vs. Right	.264	.326	.417	3765	995	199	32	104	467	333	580
Bases Empty	.266	.324	.414	3198	850	168	31	81	81	258	489
Leadoff	.280	.330	.430	1369	383	75	14	34	34	95	210
Not Leadoff	.255	.320	.402	1829	467	93	17	47	47	163	279
Runners On Base	.265	.339	.392	2392	634	131	14	48	572	275	383
First Base Only	.276	.323	.400	966	267	51	4	20	64	62	150
Scoring Position	.257	.349	.386	1426	367	80	10	28	508	213	233
Late Innings, Close	.260	.348	.398	1068	278	50	11	25	145	143	209

RBI/Opportunities			
Scoring Position		438 / 1961	(22%)
Scoring Position, 2 Out		178 / 923	(19%)
On Third, Less than 2 Out		158 / 344	(46%)
RBI in close games / RBI Total		447 / 653	(68%)

The Cardinal pitching staff produced a true team effort in the 1987 pennant campaign. Necessarily so, for no member won more than eleven games during the season. This was three fewer than the previous low individual victory total for a division winner.

Despite the lack of star performers, a superb pitching staff works in St. Louis. They deal in results, not marquee statistics. Consider this: With most squads you begin talking about pitching by discussing the starters. With the 1988 Cardinals, you begin in the bullpen. This team won more games in 1987 than any other National League team, and was second from the bottom in complete games with only ten. The Mound City Nine's closing left-right punch is arguably the very best. Ken Dayley (4 saves) and Todd Worrell (33 saves) were the perfect weapons in manager Whitey Herzog's late inning arsenal with identical 2.66 ERAs, and combined finished more than half of the Redbirds' games. Dayley was used carefully; he faced the key lefthanders while Worrell handled the righthanders. The combination was so effective that in two contests Mr. Worrell was moved to right field while Mr. Dayley operated on a leftside batter.

Righthander Scott Terry, obtained in the latter part of the season in the Pat Perry deal with Cincinnati, was a big boost. He may fill the right-handed set-up role vacated by the disabled Jeff Lahti. Lefty Ricky Horton is a rare triple threat. He can start and do both long and short relief. Other contributors in the St. Louis pen include rookie lefthander Steve Peters and righthander Lee Tunnell.

The Cardinal starting rotation, unless some trades are made, will again be mostly southpaws. Ricky Horton may join John Tudor, Greg Mathews and Joe Magrane for left-handed starts. Both Mathews and Magrane had seasons that cause fans to be optimistic about their futures. Tudor will spend his dugout time encased in plexiglass whenever Barry Lyons is on the field in the future. He figures to bounce back up to the 20 victory level this year if he can avoid kamikaze catchers. John now has a StL winning percentage of .721, the best in Cardinal history.

Danny Cox is the right-handed ace of the staff. He is 28, entering what will be his most productive years if only he can break his string of injuries from the past two years. Bob Forsch will remain with the club in a spot role if he swallows a big salary cut. If he goes, it is most likely that fans will get an early look at a rookie righty. Two likely candidates are Chris Carpenter and Ken Hill. Hill is already on the 40 man roster, and showed 90+ heat this winter with a 3–1 strikeout-to-walk ratio. Carpenter is fresh from the University of Georgia and the Pan Am games. He was the #1 St. Louis draft pick last year, and was impressive in winter ball.

The bullpen is there, and the starters will be as good as their health. If the '88 medical report contains good news, this staff could be the best in the National League this year.

Rollie Loewen and Joe May

III

THE MANAGERS

INTRODUCTION

This part of the book deals with the people many baseball fans love to hate, their home team managers. Rather than indulge in emotional evaluations of these men, we have tried to present here careful, reasoned analyses of the tendencies, the strengths and the weaknesses of these poor souls who lead their teams into battle. Of course, these guys aren't so poor anymore, as they have been getting paid much better in recent years.

In this section you will find one or two essays for each of the twenty-six major league team's skippers. There are not many statistics commonly used to evaluate the manager's, completely unlike the situation for the ballplayers whom they manage, where there are reams of stats available for the fans and analysts to argue over. Thus, these essays use many different formats and follow many different thought lines to make their points. I hope that you find the net result to be informative, thought-provoking, and—most of all—enjoyable.

Gary Gillette

MANAGER ESSAYS

Atlanta Braves
CHUCK TANNER

In the last few years, it has been difficult to separate Chuck Tanner the person from Chuck Tanner the manager. Tanner's reputation was shredded (with considerable justification) by Bill James in the 1986 *Abstract* for his non-action during the Pittsburgh drug scandal, and his previously high standing among managers has dwindled with four consecutive poor finishes. His positive outlook was once widely admired, but is not as valued in a more cynical time. Of the five things a manager does (maintain respect of his players, handle the pitching staff, lineup selection, in-game tactics, and dealing with the media), Tanner has usually been above average in four of them. But his consistently poor lineup selection throughout his managerial career has detracted from his successes in the other areas. Despite his poor talent judgement, the Braves are the first team that Tanner has not had a positive impact on.

LEADERSHIP STYLE. Chuck Tanner has always believed that a positive outlook will cure most ills. In his first job (the 1971 White Sox) his optimism was a big boost to a dispirited franchise that had not contended since 1967. The 1971 team won 23 more games than the 1970 team and the addition of Dick Allen in 1972 brought the team up to 87 wins and second place. Tanner will almost never criticize a player to the press and his players seem to like and respect him. Tanner will also almost never make a change unless forced to. The negative side of Tanner's unabashed optimism is that it blinds him to the faults and aging of his players. His pattern has been to stay with the core of his teams regardless of how they are playing. This style is most effective in a situation like he had in Pittsburgh—a core of veterans in their prime that required few changes until they got old. Tanner's style would probably be effective following a high pressure manager like a Dick Williams or Billy Martin. The low pressure managers (Jim Frey is a good example) are usually successful for a year or two by removing the pressure, but their teams seem to fade in the long run. That has been Tanner's pattern; the White Sox played good ball for two years before fading the next three years, and the Pirates were a very good team for three years (winning it all in 1979) before dropping out of contention the next six years. The Braves are the first team to not respond to Tanner's style, but he was replacing another low pressure manager (Eddie Haas) and has a team that is not suited to his style. The Braves are in dire need of change and Chuck Tanner is about the last manager you would want in a situation that requires a lot of changes.

PERSONNEL. Given how long he has managed, relatively few players have developed under him. The following notable players received their first opportunity to start under Tanner: Brian Downing, Bucky Dent, Jorge Orta, Rich Gossage, Terry Forster, Omar Moreno, Tony Pena, Johnny Ray, Don Robinson, Marvell Wynne, Andres Thomas, and Gerald Perry. It's a list that isn't particularly long on quantity or quality. Tanner will not rush rookies into the lineup like a Dick Williams, usually his rookies are reserves for a year or two before getting their chance. In 1973 Bucky Dent sat while the immortal Eddie Leon played. On the same team Downing sat in favor of Ed Herrmann and Chuck Brinkman. Andres Thomas (who had Ramirez's SS job handed to him) is the exception rather than the rule. On his Chicago rosters you can find players at the end of the line like Ron Santo, Buddy Bradford, Rick Reichardt, and Rich Morales while in Pittsburgh you can find names like Bobby Tolan, Jim Fregosi, Tommy Helms and Manny Sanguillen. His likely bench in 1988 will include Ken Griffey, Gary Roenicke, Ted Simmons, and Graig Nettles. Tanner favors a set lineup when possible, but has used platooning to good effect. In Pittsburgh, the Ed Ott/Steve Nicosia combination covered the catching position during the Family years and he had success with LF platoons involving Lee Lacy, Mike Easler, and Bill Robinson. In Atlanta, the Griffey/Roenicke platoon was successful while a platoon experiment with Dion James and Albert

Hall was aborted by injuries to Hall. The biggest problem with Chuck Tanner as a manager is his total and complete inablilty to select leadoff men. Tanner's ideal leadoff hitter was Omar Moreno, who never had an OBA higher than .339 in his career and was frequently below .300. When Moreno left the Pirates, Marvell Wynne (.310 OBA) got the job. In Chicago it was the same thing with some speed/few walks outfielders like Pat Kelly, Walt Williams, and Johnny Jeter (9 walks in 300 AB in 1973) leading off. In Atlanta Tanner used players that were slower than Moreno with even lower OBA like Ramirez, Thomas, and Moreno (again!). In 1987 Dion James become the first legitimate (.397 OBA) leadoff hitter that Tanner has used in 17 years of managing, and I'm convinced he got the job only because he looks like Moreno and the Braves organization thought that Dion was much faster than he turned out to be. Had Chuck known James was going to steal only ten bases, he probably would have batted him 7th. Entirely consistent with his past, Tanner plans to move James to the 3rd spot in 1988 so he can lead off with another fast outfielder with a so-so OBA (Albert Hall or Terry Blocker). How much has this silly conception cost his teams? I calculated his teams' runs created and discovered that seven of his teams scored significantly fewer runs than the formulas estimated. Only three of his teams ('72 Sox, '76 A's, '78 Pirates) significantly outproduced their RC estimate. After 17 years you would think that somewhere along the line someone would have tipped Chuck off that the objective of the leadoff hitter is to get on base and that you can't steal first base. If you looked at a Chuck Tanner lineup card from 1971–1986 you'd never know that.

OFFENSIVE TACTICS. In 1987, Tanner called his offensive plan "ABC Ball"—A) the batter gets on, B) he moves up, and C) he's driven in. The Braves did well in A and B (2nd in the league in OBA and 1st in SH) but flunked the C portion of the equation. Tanner is in a Catch-22 in Atlanta: In a tremendous hitters park it is usually dumb to waste outs with sacrifices, but with this group of talent there is little power outside of Murphy. Tanner likes to hit and run, primarily to break up DP possibilities. Stolen bases have always been a favorite weapon of Tanner's, but after a dismal year in 1986 (the team had a 55 percent success rate) Tanner appears to have adjusted his thinking to his talent. In 1987 the Braves stole 135 bases at a 67 percent success rate. His Pittsburgh teams usually averaged 200 SB a year, but with Stargell, Parker and others he had some power to go with the speed. His Oakland team stole 341 bases, but again they had some power to back up the speed.

DEFENSIVE TACTICS. Tanner's defensive tactics appear to have evolved over time. In the AL he used a four-man rotation almost exclusively while he now uses a 4 1/2 man rotation with two or three starters splitting the fifth spot. Tanner has usually stuck with his starters except when he had an exceptional group bullpen in Pittsburgh. He usually designates one closer and sticks with him (Forster and then Gossage in Chicago, Tekulve in Pittsburgh, and Garber in Atlanta). He plays conventional left/right percentages and issues an average amount of intentional walks. He has a strong tendency to favor junk throwers as opposed to power pitchers—Forster, Gossage, Larry McWilliams, and Jose DeLeon are the only real power pitchers he's used

518

extensively. The entire Atlanta staff threw junk in 1987—Zane Smith led the staff with 130 Ks in 242 IP.

STRATEGY. Chuck Tanner's positive impact on the White Sox and Pirates was built on defensive improvements. With the Sox, he moved Wilbur Wood from the bullpen to the rotation, eliminated some deadwood, and dropped the team's runs allowed from 822 to 597. With his Pittsburgh team he restructured his outfield, which in 1976 consisted of Dave Parker, Richie Zisk and Al Oliver. By trading Zisk, moving Oliver to LF, and playing Moreno in CF (he couldn't hit but he was a fine CF) Tanner greatly improved the his defense. Tanner is attempting to repeat the move in 1988—moving Dion James to LF and inserting Albert Hall or Terry Blocker in CF. One other noticable Tanner characteristic is his preference for offensive second basemen. He tried to make Ron Santo a second baseman at the end of his career, used Jorge Orta and Rennie Stennett as regulars (neither were much on the DP) and released Glenn Hubbard (superb defensively) to make room for more offense from Ronnie Gant. The 1987 Braves were a very atypical Tanner team—one that took walks, didn't run much, had a good leadoff hitter, and scored significantly more runs than they had in 1986.

SUMMARY. Tanner's strengths (pitching and maintaining respect) are countered by his usually poor utilization of his offensive talent. For a mediocre manager (his career record is now slightly below .500), Tanner is moving up on the career list for wins. If he finishes his current contract (which has three years to run), he could end up with with about 1600 wins, 12th on the all-time list. The 1988 Braves will require considerable rebuilding and nothing in Tanner's record suggests that he will be able to work with a rebuilding team. His work with a rebuilding Pirate team in 1985 was a disaster; the '88 Braves will be the biggest challenge of his career. (Credit Don Zminda for information on Tanner's White Sox years.)

Greg Gajus

Frankly, Chuck Tanner and the southern exposure of his recent teams are so well documented that trying to write a piece which would bring out new insights about the man is somewhat futile. So, we'll try to get a picture of where Chuck belongs alongside his contemporaries, and look at the state of the managing profession. Here's the record of Tanner and the ten other managers who have at least ten full seasons of service during the divisional play era (1969–87):

	Win Pct.	Seasons	1st's in Div.	Teams Managed
Earl Weaver	.583	15	6	1
Sparky Anderson	.576	17	7	2
Billy Martin	.550	13	5	5+
Whitey Herzog	.542	12	6	3
Tommy Lasorda	.535	11	5	1
Dick Williams	.519	14	4	6
Bill Virdon	.519	11	3	4
Chuck Tanner	.497	17	1	4
Ralph Houk	.49	14	0	3

John McNamara	.492	12	2	5
Gene Mauch	.491	15	2	3

One look at this list should dispel any myth about having to fit a particular style to hold down a job as a major league manager: these men fall all over the map. You can also see that continuing success is also not an absolute requirement. The managers in the top half of the list have both reverent fans and hard-core detractors, and it's easy to see why. Their theories on how to win serve as the basis for their actions, and, thus, feedback is almost instantaneous. Whitey trades Keith Hernandez, and it's open season on white rats. But, Whitey brings up Willie McGee and Vince Coleman, and gets credit for that, also.

On the other hand, Tanner and McNamara, among others, must be classified more as "organization" men, staying in the background, letting the team play. This approach can be successful in limited applications; for example, when a strong team is already in place or when a team is under considerable pressure and needs a low-key leader to put things in proper perspective. However, it is rarely successful for more than a year or two, because the center of the team begins to move. Without a manager who lets the team members know what is expected of them, the team flounders about in search of direction. Just look at the 1982 Reds and 1983 Angels, or, even worse, the Pirates of the early 1980s. Tanner did not inherit a bad team; neither did McNamara. Their teams just grew old on them, and they either refused to or could not identify the young talent needed to restructure their teams. Organization men can win, but their positions must be carefully chosen for them.

Major league teams have absolutely no excuse for settling for the same old choices every time a managerial position opens. Applying a statistical fact inspired by Bill James, there is a bountiful supply of "replacement-level" managers, guys who can win at least as often as the less successful managers already in the bigs. It's likely that there are some real gems waiting for a chance to show their stuff. But the same biases are still present in the thinking which dictates both roster decisions and managerial choices, especially on second-division teams. Use the proven people, even if what they have proven is absolutely nothing. The Pirates have largely scrapped conventional wisdom for two years now, and though Thrift, Leyland & Company may yet fall flat on their collective faces, there is truly a revived interest in baseball in Pittsburgh. In fact, for the first time in years, fans were talking baseball in December. Look, Minnesota broke through with a novice manager. Jimy Williams has developed well in Toronto. Williams, Lou Piniella, and Pete Rose are first of a new wave from which both good and bad managers will come—among them will be black managers, men like Willie Stargell and Bill Robinson. No doubt about it, we'll hear many of the same old complaints about this group, too.

Back to Chuck. If you accept the theory of the "organization" manager, Tanner's record doesn't surprise you. At both Chicago and Pittsburgh, success came early in his tenure. He inherited a bad team in Chicago, but quickly turned it into a contender for a couple of years. Tanner's chief strength has been molding good pitching staffs, and in his good years at Chicago, the team's improvement was largely tied to pitching. He developed a bullpen, picked up some strikeout pitchers and the staff ERA improved

markedly, from last in the AL in 1969–70 to 4th in 1971. Though this overall performance was not sustained, the strength of the bullpen did ensure a respectable staff during his Chicago years.

Unfortunately, the offense was not similarly perked up. Tanner does not generally go for strong defense at the expense of hitting, so this may come as some surprise. He does tend to settle on good double play combinations, though. The Sox did a lot of running Tanner's first two years, though they slowed down later after he got some power into the lineup. Later in his career, Tanner teams would finish among the top three teams in their league in SBs in seven consecutive seasons. Otherwise, it seems Tanner simply inserts his favorite players into the lineup and accepts whatever they produce.

This illustrates one of the strongest tendencies of Chuck Tanner—his clear preference for veterans on the bench. This is complicated by the fact that when a starting position becomes available, he then gives those veterans every chance to win the job, even when past performance is a clear indicator of their abilities. In Chicago, every position changed hands at least once during his tenure. Who filled these vacancies? Imported 26- to 30-year-olds who had to be at or near their prime, players such as Mike Andrews, Rick Reichardt, Jay Johnstone, Ed Leon, John Jeter, and Ken Henderson. Truthfully, the Sox shouldn't have been expected to win with this team, and Bob Lemon cleaned house when he arrived in 1977.

After one season in Oakland, Tanner moved on to Pittsburgh. Pittsburgh really believed that Tanner was a valuable commodity, and I'm sure they weren't alone. But basically he served as a caretaker for nine years, and all of you saw what happened.

As before, Tanner showed his knack for handling a pitching staff, though the starters didn't always like his limited expectations for them. The Pirates had strong pitching before Tanner came to town, and they maintained it throughout most of his tenure. Again, however, the workload was redistributed to emphasize the bullpen. Complete game totals went down the tubes, and the relief pitchers ran up incredible numbers for appearances. Strikeouts also jumped, with pitchers like Kent Tekulve, Enrique Romo, Grant Jackson, Odell Jones, Goose Gossage, and, later, Rod Scurry. The starters grumbled because, with names like Jerry Reuss, Jim Bibby, John Candelaria, Bert Blyleven, Bruce Kison, Rick Rhoden, and Don Robinson, they weren't exactly chopped liver. The problems of the '80s eventually wrecked the pitching as well as the hitting; nevertheless, for a pitching staff in a hitters' park, Chuck need not apologize for his handling of pitchers.

Unfortunately, Tanner couldn't keep an offense together beyond 1980. Lumber and Lightning went the way of middle age spread. As in Chicago, the bench players were largely veterans who were effective in reserve roles. In 1977, Tanner had immediately inserted Phil Garner, Omar Moreno, and Ed Ott into the lineup. Later additions would include Bill Robinson, Jason Thompson, Tim Foli, Bill Madlock, Mike Easler, and Lee Lacy. Though Tony Pena and Johnny Ray later cracked the lineup, things didn't change significantly. In 1985 alone, the team added George Hendrick, Steve Kemp, Sixto Lezcano, Al Holland, and Bill Almon. It took a change of GMs and new ownership to begin reversing this trend.

There was no doubt Chuck would find another job upon leaving the Pirates, but Atlanta was one of the last places Tanner should have gone. He fits in very well in the organization, and he's a great interview for the Superstation, but this was a team that really needed a kick in the seat and some new blood. Instead, the Braves have actually brought in Omar Moreno, Billy Sample, Ted Simmons, Graig Nettles, and Charlie Puleo, among others. They even let Bob Horner get away. They do have some guys like Murph and Glenn Hubbard who deserve much better than this, and Dion James, Gerald Perry, and Albert Hall are showing considerable promise, but it's going to take a lot more than that. The Braves need more offense in their park, and the pitching absolutely has to be revamped. Since Tanner does seem to have the ability to work on the latter, there is some hope.

Many managers never win anything, so I would never label Chuck Tanner a loser. But it is clear that the guidance he provides is minimal and that he is not a team builder like Whitey Herzog or Dick Williams. Further, with the endless pool of managerial prospects now waiting in the wings, no team should have problems finding a capable skipper to fill their needs without dipping into the old pool. Right now, I can't think of anyone who needs the organization-type manager, including the Braves. If Tanner is successful this season, it will be because he broke with some of his past practices. It could be a refreshing change.

Al Nakamura

Baltimore Orioles
CAL RIPKEN, SR.

Cal Ripken, Sr., is a man for whom timing hasn't always been the best. After the 1982 season when Earl Weaver retired, the O's had finished just a game back of Milwaukee, and it would have been a good time to take over as manager of the team. Cal didn't get the job—Joe Altobelli did—and Altobelli led the team to the World's Championship.

After 1983, things started to head downhill in Birdland. After being out of the pennant race in 1984 and the first half of 1985, Orioles' owner Edward Bennent Williams (frequently referred to as EBW) decided to make a managerial change. The new manager would not be taking over a club as good as the club that Altobelli took over, but it was still a winning team, so the new manager still had a chance to do something. Cal didn't get the chance then, either; the new manager was the old manager, Earl Weaver.

Bringing back Earl Weaver did not stop the downward spiral, though. The Orioles never really got into the pennant race in 1985, and 1986 was even worse. The team had a winning record as late as August, but they went 14–42 in their last 56 games (the pace of the 1962 New York Mets) to finish last for the first time in history. Now that the Orioles had hit bottom, they gave Cal Ripken, Sr. his chance to manage the team.

How good of a job did Cal Ripken, Sr. do in 1987? After only one season, with a team with literally no pitching, it's not really fair to judge him yet. However, there were a couple of things that need to be mentioned, if only to have the record be complete.

First is the lack of consistency in the 1987 Orioles. To explain that, one must first understand how the schedule in the American League works. The schedule is divided into four distinct parts. The first part takes approximately the first two months of the season, and in it, a team plays nine teams home and away. The second part takes about a month to play, and a team plays the other four clubs home and away. The third and fourth parts are repeats of the first and second parts. The schedule is also set up so each club visits each other club once for a weekend series and once for a weekday series each season. One team in the East is designated the "swing" team, and for scheduling purposes, they are considered a Western club. The other six Eastern clubs play the seven AL West clubs, the swing club, and one other AL East opponent in the first and third parts, and the other four Eastern clubs in the second and fourth parts. In 1987, Cleveland (the swing team) and Milwaukee were the two divisional opponents that the Orioles played in the first and third parts.

The chart below shows how the 1987 Orioles did by part of the season:

Part	Dates	W	L	Pct	GB	Place
1	4/6 to 6/3	27	25	.519	6.0	3rd
2	6/4 to 7/1	4	22	.154	18.0	6th
3	7/2 to 9/6	31	27	.534	20.0	6th
4	9/7 to 10/4	5	21	.192	31.0	6th

Yes, the Orioles, over four months had a *winning* record, 58–52 (.527). That's better than the World Champion Minnesota Twins did! For the other two months they were the most pitiful team to hit a field, 9–42 (.176)—the 1962 Mets played .250 ball. Even though the teams the Orioles played in parts one and three weren't as good as their part two and four opponents, the difference was not that great; in games not involving Baltimore, the part one and three teams had a .485 winning percentage, while the part two and four teams' percentage was .534. That is a significant difference, but nowhere near enough to explain the differences in the Orioles' play.

One of the jobs of the manager is to keep the team going throughout the entire season. The 1987 Orioles, though, had two disastrous collapses, and were not really a .527 team, but they weren't a .176 team, either. In that sense, then, Cal Ripken, Sr. did not have a successful season. When things were going bad, it seems that he was not able to bring them out of it soon enough.

The other thing that needs to be mentioned was where he had Larry Sheets batting in the lineup. Sheets had a superb season with the bat, but Ripken had Sheets down near the bottom of the order for much of the season. The two charts below show Sheets' hitting stats for 1987 and his position in the batting order when he started the game.

	AB	H	HR	BI	BA	RC	RC/G
Hitting	469	148	31	94	.316	95	7.5

	3rd	4th	5th	6th	7th	8th	9th
Position	3	1	36	15	15	52	4

Why did Cal Sr. do this? One possible explanation is Sheets big lefty-righty differential. After all, he was mostly just a platoon player before 1987. Below are Sheets' stats, broken out by lefty and righty pitchers, and his starting batting position, broken out by starting pitchers.

Hitting	AB	H	HR	BI	BA
Lefties	145	44	10	29	.303
Righties	325	104	21	65	.320

Position	3rd	4th	5th	6th	7th	8th	9th
Lefties	0	0	3	9	7	10	0
Righties	3	1	33	6	8	42	4

Actually, Sheets' hitting stats are very balanced, especially considering that he used to be platooned. He also may have hit lower in the order against lefties, but he still hit seventh or lower more than half of the time against righties.

Another logical explanation would be that Sheets got off to a slow start, and picked it up through the year. The chart below divides the season into six fairly even sections by splitting parts one and three of the season into two sections each, and gives Sheets' stats and batting position by section. TG is team games during that period.

Part	TG	AB	HR	BI	BA	3rd–6th	7th–9th
1A	23	29	1	6	.379	0	8
1B	29	89	11	26	.348	5	19
2	26	73	2	13	.247	9	10
3A	27	82	4	15	.305	9	12
3B	31	104	9	22	.337	14	14
4	26	92	4	12	.304	17	9

The stats show that Sheets actually started strong and, except for a slump during part two, hit well throughout the season. This chart also shows that eventually Ripken realized the kind of season that Sheets was having and started moving him up in the order. However, he still hit in the bottom third of the order in about a third of the games in part four, the part in which the O's went 5–21.

There is one last reasonable explanation to why Sheets hit so far down in the order so much in 1987. He might not have been able to hit well higher in the order. The last set of stats shows Sheets' batting statistics when he started the game hitting fifth or higher in the order.

	AB	H	HR	BI	BA
3rd to 5th	152	49	8	30	.322

His stats batting higher in the order are almost an exact parallel of his full season stats. There is no reason to believe that Larry Sheets hits differently if he hits in the traditional power spots.

After examining the evidence, no reason was found for Cal to be batting Larry Sheets down in the batting order so much in 1987. It seems that he was slow to react to the increase in Sheets' productivity. The jury is still out on Manager Ripken, and he deserves another chance. EBW fired the right people after the 1987 season, the general manager and the farm director. They're the people that gave Ripken that horrible pitching staff, a staff no one could have won with. However, EBW might be expecting too much out of O's in 1988; he has commented that the Red Sox went from fifth to first in one year. That is unrealistic, it would be shocking if the Orioles could finish ahead of any of the five good teams above them. EBW might take out his disappointment on his manager, and that would be unfair to Ripken. It really was Ripken's bad luck to get the Orioles only after the good times were over.

Dave Raglin

———

Cal Ripken, Sr. managed in the Orioles farm system from 1961 to 1974 and compiled a record of 983–840 (.539). He managed two years in "D" ball, five in single "A," five in double "A," and two in triple "A." Ripken spent 1975 as a scout and farm system trouble shooter, joining the parent club as a bullpen coach in 1976. In June of 1977, he took over as third base coach and stayed there until he was tapped as manager for the 1987 season.

You can't fault this guy's credentials—he's been in the Orioles' system for twenty-six years, for God's sake. Talk about paying your dues: He is reputed to be, and clearly is, "a solid baseball man." But it makes you wonder doesn't it? I mean, it's kind of like that old saying, "If he's so smart, how come he ain't rich?" Of course, part of it can be attributed to Earl Weaver's longevity in Baltimore, and part of it can be attributed to a remarkable sense of loyalty. (Twenty-six years!) When Earl left for the first time at the end of the 1982 season, Ripken was passed over in favor of Joe Altobelli. Ripken stayed on as third base coach, and when Weaver returned in 1985 . . . Ripken stayed on as third base coach. Finally, after Weaver threw in the towel (again) in 1986, Ripken was named as manager. Some cynics suggested that the fact that Cal Jr. was going to become a free agent in 1987 might have had something to do with the decision to make Cal Sr. the skipper. A more charitable view may be that he certainly deserved a shot. Whatever factors went into the decision, Cal Ripken, Sr. has been unable to apply the breaks to the Orioles' slide from the elite to the incomplete.

It is difficult to assess a man's managerial capabilities and style based on one season, particularly a season like 1987. The Most Valuable Oriole in 1986, Don Aase, disappeared onto the DL in April and did not reappear in uniform during the season, which went downhill from there.

Not noted for verbosity as a coach, Ripken became positively chatty as a manager. I can't tell you what he had to say to his players but the texts for his radio interviews were obviously prepared by some bureaucrat in the Department of Redundancy Department. Cal invariably answered every question with an insightful explanation that the key to winning ball games was to score more runs than the other team. Of course, there was the corollary: The key to winning ball games was to allow the other team to score fewer runs. Cal could paraphrase and restate these two concepts in enough ways to fill up the alloted interview time, so don't look for Cal to become a commentator when his managerial career is over.

Look, don't get me wrong. I would never imply Cal Ripken, Sr. doesn't understand the game. Cal understands the game, but he just didn't seem to understand the Orioles. After watching Weaver's patented "wait-for-a-three-run-homer" approach, Cal wanted to make things happen. He bunted, he hit-and-ran; hell, he even threw in a few double steals for good measure. Unfortunately, the Orioles aren't a team that is capable of doing any activity that requires foot speed. These guys are S-L-O-W, and I'm not entirely convinced that Cal ever reconciled himself to this fact.

But hey, you got to do something, right? The pitching staff was absolutely laughable and, although you can't blame Cal for their demise, you can't give him any credit for turning them around either. He tried everything—tried them as starters, in middle relief and in short relief. He fiddled with the rotation, he fiddled with the roster, but not much worked. He made Tom Niedenfuer his short man and never looked back. He couldn't figure what to do with Ken Dixon. He stuck with Scott McGregor for reasons only Cal can fathom. And so it goes. When a team loses 95 games, not much goes right.

The original plan was to emphasize defense, particularly outfield defense, with Ken Gerhart in left and John Shelby in center. That plan died as Gerhart looked like he would need to drop bread crumbs to find his way back to the dugout and Shelby was tattooing the ball at a .188 clip. The original plan was to shore up second base with Rick Burleson and use Alan Wiggins as DH; neither was on the roster by the end of August. The original plan was to use a rotation of McGregor, Flanagan, Dixon, Eric Bell and Mike Boddicker. Of those five, only the ones whose names start with "B" were pitching in the major leagues in June. The other three were seeing if they could get anybody out for the Rochester Red Wings.

What happened to the Orioles last season is not Ripken's fault. The Orioles know it, and that's why he's back for 1988. Unfortunately for Cal this team is not on the verge of some sort of magical turnaround and Owner Edward Bennett Williams is not a patient man. The General Manager and the Director of Minor League Operations and Scouting were canned over the winter, even though the GM had been named "Baseball Executive of the Year" in 1983. Now he's an idiot? This same logic will finish Cal Ripken, Sr. He will be gone by this time next year. He didn't break it, but he can't fix it either.

Greg Pryor

Boston Red Sox
JOHN MCNAMARA

1987 was a year of transition for the Red Sox. Three members of the 1986 post-season starting lineup were removed from the roster during last summer and five rookies became regulars. The Boston ball club was refurbished in the outfield and adjusted at catcher, with prospects of more changes at shortstop and in the bullpen. The events of the last year and the prospects of the next make these entertaining times for those fans watching John McNamara.

Mac is currently fifth in seniority in his profession behind Gene Mauch, Dick Williams, Billy Martin and Sparky Anderson, but he has received only a fraction of the publicity the other "old pros" have gotten in national sports publications. One reason is that, until 1986, he hadn't won much (the 1979 Division win with Cincinnati was his only previous first-place finish). But observers have had fifteen years to study Mac's big league management style, and some definite tendencies have been noticed.

The popular profile of Mr. McNamara is that of the quintessential organization man. That means he is not the architect of the teams he led—he is more of a supervisor. The front office provides the players and he fills out the lineup cards and lets them play. There are some hints that there is consultation by GM Lou Gorman with his manager on player moves, but off the field John is invisible.

Mac's track record is that he identifies the eight best position players and then plays them as much as possible. The only situations in which he'd play his reserves were as late-inning defense or in replacement of an injured player. When a regular had to miss a day or a week, the substitute was often just plugged into his spot in the order. For example, Ed Romero, the Sox utility infielder, often subbed at shortstop in 1986. He batted ninth, simply because the regular Boston shortstop batted last. But when he filled in for Wade Boggs in July, he moved into Boggs' (then) #2 batting slot. Apparently Mac felt that it was more important not to disturb the roles of the other eight hitters than it was to rebuild the order around a temporary substitute. Along with this rigid batting order went the determination to stay the course with his front-line players. Once he was convinced that a player would perform in the lineup, it took months to shake that conviction. The positive side of this is that his players didn't look over their shoulders when they were slumping; John would give them plenty of time to work through their problems. The negative side is that he always felt more comfortable playing the proven veteran over the untested kid. Being on the AAA affiliate of a McNamara-managed team was like being in an American Gulag—you never knew when or if your sentence would end.

In more personal terms, this commitment to his regulars both rewarded and wounded Mac in the case of Bill Buckner in 1986. Buck had had a rough season, with very little production, yet Mac kept writing his name third on the lineup card. Then came September, and the first baseman led the surge that won the division with 8 home runs and a .340 BA. Then when it was time for the series, Buckner could hardly stand on his bad ankles, yet Mac kept writing his name third on the lineup card. This time there was no late sparkle, as Bill's final Series composite box score line was 32 AB, 2 R, 6 H, 1 RBI, and he drove in just one of sixteen runners in scoring position during the seven games. When it was all over, the manager defended his player . . . Mac's way of defending his decisions.

This rigid style is carried through to the pitching staff. McNamara likes a five-man rotation, and he follows the sequence religiously, pushing everyone back for rainouts rather than having a weak pitcher skip a start and not doing any tinkering to create favorable matchups. Mac was a catcher when he played the game, but he does get good results from his rotation. One key reason is that he has not been quick to remove starters, even when he has had a bullpen. In Fenway park this is critical, because a couple of early hooks here can ruin a pitcher's confidence. John in past seasons has not let a little thing like three home runs in the same inning shift him from his dugout crouch.

Last season was an extreme case, though. With no bullpen at all, two of his hurlers were in the top eight in the league in innings pitched, and two of the top three names on the complete games list worked in Boston. As the year progressed, the relief ineptitude got to the point where he would rather have put a gun to his head than the bullpen phone receiver, but all the relievers were given many opportunities to prove just how rotten they were. Recall that in 1986 Joe Sambito came from the National League scrap pile to be a key man for the Sox, Calvin Schiraldi came from nowhere, and early in his career, Mac made Rollie Fingers a relief pitcher. So he has shown that he can identify folks who will help out the starters, and, in normal circumstances, the pitching load would be more balanced.

McNamara's record also shows that, if a change is desired by the front office, he'll clear the way for new blood. Not only the '86 Red Sox, as cited earlier, but the '84 Angels as well conducted serum replacement operations under his management. Dramatic personnel changes contradict the popular impression of John McNamara's rigidity, but they do reinforce the image of the company man.

Regarding his coaches, Mac shows no pattern of cronyism. In his first season with the Angels he retained all of previous manager Gene Mauch's staff, but when he went to Boston, hitting coach Walt Hriniak was the only holdover. His present pitching coach, Bill Fischer, was with John in Cincinnati. Once he has selected them, Mac apparently treats coaches like his players: all four of the 1987 Boston coaches were there in 1985.

Mr. McNamara is liked and respected by his players both for his low-key approach and his loyalty to them. The infamous Boyd All-Star temper tantrum in 1986 would have been followed by a quick trade in a lot of organizations; Mac handled his pitcher privately, and the squad received a sincere apology from the miscreant. After the 1986 season, Wade Boggs announced that he would prefer to bat third. A lot of folks would argue that Boggs would help the team more leading off, and Mac may indeed agree with them. Nevertheless, last year Wade was happily installed in Buckner's old lineup slot and had a terrific season. This type of management wins more ball games than all of the double switches and hit-and-run plays in the world.

People, not tactics, are Mac's forte. Once again he prefers to let his lineup do things their way. You will see him call an occasional run-and-hit play at the top of the batting order, but with the Boston park and lineup, a little bit of that can easily be too much. The ball park also dictated an adjustment in his tendency to sacrifice. He was big on bunts when he worked in big ball parks, but the Sox were eighth in the AL in SACs last year and fourth the year before. He wouldn't have his job for long if he played "one run at a time" in the Boston ball yard, but he will always bunt when he needs one run late in the game. As for defensive strategy, John was the king of the intentional walk when he managed the Angels, but again Fenway has intervened to drop him back into the pack. He routinely will pull a weak fielder after his last at-bat when Boston is leading, so Jim Rice, Tony Armas and the hobbled Bill Buckner often finished early.

Overall, John McNamara is the ideal manager for a front office that has a steady hand and a definite vision of what the club should be; thus Boston has an excellent fit between its manager and GM. Mac's career shows that he will deliver what the team is capable of consistently, with no surprises. Over 15 seasons, he rates -12 on the Bill James skipper handicapping system—that is, his cumulative record is within twelve games of the total projected performances of all his teams. Last season was something unfamiliar for him, as he experimented with a bunch of

rookies and tried out different combinations, and 1988 will also be interesting. He was not around for the second year of the California player turnover he initiated, so this year will bring some new challenges as, for the first time, he leads a team with a large number of sophomores. Watch to see if he is as patient with his newer players as he has always been with his veterans.

Fred Percival

California Angels
GENE MAUCH

1987 was the year the wheels fell off the Angels' express. It seemed that everything that could possibly go wrong went wrong in '87, just as '86 seemed to go so well.

Gene Mauch received much credit for his moves in 1986. He had some unique talents, those which he has the ability to recognize and identify. He let them do what they could to help the team win. However, in 1987, the team lost focus. Many of the things they did especially well the year before they failed to do again (draw walks, score runs, get consistent starting pitching).

In my opinion, the two main reasons for the team's sub-par performance in '87 are (1) the continued breakdown of the veterans, and (2) bad personnel decisions. Obviously, Angels manager Gene Mauch didn't cause #1, but over a period of years, the team began to become dominated by older, craftier players in the twilight of their careers. These players, like Boone, Grich, Jackson, Sutton, DeCinces, Ruppert Jones, Wilfong, and Carew, were coveted by Mauch because of their ability to concentrate and not make the kind of mistakes that young players often make. If there's one thing Mauch seems to like in a player, it's the ability to play intelligently and not make mental mistakes. He will put up with a weak bat (a Tony Taylor, a Rob Wilfong, a Bob Boone, a Bobby Wine) in exchange for good defense and good sense.

The downside is, of course, when you load a team up with old players and they begin burning out, you're *really* stuck. You can't just replace the whole team at once, and you're doomed to watch each of those older players—who may still have some value, making it hard to let them go—run down to a complete stop.

In 1987, Ruppert Jones, George Hendrick, Doug DeCinces, Don Sutton, and Bob Boone all declined from 1986. Sutton and DeCinces were finally dumped, but the damage was done. At only a few places (1B, LF, arguably 3B and CF) were the Angels better in '87 than the year before. The offense declined from '86—in absolute terms and relative to the league—and the pitching staff gave up a whopping 120 more runs than in '86. Many of 1986's most important players were either gone before the year began (Jackson, Wilfong, Grich) traded during the year (Candelaria, DeCinces) or played themselves out of their jobs (Pettis, Jones, Hendrick). Bob Boone held out until May, and Kirk McCaskill was hurt most of the season, as was Donnie Moore.

One can argue that Mauch shouldn't be blamed because some of his players got hurt or got another year older. There is merit in this line of reasoning—but this organization, which seems to be so intelligent in some ways, really hits bottom in others. For the last several years, they have had a very shaky outfield. One of their outfielders was by acclamation the majors' best defensive centerfielder, coming off his best offensive year in 1986. The Angels play in a hitters' league, in a park with an enormous outfield, and have a fly-ball staff. Yet after a poor half-year this player was benched, sent down, and after the season, traded. Why did they give up on Gary Pettis?

1987 was even worse than it should have been due to some bad personnel decisions. When the veterans on offense bombed out, Mauch replaced them with—guess what—more veterans!! The Angels mid-season acquisition list reads like a *Who's Who* from the late 1970s and early 1980s: Greg Minton, Bill Buckner, Butch Wynegar, Tony Armas, Jerry Reuss . . . it's an old bench when Johnny Ray, Gus Polidor, Darrell Miller, and Mark Ryal are the "kids."

In general, Mauch doesn't like kids crowding the bench. If there's a young player on his team, he's going to start somewhere. In 1987, Mauch had the courage (as he did with Joyner in 1986) to stick some unproven rookies into vital spots (Devon White, Mark McLemore, DeWayne Buice, Willie Fraser). Most of these moves worked pretty well. DeCinces was DHed and dumped, and third base given to Jack Howell. Howell has offensive skills and a good glove; he should work out quite well.

At second, it was a good idea to play Mark McLemore, but I'm not crazy about the acquisition of Johnny Ray. Not only did the team drop out of the race almost immediately after acquiring Ray, but Mauch didn't do McLemore's confidence any favors by benching the rookie and leaving him off the team's post-season eligibility roster. Sure, he's trying to win a pennant, but dumb's dumb. Ray's not great, and now they're stuck with a "name" player who they have to find a place for. If it's the outfield, like they're threatening, the Angels will be walking another treadmill.

The Angels, offensively, were substandard in BA, OBA, and runs. Brian Downing began the season as the leadoff man—a fine idea, but ultimately several people led off, including Pettis, White, and McLemore. The team must find a competent leadoff hitter, since the lack of a balanced offense was so evident in '87.

To try and supplement his offense, Mauch strategized. He got the running game more involved. Angel stolen bases went up by 16, while sacrifices went down by 20—a basically even trade. He had a faster team this year, and some of the better bunters—Wilfong especially—were gone. Even so, their 70 sacrifice hits led the league by seven. The trouble with using the sac and the steal in 1987 was that the rest of the league was using *firepower*. The Angels finished 11th in home runs, being outhomered 212 to 172. Anyway, offensive strategies can't work unless you get people on base, and the Angels finished last in BA, fell from 1st to 6th in walks, and ended up with a 6th-best OBA of .326—down 12 points from 1986. The Angels scored 770 runs, down 16 from 1986.

Some of the reasons for the offensive collapse were beyond Mauch's direct control—the breakdown of Hendrick, Jones, DeCinces, for example—but some of the hitting problems were exacerbated by managerial decisions. Devon White is an exciting player, but making him the center of the offense is a bad idea. A man with a .306 OBA making nearly 500 outs is not ever going to be the best player on a contending team. White's power was surprising

524

in 1987, but the question is whether he can repeat that performance.

In addition, what can be gained by playing Tony Armas, Mark Ryal, or Butch Wynegar? Even if you believe Bill Buckner's high-average hitting is valuable, is it worth acquiring *more* burned-out old players on an already elderly team? For all the personnel changes and shifting in 1987, only two position players—Downing and Joyner—could be called "improvements" from 1986.

As for the pitching, Mauch was unlucky. He compounded his bad luck with some questionable decisions.

The superb Mike Witt did a good job, but it wasn't his best year. Rookie Willie Fraser pitched pretty well—credit Mauch for using him effectively—but Don Sutton slid several more rungs down the ladder (after the year, California released him). Kirk McCaskill's injury made things tough from the start, and almost every move Mauch made to shore up his pitching blew up in his face. Mauch's designated plug-ins, Jerry Reuss and Jack Lazorko, were terrible. The middle relief—Lucas, Cook, Finley—was awful, thus making the rest of the staff look worse than it was. The staff ERA jumped up to 4.38, 7th in the league. This can partially be credited (blamed?) to a lack of clear definition of roles for the staff, caused both by injury and bad planning.

Mauch generally hasn't shown much of a preference for a finesse or power staff while he has been in Anaheim (even with softball pitchers like Forsch, Slaton, and Zahn), and the only defining feature of the 1987 Angel pitchers is that they were a "control" staff. The team led the league by only walking 504 batters. The downside to this, though, is that they finished only 7th in strikeouts. The team's home runs allowed (212, 3rd most) brings the staff into sharper focus—Mauch's pitchers in 1987 laid the ball right down the pipe. For the most part, the hurlers didn't have enough velocity to fan people, so they got hammered. Prime guilty parties included Don Sutton (38 HR, tied for third-most in league), Fraser (26 HR in 176 IP), Candelaria (17 in 117), Reuss (16 in 82), Lazorko (20 in 117), and even Kirk McCaskill (14 in 75).

Obviously, the pitchers didn't have a good year. But how long do you have to pitch Jerry Reuss and Don Sutton to know that they're not going to win you 20 games, much less 15? Not only do they not have a future, they don't even have a *present*. Between Reuss, Sutton, and Lazorko, 60 starts went out the window.

Of course, Mauch didn't know that. He was doing what he's always done—take chances. Maybe Sutton would go 15–11 again. Lazorko had some OK minor league numbers, but Reuss I find impossible to defend. I also think trading John Candelaria was a bad idea, especially when the minors aren't overflowing with young talent. Candelaria has been a good pitcher for a long time, but he's not old. He can still get people out, and even in 1987 struck out 74 men in 117 innings. A healthy McCaskill, along with Witt and Willie Fraser, comprise 3/4 of a fine young rotation—it's too bad Candelaria isn't still around.

To his credit, Mauch began the year with no bullpen—but fashioned an excellent short-man platoon out of Giants' castoff Greg Minton and rookie DeWayne Buice. This was one of the "panic moves" he was forced to make last year that worked. Buice is one of the few real flamethrowers Mauch has.

So what more can one say? Gene Mauch won't sit still. For whatever reasons, he decided that Gary Pettis wasn't going to improve. He got players for the pennant push and used them, and he once again kept an outmanned team in the race, at least for a while. The Angels do have an interesting future brewing, though. Schofield will come back; McLemore should improve. If Howell develops like the Angels think he will, they'll have a very good infield. I think their outfield is less stable. Giving up on Pettis was a bad idea. What will happen when Downing slows down? Is Johnny Ray going to play left or right? What will they do about a catcher? Obviously, there are a lot of problems the organization should address. Had the Angels started a "youth movement" a couple of years ago, 1987 may not have happened—but then again, 1986 might not have happened either.

Suffice it to say that in 1987, the Angels lived out the negative image of 1986: Most of the veterans washed out, and most of the kids disappointed. The future success of the Angels depends both on how management fills existing holes and on how the younger players develop. It would be interesting to see what Mauch could do with a really good team. The failure of the 1987 Angels doesn't make Gene Mauch a bad manager—he's a good manager who had a bad year.

Stuart Shea

Chicago Cubs
DON ZIMMER

I am a Cub fan. During the week following the Cubs' hiring of Don Zimmer as their manager for the 1988 season, I received several calls from my "friends" about Zim taking the Cubs' reins. Most of these calls demonstrated all the subtlety of children tormenting a retarded child on a playground: RING! "Hello?" "Nyanh, nyanh, the Cubs hired a gerbil! The Cubs hired a gerbil!" click. The common view—at least among my "friends"—is that Zimmer is one of those incompetent baseball insiders who is considered for every managing job because he has managed before and everyone likes him.

But what are the Cubs' prospects under Zimmer? How does he manage his teams? Will he rival the immortal Joey Amalfitano or the rotating College of Coaches for distinguished ineffectiveness at the Cubs' helm? Having not observed Zimmer in the dugout at length (see a long-suffering Red Sox fan here), the following observations are based on the statistical record of the teams he managed.

The Managing Munchkin (well, they called Connie Mack "The Tall Tactician") has directed three teams, the San Diego Padres in 1972 and 1973, the Boston Red Sox from 1976 through 1980, and the Texas Rangers in 1981 and 1982. If there is one main characteristic of Zimmer's managing style, it is moderation. Zimmer likes to sacrifice and does not like to steal, but he pursues neither predilection to excess. The Red Sox under Zimmer had moderately high sacrifice bunt totals, but these were lower than the total under Darrell Johnson. The Rangers' stolen bases dropped under Zimmer, only to be revived under Doug Rader, but it is hard to see who else could have stolen bases on the Red Sox. He appears to discourage his hitters from walking, but he is not a certified member of the Manny Sanguillen "Never-Met-a-Pitch-I-Couldn't-Hit" Club. His clubs' walk totals decline slowly over time, only reviving with a change in management.

On defense, Zimmer likes the intentional walk, but his teams have never led the league in them. His pitching staffs' strikeout and walk totals edge downward, but these changes rarely involve changing the pitchers themselves. He just appears to try to get them to throw strikes. When he has an ace reliever (Dave Campbell in 1977 and Tom Burgmeier in 1980), he will use him heavily. In those two seasons, the Red Sox' saves rose and their complete games dropped. However, all of these tendencies, offensive and defensive, are moderate; Zimmer is no Earl Weaver or Billy Martin with a burning vision of how the game must be played that he brands on his teams.

The Gerbil-Faced General loves set lineups and rotations. If Don Zimmer could find a team of nine Cal Ripkens and four Jack Morrises, he would move for a quick shift to the thirteen-man roster. His reputation comes from the ill-fated 1978 Red Sox where Butch Hobson continued to play third base despite his (rumored) need to readjust the bone chips floating around in his elbow in-between pitches. But like most good stories, this reputation is an exaggeration. He prefers a set lineup and will experiment in an attempt to find one. Mike Caldwell, Jerry Morales, and Derrel Thomas broke in as regulars under Zimmer in San Diego, and Butch Hobson became the Red Sox third baseman after Zimmer took over in mid-1976. He changes players only because the starter obviously cannot do the job (Bob Watson for George Scott in 1979) or is injured (Dave Stapleton and Glenn Hoffman for Jerry Remy and Butch Hobson in 1980).

Zimmer's decisions on pitchers are a mixed lot. He converted Charlie Hough from a reliever to a starter, a move I would rate as one of the best personnel decisions of the 1980s. But he also failed to find the proper roles for Bob Stanley and Danny Darwin after trying them as both starters and relievers (of course, no one other than Ralph Houk—for a short time—ever found the right way to use Bob Stanley either). His mishandling of Bill Lee is legendary, but you do not always have the chance to pick up Stan Papi for your best left-handed starter.

The Steel-Skulled Skipper's handling of players reflects the teams he managed. Zimmer does not tinker with his talent to squeeze maximum performance out of it, but rather his moves are driven by injuries and the incompetence of his players. The Padres were a mess, an expansion team sadly lacking talent. Zimmer probably had few other choices than playing the young talents over the no-talents. With the Red Sox, Zimmer controlled a great set lineup containing multiple Hall-of-Famers (Rice, Yaz, Fisk?, Lynn?, Evans?). Red Sox trades during this period consisted of swaps of young talent (Cecil Cooper, Don Aase, Bo Diaz, Mike Paxton, Pete Ladd) for proven regulars who they hoped would be the last piece of the puzzle (George Scott, Jerry Remy, Dennis Eckersley, Bob Watson). Obviously, Zimmer rode that lineup as hard as he could. In Texas, he presided over the collapse of a good team that was never good enough to win its division. "Crazy" Eddie Robinson's trades exacerbated the decline of the Rangers, and Zimmer found himself in a position where something had to be done and nothing helped.

What does this portend for the 1988 Chicago Cubs? It is hard to see how the Jim Frey-Don Zimmer regime can build something out of the decaying legacy of the Dallas Green era. Offensively, the Cubs are weak; after leading the NL in runs in 1984, they dropped to fourth in 1985, fifth in 1986, and eighth in 1987. Defensively, they could also improve, finishing eleventh or last in the league in runs allowed the last three years. In Wrigley Field, these numbers indicate both a weak lineup and a weak pitching staff. The Cubs on the field are a collection of players like Jody Davis, Keith Moreland, and Leon Durham that are assets as fill-in players on a great team. But with the Cubs, they are the heart of the team, and none of these three is a good enough hitter to bat clean-up (as all three have at different times over the last several seasons) for a serious team. If you do not believe me, look up their road hitting statistics elsewhere in the player section.

I do not see how the Cubs can possibly hope to compete with the Mets in the 1988 season. It is hard to see the Mets winning less than ninety-five games or the Cubs more than ninety, and that's why I think that hiring Frey and Zimmer were not bad moves. Although Dallas Green built a collection of players that is now incapable of playing championship baseball, and then blamed them when they did not win in 1986, he did build an effective minor league system and scouting organization. The Cubs' farm system is beginning to produce good players—Shawon Dunston, David Martinez, and Rafael Palmiero for example. A number of young pitching prospects—Drew Hall, Les Lancaster, Greg Maddux, and Jamie Moyer—have also emerged at the major league level. And there are more on the way (well, at least according to *Baseball America*). Hiring Frey and Zimmer should preserve the continuity of this system; none of the critical personnel left after Green's departure. Some other general manager would have cleaned house and brought in his own men. The Cubs are not going anywhere soon, and it is important not to disrupt the long-run productivity of the system. The Frey-Zimmer years should be an interlude while the Cubs wait for their players to mature and for the Mets to age.

Besides, the Cubs could have done much worse than Zimmer: They seriously considered Pat Corrales.

Jim Morrow

Chicago White Sox
JIM FREGOSI

Unlike most major league managers, Jim Fregosi was an excellent player—arguably the best player in California Angels history. Rushed to the majors at nineteen, at least in part because the expansion Angels needed "homegrown" talent to compete with the glamorous Dodgers, Fregosi began to see significant playing time a year later in 1962. Young and good-looking, he became an instant hero by hitting .291 for a club that stunned the baseball world with a third place finish. Fregosi soon became the biggest star on the team; an excellent hitter with good power, he also won a Gold Glove at shortstop. In the period from 1964 to 1970, Fregosi played in six All-Star games.

The Angels' skipper during those years was Bill Rigney, a thoughtful man who had several strong tendencies as a manager. Among them were a fearlessness about working young players, including Fregosi, into his lineup; the use of a "bullpen by committee," with a whole ensemble of relievers (Rigney was one of the first managers to use this system); a fondness for veteran role players on his bench; a strong belief in using all the players on his roster; and not much tendency toward strict left-right platooning. Rigney obviously made a big impression on his young shortstop.

Rigney lasted nearly nine seasons as the Angels' manager. Eventually he was fired, and by then Fregosi had fallen on hard times as well, due to injuries and loss of range. At the age of 30 he was dealt to the Mets, where he was expected to solve New York's eternal third base problem. When Fregosi failed and Nolan Ryan, one of the men he was traded for, became a big star, he was treated roughly and then exiled to Texas. He hung around for six years as a utilityman, retiring on June 1, 1978, when the Angels called him back to be their manager.

Fregosi has managed ever since then. He won a division title in 1979, the first in Angels' history, but was fired two years later. Subsequently he became the manager of Louisville in the American Association, a job he held until the White Sox asked him to take over for Tony LaRussa in June of '86. The Louisville experience obviously helped him grow as a manager, but for the most part Fregosi has shown similar tendencies in his stints with the Angels and White Sox. Among them are:

1. *He has shown patience with young players, especially young pitchers.* The Angels of the late seventies weren't the easiest club in the world for a man who liked to go with youngsters. Before Fregosi arrived on the scene, the club had fired Dick Williams and Harry Dalton, a manager and an executive who have been successful building with youth, because of owner Gene Autry's impatience to win a division title. Fregosi was smart enough not to swim against the tide, but he did give a lot of playing time to many of the young players he had. This was especially true of his pitching staffs. The division-winning club of '79 was typical. Four fifths of the Angel starting rotation that year was composed of pitchers who were 26 or younger (Dave Frost, Chris Knapp, Frank Tanana and Don Aase), and Fregosi's relief ace was Mark Clear, a rookie of 23. Other young pitchers whom Fregosi worked in during his Angel years included Paul Hartzell in '78, Freddie Martinez in '80 and Mike Witt in '81.

Among position players the going was tougher, as the Angels kept bringing in free agents like Joe Rudi and Bobby Grich and trading for veterans like Rod Carew. Nonetheless Fregosi helped break in Carney Lansford and Ken Landreaux in '78, used Jim Anderson and Willie Aikens extensively in '79, and gave a lot of playing time to Dickie Thon and Bobby Clark in 1980. I suppose Fregosi could be criticized for not using Rance Mulliniks more during Rance's Angels years, but Mulliniks didn't hit at all when he was put in the lineup. A more valid criticism would be over Fregosi's failure to give the shortstop job to Thon during the 95-loss season of 1980; the Angels kept playing ancient Freddie Patek. You would think that if anyone would go with a talented young shortstop, Fregosi would; maybe he was worried about getting fired. With that exception, though, his personnel decisions were similar to the moves Rigney had made with the Angels.

In Chicago the situation has been a little different. The White Sox are rebuilding and anxious to go with youth; the trouble is that the farm system to date has not produced much in the way of talent. In a year and a half Fregosi has put the still-young Jose DeLeon in his pitching rotation and stuck with him despite all the doubters; gone with Joel Davis about as long as anyone in his right mind possibly could, considering the results; made Bobby Thigpen his relief ace, though he took a while to do it; and given extensive work to Joel McKeon until McKeon, like Davis, pitched his way back to the minors. The trading of Dotson and Bannister will open up spots for pitchers like Jack McDowell and Melido Perez.

The situation has been similar for position players. Fregosi's played Daryl Boston, but Boston hasn't shown much; how many chances does he need? He gave a job to Ron Karkovice, and I'll let you decide how long a man should go with an .071 hitter. He made a regular out of Ken Williams, gave Fred Manrique his first real major league shot, and found some playing time for Steve (Psycho) Lyons. They tell me more youth is on the way, and I have no doubt that Fregosi will test it.

2. *He's spread the work out among his pitching staff—to an extreme.* During the three seasons that Fregosi finished the year as Angels manager, California never had a pitcher appear in more than 59 games or make more than 34 starts. In Chicago he's done exactly the same thing, though he seems to be changing a little; both Ray Searage (58 games) and Thigpen (51) spent about a month in the minors and would have been well over 60 except for that. Still, that's not much in this day and age; the point is that Fregosi uses his whole staff and spreads the work around. Again, this is very much like the early Angels under Rigney.

3. *He has very slowly learned to use the stolen base as a weapon.* From '78 to '80 California ranked between sixth and ninth in the league each year in SBs, with an amazing consistency to the number of attempts: 155 in '78, 153 in '79, 154 in '80; maybe the Angels tried to steal once a game unless they forgot or something. Admittedly, the Angels of those years were a pretty lead-footed team. When he went down to Louisville, Fregosi had a chance to manage Vince Coleman, and that had to open his eyes a little. The '86 White Sox attempted 169 steals, most of them coming under LaRussa. In '87, though, they attempted 190, and succeeded 138 times, for an excellent 73 percent success rate. Fregosi let Gary Redus go as much as he wanted, and he tapped the speed of Ozzie Guillen (25 of 33) and Kenny Williams (21 of 31, but better toward the end) to an unexpected degree.

4. *He uses the sacrifice bunt more often than most managers.* Bill Rigney was a power-hitting infielder who played his home games in the Polo Grounds. Nonetheless, he had a definite fondness for the sacrifice bunt; the early Angels always ranked near the top of the league in sacrifices, even when they played in little Wrigley Field. Fregosi was also a power-hitting infielder, and he also likes the bunt. From '78 to '80 the Angels ranked seventh, second and fourth in the AL in sacrifice hits. In '78 Bobby Grich had 19 sacrifice bunts, a very high total for a player with so much power. Grich didn't hit very well that year, but he did in '79, with

30 homers and 101 RBI; Fregosi still had him lay down 12 sacrifices. The White Sox ranked seventh in '86, when Fregosi took over in June, and third in '87. He's no Gene Mauch, but clearly he likes to bunt.

5. *He is pretty much of a set-lineup manager.* Fregosi didn't do very much platooning during his Angels years, and he hasn't changed with the White Sox. His use of bench players has been mostly to rest his regulars or to fill in for injured starters. At California he had several veteran role players on his bench (Merv Rettenmund, Willie Davis, Ron Fairly), but for the most part the subs were young players hoping to break into the lineup—Ken Landreaux, Dickie Thon, Bobby Clark, guys like that. In Chicago he has platooned only a little, and again his bench has been a mixture of old heads (Jerry Hairston, Ron Hassey, Jerry Royster) with young ones (Boston, Lyons, Pat Keedy); the older guys seem on the way out, though. Again, this is very similar to the Bill Rigney Angels.

6. *He is a strong personality who wants a say in personnel moves.* Despite the fact that the White Sox finished strongly in '87, they took their time about re-hiring their manager. The main reason, I think, has been Fregosi's friction with General Manager Larry Himes; it's a case of two strong men not always seeing eye to eye. Early in the year Himes wanted Bobby Thigpen sent to the minors to learn to be a starting pitcher; Fregosi wanted Thigpen to stay in his bullpen. Thigpen did get sent down, but when he came back it was as a reliever. Himes kept Ron Karkovice around, evidently thinking he should be playing; Fregosi, who didn't think the youngster could cut it, kept Karko nailed to his bench. There are other things, little things that give evidence of a power struggle. Himes, aware of the fact that the Sox farm system has been barren of prospects, has been trading veterans for minor leaguers. Naturally wanting to win now, Fregosi hasn't always approved, and he's not the sort of man who keeps his opinions to himself. The fact that Himes inherited Fregosi from the Ken Harrelson regime only adds to the problem. It strikes me that what Fregosi would like is what he saw when he managing down in the Cardinal farm system—a Whitey Herzog-type situation, with the manager being the strong man in the organization. What he doesn't want is what he saw in California—meddling from the front office, Gene Mauch lurking in the wings as an "advisor." Sensitive to his need for power, Jim Fregosi remains a manager in a precarious situation.

Don Zminda

———————

Jim Fregosi turns 45 in April with his team at a crossroads. The White Sox enjoyed a good second half in 1987 and are looking forward to 1988. However, with recent deals the team appears unsteady, and the skipper's relationship with GM Larry Himes continues to be touch-and-go. If the Sox get off to a poor start in the coming year, Fregosi could be finished with his second big league managing job. Jim has tried to establish some consistency with a franchise notorious for its hyperactive gyrations, but it may not be enough to save his job.

Fregosi was a good player who retired to manage the

Angels in 1977, and brought them a divisional crown. Further success was not forthcoming, so Fregosi was dismissed. After spending a year out of baseball, he hooked on with St. Louis' minor league organization, eventually becoming a pennant-winning manager at AAA Louisville before being hired to replace Tony LaRussa in 1986. In the off-season, Fregosi and Himes held meetings to determine the club's future, and the Sox emerged dedicated to: 1) going to youth, and 2) lowering salaries.

The White Sox offense finished 13th in runs in 1987. It finished last in on-base average. The pitchers fared a little better—4th in ERA, 6th in saves—but recent trades have gouged holes in the staff. The team continues to flounder offensively and waste some good starting and short relief with mediocre fielding, horrifying middle relief, and a hitting attack reminiscent of the '67 Sox. In short, this is a team in danger of simply fading away.

The Sox have stocked up on power recently—Ivan Calderon, Kenny Williams, and Dan Pasqua have been added just in the last year—but have continued to ignore two major problems:

1. *The Sox lack a third baseman.* At this point, they seem committed to moving Kenny Williams to 3B. Ignoring the historical failures of moves like this for a moment, *what are they doing here*? This is a centerfielder we're discussing. He can run and throw and has a good glove. Moving him to third would waste his speed and put pressure on him that could hurt his development as a hitter (and anyone with an 8–1 k/w ratio needs to develop his hitting). The Sox could have had at least an average 3B for Bannister or Dotson—Esasky, Gruber, Jacoby, Moreland, and others were on the market this winter—but Larry Himes did what he has often been accused of doing. He did a rotten job of shopping.

2. *The Sox don't score runs.* Gary Redus played in 130 games and finished 3rd on the team in runs scored. Himes has given up on Redus because of his low BA—but Himes and Fregosi continue to let the Sox plod along with a team full of guys who don't get on base. Even some of the best Sox players don't walk—but Baines, Fisk, and Williams contribute in some other ways. Guillen, Lyons, Manrique, Hill, and Boston really don't contribute very much and eat up *tons* of outs besides. The Sox have made no moves in the off-season to address this, short of acquiring a left-handed power hitter who may necessitate the trading of Greg Walker, who led the team in RBI and walks and finished 2nd in HR and runs scored.

What's tough to understand is why Fregosi plays these guys. He was a good player—he understood the value of getting on base. At times, he's had Guillen leading off or hitting second, and then complains when the Sox don't score runs. Ozzie is a fan favorite and is improving, but the man made 400 outs last year and scored 64 runs. Fregosi ran an Army barracks platoon around Ozzie last year that created no offense. After Hulett's failure at third, Fregosi played Lyons, Royster, Hill, Manrique, and Keedy at second and third. None of them was even acceptable offensively. The outfield was a pleasant surprise (without Ivan Calderon, the Sox would have finished in Buffalo). Fregosi made Kenny Williams a regular in mid-season, and he showed great promise. Gary Redus played well, though not having his best season. Daryl Boston finally convinced

Fregosi (and most Sox fans) that he's not the answer. Finally, injuries and all, Harold Baines continued to be an excellent hitter.

Fregosi's offensive strategies failed to move most fans to any emotion whatsoever. He bunted about as often as the Sox opponents did (about 55 times); Guillen was the only player over 10 sacrifices. He had a few runners going—Redus finished third in the AL in steals and was successful 80 percent of the time. Williams and Guillen ran less often and less successfully. For the year, the Sox generally ran well, posting a 70 percent success rate—further displaying a lack of clear connection between running teams and teams that score runs.

As far as the bench goes, it consisted of Jerry Hairston again. He had another good year pinch-hitting (2 HR, 10 RBI in 32 AB), but nobody else on the team did. Fregosi did have people like Hassey, Lyons, Manrique, and Royster on the team, but most of them became regulars anyway. It's interesting to note that Fregosi's bench in Chicago has been mostly veterans, whereas in California he would kill rather than stick a kid in the lineup. He played Freddie Patek at shortstop rather than stick Dickie Thon in. In Chicago, however, Jim gave jobs to Ron Karkovice, Daryl Boston, and Ivan Calderon. Karkovice and Boston lost their jobs, but Fregosi did the right thing in each situation—giving Fisk back his job and replacing Boston with another kid (Williams) rather than shopping for a Rick Manning or somebody. One would assume Fregosi's time at Louisville taught him patience and understanding with younger players.

As a major league manager, Fregosi has *always* coveted low-strikeout finesse pitchers. With the Angels, Nolan Ryan was traded after 2 years with Fregosi, and that's the closest Jim has ever been to a burner. Fregosi has always kept people like Geoff Zahn, Dave Frost, Chris Knapp, Paul Hartzell, Jim Barr, Ken Forsch, and Freddie Martinez in his rotations—having to replace them year after year.

In fact, Fregosi's greatest managerial trait is his patience. He allowed Thigpen and Greg Walker to work through early-season slumps; both players had excellent second halves and contributed to the club. At the same time, Fregosi displayed a different kind of patience with Ron Karkovice. Karkovice just wasn't ready to hit major league pitching, and Fregosi understood that sending him up to hit was just hurting the kid's confidence. Sending down Karkovice also had the added benefit of getting Carlton Fisk back in the lineup.

Patience is something that can be good and can be bad, and Fregosi's had its down side. He continues to allow Ozzie Guillen to do that voodoo that he do so well, and I don't necessarily see Ozzie's increased walk totals (from 12 to 22) as adequate offensive improvement. Fregosi didn't move decisively at second or third base last year, either.

There are quite a few questions brewing for 1988. Obviously Pasqua and new reliever John Davis (acquired from KC in the Bannister deal) will play next year, ostensibly replacing Boston/Redus and one of the relievers. The tradeoff looks OK except that the Sox also lost Dotson and Bannister and really didn't need another lefty power hitter.

Fregosi's coaches in 1987 were holdovers except for hitting coach Deron Johnson, who was fired after the season. Pitching coach Dick Bosman, another ex-finesse pitcher, was cast out acrimoniously. Do these changes bode well for strategy changes within the organization? I hope so.

Fregosi doesn't have a great team to work with. The farm system continues to stagger, trying to recover from Hawkish plundering. The front office issues communiques on sock-wearing and post-game alcoholic consumption, but can't acquire a third baseman. Does Fregosi approve of Himes' deals? If he does, I'm worried. If he doesn't, I wish he'd say something. Given a major league team, I think he'd be a good manager. Will we ever find out? Fregosi is a patient man, but a great deal about the White Sox calls out for something more like urgency.

Stuart Shea

Cincinnati Reds
PETE ROSE

The Reds and their fans were hugely disappointed by their 1987 season—another second-place finish, the third in a row. Bill Bergesch lost his job as general manager largely because he couldn't land another starting pitcher during the season the way San Francisco picked up Rick Reuschel. No one in the media or among the fans likes owner Marge Schott. Everyone blames her for things like batting coach Billy DeMars and chief scout Larry Doughty leaving. (Doughty was upset because the Reds quibbled about the laundry bills he was submitting, or some such.)

What's striking is that very few people blame Pete Rose. Fans seem to think the Reds' players failed Pete in '87, not vice versa. Yet Pete still has to show he can pinpoint weaknesses as a manager and then address them effectively.

For example, the Reds' offense in '87 suffered from a mediocre on-base percentage. Specifically, Reds hitters needed to take more walks, as they managed only 514 in '87. Yet Pete really wants to lead off his batting order in 1988 with Tracy Jones, who walked only 23 times in 359 at bats. Pete's apparent lack of appreciation for walks is odd, given the high number of them he drew during his own career. Jones is Pete's kind of guy, gung-ho, reluctant to come out of the lineup, etc. In fact, Pete took a lot of guff from Jones in '87 when Jones thought he should be playing every day. (Pete didn't accept the "play-me" complaints of Gary Redus a few years back, interestingly. The Reds shipped Redus and his propensity to take walks to the Phillies for the unlamented John Denny.) Rose relates well to ornery cusses like Jones and Denny.

On the other hand, he worries he's not getting through to quiet young players like Kal Daniels, Nick Esasky and Eric Davis. (Quiet veterans like Bo Diaz and Buddy Bell, Pete can relate to. He just puts them in the lineup and doesn't concern himself with "motivating" them, though sometimes he complains about their lack of leadership.) The Reds of the mid-1970s featured boisterous types like Rose, Morgan, Bench, Perez, Concepcion, who won all those titles. Pete seems to be one of the many managers who draw heavily from their own playing experiences when they make decisions. Hence, Pete's clear preference is for loud "leaders," and his fear that players who keep to themselves aren't giving their all.

Pete also has an inordinate faith in the experience of older players. That faith explains somewhat why he moved so slowly to give guys like Daniels and Davis a chance to blossom, and why he wasted so many at bats (207) last year on Terry Francona. Pete doesn't even like to *rest* his veterans. He finally admitted that he wore Bo Diaz down in the first half of '87; Diaz's numbers dropped drastically after he played in the All-Star game (he batted just .171 in the club's last 54 games). Dave Parker could've used an occasional breather, too, since Parker underwent surgery on his left knee after the season. Yet Pete just won't send a young player out there every day to see what the guy can do when he has a veteran he can play instead. Sometimes I wish Pete would remember how the Reds turned over second base to him, no strings attached, as a rookie in 1963.

I expected Pete to call for a lot of bunts when he became the Reds' manager, but he hasn't. He often seems content to wait for a big inning to develop. Pete likes to try to stimulate innings by the hit and run, even running players like Bell and Parker. He'd love to have a batting order of singles hitters with high batting averages (*e.g.*, Francona, Dave Collins) and maybe one guy to bat second and "hit behind the runner," with one big veteran power hitter like Dave Parker or Tony Perez to drive in runs and exert leadership.

Handling pitchers, particularly relievers, Pete sometimes relies too much on formulas and pigeonholes. Each reliever had a role in Pete's scheme, and Pete used the guy only in that role—and just one guy for each role. So he ran through his pitchers in accordance with the situations he faced and without always accounting for who needed a little rest or some work. Early in the season John Franco wasn't getting many innings in because he never pitched in anything but a save situation. Then Pete worked Frank Williams to death as his one right-handed non-closer after Ron Robinson moved into the starting rotation. I think Pete feels more comfortable dealing with—"motivating"—the hitters and so likes to rely on his formulas rather than his hunches when it comes to changing pitchers. As a result the Reds' bullpen in 1987 set a major league record for most appearances (team) in a season (392); the Reds also in '87 set a club record for fewest complete games, team, in a season with only seven. I think, however, that Rose couldn't change that: Cincinnati hasn't had a complete game-type ace since Mario Soto's arm went bad.

The Reds' staff has an abundance of not so overpowering lefthanders, like Dennis Rasmussen, Tom Browning, and Guy Hoffman. Here's a good example of Pete's managing on the basis of his experience as a player. He'd always had difficulty with the Tommy John or Randy Jones type of pitcher and so covets that type for his own staff. Last year this yearning resulted in Jerry Reuss getting 7 starts and going 0 and 5. Pete also likes his pitchers old, hence his conviction that Cincy lost the NL West title last year because the Giants obtained Reuschel and Cincinnati didn't. Rose just couldn't bring himself to go with Pat Pacillo, last year's promising rookie, either, and he's already on record as saying that Jose Rijo, the youngster the Reds got in the Dave Parker deal, probably won't start the 1988 season with the Reds.

In sum, Pete has shown a few shortcomings and blind spots as a manager so far, but he can overcome them as he grows in the job. Not many other major league managers had no previous coaching or managing experience. The Reds took quite a gamble when they hired Pete right off the active roster of the Montreal Expos. For one thing, the Reds had to wait out his chase of Ty Cobb's hit record and his desire to keep playing first base. His reluctance to hang up his spikes definitely impeded the progress of good young hitters like Daniels and Esasky, to name two, and so hurt the team in the long run. Pete seems over all that now; he just needs to lay aside a few prejudices that stem from comparing his players to himself. In the meantime, I wonder if Pete is too much of a baseball legend in Cincinnati for the Reds' brass to judge him objectively.

Mike Marrero

Cleveland Indians
DOC EDWARDS

When Cleveland finally hired Howard Rodney Edwards for 1988, studious Indians fans smiled. To many, it seemed as if the gods of fortune were making a gesture of repayment for a slew of grievous wrongs.

In his five years (1981–85) as Cleveland's AAA skipper, Doc Edwards managed many players (Karl Pagel, Jack Perconte, Steve Farr, Kevin Rhomberg, Jim Wilson) who, though they had fine credentials, never got a chance to play here. Like his players, Doc seemed to be better than his big-league counterparts: In five years, he finished second twice, third once and won a "Manager of the Year" award. Anyway, though it's a shame that his players got the shaft, it's nice to see their manager will finally be able to show his stuff in the majors.

And I think he has plenty to show. My study of Doc Edwards's track record in the minors, backed by his 75-game stint as the interim manager, leads me to the conclusion that he has an excellent chance to succeed in the majors. While I'm not crazy about his style at all, I like his results very much. If the patterns in his career hold, Cleveland should be vastly improved in 1988.

Studying a manager's minor league record is a tricky business, but it can be rewarding. While minor league managers have no control over their roster, they do make in-game strategy decisions and are allowed to play some role in developing talent. With a little deduction, you can often get a good idea of what a manager can do—or at least what he likes to do. The book on Edwards is very clear: almost a perfect Roger Craig or Gene Mauch clone. That type of manager is precisely what the Indians need.

Take, for example, the pitching. The one thing that a Doc Edwards team absolutely will not do is walk hitters. They put the ball in play at any cost; one example shows just how high a premium he puts on throwing strikes. His 1979 Rochester team was easily the worst staff in the league: last in hits, runs, homers and ERA. Only two teams allowed fewer walks—not one allowed fewer wild pitches. His teams were almost always one of the best in the league in walks allowed.

His impact on the Cleveland staff was extremely visible in 1987. Under Pat Corrales, Cleveland had allowed 4.01 walks per nine innings; they allowed 3.62 under Edwards. His mania for strikes cost him in other areas—strikeouts per nine innings fell from 5.80 to 4.88; H/9IP rose from 9.80 to 10.03—but it paid off. The team ERA under Corrales was 5.59; it was 4.93 under Edwards.

Another plus is his touch in relief. Doc is very clearly a bullpen man—starters get a lower than normal percentage of decisions; his teams are usually high in number of relief appearances—and he handles it well. Year after year in the minors, an undistinguished veteran had a fine year as his stopper; overall, Doc's bullpens are usually very effective. He got the same results in the majors. Under Corrales, the Cleveland bullpen's ERA was 6.07; it was 4.10 under Edwards.

Though the Cleveland staff needs massive infusions of talent, Edwards certainly seems to be an excellent choice to develop it. Given a healthy Greg Swindell, Scott Bailes and Rich Yett, I believe that Edwards will shave half a point from the team ERA in 1988.

Defensively, the picture is cloudy. Edwards has never had a team that helped its pitchers. Though his teams seem to have very good range, they usually make an above-average number of errors and turn very few double plays. Normally, I would ignore that (AAA managers have no control over who their regulars are), but this pattern continued in Cleveland.

Edwards seemed genuinely concerned (and rightly so) about the defense and made several changes in 1987. Pat Tabler moved from first base to DH, unless Carmen Castillo (Cleveland's weakest defensive outfielder) went into the lineup. Brook Jacoby moved to first base in September, opening a hole for Eddie Williams, who was voted the best defensive third baseman in his AAA league by *Baseball America*. Despite minimal offensive contributions, defensive whiz Tommy Hinzo became the regular second baseman after the Bernazard trade. Finally, Joe Carter (Cleveland's best defensive first baseman) began to see more action at that spot. They seemed to be sensible changes . . . but they didn't help. Errors per game rose from 0.84 to 1.08; unearned runs per game rose from .67 to .85. Perhaps it was due to the presence of the rookies—many played, and only Hinzo had good defensive stats—but the numbers show that Edwards did nothing to improve the AL's worst defense. Since nothing in his past suggests that he will be able to do so in the future, this will bear careful watching.

Offensively, the picture is also mixed. Edwards is just the kind of manager that analysts despise. He likes to advance runners with outs—his farm teams were always high in sacrifice hits and flies—which is one of the least productive ways to score runs. He adores the stolen base; so much so that it damages his offense badly. His clubs consistently lead the league in caught stealing and rarely hit the break even point (66.7 percent) on steal attempts. To make matters worse, the players who led his teams in plate appearances per game (who, one assumes, do so because they bat at the top of the order) are usually not the ones with the best OBAs—they're the dreaded "bat control" guys who bunt and steal a lot.

But there are three potentially redeeming things. First, Edwards never had a great deal of offensive talent at his disposal in the minors. He's never had the luxury of being able to just sit there and wait for runs; many managers in that situation will resort to bunting and running—whether it pays off or not. Secondly, managers who expect pitchers to not walk hitters usually insist that batters try to draw walks. The tendency is nowhere near as pronounced for hitters as it is for pitchers—but Doc's teams do draw an above-average number of walks. Finally, his decisions paid off in the minors. Edwards's teams consistently scored more runs than Bill James's Runs Created formula expected them to—as Bill notes in the 1987 *Abstract* (pp. 116, 129), that usually means that the manager is making good use of those strategies.

Very little of this musing is supported by the Indians' stats. Bunts and sac flies did go way up. Surprisingly, steal attempts went up only 1 percent; the success rate declined less than 1 percent. Though Hinzo (.296 OBA) spent a lot of time batting second, it was only when Julio Franco was injured. But, though it may be because so many rookies were playing, Cleveland hitters walked less often under Edwards. Finally, they scored 20 less runs than projected.

Frankly, I'm not worried about this. Cleveland has enough power. They have, even without Brett Butler, fine speed, and several players hit for high averages. It would be very hard to construct a lineup with serious flaws; if Edwards wants to run, he's got people he can run with. The one thing that they don't do is walk. If Edwards gets Carter, Hall and Snyder over the 50-walk plateau, it will more than offset the damage that the bunting will do. I don't see Edwards hurting the offense at all.

Finally, though a manager doesn't need to be liked in order to win, it never hurts. The players like Doc; he has a zany side that everyone enjoys. In 1986, some players were talking about shaving their heads; Doc (then the bullpen coach) cracked that he'd only do it if he was paid to. The players handed Doc $2,500 the very next day; he kept his word.

What especially impressed me was his firm stand—even when management and the media gave Doc a hard time, he didn't back down. Hair grew back, he reminded them, and $2,500 was a lot of money. Also, he said that he didn't think it would affect his ability to enforce discipline one bit, that backing down would have been worse, and that his hairstyle wasn't anyone else's business anyway. That's the kind of commonsense approach that I think every manager should have.

If you're a gambler, I'd suggest you lay money on Doc as the next AL Manager of the Year. I think he'll get the pitching under control without losing any ground offensively—if he does, Cleveland will be a .500 + team this year. The only thing that bothers me about him is his nickname—I'm going to get pretty sick of hearing the phrase "For Cleveland, Edwards is just what the doctor ordered" in 1988.

Geoff Beckman

Detroit Tigers
SPARKY ANDERSON

Sparky Anderson may be the quintessential major league manager. Judged by the traditional standards, he certainly has been a good manager, winning two World Championships with the Cincinnati Reds in the 1970s and one with the Detroit Tigers in the 1980s, as well as two other National League pennants and one other NL Western Division title with Cincinnati. The latest jewel in Sparky's crown, although it was tarnished a bit by the rude way in which the Minnesota Twins treated the Tigers in the American League Championship Series, is the 1987 AL Eastern Division title. His career winning percentage of .576 (W–1611, L–1185) puts him around 10th on the all-time list (his rank can move up or down a notch depending on how the Tigers do each season) for managers who managed at least 1000 games in the majors.

Anderson arrived on the Detroit scene during the 1979 season and brashly predicted that he would lead the Tigers to a World Series within five years. He made that prediction come true, but just barely, when the Tigers won it all in 1984. Anderson's debut in Detroit came at a time when the team's situation was strikingly similar to his debut in Cincinnati. The Tigers were a young team with lots and lots of talent in 1979, and Sparky, who the Detroit management viewed as a proven winner, was charged with teaching callow players to win.

Sparky is the only manager in major league history to win a World Championship with teams in both leagues. He is also the only manager in history to win 100 games with teams in both leagues. He achieved both these distinctions with Detroit in 1984 when the Tigers led the league from opening day to the end of the season, winning 104 games and wiping out Kansas City 3–0 in the LCS and San Diego 4–1 in the Series.

Although the Spark has had snow-white hair for many years, he is not all that old. He will be only 54 years old during the 1988 season, and he is on record as wanting to manage until he's 65 or 70 years old, and he is a good bet to do that managing exclusively in Detroit. While that may seem unlikely to some, given the short life span of managers in the big leagues today, he is in the perfect place to do it. The Detroit Base Ball Club is one of the most conservative in baseball, carrying on in the tradition of the "good old days." The President, Jim Campbell, has been with the team since the 1960s; the General Manager, Bill Lajoie, is Campbell's hand-picked successor who has faithfully continued with Campbell's previous policies; and the Manager, one George Lee Anderson, is the hand-picked choice of Campbell. While there are certainly differences of opinion and judgment between the Prez, the GM and the manager, there is never, repeat never, any public indication of friction or tension between these men. The management of the team prides itself on running a stable and steady ship, and they do. They take their business very seriously.

As a ballplayer, Anderson was typical of many of those who later became managers—that is, he wasn't very good as a player. He played in the minor leagues a total of ten years (seven at the AAA-level), making the big show only for one year with the Philadelphia Phillies in 1959. He was a regular that year at second base, playing 152 games, but he hit only .218, with a paltry 12 extra-base hits, including zero home runs, in 477 at-bats.

Interestingly enough, unlike many managers who tend to favor players who remind them of their own playing career, Sparky shows no favoritism at all for no-hit, good-field middle infielders. In fact, in Detroit he has routinely carried only one spare non-first baseman to back up in the infield, preferring to keep an extra outfielder-first baseman-designated hitter type on the roster, even if he gets very little use. Of course, the longevity and durability of his All-Stars at second base, Lou Whitaker, and at shortstop, Alan Trammell, do cut down on the opportunities for using utility players.

As for other roster decisions, Anderson is pretty conventional. He likes to keep nine pitchers, five starters, two short relievers, and two long relievers-swing men. He doesn't seem to like adding a tenth pitcher during the heat and doubleheaders of the summer, but he will do it if absolutely necessary. He normally keeps two catchers, with the rest of the roster filled up with bats who can play the outfield or first. He rarely likes to carry a strict DH, preferring to spread the DH duties around and resting his regulars. Defensively, he will replace his worst fielders in late innings in some cases, but he also leaves some very bad fielders in the game, notably Kirk Gibson.

As a tactician, Anderson is most definitely not the sabermetrician's darling. He is fond of the intentional walk and the sacrifice bunt, although he makes sparing use of the latter. One interpretation of this would be that in a power-hitter's park with a team that scores a lot of runs, bunting is not the best tactic. Another interpretation would be that Sparky's players can't bunt worth a damn, which is loudly lamented in Motown whenever some hitter fails to lay one down in a key situation. Like most old-school managers, Anderson overvalues high-average hitters. Like most other areas, though, he doesn't refuse to play hitters who walk a lot.

The strongest point in Sparky Anderson's favor when evaluating his career compared to his peers, either current or past, is his record. As they say, you can look it up, and its pretty damn good. Of course, this record was compiled with only two teams who were at the same stage of development when Anderson took over, so there isn't much evidence to look at to see how he would handle other teams in other situations. One thing is very clear to those who have watched him in Detroit, and that is that Sparky Anderson clearly thinks he is the best manager in the major leagues today.

Gary Gillette

Houston Astros
HAL LANIER: THE ASTROS' "THIRD BASE MANAGER"

Hal Lanier became the eleventh manager of the Astros at the end of the 1985 season. The son of Max Lanier (who had pitched in the majors between the 1930s and 1950s), Hal himself played ten years in the majors as an infielder, eight of them with the San Francisco Giants and two with the Yankees. Hal was known as Maxie, after his father, while playing in San Francisco. After a couple of years playing in the minors at the end of his playing career, he was signed as a manager in the St. Louis Cardinals' organization. Hal managed five years in the minors, then, in 1981, Whitey Herzog brought him up as a coach on the major league team. He spent 1981–1985 coaching for the Cardinals.

The circumstances were trying when Hal entered the Houston baseball world. Attendance had been falling ('85 attendance was the lowest since '78) ever since the controversy over Tal Smith's firing after the 1980 division-winning year. (There was even talk of the Astros moving to Washington, D.C.!) Dick Wagner (who hired Lanier) had just

been hired as General Manager of the Astros after being the GM at Cincinnati since 1977. Wagner had cut the payroll of the Reds by letting some of the top players of the Big Red Machine leave for higher-paying pastures. Thus, Wagner was credited by some with breaking up the Big Red Machine, and some in Houston felt he was coming here to break up the team, making the Astros more profitable for owner John McMullan to sell. In addition, the Astros' players had grown flat-footed, going one base at a time instead of taking the extra base. Ironically, Houston had scored more runs in '84 and '85 than in '79 or '80 (considered to be the golden years), but the stolen base totals had gone from 194 in '80 to 96 in '85.

Lanier kept three of the coaches of former manager Bob Lillis. Les Moss, a former big league catcher and manager, remained as the pitching coach; Denis Menke, a former major league infielder, stayed on as the hitting and third base coach; and Matt Galante continued as the first base coach. Lanier persuaded Yogi Berra to be his dugout coach. Yogi, of course, was a very aggressive and hard-nosed player who played on and managed winning teams. Gene Tenace was installed as the bullpen coach.

Last year, when the division races heated up, Lanier put Menke on the bench and directed the team himself from the third base coaching box (describing himself as the "third base manager"). This showed a certain lack of desire to delegate authority and lack of confidence in Menke, but Lanier told the press that he felt Menke could work with the hitters better in the dugout. The question is whether Lanier loses some objectivity by being right on the field of action.

To his credit, Lanier has attempted to solve problems on an individual basis. He has shown that he will let some players have time to work out their own problems: Dickie Thon, Glenn Davis, Jose Cruz and Bob Knepper are good examples. Thon was hit in the head in '84 (after having had a great year in '83) and has been attempting to come back ever since. He missed the first part of spring training in 1987 and came up to the Astros in May. Even though Thon got off to a bad start, Lanier continued to play him. Thon was starting to hit when he suddenly left the team in early July. Although attempts were made to get him back, they failed. Cruz and Davis both got off to bad starts in '86, but Lanier stuck with them and they both came through later in the season. In '87 Davis had a bad start, then got hot, then cooled off again. Lanier generally stuck with him, except for a couple days of benching or putting him lower in the order. Cruz got off to a good start in '87, but got hurt after the first week and never did well the rest of the season. Cruz stayed in the lineup every day until June, when he was platooned, becoming a utility player after the All-Star break. Knepper was getting bombed regularly from his first start on, yet, except for a very brief stint in the bullpen, he remained in the starting rotation throughout the year.

Nevertheless, Lanier is not always patient, and he can be equally impatient with a younger player as with an older player. For example, Phil Garner got into a slump early in '87, never pulled out of it, and was traded to the Dodgers in the middle of June. Charlie Kerfeld was out of shape when he came to spring training and was still out of shape when the season got started. He got bombed and was quickly sent down to Triple A, not to return until after the All-Star break in July. Mark Bailey was supposed to split the catching duties with Alan Ashby, but he did poorly and was shipped to the minors.

There were also times when Lanier was not only impatient, but was also painfully indecisive. A number of players were sent to the minors, while others were brought up to the majors, and then later some who came up would go back down to the minors, replaced by those who had just been sent down. Chuck Jackson, Ronn Reynolds, Bert Pena, Robbie Wine, Manny Hernandez, Dave Meads, Rob Mallicoat and Julio Solano played this elevator game.

Offensively, Lanier was equally indecisive with his batting order, as the batting order kept changing throughout '86 and into '87. For one thing, he did not know who to bat first, Doran or Hatcher. Finally on August 2, 1987, he went with Gerald Young leading off, followed by Hatcher and then Doran. It will be interesting to see if he sticks with that order in '88.

Lanier's roster and lineup selection is a mixture in all regards. Certain positions have set regulars: Davis at first, Doran at second, Bass in right, Young in center, and Hatcher in left. He wants to platoon at catcher, but since he really has no one that is as good as Ashby, he is forced to play Ashby regularly when he is healthy. Short and third have been platoon positions. Hal uses his bench and reserves mainly as pinch hitters or as replacements when he does double switches. His teams are fairly well-balanced among rookies, young players and veterans, so some of the older veterans have helped the younger players. For instance, Davey Lopes has helped Hatcher and Young with getting good starts on the steal attempts.

Lanier is also not afraid to try a rookie or non-established young player at a position at any time. He brought up Ken Caminiti in the middle of the 1987 season and tried him at third (full time for a few weeks); he put Gerald Young in center full time in early August, both at times when Houston was still in the thick of the division race. Lanier does not keep young position players up in the majors to be reserves, he prefers to give them more playing time in the minors. His offensive reserves are mostly older players or veterans like Lopes, Jim Pankovits and Terry Puhl, but his pitching reserves (long relief, spot starters) tend to be younger players.

The Astros under Lanier are supposed to be a more aggressive team in taking the extra base, stealing more often, etc. There are no figures for them taking the extra base successfully or unsuccessfully, so there is no way to gauge if they are more aggressive that way, but they have increased their stolen base totals. In 1985 they were tenth in the league in stealing, in '86 and '87 they were fifth. Their attempted steals declined, however, from '86 (238) to '87 (208) as they got smarter and were caught less in '87. The Astros grounded into far more double plays than the average National League team in '86, and in '87 they were one of the worst in the league at leaving men on base (even though they had the second-worst average in getting runners on base to begin with). Neither of the above would indicate the Astros were that aggressive in their base running. Similarly the Astros do not bunt much, and if they do, it is their pitchers who are sacrificing. They do not try bunting for base hits, either (though you think they would with Young's and Hatcher's speed), and they led the league in '86 with the lowest number of sacrifice hits. They were also one of the lowest in sacrifice flies in '86. All in all,

Lanier's prime offensive tactic, except for a few players who he lets steal, is "swing away and if you get on base run when the ball is hit."

Lanier prefers a five-man starting rotation. He tends to let his starters work out their own problems early in the game unless it just gets too far out of hand—only then will he bring in a relief pitcher. Late in a close game, he will pinch hit for the pitcher to try to score more runs. Larry Andersen is currently the setup man; Dave Smith, the closer. Smith *only* pitches if the Astros are winning a close game; Andersen will pitch middle relief or close a game himself. Lanier will use as many middle relief pitchers as necessary, once he pinch hits for a starter, to keep the Astros close in a game. He rarely pitches a relief pitcher two days in a row, much less three days in a row; therefore, he spreads the work around pretty well.

Defensively, Lanier sticks to what he has started with in the field, rarely putting a defensive replacement in or doing any fancy maneuvering. The Astros were tenth in fielding average in 1985, in 1986 they were third, and in 1987 they were tied for first, evidence that Lanier has built a strong defensive team. He likes his pitchers to challenge opposing hitters: Astros pitchers gave up the fewest intentional walks in the NL in 1986 and the fewest walks of any kind in the NL in 1986 and 1987. Lanier definitely wants his pitchers to throw strikes.

The core of the Houston Astros of 1986 and 1987 was in place when Hal Lanier took over the team after the '85 season. Only Billy Hatcher, who was added in a trade, and much later Gerald Young, brought up from the minors, were added to the core of the current team by Lanier. The Astros now have a solid foundation for Lanier to build the kind of team he wants, but Hal needs to either develop Young and Hatcher into more patient hitters (so that they have a higher on-base percentage) or find another leadoff hitter. The Astros offense needs to have men on base more than it has in the past to function better. Lanier also needs to find more right-handed punch, since only Davis and Doran consistently deliver from that side (the Astros had one of the worst won-lost records against left-handed pitching), in order to drive more runners in. Finally, the team needs to be more aggressive on the base paths—maybe a coaching change at first and third, bringing in his own men to reflect his philosophy, would encourage more aggression on the base paths. Lanier has shown a lot of patience in the past two seasons, which can be helpful for a young player adjusting to the majors but it can be detrimental to a team if it turns into indecision. In 1986 and 1987, Hal Lanier got to see a lot of different players under fire during the pennant races. This coming season, 1988, will be a year of decision for the Astros "third base manager."

Welford McCaffrey

Kansas City Royals
BILLY GARDNER/JOHN WATHAN

Billy Gardner managed the Kansas City Royals for the first 126 games of 1987. The team's inconsistent play prompted his dismissal on August 27 and the hiring of John Wathan to run the club. Gardner left the team with a record

533

of 62 wins and 64 losses, three and one-half games behind in fourth place. Wathan guided the Royals to 21 wins and 15 losses in his five week stint at the helm, and his team finished in second place, two games behind the eventual World Series champion Minnesota Twins.

Gardner and Wathan displayed several differences in managerial style. Handling the position like a custodian, Gardner tended to let the club run itself and interfered only when absolutely necessary. Meanwhile, Wathan seemed determined to leave his imprint on nearly every play. Gardner has been around for a long time and is probably familiar to most baseball fans. He managed in Minnesota from 1981 until 1985; his best season as skipper was in 1984 when the Twins finished second with an 81–81 record. On the other hand, Wathan is a newcomer to the managerial ranks and needs some introduction.

A member of the Royals for his entire professional career, Wathan first played for the team in 1976. He became a regular the next season and was a fixture on the club until his retirement in 1985. During his playing career, Wathan was a member of six American League Western Division titlists, two American League pennant winners and one World Series champion. He was primarily a catcher, but also played at first base and in right field later in his playing career. Finally, he began the 1987 season as the manager of the Royals' AAA affiliate, the Omaha Royals of the American Association.

Wathan was managed by Whitey Herzog, Jim Frey, and Dick Howser during his playing career, though Herzog appears to have had the most influence upon him. Wathan tried to mold the Royals into a team relying primarily on speed, similar to Herzog's team of the late 1970s. This also closely resembles his own approach to the game when he was a player: Wathan stole 36 bases in 1982.

When Wathan took control of the Royals at the end of August, the offense was sputtering. Under Gardner, the team's attack was based almost exclusively on power. While they were likely to score six or seven runs in a game, they were just as likely to be shut out. During one stretch early in the season, the Royals were shut out four times in a five-game span, only to score ten runs in the other game!

Feeling that this erratic scoring pattern negated the Royals' good starting pitching, Wathan undertook to realign the offensive structure of the team. He preferred to have his team score three or four runs every game than get seven runs every other day and be shut out in between. To do this, Wathan made use of many single run strategies, especially base stealing.

Wathan is a firm believer in the running game. In his 36 games at the Royals helm the team attempted 59 thefts, compared to 100 tries in 126 games under Gardner—Wathan's team ran more than twice as often. All of this running occurred despite the Royals not being fleet-footed; several relatively old players have a prominent role in the everyday lineup.

Furthermore, Wathan's Royals were more likely to use the hit-and-run than Gardner's Royals. On the other hand, Wathan does not like to make extensive use of the sacrifice bunt. Instead, he would prefer to pinch hit, steal a base, hit-and-run or even attempt a double steal. The Royals tried four double steals (three successfully) under Wathan's guidance, none under Gardner.

The stolen base might be used by Wathan at almost any time, so even the older veterans became part of the running attack. Also, he was more likely to try to steal a base or use the hit-and-run earlier in the game. However, unlike Gardner, Wathan was far more willing to use those tactics when the team was trailing by a run; Gardner would only use it when leading or occasionally when the score was tied. Generally, Wathan would use a pinch-hitter late in the game, instead of trying to steal a run or bunt a baserunner into scoring position.

Three or four rookies and several seasoned veterans were always a part of Wathan's lineup card, which was usually the same from one day to the next. The only platoon position was at catcher. This left the bench full of veterans whom Wathan used in pinch-hitting roles, usually replacing the weaker hitters at the bottom of the lineup when the Royals were trailing late in the game.

The lineup used by Wathan was designed to manufacture runs via the running game. To this end, he moved the second through fifth-place hitters down one spot and the last two batters up one position. This eliminated the slow-footed power hitters from the lower part of the order and created two openings (the second and ninth spots) which he filled with hitters having more diverse offensive skills. Two of the players to benefit from this strategy were outfielder Gary Thurman and infielder Bill Pecota, both of whom Wathan managed in Omaha.

Wathan's fondness for the running game on offense spills over to the defense as well; his offensive speedsters can cover more ground defensively. In particular, he placed Thurman in left field. When these players are combined with Frank White at second base and Willie Wilson in center field, the Royals' can cover the turf quite well.

One of the most striking differences between Wathan and Gardner is in their use of defensive tactics. Gardner had a laissez faire attitude toward difficult defensive situations—if the pitcher got into trouble, it was the pitcher's problem. Gardner's only defensive move was to change pitchers. He gave only 16 intentional passes to opponents in 126 games; Wathan issued eight in 36 games, nearly a two to one difference. If the running game was a novelty in Gardner's offense, his defense against it was even more so. The Royals used the pitchout an incredible eight times under Gardner; twelve pitchouts were used by Wathan, more than five times as often per game. Finally, Wathan used far more replacements strictly for defense, over twice as many per game than Gardner.

Due to the strong pitching and anemic hitting of the Royals, Wathan has usually had to rely on defense to carry the day. This defense is based primarily on the starting rotation, but he likes to make full use of the bullpen. Finesse pitchers seem to be preferred by Wathan instead of strike-out artists, although he has not shown a great tendency that way. His use of the recently obtained Ted Power may show how much stock he puts in hard throwers.

The pitching staff run by Wathan is well defined, so everyone on the staff has a particular role. Although the Royals' five-man starting rotation is one of the best in the majors, Wathan likes to go to the bullpen more frequently and earlier than Gardner. However, Wathan was willing to stay longer with certain starters. Charlie Leibrandt and Bret Saberhagen were likely to be allowed to work through late-inning difficulties, whereas other Royals' starters were quickly replaced. Leibrandt and Saberhagen combined for five of the eight complete games under Wathan.

Much of the wrath incurred by Gardner was due to his handling of the pitchers. His inconsistent approach from one game to the next left the staff in a constant state of confusion. Leibrandt, in particular, was visibly furious with some of Gardner's decisions.

Wathan believes in a strong bullpen led by a single stopper; Gene Garber filled this role in 1987. Either Garber, Power, or Dan Quisenberry will be called on to be the closer in 1988. Gardner's bullpen by committee produced very erratic results, although much of this was due to the unpredictable performances by the members of the Royals' bullpen.

An aggressive managerial style is one of Wathan's more distinctive traits; he attempts to solve problems immediately. A good example of Wathan's method was shown when he first took over the Royals' reins. The team had trouble scoring runs, so Wathan shuffled the lineup, introduced a new leftfielder, and began to use more aggressive base-running tactics, especially base stealing. These maneuvers helped the Royals develop a more consistent attack. The team was only shut out twice while guided by Wathan compared to 15 whitewashings while run by Gardner. Another problem area for the Royals in 1987 was the bullpen. Wathan quickly installed the newly acquired Garber as the stopper, with fine results: Garber saved eight games in September.

In Wathan's situation with the Royals he has to contend with an extreme mixture of youngsters and veterans. His job is made unique because of his past relationships with these players. Some of the younger players, those that he managed at Omaha, view Wathan as a former manager. A large number of the veterans on the club see Wathan as an old friend and a former teammate. This dichotomy might complicate interaction with the players, but Wathan cut through the confusion from the start by holding several team meetings designed to make it clear that he is a manager first and foremost.

Previous management at the triple-A level gave Wathan comprehensive knowledge of the minor league players, so he was able to bring them up to the majors with great confidence that they would fit into his game plan. The two most visible examples of this process were Thurman and Pecota, who became integral parts of the Royals in the last month of the season. While the Royals made several player moves during the winter, it is unlikely that Wathan had any direct influence on these trades. Likewise, he has had little input into the selection of the Royals' coaches. At least one new player, however, would appear to fit into his style of play very well. Shortstop Kurt Stillwell is a singles hitter who can run and has a variety of skills; Wathan is likely to use him extensively in the Royals' 1988 offense.

Wathan is the ultimate organization man. His career was born and bred in the Royals' system. He played for the team for ten years and later managed in their farm system. Early in his minor league managerial career, Wathan was pegged by the front office as the future manager of the Royals. The team's General Manager, John Schuerholz, said in June of 1987 that Wathan was being groomed for the job and that Gardner was a caretaker until Wathan was ready for the position. When Gardner could no longer be tolerated by the front office, Wathan was promoted to the major league post. Later, after Wathan was signed to a contract for the 1988 season, Schuerholz said of Wathan: "He is the consummate Royal."

Due to his short stint as manager of a major league team in 1987, Wathan was unable to truly display how he would deal with problem players in the organization. However, his past relationships with many of his current players indicate that he would be more likely to deal with any problems internally, instead of publicly criticizing the player. Besides, media battles with players are not the Royals' style, and Wathan is a prime example of a Royals' organization man.

Wathan's extensive major league experience has given him the understanding necessary to keep a steady hand through winning and losing steaks. Although he only managed the Royals for 36 games, the team had several skeins of both varieties. Throughout the streaks, Wathan did not radically alter his strategies; he was content to put his best foot forward every day and let the chips fall where they may. It remains to be seen if this approach will carry John Wathan to a long career as a major league manager.

Marc Bowman

Los Angeles Dodgers
TOMMY LASORDA

Tommy Lasorda has been the Dodgers' manager for eleven seasons now, and he has been very successful, winning one World Series, three National League pennants and five NL Western Division championships. But the Dodgers have hit the rocks recently in the eyes of many baseball observers. What role has Lasorda played in the recent failures of the Dodgers? My focus here will be on how Lasorda constructs his team, rather than on his tactical moves during games, because that is where the current failures of the Dodgers lie.

Karl Marx wrote that history repeats itself, the first time as tragedy, the second as farce. For Lasorda, the first time was no tragedy; it was a triumph of major proportions. Consider the position of the Dodgers during the winter of 1976–1977. The Big Red Machine had just won consecutive World Championships, but the cracks of age and discontent were beginning to show. The Dodgers had an excellent core of players (Steve Garvey, Davey Lopes, Ted Sizemore, Ron Cey, Bill Russell, Reggie Smith, Bill Buckner, Dusty Baker, Lee Lacy, Steve Yeager, Don Sutton, Burt Hooton, Tommy John, Rick Rhoden, Doug Rau and Charlie Hough) that was capable of beating the Reds, one of the greatest collections of talent in major league history. But how to shape this talent into a winning team?

The answer was obvious: The Dodgers had reached the World Series in 1974 by doing two things they did not do in 1975 and 1976, hitting home runs and playing a set lineup. In the off-season, the Dodgers traded to prepare their team for the 1977 season. Buckner, Ivan DeJesus, and Sizemore were sent off for Rick Monday, Johnny Oates and Mike Garman. These two trades eliminated a regular who did not have power and two infielders that might require playing time at the expense of the regular lineup and acquired a powerful centerfielder (they had been playing

Baker in center in 1976), a badly needed backup catcher, and another reliever, all three veteran players.

Lasorda then completed the strategy during the 1977 season. The Dodgers' power boomed; they were the first team with four players who hit 30 or more homers (Garvey, Cey, Reggie Smith, and Baker). Every regular except Lopes, Monday, and Yeager played in 140 or more games. The most frequently used sub was John Hale, who Lasorda turned into a defensive replacement in the outfield (a wise decision). Lee Lacy's playing time was cut, leading to his defection through free agency after the 1978 season. In 1978, when Monday developed injury problems, the Dodgers traded for Bill North to play center field instead of playing Jeff Leonard.

Lasorda also took other steps to increase the Dodgers' power. It is reported that he told Garvey to swing for the fences even if his average dropped below .300. He must have told everyone to swing for the fences—just about every regular player increased his power under Lasorda. Garvey averaged 14 homers a season before Lasorda, 25 homers a season under Lasorda; Lopes went from 7 homers a season to more than 16 under Lasorda; Cey went from 20 homers a season to more than 26; Reggie Smith posted the highest home run per at-bats figures of his career in 1977 and 1978; and Baker's power surged erratically under Lasorda. The primary offensive characteristic of Lasorda's teams is power: his teams have led the NL in homers six times (1977–1981 and 1983) in eleven seasons. After moving the fences out in Dodger Stadium in 1982, the Dodgers led the NL in road homers in 1982, 1983 and 1985. He both chooses players for their power and then encourages them to swing for the fences.

Lasorda not only loves veteran regular players, but also a veteran bench. In 1978, the Dodgers traded Jeff Leonard and Rafael Landestoy for Joe Ferguson. Both Leonard and Landestoy could have been valuable members of the bench, but Lasorda preferred Lacy and Teddy Martinez. Lasorda's bench generally has a veteran pinch hitter, like Manny Mota, Jay Johnstone or Jose Morales, because his regular lineup gives him the luxury of carrying a player who cannot play in the field.

Lasorda believes in regular starting rotations. If he has five pitchers he trusts, it will be a five-man rotation. Otherwise, he will concentrate the starts in the pitchers he trusts while experimenting to fill out the rotation. If an unestablished starter fails, he will dump him quickly for an alternative. His new candidates for the rotation have always pitched in the bullpen first; Bob Welch, Jerry Reuss, Alejandro Pena and Orel Hershiser all pitched at least a half season in relief before being promoted to the rotation. Even Rick Sutcliffe and Fernando Valenzuela pitched in relief before starting. The only exceptions are starting pitchers the Dodgers have received in trade or via free agency (Rick Honeycutt, Dave Goltz, Andy Messersmith).

The 1979 season is a good example of Lasorda's strategy in this respect. The Dodgers lost Tommy John to free agency and traded Rhoden for Reuss; Messersmith (free agent) and Welch were scheduled to take their places in the rotation. Messersmith bombed out, Welch suffered through his drinking problem, and Doug Rau had a shoulder injury that ended his career. Lasorda switched Sutcliffe into the rotation, leading to his selection as the first of a long string of Dodger Rookies-of-the-Year, and experimented with

536

Reuss and Hough as starters. In 1980, when Sutcliffe failed, Reuss was promoted to the rotation on the basis of his effective relief work that season.

In the bullpen, Lasorda does not believe in relief aces. No Dodgers reliever under Lasorda has accumulated more than 22 saves in one season (Charlie Hough in 1977 and Terry Forster in 1978). Instead, he uses two short relievers, preferably one lefty and one righty (Hough and Forster, Howe and Niedenfuer), who divide the work load. Although each may appear in 60 or more games, they almost never pitch more than 100 innings. Only Hough in 1977 and Niedenfuer in 1985 have pitched more than 100 innings in relief for Lasorda. In 1976, Hough pitched 143 innings in 77 games, which is astronomical use for a reliever; in 1977, he pitched 127 innings in 70 games; in 1978, 93 innings in 55 games. Of course, Hough was a knuckleball pitcher, so he was much less susceptible to overusage than normal pitchers. Behind his short relievers are the apprentice pitchers being groomed for the rotation.

Now Lasorda's handling of pitchers strikes me as very sensible: Don't throw untested kids into the rotation and don't burn out your good relievers. Given Lasorda was a pitcher who never received an extended shot at the majors, I believe he knows how to handle pitchers. But he sure does not know how to handle young position players.

Lasorda has three simple rules for breaking in young position players; one, always play an available veteran over the kid; two, if the kid looks good, let him sit on the bench until absolutely necessary; three, if you don't hit from day one, you're gone. In 1979, injuries to Monday and Reggie Smith opened up two spots in the outfield. Instead of playing Rudy Law and Pedro Guerrero (who in 1978 had hit over .300 and led the PCL in RBIs), he chose Gary Thomasson and Derrel Thomas. When Law was put in center in 1980, he did not hit well enough and never played regularly for Lasorda again. Guerrero did not become a regular until the second half of the 1981 season; Mike Marshall's reward for winning the PCL Triple Crown was a job as a fourth outfielder in LA. Those rookies who received and kept regular jobs (Mike Scioscia and Steve Sax) hit right from the start. Further, Lasorda will not replace a regular unless absolutely necessary; trades (and free agency) drove the replacement of three of the four members of his original infield. The fourth, Russell, held on far longer than anyone could have imagined. The great rebuilding of the Dodgers in 1983 (Guerrero to third, Marshall to left, and Brock to first) followed the dumping of Cey and Garvey.

The 1984 season is a good example of how Lasorda handles young prospects. Guerrero's back problems and other injuries created a power outage and opened spots in the outfield. He had several acceptable solutions on hand, R. J. Reynolds, Candy Maldonado, Franklin Stubbs, and German Rivera (at third with Guerrero moving to the outfield). But instead of deciding who should play and then playing him or platooning him, Lasorda gave each about 200 at-bats in an irregular fashion. None of them played well, and the Dodgers floundered. Since then, Lasorda has preferred veterans (Len Matuszek, Al Oliver, Enos Cabell, Bill Madlock, Mickey Hatcher, Phil Garner, John Shelby) as solutions to short-term problems.

Having covered the triumph of Lasorda's managing to discover his patterns and prejudices, we now turn to its repetition, the farce of the last two seasons. Massive gaps at shortstop, third base, and center field opened up in the Dodgers' lineup, and the available alternatives were prospects. Consequently, none of the prospects received an adequate trial, and the gaps were not filled. For example, when Guerrero suffered his severe knee injury at the start of the 1986 season, the Dodgers could have given two-month trials to each of their numerous outfield prospects (Franklin Stubbs, Ralph Bryant, Jose Gonzalez, Reggie Williams). None of them was a great prospect, but only Stubbs and Williams received a fair shot at demonstrating that they do not belong in the majors. Lasorda showed no conviction in his choice of players, and the Dodgers' offense floundered. The once bedrock-stable Dodger lineup became a perpetually shifting desert of fill-in players broken only by the oases of several established regulars.

In the light of this review of Lasorda's player usage, the off-season of the Dodgers make sense. They have built another set veteran lineup; every position on the field is filled by a veteran player. Alfredo Griffin at shortstop and John Shelby in center field fill two major holes. Moving Sax to third and putting Mariano Duncan at second solidifies the infield defensively. Free agents Mike Davis and Kirk Gibson complete the outfield, allowing Guerrero to be dealt away. Lasorda now has a new lefty-righty punch in the bullpen in Jesse Orosco and Jay Howell.

All these changes, however, disguise two big problems. First, the Dodgers' offense is very weak. Can Guerrero (?), Marshall, Scioscia, Davis and Gibson carry the rest of the team? Sax is a good offensive player for a second baseman, but not for a third baseman. Second, the rotation is also very weak. Valenzuela and Hershiser are the only established starters. Shawn Hillegas and Tim Belcher are talented, but if they falter, there are no obvious replacements. Given the Dodgers' losing ways of recent seasons, gambling on talented but unproven pitchers makes sense. Lasorda appears quite capable in judging pitchers, and what do they have to lose? If the gamble fails, they play .400 ball; if it succeeds, they are in contention.

Jim Morrow

Milwaukee Brewers
TOM TREBELHORN

On September 26, 1986, George Bamberger, former savior of the Milwaukee Brewers franchise, resigned (or was fired) after two listless years at the Brewers' helm. Third base coach Tom Trebelhorn was named to replace him and drew raves for his positive approach to the game as the Brewers won six of their last nine games.

Trebelhorn's task for 1987 was to mold the young Brewers players into a respectable team which could make a run at the pennant in 1989 or '90. Instead, the Brewers came out of the gate on fire, then collapsed, and later finished the season as one of the strongest teams in the league.

One of the first things that I look at to learn about a manager is the number of players and pitchers that he uses. If an AL manager uses 12 players in a game this is a PLG of 12/9 = 1.33 (12 players used to fill the 9 positions on the field). The league average for the last two years has been 1.19. The typical leader in PLG is Tony LaRussa or Bobby

Cox. Typically low in PLG are Dick Williams and George Bamberger. Bamberger, for example, had the lowest AL PLG in 1985 (1.12) and 1986 (1.09), so Trebelhorn's 1.16 indicates that the reserves got much more playing time in '87 than they did under Bamberger. Another indicator is the number of pinch-hitters (PH) used. In 1985 the Brewers' PH turned in one of the worst performances in the last 25 years. In 1986 they were much worse, collecting only 4 pinch hits in 31 AB. Trebelhorn used more than twice as many PH (85), but the Brewers' 77 PH AB were last in the AL. Trebelhorn's primary PH were Rick Manning (18 PH appearances), B. J. Surhoff (11) and Jim Paciorek (10). With Manning and Paciorek getting the call nearly a third of the time, it's not surprising that the PH totals were rather poor. Brewer PHs batted .247, 6th in the league, and drew only 4 walks, recording the second lowest OBA (.286) in the AL; their 9 RBI were lowest in the league. On the 'bright" side, Steve Kiefer did hit a home run on July 24, the Brewers first by a PH since 1983.

The second thing that I look at is the number of pitcher used per game by a manager. The AL average in 1987 was 2.73, in '86 it was 2.66. Trebelhorn used 2.74, a thoroughly unremarkable figure. Brewers' starters completed 28 games (AL avg. 26.6), but there was a clear division of labor among them. The chart below implies that Trebelhorn was making an effort to save the younger pitcher's arms.

	Age	GS	CG	ERA	IP/GS
Higuera	28	35	14	3.85	7.48
Wegman	26	33	7	4.17	6.80
Nieves	22	33	3	4.92	5.88
Bosio	24	19	2	5.22	6.44

Another notable feature was Trebelhorn's commitment to keeping the rotation stable. The best way to see this is to list the number of days rest given to a starter between starts. Below is a list of this. An "x" indicates an off-rotation start (more than 5 days), an "o" indicates a pitcher's first start of the season and a "d" indicates that the starter was coming off of the disabled list.

```
ooo  o43  304    555  4xx  xxx    x44  443  444
x45  455  454    554  544  4o4    4o3  544  446
44x  433  o44    444  445  33o    o44  44o  444
444  4x5  xxx    444  444  444    444  454  4xo
544  334  44d    544  44d  455    44x  444  444
444  444  444    445  545  x44    434  444  444
```

The two clumps of x's were caused by a rain delay and the All-Star game. The o's in line three correspond to a rash of injuries to the regular starters. For the last month (bottom line) the starting rotation was set with Higuera, Wegman, Bosio, Nieves and Barker. In all, the Brewers had 12 first starts, 2 return starts and 16 off-rotation starts.

Another way to see what a manager is doing is to divide the season into six 27-game periods and list the positions on the field and in the batting order for starters and key reserves. Space considerations prohibit giving all the tables, but a division into first and second half of the season (81 games each) and a commentary is given below. For each position in the field and in the batting order, players who started more than 9 games are listed. Frequently used pinch hitters, pinch runners and defensive replacements are also listed. For pitchers, the number of games started, finished, saved, and time of entry into game is given.

"Entry 1–3: Johnson 4" means that John Henry Johnson had 4 games in which he entered the game from the bullpen in either the 1st, 2nd or 3rd inning. Also listed are players who spent time on the disabled list (DL).

First Half (40 wins, 41 losses)

Position:		Spot in batting order:	
C	Surhoff 44, Schroeder 27, O'Brien 10	1	Molitor 34, Felder 21, Castillo 15
1B	Brock 62, Paciorek 9	2	Yount 69
2B	Gantner 47, Castillo 34	3	Cooper 41, Braggs 33
3B	Molitor 40, Gantner 25	4	Deer 39, Brock 36
SS	Sveum 74	5	Deer 17, Cooper 12, Robidoux 11, Paciorek 11
LF	Deer 57, Felder 16		
CF	Yount 73	6	Braggs 15, Brock 15, Deer 13, Surhoff 10
RF	Braggs 64, Deer 11		
DH	Cooper 60, Robidoux 10	7	Schroeder 22, Surhoff 19, Gantner 13
PH	Paciorek 10, Manning 9		
PR	Felder 7, Manning 6	8	Gantner 38, Castillo 13
DEF	Manning 31(22—RF, 6—LF,3—CF), Castillo 19 (14–2B, 5—SS) Felder 17(12—LF, 4—CF,1–2B)	9	Sveum 51, Gantner 19, Castillo 9

DL: Riles, Diaz, Cooper, Johnson, Molitor (twice), Birkbeck, Brock, Barker

GS: Higuera 19, Wegman 18, Nieves 17, Birkbeck 10, Crim 5, Ciardi 3, Barker 3, Bosio 2, Johnson 2, Clear 1, Knudson 1

GF: Plesac 32, Clear 22, Bosio 8, Mirabella 5, Crim 2, Aldrich 1

Saves: Plesac 17, Clear 2, Bosio 2

Entry 1–3: Johnson 4, Crim 3, Ciardi 1, Mirabella 1, Aldrich 1
    4–5: Crim 4, Aldrich 4, Bosio 2, Mirabella 2, Johnson 1, Clear 1
    6–7: Bosio 18, Crim 9, Clear 9, Mirabella 6, Aldrich 4, Johnson 3, Nieves 1, Wegman 1
    8+: Plesac 34, Clear 24, Bosio 7, Mirabella 6, Crim 2, Aldrich 2

Second Half (51 wins, 30 losses)

Position:		Spot in batting order:	
C	Surhoff 46, Schroeder 35	1	Molitor 71
1B	Brock 76	2	Yount 56, Felder 16
2B	Castillo 47, Molitor 18, Sveum 11	3	Braggs 40, Yount 24, Surhoff 9
3B	Riles 51, Kiefer 23	4	Brock 65, Deer 16
SS	Sveum 65, Riles 15	5	Deer 36, Surhoff 16, Brock 10, Braggs 9
LF	Deer 41, Felder 38		
CF	Yount 76	6	Sveum 17, Surhoff 15, Riles 15, Kiefer 12, Deer 11
RF	Braggs 55, Deer 13, Manning 10		
DH	Molitor 58	7	Schroeder 27, Riles 23, Surhoff 16
PR	Manning 9, Surhoff 8		
PR	Felder 10	8	Castillo 16, Sveum 15, Felder 13, Riles 11
DEF	Manning 24 (6—LF, 5—CF,13—RF) Felder 20 (15—LF, 5—CF)	9	Svuem 37, Castillo 33

DL: Diaz, Birkbeck, Gantner, Castillo, Wegman, Aldrich

GS: Bosio 17, Higuera 16, Nieves 16, Wegman 15, Barker 8, Knudson 7, Burris 2

GF: Crim 16, Plesac 15, Clear 15, Aldrich 8, Knudson 4, Mirabella 4, Burris 2, Stapleton 1

Saves: Crim 12, Plesac 6, Clear 4, Mirabella 2

Entry 1–3: Stapleton 2, Madrid 1, Aldrich 1
    4–5: Aldrich 3, Burris 3, Knudson 3, Madrid 2, Crim 2, Stapleton 1, Mirabella 1
    6–7: Crim 16, Aldrich 11, Clear 7, Mirabella 7, Plesac 5, Burris 2, Knudson 1, Stapleton 1
    8+: Plesac 17, Clear 16, Crim 12, Aldrich 6, Mirabella 5, Knudson 3, Burris 2

The Brewers played 54 games against left-handed starters and Trebelhorn did do some platooning, most notably with catchers B. J. Surhoff, who started 99 games (11% vs. LHP) and Bill Schroeder who started 66 games (64% vs. LHP). Trebelhorn also platooned at 3B for a while, with Riles started 75 games (17% vs. LHP) and Kiefer started 24 games (54% vs. LHP). Trebelhorn did some minor platooning with second basemen Gantner (76 GS, 26% vs. LHP) and Castillo (91GS, 41% vs. LHP). Backups Robidoux (17GS, 6%), Manning (22GS, 5%) and Paciorek (25GS, 84%) were also platooned.

For the first time in their history, the Brewers led the AL in stolen bases. Trebelhorn loves to hit-and-run, run-and-hit and bunt, bunt, bunt. Four of Trebelhorn's seven minor league teams led their league in stolen bases (one, led by Rickey Henderson with 95 SBs, stole 357), and another finished second. Trebelhorn had the Brewers lay down 63 SH, second only to the 'king-of-don't-swing," Gene Mauch (70 SH). But it's not just sacrifices. All sorts of Brewers were bunting for base hits, and two of the most notable were the catchers. On May 16, the Brewers were being no-hit 6–0 in the 6th inning by Charlie Liebrandt (this was in the middle of their 12-game losing streak), and with 2 out, Bill Schroeder bunted for a base hit, the only hit given up by Liebrandt. On June 6, the Brewers were tied with New York at 6 in the bottom of the 9th with 2 outs and the bases loaded when B. J. Surhoff laid down a bunt single to win the game. The speedster on third? Cecil Cooper.

Trebelhorn was given much credit for motivating the players with his positive approach to the game, but there are two situations which he handled in unusual, if not negative, manners. The first was in spring training. Dale Sveum and Edgar Diaz were battling for the starting SS job when Diaz dislocated his shoulder, giving Sveum the job. At this point Trebelhorn told reporters had Diaz not been hurt, he would have been the starting SS. Not the most encouraging start for Sveum. The second mystery was Cecil Cooper. At midseason, Trebelhorn decided that a .240 BA and .290 OBA wasn't good enough (it was the first time that I've heard a manager quote an OBA instead of a vague "ability to get on base") and benched Cooper. He kept saying, "I can't just let him sit on the bench," and then let him sit on the bench. About a month after the benching, a right-handed batter came up late in the game with a man in scoring position, a perfect spot for Cooper, but Trebelhorn didn't use him. A few nights later, the Brewers were in a blowout and Trebelhorn asked Cooper if he would like to pinch hit. Cooper, probably preferring a slightly more crucial situation declined. A friend of mine has a phrase for this, a "slap-in-the-face" offer. Why, if he wasn't going to use him, didn't Trebelhorn release Cooper (he was released this winter)?

Overall, Trebelhorn, a substitute math teacher in the off-season, did a good job of teaching the young Brewers to function as a team. He kept things interesting with his running game and six-man infields and showed an awareness of the need to get on base (Milwaukee drew 598 walks, up from 530 in '86). In this he is like Dave Johnson, another math major who took over a losing team and won better than 90 games.

The outlook for 1988 is fair. Many people are talking about the Brewers making a run for the pennant next year, but Trebelhorn cautions them by reminding them of the 1987 Indians. Molitor and Schroeder are due for large drop-offs, and Yount at age 32 may fall off some. If Molitor moves to second, what becomes of Juan Castillo and Edgar Diaz? Will Gantner be spending all of 1988 on the bench? Can Sveum repeat his 25 homer season, and if so can he improve his fielding (4.10 Range Factor, .965 FA)? Is Joey Meyer ready to be the DH? If not, will the Brewers ever find a DH? Will Nieves become the star many people expect him to become? Can Bosio become an effective starter? Who will be the Brewers' fifth starter?

With all these question marks the Brewers will probably fall off a little from their '87 performance, winning 85–89 games unless disaster strikes. If they can win 90 again, much of the credit should go to Trebelhorn.

John Rickert

Minnesota Twins
TOM KELLY

Anyone who can pilot a ball club to the World Championship in his first full season as a big-league manager (running the club from opening day through October) has to have something on the ball. However, this does not ensure greatness—eight other managers have turned the trick before Tom Kelly did so in '87. That list includes Tris Speaker (1920), Bucky Harris (1924), Rogers Hornsby (1926), Bill Terry (1933), Frankie Frisch (1934), Eddie Dyer (1946), Ralph Houk (1961), and Dallas Green (1980). Collectively, they managed their teams to a career 7396–7029 record, for a winning percentage of .513, which is the equivalent of an 83–79 mark for 162 games. Such a percentage would not come close to cracking the Top Ten career marks among managers who managed one thousand or more games in the big leagues.

It is interesting to note that, of the eight men listed above, not only were most of them considered players' managers, but five of them (Speaker, Harris, Hornsby, Terry, and Frisch) were actually player-managers. Perhaps the ability to think like a manager while acting like a player—and vice-versa—had something to do with their immediate success.

This brings us back to Mr. Kelly. Tom got his start as a player-manager for Tacoma in 1977, then was a player-coach at Toledo before taking over as manager at Visalia and then Orlando. While at Orlando he managed future Twins Randy Bush, Greg Gagne, Gary Gaetti, Tim Laudner, and Frank Viola.

It's no secret that after the Rabbit Revolt of '86 (I refer to the Ray Miller Era), many of the wimps and whiners in the Twins' clubhouse were looking to get one of their own

back into the saddle. The players wanted TK, and the players got TK.

Kelly's strength has always been his ability to communicate with his players while keeping everything on an even keel. (I called Tom to get his thoughts on managing but he was busy watching reruns of *One Day at a Time*.) He'll even go so far as to let the players think that they are in control; he does not appear to have an ego.

Kelly's coaching staff is made up of the usual suspects. Other than Oliva—whose popularity with the players and fans is a big reason for his presence on the staff—only Wayne Terwilliger can boast to his grandchildren about being an ex-major leaguer and not be ashamed to let them look at the record. Bullpen coach Rick Stelmaszek (48 games caught in three big league seasons), Rick Renick, Twig, and Kelly himself combined for a career that would look like this in seasonal notation:

6.49 YEARS 440 AB, 102 H, 19 2B, 2 3B, 7 HR, 39 RBI, .231 BA

Then, of course, there is pitching guru Dick Such (career 1–5, 7.56) who averaged nearly a walk an inning for his 50-inning career; such also compiled an 0–16 mark for York in one season. Fortunately for Dick it was not *New* York. Dick Such is widely acknowledged as being the man who made Mike Smithson and John Butcher the pitchers they are today.

There was a summer-long debate on the radio talk shows about how much credit (or blame) should go to a pitching coach. Frank Viola credits Johnny Podres with the help he needed to develop a good changeup. Bert Blyleven knew how to break off a curve when he was 18. Joe Niekro and Steve Carlton were not likely to be influenced by anyone such as Such, and the two guys on the Twins' staff who could've benefited from good coaching, Mark Portugal and Allan Anderson, were not listening to anything said by Such.

Kelly cannot be considered a tactical genius by any means. There does not seem to be any method to his madness when it comes to moves on the field. Many times he was outmaneuvered by rival skippers in late inning situations during the regular season. Of course, one is limited when there are only one or two lefties in the bullpen to choose from, and defensively there were not that many combinations to consider as long as everyone stayed healthy (which they did). Al Newman could spell either Greg Gagne or Steve Lombardozzi in the mid-infield and Gene Larkin backed up Kent Hrbek whenever the big guy was suffering from the usual aches and pains. Gaetti did not get much rest at all. One has to wonder if Kelly will be able to piece things together if any of the big guns go down for any length of time. (Give Whitey Herzog a healthy unit and he'd outmanage Kelly in series after series.)

Tom Nieto was a Kelly favorite behind the plate; the other catcher, Tim Laudner, was about the only guy on the roster to spend any time in the dog house. The only young 'uns to get any real playing time were Larkin and Davidson and neither had to bear much pressure.

Tom experimented quite freely with the lineup in 1987. At one point early in the season, when things were not going particularly well, he was asked about his decision to bat Randy Bush in the leadoff spot, with Steve Lombardozzi second instead of the other way around. TK mumbled something about getting things mixed up, then deciding that it didn't make that much difference anyway so why not? I think that all this mumbo-jumbo with the media is an effort to protect his privacy while keeping the pressure off his team, since Kelly is not in the habit of raising expectations. Good for the Twins that they don't need to rely on TK to sell tickets.

Kelly, a big horse racing fan, had the Twins running more than usual last year. However, they were not particularly good at it. They were very exciting at times, but the new wagonloads of fans are discovering that aggressive baserunning is not necessarily good baserunning.

It's hard to say at this stage how much clout Kelly carries with the front office. Although Andy MacPhail supplied him with a constant flow of veterans and castoffs (Niekro, Carlton, Baylor, *et al.*), Tom never had to go in and say "get me Joe Blow" or "I want John Doe." Everything had a way of working out for the best in 1987—it will be interesting to see how he deals with the new celebrity status of his troops this year.

Jim Rogde

Montreal Expos
BUCK RODGERS

In three seasons of Buck Rodgers' reign as Expos manager, the Expos have gone 84–77, 78–83 and 91–71. Given the loss of such stars as Gary Carter, Andre Dawson and Jeff Reardon, you have to be impressed by his record. Largely thought of as a 'player's manager," Rodgers is much more aggressive than his predecessor, Bill Virdon. Probably the most consistent difference between Virdon and Rodgers in Montreal is that Buck's teams have won more games than they should have (via the Pythagorean projection method), and Virdon's teams won fewer.

Rodgers likes to leave his star players alone, but he does believe in platooning at weak positions, as he did in centerfield (Winningham and Nichols) and at catcher (Reed and Fitzgerald). The majority of his part-time players are youngsters like Foley, Winningham and Candaele. Most of the veteran players Buck used were young veterans like Nichols and Engle or guys that Murray "The Weasel" Cook acquired (à la Wayne Krenchicki). Since Buck took over, Galarraga, Webster, Burke and Bob Sebra have taken over starting jobs. Giving Burke a job was probably Buck's best move in Montreal, because Cook probably made the decision on Webster, whom he acquired.

As previously documented by Daniel Okrent, Buck loves to tinker with the batting order. He rarely goes two consecutive games with the same order, and he loves the hit-and-run, although he usually reserves it for players in slumps and for "waking-up" the offense. The high caught stealing totals of the Rodgers era in Montreal are about 40 percent busted hit-and-runs. Rodgers' major weakness is his two-out and bottom-of-the-order tinkering in an effort to get one more run. However, the 1985 and 1987 offenses were much more efficient than any offense since Dick Williams.

Rodgers is a master at moving the ninth slot in the batting order, a National League essential lost in the Virdon era. He likes to stick with his starters, but he also uses

a 5+ man rotation, pulling someone from the rotation when they are going poorly. In the bullpen, he has a "chosen stopper" whom he does not overwork and saves for key situations (Reardon in 1985 and 1986 and Burke in 1986). Buck likes fireballers and tried to make Jeff Parrett his stopper in 1987 (until Jeff's talent took over). Maybe he just likes Jeffs?

The Expos' offense is built on speed, but that is more a function of the team's home park and personnel than of Buck's choosing. He enjoys using his entire pitching staff extensively, especially set-up men such as McGaffigan and Burke. His idea of defense is an effective pitching staff and some late-inning replacements.

Buck is a very competitive man, an ex-car salesman who wants his ballplayers to be as aggressive as he is. This caused a major rift between him and Vance Law, as Vance was a very patient hitter. Casey Candaele will replace the recently departed Vance (or at least try to). Being a very positive man, Buck has been blinded by Casey's attitude and mastery of the little things in the game.

Brent MacInnes

The charts shown below span the major league managerial career of current Expos manager Buck Rodgers along with the Montreal years of former Expos' manager Bill Virdon. The Projected columns show the team records using the Pythagorean formula for those years.

Buck Rodgers

Year, Team,		League	Projected		Actual		Game
			W–L	Pct.	W–L	Pct.	Diff.
1980	MIL A		39–31	.500	39–31	.500	0
1981	MIL A		56–53	.518	62–47	.569	+6
1982	MIL A		23–24	.496	23–24	.496	0
1985	MON N		80–81	.499	84–77	.522	+4
1986	MON N		77–84	.481	78–83	.485	+1
1987	MON N		82–80	.507	91–71	.562	+9
Career			360–350	.507	377–333	.531	+17
Seasonal			82–80	.507	86–76	.531	+4

Bill Virdon

Yrs. with Expos		Projected		Actual		Game
		W–L	Pct.	W–L	Pct.	Diff.
1983	MON N	83–79	.512	82–80	.506	-1
1984	MON N	66–65	.506	64–67	.489	-2
Career		980–936	.511	995–921	.519	+15
Seasonal		83–79	.512	84–78	.519	+1

In looking at variations from projected and actual wins and losses, one tries to make up for the difference by searching for "intangibles," which are sometimes quite tangible indeed but not specifically reflected in runs scored and allowed. For example, Bill Virdon had exceeded his projections by 7 games in 1972 (with Pittsburgh) and 8 games in 1979 and 1980 in Houston. With the Bucs, the team's differential was large (179 more runs scored than allowed). What the differential can't tell you is that the 1972 Pirates dominated the league, finishing 3rd in runs scored and allowing the fewest runs. It's hard to say a manager could have a late-inning strategic impact on a team that impressive.

In Houston, Virdon did have an impact. He had the Astros steal bases (leading the league in 1979) and used a very effective three-man bullpen in 1980. These strategies can help explain the differences in Virdon's projected and actual win differentials.

In Montreal, Virdon simply made some ridiculous decisions (as elucidated by Stan Michne in the 1985 *Bill James Baseball Abstract*). On offense, he went with prototypes of players he succeeded with in Houston (Dan Dreissen as a Bob Watson, any number of speedster outfielders—Tony Scott, Miguel Dilone—as Puhl, Cruz, Cedeno, etc). He seemed to forget how he succeeded with his bullpens in the Dome. Thus, the Expos lost two years—maybe more—of valuable time with a team that had a ton of talent (Andre Dawson, Tim Raines, Gary Carter, 1982 batting champ Al Oliver, Tim Wallach, Steve Rogers, Charlie Lea, Scott Sanderson, Bill Gullickson, and Jeff Reardon, to name a few).

Buck Rodgers changed that quickly. He doesn't look at prototypes; he looks at players. He gives new players a chance to make the team—he sees value in players like Mitch Webster, Herm Winningham, Neal Heaton, etc., that other people don't seem to see. He makes brave decisions, uses his reserves, and isn't afraid to try his players in all configurations to get the most out of their skills. Lacking Jeff Reardon, he instead utilized a relief pitching platoon that was arguably even more effective than "The Terminator" had been. His motivational skills, in-game moves and skill in using players in their best situations have allowed Rodgers to consistently win more games than the Pythagorean projection says he should. For his sake, let's hope he doesn't wind up like Gene Mauch, a great manager manning sub-par teams for the next 20 years.

Stuart Shea

New York Mets
DAVEY JOHNSON

Davey Johnson has been a rather controversial manager this past year, controversy amplified by the microscope of the New York press. It is generally thought that he and the Mets failed in 1987, although they did finish second in the NL East with 92 victories, which is two more wins than they had in 1984 when the same Davey Johnson led them out of the wilderness to a 90–72 finish. In his four years as Mets manager, he has never won less than 90 games or finished worse than second. The Mets easily have the best overall record in the majors during those four years, as their 388–260 (.599) record easily outpaces the second-best Tigers (373–274, .577). Despite this, Johnson has never won Manager of the Year, not even when the Mets won the World Series!

Why has recognition eluded Johnson? Mostly because success was always expected of the Mets. They traded for such stars as George Foster, Keith Hernandez, Bob Ojeda, and Kevin McReynolds during the '80s and brought up quality players like Ron Darling, Dwight Gooden, Len Dykstra and Wally Backman. These stars, along with other top players such as Mookie Wilson, Ray Knight, Howard Johnson, Sid Fernandez, Jesse Orosco and Roger McDowell, led to high expectations over Johnson's four years (some of the players mentioned may have been bad or invisible during 1987, but all contributed significantly during Johnson's reign). Ninety victories, a rarity in the AL West, were assumed to be an easy task, as was a divisional title in 1987. Thus, impressing critics and skeptics was not easy, despite the excellent qualifications.

Davey Johnson's leadership style involves a "tough guy" approach. He is not the ballplayers' friend, he is their manager. This is an unusual characteristic for such a young manager (45), so fresh from the player ranks. He is generally very direct with his players, letting them know exactly what he expects of them. Occasionally this breaks down and he spouts off to the press, as in his much-publicized bouts with Darryl Strawberry. Johnson's other nemesis is Ron Darling. Whereas Strawberry's problem generally involves off-field antics (lateness, missed workouts), Darling's is definitely on-field control. It appears likely that Johnson discussed these issues with both players once, then expected results. When he did not see any change, he then went to the press with his exasperation: Under stress, his communicativeness breaks down. For instance, down the stretch, Johnson failed to notify Terry Leach of his removal from the starting rotation. The problems in 1987 that caused this stress included losing McDowell and Gooden in spring training, losing Ojeda and Aguilera early in the season, Darling's early-season problems (2–4, 5.58 as of June 4), the afore-mentioned Strawberry controversy, and chasing the Cardinals from 5–10 games back all season. By the end of the season, Johnson was pretty well burned out and was not as effective as he had been in better times.

Over the course of his tenure as manager, Johnson's input into personnel decisions has been steadily decreasing. At first, he was able to bring in his Tidewater team of 1983—Wally Backman, Ron Gardenhire, and Raphael Santana. By 1987, however, he was found complaining to the press of moves being made without his consent or knowledge. His relationship with General Manager Frank Cashen, cool but cordial during the Mets rise (1984–1986), turned frigid as the 1987 season went sour. The bickering erupted publicly when Johnson let it be known that Cashen declined to extend his contract beyond 1988. Cashen reacted negatively, and it was announced that Johnson would be moved upstairs after 1988. Now, confusion reigns. During the 1986 season, Johnson had intimated that 1987 would be his last year as manager due to the effects of stress (his stomach problems and reliance on antacids are well documented). Now, however, he wants to be manager beyond 1988, and speculation about the Mets' future managerial situation runs rampant. I believe, as always, that this depends on the success or failure of the team. If the Mets win the NL East in 1988, Johnson will be offered an extension; if the Mets are below .500 by August 1, Johnson will not last the year. Anything in between, and a change will be made between seasons. Remember, you read it here first.

Despite his lack of input on personnel decisions, Johnson has been dealt quite a good hand. He has a good mix of rookies, young players, and prime players on the squad. His bench is generally made up of veterans who know their role (*e.g.,* Lee Mazzilli, Danny Heep, Larry Bowa, and Bill Almon—all current or past reserves), but always has one or two young guys trying to catch on (*e.g.,* Dave Magaden and Kevin Mitchell). Agewise, it's a perfect balance, although two prime players are inching beyond prime, Keith Hernandez (34) and Gary Carter (34 as of April 1988). Both must do some serious off-season workouts to regain their high caliber play of earlier years.

Offensively, Johnson's strategic moves are pretty standard. He employs the hit-and-run and sacrifice bunt frequently. He uses pinch hitters well and makes good use of the double switch. This is perhaps his most effective ploy, as it gets extra playing time for his platoon players and is a real offensive boost. He likes to use the bunt-and-run in certain situations, mainly with Backman or Dykstra at the plate and some speed on first. He rarely tries a suicide squeeze play.

Johnson's defensive tactics are also pretty standard. He frequently pitches around hitters; he also calls for intentional walks and pitchouts. He uses relievers well, employing the hot hand often until it cools down. He will yank a starter (based on number of pitches thrown) to protect the young arms; however, he sometimes leaves a starter in too long trying to get him to his target pitch count. He pulls relievers for one of three reasons: a bad outing, a certain situation (righty/lefty, gut feel), and to bring in his stopper. He uses a five-man rotation, and when they are going well, as happened often in 1986, his middle men get very little work. Johnson rarely makes a purely defensive substitution. His favorite defensive move is to start a shortstop with punch (*e.g.,* Howard Johnson), get a lead, and bring in Santana, but this may change if Elster shows he can hit.

Strategically, Davey emphasizes power over speed, as evidenced by the fact that the Mets generally land in the middle of the pack in stolen base totals. He seems to put equal emphasis on offense and pitching, with less emphasis on fielding. This is shown by his faithful platooning despite the gains or losses in the field. In the infield, he looks to good hands over good range as Santana, Johnson, and Backman all exemplify this. In the outfield, it is the converse—good range (Dykstra, Wilson, Strawberry) over good hands. On the mound, he'll take a power pitcher over a finesse pitcher any day, which is in line with Cashen's philosophy.

Overall, as a Mets fan, I'm pleased to have Johnson at the helm. I have talked with numerous die-hard Mets fans, and the consensus is slightly against Johnson, although the opponents are more vocal. The main dissatisfaction is with his strategic decisions; the minor one with his ability to get along with his players. I do not believe in second guessing his strategy, only first guessing while the game is in progress. When I do that, I agree with 80 to 90 percent of Johnson's moves. Some moves that I don't agree with work out; others that I do fail. But the pattern is, overall, positive. As for the latter charge, I think he gets a lot out of his players. His tactics are questionable at times (such as sniping at Darling through the media), but mostly effective.

The bottom line is that Johnson will prove to be an excellent manager. Should the Mets let him go, I predict a long and successful stint elsewhere, possibly in Atlanta.

Dave Gordon

New York Yankees
LOU PINIELLA / BILLY MARTIN

Billy Martin is once again the manager of the New York Yankees, and if he doesn't get into a drunken brawl between now and opening day he will probably be managing the team when the season begins. Lou Piniella isn't in the dugout anymore because George Steinbrenner decided that he needed to make a change. Either George has learned to be more patient (highly unlikely) or he was fearful of fan and media backlash as he waited for an unheard-of *two full seasons* before firing Piniella. That was the longest tenure for a Yankee manager since Billy I, 1975–1978.

Steinbrenner had drawn a great deal of heat from the Yogi Berra fiasco and was evidently reluctant to dismiss another fan favorite too quickly. Piniella was chosen largely due to his popularity, but he was respected by the media as a good manager. It really bothered Steinbrenner when Piniella began to get a good deal of favorable media attention last year, and he lashed out in mid-season with a bizarre statement on national television. It was obvious at that point that Piniella wouldn't be back as manager in '88 unless he delivered a world championship. Interestingly, George rationalized Piniella's firing by claiming that he had made a mistake in hiring Lou in the first place. Supposedly, Piniella lacked managerial experience and should have spent time in the minors before getting his shot with the big club, but that argument fell flat on its face when Lou was "promoted" to GM. If he didn't have enough experience to run the club on the field, how could he possibly be qualified to head the organization? It's just another example of George shielding himself from his critics; Piniella wasn't fired, he was given a more responsible position. The Yankees now have a figurehead GM named Piniella and Billy V on the field. With George running the show, things don't really change, they just get shuffled a bit.

Lou was a much more patient manager than Billy ever has been. Piniella would wait out his problems in the hope that a player would come around—he gave Steve Trout over 40 innings to straighten himself out with no success. Billy would have had Rainbow cleaning out toilets in the upper deck after two starts. Piniella watched Gary Ward and Wayne Tolleson as their seasons went down the drain and hoped that they would regain their form. He had other choices, however, that would have meant going to his younger players instead of the veterans, and Lou didn't seem to be willing to go with youngsters when he had "proven" veterans around. In contrast, Billy won't wait for anyone to come around and will go with a rookie if he thinks that he's the player who will help the team win. As one would expect, this type of approach generates fierce loyalty to Martin from some of his players as well as extreme hatred from others. Rickey Henderson loves playing for Billy, as do some of the other current Yankees; we all know about players who hate Martin. Piniella was generally liked and respected by his players, who took an "us against him" attitude when Steinbrenner began to blame Lou for all of the team's problems. One player who didn't rally around Lou was Rickey Henderson, and his attitude was hardly surprising when you consider that everyone knew that Piniella wanted Henderson traded.

As for coaches, Lou never had the opportunity to select

a coach he wanted, much less a staff. With George's penchant for firing coaches, Lou was lucky to even be on a first name basis with them. When Billy has a choice he simply looks for a good drinking buddy to coach for him, and ol' Art Fowler may be back to keep Billy company in '88.

Although Piniella was reluctant to play rookies as a manager, he's done a complete about face as GM so far. Lou has to date refused to deal away any of the Yankee's top four prospects—Al Leiter, Roberto Kelly, Jay Buhner or Hensley Meulens. Not only is this unusual for Piniella, it's also strange for the organization. The Yankees have continually dealt away their top prospects for established stars. While managing the Yankees, Piniella failed to bring along a single significant young player. He was under pressure to win and wasn't willing to place his fate in the hands of an inexperienced player.

Perhaps the best example of Piniella's impatience came when he pulled Doug Drabek out of a game against the Orioles in 1986, despite the fact that he had a no-hitter going. Players like Drabek have either been traded or left in the minors. That policy isn't due only to Piniella, as the man who owns the team calls the shots in this area, as well as most others. Billy Martin has brought along a good number of young players, Rickey Henderson and Willie Randolph being two examples, and he's always been able to motivate young players, at least for a few years.

Piniella was handicapped as the Yankees' manager by his inability to get the players he wanted in 1987. He had to wait for nearly a month to get Joel Skinner recalled from Columbus while he was being punished by George. It's difficult to say how much influence Lou had in the trade department, as George almost always had the final say. Billy always has very specific ideas about the players he wants, however, he has to deal with the same boss as Piniella did, and player moves have certainly been a major cause for the past conflicts between Billy and George. George always promises to give Billy what he needs to win, then he gets mad at Billy and refuses to make the move Martin wants. Eventually this leads to Billy calling George a @#$%?"*, which causes George to find a new manager. It's happened before and it's going to happen again.

A major difference between Billy and Lou as managers is the way they select a lineup and platoon players. Lou was obsessed with the idea that the man batting #1 had to have good speed, which led to people like Claudell Washington and Henry Cotto leading off—he even used them in the first spot on occasion when Henderson and Randolph were in the lineup. I doubt that Billy would ever make out a lineup card with Henderson and Randolph batting 5th and 7th and then rationalize the move by discussing the need to get more speed in the bottom part of the batting order. Piniella platooned on a strict left-right basis and made little allowance for a player with a hot hand. This enabled him to give most of his players fairly regular playing time, but it also meant that he was taking at-bats away from power hitters like Pagliarulo and giving them instead to players like Lenn Sakata. Martin is more likely to go with the player who's hot, and this has tended to alienate some of his bench; however, Billy has never worried about being loved by his players.

One of the trademarks of Martin's style of managing is his unpredictability. He's always willing to hit-and-run, steal, bunt, or take the extra base when it's least expected,

providing he has the personnel to make the move. Piniella often seemed afraid that he'd make a mistake, and he was thus unwilling to move runners or to take chances on the bases. He also was reluctant to pinch run for his catchers at times, worrying that he'd end up without an extra receiver; this reluctance cost him more than one game. It's difficult to manage when you have a vulture peering over your shoulder, and George Steinbrenner has a permanent perch there.

Another place where Piniella and Martin differ in managerial strategy is in the use of a pitching staff. Piniella relies heavily on his bullpen and makes use of the entire staff, while Martin places the emphasis on his starters and loads most of the work on a few arms. Billy will stick with the hot pitcher until he drops and cares little when he uses him, leading to other pitchers being almost totally ignored. In 1985, Bob Shirley went for nearly a month without getting into a game after some bad outings. Martin's reliance on his starters also had a big effect on Dave Righetti. Billy would wait until the starter got into trouble before going to his ace; the result was that Righetti would often enter the game in the middle of an inning with men on base, a situation that he isn't all that comfortable with. Piniella would bring Righetti into the game to start an inning, and this paid off with his establishing a new major league save record in 1986. Piniella was also more careful to use Righetti only in save situations and for a limited number of innings, while Martin used him for as long as needed and whenever he thought the game was on the line, be it the 5th or the 9th inning. Righetti had better be in good shape for the '88 season, because he'll get all the work he can handle while the rest of the pen gets splinters.

Lou Piniella wasn't a bad manager, and he was certainly better than Steinbrenner gave him credit for. However, he managed as if he were more concerned with not failing than he was with winning. Moreover, he would probably be a much better manager if he didn't have to contend with George. Billy Martin remains one of the best managers in the game when he's between the white lines. Unfortunately, he has to spend time off the field, too.

Craig Christman

Oakland Athletics
TONY LARUSSA

So the 1983 White Sox won the AL West by 20 games. Does that make Tony LaRussa a good manager, or the recipient of good fortune? His very talented starting rotation was healthy for the only time in their career, Greg Luzinski finished his productive days with a bang, and the AL pitchers hadn't yet figured out how to pitch to Ron Kittle. Or is Tony LaRussa considered a good manager because he has a law degree and is assumed to be smart? Whatever the answer, there is no doubt in my mind that Tony LaRussa is perhaps the AL's worst manager who might get lucky enough in 1988 to manage a division champion solely because he has been given so much talent my four-year-old niece (provided she can get the time off from nursery school) could manage them to the pennant.

Besides the intangibles, which cannot be measured, what makes a manager good or bad? In my assessment, the tangibles a manager can control are the way the pitching staff is used, the lineup (including who plays, who platoons, and in what order they bat), the choice of coaches, and the choice of tactics to employ (*e.g.,* the hit-and-run, sacrifice bunts), to name a few. With the above criteria in mind, let's evaluate Tony LaRussa, the manager.

First, lets start with the pitching staff. I could swear I read in the paper just about every day during spring training last year how LaRussa wished he had another veteran starting pitcher to complement his young starters. Then I could swear that the A's brass got him Dennis Eckersley just before the season began. Exactly how many games did Dennis Eckersley start? Two! Oh, maybe LaRussa wanted to use the veteran as the stopper in the bullpen. It wasn't until August, after Jay Howell finally proved his arm was hurting, and Gene Nelson, Greg Cadaret, and cast of thousands proved they were not the answer did LaRussa let Eckersley become the stopper. He was then replaced in late September by Eric Plunk. At this juncture you might be thinking that LaRussa didn't make Eckersley a starter because he wasn't pitching well. Wrong! Eckersley had the lowest ERA of all the A's regular pitchers throughout the entire season. However, most of his innings were pitched in mop-up roles! So why did LaRussa not make Eckersley a starter? My impression is that he gave the answer one night when he was quoted (I'm sorry, I don't remember the exact quote) in the paper when asked the same question, "I run this team. I won't allow the press to tell me who to start." (Pride doth cometh before sin).

Had enough yet? I'm not done. Let's talk about Steve Ontiveros. Before he experienced arm troubles, Ontiveros was a reliable reliever. He was extremely impressive as a reliever in 1985. When Jay Howell lost his effectiveness, the only reliever on the A's staff who had any experience saving games was Ontiveros. So what did LaRussa do? He made him a starter, of course. That left a bullpen equalled in ineptitude only by the arson squad of the Dodgers and the Orioles. Why did LaRussa choose Ontiveros to be a starter when one was needed? Was it because he had no other experienced starting pitchers? *No!* He had Gene Nelson and some guy named Dennis Eckersley. Maybe he chose Ontiveros because Onti had a history of arm troubles. Oh, that doesn't make sense. Maybe his chose Onti because he had a great breaking ball that produces a lot of double plays. (After all, who needs a double play pitcher in the bullpen to get the team out of a jam in the late innings). Oh, that can't be the reason. It also can't be because Ontiveros has a vast repertoire of pitches, because he doesn't. So why did he start Ontiveros? I wish somebody would tell me. Was it successful? For the first few games it was. Funny thing, Ontiveros usually tired by the fifth inning. Surprise! Surprise! In net, because of Ontiveros's early departures LaRussa put even more pressure on an ailing bullpen. Finally, at the end of August, the A's picked up two starting pitchers, Rick Honeycutt and Storm Davis. Did Ontiveros go back to the bullpen? Of course not. I could go on about his bungling of the pitching staff, like his wearing out Dave Stewart or rushing back Curt Young, but my editor will throw fits as to the length of this article. To his credit, LaRussa did finally convert Eric Plunk into a reliever, since Plunk never had enough pitches to be a starter.

Next, lets talk lineup; first, lets look at who played. At the end of the 1986 season, the A's had a hitter come up in

September and crash a few home runs that are still traveling. His name was Mark McGwire. Did Mark McGwire start the season as the regular first baseman? Of course not. He was platooned with Rob Nelson, a rookie who had a good spring hitting pitchers who were sent back to the minors when the season started. One of the great things about Earl Weaver is that he decided his opening day lineup during the winter. If Weaver were running the A's, McGwire would have been the starter from day one.

Platooning must be a dirty word in LaRussa's mind. Did you know that throughout his career Tony Phillips has hit lefties at about .300, and righties at around .220? This pattern has repeated itself year after year. Did you also know that Donnie Hill consistently hit righties better than lefties in his career? In 1986, Hill and Phillips were the classic platoon combination. Did they platoon? Of course not! In fact, in 1986, Hill got only 199 at-bats against righties while Phillips got 307. Phillips hit .228 against righties and Hill .291. Hill, who hit .271 against lefties, was primarily used against righties when LaRussa benched Bochte, who hit .333 (albeit in only 54 at-bats) against lefties in 1985. Lets see, to get Hill in the lineup against lefties, he moved either Phillips or Hill, both second basemen to third base, moved an excellent fielding third baseman in Carney Lansford to first base in order to take the lefty Bochte, who had no problem hitting lefties in his career, out of the lineup in favor of Hill, who did not hit lefties as well as righties. Against righties, Phillips, who couldn't hit righties, started over Hill who could hit righties. Confused? I sure am.

Now let's talk about the batting order. The purpose of a lineup is to have the guys good at getting on base in the number 1 and 2 slots to be driven in by your best hitters in the number 3, 4 and 5 slots. I'll use 1986 for example. The myriad of leadoff hitters for the A's included Alfredo Griffin and his illustrious .290 on-base percentage. Sometimes, it was Dave Collins with his .303 on-base percentage. Tony Phillips was the main leadoff hitter. This was fine against lefties, but against righties, Phillips had a .304 OBP. Who didn't hit in the top two slots? Dwayne Murphy and his 84 walks (.340 OBP), Mike Davis and his .348 OBP, and Steve Henderson (against lefties) with his .373 OBP to name a few.

Want to talk about 1987? Okay. After Tony Phillips got hurt, the A's acquired Tony Bernazard. Where did he usually bat in LaRussa's batting order? Usually sixth or seventh. Bernazard's OBP in 1986 was .362 and in '85 .361. Sounds like the perfect leadoff or number-two hitter to me. LaRussa preferred Luis (I don't believe in walks) Polonia and Alfredo Griffin, I guess. I could go on about his constantly ill-chosen batting orders which included two low-average, high-strikeout hitters (named Kingman and Canseco) back to back in the number 4 and 5 spots in 1986, but by now the editor is running amok on the length and there is plenty more to say. One other thing before I move on. When did it become obvious to you that Reggie Jackson was being awfully unproductive in the middle of the A's lineup last year and hurting the A's by continuing to play? It was obvious to me by the end of May. To LaRussa it was never obvious.

Next, on to the selection and overseeing of coaches. LaRussa insisted on Dave Duncan as his pitching coach. After all, Duncan had turned a bunch of extremely talented pitchers in Chicago like Floyd Bannister, Rich Dotson, Jose

DeLeon, Joe Cowley, Bob James, and Neil Allen—just to name a few—into Cy Young award winners. Oh, he didn't, my mistake. He also worked wonders on the talented Jose Rijo, Tim Birtsas, Bill Mooneyham, and others while with the A's. With a track record like that, who can argue with the selection of Dave Duncan?

Here's a trivia question. How many different batting stances did Jose Canseco use in 1987? My guess is around 500. How can a manager allow one of his great hitters constantly change his batting stance? What was Bob Watson, the hitting coach, doing through all this? What's most mind-boggling about this is that in spring training, Canseco used one batting stance, hit for power and average and almost never struck out. His first at-bat of the regular season, he changed his batting stance. What were LaRussa and Watson doing?

After all this and more which I could have mentioned, do you still think LaRussa is a good manager? The only manager I can think of off hand who is less aware of his players' strengths and weaknesses and who makes out worse lineups than LaRussa is Tommy Lasorda. What made Earl Weaver and makes Davey Johnson great managers is that they both know what their players can and can't do. That's why they platoon where necessary, and that's why they always had the guys who get on base at the top of the lineup and never gave up too many outs with pointless sacrifice bunts.

Ira Saltz

Philadelphia Phillies
LEE ELIA

Lee Elia has managed the Phillies for 101 games. He inherited a baseball team from John Felske whose young talent, with the exceptions of Juan Samuel and Von Hayes, was beset by nagging problems which led to underachievement. Some of the Phillies' veteran talent, particularly Glenn Wilson and Lance Parrish, also turned in seasons considerably below their normal output. This article will detail how Elia attempted to combat the Phillies' *ennui* and mediocrity by creating job competition and promoting overall team speed and athletic ability.

Managers have two primary roles. They are key members of the baseball operations and personnel part of the club, and they direct the on-field operations. I will limit myself here to Elia's on-field operations.

The first thing to note is that Lee Elia did not make, and did not have to make, wholesale changes in the starting lineup. The best Phillies were already in the majors when Elia arrived. Where Elia's different style first surfaced was in his treatment of reserves. Elia differed markedly from John Felske in his preference for certain kinds of players and in his creative use of versatile bench players. Unlike Felske, who chained certain players to the bench, Elia tried new ways to reconstitute his roster. In selecting his substitutes, Elia showed a preference for veterans like Greg Gross and Luis Aguayo. Younger players who were willing to accept part-time roles, like Rick Schu and Keith Hughes, also became important parts of the team.

Elia demanded versatility as well as patience from his reserves. Rick Schu played 28 games at first base as well as pinch hitting and spelling Mike Schmidt at third. Schu became the first baseman so that Elia could bench center-fielder Milt Thompson against lefthanders, who were holding Milt to a .160 average, and play Von Hayes in CF. This move not only spurred Thompson to hit over .300 in his last 50 AB against lefties, but kept Schmidt, Hayes and Schu all versatile enough to switch positions, which could be important if the Phillies suffer a major injury in the corners or in the outfield. Darren Daulton also played some games at first.

This kind of versatility, particularly the ability to play good defense, assures the younger players enough playing time to keep their skills up. Those players like John Russell and Jeff Stone who lack the defensive ability and the versatility, are unable to become valuable bench players under Elia. Conversely, a player like Greg Gross, who has offered strong defensive skills and versatility, has been a valuable member of the Phillies' bench for eight years. Lee Elia seems to have decided that slow men can be valuable as substitutes, but to be a starter, you can either run fast or die young. It is my guess that he will only promote younger players if he expects them to start or has a high opinion of their defensive skills and versatility.

A manager's most crucial and autonomous responsibilities are his tactical decisions. These include: Who should start in the field and on the mound? How should players be placed in the batting order? What are a team's fundamental flaws and what can be done about them? What roles will enhance or impede a player's progress? What patterns form in response to a manager's actions? How does that manager react to those patterns?

Lee Elia essentially inherited a club with starters already set. He, like any other sane man would have, continued to start Schmidt, Samuel, and Hayes every chance he could. Glenn Wilson started over 150 games, Milt Thompson started 123 while playing in 154, and Parrish played a normal starting catcher's 130 games. So Elia needed to fill holes at shortstop and left field the day he took over.

Elia's decision to make Chris James the everyday left-fielder worked like a charm. James began the season as a platoon centerfielder, and then had just returned from the minors when Elia took over. James started 77 of Elia's 101 games in left and played extremely well.

Elia deserves particular credit for this, since James seems likely to escape the Phillies' Bermuda Triangle which has sunk young outfielders like Russell, Stone, and Gary Redus in recent years. Elia's handling of James has begun to reverse the Phillies' tendency to spit on their own children and prefer the progeny of other organizations.

At shortstop, Elia experimented with fervor, sending Steve Jeltz down to the minors and trying Luis Aguayo and Ken Dowell (and by season's end, even Kenny Jackson, who is still a year or two away). Elia's problem was simple— Jeltz, even when he hits well, does not hit lefties. Aguayo hit lefties, but couldn't field. Dowell couldn't hit anybody.

Elia's approach was to toughen up on Steve Jeltz. Just as in '86, Jeltz returned from the minors leagues hitting well enough to raise his average 50 points. Elia remembered that in 1986, when Tom Foley was still with the team, Jeltz had played well. When the threat of competition was removed, Jeltz declined. First Elia tried to open up the position by giving Dowell and Aguayo a shot. They didn't have the tools, but a taste of the bus-riding minors sparked Jeltz. Elia therefore has a dire need to upgrade Aguayo's position of infield backup and keep Jeltz at his peak. As long as Jeltz remains at shortstop, the Phillies will be substandard on either offense (when Jeltz plays) or defense (when Aguayo plays) every time they face a lefty. So expect to see Shane Turner, Keith Miller, or Tommy Barrett replace Aguayo in Elia's attempt to kindle a fire under Jeltz.

Like Felske, Elia was an apologist for the sub-par seasons of Glenn Wilson and Lance Parrish. He kept writing their names onto the lineup card and simply waiting. He was rewarded by Parrish's improved defensive play in the last two months of the season; after July 22, Parrish threw out 30 percent of the opposing base stealers, improving upon a 17 percent average up until that point. Parrish also turned in decent offensive numbers after the All-Star break, but he never had the monster month Lee waited for. Glenn Wilson guaranteed himself a new home zip code by swallowing over 600 plate appearances and then burping out only 37 extra base hits and 54 RBIs. Elia is depending upon Parrish to rebound and James and Jeltz to stabilize. Here we see a preference in action: Lee has a bias against slower players (Russell, Wilson, Aguayo) in favor of faster players, who will bring more movement to the offense and hit into fewer double plays (James, Bradley, Jeltz). It is significant that all but two of the '88 starters have good speed; the exceptions are Parrish and Schmidt. For a team that was plagued by double plays, requiring your players to be fast or to be perennial All-Stars is a solid plan.

Elia's handling of pitchers is an open question so far, because he did not have any real options last year. He continued to send the same four starters in as Felske had, and they achieved about the same results as they had under Felske, except for Rawley, who is simply not a hot-weather pitcher. More to the point, Elia, who stepped in forcefully to shake up players who had performed below par in the field, continued, as Felske had, to let Claude Osteen deal with the pitchers, despite their apparent lack of progress.

By lack of progress I refer to two factors: the Phillies' inability to prevent stolen bases and the general inability of the Phillies young pitchers to make progress in their careers. While it is too early to say in the case of Bruce Ruffin and Don Carman, I don't think Kevin Gross does much of anything better these days than he did in 1983 or 1984. He still has outstanding stuff and belongs in a major league starting rotation, but he doesn't seem to have improved. Osteen also tells us that sinkerball pitcher Bruce Ruffin "pitches best when that ball is down," but was unable to get Ruffin to keep it from rising. And while Osteen has been preaching about holding runners on for three years, opposing baserunners stole 185 base in 248 attempts. I'm growing tired of Osteen naming these diseases. When does he plan to cure them? I think Elia must move ahead strongly here, and make it clear that stolen base percentages of more than 70 percent mean fewer innings and starts, and maybe a new pitching coach.

So really the only desirable changes were to add a fifth starter and to tighten up on the present crew. Neither occurred. The Phillies fifth starter was 5–17 last year, so that in all games started by the four regulars, the Phillies won 75, losing 65. This means that if newly signed David Palmer can split his decisions while the others tread water, the Phillies will improve by 5–6.

The Palmer deal should also be seen as Elia's outright endorsement of the Phillies bullpen. If the middle or late relievers fail to come through, that will prove to be a fruitless deal. Palmer, who allows hitters to hit no more than .250 in most matchups, gets lit to the tune of .390 or so after the sixth inning. For a team like the Phillies, with a strong bullpen, Palmer has value. But, unlike their other pitchers, he will require lots of relief support. This will make it crucial that Carman, Ruffin, Gross and Rawley get as many innings as possible. It will also be interesting to see if each starter now gets 32–33 starts apiece, or if the low man gets skipped when it's possible to go with four starters. When this happened last year, it was ascribed to the Phillies' utter lack of a #5 man. Now that they have a fifth starter, will Elia stick to a rotation, or adjust with the schedule, thus providing a competitive incentive for performance?

Because he was presented with a "staff *accompli*" in 1987, Elia had no opportunity to make things very competitive. Everyone who was ready and able to pitch in the bigs was there last year. Brad Brink and Bob Scanlan may be ready in '88 or '89, but it's hard to threaten the job of Kevin Gross with Tom Hume or Mike Maddux.

Even in relief pitching, the best pitchers were already set in positive roles when Elia arrived. Wallace Ritchie and Mike Jackson were in long to middle relief, with Kent Tekulve (and Elia's addition, Calhoun) setting the table for Bedrosian. This spring, with Jackson gone, probably only Teke and the Rock are assured of making the roster. Todd Frohwirth is probably the best bet to replace Jackson, given his impressive debut and his overpowering fastball. Elia seems to like to have a middle-inning flamethrower like Jackson or Frohwirth.

Uncertain, ill-defined staffs were part of the chaos Elia faced in Chicago, and it seems that he may be intentionally giving Osteen a free hand because of the clarity and order of the present situation. But seeing problems clearly is only good if it aids in solving them. Elia will have to take steps with the pitchers, just as he has done with the field players, to make them perform to their potential. In 1988, Elia must try to transform a set staff into a sound staff.

While Elia's firm style and Harry Trumanesque decision-making benefited the Phillies in most cases, one of his first decisions was his worst decision. Elia essentially robbed Juan Samuel by batting him leadoff, with Thompson second, and then rotating Hayes and James batting third; Hayes, Wilson and Parrish in the fifth position.

One effect of this batting order was the following:

LEADING OFF AN INNING

	AB	R	H	2B	3B	HR	BB	K	BA	OBA	SA
Von Hayes	89	19	31	6	0	5	16	5	.349	.440	.580
Juan Samuel	181	37	42	10	4	6	20	38	.235	.308	.439

ALL OTHER AT BATS

	AB	R	H	2B	3B	HR	BB	K	BA	OBA	SA
Von Hayes	467	65	123	30	5	16	105	72	.263	.399	.451
Juan Samuel	474	76	136	27	11	22	40	124	.282	.342	.529

In leadoff at bats from '84 to '86, Hayes hit .314, OBA of .374 and SA of .545, all better than the comparable non-leadoff number. Samuel hit .255, OBA .303, and slugged .402 over the same period when leading off innings.

Every year, Von leads off innings incredibly well, and every year, that is Sammy's worst breakdown. Now, it may be that Von doesn't like to lead off, but Sammy hates it, and reminds the manager, the media, and everyone else every year, so if they both hate it, I'd rather have the one who hits .350 getting the extra leadoff at-bats (the leadoff man usually gets about 150 more leadoff at-bats per year). Regardless of who bats leadoff, if Juan Samuel is having a great year, why would you reduce his effectiveness by guaranteeing him more at-bats in a situation where he is least effective?

Furthermore, Elia frequently talked about how Hayes needed to be more aggressive to be a proper third hitter, and advised Sammy to be more patient, to be a leadoff hitter. I would wonder why Lee just didn't stick the advice and switch their roles. I think it's because fast second basemen are supposed to hit leadoff, and first basemen are supposed to be slugging fools hitting third.

Having now noted all of that, I will give Elia credit for planning to bat Bradley first, which seems as if it will work. This will allow Hayes to bat fifth, where he accomplished the following, almost entirely under Elia:

WHEN HAYES BATTED FIFTH

	AB	R	H	2B	3B	HR	RBI	BB	K	BA	OBA	SA
SCHMIDT '87	95	27	37	7	0	12	31	12	13	.389	.457	.842
HAYES '87	116	15	30	5	1	3	14	36	14	.260	.434	.398
SCHMIDT '86	270	41	72	14	1	18	55	45	40	.266	.371	.526
HAYES '86	296	40	88	16	0	8	45	42	43	.298	.387	.432

As you can see, there was a good reason to bat Hayes at some spot other than leadoff in 1987. When Hayes hit fifth last season, Mike Schmidt did the monster mash on pitchers all over the National League. While the pattern did not hold in '86, it seems to me that if you have two fast guys who get on base .350 (Bradley and Thompson or Dernier) then Sammy, Schmitty, and Von, that does seem like an *order* to me.

One area where Felske left Elia a meager inheritance was in the execution of fundamentals. Lee inherited a team that did not bunt well, did not steal bases well despite plenty of speed, and was usually unable to advance runners in key situations. One particularly bothersome and continual failure was that, until Felske was gone, a Phillies pitcher had only twice executed a sacrifice bunt successfully. By the end of the summer, after Elia took pains not only in practice, but in the press, to end this embarrassing show, this had improved to about the level of the rest of the league.

These are the fundamentals which Elia must address. The Phillies must also turn their now overwhelming team speed into runs. Over the last few years, their speed and base-stealing have had little impact, given the number of runs which the Giants and Cardinals are able to score with less speed and less impressive personnel. The ability to add stolen runs to runs legitimately batted in has separated the Cardinals from the rest of the league throughout the '80s. They win a few extra games each year, beyond those that they win with their hitting and fielding, by executing and running. If the Phillies can get to the point where they win one out of three even when they're bottoming out, that will be a sign that Elia has turned the fundamentals around, and that the inconsistent sparkle of the last two years will give

way to a full-fledged gleam in the eyes of the Philadelphia fans.

One way to make players perform better is to enhance the level of your coaches. Elia has replaced coaches like Jim Davenport, whose reputation was founded on being "a steady man in the clubhouse and dugout" according to one scout, with men for whom coaching is teaching with vigor and with results. The only coach that Felske kept who was of managerial timber was Elia. Elia, on the other hand, has a former manager in Dave Bristol, who is well-regarded as a third base coach, Tony Taylor, a future manager, and Garry Maddox, who would make a fine manager (if he could take the pay cut), all working for him.

The point of this exhaustive survey has been to discover some tendencies to watch for in the managing style of Lee Elia. Here are some keys I would watch next year. First, I would keep track of things like stolen bases and strikeouts. How do the Phillies numbers compare to other teams? Are they throwing out opposing baserunners more than one third of the time? What kinds of streaks are developing? Are they losing three of four games at a time, or are they picking one off every series, even when nothing is going right? I would watch Elias' use of Samuel and Hayes—how does his use of them enhance or recognize their production patterns?

Who will he threaten to replace, and what will be the result? How will he maintain or create competition within positions? Will he give Phil Bradley the complete confidence that he has given to his other superior athletes, Samuel, James, and Hayes? Will he remain patient with Parrish or begin to agitate him? Will his newly acquired speed make up for the thousand or more times this Phillies team will strike out? Will he be able to teach Bruce Ruffin to keep the ball down?

Elia has compiled a team with speed, good power for the NL, a good bullpen, and middle of the road starting pitching. He will certainly make more overt demands upon his players than John Felske ever did, and it is my opinion that his approach will win 90 games for this team in 1988. The Phillies have the talent to compete, and the personal skill of Elia and his coaches should be sufficient to motivate them. Next year, there ought to be enough data to tell you how Lee does in a pennant race.

Pete DeCoursey

Pittsburgh Pirates
JIM LEYLAND

Managing a baseball team is often dictated by circumstances. While the past two years have seen the Pirates develop a team from a collection of spare parts, they've also seen Jimmy Leyland develop his managerial style based on his team.

When you analyze a manager you do so keeping in mind the roster that he has to deal with. Even with an average roster a good manager can study his players, knowing who can do what and how they can do it.

Leyland's really never had that "problem," although 1988 promises to change things. But a few ideas can be drawn from the past to see what will happen in the future.

Leyland would prefer a set lineup, both offense and

dcfense, but is not afraid to tinker until he can find it. In 1986, for example, he used (at least) 106 "variations" on a lineup. These variations were dictated by common circumstances: injuries, opposing pitchers, artificial vs. natural turf, and pure frustration. What seemed like pulling names out of a hat was really an almost two-year-long spring training of trying to fit the right player into the right hole. Johnny Ray became the third-place hitter because no one else was available that could hit third; once someone became available Ray was moved down in the lineup.

Even after the lineup was relatively set (Bonds in CF, then LF; Bream at 1B; Morrison and then Bonilla at 3B; etc.), Leyland was still tinkering, moving players up or down in the lineup to find where they belonged.

Almost paradoxically, he does like using platoons—sort of. Joe Orsulak had just come off a year hitting .300 with 24 stolen bases when it was announced that he and former Angels outfielder Mike Brown would platoon in right field. Orsulak dropped to .249, never getting untracked although he got more ABs, and is now in Baltimore. Mike Brown just dropped out of sight.

Early last year Andy Van Slyke was platooned in right field, although he was often left in the game when a lefty pitcher replaced a righty. This paid no immediate dividends, other then allowing armchair athletes to grumble that they could do better. But Leyland knew he needed Van Slyke on a regular basis, and eventually kept Van Slyke in the lineup. And Van Slyke responded with a year that would have made trading Pena for Van Slyke straight up a good deal.

Then there is Sid Bream. Yes, he hit around .275 against both lefties and righties, with actually more power against left-handed pitchers, but Bream had another midsummer slump and seemed to be dragging at the end of the year.

It could be that Leyland is trying to force Bream to produce and develop himself physically (Sid does have a problem with leg and back injuries), because Bream would fit into Leyland's offensive scheme a bit better than the alternatives. However, Mike Diaz sits on the bench while the team is in search of a right-handed power hitter.

Leyland does what he can to produce runs. Now that the Pirates have people that can produce big innings, Leyland won't have to scratch and claw so much, but will still use increased team speed and extra-base hitting ability to put runs on the board. This will never be a Baltimore Oriole "three-run homer" club.

He likes a well-stocked bench and bullpen, but then again so do most managers. Leyland reminds me of Dick Williams managing the Athletics, always with a role player, pinch hitter, or relief pitcher who can do the job. In Leyland's case it has just been a question of finding out who the players are and what they can do.

Jimmy Leyland is the on-field extension of Syd Thrift as the Pirates build their organization. Leyland has to deal with the players on a regular basis, and had a great deal to do with the movement of players like Tony Pena and Johnny Ray. He has as much as anyone to do with the Pirates now becoming a respectable team.

Mike Sopp

Jim Leyland begins his third year of managing in 1988 with a reasonably secure job. That statement alone says something quite positive about Leyland as a manager; he took over a team that was in last place and going nowhere, and has survived and even begun to prosper. His success in this job can probably be attributed primarily to two things: General Manager Syd Thrift's acquisition of more talent for him to work with, and Leyland's hard work.

Leyland is a thinking man's manager. When he makes a move, whether it's a tactical move in a game or a personnel move, he has a well thought-out reason for the move. He's always thinking and looking for new things to try to make the team better. Because he's sure of why he's making the move, he's more willing to stick by the move and give it a chance to work out, regardless of the heat he takes.

He is also capable of communicating his plan to others. The players on the Pirates understand what their role on the team is and what's expected of them. That's very important on a young team like the current Pirates.

Leyland has probably had his biggest successes and his biggest failures in the area of personnel decisions. His early personnel moves, made with players left over from the previous regime, were not very successful. He admits publicly that he mishandled Mike Brown. Leyland never could seem to decide what Brown's role should be, and naturally, Brown never knew what was expected of him, and he floundered. However, Leyland seems to have learned from his mistakes with Brown, and the young players coming along since then have begun to flourish under him. He made three major personnel moves last season, other than ones dictated by trades, and all three worked out fairly well. Moving Andy Van Slyke to center field and Barry Bonds to left improved the overall outfield defense and seemed to ignite both players offensively. Bobby Bonilla came alive with the move to third base, and while he might not become a fixture there, Leyland believes that the move from the outfield to the infield helped Bonilla. The third move was the move of Brian Fisher from the bullpen to the starting rotation. While on the surface this move might not appear to have turned out as well, as Fisher had a very up and down year as a starter, it actually was a succesful move. Fisher was becoming very discouraged in the bullpen, after not having a good year the previous season and getting off to a rocky start in 1987, and if Leyland didn't do something, Fisher easily could have been completely lost to the Pirates.

The personnel move (or non-move) that Leyland has taken the most criticism for is not getting Mike Diaz into the starting lineup, and there is some justification for the criticism. Mike Diaz hit 16 home runs, third on the team, in just 241 at-bats last season. It is true that Diaz is weak defensively, but on a team that is looking for a right-handed power hitter, you'd think that Leyland would stick him out there and see if he could keep that home run pace up. Indeed, unless Sid Bream has a great spring training in 1988, Leyland may just do that.

Still, on the whole, Leyland did a good job of getting players into the lineup. He doesn't really use a set lineup; he likes to get bench players some starts to keep them sharp. He also doesn't do a lot of simple lefty-righty platooning. Instead, he likes to sit down young players like Bonds against certain lefthanders that he considers especially tough.

He's had less success with handling the Pirates' pitchers, notably in the bullpen. The starting rotation has been reasonable, though not very deep until recently, but the bullpen has been a major problem for Leyland—one that may not yet be solved. Leyland would like to declare one pitcher to be the closer, but has had difficulty finding that pitcher. As a result, any righthander who throws hard has been given a shot at the job. Leyland seems reluctant to use a lefthander, because he's seldom had more than one left-hander in the bullpen and he likes to save the lefthander to use against the opponent's tough left-handed hitter at a key point. He also seems to prefer a hard thrower for the closer, preferring to use pitchers like Jeff Robinson and Brett Gideon in set-up roles. Jim Gott is the current designated closer, being a hard-throwing righthander who was given his chance at the job after coming over from the Giants, and he was successful in that role at the end of the season, picking up 13 saves in 25 games (1.45 ERA) with the Pirates. But this was not really an active decision by Leyland; Gott arrived and Leyland had him ticketed for the starting rotation, but he also likes to get new players into games as soon as possible, and so he brought Gott out to finish a game his first day. Gott looked good, declared that he'd like a shot at the bullpen, and since Leyland didn't have anyone else, he gave Gott the job.

Other than preferring a right-handed power pitcher for the bullpen ace, it's a little difficult to determine what kinds of players Leyland likes to have on his team. Given the situation the Pirates were in, he's had no choice but to go with young players, both in the starting lineup and on the bench.

Leyland is very much involved in the game as a manager. It is especially in the area of offensive strategy that the influence of Tony LaRussa, for whom Leyland was a third base coach, can be seen. Leyland likes aggressive base running and base stealing, he likes the hit-and-run play, and he sacrifices a fair amount. He has a strong idea of what batters he will allow to hit in a given situation and what batters he will pinch hit for. He also likes to push a opponent who is back on his heels, often calling for a steal after a team commits an error. He also employs the suicide squeeze.

Defensively, Leyland is also very much in control. He doesn't do a lot of exaggerated defensive positioning, but he is quite involved in pitcher-batter strategy and pitcher-base-runner strategy. Leyland calls all pitchouts, throws to first, and even the pitcher stepping off the rubber from the dugout. He feels that the gain from this is twofold: one, the pitcher doesn't have to think about it, and is then free to concentrate on the batter, and two, the defense against the baserunner fits into his overall plan for the game better. Much the same as he knows which batters he will leave in, he knows which pitchers he will leave in the game in a given situation and which pitchers he will get out of there. He would leave Rick Reuschel in the game in a tight situation, or even Mike Dunne, where in a similar situation he would have left Doug Drabek.

Overall, Leyland has done a good job with the Pirates. He's intelligent and hard-working and seems to be able to adapt his style to the situation at hand. This year, as the young Pirates started to mature more, he abandoned the closed-door, food-tossing clubhouse meetings of the season before, because the need for such histrionics had disappeared. Likewise, he didn't ride the umpires as much this year. For the fan, Leyland is an interesting and accessible manager, because he's been very willing to discuss his moves and the reasons for them in the press.

Sherri Nichols

St. Louis Cardinals
WHITEY HERZOG

Whitey Herzog became manager of the Cardinals on June 9, 1980, taking over a last-place team with a 19–34 record. Since then, Whitey has propelled the Cardinals into the winningest team in the majors in the 1980s.

After posting a 38–35 record as manager, Herzog moved up to general manager on August 29, naming Red Schoendienst interim manager until Whitey returned as manager in October, wearing both the manager's and general manager's hats until the spring of 1982. As GM, Herzog seemed to possess good judgment in acquiring players: Stars such as Ted Simmons, Garry Templeton and Keith Hernandez were all traded at the top of their game as Herzog acquired players who were better in the long run. Only two players still remained in 1987 from Herzog's original 1980 roster, Bob Forsch and Tom Herr.

The loss of Jack Clark this winter raises one important question—how much influence does Whitey now carry in the front office? Herzog has always enjoyed the luxury of an accommodating relationship with his general manager, so this may have been an isolated incident, a botched job of contract negotiating, but Whitey stated many times the Cards needed Clark to win, and he was surprised they held on to win after Clark's September injury.

Herzog was initially against General Manager Dal Maxvill's acquisition of former Braves slugger and Japan refugee Bob Horner, as Horner's numbers and past history were not impressive to Whitey. During Horner's nine years in the National League he hit only five home runs in Busch Stadium, an average of one every 27.8 times at-bat. During Horner's last major league season in Atlanta (1986), Horner hit 27 home runs; however, 20 of them were hit at Atlanta-Fulton County Stadium. He hit 23 home runs on grass, only four on turf. For Horner's career, he has homered every 12.6 at-bats in Atlanta, but homered only every 24.6 at-bats when on the road. Other tags attached to Horner are that he has weight problems, is slow, is prone to injuries, and is not a team player.

Another question one could ask about the Cards' front office: If Horner was so valuable, why didn't they pick him up previously to hit behind Jack Clark? These shifts in player personnel have usually in the past been up to Herzog and the Horner deal required a lot of discussion before Whitey was persuaded to accept it.

Whitey made a major lineup change in '87 by placing Ozzie Smith in the number-two spot and shifting Willie McGee to the fifth slot. The change was effective in Smith's case, as he hit over .300 for the first time; unfortunately, McGee, the former #2 man, did not work out that well hitting fifth. Although Willie had 105 RBIs, he certainly was not the threat that was needed to force pitchers to pitch to Jack Clark. McGee hit only .248 with runners in scoring position, but his overall average was .285.

Herzog began breaking in two new outfielders in '87, Curt Ford and Lance Johnson, and although they are fast and make good contact, neither is beefy enough to become the slugger the Cards so desperately need. Jim Lindeman will be relied upon for right field duties, sharing the slugging responsibilities while batting behind Horner.

Last year Herzog showed a lot of confidence in Lindeman when Whitey created an opening in right field with the trade of Andy Van Slyke. Lindeman had a miserable season, hitting only .208 with eight home runs in 75 games. Hamstring and chronic back problems caused Lindeman's troubles, and Whitey is hoping that Lindeman's .320 post-season average was an indication that Whitey's projections for Jim were not wrong.

Herzog is not the type of manager to sit on the bench and wait for home runs, *à la* Earl Weaver. Moving base runners along and solid defense are the Cardinals' strong suits. The fact that they reached the seventh game of the World Series is clear testimony to their excellence in baseball fundamentals. The Twins, on the other hand, demonstrated that they couldn't even execute a rundown play. This ability is the direct result of good management and coaching.

In St. Louis, Herzog has surrounded himself with a coaching staff that blends the years of experience of Red Schoendienst and Dave Ricketts with the youth of first base coach Rich Hacker and third base coach Nick Leyva. Leyva has managed in the Puerto Rican Winter League where he has worked with several Cardinal youngsters. Under Whitey's tutelage, Leyva at age 34 may follow former Cardinals coach Hal Lanier into the managerial ranks soon. Johnny Lewis is Whitey's hitting coach and Mike Roarke the pitching coach. These men are good teachers and spend many extra hours working individually with players to correct flaws. If Tony Pena had problems at bat last summer, it certainly wasn't for lack of attention from these coaches.

"Good pitching stops good hitting," the saying goes, and Whitey is the best at using a pitching staff effectively. Whitey won in '82 and '87 with bullpen stoppers Bruce Sutter and Todd Worrell respectively. In 1985 it was bullpen by committee, when he used Ken Dayley, Jeff Lahti, Ricky Horton, Neil Allen, Worrell and others to win a pennant. Another tactic Herzog has used more than other NL managers is to bring in a reliever to face a single batter in key situations in order to get a favorable match-up.

The starters on a Herzog staff will usually go at least six innings, even if in trouble, but rarely go the full nine. The '87 staff had only 10 complete games and no pitcher led the league in any pitching category. Herzog has not had a pitcher lead the league in victories since Joaquin Andujar was 20–14 in '84—ironically, a year the Cards didn't win.

The bench for Herzog in 1987 was led by Jose Oquendo, who was Whitey's secret weapon. Oquendo filled in defensively at every position except catcher last season and provided some timely offense, hitting .286 overall with four game-winning RBIs. John Morris was the Cards' top pinch hitter in late innings, with a .333 average in that role, and was used in double-switch situations. Steve Lake, a career backup catcher, hit .251, but during Pena's six week absence hit just under .300 and killed the Dodgers with a tenth inning GW RBI and a ninth inning home run (at 2:30 A.M.) to tie another game the Cards went on to win.

If it's frankness and honesty you want in a manager, you might get more than you bargained for with Whitey. He never dresses down his players in public and maintains a poker face whether winning or losing. A seasoned baseball man, he has held every job in baseball during his career. He has been a player, scout, coach, director of player development, manager, and general manager. Herzog has deserved every award and accolade he has received. He is among four active managers who have won over 1,000 games. Whitey has managed in the major leagues in all or part of 14 seasons, and has established himself as one of the all-time best. In the 11 full seasons in which Whitey has managed, his team has finished with the best record in its division seven times! That includes the 1981 strike season, when St. Louis was left out of post-season play by vote, rather than record.

Rollie Loewen and Tracy Thibeau

San Diego Padres
LARRY BOWA

Larry Bowa became manager of the Padres following the 1986 season in which San Diego had gone a disappointing 74–88. Bowa had managed for only one year in the minors, and clearly the Padres, only two seasons after their only World Series appearance, were thinking of 1987 as a rebuilding year. During the '86–'87 off-season San Diego traded its best home run hitter, Kevin McReynolds, to the Mets for a package of young talent; one of the players, Stan Jefferson, a speedy rookie outfielder, was expected to replace McReynolds, and another, second-year man Kevin Mitchell, would take over third base from Graig Nettles, who'd been released. San Diego also dealt another power hitter, catcher Terry Kennedy, obtaining pitcher Storm Davis and opening up a spot for rookie Benito Santiago. In addition, Bowa awarded the second base job to first-year player Joey Cora. Thus, though they were playing in what had become one of the best home run parks in the National League, the Padre attack for '87 would revolve around youth and speed.

This was the lineup Bowa chose for his first game as a major league manager on April 6:

> Marvell Wynne, cf
> Garry Templeton, ss
> Tony Gwynn, rf
> Carmelo Martinez, lf
> Kevin Mitchell, 3b
> Steve Garvey, 1b
> Benito Santiago, c
> Joey Cora, 2b
> Eric Show, p

Can we detect, uh, a few problems here? We sure can, starting from the very beginning. Wynne, the leadoff man, was taking the place of Jefferson, who had a sprained ankle. Marvell was a .260 hitter, at best, who didn't draw walks; his on base percentage in 1986 was a dismal .300. Wynne was also a poor base stealer, with a lifetime SB% of only .559, meaning his attempts were costing his team runs. However, Wynne had hit pretty well against righthanders in '86 (.289) and the opposing pitcher, Mike Krukow, was a righty, and, anyway, Jefferson was hurt—maybe Larry didn't want to break up the batting order he wanted to use.

We'll give Bowa the benefit of the doubt on this one. But how do we explain Garry "Jump Steady" Templeton in the number-two spot? Tempy was another low-average hitter who didn't draw walks; his OBA against righties in '86 had been .290. Templeton, who had lost a lot of his speed due to knee injuries—his nickname at this point probably should have been "Limp Steady"—wasn't a good base stealer either, with only 10 swipes in '86. However, he was a veteran, and he probably had good "bat control," whatever that is.

Tony Gwynn batting third was an interesting choice. Gwynn was hardly your classic number-three hitter, since he didn't have much power. On the other hand, Tony had always hit for a high average, and his performance with runners in scoring position (.341 BA from '84 to '86) was outstanding—I guess Larry took it on faith that Wynne and Templeton, or maybe one of San Diego's good-hitting pitchers, would somehow find their way into scoring position. In addition, he had a .400 lifetime BA against Krukow. So on balance the move made sense, especially given that the Padres' offense didn't have much power to begin with.

Carmelo Martinez hit fourth. Another surprise—one would think the Padres would have had John Kruk, a lefty swinger and .309 hitter in '86, in the lineup. But with the departures of McReynolds, Kennedy and Nettles, Bowa looked to Martinez as his big home run man, even though Carmelo had never hit more than 21 homers in a season. Next came Mitchell, who had some offensive potential, and Steve Garvey, whom Bowa apparently figured could provide some of the punch lost with the departure of McReynolds *et al;* otherwise Kruk would have been in the lineup in left, with Martinez playing first. Bowa closed the batting order with two rookies, Santiago and Cora, hitting in front of the pitcher. I suppose his thinking was that, whatever their potential, it was probably a good idea to take some of the pressure off the kids by putting them down in the order. This makes a certain amount of sense.

What Bowa had in mind for the Padres was a sequential offense—one that required the contributions of several players to score a run. Given the departure of the three power hitters, he had little choice but to do this, and anyway, a sequential attack can be effective, as the '85 and '87 Cardinals had proven. In fact the use of Gwynn in the third slot was somewhat similar to Whitey Herzog's choice of Tommy Herr to bat third—and in '85 Herr had driven in 110 runs, but there the similarity ends. Herzog had Vince Coleman to lead off, and though Coleman didn't have a great OBP, he did steal a ton of bases. And Herzog had Willie McGee, who hit .353 in '85, or Ozzie Smith, who had a .392 OBP in '87, batting second. Bowa had Wynne (or Jefferson) and Templeton; couldn't he see the difference? Given that Kruk was sitting and so was Tim Flannery, a lefty swinging infielder with on-base ability, I guess he couldn't.

The Padres lost the opener 4–3 in twelve innings, and that was just the beginning. San Diego lost five straight before winning their first game, and their record at various points early in the year stood at 2–11, 6–20, 9–30, and, finally, 12–42. People began comparing the Padres to the 1962 Mets, who lost 120 games, and even the 1899 Cleveland Spiders, who finished 20–134. Bowa seemed to be going crazy, holding team meetings every couple of days and taking out his frustrations on the umpires. Not only wasn't his lineup scoring runs, the pitching, with Andy Hawkins hurt, LaMarr Hoyt suspended and Storm Davis unable to get anyone out, was also a disaster. Bowa seemed a lead pipe cinch to be the first manager fired in 1987.

But, then, just when things were at their bleakest, the Padres began to turn it around. In fact they turned it around completely—from June 5 to August 11 San Diego went 34–25, the best record in the division over that period. What happened? Well, partly it was the pitching, as Ed Whitson and Eric Show steadied the staff while Davis was sent packing. Bowa also gave plenty of starts, with good results, to youngsters Mark Grant and Jimmy Jones. More fundamentally, Bowa—despite his Mr. Know-It-All manner—seemed to be learning something about managing and about his players. He stuck with Stan Jefferson as his leadoff man, but also tried Flannery and Randy Ready, a very pleasant surprise with a .423 OBP; as Ready refused to cool off, Bowa worked him into the lineup more and more. Gwynn, having a terrific year, was moved up to second and then leadoff. Garvey was finally replaced by Kruk, who also had an outstanding season. Santiago struggled early, but Bowa stayed with him, and eventually Benito turned out to be Rookie of the Year, with a 34-game hitting streak. As the season neared its end the Padres even threatened to escape the cellar; only a 2–11 finish kept them in last place. It was quite a turnaround.

Looking at Bowa's playing career, one has to marvel at what a survivor the guy was. He started out as an undrafted free agent, then made the majors at 24. He was hardly an overnight success; he batted less than .200 for his first two months, and there were cries to send him packing. Eventually he started playing better, and he never stopped working to improve himself. He wound up playing 17 years, compiling over 2,000 hits (he even hit .300 once) and winning two Gold Gloves despite limited range.

As a manager Bowa may turn out to be a survivor as well. He did seem to learn something about lineup selection as time went by, and he showed a lot of patience with young players, which is a trait San Diego is going to need. He likes the stolen base—the Padres were second to the Cardinals with 198 steals, though they were below the league average with a .685 success rate. He also seems to like the bunt, as San Diego was fourth in the league in sacrifices. Judging from '87, he does not seem to be much of a platoon manager, but did use his whole roster.

Will he be successful? A lot depends on the development of players like Jefferson, Shawn Abner, Jimmy Jones and Eric Nolte; the Padres have some other fine prospects in their farm system (including the Alomar brothers), and Bowa is obviously committed to giving them a chance. He is a very intense individual, however, and that may affect his players adversely. Early in the year he seemed to be managing as George Steinbrenner would—that is, like every game is the seventh game of the World Series—and the Padres couldn't seem to handle all the tension. They played better once they were hopelessly out of it, but at the end, when they had a chance to escape the cellar, they fell flat again. Hating to lose is one thing; learning to accept that a certain amount of losing is inevitable can be a step toward maturity. If Bowa can make this step, he may eventually be a successful manager.

Don Zminda

San Francisco Giants
ROGER CRAIG

Before Roger Craig came along, I believed there were good managers and that there were bad managers. Then, Craig made me realize that there were managers who could be good for one type of team and bad for another. At the mid-point of the 1987 season I thought Roger Craig was a good manager for a bad ball club, but a bad manager for a good club. Given that the Giants had become a good club, either Craig had to change or he had to go. He changed. He changed with help from the real star of the club's management, Al Rosen, who went and got him the players he needed.

A manager can be evaluated by four main factors: (1) the lineup, (2) how he handles the pitching staff, (3) strategy and (4) his coaches. Let's evaluate Roger Craig. (For you mathematicians, evaluating Roger Craig presents a difficulty because his performance equations contain discontinuities).

The key date in Roger Craig's metamorphosis from the wrong type of manager for the Giants to the right type is July 4. That's when the Giants obtained the final pieces of the pennant puzzle, Dave Dravecky and Kevin Mitchell. The other key event was Jeffrey Leonard severely pulling a hamstring.

Roger Craig can be commended for his patience, but sometimes he failed to respond to obvious failings. In 1986 and 1987 it took Craig much too long to get Jeffrey Leonard out of the lineup. Macho Leonard in 1986 became a singles hitter by May because of a painful wrist injury, yet lingered in the lineup and in the cleanup spot long enough to get 341 at-bats. During those at-bats, he hit a whopping 6 HRs (all in the first two weeks or so), 11 doubles, 3 triples, and 75 singles (79 percent of his hits). His slugging average was .381, which is terrible for a cleanup hitter. When Craig finally became convinced that Leonard was not productive he inserted Candy Maldonado, who probably had more HRs than Leonard in one third the at-bats, into the lineup regularly. Maldonado went on to hit 18 homers, 31 doubles, and turned in a .477 slugging percentage in 405 at bats.

The story repeated itself in 1987 when Leonard's wrist injury resurfaced. His productivity fell way off, but he stayed in the lineup and would have stayed there if not for his hamstring pull. With Leonard out, Mike Aldrete was in and a star was born. Aldrete hit .325 with an OBA of .397 and a SA of .462. Both seasons, a much more productive hitter sat on the bench while Craig sent the ailing Leonard out to bat day after day.

The acquisition of Kevin Mitchell was important to Craig. Prior to this he was stuck with unproductive hitters such as Rob Thompson or Jose Uribe near the top of the lineup. (Yes, Uribe hit .291 but he didn't walk much, unintentionally). Getting Mitchell allowed him to put a productive hitter in the number two slot and bury Thompson and Uribe at the bottom of the lineup where they belonged.

On to the pitching staff. I often judge a manager by his quotes. Coming out of spring training, Craig commented that his team didn't need a lefty in the bullpen. Is that why by year's end the bullpen had two lefties, Joe Price and Craig Lefferts, among its five members? Price was available to Craig since spring training but did not enter the picture

until August; he had the lowest ERA on the Giants' staff in 1987 and should have been on the roster from opening day.

Again, Craig's patience almost cost the Giants. He stayed too long with Mike Krukow in the starting rotation, when guys like Mark Grant, Roger Mason, and Mike LaCoss sat. However, after Rosen got Dravecky, the starting rotation stabilized. At least Craig realized Dravecky is a quality starter and not a relief pitcher (got that, Larry Bowa?). Also, how could Craig even think of making Mark Davis a starting pitcher, especially when the bullpen had no southpaw. Davis is a two-pitch pitcher, a good fastball complementing a beautiful curveball. He is devastating on lefties, but righthanders find him hittable. This sounds like the kind of pitcher who is well suited to be a short reliever against tough left-handed hitters or when a string of lefties are due up.

Once the pitching staff was completed with the acquisitions of Dravecky, Don Robinson, and Rick Reuschel, Craig used the staff very well. He took advantage of lefty-righty matchups with his relievers. He had a stable starting rotation with two lefties and three righties and a bullpen with the same ideal mix.

Strategy is where Craig had the most learning to do, and where he did. He managed the team for the first few months with 'Billyball"—sacrifice bunts, suicide squeezes, and hit-and-runs at every opportunity. He constantly put his pitchers in the hole with pitchouts. Billyball was an appropriate strategy for Billy Martin with the A's of the early '80s. That was a team which featured the likes of Dave McKay, Mario Guerrero, Jim Essian, Shooty Babbitt, and Fred Stanley. Those guys couldn't hit, so the A's needed to use trickery in order to score. They did not have the string of talented hitters that Craig had with the Giants. Observing Craig manage in the first half of the season, I thought he lacked confidence in his hitters because he was using clawing and scratching techniques to try to score runs, and the Giants probably led the league in losing runners on the basepaths. His strategy probably cost the Giants more runs than it netted. When he stopped the Billyball, he suddenly had a team that finished second in HRs only to the Cubs, who play half their games in a home run hitter's paradise. The stolen base percentages of some of his players were atrocious. The following numbers show the success (?) rate for some of Rog's players in 1986: Bob Brenly 10 for 16, Chris Brown 13 for 22, Chili Davis 16 for 29, Will Clark 4 for 11, Randy Kutcher 6 for 11, Candy Maldonado 4 for 8, and Rob Thompson 12 for 27. Ugh! He didn't do any better in 1987, either, with Clark going 5 for 22 and the team stealing successfully only 57 percent of the time.

Craig changed in the second half. He ceased with the suicide squeezes, which were backfiring left and right. He stopped sending the guys who couldn't steal and he cut down on the hit and run. As a result, the Giants' offense actually scored more runs. The Giants were no longer losing runners on the basepaths by the score.

One thing that speaks well of Craig is that many of his hitters have developed. Maldonado stunk with the Dodgers, came to the Giants and learned to hit. Kevin Mitchell was struggling with the Padres but starred with the Giants. Mike Aldrete was never expected to hit .325 in the majors, and if Chris Speier could have hit throughout his career like he did in '87, he might be going to the Hall of Fame.

With the acquisition of Brett Butler, Roger Craig finally has a leadoff hitter. If his pitchers stay healthy, the Giants stand a good chance of repeating. However, Craig must remember what he learned in 1986 and 1987 for the Giants to do that well.

Ira Saltz

Seattle Mariners
DICK WILLIAMS

The managerial career of Seattle Mariners Manager Dick Williams is fairly well known so I will mention it only briefly. Before arriving in Seattle Dick Williams had managed five other teams, the Red Sox, A's, Angels, Expos, and Padres. Four of these teams were losers before Williams (the A's the exception) and four of his teams improved their records significantly (the Angels the exception). He has made it to the World Series four times (A's 3, Padres 1), winning it twice with the A's. Along with Tigers Manager Sparky Anderson, Williams is the only manager to guide his clubs to the World Series in both the American and National Leagues. Of course, both Anderson and Williams met in the 1984 World Series between Detroit and San Diego. Since Detroit defeated the Padres for the World Championship that year, Anderson is the only manager to have his teams *win* a World Championship in both the AL and the NL.

Many managers are hired to take over losing baseball programs, but not many have a success rate of 80 percent. How does Dick Williams do it? What changes or moves does he make to turn losers into winners? Are these changes consistent among all his teams? And naturally, the important questions for Mariners fans are the following: Is he making these same changes with the Mariners, and are these changes having any effect?

In the chart below, "3 YR BW" shows the average record of the teams Williams eventually managed, in the three years before his arrival. The second line, "1 YR BW," is the average first year before Williams. "1 YR WW" is the first year with Williams, and "TOT WW" the average season of all of Dick Williams' teams. The strike year of 1981 was figured at a full 162 game season; Seattle stats are not included with the analysis presented in the first table below.

The traits of a Dick Williams' team are: a rise in team batting average without sacrificing power, an increase in stolen bases, and a decrease in errors. In pitching, he has no patience for pitchers who can't throw strikes, thus decreasing the staff's walks and increasing their walk/strikeout ratio. These are significant changes in team performance, and they naturally result in more wins.

These are the changes that have taken place in Dick Williams' previous teams, but let's see what has happened with the Mariners. Again, the data in the second table below is expressed in terms of an average 162 game season. Keep in mind the home runs and earned run average figures are a bit tainted due to the recent upsurge in home runs and scoring the past couple years.

Williams doesn't hesitate to make any personnel changes to bring about the changes in team performance he thinks necessary to build a winner. In some cases a manager is stuck with the players the front office gives him, but, at least since he's been in Seattle, Dick Williams seems to have a great influence in which players are obtained or which ones are shown the door.

A move which has been common with every team Dick has managed is his tinkering with second basemen. In Boston in 1967, he gave the second base job to rookie Mike Andrews. Oakland had Dick Green at second when Williams arrived, and he didn't make a move until the second year. Then Williams went to some kind of system where at least seven players took a turn at second base; the next year it was a Green/Ted Kubiak platoon. With the Angels he went from Denny Doyle to Jerry Remy. In Montreal he replaced Pete Mackanin with Dave Cash for two years, then went to a younger player, Rodney Scott. In San Diego the revolving door at second went from Juan Bonilla to Tim Flannery, back to Bonilla, then to Alan Wiggins. This pattern has continued in Seattle when Danny Tartabull was replaced by Harold Reynolds.

Another pattern in Williams' player moves is his willingness to give younger players a chance to play, especially if an aging veteran is taking playing time away from the younger player. Seattle players who have become regulars under him are Reynolds, Rey Quinones, Mickey Brantley, Bill Wilkinson, and Dave Valle. Others who became starters or stars under Dick Williams include Tony Gwynn, Andre Dawson, Vida Blue, Frank Tanana, Terry Kennedy, and Sparky Lyle. Williams was also the first to use Rollie Fingers exclusively out of the bullpen.

On the field, a Dick Williams team takes on the personality of a team that likes to use its speed by stealing bases, bunting for base hits and using the hit-and-run. The exception was the Red Sox—a team which he wisely kept as a power-based team, considering Fenway Park. With these types of Punch and Judy offenses, you would think he would use the sacrifice hit more often, but in fact, in 1987, M's opponents out-sacrificed the M's, 50–37.

Dick Williams strongly prefers a five-man pitching rotation, and he will go with his starters longer than most managers. This is especially true of the top couple of starters on the staff—he was second-guessed on more than one occasion in 1987 for leaving Mark Langston in the game too long. Since Williams has been with the Mariners, the AL

		W	L	PCT	RUNS	OPP RUNS	AVG	HR	SB	E	ERA	BB	K	BB/K
								Pitching						
3	YR BW	74	88	.457	611	667	.247	111	97	146	3.64	581	896	.648
1	YR BW	72	90	.444	611	677	.247	110	87	151	3.70	600	871	.689
1	YR WW	84	78	.519	674	646	.256	126	104	137	3.49	542	923	.587
	TOT WW	85	77	.525	665	630	.252	115	131	135	3.45	527	861	.612

		W	L	PCT	RUNS	OPP RUNS	AVG	HR	SB	E	ERA	BB	K	BB/K
								Pitching						
3	YR BW	68	94	.419	663	794	.253	143	110	138	4.44	599	920	.652
	TOT WW	75	87	.461	761	815	.268	159	139	132	4.58	475	910	.522

team average in complete games has been 26 per year, while the M's average 37.

In the bullpen, Williams likes to have a primary left-hander and a primary righthander for closers, although, even when he has a stopper such as Rollie Fingers, he prefers to spread the saves around a bit.

Dick Williams, as is well known, has a reputation for remaining distant from his players, and he was criticized for his lack of communication with them last year. He has certain expectations from his players, but they all know what those expectations are. He has no patience with players who are not mentally "in the game," and he won't hesitate to sit someone down a few games to emphasize this point. His players may not like Dick Williams' style of running a team, but—of course—it doesn't bother him, saying it's only those players who can't or won't perform who do the complaining.

Seattle is very fortunate to have Dick Williams as their manager. The changes he wrought on his previous teams are now being made to the Mariners, and these changes have given Seattle baseball fans good reason for optimism.

While Dick Williams has stated that 1988 will be his last year as a manager, he wants to go out as a winner. As a Mariners fan, I'd like to see him retire on a winning note, but I'll hate to see him leave if Seattle comes close to a division title in 1988 but falls short.

Steve Russell
(Stats provided by Dennis Orr, Dave Scott and Jeff Welch)

Texas Rangers
BOBBY VALENTINE

His 38th birthday will not arrive until May. He is good looking, wealthy, charismatic, envied by his peers and loved by the Dallas fans; he is Bobby Valentine. Bobby is the second-youngest manager in baseball (to Milwaukee's Tom Trebelhorn), but already he has both managed and won more games than any previous Ranger manager. Not bad for the brash kid from Connecticut who never managed a team before the Rangers, not even in Little League.

After the Rangers' disastrous 1982 season when they lost 98 games, they fired both Manager Don Zimmer and General Manager Eddie Robinson and ended the season with owner Eddie Chiles acting as the GM with the team exhaustively searching for new leadership. They found little interest in the General Manager's job, and finally selected Farm Director and former Rangers' player Tom Grieve, then just 36, mainly because no one else wanted the position. Grieve's first task was to find a field manager: He wanted Bobby Valentine, a close friend and Mets teammate in the late '70s, for the job, but Bobby had no managerial experience and was only 32. Grieve picked Doug Rader instead. Grieve and Rader looked brilliant in 1983 when the Rangers were in first place at the All-Star break, but Rader's team played .401 baseball (111–166) for the rest of his reign as manager in Texas. That record included a 9–23 start in 1985, and Grieve once again sought his friend and the Mets' third base coach, Bobby Valentine. Bobby still had no managerial experience, but was then almost 35. This time, Grieve hired him anyway.

The Rangers were in last place when Bobby took over and were still in last place at season's end, but by then they knew that they had something special. Valentine's impact was immediate. When he was hired, speculation arose that he was earning his managerial spurs for the Mets or Dodgers job when either Davey Johnson or Tommy Lasorda moved on. While flattered to be considered to manage either team, this speculation was correctly perceived by Valentine as a hindrance to his success with the Rangers. So, to show his commitment, he bought a house in Arlington within a week after becoming manager. He is now in his second home—a ten-acre spread allowing his wife to enjoy her favorite hobby: horses.

After being hired, Bobby requested $3,000 worth of video equipment be installed in the Rangers' clubhouse for scouting opponents. When denied by the financially strapped Rangers, he had the equipment installed and paid the bill himself. This man is *committed* to his work and this job. Unlike most former Rangers' managers who scooted out of town at season's end, not to be seen again until Opening Day, Valentine spends a good deal of time in the Dallas area during the winter. He is a frequent guest on radio talk shows and makes personal appearances, and he has opened two restaurants in Arlington which bear his name and are patterned after the three in Connecticut he already owns. He does much more than pay lip service to his commitment to build the Rangers, and last year it showed at the box office. Despite a last place finish, the Rangers set their all-time attendance record in Texas. Bobby Valentine is a big reason why.

COACHING STAFF: Common characteristics of Bobby's coaches include their being young and having a past affiliation with the Dodgers. The first coaches he hired in 1985 were Tom House (pitching) and Art Howe—both, like Valentine, very young. House has been the most controversial coach on the staff with his unique training methods, such as having pitchers tossing footballs to gain arm strength. House believes it is impossible to throw a spiral with a football without utilizing the proper mechanics of pitching a baseball. Going into the 1986 season, Valentine added Tim Foli and former Dodger Joe Ferguson as coaches, both only slightly older than Bobby. Valentine gives them the flexibility to do their jobs, and backs them up when they do it. Foli was initially criticized by Rangers fans for reckless decisions while coaching third; Valentine defended him all the way. House has certainly had a free reign with the pitchers, and Bobby stood behind him despite great amounts of criticism when the pitchers were hit hard early in the 1987 season.

To start 1988, Foli and Ferguson are gone. Foli, a fierce competitor, was sometimes too much of one, hurting the Rangers with his umpire baiting. Last year, Valentine ordered that any league fines Foli received were to be matched by the Rangers, in an effort to restrain Foli's temper. (This rule also applied to left fielder Pete Incaviglia.) At the Rangers' Old-Timer's game in August, Foli dropped a pop fly; later, kidding in the locker room about it resulted in a fight between Foli and some other players. This was the last straw and Foli was released at the season's end.

Ferguson was dismissed at the same time for reasons relating to his managing the La Romana team in the Dominican Republic the previous winter. The Rangers had supported the team financially, and seven Rangers played on it. One of Ferguson's assignments was to find out if Mike Stanley could catch in the major leagues in 1987. If so, the Rangers reasoned, Don Slaught could be traded for pitching help. Ferguson instead curiously chose to play Stanley at first base and DH most of the season. Consequently, therefore, the Rangers held on to Slaught. In May, with Slaught in a slump and Stanley tearing up the American Association with a .335 average, 13 home runs and 54 RBIs in only 46 games, the Rangers made Stanley their starting catcher. A suitable trade for Slaught could not be made until season's end, though, forcing the Rangers to use four roster spots with catchers the rest of the year. So, *adios,* Joe Ferguson. To Valentine's credit, criticism of Foli and Ferguson never appeared in local papers, and both firings came as a complete surprise to local fans.

Dave Oliver started last season as the Rangers "Eye in the Sky." Situated in the press box during games, he positioned the Rangers' fielders. Late in the season, Oliver coached third base on occasion, where he is targeted this year. Davey Lopes, another ex-Dodger, joins the Rangers this year, particularly to help with baserunning. Oliver at 36 and Lopes at 41 carry on Valentine's young coach tradition.

PERSONNEL: Valentine's influence on this team is most evident in the area of personnel, where he and Tom Grieve work very closely together. Among this year's projected nine non-pitching regulars, only Larry Parrish (DH) and Pete O'Brien (1B) were starting when Bobby joined the team in 1985. A lot of new faces have established themselves, and the most obvious trait of the new players is that they are *good athletes.* Almost to a man, every player on the team is muscular, the type of player that when he gets off of a bus, you know he is a professional athlete. Many have played other sports at an advanced level, such as Bob Brower, who was a running back at Duke University. Ruben Sierra and Oddibe McDowell are among the best athletes in baseball.

Grieve and Valentine's philosophy has been to build through the farm system, a good trick since the minor league cupboard was bare in 1985. They built up the farm system through trades such as Wayne Tolleson and Dave Schmidt to the Chicago White Sox for Scott Fletcher and two prospects, including Edwin Correa. They also made trades at the major league level to create an opening for a minor league player. Addition by subtraction, they call it. Thus, Gold Glove third baseman Buddy Bell moved to Cincinnati, without the team getting an established major league player or top minor league prospect, but this opened third base for Steve Buechele. This past winter they made the same type of trade, sending Don Slaught to the Yankees for pitcher Brad Arnsberg, clearing catcher for Mike Stanley.

Bobby is great with young players, largely because he shows confidence in them. When he took over in 1985, he installed rookie Oddibe McDowell in center field, *à la* Leo Durocher and Willie Mays. He gambled again in 1986, naming Pete Incaviglia his right fielder and cleanup man in the batting order. Pete had *no professional experience* prior to 1986 opening day against Toronto. In that game against Dave Stieb, the "Ink Man," as Ranger announcer Mark Holtz calls him, doubled in his third at-bat, but that was the high point of the year for his batting average. Within a week, he looked totally overmatched by major league pitching, striking out often and hitting less than .150. The local press quickly questioned Valentine about sending the Ink Man to the minor leagues, but Bobby never wavered. He vowed Incaviglia would get 150–200 at-bats, then he would assess the situation. The local writers quit asking about Inky's status, and the results speak for themselves. In two seasons, Incaviglia has hit 57 home runs with a career batting average of .260.

Valentine gives youth a chance by inserting them into the lineup and letting them play their way out of it. Moreover, Bobby believes in them and expects them to do well. Another reason for his success with young players is his talent in communicating his sound technical baseball background in a teaching situation. Unfortunately, the managerial duties do not allow him great amounts of time to teach, but when he does, the results have been good.

For example, late last season when the team's catching woes were well known, Valentine worked with Mike Stanley on his throwing. This past winter Valentine has held workouts three times each week for players in Arlington. Steve Buechele is one attendee, and particular attention has been paid to his hitting. Last January, when the Dallas area had its worst snow and ice storm in almost a decade, viewers of the local 10 P.M. news saw Buechele hitting at a local indoor facility. The batting practice pitcher, throwing quite vigorously, was Bobby Valentine (of course).

Before Valentine, a lot of talent came through this organization, never got much of a chance to play, and blossomed after moving on to other teams (*e.g.,* players such as Tom Henke.) It was a disgusting situation, and Valentine has reversed it. Unfortunately, he will not be able to give younger players such opportunity in the future unless they are pitchers, for all the positions are taken. Seven of nine starting positions are now manned by young players brought aboard by Bobby Valentine. Even the pitching staff will start 1988 with as many as eight young pitchers brought to the Rangers during Bobby's regime.

Despite the emphasis on youth with this organization, Bobby still mixes in veterans to steady the ship. The past two seasons, pinch hitters and part-time players Darrell Porter and Tom Paciorek fit that bill. They are gone, but Larry Parrish (at 34) is still around. Bobby has resisted a trade of Parrish, though such a trade makes sense on paper, because he wants an experienced hand on the roster.

The friendship of Bobby and Tom Grieve is a material force behind the turnaround of the Texas franchise. They are in tune philosophically as to how this team is to be built; only occasionally have differences of opinion surfaced regarding personnel decisions. The playing decisions on the field are an accurate reflection of the General Manager's thrust in building the team. If these two and team President Mike Stone stay together, they will field a very good team for many years.

GAME STRATEGY: Bobby Valentine wears his Dodgers' heritage on his sleeve, and his coaching experience prior to managing Texas was in the NL. He should be a National League type manager, stealing bases often, scratching runs for an early lead, and relying on a bevy of hard throwers to close out games. He should be, but he is not. He adapted to the American League style of play immediately with his arrival in Texas.

Valentine rarely runs, deferring instead to big innings. The Rangers' stolen base total last year (120) exceeded only Minnesota's among AL West teams, while succeeding in only 63 percent of the attempts (70 percent is league average), yet both figures were improvements over 1986. Even the hiring of Davey Lopes to help with baserunning signals no significant philosophical change. The Rangers have become a consummate big inning team the past two seasons. Last year, they were fifth in the American League, but first in the West in runs scored. They ranked third in the league in percentage of runs scored in innings of four or more runs.

The 1985 remodeling of Arlington Stadium coincided with Valentine's arrival. Included was a very high wall around the outfield which allowed room for a modern scoreboard and advertising. This wall is high enough to cut the persistent wind that formerly blew in toward home plate, the wind that had frustrated so many Ranger power hitters in the past, from Mike Epstein through Jeff Burroughs to Richie Zisk. Many experts thought the Rangers needed to build a team around good pitching with a bunt-and-run offense to win in this park, but the new fence made that thought passé as home runs soon flew out of Arlington Stadium at a record pace. Prior to 1985, the park record for home runs in one season was 140, while in five of twelve previous years less than 100 were hit. Over the past three seasons with manager Bobby Valentine, the Rangers have set a new team record for home runs at home *each year,* and the park total has exceeded the old record of 140 annually. Bobby Valentine's big inning offense is aided greatly by this wall.

When Bobby chooses between players at a given position, he always selects the best offensive player. There are no "good-field no-hit" players in his line-up at defensively sensitive positions. He also rarely makes defensive moves late in games when he has a lead. Most substitutions of non-pitchers are dictated by the pitching moves of the Rangers' opponents. Other than paying close attention to fielder's positioning, he utilizes no special defensive tactics. He rarely orders intentional walks (only 34 last year).

Valentine often platoons, and will do so at every position if necessary. For some players, it is a strict platoon, such as Steve Buechele and Tom O'Malley at third late last year. For others, such as Scott Fletcher and Pete O'Brien, the occasional day of rest comes when facing a pitcher that throws from their side of the plate.

Valentine's preference for hard throwers can be seen in the young pitchers joining Texas during Bobby's tenure: starters Bobby Witt, Edwin Correa and Jose Guzman and relievers Mitch Williams, Jeff Russell, and Dale Mohorcic. In his first two seasons, he was very patient with the youngsters. He often let them stay in games with big jams, especially in the early innings. While they sometimes got shelled, they often pitched out of trouble, an experience that made them stronger. Last year, Bobby seemed less willing to stick with the youngsters.

LEADERSHIP STYLE: Bobby's leadership style has gone from very outspoken in the beginning to much more subdued last year. In his first year a lot of players were shuffled between Arlington and the minors, and one of Valentine's "rules" was that a player had to play his first

day in the majors. Valentine communicates well with the players. After Valentine dropped Gary Ward from second to fifth in the batting order, Ward told reporters that Valentine had explained his reasons for the change. Ward indicated he did not agree with the decision, but that he appreciated Bobby telling him up front. This is a far cry from Valentine's predecessor's (Doug Rader) relationship with players such as catcher Jim Sundberg. Sundberg, the classiest act this franchise had for a decade, was reduced under Rader to learning of his playing status when the lineup card was posted and learning the reasons for his lessened playing time through the newspapers. Bobby can thus be characterized as a "player's manager."

This outspoken, positive attitude carried through to 1986, when in spring training, Valentine exhibited a strong work ethic. Local beat writers noted how late the staff stayed each day compared with previous staffs. It showed in 1986, as the team played more fundamentally sound baseball. They played 80 errorless games, a club record, and were fifth in the league in double plays with 160—no wonder the team spent 46 days in first place and finished second, only five games behind California. They won 25 more games than in 1985, an increase exceeded by only four other teams in baseball since divisional play began in 1969.

Bobby changed during the season, though. The team was loose and enthusiastic, often likened in attitude to an American Legion team: They looked like they were having a great time playing baseball. As the season wore on with the Rangers in contention, the pressure to win asserted itself. Somewhere, the rule about players starting their first day in the majors was forgotten. Bobby began to show less patience with the starting pitchers, and "ofer" games were often rewarded with off days.

In 1987, Bobby was much less vocal and outspoken. He later said he wanted the players to be the show, not him; he intentionally stepped into the background. He did not seem to have the same spark and enthusiasm as in 1986. He did not conduct the same stringent spring training regimen, probably assuming the problems of the past were cured. The Rangers played poor fundamental baseball, falling just short of the league lead in errors. As a manager, he made more lineup moves, especially as the season progressed. He pinch hit and substituted much more during games, often in reaction to the opponents' pitching moves, and he showed less patience with players, especially pitchers.

The 1988 team is in a new stage, one that will require a different Bobby Valentine. Forget last year's record, as the Rangers abound in offensive talent. If some pitching blooms, the Rangers can be in the division race to the end. The starting nine is to a man filled with established major league players, not youngsters trying to prove themselves. These players can and should be handled differently, for it is time for them to produce on the field. The guess in January is that Bobby will once again work very hard in the spring to cure the defensive problems he thought were cured last year. Bobby will want this team to be ready when the bell rings, as the Rangers open the season with 32 straight games against Eastern Division teams. If they are not ready, and if the 1988 season looks more like dismal '87 rather than upbeat '86, many Ranger players will realize firsthand that he is exhibiting less patience. Bobby knows it is time for the manager to produce along with this promising team.

Dic Humphrey

Toronto Blue Jays
JIMY WILLIAMS

Jimy (only one "M" please) began his career as a manager in Quad Cities of the Midwestern League in 1974; his composite winning percentage for 6 full years of managing in the minors is .535. He has had only one losing season, while he has won one league championship, that with Salt Lake City in '79. In 1980 he moved up to Toronto to become a coach. His record as a minor league manager is impressive.

In those years in the bushes one might assume Williams forged his own style of managing, yet when he assumed the reins he continued in the style of Cox, not really making any major changes and continuing to use the Jays' players in their accustomed roles. This bespeaks a security of position; if he felt he needed to impress the boss (or the media or the players) he might have been tempted to shuffle the deck for its own sake. The boat has not begun to rock, and his steady hand at the tiller has payed benefits, especially in the wake of the collapse late in the 1987 season.

In some markets a collapse of that magnitude would have had the manager tarred and feathered by noon the following day. Williams has remained unscathed and the media are taking their collective frustration out on the players, especially Barfield. This change of the expected target of opportunity may in large part be due to Williams' placid outlook.

Where did Williams begin? He was signed by the Red Sox organization off the campus of Fresno State, where he received a degree in agribusiness. The Cardinals then took him in the winter draft of 1965 and he got his proverbial cup of coffee with the Cardinals in 1966 and 1967. The problem seems to have been his bat (or the lack thereof). His fielding stats look okay (but whisper of an erratic arm), but he never hit for average (.287 was far and away his best) with little power. He was managing by the time he was 32, and he retired as a player at 33.

Taking over the Blue Jays after Cox seemed like a tough assignment: Cox had just led them to their first post-season appearance and expectations for the following season were high. Williams has proven that he is his own man by what, at the time, seemed like a subtle thing: he changed his leadoff hitter, Damaso Garcia, who follows the creed of the Dominican Republic ("Thou shalt not pass") and will swing at anything the pitcher offers. No doubt on some long, hot bus trip in the Texas league Jimy realized that a leadoff man should have a higher on-base percentage than hat size and felt that Lloyd Moseby could do that job better than Garcia. Damaso, confirming what many long thought, proceeded to pout and make a big fuss; clearly he had invested his ego in the prestige of being the Blue Jay *numero uno.* By the beginning of the following season, Damaso had been exiled to Atlanta. It's not nice to argue with Mr. Williams—Jimy had made his choice and in addition made a clear statement to the baseball world at large. This was now his ship.

This act of defiance in the spring of 1986 by Garcia had repercussions all season long in 1987 for Williams and the Jays. It seems they had gone and traded the petulant one without having really decided who his replacement was going to be. The leading candidate was Mike Sharperson, who the preceding season at Syracuse had hit .289, had a little power, a decent eye and some speed. His fielding looked okay (assists per game of 2.33), and he was at the point in his career when he needed to put up or shut up.

According to eyewitness accounts, Sharperson won the job in Florida against all comers and opened the season as the Blue Jays' second baseman. Mike had hit well in the minors, so what happened seems like a nightmare. He opens the season as the regular, and after only 96 at-bats (hitting a robust .208), he is replaced by Garth Iorg. Garth Iorg!! And besides that, what kind of trial is 96 at-bats? Since when did the Blue Jays act in a hasty manner? You see, as well as not hitting a lick, his fielding was terrible; he compiled the worse assists per game ratio of any player to play second base for the Jays all year long and by the end of May was back at Syracuse playing third base. By the end of the year, he was exiled to Los Angeles with a new second base star, Nelson Liriano, taking his place.

What happened? Gentle readers, I don't know; it does raise some questions which I also cannot answer about the way in which the decision to get rid of Garcia was made, who made it, who chose his successor, the age of the universe, and so on. If Garcia was banished because of his run-ins with Williams *and* they assumed Sharperson would easily fill in and succeed him, why was Sharperson given the ax so quickly? Ninety-six at-bats does not a fair trial make and someone with Williams' experience in the bushes would know this. If Garcia was banished because they knew that Liriano was on his way, why even fool around with Sharperson; why not just give the job to Iorg outright in the spring, announce he is just a caretaker, and wait for Liriano to get some time at triple-A before bringing him up? Surely Sharperson's trade value would have been higher *before* the season started when everyone seemed to think he could do the job than it was later after the Jays had embarrassed him in front of the world. And, if indeed Sharperson was as bad as he seems to have been and the Jays acted like he was, who made the mistake when he was given the job in the spring? I don't have the answers to these questions but someone should answer them before concluding an evaluation of Jimy Williams as a manager. The following categorical analysis attempts to develop some of these answers.

LEADERSHIP: Acts the strong silent type. He leads from the shadows, letting his players have the spotlight but making sure they know who is the boss. He'll swear at them in an attempt to motivate or discipline, and his "Born Again" players don't like it much. He does not scold his players in public; what goes on in the clubhouse is anyone's guess.

PLAYER MOVES: The Blue Jays made just 22 player moves last season. This is counting each call up or down as one move; a roster switch would be counted as two moves. This total was the least in the league; Minnesota was a close second and behind by two moves. However, those two were the suspension and reinstatement of Joe Niekro after the "hot potato" incident, so that hardly counts. Directly contrast this to one of the Blue Jays leading rivals, the Yankees, who made 76 moves.

Two things are indicated by the low total. The first is that the Jays didn't have many injuries. In fact, they only lost 55 player days and 3 pitcher starts to injuries, again a very small amount. Of Williams' 11 roster moves only 1 was made due to injury (that of subtracting Stark on April 17 and adding DeWillis). The rest were minor in importance, such as the eternal search for the tenth pitcher. The major problem was at second base. Sharperson was *so* bad (hitting only .208, adjusted assists per game only 1.93) that one has to wonder what in the hell they saw in him in the first place. Manny Lee was then called up, but Williams played not only Lee but also Garth Iorg. Now Garth is an OK third baseman but he is to second base what Jackie Gleason was to ballet. Again, what was Williams doing? If he didn't have anyone else, we could understand this stopgap move, but Lee looks like he can play. Does he have bad breath or what? Then on August 24 he calls up Nelson Liriano and then *he*'s the new second baseman. What is wrong with Manny Lee (.256, 2.43 A/G)? And is Liriano (.241, 2.22 A/G) actually better? What *is* going on here, anyway?

LINEUP: Before he obtained Juan Beniquez and signed Charlie Moore, his lineups varied little. He seemed more willing in the first part of the season to play Kelly Gruber against righties; after the All-Star break he instituted a fairly strict platoon at third. This may have been due, however, to the development of Fred McGriff. While playing sparingly in the first half he became the regular DH against righties in the second half. This moved Rance Mulliniks from DH to third, resulting in Gruber getting less time in the lineup vs. righties. Lloyd Moseby sat down sometimes against lefties; Williams does believe in a fairly strict platoon. In September with an overflowing bench he was known to make scorers crazy with his platoon system. Garcia wasn't a good leadoff hitter; Williams recognized this and set out to rectify it. However, by the end of last year he was leading off Liriano, who isn't a whole lot different an offensive ballplayer than Garcia. Hmmm.

YOUNG PLAYER DEVELOPMENT: Jimy isn't afraid to use his young players in a pennant race; his young players are used in the Baltimore tradition of "let them get their feet wet slowly and then we'll throw them in to the breach in a year or two."

OFFENSIVE TACTICS: Williams is of "the sit back and wait for it to happen" school: had the lowest total of sac bunts in the league; one must assume he doesn't like to bunt much and lives for Barfield, Bell and McGriff to tee off. Wouldn't you? His stolen base total was 5th in the AL but there was a great drop from 4th to 5th—the Blue Jays were 50 stolen bases behind the league leader. Their percentage was 72 percent, so he picked his spots well.

DEFENSIVE TACTICS: He likes to go to the bullpen, and he isn't afraid of using his pitchers. Toronto was 11th in the league in complete games, and with Tom Henke and Mark Eichhorn, could you blame him? The pitching staff led the league in intentional walks, and this total of 65 was double that of 9 other teams, so he was really exceptional in the AL in this respect. He does have some groundball pitchers, so he might've been using the IBB to set up the double play.

ROTATION: Key and Clancy started every 5th day and all other starters were shuffled around to accomplish this. Key did start on three days rest a few times in September, and this seems to have worked out rather well. In relief he sticks with Henke rather than hopping around from reliever to reliever.

STRATEGY: His offense seems balanced between power and speed with Lloyd Moseby seeming like the ideal blend of the two. The Blue Jays play the players who can hit the best, not the ones who field the best, with the exception of Iorg. George Bell and Moseby have range factors of 1.84 and 2.13, both well below average for their positions. Jesse Barfield, of course, is an exemplary right fielder, and Tony Fernandez seems as if he can do it all. His pitching staff has a good complement of both power and finesse, with his two top relievers examples of both. His bullpen and his rotation are balanced very well. His defense depends mainly on the pitchers; the fielders, on the whole are mediocre, but they have good hands.

Gerry Klug

IV

FIELDING AND BASERUNNING

INTRODUCTION

This is a new section in our book, dealing with the poor tactical and statistical stepchildren of the grand game of baseball: fielding and baserunning. At least in our case, though, it is not an intentional oversight, for we would very much like to provide comprehensive fielding and baserunning statistics as well as detailed analysis of these aspects of the game. However, as any serious baseball fan knows, the reality is that these statistics are the hardest to compile while their significance is the least understood.

It is a hoary axiom in baseball that fielding ability can't be accurately judged by fielding stats. Since most baseball people believe this to be true, the worst kinds of subjective and anecdotal evidence are used to judge fielders. Take a look at the Gold Glove awards each year and you'll see how absurd the situation has become—players get awarded Gold Gloves year after year based largely on their reputation and their *offensive* prowess, not on their defensive excellence.

For those who doubt that the above is true (most of whom probably aren't sabermetricians), I have several questions. How do you account for the fact that poor-hitting defensive specialists are almost never awarded Gold Gloves at most positions (shortstop being the prominent exception), when these no-hit but good-field players have no other reason to be playing except for their superior defensive ability? How do you account for the fact that veteran ballplayers keep getting Gold Gloves year after year while their offensive talents are clearly diminishing? Why should defensive skills be more constant than offensive ones? Why are rookies so poorly represented on Gold Glove teams?

For baserunning, the problem is not quite the same: base *stealing* statistics are duly kept and quoted, discussed and analyzed. The premier base stealers are lionized and paid accordingly, unlike most of their premier defensive counterparts who must earn their stardom and their megabucks offensively. However, practically no other base *running* stats are kept, so this interesting and important area is mostly ignored.

Why . . . why . . . why? Since this is an introduction and not a treatise, we'll leave the questions unanswered here and turn to the evidence. In the pages which follow, we have tried to shed some light on these subjects, using a combination of old and new techniques. Certainly, much more research and analysis is needed, but we think that you'll find the results interesting, and we hope that they can give some new insight into these unfairly neglected parts of our national pastime.

Gary Gillette

FIELDING TABLES

This year, we are computing a new kind of range factor that is based on balls actually fielded by the fielders instead of putouts and assists. This is particularly useful for first basemen, where putouts and assists are less useful than for other positions.

A "ball fielded" (BF) is credited to a player when he is the first to handle a ball put into play that results in an out. Thus, the player catching a fly ball or the player that starts a ground out or double play gets credit for fielding that ball.

To measure the opportunities that a player has to field balls, we measure the balls put into play by his opponents. A "ball in play" is a hit, an error, or an out, except that homeruns are not counted since they usually cannot be fielded. We compute a player's defensive equivalent games (DEQ) by counting the balls put into play while he is on the field and dividing by the league average (around 27.8 last year in the American League, 27.9 in the National). Note that it is possible for a player to have more than 162 DEQ if he plays for a team whose pitching staff allows a lot of hits or has a low stikeout total.

Given all this, we can compute a player's range factor as BF/DEQ, which is the number of balls he fields for each 28 or so that are put into play against him.

We show the raw BF/DEQ in the ratings, but we make one final adjustment for the final number used to rank the players. Players on different teams face different numbers of right- and left-handed batters due to the composition of their pitching staff, and this affects their range factors. Right-handed batters hit more ground balls to shortstops and third basemen than left-handed batters do.

We adjust for this using a method suggested by John Dewan: compute each player's range factor against lefties and righties separately, and then combine them according the to league average number of left- and right-handed batters. In the National League last year, 43% of all balls put in play were put in play by players batting left-handed, so we multiply each players range factor against lefties by 0.43 and add it to his range against right-handers, which we've multipied by 0.57. This gives the number labled "ABF/DEQ," it that's how to rank the players.

As an example, here's how Ozzie Smith's numbers work. While Ozzie was playing, St. Louis opponents put 4326 balls into play, so he played in 4326/27.87 = 155.2 equivalent games. He fielded 565 of those balls in play, for a BF/DEQ of (565/4326) × 27.87, or 3.64.

Of the 4326 balls in play, 1465 of them were hit by left-handed batters and 2861 of them by right-handers. Ozzie fielded 127 balls against lefties, for a LBF/DEQ of (127/1465) × 27.87 or 2.42. Against right-handers, he fielded 438 balls, so his RBF/DEQ is (438/2861) × 27.87 or 4.27. We combine them by multiplying the left range by 0.43 and the right range by 0.57 and adding:

$$ABF/DEQ = 2.42 \times 0.43 + 4.27 \times 0.57 = 3.47$$

In this case, the left-right adjustment brought down Ozzie's BF/DEQ, because he faced a higher percentage of right-handed hitters (66%) than the league average.

For each infielder, we give the following statistics:

G — games played
PO — putouts
A — assists
E — errors
PCT — fielding percentage, (PO+A) / (PO+A+E)
DP — double plays

Those are the official stats. Ours are

DEQ — defensive equivalent games.
BF — balls fielded
BF/DEQ — unadjusted balls fielded per equivalent game
ABF/DEQ — adjusted balls fielded per equivalent game, as described above.

For outfielders, we give roughly the same information, except that each of the outfield positions is kept distinct. The outfielder categories are:

G — games played
PO — putouts
A — assists
E — errors
PCT — fielding percentage, (PO+A) / (PO+A+E)
A/162 — assists per 162 DEQ, a way of normalizing assists totals.
DEQ — defensive equivalent games.
BF — balls fielded
BF/DEQ — unadjusted balls fielded per equivalent game
ABF/DEQ — adjusted balls fielded per equivalent game, as described above.

For catchers, we count the wild pitches and passed balls they allow, and give the rates for them based on their defensive equivalent games. Since balls put into play are not particularly relevent for catchers, we define DEQ for catchers as defensive innings / 9.

DEQ — defensive innings / 9.
WP — wild pitches allowed
WP/DEQ
PB—passed balls
PB/DEQ

Another important part of catchers' defense is their ability to throw out base stealers, and we show those numbers in the base stealing section.

CATCHERS—AMERICAN LEAGUE

name	innings	DEQ	WP	WP/162	PB	PB/162
League	20195.2	2244.0	758	54.7	267	19.3
Allanson	414.0	46.0	22	77.5	3	10.6
Bando	565.2	62.9	27	69.5	9	23.2
Boone	1036.1	115.1	39	54.9	7	9.9
Bradley S	657.0	73.0	28	62.1	2	4.4
Butera	325.2	36.2	22	98.5	9	40.3
Cerone	777.1	86.4	34	63.7	13	24.4
DeWillis	81.0	9.0	2	36.0	0	0.0
Dempsey	422.0	46.9	24	82.9	3	10.4
Fimple	32.2	3.6	0	0.0	0	0.0
Fisk	939.2	104.4	17	26.4	7	10.9
Gedman	383.2	42.6	11	41.8	8	30.4
Hassey	194.0	21.6	10	75.0	2	15.0
Heath	483.2	53.7	29	87.5	5	15.1
Karkovice	261.0	29.0	8	44.7	2	11.2
Kearney	130.0	14.4	2	22.5	0	0.0
Kennedy	1187.2	132.0	43	52.8	4	4.9
Laudner	701.2	78.0	28	58.2	10	20.8
Lowry	58.0	6.4	3	75.9	0	0.0
Marzano	425.1	47.3	9	30.8	9	30.8
Mercado	66.0	7.3	3	66.6	1	22.2
Miller D	176.2	19.6	11	90.9	3	24.8
Moore C	286.0	31.8	19	96.8	4	20.4
Nichols C	64.0	7.1	2	45.6	0	0.0
Nieto	304.1	33.8	4	19.2	0	0.0
Nokes	848.1	94.3	37	63.6	7	12.0
O'Brien C	91.0	10.1	2	32.1	1	16.0
Owen L	511.0	56.8	16	45.6	5	14.3
Petralli	407.0	45.2	16	57.3	35	125.4
Quirk	790.2	87.9	33	60.8	11	20.3
Rayford	120.1	13.4	5	60.4	1	12.1
Salas	353.2	39.3	23	94.8	10	41.2
Schroeder	542.2	60.3	23	61.8	3	8.1
Sheaffer	176.2	19.6	4	33.1	2	16.5
Skinner J	404.0	44.9	12	43.3	1	3.6
Slaught	555.1	61.7	20	52.5	20	52.5
Stanley M	466.0	51.8	22	68.8	18	56.3
Steinbach	856.2	95.2	32	54.5	14	23.8
Sullivan M	443.1	49.3	10	32.9	11	36.1
Surhoff BJ	830.1	92.3	18	31.6	9	15.8
Tettleton	582.0	64.7	20	50.1	4	10.0
Valle	627.2	69.7	17	39.5	2	4.6
Van Gorder	67.2	7.5	2	43.2	0	0.0
Whitt	1032.2	114.7	35	49.4	8	11.3
Wynegar	211.2	23.5	4	27.6	1	6.9

CATCHERS—NATIONAL LEAGUE

name	innings	DEQ	WP	WP/162	PB	PB/162
League	17379.0	1931.0	572	48.0	152	12.8
Afenir	51.1	5.7	0	0.0	3	85.3
Ashby	903.2	100.4	25	40.3	6	9.7
Bailey	151.1	16.8	3	28.9	0	0.0
Benedict	256.0	28.4	5	28.5	1	5.7
Berryhill	66.0	7.3	6	133.2	0	0.0
Bochy	158.1	17.6	6	55.2	0	0.0
Brenly	880.0	97.8	45	74.5	11	18.2
Carter G	1142.0	126.9	32	40.9	5	6.4
Daulton	298.0	33.1	9	44.0	1	4.9
Davis Jody	1014.0	112.7	36	51.7	12	17.2
Diaz B	1133.1	125.9	26	33.5	9	11.6
Fitzgerald	761.1	84.6	27	51.7	4	7.7
Lake	434.1	48.3	12	40.2	1	3.4
Lavalliere	865.1	96.1	29	48.9	2	3.4
Lyons Barry	312.0	34.7	10	46.7	4	18.7
McClendon	69.1	7.7	0	0.0	2	42.1
McGriff T	221.2	24.6	6	39.5	1	6.6
Melvin	561.1	62.4	15	38.9	4	10.4
Ortiz	490.0	54.4	29	86.4	6	17.9
Pagnozzi	105.2	11.7	0	0.0	1	13.8
Parent	55.1	6.1	2	53.1	0	0.0
Parrish Ln	1100.1	122.3	25	33.1	15	19.9
Pena T	926.0	102.9	34	53.5	14	22.0
Reed J	546.2	60.7	16	42.7	4	10.7
Reynolds Rn	262.0	29.1	9	50.1	1	5.6
Santiago	1219.2	135.5	47	56.2	22	26.3
Scioscia	1145.2	127.3	42	53.4	6	7.6
Simmons T	125.0	13.9	2	23.3	2	23.3
Stefero	122.1	13.6	3	35.7	0	0.0
Sundberg	354.2	39.4	16	65.8	1	4.1
Trevino	289.0	32.1	11	55.5	2	10.1
Virgil	1046.2	116.3	35	48.8	8	11.1
Wine	73.0	8.1	2	40.0	1	20.0

FIRST BASE—AMERICAN LEAGUE

name	G	PO	A	E	PCT	DP	DEQ	BF	BF/DEQ	ABF/DEQ
League	2529	19831	1673	174	.992	1888	2268.0	4593	2.03	2.03
BAL	165	1444	149	12	.993	154	165.8	358	2.16	2.21
BOS	185	1355	106	18	.988	137	161.6	313	1.94	1.88
CAL	171	1418	100	13	.992	145	163.1	320	1.96	1.92
CHA	172	1505	95	11	.993	149	166.8	305	1.83	1.83
CLE	174	1355	127	24	.984	115	168.1	330	1.96	1.94
DET	207	1404	145	8	.995	138	162.5	350	2.15	2.10
KC	173	1572	117	14	.992	137	161.2	330	2.05	2.14
MIL	189	1270	127	12	.991	138	165.1	290	1.76	1.81
MIN	179	1431	83	9	.994	131	157.9	325	2.06	2.03
NYA	173	1464	108	5	.997	137	164.6	333	2.02	2.19
OAK	186	1379	114	14	.991	106	160.3	318	1.98	1.93
SEA	179	1471	100	11	.993	137	162.9	298	1.83	1.82
TEX	193	1375	162	12	.992	133	153.7	366	2.38	2.31
TOR	183	1388	140	11	.993	131	154.5	357	2.31	2.37
Upshaw	146	1169	127	9	.993	114	130.6	316	2.42	2.48
Brett	83	798	50	6	.993	69	83.1	178	2.14	2.30
O'Brien P	158	1233	146	11	.992	118	138.1	322	2.33	2.27
Evans Da	105	810	100	3	.997	86	94.3	216	2.29	2.22
Mattingly	140	1239	91	5	.996	122	139.8	283	2.02	2.21
Murray E	156	1371	145	10	.993	146	157.8	334	2.12	2.18
Tabler	82	650	75	12	.984	49	79.5	170	2.14	2.09
Hrbek	137	1179	68	5	.996	112	128.2	272	2.12	2.09
Buckner	79	640	60	6	.992	54	74.0	150	2.03	1.96
McGwire	145	1173	90	10	.992	91	136.3	269	1.97	1.93
Joyner	149	1276	92	10	.993	133	145.4	285	1.96	1.92
Brock	141	1065	109	8	.993	111	137.1	248	1.81	1.85
Evans Dw	79	619	41	12	.982	72	75.2	142	1.89	1.84
Davis A	157	1386	96	9	.994	133	154.8	281	1.82	1.81
Walker G	154	1402	80	9	.994	135	154.3	278	1.80	1.81
Carter J	84	644	45	12	.983	61	82.2	141	1.71	1.72
Balboni	55	521	41	6	.989	39	51.1	93	1.82	1.90
Bergman	65	353	29	3	.992	33	42.0	82	1.95	1.92
Deer	12	48	6	1	.982	6	7.4	15	2.02	2.31
Dodson	21	99	4	0	1.000	12	12.2	23	1.89	1.86
Fielder	16	98	6	0	1.000	12	11.5	21	1.83	1.86
Lansford	17	58	9	0	1.000	5	7.6	17	2.24	2.22
Larkin G	26	165	10	2	.989	12	20.3	38	1.87	1.83
Madlock	22	167	11	2	.989	14	18.5	35	1.90	1.81
McGriff F	14	108	7	2	.983	5	11.0	18	1.63	1.67
Moses	16	51	2	1	.981	3	5.0	9	1.81	1.78
Paciorek J	21	93	6	2	.980	8	12.2	18	1.47	1.53
Paciorek	12	63	7	0	1.000	9	6.4	18	2.80	2.80
Pasqua	12	82	8	0	1.000	2	8.8	19	2.16	2.18
Robidoux	10	53	4	1	.983	9	5.8	7	1.20	1.32
Seitzer	25	183	23	2	.990	19	19.7	52	2.64	2.65
Stanley M	12	58	9	0	1.000	6	7.0	20	2.85	2.56
Ward G	15	118	8	0	1.000	11	13.1	27	2.07	2.11

FIRST BASE—NATIONAL LEAGUE

name	G	PO	A	E	PCT	DP	DEQ	BF	BF/DEQ	ABF/DEQ
League	2254	17666	1439	173	.991	1558	1942.0	3928	2.02	2.02
ATL	182	1627	113	19	.989	159	166.7	337	2.02	2.03
CIN	192	1385	100	9	.994	124	164.7	322	1.95	2.01
CHN	189	1444	88	14	.991	137	160.5	309	1.93	1.90
HOU	167	1378	121	12	.992	97	153.7	316	2.06	2.06
LA	205	1410	148	14	.991	129	158.6	332	2.09	2.07
MON	179	1476	116	13	.992	107	162.3	354	2.18	2.06
NYN	188	1457	164	15	.991	120	160.8	338	2.10	2.07
PHI	195	1428	92	14	.991	119	165.1	304	1.84	1.96
PIT	184	1497	148	21	.987	127	160.3	372	2.32	2.23
SD	189	1500	122	9	.994	126	161.3	322	2.00	1.93
SF	193	1548	122	15	.991	159	159.5	338	2.12	2.09
SL	191	1516	105	18	.989	154	168.4	284	1.69	1.84
Bream	144	1236	127	17	.988	109	130.7	315	2.41	2.30
Kruk	101	870	75	4	.996	74	91.4	209	2.29	2.18
Clark W	139	1253	103	13	.991	130	130.1	276	2.12	2.10
Galarraga	146	1300	103	10	.993	96	141.3	313	2.22	2.08
Perry G	136	1288	72	14	.990	118	130.7	266	2.04	2.08
Davis G	151	1283	112	12	.991	89	142.2	291	2.05	2.05
Hernandez K	154	1298	149	10	.993	110	145.5	296	2.03	2.00
Durham	123	1049	57	11	.990	90	111.0	222	2.00	1.96
Hayes	144	1164	78	12	.990	100	134.2	247	1.84	1.96
Stubbs	111	802	78	5	.994	65	87.7	168	1.92	1.93
Esasky	93	772	40	5	.994	72	91.1	168	1.84	1.88
Clark J	126	1151	77	14	.989	116	128.0	208	1.62	1.78
Aldrete	33	187	15	1	.995	20	18.4	38	2.06	2.00
Concepcion D	26	118	10	0	1.000	3	16.2	36	2.22	2.15
Diaz M	32	230	20	4	.984	14	25.8	51	1.98	1.95
Driessen	21	141	10	1	.993	13	15.0	25	1.66	1.87
Francona	57	373	45	2	.995	38	43.4	93	2.14	2.24
Garvey	20	138	11	0	1.000	10	15.3	25	1.63	1.61
Gross G	11	20	1	0	1.000	1	2.0	6	2.99	3.00
Guerrero	40	319	38	7	.981	30	37.0	91	2.46	2.35
Hatcher M	37	234	24	2	.992	29	25.5	58	2.27	2.20
Laga	12	66	7	2	.973	10	7.3	15	2.05	2.09
Law V	17	89	9	1	.990	5	11.9	23	1.93	1.84
Lindeman	20	118	10	1	.992	10	14.2	31	2.19	2.43
Magadan	13	71	7	2	.975	4	7.9	25	3.17	3.10
Martinez C	65	475	36	5	.990	41	53.1	88	1.66	1.63
Mazzilli	13	71	7	2	.975	4	5.8	14	2.42	2.36
Palmeiro	18	112	8	1	.992	15	15.0	26	1.73	1.76
Schu	28	169	9	1	.994	9	19.2	37	1.92	2.08
Simmons T	28	216	23	4	.984	24	23.1	43	1.86	1.73
Trillo	47	283	23	2	.994	32	34.4	61	1.77	1.74
Walling	16	95	9	0	1.000	8	11.5	25	2.17	2.16

SECOND BASE—AMERICAN LEAGUE

name	G	PO	A	E	PCT	DP	DEQ	BF	BF/DEQ	ABF/DEQ
League	2564	4785	6702	234	.980	1522	2268.0	7452	3.29	3.29
BAL	175	362	453	14	.983	129	165.8	489	2.95	2.98
BOS	170	388	531	13	.986	129	161.6	556	3.44	3.35
CAL	179	351	465	20	.976	120	163.1	528	3.24	3.19
CHA	191	326	489	12	.985	110	166.8	512	3.07	3.07
CLE	175	305	471	17	.979	92	168.1	513	3.05	3.02
DET	188	320	479	20	.976	121	162.5	496	3.05	2.99
KC	182	353	505	10	.988	103	161.2	574	3.56	3.68
MIL	191	335	467	17	.979	114	165.1	523	3.17	3.24
MIN	189	309	473	16	.980	100	157.9	540	3.42	3.36
NYA	180	393	469	17	.981	119	164.6	543	3.30	3.50
OAK	184	312	485	27	.967	86	160.3	551	3.44	3.36
SEA	170	359	522	21	.977	113	162.9	588	3.61	3.58
TEX	195	331	457	15	.981	92	153.7	525	3.42	3.36
TOR	195	341	436	15	.981	94	154.5	514	3.33	3.38
White F	152	320	458	10	.987	89	144.7	520	3.59	3.71
Phillips	87	160	260	11	.974	40	81.2	297	3.66	3.57
Reynolds H	160	347	507	20	.977	111	158.4	567	3.58	3.56
Randolph	119	286	338	12	.981	89	117.0	394	3.37	3.52
Lombardozzi	133	245	356	14	.977	77	119.9	417	3.48	3.44
Browne J	130	258	338	12	.980	66	113.2	392	3.46	3.40
Iorg G	91	139	195	6	.982	33	70.5	235	3.33	3.40
Barrett	137	320	438	9	.988	108	133.7	457	3.42	3.32
McLemore	132	291	358	17	.974	96	126.7	421	3.32	3.26
Castillo J	97	181	219	11	.973	54	83.2	258	3.10	3.16
Manrique	92	147	234	6	.984	58	76.6	239	3.12	3.08
Hill D	84	153	223	5	.987	47	78.4	237	3.02	3.07
Whitaker	148	275	416	17	.976	99	140.3	439	3.13	3.05
Bernazard	137	243	335	17	.971	61	130.4	385	2.95	2.95
Biancalana	12	9	18	0	1.000	6	6.6	21	3.19	3.21
Bonilla J	22	40	43	3	.965	10	17.6	57	3.25	3.43
Brookens	11	20	20	3	.930	10	7.4	17	2.29	2.34
Buechele	18	20	36	0	1.000	7	14.1	39	2.76	2.74
Burleson	55	112	145	6	.977	39	54.0	150	2.78	2.91
Gallego	31	49	73	4	.968	22	20.8	79	3.81	3.71
Gantner	57	95	153	4	.984	36	48.7	158	3.24	3.37
Hinzo	67	115	204	9	.973	44	67.7	211	3.12	3.03
Howell Jk	13	4	6	1	.909	2	2.5	5	2.01	2.02
Kunkel	10	17	25	2	.955	8	6.9	25	3.60	3.67
Lee M	27	51	61	4	.966	16	19.5	65	3.34	3.35
Liriano	37	83	107	1	.995	28	35.1	122	3.47	3.47
Meacham	25	40	57	2	.980	11	19.8	62	3.14	3.56
Molitor	19	35	49	0	1.000	16	17.3	56	3.24	3.36
Newman A	47	54	111	2	.988	20	33.9	111	3.28	3.10
Noboa	21	19	39	1	.983	6	14.5	40	2.77	2.64
Pecota	15	20	27	0	1.000	6	8.1	32	3.97	4.21
Ray	29	52	90	2	.986	19	29.5	94	3.19	3.22
Ripken B	58	133	162	3	.990	53	57.5	169	2.94	2.96
Romero E	29	65	81	4	.973	19	25.6	88	3.44	3.42
Sharperson	32	64	69	4	.971	16	27.3	88	3.22	3.36
Stanicek P	19	36	42	2	.975	15	18.0	53	2.94	2.93
Sveum	13	21	35	2	.966	7	13.3	41	3.08	3.08
Walewander	24	16	38	0	1.000	10	11.7	35	2.99	2.91
Wiggins	33	78	98	3	.983	21	33.4	107	3.20	3.20
Wilkerson	28	31	46	0	1.000	9	15.7	58	3.70	3.67

SECOND BASE—NATIONAL LEAGUE

name	G	PO	A	E	PCT	DP	DEQ	BF	BF/DEQ	ABF/DEQ
League	2290	4220	5924	185	.982	1276	1942.0	6336	3.26	3.26
ATL	172	344	558	14	.985	135	166.7	568	3.41	3.42
CIN	186	413	464	20	.978	102	164.7	564	3.42	3.49
CHN	182	377	488	13	.985	110	160.5	529	3.30	3.27
HOU	176	309	443	6	.992	73	153.7	511	3.32	3.33
LA	183	361	477	17	.980	99	158.6	511	3.22	3.18
MON	214	303	494	15	.982	87	162.3	533	3.28	3.16
NYN	238	337	546	23	.975	106	160.8	509	3.16	3.12
PHI	167	381	451	18	.979	101	165.1	508	3.08	3.22
PIT	174	331	542	14	.984	106	160.3	566	3.53	3.38
SD	201	322	523	16	.981	95	161.3	568	3.52	3.41
SF	203	357	485	20	.977	133	159.5	513	3.22	3.20
SL	194	385	453	9	.989	129	168.4	456	2.71	2.83
Hubbard	139	284	478	11	.986	114	138.9	485	3.49	3.50
Doran	162	300	431	6	.992	70	149.1	495	3.32	3.33
Ray	119	248	358	12	.981	84	113.8	373	3.28	3.20
Thompson R	126	246	341	17	.972	99	109.6	352	3.21	3.20
Sandberg	131	294	375	10	.985	84	127.5	411	3.22	3.19
Samuel	160	374	434	18	.978	99	161.4	492	3.05	3.19
Sax S	152	342	420	14	.982	92	143.4	454	3.17	3.13
Backman	87	131	210	6	.983	44	71.6	222	3.10	3.08
Teufel	92	138	213	10	.972	43	73.7	230	3.12	3.06
Law V	106	158	276	9	.980	47	92.4	295	3.19	3.04
Herr	137	306	350	7	.989	103	133.3	359	2.69	2.80
Almon	10	4	7	1	.917	1	3.3	6	1.80	1.92
Booker R	18	24	24	2	.960	3	9.2	22	2.40	2.50
Candaele	68	76	125	3	.985	18	38.1	128	3.36	3.28
Concepcion D	59	125	133	2	.992	36	44.9	157	3.50	3.60
Cora	66	118	192	8	.975	31	58.3	218	3.74	3.68
Flannery	84	139	207	5	.986	40	66.9	224	3.35	3.23
Foley T	39	69	93	3	.982	22	31.7	110	3.47	3.37
Gant	20	45	59	3	.972	17	19.3	60	3.11	3.18
Garner	14	6	17	2	.920	2	5.5	18	3.28	3.08
Lind	35	53	139	1	.995	12	33.7	150	4.45	4.03
Miller K	16	21	38	2	.967	6	12.0	50	4.17	4.14
Noce	36	73	99	3	.983	24	28.6	102	3.57	3.58
Oberkfell	11	13	17	0	1.000	3	7.3	19	2.60	2.52
Oester	69	183	186	10	.974	37	68.0	236	3.47	3.52
Oquendo	32	50	65	0	1.000	20	22.2	64	2.88	3.06
Ready	51	65	124	3	.984	24	36.0	126	3.50	3.27
Speier	55	80	105	2	.989	23	38.8	116	2.99	2.99
Stillwell	37	61	97	4	.975	15	32.8	106	3.24	3.25
Treadway	21	44	48	4	.958	14	19.2	65	3.39	3.42
Trillo	10	7	7	0	1.000	1	2.6	8	3.10	3.58
Wasinger	10	12	18	0	1.000	4	5.0	19	3.78	3.27

THIRD BASE—AMERICAN LEAGUE

name	G	PO	A	E	PCT	DP	DEQ	BF	BF/DEQ	ABF/DEQ
League	2697	1756	4464	312	.952	441	2268.0	5729	2.53	2.52
BAL	183	146	362	23	.957	34	165.8	476	2.87	2.82
BOS	173	125	301	15	.966	37	161.6	396	2.45	2.53
CAL	188	116	318	21	.954	37	163.1	398	2.44	2.49
CHA	185	124	337	25	.949	40	166.8	423	2.54	2.54
CLE	171	153	300	24	.950	25	168.1	420	2.50	2.53
DET	207	139	334	36	.929	21	162.5	441	2.71	2.78
KC	175	119	338	29	.940	37	161.2	423	2.62	2.52
MIL	202	122	278	26	.939	37	165.1	359	2.17	2.09
MIN	176	145	282	14	.968	28	157.9	374	2.37	2.42
NYA	180	104	349	21	.956	40	164.6	420	2.55	2.39
OAK	207	112	317	12	.973	23	160.3	401	2.50	2.55
SEA	175	136	346	21	.958	29	162.9	439	2.70	2.72
TEX	229	124	271	19	.954	25	153.7	366	2.38	2.45
TOR	246	91	331	26	.942	28	154.5	393	2.54	2.48
Knight	130	110	282	18	.956	28	128.3	366	2.85	2.80
Presley	148	113	311	21	.953	28	143.4	388	2.71	2.73
Brookens	122	85	208	14	.954	15	107.9	280	2.60	2.68
Boggs W	145	111	277	14	.965	37	141.6	361	2.55	2.61
Seitzer	141	105	292	22	.947	32	137.1	366	2.67	2.56
Gruber	119	52	168	12	.948	11	77.2	204	2.64	2.56
Buechele	123	68	175	9	.964	13	91.3	228	2.50	2.56
Lansford	142	98	249	7	.980	15	129.0	325	2.52	2.55
Jacoby	144	134	254	22	.946	19	145.1	361	2.49	2.50
Gaetti	150	134	261	11	.973	28	142.0	346	2.44	2.48
DeCinces	128	83	226	17	.948	24	118.3	277	2.34	2.41
Pagliarulo	147	96	297	17	.959	35	142.5	364	2.56	2.39
Brett	11	7	19	3	.897	3	9.9	24	2.43	2.57
Coles	36	31	63	17	.847	5	29.2	83	2.84	2.78
Gallego	24	5	24	0	1.000	1	9.6	24	2.51	2.63
Gantner	38	24	40	2	.970	8	26.8	52	1.94	1.86
Gonzales	29	18	34	2	.963	2	17.3	50	2.89	2.89
Hill D	32	14	55	9	.885	8	26.4	62	2.34	2.34
Howell Jk	48	31	85	4	.967	13	39.9	112	2.81	2.81
Hulett	61	44	118	8	.953	15	59.0	154	2.61	2.65
Iorg G	28	10	26	1	.973	3	11.6	34	2.93	2.89
Keedy	11	9	24	2	.943	2	9.3	29	3.12	2.82
Kiefer	26	15	42	2	.966	3	26.8	53	1.98	1.96
Lyons S	51	35	99	4	.971	11	46.2	128	2.77	2.71
Martinez E	12	13	19	0	1.000	1	11.1	28	2.52	2.66
Molitor	41	25	64	5	.947	8	38.8	80	2.06	1.92
Morrison	16	10	41	2	.962	1	14.4	49	3.41	3.41
Mulliniks	96	29	137	13	.927	14	64.9	155	2.39	2.35
Newman A	12	4	11	0	1.000	0	5.3	13	2.46	2.49
O'Malley	40	21	56	3	.963	3	28.3	76	2.68	2.69
Paciorek J	15	13	16	6	.829	4	10.2	26	2.54	2.53
Parrish Lr	28	19	26	4	.918	6	22.4	39	1.74	1.82
Pecota	17	7	23	3	.909	2	8.3	29	3.47	3.36
Petralli	17	8	7	2	.882	2	6.2	12	1.95	2.04
Phillips	11	3	20	2	.920	4	8.6	24	2.80	2.95
Polidor	11	1	7	0	1.000	0	4.8	8	1.66	1.78
Riles	65	41	103	10	.935	11	56.1	133	2.37	2.30
Romero E	24	13	24	1	.974	0	18.9	34	1.80	2.01
Royster	43	26	57	4	.954	6	35.3	69	1.95	1.97
Sakata	12	3	23	2	.929	1	9.5	23	2.43	2.35
Smalley	14	7	10	3	.850	0	10.6	15	1.41	1.53
Steinbach	10	1	4	0	1.000	0	3.4	4	1.17	1.20
Surhoff BJ	10	2	6	0	1.000	2	2.9	7	2.40	2.40
Walewander	17	7	11	1	.947	0	6.5	15	2.32	2.40
Washington R	20	15	40	0	1.000	3	17.1	53	3.09	3.01
Wilkerson	18	7	5	1	.923	1	4.6	8	1.75	1.78
Williams E	22	17	37	1	.982	6	19.8	49	2.47	2.73

THIRD BASE—NATIONAL LEAGUE

name	G	PO	A	E	PCT	DP	DEQ	BF	BF/DEQ	ABF/DEQ
League	2320	1440	3994	281	.951	337	1942.0	4917	2.53	2.53
ATL	190	106	322	13	.971	32	166.7	391	2.34	2.33
CIN	177	108	295	9	.978	20	164.7	371	2.25	2.18
CHN	199	110	333	34	.929	29	160.5	394	2.45	2.49
HOU	199	156	303	22	.954	31	153.7	416	2.71	2.70
LA	232	153	335	31	.940	28	158.6	441	2.78	2.82
MON	185	141	320	23	.952	23	162.3	420	2.59	2.74
NYN	190	99	320	23	.948	20	160.8	380	2.36	2.41
PHI	190	113	381	22	.957	30	165.1	441	2.67	2.47
PIT	186	108	309	22	.950	23	160.3	374	2.33	2.47
SD	192	105	341	31	.935	38	161.3	413	2.56	2.68
SF	203	114	341	21	.956	33	159.5	421	2.64	2.67
SL	177	127	394	30	.946	30	168.4	455	2.70	2.53
Wallach	150	128	292	21	.952	21	146.8	382	2.60	2.76
Mitchell K	119	73	239	15	.954	19	109.0	289	2.65	2.64
Moreland	150	99	300	28	.934	27	140.3	353	2.52	2.55
Schmidt M	138	87	315	12	.971	28	130.8	358	2.74	2.54
Brown C	80	60	132	16	.923	17	74.3	177	2.38	2.53
Morrison	82	46	151	5	.975	11	73.4	181	2.47	2.52
Pendleton	158	117	369	26	.949	27	159.2	426	2.68	2.51
Oberkfell	126	76	248	7	.979	20	121.9	299	2.45	2.42
Bonilla B	89	53	138	14	.932	12	76.0	168	2.21	2.42
Johnson H	140	82	235	21	.938	15	125.7	292	2.32	2.37
Bell B	142	93	241	7	.979	17	138.5	308	2.22	2.15
Anderson D	35	11	33	1	.978	4	14.1	42	2.99	3.03
Caminiti	61	50	98	8	.949	11	52.6	128	2.43	2.51
Coles	10	9	19	3	.903	0	9.8	24	2.46	2.65
Concepcion D	13	5	20	0	1.000	2	9.4	24	2.55	2.55
Garner	82	57	121	10	.947	5	55.6	165	2.97	3.07
Hamilton J	31	27	60	6	.935	5	23.6	81	3.43	3.43
Hatcher M	49	37	81	9	.929	7	36.1	107	2.96	2.99
Jackson C	16	6	38	2	.957	4	12.8	41	3.21	2.99
Law V	22	11	22	1	.971	2	12.6	29	2.31	2.34
Madlock	16	8	23	3	.912	2	13.8	29	2.10	2.10
Magadan	50	17	85	2	.981	5	35.1	88	2.51	2.55
Nettles	40	12	46	3	.951	6	25.6	52	2.03	2.03
Ramirez R	12	7	11	1	.947	3	10.2	15	1.47	1.58
Ready	52	30	95	12	.912	11	42.0	115	2.74	2.88
Runge	10	9	15	2	.923	3	7.9	21	2.65	2.74
Salazar L	38	17	49	3	.957	4	25.3	62	2.45	2.50
Schu	45	24	62	9	.905	2	31.9	78	2.45	2.19
Speier	44	22	84	1	.991	10	31.8	103	3.24	3.22
Spilman	10	1	6	1	.875	1	4.1	4	0.98	0.95
Stillwell	20	9	33	1	.977	1	16.1	37	2.30	2.23
Trillo	35	7	18	2	.926	2	11.8	25	2.12	2.26
Walling	79	72	109	10	.948	13	60.6	165	2.72	2.65
Wasinger	21	6	30	1	.973	4	14.5	33	2.28	2.44
Williams MD	17	6	24	1	.968	3	11.3	28	2.49	2.72
Woodson	45	36	55	4	.958	4	32.4	72	2.22	2.25

SHORTSTOP—AMERICAN LEAGUE

name	G	PO	A	E	PCT	DP	DEQ	BF	BF/DEQ	ABF/DEQ
League	2563	3650	6645	316	.970	1376	2268.0	7557	3.33	3.33
BAL	164	244	485	20	.973	105	165.8	549	3.31	3.27
BOS	174	220	445	15	.978	94	161.6	496	3.07	3.16
CAL	184	248	430	11	.984	89	163.1	501	3.07	3.11
CHA	173	297	531	20	.976	114	166.8	634	3.80	3.80
CLE	175	261	433	33	.955	83	168.1	496	2.95	2.98
DET	180	242	473	21	.971	106	162.5	543	3.34	3.37
KC	211	228	553	21	.974	93	161.2	582	3.61	3.48
MIL	176	263	435	24	.967	100	165.1	495	3.00	2.96
MIN	195	258	495	21	.973	99	157.9	556	3.52	3.57
NYA	192	244	483	25	.967	94	164.6	563	3.42	3.28
OAK	181	292	465	30	.962	87	160.3	555	3.46	3.52
SEA	175	247	484	31	.959	101	162.9	533	3.27	3.29
TEX	189	290	460	28	.964	106	153.7	511	3.32	3.38
TOR	194	316	473	16	.980	105	154.5	543	3.51	3.47
Guillen	149	266	475	19	.975	105	148.9	567	3.81	3.82
Gagne	136	194	391	18	.970	75	119.6	442	3.70	3.77
Salazar A	116	134	332	9	.981	56	92.4	345	3.73	3.61
Griffin Alf	137	245	386	24	.963	72	131.2	462	3.52	3.59
Fernandez T	146	270	396	14	.979	88	129.0	445	3.45	3.39
Trammell	149	222	421	19	.971	94	145.2	486	3.35	3.39
Fletcher	155	249	413	23	.966	98	137.0	450	3.29	3.35
Tolleson	119	162	321	15	.970	64	107.9	371	3.44	3.31
Ripken	162	240	480	20	.973	103	165.0	545	3.30	3.26
Quinones R	135	204	384	25	.959	76	132.4	424	3.20	3.23
Schofield	131	204	348	9	.984	76	129.6	401	3.09	3.14
Owen S	130	176	336	13	.975	69	126.6	381	3.01	3.12
Sveum	142	221	361	21	.965	82	137.4	420	3.06	3.02
Franco Ju	111	157	285	17	.963	53	109.8	326	2.97	2.96
Bell J	38	67	93	9	.947	22	36.5	104	2.85	3.05
Biancalana	22	12	27	5	.886	4	9.6	31	3.23	2.86
Brookens	16	14	28	2	.955	8	11.3	32	2.82	2.85
Castillo J	13	7	25	0	1.000	4	7.3	23	3.15	2.92
Diaz Mario	10	10	25	1	.972	6	6.9	22	3.20	3.45
Gallego	17	21	25	4	.920	6	9.7	30	3.10	3.09
Gruber	21	20	28	1	.980	7	10.5	38	3.62	3.62
Hoffman	16	14	49	1	.984	9	13.2	57	4.33	4.22
Jones Ro	36	42	109	4	.974	13	34.0	116	3.41	3.32
Lee M	26	26	49	1	.987	10	14.8	60	4.06	4.07
Manrique	23	29	52	1	.988	6	17.3	65	3.76	3.69
Meacham	56	70	127	8	.961	25	45.7	151	3.30	3.14
Newman A	55	62	103	3	.982	24	37.6	112	2.98	2.97
Pecota	36	40	85	3	.977	20	25.0	90	3.59	3.47
Polidor	46	42	77	2	.983	11	32.5	97	2.99	2.95
Ramos D	25	32	70	5	.953	17	22.4	84	3.74	3.67
Riles	21	35	49	3	.966	14	20.4	52	2.55	2.54
Romero E	24	22	44	1	.985	9	15.3	46	3.00	3.04
Snyder C	18	30	37	6	.918	6	15.4	48	3.11	3.11
Weiss	11	8	30	1	.974	4	8.9	35	3.92	3.97
Wilkerson	33	41	47	5	.946	8	16.8	61	3.64	3.63

SHORTSTOP—NATIONAL LEAGUE

name	G	PO	A	E	PCT	DP	DEQ	BF	BF/DEQ	ABF/DEQ
League	2341	3158	5951	333	.965	1156	1942.0	6666	3.43	3.43
ATL	178	256	549	38	.955	115	166.7	591	3.54	3.54
CIN	172	244	481	40	.948	96	164.7	531	3.22	3.15
CHN	197	282	478	24	.969	102	160.5	537	3.35	3.37
HOU	217	221	435	27	.960	59	153.7	496	3.23	3.22
LA	194	266	493	36	.955	87	158.6	552	3.48	3.51
MON	199	233	440	33	.953	88	162.3	499	3.07	3.19
NYN	205	263	506	24	.970	97	160.8	529	3.29	3.32
PHI	219	295	477	22	.972	92	165.1	595	3.60	3.49
PIT	200	280	470	23	.970	95	160.3	535	3.34	3.47
SD	176	286	500	28	.966	85	161.3	592	3.67	3.75
SF	201	275	554	26	.970	122	159.5	593	3.72	3.75
SL	183	257	568	12	.986	118	168.4	616	3.66	3.48
Templeton	146	253	447	20	.972	77	138.7	529	3.82	3.89
Uribe	95	145	286	13	.971	62	85.5	317	3.71	3.71
Thomas A	81	128	276	20	.953	56	81.0	296	3.66	3.64
Jeltz	114	191	271	14	.971	55	95.4	348	3.65	3.56
Smith O	158	245	516	10	.987	111	155.2	565	3.64	3.47
Dunston	94	160	271	14	.969	54	89.9	305	3.39	3.45
Santana	138	213	396	17	.973	82	124.1	414	3.34	3.38
Reynolds C	129	160	290	14	.970	43	101.6	334	3.29	3.27
Larkin	119	168	358	19	.965	72	114.6	381	3.32	3.19
Brooks	109	131	271	20	.953	53	103.8	306	2.95	3.09
Aguayo	78	81	154	7	.971	29	50.8	184	3.62	3.46
Almon	26	17	35	2	.963	6	10.4	33	3.16	3.19
Anderson D	65	91	169	6	.977	29	54.8	187	3.42	3.42
Belliard	71	104	176	6	.979	29	59.4	206	3.47	3.50
Berra	18	13	39	2	.963	4	13.0	45	3.45	3.41
Biancalana	16	8	16	3	.889	2	7.5	17	2.27	2.31
Blauser	50	65	166	9	.963	28	50.2	182	3.63	3.60
Brumley	34	43	93	5	.965	24	29.7	95	3.20	3.16
Candaele	25	28	48	3	.962	10	16.1	59	3.66	3.68
Dowell	15	17	36	0	1.000	7	12.3	45	3.67	3.49
Duncan	67	90	191	21	.930	37	57.9	207	3.57	3.58
Fermin	23	36	62	2	.980	13	19.6	65	3.32	3.48
Foley T	49	64	93	6	.963	21	33.3	105	3.15	3.22
Hoffman	40	70	101	6	.966	19	35.1	120	3.42	3.45
Johnson H	38	36	70	5	.955	12	25.0	74	2.96	2.94
Morrison	17	7	20	2	.931	5	4.8	20	4.19	4.25
Noce	35	43	58	2	.981	15	19.6	74	3.78	3.81
Oquendo	23	11	50	2	.968	7	12.6	49	3.88	3.57
Pedrique	80	117	192	10	.969	43	68.4	223	3.26	3.43
Pena B	19	19	35	1	.982	3	12.9	43	3.33	3.51
Quinones L	28	32	51	3	.965	9	19.4	57	2.93	2.92
Ramirez R	38	59	99	9	.946	30	32.0	102	3.18	3.24
Rivera L	15	9	27	3	.923	4	8.2	28	3.42	3.48
Salazar L	22	27	45	6	.923	7	18.4	51	2.77	2.88
Shipley	18	12	25	2	.949	2	9.3	29	3.12	3.12
Speier	22	16	40	1	.982	8	10.0	44	4.38	4.72
Stillwell	51	74	117	18	.914	22	47.7	146	3.06	3.06
Thon	31	21	53	6	.925	7	17.8	55	3.08	3.11
Williams MD	70	104	210	8	.975	49	59.8	215	3.59	3.65

LEFT FIELD—AMERICAN LEAGUE

name	G	PO	A	E	PCT	DEQ	A/162	BF	BF/DEQ	ABF/DEQ
League	2268	4560	167	124	.974	2268.0	11.9	4564	2.01	2.01
BAL	162	321	6	11	.967	165.8	5.9	323	1.95	1.98
BOS	162	293	22	9	.972	161.6	22.1	295	1.83	1.76
CAL	162	298	5	7	.977	163.1	5.0	298	1.83	1.81
CHA	162	352	16	7	.981	166.8	15.5	352	2.11	2.11
CLE	162	373	6	6	.984	168.1	5.8	374	2.23	2.22
DET	162	350	11	8	.978	162.5	11.0	350	2.15	2.11
KC	162	292	15	16	.950	161.2	15.1	291	1.81	1.85
MIL	162	375	13	8	.980	165.1	12.8	375	2.27	2.32
MIN	162	354	16	4	.989	157.9	16.4	355	2.25	2.21
NYA	162	350	6	6	.983	164.6	5.9	350	2.13	2.18
OAK	162	351	13	9	.976	160.3	13.1	350	2.18	2.13
SEA	162	286	14	5	.984	162.9	13.9	286	1.76	1.74
TEX	162	289	9	16	.949	153.7	9.5	289	1.88	1.86
TOR	162	276	15	12	.960	154.5	15.7	276	1.79	1.80
Hall M	122	263	5	3	.989	113.5	7.1	264	2.33	2.33
Gladden	105	212	9	3	.987	91.6	15.9	212	2.32	2.28
Deer	98	203	6	3	.986	93.2	10.4	203	2.18	2.22
Gibson K	119	250	6	7	.973	114.8	8.5	250	2.18	2.14
Canseco	130	267	12	7	.976	123.6	15.7	266	2.15	2.11
Redus	98	188	11	5	.975	90.8	19.6	188	2.07	2.07
Howell Jk	78	130	2	2	.985	63.1	5.1	130	2.06	2.04
Sheets	72	126	3	4	.970	66.2	7.3	128	1.93	1.94
Incaviglia	132	217	8	13	.945	115.3	11.2	217	1.88	1.87
Bell Geo	149	249	15	11	.960	135.0	18.0	249	1.84	1.86
Jackson B	94	148	8	8	.951	86.6	15.0	148	1.71	1.75
Bradley P	158	276	14	5	.983	157.1	14.4	276	1.76	1.74
Rice	94	155	12	4	.977	92.2	21.1	155	1.68	1.66
Beniquez	20	29	0	0	1.000	16.4	0.0	28	1.70	1.70
Benzinger	14	18	2	0	1.000	7.3	44.6	19	2.61	2.38
Bosley	13	12	0	1	.923	6.2	0.0	12	1.93	1.91
Boston	51	93	2	2	.979	47.1	6.9	93	1.97	2.00
Brower	45	43	1	0	1.000	26.3	6.2	43	1.64	1.63
Brunansky	58	107	5	1	.991	48.9	16.6	108	2.21	2.20
Carter J	42	87	0	3	.967	37.7	0.0	87	2.31	2.29
Cotto	15	16	0	0	1.000	9.5	0.0	16	1.68	1.74
Davidson	36	32	2	0	1.000	15.2	21.3	32	2.11	1.95
Downing	34	49	2	0	1.000	31.3	10.4	49	1.57	1.58
Ducey	18	10	0	0	1.000	6.1	0.0	10	1.64	1.61
Easler	14	23	1	0	1.000	13.0	12.5	23	1.78	1.83
Felder	80	146	7	5	.968	59.1	19.2	146	2.47	2.51
Gerhart	53	73	3	4	.950	42.5	11.4	73	1.72	1.83
Greenwell	64	119	8	4	.969	59.3	21.9	120	2.03	1.92
Grubb	21	34	1	0	1.000	13.3	12.2	34	2.55	2.33
Hairston	13	27	0	0	1.000	8.7	0.0	27	3.09	2.77
Henderson R	34	80	2	2	.976	32.1	10.1	80	2.49	2.53
Hendrick	37	43	0	1	.977	25.3	0.0	43	1.70	1.62
Herndon	32	39	4	1	.977	20.7	31.4	39	1.89	1.89
Jones Ru	53	45	1	3	.939	28.2	5.7	45	1.59	1.53
Leach R	21	16	0	0	1.000	9.9	0.0	16	1.61	1.59
Manning	21	20	0	0	1.000	9.6	0.0	20	2.09	2.18
Miller D	14	16	0	0	1.000	8.4	0.0	16	1.91	1.87
Nixon O	11	6	0	0	1.000	2.3	0.0	6	2.65	2.67
Pasqua	61	112	1	2	.983	51.1	3.2	112	2.19	2.19
Polonia	35	73	1	1	.987	28.4	5.7	73	2.57	2.45
Royster	14	22	1	0	1.000	9.3	17.4	22	2.36	2.34
Smith Lo	32	51	2	5	.914	31.7	10.2	51	1.61	1.62
Snyder C	15	16	1	0	1.000	12.2	13.2	16	1.31	1.31
Thurman	22	51	5	2	.966	20.2	40.1	51	2.53	2.53
Ward G	69	108	1	2	.982	53.1	3.1	108	2.03	2.13
Young Mike	54	109	0	2	.982	51.3	0.0	109	2.12	2.12

LEFT FIELD—NATIONAL LEAGUE

name	G	PO	A	E	PCT	DEQ	A/162	BF	BF/DEQ	ABF/DEQ
League	1942	3805	133	74	.982	1942.0	11.1	3807	1.96	1.96
ATL	161	297	8	3	.990	166.7	7.8	297	1.78	1.79
CHN	161	285	8	2	.993	160.5	8.1	285	1.78	1.76
CIN	162	342	9	10	.972	164.7	8.9	343	2.08	2.16
HOU	162	329	16	5	.986	153.7	16.9	330	2.15	2.15
LA	162	276	9	11	.963	158.6	9.2	276	1.74	1.72
MON	162	346	11	4	.989	162.3	11.0	346	2.13	2.03
NYN	162	322	8	7	.979	160.8	8.1	321	2.00	1.97
PHI	162	336	13	5	.986	165.1	12.8	336	2.04	2.07
PIT	162	358	12	5	.987	160.3	12.1	358	2.23	2.16
SD	162	321	15	7	.980	161.3	15.1	321	1.99	1.94
SF	162	300	9	7	.978	159.5	9.1	301	1.89	1.87
SL	162	293	15	8	.975	168.4	14.4	293	1.74	1.81
Bonds	101	216	10	2	.991	85.7	18.9	216	2.52	2.42
James C	96	169	4	2	.989	77.7	8.3	169	2.18	2.22
Cruz Jo	97	178	6	3	.984	82.6	11.8	179	2.17	2.19
Raines	139	290	10	4	.987	137.2	11.8	290	2.11	2.01
Daniels	94	176	5	6	.968	90.7	8.9	176	1.94	2.00
McReynolds	150	286	8	4	.987	143.5	9.0	285	1.99	1.96
Coleman	150	272	15	8	.973	151.7	16.0	272	1.79	1.86
Mumphrey	78	117	5	1	.992	63.7	12.7	117	1.84	1.84
Griffey	107	183	7	1	.995	102.3	11.1	183	1.79	1.84
Martinez C	78	116	5	4	.968	60.2	13.4	116	1.93	1.83
Leonard J	127	197	8	6	.972	111.5	11.6	198	1.78	1.76
Guerrero	109	166	4	5	.971	96.9	6.7	166	1.71	1.71
Aldrete	43	80	0	1	.988	32.5	0.0	80	2.46	2.43
Bonilla B	17	19	1	0	1.000	9.2	17.6	19	2.06	2.07
Cangelosi	27	44	1	1	.978	20.0	8.1	44	2.20	2.06
Collins	18	29	0	0	1.000	11.9	0.0	29	2.44	2.61
Davis C	18	17	1	0	1.000	7.2	22.6	17	2.37	2.39
Devereaux	11	16	1	0	1.000	9.3	17.5	16	1.73	1.67
Diaz M	28	27	0	2	.931	18.0	0.0	27	1.50	1.45
Dayett	70	64	1	0	1.000	37.1	4.4	64	1.72	1.68
Easler	30	51	4	1	.982	24.5	26.4	51	2.08	2.03
Ford C	15	4	0	0	1.000	7.3	0.0	4	0.55	0.64
Gross G	50	33	1	0	1.000	22.5	7.2	33	1.46	1.47
Gwynn C	10	12	0	0	1.000	7.5	0.0	12	1.59	1.60
Harper T	10	10	0	0	1.000	5.3	0.0	10	1.90	1.62
Hatcher W	51	79	6	0	1.000	40.2	24.2	79	1.96	1.94
Heep	17	14	1	1	.938	9.5	17.1	14	1.48	1.48
Hughes	13	17	0	0	1.000	9.7	0.0	17	1.75	1.79
James D	29	48	1	0	1.000	23.8	6.8	48	2.01	2.08
Jefferson	62	62	2	0	1.000	28.9	11.2	62	2.15	2.12
Jones T	57	99	3	1	.990	44.0	11.0	100	2.27	2.37
Kruk	29	42	3	1	.978	26.4	18.4	42	1.59	1.55
Landreaux	15	9	2	2	.846	5.8	55.7	9	1.55	1.57
Landrum T	21	16	1	1	.944	9.3	17.4	16	1.71	1.69
Martinez Da	14	6	1	0	1.000	2.5	63.6	6	2.36	2.12
Mazzilli	12	12	0	0	1.000	6.0	0.0	12	2.01	1.99
O'Neill	14	30	0	2	.938	12.7	0.0	30	2.36	2.55
Palmeiro	45	67	1	0	1.000	36.0	4.5	67	1.86	1.82
Powell A	10	13	0	0	1.000	9.4	0.0	13	1.39	1.40
Puhl	28	37	0	1	.974	14.7	0.0	37	2.52	2.48
Ready	16	30	1	0	1.000	10.2	15.9	30	2.94	2.92
Reynolds RJ	30	37	0	0	1.000	20.2	0.0	37	1.83	1.84
Roenicke G	40	55	0	2	.965	33.6	0.0	55	1.64	1.53
Roenicke R	10	3	0	0	1.000	1.5	0.0	3	1.94	1.85
Russell Jn	10	22	0	1	.957	9.2	0.0	22	2.39	2.39
Steels	17	14	1	0	1.000	6.6	24.7	14	2.13	2.15
Stone J	21	32	3	0	1.000	16.1	30.2	32	1.99	2.14
Stubbs	13	17	0	0	1.000	9.3	0.0	17	1.83	1.75
Walker C	25	29	0	1	.967	19.9	0.0	29	1.46	1.49
Williams R	16	8	0	1	.889	2.9	0.0	8	2.72	2.45
Wilson M	20	20	0	2	.909	8.8	0.0	20	2.28	2.22
Wynne	34	36	1	1	.974	17.2	9.4	36	2.09	2.07

CENTER FIELD—AMERICAN LEAGUE

name	G	PO	A	E	PCT	DEQ	A/162	BF	BF/DEQ	ABF/DEQ
League	2268	5979	90	89	.986	2268.0	6.4	5978	2.64	2.63
BAL	162	417	2	5	.988	165.8	2.0	417	2.51	2.52
BOS	162	414	15	8	.982	161.6	15.0	414	2.56	2.56
CAL	162	517	5	12	.978	163.1	5.0	517	3.17	3.16
CHA	162	468	7	7	.985	166.8	6.8	468	2.81	2.81
CLE	162	475	5	7	.986	168.1	4.8	474	2.82	2.81
DET	162	453	7	3	.994	162.5	7.0	453	2.79	2.77
KC	162	384	3	1	.997	161.2	3.0	384	2.38	2.40
MIL	162	426	5	5	.989	165.1	4.9	426	2.58	2.57
MIN	162	387	9	5	.988	157.9	9.2	388	2.46	2.45
NYA	162	475	6	8	.984	164.6	5.9	475	2.89	2.90
OAK	162	431	5	8	.982	160.3	5.1	431	2.69	2.70
SEA	162	389	8	4	.990	162.9	8.0	389	2.39	2.38
TEX	162	399	6	10	.976	153.7	6.3	399	2.60	2.60
TOR	162	344	7	6	.983	154.5	7.3	343	2.22	2.22
Pettis	131	344	2	7	.980	108.9	3.0	344	3.16	3.16
Butler	136	391	4	4	.990	138.3	4.7	390	2.82	2.81
Murphy Dw	79	183	1	3	.984	67.2	2.4	183	2.72	2.74
Williams K	111	297	6	6	.981	108.6	8.9	297	2.73	2.73
Washington C	69	165	3	2	.988	61.6	7.9	165	2.68	2.73
Lemon	145	348	4	3	.992	131.4	4.9	348	2.65	2.65
McDowell O	125	263	5	3	.989	102.1	7.9	263	2.58	2.57
Yount	150	377	4	5	.987	146.6	4.4	377	2.57	2.56
Burks	132	320	15	4	.988	125.7	19.3	320	2.55	2.53
Wilson W	143	342	3	1	.997	138.5	3.5	342	2.47	2.49
Puckett	147	343	9	5	.986	139.5	10.5	344	2.47	2.46
Lynn	102	234	2	2	.992	97.6	3.3	234	2.40	2.41
Moses	97	205	5	3	.986	86.6	9.4	205	2.37	2.34
Moseby	153	294	7	6	.980	138.9	8.2	293	2.11	2.11
Barfield	13	31	0	0	1.000	10.1	0.0	31	3.08	3.05
Bean	17	42	1	0	1.000	11.0	14.7	42	3.82	3.51
Boston	46	109	1	0	1.000	40.3	4.0	109	2.71	2.69
Brantley	51	102	2	1	.990	44.1	7.3	102	2.31	2.29
Brower	67	135	1	7	.951	49.9	3.2	135	2.70	2.72
Carter J	13	35	0	2	.946	12.2	0.0	35	2.87	2.87
Cotto	41	74	1	1	.987	26.6	6.1	74	2.79	2.79
Davidson	20	32	0	0	1.000	12.4	0.0	32	2.58	2.55
Ducey	11	18	0	0	1.000	5.3	0.0	18	3.40	3.55
Felder	22	43	1	0	1.000	16.6	9.8	43	2.59	2.59
Gallagher	14	34	1	1	.972	12.0	13.5	34	2.83	2.83
Gerhart	43	97	0	1	.990	35.8	0.0	97	2.71	2.70
Hart	29	70	0	0	1.000	25.2	0.0	70	2.78	2.79
Henderson D	29	70	0	3	.959	28.0	0.0	70	2.50	2.52
Henderson R	39	109	0	2	.982	34.8	0.0	109	3.13	3.08
Jackson B	21	30	0	0	1.000	16.1	0.0	30	1.87	1.86
Javier	52	95	3	1	.990	33.4	14.5	95	2.84	2.79
Kelly R	16	43	0	2	.956	13.4	0.0	43	3.20	3.26
Nixon D	32	75	1	0	1.000	29.8	5.4	75	2.52	2.52
Polonia	69	153	1	4	.975	59.7	2.7	153	2.56	2.58
Redus	19	40	0	1	.976	12.6	0.0	40	3.19	3.22
Sheridan	26	46	2	0	1.000	16.2	20.0	46	2.84	2.84
Ward G	30	81	1	1	.988	26.0	6.2	81	3.11	3.07
White D	66	168	3	5	.972	51.7	9.4	168	3.25	3.23

CENTER FIELD—NATIONAL LEAGUE

name	G	PO	A	E	PCT	DEQ	A/162	BF	BF/DEQ	ABF/DEQ
League	1942	4783	104	78	.984	1942.0	8.7	4786	2.46	2.46
ATL	161	361	6	4	.989	166.7	5.8	362	2.17	2.17
CHN	161	369	11	7	.982	160.5	11.1	369	2.30	2.30
CIN	162	489	10	3	.994	164.7	9.8	490	2.97	2.98
HOU	162	342	14	7	.981	153.7	14.8	342	2.23	2.22
LA	162	363	11	10	.974	158.6	11.2	363	2.29	2.29
MON	162	406	11	8	.981	162.3	11.0	406	2.50	2.50
NYN	162	415	6	8	.981	160.8	6.0	415	2.58	2.58
PHI	162	428	6	4	.991	165.1	5.9	429	2.60	2.61
PIT	162	429	11	6	.987	160.3	11.1	429	2.68	2.67
SD	162	398	3	7	.983	161.3	3.0	398	2.47	2.48
SF	162	376	5	7	.982	159.5	5.1	376	2.36	2.36
SL	162	407	10	7	.983	168.4	9.6	407	2.42	2.43
Davis E	124	378	9	3	.992	123.2	11.8	379	3.08	3.07
Thompson M	146	343	3	4	.989	126.7	3.8	343	2.71	2.70
Van Slyke	114	288	8	2	.993	107.4	12.1	288	2.68	2.65
Dykstra	117	241	4	3	.988	94.1	6.9	241	2.56	2.56
Jefferson	83	167	1	3	.982	69.0	2.3	167	2.42	2.43
Martinez Da	134	276	9	6	.979	115.0	12.7	276	2.40	2.40
Shelby	117	268	7	8	.972	113.6	10.0	268	2.36	2.36
Winningham	131	224	5	6	.974	96.1	8.4	224	2.33	2.34
McGee	152	353	8	7	.981	154.5	8.4	353	2.28	2.31
Hatcher W	94	188	9	4	.980	82.8	17.6	188	2.27	2.26
Davis C	114	204	3	5	.976	93.5	5.2	204	2.18	2.18
James D	99	212	3	1	.995	99.5	4.9	213	2.14	2.14
Aldrete	13	24	1	0	1.000	8.6	18.9	24	2.80	2.77
Bonds	46	117	2	3	.975	41.4	7.8	117	2.83	2.83
Candaele	46	87	2	1	.989	33.8	9.6	87	2.57	2.59
Cangelosi	16	24	1	1	.962	11.2	14.5	24	2.15	2.22
Dernier	72	87	2	1	.989	42.7	7.6	87	2.04	2.04
Garcia L	13	19	0	0	1.000	6.5	0.0	19	2.91	2.69
Hall A	68	149	3	3	.981	67.1	7.2	149	2.22	2.22
Hayes	29	44	1	0	1.000	17.2	9.4	44	2.57	2.87
Jackson C	12	6	0	0	1.000	5.2	0.0	6	1.15	1.07
James C	16	24	1	0	1.000	10.4	15.6	24	2.31	2.32
Jones T	34	65	1	0	1.000	25.7	6.3	65	2.53	2.63
Mack	91	158	1	3	.981	59.1	2.7	158	2.67	2.70
Milner	86	132	0	1	.992	50.1	0.0	132	2.64	2.63
Nichols	51	95	4	1	.990	32.4	20.0	95	2.94	2.88
O'Neill	10	16	0	0	1.000	6.5	0.0	16	2.48	2.50
Ramsey	38	69	2	2	.973	33.0	9.8	69	2.09	2.09
Roenicke R	15	15	1	0	1.000	7.2	22.3	16	2.21	2.21
Wilson M	88	174	2	5	.972	66.4	4.9	174	2.62	2.63
Wynne	40	60	1	1	.984	25.6	6.3	60	2.35	2.33
Young G	67	141	5	3	.980	62.9	12.9	141	2.24	2.24

RIGHT FIELD—AMERICAN LEAGUE

name	G	PO	A	E	PCT	DEQ	A/162	BF	BF/DEQ	ABF/DEQ
League	2268	4594	164	102	.979	2268.0	11.7	4594	2.03	2.03
BAL	162	336	18	5	.986	165.8	17.6	336	2.03	2.01
BOS	162	335	9	4	.989	161.6	9.0	334	2.07	2.12
CAL	162	364	16	5	.987	163.1	15.9	364	2.23	2.26
CHA	162	347	8	5	.986	166.8	7.8	347	2.08	2.08
CLE	162	345	21	9	.976	168.1	20.2	345	2.05	2.07
DET	162	317	5	8	.976	162.5	5.0	317	1.95	1.98
KC	162	251	8	7	.974	161.2	8.0	251	1.56	1.53
MIL	162	410	11	16	.963	165.1	10.8	410	2.48	2.43
MIN	162	316	6	4	.988	157.9	6.2	316	2.00	2.03
NYA	162	287	7	3	.990	164.6	6.9	287	1.74	1.69
OAK	162	289	3	15	.951	160.3	3.0	289	1.80	1.87
SEA	162	353	18	5	.987	162.9	17.9	354	2.17	2.19
TEX	162	289	18	11	.965	153.7	19.0	289	1.88	1.89
TOR	162	355	16	5	.987	154.5	16.8	355	2.30	2.27
Braggs	123	301	6	9	.972	117.6	8.3	301	2.56	2.50
White D	120	237	13	4	.984	101.1	20.8	237	2.34	2.38
Barfield	152	313	15	3	.991	132.2	18.4	313	2.37	2.34
Kingery	111	221	15	2	.992	95.9	25.3	222	2.31	2.32
Calderon	134	288	7	5	.983	136.7	8.3	288	2.11	2.11
Snyder C	134	267	16	9	.969	127.2	20.4	267	2.10	2.11
Sheridan	124	189	4	6	.970	94.4	6.9	189	2.00	2.04
Brunansky	107	164	5	2	.988	82.0	9.9	164	2.00	2.03
Davis Mike	124	210	3	13	.942	107.0	4.5	210	1.96	2.02
Lacy L	79	128	11	3	.979	64.9	27.5	128	1.97	1.97
Evans Dw	77	135	4	1	.993	70.6	9.2	135	1.91	1.95
Sierra	156	270	17	11	.963	145.3	19.0	270	1.86	1.87
Winfield	145	253	6	3	.989	144.5	6.7	253	1.75	1.69
Tartabull	150	227	8	6	.975	147.1	8.8	227	1.54	1.51
Armas	26	37	0	0	1.000	20.4	0.0	37	1.81	1.86
Benzinger	47	113	3	1	.991	46.5	10.4	112	2.41	2.56
Bosley	14	15	0	0	1.000	7.8	0.0	15	1.92	1.96
Brantley	35	49	1	2	.962	28.9	5.6	49	1.69	1.80
Bush	72	105	1	2	.981	54.0	3.0	105	1.94	1.99
Carter J	14	17	1	0	1.000	11.3	14.3	17	1.50	1.50
Castillo C	22	32	3	0	1.000	16.0	30.3	32	1.99	2.09
Christensen	41	61	1	0	1.000	29.5	5.5	61	2.07	2.02
Clark D	12	24	1	0	1.000	10.4	15.6	24	2.32	2.45
Davidson	33	38	0	0	1.000	17.7	0.0	38	2.14	2.14
Deer	29	53	4	4	.934	23.9	27.1	53	2.22	2.22
Dwyer	29	55	0	0	1.000	26.6	0.0	55	2.07	2.08
Greenwell	28	42	1	1	.977	23.1	7.0	42	1.82	1.76
Grubb	10	10	0	0	1.000	6.0	0.0	10	1.66	1.61
Harper T	13	19	0	1	.950	8.9	0.0	19	2.15	2.05
Heath	20	19	1	0	1.000	12.3	13.2	19	1.54	1.49
Henderson D	30	43	0	1	.977	18.4	0.0	43	2.33	2.33
Henderson S	28	29	0	2	.935	20.7	0.0	29	1.40	1.46
Hendrick	10	15	1	1	.941	7.7	21.0	15	1.95	1.88
Herndon	26	41	0	0	1.000	17.6	0.0	41	2.33	2.28
Howell Jk	15	19	2	0	1.000	10.3	31.5	19	1.85	1.88
Jackson Re	20	29	0	0	1.000	19.1	0.0	29	1.52	1.65
Javier	15	10	0	0	1.000	5.5	0.0	10	1.80	1.87
Jones Ru	23	32	0	0	1.000	12.0	0.0	32	2.67	2.56
Leach R	22	33	1	1	.971	16.6	9.8	33	1.99	1.87
Lusader	16	20	0	1	.952	11.5	0.0	20	1.74	1.84
Manning	52	44	1	3	.938	20.0	8.1	44	2.20	2.11
Pasqua	14	21	1	0	1.000	10.8	15.0	21	1.94	1.88
Redus	20	35	1	0	1.000	18.1	9.0	35	1.94	1.96
Ryal	15	19	0	0	1.000	8.6	0.0	19	2.21	2.10
Sheets	58	105	4	2	.982	54.0	12.0	105	1.94	1.94
Shelby	15	24	1	0	1.000	8.8	18.5	24	2.73	2.53
Simmons N	13	24	2	0	1.000	11.3	28.6	24	2.12	1.88

RIGHT FIELD—NATIONAL LEAGUE

name	G	PO	A	E	PCT	DEQ	A/162	BF	BF/DEQ	ABF/DEQ
League	1942	3710	142	96	.976	1942.0	11.8	3716	1.91	1.91
ATL	161	332	14	8	.977	166.7	13.6	334	2.00	2.00
CHN	161	285	11	4	.987	160.5	11.1	286	1.78	1.79
CIN	162	332	14	13	.964	164.7	13.8	332	2.02	1.94
HOU	162	305	11	4	.988	153.7	11.6	305	1.98	1.98
LA	162	267	9	6	.979	158.6	9.2	267	1.68	1.70
MON	162	300	9	7	.978	162.3	9.0	301	1.85	1.94
NYN	162	299	7	9	.971	160.8	7.1	299	1.86	1.88
PHI	162	343	19	13	.965	165.1	18.6	344	2.08	2.00
PIT	162	253	12	7	.974	160.3	12.1	253	1.58	1.64
SD	162	315	13	8	.976	161.3	13.1	316	1.96	1.98
SF	162	280	12	7	.977	159.5	12.2	280	1.76	1.77
SL	162	399	11	10	.976	168.4	10.6	399	2.37	2.29
Gwynn	156	300	13	6	.981	149.6	14.1	301	2.01	2.04
Wilson G	154	315	18	11	.968	150.4	19.4	316	2.10	2.01
Murphy Da	159	327	14	8	.977	164.2	13.8	329	2.00	2.00
Bass K	155	284	11	4	.987	144.0	12.4	284	1.97	1.97
Parker	142	275	12	10	.966	136.7	14.2	275	2.01	1.96
Webster	153	268	8	6	.979	146.7	8.8	269	1.83	1.92
Strawberry	152	271	5	8	.972	143.4	5.6	271	1.89	1.90
Dawson	152	269	10	4	.986	146.5	11.1	270	1.84	1.86
Maldonado	115	176	8	4	.979	105.7	12.3	176	1.66	1.69
Reynolds RJ	73	97	7	1	.990	61.2	18.5	97	1.59	1.65
Marshall	102	146	5	2	.987	96.1	8.4	146	1.52	1.54
Aldrete	31	45	2	1	.979	23.0	14.1	45	1.96	1.92
Bonilla B	35	49	0	3	.942	25.3	0.0	49	1.93	1.98
Bryant	12	12	0	1	.923	6.2	0.0	12	1.92	2.08
Candaele	16	30	1	1	.969	13.1	12.4	30	2.30	2.36
Coles	26	27	1	0	1.000	22.4	7.2	27	1.21	1.33
Davis C	36	35	1	2	.947	21.5	7.5	35	1.63	1.62
Dayett	12	8	1	0	1.000	4.6	35.0	8	1.73	1.76
Diaz M	10	18	2	0	1.000	8.5	38.3	18	2.13	2.22
Ford C	61	146	2	3	.980	49.9	6.5	146	2.93	2.78
Harper T	11	13	0	0	1.000	7.8	0.0	13	1.67	1.71
Johnson L	17	18	0	2	.900	10.7	0.0	18	1.69	1.56
Jones T	17	28	0	1	.966	12.3	0.0	28	2.28	2.12
Landreaux	45	57	2	2	.967	29.5	11.0	57	1.93	1.92
Landrum T	31	39	1	0	1.000	12.8	12.6	39	3.04	3.03
Lindeman	48	78	4	2	.976	40.6	16.0	78	1.92	1.89
Mazzilli	13	13	1	0	1.000	7.5	21.5	13	1.73	1.86
Morris Jo	68	74	0	1	.987	32.0	0.0	74	2.31	2.24
O'Neill	22	27	2	2	.935	13.1	24.7	27	2.06	1.65
Oquendo	39	43	3	0	1.000	19.6	24.8	43	2.19	2.17
Van Slyke	36	44	2	2	.958	30.6	10.6	44	1.44	1.43
Wilson M	14	13	1	1	.933	8.8	18.4	13	1.48	1.56
Youngblood	14	19	1	0	1.000	7.3	22.1	19	2.60	2.59

STOLEN BASE TABLES

The stolen base numbers here are based on success rate versus base-stealing opportunities instead of the more traditional rate versus attempts. This is to show the effect that a catcher has by preventing base stealing attempts as well as by throwing runners out.

An opportunity is defined as a plate appearance that happens when first base is occupied and second is not. For example, if Coleman walks, stays put while Smith pops out, and steals during Herr's at-bat, then he is charged with 2 opportunities: one each for being on first during Smith's and Herr's plate appearances.

The stolen base, caught stealing, and picked off categories count the events that happen to the runner on first during base-stealing opportunity situations. "Attempts" are stolen bases plus caught stealings. The percentages show the rate of each event per 100 opportunities.

As an example, let's compare Mike Scioscia and Mike LaValliere, who were both excellent at stopping the running game in 1987:

catcher	ops	attempts		stolen		caught		picked off	
Scioscia	1180	116	9.83%	75	6.36%	41	3.47%	5	0.42%
Lavalliere	871	106	12.17%	57	6.54%	49	5.63%	3	0.34%

The Scioscia numbers mean that he was behind the plate during 1,180 plate appearances in which a steal of second was possible. In 75 of those, or 6.36 percent, the runner did steal second. LaValliere did almost as well, limiting his opponents to a 6.54 percent success rate. The league average success rate was 8.97 percent.

They achieve these numbers in different ways. Runners only attempted to steal second 9.83 percent of the time against Scioscia, versus the league average of 12.37 percent, which indicates the respect base runners have for him and the Dodger pitching staff. LaValliere is a relative newcomer to the league, and runners take off for second against him at about the league rate. LaValliere keeps the success rate low by throwing out almost half the guys that try. Expect the attempt rate to go down for LaValliere as the news gets around.

These numbers are presented for all teams, both offensively (how their own baserunners fared) and defensively (how their opponents' baserunners fared), and for individual pitchers (minimum 15 games or 40 innings pitched) and baserunners (minimum 10 stolen base attempts) as well as for all catchers (minimum 10 stolen base opportunities). For the pitchers and runners, the individual success rates vary even more than they do for catchers. In eash case, exactly the same things are being counted; in all cases, the league averages and totals are also given.

Gary Gillette and Dave Nichols

catcher	ops	attempts		stolen		caught		picked off	
Karkovice	289	13	4.50%	5	1.73%	8	2.77%	0	0.00%
Kearney	114	8	7.02%	3	2.63%	5	4.39%	3	2.63%
Gedman	441	28	6.35%	16	3.63%	12	2.72%	1	0.23%
Boone	1071	72	6.72%	39	3.64%	33	3.08%	2	0.19%
DeWillis	81	8	9.88%	3	3.70%	5	6.17%	1	1.23%
Miller D	176	18	10.23%	8	4.55%	10	5.68%	0	0.00%
Allanson	475	31	6.53%	23	4.84%	8	1.68%	1	0.21%
Valle	654	50	7.65%	32	4.89%	18	2.75%	1	0.15%
Mercado	75	5	6.67%	4	5.33%	1	1.33%	0	0.00%
O'Brien C	91	13	14.29%	5	5.49%	8	8.79%	0	0.00%
Sheaffer	199	17	8.54%	11	5.53%	6	3.02%	2	1.01%
Heath	550	49	8.91%	31	5.64%	18	3.27%	2	0.36%
Marzano	467	38	8.14%	27	5.78%	11	2.36%	0	0.00%
Owen L	577	60	10.40%	34	5.89%	26	4.51%	4	0.69%
Surhoff BJ	938	87	9.28%	57	6.08%	30	3.20%	2	0.21%
Cerone	831	80	9.63%	51	6.14%	29	3.49%	5	0.60%
Sullivan M	504	48	9.52%	31	6.15%	17	3.37%	2	0.40%
Dempsey	465	46	9.89%	29	6.24%	17	3.66%	0	0.00%
Fisk	959	89	9.28%	60	6.26%	29	3.02%	3	0.31%
Skinner J	431	43	9.98%	27	6.26%	16	3.71%	0	0.00%
Steinbach	909	96	10.56%	60	6.60%	36	3.96%	1	0.11%
Nokes	889	75	8.44%	59	6.64%	16	1.80%	4	0.45%
Bando	659	61	9.26%	44	6.68%	17	2.58%	0	0.00%
Whitt	992	107	10.79%	69	6.96%	38	3.83%	4	0.40%
Schroeder	584	52	8.90%	41	7.02%	11	1.88%	1	0.17%
Wynegar	226	25	11.06%	16	7.08%	9	3.98%	1	0.44%
Bradley S	730	73	10.00%	55	7.53%	18	2.47%	4	0.55%
Tettleton	628	61	9.71%	48	7.64%	13	2.07%	3	0.48%
Hassey	216	21	9.72%	17	7.87%	4	1.85%	2	0.93%
Fimple	38	4	10.53%	3	7.89%	1	2.63%	0	0.00%
Quirk	796	92	11.56%	64	8.04%	28	3.52%	5	0.63%
Nichols C	73	8	10.96%	6	8.22%	2	2.74%	0	0.00%
Kennedy	1238	144	11.63%	102	8.24%	42	3.39%	3	0.24%
Moore C	301	31	10.30%	26	8.64%	5	1.66%	2	0.66%
Laudner	724	79	10.91%	63	8.70%	16	2.21%	3	0.41%
Butera	410	51	12.44%	38	9.27%	13	3.17%	0	0.00%
Slaught	634	79	12.46%	59	9.31%	20	3.15%	2	0.32%
Salas	388	47	12.11%	37	9.54%	10	2.58%	3	0.77%
Lowry	60	7	11.67%	6	10.00%	1	1.67%	0	0.00%
Petralli	476	69	14.50%	50	10.50%	19	3.99%	4	0.84%
Nieto	309	41	13.27%	36	11.65%	5	1.62%	0	0.00%
Rayford	135	20	14.81%	16	11.85%	4	2.96%	0	0.00%
Stanley M	537	76	14.15%	68	12.66%	8	1.49%	4	0.74%
Van Gorder	58	10	17.24%	10	17.24%	0	0.00%	0	0.00%
total	21731	2168	9.98%	1516	6.98%	652	3.00%	78	0.36%

catcher	ops	attempts		stolen		caught		picked off	
Pagnozzi	87	7	8.05%	3	3.45%	4	4.60%	1	1.15%
Parent	61	3	4.92%	3	4.92%	0	0.00%	0	0.00%
Lake	461	42	9.11%	25	5.42%	17	3.69%	2	0.43%
McClendon	70	5	7.14%	4	5.71%	1	1.43%	0	0.00%
Trevino	304	29	9.54%	19	6.25%	10	3.29%	2	0.66%
Scioscia	1180	116	9.83%	75	6.36%	41	3.47%	5	0.42%
Lavalliere	871	106	12.17%	57	6.54%	49	5.63%	3	0.34%
Melvin	626	73	11.66%	43	6.87%	30	4.79%	4	0.64%
Pena T	941	89	9.46%	68	7.23%	21	2.23%	7	0.74%
Santiago	1266	133	10.51%	92	7.27%	41	3.24%	6	0.47%
Brenly	883	112	12.68%	69	7.81%	43	4.87%	1	0.11%
Diaz B	1163	136	11.69%	95	8.17%	41	3.53%	10	0.86%
Sundberg	418	51	12.20%	36	8.61%	15	3.59%	2	0.48%
Stefero	127	13	10.24%	11	8.66%	2	1.57%	0	0.00%
Carter G	1202	147	12.23%	108	8.99%	39	3.24%	5	0.42%
Davis Jody	1113	149	13.39%	102	9.16%	47	4.22%	7	0.63%
McGriff T	210	30	14.29%	20	9.52%	10	4.76%	0	0.00%
Parrish Ln	1185	159	13.42%	115	9.70%	44	3.71%	5	0.42%
Afenir	50	6	12.00%	5	10.00%	1	2.00%	0	0.00%
Simmons T	120	17	14.17%	12	10.00%	5	4.17%	0	0.00%
Lyons Barry	338	43	12.72%	34	10.06%	9	2.66%	2	0.59%
Daulton	316	37	11.71%	32	10.13%	5	1.58%	1	0.32%
Ortiz	459	67	14.60%	48	10.46%	19	4.14%	3	0.65%
Virgil	1136	151	13.29%	119	10.48%	32	2.82%	2	0.18%
Bailey	160	24	15.00%	17	10.62%	7	4.37%	0	0.00%
Benedict	292	40	13.70%	32	10.96%	8	2.74%	0	0.00%
Reynolds Rn	287	40	13.94%	32	11.15%	8	2.79%	1	0.35%
Reed J	548	80	14.60%	63	11.50%	17	3.10%	7	1.28%
Bochy	165	20	12.12%	19	11.52%	1	0.61%	2	1.21%
Berryhill	78	10	12.82%	9	11.54%	1	1.28%	0	0.00%
Ashby	846	132	15.60%	112	13.24%	20	2.36%	1	0.12%
Fitzgerald	719	119	16.55%	100	13.91%	19	2.64%	3	0.42%
Wine	71	12	16.90%	11	15.49%	1	1.41%	0	0.00%
total	18007	2228	12.37%	1615	8.97%	613	3.40%	83	0.46%

pitcher	ops	attempts		stolen		caught		picked off	
Snell	47	0	0.00%	0	0.00%	0	0.00%	0	0.00%
Gardner	96	0	0.00%	0	0.00%	0	0.00%	0	0.00%
Lavelle	44	0	0.00%	0	0.00%	0	0.00%	0	0.00%
Sambito	41	1	2.44%	0	0.00%	1	2.44%	0	0.00%
Powell D	40	1	2.50%	0	0.00%	1	2.50%	0	0.00%
Mirabella	38	1	2.63%	0	0.00%	1	2.63%	0	0.00%
Tewksbury	36	1	2.78%	0	0.00%	1	2.78%	0	0.00%
Rodriguez R	41	4	9.76%	0	0.00%	4	9.76%	0	0.00%
Righetti	132	3	2.27%	1	0.76%	2	1.52%	0	0.00%
Dotson	241	10	4.15%	2	0.83%	8	3.32%	0	0.00%
Finley	107	8	7.48%	1	0.93%	7	6.54%	0	0.00%
McCaskill	92	6	6.52%	1	1.09%	5	5.43%	1	1.09%
Crawford	81	2	2.47%	1	1.23%	1	1.23%	1	1.23%
Schatzeder	66	1	1.52%	1	1.52%	0	0.00%	0	0.00%
Leiper	65	4	6.15%	1	1.54%	3	4.62%	0	0.00%
Searage	60	3	5.00%	1	1.67%	2	3.33%	1	1.67%
Davis Joel	58	3	5.17%	1	1.72%	2	3.45%	0	0.00%
Henneman	114	5	4.39%	2	1.75%	3	2.63%	1	0.88%
Hernandez G	55	2	3.64%	1	1.82%	1	1.82%	0	0.00%
Key	212	10	4.72%	4	1.89%	6	2.83%	5	2.36%
Witt M	263	10	3.80%	5	1.90%	5	1.90%	1	0.38%
Shirley	51	1	1.96%	1	1.96%	0	0.00%	0	0.00%
Rasmussen D	153	13	8.50%	3	1.96%	10	6.54%	1	0.65%
Bailes	152	5	3.29%	3	1.97%	2	1.32%	0	0.00%
Kilgus	99	7	7.07%	2	2.02%	5	5.05%	0	0.00%
Allen N	97	7	7.22%	2	2.06%	5	5.15%	0	0.00%
Wells	48	5	10.42%	1	2.08%	4	8.33%	1	2.08%
Vande Berg	96	5	5.21%	2	2.08%	3	3.13%	0	0.00%
Nunez	47	2	4.26%	1	2.13%	1	2.13%	0	0.00%
Reuss	91	5	5.49%	2	2.20%	3	3.30%	0	0.00%
Plesac	90	3	3.33%	2	2.22%	1	1.11%	0	0.00%
Clements P	89	2	2.25%	2	2.25%	0	0.00%	0	0.00%
Viola	244	11	4.51%	6	2.46%	5	2.05%	2	0.82%
Minton	81	2	2.47%	2	2.47%	0	0.00%	0	0.00%
Moore M	241	11	4.56%	6	2.49%	5	2.07%	3	1.24%
Jones D	117	3	2.56%	3	2.56%	0	0.00%	0	0.00%
Yett	114	7	6.14%	3	2.63%	4	3.51%	0	0.00%
Candelaria	114	9	7.89%	3	2.63%	6	5.26%	0	0.00%
Terrell	264	12	4.55%	7	2.65%	5	1.89%	0	0.00%
Farrell	73	5	6.85%	2	2.74%	3	4.11%	0	0.00%
Thigpen	104	6	5.77%	3	2.88%	3	2.88%	1	0.96%
Cerutti	135	8	5.93%	4	2.96%	4	2.96%	0	0.00%
Knudson	99	4	4.04%	3	3.03%	1	1.01%	0	0.00%
Thurmond	98	4	4.08%	3	3.06%	1	1.02%	0	0.00%
Kinnunen	32	3	9.38%	1	3.13%	2	6.25%	0	0.00%
Hurst	255	14	5.49%	8	3.14%	6	2.35%	2	0.78%
Griffin M	94	5	5.32%	3	3.19%	2	2.13%	0	0.00%
Stanley	180	11	6.11%	6	3.33%	5	2.78%	0	0.00%
Aldrich	59	5	8.47%	2	3.39%	3	5.08%	0	0.00%
Honeycutt	29	1	3.45%	1	3.45%	0	0.00%	0	0.00%
Bolton	86	6	6.98%	3	3.49%	3	3.49%	0	0.00%
Gleaton	56	6	10.71%	2	3.57%	4	7.14%	1	1.79%
Young C	191	16	8.38%	7	3.66%	9	4.71%	1	0.52%
Bannister F	203	11	5.42%	8	3.94%	3	1.48%	0	0.00%
Williams Mitch	127	13	10.24%	5	3.94%	8	6.30%	3	2.36%
Wilkinson	75	4	5.33%	3	4.00%	1	1.33%	0	0.00%
Haas	49	5	10.20%	2	4.08%	3	6.12%	0	0.00%
McGregor	121	14	11.57%	5	4.13%	9	7.44%	0	0.00%
Gordon D	48	4	8.33%	2	4.17%	2	4.17%	1	2.08%
Nelson G	117	8	6.84%	5	4.27%	3	2.56%	0	0.00%
Trujillo	69	8	11.59%	3	4.35%	5	7.25%	0	0.00%
Saberhagen	230	18	7.83%	10	4.35%	8	3.48%	1	0.43%
Hudson	157	14	8.92%	7	4.46%	7	4.46%	0	0.00%
Mohorcic	111	7	6.31%	5	4.50%	2	1.80%	0	0.00%
Musselman J	109	7	6.42%	5	4.59%	2	1.83%	0	0.00%
Flanagan	148	9	6.08%	7	4.73%	2	1.35%	0	0.00%
Sellers	168	15	8.93%	8	4.76%	7	4.17%	1	0.60%
Swindell	104	13	12.50%	5	4.81%	8	7.69%	0	0.00%
Howe S	41	4	9.76%	2	4.88%	2	4.88%	0	0.00%
Carlton	174	13	7.47%	9	5.17%	4	2.30%	0	0.00%
Rijo	114	8	7.02%	6	5.26%	2	1.75%	1	0.88%
Stieb	190	23	12.11%	10	5.26%	13	6.84%	0	0.00%
Clarke	19	2	10.53%	1	5.26%	1	5.26%	0	0.00%
Lucas	75	4	5.33%	4	5.33%	0	0.00%	0	0.00%
LaPoint	90	9	10.00%	5	5.56%	4	4.44%	1	1.11%
Crim	143	12	8.39%	8	5.59%	4	2.80%	0	0.00%
Higuera	267	23	8.61%	15	5.62%	8	3.00%	0	0.00%
Lazorko	106	12	11.32%	6	5.66%	6	5.66%	1	0.94%
Leibrandt	226	19	8.41%	13	5.75%	6	2.65%	1	0.44%
Barker	52	6	11.54%	3	5.77%	3	5.77%	0	0.00%
Bankhead	137	11	8.03%	8	5.84%	3	2.19%	1	0.73%
Black	136	10	7.35%	8	5.88%	2	1.47%	3	2.21%
Long B	136	11	8.09%	8	5.88%	3	2.21%	1	0.74%
Morgan M	229	26	11.35%	14	6.11%	12	5.24%	1	0.44%
Sutton	176	20	11.36%	11	6.25%	9	5.11%	0	0.00%
Alexander	79	8	10.13%	5	6.33%	3	3.80%	0	0.00%
Bell E	154	16	10.39%	10	6.49%	6	3.90%	0	0.00%
John	184	16	8.70%	12	6.52%	4	2.17%	0	0.00%
Jackson D	242	24	9.92%	16	6.61%	8	3.31%	3	1.24%
Andujar	60	5	8.33%	4	6.67%	1	1.67%	1	1.67%
Quisenberry	60	6	10.00%	4	6.67%	2	3.33%	0	0.00%
Langston	313	28	8.95%	21	6.71%	7	2.24%	3	0.96%
Winn	119	11	9.24%	8	6.72%	3	2.52%	0	0.00%
Tanana	207	19	9.18%	14	6.76%	5	2.42%	0	0.00%
Howell J	59	6	10.17%	4	6.78%	2	3.39%	0	0.00%
Robinson JM	131	13	9.92%	9	6.87%	4	3.05%	0	0.00%

pitcher	ops	attempts		stolen		caught		picked off	
Arnold	58	5	8.62%	4	6.90%	1	1.72%	0	0.00%
Stoddard B	58	6	10.34%	4	6.90%	2	3.45%	0	0.00%
Buice	101	11	10.89%	7	6.93%	4	3.96%	0	0.00%
Stewart S	43	3	6.98%	3	6.98%	0	0.00%	0	0.00%
Nieves	225	25	11.11%	16	7.11%	9	4.00%	0	0.00%
Harris	182	17	9.34%	13	7.14%	4	2.20%	0	0.00%
Schrom	153	17	11.11%	11	7.19%	6	3.92%	0	0.00%
King E	138	13	9.42%	10	7.25%	3	2.17%	3	2.17%
O'Connor	54	4	7.41%	4	7.41%	0	0.00%	0	0.00%
Fraser	182	18	9.89%	14	7.69%	4	2.20%	0	0.00%
Atherton	103	9	8.74%	8	7.77%	1	0.97%	0	0.00%
Ontiveros	150	15	10.00%	12	8.00%	3	2.00%	1	0.67%
Rhoden	174	25	14.37%	14	8.05%	11	6.32%	2	1.15%
Ballard	87	13	14.94%	7	8.05%	6	6.90%	0	0.00%
Guetterman	111	11	9.91%	9	8.11%	2	1.80%	0	0.00%
Huismann	49	5	10.20%	4	8.16%	1	2.04%	0	0.00%
Schiraldi	122	14	11.48%	10	8.20%	4	3.28%	1	0.82%
Wegman	216	25	11.57%	18	8.33%	7	3.24%	3	1.39%
Niekro P	144	17	11.81%	12	8.33%	5	3.47%	0	0.00%
Johnson Joe	59	8	13.56%	5	8.47%	3	5.08%	0	0.00%
Lamp	69	8	11.59%	6	8.70%	2	2.90%	0	0.00%
Clear	92	11	11.96%	8	8.70%	3	3.26%	0	0.00%
Clemens	286	38	13.29%	25	8.74%	13	4.55%	0	0.00%
Berenguer	100	12	12.00%	9	9.00%	3	3.00%	0	0.00%
Gubicza	250	36	14.40%	23	9.20%	13	5.20%	1	0.40%
Plunk	129	16	12.40%	12	9.30%	4	3.10%	0	0.00%
Nunez J	117	15	12.82%	11	9.40%	4	3.42%	0	0.00%
Eckersley	95	10	10.53%	9	9.47%	1	1.05%	0	0.00%
Dixon	94	10	10.64%	9	9.57%	1	1.06%	0	0.00%
Clancy	248	32	12.90%	24	9.68%	8	3.23%	0	0.00%
Farr	121	19	15.70%	12	9.92%	7	5.79%	0	0.00%
Camacho	20	2	10.00%	2	10.00%	0	0.00%	0	0.00%
Hough	285	40	14.04%	29	10.18%	11	3.86%	5	1.75%
Candiotti	215	27	12.56%	22	10.23%	5	2.33%	0	0.00%
Petry	175	22	12.57%	18	10.29%	4	2.29%	1	0.57%
Henke	77	10	12.99%	8	10.39%	2	2.60%	1	1.30%
Reardon	77	8	10.39%	8	10.39%	0	0.00%	0	0.00%
Williamson	125	19	15.20%	13	10.40%	6	4.80%	1	0.80%
Akerfelds	96	11	11.46%	10	10.42%	1	1.04%	0	0.00%
Bosio	163	19	11.66%	17	10.43%	2	1.23%	0	0.00%
Bordi	38	6	15.79%	4	10.53%	2	5.26%	0	0.00%
Guante	56	9	16.07%	6	10.71%	3	5.36%	0	0.00%
Niedenfuer	56	8	14.29%	6	10.71%	2	3.57%	0	0.00%
Stoddard T	102	14	13.73%	11	10.78%	3	2.94%	0	0.00%
Gullickson	37	5	13.51%	4	10.81%	1	2.70%	1	2.70%
Nipper	175	23	13.14%	19	10.86%	4	2.29%	0	0.00%
Cook M	36	6	16.67%	4	11.11%	2	5.56%	0	0.00%
Easterly	36	4	11.11%	4	11.11%	0	0.00%	0	0.00%
Russell Jf	116	16	13.79%	13	11.21%	3	2.59%	0	0.00%
Guidry	105	14	13.33%	12	11.43%	2	1.90%	0	0.00%
Mason	43	6	13.95%	5	11.63%	1	2.33%	0	0.00%
Blyleven	274	39	14.23%	32	11.68%	7	2.55%	1	0.36%
Shields	34	4	11.76%	4	11.76%	0	0.00%	0	0.00%
Loynd	93	13	13.98%	11	11.83%	2	2.15%	0	0.00%
Campbell M	50	8	16.00%	6	12.00%	2	4.00%	0	0.00%
Morris	249	37	14.86%	30	12.05%	7	2.81%	1	0.40%
Straker	166	29	17.47%	20	12.05%	9	5.42%	0	0.00%
Nielsen	74	10	13.51%	9	12.16%	1	1.35%	0	0.00%
Stewart D	251	39	15.54%	31	12.35%	8	3.19%	0	0.00%
Frazier	104	18	17.31%	13	12.50%	5	4.81%	0	0.00%
Birkbeck	48	10	20.83%	6	12.50%	4	8.33%	0	0.00%
Reed Jry	87	12	13.79%	11	12.64%	1	1.15%	0	0.00%
DeLeon J	213	34	15.96%	27	12.68%	7	3.29%	0	0.00%
Trout	68	10	14.71%	9	13.24%	1	1.47%	0	0.00%
Schmidt D	120	19	15.83%	16	13.33%	3	2.50%	0	0.00%
Boddicker	222	33	14.86%	30	13.51%	3	1.35%	1	0.45%
Habyan	94	16	17.02%	13	13.83%	3	3.19%	1	1.06%
Davis John	43	8	18.60%	6	13.95%	2	4.65%	0	0.00%
Davis Storm	35	7	20.00%	5	14.29%	2	5.71%	0	0.00%
James B	41	8	19.51%	6	14.63%	2	4.88%	0	0.00%
Guzman	208	35	16.83%	32	15.38%	3	1.44%	0	0.00%
Niekro J	155	30	19.35%	26	16.77%	4	2.58%	1	0.65%
Smithson	122	21	17.21%	21	17.21%	0	0.00%	0	0.00%
Garber	11	3	27.27%	2	18.18%	1	9.09%	0	0.00%
Portugal	60	12	20.00%	11	18.33%	1	1.67%	2	3.33%
Correa	82	19	23.17%	16	19.51%	3	3.66%	0	0.00%
Witt B	195	41	21.03%	39	20.00%	2	1.03%	1	0.51%
Eichhorn	119	30	25.21%	27	22.69%	3	2.52%	0	0.00%
total	21731	2168	9.98%	1516	6.98%	652	3.00%	78	0.36%

Pitcher	ops	attempts		stolen		caught		picked off	
Crews	29	0	0.00%	0	0.00%	0	0.00%	1	3.45%
Reuss	46	0	0.00%	0	0.00%	0	0.00%	0	0.00%
Minton	25	1	4.00%	0	0.00%	1	4.00%	0	0.00%
Hesketh	24	0	0.00%	0	0.00%	0	0.00%	0	0.00%
LaPoint	23	0	0.00%	0	0.00%	0	0.00%	0	0.00%
Candelaria	14	1	7.14%	0	0.00%	1	7.14%	0	0.00%
Horton	118	4	3.39%	2	1.69%	2	1.69%	5	4.24%
Davis R	49	4	8.16%	1	2.04%	3	6.12%	0	0.00%
McClure	49	3	6.12%	1	2.04%	2	4.08%	0	0.00%
Patterson B	47	3	6.38%	1	2.13%	2	4.26%	0	0.00%
Reuschel	216	14	6.48%	5	2.31%	9	4.17%	1	0.46%
Price	43	2	4.65%	1	2.33%	1	2.33%	0	0.00%
Calhoun	39	1	2.56%	1	2.56%	0	0.00%	0	0.00%
McDowell R	109	4	3.67%	3	2.75%	1	0.92%	0	0.00%
Lynch	130	10	7.69%	4	3.08%	6	4.62%	0	0.00%
Havens	30	1	3.33%	1	3.33%	0	0.00%	0	0.00%
Grant	178	12	6.74%	6	3.37%	6	3.37%	2	1.12%
Hershiser	257	18	7.00%	9	3.50%	9	3.50%	1	0.39%
Olwine	28	1	3.57%	1	3.57%	0	0.00%	0	0.00%
Franco Jn	81	4	4.94%	3	3.70%	1	1.23%	0	0.00%
Hawkins	130	11	8.46%	5	3.85%	6	4.62%	2	1.54%
Taylor Dorn	51	6	11.76%	2	3.92%	4	7.84%	0	0.00%
Tewksbury	24	1	4.17%	1	4.17%	0	0.00%	0	0.00%
Lefferts	95	6	6.32%	4	4.21%	2	2.11%	0	0.00%
DiPino	94	9	9.57%	4	4.26%	5	5.32%	2	2.13%
Assenmacher	47	2	4.26%	2	4.26%	0	0.00%	0	0.00%
Dunne	164	13	7.93%	7	4.27%	6	3.66%	1	0.61%
Hall D	46	5	10.87%	2	4.35%	3	6.52%	0	0.00%
Jones Ba	46	6	13.04%	2	4.35%	4	8.70%	0	0.00%
Comstock	68	5	7.35%	3	4.41%	2	2.94%	1	1.47%
Mahler R	201	21	10.45%	9	4.48%	12	5.97%	1	0.50%
Leiper	22	1	4.55%	1	4.55%	0	0.00%	0	0.00%
Tudor	87	9	10.34%	4	4.60%	5	5.75%	2	2.30%
Mason	43	2	4.65%	2	4.65%	0	0.00%	0	0.00%
Hoffman Guy	148	10	6.76%	7	4.73%	3	2.03%	2	1.35%
Sisk	82	5	6.10%	4	4.88%	1	1.22%	0	0.00%
Aguilera	122	6	4.92%	6	4.92%	0	0.00%	0	0.00%
Cox	223	19	8.52%	11	4.93%	8	3.59%	0	0.00%
O'Neal	81	8	9.88%	4	4.94%	4	4.94%	0	0.00%
Ritchie	60	3	5.00%	3	5.00%	0	0.00%	1	1.67%
Davis Mrk	160	15	9.37%	8	5.00%	7	4.37%	1	0.62%
Young Matt	60	4	6.67%	3	5.00%	1	1.67%	0	0.00%
Honeycutt	118	11	9.32%	6	5.08%	5	4.24%	1	0.85%
Valenzuela	294	22	7.48%	15	5.10%	7	2.38%	2	0.68%
Smiley	58	4	6.90%	3	5.17%	1	1.72%	0	0.00%
Baller	38	2	5.26%	2	5.26%	0	0.00%	0	0.00%
Ruffin	243	22	9.05%	13	5.35%	9	3.70%	1	0.41%
Browning	183	19	10.38%	10	5.46%	9	4.92%	0	0.00%
Robinson J	107	16	14.95%	6	5.61%	10	9.35%	0	0.00%
Mathews	188	17	9.04%	11	5.85%	6	3.19%	1	0.53%
Gossage	51	5	9.80%	3	5.88%	2	3.92%	0	0.00%
Mitchell J	135	14	10.37%	8	5.93%	6	4.44%	0	0.00%
Orosco	84	7	8.33%	5	5.95%	2	2.38%	0	0.00%
Childress	50	4	8.00%	3	6.00%	1	2.00%	0	0.00%
Williams F	99	13	13.13%	6	6.06%	7	7.07%	0	0.00%
Robinson D	115	13	11.30%	7	6.09%	6	5.22%	0	0.00%
Myers	81	7	8.64%	5	6.17%	2	2.47%	0	0.00%
Dawley	80	9	11.25%	5	6.25%	4	5.00%	0	0.00%
Forsch B	173	18	10.40%	11	6.36%	7	4.05%	0	0.00%
Trout	78	8	10.26%	5	6.41%	3	3.85%	0	0.00%
Landrum B	78	9	11.54%	5	6.41%	4	5.13%	2	2.56%
Drabek	170	18	10.59%	11	6.47%	7	4.12%	1	0.59%
Jones James	152	12	7.89%	10	6.58%	2	1.32%	1	0.66%
Dayley	75	6	8.00%	5	6.67%	1	1.33%	0	0.00%
Pena H	30	3	10.00%	2	6.67%	1	3.33%	0	0.00%
Howell K	60	5	8.33%	4	6.67%	1	1.67%	0	0.00%
Knepper	178	17	9.55%	12	6.74%	5	2.81%	0	0.00%
Meads	59	5	8.47%	4	6.78%	1	1.69%	0	0.00%
Holton	99	11	11.11%	7	7.07%	4	4.04%	0	0.00%
Burke	84	10	11.90%	6	7.14%	4	4.76%	0	0.00%
Garrelts	110	14	12.73%	8	7.27%	6	5.45%	0	0.00%
Moyer	245	30	12.24%	18	7.35%	12	4.90%	1	0.41%
Tekulve	95	11	11.58%	7	7.37%	4	4.21%	0	0.00%
Glavine	54	7	12.96%	4	7.41%	3	5.56%	0	0.00%
Rawley	247	30	12.15%	19	7.69%	11	4.45%	0	0.00%
Heathcock	39	3	7.69%	3	7.69%	0	0.00%	0	0.00%
Walk	129	16	12.40%	10	7.75%	6	4.65%	4	3.10%
Cone	116	17	14.66%	9	7.76%	8	6.90%	2	1.72%
Gott	116	15	12.93%	9	7.76%	6	5.17%	1	0.86%
Show	191	20	10.47%	15	7.85%	5	2.62%	2	1.05%
Lancaster	140	18	12.86%	11	7.86%	7	5.00%	1	0.71%
Krukow	151	22	14.57%	12	7.95%	10	6.62%	0	0.00%
Walter	25	2	8.00%	2	8.00%	0	0.00%	0	0.00%
Dravecky	187	24	12.83%	15	8.02%	9	4.81%	2	1.07%
Downs	199	24	12.06%	16	8.04%	8	4.02%	0	0.00%
Hume	99	9	9.09%	8	8.08%	1	1.01%	0	0.00%
Tunnell	86	8	9.30%	7	8.14%	1	1.16%	0	0.00%
Welch	220	31	14.09%	18	8.18%	13	5.91%	2	0.91%
Andersen L	95	8	8.42%	8	8.42%	0	0.00%	0	0.00%
Hillegas	71	9	12.68%	6	8.45%	3	4.23%	0	0.00%
Schatzeder	35	4	11.43%	3	8.57%	1	2.86%	0	0.00%
Whitson	207	23	11.11%	18	8.70%	5	2.42%	1	0.48%
Tibbs	79	10	12.66%	7	8.86%	3	3.80%	0	0.00%
Ojeda	45	6	13.33%	4	8.89%	2	4.44%	0	0.00%
Pacillo	45	5	11.11%	4	8.89%	1	2.22%	1	2.22%
LaCoss	168	18	10.71%	15	8.93%	3	1.79%	0	0.00%
Smith Z	266	27	10.15%	24	9.02%	3	1.13%	0	0.00%

Pitcher	ops	attempts		stolen		caught		picked off	
Power	220	26	11.82%	20	9.09%	6	2.73%	0	0.00%
Easley	22	3	13.64%	2	9.09%	1	4.55%	0	0.00%
Pena A	98	11	11.22%	9	9.18%	2	2.04%	0	0.00%
Murphy R	97	10	10.31%	9	9.28%	1	1.03%	2	2.06%
Magrane	168	18	10.71%	16	9.52%	2	1.19%	2	1.19%
Leary	104	14	13.46%	10	9.62%	4	3.85%	0	0.00%
Alexander	103	14	13.59%	10	9.71%	4	3.88%	0	0.00%
Nolte	72	8	11.11%	7	9.72%	1	1.39%	0	0.00%
Heaton	184	27	14.67%	18	9.78%	9	4.89%	4	2.17%
Worrell	112	13	11.61%	11	9.82%	2	1.79%	0	0.00%
Robinson R	142	21	14.79%	14	9.86%	7	4.93%	2	1.41%
Deshaies	161	27	16.77%	16	9.94%	11	6.83%	1	0.62%
McCullers	139	21	15.11%	14	10.07%	7	5.04%	0	0.00%
Scherrer	49	6	12.24%	5	10.20%	1	2.04%	0	0.00%
Smith B	155	17	10.97%	16	10.32%	1	0.65%	0	0.00%
Perry P	58	7	12.07%	6	10.34%	1	1.72%	0	0.00%
Sanderson	152	21	13.82%	16	10.53%	5	3.29%	1	0.66%
Perez P	56	9	16.07%	6	10.71%	3	5.36%	0	0.00%
Carman	191	30	15.71%	21	10.99%	9	4.71%	0	0.00%
Acker	106	15	14.15%	12	11.32%	3	2.83%	0	0.00%
Conroy	52	8	15.38%	6	11.54%	2	3.85%	0	0.00%
Darwin	201	28	13.93%	24	11.94%	4	1.99%	0	0.00%
Smith Le	92	15	16.30%	11	11.96%	4	4.35%	0	0.00%
Martinez De	137	19	13.87%	17	12.41%	2	1.46%	2	1.46%
Hammaker	177	29	16.38%	22	12.43%	7	3.95%	0	0.00%
Kipper	120	20	16.67%	15	12.50%	5	4.17%	0	0.00%
Bedrosian	96	14	14.58%	12	12.50%	2	2.08%	0	0.00%
Niedenfuer	16	2	12.50%	2	12.50%	0	0.00%	0	0.00%
Sutcliffe	236	36	15.25%	30	12.71%	6	2.54%	4	1.69%
Gullickson	149	26	17.45%	19	12.75%	7	4.70%	1	0.67%
Agosto	31	4	12.90%	4	12.90%	0	0.00%	0	0.00%
Fernandez C	155	25	16.13%	20	12.90%	5	3.23%	0	0.00%
Leach T	123	23	18.70%	16	13.01%	7	5.69%	0	0.00%
McGaffigan	127	19	14.96%	17	13.39%	2	1.57%	0	0.00%
Lopez A	36	7	19.44%	5	13.89%	2	5.56%	0	0.00%
Darling	228	36	15.79%	32	14.04%	4	1.75%	0	0.00%
Davis Storm	64	13	20.31%	9	14.06%	4	6.25%	0	0.00%
Gooden	169	30	17.75%	24	14.20%	6	3.55%	5	2.96%
Gideon	35	6	17.14%	5	14.29%	1	2.86%	0	0.00%
Rasmussen D	42	8	19.05%	6	14.29%	2	4.76%	0	0.00%
Gross K	243	43	17.70%	35	14.40%	8	3.29%	2	0.82%
Puleo	138	22	15.94%	20	14.49%	2	1.45%	0	0.00%
Jackson M	121	20	16.53%	18	14.88%	2	1.65%	1	0.83%
Booker	80	13	16.25%	12	15.00%	1	1.25%	0	0.00%
Dedmon	105	20	19.05%	16	15.24%	4	3.81%	0	0.00%
Smith D	52	8	15.38%	8	15.38%	0	0.00%	0	0.00%
Palmer D	167	30	17.96%	26	15.57%	4	2.40%	0	0.00%
Maddux G	179	36	20.11%	28	15.64%	8	4.47%	0	0.00%
Fisher	177	39	22.03%	28	15.82%	11	6.21%	0	0.00%
Bielecki	35	8	22.86%	6	17.14%	2	5.71%	0	0.00%
Scott M	204	40	19.61%	35	17.16%	5	2.45%	0	0.00%
Garber	90	17	18.89%	16	17.78%	1	1.11%	0	0.00%
Innis	22	5	22.73%	4	18.18%	1	4.55%	0	0.00%
Sebra	181	40	22.10%	33	18.23%	7	3.87%	1	0.55%
Noles	70	14	20.00%	13	18.57%	1	1.43%	0	0.00%
Kerfeld	32	7	21.88%	6	18.75%	1	3.13%	0	0.00%
Parrett	59	12	20.34%	12	20.34%	0	0.00%	1	1.69%
Ryan	200	47	23.50%	43	21.50%	4	2.00%	0	0.00%
Youmans	107	27	25.23%	25	23.36%	2	1.87%	1	0.93%
total	18007	2228	12.37%	1615	8.97%	613	3.40%	83	0.46%

def team	ops	attempts		stolen		caught		picked off	
CAL	1511	119	7.88%	66	4.37%	53	3.51%	3	0.20%
BOS	1622	132	8.14%	86	5.30%	46	2.84%	5	0.31%
CHA	1517	128	8.44%	84	5.54%	44	2.90%	5	0.33%
CLE	1627	141	8.67%	99	6.08%	42	2.58%	1	0.06%
SEA	1517	135	8.90%	93	6.13%	42	2.77%	8	0.53%
NYA	1547	152	9.83%	97	6.27%	55	3.56%	6	0.39%
DET	1574	136	8.64%	100	6.35%	36	2.29%	6	0.38%
MIL	1613	152	9.42%	103	6.39%	49	3.04%	3	0.19%
OAK	1543	158	10.24%	109	7.06%	49	3.18%	4	0.26%
KC	1490	163	10.94%	106	7.11%	57	3.83%	12	0.81%
TOR	1436	153	10.65%	104	7.24%	49	3.41%	7	0.49%
BAL	1504	182	12.10%	134	8.91%	48	3.19%	3	0.20%
MIN	1560	190	12.18%	156	10.00%	34	2.18%	5	0.32%
TEX	1670	227	13.59%	179	10.72%	48	2.87%	10	0.60%
total	21731	2168	9.98%	1516	6.98%	652	3.00%	78	0.36%

def team	ops	attempts		stolen		caught		picked off	
LA	1505	146	9.70%	95	6.31%	51	3.39%	7	0.47%
SL	1489	138	9.27%	96	6.45%	42	2.82%	10	0.67%
SF	1533	186	12.13%	113	7.37%	73	4.76%	5	0.33%
SD	1492	156	10.46%	114	7.64%	42	2.82%	8	0.54%
PIT	1424	184	12.92%	114	8.01%	70	4.92%	7	0.49%
CIN	1475	180	12.20%	125	8.47%	55	3.73%	10	0.68%
CHN	1609	210	13.05%	147	9.14%	63	3.92%	9	0.56%
NYN	1540	190	12.34%	142	9.22%	48	3.12%	7	0.45%
PHI	1560	202	12.95%	153	9.81%	49	3.14%	6	0.38%
ATL	1548	208	13.44%	163	10.53%	45	2.91%	2	0.13%
MON	1418	214	15.09%	176	12.41%	38	2.68%	10	0.71%
HOU	1414	214	15.13%	177	12.52%	37	2.62%	2	0.14%
total	18007	2228	12.37%	1615	8.97%	613	3.40%	83	0.46%

runner	ops	attempts		stolen		caught		picked off	
Nixon D	43	26	60.47%	20	46.51%	6	13.95%	1	2.33%
Redus	135	60	44.44%	50	37.04%	10	7.41%	0	0.00%
Reynolds H	150	72	48.00%	54	36.00%	18	12.00%	6	4.00%
Liriano	42	15	35.71%	13	30.95%	2	4.76%	0	0.00%
Felder	106	38	35.85%	32	30.19%	6	5.66%	2	1.89%
Wilson W	177	64	36.16%	53	29.94%	11	6.21%	0	0.00%
Kelly R	25	10	40.00%	7	28.00%	3	12.00%	0	0.00%
Henderson R	125	37	29.60%	30	24.00%	7	5.60%	3	2.40%
McDowell O	95	24	25.26%	22	23.16%	2	2.11%	0	0.00%
Molitor	154	42	27.27%	33	21.43%	9	5.84%	2	1.30%
Burks	135	33	24.44%	27	20.00%	6	4.44%	0	0.00%
Carter J	143	33	23.08%	28	19.58%	5	3.50%	1	0.70%
Moseby	198	45	22.73%	38	19.19%	7	3.54%	1	0.51%
Moses	113	36	31.86%	21	18.58%	15	13.27%	0	0.00%
White D	140	31	22.14%	24	17.14%	7	5.00%	2	1.43%
McLemore	120	27	22.50%	20	16.67%	7	5.83%	0	0.00%
Wiggins	108	23	21.30%	18	16.67%	5	4.63%	0	0.00%
Franco Ju	194	40	20.62%	32	16.49%	8	4.12%	2	1.03%
Bradley P	232	47	20.26%	38	16.38%	9	3.88%	1	0.43%
Griffin Alf	135	32	23.70%	22	16.30%	10	7.41%	2	1.48%
Polonia	155	30	19.35%	25	16.13%	5	3.23%	1	0.65%
Butler	199	49	24.62%	32	16.08%	17	8.54%	0	0.00%
Williams K	95	24	25.26%	15	15.79%	9	9.47%	0	0.00%
Smith Lo	57	12	21.05%	9	15.79%	3	5.26%	1	1.75%
Gruber	76	13	17.11%	12	15.79%	1	1.32%	0	0.00%
Gladden	135	27	20.00%	21	15.56%	6	4.44%	2	1.48%
Gibson K	132	27	20.45%	20	15.15%	7	5.30%	0	0.00%
Fernandez T	215	43	20.00%	32	14.88%	11	5.12%	1	0.47%
Boston	81	18	22.22%	12	14.81%	6	7.41%	0	0.00%
Pettis	115	21	18.26%	17	14.78%	4	3.48%	1	0.87%
Guillen	157	31	19.75%	23	14.65%	8	5.10%	1	0.64%
Davidson	64	10	15.63%	9	14.06%	1	1.56%	1	1.56%
Castillo J	108	22	20.37%	15	13.89%	7	6.48%	0	0.00%
Hinzo	66	13	19.70%	9	13.64%	4	6.06%	1	1.52%
Browne J	178	37	20.79%	24	13.48%	13	7.30%	1	0.56%
Brantley	99	16	16.16%	13	13.13%	3	3.03%	1	1.01%
Sheridan	130	28	21.54%	16	12.31%	12	9.23%	1	0.77%
Lansford	182	30	16.48%	22	12.09%	8	4.40%	0	0.00%
Davis Mike	103	19	18.45%	12	11.65%	7	6.80%	0	0.00%
Schofield	129	18	13.95%	15	11.63%	3	2.33%	0	0.00%
Newman A	110	21	19.09%	12	10.91%	9	8.18%	0	0.00%
Brower	95	17	17.89%	9	9.47%	8	8.42%	1	1.05%
Sierra	150	23	15.33%	14	9.33%	9	6.00%	1	0.67%
Jackson B	98	13	13.27%	9	9.18%	4	4.08%	1	1.02%
Braggs	131	17	12.98%	12	9.16%	5	3.82%	0	0.00%
Bush	89	11	12.36%	8	8.99%	3	3.37%	0	0.00%
Barrett	160	16	10.00%	14	8.75%	2	1.25%	0	0.00%
Yount	196	21	10.71%	17	8.67%	4	2.04%	1	0.51%
Surhoff BJ	116	18	15.52%	10	8.62%	8	6.90%	2	1.72%
Trammell	177	16	9.04%	15	8.47%	1	0.56%	1	0.56%
Brunansky	134	22	16.42%	11	8.21%	11	8.21%	0	0.00%
Bernazard	135	17	12.59%	11	8.15%	6	4.44%	1	0.74%
Calderon	140	15	10.71%	10	7.14%	5	3.57%	3	2.14%
Kingery	98	16	16.33%	7	7.14%	9	9.18%	1	1.02%
Deer	145	13	8.97%	10	6.90%	3	2.07%	1	0.69%
Canseco	131	12	9.16%	9	6.87%	3	2.29%	0	0.00%
Gaetti	122	14	11.48%	8	6.56%	6	4.92%	0	0.00%
Upshaw	155	21	13.55%	10	6.45%	11	7.10%	1	0.65%
Owen S	160	18	11.25%	10	6.25%	8	5.00%	1	0.62%
Young Mike	118	12	10.17%	7	5.93%	5	4.24%	0	0.00%
Incaviglia	137	11	8.03%	8	5.84%	3	2.19%	0	0.00%
Joyner	153	10	6.54%	8	5.23%	2	1.31%	0	0.00%
Fletcher	212	21	9.91%	11	5.19%	10	4.72%	1	0.47%
Gagne	98	10	10.20%	5	5.10%	5	5.10%	0	0.00%
Tartabull	181	13	7.18%	9	4.97%	4	2.21%	1	0.55%
Puckett	202	16	7.92%	10	4.95%	6	2.97%	1	0.50%
Phillips	113	11	9.73%	5	4.42%	6	5.31%	1	0.88%
Whitaker	190	11	5.79%	8	4.21%	3	1.58%	1	0.53%
Seitzer	252	17	6.75%	10	3.97%	7	2.78%	0	0.00%
Winfield	145	11	7.59%	5	3.45%	6	4.14%	0	0.00%
Evans Dw	151	10	6.62%	4	2.65%	6	3.97%	0	0.00%
total	21731	2168	9.98%	1516	6.98%	652	3.00%	78	0.36%

runner	ops	attempts		stolen		caught		picked off	
Coleman	217	97	44.70%	85	39.17%	12	5.53%	5	2.30%
Hall A	92	37	40.22%	31	33.70%	6	6.52%	3	3.26%
Winningham	84	35	41.67%	28	33.33%	7	8.33%	1	1.19%
Thompson M	159	54	33.96%	46	28.93%	8	5.03%	1	0.63%
Walker C	35	13	37.14%	10	28.57%	3	8.57%	0	0.00%
Jones T	104	36	34.62%	29	27.88%	7	6.73%	1	0.96%
Perry G	141	48	34.04%	37	26.24%	11	7.80%	2	1.42%
Hatcher W	170	53	31.18%	44	25.88%	9	5.29%	5	2.94%
Raines	184	52	28.26%	47	25.54%	5	2.72%	1	0.54%
Young G	91	32	35.16%	23	25.27%	9	9.89%	0	0.00%
Davis E	135	39	28.89%	34	25.19%	5	3.70%	4	2.96%
Strawberry	136	45	33.09%	34	25.00%	11	8.09%	0	0.00%
Jefferson	122	38	31.15%	29	23.77%	9	7.38%	1	0.82%
Bonds	127	38	29.92%	30	23.62%	8	6.30%	3	2.36%
Dykstra	111	30	27.03%	25	22.52%	5	4.50%	2	1.80%
Dernier	68	21	30.88%	15	22.06%	6	8.82%	0	0.00%
Johnson H	148	41	27.70%	32	21.62%	9	6.08%	0	0.00%
Daniels	117	29	24.79%	24	20.51%	5	4.27%	3	2.56%
Samuel	162	44	27.16%	32	19.75%	12	7.41%	2	1.23%
Cangelosi	82	20	24.39%	16	19.51%	4	4.88%	2	2.44%
Van Slyke	166	39	23.49%	31	18.67%	8	4.82%	2	1.20%
Gwynn	227	51	22.47%	41	18.06%	10	4.41%	2	0.88%
Ford C	63	17	26.98%	11	17.46%	6	9.52%	1	1.59%
Wynne	52	14	26.92%	9	17.31%	5	9.62%	1	1.92%
Webster	168	37	22.02%	29	17.26%	8	4.76%	0	0.00%
Santiago	116	30	25.86%	20	17.24%	10	8.62%	2	1.72%
Wilson M	115	25	21.74%	19	16.52%	6	5.22%	0	0.00%
Milner	64	19	29.69%	10	15.63%	9	14.06%	2	3.13%
Sax S	199	41	20.60%	31	15.58%	10	5.03%	1	0.50%
Cora	84	20	23.81%	13	15.48%	7	8.33%	1	1.19%
Reynolds RJ	78	13	16.67%	12	15.38%	1	1.28%	1	1.28%
Smith O	235	42	17.87%	35	14.89%	7	2.98%	3	1.28%
Uribe	74	12	16.22%	11	14.86%	1	1.35%	0	0.00%
Doran	214	41	19.16%	30	14.02%	11	5.14%	0	0.00%
Duncan	65	10	15.38%	9	13.85%	1	1.54%	0	0.00%
Larkin	109	19	17.43%	15	13.76%	4	3.67%	3	2.75%
Dunston	73	13	17.81%	10	13.70%	3	4.11%	0	0.00%
Bass K	168	28	16.67%	21	12.50%	7	4.17%	1	0.60%
Sandberg	162	21	12.96%	20	12.35%	1	0.62%	0	0.00%
Shelby	116	18	15.52%	14	12.07%	4	3.45%	0	0.00%
Thompson R	117	22	18.80%	14	11.97%	8	6.84%	0	0.00%
Leonard J	105	18	17.14%	12	11.43%	6	5.71%	0	0.00%
Davis C	128	21	16.41%	14	10.94%	7	5.47%	0	0.00%
McGee	152	19	12.50%	16	10.53%	3	1.97%	1	0.66%
Martinez Da	147	21	14.29%	15	10.20%	6	4.08%	0	0.00%
Backman	108	14	12.96%	11	10.19%	3	2.78%	1	0.93%
Morrison	81	10	12.35%	8	9.88%	2	2.47%	0	0.00%
Templeton	143	17	11.89%	14	9.79%	3	2.10%	0	0.00%
Herr	154	19	12.34%	15	9.74%	4	2.60%	0	0.00%
McReynolds	158	15	9.49%	14	8.86%	1	0.63%	1	0.63%
Thomas A	69	11	15.94%	6	8.70%	5	7.25%	0	0.00%
Anderson D	85	11	12.94%	7	8.24%	4	4.71%	0	0.00%
Kruk	183	24	13.11%	15	8.20%	9	4.92%	0	0.00%
Pendleton	171	23	13.45%	14	8.19%	9	5.26%	1	0.58%
Maldonado	107	16	14.95%	8	7.48%	8	7.48%	0	0.00%
Brenly	107	13	12.15%	8	7.48%	5	4.67%	1	0.93%
Murphy Da	176	16	9.09%	13	7.39%	3	1.70%	1	0.57%
Dawson	151	14	9.27%	11	7.28%	3	1.99%	0	0.00%
Mitchell K	112	13	11.61%	8	7.14%	5	4.46%	0	0.00%
Hayes	203	20	9.85%	14	6.90%	6	2.96%	1	0.49%
Foley T	80	15	18.75%	5	6.25%	10	12.50%	0	0.00%
Law V	107	10	9.35%	6	5.61%	4	3.74%	0	0.00%
James D	180	18	10.00%	10	5.56%	8	4.44%	2	1.11%
Pedrique	91	10	10.99%	5	5.49%	5	5.49%	0	0.00%
Bream	140	15	10.71%	7	5.00%	8	5.71%	0	0.00%
Scioscia	146	11	7.53%	7	4.79%	4	2.74%	1	0.68%
Galarraga	147	14	9.52%	6	4.08%	8	5.44%	1	0.68%
Guerrero	184	13	7.07%	7	3.80%	6	3.26%	0	0.00%
Clark W	136	16	11.76%	5	3.68%	11	8.09%	0	0.00%
Candaele	152	13	8.55%	5	3.29%	8	5.26%	1	0.66%
Griffey	127	10	7.87%	3	2.36%	7	5.51%	0	0.00%
total	18007	2228	12.37%	1615	8.97%	613	3.40%	83	0.46%

off team	ops	attempts		stolen		caught		picked off	
SEA	1498	230	15.35%	162	10.81%	68	4.54%	12	0.80%
MIL	1633	211	12.92%	154	9.43%	57	3.49%	9	0.55%
CLE	1499	185	12.34%	136	9.07%	49	3.27%	6	0.40%
CHA	1488	176	11.83%	127	8.53%	49	3.29%	6	0.40%
TOR	1573	170	10.81%	125	7.95%	45	2.86%	3	0.19%
OAK	1523	165	10.83%	109	7.16%	56	3.68%	4	0.26%
KC	1554	151	9.72%	110	7.08%	41	2.64%	5	0.32%
CAL	1524	131	8.60%	100	6.56%	31	2.03%	4	0.26%
MIN	1512	150	9.92%	96	6.35%	54	3.57%	5	0.33%
TEX	1606	154	9.59%	98	6.10%	56	3.49%	6	0.37%
NYA	1555	117	7.52%	85	5.47%	32	2.06%	6	0.39%
DET	1640	123	7.50%	84	5.12%	39	2.38%	7	0.43%
BOS	1554	115	7.40%	74	4.76%	41	2.64%	2	0.13%
BAL	1572	90	5.73%	56	3.56%	34	2.16%	3	0.19%
total	21731	2168	9.98%	1516	6.98%	652	3.00%	78	0.36%

off team	ops	attempts		stolen		caught		picked off	
SL	1585	256	16.15%	204	12.87%	52	3.28%	11	0.69%
SD	1572	241	15.33%	167	10.62%	74	4.71%	8	0.51%
MON	1452	206	14.19%	145	9.99%	61	4.20%	4	0.28%
NYN	1527	194	12.70%	152	9.95%	42	2.75%	5	0.33%
HOU	1494	188	12.58%	145	9.71%	43	2.88%	8	0.54%
CIN	1467	170	11.59%	133	9.07%	37	2.52%	14	0.95%
PIT	1517	173	11.40%	123	8.11%	50	3.30%	10	0.66%
ATL	1504	176	11.70%	121	8.05%	55	3.66%	8	0.53%
SF	1432	190	13.27%	114	7.96%	76	5.31%	5	0.35%
PHI	1469	145	9.87%	106	7.22%	39	2.65%	5	0.34%
LA	1475	150	10.17%	104	7.05%	46	3.12%	5	0.34%
CHN	1513	139	9.19%	101	6.68%	38	2.51%	0	0.00%
total	18007	2228	12.37%	1615	8.97%	613	3.40%	83	0.46%

BASERUNNING TABLES

One of the more frequently talked about aspects of baserunning is the ability of a runner to take an extra base on a hit or an out. Teams which play "station-to-station" baseball (i.e., whose runners advance only one base at a time) are often put down for their lack of speed. Unfortunately, these baserunning situation are almost never analyzed statistically, with the result being that most of this analysis is anecdotal or speculative.

Prior to 1898, the statistical category of "Stolen Bases" in baseball actually included these extra bases taken on a hit or an out, as well as the bases "stolen" in the modern sense. While it may now seem strange to combine stolen bases with extra bases taken on hits or outs, there is much merit in this methodology. Even if these different aspects of baserunning are separated statistically, more attention should be paid to these extra-base advancements.

In order to provide more information about this overlooked area, the tables in this section show how often baserunners take an extra base in each of four instances:
1) Advancing from first to third on a single.
2) Scoring from second on a single.
3) Scoring from first on a double.
4) Scoring from third on an outfield fly out.

In each case, the table shows how often the team's runners made the given advancement as a percentage of total opportunities to do so. The definition of an opportunity for each of the cases listed above is:
1) Batter singles with first base occupied and second base empty.
2) Batter singles with second base occupied.
3) Batter doubles with first base occupied.
4) Batter flies out to the outfield with third base occupied.

The only tricky situations occur in case number one, where advancements from first to third with a runner on second, who might possibly get in the way, are not separated.

For each table, the "S.1-3" column shows how often a team's baserunners advanced from first to third on a single; the "S.2-H" column shows how often they scored from second on a single; the "D.1-H" column shows how often they scored from first on a double; the "7,8,9.3-H" column shows how often they scored from third on a fly out to the outfield.

Gary Gillette and Dave Nichols

Team	S.1–3	S.2-H	D.1-H	7,8,9.3-H
BAL	28.19	65.19	26.58	60.78
BOS	33.86	64.29	23.60	80.56
CAL	35.90	67.25	41.25	75.00
CHA	32.45	67.24	37.18	85.25
CLE	34.82	71.43	34.67	78.85
DET	34.22	65.17	35.96	76.71
KC	32.50	61.71	43.68	82.35
MIL	33.58	70.43	43.37	85.00
MIN	38.57	67.92	41.03	78.72
NYA	37.34	65.33	35.37	74.51
OAK	32.76	68.48	49.38	73.85
SEA	28.43	68.72	31.51	78.33
TEX	35.87	64.43	46.51	78.46
TOR	36.32	65.03	30.00	61.40
League	33.95	66.65	37.19	76.63

Team	S.1–3	S.2-H	D.1-H	7,8,9.3-H
ATL	30.16	62.18	36.47	72.34
CHN	33.92	67.25	27.78	67.44
CIN	28.44	62.63	41.03	73.33
HOU	27.96	61.41	50.00	90.74
LA	35.78	68.85	40.58	72.22
MON	28.34	64.91	53.00	68.97
NYN	33.33	71.35	43.37	80.43
PHI	25.87	65.45	43.59	77.36
PIT	34.72	64.02	45.83	76.92
SD	37.34	63.30	40.00	72.92
SF	38.81	68.78	40.51	76.60
SL	32.05	64.47	43.68	78.12
League	32.40	65.33	42.56	75.80

Team	S.1–3	S.2-H	D.1-H	7,8,9.3-H
BAL	37.28	66.67	32.84	80.00
BOS	33.61	63.93	33.03	75.41
CAL	29.78	64.89	34.18	77.27
CHA	39.04	71.91	38.57	62.22
CLE	35.92	68.02	43.48	75.64
DET	38.24	64.97	41.18	85.45
KC	29.95	72.68	38.16	79.25
MIL	29.64	65.71	39.77	85.96
MIN	32.00	68.79	33.72	77.78
NYA	30.22	67.37	34.88	74.24
OAK	34.27	61.83	40.96	75.41
SEA	31.17	66.12	39.77	78.67
TEX	40.30	69.63	39.13	75.86
TOR	34.21	58.94	31.65	65.96
League	33.95	66.65	37.19	76.63

Team	S.1–3	S.2-H	D.1-H	7,8,9.3-H
ATL	33.48	67.20	50.00	83.05
CHN	35.96	67.54	43.18	77.78
CIN	35.08	69.68	43.18	80.65
HOU	34.27	65.61	42.11	69.39
LA	33.91	64.29	40.86	74.29
MON	30.16	61.31	41.38	81.13
NYN	31.43	67.57	31.82	81.48
PHI	31.48	59.88	38.89	75.00
PIT	23.94	59.43	52.00	63.33
SD	30.10	63.19	45.68	68.89
SF	36.89	68.48	36.11	73.47
SL	30.00	68.54	43.33	80.00
League	32.40	65.33	42.56	75.80

V

GENERAL ESSAYS

COMPUTERS IN THE DUGOUT: CLOSER THAN YOU THINK!

Arthur Margulis and Robert Merrilees

With a fleet-footed runner on first and none out, the Digitheads' third base coach looks into the dugout for a sign. But he's not searching for a man chewing tobacco and gesturing. Rather, he's watching a computer screen flash a series of bright colors. The coach sees yellow followed by blue and relays the sign to the Digitheads' runner and batter. The steal is on.

The idea of a computer making decisions for a baseball team may excite or horrify baseball fans, but with the data made available by Project Scoresheet, that is no longer a remote possibility. At the very least, the technology is available to provide today's big-league pilots with a helpful assistant. Here's how a computer could make managing decisions and how such a computer system might be implemented in the major leagues.

A computer manager would employ one powerful concept to make its decisions: win probabilities, a concept we first encountered in *The Hidden Game of Baseball* by John Thorn and Pete Palmer. A win probability is based on how often a team can expect to win given a particular game situation (the inning, the score, the number of outs and the bases that are occupied). Win probabilities are stated as percentages.

For instance, one might estimate that the Digitheads, down by a run in the bottom of the ninth with a runner on first and none out, could be expected to win 31.4 percent of the time.

Why 31.4 percent? Before Project Scoresheet, that number represented little more than educated speculation, but now it is easy to calculate such probabilities using the Project's data and a personal computer. For instance, the authors used Project data from all 1985 National League games to examine every situation during the season in which a team had a runner on first and none out. That situation arose 4,754 times. The following table lists how many runs the teams scored during the rest of the innings:

Runs	Occurrences	Percentage
0	2,795	58.8
1	933	19.6
2	549	11.5
3	267	5.6
4	128	2.7
5	50	1.1
6	15	.3
7 or more	17	.4
Total	4,754	100.0

If these numbers applied to the Digitheads, 58.8 percent of the time they would fail to score in the ninth and would lose the game. They would score one run and send the game into extra innings 19.6 percent of the time, in which case (ignoring their advantage as the home team)

they could expect to win 50 percent of the time. And in 21.6 percent of those ninth innings, they could expect to score more than once and win outright. Therefore, the Digitheads' win probability in the ninth, down a run with one on and no outs is figured:

$$.5(.196) + .216 = .314 \text{ or } 31.4 \text{ percent.}$$

Win probabilities calculated in this manner can be used to evaluate strategic alternatives during a game. For example, should the Digitheads' runner on first try to steal? If he tries and succeeds, the team will find itself with a runner on second and none out. If he fails, the Digitheads will have nobody on and one out. The win probability after a successful steal is .436; after a caught stealing, it goes to .102, based on 1985 NL data. Ignoring for simplicity other possible results, suppose the Digitheads believe their man on first will be safe on 75 percent of his steal attempts and thrown out on 25 percent. Then the expected win probability of a steal attempt is:

$$.75(.436) + .25(.102) = .353$$

The manager should call for the steal to increase his team's chance of winning from 31.4 percent to 35.3.

This example captures the essence of evaluating strategies with win probabilities. Any game situation and its potential outcomes can be considered as a combination of score, inning, outs and baserunners. A table of "expected" win probabilities can be calculated for every such combination and used to evaluate strategies. Only two sets of data are necessary: the win probability for each potential outcome, and for each strategy, the probability that each potential outcome will occur. Both can be generated from Project Scoresheet data.

Just as the Digitheads did when asking to steal or not to steal, a team should choose the strategy with the highest expected win probability.

Using 1985 National League data to calculate a decision for the Digitheads is inappropriate. Ideally, each team would start with a table of win probabilities that reflect its own performance. The differences from team to team would have a major impact on decision-making. A team with outstanding pitching and poor hitting would be more likely to benefit from playing for one-run innings, while a team of sluggers with poor pitchers might do better with "big-inning" strategies. These characteristics would be reflected in an accurate set of win probabilities.

While a team's table will contain a win probability for any situation, such as .314 for the Digitheads' ninth-inning predicament, a better estimate of a team's chance of winning can be calculated using current information. For instance, the Digitheads' .314 win probability in the above situation is based on having an average runner on first and an average batter at the plate. But if the team has a speedster on first, it is even better off trying to steal.

Expected win probabilities based on the table values for each potential outcome may not be sufficiently accurate because each potential outcome can be treated as a game situation with various possible outcomes. Expected win probabilities can be calculated for these in the same manner. If the expected win probabilities for potential outcomes are different from the table values, the overall expected win probability also will be different and will affect strategic decisions.

Suppose in the above example that the Digitheads have a singles hitter at the plate. He has a much better chance of driving the runner home from second than does a slugger with a low batting average. The .436 win probability for a successful steal is no longer accurate. All other things being equal, the stolen base attempt will now be an even more desirable strategy.

In this way, a computer manager would operate in much the same way as a chess-playing computer. The computer would look at all of its possible moves and come up with an estimated value (from the table) for each move. Then, if it had time, it would look at all the moves and countermoves that could result from each of the original moves, thereby getting a better picture of just how good its original estimated values were. It would modify those values accordingly.

In theory, this process could continue forever, but in practice, when looking ahead further than two or three batters, the differences between calculating new expected win probabilities and using values from the table have a negligible effect on the strategy choice.

Although the examples discussed so far have concerned only offensive strategy choices, win probabilities also can be used to evaluate defensive strategies such as the intentional walk, personnel moves such as pinch-hitting or pinch-running and even pitching changes. Analyzing personnel moves entails the more complicated process of expressing a player's relative abilities in win probabilities, but this too can be accomplished using player statistics.

How would a computer assistant manager work in the big leagues? We envision a setup in which a team statistician in the press box enters play results and lineup changes into a computer as they occur during the game. This data entry could also serve the purpose of compiling team statistics. The computer continually processes each new piece of information and calculates new win probabilities for each of the strategies available to the manager.

Each strategy and its corresponding win probability are displayed on a screen in the dugout. The computer looks ahead as many batters as time allows and updates its estimates of win probabilities on the dugout screen. The manager uses the information on the screen to aid his decision-making.

Would this information really improve the decision-making of major league managers? An attempt to quantify all aspects of the game as win probabilities would have advantages and shortcomings. Of course, factors such as the element of surprise can never be accurately measured, so there is some benefit to leaving the final decision to a human manager. But the computer assistant can offer an objective assessment of the subtle factors managers often cite for making their decisions (such as calling for a steal because the batter tends to ground into a lot of double plays). It can point out the unjustifiable biases that often result in bad decision-making by a human manager (such as having an inflated opinion of the sacrifice bunt or a deflated opinion of a certain pinch hitter).

The manager would be free to disagree with the choice of the computer, but he ought to have a reason for doing so, particularly when the computer selects one strategy as a clear-cut favorite.

Although this may sound far-fetched to some readers, we implemented a version of a computer manager based on these principles in our computer baseball game *Radio Baseball,* published by Electronic Arts in 1986. Several research projects remain before the computer manager will be ready for the big leagues, but most are feasible now that four seasons of Project Scoresheet data are available.

Even so, the first computer assistant may be far off because of major league baseball's traditional resistance to change—and, perhaps, the fear of being known as the "Digitheads."

THE VALIDITY OF THE QUALITY START (OR JOHNSON GAME)

David Gordon

The quality start suffers from two shortcomings that prevent it from being accepted as a valid baseball statistic: the term "quality start" itself and what I call the "4.50 syndrome."

Let's start with the name.

"Quality start" has a subjective ring to it, because quality is definitely in the eyes of the beholder. It is as if a sportswriter, or anyone who does not share your opinion, decided if a pitcher had a good or bad outing. But a quality start is an objective statistic. To earn a quality start, a pitcher must last six or more innings and give up three or fewer earned runs. Period. No subjectivity about it.

To overcome this objection, I propose a name change. Let's call it a "Johnson Game" after the great Walter Johnson, who I believe pitched more "Johnson Games" than anyone else in this century—although this is unresearched. I believe this new name lends a ring of validity to the statistic and may help speed its acceptance. But it will not be accepted until it is shown to be meaningful.

This brings up the "4.50 syndrome," the idea that a pitcher can have a 4.50 earned run average and still get credit for a quality start (three earned runs in six innings works out to an ERA of 4.50).

Yes, on occasion a pitcher has an ugly Johnson Game: six innings, four runs, three earned, eight hits, three walks. For the most part, however, Johnson Games are well-pitched. Of the 1,031 Johnson Games pitched in the National League during 1986, only 61 were of the "4.50" variety, less than 6 percent.

Among individual pitchers with three or more Johnson Games, the highest ERA in those games belonged to Mark Knudson, 3.72 in his three JGs. The 10 worst ERAs in JGs were:

PITCHER	JG	ERA in JGs
Mark Knudson	3	3.72
Larry McWilliams	5	3.38
Greg Maddux	3	3.18
Ed Whitson	4	2.93
Dennis Eckersley	16	2.76
LaMarr Hoyt	12	2.74
Chris Welsh	13	2.64
Eric Show	14	2.63
Jim Acker	8	2.59
Joel Hesketh	8	2.50

By contrast, the top 10 looked like something even the dead-ball era could not produce:

	JG	ERA in JGs
Dennis Martinez	6	0.39
Rich Anderson	3	0.50
Joe Johnson	5	1.11
Vida Blue	9	1.13
Mark Thurmond	4	1.15
Bob Ojeda	21	1.20
Nolan Ryan	15	1.29
Bob Kipper	9	1.36
Jamie Moyer	6	1.41
Tom Browning	19	1.43

Support for acceptance of the Johnson Game is overwhelming. National League pitchers overall had a 1.94 ERA in Johnson Games for 1986. For all other games, relief appearances and starts in non-Johnson Games, the ERA was a whopping 5.09. Hits per nine innings in JGs was 6.73; in other games it was 10.00. Walks per nine innings in JGs was 2.59; other games, 3.99. Only strikeouts were similar, 5.94 per nine innings in Johnson Game starts to 6.03 for other pitching.

But the bottom line is wins and losses. In the 1,031 National League Johnson Games of 1986, 682 resulted in victories, 349 in losses for a winning percentage of .661. If a team had gotten a Johnson Game every time out, it could have expected to win 107 games, good enough to take 72 of the 76 division crowns since 1969. This figure includes games where both pitchers had a JG; of course, a win and a loss are counted in there. I do not have the figures for only those games in which one pitcher had a JG and the other did not, but the won-loss record must have been awesome.

I do know that in the 907 outings that were not Johnson Games, the teams were 287–620, a .316 percentage.

The best team for JGs in the NL in 1986 was the Mets with 102; New York won 84 of these games for a winning percentage of .823, also the league best. The Mets' ERA in Johnson Games was 1.70, lowest in the NL.

The flip side in 1986 was the Cubs with only 68 JGs and a .515 percentage in those games. The Cubs fared worse in non-JGs, with a league-high 5.68 ERA.

The Braves managed a 52–32 record (.619) in Johnson Games, just a bit below the league average. Their Johnson Game ERA was 2.20, highest in the league.

The NL leader for 1986 was Mike Scott of the Astros with 31 JGs. The best record (five or more decisions) belonged to the Mets' Dwight Gooden, 14–0 in his Johnson Games. Four other pitchers were undefeated in their JGs: Greg Mathews, Cardinals, 11–0; Nolan Ryan, Astros, 10–0; Ted Power, Reds, 6–0; and Joe Johnson, Braves, 5–0. Only four pitchers with five or more decisions were below .500 in JGs: Dennis Eckersley, Cubs, 3–6; Rick Sutcliffe, Cubs, 3–5; Bob Welch, Dodgers, 6–7; and Rick Reuschel, Pirates, 7–8. Fifty-one pitchers had winning records in Johnson Games and two were at .500: Mario Soto, Reds, and Jim Acker, Braves, both 3–3.

The numbers support the Johnson Game as a valid measure of pitching ability. The figures also support the feelings of baseball men. How often has a manager said, "If he can only get me to the seventh inning . . . ?"

Indeed, bullpens are organized around setup men and stoppers, to pick up where the Johnson Game leaves off. So let's give Walter Johnson a little recognition and start taking the Johnson Game seriously.

THE STATE OF PITCHING (OR LACK OF IT), 1987

Merrianna McCully

Early in 1987, the big news in baseball was the "lively ball." Story upon story was written about it, and the issue was the subject of conversation during games on television and radio. Tests were conducted to determine how high the ball could bounce. Managers and players swore that something was different, that the ball was jumping off the bat. Broken-bat bloopers were making it into the stands, and spray hitters were setting career highs in homers. Some suggested that the air was lighter, the strike zone smaller and the hitters stronger. There was no end to the theories.

Then a few bold experts stepped forward and suggested that just maybe the pitching was thin (or just plain bad). "Oh," everyone said, and the lively ball theory slowly faded into the sunset over Candlestick Park—one flap down.

Just how thin was the pitching? How about this: Rick Reuschel, Doyle Alexander, and Dave Dravecky all pitched for two teams in '87; each pitcher had a good enough won-loss record to rank among the top five starters on both his clubs.

Pitching, or the lack of pitching, became the story. One of many articles on the subject appeared in the December edition of *Inside Sports*. In "A Farewell to Arms," Paul Ladewski dealt mostly in generalities with a few excellent stats to support several theories: the shrinking strike zone, lack in conditioning and pacing of pitchers (compared to hitters), a reluctance to throw inside, a lack of control and command by pitchers, and austerity on the part of owners. Probably the most telling point in the whole article was a simple statement by Tony Kubek: "There just aren't that many good arms around."

A combination of all of the above probably contributed to the Year of the Lively Ball and the increase in homers. While I might not have the final answer either, I do have some interesting statistics that describe the state of starting pitching in 1987. I entered every start by every pitcher for '87 (4,210 entries) into the computer, and compiled more than 300 pages of stats on starters. This article summarizes the highlights of my research.

At the beginning of the season, 129 pitchers were penciled in as starters for the 26 teams. Every team began the season with five in their rotation, with the exception of Atlanta with four. By the end of the season, the count of pitchers who had started at least one game had exactly doubled to 258. Of those 258, 16 started for two clubs and one, Phil Niekro, was fitted with three different uniforms.

In the American League, 151 starters were used by the 14 teams. That's an average of 10.79 starters per club. The Yankees' problems are reflected in the fact that they employed 15 different starting pitchers, the most of any team in the majors; on the other hand, the Tigers and Royals used only 8 different starters. In the National League, 125 pitchers started for an average of 10.42 per club. The Braves, with 13, used the most; the Astros, with 8, the fewest.

In 1987 the average major league starter made 16.32 starts, with 99.17 IP, 5.65 wins and 5.96 losses; the numbers are brought down considerably by the fact that 62 pitchers (24 percent of the total) made three or fewer starts, but isn't it sobering to ponder that the average starter had a 6–6 record? The average start lasted 6.08 innings—6.13 in the American League (with the DH), 6.02 in the National. American League starting pitchers accounted for 71.51 percent of the league's W/L decisions; NL starters accounted for 70.65 percent. Major league starters compiled a 4.40 ERA (4.52 AL, 4.25 NL). Less than half the total met the definition of "quality start" (6 or more IP, 3 or fewer ERA)—44.89 percent in the American League, 49.02 percent in the National.

With figures like that, one begins to appreciate those few hurlers who exceeded the norm by good margins. Consider the average of 16.32 starts; a pitcher with 33 starts, or twice the average, begins to look better. In the American League last year there were 25 pitchers (17.00 percent of the total) who made at least 33 starts. Charlie Hough with his "easy of the arm" knuckler had the most starts with 40, as well as the most innings pitched with 285.1. In the National League, only 15 pitchers (12.20 percent) had at least 33 starts. Shane Rawley, Mike Scott and Zane Smith shared the most starts with 36 each, although the most innings pitched was by Orel Hershiser with 262.1.

Or take that average of 6.077 IP per start. Any starter who averaged 7.5 IP/S begins to look awfully good. In the American League last year, only four hurlers met that standard:

	INNINGS	IP per start
Roger Clemens	281.2	7.824
Jack Morris	266	7.823
Bret Saberhagen	257	7.788
Mark Langston	272	7.771

In the National League, not even one pitcher could meet the 7.5 IP/S standard; that's partly because the league doesn't use the designated hitter, and maybe partly because the pitching was just plain lousy. However, one additional pitcher met the criterion. Doyle Alexander, who toiled in both leagues, also qualified:

	INNINGS	IP per start
Doyle Alexander	206	7.630

In the NL, Alexander averaged 7.354 IP per start, in the AL 8.03. The average number of wins for the splendid group of five is 17.8.

Starters who hurled over 200 innings with at least seven innings a game were Orel Hershiser, Fernando Valenzuela and Bob Welch (all Dodgers) in the NL, and Teddy Higuera, Jimmy Key, Bruce Hurst, Bert Blyleven, Charlie Hough, Dave Stewart, and Mike Moore in the AL.

Only 13 of the 258 starters (5 percent) managed to stay in enough games to go 250 or more innings: Hough (285.1), Clemens (281.2), Mark Langston (272), Bert Blyleven (267), Morris (266), Higuera (261.2), Stewart (261.1), Key (261), Saberhagen (257) and Frank Viola (251.2) did it in the AL; Hershiser (262.1), Welch (251.2) and Valenzuela (251) were the only ones in the NL. These pitchers provided quality as well as quantity: The average number of victories among the 13 was 17.3, and none had a losing record.

Of course, a pitcher usually wouldn't amass 250 innings unless he was winning more than losing. Surprisingly, though, of the 31 pitchers who had 200–249.2 innings, a whopping 41.94 percent (13) had losing records:

AMERICAN LEAGUE

	INNINGS	W–L	ERA
Mark Gubicza	241.2	13–18	3.98
Mike Moore	231	9–19	4.71
Mike Boddicker	226	10–12	4.18
Danny Jackson	219.2	9–18	4.02
Richard Dotson	211.1	11–12	4.17
Jose DeLeon	204.2	11–12	3.83
Mike Morgan	203.1	12–17	4.69
Tom Candiotti	201.2	7–18	4.78

NATIONAL LEAGUE

	INNINGS	W–L	ERA
Nolan Ryan	211.2	8–16	2.76
Eric Show	206.2	8–16	3.84
Bruce Ruffin	204.2	11–14	4.35
Ted Power	204	10–13	4.50
Ed Whitson	202.2	10–13	4.75

A few of these names have been the subject of trade rumors, and some have changed teams. Ever wonder why the likes of a Mike Moore or a Danny Jackson are so sought after with records of 9–19 and 9–18? They are among the few "horses" who did not, according to the most common analysis, play up to their full potential or fell victim to no support from the offense. In Nolan Ryan's case, no support is an understatement.

Now let's look at depth, or to be more accurate, the lack of depth, among the 26 staffs. These charts list the clubs according to the number of double-digit winners, and the number of starters with more than 200 innings pitched:

NUMBER OF DOUBLE-DIGIT WINNERS PER TEAM

NONE	ONE	TWO	THREE	FOUR
Cleveland	Atlanta	Baltimore	Boston	Mets
San Diego	California	White Sox	St. Louis	
	Minnesota	Detroit		
	Yankees	Kansas City		
	Oakland	Milwaukee		
	Texas	Seattle		
	Cubs	Toronto		
	Houston	Cincinnati		
	San Fran	Los Angeles		
		Montreal		
		Philadelphia		
		Pittsburgh		

NUMBER OF 200+ INNING PITCHERS PER TEAM

NONE	ONE	TWO	THREE	FOUR
Montreal	Baltimore	Boston	White Sox	Kansas City
Yankees	California	Milwaukee	Detroit	
Pittsburgh	Cleveland	Minnesota	Seattle	
St. Louis	Texas	Oakland	Dodgers	
San Fran	Atlanta	Toronto	Philadelphia	
	Cubs	Houston		
	Cincinnati	San Diego		
	Mets			

To judge depth, we might also pick the top three starting pitchers from each team by total innings pitched. In all but a few cases, the starters with the most innings also were the hurlers with the most wins. One exception was Baltimore, where I chose Mike Flanagan (6–8 overall) instead of Ken Dixon (7–10). Flanagan did pitch 144 innings when his Toronto numbers are added in. The other exception in the AL was Seattle, where two pitchers had better records than Mike Moore: Lee Gutterman (10–4) and Scott Bankhead (9–8). Still, Moore (9–19) threw just 13 fewer innings than Gutterman and Bankhead combined, so he had to be considered the workhorse. Seattle, Boston and Detroit were the only teams in the AL to have five starters with 100 or more innings pitched.

In the National League Chicago, Houston, Montreal, Pittsburgh and San Francisco were teams where pitchers with poorer records had more innings pitched. A case could be made for any of these clubs that one pitcher deserved to be considered over another, but for the sake of continuity, I stuck with innings pitched. Probably the biggest disparity was in leaving Mike Dunne off the list from Pittsburgh. Dunne had the best won-loss record on the team (13–6), but Fisher, Drabek and Reuschel pitched more innings and had more starts. Quite surprisingly, even with no DH, seven clubs had 5 starters with 100 or more innings: Chicago, Cincinnati, Houston, Montreal, New York, Pittsburgh and San Diego.

Even with these apparent problems, the figures provide interesting comparisons. Considering just the top three starters, the averages changed dramatically from the figures for all pitchers:

AMERICAN LEAGUE
(averages per starter, top 3 per team)

Wins (543 total)	12.92
Losses (486)	11.14
No decisions (319)	7.59
Number of starts	31.67
Innings pitched per start	6.60
Total innings pitched	208.96
ERA	4.10
Percentage of quality starts	51.58

NATIONAL LEAGUE
(averages per starter, top 3 per team)

Wins (394 total)	10.94
Losses (394)	10.94
No decisions (314)	8.72
Number of starts	30.61

Innings pitched per start 6.27
Total innings pitched 191.94
ERA 4.08
Percentage of quality starts 52.09

These numbers reflect the performance of 78 pitchers, or 30.12 percent of the total that started for the year. With a few exceptions, the top three weren't too hard to recognize. Several teams had little depth beyond the top one or two starters. Very few teams are more than three starters deep.

Another interesting way to look at pitching depth is to consider how many wins each five-man rotation accumulated. In determining the five starters, I made these cuts:

BALTIMORE—Flanagan (3–6) with his 94.2 innings, third best on the club, didn't make the top five. Baltimore's third, fourth and fifth starters together had just 12 wins, worst in the majors.

CHICAGO CUBS—Greg Maddux (6–14, 149.1 innings) was aced off the list because Scott Sanderson (7–7, 122.2), Steve Trout (6–3, 75) and Lester Lancaster (6–3, 111.2) had better won-loss records.

MONTREAL—Bob Sebra (6–15, 161) was dropped to the sixth spot because Dennis Martinez (11–4, 144.2), Floyd Youmans (9–8, 116.1) and Pascual Perez (7–0, 70.1) had much better won-loss records.

SAN FRANCISCO—Mike Krukow (5–6, 155.2) dropped to the sixth spot when Rick Reuschel (5–2, 48) appeared on the scene.

Here's how the clubs stack up in total wins, top five starters:

AL WEST	AL EAST	NL WEST	NL EAST
Royals 63	Tigers 67	Astros 52	Mets 57
Mariners 59	Blue Jays 58	Dodgers 52	Cards 52
White Sox 51	Red Sox 57	Giants 44	Expos 50
Twins 48	Brewers 54	Reds 43	Phils 50
Athletics 47	Yankees 49	Braves 38	Pirates 49
Angels 45	Orioles 32	Padres 49	Cubs 48
Rangers 44	Indians 29		

The quality sure shows here, doesn't it?—as does the lack of quality on many teams. Let's go a step further and list wins by the third, fourth and fifth pitchers on each team, eliminating big winners such as Clements, Stewart, Langston and Saberhagen.

AL WEST	AL EAST	NL WEST	NL EAST
Royals 29	Tigers 32	Astros 25	Mets 30
Mariners 28	Blue Jays 26	Reds 23	Cardinals 30
White Sox 24	Yankees 25	Dodgers 21	Expos 26
Angels 19	Red Sox 22	Giants 21	Pirates 25
Twins 16	Brewers 22	Padres 16	Phillies 20
Rangers 15	Indians 15	Braves 15	Cubs 19
Athletics 14	Orioles 12		

Depth—or lack of it—begins to show even more in this chart. Let's focus on the AL West, the division that produced the 1987 world champions. The Royals' depth is not at all surprising; the Twins' dearth of it, so well chronicled and so fortuitously unimportant in postseason, is no surprise either. The most curious team is Seattle, whose starting five includes the pitcher with the dubious honor of having the most losses in 1987, Mike Moore (9–19). Moore tallied two more wins than any starter for the Indians. Even with Moore's poor performance, the five Mariners starters were third in wins in the majors, and the team's third through fifth starters were fifth compared to the other teams. The losing record of Seattle's top five (59–61) was due mostly to the whopping 36 losses between Mike Morgan and Mike Moore. The M's pitching staff had the fewest no-decisions (31) in the majors in '87. One could say that no other pitcher, with possibly the exception of Danny Jackson, had more of an impact on his team than Mike Moore, positive and negative.

The results of this general lack of pitching depth were that many teams were guilty of robbing the minor league cradle, and a lot of 40-year-old arms were resurrected.

On the surface, the lack of good arms seemed to play a big part in causing the Year of the Lively Ball. Paul Kilgus of the Texas Rangers put it all in perspective when he told of a self-diagnosed illness he had last season: the One Stupid Pitch Syndrome.

Could it have been contagious? Did it spread rapidly throughout the leagues last year, into an orgy of Stupid Pitches?

Could be, could be!

TOP FIVE STARTERS PER TEAM—NATIONAL LEAGUE

ATLANTA	IP	QS	W	L	ND	CW	CL	TER	ERA	ST	%QS	AVG IP
Z Smith	242.0	19	15	10	11	22	14	110	4.09	36	52.78	6.722
D Palmer	152.1	9	8	11	9	12	16	83	4.90	28	32.14	5.440
R Mahler	171.0	11	6	12	10	10	18	97	5.11	28	39.29	6.107
D Alexander	117.2	8	5	10	1	6	10	54	4.13	16	50.00	7.354
R O'Neal	52.1	6	4	2	4	4	6	32	5.50	10	60.00	5.233
TOTALS	735.1	53	38	45	35	54	64	376	4.60	118	44.92	6.232

CHICAGO CUBS	IP	QS	W	L	ND	CW	CL	TER	ERA	ST	%QS	AVG IP
R Sutcliffe	237.1	22	18	10	6	22	12	97	3.68	34	64.71	6.980
J Moyer	196.1	15	11	15	7	14	19	115	5.27	33	45.45	5.950
S Sanderson	122.2	8	7	7	8	10	12	61	4.48	22	36.36	5.576
S Trout	75.0	7	6	3	2	7	4	25	3.00	11	63.64	6.818
L Lancaster	111.2	8	6	3	9	7	11	64	5.16	18	44.44	6.204
TOTALS	743.0	60	48	38	32	60	58	362	4.38	118	50.85	6.297

CINCINNATI	IP	QS	W	L	ND	CW	CL	TER	ERA	ST	%QS	AVG IP
B Gullickson	165.0	14	10	11	6	14	13	89	4.85	27	51.85	6.111
T Power	204.0	13	10	13	11	18	16	102	4.50	34	38.24	6.000
T Browning	181.0	15	10	13	8	18	13	101	5.02	31	48.39	5.839
R Robinson	105.0	10	7	3	8	10	8	44	3.77	18	55.56	5.833
G Hoffman	127.2	14	6	10	6	10	12	67	4.72	22	63.64	5.803
TOTALS	782.2	66	43	50	39	70	62	403	4.63	132	50.00	5.929

HOUSTON	IP	QS	W	L	ND	CW	CL	TER	ERA	ST	%QS	AVG IP
M Scott	247.2	24	16	13	7	19	17	89	3.23	36	66.67	6.880
J DeShaies	151.2	12	11	6	8	13	12	75	4.45	25	48.00	6.067
D Darwin	190.0	18	9	10	11	18	12	76	3.60	30	60.00	6.333
N Ryan	211.2	25	8	16	10	12	22	65	2.76	34	73.53	6.225
B Knepper	174.2	12	8	17	6	12	19	104	5.36	31	38.71	5.634
TOTALS	975.2	91	52	62	42	74	82	409	3.77	156	58.33	6.254

LOS ANGELES	IP	QS	W	L	ND	CW	CL	TER	ERA	ST	%QS	AVG IP
O Hershiser	262.1	24	16	15	4	17	18	89	3.05	35	68.57	7.495
B Welch	251.2	23	15	9	11	22	13	90	3.22	35	65.71	7.190
F Valenzuela	251.0	17	14	14	6	16	18	111	3.98	34	50.00	7.382
S Hillegas	54.0	4	4	3	3	5	5	23	3.83	10	40.00	5.400
Belcher	32.0	4	3	2	0	3	2	9	2.53	5	80.00	6.400
TOTALS	851.0	72	52	43	24	63	56	322	3.41	119	60.50	7.151

MONTREAL	IP	QS	W	L	ND	CW	CL	TER	ERA	ST	%QS	AVG IP
N Heaton	193.1	16	13	10	9	19	13	97	4.52	32	50.00	6.042
D Martinez	144.2	14	11	4	7	18	4	53	3.30	22	63.64	6.576
B Smith	150.1	13	10	9	7	13	13	73	4.37	26	50.00	5.782
F Youmans	116.1	9	9	8	6	13	10	60	4.64	23	39.13	5.058
P Perez	70.1	8	7	0	3	9	1	18	2.30	10	80.00	7.033
TOTALS	675.0	60	50	31	32	72	41	301	4.01	113	53.10	5.973

NY METS	IP	QS	W	L	ND	CW	CL	TER	ERA	ST	%QS	AVG IP
D Gooden	179.2	17	15	7	3	15	10	64	3.21	25	68.00	7.187
R Darling	207.2	16	12	8	12	17	15	99	4.29	32	50.00	6.490
S Fernandez	154.0	12	12	9	6	16	11	65	3.80	27	44.44	5.704
R Aguilera	110.2	9	11	3	3	11	6	46	3.74	17	52.94	6.510
T Leach	74.1	8	7	1	4	10	2	29	3.51	12	66.67	6.194
TOTALS	726.1	62	57	28	28	69	44	303	3.75	113	54.87	6.428

PHILADELPHIA	IP	QS	W	L	ND	CW	CL	TER	ERA	ST	%QS	AVG IP
S Rawley	229.2	21	17	11	8	23	13	112	4.39	36	58.33	6.380
D Carman	211.0	19	13	11	11	18	17	99	4.22	35	54.29	6.029
B Ruffin	204.2	14	11	14	10	15	20	99	4.35	35	40.00	5.848
K Gross	199.2	19	8	15	10	14	19	97	4.37	33	57.58	6.050
M Maddux	11.0	1	1	0	1	2	0	2	1.64	2	50.00	5.500
TOTALS	856.0	74	50	51	40	72	69	409	4.30	141	52.48	6.071

PITTSBURGH	IP	QS	W	L	ND	CW	CL	TER	ERA	ST	%QS	AVG IP
M Dunne	163.1	17	13	6	4	13	10	55	3.03	23	73.91	7.101
B Fisher	167.0	12	11	9	6	14	12	79	4.26	26	46.15	6.423
D Drabek	174.1	16	11	12	5	12	16	76	3.92	28	57.14	6.226
R Reuschel	177.0	16	8	6	11	12	13	54	2.75	25	64.00	7.080
B Walk	72.0	9	6	2	4	8	4	24	3.00	12	75.00	6.000
TOTALS	753.2	70	49	35	30	59	55	288	3.44	114	61.40	6.611

SAN DIEGO	IP	QS	W	L	ND	CW	CL	TER	ERA	ST	%QS	AVG IP
E Whitson	202.2	16	10	13	11	17	17	107	4.75	34	47.06	5.961
E Show	206.1	20	8	16	10	13	21	88	3.84	34	58.82	6.069
J Jones	125.1	8	7	7	8	10	12	60	4.31	22	36.36	5.697
M Grant	102.1	8	6	7	4	8	9	53	4.66	17	47.06	6.020
D Dravecky	54.1	5	3	4	3	3	7	22	3.64	10	50.00	5.433
TOTALS	691.0	57	34	47	36	51	66	330	4.30	117	48.72	5.906

SAN FRANCISCO	IP	QS	W	L	ND	CW	CL	TER	ERA	ST	%QS	AVG IP
M LaCoss	155.0	12	12	10	4	12	14	62	3.60	26	46.15	5.962
K Downs	167.2	15	11	8	9	14	14	72	3.86	28	53.57	5.988
A Hammaker	158.0	16	9	10	8	14	13	66	3.76	27	59.26	5.852
D Dravecky	112.2	8	7	5	6	11	7	40	3.20	18	44.44	6.259
R Reuschel	48.0	5	5	2	1	6	2	19	3.56	8	62.50	6.000
TOTALS	641.1	56	44	35	28	57	50	259	3.63	107	52.34	5.994

ST LOUIS	IP	QS	W	L	ND	CW	CL	TER	ERA	ST	%QS	AVG IP
B Forsch	174.2	12	11	7	12	16	14	86	4.43	30	40.00	5.822
D Cox	199.1	20	11	9	11	19	12	86	3.88	31	64.52	6.430
G Mathews	197.2	16	11	11	10	14	18	82	3.73	32	50.00	6.177
J Tudor	96.0	7	10	2	4	14	2	41	3.84	16	43.75	6.000
J Magrane	164.1	18	9	7	10	14	12	63	3.45	26	69.23	6.320
TOTALS	832.0	73	52	41	47	77	58	358	3.87	135	54.07	6.163

TOP FIVE STARTERS PER TEAM—NATIONAL LEAGUE (Continued)

BY ERA	IP	QS	W	L	ND	CW	CL	TER	ERA	ST	%QS	AVG IP
LA	851.0	72	52	43	24	63	56	322	3.41	119	60.50	7.151
PITTS	753.2	70	49	35	30	59	55	288	3.44	114	61.40	6.611
SF	641.1	56	44	35	28	57	50	259	3.63	107	52.34	5.994
NY METS	726.1	62	57	28	28	69	44	303	3.75	113	54.87	6.428
HOUSTON	975.2	91	52	62	42	74	82	409	3.77	156	58.33	6.254
SL	832.0	73	52	41	47	77	58	358	3.87	135	54.07	6.163
MONT	675.0	60	50	31	32	72	41	301	4.01	113	53.10	5.973
PHILA	856.0	74	50	51	40	72	69	409	4.30	141	52.48	6.071
SD	691.0	57	34	47	36	51	66	330	4.30	117	48.72	5.906
CHICAGO	743.0	60	48	38	32	60	58	362	4.38	118	50.85	6.297
ATLANTA	735.1	53	38	45	35	54	64	376	4.60	118	44.92	6.232
CINCI	782.2	66	43	50	39	70	62	403	4.63	132	50.00	5.929
TOTALS	9263.0	794	569	506	413	778	705	4120	4.00	1483	53.54	6.246

TOP FIVE STARTERS PER TEAM—AMERICAN LEAGUE

BALTIMORE	IP	QS	W	L	ND	CW	CL	TER	ERA	ST	%QS	AVG IP
M Boddicker	226.0	16	10	12	11	17	16	105	4.18	33	48.48	6.848
E Bell	154.2	9	10	13	6	12	17	96	5.59	29	31.03	5.333
K Dixon	64.2	4	5	6	3	6	8	46	6.40	14	28.57	4.619
D Schmidt	78.2	8	4	4	6	7	7	35	4.00	14	57.14	5.619
M Griffin	41.2	3	3	4	0	3	4	14	3.02	7	42.86	5.952
TOTALS	565.2	40	32	39	26	45	52	296	4.71	97	41.24	5.832

BOSTON	IP	QS	W	L	ND	CW	CL	TER	ERA	ST	%QS	AVG IP
R Clemens	281.2	23	20	9	7	22	14	93	2.97	36	63.89	7.824
B Hurst	238.2	17	15	13	5	17	16	117	4.41	33	51.52	7.232
A Nipper	174.0	11	11	12	7	13	17	105	5.43	30	36.67	5.800
J Sellers	128.0	9	7	8	7	10	12	74	5.20	22	40.91	5.818
B Stanley	127.2	7	4	12	4	7	13	72	5.08	20	35.00	6.383
TOTALS	950.0	67	57	54	30	69	72	461	4.37	141	47.52	6.738

CALIFORNIA	IP	QS	W	L	ND	CW	CL	TER	ERA	ST	%QS	AVG IP
M Witt	247.0	18	16	14	6	18	18	110	4.01	36	50.00	6.861
D Sutton	187.1	16	10	11	13	15	19	97	4.66	34	47.06	5.510
J Candelaria	116.2	9	8	6	6	12	8	61	4.71	20	45.00	5.833
B Fraser	141.0	10	7	9	7	8	15	68	4.34	23	43.48	6.130
J Reuss	79.2	4	4	5	7	8	8	46	5.20	16	25.00	4.979
TOTALS	771.2	57	45	45	39	61	68	382	4.46	129	44.19	5.982

CHICAGO W SOX	IP	QS	W	L	ND	CW	CL	TER	ERA	ST	%QS	AVG IP
F Bannister	228.2	20	16	11	7	19	15	91	3.58	34	58.82	6.725
R Dotson	211.1	16	11	12	8	12	19	98	4.17	31	51.61	6.817
J DeLeon	204.2	19	11	12	8	17	14	87	3.83	31	61.29	6.602
B Long	143.0	10	7	7	9	12	11	78	4.91	23	43.48	6.217
D LaPoint	76.2	8	6	3	3	6	6	25	2.93	12	66.67	6.389
TOTALS	864.1	73	51	45	35	66	65	379	3.95	131	55.73	6.598

CLEVELAND	IP	QS	W	L	ND	CW	CL	TER	ERA	ST	%QS	AVG IP
P Niekro	123.2	5	7	11	4	9	13	81	5.89	22	22.73	5.621
T Candiotti	201.2	12	7	18	7	9	23	107	4.78	32	37.50	6.302
K Schrom	145.1	8	6	13	10	11	18	105	6.50	29	27.59	5.011
S Bailes	92.1	8	5	7	5	6	11	47	4.58	17	47.06	5.431
J Farrell	68.0	5	4	1	4	4	5	26	3.44	9	55.56	7.556
TOTALS	631.0	38	29	50	30	39	70	366	5.22	109	34.86	5.789

DETROIT	IP	QS	W	L	ND	CW	CL	TER	ERA	ST	%QS	AVG IP
J Morris	266.0	21	18	11	5	21	13	100	3.38	34	61.76	7.823
W Terrell	244.2	21	17	10	8	19	16	110	4.05	35	60.00	6.990
F Tanana	218.2	19	15	10	9	19	15	95	3.91	34	55.88	6.431
D Alexander	88.1	9	9	0	2	11	0	15	1.53	11	81.82	8.030
J Robinson	117.0	8	8	5	8	14	7	69	5.31	21	38.10	5.571
TOTALS	934.2	78	67	36	32	84	51	389	3.75	135	57.78	6.923

KANSAS CITY	IP	QS	W	L	ND	CW	CL	TER	ERA	ST	%QS	AVG IP
B Saberhagen	257.0	19	18	10	5	21	12	96	3.36	33	57.58	7.788
C Liebrandt	240.1	22	16	11	8	21	14	91	3.41	35	62.86	6.867
M Gubicza	241.2	16	13	18	4	15	20	107	3.98	35	45.71	6.905
D Jackson	219.2	16	9	18	7	12	22	98	4.02	34	47.06	6.461
B Black	98.2	10	7	5	6	11	7	44	4.01	18	55.56	5.481
TOTALS	1057.1	83	63	62	30	80	75	436	3.71	155	53.55	6.821

MILWAUKEE	IP	QS	W	L	ND	CW	CL	TER	ERA	ST	%QS	AVG IP
T Higuera	261.2	19	18	10	7	22	13	112	3.85	35	54.29	7.476
J Nieves	194.0	13	14	8	11	19	14	106	4.92	33	39.39	5.879
B Wegman	223.1	20	12	10	11	19	14	104	4.19	33	60.61	6.768
C Bosio	122.1	7	8	7	4	10	9	69	5.08	19	36.84	6.439
L Barker	43.2	2	2	1	8	8	3	26	5.36	11	18.18	3.969
TOTALS	845.0	61	54	36	41	78	53	417	4.44	131	46.56	6.450

MINNESOTA	IP	QS	W	L	ND	CW	CL	TER	ERA	ST	%QS	AVG IP
F Viola	251.2	26	17	10	9	22	14	81	2.90	36	72.22	6.991
B Blyleven	267.0	23	15	12	10	23	14	119	4.01	37	62.16	7.216
L Straker	146.0	11	8	9	9	10	16	71	4.38	26	42.31	5.615
M Smithson	105.1	5	4	7	9	11	9	72	6.15	20	25.00	5.267
J Niekro	95.0	6	4	9	5	6	12	67	6.35	18	33.33	5.278
TOTALS	865.0	71	48	47	42	72	65	410	4.27	137	51.82	6.314

NY YANKEES	IP	QS	W	L	ND	CW	CL	TER	ERA	ST	%QS	AVG IP
R Rhoden	179.2	15	16	10	3	18	11	78	3.91	29	51.72	6.195
T John	187.2	19	13	6	14	22	11	84	4.03	33	57.58	5.687
D Rasmussen	143.0	11	9	7	9	15	10	75	4.72	25	44.00	5.720
C Hudson	98.1	6	6	5	5	7	9	45	4.12	16	37.50	6.146
R Guidry	110.1	8	5	7	5	7	10	47	3.83	17	47.06	6.490
TOTALS	719.0	59	49	35	36	69	51	329	4.12	120	49.17	5.992

OAKLAND	IP	QS	W	L	ND	CW	CL	TER	ERA	ST	%QS	AVG IP
D Stewart	261.1	25	20	13	4	20	17	107	3.68	37	67.57	7.063
C Young	203.0	17	13	7	11	20	11	92	4.08	31	54.84	6.548
S Ontiveros	125.2	7	9	6	7	12	10	56	4.01	22	31.82	5.712
J Andujar	60.2	2	3	5	5	7	6	41	6.08	13	15.38	4.667
M Haas	40.2	1	2	2	5	6	3	26	5.75	9	11.11	4.518
TOTALS	691.1	52	47	33	32	65	47	322	4.19	112	46.43	6.173

SEATTLE	IP	QS	W	L	ND	CW	CL	TER	ERA	ST	%QS	AVG IP
M Langston	272.0	21	19	13	3	21	14	116	3.84	35	60.00	7.771
M Morgan	203.1	13	12	17	2	13	18	106	4.69	31	41.94	6.559
L Gutterman	100.2	7	10	4	3	10	7	44	3.93	17	41.18	5.922
S Bankhead	143.1	12	9	8	8	12	13	83	5.21	25	48.00	5.733
M Moore	231.0	12	9	19	5	12	21	121	4.71	33	36.36	7.000
TOTALS	950.1	65	59	61	21	68	73	470	4.45	141	46.10	6.740

TEXAS	IP	QS	W	L	ND	CW	CL	TER	ERA	ST	%QS	AVG IP
C Hough	285.1	23	18	13	9	22	18	121	3.82	40	57.50	7.133
J Guzman	188.2	11	11	14	5	12	18	104	4.96	30	36.67	6.289
B Witt	142.2	11	8	10	7	13	12	78	4.92	25	44.00	5.707
G Harris	104.1	6	4	7	8	7	12	56	4.83	19	31.58	5.491
E Correa	70.0	4	3	5	7	7	8	59	7.59	15	26.67	4.667
TOTALS	791.0	55	44	49	36	61	68	418	4.76	129	42.64	6.132

TORONTO	IP	QS	W	L	ND	CW	CL	TER	ERA	ST	%QS	AVG IP
J Key	261.0	27	17	8	11	24	12	80	2.76	36	75.00	7.250
J Clancy	241.1	24	15	11	11	22	15	95	3.54	37	64.86	6.523
D Stieb	178.2	14	13	9	9	19	12	83	4.18	31	45.16	5.763
J Cerutti	108.0	10	9	4	8	13	8	57	4.75	21	47.62	5.143
J Johnson	66.2	3	4	4	6	8	6	38	5.13	14	21.43	4.762
TOTALS	855.2	78	58	36	45	86	53	353	3.71	139	56.12	6.156

BY ERA	IP	QS	W	L	ND	CW	CL	TER	ERA	ST	%QS	AVG IP
KC	1057.1	83	63	62	30	80	75	436	3.71	155	53.55	6.821
TOR	855.2	78	58	36	45	86	53	353	3.71	139	56.12	6.156
DET	934.2	78	67	36	32	84	51	389	3.75	135	57.78	6.923
CHIC	864.1	73	51	45	35	66	65	379	3.95	131	55.73	6.598
NY	719.0	59	49	35	36	69	51	329	4.12	120	49.17	5.992
OAK	691.1	52	47	33	32	65	47	322	4.19	112	46.43	6.173
MINN	865.0	71	48	47	42	72	65	410	4.27	137	51.82	6.314
BOS	950.0	67	57	54	30	69	72	461	4.37	141	47.52	6.738
MIL	845.0	61	54	36	41	78	53	417	4.44	131	46.56	6.450
SEAT	950.1	65	59	61	21	68	73	470	4.45	141	46.10	6.740
CAL	771.2	57	45	45	39	61	68	382	4.46	129	44.19	5.982
BALT	565.2	40	32	39	26	45	52	296	4.71	97	41.24	5.832
TEXAS	791.0	55	44	49	36	61	68	418	4.76	129	42.64	6.132
CLEV	631.0	38	29	50	30	39	70	366	5.22	109	34.86	5.789
TOTAL	11492.0	877	703	628	475	943	863	5428	4.25	1806	48.56	6.363

PYTHAGORAS STRIKES AGAIN

Tom Henry

One of the things we try to avoid in the *Stat Book* is making routine predictions for the upcoming season. There are plenty of other publications around for that.

However, a year ago in this publication, I wrote that the San Francisco Giants, despite having what was considered to be a surprisingly successful 1986 season, had actually been a better team that year than their final record indicated. And I predicted a further improvement in 1987.

In a similar vein, I predicted a substantial improvement in performance for the hapless Pittsburgh Pirates, a team that had finished last in the National League East in the three previous seasons, and a team which had looked progressively worse each time.

The rest is history. The Giants went on to win the National League West, and the Bucs were the "surprise" team of 1987, finishing in a tie with Philadelphia for fourth place in the National League East, just two games below .500. That came on the heels of a 64–98 finish in 1986.

The predictions were so outrageous at the time that even my local newspapers refused to give them any play. And the sports editors are friends of mine! The Giants, they said, were a fluke in 1986, and would return to the nether reaches of the NL West in short order. The Pirates were simply hopeless, they added. Besides, nobody in Pittsburgh seemed to care, so why should anyone else?

Predictably, I was vindicated.

The method behind my madness was a little known principle of baseball performance called the Pythagorean theory. Developed by Bill James several years ago, it holds that there is a direct, and measurable, relationship between the number of runs a team scores during the course of a season, the number it allows, and the team's final record. A team that scores 700 runs, and allows 700 runs, should be right around the .500 mark. You don't need a mathematical formula to figure that out. But what about the team that scores 800 runs while allowing 700? They should be over .500, but by how much? Pythagoras can help to measure that.

The numbers can get awkward, but the formula is simple: runs scored, squared; divided by the sum of runs scored, squared, plus runs allowed, squared. The math gives you a percentage figure, which is then applied to 162 games to get a won-loss record. The above fictional numbers would work out like this:

$$\frac{800^2}{800^2 + 700^2} = \frac{640,000}{640,000 + 490,000} = \frac{640,000}{1,130,000} = .566$$

which when applied to 162 games gives a record of 92–70.

OHIO BASEBALL—IT WAS THAT BAD

There were a lot of disappointed baseball fans in the state of Ohio last season. Cincinnati was the consensus choice of baseball pundits to walk through the schedule and win the National League West. After all, the division was weak, Houston couldn't repeat, the Giants would slump (see above) and the Reds had all sorts of upcoming young stars about to make their mark.

Inexplicably, many of those same pundits predicted a championship flag flying over Municipal Stadium in Cleveland by season's end. Carried away by the offensive explosion on the banks of Lake Erie in 1986, they thought that more of the same would occur, and that the pitching would improve enough to allow the Tribe to win the toughest division in baseball. Just from where that pitching was to come was not adequately explained. Pulling for the underdog is one thing, but that was ridiculous. Many of the Indians had enjoyed "career" seasons in 1986, and it was silly to think that they would all duplicate or improve their performance in 1987. The pitching was a joke. The team's 5.28 ERA was the worst in the major leagues since the 1956 Washington Senators, a team that sported a 5.33 figure. The defense was funny, too. Pre-season optimism was rewarded with 101 losses.

Were the Reds and the Indians really that bad? Sadly, the answer is yes. Both ended the season with precisely the won-loss record that the Pythagorean theory says they should have had. The Reds scored 783 runs and allowed 752 which, if you want to do the arithmetic, works out to an 84–78 record. (Note: all numbers are rounded to the nearest whole number.) Cleveland finished 61–101, and crossed the plate 742 times (or 89 times fewer than in 1986) while allowing an incredible 957 runs.

The last time somebody allowed more runs than that was in the super-rabbit-ball year of 1939 when both the Philadelphia A's and the St. Louis Browns allowed more than 1,000. Even Casey Stengel's Amazin' Mets allowed only 940 in 1962, and at least they made it fun by committing 210 errors.

So what does it mean?

It means that both the Reds and the Indians need to make changes if they hope to move up in the standings. It is interesting to note that the Reds scored exactly the same number of runs as San Francisco did last year, 783. But while Cincinnati was allowing 752, the Giants allowed only 669, an 83 run difference, or a little more than half-a-run per game. That says that the Reds need more than just one solid starting pitcher to make a serious run in 1988.

The collapse of Cleveland was total. The Tribe scored 89 fewer runs last year than in 1986, and allowed 116 more than in 1986. That is a 205 run turnaround in just one season, and they don't make any more sure-fire formulas for team collapses than that.

The two examples also are used to illustrate the accuracy of the Pythagorean method. Over the history of baseball, the vast majority of teams has come within four games of their projected Pythagorean records. In most years, no more than two or three clubs exceed that mathematical margin of error. In 1986, for example, only the Giants and

Pittsburgh were outside of the norm. In 1985, Boston substantially underperformed expectations (presaging the Red Sox 1986 World Series appearance) while Cincinnati substantially over-performed, presaging a disappointing 1986 season.

Our interest lies with those teams that are outside of the norms because the law of averages says that those teams should, under normal circumstances, return to their Pythagorean foundations the following year. That seems to be particularly true of underachievers. And that is why a year ago I predicted that San Francisco would continue to confound the skeptics and improve in the standings, and why Pittsburgh would regain some of its past respectability.

Both teams had substantially underperformed in 1986. The Giants finished eight games worse than they should have, and the Pirates were 13 games off the mark. Similarly, the '85 Boston Red Sox had underperformed their anticipated record by nine games. Knowing that in advance would have led one to conclude that the Bosox would be a substantially improved team in 1986, and maybe even a pennant contender. All of which leads to some interesting predictions for 1988.

LOOK OUT BELOW!

Some of 1987's managerial geniuses are heading into some considerably less intelligent times. Tom Kelly of Minnesota, Tom Trebelhorn of Milwaukee and Buck Rodgers in Montreal are the early nominees to spend most of the summer explaining why things aren't going very well. Ditto for Billy Martin with the Yankees; he is going to need all the magic he can find. While it may be difficult for George Steinbrenner to accept, all four of these teams ended up with records considerably better than they should have.

As an old Twins fan, it pains me to write that the Twinkies are alive and well. World Series or not, last season was a mistake, made possible by Jeff Reardon, the Homer Dome mystique and a still-weak AL West.

The Twins went to the World Series even though they were outscored last year. The last team to be substantially over .500 while being outscored was the 1984 New York Mets, featuring a very young pitching staff of Gooden, Darling, Fernandez, Orosco and Sisk. Those people were bound to become more consistent than they had been as rookies (Gooden, Darling and Fernandez), or than they had been as second-year men (Orosco and Sisk), ensuring that the Mets would not fall off their surprising 1984 rebound to respectability.

The only similarity to the Mets staff that the Twins have is Reardon in the bullpen. Juan Berenguer had his career year last season. Frank Viola is the Twins' number-one starter, but is no Gooden; Blyleven isn't getting any younger; and the number-three starter in the World Series was rookie Les Straker, not an immediate candidate for being compared with Darling or Fernandez.

The Twins' 85–77 record was fully six games above their Pythagorean projection. Put another way, the Twins should have finished below .500, and no better than fourth in the Western Division. Kansas City, Oakland and Chicago (yes, the White Sox) should have finished ahead of them.

The White Sox were one of the great underperformers in the league during the first half of the season, posting an All-Star game record seven games worse than they should have. They caught up a bit in the second half of the year, and finished just four games short of their projected 81–81 mark.

Like the Twins, Milwaukee outperformed itself by six games last year to finish at 91–71, seven games behind Detroit. A presentable bullpen headed by Dan Plesac and Chuck Crim was largely responsible. That Milwaukee was substantially improved last year is without question. What is more questionable is whether or not they can hold on to that improvement. Frankly, their chances of doing so are better than those of Minnesota, simply because they have more young pitching talent than do the Twins.

The Yankees were five games better than they had a right to be. New York's offense fell off to 788 runs, while they allowed 758. Injuries to Mattingly, Henderson and Randolph had something to do with that, but whether or not having those people healthy for an entire year will generate enough runs to overcome a weak pitching staff is problematic. St. Louis and San Francisco had plenty of injury problems, too, but won their divisions anyway. And the fact remains that New York should have ended up 84–78 last year, and that is a long way from what it normally takes to win the AL East.

But perhaps the biggest disappointment is about to happen in Montreal. Give Buck Rodgers some credit. The man has done a terrific job with mediocre talent the past two years. However, his magic is likely to disappear in 1988.

The Expos finished 91–71 last year, third in the NL East. It was a remarkable performance. Andre Dawson was gone. Tim Raines was missing until May 1. The pitching was patchwork. Vance Law was playing second base.

The Expos' record was a full eight games better than the numbers indicated it should have been. That's a big, big difference. It cannot be sustained. Tim Wallach has had his career year. Casey Candaele cannot pick up the slack. The pitching staff is still full of sore arms and drug cases. The remarkable rehabilitations of Pascual Perez and Dennis Martinez have to be viewed with a cautious eye. Can that bullpen really put together a combined total of 50 saves again? Hubie Brooks is apparently going to be moved to the outfield, but that leaves a hole at shortstop. You've got to do better than Mike Fitzgerald behind the plate. At least the Expos didn't renew Vance Law's contract. This team is mediocrity waiting to happen, and 1988 ought to be the year it does.

YOU CAN DO BETTER THAN THAT!

On the other hand, there are some teams who seem to have a chance to improve by doing nothing. None underperformed by more than five games a year ago, so the improvements may not be dramatic, but in at least one case, it won't need to be.

If it wasn't for the flopperoony the Toronto Blue Jays pulled during the last week of the season, losing their final seven games to blow a 3 1/2 game lead over Detroit, I would say that you could put a Blue Jays divisional championship in the bank right now. Pythagorically speaking, the Jays were far and away the best team in baseball last year. Their stats called for a 101–61 record, five games better than it was. By contrast, Detroit should have finished 97–65, one game worse than in real life, but four games behind the Toronto figure.

You can look for the Red Sox to begin to move up again, too. The Bosox also underperformed by five games last year, but they did so while embarking on a major youth movement. Dwight Evans isn't going to repeat in 1988 what he did in 1987, but then again, neither will Jim Rice, Rich Gedman or Oil Can Boyd. And with youngsters like Ellis Burks, Sam Horn and Mike Greenwell continuing the Boston tradition of baseball bashing, the Red Sox should start to move up again, particularly with Lee Smith in the bullpen, and Al Nipper and Calvin Schiraldi in Chicago.

Further away from contention, but still poised for an upward move, are the San Diego Padres. Talk about a youth movement! This team of kids finished five games worse than might have been expected, too. However, the law of averages says they will improve by five games next year just by repeating what they did this year, and the law of youth plus experience says their upward move could be considerably more dramatic than that. But there is still no reason for the team's management to start printing playoff tickets.

1987 ACTUAL RECORDS VS. PYTHAGOREAN RECORDS

AL EAST	ACTUAL	R	RA	PYTHAGOREAN	DIFFERENCE
Detroit	98–64	896	735	97–65	+1
Toronto	96–66	845	655	101–61	−5
Milwaukee	91–71	862	817	85–77	+6
New York	89–73	788	758	84–78	+5
Boston	78–84	842	825	83–79	−5
Baltimore	67–85	729	880	66–96	+1
Cleveland	61–101	742	957	61–101	0

AL WEST	ACTUAL	R	RA	PYTHAGOREAN	DIFFERENCE
Minnesota	85–77	786	806	79–83	+6
Kansas City	83–79	715	691	84–78	−1
Oakland	81–81	806	789	83–79	−2
Seattle	78–84	760	801	77–85	+1
Chicago	77–85	748	746	81–81	−4
Texas	75–87	823	849	78–84	−3
California	75–87	770	803	78–84	−3

NL EAST	ACTUAL	R	RA	PYTHAGOREAN	DIFFERENCE
St. Louis	95–67	798	693	92–70	+3
New York	92–70	823	698	94–68	−2
Montreal	91–71	741	720	83–79	+8
Philadelphia	80–82	702	749	76–86	+4
Pittsburgh	80–82	723	744	79–83	+1
Chicago	76–85	720	801	72–89	+4

NL WEST	ACTUAL	R	RA	PYTHAGOREAN	DIFFERENCE
San Francisco	90–72	783	669	94–68	−4
Cincinnati	84–78	783	752	84–78	0
Houston	76–86	648	678	77–85	−1
Los Angeles	73–89	635	675	76–86	−3
Atlanta	69–92	747	829	72–89	−3
San Diego	65–97	668	763	70–92	−5

SOME THEORIES ON THE POST-SEASON MYSTERIES OF THE METRODOME

Bill Jensen

In the movie *Patton,* George C. Scott surveys a battlefield shrouded in a smokey haze, turns to his aide and says: "Now I have precisely the right instrument at precisely the right moment of history in exactly the right place. . . . Like the planets spinning off into the universe, a moment like this won't come again for a thousand years."

Twins fans may have felt a similar surge of optimism in the teflon-filtered light of early afternoon last August. A four-game demolition of the division-leading Oakland Athletics and a quick study of the remaining schedule led to the realization that the best home team in baseball had the right instrument (the Metrodome) at the right time (1987). As planets spun into the universe, baseball purists spun in their graves.

Befitting a team that plays in a stadium infamous for the odd and wacky, the Twins were the subjects of many theories explaining, first, why they couldn't win, and second, their success in 1987. Most of these theories relied on "nonplayer" factors to explain the Twins; to understand why that is so, we must state the problems faced by the Twins in 1987.

A. What the Twins Overcame

Theory 1A: The Twins couldn't win because they were a bunch of smooth-faced suburban kids with no instinct for the jugular.
Advocate: Bill James ('87 *Baseball Abstract*)
What it explains: Why the acquisitions of Jeff Reardon, Juan Berenguer and Dan Gladden, three decidedly unsmooth faces, helped the team so much.
What it doesn't explain: First, how a team that won 85 regular-season games won even a division title, let alone everything; second, how the smoothest of smooth-faced traders, general manager Andy MacPhail, engineered all those trades.

Theory 2A: The Twins succeeded because, at the end of the season, they were a different team than the smooth-faced bunch that began the season.
Advocate: Tim McCarver, ABC-TV analyst.
Proof: ABC-TV presented a graphic showing the Twins' run of 18 wins and 9 losses during August and September.
Problem: The 18–9 streak included 2 extended home stands and 8 road games. The team was more impressive during a May and June streak that produced 21 wins and 7 losses. That string ended during a doubleheader against the Texas Rangers, when Berenguer's overworked arm needed time off. The Twins were better in June than October.

Theory 3A: The Twins couldn't win because they lacked depth in starting pitchers.
Advocates: Anyone who followed baseball.

Neatest Trick: Cardinals manager Whitey Herzog came close to arguing this into an advantage during the World Series. He said lack of depth wouldn't hurt the Twins because, with off-days, they could start Frank Viola and Bert Blyleven in five of the seven games.

Theory 4A: The Twins couldn't win because the current ownership had not acquitted itself well with Calvin Griffith's legacy.
Advocate: The present writer ('87 *GABSB*)
Theory: No longer applicable.

B. The Dome: The Right Weapon at the Right Time

Theory 1B: The variable jetstream. Twins hitters are aided by blowers that are turned on during the home half of the inning.
Advocates: Yankees announcer Billy Martin, Rangers manager Bobby Valentine and other amateur meteorologists.
Credibility: None. Home and away home run totals, knowledge of mechanical systems and the realization of how much wind is necessary to propel a ball out of an outdoor park discredited this theory several years ago. Its recent resurgence was short-lived.

Theory 2B: Center field spy theory. A sign-stealer stationed in center field, disguised as a fan or TV cameraman, relays the catcher's signs directly or electronically to the batter, a coach on the field or a coach in the dugout. This knowledge gives the Twins their huge home-field advantage.
Chief Advocate: Seattle manager Dick Williams
Propagandist: Sportswriter Tom Boswell
Other Support: Before the American League Championship Series, TV-analyst Don Sutton said the Brewers stole signs during the '83 season—one of those old baseball stories of the binoculars-in-the-scoreboard variety.
Counterpoint: I usually sit in center field and have never observed any clandestine activity of a baseball nature. Herzog, after studying tapes, said he was unable to find a way that the Twins were being tipped off (*The Sporting News,* Nov. 2). Finding no evidence does not disprove a theory, so expect to hear more of the same next year.

Theory 3B: Multiple Shadows Theory.
Advocates: Tony Kubek and outfielders by the dozens.
How it works: Originally this theory was restricted to explaining why outfielders lost routine fly balls. Speculation centered on a sort of Metrodome Triangle created by poor lighting. Because fielders lost track of many flyballs during the park's first years, the theory was not debated much. The humor in watching Gorman Thomas charge around center field with his arms outstretched while pleading for help was undeniable.

During the ALCS, Kubek revised and extended the poor lighting theory to explain the Twins' pitching success at home. He held that visiting teams required a game or two to adjust their batting eyes to the nightclub atmosphere. This argument is similar to attributing an advantage to a power pitcher in a poor-visibility stadium (Dwight Gooden in Shea). But the Twins do not have hard-throwing starters, and their advantage diminishes over the course of a series.

Support: From 1984 to 1987 the Twins won 70 percent of first games in home series but only 48 percent of the remaining games. On the road, the Twins were successful in about 37 percent of all games, showing no preference for first games.

Not so fast: Last season, the club won 65 percent of first games, then went on to win 70 percent of the remaining contests. With the installation of a saner if less-fun rug, much of the adjustment required in the dome has disappeared along with the kangaroo hops that bedeviled visiting fielders for five years.

Theory 4B: Little things happen. All of the above combine to provide the wide disparity in the Twins' home and road records.

Advocate: Kirby Puckett

Examples: During the AL Championship Series, Larry Herndon misplays a ball that spins demoniacally off the tarp and turf in the right field corner, resulting in a triple. During the World Series, Willie McGee and Vince Coleman lose track of the ball. (See also Team of Destiny theory.)

C. An Invisible Hand.

Theory 1C: Team of Destiny. When the Twins needed a victory, something absurd happened.

Proponents: Twin Cities television personalities and born-again baseball fans.

Example: It's Sept. 5, bottom of the eighth. The Twins, handcuffed by Brewers' pitcher Juan Nieves through seven, are trailing 1–0. With Jeff Newman on first and two outs, Puckett steps to the plate. He lines the first pitch to right center where Rick Manning (a late-inning defensive replacement in right) turns to make a routine running catch. Manning promptly trips and falls smack on his face. While Brewers fans boo and Twins fans yell, Newman scores before center fielder Robin Yount can make the play. Tom Brunansky, swinging at the first pitch to lead off the Twins' ninth, homers to center for the win. This game occurs in the middle of a starburst of one-run, late-inning thrillers and further enhances "Destiny" theory.

Critique: The theory was much in vogue after the Twins defeated the Tigers' "invincible" Doyle Alexander and Jack Morris. Like most mystical explanations, this hypothesis defies rational analysis.

Theory 2C: Homer Hanky Hell. Believers in Destiny grew weary of waiting for events to run their preordained course. They eagerly helped the Invisible Hand in its work by identifying sinners and inspiring goodness in the home team.

Advocates: *Minneapolis Star Tribune* newspaper (the Homer Hanky inventor), Team of Destiny proponents and Paul Attner of *The Sporting News*.

Accomplishments: The noise made Tigers manager Sparky Anderson ill, according to various publications, and drove visiting players and sportswriters to wearing ear plugs.

What it doesn't explain: The home-field advantage for the Twins over the last four years has been quite pronounced whether the crowds were large or small, and certainly before those pieces of cloth were waved in the indoor breeze.

Dissent: "Our fans are great; they help us a lot," manager Tom Kelly told *The Sporting News*. "But not a single one of them has hit or caught a baseball for us this year."

Theory 3C: The Invisible Hand, the Dark Side. Hubert Humphrey, Walter Mondale, Harold Stassen and Bud Grant were big-game losers; therefore, the Twins will lose.

Advocates: Pat Reusse (St. Paul sportswriter), Tom Gage (Detroit sportswriter) and the sportswriters of America.

Critique: This nonharmonic convergence of unrelated events was humorous in the first article, boring in the next 500 and reached the height of absurdity when *The Sporting News* ran several articles with the same premise and Dan Rather used it introduce a CBS News segment on the World Series.

What it explains: The episode is primarily useful in demonstrating the reasons why sportswriters are susceptible to Invisible Hand theories.

Theory 4C: The whiteness of the whale. It is the very whiteness of the evil object that is so appalling.

Advocate: Herman Melville

Proof: The roof was white. The ball was white. In 1987, a sea of white hankies blended with the whiteness of the Twins' home uniforms and shook in defiance of two white-haired managers in the white noise of the dome. Many a baseball aficionado hopes a moment like that won't come again for 1,000 years.

WHITEY HERZOG—THE PLAYER

Brock J. Hanke

When Whitey Herzog talks about his playing career, he presents himself as a modest talent who scrambled into the majors for a few brief years on the basis of being willing to work long hours of overtime. His record, however, and the facts surrounding it, paint the picture of a more talented player than that, and "thereby hangs a tale."

When Whitey entered organized baseball, according to his own autobiography, he really had two primary talents. His throwing arm was quite strong, and his speed was among the best in baseball, including the majors. He was a good hitter, though he had trouble with left-handed pitching, particularly curveballs, and didn't have much power. That's a decent centerfield prospect.

He wasn't in a real good organization (the Senators), and their responses to his hitting problems were either to platoon him or try to make a pitcher out of him. They never did try to make anything out of his speed, except to let him play center, and eventually traded him to the A's. This wasn't a much better outfit, but Whitey was making slow progress.

In 1959, hitting .293 as a platoon player (you might expect .270 or so as a full-time man), he seemed ready to establish himself. A 10+-year-career and a couple of appearances on the All-Star team did not seem out of line. A similar contemporary player might have been Jimmy Piersall. Curt Flood, too, was similar: a better flycatcher than Whitey, but with a weaker arm. Whitey's seasons from 1959 through 1962 could be prorated out to full-time play and not be out of place in either Flood's or Piersall's career. 1959 or '61 would have been the career on-base percentage high for Piersall or Flood, who didn't walk much.

Piersall and Flood, however, were never seriously injured, while Whitey took a shot to the knee which then calcified up. Trying to play through the pain, he did not give the knee time to heal properly, and lost some of his speed. He also lost his big chance to win a regular job; though, looking at his 1961 season, it's hard to see why the Orioles (he was then with Baltimore) didn't give him a bigger break. Perhaps he wasn't really fast enough for center by then. It's somewhat interesting that the very virtue that Whitey most often allows himself, the willingness to work harder than anyone else, was the attribute that most likely did his career in, but that's not what is most interesting.

Consider what would happen if Whitey Herzog were to enter the Cardinal organization as a 19-year-old right now. They'd give him a year in the Rookie League, find out he couldn't hit the lefty curve, and then say, "Right. What this kid needs to do is learn to switch-hit, so he can deal with lefties." That is what the Cardinals do, you know. Whitey, extremely bright (a talent that is not usually listed among the baseball sort, but which certainly is useful) and willing to work, presumably would learn that. Then he'd go to class A ball and the manager would say, "Right. This is my fastest player, and I'm in the Cardinal organization. He's going to learn to steal bases, and he's going to learn to play center field properly." So the baserunning gurus would be called in, and attempt to show Whitey the tricks of this trade, and he'd be out there taking an extra 100 fly balls a day. Again, Whitey learns fast and works hard.

Now he's at Arkansas, in AA ball, and hitting .320, but it's still .340 against righthanders and .280 against lefties, and there's still not much power. So they say, "Right. This kid learns to bunt and take walks, so he can bat leadoff." Whitey already takes many more walks than the average, without anyone to help him. A year in Louisville to put it all together, and Whitey's a major league leadoff man and centerfielder, like Vince Coleman with a little power. He's hitting .290 or .300, with only 8 to 12 homers a year, but with 80+ walks and 30 to 50 stolen bases. He's scoring 90 to 100 runs a year and can play center with anybody. He plays 15 years, starts the All-Star game once (in a year when no power hitter is playing center), and gets on the team 5 more times as a reserve. He wins a few Gold Gloves. He doesn't make the Hall of Fame, but he does make his team's Hall. At every stage in his development as a player, the Cardinal organization is there, with just the right emphasis as a teaching system to help Whitey's type of player.

What I want to know is when, Whitey, did you decide to build a whole organization dedicated to getting the most out of exactly the young ballplayer you were? I do understand why.

MARKOV CHAIN MODELS: AN UPDATE

Mark D. Pankin

In last year's *Great American Baseball Stat Book* (*GABSB*-1), I described a particular type of mathematical model, the Markov Chain, that can be applied to baseball analysis. The examples shown were based on a rather limited set of data, 37 Baltimore home games from 1985 and 74 Cincinnati home games from 1986, that I had input into the computer for Project Scoresheet. Since that time, I have obtained the complete 1986 data sets from the Project on floppy disks, so this year I will report my findings based on all of 1986 major league play.

Those readers wanting an extensive description of Markov Chain models, the computational techniques, and how I use the Project Scoresheet data are encouraged to read the essay I wrote last year. To summarize very briefly, the Markov Chain baseball model considers the transitions between runners and outs situations or "states" that occur during a half-inning (the half—will be left out for brevity in the rest of this paper). There are 24 such situations, which are listed below using the notation (runners, outs):

TABLE 1: RUNNERS AND OUTS COMBINATIONS

Runners:	0(none)	1	2	3	12	13	23	123
0:	(0,0)	(1,0)	(2,0)	(3,0)	(12,0)	(13,0)	(23,0)	(123,0)
Outs 1:	(0,1)	(1,1)	(2,1)	(3,1)	(12,1)	(13,1)	(23,1)	(123,1)
2:	(0,2)	(1,2)	(2,2)	(3,2)	(12,2)	(13,2)	(23,2)	(123,2)

For computational purposes, there are additional states for three outs and plays such as stolen bases and wild pitches that do not change the batter.

The Markov Chain model applies techniques of matrix mathematics to arrive at computational results that are almost impossible to achieve with other methods. The primary benefits resulting from the Markov framework are 1) the quick computation, without simplifying assumptions, of quantities useful for a variety of analytic purposes, and 2) the calculation of theoretical "strategy free" values that can be used in strategy analysis. Most other published tables of average runs scored and scoring probabilities show results computed directly from actual play, and thus they incorporate the effects of all of the strategies employed in the games. The Markov Chain model enables the computation of these values after eliminating sacrifice bunt attempts, stolen bases, times caught stealing, and/or intentional walks. Such computations provide a better basis for analyzing sacrifices and stolen bases. Unfortunately, the Project Scoresheet data files do not provide enough information to identify other strategies such as hit-and-run plays, playing the infield in, and pitching around a batter.

Tables 2 to 5 display situational data, both as observed in actual games and theoretical Markov Chain values. The simplest Markov model, which is used for almost all of the computations in the tables, assumes a sequence of identical average hitters. More realistic models are possible, but such models require greatly increased data development, more involved computations, and a considerably more detailed

TABLE 2: AVERAGE RUNS AFTER EACH SITUATION AMERICAN LEAGUE 1986 (ALL GAMES)

Situation	Number	Observed	MARKOV All Plays	MARKOV Strategy Free
1 (0,0)	21081	0.518	0.519	0.519
2 (0,1)	15000	0.272	0.281	0.281
3 (0,2)	11962	0.104	0.107	0.107
4 (1,0)	5556	0.898	0.893	0.893
5 (1,1)	6480	0.547	0.551	0.554
6 (1,2)	6456	0.237	0.230	0.229
7 (2,0)	1449	1.161	1.132	1.125
8 (2,1)	2822	0.721	0.708	0.696
9 (2,2)	3363	0.322	0.331	0.326
10 (3,0)	289	1.394	1.389	1.385
11 (3,1)	931	0.975	0.972	0.970
12 (3,2)	1378	0.390	0.400	0.397
13 (12,0)	1271	1.485	1.513	1.504
14 (12,1)	2383	0.906	0.958	0.954
15 (12,2)	2927	0.463	0.462	0.463
16 (13,0)	500	1.848	1.810	1.796
17 (13,1)	1099	1.155	1.178	1.173
18 (13,2)	1478	0.553	0.523	0.518
19 (23,0)	329	1.988	2.023	1.988
20 (23,1)	761	1.399	1.410	1.364
21 (23,2)	844	0.653	0.665	0.654
22 (123,0)	310	2.648	2.521	2.514
23 (123,1)	779	1.492	1.601	1.601
24 (123,2)	872	0.821	0.812	0.816
	90320			

exposition than this essay. One enhancement to the simplest model, which is used in the National League tables, models an average pitcher hitting next followed by a sequence of average non-pitchers. Tables 2 and 3 contain data for the average number of runs scored in the remainder of the inning following the indicated runners and outs combination.

The column headed number shows how many times each situation occurred in actual play. The next column, observed, contains the average number of runs scored in actual play after each of the situations. The final two columns contain these averages as computed using the Markov Chain model. The all plays does not eliminate any strategy plays and is presented for comparison to the observed values. There is good but not exact agreement, and the differences are due primarily to not having a sequence of identical average batters in actual play as opposed to assuming such a sequence in the Markov model. The values in the last column are computed after the elimination of intentional walks, sacrifice bunt attempts, and stolen bases and times caught stealing. These values are for the most part slightly less than the all plays Markov values, which indicates that the strategies as actually employed in the games tended to increase scoring a bit. This effect, however, is due entirely to the intentional walks. (The Markov values including

TABLE 3: AVERAGE RUNS AFTER EACH SITUATION
NATIONAL LEAGUE 1986 (ALL GAMES)

			MARKOV			
Sit'n	Number	Observed	All Plays	Strategy Free	No Pitcher	Pitcher First
1	18101	0.462	0.466	0.468	0.499	0.396
2	12985	0.250	0.243	0.244	0.264	0.185
3	10384	0.092	0.090	0.088	0.097	0.042
4	4659	0.803	0.837	0.844	0.880	0.625
5	5310	0.489	0.496	0.507	0.534	0.316
6	5226	0.216	0.212	0.208	0.225	0.122
7	1528	1.053	1.075	1.064	1.100	0.939
8	2652	0.652	0.649	0.628	0.657	0.504
9	3208	0.315	0.317	0.304	0.320	0.173
10	279	1.308	1.315	1.316	1.355	1.188
11	965	0.861	0.890	0.886	0.919	0.664
12	1363	0.342	0.355	0.345	0.362	0.217
13	963	1.405	1.468	1.462	1.505	1.376
14	1892	0.815	0.853	0.852	0.887	0.793
15	2454	0.411	0.412	0.408	0.440	0.248
16	486	1.549	1.723	1.722	1.766	1.564
17	939	1.071	1.156	1.152	1.196	0.830
18	1151	0.490	0.495	0.480	0.517	0.227
19	199	1.935	2.047	2.016	2.048	2.200
20	611	1.354	1.380	1.344	1.388	1.248
21	732	0.604	0.596	0.568	0.604	0.343
22	218	2.188	2.377	2.370	2.422	2.298
23	638	1.445	1.484	1.483	1.543	1.271
24	804	0.741	0.755	0.752	0.816	0.364
	77747					

TABLE 4: PROBABILITY OF SCORING AFTER EACH SITUATION
AMERICAN LEAGUE 1986 (ALL GAMES)

		MARKOV	
Situation	Observed	All Plays	Strategy Free
1 (0,0)	0.287	0.312	0.291
2 (0,1)	0.169	0.193	0.174
3 (0,2)	0.072	0.088	0.076
4 (1,0)	0.437	0.473	0.442
5 (1,1)	0.288	0.339	0.299
6 (1,2)	0.136	0.186	0.138
7 (2,0)	0.628	0.617	0.617
8 (2,1)	0.429	0.423	0.415
9 (2,2)	0.222	0.234	0.228
10 (3,0)	0.837	0.854	0.854
11 (3,1)	0.662	0.677	0.672
12 (3,2)	0.288	0.304	0.295
13 (12,0)	0.632	0.624	0.639
14 (12,1)	0.430	0.466	0.454
15 (12,2)	0.240	0.270	0.263
16 (13,0)	0.852	0.842	0.865
17 (13,1)	0.647	0.677	0.660
18 (13,2)	0.304	0.356	0.309
19 (23,0)	0.866	0.869	0.866
20 (23,1)	0.666	0.679	0.674
21 (23,2)	0.301	0.306	0.301
22 (123,0)	0.897	0.894	0.893
23 (123,1)	0.684	0.690	0.690
24 (123,2)	0.339	0.349	0.343

intentional walks but excluding the other strategies are not shown in these tables.) Consequently, the offensive strategies of sacrifice bunt and stolen base tries had the net effect of decreasing total scoring. Since these are usually "one run" strategies, the decrease does not necessarily mean the strategies were employed unwisely. I will return to this question later.

The first four columns after each situation are the same as in Table 2. The last two columns are provided because pitchers bat in the NL. (The DH rule does make life easier for sabermetricians!) The no pitcher column is similar to the strategy free but assuming a sequence of average non-pitchers as hitters. In pitcher first column, the assumption is that an average pitcher will hit next after the situation followed by a sequence of average non-pitchers.

Tables 4 and 5 have the same format as Tables 2 and 3 but provide data about the probability of scoring one or more runs in the remainder of the inning after each situation. These tables are of greatest interest when studying one run strategies.

Next we turn to using the data in these tables to analyze the sacrifice bunt and stolen base strategies. The most common type of analysis using situational data involves the computation of break-even success probabilities. In these calculations, usually only the two most common outcomes are considered. However, there are more than two possibilities. On a stolen base attempt, the runner may advance further due to an error. The sacrifice bunt has a richer set of outcomes, ranging from a triple or double play to the batter reaching base and runners scoring. The Markov Chain matrix framework enables the consideration of more than two outcomes with relative ease. Instead of a break-

TABLE 5: PROBABILITY OF SCORING AFTER EACH SITUATION
NATIONAL LEAGUE 1986 (ALL GAMES)

		MARKOV			
Sit'n	Observed	All Plays	Strategy Free	No Pitcher	Pitcher First
1	0.266	0.298	0.269	0.283	0.229
2	0.155	0.178	0.155	0.166	0.118
3	0.062	0.079	0.063	0.069	0.028
4	0.420	0.482	0.432	0.444	0.330
5	0.270	0.333	0.285	0.296	0.187
6	0.124	0.192	0.133	0.142	0.072
7	0.612	0.610	0.599	0.611	0.527
8	0.405	0.401	0.388	0.399	0.328
9	0.219	0.228	0.219	0.227	0.126
10	0.803	0.828	0.825	0.835	0.760
11	0.603	0.638	0.626	0.639	0.464
12	0.254	0.274	0.259	0.268	0.167
13	0.624	0.647	0.637	0.648	0.595
14	0.393	0.434	0.420	0.430	0.407
15	0.220	0.250	0.242	0.256	0.138
16	0.819	0.847	0.852	0.861	0.763
17	0.647	0.686	0.662	0.677	0.454
18	0.284	0.366	0.292	0.309	0.130
19	0.879	0.871	0.872	0.877	0.917
20	0.679	0.678	0.682	0.702	0.527
21	0.284	0.275	0.267	0.280	0.161
22	0.917	0.879	0.877	0.882	0.857
23	0.660	0.651	0.646	0.657	0.578
24	0.322	0.323	0.323	0.345	0.152

even analysis, the following tables evaluate the results of sacrifice bunt and stolen base attempts considering all outcomes according to probabilities determined by the what happened in actual 1986 play.

The sacrifice bunt with one runner on base is without a doubt a "one-run" strategy because the team is willing to trade an out, which reduces the expected scoring, for a base, which may increase the chance of that runner scoring. With two runners on, the sacrifice may be a one or a two run strategy. Table 6 shows the net results for the AL for the three most common sacrifice bunt situations.

TABLE 6: SACRIFICE BUNT ANALYSIS, AL 1986

	PROBABILITY OF SCORING		Gain or Loss
Situation	Before Bunt	After Bunt	from Bunt
(1,0)	0.442	0.378	−0.064
(2,0)	0.617	0.638	0.021
(12,0)	0.639	0.584	−0.055

Probability of scoring is the appropriate yardstick to evaluate a one-run strategy such as the sacrifice. The before bunt values are the no strategy values taken from the Table 4 strategy free column, and they represent the chance of scoring if the sacrifice (or any other strategy) is not employed in the situation. The after bunt value accounts for the probabilities of the various bunt outcomes and the probabilities of scoring after each of the resulting situations. An example of this calculation appears in my essay in *GABSB*-1. Table 5 shows the bunt was, on the average, not a good play in the AL in 1986 with a runner on first or runners on first and second. The bunt with a runner on second did show a slight improvement in the chance of scoring the runner. The bunt in the (12,0) situation also led to a decrease in the probability of scoring two runs (0.409 to 0.359).

TABLE 7: SACRIFICE BUNT ANALYSIS, NL 1986—NON-PITCHERS

	PROBABILITY OF SCORING		Gain or Loss
Situation	Before Bunt	After Bunt	from Bunt
(1,0)	0.444	0.352	−0.092
(2,0)	0.611	0.579	−0.032
(12,0)	0.648	0.623	−0.025

In this table the probabilities of scoring are computed using the no pitcher values, which are strategy free, from Table 5. We see that the bunt by non-pitchers reduced the chances of scoring in all three situations in the NL. The bunt in the (12,0) state reduced the probability of scoring two runs from 0.405 to 0.369.

For pitchers, however, the story is much different. Table 8 shows the results for no out and one out situations where there were enough bunt attempts to be meaningful.

In this table, the before bunt values are from the pitcher first column in Tables 3 and 5, and they correspond to letting the pitcher hit away rather than bunt. The after bunt values are calculated using the probabilities determined by the pitcher bunts and the no pitcher values from Tables 3 and 5 for the corresponding outcomes. We see that with the exception of the (12,1) situation, having pitchers bunt in-

TABLE 8: SACRIFICE BUNT ANALYSIS, NL 1986—PITCHERS

	PROBABILITY OF SCORING			AVERAGE RUNS		
	Before	After	Gain or	Before	After	Gain or
Situation	Bunt	Bunt	Loss	Bunt	Bunt	Loss
(1,0)	0.330	0.386	0.056	0.625	0.662	0.037
(1,1)	0.187	0.215	0.028	0.316	0.317	0.001
(2,0)	0.527	0.665	0.138	0.939	1.051	0.112
(12,0)	0.595	0.612	0.017	1.376	1.311	−0.065
(12,1)	0.407	0.285	−0.122	0.793	0.587	−0.206

creases the chance of scoring at least one run. Moreover, with only one runner on, the bunt even increases expected total scoring. Of course, this is hardly startling; pitchers are usually asked to bunt in these situations.

These results are in contrast to those presented in last year's essay based on the limited data. Then, there was evidence that bunts by non-pitchers might well increase the chances of scoring.

One problem with the above sacrifice bunt analysis is the assumption of a sequence of identical average hitters. However, the results shown can provide some general guidance. The pitcher table shows the advantage of having weak hitters bunt. Conversely, the better the hitter, the larger the loss, particularly in expected runs, from the sacrifice play. Thus, the not uncommon practice of having the lineup's number-two hitter, who usually is a decent batter, bunt after the leadoff man has reached first is almost certainly a poor strategy. This is especially true in the early innings when the main concern should be scoring a lot of runs rather than just one run.

One question that came up in last year's essay was whether pitchers were poorer bunters than non-pitchers, but I had not developed the data needed to answer it. This time, I separated pitcher and non-pitcher sacrifice attempts. To simplify a bit, group the outcomes into four categories: terrible (double play), bad (batter out, at least one runner does not advance), good (batter out, all runners advance), great (batter and all runners safe). Table 9 shows the comparison for NL play for the most frequent bunt situations.

Table 9 almost raises as many questions as it answers. Why should pitchers have a lower percentage of both the best and worst outcomes on bunt plays? Because pitchers have a higher percentage of favorable—good or great—results, I would say that the evidence points to pitchers as the better bunters, contrary to what my guess would have been. Consider that all pitchers are told to bunt, but non-pitchers who are poor bunters are rarely made to bunt. Moreover, because the DH rule is used in the minors, the NL pitchers don't even get to hit and bunt in games until they reach the majors. What's more, the defense is always looking for the bunt when pitchers bat, while non-pitchers often have the element of surprise on their side. On the other hand, the pitchers probably work more on their bunting skills. One caveat: The nature of the Project Scoresheet data files makes it very difficult to tell the score of the game when the bunts took place, so I assumed that any bunt play not scored as a sacrifice in an appropriate sacrifice situation was in fact a sacrifice attempt. I doubt that the few extra sacrifice-try transitions that resulted would qualitatively change Table 9.

Next, we look at stolen base attempts. While the stolen base is usually considered to be primarily a one run strategy, it can also be considered as a play to increase total scoring. Tables 10 and 11 analyze the play with respect to both objectives for the most common stolen base situations. These tables are similar in design to Tables 6 and 7. For the AL, strategy free Markov values are used, and for the NL, the no pitcher strategy free values are used in the calculations.

These two tables show that the stolen base should be considered a one-run strategy because as practiced, it rarely increases average total scoring. However, in some situations, it does increase the chance of scoring one run. What seems surprising is how often the steal is attempted in the (13,2) situation. Presumably, this is a steal of second base with a hoped for delayed steal of home if the defense messes up. As the table shows, with average hitters at the plate, this play doesn't work enough to justify the risk on ending the inning when two runners are on base.

In contrast to last year's essay, the tables above are generally applicable to major league play. For the most part, the results shown agree with conclusions reached by many other strategy analysts. However, I feel the Markov Chain model has advantages for this type of work, one of which is the ability to get deeper into the play-by-play data without getting bogged down in the computational complexities. One typical by-product of the Markov formulation can be seen in Table 9, which is readily available from the data developed to support the Markov Chain model. I hope this essay (and last year's) has served to enlighten, has presented results that stimulate thought and discussion, and has encouraged others to investigate the Markov model.

TABLE 9: SACRIFICE ATTEMPT RESULTS—NL 1986
(A) NON-PITCHERS

| Outcome | Runners and Outs Situation | | | |
	(1,0)	(2,0)	(12,0)	Total
Great	36(10%)	15(13%)	17(14%)	68(11%)
Good	213(58%)	75(66%)	72(59%)	360(60%)
Bad	49(13%)	11(10%)	22(18%)	82(14%)
Terrible	68(19%)	13(11%)	12(10%)	93(15%)
	366(100%)	114(100%)	123(100%)	603(100%)

(B) PITCHERS

| Outcome | Runners and Outs Situation | | | | | |
	(1,0)	(1,1)	(2,0)	(12,0)	(12,1)	Total
Great	9(4%)	8(4%)	7(16%)	7(17%)	1(2%)	32(6%)
Good	146(73%)	144(75%)	35(81%)	19(45%)	31(72%)	375(72%)
Bad	42(21%)	32(17%)	1(2%)	14(33%)	11(26%)	100(19%)
Terrible	4(2%)	8(4%)	0	2(5%)	0	14(3%)
	201(100%)	192(100%)	43(100%)	42(100%)	43(100%)	521(100%)

TABLE 10: STOLEN BASE ATTEMPT ANALYSIS, AL 1986

| Sit'n | No. of Plays | PROBABILITY OF SCORING | | | AVERAGE RUNS | | |
		Before Play	After Play	Gain or Loss	Before Play	After Play	Gain or Loss
(1,0)	405	0.442	0.475	0.033	0.893	0.845	−0.048
(1,1)	632	0.299	0.293	−0.006	0.554	0.477	−0.077
(1,2)	743	0.138	0.160	0.022	0.229	0.227	−0.002
(2,0)	14	0.617	0.563	−0.054	1.125	0.912	−0.213
(2,1)	61	0.415	0.486	0.071	0.696	0.701	0.005
(2,2)	27	0.228	0.180	−0.048	0.326	0.243	−0.083
(12,0)	18	0.639	0.608	−0.031	1.504	1.281	−0.223
(12,1)	51	0.454	0.481	0.027	0.954	0.885	−0.069
(12,2)	33	0.263	0.184	−0.079	0.463	0.368	−0.095
(13,0)	17	0.865	0.828	−0.037	1.796	1.782	−0.014
(13,1)	56	0.660	0.514	−0.146	1.173	0.970	−0.203
(13,2)	99	0.309	0.233	−0.076	0.518	0.496	−0.022

TABLE 11: STOLEN BASE ATTEMPT ANALYSIS, NL 1986

| Sit'n | No. of Plays | PROBABILITY OF SCORING | | | AVERAGE RUNS | | |
		Before Play	After Play	Gain or Loss	Before Play	After Play	Gain or Loss
(1,0)	580	0.444	0.499	0.055	0.880	0.880	——
(1,1)	769	0.296	0.283	−0.013	0.534	0.453	−0.081
(1,2)	778	0.142	0.160	0.018	0.225	0.224	−0.001
(2,0)	23	0.611	0.748	0.137	1.100	1.213	0.113
(2,1)	77	0.399	0.442	0.043	0.657	0.637	−0.020
(2,2)	51	0.227	0.214	−0.013	0.320	0.290	−0.030
(12,0)	12	0.648	0.723	0.075	1.505	1.541	0.036
(12,1)	67	0.430	0.451	0.021	0.887	0.804	−0.083
(12,2)	36	0.256	0.193	−0.063	0.440	0.371	−0.069
(13,0)	29	0.861	0.794	−0.067	1.766	1.665	−0.101
(13,1)	68	0.677	0.560	−0.117	1.196	1.053	−0.143
(13,2)	121	0.309	0.227	−0.082	0.517	0.472	−0.045

SIMPLIFIED METHOD FOR RUN CREATION MEASUREMENT

Matthew E. Lieff

Combining Markov Analysis and Run Potential theory provides a powerful method for measuring run creation from performance records expressed as state transitions. However, with 314 transitions allowed by baseball's rules, calculation of runs created seasonal totals is theoretically and arithmetically complex. This article will show that knowledge of particular state transitions is not needed to calculate run creation; rather, all that is required is the frequency of occurrence of the 24 possible initial states, and the 28 possible final states. A simple calculation technique based on these 52 frequencies, rather than the 314-element array, is presented.

First, a brief review of run creation theory. Markov Analysis describes a batter's effect through the concept of "state transitions." This is the change in state from before the plate appearance to the conclusion of the play. A state describes the number of outs and the distribution of men on base. Since there are 3 possible out situations at the beginning of a plate appearance (0, 1, or 2), and 8 possible men on base situations, there are 24 possible initial states. There are 28 possible final states because, for bookkeeping purposes, there have to be states describing the 3-out situations for plate appearances that end innings (only 4 states are added, since it does not matter which bases are occupied, only how many). For more on this, see Mark Pankin's article in *GABSB*-1.

Run potential can be defined as the expectation of the number of runs that will score following a given initial state. Palmer and Thorn introduced this idea in *The Hidden Game of Baseball* and provided potential values for the different states based on computer simulation. At SABR-17, Peter Jensen presented run potential numbers calculated from actual 1986 performance.

Gary Skoog tied the two concepts together in his article in the 1987 *Bill James Baseball Abstract*. He defined the Runs Created (RC) per plate appearance as follows:

$$RC = \text{Delta } E + RRF + K$$

Delta E is the change in run potential caused by the plate appearance; that is, the potential of the final state minus the potential of the initial state. RRF (Runs Responsible For) is the number of runs that scored on the play. K is a constant that must be added so that the Runs Created equal the actual runs scored. Since all innings starts with positive potential (.454 according to Palmer and Thorn) and most end, at 3 outs, with zero potential, there will be negative runs created if nobody scores, and in general, RC will be less than actual runs scored by .454 per inning, without a correction. (Skoog described 3 ways to do it.)

To find total runs created per season, sum runs created over all plate appearances. One way is to create an array, with the 24 initial states down the vertical axis, and the 28 final states across the horizontal axis. Each element in the array represents a particular state transition. Most will be impossible given the rules of baseball: You can't go from a 2-out state to a one-out state, for example. It is simple to calculate RC for each possible transition. The potential for the initial and final states are provided either by Palmer and Thorn or by Jensen. RRF can easily be deduced from the given initial and final states. K can be calculated most simply here by using Skoog's error correction method RC2, adding 1/3 of .454 to each transition involving one out. (Alternatively, using RC3, a constant could be added to each plate appearance at the end of the season, but this would be difficult for running totals. RC1 could be treated similarly.)

Imagine each player with a blank array on opening day. Each plate appearance puts a hash mark in one of the elements of the array. At the end of the season, the total RC for the player equals the summation, over the 314 possible transitions, of the RC value assigned to that transition multiplied by its frequency of occurrence. However, to store tables with 314 values takes a lot of memory. To calculate them from Project Scoresheet data takes a lot of computer time.

There is an easier way. To sum Runs Created (RC), the underlying transitions are not required. All that is needed are the initial and final states. To show why, let us go back to Skoog's Equation for RC totals and break it down into parts, analyzing each individually

$$\Sigma \, RC = \Sigma \, (\text{Delta } E + RRF + K)$$

over all the plate appearances of the season. This can be expanded to:

$$\Sigma \, RC = \Sigma \, \text{Delta } E + \Sigma \, RRF + \Sigma \, K$$

over all plate appearances.

The first term, Σ Delta E, is the summation of the changes in potential caused by each plate appearance; or, $\Sigma \, (E_f - E_i)$, where E_f is the final state potential, and E_i the initial state potential, of each transition. This can be expanded to $\Sigma \, E_f - \Sigma \, E_i$. To correctly calculate the value of this term, we do not need to know the actual transitions, only the final and initial states. Sum the potentials of the final states, and subtract from that the sum of the potentials of the initial states, and you get the same total as if you had summed the potential differences of all transitions. The only change is in the order of the calculation.

As for the second term in Skoog's Equation, Σ RRF can be deduced arithmetically from initial and final states alone. The Runs Responsible For per plate appearance in a transition from state i to state f can be calculated thus:

$$RRF = 1 + S_i - S_f$$

where S is the sum of the number of outs plus men on base in a particular state; S_i is that sum in state i, and S_f is the

615

sum in state f. At the end of each plate appearance, all runners and the batter must either (1) be on base, (2) be out, or (3) have scored. For a moment, exclude the batter from consideration. A runner who stays on base will not change S during the transition. A runner who makes an out will not change S either (the number of men on base is reduced, but the number of outs is increased by an identical amount). If scoring occurs, S_f will drop one for each runner that scores. Thus, excluding the batter, S_i minus S_f will equal the number of runs scored on the play. But the batter must go somewhere. If he does not score, he increases S by one, either making an out or by getting on base: if no runs score, S_f must exceed S_i by one. If one run scores, S_f must equal S_i, etc.

For example, suppose 1 out and 2 on base, so S_i is 3. If the batter walks, S_f is 4 (3 on base and 1 out), so RRF equals 1 plus 3 minus 4, or zero. If the batter strikes out, S_f is also 4 (2 outs and 2 on base) so RRF is 1 plus 3 minus 4, or zero. If the batter doubles in the 2 runners, S_f is 2 (1 out and 1 on base) so RRF equals 1 plus 3 minus 2, or two runs scored. If there is a double play, ending the inning with no score, S_f is 4 (1 for the runner who who was not doubled up plus 3 for three outs) and RRF is again 1 plus 3 minus 4, or zero.

Thus, to sum a season's RRF for a player, all that is needed are the initial and final states. For each of the 24 initial states, calculate S_i and add 1, then multiply the value obtained by the number of occurrences of that state, and sum these 24 products. Subtract from this the summation, over all 28 final states, of the values of S for each state times the number of its occurrences. The result is the SUM RRF for the season.

The final element in Skoog's Equation is the correction factor ΣK, to get Runs Created totals equal to the actual runs scored. *The specific transition states are not needed to determine ΣK using Skoog's methods RC2 or RC3.* To use RC3, a correction is added to each plate appearance in the entire season, irrespective of performance. This depends only on the number of transitions that make up an individual's performance. To use RC2, sum the number of outs in the initial states faced by the player, and subtract that from the number of outs represented by the final states. This difference is the number of outs the player has been responsible for during the season. Either way the correction does not directly depend on the actual transitions involved.

Thus, to sum Skoog's Equation for an entire season, we do not need all the data in the 314-element transition array. All we need are the frequencies of the 24 initial states and the 28 final states. It might be argued that since the frequency distribution of final states is clearly not independent of that of the initial states, performance measures can not be divorced from the actual transitions. One reply is that this dependence is reflected in the fact that not all combinations of initial states and final states are possible. The rules of baseball require that, given the initial state frequencies, there exists a finite number of sets of possible final state frequencies. For a given set of actual initial and final states, there exists a finite number of sets of actual transitions that can account for them. The Runs Created will be the same for any of these sets of transitions.

This argument appears in algebraic form in an appendix, available from the author on request. For those who do

not wish to work through the derivation, here are instructions for using the calculation technique.

The runs created for a set of plate appearances (transitions), are

$$RC = \sum_{i=1}^{24} X_i(C_i + 1) - \sum_{i=1}^{28} X_f C_f$$

where X_i and X_f are the frequencies of occurrence of initial state i and final state f, respectively, among the set of transitions for which RC is being calculated; and C is a function defined thus:

$$C_i = M_i - E_i + U_i (1 - E_a/3)$$

where M_i is the number of men on base, E_i is the run potential, and U_i is the number of outs, for state i; and E_a is the run potential of state a (no outs, no runners). These factors are all readily available either from Thorn and Palmer or Jensen, or by definition. A tabulation of the values of the calculation function C for the 28 possible states is given in Table 1.

In other words, for each of the 24 possible initial states, multiply the frequency of occurrence, times one plus the value of the function C, and take the sum of all 24 products. Subtract from that the sum, over all 28 possible final states, of the frequency times the value of C for each state. The result will be the same as if you calculated Runs Created directly from frequency data for the 314 possible transitions.

An example of how the method works is given in Table

TABLE 1. DETERMINATION OF FUNCTION "C"

State	Outs	Men on Base 1st	2nd	3rd	Run Potential (Palmer/Thorn)	Value of C *
a	0				0.454	−0.454
b	1				0.249	0.600
c	2				0.095	1.602
d	0	x			0.783	0.217
e	1	x			0.478	1.371
f	2	x			0.209	2.488
g	0		x		1.068	−0.068
h	1		x		0.699	1.150
i	2		x		0.348	2.349
j	0			x	1.277	−0.277
k	1			x	0.897	0.952
l	2			x	0.382	2.315
m	0	x	x		1.380	0.620
n	1	x	x		0.888	1.961
o	2		x	x	0.457	3.240
p	0	x		x	1.639	0.361
q	1	x		x	1.088	1.761
r	2	x		x	0.494	3.203
s	0		x	x	1.946	0.054
t	1		x	x	1.371	1.478
u	2		x	x	0.661	3.036
v	0	x	x	x	2.254	0.746
w	1	x	x	x	1.546	2.303
x	2	x	x	x	0.798	3.899
"25"	3	—0 on base—			0.000	2.547
"26"	3	—1 on base—			0.000	3.547
"27"	3	—2 on base—			0.000	4.547
"28"	3	—3 on base—			0.000	5.547

* $C = M - E + U(1 - E_a/3)$
where M = the number of men on base
E = the run potential
U = the number of outs
E_a = the run potential of state a (no outs, no runners on)

2. This table shows, for a sample of 6 plate appearances, the calculation for RC two ways: both directly from Skoog's Equation as described above, and then by the new simplified method. The agreement between the two methods is accurate to less than one tenth of one percent; this insignificant error is due to rounding off.

I would like to acknowledge the invaluable assistance of Robert Brunell of the Statistical Laboratory, Yale University, who devoted significant time to discussions with me on these ideas at SABR-17.

A COMMENT ON LIEFF'S SIMPLIFIED METHOD

The article "A Simplified Method for Runs Created Measurement" by Matthew Lieff offers what appears to be a time-saving method for the calculation of runs created. By forcing the numerical analysts among the sabermetric community to analyze their computational methods, it represents progress. There is a second benefit to his approach, which may be more important, and is also discussed here.

Before addressing these issues, the point should be made that the computational and statistical complexity is not as bad as it may appear from the first and seventh paragraphs of Lieff's article. Calling the initial state E_i and the final state E_f, there are two interesting functions defined on the 314 feasible state transitions—the transition probabilities $p(E_i, E_f)$ and the runs created $RC(E_i, E_f)$. The first of these possesses no theoretically simplified structure—p is a general function of 2 variables, with range on the interval [0,1] and which sums to 1. It is possible, though, that response surface statistical methodology may yield an empirical simplification. The other function, the focus of Lieff's article, is

$$RC(E_i, E_f) = RP(E_f) - RP(E_i) + RRF(E_i, E_f) + K$$

where RP( ) is the run potential function. The first two terms on the right-hand side suggest a decomposition of RC which is termed *additive,* or *separable.* (Generally, f(x,y) is termed separable or additive if it can be broken down into the sum of two functions, each of which depends on only one argument: f(x,y) = g(x) + h(y).) RC would be additive if $RRF(E_i, E_f)$ were additive, since the sum of additive functions is additive, and the constant function is trivially additive. Fortunately RRF is indeed additive: In Lieff's notation, S_i, the sum in state i of the outs and number of men on base, is clearly a function of E_i alone, as is S_f. Thus, RC is a separable function of its arguments, and from this Lieff's computational result follows.

Incidentally, the formula for RRF in terms of the states appears destined to be rediscovered by each sabermetrician who asks whether RRF is indeed a function at all. After presenting it in passing to an ASA meeting in Chicago, I found reference to it by Mark Pankin in the *Baseball Analyst* of 8-85. It has likely appeared before and since. Given the proper definition of state, one can, by accounting for the outs and the men on base before and after, and the batter, determine the number of runs which scored on the play.

The next question is computational efficiency. In computing runs created for the 1987 *Abstract,* for each at-bat, 2 calls to a lookup table were made along with the above accounting calculation. A league's calculations were made overnight on a personal computer. With Lieff's result, instead of the 2 lookup calls per at bat, 2 entries are added to a running count of the frequencies with which each state occurs as the initial and final state. It would appear that calculation of these 2 histograms is computationally more efficient than performing lookup table calls.

There are additional substantive lessons to be drawn

TABLE 2 SAMPLE CALCULATION

Consider a player with 6 plate appearances, with the following results (initial and final states named in parentheses):
1. 1 out, man on second (h). Batter homers, scoring 2 runs (b).
2. 1 out, man on first (e). Batter grounds into a double play (25).
3. No outs, none on (a). Batter singles (d).
4. 2 outs, man on second (i). Batter doubles, driving in the runner (i).
5. No outs, men on first and second (m). Batter sacrifices, advancing the runners (t).
6. 1 out, man on second (h). Batter strikes out, no advance (i).

Transition	BY TRANSITIONS					
	E_f	E_i	Delta E ($E_f - E_i$)	RRF	K	RC for plate appearance
h . . . . b	0.249	0.699	−0.450	2	0	1.550
e 25	0	0.478	−0.478	0	0.302	−0.176
a . . . . d	0.783	0.454	0.329	0	0	0.329
i i	0.348	0.348	0	1	0	1.000
m . . . . t	1.371	1.380	−0.009	0	0.151	0.142
h i	0.348	0.699	−0.351	0	0.151	−0.200

Total RC for all plate appearances 2.645

Initial State	BY SIMPLIFIED METHOD							
	C_i	$C_i + 1$	X_i	$X_i(C_i + 1)$	Final State	C_f	X_f	$X_f C_f$
h	1.150	2.150	2	4.300	b	0.600	1	0.600
e	1.371	2.371	1	2.371	25	2.547	1	2.547
a	−0.454	0.546	1	0.546	d	0.217	1	0.217
i	2.349	3.349	1	3.349	i	2.349	2	4.698
m	0.620	1.620	1	1.620	t	1.478	1	1.478
TOTALS				12.186				9.540

$$RC = \sum_{i=1}^{24} X_i(C_i + 1) - \sum_{f=1}^{28} X_f C_f = 12.186 - 9.540 = 2.646$$

THE TWO METHODS AGREE TO .001 IN 2.646, OR 4/100 OF 1 PERCENT ACCURACY

from the implication of separability. The first is that, for runs created, the histograms of E_i and E_s, along with the RRF count, are sufficient statistics—ways to compress the much larger primitive data without loss of information. Secondly, reporting these histograms would allow us to assess a potential source of bias suggested in the original runs created article, namely, to what extent do different hitters have different opportunities, or E_i histograms? Next, RC measures an average; averages suggest variances. Thus, other moments than the first of the histograms may be important, and we are now lead to study them. Finally, the most useful way to order the states in the histogram construction should be investigated, so that the differences in types of hitters is most clearly depicted—a problem in sabergraphics.

Gary Skoog

SON OF "OTHER BASEBALL PUBLICATIONS"

by Geoff Beckman

To a baseball fan, statistics and analysis are like cookies. You know that they warp your mind, that they're expensive and time-consuming and you try never to let anyone know just how much time and money you spend on them. But it's no use—you enjoy them so bloody much that you just can't get enough.

To make matters worse, the choices can be maddening. Like cookies, baseball analysis newsletters can and do spring up anywhere—there are an amazing variety to choose from. They also have an even shorter shelf life; in a typical year, a few new ones will spring up, a few more will collapse and others will change writers, formats and addresses. Just keeping up with everything that's going on requires some fancy footwork; not many people can do it.

Since I'm one of the few folks who do that homework, the powers that be asked me do a sequel to my piece in last year's book. What follows is an incomplete list of what's out there—incomplete for four reasons:

1. I didn't include any team-sponsored tabloids because I find them to be a complete waste of time. If you like wading your way through one-sided journalistic goo, I suggest that you call the PR director of your favorite team and ask if they publish one.

2. There are several independant, single-team, general publications around. Many do include stats and analysis, but that's not their primary focus . . . and this is, after all, *The Great American Baseball Stat Book*. If you like such things, *Dodger Dugout* and *Tiger Stripes* have addresses listed on p. 286 of the 1987 *Abstract;* if you're fond of the Red Sox, you could contact *The Buffalo Head Society* (PO Box 92, Waltham, MA 02254).

3. Call me silly, but I sorta kinda like to read something before I review it. I'm told that there's a really dynamite newsletter on the Mets out there and a pretty good one on the Padres, but I've never seen any issues—hence, no review.

4. Newsletters aren't very stable creatures. In the last year, one newsletter that was reviewed last year folded, two went on hiatus, a third cut down its publication schedule and another is considering folding. That being so, I insisted on seeing a recent issue (or, in the case of the annuals, last year's edition) before including them; several existing publications failed to meet this guideline.

Before I get to the listings, let me touch on several matters of mail-order etiquette. First and foremost: NEVER, EVER, send cash through the mails. Second, and almost as important: All of these publications are published on shoestrings of varying lengths; don't write to the editor and ask him to send you a copy "on approval." Third, for the benefit of the folks outside the border: All prices listed are in U.S. FUNDS ONLY. Lastly: Most editors like to know where their subscribers come from; it is helpful if you inform them where you heard about them in your letter.

With that out of the way, let's get on with the show. Here, in alphabetical order, are some people who know their stuff and are willing to sell it to you:

Baseball Analyst: In past years, the *Analyst* was a technical journal about general topics which featured fascinating and readable pieces cheek-by-jowl with abstruse and confusing ones. In 1987, the topics got more interesting and the articles became much more readable—partly because editor Bill James did more writing and editing for it. A bit dryer than the *Baseball Abstract,* but still worthwhile reading for anyone who doesn't mind the occasional formula. P.O. Box 161, Winchester, KS 66097—$16 for six 20-page, bi-monthly issues.

Baseball Insight: BBI is a weekly 12-page newsletter designed to help gamblers bet intelligently by providing statistics—since most of the data that gamblers want is also interesting to analysts, it's a goldmine of data. BBI features data for teams against lefties and righties both at home and away, day/night and grass/turf data, runs allowed at home and away, bullpen ERAs and unearned runs per game and also includes much of the same data for the team's top four starters as well as a page or two on current trends and analysis. If you write about baseball and need a timely source of data or simply love weekly fixes of numbers, try it. Editor Phil Erwin reports that a 1988 price change is planned; write for current info to P.O. Box 13727, Portland, OR 97213.

Baseball Insight Pitcher and Team Log: Published by the same gentleman, this is an annual roundup of all of the same stats, supplemented by analysis of the data, studies on various topics and game-by-game data for every pitcher with 20 plus starts in 1987. At $7.95, this is an excellent value and is very highly recommended; same address as above.

Baseball Insight 1987 Log: Also published by Mr. Erwin, this is basically a more detailed version of the "Day-by-day" listings for each team that are published in *The Sporting News Baseball Guide.* Along with the date, place and game score, it includes the starter, his innings pitched and earned runs allowed, the bullpen's innings pitched and earned runs allowed, unearned runs, the opposing starter and several gambling-related topics. If you're interested in doing studies, this is an invaluable time-saver. Same address as above; $9.95.

Chicago Baseball Report. This is actually two separate publications, one on the Cubs, one on the White Sox. Produced by John and Sue Dewan, the publications offer fewer stats than other reports do, but add a great deal of informed commentary. Don Zminda covers the Sox with matchless zeal, wit and insight. Mike O'Donnell, another fine analyst, does the Cub commentary. The price for either edition is $19.95 for a one-year subscription, including five regular issues and a final report. The address is

P.O. Box 46074, Chicago, IL 60646. Please specify Cubs or Sox.

Christmann Baseball Report: This annual—devoted entirely to statistics on the New York Yankees—contains full batting and pitching lines for the following categories: home/road, day/night, grass/turf, left/right, leading off innings, runners in scoring position, clutch situations and first half/second half. It also includes start/relief data for pitchers, inherited runners, full defensive stats, miscellaneous bits and pieces and a few well-chosen words of analysis. If what you're looking for isn't here, then it probably isn't important. $12.50 from 54 Old Chestnut Ridge Road, Montvale, NJ 07645.

Jays Jazz: David Driscoll's annual magnum opus on Toronto is easily the best of the statistical reports, for five reasons. First, it has all the data that the other reports do. Secondly, it adds pitch-by-pitch and base/out breakdowns. Third, it includes lengthy, perceptive and witty analyses of every player. Fourth, it's professionally bound, graphically nifty and looks great on your coffee table. Finally, it's $11.95. If you have any interest at all in baseball stats, baseball analysis or the Blue Jays, you must buy this book. Write to P.O. Box 6493, Station D, London, ONT, N5W 5S5 CANADA.

Jays Jazz Newsletter: Driscoll plans to begin a Toronto newsletter in 1988—which will, he tells me, be a timely look at topics of interest to Blue Jay fans, containing the same sort of stuff that the annual has. Though I can't recommend something that doesn't yet exist, I will say that the price— $15 for nine issues—seems like a good value. And if it is anywhere near the quality of the book, it should be a super one. Same address as above.

Outsiders' Baseball: Formerly the *Project Scoresheet Baseball Report*, *OB* is a bi-monthly collection of analytical essays on every team and essays on general topics, written by many of the people who contributed to this book and edited by yours truly. *Sport Magazine* called it "a best-buy . . . with punchy copy and inside gossip." The *Utne Reader* said it was "cheaper than a beer and a hot dog and twice as filling." Bill James said it was "witty, incisive and very knowledgeable . . . I really recommend this one highly." $12 from P.O. Box 181061, Cleveland, OH 44118. (*Outsider's Baseball* was last published in June 1987. Please contact publisher Geoff Beckman at the above address to inquire about its current status.—Ed.)

Project Scoresheet Account-Form Boxscore Books: Using the account-form boxscore (a way to shoehorn all the data on a scoresheet into a space about the size of a newspaper boxscore) to display information, these books contain a play-by-play record of every game played in a league during one season. No matter what issue you want to look at, these books give you the tools to find the answers—quite simply,

there is nothing else like them and never has been. Books are available for each league for 1984, 1985, 1986 and 1987 and cost $19.95 for non-members ($34.95 for both leagues) and $14.95 ($24.95 for both leagues) for members. Add $2.00 postage and handling for the first book and $1.00 for each additional book. PS scorers and inputters are eligible for further discounts. Order from Project Scoresheet, P.O. Box 12009, Lansing, MI 48901.

Sabermetric Review: The "Monthly Empirical Analysis of Baseball" was folded by the publisher in fall, 1987; efforts by editor Gary Gillette to resurrect it have (so far) failed. I mention this as a public service to the subscribers who were never contacted—much less offered refunds on the unpaid portions of their subscriptions. If you fall into this group, you should know that the publisher is required by law to give refunds; if you send a harsh letter to Meckler Publications, 11 Ferry Lane West, Westport, CT 06880, they will cheerlessly do so.

Seattle Baseball Bulletin: Steve Russell and his band of gypsies prove that you can so do an interesting statistical newsletter about a crummy team if you devote enough space to writing and analysis and have enough entertaining writers. Aside from its statistics, aside from the thought-provoking articles, the *SBB*'s nicest feature is its down-to-earth posture; the writers combine the fervor of the fan with the insight of the analyst. $25 for the 1987 year-end issue and monthly issues during the 1988 season; $20 for the 1988 issues only; P.O. Box 221, Redmond, WA 98073.

Tiger Tracks: Driscoll's attempt to do for Detroit what he's done for Toronto. This annual contains all of the features of *Jays Jazz* and is a badly needed antidote to the inane comments that the Tigers' management seem to specialize in. Same price and address as *Jays Jazz*.

Waseleski Baseball Report: This could be subtitled "Every Statistic that You Always Wanted to Know About the Red Sox But Were too Lazy to Figure Out for Yourself." When I write pieces about most other teams, I get my data by writing their PR office—for Boston, I get it entirely from Chuck Waseleski's fine in-season monthly. That's not unusual; virtually everyone in the working press does, too. $12.50 for the 1987 report; $50 for a full year. Write to 10 Newton Street, Miller's Falls, MA 01349.

Wild Pitches: The baby of the bunch (issue four will be out in April) is a four-page newsletter on the Minnesota Twins. Since each issue runs about twice as much commentary as stats, the pieces have to be truly outstanding in order to justify the cost; luckily for editor Jim Rogde and his staff, they are. Content ranges from critiques of management to analyses of players to historical essays—each is witty, intelligent and fun to read. Given some time, this could grow into a very fine one. $10 for 12 monthly issues from P.O. Box 2826, Minneapolis, MN 55402.

ABOUT PROJECT SCORESHEET

Gary C. Gillette, Executive Director

At its most simple level, Project Scoresheet is a nationwide organization of baseball *fans* dedicated to collecting and disseminating more and better information about baseball. Basically, the members of the Project score all of the more than two thousand major league baseball games played each season on a play-by-play basis. These scoresheets are then sent to the Project's offices, where they are checked for accuracy, filed, and computerized.

All of this effort is used to compile a comprehensive data base for each season; the Project's data base currently contains complete play-by-play information as well as dozens of statistical breakdowns for the 1984, 1985, 1986 and 1987 seasons. This information is made available to baseball fans, writers and researchers in several formats: *The Great American Baseball Stat Book,* account-form box score books for each league, computerized play-by-play files and statistics on floppy diskettes, and the original scoresheets themselves. The net result, we hope, is an increase in the enjoyment and understanding of our national pastime for baseball fans everywhere.

The Project is organized into "teams" along the lines of major league baseball. For each of the twenty-six clubs, there is a local group of members, headed by a team captain, who make sure that each of that team's games are scored. Home games are scored at the ball park and from television and radio broadcasts; road games are scored from the broadcasts, also. Of course, since there is a Project team for each club, each "home" game is also some-one else's "road" game, giving us extremely valuable back-up coverage. The Project maintains a central office to coordinate and support the efforts of the scorers and the team captains. This office administers a nationwide network of computer programmers, inputters, proofreaders, writers and editors who compile the raw scoresheets into an organized data base, and who produce statistics and analyses like this book.

Bill James, sabermetrician and author of the best-selling annual *Bill James Baseball Abstract,* founded Project Scoresheet in 1984. Bill's writing and analysis had created a loyal following of hundreds of thousands of baseball fans, and his extensive knowledge and expertise about baseball made Project Scoresheet possible. The Project is now composed of hundreds and hundreds of members who donate their scoresheets, their time and their expertise toward achieving our goals. The Project has been growing ever since its first year; 1988, our fifth season of operation, will be bigger and better than ever.

Project Scoresheet is a non-profit organization whose directors are elected by the membership. Membership in the Project is open to anyone—most of our members score games or provide other substantial in-kind service to the organization instead of paying membership dues. If you want to become a part of the Project, or if you want more information on our products and services, write to us at P.O. Box 12009, Lansing, MI 48901-2009, or call us at (517) 487–3070. We'd like to hear from you.

Project ScoreSheet

Box 12009 Lansing MI 48901
1988 Scoring Form   Copyright 1988

Date

Scorer

How | At park | TV | Radio

Visitors

Home

Start time | Time

Attendance

Umps: H | 1B | 2B | 3B

	Visiting Players	Defensive Pos In Pos In Out

Off. In

Bats

| 1 | 2 | 3 | 4 | 5 | 6 | 7 | 8 | 9 |

| 10 | 11 | 12 | 13 | 14 | 15 | 16 | 17 | 18 |

| 19 | 20 | 21 | 22 | 23 | 24 | 25 | 26 | 27 |

| 28 | 29 | 30 | 31 | 32 | 33 | 34 | 35 | 36 |

| 37 | 38 | 39 | 40 | 41 | 42 | 43 | 44 | 45 |

| 46 | 47 | 48 | 49 | 50 | 51 | 52 | 53 | 54 |

Home Pitchers	In	Out	ER	W/L Sv

Notes

Bats

GWRBI: _____

| 1 | 2 | 3 | 4 | 5 | 6 | 7 | 8 | 9 | 10 | R | H | E |

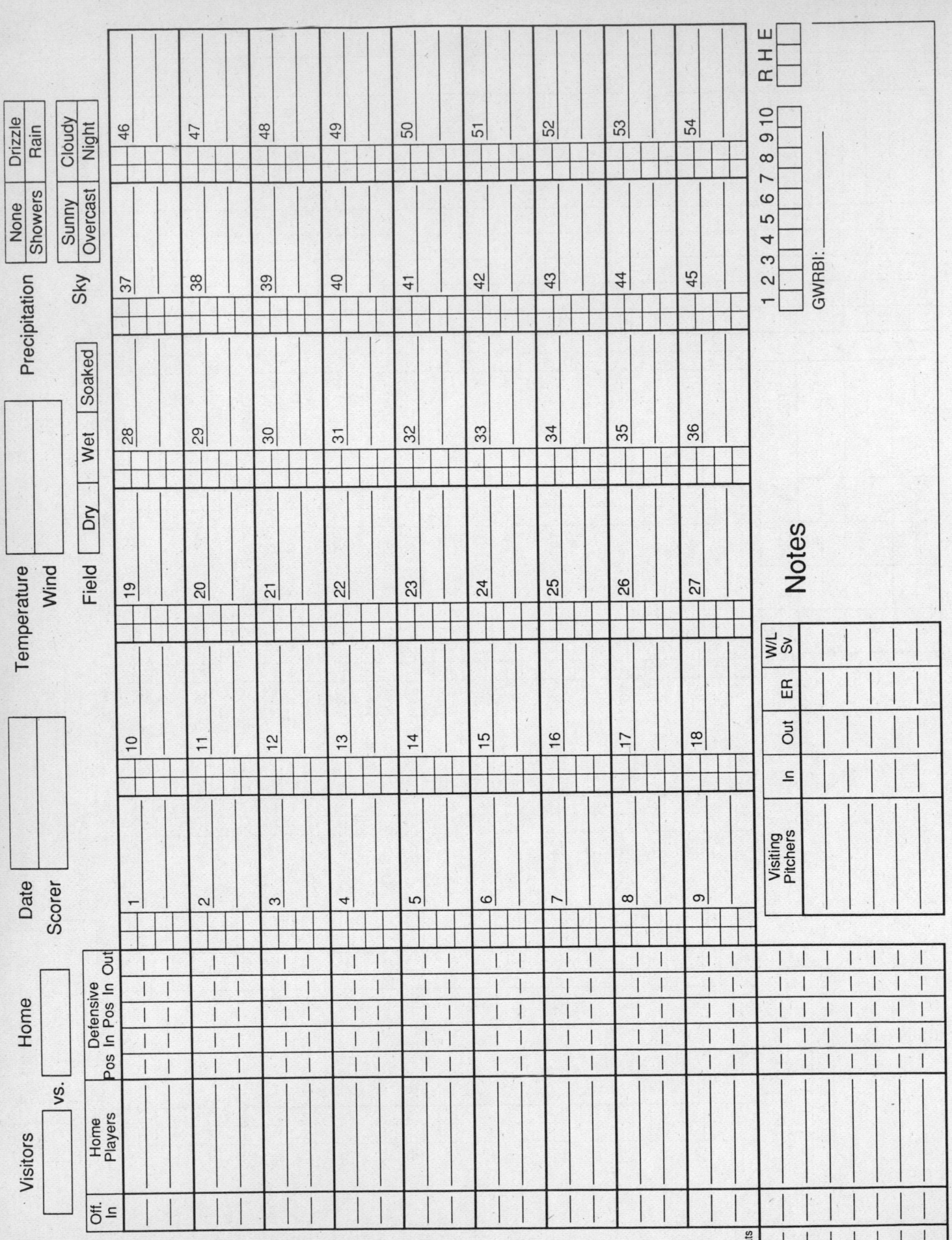